In8e

An Introductory Dictionary of
Theology and Religious Studies

An Introductory
Dictionary of Theology and
Religious Studies

Edited by

Orlando O. Espín and James B. Nickoloff

A Michael Glazier Book

LITURGICAL PRESS
Collegeville, Minnesota

www.litpress.org

A Michael Glazier Book published by Liturgical Press.

Cover design by David Manahan, o.s.b. Cover symbol by Frank Kacmarcik, obl.s.b.

1   2   3   4   5   6   7   8

Library of Congress Cataloging-in-Publication Data

An introductory dictionary of theology and religious studies / edited by
Orlando O. Espín and James B. Nickoloff.
        p.   cm.
    "A Michael Glazier book."
    ISBN-13: 978-0-8146-5856-7 (alk. paper)
    1. Religion—Dictionaries.   2. Religions—Dictionaries.   I. Espín, Orlando O.
II. Nickoloff, James B.

BL31.I68 2007
200.3—dc22

                                                                    2007030890

We dedicate this dictionary to Ricardo and Robert,

for their constant support over many years.

Contents

List of Entries

Introduction
and
Acknowledgments

College professors of religion have been discovering over the past two decades that their students are frequently unfamiliar with ideas, terms, historical events, or persons deemed important in the study of religion. *An Introductory Dictionary of Theology and Religious Studies* intends to provide basic definitions and background information on concepts, persons, objects, and events that seem to be important or useful for the academic study of the world's major religions. It is further intended for students at colleges and universities where the academic study of religion is part of the undergraduate curriculum.

This dictionary is *not* meant to take the place of the professor, or of the professor's classroom explanations, or of other required reading. It is simply intended to provide a source of information with which students may initiate or enrich their study.

The dictionary is purposely *introductory*. The entries included in this volume were not written in order to break new scholarly ground or to disseminate recent research results. The authors were asked simply to present the subject matter in synthetic form, explaining what is commonly held by mainstream specialists in the field, in language understandable to beginners.

The dictionary is not intended, furthermore, for catechesis or religious education, although it might prove helpful in those contexts as well. We have kept the college religion course in mind, and not the parish, as the primary context in which this volume might be used.

Although the dictionary reflects the Catholic heritage of many of the authors, a significant portion of entries was written by scholars from other religious traditions or from none. We hope the dictionary will be useful to students in institutions public and private, denominational and secular.

We have attempted to be as ecumenical, multicultural, and international as possible. In order to achieve this aim, we have made the following decisions:

- We have tried to reflect developing-nation and U.S. minority perspectives in the list of entries, alongside European and Euro-American perspectives.

- We have included entries on U.S. Latino/a, Latin American, African American, African, and Asian theologians, besides the expected ones on Europeans and Euro-Americans.

- We added entries on religions present in the United States but usually absent from American introductory dictionaries (for example, Umbanda, Condomblé, Santería, Vodoun, native religions from the Americas, and so on).

- We also represented European countries usually ignored in American dictionaries (for example, Spain, Portugal, Russia, and Greece).

To achieve the preceding four goals, as well as to make sure that women from across the world were included, we chose to have entries on scholars and religious leaders still living, working, and writing.

The emphasis of this dictionary is on mainstream Christianity, in particular "Catholic" Christianity, broadly understood. At the same time, we have acknowledged Protestant, Anglican, and Orthodox Christianity and have included as many entries as possible on every one of the world's other great religions. Specialists in these other traditions, often members thereof, authored the many entries on Judaism, Islam, Hinduism, Buddhism, Jainism, Santería, and so forth.

This is the first edition of the dictionary. With suggestions from professors and students, the subsequent editions can be improved, enlarged, new entries included, and others deleted. This introductory dictionary is intended as a real teaching tool for the academic study of Christian theology and world religions. We hope that it will serve its purpose well.

We also acknowledge that this first edition is not perfect. Choices were made on what to include and what to exclude, and others might agree or disagree with these choices. The students' and professors' feedback will be of great help to us in the preparation of future editions of the dictionary.

We would like to thank all the authors who wrote the entries included in this volume. Our colleagues at the College of the Holy Cross and at the University of San Diego generously participated in the long process that has finally led to the publication of this dictionary. Their support of this project, over many years, is deeply appreciated. We also thank Mark Twomey, former editorial director at Liturgical Press, and project editor Aaron Raverty, o.s.b., for their patient and gentle prodding. And we also thank the director, Peter Dwyer, and the staff of Liturgical Press for believing in this project and for shepherding it to conclusion.

We especially want to explicitly thank Professor Patricia Plovanich, of the University of San Diego, who first suggested the need for this project, and who worked with us during early editorial stages. She has remained as author of a significant number of entries.

Through the years that it took to produce this dictionary, many colleagues and friends have provided suggestions and offered support. We would like to mention in particular the help of Professors Gary Macy, Justo González, Lance Nelson, and Alana Cordy-Collins. Professor Tony Harvell (now at the University of California, San Diego) and the research librarians at the University of San Diego proved indispensable to the coeditors and to many of the authors. Finally, we offer a special word of thanks to Mary Tracy for her help at a crucial stage of this project.

Orlando O. Espín, University of San Diego

James B. Nickoloff, College of the Holy Cross

July 2007

A

AARON

The brother of Moses, the son of Amram (Exod 6:20) and the sister of Miriam who was the ancestor of the Aaronide priests who dominated the priesthood in Israel from the period of the Babylonian Exile on. The descendants of Aaron, usually called the "sons of Aaron," are presented as descended from Levi, one of the twelve sons of Jacob (Exod 6:16). The meaning of the name is uncertain.

Russell Fuller

ABBA

Recent christologies propose Jesus' use of *abba* to speak about God to indicate his unique sense of and special relationship to God. The usage derives from J. Jeremias who interpreted the term as a familial usage ("daddy") unknown to the Judaism of the era, thus unique to Jesus and suggestive of his novel teachings about God in *The Prayers of Jesus* (1967). Jeremias abandoned the interpretation, but the usage gained credence in many reconstructions of the historical Jesus, as in M. Borg's *Jesus: A New Vision* (1987). The reading allows the methodological possibility of linking the Gospels' implicit christologies to the explicit christology of dogma. Recent biblical scholarship does not support this interpretation of the word, and feminist exegetes have noted its patriarchal implications, but the christological application persists. It is an instance of a (possibly unrecognized) dogmatic interest at work in the interpretation of Scripture.

Patricia Plovanich

See also CHRISTOLOGY.

ABBASIDS

The ruling dynasty of the Islamic world (749–1258 C.E.) that came to power with the fall of the first dynasty (the Umayyads) and ended with the invasion of the Muslim empire by the Mongols. The dynasty is referred to as a caliphate because its leaders were considered spiritual and political successors of Muhammad (570–632 C.E.), Islam's founder and Prophet. The Abbasids are credited with integrating non-Arab Muslims, most notably the Persians, into the spiritual, intellectual, and political leadership of the Islamic empire. The Abbasids are also remembered for making their capital, Baghdad, a center of culture and learning where art, medicine, literature, and science flourished. Though the Abbasid caliphate was not able to exercise complete political dominance over the entire Islamic world during its

1

five-hundred-year existence, it remained a symbol of the unity and universality of Islam throughout the period. After Baghdad was sacked by the Mongols in 1258, Abbasids continued to reside in Egypt but without any significant political or military power. This last vestige of the once-great dynasty was conquered by the Ottomans in 1517.

Ronald A. Pachence

See also CALIPH (KHALIPHA)/CALIPHATE; OTTOMAN; UMAYYADS.

ABBEY

Traditional term for an autonomous monastery under the authority of an abbot or abbess. If the leader is referred to as prior or prioress, the monastery is called a priory.

Mary Anne Foley, C.N.D.

See also ABBOT/ABBESS; CONVENT/ CONVENTUAL; MONASTERY.

ABBOT/ABBESS

The title given to the leader of monasteries of men (abbot) or women (abbess) in Benedictine and most other monastic orders. The term "abbot" is derived from the Hebrew word for father, and the classical model for an abbot can be found in the second chapter of the *Rule of St. Benedict*, where it is suggested that his role is to act in the place of Christ, caring like a father for those in the monastery. During the Middle Ages, both abbots and abbesses often wielded great ecclesiastical and political authority, answerable only to the pope rather than to the local bishop.

Mary Anne Foley, C.N.D.

See also ABBA; BENEDICTINE RULE (RULE OF ST. BENEDICT); BENEDICTINES; MONASTERY; MONASTICISM IN WESTERN CHRISTIANITY; ORDERS (RELIGIOUS).

ABE, MASAO (1915–)

Contemporary Japanese philosopher and teacher and currently professor emeritus at Nara University in Japan. Abe is one of the leading representatives of the Kyoto school of philosophy and leading interpreter of Zen for the West since the death of D. T. Suzuki. He has taught extensively in the West at Columbia, Princeton, Chicago, and other places, and has also become one of the primary synthesizers of Eastern and Western philosophy. His major writings include *Existential and Ontological Dimensions of Time in Heidegger* and *Zen and Western Thought*.

G. D. DeAngelis

See also SUZUKI, DAISETSU TEITARO; ZEN.

ABELARD, PETER (CA. 1079–1142/4)

As a young man, Abelard devoted his life to the pursuit of knowledge, leaving his home near Nantes to seek out the best teachers he could find. He studied philosophy under Roscelin of Compiègne and William of Champeaux before teaching philosophy himself at Melun, Corbie, and finally at Paris. Having mastered philosophy, Abelard turned to theology, studying under Anselm of Laon. As he had earlier with William of Champeaux, Abelard soon set himself up as a rival to Anselm, and by 1113 Abelard was teaching theology in Paris. Fulbert, a canon of the cathedral of Notre Dame in Paris, hired Abelard to tutor his niece, Heloise. Abelard and Heloise soon fell passionately in love, secretly married, and produced a son, Astralabe. Fulbert, enraged by this turn of events, hired thugs who castrated Abelard. Abelard met this humiliation by joining the Benedictine abbey of St. Denis and by insisting that Heloise enter the convent of Argenteuil.

Abelard's theology also came under attack, and in 1121 he was forced by the Council of Soissons to burn his book now known as the *Theologia "Summi Boni."* Unable to get along with the monks at St. Denis, Abelard received permission to retire to his own oratory which he entitled the Paraclete. Soon a thriving school grew up at the Paraclete, but once again Abelard was forced by his enemies to retire. He spent several unsuccessful years as abbot of St. Gildas in Brittany, eventually returning to Paris to teach. In the 1130s Abelard produced a new book of theology as well as his most famous book, *The Ethics*. Led by William of St. Thierry and Bernard of Clairvaux, opposition again arose against Abelard's theology. His teaching condemned at the Council of Sens in 1141, Abelard retired to the monastery of Cluny. He died sometime between 1142 and 1144 at a priory attached to Cluny. Abelard was buried at the Paraclete where he was joined in death around 1163/4 by his wife, Heloise. The two lovers are now buried together in Père Lachaise Cemetery in Paris.

Brilliant, exasperating, and charismatic, Abelard, more than any other medieval figure, has symbolized the use of logic and dialectic to challenge existing authority. Certainly his works, especially the *Yes and No* (*Sic et Non*) and *The Ethics*, greatly influenced later thought in this regard. Yet, he was also a devout monk and concerned spiritual director as his sermons, hymns, and other writings demontrate. In the popular imagination, however, Abelard is best known for his relationship with Heloise. Their passionate affair is chronicled in Abelard's *The History of My Calamities.* Moving letters exchanged between Heloise and Abelard also exist, although doubts have been raised about their authenticity.

Gary Macy

See also BERNARD OF CLAIRVAUX; HELOISE; MEDIEVAL CHRISTIANITY (IN THE WEST); MONASTICISM IN WESTERN CHRISTIANITY; SCHOLASTICISM.

ABHIDHARMA/ABHIDHAMMA PITAKA

The collection of the early Indian Buddhist canon in which the teachings are arranged by various detailed schema. As designated by the Abhidharma's meaning, "advanced teachings," early scholastic monks collected listings of religious terms, psychological designations, and analytic elaborations of phenomena to demonstrate the application of the doctrine to all spheres of reality. By 300 C.E. numerous Abhidharmas were organized by monks in every major school to advance their understanding and presentation of the logical extensions of the Buddha's teachings. Only the Theravada canon exists in its entirety; various Sanskrit Abhidharmas endure in Chinese, Tibetan, or Korean translations. The commentary by the scholar Vasubandhu, the *Abhidharmakosha*, was the greatest, comprising a compendium of early Buddhist thought written from the Sarvastivadin school's doctrinal system.

Todd T. Lewis

See also BUDDHAGHOSA; DHARMA (IN BUDDHISM); PALI CANON; SARVASTIVADIN SCHOOL; TRIPITAKA/ TIPITAKA; VASUBANDHU.

ABHISHEKA

In Hinduism, *abhisheka* (Sanskrit, sprinkling) is a ritual of anointing, sprinkling with water, or bathing, especially as part of the coronation rites of a king or the consecration of an image of a deity in a temple. In the case of a temple icon, the ritual of consecration is said to invoke the living presence of the deity in the image. In Buddhist countries, kings and temple images are typically consecrated in similar ceremonies.

Lance E. Nelson

See also AVATARA/AVATAR; BUDDHISM; HINDUISM; IMAGES, WORSHIP OF.

ABHISHIKTANANDA, SWAMI (1910–73)

Swami Abhishiktananda was the religious name adopted by Henri Le Saux, a French Benedictine monk and priest who lived in India from 1948 until his death. Although he never abandoned his identity and faith as a Christian, Le Saux acknowledged a considerable spiritual debt to Hindu teachers, in particular the famous South Indian saint, Ramana Maharshi. As part of his spiritual quest, he took on the dress and the ascetic mode of life of a Hindu *sannyasin*, as well as his Hindu-style monastic name, meaning "the bliss of the Anointed One" (that is, of Christ). With Fr. Jules Monchanin and Fr. Bede Griffiths, Abhishiktananda was an important early pioneer of Hindu-Christian dialogue.

Lance E. Nelson

See also GRIFFITHS, BEDE; SANNYASA.

ABJURATION

The term indicates the 1917 Code of Canon Law's requirement that prospective converts or Catholics returning to the church make a formal, public rejection (before a church authority) of anything believed contrary to official Roman Catholic doctrine. The gesture is no longer required, for the new baptismal ritual for adults incorporates it in a general way.

Patricia Plovanich

ABORTION

An abortion is an intentional medical procedure to terminate a pregnancy and bring about the death of a human fetus. There has been a generally negative evaluation of this practice throughout the history of the Judeo-Christian tradition. The reasons for this negative evaluation and the circumstances in which it has been applied, however, have been varied. For example, the contemporary Roman Catholic teaching sees any direct action taken against the progress of a pregnancy—*from the moment of conception*—as a very grave offense because it deprives an innocent human person of the right to life. In the Middle Ages, however, only the abortion of a fully formed fetus was considered to be a homicide; earlier abortions were considered sinful because they were usually procured to obscure a sexual misdeed. Cultural developments and new biological insights have influenced church teaching on abortion, an issue where volatile concerns about homicide, sexual morality, and gender roles intersect.

Contemporary Concerns

After the Second World War, many persons in western Europe and North America argued for access to abortion, particularly for those cases where a new child would impose an emotional, physical, or financial hardship on the mother. Starting in the 1960s, many nations liberalized their abortion laws, and in 1973 the U.S. Supreme Court ruled in *Roe v. Wade* that laws forbidding abortion were unduly interfering in the privacy rights of women.

Since *Roe* and the resulting liberalization of abortion policy in the U.S., abortion has developed into one of the most contentious and divisive social issues of the period. It figures prominently in local and national elections as well as in the process of nominating and approving candidates for the judiciary; both sides of the debate have been effective at developing grass-roots protests and sophisticated political action organizations. At times, the controversy grows violent with abortion facilities bombed and abortion providers assassinated. The debate about the morality and legality of abortion focuses on the status of the fetus and on the moral autonomy of women. Thus, it is not a theological debate in its essence. Although Evangelical opponents of abortion may advance scriptural arguments, Roman Catholic opposition is based on natural law, which is presumed to be accessible and persuasive to all rational persons of good will.

Those in the U.S. opposed to abortion generally refer to themselves as "pro-life," while those who favor liberalized abortion policies refer to their cause as "pro-choice." Pro-life advocates argue that because fetal life is, in fact, *human* life it must be accorded the rights ascribed to persons, principally the right to life. Because the innocent may not be unjustly deprived of their lives, all abortion should be forbidden. Some pro-life advocates are willing to make exceptions, however, in cases of rape, incest, and threat to the mother's health, despite the apparent inconsistency. In addition, pro-life advocates make a "slippery slope" argument, claiming that liberalization of abortion policy undermines the sanctity of life at all stages of existence.

Although the moral status of the fetus is not the central issue for abortion rights advocates, they respond to the assertions of pro-life supporters in this regard by arguing that fetuses are not persons, that fetuses do not fulfill the criteria of personhood. Such criteria can include one or more of the following: consciousness, self-direction, communication skills, or reasoning ability, although some of these standards might exclude infants from personhood. The fetus, they argue, is "part" of the mother, and the right to bodily integrity supports the right to terminate a pregnancy. Any clash between the "rights" of a fetus and the mother's rights ought to be decided in favor of the existing person from this perspective. Pro-choice advocates in the U.S. attempt to build a positive case for abortion rights by appealing to deeply held beliefs about the freedom of conscience and the right to make private choices without government interference. Further, they argue that unless women have control over their reproductive capacities, their moral and social autonomy is effectively undermined.

Religious Perspectives

The pro-life movement in the U.S. receives strong support from those Roman Catholics and Evangelical/fundamentalist Christians who tend to favor traditional family relations and gender roles. Official teaching in those communities is solidly pro-life. Mainstream Protestant views on abortion are varied. While generally negative toward abortions, most denominations acknowledge that there are circumstances (pregnancies resulting from rape or incest, danger to the life or health of the mother, severe hardship caused by the birth of a child, or gross fetal deformity) that can justify an abortion. Thus, they support legal access to abortion. In this way, their views mirror the views of most Americans who do not support "abortion on demand" but do acknowledge circumstances where it is appropriate to end fetal life.

Brian F. Linnane, s.j.

See also CONTRACEPTION/BIRTH CONTROL; ETHICS, SEXUAL; EVANGELIUM VITAE; NATURAL LAW; SEXUALITY.

ABRAHAM

The first ancestor of Israel, presented as the father of Isaac, and the grandfather of Jacob. He is the husband of Sarah (Sarai). The stories featuring Abraham are found in Genesis 12–25. According to the biblical narratives, he is first named Abram, meaning approximately, "the father is exalted." His name is changed to Abraham by God (Gen 17:5) in conjunction with the formation of God's covenant with him and the promises of land and progeny that begin the story of the people of Israel. A popular etymology of the longer name is given in Genesis 17, "father of a multitude," but this does not correspond to known Hebrew forms. In Genesis 12, Abraham receives the command from God to journey to a new land that God will show him. His response is paradigmatic for the loyal follower of God—he leaves immediately.

Russell Fuller

ABRAHAM OF ECCHEL (OR OF HEKEL) (1600–64)

Also known as Ecchellensis, he was a Maronite Catholic scholar. Born in Lebanon, he studied and taught in Rome and Paris. He was a well-known specialist on Middle Eastern languages and liturgies and did much to recover and preserve the ancient liturgical and theological texts of the Maronite Catholic Church.

Orlando Espín

See also COMMUNION (ECCLESIOLOGICAL); EASTERN CATHOLIC CHURCHES; LITURGY (IN CHRISTIANITY); MARONITE CATHOLIC CHURCH.

ABSOLUTE

A term signifying what is infinite, ultimate, unconditioned, self-subsistent, or unrestricted, and thus an appropriate word for theological reflection about God. It is used in several ways: to designate the divine being as such (God is the Absolute); to express the adjustment of analogical concepts to represent divine existence as distinct from the finite equivalent (God's absolute love); and to express the religious conviction about the preeminence and singularity of a foundational religious experience that makes a religious group unique among other faiths (for instance, the Christian claim about an absolute revelation in Jesus Christ).

The concept's roots lie in Greek reflection on divinity's distinction from the finite realm of becoming. Scholastic theology used the term to indicate God as the independent (noncontingent) foundation of all other (finite or contingent) existence. Enlightenment philosophy's efforts to base the certitude of knowledge on empirical (or phenomenal) reality rejected the possibility of absolute religious knowledge. Kantian philosophy proposed the Absolute (God) to hold the status of a *noumenon*, a nonverifiable organizing construct. Nineteenth-century Romantic philosophers gave the term new life, using it to represent the divine existence and God's relationship to the world as the dynamic source of life that actualizes itself in history. Schelling speaks about the Absolute in history, for instance. A similar usage is found in twentieth-century process theology. A recent use of Absolute indicates the problem of the divine-human relationship as applied to problems of human historical knowledge about God, even in revelation. Inquiries into the conditions for the possibility of God may speak about the finite grasp of the infinite or absolute. A similar usage is found in theological inquiries about the mediation of God's absolute truth in historical revelation and in its inspired historical media, Scripture, tradition, and dogma.

Patricia Plovanich

See also KANT, IMMANUEL; ROMANTI-CISM; SCHELLING, FRIEDRICH WILHELM VON; SCHOLASTICISM.

ABSOLUTION

In the sacrament of reconciliation, the declaration by the priest that the penitent has been forgiven the sins he or she has confessed, as well as other sins the penitent has honestly forgotten to confess. Only in extreme circumstances can absolution be given without a prior confession of sins. In the Roman Catholic understanding, this declaration is efficacious, that is, it is the vehicle through which God forgives the sinner. This contrasts with the Lutheran view that the words of absolution are merely a reminder or declaration to a penitent that God has already forgiven one through one's faith in Jesus.

Patrick L. Malloy

See also RECONCILIATION, SACRAMENT OF.

ABSTINENCE

In general, abstinence refers to the ascetical practice of not eating certain foods (particularly meat). It is distinct from the penitential practice of fasting, which entails going without food, and sometimes even without water, for specified periods of time. The motive for abstinence is not always religious, as in the case of those who choose to be vegetarians for reasons of health and diet, or out of a conviction that animals should not be killed for human consumption. The religious justification for abstinence is hard to pinpoint;

the practice seems to rely on the belief that penance, as a sign of earnestness and contrition, adds efficacy to prayer. Some people today view abstinence and fasting as expressions of solidarity with communities of suffering.

The practice of abstaining from meat is ancient and can still be seen today in the church's annual Lenten observance when meat is not eaten on Fridays as a penitential reminder of Jesus' passion and death. Abstinence is not a uniquely Christian practice, and it may be that abstaining from meat has more to do with culture than with the Spirit. (Jesus would certainly have eaten meat as part of the Passover ritual, and there is no indication that he abstained or fasted regularly; see Mark 2:18.) Occasionally, abstinence has also referred to continence, that is, refraining either temporarily or permanently from sexual relations, and to lifelong renunciation of alcoholic beverages.

William Reiser, S.J.

See also ASCETICISM/ASCETIC; CELIBACY; FASTS/FASTING; MORTIFICATION; SACRIFICE.

ABU BAKR (573–634)

Close personal friend of the Prophet Muhammad (570–632 C.E.), the founder of Islam. After the Prophet's death, Abu Bakr became Islam's first caliph, or successor of Muhammad. He served as leader of the Islamic community for only two years—until his death in 634 C.E. Abu Bakr is remembered for his loyalty to the Prophet. He was one of the first to accept Islam and he accompanied Muhammad on his emigration (*hijra*) from Mecca to Medina in 622. Though a wealthy merchant, Abu Bakr had a reputation for compassion toward the poor and slaves. As caliph, he continued the expansion of

Islam throughout Arabia and defended the growing community against the armies of Persia and Byzantium.

Ronald A. Pachence

See also CALIPH (KHALIPHA)/CALIPHATE; HIJRA (IN ISLAM); ISLAM; MUHAMMAD.

ABUNA

Literally meaning "our father," this is the title given to the patriarch of the Monophysite Coptic Church in Ethiopia.

Orlando Espín

See also ANCIENT CHURCHES OF THE EAST; MONOPHYSITISM; NON-CHALCEDONIAN CHURCHES; PATRIARCH.

ACCIDENT

In philosophical and theological discourse, the term "accident" is used to denote any feature of a thing which is such that the thing in question could cease to possess it while still remaining the same individual thing. For example, that a table has been painted blue is an accidental feature of the table, whereas the wood of which the table is constituted is a non-accidental or "essential" feature of its existence. Any object which undergoes changes and modifications on a regular basis has many accidental characteristics. Being a student, wearing a red shirt, having brown hair are all accidents the individual possessing them will lose in the process of changing in minor or significant ways. A being which, by its very nature, does not undergo change of any sort, would not possess any accidental features. Insofar as God's nature is held to be maximally perfect, God is immutable or changeless, since an essentially maximally perfect individual can neither improve nor in any way deterio-

rate. Accordingly, on this view, God is not a possessor of accidents.

Linda L. Peterson

See also ESSENCE.

ACOLYTE

An acolyte is, broadly speaking, an assistant to the presider in a ritual or liturgical celebration. In the medieval period of Western Christianity, the office of acolyte became one of the so-called minor orders that preceded the reception of major orders (deacon, priest, bishop). These orders were structured in a hierarchy, and candidates were required to pass through each one in order to reach the last (subdeacon, until the High Middle Ages, considered a minor order) and move on to the higher offices. Today, in the Roman Catholic Church, the office of acolyte is a ministry one can exercise unofficially (as an altar server) or into which one can be formally instituted.

Joanne M. Pierce

See also LECTOR; MINOR ORDERS; ORDAINED MINISTRIES, SACRAMENT OF; ORDINATION; PRIESTHOOD.

ACTA APOSTOLICAE SEDIS

The official periodical (monthly) publication of the Vatican, started in 1908 by Pius X. It publishes the final texts of all of the Holy See's decrees, decisions, encyclical letters, and so on.

Orlando Espín

See also CURIA, ROMAN; HOLY SEE; PAPACY/PAPAL; POPE; VATICAN.

ACTA SANCTORUM

The famous collection of the lives of the saints arranged in the order of their feast days during the liturgical year. Started by the Bolllandists, a group of Jesuit scholars working under the direction of John van Bolland in the seventeenth century, work on the collections continued into the twentieth century.

Gary Macy

See also HAGIOGRAPHY; SOCIETY OF JESUS; VITA.

ACTS OF THE APOSTLES
A theological interpretation of the history of the early churches intended to complement the Gospel of Luke and written by the same author. While Acts accords with the standards of Hellenistic historical writing in its time, it is not history in the sense found in modern critical, historical documents.

Both the Gospel and Acts are addressed to a certain Theophilus, a believer in Jesus, who may have been an individual known to the author or whose name, meaning "friend or lover of God," could denote any believer. Following upon the Gospel, which describes how the salvation promised to Israel in the Old Testament was realized in Jesus, Acts tells the story of the extension of that salvation beyond the Jews to the Gentiles under the Spirit's guidance. It surveys the activities of numerous followers of Jesus, especially Peter and Paul, from the time of the Ascension of Jesus (early 30s) until the arrival and imprisonment of Paul in Rome (early 60s). This document chronicles primarily those aspects of the development and spread of the Jesus movement that caused it to spread north and west from Judea, that is, from its Jewish matrix in Jerusalem to Rome, the capital of the Roman Empire, and the Gentile milieu in which it flourished.

Because Acts concludes without indicating the outcome of Paul's imprisonment, a few have dated the writing of the text prior to his martyrdom under Nero about 65–67 C.E., although most judge it more likely written between 85–100. Among the latter it remains debated why Acts ends abruptly, for the author surely knew far more of the events of successive decades than he indicates.

While there is widespread agreement that the author of the Gospel of Luke and the author of Acts are the same writer, there is divided opinion about whether this person was actually Luke, the physician, and sometime companion of Paul. In four sections of Acts, known as the "we-passages" (16:10-17; 20:5-15; 21:1-18; and 27:1–28:16), the author switches from writing in the third person to the first person plural, implying that he was accompanying Paul. These sections may be the author's own composition or may come from his travel diary or that of another companion of Paul.

F. M. Gillman

See also GENTILES; LUKE/LUKAN; PAUL; PETER.

ADAM (AS PROPHET OF ISLAM)
The first human being created by God and, according to Muslims, Christians, and Jews alike, the father of all humans. With Jews and Christians, Muslims believe that Adam was created from the "clay" of the earth and that his wife Eve (hawwah in Arabic) was created from his rib. There are, however, two distinctively Muslim beliefs about Adam. First, Muslims accept that Adam sinned against God by eating the forbidden fruit in the Garden of Eden, but they reject the Christian belief that this act caused all subsequent humans to be born with original sin. For them the devil is responsible for sin, not Adam. Second, Muslims speak of Adam as the first prophet or messenger

of God to humankind. God is said to have revealed the Divine Word to him and made him ruler of the earth in God's name (Qur'an 2:30). All subsequent prophets of God, therefore, trace their revelations back to Adam.

Ronald A. Pachence

See also NABI (IN ISLAM); RASUL; REVELATION (IN ISLAM); SIN, ORIGINAL.

ADAM, KARL (1876–1966)

German Catholic theologian. Adam earned a doctorate in church history and patristic theology at Munich (1904), then joined the Catholic faculty at Tübingen (1919) where he studied the Latin Fathers as well as the early Tübingen theologians. He utilized the philosophical categories of Max Scheler and R. Otto to demonstrate faith's relevance for contemporary life. His work *The Spirit of Catholicism* (1924) explored the problem of unity and diversity in the church, proposed an incarnational view of church through the image of the Mystical Body. This image persists in three christological studies: *Christ Our Brother* (1931), *The Son of God* (1934), and *The Christ of Faith* (1957), which reflect Adam's grasp of the issues addressed in later studies of the "Jesus of history." A popular teacher in Germany as well as university professor, Adam anticipated and disseminated many ideas developed later in Vatican Council II.

Patricia Plovanich

See also TÜBINGEN SCHOOL.

ADAM/EVE (IN CHRISTIAN TRADITION)

There are seven references to Adam in the New Testament. These occur in Luke 3:38, Romans 5:14, 1 Corinthians 15:22-45, 1 Timothy 2:13-14.

The Lukan reference occurs in Luke's version of the genealogy of Jesus (cf. Matt 1:1-17). While the Gospel of Matthew traces Jesus' lineage back to Abraham, allowing for the assumption that the bulk of the Matthean community were Jewish converts, Luke appeals to Gentiles as well, tracing Jesus back to Adam, back to the very beginning of humankind, back to before the election of the Jews.

For Pauline theology, Adam is the person through whom sin entered the world, and through sin, death; death came to all because, in Adam, all sinned. Sin was therefore in the world before the law; the knowledge of sin came with Moses (Rom 5:14). First Corinthians 15:22 reads: "For just as in Adam all die, so too in Christ shall all be brought to life," and verse 45: "'The first man, Adam, became a living being,' the last Adam a life-giving spirit." Christ is contrasted with Adam; implicitly, Christ is the new Adam.

Only two passages in the New Testament refer to Eve, 1 Timothy 2:13 and 2 Corinthians 11:3. The 1 Timothy 2:13 passage refers also to Adam. In an effort to defend the exclusion of women from teaching and from having authority over men, the author interprets Genesis 1–3 in a manner that subordinated Eve to Adam: "For Adam was formed first, then Eve. Further, Adam was not deceived, but the woman was deceived, and transgressed" (vv. 13-14).

The Pauline reference to Eve is more traditional. She is not compared to man negatively, but she becomes the symbol of the human community vis-à-vis a faithful God. Paul is concerned that "as the serpent deceived Eve by his cunning, your thought may be corrupted from a sincere (and pure) commitment to Christ" (2 Cor 11:3). Both Adam and Eve are used by the New Testament writers in ways that diminish them.

Alice L. Laffey

ADAM/EVE
(IN THE BOOK OF GENESIS)

The Hebrew word *ʾadam* refers to the first human beings created by God, created male and female (see Gen 1:26-28).

According to the account of creation recorded in Genesis 2, "the Lord God formed man (*ʾadam*) out of the clay of the ground and blew into his nostrils the breath of life, and so that man (*ʾadam*) became a living being" (v. 7). When God determined that it was not good for man *ʾadam* to be alone (v. 18), and that none of the animals God had created was a suitable partner for the man (*ʾadam*, v. 20), "the Lord God cast a deep sleep on the man (*ʾadam*), . . . took out one of his ribs and closed up its place with flesh. The Lord God then built up into a woman the rib that he had taken from the man" (*ʾadam*, vv. 21-22). The woman (*ishah*) became a wife for the man (*ish*) (v. 24).

The term *ʾadam* comes also to refer to the first man over against the first woman. In Genesis 2:25 it is reported that the man (*ʾadam*) and his wife (*ishah*) were both naked.

The name of the first man's wife occurs only three times in the entire Old Testament, two of which are in Genesis (3:20; 4:1). In Genesis 3:20, the "Adam" calls his wife Eve (*hawwah*), because she became the mother of all the living (*hay*). The play on words accentuates the role of Eve in birthing humankind. Genesis 4:1 records Eve's becoming a mother: "The man (*ʾadam*) had relations with his wife (*ishah*), Eve (*hawwah*), and she conceived and bore Cain, saying, 'I have produced a man (*ish*) with the help of the Lord.'"

Alice L. Laffey

ADAM'S SIN

See SIN, ORIGINAL.

ADDAI

Apostle to the Syrians. According to fourth-century legends, King Abgar the Black of East Syria wrote to Jesus asking him for a cure. Jesus wrote back, explaining his mission now was to the Jews, but that help would be sent. The apostles sent the disciple Thaddeus, whose name was shortened to Addai, to cure and convert the king. The apocryphal letters between Abgar and Jesus still exist in many manuscripts. This beautiful legend symbolizes the very early Christianization of Syria by the missionary Addai and his student Mari. Little else is known of these two early Christians, except that one of the earliest Christian liturgies, still used in some communities, is named for them. The liturgy of Addai and Mari is unusual in that it appears to have lacked any words of consecration.

Gary Macy

See also CONSECRATION (CHRISTIAN); LITURGY (IN CHRISTIANITY); LITURGY OF THE EUCHARIST.

AD GENTES

This Vatican II document, The Decree on the Missionary Activity of the Church (commonly known as *Ad Gentes*, the first two words of the Latin text meaning "to the nations or peoples") was promulgated by the Second Vatican Council on December 7, 1965. It ranks among the council's most theologically innovative statements as it attempts to unify previous teachings about salvation with a new appreciation of God's presence and action in human history outside the Catholic Church. On the one hand, the decree reaffirms the church's permanent twofold missionary task of proclaiming the Word of God to all of humanity and of founding new churches in non-Christian regions of the world (no. 1). And while the bishops assert that God wills "that all people come to faith in Jesus Christ and by baptism enter the church which is his body," they recognize, on the other hand, that "God can lead non-Christians to the faith which is necessary for salvation" (no. 7). If salvation is possible outside the church (see earlier conciliar documents *Lumen Gentium* 16 and *Nostra Aetate* 1–2), then why is Catholic missionary activity necessary? The answer lies in the church's duty to purify and perfect whatever truth and grace are already found among non-Christians and, by making known the true meaning of life and the source of all grace, to draw all people into the kingdom of God (no. 9).

To carry out its mission in the world the church "must walk the road Christ himself walked, a way of poverty and obedience, of service and self-sacrifice even to death, a death from which he emerged victorious by his resurrection" (no. 5). But the council shows a keen awareness not only of Christ's poverty, but also of the poor of the world (nos. 12 and 20). The decree places the church's special commitment to the poor at the heart of its mission to be a sign of God's kingdom to all.

James B. Nickoloff

See also LUMEN GENTIUM; MISSIOLOGY; MISSION OF THE CHURCH; MISSIONARIES; MISSIONS; OPTION FOR THE POOR; VATICAN, SECOND COUNCIL OF THE.

"AD LIMINA" VISITS

Every diocesan bishop in the Roman Catholic Church must make a visit to Rome every five years, to consult with the pope and other Vatican officials. These visits are called *ad limina apostolorum* (from the Latin expression "to the threshold of the apostles") because they originally referred to visits of the bishops to the traditional tombs of the apostles Peter and Paul in the city of Rome. All bishops are required to send, prior to the visit, written reports on conditions in their dioceses.

Orlando Espín

See also BISHOP (EPISCOPACY); CURIA, ROMAN; POPE; ROMAN CATHOLIC CHURCH; ROME, SEE OF.

ADONAI

This Hebrew word literally means "my Master," but is usually translated as "Lord." It is used as the Jewish proper name designation for God.

The biblical name of God, YHWH, sometimes known as the tetragrammaton, was considered so holy that it was not pronounced aloud except on certain sacred occasions. *Adonai* was used as a substitute pronunciation for the name of God. Eventually, the original pronunciation of YHWH was lost entirely, so *Adonai* became the accepted pronunciation of God's name.

Now, even the word *Adonai* is considered so holy that it is used only in prayer —in direct communication with God. In its stead, the word *HaShem*, which means "the Name" is used to refer to God.

Wayne Dosick

ADOPTIONISM

Adoptionism means any christology that emphasizes Jesus' human existence and explains the relationship of this humanity to God as one of transformation and divinization at some historical moment, his baptism or resurrection, for instance. The adoption motif taken from Pauline theology is an apt image for conveying transformation. The earliest instances of Adoptionism are second-century Monarchian christological theories that favored the adoption imagery in order to preserve a sense of the divine preeminence and unity against the developing Logos theologies. The Antiochene bishop, Paul of Samosata (260–67) was accused of Adoptionism for resisting Origin's Logos theology, particularly his preexistence imagery. In general, the Antiochene School which emphasized the humanity of Christ preferred such christological approaches from below.

The movement took a clearer shape in eighth-century Europe when Elipandus, the archbishop of Toledo, Spain, proposed an adoptionist interpretation of the relationship between the Father and Christ's humanity. The theory did not reject Logos theology but followed an ancient Spanish tradition of affirming the genuine humanity of Christ in the manner of the Antiochene School. When the Spanish position was adopted by the Frankish theologian, Felix of Urgel, it was condemned by the Council of Frankfurt (794). The theory was soon abandoned in Spain (where it was never condemned since the country was under Moorish control). However, it persisted in northern Europe for several centuries, with versions proposed by Abelard, Gilbert of Porree, and others. Recent theologies that use an ascending formula for christological reflection and base their reflections about Christ's divinity on their study of the historical Jesus have explored the position again. Although the position is generally rejected as unorthodox, the theologians who advocated it generally understood their efforts as a corrective measure against one-sided descending christologies that ponder the divinity of

Christ to the eclipse of his real humanity. Adoptionist christologies do not necessarily, but may involve the denial of Christ's divinity.

Patricia Plovanich

See also CHRISTOLOGY.

ADORATION

Adoration (or *latria*, in Christian theology) is that characteristic of prayer and worship that expresses absolute dependence and humble submission, as a creature might offer the Creator, or a human being might offer a god. In Christianity, adoration in prayer and devotion is offered only to the Three Persons (Father, Son, and Holy Spirit) in the One God, not to other holy beings, either spiritual (e.g., angels) or human (e.g., the Blessed Virgin Mary or the saints). In Christian liturgy, some churches also hold that the bread and wine consecrated at the Eucharist (or Mass) as the Body and Blood of Christ (the incarnate Son of God) may and should also be adored, either during the Eucharist itself, or in other liturgical or private services outside the Eucharist.

Joanne M. Pierce

See also COMMUNION (LITURGICAL); CONSECRATION (CHRISTIAN); DULIA; EUCHARIST; HYPERDULIA; LATRIA; MASS; MONSTRANCE; TRINITY/TRINITARIAN THEOLOGY/TRINITARIAN PROCESSIONS.

ADULTERY

Sexual intercourse between a married man or woman with another who is not that person's spouse. *You shall not commit adultery* is the sixth (seventh in some lists) of the Ten Commandments (Deut 5:18), punishable by death in the Old Testament (Lev 20:10; Deut 22:22). Although this punishment is excessive, it clearly depicts the serious nature of the offense from the religious and social perspectives in the Old Testament. Religiously, adultery was included in one of the Ten Commandments. Socially, adultery is viewed as a direct assault upon the sanctity of the family, and therefore, the stability of society. Jesus upholds the Old Testament condemnation of adultery in the Gospel according to Matthew (5:27-30), yet the evangelist complements it with the Christian *halacha*, that is, the reinterpretation of the commandments themselves according to the fundamental law of love. No longer do we obey the commandments out of fear of divine punishment but out of love for God and neighbor. The sinful nature of adultery is a consistent teaching throughout Christian tradition.

Todd A. Salzman

See also DECALOGUE; DIVORCE (IN CHRISTIANITY); ETHICS, SEXUAL; FAMILY; GERUSHIN.

ADVAITA

An important term in Hindu and Buddhist thought, *advaita* (Sanskrit, nondualism) points to the idea that the universe and all its multiplicity are ultimately expressions or appearances of one essential reality. This one reality, to which everything else is finally reducible, is known in Hinduism as Brahman. Mahayana Buddhist forms of nondualism (*advaya-vada*) speak of overcoming the dichotomies imposed upon the world by conceptual thought, especially the dualism of subject and object and that between phenomena and the Absolute (samsara and nirvana). The term advaita is most commonly associated with the Hindu theological school known as Advaita Vedanta. There are, however, other schools of nondualistic thought within Hinduism, such as the Suddhadvaita of

Vallabha and the nondualistic schools of Kashmir Shaivism.

Lance E. Nelson

See also ADVAITA VEDANTA; DUALISM/ DUALISTIC; DVAITA VEDANTA; MAHAYANA BUDDHISM; NONDUALISM/ NONDUALISTIC; SHAIVA; VALLABHA.

ADVAITA VEDANTA

One of the most influential schools of Hindu theology, Advaita Vedanta was systematized by the theologian Shankara (seventh–eighth century C.E.), also known as Shankaracharya (Shankara the Preceptor). Advaita Vedanta teaches a radical nondualism (*advaita*) of the world, the human self (*jiva*), and Brahman, the ultimate reality. The apparent difference between the manifest world and the divine, in Shankara's view, is a false appearance caused by *maya*, the inexplicable projective power of Brahman. Maya, indeed, is the explanation of all multiplicity and all difference, including the distinctions between self and world, self and other selves, and self and God. The teaching of this school is epitomized in a verse attributed to Shankara: "Brahman is real, the world is a false projection, the individual self (*jiva*) is Brahman, nothing less." Advaita thus believes that only Brahman is real and that the essential self of each individual is fully divine. Indeed, in this way of thinking there is only one true Self, the Atman, which Shankara teaches is identical with Brahman. In this school of thought, *moksha* (liberation) is attained by the direct realization of one's identity with Atman-Brahman, through a kind of direct intuitive awareness (*jnana* or knowledge) facilitated by scriptural study and meditation.

The most authoritative works of the Advaita tradition, other than the scriptural sources themselves, are Shankara's commentaries on the major Upanishads, the *Brahma Sutras*, and the *Bhagavad Gita*. Advaita Vedanta has been and continues to be extremely influential, being the basis of much of modern Hinduism's self-understanding and the image of itself that modern Hinduism presents to the wider world. Not all Hindus, however, accept its premises.

Lance E. Nelson

See also ADVAITA; BRAHMAN; DUALISM/ DUALISTIC; DVAITA VEDANTA; HINDUISM; JIVA; MAYA; VEDANTA; VISHISHTADVAITA VEDANTA; VIVEKANANDA, SWAMI.

ADVENT

Advent (from the Latin word *adventus*, arrival) is the liturgical season that precedes the celebration of Christmas. The idea of a season of preparation before the great feast begins in Western Christianity as a parallel to the season of Lent which came to precede the feast of Easter; therefore, the origins of Lent are earlier than those of Advent. In the early Middle Ages, some parts of Gaul (much of modern-day France) kept a six-week Advent (called "St. Martin's Lent," after the great ascetic saint of Gaul/France, St. Martin of Tours, whose feast day, November 11, fell at the beginning of the period). However, the season was later restricted (according to Roman practice) to the four weeks immediately before Christmas.

The season combines a number of different themes: penance; preparation for the liturgical celebration of a major feast; a liturgical "remembering" of the "coming" of Christ, especially as seen in the writings of the prophets of the Old Testament combined with the expectation of the second coming of Christ in glory (eschatological themes). Coming as it does near the end of the year, these eschatological themes are reinforced. In many Christian traditions, the liturgical color of Advent is violet; however, in the Roman Catholic tradition, the third Sunday is celebrated as a foreshadowing of the rejoicing to come at Christmas (as is the fourth Sunday of Lent). Therefore, this third Sunday of Advent was once known as *Gaudete* (rejoice) Sunday, and the liturgical color used is a lighter violet-pink, known as rose. In medieval England, blue was commonly used for Advent, and the more penitential purple or violet was reserved for Lent.

The season begins on the first Sunday of Advent, which is reckoned to be the first Sunday of the liturgical year; the last Sunday of the year is today celebrated by Catholics as the feast of Christ the King (a feast of twentieth-century origin). In the United States, this first Sunday of Advent is often the Sunday immediately following the national holiday of Thanksgiving.

Joanne M. Pierce

See also CHRIST THE KING; CHRISTMAS; ESCHATOLOGY (IN CHRISTIANITY); LENT; LITURGICAL YEAR; VESTMENTS, LITURGICAL.

ADVENTISTS

Adventists are Christians who believe in the imminent advent or second coming of Jesus Christ. Nearly all early Christians were Adventists in that they expected the parousia, the return of Christ after his death, resurrection, and ascension. After a few years, as the parousia did not occur, hopes faded, and Christians settled in for the long haul, establishing churches, monasteries, and schools. Belief in the Second Coming declined in significance, remaining a central belief of only a few Christian groups at the outskirts of Christendom.

Adventism often included millenarianism, also known as millennialism, the belief that the Second Coming would be accompanied by a thousand-year era of peace and harmony on earth. Some Christians believed that Christ would return after the millennium (postmillennialists), while some preached that the Second Coming would precede the millennium (premillennialists). Both adventism and millenarianism are based on interpretations of biblical prophecy, especially the books of Revelation, Daniel, and Joel.

In the mid-second century, an Adventist movement arose in northern Africa and the eastern Mediterranean. Montanism was led by a former pagan priest, Montanus, and two women, Maximilla and Priscilla. Filled with the Holy Spirit, they prophesied that the new age had dawned. To prepare for Christ's return, they prescribed a rigid moral life to their followers. The majority of Christians rejected Montanism as heresy because it permitted divine revelation outside the Bible, thus threatening the authority of the church.

During the Protestant Reformation in the sixteenth century, many Anabaptists were Adventists in the Netherlands and northern Europe. Leaders included George Blaurock, Conrad Grebel, and Menno Simons. The Anabaptists believed in the radical application of the Gospel to daily life, the complete separation of church from state and society, and believer's baptism. Since many of them had been baptized as infants, their decision to become baptized again as adults earned them the scornful name "Anabaptist" or "rebaptizer." Widely considered subversive, they were persecuted and denounced as heretics.

In the nineteenth century, organized Adventism emerged in the United States. In the early 1840s, a New York farmer named William Miller (1782–1849) predicted that Christ would return in 1843. He calculated the date based on a mathematical code he discovered in Daniel and Revelation. Through revivalistic sermons and graphic charts outlining the chronology of the end of the world, he gathered thousands of followers throughout the northeastern United States. Evangelists, books, pamphlets, even a hymnal, all trumpeted the end of the world.

In January 1843, Miller announced that Christ would return between March 21, 1843, and March 21, 1844. The fervor rose. When March 21, 1844, passed, he confessed he had miscalculated and set a new date, October 22, 1844. Once again, his followers sold their possessions, donned their shrouds, and readied to go to heaven. With the second failure of Miller's predictions, his followers experienced the "Great Disappointment." Some became embittered and left the movement. Others split into a number of smaller Adventist groups. Two of these later reorganized as the Seventh-Day Adventists and the Jehovah's Witnesses.

In the twentieth century, Adventist themes have appeared in Christian groups outside the Seventh-Day Adventists and Jehovah's Witnesses, especially among fundamentalists. Billy Graham and Jerry Falwell, among others, have preached the imminent Second Coming. Hal Lindsey's 1970 best seller *The Late Great Planet Earth* traced the end of the world through contemporary global political events. Christians were exhorted to set their earthly and spiritual affairs in order before Jesus returned, to ensure the state of their souls. Adventist fervor increased as the year 2000 approached.

Evelyn A. Kirkley

See also ANABAPTISTS; FUNDAMENTALISM (CHRISTIAN HISTORICAL MOVEMENT);

JEHOVAH'S WITNESSES; MILLENARIANISM; SEVENTH-DAY ADVENTISTS.

AESTHETICS

The term refers to the study and interpretation of the beautiful in art, nature, and human life. In Western thought, the interpretation of art and beauty as a way of apprehending reality has its roots in the thought of Plato (ca. 429–347 B.C.E.) and Aristotle (384–322 B.C.E.). Aesthetics did not emerge as an intellectual discipline, however, until the eighteenth century. The term was introduced by Alexander Gottlieb Baumgarten (1714–62) in 1750, who defined it as "the science of sensory cognition." By analyzing the role of sensation, intuition, and imagination in the perception and understanding of reality, Immanuel Kant (1724–1804) located aesthetics at the very heart of the philosophical enterprise. Nineteenth-century German philosophy was greatly influenced by Kant's aesthetics. Friedrich Schelling (1775–1845), for instance, believed that art surpasses philosophy in its ability to express reality—though art itself is eventually surpassed by religious mythology. A major critic of German aesthetic philosophies was the Danish theologian Søren Kierkegaard (1813–55), who argued that the aesthetic enjoyment of the beautiful is subordinate to and subsumed within the ethical doing of the good, which is in turn subordinate to and subsumed within the religious act of faith.

In the early twentieth century, aesthetic philosophies had a great impact in Latin American countries. The Mexican philosopher José Vasconcelos (1882–1959) suggested that the most authentic form of knowledge is that expressed in "the aesthetic sense," through which reality is apprehended more immediately and more accurately than through either rational analysis or ethical behavior; in the aesthetic enjoyment of the beautiful, subject and object become "fused" as one. This fusion yields a knowledge superior to that available to reason alone; in order to know another person, one cannot simply observe and analyze him or her, but must enter into an affective, or aesthetic relationship with him or her. To think otherwise is to mistake the human person for a mere inanimate, insensate object. The highest form of "aesthetic fusion" is found in the loving union effected through religious contemplation of the divine nature.

Other twentieth-century philosophers, such as George Santayana (1863–1952), have also affirmed the possibility of a nonempirical, intuitive, imaginal kind of knowledge inaccessible to logical, scientific reason alone—precisely because the object of this knowledge is not simply the empirical, material world, but the timeless realm of spirit, imagination, and beauty manifested in and through the empirical world.

The Catholic theologian Hans Urs von Balthasar (1905–88) has articulated a more explicitly theological aesthetics that grounds the theological enterprise in Christian worship, spirituality, and contemplation of the Beauty and Glory of the Lord. He draws on the rich resources of the Christian mystical tradition, with its emphasis on the contemplation of the Divine Beauty as the heart of Christian faith and theology.

In their critique of modern reason, contemporary postmodern thinkers have also emphasized aesthetics. While logic and reason can live only in the world of abstract, universal concepts, lived reality is concrete, enfleshed, and ambiguous. Aesthetic experience, then, conveys the ambiguity of the world of feelings, the world of embodied life, better than does logical reason. The modern Western identification of aesthetics with the world of feelings has been criticized, however, by Ananda Coomaraswamy (1877–1947), who brought the Western aesthetic tradition into dialogue with Vedic, Buddhist, and Confucian thought. Taking issue with the modern Western tendency to reduce the experience of art to an emotional experience, and to make beauty an end in itself, he believed that art should serve spirituality.

Roberto S. Goizueta

See also ART, LITURGICAL; KIERKEGAARD, SØREN; LITURGY (IN CHRISTIANITY); VON BALTHASAR, HANS URS.

AETERNI PATRIS

Aeterni Patris is the encyclical issued by Pope Leo XIII (1879) establishing Thomism as the preferred philosophical system for Catholic thought. It was written to address a number of nineteenth-century issues: the challenge secular philosophies and political movements of the era posed for religious belief; general unrest in the Catholic community; and in particular, the theological pluralism of the Catholic theology faculties in Europe. Aeterni Patris attributed those problems in part to the use of erroneous philosophies for theological reflection. The letter urged Catholic theologians and philosophers to embrace anew the ancient task of defending faith against the era's errors. Noting the felicitous use of philosophy for apologetics and theological reflection by patristic and Scholastic theologians, Leo singled out the theological synthesis of St. Thomas Aquinas as the paradigmatic instance of true Christian philosophy. The letter then mandates the use of Thomist philosophy in seminaries, pontifical institutes, and by inference, in all Catholic institutions of higher learning.

The encyclical's selection of a single philosophy for theological reflection was unprecedented. It had the immediate effect of establishing one philosophical system as the primary theological language in use for a half century. In short order, Thomism, in its classical or neo-Scholastic forms, became the "Catholic" mode of thought and remains a major influence on the Catholic perception of orthodox faith and theology to the present day. Theological faculties across the church were affected. Theologians who disputed the encyclical were replaced by those who espoused its mandates; some theological faculties maintained their traditions by maintaining a low profile (the Tübingen School). The encyclical had many shortcomings, foremost its assumption about the unitary character of patristic and Scholastic thought. It was unaware of the theological diversity of the Scholastic era, and of the dynamic and experimental character of Aquinas's own thought. The happy outcome of a half-century and more of historical and textual studies of Thomas, other Scholastics, and the church fathers, was the discovery of the dynamic and historical character of the theological enterprise from its inception.

Patricia Plovanich

See also AQUINAS, THOMAS, ST.; SCHOLASTICISM.

AETIOLOGY/ETIOLOGY

As used in biblical studies, aetiology refers to a story or narrative which explains the origin of something known to the writer and their audience. Etiologies can be classified into several types depending on what they are intended to explain.

(a) persons/place names—the name Abraham, "father of a multitude," changed from Abram (Gen 17); the name "Israel" for Jacob (Gen 32); the place name Bethel, "house of El/ God" (Gen 28).

(b) custom/practice—marriage (Gen 2); the social order (Gen 3); not eating the sciatic nerve of animals (Gen 32); circumcision (Gen 17; Exod 4; Josh 5); Passover (Exod 12); the Eucharist (Mark 14; 1 Cor 11).

(c) aspects of culture—Enoch the originator of towns (Gen 4); musical instruments (Gen 4); metal working (Gen 4).

The book of Genesis is especially full of etymologies, which is reasonable since it tells the story of the origins of the physical universe (Gen 1), humanity (Gen 1 and 2); and the people of Israel.

Russell Fuller

AFRICAN AMERICAN THEOLOGY

The terms "African American theology" and "black theology" are, sometimes, used interchangeably. Like black theology, African American theology is faith-motivated inquiry and reflection that investigates the historical, cultural, religious, social (i.e., political, economic, technological), and existential experience of peoples of African descent on the continent and in the diaspora. However, these two forms of theology may be distinguished on the basis of differences of religious, cultural, historical, and social perspective and of methodological development. First, while African American theology is black theology, not all black theology is African American theology. Black theology is a form of critical reflection on the meaning of religious faith to the experience of racial, cultural, and po-

litical oppression common to the descendants of African peoples in the Diaspora —especially in the United States, the Caribbean, and Brazil—as well as on the continent—especially in South Africa. African American theology differentiates the religious, cultural, historical, and social perspective of dispersed Africans in the United States. It gives particular weight to the history of chattel slavery with its protracted influence (even into the twenty-first century) on all interpersonal, cultural, legal, political, economic relations between blacks and other racial ethnic-cultural groups, but especially between blacks and whites; and with its decisive impact on the transmission, practice, and role of Christianity in the United States. Second, without omitting black theology's sharp critique of white racist supremacy, African American theology stands as a fourfold methodological development in black theology: (a) it examines the nature and extent to which the enslaved peoples were able to retain and adapt patterns and practices of their African heritages; (b) it turns to narrative —drawing on the enslaved peoples' accounts of their experience of survival, rebellion, and endurance; (c) it engages the enslaved peoples' encounter with and critical appropriation of the Hebrew and Christian Scriptures, their rejection of the heretical, even idolatrous, Christianity of the slaveholders, and their response to divine revelation in prayer and word, song and dance; and (d) it dialogues with and utilizes the insights and discoveries of cultural anthropology, ethnography, history of religions, and literary theory.

M. Shawn Copeland

See also BLACK THEOLOGY; SLAVERY; SPIRITUALS, AFRICAN AMERICAN; WOMANIST THEOLOGY.

AFRICAN CHRISTIANITY

Christian churches were established in Africa as early as the first century C.E. Roman North Africa was the site of some of the most vigorous and creative communities during the church's patristic period. Many of the great Christian martyrs (for example, Perpetua, Felicity, Cyprian, and others) during Roman persecutions were African; and some of the greatest theologians and bishops of Christian antiquity were also from Africa (for example, Tertullian, Clement of Alexandria, Origen, Athanasius, Augustine of Hippo, and others). Indeed, some of the most important doctrinal controversies and struggles of early Christianity were mainly fought in Africa (for example, Donatism, Arianism, and so on). Most contemporary Christians forget that the church (especially the Western European church) owes to North African Christians much of what today is considered "mainstream Christianity," theologically and institutionally.

Christianity was introduced in Ethiopia (from Alexandria) in the third or fourth century, and it is still the majority religion in that country. Ethiopian Christianity (also known as Abyssinian or Coptic) has usually followed the Monophysite tradition, has survived many persecutions and periods of decline, and has managed to preserve much of the faith and customs of patristic-age Abyssinia. Its liturgical tradition is among the oldest in Christianity.

With the advent of Islam and the Arab invasions, Christianity was relegated to a small presence in the northern part of the continent, while it remained somewhat vigorous only in Ethiopia. During the fifteenth century, Portuguese Catholicism was introduced into present-day territories of Angola, Congo, and Zaire. A century later there was a Catholic bishop in Angola and soon thereafter one in the Congo. Parish churches, mission stations, schools, hospitals, and a seminary, were built in the Angolan and Congolese areas. Slavery (especially promoted by the Europeans), however, sabotaged much of the missionary effort. Further north on the western coast of Africa the Christian presence was insignificant, due also to the slave trade and the African peoples' association of slavery with Christians. It was not until the nineteenth-century abolition of slavery and its infamous commerce in human beings that, slowly, Christianity began to spread again in Africa. Roman Catholics, Anglicans, Presbyterians/Reformed, Baptists, and Methodists have been the most important denominations involved in the missionary effort. Independent, African-born churches have also been very active in the continent since the nineteenth century, sometimes inculturating the Gospel more successfully than missionary denominations from Europe or the U.S., although some of the independent churches have questionable mixtures with non-Christian beliefs.

Contemporary African Christianity has begun to significantly contribute to the worldwide church as well. Archbishop Desmond Tutu, theologian-philosopher John Mbiti, Cardinal Francis Arinze, theologian Mercy Oduyoye, and hundreds more are impacting world Christianity from the African perspective. The rapid growth of the church in the continent is a sign of the future. The Roman Catholic and Anglican Churches, on the one hand, and the recently arrived Pentecostal communities, on the other, appear to be the traditions that will have the greater impact on the future of African Christianity and that will themselves be deeply impacted by the latter. Some significant internal issues still have to be dealt with by the churches (for example, the traditional African notion of marriage, questions on the processes and criteria for ethical decision-making, truly African forms of religious leadership, the real inculturation of the liturgy and of doctrine, and so on); and Christians also have to come to terms with Islam's own missionary efforts in the continent.

Orlando Espín

See also AFRICAN THEOLOGIES; ALEXANDRIAN THEOLOGY; APOSTOLIC FATHERS; COPTIC CATHOLIC CHURCH; COPTIC MONOPHYSITE CHURCH; DOCTORS OF THE CHURCH; FATHERS OF THE CHURCH; INCULTURATION; MBITI, JOHN S.; MISSIONS; MONOPHYSITISM; SLAVERY; TUTU, DESMOND.

AFRICAN THEOLOGIES

By African theologies we mean those (professional, academic) theologies that respond to, and have been created for and by, Christians in sub-Sahara Africa. African theology, in general, is very complex—as complex as the African continent, its peoples, and its realities—and consequently, any serious understanding of this theology requires a sustained (and prior) appreciation of its birthing contexts.

It is undeniable that theology and Christianity in sub-Saharan Africa were born under the shadow of colonialism and as by-products thereof. As R. Riches has said, Christianity arrived in Africa as colonizer and not as servant, even when it presented itself as servant—because, while claiming the latter role, it had already decided (before its arrival in Africa) whom it was going to serve and how, and what the recipients of its missionary efforts really needed. Christianity was a servant who considered itself "evidently" superior to those it pretended to serve, and hence Christianity frustrated most efforts at actually listening to or learning from the recipients of its mission. Colonization and Christianity came to Africa as parts of the same Western imperial expansion, and have remained linked to one another even after the independence of the African nations. It is within this historical context that African theologies were born.

Three broad theological *movements* might be discerned in African theologies since the nineteenth century: missionary theology, African theology, and Black theology. These three movements are not to be understood chronologically (that is, as one evidently following the other in history) but rather as distinct perspectives that often overlapped during the same historical periods. Nevertheless, missionary theology seems to have appeared first.

1. *Missionary theology movement*. Influenced by, or elaborated from, the nineteenth-century German Catholic theology of mission, the missionary theology movement (crafted mostly by European missionaries) became the main Christian reflection in and for Africa at least until the 1960s and 1970s. It began by emphasizing the crucial and foremost importance of the "salvation of souls" (of the Africans' souls) as the main goal of mission, and all theological reflections (within this perspective) became justifications or explanations of that missionary goal. Thinking somewhat simplistically that "outside the church there is no salvation" (*extra ecclesiam nulla salus*) missionary theology's first thrust was to announce the Gospel to non-Christian Africans to save their souls from the (for the missionaries) evident prospect of eternal perdition. In this context, the cultures, religions, and so forth, of the recipients of mission

became ultimately irrelevant. There was no need to engage cultures or religions in dialogue, except perhaps to demonstrate their demonic side or to promote their prompt demise. Europeanization of converts, consequently, became a useful tool in the missionaries' efforts at saving the African converts' souls. What was culturally or religiously African was the alternative to be rejected by converts who accepted Christianity. Among the main proponents of this "salvation of souls" trend within the missionary theology movement were T. Ohm, K. Müller and J. Dournes—all European-born.

A variation of this first thrust of missionary theology came to be known as the theology of *plantatio Ecclesiae* ("church planting"). Beginning in the 1920s, this theological vision and justification of mission competed with the "salvation of souls" theology. The *plantatio Ecclesiae* theologians (almost all European-born) thought that what Africa and Africans needed was the effective presence of the church—understanding the "planting" of this ecclesial presence as the establishment in Africa of the European, Western model of Christianity. Again, this other trend within missionary theology disregarded all possible contributions from or dialogue with the recipients of Christian missions, assuming Europeanization as an indispensable or at least very useful outcome among converts. The church was "planted" in Africa, but as a European church among non-Europeans (that is, a church with European institutions, internal organization, and laws, liturgy and catechesis, spiritualities and religious life, theologies and theologians, and self-understanding—in brief, a church alien to Africa and among Africans). Among the main proponents of the *plantatio Ecclesiae* trend within the missionary theology

movement were J. Bruls, W. Bühlmann, and E. Loffeld.

2. *African theology movement.* Beginning in the 1950s but becoming more important and better known after the 1960s and 1970s, theologians in Africa (now many of them natives of Africa) started questioning the missionary theology movement in which they had been educated, and which had been presented to them as the best for their continent. Their questioning in time led to serious critique and rejection of both the "salvation of souls" and *plantatio Ecclesiae* models. But we must distinguish between two different trends within the African theology movement.

It seems clear that a widespread trend within late twentieth-century African theology has advocated (and still advocates) for the adaptation of Christianity to African reality. "Inculturation" has often been the key proposal of many of this trend's proponents. These theologians promote an Africanized church with an African face. The way to achieve this Africanization of Christianity is by the adaptation ("inculturation," in their understanding) of Gospel and church to African cultures, in order to make Christianity understandable for and responsive to African Christians. These theologians have insisted that Gospel and church must be adapted into non-European (African!) forms in Africa. This theological proposal found great success among pastoral agents in the years immediately following the Second Vatican Council, for example. However, a very serious difficulty faced by this trend within the African theology movement is closely associated with the problems inherent to all inculturation—is there ever (could there ever be) a non-"culturalized" Gospel or church that exists in a "pure" state among *any* group of Christians? Evidently not, and therefore it seems that the main difficulty with the "adaptation" trend within the African theology movement is that *what* it proposes to adapt in and for Africa remains *what* European Christians (in European cultural forms and terms) determined to be "Gospel" and "church." The dangers of ongoing colonization, now through "adaptation," remain intact. Among the main proponents of this trend within the African theology movement are V. Mulago, M. F. Lufuluabo and A. Kagame.

A second trend within the African theology movement could be described as an African "critical theology." The proponents of this trend understand the dangers inherent in the "adaptation" or "inculturation" model, although they have not hesitated to support it whenever the alternative has been the missionary theology movement (so explicitly associated and aligned with European colonialism). African critical theology proposes not the adaptation of Gospel and church but, rather, an effective rediscovery and retrieval of authentic African values, perspectives, (traditional non-Christian) theologies and philosophies, ritual forms, and so forth, that may then be placed in sustained dialogue with Gospel and church. From this ongoing dialogue, these theologians believe, an authentic *African* proclamation and understanding of the Christian Gospel may yet emerge, as well as the forms of a truly African church. The critical theology trend adamantly insists on the cultural contextuality and limits of all theologies. Consequently, this critical trend rejects all universal and universalizing pretensions of European (and American) theologies or philosophies. It seems clear, therefore, that the critical theology approach within the African theology movement is very much aware of the limits and dangers of inculturation. Its proposal is not one of Africanization but of the radical rebirth of Christianity in Africa as a consequence of the dialogue between today's African Christians and the continent's traditional religions and philosophies, social and cultural contexts, and the like. Among the main proponents of this trend within the African theology movement are A. N. Mushete, J. S. Mbiti, M. A. Oduyoye, and E. Messi Metogo.

3. *Black theology movement*. Mostly present in South Africa (since the early 1970s), but with important inroads in other nations of the continent, the Black theology movement began under the influence and guidance of James Cone's Black theology in the United States. After an initial period of imitation and repetition of Cone and others, South African theologians began to intimately connect the growing political, social, cultural, and economic self-awareness of black South Africans, and their increased protagonism, with a liberationist interpretation of the Christian Gospel and of the mission of the church. African Black theology, therefore, became not a proposal for the Africanization of Christianity nor for the birth of an authentically African Christianity. It is a sustained reflection on and justification for the complete liberation of all (black!) Africans. Furthermore, within the African Black theology movement, another (but as of yet less influential) current of thought wants to further distinguish between whites and blacks (worldwide, and not just in Africa) and emphatically deny legitimacy among blacks to all (cultural, religious, and so on) forms and mentalities that either come from nonblacks or that have been "tainted" by nonwhites. Finally, also within the African Black theology movement, a (small) third current of thought

employs Christian theology in order to challenge the legitimacy among Africans of (European and Europeanized) Christianity's universal claims, proposing instead a sustained, fierce critique of Christianity as it was brought to Africa and as it has grown therein, adamantly denying it universal validity among Africans. This third current has become increasingly involved with efforts to theologically justify a return to authentic, traditional African religions. Among the main proponents of the various currents of thought within Africa's Black theology movement are M. Buthelezi, A. Boesak, D. Makhatini, and O. p'Bitek.

Orlando Espín

See also AFRICAN CHRISTIANITY; BLACK THEOLOGY; CONE, JAMES H.; CONTEXTUAL THEOLOGY; CULTURE; EXTRA ECCLESIAM NULLA SALUS; GRACE; INCULTURATION; INTERCULTURAL THOUGHT; LIBERATION THEOLOGIES; MISSIOLOGY; MISSIONS; ODUYOYE, MERCY AMBA; SALVATION.

AFRICAN TRADITIONAL RELIGIONS

Religion permeates all of traditional Africa's life. There is no possible distinction there between the sacred and the secular, because all that exists is ultimately (potentially or actually) sacred. Indeed, most African languages do not even have a separate word for "religion."

Traditional religions in Africa exist for and because of the community. Individuals do not choose their religious affiliation. In traditional African society all members of the community share in their community's religion. Communal life demands total participation and, consequently, one cannot detach oneself from the beliefs, rituals, festivals, of the human community to which one belongs and which defines one's humanness. Non-Africans have a very difficult time understanding the complete participatory nature of traditional Africa's worldview and cultures. Without this holistic, religious immersion in communal reality, African individuals would find themselves in extreme meaninglessness and uprootedness. No African community could exist as African without religion.

African traditional religions do not formulate their beliefs in European-like systematic sets of dogmas that are accepted in faith. These religions are really not taught but "caught" from family and neighbors, and from frequent liturgical practices as well as from (often sophisticated) storytelling traditions. Africa's traditional religions have been called "performed religions" for good reason.

The only authorities, as to a belief's or a practice's "orthodoxy," are tradition and common sense. In these traditional religions, there are no teaching hierarchies or authorities outside the local village or town. All orthodoxy, therefore, is ultimately determined locally. There are no holy scriptures, but there is a carefully preserved oral "holy history." Traditional religions are not written down but are transmitted through memory, rite, and symbol.

Every person in an African traditional religion is a carrier and transmitter of the religion. There are religious "specialists" (priests, priestesses, storytellers, music players, and others), but these are usually local leaders serving local communities, and by no means the sole bearers of the religious traditions of their people. The traditional religions are always local or tribal, seldom national, and never universal. Rarely in Africa's history has one community's religion been propagated and adopted by another community (except fragments of belief or practice, and these usually through war, conquest, or trade). Missionary activity, therefore, is not known among them. African traditional religions have no founders and few known reformers in their very long history.

Most of Africa's traditional religions believe in some sort of original and originating supreme deity (the only one who could properly be called "god"). This supreme divinity is usually conceived of as a *deus otiosus*; although this high god is the ultimate explanation of all that is, was, or will be. Other creator beings (either a couple or a single being both masculine and feminine) are really the ones responsible for all that exists, there being no sense of natural evolution. "Time" is always religious time—the individual and the community are inevitably caught up in the unfolding of religious drama in which past and present are crucial, but the future of little consequence. Change (even a future divine intervention), therefore, is not a religious expectation. The afterlife is always (and only) conceived of and expressed in material, human terms that parallel the present.

The everyday lives of the people are under the guidance and influence of dozens of "spiritual beings" (not really "gods"). These "beings" are either personifications of the supreme god's attributes (for example, justice, wisdom), or of nature's elements and forces (for example, lightning, the sea, metals), or of the spirits of great ancestors or past leaders (for example, Shangó), or even personifications of qualities and experiences that attract or terrify (for example, fertility, death). Animals and plants are viewed as bearers of life and power, too.

Most African traditional religions engage in animal sacrifice, in food offerings, in ritual possessions, and in dozens of other rites and festivities. The purpose of the complex liturgical practices of these religions is threefold—to obtain help in dealing with specific problems in daily life; to guarantee peace with the past and with the ancestors; and to protect the present and the immediate future. Ethical/moral evil is known in the traditional religions of Africa, but it is almost always viewed as acts that either profane religious ritual or, more importantly, endanger the community's internal peace and relationships.

The advance of modern life in contemporary Africa, as well as the successes of Christianity and Islam, have created immense challenges to the continent's traditional religions. Secularization and individualism can destroy the "Africanness" of the cultures. Perhaps the Roman Catholic/Anglican communions and Islam have been spreading in Africa because they each have managed to provide complete communities (new "villages") within which converts may find total identity, life, and meaning.

Orlando Espín

See also AFRO-LATIN RELIGIONS; CAMDOMBLÉ; DIVINATION; DRUMS (IN AFRICAN AND AFRO-LATIN RELIGIONS); PALO MAYOMBE; RELIGION; SANTERÍA; UMBANDA; VODOUN.

AFRO-LATIN RELIGIONS

The religions of Africa that were brought to the Western Hemisphere (more specifically to the French, Portuguese, and Spanish colonies) and were there adapted and streamlined by the slaves. Strictly speaking, Afro-Latin religions are not African traditional religions "imported" to the Americas. Changes wrought during the colonial slavery period did not permit the straightforward continuation of the African religious universe; however, the latter was sufficiently preserved, but in streamlined fashion. The Yoruba, Fon, and Kongo-Angolan peoples (from western Africa) are the historical sources of most Afro-Latin religions.

These religions are not a mixture of Catholicism and African traditions (as too many authors like to repeat), but are the result of long and often painful processes of adaptation to and survival in the colonial realities of Latin America. The use of Catholic symbols and images has always remained peripheral to the religious core, and is more accurately understood as a successful self-defense mechanism. Catholicism has not changed —in any significant way—the worldview, liturgies, doctrines, or mythologies of these religions. Slavery (and most of what was implied in it) had a much deeper impact. In studying Afro-Latin religions, one must also remember that they are accompanied (as most religions are) by "popular" versions of themselves.

There are a significant number of these Afro-Latin religions. Some of them are sophisticated and traditional (for example, Santería, Candomblé), and have managed to successfully preserve and adapt their original (usually Yoruba) mythologies, doctrines, and liturgies, as well as priesthood. Other religions have undergone more significant changes, but still cling to the rituals and worldview of the (usually Fon) slave ancestors while suffering the loss of most of their mythologies and doctrines (for example, Haitian and Dominican Vodoun). There are some religions that exist in Latin America as separate religious traditions, while in Africa they were but one group or "fraternity" within a larger religion (for example, Abakuá in Cuba, Ayé in Venezuela, Shangó in Trinidad).

There are still some religions in Latin America that are only peripherally related to Africa, and that incorporate African elements with native and European ones. These—and only these—religions are syncretic, properly speaking (for example, Umbanda).

Although it is very difficult to know with certainty, it seems that a total of approximately forty-five million people actively participate in Afro-Latin religions throughout the world today. Most of the members of the religions have historically concentrated in Brazil, Cuba, Haiti, and the Dominican Republic, with smaller groups spread throughout the whole Caribbean Basin. Nowadays followers of Afro-Latin religions may be found in most Latin American countries, the United States, Canada, and several European countries. Many races and ethnic groups are currently represented in the religions.

Orlando Espín

See also AFRICAN TRADITIONAL RELIGIONS; CANDOMBLÉ; DIVINATION; DRUMS (IN AFRICAN AND AFRO-LATIN RELIGIONS); GROUND PAINTING (IN AFRICAN AND AFRO-LATIN RELIGIONS); HISPANIC; LATINO/A; LATINO CATHOLICISM; MACUMBA; PALO MAYOMBE; SANTERÍA; UMBANDA; VODOUN.

AGAPĒ

In the Hellenistic world there were three words for "love." The two most often used were *eros*, which meant sexual, carnal love, and *philos*, meaning friendship, meanings that might also vary depending on their context. *Agapē* was a rather unspecific term seldom employed.

The Septuagint, however, with its stress upon divine love as a gift of God, and in avoidance of the sensual associations borne by *eros*, used *agapē* somewhat and even more so its verb form *agapao*, "to love," when speaking theologically of love.

In contrast to normal Greek usage, but in keeping with and further developing the trend in the Septuagint, *agapē* is the most frequently used word for "love" in the New Testament, with *philos* still used as well, and *eros* not at all.

Agapē in the New Testament refers both to the unconditional love of God for humanity shown in the sending of Jesus as Redeemer and to the love Christians must have for each other. A discussion of agapaic love is found, for example, in 1 Corinthians 13. *Agapē* in Greek was usually translated into Latin as *caritas*, thus supplying the original meaning of "charity" in English.

By extension, one early Christian use of the term *agapē* was to name certain fellowship meals. These reflected the concrete practicality of the expression of Christian love by offering occasions for charity toward poorer church members. Such *agapē* meals, or love feasts, as are mentioned in Jude 12, came to be associated with eucharistic celebrations in early Christian practice (see 1 Cor 11:18-34).

F. M. Gillman

See also EUCHARIST; LOVE (IN GENERAL); SEPTUAGINT.

AGGADAH

(Alternative: Haggadah). In Judaism, a Hebrew term referring to homiletical tales or expositions of Scripture; contrasted with Halakhah or legal discussions. Aggadah is found throughout the Talmud, but is the particular province of the Jewish literature of scriptural exegesis known as Midrash. Alongside line-by-line interpretations of Scripture, the Aggadic literature presents folkloristic stories, allegories, anecdotes, and maxims of the sages and common people alike.

Alan J. Avery-Peck

See also ALLEGORY IN JUDAISM.

AGGIORNAMENTO

Italian for "bringing up to date." This word was used by Pope John XXIII in announcing the Second Vatican Council (1962–5). In using this word, the Pope indicated that the council's emphasis would be on "renewal" rather than condemnation of heresy or defensive definitions of dogma.

Mary Ann Hinsdale

See also COUNCIL, ECUMENICAL; JOHN XXIII, POPE; VATICAN, SECOND COUNCIL OF THE.

AGNI

The Hindu god of fire and associated phenomena, Agni was especially important in the *Rig Veda* and Vedic religion as the power of life and conveyer of sacrificial offerings to the gods. In post-Vedic Hinduism, Agni is less important, but he still figures significantly in the domestic rites of ritually observant Hindus belonging to the three uppercaste categories (*varnas*).

Lance E. Nelson

See also HINDUISM; VEDAS; YAJNA.

AGNOSTICISM

The position "I do not know" regarding the proposition, "God exists," thus neither affirming nor denying the existence of God. More generally, the term is used to describe a skepticism regarding religious claims.

J. A. Colombo

AGRICOLA, JOHANN
(CA. 1494–1566)

Born in Eisleben Saxony-Anhalt (Germany), Agricola studied under Martin Luther at Wittenberg. He returned to spread the Reformation message in his home town and also in Frankfurt. He and Luther disagreed when Agricola espoused Antinomianism. In 1540 Agricola moved to Berlin where he recanted his earlier views on Antinomianism. The recantation, however, did not appease Luther. He was appointed court preacher and General-Superintendent in the court of Brandenburg, influential posts he held until his death in 1566. Agricola is also famous for being the first person to publish books of German proverbs.

Gary Macy

See also ANTINOMIANISM; LUTHER, MARTIN.

AHIMSA

An ideal highly valued in all Indic religions, ahimsa (Sanskrit, noninjury) was first articulated in non-Vedic ascetic traditions, in opposition to the Vedic practice of animal sacrifice. It emerged as a dominant ethical principle in Jainism and Buddhism, and was also incorporated into Hinduism, where it is identified as "the highest dharma" (moral duty) in the Mahabharata and the first of the ethical precepts (yama) in the Yoga Sutras. The doctrine of ahimsa teaches that harm to living beings should be carefully avoided, to the maximum extent possible. This is in part out of compassion for other creatures, in a religious context in which all beings in the transmigratory process have equal spiritual potential, and in part out of the desire to avoid the bad karma that would accrue to the injurer. Vegetarianism is an ideal typically associated with its practice. Jainism is known for observing the principle of nonviolence most strictly; Jains are required to be strict vegetarians and encouraged to actively protect animals, even insects and smaller life forms, from harm. Mohandas Gandhi, who developed the ideal of ahimsa into a force for political change that he called satyagraha, grew up in a part of India where there were many Jains, and was deeply influenced by their teachings.

Lance E. Nelson

See also BUDDHISM; DHARMA (IN HINDUISM); GANDHI, MOHANDAS K.; HINDUISM; JAINISM; KARMA; SATYAGRAHA; VEDAS; YAJNA; YAMA (PRACTICE); YOGA SUTRAS.

AHL AL-KITAB
("PEOPLE OF THE BOOK")

The term used by Muslims for those who believe in the Qurʾan, who follow the Jewish Scriptures, the Sabians, and the Christians, indeed are people "who believe in God and the Last Day, and work righteousness" (Qurʾan, 5:69; see also 5:51). Though the reference to the Sabians is ambiguous, it is clear that all Jews and Christians are included in this designation. By "the Book," Muslims mean the revelation of God as given to prophets from Adam, the first prophet, to Muhammad (d. 632), the last prophet. In effect, "People of the Book" are believers in the one God, and whether these people profess Islam or not, Muslims are commanded to treat them with respect. Throughout their history, Muslims have honored this teaching by allowing Christians and Jews in conquered lands to practice their religion without interference from Islamic authorities.

Ronald A. Pachence

See also ADAM (AS PROPHET OF ISLAM); DHIMMI; QURʾAN.

AHMADIYYA

Also referred to as the Ahmadis, the Ahmadiyya is an officially recognized sect of Islam found mostly in northern India and Pakistan, though there are also Ahmadis in Iran, Africa, Saudi Arabia, and Afghanistan. Established in the Punjab (India) in 1882 by Mirza Ghulam Ahmad (1835–1908), Ahmadiyya began as a reaction against Christian missionary and Western colonizing efforts in the Islamic world. Mirza Ghulam did not advocate violence against the West. Rather, he called for peaceful resistance, claiming to be the *Mahdi*, "the guided one" whom some Muslims believe will appear to establish universal peace just before the end of time. He also announced that he was Jesus Christ returned to earth and an *avatar* of the Hindu deity Vishnu. Not long after Mirza Ghulam's death, Ahmadiyya split into two rival groups, the Qadianis and the Lahorites in a dispute over interpretations of the founder's mission. They remain united, however, in their fierce opposition to Christianity, which they say has deviated from the original revelation of Jesus.

Ronald A. Pachence

See also AVATARA/AVATAR; MAHDI.

AHRIMAN

See ANGRA MAINYU; ZOROASTRIANISM.

AHURA MAZDA

The quasi-monotheistic Supreme Deity of Zoroastrianism, Ahura Mazda (Lord Wisdom) is the creator of the world, all-knowing and all-good. He commands the forces of good in the battle against cosmic evil. The Avestan name Ahura Mazda is, in the later tradition, shortened to Ohrmazd.

Lance Nelson

See also DUALISM/DUALISTIC; ZOROASTER; ZOROASTRIANISM.

AL-ASHʾARI/ASHʾARISM

Abu-l-Hasan al-Ashʾari (873–935 C.E.), an Islamic theologian, is often described as the founder of Sunni Muslim theology. He began his intellectual career as a Muʾtazilite, a rationalist school of Islamic thought that challenged such revealed Qurʾanic doctrines as the uncreated nature of the Qurʾan, predestination, and the attributes of God. Though he never lost his interest in the logical foundation of Muʾtazilite philosophy, he came to recognize the transcendent dimension of his faith and the inability of rational discourse to fathom the mystery of the divine. A prolific writer, al-Ashʾari made a public confession of his errors and spent the rest of his life using his knowledge of the philosophical method to refute the errors of rationalist Muslim scholars. He is credited with the substance of *Fiqh Akbar II*, a creed or profession of Muslim belief, in which the major tenets of orthodox Islam are presented in clear, simple statements. An important affirmation of this creed summarizes al-Ashʾari's post-Muʾtazilite position: "We do not question: in what sense?" When revealed truth seems to contradict human logic, he was saying, the problem is not with the truth. It lies with the poverty of the intellect.

Ronald A. Pachence

See also AL-MATURIDI; KALAM; MUʾTAZILITES; SUNNA/SUNNI/SUNNISM.

ALAYA VIJNANA

"Storehouse consciousness," a term that the Yogachara Buddhist school employed to explain the means of connecting past, present, and future karmic accumulations.

Alaya vijnana is described as a subconscious "stream," with later philosophers identifying it with the ultimate reality from which the individual constructs the world. It is into this storehouse consciousness that the "seed-like" effects of actions (*karma*), habit energies, and personality dispositions are deposited to "sprout" and shape the future.

Todd T. Lewis

See also ASANGA; CITTAMATRA; LANKAVATARA SUTRA; YOGACHARA.

ALBERT THE GREAT (CA. 1200–80)

A theologian, philosopher, scientist, and bishop, the Dominican friar Albert was considered one of the greatest minds of his time. Albert was born in Germany, but studied in Bologna and Padua where he joined the Dominicans in 1222. Albert taught in several Dominican houses in Germany before going to Paris in the early 1240s. He held the Dominican chair in theology at Paris from 1245 to 1248. From 1248 until 1253, Albert taught at the new Dominican school in Cologne. The famous Dominican theologian, Thomas Aquinas, was a student of Albert's both in Paris and in Cologne. Albert took over as provincial of the German Dominicans in 1253, and became bishop of Regensberg from 1260 to 1262. In 1262 he returned to teaching for the Dominicans. Albert contributed greatly to the understanding and acceptance of Aristotle's metaphysics and natural philosophy (science). He commented on most of Aristotle's writing, as well as on the *Sentences* of Peter Lombard and on Scripture.

Gary Macy

See also AQUINAS, THOMAS, ST.; ARISTOTLE; MEDIEVAL CHRISTIANITY (IN THE WEST); SCHOLASTICISM.

ALBIGENSIANS

The city of Albi in southern France was seen in the twelfth and thirteenth centuries as the center of heretical activity in Europe. The term "Albigensian" came to refer to heretics in general, but particularly to the Cathars and Waldensians. Albi was, in fact, the see of the first Cathar bishop. Most modern historians use "Albigensian" to refer only to the Cathars.

Gary Macy

See also CATHARS; CRUSADES; HERESY; MEDIEVAL CHRISTIANITY (IN THE WEST); WALDENSIANS.

ALBRIGHT, WILLIAM FOXWELL

William Foxwell Albright was one of the most important and influential figures in the areas of Old Testament Studies and biblical archeology in the twentieth century. He received his doctorate from Johns Hopkins University in 1916 and became professor of Semitic Languages there in 1929. He was the director of the American School of Oriental Research in Jerusalem from 1920–9 and 1933–6. He recognized the importance of integrating archaeological and inscriptional data from the ancient Near East for improving the understanding of the origins and history of the Hebrew Bible and the religion of ancient Israel. He was one of the first scholars to recognize the antiquity and importance of the Dead Sea Scrolls for biblical studies and the study of early Judaism and Christianity.

Russell Fuller

ALCUIN (CA. 730–804)

Alcuin is best known as the head of the palace school of Charlesmagne from 782 until 792. His career as a scholar starts much earlier, however. He was a student at the cathedral school of York where he started teaching in 768. Alcuin became the head of that school in 778. Charlesmagne asked Alcuin to take over the imperial palace school in 782 and from that point, Alcuin became the leader of band of scholars who saw themselves as the "new Athens" of Christian learning. From this post, Alcuin was in an important position to influence and implement the reforms Charlesmagne wished to impose on his vast empire. Alcuin established a course of studies based on the classical *trivium* (grammar, rhetoric, and dialectic) and *quadrivium* (arithmetic, geometry, music, and astronomy). Alcuin also worked to correct the Latin text of the Bible, wrote scriptural commentaries, and was involved in the Adoptionist and iconoclast controversies. In order to write more quickly, the scribes of the palace developed a cursive form of writing called the Carolingian minuscule, the forerunner of our present cursive writing. Alcuin also aided Charlesmagne to provide a uniform liturgy for the empire. Alcuin retired from the palace school in 796 to become the abbot of St. Martin's in Tours. There he continued his scholarly work until his death on May 19, 804.

Gary Macy

See also ADOPTIONISM; CHARLESMAGNE; ICONOCLASTIC CONTROVERSY; MEDIEVAL CHRISTIANITY (IN THE WEST).

ALEGRE, FRANCISCO XAVIER (1729–88)

Mexican philosopher. A member of the Society of Jesus (Jesuits) since 1747, Alegre had been born in the city of Veracruz. He studied in Jesuit schools in Puebla and Mexico City, and later taught both in his native Mexico and in Cuba. In 1767 he was expelled by royal decree, together with all other Jesuits in the Spanish colonies, and was sent to Italy where he lived (in Bologna) until his death. Most of his writings were published in Venice after 1788. Alegre today might be called a "legal philosopher," or a philosopher of the law. In his works he discussed the foundations of law and of legal systems, and theorized on the natural law. His thought, even though rooted in his eighteenth century, was clearly ahead of his time. Indeed, Alegre was both a proponent of modernity and the Enlightenment, as well as one of its earlier and more insightful critics in Mexico. Much of what he critiqued in modernity has been repeated by many of today's postmodern theorists. Some of his philosophical and legal thought is found in his *Institutiones theologicarum* (1789).

Orlando Espín

See also CLAVIGERO, FRANCISCO XAVIER; ENLIGHTENMENT (IN WESTERN HISTORY); GUADALUPE, VIRGIN OF; LATIN AMERICAN CATHOLICISM; METHOD IN THEOLOGY; MODERNITY; POSTMODERNITY; SOCIETY OF JESUS.

ALEXANDER OF ALEXANDRIA (312–28 C.E.)

Patriarch of Alexandria. Alexander became the head of the Alexandrian church during troubled times. His predecessor, Peter, had been martyred and a schism resulting from the persecution split the community. To make matters worse, one of Alexandria's most learned and popular priests, Arius, began expounding the teaching that the Logos, or Son of God, was not equally divine with the Father. Alexander assembled a synod of one hundred bishops that condemned the teaching of Arius. Arius appealed to his powerful friends among the Eastern bishops, especially his classmate, Eusebius of Nicomedia. Arius's teaching was formally condemned at the Council of Nicaea in 325. Alexander died a few years later, to be succeeded as patriarch by his secretary, Athanasius.

Gary Macy

See also ALEXANDRIAN THEOLOGY; ARIUS; ATHANASIUS, PATRIARCH OF ALEXANDRIA; NICAEA, FIRST COUNCIL OF.

ALEXANDER OF HALES
(CA. 1186–1245)

Born in Halestown, England, Alexander studied philosophy and theology at the University of Paris, where from around 1220 until his death he was a regent master of theology. Roger Bacon, a fellow theologian of the time, called him "a good and rich man, and also a great master of theology in his time." In 1236, to the wonder of everyone, he gave up his wealth and became a Franciscan. He kept his position as a theologian, however, and so the Franciscans now had their first chair of theology at Paris. Alexander was one of the first theologians in Paris to use the *Sentences* of Peter Lombard as the textbook for theology, and his teaching greatly influenced succeeding generations of scholars.

Gary Macy

See also FRANCISCANS; MEDIEVAL CHRISTIANITY (IN THE WEST); SCHOLASTICISM.

ALEXANDER THE GREAT
(356–323 B.C.E.)

(A.k.a. Alexander III). Alexander was born in Macedonia in 356 B.C.E., the son of Philip of Macedon. He was arguably one of the greatest generals and military strategists of the ancient world. Between 336 and 323 he conquered the Persian Empire and most of the known world. His conquests extended from Greece to India and included Syria-Palestine and Egypt. Wherever Alexander went he founded cities (reportedly over seventy) based on the Greek model. He fostered the spread of Greek or Hellenistic culture and the Greek language. He died in Babylon in 323 B.C.E. apparently of a fever following a drinking party. His generals fought until 275 B.C.E. over who was to succeed him. Three empires emerged led by three of his generals; the Antigonids ruled in Macedon until 168 B.C.E.; the Seleucids ruled in Syria until 64 B.C.E.; and the Ptolemies ruled in Egypt until 31 B.C.E. The influence of Alexander on the ancient world is briefly told in 1 Maccabees 1.

Russell Fuller

ALEXANDRIAN THEOLOGY

Founded by Alexander the Great in 331 B.C.E., the city of Alexandria in Egypt with its museum and great library established by Ptolemy I in 280 B.C.E. was a major center of Greek learning. Within a few years of its establishment Alexandria had a large Jewish population. The Alexandrian Jewish community in the second century B.C.E. had the Hebrew Scriptures translated into a Greek version known as the Septuagint. Here in the first century the great Jewish religious thinker Philo lived and worked. Christianity arrived early at Alexandria. In the second century the city's large Christian population benefited from a cathechetical school founded by Pantaenus. Under its directors Clement of Alexandria and Origen a specifically Alexandrian style of theology began to emerge. Alexandrian Christian theology attempted to show how the Greek literary and philosophical tradition could support Christian doctrine. Following Philo's example, Alexandrian theology imitated his use of the allegorical method to understand Scripture. Though eclectic in borrowing from the Greek tradition of philosophy, Alexandrian theology generally adopted Platonic or Neoplatonic philosophical positions.

Simultaneously employing both allegorical biblical interpretation and Platonic philosophy, Alexandrian theology upheld the divinity of the eternal Logos and the physical reality of the incarnate Word. St. Athanasius and St. Cyril of Alexandria are major orthodox exemplars of Alexandrian theology. Athanasius defended the divinity of the eternal Logos against Arius. St. Cyril championed against Nestorius the physical reality of the union of the Word with the human nature the Word assumed in the Incarnation. Some proponents of the Alexandrian theology carried its theological concerns to extremes. Apollinaris (d. ca. 390), bishop of Laodicea in Syria, a friend and supporter of Athanasius, insisted on the immediate union of the Logos with physical humanity in Christ. However, Apollinaris did so in such a way that he made the Logos the very life-principle or intellect of Jesus. For Apollinaris Christ is one composite nature with Christ's body so knit together with the Godhead that Jesus was not really a human being because he lacked a human intellect, will, and self. The Council of Constantinople in 381 condemned Apollinaris. In 449 Eutyches, misinterpreting the terminology of St. Cyril of Alexandria which Cyril himself had changed in 433 in an agreement with John of Antioch, advanced a position known as Monophysitism (*monos* = one, *physis* = nature). Eutyches held that, before the Incarnation, Jesus and the Logos were two natures, but after the Incarnation only one nature. Though condemned at the Council of Chalcedon in 451, Monophysitism, recycling Apollinaris' and Eutyches' ideas in a variety of forms (Monergism = "one energy"; Monothelitism = "one will") resurfaced for several hundred years after the Council of Chalcedon and caused doctrinal controversies that were not resolved until the end of the seventh century.

Herbert J. Ryan, s.j.

See also APOLLINARIANISM; ARIANISM; ATHANASIUS, PATRIARCH OF ALEXANDRIA; CLEMENT OF ALEXANDRIA; CYRIL OF ALEXANDRIA; LOGOS/WORD; MONOPHYSITISM; NEOPLATONISM; NESTORIANISM; ORIGEN; PHILO OF ALEXANDRIA; PLATONISM; SEPTUAGINT.

AL-FATIHAH

Arabic term for "the opening" of the sacred scripture of Islam, the Qur'an. It is the first sura (chapter) of the 114 suras in the Qur'an. Its importance derives not only from its beauty and simplicity, but also from its centrality in the daily prayer life of practicing Muslims. For this reason, its seven verses are among the most frequently recited passages of the Qur'an. In the translation of Abdullah Yusuf Ali (*The Meaning of the Holy Qur'an*, revised edition, 1991), al-Fitiha reads:

In the name of Allah, Most Gracious
    Most Merciful.
Praise be to Allah, The Cherisher and
    Sustainer of the Worlds;
Most Gracious, Most Merciful;
Master of the Day of Judgement.
Thee do we worship, and Thine
    aid We seek.
Show us the straight way.
The way of those on whom
    Thou hast bestowed Thy Grace,
    Those whose (portion) is not
    wrath, and who go not astray.

Ronald A. Pachence

See also MUSLIM; QUR'AN.

AL-GHAZALI (1058–1111 C.E.)

Abu Hamid Muhammad al-Ghazali, a Persian Muslim who studied and taught in Baghdad, the intellectual center of Islam at the time, is described by historians as a lawyer, a philosopher, a theologian, and a mystic. This description reflects al-Ghazali's diverse intellectual interests and his effort to synthesize the many spiritual and academic disciplines current in the Muslim world. Like al-Ash'ari (873–935) some two hundred years earlier, al-Ghazali eventually became suspicious of philosophy and its value in the quest for truth. He wrote *The Inconsistency of the Philosophers* in which he demonstrated that philosophers could not logically prove the validity of their philosophical systems. Before his death in 1111, al-Ghazali embraced the mystical spirituality of Sufism—a religious path that preferred intuitive knowledge of God over intellectualism. In his own words: "I arrived at Truth, not by systematic reasoning and accumulation of proofs, but by a flash of light which God sent into my soul."

Ronald A. Pachence

See also AL-ASH'ARI/ASH'ARISM; SUFI/SUFISM.

AL-HALLAJ (857–922 C.E.)

Husayn ibn Mansur al-Hallaj was a Persian-born Muslim mystic and poet. He is associated with the spiritual path of Sufism and its quest for the experience of God's presence and unity with the divine in this life. To his detractors, al-Hallaj was a dangerous innovator, a demagogue, and a heretic (teacher of false doctrine) whose reported miracles and esoteric teachings threatened the unity of orthodox Islam. To his followers, he was a saint and a sage who offered them a path straight to God. In the end, it was his controversial statement "*Ana al-Haqq*" ("I am the Truth") that led to his arrest and execution by religious authorities in Baghdad. They considered this statement to be a blasphemous claim by al-Hallaj that he was God. Others, more sympathetic to Sufism, say that al-Hallaj's words simply stated the obvious for a Sufi: that a person's own ego-centered self must be annihilated (*fana*, in the teaching of Sufism) to make room for God ("the Truth") in his or her life. At that point, the "I" ceases to exist. It is supplanted by *al-Haqq*—the Truth—God.

Ronald A. Pachence

See also FANA; MUSLIM; SUFI/SUFISM.

ALI (598–661 C.E.)

Fourth caliph (early leader) of the Islamic community who assumed the leadership after the assassination of Uthman in 556. Related to the Prophet Muhammad by birth (cousin) and by marriage (son-in-law, husband of the Prophet's daughter, Fatima), Ali ibn Abi Talib was one of the early converts to Islam, a military leader during the early years of Islam and a personal friend of Muhammad. Because of his close family ties to the Prophet, some Muslims thought that Ali should have succeeded Muhammad instead of Abu Bakr. This partisanship of Ali continued until and, tragically, long after Ali eventually became caliph. Ali will always be remembered as the symbol of Islam's struggle with the issue of succession.

Before being elected caliph, he was accused by his enemies of not defending Uthman against the enemies who put him to death. As caliph, he was faulted for his decision to arbitrate a long and bloody dispute with the rebel army of his rival, Mu'awiya, governor of Damascus.

After being deposed by Mu'awiya's negotiator, he confronted another splinter group, the Kharijites, and in 661 was assassinated by a member of that group. Ali's sons, Hasan and Husayn, carried on the struggle with Mu'awiya, but without success. Hasan was poisoned and Husayn died in battle.

The Shi'ite sect of Islam traces its history back to Ali. They are the *shi'at* (party) of Ali. Shi'ites hold that Ali was deprived of his right to succeed Muhammad and that his son, Husayn, was a martyr in the cause of Islam. For the majority of Muslims, the Sunnis, Ali is respected for his efforts to guide Islam through a difficult period of their early history. For the Shi'ites, about 10 percent of the Islamic population today, he is a saint who had special spiritual knowledge passed on to him and other designated leaders (*imams*) through the Prophet Muhammad. The Sufis also claim Ali as an inspiration for their spiritual tradition and a source of special wisdom.

Ronald A. Pachence

See also ABU BAKR; CALIPH (KHALIPHA)/ CALIPHATE; HUSAYN; KHARIJITES; MUHAMMAD; SHI'A/SHI'I/SHI'ITE/ SHI'ISM; SUFI/SUFISM; SUNNA/SUNNI/ SUNNISM; UTHMAN.

ALIYAH

This Hebrew word literally means "to go up." It has two distinct and important meanings in Jewish life.

When the Torah is read at Jewish worship services, that particular Torah portion is subdivided into a specific number of parts. Each part is called an *aliyah*, because for each part, a member of the congregation is called up to the Torah to recite a blessing both before and after that part is read. Coming to the Torah to recite the blessing is called having an *aliyah*, because it involves "going up" to the pulpit where the Torah is being read. There are a different number of *aliyot* (plural) on different days in the liturgical year. For example, on the Sabbath, the main Torah reading day each week, there are seven aliyot. The first *aliyah* usually goes to a *Kohen*, a descendant of the priestly tribe; the second to a *Levi*, a descendant of the assistants to the priests; and all others to a *Yisrael*, a member of the Jewish people who is neither a *Kohen* or a *Levi*.

The second meaning of *aliyah* is to "go up" to live permanently in Israel. The term *aliyah* is used because going to live in Israel is like making ascent to a place of spiritual holiness. Anyone who goes to live permanently in Israel is said to be "making *aliyah*."

In modern times, there have been concentrated periods of immigration to Israel, beginning with the First Aliyah in the early 1880s. The Second Aliyah (1904–14), the Third Aliyah (1919–23), the Fourth Aliyah (1924–8), the Fifth Aliyah (1929) and the immigration during World War II were all in prelude to Israeli statehood. Since the establishment of the modern State of Israel in 1948, more than 1.5 million Jews have "made *aliyah*."

Wayne Dosick

See also ERETZ YISRAEL; KERIAT HATORAH; KOHEN; LEVITE; MEDINAT YISRAEL; SEFER TORAH; TORAH; YISRAEL.

ALLAH (ISLAM)

In Arabic, a contraction of *al* (the) and *ilah* (God or Divinity). Though most commonly associated with Islam, Allah should not be considered "the God of the Muslims." Arabic-speaking Christians also refer to God as Allah, and though there are important differences between the Islamic and Christian understandings of the one God, both groups acknowledge that they and the Jews worship the same Supreme Being. Theologically, Muslims hold that Allah is the creator and sustainer of the universe. He (Muslims always use the masculine pronoun when referring to Allah) will judge all people according to their deeds, rewarding believers with eternal paradise and condemning unbelievers to everlasting punishment.

Islam recognizes ninety-nine "Most Beautiful Names" for Allah including *ar-Rahman*, "the Merciful" and *ar-Rahim*, "the compassionate." Every sura or chapter of the Islamic scripture, the Qur'an, begins with the words, *Bismi-Llahi-r-Rahmani-r-Rahim*: "In the Name of God, the Merciful, the Compassionate." These words are also spoken frequently throughout the day, especially at meals.

Followers of Islam define their religion in terms of their relationship to Allah. The word "Islam" means "submission" and the "peace" one achieves through submitting oneself to Allah's will. Obedience to God, therefore, is the heart and soul of Islam. Muslims reject the Christian doctrine of the triune God. For them, it is blasphemy to say that Allah has a son or that the Spirit is God. According to Sura 5:73, "They do blaspheme who say: Allah is one of three in a Trinity: for there is no God except One God."

Ronald A. Pachence

See also ISLAM; MONOTHEISM (IN CHRISTIANITY AND ISLAM); MUSLIM; QUR'AN; SURA; TRINITY/TRINITARIAN THEOLOGY/TRINITARIAN PROCESSIONS.

ALLEGORY (MEDIEVAL)

Medieval exegetes built upon the solid foundation of the classical Latin writers.

Distant from Origen's philosophic explanation of the purposes of allegory, they continued to use it because it was sanctified by the tradition but, more especially, because of its pastoral usefulness. They took their understanding from Gregory the Great who, in the *Moralia in Job*, consistently interpreted each biblical text according to its literal, mystical and moral meaning. Like Gregory, medieval exegetes generally emphasized the moral implications of a text although later monastic authors, especially the Cistercians, would develop a skill and fondness for the mystical meaning. Medieval writers were also greatly influenced, in their use of allegory, by the liturgical context of the proclamation of Scripture. Although they read and studied biblical books in their entirety, their interpretation of individual passages was often shaped by the position of the text in the program of readings chosen for use in the Eucharist and the Divine Office (the lectionary system). This meant, first, that the meaning of the text was influenced by the feast or season at which it was read in the liturgy and, second, that the exegete often interpreted the passage for the specific needs of a particular worshiping community, whether parochial or monastic.

Medieval allegory is often criticized for its extravagance in which meanings culled from the text bear no connection whatever to the intention or setting of the original author. But where liturgical influences were strong, such as in the monastic exegete Bede, allegory was tempered by liturgical *typology*, a way of understanding the connections between the Jewish Scriptures, the New Testament and the contemporary worshiping community as points on a continuum of salvation history. Thus Bede, commenting on the story of the Syro-Phoenician woman (Mark 7:24-30;

Matt 15:21-28), sees her as a *type* of the Englishmen of his own day, newly crossing over from borderlands of paganism to the kingdom of faith, and Aelred of Rievaulx will interpret the stories of Abraham (Gen 2) and Mary, the Mother of God (Luke 1), in relation to each other and to the lives of the monks in his monastery who leave their homes in an act of obedient faith. Allegory remained the predominant method for interpreting the Scriptures long after the Middle Ages. It was used by the great scholastic theologians as well as by the Reformers, especially Luther and Calvin. It was only significantly displaced by the advent of the historical critical method in the eighteenth century.

Marie Anne Mayeski

See also BEDE THE VENERABLE; EUCHARIST; GREGORY I, THE GREAT, POPE; LECTIONARY; LITURGY OF THE HOURS; TYPE/TYPOLOGY.

ALLEGORY IN JUDAISM

In the rabbinic literature, allegories most frequently appear in exegetical contexts, shedding light on God's actions depicted in a particular biblical verse by comparing those actions to those of an earthly king. Through allegories, the rabbis depicted God as a three-dimensional figure, a king who, like other kings, judged his subjects, argued with the members of his court, fought and killed his enemies, and worked to assure justice for all people. While using images intelligible to a nation familiar with the ways of earthly kings, the rabbinic allegories ultimately define the unique power and place of God who, as the King of kings, created and rules over the entire world. Allegory has no unique meaning or significance in modern Judaism.

Alan J. Avery-Peck

ALLELUIA (IN CHRISTIANITY)

The word "alleluia" has been used as a biblical and liturgical exclamation or acclamation of praise and rejoicing in both Judaism and Christianity. One can see the use of the word in the book of Revelation (19:1, 3, 4, 6) in the New Testament. In addition, the use of the word (often elongated by a longer phrase called a verse) can be found in some Christian liturgy on ordinary Sundays (as an acclamation accompanying the reading of the Gospel at Mass) and especially pronounced during certain joyful liturgical feasts (for example, the Ascension) or seasons (for example, the Easter or Christmas season). During penitential seasons, such as Lent or Advent, the use of the Alleluia was often prohibited; today, in the Roman Catholic tradition, it is only omitted in Lent. The solemn triple chanting of the Easter Alleluia is a liturgical high point in some Christian traditions.

Joanne M. Pierce

See also CHANT (IN CHRISTIANITY); EASTER; GOSPEL; LECTIONARY; LENT; LITURGICAL YEAR; PASCHAL.

ALLELUIA IN JUDAISM

(Hebrew, Praise the Lord). A liturgical expression appearing frequently in biblical psalms, the term Alleluia has no independent significance in postbiblical Jewish religion.

Alan J. Avery-Peck

AL-MATURIDI (?–944 C.E.)

Though less well known than his contemporary, al-Ashʾari (873–935), Abu Mansur Muhammad al-Maturidi is recognized as one of Islam's early theologians and a defender of orthodox Islam against the Muʾtazilite philosophers. There are few differences between the theological system of al-Maturidi and al-Ash'ari, though scholars note that al-Maturidi was more willing to pursue difficult theological questions despite the limitations of human reason. For example, when confronted with the apparent contradiction between the Islamic doctrine of free will and predestination, al-Ash'ari was content to conclude that we cannot probe the mind of God in this or any other theological question. For him, no further discussion of the subject was useful. Al-Maturidi, however, defended both doctrines, giving no more weight to the one than to the other, without making any attempt to reconcile the logical contradiction between the two.

Ronald A. Pachence

See also AL-ASH'ARI/ASH'ARISM; FREE WILL; MU'TAZILITES; PREDESTINATION (IN ISLAM).

ALONSO-SCHOEKEL, LUIS (1920–98)

Jesuit priest whose leadership in biblical scholarship is internationally recognized. Born in Spain of a German father and a Spanish mother, Luis Alonso-Schoekel was trained in literary studies and brought keen literary sensitivity to his study of the Bible. Most of his professorial life was spent at the Pontifical Biblical Institute in Rome.

Professor Alonso-Schoekel was the author of many books and innumerable articles. His monographs include *The Inspired Word*, a Spanish translation of the Bible for Latin America, a set of commentaries in Spanish on the entire Old Testament, more extensive commentaries on the books of the Prophets and the book of Job, and a Hebrew-Spanish dictionary of the Bible.

He lectured widely throughout the world, making the fruit of biblical scholarship available to other academics in university settings as well as to ecclesiastical communities of all sorts. His original scholarship and his persistent application of literary and linguistic methodologies set him apart from most of his contemporaries who employed historical criticism.

Alice L. Laffey

ALPHONSUS LIGUORI (1696–1787)

St. Alphonsus Liguori, the founder of the Congregation of the Most Holy Redeemer (the Redemptorists; their initials are C.SS.R.), was born near Naples. While remembered for his preaching, his pastoral concern for the poor, and his devotional and spiritual writings, Alphonsus is perhaps best known for his work *Theologia Moralis* (Moral Theology), which began appearing in 1748. With respect to whether or not a specific course of action was permissible, he advanced what is called "equiprobabilism." Alphonsus believed that in the case of two equally valid opinions, one taking the side of the law and the other favoring the individual's liberty, a person is free to make his or her own decision. He is thus known as a champion of conscience. Alphonsus was declared a saint in 1839.

William Reiser, S.J.

See also MORAL THEOLOGY/CHRISTIAN ETHICS; PROBABILIORISM; PROBABILISM.

AL-QAEDA

See ISLAMIC RADICALISM (FUNDAMENTALISM).

ALTAR

The term is derived from the Latin (*altaria*, plural of *altus*, high) meaning a structure placed upon a pagan altar (*ara*), but by association came to mean a high altar itself, altars, or an altar top; Christian usage formulated the singular, *altare*. In its broadest meaning it is a place designated by tradition or custom for the offering of sacrifices or other gifts to superhuman beings, for example, God, spirits, ancestors, and so on, in an attempt to communicate with and influence or honor such beings. The use of sacrifices is much older and broader than the use of altars (some societies simply slaughter the victim in some manner and leave it in the open). Altars are first found in pastoral or agricultural societies as either a special place for the killing of a sacrificial victim, or a place where the sacrificial part of the victim is burnt to be made available to the deity or others in the spirit world, or a place of offering holding the victim before it is consumed, or the place where the participants (priests and other worshipers) actually consume the victim in a sacrificial meal.

Early Christian Use

In Christian use the first altars were tables associated with the paschal meal of Jesus which anticipated his death and resurrection (Last Supper accounts), his postresurrection meals with the disciples (cf. Mark 16:14; Luke 24:13-35, 41-43; John 21:9-14), and with the theme of the messianic banquet found in the tradition of Israel and in the life and teaching of Jesus (for example, the wedding banquet, the multiplication of the loaves and fish). The first clear reference to a Christian altar (Heb 13:10) was metaphorical, distinguishing the sacrifice of Christ and probably the Eucharist from Jewish animal sacrifice, and referred to the sacrifice of praise based on interior disposition of heart, often associated with ritual (unbloody) meals and the prayers that

accompanied them. Thus the "altar" of Hebrews 13 is probably the Christian eucharistic table. Early Christians rejected the sense of altar in Jewish Levitical sacrificial practice and in Greco-Roman pagan religions as a model for the Eucharist or Lord's Supper, instead emphasizing the spiritual sacrifice of praise. Thus, initially the eucharistic table was moveable and wooden, variously shaped (square, semicircular, or round) and in itself treated as little more than a place of convenience for a ritual meal. However, Greek and Roman Christian authors of the first four centuries use altar and table interchangeably for the place of the eucharistic action, and as late as the fifth century, Augustine of Hippo uses *altare* in reference to a wooden table. Nevertheless, the table was thought of as a different kind of altar than that associated with bloody sacrifice.

The fourth century marked the transition from wooden table to stone altar with several influences involved. The end of persecution negated the need for portable tables. The legalization of Christianity led to the building of public churches as basilical gathering places. These new (or adapted) Christian structures, most often built of stone, aesthetically seemed to warrant an altar table also made of stone. No doubt the biblical theme of the rock or stone was a factor, along with increased reverence for the altar itself. These stone altars remained small, with only enough table space for bread, chalice, and book. This remained so until the Carolingian era. They were generally covered with a ciborium as a mark of respect and as a visual means of enlarging their proportion.

However, the most significant influence for the transition from wooden table to stone altar began with the early practice of celebrating the Eucharist on portable tables placed on or near the tombs of martyrs, or less frequently on stone tables constructed within catacombs for very small gatherings. This practice was rooted in the association of the sacrifice of Christ commemorated in the Eucharist with the sacrifice of the martyrs, in the notion of the communion of saints being present at the Eucharist, and in the emphasis on the intercessory power of the saints and their commemoration in the eucharistic prayer as forebears in the faith. This development of thought was further popularized by the written, often legendary accounts of martyrdoms (passions of the martyrs). This cult of the martyrs found its fullest expression beginning in the fourth century with the construction of public shrine churches on the tombs of the great martyrs and the practice of public pilgrimage that ensued. The notion of a shrine demanded a fixed, stone altar placed above the martyrs tomb, with access to the tomb itself provided by a confessional (an opening in front of the altar with steps leading down to the tomb).

Due to the intense popularity and the rapid spread of the cult of martyrs, communities without the whole body of a martyr/saint sought to entomb divided and translated relics within a hollowed out area of the altar mensa (table top) or in its main support. This practice was slow to come to Rome, but prevailed in the East and in Gaul. From the ninth to the fourteenth centuries even second-class relics, that is, things associated with the saint or cloths touched to the body were entombed, and in some places where relics were unavailable a consecrated host or even a corporal (which touched the host) was substituted. The entombment of relics in altars influenced their shape to be cubed, box-like, often with openings to see or to have access to the relics within. However,

only in the sixteenth century in baroque and rococo design were altars shaped as actual sarcophagi. Also by the sixteenth century all altars were required to have relics. This requirement is abrogated in the reforms of the Second Vatican Council.

Originally only one altar was permitted in a church. As the multiplication of masses occurred with the ordination of monks in the seventh century and the popularization of private Masses offered for particular intentions, so too the number of altars in a church. Nevertheless, the principle of one main altar/sanctuary in a church has prevailed. Through the pre-Carolingian period that altar was always visible to the congregation, located at the edge of the apse away from the wall or in the nave itself, sometimes on an elevated platform (except probably for the East Syrian churches where the altar was located against the apse). Some have thought this to be evidence for the presider to face the community at the altar. However, beginning with Tertullian the preponderance of evidence is that all, including the presider, faced east during prayer.

Medieval Use

In the Middle Ages several influences combined to remove the altar from proximity to the people. The churches of the East and of Gaul had the custom of orienting the apse of the church toward the east. (In Roman basilical style the east-west axis was maintained, but with the apse generally to the west.) In such instances it seems that even though the altar was out from the apse, all surrounded the altar and faced east with the presider. Gradually this facilitated the placement of the altar in the apse itself. This practice arrived in Rome in the tenth century with the adoption of liturgical books from the north which combined Gallican and

Roman rites. With the development of eucharistic controversies and popular eucharistic devotions of adoration, monstrances exposing the consecrated Host were placed on the altar for veneration. Also with the medieval emphasis on the cult of the saints and the veneration of relics further increasing, reliquaries, often quite large, were also displayed on the altar. Originally these devotions were occasional, but eventually became so routine that the montrances and reliquaries became permanent fixtures designed into a retable behind the altar. In churches without first-class relics the retable was often used to depict painted or carved scenes of the lives of the saints. In cathedral churches this blocked the view from the bishop's chair located in the apse, causing it to be moved forward, and the altar with its retable to be positioned against the wall of the apse. Other churches soon imitated the practice. Eventually this altar so positioned became elongated, in some places to as much as sixteen feet. It served as a kind of stage for a sacred allegorical drama, as the Mass became so interpreted, depicting the life of Christ and illustrating Christian doctrine for a congregation piously watching at a distance. No doubt the growing reverence for the Eucharist, the diminishment of regular Communion by the whole congregation, and the continuing rise of a marked distinction between clergy and laity contributed as well. Eventually this division became an architectural barrier in the iconostasis of the Byzantine East and the rood screen or chancel of the West (whose use generally declined due to baroque influence). However, in the West in the sixteenth century the placement of the tabernacle on the high altar became normative, further obscuring the altar, especially with the addition of gradines or pedestals for further decoration with flowers, candles, statues, paintings, and additional reliquaries.

At the time of the Reformation, many stone altars were destroyed because of their association with a perceived interpretation of the Eucharist as a bloody sacrifice and replaced with wooden tables, often moveable. Through contemporary biblical scholarship and ecumenical dialogues on eucharistic theology, Christian understanding of the altar table has moved beyond the limitations of the position generally maintained by the Reformers (Eucharist as only a commemorative meal) and that of medievalists and Counter-Reformers (Eucharist as sacrifice almost exclusively associated with immolation and death) to embrace a sense of the Eucharist as a recalling, offering of, and participation in all the saving events of Christian salvation, Christ's life, death, resurrection, ascension, and coming in glory.

Modern Use

Current Catholic theology and practice regarding the altar table is found in *The Roman Pontifical: Rite of the Dedication of a Church and Altar* (1977), especially chapter four, "The Rite of Dedication of an Altar." It emphasizes Christ as the victim, priest, and altar of his own sacrifice, the Christian as a spiritual altar, offering the sacrifice of a holy life to God in union with Christ, the altar as both the table of the sacrifice and of the paschal meal, the altar as a sign of Christ, and the altar as a means of honoring the martyrs whose sacrifice was a witness to Christ and undertaken in union with him as their head. Normatively, there is to be only one altar, fixed, ordinarily of natural stone or other approved, suitable and becoming, finely wrought material, freestanding so that the priest can easily walk around it and celebrate mass facing the people; statues and pictures of saints may not be placed above the altar in new churches; relics should not be placed on the altar table for veneration; authentic relics of sufficient size may still be placed beneath the altar but not set in the table of the altar. Further commentary is found in the *General Instruction of the Roman Missal* (Third Typical Edition, 2002), nos. 296–308, and (for usage in the U.S.) *Built of Living Stones: Art, Architecture, and Worship* (NCCB/USCC [now USCCB], 2000), nos. 56–60.

Furthermore, the current legislation and theology of reservation of the Blessed Sacrament indicates that it is most appropriately reserved in a special chapel for devotional purposes, in a wall niche or eucharistic tower or pillar, and not on an altar which is to be reserved for the eucharistic action itself.

Dennis W. Krouse

See also ALLEGORY (MEDIEVAL); ANAPHORA; ART, LITURGICAL; BALDACHINO; BASILICA; CLERICALISM; EUCHARIST; EUCHARISTIC PRAYER; HOST; ICONOSTASIS; MARTYR/MARTYRDOM; MASS; MEDIEVAL CHURCH; MONSTRANCE; RELIC (IN CHRISTIANITY); SACRIFICE; SACRIFICE OF THE MASS; SANCTUARY (PLACE).

ALTHUSSER, LOUIS PIERRE (1918–90)

Algerian-born French Marxist philosopher. He studied at the Paris' École Normale Supérieure, and in time became professor of philosophy there. A devout Roman Catholic progressive, during World War II Althusser was taken prisoner by the Germans, and while a prisoner of war came in contact with Marxism, to which he turned his attention and his personal commitment. His brand of Marxism was closer to the orthodox views of the Chinese Communist party and not always popular with French Communists (although later in life he "corrected" earlier views and adopted much of the new orthodoxy of the French Communist party). He murdered his wife in 1980, spent three years in a psychiatric hospital, and then lived as a recluse until the end of his life. Althusser thought that Marx's thought had been misunderstood and therefore condemned most interpretations of Marx's works; he then proceeded to elaborate what he thought was the correct understanding of Marx's thought as a groundbreaking epistemology based on the rejection of every subject-object dichotomy. Among Althusser's most influential works are *Reading Capital* (on Marx's *Das Kapital*), his *Ideology and Ideological State Apparatuses*, and *On the Young Marx*. His thought had some importance among French structuralists.

Orlando Espín

See also MARX, KARL; MARXISM; SOCIALISM.

ALTIZER, THOMAS, J. J.

See DEATH OF GOD THEOLOGY.

ALUMBRADOS/ILUMINATI

"Alumbrados" (in Spanish) or "Iluminati" (in Latin) means "enlightened" and was the name given to a group of mystics in Spain who claimed to have attained the direct vision of God through meditation. The name was first applied to them in 1494, and references to followers of this movement continue into the seventeenth century. The movement was condemned as heretical and pursued by the Spanish Inquisition. According to the Inquisition accounts, the Alumbrados claimed that the vision of God attained through meditation caused immediate salvation and removed any need for rituals, or charitable acts, or even morality. The movement seems to have occurred only in the dioceses of Cadiz and Seville, but the wariness of later theologians toward mysticism may have been, in part, a reaction to the notorious reputation given the Alumbrados by the Spanish Inquisition.

Gary Macy

See also INQUISITION; MEDIEVAL CHRISTIANITY (IN THE WEST); MYSTICISM/MYSTICS (IN CHRISTIANITY).

ALVES, RUBEM (1933–)

Brazilian Protestant theologian and philosopher. Educated in Presbyterian theology both in Brazil and in the U.S., Alves made his first important contribution with the publication of his *A Theology of Human Hope* (1969). He has since written several other books (for example, *Tomorrow's Child: Imagination; Creativity, and the Rebirth of Culture;* and *Religión, ¿instrumento de liberación?*) and numerous articles. Alves was a professor at the University of Campinas, in the Brazilian state of São Paulo. Beginning with the theology of hope, interpreted from a Latin American perspective, Alves' thought has since moved through utopian humanism to a difficult and anxious hope in a good future.

Orlando Espín

See also LATIN AMERICAN PROTESTANTISM; LATINO THEOLOGY (-IES); LIBERATION THEOLOGIES; MODERNITY; PHILOSOPHICAL THEOLOGY; POSTMODERNITY.

AMALADOSS, MICHAEL (1936–)

Indian Catholic theologian and missiologist, and member of the Society of Jesus (Jesuits). Amaladoss (at times spelled Amaladas) became professor and dean at the Jesuit school of theology in Delhi, after several years in Rome as a member of the central council of the Jesuits. He has contributed to a deeper understanding of inculturation and missiology. His thought, powerfully conveyed through conferences and in the classroom, has been very influential (through his students) in contemporary developments of the theology of inculturation. One of his more recent books is *Challenges to Mission* (1994).

Orlando Espín

See also INCULTURATION; MISSIOLOGY; MISSIONS; SOCIETY OF JESUS.

AMATERASU

(Japanese, O-Mikami, "heaven illuminator"). The primary deity in Shinto belief, popularly known as the Sun Goddess and protector of the nation. She is portrayed in the early mythologies as the daughter of the primordial couple Izanami and Izanagi. In the Nihongi she came to play a central role for the Japanese people as the tutelary *kami* of the Imperial clan. It was believed that Japan's imperial line began when Amaterasu sent her grandson, Ninigi, to rule Japan and his great grandson, Jimmu Tenno, became the legendary first emperor in 663 B.C.E. Up until modern times, all Japanese emperors have traced their descent back in an unbroken line to Amaterasu, leading to the belief in the divine descent of the emperor. It is also believed that Amaterasu resides at the Grand Shrine at Ise which continues to serve as Japan's primary pilgrimage location for both the emperor and the Japanese people. In addition to her imperial role, Amaterasu has also served as the primary nature deity, supreme ancestor, dispenser of fertility, and the bringer of good fortune.

G. D. DeAngelis

See also ISE; IZANAGI; IZANAMI; KAMI; NIHONGI; SHINTO; SHRINE.

AMBROSE OF MILAN (CA. 339–97)

Ambrose of Milan, one of the four great Latin Doctors of the Church (Ambrose, Jerome, Augustine, and Gregory the Great), was born at Trier. His father was the praetorian prefect of Gaul, and Ambrose, after a successful legal career in Rome, was appointed in 370 to be governor of Aemilia-Liguria. Ambrose governed his populous and wealthy province from Milan, which was the capital of both Aemilia-Liguria and the western Roman Empire. In 374, though only a catechumen, Ambrose acceded to the requests of the Catholic laity that he succeed Auxentius, an Arian, as the bishop of Milan. In short order, Ambrose was baptized and ordained. In his early years as bishop he studied theology under the guidance of Simplicianus who became Ambrose's successor to the see of Milan. Ambrose's early theological writings dealt with Christian ethics and the promotion of the ascetic movement. Through his contact with the rulers of the Empire, Valentinian II and Theodosius I, Ambrose fought against paganism and Arianism while upholding the independence of the church from the Empire. He protested against Maximius's execution of the Priscillianist heretics and excommunicated the emperor Theodosius I for causing a massacre of civilians in Thessalonica as a punishment for the murder of an imperial officer in that city. Ambrose had a good command of Greek, and his Latin treatises, sermons, and letters show how frequently Ambrose borrowed from Greek theological thought and popularized it in the Latin West.

Herbert J. Ryan, s.j.

See also ARIANISM; ASCETICISM/ASCETIC; AUGUSTINE OF HIPPO; DOCTORS OF THE CHURCH; PRISCILLIANISM.

AMBROSIAN RITE

The Ambrosian Rite, also known as the Milanese Rite, is the form of liturgical celebration of the ancient metropolitan province of Milan and one of the few to survive outside the Roman Rite in the West. It derives its name from St. Ambrose, bishop of Milan from 374 to 397, who no doubt contributed to its euchological development, but who is only one of several significant influences. The rite shows some Byzantine tendencies, but is predominantly Western and Roman in substance. It uses a slightly altered version of the Roman Canon with its own collection of variable prefaces so that a different preface is used for each Mass. It has its own collection of insertions for the canon as well as two other eucharistic prayers for use on Holy Thursday and the Easter Vigil respectively. (Currently it also employs the other eucharistic prayers approved for Roman usage in the reform of Vatican II.) It developed its own musical compositions, known as Ambrosian chant, which are in general less rigid in modality and more diversified than the Gregorian chant of the Roman Rite. According to some specialists, the Milanese chants represent a more primitive style than the Gregorian, possibly predating the Carolingian period, even though the oldest extant annotated manuscripts date only from the twelfth century.

The revision of liturgical books mandated for the Roman Rite by the Constitution on the Sacred Liturgy of the Second Vatican Council influenced the publication of revised Ambrosian liturgical books that began in 1976, including a lectionary and a missal. Significant differences from the Roman Rite are minimal, but include placement of the Creed after the preparation of the gifts, the washing of the hands within the eucharistic prayer before the words of institution, the fraction rite with a chant proper to the day (*Confractorium*) prior to the Lord's Prayer, and differences in calendar observances.

Dennis W. Krouse

See also CHANT (IN CHRISTIANITY); RITUAL; WESTERN CATHOLIC CHURCHES.

AMBROSIASTER

Active ca. 350. The name given by sixteenth-century scholars to an anonymous Scripture scholar of the mid-fourth century. His or her most famous extant work, a commentary on the thirteen Pauline Epistles, was commonly but wrongly attributed to Ambrose of Milan. Augustine was the first of many scholars to use these commentaries, although Augustine thought they were written by Hilary of Poitiers. In general, the author avoids allegorical interpretations of Scripture and shows a profound knowledge of Jewish institutions.

Gary Macy

See also AMBROSE OF MILAN; AUGUSTINE OF HIPPO; HILARY OF POITIERS.

AMERICANISM

An alleged heresy in the American Church condemned by Pope Leo XIII in *Testem Benevolentiae* (1899). The term also refers to a movement among some bishops and intelligentsia to foster Catholic adaptation to the U.S. culture. A related issue, the so-called Americanist crisis, indicates the late nineteenth-century debates about the shape and future of U.S. Catholicism.

The conflict was created by a number of issues: rapid increase in Catholic population due to immigration; the expansion of ecclesiastical structures (dioceses, institutions, and so on); the education of Catholic children; ethnic parishes; and always in the background, anti-Catholic

(nativist) sentiment. Bishops of the Americanist persuasion (John Ireland, John Keane, James Cardinal Gibbons) espoused the Manifest Destiny vision of the national future and believed the Catholic Church would contribute to its achievement. Encouraged by the writings of O. Brownson and I. Hecker, they urged Catholic adaptation to American culture. Their opponents, including many German bishops and lay leaders as well as Irish prelates in New York and New England, believed their congregants' faith to be linked to preservation of ethnicity and were wary of forays into the hostile arena of American Protestant culture. The issue did not remain within national borders but engaged the European church when lobbyists for both viewpoints solicited Vatican approval, among them, Dennis O'Connell, rector of the American College in Rome and supporter of the Americanist position.

Vatican support seemed to lie with the Americanizers at first, particularly when an apostolic delegate joined Keane and Ireland at the World Parliament of Religions in Chicago (1893). The tide turned when a French apologist attacked the orthodoxy of Americanist thought as he interpreted it through a French translation of Isaac Hecker's biography. The Vatican initiated an inquiry into Americanist affairs soon after, and Leo XIII's 1899 letter to Cardinal Gibbons, *Testem Benevolentiae*, cautioned the Americans about certain errors it termed Americanism, among them aspects of Hecker's thought. The movement's opponents hailed the letter as a vindication of their concerns. The Americanists voiced support for the document, denying that the positions described existed, for the letter did not portray Hecker's or the Americanizers' positions accurately. As no persons were censured, the surface of American Church life appeared undisturbed. The letter's consequences would be seen only with time as church leadership fell to conservative bishops, the Americanists' intellectual initiatives faded, and the American Church proceeded to think about its identity as somehow distinct from American culture for a half century more.

Patricia Plovanich

See also BROWNSON, ORESTES; ECCLESI-OLOGY; HECKER, ISAAC; LEO XIII, POPE; MODERNISM.

AMITABHA/AMIDA

A supramundane Buddha thought by many Mahayana Buddhists to have created with his merit a celestial paradise (Sukhavati) designed to facilitate the enlightenment of faithful devotees who secure rebirth there. Accounts in texts such as the *Larger and Smaller Sukhavativyuha Sutras* and the *Amitayurdhyana Sutra* record that a supramundane bodhisattva in the Mahayana cosmological tradition made vows to create a paradise with many auspicious qualities. Most significant are those making rebirth there available to devotees who practice various devotions, including those specifically dedicated to being reborn there. For Pure Land practitioners, Amitabha (also called Amitofo [China] and Amida [Japan] in East Asia) is expected to appear before the devout at death and guide their passage to paradise. Later Buddhist cosmology identified Amitabha and his paradise residing in the western direction; this Buddha is also said to be the spiritual "father" to the bodhisattva Avalokiteshvara, who assists in the work of salvation.

Todd T. Lewis

See also BARDO; BODHISATTVA; HONEN; MAPPO; MERIT (PUNYA); SHINRAN.

AMRAM BEN SHESHA HAGAON (D. CA. 875 C.E.)

A great sage of the Talmudic academy of Sura. He is most noted for formally outlining the first basic rubric of Jewish prayer, and the first systematic Jewish prayer book.

Wayne Dosick

See also SIDDUR.

AMULET

Any object that supposedly protects a person from harm, or brings her or him good luck. Most human cultures believe in the power of amulets, and some might have specific rituals to turn objects into amulets. Just about any object, animal, plant, or word could be or become an amulet (the choice depending on the cultural assumptions of the user). Some religions employ amulets while others "officially" disdain them, although the use of amulets does not seem to be automatically deterred by any religion's condemnation of their use.

Orlando Espín

See also CHARM OR SPELL; FETISH.

ANABAPTISTS

In the sixteenth century, some Christians in Switzerland, the Netherlands, and Germany criticized Martin Luther and Ulrich Zwingli for not going far enough to reform the church. These Christians sought a more radical Reformation, including the application of the Bible to daily life, restoration of first-century Christian belief and practice, and a clear separation of the church from state and society. They became known derogatively as "Anabaptists" or "rebaptizers" because they believed in believer's baptism and, believing their infant baptism invalid, became baptized again as adults upon a profession of faith. In 1525 George Blaurock and Conrad Grebel baptized one another at the fountain square in Zurich, Switzerland.

A loose collection of Reformers held together by commitment to adult baptism and the creation of a pure church, Anabaptists' practices varied from one group to another and from region to region. Some preached pacifism while others promoted revolution to usher in the kingdom of God. Some practiced communalism and egalitarianism, while others created hierarchical structures. Some baptized by immersion, others by pouring. Most Anabaptists believed that the Second Coming was imminent and that Christians must prepare for Christ's advent through absolute obedience and piety. Obedience to God often led to civil disobedience: Anabaptists refused to serve in the military, swear oaths, or pay taxes. They also repudiated the church's corruption by the world, insisting the church was a voluntary community of believers. Considered subversive to both state and church, they were persecuted and denounced as heretics. Many Anabaptists were drowned or burned for their beliefs. The heroism of the martyrs attracted more people to the movement.

In 1534–5, the movement turned violent. Inspired by Melchior Hoffman, imprisoned for Anabaptist beliefs, John Matthys and John of Leiden preached that the end of the world was now, and that Jesus was coming to establish the New Jerusalem in Münster, Germany. Anabaptists took over the city by force and expelled all Catholics, who in turn gathered an army and laid siege to the city. Inside the city, adherence to biblical norms was decreed, including polygamy and communism. Religious paintings and sculptures were destroyed as sacrilegious icons. Ultimately, on the verge of starvation, the city fell, and the leaders of the rebellion were tortured and executed. Although the Münster rebellion was atypical of the movement, after it, Anabaptists gained the reputation as fanatics and lost support.

After the fall of Münster, Anabaptists stressed practicing the Sermon on the Mount without instigating conflict with civil authorities. The Mennonites, Amish, Moravians, and Brethren grew from this emphasis. The Mennonites were followers of Menno Simons, a Dutch Catholic priest who became an Anabaptist in 1536. Jacob Amman, a Swiss Mennonite leader, criticized the Mennonites for laxity and formed his own group that came to be known as the Amish. The Amish practiced strict discipline and rejection of all worldly standards. The Moravians descended from followers of John Hus, burned as a heretic in 1415. Stressing pacifism and pietism, they thrived in Moravia and Bohemia in the eighteenth century under the leadership of Count Nicholas von Zinzendorf. Also in the eighteenth century, the Church of the Brethren emerged in Germany led by Alexander Mack who had been influenced by Pietists and Mennonites.

Still persecuted in western Europe, many Anabaptists moved to North America in the eighteenth century, finding freedom in Pennsylvania, where religious toleration was law. Others scattered across eastern Europe, especially Russia. In the nineteenth and twentieth centuries, many settled in South America where they could practice pacifism in peace.

Evelyn A. Kirkley

See also ADVENTISTS; BOHEMIAN BRETHREN / MORAVIANS; MENNONITES.

ANALECTS

(Chinese, Lun Yu, "selected sayings"). This is one of China's most admired classics. It is a collection of the sayings, conversations and aphorisms of Confucius, put together by his close followers. It represents Confucius' views on life, society, relationships, morality, governance, community, human nature, ritual, and so on. In time it became one of the Chinese classics and an integral part of the Chinese educational, governance, and religious systems. While it is uncertain what can actually be attributed to Confucius in this text, it certainly represents the teachings of the early Confucians and has had an extraordinary impact on nearly every aspect of Chinese society for over two thousand years.

G. D. DeAngelis

See also CHU HSI; CHUN-TZU; CHUNG YUNG; CONFUCIUS; FILIAL PIETY; JEN; LI; MENCIUS.

ANALOGIA ENTIS (ANALOGY OF BEING)

The *analogia entis* or analogy of being is a principle guiding metaphorical language about God. It presumes some similarity or proportionality (or ontological correspondence) between God's existence and that of the world because of the Creator– creature relationship. This correspondence means that created existence has a capacity to represent divine reality, although in a finite imperfect way. Such analogical usage is rooted in the biblical practice of proposing images from ordinary life as symbols for the character of divine life. Its philosophical refinement is derived from the principles Plato and Aristotle proposed to guide analogical usage to explore the unknown. Plato devised the use of metaphors to explore reality as yet unknown. Aristotle noted the metaphorical potential of concepts whose similarity (or proportional participation in being) allowed comparison despite the entities' dissimilarity. Medieval discussions of analogical usage led to the triadic schema proposed by the Fourth Lateran Council (1215), which has governed the analogy of being since that time.

In practice, the analogy of being involves three stages or steps. The first step or the way of affirmation (*via affirmativa*) proposes a metaphor or image to hold similarity to divine being. The second step (*via negativa*) notes the dissimilarity between image and God, a dissimilarity greater than the similarity. This cautionary and purifying step recognizes the finite character of the analogue and its inability to represent God as God is. The final stage is the way of eminence (*via eminentiae*) that reconsiders the analogue and proposes it to function in a superlative or absolute way that surpasses human understanding. Thus one may speak about the absolute mercy of God.

The analogy of being is an honored practice in Roman Catholic theology, although the proposed knowledge about God is always surpassed by revelation. The metaphorical potential of this analogy is the foundation of natural theology. The analogy was criticized severely by Karl Barth who stressed the infinitive qualitative distinction between God and world that requires positive revelation for true speech about God. Modern Catholic thinkers who responded to the Barthian critique have refined the medieval doctrine, among them Erich Przywara and Hans Urs von Balthasar. Recent discussions of religious language have urged a more imaginative approach to analogical language, one open to the categories of contemporary experience (Sally McFague, David Tracy, and others).

Patricia Plovanich

ANALOGIA FIDEI (ANALOGY OF FAITH)

The *analogia fidei* or analogy of faith is a cautionary theory of religious language that recognizes the limited capacity of human experience and language to represent the divine mystery. This analogy proceeds as a reflection on positive revelation, exploring the meaning of God, world, and so on, from the viewpoint of revelation, not human experience. There is both a Catholic and a Reformed approach to the analogy of faith.

The Catholic approach to the analogy of faith is explained in *Dei Filius*, the Vatican Council I treatise on faith. The treatise notes the limits of human testimony about God that, even in revelation, affords only partial insight into the divine mystery. Thus, no single Scripture yields a complete sense of divine truth, but the reference of any topic to the whole of biblical testimony yields patterns which reflect the character of divine life and truth. The interpretation is closely related to the concept of tradition, and as a method of discernment of divine truth it is used in all official church statements which propose a relationship between revealed truth and later historical concerns.

Karl Barth, the twentieth-century neo-orthodox theologian, proposed a stricter meaning of the analogy of faith. An unrelenting critic of natural theology and of the analogy of being, Barth's theology recognized the human tendency to project human meanings as God's Word. His early works reject analogical language entirely and proposed discerning divine truth through a method of dialectical opposition between divine revelation and human experience. Barth nuanced the position in later works, proposing an analogy of faith that shines the light of revelation, particularly the example of Christ, on all topics. In practice, Barth reversed the analogical process, arguing that human concepts did not disclose the character of God, but that the meaning found in Scripture disclosed the true meaning of human concepts. An example of this principle would suggest that the image of human fatherhood discloses nothing about God, but the experience of God as father/parent reveals the true meaning of human parenting. In all cases, for Barth the divine analogue has primacy over human reality and is the single source of the true meaning and identity of creation. Although Barth tempered his severe criticism of liberal theology later in life, his interpretation of the analogy of faith remains a strong caution about the care required when speaking about God.

Patricia Plovanich

See also BARTH, KARL.

ANALOGICAL IMAGINATION

This phrase, used by David Tracy in *The Analogical Imagination* (1981), is similar to analyses of religious language by Gordon Kaufmann in *The Theological Imagination* (1981) and Julian Hartt in *Theological Method and Imagination* (1977). The term indicates the effort of systematic theologians to broaden the possibilities of the theological use of analogy as delineated in traditional theological literature. It intends a cogent contemporary communication of faith experience as embodied in a religious classic (which can be an event, symbol, or traditional text). However, it recognizes the inherent historicity of theological statements, is aware of the diversity of theological systems, and acknowledges the restrictive, even oppressive interpretations of traditional analogical usage (in metaphors for God, for instance). Therefore, it seeks a wider field of analogical referents and applications than the classic doctrine of analogy permits.

Patricia Plovanich

See also ANALOGIA ENTIS (ANALOGY OF BEING); TRACY, DAVID.

ANAMNESIS

This scriptural and liturgical term comes from the Greek word *anamnesis*, meaning memorial or remembrance. In the New Testament, the word is found in one of the letters (epistles) of St. Paul, in reference to the celebration of the Eucharist: "Do this in remembrance of me" (1 Cor 11:24f.; Luke 22:19). Therefore, one of the important applications of this concept deals with the eucharistic liturgy (known to Roman Catholics and some others as the Mass). The Eucharist can be understood theologically as a memorial or a remembrance of Jesus Christ.

However, this remembrance or memorial aspect of the eucharistic liturgy (and, more broadly, of Christian liturgy in general) is not simply a passive process. *Anamnesis* does not merely suggest a group of interested persons collected in a room thinking about someone they all know; it is understood to be a more active process, one by which the Christian can be said to actually enter into the paschal mystery, the life, passion, death, and resurrection of Jesus Christ. In the liturgy, this paschal mystery is understood to be made present in a real way; the Christian does not simply remember an event that happened more than two thousand years ago, but instead enters personally into

that saving act of Christ in the here and now, as it is actualized and made present to him or her in the liturgy.

Since this commemorative function of the liturgy is experienced most fully in the Eucharist (or Mass), the eucharistic prayer (or *anaphora*) can be understood on one important level to be *anamnetic*. More specifically, most eucharistic prayers contain one section that can be called technically the *anamnesis*. This section often refers to the abovementioned citation from Paul, which repeats Christ's command to "do this" (that is, offer the bread and wine in the Eucharist) "in remembrance of me."

Joanne M. Pierce

See also ANAPHORA; EPICLESIS; EUCHARIST; EUCHARISTIC PRAYER; LITURGICAL MOVEMENT; PASCHAL MYSTERY.

ANAPHORA

From the Greek meaning "offering," it is the standard Greek term for the eucharistic prayer, that is, prayer of thanksgiving, as distinguished from the "prosphora," meaning the gifts offered, ostensibly the bread and wine, but in some traditions including the offering of Christ in his paschal mystery and thus of the offering of the church. The generally acknowledged earliest text, found in the *Didache*, alludes to the universal sacrifice of Malachi 1:11, and also evokes the sense of the Jewish interior sacrifice of praise (for example, Pss 50, 51). Thus the Eucharist is not merely the outward ritual of offering, but the interior disposition of communal and individual surrender of self to God in imitation of Jesus. The literary form of the anaphora has developed differently in various traditions, but is generally understood to include the introductory dialogue of invitation, the narration of the blessings of creation and of salvation history punctuated with the popular singing of the angelic hymn (*Sanctus*), the words of institution (from the Last Supper accounts, the notable exception being the Anaphora of Addai and Mari), the anamnesis (memorial) of Jesus' death and resurrection, the epiclesis (invocation) of the Holy Spirit or the Logos to consecrate the gifts of bread and wine as well as the community of the church for a fruitful communion, intercessions and commemorations (especially in later traditions), and a final doxology with a concluding Amen of the people. Significant historical examples include the Anaphora of St. Hippolytus (*Apostolic Tradition*), *Apostolic Constitutions*, bk. viii, Anaphora of St. James, Anaphora of St. Basil, Anaphora of St. John Chrysostom, Anaphora of St. Mark, and the over one hundred anaphorae of the Syriac tradition.

Dennis W. Krouse

See also ANAMNESIS; EUCHARIST; EUCHARISTIC PRAYER; MASS; SACRIFICE.

ANATHEMA
A Latin word meaning "condemned." In the Catholic tradition, it occurs usually in the phrase *anathema sit*, meaning "Let that one be condemned." Church councils and other ecclesial authorities have used this phrase to publicly condemn those who hold or teach certain theological positions contrary to what is considered to be orthodox, that is, correct. The word anathema can also be used as a noun meaning the condemnation itself, as in the sentence: "An anathema has been declared against those persons and their teachings." In making such declarations, the church does not intend to pass judgment on whether or not the person will be saved. It merely intends to pass

judgment on the theological opinion of the person, and to exclude the person from most aspects of active membership in the church.

Patrick L. Malloy

See also DENZIGER, THE.

ANATMAN DOCTRINE
"No-*atman*" or "no-soul," a term designating the Buddhist rejection of an essential, unchanging interior entity that endures as the essence of a person's long-term identity. (The Pali term is *anatta*.) The *"atman"* rejected is the "soul" and the specific technical term used is that found in the Upanishads and subsequent Hinduism that transmigrates and "centers" the psychophysical nature of all beings.

Within the early philosophical schools, the Buddhist scholars argued that the doctrine of impermanence, one of the three marks of existence, certainly included the phenomenon of the human person. As a result, they analyzed the human "being" as the continuously changing, interdependent relationship between the five *skandhas* ("heaps"), the five base elements, or in terms of longer lists of constituents. The spiritual purpose of Buddhists breaking down any essential, unchanging locus of individuality, beyond the extension of their ontology of impermanence into the personal sphere, has been the attempt to demonstrate that there is no thing to be attached to or invest one's desire in, ultimately speaking.

The *anatman* doctrine, however, presented one of the enduring doctrinal and moral theory problems for Buddhists: how can the doctrine of *karma*, with its emphasis on moral retribution, operate without the mechanism of the soul (as in Hinduism or Christianity)? Early texts show that this question was clearly posed to Shakyamuni Buddha: if there is no soul, how can the karma "fruits" of any good or evil act pass into the future of this life or in a later incarnation? The standard explanation given is that karma endures in habitual mental energies (*samskaras*) that are impressed in the fifth skandha, *vijnana* ("consciousness"); although always evolving, vijnana endures in this life and is what passes over into the next.

Although among the philosophical elite this doctrine was at the center of Buddhist thought, householders across Asia nonetheless typically conceive of their bodies and spiritual life in terms of a "soul," with terms for "soul" common in most vernacular languages.

In the Mahayana philosophical systems, the *Tathagatagarbha* doctrine that holds that all beings have the Buddha nature (particularly important in the Hua-yen and Yogachara schools) seem to have articulated an ultimate reality that might be compared to a soul. It is not surprising, therefore, that by the time of its domestication in East Asia, Buddhism is thought different from indigenous religious systems based upon its teaching concerning the immortal soul. The *Tibetan Book of the Dead*, a fifteenth-century text, develops an elaborate teaching based upon preparing the human being for the after-death consciousness experience and winning salvation through skillful afterlife.

Todd T. Lewis

See also PRATITYASAMUTPADA; SKANDHA; TATHAGATAGARBHA DOCTRINE.

ANAWIM (POOR OF YAHWEH)

The Hebrew term, transliterated "anawim," is best translated "poor" or "oppressed," or "lowly." This is a category of people described in the Hebrew Scriptures as frequently having been unfairly treated, even by the Lord's own people. The "anawim" are referred to especially in the preexilic prophets and the psalms. See, for example, Isaiah 3:15; 29:19; 32:7, but also Psalms 9:19; 10:12, 17-19; 37:11 and 69:33. They are depicted as being faithful and as deserving of just treatment and protection. Just as the Lord had compassion on the Hebrew slaves (Exod 3), so the prophets believe that the Lord is particularly on the side of the "anawim."

Alice L. Laffey

ANCESTORS, CHINESE

The traditional belief in Chinese folk religion is that one's deceased family members continue on after death in a spiritual realm existing parallel to the temporal world. These deceased ancestors are believed to be living and powerful spirits who can impact the well-being of family members in this world. The relationship between family and ancestors is reciprocal, with ancestors having the power to bring blessings and good fortune to the family, while the family, through worship, remembrance, and reverence is capable of keeping the ancestors tied to the temporal world and involved in family affairs. Ancestor worship has served to perpetuate family solidarity by emphasizing lineage and cohesion and has helped to reinforce the centrality of the family in China back to the Shang Dynasty (1766–1122 B.C.E.). Traditionally, many homes have kept an ancestral shrine and have engaged in the practice of recounting ancestral names and deeds. More affluent families have maintained ancestral temples.

G. D. DeAngelis

See also CH'ING MING; FENG-SHUI; FILIAL PIETY; HUN; KUEI.

ANCHORITES

The term comes from a Greek word that means to withdraw from the concerns of the world. The feminine form is anchoress; it would apply to a fourteenth-century figure like Julian of Norwich, who spent her religious life in a small cell attached to a village church. The anchorites were essentially hermits. In the fourth century, they retired to desert caves (St. Antony was one of the best known). In certain religious orders (such as the Camaldolese, founded in the early eleventh century), members not only withdrew from the world into solitude; they also lived in isolated dwellings rather than in a community building. The influential twentieth-century Cistercian monk Thomas Merton withdrew to a hermitage for a period of time, although he was hardly out of contact with the world. The anchoritic impulse is not basically antisocial, since the love of solitude does not automatically imply a disregard for human community. In fact, often the anchorites and anchoresses became sources of spiritual support for others.

William Reiser, S.J.

See also FATHERS / MOTHERS OF THE DESERT; HERMIT; JULIAN OF NORWICH; MERTON, THOMAS; MONASTICISM IN EASTERN CHRISTIANITY; MONASTICISM IN WESTERN CHRISTIANITY.

ANCIENT CHURCHES OF THE EAST

General name used for the Eastern churches that have *not* accepted some key doctrinal decisions of the first seven ecumenical councils of undivided Christianity (especially the Councils of Chalcedon and Ephesus). Doctrinally, these churches would be considered Monophysite and Nestorian. The Ancient Churches of the East are: the Assyrian Oriental Church, the Armenian Church, the Coptic Church in Egypt, the Ethiopian Coptic Church, the Syrian Church, and the Syrian Church of India. There are approximately eleven million Christians throughout the world who belong to these churches.

Orlando Espín

See also APOSTOLIC FATHERS; CHALCEDON, COUNCIL OF; CHALCEDONIAN CHRISTIANS; COUNCIL, ECUMENICAL; EASTERN CATHOLIC CHURCHES; EPHESUS, COUNCIL OF; FATHERS OF THE CHURCH; MONOPHYSITISM; NESTORIANISM; NESTORIUS; ORIENTAL CHURCHES; ORTHODOX CHURCHES; PATRISTICS / PATROLOGY.

ANDEAN / AYMARA / QUECHUA TRADITIONAL RELIGION

Quechua and Aymara peoples represent the largest native culture in the Americas with approximately two million Aymara speakers and eight million Quechua speakers. Contemporary Andean religion is a synthesis of Christianity, pre-Incaic traditional beliefs and practices, and Inca state religion. Pre-Incaic Andean religion centered around sacrificial exchange between humans and mountains, lakes, and earth in return for crops, rain, animals, health, and good fortune. The Incas introduced to the Andean region a theocratic state that involved worship of the sun and moon, which the Inca rulers embodied, a system of tribute to the state that mimicked the pre-Incaic logic of sacrifice, and an annual calendar of state rituals. The religion imposed by the Incas on peoples that they subjugated played a significant role in imperial expansion and state organization. The Inca religion differed from the more localized earlier traditions in that it imposed a system of state control, bureaucracy, and tribute payments centered in Cusco over the previous system of exchange to the earth and mountains. The Incas also created an elaborate calendar of state and local rituals linked to the agricultural cycle and to the political aims of the state. The Inca state religion centralized all local shrines, sacrifices, tributes, and rituals by linking them along a system of lines that radiated out of Cusco and extended throughout the empire.

In 1536, when the Spanish executed the Inca ruler Atahualpa, Christianity was introduced to the region. The Spanish dismantled and destroyed many of the temples, local shrines, and religious paraphernalia, and established missions and schools to educate the indigenous people in Spanish and Christianity. But native practices and beliefs adapted and survived. Some aspects of Christian beliefs and practices were incorporated into Andean patterns. Most Andean natives now identify themselves as Catholics and pay tribute to local saints. In many ways, Andean religious practice resembles so-called "folk Catholicism." However, other beliefs and practices remain salient. For example, the various cults, shrines, and pilgrimages to the Virgin, Christ, and the saints are clearly tied to regional, sacrificial exchange patterns with mountains and earth spirits. Many of the places where a particular vision of Christ or the Virgin occurred are at sites of previous religious significance such as the tops of mountains, large rocks, caves, or springs.

Andean religious practitioners include healers or shamans who mediate the exchange of the flow of the vital essence of life between humans and mountain spirits. Shamans prepare a mesa, or altar, on which they lay out items with symbolic importance. On the altars, they prepare offerings that are fed to the mountains or earth and burn them in exchange for the maintenance of health and well being for people, animals, and crops. Offerings are made to mountains, or saints, or the earth mother, or the Christ of a particular mountain for good fortune, health, fertility of animals, abundance of crops, and other everyday necessities and desires. In these practices, the syncretism of pre-Incaic, Incaic, and Christian traditions is apparent.

Christine Greenway

See also MAYA TRADITIONAL RELIGION; NAHUA TRADITIONAL RELIGION; POPULAR CATHOLICISM; SACRIFICE; SHAMAN; SYNCRETISM; THEOCRACY.

ANDREW OF ST. VICTOR

Died 1175. Andrew became a canon of the abbey of St. Victor in Paris before 1141. A student of Hugh of St. Victor, Andrew became famous for his biblical commentaries on the books of Hebrew Scripture. Andrew tried to uncover the literal and historical meaning of the texts and would not only consult, but also often accept, the interpretations of the Jewish rabbis of Paris. Andrew spent his last years as abbot of Wigmore in England.

Gary Macy

See also EXEGESIS/EISEGESIS; HUGH OF ST. VICTOR; MEDIEVAL CHRISTIANITY (IN THE WEST).

ANGEL

"Angelos" is the Greek word for messanger and refers to supernatural beings who do the bidding of God. Angels are referred to in both Hebrew and Christian Scripture, playing a particularly important role in the book of Revelation. Discussion of the role and nature of angels received little attention until Pseudo-Dionysius' *Celestial Hierarchy* ranked and named the different kinds of angels. In the Middle Ages, "angelology" (the study of angels) became important as a means of discussing the role of the intellect in itself, since angels were held not to have corporeal bodies. According to postbiblical writings, the devil and his followers are also angels who have fallen from heaven due to their revolt against God.

Gary Macy

See also GUARDIAN ANGELS; DIONYSIUS THE AREOPAGITE (PSEUDO).

ANGLICAN COMMUNION

The fellowship of self-governing churches throughout the world that trace their roots more or less directly to the Church of England and find their focus of unity in the see of Canterbury, acknowledging its archbishop as "first among equals" with all its other bishops.

The Communion does not understand itself as a distinctive church because it claims no distinctive faith other than that of the "one, holy, catholic, and apostolic" church. There are no particular documents, like the Lutherans' Augsburg Confession, to which Anglicans are required to subscribe. The Thirty-Nine Articles are important but not authoritative.

Anglicans consider their Communion as a branch of the one Church of Christ: catholic in its adherence to the early Creeds, patristic traditions, and Latin Rite liturgical elements; reformed in its affirmation of the primacy of Scripture and rejection of papal primacy. Insofar as Anglicanism embodies characteristics found in the other main branches of Christianity (Catholicism, Orthodoxy, and Protestantism), many Anglicans hold that the Communion's particular and historical vocation is to help reunite the one church of Christ.

For most of its history, the Communion has been distinctively British. It originated in the Act of Supremacy (1534) declaring Henry VIII head of the Church of England. Its early character and thought were shaped during the reigns of Henry, Edward VI (1546–53), Mary Tudor (despite her effort to restore Roman Catholicism, 1553–8), and Elizabeth I (1558–1603). In its next phase, the Church of England simply followed the spread of the British Empire and established outposts in lands that came under British sovereignty. In the third phase, the nineteenth and early twentieth centuries, the church grew mainly by missionary outreach. The farflung colonies of the mother church gradually acquired independent status on account of communication difficulties and the rise of nationalism. The impetus toward independence and the development of culturally distinctive forms of Anglicanism increased after World War II and the fading of European hegemony in the Third World. Even today, roughly 90 percent of its seventy to eighty million members live in lands where English is the official language.

Governance of each of the roughly 500 dioceses spread across 164 nations is synodical, that is, shared among elected representatives of the laity and the clergy along with the bishop, since each recognizes the authority of the bishop as necessary to the life of the church. The dioceses in turn are organized into thirty-one (as of this writing) independent churches, also called regions or provinces. These, too, are governed synodically and headed by a bishop, called its Primate. This structuring of church life is seen to be most faithful to the pattern of early Christianity, as well as most appropriate for an age where democratic governance has the most legitimacy.

Still, the independence of these churches frequently produces concern about the cohesion of the Communion. The Book of Common Prayer once used everywhere was the symbol and instrument of unity. Now many of the churches, like the Episcopal Church in the United States, have the Book of Common Prayer in the vernacular. Periodic suggestions that some central authority be established to foster unity and govern all the Anglican churches are rejected; for instance, the 1930 Lambeth Conference formally refused to establish a central authority, deciding instead for regional autonomy.

Unity is, however, promoted by other means. The Lambeth Conference is a meeting of all the bishops of the Communion every ten years for prayer, friendship, and mutual consultation. It has been held thirteen times since 1867. Five hundred bishops came to Lambeth 1988. The conference will convene again in 2008. The Anglican Consultative Council was established in 1968 and first convened in 1971. It includes clergy and lay representatives and functions as the Communion's executive commitee. The full council meets every two to three years and its Standing Committee meets annually. The Primates of the independent churches have been meeting regularly since 1979. The archbishop of Canterbury presides over these organizations.

The Anglican Communion is in full communion with the Old Catholic churches, the Phillippine Independent Church, and the Mar Thoma Syrian Church of Malabar. It maintains formal dialogues aimed at the establishment of full communion with partners like the Lutheran World Federation and the Roman Catholic Church. The first Anglican-Roman Catholic International Commission (ARCIC) reached landmark agreements on the Eucharist, ministry, and authority. The second International Commission (ARCIC II) produced the first ecumenical agreed statement devoted to ethics, *Life in Christ*. Dialogues are also maintained at the provincial level; thus, the Episcopal Church in the United States is a partner in ARC–USA (the Anglican-Roman Catholic Consultation in the United States) and passed a proposal for full communion with the ELCA (the Evangelical Lutheran Church of America) in 2000.

Jon Nilson

See also BOOK OF COMMON PRAYER; CANTERBURY, SEE OF; EPISCOPAL CHURCH; LAMBETH CONFERENCES; THIRTY-NINE ARTICLES.

ANGLICAN ORDERS, CONTROVERSY OVER

The debate over the validity of ordained ministries in the Church of England and other churches that stem from it.

Its first phase, from the Reformation to 1964, was marked by Pope Leo XIII's declaration in *Apostolicae Curae* (1896) that Anglican orders were "absolutely null and utterly void." This remains a major obstacle to the reconciliation of the Roman Catholic Church and the Anglican Communion, as well as to more cordial relations between Anglicans and Roman Catholics.

Leo XIII's judgment was based upon his perception of a "defect of form." Since the ordination rite of the Book of Common Prayer of 1552 omitted reference to the power of the priest to offer the Eucharist as Christ's sacrifice on the cross, it lacked something essential. Those who ordained by means of this rite clearly intended to confer an office different from the priesthood as understood by the church. Thus, the Ordinal was held to be defective in its "native character and spirit"; Anglican orders were invalid.

The archbishops of Canterbury and York replied in 1897 (*Saepius Officio*) that the Church of England intended to confer the priesthood instituted by Christ with all that belongs to it. They argued that the form and rite demanded by *Apostolicae Curae* are not found in the earliest Roman ordination rites. Thus, if Anglican orders are voided by a defect of form, orders in the Church of Rome are questionable, too. In 1922 the ecumenical patriarch of Constantinople recognized the validity of Anglican orders. Yet Anglican priests accepted for service as Roman Catholic priests are absolutely, not conditionally, "re-ordained" even today.

In the second phase, possible ways beyond the impasse created by *Apostolicae Curae* have developed. A "new context" has emerged. It began with Vatican II's Decree on Ecumenism (*Unitatis Redintegratio*) and its recognition that the rites of non-Catholic Christians can confer grace. Further progress has been achieved by ecumenical agreements, such as the Lima Report (*Baptism, Eucharist and Ministry*) and the first Anglican-Roman Catholic International Commission's *Final Report*, which claimed to have reached "substantial agreement on eucharistic faith." Also, records from the Vatican Archives reveal that the commission Leo XIII had appointed to advise him was more divided on the issue than was previously thought.

The Anglican-Roman Catholic Consultation in the U.S. has documented the elements of this new context and proposed that Rome formally reexamine the verdict of *Apostolicae Curae*.

Jon Nilson

See also BOOK OF COMMON PRAYER; UNITATIS REDINTEGRATIO.

ANGRA MAINYU

In Zoroastrianism, Angra Mainyu is the Evil One, an uncreated and extremely powerful evil spirit that stands in conflict with Ahura Mazda, the Supreme Deity and power of good. In Zoroastrian mythology, Angra Mainyu leads the forces of evil. The Avestan name Angra Mainyu is, in the later tradition, shortened to Ahriman.

Lance E. Nelson

See also AHURA MAZDA; ZOROASTER; ZOROASTRIANISM.

ANICCA/ANICCHA

The Pali word for "impermanence," *anicca* (Sanskrit, *anitya*) is in Buddhist teaching a characteristic of all conditioned existence. Along with unsatisfactoriness (*dukkha/duhkha*) and absence of substantial self-hood (*anatta/anatman*), the Buddha included impermanence (*anicca*) as one of the "three marks" of ordinary human experience that ought to be acknowledged and meditated upon by anyone seeking a way beyond the suffering of life.

Lance E. Nelson

See also ANATMAN DOCTRINE; BUDDHA; BUDDHISM; DUHKHA; PALI.

ANIMISM

This concept was created in the field of anthropology in the nineteenth century to name the diverse beliefs that had been discovered among indigenous peoples. As such, it belongs neither to the world of religious traditions nor to the self-awareness of native peoples. Nevertheless, it has become a commonly used word in the field of religious studies, and thus deserves comment in recognition of its broad usage.

As used by early scholars, E. B. Tylor and others, it referred to the widely encountered belief that sacred power pulses through all living things. Thus nature in all its aspects was perceived to manifest the divine, sometimes vividly, at others in a veiled manner. This is the description actually given from sources interviewed by Owen Dorsey, James Walker, Ruth Benedict, and others, when they were seeking to analyze the form and content of Native American tribes' beliefs in the beginnings of American anthropology. The overriding context and structural principles of the newly emerged social sciences, however, rested on the Enlightenment critique of religion and had given to this term a derogatory sense. The Darwinian view of evolution, applied to culture and intellectual history, made almost necessary the evaluation that early religious cultures had unsophisticated and crude perceptions of the Sacred, in comparison with the "higher" cultures that produced monotheism. Therefore our comments on animism will approach it with sensitivity to the experience that led to a rich analysis of divine presence.

Indigenous peoples are often classified as "primal" in terms of their religious experience. Thus their perceptions are seen as partaking of the freshness of the beginnings, of nearness to a time in human history when people lived in closer relationship to the natural world. Their vision was awake to the depth of things, and to sights and sounds that we have gradually lost. Their awareness that everything is alive is rooted in practical experience that becomes closer to modern physics than to mysticism. Their conclusion, however, is expressed in religious language, specifically terms relating to "spirit." Thus myth and ritual image a world in which the sacred is not only present, but visible and communicating through the elements of creation—the sky, clouds, stars, animals, birds, waterfowl, ocean mammals, and so on. This is accompanied by the power of any of the sacred beings to shift shape and appear in a myriad of forms. Ultimately, the recognition that is called animism indicates a specific experience of the Sacred and a related naming of it that is linked worldwide to mythic consciousness, visions, and cosmic mysticism. It is an element in all religious traditions (though in strictest monotheism, is perceived as heterodox), but belongs in a specific sense to the traditional indigenous religions.

Kathleen Dugan

See also MONOTHEISM (IN CHRISTIANITY AND ISLAM); MONOTHEISM (IN JUDAISM); MYTH; PANTHEISM; REVELATION; VISIONS (IN CHRISTIAN MYSTICISM).

ANITYA
See ANICCA/ANICCHA.

ANKH
A cross with a circular top used to symbolize a variety of themes and deities in ancient Egypt.

Todd T. Lewis

ANNULMENT
A popular term referring to a decree by an ecclesiastical authority that declares that a particular marriage is invalid, that is, the marriage was null and void from the very beginning. The term is also applied to the judicial process of investigation and recognition that a marriage never came into being despite appearances and a wedding celebration to the contrary. Thus annulment is not the termination of a valid marriage but rather an official declaration that a marriage

union never validly existed. This distinguishes annulment from divorce when it is recognized in other churches, and from a declaration of dissolution of the marriage bond (Petrine privilege, Pauline privilege, nonconsummation) in Roman Catholic canonical procedure. Dissolution of the bond is, in fact, a form of divorce, that is, a breaking of a valid marriage union that is either nonsacramental (one or both parties are not baptized) or incomplete (nonconsummation). Since most churches not in union with Rome recognize divorce and remarriage, annulment procedures are primarily a Roman Catholic concern.

The Code of Canon Law of 1983 offers a considerably more pastoral approach that is speedier, simpler, and more just in the judicial procedures involving annulment cases than did the Code of 1917. The new Code gives three categories of reasons for annulment: (1) diriment (invalidating) impediments (Canons 1083–1094), that is, unlawful age; antecedent and perpetual sexual impotence; marriage to a person in a valid previous marriage; marriage without a dispensation to an unbaptized person, or to a person in sacred orders, or to a person with perpetual vow of chastity; abduction of the intended spouse; the killing of one's spouse or that of another in order to marry; marriage involving relationships of consanguinity, affinity, public propriety, or adoption; (2) defects in matrimonial consent (Canons 1095–1107), for example, insufficient use of reason or discretion regarding marriage responsibilities; psychological inability to assume the essential obligations of marriage (generally interpreted to include sociopathic or psychopathic personality, schizophrenia); lack of intention to form a permanent relationship of love for life ordered to procreation of children through sexual cooperation; substantial error about the person to be married; marriage entered into through deceit regarding a quality which by its nature can seriously disrupt conjugal life; and marriage entered into through force or great fear; (3) defects in the canonical form of marriage (Canons 1108–1123); ordinarily the parish priest or deacon or their delegate and two witnesses (Canon 1127 allows two significant exceptions: Catholics can validly marry non-Catholics of an oriental church in the marriage rite of that church, but for lawfulness should have their ordinary's permission; for a serious reason the local ordinary can grant a dispensation for a Catholic to marry a non-Catholic in another public form, for example, in a civil or non-Catholic service).

A public annulment process by a church court (tribunal) is said to take place in the "external forum," that is, the proceedings are a matter of record, rendered according to canon law. When such a trial is not possible due to lack of cooperation from the former spouse or from witnesses, or due to excessive emotional strain, many authors maintain that an "internal forum" solution in conscience can be made to enter into a second marriage and return to the sacramental life of the church after consultation with a confessor or competent priest. These authors usually list conditions for such a decision in conscience to be legitimate; for example, a *bona fide* attempt at an external forum solution; avoidance of serious scandal; fulfillment of obligations to the spouse and children of the first marriage (including alimony, child support and sorrow for any sin involved in the failure of the marriage); if a second marriage has been attempted, acceptance of those marriage and family responsibilities; and a desire for sacramental participation is rooted in genuine Christian faith. Although an internal forum solution is not directly supported by the Code of Canon Law and has been criticized by magisterial statements, many Catholic moralists maintain its legitimacy.

Dennis W. Krouse

See also CONSCIENCE; DIVORCE (IN CHRISTIANITY); INDISSOLUBILITY; MARRIAGE IN CATHOLIC PERSPECTIVE; PAULINE PRIVILEGE; PETRINE PRIVILEGE.

ANNUNCIATION

The message of the incarnation given by the angel Gabriel to the Virgin Mary and the event of the conception of Christ which is recorded in Luke 1:26-38. (This text should be read in comparison with the parallel annunciation of the birth of John the Baptist in Luke 1:5-25.) Both annunciation accounts show clear signs of Jewish midrashic composition. Another account of the annunciation of the birth of Jesus to Joseph is found in Matthew 1:18-25.

The Annunciation also refers to the feast in honor of the angel Gabriel's announcement of the birth to Mary and the conception of Jesus which is observed on March 25, and is related to the establishment of the feast of the Nativity on December 25. The feast may have been observed as early as the fifth century in the East, but is known only with certainty in the West in the seventh century from texts found in the Gelasian Sacramentary. In the East, the Council in Trullo (692) exempted it from the ban of feasts celebrated in Lent. In order to avoid conflict with Lenten observance, the Council of Toledo remanded the celebration in Spanish (Mozarabic) usage to December 18, a week before Christmas. By the eighth century the feast was observed universally throughout the West on March 25. While the original observance was a feast in honor of Christ, for over a millenium it has been celebrated in honor of Mary until the revised Roman Calendar (1969) that regards the Annunciation as a feast primarily in honor of Christ and changed its name from the Annunciation of Mary to the Solemnity of the Annunciation of Christ.

The Syrian tradition, both East and West (including the Maronites, Chaldeans, Nestorians, Syrian Jacobites, Malankarese, and Malabarese) celebrates a season of annunciations or announcements similar to Advent in the West. During four or five weeks they celebrate in succession the annunciation to Zechariah, the annunciation to Mary, the annunciation to Elizabeth (visitation), the birth of John the Baptist, and the annunciation to Joseph. Even Christmas is called by some the annunciation of the angels.

Dennis W. Krouse

See also MARIAN DEVOTIONS; MARIOLOGY.

ANOINTING OF THE SICK, SACRAMENT OF

Healing has been a key component of Christian life and ministry from the earliest writings of the New Testament. The Gospels record many instances of Christ healing the sick, healing which is often accompanied by a statement of forgiveness of sin (for example, Mark 2:3-12, and parallel passages Matt 9:1-8 and Luke 5:17-26). Paul refers to those with the gift of healing in the earliest Christian communities (1 Cor 12:9). However, an even more explicit reference to prayers for the sick can be found in one of the Pastoral Epistles (James 5:14-15). Here, the "elders" of the church are to pray over the sick person and anoint him or her "with oil in the name of the Lord."

Thus, prayer for the sick was almost from the first connected with anointing with oil, a logical connection since oil was often used for medicinal purposes, as well as to promote health and vigor in those who were well (athletes, for example). As the Christian churches grew and developed, the actual liturgical rites used for the sick also became more elaborate and formal. In earlier centuries, anointing by laypeople was apparently customary (at least in some places); however, anointing was eventually restricted to priests, and the rite was increasingly reserved for those suffering serious illness. The reception of a "last Communion," called *Viaticum* (from the Latin, "traveling supplies/provisions"), was considered to be an important component of the rites for the seriously ill.

During the medieval period, the focus of the rite shifted from anointing of the sick to anointing of the dying. The earlier rites referred to recovery from illness, and health in mind and body; the later ritual form centered on preparation for death. The name of the sacrament itself reflected this change: *Extreme Unction* (later commonly referred to as "last rites"). The theological theme of the anointing and prayer texts also shifted and became increasingly penitential in tone. The number of ritual anointings and their placement on certain parts of the body was strictly defined, and the multiplicity of gestures (anointings and signs of the cross) was associated with a forgiveness of any sins that had been committed through the five senses. The emphasis on Viaticum, the final reception of Communion, gradually gave way to an emphasis on a final confession of sin (although Viaticum was never dropped from the rite). It was during this medieval period that theologians singled out certain liturgical acts as having a kind of primacy; thus, this rite became listed in the Western church as one of the seven official sacraments. A particular type of oil was consecrated (traditionally, by the bishop on Holy Thursday) for sacramental use: the oil of the sick.

In many Eastern churches, the rite was to be performed not only by one priest but by several, inside the church building (not in the home, as in the West). In some traditions, the oil was taken from lamps burning in the sanctuary; hence, the rite was called the "Rite of the Lamp."

The rite was dropped from most of what would become the Protestant churches during the Reformation. Since the Reformers stressed the authority of the Scriptures, the only rites accepted as sacraments (by most) were baptism and Eucharist, since they alone had been "instituted" by Christ in the Gospels. Luther, for example, questioned the scriptural authenticity of the Letter of James, and thus, of the scriptural "warrant" for a sacrament of the anointing of the sick. Prayer for the sick and Communion of the sick, however, were retained in many of these churches, and (in a few) an absolution was kept as well. The Roman Catholic Church retained the rite as a sacrament in its liturgical books (*Rituale Romanum*, 1614).

When the Roman Catholic liturgy was reformed after the Second Vatican Council (1962–5), the sacrament of *Extreme Unction* was revised as well. The more ancient context of the sacrament, as anointing of the sick (even the chronically ill) rather than the rite for the dying, was restored. The ritual was simplified, and set more closely into the wider network of the "Pastoral Care of the Sick"; a communal celebration of the rite within the celebration of Mass was included as an option. Current theological reflection on the rite often involves a new perspective on illness and the role of the sick in the church: that to suffer illness is itself a vocation, a call to a share in the ministry of Christ as Suffering Servant.

Joanne M. Pierce

See also BURIAL (IN CHRISTIANITY); RECONCILIATION, SACRAMENT OF; SACRAMENT; UNCTION; VIATICUM.

ANONYMOUS CHRISTIANITY

This term, which entered the contemporary theological mainstream through the writing of Karl Rahner reflects an effort to square Christian belief in God's universal saving will with the church's traditional teaching that salvation is impossible apart from Christ (see Matt 28:18-20). Since the attainment of salvation requires obedience to the moral law, wherever human beings follow their conscience and live authentically human lives, there God's grace in Christ is present. Drawing on a form of Christian existentialism, Rahner essentially defined moral goodness, human perfection and authenticity in terms of Christ. For Rahner, Christ reveals and expresses in his own life what authenticity and perfection consist of. Yet there are people who follow God's will even though they do not explicitly call upon Christ. The Gospel text of major importance here is Matthew 25:31-46. In that passage, the righteous are admitted to blessedness because they came to the rescue of those in need, with whom Christ identified himself. Thus they served Christ who is "anonymously" present in the poor, the imprisoned, the hungry, and so on.

Rahner's idea found its way into The Dogmatic Constitution on the Church (*Lumen Gentium*) of Vatican II, where the council taught that salvation was available not only to those who have never known Christ, but even to those who have no explicit knowledge of God (no. 16). As Catholic theology, since the council, has become more ecumenically sensitive, a number of theologians have found the term "anonymous Christianity" triumphalistic. But Rahner's work had bridged the narrow theology that portrayed salvation as exclusively and explicitly bound to Christ with the growing conviction that the other world religions are also instruments of grace.

William Reiser, s.j.

See also AD GENTES; BAPTISM OF DESIRE; RAHNER, KARL; REVELATION; SALVATION.

ANSELM OF CANTERBURY (1033–1109)

Anselm is one of the most famous philosophers and theologians of the Middle Ages. Born in Italy, Anselm joined the monastery of Bec in France in order to study with the great teacher, Lanfranc. Anselm succeeded Lanfranc as prior of Bec in 1063, eventually becoming abbot of Bec in 1076. Anselm was ordained archbishop of Canterbury in 1093 and held that post until his death. Although Anselm was known during his lifetime for his strong stand in support of the papacy during the investiture struggles, he is best known today for his theological and philosophical treatises. In the *Monologion* (*Monologue*) and *Proslogion* (*Dialogue*), Anselm sought to argue on the basis of reason alone for the existence of God. His arguments, which were meant to show that faith in God was reasonable, have continued to fascinate philosophers down to the present day. In Anselm's book *Cur Deus Homo* (*Why God Became Human*),

Anselm argued that the incarnation took place out of God's love in order that a human being could make satisfaction to God for original sin. Anselm through this argument rejected Augustine's argument that the Incarnation took place to ransom humans back from the devil. Although these three works are the best known of Anselm's works and have most influenced later writers, Anselm wrote many other treatises, letters, and prayers that show not only a brilliant mind, but a deep devotion, particularly to Mary, the mother of Jesus.

Gary Macy

See also AUGUSTINE OF HIPPO; INVESTITURE CONTROVERSY; LANFRANC; MARIOLOGY; MEDIEVAL CHRISTIANITY (IN THE WEST).

ANTHROPOLOGY, THEOLOGICAL
See THEOLOGICAL ANTHROPOLOGY.

ANTHROPOMORPHISM
(From the Greek *anthropos*, "human being" + *morphe*, "shape or form"). Anthropomorphism is the term used to describe the attribution of human characteristics or features to something that is not human. In biblical studies, anthropomorphism usually refers to the attribution of human features or characteristics to God. This tendency varies depending on the biblical tradition in question. The J (or "Yahwist") tradition of the Pentateuch/Torah presents a God who apparently has human form, who, in Genesis 3, walks in the Garden of Eden in the cool of the day, and whose knowledge is limited. Other traditions speak of the "arm" of God, and ancient poetry in the Hebrew Bible, such as Exodus 15, assumes a God whose shape is human. Later traditions, such as the

Priestly tradition and later still the Septuagint translators, tend to avoid blatant anthropomorphisms.

Russell Fuller

See also PRIESTLY SOURCE; YAHWIST SOURCE.

ANTICHRIST
Several interpretations of this biblical figure have developed in church history. In a broad sense, Antichrist indicates particular persons or forces opposing God's plan for history or persons or groups who lead believers into error or persecute them. It can apply to historical persons (Nero, for instance) or movements (the Arians) who oppose the Christian community. A particular usage coined in the Reformation identifies the institutional Roman Catholic Church and/or papacy as the Antichrist. The term is sometimes used without specific connections to the church, signifying persons responsible for unleashing destructive forces in history (for example, Hitler). Finally, the term can hold an apocalyptic connotation, indicating a future figure who will appear in the end time (*eschaton*) and obstructs God's ultimate goal for history.

Patricia Plovanich

ANTINOMIANISM
The term antinomianism (from the Greek *nomos* or law) means those interpretations of Christian life which propose that the freedom won in the Christ event exempts Christians from observing the law, whether moral, ecclesiastical, or civil law, because salvation comes through faith. This interpretation of Christian life is taken from the Pauline argument about the Christian's freedom from Mosaic Law (Rom 3:21ff.). The central problem

in the antinomian view is understanding the necessity of spiritual discipline and moral life when salvation is already achieved in Jesus Christ. Gnostic extremists in early Christianity who justified their licentious behavior by appealing to the spiritual character of salvation were designated antinomians. The problem occurs in the Reformation era because of the Reformed emphasis on the salvific nature of faith distinct from that of good works, a conviction expressed as the contrast between faith and works, Gospel and law. Roman Catholic critics deemed this view antinomian. Reformed theology did not reject the beneficial effects of moral law and Christian discipline, but the Gospel/law contrast prompted movements within Reformed Churches that interpreted the doctrine of justification to mean exemption from all forms of law. Luther criticized his own follower, Johann Agricola, as antinomian for failing to teach the necessity for moral behavior to further the project of sanctification. The term can have a more general application and indicate any movement or theology whose understanding of Christianity is so spiritual that it challenges the validity of the church's institutional life, its sacramental structures, or its exercise of moral authority. It can also indicate any Christian movement guided largely by spiritual enthusiasm.

Patricia Plovanich

ANTIOCHENE THEOLOGY

While Antioch does not seem to have had a formal school of theology like that of Alexandria, the city did witness a flourishing of a particular form of theology under a series of great masters during the late fourth and early fifth centuries. "Antiochene theology" refers especially to the theology developed during this period by Diodore of Tarsus, Theodore of Mopsuestia, John Chrysostom, and Theodoret of Cyrrhus.

Antiochene theology is usually described in distinction to that of Alexandria, which the theologians of Antioch often strongly opposed. First, theologians in Antioch took a more literalist approach to reading Scripture, rejecting, for the most part, the allegorical approach taken to Scripture in Alexandria. Secondly, and most controversially, the Antiochene theologians insisted on the full humanity of Jesus in the Incarnation. While Alexandrian theologians stressed the divinity of the Christ to the point of subordinating the human side of Jesus, the Antiochenes argued that Jesus must have been a fully human, self-sufficient being.

During the Arian controversy, the Antiochenes took a strongly anti-Arian stance, eventually supporting the christology of Basil the Great. Nestorius, Patriarch of Constantinople and focus of the Nestorian controversy, was trained in Antioch. While his insistence on the full humanity of Jesus might represent a more extreme Antiochene position, the theology of Theodore of Mopsuestia and Theodoret of Cyrrhus contained a similar insistance. Alexandrian theologians, under the leadership of Cyril of Alexandria, argued that the divinity of the Christ overshadowed a subordinated humanity. A prolonged and sometimes vicious struggle broke out between the theologians of Alexandria and those of Antioch over the proper explanation for the incarnate Christ.

The statement of faith reached at the Council of Chalcedon in 451, which proclaims the full humanity as well as the full divinity of the incarnate Christ, is considered the standard orthodox position in the majority of Christian churches. This statement owes more to Antiochene christology than to that of Alexandria and it is particularly in this regard that Antiochene theology has had its greatest impact. The controversy did not stop there, however, and during the Monophysite controversy, the works of Theodore of Mopsuestia and Theodoret of Cyrrhus were included as two of the Three Chapters condemned by an edict of Justinian around 544. The condemnation received strong opposition in the West, however, and both Theodore and Theodoret are accepted as orthodox by the majority of Christians.

Gary Macy

See also ALEXANDRIAN THEOLOGY; ARIANISM; CHRISTOLOGY; CYRIL OF ALEXANDRIA; JOHN CHRYSOSTOM; JUSTINIAN; MONOPHYSITISM; NESTORIANISM; NESTORIUS; THE THREE CHAPTERS; THEODORE OF MOPSUESTIA; THEODORET OF CYRRHUS.

ANTIPOPE

A person who declares himself to be Bishop of Rome (that is, "pope") in place of the individual already legitimately elected to that ministry. The exact number of antipopes in the church's history is not known, because sometimes there has been honest doubt as to the legitimacy of a pope's election (for example, the Great Western Schism). Even so, it is possible to say that there have been about thirty-five individuals in history who are considered antipopes.

Orlando Espín

See also BABYLONIAN CAPTIVITY; CARDINAL; CONCLAVE; PETRINE MINISTRY; POPE; SCHISM, GREAT WESTERN.

ANTI-SEMITISM

Hatred of Jews, or unreasonable hostility or prejudice toward them.

Throughout history, many in the non-Jewish world have held a great animosity toward Jews and Judaism. This blind bigotry and hatred has been manifest in tyranny and persecution against Jews. Well-known examples from the last millennia alone include the Crusades, the Spanish Inquisition, the blood libels, the edicts of the Czar, and the horrific genocide of the Nazi Holocaust. Lesser-known but equally powerful prejudices and persecutions kept Jews from owning land, homes, and businesses, joining guilds, and having civil rights and political equality in the lands of their sojourn.

Many political and sociological theories have been offered for the reasons for anti-Semitism. Three overriding causes seem to be at the root and source: (1) Religion: With the advent of Christianity, Jews were accused of deicide. Even when not denounced as Christ-killers, Jews were derided infidels for not accepting Jesus as Lord and Savior. (2) Economics: Unable to own property or join the guilds, Jews were forced to make their livings as small merchants, traders, jewel dealers and moneylenders. When a society began to fall on hard economic times, the Jews—outsiders who were wrongly perceived as wealthy—were always hated when jobs, income, and sustenance became scarce. (3) Morality: Jews were chosen by God for the special responsibility of receiving, living, and transmitting God's ethical mandate. Few want the mirror of morality constantly held in their faces. But rather than rejecting the moral code, it is easier to sweep away the mirror and those holding it.

While simple ignorance and prejudice do not constitute anti-Semitism, hateful and virulent attacks against Jews—usually just for being Jewish—is an insidious disease that still grips much of the world. While men and women of peace and good will of every ethnic group, religion, and creed are deeply committed to wiping out anti-Semitism, its continuing existence makes Jews ever vigilant for their acceptance and safety.

Wayne Dosick

ANTONY OF EGYPT (251?–365)

One of the forerunners of Christian monasticism. As a young man, Antony gave away all he owned and dedicated his life to prayer and penance, seeking God in the desert of Egypt. Although he was not the first hermit, his holiness and sense of self-discipline attracted followers whom he organized in a loosely bound community. He was very supportive of Athanasius of Alexandria and of the decisions of the First Council of Nicaea (325) during the Arian controversy. Antony's fame spread during his lifetime, which, in turn, greatly contributed to the growth of eremitical monasticism throughout Christendom.

Orlando Espín

See also ANCHORITES; ARIANISM; ASCETICAL THEOLOGY; ASCETIC/ASCETICISM; ATHANASIUS, PATRIARCH OF ALEXANDRIA; HERMIT; MONASTICISM IN EASTERN CHRISTIANITY; MONASTICISM IN WESTERN CHRISTIANITY; NICAEA, FIRST COUNCIL OF; NUN; PACHOMIUS.

APOCALYPSE

A type of literature; from the Greek apokalypsis, "reveal" or "uncover." There has been much discussion of the definition of apocalypse (see especially Apocalypse—The Morphology of a Genre by John J. Collins). There are two apocalypses in Christian Bibles, the book of Daniel in the Old Testament and the book of Revelation in the New Testament. Apocalypses generally show similar characteristics such as a heavenly journey, cosmological speculation, and a description of God's plan for human history from the beginning of creation to the time of the writer and beyond. Some scholars have suggested that apocalyptic literature always arises out of a situation of persecution and hopelessness for the writer and their community or group, but there is now no consensus on this. Certainly the book of Daniel seems to date from the time of the persecutions of Jews and Judaism under Antiochus IV Epiphanes around 164 B.C.E.

Russell Fuller

APOCATASTASIS

The name of an early Christian doctrine that held that all humans (and angels and devils) will be ultimately saved. It was held by Clement of Alexandria, Gregory of Nyssa, and Origen, although it has been more commonly associated with the last. It was firmly opposed by Augustine of Hippo, and formally condemned as heretical by the Council of Constantinople in 543 C.E. In more recent times, Friedrich Schleiermacher and others have favored it again.

Orlando Espín

See also AUGUSTINE OF HIPPO; CLEMENT OF ALEXANDRIA; GRACE; GREGORY OF NYSSA; ORIGEN; SALVATION; SCHLEIERMACHER, FRIEDRICH.

APOCRISIARIOS

The official ambassadors or legates of the Ecumenical Patriarch of Constantinople. Up to the ninth century, an apocrisiarios was the representative sent on official business by any of the patriarchs (usually to other patriarchs or to the imperial court). The term *apocrisiarios* is derived from the Greek verb *apokrinomai* (meaning "to respond").

Orlando Espín

See also CONSTANTINOPLE, SEE OF; ECUMENICAL PATRIARCH; PATRIARCH.

APOCRYPHA

From the Greek meaning "hidden" books. The term refers to those books and portions of books included in the collection of writings in the Septuagint and the Vulgate and accepted as Sacred Scripture but not found in the Hebrew Scriptures or accepted into the Jewish canon of Scripture. In preparing the Vulgate around 400 C.E., Jerome followed the Hebrew canon (the *hebraica veritas*). He separated those works that were found in the Septuagint but not in the Hebrew Scriptures into a separate corpus, which he labeled, "apocrypha." Roman Catholics, Orthodox and Protestant Christians all have different understandings of the "Old Testament Apocrypha." The apocryphal books of the Old Testament include:

(1) Tobit; Judith; The Wisdom of Solomon; Ecclesiasticus, also called the Wisdom of Jesus, the son of Sirach. All of these were accepted as canonical by the Eastern Church at the Synod of Jerusalem in 1672.

(2) Baruch; The Letter of Jeremiah (in the Septuagint these two writings appear as additions to the book of Jeremiah); The Prayer of Azariah and the Song of the Three Young Men; The Story of Susanna; Bel and the Dragon (in the Septuagint the last three appear as additions to the book of Daniel); 1 and 2 Maccabees. All of these writings as well as those listed above in (1) were confirmed as canonical by the Council of Trent in 1548. They were labeled as deuterocanonical because they do not appear in the Hebrew Scriptures. The Protestant Reformers accepted only those books as part of the canonical Old Testament that were in the Hebrew Scriptures; thus, the writings listed in (1) and (2) were not accepted.

(3) 1 Esdras (= Esdras A in the Septuagint and III Esdras in the Vulgate; 2 Esdras (= IV Esdras in the Vulgate; also known as "The Ezra Apocalypse"); V Esdras; the Prayer of Manasseh. All of these were not confirmed as canonical by the Council of Trent and may appear in Catholic Bibles in an appendix. Modern, ecumenical Bibles may include all of these writings as part of the Apocrypha.

Russell Fuller

APOLLINARIANISM

The teaching of Apollinaris of Laodicea (ca. 310–ca. 390) which was condemned by synods at Rome in 377, at Antioch in 379, and at the ecumenical Council at Constantinople in 381. In its essence, Apollinarianism asserts that there is only one mind, will, and soul in Christ, and that is the mind, will, and soul of the Second Person of the Trinity. The human aspect of the human Jesus is limited solely to his bodily flesh.

Apollinaris and his students were concerned that if the human is separated from the divine in Christ, a merely human person could not redeem us, save us from our sins or raise us from the dead. If Jesus was just an ordinary man indwelt by the Spirit, then he must have been fallible, and therefore unable to redeem the human condition. They therefore asserted that the Incarnate is "one nature composed of impassible divinity and passible flesh." The Body of Christ cannot exist of itself as an independent nature, so it had to be conjoined with and animated by spirit, which was the Logos. The frankly acknowledged presupposition of this argument is that the divine Word was substituted for the normal human psychology in Christ. The Logos actually becomes the vivifying and animating spirit of Jesus' earthly actions. Apollinaris accepted that Jesus was different from other people; in fact, the exclusion of a human psychology had the advantage of removing any possibility of sin in Jesus, and the possibility of two contradictory wills and intelligences in Jesus. Jesus was therefore immune to earthly passions, and not only invincible to death, but able to destroy it.

This theory, though condemned in 381, continued to influence theological debates since several Apollinarian writings were wrongly attributed to Athanasius and continued to circulate under his name. The question of the relationship between the human Jesus and the Second Person of the Trinity initiated by Apollinariansim continued to divide Christianity during the Nestorian controversy and still separates the different Christian churches of the East.

Gary Macy

See also APOLLINARIS; ATHANASIUS, PATRIARCH OF ALEXANDRIA; NESTORIUS.

APOLLINARIS OF LAODICEA (CA. 318–CA. 392)

Apollinaris became friends with Athanasius of Alexandria when Athanasius stayed with Apollinaris and his father in 346 during one of Athanasius' many exiles. Apollinaris strongly supported his friend, Athanasius, in opposition to the teaching of Arianism. The opponents of Arianism

split, however, over the understanding of the Council of Nicaea and political battles between the two groups ensued. Apollinaris was chosen bishop of his hometown of Laodicea by those in his community who supported Nicaea. By 363, Apollinaris was the undisputed bishop of Laodicea and a teacher of some renown, but continued political strife would cost Apollinaris the friendship of Basil the Great and Damasus of Rome. Apollinaris developed his own particular understanding of the relationship between the Logos and the person of Jesus. The teaching, Apollinarianism, was condemned at a synod at Rome in 377, at Antioch in 379, and at Constantinople in 381. Apollinarianism continued to find support in Antioch until 425 despite an imperial edict against it in 388.

Gary Macy

See also APOLLINARIANISM; ARIANISM; ATHANASIUS, PATRIARCH OF ALEXANDRIA; BASIL THE GREAT; DAMASUS I OF ROME.

APOLOGETICS (PATRISTIC PERIOD)

Apologetics is a term which derives from a Greek word meaning to answer, account for, defend, or justify some idea, viewpoint, theory or belief. In this sense the whole Old Testament could be seen as a sophisticated accounting for Yahweh's actions on behalf of the chosen people. The New Testament is also filled with apologetic argument, helping Christian believers give reasons for the faith they possess. The Christian apologists of the second century rely heavily on the Old Testament's arguments to show the religious superiority of monotheism over pagan polytheism. Writing in the middle of the second century, Justin Martyr in the *Dia-*

logue with Trypho the Jew widens the scope of apologetics. Justin claims that God's revelation to the Jewish prophets better fulfills the philosopher's search for wisdom than even Platonic philosophy. Moreover, the Jewish prophets, when properly understood, indicate that God's very Word or Wisdom is present in Christ. In the *Apology*, written about 150 C.E., Justin answers the three charges of atheism, sedition, and immorality that pagan writers classically leveled against Christians. Justin replied that Christians are not atheists because they worship the one true God. They are not seditious since the kingdom they seek is not of this world. Far from being immoral, Christians strictly adhere to an honorable moral code. Justin's identification of Christ the incarnate Word with the very principle of the intelligibility of the cosmos laid the foundation for all subsequent types of Christian apologetics with different cultures, philosophies, and religious traditions. In the third century, Origen's *Contra Celsum* followed Justin's lead in presenting a defense of Christianity that appealed to Hellenistic culture and philosophy. In the medieval period, Abelard's *A Dialogue between a Philosopher, a Jew and a Christian* developed Justin's idea of the moral superiority of Christianity over other religions and Aquinas's *Summa Contra Gentes* was a reasoned answer to the challenges put to Christianity from the scientific Greco-Arabic world. Contemporary Christian apologetics, which is open to interreligious dialogue, owes to Justin Martyr its insistence that cultural traditions do not simply explain religious experience but they deeply influence it and help to shape it.

Herbert J. Ryan, s.j.

See also APOLOGISTS; AQUINAS, THOMAS, ST.; ATHENAGORAS; CELSUS; JUSTIN MARTYR; LOGOS/WORD; ORIGEN; PHILO OF ALEXANDRIA; TERTULLIAN.

APOLOGISTS

Apologists is the name given by historians to some Christian writers of the second and early third centuries. The name derives from a Greek literary genre, an *apologia* or "speech for the defense." The apologists attempted a reasoned defense of Christianity and the promulgation of its religious viewpoint. These writers include Quadratus, Aristides, Justin Martyr and his disciple Tatian, Melito of Sardis, Athenagoras, Theophilus of Antioch, Minucius Felix, and Tertullian. Among the apologists, only Justin Martyr and Tertullian rank as theologians. The other apologists are skilled rhetoricians who try to persuade their readers to consider Christianity seriously. They present the case for Christianity by employing classical forms of argument with which the educated elite of the period would have been impressed.

Herbert J. Ryan, s.j.

See also APOLOGETICS (PATRISTIC PERIOD); ATHENAGORAS; CELSUS; JUSTIN MARTYR; PHILO OF ALEXANDRIA; TERTULLIAN.

APOPHATIC THEOLOGY

A type of mystical theology which emphasizes the difference between God as Creator and the human person as creature, yet encourages knowledge and experience of God by means of negation. Apophatic (Greek *apophatikos* = negative) spirituality is often contrasted with kataphatic (Greek *kataphatikos* = affirmative) which stresses the idea that God manifests the divine Self in the world and can be known by means of created things.

Mary Ann Hinsdale

APOPHTHEGM

A term taken from Greek literature denoting a short, pithy, and instructive saying. From the perspective of form criticism, Rudolf Bultmann applied the term to describe a unit of the Gospel traditions that consists of a saying or sayings of Jesus set in a brief context. He outlined three different types of apophthegms, according to the different settings or causes for the sayings: controversy dialogues (occasioned by Jesus' conduct or his healings); scholastic dialogues (suggested by questions from opponents); biographical apophthegms (embedded in the form of a purportedly historical report about Jesus).

In determining the historicity of such units, many would hold that only the pronouncement might have come authentically from Jesus, while the context is a creation of the ecclesial community.

F. M. Gillman

See also BULTMANN, RUDOLF; FORM CRITICISM.

APOSTASY

The willful rejection and abandonment of Christianity by a baptized person.

Orlando Espín

APOSTLE

Today, the term "apostle" is a title that is almost exclusively reserved to the twelve disciples of Jesus' inner circle as well as Paul, who called himself an apostle to the Gentiles (Rom 11:13). In classical Greek literature the adjective *apostolos* (from the verb *apostello*, to send) occasionally appears in references to an envoy or messenger. The primitive Jesus movement appropriated the term as a noun to designate a title and office. Paul's letters, the earliest extant Christian texts, presume that readers would be familiar with the term as a component of Christian vocabulary.

In the New Testament the word apostle identifies a variety of individuals and is associated with a wide range of functions. Attempts to provide a precise definition of the term apostle in New Testament and patristic texts have always been disputed. Apostle is used to identify representatives of specific communities (2 Cor 8:23), some missionaries and preachers of the Gospel (Acts 1:21-26; 13:1-3), as well as administrators and founders of new churches (1 Cor 9:5, 12:28; Eph 2:20; 3:5, 4:11; Rev 18:20; *Did.* 11.3-6). Paul introduces himself (Rom 1:1; 1 Cor 1:1; 2 Cor 1:1, Gal 1:1; see also Eph 1:1; Col 1:1; 1 Tim 1:2; 2 Tim 1:2; Titus 1:1) and makes other references to his identity as an apostle (Rom 11:13; 1 Cor 9:1-2, 15:9; see also 1 Tim 2:7; 2 Tim 1:11). Paul also calls some of his unnamed opponents "super apostles" (2 Cor 11:5; 12:11) or "false apostles" (2 Cor 11:13). In addition, Barnabas (Acts 14:14), Andronicus, and Junia (Rom 16:7), James, the brother of the Lord, and an unnamed group (1 Cor 15:7) are identified as apostles. Of these, Junia, the name of a woman that appears in the earliest manuscript of Paul and in a few other places, was "corrected" to "Junias" by a scribe who could not conceive that women could also be called apostles. Jesus is also called an apostle in Hebrews 3:1.

If the term apostle had a wide range of applications in the early church, a very different understanding was introduced as the title came to be associated with the inner circle of twelve disciples of Jesus. Although the number twelve is fixed, there are discrepancies among the lists that name the Twelve (Mark 3:16-19; Matt 10:2-4; Luke 6:14-16; Acts 1:13, 23, 26;

John 6:71, 12:4, 20:24; Acts 6:2). Since twelve corresponds to the twelve members of Jesus' inner circle to the twelve tribes of Israel, the theological significance suggests that it is very likely the number is a construct of the early church that was introduced before the twelve were identified as apostles. This thesis accounts for the inconsistencies in New Testament use of the term apostle as well as the various lists of the Twelve.

Regina A. Boisclair

See also DISCIPLE.

APOSTLES' CREED

(*Symbolum apostolorum*). The Apostles' Creed is one of the most beloved creeds in Western Christianity but is not an apostolic creation. It is a descendent of an ancient baptismal creed from the late second century, the Old Roman Creed (or R–*textus Romanus*). A commentary on R by Rufinius attributed it to the apostles, and later legend embellished the story by ascribing each article of the creed to one of the Twelve. An eighth-century manuscript by the monk Pirminius describes the later creed, by then widely used in the Western Church for baptism, the Divine Office, and personal prayer. Largely unknown in the Eastern Church, the creed's success in the West can be attributed to Charlemagne's liturgical reforms. Its simplicity, clear trinitarian structure and succinct articulation of the tradition's trinitarian theology recommend its use as a short formula for faith or a popular profession of faith. It is faithful to the contours of the Nicene-Constantinople Creed with a few emendations. In the late creed, the salvific scope of the Christ event is widened to include a descent into hell. Jesus' conception and Christian salvation in history are attributed to the Holy Spirit. These slight emen-

dations illustrate the subtle transformation of ancient tradition over time. The legendary reference to apostolic roots demonstrates the constant effort to understand faith as connected to its origins in Christ. Not in wide use today, the Apostles' Creed may be used in baptism if requested.

Patricia Plovanich

See also CREED/SYMBOL OF FAITH.

APOSTOLIC

In addition to its application to the church as a whole, the term "apostolic" has been used to refer to the way specific groups of Christians lived. Although it always implied imitation of the apostles, at different points in history different aspects of "apostolic" life were emphasized. Thus, in the twelfth and thirteenth centuries the sharing of goods in the Jerusalem community as described in Acts 2:44-45; 4:32-35 was interpreted by many to call for a renunciation of property and often of marriage as well. By the time of the Reformation, missionary groups of men like the Jesuits were considered apostolic because of their willingness to travel in order to preach the Gospel. Eventually the term was also applied to women in religious congregations dedicated to active service, so that now it is used to distinguish this form of religious life from contemplative religious life, a life dedicated primarily to prayer.

Mary Anne Foley, C.N.D.

See also APOSTOLICITY; CONGREGATIONS (ORDERS); CONTEMPLATIVES; COUNTER-REFORMATION/CATHOLIC REFORMATION; MENDICANTS; SOCIETY OF JESUS.

APOSTOLICAM ACTUOSITATEM

This Vatican II document, the Decree on the Apostolate of the Laity, commonly known as *Apostolicam Actuositatem* (taken from the first two words of the Latin text meaning "apostolic activity") was approved by the bishops of the Second Vatican Council on November 18, 1965. The "lay apostolate," as the Catholic Church commonly refers to the mission or duties of non-ordained members of the church, stands at the center of the council's hopes for renewal of the church as expressed in its most important documents, the dogmatic constitution *Lumen Gentium* (on the church) and the pastoral constitution *Gaudium et Spes* (on the church in the modern world). Fundamentally, the decree calls on the laity to exercise their Christian vocation to participate in the work of the church. Though divided into eight chapters, *Apostolicam Actuositatem* takes up three issues: (1) the definition of the lay apostolate; (2) its basis; and (3) methods for its greater effectiveness.

First, all members of the church share in the mission of Christ to make God's love present in the world; as believers and as citizens of the world (no. 5), lay people are specifically called to be "a leaven in the world" (no. 2). Among Christians, then, there is a diversity of service (lay and clerical) but a unity of purpose in the apostolate. Second, the foundational principle is clear: "from the fact of their union with Christ the head flows the laity's right and duty to be apostles" (no. 3). This union is achieved in the sacrament of baptism, strengthened in the sacrament of confirmation, and nourished by the sacrament of the Eucharist (no. 3). While the Holy Spirit gives gifts to all Christians for the service of the church and the world, such gifts must be examined, and their use directed, by the church's pastors (bishops) (nos. 23–24). Finally, the decree outlines the various fields of apostolic activity. These include the church itself; the family, society, and the nation in which Christians live; and the international sphere. Lay Catholics are called to "infuse the Christian spirit" in all these arenas (no. 13). The important role of women and young people in the church's apostolate is singled out for special mention (nos. 9 and 12). The lay apostolate is to be carried out by both individuals and by organizations properly regulated by church authorities (nos. 15–27). *Apostolicam Actuositatem* closes with a mandate for the careful training and instruction of Catholics for the lay apostolate. It also calls for the promotion of a spirituality that corresponds to lay life (nos. 28–33).

James B. Nickoloff

See also LAY MINISTRY; VATICAN, SECOND COUNCIL OF THE.

APOSTOLIC CONSTITUTION
A type of official document issued by a pope for the purpose of clarifying a point of doctrine or, more frequently, for legislative purposes within the church.

Orlando Espín

See also APOSTOLIC EXHORTATION; AUTHORITY; CANON LAW; ENCYCLICAL; MAGISTERIUM, ORDINARY; POPE; ROMAN CATHOLIC CHURCH.

APOSTOLIC EXHORTATION
A type of document issued by a pope, similar in importance to an encyclical today, for the purpose of clarifying or introducing reflections on a doctrinal or pastoral subject. It is frequently designed to encourage discussion of the subject within the church.

Orlando Espín

See also APOSTOLIC CONSTITUTION; AUTHORITY; CANON LAW; ENCYCLICAL; MAGISTERIUM, ORDINARY; POPE; ROMAN CATHOLIC CHURCH.

APOSTOLIC FATHERS

A title given, since the seventeenth century, to some ecclesiastical writers and church leaders of the period immediately following (or even contemporary with) the writing of the New Testament. An effort is currently being made to find and use another expression that would avoid the gender-bound, misleading character of the title.

Orlando Espín

See also DOCTORS OF THE CHURCH; PATRISTICS/PATROLOGY; TRADITION (IN CHRISTIANITY).

APOSTOLICITY

A "note" or "mark" of the church. Along with unity, holiness, and catholicity, apostolicity represents an essential mark of the true church of Christ. By being linked to the original *apostles* (that is, those who witnessed the resurrection of Christ, were appointed his messengers, and were seen as pillars of the early Christian community), the church is "apostolic." Because the first apostles founded a tradition that is considered forever normative and salvific, salvation in Christ is available through union with Christ's messengers and their saving tradition. The church's apostolicity means that error will not prevail (Matt 16:18) and that the church, despite the sinfulness of all its members, will be preserved as a universal means of salvation. The church's apostolicity is supported by the New Testament (see 1 Tim 1:3-5; 2 Tim 1:13, 2:2, and 3:14ff., and 4:5; Titus 1:1-5; Eph 2:20; Matt 16:18; Rev 21:14) and is made explicit in the Nicene Creed (381 C.E.) and at the Second Vatican Council (*Lumen Gentium* 20; *Dei Verbum* 7–8). Nearly all Christian churches today agree that apostolicity is essential to the church's identity. They differ, however, in understanding how apostolicity is maintained. During the sixteenth-century Reformation, Protestant leaders emphasized the apostolicity of doctrine (that is, continuity with the original teaching of the apostles) while Catholics stressed the apostolicity of ministry guaranteed by the unbroken chain into which bishops are ordained (and through them, priests and deacons) through the laying on of hands. Today the Catholic Church recognizes the apostolicity of both doctrine and ministry as well as the duty of all members of the church to maintain the link to the apostles through service and witness to the Gospel.

James B. Nickoloff

See also CATHOLICITY; HOLINESS; NOTES OF THE CHURCH; UNITY.

APOSTOLIC SUCCESSION

Apostolic succession refers to the belief that the Christian community stands in continuity with the faith of the apostles. Different Christian denominations have understood this continuity variously: some stress a more "invisible" connection of faith between the apostles and the communities descended from them (Protestant Christianity); others stress a more visible, historical connection based upon a validity of "orders" (episcopal and priestly ordination) which can be traced back to Peter, the first apostle (Orthodox/Roman Catholic).

Mary Ann Hinsdale

See also BISHOP (EPISCOPACY); CANON, BIBLICAL; CHURCH; COMMUNION (ECCLESIOLOGICAL); DEVELOPMENT OF DOGMA/OF DOCTRINE; INSPIRATION; ORDINATION; REVELATION; SENSUS FIDELIUM/SENSUS FIDEI.

APPARITIONS

Although more frequently associated in the last two centuries with manifestations of Mary, many claims of apparitions of Jesus, of the Holy Spirit, and of numerous saints have been made throughout most of Christian history. Wrongly assumed to happen only within the Roman Catholic milieu, apparitions have been reported among all major Christian traditions, and indeed, in most religions known to humanity. In Catholicism no apparition has ever been or could ever be given the importance of revelation, or of "adding to" revelation. Such a notion would be heretical in the Catholic tradition. At best, apparitions can be thought of as "visualized messages" granted by God to individuals for their own private spiritual progress, without ever requiring assent or acceptance on the part of the church or other individual Christians. Belief in apparitions is certainly not necessary in any of the major Catholic, Anglican, Orthodox, or Protestant Churches.

Orlando Espín

See also MARIAN DEVOTIONS; MARIOLOGY; POPULAR CATHOLICISM.

AQUINAS, THOMAS, ST. (1224–74)

St. Thomas Aquinas is one of the most well-known and influential Catholic theologians and philosophers of all time. He lived only approximately fifty years, which makes the size of his literary output truly amazing. He wrote several theological treatises, commentaries on books of the Bible, and commentaries on treatises of Aristotle and other philosophers. He entered the Dominican Order of Preachers in 1244 after a conflict with his parents who wanted him to become a Benedictine. He studied philosophy and theology at Paris and Cologne (under Albertus Magnus). Eventually, he joined the theology faculty at the University of Paris. Aquinas attempted to accommodate Aristotelian metaphysics (theory of the ultimate nature of reality) and epistemology (theory of knowledge) to a systematic Christian philosophy and theology. He followed Aristotle in rejecting Plato's doctrine of innate knowledge and in holding that knowledge in human beings has its ground or basis in sensory experience. According to Aquinas, the intellect, at birth, is a *tabula rasa* or "blank slate." Concepts are acquired by abstraction from sensory images or *phantasmata*.

Since we have no direct sensory experience of God in this life, we can only know about God's nature through the process of attending to *analogies* drawn from sensory experience. When we predicate certain attributes of God, for example, wisdom, goodness, and justice, we must acknowledge that our understanding of these attributes does not constitute knowledge of the Divine Essence as it is in itself. Aquinas's doctrine of Analogical Predication is midway between the view that attributes are predicable of God and creatures *univocally* (so that "wise" means the same thing whether attributed to God or humans) and the alternative position that attributes are *equivocally* predicated of God. On this latter view, "wise" in "God is wise" does not carry the same meaning as it does in ascriptions of wisdom to humans. Aquinas rejects both of the foregoing positions regarding attributing properties to God. Univocal predication implies that we can know as much about God as we know about ourselves, which is false on his view. Equivocal predication implies that we can know nothing about God in a positive way. Aquinas maintains that we need to be aware that, while we can have some understanding of God's nature in this life, it is an understanding that is limited by being filtered through the lens of sensory experience.

Aquinas's famous "Five Ways"—five arguments for the existence of God—reflect his epistemological stance. All of these arguments are *a posteriori* (grounded in experience). The "First Way" is based on Aristotle's reasoning leading to the conclusion that an Unmoved Mover must exist in order to account for the fact of our experience of motion in the world order. Aquinas's account of the nature of the human soul is also Aristotelian, though there is some question about whether Aristotle held that the soul is capable of surviving the death of the body. For Aquinas, the soul's postmortem immortality was a matter of religious faith as well as philosophical speculation. He held that the soul is the "substantial form" or basic organizational principle of the material body. Yet the soul is an immaterial form, on Aquinas's view, that can survive independently of the body after death since it has an intellectual activity that it can perform independently of matter.

Aquinas's positions on God, the creation of the world, the nature of physical substance, the relation of God to the created order, the moral and religious life of humans, and many other topics can best be studied by reading his two most famous treatises, the *Summa Theologiae* (in three parts) and the *Summa Contra Gentiles* (Books I–IV).

Linda L. Peterson

See also ARISTOTELIANISM; HYLOMORPHISM; SCHOLASTICISM; SUMMA CONTRA GENTILES; SUMMA THEOLOGIAE.

AQUINO, MARÍA PILAR (1956–)
Latina feminist theologian, currently a professor at the University of San Diego.

Aquino was raised on the U.S.-Mexico border, and educated in Mexico and in Spain. She was the first Catholic woman to earn a doctorate in theology from the Pontifical University of Salamanca. Former president of the Academy of Catholic Hispanic Theologians of the U.S., she has been influential in developing Latin American and U.S. Latina feminist theologies, critiquing male Latin American and Latino theologians for their frequent disregard of women's epistemologies and perspectives. Her greater contributions have been in the areas of epistemology and method. Besides numerous articles in journals and collective works, Aquino has published *Our Cry for Life* (1993), and *La teología, la Iglesia y la mujer en América Latina* (1994).

Orlando Espín

See also FEMINIST THEOLOGIES; LATIN AMERICAN CATHOLICISM; LATINO/A; LATINO CATHOLICISM; LATINO THEOLOGY (-IES); LIBERATION THEOLOGIES.

ARAHANT
An ancient Indic term meaning literally "Worthy One" that originally was applied to the Vedic gods. In early Buddhism and Jainism, Arahant (Pali, Arhat; Chinese, Lohan) came to designate a person who has realized the highest goal, nirvana, cut off all karma accumulations, destroyed desire and attachment, fully developed insight (*prajna*), and experienced enlightenment via meditation. Although the attained nirvana of Arahants and Buddhas is not different, a Buddha is superior based upon his possessing a host of supramundane powers and other perfections.

The early Buddhist path to the Arahant stage passes through the taking of the "three refuges" (Buddha, Dharma, Sangha);

then on to the *srotapanna* ("Stream Enterer") who would have no more than seven more human incarnations. Next comes the *sakridagamin* ("Once-returner") destined to only one more human birth, followed by the *Anagamin* ("Non-returner") destined for rebirth in a "formless realm" reserved for advanced meditators; and finally the Arahant who has completely cut off all the *asravas* ("defilements": sensual desire, desire for continued existence, false views, ignorance). In the Nikaya schools, attaining Arahant status was seen as only possible—with rare exceptions—for monks or nuns; later canonical texts assert that any householder who realized Arahantship had to be ordained that day or pass out of life into parinirvana. Arahants are also celebrated in the early texts for their supramundane powers (*siddhis*). Early controversies in the first centuries disputed whether individual Arahants can regress out of salvation.

The development of the Mahayana schools was distinguished above all by the exaltation of the bodhisattva at the expense of the Arahant: early texts criticize the Arahant's pride, characterize the isolated individual-centered quest for nirvana as selfish, and deride the Arahant's spiritual attainment as partial and inferior. The *Lotus Sutra*, for example, describes the Arahants as being astonished at hearing the "higher revelations" taught by Shakyamuni; they become so confused and angry by these teachings that they walked out! Other Mahayana texts (such as the *Prajnaparamita*) make Arahants the object of ridicule and exhort them to deeper understanding of the Buddha's teaching.

Across the Sino-Japanese regions where Mahayana Buddhism dominated, many large monastery temples have halls that enshrine a set of "Sixteen Lohans." This perhaps indicates their assimilation with the bodhisattva ideal such that all are thought to be still present in samsara to protect the faith until the coming of the next Buddha, Maitreya. In modern Theravada societies, the rarity of new Arahants is often interpreted as a sign of the religion's decline.

Todd T. Lewis

See also BODHI; BODHISATTVA; BUDDHA; HINAYANA; MAHAYANA BUDDHISM; PRAJNA.

ARAMAIC

A Northwest Semitic language related to Hebrew that was spoken and written in parts of Mesopotamia and Syria-Palestine as early as the ninth or tenth century B.C.E. Aramaic was written using the Phoenician alphabet that was also used for Hebrew and other languages of Syria-Palestine. Aramaic became the most widely used language in Mesopotamia from about the sixth century B.C.E. on. It eventually became one of the official languages of the Persian Empire. Because of this widespread usage, some parts of the Hebrew Bible were written in Aramaic (Ezra 4:8–6:18; 7:12-26; Dan 2:4b–7:28, and isolated words and phrases elsewhere). Aramaic survived as a spoken language well into the Roman period in Syria-Palestine. From the second century B.C.E. through the second century C.E. much Jewish literature was composed in Aramaic, including materials found at Qumran; the Targumim (translations of biblical writings into Aramaic); and midrashim (interpretations of Scripture). In the first century C.E. Aramaic was in general use in Palestine, especially in Galilee. As a Galilean, Jesus spoke Aramaic and some of the words attributed to him in the Gospels are Aramaic; for example, Mark 5:41, *ta-*

litha cum and the citation of Psalm 22 in Mark 15:34, *eloi eloi lama sabachthani*. Many Aramaic documents have survived from the first and second centuries C.E. Syriac, a dialect of Aramaic, became the standard language of Eastern Orthodox churches.

Russell Fuller

ARAMAIC MATTHEW

An early tradition stemming from Papias (ca. 130), bishop of Hierapolis in Asia Minor, is quoted in the fourth century by Eusebius (*HE* 3.39.16), stating that "Matthew collected the oracles [the sayings of Jesus?] in the Hebrew language, and each interpreted them as best he could." By Hebrew, Papias possibly meant Aramaic, the language Jesus and his followers would commonly have spoken. The collection of oracles may refer to a document with a genre like that of Q or the later Gospel of Thomas.

The Papias tradition has been used in theorizing that Matthew, as a collector of oracles, was the first evangelist to write a gospel, and that it must have been in Aramaic. This concept of Aramaic Matthew has been brought into many discussions of the literary relationships among the Synoptic Gospels.

Papias' statement, however, does not support the existence of Aramaic Matthew as a gospel since it refers only to a collection of sayings, presumably those of Jesus, although even that is not certain. Furthermore, while the apostle Matthew may somehow have been at the origins of the Gospel tradition if he collated the sayings of Jesus in a document like Q, scholars widely agree that the full Gospel of Matthew in Greek as it has been transmitted to us is not a translation from an Aramaic original.

F. M. Gillman

See also ARAMAIC; EUSEBIUS OF CAESAREA; MATTHEW/MATTHEAN; Q SOURCE; SYNOPTIC GOSPELS; SYNOPTIC PROBLEM; THOMAS, GOSPEL OF.

ARBAᵓAH TURIM

Literally, "Four Rows." A compilation of Jewish law written by Jacob ben Asher in Toledo, Spain, in 1475.

Known simply as the Tur, this compendium of Jewish law is the author's attempt, in his time and place, to resolve differences of opinion about Jewish law, and to spell out clearly and concisely how the law was to be observed by each Jew.

It gets its name from its structure. It is composed of four major books, each dealing with a different aspect of Jewish law: *Orach Chayim*, The Path of Life, deals with the laws and liturgy of prayer and the festivals. *Yoreh Deᵓah*, The Teachings of Knowledge, deals with ritual laws of everyday life. *Eben HaᵓEzer*, The Stone of Help, deals with the laws of marriage and divorce. *Choshen HaMishpat*, The Breastplate of Judgment, deals with Jewish civil law.

Wayne Dosick

See also HALACHAH.

ARCHBISHOP

This title originated in the fourth century. Today, it refers to a bishop responsible for an archdiocese. Occasionally the title is used as a way of honoring a bishop who does not lead an archdiocese but has contributed distinguished service to the church.

Orlando Espín

See also BISHOP (EPISCOPACY); DIOCESE/ARCHDIOCESE; ECCLESIASTICAL PROVINCE; EPARCH.

ARCHDIOCESE

See DIOCESE/ARCHDIOCESE.

ARCHIMANDRITE

In many Eastern Churches, this is a title roughly equivalent to the Western term "abbot."

Orlando Espín

See also ABBOT/ABBESS; EASTERN CATHOLIC CHURCHES; ORIENTAL CHURCHES; ORTHODOX CHURCHES.

AREOPAGUS

A hill that juts out from but is still part of the Acropolis, in Athens. In time the term became associated with the council that met on the hill to dispense justice and influence the course of city politics. Under the Roman Empire, the council was increasingly concerned with religious matters. The apostle Paul was brought to the Areopagus to explain his teachings (cf. Acts 17:19).

Orlando Espín

See also GRECO-ROMAN RELIGION; PAUL.

ARIANISM

Arianism was a theological movement within Christianity that so stressed the unity and transcendence of God that it denied the divinity of the Logos/Son. Thus Arians maintained that Jesus, the incarnate Logos, was not God. The movement takes its name from the Alexandrian priest Arius, the first proponent of this position. Arius held that monotheism required the Logos/Son could not be the same in substance as the Father because the Logos/Son is begotten, and the Father is unbegotten. Moreover, Arius held that "there was a moment when the Logos/Son was not." For Arius, the Logos/Son, though above all other created beings, was still only a creature and not God. Though condemned at Alexandria in 320, Arius's views nevertheless spread throughout the Christian East. The Council of Nicaea in 325 condemned Arius's teachings as blasphemous. The council taught that the Logos/Son was "from the substance of the Father," "true God from true God, begotten not made, and of one substance with the Father (homoousion)." For more than fifty years after the Council of Nicaea, various forms of Arianism surfaced to trouble the church. The root cause of this resurgence was the fear among many Greek-speaking bishops that Nicaea had so stressed the consubstantiality of the Father and the Logos/Son as to eradicate the difference between them. To stress the difference, many local councils of bishops proposed that the Logos/Son was "unlike the Father" or simply "like the Father." St. Athanasius opposed these proposals and wrote many theological works in which he carefully explained the meaning of the formula of the faith adopted at Nicaea. Eventually, the bishops saw that their alternate formulas were denying the divinity of the Logos/Son who was "like the Father in regard to substance." Once the bishops grasped this insight, they were ready to accept what Nicaea had taught. At the Council of Constantinople in 381, the Father, Son/Logos, and Holy Spirit were all seen to be "one substance" (homoousios) and the Christian doctrine of the Trinity was clearly articulated.

Herbert J. Ryan, s.j.

See also ARIANISM; ATHANASIUS, PATRIARCH OF ALEXANDRIA; CAPPADOCIANS; CONSTANTINOPLE, FIRST COUNCIL OF; CONSTANTINOPLE, SECOND COUNCIL OF; CONSTANTINOPLE, THIRD COUNCIL OF; HOMOIOUSIOS TO PATRI; HOMOOUSIOS TO PATRI; LOGOS/WORD; NICAEA, FIRST COUNCIL OF; SUBORDINATIONISM; TRINITY/TRINITARIAN THEOLOGY/ TRINITARIAN PROCESSIONS.

ARISTOTELIANISM

Very little of the actual literary output of the ancient Greek philosopher Aristotle (384–322 B.C.E.) survived into the Middle Ages, but his work had a profound influence on the development of medieval theology and philosophy. The Roman philosopher Boethius (480–524) had completed Latin translations of some of Aristotle's works on logic and rhetoric. Notes and commentaries on Aristotle's work had been translated into Hebrew and Arabic, and these became available in Europe during the twelfth century. By 1255, Aristotelianism was included in the required course of study at the University of Paris.

The introduction of Aristotelian thought in European universities was the initiation of a series of vigorous debates that were carried on for centuries. Some Christian thinkers, most notably St. Thomas Aquinas (1224–74), attempted a synthesis of Aristotle's philosophy and Christian theology. Aquinas's interpretation of Aristotle's thought was sometimes in conflict with the interpretations developed by Islamic and Jewish philosophers who had no interest in rendering Aristotle's teaching compatible with Christian doctrine. The Islamic philosopher Averroes (Cordoba, twelfth century) was among the most influential commentators on Aristotle's work. One of the more significant debates in the history of theology arose out of conflicting interpretations of Aristotle on the part of Averroes and Aquinas. Averroes' followers at the University of Paris held that, according to Aristotle, the human intellect is necessarily immaterial, yet the soul is the substantial form (or basic organizational principle) of the body. Since the form of the body must be a material form, the human soul, the Averroists reasoned, cannot be immaterial. Hence, the soul does not contain the intellect. Instead, according to the Averroists, there is one singular immaterial intellect through which all human beings understand. This singular intellect exists apart from the physical world, but each human being is somehow in contact with it through the intermediation of sensory experiences. For the Averroists, this conclusion about the singularity of the human intellect followed necessarily from an accurate interpretation of Aristotle's thought.

Though the idea that all humans share a single immaterial mind has to be one of the most fascinating ideas ever put forward, it is clearly at odds with certain Christian beliefs and Aquinas was quick to point this out. Aquinas agreed with the Averroists that Aristotle must be interpreted as holding that the intellect is immaterial. He also agreed that, according to Aristotle, the human soul is the substantial form of the living human organism. Yet, according to Christian doctrine, each individual human soul is said to survive the death of the body. If the soul is regarded as a material form, Aquinas reasoned, it would degenerate with the body at death. Life after death would be impossible and there would be no postmortem judgment, heaven, or hell. Accordingly, on Aquinas' interpretation of Aristotelian thought, the human soul is immaterial and capable of surviving the death of the body. Aquinas criticized the Averroists claiming that, on their rendering of Aristotle's view, it would be impossible to account for the fact that different human beings understand things differently. If all humans share a single mind, as the Averroists maintained, it would seem to follow that we would all understand things in precisely the same way, which is contrary to what is observed. Aquinas's arguments against the Averroists are found in his treatise *De unitate intellectus contra averroistas*. This treatise had an enormous impact on subsequent theorizing, among Christian philosophers and theologians, concerning the nature of the soul's relation to the body and the possibility of the soul's surviving death.

Linda L. Peterson

See also AQUINAS, THOMAS, ST.; ARISTOTLE.

ARISTOTLE (384–322 B.C.E.)

Aristotle would appear on anyone's list of the greatest philosophers of all time. He was a student of Plato and, together with his teacher, had a lasting influence on the development of all subsequent philosophical and theological theorizing. His work profoundly influenced the thinking of St. Thomas Aquinas in all areas of philosophy and theology. Aristotle's theory of the ultimate nature of reality departed significantly from the view of his teacher, Plato. While Plato held that the ultimate principles of reality, the Forms, exist separately from the physical world of our experience, Aristotle brought the Forms into the physical world with his hylomorphic account of the natures of natural kinds. According to Aristotle, each natural substance has a form or basic structure that makes it a member of its species. Forms, for Aristotle, are immanent rather than transcendent.

Aristotle's influence circumscribes almost every area of intellectual inquiry. He wrote books on logic, the physical sciences, psychology, natural history, ethics, politics, rhetoric, and poetry. His best-known contribution in the area of theology is his account of the Unmoved Mover. In Aristotle's view, God, or the Unmoved Mover, is responsible for all motion. Since

he holds that the world exists eternally, he does not regard God as the world's creator. God, for Aristotle, is a metaphysical principle which moves all else in reality through being the ultimate object of desire (or "final cause"). Aristotle defines God as "Thought of Thought." God's activity is purely intellectual, in his view, and God does not interact with the world. God only thinks about God; that is, on this theory, God is the only proper object of God's thought.

Linda L. Peterson

See also AQUINAS, THOMAS, ST.; ARISTOTELIANISM; HYLOMORPHISM; PLATO.

ARIUS (?–336)

Arius was a student of Lucian of Antioch, the influential priest, teacher, and martyr. Arius became a deacon and then a priest in Alexandria, where he became a popular preacher in one of the major churches of the city. He began to spread the teaching that the Logos, the Second Person of the Trinity, was a lesser divinity, subordinate to the Father, who came into being after the Father. Arius' theology was condemned by the patriarch of Alexandria, Alexander, but Arius appealed for support from, among others, his influential fellow student, Eusebius, bishop of Nicomedia. The emperor Constantine tried to end the controversy by sending Hosius, bishop of Cordova, to Alexandria in an attempt to intervene. The attempt failed and Constantine called for a conference to meet at Nicaea to settle the issue. The council met in 325 with an attendance of some two hundred and fifty bishops. The teaching of Arius was condemned, and the phrase *homoousios* (one in substance) was included in the creed agreed upon by the council to specifically exclude the teaching of Arius. Arius was banished by the emperor, but, through the influence of Eusebius of Nicomedia, was restored to Alexandria around 334. However, the new patriarch of Alexandria, Athanasius, refused to accept Arius back into communion, and Arius died in Alexandria shortly thereafter in 336. The teaching that the Son was subordinate to the Father, called Arianism, and considered heretical by its opponents, continued to be defended by many Christians for at least another century.

Gary Macy

See also ALEXANDER OF ALEXANDRIA; ARIANISM; ATHANASIUS, PATRIARCH OF ALEXANDRIA; CHRISTOLOGY; CONSTANTINE I THE GREAT; CREED/SYMBOL OF FAITH; HOMOOUSIOS TO PATRI; LOGOS/WORD; NICAEA, FIRST COUNCIL OF; NICAEA, SECOND COUNCIL OF; NICENE CREED; SUBORDINATIONISM; TRINITY/TRINITARIAN THEOLOGY/ TRINITARIAN PROCESSIONS.

ARJUNA

A central figure of the *Mahabharata*, the great Hindu epic, Arjuna is a warrior renowned in Hindu lore for his prowess in battle. He is most widely known in the West as the pupil of Krishna in the *Bhagavad Gita*.

Lance E. Nelson

See also BHAGAVAD GITA; KRISHNA; MAHABHARATA.

ARK OF NOAH

Box-dwelling made of gopher wood which, according to the account in Genesis 6–9, housed Noah, his family, and male and female representatives of all the living creatures of the earth during a cosmic flood that destroyed all the other living creatures God had created. According to the narrative, human beings had sinned. As punishment, God determined to destroy them. However, Noah was a righteous man, so God provided that he and his family should be saved. God therefore commanded Noah to build an ark. Those taken into the ark were preserved from drowning. After the Flood, those who had been saved in the ark repopulated the earth. God made a covenant with all creation promising never again to destroy the world with water. As a sign of the covenant God placed a rainbow in the sky.

Genesis 6–9 is believed to contain Yahwist and Priestly sources. Different authors account for discrepancies in the duration of the Flood, the numbers of animals taken into the ark, and other details of the narrative.

Many other ancient Near Eastern peoples also had flood stories among their traditions, the most famous of which is the Akkadian Gilgamesh epic. Historical scholars believe that the ancient Israelites were familiar with these other flood stories and incorporated aspects of them into their own story.

There is only one other reference to the ark of Noah in the Old Testament. In the book of Wisdom, Wisdom is credited with saving the earth, "piloting the just man on frailest wood" (10:4). In the New Testament, the building of the ark in which a few persons were saved is said to prefigure baptism through which believers in Jesus are saved (1 Pet 3:20).

Alice L. Laffey

ARK OF THE COVENANT

(Hebrew, 'aron hab-berit). The ark of the covenant was a sacred artifact of the ancient Israelites that symbolized the presence of YHWH. The ark was also called the ark of God, or the ark of the Lord. According to Exodus 25:10-22 the ark was to be constructed of acacia wood and overlaid with gold. It was to be a rectangular box approximately 1 X 0.7 X 0.7 meters. It was transportable, and there were rings on the sides through which poles could be placed. The Levites were given the task of carrying the ark. According to Deuteronomy 10:5, the tablets with the Decalogue were placed by Moses in the ark. In early stories the ark is a powerful object that could be carried into battle as a symbol of the presence of YHWH. If the ark was present, then YHWH was fighting for the people. The ark was so sacred that if it were touched by unauthorized persons they would die (2 Sam 6:6-7).

Russell Fuller

ARMENIAN CATHOLIC CHURCH

Armenia was the first country to accept Christianity as its official religion (in 303 C.E.). For a number of reasons, the Armenian Church rejected the definitions of the Council of Chalcedon (451 C.E.); and yet Armenians were never in full communion with other Monophysite churches. During the eleventh and twelfth centuries, the whole Armenian Church was in communion with Rome, but then separated until a significant group again united with Rome in 1740 and formed the Armenian Catholic Church; but most Armenian Christians did not join. Turkish persecution of Armenians during World War I helped spread the Armenian Catholic Church throughout the world. Its liturgy is substantially that of St. Basil, yet it is considered an older version of the Byzantine Rite with Antiochene and Latin influences. The Armenian Catholic Church has some 200,000 members worldwide under the overall jurisdiction of the Patriarch of Cilicia.

Orlando Espín

See also ANCIENT CHURCHES OF THE EAST; BYZANTINE CATHOLIC CHURCHES; BYZANTIUM/BYZANTINE; CATHOLIC TRADITION; CHALCEDON, COUNCIL OF; EASTERN CATHOLIC CHURCHES; MONOPHYSITISM; ORIENTAL CHURCHES; ORTHODOX CHURCHES; ROME, SEE OF.

ARMINIANISM

Associated with Dutch minister Jacob Arminius (1560–1609), this theological movement challenged a Calvinist interpretation of predestination. The Remonstrance of 1610, a manifesto drawn up by disciples of Arminius, asserted the compatibility of human free will with divine sovereignty. At the Synod of Dort of 1618–9, the Dutch Reformed Church rejected the Remonstrance and affirmed in five articles: the total depravity of humanity; the unconditional election of those predestined to salvation; the atonement effected by Christ limited to the elect; the irresistibility of grace; the perseverance of the elect. These articles reaffirmed the doctrine of predestination to salvation or damnation without regard for human merit of any kind.

Arminianism continued, however, to influence Reformed Churches in Holland, France, England, and elsewhere. John Wesley (1703–91), founder of the Methodists, figures among prominent Arminians.

Thomas Worcester, S.J.

See also ARMINIUS; CALVIN, JOHN; CALVINISM; GRACE; MERIT; PREDESTINATIONISM (CALVINIST); REFORMED CHURCHES; REFORMED THEOLOGY (-IES); WESLEY, JOHN.

ARMINIUS, JACOB (1560–1609)

A Dutch Reformed minister, Arminius was accused of Pelagian heresy when he challenged the Calvinist interpretation of grace and predestination. Professor at Leiden (Holland), Arminius sought changes in two key doctrinal formulations: the Belgic Confession and the Heidelberg Catechism. Theologians inspired by Arminius continued to pursue doctrinal reformulation after his death.

Thomas Worcester, s.j.

See also ARMINIANISM; CALVIN, JOHN; CALVINISM; PELAGIANISM; PREDESTINATIONISM (CALVINIST); REFORMED THEOLOGY (-IES).

ARNAULD, ANGÉLIQUE AND ANTOINE

Sister and brother, these two members of a prominent French family played important roles in the early stages of the Jansenist movement.

Angélique (1591–1661) was abbess of the convent of Port-Royal. From 1608 she undertook a rigorous reform of this house, eventually removing it from the Cistercian order and bringing it under the spiritual direction of Saint-Cyran, friend and collaborator of Jansen.

Antoine (1612–94) was ordained a priest in 1641 and published two years later his most famous work, *De la fréquente communion*. For Antoine Arnauld, not only must confession precede Communion, but a period of penitential preparation should intervene between confession of sins and absolution. The effect of this approach to penance was not frequent but infrequent Communion. Opposed to Jesuit sacramental practice, Arnauld's work generated enormous controversy in the seventeenth century and well beyond. Defense of Arnauld plays a role in Pascal's *Provincial Letters*. It was not until the early twentieth century that Arnauld's perspective was definitively rejected by the church, when Pope Pius X established and encouraged the practice of frequent reception of Communion.

Thomas Worcester, s.j.

See also EUCHARIST; JANSEN, CORNELIUS; JANSENISM; PASCAL; PIUS X, POPE; RECONCILIATION, SACRAMENT OF; SAINT-CYRAN, ABBOT OF; SOCIETY OF JESUS.

ARNOBIUS OF SICCA
(FOURTH CENTURY C.E.)

A teacher of rhetoric in North Africa for many years, Arnobius was at first an opponent of Christianity. He was converted by opponents late in life, and defended his new beliefs in *Against the Nations*, his only surviving work. The treatise shows a remarkable command of classical literature, but surprisingly contains very few references either to Scripture or to other Christian writers.

Gary Macy

See also APOLOGISTS.

ARON HAKODESH

(Hebrew, holy ark). In a synagogue, the receptacle in which the Torah scrolls are kept. In the Western Hemisphere, the ark normally is located on the eastern wall of the synagogue, so that the congregation in prayer faces both the ark and Jerusalem. Second to the scrolls themselves, the ark is considered the holiest part of the synagogue.

The earliest arks were movable chests, often placed in a niche in the synagogue wall. Later the ark became a permanent fixture in which the scrolls stand upright, covered in elaborate cloth wrappers and topped with decorative finials. The ark's doors or decorative curtains remain closed during the majority of the worship service. They are opened when the scrolls are to be removed for reading and at other particularly important points in the prayer service. At these times, the congregation stands and so confronts God through the divinely revealed Torah observed within the ark.

Alan J. Avery-Peck

See also SYNAGOGUE; TORAH.

ART, LITURGICAL

The term refers to art whose function is use in the public worship of the church. It is distinguished from other generally broader terms which suggest art with a particular theme or subject matter, for example, sacred art, religious art, or Christian art, which may or may not be appropriate for liturgical use. The term sacred art, although long used especially among Europeans for both liturgical art and for any art with the capacity to reveal the mystery of God, is problematic (as are the similar terms, sacred place, sacred music, sacred time, and so on) due to the dualistic suggestion that "nonsacred" art is somehow not holy or not a means of disclosing the infinite beauty of God. The term "liturgical art" is more precise and restrictive. It refers to art governed by two basic criteria: (1) quality, including, for instance, honesty and genuineness of materials, care in execution, the artistic gift for producing a harmonious whole; (2) appropriateness for use in the liturgy, that is, the work of art must "must be capable of bearing the weight of mystery, awe, reverence, and wonder which the liturgical action expresses, [and] it must clearly *serve* (and not interrupt) ritual action which has its own structure, rhythm

and movement" (United States Conference of Catholic Bishops, *Environment and Art in Catholic Worship*, 24). Thus liturgical art includes any art form that might be employed in the action of public worship or in its environment: music, architecture, sculpture, painting, furniture-making, pottery-making, glass-blowing, audiovisuals, ritual movement and gesture, dance, mime, and drama.

Sometimes the term is used more specifically to indicate liturgical architecture and the decorative arts needed for liturgy, that is, the design, construction/renovation and decoration of churches, other liturgical spaces, and of specialized areas within the church building, for example, gathering space, area for the assembly, baptistry, chapels or areas for the sacrament of reconciliation, reservation of the Eucharist, particular devotions, and so on. Liturgical art also includes the design and fashioning of the following: furnishings of the worship space, especially the altar or holy table, ambo, presider's chair, baptismal font; liturgical vessels, for example, chalices, flagons for water and wine, bread plates and ciboria; liturgical vestments, for example, chasubles, albs, copes, stoles, choir robes, etc.; other items for liturgical use, for example, processional cross, candlesticks, liturgical books (design of covers and layout); decorative art or images for placement in the liturgical space, for example, paintings, icons, murals, and tapestries, cloth hangings, and sculpture.

The Second Vatican Council's Constitution on the Sacred Liturgy (pars. 122–30) deals with the use of the arts in worship only in a general way, leaving to postconciliar liturgical documents the delineation of specific norms. However, it makes the following points of special significance: (1) reassertion of the church's role as patron of the arts; (2) acceptance in principle that all styles of art "be given free scope in the Church," including contemporary art and art "from every race and country," provided they express appropriate "reverence and honor"; and (3) the mandate for bishops to encourage art of "noble beauty," to avoid that of "sumptuous display," to remove any art from churches lacking in artistic merit or offensive because of "mediocrity or pretense," and to take great care when building churches that "they be suitable for the celebration of liturgical services and for the active participation of the faithful." Current norms for the application of the Constitution can be found in documents from the Congregation for Divine Worship and Discipline of the Sacraments: *General Instruction of the Roman Missal* (Third Typical Edition, 2002), nos. 288–318, 325–51; and *Redemptionis Sacramentum*, nos. 117–28 (2004). For usage in the U.S. see *Built of Living Stones: Art, Architecture, and Worship* (NCCB/USCC [now USCCB], 2000). Many liturgical scholars and consultants see these documents as a step backward from earlier ones, for example, previous editions of the General Instruction and (for usage in the U.S.) *Environment and Art in Catholic Worship* (Bishops' Committee on the Liturgy, NCCB, 1978).

Dennis W. Krouse

See also CHANT (IN CHRISTIANITY); LITURGY (IN CHRISTIANITY).

ARTHA
Artha (Sanskrit, material well-being, prosperity) is one of the four goals of life recognized in Hindu ethics as legitimate human pursuits, along with *dharma* (social and religious duty), *kama* (pleasure), and *moksha* (spiritual liberation). In order to carry out one's obligations to society and lead a religious life, Hindus believe, the layperson must first have a minimal standard of material well-being. Artha also includes political strategy and statecraft, concerns that received their classical textual articulation in the *Arthashastra*, the "Science of Politics."

Lance E. Nelson

See also DHARMA (IN HINDUISM); HINDUISM; KAMA; MOKSHA.

ARTICLES OF FAITH
Individual and distinct statements of truth that together make up the basic content of Christian faith. Although there is ongoing discussion among theologians, and certainly among different Christian denominations, about the precise content to be included among such statements, there is general agreement by most Christians that the ancient creeds (for example, the Nicene-Constantinopolitan Creed and the Apostles' Creed) contain the most basic articles of faith.

William A. Clark, s.j.

See also CREED/SYMBOL OF FAITH.

ARYAN
The Aryans (from the Sanskrit, *arya*, noble) were an Indo-European-speaking people known to scholars as the Indo-Iranians. One branch of this group migrated into the Indian subcontinent, by best estimates, around middle of the second millennium B.C.E. Their priests, known as *rishis*, were the inspired poets of the Vedas, which came to be regarded as the most sacred scriptures of Hinduism. The other branch of the Indo-Iranians, who also called themselves Aryans, settled in what is now Iran (a word ultimately derived from the term *Aryan*). They composed the bulk of the

Avesta, a text closely related to the *Rig Veda* in language, content, and time of composition. The Avesta later became the scripture of Zoroastrianism. As is well known, Adolf Hitler misappropriated the term Aryan to designate his imagined racially pure Nordic "master race." Neither the Indo-Iranians nor Hindu or Zoroastrian religious teachings have, of course, any actual historical connection with Nazism.

Lance E. Nelson

See also AVESTA; HINDUISM; RISHI; VEDAS; ZOROASTER; ZOROASTRIANISM.

ARYA SAMAJ
See DAYANANDA, SWAMI.

ASANGA (310–90?)
Indian Buddhist monk-philosopher of the fourth century C.E. associated with the Yogachara school of "Consciousness-Only." Both he and his brother Vasubandhu were influential in the scholastic traditions of Gandhara, in Northwest India; Asanga reputedly converted his younger brother away from the Sarvastivada school to the Mahayana. Legendary accounts of Asanga's exposition of Yogachara doctrine describe his instruction by the future Buddha Maitreya after a twelve-year period of forest meditation retreat. Texts attributed to him include the *Mahayanasamgraha*, the *Mahayanasutralankara* and the *Yogacarabhumishastra*. In the last text, Asanga develops his influential elaboration of the stages (*bhumi-s*) through which a bodhisattva progresses on the way to Buddhahood. Asanga's explication of the Consciousness-Only doctrine emphasized the importance of Yoga practice and the avoidance of extremes: either of taking the external constructs of mind as ultimately real or of neglecting to see that only consciousness truly exists.

Todd T. Lewis

See also ALAYA VIJNANA; CITTAMATRA; LANKAVATARA SUTRA; YOGACHARA.

ASBURY, FRANCIS (1745–1816)
Born in England, Asbury has been called the "patron saint" of American Methodism. In 1769, while Methodists were still part of the Church of England, he was appointed by John Wesley to organize Methodist societies in the thirteen colonies. Remaining in the colonies at the outbreak of the American Revolution, he was instrumental in laying the foundation for the independent organization of the Methodist Church in 1784. Ordained a deacon and elder at the founding conference known as the "Christmas Conference," Asbury was elevated to bishop in 1787. Asbury pioneered the practice of circuit-riding, itinerant preaching across a geographical "circuit" to plant new Methodist churches and strengthen existing ones. During his career, Asbury logged more than a quarter million miles on horseback along the eastern seaboard. Although he had an authoritarian leadership style, he sought to broaden the constituency of the church by appealing to the poor and less formally educated, using easily understood language, and creating a sense of family, all of which made Methodism the fastest-growing U.S. religious group in the first half of the nineteenth century.

Evelyn A. Kirkley

See also METHODIST CHURCHES; METHODIST THEOLOGY; WESLEY, JOHN.

ASCENSION
The beliefs that the risen Christ was bodily taken up, enthroned at the right hand of

God, and exalted as Lord are integral aspects of the doctrine of the Ascension. This major tenet of Christianity is included in the Apostles' Creed and all the major creedal summaries (for example, Hippolytus [ca. 215], Nicaea [325] Constatinople [381]). Since the Crucifixion and Resurrection are considered two acts of a single drama, the Ascension, enthronement, and exultation of Christ represent subsequent scenes in the act of the Resurrection.

Enoch (Gen 5:24; Sir 44:16; 49:14) and Elijah (2 Kgs 2:11; Sir 48:12; 1 Macc 2:58) were "taken up" to be with God before death. Jesus was not only raised to the life he enjoyed before his death on the cross, but he also entered a completely new kind of transcendent existence with God. The destiny of Christ foreshadows the destiny of his faithful believers. Christians assume that Christ will remain with God until he returns as judge at the end of time. However, Christ's present glorified transcendent existence also enables his abiding presence in the church.

The Ascension, enthronement, and/or exaltation are alluded to or presupposed in many New Testament texts (for example, John 1:18; 3:12-15; 6:62; 20:17; Phil 2:11; Col 3:1-2; Heb 1:3; 4:14, 6:19; 9:24, and others). Descriptions of the ascent of the Risen One into heaven in the presence of witnesses are found only in Luke (24:51), Acts (1:9-11), and the canonical ending of Mark (16:19). Although these reports explain why the resurrection appearances ceased, the Ascension has as much to do with Christ's present existence and status as Lord who intercedes for his followers (Rom 8:34) as it does with his disappearance from historical time and space.

Taking into consideration all relevant New Testament passages, the tradition inherently links Christ's ascension with his exaltation as Lord of creation (Phil 2:5-11; Eph 4: 7-11; 1 Pet 3:22b) as prelude to the sending of the Spirit who empowers the mission of the church (John 16:7; Acts 1:8; 2:32). In his present heavenly existence, Christ is the firstfruits that guarantees the ultimate salvation of believers (1 Cor 15:20; Col 1:15, 18) already united with him by faith and baptism (Eph 1:22; 4:15; Col 1:18; 2:10, 19) in the new and final age.

It seems likely that the conviction that Christ ascended and was enthroned and/or exalted stems from deep and early reflections on texts such as Psalms 8:6 and 110:2 in light of the resurrection experiences. The accounts and allusions to Jesus' ascent into heaven presuppose a three-story universe derived from an ancient, outdated cosmology and are overlaid with theological insights informed by early Christian experience and their subsequent interpretation of the religious writings of Israel. Today, in an age of space travel, the ascension should be recognized as a metaphorical way to express Jesus' transcendent destiny.

Regina A. Boisclair

ASCETICAL THEOLOGY

What today generally goes by the name of spiritual theology, or simply Christian spirituality, used to be referred to as ascetical and mystical theology. The root meaning of the word "ascetical" is exercise, practice, or training, and ascetical theology was variously called "spiritual science," "the art of perfection," "the science of the saints." Its primary concern was the steps which a person had to take in order to attain the perfect imitation of Christ.

The effort to reduce the practice of perfection to a science typified a manner of doing theology that held sway prior to the modern biblical movement. Vatican II marked the emergence of a theological style that was more pastorally oriented, more scripturally based, more comfortable with the category of experience, more contextualized in terms of history, more ecumenical, and less dogmatic. Ascetical theology felt the impact of those developments; it could not escape its association with negativity (the "soul's" pursuit of perfection entailed self-denial, mortification and renunciation) and its suspicion of the world and the body as sites of temptation. The term "Christian spirituality" or "spiritual theology" thus replaced it.

William Reiser, s.j.

See also ASCETICISM / ASCETIC; PERFECTION; SPIRITUALITY.

ASCETICISM / ASCETIC

By definition, an ascetic is someone who practices asceticism, and asceticism generally denotes the rigorous pursuit of holiness through discipline of mind and heart, thoughts and affections, by means of prayer, penance, and good works. Growth in perfection or holiness usually entails spiritual direction and discernment in order to safeguard the individual against self-deception and false humility, and to ensure that one's experience of God does not become idiosyncratic. Although many people would associate asceticism with monastic life or with the severe penitential practices of the Desert Christians of the fourth century, there is an asceticism proper to ordinary Christian living which could be summed up in the text: "If any want to become my followers, let them deny themselves and take up their cross daily and follow me" (Luke 9:23).

The history of asceticism is basically the history of Christian spirituality itself.

Inherent in the notion of asceticism, however, is the note of cultural resistance. What it means to be a Christian ascetic today is being determined by the challenges and dangers within contemporary society. While we have a far more positive view of human bodiliness than Christians of late antiquity, for example, we still need to develop a spiritual strategy that keeps us chaste, sensitive to the value of all human life, alert to the seductions of consumerism, leisure, and monetary success, ecologically responsible, and that preserves us from becoming selfish or isolationist in our attitudes toward weaker members of society. Contemporary asceticism, therefore, is not being construed in terms of the solitary individual before God in a private ascent to holiness, but in terms of an ascesis or practice that has social, political, and economic dimensions. Perhaps the form and meaning of Christian asceticism today is best expressed in the preferential option for the poor.

William Reiser, s.j.

See also DISCERNMENT; OPTION FOR THE POOR; SPIRITUAL DIRECTION; SPIRITUALITY.

ASHARIYYAH (TWELVERS)

See TWELVERS (IN ISLAM).

ASHKENAZIM

Since the Middle Ages, there have been three groups of the Jewish people, designated by the geographical area from which they come: Ashkenazim, Sephardim, and Edot HaMizrach.

The word "Ashkenaz" means "Germany." It is used to designate Jews who are descendants of the Jewish communities of Germany, Central Europe, and Eastern Europe, including Poland, and Russia.

All Jews share basic beliefs and practices. The differences revolve around custom, usually stemming from the cultural influences—food, dress, music, dance—of the countries and communities of origin.

The majority of Jews in the United States are Ashkenazim, that is, they are first-generation immigrants or second-, third-, or fourth-generation descendants from the Ashkenazic countries. For most of the history of the modern state of Israel, the majority population was Ashkenazic. In the late 1970s, the Sephardic population became the majority. With the large influx of Jews from the Former Soviet Union (mid 1990s), the majority population in Israel has once again become Ashkenazic.

Wayne Dosick

See also EDOT HAMIZRACH; SEPHARDIM.

ASHRAM

See ASHRAMA/ASHRAM.

ASHRAMA (LIFE STAGES)

In Hinduism, an *ashrama* (Sanskrit, place of striving) is a stage of life, one of the four stages of life recognized by classical Hindu law books as forming an ideal pattern to be followed by males of the three uppercaste categories. The stages include that of the student (*brahmacharin*), the householder (*grhastha*), the religious retiree (*vanaprastha*, literally, "forest dweller"), and the renouncer (*sannyasin*). The idea appears to have been that a male of one of the three uppercaste categories should first devote his energies to fulfilling his worldly duties (*dharma*), and then only should he begin to focus on the quest for spiritual liberation (*moksha*). In practice, only a minority have ever lived out the four stages according to this pattern, and some law books restrict access to sannyasa to brahmins alone. Nevertheless, it remains an important ideal.

Lance E. Nelson

See also BRAHMACHARIN; HINDUISM; SANNYASA.

ASHRAMA/ASHRAM

In Hinduism, an *ashrama* (or *ashram*) is a center for religious study and concentrated spiritual practice, a place where religious seekers gather in a residential setting to study with a *guru* who imparts spiritual blessings, wisdom, and practical instruction. Residents, who may be either laypersons or monastics, use their time in the ashrama to engage in spiritual practice, especially meditation. Like spiritual retreat centers in the West, ashramas tend to be located in quiet rural settings, as tranquility is felt to be conducive to meditation.

Lance E. Nelson

See also GURU; HINDUISM; RAJA-YOGA; YOGA.

ASH WEDNESDAY

Since the fourth century C.E., Ash Wednesday has been considered the traditional beginning of the Christian liturgical season of Lent (forty days of prayer and penitence before the joyful celebration of Easter). In many Christian churches today, ashes are distributed to the faithful during a liturgical service; the presider and/or assisting ministers dip the thumb in a small container of ashes, and mark the sign of the cross on each person's forehead. The placing of ashes on the head has its roots in Jewish and early Christian tradition; the original meaning seems to be an expression of mourning or sorrow, which developed gradually into the sense of sorrow for sins, a sign of penitence. In the Roman Catholic Church, the distribution of the ashes is accompanied by a short verse, or formula; the older version, "Remember, man, that you are dust and unto dust you shall return" has been replaced since the reforms of Vatican II by "Repent and believe the Good News."

Joanne M. Pierce

See also EASTER; LENT; LITURGICAL YEAR; RECONCILIATION, SACRAMENT OF.

ASIAN (CHRISTIAN) THEOLOGIES

Asian Christianity is as old as its founder, since Jesus is, as Pope John Paul II reminds us, an Asian, born as he was in the Middle East. Furthermore, early Christian missions were carried out not only in the western parts of the Roman Empire but also in its eastern parts and in the Persian Empire and beyond. The names of Addai, Aggai, and Mari figure among the most illustrious missionaries who brought the Christian faith beyond the eastern borders of the Roman Empire to the Persian Empire of the Parthians (Iran) and its client-kingdoms of Osrhoene, Adiabene, and Armenia. According to the *Acts of Thomas*, the apostle Thomas brought the Gospel to India not long after Jesus' resurrection and ascension. Toward the end of the third century, the learned theologian of Alexandria, Pantaenus, was sent on a mission to India by his bishop Demetrius. One of the attendees at the Council of Nicaea (325) was a certain bishop "John . . . of Persia and in the great India." Missionaries from the Persian church—among whom a certain Thomas of Cana—went to India, where later many Persian Christians ("Nestorians") took refuge during the so-called Great Persecution (340 to 380). By the middle of the fourth century, the

Indian church had many congregations with its own local clergy and indigenized liturgy in Syriac. The same "Nestorian" or East Syrian Church (or the Church of the East) pushed its mission farther into China in 635, as the Xi'an Stele, erected in 781, testifies.

The Catholic Church entered Asia for the first time in the thirteenth century during the Yuan (Mongolian) dynasty but did not survive. At the beginning of the sixteenth century, Catholic missions, even though tainted by their connections with European colonialism, were resumed with remarkable success, especially in India, China, Japan, Vietnam, and the Philippines, thanks to a great number of missionaries, mostly Jesuits, Franciscans, and Dominicans. Unfortunately, with the condemnation of the so-called Chinese Rites, that is, the veneration of ancestors, and the suppression of the Society of Jesus in 1773, Catholic missions in Asia suffered a severe setback and did not recover until the third decade of the nineteenth century. Meanwhile, Protestant Churches rivaled Catholics, as missionaries of various denominations poured into Asia, especially from Holland (Indonesia, Taiwan, and Sri Lanka), Denmark and Germany (India), England (India, China, Sri Lanka, and Singapore), and the United States (the Philippines, Korea, Japan, Thailand, Burma/Myanmar, and Malaysia). Christian missions, both Catholic and Protestant, were so successful that the years 1784–1860 are often called "The Great Century" in the history of missions. Recently, the dramatic increase in the number of the Charismatics/Pentecostals in Asia is an event of major consequences for Christian missions. For Catholicism in Asia, as well as elsewhere, Vatican II marks a watershed renewal movement, and its most long-lasting fruit is the founding of the Federation of Asian Bishops' Conferences (FABC) in 1970.

Theological Elaborations

A certain theology always undergirds liturgical, ecclesiastical, and missionary practices, and in this sense an Asian theology has been present since the very beginnings of Asian Christianity. Thus, early Indian Christianity is said to be "Hindu in culture, Christian in faith, and oriental in worship." All theologies are necessarily contextual; they have to make use of local languages and thought forms to make the Christian faith accessible to people in new sociopolitical, cultural, and religious environments. The Asian context is often represented as characterized by extreme poverty, cultural diversity, and religious pluralism, and Asian theologies can be viewed as self-conscious attempts to respond to these three features: liberation (to poverty), inculturation (to cultural diversity), and interreligious dialogue (to religious pluralism). Chronologically, the introduction of Asian Christian theologies began with inculturation, followed with liberation, and ended with interreligious dialogue.

Dialogue with Culture. The first to attempt a systematic expression of the Christian faith in indigenous cultural terms belongs to the Nestorian/East Syrian missionaries during the T'ang dynasty. As can be seen from the inscription on the Xi'an stele, its author, Jing-jing, made a creative use of Buddhist, Confucianist, and Daoist concepts and terms to expound the Trinity, creation, the original fall, Satan's rule, the Incarnation, salvation, the Bible, baptism, evangelization, ministry, morality, fasting, the Liturgy of the Hours, and the Eucharist. Similar borrowings can be found in the so-called Duahuang Cave Documents such as the *Book of Jesus-Messiah, Discourse on Monotheism,* and *Book of Mysterious Rest and Joy.*

In the seventeenth century, under the influence of Alessandro Valignano (1539–1606), the Jesuits carried out an extensive work of inculturation, particularly in China, Japan, Vietnam, and India. In China, Matteo Ricci's (1552–1610) use of Confucianism, for example, in his famous *Tianzhu shiyi* [The True Meaning of the Lord of Heaven] and his adoption of the controversial practice of ancestor veneration, the work of Giulio Aleni (1582–1649), and the writings of the *figurists* (who believed that Christian doctrines were "prefigured" in Chinese philosophy and culture), were path-breaking in formulating an Asian theology. In India, Roberto de Nobili lived as a sannyasi and taught the Christian faith using the philosophical and religious categories of Hinduism. In Vietnam, Alexandre de Rhodes (1593–1660) wrote a catechism in Vietnamese.

In more recent times, the focus has been, especially in the Catholic Church, on liturgical inculturation, with the adoption of indigenous rituals, vestments, music, dance, and architecture. Here the experiments of Indian liturgists are highly significant. Another extremely important achievement is the translation of the Bible into local languages, which is in itself a work of inculturation, to which Protestant missionaries have made an enormous contribution. Also, extremely interesting and original is the use of Asian myths and stories to convey the Christian message (Anthony de Mello, Choan-Seng Song, and Kosuke Koyama). In biblical hermeneutics, the works of Rasiah S. Sugirtharajah and Archie Lee are influential.

Dialogue with the Poor. Even though Asian Christian theology had not ignored the sociopolitical and economic dimensions of the Asian context, it was only in the 1970s, under the influence of Latin American liberation theology, that Asian theologians began developing indigenous forms of liberation theology. The sources of Asian liberation theology are drawn less from Marxist theories than from the experiences of those who were oppressed by colonialism and military dictatorships. In Korea, *minjung* theology was elaborated to defend the people (*minjung*) against human rights abuses, especially under President Park Jung Hee's regime, and to seek release from the collective bottled-up anger due to oppression (*han*). The *minjung* is identified with the crowd (*ochlos*) of the Gospels, and Jesus is presented as a member of the *minjung* (David Kwangsun Suh, Suh Nam Dong, Ahn Byung Mu, Kim Yong Bock, Hyun Young Hak).

In the Philippines, the "theology of struggle" was developed during the years of martial law imposed by President Ferdinand Marcos; it reclaimed the tradition of Filipino nationalist movements and emphasized the process and spirituality of the struggle rather than its outcome of liberation (Eleazar Fernández). In India, *dalit* (broken) theology was developed to combat discriminations perpetrated by the caste system (Arvind P. Nirmal, V. Devasahayam, James Massey). In India, too, tribal theologies were developed to draw attention to abuses of tribal rights, especially land rights, by colonialism and the central governments that followed (Nirmal Minz). In Taiwan, "homeland theology" and *Chhut Thau Thin* theology supported the right of the Taiwanese people to self-determination (Huang Po-Ho). One important recent development in Asian liberation theologies is Asian feminist theology, which combats the patriarchy and androcentrism prevalent in many Asian cultures, and seeks to foster the full flourishing of Asian women (Chung Hyun Kyung, Kwok Pui-lan, Mary John Mananzan, Virginia Fabella).

Dialogue with Asian Religions. Asia is the cradle of most of the world's major religions, and Christians have been very active in dialogue with the followers of these other faiths, even in the earliest centuries, particularly in China and India. Today, such dialogues, according to the FABC, should include four aspects: life, action, theological reflection, and spiritual experience. In the recent past, these fourfold dialogues were carried out especially by Western monks and clerics, including Jules Monchanin, Henri Le Saux, Francis Mahieu, Bede Griffiths, and Thomas Merton, many of whom lived as sannyasis in ashrams. In systematic theology, the focus has been on the doctrines of God, the Trinity, christology, mission, and spirituality (Michael Amaladoss, Felix Wilfred, Jacob Kavunkal, John Mansford Prior, Wesley Ariarajah, Jacob Parapally, Samuel Rayan, Tissa Balasuriya, Johannes B. Nanawiratma, Carlos Abesamis, James H. Kroeger). Also relevant are the works of Raimundo Panikkar (with Hinduism), Aloysius Pieris (with Buddhism), William Johnston (with Zen Buddhism), Jung Young Lee, Peter Phan, and Heup Young Kim (with Confucianism), and Joseph Wong (with Daoism).

In the ongoing dialogue of Christianity with Asian religions, the Christian God is interpreted using Emptiness, Brahman, and Dao; the Trinity is interpreted in terms of the Trimurti and Heaven-Earth-Humanity; Christ is interpreted in terms of monk, guru, avatar, buddha, and teacher; and spirituality in terms of contemplation, monasticism, yoga, *wu-wei, ren,* and *yin-yang*. Asian theology is on a fruitful course as it responds to the triple challenges of inculturation, liberation, and interreligious dialogue. A host of younger theologians are taking on the challenging task of creating a Christianity with an Asian face and a truly Asian theology, with great imagination and creativity (Andrew Park, Jonathan Tan, José de Mesa, Christina Astorga, Edmund Chia, Amos Yong, Gemma T. Cruz, Namsoon Kang, Hee An Choi, and others).

Peter C. Phan

See also AMALADOSS, MICHAEL; BUDDHISM; CONTEXTUAL THEOLOGY; CULTURE; DALIT; DE MESA, JOSÉ M.; DE NOBILI, ROBERTO; HINDUISM; INCULTURATION; INTERCULTURAL THOUGHT; KOYAMA, KOSUKE; METHOD IN THEOLOGY; MINJUNG THEOLOGY; PANIKKAR, RAIMUNDO; PHAN, PETER C.; RICCI, MATTEO; SANNYASA.

ASOKA/ASHOKA (269–232 B.C.E.)

Important ruler of ancient India, third in line of the Maurya dynasty, whose remorse after conquering the Kalinga kingdom led to his conversion to Buddhism. His over forty inscriptions proclaimed his wish to rule by moral practice, not authoritarian force. Buddhists in later history held him up as the ideal ruler who supported the faith and ruled compassionately.

Todd T. Lewis

See also BUDDHISM.

ASPERGES

The Latin word for sprinkle. In a number of liturgical services, the presider sprinkles the people with water to remind them of their baptism. This rite is called the *Asperges* because Psalm 51:7 has traditionally been sung during the actual sprinkling: "Sprinkle me, O Lord, with hyssop that I may be purified, wash me and I shall be whiter than snow." The Sacramentary allows the *Asperges* in place of the penitential rite at Mass on Sundays and at Sunday Masses celebrated on Saturday evenings. It is an integral part of the Easter Vigil and the Masses of Easter Day, where it is linked to the renewal of baptismal promises. In the anointing of the sick and in various rites of blessing, holy water is also sprinkled on persons. Some rites for the blessing of objects also includes the sprinkling of water. In this case, the imagery is not of baptism but of purification or setting apart for a sacred purpose.

Patrick L. Malloy

See also ANOINTING OF THE SICK, SACRAMENT OF; BLESSING (CHRISTIANITY); HOLY WATER; SACRAMENTARY.

ASSEMANI

The Syriac name "Simon." Its use is frequently limited to four members of an eighteenth-century Maronite Catholic family, famous for their learning. All four were great promoters of eastern liturgical and theological texts in western Europe, and were equally held by their contemporaries to be the authorities on Syriac traditions. The first and most famous of the four was Joseph Assemani (1687–1768) who was educated in Rome, became director ("prefect") of the Vatican Library, was elected archbishop of Tyre, was also a very active member of the Maronite National Council, and was mostly responsible for bringing the Syriac liturgical and theological traditions to Europe's attention in the first place.

Orlando Espín

See also EASTERN CATHOLIC CHURCHES; MARONITE CATHOLIC CHURCH.

ASSEMBLIES OF GOD

The Assemblies of God constitute the largest Pentecostal Christian denomination in the United States. A predominantly Euro-American group, it was founded in 1914 from a merger of Pentecostal groups in Texas, Alabama, Ohio, and Illinois. Although it began as a denomination of the disadvantaged and disinherited, it has become more mainstream and middle class in recent years. Like other Pentecostal groups, the Assemblies believe in biblical inerrancy, the fulfillment of biblical prophecy through premillennial dispensation, strict standards of ethical and moral conduct, and the manifestation of the Holy Spirit in faith healing and glossolalia, the spiritual gift of speaking in tongues. However, the Assemblies of God differ from other Pentecostal groups in that they are less Wesleyan and more Reformed in theology. They stress sanctification as a lifelong process rather than an instantaneous work of grace that follows on the experience of salvation. For them, glossolalia is not a sign of sanctification, but an independent manifestation of the Holy Spirit.

The Assemblies of God grew quickly in the twentieth century. They are aggressive missionaries and have established churches all over the world. While other Christian denominations have declined in membership in recent years, the Assemblies experienced steady growth through the 1970s–1990s. Their conservative morality, literal approach to the Bible, and clear-cut answers to theological questions, combined with a vibrant, charismatic spirituality have been the predominant reasons for their appeal.

In the 1980s, the Assemblies experienced two blows to their public image. Two prominent televangelists and Assemblies of God ministers became embroiled in controversy. Jim Bakker, host with his wife Tammy Faye of the "PTL Club," a popular television ministry with a variety/talk show format (PTL stands for "Praise the Lord" or "People That Love"), was accused of sexual and financial improprieties and went to prison for the latter. He was forced to resign as head of the PTL Club. Jimmy Swaggart, an old-style revivalist who shouted and cried during his TV sermons, was suspended from the Assemblies of God and stripped of his ministerial credentials for his relationship with a prostitute. He resigned in disgrace. Despite these setbacks, or perhaps because of the swift action taken by the denomination to deal with these miscreants, the Assemblies of God have continued to increase in membership and financial resources.

Evelyn A. Kirkley

See also FRUITS OF THE SPIRIT; GLOSSOLALIA; PENTECOSTALISM.

ASSMANN, HUGO (1933–)

Brazilian theologian and philosopher, Assmann was educated in Catholic theology in Brazil and in Rome, and in sociology. He has taught in universities in Brazil, Germany, and the U.S., and for many years was professor at the National University of Costa Rica. He has taught at the Methodist University of Piracicaba (Brazil). Assmann has written extensively on liberation theology and from the liberation perspective, having been deeply influenced by Marx's method of social analysis; this influence frequently placed him on the more "left-leaning" wing of Latin American theological thought during the past three decades. Among his more influential books are *Teología desde la praxis de la liberación* (1973), *Opresión-liberación, desafío a los cristianos* (1971), *Crítica à lógica da exclusão: Ensaios sobre economia e teologia* (1994), and the monumental *Sobre la religión* (1974–5), which he edited with Reyes Mate, gathering for the first time most texts by Marxist and other socialist authors on religion.

Orlando Espín

See also LATIN AMERICAN CATHOLICISM; LIBERATION THEOLOGIES; MARX, KARL; MARXISM.

ASSUMPTION OF MARY

The belief that Mary of Nazareth, after completing her life on earth, was bodily taken to heaven ("assumed") by God. It was defined as a dogma of the Catholic Church by Pope Pius XII in 1950. The Eastern Orthodox Churches usually hold the same belief (called *Koimesis*, or "Dormition," by them), but without official definition as to its precise dogmatic status or content.

It is generally agreed that this belief was unknown to the early church, appearing first in Eastern Christian circles during the fourth century. In the West the doctrine is taught from at least the sixth century. Liturgical celebrations recalling the "Dormition" (the "falling asleep") of Mary appear in the East sometime in the sixth century, and in the West after the seventh. From Rome the liturgy for the feast of the Assumption spread throughout western Europe. During the Middle Ages it became a very popular celebration. Some important medieval theologians (like Albert the Great, Thomas Aquinas, and Bonaventure) held that it was possible to think that God could have brought Mary bodily to heaven, because it was possible to think that Mary—as the model disciple of her son—could already be participating in the glory of the Resurrection. The assumption of Mary was a popularly held doctrine throughout most of the Catholic Church's history, but without official dogmatic definition until 1950.

Contemporary theologians, often considering Mary in her traditional role as symbol of the church, tend to view the doctrine of the Assumption on more ecclesiological grounds, as foreshadow of the church's full share in the life of the Resurrection. In countries where persecution of the church has occurred, the doctrine of the assumption of Mary often became a symbol for the hope that those suffering and despised today will one day share in the glory of the Resurrection.

Orlando Espín

See also DE FIDE; DEFINITION (OF DOCTRINES); DEVELOPMENT OF DOGMA / OF DOCTRINE; MARIOLOGY; MARY OF NAZARETH; TRADITION (IN CHRISTIANITY).

ASTARTE

(Ashtoreth, Ashtaroth). The Greek form of Ashtart, one of three Canaanite goddesses.

Russell Fuller

ASTROLOGY

The study of the supposed influence of stars and planets on human life. Astrology was very popular in the ancient world. Under the influence of Christianity, it was suppressed within the Roman Empire, but it reappeared in the West through the works of Muslim and Jewish writers. Astrology became popular in the sixteenth century among both Protestants and Catholics, but the Enlightenment again brought a decline in interest. Currently there is some revival in astrology's popularity.

Orlando Espín

See also MAGIC; POPULAR RELIGIONS.

ASURA

Related to the Avestan *ahura*, the Sanskrit word *asura* means "spiritual being." In the early hymns of the Vedas, the asuras were gods. In later Vedic texts and Hindu mythology, however, a shift of meaning occurred, and asuras came to be understood as demons, typically dwelling in the underworld, who seek in various ways to increase their own power in the cosmos at the expense of the gods, or *devas*. The asuras are not satanic, however, in the Western sense of being purely evil. They are rather examples of reincarnating beings, not essentially different from human beings or the gods, who have descended to a level of extreme egoism and blind power-seeking. A curious fact of Hindu myth is that particularly powerful asuras are more often than not launched on their destructive careers by boons bestowed upon them by deities such as Brahma, as the result of the demon's successful performance of ascetic disciplines. This indicates that, underlying the apparent conflict between the devas and the asuras, there is believed to be a mysterious and unspoken commonality of purpose that belies the common Western dualism of good and evil.

Lance E. Nelson

See also BRAHMA; DEVA/DEVI; DUALISM/DUALISTIC; HINDUISM.

ATATÜRK, MUSTAFA KEMAL (1881–1938)

Founder and first president (1923–38) of the Turkish Republic, established after the defeat of the former Ottoman Empire in World War I. Atatürk's given name was Mustafa Kemal but he is best known by his title, Atatürk, or "Father of the Turks." Much loved by his people, he is best known for his efforts to make Turkey a modern Islamic state and one that welcomed Western ideas. He also encouraged Turks to celebrate what was unique to Turkish culture and to avoid the influence of Arab culture as much as possible. For example, he "Turkified" the Turkish language by replacing old Arabic words with ones of "pure" Turkish origin. He also changed the alphabet used in written Turkish from Arabic to Latin. This had the effect of making it much easier for people to learn reading and writing. Though he did not advocate abandoning Islam, Atatürk believed that Turkey should adopt a Western-style constitutional democracy as its government, thereby diminishing the political influence of religious leaders on matters of state.

Ronald A. Pachence

See also OTTOMAN.

ATHANASIAN CREED

The creed, attributed to St. Athanasius and thus called the Athanasian Creed, was, in fact, composed in Latin about the beginning of the sixth century. Its opening words in Latin *Quicumque vult* ("Whoever would be [saved]") gives the creed its distinctive, scholarly name. The Latin text of this creed is a rhythmic paraphrase of St. Augustine's *De Trinitate* (I. IV. 7). Modern scholarship points to St. Caesarius of Arles as the author of this creed which was composed to guide the clergy of sixth-century southern France away from a form of Arianism resurfacing in that region. This creed attributed to Athanasius was never used in the baptismal liturgy. It was, however, recited at the hour of Prime during the Liturgy of the Hours. In the reform of the liturgy for the Catholic Church after Vatican Council II, the Office or Breviary was shortened and the recitation of this creed was dropped from the Liturgy of the Hours. The *Quicumque*, however, still remains in the service books of both the Lutheran and Anglican families of churches.

Herbert J. Ryan, s.j.

See also APOSTLES' CREED; ARIANISM; ATHANASIUS, PATRIARCH OF ALEXANDRIA; CREED/SYMBOL OF FAITH; LITURGY OF THE HOURS; NICENE CREED.

ATHANASIUS, PATRIARCH OF ALEXANDRIA (328–73)

Patriarch of Alexandria. Athanasius was the leader of the opposition to Arianism, insisting throughout his long life that the Son of God incarnate in Jesus was fully divine. Athanasius suffered much for his beliefs, spending over fifteen years of his episcopate in either exile or hiding. Beloved by his community, he was never handed over to the authorities while in hiding, and often he found his way out into the desert, where the famous monk, Antony, supported his cause. Along with his numerous writings against Arianism, Athanasius wrote a famous life of Antony that did much to popularize monasticism. Athanasius attended the Council of Nicaea in 325 as secretary for Alexander of Alexandria, and late in life, as one of the few who remembered the council first hand, helped to forge an agreement between those who accepted Nicaea and those who did not.

Gary Macy

See also ALEXANDER OF ALEXANDRIA; ARIANISM; NICAEA, FIRST COUNCIL OF.

ATHARVA VEDA

See VEDAS.

ATHEISM

The explicit and reasoned denial of the proposition, "God exists."

J. A. Colombo

See also RELIGION, CRITIQUE OF.

ATHENAGORAS

Second-century apologist. Little is known of Athenagoras' life. A professional philosopher in Athens, Athenagoras wrote a defense of Christianity called the *Embassy for the Christians* sometime between 176 and 180 C.E. In it he tried to convince Emperor Marcus Aurelius of the value of Christianity. He is considered the best of the apologists.

Gary Macy

See also APOLOGISTS.

ATMAN

In Hinduism, the *atman* (Sanskrit, self) is the authentic spiritual identity of each being, human and nonhuman. The essential self, it is usually said to consist of pure, blissful, undifferentiated consciousness. As such, the atman excludes all empirical components of the individual—including mind, memory, emotions, and karmic traces—indeed, everything that would distinguish it as belonging to a particular being. It is therefore misleading to translate it as "soul." Note that, for most schools of Hindu thought, the atman in animals and even in plants is the same, having the same spiritual potential as that found in human beings. In the theistic Vedanta of such theologians as Ramanuja and Madhva, there is a plurality of atmans, each individual being having its own discrete spiritual self. These many atmans are conceived of as parts, emanations, or creations of God, and the essential spiritual task is to disengage the atman from material entanglements and relate it properly to God. In the Advaita (nondualistic) Vedanta of Shankara, there is only one atman, which is understood to be identical with Brahman, the ultimate reality. In that context, "Atman" and its translation "Self" are appropriately capitalized, since they refer to the Absolute.

Lance E. Nelson

See also ADVAITA VEDANTA; MADHVA; UPANISHADS; VEDANTA; VISHISHTADVAITA VEDANTA.

ATONEMENT, CHRISTIAN

Atonement refers to the means by which sinful humanity is reconciled with God through the death and resurrection of Jesus. This theme pervades the New Testament. For example, in the writing of Paul, who states that "all have sinned and fall short of the glory of God" (Rom 3:23), the initiative in bringing about at-one-ment between God and humanity is shown to be from God (Rom 5:10-11; 2 Cor 5:18). Christ's death and resurrection are described as the means by which believers are redeemed from sin, from condemnation, and from death, and raised to new life. According to Romans 6:3-11, one of Paul's most developed passages on the believer's relationship with Christ, it is through faith in Jesus Christ, expressed in baptism, that a Christian is baptized into the death of Jesus, that is, is buried with him, so that just as Christ was raised from the dead, so also the believer is raised to walk in newness of life.

Ephesians conveys the sense that the atonement God brings about in Christ has various dimensions, that is, "horizontally," Gentiles and Jews "who once were far off have been brought near by the blood of Christ" (2:13) and "vertically," Christ has reconciled "both groups to God in one body through the cross" (2:16).

Among the numerous Gospel traditions reflecting early Christian thought on atonement are the statement in Mark 10:45 that Jesus came to give his life as "a ransom for many," and the declaration in John 1:29 that Jesus is "the Lamb of God who takes away the sin of the world."

In addition to the atonement effected between God and humans, thus the anthropological effects of the Christ event, the New Testament refers to a cosmological dimension of reconciliation as well. According to 2 Corinthians 5:19, "in Christ God was reconciling the world to himself," a clear denotation that the effects of atonement extend even to the kosmos itself (see also Col 1:20).

The concept of atonement or reconciliation in itself has nothing to do with cultic or sacrificial terminology, and must therefore not be equated with either expiation or propitiation.

F. M. Gillman

See also JUSTIFICATION; PROPITIATION; RECONCILIATION; REDEMPTION, CHRISTIAN; SALVATION; SANCTIFICATION (IN CHRISTIANITY).

ATONEMENT, HEBREW

(Hebrew, kapparah). The forgiving of sin by God. In Judaism, God offers atonement to those who engage in acts of repentance, a process designated by the Hebrew term teshuvah, which means, literally, "return," and refers to the individual's break from sinful conduct and return to proper behavior before God. Judaism thus sees the process of repentance, rather than God's offering of atonement, as central to religious and social life. Repentance is listed as one of the seven things God made before creation (Babylonian Talmud Nedarim 39b) and is seen as equivalent to the rebuilding of the Jerusalem Temple and restoration of the sacrificial cult (Babylonian Talmud Sanhedrin 43b), which are the highest goals of Jewish religious life. Repentance is viewed as the most direct and efficacious manner of placating God and assuring God's continued protection.

In light of this, even the Day of Atonement (Yom Kippur), the occasion on which God annually judges and forgives the people, is significant primarily in that it leads people to focus upon the process through which they must repent and correct their ways. On the Day of Atonement, God is believed to grant forgiveness only to those who already have repented; a simple profession of faith or promise to behave correctly in the future is not sufficient (Mishnah Yoma 8:8).

Judaism holds that forgiveness is available to all who repent, and that the hand of God is continually stretched out to those who seek atonement (Babylonian Talmud Pesahim 119a). Moreover, recognizing the dramatic change of behavior and intense commitment to God's will that stand behind true repentance, Judaism praises those who have sinned and repented even beyond those who have never sinned: "In a place in which those who repent stand, those who are completely righteous cannot stand" (Babylonian Talmud Berakhot 34b).

In Jewish thought, repentance always is possible, even on the day of death. The only requirement is that the desire to repent be serious and that the individual forsake his or her sinful ways. By contrast, one who continually repents but then sins again is not granted God's forgiveness, even on the Day of Atonement (Mishnah Yoma 8:9). Atonement is not achieved through the pronouncing of a linguistic formula or through simple participation in a rite of expiation. It depends, rather, upon a true commitment to changing one's life, turning from sin, and engaging in proper behavior before God.

Alan J. Avery-Peck

See also YOM KIPPUR.

ATTRITION

Attrition is repentance for one's sins out of fear of punishment or general repugnance of one's action rather than out of contrition, a repentance motivated by love for God and/or one's neighbor. The contrast between attrition and contrition involved a contentious theological debate (particularly between Dominicans and Franciscans) about which was sufficient as preparation for the sacrament of penance (currently called the sacrament of reconciliation). Scholastic theologians generally regarded attrition as a preparation for the more perfect contrition. Thus attrition was called imperfect contrition. Reformers (for example, Martin Luther) criticized much of the discussion about attrition and contrition as a misplaced Catholic emphasis on salvation by works. The Council of Trent declared that attrition and contrition were both a movement of God in the sinner to seek forgiveness in the sacrament of penance.

Michael J. Hartwig

See also CONTRITION; RECONCILIATION, SACRAMENT OF.

AUGSBURG CONFESSION

Composed by Philip Melanchthon and other Lutheran theologians, this doctrinal summary was presented to Emperor Charles V at the imperial Diet of Augsburg in 1530. Designed as a relatively moderate and somewhat conciliatory formula, it was nevertheless rejected by Catholic theologians present at the diet. The Augsburg Confession became and remains an important, authoritative document for Lutheran Churches. In the late twentieth century it became a focus of ecumenical discussions between Catholics and Lutherans.

Thomas Worcester, s.j.

See also CONCORD, FORMULA AND BOOK OF; LUTHER, MARTIN; LUTHERAN THEOLOGY; LUTHERANISM; MELANCHTHON, PHILIP; REFORMATION.

AUGUSTINE OF CANTERBURY (?–604)

Augustine, the prior of a Benedictine monastery, was chosen by Pope Gregory I, the Great, to lead a missionary effort to the Anglo-Saxons in England. Augustine and his party arrived in Kent in England in 597. Fortunately for the missionaries, the king of Kent, Ethelbert, was married to a Christian, the Frankish princess, Bertha. Aided by Bertha, Augustine not only succeeded in his missionary efforts, but also introduced Benedictine monasticism to southern Britain. He was appointed archbishop of Canterbury and, as such, the leader of the British church. This designation was not accepted, however, by the Celtic Christians already present in Britain, who rejected the Roman practices introduced by Augustine. Augustine died before these differences were reconciled.

Gary Macy

See also BENEDICTINES; GREGORY I THE GREAT, POPE; MEDIEVAL CHRISTIANITY (IN THE WEST); MISSIONARIES; MONASTICISM IN WESTERN CHRISTIANITY.

AUGUSTINE OF HIPPO (354–430)

One of the greatest of the Latin Christian writers, Augustine was born in North Africa in 354 C.E. His mother was a fervent Christian and his father was a pagan. Both agreed that Augustine should become a successful rhetor (lawyer). By the age of thirty, Augustine had succeeded beyond his parents' dreams in becoming rhetor of the city of Milan. Disillusioned with the Manichaeism he had picked up in his youth, Augustine was converted to Christianity by reading Neoplatonism and listening to the sermons of Ambrose of Milan. Augustine was baptized in 387. He retired as a rhetor and eventually become bishop of the North African city of Hippo (modern Annabis) in 395. He died at the age of seventy-six while the city of Hippo was under siege by the Vandals.

Augustine's most widely read books are his *Confessions*, an autobiographical work praising God for intervening in his life to save him, and *The City of God*, a book written to explain how it was possible for God to allow Rome to fall to the barbarian tribes. Augustine wrote, however, on almost every important topic of the time and influenced not only the North African Church, but the entire Western church. He wrote important treatises against the Donatists and against the Pelagians. His theology of the Trinity was original and central to later theology in the West. Augustine also wrote sermons, biblical commentaries, and catechecal lectures.

Gary Macy

See also AUGUSTINIANISM; DONATISM; PELAGIANISM.

AUGUSTINIANISM

Augustinianism refers to theologies that have been heavily influenced by the thought of Augustine of Hippo, the famous Christian writer of the fourth and fifth centuries. Augustine, however, wrote a great deal on many subjects, and his writings were some of the most influential in all of Western Christian thought; therefore, it is difficult to enumerate all the different theologies that might be called "Augustinian." Most commonly, "Augustinianism" refers, however, to two movements in theology. A series of twelfth-century theologians, particularly the Victorines and their students, relied heavily on Augustine for their approach to theology and their theological method was continued by the Franciscan theologians of the thirteenth and fourteenth centuries. This theology stressed the role of the will and of love over the role of the intellect, and has been contrasted with the Aristotelianism of Thomas Aquinas and the Dominicans. A second form of Augustinianism stresses Augustine's teaching on divine election and predestination. Here the strongest advocates of this form of Augustinianism would be Martin Luther, John Calvin, and the Jansenists.

Gary Macy

See also ANDREW OF ST. VICTOR; AQUINAS, THOMAS, ST.; AUGUSTINE OF HIPPO; CALVIN, JOHN; DOMINICANS; FRANCISCANS; HUGH OF ST. VICTOR; JANSENISM; LUTHER, MARTIN.

AUROBINDO, SRI

See GHOSE, AUROBINDO.

AUTHORITY

The term (from Latin *auctor*, "cause, creator, author"; and *augere*, "to increase, enrich") originated in ancient Rome's culture of law. Today we commonly distinguish between personal (or subjective) and official (or objective) authority. The first refers to the moral excellence or distinctive gifts of a person, while the second points to the office or role a person has in society. The authority of things such as books (for example, the Bible), laws, or symbols, derives from the personal or official authority of the people who stand behind them. *Theologically*, all authority, whether personal or official, comes from God. For Christians, this has meant that human authority is always and necessarily limited and is best understood as service (Greek: *diakonia*) to other members of the community or of the human family (Luke 22:24-27). Using authority for any other purpose is illegitimate, for it limits or even eliminates the freedom of others. When Christians speak of authority, they are usually referring to Scripture, church tradition (which includes the profession of faith and dogmas), the people of God, church councils, official ministers, theological consensus, or all of these.

Christians have long debated the link between human and divine authority, and this question led to such major schisms in Christianity as the division between Eastern Orthodoxy and Roman Catholicism (eleventh century) and between Catholicism and Protestantism (sixteenth century). The Roman Catholic tendency to borrow authoritarian models from feudal political society reached a high-water mark at the First Vatican Council (1869–70) with the official declaration of papal infallibility. At the Second Vatican Council (1962–5), the church significantly modified its view of authority by emphasizing ministry, or service (see *Lumen Gentium* 24) and by linking papal authority to the college (body) of bishops as successors of the apostles (see *Lumen Gentium* 22–23).

James B. Nickoloff

See also ECCLESIOLOGY; SCRIPTURES (GENERIC); TRADITION (IN CHRISTIANITY).

AUTOCEPHALOUS CHURCHES

The term was originally used for and by the few Christian Churches that were not under the jurisdiction of any one of the five major patriarchates of undivided Christianity (prior to 1054). In its contemporary sense, "autocephalous" are the various national, self-ruling churches that are in full communion with the see of Constantinople and with each other, and which are also commonly called Orthodox Churches.

Orlando Espín

See also CONSTANTINOPLE, SEE OF; ORTHODOX CHURCHES; PATRIARCH; SCHISM, GREAT EASTERN.

AUTO DE FE

Ceremony of the Spanish Inquisition in the midst of which sentences were read against those accused and convicted of heresy and other serious crimes against religion. Those condemned to die were handed over to civil authority. The Portuguese Inquisition had the same ceremony and called it *auto da fe*.

Orlando Espín

See also HERESY; HERETIC/HERETICAL; INQUISITION.

AUTO SACRAMENTAL

A type of theatrical production, very popular in Spain in the fifteenth and sixteenth centuries. With roots dating back into the Middle Ages, the *autos sacramentales* were frequent religious entertainment in Spanish villages and towns. Usually associated with biblical and doctrinal themes, the *autos sacramentales* in turn became very popular and important tools in the evangelization of native populations in Spanish America.

Orlando Espín

See also DRAMA IN CHRISTIANITY; EVANGELIZATION; INCULTURATION; LATIN AMERICAN CATHOLICISM; LATINO CATHOLICISM; MISSIONS; POPULAR CATHOLICISM.

AVALOKITESHVARA

The celestial bodhisattva at the center of popular Mahayana Buddhism throughout its entire history in Asia. Avalokiteshvara ("Lord who looks down [on humanity]") is the Sanskrit name used in the Mahayana school's Indic genesis; in each country, a regional name evolved in common usage: Chinese referred to Kwan Yin or Kwan-shih Yin ("Cry Regarder"), Japanese to Kannon, Tibetans to Chenrizig. Exemplary among bodhisattvas vowing to assist all beings reach salvation before enjoying their own individual release, Avalokiteshvara has returned to samsara to share his vast merit with all who request it. This compassionate capacity is rendered in art through multiple arms that reach out bearing tools of deliverance.

In later Mahayana cosmology, Avalokiteshvara is identified as the spiritual "son" of the Buddha Amitabha and associated with his Pure Land, Sukhavati. In Mahayana meditation traditions, Avalokiteshvara's form is visualized as the embodiment of compassion and enlightenment; this, too, is expressed in the central iconography in which the bodhisattva holds a lotus blossom, symbolic of the teachings and of revelation, in the left hand. The mantra of Avalokiteshvara, *"Om Mani Padme Hum,"* is likely the most often repeated Buddhist utterance in Mahayana societies.

Todd T. Lewis

See also AMITABHA/AMIDA; BODHISATTVA; LOTUS SUTRA; PURE LAND BUDDHISM; SUKHAVATI; TRIKAYA (DOCTRINE OF).

AVATARA/AVATAR

The Sanskrit term for a divine incarnation, *avatara* means literally "descent." In Hinduism, the Supreme Being—most especially Vishnu—is said to descend to earth periodically, whenever forces of irreligion and immorality (*adharma*) are threatening to overwhelm righteousness. The purpose of the avatara, as stated by Krishna in the *Bhagavad Gita* (4.1-9), is to defeat the forces of moral chaos and restore authentic religious and moral observance (*dharma*). The avatara is, however, also said to come to earth simply to give joy to those who love God. There are in the Puranas various lists of avataras of Vishnu, past and future. The most popular consists of ten, the *dashavatara*, of which the most important are Rama and Krishna. Sometimes Krishna himself is said, by Krishnaite theologians, to be the source of all avataras, replacing Vishnu in this capacity. Additionally, any highly respected saint, male or female, may be regarded by his or her devotees as an avatara of God or the Goddess. The divine is also said to incarnate in images in Hindu temples; this sacramental incarnation is referred to as an *arcavatara*, a "descent for worship." It should be noted that the word *incarnation* is not a precise translation of avatara, since the deity's embodiment is often thought to be only apparent, a projection of the divine creative power (*maya*) or the manifestation of a pure celestial substance (*shuddha-sattva*). In either case, at least for the theologically sophisticated, the avatara's embodiment is not really physical.

Lance E. Nelson

See also BHAGAVAD GITA; HINDUISM; IMAGES, WORSHIP OF; KRISHNA; MAYA; PURANA; RAMA; YUGA.

AVERROES (1126–98)

"Averroes" is the Latin name for the Islamic Spanish philosopher, theologian, lawyer, and physician Abu al-Walid Muhammad ibn Ahmad ibn Rushd. Ibn Rushd was born in Cordoba to a distinguished family of lawyers. He himself became a judge in Cordoba in 1171, but by 1182 was appointed court physician, a position he held with one short break until his death in 1198. Although Ibn Rushd wrote medical and legal texts, he is most famous for his commentaries on the works of Aristotle and for his defense of philosophy. His philosophical works were soon translated into Latin from their original Arabic and, together with the work of the philosopher, Avicenna, were an important source for Christian philosophy and theology in the thirteenth century. Ibn Rushd's works were so popular that he was simply known as "The Commentator" by medieval Christian theologians.

Gary Macy

See also ARISTOTLE; ARISTOTELIANISM; AVERROISM; AVICENNA; SCHOLASTICISM.

AVERROISM

Starting in the early thirteenth century, philosophers at the University of Paris began to teach Aristotle's philosophy using Latin translations of the commentaries on Aristotle by the Islamic philosopher, Ibn Rushd (known in Latin as Averroes). Based on the ideas of Ibn Rushd, some philosophers, notably Siger of Brabant, began to teach that faith and philosophy were radically separate, so that things true in philosophy are not necessarily true in faith. Two of the philosophical truths, based on Averroes, that contradicted Christian faith were, first, the understanding of all intellects as basically one, that is, there are no individual minds; and secondly, that the universe is eternal rather than created. If these two propositions were true, it would mean first, that there there is no individual salvation because we would all be one "mind" in heaven; and secondly, that God did not create the universe from nothing, but that each species was eternal. The advocates did not deny that, in faith, it is true that individual salvation could occur, or that, in faith, it could not be true that God created the universe at some point in time. They argued that there was a "double truth": one in philosophy and one in faith. Albert the Great, Thomas Aquinas, and Bonaventure all wrote against these teachings, and the bishop of Paris condemned "Averroist" teaching in 1270 and again in 1277. Proponents of these propositions continued to teach, however, until the sixteenth century.

Gary Macy

See also ALBERT THE GREAT; AQUINAS, THOMAS, ST.; ARISTOTLE; ARISTOTE-LIANISM; AVERROES; BONAVENTURE; MEDIEVAL CHRISTIANITY (IN THE WEST); SCHOLASTICISM.

AVESTA

The Avesta is the principle scripture of Zoroastrianism. It is written in a dialect of Old Iranian of which the Avesta itself is almost the only surviving example. This dialect, an Indo-European language closely related to that of the *Rig Veda*, is therefore called "Avestan." The Avesta consists mostly of liturgical prayers and hymns, which have for centuries been chanted by Zoroastrian priests as part of their ceremonial worship. The present text of the Avesta appears to have been finalized and written down between the third and seventh centuries C.E., but much of it is the product of an oral tradition that goes back considerably earlier. Indeed, portions of the Avesta, especially a section known as the *Gathas*, go back to Zoroaster (about 1200 B.C.E.) himself. It

should be noted, however, that Zoroastrian tradition believes that the whole of the Avesta was revealed to Zoroaster by Ahura Mazda. By the first millennium C.E., or even earlier, Avestan was already an archaic language, unintelligible to ordinary believers. Since almost all Zoroastrian prayers are in Avestan, this would appear to create a problem. The prayers are, however, regarded as sacred *manthras* and, like the *mantras* of the *Rig Veda*, regarded as potent, when correctly chanted, for their sound quality alone, over and above their semantic value.

Lance E. Nelson

See also ARYAN; GATHAS; ZOROASTER; ZOROASTRIANISM.

AVICENNA (980–1037)

"Avicenna" is the Latin name for the Islamic philosopher, scientist, physician, and mystic Abu al-Husayn ibn Abdallah ibn Sina. Born in Bukhura in Persia, Ibn Sina was an extraordinarily precocious young man, mastering the Qur'an and most of Islamic learning by the age of sixteen. By the time he was twenty-one, he was already famous as a physician and scholar. Despite a tumultuous life wandering from city to city looking for a quiet place to continue his studies, Ibn Sina wrote an extraordinary amount. He is perhaps the most famous Islamic physician, and his philosophical and theological works are major contributions to Islamic thought. Ibn Sina also made contributions to chemistry and astronomy. In western Europe, the philosophy of Ibn Sina influenced many important writers, including Thomas Aquinas and John Duns Scotus.

Gary Macy

See also AQUINAS, THOMAS, ST.; AVERROES; DUNS SCOTUS, JOHN; SCHOLASTICISM.

AVIGNON (PAPACY AT)

For nearly seventy years, the pope and the papal court resided not in Rome, but in the city of Avignon in France. This odd state of affairs began when Pope Boniface VIII died in the midst of a struggle for power with Philip IV, the king of France. The next pope, Benedict XI, lived only a short time. His successor, Clement V, himself a Frenchman, was in France when he was elected pope in 1305. Because of political problems in the city of Rome and in order to prepare for the Council of Vienne, Clement decided to move the papal court to Avignon, a city which technically was part of the Holy Roman Empire, but sat on the border with France. Philip IV had a much easier time getting Clement V to go along with him politically, especially in his condemnation of the Knights Templar at the Council of Vienne in 1311. Despite the great expense of maintaining the papal court at Avignon and the scandal of the Bishop of Rome not living in Rome, Popes John XXII, Benedict XII, Clement VI, Innocent VI, Urban V, and Gregory XI all continued to rule the papal court in Avignon. Pope Gregory was finally persuaded to return to Rome in 1377, particularly due to the influence of Catherine of Sienna. When Gregory died in Rome, the troubled election of Pope Urban VI started the Great Schism of Western Christianity.

Gary Macy

See also BONIFACE VIII, POPE; CATHERINE OF SIENNA; JOHN XXII, POPE; MEDIEVAL CHRISTIANITY (IN THE WEST); MILITARY ORDERS; SCHISM, GREAT WESTERN.

AVOT

See ETHICS OF THE FATHERS.

AYA

Arabic term used for "verse" or reference to a small part of a *sura* (chapter) in the Qurʾan, the sacred scripture of Islam. References to *sura* and *aya* are similar to biblical references, though unlike the Bible, the Qurʾan has no "books," just one hundred and fourteen suras. For example: The first sura of the Qurʾan, called al-Fatihah ("The Opening"), has only seven aya. Reference to the sixth aya would be cited this way: Qurʾan 1:6 (sometimes Qurʾan 1.6).

Ronald A. Pachence

See also AL-FATIHAH; QURʾAN; SURA.

AYATOLLAH

A title used by Shiʿite Muslims for a distinguished member of the *ulama* (the body of Islamic religious and legal scholars). The term literally means "sign of God," indicating that the *ayatollah* is thought by his followers to have special authority invested in him by Allah. The title was unknown before the twentieth century and even now, it is not common among Shiʿites. One becomes an ayatollah when recognized as such by other ayatollahs and by one's followers.

Ronald A. Pachence

See also SHIʿA/SHIʿI/SHIʿITE/SHIʿISM; ULAMA/ULEMA.

AZTEC TRADITIONAL RELIGION

See NAHUA TRADITIONAL RELIGION.

B

BAAL

Hebrew word meaning "master, husband, lord." The term refers to the Canaanite god of fertility who manifests himself in many different places in many different ways. From the perspective of the authors of the Hebrew Bible, when used in the plural, the term refers to gods other than Yahweh, that is, foreign gods, false gods, idols. In the singular, the term may refer to a particular god or to the god of a particular place, for example, the Baal of Peor (Num 25:3, 5; Deut 4:3; Ps 106:28), the Baal of Berith (Judg 8:33; 9:4), and the Baalzebub (2 Kgs 1:2-3).

The Deuteronomic History portrays Baal worship as a serious threat to Yahwism in Israel. The evil king of Israel, Ahab, built a temple of Baal in Samaria and erected in it an altar to Baal (cf. 1 Kgs 16:32). The prophet Elijah, however, confronted the prophets of Baal on Mount Carmel, and in the contest that ensued Yahweh emerged victorious (1 Kgs 18:25-40). Jehu is credited with rooting out the worship of Baal from Israel (2 Kgs 10:28).

In the patriarchal society of ancient Israel, one's husband was one's baal. One owned one's wife, so that in the context of ancient Israelite marriage, a wife's master and husband were one and the same. See, for example, Genesis 20:3, Deuteronomy 22:22, and 24:4.

The Hebrew term is used to describe Yahweh's relationship with Israel in Jeremiah 31:32. Scholars differ regarding the appropriate English translation of the term in that context. Perhaps the term was used intentionally to include both the lordship of God over Israel and also the covenant relationship of Israel and God depicted elsewhere in Jeremiah and in Hosea as a husband–wife relationship.

In the New Testament, the term "Baal" appears only once, in Romans 11:4, with reference to an idol, a god other than the Father of Jesus Christ.

Alice L. Laffey

BAAL SHEM TOV

Hebrew, meaning "Master of the Good Name" is the title and name-designation bestowed on Israel ben Eliezer (1700–60), the founder of the Jewish religious movement Hasidism.

Born in the south of Poland, ben Eliezer was orphaned as a young child. He received little formal education, but was drawn to Judaism's mystical teachings. He became an itinerant healer who was well known for his "miracle" cures, and was considered by many as a spiritual master.

Ben Eliezer lived for many years in the town of Miedzyboz, where disciples gathered around him. The Baal Shem taught that the spiritual quest centers on creating a deep, personal, intimate relationship with God. His primary teaching was that God can be approached through joy. This translated into prayer services that were filled with deep, focused concentration, and fervent song and dance. Although prayer is the most natural vehicle for coming to God, the Baal Shem taught that God can also be approached in joy through normal, everyday activities such as eating, drinking, and conversation. The Baal Shem taught through parables and examples, and many stories about his own life and deeds now are part of the corpus of his teachings.

The Baal Shem's unique approach to God—in a Jewish world that was used to meeting God through study and the meticulous performance of law and ritual—attracted many followers, and led to the birth and the growth of the Hasidic Movement. In times when the prevailing political powers repressed Jews and Judaism, Hasidism, which revolved around charismatic rabbis in various cities and "courts," gave Jews and Judaism renewed vigor and hope.

Though vehemently opposed by Jews who held to the primacy of law, Hasidism carved out and still holds a major place in Jewish life. The Baal Shem Tov remains revered as the visionary founder of the movement.

Wayne Dosick

See also HASIDISM.

BABEL, TOWER OF

At Genesis 11:1-9, Babel is a city featuring a tower, the completion of which God thwarts in order to prevent the people from gaining such strength and reputation as to be able to accomplish anything they desire. Apparently seeing this as a challenge to his own authority, God confuses the people's language and scatters them across the land, exactly what they had hoped their fortified city would prevent from happening. God's confusing of their language, which serves in Scripture to explain the world's diverse language groups, also stands behind the name of the city, since Babel derives from the Hebrew root meaning "to confuse."

Within Christianity, the Pentecost narrative in Acts 2:5-13 may be meant to represent God's reversal of the chaos created at Babel. At Babel, the proliferation of languages caused confusion and prevented people from "making a name for ourselves"; in Jerusalem, the Holy Spirit made it possible for many different languages to be understood as one, which led to the pronouncement of "the mighty works of God." The scattering of the people from Babel constituted God's judgment against their deeds; the scattering of people from Jerusalem (Acts 8:1, 4) would lead eventually to worldwide unity.

Alan J. Avery-Peck

BABYLON

Name of ancient city and empire located in southern Mesopotamia. The name Babylon is derived from the Akkadian *bab ili* "gate of the gods." Babylon is important in biblical studies because it dominated the ancient Near East (including Palestine) in the sixth century B.C.E. and thus was responsible for the political history of the kingdom of Judah from approximately 605 B.C.E. until 538 B.C.E. In 597 and again in 587 Babylon deported elements of the population of Judah to Babylon and other areas of its empire in

Mesopotamia. These populations, especially the group in Babylon, were largely responsible for the final stages in the production of the Hebrew Bible during the sixth and fifth centuries B.C.E. The Jewish communities first established, beginning in the sixth century B.C.E., remained important centers of Jewish learning and culture well into the first millennium C.E. During the period of the Babylonian Exile (587–538 B.C.E.), Babylonian thought probably strongly influenced the redactors of the Hebrew Bible. This influence surfaces in such passages as the first creation story in Genesis, chapter 1, which may deliberately contrast with the Babylonian epic, *Enuma Elish*. Such influence may also be seen in other exilic compositions such as Second Isaiah (chapters 40–55).

Russell Fuller

BABYLONIAN CAPTIVITY

An expression used for three very different historical circumstances: (1) the Exile of many from the southern Jewish kingdom, under Babylonian rule, about the sixth century B.C.E.; (2) metaphorically, it was used for the years (from 1309 to 1377) the popes lived in the French city of Avignon; and (3) it was the title of a book by Martin Luther (*The Babylonian Captivity of the Church*, 1520) in which he attacked the liturgical practices and theories that he believed were enslaving the church.

Orlando Espín

See also AVIGNON (PAPACY AT); BABYLON; EXILE; LUTHER, MARTIN.

BAHA'I

A religion in its own right, Baha'i traces its origin to the *Babi* sect of Islam and through the *Babis*, to Twelver Shi'ite Islam. Baha'i was founded by Mirza Husayn Ali Nuri (1817–92), better known by his title,

Baha'u'llah ("the Splendor of God"). As a *Babi*, Baha'u'llah declared himself to be the one promised to come by *Babi* prophets, and on this authority he founded the new religion called Baha'i today. The tomb of Baha'u'llah, located in Haifa, Israel, is an important Baha'i shrine. The Baha'is preach a universal religion based on peace among all people, spiritual solutions to economic problems, a universal auxiliary language, and love for all women and men. Members are expected to make a substantial financial contribution to sustain the community. Baha'is are found in many countries throughout the world; from Iran, where they are a persecuted minority, to Europe and North America.

Ronald A. Pachence

See also REVELATION (IN BAHA'I); TWELVERS (IN ISLAM).

BAHA'U'LLAH

See BAHA'I.

BAIUS, MICHEL (MICHEL DE BAY) (1513–89)

Belgian Catholic theologian, educated at the University of Louvain where he also taught for many years. After 1550 he began to teach certain doctrines on grace and original sin that brought him into confrontation with church authorities. He was never personally condemned for heresy, but some of his doctrines were (in 1567 and again in 1579). Baius remained a member of the Catholic Church, although he seems to have held on to his teaching while trying to reconcile it to the more mainstream Catholic views. His teaching is often considered an anticipation of Jansenism.

Orlando Espín

See also GRACE; JANSENISM; SIN, ORIGINAL.

BALAAM

At Numbers 22–24, a professional diviner called upon by Balak, king of Moab, to curse the people of Israel so that Balak can defeat them in war. Despite Balak's instructions and the elaborate sacrifices Balaam instructs him to prepare, Balaam is able to speak only the words put in his mouth by the Israelite God. Instead of cursing Israel, he therefore pronounces oracles that bless them and that predict Balak's defeat. In these materials, the story of Balaam's ass, which, unlike its master, sees a messenger of God blocking Balaam's path on his way to Balak, is particularly poignant.

While Balaam at Numbers 22–24 is true to the Israelite God, sympathetic to the Israelite cause, and able to prophesy only what Yahweh instructs, other Old Testament passages see him in a wholly negative light. Numbers 31:8 and 16 state that at Peor, Balaam counseled the Israelites to apostatize, causing God to bring a plague against the people; according to this tradition, those who remained true to God later killed Balaam in their war against Midian. Contrary to the account in Numbers 22–24, Deuteronomy 23:4-5 implies that Balaam indeed tried to curse Israel, but that God did not heed his words. Micah 6:5 refers to the incident of Balak and Balaam ambiguously, calling on the people of Israel to remember Balaam's actions, but not stating clearly whether these are to be viewed positively, as at Numbers 22–24, or negatively, as at Deuteronomy 23:4-5.

Later Jewish and Christian writings, including Philo, Josephus, and the New Testament, where he is mentioned three times, uniformly view Balaam in a negative light. In the rabbinic literature and later Judaism, Balaam comes to symbolize the nations of the world that oppress the Jewish people.

Alan J. Avery-Peck

BALDACHINO

Or *baldachin* is derived from the Italian word for the city of Baghdad (*Baldacco*) from which finely woven fabrics of silk and metal threads were imported at the beginning of the Renaissance for use as a canopy hung over an altar, especially when it was attached to a wall, or for carrying over a sacred object, for instance, the Blessed Sacrament. Fabric baldachins were also placed over the thrones of bishops and royalty. By extension, the term has also come to be used for what is more properly known as a ciborium, that is, a canopy made of wood, stone, or metal, resting on four columns, whose Christian origin is in the ancient basilicas. Ciboria were used over altars, baptismal fonts, and eventually as a support from which to hang a pyx that contained the reserved eucharistic bread. The oldest example of a ciborium is from the ninth century in Ravenna. The largest example is Bernini's canopy on twisted columns over the principal altar of St. Peter's Basilica in Rome. The Reformers generally rejected the use of baldachins or ciboria because they tended to make the table for the Lord's Supper too much of a special fixture. While it is no longer required in Catholic usage, a carefully designed baldachin or ciborium, or the architectural suggestion of one, can be appropriately used to highlight any area needing emphasis, for example, the altar table, especially if it is reduced in proportions to be more accessible, the baptismal font, or the tabernacle in a reservation chapel.

Dennis W. Krouse

See also ALTAR; ART, LITURGICAL.

BALFOUR DECLARATION

The document through which the British, on November 2, 1917, officially declared sympathy with the Jewish-Zionist aspiration to create a Jewish homeland in Palestine. The Balfour Declaration resulted from negotiations beginning as early as 1914 between the British foreign secretary Arthur James, earl of Balfour, and Zionist leaders, including Chaim Weizmann, Nahum Sokolow, and others. The formal proclamation of the Balfour Declaration, which took the form of a letter from Arthur James Balfour to Lord Rothschild, was ultimately facilitated by U.S. President Woodrow Wilson's agreement to the proposed document.

The Balfour Declaration was later incorporated into the terms of the British Mandate over Palestine. It reads: "His majesty's government view with favour the establishment in Palestine of a national home for the Jewish people, and will use their best endeavors to facilitate the achievement of this object, it being clearly understood that nothing shall be done which may prejudice the civil and religious rights of existing non-Jewish communities in Palestine, or the rights and political status enjoyed by Jews in any other country."

In subsequent negotiations between the Zionists, British, and League of Nations concerning the actual creation of a Jewish homeland, the words "establishment *in* Palestine" became a point of contention. The Zionists insisted that the British had promised Palestine as a homeland for the Jews, while the League of Nations understood the Balfour Declaration to have proposed only the use of *some portion of* Palestine as the Jewish homeland. That reading of matters resulted in the Partition Plan of 1948, which divided Palestine into two states, one Jewish and one Palestinian.

Alan J. Avery-Peck

See also ZIONISM.

BALTIMORE, COUNCILS OF (1829–84)

The Councils of Baltimore were the first official conferences held by the United States Catholic hierarchy to discuss and regulate ecclesial life in the young national church. The ten councils held between 1829 and 1884 reflect the bishops' efforts to continue the collegial traditions of John Carroll and John England and the rapid growth of the nineteenth-century church. The first seven provincial councils (1829–49) represented one archdiocese, Baltimore. The three Plenary Councils (1852–84) reflected a vastly changed church that by 1884 had seven archdioceses, seventy-two dioceses, and whose Catholic population of several million made it the largest denomination in the United States. The conciliar agendas chronicle the many challenges confronting the church of the era.

Perennial issues preoccupied all councils: clerical recruitment, education and regulation; the establishment of new churches; regulation of canonical and sacramental life; the education of Catholic children; and the erection of educational institutions. The adaptation of ecclesial and personal life to the American situation required repeated reflection: Catholic membership in secret societies; regulation of mixed marriages; responses to anti-Catholic sentiment; and the continuing struggle with problems stemming from the lay trustee form of parish administration. From the Third Provincial Council (1837) on, the bishops worked to meet the challenges posed by Catholic immigration to the United States.

Special concerns of some councils also shed light on the identity of the church of the era. The First Provincial Council (1829) featured the sole instance of lay participation, lawyers who advised on matters of legal incorporation, including Roger B. Taney, future Supreme Court justice. The Third (1837) issued a pastoral letter about nativist attacks on the church, protesting the persecution of Catholics, and asserting Catholic allegiance to the state; but it maintained silence about attacks on church property. The First Plenary Council (1852), which praised the government's noninterference in church affairs, said nothing about the impending civil conflict or slavery. The Second (1866) urged care for former slaves and the erection of separate churches for black Catholics. The Third Plenary Council (1884) confirmed decrees of Vatican Council I, urged the establishment of Catholic schools, the creation of a Catholic University, and a common catechism (the Baltimore Catechism) to regularize national religious instruction. This council anticipated the challenges of the next half century: ministry to immigrant communities and the ethnic character of Catholic communities, clergy, and hierarchy; and the continuing growth of church population and institutions. Divergent views of the participants in the last council presaged the divisions among the hierarchy over the issue of Americanization and the end of the collegial vision of the Baltimore councils.

Patricia Plovanich

BÁÑEZ, DOMINGO

Spanish Catholic theologian (1528–1604) and prominent member of the Dominican Order. He taught at the universities of Avila, Alcalá, and especially at Salamanca. Báñez earned a widespread reputation as a very able exponent of Thomist, Scholastic theology. He became a major figure in the sixteenth-century controversy on grace between Dominicans and Jesuits, and was confessor and advisor to Teresa of Avila. His greatest contribution did not come from the originality of his thought, but from his extraordinary ability to synthesize and teach what others had first proposed, and from his gift as a great polemicist in an age of great polemics.

Orlando Espín

See also DOMINICANS; GRACE; MOLINA, LUIS DE; SCHOLASTICISM; THOMISM/ TRANSCENDENTAL THOMISM.

BAPTISM BY BLOOD

An expression occasionally used in reference to those persons who, through no fault of their own, were never actually baptized, but nevertheless died a martyr's death because of their Christian faith.

Orlando Espín

See also BAPTISM OF DESIRE; BAPTISM/ CONFIRMATION; FAITH; GRACE; MARTYR/MARTYRDOM; SALVATION.

BAPTISM/CONFIRMATION

The word baptism (from the Greek, *bapto*, *baptizo*, "dip") refers to part of the Christian ritual of initiation, specifically, the ritual moment in which the candidate is literally "dipped" in water. The use of water at baptism is rooted in a deep layer of symbolic meanings. Water communicates life, birth, cleansing, as well as death, chaos, and dissolution. Christian baptism traces back to Jewish use: Judaism used a baptismal ceremony for adult converts to Judaism. In the Gospels, John the Baptist is recorded as offering baptism; this baptism was understood as a sign of repentance in preparation for the coming of the Messiah.

But even more clearly, the Christian practice is rooted in the Gospel narratives of the baptism of Jesus in the Jordan by John the Baptist at the beginning of Jesus' public ministry (Mark 1:4-11; Matt 3:1-17; Luke 3:1-22; cf. John 1:19-34). Several other texts in the New Testament point to the importance of baptism as the normative, or key, event of Christian initiation: for example, the eleven disciples are told by Christ after the resurrection to "make disciples of all nations" by baptizing them (Matt 28:16-20); Gentiles as well as Jews were among the earliest believers to be baptized (see Acts 8:36-38; 12:44-48); baptism is seen by Paul as uniting the believer with the death and resurrection of Christ (Rom 6:3-11).

The practice of initiating converts through baptism continued as part of the Christian tradition after the time of the apostles. Throughout antiquity, the use of large containers or pools of water (called *fonts*) was common; after the legalization of Christianity, these were often placed in round or eight-sided buildings (called *baptisteries*) separate from the main basilica used for the celebration of the Eucharist. Candidates were usually adults, and were prepared for baptism by having enrolled in the order of *catechumens* for a period of time (perhaps as long as three years). Those who were close to the end of this preparation period were singled out for a final period of more intense prayer and fasting immediately before their initiation (which was usually held during the vigil of the great feast of Easter); this was one of the roots of the season of Lent.

Baptism itself was administered while the main body of the community was gathered in the basilica, keeping a vigil of prayer, song, and readings; those to be baptized, along with the bishop, presbyters (that is, priests), and deacons/deaconesses, gathered at the baptistery. The candidates for baptism took off their clothes, renounced Satan, and accepted Christ; they next moved to the font itself. One by one, after being anointed, they were immersed in the warm water of the large, tub-like font, while the bishop presided by reciting the baptismal questions ("Do you believe in God the Father?") and the trinitarian formula (the person was baptized "in the name of the Father, and the Son, and the Holy Spirit"). In some areas, the newly baptized person (or neophyte) was anointed again after baptism, and put on a clean, white robe or garment; often they held lit candles or lamps as well. The ceremony of initiation was completed in some areas by an anointing by the bishop in front of the whole community (see below), and then by the neophytes' participation in the Easter Eucharist, during which they would receive Communion (that is, the consecrated bread and wine) for the first time.

In late antiquity and the early Middle Ages, baptism was administered not usually to adults, but to infants. This shift to infant baptism changed several elements in the Western rite: the catechumenate fell into practical disuse; Communion was not administered unless the infant had been confirmed at the same time (see below); and the postbaptismal anointing that was to become confirmation was often separated from the "water-event" of baptism. Fonts became smaller, and immersion was dropped in favor of pouring or sprinkling the infant's head with water. During the Reformation, some of the more radical Reformers insisted on restoring adult baptism (called "believer's baptism") on scriptural grounds; they held that one had to make a personal profession of faith before baptism. These Anabaptists (so called because they taught that infant baptism was invalid) were often persecuted by other Protestant groups and Catholics alike.

Today, some Protestant churches have adopted this practice (for example, the Baptists) and others are direct descendants of the original Anabaptists (for example, the Mennonites and the Amish). Most Protestant churches do practice infant baptism (for example, Lutherans), as do the Roman Catholic and Orthodox churches. The Roman Catholic Church has, however, also revived the ancient catechumenate in its reformed baptismal liturgy: the Rite of Christian Initiation of Adults (RCIA) provides for older candidates for baptism and confirmation. RCIA programs can be found in most parish churches and often as part of college campus ministry programs as well.

Confirmation (from the Latin, *confirmare*, to confirm or strengthen) was originally part of the unitive rite of Christian initiation. In Rome, the baptismal process was "sealed" by a public anointing of the neophytes (newly baptized) by the bishop, after the water ceremony in the baptistery. The neophytes then participated in the Easter Eucharist, where they received Communion for the first time (see above). In the West, however, after the shift had taken place from adult to infant baptism, this postbaptismal anointing was still reserved to the bishop, while the administration of baptism (the water-event) was delegated to the local parish priests. In this way, confirmation became a separate sacrament: while most babies were baptized by a priest rather soon after birth, they had to wait, often for years, before the bishop visited their town or village to be confirmed.

The Protestant Reformers generally did away with confirmation as a separate sacrament, on the grounds that it could not be found in the Scriptures (the New Testament). Some churches did tie reception of Communion to a statement or confession of faith made by older children, while others were content to permit small children to receive Communion without such a public examination. Later, in the early twentieth century, the Roman Catholic practice changed once again: children were permitted to receive Communion for the first time at the age of reason (usually about the age of seven) without having to wait for the reception of confirmation. Today, confirmation in the Roman Catholic tradition is administered in one of two ways: as part of a school or parish program of education (often set on a particular grade level, like eighth grade, or sophomore year in high school), or as part of the RCIA (usually for young adults who did not participate in a school program, or adults converting to Catholic Christianity from another church or faith).

Joanne M. Pierce

See also COMMUNION (LITURGICAL); EASTER; IMMERSION; PASCHAL MYSTERY; SACRAMENT; SACRAMENTAL THEOLOGY.

BAPTISM IN THE SPIRIT

An expression used to refer to a religious experience among some groups of charismatic or Pentecostal Christians, wherein they believe they have received the Holy Spirit in a significantly special and new way. This expression, however, cannot be meant to imply that the sacrament of baptism was somehow insufficient or deficient, or that the Holy Spirit was absent from or inactive in the sacrament of baptism. At best, the expression is a means of naming a profound experience of the Spirit of God in a baptized Christian's life, marking his or her existence thereafter with a renewed and deeper commitment to God and Gospel, and with a better awareness of the Spirit's actions in the world. Sometimes the "baptism in the Spirit" is accompanied by external signs such as speaking in tongues.

Orlando Espín

See also BAPTISM/CONFIRMATION; CHARISMATIC MOVEMENT; GLOSSOLALIA; HOLY SPIRIT; PENTECOST (IN CHRISTIANITY); PENTECOSTALISM.

BAPTISM OF DESIRE

An expression occasionally used today, but frequently in the past, to explain how it was possible for unbaptized persons to share in salvation. There were two groups of these unbaptized persons: to one belonged those who had never heard the Christian message but were sincerely attempting to lead honest, moral lives according to their consciences; and to the other group belonged those who heard the Christian message and sincerely sought baptism but died before actually being baptized. Most of the theological reflection (starting as far back as the third and fourth centuries), however, focused on the persons of good will who had never heard of Christ. Contemporary theology has moved beyond the terminological and conceptual boundaries of "baptism of desire" and developed other systematic reflections along the lines of a theology of religions, of the "anonymous Christians," and so on. Much of the current discussion on the issues raised by "baptism of desire" is focused on the nature, universality, accessibility and meaning of faith and salvation, and on grace.

Orlando Espín

See also BAPTISM BY BLOOD; BAPTISM/ CONFIRMATION; FAITH; GRACE; SALVATION.

BAPTIST CHURCHES/BAPTIST CONVENTIONS

There are two theories about Baptist beginnings. One is that Baptists descended from Anabaptists, sixteenth-century advocates of radical Protestant Reformation in Switzerland, the Netherlands, and Germany. Anabaptists sought to apply the Bible to daily life and instituted believer's baptism by immersion because they believed it followed biblical practice. The second theory about Baptist origins, one advocated by most historians, is that they emerged in England in the seventeenth century among radical Puritans known as Separatists. They believed not only that the Church of England should be purified of "popishness," but also that baptism should be restricted to those who could give testimony of their experience of saving grace, that is, adults. They also believed in simple, sermon-centered worship and congregational polity.

The first identifiable Baptist church was founded about 1609 in Amsterdam, Holland, by British Separatists John Smyth and Thomas Helwys who had parted from the Separatists who would later emigrate to the North American British colonies on the *Mayflower*. The first Baptist church on British soil was established in London in 1611 from a segment of the Amsterdam congregation. The first Baptist church in the British colonies was founded in 1639 in Providence, Rhode Island, by Roger Williams, an exile from the Puritan Massachusetts Bay Colony for advocating absolute purity and the separation between church and state. Although Williams left the Baptist fold thereafter, Baptist churches grew in New England

and the Middle Colonies. The first association of Baptist churches was the Philadelphia Baptist Association in 1707, which eventually linked churches in seven colonies of the eastern seaboard and engaged in vigorous missionary activity.

Baptists in the United States grew prodigiously as a result of revivalism in the First and Second Great Awakenings. Baptists expanded especially in the South and along the western frontiers of Kentucky, Ohio, and Tennessee. In 1755 Shubal Stearns and Daniel Marshall founded a Baptist church in Sandy Creek, North Carolina, that became the center of missionary activity in North and South Carolina and Virginia. In 1801 Baptists attracted thousands of converts in the revival camp meeting at Cane Ridge, Kentucky. Although frontier churches were more emotional and less genteel than those along the eastern seaboard, most affiliated with the Philadelphia Association. Along with Methodists, Presbyterians, and Congregationalists, Baptists became a leading Evangelical denomination, participating in the educational, missionary, and social reform efforts of the "Benevolent Empire." Baptists were instrumental in the formation of the American Board of Commissioners for Foreign Missions in 1810, and Adoniram Judson and his three successive wives were among the earliest foreign missionaries, working in India and Burma.

As the nineteenth century progressed, Baptists became more numerous, diverse, and fragmented. Slavery split Euro-American Baptists, as it did the Methodists and Presbyterians. The Southern Baptist Convention (SBC) formed in 1845, primarily because northern Baptists refused to appoint slave-holders as missionaries, and secondarily to centralize and coordinate evangelism. The SBC became a, if not the, dominant religious group in the South and strongly identified with Southern culture, a phenomenon historian John Eighmy called the "cultural captivity" of Southern Baptists. African Americans became Baptists in large numbers, both before and after the Civil War. The first black Baptist church was reportedly formed in Silver Bluff, South Carolina, around 1773. Baptists appealed to African Americans due to their evangelical theology of being born again, emphasis on experiential, liberative religion, congregational autonomy, and the opposition to slavery among Northern Baptists. While many enslaved Africans attended Baptist churches with their masters and mistresses before emancipation, after the Civil War they founded numerous independent congregations. Early black Baptist leaders included Andrew Bryan, George Lisle, David George, John Jasper, and Nannie H. Burroughs.

A variety of Baptist conventions existed in the United States in the twentieth century, divided along racial and theological lines. The largest Euro-American groups are the SBC and the American Baptist Churches in the U.S.A. (ABC). The SBC is the largest Protestant denomination in the U.S., strongest in the South, but with churches in every state and numerous countries. The SBC has historically been conservative Evangelical, but tolerant of diversity. However, in 1979, a group of fundamentalists took over SBC leadership and determined to rid the denomination of what they perceived as liberals. They systematically began to pressure SBC seminaries and agencies to adhere to biblical literalism and inerrancy; the takeover has spawned several smaller Southern Baptist groups committed to tolerance, including the Southern Baptist Alliance and Cooperative Baptist Fellowship.

The former Northern Baptist Convention renamed itself the American Baptist Convention in 1950 and American Baptist Churches in 1972. The name changes reflect the decreasing regionalism and increasing pluralism and diversity of the denomination. The ABC is a liberal progressive denomination which counts among its forebears Social Gospel theologian Walter Rauschenbusch, liberal theologian William Newton Clarke, and modernists Shailer Mathews and Harry Emerson Fosdick. It is strongest in the northeastern United States and Upper Midwest. Smaller Euro-American Baptist groups include the General Association of Regular Baptists, Conservative Baptists of America, Seventh-Day Baptists, and Primitive Baptists. A number of independent Baptist congregations exist, notably Liberty Baptist Church in Lynchburg, Virginia, pastored by Jerry Falwell, founder of the Moral Majority.

Baptist groups exist in nearly every ethnic and racial group. The first national group of African American Baptists was the National Baptist Convention (NBC) formed in 1895. It sponsored home and foreign mission boards, a publication board, colleges, and seminaries. Due to struggles over control of the publication board in 1915, the NBC split into the National Baptist Convention of America and National Baptist Convention of the USA, Incorporated. Controversies in the latter denomination over the role of the president, convention structure, and approaches to the civil rights movement led to the 1961 formation of the Progressive National Baptist Convention (PNBC), whose leaders have included Gardiner Taylor and Martin Luther King Jr. Although historically independent and schismatic, cooperative Baptist efforts include the Baptist Peace Fellowship of North America and Baptist World Alliance.

Evelyn A. Kirkley

See also ANABAPTISTS; BAPTIST THEOLOGY; EVANGELICAL THEOLOGY; EVANGELICALS; GREAT AWAKENING(S) (EURO-AMERICAN RELIGIOUS HISTORY); KING, MARTIN LUTHER, JR.; PURITANISM; RAUSCHENBUSCH, WALTER; REVIVALISM; SOCIAL GOSPEL.

BAPTIST THEOLOGY

The most distinctive feature of Baptist theology from other Protestant Christians is believer's baptism by immersion. This belief has two aspects. First, Baptists believe that an individual should only be baptized upon a profession of faith, after having repented of sin and accepting salvation. Thus, Baptists argue that infants should not be baptized because they cannot profess the Christian faith (although baptism of children as young as six is not uncommon). Second, Baptists believe that the appropriate mode of baptism is full bodily immersion, as opposed to effusion or sprinkling. They defend believer's baptism as following the scriptural norm, as evidenced by Jesus' baptism by John the Baptist.

Besides believer's baptism by immersion, there are other Baptist distinctions. Baptists have been among the loudest proponents of religious freedom and the separation of church and state in the United States. Roger Williams in the seventeenth century and Isaac Backus in the eighteenth opposed state establishment of any religious group. They have also advocated congregational autonomy, vigorous missions and evangelism, and faithfulness to the Bible. Britisher William Carey, Euro-American Adoniram Judson, and African American Lott Cary were pioneers of foreign missions in the eighteenth and nineteenth centuries; Cary helped found the African nation of Liberia. Euro-Americans Lottie Moon and Annie Armstrong were prominent women supporters of home and foreign missions in the late nineteenth and early twentieth centuries.

At the same time, Baptists have historically been individualistic and nonconformist, and their theology is no exception. They have had significant theological controversies. Early British Baptists were divided between Calvinists, called Particular Baptists because they believed in "particular atonement," that Christ had died only for the elect, and non-Calvinists, called General Baptists, who held that Christ died for all. In the United States, non-Calvinist Baptists came to predominate as a result of revivalism and evangelical theology in the eighteenth and nineteenth centuries. Baptist theology moved in a decidedly Arminian direction, affirming that the believer plays a critical role in effecting salvation.

In the late nineteenth and early twentieth centuries, liberal and fundamentalist theologies divided Baptists in the United States. William Newton Clarke of Colgate University and Shailer Mathews of the University of Chicago pioneered evangelical liberalism and modernism respectively. Walter Rauschenbusch of Rochester Theological Seminary was the premier theologian of the Social Gospel. Harry Emerson Fosdick was a pastor and pulpit orator at Riverside Church in New York City. Fundamentalist Baptist leaders included J. Frank Norris, pastor in Fort Worth, Texas; William Bell Riley, pastor in Chicago and Minneapolis; and Augustus H. Strong, president of Rochester Theological Seminary. They sought to save Baptist theology from the influence of secular humanism and Unitarianism. In 1878 Crawford Toy, professor at Southern Baptist Theological Seminary in Louisville, Kentucky, was forced to resign for teaching historical criticism of the Bible.

In the late twentieth century, Baptist theology ranged from liberal evangelical to fundamentalist. The American Baptist Churches in the U.S.A. and Progressive National Baptist Convention are fairly liberal, while the National Baptist Convention of America, National Baptist Convention of the U.S.A., Incorporated, and Southern Baptist Convention are more conservative. Since the 1950s, African American Baptists, including Martin Luther King Jr. and Howard Thurman, have been in the forefront of civil rights and black liberation theology. Between the 1970s and 1990s, Baptist conventions have experienced severe conflicts over the ordination of women, gay men, and lesbians.

Due to diverse theologies and congregational polity, Baptist worship can vary significantly from church to church. In general, worship is simple, and the sermon is the focus of the service. Music is often a significant element as is an evangelistic invitation to discipleship known as an altar call. Baptist worship is not sacramental; Baptists practice two ordinances, baptism and Communion, understanding them as symbolic representations of biblical events. Their view of ministry is of pastor rather than priest, a leader called out from and yet living among the people; there is little division between clergy and laity.

Evelyn A. Kirkley

See also BAPTIST CHURCHES/BAPTIST CONVENTIONS; CALVINISM; CONGREGATIONAL CHURCHES; EVANGELICAL THEOLOGY; EVANGELICALS; GREAT AWAKENING(S) (EURO-AMERICAN RELIGIOUS HISTORY); PURITANISM; REVIVALISM; SOCIAL GOSPEL.

BARAKA/BARAKAH

Arabic word for "blessing," "spiritual power," or "grace." Any spiritual gift one has received from Allah, Muslims would call *baraka*. Since Allah's presence is universal and all-powerful, persons or things —even special places—can be experienced by believers as blessings sent freely from God. A popular way of saying "thank you" among Arabic-speaking Muslims includes this term: *Baraka'Llahu fik*, "May God bless you."

Ronald A. Pachence

BAR/BAT MITZVAH

Hebrew, meaning "son of/daughter of the commandment(s)," is Jewish coming of age.

At the age of thirteen, a Jewish boy reaches the age of majority, and becomes obligated to fulfill both the privileges and the responsibilities of the *mitzvot*, the commandments of God. He becomes personally responsible for his own conduct in fulfilling the ethical commands, and assumes responsibility for fulfilling the ritual commands such as being counted in a *minyan*, and being called to the Torah for an *aliyah*. On reaching the age of thirteen, the young man automatically becomes a Bar Mitzvah. Whether or not he exercises them, the privileges and responsibilities of Jewish adulthood are his.

The first public act marking the age of majority is usually the Bar Mitzvah ceremony. The ceremony as it is known today came into Judaism in the Middle Ages. The central act is being called to the Torah for an *aliyah*. Thus the Bar Mitzvah can take place anytime the Torah is read. In practice, most Bar Mitzvah ceremonies take place on Shabbat morning.

In addition to coming to the Torah for an *aliyah*, the Bar Mitzvah often reads directly from the Torah, chants the *haftarah*, and leads parts of the worship service. He may give a short speech commenting on the Torah portion and expressing personal feelings.

The age of Jewish majority for girls is twelve years and one day. In traditional Judaism—where women do not have the same ritual obligations as men—there is no need for a Bat Mitzvah ceremony. In liberal Judaism, where the first Bat Mitzvah ceremony in the United States took place in 1921, the Bat Mitzvah ceremony for girls is virtually identical to the Bar Mitzvah ceremony for boys.

The Bar/Bat Mitzvah ceremony is public recognition of a young person's new status within Judaism, and is a time for personal growth and evolving maturity.

Wayne Dosick

See also ALIYAH; HAFTARAH; KERIAT HATORAH; MINYAN; MITZVAH; SHABBAT.

BARCELONA, CIRILO DE
(1731–99)

Catholic missionary in Louisiana. First Roman Catholic bishop to canonically reside in the United States (five years before John Carroll was appointed bishop of Baltimore). Although technically an auxiliary bishop first of Santiago de Cuba and later of Havana, Cirilo de Barcelona was the first bishop to actually have canonical jurisdiction (as apostolic vicar for West Florida and Louisiana since 1784) exclusively over a territory that would later become the United States.

Orlando Espín

See also BISHOP (AUXILIARY, SUFFRAGAN); LATIN AMERICAN CATHOLICISM; LATINO CATHOLICISM; MISSIONARIES; MISSIONS.

BARDO

A Tibetan term indicating the "intermediate state" between death and rebirth. While all Buddhist schools emphasized the necessary continuity of individual karma within disembodied consciousness across the after-death period, it was in Tibetan Buddhism that specific practices developed to guide very explicitly the consciousness toward enlightenment or at least a most favorable rebirth. A fourteenth-century "rediscovered text" (Tibetan, *terton*), *The Tibetan Book of the Dead* (Tibetan, *Bardo Thodol*), articulates a forty-nine-day recitation of assurance and guidance to the deceased in the *bardo* state; ideally, the devotee begins spiritual practices associated with this tradition before death to guide her death experience as well.

Todd T. Lewis

See also BODHI; DHARANI; TANTRIC BUDDHISM.

BAR KOCHBA

Leader and messianic figure in the second Jewish war against Rome, 132–5 C.E. The name Bar Kochba means "son of the star," a messianic title based on Numbers 24:13. Rabbi Akiba, the leading Jewish scholar and teacher of his day, was apparently convinced that Bar Kochba was the messiah. After the failure of the rebellion, he was referred to as Bar Kosiba, "son of the lie."

Russell Fuller

BARK OF PETER

A somewhat poetic phrase, sometimes used by Catholics, to refer to the church. Since the apostle Peter was a fisherman, and since he is believed to have been appointed by Jesus as visible head of the earthly church, the latter is then imaged as "Peter's boat." An evident reference is also being made to the Peter passages in Matthew 13 and John 21.

Orlando Espín

See also POPE; ROME, SEE OF.

BARNABAS, LETTER OF

Written in the late first or early second century, this theological treatise in the form of a letter was considered part of Christian Scripture by some earlier writers, including Origen. The letter consists of two sections: a long anti-Jewish polemic, and a shorter treatise on the two paths of light and darkness. Modern scholars suggest that this work originated among the early Christian communities in Syria or Asia Minor. Since the letter already cites the Gospel of Matthew as Scripture, it must have been written much later than the time of the apostle Barnabus, who cannot therefore be considered its true author.

Gary Macy

See also MATTHEW/MATTHEAN; ORIGEN.

BAROQUE

The art/architectural style known as the baroque flourished from the late sixteenth through mid-eighteenth centuries. Much used during the period of the Catholic Reformation, and frequently (but not exclusively) associated with Jesuit buildings and churches, the baroque style features a fluid, almost rippling, sense of movement in stone entryways (*façades*) and statuary. It has been vividly described as brilliant, ecstatic, opulent, theatrical, passionate, and versatile. This monumental style can be associated with a kind of Catholic triumphalism over the challenges of the Protestant Reformation. The

Church of the Gesù in Rome and parts of St. Peter's Basilica (especially the altar and baldachino) are prominent examples. Baroque sculpture shares many of these same dynamic and dramatic qualities, for example, *The Ecstasy of St. Theresa* (Bernini, 1652). Two of the most important architects and sculptors of the period are Gianlorenzo Bernini (1598–1680) and Francesco Borromini (1599–1667).

Joanne M. Pierce

See also ALTAR; BALDACHINO; BASILICA; CATHEDRAL; GOTHIC; ROMANESQUE.

BARRETT, C. K. (1917–)

Charles Kingsley Barrett, Emeritus Professor of Divinity at Durham, England, where he spent most of his teaching career (1958–82), is especially known for his many publications on Paul and Pauline Studies. An international authority as well on Johannine and Lukan scholarship, Barrett is a Fellow of the British Academy (1961) and has had a lengthy preaching service in the Methodist ministry (1943–).

F. M. Gillman

BARTH, KARL (1886–1968)

Swiss theologian. A "founder" and central figure of neo-orthodox theology, Karl Barth defended the "sovereignty of God" against liberal theology in a series of lectures and papers following the First World War— collected in *The Word of God and the Word of Man* (1924)—and the second edition of his *The Epistle to the Romans* (1921). These works were largely cast in dialectical language, that is, they emphasized God as "Wholly Other," the "infinite qualitative difference between time and eternity," and God's Word as a *krisis* ("judgment") on the world. A turning point enabling his magisterial *Church Dogmatics* occurred

with his "discovery" of the possibility of an *analogia fidei* ("analogy of faith") in his book *Anselm: Fides Quaerans Intellectum* (1931). Over the next three decades Barth labored over his *Church Dogmatics* (1932–60), attempting to articulate a strictly Christocentric theology. Uncompleted at the time of his death, *Church Dogmatics* ran well over eight thousand pages and included volumes treating the doctrines of the Word of God, God, Creation, and Reconciliation. Barth's influence on twentieth-century theology cannot be overestimated and can be seen today in the work of such diverse authors as Gerhard Ebeling, Eberhard Jüngel, Hans Urs von Balthasar, Heinrich Ott, Hans Küng, Hans Frei, and George Lindbeck.

J. A. Colombo

See also NEO-ORTHODOX THEOLOGY.

BARTHES, ROLAND (1915–80)

French philosopher and literary critic. He taught at the École Practique des Hautes Études and at the Collège de France. Influenced by Marx and by French existentialism, Barthes' reflection moved from studying the relationship between text and author to the relationship between text and reader. He is often regarded as one of the founders of contemporary literary criticism. His thought has influenced a generation of biblical scholars. Among his main publications are *Writing Degree Zero* (1953) and *Mythologies* (1957).

Orlando Espín

See also BIBLICAL CRITICISM; EXISTENTIALISM; MARX, KARL.

"BASIC" ECCLESIAL COMMUNITIES

The term "'basic' ecclesial communities" (a translation of the Spanish *comunidades eclesiales de base;* thus the common acronym CEBs), or "base Christian communities," began to be used in church circles and by theologians in Latin America in the 1960s. Each word in the term carries a specific meaning from the Spanish, which is sometimes overlooked by people outside Latin America. "Basic" refers to the base of society, that is, to the people without social, economic, or political power, and/or those who are oppressed because of their ethnic or cultural identity or because of their gender. Members of CEBs commonly come from the poor and working-class sectors of society; nonpoor members are those who have chosen to live and work in solidarity with people at the base of society. "Ecclesial" refers to the organic link such communities have to the church (usually the Catholic Church). They are not separatist or sectarian in purpose; indeed, they are officially recognized subcommunities in many parishes whose aim is to build up the church. Criticism of the church arises in CEBs when the institution lends its support to oppressive political regimes or fails to promote the liberation of the poor. Less frequently are the church's internal structures themselves the subject of criticism, though this sometimes occurs. Finally, "community" signifies a relationship of profound commitment of members (usually between ten and thirty) to God and to each other that goes far beyond what is found in voluntary associations common to Christian parishes in affluent societies. The CEBs of Latin America are not primarily a way for people in large, impersonal parishes to get to know each other better.

People normally join a CEB as a way of committing themselves to a life of Christian discipleship in union with others. This is carried out by frequent meetings of the community during which the meaning of people's individual lives, of their life as a community, and of the current historical context is understood in dialectical relation to the Word of God (found in Scripture and the church's teaching). This means that Bible study, prayer, Christian doctrine, and current events all influence the ongoing life of the community. In the process, the spiritual and political consciousness of members tends to grow. The raising of political awareness has led some critics to consider CEBs groups whose aim is political training. Yet, in the context of multifaceted oppression and institutionalized injustice suffered by the majority of Latin Americans, supporters of CEBs claim that the Gospel of Jesus Christ cannot help but have consequences in all areas of personal and social life, including the political realm.

The number of "basic" ecclesial communities in Latin America cannot be known with any certainty, though there are certainly thousands of such groups in many countries. Whatever their number, the CEBs represent—in the words of the Catholic bishops at their third general conference in Puebla (1979)—"one of the causes for joy and hope in the Church" (no. 96); they "embody the Church's preferential love for the common people" (no. 643); and they have "helped the Church to discover the evangelizing potential of the poor" themselves (no. 1147).

James B. Nickoloff

See also LATIN AMERICAN CATHOLICISM; LIBERATION THEOLOGIES; PUEBLA DOCUMENT.

BASILICA
After the legalization of Christianity by Constantine, a new style of church building which could accommodate a large

number of worshipers was needed; the older house-church, designed on the plan of a smaller domestic building was no longer adequate. The style chosen was that of the *basilica* (from the Greek, meaning royal palace/hall), a building plan used less for private palaces than for law courts or other public buildings.

The plan or design of the basilica included a large central hall (the *nave*), sometimes subdivided into side aisles by rows of pillars running the length of the building. The front of the hall, or *apse*, was semicircular, and was reserved in Christian churches as the sanctuary area, containing the altar and seats for the bishop and presbyters. It was often set off from the main nave by steps and/or a low railing or chancel barrier. The half-dome of the apse ceiling was often decorated with mosaics, small colored tiles that could be arranged in any kind of a pattern; the theme was usually Christ as emperor or savior. Other features included an open courtyard at the entrance (the *atrium*), a small entryway inside of the main doors (the *narthex*), and, on occasion, smaller extensions off the sides of the building on the apse end (*transepts*), resulting in a cross-shaped floor plan.

Joanne M. Pierce

See also BAROQUE; CATHEDRAL; GOTHIC; ROMANESQUE.

BASILIDES (SECOND CENTURY)

Basilides taught a Gnostic form of Christianity in Alexandria during the first half of the second century. Almost all our information about Basilides comes from his orthodox opponents, and so is not above suspicion. According to them, Basilides claimed to have learned the secret teaching of the apostle Matthias from Glaucias, Peter's interpreter. This teaching included a complex and elaborate cosmology, Docetism, and the belief that Simon of Cyrene, rather than the spirit Jesus, was crucified at Calvary.

Gary Macy

See also DOCETISM; GNOSIS/GNOSTICISM; PETER.

BASIL THE GREAT (330?–79)

Born in Cappadocia (now central Turkey), Basil received his grounding in Christianity from his grandmother, Macrina the Elder. Basil was educated in Caesarea, Constantinople, and Athens in preparation for a career in the imperial service. He gave up his career, however, to lead the life of a hermit. Only when his bishop asked him to debate the Arian emperor, Valens, did he come out of his retirement. He was elected bishop of Caesarea in 370 and spent the rest of his life defending orthodoxy against the claims of the Arians. Basil was also an excellent administrator and organized the monastic communities in Turkey. He convinced both his brother (Gregory of Nyssa) and his good friend (Gregory Nazianzus) to aid him in his efforts. Together, these three great Christian leaders are known as the "Cappadocians" since this was the region in which they lived. Basil also built one of the first "hospitals," actually a vast complex to house and care for not only the sick, but also the poor, the unemployed, the elderly, and any in need of hospitality. He died in 379 C.E. shortly before the Arian controversy was settled at the Council of Constantinople. Basil is considered one of the great Doctors of the Eastern Church.

Gary Macy

See also ARIANISM; CAPPADOCIANS; DOCTORS OF THE CHURCH; GREGORY NAZIANZUS; GREGORY OF NYSSA; MACRINA.

BASLE-FLORENCE-FERRARA (COUNCILS OF)

The Council of Constance (1414–18) had decreed that a general council should be called in five years, another in seven years, and then every ten years after that. Pope Martin V, chosen at the Council of Constance to end the Western Schism, acquiesced to this decree by calling the short-lived and ineffective Council of Pavia in 1423. Before Martin died in 1431, he had already arranged for a second council to meet in Basle which it did that same year. The new pope, Eugenius IV, was opposed to the council from the first, and in December of 1431 ordered the council to dissolve. The strong reform decrees the council had passed, as well as its successful negotiations with the Hussites, won it the respect of most of the cardinals, including the respected theologian, Nicolas of Cusa. The Pope relented, and in 1433 nullified his early dissolution. The Pope refused to enact the reforms proposed, however, and the council responded by reasserting its authority as defined by the Council of Constance. Eugenius pressed the council to move to the city of Ferrara in Italy, and when a minority of the members sided with the Pope and did so move, Eugenius declared them the true council. The council then split. The papal camp met in Ferrara, and then in 1439 moved to Florence, while the conciliar majority remained in Basle. The Council in Ferrara-Florence met with representatives of the Greek church and negotiated a reunion of the Eastern and Western churches that was proclaimed in the decree *Laetentur Coeli*. The agreement was a real coup for the Pope, but the council was transferred once again, this time to Rome where it petered out. Meanwhile in Basle, the council proceeded to suspend Eugenius from office and depose him as a heretic and schismatic. A new pope with the name of Felix V was elected to succeed him. The movement was a failure. No one wanted another Western schism of Christianity, especially as it seemed the older Eastern schism had just been healed. On April 25, 1449, the Council of Basle moved to Lausanne, finally gave up, and decreed its own dissolution. The question of whether Basle should be included among the ecumenical councils is much discussed. Roman Catholics tend either to reject it altogether, or to accept only the session that met before the move to Ferrara.

Gary Macy

See also CONCILIARISM; CONSTANCE, COUNCIL OF; COUNCIL, ECUMENICAL; HUSSITES; MEDIEVAL CHRISTIANITY (IN THE WEST); POPE; SCHISM, GREAT EASTERN.

BAUER, BRUNO (1809–82)

German theologian, historian of religions, and political publicist. Philosophically, Bauer was at first a right-wing and then a radically left-wing "young Hegelian." In 1835 and 1836 Bauer published important reviews of D. F. Strauss's *Life of Jesus*, and in 1838 he published *Kritik der Geschichte der Offenbarung* (*Critique of the History of Revelation*). He began his teaching career in Berlin in 1834 and moved to Bonn in 1839. In 1842, when his work came under close critical scrutiny, Bauer was forced out of teaching, and in 1843 he reacted to this negative treatment by writing *Das entdeckte Christentum* (*Christianity Exposed*). He then turned his attention to historical and philosophical research, writing on the French Revolution, Napoleon, eighteenth-century Illuminism, and partisan political struggles in Germany. In the 1850s, Bauer returned to theological research. Albert Schweitzer identifies Bauer as the author of the first skeptical life of Jesus, writing that Bauer's *Critique of the Gospels and History of their Origins* (*Kritik der Evangelien und Geschichte ihres Ursprungs*, 1850–1) "is worth a good dozen Lives of Jesus, because his work . . . is the ablest and most complete collection of the difficulties of the Life of Jesus which is anywhere to be found" (*The Quest of the Historical Jesus*, 159). His New Testament research became increasingly skeptical, ultimately leading him to deny the historical existence of Jesus.

Jean-Pierre Ruiz

See also HEGEL, G.W.F.; JESUS OF HISTORY; SCHWEITZER, ALBERT.

BAUM, GREGORY (1923–)

Canadian Roman Catholic theologian, ecumenist, and social ethicist, Baum was born in Berlin, Germany. The son of secular Jewish parents, he escaped from Nazi Germany at the age of sixteen. Under the sponsorship of a Christian British woman, he was interred in Canada during WWII with other German nationals. After becoming a Catholic, Baum entered the Order of St. Augustine in Ontario and studied mathematics at Ohio State and theology at the University of Fribourg. At Vatican II he served as *peritus* to the Canadian bishops, where he was instrumental in drafting the Decree on Ecumenism (*Unitatis Redintegratio*) and the Decree on the Relationship of the Catholic Church to Non-Christian Religions (*Nostra Aetate*).

From 1960–86 he taught in the Institute of Christian Thought at the University of St. Michael's College in Toronto. In 1978 he left the Augustinians and married Shirley Flynn. Moving to McGill University in Montreal in 1986, Baum taught social ethics until his retirement in 1994.

Baum's earlier writings concern chiefly the areas of fundamental theology (revelation, development of doctrine) and ecumenism. In the late 1960s he studied depth psychology and spent two years studying critical social theory at the New School of Social Research. These perspectives inform his writing throughout the 1970s and 1980s, especially *Religion and Alienation: A Theological Reading of Sociology* (1975) and *Theology and Society* (1988). Embracing political and liberation theologies, Baum has continued to espouse a "critical theology" that seeks to uncover the passionate longing for compassion and solidarity hidden in the great religious traditions. An ardent advocate of Catholic Social Teaching, he believes it is the duty of Christians to translate these desires into action on behalf of and in solidarity with the poor and marginalized.

Having served from 1962–2004 as editor of *The Ecumenist*, as well as a codirector of the international Catholic review *Concilium*, Baum's most recent works include *The Twentieth Century: A Theological Overview* (1999) and *Amazing Church: A Catholic Theologian Remembers a Half-Century of Change* (2005). Named to the Order of Canada in 1990, Baum continues to work as a research associate in the Centre Justice et Foi, the Jesuit social justice center in Montreal.

Mary Ann Hinsdale

B.C./A.D.

See C.E. / B.C.E.

BEA, AUGUSTINE (1881–1968)

German-born cardinal of the Catholic Church, and member of the Society of Jesus (Jesuits), he was a respected biblical scholar and university professor, very instrumental in promoting the agenda of the Second Vatican Council. As a cardinal, he was responsible for promoting unity among separated Christians. He was successful in breaking down many old barriers of mistrust between Protestants and Catholics, as well as in promoting serious biblical scholarship within the Catholic Church.

Orlando Espín

See also CARDINAL; COUNCIL, ECUMENICAL; CURIA, CONGREGATIONS OF THE (ROMAN); ECUMENICAL MOVEMENT/ECUMENISM; SOCIETY OF JESUS; VATICAN, SECOND COUNCIL OF THE.

BEATIFICATION
In the Roman Catholic Church, this is an act whereby the pope, after a long and thorough examination of a (deceased) Catholic's life and beliefs, recommends that he or she may be venerated within particular dioceses, nations, or religious congregations, or (nowadays) throughout the entire church. Before the seventeenth century, it was customary for local bishops to beatify deceased Christians who could be venerated within their dioceses only. A beatified person is called "blessed." Beatification is not the same as canonization. Some Orthodox Churches have a custom similar to beatification.

Orlando Espín

See also CANONIZATION; ORTHODOX CHURCHES; POPE; SAINT; SAINTS (CHRISTIAN), DEVOTION TO.

BEATIFIC VISION
The beatific vision is a traditional metaphor for the personal experience of God after death. The image suggests the transformed and perfected condition of existence with particular emphasis on knowledge of God. The idea is rooted in the Christian confidence in Jesus' resurrection. The emphasis on vision comes from the Pauline imagery of a present dim vision of God, contrasted with a face-to-face vision in the Resurrection (1 Cor 13:12). St. Thomas Aquinas understood the vision metaphor as completeness of knowledge, knowing God as God is. Contemporary theology understands the beatific vision as a relational metaphor. The destiny of personal life is to be in relationship with God; the beatific vision signifies the complete openness to God that is the condition of participation in God's life. The Christian emphasis on the personal free option for God cautions that the beatific vision is not the only possible end to life.

Patricia Plovanich

See also HEAVEN; HELL; PURGATORY.

BEATITUDES
The popular designation for the collection of eight sayings of Jesus that introduce Matthew's Sermon on the Mount (Matt 5:3-10). The word is derived from the first word in all eight sayings in Latin (*beati*), translated as "blessed" or "happy." Four of these sayings also appear in Luke's Sermon on the Plain (Matt 5:3 = Luke 6:30b; Matt 5:4 = Luke 6:21b; Matt 5:6 = Luke 6:21a; Matt 5:11 = Luke 6:22).

Although the more technical name is "macarism" (from the Greek, *makarios*, "blessed" or "happy"), the term "beatitude" identifies many sayings in Egyptian, Greek, Jewish, and Christian literature that have a similar form. Macarisms or beatitudes are brief, often isolated statements that praise those whose conduct, attitudes, or qualities render them happy or blessed. Since they praise human qualities, beatitudes must be distinguished from blessings that come from God. There are four types of macarisms: secular, religious, wisdom, and satirical.

There are forty-five beatitudes in Hebrew Scripture: Deut 33:29; 1 Kgs 10:8; 2 Chr 9:7; Isa 30:18; 32:20; 56:2; Pss 1:2; 2:12; 32:1, 2; 33:12; 34:9; 40:5; 41:2; 65:5; 84:5, 6, 13; 89:16; 94:12; 106:3; 112:1; 119:1, 2; 127:5; 128:1, 2; 137:8, 9; 144:15; 146:5; Job 5:17; Prov 3:13; 8:32, 34; 14:21; 16:20; 20:7; 28:14; 29:18; Eccl 10:17; Dan 12:12; and fourteen beatitudes from the Septuagint are also included in Catholic and Orthodox Bibles (Tob 13:14; Wis 3:13; Sir 14:1, 2, 20; 25:8, 9; 26:1, 28:19; 31:8; 34:15; 48:11; 50:28). Some claim that beatitudes emerged in Israel in cultic settings; most believe they originated in the Wisdom tradition. Although wisdom beatitudes predominate in biblical texts, religious macarisms with eschatological overtones are prominent in Jewish postbiblical apocalyptic literature (1 Enoch 58:2; 81:4; 82:4; 99:10; 103:5; 2 Enoch 41:1; 42:6-14; 44:4; 48:9; 52:1-14; 61:3; 62:1; 66:7).

There are thirty-seven beatitudes in the New Testament: Matt 5:3, 4, 5, 6, 7, 8, 9, 10, 11; 11:6; 13:16; 16:17; 24:46; Luke 1:45; 6:20, 21, 22; 7:23; 10:23; 11:27, 28; 12:36, 43; 14:15; 23:29; John 20:29; Rom 4:7, 8; 14:22; Jas 1:12; Rev 1:3; 14:13; 16:15; 19:9; 20:6; 22:7. Since seven in Matthew are also found in Luke and the two in Romans 4:7-8 are a citation of Psalm 32:1-2, the New Testament actually includes twenty-eight different macarisms. Of these, seventeen are sayings of Jesus.

The four Beatitudes found both in Matthew's Sermon on the Mount and Luke's Sermon on the Plain were derived from Q. Many believe the substance of these four Beatitudes goes back to the proclamation of the historical Jesus. Three appear in modified form in the Gospel of Thomas (Matt 5:4 = Thomas 54; Matt 5:6 = Thomas 69b; Matt 5:11 = Thomas 68-69a).

The canonical forms of the Beatitudes in Matthew 5 and Luke 6 betray the redactional activity on the part of both evangelists. Matthew spiritualized the first and fourth Beatitudes and shaped the fifth, sixth, and seventh to provide the collection with the characteristics of a church exhortation. Matthew's Beatitudes praise those who adopt the ideals of the believing community. Luke's beatitudes address those who are literally deprived. Luke also intensifies his social concerns by juxtaposing the four Beatitudes with four corresponding antithetical woes. In Luke, those who are declared blessed are to be comforted in their present realities by the happiness they are assured in an eschatological future.

Regina A. Boisclair

See also Q SOURCE; REDACTION CRITICISM.

BEDE THE VENERABLE (672/3–735)

A Benedictine monk at Jarrow and Wearmouth in Northumbria (present-day Yorkshire), Bede recorded the essential facts of his life at the end of his most well-known work, the *History of the English Church and People,* which narrates the story of the evangelization of England from the period of the Roman conquest to the full institutionalization of church authority in all of the Saxon kingdoms (about 731). He was entrusted to the monks at the age of seven for his education, and remained in the monastery where, in his own words, his "chief delight [had] always been in study, teaching, and writing." At a time when much of western Europe was struggling to retain the rudiments of learning and to preserve the limited store of classical Christian texts still available, Bede exhibits theological originality and a profound respect for history as the continuing story of God's plan for salvation. His other written works include commentaries on many books of Scripture, school texts (for example, on spelling and composition techniques), and the lives of saints and abbots important to his locale.

Marie Anne Mayeski

See also EXEGESIS / EISEGESIS; MEDIEVAL CHRISTIANITY (IN THE WEST); MONASTICISM IN WESTERN CHRISTIANITY.

BEGUINES

At the end of the twelfth century, a century of religious fervor and a good deal of experimentation with forms of religious living, various women in the Netherlands began to combine a life of chastity and prayer with pious activity in the world in ways that were considered new, and somewhat dangerous, by their contemporaries. Seeking both a freedom from social constraints (represented by the obligations of marriage) and from ecclesiastical constraints (represented by the imposition of canonical rule), these women, called Beguines by their contemporaries, lived alone or in small groups, supported themselves by the work of their own hands, and sought to serve the poor and the sick. But they followed no specific rule, took no formal vows, and observed the round of religious services in the parish church like the laypeople they were. Though they seemed to have chosen religious counselors from among the canons of St. Augustine, and though there was a comparable male movement (the Beghards) that imitated their example, the Beguines rejected all forms of male control, either in marriage or through ecclesiastical structures. Their small communities were only loosely connected to one another; their devotion to ascetical poverty (they were free to hold private property, in fact)

and their commitment to urban locales were the common threads that united them. The rapid spread of the Beguine ideal and the flourishing of their establishments were phenomenal. At the end of the thirteenth century in Cologne, there were fifty-four "beguinages," while in many towns in the Low Country they created virtual enclaves for themselves.

Historical interpretation of the Beguines has largely been determined by the *Life of Mary of Oignes*, written by James de Vitry around 1215 (*Acta Sanctorum*, June, 5:542-88). James, it would seem, wanted to deflect ecclesiastical censure from his friend (who had just died) and also wanted to use his account of her life to demonstrate to devout women, drifting toward the greater freedom offered by the Cathari and Albigensian movements, that an orthodox path to that freedom existed in Catholicism. His strategies were not entirely successful: the novelty of their life, their social ideals and commitment to poverty, and their mysticism—all brought upon them the scrutiny and suspicion of the church authorities. The so-called "teaching" of the Beguines was condemned by the Council of Vienne in 1311.

Marie Anne Mayeski

See also ALBIGENSIANS; ASCETICISM / ASCETIC; CATHARS; MYSTICISM / MYSTICS (IN CHRISTIANITY); RULE (MONASTIC / RELIGIOUS); VOWS (RELIGIOUS).

BEIT DIN

(Hebrew, house of judgment). In Judaism, the panel of as few as one or as many as seventy-one judges needed to try criminal or civil cases. In premodern times, a court of three judges had jurisdiction in civil matters, including divorce, conversion, and absolution from vows, and was empowered to penalize a defendant through fines, flogging, or even enslavement. Courts of twenty-three adjudicated in criminal matters, including capital cases, and a court of seventy-one judges had essentially unlimited legislative, administrative, and judicial power, including the authority to elect a king or high priest. Since, even in rabbinic times, the Jewish government had only limited autonomy, its courts could not exercise many of the functions described here. This was so particularly in capital cases, in matters involving a Jew and non-Jew, and in cases in which a Jew chose of his own volition to resort to a non-Jewish court. In modern practice, and in particular in the state of Israel, a beit din is normally a panel of three rabbis that has jurisdiction in matters of personal status, especially conversion and divorce.

Alan J. Avery-Peck

BEIT HAMIKDASH

(Hebrew, house of sanctification). In Judaism, the Hebrew designation for the Jerusalem Temple, where the Israelite cult was carried out from the time of Solomon until the Temple's destruction by Rome in the Jewish war of 66–70 C.E. Contemporary Orthodox Judaism continues to look forward to God's restoration of the Beit HaMikdash in the messianic age.

Alan J. Avery-Peck

See also ESCHATOLOGY (IN JUDAISM); TEMPLE OF JERUSALEM.

BELLAH, ROBERT N. (1927–)

A sociologist of religion and professor at the University of California at Berkeley, he has made two significant contributions to understandings of contemporary U.S. religion. In 1967 he published a landmark essay describing what he called the "civil religion" of the United States. He defined civil religion as the religion of patriotism, with sacred scriptures (the Declaration of Independence), sites (the Washington Monument or Lincoln Memorial), and icons (the flag). He envisioned civil religion as a unifying force in an increasingly pluralistic culture. Second, he has examined individualism and community in U.S. religious life. In *Habits of the Heart* (1985), he and coauthors identified a popular strain of modern religion they dubbed "Sheilaism," a highly individualistic belief and practice detached from any organized community. In *The Good Society* (1991), they countered this radical individualism by urging the revitalization of responsibility and morality in public institutions. Since Bellah, many scholars have analyzed the scope and impact of civil religion and religious affiliation in the United States.

Evelyn A. Kirkley

See also CIVIL RELIGION; PLURALISM.

BELLARMINE, ROBERT (1542–1621)

Canonized as a saint in 1930, Bellarmine was an Italian Jesuit, a theologian, a cardinal and a bishop. Professor of theology at Louvain and then in Rome, he produced volumes of controversial theology in which he sought to refute Protestant doctrine and demonstrate the "truth" of Catholicism. He also participated in the revision of the Vulgate (Latin Bible) and in some of the controversies surrounding Galileo. In contrast to some political theorists, Bellarmine held that the pope should play but an indirect role in temporal (secular) matters.

Thomas Worcester, s.j.

See also COUNTER-REFORMATION / CATHOLIC REFORMATION; SOCIETY OF JESUS.

BENEDICTINE RULE (RULE OF ST. BENEDICT)

The *Rule of St. Benedict*, written by Benedict of Nursia for use by his monks, is a guidebook describing how monks should organize their monastery and their lives. The *Rule* is not original, but draws on several earlier rules, especially the anonymous *Rule of the Master*. Benedict's *Rule* is remarkable for its simplicity, brevity, and moderation. The motto of the *Rule* is "Pray and Work" (*Ora et Labora*), the two actions that were to make up the monastic life. Although at first the *Rule of St. Benedict* was only one of many rules monks used in organizing their lives, Benedict of Aniane in the ninth century, supported by Emperor Louis the Pious, urged that all monks use the one *Rule of St. Benedict*. By the middle of the eleventh century, nearly all the monks in Western Christianity used the *Rule of St. Benedict*. Indeed, this period has been called "The Benedictine Age" by some scholars. The Benedictine monks still follow the *Rule of St. Benedict* to this day.

Gary Macy

See also BENEDICT OF NURSIA; BENEDICTINES; MONASTICISM IN WESTERN CHRISTIANITY.

BENEDICTINES

"Benedictine" is a term used to refer to the men and women who follow the *Rule of St. Benedict* in their monastic lives. There really is not a "Benedictine Order," since each monastery is independent of the others and since there are several "groupings" of Benedictine monasteries based on the different reform movements that have taken place during the long history of the Benedictines. The Benedictines, however, do form a kind of "confederation" and meet every four years in Rome to discuss common issues.

The Benedictines started in the fifth century when Benedict of Nursia put together a guidebook for organizing monastic life. At first, this code was just one of many available to monks in Western Christianity. However, its simplicity and common sense soon made it very popular. In the ninth century, Charlemagne and particularly his son, Louis the Pious, supported the monk Benedict of Aniane in his efforts to organize all monks under the Benedictine Rule. By the eleventh century, this movement was generally successful, and especially under the influence of the powerful monastery of Cluny, the *Rule of St. Benedict* was, for practical purposes, the only monastic Rule used in Western Christianity. Indeed, the tenth, eleventh, and twelfth centuries saw the greatest flowering of Benedictine life that it has ever known. Monasteries were the centers of learning and devotion. Great saints and scholars, like Hildegard of Bingen and Bernard of Clairvaux, came from Benedictine monasteries.

By the beginning of the thirteenth century, new ways of religious life began to compete with the Rule. Francis of Assisi, Dominic de Guzman, and others offered an alternative to the monastic life, and the new universities took over from the monastic schools. The Reformation of the sixteenth century brought the closure of most Benedictine houses in northern Europe, but the eighteenth century saw a revival of scholarship among the Benedictines and a renewal of interest in their way of life. Today there are some 1200 monasteries and houses around the world still living according to the *Rule of St. Benedict*.

Gary Macy

See also BENEDICT OF NURSIA; BENEDICTINE RULE (RULE OF ST. BENEDICT);

MEDIEVAL CHRISTIANITY (IN THE WEST); MONASTICISM IN WESTERN CHRISTIANITY; RULE (MONASTIC/RELIGIOUS).

BENEDICTION WITH BLESSED SACRAMENT

A ceremony in which a priest or deacon blesses an assembly by making the sign of the cross over it using the eucharistic Bread. The blessing is usually preceded by a service of praise and thanksgiving made up of hymns, readings, a litany, and sometimes preaching. Strong nonverbal symbols—vestments, a large number of lighted candles, and burning incense—figure prominently in the service. During the service, the eucharistic Bread is almost always placed in a vessel called a monstrance. This vessel is less frequently called an ostensorium. Both of these words come from Latin roots, meaning "to show." A monstrance holds the eucharistic Bread behind a small glass window in such a way that it is shown to those assembled for the service. The custom of displaying the Eucharist in this way is called Exposition of the Blessed Sacrament.

Patrick L. Malloy

See also BLESSING (CHRISTIANITY); LITURGY OF THE EUCHARIST.

BENEDICT OF NURSIA (480?–547?)

Benedict is most famous as the founder of Benedictine monasticism. Sent by his wealthy family to study in Rome, Benedict rejected the worldly and corrupt city for a solitary life near Subiaco. Benedict's followers and admirers grew in number and included the later Pope Gregory I, the Great. In all, twelve monasteries were founded by Benedict, including Montecassino, to which Benedict himself moved around 529. The "Rule" Benedict wrote for his monks became the most influential monastic rule in Western Christianity.

Gary Macy

See also BENEDICTINE RULE (RULE OF ST. BENEDICT); BENEDICTINES; GREGORY I THE GREAT, POPE; MONASTICISM IN WESTERN CHRISTIANITY; RULE (MONASTIC/RELIGIOUS).

BENEDICT XVI, POPE (1927–)

Born Joseph Ratzinger, Benedict was earlier *peritus* (expert) at Vatican Council II; professor for theology at Bonn (1959), Münster (1964), Tübingen (1966) and Regensburg (1969); archbishop of Munich–Freising (1977); Prefect of the Congregation for the Doctrine of Faith (1981). Ratzinger's doctoral studies in dogmatic theology and history generated his interest in historical theology. Early studies of Augustine and Bonaventure examine the relationship between philosophy, theology, and salvation history. Other works after Vatican Council II are cogent expositions of conciliar themes. *Introduction to Christianity* (1969), his meditation on the Apostles' Creed, uses a more traditional dogmatic approach and expresses reservations about the historical-critical method. In his role as senior official in the Congregation for Faith, Ratzinger's concern about historical thought, theological pluralism, and the orthodoxy of many new theological approaches has resulted in the examination of many theologians (Hans Küng, Edward Schillebeeckx), and the censure of others (Charles Curran, Leonardo Boff, and Piet Schoonenberg).

Benedict was elected Pope in 2005. His papal activities have featured interreligious dialogue and the interface between faith and the secular spirit of modernity. His first encyclical is *Deus Caritas Est (God Is Love)*.

Patricia Plovanich

BERENGAR OF TOURS (1010?–88)

Born of an influential family from Tours in France, by the age of twenty he already held a post in the church there. A very popular and successful teacher of grammar and rhetoric, he turned to the teaching of theology in his later years. His teaching on the Eucharist aroused a great deal of opposition and was condemned in several councils, the most important being those held at Rome in 1059 and in 1079. Lancfranc, the abbot of Bec, was one of Berengar's strongest opponents. Berengar died in retirement in 1088. He was accused of denying the Real Presence of the risen Christ in the Eucharist, and the condemnations of his teaching were included in the important canon law collection of Gratian, the *Decretum*. Theologians of later generations, therefore, knew of the condemnation of Berengar and continued to discuss it. The debate over Berengar's teaching helped to develop the technical language that would be used in later centuries in elaborating the theory of transubstantiation.

Gary Macy

See also CHRIST OF FAITH; EUCHARIST; MEDIEVAL CHRISTIANITY (IN THE WEST); REAL PRESENCE; RESURRECTION OF CHRIST; TRANSUBSTANTIATION.

BERGER, PETER L. (1929–)

American sociologist of religion, he has made important contributions to his field, especially through the publication of *The Social Construction of Reality* (1966, written with T. Luckmann), *The Sacred Canopy* (1967), and *A Rumor of Angels* (1969). Berger influenced American theological thought on secularism and the survival of religion in secular contexts. To Latin American theology he contributed his reflections on the impact of socially constructed reality on religious formations and thought.

Orlando Espín

See also CIVIL RELIGION; ETHICS, SOCIAL; IDEOLOGY (IDEOLOGIES); LUCKMANN, THOMAS; MODERNITY; POSTMODERNITY; PRIVATIZATION OF RELIGION; SECULARIZATION/SECULAR/SECULARIZED; VALUES.

BERGSON, HENRI (1859–1941)

French philosopher and one of the founders of process philosophy/theology, in 1927 he won the Nobel Prize for literature.

Bergson was heavily influenced by Darwin's *The Origin of Species*, published in the year of Bergson's birth, but he came to criticize the theory of natural selection because, he thought, merely random mutations could never result in changes that were coadapted to an existing organism, and also because it failed to explain why evolution produces ever more complex organisms which, because they are more fragile, are less adapted to survival. He concluded that internal to the evolutionary process, an *élan vital* (vital impulse) was operating that accounted for continuity of functioning and increased complexity of organization.

In regard to human evolution, Bergson argued, natural selection presented only half the picture, yielding a view of humankind as toolmakers. Tool-making is linked with survival and practicality. The organ of tool-making is the intellect, which proceeds by analysis. In order to function properly, the intellect must render the surrounding world as a collection of static things that are easily susceptible of manipulation. The other half of the picture can be reached only through intuition, in which the mind suspends its concern with the practical and turns inward toward the core of the self. There the mind encounters a reality that is both continuously mobile and profoundly integrated. This reality is pure duration, and is closely associated with the *élan vital*.

Philosophy's excessive concentration on the intellect and its method of analysis has, Bergson argued, produced theories that render reality as both static and fragmented. Plato's Forms and Kant's concepts of the understanding are two examples. In contrast, the method of intuition places the mind in immediate contact with true reality, which is both mobile and integrated. Also, the method of analysis has yielded a multiplicity of conflicting systems, each of which captures, at best, only a single aspect of reality. Intuition penetrates beneath this multitude of conflicting systems and provides a view of reality in its concrete fullness. Analysis, of course, is also the method of the sciences, and as a result, science, at best, can only provide a view of reality that is relative to some perspective. Metaphysics, on the other hand, provides an absolute knowledge of reality.

Another casualty of the dependence on intellect is a distortion of the true reality of time. Intellect yields a view in which time is reduced to a sequence of static moments each of which exists simultaneously with all the rest. This is time as spacialized, the time that is represented in mathematical graphs. This view of time inevitably leads to the triumph of determinism over freedom, because it always views human choice as something after the fact instead of something in the making. Time in the true sense is apprehended only through intuition where it appears as lived duration. Duration is time in the concrete, a flowing, irreversible succession of states in which the future unfolds from the present and the past wraps up in the present. When placed in the context of duration, human choices are seen as moments of creativity in which the outcome is literally brought into existence by the act of choosing. Only when viewed in this way can human choices be free.

Duration is otherwise called spirit, and is the proper object of metaphysics, whose method is intuition. Frozen spirit is otherwise called matter, and is the proper object of the several sciences, whose method is analysis. By applying time in the spacialized sense to matter, science is able to interpret matter in terms of numerous deterministic laws. But at best, the sciences yield views of reality that are relative to their various outward perspectives. In contrast, by approaching reality from its inward core, which is suffused with duration, metaphysics yields a view of reality that is absolute.

Bergson's view of God is that of a being closely related to the *élan vital*, which is active throughout the cosmos, continually driving it to ever higher forms of complexity and organization. The idea of God as an omnipotent, omniscient, and all-perfect being that transcends the physical universe is absent from Bergson's philosophy. Humans can contact God through a special form of intuition characteristic of the mystical experience. As so experienced, God appears as pure creative activity that is identical to love.

Bergson extends the contrast between intuition and intellect to an interpretation of religion and morality. The closed religion is heavily dependent on the products of the intellect, and it concentrates on static dogma and repetitive, mechanical rituals. It is resistant to change and subject to authoritarian leadership. Like the various systems of philosophy, the closed religion tends to become fragmented into groups that continually battle one another over theological details. In contrast, the open religion, grounded in intuition, is flexible and open to change. It places maximum value on freedom, and minimizes the importance of mechanical ritual. It is inclusive of all humankind and encourages diversity among its members. As its principal source of illumination, it looks not to dogma but to the mystical spirit, which provides the only true access to God.

Bergson's more important writings include *Time and Free Will* (1889), *Matter and Memory* (1896), *Introduction to Metaphysics* (1903), *Creative Evolution* (1907), and *The Two Sources of Morality and Religion* (1932).

Patrick J. Hurley

BERKELEY, GEORGE (1685–1753)

Irish philosopher and Anglican bishop of Cloyne, Berkeley advocated a form of idealism in which the entire corporeal universe is reducible to collections of ideas. The city of Berkeley, California, was named after him in recognition of his contributions to education in the American Colonies.

Berkeley was a deeply religious thinker who sought to rescue religion and morality from the hands of skeptics and atheists spawned by the scientific revolution. Berkeley's procedure was to accept at face value the theory of perception created in the wake of the revolution and to show that it logically entailed the impossibility of the existence of matter. This removed the foundation for skepticism. Then, Berkeley showed that this theory of perception required the existence of an omnipotent deity, which countered the charges of the atheists.

The theory of perception that served as Berkeley's starting point was the one advocated by Locke, and earlier by Descartes and Galileo. According to this theory, the only qualities that actually exist in corporeal things are the primary qualities—extension, figure, and motion. The secondary qualities—color, taste, fragrance, sound, warmth, coldness, and so on—do not actually exist in corporeal things, but are produced by the mind in response to the action of bodies on the sense organs. This view was supported by observations such as the following. The same object can feel cold to one hand and warm to another, but the object itself is not both warm and cold; and the color of an object depends on lighting conditions and the state of the perceiver, but these factors do not affect changes in the object perceived. Therefore, warmth and color are not in the object, but they exist only as ideas in the mind of the perceiver.

According to this theory the sensory object is known not directly, but only through the ideas we have of its qualities. Berkeley was quick to point out that this theory led to skepticism, because the mind is unable to determine if these ideas represent the object as it really is. In other words, the mind is not able to climb outside of itself and compare the ideas with the object, so the mind can never be assured that its ideas are truly representative. For all we know, the corporeal world might be completely different from the way we perceive it, and this is the basic attitude of skepticism.

Now, accepting the scientific theory of perception for what it says, Berkeley observes that the primary qualities are inseparable from the secondary qualities and are unknowable without them. For example, the extension of an apple is unknowable apart from its color or tactile qualities, the motion of a ship at sea is dependent on the perceiver's selection of some point of reference, and the figure of an object, such as a coin, is dependent on the perspective of the perceiver. Thus, if the secondary qualities exist only as ideas in the mind of the perceiver, then so do the primary qualities.

Next, Berkeley asks, what is there left that might support the claim that the perceptual object exists outside the mind? If the respondent answers "matter," Berkeley replies that any such matter is unknowable apart from its extension, figure, and motion, and these have been shown to be mere ideas in the mind of the perceiver. Thus, there is nothing at all outside the mind of the perceiver that answers to the term "matter." In other words, matter simply does not exist. As a result, all perceptual objects are immediately present to the mind. This conclusion destroys the ground of skepticism.

Berkeley reinforces his conclusion that perceptual objects exist only in the mind of the perceiver by observing that any other conclusion is inconceivable. Colors cannot be heard, nor sounds seen, nor fragrances tasted, but these qualities are meaningful only in connection with the proper sense of the perceiver. This conclusion is expressed in the famous claim *Esse est percipi*—the very being of the perceptual object is identical with its being perceived. Perceptual objects such as tables, houses, and mountains have no existence whatsoever independent of the perceiver, but they exist as mere collections of ideas in the perceiver's mind.

Finally, Berkeley observes, there are some ideas, such as the idea of a purple cow, that we create for ourselves, and we are aware of the act of creating them. But with ordinary perceptual objects there is no attendant creative effort. Surely we have no reason to think that the chair passes out of existence the moment we stop perceiving it and begins existing once again when it reenters our perception. The conclusion is that there must be an active perceiver who creates these ordinary objects through the act of perceiving them, and who then sends these perceptions to us. This active perceiver can only be a supremely powerful mind who creates the perceptions of the entire cosmos. We call this perceiver God.

In our communications with other finite perceivers, God acts like an all-observant telegraph exchange, receiving the perceptions from the mind of the speaker and immediately conveying them to the mind of the listener. God, for Berkeley, thus serves a function not so different from the divine monad in Leibniz's theory. Just as Leibniz's God attunes every monad with every other monad through preestablished harmony, so Berkeley's God provides the essential link between one human perceiver and another.

Berkeley's more important works include *An Essay Toward a New Theory of Vision* (1709), *A Treatise Concerning the Principles of Human Knowledge* (1710), *Three Dialogues Between Hylas and Philonous* (1713), *Alciphron* (1732), *The Analyst* (1734), and *Siris* (1744).

Patrick J. Hurley

BERNARD OF CLAIRVAUX (1090–1153)

One of the most important religious and political figures of the twelfth century, Bernard joined the fledgling reform monastery of Cadets in 1113 and became founder and abbot of Clairvaux two years later. He was formative in founding the military order of the Knights Templar (1128) and preached the Second Crusade.

He was strictly orthodox in theology and fierce in protecting what he believed; he savagely attacked Peter Abelard and influenced the Council of Sens (1140) to condemn him for heresy. His exegetical and theological writings (*Commentary on the Song of Songs*; *Treatise on Loving God*; *Concerning Grace and Free Will*) exhibit the characteristics of Cistercian thought with its emphasis on the human nature of Christ, the soul as the image of the Trinity, and the primacy of love.

Marie Anne Mayeski

See also ABELARD, PETER; CISTERCIANS; CRUSADES; MEDIEVAL CHRISTIANITY (IN THE WEST); MILITARY ORDERS.

BÉRULLE, PIERRE DE (1575–1629)
Cardinal and theologian, Bérulle was one of the most important figures of the French Catholic Reformation. Instrumental in bringing the reformed (Discalced) Carmelites to France, Bérulle created, in 1611, the congregation of diocesan priests known as the Oratory. Modeled on Philip Neri's Roman Oratory, Bérulle's foundation served to promote a spirituality for clergy that was focused on the person of Christ. Bérulle thus played an important role in implementing the Council of Trent's decrees on the reform of priests. His most important book is the *Grandeurs de Jésus*, first published in 1623, in which devotion to Christ as Word incarnate is developed at length.

Thomas Worcester, S.J.

See also CARMELITES; COUNTER-REFORMATION/CATHOLIC REFORMATION; ORATORY/ORATORIANS; TRENT, COUNCIL OF.

BEZA, THEODORE (1519–1605)
Successor to Calvin as leader of the Reformation in Geneva, Beza, like Calvin, was born and educated in France. After studies in Paris, Orléans, and Bourges, Beza moved to Geneva in 1548 in order to participate in the Reformation underway there.

Beza's studies had exposed him to humanism; as professor in Lausanne and then Geneva his publications included a Latin translation of the Greek New Testament and a new edition of the Greek text. Discoverer of a fifth-century manuscript of parts of the New Testament, Beza is still honored today by designation of this text as the Codex Bezae. Beza also produced, in 1560, an important summary or confession of the Christian faith.

Calvin died in 1564; from that date until his own death some forty years later, Beza was the most influential of Genevan reformers. In the 1590s Francis de Sales visited Beza several times in the hope of convincing him to return to Catholicism. These efforts came to nothing.

Thomas Worcester, S.J.

See also CALVIN, JOHN; CALVINISM; DE SALES, FRANCIS; HUGUENOTS; REFORMATION; REFORMED CHURCH; REFORMED THEOLOGY (-IES).

BHAGAVAD GITA
One of the most popular scriptures of Hinduism, the *Bhagavad Gita* contains the instruction given to Arjuna, the warrior hero of the *Mahabharata*, by the *avatara* and divine teacher Krishna. The text, which was probably composed sometime between 200 B.C.E. and 200 C.E., in fact, forms part of the *Mahabharata*. The setting of the *Bhagavad Gita* is significant: it takes place on the battlefield, just as Arjuna is about to enter into a battle of monumentally tragic proportions. Krishna teaches his disciple that, if he carries out his *dharma* (sacred duty) as a warrior without attachment, as an offering to God, his actions

will not create karmic bondage. Krishna also tells Arjuna that he, as God, will grant *moksha* (liberation) to all those who surrender their lives completely to him in love. Thus the *Gita*, as it is frequently called, is the primary source for Hindus of the teachings of *karma-yoga*, the path of nonattached action, and *bhakti-yoga*, the path of loving devotion. It thus offers the possibility of genuine spiritual life to laypeople, unlike Jainism, early Buddhism, and the renouncer traditions within Hinduism, which opened the highest spiritual goals with rare exceptions only to ascetics. Still, Krishna's teaching ranges over the entire gamut of Hindu spirituality as it was practiced at the time, including what was later called *jnana-yoga*, the path of knowledge, and meditative practices similar to those described in the *Yoga Sutras*. The *Bhagavad Gita* climaxes in its eleventh chapter, one of the most dramatic passages in the religious literature of the world, in which Krishna grants Arjuna a vision of his universal form (*vishva-rupa*) as Lord of the universe.

Lance E. Nelson

See also ARJUNA; BHAKTI-YOGA; BUDDHISM; JAINISM; JNANA-YOGA; KRISHNA; MAHABHARATA; YOGA SUTRAS.

BHAGAVATAM
See BHAGAVATA PURANA.

BHAGAVATA PURANA
The *Bhagavata* is perhaps the most widely popular of the Hindu Puranas. Like most texts of this genre, it considers a diverse collection of topics, including the origins and history of the cosmos and the careers of the various *avataras* or divine incarnations that have appeared on earth, all from a Vaishnava perspective. Composed around the ninth century C.E., this text is especially beloved for its description, in highly poetic and sensuous language, of the life of Krishna, particularly his childhood pranks and his adolescent love-play with young women of his village, the *gopis*. Because it evokes a highly emotional, even ecstatic love of the divine as Krishna, it has become a favorite of the Krishnaite *bhakti* movements, some of which hold the text in such high esteem that they regard it as having an authority equal to the Vedas.

Lance E. Nelson

See also AVATARA / AVATAR; BHAKTI; BHAKTI-YOGA; GOPI; HINDUISM; KRISHNA; PURANA; VAISHNAVA; VEDAS.

BHAKTI
As a spirituality of loving attachment to God, *bhakti* (Sanskrit, devotion) is a central theme of Hinduism and Mahayana Buddhism from classical times to the present. While the renouncer traditions of Hinduism—the *sannyasins* and *yogins*—have emphasized a world-denying, ascetic spirituality, the vast majority of Hindus, scholars as well as common folk, have practiced a religion of bhakti. This means that they approach the divine in loving devotion and trusting surrender, conceiving God in intimate, personal terms as a merciful and benign savior. The classical texts of Krishnaite bhakti are the Sanskrit *Bhagavad Gita* and *Bhagavata Purana*, but perhaps even more important in the lives of people are the songs of numerous poet-saints who evoked intense love of God and conveyed profound points of theology in simple but striking poetic images in the various regional vernaculars understood by the common people. Krishna, however, is not the only deity important in bhakti Hinduism. The

particular deity regarded as supreme, and hence the object of devotion, depends upon the traditional denominational affiliation of the individual Hindu's family and caste or, sometimes, upon personal choice. While the traditions of Krishna bhakti are most widely known and studied in the West, there are also strong and equally important traditions within Hinduism of devotion to Shiva and the Goddess (Shakti or Devi), each with their own saints and literature. The most typical practices of bhakti spirituality are chanting the name of the deity by means of a *mantra*, temple worship, and pilgrimage. These and other practices constitute the way of devotion, *bhakti-yoga*.

Lance E. Nelson

See also BHAGAVAD GITA; BHAGAVATA PURANA; BHAKTI-YOGA; DEVA/DEVI; HINDUISM; KRISHNA; MANTRA; SANNYASA; SHAKTA; SHAKTI; SHIVA; VAISHNAVA; VISHNU; YOGA.

BHAKTIVEDANTA, SWAMI
(1896–1977)
The founder of the Hare Krishna Movement, Swami Bhaktivedanta was born Abhay Charan De in Calcutta. Known to his followers as Shrila Prabhupada, Bhaktivedanta became a *sannyasin* in 1959 and came to the U.S. from India in 1965. He began what has grown into a respected, worldwide religious movement by preaching to "hippies" in the streets of New York City's East Village.

Lance E. Nelson

See also BHAKTI; HARE KRISHNA MOVEMENT; HINDUISM; SANNYASA; VAISHNAVA.

BHAKTI-YOGA
The way of loving devotion, *bhakti-yoga* is one of the four classically recognized spiritual paths of Hinduism, known as the four *yogas* (disciplines) or *margas* (paths). The way of bhakti is based on cultivating an attitude of loving devotion and trusting surrender to a grace-bestowing savior deity, which—depending on one's family and caste tradition or, sometimes, on one's choice—could be Vishnu (or one of his incarnations, especially Rama or Krishna), Shiva, or the Goddess (Shakti, Devi). Characteristic practices of bhakti-yoga would include: constant chanting the name of the deity in the form of a *mantra*, singing devotional songs, reading devotional scriptures (such as the *Bhagavad Gita* or the *Bhagavata Purana*), visiting temples, maintaining a home altar, and going on pilgrimage. Like *karma-yoga*, bhakti spirituality is very much open to the laity as well as practiced by monastics.

Lance E. Nelson

See also BHAGAVAD GITA; BHAGAVATA PURANA; BHAKTI; DEVA/DEVI; HINDUISM; KARMA-YOGA; KRISHNA; MANTRA; MARGA; RAMA; SHAIVA; SHAKTA; SHAKTI; SHIVA; VAISHNAVA; VISHNU; YOGA.

BHIKSHU/BHIKSHUNI
Terms used in Buddhism and Jainism usually translated as monk/nun in English. The terms derive from the root meaning of "beggar," an attribute of those who entered the early ascetic communities (*sanghas*) and adhered to their rules which required daily alms rounds to obtain one's subsistence. In Buddhism, *bhikshu* designated the status of a fully ordained member of the sangha who had vowed to follow the rules of the *Vinaya* that regulated communal life. These included rejecting certain activities associated with the householder's life such as sex and cohabitation with a spouse, while wearing simple robes, having few

possessions, eating solid foods between dawn and midday, and attending the fortnightly recitation of the *Pratimoksha*, a summary of the code of conduct. To maintain one's membership also meant submission to the spiritual and procedural authority of monks who had longer tenure "in the robes." Patriarchy in Buddhism was expressed in the rule that all women ordained as *bhikshunis*, regardless of seniority, still had to accept inferior status to even the most junior bhikshus. (The Pali terms of Theravada Buddhism are *bhikkhu/ bhikkhunii*.)

Todd T. Lewis

See also MONASTICISM (OUTSIDE CHRISTIANITY); SANGHA; VOWS.

BIBLE

The name of the collection of the sacred writings of Christianity and Judaism. The Greek word *biblia*, literally, "little books," was derived from the Phoenician city of Byblos, where papyrus was cut and dried in strips for use in writing. In the ancient world *biblia* referred to "scrolls"; however, with the development of codices, it became possible to bind texts together into a volume. While Jews continue to use scrolls in synagogue services, Christians use a codex Bible in liturgy. Both Christians and Jews use codex Bibles for private reading and study.

The Jewish Bible contains the sacred texts that Israel shaped over a long period of oral and written transmission before they became fixed into a final, canonical form. The canon of twenty-four books dates from the late first century C.E. The Jewish Bible incorporates three collections: the *Torah* (Law); the *Neviim* (Prophets: subdivided into the Former Prophets and the Latter Prophets); and the *Kethuvim* (Writings). Jews refer to the Bible as the *Tanak*, an acronym derived from the first letters of each section.

The Christian Bible has two major divisions, traditionally called the Old Testament and the New Testament. Although it contains the sacred texts of Israel, the Old Testament is not identical with the *Tanak*. When the Jesus movement expanded beyond Palestine, Greek-speaking Christians adopted the Greek translation of the Scriptures known as the Septuagint (abbreviated, LXX). The LXX used a different arrangement and numbering of the books and included some texts that were not later included in the Jewish canon. Thus, the religiously significant texts of the Jewish diaspora were considered Christian Scripture long before the end of the first century. However, the early extant lists of Christian sacred texts indicate that some communities questioned the authority of some of the books that were accepted by others. While some small Christian groups, such as the Ethiopian Church, settled on more extensive canons, since the fifth century, most Eastern churches have followed a fifty-book Old Testament while the whole Western church adopted a forty-six-book Old Testament.

For a variety of reasons, the sixteenth-century Reformers rejected seven deuterocanonical books and passages in Esther and Daniel that were not in the Jewish Bible. They identified these texts as apocrypha. Subsequently, although Protestant Bibles continued to follow the order and numbering of texts of the LXX, their thirty-nine-book Old Testament only contains the texts that are found in twenty-four books in the Jewish Bible.

The early Christians also wrote, collected, and preserved their own literature. By the end of the second century C.E., four Gospels and some epistles were invested with the same sacred authority as the LXX. By the end of the fourth century c.e., there was a general acceptance of a twenty-seven-book New Testament.

Christians traditionally call the collection of texts that stem from Israel, the Old Testament and identify the collection of their own writings, the New Testament. Today, a number of English-speaking Christian scholars prefer to refer to these collections as the First Testament and Second Testament. This represents an effort to diminish an anti-Judaic presupposition that may be associated with the traditional names.

Regina A. Boisclair

BIBLE (VERSIONS)

Whether ancient or modern, every translation of the Bible from the original languages is called a version. Postexilic Israel produced versions in Aramaic, Greek, and probably Syriac. The Greek version, called the Septuagint (abbreviated, LXX), is uniquely important to Christians. As "the Bible" of the early church, many words, concepts, citations, and allusions in the New Testament come from the LXX.

In the third century Christians began to translate the two Testaments into Latin using the LXX as the basis for the Old Testament. The Old Latin Version, characterized by its lack of uniformity, underwent a number of revisions before an official Vulgate stabilized in 1592. The Old Testament of the 1592 Vulgate synthesized the best existing Latin translations with those that St. Jerome had provided from Hebrew texts (ca. 406 c.e.). Until 1948 the Vulgate was the official Bible of the Roman Catholic Church and served as the basis of all Catholic vernacular versions. Today, a Neo-Vulgate Version (1979) provides the official Latin text of the Bible for pontifical documents.

Versions in modern vernacular languages began to appear shortly before the Reformation. The Reformers were convinced of the importance of using the original languages as the basis for these translations, while the Catholic Church remained committed to the Latin text. Although the first complete English Bible, credited to Wycliff (1382), was a translation from the Latin, it was condemned by Catholic authorities as was Tyndale's translation of the New Testament from the Greek (1525). *The Coverdale Bible* (1535), *Matthew's Bible* (1537), *Taverner's Bible* (1537), *The Great Bible* (1539), *The Geneva Bible* (1560), and the *Bishops Bible* (1568) gave way to the highly polished English in the *King James* or *Authorized Version* (1611).

Catholic authorities responded somewhat reluctantly to the growing demand for an English Bible. The New Testament (Rheims, 1582), the Old Testament (Douay, 1609), and their revisions by Bishop Richard Challoner (1763), were all based on the Vulgate. *The Douay-Rheims-Challoner Version* was the official Catholic English Bible until Pope Pius XII, in his 1943 encyclical *Divino Afflante Spiritu*, authorized new versions based on manuscripts in the original languages.

Nineteenth-century advances in text criticism demonstrated that the manuscripts used for the *King James* version did not always provide the most likely original reading. This led to the production of *The Revised Version* (1885), *The American Standard Version* (1897) and *The Revised Standard Version* (1952). More recently, *The New American Standard Bible* (1970), *The New English Bible* (1976), *Today's English Version* (1976), *The New International Version* (1978), the *New King James Version* (1982), the *Revised English Bible* (1989), and *The New Revised Standard*

Version (1990) were produced, largely under Protestant sponsorship, although Catholics served on the committee that produced the NRSV.

La Bible de Jérusalem (1956), translated by scholars and associates of the École Biblique de Jérusalem was the first Catholic vernacular version based on the original languages. However, its English translation, *The Jerusalem Bible* (1966), was based largely on the French text. The second English edition, *The New Jerusalem Bible* (1985), was a translation based on texts in the original languages. *The New American Bible* (1971) was the work of members of the Catholic Biblical Association of America. The NAB subsequently incorporated a revised translation of the New Testament (1987); a revision of the Old Testament awaits approval by the USCCB (United States Conference of Catholic Bishops).

There are no significant differences between modern Catholic and Protestant versions. The RSV is approved for use in Catholic liturgy. However, there is a difference between dynamic equivalent versions that seek to approximate ancient idioms in contemporary English and verbal correspondence versions that seek to use words that match as precisely as possible those in the original languages. *Today's English Version* is the most obvious example of the former, while most scholars consider *The Revised Standard Version* the best example of the latter. To varying degrees, the most recent versions (NRSV, NJB, REV, and the second edition of the New Testament and Psalter of the NAB) also provide gender-inclusive language in their translations.

Regina A. Boisclair

See also PESHITTA; SEPTUAGINT; TARGUM; VULGATE.

BIBLICAL CRITICISM

Derived from the Greek term *krinō*, "to judge," biblical criticism is the study and analysis of biblical writings in order to make careful judgments about the texts. Biblical criticism functions analogously to literary criticism, music criticism, and art criticism, and the like, all of which have as their purpose the carefully informed study of products in their area.

With respect specifically to biblical criticism, among its concerns are: the manuscript history of the texts; the origin of each biblical writing, including when and where it originated, how, why, by whom, and for whom it was composed and edited; the genre and content of each document, including sources used and influences operative upon the author(s) and the text; the literary, historical, and theological meaning of the documents; the reception of the text by its hearers and readers from the time of the text's origins and throughout its existence; and the role of the book within the whole biblical canon. These concerns form the basis for the various interconnected branches of biblical criticism.

F. M. Gillman

See also FORM CRITICISM; HISTORICAL CRITICISM; NARRATIVE CRITICISM; REDACTION CRITICISM; SOURCE CRITICISM; TEXT CRITICISM.

BIBLICAL REFERENCES

The standard way to refer to a specific passage in the Bible is to identify the book, chapter(s), and verse(s) in which the passage appears. Scholarly works often provide these references without introducing the text of the passage. However, it is customary to note the book, chapter(s), and verse(s) before or after a biblical passage is written out or read, although such references may only identify the biblical book in a liturgical context.

The division of biblical literature into books stems from antiquity. The division of the biblical books into numerical sequences of chapters and verses that are used today was devised in two stages. Stephen Langton, an archbishop of Canterbury and chancellor of the University of Paris, introduced the numerical sequence of chapters in a copy of the Vulgate in 1226. Robert Estienne, a Parisian printer, subdivided Langton's chapters into a numerical sequence of verses that first appeared in his 1551 New Testament. These divisions were quickly adopted and are now printed in every language and version of the Bible. However, text-critical research and editorial decisions introduced minor differences in some of the verses in contemporary versions of the English Bible.

There are standard forms to abbreviate and punctuate biblical references. The following examples are from Genesis: Gen 2:4 identifies the fourth verse in second chapter; Gen 2–4 identifies the second through fourth chapters; Gen 2:1-4 identifies the first through fourth verses of chapter two, while Gen 2:1-4, 15-17 skips from verse four to verses fifteen through seventeen. In the more complicated citation: Gen 1:26-30; 2:18-23; 5:2, the semicolons mean "skip to." This notation identifies passages in three different chapters that speak of human creation.

Although the traditional chapter and verse divisions are a universal "shorthand," chapters frequently separate integral parts of a passage, while some verses are too short and others are too long to make sense. They should be ignored when trying to identify a pericope. In addition, scholars frequently subdivide a verse into an alphabetical sequence to provide greater precision. An example of this practice is found in noting that the first creation account is found in Genesis 1:1–2:4a. This reference presumes that readers will recognize that the complete sentence that begins Genesis 2:4 is Genesis 2:4a; the remainder of Genesis 2 begins a sentence that does not end until Genesis 2:9.

Regina A. Boisclair

See also BIBLE (VERSIONS).

BIBLICAL THEOLOGY

The major task of biblical theology is to help believers mediate between the religious experience of people of the past and those of the present. Using the results of critical biblical scholarship, biblical theology evaluates what the Bible says, for example, about what ancient Israelites or early Christians believed about God and how they responded to God. Without stopping at that point, however, biblical theology proceeds to see what light that information can shed upon contemporary experience of God and articulation of faith. Thus, biblical theology evaluates current belief in light of the biblical tradition. It is a process in which the biblical text is allowed to inform or challenge current understandings of self, others, the world, and God. As such, this work must be redone in each generation.

The dynamic described here cannot be based upon an uninformed reading of the text. Biblical theologians rely upon the results of critical exegesis for help in determining the various theological perspectives within the biblical material. While at some times in the past it was generally assumed that the whole Bible, both Old and New Testaments, offered a unified theology, it is now widely recognized that there is a diversity or plurality of theological perspectives within Scripture.

F. M. Gillman

See also BIBLICAL CRITICISM; HEILSGESCHICHTE; JOHANNINE CORPUS; PAULINE THEOLOGY.

BINGEMER, MARIA CLARA (1949–)

Brazilian Catholic theologian, professor, and dean in the school of theology at the Pontifical Catholic University of Rio de Janeiro. Bingemer did her undergraduate studies in communications and journalism, completing her first graduate degree in theology at the Pontifical Catholic University in Rio. She earned the doctorate in theology at Rome's Gregorian University. She has focused her research and publications on the theology of laity, on (Ignatian) spirituality, and on a feminine reading of Christian doctrines of God. Her personal commitments and theological work have incorporated methodological and other contributions from Latin American liberation theology. Among her best publications are *Alteridade e vulnerabilidade* (1993) and *Segredo feminino do Mistério* (1994).

Orlando Espín

See also FEMINIST THEOLOGIES; IGNATIUS LOYOLA; LAITY; LATIN AMERICAN THEOLOGIES; LIBERATION THEOLOGIES; OPTION FOR THE POOR; SPIRITUAL EXERCISES.

BIOETHICS

Bioethics is the systematic consideration of ethical or moral issues associated with health care, medical research, and life sciences. Ethics is the study of what is good (usually what is considered good or well-being for humans) and what actions and personal dispositions (virtues and vices) tend to bring about or undermine such goodness. Bioethics, then, studies how various practices in health care, medical research, and application of various life sciences tend to enhance or detract from human well-being. Bioethics examines specific actions, practices, professional and personal virtues and vices with the attempt to assess whether they are likely to promote or jeopardize the good of those involved.

Typical issues considered in bioethics include the right of patients to make informed decisions about treatment; the right of human subjects to be informed of risks associated with medical research (informed consent); health care professionals' obligations to patients; euthanasia; organ transplants; reproductive technologies (that is, contraception, in-vitro fertilization, embryo freezing, surrogacy, abortion); allocation of health care resources, genetic research and therapy/ enhancement; questions concerning use of animals for medical research; and impact of human activity on the overall well-being of the biosphere.

Michael J. Hartwig

See also ETHICS.

BIRKATH HAMINIM

In the daily Jewish liturgy, the twelfth benediction of the Shemonah Esreh ("Eighteen Benedictions"), invoking God's wrath against heretics, slanderers, and enemies of the Jewish people. In its original formulation in the second century B.C.E., the prayer was directed against Jews sympathetic to Hellenization and the Syrian assault against traditional Jewish practice. After the destruction of the

Second Temple in 70 C.E., it was applied to Sadducees, heretics, and apostates in general. This prayer is omitted from the contemporary Reform liturgy.

Alan J. Avery-Peck

See also LITURGY (IN JUDAISM); REFORM JUDAISM; SHEMONAH ESREH.

BIRTH CONTROL
See CONTRACEPTION/BIRTH CONTROL.

BISHOP (AUXILIARY, SUFFRAGAN)
An "auxiliary" bishop assists the "ordinary" in a Roman Catholic diocese. Both are ordained to the episcopate, but they differ in jurisdictional authority. All bishops have the power to ordain and are the usual ministers of the sacrament of confirmation.

Mary Ann Hinsdale

BISHOP (EPISCOPACY)
The office of bishop (Greek = episkopos) in the New Testament refers to the role of an "overseer" in the early Christian community. It is often used interchangeably with the office of "elder" (Greek = presbyter) in the Pastoral Letters (1 and 2 Tim; Titus). A monarchical office developed gradually in the early church and can be found in the second-century letters of Ignatius of Antioch. The bishop is the symbol of unity in the church (Ignatius of Antioch: "where the bishop is, there is the church").

Mary Ann Hinsdale

See also APOSTOLIC SUCCESSION; CHURCH; COMMUNION (ECCLESIO- LOGICAL); DIOCESE/ARCHDIOCESE; EPISCOPAL CONFERENCES; EPISKOPOS; IGNATIUS OF ANTIOCH; MAGISTERIUM, ORDINARY; ORDINARY (CANONICAL); ORDINATION; PRIESTHOOD.

BISHOP (ORDINARY)
The "ordinary" is a bishop who heads a Roman Catholic diocese. He is the chief authority in the diocese and has the power to make laws (jurisdiction) for the local church. In most cases, he is appointed by the pope and serves for life, unless he resigns or is transferred to another diocese. An auxiliary bishop who is appointed to a diocese with the status of "coadjutor" or "with the right of succession" becomes an "ordinary" upon the resignation or death of the current ordinary.

Mary Ann Hinsdale

See also BISHOP (AUXILIARY, SUFFRAGAN); BISHOP (EPISCOPACY); CANON LAW; DIOCESE/ARCHDIOCESE; LOCAL CHURCH.

BISHOP OF ROME
See POPE.

BLACK CHRIST, THE
In Black Liberation Theology, Jesus Christ is depicted as black, either physically (Albert Cleague), ontologically (James Cone), or symbolically (J. Deotis Roberts). Womanist theologians, such as Jacquelyn Grant and Kelly Brown Douglass, also speak of the Black Christ in their discussions of Christ's significance for black women.

Christ as black is of critical importance for black (African) Americans in terms of his salvific stance of liberation of those unjustly oppressed. Jesus Christ is the Black Christ because he has identified himself in his incarnation with the poor and the marginalized in society. In the United States, those who have historically been poor and oppressed are black (African) Americans. As their oppression is due, most specifically as their enslavement was, to their blackness, then the christological importance of Jesus Christ must also be found in his blackness. In order to save black people, Jesus Christ must himself partake of their life situation. As Jesus was Jewish in his actual birth, for contemporary black (African) American Christians, Christ must be and is black. By sharing in their marginalization because and only because of their skin color, the Black Christ in his death and resurrection thereby saves and liberates all blacks from the chains of oppression.

For most black and womanist theologians, the actual historical skin color of Jesus Christ is not a factor. Christ's blackness is not exclusively salvific for blacks (African Americans) alone, but is expressive of the present reality in the United States today, a society in which the victims of poverty, oppression, and marginalization are most often people of color. Thus, Christ can also be seen as brown, red, and yellow. The Black Christ, however, as one united in suffering with black (African) Americans, is liberating for all who suffer unjustly due to racial stigmatization and oppression.

Diana L. Hayes

See also AFRICAN AMERICAN THEOLOGY; AFRICAN TRADITIONAL RELIGIONS; CONE, JAMES H.

BLACK ELK (1863?–1950)

Perhaps one of the best-known spiritual leaders of the Plains Indians during their final period of struggle to retain their freedom, his long life witnessed the last days of his people's free-roaming life as buffalo warriors. In the narrative he confided to John Neihardt (*Black Elk Speaks*), he described taking part with his clansmen, one of whom was the famous medicine man, Crazy Horse, and the Cheyenne in the epochal Battle of the Little Bighorn,

where Custer and his cavalry were totally defeated. More tragically, he also saw his people confined to reservations and the awful events of the massacre at Wounded Knee.

His own path led him, by sacred initiation, to the vocation of a medicine man. All his life was spent serving his people. At one point, that desire led him to convert to the Catholic faith, and to the role of catechist. Thus he is remembered in his own community as a faithful witness to the life of the spirit, and also as a faith-keeper of the traditions of his people, the Lakota. He fulfilled the latter role in a special way when he entrusted to Joseph Epes Brown his detailed account of the major rites of his people. This was eventually published as *The Sacred Pipe*. His position in history and his profound spiritual life have made him a universal teacher in the late twentieth century.

Kathleen Dugan

See also SHAMAN.

BLACK THEOLOGY

Black theology is a global movement thematized primarily in the United States and South Africa, but to some extent also in the Caribbean and in Brazil. Like all Christian theology, black theology strives to discern, to understand, to interpret, and to impart the word of God and its meaning in cultural and social (that is, political, economic, technological) contexts. However, black theology explicitly addresses the historical, cultural, structural subordination of black peoples within social contexts dominated by white supremacist rule and explicitly exposes and critiques the idolatrous use of the Hebrew and Christian Scriptures, of Christian doctrines, and of theology to justify that subordination.

The Roots of Black Theology

Black theology both in the United States and in South Africa can be linked to legacies of African peoples' negotiated and armed struggles for civil and human rights in societies ordered by racial preference, discrimination, and apartheid. It can also be linked to African peoples' analysis and critique of their subjugation and oppression in light of the message and ministry of Jesus of Nazareth and their affirmation of their culture, history, and identity. This historic struggle, analysis, and affirmation constitute not only the roots of black theology, but the conditions for its possibility as well.

The Development of Black Theology in the United States (BTUSA)

The first phase of BTUSA (1960–9) coincides with the modern civil rights movement and the irruption of the black power movement. Under the leadership of the Rev. Dr. Martin Luther King Jr., the civil rights movement practiced non-violent protest in the face of white racist supremacist brutality. Despite more than ten years of verbal abuse, physical humiliation, fire hoses, cattle prods, dogs, shootings, and bombings by white segregationists, the protesters held to King's doctrine of Christian suffering love. But by the summer of 1966, members of the Student Non-violent Coordinating Committee (SNCC or "Snick") began to embrace "black power." Their action ruptured the precarious relationship King had forged between blacks and whites and polarized black pastors, clergy, and laity. During this same period, the strategic and moral potency of the civil rights movement had come under assault not only by Muslim Minister Malcolm X, but by protracted police and FBI probes of various black leaders and organizations. When,

instead of denouncing "black power," the National Committee of Black Clergyman (NCCB) published the "Black Power Statement" in the *New York Times*, July 31, 1966, their endorsement ushered in a radical religious movement among black Christians and paved the way for the appearance of James Cone's *Black Theology and Black Power.*

In its second phase (1970–6) BTUSA was read and taught in seminaries and universities; professors, black and white, explored the meaning of black theology in monographs and articles and organized conferences and seminars. In 1970 black scholars in religion and theology organized the Society for the Study of Black Religion (SSBR) to promote and sustain rigorous dialogue about black theology and the religious experience of African Americans.

BTUSA in its third phase (1977 to 1989) dialogued with several groups, including Latin American liberation theologians, and in a special way, Theology in the Americas (TIA) provided that opportunity. Under the leadership of Chilean priest, Sergio Torres and Filipino Maryknoller, Virginia Fabella, TIA sponsored the first of two national conferences in Detroit, Michigan, in August of 1975. This meeting brought together theologians, church workers, social theorists, and activists from Latin America and the United States. Out of this assembly came several "affinity groups" committed to exploring the relation of theology to racial or cultural-ethnic or gender or class critiques. Two years later, in Atlanta, Georgia, TIA's Black Theology Project sponsored the first national ecumenical consultation on black theology under the theme, "The Black Church and the Black Community." Cone, in the conference's keynote address, proposed two new priorities for black theology: (1) reappraisal of the use of Marxist economic and social categories to critique U.S. capitalism, and (2) linking the struggle for justice by U.S. blacks to the struggle for justice by oppressed peoples around the globe.

Finally, during this third phase, black women theologians began to comment on the sexist bias of black theology. In particular, Katie Cannon, Jacquelyn Grant, and Delores Williams, along with sociologist of religion Cheryl Townsend Gilkes, began to critically engage the experience of black women as a source for theological reflection. Taking up a familiar African American cultural expression (*womanish*) that had been popularized by novelist Alice Walker, they coined the phrase "womanist theology." They meant to differentiate black women's theology from that of black male theologians and white liberal feminist theologians, both of whom had taken the presence and physical labor of black women (labor that had made it possible for these men and women to theologize) for granted, ignoring black women's intellectual work, silencing their distinctive perspective.

In this current fourth phase, BTUSA seems to be configured in three models. A first model has turned black theology toward narrative, thus making a distinct African American theology possible. Major sources for this theology are the recovery of precolonial African cultures, the religious practices of the enslaved peoples, the spirituals, and slave narratives. Recent work by Will Coleman, Dwight Hopkins, Riggins Earl Jr., and Theophus Smith are good examples. A second model responds to theology's systematic exigence. Here black theology interrelates and synthesizes major Christian doctrines in light of the historical, religious, cultural, and social experience of black people. The possibilities of this model are shown in the work of James Cone, J. Deotis Roberts, James Evans, Jacquelyn Grant, Jamie T. Phelps, Diana Hayes, and Delores Williams. The third model of black theology interrogates the social situation of black peoples in postmodern, postindustrial United States. The ever more egregious cultural and social conditions of the masses of black peoples calls black theology to come to terms with the interaction and mutual conditioning between racism, sexism, class exploitation, and imperialism; to sharpen its understanding of economic and political decline on the national and global scales; to respond to pressing psychological and spiritual needs of black peoples; and thereby assist the black church in the articulation of a program for concrete intelligent ministerial practice.

The Development of Black Theology in South Africa (BTSA)

In South Africa, the first phase of black theology can be dated from about 1970 to 1977. Black theology seems to have been introduced into South Africa in the early 1970s through the efforts of the multiracial University Christian Movement (UCM). But no understanding of black theology in South Africa is possible without considering the Black Consciousness Movement (BCM) and its charismatic leader Steve Biko. For Biko, the heart of black consciousness was the realization by blacks that the most potent weapon in the hands of the oppressor is the mind of the oppressed. Arguing, even with the sacrifice of his life, for the renewal of culture, education, religion, and economics in light of African genius and creativity, Biko set the philosophic and cultural stage for the development of black theology in South Africa.

The first formal seminar on black theology was held in 1970. It met not only with the rejection of some black and white scholars, but also with government interference and restrictions. Although the proceedings from that conference were banned in South Africa for "security reasons," the participants published them as a book abroad. A second conference was attempted in 1975, but floundered under government pressure. The first full-length scholarly discussion of black theology in South Africa appeared in 1977 with the publication of *Farewell to Innocence: A Socio-Ethical Study on Black Theology and Black Power* by Allan Boesak.

The second phase of black theology in South Africa extends from about 1978 to 1989; it is a fertile period marked by growth and consolidation. Frank Chicane, Sigibo Dwane, Bonganjalo Goba, Simon Maimela, Itumeleng Mosala, and Takatso Mofokeng developed a considerable and rigorous body of theological literature. Themes most characteristic of BTSA in this phase include: interrogation of the role of traditional religious and cultural practices; use of Marxist analytic categories; critical reinterpretation of violence in the black townships in the light of the structural violence of state apartheid; attentiveness to the condition of the black poor and black workers; and ongoing self-criticism. Still, what was most challenging during this period, was black theology's demand for redistribution of land.

One important institutional outcome of black theology in this second phase was the Institute for Contextual Theology (ITC); Chicane served as its first general secretary. In 1985, under ITC auspices, a multiracial group of lay and ordained Christians responded to South Africa's state of emergency with the *Kairos Document*. This theological statement defined and critiqued two types of church-state relations and their corresponding theologies: the one, a racist "state theology" spawned from the collusion of the Dutch Reformed Church and the Afrikaner government; the other, an equivocating "church theology," put forward by the liberal rhetoric of white English-speaking churches, but ignoring the difficult concrete work of justice to the victims of institutionalized violence. The alternative the *Kairos Document* advanced was a biblically rooted, action-oriented "prophetic theology" that would contest both external (white) and internal (black) oppressions and utilize critical social analysis to comprehend the totality of the racial-political-economic capitalism.

Like its U.S. counterpart, BTSA has not been free of sexist bias. In 1984 the ITC sponsored a conference on feminist theology that dealt with a range of issues including the male image of God projected by theologians and the church in its ritual practices, cultural and social practices that exploit women, educational discrimination against women, and the oppression of women by women. Bernadette Mosala and Bonita Bennett have argued that black women in South Africa endure a fourfold oppression: women are discriminated against and oppressed as black people (race), as workers (class), as women (gender), and by one another as women both as individuals and a group. Thus, B. Mosala insists that an authentic black theology is morally bound to eradicate the oppression of women in church and society.

In 1990 South Africa itself embarked on a new phase with the release of Nelson Mandela, the lifting of the ban against the ANC and other activist groups, culminating in the first multiracial elections which brought Mandela to the presidency of

South Africa. Given the seriousness with which it has regarded the political situation, BTSA has been projected into a current and third phase. Despite the political enfranchisement of South Africa's black majority, the economic and educational situation of ordinary black people lags far behind that of whites and other groups. Perhaps, the future of black theology in South Africa lies in its ability to incarnate a prophetic political theology of liberation: biblically rooted, action-oriented theology of oppressed people—healing the deep wounds against black humanity and nourishing black culture; committed to land reform and redistribution; utilizing social analysis to deconstruct the oppressions of race, gender, and class; and promoting a vision of a just society that yields only to the reign of God.

M. Shawn Copeland

See also AFRICAN AMERICAN THEOLOGY; CANNON, KATIE GENEVA; CONE, JAMES H.; WOMANIST THEOLOGY.

BLASPHEMY

The showing of contempt or a lack of reverence for God. According to Leviticus 24:16, "Whoever blasphemes the name of the Lord shall be put to death. The whole community shall stone him; alien and native alike must be put to death for blaspheming the Lord's name." This law is closely connected with the teaching that "You shall not take the name of the Lord, your God, in vain" (Exod 20:7; Deut 5:11).

In the New Testament, Jesus is believed by some of the scribes to be blaspheming when he says to a paralytic that his sins are forgiven since Jesus has attributed to himself a power believed to be reserved to God alone (Mark 2:7). Later in the Gospel, and in Matthew's account also, Jesus is condemned for blaspheming when he admits to Caiphas, the high priest, in the hearing of the Sanhedrin, that he is the Messiah, the son of the Blessed One (14:61-62; cf. Matt 26:63-65). By claiming such an identity, in the minds of those who accuse him of blasphemy, Jesus is showing contempt for God.

The Gospel of John, like those of Mark and Matthew, portrays Jesus as accused of blasphemy because of his identification with the Messiah. However, the setting for John's account is earlier in Jesus' life, before his arrest. Nevertheless, the consequence of Jesus' testimony is the same. Had Jesus not escaped from their power, they might have stoned him, in accordance with Leviticus 24:16, for blasphemy (John 10:24-33).

The Synoptic Gospels portray Jesus as claiming that every sin including blasphemy will be forgiven people, but blasphemy against the Holy Spirit will not be forgiven (Matt 12:31; Mark 3:28-29; cf. Luke 12:10).

Alice L. Laffey

BLESSING (CHRISTIANITY)

A blessing is a prayer addressed to God asking for divine favor, or a wish addressed to a person or persons that God will grant them divine favor. Blessings are invoked by religious authorities, and may be imparted to persons, other living creatures, or inanimate objects. In blessing people, the minister invokes God's favor directly upon them. The request may include, either implicitly or explicitly, the spiritual, emotional, and physical good of the person. At the end of many liturgical rites, the ordained minister invokes a blessing upon the assembly, perhaps making the sign of the cross over the persons being blessed. A layperson who presides over a liturgical service does not use such authoritative blessings because the layperson ministers as an equal among equals. In these cases, the leader does not impart a blessing ("May almighty God bless you . . .") but asks God's blessing ("May almighty God bless us . . ."). Parents and other adults sometimes invoke a blessing upon children, by virtue of their authority or seniority. In some cultures, the one blessing the child marks him or her with a small sign of the cross. The *Book of Blessings*, the liturgical book containing the rites for various kinds of blessings, reveals that all blessings, even of inanimate objects, refer ultimately to human beings. The service for the blessing of animals, for instance, asks God to "grant that these animals may serve our needs" (no. 958). The blessing of a gymnasium likewise focuses on the human persons who will use the facility. "Grant that all who meet here may find the enrichment of companionship and together offer you the praise that is due" (no. 847). All blessings, therefore, are indirectly for the sake of humans. In blessing persons, animals, or objects, Christians do not imply that these things were profane or evil before the blessing.

Patrick L. Malloy

See also EPICLESIS.

BLESSING (JUDAISM)

(Hebrew, *berakhah*). In Judaism, the central way in which God is thanked for sustaining the world and human beings. The blessing-formula stands at the foundation of the daily and festival liturgy, and blessings are recited as well (1) before the performance of each religious obligation (mitzvah), (2) at moments of thanksgiving or sorrow, and (3) before the enjoyment of food. Blessings preceding the fulfillment of a religious commandment are introduced, "Blessed are you, Lord our God, sovereign over the universe, who has sanctified us with his commandments and commanded us to . . ." A description of the specific obligation to be fulfilled follows, for example, "to kindle the Sabbath light." Blessings in the other categories are introduced, "Blessed are you, Lord our God, sovereign over the universe . . .," followed by a statement of that for which God is being recognized. Prior to a meal, for instance, one adds "who has brought forth bread from the earth"; upon hearing thunder, the formula is, "whose strength and might fill the world"; upon hearing of a death, one states "who is a true judge." So that God's role in the world and the bounty God provides might constantly be recognized, the Talmud enjoins each Jew to recite a minimum of one hundred such blessings each day.

Alan J. Avery-Peck

See also LITURGY (IN JUDAISM).

BLOCH, ERNST (1885–1977)

German philosopher. A Marxist, Bloch was very well acquainted with Christianity and Judaism, especially with eschatological and utopic traditions in both. He was an influence on the so-called "theology of hope" movement and on later political theologies, including Latin American liberation theology. He wrote a number of books, the most important of which are the three volumes of *Das Prinzip Hoffnung* (*The Hope Principle*) (1954–9).

Orlando Espín

See also ESCHATOLOGY (IN CHRISTIANITY); ESCHATOLOGY (IN JUDAISM); HOPE (IN CHRISTIANITY); LIBERATION THEOLOGIES; MARXISM; METHOD IN THEOLOGY; PRAXIS; UTOPIA.

BLONDEL, MAURICE (1861–1949)

French Catholic philosopher. Blondel tried to construct a Christian philosophy demonstrating Christianity's credibility against the rationalist philosophies of his day. His doctoral thesis, *L'action*, an original effort in fundamental theology, attempts to explain the human potential for knowledge of God. The thesis considers the dynamic character of human volition, argues the inability of natural objects to satisfy human desire, thus indicating the supernatural orientation of human will that is satisfied only through an encounter with God. Blondel's argument proposed a dynamic concept of intellect and will, a new approach to the nature–grace relationship and prefigured similar efforts by the transcendental Thomists. His work makes an important contribution to twentieth-century apologetics and fundamental theology as it demonstrates the possibility of religious experience in the midst of ordinary life.

Patricia Plovanich

See also THOMISM / TRANSCENDENTAL THOMISM.

B'NAI BRITH

(Hebrew, "Sons of the Covenant"). Founded in New York in 1843, the world's largest Jewish service organization. Principal arms of the B'nai Brith promote Jewish education, commitment, and the protection of Jewish interests. The Anti-Defamation League (ADL) was founded in 1913, dedicated to fighting anti-Semitism, protecting the rights of Jews, and strengthening relationships between Jews and non-Jews. The B'nai Brith Hillel Foundation, created in 1923, funds Jewish organizations on college campuses to encourage college students' practice of and commitment to Judaism. The B'nai Brith Youth Organization (BBYO), comprised of separate divisions for boys, girls, and young adults, was formed in 1924. Principally a men's organization, the B'nai Brith's women's arm, B'nai Brith Women, was founded in 1897.

Alan J. Avery-Peck

BODHI

A Sanskrit Buddhist term derived from the verbal root "awaken" and usually translated "enlightenment." *Bodhi* is a quality of mind (*bodhicitta*) associated with the cessation of karmic bondage and the implication of utter clarity in discerning reality with insight (*prajna*), seeing it marked by suffering, impermanence, and soul-lessness. As implied by its use by Buddhists for traditional names of spiritual beings (for example, *bodhisattva*, literally "enlightenment being" or "Buddha-to-be") and historical figures (for instance, Bodhidharma, Chan/Zen patriarch), achieving bodhi is definitive of salvation.

The Abhidharma scholastics identified three forms of bodhi, in order of increasing scope: that of disciples (*shravakas*), that of private Buddhas (*pratyekabuddhas*), and that realized by Buddhas. The last, called *samyak sambodhi* ("completely perfect enlightenment"), is cosmic in scale, independently gained but shared with others. The early Pali Nikaya tradition identified the "Seven Limbs of Enlightenment" (*bojjhanga*) in practice: mindfulness, doctrine investigations, energy, zest, calmness, concentration, equanimity. Another longer formulation is its list of "thirty-seven qualities of *bodhi*" (*bodhipaksha dharmas*), a list that came to be used as a summary of Buddhist spiritual training. In the Mahayana schools, the realization of bodhi was measured by the ability to see the ultimate emptiness of all phenomena.

Todd T. Lewis

See also BODHI; BODHISATTVA; BUDDHA; NIRVANA; PRAJNA.

BODHISATTVA

A "Buddha to be," aspiring to complete enlightenment and the teaching of humanity. All Buddhist schools have believed in the *bodhisattva*, a figure who through many incarnations—as animal, spirit, human being—develops spiritual qualities and good *karma*, a cumulative achievement that eventually culminates in the realization of Buddhahood. These previous lifetimes have been of great interest to Buddhists throughout history, making stories of these lives (called *jatakas*) the most popular literature in the Buddhist world. (Over six hundred of these exist in the myriad collections.)

In the Hinayana schools, to speak of "the bodhisattva" usually refers to the previous lives of Gautama, the Buddha of this historical epoch. In later texts, the career of this bodhisattva is said to begin with a vow someday to reach Buddhahood "for the welfare of all beings." Eight conditions are also specified for the successful completion of the vow, including male birth, asceticism, unhesitating self-sacrifice, and unswerving resolve. Many thousands of lifetimes are needed to complete the task; a long incarnation in the heavenly realm called Tushita is said to be the norm for the last existence before human birth and final realization of Buddhahood.

In Mahayana schools, the understanding of what a bodhisattva is expands greatly. Consistent with its doctrinal explication of myriad universes and Buddhas existing in all spheres, it is bodhisattvas who assist in each Buddha-realm by preaching and compassionate action. Following from the Mahayana doctrine of the ultimate interdependence of all reality, Mahayana texts describe the bodhisattva ideal as one necessarily involving the pursuit of one's own enlightenment simultaneous with assisting all others reaching nirvana. This involves moving through various perfections (*paramitas*) including giving, patience, skillful means, and *prajna*, salvific insight.

Because of the eons involved in this process, some bodhisattvas can accumulate immeasurable merit allowing rebirth as celestial deities who can use their vast powers to assist humanity in all spheres. Thus, in Mahayana cultures, Buddhists have taken special refuge in these supramundane bodhisattvas who can be invoked to guide one's meditations, assist in the teaching of the doctrine, ease the path at death toward a better rebirth, and provide relief from every type of suffering.

The most popular celestial bodhisattva known in every Buddhist society is called Avalokiteshvara in Indic traditions, Kwan-Yin in Chinese, Kannon in Japanese, Chenrizig in Tibetan. Others include Manjushri (bodhisattva of learning), Samantabhadra (supporter of vows made), Tara (the feminine emanation of Avalokiteshvara), and Kshitigarbha (Jap., Jizo), who specializes in protecting children and rescuing beings from hells. While the celestial bodhisattvas inspired the development of Buddhist temples, rituals, and pilgrimage to sites associated with their grace, the bodhisattva ideal also inspired individual spiritual pursuits: common forms of meditation involve visualizing the divine form and repeating mantras designed to "attain the qualities of Avalokiteshvara." Buddhists were also motivated to identify themselves as bodhisattvas and perform acts of selfless service on behalf of their communities.

Todd T. Lewis

See also BUDDHA; JIZO; KARUNA; KUAN-YIN; MAHAYANA BUDDHISM; PARAMITA; UPAYA.

BODY
The term body refers to the physical organic reality of human life. Religious approaches to the body usually include a consideration of the relationship between the body and soul, spirit, mind or subjectivity. Is the individual a body or does the individual have a body? Since the body represents so-called irrational desires and urges, there has been a tendency in a number of religious systems to view the body as a problem or hindrance to the perfection and integrity of the soul. Liberating the soul or the spirit from the vagaries of bodily life has often been considered critical for personal holiness (cf. Plato). The view that the body and soul are at odds or that the soul could and should ideally be free from the body is considered a dualistic theory. On the other hand, modern philosophy has shown that the very experience of soul or spirit requires a body in which consciousness and action are possible. This nondualistic view has roots in Aristotle's idea of a union between body and soul.

St. Paul contrasted life in the Spirit with life of the "flesh." Paul's use of the term "sarx" (flesh) should not be identified with the body. Rather "sarx" refers to a disorientation of one's desires (as a result of sin) such that one doesn't love what is genuinely good. Indeed, Paul's teaching on the resurrection includes the idea of a spiritualized body.

Despite the relative absence of pejorative views of the body in Christian Scripture, and despite the centrality of the doctrine of the Incarnation (God assuming bodily existence in Jesus), it is ironic that the Christian tradition developed such a dualistic approach to the body. Severed from its roots in Palestinian Judaism (which was less dualistic), Christianity quickly assumed the philosophical tendencies of Gnosticism, Platonism, and Stoicism, where the body was viewed more suspiciously. Much of Christian spirituality and sexual ethics included efforts to liberate the soul or spirit from the emotions and desires of bodily existence. This has been viewed by many contemporary psychologists and theologians as unhealthy and counterproductive. Consequently, contemporary reform of sexual ethics and spirituality invariably includes a renewed appreciation for the body as integral to human flourishing and the development of spirituality.

Michael J. Hartwig

See also DUALISM/DUALISTIC; ETHICS, SEXUAL; FLESH/SARX; PLATONISM.

BODY OF CHRIST (IN CHURCH USE)
Christians use the expression "Body of Christ" to refer to (1) the actual body which Jesus had while on earth, which rose from the dead and ascended to heaven; (2) the entire Christian community now enlivened by the risen Christ; and (3) the presence of Christ in the Eucharist, especially that presence symbolized by the consecrated bread. Paul already made use of the second meaning of the term in his First Letter to the Corinthians. Augustine of Hippo, among others, closely identified the second and third meanings, urging his community to understand that when

they received the Body of Christ (no. 3, above), they are receiving themselves (no. 2, above). The theologian Paschasius Radbertus identified the Body of Christ received in the Eucharist (no. 3, above) with the body Jesus had on earth (no. 1, above). This identification became extremely important in late medieval and Roman Catholic devotion, while it was denied particularly by Protestants in the Calvinist tradition. All Christian groups, however, stress the importance of the Christian community as the "Body of Christ" now active in the world and enlivened by the risen Christ. The twentieth-century Catholic scholars Bernard Cooke, Karl Rahner, and Edward Schillebeeckx wrote particularly movingly on this issue.

Gary Macy

See also AUGUSTINE OF HIPPO; CHRIST OF FAITH; COOKE, BERNARD; CORPUS CHRISTI; EUCHARIST; PAUL; RAHNER, KARL; REAL PRESENCE; RESURRECTION OF CHRIST; SCHILLEBEECKX, EDWARD; TRANSUBSTANTIATION.

BODY OF CHRIST (IN SCRIPTURE)

"Body of Christ" is an expression used in three interrelated senses in the Pauline and deutero-Pauline literature of the New Testament: (1) the crucified body of Jesus; (2) the eucharistic bread as "body of Christ"; (3) the church as the "body of Christ."

Paul uses the expression in the first sense, as a reference to the crucified body of Jesus, in Romans 7:4: "you have died to the law through the body of Christ, so that you may belong to another, to him who has been raised from the dead in order that we may bear fruit for God." Colossians 1:21-22 also uses "body" in

this sense in a soteriological expression: "And you who were once estranged and hostile in mind, doing evil deeds, he has now reconciled in his fleshly body through death, so as to present you holy and blameless and irreproachable before him."

"Body of Christ" in the second sense, as a designation of the eucharistic bread, draws upon the first sense insofar as the eucharistic sense of the expression is based on the words spoken by Jesus over the bread at the Last Supper on the night before his crucifixion, particularly in their Lukan form: "This is my body, which is given for you" (Luke 22:19; see also Matt 26:26; Mark 14:22). In the New Testament, this eucharistic sense of "body of Christ" is employed most extensively in 1 Corinthians. In 1 Corinthians 10:16-17, Paul explains: "The cup of blessing that we bless, is it not a sharing in the blood of Christ? The bread that we break, is it not a sharing in the body of Christ? Because there is one bread, we who are many are one body, for we all partake of the one bread." Arguing that the Christian celebration of the Eucharist both symbolizes and effects the unity of those who partake in it, Paul urges the Corinthians not to participate in the ritual meals that took place in temples, exhorting them to "flee from the worship of idols" (1 Cor 10:14). For Paul, participation by Christians in such banquets would send mixed messages about the sincerity of their commitment to the community of believers and about the strength of their religious convictions.

Later on in 1 Corinthians, Paul emphatically deploys "body of Christ" in a third sense, as a metaphor for the church, in order to address serious problems of ecclesial unity that were manifesting themselves during the worship of the Corinthian church. Addressing what were in all likelihood divisions that had to do with the diversity of socioeconomic classes represented among the members of the Corinthian church, Paul cites the words of Jesus over bread and wine at the Last Supper, "This is my body that is for you. Do this in remembrance of me. . . . This cup is the new covenant in my blood. Do this, as often as you drink it, in remembrance of me" (1 Cor 11:24-25). Paul warns the Corinthian Christians, "All who eat and drink without discerning the body, eat and drink judgment upon themselves" (1 Cor 11:29). "Discerning the body" involved awareness of one's relationship with other members of the Christian community which was constituted as the "body of Christ" by its sharing in the one eucharistic bread. Clearly the third sense of "body of Christ" as a metaphor for the church builds on the eucharistic sense of the expression, though Paul may well have been aware of Hellenistic philosophers' use of "body" as a political metaphor for the state, the "body politic," a notion found as early as Aristotle (*Politics* 1302b, 35-36).

In the following chapter, Paul expands the metaphor of the body to describe the diversity and the mutual interdependence of the members of the church: "just as the body is one and has many members, and all are members of the body, though many, are one body, so it is with Christ" (1 Cor 12:12), concluding "Now you are the body of Christ and individually members of it" (1 Cor 12:27). The distinct individuals who belong to the church can dispense with each other no more than the eye can say that it does not need the hand (1 Cor 12:21). This theme of the unity-in-diversity of the Body of Christ, composed of many members, recurs in Romans 12:4-5, where Paul accents the variety of gifts and talents distributed among the various members of the church.

In the deutero-Pauline epistles, the notion of the church as the Body of Christ is developed further, with Christ described as head of the body so as to emphasize Christ's leadership over the church. In the christological hymn found in Colossians 1:15-20, a redactional insertion highlights this theme: "He is the head of the body, *the church*." The image of the Church as a body which has Christ as its head is a key theme throughout Colossians (1:24; 2:19; 3:15), as well as in Ephesians (1:22-23; 4:15-16; 5:23).

Jean-Pierre Ruiz

See also BODY; CHURCH; EUCHARIST; LAST SUPPER; PAUL.

BOEHME, JACOB (1575–1624)

German Lutheran mystic, early Theosophist, and author of numerous treatises on mysticism. Boehme's writings explore the mystery of God and the relationship of God to humanity and nature through reflection on his own mystical experience. He made bold use of ideas from Neoplatonism, the Jewish kabbalah, and from alchemy to explain his ideas. His treatises on the divine mystery are instances of theosophical thinking rather than confessional theology. Relatively unknown in his time, his influence continued later as his ideas were adopted by German idealists such as Schelling and Hegel and by English romantics such as Coleridge and Blake.

Patricia Plovanich

See also KABBALAH; NEOPLATONISM.

BOETHIUS (475/80–524/6)

Anicius Manlius Toquatus Severinus Boethius. Boethius came from a noble

Roman and Christian family. After an excellent education, he embarked upon a successful political career under Theodoric, king of the Ostrogoths. In 522, after holding many other important posts, Boethius was granted general oversight of Theodoric's affairs. Within two years, however, Boethius found himself accused of treason, imprisoned, and eventually executed by Theodoric. Boethius' influence as a scholar has been immense. He translated, commented upon, or summarized in Latin many important Greek texts, thus creating the basic textbooks for the early medieval period. He also wrote theological treatises, and is probably best known for his remarkable treatise *The Consolation of Philosophy*, written while waiting in prison for his own execution.

Gary Macy

See also MEDIEVAL CHRISTIANITY (IN THE WEST); SCHOLASTICISM.

BOFF, CLODOVIS (1944–)

Brazilian Catholic theologian and member of the Servite Order. He has written on a number of subjects, but his main publication is a book on theological method, *Theology and Praxis* (1978). He places himself in the liberation theology current, and is quite insistent on spending considerable time among the poor as precondition for a theology methodologically responsive to them. His brother Leonardo is better known internationally.

Orlando Espín

See also BOFF, LEONARDO; LATIN AMERICAN CATHOLICISM; LIBERATION THEOLOGIES; OPTION FOR THE POOR.

BOFF, LEONARDO (1938–)

Born in Concórdia, Brazil, into a family of Italian descent, Leonardo Boff received degrees in philosophy in 1961 (Curitiba, Brazil) and theology in 1965 (Petrópolis, Brazil) before receiving the doctorate in theology in 1970 (Munich, Germany). Ordained a Franciscan priest in 1964, he became a central figure in the development of liberation theology in the 1970s and 1980s. He served as professor of systematic theology at Petrópolis and as editor of the Brazilian theological journal *Vozes*. His theological interests include christology, the doctrine of grace, ecclesiology, and spirituality—all in relation to human liberation. Among the most important of the over thirty books he has published are *Jesus Christ Liberator* (1976), *Liberating Grace* (1979), *Ecclesiogenesis* (1983), and *Church: Charism and Power* (1985). The last book gave rise to a public disagreement with the Vatican over Boff's twofold contention that a hierarchically structured church both distances the church from the poor of society and perpetuates injustices within the church itself. This dispute led to Boff's official silencing for one year (1985–6). In 1992 Boff left the Franciscans and the priesthood but continued his research, writing, and teaching.

James B. Nickoloff

See also LIBERATION THEOLOGIES.

BOGOMILS

The Bogomils were a heretical sect that arose in the Balkans in the eighth century. Thoroughly dualistic, the Bogomils believed that matter was a creation of an evil god who captured the life principle from the good god in order to vivify material creation. The evil god was identified with the god of the Old Testament whom the Bogomils rejected. The Bogomils understood Jesus as the emissary of the good god, but in a thoroughly docetic fashion, since the Bogomils were appalled by the idea that Jesus could have a material body. The Bogomils also rejected anything material as evil, including sexuality, marriage, and any ritual other than serial repetitions of the Lord's Prayer and a "spiritual baptism" administered on the deathbed. Bogomils spread their teaching to Constantinople, Greece, Bosnia, and eventually to France and Italy where Bogomil missionaries were an essential catalyst in the spread of the Cathars. The Bogomils survived in the Balkans until the seventeenth century.

Gary Macy

See also ALBIGENSIANS; CATHARS; DOCETISM; HERESY.

BOHEMIAN BRETHREN/ MORAVIANS

The Bohemian Brethren formed in the fifteenth century around John Hus (ca. 1373–1415). Hus was an evangelical preacher in Prague who sought reform in the Christian Church and anticipated many of Martin Luther's ideas. He believed the church should aspire to its highest ideals, and on that basis, he rejected the Crusades, sale of indulgences, and the authority of any church leader who did not obey the Bible, including the pope. Hus was burned at the stake as a heretic in 1415. His followers formed the *Unitas Fratrum* (literally, "Unity of the Brethren"), advocating communion in both kinds for the laity, voluntary poverty for clergy, and strict standards for morality. They grew in Bohemia and Moravia.

The Brethren established close ties with Lutherans during the Protestant Reformation and were strenuously persecuted by the church. They dispersed and almost disappeared. In the 1720s, many took refuge at the Moravian estate of Count Nicholas von Zinzendorf (1700–60), a Lutheran nobleman turned Pietist. Reacting to the lifelessness of Reformed Protestantism, Pietism emphasized the experience of Christianity over theological doctrine. Zinzendorf welcomed to his estate any Christians seeking to recover the authentic spirit of Christianity through prayer, singing, and Bible study. The Brethren thrived with Zinzendorf's protection, and along with other Pietists drawn to him, became reborn as the Moravians. In 1737 Zinzendorf was consecrated as bishop of the Moravian Church.

Under his leadership, the church undertook an aggressive evangelistic effort to unite Christians into a single community. In the 1730s they engaged in missionary activity in Africa, India, and South and North America, the last among Native and African Americans in the British colony of Georgia. In 1740, faced with civil opposition to their activities, they moved to Pennsylvania, a colony known for religious toleration, and established the towns of Nazareth and Bethlehem. Moravians also settled in Salem, North Carolina. Expelled from Moravia in 1738 for his radical religious activities, Zinzendorf embarked on a missionary tour of the North American British colonies in 1741. Although he was unsuccessful in uniting Pietists under the Moravian banner, he did establish churches and expanded missionary activity among Native Americans.

Moravians sought to apply the Gospel to everyday life. They lived a semicommunal existence, sharing their material goods, working together in "choirs" divided by age, gender, and marital status. Their work centered on agriculture and crafts. They stressed a simple, non-ornate lifestyle. Their worship stressed music and the suffering and death of Jesus Christ.

In the nineteenth and twentieth centuries, Moravians gradually abandoned the communal ideal and began to resemble other Protestant denominations. The church's headquarters is in Bethlehem, Pennsylvania, and it supports colleges in Pennsylvania and North Carolina.

Evelyn A. Kirkley

See also ANABAPTISTS; HUS, JOHN; MENNONITES; PIETISM.

BONAVENTURE (1215/17–74)

Giovanni di Fidanza was born in Bagnoregio and studied liberal arts in Paris. He joined the Franciscan Order in Paris after finishing his bachelor's degree, and at this time he took the religious name, "Bonaventure." He studied theology under the Franciscan masters, most notably Alexander of Hales. Bonaventure himself became the Franciscan master of theology in Paris in 1254 and held this post until 1257. In 1257 Bonaventure was elected minister general of a Franciscan Order dangerously split by the dispute between the Spiritual and the Conventual Franciscans. He worked and traveled tirelessly to reunite the order, an effort that was ultimately unsuccessful. In 1272 Pope Gregory X requested Bonaventure's help in preparing the agenda for an ecumenical council called to reform the church and reunite Eastern and Western Christianity. Bonaventure was made cardinal of Albano the following year, resigning as minister general in 1274. That same year, he attended the Council of Lyons where he preached the sermon celebrating the reunification, albeit short-lived, of Eastern and Western Christianity. He fell ill almost immediately afterward and died on July 15, 1274. Bonaventure was canonized in 1482, and declared a Doctor of the Church in 1587. The Seraphic Doctor, as he is called, is famous not only for his theology, but also his mytical writing, his famous life of St. Francis, and for his many sermons.

Gary Macy

See also ALEXANDER OF HALES; DOCTORS OF THE CHURCH; FRANCIS OF ASSISI; FRANCISCANS; FRIARS; MEDIEVAL CHRISTIANITY (IN THE WEST); SCHISM, GREAT EASTERN; SCHOLASTICISM; SPIRITUAL FRANCISCANS.

BONHOEFFER, DIETRICH (1906–45)

A German Lutheran pastor, the theologian of the Confessing Church, who was killed by the Nazis for his involvement in a plot against Hitler's life. Born in Berlin, Bonhoeffer studied theology at Halle under Adolf von Harnack and other liberal Protestants. After pastoral work in England and Switzerland, he spent a year at Union Theological Seminary in New York City, where he also worked in Harlem. He returned to Germany in 1939. With other professors and students who refused to support the pro-Hitler *Deutsche Christen* ("German Christians"), Bonhoeffer was dismissed from the university faculty. He assumed the leadership of a Confessing Church seminary near the North Sea, the setting that informs his inspirational works *The Cost of Discipleship* and *Life Together*.

Influenced by the dialectical theology of the Swiss Reformed theologian Karl Barth, Bonhoeffer sought to preserve God's transcendence in "a word come of age" by insisting upon the "worldliness" of the world, that is, the autonomy of created reality.

Mary Ann Hinsdale

See also BARTH, KARL; CONFESSING CHURCH.

BONIFACE VIII, POPE (1235?–1303)

Pope from 1294 until 1303, he was born Benedict Gaetani. Boniface rose rapidly through the ranks of the papal Curia, becoming cardinal deacon in 1281 and cardinal priest in 1291. In 1292, when a successor was to be chosen to succeed Pope Nicholas IV, over two years passed before the cardinals could agree on a new pope, chosing the elderly and pious hermit, Peter of Marrone, as Pope Celestine V. Celestine was a holy but inept leader who decided to resign the papacy, which he did on December 13, 1294. Celestine remains the only Pope who has ever voluntarily resigned from office. Within a few days, Benedict Gaetani was chosen as Pope Boniface VIII. A difficult and proud man, Boniface was faced immediately with serious problems. First of all, the Spiritual Franciscans, whom Clement had supported, were claiming that Clement could not abdicate his office. Boniface responded by imprisoning Clement and proclaiming the Spiritual Franciscans to be heretics. Even more serious, and in the end, deadly for Boniface was his struggle with King Philip the Fair of France. Philip wished to tax the clergy of France, an act that Boniface felt interfered with the rights of the church. Tensions increased, culminating in Boniface publishing the famous papal bull *Unam Sanctum*, in which he declared it "altogether necessary to salvation for every human creature to be subject to the Roman Pontiff." Philip in turn proclaimed Boniface to be a heretic and sent troops to arrest the Pope. Boniface was taken prisoner and then released, but the experience ruined his health and he died soon afterward.

Gary Macy

See also MEDIEVAL CHRISTIANITY (IN THE WEST); POPE; SPIRITUAL FRANCISCANS; UNAM SANCTAM.

BOOK OF COMMON PRAYER

The official service book of a particular church (or province) belonging to the Anglican Communion that contains the prayers and rites mandated for use in public worship and the celebration of the sacraments.

Anglicanism has no distinctive doctrines or central teaching authority. Instead, Anglicans hold that "the law of prayer is the law of belief" and point to the Prayer Book as the most authoritative guide to their belief and practice.

The first Prayer Book, mainly the work of Thomas Cranmer, appeared in 1549. It drew heavily on the Sarum Rite, a modification of the Latin liturgy then used in most of the dioceses in England. Since it was acceptable to few, the Prayer Book was revised and a new version was issued and mandated by the Act of Uniformity in 1552. Likewise, adaptations were published in 1559, 1604, and 1662, also mandated by Acts of Uniformity. In 1927 Parliament rejected a new Prayer Book, although it had been approved by the bishops. Thus, the 1662 version is still the official prayer book of the Church of England. An Alternative Service Book (1980), however, is widely used.

Typically, the Prayer Book contains Morning and Evening Prayer with the appointed psalms and Scripture readings, rites for the adminstration of sacraments, and the Psalter. The American BCP also contains the Catechism, the calendar of the church year, "Prayers and Thanksgivings," and important historical documents.

Since the provinces of the Communion are autonomous, each has its own version of the Book of Common Prayer. Many provinces have adapted the English Prayer Book or use it along with an authorized "Alternative Services" book. Yet each is free to develop its own liturgy in and for the culture(s) of its particular part of the world. Thus, the Prayer Book is always in the vernacular. Some Anglicans worry that the use of different Prayer Books will weaken the cohesion of the Communion.

In 1789 the Episcopal Church in the United States approved its own Prayer Book. The Scottish liturgy of 1764 was a major source since the church's first bishop, Samuel Seabury, had been consecrated by Scottish bishops. By order of the General Convention, revised Prayer Books were issued in in 1892, 1928, and 1979. Additional rites have subsequently been authorized for use.

Jon Nilson

See also ANGLICAN COMMUNION; CRANMER, THOMAS; EPISCOPAL CHURCH; UNIFORMITY, ACTS OF.

BORNKAMM, GÜNTHER (1905–90)

Günther Bornkamm was Professor of New Testament Exegesis at Heidelberg University. A pupil of Rudolf Bultmann, he forged new paths beyond his mentor along with other post-Bultmannians, also known as the "old Marburgers." With their special interest in the historical Jesus, they contributed extensively to scholarly literature on the Gospels and Paul in the "New Quest of the Historical Jesus." Bornkamm's *Jesus of Nazareth* (1956) was one of the first publications of the post-Bultmannian movement.

F. M. Gillman

See also BULTMANN, RUDOLF; CONZELMANN, HANS; FUCHS, ERNST; KÄSEMANN, ERNST.

BORROMEO, CHARLES (1538–84)

Archbishop of Milan and cardinal of the Catholic Church. Educated for the priest-hood from an early age, and trained in civil and canon law, Borromeo seemed destined to benefit from his family's position and wealth. His uncle was Pope Pius IV, who appointed him cardinal and archbishop at the age of twenty-two. Borromeo became an active promoter of the Council of Trent, and was influential during the council's last session. Indeed, he was charged by that council with heading the commission that wrote what came to be known as the *Roman Catechism* that was to have great influence in Catholicism after Trent. Under his leadership, Milan established the first European seminary and the first school of catechists. He was a reforming bishop in his diocese, supporting the work of the Society of Jesus, and taking particular care of the poor and sick. Borromeo's letters and other writings indicate that he believed that Trent's reforms would be successful only if accompanied by the church's renewed commitment to prayer, poverty, and the poor. His reform work provoked great hostility against him within the church. He was canonized in 1610.

Orlando Espín

See also ARCHBISHOP; BISHOP (EPISCO-PACY); CANONIZATION; CARDINAL; CATECHISM; COUNTER-REFORMATION / CATHOLIC REFORMATION; DIOCESE / ARCHDIOCESE; OPTION FOR THE POOR; ROMAN CATHOLIC CHURCH; SEMINARY; SOCIETY OF JESUS; TRENT, COUNCIL OF.

BOSSUET, JACQUES BÉNIGNE (1627–1704)

Bishop and preacher, writer and ecclesiastical politician, Bossuet played a leading role in the French church under King Louis XIV. Admired for elegant pulpit oratory, funeral orations in particular, Bossuet was bishop of Condom from

1669, then of Meaux from 1681. He was a principal architect of the Four Gallican Articles, adopted by the assembly of the French clergy in 1682. These articles affirmed French independence from papal authority. Favorable to the 1685 Revocation of the Edict of Nantes (the decree that had permitted Protestants the exercise of their religion in France), Bossuet opposed toleration of religious diversity. He also opposed both Fénelon's quietism, and any efforts to study the Bible as literature from a particular historical context. For Bossuet, Scripture demonstrated the central role of providence in human life; Scripture also provided a sure guide to politics and a clear affirmation of the divine right of kings.

Thomas Worcester, s.j.

See also COUNTER-REFORMATION/ CATHOLIC REFORMATION; FÉNELON, FRANÇOIS; GALLICAN ARTICLES; GALLICANISM; PROVIDENCE.

BRAHMA

Brahma is the deity in Hinduism who oversees the cyclic remanifestation of the cosmos after it has been through a period of rest. Although he was worshiped as the Supreme Being in the late Vedic period, and is sometimes spoken of as part of the Hindu "trinity" (*trimurti*) of Brahma, Vishnu, and Shiva, Brahma is no longer a major deity. In classical Hindu mythology, he becomes a reincarnating soul like the other lesser gods of Hinduism, the *devas*, albeit one that has earned a very high position in the cosmos, a good deal of power, and a very long life. He will, at the end of the cosmic cycle or *kalpa*, die as the universe enters another period of dissolution, and, at the world's reemergence, another soul will fill his office. In all this he is to be distinguished from the great Gods, and the Goddess, of Hinduism—Vishnu, Shiva, and Shakti—who are, for their respective followers, Supreme Beings in the fullest sense. Brahma (masculine) is to be distinguished from Brahman (neuter), the ultimate reality of the Upanishads and Vedanta. This is sometimes confusing for students, especially as *Brahman* is sometimes also written *Brahma*, without the final "n."

Lance E. Nelson

See also BRAHMAN; DEVA/DEVI; HINDUISM; KALPA; SHAKTI; SHIVA; TRIMURTI; VISHNU.

BRAHMACHARIN

In Hinduism, a *brahmacharin* (or *brahmachari*; Sanskrit, living with the sacred) is a celibate student in the first of the four classically recognized life stages or *ashramas*. A brahmacharin was expected to master, to a degree appropriate to his caste standing, the learning associated with one or more of the Vedas. A novice monk, preparing to take final vows as a *sannyasin*, is also called a brahmacharin.

Lance E. Nelson

See also ASHRAMA (LIFE STAGES); HINDUISM; SANNYASA.

BRAHMAN

Brahman is the Hindu word for ultimate reality, a usage derived especially from the Upanishads. In earlier Vedic literature, the word *brahman* had meant something like "holy power." In their interpretation of the Upanishads, theistic Hindus understand Brahman to be a personal God, equated—according to particular denominational traditions—with Vishnu (or one of his incarnations), Shiva, or the Goddess. According to the nondualist Advaita Vedanta, however, Brahman is an impersonal Absolute, in relation to which the personal God (*Ishvara*) is a secondary, penultimate reality. According to this tradition, the essential nature of Brahman is defined in the formula *sat-cit-ananda*, Being-Consciousness-Bliss. Because the Advaita tradition had historically set the terms of the debate and remains extremely influential in modern Hinduism, as well as better known in the West, the word Brahman in scholarly writing on India, unless otherwise specified, typically refers to the impersonal absolute as conceived by the nondualist tradition.

Lance E. Nelson

See also ADVAITA VEDANTA; BRAHMA; HINDUISM; NIRGUNA BRAHMAN; SAT-CHIT-ANANDA; SHIVA; UPANISHADS; VEDAS; VISHISHTADVAITA VEDANTA.

BRAHMANA

In Hinduism, the Brahmanas are a class of texts attached to, and regarded as forming a part of, each of the four Vedas. The Brahmanas (about 1100–700 B.C.E.) are distinguished from other Vedic literature by their subject matter: they predominate in descriptions and symbolic interpretations of the elaborate Vedic rituals, known as *yajnas*, that were performed by a highly trained class of priests. Somewhat confusingly, the same word is used to designate these priests—the *brahmanas*.

Lance E. Nelson

See also BRAHMANA/BRAHMIN; VEDAS; YAJNA.

BRAHMANA/BRAHMIN

In addition to being the name of a class of Vedic texts, *brahmana* is the Sanskrit name for the priests who traditionally performed the Vedic rituals described in the texts. The *brahmanas*, as a social group, continued to function as the priestly caste category (*varna*) in classical Hinduism. The traditional occupations of brahmanas have been priest, scholar, and teacher. In the varna hierarchy, the brahmanas are ranked highest, above the *kshatriyas*, *vaishyas*, and *shudras*. Classified within this varna are many brahmana castes (*jatis*) that are often further divided into smaller groups. Brahmana is often written as *brahman*, to suggest its pronunciation in modern Indian languages, or as "brahmin," using its anglicized spelling. The latter form has the advantage of distinguishing brahmana (the caste category) from both Brahmana (the texts) and Brahman (the ultimate reality in Hinduism), thus avoiding confusion. For this reason, it is used throughout this volume in place of brahmana.

Lance E. Nelson

See also CASTE; HINDUISM; KSHATRIYA; SHUDRA; VAISHYA; VEDAS; YAJNA.

BRAHMA SUTRAS
See VEDANTA.

BRAHMIN
See BRAHMANA/BRAHMIN.

BRAHMO SAMAJ
See ROY, RAM MOHAN; SEN, KESHAB CHANDRA.

BREAD, UNLEAVENED

The Christian use of unleavened bread at the Eucharist traces back to the Jewish custom of using unleavened bread at Passover. Unleavened bread, that is, bread made without yeast (and without its "rising action" in the dough) is used for the *matzah*, the "bread of affliction," at the Passover Seder. Christians continued to use unleavened bread during early celebrations of the Eucharist because of the connection between the Last Supper and the Passover season. The Synoptic Gospels have the Last Supper as a Passover Seder celebrated by Jesus and his disciples/apostles; the Gospel of John sets it as a fellowship (*[c]haburah*) meal the night before Passover.

Christian practice in the early centuries was to use ordinary bread for the Eucharist. However, as time went on, the Eastern churches tended to retain the use of leavened bread for the Eucharist, while the Western churches returned to the use of loaves of unleavened bread. In the Middle Ages, this bread was specially produced for the celebration of Mass, and was baked in round, flat wafers, which were known as *hosts* (from the Latin, *hostia*, or "victim"). This discrepancy was one of the many sources of tension between the Western church (of Rome) and the major Eastern church (of Constantinople, the Byzantine tradition), although some of this seems to have dissipated by the time of the Council of Florence (1439).

In the West, the liturgical developments of the Reformation led to the use of leavened bread by some of the Protestant churches; others kept to unleavened bread (for example, the Anglican churches). The flat host was retained by the Roman Catholic Church; because of the stress on transubstantiation and the real presence of Christ in the Eucharist, the adoration of the consecrated Host (exposed to the view of the faithful in a gold stand or *monstrance*), became very widespread during this Baroque period. The Roman Catholic Church still mandates the use of unleavened wheat bread at Mass (GIRM 2003, n. 320); however, it can be baked privately, or purchased in the form of hosts through church supply establishments. It must, however, actually have the appearance of food (GIRM 2003, n. 321), even if a more traditional host is used: the bread must be fresh and capable of being broken piecemeal and distributed (GIRM 2003, n. 321). Thus, the primary ritual/theological action of communion from the one loaf (1 Cor 10:16-17) is at least partially retained, even if separate hosts must be used in addition for practical reasons.

Joanne M. Pierce

See also ADORATION; BAROQUE; COMMUNION (LITURGICAL); CONSECRATION (CHRISTIAN); EUCHARIST; MASS; MATZAH; MONSTRANCE; PASSOVER; SACRAMENT; TABERNACLE (CHRISTIAN LITURGICAL); VIATICUM.

BREAKING OF A GLASS

The last ritual of a Jewish wedding ceremony is the breaking of a glass. Part of the ceremony through custom rather than by law, the groom steps on a glass—that has been wrapped in a protective cloth—and shatters it.

Many explanations have been given for this quaint custom, the most compelling—and, most likely, historically accurate—is that even at moments of greatest joy, Jews remember the destruction of the Holy Temple and Jerusalem, and the exile they have been forced to endure.

Wayne Dosick

BREAKING OF BREAD (IN CHRISTIANITY)

"Breaking of bread" is the term used in Luke and the Acts of the Apostles to refer to the ritual meal the early Christian community shared in memory of the risen Christ. It was in the "breaking of the bread" that the disciples recognized the risen Christ (Luke 24:30-31) and this same "breaking of bread" appears in Acts as the central ritual of the early community (Acts 2:42, 46; 20:7; 27:35).

Gary Macy

See also ACTS OF THE APOSTLES; CHRIST; COMMUNION (LITURGICAL); EUCHARIST; LUKE/LUKAN; RESURRECTION OF CHRIST.

BRIT

See COVENANT (IN JUDAISM).

BRIT MILAH

(Hebrew, covenant of circumcision). In Judaism, the removal of the foreskin of the penis. This common ancient Near Eastern practice served in the Hebrew Scriptures as a symbol of the Israelite male's participation in the covenant with God. Later Judaism retains circumcision's metaphorical significance as the sign of the covenant, while focusing as well upon its role as a physical indicator that a person is a member of the Israelite nation. To assure that circumcision serves this purpose, Jewish law requires that the foreskin be completely removed, so as to reveal entirely the head of the penis (Mishnah Shabbat 19:6). Leaving even small shreds of skin that slightly conceal the head of the penis renders the circumcision invalid. This concern for the complete removal of the foreskin appears to respond to the Hellenistic influence that, by Maccabean times, had led some Jews to hide the physical evidence of their circumcision. Later Judaism responds by stating that one who obliterates this sign of the covenant has no share in the world to come (Mishnah Abot 3:11).

While in the Western world today circumcision is commonly performed by doctors on Jewish and non-Jewish newborn boys, many Jewish families continue to have the procedure performed by a Jewish functionary called a "mohel," trained both in the medical aspects of circumcision and in the attendant Jewish ritual. The circumcision ritual includes (1) the reading of Numbers 25, which concerns Pinchus's killing of Israelites who engaged in inappropriate conduct, a deed for which he received God's covenant of peace; (2) reading of 1 Kings 19:10-14, where the prophet Elijah complains that the Israelites have neglected the covenant; (3) the actual circumcision; and (4) the recitation of a benediction that refers to God's sanctifying of the beloved of the womb.

Alan J. Avery-Peck

BROWN, RAYMOND E. (1928–98)

A Roman Catholic Sulpician priest, Brown was one of the most influential biblical scholars of the latter half of the twentieth century. Raymond Brown produced a number of highly acclaimed biblical commentaries, including three for the Anchor Bible series (*The Gospel According to John* [two volumes]; *The Epistles of John*) as well as *The Birth of the Messiah* (1977) and *The Death of the Messiah* (two volumes, 1994). Additionally, he was one of the three editors of *The New Jerome Biblical Commentary* (1990), a thoroughly revised and improved reference work of the original edition (1968), which he also coedited.

Brown is well known for the rigor and thoroughness of his biblical scholarship, a clarity of writing, and the balanced perspectives he espouses. As Auburn Distinguished Professor Emeritus at Union Theological Seminary (NYC), he had also been a past president of the *Studiorum Novi Testamenti Societas* (Society for the

Study of the New Testament) and a member of the Pontifical Biblical Commission. Brown held over twenty honorary doctorates from both Catholic and Protestant universities.

John Gillman

BROWN, ROBERT McAFEE (1920–2001)

Robert McAfee Brown, prominent U.S. Presbyterian theologian, described his life as one of "creative dislocations." Born in Summit, New Jersey, he was educated at Amherst College, Union Theological Seminary, and Columbia University, from which he received a doctorate in theology. An ordained Presbyterian minister, he taught at Union Theological Seminary, Macalester College (Minnesota), Stanford University, and the Pacific School of Religion (California). He attended the second session of the Second Vatican Council of the Catholic Church as an official observer in 1963 and wrote about the fourth session (1965) as a journalist. His primary intellectual debts were to Reinhold Niebuhr, Karl Barth, and Gustavo Gutiérrez, a combination that strengthened his own bent to be active in social and political struggles for justice (including the U.S. civil rights and antiwar movements) and, within the church, to promote the ecumenical movement. In later years he became a leading expert on, and proponent of, Latin American liberation theology. His major works include *Religion and Violence* (1973), *Theology in a New Key: Responding to Liberation Themes* (1978), and *Unexpected News: Reading the Bible with Third World Eyes* (1984).

James B. Nickoloff

BROWNSON, ORESTES (1803–76)

Writer, lay theologian, and Catholic convert, Brownson was an astute observer of events shaping the nineteenth-century American church. A political and social progressive, Brownson used his talents as writer and editor for the *Boston Quarterly Review* (1838–42) and his own *Brownson's Quarterly Review* (ca. 1844–66). Through these publications, he wielded influence in national and church affairs. A staunch defender of Catholicism against anti-Catholic opponents, he was an outspoken critic of American bishops when he found their positions objectionable, as in their support of slavery. He urged the Americanization of the church to the ire of Catholic ethnic communities. Early writings propose a progressive view of the church expressed in the ecclesial imagery of Body of Christ and Communion, unusual for the time. His disillusionment with aspects of American and church life led him to support Ultramontane ideas in his later years.

Patricia Plovanich

See also AMERICANISM; ULTRAMONTANISM.

BRUNNER, EMIL (1899–1966)

Noted Swiss theologian and professor of theology at Zurich who joined Karl Barth and Friedrich Gogarten in criticizing German liberal Protestant theology for seeking positive knowledge about God through philosophy. Brunner also opposed mystical claims that one can only speak of what God *is not*. Like Barth, Brunner stressed the superiority of Christian revelation over human reasoning. His "dialectical" theology uses conflicting philosophical ideas to rise above our limited human reason in response to divine revelation, which he sees as God's personal self-disclosure, not a list of intellectual statements. Unlike Barth, Brunner believes philosophy can help answer God's personal call by marking the limits of reason while engaging our human aptitude for speech. Brunner accepts a valid but limited moral role for strictly human social institutions and ethics that restrain sin. Modern stress on autonomy, individualism, and technology increases human sinfulness by inducing us to treat others as mere objects, ideas, or tools, rather than as reflecting God's personhood. But God's love, shown in Christ's self-sacrificing action, defeats such depersonalization in ways human ethics can not. We reach true personhood by responding to God's self-revelation, which calls us to oppose all totalitarian systems and reassert the personal character of social life.

Francis D. Connolly-Weinert

BRUNO, GIORDANO (1548–1600)

Italian philosopher and one-time member of the Order of Preachers, Bruno was a pantheist in his philosophy and theology and a victim of the Roman Inquisition. Imprisoned in 1592, he was condemned as a heretic and burnt at the stake in Rome on February 17, 1600. Bruno is perhaps better known as a symbol or symptom of Counter-Reformation intolerance and violence than as a major philosopher. He has often been seen as a kind of martyr for liberty of thought, and has been a popular figure in the arsenal of anticlerical polemicists, particularly in Italy.

Thomas Worcester, s.j.

See also COUNTER-REFORMATION/
CATHOLIC REFORMATION; DOMINICANS;
PANTHEISM.

BUBER, MARTIN (1878–1965)

Foremost modern Jewish theologian, philosopher, and Zionist thinker, Buber was born in Vienna, the grandson of Solomon Buber, an important scholar of Midrashic and other Jewish literatures. He studied at the universities of Vienna, Leipzig, Zurich, and Berlin, under the philosophers Wilhelm Dilthey and Georg Simmel. As a young student, he joined the wing of the Zionist movement that advocated the renewal of Jewish culture. In opposition to Theodor Herzl's political Zionism, he thus focused upon education rather than political action. As a Hebrew humanist, he additionally called for peaceful coexistence with the Arabs. Buber was appointed to a professorship at the University of Frankfort in 1925, but when the Nazis came to power he received an appointment at the Hebrew University of Jerusalem where, in 1938, he became a professor of social philosophy.

At age twenty-six, Buber became interested in Hasidic thought, and he was subsequently responsible for bringing Hasidism to the attention of young German intellectuals who had previously scorned it as the product of ignorant eastern European Jewish peasants. Hasidism had a profound impact on Buber's thought, and he credited it as the inspiration for his theories of spirituality, community, and dialogue. Indeed, Buber's work created a new system of Jewish religious belief, referred to as neo-Hasidism. Buber also wrote about utopian socialism, education, Zionism, and respect for the Palestinian Arabs; with Franz Rosenzweig, he translated the Hebrew Bible into German.

Buber is known today for his theological writings, which proposed a dialogue-theory in which all relationships, including those between people and God, can be classified as I–Thou or I–It. This theory has been influential in Christian as well as Jewish theological thinking.

Alan J. Avery-Peck

See also HASIDISM.

BUCER, MARTIN (1491–1551)

Born in Germany, Martin Bucer played an important role in the Reformation in Switzerland, southern Germany, and England. A member of the Order of Preachers from 1506 to 1521, Bucer left the Dominicans, married, and joined the Reformation underway in Zurich. After Zwingli's death in 1531, he became for a time a leader of the Reformed Church in Switzerland and Germany. In 1549, in the reign of King Edward VI, Bucer was named Regius Professor of Divinity in the University of Cambridge. Holding that post until his death two years later, he helped to promote church reform along the lines adopted in Zurich and Geneva. After Mary, the Catholic daughter of King Henry VIII, acceded to the English throne, Bucer's body was unearthed and publicly burned in Cambridge.

Thomas Worcester, S.J.

See also REFORMATION; REFORMED CHURCH; ZWINGLI, ULRICH.

BUDDHA

At the turn of the sixth century B.C.E., North India was a place of spiritual questioning and ascetic searching. In remote retreats and in areas proximate to the emerging urban centers, there were many hundreds of renunciant seekers called *shramanas* who pursued ascetic practices (*yoga*) in hopes of realizing the true essence of life, reality, consciousness, or to amass magical power.

The most famous man ever to become a shramana was born the son of a warrior-caste father and mother who ruled one of the small states in the foothills of the Himalayas. According to the legendary accounts, this boy's birth was accompanied by auspicious celestial signs and a wise man's prediction that he would either be successful as a universal monarch or a great ascetic. (The personal name given as a result, "Siddhartha," means "the one who attains the goal.") After his mother died a week after giving birth, the young prince grew up in a palace where his father did everything in his power to insure the first destiny. He was trained in the martial arts, isolated from life's unpleasantries, and pampered with all the pleasures of rule, including marriage, a harem of concubines, and every form of artistic distraction.

Siddhartha's life changed when he followed his inclination to see the world beyond the palace walls, going with his faithful chariot driver out into the world. All the textual legends describe the profound impact that seeing a sick man, old man, dead man, and shramana had upon him (called the "four passing sights"), shaking his rosy assumptions about life and also suggesting a path he could take to escape his sheltered existence. Within days and at the age of twenty-nine, Siddhartha had left his palace and family behind to embark on his search for a teacher among the forest-dwelling ascetics.

He soon found shramana gurus who taught forms of meditation that allowed one to reach a state of "neither perception nor nonperception," and Siddhartha soon mastered them. But he recognized them as limited accomplishments. He then joined five other ascetics committed to intense ascetic practices involving fanatical fasting and spending long periods seated in unmoving meditation. Siddhartha conformed to these rigors, but eventually rejected them because they were too extreme. Through these experiments, Siddhartha did come to understand that the spiritual life is best undertaken as a middle path between the extremes of sense indulgence (the life in the palace) and over-zealous asceticism (of the forest). One name for Buddhism, the Middle Way, resulted from this experience.

Although he lacked bodily strength, Siddhartha soon was buoyed by a gift of food from a village woman. He then sat beneath a great tree by a river outside the town of Gaya where he vowed either to find success or death. The legendary accounts relate that his revitalized meditations were soon disturbed by Mara, a supernatural being regarded by Buddhists as the personification of death, delusion, and temptation; his minions appeared as armies to elicit fear and as alluring females to arouse lust. Siddhartha's gesture of touching the right hand to earth, asking it to bear witness to his merit and eventual success, brought forth earthquakes and a cooling stream that washed away Mara and his hordes. (The earth-touching gesture is one of the most common depictions of the Buddha in art.)

Later that night, after Siddhartha resumed his meditations, he reached more subtle and blissful perceptions and then the attainment of superfaculties such as memory of his former lives and telepathy. Finally, he completely extinguished all desire and ignorance by fully awakening his insight (*prajna*). This "awakening" to the nature of reality provides the root meaning of the term "Buddha" which from this moment onward we can properly apply to Siddhartha. The references to him have assumed many other forms: using his family surname, "Gautama Buddha"; adopting his clan name to inflect Shakyamuni, "the sage (*muni*) from the Shakyas"; *Mahashramana*, "The Great Ascetic"; *Tathagata*, "the one who has come thus," and *Jina*, the "conqueror" (that is, of *karma*, ignorance, death, and so on).

For seven weeks, the Buddha remained in the vicinity of the Bodhi Tree ("Enlightenment Tree"), enjoying the bliss of nirvana. He then walked first to Sarnath, a deer park outside the city of Varanasi, where he found his former five ascetic colleagues; after he taught them the Four Noble Truths, each was enlightened. These ascetics were ordained as the first members of the *sangha*, and they were then instructed to share the *Dharma* with others and to travel to different places in the four directions to do so.

For the next forty or so years, the Buddha empowered his enlightened disciples called Arahants ("Worthies") to act on his behalf, to admit seekers into the sangha, guide those who wished to meditate, and teach the Dharma to whomever wished to hear the teachings. All traditions state that the Buddha's faculty of psychic knowledge allowed him to preach according to the exact capacity of his audience. Slowly the movement grew as the Buddhist shramanas found an interested audience primarily among the urban populations. Shakyamuni traveled almost continuously, except for the period of the monsoon rains when he remained in one place.

As the Buddhist movement grew, new situations arose that required adaptation, so that, in addition to his skill at teaching, the Buddha also managed the successful creation of the sangha as an entirely new institution in ancient India. After much urging, Shakyamuni also gave permission for the creation of a *bhikkhuni sangha* of female renunciants. In allowing the sangha to receive lands, buildings, and other communal resources donated initially to make the rains retreat well-observed, the Buddha's concession established the means by which the sangha shifted its focus over time from wandering to settled cooperative communal existence.

The Buddha, in old age, began to suffer from various ailments, and in 483 B.C.E. died in Kushinagar, a rural site. He was cremated, and after his ashes were divided, they were placed in mounds (*stupa*), as these shrines became the focus of Buddhist ritual and the visible symbol of the Buddha's presence in the world.

Shakyamuni's life story became for Buddhists a paradigmatic example of an individual's quest for enlightenment, and his exemplary role for subsequent generations was elaborated in hundreds of didactic stories that describe incidents from his previous births as human, animal, or spirit; these narratives called *jatakas* along with stories of his final ascent to Buddhahood inspired vernacular arts and literatures across Asia that conveyed the essential doctrines in explicit, personified form. The Buddha, thus, embodied the Dharma, the ultimate truth and its formulation in teachings.

Finally, it should be noted that Shakyamuni is not the only Buddha in Buddhism: Buddhas are born into the world regularly and the recurring reality of "Buddhahood" is thought by all Buddhists to be a distinguishing characteristic of this universe. Cosmic notions of Buddhahood and Shakyamuni Buddha were developed in the Mahayana texts. Their most common doctrine concerned the "Three Bodies of the Buddha" (*trikaya*) and divine bodhisattvas.

Todd T. Lewis

See also ASANGA; DHARMA (IN BUD-DHISM); MAITREYA; REFUGE, THREE-FOLD; SIGHTS, FOUR PASSING; TRIKAYA (DOCTRINE OF); TRUTHS, FOUR NOBLE.

BUDDHAGHOSA (CA. 380–440 C.E.)

One of the most influential scholar-monks in Theravada Buddhist history, Buddhaghosa was regarded as the definitive interpreter of the Pali Canon throughout the subsequent history of this school. Born in Andra (south India) where he was ordained, Buddhaghosa traveled to Sri Lanka where he settled in the Mahavihara in Anuradhapura, the great royally endowed center of scholarship. There he wrote and synthesized earlier commentaries on most of the canonical texts, adding popular stories that by tradition had become associated with specific narratives. It was Buddhaghosa's assimilation of doctrinal texts in his masterly treatise, the *Visuddhimagga* ("The Path Toward Purification"), that ordered the Theravada path into the three stages of morality, meditation, and insight. In addition to valorizing Pali as the language of later Theravada scholarly discourse, Buddhaghosa effectively established the school's normative approach to systematic philosophy and doctrinal interpretation.

Todd T. Lewis

See also NOBLE EIGHTFOLD PATH; PRAJNA; SOUTHERN BUDDHISM; THERAVADA BUDDHISM; VIPASHYANA/ VIPASSANA.

BUDDHISM
Introduction

For over two thousand years, the simple recitation of "going for refuge"—*Buddha Saranam Gacchami* ("I go for refuge in the Buddha"), *Dharma Saranam Gacchami* ("I go for refuge in the Teachings"), and *Sangha Saranam Gacchami* ("I go for refuge in the Community")—has marked an individual's conversion to Buddhism and the start of Buddhist rituals. Today these three repetitions are still heard across Asia and increasingly beyond, in Japan and Nepal, from Mongolia to Thailand, by immigrants and converts in the West.

Buddhism's journey begins in its homeland of South Asia, travels into the high Himalayas, across the tropical states of Southeast Asia and over the central Asian deserts, and finds millions of followers throughout the imperial domains of China, Korea, and Japan.

Unlike the other trans-ethnic world religions, Buddhism has but a few universally accepted doctrinal formulae. Beyond sharing the refuges above, Buddhists have adopted varying subsets of the Buddha's teachings and many rituals, always integrating the monastic community (the sangha) as the central institution in its midst. Pluralism complicates the study of Buddhism: all schools believe that the Buddha taught many doctrinal formulations and advocated different practices that could lead every sort of individual toward the state of salvation called nirvana. Within the first thousand years after the death of Shakyamuni (563–483 B.C.E.), there were dozens of doctrinal schools that aligned themselves under two main divisions, those of the "elder traditionalists" called Sthaviras (the sole surviving school of which is called Theravada) and those of the "Great Vehicle" calling themselves the Mahayana (among which many schools survive today such as Pure Land and Zen).

Since the Buddha also disallowed having any one sangha or institutional authority define a single canon or rule on the orthodoxy of doctrinal interpretations (the opposite extreme of premodern Christianity in this matter), it is in some respects quite artificial to posit a single "Buddhism" based upon a common code, text, or catechism of belief. In every land, practices developed independently that led to the faith's twin classic goals: worldly blessings and nirvana.

Historical Overview

In the first sermon after his enlightenment, Shakyamuni Buddha told his first five monks to spread the teaching (Dharma) so that from its inception Buddhism was a missionary religion (the first in the world) that taught a message directed to and thought suitable for all peoples. In its early centuries, Buddhism spread to places similar to where it began, among the urban peoples becoming part of the first regional states that formed to govern the subcontinent. Within the first millennium, Buddhism had spread throughout South Asia and far beyond it into Central Asia via the overland routes, via maritime trade to Sri Lanka, and across continental and insular Southeast Asia. By 500 C.E., while its monasteries welcomed all who would observe the rules of residence, the community split into more than twenty schools of doctrinal interpretation, roughly divided among the Sthavira traditionalists and Mahayana interpreters. Thus, from soon after the Buddha's death, throughout its subsequent 1500 years in its Indic homeland, then in diaspora, Buddhism never could be characterized as a unified faith.

In East Asia, the successful adaptation of Buddhism was achieved in a culture that had equally venerable and strong roots in very different religious traditions: Confucianism and Daoism. The partial conversion of China to Buddhism constitutes one of the greatest instances of mass cross-cultural transmission and conversion in world history, parallel in scope only with the transformations wrought by the world's other great missionary faiths, Christianity and Islam. Buddhists also overcame obstacles in the East Asian culture area based upon them: prejudice against "barbarian" cultures and particularly the Confucian suspicion against

Buddhist monasticism's rule of celibacy that made it seem unnatural and inimical to family values. What did attract East Asians was the doctrine of reincarnation and karma, the highly developed pantheon of Indic Buddhism, and rituals reciting the Buddha's words designed to insure health, wealth, and prosperity.

The bewildering complexity of the Indic legacy was resolved in East Asia by schools that considered one text or teaching as the most authoritative. Over time, it was the Mahayana ("Great Vehicle") that dominated in the successful transplantation of the faith in northern and eastern Asia. At the courts of the great capitals (often with strong support by women at court), some saw the utility of Buddhist rituals and morality, while others were drawn to unique forms of spiritual practice and experience. Until the extinction of the great Buddhist centers of north India by 1200 C.E., there was for over eight hundred years a great, international network of trade centers and Buddhist monasteries, as monks from South Asia, Central Asia, and East Asia traveled in search of texts, relics, and teachers.

After several centuries of assimilation under the weak regional governments preceding the T'ang Dynasty, Buddhism moved east and again it was imported via imperial initiative to Korea (by 400 C.E.) and via Korea to Japan (by 580 C.E.). In the first centuries after its introduction to these countries, Buddhism was adopted almost exclusively by aristocrats and literati, although the elites' motives were primarily for adopting Buddhist rituals to protect the courts, and its moral teachings to enhance the quest for national unity in their newly established states. In East Asia, governments established considerable jurisdiction over the sangha.

Transmitted to Korea and Japan initially were the branches of the early Chinese schools; later, great figures in each country followed their own interpretations of the doctrine and started indigenous schools.

Buddhism also found successful transplantation in the Himalayas and beyond in the highlands of the Tibetan plateau about the same time it reached Japan. The first installation of Buddhism in the Tibetan state, instituted via royal imposition around 600 C.E., established rich legends but did not endure with the disintegration of the state; the second era (after 1000) saw the evolution of large monastic schools that competed for political dominance across the region, with one, the school of the Gelugpas headed by the Dalai Lamas (after 1500), dominating in the formation of the early modern state. Starting in 1253, several Tibetan schools established ties with the resurgent Mongols, converting them to their form of Mahayana–Vajrayana Buddhism; the institutions of Mongolian Buddhism were founded later via relationships with the Dalai Lamas.

Sangha and Monastery: The Institutional Vehicle of Buddhism's Expansion

What does provide the strongest common thread in the history and practice of Buddhism across Asia is the sangha, the community of monks, nuns, and devout lay followers who established durable monasteries and shrines that rooted the faith in every locality. When Buddhist monasticism spread across Asia, it introduced independent, corporate institutions that transformed local societies and regional polities. In early India, the sangha disregarded caste as a spiritual or social category for its members; in Buddhism's subsequent missionary migrations, the sangha provided a refuge for spiritual and educational advancement that for most individuals in these societies was otherwise unavailable.

The key to understanding Buddhism in society is to note the essential complementary role householders played in maintaining the faith: donations to the sangha earned them merit to improve their karma and worldly blessings for themselves as well as their families and communities. It was this central exchange maintained between sangha and society as well as these dual goals that kept Buddhism vibrant:

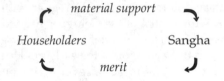

material support

Householders   Sangha

merit

Major Schools of Buddhism

While one may emphasize the intellectual division into Traditionalists and Great Vehicle adherents that grew among Buddhists by the end of the faith's first millennium, it must always be remembered that for the lay majority such disputes were mostly irrelevant to their focus on merit and blessings; for them as for the sangha, conformity to the Vinaya code of discipline was the central concern since only monks and nuns of integrity guaranteed that householders would earn merit by making donations to them. All Buddhists, regardless of doctrinal inclination, also share a common ritual focus: circumambulating *stupa* shrines and making offerings at Buddha images; gathering at the monastery for preaching on the weekly holy days; making donations marking the observance of the sangha's three-month rain retreat.

Sthaviravadins and Mahayanists

The great divide within Buddhism had its origins in dissent about core doctrinal interpretations: the nature of Buddhahood, the ultimate explanations of impermanence and no-soul teaching, the formulation and implications of interdependence. There also seems to have developed a reaction against the conservative scholasticism that arose among the prominent traditionalist monks (Sthaviras) who claimed that as Enlightened Arahants their interpretations were infallible and their status was the highest in the sangha. Another difference developed regarding whether meditation techniques, rituals, or mantra recitations discovered by non-Buddhist *shramanas* or Hindus could be adopted. The divide between traditionalists and Mahayanists seems to reflect a universal tendency for humans to divide between those inclined to either a literal approach holding to the letter within a conservative tradition or else a more open-ended, experimental, and expansive approach to the spiritual that finds "keeping the spirit" essential. (The Mahayana in this domain might be compared to the Sufis in Islam as opposed to the legalistic theologians; the Christian analogy would be the Gnostics as opposed to the authoritarian church.)

On the philosophical level, there were fiercely contested disagreements that we know of chiefly from the Mahayana side. For the most part, the traditionalists ignored their opponents' polemics except to point out that their texts were invented and that the teaching of emptiness [see below] undermined the tradition. The term found in the Theravada commentaries for the Mahayanists, *Vaitulika* ("Illusionists"), perhaps refers to their view of Mahayana Buddhology or their dismissal of the arguments raised. The label the Mahayanists applied to their opponents, Hinayana ("Lesser Vehicle"), suggested diminished religious effectiveness, commitment, vision. What were the reasons for this pejorative name?

Among the earliest Mahayana sutras attributed by this school to the Buddha are those called *Prajnaparamita* ("Perfection of Wisdom"). These texts of varying length set out to poke fun at the Arhants and seek to poke holes in their scholasticism. Their main target is the traditionalist's scholasticism that tried to classify all reality according to physical and psychological units called *dharmas;* although the traditionalist's *Abhidharmas* asserted that these were impermanent, passing phenomena, the Mahayana critics saw such attempts as defying the central no-soul doctrine and the teaching of dependent arising. For them, true *prajna* ("insight") involved the thoroughgoing perception of reality as empty of all independent reality-units, to which they applied the adjective *shunya.*

This opposition to the Traditionalists coalesced in the writings of one of India's greatest philosophers, Nagarjuna (born ca. 120 C.E.), who developed this deconstructive view via dialectical argumentation, and applied it to create a systematic school of thought that became known as the Madhyamika. In one of the most courageous philosophical explorations in the history of religions, Nagarjuna argued that all language is conventional and all oppositions set up by it are mere constructions, including even the Buddhist "nirvana" and "samsara." The announced purpose in this was religious: to clear away all false assumptions and even the subtle attachment to language and scholastic categories, finding true refuge and enlightenment only via meditation.

Another major school of Mahayana thought continued from this Madhyamika

standpoint: the Cittamatra ("Consciousness Only") school largely agreed with this critique of external human experience and asserted that the real arena of spiritual transformation and causality therefore must occur within the workings of consciousness. This school's great thinkers were the brothers Asanga and Vasubandhu (active ca. 320 C.E.). Yet another Mahayana school also grew from Madhyamika roots: the Buddha Nature (Tathagatagarba) school. They held that if it is true that nirvana and samsara cannot be separated in any meaningful way, then nirvana interpenetrates all reality. And if this is so, then one might say that all beings have a portion of it and so possess the latent potential for nirvana-realization or enlightenment. The buddha nature doctrine appeared to some as a "back-door" admission of soul theory into Mahayana thought; it did reinforce the need for traditional meditation practices.

The most popular Buddhist scripture in the world, and likely the earliest Mahayana text composed, was the *Lotus Sutra.* The *Lotus* develops another important and popular avenue of Mahayana doctrine: the theory of cosmic Buddhahood. Through parable, astounding miraculous display, and polemic, the text recounts how the human Buddha the Arhants are so attached to is, in fact, the embodiment of a more universal Buddha reality that can materialize in many forms simultaneously throughout the cosmos. The *Lotus* describes the Buddha's preaching various teachings to suit the level of the audience, even dying just to encourage the active practice of devotees.

The religious ideal in the *Lotus* and in other Mahayana texts shifts from the Arahant to the bodhisattva, "future Buddha." Disciples are encouraged to see that, given the reality of interdependence, no one can be enlightened independent of others; bodhisattvas should therefore vow not to enter final nirvana until all beings are realized, a mind-boggling, long-term commitment. This Mahayana vow has given many Buddhists over the millennia a profoundly challenging spiritual ideal, one of the most altruistic articulated in the history of religions.

The *Lotus Sutra* is only the most popular among a large class of texts that focus on bodhisattvas who have garnered the merit necessary to find rebirth as divinities. These "celestial bodhisattvas" continue to serve humanity by offering compassionate intervention to secure worldly blessings and even the means to salvation. In the popular imagination, they became the Buddhist parallels to Hindu or Chinese deities by the end of the faith's first millennium. The most popular and universal of these was Avalokiteshvara who came to be known as Kwan-Yin in China, Kannon in Japan, Chenrizig in Tibet, and Karunamaya in Nepal.

Perhaps as an extension of Shakyamuni Buddha's injunction that the sangha should "show the way to heaven," yet another "cabin" in the Great Vehicle was the Pure Land School. This school's texts describe how certain bodhisattvas vowed to create celestial paradises upon their reaching Buddhahood, "Pure Lands" dedicated to supplying all requisites for the enlightenment of individuals reborn there.

The most important and highly developed of these traditions was that associated with Amitabha Buddha (Chinese Amitofo, Japanese Amida) and the paradise Sukhavati. T'an Luan (476–542), regarded as the first patriarch of China's Pure Land School, first systematized the school's characteristic practice of chanting Amitabha's name [*"Namo A-mi-t'o Fo"*] and its doctrine of this Buddha's distinctive "other power" that could save even those with bad karma. Still later in Japan (by 1100 c.e.), Pure Land Buddhism continued to evolve as a separate school that emphasized human inadequacy, the "other power" of Buddhas and bodhisattvas, and rituals at death dedicating an individual's merit to find rebirth there. Eventually, these schools de-emphasized the requirement of celibacy to join the ordained sangha.

In response to the Pure Land emphasis on "other power," a more "traditionalist Mahayana" school called Ch'an also arose about 500 c.e. in China that insisted on "self power" as the true Buddhist teaching. Ch'an stressed meditation, this-life realization, and its patriarchs from Shakyamuni onward passing on the wordless "mind to mind" transmission of enlightenment. This tradition later known as Zen in Japan also developed in monasteries upholding strict monastic rules.

One final school that had emerged among the Mahayanists after the faith's first millennium was the Vajrayana, a wing that some scholars would highlight (as did later Tibetan scholastics) as a third division of the faith. The development of this tradition was part of a religious movement called *tantra* that affected all South Asian traditions, including Hinduism and Jainism; it was centered among the wandering mendicants whose spiritual seeking on the fringes of society began in the Buddha's era and continues up to the present. Tantric traditions emphasize realization in this lifetime. Tantric Buddhism is also called *Vajrayana* ("Thunderbolt Vehicle") or *Mantrayana* ("Mantra Vehicle"), terms indicating the esoteric spiritual traditions that developed principally within later Mahayana

Buddhism and as part of the pan-Indic yoga movement that sought lightening-quick enlightenment in this lifetime via both standard and unorthoprax means under the guidance of an accomplished teacher (*siddha*). Tantric Buddhism arose in continuity with the philosophical trends within Mahayana philosophy that equated samsara with nirvana, agreed that all beings partake of the buddha nature (Tathagatagarba doctrine), and pursued this ultimate goal by whatever means necessary.

The central experience of tantric Buddhism is *sadhana*, communion with a celestial Buddha or bodhisattva through the experience of identification with his (or her) body, speech, and mind. Based upon the assumption that the siddha who discovered each path had experienced the deity as the embodiment of enlightenment, an initiate is taught to place the deity (with entourage) in her minds' eye, repeat *mantras* that resonate with that form, and build an existential connection with it. When complete, one's identification ultimately implies the attainment of enlightenment coequal with the divine form.

Todd T. Lewis

See also ARAHANT; BODHI; BUDDHA; DHARMA; HINAYANA; HUA-YEN BUDDHIST SCHOOL; MAHAYANA BUDDHISM; NIRVANA; NOBLE EIGHT-FOLD PATH; NORTHERN BUDDHISM; PALI CANON; PRAJNA; REFUGE, THREE-FOLD; SANGHA; TANTRIC BUDDHISM; THERAVADA BUDDHISM; TRUTHS, FOUR NOBLE; VINAYA.

BULGAKOV, SERGEI (1871–1944)

Russian Orthodox theologian and philosopher. As a result of his reading Hegel's works, he became a skeptic and turned to Marxist thought. After 1905 he returned to the Russian Orthodox Church and was later ordained a priest. He was expelled from Russia in 1922, moving then to Paris where he became dean of the Orthodox Theological Seminary until his death. Committed to Christian union, he critically promoted the ecumenical movement in his church. His theology centered around Divine Wisdom (*Sophia*), continuing the tradition that dated back to the early Eastern Churches. Although the Moscow patriarchate condemned his teaching in 1935 for political reasons, he remained a highly regarded scholar within and outside his own church in both Europe and the Americas. His main publications were *The Orthodox Church* (1935), *The Wisdom of God* (1937), and *Le Paraclet* (1947).

Orlando Espín

See also LOSSKY, VLADIMIR; MARXISM; ORTHODOX CHURCHES; RUSSIAN ORTHODOX CHURCH; WISDOM.

BULL

The seal (Latin, *bulla*) affixed to papal church documents that indicates the level of authoritativeness the document possesses. The most authoritative are sealed with lead. Lesser documents may be sealed with wax or ink stamps.

Mary Ann Hinsdale

BULTMANN, RUDOLF (1884–1976)

Held by many to have been the most influential figure in twentieth-century New Testament scholarship, during most of his career he was professor of New Testament at the University of Marburg, Germany (1921–51). His teaching combined vast knowledge and scholarship with a concern to preach a relevant message to his contemporaries in a world where faith is difficult. Two major influences permeated Bultmann's work: thorough-going Lutheranism and the existentialism of Martin Heidegger. Deep skepticism on Bultmann's part concerning the historicity of the Gospels, to which he applied a rigorous form criticism, correlates with his dehistoricizing of the kerygma. He held that the only history to be found in the kerygma is the *Dass*, the fact of the existence and crucifixion of Jesus. Thus, in his view, the Word that addresses individuals in the kerygma is both the ground, as well as the object of faith. His notion of kerygma effectively ended the so-called Quest of the Historical Jesus, that is, the various eighteenth- and early nineteenth-century attempts to compile a history of the life of Jesus. Bultmann's disciples, the post-Bultmannians or "Old Marburgers," for example, G. Bornkamm, H. Conzelmann, E. Fuchs, E. Käsemann, H. Koester, and J. M. Robinson, have carried forth his work, yet with enough independence to cause new trends in exegesis.

F. M. Gillman

See also BORNKAMM, GUNTHER; CONZELMANN, HANS; EXISTENTIALISM; FORM CRITICISM; FUCHS, ERNST; HEIDEGGER, MARTIN; KÄSEMANN, ERNST; KERYGMA.

BURIAL (IN CHRISTIANITY)

In the Christian tradition, the dead are usually interred in some way, or buried. In antiquity, Christians generally followed Jewish or Greco-Roman practice in the final arrangements for the dead: often, the dead were entombed in crypts or sarcophagi, or were cremated (the body burned to ashes). The underground burial areas of Rome, called the catacombs, were important burial sites in antiquity, and offer some moving examples of early Christian art (many frescos and some mosaics).

The early Christian burial service (or funeral, from the Latin word *funus*) covered a number of important moments in the event of dying. Many of these were domestic rites, that is, liturgical activities carried out at home. There were prayers and readings from Scripture at the deathbed, and especially vital was the reception of the *viaticum*, or the "last" or "final" Communion, by the dying person. The moment of death was marked by other special prayers, as was the preparation of the body for burial (this washing and dressing of the body was also done at the home). The body was then brought to the church in a procession, accompanied by the chanting of psalms; a short service followed (later, a celebration of the Eucharist or Mass), and the body would then be buried. It became customary for bodies to be buried inside the church, and later, outside on church property (the churchyard). The deceased would also be remembered at special celebrations of the Eucharist (or Mass) after the funeral, following the Roman pagan practice of celebrating a special funeral meal in memory of the departed on certain days: most commonly, these would be on the third (or fourth) day after the funeral, then on the thirtieth (or fortieth) day after the funeral, and then after one year had passed (the anniversary).

In the Middle Ages, a number of changes took place. The dying person would still receive Communion (the Viaticum) on his or her deathbed, but due to shifts in Christian spirituality, the ritual of anointing the dying person and absolving him or her of sin became much more important in the rites of the dying. The rituals performed in the church became more important as well: the celebration of a special Mass for the dead (called a *Requiem Mass*) became common, and the dead were more frequently buried in a churchyard or cemetery outside of the church, so that an additional procession to the grave became a more important element in the funeral liturgy. Masses "said for the dead" began to multiply, and became a key element in popular spirituality.

Today, Christian burial in the United States does retain some of these earlier elements. While the funeral home has replaced the family home as the place for the preparation of the body and the place to pay final respects to the person and the family (the "wake"), the church still remains the primary location for the liturgical rites of burial. A procession is still formed after the funeral, but because of changes in burial customs, it is usually made up of cars traveling to a more distant cemetery for the committal at the grave. In the Roman Catholic tradition, the liturgical emphasis has been shifted from the mourning themes accentuated by the use of black vestments to a focus on the resurrection promised in the person's baptism, accentuated by the use of white vestments and the paschal candle.

Joanne M. Pierce

See also ANOINTING OF THE SICK, SACRAMENT OF; DEATH (CHRISTIAN); PASCHAL CANDLE; RECONCILIATION, SACRAMENT OF; UNCTION; VIATICUM.

BURIAL (IN JUDAISM)

In line with Judaism's reading of Genesis 3:19 ("you are dust, and to dust you shall return"), Jews prohibit embalming or other methods of preserving a corpse, requiring instead that the corpse be buried in the ground in a wooden casket in a manner that does not prevent decomposition. Since the body is meant to decompose naturally, cremation and the use of mausoleums are forbidden by traditional Judaism. On the principle that Jews must follow the law of the land in which they live, however, embalming and the use of burial vaults or copings are permitted where required by state law. Out of respect for the corpse, in Judaism burial normally takes place as quickly after death as is practicable. Viewing the corpse is not a Jewish custom.

Alan J. Avery-Peck

See also CHEVRAH KADESHA; DEATH (IN JUDAISM); KADDISH; KERI'AH; SHIVAH; TACHRICHIN; TAHARAH.

BURIAL MOUND

In the prehistoric civilizations of North America, the great earthworks that dot the valleys of the Ohio and Mississippi Rivers served as places of burial for their dead. Archeological studies have discovered that these impressive structures were raised at the cost of considerable labor to serve as tombs and monuments for the dead. They are especially remarkable for their height and extension, as well as their carefully designed geometric patterns. The recently achieved ability to view them from above has raised an interesting question: how, with the available technology of that time, did they manage to execute accurate designs on such a large scale? We may never know the answer to this, but what is left of their material culture indicates a highly intelligent people, and a refined form of civilization. This has produced an excellent foil to the opinion that only "savages" inhabited the northern half of the continent. Above all, it reveals a capacity to reflect on life and death and transform them into art.

Kathleen Dugan

See also ANCESTORS, CHINESE; DEATH (CHRISTIAN); DEATH (IN JUDAISM); ESCHATOLOGY (IN CHRISTIANITY); ESCHATOLOGY (IN JUDAISM).

BUSHIDO

(Japanese, way of the warrior). This is the code of conduct and ideal of behavior for the warrior class of feudal Japan, which became codified during the Tokugawa Period (1600–1868). It was a code influenced by Shinto, Zen, and Neo-Confucian beliefs and practices, emphasizing devotion to country, obedience to superiors, honor, courage, and loyalty. While this practice of devotion to duty and self-cultivation was initially limited to the warrior class (samurai), in time it spread to the rest of society and was supported by the strong Neo-Confucian influence of the period.

G. D. DeAngelis

See also NEO-CONFUCIANISM; SHINTO; TOKUGAWA PERIOD; ZEN.

BUSHNELL, HORACE (1802–76)

Born near Litchfield, Connecticut, Bushnell spent most of his adult life as a Congregational pastor and theologian in Hartford, Connecticut. He made two significant theological contributions that undermined evangelical Protestantism. First, he critiqued revivalism by denying that Christians must experience a cataclysmic conversion from sin to grace. In A Discourse on Christian Nurture (1847), he argued that a child raised in a Christian home could gradually grow into realization of God's grace. Second, in God in Christ (1849), he stated that theological

language is imprecise and poetic rather than literal. Creeds, confessions, and even the Bible must be understood as attempts to articulate what is essentially inarticulable. He pioneered metaphorical interpretations of sacred texts as approximations of divine truth. Influenced by the Romanticism of Samuel Coleridge and Friedrich Schleiermacher, Bushnell mediated evangelical Protestantism and the emerging theology of liberalism.

Evelyn A. Kirkley

See also CONGREGATIONAL THEOLOGIES; EVANGELICAL THEOLOGY; EVANGELICALS; REVIVALISM.

BUTSUDAN

The name of the "Altar of the Buddhas," the traditional shrine in a Japanese Buddhist house that is usually kept separate from the kamidan, the shrine for the local/national gods (kami). The butsudan may be a simple box or an elaborate gilded altar. Regardless of style, most butsudan hold tablets of deceased family members placed alongside the particular symbols of the Buddhist faith revered in the particular family; it is here, too, where amulets brought home from pilgrimages are kept. It is before the butsudan that the Buddhist family priest will perform the yearly death anniversary rites.

Todd T. Lewis

See also KAMIDANA.

BYZANTINE CATHOLIC CHURCHES

The Byzantine Churches were established originally from or came under the influence of the Patriarchate of Constantinople (known as Byzantium before Emperor Constantine the Great changed the city's name). The several Byzantine

Catholic Churches were formed as Orthodox groups and established full communion with Rome during the last five centuries. There are fourteen Byzantine Catholic Churches—the largest of which are the Ukrainian, the Melkite, and the Ruthenian.

Orlando Espín

See also BYZANTIUM/BYZANTINE; CATHOLIC TRADITION; CONSTANTINOPLE, SEE OF; EASTERN CATHOLIC CHURCHES; GREEK CATHOLIC CHURCH; MELKITE CATHOLIC CHURCH; ORTHODOX CHURCHES; ROME, SEE OF; RUTHENIAN CATHOLIC CHURCH; UKRAINIAN CATHOLIC CHURCH.

BYZANTIUM/BYZANTINE

Byzantium was the ancient name of the city on the Bosphorus Straits renamed Constantinople by Constantine when he moved the capital of the Roman Empire there in 330. The adjective "Byzantine" and the noun "Byzantium" came to refer to the eastern part of the Roman Empire, particularly after the western part of the empire effectively split with the East by the ninth century. The religion of Byzantium was the Christianity espoused by the Councils of Nicaea (325) and Chalcedon (451), and the official language, Greek, although the empire included a wide range of cultures and languages. Byzantine theology is strongly marked by the influence of Platonism and reflects the ongoing christological conflicts that continued to shake Eastern Christianity. The emperors, together with the patriarch of Constantinople, were considered to be the leaders of Byzantine Christianity, especially as the the power of the other Eastern patriarchs waned following the Muslim invasions.

The Byzantine Empire survived a series of crises, including the sacking of Constantinople during the Third Crusade in 1203–4, to endure as a potent political force in the eastern Mediteranean until Constantinople fell to the Turks in 1453. The Byzantine Church maintained, preserved, and developed the classic Christian teachings of the fourth and fifth centuries. The successors to this tradition are the Orthodox Churches of Christianity. Although relations between the Orthodox tradition and the Western tradition began to fray by the ninth century, an important step was taken in separating the two churches when the Roman Church and the Byzantine Church officially excommunicated each other in 1054. The split was not seen as irreconcilable at the time, and several attempts were made in subsequent centuries to bring the churches into union, but the differences were too great and reconciliation was never successful.

Gary Macy

See also CONSTANTINE I THE GREAT; CRUSADES; ORTHODOX CHURCHES; ORTHODOX THEOLOGY.

C

CADBURY, HENRY J. (1883–1974)
Born in Philadelphia, Pennsylvania, to a Quaker family, Henry Joel Cadbury was a biblical scholar who pioneered the Christian peace movement and introduced significant aspects of German historical criticism to the United States. With degrees from Haverford College and Harvard University, in 1910 he joined the faculty at Haverford College, teaching subsequently at Andover Theological Seminary, Bryn Mawr College, and Harvard University. In 1915, as World War I loomed, Cadbury organized a conference of Quakers to advocate peace, leading to the formation of the American Friends Service Committee, in which Cadbury was active the rest of his life. In 1923 he introduced to U.S. audiences form criticism of the Bible, a method of studying biblical genres, such as parables, miracles stories, poetry, and so on. He applied form criticism to the Gospels in *The Making of Luke-Acts* (1927). In *The Perils of Modernizing Jesus* (1937) and *Jesus, What Manner of Man* (1947), he examined the historical Jesus, concluding that he must be studied as a first-century Jew as free as possible of anachronism. Late in life he turned to Quaker history, editing works on George Fox and John Woolman in 1972.

Evelyn A. Kirkley

See also FOX, GEORGE; HISTORICAL CRITICISM; QUAKERS.

CAESAROPAPISM
Name of a system whereby a ruler exercises supreme power over the church within his or her domains. This power is carried even into doctrinal and liturgical matters. This type of absolute royal control over the doctrine and life of the church was often practiced by rulers of the Byzantine Empire, and has been attempted a few times in the West.

Orlando Espín

See also BYZANTIUM/BYZANTINE; ECCLESIOLOGY; ERASTIANISM.

CAHILL, LISA SOWLE (1948–)
American Catholic lay theologian. A native of Philadelphia, Cahill was educated at Santa Clara University and at the University of Chicago, where she earned her doctorate. She is currently professor of Christian Ethics at Boston College. Cahill is one of American Catholicism's leading moral theologians. She has contributed to social and sexual ethics, genetics, and to feminist ethical theory. Cahill has blended excellence in theology with a precise awareness of contemporary American social realities. Among her best

publications are *Women's Sexuality* (1992), *Love Your Enemies: Discipleship, Pacifism, and Just War Theory* (1994), and *Sex, Gender, and Christian Ethics* (1996).

Orlando Espín

See also ETHICS, SEXUAL; ETHICS, SOCIAL; FEMINIST THEOLOGIES; HERMENEUTICS; MORAL THEOLOGY/CHRISTIAN ETHICS.

CAITANYA/CHAITANYA (1486?–1533?)

An important Hindu saint who inspired a revivalist Krishnaite *bhakti* movement in Bengal in Northeast India, Caitanya is known especially for advocating the practice of *kirtana*, the chanting of the "Hare Krishna" *mantra* with great feeling. His followers came to regard him as a divine incarnation, or *avatara*, of both Krishna and Radha in the same body. Caitanya was the founding inspiration of Bengal (Gaudiya) Vaishnavism, an important bhakti tradition, of which the Hare Krishna movement is a modern outgrowth.

Lance E. Nelson

See also AVATARA/AVATAR; BHAKTI; BHAKTI-YOGA; HARE KRISHNA MOVEMENT; HINDUISM; KRISHNA; MANTRA; VAISHNAVA.

CAITYA

An ancient Sanskrit term meaning "shrine." In early Buddhism, *caitya* and *stupa* were often used as synonyms in inscriptions and literature. But definitions on usage varied: the Mahasamghika school's *Vinaya* commentary suggested the existence of a technical distinction between Buddhist shrines with relics (stupa) and shrines without them (caitya). A sixth-century Chinese pilgrim to India gives a definition of the myriad forms the shrine assumed: "Again, when the people make images and caityas which consist of gold, silver, copper, iron, earth, lacquer, bricks, and stone, or when they heap up the snowy sand, they put into the images or caityas two kinds of 'bodies': the relics of the Great Teacher or inscribed words with the chain of causation" (Takakusu, 1896). Buddhists revere their shrines by clockwise circumambulation, leaving offerings, and using them as templates for meditation visualizations. Caitya/stupa worship thus became the chief focus of Buddhist ritual activity linking veneration of the Buddha's "sacred traces" to an individual's attention to managing karma destiny and mundane well-being.

Todd T. Lewis

See also MERIT (PUNYA); STUPA.

"CAJETAN," THOMAS DE VIO (1469–1534)

Known best by his nickname, "Cajetan" or "Gaetano" because he came from the city of Gaeta in Italy, Thomas de Vio became a Dominican in 1484. He taught philosophy and theology in Padua, Pavia, and Rome before becoming master general of the Dominicans in 1508. By the time he stepped down from this post in 1518, he had been appointed cardinal and in 1519, bishop of Gaeta. Cajetan used his position as cardinal and bishop to push for the cause of reform in the church. He tried to reach agreement with Luther in 1518 and opposed the divorce of Henry VIII in 1530. Cajetan's scholarly output was as impressive as his political career. His extensive commentary on the *Summa Theologiae* of Thomas Aquinas marked the beginning of Neo-Scholasticism and continues as a classic representative of that movement.

Gary Macy

See also AQUINAS, THOMAS, ST.;
DOMINICANS; LUTHER, MARTIN;
NEO-SCHOLASTICISM; REFORMATION.

CAKRA/CHAKRA

The Sanskrit word *cakra* (or Pali, *cakka*) means "wheel" or "circle." In Buddhism the symbols of the Dharma-*cakra*, the "Wheel of Truth" (symbolizing the Buddha's teachings) and the *bhava-cakra*, the Wheel of Rebirth (an image of the various realms within samsara), are important. The term cakra also refers to one of several spiritual centers in the body recognized in the mystical physiology of Hindu and Buddhist Tantra. The most commonly known scheme has seven *cakras*, each associated with a different level of spiritual development, located at the base of the spine, the genitals, the solar plexus, the heart, the throat, between the eyebrows, and the crown of the head. The cakras are said to be connected by subtle channels through which the spiritual energy known as *kundalini* rises as the practitioner progresses toward higher states of awareness.

Lance E. Nelson

See also BUDDHISM; DHARMA (IN BUDDHISM); HINDUISM; KUNDALINI; REINCARNATION; SAMSARA; TANTRA; TANTRIC BUDDHISM; TANTRIC HINDUISM.

CALENDAR (LITURGICAL)

The liturgical calendar orders Christian worship into annual commemorations of Jesus' birth, ministry, death, and resurrection. The basic pattern stabilized in the seventh century. It evolved from first-century observances of an annual Pasca and weekly Sunday gatherings. While there are many variations among the calendars of Eastern and Western churches and rites, Christian calendars follow the same basic pattern.

The liturgical calendar separates the year into two cycles. The first cycle is divided into the seasons of Advent, Christmas, and Epiphany. The second cycle includes the seasons of Lent, Easter, and Pentecost. The most recent revision of the Roman Catholic calendar retained the feasts of Epiphany and Pentecost, but replaced their seasons with a sequential sequence of "Sundays of the Year," often called "Ordinary Time."

Advent begins four Sundays before the fixed date of Christmas. The sequence of Sundays following Christmas adjusts to accommodate the moveable date of Easter Sunday and the first Sunday of Advent on the following year. In addition to an annual rotation of Sundays and Major Solemnities, some major feasts, which are assigned to specific dates (for instance, the Transfiguration of the Lord on August 6), replace a sequential Sunday observance whenever the date falls on a Sunday. The following Sunday skips over the Sunday that had been displaced.

The recent Roman Catholic calendar reform had an enormous influence on other North American churches that adopted modestly revised lectionaries based on the Roman Lectionary of 1969. For some (for example, the United Church of Christ), a detailed calendar was a major innovation. Others who had always followed the traditional calendar (for instance, Lutherans, Episcopalians), retained the traditional designations of Sundays "After Epiphany" or "After Pentecost."

Regina A. Boisclair

CALIPH (KALIPHA)/CALIPHATE

In Islam, caliphs were the successors of the Prophet Muhammad (570–632). Their role was to provide spiritual and political leadership for the Islamic community after the Prophet's death. Caliphate refers to the office or institution of the caliphs, as in the sentence, "The caliphate developed immediately after Muhammad's death." The first four caliphs (Abu Bakr, Umar, Uthman, and Ali) are known as the Patriarchal Caliphs or the Rightly Guided Caliphs. These descriptions refer to their status as close companions of the Prophet Muhammad and the important role they played in the spiritual development of Islam. Shi'ite Muslims recognize the legitimacy of only the last of these four leaders, Ali. After Ali, the caliphate became a dynastic institution, passing first to the Umayyads (661–749), then to the Abbasids (749–1258). In the meantime, other splinter caliphates emerged, most notably in Spain, Egypt, and Persia. With the invasion of the Mongols in the thirteenth century C.E., the caliphate ceased to exist as an institution in Islam.

Ronald A. Pachence

See also ABBASIDS; ABU BAKR; ALI; SHI'A/SHI'I/SHI'ITE/SHI'ISM; UMAR; UMAYYADS; UTHMAN.

CALLISTUS II OF ROME (?–1124)

Callistus II was Pope from 1119 until 1124. Guido of Burgundy was the son of the Count of Burgundy and rose to power in the papal chancellory as a strong opponent of Emperor Henry V during the investiture controversy. Guido was chosen as Pope Callistus II by a group of cardinals in exile at Cluny because Henry V had set up the antipope Gregory VIII in Rome. Upon becoming Pope, Callistus began to work to establish peace with the empire and to return to Rome. He accomplished the return to Rome with the help of the Normans in 1119, but peace with the emperor proved more elusive. A compromise between Rome and the empire was reached in the famous Concordat of Worms in 1122, bringing to an end the long investiture controversy. The agreement at Worms was ratified by the First Lateran Council of 1123, presided over by Callistus. This council is also important for its decrees against clerical marriage and simony.

Gary Macy

See also CELIBACY; GREGORIAN REFORMS; INVESTITURE CONTROVERSY; MEDIEVAL CHRISTIANITY (IN THE WEST); POPE; SIMONY; WORMS, CONCORDAT OF.

CALUMET

The calumet, or peace pipe, is a central sacrament in the religious traditions of North America. When it was first noted as a ritual object, the early Jesuits recognized it as a sacred object. They also realized that it was used to symbolize the act of pledging peace. Its frequent presence in treaty-making influenced the common view that it was an object that held political reference. Though this is undoubtedly one of its meanings, its full significance can only be understood along the lines of the Jesuit insights. It was Black Elk who allowed the outside world to glimpse some of the depths of its meaning. In reciting for Joseph Brown the narrative description of his people's major rites, he placed the pipe at the very center. Some aspects of his description show why. As he informed Brown, the Sacred Pipe of the Oglala was a unique sacred gift from the Sacred White Buffalo Woman who came to the Lakota in the early stages of their modern history. As a messenger from Wakan Tanka, she bore the Creator's blessing and instruction which was embodied in a sacred gift. This was the origin of the Sacred Pipe, and they were told how to use it in prayer, and urged to use it unfailingly. As the first gift, it not only has unique status, but is also the gate to all the other rites.

In the beautiful instruction she imparted, the Buffalo Calf Woman revealed some of the profound symbols the pipe holds. It is considered both Revelation, and the means of continuing revelation. It is inherently linked with the gift of the buffalo, which she also gave in a time of great starvation. It is sacrosanct, as its origin story shows, with a holiness not unlike the ark of the covenant. As such, it dwells among the people as a lasting sacrament of the Creator's loving presence. The role of keeper is heredity, and exists today in the family of Elk Head on the Lakota reservation. Interestingly, this sacred object has proven able to touch others, outside of the People, and convince them of its power and sacredness. Thus, it continues to exist and be regarded with great reverence.

Kathleen Dugan

See also RITUAL; SACRAMENT.

CALVIN, JOHN (1509–64)

A native of the French town of Noyon, Calvin was educated in France before going to Geneva, where he undertook a thorough reform of the church and became one of the most important figures of the Reformation. By the time of his death, the Reformation in Geneva had become the model and norm for the Reformation in many parts of Europe.

As a young man, Calvin studied theology at the University of Paris. There he was exposed to both the traditions of medieval theology and to the new, humanist emphasis on languages and study of Scripture. In 1528 Calvin began the study of law at Orléans and Bourges. Sometime in 1533, he felt called by God to "restore" the church.

As the French monarchy was increasingly hostile to church reform, Calvin left France for the city of Basle in 1535, and then in 1536, Geneva. William Farel had already begun to reform the Genevan church and Calvin remained in Geneva to assist with this work. The year 1536 also saw the first edition of Calvin's most important publication, *Institutes of the Christian Religion*. Two years later, however, a political conflict between Geneva and the city of Berne led to Calvin's expulsion from Geneva and his move to Strasbourg.

In Strasbourg, Calvin produced a second, enlarged edition of the *Institutes*, as well as a letter of "reply" to Cardinal Sadoleto. The *Institutes* were a summary of Christian doctrine, a summary that placed great emphasis on the sovereignty of God, on salvation through grace alone, and on the structure and discipline of the church. After Calvin left Geneva, the religious situation there was uncertain for a time. Sadoleto, a bishop and cardinal in France, wrote a letter to the Genevans urging them to return to the Roman Catholic Church. In Calvin's reply, he argued that Rome had led people away from Scripture and away from the example of the early church; Rome was guilty of idolatry and of leading the flock of Christ astray.

Returning to Geneva in 1541, Calvin put into effect the reform of the church he had begun earlier. Unlike Luther, for whom the doctrine of justification by faith was the heart and soul of reform, Calvin saw reform of church structures as equally significant. Calvin rejected not only the pope but also the bishops. In place of a structure centered on the episcopacy, Calvin delineated four offices in the church: pastor, doctor, elder, deacon. These Calvin found in the New Testament and in the practices of the early church. Like Zwingli's reform in Zurich, Calvin's reform included also a zealous destruction of images considered idolatrous, and a rejection of the Mass as idolatry.

Calvin remained leader of the church in Geneva until his death in 1564. Dissent was not always tolerated: In 1553 Michael Servetus was executed for his denial of the doctrine of the Trinity. Church and city government worked together closely. Support for Calvin grew, and his influence spread from Geneva to parts of Switzerland and Germany, and especially to France, Holland, England, and Scotland. Education of clergy competent to expound Scripture and teach sound doctrine was a priority for Calvin: in 1559 he founded the Academy of Geneva for the purpose of such education. Moral standards were also promoted, with Geneva thus serving as an example of sound doctrine and sound discipline.

Today, the term "Reformed Church" commonly refers to a church that sees itself as in the tradition of Calvin's reform.

Thomas Worcester, s.j.

See also BEZA, THEODORE; CALVINISM; INSTITUTES OF THE CHRISTIAN RELIGION; PREDESTINATIONISM (CALVINIST); REFORMATION; REFORMED CHURCH; REFORMED THEOLOGY (-IES); ZWINGLI, ULRICH.

CALVINISM

The work of churches and individuals to perpetuate and spread the Reformation as implemented by John Calvin, Calvinism includes theological as well as political and social dimensions. If Luther's Reformation was adopted chiefly in parts of Germany and in neighboring Scandi-

navia, Calvin's model of reform was followed in a greater diversity of places.

Theology

Calvin's *Institutes of the Christian Religion*, along with his Scripture commentaries and other works, are the theological foundation of Calvinism. Prominent themes and/or principal doctrines are: the sovereignty, power, and glory of God; God's predestination of the elect for salvation; justification by faith alone; the symbolic presence of Christ in the Eucharist; the holy and disciplined lives of genuine Christians; the elimination of images considered idolatrous; the testimony of the Holy Spirit that confirms the true meaning of Scripture. Various confessions and statements of belief helped to articulate these doctrines and practices in a concise and catechetical form. The Helvetic Confessions of the mid-sixteenth century are among the earliest of Calvinist confessions; others followed.

By the early seventeenth century, the predestination of a disciplined and holy elect took a place of honor in many Calvinist summaries of doctrine; what became known as "Calvinist orthodoxy" highlighted God's predestination of some for salvation, and many for damnation. The possible means of distinguishing the elect from the non-elect (the "reprobate") was an inevitable question, albeit one that Calvin himself had not developed. Seventeenth-century Calvinists frequently looked to holiness of life for evidence of predestination.

Calvinist theology was challenged in the Enlightenment by a new emphasis on the goodness of all human beings and the beneficence of a God who desired salvation for all. If the nineteenth century saw continued dominance of Enlightenment theology in many Protestant churches, in the twentieth century there was a Calvinist revival. The most eloquent spokesperson for this return to "orthodoxy" was the Swiss theologian Karl Barth, though his theology excludes a doctrine of predestination to damnation.

Politics and Society

Churches tracing their spiritual roots to Calvin are known as Reformed Churches. In Calvin's Geneva, the church and the city government worked together closely to reform the church and to defend Geneva from the princes of Savoy who claimed it as part of their territory. In fact, in many places where the Reformed Church was established, its adherents were opponents of centralized power. Politically, Calvinism has been associated, from its origins, with movements seeking de-centralization and, at least to some degree, democratization of power. The Reformed Church itself is organized chiefly on the local level, without bishops, and with a considerable degree of authority reserved for the laity. This type of church government provided a useful model for those seeking reform of civil government in early modern Europe.

Historians also identify "Calvinist" contributions to social and economic developments. With its married clergy and its emphasis on order and discipline, moral probity, and exemplary lives, the Reformed Church may have helped to foster family life and the hard work necessary for economic growth. Max Weber, in *The Protestant Ethic and the Spirit of Capitalism*, draws connections between Calvinism and the advancement of capitalist economies since the sixteenth century. Nations where the Reformed Church was influential, such as Holland, led the way in creating a modern economy based on accumulation of capital. With salvation dependent solely on the eternal will of an inscrutable God, one could devote one's energies to earthly pursuits such as acquisition of wealth.

Geography

From Geneva, Calvinism spread rapidly, already in Calvin's own lifetime. The printing press was a particularly effective tool in this expansion, with Bibles in various languages, and editions of Calvin's writings providing the basis, in print, for church reform. In addition to Switzerland and Germany, Holland, England, Scotland, and Calvin's native France, soon had active Reformed Churches.

Calvinist theology and politics were at the heart of many conflicts in early modern Europe. From the 1560s to 1590s France was engulfed in the Wars of Religion between Catholics and Calvinists. Calvinists also played an important role in the Thirty Years War in central Europe from 1618 to 1648. Dutch Calvinists led the way in attaining Holland's independence from the Spanish empire. Puritans, another branch of Calvinists, were at the forefront of the English Civil War that led to the execution of King Charles I and (temporary) elimination of monarchy in seventeenth-century England. In Scotland the Reformed Church became the established church, thus marginalizing both Roman Catholics and Anglicans.

English and Dutch Calvinists brought the Reformed Church to what would later become the United States. From 1620, English Puritans strove to make Massachusetts a Christian commonwealth; Boston was to be a kind of new Geneva; the new world was imagined as a new Israel in which a new elect people had found its home. Politics and religion in the United States have always been informed, at least in part, by these ideas. Thus some understanding of Calvinism is essential for comprehension of U.S. history.

Thomas Worcester, s.j.

See also BARTH, KARL; BEZA, THEODORE; BUCER, MARTIN; CALVIN, JOHN; ENLIGHTENMENT IN WESTERN HISTORY; HELVETIC CONFESSIONS; INSTITUTES OF THE CHRISTIAN RELIGION; KNOX, JOHN; OCHINO, BERNARDINO; PETER MARTYR (REFORMER); PREDESTINATIONISM (CALVINIST); PROTESTANTISM; PURITANISM; REFORMATION; REFORMED CHURCH; REFORMED THEOLOGY (-IES); WEBER, (KARL EMIL MAXIMILIAN) MAX.

CAMUS, ALBERT (1913–60)

French writer and philosopher. Born in French-occupied Algeria, he went to mainland France in 1938, and soon became a member of the Resistance against the Nazis. His writings conveyed a sense of despair and absurdity, rejecting both Christianity and Marxist communism. He is usually placed within the philosophical currents of existentialism. He had immense influence over a generation of Christian theologians attempting to answer his philosophical, existential challenge. Camus died in an automobile accident. He had received the Nobel Prize for literature. His more important writings are *The Myth of Sisyphus* (1942), *The Stranger* (1946), *The Plague* (1948), and *The Fall* (1951).

Orlando Espín

See also EXISTENTIALISM; IDEOLOGY (IDEOLOGIES); MARCEL, GABRIEL; MARXISM; MODERNITY; POSTMODERNITY; SARTRE, JEAN PAUL; SECULARIZATION/SECULAR/SECULARIZED.

CANAAN

A grandson of Noah who is a son of Ham. Because of his father's indiscretion, Canaan is cursed and destined to be a slave (Gen 9:25). The genealogy in Genesis 10 includes Canaan and suggests that he and his brothers represent peoples in the ancient Near East, for example, Put (Libya), Cush (Ethiopia), and Mizraim (Egypt). Canaan, then, is also the land of the Canaanite people, the land that would later become Israel.

The Canaanites are a people despised by the Israelites. In fact, because of what the Israelites considered evil religious practices, Israel would obliterate them. According to Deuteronomy 20:16-18, the Israelites are to exterminate all the peoples in the cities of those nations the Lord is giving them as an inheritance, including the Canaanites, "lest they teach you to make any such abominable offerings as they make to their gods, and you thus sin against the Lord, your God."

Canaanite religion emphasized sexuality and fertility. Because of the Canaanites' dependence on agriculture, and the dependence of a successful harvest on rain, the Canaanite storm god Baal was central to their pantheon. Fertility rites were central to religious practice; if the gods and goddesses mated successfully, then there was hope that the people and the cattle and the crops would produce many offspring.

Historical scholars today would posit that many of the Canaanites became Israelites. According to one theory of how the Hebrews/Israelites came to possess Canaan, the process was long and slow. The Hebrews slowly immigrated into the land, at first inhabiting the uninhabited and least desirable land, all the while professing faith in the God who brought them out of bondage. Those people were soon joined by Canaanites who were themselves oppressed in their own city-states and to whom a God who brings out of bondage was quite attractive. It has even been suggested that most of the people who became Israel were Canaanites; the profession of faith to a God who brings out of slavery was the unifying energy in creating the people Israel.

Alice L. Laffey

See also ISRAEL.

CÁNCER DE BARBASTRO, LUIS (1504–49)

Spanish missionary and member of the Dominican Order. In 1549 he led a small group of Dominicans from Mexico and Guatemala to the Tampa Bay area of Florida. Their intention was to establish contact with and evangelize natives who had not been antagonized by earlier Spanish armed incursions. Four Dominicans were killed by hostile natives (clearly for religious reasons), thereby becoming the first Christian martyrs to die in present-day United States territory.

Orlando Espín

See also DOMINICANS; LATIN AMERICAN CATHOLICISM; LATINO CATHOLICISM; MISSIONARIES; MISSIONS.

CANDLES, LIGHTING OF

The lighting of candles, now a largely symbolic gesture, was a practical one in the ancient world. Having no electrical lighting, families lighted candles or oil lamps each evening. During the lamp-lighting, Christians prayed and sang hymns in praise of Jesus, the light of the world. This custom survives in the lighting of the paschal candle at the Easter Vigil, and in a similar ceremony called "lucernarium" sometimes used at Evening Prayer. Christians may have used lighted candles even at daytime liturgies as early as the second century. By the fourth century, they certainly did, perhaps in imitation of the Romans who used candles during imperial ceremonies, no matter what time of day. In the thirteenth century, it became customary to keep a lamp constantly burning near the place where the Blessed Sacrament was kept in the church.

Patrick L. Malloy

See also EASTER TRIDUUM.

CANDOMBLÉ

Name of an important Brazilian religion of West African roots. Candomblé is a descendant of the traditional Yoruba religion of Nigeria. The experience and realities of slavery forced some modifications and, more significantly, some simplifications of the Yoruba traditions. Candomblé is found in many Brazilian states, but especially in Bahia. It has begun to spread to other South American countries. Afro-Cuban *Santería* is its sister religion, and very similar (differences between the two are superficial). However, Candomblé is different from and substantially unrelated to another Brazilian religion called Umbanda. It has little connection with Haitian Vodoun, or with Macumba.

Orlando Espín

See also AFRICAN TRADITIONAL RELIGIONS; MACUMBA; PALO MAYOMBE; SANTERÍA; UMBANDA; VODOUN.

CANDRAKIRTI (600–50 C.E.)

A monk who shaped Mahayana philosophical discourse, whose interpretation of Madhyamaka doctrine founded the influential Prasanghika school. In the *Prasannapada*, his commentary on Nagarjuna's *Madhyamakakarika*, Candrakirti argues that the proper understanding of the Buddha's teachings on causality is that it is only a provisional teaching; for him, too, "empty" must also be applied even to the dual construct "ultimate"/ "conventional existence." His *Madhyama-kavatara* and its commentary were also influential in articulating how to integrate Mahayana spiritual practices with the emptiness doctrine: reality must be found in going beyond all verbal and mental constructs. Here, too, Candrakirti articulates the path of the bodhisattva as one who realizes this, yet works compassionately to have others see reality clearly. These works became the "official" sources for later Tibetan academic studies of Madhyamaka philosophy.

Todd T. Lewis

See also MADHYAMAKA/MADHYAMIKA SCHOOL; MAHAYANA BUDDHISM; NAGARJUNA.

CANISIUS, PETER (1521–97)

Jesuit preacher, teacher, catechist, and administrator, Canisius was perhaps the most significant figure in the German-speaking Counter-Reformation. Born in Holland, the young Canisius undertook theological studies in Cologne and Mainz. He then entered the Society of Jesus and was soon actively promoting a Catholic revival in Prague, Bavaria, and Austria. As provincial superior of the Jesuits, he founded colleges in Augsburg, Innsbruck, Munich. He also composed several catechisms designed for various age groups and intellectual capacities that went through many editions and were translated into several languages. Canisius was canonized as a saint in 1925.

Thomas Worcester, S.J.

See also COUNTER-REFORMATION/ CATHOLIC REFORMATION; SOCIETY OF JESUS; TRENT, COUNCIL OF.

CANNON, KATIE GENEVA (1950–)

Ordained Presbyterian minister, womanist ethicist. Born and raised in segregated Kannapolis, North Carolina, Cannon was educated in the elementary schools in Kannapolis, attended Barber Scotia College, and Atlanta's Interdenominational Theological Seminary. Cannon is the first African American woman to receive the doctoral degree in ethics (1989) from Union Theological Seminary and, currently, is tenured associate professor of Christian social ethics at Temple University in Philadelphia.

An internationally recognized educator, ethicist, and lecturer, Cannon is the author of two books and more than fifty book chapters and journal articles. Her theological research and writing focuses on womanist ethics and explores such topics as slave ideology and biblical interpretation, moral wisdom in the black women's literary tradition, and appropriation and reciprocity in womanist ethics. Cannon leads the Womanist Approaches to Religion and Society group at the American Academy of Religion, and is an elected member of the Society for the Study of Black Religion.

M. Shawn Copeland

See also BLACK THEOLOGY; WOMANIST THEOLOGY.

CANO, MELCHOR (1509–60)

Spanish theologian, and member of the Dominican Order. He became (1543) the first professor of theology at the University of Alcalá, and in 1546 succeeded his teacher Francisco de Vitoria as professor in Salamanca. Cano was very active at the Council of Trent, especially in the debates concerning the sacraments of reconciliation and Eucharist. He was adamantly opposed to the Jesuits, and quite involved in the Spanish ecclesiastical politics of his day. His best-known work is *De locis theologicis*, published in 1563, three years after his death. Cano has today come to be understood better for his contributions to ecclesiology and to the theology of Tradition.

Orlando Espín

See also DOMINICANS; EUCHARIST; RECONCILIATION, SACRAMENT OF; SOCIETY OF JESUS; TRENT, COUNCIL OF; VITORIA, FRANCISCO DE.

CANON, BIBLICAL

Canon is derived from the Greek word *kanon* meaning "rule." The Greek may be related to the Semitic form *qaneh* meaning "reed," but in developed usage referred to a measure or rule. The term canon came to be applied within Christianity to those writings that contained the rule of faith and the authentic teaching of the apostles. As used in this sense, canon refers to lists of writings that were considered authentic, or sacred. The idea of canon developed slowly, but was given a major impetus in the second century C.E. by the position and writings of Marcion who argued for a much reduced and heavily edited list of sacred writings. The resulting controversy led to the eventual establishment of a canon of Scripture that was shared by many Christians. Within Christianity the so-called "Old Testament" or the inherited Scriptures became the first section of the canon. The second section was and is made up of Christian writings. There was little further discussion of canon within Christianity until the Protestant Reformation. The Reformers chose to return to an Old Testament canon that was identical in content, although not in order, with the authoritative collection of Judaism. In response, at the Council of Trent, the Catholic Church reiterated the inspired nature of those books the Reformers had rejected and also were not contained in the Jewish Bible.

Russell Fuller

CANON, LITERARY

In the twentieth century, scholars in humanities disciplines have adapted the religious notion of canon (mainly used to identify a list of sacred books recognized as authoritative by a believing community), employing it in an extended sense to describe the list of literary works recognized as significant by the academic community for inclusion in the educational curriculum. Beginning in the 1980s, the literary canon came to be the focus of intense debate in the United States because, as John Guillory points out, "In recent years many literary critics have become convinced that the selection of literary texts for 'canonization' (the selection of what are conventionally called the 'classics') operates in a way very much like the formation of the biblical canon. These critics detect beneath the supposed objectivity of value judgments a political agenda: the exclusion of many groups of people from representation in the literary canon" ("Canon," 233).

According to Charles Taylor, "The main locus of this debate is the world of education in a broad sense. One important focus is university humanities departments, where demands are made to alter, enlarge, or scrap the 'canon' of accredited authors on the grounds that the one presently favored consists almost entirely of 'dead white males.' A greater place ought to be made for women, and for people of non-European races and cultures" ("The Politics of Recognition," 97). Recognizing that canons serve to exclude (whether consciously or unconsciously) as well as include, to discredit as well as validate, critics voiced grave concern that the conventional canon of European and North American literature left out many authors and their works on the basis of gender and race, leaving literature by women and persons of non-European descent beyond the margins of the higher educational curriculum. They contend that such exclusion has serious political ramifications and that even the notion of a literary canon is in urgent need of rethinking in the direction of greater openness and flexibility.

The analogy between the biblical canon and the canon of literary "classics" breaks down when it is recognized that the academy does not provide the secular literary canon with the permanence that the authority of the church guarantees for the biblical canon. The literary canon is necessarily open-ended and flexible. Frank Kermode writes that "Canons . . . which are instruments of survival built to be time-proof, not reason-proof, are of course deconstructible; if people think there should not be such things, they may well find the means to destroy them. Their defense cannot any longer be undertaken by central institutional power; they cannot any longer be compulsory, though it is hard to see how the normal operation of learned institutions, including recruitment, can manage without them" (*Forms of Attention*, 78). Addressing himself to the difference between the notion of literary canon and the biblical/religious use of the term, Harold Bloom notes, "The Canon, once we view it as the relation of an individual reader and writer to what has been preserved out of what has been written, and forget the canon as a list of books for required study, will be seen as identical with the literary Art of Memory,

not with the religious sense of canon" (*The Western Canon*, 17).

The debate over the literary canon and its contents has generated heated polemic both from its critics and from its defenders, with each group taking sides in these "culture wars" involving feminism and multiculturalism. At opposite ends of the very broad spectrum of argument we find on the one hand those defenders of the conventional canon who hold that inclusion and exclusion depend solely on the intrinsic, enduring worth of a literary work. At the other extreme we find those critics of the canon who maintain that selection takes place according to the political interests of those who belong to particular social groups (either those who seek to maintain the status quo or those who seek to challenge and transform it).

Beyond the polemical fallout generated by arguments between right and left over the shape of the literary canon, the debate has produced some positive results. Among the most significant of these outcomes has been the proliferation of new academic departments and programs reflective of the ever-increasing heterogeneity of contemporary society, and attentive to the ever more diverse literature being generated and read both within and beyond the academy.

Jean-Pierre Ruiz

See also CANON, BIBLICAL; CULTURE; LITERARY CRITICISM.

CANONICAL CRITICISM

Canonical criticism has been used to designate two critical approaches introduced in the late 1970s. One was devised by Brevard Childs, the other by James A. Sanders. Both distinguish the canonical process from the canonical text, avoid investing the earliest layer of tradition with the greatest authority, and identify with the function rather than the formation of the canon, but their foundational premises, methods, and goals are different. Childs seeks to determine the theological thrust in each book of the Bible that is established by its canonical form. Sanders seeks to determine the insights that gave shape to a canonical text through every stage of its formation—from oral traditions to stabilized texts as well as its subsequent use in believing communities.

According to Childs, canonical texts incorporate their own interpretation. While his approach is called canonical criticism, Childs himself resists the term "criticism" in order to distance what he considers his "holistic reading" from any historical and literary methods or contemporary theories of interpretation. Until the Reformation, no one looked for the principles of interpretation of the Bible in the Bible, but Childs is convinced that the individual books provide an authoritative "inner theological dialectic" that discloses how they should be understood. Although Childs invests the Masoretic Text with more authority than text critics allow and isolates canonical books from the history of their formation, his approach is a useful corrective to those who turn the biblical witness into an archaeological tell or the focus of research comprehensible only by scholars.

Sanders considers his understanding of canonical criticism the next stage in the development in critical methodologies. He recognizes that each canonical text is the product of a long history of oral and written transmission during which traditions were repeatedly reshaped and adapted to new and changing needs of the community. This process of re-presentation introduced varying degrees of multivalency into traditions as they were adapted to new situations. Thus, in turn, multivalency became a quality of the traditions themselves making other applications possible. While Sanders claims that traditions that survived and were used only did so because they were adaptable to new circumstances, he overstates his case, since some degree of chance must be acknowledged. However, Sanders rightly recognizes that once the traditions were set in written form, they were portable and thus indestructible. For Jew, the canonical process insured their survival as community after they had neither the land nor the Temple.

Sanders identifies five hermeneutical tendencies that shaped the canon as a whole. (1) It preserves monotheizing literature that incorporates (2) a broad theocentric hermeneutic and (3) a tendency to illustrate how God's grace works in and through human sinfulness, since many of the events are ultimately consequences of human failures. In addition, (4) the traditions that were preserved have a tendency to portray God as one who identifies with the poor and the powerless, although there is not a pervasive divine bias for the weak and dispossessed. Finally, (5) the wisdom of others that could be depolytheized, monotheized, Yahwized, and Israelitized was adapted and resignified by the canonical process.

For Sanders there is a clear connection between the historical process of canon formation and continued re-application of the Bible in the ongoing life of the synagogue and the church. His appreciation of a continuing canonical process makes Sanders' method compatible with other methods that take either a literary or historical approach and is most amenable to a critical study of lectionaries.

Regina A. Boisclair

CANONICAL FORM
(OF MARRIAGE)

A term referring to the required manner for entering into a valid marriage according to Roman Catholic canon law. The current legal requirements for the Latin rite are found in The Code of Canon Law (1983), Canons 1108–1123. Ordinarily the canonical form of marriage for a Roman Catholic is marital consent expressed before the local ordinary, the parish priest, or another priest or deacon delegated by either of them, in the presence of two other witnesses. In order for the marriage to be valid, the one assisting at the marriage (ordinary, that is, the diocesan bishop or priest with ordinary jurisdiction over a territory, parish priest, or priest or deacon delegated by either of them) must ask for the consent and receive it in the name of the church (Can. 1108). Exceptions include the following: the delegation of suitable laypersons to assist at marriage under special circumstances (Can. 1112); consent can be exchanged in the presence of only two witnesses for a valid and lawful marriage when there is danger of death, or when one competent by law to assist at the marriage cannot be present or be approached without grave inconvenience, when it is foreseen that this situation will continue for a month (Can. 1116); a Catholic can enter a valid (although unlawful without permission) marriage to a non-Catholic of an Oriental church provided it is with the "intervention of a sacred minister," that is, it is celebrated according to the norms of the Oriental church (Can. 1127:1); for serious reason, the local ordinary can dispense a Catholic marrying a non-Catholic from the canonical form of marriage provided that the marriage is celebrated in some public form (Can. 1127:2). This legislation, with its broader possibilities of exception, deports from the narrower and revolutionary Tridentine decree *Tametsi* of 1563, which, for the first time, required that for validity a Catholic be married before the local ordinary, pastor, or a priest delegated by either them, and two witnesses.

The valid form of marriage has not always been so narrowly construed. The earliest evidence through the early fourth century indicates that Christians married according to local (civil) custom, cleansed of anything superstitious or inappropriate for Christians. The fact that both were baptized made their marriage holy, one undertaken "in the Lord." Roman practice had included many customs, such as the exchange of dowry and wedding rings, the carrying of the bride over the threshold, the bride's eating of a wedding bread (later to become the wedding cake) in the home of her husband, and so on. In the midst of confusion as to what made the marriage legal and binding (especially for purposes of property and inheritance rights), the pagan emperor Diocletian (284–305) decreed that consent of the parties or of their parents made the marriage valid. This was later repeated in the Code of Justinian (529), a Christian emperor, and has been a great influence on Christian practice to this day.

Some early Christian writers advise consultation with or even permission from the bishop before marrying, especially for marriage of clerics or catechumens. The first indication of a Christian ceremony is only from the mid-fourth century, and consists of a clerical blessing at the end of what is in actuality a civil and domestic affair. A century later, in Rome, we find the first evidence of a wedding associated with the celebration of the Eucharist. The vast majority of Christian marriages, however, continued to be celebrated according to local custom that varied greatly according to geography: the handing over (*traditio*) of the bride (in a sense owned) by her father or guardian among the Germans; the purchase of the bride among the Anglo-Saxons; the exchange of gifts (negotiation of the dowry of the bride and groom's endowment to the bride) among the Franks; or in some places the beginning of cohabitation or the birth of a child if there was no dowry. These practices, especially of treating the bride as virtual chattel, came into conflict with the Roman practice of consent as the only required element. This emphasis on consent was often abused since it easily allowed for secret weddings. These were frequently forbidden by law, but nevertheless considered valid. Secret marriages often went against parental authority, allowed couples to cohabit under pretense of a secret marriage, or led to a second marriage even though one was already secretly married. From the ninth through the thirteenth centuries, the church enacted more and more laws regarding marriage, especially regarding the abuses of secret marriage, and in practice integrated many transalpine customs with consent, and eventually included the necessity of consummation for a marriage to be complete (and indissoluble). By the twelfth century, most marriages were conducted on the porch of the church (*in facie ecclesiae*) and included the priest's inquiry about consent, the exchange (or reading of a list) of the dowry, the handing over of the bride, the blessing and giving of a ring to the bride, and the groom's giving of gold or silver coins (*arrhae*) to the bride as a sign of support. If a nuptial Mass was celebrated, the bridal party entered the church bearing candles, and gave an offering at the offertory; the priest gave the bride the nuptial blessing after she was veiled (the veil was laid on the head of the bride and on the shoulders of the groom). In many places the priest's blessing of the bridal chamber and the enclosing of the couple followed in an effort to ensure the completion of marriage through consummation.

In the Oriental churches, by the fifth century and perhaps earlier, it was customary to marry before a priest. The nuptial blessing, and especially the crowning of the couple, came to be viewed as very important, and by the ninth century was required for validity in the Byzantine tradition. Consent was presumed present by the fact of the liturgical ceremony alone. Nor was any importance attached to the juridical status of the priest, suffice that he blessed (consecrated by invoking the Holy Spirit) and crowned the couple. Eastern churches in union with Rome gradually came to include an explicit exchange of consent out of influence from the West and direction from the papacy.

The churches of the Reformation, while generally accepting a civil marriage as valid, for the most part have developed wedding ceremonies that include many of the traditional Western elements. (For a good summary of the forms used for marriage in the various Protestant churches see "Marriage" in J. C. Davies, ed., *The New Westminster Dictionary of Liturgy and Worship* (Philadelphia: Westminster Press, 1986) 349–64.

Dennis W. Krouse

See also ANNULMENT; DIVORCE (IN CHRISTIANITY); INDISSOLUBILITY; MARRIAGE IN CATHOLIC PERSPECTIVE; PAULINE PRIVILEGE; PETRINE PRIVILEGE.

CANONIZATION

In the Roman Catholic Church, it is the official declaration, made by a pope, that a deceased member of the church (already beatified) is indeed sharing in eternal glory. The usual consequence of this declaration is that the person so canonized is henceforth venerated as a saint throughout the whole church. The Orthodox churches also have a process of canonization, but the official declaration of sainthood is usually made by the synods of bishops.

In the early church, the custom of venerating admirable deceased Christians began the veneration given the martyrs. After the fourth century, it was extended to others who had not been martyred. During the early Middle Ages, the popes began to demand, because of local abuses, that certain requirements be observed before declaring that someone could be venerated as a saint. Today the process of canonization is long, thorough, and demanding.

Orlando Espín

See also BEATIFICATION; SAINT; SAINTS (CHRISTIAN), DEVOTION TO; POPE.

CANON LAW
Canon law refers to the code of laws that govern the Roman Catholic Church. Originating in the twelfth century as Gratian's Decrees, the legal rulings of the church were not codified into a coherent system until 1917. The Second Vatican Council mandated a revision of canon law which was accomplished in 1983.

Mary Ann Hinsdale

See also GRATIAN.

CANON OF THE MASS
The word canon, derived from the Greek (*kanón*, measuring stick or ruler), refers to "that which measures up" or is fixed and approved; in this case, the consecratory or eucharistic prayer (anaphora) of the Roman Rite Mass, also known as the Roman Canon. It is an obsolete term refer-

ring to what is now known in the Roman rite as Eucharistic Prayer I of the *Roman Missal* (1969). There are various opinions regarding the origin and the apparently unique style of this anaphora. It shows some structural similarities to eucharistic prayers of Alexandrian (Egyptian) origin and linguistically was influenced by the Latin usage of the imperial Roman court. It was probably based on an earlier Greek eucharistic prayer and came into Latin usage in the fourth century under the vernacularization of Roman liturgy by Pope Damasus I. It is quoted in a related form by St. Ambrose (d. 397) in his *De Sacramentis*. Pope Gregory I (590–604) further modified it, giving it substantially the form it has today. Some of its earliest extant occurrences are in the Gelasian and Gregorian Sacramentaries, the Bobbio Missal, and the *Missale Francorum*.

Since the Roman prefaces were variable, the canon or fixed prayer was understood to begin with the *Te igitur* which immediately follows the *Sanctus* ("Holy") and continues through the *Per ipsum* ("Through him, with him") with the assenting Amen of the people (Great Amen). The canon itself was viewed as a series of prayers often concluded with *"per Christum Dominum nostrum. Amen"* ("through Christ our Lord. Amen"), with the words of institution as the central apex of the series. From the late eighth or early ninth century the Roman Canon was prayed silently with the exception of three words, *Nobis quoque peccatoribus* ("For us sinners also"), and the conclusion to the doxology, *per omnia saecula saeculorum*. Since 1967, as a result of the initial liturgical reforms of the Second Vatican Council, the canon was once again to be recited or chanted aloud. Since 1969, options in the use of the Roman Canon have given greater literary unity to the prayer by allowing the omission of prayer conclusions within the text and an abbreviation of the two listings of the saints.

It is especially significant that the Roman Canon was almost universally the only eucharistic prayer in the West for well over a millennium, unlike other rites that have had a variety of eucharistic prayers to choose from. However, in the *Roman Missal* of 1969 are added three other eucharistic prayers. Since that time in the United States two Eucharistic Prayers for Reconciliation, three Eucharistic Prayers for Masses with Children, and four Eucharistic Prayers for Various Needs and Occasions have been added to the Sacramentary. Other national conferences have additional eucharistic prayers available. In recent years the International Committee on English in the Liturgy (ICEL) prepared other eucharistic prayers for English-speaking Catholics of the Latin rite. These need approval from episcopal conferences and confirmation by the Vatican, which does not seem to be forthcoming in the near future.

Dennis W. Krouse

See also ANAPHORA; EUCHARIST; EUCHARISTIC PRAYER; MASS.

CANTERBURY, SEE OF

The chief diocese of the Church of England, founded by St. Augustine of Canterbury in 597 and located about fifty-five miles southeast of London. As such, it is also the see of the archbishop of Canterbury, who symbolizes and promotes the unity of the Anglican Communion and is held as "first among equals" among the Communion's bishops.

Augustine chose Canterbury over London since it was the city of the Christian king Ethelbert, who reigned over the most powerful Anglo-Saxon realm of the time. The site of the cathedral, Christ Church, has been used for worship since Augustine's time. Now, however, the principal residence of the archbishop of Canterbury is Lambeth Palace in London, although he also retains one at Canterbury.

In 753 York became the second metropolitan see in England, but in 802–3 the pope and a provincial council established the supremacy of Canterbury. Thus, its archbishop is Primate of All England. Prior to the English Reformation, he commonly served also as papal legate to the Church in England. As this church spread throughout the world, he became the focus of unity for the emerging worldwide Anglican Communion. As such, he convokes the Lambeth Conference roughly every decade. His decisions, like those of the conference, must be adopted by each region or province of the Anglican Communion to become binding there.

Canterbury's unbroken line of more than 100 archbishops is notable for men of extraordinary ability and holiness, for example, Stephen Langton, St. Thomas à Becket, St. Anselm, Thomas Cranmer, Robert Hugh Benson, William Temple, and Michael Ramsey.

Like other Anglican dioceses, Canterbury is governed by clerical and lay representatives with the archbishop presiding. From the beginning, synods of clergy or their representatives played an influential role in English church life. These meetings, known as the Convocations of Canterbury, continue today, although their proceedings have become more formal than substantive.

Jon Nilson

See also ANGLICAN COMMUNION; CANTERBURY, CONVOCATIONS OF; PRIMATE/PRIMATIAL SEE; RAMSEY, ARTHUR MICHAEL.

CANTOR (IN CHRISTIANITY)

From the Latin *cantare*, to sing: the leader of congregational song, and the singer of solo parts of liturgical services. During the first Christian centuries, liturgical roles seem to have been shared so fully that there was no ministry equivalent to that of a cantor. By the fourth century, however, Christians in the East and the West began to rely on specially trained singers to lead—and sometimes to replace—the congregation in singing. Women were generally excluded from these musical leadership roles. As the music of the liturgy became more and more complex, ordinary worshipers were increasingly excluded from most liturgical singing. Then, when King Pepin (714–68) and Emperor Charlemagne (ca. 742–814) imposed the Latin-language Roman liturgy on the entire realm, people in non-Latin-speaking northern Europe found themselves worshiping in a language they did not understand. This affected the sung as well as the recited parts of worship, further rendering the worshipers silent. Music for worship was provided by the cantor (a solo singer) and the *schola cantorum* or choir. This pattern continued in the Roman Catholic tradition through most of its history. One of the aims of the liturgical movement, however, and of the Second Vatican Council, has been the full, active, and conscious participation of the entire church in liturgical worship, including liturgical music. The role of the cantor has been revived and rehabilitated as one tool for encouraging and enabling such participation. While in an earlier day the cantor may have usurped the musical role of the other worshipers, the cantor's role in today's liturgy is quite the opposite. The 1972 American document, *Music in Catholic Worship*, portrays the cantor as one who leads, but does not replace, the song of the entire assembly. "While there is no place in the liturgy for display or virtuosity for its own sake, artistry is valued, and an individual singer can effectively lead the assembly and attractively proclaim the Word of God in the psalm sung between the readings, and take his or her part in other responsorial singing" (no. 35). The document goes on to quote the Vatican document *Musicam Sacram*, which says that each church should have one or two cantors to carry out this ministry in collaboration with a choir or, in some cases, in place of one (*Musicam Sacram*, no. 21).

Patrick L. Malloy

See also MINISTRY/MINISTERIAL; RESPONSORIAL PSALM.

CANTOR (IN JUDAISM)

(Hebrew, *chazzan*). In Judaism, the clerical officiant who chants the liturgy in the synagogue. In Talmudic times, the title *chazzan* referred to a community leader in general; in early medieval times it came to connote a permanent prayer leader, the need for which developed in response to the growing complexity of the liturgical tradition and the decline in the general public's knowledge of Hebrew. Since the *chazzan* represented the community in prayer, the position was viewed as extremely important and often was held by highly regarded rabbis. From the earliest period, a chief qualification of the *chazzan* was a pleasant voice. This aspect of the position has grown in importance in the nineteenth and twentieth centuries, as the cantorial repertoire has been increasingly influenced by European musical trends. In this period, cantors have gained high regard for their vocal skills as well as for their piety and knowledge of Jewish tradition.

Today, individuals trained in schools of sacred music at the seminaries of the Reform, Conservative, and Orthodox movements are invested by those movements as cantors. ("Investment" of a cantor is parallel to "ordination" of a rabbi.) Judaism, however, does not require that its liturgy be chanted by such a cantor. Accordingly, within all three movements, liturgical rites frequently are chanted by lay leaders or by professionals who have not received formal training and investment. Such individuals are referred to as *chazzan, shaliach tzibbur* (literally, "representative of the community"), or, in the Reform movement in particular, as "cantorial soloist"; by contrast, the English title "cantor," is normally reserved for those who have been invested by a seminary. In traditional forms of Judaism, only men are permitted to lead the congregation in prayer; today, in the contemporary Reform movement and in most Conservative synagogues, women as well may receive this honor.

Alan J. Avery-Peck

CAPITAL PUNISHMENT

The United States is the only Western nation to execute its citizens, with thirty-eight states allowing capital punishment.

The death penalty has been traditionally supported in Catholic teaching as one of several exceptions to the prohibition against taking human life. Since the early 1980s, however, efforts by U.S. Catholic bishops to link opposition to war, euthanasia, abortion, and capital punishment in a "consistent ethic of life" have strengthened critical views against capital punishment. A "consistent ethic of life" teaching is particularly the work of Cardinal Joseph Bernardin who chaired the committee that prepared the 1983 bishops' pastoral,

"Challenge of Peace: God's Promise and Our Response," that links opposition to abortion with capital punishment.

Since this time there has been increased Catholic visibility in opposing the death penalty, including the 1995 encyclical by John Paul II, *Evangelium Vitae* ("Gospel of Life") that strongly condemns abortion, euthanasia, and capital punishment. The fundamental right to human life applies to the unborn as well as to those convicted of the most heinous crimes.

Mary E. Hobgood

See also JUST WAR THEORY.

CAPPADOCIANS

The "Cappadocians" were three fourth-century saints and theologians who came from the Roman province of Cappadocia (now in modern Turkey). The eldest was Basil, bishop of Caesaria in Cappadocia (b. ca. 330; d. 379). Basil received an excellent eduction with hopes of entering the Roman government. He gave up his career, however, to lead a monastic life. He was elected bishop of Caesarea in 370 and spent the rest of his life defending orthodoxy against the claims of the Arians. Basil was also an excellent administrator and organized the monastic communities in Turkey. Gregory, bishop of Nyssa (b. ca. 335/40; d. after 394) was the younger brother of Basil and was educated by Basil and his learned sister, Macrina. Gregory married and originally practiced law as a Roman rhetor. In 371 he was consecrated bishop of Nyssa, and after the death of his brother assumed the leadership in defending the orthodox faith against the Arians. Much in demand as a preacher, he traveled a great deal in his later years. The third of the Cappadocians was Gregory Nazianzus. Born around 330, Gregory was the son of the bishop of Nazianzus in Cappadocia. He was a fellow student of Basil of Caesarea in Athens. Gregory followed Basil of Caesarea into the monastery. Truly of a monastic spirit, Gregory was ordained and became bishop of the small village of Sasima in 372, but only under duress. He never even visited Sasima, but helped his father in Nazianzus until his father died in 374. In 379 Gregory attended the Council of Constantinople, where he was elected patriarch, but resigned after the council, returning to the monastic life until his death in 389. These three writers, although best known for their defense of orthodoxy against the Arians, also produced scriptural commentaries, sermons, and theological treatises. They are three of the most influential theologians in Greek Christianity.

Gary Macy

See also ARIANISM; BASIL THE GREAT; CONSTANTINOPLE, FIRST COUNCIL OF; GREGORY NAZIANZUS; GREGORY OF NYSSA; MACRINA; MONASTICISM IN EASTERN CHRISTIANITY.

CARDINAL

A title bestowed today usually (but not always) on about 120 bishops of the Catholic Church. All cardinals are appointed by the pope and serve as his advisors and main assistants in the central administration of the church. Some cardinals reside in Rome and work at the Vatican, while others are bishops of dioceses throughout the world. Cardinals are the electors who choose the pope, but they are not allowed to vote after they turn eighty years old. The term "College of Cardinals" is frequently used to refer to the whole group of the cardinals as a single corporate body.

Orlando Espín

See also BISHOP (EPISCOPACY); CONSISTORY; CURIA, ROMAN; DIOCESE/ ARCHDIOCESE; PETRINE MINISTRY; POPE.

CARGO CULTS

A Melanesian religious movement whose participants awaited the arrival of an abundance of goods and a utopian society. Cargo cults were named for their focus on the acquisition of Western goods that were introduced by missionaries, traders, and colonists. In the pidgin English of New Guinea, cargo is the word for trade goods. But it also came to signify a fair, just, and equal world in which all people, including indigenous natives, would ultimately partake of material well-being.

Cargo cults were prevalent in Melanesia after the first colonial contact. A cult emerged in Irian Jaya in 1860 and in 1877 a cult in Fiji in which a reversal of the roles of the British and the indigenous people was prophesied. In 1931, on Buka in the Solomon Islands, a native religious cult with particular characteristics emerged. Prophets predicted that a deluge would engulf the white settlers. This event would be followed by the arrival of a ship with European goods that would belong to the natives. Believers in the prophesy began to construct a storehouse for the anticipated goods. Because they believed that the ship would arrive only when they had depleted their own supplies, they stopped working in their fields. The leaders of the cult were arrested but similar movements continued for some years. Cults declined after the independence of most Melanesian countries happened in the 1970s and 1980s; some movements developed into independent churches.

The activity in the Solomon Islands was not an isolated incident. Other similar movements that have promised the resurrection of the dead, the destruction of Europeans, the coming of utopian riches, and the return of a more harmonious and just past have arisen sporadically throughout Melanesia, Africa, and the Americas since the beginning of the twentieth century. Interestingly, cults that are separate in terms of the time, location, and cultures involved share a number of similar characteristics. The emergence of such beliefs and practices is linked to a similar pattern of social conditions, most typically that of rapid social, economic, and religious change. For example, the uprooting of traditional cultures of indigenous peoples and the introduction of Christianity during periods of colonial expansion are precursors to cargo cults. The presence of Europeans or European-influenced natives with power also stimulates the development of cargo cults as a rational means within a religious perspective of reality of attempting to alter inequities in wealth and power. Natives became aware of their lack of political and economic power in relationship to Europeans as they were employed in unloading, storing, and distributing Western-made goods with no hope of attaining such products for themselves. When frustration about the disparity between social groups escalates and there is no other hope of bringing about change, religion offers a solution. Such belief systems have been common in a variety of cultures. For example, the revitalization movements in Papua, New Guinea, were tied to a belief that Western goods are produced by supernatural forces. Cargo cults combined elements of indigenous beliefs, Christianity, and encounters with modern technology. Movements such as the Ghost Dance Religion among Native Americans in the United States share many features in common with cargo cults and other nativistic, millenarian, or revitalization cults.

Christine Greenway

See also GHOST DANCE; MILLENARIANISM; SACRIFICE; SHAMAN; THEOCRACY.

CARMELITES

A religious order founded in the twelfth century by a group of Christian hermits living in the Holy Land. The name comes from Mount Carmel in northern Palestine, not far from the modern city of Haifa and about twenty miles west of Nazareth. The Carmelites tried to maintain their essentially eremitical lifestyle, even as they spread into Europe, but the changing social circumstances of the Middle Ages and the pastoral needs of the church forced them to become actively engaged in teaching, preaching, and sacramental ministry. They thus developed into a mendicant order.

While there is no special founding personality among the Carmelites, the biblical figures of Elijah (the legendary prophet who dramatically proved on Mount Carmel the hollowness of the god Baal [1 Kings 18]) and Mary, the mother of Jesus, have played major roles in the development of Carmelite spirituality, which tends to be deeply contemplative and mystical. In the sixteenth century, a major reform movement took place among the Carmelites through the inspiration and guidance of Teresa of Avila and John of the Cross, the two saints who it might be said refounded the order.

William Reiser, s.j.

See also JOHN OF THE CROSS.

CARR, ANNE (1934–)

Anne E. Carr, B.V.M., was born in Chicago, Illinois. She received her Ph.D. from the

University of Chicago Divinity School, where she wrote a thesis on the method of theologian Karl Rahner. A feminist theologian, she has been active in Concilium, an international group of scholars committed to post–Vatican II theological trends. Her book *Transforming Grace* (1988) is one of the first systematic expositions of Christian feminist theology.

Mary Ann Hinsdale

See also FEMINIST THEOLOGIES; RAHNER, KARL.

CARRASCO, DAVID (1949–)

Historian of religions and one of the foremost scholars of Mesoamerican religions and cultures. After earning the doctorate at the University of Chicago, he taught at the University of Colorado until 1993. That year he joined the faculty at Princeton University, and then in 2001 went to the Divinity School at Harvard University. Carrasco is the founder and director of the Moses Mesoamerican Archive and Research Project. His work on the Nahua and Maya traditional religions has focused on the symbolic and ritual role of cities, on violence and its relation with the sacred, on ancient Mesoamerican myths, and on more modern expressions and structures of Mexican and U.S. Latino/a religion. Carrasco remains actively involved in social issues impacting the U.S. Latino/a communities. Among Carrasco's long list of distinguished publications we find the award-winning three-volume *Oxford Encyclopedia of Mesoamerican Cultures* (2001), of which he was editor in chief; and also *Quetzalcoatl and the Irony of Empire* (1992), *Religions of Mesoamerica* (1998), and *City of Sacrifice* (1999).

Orlando Espín

See also CULTURE; HISTORY OF RELIGIONS; MAYA TRADITIONAL RELIGION; NAHUA TRADITIONAL RELIGION.

CARROLL, JOHN (1736–1815)

First Catholic bishop for the United States. A Marylander, educated in Belgium and a Jesuit until the Society's suppression in 1773, Carroll served the Catholic missions in Maryland and Virginia after returning home, then assumed a diplomatic role on behalf of the revolutionary movement. His work to organize the American mission led to his nomination as bishop in 1789 (consecrated the next year). Carroll's vision of an American church prompted him to adopt the lay trustee system of parish leadership, to commission an English translation of the Bible, to establish Catholic schools (the Georgetown Academy for males in 1791), and a seminary for the education of priests (St. Mary's Seminary, Baltimore). His understanding of the American project and his dream of an American church adapted to the national reality, of better ecumenical relations, for a national clergy, remained unrealized for more than a century after his death.

Patricia Plovanich

See also LAY TRUSTEEISM.

CARTHUSIANS

One of a number of monastic reforms that took place during the twelfth century, the Carthusian movement actually had its roots in the eremitical life. In 1106 Guigo, the dean of Grenoble, joined a small group of hermits that were pursuing a life of solitude high up in a valley in the Alps. Through Guigo's wide circle of friends and correspondents, the hermitage became well known and attracted many new recruits; by 1130 Guigo was forced to compile some sort of written rule or charter for the original colony and the many that sprang forth from it. He culled the elements he found helpful from the Benedictine Rule and other twelfth-century monastic documents: liturgical prescriptions came from the Rule and, from the Cistercians, the practice of an annual chapter attended by all the abbots of the order. The unique genius of this community, however, named after the ultimate location of its original community, La Grande Chartreuse, lay in its blend of hermitage and community. Each monk had his own stone cell, complete with small garden and latrine; these were all grouped around a central cloister walk. Community gatherings were limited: daily the monks celebrated Vespers and the night Office together in the monastery church; on Sundays they were together for Mass, a chapter meeting and dinner, which was followed by a period for conversation. All other observances, including the one or two simple daily meals permitted, were performed apart and in silence. The physical life of the monks was more austere than that allowed by the Benedictine Rule. Meat was excluded from the diet, and on the many fast days in the monastic calendar, the monks sustained themselves only on bread and water.

Sustaining such a self-enclosed community required outside help. The rule provided for a supporting community of lay brothers (*conversi*) who supplied the physical labor needed by the monastery and mediated all contacts with the outside world. The brothers had a separate prayer life, set up on the premise that they would generally be illiterate. Aside from the small amount of gardening which each monk did in his own cell's plot, the work of the monastery was the preparation of books. Each cell was, in fact, a scriptorium. The Carthusian founders had many connections to the university world; they believed that books were essential to contemplation as well as theology and that they had a missionary function as well, disseminating the Word of God. Their production was a great service the Carthusian Order provided for the ecclesiastical community outside its walls.

Marie Anne Mayeski

See also ASCETICISM/ASCETIC; BENEDICTINE RULE (RULE OF ST. BENEDICT); CLOISTER; FATHERS/MOTHERS OF THE DESERT; MONASTICISM IN WESTERN CHRISTIANITY.

CASSIAN, JOHN (360?–432/3?)

After receiving a good classical education, Cassian entered a monastry in Bethlehem. From Bethlehem, he journeyed to Egypt in order to study monastic life there. When the theological disputes surrounding Origenism broke out in Egypt, Cassian moved to Constantinople. At Constantinople he was charged with delivering a letter from John Chrysostom to Innocent, patriarch of Rome. Cassian stayed at Rome where he befriended Leo the Great. The last part of his life was spent at Marseilles where he founded a monastery and a convent. Cassian wrote two main works, the *Institutions* and the *Collations*, both of which are concerned with monasticism, its theology and its practice.

Gary Macy

See also JOHN CHRYSOSTOM; LEO THE GREAT, POPE; MONASTICISM IN EASTERN CHRISTIANITY; MONASTICISM IN WESTERN CHRISTIANITY; ORIGENISM.

CASSIODORUS (485/90?–580?)

Flavius Magnus Aurelius Cassiodorus. During his long life, Cassiodorus participated fully in both secular and religious life. Coming from a senatorial family in

Calabria, Cassiodorus early gained the favor of the Gothic king, Theodoric, succeeding Boethius as Theodoric's master of court affairs in 523. Cassiodorus copied his palace correspondence into a single collection that provides valuable insight into the workings of the Gothic court. He also produced a history of the Goths and a chronicle reaching from Adam until the year 519. Cassiodorus retired from public life around 537/8. He attempted to establish a Christian school and library in Rome with the help of Pope Agapetas but without success. Cassiodorus met with better luck founding the monastery of Vivarium in Calabria. There monks could work or study in Vivarium's famous library. While at Vivarium, Cassiodorus wrote the *Institutes*, a guide to sacred and profane literature, as well as translations of Greek works and an introduction to writing and grammar.

Gary Macy

See also BOETHIUS; MONASTICISM IN WESTERN CHRISTIANITY.

CASSIRER, ERNST (1874–1945)
Neo-Kantian German philosopher who is recognized for his historical adaptation of the Kantian proposal of a priori categories as preconditions for objective thought. Cassirer argued that thought came to expression through culturally and historically conditioned symbols. These symbol systems representing the world for thought also exercise a constitutive function for consciousness. Thus human intellection is dynamic, historical, and, throughout history, creates a plurality of symbol systems to express the world's reality. Cassirer's interest lay not so much in the scientific and epistemological study of symbolization but in the phenomenon as it occurred in art, language, religion, and mythology.

His interest in religious thought was thus directed more to personal religious experience than to theories about religion. His works have played an influential role in later theological studies, which consider the potential that imagination holds for developing theological language.

Patricia Plovanich

See also ANALOGICAL IMAGINATION.

CASTE
The term caste, derived from the Portuguese *casta* (race), refers to the hierarchically arranged groups that make up the Hindu social system. Most commonly, it is used to designate one of four great social categories or estates (*varna*, color) into which traditional Hinduism divides society. As described in the Hindu texts dealing with religious law (*dharma*), the four varnas are (1) the *brahmins*, traditionally the priests, scholars, and teachers; (2) the *kshatriyas*, the rulers, warriors, and administrators; (3) the *vaishyas*, the merchants and farmers; and (4) the *shudras*, the manual laborers. Castes in the three higher categories are referred to as "twice-born" (*dvija*) castes, since males belonging to them are eligible to undergo the sacrament (*samskara*) of investiture with the sacred thread, the *upanayana* ritual, which is understood as a second birth.

The *Rig Veda* (10.90) presents the four great caste categories as originating in the sacrifice of a primordial cosmic Person (*purusha*); in the *Bhagavad Gita* (4.13), Krishna as God proclaims that he created the fourfold system to accord with different personality types and karmic destinies. Traditionally, one's position in the system was fixed by birth, as determined—and justified—by one's karma. Carrying out the calling of one's varna conscientiously was considered a holy obligation of dharma (religious duty). The system was thus fully supported by a complex network of religious ideas.

Caste is also used (many scholars believe more correctly) to translate the term *jati* (Sanskrit, birth group) that designates one of the innumerable hereditary, endogamous communities that function as regionally limited subgroups within each of the four pan-Indian varnas. The jatis are constituted according to such considerations as profession and sectarian affiliation, as well as region and language, and are frequently divided into smaller subdivisions. In the traditional system, there were severe restrictions on dining with persons outside of one's jati, as well as on marriage. Mobility of individuals within the system was scarcely possible; entire jatis, as a result of increase in wealth, prestige, or ritual status, could achieve a higher position in the hierarchy, or even be classified in a higher varna, but this would usually take several generations.

There was also a class of persons known as the untouchables (*asprishya*), sometimes considered a fifth varna, who performed tasks—such as cleaning latrines, managing cremation grounds, working with leather, and brewing alcoholic beverages —considered so impure that no caste Hindu would do them. Gandhi made great efforts to transform Hindus' ideas about the untouchables, whom he called Harijans, "children of God."

It should be noted that untouchability and discrimination based on caste were outlawed by the Indian constitution of 1950, and the interrelations among castes are changing rapidly under such pressures as urbanization and industrialization. Still, much of the traditional system remains intact, especially in rural areas, and caste consciousness remains very much a factor of life and politics in contemporary India. The untouchables—who nowadays may prefer to be referred to as *dalits*, "the downtrodden"—remain a large but disadvantaged group, and in villages are still typically forced to live separately from caste Hindus. The lower castes and dalits are, however, becoming increasingly active politically.

Finally, students should be warned that in the literature on Hinduism the term "caste" is used as a translation of both varna (as in "the brahmins are the highest caste") and jati. To avoid confusion, varna has been translated consistently in this volume as "caste category" and jati as "caste."

Lance E. Nelson

See also BRAHMANA/BRAHMIN; CASTES, SCHEDULED; DHARMA (IN HINDUISM); HINDUISM; JATI; KSHATRIYA; MANU SMRITI; SAMSKARA; SHUDRA; VAISHYA.

CASTES, SCHEDULED

The scheduled castes are groups formerly identified as untouchables in the Hindu social system, also known as Harijans (children of God), a term coined by Gandhi. Nowadays, some prefer to be known as *dalits* (the downtrodden). The term "scheduled" derives from the fact that these groups are listed in the 1950 Indian Constitution, which abolished untouchability, as recipients of special protections from the state. These protections include the reservation of places in universities, government jobs, and legislatures, a process not unlike that known as "affirmative action" in the U.S. Tribal groups in India, called *adivasis* (original inhabitants), were given similar protections, and are hence referred to as scheduled tribes.

Lance E. Nelson

See also CASTE; GANDHI, MOHANDAS K.; HINDUISM.

CASUISTRY

(From Latin, *casus:* a case). A method in ethics that seeks to resolve moral problems (cases of conscience) by means of an analysis considering *both* the relevant moral norm(s) and the particularities of a given case. It is premised on the understanding that moral rules are generally universal and abstract, and if these rules are to be helpful, they must be interpreted in light of concrete cases. In addition, similar cases already satisfactorily resolved can be brought to bear on the solution of the problematic case by means of analogy. Casuistry has played a dominant role in Roman Catholic moral theology, although it has been largely rejected by Protestants and philosophical ethics since the seventeenth century and the controversy over probabilism. It has been viewed by these critics as a method that enables moral laxity by means of overly fine distinctions and sophisticated argument. The method has seen a major revival in medical ethics since the mid-1980s.

Brian F. Linnane, s.j.

See also BIOETHICS; ETHICS; MORAL THEOLOGY/CHRISTIAN ETHICS; PROBABILIORISM; PROBABILISM.

CATACOMBS

Underground cemeteries formed by labyrinths of tunnels, vaults, and galleries. The term probably is derived from the Greek phrase *kata kumbas,* "at the ravine," the name given in the fourth century to the cemetery at San Sebastiano in Rome and applied by the ninth century to many similar subterranean burial places. The most famous and extensive catacombs are in Rome, where the approximately forty that have been found run several hundred miles in length. Similar burial places are known elsewhere in Europe, North Africa, and Asia Minor.

Catacomb excavations indicate that these areas were used by a cross-section of Roman society, including Christians and Jews. The development of the great series of Christian catacombs began about 150 C.E. and continued until the fifth century. After the siege of Rome under Alaric in 410, and due to fear of barbarian invasions, catacomb burials ceased. Gradually, the relics of the martyrs were transferred from their tombs to the churches throughout Rome. The catacombs were forgotten during the Middle Ages until a chance discovery of one of them in 1578 led to exploration.

While the early Christians especially frequented the catacombs to visit the tombs of martyrs and of their own families, the once widely held idea that Christians regularly worshiped and hid in them is now judged erroneous.

F. M. Gillman

See also MARTYR/MARTYRDOM; RELIC (IN CHRISTIANITY).

CATECHESIS/CATECHETICAL

(Greek, *katecheiesis*, from *kateachein*, to teach, to echo). *Catechetical* refers to materials, processes, and methodology used in providing *catechesis*. Catechesis, a basic element in the ministry of the Word, is the term used to designate the presentation of the basic teachings and lifestyle of the church to adults and children in preparation for initiation into the church and formation for sacraments.

Since the publication of the *National Catechetical Directory* in 1979, the use of the word has broadened. Historically, catechesis concerned the whole process of making disciples of Jesus. Later, the word meant the organic and systematic education of children and converts to the faith. The process included the use of small books of questions and answers called *catechisms*. The methology included memorizing both questions and answers that were repeated to a *catechist* who was trained in methodology or *catechetics*. Today, the concept embraces a continuing spectrum of both proclamation and systematic education by both word and the life of the whole community. The U.S. bishops have stated in *To Teach as Jesus Did* (1973) and in *Catechetics in Our Time* (1977) that, after parents, the first catechists, the community and its living of the Gospel become the major catechist of both children and adults.

The main purpose of catechesis is instruction of adults and children in the basic tenets of the Catholic Church and provision of support for the process of their conversion. *Religious education* has a broader meaning that includes many different aspects of religion and the tenets of other religions. Catechetics also differs from *theology*, a form of religious education. *Theology*, directed toward scholars and those mature in the faith, involves research, scholarly methodologies, and speculation. *Praxis*, a methodology, refers to critical reflection on actions already taken in relation to the Gospel and the action resulting from that reflection. *C.C.D.*, initials used for Sunday school, or children's religious education classes, actually refer to the *Confraternity of Christian Doctrine*. A parish structure involving parish welcoming, visitation, census-taking, religious education, transportation, and other functions, the confraternity structure rarely exists in parishes today. However, most of these ministries continue to give services with different structures and titles.

A new international *Catechism of the Catholic Church* (1994) to be used as a reference tool and guideline for bishops, publishers, and diocesan directors in the formulation of catechetical materials for children, youth, and adults entering the church.

M. Jane Gorman

See also RELIGIOUS EDUCATION.

CATECHISM

A term used, especially since the sixteenth century, to refer to manuals of fundamental Christian doctrines, written (often in question-answer format) for the religious education of the laity. The idea of written texts for religious education preceded the sixteenth century, of course, but the earlier texts seem to have been more like collections of creeds, prayers, devotions, and the like, and not quite the systematic presentation and explanation of doctrines that later catechisms intended to be. The fact that most Christian laypeople were illiterate must be taken into account when considering the effectiveness of the written catechisms, as it also explains why earlier catechisms were frequently pictographic. Catechisms did become popular and important in most Christian churches during and after the various sixteenth-century Reformations. They are still in use, although in many different formats, and with varying degrees of theological and pastoral quality.

Orlando Espín

See also BALTIMORE, COUNCILS OF; CANISIUS, PETER; CATECHESIS/ CATECHETICAL; CATECHUMEN; CATECHUMENATE; EVANGELIZATION; MISSIONS; TRENT, COUNCIL OF.

CATECHUMEN

An unbaptized person who, after a period of inquiry, makes a public declaration of intention to enter the church and celebrates the Rite of Welcome that marks the person as "joined to the Church and . . . part of the household of Christ" (*Order of Christian Initiation of Adults*, art. 18). The catechumen receives a sponsor to join in the journey of learning the life and teachings of the church while experiencing that life with the community. The sponsor accompanies the catechumen, giving support, answering questions, making introductions into the community, and assisting in the determination of the person's readiness for the sacraments of baptism, confirmation, and Eucharist. Upon approval, the catechumenate comes to an end when the catechumen goes before the bishop for the Rite of Election. The catechumen's name enters the Book of the Elect, and the third stage of "retreat" or final preparation for sacraments begins.

M. Jane Gorman

See also CATECHUMENATE; RITES OF CHRISTIAN INITIATION (RCIA).

CATECHUMENATE

(Greek, *katechein*, to echo). Also referred to as the RCIA (Rite of Christian Initiation of Adults), this word often denotes the four stages of the initiation process that was restored in 1972 for the unbaptized. After a period of "inquiry" about the faith, a person publicly states the intention of joining the community and enters a period of formation. The actual catechemenate (second stage) begins with the Rite of Welcome. While participating in the life and work of the community, assisted by a sponsor, the catechumen learns the basic aspects of church mission, teachings, prayer, forms of reflection, and sharing of faith. The length of the catechumenate is indefinite. When deemed ready, the pastor recommends the person

to the bishop. The Rite of Election takes place with the bishop, usually at the beginning of Lent. The bishop "elects" or calls the catechumens forth, places their names in the records of the church, and the "elect" enter the period of *purification* and *enlightenment* (stage three).

M. Jane Gorman

See also BAPTISM/CONFIRMATION; CATECHUMEN; RITES OF CHRISTIAN INITIATION (RCIA).

CATEGORICAL IMPERATIVE

The "categorical imperative" is Immanuel Kant's formulation in the *Groundwork of the Metaphysics of Morals* of "the supreme principle of morality" that unconditionally applies to all moral agents. Behind this principle—always act in such a way that the maxim or rule by which Kant acts should become universal law—defends the insight that genuine morality is that which is universalizable, that is, applies to all agents in similar circumstances with no distinction of persons. How well-formed maxims are constituted and whether there are genuine exceptions to such an imperative are issues that beguile Kant's formulation.

J. A. Colombo

See also KANT, IMMANUEL.

CATHARS

The Cathars were a heretical movement that achieved its greatest influence in the twelfth and thirteenth centuries in Italy and southern France. The group got its name from the Greek word *katharos*, meaning "perfect," a title given to the leaders of the movement. Although a few Cathar books survive, most of the information about the Cathars comes from their enemies. There remains, therefore, scholarly disagreement about Cathar history, organization, and beliefs. The Cathars themselves were divided into different sects with differing beliefs, but several common features of Cathar belief do emerge from the sources. The Cathars were dualists, that is, they believed in two divine forces in the universe. Only the spiritual force was good; the material universe being the creation of Satan, variously interpreted as Christ's brother or as a second evil god. Souls were angels trapped in matter, and the whole point of Cathar practice was to free this angel once and for all from its material prison. Angels who sinned were forced upon death to be reborn in another body. Cathars, therefore, rejected everything to do with matter, especially procreation, since this continued the evil force's work of trapping souls in matter. Most Cathars believed Jesus to be a pure spirit sent to lead the angels back to heaven. Cathars rejected Christian sacraments, retaining only the laying on of hands, a ceremony that elevated a member to the status of a Perfect (Cathar). This ritual, called *consolamentum*, could happen either after a long period of probation or on one's deathbed. The Perfects lived lives of strict chastity and asceticism, eating no meat, cheese, milk, or eggs. The effectiveness of consolamentum depended on the purity of the Perfect who administered it, and if, at any later date, the celebrant sinned, then all those whom he or she had consoled (even if already in heaven) immediately lost their status as Perfects. This was extremely important as only the Perfects could attain salvation. The similarity of Cathar teaching to earlier heresies, including dualism, Docetism, and a form of Donatism, caused contemporaries to describe them as a new form of Manichaeism.

It is difficult to determine exactly when Cathars arose in Europe; but certainly when Niketas, a missionary from the Bogomil Church, arrived in Italy in the third quarter of the twelfth century, the Cathars were already well established. By the thirteenth century, the Cathars had a church structure including regional bishops, mirroring that of the orthodox community. Response to the Cathars on the part of the orthodox community was slow in coming, since each individual bishop was left to counter the heretics in his own diocese. The first major blow against the Cathars came in the form of a crusade against them called by Pope Innocent III and ruthlessly carried out by the northern French lord, Simon de Montfort. The war devastated the southern French strongholds of the Cathars. In 1231 Pope Gregory IX appointed special agents to seek out heretics in the Cathar regions. This was the beginning of the papal Inquisition. Finally, a new religious order, dedicated to debating and converting the heretics, was founded by the Spaniard, Dominic de Guzmán. The Order of Preachers, or Dominicans, soon became the preferred officers of the papal Inquisition. These forces dramatically reduced the Cathars' numbers. The last-known Cathar leader was captured in 1321, and from that point, the Cathars disappear as a force in European history. Their legacy lives on, however, as one source of later movements of extreme asceticism, especially in their rejection of sexuality as intrinsically evil.

Gary Macy

See also ALBIGENSIANS; CRUSADES; DOCETISM; DOMINIC DE GUZMÁN; DOMINICANS; DONATISM; INNOCENT III, POPE; INQUISITION; MANICHAEISM; MEDIEVAL CHRISTIANITY (IN THE WEST); WALDENSIANS.

CATHEDRAL

Usually the central, and largest, church of a diocese, the Christian cathedral takes its name from the fact that the bishop's throne (*cathedra*) is located there (although occasionally today the word is used simply to denote a very large church building). They often have smaller side spaces or rooms (*chapels*) for quiet prayer or worship with smaller groups. Cathedrals can be found in most major cities (and sometimes in smaller towns) throughout the world, but most commonly in Europe and other European-influenced areas. Because of their stunning architectural styles, the medieval cathedrals of Europe in particular are often centers of tourist activity as well as Christian worship.

Joanne M. Pierce

See also BAROQUE; BASILICA; CHAPEL; GOTHIC; ROMANESQUE.

CATHERINE OF GENOA (1447–1510)

A medieval mystic, Catherine was born in Genoa, Italy. She was married at the age of sixteen to a self-indulgent nobleman, Giuliano Adorno. After ten miserable years of marriage, she underwent a religious experience that radically changed her. Her rich interior life was complemented by service to the sick and poor at the hospital of the Pammatone, where she ministered with her husband, who himself experienced a conversion and had become a Franciscan tertiary. Although there is no evidence that Catherine herself wrote down her thoughts, her spontaneous utterances were recorded by her spiritual followers. Most significant of the works ascribed to her are her *Spiritual Dialogues* and the *Treatise on Purgatory* (originally part of a larger work, *Life and Doctrine*).

At the turn of the twentieth century, interest in her was revived by the work of Baron Friederich von Hügel.

Mary Ann Hinsdale

See also MYSTICISM/MYSTICS (IN CHRISTIANITY).

CATHERINE OF SIENA (1347–80)

Born in Siena, Italy, Caterina Benicasa joined the Dominican third order at the age of sixteen. She lived at home, in seclusion, until the age of nineteen when she experienced a mystical vision of Christ inviting her to undertake an apostolic life. She worked with the sick, the imprisoned, and accompanied prisoners sentenced to death to the gallows. She had many spiritual disciples, including many priests. Her letters of spiritual instruction included critical appraisals of the political and ecclesiastical troubles of her time. One of her most notable political achievements was persuading Pope Gregory XI to transfer the papacy from Avignon, France, back to Rome in 1377.

Catherine's spirituality centered on the love of God, symbolized by the Blood of Christ. She herself received the stigmata, the bleeding wounds of Christ, in a vision before a crucifix in 1355. Her theological views on the church and the sacraments can be found in *The Dialogue* (1378). Gregory's successor, Urban VI, summoned Catherine to Rome to help bring an end to the Great Schism that had followed the election of Urban IV. On the journey she became sick and died at the age of thirty-three. In 1970, along with St. Teresa of Avila, she was declared a Doctor (Teacher) of the Church—one of only three women "doctors" in the history of the church.

Mary Ann Hinsdale

See also DOCTORS OF THE CHURCH.

CATHOLICITY

("Note" of the church). While the term *catholic*, meaning universal, complete, or all-embracing (from the Greek *kata*, according to, and *holos*, the whole) is not found in the Bible, the idea of the church's universality is present in the New Testament (see, for instance, Mark 16:15; Matt 5:14-16 and 28:19). In Christian theology, the term describes an essential characteristic of the Christian Church, one closely linked to the "note" of unity. It came to designate the Church of Rome (Roman Catholic Church) after the East-West Schism of the eleventh century, and it is also generally applied to those Christian Churches (such as the Anglican Communion) that maintain an episcopal ministry (bishops) founded on the apostolic succession and celebrate the sacramental life.

Christians express the church's catholicity (universality) by proclaiming the divine call to all nations to join the people of God. At the Second Vatican Council (1962–5), the Catholic Church acknowledged that all human beings are already related to the church in a variety of ways because all are called to salvation by the one God (*Lumen Gentium* 14–16). In Christ and through the Holy Spirit, the Triune God accomplishes a universal reconciliation of humanity of which the church is a sign to the degree that it welcomes into itself the special gifts of all peoples. To the pope falls the task of protecting legitimate differences among local churches as well as preventing these from becoming divisive (*Lumen Gentium* 13). Thus the Catholic Church today conceives of catholicity as a "unity-in-diversity," and has moved away from an earlier emphasis on uniformity in external practices.

James B. Nickoloff

See also APOSTOLICITY; HOLINESS; NOTES OF THE CHURCH; UNITY.

CATHOLIC REFORMATION

See COUNTER-REFORMATION/CATHOLIC REFORMATION.

CATHOLIC SOCIAL TEACHING

A tradition of teaching contained in the pastoral letters of national and regional bodies of bishops and the encyclical letters of popes. Catholic social teaching focuses on the relationship between God, people, and the world. It pays specific attention to issues of family, and economic, political, and cultural life.

A significant portion of Catholic social teaching has exhibited concern for those marginalized in societies dominated by capitalism. Dating from the late nineteenth century, modern Catholic social teaching was first a response to the socialist aspirations of people who were enduring the economic suffering and social dislocation of newly emerging industrial capitalist societies. By the mid-twentieth century, it was addressing the plight of the poor in the so-called Third World nations. Most recently, it has responded to the economic suffering caused by the creation of Third World conditions, such as structural unemployment, underemployment, and economic insecurity, in First World countries.

Even though Catholic social teaching largely (although not totally) affirms capitalist market relations, it has been critical of capitalism for its support of individualism and its lack of concern for the common good. The tradition of Catholic social teaching has insisted on norms of social justice, such as the social responsibility of property, the priority of labor over capital, and a preferential option for poor people who exhibit human dignity by struggling against the injustice in their lives. These principles of social justice privilege communal well-being over individualistic conceptions of happiness. In the tradition of the Second Vatican Council (1962–5), Catholic social teaching endorses a world in which the joys and hopes of people, especially the poor, are nurtured and celebrated in community, and their griefs and anxieties are addressed and borne in solidarity.

Mary E. Hobgood

See also ECONOMIC JUSTICE FOR ALL; JUSTICE; MATERIALISM; POVERTY; QUADRAGESIMO ANNO; RERUM NOVARUM; SOLIDARITY; THIRD WORLD; USURY.

CATHOLIC TRADITION
The term "catholic" comes from the Greek word for "universal." Ignatius of Antioch (d. 107 C.E.) used it first in reference to Christianity. Historically, the adjective "Catholic" was applied to the entire Christian Church before its divisions, and to the universal church as distinct from the local congregations. It has also been used, especially after the Reformation, to distinguish the Christians who remained in communion with the Bishop of Rome from the Christians who separated from this communion. More recently the term "Catholic" has generally referred to Anglicans, Catholics (Roman and Eastern), and Orthodox, because they are believed to represent and embody, together, the church of undivided Christianity and its apostolic belief and tradition. It is in this latter sense that today many speak of a broad and ancient Catholic tradition that is still shared and lived by the vast majority of Christians. This tradition is found in the three Communions (Anglican, Catholic, and Orthodox), even if they disagree among themselves on some important doctrinal issues. The Catholic tradition, thus understood, assumes as necessary (at least) the normative centrality of the Scriptures, the acceptance of the doctrinal definitions of the first seven ecumenical councils, the apostolic succession of bishops, the preeminent role of the liturgy and the sacraments, and the indispensable hermeneutic and sacramental role of the church. This understanding of Catholic "tradition," however, should not be confused with the ecclesiological opinion that the Catholic "Church" subsists in three branches—Anglican, Catholic (Roman and Eastern), and Orthodox.

Orlando Espín

See also ANGLICAN COMMUNION; CANTERBURY, SEE OF; CONSTANTINOPLE, SEE OF; DOCTORS OF THE CHURCH; EASTERN CATHOLIC CHURCHES; FATHERS OF THE CHURCH; ORTHODOX CHURCHES; PATRISTICS/PATROLOGY; ROMAN CATHOLIC CHURCH; ROME, SEE OF; WESTERN CATHOLIC CHURCHES.

CAUSALITY
The ancient Greek philosopher Aristotle developed a doctrine of the nature of causality that influenced thinking about the subject for centuries. On Aristotle's account, it is possible to distinguish among four types of causality. An *efficient cause* is whatever is responsible for producing a thing or making an event occur. The *final cause* of an event or thing is its purpose, the reason for which the thing was made, or the goal of the event's occurrence. He made a further distinction between *formal* and *material* causes which derives from his view that substances are subject to hylomorphic composition, that is, they have matter (the "stuff" of which they are made) and form (their organizational principle or structure) as their ultimate metaphysical constituents. Accordingly,

a thing's *formal cause* is its basic structure, and a thing's *material cause* is the matter on which that structure is imposed. On Aristotle's account, each of the four causes can be specified when attempting to explain the production of anything. So, for example, a shirt has the fabric of which it is made as its material cause, the design or pattern from which it was constructed as its formal cause, the tailor as its efficient cause, and the purpose for which it was made (for example, to be worn) as its final cause.

Aristotle's doctrine of the Four Causes played a significant role in the construction of arguments for the existence of God throughout the Middle Ages and into the modern period. The world and all natural substances in it can be viewed as being an artifact or something that had been made or produced. Many philosophers held that it was possible, through examination of the artifact or thing made, to determine the existence of a divine artificer or maker. Such arguments typically proceed by way of drawing an analogy. The universe, it is claimed, resembles an artifact, for example, a clock, in its intricacy and organizational structure. The intricacy and organizational structure of a clock is due to its having a designer who invented and constructed it. Likewise, so the reasoning goes, the universe must be the product of intelligent design as well. God, then, is held to be both the final and efficient cause of the universe.

An important challenge to arguments for God's existence based on causal reasoning came from the Scottish philosopher David Hume (1711–76). Hume's challenge was based on a critique of the assumption that causes necessitate their effects so that, given an understanding of an effect, one could draw inferences back to the requisite cause. Hume denied that there is any necessary connection between causes and their effects. His argument against causal necessity has its grounds in his empiricist epistemology. On Hume's view, our knowledge of causal relations must be grounded in what we are able to observe via sensory experience. What we observe is simply a certain regularity in the order of occurrence of events of certain types. For example, we observe that putting salt in water is always followed by the salt dissolving. We conclude, on the basis of repeated observations of this sort, that an event of the first type (salt placed in water) is the cause of an event of the second type (salt dissolving). There is no observation of any logical necessity between the two types of events. There is simply the awareness of a regular succession or "constant conjunction" of two types of events. Hence, Hume held that one could never, through observation and examination of the world, deduce that necessarily the world is the product of an intelligent designer. We have no direct experience of the origin of worlds and so no experiential basis from which to make such an inference.

Linda L. Peterson

See also ARISTOTLE; HYLOMORPHISM.

C.E./B.C.E.

In 532 C.E., Denys le Petit suggested that history be divided into two eras calculated from the year he believed that Jesus was born. When this schema was adopted in Christian countries, about three of four centuries later, the years before Christ were calculated by subtraction and designated as A.C. (*Ante Christum*), later translated to B.C. (*Before Christ*). Then, the years following Jesus' birth are added and designated A.D. (*Anno Domini* or Year of the Lord). This order of years was first applied to the Julian calendar. In 1582, when the Gregorian calendar adjusted the Julian year to the solar year, the sequence of historical years and eras remained unchanged.

Today, although many religions continue to follow other calendars, the Gregorian calendar has become the international standard. However, in a pluralistic world it is increasingly recognized that it is inappropriate to make the birth of Christ the axis of history. Since revising traditional dating would bring needless confusion, many have adopted the designations B.C.E. (Before the Common Era) and C.E. (Common Era). These alternatives for A.C./B.C. and A.D. were introduced in the Jewish community in order to avoid implicit christological affirmations when referring to dates in the civil calendar. Although the actual sequence of years remains based on a year once assumed to be that of Christ's birth, the move to identify each era in a way that is not simultaneously a Christian presupposition is a practical solution.

Regina A. Boisclair

CELAM

The Consejo Episcopal Latinoamericano, or Latin American Bishops' Council (known by the Spanish acronym CELAM), was formed in 1955 by the Roman Catholic bishops of all the countries of Latin America and the Caribbean. It marked an important step in ending the isolation of local churches and the beginning of a genuinely Latin American Church. CELAM has held five general conferences. At the first in Río de Janeiro (1955), the bishops confronted the reality of the large population in their countries which, despite centuries of nominal Catholicism, remained effectively unevangelized. In 1968 at Medellín (Colombia), the bishops reversed nearly five centuries of ecclesiastical acquiescence in, or even outright support for, social and political structures that favored a tiny minority at the expense of the masses of people. In 1979 at Puebla (Mexico), CELAM reaffirmed Medellín's call for solidarity with the poor and oppressed of the continent and officially proclaimed the church's "preferential option for the poor." In 1992 at Santo Domingo (Dominican Republic), recalling the five-hundredth anniversary of the conquest of the Americas by Europeans and the arrival of Christianity, CELAM endorsed Pope John Paul II's call for a "new evangelization" of Latin America and the creation of a "civilization of love," and asked forgiveness for the church's cooperation with injustice. CELAM had its fifth general conference in Aparecida (Brazil) in 2007.

James B. Nickoloff

See also EPISCOPAL CONFERENCES; LATIN AMERICAN CATHOLICISM; LATIN AMERICAN THEOLOGIES; OPTION FOR THE POOR.

CELEBRATION

(Latin, *celebrare*). A religious ceremony or liturgical rite. In common usage, celebration designates festivals that mark happy events. The word is less restricted in its liturgical usage, however, and can indicate a rite marking even a painful reality, for example, the celebration of a funeral.

Patrick L. Malloy

CELIBACY

The vow of celibacy corresponds to the second of the three evangelical counsels (poverty, chastity, and obedience). Its observance is also required for priests ordained in the Latin Rite. Celibacy means foregoing all sexual activity and relationships. Strictly speaking, celibacy is different from chastity, since the virtue of chastity ought to characterize every Christian's life, whether married or single. As an ascetical discipline, the practice of celibacy can be found among the world's major religions. Ideally, like poverty, celibacy is meant to help the individual concentrate on what is essential to the interior life; paradoxically, the renunciation of sexual relationships, when undertaken for religious motives, can lead to a love or compassion that is both deep and universal. The practice of celibacy does not mean the denial of one's sexuality, however; denial would eventually bring about a distortion of a person's very humanity as well as a lopsided spirituality.

What makes celibacy evangelical, therefore, is that it is patterned after the life of Jesus. Yet, for Jesus, celibacy was not an end in itself, but a means; or rather, an expression of his wholehearted dedication to the kingdom of God. Like voluntary poverty, celibacy becomes evangelical when it leads to a thoroughgoing solidarity with the poor and oppressed. Although celibacy exists among the various world religions, it does not reflect a universally esteemed value; some cultures disparage it. Selfless, heroic love and commitment, however, are the values that make celibacy shine; but one need not be single to be either selfless or deeply committed. The practice of celibacy in the church should probably be seen as complementary to marriage in giving full sacramental expression to the richness of God's love for the world.

William Reiser, s.j.

See also CHASTITY; COUNSELS (OF PERFECTION); MARRIAGE IN CATHOLIC PERSPECTIVE; OBEDIENCE; POVERTY; SEXUALITY.

CELSUS (SECOND CENTURY C.E.)

A Platonist philosopher who, about 178, published one of the most cogent pagan attacks on early Christianity, *On True Doctrine*. This work was so highly regarded in pagan literary circles that Origen wrote *Against Celsus*, a point-by-point refutation of it. No independent copy of *On True Doctrine* survives. However, so closely does Origen's work follow Celsus' text that Origen's *Against Celsus* contains 90 percent of Celsus' famous work. Celsus believed that Christianity repeated the worst features of Judaism, namely, monotheism and exclusivism. He held that the Gospel portrayal of Jesus is inconsistent and absurd, and that the Christian notion of God fails to grapple with the existence and increase of evil. Celsus maintained that Christians unwittingly contradict themselves in believing their God is both Creator and Redeemer. Celsus mocked Christians for holding the resurrection of the flesh, a doctrine he thought philosophically impossible.

Herbert J. Ryan, s.j.

See also APOLOGISTS; JUSTIN MARTYR; ORIGEN; PLATONISM.

CENTESIMUS ANNUS

On May 1, 1991, the memorial of St. Joseph the Worker in the Catholic Church, Pope John Paul II issued the document *Centesimus Annus* to commemorate the one-hundredth anniversary of Pope Leo XIII's encyclical on "The Condition of Labor" (*Rerum Novarum*, 1891), commonly considered the foundational document of modern Catholic social teaching. After pointing out the highlights of *Rerum Novarum* and reminding his readers of its significance in the history of the church's commitment to socioeconomic justice (chapter 1), John Paul II examines the "new things" of the present moment in human history (chapter 2) that include the collapse of state socialism in Europe, the rise of consumerism in affluent Western countries, and the growing poverty of the Third World. In chapter 3, the pope examines in detail the "events of 1989" that ended the long Cold War in Europe with the apparent victory of capitalism. He suggests that because totalitarianism and authoritarianism deny both God and the intrinsic dignity of human beings (itself rooted in humanity's openness to transcendent reality), they are ultimately doomed to failure.

The Pope devotes the fourth and longest chapter of the encyclical to a discussion of "private property and the universal destination of material goods." Here we see why capitalism's victory is only "apparent." While celebrating the fall of socialism, the Pope issues a stern warning to those who believe that the free market alone can meet all human needs (no. 34). The chapter's title itself suggests John Paul II's desire to remind readers that if the fundamental dignity of human persons requires the right to possess material goods, this right belongs to *all* people. Thus the "inhuman exploitation" of the weak by the strong, including the "unbearable sacrifices" required of the poor in Third World countries required to pay foreign debts (no. 35), violates God's law. As Vatican II affirmed, "we ought to regard [lawfully held material possessions] not just as our own but also as common, in the sense that they can profit not only the owners but others too" (no. 30). He warns that consumer societies built on "having and enjoying" material goods produce alienation. Only when a society promotes the "being and growth" of persons does it fulfill its true purpose (no. 37).

In the fifth chapter, John Paul II affirms the role of the state in promoting (but not controlling) economic development and, along with individuals, groups, and associations, in guaranteeing economic security for all members of society (no. 48). Only when injustice and poverty are overcome will a culture of peace be possible (no. 52). In the sixth and final chapter, the Pope reaffirms the church's unchanging commitment to the temporal well-being and eternal salvation of the entire human family. He notes that such a commitment, which has grounded the church's social teaching for the past century, requires a preferential option for the poor of the world (no. 57).

James B. Nickoloff

See also CATHOLIC SOCIAL TEACHING; JOHN PAUL II, POPE; OPTION FOR THE POOR; SOCIALISM.

CHADO

(Japanese, *cha-no-yu*, the way of tea). Generally referred to as the tea ceremony, *Chado* originated in China as a ritualized form of tea serving and drinking. The practice of drinking green powdered tea was brought to Japan by Buddhist monks in the twelfth century C.E. At that time, it was used in Zen monasteries for both medicinal purposes and as an aid to meditation. Over a long period of time, chado became widely integrated into Japanese culture as both a social and aesthetic form as well as a meditative practice. However, for the most part, chado has mainly been associated with Zen practice, and under the creative guidance of Sen Rikyu (1522–91) it became a way of life manifesting the basic principles of harmony, respect, purity, and tranquility.

These four principles underlie all of tea practice and constitute its highest ideals. Ultimately these principles of the way of tea are directed toward every aspect of one's life.

G. D. DeAngelis

See also NAKA IMA; ZEN.

CHADOR

A long black garment that covers the entire body of a woman, including her head. In some Muslim countries, most notably Iran, wearing of the *chador* is expected of all adult women. In other Islamic countries women cover most of their bodies and wear a veil, but leave their faces uncovered. The practice of wearing the chador is sometimes called *purdah*. One of the Qur'anic references used to explain this custom is found in 33:59, where the Prophet Muhammad is told by God: "Tell thy wives and daughters, and the believing women, that they should cast their outer garments over their persons when abroad." Whether Islamic women fully cover their bodies or not, they are expected to "guard their modesty" (Qur'an 24:31) at all times. Some Hindu women also wear this kind of garment.

Ronald A. Pachence

See also PURDAH; QUR'AN.

CHALCEDON, COUNCIL OF

The Fourth Ecumenical Council held in 451. The newly chosen emperor, Marcian, summoned a council to meet to solve the problem of how to describe the relationship between the divine and human existence of Jesus as the incarnation of the Logos. The decrees of the earlier Council of Ephesus (449) on this subject were strongly opposed, especially by Pope Leo I, because of the council's irregular proceedings as well as its apparent support of Monophysitism (the teaching that Jesus as the incarnate Logos has only one divine nature). The council originally met at Nicaea, but was moved to Chalcedon to be closer to the capital, Constantinople. After extensive discussion, the bishops at Chalcedon reaffirmed the creeds of the Council of Nicaea (325) and of the Council of Constantinople (380), nullified the decrees of Ephesus, and reasserted the teaching that Jesus has two natures, human and divine. The debate over the relationship between the divine and human natures of Christ continued for centuries, and the decrees of the council were rejected by the Armenian, Coptic, Ethiopian, and Syrian Orthodox Churches. Only recently did the Catholic Church and the Coptic Church (1973) and Syrian Orthodox Church (1984) reach agreements on the issue of christology. The council also decreed that Constantinople was second only to Rome among the patriarchates. This decree was opposed by Leo I and never accepted in the West.

Gary Macy

See also CHALCEDONIAN DEFINITION; CHRISTOLOGY; CONSTANTINOPLE, FIRST COUNCIL OF; CONSTANTINOPLE, SEE OF; COPTIC MONOPHYSITE CHURCH; COUNCIL, ECUMENICAL; CREED/SYMBOL OF FAITH; EPHESUS, COUNCIL OF; LEO I THE GREAT, POPE; LOGOS/WORD; MONOPHYSITISM; NICAEA, FIRST COUNCIL OF; NICAEA, SECOND COUNCIL OF; NICENE CREED; ROMAN CATHOLIC CHURCH; ROME, SEE OF.

CHALCEDONIAN CHRISTIANS

Members of all the Orthodox, Catholic, and Anglican Churches, of the East and the West, that accept as normative and binding the doctrinal definitions of the Council of Chalcedon in 451 C.E. Monophysite, Nestorian Christians do not accept these doctrinal definitions.

Orlando Espín

See also ANGLICAN COMMUNION; CATHOLIC TRADITION; CHALCEDON, COUNCIL OF; EASTERN CATHOLIC CHURCHES; FATHERS OF THE CHURCH; MONOPHYSITISM; NESTORIUS; ORTHODOX CHURCHES; ROMAN CATHOLIC CHURCH.

CHALCEDONIAN DEFINITION

At the Council of Chalcedon (451), an agreement was reached by the majority of bishops in attendance on the relationship between the divine and human existence of Jesus. This settlement was accepted by both Eastern and Western Christians with the exception of the Armenian, Coptic, Ethiopian, and Syrian Orthodox Churches that continued to assert that Christ has one nature (Monophysitism). The council reaffirmed the creeds of the Council of Nicaea (325) and of the Council of Constantinople (380), accepted the title of Mother of God (*Theotokos*) for Mary, the mother of Jesus, and nullified the decrees of the Council of Ephesus (449). Christ was held to be consubstantial (*homoousios*) with the Father regarding Christ's divinity and consubstantial with us regarding his humanity. The divine and human natures of Christ exist without confusion, without change, without division, and without separation in one nature (*hypostasis*) and one person (*prosopon*). The settlement was a compromise that sets limits to the discussion concerning the divine and human existence of Christ rather than defining with any precision how Christ could be both divine and human.

Fundamentally, the Council of Chalcedon stated that Christ was both fully divine and fully human while remaining one individual.

Gary Macy

See also CHALCEDON, COUNCIL OF; CHRISTOLOGY; CONSTANTINOPLE, FIRST COUNCIL OF; CONSTANTINOPLE, SECOND COUNCIL OF; CONSTANTINOPLE, THIRD COUNCIL OF; COPTIC MONOPHYSITE CHURCH; CREED/SYMBOL OF FAITH; EPHESUS, COUNCIL OF; HYPOSTASIS; HYPOSTATIC UNION; MONOPHYSITISM; MOTHER OF GOD/THEOTOKOS; NICAEA, FIRST COUNCIL OF; NICAEA, SECOND COUNCIL OF; NICENE CREED; PERSON/PROSOPON.

CHALDEAN CATHOLIC CHURCH

This church was established originally from, or came under the influence of the Patriarchate of Antioch. Although dependent on Antioch in many ways, the Chaldean Christian tradition became known for its rejection of the Hellenizing influences of Antioch, preferring to adopt (and adapt) Palestinian Christian traditions instead. The Chaldean Church was involved in the Nestorian schism that followed the Council of Ephesus in 431 C.E., while it continued its missionary activity in Persia (present-day Iran), China, and India. Two groups of Chaldean Christians established full communion with Rome in 1551 and in 1830. Today, most Chaldeans are members of the Catholic Church under the overall jurisdiction of the patriarch of Babylon (in Baghdad). There are some 360,000 Chaldean Catholics worldwide.

Orlando Espín

See also EASTERN CATHOLIC CHURCHES; NESTORIUS; ORTHODOX CHURCHES; PATRIARCH; ROME, SEE OF.

CHALICE

The word chalice (from the Latin *calix*) originally meant goblet or drinking vessel. In Christian liturgy, the term is used to refer to the cup that holds the wine to be used at the celebration of the Eucharist (or Mass). The chalice is more specifically the cup actually placed on the altar; the wine inside would then be consecrated, understood to be transformed in some way into the Blood of Christ; or, in some Protestant traditions, spoken of as a sign or symbol of the Blood of Christ. Additional cups, or chalices, may be used in distributing Communion to the congregation, in some traditions.

The design of the chalice has changed over the centuries. Originally made from a variety of different materials (horn, wood, glass), the use of precious metal (such as gold or silver) came to be preferred. Often, the laity would receive the consecrated wine by drinking directly from the chalice until this custom fell into disuse in the medieval period. Thus, the size could vary according to the size of the community and the historical date: well into the medieval period, for example, chalices could be double-handled cups of some size, while from the sixteenth to the early twentieth centuries, some traditions (for example, Roman Catholics) used chalices that had rather small and shallow bowls on long and ornate stems. Contemporary chalices have moved back to a deeper bowl on a somewhat shorter stem, and may be made of many materials (metal, glass, ceramic, wood), as the reception of the consecrated wine by the laity from the chalice becomes more common in some Christian churches.

Joanne M. Pierce

See also COMMUNION (LITURGICAL); CONSECRATION (CHRISTIAN); EUCHA-RIST; MASS; TABERNACLE (CHRISTIAN LITURGICAL).

CHALLENGE OF PEACE: GOD'S PROMISE AND OUR RESPONSE

The 1983 U.S. bishops' letter that continued the tradition of Pope John XXIII's *Pacem in Terris* and the Second Vatican Council's *Gaudium et Spes* in challenging the morality of U.S. military policies. Both this document and its ten-year anniversary "reflection," *The Harvest of Justice Is Sown in Peace*, affirmed the morality of selective conscientious objection for Catholics while reaffirming the validity of a traditional just war theory. This pastoral claimed that war is not inevitable, and that peace is both a gift from God and a work of human construction. It called for support of human rights and democracy as essential components of peace.

The pastoral also gave "strictly conditioned moral acceptance" of nuclear deterrence, if it was part of a progressive process of disarmament. Critics have charged that the bishops did not make clear that world peace is most fundamentally a matter of just social, political, economic, and legal structures. Nor did the pastoral address the problems for Christians in dealing with military policy that acknowledges neither selective objection to particular wars nor selective obedience to military orders. There is also criticism about the lack of effort to promote the pastoral or to provide adequate facilities for the formation of conscience and behavior in accord with the pastoral's teachings. Nevertheless, this pastoral, and its 1993 follow-up letter, is important for its critique of militarism and its support not only of conscientious objectors to all wars, but its support of Catholics who choose to be conscientious objectors to particular wars.

Mary E. Hobgood

See also CONSCIENTIOUS OBJECTION; JUSTICE; JUST WAR THEORY; PEACE; WAR.

CHAN
Chinese.
See ZEN.

CHANCELLOR
The chief representative of the bishop in the daily administration of a diocese. Although canon law allows lay men and women to be appointed diocesan chancellors, often they are priests. The office of the chancellor is called the chancery, a name often extended to the complex of diocesan administrative offices.

Orlando Espín

See also ARCHBISHOP; BISHOP (EPISCOPACY); DIOCESE/ARCHDIOCESE.

CHANCERY
See CHANCELLOR.

CHANGING WOMAN
Among the Holy People who guided and protected the Navajo in their long journey of Emergence, Changing Woman is the only one whose dependability and benevolence remained constant. When she appears in the myth of origins, she is described as daughter of the Sun and the vessel chosen to bear his children, the twins Monster-Killer and Born-of-Water. It is they who will perform the great service of ridding the earth of monsters and making it possible for the People to live upon the Earth's surface. Among the many beautiful descriptions of Changing Woman, there is one that explains her name. Like the earth, she changes her appearance with the seasons: newborn in the spring, adolescent in the summer, mature person in the fall, and descending into old age in the winter. But she is immortal, and like the earth she begins the cycle anew with each spring. For that reason, she is a symbol of immortality (as another of her names, White Shell Woman, suggests), and the living symbol of life and its goodness.

In a society that esteems women as highly as men, she is the example of what every young Navajo woman is called to become. This is part of the instruction of the girls, and it reaches its fullest communication in the female initiation ritual called Kinaalda. In this exemplary rite of initiation, every gesture and prayer affirms the young woman's close relation to Changing Woman, and she is called to be what she is—heroic, generous, lifegiving, virtuous, and mother of her people. She is assured that her fidelity to this call will bring her an immortal place in the universe, and that she will be the personification of "beauty."

Kathleen Dugan

See also CHANTWAY; INITIATION (NON-CHRISTIAN).

CHANT (IN CHRISTIANITY)
In general, the traditional style for liturgical singing in Christianity, sometimes known as plainchant or plainsong. There are multiple parallels for different rites of the church as well as for different historical periods. In the West, the most common form is that of the Roman Rite called Gregorian chant, after Pope St. Gregory the Great, although his actual contribution is a matter of some dispute. Other forms include Ambrosian (Milan), Gallican (France), Mozarabic (Spain), Old Roman (generally thought to be prior to the Car-

olingian reforms and without Gallican influence), Byzantine (varies according to linguistic/ethnic lines), and the chant styles employed by the other churches of Eastern Christianity. Chant styles are generally characterized by being: (1) monophonous or monodic, that is, having a single, melodic line; (2) purely vocal and generally unaccompanied—although instrumental accompaniment is sometimes used, depending on the rite and the historical period; (3) prose rather than verse, with the rhythm reflecting the irregular stresses of speech rather than adhering to strict time values as in metered poetry. No doubt a number of influences converged to produce the various styles of chant that have developed in Christianity, including the ancient Hebrew and Greek (Diaspora) chant of the synagogue, especially for psalmody, and the musical systems of the Syriac and Hellenized communities of the Near East basin that were the first to embrace Christianity. Chant has remained the normative form of liturgical music in the churches of the East, though not without strong influence at times from the musicological developments within their respective cultures. In the West, chant began to decline with the development of polyphony and later more elaborate forms of music. Today it is all but absent from the worship found in most Christian communities, outside of some monasteries and convents.

Dennis W. Krouse

See also EUCHARIST; GREGORIAN CHANT; LITURGY (IN CHRISTIANITY); LITURGY OF THE HOURS; MASS.

CHANT (NATIVE AMERICAN)

As in Christianity, specialized forms of music developed within the religious cultures of North America. The proper locus of chant has always been ritual, where it serves to support the narrative telling of the underlying story which is the ritual's source, and to uphold the disciplined movement of the dancers. With song in general, it is believed to emanate from the depths of the human spirit and from the rich embodiments of sacred life found in the natural world. There is a perceptible link between the forms of chant and the rhythms of living creatures. It is their voices the people sought to imitate as a gesture of true respect and admiration, but also in the belief that such harmony pleases the Creator. From the sound of birds and animals, to the wordless speech of the earth, and the groanings of the human spirit, such ritual practice aimed first of all to speak gratitude for all of life, and to affirm the intricate relationships that unite all into one.

There is a special characteristic to Native American chant that marks it as unique. All songs were understood to have their origin in a vision or a dream. These were the time-honored channels through which revelation occurred. The significance of this should be recognized. It represents the belief that communications were to be sought and expected by all in the process of growing to adulthood. Thus direction, strength, and the skills to live a good and productive life were sought in this way, and the sign of acceptance of them was often signified in the gift of a song. Not all songs emerged into the public forum, but those with universal import did, and they added to the growing store of sacred knowledge imparted to the people. Thus, in a singular way, they represent the living voice of the sacred in its dialogue with creation.

Kathleen Dugan

See also CHANTWAY; INITIATION (NON-CHRISTIAN); REVELATION; RITUAL.

CHANTWAY

For the Navajo, a communal ritual centers largely on the rituals of healing in which the ill person is placed in a sacred space created by the intricate construction of a sand painting (more properly called a "ground painting") that expresses a section of the Emergence story. An essential part of this ritual is the perfect narration of the myth in a formalized chant. Thus the leader of the ritual is given the title "Hataali" (singer), and his responsibility is the process that draws the sacred beings into the ritual space, assisting the patient in becoming identified with the narrative and its powers. As he intones the chant, he and the patient are drawn into intimate participation in the life and energy of the drama, and the expected result is a transformation that brings the sick person back to health and harmony with all creation. Though every element of this ritual is meaningful, the chant is the most powerful agent of transformation and directs the whole. The elemental power of sound fused with harmonic music echoes an ancient recognition of a primal source of power. Thus, instead of simply being called a ritual, this action is named for its primary component, and is known as a Chantway. Perhaps one of its most frequent forms reveals best its essence. In the rite called Blessingway, used for a general access to every kind of blessing, we find an alternate name—the Way of Good Hope.

Kathleen Dugan

See also CHANGING WOMAN; CHANT (NATIVE AMERICAN); SHAMAN.

CHAPEL

A chapel (from the Latin word *capella*) is usually a small church building containing an altar, which is not used regularly as a site for parish worship. In the early Middle Ages, such buildings were erected to house relics (the earliest seems to have held the cloak, or *cappa*, of St. Martin of Tours), and became small shrines for prayer and occasional liturgical celebrations. In addition, larger church buildings may have smaller rooms along the sides or in the basement; these areas, set aside for worship, and containing their own smaller altars or "side altars," are also called chapels. Chapels are often used for private prayer or for the celebration of the Eucharist by smaller groups for certain occasions. In certain Christian traditions, for example, Roman Catholicism, an early morning daily Mass may be celebrated in a chapel, not the main body of the church. In addition, since the liturgical reforms of Vatican II, it has become a frequent custom for the reserved sacrament to be kept in a tabernacle housed in a side chapel.

Joanne M. Pierce

See also CATHEDRAL; GOTHIC; ROMANESQUE; TABERNACLE (CHRISTIAN LITURGICAL); VATICAN, SECOND COUNCIL OF THE.

CHAPTER (RELIGIOUS)

Religious chapter refers to the governing body of a religious institute or community; it may be local (a "provincial" chapter) or universal (a "general" chapter). The scope and nature of their authority are determined by the law and constitutions of each congregation, order, or institute. According to the church's law, the principal duty of the general chapter is "to protect the patrimony of the institute" and to "promote suitable renewal in accord with this patrimony, to elect the supreme moderator, to treat business matters and to publish norms which all are bound to obey" (Can. 631).

William Reiser, s.j.

See also CANON LAW; CONGREGATIONS (ORDERS); RULE (MONASTIC/RELIGIOUS).

CHARACTER (SACRAMENTAL)

The word originally referred to a mark, carving, or seal that was a sign of ownership, but eventually assumed the notion of a permanent, distinguishing quality that differentiates one thing from another. Regarding the sacraments, character refers to that dimension of the sacrament that permanently sets one aside in relationship to God and the church. Thus, one is said to be "marked" or "sealed" by the Holy Spirit through the sacraments of baptism, confirmation, and holy orders. The notion of a permanent sacramental character is rooted in the church's practice never to repeat these three sacraments. While early church writers identified the character of a sacrament as the experience of the sacramental ritual itself, in the Middle Ages it became associated with the Scholastic notion of *res et sacramentum* (the lasting effect of any of the sacraments; for example, the indissoluble bond in marriage, the presence of the Body and Blood of Christ in Eucharist), as distinguished from the ritual (*sacramentum tantum*, the "sign alone") and that which it ultimately points to and communicates, namely, the particular sacramental grace (*res tantum*, the "reality alone").

Modern theologians, beginning with Mattias Scheeben (1835–88) in *The Mysteries of Christianity*, tend to view both sacramental character and *res et sacramentum* from a more ecclesial perspective and as a means of establishing ecclesial relationship and status, in contradistinction to the medieval and Tridentine view of an individual "mark on the soul." Anthropologists such as Victor Turner and Mary Douglas have indirectly helped theologians to see the sacramental character as induced by the ritual process itself. Behavioral studies of rituals, especially initiation rites, reveal a fourfold process: (1) separation from old patterns; (2) a period of liminality or marginality, including continuing isolation, a theoretical and practical indoctrination in new mores and responsiblities in the community, and testing or ordeal to determine competence and dependability; (3) reintegration into the community at a new level of social existence; (4) resulting in "communitas"—the renewal of the whole community due to its direct and vicarious participation in the initiation process. Anthropologically this social process changes ("marks") the initiate and continues to change ("mark") the entire community. This provides a more communal (ecclesial) basis for understanding sacramental character imparted by the Holy Spirit first present and operative in the whole community. Classical Christian initiation rites and the modern reintroduction of the catechumenate help us to appreciate how sacraments function in transforming ("characterizing") individuals into members of the Body of Christ with new identities and ministerial responsibilities in the community.

Dennis W. Krouse

See also BAPTISM/CONFIRMATION; LIMINAL/LIMINALITY; ORDAINED MINISTRIES, SACRAMENT OF; RITES OF CHRISTIAN INITIATION (RCIA); RITUAL; SACRAMENT; SACRAMENTAL THEOLOGY.

CHARISMATIC MOVEMENT

The origins of this movement can be traced, among Protestants, to an Episcopalian church in Van Nuys, California, in

1958, and among Catholics to a retreat at Duquesne University in 1967. The movement is essentially characterized by an intense outpouring of the gifts of the Spirit (or "charisms"), particularly the gift of tongues (glossolalia), which Paul mentions in 1 Corinthians 12:4-11; Luke associated some such gift with the first Christian Pentecost (Acts 2:1-13). The celebrated "gifts of the Spirit" or "pentecostal gifts" thus date back to the origins of Christianity, and from time to time during its history those gifts (and others) have reappeared.

But also characteristic of the movement would be the regular gathering in small prayer groups, enthusiasm for the life of the Spirit, an ecumenical openness rooted in the experience of the Spirit that blows wherever it wills, even across confessional and denominational lines, and leadership based on charism rather than on office. Baptism in the Spirit, spontaneous utterances or prophecies, and healings and inspired hymns commonly occur during the prayer meetings. Three criticisms sometimes made of the charismatic movement are (1) its tendency toward a fundamentalist reading of the Bible; (2) its favoring the intense, intimate experience of prayer groups at the expense of social concern; and (3) the emotionalism that often characterizes charismatic prayer.

One has to distinguish, however, the charismatic movement from the charismatic nature of Christian religious experience. Safeguarding the charismatic dimension of Christian faith requires vigilance. On the one hand, there lies the danger of sectarianism and losing a sense of communion with the wider church; while on the other hand, there is the tendency of the wider church to attempt to contain and impose an institutional stamp on what is essentially free and uncontrollable. A number of religious congregations began as charismatic movements; indeed, religious life ought always to be a manifestation of the Spirit. It could even be argued that the church itself is fundamentally a charismatic reality, founded at Pentecost.

William Reiser, s.j.

See also BAPTISM IN THE SPIRIT; CHARISM/CHARISMATIC; CHURCH; GLOSSOLALIA; HOLY SPIRIT; PENTECOST (IN CHRISTIANITY); PENTECOSTALISM; SPIRIT.

CHARISM/CHARISMATIC

These terms derive from the Greek word *charisma*, meaning gift or grace. In the Bible, primarily the New Testament, charism is seen as a gift, of which there are many, from the one Spirit to believers. The term charismatic, as used, for example, in the phrase, "charismatic leader," names the quality of possessing a concentration of exceptional powers or qualities that set one apart from the ordinary person. These exceptional powers are viewed as divine in origin.

Although the term charism does not appear in the Old Testament, the concept is there, especially in reference to certain individuals who are empowered by the Spirit of the Lord to do extraordinary feats. Primarily, this divinely given spiritual power enables leaders to be victorious militarily (for instance, Othniel in Judg 3:10; Gideon in Judg 9:39), or to demonstrate unusual physical strength (for example, Samson in Judg 14:6). With the dawn of the monarchy, the spirit was understood to reside permanently in the kings, although not all manifested remarkable qualities.

In the New Testament, charism is used occasionally to refer to the "one person Jesus Christ" (Rom 5:15) or to "eternal life" (Rom 6:23). More commonly, it refers to specific spiritual gifts. Two Greek expressions used for "spiritual gifts" are *ta pneumatika* and *pneumatikon charisma*, both terms emphasizing the origin of the individual gifts, namely the Spirit (*pneuma*). They are freely and diversely given to members of the Body of Christ to be exercised for building up the community, the church.

There are several lists of spiritual gifts in the Pauline literature (1 Cor 12:4-11, 28-30; Rom 12:6-8; Eph 4:1-12; cf. 1 Pet 4:10-11), all of which are different, clearly suggesting that no one list is definitive or exhaustive.

The various gifts may be organized into three different groups. (1) There are *gifts of utterance*, including prophecy, exhortation, instruction, speaking in tongues, the ability to interpret tongues, the ability to distinguish between true and false prophecy. (2) The *gifts of practical ministry* include care for the needy, financial contribution, acts of mercy, administration, and teaching. (3) Finally, there are *gifts of wonderworking*, including healing and performing miracles.

Paul articulates some basic tenets about the spiritual gifts in 1 Corinthians 12–14. He affirms that the variety of charisms, though many, are from the one source: the same Spirit, the same Lord, the same God (see 1 Cor 12:4-6), and hence their exercise is to foster unity, not division. Further, Paul stresses that every person has received some "manifestation of the Spirit" (12:7). Paul emphasizes the importance of love, calling it the greatest of all gifts (1 Cor 13).

The person who stands at the origin of a religious movement is often endowed with remarkable spiritual gifts, and thus hailed as a charismatic leader. However, as Max Weber has pointed out, in the transition to subsequent generations of such a movement, the charisma of the founder is "routinized," structures emerge, and institutionalization takes place. Then, the challenge for the religious community is to find ways to remain faithful to the original charism of its founder.

John Gillman

See also GIFTS OF THE SPIRIT; HOLY SPIRIT; MINISTRY/MINISTERIAL; PNEUMA; PROPHECY.

CHARITY

The words charity and love are often used interchangeably, but charity sometimes carries the added note of service of one's neighbor, as in the phrase "works of charity." While all truly Christian service proceeds from love, charity connotes love in action or practice. Scripture should be the starting point for understanding the meaning and range of usage of charity. Three important texts are: (1) Mark 12:28-33, where love of God and love of neighbor are intimately linked; (2) 1 Corinthians 13, where Paul explains the priority of charity in Christian living (in Gal 5:22 charity is referred to as a fruit of the Spirit); and (3) 1 John 4:7-21, where God is defined as love. Charity, therefore, is the concrete confirmation and demonstration of the presence of God in a person's life.

Love (or charity) considered as a moral virtue falls under the domain of ethics and moral theology, while love or charity as a properly theological virtue is treated in systematic theology, since one cannot talk about God apart from God's charity toward humanity, and one cannot adequately describe the human being apart from its capacity to love and be loved (love being the verbal form of the noun charity). Thus, a person who has never known or experienced love would be unable to know God, because "Whoever does not love does not know God, for God is love" (1 John 4:8). This statement has far-reaching implications. Wherever men and women truly love, there the Spirit of God is present, whatever their religious tradition.

William Reiser, S.J.

See also HOLINESS; LOVE (IN GENERAL); PERFECTION; THEOLOGICAL VIRTUES; VIA UNITIVA.

CHARLEMAGNE (742?–814)

Charles "the Great" was the son of Pippin, the king of the Franks. When his father died in 768, Charles inherited the throne along with his brother, Carloman. When Carloman died in 771, Charles became sole ruler and began a consolidation and expansion of the Frankish kingdom which, at its furthest extent, embraced much of what is now modern western Europe. Charles undertook an ambitious reform of these territories, both secular and religious. His educational reforms were spearheaded by the famous scholar Alcuin of York. Charles also initiated important reforms in the liturgy and attempted reforms in church discipline and teaching. On Christmas day in the year 800, Charles was crowned Roman Emperor by Pope Leo III, thus, in theory, replacing Empress Irene in Constantinople. Charlemagne did not acknowledge this usurpation, however, and the title, which was passed on through Charlemagne's descendents, was modified to "Holy Roman Emperor." Charlemagne's empire began to fall apart after his death, but not all his reforms died with him, and his reign is considered by some historians to be the beginning of modern Europe.

Gary Macy

See also ALCUIN; MEDIEVAL CHRISTIANITY (IN THE WEST).

CHARM OR SPELL

A set of words that, with or without an accompanying gesture, have the power to significantly affect a person, an animal, or an object. The affected person, animal, or object might acquire certain properties or powers unavailable to it without the effects of the charm or spell. A charm or spell can also harm or control the person, animal, or object against which it is directed. Frequently uttered by persons who have a special knowledge or power, sometimes a charm or spell bears its power in the very utterance of the words and thus could be effective as uttered by anyone. Some religions believe, or have in the past believed, in the reality of charms or spells, while others do not. It should be clear that sometimes the word "charm" is not used to mean a spell but to mean an amulet.

Orlando Espín

See also AMULET.

CHARVAKA

Charvaka (Sanskrit, Sweet Talker) is the name of an ancient Indian school of skeptical, hedonist, materialist philosophy, the Charvakas, as well as the name of a philosopher said to be its founder. The major work attributed to Charvaka, the *Brihaspatya Sutras*, is no longer extant. Charvaka—if he was a historical person—and his school (the Charvakas) flourished around the middle of the first millennium B.C.E. The only evidence we have of his teachings are references to him in Hindu, Buddhist, and Jain texts, in which he is vigorously criticized as a teacher of pernicious doctrines and held up as a symbol of irreligion. According to these sources, he ridiculed the Vedas and denied the possibility of any existence after death. Believing that sense experience is the only valid source of knowledge, we are told, he taught that the goal of life is to maximize physical pleasures and minimize pain.

Lance E. Nelson

See also ATHEISM; MATERIALISM; VEDAS.

CHASTITY

Although "chastity" names the second of the traditional religious vows, the word has a broader meaning. Chastity is the virtue that directs human sexual behavior, whether we are single, married, or vowed religious. Every expression of human love ought to be chaste, that is, it ought to proceed from a heart whose first love is the word of God. As a virtue, chastity refers to the need for restraint and moderation in the exercise of one's sexual appetite; it is something to which all Christians are summoned by reason of their being baptized into Christ Jesus.

The development of chastity is part and parcel of a person's overall growth in the Spirit. As the mind and heart become purified in the mystery of dying with Christ, and as they become liberated in the mystery of rising with him, our affections and desires likewise become transformed by his life. Chastity is a sign of the human spirit's freedom, of love purified and liberated. According to the *Catechism of the Catholic Church*, chastity falls under the category of temperance. Paul viewed self-control as a fruit of the Spirit's presence in our lives (Gal 5:23). From a Christian standpoint, chastity is as much an expression of healthy psychological integration and moral development as it is of spirituality.

William Reiser, S.J.

See also CELIBACY; OBEDIENCE; POVERTY; SEXUALITY; VIRTUE; VOWS (RELIGIOUS).

CHÁVEZ, CÉSAR (1927–93)

Catholic layman and labor leader. Born in Yuma, Arizona, Chávez later moved to California's San Joaquín Valley. A farm worker and devout Catholic himself, in 1962 he began to organize (with Dolores Huerta) the United Farm Workers Union. He was quite active in promoting the rights of migrant and other agriculture field workers. His Latino Catholic roots became apparent in his prominent display of the religious symbols of the mostly Catholic Mexican and Mexican-American farm workers, in his active nonviolence, and in his explicit and unwavering justification of the farm workers' movement along the broad lines of Catholic social doctrine. His impact on U.S. Latino Catholic circles has been immense, awakening the Christian social conscience of many. Chávez is regarded as a model of Catholic lay involvement in social struggles for justice. He died still fighting for the farm workers.

Orlando Espín

See also CATHOLIC SOCIAL TEACHING; ECONOMY; ETHICS, SOCIAL; JUSTICE; LATINO CATHOLICISM.

CHAZZAN

See CANTOR (IN JUDAISM).

CH'ENG HUANG

(Chinese, god of walls and ditches). This is a general classification referring to an ancient form of popular patron deity in

Chinese folk religion. In the bureaucratic hierarchy of the spiritual realm, he is perceived as the minister of justice and the spiritual magistrate in charge of bereaved spirits. In folk practice, he is honored as the spiritual mayor of a town or city and prayed to for the town's general well-being, as well as for help with difficult legal cases.

G. D. DeAngelis

See also T'U TI KUNG.

CHENU, MARIE DOMINIQUE (1895–1990)

French Dominican theologian and historian. Chenu was professor and later rector at the French Dominican House of Studies at Le Saulchoir and a founder of the New Theology movement advocating the study of tradition history in service of contemporary theological reflection. Chenu urged the use of textual studies and the historical-critical method for the study of medieval thinkers. Chenu's studies of Thomas Aquinas revealed the innovative and dynamic character of Thomas's thought. As his convictions about the social character of faith led to his support of the French Catholic Action and the worker priest movements, his views came under suspicion. His writings were placed on the Index, and Chenu was forbidden to teach in 1942. An invitation to serve as expert (peritus) to Vatican Council II reinstated him, and his hand can be seen in the conciliar document Gaudium et Spes. Yves Congar is perhaps his best-known student.

Patricia Plovanich

CHERUBIM

(Hebrew, plural of "cherub"). Winged celestial beings stationed at the entrance to the Garden of Eden to guard the path to the tree of life (Gen 3:24). Three-dimensional images of cherubs were found in the tabernacle the Israelites carried with them in the wilderness (Exod 25:19) and in Solomon's Temple (1 Kgs 6:25-27). In these settings, the cherubim apparently represented the resting place of the invisible glory of God. Cherubim figure prominently in Ezekiel's vision of God's celestial throne room (see, for example, Ezek 10:7-14) and are well known in the art and symbolism of the ancient Near East. They combine the features of humans and animals and, because of their wings, have complete mobility. They therefore were appropriate representations of deities who were viewed as neither animal nor human and who moved where people could not. The cherubim described in the Bible are in no way similar to the round-faced infants that commonly represent cherubim in Western art.

Alan J. Avery-Peck

CHESTERTON, GILBERT KEITH (1874–1936)

Prolific English writer and convert to Catholicism, Chesterton saw himself as a defender of Christian orthodoxy in a de-Christianized world. His publications included Heretics (1905) and Orthodoxy (1908); biographies of Thomas Aquinas and Francis of Assisi; an autobiography in 1936; poems and newspaper columns; and numerous novels, including those in a "Father Brown" series. He also broadcast regularly on BBC radio. Though Chesterton left the Church of England for the Roman Catholic Church in 1922, his influence continued to be felt widely in Britain, beyond the limits of Catholic circles.

Thomas Worcester, S.J.

See also MODERNITY; OXFORD MOVEMENT.

CHEVRA KADESHA

(Hebrew, "holy brotherhood"). Originally, a name for Jewish charitable societies in general; among Ashkenazic Jews, the term now indicates, in particular, a voluntary society that accepts responsibility for the proper burial of Jewish dead. The Chevra Kadesha's tasks generally include washing the corpse, accompanying it to the grave, and completing the burial. Since Judaism deems fulfillment of these religious obligations to be particularly meritorious, membership in the Chevra Kadesha is a coveted honor. While the term Chevra Kadesha appears as early as the Talmudic period, its current use as the title for a burial society emerged in medieval times.

Alan J. Avery-Peck

See also BURIAL (IN JUDAISM); TACHRICHIN; TAHARAH.

CH'I

(Chinese, *qi*, vital energy). This is a traditional primary concept in Chinese cosmology based on the religious, philosophical, and scientific tenet that there is an active energy in all living things in the universe. This energy is both the basic substance of all creation and the life force, and is often referred to popularly as cosmic breath. This energy is considered raw and wild and, as such, needs to be controlled or harnessed. A great deal of traditional Chinese medicine, martial arts, meditative practice, and *feng-shui* practice are based on this theory of vital energy and the beneficent effects that can be brought about if one learns to control it. From both a Taoist and Confucian perspective, it is important to align one's *ch'i* with the *ch'i* of the universe or Tao for balance, order, and harmony in one's life. For Confucians, this was perceived as moral cultivation, while Taoists considered it a physical realignment of energy through meditation, breath control, and diet.

G. D. DeAngelis

See also CONFUCIANISM; DAOISM; FENG-SHUI; T'AI CHI; TAO; YIN AND YANG.

CHILDREN OF ISRAEL

See ISRAEL.

CHILIASM/CHILIASTIC

From the Greek word for "thousand," chiliasm is a form of millenarianism, the Christian belief in the future thousand-year reign of Jesus the Christ in peace and justice. Related to adventism and synonymous with premillennialism, chiliasm is the belief that the second coming of Jesus will occur prior to the millennium, and that Christ will preside over it in corporeal form. Not adopted by all Christians, chiliasm is most often believed by fundamentalists and scriptural inerrantists. It is based on literal interpretations of the biblical books of Daniel and Revelation, especially Revelation 20.

Evelyn A. Kirkley

See also ADVENTISTS; FUNDAMENTALISM (ATTITUDE); MILLENARIANISM.

CH'ING MING

(Chinese, *ching-ming*, clear and bright). This is one of the most important festivals on the Chinese religious calendar, and one of the more persistent throughout Chinese history. Sometimes referred to as the Rites of Spring Festival, it is a form of ancestor worship where the kinship ties between the living and the dead are renewed. This celebration takes place one hundred and five days after the winter solstice in the third lunar month, and symbolically represents a coming back to life of both the earth and the ancestral spirits. It is a family reunion of sorts between living members and deceased ancestors, in which gravesites are cleaned and tombs restored in a festive atmosphere. It is the most important of the three special occasions of the year for visiting ancestral tombs and graves. It is one of the few universal religious practices found throughout China.

G. D. DeAngelis

See also ANCESTORS, CHINESE; FENG-SHUI; FILIAL PIETY.

CHOL HAMOED

(Hebrew, "the secular days of the festival"). In Judaism, the intermediate days of the weeklong festivals of Passover and Tabernacles. The first and last days of these holidays are designated "holy convocations" on which work is entirely forbidden (see Exod 12:15-16, regarding Passover, and Lev 22:34-36, regarding Tabernacles). While on the days between these holy convocations work is not entirely forbidden, certain restrictions continue to apply. First and foremost, during this period, the central obligations of the festival must be observed: during the intermediate days of Passover, leavened products may not be eaten, and during the intermediate days of Tabernacles, people continue to dwell outdoors in huts. Additionally, during Chol HaMoed, as on the preceding and following days of holy convocation, marriages may not be performed, mourning rituals are forbidden, and, during daily worship, portions of the liturgy appropriate to the particular holiday are recited. Finally, although during Chol HaMoed, unlike on the holy convocations, work is not entirely prohibited, in recognition of the holiday, only work that is absolutely essential is carried out.

Alan J. Avery-Peck

See also PASSOVER; TABERNACLES, FEAST OF.

CHORIEPISKOPOS

In the early church, this was the name of the bishop with jurisdiction only over a rural district, but in turn always dependent on an ordinary diocesan bishop. In the Eastern Churches (Orthodox and Catholic), they were eventually replaced by deacons and priests without episcopal ordination. The choriepiscopal ministry survived, but very limited in scope, until the thirteenth century, remaining today only as an honorary title in some of the Eastern Churches. In the West, they were especially popular as missionary bishops in Germany during the eighth and ninth centuries, but the ministry was eventually replaced by priests without episcopal ordination by the twelfth century. In the West, the liturgical functions of the choriepiskopos survive in the those of the mitered abbots.

Orlando Espín

See also ABBOT/ABBESS; BISHOP (EPISCOPACY); BISHOP (ORDINARY); DEACON; ORIENTAL CHURCHES; PRIESTHOOD.

CHOSEN PEOPLE

See COVENANT (IN JUDAISM).

CHOU DYNASTY

See ZHOU DYNASTY.

CHRISM

One of the three liturgical oils. The others are oil of the sick (used in the sacrament of the sick) and oil of catechumens (used in the rites of the catechumenate and in baptism). All three are blessed by the bishop, usually during Holy Week, at the Chrism Mass. Chrism is used in baptism, confirmation, and priestly ordination, and in the dedication of an altar. The words chrism and Christ come from the same Greek root, meaning "to anoint." Just as God anointed Jesus, giving him a unique identity, mission, and dignity, so those anointed with chrism in baptism, confirmation, and ordination are understood to share this identity, mission, and dignity. The rite for the dedication of an altar explains that "the anointing with chrism makes the altar a symbol of Christ . . . the Anointed One" (no. 22). Chrism is made of olive oil mixed with balsam, giving it a distinct evergreen aroma. The other two liturgical oils are olive oil alone.

Patrick L. Malloy

See also ANOINTING OF THE SICK, SACRAMENT OF; BAPTISM/CONFIRMATION; CHRIST.

CHRIST

The term Christ comes from the Greek translation of the Hebrew word *masiah* which means "the anointed (of Yahweh)." The Hebrew anointing image conveyed a sense of vocation or mission from God. Thus, the New Testament kerygma that proposed Jesus as Christ reflected the early Christian conviction that Jesus was the messianic figure. This meaning disappeared late in the first century when Gentile Christians used Christ as Jesus' own (proper) name. In time, the two names, Jesus and Christ, became interchangeable. In popular Christian piety, the name Christ is often understood to indicate Jesus' divinity. Recent theological efforts to gain a greater sense of the human person, Jesus of Nazareth, through use of historical-critical methods, distinguish the real Jesus

from his designations as the Christ, which means the interpretative perspectives in the New Testament that explain Jesus' mission or identity. By extension, the term Christ can indicate all later theological interpretations of Jesus' meaning and being.

Patricia Plovanich

See also CHRIST OF FAITH; CHRISTOLOGY; JESUS OF HISTORY.

CHRISTENDOM

From the eleventh century until the modern period, the English word "Christendom" referred either to the state of being Christian, Christianity itself, or to the countries professing Christianity taken as a whole. During more recent times, the word has taken on a pejorative connotation, referring to the society that resulted from the merging of Christianity with the secular government and/or with secular society. The constrast was made, for instance, by Søren Kierkegaard between Christianity and the religious establishment supported by the state that Kierkegaard calls "Christendom." He claimed that Christendom is not and cannot be Christian since it identifies being "Christian" with merely being a member of a particular society with no further spiritual or moral claims. In this sense of the word, "Christendom" began when Constantine adopted Christianity as his favored religion and began to incorporate it into the structure of the Roman government. This second sense of the word nearly reverses the sense of the early usage, since "Christendom" in the modern sense can never be truly Christian and is, in fact, a perversion of true Christianity.

Gary Macy

See also CHRISTIANITY; CONSTANTINE I THE GREAT; KIERKEGAARD, SØREN.

CHRISTIAN

A name originally given to followers of Jesus, most likely by outsiders, and perhaps initially used in a derogatory sense. From Acts 11:26 it is evident that *Christianoi* was first used for disciples in Syrian Antioch in the early 40s. The term literally means "Christ's adherents," those who belong to him. It reveals, however, that those who coined it thought of *Christos* as a proper name rather than as the title it was, *ho Christos*, that is, the Messiah or Anointed One.

In the New Testament this epithet is found only in two other places: Acts 26:28, where Agrippa suggests Paul wants him to become a Christian; and 1 Peter 4:16, which envisions that a believer might suffer punishment as a Christian. According to Tacitus, *Annals* xv.44, those blamed and persecuted for the conflagration in Rome in the Neronian persecution of the mid 60s were called Christians by the populace of Rome. This generally applied label then became the official Roman designation for members of the church, and it was during times of persecution that a believer was thus challenged with the confession or denial of this name.

In their own writings, Christians long avoided the term, except when referring to their conflicts with paganism and the charges that might be brought against them (as in 1 Pet 4:16). They called themselves, among other terms, Nazarenes, brethren (a masculine plural which included women), disciples, and believers. Apparently no attempt was made to form a title from the name of Jesus.

Over time, since "Christian" was indeed the name martyrs suffered and died under, and because it contained the name of the Christ, the term, in fact, supplied what the members of the churches needed to distinguish themselves as followers of Jesus from other Jews and pagans, as well as in later centuries from many other religious traditions.

Today, the name Christian is used by every form of belief deriving from early Christianity.

F. M. Gillman

See also CATHOLIC TRADITION; CHRISTIANITY; ORTHODOXY (IN CHRISTIANITY); PROTESTANTISM/ PROTESTANT.

CHRISTIANITY

Christianity can be understood as a family of faith traditions united in their monotheism and in their belief in the central role of Jesus of Nazareth in redemption. Taken together, this family of traditions makes up the largest faith grouping in the world today, with some two billion members or just under a third of the world's population. Christians can be found on all continents, and because Christianity has had and continues to have such a wide range of customs, beliefs, and institutional structures, any brief synopsis will necessarily undervalue the richness of Christianity as it is actually lived, so that the best the following article can hope to present are the shadowy outlines of the majority consensus about Christianity and its beliefs and practices.

Brief History

Christianity began as a sect of Judaism in the first century C.E. that believed that Joshua ("Jesus" in Greek) from the town of Nazareth was the Messiah ("Christos" in Greek) promised in the Hebrew Scripture. He had been a teacher, healer, and miracle worker executed by the Romans for sedition, and was believed by his followers to have been raised from the dead. Members of the group held that they shared in the life of their risen leader and that they would also eventually share in a future kingdom ruled by Jesus if they lived up to the teachings and example of Jesus. Christians preached the equality of all peoples and were known for their remarkable generosity. Their beliefs spread among both Jews and Gentiles throughout the cities of the Roman Empire. Christians gradually separated themselves from Judaism and established themselves as an independent group. Despite sporadic, but often harsh, persecution by the Roman government, the movement spread rapidly. During this time, educated Christians began to express their beliefs in the language of the reigning philosophies of the day, especially that of Platonism. The translation, or perhaps more accurately, the integration, of Christian beliefs into Platonic thought and language would be a centuries-long struggle, but the end result would be a fusion that informs the basic creeds of Christianity to the present day.

By 324, Emperor Constantine ended the persecution of Christianity and adopted Christianity as his favored religion. This imperial sponsorship continued unbroken except for the brief reign of Julian the Apostate, and marked a monumental shift in the history of Christianity. Christian communities and leadership were integrated into the Roman government, a move some Christians welcomed. Others, however, withdrew from Roman society, believing that the true Christianity could only live free from the constraints of any political or social system. This tendency toward separation would continue to drive some Christians throughout history to experiment with new social groupings that stood over against the social, cultural, and historical structures of their day. Christians were never a united group, but their dissension took on political importance once they were integrated into

the Roman government. The Arian and then Nestorian controversies rocked the church and the Empire in the fourth and fifth centuries as Christians debated how to express in Platonic language their belief that the one God of all had been uniquely expressed in the person of Jesus. Although a majority consensus on these issues was reached at the Council of Chalcedon in 451 C.E., the Nestorian and Monophysite Christians refused to accept that compromise and still remain separate Christian communities. In main, however, this was a time of stabilization for Christianity. Its central creeds were produced at the Councils of Nicaea, Constantinople, and Chalcedon. The corpus of Christian Scripture was determined and, with few variations, has remained fixed throughout Christian history.

The expansion of Islam in the seventh and eighth centuries gradually removed Christianity as a force in the Middle East, concentrating Christian communities into two distinct faith groupings. One group centered on Constantinople where the Roman Empire, now much reduced, continued the traditions of the fourth and fifth centuries. A lively missionary effort brought this tradition to Russia and the countries of Eastern Europe from which a series of autonomous churches united with the patriarch of Constantinople came to make up Eastern or Byzantine Christianity. Eastern Christianity was shaken in the eighth and ninth centuries by the iconoclast controversy, the resolution of which helped to establish the important central role in Eastern Christianity, both of the liturgy and of monasticism. In the Western Empire, Christianity faced waves of Teutonic tribal invasions, from the Gothic tribes in the sixth century through the Nordic invasions of the tenth century. The immediate concerns of Western

Christians were evangelization of the tribes, preservation of Christian traditions and learning, and overcoming the trauma caused by the invasions. When the imperial government could no longer provide protection from the invaders, the Bishops of Rome took their own initiative in negotiating with the tribes. The independence of the Western Empire was complete with the crowning of a Frankish lord, Charlemagne, as emperor by the pope in 800 C.E.

For two centuries, Western Christianity paled in comparison with the Christianity of the East. Only with the Gregorian reforms did the Western church begin to recover from the effect of the Teutonic invasions. Under the leadership of a reformed and reforming papacy, a separate and fairly independent ecclesiastical culture grew up in the West, centered on Rome. Eastern and Western Christianity continued to drift apart linguistically and theologically until, in 1054, mutual misunderstanding led to mutual excommunication, and a rupture between Eastern and Western Christians became explicit. Despite several attempts at reunion, this split, referred to as the Great Schism, has not yet been healed. This was a time of growth for Western Europe. Not only did Christianity expand geographically to the north, east, and south, but advances were made in learning, art, literature, and law. New forms of Christianity emerged, some judged orthodox and others not. The question of authority was raised with growing urgency, especially when the papacy itself experienced its own internal schism with the election of two popes in the late fourteenth century.

The question of authority reached a crisis point in the early sixteenth century when Western Christianity itself split into several independent religious groupings in a process known as the Reformation. The Lutheran, Anglican, and Calvinist churches were only the largest of the churches that ceased to see Rome as the center of authority for Western Christianity, and instead advocated a return to the Bible as the center of Christian life. Those Christians who remained loyal to Rome themselves regrouped at the Council of Trent (1545–63), offering their own form of reformed Christianity. The fissions that began in the sixteenth century continued with more or less hostility down to the mid-twentieth century when a movement to reunite Christians of both the East and the West gained widespread support.

Before the Reformation began, however, Christianity had spread to the Americas where Spanish and Portuguese missionaries established what would eventually become the largest Christian grouping in the world. The Catholicism that developed in southern North America, Central, and South America was slow to adopt the reforms of Trent and continued many late medieval devotional practices, merging them with indigenous religiosity as well as practices and beliefs brought from Africa by the slave trade.

Protestant and Anglican Christianity was brought to North America in the seventeenth century, while Portuguese and Spanish missionaries spread Christianity to Asia. The great period of missionary activity for Christianity accompanied European empire building in the eighteenth and nineteenth centuries, and gradually Christianity spread to sub-Saharan Africa, Asia, and Australia. Meanwhile, in Europe, Christianity was being challenged first by the Enlightenment and by different theories of materialism. The power of Christianity to convince was disappearing in Europe just as it was spreading in other parts of the world.

Christianity today is stronger in North and South America than in Europe and is growing in Africa and Asia, while many of the Eastern Christian communities are just beginning to emerge from seventy-five years of Communist domination. The future of Christianity would seem to lie outside Europe, since, for the first time since the seventh century, the majority of Christians are not of European origin. It may well be that Christianity once again faces a period of adaptation.

Beliefs

Central to Christianity is a historical person, Jesus, rather than an idea or set of ideas. This means that Christianity was and remains first of all a way of life and only secondly a set of dogmatic beliefs. Christians celebrate and hope to imitate the life, death, and resurrection of Jesus. Therefore the central focus of Christianity is on actions. When Christians are living up to their own ideals, they are called to be compassionate, charitable, forgiving, and loving. Historically, Christians have usually only pursued dogmatic questions when tension in the community demanded it. Having said that, however, we must acknowledge a set of central Christian beliefs to which most, but not all, Christians would adhere.

Christians, following Judaism, are monotheists. They believe there is but one God who is the Creator and Redeemer of the universe. This creates a series of problems for Christians when they speak of the exact relationship of Jesus to the one God. Christians insist that Jesus is both a real human being and a full revelation of the divine. This central concept of the Incarnation encapsulates the Christian belief in a God so loving that God would suffer death to make our salvation possible. Once one makes such an assertion, how-ever, explaining it becomes extremely difficult. Using Platonic categories, Christians of the fourth and fifth centuries hammered out a compromise language which asserts that Jesus as the Christ is both fully divine and fully human. Further, the divinity in which Jesus partakes is not different from the divinity of the one God, that is to say, Jesus as the Christ is not in any sense another God. The use of Platonism further complicates Christian ideas of God, however, since the unchanging nature of the Platonic God clashes with the notion of God active in history both in the life of Jesus and in the life of the Christian community. Christians have offered and continue to offer more or less convincing explanations for this belief, but it remains a tension in Christianity. The most enduring explanation of how the actions of the one God can be mediated through Jesus as Christ, as well as through the Christian community, remains the Christian dogma of the Trinity.

Equally central to Christian belief is the assertion that the life, death, and resurrection of Jesus are of decisive significance in overcoming sin and evil. Since Jesus did not immediately return to establish his kingdom on earth after his resurrection, Christians have developed several different but overlapping understandings of how evil has been and will be overcome. On one hand, Christians have understood salvation as personal and immediate. The life of the risen Christ is explained as transforming believers' lives here and now, allowing them to live a life of charity and trust in God modeled after that of Jesus. Christians may also speak of an afterlife where good and evil are judged and rewarded or punished. Some Christians look forward to the establishment of the kingdom of Christ on earth—either a kingdom built by the political and social action of Christians themselves, or one imposed by the returning Christ come to judge the world.

Finally, most Christians join together ritually to experience the empowering presence of the risen Christ in the community. This gathering can range from the extremely simple Quaker meeting to the elaborate and spectacular Eastern liturgies. Most Christians share two central liturgical celebrations. First, there is an initiation into the Christian community through a ritual washing or baptism. Again, this ritual can be very elaborate or very simple, but most Christians consider some form of baptism essential to the beginning of the Christian life. Christians also share a ritual meal in which they believe they share in a renewal of the empowering presence of Christ. The ritual includes two parts: a reading of Scripture and a sharing in consecrated bread and wine. For most Protestant groups, the reading of Scripture followed by a commentary upon it is felt to be the best way to mediate the presence of the risen Christ. For Roman Catholics and Eastern Christians the partaking of the bread and wine are considered a more intimate way in which to share in the life of Christ. This once decisive and divisive difference has lessened in the last fifty years, as Christians have attempted to resolve this as well as other divisive issues of doctrine and practice as part of the ecumenical movement.

This overview of Christianity is necessarily vague, cursory, and lifeless. Christianity, like all families of faith communities, is much more diverse, much more alive. Few Christians will see their own beliefs precisely mirrored here. Further information on all branches of Christianity is readily available, however, and, then, of course, the only real way to know Christianity is to get to know those who profess their faith in Christ.

Gary Macy

See also AFRICAN CHRISTIANITY; ANGLICAN COMMUNION; ARIANISM; BAPTISM/CONFIRMATION; BIBLE; BISHOP (EPISCOPACY); BYZANTINE CATHOLIC CHURCHES; BYZANTIUM/ BYZANTINE; CALVINISM; CANON, BIBLICAL; CATHOLICISM/CATHOLIC TRADITION; CHALCEDONIAN CHRISTIANS; CHALCEDONIAN DEFINITION; CHARLEMAGNE; CHRIST; CHRISTIAN; CHURCH; CLERGY; CONGREGATIONAL CHURCHES; CONSTANTINOPLE, SEE OF; COUNTER-REFORMATION/CATHOLIC REFORMATION; CREED/SYMBOL OF FAITH; DOCTRINE; DOGMA; EASTERN CATHOLIC; ECUMENICAL MOVEMENT; ESCHATOLOGY (IN CHRISTIANITY); EUCHARIST; EVANGELICALS; FAITH; GOD; GOSPEL; GREGORIAN REFORMS; HEBREW SCRIPTURES; HERESY; HETERODOXY; HISPANIC; HYPOSTATIC UNION; ICONOCLASTIC CONTROVERSY; JESUS OF HISTORY; JUDAISM; LATINO/A; LITURGY (IN CHRISTIANITY); MEDIEVAL CHRISTIANITY (IN THE WEST); MISSIONARIES; MONASTICISM IN EASTERN CHRISTIANITY; MONASTICISM IN WESTERN CHRISTIANITY; MONOTHEISM (IN CHRISTIANITY, AND IN ISLAM); MUSLIM; NEW TESTAMENT; OLD TESTAMENT; ORDERS, RELIGIOUS; ORTHODOX CHURCHES; ORTHODOXY (IN CHRISTIANITY); PAPACY/ PAPAL; PERSECUTION (IN CHRISTIANITY); PLATONISM; PREDESTINATION (IN CHRISTIANITY); QUAKERS; RATIONALISM; REDEMPTION, CHRISTIAN; REFORMATION; REFORMED CHURCHES; RELIGION; RELIGION, CRITIQUE OF; RESURRECTION OF CHRIST; REVELATION (IN CHRISTIAN PERSPECTIVE); ROMAN CATHOLIC CHURCH; ROME, SEE OF; SALVATION; SECULARISM; SYNCRETISM; THEISM/THEISTIC; TRIDENTINE.

CHRISTIAN SCIENCE CHURCH

Officially known as the Church of Christ, Scientist, the Christian Science movement was founded in Lynn, Massachusetts, by Mary Baker Eddy (1821–1919). Eddy was a sickly woman who suffered several unhappy marriages and studied various healing techniques. In 1866 she slipped on an icy pavement and nearly died. After three days, she miraculously recovered after receiving a revelation of divine healing. In 1875 she published *Science and Health with Key to the Scriptures*, her teachings about scientific healing based on the New Testament, considered authoritative scripture by church members, along with the Bible. She began instructing students in healing, and in 1879 she organized the Church of Christ, Scientist. In 1881 she founded a metaphysical college; in 1883, a journal; and in 1886, a national association.

The central affirmation of Christian Science is the reality of spirit and unreality of matter, sin, and death. God is perfect spirit, impersonal ideal of life, love, and mind. Illness is the result of belief in evil; quite literally, to Christian Scientists, illness is all in one's head. Healing consists in realizing this truth through reading and prayer. While church members consider themselves authentically Christian, most Christians do not. Christian Science has been especially attractive to women, the elderly, and to those struggling with chronic illness. A high percentage of Christian Science practitioners were women, finding in the church personal empowerment and leadership.

The church has been beset by internal and external controversies from its foundation. Several of Eddy's early students broke away from her and established their own mental healing movements. Toward the end of her life, Eddy became convinced she was the victim of "malicious animal magnetism," harmful thoughts directed at her from her enemies. Eddy responded to criticism by standardizing her teachings and establishing a hierarchical organization headquartered in Boston. Doctors also opposed Christian Science, claiming that its healing techniques were fraudulent and life-threatening. Christian Scientists have fought numerous legal battles to gain the right to refuse conventional medical treatment. In recent years, court cases have focused on the rights of Christian Science parents to deny conventional medical treatment for their children. The church is also well known for its periodicals, and particularly its newspaper the *Christian Science Monitor*, and its reading rooms located in most U.S. cities.

Evelyn A. Kirkley

CHRISTMAS

The Christian feast of Christmas celebrates the Incarnation, the first movement in the theological understanding of Christ's redemptive action, the paschal mystery; more specifically, the feast focuses on the nativity, or birth, of Jesus Christ.

In the early church, the celebration of Sunday was the initial feast, which contained within it a large number of theological themes. During the second century, the central feast known as Easter began to be celebrated as a separate festal event in the church's liturgy. During that same century, another great feast began to be celebrated in the Christian East: Epiphany (January 6), which commemorated many of Jesus Christ's initial "appearances" or manifestations in the world (for example, Nativity, the visit of the Magi, more popularly known as the Wise Men or Three Kings, and Christ's baptism in the Jordan). During the fourth century, Epiphany was also celebrated in the Christian West, along with another important feast commemorating the actual nativity of Jesus Christ: the feast of Christmas (from the Middle English for "Christ's Mass"), set on December 25. The feast may have been celebrated in Rome as early as 330 C.E. Some conjecture that the feast of Christmas (and possibly Epiphany) may have been instituted to offset other pagan celebrations of the winter solstice held at this time.

Roman liturgy was much influenced by the demands of the papal liturgy, that is, the calendar and forms of liturgical celebration prescribed for the pope. One of these expectations was the practice of the pope celebrating liturgy at different Roman churches on different days of the liturgical year (*stational* liturgy). That is why, by the beginning of the seventh century, it was the custom in Rome to celebrate three Masses (or Eucharists) on December 25: one "at night," which became the traditional Midnight Mass; one at dawn; and one during the day. This practice spread throughout western Europe as the Roman liturgy became widely used.

Other medieval developments included the celebration of the "feast of fools," around January 1; the use of the Christmas *crèche*, or nativity scene in the stable; and the connection of St. Nicholas (feast day, December 6) with the practice of gift-giving during the Christmas season. This served as the beginning of the modern American concept of Santa Claus (in England, the figure is known as Father Christmas).

Due to the riotous feasting and carousing associated with the celebration of Christmas in sixteenth-century England, the celebration of the feast was originally forbidden in Puritan New England. However, it quickly became a cultural as well as a religious holiday in the United States; today, the emphasis is largely on the season, not the religious content, in general American society. Greeting cards (Christmas cards) are often mailed to family and friends, and the U.S. Post Office issues yearly stamps with Christmas and seasonal themes. In many Christian traditions, it is the custom to attend church on that day; the liturgical color, for those churches who use them, is white for rejoicing. Some traditions also continue the early medieval practice of celebrating a service at midnight, for instance, the Roman Catholic Midnight Mass.

Joanne M. Pierce

See also LITURGICAL YEAR; PASCHAL MYSTERY.

CHRISTOCENTRIC

The term Christocentric means Christ-centered and designates a worldview or emphasis which interprets person, society, world, indeed, history itself from the standpoint of God's plan for salvation which is revealed in Jesus Christ. The viewpoint is found in New Testament imagery that proposes Jesus as the second Adam (Rom 5:15-21), the revelation of God (Col 1:15), or the model for creation (Col 1:16; John 1:3). It can be a principle in personal spirituality understood as the Imitation of Christ or the motivating principle in spiritual or ecclesial reform, in the development of Franciscan and Jesuit spirituality, for instance, or in Reformation spirituality and theology that is decidedly Christocentric. Theologies that propose Jesus as the model for redeemed creation, most recently Teilhard de Chardin and Wolfhart Pannenberg, are Christocentric. The perspective is distinguished from a theocentric or anthropocentric point of view.

Patricia Plovanich

CHRIST OF FAITH

This expression is frequently heard in conjunction with "Jesus of history." Since the eighteenth century, there has been an effort among biblical scholars to understand the figure of Jesus without viewing him through the lens of church dogma. Dogmatic or doctrinal expressions of faith about Jesus as Son of God tended to eclipse his humanity and also led to reading the Gospels in an unhistorical fashion. In order to retrieve the human, historical, "unfiltered" Jesus, biblical scholars engaged in a "quest" for the Jesus of history. This search entailed bracketing the Christ of the church's creeds and the many statements confessing Jesus to be Lord or Son of God which are found in the New Testament. Those scholars were mainly Protestant, since Catholic Scripture scholars were constrained by their church's unreadiness to see that doctrinal expressions are conditioned by history.

"Christ" was the title applied by the early church to Jesus on the basis of its faith in him as God's "anointed"; the Greek word *christos* translated the Hebrew word *messiah*. Juxtaposing the Christ of faith with the Jesus of history (where "Jesus" stands for the Jewish prophet from Galilee before he was colored and transfigured by the community's belief about him) can be misleading. The eighteenth-century German philosopher Immanuel Kant had argued that there is a difference between things as they appear to us and things as they are in themselves; and since we can only know things as they appear to us, reality as it is "in itself" is inaccessible to the human mind. Kant was right in saying that knowledge is a human construction, but he was mistaken in saying that there exists such a thing as "reality in itself." In some ways, the search for the Jesus of history—the reality in itself—was an illusion; it was based on an inadequate understanding of how human knowing works. As the contemporary New Testament scholar James Dunn has explained, the only Jesus we can know is the Jesus remembered by his early followers. The portraits of Jesus that emerge from a study of the Gospels are portraits drawn by believers.

The "Christ of faith" should not be identified in an abstract way with the Christ of the dogmatic propositions found in the Creed or the faith expressions that pervade the entire New Testament. Jesus, whom the church confesses to be Lord, Messiah, and Son of God, was himself a person of faith, a believer, a man who prayed and who made loving and serving God the most important thing in his life. Behind Jesus stands God. As a result, historical research into the figure of Jesus sooner or later encounters the faith of Jesus as an important datum. The Jesus of history is at the same time the Jesus who is himself a believer; one cannot study Jesus and understand him without eventually raising questions about the God he served. Faith and history can be distinguished, but in the end they cannot be separated.

William Reiser, s.j.

See also CHRISTOLOGY; JESUS OF HISTORY.

CHRISTOLOGY

That area of systematic or doctrinal theology devoted to the study of Jesus Christ is called christology. Not every study of Jesus is expressly theological. Some New Testament scholars, for example, confine themselves to the historical study of Jesus as a first-century Jew from Galilee; their historical interest usually includes sociological and cross-cultural approaches in researching Jesus and examining the New Testament texts. To talk about theology, however, is to speak about the mystery of God. The entire Gospel story presupposes the ongoing historical and redemptive involvement of the God of Israel on behalf of Israel itself and of the whole human family. That it is the Father's initiative and plan which guide the Gospel narrative becomes evident through the heavenly voice speaking in the baptism and transfiguration scenes, but above all in the Resurrection, since it is God who raises Jesus from the dead (Acts 2:24). Thus the Gospel story can be said to be as much about the God of Israel as it is about Jesus. One cannot think about Jesus without thinking about God for two reasons: first, because Jesus as a devout Jew stood in a faith relationship with God and proclaimed God's reign or kingdom; and second, because the process of God's self-revelation started long before Jesus was born.

Christology is concerned with the Christ of the church's faith and with the faith of the historical Jesus. For the sake of analysis, theologians have tended to examine Jesus from two aspects, his person (christology) and his work or mission ("soteriology," from the Greek word for savior). In reality, as one studies the New Testament texts, person and mission are inseparable since who Jesus is remains firmly connected to what he has done. In recent years theologians have noted the difference between christology "from above" and christology "from below." The difference is largely methodological. Christology from above generally starts with the classic expressions of faith about Jesus Christ located in the ancient creeds and in the liturgy. Christology from below generally starts from what the New Testament tells us about Jesus of Nazareth in his religious, social, cultural, and historical context. Christology from below, consequently, tends to highlight the humanness of Jesus, whereas christology from above draws attention to his exalted and divine status. Sound theology takes both approaches into account.

Christology is concerned with more than how the humanity and divinity of Jesus are to be understood and related. At stake, ultimately, is how salvation takes place. Human beings cannot be expected to follow someone as disciples who is so perfect and divine that one can never reasonably hope to imitate him; yet if Jesus is simply a good and holy human being, then salvation, as the New Testament understands it, has not really been accomplished. In short, christology has a great bearing on Christian practice or discipleship.

William Reiser, s.j.

See also CHRIST OF FAITH; FILIOQUE; HYPOSTATIC UNION; INCARNATION; JESUS OF HISTORY; MODALISM; SALVATION; SUBORDINATIONISM.

CHRIST THE KING

Originally instituted in the Roman Catholic tradition by Pope Pius XI in 1925, the liturgical feast day of Christ the King was at first celebrated on the last Sunday in October. Since the reforms of Vatican II, it has been moved to the last Sunday of the liturgical year, the week before the first Sunday of Advent (therefore, around the end of November). It is a feast of the Lord, that is, one that commemorates some Gospel event or theological theme about Jesus Christ. On this Sunday, the focus of the liturgy is to emphasize the sovereignty of Jesus Christ over creation and over time. Unlike the earlier texts of the feast (which stressed the Lordship of Christ over governments and nations), the current prayers and readings carry an eschatological tone, one which will be picked up strongly in the following season of Advent.

Joanne M. Pierce

See also ADVENT; FEAST; LITURGICAL YEAR.

CHRISTUS DOMINUS

This Vatican II document, The Decree on the Bishops' Pastoral Office in the Church, usually known as *Christus Dominus* (the first two words of the Latin text meaning "Christ the Lord"), was promulgated on October 28, 1965, during the fourth session of the Second Vatican Council. Because the work of the First Vatican Council (1869–70) was interrupted by political crisis in Italy, its treatise on the church considered only the pope and not the role of other bishops, priests, or laypeople in the Catholic Church. Vatican II corrected this imbalance by placing its discussion of the role of pope and bishop in the framework of the "people of God" within which all baptized Catholics are equal. Regarding bishops, *Lumen Gentium* (Dogmatic Constitution on the Church) directed its attention to the theological basis of the episcopacy while *Christus Dominus* dealt with the practical exercise of the episcopal office. Beginning with the recognition of the primacy of the pope in the Catholic Church, the decree calls attention to the role of the bishops who, "designated by the Holy Spirit . . . take the place of the apostles as pastors of souls, and together with the Supreme Pontiff and subject to his authority . . . are commissioned to perpetuate the work of Christ"

(no. 2). In the decree's three chapters, the council sets forth the role of individual bishops (1) in the universal church, (2) in their own particular churches (dioceses), and (3) in regional associations of particular churches or dioceses (episcopal conferences). In detailing the functions of bishops, the decree clearly emphasizes service over privileges.

James B. Nickoloff

See also BISHOP (AUXILIARY, SUFFRAGAN); BISHOP (ORDINARY); ECCLESIOLOGY; EPISCOPACY; LUMEN GENTIUM; VATICAN, FIRST COUNCIL OF THE; VATICAN, SECOND COUNCIL OF THE.

CHUANG TZU (365?–290? B.C.E.)

(Chinese, Zhuang Zi). Known as Master Chuang, his personal name was Chuang Chou, and he was believed to be a native of Meng in the state of Sung (eastern Hunan Province). Next to Lao-Tzu, he was the most renowned Taoist philosopher in Chinese history and one of the great thinkers and writers of the Classical Period. He is believed to be the composer of one of the two seminal texts, along with the *Tao Te Ching*, of philosophical Taoism. His teachings, found in the text bearing his name, tend to be more mystical and more anarchistic than Lao-Tzu. He was interested in the practical consequences of living the Taoist life, and while popularizing the teachings of his master, Lao-Tzu, he gave more emphasis to the Tao as the focus of one's life. He also encouraged the rejection of social and political life in order to develop one's inner life in communion with nature and attunement with the Tao. The text itself is a blend of aphorisms, poetry, anecdotes, conversations, and allegory marked by the characteristically Taoist use of humor, skepticism, and paradox. While concentrating on the issue of how one should live, Chuang Tzu places more emphasis on transformation rather than on the adjustment of Lao-Tzu, and delineates a mystical vision of freedom from the world and conventional values. The writings of Chuang Tzu have had a significant impact on both the Chinese character and Chinese culture in general.

G. D. DeAngelis

See also DAOISM; LAO-TZU; TAO; WU-WEI.

CHU HSI (1130?–1200?)

(Chinese, Zhu Xi). The leading Sung Neo-Confucian whose commentaries on the Confucian Classics became authoritative. Chu Hsi's reasoned defense of Mencius and his followers against the attacks of Hsun Tzu, whom he characterized as a heretic for departing from Confucius' belief in the innate goodness of human nature, established Mencius as the orthodox interpreter of Confucianism. He was also an important contributor to the Confucian school in clarifying the orthodox attitude toward themes in Taoism and Buddhism and leading the Neo-Confucian movement in debating with rival schools and adopting what was sound.

He was considered a synthesizer of the Sung School of Principle (Li-Hsuen) whose approach was one of "philosophical realism" in which he engaged in the study of the nature of things to discover the basis and principles of goodness. In his metaphysical and ontological theory, he advocated self-development through the use of *ch'i* and attuning oneself to the Tao. He was the consummate Confucian in advocating service to society, and his commentaries on the scriptures of Classical Confucianism constituted the basis for the Chinese civil service exam. Chu Hsi had the most lasting influence on Chinese religion, philosophy, and political life of all the Neo-Confucians.

G. D. DeAngelis

See also CONFUCIANISM; CONFUCIUS; JEN; LI; MENCIUS; NEO-CONFUCIANISM; WANG YANG-MING.

CHUNG YUNG

(Chinese, *zhong yong*, centrality and normality). An early Confucian text that came to be considered one of the Four Books of Confucianism, along with the Analects, Mencius, and Great Learning. Supposedly written by Tzu Ssu, grandson of Confucius, and originally a part of the *Li Chi* (Book of Rites), it was an essay on the relationship of moral man to a moral universe. This is the closest one comes to a Confucian metaphysics as it delineates the Doctrine of the Mean (*chung*) or the Central and Universal Moral Law. It establishes the basic norm of human behavior that will bring human beings and their actions into harmony with the whole universe, claiming that moral and cosmic order are one. The Doctrine of the Mean manifests the central Confucian tenet of the relationship between the underlying reality or truth of the universe and what is most essential and real in humanity. This is brought about through ethical development in which the individual becomes one with heaven and earth. The underlying metaphysical principle in this theory is sincerity, perceived to be the "Way" (Tao) of both human beings and heaven. Thus, the moral person is the sincere individual who stands in the middle, encourages compromise, and establishes harmony and balance. Chung Yung, literally, "middle and constant," makes clear that we live in a moral universe. This doctrine was an important part of the eleventh-century C.E. Neo-Confucian response to the threat of Buddhism and Taoism.

G. D. DeAngelis

See also CHU HSI; CONFUCIANISM; CONFUCIUS; LI-CHING; NEO-CONFUCIANISM; TAO; TE; WANG YANG-MING.

CHUN-TZU

(Chinese, *jun zi*, lit., son of a ruler). This term refers to a gentleman, or a member of upper classes. Within Confucian thought, this points to the Superior Man, that is, the ideal man all should aspire to become for a just and orderly society to prevail. For Confucius, the Superior Man was not a condition of birth and class, but of learning. He was the individual whose mind was perfectly clear about names and duties, human-hearted (*jen*), knew ceremony and correct ritual form (*li*), and displayed the five constant virtues. This was a man who incorporated wisdom and compassion and had achieved a balance between his actions and ideals. He practiced moderation in his conduct and opinions, did nothing in excess, was sincere and genuine, and always maintained a strong sense of duty and commitment to the ruler. His moral vision enabled him to see beyond personal profit and act in the best interests of the community, state, and humankind. According to Confucius, the "ordinary man knows what is profitable, the superior man knows what is right." Confucius believed that order and harmony would be restored in society by the emergence, through learning, of superior men.

G. D. DeAngelis

See also ANALECTS; CHUNG YUNG; CONFUCIANISM; CONFUCIUS; JEN; LI.

CHUPPAH

In Judaism, a canopy, symbolizing the couple's future home, under which the wedding ceremony takes place. The chuppah normally consists of a cloth spread over four staves, either fixed in the ground or supported by attendants. In common parlance, the term chuppah is also used to refer to the wedding ceremony itself.

Alan J. Avery-Peck

See also MARRIAGE (IN JUDAISM).

CHUPUNGCO, ANSCAR (1931–)

Filipino Catholic liturgist and Benedictine monk. Chupungco was professor at universities both in Manila and in Rome, and is a specialist on liturgical inculturation. He is considered one of the world's authorities in his field. As part of his studies on liturgy and culture he has also examined popular religion, catechesis, and the so-called sacramentals. His best books are *Liturgies of the Future* (1989) and *Liturgical Inculturation* (1992).

Orlando Espín

See also BENEDICTINES; CATECHESIS/CATECHETICAL; CULTURE; INCULTURATION; LITURGY (IN CHRISTIANITY); SACRAMENTALS.

CHURCH

Originally from the Greek *ekklesía* and the Latin *ecclesia* (by way of the German *Kirche*), the term "church" at first referred —in the Greco-Roman world—to the community of citizens in a self-governing city. The Septuagint used it to mean the assembly of the whole people of Israel. The New Testament employs the term to mean exclusively the community of Christians. Only much later did the word "church" come to also be used for buildings or for what today we may say by "denomination." Consequently, today "church" means the whole community of Christians (the universal Christian church), or one specific branch of Christianity (the Roman Catholic Church, or the United Methodist Church), or a local congregation (a parish), or the building where a local congregation meets. Unfortunately, "church" is also frequently used to designate the institution or clergy of a specific branch of Christianity, but this is an inaccurate and misleading use of the term.

Orlando Espín

See also CLERICALISM; DENOMINATION; ECCLESIOLOGY; LAITY; NEW TESTAMENT; SEPTUAGINT.

CHURCH OF JESUS CHRIST OF LATTER-DAY SAINTS

The Mormons, officially named the Church of Jesus Christ of Latter-Day Saints, were founded by Joseph Smith Jr. (1805–44) in 1830 in upstate New York. As a young man, Smith was bewildered by the proliferation and competition of Christian groups; he sought the true church. His confusion was dispelled in 1820, when he received a vision from God the Father and Jesus who told him that no existing church preached the truth. In 1823, he was visited by the angel Moroni, who directed him to a hill near Palmyra, New York, to discover golden plates inscribed with ancient writings. Smith translated these plates and in 1830 published them as the Book of Mormon, which the Mormons consider sacred scripture along with the Bible.

The new Church immediately attracted followers and opposition. They seemed to invite persecution due to their exclusivity and self-righteousness. Civic leaders were threatened by the Mormons' size and solidarity. In 1831, Smith, by now designated Prophet of the Church, moved the group to Kirtland, Ohio; in 1838 to Independence, Missouri; and in 1839 to Nauvoo, Illinois, which soon became the largest city in the state. In Nauvoo, he received a revelation to revive the Old Testament practice of polygamy (more accurately, polygyny, the practice of multiple wives rather than multiple husbands). The practice spread among Church leaders and created intense internal and external hostility. In 1844 Smith was murdered by an angry mob in Carthage, Illinois, where he was awaiting trial on charges of fomenting civil unrest.

After the Prophet's death, the church splintered into several groups. The two most important were the non-polygamy-practicing Reorganized Church of Jesus Christ of Latter-Day Saints, led by Joseph Smith III, ultimately headquartered in Independence, Missouri, and the larger Church of Jesus Christ of Latter-Day Saints led by Brigham Young, one of the Prophet's lieutenants. In 1848 Young led the latter group in a forced migration westward to Utah.

In Utah, the Mormons continued to arouse public outrage due to the increasingly public practice of plural marriage. The first federal legislation against polygamy was enacted in 1862, and the U.S. government refused to grant Utah statehood until it was outlawed. In 1890 Church president Wilford Woodruff received a divine revelation to reverse Church policy on plural marriage, and by 1904, any polygamous Mormon faced excommunication. Several Mormon groups split from the Church and continued the practice.

The Church is one of the few religious groups indigenous to the United States and one of the fastest growing in the world.

While most Christians do not consider Mormons Christian, Mormons consider themselves members of the true church, a chosen people who have restored the authentic first-century Christian church. The Church is organized into wards, roughly equivalent to a local parish, presided over by a bishop, a layman with a secular job. The bishop oversees worship, religious education, social life, and charitable activities in the ward. Worship occurs weekly and includes hymn-singing, informal talks by congregation members, and a eucharistic sacrament of bread and water. Wards are organized into larger units called stakes. Other distinctive Mormon rituals, such as marriage and baptism of the dead, in which a living person is baptized to enable the deceased to join the Church, occur in regional temples.

Mormons have a distinctive lifestyle. They are expected to abstain from caffeine, tobacco, and alcohol. They are strongly committed to patriotism, evangelism, and family life, defined as heterosexual nuclear families with children. The Church has taken strong positions against abortion, feminism, and homosexuality; however, Utah was one of the first territories to grant women the right to vote. In the United States today, the Church is strongest in the Rocky Mountain region, with headquarters in Salt Lake City, Utah.

Evelyn A. Kirkley

See also MORMON, BOOK OF.

CISTERCIANS

In 1098, a group of monks from Molesme who wanted a more primitive observance of the Rule, received permission to start a small community in a remote Burgundian site called Cadets. Though the beginnings were not auspicious, the arrival of Bernard of Clairvaux with a group of about thirty other men (family and friends) put Cadets "on the map," as it were, and the new community began to grow and expand with extraordinary rapidity. By the time of Bernard's death in 1153, there were 343 Cistercian abbeys in all parts of Europe.

The early Cistercians believed they were returning to the true and original Rule of Benedict (though they could not know a great deal about the actual historical situation of sixth-century monks). They rejected the elaborate liturgical life and rituals that had become the main "work" of Benedictine monks after Cluny. They simplified the structure of the Divine Office, lengthened the time devoted to *lectio divina* (prayerful reading of the Bible) and contemplation, and required the monks to provide for all their own needs by the work of their hands; manual labor thus regained the central place it had in early Benedictinism. One of the most important elements in the success of the Cistercians was the system of governance and accountability provided for by the *Carta Caritatis*. The Cistercian model allowed each monastery its autonomy (a feature of Benedictinism that had been lost under the Cluniac Reform), but provided for mutual visitation of abbots who were to hold each other to account for fidelity to the Rule. Out of these mutual visitations grew the institution of the general chapter, a yearly meeting of all Cistercian abbots in a system of federation and representation that anticipated later changes in religious governance.

But Cistercianism transcended legal and structural reforms. The many thoughtful and well-educated Cistercian monks of the early generation, Bernard, Aelred of Rievaulx, William of St. Thierry, and Isaac of Stella, created a body of religious literature that reflects common themes: the importance of the humanity of Christ in salvation and spiritual perfection; a positive understanding of human nature as the "image of God" designed "by nature" for union with God; and the centrality of love, both in its volitional and affective sense, in human life. This Cistercian "school" was reflected in its architecture; Bernard called for a simplicity in stone that matched and promoted true simplicity of life. Many monasteries founded during his lifetime, such as Fontenay in Burgundy or Le Thoronet in Provence, remain today as visual expressions of Cistercianism.

Marie Anne Mayeski

See also ABBEY; ASCETICISM/ASCETIC; BENEDICTINE RULE (RULE OF ST. BENEDICT); BERNARD OF CLAIRVAUX; MERTON, THOMAS; MONASTICISM IN WESTERN CHRISTIANITY.

CITTAMATRA

A term that designates the "dynamic idealism" Mahayana school. The Cittamatra ("Mind-Only") also became known by the Yogachara ("Yoga Practice"). Beginning with the *Samdhinirmocana Sutra*, texts of this school build upon Madhyamaka doctrines that deconstruct all phenomena as inherently empty; but they assert that this is not the Buddha's highest teaching. Cittamatra exponents argue that this realization of emptiness occurs within the mind and that the flow of experience in the mind, as well as the mental participation in that process, is what has ultimate reality.

The Indian monk Vasubandhu, a powerful early Cittamatra exponent, likened the mind to a flowing river that was ever changing, but kept its identity. In his view the mind is the basis of samsara bondage by its false assumption of an exterior du-

ality of self/world. Cittamatra exponents likewise regarded the mind experience positively, that is, as the substratum for enlightenment. Thus, meditation leading to the experience of "signless cognition" (*vijnaptimatra*) was central to experiencing nirvana (hence the alternative name "Yogachara"). The school's doctrinal developments, for example, the explanation of karma in terms of seeds (*bijas*) deposited in and then influencing the baseline "store consciousness" (*alaya vijnana*), likewise must be understood as provisional attempts to explain human experience and the basis of spiritual release.

Todd T. Lewis

See also ASANGA; MAHAYANA BUDDHISM; VASUBANDHU.

CIVIL RELIGION

Civil religion is the religion of United States patriotism, the "cult of America." The term was popularized in 1967 by sociologist of religion Robert N. Bellah, who envisioned civil religion as a unifying force in an increasingly pluralistic U.S. culture. Although civil religion is an amorphous concept, Bellah and other scholars have described it in terms similar to other organized religious systems. Its theology elevates the values of freedom, democracy, and equality. The United States has been chosen by God for a special destiny. It is a beacon of liberty to the nations of the world, the site of the millennium, the thousand-year reign of Christ on earth. It is also the redeemer nation, charged with the responsibility to serve other nations in humility and grace. In short, America is God's country.

Civil religion also communicates a distinct ethics. Americans have a unique covenant relationship with God and must obey divine commands or face punishment and the loss of their elect status. Therefore, Americans have a responsibility to act with "liberty and justice for all." They must treat others fairly, adhering to the letter and spirit of the law, including the assumption of innocence until proven guilty. They should behave with compassion and empathy. At the same time, individualism, pragmatism, and the desire to win are hallmarks of American ethics. From the Olympics to Wall Street to global politics, U.S. citizens compete to be number one. Throughout runs the assumption of the righteousness and moral superiority of the nation and its citizens.

The theology and ethics of the "cult of America" are expressed in an elaborate network of rituals and icons. It celebrates national holy days, including the Fourth of July, Labor Day, Thanksgiving, and Memorial Day. It has sacred scriptures—the Declaration of Independence and Constitution—and a creed, the Pledge of Allegiance. Sacred sites include the Washington Monument, Lincoln Memorial, Mount Rushmore, and the Statue of Liberty. Its hymns are "America the Beautiful," "My Country 'Tis of Thee," "The Star-Spangled Banner," and "The Battle Hymn of the Republic," and its icons include the flag and bald eagle. It even has sacred colors: red, white, and blue.

Civil religion is replete with biblical and classical imagery. "America" is portrayed as the Garden of Eden and New Jerusalem. George Washington and Abraham Lincoln are compared to Joshua and Moses, leaders of the Israelites in the Old Testament. Washington has also been identified with Cincinnatus, a Roman general who refused to become king after his military victories. The Great Seal of the United States, replicated on the dollar bill, depicts a pyramid and two Latin inscriptions, *Novus Ordo Seclorum* ("the new order of the ages"), and *Annuit Coeptis* ("He has prospered our undertaking"). It also includes the motto "In God We Trust."

Since the 1960s, civil religion has fragmented. Its icons no longer receive the respect formerly accorded them. The American flag is made into bikinis and bath towels, and the Statue of Liberty is depicted as Marilyn Monroe with wind blowing up her skirt. Since Watergate, political leaders no longer receive unconditional admiration and loyalty, and the peccadilloes of public figures have been exhaustively investigated. The gap between the preaching of civil religion and its practice has been revealed, especially the injustices inflicted on women, Native Americans, African Americans, Latino/a Americans, and gay men and lesbians, in a country that champions "life, liberty, and the pursuit of happiness." Attempts in the 1980s to pass a constitutional amendment banning flag-burning tried to restore an outdated version of civil religion. In many respects, the United States has betrayed the precepts of civil religion and has yet to reconstruct a civil religion for the twenty-first century.

Evelyn A. Kirkley

See also BELLAH, ROBERT N.; MILLENARI-ANISM; RELIGION, FREEDOM OF.

CLAN BUNDLE

The process of socialization in the native peoples of North America resembled the same process in primal cultures all over the world. It is a form of identification and differentiation not merely part of the ancient past of humanity, but that also survives into the present in traditional peoples all over the world. Among the hunters, a specific element of this organizational process was the tracing of the origin of a clan back to the earliest phase of existence, to a time when animals ruled the earth. Each story differs, but all speak of a moment when certain animals, gifted with spiritual power, transformed themselves into human persons and began a lineage of like persons who are the ancestors of the tribe. This early alliance of humans and animals was not destined to last in a material way, but the primogenitor allied itself with the people in a permanent way. Thus, it became the guardian spirit of that group. In subsequent history, a member of the clan would encounter the guardian animal in a vision, and the relationship would be renewed in each generation. The early fieldwork of Paul Radin, James Owen Dorsey, and Lewis Morgan show that this relationship was manifested in a special medicine bundle kept by an individual and family; but, in reality, its possession was extended to all the clan. The sacredness of such an object was met with the profound respect and ritual propriety it deserved as a sacrament of the loving protection of the sacred. Such bundles functioned in many societies as spiritual armor in war, and were honored before a battle and actually carried into combat. Such bundles were sometimes called War Bundles, as among the Winnebago, or retained their original designation, as the Sacred Arrows bundle among the Cheyenne. Their presence is still the spiritual center of their people, where they have survived.

Kathleen Dugan

See also FETISH; MANA; SACRAMENT.

CLARE OF ASSISI (1194–1253)

A noblewoman of Assisi, Italy, Clare came to accept Francis of Assisi's vision of the Christian life, particularly his devotion to poverty. Rather than embracing the itinerant life of the Franciscan Friars, with Francis's encouragement she founded a monastery of women and struggled for a number of years to obtain approval for their rule of life that included a vow of absolute poverty. In the end, the condition for papal recognition of such a rule was the sisters' acceptance of very strict cloister. Monasteries of women following this way of life, though officially known as the Second Order of St. Francis, are often popularly called Poor Clares. Clare's spirituality is particularly marked by devotion to the Eucharist.

Mary Anne Foley, C.N.D.

See also CLOISTER; FRANCIS OF ASSISI; FRIARS; MONASTICISM IN WESTERN CHRISTIANITY; POVERTY (RELIGIOUS VOW).

CLARK, J. (JOHN) MICHAEL (1953–)

American gay theologian, Clark has developed his theological career and thought outside the usual institutional settings. Although he has spent much of his professional life employed in other fields by several universities, the theological profession (probably due to misconceptions and lingering prejudice) has not been eager to support his research. He has written and published twelve books and numerous articles, all dealing with gay theological themes, including sexual ethics, the problem of suffering, HIV/AIDS, and with what he calls gay "ecotheology." Through his writings, his organizing efforts (for example, he cofounded the Gay Men's Issues in Religion Group within the American Academy of Religion), and through his editorial work at the *Journal of Men's Studies*, Clark has significantly contributed to the creation of contemporary gay theology in the U.S., and is successfully and unapologetically bringing the theological mainstream to dialogue with it. Among his best books are *A Place to Start: Toward an Unapologetic Gay Liberation Theology* (1989), *Beyond Our Ghettos: Gay Theology in Ecological Perspective* (1993), and *Queering the Darkness: Theology in the Shadows* (1997).

Orlando Espín

See also CULTURE; DISCRIMINATION; ECOLOGY; ETHICS, SEXUAL; JUSTICE; SEXUALITY.

CLASSISM

The term given to attitudes, cultural ideology, and social structures that promote admiration, emulation, and support of the affluent or socioeconomically powerful, and hatred, fear, and abandonment of poor people, or the socioeconomically powerless. The popular view of class, supported by neoclassical economic theory, has to do with *income stratification*. Hierarchies of power and prestige according to income and wealth are set up between the so-called upper, middle, and lower classes.

Another view, taken from the neo-Marxist tradition, understands class as *a hierarchical relationship among groups of people* determined by the social processes of production. In its simplest form, class relations are understood to be primarily between those who own and control the means of producing social wealth, and those who sell their labor for a wage. For example, the capitalist class, comprised of fewer than 10 percent of the U.S. population who own and control the means of production, not only possess over two-thirds of the nation's wealth. More importantly, they also possess greater social and political power than those who must sell their labor for a wage or those who remain unemployed. They basically de-termine the shape of the political economy, including deciding what work will be done, how it will be done, and how the surplus from that work will be reinvested in the society or elsewhere.

In its more complex forms, class remains a product of specific capitalist relations and is highly stratified depending upon a group's amount of control, subordination, and degree of autonomy at work, including the amount of unemployment some groups must endure to keep inflation at acceptable levels and wages down. The relational view of class also claims that class is both gender and racially stratified. That is, white women and people of color will be more heavily represented in the lower tiers of the working class and the underemployed and the unemployed than in the capitalist class.

Those who hold the income stratification view of class believe that classism can be addressed by upward mobility, that is, by moving people from the lower working class to the upper income working class through such means as increasing their education and job skills. Those who hold the second, relational notion of class, believe that capitalist economics require that some people remain in the subordinate sectors of the working class and that the social degradation of classism cannot be solved without fundamental change in the structure of the political economy itself.

Mary E. Hobgood

See also ECONOMY; MATERIALISM; POVERTY; RACISM; SEXISM.

CLAVIGERO, FRANCISCO XAVIER (1732–87)

Mexican philosopher and a member of the Society of Jesus (Jesuits) since 1748, Clavigero was born at the city of

Veracruz. He studied in Jesuit schools in Puebla and Mexico City. While in the seminary, he studied ancient Nahua (Aztec) manuscripts, and as a priest became a renowned historian of Mexican antiquities. In time, he became a professor of history and philosophy in several of his order's institutions in various Mexican cities. Many of his philosophical works have been lost, but a few historical texts have survived (especially his *Historia antigua de México*). Committed to the defense of Mexico's native history and cultures, he promoted ideas that a few decades later became foundational to Mexican independence from Spain. Indeed, there is the distinct historical possibility that Miguel Hidalgo (who proclaimed Mexican independence) was one of Clavigero's students. His writings also show him to be, like his Jesuit contemporary Francisco Xavier Alegre, a proponent as well as an early critic of modernity and the Enlightenment. Together with all Jesuits in the Spanish colonial empire, Clavigero was expelled from his native Mexico by royal decree, in 1767, and was then sent to Italy. He died in Bologna twenty years later.

Orlando Espín

See also ALEGRE, FRANCISCO XAVIER; ENLIGHTENMENT IN WESTERN HISTORY; GUADALUPE, VIRGIN OF; LATIN AMERICAN CATHOLICISM; MODERNITY; NAHUA TRADITIONAL RELIGION; POSTMODERNITY; SOCIETY OF JESUS.

CLEMENT OF ALEXANDRIA
(150?–215?)
Titus Flavius Clemens. As a young man, Clement seems to have attended several philosophical schools, searching for wisdom. He found the teacher he was looking for at Alexandria in the person of the Christian, Pantaenus. Clement not only converted, but opened a famous Christian school in Alexandria in which he taught a form of Christianity and Greek philosophy that attracted the educated classes of Alexandria. Clement left Alexandria in 202/3 to avoid the persecution of Septimus Severus. Clement's most famous student, the young Origen, took over the school. In 215/6 Origen received a letter from the bishop of Jerusalem informing him of the death of his teacher. Clement's most famous works are the three long treatises, the *Introduction*, the *Teacher*, and the *Miscellanies*. In these works, Clement demonstrates a high regard for Greek philsophy which he considers to be compatible with and even an introduction to Christianity. His gentle, cultured, and essentially ethical writings have long been held in high esteem by Christians.

Gary Macy

See also ALEXANDRIAN THEOLOGY; ORIGEN; PERSECUTION (IN CHRISTIANITY).

CLEMENT OF ROME
Very little is known of this first-century Christian writer apart from the witness of Hermas, who described Clement as the scribe or letter-writer of the Christian community. One of Clement's letters survives, written to the church of Corinth around 96/8. The letter is an invaluable guide to the life of the first-century Roman church. Clement wrote to plead with the Corinthians to avoid splits in the community and to follow their presbyters, who, it appears, had been unjustifiably dismissed by a younger group within the Corinthian church. The letter demonstrates both knowledge of Hebrew Scripture as well as of Greek culture.

Other "letters" attributed to Clement are not genuine.

Gary Macy

See also HERMAS.

CLERGY

The Greek word *kleros* originally meant "chosen by lot," and was used of the Levites (Deut 18:2) in the Greek translation of the Hebrew Scriptures known as the Septuagint. The word was transferred to the Christian leadership and came in time to be applied primarily to the *episkopos*, *presbyteros*, and *diakonos*. Clergy now refers to those who have been set aside by their communities to lead them in worship. The opposing term, referring to those who are not set aside is "laity." Although the term originated with Jewish and later Christian communities, the term came to be used of the leaders of any religious community. The understanding of the role of the clergy differs greatly among religious communities; some stress the difference between the clerical and lay state while others insist that there is no fundamental distinction between the clerical and lay state.

Gary Macy and Wayne Dosick

See also BISHOP (EPISCOPACY); CHRISTIANITY; DEACON; EPISKOPOS; JUDAISM; LAITY; MINISTRY/MINISTERIAL; PRESBYTEROS (IN THE NEW TESTAMENT); PRIESTHOOD; RABBI.

CLERICALISM

An attitude on the part of ordained ministers to maintain or increase power within hierarchical structures of religions. Historically, clericalism was a hostile term used against Catholicism that referred to supposed attempts on the part of the hierarchy to maintain secular power and control of its lands during the periods of nationalization of city-states and the Papal States. In Italy and France it came to mean any attempt of the papacy or bishops to gain power or influence over the state.

Today, the term is used both inside and outside the church to refer to a vision of church that embraces institutional, patriarchal structures and the privileges of both the ordained clergy and religious who maintain a status separate from the laity. Such status gives clergy power over the laity. These structures and clergy generally "rule" rather than serve the community and keep women in places of subjection.

M. Jane Gorman

CLOISTER

Connected in meaning to the verb "to close" and the noun "enclosure," the cloister, in religious terminology, is an enclosed space destined for the use of persons seeking a religious way of life, apart from worldly conversation and activities. It also came to be the term used for one of the most important architectural elements in a monastery or convent: the covered walkway surrounding the central courtyard and connecting the major buildings of the establishment. Monks and nuns could use the cloister in inclement weather to move from building to building and to get a bit of simple exercise between religious services. Most generally, it designates all the legal and physical restrictions that, together, make religious or monastic life one of seclusion, contemplation, and separation.

Marie Anne Mayeski

See also ABBEY; MONASTERY; MONASTICISM IN EASTERN CHRISTIANITY; MONASTICISM IN WESTERN CHRISTIANITY; NUN.

CLOVIS

The name "Clovis" refers to the projectile points discovered at Sandia, New Mexico, and also to the culture that created this effective weapon for hunting in Paleo-Indian prehistory in the new world. Archeologists have dated this tool's emergence to around 11,600 years ago, probably as a derivation by the big-game hunters who were the earliest culture in North America, and who are currently traced to the emigration over the Bering Strait. At the time of its creation (in a Stone Age process called flaking), it was a quantum leap in subsistence hunting. The food animals were the ancient herds of mammoths, bison, horses, caribou, and others, which were more than a match for men on foot. So efficient were these stone points (probably attached to spears and lances) that the possibility of human survival was dramatically enhanced. The wide diffusion of this culture is the best evidence for this. Indeed, in a short time they spread throughout the Americas. In historic times, their descendants were still present in the hunting cultures that survived unchanged until the last Plains wars of the nineteenth century.

Kathleen Dugan

See also INDIGENOUS RELIGIOUS TRADITIONS.

CLOWN SOCIETIES

A distinctive feature of primal religions is the role that the image of the clown has in religious ritual. It is a deeply perceived fact that humor has an essential place in even the most sacred of human activities. This insight was also present in medieval religious events, but was displaced into the realm of theater. For primal societies, that connection has been preserved in several forms. The role of the clown, for example, in Hopi and Zuni ritual, is entirely sacred. For these peoples, the sheer terror of sacred mystery must be counterbalanced by representing the all-too-human dimensions of our lives. One effect of this is to contextualize the sacredness of the ritual in the ordinary—a basic corollary to the view that all is sacred. Yet another allows levity to balance the awe.

In another example, the skillful use of masks to show the distorted features of the False Faces among the Iroquois brings the viewers to recognize the sheer difference between the Spirits that roam the forests and have so much power that they can heal the wounds of the community. They are on the Creator's side and share the quality of true transcendence.

There are wonderful examples of individual calls to this ceremonial, such as the sacred vocation of the Heyoka among the Lakota, and the Contrary among the Cheyenne, but among the agrarian tribes, these individuals were organized into sacred societies that had prescribed ritual duties. In all cases, they are the necessary complement to the awesome mystery acknowledged in ritual.

Kathleen Dugan

See also CELEBRATION; RITUAL.

CLUNY, ABBEY OF

Founded by Duke William of Aquitaine in 909, Cluny became the center of monastic reform in the Middle Ages. William and Berno, its first abbot, gave Cluny a constitution that provided the opportunity for significant growth and influence. The monks were allowed to elect their own abbot, without any lay influence, an unusual degree of independence in monastic foundations. Additionally, and to insure freedom from lay manipulation, William gave the apostles Peter and Paul proprietary control of the monastery, placing it under the direct authority of the Holy See. Although it was not unique and largely symbolic at the time, a series of exceptionally gifted abbots who ruled Cluny from 926 to 1109 helped to turn this relationship with Rome into an opportunity for extraordinary influence and for the centralization of power.

The reforming zeal and spiritual fervor of Cluny became widely known under its first two abbots: by 931, Cluny was accepting monks who left other monasteries in search of a stricter observance of the Rule. Soon secular rulers outside of France invited the abbot of Cluny to reform the monasteries within their borders. By the beginning of the eleventh century, a network of Cluniac monasteries, all of them under control of the abbot of Cluny, had emerged, added to by lay patrons who wanted their monasteries to be part of the increasingly prestigious Cluniac family. In 1024 the power and independence of Cluny reached its peak: in this year, Abbot Odilo obtained a papal exemption from local episcopal control for all Cluniac monks. Henceforward, they owed submission only to the abbot of Cluny and, through him, the pope. Indeed, the growth of Cluny was parallel to, and generally supportive of, the growing centralization and reforming zeal of the eleventh-century popes. Gregory VII, architect of the Gregorian Reform, was himself a monk and sought support from Hugh, then abbot of Cluny (whose loyalties were somewhat divided by the long-standing generosity of secular princes to Cluny).

Cluny's influence was not entirely, nor even primarily, political and papal, however. At the spiritual heart of Cluny lay the conviction that the world was hopelessly sinful, that sure salvation lay only within the monastic vocation (convictions shaped by the attitudes and anxieties of the end of the first millennium). Laypeople were encouraged to seek salvation by various spiritual and material associations with Cluny. To respond to the spiritual needs of the laity, Cluny developed the Divine Office into a virtual continuum of liturgical and vocal prayer. Anxious petitioners and grateful recipients alike contributed to the immense wealth that Cluny (and its larger dependencies) acquired and dispensed in building and artistic programs.

Marie Anne Mayeski

See also ABBEY; BENEDICTINE RULE (RULE OF ST. BENEDICT); LITURGY (IN CHRISTIANITY); LITURGY OF THE HOURS; MEDIEVAL CHRISTIANITY (IN THE WEST).

COCHISE (CA. 1805–74)

The charismatic leader of the Chiricahua Apache who struggled against the American army to preserve the freedom of his people. His path to this role was unusual. At first, he had not objected to the movement of settlers through his land, but he was seen as hostile and escaped capture in a skirmish in which he was wounded. Members of his family were murdered in reprisal, and this unleashed two decades of battles in which the Apaches fought courageously for their land and freedom. Cochise was joined in this by other leaders (for instance, Mangus Colorado, and Geronimo) who are also legendary. Finally, blockaded and ill, Cochise was forced to surrender to General Howard in 1872. His condition for surrender was that Howard promise to let the Apaches return to live in peace on their own land. But Cochise had no confidence in the white man's promises, which had thus far only been lies. And when he died in 1874, his pessimism was justified.

Kathleen Dugan

CODEX

(Plural: codices). A codex is an ancient manuscript in book form. A codex may be made from either vellum or papyrus. Codices were introduced into usage as early as the second century C.E. and were favored by Christians as an alternative to the scroll that had been used for Scripture and other works of literature. The codex may have facilitated both the finding of a specific text, since the order was fixed, as well as the eventual development of a fixed order of books.

Russell Fuller

COHEN GADOL

See HIGH PRIEST (IN JUDAISM).

COLERIDGE, SAMUEL TAYLOR (1772–1834)

English poet, writer, contemporary of William Wordsworth, Coleridge's early studies in theology and philosophy whetted his appetite for the subjects throughout his life. His interest in the German idealists, Kant, Schelling and Fichte, resulted in the introduction of their philosophical ideas in England. Under the influence of Schelling's romantic idealism, Coleridge developed an interest in imagination as a primary source of knowledge that he explored in later studies of the relationship between language and imagination.

Patricia Plovanich

See also ANALOGICAL IMAGINATION.

COLLEGIALITY

Collegiality refers to the relationship between the pope (the Bishop of Rome), and the other bishops. In the Roman Catholic church the bishops and the pope comprise a "college" (Latin = *collegium*). In the medieval and Tridentine period, the Catholic Church's ecclesiology stressed the primacy of the pope to such a degree that the authority of the bishop in the local church was eclipsed. *Lumen Gentium*, Vatican II's Dogmatic Constitution on the Church, redefined the relationship between the bishops and the pope so that together they have responsibility for the governance of the church, though it qualified episcopal authority (the bishops can never act independently of the pope) and preserved the autonomy of the papal teaching office (the pope did not need the consent of the bishops to teach).

Mary Ann Hinsdale

See also BISHOP (EPISCOPACY); GALLICANISM; PAPACY/PAPAL; PETRINE PRIVILEGE; PRIMATE/PRIMATIAL SEE.

COMBLIN, JOSEPH (1923–)

Belgian-born theologian, better known for his work and writings in Latin America. Comblin has taught at universities in Chile, Brazil, and Ecuador. He has written extensively, but perhaps his more theologically influential publications have been *Teología de la revolución* (1973), *Hacia una teología de la acción* (1968), and *El Espíritu Santo y la liberación* (1986). Clearly within the currents of Latin American liberation theology, Comblin has attempted to keep a deep sense of the spiritual as a foundation for militant theology and pastoral action.

Orlando Espín

See also LATIN AMERICAN CATHOLICISM; LATIN AMERICAN THEOLOGIES; LIBERATION THEOLOGIES; SPIRITUALITY.

COMENIUS, JOHANNES AMOS (1592–1670)

Bohemian theologian and educator, and pastor of the Church of the Moravian

Brethren. A committed Christian educator, he published a number of works promoting his theories and his conviction that education was the best way to bring about a united Christian Church. He was far ahead of his age in promoting modern teaching methods. His ideas had considerable influence in the nineteenth century. His best published works were *Didactica magna* (1657) and *Unum necessarium* (1668).

Orlando Espín

See also BOHEMIAN BRETHREN/MORAVIANS; HUS, JOHN; REFORMATION.

COMMANDMENT IN JUDAISM
See MITZVAH.

COMMANDMENTS
Statutes, laws, ordinances, and teachings of a particular community. Commandments may be absolute, positive and negative imperatives, or casuistic, declaring what constitutes faithful or unfaithful, permissible or forbidden, behavior in certain specified circumstances.

In the Hebrew Scriptures, the commandments are traditionally ten, dictating what constitutes a proper posture before God (monotheism and faithfulness) and appropriate behavior among God's people (respect for parents, no killing, no adultery, no stealing, no lying, no coveting). Those who love God are those who obey God's commandments (Exod 20:6; Deut 5:10). Most of the commandments are contained in the Torah/Pentateuch of the Hebrew Scriptures. They are the teaching, broadly conceived, of God's covenant people.

Jesus is depicted as summarizing the commandments of the Hebrew Scriptures with two commandments: love of God and love of neighbor. According to Matthew 22:37-40, when asked by a Pharisee which was the greatest commandment, Jesus answered, "You shall love the Lord, your God, with all your heart, with all your soul, and with all your mind. This is the greatest and the first commandment. The second is like it: You shall love your neighbor as yourself. The whole law and the prophets depend on these two commandments."

Alice L. Laffey

See also PENTATEUCH; TORAH.

COMMANDMENTS OF THE CHURCH
Although the number of "commandments of the church" has varied over time, generally speaking, most twentieth-century Catholics learned that there are six "precepts" of the church: (1) to attend Mass on all Sundays and Holy Days of Obligation; (2) to fast and abstain on the days appointed; (3) to confess all mortal sins at least once a year; (4) to receive Holy Communion during the Easter time; (5) to contribute to the support of the church; and (6) to observe the laws of the church concerning marriage. Saints Peter Canisius and Robert Bellarmine list these laws in the sixteenth century; however, neither the Council of Trent nor Vatican II mentions them. Their purpose was to maintain discipline by prescribing the minimal external behaviors expected of members of the Catholic Church. This list of six is derived from the U.S. bishops at the Third Plenary Council of Baltimore in 1886. *The Catechism of the Catholic Church* (1994) lists only five, dropping the sixth commandment concerning marriage.

Mary Ann Hinsdale

COMMON GOOD
A beneficial way of life for a society and its members; the social conditions that

improve citizens' well-being and help them live together peaceably. The term originated in ancient Greek philosophy and conveys the Greeks' insight that humans are social and political animals. Plato said the common good obtained when the citizens lived virtuously and each social class fulfilled its proper functions. Similarly, Aristotle described it as a society that helps its citizens to live well, particularly by educating them in virtue and empowering them to participate in political and intellectual activities. Justice and equality were important components of the common good for these philosophers; yet in ancient Greece the benefits of the common good were reserved for male citizens who owned property.

The notion of the common good gained currency in Christianity first through the influence of Roman legal thought, and later when Aristotle's writings were reintroduced to the West in the thirteenth century. Thomas Aquinas gave it a prominent place in his political thought, claiming that "a government will be just and fitting to free persons if the ruler orders it to the common good of the people" (*On Kingship* I.1). The common good remains prominent in modern Catholic social teaching, where it has received philosophical articulation by Jacques Maritain (*The Person and the Common Good*, 1947) and official expression in church documents (*Gaudium et Spes*, 26 and 74). The common good has been spoken of mostly in Catholicism; Protestantism and other religions use allied concepts like community, covenant, and brotherhood. However, these terms do not capture the political and institutional elements of the public project as well as "common good" does. An ecumenical and interdisciplinary revival of interest in the common good began in the mid 1980s, sparked by religious writers both Catholic (David Hollenbach, Michael Novak) and Protestant (Max Stackhouse), and enriched by creative works in philosophy (Alasdair MacIntyre, Charles Taylor) and sociology (Robert Bellah, Amitai Etzioni).

Brian Stiltner

See also AQUINAS, THOMAS, ST.; ARISTOTLE; BELLAH, ROBERT N.; GAUDIUM ET SPES; MARITAIN, JACQUES; PLATO; PLURALISM; POLITICS; SOCIAL JUSTICE.

COMMUNICATIO IDIOMATUM

The term *communicatio idiomatum* comes from the words *communicatio* (sharing, participation, or exchange) and *idiom* meaning properties or attributes. The phrase means "the exchange or sharing of attributes." The concept, developed in fifth-century christological debates, explained the relationship between Christ's divine and human natures. In practical terms, the *communicatio idiomatum* explains how the two natures coexist and the significance of one nature for the other. It proposes a genuine exchange of attributes so that the qualities of one nature can be predicated of the other. The *Theotokos* theology applies the concept, for only if the properties of divinity are ascribed to Jesus' humanity can Mary be designated God-bearer. The limits of idiom were tested in the Theopaschite controversy by theologians proposing to speak about God's suffering in the crucifixion, but the usage was never considered orthodox. Reformation theologians invoked the concept in their eucharistic theology to designate the reality of divine presence in the symbols of bread and wine.

Patricia Plovanich

See also HYPOSTATIC UNION; TRINITY/ TRINITARIAN THEOLOGY/TRINITARIAN PROCESSIONS.

COMMUNION (ECCLESIOLOGICAL)

Communion, in the ecclesiological sense, refers to the relationship between a local church and the See of Rome (that is, the Vatican). Christian communities (churches) "in communion" with Rome recognize the primatial authority of the pope and accept the sacramental and canonical systems of the Roman Catholic Church. Thus, for example, the Maronite and Byzantine Churches are in communion with the Roman Catholic Church.

The theological understanding of the church as a communion (Latin = *communio*) reemerged in the Roman Catholic Church after the Second Vatican Council. Communion ecclesiology stresses unity of the baptized symbolized by the bishop in the local church, and the unity and universality of the local churches symbolized by the communion of the bishops with the bishop of Rome.

Mary Ann Hinsdale

See also CHURCH; CONGAR, YVES; ECCLESIOLOGY; LOCAL CHURCH.

COMMUNION (LITURGICAL)

The word *Communion* in Christian liturgical use designates first an action, and second, the elements consumed during that action. The reception of Communion takes place during the celebration of the Eucharist (or Mass), after the recitation of the eucharistic prayer. The altar bread (or *host*, in some traditions) and the wine (in the chalice) are understood to be in some way consecrated during/by this prayer, and the presider and congregation then prepare to follow the command of Jesus Christ to take and eat/drink (see 1 Cor 11:23-26; Matt 26:26-29; Mark 14:22-25; Luke 22:17-20). There is a short preparation rite (the "Communion Rite") which,

in the Roman Catholic tradition, consists of the Lord's Prayer, the greeting of peace, the *fraction* (breaking off a small piece of the host and placing it into the chalice of consecrated wine), and the liturgical acclamation *Lamb of God* (*Agnus Dei*). There follows a brief ritual verse (an invitation to Communion), and a short response by the congregation. Usually the presider and other ministers and/or assistants take Communion first, then distribute it to the congregation.

Usually, those assembled approach the altar in a procession, and either stand or kneel to receive a Host (or consecrated bread) either on the tongue or in the hand. In some traditions, the communicants then may take a sip of wine from the cup held by an assisting minister or minister of Communion. In Eastern churches, Communion is often distributed by intinction, that is, pieces of the consecrated bread are placed in a large chalice of consecrated wine, and each communicant receives a piece of that bread that is placed in the mouth by a priest using a special spoon. In some Protestant churches, the congregation remains seated for Communion; trays of bread (cut into cubes) and small glasses of wine or grape juice are passed around to everyone in the pews; then all eat the bread and drink the wine or juice at the same time.

Joanne M. Pierce

See also ADORATION; CHALICE; CONSECRATION (CHRISTIAN); EUCHARIST; MASS; MONSTRANCE.

COMMUNION OF SAINTS

The communion of saints is the unity that all those who will be and are saved share with Christ. Through their unity with Christ, all the saved then are linked to one another in a bond of sanctity. Belief in the communion of saints dates from at least the fourth century C.E., as it makes up the ninth article of the Apostles' Creed. The communion of saints came, in time, to be understood as comprised of three groups: those already in heaven (the Church Triumphant), those on earth (the Church Militant), and those in purgatory (the Church Suffering, or Expectant). Especially in medieval and later in Roman Catholic theology, the three groups were understood to be of mutual benefit to one another. Those on earth could pray for the release of members from purgatory as well as pray for aid from members already in heaven. Those in heaven could be and indeed were expected to help those on earth as well as those in purgatory. Protestant writers in general would not accept the role of intercession within the communion of saints, nor of the existence of purgatory. Early and medieval Christian writers tended to identify the church with the communion of saints, that is to say that the true church can be defined as of all those who are or will be saved. This understanding of the church still has great influence on modern ecclesiology.

Gary Macy

See also APOSTLES' CREED; CHURCH; ECCLESIOLOGY; HEAVEN; PURGATORY; SAINTS (CHRISTIAN), DEVOTION TO; SALVATION.

COMPARATIVE RELIGION

The practice of "comparing religions" is probably as old as religion is, as individuals and communities have always been intrigued by how their identities, moral beliefs, and understandings of ultimate reality compare with others outside their own society's circle. With the rise of the world religions, especially the missionary faiths (Buddhism, Christianity, Islam), interest in comparative religion was centered in the discovery of falsehood, establishing the grounds for spiritual conquest, and the promotion of conversion.

The modern pursuit of comparative religion originates in the Euro-American area with the Enlightenment, the Protestant Reformation, and global contacts between faiths begun with colonialism. Although many figures within the different world religions have continued to adopt the pre-Enlightenment triumphalism approach to other faiths, liberal factions have joined positivist scholars in pursuing modern comparative religious inquiries. Comparative religion has been closely connected with the development of the history of religions as a scientific discipline as the texts, arts and architecture, spiritual practices, and ethnographic accounts distinctive of each of the world religions have been identified, translated, and explored. It was Indologist and comparative linguist Max Müller who captured the early spirit of comparative religion's forceful methodological claim: "The person who knows only one religion understands none."

The early predominant concern among nineteenth-century comparativists was to establish an evolutionary schema of religion in human history. The sequence proposed early—animism → pantheism → polytheism → monotheism—has been shown not to be universal, arbitrarily reductive, and based upon faulty data. Interest in finding the logic of patterns of change in one tradition with reference to other faiths and world regions nevertheless endures in religious studies.

The strategy of discovering or adopting a single theme for comparative religion inquiry also has a long history and continuing relevance for the field. Only a few representative examples can be cited here. Protestant theologian Frederick Schleiermacher (1768–1834) articulated the notion that the essence of all religion was the feeling of "absolute dependence" on God. This was an influential approach that has been taken up by many in the study of comparative mysticism; in a more hermeneutical mode, Rudolf Otto (1896–1934) developed the categories of "the Holy" and "the numinous" to refer to the universal human experience of transcendent reality, employing such terms as "the absolute," "immortality," or "freedom" to refer to it. More recently, the phenomenological approach of Mircea Eliade (1907–88) focused upon finding the universal pattern of religions demarcating the "sacred" from the "profane" in terms of space, time, and human experience. Interest in comparing religions on the basis of simple phenomenological types—symbolism, myth, ritual, functional patterns—continues in the field of anthropology. In psychology, the interpretations of Freud, William James, Jung, and Maslow have also informed comparative religious inquiries.

As early theologies, texts, and community practices in the world religions have been further clarified, problems in comparative religions approaches have been voiced. Among these, the assumption of the universal viability in even the use of the concept of "religion" has been questioned; the notion of exclusive religious preference has been shown as a Western construction not applicable to Asian faiths. The problem of privileging the Euro-American voice in framing comparisons has been critiqued for ethnocentric bias.

Todd T. Lewis

See also HISTORY OF RELIGIONS; RELIGION, THEORIES OF.

COMPLUTENSIAN POLYGLOT

The name of the first polyglot (i.e., multilingual: Hebrew, Greek, Latin, with some Chaldean) edition of the whole Bible. It was begun in 1502 and finally printed in six volumes between 1514 and 1517. The edition was the work of a group of experts at the University of Alcalá (Spain), brought together by Cardinal Francisco Jiménez de Cisneros. It is called "Complutensian" because, in Latin, that is the adjective for the city of Alcalá.

Orlando Espín

See also BIBLE; JIMÉNEZ DE CISNEROS, FRANCISCO.

COMPOSTELA

A city in northwestern Spain, in the region of Galicia, where tradition says that the apostle James was supposedly buried. During the Middle Ages, and especially after the eleventh century, the tomb of James in Compostela became one of Europe's most important religious sites and the reason for many pilgrimages. To travel to "St. James of Compostela" (in Spanish, *Santiago de Compostela*) became a very popular devotional practice across Christian Europe during most of the Middle Ages. St. James became the most important religious symbol, and his legendary tomb the most important shrine, in Christian Spain's eight-century struggle against Muslim rule over much of the Iberian peninsula.

Orlando Espín

See also DEVOTIONS; MEDIEVAL CHRISTIANITY (IN THE WEST); MEDIEVAL CHURCH; PILGRIMAGE; POPULAR CATHOLICISM; SAINT; SAINTS (CHRISTIAN), DEVOTION TO.

COMTE, AUGUSTE (1798–1857)

Founder of French positivism, Comte is also considered one of the founders of modern sociology. He was educated in science and mathematics, and early in life lost his religious faith. He proposed the "law of three stages" through which he attempted to explain the phases of humanity's development in history. He unsuccessfully attempted to create a new religion based on "positive," "scientific" ideas. His two fundamental writings were the six-volume *Cours de la philosophie positive* (1830–42), and *Système de politique positive* (1848).

Orlando Espín

See also MODERNITY; POSITIVISM; POSTMODERNITY; SECULARISM; SECULARIZATION/SECULAR/SECULARIZED.

CONCELEBRATION

In general, the joint celebration of any liturgical action by several ministers; for instance, the blessing of Holy Oils at the Chrism Mass, and the Byzantine practice of several priests celebrating the anointing of the sick. However, the term more commonly refers to the joint celebration of the Eucharist by several bishops and/or presbyters, one of whom functions as presider. Eucharistic concelebration has ancient roots (Hippolytus, *Apostolic Tradition*, early third century) and was practiced primarily as a sign of ecclesial unity of the local church and of union with other churches when eucharistic hospitality was offered to visiting bishops or presbyters. The practice of concelebration generally continued uninterrupted in Eastern churches, but fell into disuse in the Roman Rite during the twelfth century except for episcopal and presbyteral ordinations. The practice was revived by the Second Vatican Council in 1963.

Current norms for eucharistic concelebration in the Roman Rite require either verbal participation in a subdued tone or unison singing for essential parts of the eucharistic prayer (epiclesis, words of institution, anamnesis, and petition for fruitful Communion) by concelebrants. Unison gestures are also required; for example, extension of hands in the orans position, imposition of hands during the epiclesis (during the words of institution the pointing to the bread and wine is optional), and bowing. Historically and currently, the practices of Eastern churches admit of silent concelebration, or a division of various parts of the eucharistic prayer, including the words of institution (*Didascalia Apostolorum*, fourth century).

Today, theological discussion regarding concelebration centers on balancing the various meanings of the practice: unity of the people of God hierarchically assembled and acting, the unity of the sacrifice of Christ, and the unity of the ministerial priesthood. Most commentators point out that present practices, including verbal co-recitation of the eucharistic prayer, disruption of the inherent unity of the eucharistic prayer by dividing up its parts, confusion of presider and concelebrant roles, and concelebration in exclusively male religious communities or presbyteral gatherings without participation of the faithful, tend to emphasize clerical unity, even clericalism, at the expense of the other, more important meanings of the rite.

Dennis W. Krouse

See also ANAPHORA; CHURCH; CLERGY; CLERICALISM; ECCLESIOLOGY; EUCHARIST; EUCHARISTIC PRAYER; MASS; PRIESTHOOD.

CONCILIARISM

The doctrine of conciliarism teaches that a general council wields supreme authority in the church or, at least, holds concomitant power with the pope. Although forms of conciliarism had been suggested by earlier writers and canonists, this theory came to prominence during the fourteenth and fifteenth centuries in an attempt to heal the the Western Schism. Faced with the problem of two popes, one in Avignon and one in Rome, theologians and canonists struggled with the issue of authority within the church. Based to some degree on earlier canonical speculation on this matter, a group of scholars suggested that a general council could be called without papal sanction to heal the schism. The most prominant proponents of conciliarism were the famous theologians Pierre d'Ailly and Jean Gerson and the canonist Francesco Zabarelli. Although the theories put forward by the conciliarists differ, they all agree that the church as a whole possesses more authority than the local Roman church, and therefore a general council once assembled would wield supreme authority even over the pope. This theory was given practical application when a group of cardinals, backed by most of the secular rulers, called a conference at Pisa in 1409. The council proceeded to depose both the pope in Avignon and the pope in Rome and elect a new pope, Alexander V. The action was defended by Gerson and d'Ailly, but did not have the desired effect as neither of the deposed popes stepped down and Europe was faced with the prospect of three popes. The successor to Alexander, John XXIII, called for another council to be held at Constance. A large and representative body assembled in 1414, and when John XXIII fled the council under fear for his own authority, the assembly passed the decree *Haec Sancta* which declared that "[this council] has its power directly from Christ; [therefore] every person of whatever status or dignity, be it even papal, has to obey [this synod]. . . ." The council proceeded to depose John and the pope in Avignon, while the pope in Rome resigned. A new pope, Martin V, was elected by the council in 1417. The council went on to estabish in the decree *Frequens* that another general council should meet in five years, a second in seven years, and thereafter, general councils should meet every ten years. The Council of Constance in effect set up the framework for a government of the church by general council. This was the high point of the conciliar theory. Martin V soon turned against conciliarism, however, and in 1418 refused to recognize a general council's right to override a papal position or decision. A council was convoked by Martin to meet in Basle in 1431, but the new Pope Eugenius IV attempted to dissolve it. The council refused to disband, appealing to the decree *Haec Sancta* of Constance. The Pope then ordered the council moved from Basle to Ferrara. A few of the holdouts in Basle attempted to depose Eugenius and set up a new pope in his place, but the attempt failed. In 1460 Pope Pius II forbade appeals of papal decisions to a general council, thus, in effect, condemning conciliarism. Conciliarism continued to have its advocates, especially among those espousing Gallicanism. It is considered a heresy by the modern Roman Catholic Church, especially since the decree on the infallibility of the pope by Vatican I.

Gary Macy

CONCLAVE

Name of the formal meeting of the cardinals of the Catholic Church, held after the death or resignation of a pope, for the sole and express purpose of electing a new pope. The cardinals are literally locked in the set of rooms where the election is to take place (hence the word "conclave," which means "with a key"). No one is allowed in or out until the final choice has been made. The actual procedures for election of new popes, in the conclaves, have changed throughout the centuries.

Orlando Espín

See also CARDINAL; CATHOLIC TRADITION; CONSISTORY; POPE; ROMAN CATHOLIC CHURCH; ROME, SEE OF.

CONCORD, FORMULA AND BOOK OF

After Martin Luther's death in 1546, diverse interpretations of his theology frequently divided those who considered themselves faithful to the Reformation he had begun. Debated issues included the place of optional rites and ceremonies in the church, the doctrine of the Eucharist, the relationship between law and grace, and the use of philosophical language and categories by theologians. Efforts to achieve and articulate theological consensus included the Formula of Concord, a confession of faith produced in 1577 by Lutheran theologians, including Jakob Andreae, Martin Chemnitz, and Nikolaus Selnecker.

In 1580 the Book of Concord was issued in Dresden. First published in German, its later editions appeared in Latin as well. The Book of Concord included the 1577 Formula of Concord, the *Augsburg Confession* of 1530, two catechisms by Luther himself, and several other doctrinal statements. "Concord" remained, however, a goal rather than an achievement, as controversy continued to divide Lutheran theologians.

Thomas Worcester, s.j.

See also AUGSBURG CONFESSION; LUTHER, MARTIN; LUTHERANISM; LUTHERAN THEOLOGY; REFORMATION.

CONCORDANCE

An alphabetical list of all or all the principal words in an important text, or the collected works of an author that identifies every instance that each word appears. A biblical concordance is an importance resource for students, pastors, and theologians; it is an indispensable tool for biblical scholars. In a biblical concordance each term in the Bible is followed by a list of all its occurrences in canonical order. A concordance includes a few of the words that appear before and after each occurrence of the term and provides the reference locating each citation.

One popular use of a biblical concordance is to identify where a half-remembered verse or saying is found in the Bible. A more serious use is to identify every occurrence of a term in one or more biblical texts for any number of applications. Biblical scholars use concordances based on the original languages to locate words and word groups; they can then determine the range of the word's possible meanings by considering its use in various contexts. It is generally advisable to consult the concordance based on the version of the Bible being used. Those with only a limited knowledge of the ancient languages will find that by using analytical concordances it is possible to identify and separate the various Greek or Hebrew terms translated by the same English word.

Computerized concordances are beginning to replace printed concordances. It is too soon to determine which, if any, of the machine applications presently available will become the standard. Second Testament and patristic scholars will find the *Thesaurus Lingua Graecae* (TLG) on CD ROM essential, since it will search all (or a selection of) Greek texts from Homer (B.C.E.) to 600 C.E., including the Greek New Testament and the Septuagint (LXX).

Regina A. Boisclair

See also BIBLICAL REFERENCES.

CONCORDAT

A legally binding agreement or treaty between a civil government, representing a nation, and the See of Rome, representing the Catholic Church within that nation.

Orlando Espín

See also CURIA, ROMAN; POPE; ROMAN CATHOLIC CHURCH; ROME, SEE OF; VATICAN.

CONCUPISCENCE

Human beings are in fundamental conflict: we are finite beings with a desire for the infinite. In the most general terms, this conflict between the finite and infinite within us is called "concupiscence." It is a notion that appears with different names in many different philosophies such as existentialism and Marxism.

In Christian Scripture, especially in Paul's Epistle to the Romans, chapter 7, the conflict takes on a religious character: the person's resistance to the loving call of God in Christ. This "separation" of the self from God, this "division" within the self as a result of desires opposed to the desire to follow God, leads to sin (from the German word, *Sunde*, "sunder-

ing," "separation"). Eventually, borrowing from the Hebrew Scriptures, Catholic doctrine at Trent defined concupiscence as something that "comes from sin and induces to sin" (*D* 792).

We must be careful, however, to attend to the nuances of concupiscence, especially in Catholic thought. First, Catholic theology has always held that, as created by God, human beings are fundamentally good. Even the fall of Adam and Eve did not change this fundamental goodness of human nature (although it obscured it, and deprived it of a true vision of the Good). Therefore, concupiscence, as a "natural" conflict in human beings, is not in itself evil (cf. Rom 7:8-9, *D* 792), and with God's grace, can become a longing for self-integration and true communion with others through union with God (cf. Pss 5; 6; 13; 30; and esp. 22; 32; 38; 42–43). Regarding that natural longing, Thomas Aquinas makes unique use of the notion of "Concupiscence" in his *Treatise on the Passions* (*ST* I–II.22-48, qq. 30ff.). He considers the Latin etymology of the concupiscence: "con" ("with") and "cupiditas" ("desire"). He then shows that (a) concupiscence is the concerted desire of the whole person that can lead to integration; (b) concupiscence is also the shared desire of lover and beloved for each other.

G. Simon Harak, S.J.

See also SIN, ORIGINAL.

CONE, JAMES H. (1938–)

A minister of the Christian Methodist Episcopal Church, James H. Cone is arguably the most influential U.S. theologian of the twentieth century. Cone broke new and controversial ground with his originative use of the term "black theology" and generated one of the most innovative and fertile movements in North

American Christian thought. Since 1969 Cone has been a member of the faculty of Union Theological Seminary where he is currently the Charles A. Briggs Professor of Systematic Theology. He is the author of numerous important theological works.

Brought up in rural Arkansas and educated at historically black Philander Smith College, Cone was an active participant in the civil rights movement and was influenced by both the Rev. Dr. Martin Luther King Jr. and Malcolm X. Cone received his doctorate in systematic theology in 1965 from Garrett Biblical Institute (now Garrett-Evangelical Theological Seminary). After a brief teaching stint at Philander Smith, Cone taught at Methodist Adrian College. Already at Philander Smith, Cone had grown disillusioned with theology; it lacked, he argued, a structure and a language by which to engage and express the oppression and suffering of black women and men. King's assassination and the rebellious aftermath, literally, forced him to write *Black Theology and Black Power* (1969). Cone's intent in that first of eight books was to demonstrate that the politics and healing work of black power embodied the message of Jesus to twentieth-century America. Just as Jesus put his ministry at the service of the blind, the lame, the hearing and speech impaired, the outcast, and the poor, so too, black power was committed to the liberation of black people from oppression. Not surprisingly, Cone's work met hostile responses from white and black critics who charged him with distorting Christianity; but others, white and black, found in his message both a challenge and a springboard for further reflection and action.

M. Shawn Copeland

See also BLACK THEOLOGY; KING, MARTIN LUTHER, JR.; MALCOLM X; WOMANIST THEOLOGY.

CONFESSING CHURCH

The Confessing Church (German = *Die bekennender Kirche*) was the name given to the German Lutheran pastors and congregations who did not support Hitler during the Nazi regime. Those Christians who swore allegiance to Hitler and the Nazi state were called the German Christians (*Deutsche Christen*). Karl Barth, Dietrich Bonhoeffer, and others were members of the Confessing Church. The "Barmen Declaration," issued in 1934 and drafted by Karl Barth and Hans Assmussen, contains the basic principles, or creed, that grounded their stance against Hitler and his policies.

Mary Ann Hinsdale

See also BARTH, KARL; BONHOEFFER, DIETRICH.

CONFESSION

See RECONCILIATION, SACRAMENT OF.

CONFESSION OF FAITH

The confession of faith is a formal public statement of faith, usually a summary of a group's core convictions, and sometimes a regulatory statement. The faith confession expresses acceptance of the community's faith and allegiance to the faith community. Biblical examples of faith confessions are the Shema (Deut 6:4) and the christological kerygma (see Acts 2:25). The ancient baptismal creeds were confessions developed as catechetical tools and declarations of faith in initiation rituals. Some faith confessions are rules of faith. The christological dogmas, crafted to demarcate orthodox from erroneous faith, served as faith confessions as well; for instance, the Nicene Creed. In the sixteenth century, Reformed churches developed another type of faith confession, doctrinal summaries that clarified a group's theological convictions; for instance, the Lutheran *Augsburg Confessions* (1534). All these faith confessions have the character of theological formulae expressing the public affirmation of a group's religious vision.

Patricia Plovanich

See also CONCORD, FORMULA AND BOOK OF.

CONFESSOR

The term has two meanings in Catholicism. First, it referred in the early church to anyone who suffered for "confessing" his or her Christian faith, without leading to the person's martyrdom. After the fourth century, it came to be applied to admirable and holy Christian men. Second, and more frequent today, the term refers to the priest who hears private confessions.

Orlando Espín

See also CATHOLIC TRADITION; MARTYR/ MARTYRDOM; RECONCILIATION, SACRAMENT OF; SAINT; SAINTS (CHRISTIAN), DEVOTION TO.

CONFIRMATION

See BAPTISM/CONFIRMATION.

CONFLICT

A serious controversy or confrontation. The notion of conflict has been important, under many descriptions and labels, in some modern philosophies and social analyses. Through these it has influenced a number theological currents and schools in Christianity. Indeed, it would be difficult to explain messianic and millenarian movements, liberation theologies, the struggle for human and civil rights, and even Catholic social doctrine, without underlying notions of conflict. Positively, social and cultural conflicts have greatly (even if at times painfully) contributed to the development of Christian doctrines and institutions, and led to Christian involvement and specific commitments in society. Unfortunately, theologians often refuse to systematically reflect on conflict. There seems to be some difficulty in publicly acknowledging the reality and grip of conflict in both civil and ecclesial contexts. The existing theological reflection on conflict has been mostly done by moral theologians and pastoral agents, with the unspoken (and false) implication that systematic theology has little to do with or learn from conflict.

Orlando Espín

See also CATHOLIC SOCIAL TEACHING; CULTURE; ECONOMY; ETHICS, SOCIAL; JUSTICE; LIBERATION THEOLOGIES; MARXISM; MESSIANIC MOVEMENTS; MILLENARIANISM; SOCIALISM.

CONFUCIANISM

The Confucian tradition is usually traced to the life and teachings of Kongzi (ca. 551–479 B.C.E.), who was born in the state of Lu in central China. In fact, its roots extend to an ancient tradition of wisdom and ethical behavior that Kongzi and other philosophers preserved, elucidated, and transmitted to future generations. This tradition, which incorporates individual character development, social ethics, and political philosophy, has been central to the Chinese worldview and, further, has deeply influenced the cultures of China, Korea, Japan, Taiwan, Singapore, and Vietnam.

According to legend, Kongzi lost his father at a young age and was raised by his mother, who made many sacrifices so that he could receive a good education. Living in an era of great turmoil, he observed many instances of brutality, discord, injustice, and corruption in human society. These experiences led him to believe that human nature is basically benign, but, like refined rice, human beings become good through being educated and trained in the virtues that build good character.

Kongzi eschewed offerings to the gods and speculation about the existence of an afterlife, advocating instead a life of moderation and virtue. Kongzi emphasized five key human values: *ren* (benevolence), *xiao* (filial piety), *li* (propriety), *shu* (reciprocity), and *wen* (learning and culture). He taught that human harmony is ensured by observing the conduct appropriate to the five human relationships: ruler/subject, father/son, husband/wife, elder/junior, and friend/friend. The nature of these relationships is both hierarchical and reciprocal, entailing mutual obligations and benefits. The goal for a human being is to become a *junzi*, a person who is noble by virtue of wisdom and good moral character. Such a person accords with the will of Heaven (*tian*) by observing the rites of propriety that ensure social harmony and continuity of the moral order. Proper behavior includes rites and rituals, particularly ritual reverence for ancestors.

Kongzi's philosophy extends to the political dimension as well as the social. Although Kongzi never achieved his goal of becoming an advisor to the highest ranks of government, he traveled widely for more than ten years, advising local rulers in line with his social, ethical, and political philosophy. He taught that rulers have a special responsibility to cultivate virtue and enact their duties with wisdom

and benevolence. A ruler who does so is said to possess the Mandate of Heaven. When a ruler becomes corrupt and dissolute, a change of government occurs, sometimes in the form of a rebellion or coup, and the Mandate of Heaven passes to a successor. The highest ruler of the land, the Son of Heaven, was traditionally responsible for performing annual ritual sacrifices at the Temple of Heaven in Beijing. Additional rituals and temples were developed to honor Kongzi and other sages and historical figures.

Early Confucianism took as its canon the *Five Classics*: the *Book of Changes (Yijing)*, *Book of History*, *Book of Poetry*, *Book of Rites*, and the *Spring and Autumn Annals*. Over time, Kongzi's ideas were systematized and developed by other thinkers, such as Mengzi and Xunzi, during the third century B.C.E. During the Song Dynasty, Neo-Confucian scholars emphasized a smaller number of works, the *Four Books*, to represent the heart of the tradition: the *Analects* of Kongzi, the *Book of Mengzi*, the *Great Learning*, and the *Doctrine of the Mean*. An imperial examination system established in 125 B.C.E. and based on the *Five Classics* ensured the dominance of Confucian ideology in matters of state for two millennia.

Many schools of Confucianism arose over time. For example, Neo-Confucianism emerged in response to the introduction of Buddhism in the early centuries of the Common Era and its development was strongly influenced by both Daoist and Buddhist thought. This spiritually oriented approach to Confucianism was emphatically critiqued by nationalists during the early twentieth century and communists from the 1940s on. Even so, credit for the economic successes of China—as well as Japan, Hong Kong, Singapore, and Korea —is often attributed to Confucian ideals such as loyalty, thrift, diligence, and social harmony.

Karma Lekshe Tsomo

See also ANALECTS; ANCESTORS, CHINESE; CHU HSI; CHUN-TZU; CHUNG YUNG; CONFUCIUS; FILIAL PIETY; HSUN-TZU; JEN; LI; LI-CHING; MENCIUS; NEO-CONFUCIANISM; TAO; TE; T'IEN; WANG YANG-MING; ZHOU DYNASTY.

CONFUCIUS (551–479 B.C.E.)

(Chinese, *K'ung Fu-tzu, K'ung Chung-ni,* Master K'ung). The nominal founder of the Confucian School in China; born in Ch'u-fu in the state of Lu (Shantung Province) during the Zhou Dynasty. Confucius was a social reformer, teacher, and philosopher who lived during a period of social chaos in China and sought to restore order and harmony to society. He has been characterized as an optimistic humanist who found the secret of life in men and their better relationships and saw a direct correlation between social order and cosmic order. Note: Confucius and Confucianism, in general, frequently refer to man or men, and this is not used in a generic sense for the most part. The Confucian writings reflect the patriarchal nature of Chinese society at that time, and consequently, the term men or man has been used in this volume (in the China entries) to reflect the traditional intent of Confucius. He was a social philosopher whose teachings had profound religious implications, in claiming that a heavenly source of correct moral and social behavior existed within each individual in an inner organ called the *hsin* (mind heart). While his teachings were not particularly popular during his lifetime, no other individual has had such a profound impact on the life and thought of China. He was more of a creative interpreter and trans-

mitter of ancient Chinese beliefs than an original thinker, but his humanistic and rationalistic approach placed less emphasis on supernaturalism and more on man's capacity to bring about order and harmony. His answer to disorder was the recovery of *li* (correct forms and patterns of social relationships) in man's behavior supported by *jen* (human-heartedness, sincerity). He firmly believed that the right balance of *li* and *jen* in men's individual lives would lead to the recovery of harmony in social life and then in political life. His teachings, found primarily in the *Lun Yu* (Analects), along with the other texts that he edited, came to be known as the Confucian Classics, and had a tremendous influence on Chinese thought, social customs, government institutions, literature, and the arts from the first century C.E. up to the present time. These teachings have also had a significant impact on other Asian societies, for example, Japan, Korea, Vietnam, and others. While Confucius' teachings appear to be overly formalistic at times, the keys to his philosophy of life are humaneness, virtue, kindness, and sincerity.

G. D. DeAngelis

See also ANALECTS; CHUANG TZU; CHU HSI; CHUNG YUNG; CONFUCIANISM; FILIAL PIETY; HSIN; HSUN-TZU; JEN; LI; MANDATE OF HEAVEN; MENCIUS; NEO-CONFUCIANISM; RECTIFICATION OF NAMES; TAO; TE; WANG YANG-MING.

CONGAR, YVES (1904–95)

French Dominican theologian and one of the seminal Catholic thinkers in the twentieth century, Congar is known for his studies in ecclesiology and tradition. Trained at Le Saulchoir by M.-D. Chenu, Congar taught fundamental and dogmatic theology there. A proponent of the

New Theology, Congar was committed to theological renewal from the study of the original sources. His study of the history of ecclesiology retrieved an ancient image of church as people of God and as *communion*, which enabled Congar to promote a broader vision of ecclesial reality as in the study *Lay People in the Church* (1957), for instance. Congar's interest in ecumenism and the problem of ecclesial unity and diversity prompted his study of tradition in the classic work *Tradition and Traditions* (1966). Prohibited from teaching and publishing in 1954, Congar remained in seclusion until his appointment as expert (*peritus*) for the Vatican Council II. He was named a cardinal in 1994.

Patricia Plovanich

See also CHENU, MARIE DOMINIQUE; TRADITION.

CONGREGATIONAL CHURCHES

In a general sense, a congregational church is one that practices congregational polity. This means that the individual congregation is completely autonomous; it governs itself, hires and fires its staff, manages its budget, and creates policy, all without answering to or receiving help from ecclesiastical authority. Baptists, Disciples of Christ, and the United Church of Christ are all congregational churches in this sense. At the same time, Congregationalists are a mainline Protestant Christian denomination in the United States, one with varied names and theologies over the years, but consistently maintaining congregational polity. Congregationalists are a quintessential "American" denomination: independent, pragmatic, conscientious, and involved in the major theological, social, and political developments in U.S. history.

The earliest Congregationalists were seventeenth-century Puritans who believed that congregational polity was closer to scriptural directives than presbyterian. A reform movement seeking "purity" within the Church of England, Puritans first emigrated to New England in 1630 and established three colonies: Massachusetts Bay, Connecticut, and New Haven. The latter two eventually merged. They were Calvinists, affirming unconditional election, limited atonement, and irresistible grace. They sought to establish a biblical commonwealth based on Old Testament norms and believed that, like the Israelites, they were chosen by God for a special covenant relationship. Congregational churches were autonomous but not independent from one another; all were part of the state church. The state supported the churches and enforced religious law, and, in turn, church membership and gender determined who could vote.

In the mid-eighteenth century, New England Congregationalists encountered dissension over revivalism in the First Great Awakening. Some, like Jonathan Edwards of Northampton, Massachusetts, enthusiastically endorsed it, seeing it as the Holy Spirit's method of reviving flagging church membership and reinvigorating the "Puritan experiment." Others, like Charles Chauncy of Boston, vigorously opposed its emotional excesses and lack of intellectual rigor. Congregationalists divided into a pro-revivalist faction called New Lights and anti-revivalists called Old Lights. The most radical New Lights became Baptists, and the most radical Old Lights, Unitarians. Most Congregationalists remained in the middle, advocating moderate Calvinism and moderate revivalism. Despite the separation of church and state guaranteed by the Constitution, Congregationalism remained the established religion, albeit nominally, until 1818 in Connecticut, 1819 in New Hampshire, and 1833 in Massachusetts.

Most Congregationalists were in the mainstream of political, intellectual, and cultural events. They founded Harvard and Yale Colleges, supported independence during the Revolutionary War, and were active in nineteenth-century social reforms like abolitionism, women's rights, temperance, and anti-prostitution. They were avid advocates of evangelicalism during the Second Great Awakening; revivals at Yale College in 1801 were conducted by Congregationalists Timothy Dwight and Asahel Nettleton. They cooperated with Presbyterians on evangelistic efforts and home missions among African and Native Americans. The first woman ordained to the ministry was Congregationalist Antoinette Brown in 1853.

Concentrated in New England and the Great Lakes region, most staunch abolitionists, Congregationalists were one of the few Protestant denominations that did not divide between Northern and Southern branches over slavery prior to the Civil War. They grew slowly but steadily, especially among educated, urban, middle-class Euro-Americans. One of the most remarkable families of the nineteenth century were Congregationalists: the Beechers. The patriarch of the clan was Lyman Beecher, pastor, president of Lane Seminary, and evangelical leader. Children included Catherine Beecher, pioneer for women's education; Henry Ward Beecher, pulpit orator, liberal, and object of a sex scandal in the 1870s; Isabella Beecher Hooker, suffragist and women's rights activist; and Harriet Beecher Stowe, author of the best-selling abolitionist novel *Uncle Tom's Cabin*.

In the second half of the nineteenth century and early twentieth, most Congregationalists advocated liberalism over fundamentalism. Pastor of Plymouth Church in Brooklyn, Henry Ward Beecher was the most famous preacher of the era, succeeded by Lyman Abbott. Both expounded liberal themes: the benevolence of God, brotherhood of humanity, centrality of religious feelings, and acceptance of recent intellectual developments such as Darwinism and historical criticism of the Bible. Congregationalists were also active in the Social Gospel, especially Columbus, Ohio, pastor Washington Gladden, called the "father of the Social Gospel" for his activism on behalf of workers and recently formed labor unions.

In the mid-twentieth century, Congregationalists became involved in ecumenical efforts. They supported the formation of the National and World Councils of Churches for interdenominational cooperation and support. In 1931 they went even further, actually merging with another congregationalist denomination, the Christian Churches, to form the Congregational Christian Churches (CCC). In 1957 the CCC merged with the Evangelical and Reformed Church to create the United Church of Christ (UCC). The UCC has continued many Congregationalist emphases: congregational polity, commitments to justice and societal transformation, and a tendency to introspection and self-righteousness. Although their membership declined from the 1970s to the 1990s, the UCC nonetheless remains a mainstream progressive Protestant denomination.

Evelyn A. Kirkley

See also CONGREGATIONAL THEOLOGIES; EDWARDS, JONATHAN; EVANGELICALS; EVANGELICAL THEOLOGY; PURITANISM; SOCIAL GOSPEL; UNITED CHURCH OF CHRIST.

CONGREGATIONAL THEOLOGIES

As a distinctive Protestant denomination in the United States, Congregationalists have made significant contributions to Christian theology. In fact, they have shaped U.S. religious movements of Puritanism, evangelicalism, and liberalism. Jonathan Edwards, Nathaniel William Taylor, and Horace Bushnell were not only exponents of prevailing Congregationalist theological currents, but also shaped U.S. theology for generations after their deaths; their influence is still palpable in U.S. religious culture.

Edwards (1703–58), pastor in western Massachusetts and revivalist during the First Great Awakening, integrated Puritanism, Enlightenment philosophy, and revivalism. He reinterpreted Puritan categories in light of contemporary science and psychology, forging a synthesis of John Locke, Isaac Newton, and John Calvin. He stressed God's sovereignty and human sinfulness, traditional Calvinist doctrines, but Edwards individualized them, making sin a more personal, interior state than the communal emphasis of the Puritans. He argued that reason must be accompanied by "religious affections," spiritual emotions combined with volition, aroused by the presence of the Holy Spirit. He speculated that revelations of grace in the Awakening were signs of God's favor to "America" and of its divinely ordained destiny.

Like Edwards, a graduate of Congregationalist Yale College, unlike him a professor there and pastor in New Haven's First Congregational Church, Taylor (1786–1858) pioneered evangelical theology in the first half of the nineteenth century. "Taylorism," "New Divinity," or "New Haven theology," as Taylor's system was variously called, adapted Calvinist orthodoxy to revivalism and social reform and influenced evangelical leaders such as Lyman Beecher and Charles Grandison Finney. Instead of total depravity, the ineffable depths of human sinfulness, Taylor stressed the human capacity to do good. Although people did sin, sinfulness was neither inevitable nor intrinsic to the human condition; it was a choice. Instead of God's unfathomable sovereignty, he emphasized the "moral government" of the universe in which God acted with justice and benevolence. Taylor mitigated the harsh edges of orthodox Calvinism, making it more palatable to people who could no longer accept the notion that God damned innocent infants. However, in the process, Taylor fundamentally changed Calvinism.

Bushnell (1802–76), another Connecticut pastor, further mitigated Calvinist orthodoxy and anticipated liberal Protestant theology, in effect bridging evangelicalism and liberalism. A Congregationalist pastor in Hartford, he argued that conversion was not necessarily a cataclysmic experience, a radical shift from evangelical theology. For a child raised in the Christian faith, conversion might be gradual; in fact, such a person might never have the consciousness of not being Christian. In so doing, he stressed the centrality of religious feelings and ethical living, and downplayed the importance of revivalism. These would all become liberal emphases. Second, Bushnell argued for a metaphorical interpretation of the Bible in contrast to a literal one. In suggesting that biblical and creedal language is evocative and imprecise, he anticipated the historical-critical interpretation of the Bible by liberals: their belief that the Bible attempts to express the inexpressible, the experience of individuals and communities with the divine.

Evelyn A. Kirkley

See also BUSHNELL, HORACE; CONGRE-
GATIONAL CHURCHES; EDWARDS,
JONATHAN; EVANGELICALS; EVANGELI-
CAL THEOLOGY; GREAT AWAKENING(S)
(EURO-AMERICAN RELIGIOUS HISTORY);
REVIVALISM.

CONGREGATIONS (ORDERS)

Vowed religious men and women in the
Roman Catholic Church belong to communities known as "congregations" or
"orders." The term "congregation" is
usually applied to a canonically recognized community of persons with simple
vows. Members of an "order" take solemn
vows. Examples of religious congregations
include: the Brothers of the Christian
Schools, founded by John Baptist de la
Salle (F.S.C.); the brothers and priests of the
Congregation of the Holy Cross (C.S.C.);
Congregation of the Sisters of St. Joseph
(C.S.J.). Examples of religious orders include: the Jesuits (the Society of Jesus =
S.J.); the Dominicans (the Order of Preach-
ers = O.P.); and the Franciscans (Order of
Friars Minor = O.F.M.; Order of Sisters of
St. Francis = O.S.F.).

Mary Ann Hinsdale

See also BENEDICTINES; DOMINICANS;
FRANCISCANS; ORDERS, RELIGIOUS;
RELIGIOUS (VOWED); SOCIETY OF JESUS.

CONSCIENCE

Conscience refers to a sense of duty or
accountability for decisions of moral importance. More specifically, it is the human
faculty of judging the rightness or wrongness of particular actions. Thomas Aquinas
refers to conscience as "the mind of the
human person making moral judgments."
Conscience is technically distinguished
from "synderesis" which refers to knowledge of moral principles. Conscience refers
to the ability of the human mind, in the
exercise of practical reason, to apply moral
principles to concrete circumstances.

Conscience sometimes refers to an
inner voice of moral authority, or, as some
put it, to an inner voice of God calling
people to moral responsibility. Whether
the actual source of conscience is God or
an innate human faculty, it is generally
believed that it must be followed, since,
without it, people are unable to make
moral decisions or feel any sense of moral
accountability. The problem, of course, is
that sometimes people suffer from an erroneous conscience.

A conscience can err when it makes an
error of factual judgment about relevant
circumstances of a moral decision-making
situation, when it is overwhelmed by
emotions that cloud reason, or when the
conscience's knowledge of moral principles is corrupted.

Contemporary psychology and theology have come to appreciate that conscience probably does not inherit a
knowledge of moral principles, but acquires them through moral education. If
one's moral education is inadequate, conscience can be misinformed and make
objectively erroneous moral judgments.
Thus, an individual "in good conscience"
could make a decision that actually compromises some genuine moral good (*error
invincibilis* = invincible ignorance). A
vincible ignorance (*error vincibilis*) refers
to the conscience of an individual who
negligently refuses to inform himself or
herself about moral principles or facts
relevant to a moral decision. Contemporary moral theology and church teaching
(for example, Vatican Council II) consider
it imperative that persons follow their
consciences, even if at odds with particular moral norms, since, again, this is the
faculty by which moral accountability is
experienced. Disregarding conscience

jeopardizes future moral judgments. An individual has a responsibility, however, to seriously consider the moral wisdom of his or her tradition when contemplating a decision "in good conscience" that differs from explicit moral norms.

Michael J. Hartwig

See also MORAL THEOLOGY/CHRISTIAN ETHICS.

CONSCIENTIOUS OBJECTION

Objection to participation in war for moral reasons was officially supported in 1965 in *Gaudium et Spes* (Pastoral Constitution on the Church in the Modern World) of the Second Vatican Council (nos. 78–79); by the U.S. bishops in the 1968 pastoral *Human Life in Our Day*; in the 1983 pastoral *The Challenge of Peace : God's Promise and Our Response*; and the 1993 reflection letter *The Harvest of Justice Is Sown in Peace*. In contrast to the U.S. armed forces, which recognize only opposition to war in any form, the U.S. bishops have recently insisted upon respect for, and legislative protection of the rights of, both total *and* selective conscientious objection.

Mary E. Hobgood

See also CHALLENGE OF PEACE; JUST WAR THEORY; PEACE.

CONSECRATION (CHRISTIAN)

The word consecration comes from a Latin word (*consecrare*) meaning to make sacred or to dedicate to a god. The Christian tradition, more specifically, the Roman Catholic tradition, uses the term in several important ways: first, the consecration of the bread and wine into the Body and Blood of Christ at the Eucharist (or Mass); the consecration (or ordination) of a bishop; the consecration (or dedication) of a church; and the consecration of vir-

gins (which had fallen into disuse but was revised in 1970, during the liturgical reforms of Vatican II). Chrism, a special kind of blessed oil, can also be said to have been consecrated, as can an altar.

The first three of the above are perhaps the most important. To begin with the third, the consecration of a church (and the altar within it) is a liturgical ceremony that sets the building apart, hallows it, and dedicates it for use in the worship of God. The next use, the consecration of a bishop, is a phrase used to refer to the ceremony in which the bishop is ordained to that office (today, from the ordained order of *presbyter*, or priest); the candidate's head is anointed during the Roman Catholic rite by the consecrating bishops.

Perhaps the most important use, however, is as a description of what happens during the Eucharist (or Mass) to the elements of bread and wine. These gifts, which have been placed on the altar at the offertory (or presentation of gifts), are said in some Christian traditions to be consecrated, or transformed, into the Body and Blood of Christ during the recitation of the eucharistic prayer. Theological explanations of the nature and degree of this transformation vary among the various Christian denominations. Some traditions (for instance, Roman Catholicism) have also historically focused on defining not just the manner but the exact "moment" or point during the eucharistic prayer at which the bread and wine can be said to have been "consecrated," or transformed: for example, in the past, Roman Catholic theology pinpointed the recitation of the *verba*, or words of Christ at the Last Supper ("This is my Body . . . This is my Blood") as the moment of consecration, thus calling these phrases the "words of consecration." Since the reforms of Vatican II, this kind of analysis has been de-emphasized in favor of a more holistic view of the "consecratory" function of the prayer, and the liturgy itself, as a unitive experience.

Joanne M. Pierce

See also ANAMNESIS; ANAPHORA; COMMUNION (LITURGICAL); EPICLESIS; EUCHARIST; EUCHARISTIC PRAYER; MASS; ORDAINED MINISTRIES, SACRAMENT OF; ORDINATION; REAL PRESENCE.

CONSERVATIVE JUDAISM

Conservative Judaism is a modern branch/denomination/movement of Judaism that has its roots in mid-to-late nineteenth-century Europe, and was transplanted to the United States in the late nineteenth and early twentieth centuries.

While throughout Jewish history there has never been a unilateral approach to Jewish beliefs and practices, the core teachings of Judaism were widely accepted by most Jews. In the mid-nineteenth century, Reform Judaism was born in Germany and Central Europe. Responding to the Enlightenment, the Emancipation, and scientific scholarship, Reform Judaism rejected the concept of divine revelation, and instead, attributed the authorship of Torah to divinely inspired human beings. Torah law, therefore, for Reform Jews, became instructive and inspirational, but not binding. Early Reform practices modernized the worship service, and eliminated many ritual practices.

The founders of Conservative Judaism accepted the Reform notion that change in Jewish belief and practice is necessary in an ever-changing world, but they felt that the reformers had gone too far, had eliminated too many basic Jewish practices. So they wished to conserve, to retain, some of the theology and rituals that Reform had eliminated.

The Conservative motto became "tradition and change," indicating the principle that Jews are still bound to observing Torah and Rabbinic law, but that the interpretation and application of the law is ever-evolving, based on careful study of its origin and historical development, and its function in modern circumstance.

The main institutions of Conservative Judaism are the Jewish Theological Seminary in New York and the University of Judaism in Los Angeles, the seminaries for training Conservative rabbis, cantors, and educators; the United Synagogue of Conservative Judaism, the organization of synagogues and lay leaders; and the Rabbinical Assembly, the international organization of Conservative rabbis.

Wayne Dosick

See also JEWISH RENEWAL MOVEMENT; JUDAISM; RABBINIC JUDAISM; RECONSTRUCTIONIST JUDAISM; REFORM JUDAISM.

CONSISTORY

In the Roman Catholic Church, this is the name of the official meetings of the pope with the "college" (that is, the whole group) of cardinals. There are several kinds of consistories, depending on their purpose (for example, to approve or promote canonization procedures, to invest new cardinals, to receive foreign ambassadors, and so on). In some churches of the Anglican Communion, a consistory is a type of ecclesiastical court of law.

Orlando Espín

See also ANGLICAN COMMUNION; BEATIFICATION; CANONIZATION; CARDINAL; CONCLAVE; CURIA, ROMAN; ROMAN CATHOLIC CHURCH; ROME, SEE OF.

CONSTANCE, COUNCIL OF

After the failure of the Council of Pisa to end the Western Schism, Pope John XXIII, the second pope in the Pisan line, convened a council at Constance in 1414 under the auspices of Emperor Sigismund. When John fled Constance in disguise on March 20, 1415, the council decided to assert its own authority, declaring in the decree *Haec Sancta* that "[this council] has its power directly from Christ; [therefore] every person of whatever status or dignity, be it even papal, has to obey [this synod]. . . ." The council proceeded to depose both John and Benedict XIII, the pope of the line of Avignon. The Roman pope, Gregory XII, resigned under the condition that he be permitted to officially convoke the council, a request the council leaders granted. Electors chosen by the council, and including cardinals from all three papal lines, then elected a new pope, Martin V, thus ending the Western Schism. The council proceeded to other matters, including the condemnation and ultimately the burning of the Czech reformer Jan Hus for heresy, as well as the formal condemnation of the teachings of John Wycliff. A further decree, *Frequens*, provided for future councils to meet periodically for the reform of the church. The council formally closed on April 22, 1418. The Council of Constance is reckoned by Western Christians as the sixteenth ecumenical council, although Roman Catholics do not recognize the decree *Haec Sancta* as valid.

Gary Macy

See also AVIGNON (PAPACY AT); COUNCIL, ECUMENICAL; MEDIEVAL CHRISTIANITY (IN THE WEST); PISA, COUNCIL OF; SCHISM, GREAT WESTERN.

CONSTANTINE I THE GREAT (?–337)

The son of the emperor Constantius Chlorus and St. Helena, Constantine was proclaimed emperor in 306 upon the death of his father. He defeated his chief rival in the West, Maxentius, at the battle of Milvian bridge. According to tradition, Constantine adopted the Christian cross as his battle standard before this important battle. Shortly afterward, in 313, Constantine and the Roman ruler in the East, Licinius, jointly proclaimed the "Edict of Milan," giving religious freedom to Christians. By 324, Constantine was sole ruler of the Empire. He intiated several important administrative reforms throughout the Empire, perhaps the most dramatic the dedication of the new city of "Constantinople" (Constantine's city) as the new capital of the Empire. Constantine, although not baptized until his death in 337, supported Christianity as his favored religion. He worked to integrate the Christian faith into Roman law and society and gave generously to the construction of basilicas for Christian worship. He also felt no compunction in intervening in theological disputes, both by calling the Council of Nicaea in 325 and by attempting to settle the Donatist controversy in North Africa. Constantine's belief that the Emperor also played an important leadership role in the Christian church did much to develop the theory of caesaropapism.

Gary Macy

See also CAESAROPAPISM; DONATION OF CONSTANTINE; DONATISM; NICAEA, FIRST COUNCIL OF.

CONSTANTINOPLE, FIRST COUNCIL OF

The Second Ecumenical Council held in 381. The council was called by Emperor

Theodosius I to settle the Arian controversy. This controversy was named for the presbyter of Alexandria, Arius, who taught that the Logos, the Second Person of the Trinity, was subordinate to the Father in divinity. This issue had been addressed by the Council of Nicaea (325) where the teaching of Arius was condemned. The issue continued to be debated, however, and the emperor wished to establish doctrinal uniformity based on the creed of Nicaea. The council, in fact, reaffirmed the creed of Nicaea, thus again condemning Arianism. While Arianism continued among some of the Germanic tribes, the end of the Arian controversy is usually marked by the First Council of Constantinople. The council also affirmed the full divinity of the Spirit, and condemned the teaching of the Pneumatomachians that the Spirit was a lesser being than the Father and the Son. The council further condemned the teaching of Apollinaris, the bishop of Laodicea, who denied that Jesus has a human mind or soul. The creed endorsed by the council has become the basis for creeds used by both Eastern and Western Christians.

Gary Macy

See also APOLLINARIANISM; APOLLINARIS; ARIANISM; ARIUS; CHRISTOLOGY; COUNCIL, ECUMENICAL; CREED/SYMBOL OF FAITH; NICAEA, FIRST COUNCIL OF; NICAEA, SECOND COUNCIL OF; NICENE CREED; PNEUMATOMACHIANS; SUBORDINATIONISM; TRINITY/TRINITARIAN THEOLOGY/TRINITARIAN PROCESSIONS.

CONSTANTINOPLE, SECOND COUNCIL OF

The Fifth Ecumenical Council held in 553. The council was called by Emperor Justinian to settle the controversy over the "Three Chapters." The issue at stake was whether Theodore, bishop of Mopsuestia (392–428), Theodoret, bishop of Cyrrhus (423–ca. 460), and Ibas, bishop of Edessa (435–49, 451–7), ought to be condemned for teaching Nestorianism (the belief that there are two natures and two persons in Christ). The emperor had already condemned them and their teaching in the so-called "Three Chapters," a decree issued in 543–4 in an attempt to impose unity of belief on the empire. The council upheld the decree of the emperor by condemning all three theologians and their teaching. Pope Vigilius opposed the condemnation by both emperor and council, although, in the end, under pressure from the emperor, he accepted the decision of the council.

Gary Macy

See also CHRISTOLOGY; COUNCIL, ECUMENICAL; HYPOSTATIC UNION; JUSTINIAN; NESTORIANISM; THE THREE CHAPTERS; THEODORE OF MOPSUESTIA; THEODORET OF CYRRHUS; VIGILIUS OF ROME.

CONSTANTINOPLE, SEE OF

The city of Constantinople was established by Emperor Constantine the Great in 330 C.E. on the site of an already existing town called Byzantium. The latter had had a Christian community for about two hundred years before Constantinople was established. Because of the city's role as the new imperial capital, its bishops received patriarchal honors. The First Ecumenical Council held at Constantinople (381 C.E.) raised this see to preeminence, only after the see of Rome. For over a century, the bishops of Alexandria and of Constantinople fought for supremacy in the East, with Constantinople the clear winner. Since the sixth century, the bishop of Constantinople is recognized and respected as the "Ecumenical Patriarch," that is, as the first in rank among all the bishops of the Eastern Orthodox Churches. After a long, gradual estrangement from the see of Rome and the Western Churches (due to a series of cultural, political, and ecclesiastical causes), Constantinople finally broke with Rome in the year 1054. Istanbul is the modern name of the city of Constantinople.

Orlando Espín

See also BYZANTIUM/BYZANTINE; CATHOLIC TRADITION; ECUMENICAL PATRIARCH; FATHERS OF THE CHURCH; ORTHODOX CHURCHES; PATRIARCH; PATRISTICS/PATROLOGY; SCHISM, GREAT EASTERN.

CONSTANTINOPLE, THIRD COUNCIL OF

The Sixth Ecumenical Council held in 680–1. The council was called by Emperor Constantine IV in order to settle the question whether Christ had a single will or two wills, one divine and one human. With the support of Pope Agatho, the emperor, and the patriarchs of Constantinople and Antioch, the council condemned the teaching that Christ had only one will (Monothelitism). The principal adherents to this teaching, including Pope Honorius (625–38), were also anathematized.

Gary Macy

See also ANATHEMA; CHRISTOLOGY; COUNCIL, ECUMENICAL; HONORIUS I OF ROME; HYPOSTATIC UNION; MONOTHELITISM; PATRIARCH.

CONSTRUCTIVE THEOLOGY

A contemporary theological reflection with roots in the "liberal theology" of the late nineteenth and early twentieth centuries, constructive theology addresses the irrelevance of Christianity by constructing Christian teaching and practice based on modern philosophies, cultures, and social practices. As R. Gruenler explains in his article in *The Evangelical Dictionary of Theology*, it uses a Hegelian method of *thesis*, a brief history of a doctrine; *antithesis*, a critique of the irrelevance of the doctrine to moderns; and *synthesis*, a restatement of the doctrine in contemporary terms. As Gordon Kaufman conceives of it (see also Edward Farley, Schubert Ogden, David Tracy, Sally McFague, among others), theology must rethink notions of truth, person, God, and Jesus Christ. Religious truth about the source and meaning of all reality comes through dialogue, is pluralistic, and must be practical and apply to human beings as they engage with their everyday world. The interconnectedness of humans with all life, their own coming to terms with guilt, anxiety, and the social realities of oppression and disorder, and the cosmic reality of a chance universe in process, require that God and images of God extend along a continuum from myths to the source of all that is. For Kaufman the way we understand person and God determines how we understand Jesus Christ. Necessarily he wants to reexamine christological terms, but embraces the crucified Christ as the image of God who suffers with his people and in whose resurrection a new community of peace comes to life.

Thomas McElligott

See also GOD; JESUS OF HISTORY; METHOD IN THEOLOGY; PERSON/ PROSOPON; PLURALISM.

CONSUBSTANTIATION

A metaphysical theory that explains how the risen Lord becomes present in the bread and wine of the Eucharist. Consubstantiation argues that the substance of the bread and wine coexist with the substance of the Body and Blood of the risen Lord. This was one of three explanations of transubstantiation in the late twelfth and thirteenth centuries. By the end of the century, few theologians accepted consubstantiation, and John Quidort of Paris in the early fourteenth century was the last of the medieval theologians to defend it.

Consubstantiation is also used inaccurately to describe the theology of Martin Luther. Luther did not wish to use Aristotelian philosophy at all in describing the Real Presence. Luther felt transubstantiation to be "an unfortunate superstructure [built] on an unfortunate foundation." Scripture, not Aristotle, should be the foundation for all Christian thinking on the Eucharist. Luther preferred the teaching known as "ubiquity," that is, that the Body of the risen Lord could be present anywhere, since the divine nature of the Lord was present everywhere (*ubique* in Latin). Since Luther did teach, however, that both the Body and Blood and the bread and wine are present in the Eucharist, his teaching has often been called consubstantiation by his opponents. Since consubstantiation depends on Aristotelian metaphysics, though, this is not really an accurate description.

Gary Macy

See also ARISTOTELIANISM; ARISTOTLE; EUCHARIST; LUTHER, MARTIN; REAL PRESENCE; SUBSTANCE; TRANSIGNIFICATION; TRANSUBSTANTIATION; UBIQUITARIANISM.

CONTEMPLATION

The words "meditation," "prayer," and "contemplation" are often used interchangeably, but there are shades of difference among them, based on Christian religious experience. Contemplation, as a form of prayer, generally refers to a prayer more from the heart than from the head, a looking at the holy mystery of God, even being absorbed by that mystery, in a quiet act of love. Contemplation thus names an interior state of being united with the mystery of God through love. As such, it sounds very close to what is commonly meant by mysticism. But interior states are not easily mapped; there can be considerable overlapping in the activities of mind, heart, and imagination. The state of being in love with God cannot prescind completely from idea and image in favor of pure feeling, even though the individual might not be consciously thinking or imagining. Often, however, the term "contemplation" is intended to convey an attitude of letting God become present to us, for the divine presence cannot be forced, figured out, or controlled in any way. In a culture that prizes technology and scientific reasoning, contemplation becomes difficult; it demands an interior shift, more akin to what happens when we enjoy a work of art, become caught up in a piece of music, or are drawn to an experience of wonder over the beauty in creation. Contemplation thus involves the creation of an interior "space" (or attitude) where the mystery of God can show itself. Normally, creating that inner space calls for meditation, asceticism, and discipline— "exercises of the spirit," as it were. The contemplative experience cannot be rushed, but neither is it reserved only for a few.

William Reiser, s.j.

See also CONTEMPLATIVES; MEDITATION (CHRISTIAN); PRAYER.

CONTEMPLATIVES

The designation "contemplative" has both a narrow meaning and a broad meaning. Members of contemplative religious communities, such as the Cistercians and Carthusians, live apart from the world in order to devote themselves completely to the pursuit of God. They assemble for the recitation or singing of the Liturgy of the Hours and for the Eucharist, engage in periods of manual work and study, and live very simply, even austerely. Such a lifestyle frequently produces men and women so centered on the mystery of God that they become joined to that mystery in heart, mind, and soul.

In the broader usage, men and women with the facility of finding or seeing God in all things are properly called contemplatives, whether they live in religious communities or not. The contemplative does not impose God on everything like a transparency, but has acquired a lived sense of God's nearness, faithfulness, and love. That sense permeates the contemplative's way of relating to other men and women and to the created world. The contemplative state may not be much different from mysticism, and it is ordinarily not attained without everyday attentiveness to the presence of God in one's life. In the church, there is nothing exceptional about one's becoming contemplative; a good example is the Mary who sat at the feet of Jesus and listened to him (Luke 10:39). With its stress upon Jesus' constant union with the Father (for example, John 14:11-12) and the believer's lifelong union with Jesus (for example, John 15:1-11), the Fourth Gospel apparently assumes that the contemplative attitude ought to be the rule.

William Reiser, s.j.

See also CONTEMPLATION; MEDITATION (CHRISTIAN); PRAYER; RELIGIOUS (VOWED).

CONTEXTUALIZATION

Contextualization is a theological method that seeks to locate the process of theological reflection in the concrete, lived experience of a particular culture.

Mary Ann Hinsdale

CONTEXTUAL THEOLOGY

More than a specific theological content or method, this expression refers to theologies consciously and acknowledgedly constructed from a specific social location (recognizing—as part of location—the theologian's culture, gender, race, ethnicity, class, and so forth). However, all theologies—whether they acknowledge it or not—are contextual because all theologies (and the theologians who construct them) are always and inescapably socially, historically, and culturally located and contextualized.

Orlando Espín

See also CONTEXTUALIZATION; CULTURE; INCULTURATION; INTERCULTURAL THOUGHT; METHOD IN THEOLOGY.

CONTINENTAL THEOLOGY

Continental theology means the systematic theologies that take their leading questions and develop their premises, structures, and philosophical categories with reference to the religious, cultural, and political situation in the various nations of Europe. Examples of such theologies are the works of Rudolph Bultmann and Karl Rahner, who utilized the existential philosophical concepts of Martin Heidegger to forge their theological systems, or Karl Barth and Paul Tillich who adopted the dialectical categories of Idealist philosophy for their theological work.

Patricia Plovanich

CONTINGENT

A being such that it is possible for the being to exist and possible for the being to not-exist.

J. A. Colombo

CONTRACEPTION/BIRTH CONTROL

These terms generally refer to any attempt to render heterosexual intercourse sterile or prevent the conception of a child by *artificial* means. There are two basic types of contraception: those that inhibit the union of the sperm and ovum (by imposing a barrier such as condoms or cervical caps or prevent ovulation as in birth control pills); and those that prevent the implantation of a fertilized ovum (intrauterine devices or IUDs). The latter methods are, strictly speaking, abortifacient rather than contraceptive.

Until the twentieth century, recourse to contraception was viewed in a negative light and so forbidden by the Christian traditions. There are three reasons that explain this prohibition. First, St. Augustine held that offspring was one of the three goods of marriage that validated marital sexual intercourse, a practice otherwise considered to be sinful. Second, according to St. Thomas Aquinas, contraception frustrates the natural purpose of sexual intercourse, that is, procreation. Thus it is contrary to natural law and a rebellion against its divine author. Third, until the time of the Industrial Revolution (later in agricultural societies), the birth of children and, indeed, large families were viewed as economically and socially beneficial. Thus the use of contraception has traditionally been linked not with attempts to space or avoid the birth of children, but rather with attempts to hide illicit sexual unions.

The Church of England reversed the traditional negative evaluation of contraception in 1930 and other Protestant denominations soon followed. Not bound by a strictly procreative sexual ethics, many Protestants would argue that planning pregnancies for opportune times promoted the stability of family life. The Roman Catholic Church rejected the Church of England's liberalization on contraception in 1930 and reaffirmed its official opposition to artificial birth control with the encyclical letters *Humanae Vitae* in 1968 and *Evangelium Vitae* in 1995. Modern popes have seen that there can be valid reasons to postpone or avoid the birth of children. This can only be achieved licitly by abstinence from sexual intercourse or by using a method of natural family planning that helps couples avoid intercourse during the time of fertility in the woman's menstrual cycle. Critics of this stance have argued, however, that there is no moral difference between artificial and natural methods.

Humanae Vitae, which dealt solely with questions of birth control, was greeted with considerable dissent among theologians and skepticism among the faithful. It generated a decline in the church's authority in sexual matters. Indeed, a very large majority of Roman Catholic married couples use some form of artificial birth control. The widespread acceptance of contraception among Christians can be explained by a number of factors, including: the dangers of national and global overpopulation; the economic burdens of large families and children generally; the increased social and economic role of women; and a change in the perception of the meaning of sexual intercourse from essentially procreative to expressive of interpersonal love. From a religious perspective, those who oppose artificial contraception argue that it frustrates the natural and interpersonal purposes of human sexuality as created by God. Further, it is a manifestation of selfishness that functions as a rebellion. Critics are also concerned about negative social consequences, such as increased marital infidelity and promiscuity, the degradation of women, and a negative attitude toward children—the so-called contraceptive mentality in which the conception of a new life is to be avoided at all costs instead of being welcomed as a great gift.

Brian F. Linnane, s.j.

See also ETHICS, SEXUAL; EVANGELIUM VITAE; HUMANAE VITAE; NATURAL LAW; SEXUALITY.

CONTRITION

In general, a sorrow for wrongdoing and a resolution not to repeat the wrong action. Catholic doctrine at Trent defined contrition as "sorrow (*dolor*) of heart and detestation (*detestatio*) for sin committed, with the resolution not to sin again" (*D* 897, 915). Christian theology has always held that, with God always offering forgiveness, contrition is necessary to obtain forgiveness from sin. That is because the human being is free to accept or reject God's grace. Thus, though instigated by God's offer, contrition must entail facing one's past, accepting responsibility for one's wrongful action or attitude, and firmly rejecting it from one's life. The latter can involve commitment to long struggle, especially in the case of bad habits or addictions.

Motivation for contrition became a concern for Catholic theology in the twelfth century. Imperfect contrition (*attritio*) was contrition because of fear of loss of one's soul, or of hell. [Note: fear of physical punishment is always insufficient.] Per-

fect contrition (*contritio*) came from love of God who had been offended. The question: was "imperfect contrition" sufficient to receive absolution in confession? Pope Alexander VII in the mid-seventeenth century finally declared that one could hold either position. Modern thinkers tend to include acts of apology and/or reparation to the *community* as a necessary sign of contrition.

G. Simon Harak, s.j.

See also FORGIVENESS; MERCY; RECONCILIATION.

CONVENIENCE, ARGUMENT FROM

A fallacious form of argument that claims something is in fact the case, or a proposition is true, solely because one needs, wants, or would like it to be the case or true.

J. A. Colombo

CONVENT/CONVENTUAL

A convent is the name of the canonically approved house in which members of religious orders or congregations live. The term is applicable to the dwelling of both male and female religious. Despite its more common usage for female religious houses, monastic women are returning to the use of the term monastery.

Mary Ann Hinsdale

CONVERSION

The Latin term *convertere* (to turn around) corresponds to the Hebrew *shub* (to turn, to return) and Greek *metanoĕō* (I change my mind). In everyday usage, the term "conversion" usually refers to a person's changing his or her religion (or denomination within the same religion). Nevertheless, in theological usage, it designates the redirection of an individual's, or community's, commitment in response to God's call or, even more precisely, to God's self-gift in love. Thus conversion means turning one's life around and moving in a new direction, namely, toward God. Some Christian writers think of conversion as a once-in-a-lifetime experience, while others see Christian life as an ongoing process of personal and communal conversion. While contemporary theologians have followed Bernard Lonergan's breakdown of conversion into distinct types (affective, moral, intellectual, and religious), the term continues to be used primarily in reference to spiritual experience.

James B. Nickoloff

See also GERUT; LONERGAN, BERNARD.

CONVERSION IN JUDAISM

See GERUT.

CONVOCATIONS OF CANTERBURY

Originally, synods of elected representatives of the clergy of the province of Canterbury in England. Parallel to them were the Convocations of the other province, York. These Convocations spoke for the clergy of the Church of England.

By the seventh century, synods were common in Britain and modeled upon the participatory governance structures of the religious orders. In 1226 Archbishop Stephen Langton convened a Convocation of Canterbury that included bishops, abbots, deans, archdeacons, two representatives of the clergy of each diocese, and one representative of each cathedral chapter. Canterbury's composition thus matched that of the Convocation of York and soon became normative.

Henry VIII obtained the "Submission of the Clergy" from the Convocation in 1532, which ended its independence from the state. Like her father, Elizabeth I used the Convocation to consolidate the gains of the English Reformation. After the Acts of Supremacy (1559) and Uniformity (1660), the Convocation's influence upon the life of the church was closely monitored and controlled by the state.

The monarchs effectively suspended the Convocation from 1717 to 1852 on account of its contentiousness. It formally convened during this period but enacted no measures. Then Convocation was revived as part of the renewal of English church life stimulated by the Oxford Movement. Likewise, the Convocation of York began again in 1861.

In 1885 a representative House of Laymen started meeting concurrently with the exclusively clerical Convocation. The concurrent meetings soon evolved into the Representative Council in 1904. In 1919 Parliament established the inclusive Church Assembly, which superseded the Representative Council. In 1969 Parliament's Synodical Government Act transferred all the functions of the Church Assembly and nearly all the functions of the Convocations to the General Synod. The Synod is composed of three "Houses": bishops, clergy, and laity. The archbishop of Canterbury presides over this, the highest authority of the Church of England.

The Convocation still meets, but its proceedings are more formal than substantive.

Jon Nilson

See also OXFORD MOVEMENT.

CONZELMANN, HANS (1915–89)

German Lutheran Evangelical biblical scholar, student of Bultmann, and professor of New Testament at Heidelberg,

Zurich, and Göttingen. Conzelmann is best known for his pioneering work in redaction criticism, *Die Mitte der Zeit* (*The Theology of St. Luke*). Here he argues that Luke's use of literary sources and spatial cues reveals a distinct theological mindset. For Luke, God's saving plan advances in three main ages, that of Israel, of Jesus' public career as "the center of time," and of the church between Christ's departure and final return. Scholars since Conzelmann have challenged his views about Luke's approach to history, Jesus' salvific role, the church, and the delay of Jesus' return. Recent sociocultural, narrative, rhetorical, and aesthetic trends have reduced current interest in Conzelmann, but his work remains a benchmark in twentieth-century Lukan studies. His other major studies include books on Acts, the Pastoral Letters, 1 Corinthians, and a complete study of the New Testament writings.

Francis D. Connolly-Weinert

COOKE, BERNARD J. (1923–)

Bernard J. Cooke is an American theologian who specializes in historical and systematic theology. Born in Wisconsin, he entered the Wisconsin province of the Society of Jesus (Jesuits) in 1939. After completing his B.A. (1944) and M.A. (1946) at St. Louis University, he earned a doctorate in theology from the Institut Catholique de Paris (1956). A leader in the post–Vatican II theological renewal in the U.S., Cooke chaired the Theology Department at Marquette University during the 1960s. Under his influence Marquette became one of the leading North American graduate theological programs. Leaving the Jesuits in 1969, Cooke has also taught at Yale University, the University of Calgary (Canada), the University of Windsor (Canada), the College of the Holy Cross (Worcester, MA), the University of the Incarnate Word (San Antonio, TX), and the University of San Diego (CA). Author of numerous books on sacramental theology and christology, Cooke is known for his ability to combine historical erudition with personalist philosophy and psychology. Among his best-known books are *Christian Sacraments and Christian Personality* (1965), *Ministry to Word and Sacraments* (1976), *Sacraments and Sacramentality* (1983), *Reconciled Sinners: Healing Human Brokenness* (1986), *The Distancing of God* (1990), *God's Beloved: Jesus' Experience of the Transcendent* (1992), *Why Angels?* (1996), and *Power and the Spirit of God* (2004).

Mary Ann Hinsdale

COPELAND, M. SHAWN (1947–)

A Catholic systematic theologian, Copeland was born in Detroit, Michigan. She received her B.A. degree in English from Madonna College and Ph.D. in systematic theology from Boston College.

Dr. Copeland was active in the beginnings of Black Liberation Theology in the United States, serving as program director for the first national consultation on Black Theology sponsored by the TIA Black Theology Project in 1977. She was also a founding member of the Black Catholic Theological Symposium and the Institute for Black Catholic Studies.

Her theological work has been influenced by Bernard Lonergan for whom she served as a teaching assistant and focuses particularly but not exclusively on methodology and critical thought. Lonergan's methodology is used as a lens through which she attempts to critically analyze the black (African) American situation in the United States today. The author of many articles, she has served as the coeditor of the Feminist Theology series for Concilium, *The International Theological Review*, and as president of the Catholic Theological Society of America.

Diana L. Hayes

See also AFRICAN AMERICAN THEOLOGY; WOMANIST THEOLOGY.

COPTIC CATHOLIC CHURCH

This church is a descendant of the ancient Patriarchate of Alexandria in Egypt. There is a tradition claiming that Mark the Evangelist founded the see of Alexandria. Whatever the historical accuracy of that claim, the fact remains that Egypt gave Christian monasticism to the world, and that the Coptic/Alexandrian Church was one of the great centers of theological learning in Christian antiquity. The Coptic Church broke with most of Christianity when it rejected the definitions of the Council of Chalcedon (in 451 C.E.), joining the Monophysite schism. In 1741 a group of Copts established full communion with Rome, accepted Chalcedon, and thereby established the Coptic Catholic Church. Today there are about 200,000 Coptic Catholics worldwide under the overall jurisdiction of the patriarch of Alexandria (in Cairo). The name "Copt" comes from an Arabic mispronunciation of the Greek word for "Egyptian."

Orlando Espín

See also AFRICAN CHRISTIANITY; ANCIENT CHURCHES OF THE EAST; CHALCEDON, COUNCIL OF; COPTIC MONOPHYSITE CHURCH; EASTERN CATHOLIC CHURCHES; MONOPHYSITISM; PATRIARCH; ROME, SEE OF.

COPTIC MONOPHYSITE CHURCH

The main descendant of the ancient Patriarchate of Alexandria in Egypt, the Coptic Church claims to have been founded by Mark the Evangelist. Traditionally led by Alexandria, Egyptian Christians were responsible for the birth of Christian monasticism, and for a proud history of theological and catechetical innovations and development. The Coptic Church officially joined the Monophysite schism when it rejected the Council of Chalcedon in 451 C.E. This church has had to suffer great periods of persecution ever since the Muslim conquest of Egypt. The Coptic Church in Ethiopia was established from this Egyptian Church and is now autonomous and self-ruling. The Coptic Church substantially follows the Liturgy of St. Basil. There are some ten million Coptic Monophysite Christians today. The name "Copt" comes from an Arabic mispronunciation of the Greek word for "Egyptian."

Orlando Espín

See also ANCIENT CHURCHES OF THE EAST; CHALCEDON, COUNCIL OF; COPTIC CATHOLIC CHURCH; FATHERS OF THE CHURCH; MONASTICISM IN EASTERN CHRISTIANITY; MONOPHYSITISM; PATRIARCH.

CORNELIUS A LAPIDE (1567–1637)

Cornelius Carnelissen van den Steen was born near Liège and educated at Maastricht and Cologne. He became a Jesuit in 1592, and professor of biblical studies first at Louvain (1596–1616) and then in Rome. Cornelius commented on nearly every book in the Bible during his long career. His commentaries, published several times since his death, have an enduring quality and are still sometimes read for their spiritual insights.

Gary Macy

See also SOCIETY OF JESUS.

CORNELIUS OF ROME (?–253?)

Elected Bishop of Rome in March of 251, during the Decian persecution, Cornelius succeeded Fabian after a fourteen-month vacancy. The learned presbyter Novation, who had been serving as interim bishop, did not accept Cornelius's election and had himself ordained Bishop of Rome by three other Italian bishops. Novation also opposed Cornelius's forgiving attitude toward the *lapsi*, those who had given up the faith during the persecution. Cyprian, bishop of Carthage, himself tending toward a more rigorous approach to the *lapsi*, nevertheless supported Cornelius, as did a synod of sixty bishops held in Rome. The synod excommunicated and expelled Novation, whose followers formed a schismatic church in Carthage. Cornelius was exiled under the renewed persecutions of Gallus and was probably martyred in 253.

Gary Macy

See also CYPRIAN OF CARTHAGE; NOVATION OF ROME; NOVATIONISM; PERSECUTION (IN CHRISTIANITY).

CORPUS CHRISTI

Corpus Christi in Latin means "Body of Christ," and the feast of Corpus Christi is celebrated in honor of the Real Presence of the risen Christ in the Eucharist by Catholics on the Sunday following Trinity Sunday. The feast has its origin in the city of Liège where Juliana of Cornillon, a Beguine, had a dream in which Christ revealed to her that he wished a feast celebrated to honor his presence in the Eucharist. The feast was established in the diocese of Liège in 1246 and was supported by such luminaries as the Dominican theologian Hugh of St. Cher, and the papal legate Jacques Pantaleon. When Jacques was chosen Pope Urban IV in 1261, he moved to promulgate the feast for the entire church, which he did in the bull *Transiturus* in 1264. Urban died soon after promulgating the feast, however, and few of the letters so doing were ever sent out. The feast of Corpus Christi spread slowly in the thirteenth century, but only gained popularity when *Transiturus* gained widespread circulation through its publication in the new book of canon law issued by Pope John XXII in 1317. The feast was very popular in the fourteenth and fifteenth centuries, but was dropped by the Protestant Reformers in the sixteenth century. The central celebration of the feast is a procession carrying a consecrated Host. In some churches, this is accompanied by a period of public adoration and/or a parish festival.

Gary Macy

See also BEGUINES; CHRIST OF FAITH; EUCHARIST; JOHN XXII, POPE; MEDIEVAL CHRISTIANITY (IN THE WEST); REAL PRESENCE; RESURRECTION OF CHRIST.

COSMOGONY

A term having to do with the origin and development of the universe. In the ancient Near East, explanations of how the cosmos came to be always involved gods, usually power struggles between gods. These explanations can be found in works such as the Babylonian *Enuma Elish*. The ancient Israelites put forth their own theories about how the earth came to be, and these are found in Genesis 1 and 2.

The first account of Creation, found in Genesis 1, probably the later account, is thought to date from the sixth century B.C.E. The Priestly source names God/Elohim as the source of all that is. Further, it describes the coming to be of Creation in six days with God creating humankind, male and female, on the sixth day, and God resting on the seventh day. All takes place in an orderly fashion. Everything that God creates is good.

The second account of Creation, found in Genesis 2, is thought to date from the tenth century B.C.E. The Yahwist source names Yahweh as the source of all that is. Although Yahweh creates ʾadam at the beginning, only after God has produced many other creatures and not found any suitable partner for ʾadam does Yahweh create a woman from the rib of Adam. Despite differences in the two creation accounts, both presume that Yahweh God is the source of all.

Closely allied to cosmogony in the ancient Near East was cosmology, which has to do with the order of the universe. According to ancient belief, there existed waters above the earth and waters below the earth. The waters above the earth fell down upon the earth as rain. They watered the earth and made it fertile. They provided water for all the living creatures to drink. However, extraordinary and extensive rainfall could cause destructive flooding.

The waters below the earth, including the seas, the rivers, and streams, could also be helpful to living creatures. These bodies of water had boundaries set by God/the gods, over which they were not meant to transgress. The boundaries accounted for the separations between the dry land and the seas, the rivers and the streams. Timely overflowing of the waters onto the dry land provided natural irrigation; untimely and extensive overflowing of the waters onto the dry land could occasion destructive flooding.

Directly above the earth were the heavens in which dwelled the bodies that gave light to the earth. The larger body, the sun, "ruled the day" while the smaller body, the moon, "ruled the night." Smaller bodies of light, the stars, often accompanied the moon and gave lesser light.

That there was order in the cosmos that could be depended on was essential to the life of early peoples. It made possible planting with the expectation of a harvest. Though sun and rain could not be programmed, their coming and going in appropriate rhythms was essential for the fertility of land and crops.

Alice L. Laffey

COSMOLOGICAL ARGUMENT

The cosmological argument seeks to demonstrate that the existence of God is necessary to fully explain some aspect of the world directly accessible to human experience. This argument usually appeals to some form of the "principle of sufficient reason," that is, nothing takes place without a reason sufficient to determine why a thing is the way it is and not otherwise. Because the cosmological argument proceeds from the visible world to the existence of an invisible God, it is termed an *a posteriori* argument. Aquinas's arguments from "motion," "efficient causality," "contingency of existence," and "the gradation of 'perfections,'" are classic statements of the cosmological argument.

J. A. Colombo

COSTAS, ORLANDO E. (1942–87)

Latino Protestant theologian. Born in Puerto Rico, Costas earned his doctorate in theology at the Free University of Amsterdam. He was very active in the World Council of Churches and was particularly influential at the WCC's 1974 Lausanne conference. He worked in several Latin American countries and spent the last third of his life in the U.S. Here, he was professor at Eastern Baptist Theological Seminary, as well as academic dean at

Andover-Newton Theological School. Costas authored sixteen books and numerous articles. Costas influenced Latino Protestant thought in the U.S. and Latin America as few others have. Personally committed to the poor and their rights, he developed a type of Protestant Evangelical theology that was culturally and socially engaged, solidly biblical and missionary, and publicly on the side of the marginalized groups within American (and Latin American) society.

Orlando Espín

See also LATIN AMERICAN PROTESTANTISM; LATIN AMERICAN THEOLOGIES; LATINO PROTESTANTISM; LIBERATION THEOLOGIES; WORLD COUNCIL OF CHURCHES (WCC).

COUNCIL, ECUMENICAL

An ecumenical council is a worldwide gathering of bishops in communion with the Roman Catholic Church. According to this definition, there have been six ecumenical councils: Nicaea I (325), Constantinople I (381), Ephesus (431), Chalcedon (451), Constantinople II (553), and Constantinople III (680). These are accepted by all Christians of both East and West. In the Catholic reckoning, there have been twenty-one ecumenical councils. Until Vatican II, ecumenical councils were largely European in makeup. Because of its large, worldwide representation, many theologians believe that Vatican II was the first truly ecumenical council.

Mary Ann Hinsdale

COUNCIL OF CHURCHES (WORLD, NATIONAL)

Councils of churches at the local, national, and global levels have emerged in the twentieth century as an expression of the ecumenical movement. Ecumenism, from the Greek word for "the inhabited world," is a movement to unite Christians in joint projects and in discussion of theological and liturgical similarities and differences. Many cities have ecumenical councils that sponsor worship services and cooperate on social and political issues. The ecumenical movement has two aims: to nurture solidarity among Christians and to envision a worldwide church.

The World Council of Churches (WCC) was founded in 1948 through the united efforts of the Faith and Order movement, which sought honest discussion on theology, sacraments, ordination, and polity; and the Life and Work movement, which engaged in the practical task of applying Christianity to modern social problems. Since its foundation, the WCC has adopted controversial stands, advocating labor organization, political freedom for dissidents, and the equalization of wealth, while opposing imperialism, totalitarianism, and the excesses of industrial capitalism. In the 1950s, it was accused of collaborating with Communists.

The United States Federal Council of Churches (FCC) was formed in 1908 and renamed the National Council of Churches (NCC) in 1950. Originally composed of more than thirty Protestant denominations, the FCC organized to coordinate foreign and home missions, especially among Native Americans, and to address contemporary social issues. A supporter of the Social Gospel, it issued a report on the 1910 Bethlehem, Pennsylvania, steel strike that criticized the exploitation of workers by the steel industry. The NCC discontinued mission activity and expanded its membership to include mainline white Protestant groups, African American denominations, many Orthodox communions, including Greek and Russian, and smaller groups such as the

Church of the Brethren. It focuses on interdenominational cooperation in evangelism, education, and social action. During the 1950s, the NCC was a strong supporter of the civil rights movement, eliciting criticism from many white Southerners.

Both WCC and NCC have been supported largely by liberal Protestants. Most evangelical and fundamentalist groups do not participate, most notably the largest Protestant denomination in the United States, the Southern Baptist Convention. Since the Second Vatican Council, the Roman Catholic Church, although not a full member, has held observer status and cooperated in joint projects. In recent years, the participation of the Universal Fellowship of Metropolitan Community Churches, a denomination composed primarily of gay men, lesbians, and bisexuals, has created conflict, Orthodox communions threatening to leave if the UFMCC is granted observer status.

Evelyn A. Kirkley

See also ECUMENICAL MOVEMENT/ ECUMENISM; WORLD COUNCIL OF CHURCHES (WCC).

COUNSELS (OF PERFECTION)

The evangelical counsels refer to the longstanding observance of poverty, chastity (or celibacy), and obedience by men and women who have promised or vowed to lead lives in close imitation of Jesus. The promise to live poor, chaste, and obedient has traditionally been seen as a response to the Spirit's invitation rather than something enjoined by Jesus on all his followers. For that reason they are called "counsels" and not "commands." The classic Gospel text is given in Jesus' reply to the rich young man who wanted to know what more he might do to gain eternal life in addition to keeping the commandments: "If you wish to be perfect . . ." (Matt 19:16-22). Thus arose the association between being perfect and the voluntary renunciation of material goods. The counsels are sometimes called evangelical because it was believed that poverty, chastity, and obedience were radical expressions of the spirit of the Gospel. A person who followed the counsels embodied "the secrets of the kingdom of God" (Luke 8:10).

But the evangelical counsels are not the only route to Christian perfection, nor even the most effective one. For the Gospel enjoins all to be perfect as the Father is perfect (Matt 5:48), and perfection consists of loving one's enemies (Matt 5:44; Luke 6:27). In Luke, perfection consists of compassion (Luke 6:36); in the First Letter of John, it consists of love, in imitation of God (1 John 4:7-12). Vatican II teaches that "all the faithful of Christ . . . are called to the fullness of the Christian life and the perfection of charity" (*Lumen Gentium* 40).

William Reiser, S.J.

See also CHARITY; CHASTITY; HOLINESS; OBEDIENCE; PERFECTION; POVERTY (RELIGIOUS VOW); RELIGIOUS (VOWED).

COUNTER-REFORMATION/ CATHOLIC REFORMATION

In describing the Roman Catholic Church contemporary with the Protestant Reformation, historians distinguish a response to the Reformation and an internal reform and renewal of the Catholic Church. Thus the "Counter-Reformation" refers to efforts to refute Reformation theology and to defeat politically and militarily those civil rulers who supported the Reformation. The "Catholic Reformation" refers to efforts to reform the church from within, through means such as the education of the clergy and laity in Catholic doctrine.

If the Reformation began in 1517 with Luther's posting of his "Ninety-Five Theses," the Catholic Reformation may be considered to have begun somewhat earlier. Such early endeavors, however, had seen few results. It was not until the 1530s that the papacy took seriously the need for internal church reform.

Terms such as "early modern Catholicism" or "Catholicism in the Reformation era" are sometimes used to include both the Counter-Reformation and the Catholic Reformation, two efforts that were, indeed, in many ways interrelated. Like the Reformation, the Counter-Reformation and/or Catholic Reformation entailed many theological as well as political and social dimensions.

Theology and Reform

The reign of Pope Paul III (1534–49) is usually considered a watershed for Catholicism and reform. Paul III named several new cardinals seriously committed to reform of the clergy in particular; among these cardinals was Gasparo Contarini (1483–1542). Contarini headed a commission that produced, in 1537, a list of issues for urgent attention by the pope and bishops. It recognized that clergy needed better education and needed to maintain higher moral standards. The commission's recommendations later had considerable impact on the Council of Trent in its deliberations. Trent would insist that preaching was the principal duty of bishops, and that priests must obtain the education necessary for pastoral ministry. Contarini was also the cardinal who introduced Ignatius of Loyola (1491–1556) and the early Jesuits to Paul III; it was Paul III who gave approval to the foundation of the Society of Jesus in 1540.

Convoked by Paul III, the Council of Trent met periodically between 1545 and 1563. The theological pronouncements of this gathering of bishops were divided into decrees and canons: decrees attempted to articulate what was Catholic belief on a particular point of doctrine, while canons condemned beliefs that were considered at odds with Catholic doctrine. Concerning sources or norms for doctrine, the council rejected the Reformation's insistence on Scripture alone, affirming rather that both Scripture and tradition were normative for doctrinal formulations. By "tradition" the council understood beliefs and practices originating in the age of the apostles, but handed on orally from generation to generation of Christians.

Among the traditions affirmed by the council were seven sacraments. Many of the decrees of Trent explain and defend these as divinely instituted signs that effect what they signify. Thus, for instance, the sacrament of penance is affirmed as not merely a sign of forgiveness but as a sign that effects forgiveness of the sinner. Emphasizing the power of ordained priests to absolve sins and to consecrate bread and wine, Trent also defended the doctrine of the Real Presence of Christ in the Eucharist. Trent asserted that, at the words of consecration, the substances of bread and wine become the Body and Blood of Christ, in all but appearances. Though Luther, among Protestant Reformers, had remained relatively close to Roman Catholicism in his doctrine of the Eucharist, he nevertheless rejected an explanation of the Real Presence that depended on a distinction between substances and appearances.

If Luther and other Reformers stressed the sinfulness of humanity, and asserted that salvation came through grace alone, Trent declared that human cooperation with grace was possible, through good works, and indeed was necessary in order to be saved. Though Trent rejected Renaissance "humanism" in its exaltation of Scripture in its original Hebrew and Greek—Trent affirmed rather the authority of the Latin translation of the Bible—the council nevertheless echoed the affirmation of human goodness that also characterized the "humanism" of the Renaissance. For Trent, despite original sin, human beings remain free to accept or reject the gift of grace; human beings remain free to respond to that gift not only with faith, but also with works of love. In Trent's teaching, it is not faith alone, but faith formed by love that saves.

The theological perspectives of early modern Catholicism also shaped its theology of mission. If the Reformation accentuated St. Paul's teaching on justification by faith, Catholicism in the Reformation era highlighted Paul's itinerant preaching as a model to be imitated. As Paul traveled about the Mediterranean world preaching the Gospel to Jews and Gentiles of all sorts, so now missionaries were to go to the entire world. As Christ had sent apostles to preach and baptize, so now Christ, through the pope as universal pastor, was sending new apostles. Not only the Jesuits, but also many other religious orders zealously embraced such missions. Of the Jesuits, Francis Xavier (1506–52) gained greatest recognition as a model of the new missionary with his work in India and Japan.

Both diocesan clergy and religious orders experienced renewal in the sixteenth century. If many religious were sent on foreign missions, others devoted their energies to renewal of contemplative life at home. Teresa of Avila (1515–82) is an outstanding example. A Spanish Carmelite, she worked successfully for the reform of her order through a return to a simple lifestyle of prayer and humble service in community. Reform of the episcopate was given exemplary models in the work of Charles Borromeo (1538–84) and Francis de Sales (1567–1622). Archbishop of Milan, Borromeo founded seminaries and schools of Christian doctrine; he visited his diocese and disciplined clergy who were not up to standards; he preached regularly and cared for the sick in time of plague. Gentler than the severe Borromeo, Francis de Sales was bishop in Annecy (Savoy). He, too, visited his diocese and preached regularly; he wrote spiritual treatises designed to give the laity full access to a life of devotion; he assisted Jane de Chantal in founding the Order of the Visitation.

Politics

The pope and the bishops sought the help of secular authorities in curbing the spread of the Protestant Reformation. The Counter-Reformation thus included not only theological polemic but also diplomatic, military, and judicial policy. Particularly in Germany and central Europe, the combination of the coercion of the state and the pastoral zeal of a clergy committed to propagation of the decisions of the Council of Trent was successful in the late sixteenth century in regaining for the Catholic Church some territories that had for a time implemented the Reformation.

The repressive side of the Counter-Reformation included persecution of "heretics." Since the thirteenth century, various forms of "inquisition" had existed for uncovering and punishing what was considered heretical. Torture and executions were a part of the judicial arsenal put to use. Reasons of state often mattered most, for heretics were seen by many rulers as introducing division and dissent in place of political unity. The Spanish Inquisition, a royal rather than ecclesiastical institution, functioned in this way. Not without difficulty, some of the popes of the sixteenth century attempted to assert greater ecclesiastical control of inquisitorial proceedings. However, inquisition was especially valued by Pope Paul IV (reign 1555–9); he also created the Index of Forbidden Books in an attempt to proscribe works seen as dangerous for the integrity of Catholicism.

In the early modern period, the Hapsburgs were the ruling house not only of Austria and the Holy Roman Empire, but also of Spain and its many territories in Europe and in the Americas. The Hapsburgs put themselves forward as the most powerful and most capable defenders of the Catholic faith; Hapsburg ideology spoke of a universal, Catholic monarchy, one able not only to defeat the Protestants, but to save Europe from the power of the Turks in the East, and to spread the "true" religion in the New World. Such pretensions were the source of a series of conflicts, not only with Protestant powers and with the Turks, but also with rival Catholic princes, including several popes. The Thirty Years War of 1618–48 saw Catholic France ally itself with Protestant princes in Sweden and Germany in order to contain Hapsburg power.

France itself suffered a series of civil wars in the late sixteenth century, wars that pitted Catholics against Protestants, as well as moderate Catholics willing to make peace with the Protestant minority in France against Catholic fanatics determined to annihilate "heresy" at all costs. Catholic preachers played a key role in promoting fanaticism, proclaiming that God would punish France if it tolerated the heretics. The moderates, however, triumphed with the Edict of Nantes of 1598. This royal decree extended religious toleration to Protestants in France, a kind of toleration that, though limited, was far more generous than that enjoyed by most religious minorities in the Reformation and Counter-Reformation era.

Society

The Council of Trent decreed that bishops were to create seminaries for the education of clergy. Though implementation of this decree was not widespread until the second half of the seventeenth century, seminaries eventually produced a new type of parish priest, one that was well formed in doctrine, disciplined in his personal life, genuinely celibate, and more remote from his flock than had been medieval clerics. Among the consequences of seminary education was a growing division in Catholic society between the literate religion of a spiritual elite, and what that elite considered to be the superstitious ways of the mass of common, ignorant people. Armed with catechisms that explained the doctrines of Trent in relatively simple terms, missionaries set out, not only for foreign lands, but also for rural Europe.

The educational agenda of the Catholic Reformation concerned both clergy and laity. The Jesuits gained a reputation as excellent teachers in their many colleges. Yet even before the founding of the Jesuits in 1540, the Ursulines had been established with the goal of educating women. Founded by Angela Merici (1474–1540) in 1535, this order overcame much conservative opposition to open the way for female education.

Religious art and architecture also prospered in the age of the Counter-Reformation/Catholic Reformation. The "Baroque" style is often considered characteristic of the period. The present Basilica of Saint Peter in Rome, as well as a number of other buildings that make up

Vatican City, were built in the sixteenth and seventeenth centuries. If some Protestants rejected as idolatry the Catholic predilection for images, early modern Catholicism reveled in proliferation of images designed to instruct the mind in Catholic doctrine and to rouse the will to perform good works of charity for one's neighbor.

Most historians consider the era of the Counter-Reformation/Catholic Reformation to have ended by the early eighteenth century with the rise of the Enlightenment's critique of traditional Christianity, whether it be Protestant or Catholic.

Thomas Worcester, s.j.

See also BAROQUE; BELLARMINE, ROBERT; BÉRULLE, PIERRE DE; BRUNO, GIORDANO; CANISIUS, PETER; DE SALES, FRANCIS; ERASMUS OF ROTTERDAM; GOOD WORKS; GRACE; IGNATIUS LOYOLA; LEFÈVRE D'ÉTAPLES, JACQUES; MERICI, ANGELA; PIUS V, POPE; REFORMATION; RENAISSANCE; SOCIETY OF JESUS; TRANSUBSTANTIATION; TRENT, COUNCIL OF; TRIDENTINE.

COVENANT IN CHRISTIANITY

A covenant is an agreement between two parties. In the Hebrew Bible, the covenant with God consists of the law given to the people of Israel through Moses, and in God's statement, "And I will take you for my people and I will be your God" (Exod 6:7). In the New Testament Gospels and letters, the new covenant represents a Christian dispensation, brought about by Christ's passion, death, and resurrection. The New Testament authors, especially Paul, make the distinction between the old dispensation (that of the law; the letter that kills as in 2 Cor 3:6), and the new dispensation (that of Christ and the Spirit that is life-giving). The distinction between old and new, in this view, is between a dispensation that condemns and one that justifies. In spite of these distinctions, the theology of covenant throughout the Bible is one of divine promise. *Covenant Theology*, which brought this covenantal promise to the foreground, was the dominant Calvinist theology in North America and England throughout the seventeenth century.

Robert D. McCleary

COVENANT IN JUDAISM

(Hebrew, *brit*). In Judaism, the agreement between God and the people of Israel that calls for the Jews to follow God's law embodied in Torah, in return for God's fulfillment of the promise to make of them a great nation dwelling in peace in the Promised Land. Judaism understands God to have entered into a number of covenants with the people of Israel, beginning with the covenant in which God promised to make of Abraham a great nation (Gen 12:1-7; 17; 22), and culminating with the covenant sealed between God and the nation of Israel as a whole at Sinai, following the Exodus from Egypt (Exod 19–20). The significance in Judaism of the Sinaitic covenant derives from the fact that the terms of this covenant included both those present at Sinai and all future generations of Jews (Deut 29:14-15). Additionally, Jews understand the totality of what would emerge over the ages as Jewish ritual, social norms, and ethical law to have been presented by God to Moses as part of this covenant. Observing this law is understood to be the Jews' particular obligation under the terms of the covenant.

While some contemporary forms of Judaism reject the continuing applicability of certain elements of Jewish law, virtually all forms of Judaism continue to see as central to Jewish faith the notion that

God chose the people of Israel, entered into a covenant with them, and that this covenant separated the Jews from the other nations of the world, making them subject to unique ethical and religious standards. The Jews' covenant with God, however, is not understood to offer the Jews alone salvation. This, Jews believe, is available to all people who accept the existence of the one God and follow certain minimal ethical requirements.

Alan J. Avery-Peck

See also GENTILES; MIZVAH; TORAH.

COX, HARVEY (1929–)

Born in Malvern, Pennsylvania, Harvey Cox received his bachelor of arts degree from the University of Pennsylvania in 1951, his bachelor of divinity degree from Yale University in 1955, and his doctorate in history and philosophy of religion from Harvard University in 1963. He was ordained a minister of the American Baptist Church in 1957 and has taught at Harvard Divinity School since 1965. His research has focused on urbanization, theological developments in world Christianity, and the ministry of the church in the global setting (especially Latin America). His best-known work is *The Secular City* (1965); other important works include *Religion in the Secular City* (1984), *The Silencing of Leonardo Boff* (1988), *Many Mansions: A Christian's Encounters with Other Faiths* (1988), *Fire from Heaven: The Rise of Pentecostal Spirituality and the Reshaping of Religion in the Twenty-First Century* (1995), and *When Jesus Came to Harvard: Making Moral Choices Today* (2004).

James B. Nickoloff

See also BOFF, LEONARDO; PENTECOSTALISM; SECULARISM; SECULARIZATION/ SECULAR/SECULARIZED.

CRANMER, THOMAS (1489–1556)

Archbishop of Canterbury, 1533–53. His view that the monarch was the rightful temporal head of the Church in England helped win him appointment as archbishop. As papal legate he supported Henry VIII by declaring his marriage to Catherine of Aragon invalid and by approving the Act of Supremacy in 1534. A year later he pronounced the marriage to Ann Boleyn invalid as well. Consistently, he later supported the policies of the Catholic queen Mary Tudor. As compiler of the first two Books of Common Prayer (1549, 1552), he is considered the chief liturgical architect of Anglicanism. His patristic scholarship helped him to inculcate a dignified simplicity in his vernacular liturgy, shorn of medieval accretions. Cranmer also mediated the thought of Zwingli, Calvin, and Luther to England. He was martyred with Latimer and Ridley under Mary Tudor. The Episcopal Church commemorates him on October 16.

Jon Nilson

See also BOOK OF COMMON PRAYER; LATIMER, HUGH.

CREATION

There are two formal creation stories in the Hebrew Bible/Old Testament, the priestly tradition in Genesis 1:1–2:4a and the earlier Yahwistic account in Genesis 2:4b-25. In addition there are numerous allusions to other stories of the beginning found primarily in poetic texts scattered throughout the Hebrew Bible. Genesis 1:1–2:4a, the priestly story of creation, may have been composed both to introduce Genesis as well as the primary history (Genesis–2 Kings). Whether or not it was composed in the period of the Babylonian Exile (587–538 B.C.E.), that experience quite probably influenced the final form of the story. The similarities between the Babylonian "story of the creation," *Enuma Elish*, and the story of Genesis 1:1–2:4a have long been noted, but of equal importance are the differences.

In *Enuma Elish*, the Babylonian god Marduk attains the kingship over all the gods after he successfully defeats and slays the matriarch of the older gods, Tiamat. He uses her body for the building materials of the universe that he then puts in order. He then conceives of the creation of humans to take over the work of the raising and preparing the food of the gods. This composition was recited annually at the Babylonian New Year (*akitu*) festival. The Israelites in Exile were probably exposed to this composition and the claims of Marduk's power and role in creation. The priestly creation story in Genesis 1:1–2:4a can be seen in its final form as a response to *Enuma Elish*. God (*Elohim*) creates without any conflict simply by speaking. There are no other deities in evidence in the story. Humans are the last living beings created and are blessed and commanded to multiply and fill the earth and to "rule" over the other creatures God has created. They are given all fruit-bearing plants as food. The story in Genesis 1:1–2:4a asserts the power of the God of Israel over all creation and by implication over history as well. God emerges as the powerful Creator of human beings. For the Israelites in Exile this story might have represented a counter to the claims of their Babylonian overlords.

The Yahwistic story in Genesis 2:4b-25 begins with the earth already in existence, but without vegetation or water. The earth is watered and then the first human is created, a sexually undifferentiated being formed from the earth itself (*adam*). Unlike the first story of creation, the God of this story, Yahweh, forms the human from the earth as a potter would a vessel, and then breathes into it the breath of life to animate it. All other living creatures are formed subsequently, and finally the woman is built from the man's rib. This is the climax of the story. Neither of these stories is referred to elsewhere in the Hebrew Bible other than the reference to the priestly story in Exodus 20:11.

Russell Fuller

See also COSMOGONY.

CREATIONISM

Creationism is the theory that God created the world in seven twenty-four-hour days, as recorded in the first chapters of Genesis, the first book of the Bible. It is prevalent among fundamentalist Christians who hold the Bible is literally true and inerrant, including many Missouri Synod Lutherans and Southern Baptists. Also known as creation science, creationism posits that evolution and the Bible are mutually exclusive and antithetical explanations of creation. One may be a Christian or an evolutionist, but not both. Not the belief of crackpots, creationism is based on the Enlightenment philosophy of Scottish Commonsense Realism, which argues that reality is straightforward, perspicuous, and empirically verifiable. Truth is a set of properly classified and organized propositions. In this view, the Bible is an infallible science textbook. Creation expresses God's divine design, a testament to God's glory, power, and benevolence.

Until Charles Darwin, nearly all Christians were creationists. Charles Darwin's theories of evolution, first published in *The Origin of Species* in 1859, were initially received negatively by most Christians. Believing Darwinism meant accepting a brutal, capricious world marked by an endless struggle for survival. In his erudite repudiation of Darwinism entitled *What Is Darwinism?* (1874), Princeton professor Charles Hodge argued that natural selection contradicted an omnipotent, omniscient Creator. However, as evidence mounted and Darwinism became part of the dominant intellectual paradigm of the twentieth century, many Christians accepted it as the way God had created the world and Genesis as a metaphorical account of it. However, some Christians refused to compromise. The controversy culminated in the 1925 Scopes trial in Dayton, Tennessee, in which a high school science teacher was accused of breaking a state law against teaching Darwinism in public schools. Although John Scopes was convicted, creationism was discredited during the trial.

Although battered, creationism survived. The Creation Research Society was founded in 1963 and is now known as the Institute for Creation Research with headquarters near San Diego, California. The ICR stresses the number of Ph.D.s in its membership, including many engineers and applied scientists. Creationists further emphasize the scientific credibility of their theories. They work to substantiate the "big bang" theory and the analysis of fossils that undermine evolution. In 1981 creationists passed laws in Louisiana and Tennessee mandating public school science teaching that balanced evolution and creationism. Both laws were struck down by higher courts as violating the separation of church and state. These setbacks discouraged the movement but have not destroyed it.

Evelyn A. Kirkley

See also DARWINISM; EVANGELICALS; EVANGELICAL THEOLOGY; FUNDAMENTALISM.

CREED/SYMBOL OF FAITH

The word "creed" (from the Latin *credo*, "I believe"), is a concise, formal statement of belief. The Greek word *symbolon* (sign) emphasizes the sacramental character of creedal affirmations. Creeds are formal summaries of a community's convictions about God and human life developed for public or ceremonial use. Creeds have served several purposes: as confessions of faith, as catechetical instruction or baptismal creeds, as doxologies for worship, or as dogmas that regulate the contours of right belief.

Examples of creedal statements in Scripture are the Shema (Deut 6:4), the resurrection kerygma (Acts 2:36), and the trinitarian baptismal formula (Matt 28:19a). The patristic era developed creedal formulae as rules of faith, expressions of correct belief. The great conciliar dogmas of the fourth and fifth centuries are theological formulae forged to clarify the church's convictions about the nature of divine life and the character of God's deed in Christ. These dogmas became creeds in the church, serving not so much a regulative as a doxological purpose. The Apostles' Creed, intended as a baptismal confession, became a popular prayer in the Middle Ages. A different conception of creed developed in Reformation Churches that formulated Confessions or summaries of dogmas to clarify the religious convictions of particular groups. In recent years, the creed served as an instrument for pastoral guidance in Pope Paul VI's publication, the *Credo of the People of God* (1967).

Patricia Plovanich

See also APOSTLES' CREED; ATHANASIAN CREED; CONFESSION OF FAITH; NICENE CREED.

CRITICAL THEORY

Term used to refer to the work of those scholars—especially Max Horkheimer, Theodor Adorno, Friedrich Pollak, Leo Lowenthal, Erich Fromm, and Herbert Marcuse—who were members of the Institüt für Sozialforschung (1932–41) in Frankfurt and, after forced emigration in 1935, in the United States.

Also referred to as the "Frankfurt School," the Institüt was distinguished by a twin commitment to a revisionist Marxism, as well as a multi- and interdisciplinary approach to understanding contemporary society as a "totality." Its specific understanding of this totality was stamped by two contemporary historical developments: the collapse of a truly emancipatory, organized Marxist movement in Europe and the Soviet Union, and the rise of National Socialism in Central Europe. This historical context led to the central thesis of Horkheimer's and Adorno's principal text, *Dialectic of Enlightenment* (1944): under the hegemony of capitalism, the telos of modern society toward "enlightenment" had mutated into the domination of self, society, and nature. The themes elaborated in *Dialectic* and other contemporary works, for example, the regressive power of mass culture and the culture industry, anti-Semitism, the authoritarian personality, the relation between "late capitalism" and totalitarianism, the liberative potential of the authentic work of art, and the complementarity of Freud and Marx, remained characteristic of the work of Horkheimer and Adorno after their return to Germany following World War II, albeit on a more abstract level of philosophical investigation.

The Institüt's work was "rediscovered" by the student protest movement of the late 1960s, and its legacy is discernable today in the work of Jürgen Habermas and Albrecht Wellmer as well as in the reflections on the contradictions of modern, capitalist society in the work of Johann Metz and Jürgen Moltmann.

J. A. Colombo

See also MARX, KARL; MARXISM.

CROCE, BENEDETTO (1866–1952)

Italian philosopher, influenced by Hegel, who developed a type of "creative" Idealism that became important in European thought in the early twentieth century, and that challenged both Christian theologies and Marxist philosophies. Croce's system attempted to describe and explain the forms taken by the "life of the (human) Spirit" in history. Many theologians, as well as Antonio Gramsci and other Marxist thinkers, considered Croce an intellectual force to be dealt with. Croce's main work is his multivolume *Filosofia dello spirito* (1902–17).

Orlando Espín

See also GRAMSCI, ANTONIO; IDEALISM, CLASSICAL GERMAN; MARXISM; MODERNITY; POSTMODERNITY.

CROSS, SIGN OF THE

In making the sign of the cross, one traces the shape of a cross on one's own body, or over another person or object. The shape that is traced can be quite small, as when one uses a thumb to trace a cross on another person's forehead. This form of the sign of the cross is used, for example, in the celebration of baptism. The shape can also be a triad of small crosses: one on the forehead, one on the mouth, and one on the breast. This sign of the cross is commonly used at the beginning of a reading from the Gospels in a liturgical ceremony. The most common form of the sign of the cross, however, is traced across one's own upper body, moving the hand from forehead to chest, and then from shoulder to shoulder (right to left in Eastern Christianity and left to right in Western Christianity). During this gesture, the person says, "In the name of the Father and of the Son and of the Holy Spirit." As early as the second century, Tertullian mentions the use of the sign of the cross in baptism. During the Middle Ages, the sign came also to be associated with exorcisms, blessings, and dedications.

Patrick L. Malloy

CROSS, THEOLOGY OF THE

The theology of the Cross is the effort to explain the meaning of Jesus' death in relationship to the mystery of God and to human beings. It must always be understood, however, that in Christian theology and spirituality the Cross does not stand independently of the resurrection and the ministry of Jesus. If Jesus had not been raised from the dead, then his death could only be interpreted in terms of the Bible's wider reflection about the meaning of the suffering and death of the martyrs for justice and faith who came before Jesus— the prophets, the Maccabean brothers, or the righteous servant of Isaiah 53. In trying to understand the significance of Jesus' death, theology has to begin with what his death meant in historical terms. For what reasons were people in the Roman imperial world crucified, and what exactly had Jesus been doing and teaching that created such hostility toward him and his message? In other words, Jesus' death cannot be divorced from its historical circumstances.

The confessional statement "Jesus died for our sins" expresses what the death of Jesus is believed to have accomplished, namely, forgiveness of sins, reconciliation with God, redemption, and everlasting life. The first Christian communities drew heavily from the Hebrew Bible—the Christian Old Testament—as they searched for ways to make sense of the death of Jesus. Indeed, Jesus himself would have turned to his people's Scriptures as a way of interpreting his life and mission. Given the prominence of sacrifice in Jewish worship, it is no surprise that Jesus' death was interpreted in sacrificial terms. His death (John the Baptist calls him "the Lamb of God" in John 1:36) was viewed as taking away sins (Matt 26:28), in the same way that sacrifices and sin offerings had done (see Hebrews 10). Nevertheless, as rich as it is, the mystery of sin and forgiveness is not the only perspective within which to contemplate the crucified Jesus.

In recent years, theologians (particularly though not exclusively from Latin America) have increasingly turned their attention to how the Cross reveals Jesus in solidarity with all victims. In fact, this relationship or connection becomes a matter of divine solidarity in light of the Resurrection. The Cross brings to mind in an astonishing, effective way, not so much human suffering in general, but the historical forms of suffering caused by injustice. Jesus lived and died as a Jewish prophet, or as some writers have said, a martyr for justice. To contemplate the crucified Jesus, then, is to become aware of the countless women, men, and children who have been "crucified" by poverty, intolerance, racism, greed, and powerful social and economic elites; it is to appreciate God's terrifying, yet compassionate, oneness with those "on the bottom" or consigned to the margins of national and international attention.

As a religious symbol, the Cross also speaks to believers in moments of suffering that are not tied to injustice. On the one hand, as their interior lives develop, those who follow Jesus will discover themselves wanting to be with Jesus where he is. If Jesus is headed to the Cross, then they will experience a desire to share his suffering (see John 11:16). Concretely, this desire will eventually lead them into deeper solidarity with the world's victims. But for Catholic sacramental imagination, the Cross also represents God's "desire" to be with men and women in the particular circumstances of their lives. And so, on the other hand, the Cross has been a precious sign of how much God both understands and even experiences what human beings frequently have to endure. There is deep solace in the contemplative awareness that God, through the mystery of the Word made flesh, "knows" human suffering from the inside.

William Reiser, s.j.

See also CHRISTOLOGY; INCARNATION; LIBERATION THEOLOGIES; REDEMPTION, CHRISTIAN; RESURRECTION (IN CHRISTIANITY).

CROSS, VENERATION OF THE

The service of the veneration of the cross is part of the liturgy of Good Friday in some Christian traditions. The earliest form of the service can be traced to the fourth century in Jerusalem: a relic of the True Cross would be venerated (that is, kissed) by a worshiping community gathered in a church built on the supposed site of Christ's crucifixion. Later, a structured order for the service can be found in Roman liturgical books dating to the seventh century.

As the medieval period advanced, the service of the veneration of the cross became more elaborate: the veiled cross (or a crucifix in many places, that is, a wooden or metal cross with the *corpus*, or body, of Christ hanging on it) was brought in formal procession into the church, accompanied by sung acclamations; the presider (priest or bishop) and the ministers approached the cross with ritual genuflections and verses, and would then kiss or otherwise venerate it; and finally, the people would approach and venerate it.

Gradually, the veneration of the cross became a popular focus for devotion outside the Good Friday liturgy. One of the most enduring of these services is known in the Roman Catholic tradition as the "Way of the Cross," or the "Stations of the Cross." Dating from the later Middle Ages, this service centered on specific moments in the passion of Christ, leading up to and including the process of Christ's crucifixion and death. Fourteen of these moments, or "stations," were finally included in the devotional service; often small crosses (and later, pictorial representations in paint or statuary) would be placed at an outdoor site, or inside, on the walls of a church building. A fifteenth station, for the Resurrection, is often added in contemporary use.

The Stations of the Cross can be celebrated individually or by a group of believers gathered together; it is still in use today in many Catholic parishes, especially during the season of Lent or on Good Friday itself.

Joanne M. Pierce

See also CROSS, THEOLOGY OF THE; EASTER; HOLY WEEK; LENT; STATIONS OF THE CROSS.

CRUCIFIXION

A form of capital punishment introduced in Persia in the sixth century B.C.E. that was soon adopted by other peoples in the Mediterranean basin. Roman writers indicate that crucifixion was recognized to be such a cruel form of execution that Roman citizens were normally exempt, regardless of the offense. The Romans used crucifixion extensively for mutinous troops, subjugated peoples, violent criminals, and slaves. The practice ceased after it was banned by Constantine in the fourth century C.E. Jesus of Nazareth is the most prominent victim of this form of execution, although thousands of others suffered this extraordinarily painful form of death.

While there were variations, crucifixion most frequently involved nailing or tying the extended arms of the condemned onto a vertical beam (*patibulum*) that was placed either into a groove across the top of a horizontal stake (*crux commissa*) or into a notch situated below the top of the upright stake (*crux immissa*). Since the full weight of a human body hanging by the arms prevents the lungs from functioning, death by asphyxiation or heart attack should arrive quickly. However, to prolong their suffering, victims were seated onto a wooden block or peg (*sedile*) that was affixed in the horizontal stake, and their legs, feet, or heels were bound or nailed to the upright beam. In this position no vital organs were damaged, and death could take several days while the victims suffered in agonizing pain. Romans favored crucifixions along busy roadways where the horizontal stake(s) were always left in position at the site. They also preferred to leave the bodies to rot and to be eaten by birds as an additional way to disgrace the condemned and to provide a warning to others.

Crucifixions occurred in Judea during the Hellenistic, Hasmonean, and Roman eras. In 267 B.C.E. Antiochus IV crucified some Judeans who, in defiance of the Seleucid Hellenization policies, remained faithful to the Jewish laws. The Hasmonean Sadduccee high priest, Alexander Jannaeus (103–76 B.C.E.), crucified eight hundred Pharisees. A reference in the Qumran scrolls indicates that the Essenes may have also crucified for serious crimes. Drawing from Deuteronomy 21:22-23, many Jews at the time considered those who died by crucifixion accursed by God. Paul used this tradition to argue that by the very manner of his death Jesus was cursed (cast out) by the law (Gal 3:13) so that by the law, those who believe in Jesus have died to (been cast out of) the law (Gal 2:19).

The accounts of Jesus' execution in the four Gospels conform to what is known about Roman crucifixions (for example, scourging, posting a placard with the name and crime of the victim), their dealings with subjugated peoples, and some concessions made in Judea to accommodate Jewish sensibilities (for instance, removal of the bodies). The passion narratives were fashioned from traditions drawn from the knowledge of Roman practices and bits and pieces of what may be actual memories. Each evangelist shaped his account to highlight particular theological insights. In light of the proclamation of his resurrection, one of the important features that all the passion narratives seek to establish is that Jesus really died.

Since crucifixion was such an ignominious form of execution, Paul did not engage in hyperbole when he claims that the cross was "a stumbling block to Jews and folly to Gentiles" (1 Cor 1:22-23; Gal 5:11). For most of Paul's contemporaries, the claim that someone crucified was the Messiah, Son of God, and universal Lord, was inconceivable. Christians came to consider the crucifixion of Jesus as God's decisive act of love that transforms the world, redeems humanity from sin and death, and empowers believers to become children of God and heirs of eternal life.

Regina A. Boisclair

CRUSADES

The term "Crusade" is used most often to refer to the series of wars fought by Christian armies in order to gain or retain possession of the Holy Land from Islam. The crusading ideal first developed in the battles against Islam fought in Sicily and especially in Spain, where the long battle to regain Christian possession of the penisula is called the "Reconquista." The word "crusade" developed in the thirteenth century in reference to the cross (in Latin, *crux*) worn by the Crusaders. Although the crusading movement was really an ongoing affair, most historians enumerate the major armed movements in the following order.

The First Crusade (1096–9) was called by Pope Urban II in 1095 at the request of the Byzantine emperor. His call was enthusiastically received for many reasons. First, the Holy Land was a popular pilgrimage site that people wanted to visit in peace and safety. Second, the Crusades were a way to harness the warrior cult of the Teutonic tribes to what was deemed by most people of the time a more noble purpose. Third, the Pope offered a plenary indulgence, that is, complete remission of all temporal punishment due to sin, to all those who volunteered to go on crusade. The First Crusade was the most successful of all the Crusades. Antioch fell to the Crusaders in 1098 and Jerusalem itself in 1099.

For several years, the Crusader states stood and even expanded, but the Muslim armies regrouped and took Edessa in

1144. As a result, the Second Crusade was called for by Pope Eugenius III in 1144, a call taken up in earnest by Bernard of Clairvaux. His preaching attracted King Louis VII of France and Emperor Conrad of Germany. The crusading army reached the Holy Land in 1147. But in 1148, the Crusaders left without retaking Edessa or, indeed, making a significant advance.

The Third Crusade (1189–92) was called when an Islamic army under the leadership of Saladin retook Jerusalem in 1187. Three of the most powerful lords of Europe, Emperor Fredrick I (Barbarosa), Richard the Lionhearted of England, and Philip II of France, took control of the crusading armies. Frederick died on the journey, but Philip and Richard, despite constant quarrelling, managed to take the city of Acre in 1191. Philip returned to France that same year, but Richard stayed on and was able to negotiate a truce with Saladin that allowed safe passage for pilgrims and guaranteed what was left of the Crusader states.

Innocent III called for a fourth Crusade to retake Jerusalem in 1198. The Fourth Crusade (1202–4) went dreadfully wrong, however, and instead of attacking the Islamic armies in the Holy Land, the crusading army attacked and captured the Christian city of Constantinople. Much to the chagrin of the Byzantines, the Crusaders set up a Latin kingdom in Constantinople that lasted until 1261. After this disaster, Innocent called for a new Crusade in 1213, but a crusading army was not gathered until 1217. This was the beginning of the Fifth Crusade (1217–21). After initial success in taking the city of Damietta, the crusading armies stalled and ultimately failed to hold any territory.

Fredrick II of Germany undertook yet another Crusade in 1228, but rather than engage in battle, he negotiated a ten-year truce with the Muslims as well as gaining control of the cities of Bethlehem, Nazareth, and Jerusalem itself. Jerusalem fell into Muslim hands again in 1244, never again to return to control of the Crusaders.

The crusading spirit declined, but Crusades continued to be promulgated. Expeditions were led, for example, by Louis IX against Egypt (1249–54) and Tunisia (1270), but all failed to regain the Holy Land. Crusades were also called against the Turkish armies invading eastern Europe in the fourteenth century. On the whole, however, the Crusades had lost their popularity.

The term "crusade" was used for purposes other than the raising of armies to regain the Holy Land, however. Crusades could also be called against heretics, as in the case of the Albigensian Crusade in the thirteenth century or the crusade against the Hussites in the fifteenth century. The Reconquista of Spain was considered a crusade, a continuation of which was the conquest of the New World by the Spanish armies. The term "crusade" continues to be used by Christian movements, especially to describe evangelical revivals.

Gary Macy

See also ALBIGENSIANS; BERNARD OF CLAIRVAUX; BYZANTIUM/BYZANTINE; CATHARS; HUSSITES; INDULGENCES; INNOCENT III, POPE; ISLAM; MEDIEVAL CHRISTIANITY (IN THE WEST).

CULLMANN, OSCAR (1902–99)

Born in Strasbourg, this Alsatian Lutheran New Testament scholar and biblical theologian pursued undergraduate and graduate studies at the University of Strasbourg, completing a doctorate in theology in 1930 with a dissertation on the Pseudo-Clementine writings. From 1930 to 1938, Cullmann was professor at the University of Strasbourg, and in 1938 he became professor of New Testament and church history at the University of Basel in Switzerland. In *Christ and Time: The Primitive Christian Conception of Time and History* (1945) and *Salvation in History*, Cullmann made his case for viewing *Heilsgeschichte*, salvation history, as the key to New Testament theology. Cullmann's active involvement in Protestant-Catholic ecumenical efforts found expression in several publications, including his books *Catholics and Protestants: A Proposal for Realizing Christian Solidarity* (London: Lutterworth, 1959) and *Vatican Council II: The New Direction* (New York: Harper & Row, 1968).

Books by Cullmann translated into English include *Peter: Disciple, Apostle, Martyr: A Historical and Theological Essay* (Philadelphia: Westminster, 1953; 1962) and *The Johannine Circle: Its Place in Judaism, Among the Disciples of Jesus and in Early Christianity: A Study in the Origin of the Gospel of John* (London: SCM, 1976).

Jean-Pierre Ruiz

See also HISTORY; SALVATION.

CULT, LITURGICAL

In general, cult refers to external behavior by which the excellence or superiority of another is acknowledged. Catholic theology has traditionally recognized three ranks within the Christian cult: *latria*, that cultic behavior due only to the Persons of the Trinity and the presence of Christ in the Eucharist; *dulia*, the honor shown to the saints and angels; and *hyperdulia*, the cult accorded only to the Blessed Virgin. While *latria* is adoration, *hyperdulia* and *dulia* are honor. Each of these three levels of cult has private and public manifestations. The public cult, in turn, has two divisions: liturgical and nonliturgical public cult. This distinction between liturgical and nonliturgical is by no means clear. Canon law says that the liturgical cult and its books are those that are under the supervision of the pope and, in individual dioceses, the bishop (Can. 838). This implies that other rites are nonliturgical. Some would argue, however, that any service presided over by an ordained minister as part of the public worship of a parish can be considered liturgical, whether or not the rite has been mandated or approved by the Vatican or the local bishop.

Patrick L. Malloy

See also ADORATION; LATRIA; RITUAL.

CULTS

In the language of the sociology of religion, the term "cult" refers to a new religious movement that has arisen from an older established form of religion. Insofar as it is new, it consciously stands over against the older forms, and is frequently seen, both by its members and by outsiders, as competing with it. Cult is a distinctly modern referent, supplanting the earlier term, "sect," and seems to have been necessitated by the characteristics of recent modern forms of religion. As Catherine Albanese notes in *America: Religions and Religion*, cults are described as "emerging from the experience of a charismatic leader, a person who claimed authority because of that experience, and carrying a new revelation. It encourages the individual to verify the leader's experience by seeking to realize it personally. Unlike a sect, it grows away from the older traditions, often in radical ways. Like a sect, however, it sets careful boundaries, thus demarcating its reality from the rest of society. The

benefit to its members is the heightened sense of community that it provides" (1981:127, 128).

The study of cults has taken place in the field of the Scientific Study of Religion, a scholarly body that arose when social scientific theory was being applied to the phenomenon of religion. In America, this group has been focused on the cults, or, to name them more correctly, new religious movements, since the early 1970s, when a burgeoning number of these communities arose. Their analysis (by authors R. Bellah, T. Robbins, A. Shupe, and others) has clarified the societal causes and connections, and helped to chart a renewal of religious enthusiasm in the twentieth century. It is essential to note that modern cults have important predecessors in the Holiness movements of the Protestant tradition, and in their close relatives in the Mormon Church, the Adventists, and the Church of Christian Science. Those precedents show that many of the characteristics of the contemporary cults were shared by the early examples—rigid discipline, requirement of full obedience to the law of the community and its leader, and a tendency to be separatist yet proselytizing.

The more esoteric and separatist a community becomes, the more it attracts the attention and often the resentment of the mainstream society. Thus, the last two decades have seen the new religions become the target of legal actions, and the phenomenon of scholars of religion defending them under the First Amendment. Interest in religion in the public sphere is striking in a world so recently evaluated as secular. At this point, the new religions seem here to stay, and they seem to be fulfilling fundamental spiritual needs some cannot satisfy in the older church traditions—specifically, the thirst for profound religious experience and nurturing community.

Kathleen Dugan

See also AUTHORITY; CHARISM/CHARISMATIC.

CULTURE

Scholars argue about the most adequate description or definition of what is "culture," but in fact they are attempting to discover common denominators among diverse, shared "styles of humanness" (or of *praxis*) in living human communities. Culture is, more fundamentally, the historically shared means and ways through which a people unveil themselves (to themselves, and only secondarily to others) as *human*. The most basic means and ways for this unveiling are the social construction of reality and the discovery of meaning within and through that socially constructed reality.

The very *act of defining* culture, however, is problematic. It would be naive (to say the least) to assume that the act of defining what is "culture" is not, in itself, a cultural act. Furthermore, and more importantly, the act of defining culture—either in reference to cultures other than one's own, or in reference to the culture of one's own society—grants the definer an extraordinary power over meaning, reality, and truth. Therefore, much more crucial and substantive than the scholarly discussions about the more adequate *definition* of "culture" is an investigation of the meaning, function, and possibility of the *act of defining* culture and of those who exercise it.

Orlando Espín

See also DISCRIMINATION; GRACE; HUMAN BEING; IDEOLOGY (IDEOLOGIES); INCULTURATION; INSPIRATION; JUSTICE; LATINO CATHOLICISM; LIBERATION THEOLOGIES; MISSIONS; POPULAR CATHOLICISM; PRAXIS; REVELATION; THEOLOGICAL ANTHROPOLOGY; THIRD WORLD THEOLOGIES; TRADITION AND TRADITIONS.

CULTURE HERO

The figure of the *culture hero* is a familiar character in the myths of primal peoples. He or she is usually introduced at an early stage of the narrative and acts in concert with the Creator to assist in the making of civilization. Their qualities identify beings who possess supernatural power and whose authority is recognized by their closeness to the sacred. Thus the hero/heroine is regarded with respect and is given attention; this is necessary if we are to benefit from their knowledge and power. Because they are of a different nature than humans, being older, more primary, their wisdom is welcomed, even when it is sometimes accompanied by trickery and deviousness. In his study of the Winnebago Trickster cycle, Paul Radin relates the wonderfully humorous story of this tribe's culture hero, while noting that his place in creation is very high. He is called from his meanderings by the Creator who fondly reminds him that, as Elder Brother, he has a duty to perform in finishing important details in the work of creation.

One of the great female culture figures is Spider Woman. She is considered to be a medicine person in her own right and to be gifted with the ability to make other persons sharers in sacred power. In a special way, she is the instructor of women who are called to the creative work of weaving, beadwork, and sewing, and also for those who are given the invitation to work in the healing arts as specialists and shamans. This latter is a fearsome call, and Spider Woman's power is directly linked with the field of energy that makes healing possible. Her presence in visions and dreams is a call to adult initiation of the highest kind. A story from the Cherokee helps to demonstrate her high place. In it she, as a very small creature in her physical form, is the only one who can save the other creatures by stealing back the sun from the selfish ones who have contrived to keep it on the other side of the world. In the language of myth, then, she is solely responsible for the second great empowering gift of creation—the sun—and as such shows herself to be linked with the power to give life. As a class, these characters are essential to indigenous myth.

Kathleen Dugan

See also CREATION; TRICKSTER.

CURATE

A priest who is responsible for the "pastoral care" (in Latin, *cura pastoralis* or *cura animarum;* hence the term) of the people of a parish. However, in English-speaking countries, the term has come to refer to associate or assistant pastors.

Orlando Espín

See also PARISH; PASTOR; PASTORAL; PRIESTHOOD.

CURIA, CONGREGATIONS OF THE (ROMAN)

A group of agencies in Rome that assist the pope in the central administration of the Catholic Church. All curial congregations function under the pope and by authority granted them by the incumbent pope. There are currently nine "congregations" of the Curia, each led by a cardinal. These have responsibility over the most sensitive areas in the church's life. The nine "congregations" are: Doctrine of the

Faith (guards the doctrines of the church, and examines doctrinal and ethical questions); Oriental Churches (has competence over matters that concern all Eastern Catholic Churches); Bishops (recommends appointments of bishops to the pope, and supervises the bishops and their ministry throughout the world); Divine Worship (supervises everything regarding the celebration of the liturgy); Causes of the Saints (handles all matters connected with the processes of beatification and canonization); Clergy (has two main areas of competence: the life and ministry of the clergy, and matters relating to catechesis and religious education); Institutes of Consecrated Life (handles everything concerning religious congregations and orders, and secular institutes); Catholic Education (has competence over seminaries, and supervises Catholic schools and universities everywhere); and Evangelization of Peoples (directs and coordinates missionary work throughout the world).

Orlando Espín

See also BEATIFICATION; BISHOP (EPIS-COPACY); CANONIZATION; CARDINAL; CATECHESIS/CATECHETICAL; CONCLAVE; CONSISTORY; CURIA, ROMAN; DEFINI-TION (OF DOCTRINES); DOCTRINE; DOGMA; EASTERN CATHOLIC CHURCHES; ECCLESIOLOGY; EVANGELI-ZATION; LAITY; LITURGY (IN CHRISTI-ANITY); MISSIONARIES; MISSIONS; PETRINE MINISTRY; POPE; PRIESTHOOD; RELIGIOUS, VOWED; RELIGIOUS EDUCA-TION; ROMAN CATHOLIC CHURCH; ROME, SEE OF; TRIDENTINISM; UNIVER-SITY, CATHOLIC; VATICAN; VATICAN, SECOND COUNCIL OF THE.

CURIA, ROMAN

The collective name of the central administrative offices of the worldwide Catholic Church. The Curia exists for the sole purpose of assisting the popes in their work, and to the extent authorized by the popes. The Curia evolved gradually throughout the centuries, achieving a shape resembling the current one only in the latter half of the sixteenth century. According to its present form (mandated by John Paul II in 1989, but which any future pope could change), it consists of the Secretariat of State, nine congregations, three tribunals, twelve pontifical councils, and several other offices. The term "curia" can also refer, by extension, to the administrative offices of any diocese.

Orlando Espín

See also BISHOP (EPISCOPACY); CARDINAL; CONCLAVE; CONCORDAT; CONSISTORY; CURIA, CONGREGATIONS OF THE (ROMAN); DIOCESE/ARCHDIOCESE; EASTERN CATHOLIC CHURCHES; ECCLESIOLOGY; JOHN PAUL II, POPE; JOHN XXIII, POPE; LAITY; MEDIEVAL CHURCH; PAUL VI, POPE; PETRINE MINISTRY; POPE; ROMAN CATHOLIC CHURCH; ROME, SEE OF; TRIDENTINISM; VATICAN; VATICAN, SECOND COUNCIL OF THE.

CURRAN, CHARLES E. (1934–)

After earning two doctorates at Rome's Lateran and Gregorian Universities, Curran began teaching moral theology at The Catholic University in Washington, D.C., in 1965. The author of over forty books (several coauthored with Richard McCormick), Curran takes a consistently pastoral approach to his ethics, attending to the historical realities, actual practices, and ordinary needs of believers, calling for "a living Church and a living tradition." In general, he might be said to take a "common law" approach to ethics, as opposed to a "Roman law" approach, which stresses the duty of a community to form a moral character in light of a certain explicit ideal.

Curran treats of a variety of subjects, including the magisterium, dissent in the church, academic freedom, sexual ethics, and the use of military force. He does not ignore tradition but invites the believer to "creative fidelity to the word and work of Jesus." He challenges the Catholic Church's magisterium for frequently stifling that creativity, and calls for the magisterium to apply the methodology of its rich tradition of social doctrine to its own structure and teaching function.

The conflict between the two approaches to ethics, and his own explicit challenge to *Humanae Vitae* in 1968, led to prolonged conflict with the Vatican. On August 18, 1986, the Vatican dismissed Curran from his post at The Catholic University (a Pontifical Institute), the first American theologian to be so disciplined. He currently (2006) teaches at Southern Methodist University.

G. Simon Harak, s.j.

See also DISSENT; HUMANAE VITAE; MCCORMICK, RICHARD A.

CURSES (IN JUDAISM)

Scripture and later Judaism understand a curse to express a hope upon which God might or might not act. While Scripture understands curses to be ineffective unless deserved, Talmudic Judaism sees them in all events as extremely powerful. They are particularly effective when uttered by well-educated rabbis, believed to have a close connection to God, but must be taken seriously even when spoken by an ignorant or impious person. Rabbis were believed able to curse through an angry stare that would reduce their victim to poverty or even death. Ancient Judaism permitted cursing for religious reasons, for instance, against those who mislead the people by calculating the time of the arrival of the messiah or who promoted heresy. Cursing plays no role in contemporary Jewish practice.

Alan J. Avery-Peck

CURSILLO MOVEMENT

A Roman Catholic lay organization founded in Spain in the middle of the twentieth century for the purpose of stimulating and empowering lay persons to engage in active Christian living, in society, and in the church. The Cursillo movement's method centers around an intense three-day weekend workshop (called *cursillo* in Spanish) and a post-cursillo follow-up. The movement has had extraordinary influence among the laity all over the world and it has been instrumental in the renewal of many parishes and dioceses.

Orlando Espín

See also ECCLESIOLOGY; EVANGELIZATION; LAITY.

CYCLE/CYCLICAL

Although these terms are applied to any recurring pattern, what follows applies to biblical studies and religious observances.

In the Bible, the term cycle designates accounts that can be isolated from an overall narrative in which there are recurring motifs. For example, "The Jacob Cycle" that recounts stories of Jacob and his children incorporates a pattern of deceptions (Gen 25:19–50:26). Some also isolate "The Joseph Cycle" (Gen 37–50, [except 39 and 49]), a novella in which Joseph's ability to interpret dreams is a separate pattern that is integrated into the Jacob cycle. Another example is that of "The Elijah and Elisha Cycles" (1 Kgs 17–2 Kgs 1; 2 Kgs 2–13, respectively), complexes that recount the events and

miraculous occurrences in the story of Elijah and are more or less repeated in the story of Elisha.

Since antiquity, religions have ordered their observances and rituals by a calendar. For example, the calendars of Judaism, Islam, and Christianity establish a cycle of weekly observances at seven-day intervals that are set into annual cycles of seasons and/or feasts and fasts. Particular observances follow a cycle of rituals peculiar to each occasion. All Jews and most Christians also incorporate into their ritual observances a cycle of predetermined readings from the sacred texts. In Judaism the readings are distributed so that the entire Torah is read over the course of each year; each Torah portion is also assigned a related selection from the Prophets. Although Orthodox and Eastern-rite churches follow a one-year, two-reading lectionary cycle, many Western churches have adopted a three-year, three-reading cycle of lectionary readings. In this scheme, the same cycle of observances recurs each year. However, the readings appointed for the first year are repeated only after the three-year cycle of readings has been completed.

Regina A. Boisclair

CYPRIAN OF CARTHAGE (?–258)

Thascius Caecilianus Cyprianus was a wealthy landowner and rhetor in North Africa who converted to Christianity in 246, and became *episokopos* (bishop) of Carthage in 249. Almost immediately faced with the Decian persecution, Cyprian led his congregation while in hiding. He used his wealth to assist the poor during both persecution and plague. While Cyprian supported Cornelius of Rome against the claims of Novatian, he strongly and publicly disagreed with the Roman practice of accepting as valid, baptism administered by heretics. Cyprian wrote several letters and treatises, including *De unitate ecclesiae* (*On the Unity of the Church*), probably the first Christian writing on this topic. His work was popular and much admired for its practical and pastoral approach. He was one of the first Latin theologians of Christianity. Cyprian met a martyr's death in the persecution of Valerian in 258.

Gary Macy

See also CORNELIUS OF ROME; MARTYR/ MARTYRDOM; NOVATIANISM; NOVATIAN OF ROME; PERSECUTION (IN CHRISTIANITY).

CYRIL (827–69) AND METHODIUS (826–85)

Constantine (Cyril was Constantine's monastic name) and Methodius were brothers who were Byzantine Christians sent as missionaries to the Slavs in 863 by the Byantine emperor and the patriarch of Constantinople. The brothers translated the Christian Scripture and liturgy into the Slavic language, inventing a new alphabet in order to do so. This alphabet, called Glagolitic, was developed by Cyril and Methodius' students into the Cyrillic alphabet used in Eastern Europe and Russia to the present day. When conflicts arose with Frankish clergy in Moravia over the use of Slavic rather than Latin in the liturgy, the brothers appealed to the pope, who not only supported them, but appointed Methodius archbishop of Sirmium with jurisdiction over the Slavs. Cyril died in Rome in 869, but Methodius carried on his missionary efforts, supported by both Rome and Constantinople until his death in 885.

Gary Macy

See also BYZANTIUM/BYZANTINE; MISSIONARIES.

CYRIL OF ALEXANDRIA (370/80?–444)

Cyril succeeded his uncle as patriarch of Alexandria in 412. Cyril, ambitious and energetic, immediately initiated a harsh policy against heretics and pagans in Alexandria. When the new patriarch of Constantinople, Nestorius, suggested that the term *Theotokos* (Bearer of God) would be inappropriate for Mary, since Mary was mother only of the human Jesus, Cyril immediately protested. This would be the beginning of the Nestorian controversy, a bitter dispute about the relationship of the human and divine natures in Christ that would last until the Council of Ephesus in 451. The teaching of Nestorius was referred to the church of Rome, where Pope Celestine condemned it and asked that Cyril convey this decision to Nestorius. Cyril not only sent Nestorius word of the condemnation, but added his own twelve condemnations, deliberately written in a way to infuriate any Antiochene theologian. Nestorius appealed to the emperor, Theodosius II, who called for a council to be held at Ephesus in 431. Cyprian arrived at Ephesus first, and immediately condemned and deposed Nestorius before the Antiochene bishops could arrive. When Nestorius and his supporters got to Ephesus, they held their own council and deposed Cyprian. The emperor at first accepted both depositions but Cyprian soon evaded the condemnation. Once Nestorius was removed from office, Cyprian was willing to accept a theological compromise with the Antiochene theologians. A Pact of Union was signed in 433, and Cyril supported it until his death in 444. Although Cyril's political ambitions and occasional lack of scruples in pursuing his ends are not to be admired, his theology is perhaps the best representative of the Alexandrian approach to the problem of the nature of Christ. It is for this theology and for his sermons, letters, and scriptural exegesis that he is mainly admired.

Gary Macy

See also ALEXANDRIAN THEOLOGY; ANTIOCHENE THEOLOGY; CHRISTOLOGY; EPHESUS, COUNCIL OF; NESTORIANISM; NESTORIUS.

CYRIL OF JERUSALEM (315?–386)

Cyril was patriarch of Jerusalem from around 349 until his death in 386. On three different occasions, Cyril was banished during the Arian controversy because of his faith. Although slow to accept the term *homoousion* (one in substance), Cyril defended the Council of Nicaea against the Arians. He is best known for a series of catechetical lectures that describe in great detail the rituals and understanding of both baptism and the Eucharist as used in Jerusalem during the fourth century.

Gary Macy

See also ARIANISM; BAPTISM/CONFIRMATION; EUCHARIST; HOMOOUSIOS; LITURGY (IN CHRISTIANITY); NICAEA, FIRST COUNCIL OF.

D

D'AILLY, PIERRE (1350–1420)

Doctor of theology from the University of Paris, D'Ailly was, successively, chancellor of the university, bishop of Le Puy, and bishop of Cambrai. Made a cardinal in 1412, he played a prominent role at the Council of Constance (1414–8), the council that brought an end to the Great Schism in the West.

D'Ailly was, like many late medieval churchmen, a "nominalist" in philosophy and theology. He thus taught that the existence of God could not be proven by reason, and that sins were sins solely because God willed it so. There was nothing that could be shown to be inherently evil.

The Great Schism had seen the papacy divided first by two, then by three rival popes. It was in this context that D'Ailly developed an ecclesiology that would later be known as Gallicanism. For D'Ailly, bishops and priests received jurisdiction from Christ directly, not through the intermediary of the pope. Also, neither the pope nor a council of bishops could be considered infallible. Among D'Ailly's students was John Gerson (1363–1429).

Thomas Worcester, s.j.

See also ECCLESIOLOGY; GALLICANISM; GERSON, JOHN; NOMINALISM; SCHISM, GREAT WESTERN.

DALAI LAMA

Leader in the Tibetan Gelugpa school and ruler over traditional Tibet for roughly the last four hundred years. The title Dalai Lama ("Ocean [of Wisdom] Teacher") was bestowed by Mongol patron Altan Khan in 1578 on the already established "reformed" Gelugpa school leader Sonam Gyatso. (Since the term was applied retrospectively back to 1445, he was the third Dalai Lama.) One of many hundreds of reincarnating bodhisattva lineages in Tibet, the Dalai Lama is regarded as the continuing incarnation of the celestial bodhisattva Avalokiteshvara (Tibetan, Chenrizig).

Each Dalai Lama reincarnation is found by consulting the last messages of the previous Dalai Lama as to his next birth, by following the revelations of state oracles, and then subjecting candidates to tests regarding their recognition of objects used in the former birth. The Dalai Lama has resided in the Potala palace in Lhasa since the time of the Great Fifth Dalai (1617–79), a figure who gained political control over all Tibet in alliance with the Mongols and the Chinese emperor. It was this figure, too, who established the notion that the Dalai Lama was during his youth religiously subordinate to the Panchen

Lama; the Great Fifth identified the Panchen as an incarnation of Amitabha Buddha who, as head of the Gelugpa monastery Tashilhunpo, ruled over the region of western Tibet with the town of Shigatse as its capital. The current Dalai Lama, Tensing Gyatso (1933–), is the fourteenth; he has ruled the Tibetan government in exile from Dharamsala, India, since 1959.

Todd T. Lewis

See also AVALOKITESHVARA; BODHISATTVA; LAMA; TULKU.

DALIT
See CASTE; CASTES, SCHEDULED.

DALY, MARY (1928–)
Mary Daly, American feminist philosopher, was born in Schenectady, New York. She was educated at the College of St. Rose in Albany, New York, and received an M.A. in theology from the Graduate School of Sacred Theology at Saint Mary's College, Notre Dame, Indiana. She was awarded two doctorates, one in philosophy and one in theology from the University of Fribourg in Switzerland. From 1966 to 1999 she taught in the Theology Department at Boston College. Her first book, *The Church and the Second Sex*, is a historical treatment of women in the Catholic Church. Since its appearance in 1968, the book has been published with a post-Christian feminist introduction and a "new archaic" afterword. These emendations chart Daly's course from initial optimism concerning reform of the church's teaching about women to her increasing disenchantment and departure from Catholicism. Her 1975 book, *Beyond God the Father*, has been acclaimed as a classic argument for the feminist critique of patriarchal religions. Since

then she has been concerned with emancipating women from the hegemony of patriarchal symbolism and language by creating a philosophy and language based upon women's experience, a task which occupies her subsequent publications: *Gyn/Ecology, Pure Lust, Wickedary, Outercourse, Quintessence,* and *Amazon Grace.*

Mary Ann Hinsdale

DAMASUS I OF ROME
Damasus's father belonged to the Roman clergy, and both his mother and sister had taken vows when Damasus became a deacon under Bishop Liberius of Rome. Damasus himself was chosen Bishop of Rome in the midst of controversy. His election was opposed by the rigorist deacon Ursinus. The fighting became so intense that eventually the emperor intervened on Damasus's behalf. He was pope from 366 to 384. Damasus is best known for his contributions to the development of the papacy. He was the first pope to appeal to Matthew 16:18 as a claim for papal prerogatives, and insisted that the pope could be judged only by the emperor. Damasus opposed the designation of Constantinople in 381 as a "second Rome," thus rejecting equal status for the patriarchs of Rome and Constantinople. Damasus also took a firm stand against Apollinarianism and in favor of the full divinity of the Holy Spirit.

Gary Macy

See also APPOLLINARIANISM; CLERGY; PATRIARCH; POPE; VOWS (RELIGIOUS).

DAMNATION
This term expresses the idea of condemnation, penalty, or punishment. In theological usage, it has an eschatological significance, expressing the idea of personal loss of community with God after death, and

more, estrangement from God as a consequence of one's choices during life.

Patricia Plovanich

See also HELL.

DANIÉLOU, JEAN (1905–74)

French Jesuit, professor at the Institut Catholique (Paris), patristic scholar, later bishop and cardinal. Daniélou was a member of the New Theology movement advocating study of the original sources of theology to explore their contemporary significance. Convinced of the value Christianity and its tradition held for modernity, Daniélou advocated and pursued the study of Scripture, liturgy, and especially the patristic era. He was cofounder and contributor to *Sources Chrétiennes*, a series devoted to translations of patristic texts. He distinguished himself not only as a patristic scholar but as cogent interpreter of the tradition for contemporary reflection. The caliber of his scholarship was recognized in his nomination to the Académie Française (1972–3), in his appointment as expert (*peritus*) to Vatican Council II, and his appointment as cardinal in 1974. He became critical of many post–Vatican II theological developments, however.

Patricia Plovanich

DAO
See TAO.

DAODEJING
See TAO TE CHING.

DAOISM

The term Daoism refers to a wide variety of ancient Chinese philosophical beliefs and religious practices. The seminal literary source for the philosophical tradition is a short, evocative text known as the *Daodejing*. The work is attributed to Laozi, a semimythical sage who is said to have lived around the sixth century B.C.E., although the text itself dates to the early third century B.C.E. In cryptic, poetic verses, the *Daodejing* describes the Dao (literally, "way") as the source of all things as well as their manifestation. A second source for the philosophical tradition is the *Zhangzi*, a text compiled in the fourth century B.C.E. and attributed to an antinomian figure named Zhangzi, also thought to have lived around the sixth century B.C.E. In whimsical, paradoxical language, the *Zhangzi* raises the primordial questions of life and death. It also reminds us to keep things in perspective. The world looks different to a human and a fish, as perceptions of the world are relative to the perceiver.

The Dao is subtle and mysterious, beyond classification or categorization. Although the Dao is beyond naming and characterization, the term hints at a primordial unity, a cosmic potential, or the totality of myriad phenomena. The Dao encompasses two fundamental and complementary principles of the universe: *yin*, associated with shade, cold, weakness, and receptivity; and *yang*, associated with light, heat, strength, and activity. Ultimately the Dao symbolizes the creative, spontaneous, natural ground of all being —the unity of all dichotomies. For human beings, to be in harmony with the Dao is to accord with one's own true nature. Peace and harmony are achieved through balancing the interdependent, mutually complementary forces within oneself, with others, and with nature. Without grasping or resisting, holding on to expectations or disappointments, one lives simply, like an "uncarved block" that takes form in relation to circumstances.

Living in harmony with the natural world is especially important to Daoists. The cycles of night and day, expansion and contraction, life and death, winter/spring/summer/fall are all natural processes. Living simply, away from the artifice, intrigue, and cacophony of population centers, one becomes attuned to the natural rhythm of the universe. Daoists reject education in the form of book learning and character development in favor of *wu-wei*: nonaction, nonresistance, nonstriving. To be genuine, rather than striving to be what one is not, is to live in accord with the Dao.

Whether the tradition referred to as Daoism is religious in nature depends on what definition one uses. Although it lacks a specific set of beliefs, it presents a worldview that fosters inquiry about theological questions. Daoism lacks a supreme being, yet the Dao is portrayed as a first cause of the cosmos and life force of all things. It lacks a clearly defined code of ethics, yet it sets forth a clear path for human conduct, values of gentleness and simplicity, and a prototype for a cogent environmental philosophy. Daoism is called mystical because it is a path of discovery that relies on inner experience rather than scriptural knowledge or discursive thinking.

It is often assumed that philosophical Daoism gave way to popular or religious Daoism in response to the importation of Buddhism, but the religious practices now associated with Daoism were probably popular in China long before Buddhism arrived. These practices include divination, meditation, holistic healing, alchemy, and reverence for ancestors. They involve spirit mediums, talismans, and a vast pantheon of celestial beings and immortals. A range of practices that balance the vital energies (*qi*) are utilized in the quest for longevity and immortality. Spirit mediums are believed to have access to an invisible world of spirits and ancestors. The rituals they perform are designed to facilitate communication between the living and the dead, with the aim of maintaining harmony between them. When human beings act appropriately and honor their ancestors, the ancestors are pleased and express their approval by bestowing health, longevity, and prosperity. When human beings act otherwise, the ancestors are displeased and may intervene in ways that are disruptive or destructive. At ritual intervals, especially at Qing Ming, an annual ceremony to commemorate the dead, human beings summon their ancestors with incense, make offerings to them, and request their blessings.

There have been innumerable Neo-Daoist movements, beginning from the third century. Some of these have taken the form of political protest movements or rebellions in response to corruption and oppression on the part of Confucian rulers and functionaries. Daoism remains popular in China, Korea, Vietnam, and the Chinese diaspora up to the present day.

Karma Lekshe Tsomo

See also ANCESTORS, CHINESE; CH'I; TAO; TAO TE CHING; WU-WEI; YING AND YANG.

DAR AL-HARB

In Islam, the "Abode of War," contrasted according to Islamic law with *dar al-Islam*; the "Abode of Peace" through submission (to Islam). More specifically, the *dar al-Islam* encompasses the lands where Islamic faith is practiced and Islamic law is observed, and the *dar al-Harb* is the non-Islamic world—the house of unbelievers. In theory, designating non-Muslim peoples as the Abode of War suggests that Islam is at least potentially at war with all who do not accept Islam. Indeed, the Qur'an enjoins Muslims to "strike terror into (the hearts of) the enemies of Allah" (8:60). In practice, however, Islam has traditionally recognized that such an adversarial response to non-Muslims is appropriate only in legitimate self-defense, and that the message of Islam and the *dar al-Islam* are better served by the dissemination of information about Muslim faith. Despite the actions of Muslim terrorist groups in recent years, it would, therefore, be inaccurate to conclude that the idea of *dar al-Harb* and *dar al-Islam* necessarily imply hostility or militancy toward Jews, Christians, and adherents of other faiths.

Ronald A. Pachence

See also AHL AL-KITAB; JIHAD; QUR'AN.

DAR AL-ISLAM
See DAR AL-HARB.

DAR AL-SALAM
Arabic term for the "Abode" or "Home of Peace (in the afterlife)." In Islam the Abode of Peace is paradise—the eternal life with Allah (God) that the just will enjoy after this life has ended. It is the "heavenly" reward of those who placed obedience to God over earthly pleasures in this world. Sura 10:25 of the Qur'an says that Allah calls whom He wills to the Abode of Peace, and in 6:127, believers are told that because they practice righteousness, they will be Allah's friends and will live forever in the divine presence in the *dar al-Salam*.

Ronald A. Pachence

See also ALLAH (ISLAM); DAR AL-HARB; DAY OF JUDGMENT (IN ISLAM); PREDESTINATION (IN ISLAM); QUR'AN; SURA.

DARK NIGHT OF THE SOUL
The phrase is drawn from the title of a mystical writing by the sixteenth-century Carmelite John of the Cross. Originating within his own experience of arrest and nine-month imprisonment by religious authorities under dungeon-like conditions, John's poem ("The Dark Night") and his treatise or commentary on that poem bear eloquent testimony to a person's ability to encounter God in the most desperate of circumstances. The theme of the work is contemplative or mystical union with God through love, a process that requires passing through the "dark night" of intense purification. Human senses, imagination, thought processes, affections, willing, and loving, all must be purified and radically emptied prior to a person's being joined with "the eternal being of God." One cannot predict how long the "dark night" will last. John's experience often speaks to those whose approach to God feels "negative." That is, they sense the inadequacy of traditional ideas and images about God, and are led by the Spirit to finding God in darkness.

William Reiser, s.j.

See also APOPHATIC THEOLOGY; CARMELITES; JOHN OF THE CROSS; VIA NEGATIVA.

DARSHANA (PHILOSOPHY)
Darshana (Sanskrit, seeing, vision) is the Hindu term for a system of thought. Six orthodox darshanas or schools of "philosophy" (literally, "ways of seeing") are recognized. These include Nyaya (logic), Vaishesika (realistic pluralism), Samkhya, Yoga, Mimamsa (ritual exegesis), and Vedanta. The most important of the darshanas for modern Hindus are Vedanta and Yoga. There is some debate as to whether darshana in this sense should be

translated as "philosophy" or "theology," for the kind of thought it designates combines elements of both Western concepts.

Lance E. Nelson

See also HINDUISM; PATANJALI; SANKHYA; VEDANTA; YOGA.

DARSHANA/DARSHAN

Darshana in this sense is an important devotional act in Hinduism involving the"seeing" of a holy image, place, or person. By being in the presence of a sacred icon in a temple, or having an audience with a saint, Hindus expect to receive a blessing that will uplift them spiritually. Devotees may also hope that blessings received from darshana of temple deities or saints, accompanied by prayer, will lead to some worldly benefit. In transcribing modern Indian languages, darshana is typically written as *darshan*, without the final "a."

Lance E. Nelson

See also BHAKTI; BHAKTI-YOGA; GURU; HINDUISM; IMAGES, WORSHIP OF.

DARWIN, CHARLES (1808–82)

English scientist and main proponent of the theory of evolution. Educated at Cambridge, he sailed to South America on a scientific mission. The evidence he collected on this trip later led him to argue that all living things developed from simpler forms through a process of natural selection that rewards (with survival) the strongest, fittest, and best adapted. His theories caused much controversy among scientists and theologians during the nineteenth century and thereafter, because evolution was perceived by some as challenging the biblical account of creation and thus the traditional understanding of revelation. Darwin's basic arguments,

however, have been amply substantiated by later science. Some Christians (mostly fundamentalists) still refuse to accept the scientific evidence for evolution, although most Christian theologians and churches (most branches of Christianity) have acknowledged that evolution is a fact, and that it does not contradict or endanger revelation. Darwin's main publications were *The Origin of Species* (1859) and *The Descent of Man* (1871).

Orlando Espín

See also CATHOLIC TRADITION; CREATION; CREATIONISM; DARWINISM; EVOLUTION; FUNDAMENTALISM (CHRISTIAN HISTORICAL MOVEMENT); REVELATION; SCIENCE, AUTONOMY OF; SCIENCE AND THEOLOGY.

DARWINISM

Darwinism is an explanation for the evolution of animal and human species developed in the mid-nineteenth century by Charles Darwin, an English naturalist. Although Darwin's was not the first theory of evolution, his was the most influential. In works such as *The Origin of Species* (1859) and *The Descent of Man* (1871), Darwin argued that varieties of life evolved through natural selection, the gradual adaptation of physiology to environment. Physical traits that enable a species to adapt to its natural environment persist and are passed from generation to generation; in short, the most adaptable species survive.

Even though Darwin did not relate his argument to religion, his theories had profound implications for Christianity. First, Darwinism called into question creation accounts in the first chapters of the biblical book of Genesis that state that God created the world in seven days by calling it into being. Darwinism implied that creation by divine fiat was untrue. Second, Darwinism made a godless world scientifically possible. Religion, or a divine creator, was not necessary to explain how the world worked. While previously science and Christianity had buttressed one another, after Darwin they collided more and more often. Third, Darwinism implied that the world was completely arbitrary. Creation was not directed by a divine will, but humans drifted aimlessly, molded by capricious forces beyond their control. People were no different from animals, fighting to survive in a hostile world.

Fourth, Darwinism was especially troubling when applied to society. Social Darwinism, as promulgated by sociologist Herbert Spencer and others, argued that, in society as well as in the natural world, only the fittest survived. Many in business and industry concluded that the most capable "naturally" became wealthy, while the poor just didn't have what it took to succeed. This theory implied that the rich were destined to be rich and the poor, poor, and it justified virtually any means to get ahead.

The implications of Darwinism sparked a crisis among all Christians, but especially Protestant Evangelicals. Some believed that Darwinism and the Genesis creation accounts were not contradictory and could be reconciled with one another; they saw Genesis as metaphorical rather than scientifically factual. Others argued that Darwinism and the Bible were fundamentally incompatible; one or the other was true, but not both. These Protestants rejected Darwinism and adhered to a literal, inerrant view of the Scriptures. The former group were often liberals, and the latter, fundamentalists. As to Social Darwinism, it found adherents among both liberals and fundamentalists. Scientific Darwinism sparked public controversy in the 1925 Scopes trial in Dayton, Tennessee, in which a high school science teacher was charged with teaching Darwinism. He was convicted, but fundamentalism was discredited. As Darwinism became part of the scientific paradigm of the twentieth century, few Christians disbelieved it entirely; however, those that do are vociferous advocates of creationism.

Evelyn A. Kirkley

See also CREATIONISM; EVANGELICALS; EVANGELICAL THEOLOGY; FUNDAMENTALISM (CHRISTIAN HISTORICAL MOVEMENT); SOCIAL GOSPEL.

DAVID

First king of a united Israel who ruled from approximately 1000 B.C.E.–960 B.C.E. According to 1 Samuel 16:13, he was chosen by God. He is idealized in the books of Samuel and especially in 1 Chronicles. God promises David a dynasty (2 Sam 7). God forgives him for his treatment of Uriah in the Bathsheba affair (2 Sam 12). Second Samuel 24 depicts him as wanting the welfare of his people more than his own. David is the king for the sake of whom God preserves the kingdom of Judah (1 Kgs 11:32; cf. 2 Kgs 19:34; 20:6).

Historical scholars doubt that the contrast between Saul and David presented in the Deuteronomic History is an accurate one. Saul sins and is rejected by the Lord. David also sins, but acknowledges his sin and is forgiven. By the time of the earliest editing of the History, Saul was dead with no heir on the throne. David, however, had emerged as Saul's successor. David's house ruled Judah for about four hundred years. The depiction of David in relation to Saul is therefore colored by David's success and the endurance of his dynasty.

Using a similar methodology, historical scholars note the crafting of 1 Chronicles in contract to the portrait of David in 1–2 Samuel. The Chronicler's account, presumed later than the deuteronomic, omits all reference to David's affair with Bathsheba. Moreover, it is David who prepares for the building of the Lord's Temple. All Solomon does is execute David's preparations. From an exilic perspective, David emerges as greater than his son Solomon, and is recalled with increased devotion as the symbol of Israel's past success.

Later Jewish tradition and its incorporation into the New Testament further enhance the portrait of an idealized David. Tracing one's lineage back to David was clearly meant to legitimate one's ancestry. The Gospel of Matthew takes pains to identify Jesus as a descendent of David (Matt 1:1-20). In each of the Gospels, Jesus is frequently identified as Son of David (for example, Matt 9:27; 15:22; 20:30-31; Luke 18:38-39). The theological significance of this appellation cannot be underestimated. The Messiah who would come to deliver Israel would be a descendent of David (for example, Jer 23:5; 33:15; Ezek 34:23-24; 37:24-25). Jesus is thus identified as the Messiah, and as king, par excellence. He does not so identify himself, but that is the judgment of those who approach him for help (for example, Mark 10:47-48) and those who honor him as he enters Jerusalem to celebrate the Passover with his disciples (for example, Matt 21:9).

Alice L. Laffey

DAVIES, WILLIAM D. (1911–2001)

A New Testament scholar who recognized that Judaism in the first century C.E. was the primary intellectual matrix of early Christianity. Davies was a major influence on a number of scholars who have made the recovery of the Jewish Paul and the Jewish Jesus among the major thrusts of New Testament research since the early 1980s.

William David Davies was born in Wales, and studied at the University of Wales (B.A., 1934; B.D., 1938; D.D., 1948) and Cambridge University (M.A., 1942). After serving on the faculties of Duke, Princeton, and Union Theological Seminary in New York (1955–66), he was appointed the George Washington Ivey Professor of Advanced Studies and Research in Christian Origins at Duke University (1966–81). His writings include: *The Setting of the Sermon on the Mount* (1966), *Paul and Rabbinic Judaism* (1970), and *The Gospel and the Land: Early Christianity and Jewish Territorial Doctrine* (1974). A number of his important articles were republished in *Jewish and Pauline Studies* (1984).

Regina A. Boisclair

DAVIS, CYPRIAN (1930–)

Father Davis is the leading historian of Black (African) American Catholic Church history in the United States. A native of Washington, D.C., and a Benedictine monk of St. Meinrad Abbey (Indiana), he also serves as a professor of church history at St. Meinrad Seminary.

After receiving his Ph.D. from the Catholic University of Louvain (Belgium), Davis embarked upon a scholarly career which has included numerous articles on monastic history, black Catholic history, and black spirituality as well as a high school textbook on church history. He has been preeminent in his work on black Catholic spirituality, contributing monographs, lectures, and other works that retrieve, contextualize, and interpret both black and Catholic models of sanctity and spiritual traditions. A founding member in the early 1960s of the National Black Catholic Clergy Caucus, Davis also served as a consultant and writer for *Brothers and Sisters to Us: The U.S. Bishop's Pastoral Letter on Racism in Our Day* (1979) and *What We Have Seen and Heard: The Black Bishops' of the United States Pastoral Letter on Evangelization* (1984).

His most significant contribution has been the recovery of the history and contributions of Africans and African Americans in the Roman Catholic Church. His book, *The History of Black Catholics in the United States* (1993), the first full-length treatment of that history to be published in modern times, is based on years of primary research in the United States and throughout the world, including the Vatican archives. This work traces the history of the African presence in the early church and chronicles the involvement and contributions of English-, French-, and Spanish-speaking Catholics of African descent in the church in the United States.

Diana L. Hayes

DAY, DOROTHY (1897–1980)
Born in Brooklyn, New York, on November 8, 1897, Dorothy Day was raised in Chicago in a lower-middle-class Episcopalian family. As a young woman, she espoused political radicalism and the worldwide cause of workers to which she contributed as a professional journalist. Soon after her conversion to Catholicism in 1927, Day met the French Catholic social philosopher Peter Maurin with whom she founded the Catholic Worker Movement. Through the newspaper of the same name, they attempted to spread Catholic social teaching, houses of hospitality to carry out the works of mercy for the urban poor and the homeless, and farming communes in the country as an alternative to life in industrial society. Gradually, Day developed a philosophy

of Catholic anarchism, which embraced pacifism, voluntary poverty, and prayer. Her combination of political activism and mysticism continued to challenge the conscience of American Catholics even after her death on November 29, 1980. While many Catholics already consider Day a saint, the formal process leading to canonization began in 2000.

James B. Nickoloff

DAYANANDA, SWAMI (1824–33)
Swami Dayananda, the founder of the Arya Samaj (Society of Noble Persons), was an important eighteenth-century Hindu reformer. He believed that the Vedas contained all truth and could provide a basis for a renewed Hinduism, purified of the complex polytheism, image worship, and post-Vedic social and ritual practices so much criticized by Western missionaries. Identifying a good deal of contemporary Hindu belief and practice as a false accretion that distorted the Vedic revelation, he argued strongly for improving the lot of Hindu women and eliminating the evils of the caste system. An early Hindu nationalist, Dayananda did much to restore Hindu pride after years of conquest and colonial domination. Militant in temperament, he engaged in a vigorous polemic against Islam and Christianity, and he is known in particular for instituting a ritual known as *shuddhi* (purification), whereby Hindus who had converted to one of those faiths could be reinstated in their traditional religion. Unlike the Brahmo Samaj, Dayananda's Arya Samaj remains an important and influential movement in modern India.

Lance E. Nelson

See also HINDUISM; RAMAKRISHNA, SRI; ROY, RAM MOHAN; VEDAS; VIVEKANANDA, SWAMI.

DAY OF JUDGMENT (IN ISLAM)

In Arabic, *Yawm ad-Din*, which literally means "day of religion," is the Islamic belief in the last day of this world, when the dead are reunited with their bodies and all peoples are judged according to their deeds. Those whom Allah judges worthy are admitted to paradise and evildoers are condemned to eternal punishment. The Qur'an is full of references to the Day of Judgment, indicating its centrality to Islamic faith and practice. A typical aya (verse) from Sura (chapter) 3 reads: "Every soul shall have a taste of death: And only on the Day of Judgment shall you be paid your full recompense" (3:185).

Ronald A. Pachence

See also AYA; DAR AL-SALAM; QUR'AN; SURA.

DAY OF THE LORD/DAY OF YAHWEH

In the Hebrew Bible/Old Testament the Day is a concept that is ancient and undergoes changes over time. Initially, the Day referred to the time when Yahweh would appear to fight for the people of Yahweh. Since Yahweh had to appear to fight the battle, the Day was considered to be a day of light and salvation (= military victory). The imagery associated with theophany was associated with the Day (compare Deut 33, Judg 5, and so on), light, brightness, connected with Yahweh shining forth. In the eighth century B.C.E., in the writings of the prophet Amos, we find this concept of the Day assumed and somewhat modified. Amos warns his audience that the Day will not be a day of light for them, but rather a day of darkness (Amos 5:18-20; 8:9-10). Amos redefined the Day only slightly by asserting that part of the Israelite population would be considered as the enemies of Yahweh

and would be destroyed. Inherent in this idea is that, before the destruction of the enemies, Yahweh would judge to determine who was his enemy and who was his loyal follower. Thus the idea of judgment comes to be associated with the Day. This presentation of the day is continued in prophetic literature down to the fifth century B.C.E. The time of Yahweh's intervention is gradually projected more and more into the future.

Russell Fuller

DAY OF YAHWEH

See DAY OF THE LORD.

DEACON

See DIAKONIA.

DEACONESS

Based on the Greek term *diakonissa*, a word that did not come into use until the fourth century C.E., it denoted an office held by women that developed especially in the third and fourth centuries, whereby a deaconess cared for other women, especially the sick or poor, instructed female catechumens, and assisted at their baptism. When adult baptisms declined, the office of deaconess faded in importance, although it is found in some places until the eleventh century.

Due to the late development of the term, and the restriction of the ministry of deaconess to other females, it is incorrect and anachronistic to translate references to women who are called *diakonos* in the New Testament as "deaconess." For example, Phoebe in Romans 16:1-2 should be denoted in translations as a deacon.

In the nineteenth century, the office of deaconess was restored in a modified form among some Protestant communities, notably in Germany, England, Scotland, and the U.S.A. In contemporary Roman Catholicism the office has not been revived.

F. M. Gillman

See also DIAKONIA.

DEAD SEA SCROLLS

Refers to those manuscript discoveries (1947–55) in the vicinity of the Dead Sea, especially those manuscripts found in Caves 1–11 near Khirbet Qumran. Most scholars associate the scrolls with the community (-ies) resident at Qumran between about 150 B.C.E. and 68 C.E. The community is most often thought to have been affiliated with the Essenes, a Jewish group known from ancient sources. The manuscripts range in date from around 275 B.C.E. to approximately 68 C.E. They were written primarily in Hebrew and Aramaic, with some scrolls in Greek. The scrolls were usually composed of parchment (leather) with some of papyrus. The manuscripts fall into two categories: (1) biblical scrolls and (2) nonbiblical compositions. The majority of the manuscripts and the oldest (around 275 B.C.E.) are biblical. The biblical manuscripts are of importance because they allow us to trace the history and the transmission of the Hebrew text from the third century B.C.E. until the first century C.E. on the basis of manuscript evidence. The oldest manuscripts of the Hebrew Bible from Qumran are older by nearly one thousand years than the next oldest manuscripts of the Hebrew Bible. This is a period of time when the text and the order of material is still in a state of flux. The nonbiblical manuscripts also fall into two major groups: (1) previously known compositions such as the apocrypha and pseudepigrapha of the Hebrew Bible, and (2) compositions whose existence we knew little or nothing about such as the Manual of Discipline and the Temple Scroll, both of which have become important sources of information about the community. The previously unknown compositions are important because they are assumed to derive from the community settled at Qumran from approximately 150 B.C.E. until about 68 C.E. Thus, they are primary sources for the religious beliefs and practices of the Essene community at Qumran and elsewhere. These sectarian compositions, as they are also called, provide information on the wide variety of religious beliefs and practices within Judaism during the last two centuries B.C.E. and the first century C.E. They thus allow us to understand the antecedents of many early Christian and Jewish beliefs and practices that date from this period.

Russell Fuller

DEATH (CHRISTIAN)

For a Christian, death marks the definitive transition from human history to God's eternity. In itself, death is not our common enemy, for death is a natural feature of creation, which God in the beginning pronounced good; but under the dominion of sin, death becomes fearful, even terrifying. Christians believe that through the death and resurrection of Jesus, the power of sin has been broken and has lost its power to keep us slaves to fear (Rom 8:15). Christians also believe that one who has been joined to the mystery of the dying and rising of Christ through baptism has already "died" to the old self of sin (Rom 6:1-14). The actual end of one's life, accepted as part of God's plan for each of us, can become a prayerful surrender into the loving hands of God (Luke 23:46).

For Paul, death and life are mutually defining existential categories: whoever is alive in the Spirit is automatically dead to sin, while those who refuse to acknowledge their sinfulness may be physically alive, but they are spiritually dead. Those who refuse to follow God's commandments are walking the way of death, while those who put God's word into practice have chosen the way of life (Deut 30:15-20). For a Christian, death's sting is not removed by belief in an afterlife, but through the liberation of heart, mind, and soul that comes from "dying ahead of time," that is, from the daily letting-go that takes the form of becoming poor in spirit, compassionate, selfless, and humble. The grain of wheat that falls into the ground and dies, dies not once, but many times in the course of a lifetime (John 12:24).

William Reiser, s.j.

See also BAPTISM / CONFIRMATION; DESCENT INTO HELL; ESCHATOLOGY (IN CHRISTIANITY); ETERNAL LIFE; ETERNITY; SIN, PERSONAL.

DEATH (IN JUDAISM)

While recognizing that the ultimate reason for the existence of death is Adam's sin, Judaism understands the proximate cause of each person's death to be his or her own personal sin. No person on earth is totally without sin, and therefore, like Adam, each dies on account of his or her own actions during life (Babylonian Talmud Shabbat 55a-b; cf., Exodus Rabbah 2). The notion that the individual is responsible for his or her own death is modified only to explain the death of the obviously innocent, for example, children, who are understood to die because of sins of others, for instance, unfilled vows made by their parents (Babylonian Talmud Shabbat 32b).

Viewing death as the result of sin, Judaism considers death, in conjunction with repentance, to be the greatest act of atonement (Mishnah Yoma 8:8). Death does not, however, lead invariably or immediately to heavenly life. Rather, Judaism describes the first year after death as a period of judgment, during which the soul remains in contact with the disintegrating body (Babylonian Talmud Shabbat 152b-153a) and during which prayers of mourners can sway God's decision. After this period of judgment, the souls of the righteous go to paradise ("Gan Eden," the Garden of Eden) and the souls of the wicked go to hell (*gehinnom*). At the eventual coming of the messiah, the souls of the righteous will be reunited with the bodies that they once occupied.

Alan J. Avery-Peck

See also SOUL (IN JUDAISM).

DEATH OF GOD THEOLOGY

A theological movement of the 1960s—associated with William Hamilton, Paul van Buren, Thomas J. J. Altizer, and Gabriel Vahanian—that sought to incorporate an explicit and principled atheism within the possibilities of Christian faith (or, in the case of Richard Rubenstein, within the possibilities of Jewish faith). Appealing to a diverse set of sources, for example, William Blake, Mircea Eliade, Friedrich Nietzsche, and Dietrich Bonhoeffer, death of God theology argued that orthodox theism is inherently supernaturalistic and thus incompatible with both the reality and full affirmation of contemporary secularism. Further, all forms of theism are ultimately supernaturalist. Thus, to acknowledge and embrace the reality of secularization is to reject theism as such. In the absence of explicit talk about God, the figure of "Jesus"—whose crucifixion was the "death of God"—became the major focus of this theology's reflection, albeit a Jesus understood a-theologically, that is, apart from the reality of God. As a theological movement, death of God theology was extremely short-lived, succumbing quickly to charges of incoherence in critiques such as that of Langdon Gilkey.

J. A. Colombo

See also GILKEY, LANGDON.

"DE AUXILIIS" CONTROVERSY

See GRACE; MOLINA, LUIS DE.

DEBORAH

A female character of the Old Testament whose story is found in Judges 4–5. She is the only woman credited with being a judge. Because of the likely age of the poetic account in Judges 5 (twelfth century B.C.E.), scholars believe there is a kernel of historical accuracy in the account. Judges 4 provides a duplicated prose account of her role in the defeat of Sisera. Deborah is also one of only four women in the Old Testament identified as a prophet (cf. Miriam, Huldah, and Noadiah).

Feminist historical critics, in particular, stress that women in Israel's earliest history most likely assumed more positions of leadership than they came to have during the monarchy.

Alice L. Laffey

DECALOGUE

(Hebrew, *Eseret HaDibbrot*, "the ten words"). The Ten Commandments, a collection of laws found at Exodus 20:1-17 and, in a slightly different form, at Deuteronomy 5:6-21; understood by Judaism and Christianity to be the foundation of all proper moral and religious behavior. While honoring the Ten Commandments as central to religious life, Judaism views these rules within the context of the longer legal codes in which they appear. In this way, Jewish theologians and legal thinkers have combated the idea that the Decalogue alone was given by God or that only these ten rules are obligatory. Jewish authors (other than Philo) thus do not use the Ten Commandments as headings under which the remainder of the law can be classified. Christians, by contrast, who view the law to have been abrogated by Jesus, tend to see in the Ten Commandments a complete statement of God's ethical demands. Beginning in medieval times, Roman Catholic thinkers in particular have viewed the Decalogue as a condensation of all of natural law.

The Decalogue has been interpreted in a number of ways, with Jews and groups within Christianity suggesting divergent enumerations of the ten individual commandments. These distinct interpretations yield, as well, different accounts of the number of commandments that pertain to the relationship between people and God and the number that control the relationship among people in society.

Alan J. Avery-Peck

DECLARATION (DOCUMENT)

A declaration is a church document issued by an ecumenical council or a Roman curial congregation. Its canonical status is such that it is not a definitive statement. In a canonical understanding of the authority of church documents, declarations are not considered infallible utterances of the magisterium.

Mary Ann Hinsdale

See also CANON LAW; CURIA, ROMAN.

DECONSTRUCTION

Deconstruction names both a philosophical school and a type of Anglo-American literary criticism closely associated with poststructuralism and postmodernism. Deconstruction's influence is felt in fields ranging from architecture to anthropology, theater to theology. Created by the French philosopher Jacques Derrida, deconstruction exposes the way Western metaphysical thought has misunderstood the nature of language, thus yielding the idea that texts possess unchanging, unambiguous meaning. As philosophical activity, deconstruction designates a certain way of interrogating the self-evident concepts and ruling axioms that undergird traditional Western metaphysical or "logocentric" thought (for example, reason, truth, the good, God, essence) as well as institutional structures that embody those concepts today (such as democracy, market economy, and monotheistic religion). Western thought features a binary structure (presence/absence, divine/human, transcendence/immanence) and a hierarchy of violence that suppresses one term of the opposition at the expense of the other. Attending respectfully to the language of texts, deconstruction intervenes in those very structures of authority that shape Western thinking. It is most interested in what is marginal or excluded by the structure. Accused often of being nihilistic, deconstruction, Derrida insists, is a positive action. Deconstruction aspires to think through and to take responsibility for the way language is used in the world.

As one strategy for reading texts, deconstruction ordinarily proceeds in two stages. The first exposes the value-laden hierarchies expressed in a text (for instance, male over female, inside over outside, spirit over flesh) and the relationship of mutual dependency one term has with the other. The second inverts and disrupts this hierarchy. The aim is to exploit the pro-ductive tension that exists between these terms. Thus, deconstructive reading opens up the text for a new intelligibility. In this way, it deliberately searches out unexamined or marginalized meanings that a text harbors—the surplus of meaning that ever exceeds what an author might intend or a reader might discover. Deconstruction differs from traditional forms of interpretation interested in finding that one, true, original meaning of a text. Rather, it is concerned with the generative process by which texts produce meaning over and over again. Deconstruction and deconstructive literary criticism, when directed to religious texts such as the Bible, help expose the way the Bible as a text continues to offer powerful new, even contradictory, meanings, and why critical readers have an ethical responsibility to read between the lines.

Gary A. Phillips

See also DERRIDA, JACQUES; LITERARY CRITICISM; POSTMODERNITY.

DECRETALS

Decretals are papal letters (canonical documents) that are used as sources for church law. Starting in the eleventh century, papal letters were included in collections of canon law. Not all papal letters were included, since some dealt with particular local issues, or simply weren't available to the compiler. Once a letter was included in a collection, however, it was considered a source for the law. Gratian included many decretals in his *Decretum*, but canonists soon started new collections made up of papal letters written after the time of Gratian. The most important of these collections were those made for canon law courses at the University of Bologna and approved by the papacy. A compilation of these collections was made in 1234 and issued as a papal lawbook. This compilation, the *Decretals of Gregory IX*, is included with Gratian's *Decretum* and, together with later collections of decretals, makes up the *Corpus juris canonici*, the law book used by the Roman Catholic Church from the thirteenth century until a new set of canon law was introduced in 1917.

Gary Macy

See also CANON LAW; GRATIAN; POPE.

DEER DANCE

The deer dance of the desert Southwest is represented in a powerful way by its performance among the Yaqui. It refers to the time in a not-so-distant past when the presence of deer was sufficient to allow hunting the species for subsistence. But the number of deer was severely impacted by colonization of the native lands, first by the Spanish, and later by the Americans. Reduced to a level of poverty, the Yaqui people continue to celebrate the gift of a beautiful creature and entreat it to surrender to their need. At the same time, they exemplify the attitude of reverence that should guide the hunter.

In the dance, a highly trained person evokes the presence of the deer by his costume, but especially by his demeanor and movements. Young boys play the role of the coyotes, and the dance ritually imitates the pursuit of the deer that is chased to exhaustion, and the febrile but annoying actions of the pursuers. All the while, the deer is beseeched to yield itself. The drama transports the saga of the hunted and the hunters to a cosmic plane on which the final surrender of the deer is an act of grace and love. The great circle of creation in its rhythms of life and death is affirmed as the central meaning of reality.

Kathleen Dugan

See also RITUAL.

DEFENSE

Distinct from a theodicy, a defense is a rebuttal to the claim that the problem of evil constitutes a proof of the nonexistence of God, that is, the propositions "God exists" and "Evil exists" are logically inconsistent. Let *p* be "An omnipotent and omnibenevolent being, God, exists" and let *q* be "Evil exists." To demonstrate that *p* and *q* are logically consistent, the defense seeks some proposition *r* that is consistent with *p*, and together with *p* entails *q*. In order to demonstrate logical consistency, *r* needs only to be *possibly* true. Alvin Plantinga is the foremost exponent of this position in his "free will defense."

J. A. Colombo

See also EVIL, PROBLEM OF; THEODICY.

DE FIDE

Latin phrase that literally means "of the faith," or "belonging to the faith." In Roman Catholic theology, any doctrinal statement is called *de fide* that has been explicitly and officially defined and declared as true by the church (that is, "true" because it is and has always been part of revelation). To deny or expressly contradict a *de fide* doctrinal statement would be considered heresy.

Orlando Espín

See also COUNCIL, ECUMENICAL; DEFINITION (OF DOCTRINES); DEVELOPMENT OF DOGMA/OF DOCTRINE; DOCTRINE; DOGMA; DOGMATIC THEOLOGY; FAITH; HERESY; PETRINE MINISTRY; REVELATION; RULE OF FAITH; TRADITION (IN CHRISTIANITY).

DEFINITION (OF DOCTRINES)

A solemn judgment made by an ecumenical council or the pope speaking *ex cathedra* ("from his chair," meaning with his full authority) that a truth has been revealed by God and has been definitively taught as such by the teaching office (magisterium) of the church.

Mary Ann Hinsdale

See also DOGMA; EX CATHEDRA; INFALLIBILITY.

DE FOUCAULD, CHARLES (1858–1916)

After a period of dissolute living and two brief stints in the French military in North Africa, Charles de Foucauld experienced a conversion that brought him first to the Trappists (1890) and then to embrace the life of a hermit in the Sahara. Born in Strasbourg, he was twenty-nine years old when he responded to the "call of the desert." Missioned to a poor monastery in Syria, Charles grew dissatisfied because he did not find the Trappists sufficiently austere. Struck by the severe poverty in which an Arab family was living, he determined to settle in Nazareth and lead a poor, simple life in the place where Jesus had lived. In 1901 he returned to North Africa where he lived and worked among the Tuareg people in the Sahara desert. His hermitage became a symbol of Christ's presence among poor, nomadic tribes in a Muslim world. Caught in what was probably a conflict of cultural identity and loyalties, he was killed in 1916. Although he had no followers during his lifetime, his writings and example provided the impulse for the founding of the Little Brothers of Jesus (1933), and then the Little Sisters of Jesus (1936).

William Reiser, s.j.

See also FATHERS / MOTHERS OF THE DESERT; INCULTURATION; MUSLIM; TRAPPISTS.

DEGANAWIDAH

In the great story of the founding of the League of the Iroquois, Deganawidah is the central hero. As the story tells, he was born among the Huron, and thus among an enemy people, at a time when all the Iroquois peoples were warring among themselves and with all others. When he grows to manhood, he leaves his family and tells them that he must go on a mission into the land of the enemy. In the course of his travels, that include marvels, he makes two converts who will help him. First, there is an old woman who becomes the first to accept the good news he brings. The second, the cannibal warrior Hiawatha, becomes his disciple and companion. The great obstacle to the acceptance of the message, that is essentially the way to peace, is the great chief Atotarho; he must be tamed and converted by the symbolic task of combing the snakes out of his hair. With Deganawidah's help, Hiawatha eventually succeeds in doing this. This is the key to all the tribes of the Iroquois, and so the principles of the good news become the foundation for the first democracy in the new world—the League of the Iroquois. Deganawidah, having finished the work for which he had come, departs mysteriously, but the league continues to support and guide the Iroquois nation as it has for at least four hundred years.

Kathleen Dugan

See also MYTH; REVELATION (IN OTHER RELIGIONS).

DEIFICATION

See DIVINIZATION; GRACE.

DEI FILIUS

Dei Filius is the Vatican Council I document on revelation and faith, written to clarify the church's position on these topics in view of modern philosophies and theologies considered contrary to traditional teaching. The document's exposition contrasts orthodox church teaching with erroneous interpretations. It delineates the classical nineteenth-century approach to the topic, defending the capacity of human reason for natural knowledge of God against atheism, agnosticism, fideism, and traditionalism. Against humanism and rationalism, it describes the human capacity (obediential potency) for revelation that perfects fallen human nature. Faith is proposed as an assent to revelation, assent to mysteries beyond human ken, that perfects humanity. The document identifies two fonts of revealed knowledge, Scripture and tradition, and explains the church as the sign and defender of revealed truth in the world. The document holds the positivist and ahistorical view of revelation and faith generally accepted in the nineteenth century, a view different from the dynamic historical view of revelation promoted by Vatican Council II in its document, *Dei Verbum*.

Patricia Plovanich

See also DEI VERBUM; FAITH; MAGISTERIUM, ORDINARY; REVELATION; TRADITION; VATICAN, FIRST COUNCIL OF THE; VATICAN, SECOND COUNCIL OF THE.

DEISM

The distinctive product of the European Enlightenment at the end of the seventeenth and beginning of the eighteenth centuries, the Deists—for example, Lord Herbert of Cherbury, Charles Blount, John Toland, Anthony Collins, Matthew Tindal, Voltaire, Hermann Reimarus—represented an attempt to rationally reconstruct religion (Christianity), to fit the emerging realities of nation-states, religious and confessional pluralism, and the empirical sciences.

In its negative task, the Deists were advocates of toleration (including "free-thinking") in a world of conflicting confessional beliefs that issued in the devastating religious wars of seventeenth-century Europe. Thus, they were ruthless critics of "priestcraft" and both dogmatic and scriptural sources of religious "mystery" that amounted, in their estimate, to little more than a sacrifice of common sense. In its positive task, the Deists argued that, correctly understood, Christianity was identical with a "rational religion" that was often equated with a primordial monotheism and whose hallmarks were the affirmation of the existence of God as the Creator, the universality of the natural moral law, and the immortality of the soul.

In fact, however, the reasonable Christianity of the Deists was an optimistic piety of confidence in the abilities of human nature, based on the axiom that "man is the measure of all things," and secured only at the price of isolating the Creator from creation. The methodological impetus of Deism, for instance, the mediation of Christian faith and modernity, was carried on in a subsequent movement, liberal theology.

J. A. Colombo

See also ENLIGHTENMENT IN WESTERN HISTORY.

DEI VERBUM

This document of Vatican Council II contains the council's teaching on the doctrine of revelation and its historical transmission to the church. Published after four years of debate (1965), the constitution signaled a significant shift in the

Catholic understanding of revelation. It abandoned Vatican I's positivist position in favor of a dynamic historical and interpersonal view of revelation. While it reiterates the traditional teaching of two sources of revelation (Scripture and tradition), it supports Scripture's primacy in the church that teaches as servant of the Word. The document paints a broad view of the Word of God that is active not only in doctrine and tradition, but in church life, liturgy, Christian practice, and so on. It approved of modern historical methods of biblical study and encouraged ecumenical cooperation in translating Scripture from the original languages. It names Scripture more clearly as a primary source of faith and life in the church and encouraged its study for ministry and for ordinary Christian life. The conciliar declaration has fostered Scripture study in the Roman Catholic community.

Patricia Plovanich

See also REVELATION; TRADITION; VATICAN, SECOND COUNCIL OF THE.

DE LA CRUZ, JUANA INÉS (1648/1651–95)

Mexican poet, dramatist, and theologian, Sor Juana Inés de la Cruz was the most significant colonial voice in Latin American letters. Her writings interwove a variety of sources, including Spanish literature, Christian theology, Greco-Roman mythology, and Hermetic philosophy. Sor Juana became an internationally recognized scholar during her lifetime, and she lived to see the majority of her works published in Spain. This occurred despite the fact that she spent the greater part of her life as a cloistered nun in Mexico. She was (and is still) known for her brilliant writings and her captivating life story. Unwilling to accept the exclusion of women from theological and philosophical discourses, Sor Juana challenged the gendered construction of these disciplines and pursued scholarship in both fields. While the details of the final years of her life remain murky to modern scholars, this brazen behavior led to the eventual silencing of her voice under what many interpret as ecclesial pressure. Among her most important works are *La Respuesta* and *El Divino Narciso*. Her *Obras Completas* (complete works) were edited by Alfonso Méndez-Plancarte and Alberto G. Salceda, in four volumes (Mexico City, 1995).

Michelle González

See also FEMINISM; FEMINIST THEOLOGIES; LATIN AMERICAN THEOLOGIES.

DE LUBAC, HENRI (1896–1991)

French Jesuit, theologian, professor of fundamental theology and the history of religions at the Institut Catholique in Lyons. A member of the New Theology movement, de Lubac was dedicated to retrieving the theological views of the patristic era and the Middle Ages. His major study, *Surnaturel* (1946) rethought the doctrine of grace and the relationship of nature and grace, not in the rationalist framework of Neo-Scholasticism, but with reference to early Christian sources. The study disputed the New-Scholastic category of "pure nature," explaining grace as the dynamic relationship of God to human persons who are created with an intrinsic desire for God. His discussion of faith's significance for modern atheism is seen in *The Drama of Atheistic Humanism* (1963). He was censured by Roman authorities for his views but vindicated when made a *peritus* (expert) to Vatican Council II. He was made a cardinal in 1983.

Patricia Plovanich

DE MARILLAC, LOUISE (1591–1660)

Saint Louise de Marillac was born in Paris, France, on August 12, 1591, natural child of Louis de Marillac, mother unknown. Louise married Antoine Le Gras in 1613, and bore a son, Michel. Upon Antoine's death in 1625, Louise took a vow of widowhood. By 1628, Vincent de Paul had given Louise the supervision and formation of the "Charities" he had formed during his missions to serve the village poor and sick. Eventually, women emerged to minister full-time. Louise formed the first Daughters of Charity that grew to become the largest women's "active congregation" in the world. While Vincent gave his time to the formation of priests, Louise, with Vincent, laid the foundation for the first of many active congregations of women to live and work outside the cloister. Canonized in 1934, Louise is patron saint of all Christian social workers. She died on March 15, 1660.

M. Jane Gorman

See also DE PAUL, VINCENT.

DE MESA, JOSÉ M. (1946–)

Filipino Catholic lay theologian, born in Manila. De Mesa earned his doctorate in systematic theology at the University of Louvain (Belgium). He currently teaches systematics at Manila's East Asian Pastoral Institute. De Mesa's theological work has centered around the relationship between religion and culture (more specifically Filipino culture), having created a very respected body of literature on those issues as well as on theological inculturation. His methodological contributions to the field of theological inculturation are among the most original anywhere within the past few decades. Among his best works are *In Solidarity with Culture: Studies in Theological Re-Rooting* (1987), and *Doing Christology: The Re-Appropriation of a Tradition* (1989).

Orlando Espín

See also INCULTURATION; METHOD IN THEOLOGY.

DEMIURGE

Used by Plato to describe God as the Creator, the term was used by some Gnostic groups for the lesser divine being who created the material universe in order to distinguish this being from the highest God of pure spirit. The demiurge in Gnostic usage would refer, then, to the God of the Old Testament.

Gary Macy

See also GNOSIS/GNOSTICISM; PLATO.

DEMON (IN THE BIBLE)

The Greek word *daimones* (masc.) or *daimonion* (neut.) denoted superhuman powers, good or evil, that are less than fully divine. Although the Septuagintal Old Testament Greek translation employs it scornfully for foreign gods, earlier biblical Hebrew usage is spotty and unclear. Scholars disagree whether such usage represents hostile (or neutral) superhuman beings, or poetic personification of uncanny natural events (plague, fever, frost, lightning, night sweats, dreams), wild animals with eerie traits, dead ancestors, or foreign gods. Jewish belief in God's cosmic rule impeded borrowing from popular Egyptian and Greek demonology, or Zoroastrian dualistic views of the spirit world. By the first century C.E., however, Judaism itself had developed an elaborate belief in an active swarm of unholy spirits or angels who plague humanity.

The New Testament writings, which view such demonic action as causing all sorts of human suffering, often blur the line between sickness and possession. The Gospels cite Jesus' dramatic success in breaking the grip of demons as confirming his claim that the domain of their leader Satan was collapsing under God's imminent reign. Jesus shares this power with his disciples in handing on his mission, and the struggle goes on in the early church. Acts offers several cases of exorcisms by Peter, Paul, and others, without the stress on names, techniques, and spells found in standard Hellenistic magic. Christian exorcists thus emerge as human agents of God's immediate, final rule. John's Gospel notably lacks any exorcisms, but still presumes the final collective downfall of such forces and their prince (12:31). The Pauline tradition and Revelation view demons in more moral, cosmic terms as the unseen spiritual forces that mislead believers, inspire secular rulers to oppose God, and provoke final divine judgment on the whole world. Patristic, medieval, and Reformation thought all see demons as a lower, debased angelic form of God's creation. Modern efforts to interpret such references in psychological, sociopolitical, mythological, or philosophical terms must wrestle with the limited but significant role they play in our sources.

Francis D. Connolly-Weinert

DEMON (IN WORLD RELIGIONS)
This is an ambiguous term that refers to any spirit. It is frequently attributed, however, to an evil spirit. Often, the term has been applied ethnocentrically to refer to spirits in non-Christian religious traditions. Typically, however, in a number of cultures, a demon is a superhuman being midway between humans and gods and often in a category of beings capable of either malevolent or beneficent acts. Demons may aid humans. But they are generally held responsible for disease, injuries, and personal and group disasters (both minor or catastrophic). In some cultures, demons are held to be more powerful than humans, but less so than gods or ancestors. Their characteristics, appearance, and behavior differ in various belief systems.

In Japanese religious beliefs, there are numerous kinds of demons. *Oni* are monstrous ghosts of the dead. The Yamauba is a "mountain hag," a cannibal who consumes children. Other demons in Japanese beliefs prey on women or are mischievous. Some are fierce, hideous, and horrible smelling, while others appear as humans. In many systems of belief, demons inhabit lonely, isolated, and often mountainous places. Hindu demons belong to castes, a social order that reflects that of Hindu humans. The categories of demons, then, reflect human classes and behavior. There are celestial and earthbound demons in Hindu belief. The earthbound ones are antihuman; they steal or defile the sacrifice and bother sacrificers. They wander at night and include *pishachas* (flesheaters).

In Greco-Roman and Hebrew thought, a connection was made between sorcerers and their spirit aids—*daimones.* In Greek cosmology, a demon could be malevolent or benevolent. Demons were identified as either almost a god (*theos*) or simply a spirit. Neoplatonists defined demons as between humans and gods. In Hebrew thought, the idea of the *mal'akh* emerged as an independent spirit sent as a messenger by God. In the Greek translations of the Hebrew, this term was *angelos*—messenger. But during the Hellenistic period (200 B.C.E.–150 B.C.E.), the belief in evil spirits led by Satan, the

Lord of Evil, became important. Christians divided the Greek *daimones* into two groups: the good angels and the evil demons. The demons were angels who turned against God as a result of Satan's influence. Ideas about demons, their link to Satan, and their propensity for evil-doing were tied to the development of ideas about witchcraft in Christian societies. During colonial encounters between Western and non-Western peoples, the Western notion of demon was used to label a variety of spirits, deities, and other entities that did not coincide with Christian beliefs.

Christine Greenway

See also ANGEL; COSMOLOGY; HINDUISM; MYTH; WITCHCRAFT.

DEMYTHOLOGIZATION

A critical method of interpretation of New Testament texts and Christian theology that was introduced by Rudolph Bultmann in his 1941 essay, "New Testament and Mythology: The Problem of Demythologizing the New Testament Proclamation." In this essay, Bultmann set the agenda for vigorous international, interdenominational, and inter-disciplinary debates among scholars for the next three decades. In this and subsequent studies Bultmann insisted that since the mythological world view presupposed and developed in the New Testament is obsolete, it is not only incredible but it is also an obstruction to faith and a betrayal of the essence of the New Testament.

Bultmann proposed that it was essential (1) to decode the mythological framework and imagery of the New Testament, and (2) to reinterpret its foundational kerygma in an existentialist way. Bultmann identified the first process as demythologizing.

He drew from the anthropological categories of Martin Heidegger for his existential reinterpretations.

It is essential to recognize that when he spoke about myth, Bultmann did not mean imaginary stories. He recognized myth as the images used in a prescientific age to express understandings of the nature of the universe and of other realities that informed the worldview that was presupposed by earlier cultures. Bultmann's intentions were profoundly pastoral. He recognized it was impossible for contemporary individuals to accept such constructs as a flat world and a three-story universe that are assumed in biblical texts. Bultmann was convinced that by eliminating these constructs, it would be possible to focus on the essential kerygma of the Gospel: the life and death of Jesus Christ as the ultimate act of God for humanity. He sensed that the process of demythologizing was already present in Paul and John, especially as they appeal to realized eschatology to emphasize the transformed nature of Christian life here and now even more than awaiting a final parousia.

While fundamentalist Christians completely rejected demythologization, critical scholars agree that Bultmann identified the very real problem of how to communicate the Christian message in the twentieth century. The negative reactions of critical scholars were not directed at the need to decode and reinterpret the mythical imagery, but against Bultmann's understanding of what are unacceptable myths. For example, Bultmann assumed that the resurrection of the dead and the miraculous are no longer tenable. Other scholars disagree.

Regina A. Boisclair

See also BULTMANN, RUDOLPH; MYTH.

DE NOBILI, ROBERTO (1577–1656)

Roberto de Nobili, born in Rome of a noble family, became a Jesuit missionary whose work in India from 1604 to his death in 1656 challenged the prevailing Catholic approach to evangelization of his day. Ordained a priest in 1603, de Nobili followed the lead of fellow Jesuits Alessandro Valignano (superior of the Asian missions) and Matteo Ricci in China who, instead of demanding that Asians adopt European culture along with Christian faith, urged missionaries to adopt the local language, dress, and culture as a way of drawing the upper classes of native society to Christianity. These elites, in turn, it was believed, would bring about the conversion of the masses. De Nobili thus became a *raja sannyasi*, or noble holy man, and had considerable success among the Indian nobility. In Europe, however, this method of "adaptation" to the local culture gave rise to years of controversy that only ended in 1623 when Pope Gregory XV and the grand inquisitor of Portugal both approved it. De Nobili's most important work *Gnaopadesam* (Spiritual Teaching) was written in Tamil.

James B. Nickoloff

DENOMINATION

A term that is frequently used, in public discourse, to refer to a branch of Christianity. It is often but inappropriately confused with "church."

Orlando Espín

See also CHURCH.

DENZINGER, THE

The frequent way of referring to the *Enchiridion symbolorum, definitionum et declarationum de rebus fidei et morum*, a comprehensive collection of the creeds, definitions, and declarations by/from popes and councils throughout the history of the church. This collection, first published in 1854, has been updated and enlarged in many subsequent editions. It has become a standard reference work among Catholic theologians who simply refer to it as "the Denzinger," because the original compiler and editor was the German Jesuit Heinrich Denzinger (1819–83).

Orlando Espín

See also COUNCIL, ECUMENICAL; CREED/SYMBOL OF FAITH; DE FIDE; DEFINITION (OF DOCTRINES); DOCTRINE; DOGMA; RULE OF FAITH.

DEONTOLOGICAL

From the Greek *deon* meaning "duty," deontological ethics refers to a branch of ethics advanced by eighteenth-century German philosopher Immanuel Kant that centers on identifying and fulfilling moral duties and obligations. Based on Kant's two formulations of the categorical imperative, the rightness of an act in a duty-based ethic is determined based on an intrinsic quality of the act, in this case, conformity to a universal moral principle regardless of real-life contexts and consequences, and respect for the intrinsic value of human persons as ends-in-themselves rather than means-to-other-ends. Deontological ethics, therefore, contrasts with utilitarian ethics or, as it is sometimes called, consequentialist ethics.

A duty-based ethic supports absolute moral principles, at times with mixed results. For example, a universal moral principle derived from natural law and demonstrated by universal human reason can help articulate shared human rights, goods, and responsibilities on the one hand, as well as simultaneously produce a more reified, restrictive moral law and/

or conflicting moral principles on the other. To mitigate these problems, especially with conflicting moral principles, modern and contemporary deontic ethicists introduce the notion of *prima facie* ("other things being equal") duties. That is to say, a *prima facie* approach to duty ethics rejects moral absolutist principles, and instead critically examines possibly conflicting principles in order to prioritize the principle that carries more moral weight. With the global rise of experiential, contextual, and indigenous theologies and ethics in the twentieth and twenty-first centuries, deontological ethics will need to deal more sufficiently with the possibility of conflicting moral absolutes (within and across societies) and to open up moral space for contextual concerns to play a more significant role in moral decision-making and action.

Rosemary P. Carbine

DE PAUL, VINCENT (1581–1660)

St. Vincent de Paul, patron saint of the poor, was born of Jean de Paul and Bertrande de Moras on April 24, 1581, in Pouy near Dax, France, and died on September 27, 1660, in Paris. Vincent founded the Congregation of the Missions (Vincentians or Lazarists) to serve the spiritual needs of the rural and urban poor and to assist in the reformation of the clergy through seminaries and ongoing education. With Louise de Marillac, Vincent established "Charities," groups of the laity, to care for the sick and poor throughout France. From these groups, the Ladies of Charity were formed both to serve the poor and to provide funds for the works. The Ladies continue to serve throughout the world. Louise and Vincent also founded the Daughters of Charity, the first organized group of vowed women to live in community among the people in order to care for the sick and the poor.

M. Jane Gorman

See also DE MARILLAC, LOUISE; VINCENTIAN FATHERS.

DEPOSIT OF FAITH

Derived from the Greek *paratheke*, "deposit" of faith is a specific term in modern and contemporary Catholic theology that refers to the full, complete, definitive revelation or self-disclosure of God in Jesus Christ reflected in Scripture and tradition, and that the church has received, professed, and handed on since the apostolic age. The deposit consists of the person and work of Jesus Christ for the sake of salvation as well as the treasury of Christian Scriptures (both the Old and the New Testaments), official teachings, and traditions, including liturgical traditions associated with the Eucharist, that are entrusted to the whole church.

Although used at the Council of Trent (1545–63), the term "deposit of faith" was introduced into common theological language in the mid-to-late nineteenth century. The First Vatican Council (1869–70) articulated the term narrowly to mean Christian doctrines as well as infallible papal teachings and other official teachings. Vatican I defended an objectified understanding of the deposit in response to (1) the European Enlightenment that consistently questioned all traditional authorities not grounded on reason, and (2) the rise of modern historical consciousness that challenged allegedly timeless religious truths. However, the limitation of the deposit to doctrines and other official teachings largely excluded nonordained, nondominant laity as well as women, especially marginated women, from the process of receiving, rearticulating, and transmitting the deposit to present and future Christians.

Vatican II (1962–5) rejected an objectified and propositional understanding of the deposit of faith as well as its associated institutional model of the church as an elite clerical guardian of orthodoxy for the majority of the laity. In the document *Dei Verbum*, the council fathers defined the term according to the scriptural understanding of sacred trust (1 Tim 6:20; 2 Tim 1:12, 14), with the Catholic Church acting as the trustee and interpreter of the sacred treasure, now understood as the living Word of God. The church regards itself as the trustee of this deposit, and seeks to preserve and profess it to and for all peoples and all times. In its understanding of its mission as trustee, the church cannot substantially alter this deposit, but can further interpret and expound on it regarding particular sociohistorical contexts and concerns. To curb the strong institutional dualism of Vatican I between clergy and laity, Vatican II proposed that not only the magisterial and clerical hierarchy, but also theologians and the entire church as a whole, bear responsibility for preserving, interpreting, and professing this deposit. This takes place, for example, in the reformulation of doctrines, in preaching, in the various methods of biblical and scriptural exegesis, and in the celebration of the liturgical life of the church, especially in the Eucharist that witnesses to the life, death, and resurrection of Jesus Christ for the purpose of the sanctification or growth in holiness of Christians. Of particular interest is that the more recent Vatican II notion of the deposit of faith, grounded in the total Christ event, recognizes rather than restricts the ongoing historical development of doctrine and tradition, as Vatican I attempted to do.

Rosemary P. Carbine

DERRIDA, JACQUES (1930–2004)

Jacques Derrida, French philosopher born in El-Biar, Algeria, the father of deconstruction, taught philosophy at the École Normale Supérieure in Paris from 1965 to 1984, the Sorbonne in Paris from 1960 to 1964, and at various universities in the United States, including Johns Hopkins, Yale, and the University of California at Irvine.

Noted widely for his unique style of critical reading of philosophical, literary, and historical texts, Derrida's deconstructive criticism exposes the way Western metaphysical thought has misunderstood the nature of language, thus yielding the idea that texts possess unchanging, clear, unified meanings. Deconstruction is a wide-ranging, interdisciplinary critique of this view of meaning and an effort to expose, interrogate, and change those institutional structures that sustain this view.

A prolific author, Derrida first laid out his deconstructive project in *Speech and Phenomena* (1967), *Of Grammatology* (1967) and *Writing and Difference* (1967), and subsequently in *Dissemination* (1981), *Glas* (1986), *The Post Card* (1987), *Spectors of Marx* (1994), and *Rogues: Two Essays on Reason* (2004).

Gary A. Phillips

See also DECONSTRUCTION; LITERARY CRITICISM.

DERVISH (DARWISH)

Originally, the term indicated the person who possesses spiritual poverty, and it was used in early Sufi texts for the one who was an ascetic or a hermit. In the context of virtue, it was associated with self-discipline, charity, humility, and truthfulness. Its most dominant meaning refers to the masters of Sufi discipline. From the thirteenth century, in the progressive decline of Islamic society, people turned to the Sufis for religious guidance. The orders became the primary vehicle for the teaching of popular religion and for inspiration in its practice. Each order is headed by a master (shaykh) who is credited with supernatural powers and knowledge. This person is the spiritual guide of each member. Initiation can direct a candidate to either a vocation in the world or as member of the ascetic discipline of the Sufi inner community. The ideal includes continual initiation in prayer and into the most advanced doctrines and techniques of spiritual practice.

The highly mystical tendencies of the community had produced mystics whose attainment in prayer became manifest in poetry and ecstatic dancing. In the latter, a state of deep meditation, even trance, is reached, and the individual is led by the Sufi leader into a ritually patterned dance. Seen in their striking white robes as they demonstrate a profound attunement to the Spirit at work within them, the "whirling Dervishes" make a lasting impression of spiritual virtuosity. Yet they have always had a very practical side, providing social functions, trade guilds, and education in the community, and serving in politics when there was a dearth of leadership. Primarily, however, they represent a mystical dimension in the wide spectrum that is Islam.

Kathleen Dugan

See also ASCETICISM/ASCETIC; ISLAM; MYSTICISM/MYSTICS (IN WORLD RELIGIONS); WHIRLING DERVISHES.

DE SALES, FRANCIS (1567–1622)

Preacher, bishop, and spiritual writer, de Sales was a native of Savoy whose influence spread throughout Europe. In the 1590s, he was an itinerant preacher in the Chablais region near Geneva, succeeding in his efforts to convince the population to return to the Catholic Church. De Sales was named bishop of Geneva in 1602, but resided in Annecy, as Geneva remained faithful to Calvin's reform. Efforts by de Sales to convert Theodore Beza, Calvin's successor in Geneva, were not fruitful.

In 1610 de Sales helped Jane de Chantal found the Order of the Visitation, a congregation designed, at least initially, to care for the poor and the sick, as well to lead a life of prayer.

As a writer, de Sales was concerned to help the laity lead lives as Christian as those of members of religious orders. In 1609 he published *Introduction to the Devout Life*; in 1616, *Treatise on the Love of God*. Both went through many editions and were translated into most European languages. The spiritual life, as articulated by the bishop of Geneva, was one of moderation and gentleness, one of progress in the love of God and of one's neighbor. Canonized in 1665, St. Francis de Sales served as a model of a bishop and pastor who implemented, in his life and work, the decrees of the Council of Trent on the reform of clergy.

Thomas Worcester, S.J.

See also BEZA, THEODORE; CALVIN, JOHN; COUNTER-REFORMATION/ CATHOLIC REFORMATION; SALESIANS; TRENT, COUNCIL OF.

DESCARTES, RENÉ (1596–1650)

French philosopher and mathematician, and inventor of analytic geometry, Descartes is generally considered the father of modern philosophy because he succeeded in directing the attention of the philosophical community away from external entities and toward the experiencing subject as providing the starting point for philosophical inquiry.

In response to the skeptics of his day, Descartes sought to provide an indubitable starting point for his philosophy, and he claimed to have accomplished this through the application of his famous method of doubt. This method serves as a kind of sieve that separates things that are doubtable from things that are not. In the *Meditations*, he applies the method first to distant and very small things in the outside world, and he concludes that it is easy to doubt things of this sort. The possibility that he might be dreaming allows him to doubt the existence and nature of nearby things, including his own body. Finally, the possibility that a supremely powerful and malicious demon is deceiving him allows him to doubt even the operations of his own memory. However, as long as he is thinking, he finds that it is impossible to doubt the existence of his own mind. This intuition, expressed in the famous dictum, "Cogito, ergo sum." (I am thinking, therefore, I am), provides Descartes with the absolutely certain starting point that he had been seeking.

Upon examining the content of his own mind, the existence of which he is now assured, Descartes now finds that he possesses an idea of an infinitely perfect being. This discovery leads to three arguments for the existence of God. The one that is most uniquely Descartes' proceeds by distinguishing the formal reality of this idea from the objective reality. The formal reality is merely the idea as an entity in his mind, while the objective reality is what the idea is *of*—that is, an infinitely perfect being. According to the

principle of causality, this objective reality needs a cause, and the cause must be as perfect and real as the effect—that is, infinitely real and infinitely perfect. We call this infinitely perfect cause "God."

Proceeding, Descartes concludes that God is responsible for his (Descartes') very being. Furthermore, given that God is infinitely perfect, it follows that he is infinitely veracious. Thus, Descartes can be assured that he is not being deceived as long as he uses every effort to avoid deception. To conclude otherwise would imply that God is responsible for deception, which is impossible. An analysis of the nature of error leads Descartes to conclude that he will avoid deception if he bases all his judgments on ideas that are clear and distinct. Thus, memories that are clear and distinct are trustworthy, and this conclusion eliminates the possibility of universal deception by a malicious demon.

Proceeding further, Descartes finds that he has many ideas of physical objects in a world existing outside of his mind. However, the only clear and distinct ideas that he has of these objects are those that are describable in terms of the so-called primary qualities—extension, figure, and motion. In contrast, the ideas of these objects as qualified by the secondary qualities (color, sound, taste, fragrance, warmth, coldness, and so on) are not clear and distinct. Thus, Descartes is justified in concluding that an outside world exists, but only an outside world qualified by the primary qualities (the qualities measurable by mathematics). Colors, sounds, tastes, and the like, do not actually exist in the outside world, but are produced by the activity of the mind itself.

As a result of this procedure, Descartes is left with two fundamentally different kinds of substance (in addition to the divine substance)—body, which is extended and material, and mind, which is unextended and immaterial. This bifurcated universe leads to the famous mind–body problem that concerns the apparent impossibility of any interaction between the extended, material human body and the unextended, immaterial mind (there being no point of contact between the two). Descartes attempted to mitigate the seriousness of this problem by situating the mind in the pineal gland of the brain, and by endowing that gland with subtle humors that were supposed to provide a medium of interaction. However, it was immediately apparent to most philosophers of the time that this appeal to the pineal gland solved nothing.

In Descartes' system, God serves as the bridge between the mind and the outside world. Should any defect exist in his arguments for the existence of God, Descartes is left with solipsism, which is the condition of being totally isolated from an independently existing physical world. In such a condition, all Descartes' ideas, with the sole exception of *Cogito ergo sum*, become mere illusions. This fact had serious repercussions for Descartes' successors in the modern period, and it constitutes an important challenge for any attempt to commence philosophical inquiry with an analysis of the experiencing subject.

Descartes' more important writings include *Rules for the Direction of the Mind* (written in 1628 or 1629, published posthumously in 1701), *Geometry* (1637), *Discourse on Method* (1637), *Meditations on First Philosophy* (1641), *Principles of Philosophy* (1644), and *Passions of the Soul* (1649).

Patrick J. Hurley

DESCENT INTO HELL

This term refers to Jesus' descent into hell, an article in the Apostles' Creed (eighth century) that asserts an event omitted in the Nicene-Constantinople Creed, a state or stage between Jesus' death and resurrection associated with Sheol, the place of death in ancient Judaism. The phrase is not rooted in the biblical resurrection tradition, but suggests an interpretation of the soteriological significance of Jesus' death. It emphasizes the reality of Jesus' death (he enters the place of the dead) and thus his solidarity with the human condition (as opposed to the Nicene silence on this event). A later interpretation of the article proposed his appearance to ancient holy persons whose salvation was incomplete until the Christ-event. This legendary tradition is not related to early convictions about the human reality of Jesus' death, but it suggests the historical inclusiveness of the Christ-event and the cosmological shift it engendered, namely, the victory over death and the beginning of the perfection of all creation, signaled in the Resurrection.

Patricia Plovanich

DETERMINISM

A general name given to a number of diverse philosophical systems and doctrines that share a common belief in humankind's (or even the universe's) subjection to rigid laws. These laws would make chance impossible and human free choice ultimately pointless, according to determinism. Evidently, if determinist philosophies were correct, all ethics and morality would be meaningless, and the social status quo must be judged impermeable to human-chosen change. Some Christian theological views seem to espouse some form of determinism, especially in reference to predestination.

Orlando Espín

See also ELECTION (DOCTRINE OF); ETHICS; FREEDOM; FREE WILL; IDEOLOGY (IDEOLOGIES); JUSTICE; PREDESTINATION (IN CHRISTIANITY).

DEUS ABSCONDITUS
A Latin phrase that means "hidden god." It is used in the study of religions to describe the "hidden" character or nature of the gods and/or of divine activity. The Judeo-Christian God is at times also referred to as a "hidden God" in Scripture (for instance, Pss 10; 102; 104). Olódùmarè (the supreme god of Yoruba traditional religion, and of Santería and Candomblé) is also considered a *deus absconditus*.

Orlando Espín

See also AFRICAN TRADITIONAL RELIGIONS; AFRO-LATIN RELIGIONS; CANDOMBLÉ; DEUS OTIOSUS; GOD; HIGH GOD/SUPREME GOD; OLÓDÙMARÈ; RELIGION; REVELATION; SANTERÍA.

DEUS EX MACHINA
In Greek and Roman theater, a god lowered to the stage by a machine to rescue the hero from difficult circumstances or to resolve an impasse in the plot. The phrase is used with a negative connotation to describe an arbitrary resolution by God of some theological or religious difficulty. More broadly, the phrase is used to describe a popular and naive supernaturalistic theism where God intervenes only as a last resort in the world or human affairs when these have arrived at the limits of their ability to resolve difficulties.

J. A. Colombo

DEUS OTIOSUS
A Latin phrase that means "idle god." It is used in the study of religions to describe the "idle" or "distant" character (or nature) of the supreme or highest God. For example, Bondyé (the supreme God in Vodoun) is a *deus otiosus* who created the world but left its daily workings to lesser divinities or spirits.

Orlando Espín

See also AFRICAN TRADITIONAL RELIGIONS; AFRO-LATIN RELIGIONS; DEUS ABSCONDITUS; GOD; HIGH GOD/SUPREME GOD; RELIGION; VODOUN.

DEUS PRO NOBIS
A Latin phrase that means "God for us." It has been used in Christian theology in various contexts and times, and by many authors.

Orlando Espín

See also CHRISTOLOGY; COUNTER-REFORMATION/CATHOLIC REFORMATION; CROSS, THEOLOGY OF THE; FAITH; GRACE; JUSTIFICATION; LUTHER, MARTIN; REFORMATION; REVELATION (IN CHRISTIAN PERSPECTIVE); SALVATION; TRENT, COUNCIL OF.

DEUTEROCANONICAL
Within biblical studies, deuterocanonical refers to those compositions and parts of compositions that existed in the Greek Septuagint and thus in the Latin Vulgate, but not in the Hebrew Bible. They were thus not a part of the Jewish biblical canon and the Protestant canon of the Old Testament. These compositions were affirmed as canonical by the Council of Trent in 1548, but secondarily so since they were not a part of the "proto canon" in Hebrew. The deuterocanonical books include: Tobit; Judith; The Wisdom of Solomon; Ecclesiasticus (= The Wisdom

of Jesus the son of Sirach); Baruch; the Letter of Jeremiah (= Baruch 6); the Prayer of Azariah, and the Song of the Three Young Men; The History of Susanna; Bel and the Dragon; 1 and 2 Maccabees.

Russell Fuller

DEUTERONOMIC HISTORY

The account of the history of the people of Israel as it is relayed in the biblical books of Joshua through 2 Kings. The historical-critical scholar Martin Noth proposed, in the mid-twentieth century, that those books the Jews traditionally refer to as "the books of the former prophets" and that Christians consider "historical books," are really a unified history, composed of various sources, to be sure, but a unified history nevertheless. This literature traces the life of the people of Israel from their conquest of Canaan through the period of the judges, the establishment of a monarchy and then a dynasty, the division of the kingdom into north and south (Israel and Judah, respectively) and then to the fall of Israel to Assyria in 721 B.C.E. and of Judah to Babylonia in 586 B.C.E. What holds this history together is Deuteronomic Theology.

The Deuteronomic History (sometimes also referred to as Deuteronomistic, allowing for additional levels of redaction) incorporates several sources. One notes, for example, the repetition and seeming contradictions between the end of the book of Joshua and chapter 1 of the book of Judges. One notes also a bit of confusion about the competing and/or complementary roles of the northern prophets Elijah and Elisha. There seems also to be a Saul source and a Samuel source, each highlighting its "hero." And there are duplications in how Saul and David came to meet, how Saul sins to deserve to be re-

jected as monarch, and so forth. Though the book of Deuteronomy is not actually a part of what is termed the "Deuteronomic History," the history is dependent on it. Israel's history and its actors are judged by their faithfulness and/or unfaithfulness to Israel's God, that is, by their obedience and/or disobedience to the teachings and laws of God as expounded in the book of Deuteronomy.

Alice L. Laffey

DEUTERONOMIC THEOLOGY

The articulation of the covenant of God with Israel in terms of God's *hesed* (compassion) and Israel's faithfulness/obedience. The theology is conditional, whereby Israel is understood as being blessed by God (that is, long life in their land, fertility, and prosperity) as long as they remain faithful to God's teaching; on the other hand, if they are disobedient, that is, unfaithful to God's law, they will be cursed and punished. They will lose the land (Josh 23:16, for example). This theology is implicit in the Decalogue itself and in the case laws following the Decalogue. Deuteronomy 28 provides a clear articulation of the blessings the people will receive for their faithfulness, and the curses for their unfaithfulness.

Within the Deuteronomic History, this theology is most succinctly seen in the book of Judges. As long as a judge is leader of the people, these people are faithful to their God; when, however, the judge dies, these people fall into idolatry, provoking God's anger; God then punishes the people; God sells the people into the hands of an enemy who oppresses them; in their distress they cry out to God for deliverance. God hears their prayer and sends a savior/judge. All goes well, that is, the people are faithful and prosper until the death of the leader. The cycle repeats itself again and again.

The theology appears in 2 Samuel also. Because of David's sin of taking Bathsheba, his punishment, announced to him by the prophet Nathan (2 Sam 12), is that the sword will never depart from his house. The remainder of the Deuteronomic History chronicles the "sword's presence" in David's family (the rape of his daughter Tamar, the killing of his son Amnon by his son Absalom, the death of his son Absalom, the death of his son Adonijah, and so on) and in David's dynasty (political difficulties leading to the fall of Judah in 586 B.C.E.). Nevertheless, David is represented as being more faithful than Saul, for which reason he is chosen in place of Saul, and it is because of David's faithfulness that one part of the kingdom remains with his dynasty.

Alice L. Laffey

See also DAVID; DECALOGUE.

DEVA/DEVI

A *deva* (Sanskrit, shining one) is a god or deity in Hinduism. Although High Gods such as Vishnu and Shiva are sometimes addressed as Deva or Mahadeva (Great God), when Hindus speak of "the *devas*" in the plural they are speaking of the many lesser gods recognized by the tradition. The devas are powerful spiritual beings, somewhat like angels in the West, who have certain functions in the cosmos and live immensely long lives. Certain devas, such as Ganesha, are regularly worshiped by the Hindu faithful. Note that, while Hindus believe in many devas, many are also monotheistic to the extent that they will recognize only one Supreme Being, a God or Goddess who is the source and ruler of the devas. The feminine form of deva is *devi*, "goddess."

The great Goddess—Shakti or Parvati—is often referred to as the Devi.

Lance E. Nelson

See also GANESHA; HINDUISM; MONOTHEISM (IN CHRISTIANITY AND ISLAM); POLYTHEISM; SHAKTI; SHIVA; VISHNU.

DE VAUX, ROLAND (1903–71)

French Dominican archeologist and biblical scholar, resident at the Ecole Biblique et Archéologique in Jerusalem. Fr. de Vaux was well known as an archeologist who excavated Khirbet Qumran and led the international team of scholars assigned to edit the Dead Sea Scrolls. De Vaux was also known as an excellent teacher and biblical scholar. His widely used volume *Ancient Israel* grew out of his teaching at the Ecole.

Russell Fuller

DEVELOPMENT OF DOGMA/OF DOCTRINE

The question of development is basically whether it is truth itself that changes or whether it is our understanding of the truth that expands and deepens. The Catholic Church insisted for centuries, under the influence of a static view of truth and the way human understanding works, that there could not be a change in or evolution of dogma. But such a position proved increasingly vulnerable to historical study of church doctrines. And as the modern science of hermeneutics has shown, human understanding itself is profoundly historical; the notion of "timeless truths" is misleading.

The idea of doctrinal or dogmatic development received classic formulation and resolution from Cardinal Newman in the nineteenth century, although in the early twentieth century, in the midst of the Modernist crisis, the official church rejected the notion of development altogether. When Pope John XXIII, in convening the Second Vatican Council, said that it was necessary to distinguish between the substance of the faith and the manner in which that faith has been expressed, some people concluded that he had been contaminated by the Modernist heresy. Cardinal Newman had argued for an organic model of doctrinal development: growth was a feature of living organisms that manage to maintain their identity even though they change; a proper understanding of how the mind works helps us to see that ideas and beliefs also develop organically.

The idea of doctrinal development helped theologians resolve the tension between the church's age-old profession of faith and the fruits of modern critical research into the history of doctrine. From a theological viewpoint, it enabled the church to enter the world of modern historical consciousness in which understanding is anything but static and impervious to change. At the same time, the notion of doctrinal development has perhaps been a bridge idea. The fact of development, even in matters of doctrine, is at this point beyond debate. Moreover, modern biblical studies have shown convincingly both the theological diversity to be found in the charter documents of Christian faith and a genuine development of belief within the first few generations of believers.

As historical consciousness has taken firmer hold, the idea of doctrinal development has receded in theology; scholars are increasingly investigating the social, cultural, political, and economic circumstances under which doctrines appeared, grew, and evolved. As Karl Rahner pointed out, the major christological dogmas of Christian faith, for example, should not be viewed as end points of theological reflection, but as points of departure for further understanding and integration with the totality of belief. One might argue further, however, that the term "development" does not accurately describe what took place in the course of the church's reflection on Jesus. "Development" implies growth and advance, but it would be very difficult to prove that the christological doctrines of the fourth and fifth centuries represent an improvement upon the New Testament. Not every change in understanding or expressing Christian faith is automatically a "development" of doctrine.

William Reiser, s.j.

See also DEFINITION (OF DOCTRINES); DOCTRINE; DOGMA; HERMENEUTICS; HIERARCHY OF TRUTHS; MODERNISM; PLURALISM.

DEVIL

Name commonly given to the source of evil and the personified adversary of God, primarily in the Christian and Islamic traditions. Muslims call the devil Iblis (from the Greek, *diabolos*) or Shaytan ("Satan" or "the adversary"). Christians have referred to the Evil One as Satan, Father of Lies, Lucifer, and Beelzubub. Both Islam and Christianity teach that the devil has no power to make people sin. Each person freely chooses either to do evil, thereby embracing the cause of the devil, or to live in accord with the will of God. In both Christianity and Islam, allegiance with the power of evil condemns one to eternal punishment after death (hell), and those who reject the devil's enticements earn the everlasting reward of heaven (Christianity) or paradise (Islam).

Theologians note that the concept of the devil is not prominent in the Hebrew Scriptures and that the five books where the devil is mentioned were probably written after 538 B.C.E. This is significant because between 587 and 538, a prominent segment of the Jewish population was exiled in Babylonia until they were repatriated by the Persians who defeated the Babylonians. This means that during this period of the Babylonian Exile and the years after their return to Palestine, the Hebrew people were exposed to "foreign" religious traditions (especially Persian Zoroastrianism) which, in contrast with earlier Jewish thought, embraced a dualistic worldview and a belief in an evil power that rivaled and competed with the power of good. Yet even when mentioned by the Hebrew authors of these biblical texts, the devil (or Satan) is not portrayed as anything more than an adversary or a trickster. Association of the devil with the snake in the story of Adam and Eve's fall in the Garden (Gen 3:1-16) was made later by some Christian and Jewish writers.

The Christian New Testament makes frequent reference to the devil and to devils. In this Scripture, the devil tempts Jesus three times in the desert, causes illnesses of mind and body, and takes possession of people—even animals. We are also told that Jesus cast out evil spirits, and that it was after the devil had entered Judas' heart that he betrayed Jesus. These stories indicate a more developed belief in the power of evil among first-century C.E. Jews than is evident in the Hebrew Scriptures. It is also clear, however, that as powerful as the devil may be, New Testament authors record that demons always submit when confronted by Jesus and the Word of God. This suggests that while the early Christians certainly ac-

cepted the reality of evil and its devastating effects on the world and humans, they also understood that it is subordinate to God and will eventually be defeated by God.

In the Western world, many of the popular images of the devil as a fallen angel, the master of hell, and personal enemy of both God and people are derived largely from two sources. The first is the book of Revelation (New Testament) that speaks of "the huge dragon, the ancient serpent known as the devil or Satan" (12:9) who fought and lost a war with "Michael and his angels" (12:7) and was cast into the abyss of hell (20:3, 10). The other source is the epic *Paradise Lost* (1667) by John Milton, where Satan is depicted as having considerable influence over people and the world. Many Christian theologians today interpret the devil as a symbol of the reality and power of evil that manifests itself wherever injustice, violence, greed, or destructive behavior of any kind is found. Many other Christians, and virtually all Muslims, hold to the more literal view that the devil is a "spiritual person" and a fallen angel who is actively involved in human affairs and who constantly seeks new recruits for the realm of hell.

Ronald A. Pachence

See also DAMNATION; DEMON; EVIL; HELL; IBLIS; SATAN; ZOROASTRIANISM.

DEVOTIO MODERNA

The Latin phrase means the "new devotion" and refers to a renewal of spirituality that spread from Holland to Germany, France, and Italy in the fourteenth century. The leader of the movement was Geert de Groote, a preacher and writer who founded the Brethren of the Common Life. The classical expression of the *Devotio moderna* is found in Thomas à Kempis' *The Imitation of Christ*. The *Devotio moderna* is marked by a strong interior life with emphasis on contemplation, especially on the passion of Jesus.

Gary Macy

See also CONTEMPLATION; IMITATION OF CHRIST (BOOK, CONCEPT); MYSTICISM/MYSTICS (IN CHRISTIANITY).

DEVOTIONS

Acts of piety by individuals or communities, in public or private, to express their commitment to the Divine (divinities) and religion, or to seek specific favors, or to beg for mercy. Most religions know and encourage devotions. Although devotions might not be considered necessary to religion, the "devout" attitude (however it may be explained) is usually deemed essential. In some religions, devotional practices have become very important in the daily lives of the people and as support for their beliefs.

Orlando Espín

See also BUDDHISM; CATHOLIC TRADITION; HINDUISM; ISLAM; LATINO CATHOLICISM; POPULAR CATHOLICISM; POPULAR RELIGIONS; POPULAR RELIGIOSITY; RELIGION; SAINT; SAINTS (CHRISTIAN), DEVOTION TO; SANTERÍA; SENSUS FIDELIUM/SENSUS FIDEI.

DE WETTE, W.M.L. (1780–1849)

German Protestant biblical scholar who pioneered the application of historical-critical method from the study of literature to biblical studies. Arguing against the use of dogmatic premises for biblical exegesis, De Wette proposed that the discovery of the original meaning of biblical texts lay in authentic exegesis that required understanding biblical texts in relationship to their historical origins. He also encouraged the interpretation of documents based on their historical interrelationship, an interpretative method he utilized in his study of the relationship between the Pentateuch and the book of Kings. De Wette was a major figure in the early nineteenth-century movement toward the use of historical criticism in biblical studies.

Patricia Plovanich

DEWEY, JOHN (1859–1952)

Educated at the University of Vermont and Johns Hopkins University, a faculty member at the University of Michigan, University of Chicago, and Teachers College of Columbia University, Dewey was an educator, educational theorist, and philosopher. He contributed to U.S. religious life as an advocate of pragmatism and secular humanism. Although raised as an evangelical Congregationalist, he stopped attending church as an adult and was a signer of the "Humanist Manifesto" in 1933. However, he remained convinced of religion's importance in promulgating social and ethical values. His primary religious work was *A Common Faith* (1934) in which he argued for a democratic, natural faith. God was the idea that human beings could harmonize themselves with the universe. To Dewey, churches and synagogues were nonreligious when they excluded those who did not believe like them. He did not reject organized religion, but saw it as a vehicle for expounding the public good. Convinced theism and supernaturalism would be eclipsed by a reasonable, scientific faith, Dewey believed humanism was the religion of the future. Although Dewey was simply an infidel blasphemer to many devout believers, his ideas influenced not only humanists, but also many liberal Protestants, Catholics, and Jews.

Evelyn A. Kirkley

See also HUMANISM; PRAGMATISM; SECULARISM.

DHARANI

A Sanskrit term for a phrase that is chanted for mundane and spiritual effect, used by some authors as synonymous with *mantra*. The term's use was particularly popular in Mahayana Buddhism, showing the tradition's acceptance of theories associating sound and consciousness transformation via recitation that developed in later Vedic Hinduism. Some *dharanis* were described in Mahayana texts as a Buddha-derived recitations aiding study and essential to meditation; others were directed to the creation of a spiritually auspicious environment by attracting protective deities and/or exorcising evil beings. Still other early dharanis originated in efforts to strengthen the scholar's mind when memorizing and explicating texts.

In the visualization exercises of Mahayana Buddhism, the meditator places the enlightened figure in the mind's eye, then recites the dharani specific to that being in the quest to acquire the "divine realization." The most famous of such dharanis would be the *"Om Mani Padme Hum"* of Avalokiteshvara. In some cases, dharanis represented distillations of longer works, and the meaning of the words has relevance; in others, there is no ostensible meaning conveyed, although the tradition records episodes of revelation or meditation that explains their genesis and efficacy.

Todd T. Lewis

See also MANTRA; TANTRIC BUDDHISM.

DHARMA (IN BUDDHISM)

In Buddhism, the term *Dharma* (Pali, *Dhamma*) has meanings that vary from the general to the technical. The (usually capitalized) "Dharma" is one of the "Three Refuges" or "Three Jewels" to which Buddhists affirm their loyalty on every ritual occasion. As such it can refer to the Buddha's teachings as a whole, and mean as well "the Universal Truth" that is the basis of the Buddhist path's ascent to salvation. In all Buddhist schools, the Dharma as "Universal Truth" exists independently, as it is rearticulated by every Buddha and therefore existed before Shakyamuni, the current era's Buddha. Each Buddha is said to "Turn the Wheel of the Dharma" by proclaiming the Four Noble Truths.

In some textual passages, it can also refer to the religion overall. "Following the Dharma" or "Doing Dharma," common expressions in all Buddhist societies, mean faithfully acting according to the Buddhist Eightfold Path's moral and meditative regime.

In the early scholastic Abhidharma texts of the Nikaya schools, "dharma" (usually rendered in lower case) refers to an "ultimate constituent" of reality when experience is broken down to the simplest material and psychological components. Each dharma was said to have its "own nature" (*svabhava*) and to consist of a patterned continuum of momentary events of a particular kind. The most influential Abhidharma in North India, that of the Sarvastivada School, identified 75 *dharmas;* the Theravadin Abhidhamma identified 72.

It was this systematic formulation of reality in terms of permanent phenomena and atomic units that was strongly attacked by early Mahayana texts as transgressing the teaching of impermanence. Later Mahayana schools and texts, however, in their cosmological formulation of the "Three Bodies of the Buddha," defined the "Dharma Body" in two senses: as the inner nature shared by all Buddhas, particularly their supreme and perfect knowledge; and as the single, inner truth and essence of all reality, the Buddha nature within all beings and phenomena.

Todd T. Lewis

See also ABHIDHARMA/ABHIDHAMMA PITAKA; HINAYANA; MAHAYANA BUDDHISM; SARVASTIVADIN SCHOOL; TATHAGATAGARBHA DOCTRINE; TRIKAYA (DOCTRINE OF); VASUBANDHU.

DHARMA (IN HINDUISM)
In the Hindu tradition, *dharma* (Sanskrit, that which sustains) is an important term, but one that carries a wide range of meanings. Most commonly, it means "religious and social duty" or, more precisely, "religiously sanctioned ways of life and obligations." With *artha*, *kama*, and *moksha*, dharma is one of the classically recognized four goals of life (*purusarthas*) in Hinduism. As such, dharma evokes the idea of fulfilling one's duty to family and the wider society. The term *varna–ashrama–dharma*—the "duties (dharma) of caste category (varna) and stage of life (ashrama)"—reflects the Hindu idea of society as a social organism in which everyone plays a prescribed role (their dharma), as determined by their age, gender, marital status, family profession, caste category, and other factors. Hindu law books (Dharma shastras), such as the *Manu Smriti*, describe the dharma (duties and correct behavior) proper to each caste category, life stage, and so on in great detail. More broadly, dharma can mean "cosmic order," the principles by which the universe is sustained, corresponding roughly to concepts like natural law and Logos (in the West), and Tao (in Chinese religion). By extension, dharma can mean "behavior in accord with the law of the cosmos," thus "lawful behavior," "righteousness," or even (ethical) "goodness." In a famous passage in the *Bhagavad Gita*, Krishna explains that he, as God, comes to earth as *avatara* whenever dharma is in decline and social chaos (*adharma*) is on the rise. Finally, in modern discourse in India, the word dharma has come to be used as a translation for the Western term *religion*. Thus Hinduism is often referred to as the *sanatana–dharma*, the "eternal religion."

Lance E. Nelson

See also ARTHA; ASHRAMA (LIFE STAGES); AVATARA/AVATAR; BHAGAVAD GITA; KAMA; LOGOS (PATRISTIC TIMES); MANU SMRITI; MOKSHA; NATURAL LAW; TAO.

DHARMADHATU
Literally meaning "Dharma realm," this Mahayana term refers to the world as perceived by enlightened Buddhas, that is, where all phenomena are perceived as empty of independent existence, impermanent, in interpenetrating flux. It is the Hua-yen school of China, and particularly the *Avatamsaka Sutra*, that attempts to provide systematic explanations of the *dharmadhatu*. It emphasizes that the ultimate is not elsewhere than here and now, even in the most minute entity. To experience the world in this way is the goal of an advanced bodhisattva's meditation.

Todd T. Lewis

See also HUA-YEN BUDDHIST SCHOOL; PRAJNA.

DHARMAKAYA
The "Body of Dharma," a term originally used to distinguish Shakyamuni Buddha's

teachings as opposed to his physical body. In the first millennium, this term was given a metaphysical interpretation, first by the Sarvastivadins, later as part of the "Three Body" formulation of Mahayana metaphysicians. In the latter, the *dharmakaya* becomes the essential reality of Buddhahood itself, the inner nature shared by all Buddhas transcending all perceivable forms and limitations, an ultimate reality that can be discerned only by Buddhas. Aspiring bodhisattvas seek the dharmakaya in their quest for Buddhahood. Among the advocates of Buddha nature theory, such as the authors of the *Shrimala Sutra*, this is possible because dharmakaya is "beginningless, uncreate, unborn, undying, permanent, steadfast, calm, eternal." This text also proposes that the *tathagatagarbha* ("Buddha-womb") or *bodhicitta* within each being can be equated with the dharmakaya. In later Mahayana Buddhist iconography, the dharmakaya is symbolized by Vairocana, "the Resplendent One" who adopts the teaching pose.

Todd T. Lewis

See also BUDDHA; TATHAGATAGARBHA DOCTRINE; TRIKAYA (DOCTRINE OF).

DHIKR

An Islamic term meaning "remembering" or "mentioning." It is a practice particularly popular among Sufis, though all Muslims recognize its spiritual value. In general, *dhikr* involves calling to mind the glory of Allah (God), sometimes accompanied by the repetition of one of God's "Beautiful Names" or some other expression of one's faith. One can practice dhikr at any time (in contrast with the five daily prayers which must be offered at prescribed times) simply by reflecting on God's mercy or kindness or one of God's other qualities. Some believers use prayer

beads (like the Catholic rosary) to encourage frequent dhikr. In Sufism, dhikr has been formalized into a number of more elaborate prayer forms and methods of prayer. Under the guidance of their spiritual masters, Sufis have developed three major kinds of dhikr. The first consists of sets of phrases recited each day. The second involves remembrance coupled with breath control techniques. The third is a kind of group meditation that utilizes chant, music, and dance. Unlike the general practice of dhikr among all Muslims, Sufis rely heavily upon a guide or a recognized Sufi master called a *shaykh* or *pir* in their use of this kind of prayer.

Ronald A. Pachence

See also ALLAH; PIR; SHAYKH; SUFI/ SUFISM.

DHIMMI

This term refers to a protected class of non-Muslims living under Islamic rule. The *dhimmi* include all monotheists or, as Muslim law refers to them, *ahl al-kitab* (People of the Book), particularly Jews and Christians. As the etymology of the term suggests, the dhimmi enjoy a *dhimma* or "covenant of protection" as minority people in an Islamic territory. This indicates their kinship to, and hence right of protection by, their Islamic rulers as long as they fulfilled certain obligations like the payment of additional taxes. These taxes were imposed since the dhimmis were exempt from the alms (*zakat*) every Muslim citizen was expected to pay.

Ronald A. Pachence

See also AHL AL-KITAB; ZAKAT.

DHUODA OF SEPTIMANIA

Dhuoda was an aristocratic laywoman during the later Carolingian period. Deprived of her sons by the fortunes of war, she determined to influence their education and Christian formation by writing a book. The *Liber Manualis* (Handbook), completed in 842, contains brief narratives of her sons' family background, an exposition of the seven gifts of the Holy Spirit and the Beatitudes, a short treatise on the virtues and vices, and a structured program for developing the kind of Christian life appropriate to a civic and secular leader obliged to military and political duties. The heart of her text is an interpretation of the Scriptures, essentially a reading of the texts from the perspective of contemporary life. The tone of her book is both personal and didactic; self-revelatory, it has become an important source for social historians interested in the lives of women and the religious thought of the laity in the early Middle Ages.

Marie Anne Mayeski

See also CHARLEMAGNE; EXEGESIS/ EISEGESIS; LAITY; MEDIEVAL CHRISTIANITY (IN THE WEST).

DHYANA

In Hinduism, *dhyana* is the Sanskrit term for meditation. The classical description of dhyana is to be found in Patanjali's *Yoga Sutras*, where it is defined as an uninterrupted flow of the mind toward an object. Dhyana is the seventh of the eight disciplines (*anga*, "limbs") of classical *raja-yoga*, as defined by Patanjali. It is to be preceded by sense-withdrawal (*pratyahara*) and followed, if successful, by a state known as "absorption" (*samadhi*), a complete immersion in the object of meditation that leads to a mystical state of transcendence, in which one becomes aware of one's true Self (*atman, purusha*). The word dhyana is related to the Pali

word *jhana*, the Chinese *ch'an-na*, and the Japanese *zen*, all of which mean, roughly, "meditation."

Lance E. Nelson

See also ATMAN; HINDUISM; PALI; PATANJALI; PURUSHA; RAJA-YOGA; SAMADHI; YOGA; ZEN.

DIAKONIA

The Greek terms *diakonein*, "to serve," *diakonia*, "service," and *diakonos*, "servant," form a word group widely used within the New Testament to refer to service and ministry.

As reflected in the Gospels, which portray the ministry of Jesus as fundamentally one of freely given service, *diakonia*, his followers likewise are to pattern their lives on Jesus, to be servants, *diakonoi*, as well (Mark 9:35; Matt 20:26-28).

First Corinthians 12:4-11 makes it clear that the early churches understood the Spirit to be active in each believer, giving different gifts and ministries to each. Ministry is therefore the responsibility of each Christian, depending upon what the Spirit grants to each.

At the same time, within the context of ministry by all, Paul also uses *diakonos*, deacon, to denote certain individuals, both male and female, including himself, who had leadership roles in various churches. For example, in Romans 16:1, Phoebe is described as a deacon of the church of Cenchreae. (On the inaccuracy of calling her a deaconess, see the entry "Deaconess.")

In Philippians 1:1, within a greeting to all the Christians at Philippi, Paul links deacons with bishops, indicating both groups were in some way church leaders, although the sense remains ambiguous. It is significant to point out that the passage in Acts 6:1-6, the choosing of the seven (who are *not* called *diakonoi* in the text), is often mistakenly brought into discussions of the New Testament diaconate. In fact, the function of the seven, as reflected in the various stories in Acts about Stephen and Philip, had more to do with the role of evangelist (see Acts 21:8).

In the latter part of the New Testament period, as seen in 1 Timothy 3:8-13, the term *diakonos*, deacon, carries the nuance of being a specific office within the church structures emerging at that time. The writer of 1 Timothy in 3:1-7 describes the qualities that bishops (equated with elders in Titus 1:5-9) should have, followed in 3:8-13 by those of deacons. Timothy 3:11 lists qualities specific to women, referring either to those holding the office of deacon, or to the wives of deacons. If the text does refer to female deacons, some theorize that the need to list specific qualities for them (vs. no distinctions being made in the earlier period) hints at the gradual alienation and exclusion of women from key ministerial roles in the churches as more solidified leadership structures were developed.

In the case of each of the leadership roles mentioned here—bishops, elders, and deacons—it is not possible to tell from the New Testament precisely what their different duties were.

F. M. Gillman

See also DEACONESS; EPISKOPOS; PRESBYTEROS (IN THE NEW TESTAMENT).

DIASPORA

(Hebrew, "Golah," or Galut"). The term designating Jewish areas of settlement outside the land of Israel from the period of the Babylonian Exile of 586 B.C.E. and on (see, for example, Jeremiah 28:6; 2 Chronicles 36:20). Following the destruc-

tion of the Second Temple in Jerusalem (70 C.E.) and the failed Bar Kokhba revolt (133–5 C.E.), events that marked the end of any Jewish hope for renewed political control over the Promised Land, Jews grappled with the fact that Judaism in the foreseeable future would be a diaspora religion. In the face of the devastating wars caused by attempts to regain Jewish political control, rabbinic leaders rejected the use of military means to effectuate a return to the Promised Land. At the same time, they continued to dream of an end to the Exile, to be marked by the return of Israelite sovereignty over the land of Israel, the rebuilding of the Temple, and the reinstitution of animal sacrifice. Rejecting the political approach to these aspirations that had led, for instance, to the devastating Bar Kokhba revolt of 133–5, rabbis increasingly envisioned the end of the Diaspora and the return to the land of Israel in messianic terms, as events to be brought about directly by God in response to the Jewish people's proving themselves worthy of redemption.

In line with this approach, the rabbis frequently expressed their belief that the Diaspora was undesirable, the consequence of the people's sin (see Numbers Rabbah 7:10, Mishnah Avot 5:9, for example) and that the return of all Jews to the land of Israel was the ultimate goal of Jewish life (Genesis Rabbah 98:9). At the same time, just as they believed the Diaspora was a divine punishment for the people's sins, so they saw life in exile as an act of repentance (Babylonian Talmud Berakhot 56a). They described the suffering of life in exile as tantamount to all the other tribulations the people had endured combined (Sifre Deuteronomy 43). The suffering created by life in the Diaspora was so great that even God was understood to lament having had to respond to his people's sins by destroying the Temple and sending them into exile (Babylonian Talmud Berakhot 3a).

This negative attitude toward the Diaspora was balanced by the creation of religious behaviors and attitudes that would allow the Diaspora community to find meaning and closeness to God in its current life. Thus a central focus of the rabbinic movement was the creation of a Judaism that could be carried out independently of priestly activities and nationalistic governance that had defined Jewish life in the land of Israel. In particular, the rabbis legitimated Diaspora life by arguing that the Jerusalem Temple had never been the only place in which God could be found. God, rather, was everywhere (see Leviticus Rabbah 4:8 and Babylonian Talmud Berakhot 10a, for example). Even the question of whether God's presence had dwelled in the Second Temple at all was subject to debate (Pesikta Rabbati 160a). To lessen the centrality of the Temple cult in Jewish life, the rabbis imputed to a wide range of human activities that could be carried out in the Diaspora the power previously granted only to sacrifice. Along with daily prayers corresponding to the prior sacrificial worship, the rabbis saw in acts of loving kindness and study of Torah direct replacements for animal offerings (see, for example, Deuteronomy Rabbah 5:3, Mishnah Avot 3:2, and Babylonian Talmud Shabbat 199b).

Initiating a trend that would mark later forms of Judaism's response to Diaspora, the rabbis even identified positive consequences of exile, for example, in increasing the number of converts to Judaism (Babylonian Talmud Pesahim 87b) and in making the name of the people of Israel great throughout the world (Song of Songs Rabbah 1:4). In the contemporary period, such understandings of the significance of Jewish life in the Diaspora are commonplace, represented in particular in the notion that the Jews' mission to be a light to the nations can be fulfilled only if they live among non-Jews. The majority of Jews today—in particular those living in freedom in the Western world—do not in any way feel they belong in other than the country in which they live out their lives.

Judaism thus provides a multifaceted response to life in the Diaspora. On the one hand, as a punishment for the people's sin, exile historically has been viewed as temporary and a source of great suffering and degradation. On the other hand, the comfort and ease with which Jews have adjusted to life outside the land of Israel and the fact that the vast majority of Jews throughout history have not desired to return to the Promised Land have led Jewish thinkers to define modes of Jewish existence and to establish a theological foundation that allows Diaspora Jews to make sense of and find meaning in productive and happy lives far from the land of Israel.

Alan J. Avery-Peck

DIBELIUS, MARTIN F. (1883–1947)

Martin Dibelius was professor of New Testament exegesis and criticism at the University of Heidelberg, Germany, from 1915 until his death. Especially known for his pioneer studies in the form criticism of the Gospels, Dibelius was responsible for the term *Formgeschichte* (critical study of literary forms). His major work, *Die Formgeschichte des Evangeliums* (= *From Tradition to Gospel*), originally appeared in 1919.

F. M. Gillman

See also BULTMANN, RUDOLF; FORM CRITICISM.

DIDACHE, THE

The name of a brief manual on church practice and morals written around the year 60 C.E., probably in Syria, by and for an early Christian community contemporary with (or even earlier than) the Gospels. The *Didache* is immensely important for the study of early Christian doctrine, liturgy, and ministries.

Orlando Espín

See also APOSTOLIC FATHERS; CATECHESIS/CATECHETICAL; CHRISTIANITY; DEVELOPMENT OF DOGMA/OF DOCTRINE; DOCTRINE; ECCLESIOLOGY; FATHERS OF THE CHURCH; LITURGY (IN CHRISTIANITY); MINISTRY/MINISTERIAL; PATRISTICS/PATROLOGY.

DIDASCALIA APOSTOLORUM, THE

The name of an early Christian book that claims to be the "teaching of the apostles" (hence the name). It was probably written in Syria by a Jewish Christian about the year 210 C.E. In a disorderly fashion, the author discusses and copies liturgical texts and customs, moral teaching, doctrinal questions, and the like.

Orlando Espín

See also APOSTOLIC FATHERS; CATECHESIS/CATECHETICAL; CHRISTIANITY; DEVELOPMENT OF DOGMA/OF DOCTRINE; DOCTRINE; ECCLESIOLOGY; FATHERS OF THE CHURCH; LITURGY (IN CHRISTIANITY); MINISTRY/MINISTERIAL; PATRISTICS/PATROLOGY.

DIDYMUS THE BLIND
(310 OR 313–98 C.E.)

Blind since childhood, Didymus taught Christianity and philosophy in Alexandria, possibly as a distant successor to Origen at the catechetical school of Alexandria. Certainly, Didymus' many works depend on the earlier Alexandrian scholar. A prolific and long-lived author, Didymus produced commentaries on many of the books of the Bible (some of which now exist only in fragments), a book written against the Manichees, another against the later Arians, and a treatise on the Holy Spirit.

Gary Macy

See also ARIANISM; MANICHAEISM; ORIGEN.

DIGNITATIS HUMANAE

This Vatican II document, The Declaration on Religious Freedom (officially known as *Dignitatis Humanae*, the first two words of the Latin text meaning "human dignity") was promulgated by the Second Vatican Council on December 7, 1965. It was overwhelmingly approved after a sharp debate in the council that took up the Catholic Church's longstanding ambivalence about the doctrinal and pastoral implications of religious freedom. In its final form, the declaration affirms (a) religious freedom as a personal and collective human right (no. 2); (b) the duty of civil authorities to protect religious freedom (nos. 2 and 6); and (c) the church's right to proclaim the Gospel in every civil society (no. 13). In this way, the council overcame the historical inconsistency between the church's promotion of religious freedom in some instances and its opposition to it in others, depending on whether Catholics were a minority or the majority in society. Doctrinally, the declaration is significant because it simultaneously asserts religious freedom and religious truth. While the church remains committed to preaching what it holds to be the absolute truth of Christian revelation, it is equally convinced that religious coercion, by the state or the church itself, contradicts the very Gospel it proclaims (no. 12).

Another question addressed indirectly by *Dignitatis Humanae* is that of doctrinal change in the Catholic Church. Because it represents a significant shift on the question of religious freedom from the position asserted by Pope Pius IX in the *Syllabus of Errors* (1864), the Declaration on Religious Freedom demonstrates the possibility and legitimacy of doctrinal evolution.

James B. Nickoloff

See also DEVELOPMENT OF DOGMA/OF DOCTRINE; FREEDOM; PIUS XI, POPE; SYLLABUS OF ERRORS; VATICAN, SECOND COUNCIL OF THE.

DIGNITY

The value or worth that human persons intrinsically possess. Championing the dignity of persons, rooted in their creation in the Divine image and their vocation to nurture and sustain human life, and indeed all life on the planet, is the goal of social justice. Human dignity has traditionally been understood to be dependent upon the exercise of individual human rights. In their efforts to protect and achieve universal human dignity, Popes John XXIII, Paul VI, and John Paul II have enunciated in their encyclicals an order of human rights that includes not only basic civil rights characteristic of liberalism, but socioeconomic rights such as rights to a job, food, shelter, clothing, and medical care. In addition, the encyclicals of John Paul II insist that human dignity also entails one's participation in determining the structures of political economy that shape human life. For example, human labor is a necessary expression of human dignity and must be self-directed. These encyclicals claim that the dignity of persons will be achieved when social structures protect and pro-

mote these individual civil and economic human rights.

Recent work in feminist ethics extends this notion of human dignity by deepening awareness of the connections between civil and economic rights and friendship/sexual rights. For example, feminist ethicists wish to recover a respectful appreciation for the centrality of community and of pleasure and sexual well-being as basic to personal dignity. Their efforts are critical of the absence of mutuality and attention to community in the human rights tradition. This tradition, shaped by the Enlightenment and patriarchal Christianity, has been centered on autonomy, freedom from dependency, and the notion that self/other relations are nonmutual and can do without common goods, including friendship, pleasure, and self-esteem. In the feminist view, dignity is not only the achievement of individual human rights; it is something we bestow upon one another through interdependence in community.

Mary E. Hobgood

See also SEXUALITY; SLAVERY; VICTIM; WAR; WORK/EMPLOYMENT.

DIN

The Arabic word used in Islam for the practice of religion. Because Islam understands itself as a way of life involving every sphere of human existence, *din* applies to far more than spiritual concerns and matters of theological interest. This usage may be illustrated by contrasting how the adjective "religious" is commonly understood in the West with its application in Islam. When Westerners hear that a book or movie, for example, has a "religious" theme, they assume that it is about God or church or some spiritual subject. Muslims, however, would use "religious" to describe their entire outlook on life, from lifestyle to law, from piety to politics, from sacred to social concerns. Everything Muslims do is governed by their allegiance to *din*—the religion (Islam) chosen for them by God (Qur'an 5:3).

Ronald A. Pachence

See also ISLAM; QUR'AN; REVELATION (IN ISLAM).

DINNAGA

An Indian Buddhist logician of the fifth to sixth century C.E. and reputed disciple of Vasubandhu and Asanga, Dinnaga developed a formal system of logic called *Buddhist Nyaya*, derived from the Indic rules of orderly debate. The motive for Dinnaga's systematic development of argumentation was, in part, a response to the institution of royal disputation in which Buddhists had to defend the faith against opponents of other schools. His main works, including the *Pramana-sammuccaya* (*Compendium of the Theory of Knowledge*), became a standard text among later generations of scholar–logicians. Dinnaga was a proponent of the Yogachara school, although he reinterpreted the central arguments of Asanga in a manner that appealed to later Madhyamaka scholastics. He developed a theory of knowledge in which perception and inference are shown to be the only reliable means of understanding reality. Critiquing the naive assumption that words correlate with reality, Dinnaga sought to demonstrate that the Buddha's Four Noble Truths could be verified by perception and inference alone; the tradition's meditative traditions likewise were supported as they were argued to produce pure perceptions.

Todd T. Lewis

See also MADHYAMAKA/MADHYAMIKA SCHOOL; PERFECTION OF WISDOM SUTRAS; TRUTHS, FOUR NOBLE.

DIOCESE/ARCHDIOCESE

In many Christian churches (for example, in the Catholic Churches in communion with Rome, in the Churches of the Anglican Communion, and so on) a diocese is a territory governed pastorally by a bishop. In Orthodox Churches it would frequently be synonymous to the Western meaning of "parish." In Western (Catholic and Anglican) churches, an archdiocese is an important diocese that heads an "ecclesiastical province." An archdiocese is pastorally governed by an archbishop who, consequently, is that ecclesiastical province's "metropolitan." A diocese or archdiocese (especially in Catholic usage) bears the name of the city, within its territory, where the bishop has his cathedral.

Orlando Espín

See also ANGLICAN COMMUNION; ARCHBISHOP; BISHOP (EPISCOPACY); CATHEDRAL; CHANCELLOR; EASTERN CATHOLIC CHURCHES; ECCLESIASTICAL PROVINCE; EXARCH; METROPOLITAN; ORTHODOX CHURCHES; PARISH; PATRIARCH; ROMAN CATHOLIC CHURCH.

DIOCLETIAN

Roman emperor who led the last systematic persecution of the Christians in the earlier years of the fourth century (303–5). Dalmatian by birth, Diocletian rose to power in 284 when the emperor Numerian was killed in battle. The soldiers proclaimed Diocletian emperor, a role he assumed in 286 after the death of the co-emperor, Numerian's brother Carinus. Diocletian undertook a thorough reorganization of the Roman Empire in all its aspects, administrative, finanacial, military, and religious. He initiated an elaborate and elective form of rule, dividing the empire among two Augusti and two Caesars. To support the government, Diocletian associated all four rulers with the mantle of divinity, himself claiming descent from Jove. The persecution of his last years, one of the most brutal and systematic the Christians would experience, fit his plans to reunite the state under a single religious aura. Diocletian abdicated in 305, returning briefly to power in 308 in an attempt to support his already crumbling system of government.

Gary Macy

See also CHRISTIANITY; PERSECUTION (IN CHRISTIANITY).

DIOGNETUS, LETTER TO

Not a letter at all, the "Letter to Diognetus" is an explanation and defense of Christianity dating from the late second or early third century, possibly written in Alexandria. The anonymous author purports to answer questions put to him by the unidentified pagan, Diognetus. The only manuscript of this work was found in 1436 in Constantinople and destroyed in 1870 in Strasbourg in a military bombardment. Fortunately, good copies of the text had already been made. The author concentrates on the positive attributes of Christianity, pointing out the communal life of love Christians live and likening the enlivening action of Christians in the world to that of the soul in the body.

Gary Macy

See also APOLOGISTS; CHRISTIANITY.

DIONYSIUS THE AREOPAGITE (PSEUDO)

The author of several influential theological works who wrote under the pseudonym of the apostle Paul's disciple, "Dionysius" appears to have been a member of the school of the Platonic philosopher Proclus in Athens. Writing between 482 and the beginning of the sixth century, he produced *The Celestial Hierarchy*, the *Ecclesiastical Hierarchy*, the *Divine Names*, a *Mystical Theology* and ten letters. These works are marked by a preference for negative or apophatic theology, emphasizing the absolute transcendence of the divinity. "Dionysius" understands the entire universe to be ordered by the divine influence, and this same order ought to be reflected in the church. Thought to be actually written by the Athenian disciple of Paul (who was believed to have later converted the Franks), the works of Pseudo-Dionysius were extremely influential in the Middle Ages, especially among writers of a mystical bent.

Gary Macy

See also APOPHATIC THEOLOGY; MYSTICISM/MYSTICS (IN CHRISTIANITY); PAUL; PLATONISM.

DIRECTIONAL SPIRITS

In the image of the world that is an essential part of the Native American worldview, the earth is seen as the home of the earth surface people and the rest of creation. But there are other inhabitants who are pure spirits, and whose function has been to participate in the original creation/emergence and (usually) the migrations that follow. The directional spirits have a specific role; they are the guardians of the Four Directions, and they are understood to be persons responsible for the safety of the earth and its inhabitants. Their beneficent presence is acknowledged and invoked in every ritual and every act of prayer. As inherent structural powers, they are greatly revered. There is an alternate matrix that names six directions, adding the Above and the Below to the cardinal directions. This can be extended to seven by referring last to the "I" who speaks. The resulting image sees human life embraced by the cosmic powers and immeasurably blessed.

Kathleen Dugan

See also PRAYER; RITUAL.

DISCERNMENT
The development of the interior life obeys a logic long familiar to Christian saints and ascetics, but learning that logic can be a long, tedious, and often painful process. It is not always easy to tell whether the "movements" or "inspirations" one feels or experiences come from the Spirit. Often, an idea, image, intuition, feeling, and the like, seem to be clearly and unmistakably from God; so much so that one might believe the experience to be a vision, revelation, or interior "word" spoken by God. On reflection, however, it may turn out that the interior movement was not of God, but a subtle temptation or a delusion, or simply a mistake. The process of determining what is and what is not of the Spirit is called discernment. One of the best-known considerations of discernment for someone who is seeking the will of God can be found in the *Spiritual Exercises* of Ignatius Loyola, although contemporary writers normally update Ignatius's language and insight.

The basic criterion for discriminating between what is and what is not of the Spirit is perhaps summed up best in the text of Deuteronomy 30:15-20. What is of God promotes life, and what is not of God leads to death. That leaves the question open, of course, as to what life and death mean, and thus there emerges another set of categories. Whatever leads to deeper freedom, joy, peace, communion, love, and passion for justice is, by definition, life-giving. Whatever leads to confusion, discord, self-absorption, isolation, pride, and so forth, is death. In the language of discernment, the terms "life" and "death" are not biological terms but existential and spiritual ones. Discernment presupposes prayer and serious effort at leading a life of faith. Since discernment normally requires considerable attentiveness to one's inner experience, there arose the practice of spiritual direction to assist people in the development of their interior life. The need for discernment is not limited to individuals. Groups, communities, and even the universal church are to some degree always involved in the process of learning what is truly of God and responding accordingly. Thus Vatican II spoke of scrutinizing and interpreting the "signs of the times" (see the Pastoral Constitution on the Church in the Modern World, no. 4).

William Reiser, S.J.

See also EXAMINATION OF CONSCIENCE; SPIRITUAL DIRECTION.

DISCIPLE
Although the Gospels occasionally refer to disciples of John the Baptist, the word "disciple" (*mathetes*) generally applies to those who were followers of Jesus during his ministry. In Acts, the term refers to Christians. While the word disciple appears in the Gospel and Acts, the word *akolouthein*, "to walk behind" or "to follow" is found in the Gospels and elsewhere in the New Testament. Following Jesus is the best definition of discipleship.

There are some similarities between the relationship of Jesus to his disciples with the traditions associated with student–teacher relationships in philosophy or religious circles in the ancient world. Students learned by imitation of a master with whom they lived for a period of time to learn the appropriate teachings and lifestyle. This practice was followed by the scribes in postexilic Israel and later by the rabbinic schools of Judaism. However, the rabbis were petitioned by prospective students; Jesus alone called individuals to follow him. In addition, the disciples in the Gospels are not so much engaged in learning his teachings as by learning how to respond to Jesus as a person.

The term "disciple" refers especially to those who were among the inner circle of Twelve; it also applies to other men and women who made up Jesus' larger inner group of followers. Just as Jesus is understood as being sent into the world by God, so his disciples are those Jesus sends out to others. In the process of proclaiming his Gospel, his disciples memorialized his life and teachings. Some experienced rejection, persecution, and even death as part of their commitment to follow him. All who also sense themselves called into a relationship with Jesus learn by the teaching and witness of the first disciples and their early followers, which are recounted in the New Testament, the cost and nature of discipleship.

Regina A. Boisclair

See also DISCIPLESHIP.

DISCIPLESHIP
Discipleship summarizes the whole ideal of Christian life. It is first and foremost a lifetime commitment to Jesus. Such a commitment means consistently reordering one's heart and life in accordance with the will of God as interpreted by Jesus. It is a commitment that may lead one to a radical way of life in imitation of Jesus. This is illustrated in the Gospels when some of the individuals Jesus called left their families and livelihood to follow him.

During his ministry, Jesus taught his listeners that they had an urgent obligation to seek first the reign of God. He used parables to illustrate how God's reign is realized. He insisted that the poor, sinners, and others, marginalized by the social and religious constructs of his times, were welcomed in God's reign. In other instructions, Jesus clarified what it meant to follow him as a disciple. He indicated that those who seek to follow him must show the same outgoing love, acceptance, and service that marked his own ministry. In other words, discipleship must be characterized by self-denial, carrying one's cross, and following after him.

Many of the disciples of the historical Jesus would later also engage in an itinerant preaching ministry. They all experienced rejection and many suffered and died like Jesus. However, the Resurrection changed the focus of their proclamation. Jesus proclaimed the imminent inbreaking of God's reign. The disciples proclaimed their memories of Jesus' life, death, and resurrection. In their proclamation, Jesus' words and deeds became prototypes for Jesus' followers of all ages.

Discipleship today is the extension in time and space of those whom Jesus called to follow him during his ministry. It is manifested in engagement as healers in the world more than in theoretical discourse. It has social as well as spiritual ramifications and is corporate as well as individual. Discipleship still involves a break with anyone or anything in one's past that distances one from following

Jesus. It also means being open to the promptings of the Spirit. It is chiefly characterized by forgiveness of others as well as repentance for every failure to live as Jesus lived—in harmony with God and dedicated to loving service to others. It is comforting, however, to recognize that the inadequate responses of the disciples in the Gospels did not cancel their discipleship.

Regina A. Boisclair

DISCIPLES OF CHRIST/ CHURCHES OF CHRIST

The Disciples of Christ is a Protestant Christian denomination in the United States that formed in the 1830s from the fires of the Second Great Awakening. It began as a restorationist group on the Kentucky frontier, led by disaffected Presbyterians Barton Stone and Alexander Campbell. Stone's followers were converted in the Cane Ridge revivals of 1801 and called themselves simply "Christians." Alexander Campbell, his father Thomas, and others, formed the similarly named "Christian Association" in 1807–8. They sought to recover the pure, pristine New Testament church that would erase denominational division and unite Christian groups under the banner of "Christian."

In 1831–2, the Stone and Campbell groups united. To avoid a single, restrictive name, they were known variously as Christians, Churches of Christ, and Disciples of Christ. They adopted the Bible as their only guide for belief and practice. Thomas Campbell's dictum became authoritative: "Where the Scriptures speak, we speak; and where the Scriptures are silent, we are silent." They differed from the more emotional Baptists and Methodists by taking a rationalistic, even legalistic approach to the Bible. Although their roots were in revivals, they gradually moved away from dramatic conversion experiences. After prolonged discussion about proper New Testament worship forms, they agreed on believer's baptism by immersion, congregational polity, and weekly Lord's Supper. They avoided creeds and institutional structures, although they did establish schools and a missionary society. They spread through the South and West by word of mouth and the work of lay preachers.

Although they affirmed unity and the transcendence of denominational differences, the Christians ironically ended up creating yet another series of denominations. In the late nineteenth century, the movement experienced conflict between urban liberals and rural conservatives. In 1906, a sizeable group of rural, conservative churches left to form the Churches of Christ; this group is distinctive in prohibiting instrumental music in worship services. By 1952 another schism had occurred, leading to the formation of the conservative Christian Churches and Churches of Christ. The remaining group is now officially known as the Christian Churches (Disciples of Christ). In the 1960s, the Disciples contravened earlier policy and established a denominational structure similar to the United Church of Christ. Although they maintained congregational polity and authority, they created regional coordinating structures and a national General Assembly. The General Assembly has only advisory power over local congregations and coordinates mission organizations and denominational bureaucracy. National headquarters are in Indianapolis, Indiana.

Today the Disciples are a middle-class, middle-of-the-road Protestant denomination. Due to congregational polity, worship varies from elaborate to simple, generally following the Reformed pattern. Little distinction is drawn between clergy and laity, and laity can administer the Lord's Supper. Women have been ordained since the nineteenth century. Due to their legalistic approach to the Bible, there is less theological variation than other congregational denominations such as the United Church of Christ. The Disciples are concentrated in the middle of the United States, with large populations in Texas, Oklahoma, Arkansas, Tennessee, Kentucky, Indiana, Ohio, and Missouri. Like other Euro-Protestant denominations, they declined in membership between the 1960s and 1990s and have pursued ecumenical discussions with other groups since the 1980s, especially the United Church of Christ. The most prominent Disciple in recent years was former President of the United States Ronald Reagan, who had a Disciples background, but a rather shadowy religious affiliation as an adult, despite being a favorite of the Religious Right.

Evelyn A. Kirkley

See also EVANGELICALS; EVANGELICAL THEOLOGY; GREAT AWAKENING(S) (EURO-AMERICAN RELIGIOUS HISTORY); REVIVALISM; UNITED CHURCH OF CHRIST.

DISCIPLINE

This term can refer to a small whip used by monks and religious as a means of doing penance by inflicting bodily pain on oneself (a form of "mortification"). More commonly, discipline refers to the system of rules, norms, and customs governing the life of the church. The content of ecclesiastical discipline is contained in canon law. In religious communities, discipline likewise means the regulations and customs that constitute their way of proceeding: their daily order or routine, their mission or apostolate, formation program, ascetical practices, and the like.

The Latin word *disciplina* usually means teaching or instruction. Thus both religious and ecclesiastical discipline carry the note of order for the sake of instruction and growth. The goal of discipline, therefore, is not merely to ensure orderly conduct, but to help men and women advance in holiness (see Hebrews 12:4-11). The notion of discipline, whether ecclesiastical or religious, should always be situated within the framework of the church as a communion of life and of love.

William Reiser, S.J.

See also CANON LAW; MORTIFICATION; RULE (MONASTIC/RELIGIOUS).

DISCRIMINATION

Understood as a process of making distinctions between and among things, discrimination functions as a necessary basis for human decision making. However, this basic epistemological tool has been and continues to be used by individuals and groups who possess social power in order to separate, exclude, and marginalize individuals and denigrate the dignity of their humanity based on their group identification with, for example, a particular sex, gender, sexual orientation, race, class, nationality, or religion. When discrimination happens, the discriminated-against individual is treated and understood only as a member of her or his particular group or groups, with the attendant antipathy toward that group that the discriminator harbors. The goal of discrimination is to create, maintain, and enhance the social power and personal value of the discriminator, a self-assertion and self-perpetuation that come at the expense of the discriminated-against.

Discrimination is and has been perpetuated by individuals, social groups, and governments, through informal as well as government-sanctioned legal means. It is particularly insidious because although efforts can be and have been made through positive law to combat discrimination (for example, government nondiscrimination laws), nevertheless individuals, even the most well intentioned, can continue to harbor discriminatory thoughts and feelings that can manifest themselves in daily interpersonal interactions as well as in public-policy decisions. It is also unfortunately true that historically discriminated-against individuals and groups, who fail to recognize internalized self-denigration and/or a system of interlocking oppressions, can discriminate against others.

In a Christian theological context, discrimination is tantamount to heresy. In discriminating against individuals because of constructs such as sex, gender, and race, one rejects the *good* (as Genesis states) creation of God who made *all* humans *imago Dei* (in the image of God). The Christian church, unfortunately, has been complicit in not only establishing and perpetuating but also dogmatizing discrimination, most notably against women. While various Christian denominations, with different degrees of success, have attempted to overcome discrimination both within and without church walls, it seems painfully ironic to many that the church of Jesus Christ, a messiah who preached freedom from oppression, continues to reify discrimination.

Meghan T. Sweeney

See also PATRIARCHY; SEXISM; SIN (SOCIAL, STRUCTURAL); SOCIAL JUSTICE; THEOLOGICAL ANTHROPOLOGY.

DISPENSATION (CANONICAL DOCUMENT)

A permission or license granted by ecclesiastical authority to an individual or group within the church. A dispensation allows the recipient to do what would otherwise be unacceptable according to canon law.

Orlando Espín

See also CANON LAW; INDULT.

DISPENSATIONALISM

A variant of adventism, dispensationalism is a belief characteristic of Christian fundamentalism. It reacted against optimistic predictions of world Christianization and explained the decline of Christianity and turmoils in the church in the nineteenth century. A theory of human history based on biblical prophecy in Daniel and Revelation, dispensationalism posits that the earth's history is divided into seven chronological dispensations. In each dispensation, God initiates a covenant relationship with humanity for its salvation. In each one, humanity disobeys the covenant, and the dispensation ends with divine judgment, catastrophe, and the loss of human life. Then God begins a new dispensation. Despite humanity's consistent failure to live up to God's requirements, God never gives up and never entirely destroys humanity.

Although dispensationalists disagree on the details, they agree that the first dispensation occurred in the Garden of Eden. There God made a covenant with Adam and Eve that they would be blessed as long as they did not eat the fruit of the tree of the knowledge of good and evil. Adam and Eve disobeyed and were punished by expulsion from the Garden. The second dispensation ended with the Great Flood, the third with the Tower of

Babel, and so on. Currently, humanity lives in the sixth dispensation, the age of the church. It will end with the appearance of the Antichrist, tribulation, rapture, Second Coming, and Armageddon, the cosmic battle between Christ and the forces of evil. After vanquishing Satanic forces, Christ will reign for a thousand years in an earthly kingdom of peace. In the twentieth century, most dispensationalists were also premillennialists, believing that the Second Coming would occur before the millennium.

Pioneered in the 1820s by John Nelson Darby, a leader of the British sect Plymouth Brethren, dispensationalism was popularized transdenominationally among evangelical Protestants in the United States and Europe through Bible conferences, the preaching of revivalist Dwight Moody, and *The Scofield Bible* (1909), an influential fundamentalist biblical translation. Dispensationalists initiated the publication of *The Fundamentals* in 1910–5, a twelve-volume series of pamphlets articulating the fundamentals of the Christian faith, giving the fundamentalist movement its name.

Late twentieth-century fundamentalists continued to promulgate dispensationalism. It is taught at Moody Bible Institute in Chicago, the Bible Institute of Los Angeles, and Dallas Theological Seminary. It is intensely antimodernist, rejecting historical scholarship of the Bible in favor of scriptural literalism and inerrancy. Assuming God's omnipotence and human sinfulness, dispensationalism is a pessimistic interpretation of human history in which change occurs through divine intervention and supernatural cataclysm.

Evelyn A. Kirkley

See also ADVENTISTS; FUNDAMENTALISM (CHRISTIAN HISTORICAL MOVEMENT); MILLENARIANISM; RAPTURE (IN AMERICAN PROTESTANTISM).

DISSENT

Dissent involves the inability in conscience to accept the teaching of the church on a particular matter. Catholic Church teaching has a variety of levels of authority, and appropriate response to church teaching demands an understanding of these degrees of authoritativeness. The church teaches "infallibly" when the pope, or the bishops together with the pope, exercise their teaching office in proposing a matter of revealed faith or morals. Such pronouncements are extremely rare. A Catholic may not dissent from an infallible dogma. The day-to-day authoritative teaching of the magisterium enjoys the presumption of truth, since the pope and bishops are entrusted with the charism of teaching and are believed to receive the guidance of the Holy Spirit in the exercise of their office. Such teaching is said to be "authoritative" but non-infallible. Vatican II said that the proper response to non-infallible teaching was "religious assent of mind and will" (*Lumen Gentium* 25). Since the encyclical *Humanae Vitae* (1968) there has been considerable debate about the possibility of dissent from non-infallible teaching. Some theologians have taught that legitimate dissent from non-infallible teaching is possible, distinguishing between the application (non-infallible) and the moral principles (infallible) themselves. The U.S. Bishops in "Human Life in Our Day" (1968) presented the following criteria for legitimate dissent: it must (1) be based upon serious reasons; (2) be respectful of the magisterium's teaching authority; (3) not cause scandal.

Mary Ann Hinsdale

See also CHARISM; HUMANAE VITAE; INFALLIBILITY; MAGISTERIUM, EXTRAORDINARY; MAGISTERIUM, MINISTRY OF THE; MAGISTERIUM, ORDINARY.

DIVALI/DIWALI

The Hindu festival of lights, Divali is a popular celebration throughout India. Its name is a vernacular version of the Sanskrit *dipavali* (garland of lamps). Falling on the new moon between late October and mid-November (the exact date is determined by the Hindu lunar calendar), Divali is celebrated by the lighting at night of rows of numerous small oil lamps (or, nowadays, strings of small electric lights) that illuminate homes, temples, and streets. In preparation, houses are cleaned and new clothes are worn. Hindus in different parts of India look to different stories to articulate the festival's meaning: the most popular explanation is that it celebrates Rama's return to the city of Ayodhya after his victory over the demon king Ravana. On Divali night, Lakshmi, the goddess of fortune, is said to visit every house.

Lance E. Nelson

See also HINDUISM; LAKSHMI; RAMA; RAMAYANA; RAVANA.

DIVINATION

The practice of discovering the hidden causes of problems or foretelling future events through ritual techniques that somehow tap into the spiritual dimension, in which past, present, and future are experienced as being not quite as distinct as they are in the visible world. Divination may involve reading seemingly accidental circumstances such as the cracks of bones that have been ritually heated, the appearance of the organs of eviscerated animals, or the patterns formed by ritually cast objects or the flight of birds. Palmistry and the reading of tea leaves are examples of divination. Divination may also involve states of oracular trance or spirit possession. The use of divination was common in the religions of the ancient world, and is still important in indigenous religions, as an aspect of the great religious traditions of Asia, and in popular religious practice elsewhere.

Lance E. Nelson

See also CANDOMBLÉ; INDIGENOUS RELIGIOUS TRADITIONS; OMEN; ORACLE; POPULAR RELIGIONS; RELIGION; SANTERÍA; SHAMAN.

DIVINIZATION

To become a god, or to become god-like. (For the use of this term in Eastern Christianity's theology of grace, see "Grace.")

Orlando Espín

DIVINO AFFLANTE SPIRITU

An encyclical issued in 1943 by Pope Pius XII that represents a watershed in Catholic biblical studies and interpretation. *Divino Afflante Spiritu* (hereafter: DAS) was issued to mark the fiftieth anniversary of the 1893 encyclical *Providentissimus Deus* (hereafter: PD). In PD, Pope Leo XII stressed the dangers of higher criticism and insisted that the Latin Vulgate was the primary text. DAS not only endorsed the developing methods of critical exegesis, but also called for new translations of the Bible from the original languages. DAS encouraged Catholic exegetes to consider difficult questions using source and form criticism and the new insights of archeology, science, history, and social research. While PD had cautioned exegetes that their research could neither call into question traditional interpretations nor those that represented the unanimous consent of the fathers, DAS recognized that very few biblical texts had an authoritative interpretation or patristic consensus.

Regina A. Boisclair

DIVORCE (IN CHRISTIANITY)

Divorce refers to an official or legal ending of a marriage. Divorce is distinguished from an annulment, a declaration of the invalidity of a marriage. An invalid marriage is one that has from its beginning lacked something essential to marriage (proper ceremonial form, consummation, free and complete commitment, or psychological capacity to sustain a marital relationship). Divorce only involves the decision on the part of one or both parties to end the relationship.

Most religions include some norms regarding divorce. In Judaism, divorce was permitted when a woman was infertile or when there were allegations of sexual infidelity. Jesus is reported to have prohibited divorce, setting in motion a more restrictive set of norms in Christianity. For many centuries, divorce was grounds for excommunication from the Catholic Church. Today, most Christian denominations permit members to divorce and remarry. Some, notably the Episcopal Church and Orthodox Church, require a conversation with a priest where discernment about freedom to remarry is resolved in a nonjuridical manner. The Roman Catholic Church still prohibits divorce and remarriage but has made the process of obtaining an annulment easier.

Michael J. Hartwig

See also ANNULMENT; MARRIAGE (IN JUDAISM); MARRIAGE IN CHRISTIAN PERSPECTIVE.

DIVORCE (IN JUDAISM)

See GERUSHIN.

DO

(Japanese, *michi*, way, path). This is an important expression of Japanese religious life indicating that as a Way or Path, religion should be conceived as a way of living and being or acting as opposed to religion as an institution or institutional form; for example, *Shen Do* (Shinto), the way of life honoring the *shen* (spirits), and *Butsudo* (Buddhism), the way of the Buddha. It is also applies to a broader range of practices, for instance, *Chado* (tea) and *Judo* (way of the gentleman) that also lead to deeper levels of spiritual awareness.

G. D. DeAngelis

See also BUSHIDO; SHINTO; TAO.

DOCETISM

Docetism, related to the Greek verb *dokein*, meaning "to appear" or "to seem," refers to an early heterodox christological belief that questioned the full humanity of Jesus Christ. A docetic christology supported the full divinity of Jesus Christ, but claimed that he only seemed to suffer death, and thus only appeared to have a physical body or to be fully human. The Gnostics may have professed a docetic christology to safeguard the divinity of Christ from interacting with materiality, including physicality and bodiliness that were often associated with corruption, sin, and evil.

In the late first to early second century, theologian and martyr Ignatius of Antioch (d. ca. 110) took the opportunity in his letters to churches in Asia Minor, now Turkey, to strongly object to Docetism because it contradicted basic Christian teachings about the real human nature of Jesus. The Gospels portray Jesus as a historical person who was born into a certain lineage, born of Mary, was an early first-century Jew, matured and lived in Nazareth, became an itinerant preacher, and experienced all the features of human life, with the exception of sin. Similar to this scriptural portrait, Ignatius refuted Docetism and defended the full humanity of Jesus by stating that Jesus was "truly" born of Mary, persecuted under Pontius Pilate, crucified and died, and raised from the dead. Ignatius stressed the real humanity of Jesus from birth to everyday life to death to resurrection in order to uphold the salvation of human beings in all aspects of humanity.

Docetism fundamentally undermined a central Christian teaching about the person of Jesus, namely, the incarnation of the Son of God as a fully human being in Jesus Christ. Moreover, the claim that Jesus only seemed to suffer challenged the soteriological significance of Jesus' death and resurrection for the redemption of all humanity. The person and work of Jesus for the sake of salvation are inextricably interrelated. As noted by the fourth-century theologian Gregory Nazianzus (d. 390), "what has not been assumed has not been healed." Who Jesus is cannot be separated from what Jesus does. If Jesus did not totally take on, assume, or unite with a fully human nature, if he did not experience full solidarity with the human condition with the exception of sin, then he cannot recreate and redeem all of humanity.

Rosemary P. Carbine

See also HERESY.

DOCTORS OF THE CHURCH

A title given in the Catholic Church, and in some Anglican and Orthodox Churches, to a few canonized Christians (that is, "saints") who are also recognized as great theologians and teachers from, and whose writings have had a significant impact on Christian thought. In the Roman Catholic Church, these are the "doctors" (in alphabetical order): Albert the Great (1220–80), Alphonsus Liguori (1696–1787), Ambrose of Milan (340–97), Anselm of Canterbury (1033–1109), Anthony of Padua (1195–1231), Athanasius (297–373), Augustine of Hippo (354–430), Basil the Great (329–79), Bede the Venerable (673–735), Bernard of Clairvaux (1090–1153), Bonaventure (1217–74), Catherine of Siena (1347–80), Cyril of Alexandria (376–444), Cyril of Jerusalem (315–86), Ephraem of Edessa (306–73), Francis de Sales (1567–1622), Gregory Nazianzus (330–90), Gregory I the Great (540–604), Hilary of Poitiers (315–68), Isidore of Seville (560–636), Jerome (343–420), John Chrysostom (347–407), John of Damascus (675–749), John of the Cross (1542–91), Lawrence of Brindisi (1559–1619), Leo I the Great (400–61), Peter Canisius (1521–97), Peter Chrysologus (400–50), Peter Damian (1007–72), Robert Bellarmine (1542–1621), Teresa of Avila (1515–82), and Thomas Aquinas (1225–74).

See also the entries under the individual doctors.

Orlando Espín

See also APOSTOLIC FATHERS; CHURCH; COUNTER-REFORMATION / CATHOLIC RE- FORMATION; DEVELOPMENT OF DOGMA / OF DOCTRINE; DOCTRINE; DOGMA; FAITH; FATHERS OF THE CHURCH; MEDIEVAL CHRISTIANITY (IN THE WEST); MEDIEVAL CHURCH; ORTHODOX CHURCHES; PATRISTICS / PATROLOGY; REFORMATION; SAINT; WESTERN CATHO- LIC CHURCHES.

DOCTRINE

A doctrine is an official teaching or interpretation of faith, often in prepositional form, by persons or groups holding teaching authority in the church—bishops, the pope, church councils, or synods. Examples of doctrine in the earliest Christian tradition are the New Testament kerygmatic formulae that summarize the community's convictions about Christ. The formulation of faith in doctrinal form is rooted in the church's mission to proclaim the Gospel for all ages. As faith that is interpreted and applied for a later Christian generation, doctrine has two references: the experience of God or the Christ-event and the concerns of the present age.

There is a dogmatic form of doctrine, teaching officially proclaimed or later confirmed as a privileged expression of revealed truth. Not all doctrines are dogmas, however; the term dogma applies only to doctrines proclaimed as such in a formal declaration of an ecumenical council or the Roman pontiff. There has been a proliferation of doctrines in Christian history, and because they are directed to and formulated in historical situations, doctrines contain a historical and cultural reference. Thus, doctrines have their "hour"; some remain significant, some are forgotten, others regain importance, a few are consigned to archives or theological compendia.

It follows that the interpretation of doctrine requires guiding principles. One principle is the ranking or hierarchy of doctrines. This principle means that teachings from the apostolic era hold a privileged status over later eras. The principle also means that some doctrines (dogmas) such as the Trinity or Incarnation, express the foundation of faith. The significance of other doctrines is determined by their relationship to scripture and to the central symbols of faith.

Second, the study of the history of doctrines suggests that there are developments or changes in the understanding of faith. This gives rise to the idea of the development of doctrine. The concept proposes that because divine revelation is greater than human language can express, each dogma or doctrine unfolds some aspect of divine truth, but not the entirety of it. The history of dogma is the gradual or continuing unfolding of the experience of God, understanding that comes slowly in time. Finally, Karl Rahner has suggested that doctrine's ultimate purpose is the *reduction ad mysterion*, the recognition of the symbol's mysterious capacity for re-presentation. Beyond its confessional and regulative purposes, the final goal of doctrine is to open minds and hearts to the mystery of the divine presence among us.

Patricia Plovanich

See also DEVELOPMENT OF DOGMA/OF DOCTRINE; DOGMA.

DOCTRINE OF THE MEAN
See CHUNG YUNG.

DODD, CHARLES HAROLD (1884–1973)
Described as the greatest British (Welsh) New Testament scholar of the twentieth century, C. H. Dodd published more than twenty books and more than seventy scholarly lectures, essays, articles, and reviews during his long and distinguished career. Born April 7, 1884, at Wrexham, in North Wales, Dodd undertook classical and theological studies at Oxford and was ordained in 1912. He then spent three years as minister of the Congregational Church in Warwick before returning to Mansfield College at Oxford, where his own theological training had taken place, as Yates Lecturer and then Yates Professor of New Testament Greek and Exegesis. In 1930 he became Rylands Professor of Biblical Criticism and Exegesis at the University of

Manchester, and in 1935 Dodd was elected Norris-Hulse Professor of Divinity at Cambridge. After his retirement in 1949, Dodd came to the United States where, among other appointments, he was visiting professor in biblical theology at Union Theological Seminary in New York. In 1950 he returned to England, becoming general director of the *New English Bible*. Dodd died in Oxford on September 21, 1973.

The clearest instances of Dodd's lasting influence on New Testament studies are in the expression "realized eschatology," which he coined, and in the term *kerygma*, to the significance of which he devoted considerable attention. Among Dodd's important works are *The Meaning of Paul for Today* (1920); *The Parables of the Kingdom* (1935); *The Apostolic Preaching and Its Developments* (1936); *History and the Gospel* (1938); *The Coming of Christ* (1951); *The Interpretation of the Fourth Gospel* (1953); *Historical Tradition in the Fourth Gospel* (1963); and his last book, *The Founder of Christianity* (1970).

Jean-Pierre Ruiz

See also ESCHATOLOGY (IN CHRISTIANITY); ESCHATOLOGY (IN JUDAISM); ESCHATON/ESCHATOLOGICAL; KERYGMA.

DOGEN (1200–53)

Japanese Zen master who brought from China the sitting zazen method and founded the Soto school he promulgated in Kyoto as teacher and author. His most famous work, the *Shobogenzo*, became one of the landmarks in Japanese Buddhist intellectual history. Dogen emphasized the unity of daily life activities and the attainment of enlightenment, and he argued for the preeminence of zazen as a means for realizing Buddha nature as a changing presence in every human life.

The idea of *mappo* (the onset of a decadent spiritual age) was rejected by Dogen in his attempt to revive Buddhist practice; he insisted that a celibate order could still transmit the truth from mind to mind.

Todd T. Lewis

See also MAPPO; MINDFULNESS; TATHAGATAGARBHA DOCTRINE; ZEN.

DOGMA

Dogma (from the Greek for "what seems good") has had several meanings in Christian history. In early Christianity, it was nearly synonymous with doctrine, indicating the church's beliefs and teachings in an inclusive way. Thus doxologies, creeds, and conciliar decrees were all instances of dogma. Vincent of Lérins (d. 450) gave some precision to the concept by defining dogma as truths with a universal reference: believed at all times, in all places, by everyone. Basil (d. 364) and Chrysostom (d. 407) further defined the concept by designating dogmas as truths beyond reason accepted because of their christological origin. Thomas Aquinas held a propositional view: dogmas were articles of faith. Several meanings combined in the modern era to yield what is termed the propositional view of revelation, the teaching proposed in *Dei Filius*, the Vatican Council I constitution on faith. The council proposed dogmas as revealed truth expressed in clear statements, articles of faith divinely revealed and universally held. The proposal of divine origin and catholicity (universality) did not note ecumenical differences in the matter of dogma, of Christian churches who hold the same core dogmas, but have separated because of differences about dogmas later interpreted or proposed.

Recent studies of the history of dogma have proposed a more dynamic and historical meaning to the concept. First, the validity of dogma lies in the church's conviction about the divine origin of its faith. It is rooted in the social character of ecclesial life and can express commonly held convictions, or act to regulate expressions of faith when doctrinal differences threaten the unity of ecclesial faith and love. Finally, recent studies have noted the pedagogical, historical, and doxological character of dogma. Dogmas arise from the church's effort to interpret the experience of God and Christ for a particular historical age. A dogma expresses enduring truth, but formulated in the cultural categories of the era, it will exhibit a historical influence or index as well. Because historical eras bring different questions and insights to faith, dogmas are best understood as the truth stations along the path the church walks in history, formulations fostering faith in the present age and contributing to faith's futurity. In this view, dogmas are not studied merely for their regulatory meaning or to elicit consent to mysteries beyond human ken. They are symbols that express the mystery of divine presence among humanity throughout history.

Patricia Plovanich

See also DEI FILIUS; DEVELOPMENT OF DOGMA/OF DOCTRINE; METHOD IN THEOLOGY.

DOGMATIC THEOLOGY

A branch or type of Christian theology that studies the doctrines of the church, and more specifically those doctrines contained in or derived from revelation. Even though the term "dogma" is usually employed to refer only to doctrines specifically contained in the Scriptures, or those officially defined by the church as part of revelation and consequently as necessary,

dogmatic theology historically developed as a discipline interested not only in dogmas (in the strict sense of this term) but also in all Christian doctrines. Today it is often equated with systematic theology or doctrinal theology, although some distinctions between them can be made.

Orlando Espín

See also CONSTRUCTIVE THEOLOGY; DEVELOPMENT OF DOGMA/DOCTRINES; DOCTRINE; DOGMA; REVELATION (IN CHRISTIAN PERSPECTIVE).

DÖLLINGER, JOHANN J.
(1799–1890)

German Catholic theologian and church historian, appointed professor of theology and church history at Munich in 1829. Döllinger was known both for his broad interests in historical studies and church history and his active participation in the political questions of the age. He advocated the concept of freedom in the church as Pius IX's pontificate became increasingly conservative, a time of a widening gap between church and world. Döllinger argued publicly against the increasing Roman influence in the European church at the Munich Congress in 1863. An opponent of the infallibility movement, Döllinger remained critical of Vatican Council I. His book criticizing papal authority was placed on the Index of Forbidden Books in 1869, and he was excommunicated in 1871. Removed from his Catholic professorship, Döllinger remained active at the university, but founded a separatist movement called the Old Catholic Church.

Patricia Plovanich

See also INFALLIBILITY; OLD CATHOLICS; PIUS IX, POPE; VATICAN, FIRST COUNCIL OF THE.

DOME OF THE ROCK

In Arabic, *Qubbat* (or *Kubbat*) *as-Sakhra*. Located in Jerusalem, the Dome of the Rock is a Muslim shrine completed in 691 C.E. by Caliph Abd al-Malik ibn Marwan. It stands on a site that Jews claim was the Holy of Holies, the most sacred part of the Jewish Temple of Solomon. The rock enshrined in this octagonal domed structure is believed by Muslims to be the one from which Muhammad ascended into heaven during his *mi'raj* or Night Journey. This makes the Dome of the Rock the second most holy shrine of Islam, after the Ka'ba in Mecca. Though it is not a mosque, the structure does include areas where pilgrims can offer prayers.

Ronald A. Pachence

See also HOLY OF HOLIES; KA'BA/KAABA; MIRAJ/MI'RAJ; MOSQUE/MASJID.

DOMESTIC CHURCH

This is the term employed in *Lumen Gentium* to designate the Christian family. The fourth-century Greek theologian John Chrysostom seems to have been the first to speak of the family as a kind of "little church," in which the father fulfills the ecclesial functions of teaching, governing, and sanctifying the members of the household. Augustine further developed this understanding, and after the Reformation the phrase was taken up by Protestants who at times claimed that both parents exercised those functions. Since the Second Vatican Council, this approach to the family has been pursued in such Roman Catholic documents as John Paul II's Apostolic Exhortation on the Family, where it is suggested that all family members and the family as a whole can exercise those roles in some ways. As a result, efforts have been recently made to allow a "family perspec-

tive" to transform the functioning of church on a parish level.

Mary Anne Foley, C.N.D.

See also AUGUSTINE OF HIPPO; ECCLESIOLOGY; FAMILY; LUMEN GENTIUM.

DOMINICANS

"Dominican" is the common name for the religious family of orders of priests, nuns, brothers, members of secular institutes, and laypeople associated with the Order of Friars Preachers, started by Dominic de Guzmán and approved by Pope Innocent III in 1216. The order grew out of the preaching mission of the founder, Dominic de Guzmán, to the Cathars. Beginning in 1206, Dominic and his bishop, Diego de Azevedo of Osma, decided that their missionary effort demanded that they adopt a life of strict evangelical poverty. In 1215 Dominic approached Pope Innocent III for approval of his new organization. Like his contemporary, Francis of Assisi, Dominic was suggesting a radical new form of Christian life entailing voluntary poverty, extensive study, and wandering preaching against heresy. Up to that time, most religious orders were monastic. On the condition that Dominic take the Rule of St. Augustine for his order, Innocent approved the new group in 1216. Dominic and later the Dominican canonist Raymond of Peñafort proved to be excellent organizers, and the Dominican system of election of superiors and of annual general chapters proved highly successful and was adopted by other mendicant groups.

The Dominicans grew rapidly. By 1256 there were approximately 13,000 friars, and by 1347 probably more than 21,000. From the very beginning, Dominic intended that his friars should have the best education possible. He sent friars to study and start priories in the university cities of Paris (1217), Bologna (1218), Palencia (1220), Montpelier (1221), and Oxford (1221). Study itself was considered a form of prayer, and superiors could dispense students and professors from religious exercises if they needed the time for reading or writing. The approach paid off, and the Dominicans attained their first chair of theology at Paris in 1229, and a second in 1230. By 1248, the Dominicans also had a chair of theology at Oxford. The people who filled those chairs were of exceptional quality and made up a veritable "who's who" of great thirteenth-century theologians. Hugh of St. Cher, Albert the Great, and Thomas Aquinas at Paris, and Richard Fishacre and Robert Kilwardy at Oxford are only the most outstanding of these scholars. Despite condemnations of some of his ideas both at Paris in 1277 and at Oxford in 1284, the teaching of Thomas Aquinas became the theology of the order, and Dominicans were commanded to teach his theology in all their schools. Thomas's theology was revived in the sixteenth century by a series of brilliant commentaries on his work by the Dominican theologians Francesco de Vitoria and Cajetan (Thomas de Vio).

Dominicans were not just theologians, however, but also physicians, canonists, and of course, preachers. One of the most prized titles among the Dominicans was that of "preacher general," a title denoting the centrality of preaching in Dominican life. Dominicans built their churches especially for preaching and not only led preaching missions, but prepared preaching manuals. It was this very mission, however, that caused problems, not only for the Dominicans but for their fellow mendicants. Secular clergy did not appreciate having their congregations (and in-

comes) stolen away by the better-trained and more entertaining mendicant preachers. Several attempts were made to withdraw from the mendicants the right to preach and to hear confessions. The conflict continued throughout the Middle Ages and was only definitively settled by the Council of Trent that ruled that preaching or hearing confessions needed the permission of the local bishop. Because of their role as preachers against heresy, Dominicans almost inevitably also played a prominant role in the inquisitions. The Dominicans Bernard Gui, Nicolas Eymeric, and Tomás de Torquemada are perhaps the most famous (or infamous) of the inquisitors.

Although the Dominicans saw a relaxation in discipline starting in the fourteenth century, a series of reform movements supported by the Dominican leadership resulted in a vigorous and renewed order in the sixteenth century. The Dominicans suffered none of the bitter controversies that mar Franciscan history. The greatest decline in Dominican vocations and houses came in the late eighteenth and early nineteenth centuries when a number of Dominican houses were forced to close either through decline in numbers or through political suppression.

Women have played an important role in Dominican history right from the start. Dominic founded the first nunnery in 1207, and three others were started before his death. Dominican nuns are affiliated but independent of the friars. Far more numerous are the congregations of religious women who affiliated themselves with the Dominicans as members of the third order. There are over a hundred such congregations, and among their number are included such great saints as Catherine of Siena and Rose of Lima. Dominicans have been particularly noted for their spirituality, particularly Catherine of Siena and the influential fourteenth-century Dominican mystic Meister Eckhart.

Gary Macy

See also ALBERT THE GREAT; AQUINAS, THOMAS, ST.; CATHERINE OF SIENA; DOMINIC DE GUZMÁN; ECKHART, J. (MEISTER); FRIAR; INNOCENT III, POPE; MEDIEVAL CHRISTIANITY (IN THE WEST); MENDICANTS; MYSTICISM/MYSTICS (IN CHRISTIANITY); POVERTY (RELIGIOUS VOW); PREACHING; TORQUEMADA, TOMÁS.

DOMINIC DE GUZMÁN (1171?–1221)

Dominic (Domingo in Spanish) was born in the village of Caleruega in Castile, Spain. He attended school at Palencia and became canon of the church of Osma around 1196. In 1206 Dominic joined Bishop Diego de Azevedo of Osma in an effort to convert the Cathars of southern France through preaching. The mission met with success, and Dominic continued his efforts at peaceful conversion during and after the Albigensian Crusade. In 1216 Dominic gained permission from Pope Honorius III to start a new religious order dedicated to preaching. This was really a new idea since previously only bishops had the right to preach or to grant permission to preach. Dominic's order would also be a mendicant (that is, begging) order like that of his contemporary, Francis of Assisi. The "friars" (brothers) would travel through the world preaching and begging for a living. This Order of Preachers, better known as the Dominicans, insisted on a rigorous program of education in preparation for their preaching, and they were soon attending the best theological schools in Europe. Dominic won many converts to this new way of life through his preaching and simplicity of life. Dominic was also an excellent administrator, and the Dominicans developed one of the first organizations in Europe whose leaders were democratically elected. Although the wandering preachers were men, Dominic also organized an order for women whose role was educational as well as contemplative. Dominic was canonized in 1234, just thirteen years after his death.

Gary Macy

See also CATHARS; CRUSADES; DOMINICANS; FRIAR; FRANCISCANS; FRANCIS OF ASSISI; MEDIEVAL CHRISTIANITY (IN THE WEST); MENDICANTS; POVERTY (RELIGIOUS VOW).

DONATION OF CONSTANTINE

A document that appeared in Western Christianity in the eighth century describing how Constantine turned control of Italy and the western provinces of the Roman Empire over to Pope Sylvester. The document was considered genuine up to the fifteenth century and was used to justify the temporal rule of the pope over the Papal States as well as the supremacy of the pope over the emperor. The scholar and later Pope Pius II, Aeneas Sylvius Piccolomini, first suggested that the document was inauthentic in 1433. The donation was soon conclusively shown to be a fake by Reginald Pecock, Nicholas of Cusa, and Lorenzo Valla.

Gary Macy

See also CONSTANTINE I THE GREAT; NICHOLAS OF CUSA; PAPACY/PAPAL; POPE.

DONATISM

Donatism is the teaching of the schismatic North African church that flourished in the fourth and fifth centuries. During the persecution of Diocletian, clergy were ordered to hand over sacred books to the authorities, and indeed some clergy did do so. Other Christians defended their beliefs and their texts to their imprisonment and death. Those who remained faithful condemned as traitors (*traditores*) the clergy who had given in. When the persecution ended, Caecilian, a deacon suspected of supporting the traitors, was elected bishop of Carthage. Immediately, those who had resisted the Romans objected, and the church of North Africa split into two camps. Around 313, Donatus was elected as the bishop and leader of the schismatics in Carthage and it is for him that the schism is named.

Despite strong opposition from Constantine I and condemnations by the Roman Church, the Donatist community grew, especially in Numidia. Basing themselves on the teachings of Cyprian of Carthage and Tertullian, the Donatists believed that the church should be a society of the holy, dedicated to the ideal of martyrdom. Further, only those clergy whose lives were blameless could worthily administer the sacraments, especially baptism. True Christianity remained, therefore, only within the Donatist community. Any other Christian who wished to join their community would need to be rebaptized, since any earlier baptism would have been invalid.

In the early fifth century, under the leadership of Augustine of Hippo, a concerted effort was made to end the Donatist schism. A conference was held in Cathage in 411 to decide which of the two churches was the true church of North Africa. The Catholic group prevailed and the Roman government began to enforce decrees banning Donatism and confiscating its churches. Donatism began to decline and gradually disappeared when faced with the invasion first of the Vandals and then of the Arabs.

Gary Macy

See also AUGUSTINE OF HIPPO; CONSTANTINE I THE GREAT; CYPRIAN OF CARTHAGE; PERSECUTION (IN CHRISTIANITY); TERTULLIAN.

DOSTOYEVSKY, FEODOR M. (1821–81)

Russian writer. From a Russian Orthodox family, he espoused revolutionary ideas that landed him in forced labor camps and brought him close to death more than once. Although he earned a living as a journalist, he is better remembered through his very influential novels. He was, in his own way, a deeply religious person who discussed crucial theological and religious experiences and concepts in his novels, especially questions of salvation, grace, compassion, free will, and reason. He considered the institutions of the church as often inimical to the Gospel. Dostoyevsky had great influence on European and American theological and philosophical thought during most of the twentieth century, especially during the heyday of existentialism.

Orlando Espín

See also EXISTENTIALISM; ORTHODOX CHURCHES; RUSSIAN ORTHODOX CHURCH.

DOUBLE EFFECT

This principle of ethics deals with an action that has both an evil and good effect, and stipulates the circumstances under which such an action can be allowed. In other words, it specifies the circumstances under which one may knowingly cause evil. It is most often associated with Roman Catholic moral theology, but the principle has proven useful to many persons in Protestant and secular ethics—bioethics (abortion, euthanasia) as well as in questions of military strategy. The principle holds that one may rightfully cause evil if four conditions are present: first, the action itself is good or at least neutral; second, the good effect is what the agent sincerely intends (it is the object of his or her *direct* intention, the evil effect is merely permitted or tolerated); third, the good effect and the evil effect must occur simultaneously (the evil effect may not be a means to the good effect); and fourth, the good effect must be proportionately greater than the evil effect, or there must be a proportionately grave reason for permitting the evil effect to occur.

There are two major suppositions of the principle that are of interest to contemporary ethicists: that there is a morally significant difference between intending evil and permitting evil, and that one may not use evil means to achieve a good end (good ends cannot justify evil means). Some argue that the principle simply serves to ease individual consciences about the "dirty hands" problem; others claim that the principle serves to limit the moral ambiguity in difficult cases by specifying objective grounds for determining to what extent we can cause evil in the pursuit of good.

Brian F. Linnane, s.j.

See also BIOETHICS; ETHICS; MORAL THEOLOGY / CHRISTIAN ETHICS; PROPORTIONALISM; SCRUPULOSITY.

DOUBT

In general, doubt is the recognition of a particular thesis as uncertain. John Henry Newman in his writings considers doubt in the context of faith. He calls doubt a "suspension of mind" such that one withholds assent from either a proposition or its contrary. Thus, for example, if one doubts the proposition that God exists, one neither assents that God exists, nor assents that God does not exist. Defined in such a way, doubt is incompatible with faith, since faith is construed as unqualified assent or at least qualified assent (inference) of a faith proposition.

One must be careful, however, to distinguish this technical definition of doubt from the true assertion, for example, that one cannot logically conclusively prove the existence of God. Further, the acknowledged and theologically affirmed inability of a human mind (or community) to fully grasp truth should prevent a descent into moralism or dogmatism as a response to doubt. Finally, one cannot remove the element of risk from putting practical faith in God in one's life. Often what we commonly call doubt is really fear of encounter with God and the effect God will have on our life.

G. Simon Harak, s.j.

See also FAITH; TRUTH.

DOUGLAS, MARY (1921–)

English anthropologist, trained at Oxford; she did fieldwork in Zaire. She has taught in British and American universities. Douglas is important because of her studies on symbols. She understands that there are few if any common symbols in today's societies, and this explains why there is such a weakened sense of social belonging in the modern world. Her studies led her to theorize on "group" (the experience of being and belonging to a social unit) and "grid" (the rules implied in relating one individual to another on an ego-centered basis). Douglas believes that contemporary European and North American societies have favored "grid" over "group." Her two most influential books are *Natural Symbols* (1970) and *Purity and Danger* (1966).

Orlando Espín

See also CULTURE; LITURGY (IN CHRISTIANITY); SOCIETY; SOLIDARITY; SYMBOL.

DOXOLOGY

The word doxology (from the Greek *doxa*, meaning "glory") can refer to the general Christian theological theme of the praise and glorification of God, or, more narrowly, to a specific liturgical formulation expressing that idea in prayer. The liturgical text *Glory to God in the highest* (taken from the song of the angels before the shepherds at the birth of Christ; see Luke 2:14) is referred to in some Christian traditions as the "Greater Doxology." In addition, the concluding phrase at the end of some types of liturgical prayer is also called a doxology (for example, the lines "Glory be to the Father, and to the Son, and to the Holy Spirit, as it was in the beginning, is now, and ever shall be, world without end. Amen"). The concluding section of the preconciliar Roman Catholic eucharistic prayer (the *Roman Canon*), as well as of the new eucharistic prayers composed after Vatican II, is also called a doxology: "Through him [that is, Christ], with him, and in him, all glory and honor are yours, almighty Father, now and forever. Amen."

Doxology can be considered in a broader sense to be the underlying theological understanding behind Christian public worship (liturgy) and private prayer (for example, private devotions like the recitation of the rosary). Christian liturgy is the action of the church that, in a real sense, makes it church, the Body of Christ, the Presence and Sacrament of Christ in the world: the church becomes most fully what it is by engaging in the corporate and communal praise and glorification of God, as Father/Creator, Son/Redeemer, and Spirit/Sanctifier.

Joanne M. Pierce

See also ADORATION; LITURGY (IN CHRISTIANITY); SACRAMENT; SACRAMENTAL THEOLOGY; TRINITY/ TRINITARIAN THEOLOGY/TRINITARIAN PROCESSIONS; WORSHIP.

DRAMA IN CHRISTIANITY

Because of drama's origins in Greco-Roman religion and in questionable moral contexts of the Roman Empire, early Christianity was adamantly opposed to participation in any and all dramatic presentations. With the collapse of the Western Roman Empire, pagan drama ceased to exist; but by the ninth and tenth centuries, some Christian writers began composing plays around biblical themes and scenes for the education and edification of townsfolk. Soon afterward, plays were created to teach and extol the goodness of the virtuous life, as well as the biblical commandments. During the later Middle Ages and into the modern period, religious drama became a very important means through which religious education was offered, as well as a means through which Christian communities could join in expressing their faith life and commitment. Religious drama became a crucial means of evangelization during the colonial period in Latin America and the Philippines. And it is still popular in many Catholic communities in Europe, Latin America, the Philippines, and the U.S. (especially among Latinos). This explicitly Christian theater lies at the origin of the late medieval European revival of secular drama.

Orlando Espín

See also AUTO SACRAMENTAL; CATE-CHESIS/CATECHETICAL; EVANGELIZA-TION; LATIN AMERICAN CATHOLICISM; LATINO CATHOLICISM; LITURGY (IN CHRISTIANITY); MEDIEVAL CHRISTIAN-ITY (IN THE WEST); MEDIEVAL CHURCH; POPULAR CATHOLICISM; POPULAR RELIGIONS; RELIGIOUS EDUCATION; SACRAMENT; SYMBOL.

DRAVIDIAN

A large language group comprising some twenty-five languages, Dravidian languages are spoken primarily in South Asia (especially South India and northern Sri Lanka). Tamil, Telugu, Kanada, and Malayalam are the four most prominent languages of this family. Although *dravidian* designates a linguistic and not a racial group, peoples who speak Dravidian languages are commonly referred to as Dravidians. Dravidian-speaking peoples are widely believed to have inhabited the South Asian subcontinent prior to the arrival of the Aryans around the middle of the second millennium B.C.E.

Lance E. Nelson

See also ARYAN.

DREAM DANCE

Part of the period of religious revitalization that emerged to counter the devastation of the Plains wars of the nineteenth century, the Dream Dance originated among the Dakota. The story tells of a young girl who belonged to a band captured by American soldiers. She escaped the carnage that followed by hiding in water (a lake or a river). She remained there in terror about ten days, and in her weakened state she received a vision in which she was directed to create a new dance, a significant element of which was to be a special drum. She was told how to build it, and was urged to spread the ritual to her own people and beyond. She was assured that it would provide a means of protection against the whites. She did so, and it was carried widely to other tribes. Its teachings promoted reaffirmation of traditional communal ethics, and, with other late nineteenth movements, it created pan-Indian friendships.

Kathleen Dugan

See also RITUAL; VISIONS (IN CHRISTIAN MYSTICISM).

DREAMS

In ancient Israel and thus in the Hebrew Bible, dreams were a frequent means of communication between God and humans. Abraham, Jacob, and Joseph are notable dreamers in the book of Genesis. As the stories of Joseph and Daniel show, dreams sometimes needed interpretation to make their meaning clear. In both these cases, the meaning is clear to the faithful follower of Yahweh and unclear to the non-follower. Dreams were also a means used by God to communicate with prophets other than Moses. The assumption ancient Israel shared with the rest of the ancient Near East seems to have been that God/ the gods could choose to communicate with humans in a variety of ways, some of them "coded" and thus in need of one of the faithful (in the Israelite context) or a specialist to provide the recipient with the meaning. We have records of dream communication at least as early as the time of Gudea of Lagash who received the command to rebuild a temple through a dream interpreted for him. He later received the plans for the temple also in a dream.

Russell Fuller

DREIDEL

Yiddish, meaning "spinning top." In Hebrew it is called *sevivon*.

This toy is traditionally used on the Jewish festival of Hanukkah to play a game that provides a few moments of lighthearted fun to the members of the family while the Chanukah candles are burning.

The *dreidel* has four sides, each of which contains a Hebrew letter standing for the phrase that means "a great miracle happened there." (In Israel, the fourth letter is changed so that the phrase means "a great miracle happened *here*.") Players take turns spinning the top, and often add to the game's enjoyment by making small wagers of pennies or toothpicks on the outcome of the spins.

Wayne Dosick

See also HANUKKAH; MENORAH.

DREXEL, KATHERINE (1858–1955)

Born the daughter of a wealthy Philadelphia family that had made its fortune in banking, Katherine Drexel wanted to donate her fortune to the missionary work among African American and Native American peoples mandated by the Third Plenary Council of Baltimore (1884). At the suggestion of Pope Leo XIII, she decided to become a missionary herself. After completing a novitiate with the Pittsburgh Sisters of Mercy, she and some companions founded the Sisters of the Blessed Sacrament for Indians and Colored People (S.B.S.) in 1891. Soon requests came for sisters to staff missions in the Southwest and the South, and eventually Drexel opened convents and schools in major cities (Chicago, Boston, Harlem in New York City). In 1915 she founded Xavier University in New Orleans, the first and only Catholic university for African Americans in the

U.S. She was canonized by Pope John Paul II in 2000.

Mary Ann Hinsdale

DRUM CHIEF

One of the ritual functionaries of the Peyote Cult that began as a new religious movement in the mid-nineteenth century, and, despite many challenges, has continued to serve the spiritual needs of the Native American community in the debilitating conditions in which so many live. The symbolism of the drum is cosmic (the earth) and traditional, in that it has been the supporting sound of ritual from ancient times. In the peyote ritual, these traditions are not supplanted but reaffirmed and linked with new forms in which the goal remains the same—to gain spiritual power for life. The role of the Drum Chief is an honored one, and is given to one whose spiritual intent and practice is unwavering. This is a true ritual of regeneration, and those who serve in it serve the entire community.

Kathleen Dugan

See also DRUMS (IN AFRICAN AND AFRO-LATIN RELIGIONS); PEYOTE.

DRUMS (IN AFRICAN AND AFRO-LATIN RELIGIONS)

African and Afro-Latin religions revere some drums, frequently associated with ritual use, as the voices of the divinities. Sometimes the drums also act as means of calling and greeting the divinities or even special (human) guests of the community. Ritual drums are handled with extreme care and respect, but must first be especially consecrated by a priest or priestess so that they may receive the religious power that will allow them to perform their religious function. Those who play the drums ritually undergo a long and careful spiritual and liturgical preparation, and are held in high esteem by other members of the community. Without drums there would be no ritual life in African and Afro-Latin religions.

The ritual drums are usually three, of different sizes and widths, called by names proper to each. Always made of natural materials and animal skins, the group of drums is jointly known by different names in the Afro-Latin religions—*atabaques, atabales, bataá,* and so on.

Orlando Espín

See also AFRICAN TRADITIONAL RELIGIONS; AFRO-LATIN RELIGIONS; CANDOMBLÉ; CULTURE; DIVINATION; INCULTURATION; RITUAL; SANTERÍA; UMBANDA; VODOUN.

DUALISM/DUALISTIC

Dualism is a term used to designate a way of thinking in philosophy or theology, or a mythic vision, that sees reality as consisting of either (a) two fundamentally different *kinds* of existence, neither of which can be reduced to the other, or (b) two fundamentally *antagonistic realms* of existence in conflict with each other. The first may be termed philosophical or metaphysical dualism; the second becomes, in practice, what may be called ethical dualism. Examples of philosophical dualisms would be those between spirit and matter, soul and body, and— sometimes—God and the world. In opposition to dualism of this metaphysical type stands monism or nondualism, a philosophical or theological view that sees all things as reducible to one essential reality. In Hindu theology, for example, there is a school of Vedanta that calls itself Dvaita (Dualism). Dvaita Vedanta, in opposition to the nondualistic Advaita

Vedanta, champions the idea that God and the world are eternally distinct. Dualisms of the second type (b) take on an ethical overtone. In them, the moral dimension is highlighted instead of or in addition to the metaphysical, and an inherent situation of conflict between good and evil, or light and darkness, is envisioned. The world and history are then seen as the working out of the struggle between these antagonistic forces. Zoroastrianism and Manichaeism are examples of this kind of dualistic thinking.

Lance E. Nelson

See also ADVAITA VEDANTA; DVAITA VEDANTA; GNOSIS/GNOSTICISM; MADHVA; MANICHAEISM; NONDUALISM/NONDUALISTIC; VEDANTA; ZOROASTRIANISM.

DUALISTIC VEDANTA

See DVAITA VEDANTA.

DUCHEMIN, THERESA MAXIS (1810–92)

Cofounder of the Sisters, Servants of the Immaculate Heart of Mary (Monroe, Michigan, and Immaculata, Pennsylvania) and foundress of the Scranton branch of this order. An illegitimate child of a white British father and a biracial Haitian mother, she entered the fledgling Oblate Sisters of Providence in Baltimore, a community founded to educate Catholic children of color. In 1845, accompanied by Oblate Sister Ann Constance Shaaff, Duchemin left the Oblates for Michigan at the invitation of a Redemptorist priest, Louis Florent Gillet, to undertake the religious education of the daughters of the French frontier families settling in the area around Monroe, Michigan. Under the aegis of Gillet, Teresa Renaud of Grosse Pointe, Michigan, joined Duchemin and

Shaaff. They took private vows, forming a religious community known as Sisters of Providence (later to become the Sisters, Servants of the Immaculate Heart of Mary).

Disturbed by the slow growth of the religious community, the inhospitable climate, and the living conditions in Michigan, and the seeming desertion of Gillet, Duchemin sought new recruits in Pennsylvania. Her independent activities irked the bishop of Detroit, Peter Paul Lefevere. Lefevere, who had known Duchemin's racial background, complained to John Neumann, bishop of Philadelphia, about his laissez-faire handling of the matter. Caught between ecclesiastical egos, in 1859 Duchemin was removed from office and her sisters in Michigan and Pennsylvania were instructed to have no contact with each other. Exiled by the bishops from both branches of the community, Duchemin was taken in by the Grey Nuns of Ottawa. After several fruitless attempts to be reunited with any I.H.M. congregation, in 1885 she was allowed to return to the motherhouse of the Philadelphia I.H.M.s in West Chester, Pennsylvania. She died there in 1892. Today, Theresa Maxis Duchemin is honored by all three congregations who trace their roots to her: Monroe, Michigan, and Scranton and Immaculata, Pennsylvania.

Mary Ann Hinsdale

DUCHESNE, LOUIS (1843–1922)

Born in Saint-Servan, France, Duchesne was a historian, archeologist, and prelate in the Roman Catholic Church. After theological studies in Rome and ordination in 1867, he taught church history at several institutions including the Institut catholique of Paris and the Ecole supérieur des lettres. From 1895 to his death, he was director of the Ecole archéologique française de Rome. Using archeological and archival evidence he unearthed in his research, Duchesne studied the history of the early Christian church. Analytical, precise, and at times ironic, he was sharply criticized by conservatives for using the historical-critical method. Duchesne was especially skeptical of claims to apostolic origins of the church in France. His three-volume *Histoire ancienne de l'Eglise chrétienne* (1906–10), published in English as *Early History of the Church*, went through numerous reprintings and served as the standard introduction to the early church for many years. Duchesne's careful research, integrity as a historian and cleric, and perseverance despite opposition from anti-Modernists, make him a significant figure among church historians.

Evelyn A. Kirkley

See also HISTORICAL CRITICISM; MODERNISM.

DUHKHA

The Sanskrit term (Pali, *dukkha*) meaning "suffering." In Buddhist doctrine, it occupies a central place: just as the awareness of *duhkha* brought upon a crisis that led the future Buddha Gautama to depart from the householder life on his spiritual quest, the recognition of suffering is the starting assertion of the Four Noble Truths, with the Buddha's path designed to help individuals overcome it. Another central Buddhist definition of reality, "The Three Characteristics of Existence," includes duhkha as well as impermanence and no-soul. Seeing suffering in every arena of human experience is necessary for enlightenment; it is possible only with the development of *prajna* ("insight"). Buddhist analysts argued that suffering is present in all human experience, both physical and mental. The early Buddhist texts argued *against karma* determining all suffering, with natural causality recognized. There was also an early classification of duhkha in specific areas: the "ordinary suffering" of birth, disease, old age, and death; separation from loved ones and pleasant conditions; "suffering produced by change," that is, when favorable conditions are reversed; and "suffering via the *skandhas*," namely, the five basic units of a human being. Buddhists have not traditionally viewed their doctrine's emphasis on duhkha as pessimistic but as simply realistic and essential to facing life's spiritual possibilities fully.

Todd T. Lewis

See also PRAJNA; SKANDHA; TRUTHS, FOUR NOBLE; VIPASHYANA/VIPASSANA.

DULIA

This technical Christian theological term refers to the veneration that might be given to the saints (as distinct from *latria*, or the worship due only to God). *Dulia* becomes an important concept in a number of theological controversies. Perhaps the most important was the *iconoclast* controversy which embroiled Eastern Christianity during the eighth and ninth centuries: the issue was whether or not icons could be venerated as part of Christian worship and spirituality.

Joanne M. Pierce

See also ADORATION; HYPERDULIA; ICONOCLASTIC CONTROVERSY; LATRIA.

DULLES, AVERY (1918–)

Born in 1918 in the United States, Avery Robert Dulles is a Jesuit priest and theologian who is best known for his work in Catholic ecclesiology. In his minor classic *Models of the Church* (1974), Dulles proposed five "models," or types, for analyzing the diverse understandings of the church's life and mission which exist among, and even within, Christian denominations: the church as institution, mystical communion, sacrament, herald, and/or servant. He later added a sixth model: the church as community of disciples. He used a similar typology for analyzing diverse approaches to the Christian doctrine of revelation in his 1983 work *Models of Revelation*. All his works demonstrate a loyalty to Catholicism as well as a concern for genuine ecumenical dialogue. He has taught at Woodstock College (Maryland), The Catholic University of America (Washington, D.C.), and Fordham University (New York). He was made a cardinal of the church in 2001.

James B. Nickoloff

See also ECCLESIOLOGY; REVELATION (IN CHRISTIAN PERSPECTIVE).

DUNS SCOTUS, JOHN (1266?–1308)

John was born in Duns, Scotland, and hence his name, literally "John, the Scot from Duns." John is most often referred to as "Scotus,"or "Duns Scotus," however. He entered the Franciscan order when he was fifteen. Starting his studies at Oxford, Scotus moved to Paris where he was a student from 1293 to 1296. Returning to Oxford, Scotus taught at the University until 1302 when he returned to Paris. He became Franciscan master of theology at Paris for only one year in 1307 before he went to Cologne where he died in 1308 at the age of forty-two. Called the subtle doctor, he is best known for his insightful, if sometimes torturous, use of logic. Scotus so frustrated some readers that his name, "Duns" became in English "dunce," the word for someone stupid. In reality, however, it would be his detractors, not Scotus, who deserve that title. Scotus strongly influenced later theologians, even if they couldn't always understand him.

Gary Macy

See also FRANCISCANS; MEDIEVAL CHRISTIANITY (IN THE WEST); NOMINALISM; SCHOLASTICISM.

DURA EUROPOS

An ancient city located on the west bank of the Euphrates River halfway between Aleppo and Baghdad. It was founded in the third century B.C.E. by the Seleucids and was destroyed in 256 C.E. by the Sassanid ruler Shapur I. Dura Europos is well known especially for the art work preserved there. There are paintings from the Temple of the Palmyrene Gods, the Mithra temple in the Roman camp, the Jewish synagogue, and the Christian church. The paintings from the synagogue have been extensively studied and are of great importance. There is great religious diversity evident in the paintings that depict fifty-eight biblical scenes. Among the biblical figures represented are Abraham, Isaac, Jacob, Moses, Aaron, Samuel, Elijah, Ezekiel, David, and Solomon.

Russell Fuller

DURGA

An important Hindu goddess, Durga is typically regarded as a form of Shakti, the spouse and feminine counterpart of Shiva. She is worshiped by Shaktas as the Supreme Being, eclipsing her husband Shiva in importance. Other mythic forms of what is, on most accounts, the same goddess include Parvati and Sati. The focus of the famous Durga Puja festival in Calcutta, usually falling in October, Durga displays in myth both benevolent

aspects (as compassionate Mother) and fearsome aspects (as destroyer of evil, especially evil as personified in Mahisasura, the Buffalo Demon).

Lance E. Nelson

See also HINDUISM; KALA; PARVATI; SHAKTA; SHAKTI; SHIVA.

DURKHEIM, ÉMILE (1858–1917)

French sociologist. A university professor at Bordeaux and Paris, he taught that the laws of human social behavior should not be deduced or inferred from biological laws. He theorized on what he called human "collective consciousness/conscience." In the area of religion he is best known for his very important and groundbreaking work The Elementary Forms of the Religious Life (1912), in which he explained religion in general and ritual in particular as symbols of social bonds.

Orlando Espín

See also INDIGENOUS RELIGIOUS TRADITIONS; MODERNITY; POSITIVISM; POSTMODERNITY; RELIGION; SACRED/SACRAL/SACRALIZED; SYMBOL.

DUSSEL, ENRIQUE (1934–)

Enrique Dussel is one of the major figures of Latin American liberation theology. He received a doctorate in philosophy from the University of Madrid (1957) and in church history from La Sorbonne (1965). During 1959–61, Dussel worked as a carpenter and angler in the Holy Land, an experience that made a lasting impression on him. Here he began to understand the "otherness" of the poor and to reflect on the philosophical and theological significance of the poor as "the Other" —a theme he would develop extensively in his writings. After returning to Argentina and teaching at the National

University of Cuyo for several years, Dussel was blacklisted by the military regime. In 1975 he and his family went into exile in Mexico. Since then, he has lived in Mexico and currently teaches at the National Autonomous University of Mexico. Dussel has served as president of the Commission for the Study of the History of the Church in Latin America (CEHILA) and has authored more than forty books in Latin American church history, ethics, philosophy, and theology.

Roberto S. Goizueta

See also LEVINAS, EMMANUEL; LIBERATION THEOLOGIES; MODERNITY.

DVAITA VEDANTA

A theistically oriented Hindu school, Dvaita (dualistic) Vedanta was founded by the Vaishnava theologian Madhva (twelfth century C.E.). Holding that *bhakti* is the surest path to God, Dvaita holds that Brahman, the ultimate reality described in the Upanishads, is identical with the Supreme Being Vishnu, who is a loving personal deity. In asserting that God, the human soul (*jiva*), and the world are absolutely and forever distinct, Madhva's dualism rejects not only the trans-theistic nondualism of Shankara's Advaita Vedanta, but also the theistic "qualified nondualism" of Ramanuja's Vishistadvaita Vedanta. Dvaita teaches that the world is fully real and composed of a plurality of fully real entities, but it denies the typically Vedantic idea that the world is a manifestation of Brahman's own substance. Unlike all other schools of Vedanta, Dvaita teaches that souls are different in their essential nature, enjoying different degrees of bliss in moksha, with some destined to undergo everlasting reincarnation or even eternal damnation.

Lance E. Nelson

See also ADVAITA VEDANTA; BRAHMAN; HINDUISM; JIVA; VAISHNAVA; VALLABHA; VEDANTA; VISHISTADVAITA.

E

EARTH DIVER

This is a major character in the creation stories of the Algonkian peoples, and of some others who lived near them. Typically, the Earth Diver is a creature who comes to the assistance of a human being who is lost in the universe and desperately needs to find solid land on which to live. The story proceeds when the human asks for volunteers in the search. Several of the larger creatures try and fail, but our hero has the courage and willingness to go where others have not succeeded, and always finds the material needed. This is accomplished by diving deep beneath water and retrieving a piece of earth he brings to the surface. Frequently, the effort is so great that he loses his life in the process, but is revived by the human. The meaning is clear; this is the price for life's continuation, and justly is the one who makes the sacrifice revered and loved. The form of the Earth Diver varies from tribe to tribe, and typically is one familiar to the local geography. Thus it could be a water bird, or a muskrat, or others.

Kathleen Dugan

See also MYTH.

EAST, ANCIENT CHURCHES OF THE

See ANCIENT CHURCHES OF THE EAST.

EASTER

Since the early eighth century (St. Bede the Venerable), the word was thought to be derived from the Anglo-Saxon goddess of spring, Eastre, but is more likely related to the German word for dawn, and has been the usual English expression for the celebration of Christ's resurrection, that is, the Easter Vigil, Easter Sunday, and the Season of Easter. The word often translates the Latin, *Dominica resurrectionis* (Sunday of the Resurrection), and the Greek/Latin term, *pascha* (Pasch) which, in turn, is a transliteration of the Aramaic *pesach* (Passover).

The New Testament, while unclear as to a specific Christian feast celebrating the Pasch (see 1 Cor 5:7-8), nevertheless consistently associates the death/resurrection of Jesus with the Jewish feast of Passover. This is true even in the case of John's Gospel with its different dating of the events of Jesus' last days (Jesus dies on the Jewish fourteenth of Nisan, the day before Passover, celebrated on the eve of Nisan 14/15, instead of on the day of Passover,

Nisan 15, as in the Synoptics). The earliest clear references to an annual celebration of the Pasch of Jesus are early second century (for example, *Epistula Apostolorum*, between 130–140, Apollonius of Hierapolis, before 170), and Melito of Sardis, before 190. It was a unitive celebration of both the death and resurrection of Jesus, observed annually on the Sunday after the fourteenth of Nisan by a daylong fast (Saturday) and an all-night vigil that became the normative time for baptism (Tertullian, *On Baptism*, about 200; and Hippolytus, *Apostolic Tradition*, around 215). The vigil was concluded with the Eucharist on Sunday morning. Since the sixth century and until the liturgical reforms of the Second Vatican Council, the West has emphasized Easter more as a celebration of the historical moment of the Resurrection, and Good Friday as the commemoration of Christ's suffering and death. The reforms resulting from Vatican II tend to view Easter as a more unitive celebration of the paschal mystery spread over the Easter Triduum, with Holy Saturday night once again the time par excellence for the celebration of Christian initiation.

An important part of the development of Easter is the paschal controversy of the latter half of the second century, centering around the practice of the church in Asia Minor (present-day Turkey), that observed the fourteenth of Nisan (hence, the "Quartodeciman" Controversy, recorded for us by Eusebius of Caesaria, *Ecclesiastical History*, 5.23-25, early fourth century) as a fast in commemoration of the death of Jesus. The observance was concluded with a eucharistic meal and celebration in the evening that may also have emphasized the Resurrection. This practice meant that when the fourteenth of Nisan fell on a Sunday, the fast would still be kept. Such a Sunday fast was con-trary to the practice of other churches that observed every Sunday as the Lord's Day, and reserved it for celebrating the whole of the paschal mystery in the Eucharist. Earlier in the second century, the Asian practice was at least tolerated by other churches, including Rome. Sometime after 190, Pope Victor excommunicated the Asian churches for the practice, despite a reminder from Irenaeus of Gaul and other bishops that earlier popes had lived in peace with a variety of paschal practices and lengths of fasts.

The First Council of Nicaea (325) gave final suppression to the Quartodeciman practice by opting for an Alexandrian computation of the "Paschal Moon" (first full moon after the vernal equinox, with Easter celebrated on the following Saturday night/Sunday). In so doing, the council also voted against the Antiochene practice that relied on Jewish computation for Passover with Easter celebrated on the following Sunday. However, divergent practices for the date of Easter continued through the seventh century due to differences in calendrical computation, notably in Rome, Alexandria, Gaul, Britain, and Ireland. Differences in dating Easter were again introduced by the adoption of the Gregorian calendar (1582, with later dates in the Reformation churches) over the Julian calendar, and continue today between Western churches and the Orthodox. In the twentieth century, various attempts were made to establish a uniform date for Easter. The Second Vatican Council stated it was not opposed to such a reform provided there was agreement among all Christian churches. Agreement is not likely until there is acceptance by the Orthodox at a future, as yet unscheduled, pan-Orthodox council.

Dennis W. Krouse

See also CALENDAR (LITURGICAL); EASTER TRIDUUM; PASCHAL; PASCHAL MYSTERY; PASSOVER; RESURRECTION (IN CHRISTIANITY); RESURRECTION OF CHRIST; RESURRECTION OF THE BODY.

EASTER TRIDUUM

The Easter Triduum, also known as *Triduum Sanctum* and considered by Christians to be the three most solemn days of the year, celebrates the whole paschal mystery of Jesus. Originally, the sense of the three days was rooted in the symbolism of Jonah's three days in the belly of the whale, applied to Christ's three days in the tomb (actually two nights and a day, that is, Good Friday evening to Easter morning; cf. Jonah 2:1; Matt 12:40; 16:4; Luke 11:30; 1 Cor 15:4).

Historical Overview

In the first centuries after Christ, these three days were marked liturgically by fasting and prayer with an all-night vigil on Holy Saturday that concluded with the celebration of baptism/confirmation and the Eucharist at dawn on Sunday. Many of the other distinctive liturgical practices of these days can be traced to the historicizing tendencies of the liturgies developed in late fourth-century Jerusalem to reenact the major events of the life of Christ, often in what was considered to be their actual location; for instance, the introduction of an afternoon Eucharist on Holy Thursday (up to then a non-eucharistic day) in memory of the Last Supper, readings of appropriate parts of the passion narrative and prayer at various stations from Thursday evening through Good Friday (Garden of Olives, the Cenacle or Upper Room, Calvary), and veneration of the relic of the cross with other relics on Friday afternoon at Golgotha. As other churches adopted these creative practices and adapted them to their own liturgical spaces, the Triduum gradually came to be viewed as including all of Holy Thursday, Good Friday, and Holy Saturday.

Holy Thursday is also known as Maundy Thursday (from *mandatum*, the new commandment of John 13:34). In Rome, beginning in the fourth century, the day primarily emphasized reconciliation of penitents during a Mass. There was no Mass for the commemoration of the Last Supper. Other churches adopted the Jerusalem custom of the Mass of the Last Supper, including North Africa (witnessed by Augustine) and Gaul. This often meant two Masses, one in the morning to conclude the Lenten fast (the paschal fast of Good Friday–Holy Saturday was usually seen as distinct), and one in the afternoon or evening for the Last Supper. In seventh-century Rome, churches served by presbyters adopted this two-Mass practice. At the same time, the pope began celebrating a midday Mass that commemorated the Last Supper and included the blessing of oils and consecration of chrism to be used for the initiation rites of the Holy Saturday vigil, in addition to the Mass for reconciliation. By the eighth century, the pope began celebrating three Masses: one for reconciliation (now long in disuse with the rise of private confession), another for the blessing of oils, and a third for the Last Supper. The latter two had no Liturgy of the Word. Presbyteral churches celebrated only one Mass, that of the Lord's Supper, its hour varying throughout the day according to local usage. After the sixteenth century, Tridentine reforms (Missal of Pius V) prohibited Masses after noon, so the Mass of the Lord's Supper was only celebrated in the morning. This shift clearly made the Triduum all day Thursday through Saturday, omitting

Easter Sunday itself, contrary to earlier tradition.

The *pedilavium* or washing of the feet (John 13) associated with Holy Thursday was initially a part of baptismal practices for Holy Saturday in many churches other than Rome. It was generally popular as a monastic service to the poor or as a gesture of communal love in religious houses. It is first mandated on Holy Thursday by the seventeenth Council of Toledo (694) for bishops and clerics, and found in the Roman Liturgy by the twelfth century as a separate service. The Missal of Pius V places it at the end of the morning Mass of the Lord's Supper, requiring it only in cathedrals and abbey churches.

The earliest reference to a unique liturgical celebration for Good Friday is found in the late fourth century in Egeria's diary of her pilgrimage to Jerusalem. Stational observances from Thursday night included readings from the prophets, passion accounts from the Gospels, the singing of psalms, and prayers. In the afternoon, all met on Calvary where the bishop presented the wood of the cross for veneration. It was guarded by two deacons to prevent theft (after a pilgrim had once bit off a piece of the relic!).

The first evidence for a liturgy for Good Friday in Rome dates from the seventh century. The papal liturgy consisted of readings, the Passion according to John, and the ancient form of the prayers of the faithful. The presbyteral churches first displayed a cross on the altar, followed by the same Liturgy of the Word used in the papal liturgy, followed by a liturgy of the presanctified Eucharist (of Byzantine origin). The presanctified service included a veneration of the cross by the priest while deacons brought the Eucharist reserved from the Liturgy of the Lord's Supper the day before; all recited the Lord's Prayer,

received Communion, and venerated the cross. By the eighth century, the papal liturgy included the veneration of the cross, but with no Communion service. In the thirteenth century, a shift occurred that prevailed until the twentieth century, namely, only the priest received Communion, which included taking a particle of the consecrated Host and placing it in a chalice of unconsecrated wine that was then consumed, a relic of the medieval practice of consecration by contact. Originally, these Good Friday services were celebrated in the afternoon in replication of Christ's death on the cross. Gradually, due to the popular desire to end the day's fast earlier, the time for the service was moved to the morning. Sixteenth-century reforms mandated a morning service which continued until the reforms of 1951/1955.

Holy Saturday commemorates the repose of Jesus in the tomb, his descent to hell (1 Pet 3:19-20; 4:6), and opening the gates of heaven. Aside from the Liturgy of the Hours, the day has never assumed any special liturgical celebration. It was a day of fasting and personal prayer. When baptisms were celebrated at the night vigil, there was an afternoon service for the "giving back of the creed" that had been memorized by the catechumens. The liturgical "void" of the day gradually came to be filled by earlier celebration of the vigil, again to terminate the fast sooner, until, in the sixteenth century, the vigil itself was celebrated in the early morning hours of Saturday. This continued until 1951/1955.

The Easter Vigil, which Augustine calls the "mother of all vigils," was originally an all-night service of readings, psalms, reflection, and public prayer, completed by the Liturgy of the Eucharist at dawn. It functioned as the closure of the Easter fast of Good Friday and Holy Saturday. It was the original and primary celebration for Easter Sunday, with no other Eucharist being celebrated. The earliest evidence associates the vigil with Christian initiation during which catechumens for the first time, and the community by way of renewal, participate sacramentally in the paschal mystery of Christ. At least by the fourth century, and probably earlier, a light service (*lucernarium*), similar to that used at cathedral Vespers, and possibly associated with the Friday night blessing of the Jewish Sabbath meal, introduced the vigil. Elaborate diaconal proclamations of thanksgiving for Easter joy and light developed in the fourth century. The one used today, the *Exultet*, was probably composed by Ambrose in the late fourth century.

Modern Reforms

The reform of the Easter Triduum began in 1955 (done experimentally in various places beginning in 1951). It included the restoration of an evening celebration for the Mass of the Lord's Supper on Holy Thursday, and an afternoon celebration of the Good Friday service that also restored the Communion of the people (with no use of the chalice for priest or people). The reform restored the Easter Vigil as an actual vigil, to begin after sunset on Holy Saturday, and as the time par excellence for baptism. It also included for the first time a renewal of the baptismal promises of the faithful. The effect of this reform was primarily greater simplification of the rites. Its general thrust was employed in the liturgical reforms mandated by the Second Vatican Council (*Sacrosanctum Concilium*, 1963) that resulted in the publication of the *Missale Romanum* in 1970. The English version, *The Sacramentary*, was available in 1974. There can be no substitute for a careful reading of the liturgical texts themselves. In 2002 the Congregation for Divine Worship and Discipline of the Sacraments published a revision of the *Roman Missal* (*Missale Romanus, editio typica tertia*) that included some further changes in the liturgies of the Triduum. (The International Committee for English in the Liturgy has completed a translation that requires approval of the English-speaking episcopal conferences of the world and final approbation of the Holy See, expected at the end of 2007.) The following outlines reflect these changes:

Holy Thursday—
Evening Mass of the Lord's Supper
Introductory Rites (standard)
Gloria (church bells are rung, then remain silent until the *Gloria* of the Easter Vigil)
Liturgy of the Word (standard)
Washing of the Feet (after the homily)
Liturgy of the Eucharist (standard, except for a proper preface and for a special collection for the poor to be taken up during the preparation rites—the only one mentioned in the missal)
Transfer of the Holy Eucharist
Incensation of the Blessed Sacrament
Procession to the Place of Reposition
Adoration by the Faithful (until midnight)
(No Dismissal Rites)

Good Friday—
Celebration of the Lord's Passion
Introductory Rites
Reverence to Altar
Prostration or Kneeling in Silent Prayer
Opening Prayer

Part One: Liturgy of the Word (standard)
Reading of the Passion according to John (no lights or incense; multiple readers, including laypersons, may be used for the various parts; it may also be chanted)
Brief Homily
General Intercessions (in classic Roman style using a thematic invitation to prayer, silence and a collect for each of ten petitions)

Part Two: Veneration of the Cross
Showing of the Cross and Invitation

Procession of Veneration (various songs can be used including the traditional Trisagion ("Holy God, Holy Strong One . . ."; the Reproaches are often substituted because of possible anti-Semitic interpretation)

Part Three: Holy Communion
Our Father
Invitation to Communion
Distribution of Communion
Prayer after Communion
Prayer over the People
Departure in Silence

Easter Sunday—During the Night—The Easter Vigil (must not begin until nightfall—45 minutes after sunset, and must conclude by daybreak—45 minutes before sunrise)

Part One: Solemn Beginning of the Vigil:
The Service of Light
Sign of the Cross
Blessing of the Fire and Lighting of the Paschal Candle (Preparation of the Candle is optional)
Procession (into church)
Easter Proclamation (*Exsultet*)

Part Two: Liturgy of the Word
(Seven Readings from the Old Testament, each followed by a responsorial psalm/canticle, and/or silence, and a collect; a minimum of three readings are required)
Gloria (church bells are rung)
Prayer
Epistle
Alleluia
Gospel (incense may be used, but not candles)

Part Three: Liturgy of Baptism
Litany of the Saints
Blessing of Water
Baptism and Confirmation (of those past the age of reason)
Renewal of Baptismal Promises and Sprinkling with Blessed Water

Part Four: Liturgy of the Eucharist
(standard, except for proper preface)
Blessing and Dismissal (standard, except for double alleluia)

With this reform of the Second Vatican Council, the Easter Triduum is restored to its primitive, three-day clarity. It begins with the Mass of the Lord's Supper on Holy Thursday after sunset and concludes on Easter Sunday with the celebrations of the Mass of Easter Sunday, Evening Prayer, and Compline at night.

Dennis W. Krouse

See also CALENDAR (LITURGICAL); EASTER; FASTS/FASTING (IN CHRISTIANITY); HOLY WEEK; LITURGY OF THE HOURS; PASCHAL; PASCHAL CANDLE; PASCHAL MYSTERY; PASSION NARRATIVES; PASSOVER; RESURRECTION (IN CHRISTIANITY); RESURRECTION OF CHRIST; RESURRECTION OF THE BODY.

EASTERN CATHOLIC CHURCHES

The churches that form the one worldwide Catholic Church are in some ways very different from each other. Each church has its own theological and doctrinal traditions and styles, its own liturgy and religious practices, its own patriarch and bishops, priests and deacons, its own canon law and ecclesiastical organization, its own parishes, and so on. However, every one of these churches shares, with all of the others, the same doctrinal beliefs, the same sacraments, the same mutual recognition of their having preserved the apostolic succession, and so on. Their diversity is seen by them as a healthy sign of catholicity and not as a hindrance to their unity. Among them there is no distinction (and there can never be any such distinction) as to which of these churches is "more Catholic." They are *all equals.* They are all "in full communion" with each other and with the Church of Rome and its bishop.

From roots in Palestine, Christianity spread to other areas in the ancient Mediterranean world, where a few cities slowly emerged as key centers of Christian life and understanding, with great influence over the local churches in their general vicinity. These centers were Jerusalem, Alexandria, Antioch, and Constantinople (all in the eastern Mediterranean region), and Rome (in the western Mediterranean region). The bishops of these five cities became very influential, too, and eventually became known as "patriarchs," and their sees (and areas of influence) "patriarchates."

In time, the church spread throughout the world under the influence of these five traditional patriarchates. Local churches (with some exceptions) were established as heirs to one or another of these five Christian traditions, depending on the church of origin of its founding missionaries.

The "Eastern Catholic Churches" are the twenty-three churches, in full communion with Rome and with each other, that trace their liturgical and doctrinal ancestry back to the traditions of the patriarchal sees of the ancient eastern Mediterranean region. With few exceptions, these Catholic Churches were separated from Rome in the past, and often represent groups from within Orthodox Churches that left the latter in order to reestablish full communion with Rome. As in the Orthodox Churches, the liturgy plays an eminent role in ecclesial life and self-understanding.

The largest group of Eastern Catholic Churches are those of Byzantine tradition. These were established originally from or came under the influence of the patriarchate of Constantinople (known as Byzantium before Emperor Constantine the Great changed its name; it is the present-day Istanbul): for example, the Albanian, Bulgarian, Greek, Italo-Albanian, Melkite, Rumanian, Russian, Ruthenian, and Ukrainian Churches.

There are two Catholic Churches of the Alexandrian tradition. They were established originally from or came under the influence of the patriarchate of Alexandria. There is a legend that claims that the evangelist St. Mark founded the see of Alexandria in Egypt. Whatever the historical accuracy of this claim, the fact remains that Egypt gave Christian monasticism to the world, and that the Coptic/Alexandrian Church was one of the great centers of theological learning in Christian antiquity. The missionary activity of Alexandria reached deep into Africa until the Islamic conquests of the seventh century. The two churches are the Coptic (or Egyptian) and the Ethiopian (or Abyssinian). The name Copt comes from an Arabic mispronunciation of the Greek word for "Egyptian."

There is but one Catholic Church of Armenian tradition (the Armenian Catholic Church), while there are a handful of Catholic Churches of the Antiochene tradition. The latter were established originally from or came under the influence of the patriarchate of Antioch in Syria. The so-called *Apostolic Constitutions* and the Liturgy of St. James of Jerusalem had great influence in the patriarchate of Antioch, and shaped the liturgy and traditions of the churches in its area of influence. The largest of the Catholic Churches of Antiochene tradition is the Maronite Church.

There are three Catholic Churches of the Chaldean tradition. These were also established originally from or came under the influence of the patriarchate of Antioch, but by way of the Assyrian Oriental Church. This particular church tradition, although dependent on Antioch, developed to the east of this city and became known for its rejection of the Hellenizing influences of the Antiochene patriarchate. It adopted Palestinian Christian traditions instead. Involved in the Nestorian schism that followed the Council of Ephesus in 431 c.e., these churches separated from the rest of Christendom and continued their missionary activity in Persia (present-day Iran), China, and India. Most Christians of this tradition are now in full communion with Rome. The three Catholic Churches of the Chaldean tradition are the Chaldean, the Malabar, and the Malankarese.

Orlando Espín

See also AFRICAN CHRISTIANITY; ALEXANDRIAN THEOLOGY; ANCIENT CHURCHES OF THE EAST; ANTIOCHENE THEOLOGY; APOSTOLIC FATHERS; ARMENIAN CATHOLIC CHURCH; BYZANTINE CATHOLIC CHURCHES; BYZANTIUM/BYZANTINE; CAPPADOCIANS; CATHOLIC TRADITION; CHALDEAN CATHOLIC CHURCH; CONSTANTINOPLE, SEE OF; COPTIC CATHOLIC CHURCH; EPARCH; EXARCH; FATHERS OF THE CHURCH; GREEK CATHOLIC CHURCH; MAJOR ARCHBISHOP; MALABAR CATHOLIC CHURCH; MALANKARESE CATHOLIC CHURCH; MARONITE CATHOLIC CHURCH; MELKITE CATHOLIC CHURCH; ORTHODOX CHURCHES; PATRIARCH; PATRISTICS/PATROLOGY; PETRINE MINISTRY; PRIMACY; ROME, SEE OF; RUTHENIAN CATHOLIC CHURCH; SCHISM, GREAT EASTERN; SYRIAN CATHOLIC CHURCH; UKRAINIAN CATHOLIC CHURCH; WESTERN CATHOLIC CHURCHES.

EASTERN CHURCHES

See AFRICAN CHRISTIANITY; ALEXANDRIAN THEOLOGY; ANCIENT CHURCHES OF THE EAST; ANTIOCHENE THEOLOGY; APOSTOLIC FATHERS; BYZANTIUM/BYZANTINE; CAPPADOCIANS; CATHOLIC TRADITION; COMMUNION (ECCLESIOLOGICAL); CONSTANTINOPLE, SEE OF; EASTERN CATHOLIC CHURCHES; ECUMENICAL PATRIARCH; EPARCH; EXARCH; FATHERS OF THE CHURCH; MAJOR ARCHBISHOP; ORTHODOX CHURCHES; PATRIARCH; PATRISTICS/PATROLOGY; PETRINE MINISTRY; ROME, SEE OF; SCHISM, GREAT EASTERN; UNIATES; WESTERN CATHOLIC CHURCHES.

E.A.T.WO.T.

These initials stand for the Ecumenical Association of Third World Theologians. EATWOT gathers representative theologians of most Christian denominations from across the globe, including African American and Latino theologians from the U.S. It also has a strong list of publications to its credit. It regularly holds international congresses and symposia on specific topics of interest to the worldwide theological community.

Orlando Espín

See also AFRICAN CHRISTIANITY; FEMINIST THEOLOGIES; LATIN AMERICAN CATHOLICISM; LATIN AMERICAN PROTESTANTISM; LATINO CATHOLICISM; LATINO PROTESTANTISM; LIBERATION THEOLOGIES; MUJERISTA THEOLOGY; THIRD WORLD THEOLOGIES; WOMANIST THEOLOGY.

EBELING, GERHARD (1912–2001)

Professor of historical, systematic, and New Testament theology at Tübingen and Zurich. His work figured prominently in German discussions during the 1960s about the "New Quest" for the historical Jesus. Following the lead of biblical scholars like Bornkamm, Ebeling challenged the modern pessimistic reluctance to pursue historical questions about Jesus, striving to push such discourse in a more positive way. Ebeling's book *Wort und Glaube* (*Word and Faith* [1960]) perceptively explores the background, meanings, and possibility of "biblical" theology from the standpoint of systematic theology.

Francis D. Connolly-Weinert

See also JESUS OF HISTORY.

EBIONITES

The name used for groups of Christians who continued to follow Jewish laws and customs. Called "Ebionites" from the Hebrew word for "poor," some Christian writers, not knowing Hebrew, mistakenly thought that they had been founded by a person named "Ebion." As Christians lost touch with the Jewish roots of Christianity, these Jewish-Christian groups became smaller and more marginalized. Already in the second century, Irenaeus and Tertullian referred to them as heretics for teaching that Jesus was a mere man. Origen quoted from a "Gospel to the Hebrews" used by the Ebionites, and Epiphanius mentioned other Ebionite books, now lost. There appears to have been more than one group of Jewish Christians whom different early writers lump together as Ebionites. Among the beliefs and practices ascribed to these groups (apart from those already mentioned) are the use of unleaven bread for the Eucharist, the rejection of the apostle Paul and/or of the prophets, the avoidance of Gentiles, and ritual purification. Eusebius described the Ebionites as the descendents of the Christian community who had fled from Jerusalem after the destruction of the Temple by the Romans. Some forms of Ebionite Christianity lasted at least into the fourth century, and some of these communities may have adopted Gnostic views. It is difficult, however, to be sure of what the Ebionites actually believed since most of our information about them comes from unsympathetic writers who considered them heretical.

Gary Macy

See also EPIPHANIUS; EUSEBIUS OF CAESAREA; GNOSIS/GNOSTICISM; HERETIC/HERETICAL; IRENAEUS OF LYONS; TERTULLIAN.

ECCLESIAM SUAM

An encyclical issued by Pope Paul VI on August 6, 1964, this was Pope Paul's first encyclical and was issued while the Second Vatican Council was still in session. It exhorts the church to greater self-knowledge by seeing itself as Christ sees it (hence the title, "His Church"). The result of this self-knowledge will be the realization that the church is in need of renewal. Finally, the Pope calls upon the bishops to be courageous in undertaking renewal and to seek ways to present the Gospel in a spirit of "friendly dialogue" with both those within and without the confines of the church.

Mary Ann Hinsdale

See also ENCYCLICAL; PAUL VI, POPE.

ECCLESIASTICAL PROVINCE

In the Roman Catholic Church, an ecclesiastical province is the name of a specific territory comprised by several dioceses (called the "suffragan" dioceses of the province) and one archdiocese (called the "metropolitan see" of the province). The "metropolitan" archbishop has some rights and obligations over the province.

Orlando Espín

See also ARCHBISHOP; BISHOP (AUXILIARY, SUFFRAGAN); BISHOP (EPISCOPACY); DIOCESE/ARCHDIOCESE; METROPOLITAN; ROMAN CATHOLIC CHURCH.

ECCLESIOLOGY

The English word "church" is derived from the Greek adjective kuriokos which means "of the Lord," and is short for kuriakos domos, or "the Lord's house." In the New Testament, the Greek word ekklesia refers to an assembly of people and is used to translate the Hebrew term *qahal* which means a convoked assembly. Ecclesiology, then, is the study (or doctrine) of the assembly of Christian believers. In the New Testament, *ekklesia* usually signifies a local community modeled on a Jewish synagogue that gathers for worship (see 1 Cor 1:2). Less frequently it refers to the Christian community at large (see Eph 1:22). While historical and sociological studies of Christianity and the Christian church shed light on important aspects of these phenomena, theological analysis alone can uncover what for Christian believers is the heart of the matter: the church's true origin, nature, and mission. The theological study of the church (ecclesiology), then, attempts to understand the church in relation to God. Efforts to do this began with the early church, and while there is no systematic ecclesiology developed in the New Testament, there are diverse images used to portray the fundamental meaning and purpose of the Christian community. Some of these include the temple of God (or Holy Spirit; see 1 Cor 3:16; 2 Cor 6:16; Eph 2:21); the "new Zion" or "new Jerusalem" (that is, the perfect kingdom of God of the future; see Rev 21:2); the Bride of Christ (Eph 5:25-32; 2 Cor 11:2; Rev 21:2; 22:17); the Body of Christ (Rom 12:4-5; 1 Cor 12:27; Eph 1:22-23; 4:12; Col 1:18, 24); the people of God (1 Pet 2:9-10; Rom 9:25); and the inauguration (but not the fullness or completion) of the kingdom of God (Rev 1:6; 5:10).

Early Christians did not first produce a theoretical notion of the church and then set out to bring their conception to realization. Instead, they believed that they had been assembled by the Holy Spirit of the Risen Christ. In pondering the meaning and implications of their already-existing assembly, they produced the first ecclesiological reflections. Yet,

because the community of faith exists in changing sociohistorical circumstances, not only has the outward form of the church changed over time but its self-understanding has grown and developed as well.

Major ecclesiological shifts in the history of the church include the following. From the death of Jesus to the fourth century, Christianity dramatically passed from being a persecuted Jewish sect to the official state religion of the empire (381 C.E.), thanks to the conversion of the Roman emperor Constantine. In this same period, the church adopted the first commonly accepted creed (Nicene Creed, 325 C.E.), established the canon of the New Testament, and instituted ecclesiastical structures centered on the episcopate (office of bishop) as a way of maintaining continuity with its origins. From the fifth to the sixteenth centuries, the church became self-consciously hierarchical and sacralized, and the church at Rome rose to a position of practical and theoretical primacy among the local churches. Its life was largely modeled on a feudal monarchy, with the pope at its head. In the context of continuous conflict between the church's spiritual power and the secular power of emperors and the nobility, the church employed the framework of Roman law in its self-understanding and practice. Yet, even in a highly structured institution, theologians continued to make use of New Testament images in describing the church such as the Body of Christ, Temple of the Holy Spirit, and people of God. From the sixteenth to the twentieth centuries, the church faced the multiple challenges posed by science (reason), democratic thought (as seen in the French Revolution), the struggle for individual rights (liberalism), and religious pluralism (Protestant Reformation)—in short, by the modern world. The Reformation challenged not only the corruption of some Catholic practices but the heart of Catholicism's self-understanding as well, especially the primacy of the pope. Catholic retrenchment and resistance to any accommodation to modernity, made manifest in the proclamation of papal infallibility in matters of faith and morals at the First Vatican Council (1869–70), was maintained until the Second Vatican Council (1962–5). At Vatican II, the Catholic Church attempted to reconcile its tradition with modern thought and mandated reform in many areas of its life. For this purpose, the council emphasized the biblical image of the church as the people of God and creatively employed the notion of sacrament (sign and instrument of God's grace) to describe the church's essence.

Today, Christians recognize a variety of ecclesiologies present in the church(es). The Catholic theologian Avery Dulles has proposed six distinct but not necessarily incompatible "models" of the church: institution, mystical communion, sacrament, herald, servant, and community of disciples. In each model, the mission (or purpose), ministry (or means of accomplishing the mission), and membership are understood in a slightly different manner. When the church is understood principally as an institution, its mission is often conceived as the salvation of souls, its ministry as the celebration of the sacraments, and its membership as those who are baptized sacramentally. Those who envision the church primarily as a mystical communion see its mission as the achievement of spiritual union among the members and between them and God, the ministry as those activities that foster such union, and membership as open to all who enter into such union. If the church itself is perceived primarily as a sacrament (and thus the ground of the seven traditional sacraments), its mission is to be a sign of God's grace in the world and to make that grace present, ministry is any activity that accomplishes this purpose, and membership includes those who accept the call to be themselves sacraments of God's love. Christians who envision the church as the herald of God's word take its mission as the proclamation of that word, its primary ministry as preaching that word, and the church's membership as consisting of those who make the task of proclaiming God's word central in their lives. Those who take servant as the best description of the church usually see its mission as serving the whole world, particularly by promoting social consciousness and social transformation so that God's kingdom may come to be "on earth as in heaven." These Christians define ministry in broad terms as all activities that support such a transformation of the world and see as full members of the church those who take up such a task. Finally, we must note that none of the above models is mutually exclusive of the others; that is, aspects of any one of the models may be incorporated into the others so that in reality the ecclesiology of most Christians is a blend of the models and not "pure." This might be especially true of the last group, those who envision the church primarily as a community of disciples. Here the mission is seen as the formation of a spiritually united community, but one that also recognizes its duty to imitate Christ by going out into the world to serve. Ministry is discipleship, that is, the replication of Jesus' words and deeds. The membership of the church consists of those who commit themselves to being such disciples.

While most Christian churches emphasize one understanding of the church over others, it is also true that elements of the foregoing models are found in the Catholicism of Vatican II, in many Protestant churches, and even in the relatively traditional Orthodox Church. The future of ecclesiology, like its past, will likely be complex and creative.

James B. Nickoloff

See also CHRISTIANITY; DEVELOPMENT OF DOGMA/OF DOCTRINE; VATICAN, SECOND COUNCIL OF THE.

ECK, JOHANN OF (1486–1543)

Johann Meier was born in Egg an der Günz and thus received his name "Eckius" or "from Eck." Johann was professor of theology at Ingolstadt from 1510 until his death. Much influenced by humanist scholarship, Johann was a friend of Martin Luther until the indulgence controversy of 1517. From then on, he took the lead in opposing Luther, debating him in 1519 and playing an influential role in Luther's excommunication in 1520. Johann wrote a defense of the papacy in 1521, attacked the *Augsburg Confession* in 1530, and produced a German translation of the Bible for Catholic use in 1537.

Gary Macy

See also AUGSBURG CONFESSION; HUMANISM; LUTHER, MARTIN.

ECKHART, J. (MEISTER) (1260?–1328)

Meister (Master) Eckhart was a Dominican theologian, preacher, and mystic. Eckhart had joined the Dominican order by 1277 when he was a student in Paris. He later studied in Cologne and held several important posts in the Dominican Order. Although during his lifetime he was re-

nowned for his learning, holding chairs of theology at the University of Paris in 1302–3 and again in 1311–3, Eckhart is best known for his sermons written in German. Here he expounded a mystical theology of "emptiness," by which he meant that Christians should empty themselves of all desire and all will so that, by becoming nothing, humans can touch the nothingness that is God. In this way, God and the soul become one while yet retaining their distinct identities. Toward the end of his life, this teaching got Eckhart in trouble, and he was the first Dominican accused of heresy. Eckhart recanted those parts of his work that were considered a problem before his death in 1328. Eckhart is considered one of the greatest of the medieval mystics. His works influenced not only other medieval mystics, but also Martin Luther, and even modern philosophers.

Gary Macy

See also CHRISTIANITY; DOMINICANS; LUTHER, MARTIN; MEDIEVAL CHURCH; MYSTICISM/MYSTICS (IN CHRISTIANITY).

ECOLOGY

From the Greek word *oikos*, meaning "household," "home," or "place to live," ecology is the study of the multiple relationships of coexistence, production, and consumption in environments composed of living and nonliving things. The interactions among organisms and between organisms and their environment are considered ecological systems (ecosystems) or the economy of nature. Traditionally, ecological studies have focused on the population dynamics of various organisms—considering the relationship among different species (whether it represents symbiotic cooperation, predatory, or coexistence), and also considering the environmental factors affecting specific populations over a period of time. Population dynamics also take into consideration the different factors affecting the equilibrium of a population of organisms in an environment over a period of time with respect to the availability or scarcity of resources. For this reason ecology encompasses both geographic and historical (intergenerational) dimensions. Another traditional area of study has been the flow or transfers of energy within a system—how food energy is developed by plants and transferred through different levels of consumption throughout the system. Because of the difficulty of controlling all the variables existing in an open environment, many ecological studies have been limited to observation, statistical prediction, and descriptive analysis of ecosystems. Contemporary studies allow the use of experimental methods that can control for one or more variables in an enclosed system. Ecological studies have developed into a multidisciplinary science, including the branches of genetics, taxonomy, biology, geology, anthropology, sociology, and mathematics. It has also expanded to include the interrelationship among organisms and their environment beyond the Earth's surface to explore the relationship among the planets and other components of the cosmos. Ecological studies have become an important field within politics and economics because of the interrelationship between environmental sustainability, economic development, consumption, dependence on fossil fuels, global warming, water scarcity, growing urban populations, human waste management, and other elements affecting the balance of the human population and the Earth's environment. The growing fields of environmental theology and ethics look at the relationship of the world's religious traditions and the environment throughout their sacred texts, the histories of the different traditions, and their intersection with contemporary reflections on the environment. Judaism, Christianity, Islam, Buddhism, native or indigenous traditions, and other world religions include a consideration of the transcendent or sacred dimensions of the relationship between humanity and its environment as well as of the delicate balance among all living things. Ecological or environmental ethics assesses how the direction of a number of interrelationships in the ecosystem are unjust or oppressive to some of its members—such as populations of humans and animals suffering from pollution, overcrowding, scarcity of resources, and ecological degradation and spoliation—as well as presenting the natural environment as an oppressed member of the human social environment that must be protected and restored.

María Teresa Dávila

See also CATHOLIC SOCIAL TEACHING; ECONOMY; SCIENCE AND THEOLOGY.

ECONOMIC JUSTICE FOR ALL: CATHOLIC SOCIAL TEACHING AND THE U.S. ECONOMY

In 1986 the Catholic bishops of the United States published a letter that addressed economic suffering, including rising unemployment, underemployment, and escalating poverty for many despite full-time employment. In highlighting the misery of millions because of current economic arrangements, the letter defined injustice as marginalization and justice as participation with dignity in the economy.

The bishops said that achieving "basic justice for all is not an optional expression of largesse, but an inescapable duty for the whole of mankind." Remaining within the neoclassical economic tradition, the bishops assumed that members of capitalist societies could reform unjust conditions through liberal social welfare policies, increased education and job creation, and a mutual partnership between capital and labor.

Critics have suggested that, unlike similar letters issued by the Canadian bishops during the 1980s, a fundamental flaw in the encyclical is its inadequate treatment of economic power and the morality of that power. Even though such an analysis is missing, it is nevertheless true that this letter challenged what most people in the U.S. have been taught to assume—the justice of current economic arrangements. The bishops advocated "a new American experiment" in economic democracy that would include a majority of workers becoming "owners, at least in part, of the instruments of production." This pastoral letter said that the justice of an economy should be measured by its effect on people, especially those at the bottom of the economic ladder.

Mary E. Hobgood

See also CATHOLIC SOCIAL TEACHING; ECONOMY; QUADRAGESIMO ANNO; RERUM NOVARUM.

ECONOMY

Derived from the Greek word "oikos" or "house," the word economy shares the same root as the words ecumenical and ecology. Economy, then, means providing for the needs of the whole household, the whole society and the planet itself.

Modern neoclassical economic theory, however, has been centered on a view of the economy as society organized by exchange, that is the profit-maximizing choices of autonomous rational agents. Critics claim that this view has lost the sense of the true purpose of the economy —to provide for the whole human family, or even for the whole ecosphere. An economic system organized around the profit-maximizing choices of autonomous rational agents is especially inhospitable toward those not primarily defined by these characteristics, like children, women, the disabled and others who participate in the subordinate socioeconomic classes, as well as the planet itself.

In the discussion about the economy by religious thinkers, three views are prominent. Some advocate the moral self-sufficiency of the market economy for human provisioning, while others support the market but believe a strong welfare state is necessary to make the market morally tolerable. Finally a third group, more prominent in the industrialized states with a wider economic spectrum than the United States, argues that a radical restructuring of the political economy is necessary to make just provision for the whole human race while preserving the integrity of other earth creatures and the planet itself.

Mary E. Hobgood

See also CATHOLIC SOCIAL TEACHING; CLASSISM; ECONOMIC JUSTICE FOR ALL; JUSTICE; MATERIALISM.

ECONOMY OF SALVATION

A Christian theological term that refers to the whole of God's activity in the world, specifically for the benefit of humankind (for humanity's "salvation"). In Orthodox Churches the term may be found in reference to dispensations from ecclesiastical law.

Orlando Espín

See also FAITH; GOD; GRACE; JUSTIFICATION; SALVATION; SOTERIOLOGY.

ECSTASY

Literally, ecstasy means "standing outside" of oneself. The state of ecstasy is one in which "the concentration of interest on the Transcendent is so complete, the gathering up and pouring out of life on this one point so intense, that the subject is more or less entranced, and becomes, for the time of the ecstasy, unconscious of the external world. . . . In ecstasy [the subject] cannot attend to [the external world]. None of its messages reach him; not even those most insistent of all messages which are translated in terms of bodily pain" (Evelyn Underhill, *Mysticism*, 358).

Ecstasy is generally an intensely joyous experience; for Christians, it is the state of being seized by the Spirit and thus frequently a feature of charismatic prayer. Among mystics, ecstasy is the experience of being grasped and lifted outside of oneself, as it were, by divine love. Paul seems to be describing such an experience in 2 Corinthians 12:1-4. Yet there may also be something "ecstatic" about the experience of self-emptying (see Phil 2:7, where Paul speaks of Christ Jesus as having "emptied" himself). In this case, however, Christ is seen to have concentrated his attention outward and on the world out of love for us, letting go of his equality with God and taking the form of a slave. Thus, it would not be incorrect to see an ecstatic aspect to service and the practice of humility.

William Reiser, s.j.

See also CHARISM/CHARISMATIC; CHARISMATIC MOVEMENT; KENOSIS; MYSTICISM/MYSTICS (IN CHRISTIANITY); RAPTURE (IN AMERICAN PROTESTANTISM); VIA UNITIVA.

ECUMENICAL COUNCIL

See COUNCIL, ECUMENICAL.

ECUMENICAL MOVEMENT/ ECUMENISM

Ecumenism differs from interreligious dialogue, or dialogue among different world religions. Drawn from the Greek *oikoumene*, meaning "inhabited world," ecumenism refers to inter-Christian relations among worldwide Catholic (Roman and Eastern), Protestant, and Orthodox Churches for the purpose of deeper understanding, cooperation, mutual recognition, and possibly full communion (Greek, *koinonia*).

The twentieth century is commonly considered the ecumenical century by historians of Christian thought, given the flowering of many ecumenical movements devoted to prayer, dialogue, and/or social justice among Christian churches. The World Missionary Conference in 1910 at Edinburgh is widely regarded as the beginning of the modern ecumenical movement. The World Council of Churches (WCC), formed in 1948 and headquartered in Geneva, Switzerland, understands itself to already partly signify and to be working toward a full realization of unity in faith and fellowship among Anglican, Orthodox, and Protestant traditions and more recently Coptic and other African churches. The WCC has held several general assemblies across the globe since its inception, including Europe, the United States, Asia, Africa, Canada, and Australia. Assembly topics vary widely; of particular interest is the Ecumenical Decade of the Churches in Solidarity with Women (1988–98), which addressed such topics as gender and power in institutional structures, theologies, and practices of member churches, as well as global trends in poverty, racism, sexism, and violence against women and girls.

In regard to Catholic traditions, Pope John XXIII initiated the Pontifical Secretariat for Christian Unity, as well as invited non-Roman Catholic observers to attend Vatican II (1962–5). After Vatican II, the Secretariat (now Council) began bilateral dialogues with Orthodox, Anglican, and Protestant churches (Lutheran, Reformed, Methodist, and so on). The conciliar decree *Unitatis Redintegratio* from Vatican II (1962–5) outlined a theological rationale for dialogue with Eastern churches (some already and some not yet in official union with Rome) and with Protestant churches separated from Rome either during or after the European Reformation in the sixteenth century. Moreover, in the conciliar decree *Lumen Gentium* (no. 8), the council fathers argued that the true church "subsists in" but not only in the Roman Catholic Church, thus blazing a theological trail for future ecumenical dialogues among Christian churches based on mutual recognition. Expanding on this ecclesiology or theological self-understanding of the church, in 1995 Pope John Paul II issued two major encyclicals, *Orientale Lumen* and *Ut Unum Sint*, both of which officially recognized the equal dignity and rights of Eastern Catholic Churches and Orthodox Churches as "sister" churches.

The goal of these and other ecumenical movements, especially the ongoing Lutheran-Catholic dialogue that culminated in the 1999 Joint Declaration on the Doctrine of Justification (that is, the forgiveness of sin and the restoration of right relations with God, others, and the earth by grace through faith that leads to good works), is to express more fully and visibly the mark of the unity of the church described in the Gospels (John 17:11, 20-23) and professed in the Nicene-Constantinopolitan Creed of 381 (one, holy, catholic, and apostolic church). In regard to Christian theology, ecumenism takes the form of global congresses and

assemblies among theologians, sponsored for example by the Ecumenical Association of Third World Theologians (EATWOT), which was founded in 1976 for the purpose of fostering theological reflection and solidarity across Christian traditions and communities in the two-thirds world.

Rosemary P. Carbine

See also COUNCIL OF CHURCHES (WORLD, NATIONAL); ECCLESIOLOGY; UNITATIS REDINTEGRATIO; VATICAN, SECOND COUNCIL OF THE.

ECUMENICAL PATRIARCH
A title of honor and dignity used by the Orthodox bishops of Constantinople since the sixth century.

Orlando Espín

See also BISHOP (EPISCOPACY); CONSTANTINOPLE, SEE OF; ORTHODOX CHURCHES; PATRIARCH.

EDDY, MARY BAKER
See CHRISTIAN SCIENCE CHURCH.

EDOT HAMIZRACH
(Hebrew, "Communities of the East"). Term used to designate the Jewish communities of Yemon, Ethiopia, and other eastern countries. The religious rituals and culture of Jews from these areas are distinguished from those of Sephardic Jews, who originate in the Mediterranean and Arab world (as well, more recently, as South and Central America) and from those of Ashkenazic Jews, who originated in the communities of eastern and western Europe, including Russia. Best known today among the Jews of the Edot HaMizrach are the Falashas (Amharic: "exiles"), a Jewish ethnic group originating in Ethiopia that follows a form of

Judaism based upon the Bible, certain books of the Apocrypha, and other religious writings. Originally living in the provinces surrounding and to the north of Lake Tana, beginning in 1975, members of the group came to Israel, where a large community of Ethiopian Jews now resides.

Alan J. Avery-Peck

See also ASHKENAZIM; SEPHARDIM.

EDWARDS, JONATHAN (1703–58)

Born in East Windsor, Connecticut, Edwards was a theologian and preacher of the First Great Awakening. Educated at Yale College, he became a Congregational pastor in Northampton, Massachusetts, in 1727. In 1734–5, the church experienced a dramatic increase in conversions. The flames of revival spread through western Massachusetts and the eastern seaboard. While Edwards interpreted the revivals as miraculous outpourings of the Holy Spirit, they were also due to his preaching on religious affections, those emotions or sensations that he argued were signs of God's grace. Edwards believed in God's absolute sovereignty, the sinfulness of humanity, and unmerited election, but he reinterpreted those Calvinist doctrines through the lenses of psychology and Enlightenment philosophy. He developed a brilliant synthesis of John Locke, Isaac Newton, and John Calvin, in the process shifting the focus of Puritanism from societal theocracy to God's relationship to the individual. His works included *A Faithful Narrative of the Surprising Work of God* (1737), *Treatise Concerning Religious Affections* (1746), and *Freedom of the Will* (1754). Edwards' thought influenced evangelical theology and revivalism for the next two hundred years. He died shortly after his appointment as president of the College of New Jersey, later Princeton University.

Evelyn A. Kirkley

See also CALVINISM; ENTHUSIASM/
ENTHUSIASTIC; EVANGELICAL
THEOLOGY; GREAT AWAKENING(S)
(EURO-AMERICAN RELIGIOUS HISTORY);
PURITANISM; REVIVALISM.

EFFICACY, SACRAMENTAL

The question of sacramental efficacy concerns how the sacraments *work*. It asks whether the sacraments have a power in themselves, or whether their power depends on the condition of the ones receiving and administering them. St. Augustine (354–430) faced these questions in his disputes with the Donatists. The Donatists held that sacraments administered by sinful ministers have no effect. Augustine countered that the efficacy of a sacrament does not depend on the minister but on God, the real actor in the sacrament. Concerning baptism, Augustine wrote, "Baptism does not have its value from the merits of the one who administers it or even of the one who receives it, but by reason of its own holiness and efficacy, communicated to it by him who instituted it" (*Contra Cresconium* 4.19). In the thirteenth century, theologians began to speak of this distinction using the terms *ex opere operantis*, and *ex opere operato*. Catholic tradition holds that the sacraments do not have their effect *ex opere operantis* (by virtue of the one who does the action) but *ex opere operato* (by virtue of the action simply being done). This does not imply that the sacraments are magic, or that God forces Godself upon humans. It merely means that the sacraments are a genuine gift that God promises and faithfully gives to the church whenever it asks. The recipient of a sacrament can place an obstacle in God's way, so that the sacrament does not become *fruitful* in the person's life. Still, the disposition of the recipient can neither cause nor destroy God's presence in the sacrament. One problem remains concerning sacraments that can be received only once: baptism, confirmation, and holy orders. If a person is not receptive to God's grace at the time when he or she receives these sacraments, is that person doomed never to receive the grace offered? The tradition answers that, in sacraments that can be received only once, God places a spiritual seal or "character" upon the person. If the person eventually becomes receptive to what God has offered, there will be a "reviviscence" of the sacrament, that is, a return to life of the grace that God offered the person once and for all.

Patrick L. Malloy

See also AUGUSTINE OF HIPPO;
CHARACTER (SACRAMENTAL);
DONATISM; EX OPERE OPERANTIS;
EX OPERE OPERATO.

ELDER (IN CHRISTIANITY)

An elder is a church officer primarily in the Protestant Christian tradition. In the sixteenth century in Geneva, John Calvin instituted "elder" as a church office along with pastors, teachers, and deacons. Elders were laymen charged with maintaining moral discipline in the community. This system was modified and adapted by New England Puritans and Presbyterians. Among the former, elders were not only lay overseers of congregational discipline, but also exhorters who delivered homilies when the pastor or teacher was unavailable. In the Presbyterian tradition, elders and pastor form the session, the decision-making body for a congregation, with oversight over worship, programs, and pastoral care. Elders are laity elected by the congregation and ordained to their position, although they have no priestly function.

By contrast, in the Methodist tradition founded by John Wesley, elders are not laypeople but part of the professional ministry. Elders are full members of a conference, a group of congregations in a geographical area. They have completed all ordination requirements and have served in a ministerial capacity for a specified length of time. After ordination as an elder, a Methodist pastor is guaranteed ministerial appointments for life. The Church of Jesus Christ of Latter-Day Saints, known as the Mormons, also has the office of Elder. It is the first stage in the Melchizedek Order of the Priesthood, to which young men are ordained at the age of nineteen. As Elders, they are recognized as adults and are commissioned as missionaries for two years. Although, historically, elders in all traditions were men, in recent years women have been ordained as Presbyterian and Methodist elders.

Evelyn A. Kirkley

See also CHURCH OF JESUS CHRIST OF
LATTER-DAY SAINTS; METHODIST
CHURCHES; PRESBYTERIAN CHURCHES;
PURITANISM.

ELDER (IN JUDAISM)

In the Hebrew Bible, the term "elder" (Hebrew, *zaqen*) refers to leaders of kinship groups at different levels of Israelite society larger than the nuclear family. The system of kin or lineage-based structures seems to have come into existence before the development of the Israelite kingdom under David. The royal administration may have displaced the role of elder in part, but probably not completely, since they are mentioned in seventh-century compositions such as Deuteronomy and in postexilic writings as well. The role of elder thus probably survived the establishment of a centralized state under the kings as well as foreign rule and exile. As far as we know, elders were males from powerful families. Elders are also mentioned in the narratives of the Israelites wandering in the wilderness, where they seem to share some responsibility with Moses for governing the Israelites. The seventy elders accompany Moses to the top of Sinai in the covenant ratification ceremony in Exodus 24. Elders are also mentioned in the New Testament.

Russell Fuller

ELECTION (DOCTRINE OF)

This Christian doctrine refers to the belief that God has chosen some people to be special recipients of God's mercy and revelation. In the Hebrew Scriptures, the people of Israel are the chosen ones, and in the New Testament the church (as a new Israel) is the elect. Later Christian reflection, however, connected the term with the notion of predestination. Most of the early theologians (first six centuries) made little or no distinction between the concepts of election and predestination. But Augustine of Hippo (d. 430) and many others since (for instance, Thomas Aquinas), believed that predestination assumes a prior divine free act of election in favor of those predestined. In the sixteenth century, Calvin taught that God elects individuals and predestines them for salvation without regard to either their faith or their good works. Everyone else who is not so elected, said Calvin, is doomed to damnation no matter what

one may do or believe. Most mainstream Christian theologians, however, have rejected such rigorist views. Today, most theologians consider that such narrow interpretation of the concept of election would actually contradict the much more fundamental beliefs in God's loving mercy and in God's offer of salvation to all. Indeed, a widespread theological view today is that God has in fact elected all who are the intended recipients of God's offer of salvation, and since *all* human beings are the intended recipients of this offer, then all human beings have been elected by God. Notice, however, that this universal election does not imply universal predestination to salvation ("apocatastasis"), because, although elected by God for salvation, humans still have the choice of freely accepting or rejecting that election. Therefore, the narrow, rigorist understanding of either predestination or election is rejected by most contemporary, mainstream Christian theologians.

Orlando Espín

See also APOCATASTASIS; AQUINAS, THOMAS, ST.; AUGUSTINE OF HIPPO; CALVIN, JOHN; CALVINISM; DETERMINISM; FREE WILL; GRACE; JUSTIFICATION; LUTHER, MARTIN; LUTHERANISM; ORIGINAL JUSTICE; PREDESTINATION (IN CHRISTIANITY); SALVATION; SIN, ORIGINAL; THEOLOGICAL ANTHROPOLOGY; TRENT, COUNCIL OF.

EL/ELOHIM

A Hebrew term for God/gods/the God of gods. The text of the Hebrew Bible designates the God of the Israelites in several ways. "He" is YHWH, the God who tells Moses, "I am who am" (Exod 3:14). God is Abram's "God Most High" (el elyon in, for example, Gen 14:22), and his "God the Almighty" (el shadday in, for example,

Gen 17:1); God is Isaac's "Awesome One" (*pahad* in Gen 31:42). Whereas El can be used to designate the God of Israel, more frequently the plural term Elohim is used. Scholars consider the form to be a plural of majesty, indicating the superior nature of Israel's God over the gods of other peoples.

The plural form is also frequently used in the Hebrew Bible for gods other than the God of Israel. In Genesis 31, for example, Laban asks Jacob why he, when returning to Canaan from Haran, took with him Laban's gods? (v. 30). The text suggests a period in Israel's history before monotheism. In Genesis 35 the term *elohim* occurs in succeeding verses (4 and 5), indicating first "foreign gods" (*elohe hannekar*) and then Israel's God (*elohim*).

Historical scholars came to recognize strands of narrative in the Pentateuch that use "Elohim" as the designation for Israel's God in contrast to other strands of narrative that use the term "Yahweh." This observation was part of what led to the development of what has been termed the "Source Theory," a hypothesis asserting that at least four literary strands or sources make up the Pentateuch.

Alice L. Laffey

See also ELOHIST SOURCE.

ELIADE, MIRCEA (1907–88)

A European scholar whose phenomenological approach to the study of religion came to dominate the field of religious studies from the mid-twentieth century onward. Based upon his own fieldwork in India, and in-depth textual studies on both yoga and shamanism, Eliade and his associates at the University of Chicago sought to use comparative studies of religious belief and practice to trace the dichotomy between the "Sacred" and the "Profane."

They argued that any expression of religion as lived reality can be understood when showing how a local tradition expresses a universal pattern of religious life, or archetype. Religion's effect on how humans experience space, time, symbols, myth, and ritual, he argued, can be revealed using this comparative phenomenological approach. Among his better-known works are *Traité d'histoire des religions* (1949); *Cosmos and History: The Myth of the Eternal Return* (1954); *The Sacred and the Profane* (1957); *Rites and Symbols of Initiation* (1958); *The Quest* (1969); and *A History of Religious Ideas* (two volumes, 1982 and 1985).

Todd T. Lewis

See also COMPARATIVE RELIGION; HISTORY OF RELIGIONS; MYTH; RITUAL; SHAMAN.

ELIJAH

(1 Kings 17–2 Kings 2). Elijah is one of the paradigmatic prophetic figures in the Hebrew Bible/Old Testament. He causes a drought, calls down fire from heaven to consume a sacrifice to Yahweh or royal troops, he multiplies food, and raises the dead. Finally, Elijah is one of two characters in the Hebrew Bible/Old Testament who do not die. Elijah is taken directly up to heaven in a chariot of fire drawn by fiery horses. It is no wonder that this character has caught the interest of readers of these texts for centuries. The original form of the narratives concerning Elijah probably dates to the ninth century B.C.E., since he is described as the contemporary of Ahab (869–850 B.C.E.). By the fifth century B.C.E., the belief that Elijah would return before the Day of the Lord had achieved written form in the book of Malachi (Mal

4:5-6). He is described as having the task of reconciling fathers and sons (NRSV—parents and children) before the Day of the Lord. The belief continued and developed in the third century B.C.E. Jesus, the son of Sirach, wrote that Elijah would also restore the tribes of Jacob (Sirach 48:10). In the New Testament, John the Baptist is identified as Elijah returned, the intended precursor of Jesus.

Russell Fuller

ELIJAH BEN SOLOMON (1720–97)

One of the greatest Jewish thinkers, legal authorities, and spiritual leaders of early modern times, known as the Vilna Gaon or, in Hebrew, as *HaGra* (*HaGaon Rabbi Eliyahu*; "The Gaon, Rabbi Elijah"). The author of over seventy works on a vast range of topics, he is best known for his commentaries on the Hebrew Bible and the Mishnah and, in general, for his use of philological methods in the critical study of traditional texts.

An unassuming person who continually declined offers of appointment to the office of community rabbi, the Vilna Gaon made his authority felt only in the struggle that emerged in his day between the then normative rabbinic-legal tradition and the mystical, antischolastic Hasidic Judaism that had emerged in the backwaters of Poland and was now seeking followers even among the Jews of Elijah Ben Solomon's own city. He responded by declaring adherents of Hasidism among Vilna's Jews to be excommunicated and by sending letters to all other large communities urging this same action. After this struggle that took place in 1777–81, Elijah returned to his ascetic and private life and took no further part in public affairs.

Alan J. Avery-Peck

See also HASIDISM.

ELIZABETH

A woman portrayed in the New Testament as recognizing the identity of the child her pregnant cousin Mary was carrying. She is described as "righteous in the eyes of God, observing all the commandments and ordinances of the Lord blamelessly" (Luke 1:6). Elizabeth is identified as the wife of Zachariah, a Jewish priest, a woman barren and "advanced in years" (v. 7). Like many of her Jewish foremothers depicted in the Scriptures, she can only become pregnant if God overcomes the obstacles. God acted for Elizabeth as he had done for Sarah, for Rebecca, for Rachel, and for Hannah. Just as God sent messengers/angels to Abraham (Gen 18), God sent the angel Gabriel to Zachariah to declare that his wife would bear a child. Elizabeth became the mother of John the Baptizer.

Elizabeth's language contrasts her unbelieving husband with Mary's belief that what was spoken to her by the Lord would be fulfilled. Whereas Zachariah was "speechless and unable to talk" until after the birth of his child because he "did not believe" the words of the angel that would "be fulfilled" at their proper time (Luke 1:20), Elizabeth praises Mary because she "believed that what was spoken" to her by the Lord "would be fulfilled" (v. 45). This profession to Mary occasions what is commonly called "Mary's Magnificat," a prayer of praise seemingly based on Hannah's prayer in 1 Samuel 2:1-10.

Alice L. Laffey

ELIZONDO, VIRGILIO (1935–)

Latino Catholic theologian. After seminary education in his native San Antonio, Texas, Elizondo earned graduate degrees in Manila and later a doctorate in Paris.

He founded and directed the Mexican American Cultural Center, has been rector of San Fernando Cathedral (in San Antonio), and was one of the founders of the Academy of Catholic Hispanic Theologians of the U.S. Elizondo has taught at several American and European universities, and has received frequent international recognition for his theological work. He is considered the "father" of U.S. Latino theology, beginning his work in this field in the 1960s. Few individuals have influenced a whole generation of theologians as he has in the U.S. Latino context. Among his most important and permanent contributions are his work on *mestizaje* (the biological and cultural mixing of different racial and ethnic groups) as a theological category, and his reflections on the relationship between culture and Gospel. He has written extensively on Our Lady of Guadalupe as a cultural, social, and evangelizing symbol. Among his more important books are *Christianity and Culture* (1975), *La Morenita: Evangelizer of the Americas* (1980), *Galilean Journey: The Mexican American Promise* (1985), and *The Future Is Mestizo* (1988).

Orlando Espín

See also CULTURE; GUADALUPE, VIRGIN OF; INCULTURATION; LATIN AMERICAN CATHOLICISM; LATINO/A; LATINO CATHOLICISM; LATINO THEOLOGY (-IES); LIBERATION THEOLOGIES; POPULAR CATHOLICISM.

ELLACURÍA, IGNACIO (1930–89)

Born in Spain, Ignacio Ellacuría entered the Society of Jesus (Jesuits) in 1947, went to work in El Salvador from 1955 to 1958 as a Jesuit seminarian, and then traveled to Innsbruck (Austria) where he studied theology with Karl Rahner. He was ordained a priest in 1961, and, upon re-

ceiving his doctorate in 1967 in Madrid under Xavier Zubiri, he returned to El Salvador to teach at the University of Central America (UCA). As he became more and more involved in the struggle for justice in El Salvador (of which he became a citizen in 1975), Ellacuría helped mold the university along the lines of liberation theology, turning it into a critical conscience of the country. As he became a more public advocate for justice, he (and the university of which he became president in 1979) came to be seen as an enemy by the government. Ellacuría was among the six Jesuits who were assassinated in their residence on the night of November 16, 1989, by Salvadoran soldiers along with their cook and her daughter, a crime that provoked worldwide revulsion.

James B. Nickoloff

See also LATIN AMERICAN CATHOLICISM; LATIN AMERICAN THEOLOGIES; LIBERATION THEOLOGIES; ROMERO, OSCAR ARNULFO; ZUBIRI, XAVIER.

ELLIS, JOHN TRACY (1905–92)

Priest, educator, historian of the American Catholic Church. Ellis earned a doctorate in history from The Catholic University of America in 1930, then became professor of American Catholic history at C.U.A. when Peter Guilday retired. Ellis advocated the reconstruction of history from documentary sources, a method modeled in his biography, *The Life of James Cardinal Gibbons* (1952). With his students' assistance, he published a collection of early church documents, *Documents of American Catholic History* (1956) which, through several revisions, has remained a standard text in the study of the American Church. He was managing director of the *Catholic Historical Review* (1941–63), and a driving force in the American Catholic Historical Association. He engaged in the mid-1950s examination of the intellectual caliber of Catholic colleges and universities, and remained a staunch advocate of higher standards for the same. After a brief tenure at the University of San Francisco, he returned to C.U.A. in 1976. Ellis contributed numerous studies to the history of the American Catholic Church.

Patricia Plovanich

ELOHIST SOURCE

One of at least four "authors" or literary strands believed to make up the Pentateuch. (Others include the Yahwist, the Deuteronomic, and the Priestly sources.) The Elohist source may have originated in the northern kingdom, Israel, during the mid-ninth century B.C.E. When combined with the Yahwist source, which may be the product of the southern kingdom, Judah, in the mid-tenth century B.C.E., it came to form what historical scholars refer to as Israel's "Old Epic Tradition." The old epic narrative is found in the primeval history (Gen 1–11), the ancestral history (Gen 12–50), and the people's history (Exodus–Numbers).

The Elohist source may have been composed in Israel not too long after the kingdom was divided (932 B.C.E.). Israel needed its own articulation of its people's story just as they needed their own expressions of the God who brought them out of Egypt—the shrines at Bethel and Dan in place of the Temple at Jerusalem —if it was to survive as an independent nation. Yet Israel in fact shared much of its past—its oral traditions and memories— with the people of Judah. It is believed that the northern expressions of Israel's past, what became the Elohist source, were quite similar to Judah's Yahwist source

but with variations. One such variation is the predominance of the term "Elohim" for God instead of the term "Yahweh." The Elohist source also seems to have preferred to depict encounters with God as occurring through intermediaries, that is, messengers or angels. This corresponds to its approach to God as exalted, transcendent, and awesome. Other variations include the naming of the mountain where Moses received God's teaching (Horeb, not Sinai) and the name of his father-in-law (Reuel, not Jethro). The Yahwist source seems to dominate the old epic material with additions from the Elohist source.

Alice L. Laffey

ELOISE

See HELOISE.

ELVIRA, COUNCIL OF

Among the earliest perserved records of a council of Christians are those ascribed to the Council of Elvira, held outside Granada about 300/3. The acts of the council describe early Christian life in Spain and are noted for the rigorous decrees against maintaining links with Roman religion or Judaism. The most famous of all the decrees of Elvira, however, is Canon 33 that forbids marriage to those in ministry. This act, if it is geniune, would be the earliest such law in Christianity. Since the record, as we now have it, dates from a much later period, there have been doubts raised about the authenticity of all eighty-one laws ascribed to the council.

Gary Macy

See also CELIBACY; JUDAISM.

ELYSIUM

In Greek mythology, Elysium, also known as the Elysian Fields, the Elysian plain, or the Isles of the Blessed, was the dwelling place after death of virtuous mortals. Here, beyond the river Okeanus at the edge of the earth, the blessed dead enjoyed a happy life in eternal sunshine. The Odyssey describes Elysium in these words: "No snow is there, nor heavy storm, nor rain ever, but always Ocean sends forth the breezes of clear-breathing Zephyr to bring refreshment to men." The Greek poets Homer, Hesiod, and Pindar tell that Elysium was ruled by Kronos, father of Zeus, and by Rhadamanthys, brother of King Minos of Crete. Because Kronos is even older than Zeus, and the advanced culture of Crete was the oldest of the cultures of the Greek complex, scholars believe that the idea of Elysium occurred quite early—by at least 1800–1600 B.C.E.—as a pre-Greek notion. By the time of the Roman poet Virgil, Elysium had become a part of Hades, the underworld itself. The judges of the dead decided whether a soul would go to the Elysian Fields, for the virtuous; or to Tartarus, a place of punishment for the wicked. In some stories, Elysium is identified with real islands in the Black Sea, where Helen of Troy and the heroes of the Trojan War lived on after death.

Helen deLaurentis

See also HOMER; MYSTERY RELIGIONS.

ENCYCLICAL

Originally a term that meant that a pastoral letter, written by a local bishop, was being circulated around his diocese. But in today's Roman Catholic usage, the term refers only to letters written and sent by popes to the entire church, dealing with an important issue. In the Anglican Communion, and only since the last century, the term refers to the joint letters issued by the bishops at the conclusion of a Lambeth Conference.

Orlando Espín

See also ANGLICAN COMMUNION; BISHOP (EPISCOPACY); DOCTRINE; LAMBETH CONFERENCES; PETRINE MINISTRY; POPE; ROMAN CATHOLIC CHURCH; ROME, SEE OF.

ENLIGHTENMENT (IN BUDDHISM)

See BODHI.

ENLIGHTENMENT IN WESTERN HISTORY

From the second half of the seventeenth century through the late eighteenth century, a philosophical and theological movement in western Europe sought to shed the "light" of reason on the meaning of human and divine existence. Eventually referred to by historians as the "Enlightenment," this movement subjected religion to a rational analysis and criticism that marginalized or eliminated altogether the significance or possibility of a divine revelation distinct from what could be known through human reason. Rejecting in particular the doctrine of original sin, as it had been taught by Protestant or Catholic theologians, Enlightenment thinkers emphasized the goodness of nature, human nature included, and the happy progress of humanity toward perfection. Such progress would leave behind superstition and credulity by espousing science, reason, and nature.

Though atheism gained some adherents in the Enlightenment, "deism" was the form of religion that grew most rapidly. Deists, like the Socinians of the sixteenth century, rejected the doctrine of the Trinity in favor of a simpler affirmation of the goodness and providence of the one deity. God was the beneficent Creator who had made an agreeable world for humanity to enjoy. Human beings had but to praise God, love one another, and prosper freely. German philosopher G. W. Leibniz (1646–1716) helped to encourage this point of view, with his suggestion that this was the best of all possible worlds.

Fear of hell and of other divinely sanctioned punishments declined in eighteenth-century Europe, at least among the educated classes. The "enlightened" image of God was not one compatible with a concept of eternal torment. At the same time, many Enlightenment thinkers called for elimination of torture and gruesome judicial penalties; some also appealed for elimination of the death penalty. As God was not one who tormented his creatures, earthly authorities should put aside cruelty and mirror divine clemency.

Individual liberty and equality before the law were major goals of Enlightenment thinkers. Such liberty and equality, they argued, must include toleration of religious diversity. In his *Letters on England*, published in 1734, the Frenchman Voltaire (1694–1778) praised the variety of religious denominations in England and castigated France's intolerance of Protestants. In most parts of Europe, the Enlightenment era did put an end to violent hostility between Catholics and Protestants.

The Enlightenment's criticism of traditional Christianity gained the favor of some of Europe's monarchs. So-called "enlightened despotism" was the effort of these rulers to impose an Enlightenment agenda on their territories.

The Enlightenment, like the Renaissance, was an elite, intellectual movement. While the Renaissance had looked to the past for a golden age, the Enlight-enment looked ahead to a perfect future, a future that could be achieved through human effort.

Thomas Worcester, s.j.

See also ATHEISM; DEISM; JOSEPHINISM; LEIBNIZ, GOTTFRIED WILHELM; PASCAL, BLAISE; RATIONALISM; RENAISSANCE; REVELATION; SIN, ORIGINAL; SOCINIANISM; TOLERATION; UNITARIANISM.

ENOCH, BOOKS OF

In Genesis 5:24, Enoch is said to have walked with God, "and he was not, for God took him." This is the starting point for the tradition that Enoch did not die but was taken bodily to heaven where all the secrets of the cosmos, including all of God's future plans, were revealed to him. This, in turn, gave rise to the development of a literature pseudepigraphically attributed to Enoch that sought to describe various aspects of the history of the cosmos and its mysteries. Remains of this Enochic literature survive in several different languages and versions. There are "books" of Enoch in Hebrew, Greek, Latin, Ethiopic, and Old Church Slavonic. Fragments of Enochic literature have been found at Qumran where it was apparently popular.

Russell Fuller

ENTHUSIASM/ENTHUSIASTIC

From the Greek word for "inspired," enthusiasm refers to the emotional aspect of religion. Enthusiasm wells up in the heart, aroused by music, word, prayer, dance, or trance. Broadly speaking, enthusiasm is synonymous with zeal, passion, and ardor; it may express either sorrow or ecstasy. Applied to Christianity specifically, enthusiasm is infusion of passion by the Holy Spirit. Honoring heart over head, experience over doctrine, enthusiasm is integral to spirituality, and is both cause and result of piety and devotion.

Enthusiasm has been a central feature of several Christian movements, particularly pietism, evangelicalism, and revivalism. Pietism, the late seventeenth-century renewal movement in Germany, stressed enthusiasm as a critical characteristic of the Christian life. Pietists like Philipp Spener urged Christians to nurture a deep personal faith and to take seriously their call to daily discipleship. In the 1730s, pastor and revivalist Jonathan Edwards perceived the "surprising work of God" in the enthusiastic revivals occurring in his congregation in western Massachusetts. In his 1746 *Treatise Concerning Religious Affections*, Edwards defined enthusiasm as supernatural stirrings in the heart and will that enabled one to become infused with God's grace and convinced of salvation. To early nineteenth-century revivalist Charles G. Finney, writing in *Lectures on Revivals of Religion* (1835), enthusiasm was less a miraculous event and more a human affair, engineered by the application of his sure-fire evangelistic techniques.

For many, enthusiasm is a positive feature of Christianity, reviving dead, dried-up doctrine. However, for others, enthusiasm is dangerously close to fanaticism. In *Seasonable Thoughts on the State of Religion in New England* (1743), Charles Chauncy, Boston Congregationalist pastor and opponent of Jonathan Edwards, attacked revivalism for its excessive emotionalism and neglect of rationalism. A hundred years later, in *The Anxious Bench* (1843), John W. Nevin, a German Reformed seminary professor, deplored Finney's "new measures" as inimical to intelligent piety, damaging to true worship, and contrary to the authen-

tic work of the Holy Spirit. Chauncy and Nevin had a point. Enthusiasm in the First Great Awakening led to book-burnings, suicides, and the declaration that at least one revivalist was insane. In the Second Great Awakening, enthusiasm resulted in twitching, barking, and jerking. Although a key aspect of religion, enthusiasm must be handled with care.

Evelyn A. Kirkley

See also EVANGELICAL THEOLOGY; EVANGELICALS; GREAT AWAKENING(S) (EURO-AMERICAN RELIGIOUS HISTORY); PIETISM; REVIVALISM.

EPARCH
In many Eastern Churches (Catholic and Orthodox alike), it is frequently the episcopal title that is equal to the Western term "metropolitan archbishop." An eparch is the chief bishop in an eparchy, which in turn is similar to an ecclesiastical province in the West.

Orlando Espín

See also ARCHBISHOP; BISHOP (EPISCOPACY); DIOCESE/ARCHDIOCESE; EASTERN CATHOLIC CHURCHES; ECCLESIASTICAL PROVINCE; METROPOLITAN; ORTHODOX CHURCHES.

EPHESUS, COUNCIL OF
The Council of Ephesus is the third ecumenical council of the church. It was summoned by the emperors Theodosius II and Valentinian III at the request of Nestorius, the bishop of Constantinople. Nestorius had been condemned at Rome at the instigation of Cyril of Alexandria on August 11, 430, for denying that the Virgin Mary could properly be called *Theotokos*, Mother of God. This condemnation occurred only after an exchange of bitter letters between Nestorius and Cyril, in which Nestorius insisted that

Mary was mother only of the man Jesus and in no way could be called Mother of God. The council was to have opened on the feast of Pentecost at Ephesus on June 7, 431. Before the arrival of either the legates of the Pope or the Eastern bishops led by John of Antioch, Cyril of Alexandria began the council. One hundred ninety-five bishops immediately subscribed to the condemnation of Nestorius and his teaching. Shortly afterward, John of Antioch and the Eastern bishops arrived at Ephesus. They refused to join the council Cyril chaired. The Pope's delegates arrived at Ephesus some days later, joined Cyril's council, confirmed the condemnation of Nestorius, and on July 17, 431, excommunicated John of Antioch and the bishops who refused to join Cyril's council. On April 23, 433, after two years of negotiation, John of Antioch and Cyril of Alexandria reached agreement on the central issue of the council. The bishops removed their mutual condemnation of one another and, in their Formula of Union, John and Cyril agree that Mary is *Theotokos* and that, in Christ, there are two natures united in one Person. Theologians dispute which documents of the council express the teaching of the church. Two of the seven documents associated with this council are generally agreed to represent the church's definitive statement regarding Mary's being *Theotokos*: the second letter of Cyril to Nestorius and the condemnation of Nestorius. Moreover, the Formula of Union between John of Antioch and Cyril of Alexandria and Cyril's letter to John expressing his agreement with the Formula were read at the Council of Chalcedon as proper expressions of the orthodox faith.

Herbert J. Ryan, s.j.

See also CYRIL OF ALEXANDRIA; COUNCIL, ECUMENICAL; MOTHER OF GOD/THEOTOKOS; NESTORIANISM; NESTORIUS.

EPHRAEM OF SYRIA (306?–73)

Ephraem was born in Nibisis in Syria where he established a theological school. Due to Roman intervention, Ephraem was forced to move to Edessa where he continued his theological work until his death. Ephraem lived as a deacon and "son of the covenant," meaning he took vows of abstinence and virginity. The most beautiful poet of the early years of Christianity, and perhaps of all of Christianity, Ephraem's works still influence Eastern Christian liturgy. His theology, contained mostly in scriptural commentaries, letters, and hymns, is far closer to early Jewish Christianity than is that of his contemporaries in the Greek-speaking East. Ephraem rejected Arianism without adopting the fundamentally philosophic stance of Arian's opponents. Ephraem tries, rather, to preserve the mystery of God through the use of a multiplicity of images to describe the Divinity.

Gary Macy

See also ARIANISM; LITURGY (IN CHRISTIANITY); ORTHODOX THEOLOGY.

EPICLESIS

An epiclesis (from a Greek word meaning to "call upon" or invoke) is a prayer or section of a longer prayer that calls down the Holy Spirit upon persons or objects, in order for them to be prepared, consecrated, made holy, blessed, or sanctified. The most important Christian example of an epiclesis can be found in the genre of prayer known as the eucharistic prayer, that is, the prayer used over the elements of bread and wine during the celebration of the Eucharist (or Mass). Some may have one (over the gifts of bread and wine, a *consecratory epiclesis*) or two (another over the community as well, often in preparation for Communion, a *communion epiclesis*). The epiclesis prayer form can also be found in other longer benedictional prayers, for example, the blessing of the baptismal font during the Easter Vigil.

Joanne M. Pierce

See also ANAMNESIS; ANAPHORA; CONSECRATION (CHRISTIAN); EUCHARIST; EUCHARISTIC PRAYER; HOLY SPIRIT; MASS.

EPICTETUS OF CORINTH
(50?–130 C.E.)
A contemporary of Athanasius and fellow opponent of Arius, Epictetus wrote to the bishop of Alexandria to explain the christological problems that had surfaced in Corinth. Athanasius responded in detail to the different positions outlined by Epictetus. Apart from this correspondence, scholars know little else about him.

Gary Macy

See also ARIUS; ATHANASIUS, PATRIARCH OF ALEXANDRIA.

EPIPHANY
A Greek term meaning "manifestation." On January 6, Christians in the West celebrate a feast called Epiphany. The feast has a rather complex history. In the fourth century, Christians in various parts of the world began to celebrate an annual feast recalling how God became humanly manifested in Jesus. In southern Europe and Africa, the feast was observed on December 25, while in parts of northern Europe and in Asia Minor it was celebrated on January 6. The feast commemorated the earliest events in Jesus' life that showed him to be a manifestation of God: his birth; the proclamation by the Magi that Jesus was a king; the voice at Jesus' baptism proclaiming him to be God's son; and the changing of water to wine at Cana. Scholars agree that neither December 25 nor January 6 is actually the anniversary of any of these events. Research suggests that Christians essentially borrowed these dates from pre-Christian cultures that already celebrated a feast on those days in honor of the sun god. These dates were appropriate for such a feast because they roughly coincided with the winter solstice. After the winter solstice, the short winter days begin gradually to lengthen. Many early civilizations saw these longer days as a manifestation or epiphany of the sun god's triumph over his enemy, darkness. According to a widely accepted theory, Christians claimed that their God, not the sun god, was the true conqueror of darkness, and that God had become manifest in Jesus. They came to celebrate this fact on December 25/January 6, thereby setting up a feast in competition with the older solstice feast. Once the Christian form of the feast was established, it developed in two distinct forms. In the West (Europe and Africa), the feast split into a number of distinct feasts. December 25 marks the birth of Jesus, January 6 (now called Epiphany) celebrates the visit of the Magi, and the Sundays following commemorate the Baptism of Jesus and the Wedding at Cana. In the East, however, the original form of the feast is maintained, so that the various aspect of Jesus' manifestation as the Son of God are all celebrated together on 6/7 January.

Patrick L. Malloy

See also CHRISTMAS; HIEROPHANY.

EPISCOPAL CHURCH

The church, formerly known as the Protestant Episcopal Church in the United States, belongs to the worldwide Anglican Communion. It is headed by the Presiding Bishop and ordered by the General Convention.

In the colonial period, the church was under the jurisdiction of the bishop of London. After the American Revolution, it was not only disestablished but distrusted as an English institution. Yet it was soon revitalized. After his election by the clergy of Connecticut, Samuel Seabury went to Europe to be consecrated as the first bishop in the United States in 1784. He could not be consecrated in England because the English rite required an oath of allegiance to the Crown. So he sought and received consecration from four Scottish bishops. Independence from London and the church's "Americanization" were completed by its first General Convention and the adoption of its own Book of Common Prayer in 1789.

Like the Anglican Communion of which it is part, the Episcopal Church claims officially no distinctive faith other than that of the "one, holy, catholic, and apostolic" church; it is a branch of the one church of Christ. As such, the Apostles' Creed and the Nicene Creed figure prominently in Morning and Evening Prayer and the Eucharist. There are no further confessional documents to which Episcopalians must subscribe. Many Episcopalians hold that their church's particular and historic vocation is to promote the reunion of the one church of Christ. They see their church as comprising the best elements of the Catholic and Evangelical traditions of Christianity: a *via media* or "middle way."

The basic unit of the church is the parish, headed by the rector, who is a priest; the wardens and the vestry, elected representatives of the parish; and the trustees of the parish corporation, who are also elected.

Parishes belong to dioceses governed by synodical bodies called Conventions and headed by bishops. Larger dioceses may have one or more suffragan, or assistant, bishops. The bishop is elected by clergy and lay representatives of the entire diocese, but his or her election must be approved by a majority of the Episcopal bishops with jurisdiction over dioceses and of the Standing Committees of all the other dioceses of the church. Only then may the bishop be ordained and take office.

The church presently numbers about 2.5 million members and 120 dioceses grouped into nine provinces. Its headquarters are located at 815 Second Avenue in New York City. There are eleven seminaries; the oldest and only one founded by the General Convention is The General Theological Seminary (1817) in New York City.

The highest authority in the church is the General Convention that meets every three years. It is composed of a House of Deputies (elected lay and clergy representatives) and a House of Bishops. All measures binding on the church must be passed by both Houses. The General Convention elects the Presiding Bishop, who symbolizes and fosters the unity of the church, as well as serving as its chief administrator and President of the House of Bishops. As Primate, the Presiding Bishop represents the Episcopal Church to the other churches of the Anglican Communion.

The church belongs to the World Council of Churches and the National Council of Churches of Christ. It also maintains formal dialogues aimed at establishing full communion with the Roman Catholic Church, the United Methodist Church, the Polish National Catholic Church, and others. The church also works closely with the Russian Orthodox Church in its rebuilding efforts. In 2000, the General Convention voted on a proposal for full communion with the ELCA (the Evangelical Lutheran Church of America).

The Episcopal Church has played a leading role in the shaping of the whole Anglican Communion. In 1886 its House of Bishops approved the Quadrilateral, a statement of the fundamentals of the faith to serve as the basis for efforts to reunite the church of Christ. The Lambeth Conference of 1888 revised and approved this text that has since become authoritative for Anglican participation in the ecumenical movement. In 1976 the church became the third province of the Anglican Communion to approve the ordination of women to the priesthood and the episcopate. The Church of England began to ordain women in 1994. This action and its effects, however, remain causes of contention even today. In 1988 the church approved the ordination of a woman as a bishop in the Communion, the first to take up episcopal ministry among the three branches of Orthodoxy, Anglicanism, and Roman Catholicism.

Jon Nilson

See also ANGLICAN COMMUNION; BOOK OF COMMON PRAYER; LAMBETH CONFERENCES; LAMBETH QUADRILATERAL.

EPISCOPAL CONFERENCES
In the contemporary Catholic Church, permanent regional or national organizations of bishops structured for regular deliberation on pastoral questions and problems common to the church in their various dioceses. In the early church, regional synods or consultations of bishops, deliberating on matters of both doctrine and discipline, were common and very important to the overall governance of the church. In western Europe, however, such gatherings declined in frequency and authority over the centuries in the face of the strong role of the papacy. Nonetheless, in the United States during the late nineteenth and early twentieth centuries, various structures of cooperation among the American bishops emerged, including several national synods (one of which authorized the famous Baltimore Catechism). The establishment of permanent conferences throughout the world was authorized by the Second Vatican Council, along with regularly scheduled international synods of representative bishops at Rome. These were to be practical expressions of the "collegiality" (shared pastoral responsibility) of the bishops, which was an important theme of Vatican II. During the 1970s and 1980s, national and regional conferences of bishops made significant contributions to the development of the church in various regions of the world, issuing pastoral letters on urgent social topics, supporting new theological and pastoral movements, and in some cases directly challenging civil authorities in matters of justice. In the latter part of the papacy of John Paul II, a much more cautious approach to the role of the episcopal conferences prevailed in Rome. A papal statement in 1998 reminded bishops that the authority of episcopal conferences is limited, and required that their decisions and statements be both unanimously adopted and subsequently approved by the Vatican.

William A. Clark, S.J.

See also ECCLESIOLOGY.

EPISKOPOS

A Greek word meaning "overseer," the root of the English word "bishop." In the New Testament (Acts, Philippians, 1 Timothy, Titus) it designates an elder of the local church community who has moral authority within the community and is charged with various duties that recall both Jesus' commission to his apostles and the duties of a head-of-household in Greco-Roman society. By the early to mid-second century, a clear distinction was emerging between the *episkopos* and the other elders (*presbyteroi*) of the community, who were more and more seen as advisors to the bishop. Through at least the fifth century, the leadership of the *episkopos* remained focused on the united community of Christians within a particular city or town, where he would preside over all important functions of the community, particularly Eucharist and baptism. The development of larger episcopal territories (dioceses) that included many individual parishes served by priests accountable to the bishop alone did not begin until around the seventh century. From very early in Christian history, though, the *episkopoi* concerned themselves with the wider church by consulting one another and by presiding over the installation of new bishops in nearby communities.

William A. Clark, s.j.

See also BISHOP (EPISCOPACY); ECCLESIOLOGY.

EPISTEMOLOGY

Epistemology, one of the main branches of Western philosophy, investigates the foundations, methods, methodologies, and limits of human knowledge. As the scientific method has shown, because tools and approaches for knowing determine the extent and depth of what can be known, that is, because *how* humans know (epistemology) determines *what* humans know, there is an inherent relationship between knowledge and truth.

In the mid-twentieth century, Michel Foucault in his *episteme* made evident the inseparable relationship between knowledge and power, demonstrating that knowledge linked to power is based in, makes use of, reproduces, and is a function of power in order to maintain and further itself, and to make itself and its claims true. When his theory is applied in a theological context to such questions as, "What experiences and understandings count as knowledge and truth?" and "Who is allowed to participate in determining what knowledge and truth are?" it becomes evident that those who have ecclesial power hold sway, thus reinscribing the "truthfulness" of their positions. Indeed, the inherent relationship among power, knowledge, and truth is at the core of all discussions of heresy.

Although many different theological liberationist epistemologies have developed out of Foucault's insights, all liberationist epistemologies are concerned with investigating, empowering, and validating the experiences, insights, and understandings of individuals and groups whose knowledge historically has been discounted, ignored, maligned, or erased. The purpose of such liberationist epistemologies is not only to deepen knowledge in order to more fully understand God and God's workings in the world, but also to validate the personhood of the individual knower or group of knowers.

Meghan T. Sweeney

See also HUMAN BEING; THEOLOGICAL ANTHROPOLOGY.

EPISTLE

Derived from Greek (*epistole*), a written communication or letter.

It was once fashionable to consider that the term epistle distinguished public, formal correspondence from private letters. However, in the Hellenistic period, all forms of correspondence were called epistles. Today, the term epistle is generally reserved to designate twenty-one books in the New Testament and several patristic writings. Letters are also found in 2 Samuel 11:14-15; 1 Kings 21:8-11; 2 Kings 10:1-2; Ezra 7:12-24; Acts 15:23-29; 23:26-10; and Revelation 2–3.

All the undisputed works of Paul (Rom, 1 and 2 Cor, Gal, Phil, 1 Thess, Phlm), most disputed letters (Col, 2 Thess, the Pastorals: 1 and 2 Tim, Titus), as well as 1 Peter, and 2 and 3 John, are true letters. The New Testament letters generally follow closely the standard conventions for letters of the period. These formal features include: (1) an opening (identifying the sender and recipient in a greeting); (2) a thanksgiving or blessing; (3) the body; (4) applications (paraenesis); (5) the closing (including greetings and a blessing). Of the remaining New Testament books traditionally called "epistles," Hebrews and 1 John are sermons; James, 2 Peter, and Jude are exhortations with an epistolary greeting; Ephesians is a treatise set into the standard opening and closing of a letter.

Regina A. Boisclair

ERASMUS OF ROTTERDAM (1469?–1536)

A native of the city of Rotterdam, Erasmus left Holland to become an itinerant scholar and renowned humanist. After studies in Paris, Erasmus went to England in 1499 where he met John Colet and other humanists; later he would return to England and teach for a time at the University of Cambridge. His circle of friends included Thomas More.

On the continent, Erasmus lived mostly in Basle in the 1520s and 1530s, collaborating with the printer Froben. The publications that helped to build the reputation of Erasmus as a humanist scholar and as a critic of the late medieval church include *Handbook of a Militant Christian* (1504), *Praise of Folly* (1509), and a Greek edition of the New Testament (1516). In his writings, Erasmus criticized a piety that was external, focused on fasts, pilgrimages, or ritual acts. In place of this, he urged an interior piety of the heart, a simple love of God and neighbor based on the teachings of Jesus as found in the Gospels. In 1524 Erasmus distinguished his approach to reform from that of Luther by publishing a treatise on free will. Whereas for Luther free will was destroyed by the fall of Adam, Erasmus argued that some degree of free will remained, the free will by which human beings could accept or reject God's offer of grace and salvation. Despite this disagreement between Luther and Erasmus, most historians stress the Reformation's link with humanism and its continuity with much of Erasmus's reform agenda.

Thomas Worcester, s.j.

See also HUMANISM; LUTHER, MARTIN; MORE, THOMAS; REFORMATION; RENAISSANCE.

ERASTIANISM

The name given to a theory proposed by Swiss theologian Thomas Lüber, also called Erastus (1524–83). He suggested that the rulers of states with one religion have the right and duty to control both civil authorities and the church within their states. According to this theory, rulers have the right to decide on doctrinal issues as well as on questions of orthodoxy and heresy. Erastianism, under several guises, became very influential in England and in colonial British North America. Erastus' book *Explicatio gravissimae quaestionis* (1589) was translated and published in English in 1659 under the title *The Nullity of Church Censures*.

Orlando Espín

See also CAESAROPAPISM; ECCLESIOLOGY; REFORMATION.

ERETZ YISRAEL

Hebrew, meaning the Land of Israel.

The covenant God made with Abraham included the promise of a piece of land—which eventually come to be known as Eretz Yisrael, the Land of Israel—as an everlasting homeland for the Jewish people (Gen 12:7; 13:14-15, 17; 17:8). When God told Moses to tell Pharaoh to free the captive Hebrews, it was so God would be able to fulfill the promise to Abraham to bring Abraham's descendants to "a land flowing with milk and honey, unto the place of the Canaanite" (Exod 3:8). To make sure that there would be no doubt where the land is located, God gave Moses precise geographical boundaries (Num 34:2-12), and reiterated those specifications to Joshua, the successor of Moses, who would lead the Children of Israel into the Promised Land (Josh 1:4-5).

From the moment Joshua entered the land (around 1200 B.C.E.), Jews have lived in the Land of Israel—sometimes free and independent, sometimes ruled by others. Israel has been and continues to be the physical homeland for millions of Jews, and the spiritual homeland of every Jew.

In approximately 1030 B.C.E., the Jewish monarchy was established in Israel with the appointment of Saul as first king. In about 1010 B.C.E., King David established Jerusalem as the political and spiritual capital of the land. In 950 B.C.E., King Solomon built and dedicated the Holy Temple as the centralized sacred place for worshiping God. It was in the Land of Israel that the prophets taught the enduring values of spiritual faithfulness and social justice.

The Land of Israel has often been the target of foreign invaders. In 722 B.C.E., the Assyrians destroyed the kingdom of Israel, leaving only the small kingdom of Judah as the independent Jewish homeland. In 586 B.C.E., the mighty Babylonians conquered the land, destroyed the Holy Temple, and sent the people into exile. Yet this was not an exile that was to last long. In 536 B.C.E., the Persians, who had defeated the Babylonians, permitted the Jews to return to the Land of Israel. There, the Holy Temple was rebuilt, religious reformation took place, and sovereignty was eventually reestablished.

As the Greek world spread its influence throughout the ancient Middle East, Israel came under Hellenistic and then Roman domination and rule. In 70 C.E., the Romans conquered the land, the second Holy Temple was destroyed, and the people sent into exile again. This would be a long exile, lasting almost two millennia. During those years, Israel was ruled by many different powers, but there was never one day when Jews did not live in the land. Jews outside the land prayed every day for return and restoration.

In 1948, exile ended when the Third Jewish Commonwealth, the modern State of Israel, was established.

The Land of Israel has always been a nation-state of the world, but for Jews it has been even more. It is a near-mystical place, a place of special holiness, a place where past, present, and future meet, a place where there is a sacred union with God. The Land of Israel is the heart and the soul of the Jewish people; it is for Jews a land like no other.

Wayne Dosick

See also BEIT HAMIKDASH; KOTEL HAMA'ARAVI; MEDINAT YISRAEL; WAILING WALL.

ERIKSON, ERIK H. (1902–94)

Erik Homburger Erikson was a German-born psychoanalyst who emigrated to the United States in 1933. He was associated with Harvard University, Yale University, and the University of California at Berkeley and San Francisco. Erikson came to believe that while Sigmund Freud's contribution had been to study human beings from a perspective that moved "inward, downward, and backward," his own work complemented Freud's by examining the human ego as it moved "outward, upward, and forward." Thus, in his dozen books, Erikson describes the social (outward), spiritual (upward), and evolutionary (forward) development of the human ego. Erikson's writings on religious personalities include the psychohistories *Young Man Luther* (1958), which examines Luther's identity crisis, and *Gandhi's Truth* (1969), which describes the defining characteristics of the religious person. Other works deal with the development of the ego through eight stages, development of personal virtue, the significance of ritual, the nature of ethics, and the sayings of Jesus.

Helen deLaurentis

See also FREUD, SIGMUND; FROMM, ERICH.

ESCHATOLOGY (IN CHRISTIANITY)

In Christianity, eschatology is theological reflection on the ultimate destiny of the individual and world. Christian reflection on the future is guided by confidence in Christ's resurrection as a sign of God's commitment to creation and as a symbol of the transformation of persons and cosmos that will occur in the end time. Early Christian reflection on the resurrection of individuals ponders the fate of persons after death. This personal eschatology is summarized as the Last Things or final events in personal destiny: death, judgment, heaven or hell. Recent biblical studies recovered the eschatological dimension of Old and New Testament teaching considering the fate of persons and also that of society, world, and cosmos and fostered a new collective eschatology. This is seen in the reflection on the dynamic effect of the Christ event in theologies of history (Wolfhart Pannenberg) and evolutionary theologies (Teilhard de Chardin). Political theologies (Johann Metz), theologies of hope (Jürgen Moltmann), and the many liberation theologies reflect eschatology with an immanent concern, the power of divine presence which transforms the world here and now.

Patricia Plovanich

ESCHATOLOGY (IN JUDAISM)

Judaism envisions a future fulfillment of God's promises at a time when God will judge all human beings and initiate a messianic age. Classical Judaism holds that this age, referred to as "the world to come," will be introduced by a distinct period, called "the days of the messiah," that will occur in a time of devastating political and social upheaval (Mishnah

Sotah 9:15), leading ultimately to the destruction of the current world (Babylonian Talmud Sanhedrin 97b). This conception of the travail to accompany the coming of the messiah means that the messianic age was never an object of intense religious concern or longing. Classical Jewish texts reflect that, however much people might long for messianic redemption, they do not wish themselves to be alive at that time (Babylonian Talmud Sanhedrin 98b).

Rabbinic masters calculated the advent and duration of the days of the messiah and world to come. According to different rabbis, the former would last 40, 70, 365, or 400 years (Babylonian Talmud Sanhedrin 99a; see Babylonian Talmud Abodah Zarah 9b). Babylonian Talmud Sanhedrin 97a-b holds that the world will exist for six thousand years: "For two thousand it will be desolate, two thousand years will be the time of Torah, and two thousand years will be the days of the messiah." The same source holds that, on account of the Israelites' sins, the messiah has tarried. Part of what should already be the messianic age therefore has been lost.

While some rabbis speculated on the exact date on which the messiah will come (see Mekhilta Pisha 14), Jewish thinkers in general condemned those who engage in such predictions. Their concern was that the failure of such messianic predictions to come true might lead people to deny that the messiah ever will come. The Talmud thus lists the exact date of the messiah's coming among things God has hidden from the people (Babylonian Talmud Pesahim 54b; Babylonian Talmud Sanhedrin 97a) and states that, instead of being predetermined, the coming of the messiah depends upon the Israelites themselves. When they conform to the will of God—repenting and performing good deeds, or even simply correctly observing one Sabbath—the messiah will come (Babylonian Talmud Sanhedrin 97b; Jerusalem Talmud Taanit 4:8, 68d; Exodus Rabbah 25:12). In the meantime, the people are admonished not to attempt forcibly to hasten the coming of the end of time (Babylonian Talmud Ketubot 111a).

Judaism perceives the messianic age to be marked by the fulfillment of the promises God made to the Israelites in the Hebrew Scriptures. In particular, the Israelite nation will be restored to the Promised Land, where the priesthood and sacrificial worship will resume in a rebuilt Temple. The cult will be different from that of the current world only in small ways, for instance, by the fact that the harps played in the Jerusalem Temple will have more strings (Tosefta Arakhin 2:7). In this period, the transplantation of the Babylonian rabbinic academies to the land of Israel is imagined (Babylonian Talmud Megillah 29a). But this period is not marked by the end of sin, for the riches of the days of the messiah will lead people to transgression (Sifre Deuteronomy 318). Modes of expiation such as study and observance of the law therefore will still be required.

By contrast to the age of the messiah, the conditions of the world to come—after the final judgment and the resurrection of the dead—are understood to be very different from those of current life. "The world to come is not like this world. In the world to come there is neither eating nor drinking nor procreating nor business negotiations nor envy nor hatred nor competition. But the righteous are enthroned with their crowns on their heads, enjoying the splendor of the Presence of God" (Babylonian Talmud Berakhot 17a). This age will be like a continual Sabbath

(Abot deRabbi Nathan 1:13), and there will be no death, sorrow, or tears (Mishnah Moed Qatan 3:9). What will remain is study and observance of the law, taught now by God himself (Tanhuma, Yitro 13; Tanhuma Vayiggash 12).

Central to this concept of the world to come is the doctrine of the resurrection of the dead (*Tehiyat HaMetim*) that developed in Judaism from postbiblical Israelite and Greco-Roman thought. The Hebrew Bible expresses no such doctrine. It views God as the source of life and death, who may rescue a soul from deadly-danger (for instance, Psalm 49:15), but who does not actually revive people from death. The rabbinic view, by contrast, depends upon the single biblical reference to resurrection (Daniel 12:2: "Many of those who sleep in the dust will awake"), and takes up an emerging postbiblical concern with this concept (see, for example, 2 Maccabees 7:9; 1 Enoch 22; 90:33; 91:10; 92:3, and the probably later chapters 30–31). Based upon this foundation, the rabbinic doctrine of resurrection took firm hold with the ascent of Pharisaism after the destruction of the Second Temple in 70 C.E., in particular with the decline of the Sadducees, who had rejected the notion of resurrection (see Acts 23:8; Matthew 22:23).

The centrality of resurrection in Jewish thought is indicated by M. Sanhedrin 10:1 that lists as the first of those who have no portion in the world to come anyone who denies the origin in the Torah of belief in resurrection of the dead. Other sources dispute not the fact of resurrection but its mechanics. Babylonian Talmud Rosh Hashanah 16b-17a states that, on the day of judgment, three groups will arise: the thoroughly righteous, the thoroughly wicked, and those in the middle. The righteous immediately are sealed for eternal life, while the wicked are assigned to hell. The fate of those in the middle, however, is subject to dispute. Some authorities hold that they first are sent to hell, where they scream in prayer and are redeemed; others hold that, as a result of God's mercy, they share the fate of the thoroughly righteous. Elsewhere, the Talmud describes the process of resurrection as like the growth of a grain of wheat (B. Sanhedrin 90b; B. Ketubot 111b). B. Berakhot 60b describes resurrection as the reunion of the soul with the dead body, and some sources hold that a small, incorruptible part of the body, or even a small amount of rotted flesh, will serve as the material from which a new body is fashioned.

Despite the classical rabbis' own speculation regarding the nature of the messianic age, day of judgment, and world to come, Jews have generally discouraged concrete messianic thinking, which might threaten the community's stability by instigating a deadly political revolt against the nations under whom the Jews lived. When, in the second century C.E., Rabbi Aqiba declared Bar Kokhba to be the messiah, Yohanan b. Torta reportedly told him, "Aqiba, grass will grow from your cheeks and He will still not have come" (Lamentations Rabbah 58; Jerusalem Talmud Taanit 4:8, 68d). Similarly, the rabbis instruct a person who, while plowing his field, is told that the messiah has arrived to complete his work and only then to investigate.

The doctrine of resurrection has a prominent position in Jewish liturgy, forming the focus of the second benediction of the Amidah, recited in all worship services. This prayer proclaims that God "causes death, gives life, and makes salvation spring forth, he makes the dead live and keeps faith with those who sleep in the dust." It concludes by praising God as one who resurrects the dead.

Alan J. Avery-Peck

ESCHATON

A word derived from the Greek *eschatos* meaning "last," *eschaton* indicates the final destiny or last age of the world, the end time. The term in Hebrew prophets expressed the postexilic hope of the restoration of Jerusalem and the Temple (Ezek 40–48) or the fulfillment of Israel's destiny as God's people in the day when Yahweh rules the nations (Isa 40–55). Eschaton in Pauline theology has a present connotation, the transformation of the world already begun in the Christ event. The term sometimes has an apocalyptic meaning presenting the eschaton as the new creation, the ideal future achieved through God's power in history.

Patricia Plovanich

See also ESCHATOLOGY (IN CHRISTIANITY); ESCHATOLOGY (IN JUDAISM); PAROUSIA.

ESCOBAR, SAMUEL (1934–)

Peruvian Protestant theologian and missiologist. Escobar is one of the leading voices of the Protestant, Evangelical churches of Latin America. He studied in his native Peru and later earned his doctorate at Madrid's Universidad Complutense. He is an ordained minister of the Baptist Church of Peru. Internationally recognized as one of the main drafters of the World Council of Churches' Lausanne Covenant (1974), Escobar was also instrumental in establishing the Latin American Theological Fraternity—an association of Protestant theologians. He has taught at universities in Latin America, Europe, and the U.S. He has written numerous pastoral and scholarly articles and several books.

Orlando Espín

See also BAPTIST CHURCHES / BAPTIST CONVENTIONS; BAPTIST THEOLOGY; COSTAS, ORLANDO E.; ECUMENICAL MOVEMENT / ECUMENISM; LATIN AMERICAN PROTESTANTISM; LATINO PROTESTANTISM; LATINO THEOLOGY (-IES); PROTESTANTISM / PROTESTANT; THIRD WORLD THEOLOGIES; WORLD COUNCIL OF CHURCHES (WCC).

ESDRAS, BOOKS OF

1 Esdras and 2 Esdras are made up of very diverse material. 1 Esdras may be viewed as a "historical" book that is an alternate version of the canonical book of Ezra with the addition of a section from the book of Chronicles at the beginning and the addition of a section from the book of Nehemiah at the end. The narrative begins with the Passover celebration of Josiah and ends with the public reading of the Torah brought to Jerusalem by Ezra. 1 Esdras is not considered canonical in the West and appears in the Apocrypha under the title 3 Esdras.

2 Esdras is found in the Apocrypha where it is commonly titled 4 Ezra. Chapters 3–14 consist of a Jewish apocalypse probably from around 100 C.E. written originally in Hebrew or Aramaic. The protagonist of the book is Ezra who, in a series of discussions with an angel, probes questions of human sin, destiny, and God's mercy.

Russell Fuller

See also BIBLE.

ESPÍN, ORLANDO (1947–)

Orlando Oscar Espín, U.S. Latino Catholic theologian, was born in Cuba. Raised in the United States, Espín was educated in Florida and in Brazil where he earned a doctorate in systematic theology (1984). He is currently professor at the University of San Diego. Extensive experience among the poor in the Dominican Republic has had a deep impact on his thought. Espín has focused his theological work on popular Catholicism, raising serious questions on the relationship between culture, religious experience, and faith. He has made important contributions, from the perspective of Latino popular religion, on the theologies of tradition, the *sensus fidelium*, and grace. He was one of the original members of the Academy of Catholic Hispanic Theologians of the U.S. (ACHTUS), and has twice been president. Espín founded the *Journal of Hispanic/ Latino Theology*, and was its first editor in chief. He has written numerous scholarly articles, and among his books is *The Faith of the People: Theological Reflections on Popular Catholicism* (1997).

James B. Nickoloff

See also LATINO THEOLOGY (-IES); POPULAR CATHOLICISM; POPULAR RELIGIONS; POPULAR RELIGIOSITY.

ESSENCE

A thing's essence consists of all those properties or features of the thing that define it and are necessary for its very existence. Any property a thing could not lose without ceasing to exist altogether is one of its essential or defining characteristics. For example, a particular cat will always have the properties being-an-animal and being-a-mammal regardless of any changes it may undergo. In the case of very complex beings, such as human beings, there are a wide variety of opposing views about which properties belong to the essential or intrinsic nature. Some

philosophers and theologians have held that human beings are essentially spiritual beings. On some accounts, the soul or spirit, which is able to survive death, is regarded as being the individual's essence. The body that is destroyed at death is held, on this view, to be an unnecessary or merely "accidental" feature of the human being. Alternatively, materialists hold that human nature is essentially physical and that there is nothing to a human's essence apart from biological and physiological characteristics.

Linda L. Peterson

See also ACCIDENT.

ESSENES

An ancient Jewish group known both from secondary sources of the first century C.E. as well as from primary sources of the second and first centuries B.C.E. and the first century C.E., although there is some disagreement about this. Before the discovery of the Dead Sea Scrolls, most of our information about the Essenes was derived from Josephus and Pliny the Elder. With the discovery of the Dead Sea Scrolls, the theory developed that the community resident at Khirbet Qumran was a group of the Essenes. This theory still dominates the field of Qumran studies, and therefore most scholars feel justified in using the "sectarian compositions" found at Qumran as sources of information on the beliefs and practices of the Essenes, or at least that group of Essenes. Some of the most important documents here are the Manual of Discipline, the Damascus Document, the Temple Scroll, and the War Scroll. When these compositions are combined with the information provided by Josephus, with which they agree for the most part, a fairly good picture of the Essenes at Qumran emerges. They were an apocalyptic group that lived in expectation of the imminent end of the world as it was. They thought of themselves as living in the "end of days." According to the War Scroll, they lived in "hope" of a series of battles between the forces of good and the forces of evil in which they would fight beside the angels of heaven. They called themselves the "sons of light," and their community was called the "Community" (Hebrew, *yahad*). They organized themselves into a hierarchical community divided into two groups, the priests and the nonpriests. The community was dominated by the priest members who presided at the communal sacred meals. This dominance is also reflected in the messianic expectations of the community. According to the Community Rule, they expected both a priestly messiah and a lay messiah, probably descended from David. The priestly messiah seems to have taken precedence over the Davidic messiah in the eschatological sacred meal and to have served as an advisor to him. The community may also have expected a prophet, but the role of this figure is not defined, and the relationship to the two messiahs is unclear. Ritual purity was also of extreme importance to this group, as were the Laws of Moses in general. They had developed their own understanding of the observance of these laws that were sometimes at variance with the understanding of other groups within Judaism in this period. This conflict over *halakhah*, or the correct observance of the Torah, is in part revealed by the important early composition entitled *Miqstat Ma'aseh Hat-Torah* (4QMMT). In that composition, which some scholars think was a letter from the community at Qumran to religious leaders in Jerusalem about their disagreements over *halakhah*, the Qumran community explains their disagreements and attempts to convince their opponents of the correctness of their views. Laws concerning ritual purity are central to that part of 4QMMT.

Russell Fuller

ETERNAL LIFE

Eternal life is a metaphor for the condition of human life after death or an image of the risen life of the faithful. The concept is distinguished from the Greek idea of immortality, for the phrase comes from biblical imagery for the relationship with God and from the experience of Christ's resurrection understood to be the destiny of all humanity, life completed and transformed through communion with God. Descriptions of such existence abound in popular piety; theological speculation has drawn on Scripture to explain such conditions as the beatific vision. Secular critics of religion have judged the concept to distract believers from the task of ameliorating the inequities of the present age, a theme noted by contemporary theologies of hope and liberation. In systematic theology, the discussion of eternal life belongs to the topic theological anthropology and its reflection on the meaning of human life.

Patricia Plovanich

See also BEATIFIC VISION; HEAVEN; RESURRECTION OF THE BODY; THEOLOGICAL ANTHROPOLOGY.

ETERNAL LIGHT

See NER TAMID.

ETERNITY

In common usage, eternity can designate eternal life or heaven, the condition of human life with God after death. Generally, however, the term designates a divine attribute. The concept from Greek philosophy contrasts the imperfection and mutability of finite existence with the immutable or timeless perfection of the divine being. The discussion of God's eternity in fundamental theology involves the question about God's real relationship to the world, particularly to suffering. The classical discussion generally resolved the dilemma on the side of divine disengagement or transcendence. However, this interpretation is a problem for theology based on biblical testimony about God who intervenes in history and engages in relationships with human beings. The patristic discussion of the Incarnation that expresses God's immersion in human life in Jesus Christ was at pains to link Jesus' human birth, suffering, and death with the eternal Logos' immutability. Many theologians today propose dynamic and interpersonal categories as attributes faithful to biblical testimony and honor engagement and relationship as higher perfections than immutability.

Patricia Plovanich

ETHERIA (THE PILGRIMAGE OF)

The Pilgrimage of Etheria (or Egeria) is a late fourth- or early fifth-century description of the journey of a Spanish woman to the Holy Land, Egypt, Syria, Asia Minor, and Constantinople. All scholars know about the author comes from internal evidence. She was wealthy, of high social standing, and a member of a religious community to which she addresses her work. The first half of the *Pilgrimage* describes Etheria's visit to biblical sites, while the second half of the work concentrates on liturgical descriptions. The treatise is extremely valuable as a witness to the devotions and liturgy of the time.

Gary Macy

See also HOLY LAND; LITURGY (IN CHRISTIANITY); PILGRIMAGE.

ETHICS

In general, morality is what is presented by one's community as right or wrong. One receives a sense of appropriate or inappropriate behavior by narratives of heroes or villains, by direct or indirect instruction from family, school, church, and other formative organs of society (such as media), and even by slogans or maxims. Ethics is the disciplined study of the nature of such formators, and of the resultant actions and passions by the moral person (agent) and the moral community. As such, the study of ethics can in turn influence the moral practices of the community. Further, it can open one to the study of the moral practices of other communities.

In the last twenty years, especially, many theologians have been attending to the truth claims of particular faith communities, how they are distinguished from the truth claims of other communities (particularly those of the dominant "secular" culture), and what special actions and passions those beliefs would effect. This has led to the development of the term "theological ethics," which seeks to answer the question, "What difference does believing in [this] God make to how I live my life?" Thus, for example, we might consider that confessing Christians should practice an ethic of nonviolence, since Jesus, as the divine Word in Christianity, commands Christians to love their enemies.

G. Simon Harak, s.j.

ETHICS, SEXUAL

Christian moral reflection on human sexual behavior is characterized by both a genuine appreciation for human sexuality as a gift from God for human well-being and by a profound suspicion of sex and especially of sexual pleasure due to its capacity to distract persons from their obligations to love God and neighbor. It has been this wariness of sex and sexual pleasure that has been dominant in Christian sexual ethics. While most contemporary authors agree that this suspicion has generated an overly negative evaluation of sexuality by the Christian tradition, it is by no means wholly unfounded in light of the capacity of irresponsible sexual behavior to inflict grave harm on persons. Christians have historically attempted to limit the prospects for such harm by understanding human sexuality within the context of marriage and in light of its procreative capacity. Legitimate sexual activity, then, was limited to marriage with a view toward producing new life. Nonprocreative sexual activity —masturbation, same-sex relations, oral or anal sex, and the use of contraceptive or birth control devices—has been traditionally proscribed as has any sexual activity outside of the bonds of monogamous, permanent marriage.

Sources of the Tradition

The New Testament. The authors of the Christian Scriptures expected an imminent second coming of Christ and end of the world. They did not, then, tend to emphasize ethical questions or attempt to generate a wholly new morality. Instead, these writers emphasized the love commandment and conversion to Christ, and the coming of God's kingdom that it necessarily implies. Although Jesus does address the question of divorce (Mark 10:2-12/Matt 19:3-9) and reinforces the prohibition against adultery (Matt 5:27-28; John 18:11), the Gospels do not record any extended discussion of sex or sexual morality on his part.

There are references in the letters of Saint Paul to certain questions of sexual morality; indeed, 1 Corinthians 7 contains the only extended treatment of sexual morality in the New Testament. As he expects an imminent end of the world, Paul generally encourages persons to stay remain in their present state. He does, however, voice a decided preference for celibacy and virginity. Paul advocates marriage only as an antidote to lust or temptation to the sin of fornication (extramarital sexual activity); "If they cannot exercise self-control, they should marry. It is better to marry than to be on fire" (1 Cor 7:9).

Most New Testament scholars urge caution in interpreting the specific Pauline norms and attempting to apply them to contemporary experience due to vast historical and cultural differences. Paul's consistently negative evaluation of homogenital activity (Rom 1:23-28; 1 Cor 6:9) is a good example of the problem. Paul saw sexual activity between persons of the same sex as paradigmatic of the type of behavior that results from a refusal to recognize the one, true God. His condemnations often appear in vice lists that are similar manifestations of this error. In some passages, the exact nature of the behavior Paul refers to is unclear. When it is clear, as in the letter to the Romans, John Boswell has argued that, because homosexuality is a modern concept unknown to Paul and his culture, what Paul is actually criticizing is homogenital actions committed by persons who are heterosexual. Because he is unaware of the existence of persons "constitutionally" homosexual or gay, he is not in a position to offer a critique of gay sexual expression. Others counterargue that Paul's sexual ethic implicitly affirms heterosexuality as normative and that there is no reason to believe that if Paul had been aware of the homosexual orientation he would change his evaluation of homo-genital acts.

The role of Stoic philosophy. In the ancient Greco-Roman philosophy of Stoicism, early Christian thinkers found a view of sexuality consistent with their own concerns about the power of sexual desire to undermine commitment to the Gospel and its dual love command. The Stoics understood that a worthy, moral life was eminently reasonable; therefore, they distrusted the emotions and physical passion. Sexual intercourse, with its attending bodily passion, could only be morally acceptable insofar as it had a rational purpose. For the Stoics, the only rational purpose for sexual intercourse was the propagation of the human species; thus, a procreative intent was necessary for morally acceptable intercourse. This procreative intention, based on rationality, became the cornerstone for Christian sexual ethics up until the time of the Protestant Reformation and beyond.

The influence of Augustine. The thought of Saint Augustine (354–430) has exerted a powerful influence in the development of Christian theology and ethics in the West. In many ways, his own thought on sexual matters was shaped in reaction to his theological opponents. Against the dualistic heresy of the Manicheans, which denigrated the physical and so procreation as a manifestation of spirit being trapped by the physical, Augustine asserted the good of marriage and its procreative dimension. Indeed, Augustine saw that marriage had three "goods": offspring, the faithfulness of the married couple, and the sacramental bond. Against the more optimistic heresy of Pelagianism, which claimed that human persons were able to save themselves—in theory, at least—without the assistance of divine grace, Augustine asserted the great, destructive power of original sin. For Augustine, the effects of original sin were nowhere more evident than in the passion that necessarily accompanies human sexual activity; a passion that completely undermines that spark of the divine in humans that Augustine equates with rationality. Sexual passion is, by its nature, beyond rational control; thus, following the Stoics, it is morally permissible only with a procreative intent. Sexual desire, then, has been affected by sin in Augustine's account. For a married couple to engage in sexual activity for pleasure or the release of sexual tension is sinful in Augustine's account, although not mortally so.

The contributions of Thomas Aquinas. Thomas Aquinas (around 1225–74), while denying that any spontaneous inclination or desire such as sexual desire could be sinful in itself, argued strongly for the procreative norm as encountered in Augustine. Consistent with his own theory of natural law that continues to exert a strong influence on Roman Catholic sexual ethics, Aquinas develops two different sorts of reasons for restricting sexual activity to the marital and the procreative. On the one hand, he emphasizes the importance of bodily structures when he argues that the anatomy and physiology of the human sexual organs demonstrate that sexual activity is ordered, or finds its goal, in reproduction. Intentional nonreproductive sexual activity is contrary to the nature and purpose of the sexual faculties. Thus he rejects masturbation, same-sex relations, and contraception. On the other hand, Aquinas argues that nonmarital sexual relations are unnatural because they are irrational. They are irrational in that they deprive possible offspring of the stable family setting he believed childrearing required. Thus premarital and extramarital sexual relations, as well as divorce, are proscribed in Aquinas's account.

Like most of his predecessors, Aquinas privileged virginity and the celibate state. This helped to perpetuate the view of marriage as a "lesser calling." Nonetheless, in some of Aquinas's writings, there are the foundations for integrating marital sexuality with interpersonal love and companionship. Although not developed by Aquinas, later writers will pursue this theme. Similarly, it will be a dominant theme in Reformation thought on marriage and sexuality.

Reformation perspectives. The contributions to Christian sexual ethics by the fathers of the Protestant Reformation, Martin Luther (1483–1546) and John Calvin (1509–64), were characterized by the centrality of the Scriptures, an Augustinian awareness of the power of original sin, and profound suspicion of the pride-of-place given to celibacy in the Christian tradition. Both rejected any preference for celibacy, arguing that it was an extremely rare calling. Indeed, for Luther, marriage was viewed as a worthy "estate" to which most persons were called. Unlike earlier traditions in Christian sexual ethics, Luther's contribution was not procreation-centered. Sexual desire and pleasure as part of God's plan were good, although because of original sin these goods could interrupt the proper ordering of the human-divine relationship. Marriage served to direct and channel sexual pleasure and link it to the related goods of marital companionship and offspring. Luther's own happy marriage encouraged him to think of marriage as a school of virtue in which both partners grew in the Christian life. John Calvin, too, emphasized the dignity of marital companionship and its potential for promoting human flourishing.

Modern developments. Until the twentieth century, the actual moral norms for sexual behavior were similar for both Protestants and Roman Catholics, although the justifications for these norms might, as we have seen, be quite dissimilar. Notable exceptions to this convergence included questions of celibacy and divorce. For both groups, sexual expression was confined to lifetime, monogamous, heterosexual marriage. Premarital sex, adultery, homosexual relations, masturbation, and the use of birth control were all proscribed by the Christian churches.

A major shift among Protestants occurred with the Lambeth Conference of the Anglican Communion (of which the Episcopal Church in the U.S. is a branch) in 1930 that lifted the traditional ban on birth control. Other Protestant denominations followed while official Roman Catholic opposition continued. Indeed, the Anglican decision in 1930 was an important fact in Pius XI's decision to issue the papal encyclical letter *Casti Connubii* later that year. In addition to reaffirming the immorality of contraception, the encyclical affirmed the good of marital love, albeit as a secondary good to the good of procreation. There was also some openness to "natural" forms of birth regulation or rhythm (CC 85), although it was not until 1951 that Pius XII approved the practice unambiguously. In the 1968 encyclical *Humanae Vitae*, Paul VI argued that there were two equal goals to marital sexual expression: procreation and unifying the couple in love. Thus, even within the Roman Catholic tradition, there was some slight weakening of the procreative ethic as well as an assertion of the relation between sex and love. Indeed, in contemporary articulations of Christian sexual ethics, committed, interpersonal love often plays a decisive role in generating moral assessments.

A number of circumstances resulted in sweeping changes in Christian sexual ethics from the 1960s and beyond. Psychological, biological, and sociological studies offered new insights into the human person and human sexuality that in turn raised significant questions about traditional sexual morality. Similarly, theological and ecclesiological shifts raised questions about the scope and limitations of church authority and competence in the area of sexual ethics. For Catholics, the issue of birth control was again determinative.

Following Vatican II, a commission was established to review the traditional ban on artificial contraception, with many Catholics anticipating a liberalization. However, the encyclical *Humanae Vitae* reaffirmed Pius XI's earlier ban. The resulting controversy—within the clerical, theological, and lay communities—continues to be felt. As a result, official Catholic teaching on sexual matters has been perceived to be less than credible in some quarters. Many believe that Catholic authorities continue to assert a sexual ethics based on a physicalist natural law, no longer adequate in light of new understandings of moral theology, notably personalism. Others argue that the Catholic Church, by maintaining its traditional norms in the area of human sexuality, is staunchly resisting the dehumanizing tide of materialism and consumerism in a way consistent with its teachings on human dignity and human rights. In any case, recent authoritative teachings rearticulating traditional views on same-sex relations, clerical celibacy, and the status of women, have generated theological controversy and division among the laity.

Protestant denominations, particularly the mainstream denominations like Episcopalians, Presbyterians, and Lutherans, have also experienced significant development and division. Although officially sanctioning sexual relations within heterosexual marriage only, each of these denominations in the U.S. has launched commissions to examine questions of sexual morality. As with Catholics, the moral evaluation of homosexual relationships and homogenital acts remains particularly problematic.

Finally, traditional Christian sexual ethics must respond to questions arising from feminist theory and cultural studies. Feminist studies suggest that the sexual norms have placed women at a distinct disadvantage, allowing women to be objectified and abused. Cultural studies suggest human sexuality and related norms do not reflect an objective reality, but rather are "constructed" by particular cultures and so reflect power relationships. Nonetheless, the Western Christian tradition, with its emphasis on the centrality of love and the intrinsic value of every person, surely has an important contribution to make in this key arena of human experience.

Brian F. Linnane, s.j.

See also CONTRACEPTION/BIRTH CONTROL; MORAL THEOLOGY/CHRISTIAN ETHICS; NATURAL LAW; PERSONALISM; SEXUALITY.

ETHICS, SOCIAL

The discipline of social ethics evaluates the morality of our lives together as persons who participate in cultural, political, and economic structures. The goal of social ethics is to articulate what is necessary to achieve justice or right relationships between persons, other earth creatures, and planetary systems and the institutions that mediate relations between these entities.

The struggle to achieve justice or right relationships is the struggle to achieve mutuality, interdependence, and cooperation between and among persons, groups, ecosystems, and institutions in society. The goal of social ethics proceeds from the understanding that an individual can never fully flourish, or achieve who he or she ought to be, unless all others are also flourishing and becoming who they ought to be. The work of social ethics is the work of justice-making; the work of achieving authentic community in which there are no excluded ones, and the society is open to new truths, self-criticism, and different others.

Among the resources used to create Christian social ethics are the following: (1) social theories or the various forms of social analysis that evaluate larger social systems or structures; (2) the vision of what constitutes a moral society drawn from theology, Scripture, and various ecclesial, literary, or other traditions; (3) praxis or the struggle to enact principles or norms that increases ethical perception; (4) the context of persons or groups who do social ethics and their ideological commitments.

Given the wide spectrum of theory, vision, praxis, and context utilized by and pertinent to social ethicists, the body of social ethics is profoundly pluralistic in its content. Much of the literature in the field consists of discussions about what constitutes appropriate resources for doing Christian social ethics.

Mary E. Hobgood

See also FREEDOM; JUSTICE; SOLIDARITY.

ETHICS OF THE FATHERS

(Hebrew, *Pirke Avot*, "The Chapters of the Fathers"). A section of the Mishnah normally recited on Sabbath afternoons in the months following Passover. Avot describes the chain of tradition through which the oral law embodied in the Mishnah was transmitted from God to Moses in the revelation at Mount Sinai and then to the sages of successive generations and, finally, to the rabbis of the first centuries C.E. Following the chain of tradition, the tractate presents a collection of statements of wisdom essential to leading a moral and pious life. This content has made Avot one of the most popular religious works in Judaism.

Alan J. Avery-Peck

See also MISHNAH.

ETROG

A citrus fruit (citron), resembling a lemon, used on the Jewish festival of Tabernacles as "the fruit of goodly trees," one of the four species referred to at Leviticus 23:40 ("And you shall take on the first day the fruit of goodly trees, branches of palm trees, and boughs of leafy trees, and willows of the brook; and you shall rejoice before the LORD your God seven days"). Scripture views these species as representing the bounty of the land and so as appropriately used in a celebration of the harvest season.

Alan J. Avery-Peck

See also TABERNACLES, FEAST OF.

EUCHARIST

The word "Eucharist" comes from the Greek "to give thanks" and is one of many expressions used to refer to the Christian ritual meal. The ritual itself is modeled on Jewish ritual meals, particularly the

Passover meal. In the Synoptic Gospels, Jesus is described as blessing bread and wine at the Passover meal before he died, and then distributing them to his disciples, exhorting them to repeat this action in his memory. This meal in Jesus' memory was from the beginning one of the most important Christian rituals, described by Paul, and called in the Acts of the Apostles the "breaking of the bread." Originally, the ritual consisted of an entire meal, but soon was reduced to the reception of blessed bread and wine to which water was frequently added. A second Jewish ritual was joined to the meal, that of the reading and explanation of a passage from Scripture. Christians not only read Jewish Scripture, but added new writings of their own. The reading of Scripture and the ritual meal of bread and wine still make up the heart of the Christian Eucharist. At first, the ritual seems to have had no fixed celebrant, but by the third century, the usual celebrant of the Eucharist was the *episkopos* and/or the *presbyteros*.

During the Eucharist, Christians believe that they encounter and are empowered by Jesus, now the risen Christ. So powerful is this experience that the community thinks of itself as the Body of Christ present on earth. In this capacity, they pledge themselves by participation in the Eucharist to model their lives after that of Jesus. The commitment made in the Eucharist is very serious and only those who are members of the community may participate. Removal from the Christian community often has taken the form of excommunication, that is, refusal to allow an individual to share in the reception of the consecrated bread and wine.

The actual ritual, or liturgy, of the Eucharist has varied considerably over the centuries, while retaining the basic ac-

tions of scriptural reading and reception of consecrated bread and wine. During the fourth and fifth centuries, elaborate rituals based on Roman imperial practice were added to the ceremony. In Western Christianity, a number of penitential prayers were added in the early Middle Ages, while in Eastern Christianity, an element of mystery was added as parts of the ceremony were withdrawn behind a screen, often covered with icons. The liturgy in the West remained in Latin long after it was no longer the spoken language of the uneducated. For Roman Catholics, this remained the language of the liturgy until the twentieth century. The Eastern Church not only used ancient Greek and Syrian liturgies, but also translated the liturgy into the Slavic languages.

The Eucharist underwent important changes in the medieval West. Some of the communal aspect of the Eucharist was lost with the introduction of liturgies for the celebrant and his assistant alone. The liturgy came to be seen as the preserve of the clergy, who could offer Masses both for the living and the dead. On the other hand, lively lay devotion accompanied the liturgy. Enactment of the scriptural readings in the liturgy led in time to modern Western drama. Much Western music owes its origin to the elaborate scores developed for use in the Eucharistic Liturgy.

In reaction to these developments, the sixteenth-century Reformers argued for a return to what they understood to be the liturgies of early Christianity. They reduced or eliminated the distinction between celebrant and laity and placed more emphasis on the scriptural reading and sermon, shifting focus away from the ritual meal. While the Lutheran and Anglican communions retained a significant Communion service, the Calvinist communions greatly reduced its importance. In the twentieth century, due to the ecumenical movement and to a renewed interest in liturgical studies, differences between Protestant, Roman Catholic, and Anglican liturgies are gradually fading. The Eucharistic Liturgy appears to be entering a new and lively phase, however, as the cultures of Latin America, Asia, and Africa more and more influence Christianity.

Not only have Christians differed over the proper celebration of the Eucharist, but have disagreed equally strongly over its meaning and function. While all Christians would agree that the Eucharist pledges them to live as Jesus lived, and that in the celebration the Christian community is empowered by the risen Christ, the precise understanding of how the risen Christ is present and who may celebrate an efficacious liturgy have been and remain divisive issues. The Reformation debates of the sixteenth century focused on both these issues. Roman Catholics insisted both on transubstantiation as proper explanation for the Real Presence and on an ordained clergy (ordinarily celibate) as the proper celebrants of the Eucharist. Lutherans and Anglicans rejected transubstantiation, but held to a strong sense of Real Presence; both groups continued ordinations but did not consider it a sacrament nor did they insist on celibacy. Calvinist churches on the whole minimized any sense of Real Presence, and further reduced the division between minister and laity, although they too retained a ritual ordination.

While these and other questions continue to vex Christian unity, the Eucharist continues to play the lively central role in Christianity it has from its beginning. Despite the wrangling over the proper administration and understanding of this ritual, the Eucharist remains first and foremost something one does, not something about which one talks, and daily, all over the world, there are Christians from all congregations who pledge themselves in the ritual meal to a live of faith and love to which they daily aspire. In the life and in that pledge, their claim is that they there encounter the risen Christ.

Gary Macy

See also ACTS OF THE APOSTLES; ANGLICANISM; BODY OF CHRIST (IN CHURCH USE); CALVINISM; CHRIST; CLERGY; CORPUS CHRISTI; ECUMENICAL MOVEMENT; ECUMENISM; EPISKOPOS; EXCOMMUNICATION; HOST; JESUS; LITURGY (IN CHRISTIANITY); LUKE/LUKAN; LUTHERANISM; MASS; MINISTRY/MINISTERIAL; ORTHODOX CHURCHES; PAUL; PRESBYTEROS (IN THE NEW TESTAMENT); PRIESTHOOD; REAL PRESENCE; REFORMATION; REFORMED CHURCHES; ROMAN CATHOLIC CHURCH; TRANSUBSTANTIATION; VALIDITY, SACRAMENTAL.

EUCHARISTIC PRAYER

The word eucharistic is from the Greek *eucharistein*, to give thanks. The eucharistic prayer is the lengthy prayer offered over the bread and cup during the celebration of the Lord's Supper, the principal Christian act of thanksgiving. The deepest roots of the eucharistic prayer are Jewish. Scholars are engaged in an ongoing debate about which specific Jewish custom gave birth to the eucharistic prayer, but most agree that it is an outgrowth of the *birkat ha-mazon*, Jewish meal prayers. These *birkat ha-mazon* prayers contained three sections: praise of God, thanksgiving for God's gifts, and intercessions. All three of these elements are present in even the oldest eucharistic prayers. As early as the end of the first century, some authors had committed what seem to be model eucharistic prayers to writing. In general, however, during the first centuries after Christ, the one presiding at the liturgy would have prayed the eucharistic prayer extemporaneously, following a general outline. Gradually, written texts multiplied, and as more and more presiders used such forms, variety gave way to uniformity. The oldest known complete eucharistic prayer comes from third-century Rome, the work of the bishop Hippolytus. Most subsequent eucharistic prayers share Hippolytus' basic format, and make only minor structural additions. Generally, eucharistic prayers have six distinct parts: (1) a dialogue between the presiding minister and the assembly ("The Lord be with you. Lift up your hearts. Let us give thanks to the Lord our God"); (2) a memorial of God's deeds throughout history for which Christians are grateful, especially the life, death, and resurrection of Jesus, including mention of his command at the Last Supper to "do this in memory of me"; (3) an acclamation by the entire assembly (*Holy, holy, holy*); (4) a petition that God will send the Holy Spirit to transform the community, and its bread and wine; (5) intercessions, including a petition for the salvation of the members of the assembly; (6) and a concluding doxology, ending with amen. This is sometimes called the Great Amen since it concludes the great prayer of thanksgiving. Theologians have pointed out that the eucharistic prayer presents a concise summary of Christian belief. It speaks of God's creating and saving actions, the redeeming work of Jesus, the presence of the Holy Spirit with believers, and Christian hope for eternal life. In this way, it parallels the Creed.

Patrick L. Malloy

See also ANAMNESIS; ANAPHORA; CREED/SYMBOL OF FAITH; LAST SUPPER; LITURGY OF THE EUCHARIST.

EUDOXIA

There were two Roman empresses of this name who enter into Christian history. The first, the wife of Emperor Arcadius, took the title of "Augusta" in the year 400 and ruled alongside her husband. When the newly chosen patriarch of Constantinople, the famous preacher John Chrysostom, attacked the morals of the court (and more particularly those of Eudoxia), she helped engineer his condemnation in 403. After a first futile attempt, Eudoxia managed John's exile in 404.

The second Eudoxia was the highly educated wife of Emperor Theodosius II. Originally named Athenaïs as a pagan, she took the name Eudoxia upon baptism. Two years after her marriage in 421, she too was proclaimed "Augusta." She was a supporter of the patriarch of Constantinople, Nestorius, against the attacks of Cyril, the patriarch of Alexandria. In the midst of the politically charged Nestorian controversy, she was accused of infidelity in 442 and banished to Jerusalem where she died in 460. Several of her poems survive, including paraphrases of Zechariah and Daniel.

Gary Macy

See also CYRIL OF ALEXANDRIA; JOHN CHRYSOSTOM; NESTORIANISM; NESTORIUS.

EUNOMIANISM

The most radical form of Arianism as taught by Eunomius, the bishop of Cyzicus, from 360 until his exile by Emperor Theodosius in 383. Eunomius had been the student and secretary of Aetius, the philosopher and founder of Eunomianism. According to Aetius and Eunomius, the Son cannot share in the ungenerate nature of the Father; it would be logically impossible for the Son to be both generated from the Father and share the Father's ungenerate nature. Called "anomoeism (unlikeism)" by its opponents, this theology claims that the Son is "unlike" the Father by nature. The Son, then, does not share in the utter transcendence of the Father, has a definite beginning, and remains clearly inferior to the Father. The Spirit is not considered divine at all by Eunomius, but rather the most perfect of creatures.

This theology, based on the earlier position of Arius, came into its own in the fifth decade of the fourth century. Under the leadership of Valens, bishop of Mursa, religious advisor to Emperor Constantius, Athanasius was condemned and forced to flee into hiding in the desert. Athanasius' supporters, including Liberius, the Bishop of Rome, were exiled. At a meeting held in Sirmium, a creed was propounded that condemned the use of both *homoousios* and *homoiousios*, thus tacitly supporting the Eunomians. Eunomianism never had popular support, however, and the more moderate Arians, incuding Valens, began to distance themselves from Aetius and Eunomius. Under Emperor Julian, Eunomius and Aetius established a separate schismatic church. With the succession of Emperor Theodosius in 379, however, the Eunomians fairly rapidly disappeared as a force in Christianity.

Gary Macy

See also ARIANISM; ARIUS; ATHANASIUS, PATRIARCH OF ALEXANDRIA; CHRISTOLOGY; HOMOIOUSIOS; HOMOOUSIOS; JULIAN THE APOSTATE.

EURO-AMERICAN THEOLOGIES

In the United States, the dominant Euro-American Christian theologies have been Puritanism, Evangelicalism, liberalism, fundamentalism, neo-orthodoxy, and postmodernism. Although promulgated largely by Protestant males, most U.S. residents have subscribed to one or more of these theological systems and many still do; all have been affected by them. And while these six theological systems have often justified the hegemony of wealthy, educated, Anglo-Saxon Protestant men, they have nonetheless shaped the culture, ethos, and ideology of "America" over the last three hundred years.

In the seventeenth and early eighteenth centuries, Puritanism was the most influential Euro-American theology in the colonies. Centered in Massachusetts and Connecticut, Puritanism was followed by Calvinists seeking to purify the Church of England. They incorporated Calvinist precepts of unconditional election and irresistible grace into a covenant theology that applied to individuals, families, and nations. Puritan theologians included John Cotton, Cotton Mather, and Jonathan Edwards. Puritans bequeathed to American culture a commitment to education, legalism, self-righteousness, intense introspection, and the notion of Americans as God's chosen people.

From the mid-eighteenth to mid-nineteenth centuries, the dominant Euro-American theological mode was Evangelicalism. It was the theology of being born again, stressing an individual's intense conversion experience of repentance, justification, and sanctification. Conversions were stimulated through the medium of revivalism, which created an environment in which the sinner could become aware of God's gift of salvation through Jesus the Christ. Prominent

Evangelical theologians included Nathaniel William Taylor and Horace Bushnell. Evangelicalism contributed to U.S. culture a pragmatic approach to Christianity, missionary fervor, emotional enthusiasm, and a network of reform and social organizations designed to Christianize the country, including abolitionist, temperance, women's rights, and anti-prostitution societies.

Liberalism and fundamentalism emerged out of conflicts Evangelicals experienced in the late nineteenth century. Confronting immigration, urbanization, and industrialization, and clashing over Darwinism and new biblical scholarship, Evangelicals divided into two camps. One group, which came to be known as liberals, sought to reconcile the new social and intellectual developments with Christianity. They adopted a metaphorical approach to the Bible, an optimistic view of humanity, and the centrality of religious feelings. Theologians of liberalism included Walter Rauschenbusch, William Newton Clarke, and Borden Parker Bowne, while institutional manifestations were the Social Gospel and ecumenical movement. The legacy of liberalism was an emphasis on applying Christianity to human suffering, an understanding of the Bible as literature, and tolerance of the truth claims of other religions.

Other Evangelicals, who came to be known as fundamentalists, refused to compromise Christianity with modern scholarship. They asserted the literal truth of the Bible as written, adopted a theory of interpreting biblical prophecy called premillennial dispensationalism, and stressed fundamental doctrines as essential to Christian belief, such as the virgin birth, miracles, and physical resurrection of Jesus from the dead. The most prominent fundamentalist theologians were Charles Hodge and J. Gresham Machen. The fundamentalist legacy is an emphasis on right belief, the importance of conserving tradition, Pentecostalism, and a commitment to Enlightenment commonsense philosophy.

Along with liberalism and fundamentalism, neo-orthodox and postmodern theologies have diversified the twentieth-century theological landscape. Neo-orthodoxy reacted to liberalism's optimism and its stress on God's immanence by asserting the reality of sin and God's transcendence. Neo-orthodox theologians like Reinhold and H. Richard Niebuhr argued for a new Christian realism and critiqued churches for failing to realize their prophetic potential. Postmodern theology is not a monolithic system but a collection of responses to modernity. Death-of-God theologians William Hamilton and Thomas Altizer emphasized the irrelevance of conventional ideas of deity in the late twentieth century. Process theologians like John Cobb applied insights of existentialism and process philosophy to Christianity. Jürgen Moltmann emphasized realized eschatology in the theology of hope. The predominant contributions of neo-orthodoxy and postmodernism are a renewed sense of the systemic nature of evil, the unquenched desire for community, the fragility of humanity, and pluralism.

Evelyn A. Kirkley

See also BUSHNELL, HORACE; CIVIL RELIGION; DISPENSATIONALISM; EDWARDS, JONATHAN; EVANGELICAL THEOLOGY; FUNDAMENTALISM (CHRISTIAN HISTORICAL MOVEMENT); NEO-ORTHODOX THEOLOGY; NIEBUHR, H. RICHARD; NIEBUHR, REINHOLD; PURITANISM; RAUSCHENBUSCH, WALTER; REVIVALISM.

EUSEBIUS OF CAESAREA (265?–339/40? C.E.)

Eusebius was educated in Caesarea at the school founded by Origen. A student of Pamphilus, himself a student of Origen, Eusebius worked with his master to restore the school and its great library. During the persecution of Diocletian, Pamphilus was martyred, and Eusebius fled first to Tyre and then to Egypt. Arrested in Egypt, he was freed in 311 when the persecution ended. He was elected bishop of Caesarea in 313 and became immediately embroiled in the Arian controversy, at first openly siding with Arius. Eusebius signed the creed at Nicaea in 325, but remained unhappy with the *homoousios* and the theology of Athanasius. Until his death, he supported attempts to remove the *homoousios* from the Creed. Eusebius wrote extensively in theology and Scripture, but he is best known for his historical works, especially his *Ecclesiastical History*. The work covers the period from the beginnings of Christianity until the victory of Constantine over Licinius in 324. Eusebius is intent on showing the ultimate triumph of Christianity over the Roman Empire. The work is an invaluable source for the history of the early church, despite its undeniably polemical purpose.

Gary Macy

See also ARIANISM; ARIUS; ATHANASIUS, PATRIARCH OF ALEXANDRIA; DIOCLETIAN; HISTORY; HOMOOUSIOS; NICAEA, FIRST COUNCIL OF; NICAEA, SECOND COUNCIL OF; ORIGEN.

EUTYCHES (378?–454)

A monk for over seventy years, Eutyches was a friend and supporter of Cyril of Alexandria and of his successor, Dioscurus. In 448 Eutyches was con-demned by Flavian, the patriarch of Constantinople, at a synod in Constantinople. Eutyches was accused of teaching a form of Monophysitism. Clearly, he believed that there was only one nature in Christ, but even contemporaries were confused by Eutyches' garbled defense. With the support of his powerful friends, especially Dioscorus, however, Eutyches was able to get this decision reversed at the Council of Ephesus in 449 (a council later referred to as the "den of thieves" by Pope Leo I). At the same council, Dioscurus further insisted on the condemnation of Flavian and of the teaching that there are two natures in Christ. The decisions of this council did not last, however, and Eutyches was again condemned by the Council of Chalcedon in 451.

Gary Macy

See also CHALCEDON, COUNCIL OF; CYRIL OF ALEXANDRIA; MONOPHYSITISM.

EVANGELICAL

This term has three distinct meanings. (1) It signifies that something pertains to, or is in accordance with the Christian Gospel (in Greek, *evangelion*). In this sense, it is employed by all churches. (2) It is also part of the name of some particular Christian denominations worldwide, for instance, the Evangelical Lutheran Church. The inclusion of the term "Evangelical" in a mainstream denomination's name does not usually imply that it regards all other Christian churches as not "evangelical" (in the first sense of the term). (3) The term "evangelical" also refers to a particular Christian movement, and its offshoot denominations, that trace their roots (directly or indirectly) to England's 1735 "Evangelical Revival," and/or to

"The Great Awakening" of 1740 in the United States.

Orlando Espín

See also CHRISTIANITY; CHURCH; ECCLESIOLOGY; EVANGELICALS; EVANGELICAL THEOLOGY; EVANGELISM; GOSPEL; GREAT AWAKENING(S) (EURO-AMERICAN RELIGIOUS HISTORY); PROTESTANTISM; REVIVALISM.

EVANGELICALS

An evangelical is an adherent of evangelical Christian theology. Broadly speaking, evangelicals believe the Good News that Jesus of Nazareth is the Christ; more narrowly, they proclaim that sinful individuals must be born again in a dramatic conversion experience. Evangelicals stress conversion through revivalism and sanctification through discipleship. They commit themselves to holy living and to transforming society in conformity with the Bible. Since anyone can be born again, regardless of birth, wealth, race, or gender, evangelicals preach the leveling of social distinctions. Their commitment to Christianizing society gives a strong impetus to reform movements.

This egalitarianism and democratizing effect helped Evangelicalism become the dominant Christian ethos in the United States beginning in the eighteenth century, expanding in the nineteenth, and continuing in the twentieth. Evangelicalism was so influential that it became virtually synonymous with Protestantism; it shaped every U.S. religious group, including Catholics and Jews, but especially Baptists, Methodists, Congregationalists, Presbyterians, and Disciples of Christ. Evangelicalism began with the Great Awakenings of the mid-eighteenth- and early nineteenth centuries. Leaders of the First Great Awakening in the 1730s and 1740s included revivalist George Whitefield, the "Grand Itinerant"; pastor and revivalist Jonathan Edwards, theologian of "religious affections"; and John Wesley, founder of the Methodists. During the Second Great Awakening, Charles G. Finney implemented the "new measures," effective evangelistic techniques, and became known as the father of modern revivalism.

Fired up by the revivals of the early nineteenth century, evangelicals cooperated transdenominationally and created the "Benevolent Empire," a vast network of organizations devoted to foreign and home missions, Sunday Schools, Bible and tract distribution, and social reforms ranging from temperance and antidueling to abolition, women's rights, and antiprostitution. However, after the Civil War, evangelicals experienced conflict over social and intellectual challenges to their hegemony. Social changes such as urbanization, industrialization, immigration, and technology strained evangelical unity. More critical, Darwinism and higher criticism of the Bible questioned the divine order of the universe and scriptural truth as evangelicals had accepted them.

Gradually, evangelicals divided into two groups: liberals who accommodated modern culture and scholarship, and fundamentalists who refused to compromise the Christian faith to modernity. Heresy trials were held in seminaries, denominations split, and the 1925 Scopes trial on evolution discredited fundamentalism. Liberal leaders included Henry Ward Beecher, Congregationalist pastor and pulpit orator; Walter Rauschenbusch, seminary professor and theologian of the Social Gospel; and Harry Emerson Fosdick, pastor and pulpiteer in New York City. Fundamentalist leaders were Charles Hodge, Princeton professor and theologian; Dwight Moody, widely popular revivalist; and J. Gresham Machen, theologian and author of *Christianity and Liberalism* (1923).

In the mid-twentieth century, liberal and fundamentalist Christians were joined by a third group calling themselves evangelicals or neo-evangelicals. Seeking middle ground, they believed liberals had accommodated too much and diluted Christian essentials and that fundamentalists were too rigid, overly concerned with theological minutiae such as premillennial dispensationalism. In contrast, they affirmed traditional evangelical emphases on conversion, revivalism, and missions. They formed the National Association of Evangelicals in 1942, a loose conglomeration of evangelical organizations and individuals united to promote evangelism. Their champion is Billy Graham, internationally famous revivalist of the 1950s–1980s. In the late twentieth century, many evangelicals blurred their differences with liberalism and fundamentalism. Evangelicalism has become a diverse mosaic of organizations and individuals, including the Sojourners Community, Campus Crusade for Christ, and Intervarsity Fellowship.

Historically, many evangelicals have been people of color and women, attracted to the messages of liberation and societal transformation. African American evangelicals include Richard Allen, founder of the African Methodist Episcopal Church; Charles Mason, founder of the Church of God in Christ; Martin Luther King Jr., Baptist pastor and leader of the civil rights movement; and Jesse Jackson, Baptist preacher and social activist. Women evangelicals include Phoebe Palmer, founder of the Holiness movement; Frances Willard, leader of the Women's Christian Temperance Union; Sojourner Truth,

African American abolitionist and woman's rights advocate; and Marabel Morgan, antifeminist and author of *The Total Woman* (1973).

Evelyn A. Kirkley

See also EVANGELICAL THEOLOGY; EVANGELISM; FUNDAMENTALISM (CHRISTIAN HISTORICAL MOVEMENT); GREAT AWAKENING(S) (EURO-AMERICAN RELIGIOUS HISTORY); REVIVALISM; WITNESS/WITNESSING.

EVANGELICAL THEOLOGY

Deriving from the Greek word for good news, "evangelical" theology is, broadly speaking, concerned with receiving and proclaiming the Good News that Jesus of Nazareth is the Christ. Using that definition, it applies to all Christians. However, the term is more often used with a more specific meaning. Evangelical theology emerged in the United States and Europe in the mid-eighteenth and nineteenth centuries in the work of John Wesley, Jonathan Edwards, George Whitefield, and Charles G. Finney, among others. It is the dominant theology for many contemporary Baptists, Methodists, Presbyterians, Disciples of Christ, and even some Episcopalians and Lutherans. Evangelical theology is not synonymous with Protestant Christianity, but is a particular interpretation of it.

Evangelical theology is the theology of being born again. It is individual, experiential, pragmatic, and adaptive. First, it stresses the vertical relationship between the individual and Christ rather than the horizontal relationship of believers in community. It presumes original sin and the necessity of individual conversion. Second, conversion is a dramatic experience in which the individual encounters the love and power of the risen Christ.

Revivalism is the most prevalent method of stimulating conversions. Third, Evangelical theology is success-oriented. Revivalism is popular because it works: it effectively converts large numbers of people. Fourth, Evangelical theology adapts to change. Through revivalism, it shifted from a Calvinist to an Arminian orientation. Instead of unconditional election and irresistible grace, it stresses the individual's role in achieving conversion. More recently, Evangelicals have adopted modern technology and mass media as vehicles for revivalism.

The center of Evangelical theology is the conversion experience consisting of three steps: repentance, justification, and sanctification. First, the individual recognizes how far he or she has strayed from God's will and becomes convicted of sin. Repentance involves sincere contrition, receipt of forgiveness, and the pledge to avoid intentional sin in the future. Second, the individual is justified through faith. Evangelical theology posits a substitutionary theory of the atonement, that Christ died as a substitute for sinful humanity. An individual is justified, or made right in God's eyes, when he or she accepts God's gift of grace freely given. Third, conversion results in sanctification, a commitment to an ethics of holy, righteous living as disciples of Christ. They testify to the authenticity of their conversion by emulating Christ in their words and behavior. Sanctification also entails witnessing, evangelizing others about Christ's work in one's life.

Evangelical conversion leads to a radical change not only in individuals, but also in society. Seeking universal application of the Gospel, Evangelicals strive to eliminate sin from society as well as from their own lives. They believe they have a responsibility to Christianize their cul-ture, to transform it by living a sanctified life. As a result, Evangelicalism has spawned such diverse movements as the Social Gospel, fundamentalism, and Pentecostalism, and undergirded reform movements including abolition, women's rights, and civil rights.

Evelyn A. Kirkley

See also EVANGELICALS; EVANGELISM; FUNDAMENTALISM (CHRISTIAN HISTORICAL MOVEMENT); GREAT AWAKENING(S) (EURO-AMERICAN RELIGIOUS HISTORY); PENTECOSTALISM; REVIVALISM; SOCIAL GOSPEL; WITNESS/WITNESSING.

EVANGELII NUNTIANDI

Name of an "apostolic exhortation," written by pope Paul VI in 1975, on the "proclamation of the Gospel" in the modern world (hence the name of the document in Latin). *Evangelii Nuntiandi* is a very important document for understanding Catholic evangelization. In this text Paul VI emphasized the intimate relationship between culture and evangelization, social issues and Christian faith, and discussed the role of base communities, the importance of inculturation, etc. This apostolic exhortation has had significant influence in modern Catholic pastoral work, especially in the Third World.

Orlando Espín

See also APOSTOLIC EXHORTATION; "BASIC" ECCLESIAL COMMUNITIES; CATECHESIS/CATECHETICAL; CULTURE; ECCLESIOLOGY; EVANGELIZATION; FAITH; INCULTURATION; JUSTICE; MISSIOLOGY; MISSIONS; PAUL VI, POPE; PETRINE PRIVILEGE; POPE; ROMAN CATHOLIC CHURCH; ROME, SEE OF.

EVANGELISM

Deriving from the Greek word for good news, Christian evangelism is proclaiming the Good News that Jesus of Nazareth is the Christ. It began when Mary Magdalene discovered the empty tomb, saw the resurrected Jesus, and told the other disciples. Beginning with Mary, and later Paul, evangelism's purpose is to lead others to Christ and to the church by convincing them of the truth of Christianity. It results in planting churches or refers to individuals affiliating with churches already established. In the early centuries of the church, martyrdom and monasticism were forms of evangelism, ways to testify to Christianity's authenticity, even to the sacrifice of one's life.

In recent centuries, dominant forms of evangelism have included catechesis, sacramentalism, revivalism, and nurture, each reflecting different Christian theologies. Catechesis is the most intellectual form of evangelism. It consists of mastering questions and answers that encompass the essentials of theology and ethics and integrating them into oneself. Catechesis is most common in Roman Catholicism and the Church of England.

Sacramentalism is the appropriation of Christian faith through the sacraments, usually baptism, confirmation, Eucharist, and/or reconciliation. It is the most mystical means of evangelism, as an individual or group receives the evangel through divine grace in the process of receiving the sacrament. It is typical of Catholicism, Anglicanism, Lutheranism, and other highly liturgical traditions.

Revivalism focuses on the heart, seeking to provoke an experiential and dramatic encounter with Christ. Through protracted meetings and exhortatory preaching, revivalism convicts an individual of sin, convinces him or her of salvation, and persuades one to become a disciple of Christ. Revivalism is most common among Evangelical and funda-

mentalist Protestants, among them Methodists, Presbyterians, Baptists, and Disciples of Christ.

Being nurtured in the Christian faith without a dramatic conversion experience was pioneered by Congregationalist pastor and theologian Horace Bushnell in *A Discourse on Christian Nurture* (1847). It consists of raising a child to intellectual and emotional understanding of the Christian faith through words and example. Liberal Christians, both Catholic and Protestant, utilize nurture as a form of evangelism.

Evangelism can occur in church, through a sermon, liturgy, or Sunday school. It is conducted by both clergy and laity; most Christians believe that all Christians bear a responsibility for evangelism. Some clergy are vocationally set apart solely for evangelism; they are called missionaries or evangelists. Evangelism can also take place outside a church, through extemporaneous preaching on street corners or door-to-door distribution of tracts. Evangelism also occurs informally, as friends and family share with one another the significance of their faith.

Evelyn A. Kirkley

See also BUSHNELL, HORACE; EVANGELICALS; EVANGELICAL THEOLOGY; GREAT AWAKENING(S) (EURO-AMERICAN RELIGIOUS HISTORY); REVIVALISM; WITNESS/WITNESSING.

EVANGELIST

Literally, one who proclaims the Good News. In the New Testament, Christian missionaries who traveled from place to place to spread the story of Jesus are called evangelists (Acts 6:1-5; Eph 4:11; 2 Tim 4:5). Contemporary individuals, like Billy Graham, who are engaged in a traveling ministry, preaching the Christian message, are also called evangelists.

The title "evangelist," however, applies especially to the authors of the four canonical Gospels. These four evangelists were actually the final redactors who arranged, revised, edited, and otherwise shaped oral and written traditions about Jesus into the final form of each Gospel. None of the canonical Gospels identifies its evangelist, although sources from the second century assigned the names—Matthew, Mark, Luke, and John—to the four texts, respectively. Since there is no way to verify the names of the authors, these traditional names continue to be used. There are a number of extracanonical gospels that were never accepted by the whole church as Scripture. The authors to which these texts are attributed are not considered evangelists.

Regina A. Boisclair

See also GOSPELS (TEXTS).

EVANGELIUM VITAE

("The Gospel of Life"). An encyclical letter on the dignity of human life in all its forms by Pope John Paul II, issued in March 1995. To be true to the teachings and spirit of Jesus Christ in the contemporary world, the Pope argues, requires a proclamation of the Gospel of life to a culture of death; that is, a culture in which life, particularly vulnerable life, is relativized and so threatened. The encyclical reaffirms teaching on the sacredness and inviolability of human life and against abortion, artificial birth control, euthanasia, and homicide in the strongest terms.

The strength of the condemnations of the perceived crimes against life is of particular interest to moral theologians and to ecclesiologists. Pope John Paul asserts the seriousness of these offenses by invoking a claim to universality—that is, that bishops, always and everywhere, are in agreement with his assessment. Such a claim would seem to indicate that church teaching on these matters is infallibly correct and so not subject to reform or revision. This would be an unprecedented situation in the area of Catholic moral teaching. The eminent ecclesiologist Francis A. Sullivan, s.j., has asserted, however, that the evidence suggests that infallibility has not been invoked in this letter, and so that the teaching is an authoritative one of the ordinary magisterium.

Brian F. Linnane, s.j.

See also ABORTION; BIOETHICS; CONTRACEPTION/BIRTH CONTROL; EUTHANASIA; HUMANAE VITAE; INFALLIBILITY.

EVANGELIZATION

(Greek, *euangelion*; Latin, *evangelium*; Gospel, Good News). Evangelization began when Jesus preached the Good News of God's love, cured the sick, and sent his disciples into the countryside to do the same (Luke 9:1-10). After his resurrection, Jesus commissioned his disciples to make disciples of the whole world (Matt 28:16ff.; Mark 16:15-19; Acts). Through the ages, the church responded to Jesus' mission by sending missionaries into areas that had not heard the Gospel. Pope John Paul II's 1990 encyclical, "The Permanent Validity of the Church's Missionary Mandate," insisted that the church must always remain "missionary."

Besides preaching and teaching, evangelization occurs in liturgy, sacraments, catechesis, devotions, and striving for social justice. The Vatican II document, *Lumen Gentium* (Dogmatic Constitution on the Church, no. 17) clearly states the duty of every disciple to evangelize, not just clergy and religious. *Lumen Gentium* (no. 17) instructs the church to send missionaries only until the new churches can carry on the work of evangelization themselves. *Ad Gentes Divinitas* (The Decree on the Church's Missionary Activity) reminds the church of its duty to evangelize by also listening and learning from the people who are receiving the Gospel. *Dignitatis Humanae* (The Declaration on Religious Liberty) demands that the church respect the culture of others and never use coercion in forcing people to become followers of Jesus or members of the Catholic Church. *Gaudium et Spes* (The Pastoral Constitution on the Church in the Modern World) states clearly that evangelization is about bringing justice and peace into the world.

During the age of discovery (sixteenth and seventeenth centuries), colonialism often turned zeal for converts into oppression while destroying native peoples, their cultures, traditions, and artifacts in God's name. Pope Paul VI wrote in his encyclical *Populorum Progressio* (Progress of Peoples, 1967) that the humanization of peoples and social justice must accompany the process of teaching the Gospel. He insisted that evangelizing consists in giving witness to the Good News through liberation from sin and oppression, not just preaching and formal teaching. Later in *Evangelii Nuntiandi* (On Evangelization in the Modern World), Paul VI repeated that evangelization must include not only the coming of the reign of God as liberation "from sin and the Evil One," but from all forms of economic, social, and political oppression as well (nos. 9, 29). Pope Paul also made it clear that the reign of God must be witnessed to in the present, and not waited upon in the future.

M. Jane Gorman

See also MISSIONARIES; MISSIONS; VATICAN, SECOND COUNCIL OF THE.

EVANS-PRITCHARD, EDWARD E. (1902–73)

British anthropologist. Educated at Oxford and at the London School of Economics, Evans-Pritchard was deeply influenced by his teacher, Bronislaw Malinowski. His research on Sudanese Nuer religion was important in expanding the field of mythology studies, showing that there is rationality in myth-making and in mysticism. He converted to Christianity in 1944, and then began reflecting on the possibility of comparative sociology, and on whether there were laws of human social behavior. His studies on Nuer religion, published between 1940 and 1956, remain his best work.

Orlando Espín

See also MYSTICISM / MYSTICS (IN WORLD RELIGIONS); MYTH.

EVIL

Descriptively, evil is any instance of pain or conscious suffering endured by a sentient creature. When pain or conscious suffering is the result of human (individual or social) agency ("sin"), such evil is called "moral" evil. When pain or conscious suffering is the result of nonhuman agency (acts of nature), such evil is called "natural" evil. Some also distinguish between "prima facie" and "genuine" evil. The latter is a subset of the former and includes only those instances of pain and suffering that are truly absurd, that is, cannot be conceived as means to a greater good.

Because each being's created existence is limited by that being's "measure, form, and order," some maintain that the created finitude of being is itself a species of evil: "ontological" evil. Overwhelmingly, the Christian tradition has rejected this as a genuine form of evil, in the conviction that the world as created is good and that a plentitude of good/being resides in creation as a whole.

Ontologically, the Augustinian and Thomist traditions define evil as *privatio boni*, an "absence of the good" properly belonging to a being according to that being's created measure, form, and order. Thus viewed, evil is parasitic on the proportionate good that is each thing's created being. In itself, evil is nothing. In the Irenaean traditions (including Schleiermacher and Hick), evil is understood as a necessary means of "soul-making," that is, a means toward attaining some future good that has not existed in the past.

J. A. Colombo

See also DEFENSE; EVIL, PROBLEM OF; SIN (SOCIAL, STRUCTURAL); SIN, PERSONAL; THEODICY.

EVIL, PROBLEM OF

The problem of evil varies according to each religion's understanding of ultimate reality and its relation to the world and self. Thus, the problem of evil for Christianity may not be identical to the problem of evil, for example, in Hinduism. For each religious tradition, the problem of evil is twofold: "How does one understand the possibility of evil within this specific religious tradition?" and "How does one live authentically in relation both to evil and to the ultimate reality within this specific religious tradition?"

The traditional formulation of the problem of evil focuses on the first question and arises from Christianity's specific understanding of God. If God is omnipotent and God is omnibenevolent, then whence evil? The existence of evil is a problem because a being with essentially unlimited power *could* eliminate evil and an all-loving being *would* eliminate evil. The response to this problem in the form of supplying a reason why God permits evil is called theodicy.

Slightly reformulated, some (for instance, J. L. Mackie) argue that the problem of evil is a proof of the nonexistence of God; that is, the propositions "God exists" and "Evil exists" are logically inconsistent. Assuming omnipotence and omnibenevolence are essential to the being of "God": If God exists, then there is no evil, because an omnipotent being could eliminate evil and an omnibenevolent being would eliminate evil. But evil exists. Therefore, God is either not omnipotent or not omnibenevolent. If God is either not omnipotent or not omnibenevolent, then by definition, "God" does not exist. The response to this problem is called a "defense."

J. A. Colombo

See also DEFENSE; EVIL; THEODICY.

EVOLUTION

The modern idea of the evolution of species has developed within the scientific community following the work of Charles Darwin in the areas of biology and paleontology. Evolution had no parallels during biblical times. In the modern period, the theory of evolution has dominated the relevant scientific fields almost without contest.

Russell Fuller

EXAMINATION OF CONSCIENCE

In the *Spiritual Exercises*, Ignatius Loyola recommends the practice of the examination of conscience at midday and again before retiring. The purpose of this brief, prayerful exercise is to help an individual become aware of particular areas of his life needing improvement. Ignatius suggests (1) beginning with giving thanks to God for goodness received; (2) asking God for insight into one's actions, behavior, motives, and so forth, in order to spot what was not of God (and thus disordered or sinful); (3) reviewing one's life since the previous examination; (4) begging healing and forgiveness; and finally (5) resolving, with God's help, to do better. Ignatius distinguished the "particular examen" from the "general examen." The former was a means of correcting a specific fault or advancing in a specific virtue, while the latter was concerned with one's overall sensitivity to God's presence or absence.

The practice of the general examen has frequently been adopted outside the context of a retreat as a means of recentering one's attention on the presence and action of God in one's life. Some commentators have suggested that "consciousness" or "awareness" would be closer to Ignatius's purpose in proposing this particular exercise than "conscience," since the desired effect is to render a person more reflectively aware of how various circumstances, events, remarks, relationships, encounters, moods, feelings, and so forth, are affecting her sense of the presence of God. The practice can play an indispensable role in ongoing discernment.

William Reiser, s.j.

See also CONSCIENCE; DISCERNMENT; SPIRITUAL EXERCISES.

EXARCH
In many Eastern Churches (Catholic and Orthodox alike), this is frequently a title given to bishops who are not patriarchs but who have responsibility and dignity over eparchs. In church usage (during the late Roman Empire), the title originally referred to the chief bishop of a civil diocese that included several eparchies.

Orlando Espín

See also ARCHBISHOP; BISHOP (EPISCOPACY); DIOCESE/ARCHDIOCESE; EASTERN CATHOLIC CHURCHES; ECCLESIASTICAL PROVINCE; EPARCH; METROPOLITAN; ORTHODOX CHURCHES; PATRIARCH.

EX CATHEDRA
Literally, this phrase means "from the chair" (Latin, *sedes*) and refers to the authoritative teaching of the pope. The term recollects the practice of a presiding bishop who preached and presided from his chair near the altar. Vatican I used it to refer to one of the criteria for papal infallibility. Thus, it refers to the highest level of papal teaching on faith and morals. An *ex cathedra* teaching requires assent from all Catholics.

Mary Ann Hinsdale

See also INFALLIBILITY.

EXCOMMUNICATION
The ancient Jewish custom of excluding from the community those who seriously violate God's law has carried over in modern times in both Judaism and Christianity. In Christian churches, a twofold practice developed. First, total excommunication by legitimate ecclesiastical authority for those who commit serious moral failure or hold heretical doctrinal views means that such persons are no longer considered members of the faith community. Second, temporary exclusion for those guilty of less serious moral or doctrinal failings is intended as a corrective discipline. In the Catholic Church, excommunicated persons in the second sense may not receive the sacrament of

Communion. Scriptural bases for the practice of excommunication include Leviticus 18:29; Deuteronomy 13:6-11; Matthew 16:19 and 18:18; and 1 Corinthians 5:1-13.

James B. Nickoloff

See also COMMUNION (LITURGICAL); HERESY; SIN (IN JUDAISM); SIN, PERSONAL; SIN (SOCIAL, STRUCTURAL).

EXEGESIS/EISEGESIS

Exegesis, from the Greek word *exegeōmai*, "to lead out of," denotes the reading out of the meaning of a text. Applied to the Bible, it is the process of understanding and explaining the biblical text. This may involve translation, paraphrase, and commentary on the meaning, with the goal being to set forth the original sense of the document. It is the task of biblical theology to relate the results of exegesis to contemporary life. The procedures of exegesis are determined by the science or art of hermeneutics.

Eisegesis, in contrast, is a misguided form of biblical interpretation that involves reading meaning into a text. In this process an interpreter imposes on the text a meaning alien to it.

F. M. Gillman

See also BIBLICAL CRITICISM; BIBLICAL THEOLOGY; HERMENEUTICS.

EXILE

A term usually associated with the deportation of influential people of Judah out of Judah to Babylon in 586 B.C.E. Though people of the northern kingdom were also taken into exile, into Assyria and elsewhere, in 721 B.C.E., the fall of the kingdom of Judah is understood to be "the" exile, the end of political independence in the land for any of the people who would trace themselves back to their ancestors Abraham, Moses, and King David. With the exception of approximately eighty years, the Jewish people did not again experience independence in the land until 1948.

The history behind the Exile, according to the Deuteronomic History, is one of repeated unfaithfulness to God culminating in the very evil reign of King Manasseh. From a historical perspective, Babylon was on the rise for quite some time, and its defeat of Assyria, Assyria's conquered territories, and beyond, was inevitable.

Psalm 137 attempts to capture the sentiment of the people in exile:

By the streams of Babylon we sat and wept when we remembered Zion.
On the aspens of that land we hung up our harps.
Though there our captors asked of us the lyrics of our songs,
And our despoilers urged us to be joyous: "Sing for us the songs of Zion."
How could we sing a song of the Lord in a foreign land? (vv. 1-4)

The book of Lamentations uses the symbol of widowhood to depict the experience of the people at the time of the fall of Judah.

Many Jews did not return to what had been the kingdom of Judah after the Persian conquest of the Babylonian Empire allowed them to do so, but rather remained dispersed in other lands. This period, then, technically speaking from 586–539 B.C.E., marks the beginning of reshaping the theology of the people of Israel. An exilic theology tends to be more universalist, since the people are scattered and exist as a minority in other peoples' lands. An exilic theology also seeks purpose in the Exile; Israel, for example, becomes the Suffering Servant for the sake of the other nations, a light for the nations (for example, Isaiah 42; 52–53). For those who remained in the land and those who returned, "the Exile" per se, marked the beginning of colonial rule.

Alice L. Laffey

EXISTENTIALISM

The name of a European philosophical movement, very influential during the period before and after World War II (roughly, 1920–75). The term "existentialism" was coined by Søren Kierkegaard (d. 1855). It commonly refers to the philosophies that emphasize or focus on human freedom and responsibility, and on the concrete existence of the individual person. Existentialism stood in opposition to all sorts of massification of human life, to claims of objective standards, and to abstract constructs of humanness. It promoted notions of authenticity, hope, and individuality. The term "existentialism," however, covers such a diverse array of authors that the label must always be used cautiously. Nevertheless, there seem to be two main groups of existentialists: the "secular" (for example, M. Heidegger, J. P. Sartre, C. Merleau-Ponty) and the "religious" (for example, S. Kierkegaard, G. Marcel, K. Jaspers). Existentialism has had a profound influence on both Protestant (for example, R. Bultmann) and Catholic (for example, K. Rahner) theologians, and on other philosophers who cannot be properly interpreted as belonging to this movement (for example, X. Zubiri).

Orlando Espín

See also BULTMANN, RUDOLF; CAMUS, ALBERT; DEVELOPMENT OF DOGMA / OF DOCTRINE; DOCTRINE; DOGMA; DOSTOYEVSKY, FEODOR M.; FREEDOM; FREE WILL; HEIDEGGER, MARTIN; HUMAN BEING; HUMAN RIGHTS; JASPERS, KARL; KIERKEGAARD, SØREN; MARCEL, GABRIEL; MERLEAU-PONTY, MAURICE; RAHNER, KARL; SARTRE, JEAN-PAUL; ZUBIRI, XAVIER.

EXODUS

The event associated with the book of Exodus in the Bible, that is, the liberation of *'apiru* (slave community) from bondage in Egypt by a god who came to be known by the liberated people as their god, "the God who brought us out of Egypt." This act of deliverance by God is dramatically portrayed in Exodus 1–15. It led to the establishment of the people of "the God who brought us out of Egypt" and the covenant relationship whereby God became Israel's God and Israel became God's people (for example, Exod 20:2-3).

Historians believe that only a small portion of the people who became Israel were part of the original Exodus experience. In fact, there is no record of an escape of slaves from Egypt in extant Egyptian records from that period. It is theorized, however, that *'apiru* slowly immigrated into Canaan, and over time, poor Canaanites who had been exploited became associated with them and came to understand that the God who sided with the enslaved, the *'apiru* God, could also be their God. They came to claim this God as their own.

New Testament writers use the Exodus as a symbolic event. Just as the Hebrews were delivered from bondage in Egypt, those who came to believe in Jesus were likewise delivered—from the bondage of sin and death into the freedom of the children of God (cf. Rom 6; 8:21).

The event of Exodus has become a symbol of deliverance for enslaved peoples elsewhere. It has been paradigmatic for liberation theologies in Latin America, Asia, and Africa. While the New Testament is central to liberation theology—the role of Jesus as especially articulated in Luke 4:18-19—the Exodus narrative/event also functions as a source of empowerment.

Alice L. Laffey

EX OPERE OPERANTIS/ EX OPERE OPERATO

Latin expressions that mean (respectively) "by means of the one performing the action" and "by means of the action itself." The phrases refer to two different ways of understanding what makes a Christian ceremony effective. According to the first understanding (*ex opere operantis*), a ceremony is only effective when the person performing the ceremony is free from impurity or sin. According to the second understanding (*ex opere operato*) a ceremony is effective whenever it is properly performed, regardless of the moral state of the celebrant. The first form of thought was adopted by the Donatists and by the Waldensians, to give but two examples, in order to safeguard the purity of the Christian community. The second position, that advanced by Augustine and upheld by the majority of Christians, argues that it is God who is acting by means of the ceremony and therefore the efficacy of a ceremony depends on the power of God, not on the moral state of the celebrant, who is merely instrumental in the process of sanctification.

Gary Macy

See also AUGUSTINE OF HIPPO; DONATISM; VALIDITY, SACRAMENTAL; WALDENSIANS.

EXORCISM

A ritual performed to expel demons or evil spirits from the human body or a place. It is found in religious systems that have ideas about supernaturalism or possession by spirits. It involves the driving away of evil spirits such as demons by chanting, praying, commanding, or other ritual means. Exorcism is found throughout the world in a variety of traditions. In some cultures, the belief that an evil spirit causes illness by entering a person's body leads people to cure by expelling the spirit. A belief in exorcism assumes a related belief in the power of ritual to move an evil spirit from one place to another, preferably out of an individual's body. William Howells describes several techniques reported around the world for exorcising evil spirits and diseases. These techniques include sweat baths, cathartics, emetics, trephining (cutting a hole in the skull), manipulating and massaging the body, sucking out the spirit, scraping or sponging the illness off the body, magical spells, coaxing, singing songs, tempting with a meal or other diversion, keeping the patient, and thus the possessing spirit, uncomfortable by beating the patient, lighting a fire under the patient, or exposing the patient to foul smelling odors.

In Christianity, exorcisms play a role in the descriptions of the ministry of Jesus. Exorcism is used in various ways in Christian rituals. For example, it appears in baptismal liturgies to symbolize an individual's departure from sin and entrance into the body of Christians. It is also used in the Christian context as a ritual that aims to free a person from demonic possession. In the Catholic Church this ritual can be done only with authorization, and exorcisms by the Catholic Church continue to be approved in the present day. In fundamentalist Christian groups, exorcism is accomplished with the laying on of hands, prayer, and Scripture reading.

In the Japanese religious tradition, exorcism is an important concept in myth and Shinto ritual. Exorcism was linked to purification. In classical Japan the Great Purification, or Great Exorcism, was held twice a year to purify the imperial court and thus the nation. A version of this purification ritual is today the beginning of each Shinto ceremony. The Incas also used state exorcisms, the banishing of evil spirits from the empire with fire rituals, to cleanse the entire society of the presence of harmful agents.

Christine Greenway

See also DEMON; POSSESSION.

EXORCISM (IN CHRISTIANITY)

From the Greek *exorkismos*, administration of an oath. The casting out of evil spirits, or prayer asking God to free a person from evil influences and desires. In Christianity, exorcism is rooted in the ministry of Jesus, who expelled demons and thereby restored physical, psychological, and spiritual health (for instance, Matt 12:22; Mark 1:23-27). Jesus commissioned his disciples to continue his work (Luke 9:1; Mark 16:17). The rites of the catechumenate and baptism include prayers of exorcism that ask that the candidate be set free from whatever stands in the way of a total commitment to Christ, and that he or she be filled with God's Spirit. The sort of exorcism popularized by the media, in which demons are driven from a possessed person, are quite rare and are carefully regulated by canon law (Can. 1172).

Patrick L. Malloy

See also BAPTISM / CONFIRMATION; POSSESSION.

EXORCISM (IN JUDAISM)

Talmudic Judaism only infrequently refers to the notion of an evil spirit entering a person; as a result, exorcism is rarely discussed. Still, the procedure is known, referred to, for instance, by Yohanan b. Zakkai, who recommends exorcising a demon by burning certain herbs under the affected individual and then surrounding him or her with water (Pesikta deRab Kahana 40a). Simeon b. Yohai is said to have driven a demon named Ben Temalion from the daughter of a Roman emperor (Babylonian Talmud Meila 17b).

Concern for demonic possession and methods of exorcism increased somewhat in late medieval Judaism under the influence of Kabbalah and then Hasidism. In the wide range of contemporary forms of Judaism, however, neither the belief in demons nor the notion that evil spirits may enter people and need to be exorcised has any currency.

Alan J. Avery-Peck

See also DEMON; POSSESSION.

EXTRA ECCLESIAM NULLA SALUS

A Latin phrase meaning "outside the church, there is no salvation." The phrase comes originally from a letter of Cyprian, the third-century *episkopos* (bishop) of Carthage. Cyprian was arguing that baptism by heretics and schismatics was not valid, a position opposed by Stephen, the *episkopos* of Rome. Although the Roman opinion on this particular issue won the day among the majority of Christian groups, Cyprian's phrase has been used by many Christians down through the centuries to describe the church's relationship to salvation. The meaning of the phrase depends, of course, on how the church is defined. If, for instance, the church is defined as the body of all those who will be saved, then the phrase is a mere tautology. If, on the other hand, one defines the church as only those who belong to a particular confessional or institutional form of Christianity, then the membership in that confession or institution is considered mandatory for salvation. The quotation from Cyprian can and has been used in both contexts as well as in descriptions of the relationship between the church and salvation that fall between these two extremes.

Gary Macy

See also CHURCH; CYPRIAN OF CARTHAGE; EPISKOPOS; NOVATIAN OF ROME; NOVATIANISM; SALVATION; STEPHEN I OF ROME.

EZEKIEL

A prophet of the sixth century B.C.E. (active perhaps from 593–563 B.C.E.). Ezekiel was a priest who was part of the exile of 597 B.C.E. when the Babylonians deported the young king Jehoiakim to Babylon following the collapse of the rebellion begun by his father, Jehoiachin. Ezekiel was thus active, presumably in Babylon, from shortly after the exile of Jehoiakim in 597 B.C.E. until after the fall of Jerusalem in 587 B.C.E. His oracles can thus be divided into two periods: those from before the fall of Judah, frequently negative in tone; and those after the fall of Jerusalem and the beginning of the Babylonian Exile (587–538 B.C.E.) that are more hopeful. The book of Ezekiel has been heavily edited in the opinion of most scholars; oracles are usually dated. There is a close connection between the book of Ezekiel and the Priestly Tradition found in the Pentateuch/Torah in terms of concepts and language. Ezekiel has an idealistic program for the restoration of Jerusalem and Judah and the rebuilding of the Jeru-

salem Temple found in chapters 40–48. His vision did not find fulfillment.

Russell Fuller

EZRA

In Ezra 7:6, Ezra is described as "a scribe skilled in the law of Moses." Ezra was also a priest, and his genealogy going back to Aaron, the brother of Moses, is also given in Ezra 7 when he is first introduced in the narrative. He was active in the fifth century B.C.E. during the period of Persian hegemony. He is linked, perhaps artificially, with the figure of Nehemiah who was apparently appointed governor of the province of Yehud (= Judah) during the reign of Artaxerxes I (464–423 B.C.E.) in approximately 458 B.C.E. There are numerous chronological difficulties concerning the relative order of Ezra and Nehemiah, and the reader is referred to the appropriate commentaries for a complete discussion of the issues. Ezra was a champion of the Law of Moses, the Torah, which he was apparently empowered to establish as the law of the land by the Persians. He became an important figure in Jewish tradition, ranking with Moses in terms of importance. An extensive literature developed that was attributed to him in the fourth through the second centuries B.C.E.

Russell Fuller

EZRAT NASHIM

(Hebrew, women's gallery). In the synagogue, this is the area set aside for the seating of women, who, in traditional Jewish practice, pray separately from men. In the earliest synagogues, the women's gallery was usually a balcony. In later synagogue architecture, it may also be an area at the back of the sanctuary or, especially in contemporary Orthodox synagogues, may even be located alongside the area reserved for men. In all of these configurations, the men's and women's areas are demarcated by a cloth or wooden divider (Mehitzah) that prevents the two sexes from seeing each other during prayer.

The practice of separate seating areas for men and women was dropped in the mid-nineteenth century by Jewish re-formers, who instituted the practice of family pews, common in Protestant churches. Contemporary Reform, Conservative, and Reconstructionist congregations do not require or provide for the separate seating of women.

Alan J. Avery-Peck

See also SYNAGOGUE.

F

FAITH

Derived from the Latin *fides*, meaning "belief," faith carries both epistemological and experiential meanings in Christian theology. It consists of the acceptance of religious doctrines and teachings about God, the active cultivation of a personal relationship with God that is lived out with others and the earth. In Western Christian theology, faith is a free gift from God that addresses and impacts the whole person (an integrated union of soul and body) and her or his way of life in given as well as chosen multiple communities of belonging. It involves a free response of the whole person, in grace, to the gratuitous self-disclosure of God in revelation, both in general revelation, expressed in the sacramentality of creation, history, and ordinary life, and in special revelation, embodied in Jesus Christ and in Christian texts, teachings, and traditions.

One major debate in Western Christian theology addresses the relationship between faith and reason, sometimes construed as the relationship between theology and philosophy. Some medieval European Scholastic theologians like Aquinas (d. 1274) argued that theology is a kind of science that outranked and completed all other kinds of sciences, especially philosophy, regarding knowledge of God. Some theologians and philosophers during the eighteenth-century European Enlightenment contended that reason can either demonstrate or undermine faith. Modern theology either utilized reason to explain Christian faith in a more widely intelligible way on philosophical grounds (like German philosopher Immanuel Kant) or challenged the ability of reason to support traditional Christian faith claims, for example, in an all-loving God (like British philosopher David Hume).

For the most part, Christian theology holds that faith, or belief in God or in a divine reality, is coextensive with reason; faith and reason are considered mutually supportive because of their common theocentric origin. Based on early Christian theologians like Augustine, the fourth- to fifth-century bishop of Hippo in North Africa, and medieval theologians like Anselm, the eleventh- to twelfth-century monk and pioneer of medieval European Scholasticism, Christian theology is best defined as "faith seeking understanding." For Augustine, theology involved the use of reason (and the critical appropriation of philosophy) in an ongoing

443

quest for a deeper love of God and understanding of faith. For Anselm, theology did not provide a rational foundation for faith, but placed reason in the context of faith to gain a deeper understanding and perhaps contemplation of God. Faith takes its starting point from God, not reason; nevertheless, reason plays an important role in the ongoing quest to understand God more deeply, to more carefully interpret biblical and scriptural texts, and to more adequately respond to the challenges that affect everyday life from a faith-based perspective.

Faith does not provide once-and-for-all answers about God and human life apart from reasoned reflection; faith in many ways needs reason. For example, in more contemporary theology, Pope John Paul II (d. 2005) addressed the integrity and unity of faith and reason in the encyclical *Fides et Ratio* (1998), in which he noted that the magisterium, or teaching office of the Catholic Church, sees as the limitations of reason (and of certain kinds of philosophy) and yet promoted the use of reason in interpreting revelation or encounters with God that ultimately remain an infinite mystery. Reason on its own cannot arrive at the truths about God found in special revelation, but the truths about God found in special revelation still lay beyond human understanding, fragmentary and fallible as it is. Thus, special revelation (given in Christ, Scripture, doctrines, and traditions) does not trump the use of reason; reason is integral to uncovering and more deeply understanding the truths of special revelation. Since God or the divine is the object of faith, and God is an inexhaustible mystery or an ever-receding horizon in human experience as described by the twentieth-century German Jesuit theologian Karl Rahner, then reason is absolutely integral to faith.

Reason promotes ongoing critical inquiry into ultimate questions about God from within a living faith, that is, a faith lived out in particular contexts as well as in new, challenging situations.

Predominant Western Christian definitions of theology, such as faith seeking understanding, can overemphasize a rational response to God's self-offer in revelation. Faith does not amount only to an individual intellectual assent to religious creeds, teachings, and practices. Faith is not reducible to fideism—a passive, blind obedience to Christian texts, doctrines, and practices apart from reasoned reflection on them. Rather, faith shapes and is shaped by the situatedness of persons in communities; it implies a living faith situated in particular religious communities as well as applying to real human life situations.

Moreover, a living faith implies a whole way of life in responsive relation to God, to others, and to the earth. In Pauline theology and in the theologies of the sixteenth-century European Reformation, living faith is described through the interrelationship of faith and works; faith necessarily and inherently produces works (James 2:17). More contemporary theologians attempt to derationalize and deprivatize faith by emphasizing that faith is deeply committed to an active engagement with society and to justice. For example, liberation theologies strive to articulate a responsible theology that critically reflects on the lived faith and struggles of oppressed peoples for the purpose of personal, social, and religious transformation. In liberationist theologies, praxis figures as an integral part of faith. Praxis stresses the mutual interconnections between faith and daily life; Peruvian priest and Latin American liberation theologian Gustavo Gutiérrez defines praxis as the mutual interrelation of action and reflection in the light of the Gospel for the purpose of seeking and sustaining justice. To capture more adequately the emphasis on the praxis of faith in contemporary theologies, African American womanist theologian Delores Williams offers a new spin on the traditional definition of Christian theology by claiming that theology has to do with faith seeking understanding "from below," from the perspectives of oppressed peoples and their spiritual and political "works" or struggles for personal and social survival as well as salvation.

Rather than an irrational, ruggedly individual and privatized reality, faith refers to a rational, communal, and socially engaged reality that takes it starting point from the voluntary, communal, and socially engaged self-disclosure of God to humanity, described in, for example, the liberation of the enslaved Israelites and the liberation of all humanity from sin, both personal and structural, in Jesus Christ.

Rosemary P. Carbine

See also GRACE; JUSTIFICATION; REVELATION; TRADITION.

FALASHAS

See EDOT HAMIZRACH.

FALL, THE

This term is used in theology to refer to the result of the events narrated in Genesis 3:1-24. Pentateuchal scholars usually attribute this story to the J or Yahwistic Tradition that is dated by many scholars to the early period of the monarchy, and by others to the seventh century B.C.E. or later. The story of Genesis 3 builds on the creation story of Genesis 2 and tells how the first man and the first woman were tempted to eat of the tree of the knowledge of good and evil in the center of the Garden where Yahweh had placed them. In Genesis 2, Yahweh had commanded the man, before the creation of the woman, not to eat of the tree, but together with the woman he is persuaded by the serpent, and they both eat. The text describes their transformation in verse 7, "Then the eyes of both were opened, and they knew that they were naked." They had become like God, knowing good and evil as the serpent said they would. The consequence of this action for all three characters is swift and harsh, especially for the serpent and the woman. In addition to the punishments listed in verses 14-19, the human couple is expelled from the Garden as a means of keeping them from the tree of life, for Yahweh fears that they will also eat from that tree, "and live forever." The transition from an "innocent" state of being to one where they knew the difference between good and evil is what is usually described as "the Fall." The assumption is that before the humans ate of the tree, they were in a state God intended when they were created. After they had eaten of the tree, they are in a corrupted state. The story is an etiology, a story that attempts to explain how the human condition and Israelite society came about. There is actually no mention of, or allusion to, this story elsewhere in the Hebrew Bible (besides Ezekiel 28:11-16, part of a lament over the fall of Tyre).

The Priestly Source or Tradition also has an idea somewhat similar to that of the Eden story of humans moving from an ideal created state to a "normal" state. In the P tradition's creation story, there are no creatures who eat flesh, including humans. In the Priestly Tradition, it is only after the Flood that humans (and presumably other animals) are given permission to eat flesh, and for humans there is the added constraint that the blood of the animal must not be consumed.

Russell Fuller

FAMILY

"The Christian family is a communion of persons, a sign and image of the communion of the Father and the Son in the Holy Spirit" (*Catechism*, §2205). This definition of the family depicts the relational aspect of family as community, as well as its sacred character as a sign and image of the Trinity. The cornerstone of society is the family that finds its roots in the Old Testament. The *Bêt-ʾab* (Father's House) was the fundamental unit of ancient Israel that comprised the nuclear family as well as the extended family and nonrelated dependents such as slaves and employees. Members of this unit were dependent upon it for economic support, judicial representation, guidelines for behavior both internally within the *Bêt-ʾab* and externally among society, and for didactic or teaching purposes, that is, passing on the faith, history, and sacred traditions of the nations. The glue that held these aspects of the *Bêt-ʾab* together and grounded it in the transcendent was the covenantal relationship between the Jewish people and Yahweh. The people's relationship with God was manifested in the most fundamental way within the *Bêt-ʾab*. If this unit was in any way threatened due to internal strife or external threats such as war or famine, so, too, was the covenantal relationship with God as well as the stability of society. Hence, the protection and preservation of the *Bêt-ʾab* was of utmost importance within ancient Israel.

The fundamentally relational aspect of the family and its sacred character are supported within the New Testament as well with a notable exception. Whereas Moses allowed for divorce in the Old Testament (Deut 24:1-4), Jesus regards marriage as a sacred relationship where two become one (Mark 10:6-9), instituted by God by the very nature of his creation of male and female (Gen 1:27; 2:24; 5:2), which may not be violated. The concept of family is designated by two words in the New Testament: *patria*, which indicates male historical descent or lineage; and *oikos* (house), which signifies the family as household. The latter term is the Greco-Roman equivalent to the Old Testament *Bêt-ʾab*, and designates a similar social unit.

The central importance of the family unit in maintaining the stability of society and as a manifestation of our relationship with God and one another is clear from this brief interlude on the scriptural foundations and understanding of the family. The current demise of social mores is often traced, in large part, to the breakdown of the family that challenges us to renew our commitment to support and nurture the family as the *"original cell of social life"* (*Catechism*, §2207).

Todd A. Salzman

See also ADULTERY; GAUDIUM ET SPES; MARRIAGE IN CATHOLIC PERSPECTIVE.

FAMILY PURITY

See TAHARAT HAMISHPACHAH.

FANA

In Sufism, the annihilation or extinction of the ego or self. Sufis employ a variety of spiritual disciplines, including meditation and mystical practices, on their journey toward this experience. Once *fana* is achieved, Sufis believe that what remains of their earthly lives is the abiding, eternal presence of God—not their individual selves. In a sense, during the periods when Sufis experience *fana*, they are no longer in this world. They are united with God and it is only with great pain and suffering that they "return" to their normal routine of daily life.

Ronald A. Pachence

See also SUFI/SUFISM.

FANATICISM

Fanaticism is defined as an intense commitment to religion that results in behavior dangerous to oneself and/or others. Fanaticism is characterized by excessive enthusiasm and uncritical devotion; it often appears threatening, maniacal, or frenzied. Although simple to define, fanaticism has not been easy to identify in a religious movement. In a sense, fanaticism is in the eye of the beholder; what is fanaticism to one may be devotion to another. In its early history, Christianity was considered a fanatical religion, since it prompted its adherents to persecution, martyrdom, and monastic deprivation. In the Middle Ages, Christian saints regularly starved themselves, wore hair shirts, and otherwise punished their bodies.

More recently, religious groups outside the mainstream have been called fanatical. Any group that demands behavior from its members beyond the conventional is open to the charge. In the eighteenth and early nineteenth centuries in the United States, the enthusiasm of Evangelicalism and revivalism led to barking, jerking, and charges of fanaticism. In the nineteenth century, groups labeled sect or cult were accused of fanaticism; members of the Church of Jesus Christ of Latter-Day Saints because they practiced polygyny and demanded complete loyalty; Spiritualists because they conducted séances; and Christian Scientists because they refused conventional medical treatment. Communitarian groups, such as the Oneida Perfectionists and Shakers, were considered strange for their withdrawal from the world in self-contained communities. Moreover, they attracted criticism for their unusual sexual ethics; the Oneida Perfectionists practiced plural marriage while the Shakers were celibate.

In the early twentieth century, fundamentalists were widely perceived as fanatics because some relied on faith healing rather than doctors. Jehovah's Witnesses not only refused medical treatment, but also refused to salute the flag and serve in the military, and they persisted in evangelism many considered a public nuisance. A group is likely to be charged with fanaticism until it has become established and institutionalized over several generations.

In the more pluralistic climate of the late twentieth century, charges of fanaticism are most often reserved for religious groups perceived as violent and abusive. The Nation of Islam has been accused of separatism and inciting violence against people of European descent. The Unification Church, International Society for Krishna Consciousness (Hare Krishna), and the Church of Scientology, among others, have been accused of brainwashing their members through abuse and deprivation. These accusations have justified kidnapping members and attempting to "deprogram" them.

Two recent events have alerted the public to the danger of fanatical charismatic leaders. In 1978, more than nine hundred women, men, and children, members of the People's Temple, committed suicide in Jonestown, Guyana, at the direction of their leader Jim Jones, when threatened by governmental investigation and press exposure. Sixteen years later, David Koresh and his followers, the Branch Davidians, surrounded by federal authorities, refused to surrender and instead chose to die by setting fire to their compound in Waco, Texas. These tragedies make fanaticism a critical issue for all persons of faith.

Evelyn A. Kirkley

See also ENTHUSIASM/ENTHUSIASTIC; FUNDAMENTALISM (ATTITUDE).

FAQIH

An Arabic term used by Muslims to refer to a person who possesses extensive knowledge of Islam. It can be applied to a theologian, a distinguished leader, or an expert in *sharia*, Islamic law.

Ronald A. Pachence

See also FIQH; ISLAM; SHARIA/SHARI'A.

FAQIR

An Arabic term that literally means poor or needy. In Sufism, a *faqir* is a person who seeks detachment from the world so that he or she becomes "empty" of all desires and attachments except for the love of God. The Persian word *darwish* (dervish in English) is synonymous with faqir and is sometimes used in the same sense as the Arabic term, as in the case of the Whirling Dervishes—a Turkish Sufi order.

Ronald A. Pachence

See also DERVISH (DARWISH); SUFI/SUFISM; WHIRLING DERVISHES.

FARLEY, MARGARET A. (1935–)

Gilbert L. Stark Professor of Christian Ethics at Yale University. Drawing on such diverse sources as feminist theory, traditional and contemporary Roman Catholic moral reflection, and Protestant sources and continental philosophy, Farley was an important influence on U.S. religious ethics during the late twentieth century. She has written extensively on the ethics of commitment and sexuality, healthcare ethics, ethical methodology, and feminist ethics.

Brian F. Linnane, S.J.

See also FEMINIST THEOLOGIES; MORAL THEOLOGY/CHRISTIAN ETHICS.

FASTS/FASTING
(IN CHRISTIANITY)

The Christian practice of fasting has its roots in Judaism. In early Christianity, believers would fast twice a week (that is, eat only one meal, usually toward the end of the day) on Wednesdays and Fridays (and, in some places, also on Saturday), as well as engage in almsgiving and prayer at certain times each day. These days seem to have been chosen because of their associations with the passion of Jesus Christ: his arrest on a Wednesday, and his crucifixion on a Friday. Over the centuries, these fast days were reduced until (with the exception of certain particular days of the year, like Ash Wednesday or the Ember Days) only Friday remained as a weekly day of abstinence in the Middle Ages.

Fasting was understood to act as an aid to prayer and as an expression of repentance. Fasting became associated with penance, as a sign of sorrow, or mourning, for sin, in two ways: first, as a penitential practice for individuals engaged in public or canonical penance, hoping for official reconciliation with the church community as a whole; and second, as a prayerful practice for that entire community, a practice that came to be associated with certain periods or seasons in the liturgical year associated with preparation for the celebration of great feasts (for example, Lent and Easter). Later, fasting from food (and from other pleasurable activities as well like sex or bathing) became a discipline associated with monastic asceticism, and the control of the human "appetites" was viewed as an element in the quest for spiritual perfection through the monastic "white martyrdom" (especially after the legalization of Christianity in the early fourth century, and with it, the cessation of imperial persecution).

Several seasons and specific days were set aside as times for fasting in the medieval West (for example, Lent, the Ember Days, Ash Wednesday). This practice was discontinued by many Protestant churches during the time of the Reformation, since one major point of Protestant theology was the tenet that the believer could attain salvation only by faith, not by "works" (such as fasting, attendance at Mass, or indulgences). Since the liturgical reforms of Vatican II, only two fast days remain in the Roman Catholic Church as part of the liturgical year: Ash Wednesday and Good Friday. Abstinence is a related practice. At various times in the medieval period, refraining from eating certain types of food (for instance, meat, wine, dairy products) was practiced during Lent or for other penitential/ascetic reasons. Abstinence, interpreted more narrowly as refraining from the eating of meat, was observed by Roman Catholics before Vatican II on every Friday of the year, but is today required only on the Fridays of Lent.

Joanne M. Pierce

See also ADVENT; ASCETICISM/ASCETIC; ASH WEDNESDAY; FEAST; LENT; MONASTICISM IN EASTERN CHRISTIANITY; MONASTICISM IN WESTERN CHRISTIANITY; RECONCILIATION, SACRAMENT OF; VATICAN, SECOND COUNCIL OF THE.

FASTS/FASTING (IN JUDAISM)

(Hebrew, Tzom, Taanit). In Judaism, fasting is practiced as an aspect of repentance, as a sign of mourning, or to request divine assistance. Two annual fasts are observed for a full twenty-four hours, from sundown to sundown: the penitential fast of the Day of Atonement (Yom Kippur) and the fast of the Ninth of Av (Tisha B' Av) that commemorates the destructions of the First and Second Temples in Jerusalem. Other fasts are observed from sunrise to sunset. These include the fast of the seventeenth of Tammuz that recalls the breaching of the walls of Jerusalem prior to the Temple's destruction; the Fast of Gedaliah on the third of Tishre that marks the events described at 2 Kings 25:22-25; the Fast of Esther (see Esther 4:16); and the Fast of the First Born that precedes Passover. Private fasting is not common in Judaism, with such fasts observed primarily to mark the anniversary of a near-relative's death, on one's wedding day, prior to the ceremony, and by those who are present when a Torah scroll is dropped.

Alan J. Avery-Peck

See also TISHA B'AV; YOM KIPPUR.

FATE (IN JUDAISM)

Judaism presents a largely deterministic point of view, expressed in the statement of Babylonian Talmud Hullin 7b that "A person does not hurt his finger on earth unless it has been decreed from above." Similarly, Babylonian Talmud Taanit 25a reports that when the impoverished Eleazar b. Pedat questioned how long he would suffer, God responded that, since Eleazar's poverty was predetermined,

God could not remedy it without over-turning the entire world.

Despite this deterministic point of view, Judaism posits the existence of free will and understands people to be responsible for their actions and fate. Rabbi Aqiba (Mishnah Avot 3:15) expressed this in the paradoxical maxim, "Everything is fore-seen, yet free choice is given." Similarly, the Talmud notes that "All is in the hands of Heaven except for the fear of Heaven" (Babylonian Talmud Megillah 25a; Baby-lonian Talmud Berakhot 33b; Babylonian Talmud Niddah 16b). Judaism thus dis-tinguishes between material existence, in which everything is predetermined, and spiritual life, in which people have the choice of abiding by or rejecting God's will.

Alan J. Avery-Peck

See also DETERMINISM.

FATHERS/MOTHERS OF THE DESERT

For reasons still debated by scholars, lay men and women early in the fourth cen-tury began to leave the cities of Syria and Egypt in increasingly large numbers to seek solitude and austerity in surround-ing deserted places. They were probably attempting to find a kind of "living mar-tyrdom" once the legalization of Chris-tianity closed that door to sanctity. They may also have wanted a more intense and spiritual form of Christian life than was offered by an urban faith now popu-lar and politically acceptable. Whether in complete isolation or in small groups, liv-ing a minimalist form of community life, the desert dwellers captured the imagina-tions of Christians generally and made the practice of silence, prayer, poverty of spirit, spiritual warfare, and the renun-ciation of all physical pleasure issues of

intense interest and debate throughout the Christian world. The Desert Mothers and Fathers exercised an enormous influ-ence on the ideals and theology of the church.

Among the more well known of the early ascetics are Anthony of Egypt, Paul the Hermit, Pachomius, and the Cappa-docian bishops Basil of Caesarea and Gregory Nazianzus. Important women of the desert include Mary of Egypt, Pelagia, Thais and Mary, the Niece of Abraham. The texts associated with the desert move-ment were extremely important in the formation and spread of Christian life and faith. Athanasius, bishop of Alexan-dria, wrote the *Life of Anthony*, one of the first Desert Fathers, in which he extolled both the ideals of asceticism and an anti-Arian christology. Through his several exiles, he disseminated his book and spread the ideals of asceticism and mo-nasticism to Rome, Carthage (where it influenced the conversion of Augustine), and Gaul. Jerome promulgated the ascetic life in Rome where he won many wealthy women to its pursuit; he also wrote the life of Paul the Hermit. Cassian visited the Egyptian desert where he recorded in detail the deeds and wisdom of the an-cient and contemporary solitaries; years later in Gaul, he distilled his notes into his *Conferences* and *Institutes*, works that became staples of the Western monastic tradition and carried the example and experience of the desert dwellers even into modern times. For the most part, it was a community form of monasticism that predominated in the West, but the solitary, ascetic life has remained popular in the East and long remained an ideal in England and Ireland, as Julian of Nor-wich witnesses.

Marie Anne Mayeski

See also ANCHORITES; ARIANISM; ASCETICISM/ASCETIC; ATHANASIUS, PATRIARCH OF ALEXANDRIA; AUGUSTINE OF HIPPO; HERMIT; JEROME; MONASTICISM IN EASTERN CHRISTIANITY; MONASTICISM IN WESTERN CHRISTIANITY; PACHOMIUS.

FATHERS OF THE CHURCH

Up until the seventeeth century, the "Fathers" of the church were considered to be those writers whose theology was considered to be a model of orthodoxy and insight. Medieval writers appeal to both ancient and modern "Fathers." Starting in the seventeenth century, the term was applied more narrowly to the the writers of the early church, especially the great thinkers of the fourth and fifth centuries. Although one often sees references to the "Fathers," the term is used with less and less frequency, due to its obvious sexist bias.

Gary Macy

See also PATRISTICS/PATROLOGY.

FATWA

In Islamic jurisprudence, an opinion or official ruling on a particular topic issued by a local expert or an Islamic court. Once a *fatwa* is published, it becomes precedent for decisions rendered in subsequent cases of a similar nature. In 1989, for example, Iranian leader Ayatollah Ruhollah Khomeini issued a fatwa in which he sentenced author Salman Rushdie to death for his 1988 novel, *The Satanic Verses*. Khomeini decreed the work's portrayal of the Prophet Muhammad to be blasphemy, highly offensive to Muslims, and worthy of death. The fatwa also applies to others who were responsible for the book's translation and publication. Though Rushdie lives outside of Iran, this ruling directs all Muslims to take any opportunity they have to carry out the sentence.

Ronald A. Pachence

See also MUFTI; SHARIA/SHARI'A; ULAMA/ULEMA.

FEAR OF GOD

Fear is a major biblical theme. Specifically, the fear of God defines those aspects of the human encounter with the divine in which one feels both the seemingly contradictory need to turn away in terror from the awesomeness of God, yet also an attraction and love for God. With diminishment of the sense of terror, "to fear God" can also mean to live in piety toward God, that is, to obey and worship God. In this sense, the "fear of the Lord" can be held to be true religion (see Ps 34:12). Thus, for example, King Jehoshaphat wants the fear of the Lord to arise among his people so that they will serve God faithfully and wholeheartedly (1 Chr 19:7-9). Similarly, the early church is described as one that "walked in the fear of the Lord" (Acts 9:31). To fear God, that is, "to stand in awe," preserves believers from becoming haughty (Rom 11:20) and reminds them of their reliance upon God and the coming judgment. Even from these few examples, it is clear that, from the biblical perspective, fear on the part of humans toward God is not paralyzing and destructive, but rather helpful and hope-inspiring.

F. M. Gillman

See also DAY OF THE LORD/DAY OF YAHWEH.

FEAST

The Christian feast is part of the rhythm of the liturgical year; fasts alternate with feasts, and with seasons that are strictly neither (called *Ordinary Time* in some traditions). In the widest sense, every Sunday is a liturgical feast; the original Christian feast can be said to be the weekly observance of Sunday. Specific feasts or celebrations of various degrees in the liturgical year developed more gradually over the course of Christian history. The earliest of these include a number of occasions common to most Christian traditions. The most important group are the "feasts of the Lord" that commemorate some important event in the life and ministry of Christ; for example, Easter (developed by the second century as the celebration of the resurrection of Jesus Christ, set in the early fourth century on the first Sunday after the first full moon in spring); and Christmas (set in the early fourth century as the celebration of the nativity, or birth, of Jesus Christ, on December 25). These two feasts also illustrate another important element: some feasts vary as to exact date, depending on the lunar calendar, while others have been set on specific days of the year. In addition, Easter is always celebrated on a Sunday, while Christmas may fall on any day of the week; this is true of other Christian feasts as well, for instance, Pentecost (Sunday), or the feast of All Saints on November 1 (any day of the week).

In several Christian traditions, feast days of Mary (some on Sundays, others on specific calendar dates) and the saints (on a specific calendar date, usually the supposed date of death) are also celebrated. In some churches, certain Sundays are also assigned specific festive theological or christological themes, as is Christ the King or Trinity Sunday. Moreover, some of these feasts are specific to certain churches, like Reformation Sunday (the last Sunday in October), an important celebration for a number of Protestant denominations.

Joanne M. Pierce

See also ADVENT; ASCENSION; CHRIST THE KING; CHRISTMAS; EASTER; FASTS/FASTING (IN CHRISTIANITY); LENT; LITURGICAL YEAR.

FEAST OF WEEKS
See SHAVUOT.

FEBRONIANISM
Febronianism is the name of a nineteenth-century German Catholic movement that promoted the theory that church power was vested in the community, and church jurisdiction was exercised rightfully by local bishops. The movement, similar to French Gallicanism, supported episcopal authority over that of the pope, who was described as a bishop among equals whose power was subject to ecumenical councils. The papacy's unique role was preservation of church unity and enforcement of conciliar decrees. Papal primacy was merely an honorific concept. The movement was provoked by church–state tensions in Germany exacerbated by Pope Pius IX's promulgation of the *Syllabus of Errors* and the Vatican Council I declaration of papal infallibility. The name comes from the pseudonym Justinus Febronius used for a treatise penned by Bishop Johann N. V. Hontheim. An offshoot of the movement, Josephinism, developed in late nineteenth-century Austria that proposed the supremacy of the Austrian emperor over church affairs in that nation.

Patricia Plovanich

FELLOWSHIP
In the Christian tradition, a fellowship (used as a noun) is a gathering of believers. Neither a church nor a denomina-

tion, it is a group united by a common purpose in addition to their commitment to Christianity. Led by laity rather than clergy, a fellowship is usually an inter-denominational group that does not require its members to disaffiliate from their churches. The United States provides numerous examples. During World War I, the Fellowship of Reconciliation formed to promote Christian pacifism; in the 1920s, it shifted its focus to labor and the Social Gospel. Similarly, the Fellowship of Socialist Christians was created in 1930 to advocate the radical restructuring of the social order to eliminate class oppression. Reinhold Niebuhr played a leading role in its early years. The Full Gospel Businessmen's Fellowship International was founded in 1951 to promote Pentecostal renewal among laymen apart from clerical oversight. Interdenominational fellowships are common on college campuses; the Fellowship of College Athletes and Intervarsity Christian Fellowship are two evangelical student groups that meet for singing, prayer, Bible study, and socializing.

Used as a verb, fellowship means to join with a church or community of believers. In the last twenty years, individuals and congregations have been disfellowshiped, or expelled, from their churches and denomination for violating the formal or informal rules of the body; for example, ordaining women and homosexuals as ministers.

Evelyn A. Kirkley

FEMINISM

Feminism is a belief and political philosophy that upholds the full humanity of women. It desires to transform all social structures that hinder the realization of this goal in any way. Liberal feminism insists upon equal rights and opportunities for women. Socialist feminism focuses upon the patriarchal structures of society, especially marriage, the family, and women's work, drawing attention to the economic and social consequences for nondominant races, genders, and social classes. Radical feminism advocates separation from the patriarchal system in order for women to create their own liberating structures. Another version of feminism may be termed "romantic," such as nineteenth-century Victorian feminism, which looked to women's "humanizing" presence as the remedy for such social evils as alcohol consumption and prostitution.

The struggle for women's rights in modern Western countries began with Mary Wollstonecraft's 1792 publication, *A Vindication of the Rights of Women*. In the U.S. in 1848, largely through the efforts of Elizabeth Cady Stanton and Susan B. Anthony, the first Women's Rights Convention met in Seneca Falls, New York. Women's suffrage in the U.S.A. was achieved in 1920 and the American feminist movement fell into decline. Revived in 1963 with Betty Friedan's book *The Feminine Mystique*, the women's liberation movement of the 1960s and 1970s represented a "second wave" of feminism. In addition to gender oppression, the contemporary feminist movement has become much more conscious of the intersection of oppressions such as those based upon race, class, sexual orientation, and physical disability. It is therefore more appropriate to speak of "feminisms."

Mary Ann Hinsdale

See also AFRICAN AMERICAN THEOLOGY; FEMINIST THEOLOGIES; LATINO THEOLOGY (-IES); LIBERATION THEOLOGIES; PATRIARCHY; SEXISM.

FEMINIST THEOLOGIES

The term "feminist theology" is often used to describe what, in reality, is plural. Feminist theolog*ies* emerge from a liberationist perspective on the faith experience of a particular class of people, in this case, women. Feminist theologies belong to the larger family of "liberation theologies," sharing particularly in liberation theology's critical task of exposing the failure of so-called "universal" theology to attend to economic exploitation, structural injustice, cultural domination, ecological degradation, and patriarchal violence. Feminist theologies take women's experience as their reflective starting point. They critique both past and present theology and church praxis for distorting, or rendering invisible, the contributions of women.

As does liberation theology, all feminist theologies are inspired by a vision of an alternative society that sustains concrete life, justice, and the well-being of all creation. The strategies leading to the creation of such a society are diverse, just as the actors and historical realities are. The worldwide reach of feminist theologies is such that today it is possible to speak of European, North American, Pacific Island, South Asian, African, and Latin American feminist theologies. Feminist theology is usually done from within a patriarchal religious tradition; hence, one can speak of Christian, Jewish, Buddhist, and so forth, feminist theologies. The intent of feminist theology is to recover the emancipatory force of the particular religious tradition, and to rehabilitate and reconstruct the tradition from the contextualized perspective of a particular group of women.

In the U.S., nineteenth-century women such as Elizabeth Cady Stanton (author of *The Women's Bible*), Susan B. Anthony, Anna Howard Shaw, and Matilda Joslyn Gage, represented the "first wave" of feminist theology in their realization that women as well as slaves were unequal in the eyes of white male society. The "second wave" is considered to have begun in 1960 with Valerie Saiving's essay "The Human Situation," which argued that a theology stressing pride as "sin" had been done from the perspective of male experience. Mary Daly (1973) radically challenged the patriarchal conception of God in *Beyond God the Father*, which also served as a demarcation point, separating biblical from postbiblical religious feminists. For Daly, if God was male, then male was "God."

In unmasking the universal narratives of theology, many postcolonial feminists raised criticisms of white, middle-class, feminist theology that failed to attend to race and class in its critical and constructive strategies. Thus, "womanist" (the term adopted from Alice Walder to describe black feminists), "mujerista," "Latina," "Chicana," "lesbian," "Asian," and "African" now serve as qualifiers to feminist theology developed from the experience of women of color and non-dominant groups of women, in order to give voice to the women made "other" by patriarchy *and* by middle-class, Euro-American feminism.

The most recent expressions of feminist theology include Ecofeminist theology and Indigenous feminist theology. The connection between ecology and feminism derives from the feminization of nature and the subsequent degradation of the environment. The socioreligious experience of native peoples and cultures in Latin America, North America, and Australia has given rise to Indigenous feminist theology.

Mary Ann Hinsdale

See also AFRICAN AMERICAN THEOLOGY; CONTEXTUALIZATION; ECOLOGY; ETHICS, SEXUAL; HERMENEUTICAL SUSPICION; LIBERATION THEOLOGIES; MUJERISTA THEOLOGY; PATRIARCHY; SEXISM; SOCIAL JUSTICE; WOMANIST THEOLOGY.

FÉNELON, FRANÇOIS DE SALIGNAC DE LA MOTHE (1651–1715)

French preacher, bishop, and spiritual writer, Fénelon was one of the most prominent clergymen in the age of Louis XIV. From 1688, Fénelon defended Madame Guyon, a mystic whose spirituality gained the name of Quietist. Quietists emphasized the need for human passivity before God and as a response to the workings of God's grace. Archbishop of Cambrai from 1695, Fénelon was criticized for his support of Madame Guyon by the bishop of Meaux, Jacques Bossuet. With the backing of both King Louis XIV and the Holy See, Bossuet was victorious, and Fénelon accepted condemnation of Quietism.

Thomas Worcester, s.j.

See also BOSSUET, JACQUES BÉNIGNE; MYSTICISM/MYSTICS (IN CHRISTIANITY); SPIRITUALITY.

FENG-SHUI

(Chinese, lit., wind and water). This is a traditional Chinese folk practice known as geomancy used to determine the placement of homes, buildings, tombs, temples, and the like. A system of divination for locating the most auspicious spiritual/physical site for human dwellings, it is based on the theory that topographical characteristics of earth and meteorological elements manifest *yin* and *yang* (positive and negative energy) in varying degrees, and that the most auspicious dwelling places are where these forces are found

to be in balance, "the point of tranquil harmony of all terrestrial and heavenly elements." Diviners, known as *feng-shui* masters, are used to determine where these sites might be, where humans and nature are in balance.

G. D. DeAngelis

See also I-CHING; T'AI CHI; TAO; YIN AND YANG.

FERNÁNDEZ DE SOTOMAYOR, JUAN (1777–1849)

Colombian Catholic theologian and patriot. Born in Cartagena de Indias and educated in Bogotá, he was ordained to the priesthood in 1801. Persecuted by Spanish colonial authorities for his active support of Colombian independence, he became one of the key ecclesiastics in the new republic. Fernández de Sotomayor died while serving as bishop of his native city. His *Catecismo popular* (1814), published during the struggle for independence, theologically justified Colombia's right to independence and explained why Catholics had the obligation to fight for freedom and human rights. This book and its author stand as precursors of contemporary liberation theology.

Orlando Espín

See also LATIN AMERICAN CATHOLICISM; LATIN AMERICAN THEOLOGIES; LIBERATION THEOLOGIES.

FESTIVALS, INTERMEDIATE DAYS

See CHOL HAMOED.

FETISH

A "power object," an object that can focus and transmit sacred power for human use, for example, for healing or success in hunting or battle. The term is most commonly used in relation to the religions of indigenous peoples. Various natural objects (for example, stones, feathers, shells) and man-made instruments (such as rattles, shields, or masks) can be used in this way, typically in a ritual context. Indigenous art is typically not creative in the modern sense: song, dance, masks, and visual designs do not express the individuality of the artist but reproduce sacred patterns seen or heard in visions. By so doing, they are understood to forge sacramental, even magical, links with the spirit world. A fetish may also be understood to be the dwelling place of a powerful spirit. In any event, fetishes are typically thought to be dangerous. If they may be handled at all, it must be by a qualified individual, such as a shaman or designated owner. The popular use of this term in a wider, psychological sense is related to, but not to be confused with, its technical use in religious studies and anthropology.

Lance E. Nelson

See also AMULET; INDIGENOUS RELIGIOUS TRADITIONS; SHAMAN.

FEUERBACH, LUDWIG (1804–72)

German philosopher. Although he began his studies expecting to become a theologian, he turned to philosophy under Hegel's influence. Feuerbach rejected Christianity (which he came to consider an illusion) and all belief in transcendence. He thought that both theology and philosophy were ultimately only concerned with humankind, "God" being no more than a projection of the most fundamental traits and quests of humanity. His writings, especially *The Essence of Christianity* (1841), were very influential on Nietszche and Marx.

Orlando Espín

See also ATHEISM; ENLIGHTENMENT IN WESTERN HISTORY; GOD; HEGEL, G.W.F.; IDEALISM, CLASSICAL GERMAN; MARX, KARL; MARXISM; METHOD IN THEOLOGY; MODERNITY; NIETSZCHE, FRIEDRICH; POSTMODERNITY.

FICHTE, JOHANN GOTTLIEB (1762–1814)

German "Idealist" philosopher. He first studied theology at the universities of Jena and Leipzig, and then became fascinated with Immanuel Kant's philosophical system. After teaching at Jena, in 1809 he became professor of philosophy in Berlin. Famous and influential for his commitment to German nationalism (especially against Napoleon), Fichte was also committed to what he believed to be the development of Kant's thought. His philosophy has been called "ethical pantheism" because he promoted and philosophically argued for a society in which morality was the norm. His reflections on "God" were intended as foundation for the new moral order. Fichte thought that once the stage of social morality was achieved, the "churches" (meaning "organized religion") would become obsolete. His most influential publication on the philosophy of religion was *Anweisung zum seligen Leben* (1805).

Orlando Espín

See also CATEGORICAL IMPERATIVE; HEGEL, G.W.F.; IDEALISM, CLASSICAL GERMAN; KANT, IMMANUEL; MODERNITY; PANTHEISM; POSTMODERNITY; SCHELLING, FRIEDRICH WILHELM VON.

FICINO, MARSILIO (1433–99)

Florentine humanist and philosopher, Ficino was an important scholar of Greek. A prominent figure in the Italian Renaissance, Ficino was responsible for a new translation of Plato from Greek into Latin, as well as for Scripture commentaries. His interest in Plato points to a late medieval and Renaissance interest in ancient philosophy that went beyond the limits of Aristotelianism.

Thomas Worcester, S.J.

See also ARISTOTELIANISM; HUMANISM; PLATO; PLATONISM; RENAISSANCE.

FIDEISM

Most broadly, the term refers to the position that there can be no knowledge of God apart from supernatural revelation. More specifically, the term refers to specific reaction to Scholastic rationalism in nineteenth-century Roman Catholic theology as found in the works of Joseph de Maistre, Louis de Bonald, Félicité de Lamennais, and, above all, Louis Bautain. This position was definitively rejected in the second chapter of the apostolic constitution *Dei Filius* at the First Vatican Council (1870).

J. A. Colombo

See also DEI FILIUS; LAMENNAIS, FÉLICITÉ ROBERT DE.

FIDES FIDUCIALIS

Martin Luther taught that salvation comes through faith alone. This "faith," however, is not simply a matter of intellectual assent to a creed or list of doctrinal propositions. Faith, for Luther, is "trusting faith" (in Latin, *fides fiducialis*). This faith constitutes a personal relationship with Christ as one's redeemer. Such faith comes from the heart and is a gift from God.

Much of the sixteenth-century controversy about the role and meaning of faith, controversy that divided Catholics from Lutherans, had to do with this question. For Catholics, "faith" usually meant intellectual assent to doctrine, and

was not seen as sufficient, in itself, for salvation.

Thomas Worcester, S.J.

See also FAITH; JUSTIFICATION; LUTHER, MARTIN; REFORMATION; SALVATION; SOLA FIDE.

FIDES QUA/FIDES QUAE CREDITUR

The Latin phrases *fides qua creditur* and *fides quae creditur* express the subjective and objective character of the one experience of faith. The active *fides qua creditur* is the act of believing or believing faith, the subjective experience of faith or the personal disposition toward the encounter with God. Personal faith also has an objective dimension that signals the objectivity or "otherness" of revelation. Thus the *fides quae creditur* means the content of faith or the faith that is believed, the objective expression of faith. While the ultimate object of faith is God revealed in Jesus Christ, the *fides quae* also means the objective testimony about revelation or the faith tradition. The two terms convey different aspects of faith and signal the importance both of the objective reality of divine revelation and the significance of the personal faith response to that revelation.

Patricia Plovanich

FIELD, RACHEL (1894–1942)

Born in New York City, Rachel Lyman Field was a poet, novelist, and writer of children's literature. While attending Radcliffe College as a special student from 1914–8, she took courses in literature, composition, and playwriting. After five years working in the editorial department of a film company, writing synopses of books and plays, she turned to her own writing, dividing her time between New

York and an island off the coast of Maine. Her fiction often reflected Christian themes of repentance and redemption. Her novel for children, *Hitty, Her First Hundred Years* (1929), that told the story of a wooden doll and the children who loved her, won the Newberry Medal as the most distinguished children's book of the year, and established children's literature as a viable literary genre. Her adult fiction *Time Out of Mind* (1935) was awarded the National Book Award, and *All This, and Heaven Too* (1938) was a bestseller and made into a successful film. The latter was based on the story of Field's great-uncle, Reverend Henry Field, who married a woman accused of complicity in a murder.

Evelyn A. Kirkley

FILIAL PIETY

(Chinese, *hsiao/xiao*). The central ideal in Confucianism of respect for one's elders or serving one's parents. This term originally meant piety toward ancestors, but Confucius shifted the focus to parents, indicating his primary concern with life in the here and now. From the Confucian perspective, mainly fostered by Mencius, respect and concern for one's parents were essential for order and harmony in the family. While filiality was seen as the foundation of family government, it was also recognized by Confucian thinkers as a natural basis for all moral and political behavior and as such an ideal principle for society and the state. Confucius believed that "only after learning how to serve one's parents reverently and obediently can one serve the ruler and society." While filiality has helped to keep the family as the central focus in Chinese society, it has also had a great impact on society and governance.

G. D. DeAngelis

See also CONFUCIANISM; CONFUCIUS; LI; MENCIUS.

FILIOQUE

This expression comes from the Latin version of the Creed; it means "and from the Son": "We believe in the Holy Spirit, the Lord, the giver of life, who proceeds from the Father *and the Son [qui ex Patre Filioque procedit]*." The expression has a long and polemical history; it is a major reason for the division between the church of the East and the West (the Western church inserted *filioque* into the Creed of Nicaea–Constantinople, the Eastern church rejected it). The dispute was essentially over how to interpret Scripture. The Fourth Gospel makes it abundantly clear that Jesus was "sent" into the world by God (John 3:17, 34; 4:34; 5:30; 8:18, and others), and it states further that the Father will send the Holy Spirit in Jesus' name (John 14:26). Yet, does the Holy Spirit come from the Father alone, or jointly from the Father and the Son? Jesus says, "When the Advocate comes, whom I will send to you from the Father, the Spirit of truth who comes from the Father, he will testify on my behalf" (John 15:26; see also 16:7ff.). It appears, then, that the Spirit "comes" from both the Father and the Son, since Jesus as Son does the sending. Jesus "proceeds" from the Father, and the Spirit "proceeds" from the Father and from Jesus; hence, the Spirit can even be referred to as the Spirit of Jesus (Acts 16:7) or the Spirit of the Lord (2 Cor 3:17).

Texts such as John 15:26 affect the church's understanding of the trinitarian nature of God because they identify so distinctly three "Persons" within the divine mystery and speak of "sending." Christian thinkers reasoned that how God appears in space and time, in history, reflects how God must be outside of space and time, even before history began. The "sendings" mentioned in the New Testament, they reasoned, are based on something that is always going on inside the mystery of God. "Sending" became "procession." But biblical language is not conceptually precise. Thus, while the New Testament speaks of Father, Son, and Spirit, it does not provide a technical explanation of how these three figures are related. The effort to make the meaning of scriptural language more precise, however, is not always successful. The Eastern church viewed the Western insertion of *filioque* as compromising the divine unity.

William Reiser, S.J.

See also GOD; HYPOSTATIC UNION; TRINITY / TRINITARIAN THEOLOGY / TRINITARIAN PROCESSIONS.

FINITUDE

The condition of being "limited." The term is used to describe the ontological nature of worldly (created) being. These beings can be described as limited or finite in any or all of three ways. First, a being belongs to a particular class of things and is thus limited because it does not belong to some other class. For example, to be a cat is not to be a dog, a begonia, and so on. Second, a being is one instance of a class and is thus limited by not being some other instance of the same class. For example, "this" cat is not "that" cat. Third, a being is temporally limited by either its beginning and/or end.

J. A. Colombo

FIQH

An Islamic term that originally meant religious law and theology, but according to current usage refers to human understanding of the law, legal processes, and application of Islam's complex legal code

called the *Sharia*. Fiqh is often translated as the science of jurisprudence, or science of the law. It differs from *Sharia* (the law itself) in that the law comes from Allah (God) and may never be changed. Fiqh was produced by the human mind and, therefore, continues to develop as understanding of divine revelation progresses over the centuries.

Ronald A. Pachence

See also FAQIH; SHARIA / SHARI'A.

FIVE PILLARS (IN ISLAM)

In Arabic, *arkan ad-din* or the foundation / supports of the religion. The pillars express in summary fashion the basic beliefs and practices of all Muslims.

1. *Shahadah:* Faith profession—"There is no god but God (Allah) and Muhammad is the Messenger (*rasul*) of God."
2. *Salat:* Prayer—All Muslims are to pray at five prescribed times each day.
3. *Zakat:* Almsgiving—Believers are expected to give 2½ percent of their liquid assets held for one year as alms for the poor and needy.
4. *Sawm:* Fasting from dawn to sunset during the month of Ramadan, the ninth month of the Islamic calendar.
5. *Hajj:* Pilgrimage to the holy city of Mecca (in Saudi Arabia) at least once in a Muslim's life, providing he or she can afford the trip.

Some Muslims add a sixth pillar, *jihad* or "striving in the way of God." While jihad is often translated as "holy war" in defense of Islam, it also involves the personal struggle with the powers of evil within oneself.

Ronald A. Pachence

See also ALLAH (ISLAM); HAJJ; JIHAD; MUHAMMAD; RAMADAN; RASUL; SALAT; SAWM; SHAHADAH; ZAKAT.

FLESH/SARX

Sarx, the Greek word for "flesh," is a term used in the Bible to refer to the natural earthly realm, the human realm, and is sometimes employed as a synonym for body. It can have a neutral sense, referring simply to a created being, or it can have a more negative connotation, naming that which gives rise to self-righteousness or to the vices. In this latter sense, the works of the flesh are opposed to the Spirit of God. For the most part, *sarx* is not used in a dualistic sense, characteristic of Greek thought, where it names the material part of a living being as opposed to the spirit of the living being.

In the Old Testament "all flesh" can denote "all of us," that is "all human beings." More broadly, it can comprise all living beings: angels, humans, and animals. Thus, flesh is the link that living beings, especially humans, have with the earth and with one another. The creaturely dimension is underscored by such phrases as "skin and flesh" (Job 10:11), "flesh and bone" and "heart and flesh" (Ps 84:2). "Flesh and bone" is also a customary way of expressing kinship.

In the flesh are manifested "deeds of iniquity" (Ps 65:2-3). This same text, "to you all flesh shall come" (v. 2), indicates that flesh is drawn toward God. Nonetheless, flesh remains mortal, as Isaiah vividly says: "All people [flesh] are grass, their constancy is like the flower of the field" (Isa 40:6).

In the New Testament, *sarx* is used to refer to the Incarnation, as in John 1:14, "the Word became flesh" (cf. 2 Cor 5:16). The term also functions as a synonym for body (1 Cor 6:16; 15:39; 2 Cor 7:1). When Paul says that God sent Jesus "in the likeness of sinful flesh" (Rom 8:3), he does not say that Jesus came "with sinful flesh," but that he experienced the effects of sin and suffered death.

The flesh is a battleground where sin is manifested. Hence, believers are called to "walk not according to the flesh but according to the Spirit" (Rom 8:4). The contrast between flesh and Spirit is regularly drawn. Setting one's mind on flesh is death, whereas setting the mind on the Spirit brings life and peace (Rom 8:6). The desires of the flesh and its works are opposed to the Spirit and its fruits (Gal 5:16-26).

The flesh/spirit antithesis is taken up in the Fourth Gospel. Jesus instructs Nicodemus: "What is born of the flesh is flesh and what is born of the Spirit is spirit" (John 3:6). Only the Spirit can give life (John 6:63); humans judge "according to the flesh" (John 8:15). In all these passages, flesh stands for the human way of thinking as opposed to God's life-giving ways.

John Gillman

See also PAULINE THEOLOGY; SOMA (GREEK); SPIRIT.

FLORENCE-FERRARA-BASLE (COUNCILS OF)

See BASLE-FLORENCE-FERRARA (COUNCILS OF).

FLORISTÁN, CASIANO (1926–2006)

Spanish Catholic theologian. Born in Navarre, Spain, Floristán began studying to be a chemist until he felt called to the priesthood, to which he was ordained in 1956 after studies in Salamanca and Innsbruck. While in Austria (Innsbruck) he studied under Josef Jüngmann, and both Hugo and Karl Rahner. He then earned his doctoral degree in practical theology at Tübingen. Specialized in pastoral/practical theology and in liturgy, Floristán held (for thirty-six years, beginning in 1960) the chair in Pastoral Theology at the Pontifical University of Salamanca. He was a *peritus* ("expert") at the Second Vatican Council, and for many years a board member of the prestigious journal *Concilium*. Casiano Floristán impacted, through his teaching and research, an entire generation of Spanish and Latin American theologians, and was well known and very highly respected in U.S. Latino/a theological circles. Admired for his kindness and personal integrity, he was clearly committed to the goals of liberation theology. Floristán spearheaded the methodological renewal of pastoral/practical theology in the Spanish-speaking world after Vatican II. Among his most influential books are *Criteriología de la acción pastoral* (1968), *El catecumenado* (1972), and *Teología práctica* (1991).

Orlando Espín

See also LAITY; PRACTICAL THEOLOGY; VATICAN, SECOND COUNCIL OF THE.

FORGIVENESS

A multifaceted term, understood best as one of a constellation of attitudes and practices such as contrition, mercy, and reconciliation. Forgiveness attends specifically to the response of a wronged person(s) to the wrongdoer(s). As such (unlike reconciliation, for example), it can (though not necessarily) be unilateral—not requiring any change on the part of the wrongdoer(s). Thus, for example, God is always forgiving, though people may not receive it. Forgiveness can also be mutual (unlike mercy, for example). By its very nature, forgiveness admits that a wrong has been done. Thus, "Don't bother, it was nothing" is not forgiveness.

Forgiveness is often associated with "pardon" and "amnesty," and in some

ways rightfully. However, Christian commentators are careful to avoid "robbing the cross of Christ of its power," in so doing. That is, such commentators are wary of the notion that any wrongdoing has "automatic" forgiveness from God. Such an attitude deprives the wrongdoer of the chance to mature into full responsible personhood and, more importantly, "cheapens" the passion of Christ who suffered to bring us this gift. It is best, then, to look at forgiveness as a feature of an ongoing personal relationship with the trinitarian God.

Internally, forgiveness seeks to overcome resentment. Externally, it can forgo (or possibly commute) punishment due. Interpersonally, it seeks to see the wrongdoer(s) as more than the wrong they have done, or as part of a greater plan for good. It is in this area of interpersonal relationship that forgiveness is best understood, because forgiveness seeks to reestablish the personhood of each party involved in the wrong. That is, both the wrongdoer and the wronged have suffered diminishment of their personhood. Forgiveness seeks to restore (or even enhance) that lost personhood, especially through mutual acknowledgment of personal dignity. This recognition of the personal dignity of the other can involve acts of reparation, atonement, or sorrow—acts that in the rite of reconciliation might be called "penance." In speaking of forgiveness, however, those acts are characteristically undertaken *after* forgiveness is granted, and undertaken voluntarily to "fill up" the re-turning toward the now restored or deepened interpersonal relationship of mutual respect.

Sometimes forgiveness is thought to occur after the wrongdoer has suffered punishment or performed some act of restorative justice, but this is more properly *reconciliation*, which, in one of its forms, can be a psychological acceptance that justice has been done and the proper balance of the relationship has been restored.

Sometimes forgiveness among human beings seems to be instantaneous and complete, but most times it requires a long process, depending on the depth of the injury. In that case forgiveness can be thought of as "first in intention (we intend, and even say, "I forgive you,") but last in execution (a final freedom from resentment and the desire to punish)."

G. Simon Harak, s.j.

See also CONTRITION; MERCY; RECONCILIATION.

FORMATION
While formation can refer to any number of programs of instruction and training, it is frequently used in a technical sense to designate the process by means of which men and women are assimilated into religious life. Following the general directives on religious life decreed by Vatican II, each religious community (variously referred to as an "institute," "congregation," or "order") has attempted to adjust its plan of training and instruction in ways that both respect its founding charism and take into account the circumstances of today's world.

While the novitiate is a particularly formative moment in the life of a religious, formation generally continues through a plan of studies, apostolic or ministerial experiences, prayer and spiritual direction for a number of years until final profession. In fact, today formation is often viewed as a lifelong process. Since religious life is basically a charismatic reality, formation above all means growth in the life of the Spirit. Religious formation is thus geared above all to fos-

ter interior freedom, discernment, and a readiness to follow the Spirit's lead. Formation, then, does not mean becoming institutionalized, and it does not bring about a loss of spontaneity and imagination but a channeling of these gifts for the good of God's people.

William Reiser, s.j.

See also NOVICE; NOVITIATE; PERFECTAE CARITATIS; PROFESSED; RELIGIOUS (VOWED).

FORM CRITICISM
Form criticism is the classification and study of individual units of traditions in the Bible by literary genres. Form critics recognize: (1) that biblical texts are made up of separable units; (2) that each unit can be classified according to its literary genre; (3) that the genre (or form) in which a tradition is preserved suited the context in which the unit was shaped; and (4) that each genre betrays something about the particular life setting that shaped the tradition. Since context sheds light on content and intention, form critics seek to identify the circumstances in the life (*Sitz im Leben*) of the believing community that led to the formulation of each unit into its particular genre. Form critics also realized that many units underwent changes as they were preserved and transmitted in the oral and written strata antecedent to the canonical texts.

The application of form criticism to the Old Testament is vastly more complicated. Hundreds of years of oral and written revisions lie behind the canonical texts. While form criticism has been applied to every text of the New Testament, it remains most significant in the study of the Gospels. Form critics classify units of the Gospels into miracle stories, narratives, legends, sayings, parables, and so on, although a great variety of subdivisions of these major forms has been suggested. Form critics seek to get behind the written sources to identify and describe what was happening as the traditions were developing. They consider what was introduced and why it was introduced, and distinguish the literary shape from the memories of what might go back to historical events.

The major weakness of the original understanding of form criticism was that it neglected the contribution of the evangelists or the authors of other texts. While this was rectified with the development of redaction criticism, many premises of the first generation of form critics have been rightly challenged. For example, scholars now realize that a uniform passion narrative was not set within a few years after Jesus' death. It is also now recognized that reconstructions are hypothetical, and it is not really possible to claim one has established "assured results" based on the reconstructed oral traditions.

Despite the limitations and hypothetical nature of the enterprise, form criticism is an enduring feature of biblical scholarship. It is no longer possible to ignore the fact that biblical texts are composites of discrete units of various forms of literature that took their shape from particular circumstances. These forms have specific characteristics that reflect a "situation in life" in which they were shaped, be it of worship, preaching, or the like. Form criticism is an integral aspect of the historical-critical method. In addition, a number of scholars have joined form criticism with rhetorical criticism or aesthetic criticism to sharpen an appreciation of the written forms as literary units as they appear in the text.

Regina A. Boisclair

See also HISTORICAL CRITICISM; REDACTION CRITICISM.

FORNET-BETANCOURT, RAÚL (1946–)

Fornet-Betancourt is a philosopher who was born in Holguín, Cuba, and is currently professor of philosophy at the University of Bremen, Germany, and director of the Latin American section of the *Missio* Institute of Missiology in Aachen. He is also a frequent visiting professor at various European and Latin American universities. Fornet-Betancourt received a doctorate in philosophy from the University of Salamanca, and then studied at the Sorbonne (Paris) under Jean-Paul Sartre. He earned another doctorate in philosophy (with secondary specializations in linguistics and theology) at the University of Aachen, Germany. He is very active in various professional associations throughout the world, having been the inspiration for a number of philosophical societies interested in intercultural thought. In 1982 he founded (in Germany) the journal *Concordia* as an international philosophical quarterly. Educated in the contemporary philosophies of Europe and Latin America, and with an impressive list of publications in both, Fornet-Betancourt has been mainly responsible for the creation of today's intercultural philosophy (and theology) as method. He is currently regarded as one of the world's most influential and creative thinkers. Among his important publications are: *Problemas actuales de la filosofía en Hispanoamérica* (1985); *Comentario a la Fenomenología del Espíritu de Hegel* (1987); *Aproximaciones a José Martí* (1998); *Hacia una filosofía intercultural latinoamericana* (1994); *Interculturalidad y globalización* (2000); *Transformación intercultural de la filosofía* (2001); *Interculturalidad y filosofía en América Latina* (2003); *Resistencia y solidaridad* (2003); *Crítica intercultural de la filosofía latinoamericana actual* (2004); and *Filosofar para nuestro tiempo en clave intercultural* (2004).

Orlando Espín

See also CULTURE; INCULTURATION; INTERCULTURAL THOUGHT; METHOD IN THEOLOGY.

FORTITUDE

In general, fortitude is the power to stand up for one's beliefs, even in the face of dire consequences, including death. One thinks, for example, of the American story of Nathan Hale. In classical ethics, fortitude is considered one of the four cardinal (*cardo*, "hinge") virtues from which all other virtues flow. As a virtue, it is also necessary for Christians in their beliefs (as martyrs and confessors, for example). Thomas Aquinas points out that such "endurance" is not mere passivity, since it involves a vigorous grasping of and clinging to the good. Joseph Pieper points out that an important characteristic of the Christian virtue of fortitude is what we might now call "counterattack."

Thomas Aquinas and John of St. Thomas point out that fortitude is also mentioned in Isaiah 11:2 as one of the seven gifts of the Holy Spirit. As a *gift*, they say, it goes beyond even the virtue of courage to its "full scope." The virtue of fortitude is moderated by prudence as are all other virtues. But through the gift of the Holy Spirit one can face superhuman difficulties because the gift of fortitude draws on the power of God. Thus Michael, for example, was able to defeat the more powerful Lucifer. And in Isaiah 39:30-31, we read, "Young men may grow weary and faint, youths shall stumble and fall. But those who look to the Lord will renew their strength; they will run and not grow weary, they will walk and not grow faint."

G. Simon Harak, s.j.

See also GIFTS OF THE SPIRIT; PRUDENCE; VIRTUE.

FOUCAULT, MICHEL (1926–84)

French philosopher. A professor at the prestigious Collège de France in Paris, Foucault contributed to the so-called postmodern movement in both Europe and North America. He critiqued universal claims and insisted on examining their roles and uses in society. He taught that knowledge is power, and the need to understand how that power is socially and culturally used. Foucault has been important to theologians and theologies that participate in the postmodern critique of culture. His more influential books are *Madness and Civilization* (1961), *The Archaeology of Knowledge* (1972), and *The History of Sexuality* (1976).

Orlando Espín

See also CRITICAL THEORY; CULTURE; EPISTEMOLOGY; HISTORICAL CRITIQUE; MODERNITY; POSTMODERNITY.

FOUR-SOURCE THEORY (OF SYNOPTICS)

The four sources of the Synoptic Gospels to which this theory refers are Mark, Q, Luke's special material, and Matthew's special material. The concept builds on the Two-Source Theory or Two-Source Hypothesis, by which titles it is far more widely known and under which entry it is described in this volume.

F. M. Gillman

See also TWO-SOURCE THEORY (OF SYNOPTICS).

FOUR YOGAS

See BHAKTI-YOGA; JNANA-YOGA; KARMA-YOGA; RAJA-YOGA; YOGA.

FOX, GEORGE (1624–91)

Born in Fenny Drayton, England, Fox founded the Society of Friends, popularly known as the Quakers. Disturbed by Christian hypocrisy and superficiality, he was a spiritual seeker and became convinced in 1646 that humanity has been endowed by God with a measure of "Inner Light." If humans follow this light, they will encounter divine truth. Revelation is not limited to the Bible; God speaks to those who earnestly listen. Fox preached that true Christians had no need for ordained clergy, formal worship, worldly titles, oaths, or military service. Aided by his wife, Margaret Fell, he also preached that women had the same access to the Inner Light as men. Fox's message attracted followers, especially among the Puritans, and by 1652 the first Quaker meeting was organized in northern England. Through aggressive missionary efforts, the movement spread to Germany, Austria, Holland, the West Indian islands, and the North American British colonies. His individualism, pacifism, and egalitarianism brought him into conflict with church and civil authorities, and he and many Quakers were systematically persecuted. By the time of Fox's death, however, the Society of Friends had become firmly established.

Evelyn A. Kirkley

See also QUAKERS.

FRANÇA MIRANDA, MÁRIO DE (1936–)

Brazilian Catholic theologian and member of the Society of Jesus (Jesuits). França Miranda studied in his native country as well as in Germany and Italy. Upon return to Brazil, he taught in Rio de Janeiro and in the prestigious Jesuit house of studies in Belo Horizonte. He is currently professor at the Pontifical Catholic University of Rio de Janeiro. França Miranda's contribution and publications have been mostly about the theology of grace. Influenced by Karl Rahner and by liberation theology, he links contemporary European (Catholic) thought on grace with the social justice demands of Latin American theology. He has developed an interesting theological understanding of Afro-Brazilian religions. His best books are *O Mistério de Deus em nossa vida* (1978) and *Libertados para a práxis da justiça* (1980).

Orlando Espín

See also AFRO-LATIN RELIGIONS; ELECTION (DOCTRINE OF); FREE WILL; GRACE; JUSTICE; JUSTIFICATION; LATIN AMERICAN CATHOLICISM; LATIN AMERICAN THEOLOGIES; LIBERATION THEOLOGIES; SALVATION; SOTERIOLOGY.

FRANCISCANS

"Franciscan" is the common name for the religious family of orders of priests, nuns, brothers, members of secular institutes, and laypeople associated with the Order of Friars Minor, started by Francis of Assisi and approved by Pope Innocent III in 1210, or associated with the Order of Poor Clares started by Francis's friend, Clare of Assisi, in 1212 for women.

The history of the Franciscan Order is marked by controversy starting during the lifetime of Francis himself. The movement spread rapidly, and there were several hundred members in Italy by the year 1215. Franciscans spread to Spain in 1217, to France in 1218, to Germany in 1221, to England in 1224, and to Hungary in 1228. The need to organize such a large body caused a gradual relaxation of the strictness of poverty desired by Francis as well as a loss of the exuberant spontaneity of the early Franciscans. The first serious disputes came over ownership of property and over the role of university study within the order. Pope Gregory IX ruled in the bull *Quo elongati* that the order could own houses, books, and other possessions. This ruling, and the autocratic leadership of the minister general, Brother Elias, led eventually to a formation of a group of Franciscans, including some of the original followers of Francis, who followed the strict lifestyle envisioned and lived by Francis. The "Spiritual Franciscans" as they were called, continued to protest as the papacy once again cooperated with the minister general in relaxing the ideals of St. Francis. In 1245, in the bull *Ordinem vestrum*, Pope Innocent IV ruled that property could be owned for the Franciscans by the papacy, and that finances could be handled for the friars by agents outside the order.

Dissension within the order was joined by opposition from without. The masters at the University of Paris objected first to the new chairs of theology granted to the Franciscans and Dominicans, and then challenged the very existence of the friars. Some of the Spirituals, meanwhile, were inspired by the teaching of Joachim of Fiore to predict that the final age of the Spirit had opened with the appearance of the friars, and that the age of the clerics was passing. This attack on the clergy fueled opposition to the friars. At this critical juncture, Bonaventure became minister general of the order. He cracked down on the Spirituals, but also strengthened the commitment to a simple life of poverty. Bonaventure's moderate line was strengthened by Pope Nicholas III in 1279 by the bull *Exiit qui seminat*, but the

Spirituals persisted in their criticism of the rest of the order, now referred to as "Conventuals."

The Spirituals suffered imprisonment and exile before they were allowed to form their own order, called the Poor Hermits of Pope Celestine, during the short reign of the Pope of the same name. Pope Celestine V's successor immediately suppressed the new order, and once again hostilities broke out between Spirituals and Conventuals. Serious persecution of the Spirituals was undertaken by Pope John XXII in 1317, with the result that four of the Spiritual Franciscans were burnt as heretics. Pope John went even further, however, and declared that it was heresy to teach that Jesus and his followers lived a life of voluntary poverty, and the papacy would no longer hold Franciscan possessions for them. Ownership was turned directly over to the Franciscans. The minister general of the order, Michael of Cesena, was forced to flee to the emperor for protection and was excommunicated. The Conventuals seemed to have triumphed completely. The few groups of Franciscans who tried to revive the Spirituals' concern with poverty were forced to disband.

The Franciscan ideal of poverty was impossible to stifle, however, and in 1368 a network of Franciscan houses began to grow up that followed a stricter way of life. Called the Friars Minor of the Observance, or simply "Observants," they numbered some twenty-five houses by the year 1400. In 1415, at the Council of Constance, they received permission to elect their own vicar general and to elect vicars for each province. The Franciscans had now split into two orders, even if the fiction of unity still remained. Attempts at unity failing, the two groups definitely split into separate orders in 1517, the

Observants by now being the larger of the two orders of Franciscans.

The splintering was not yet complete, however. In the sixteenth century, the Observants themselves were further divided by four reform movements that claimed the right to have their own leaders. They are known as the "Discalced" (shoeless) Franciscans, Reformed Franciscans, the Recollects, and the Capuchins. Each of these movements was an attempt to further reform the Observants. The Capuchins constitute a separate Franciscan Order from either the Conventuals or the Observants, while the Discalced, the Reformed, and the Recollects were united into a single Observant Order in 1909. The Conventuals also constitute a separate Franciscan Order.

The order founded by Clare of Assisi underwent a similar, if not so violent and persistent division. Clare, after a long and arduous struggle, managed to convince Pope Innocent IV to approve an order linking her order to that of Francis's and embracing the ideal of poverty that drew her to this life in the first place. In 1264 the order split when Pope Urban IV imposed a new rule on the Poor Clares that granted concessions of ownership Clare herself had fought hard to reject. Those who accepted the new rule were called "Urbanists" (for the Pope), and those who rejected it "Primitives" (since they followed the original Rule of Clare). A further reform of the Poor Clares was undertaken by St. Collette of Corbie in the fifteenth century, and this branch of the order is called the Colettine Poor Clares. Since, however, each monastery of Poor Clares is independent, they are today considered different branches of the same order.

Francis and Clare inspired many other religious orders of women, however, and there are today over fifty religious orders

of women in the Franciscan tradition. Many of these come from the "third order" of the Franciscans, an organization established to allow people living in the world to live the Franciscan life. The many varieties of Franciscan life operative today are perhaps the best testament to the powerful models for experimentation, devotion, and enthusiasm that Francis and Clare offer to all ages.

Gary Macy

See also BONAVENTURE; BONIFACE VIII, POPE; FRANCIS OF ASSISI; FRIARS; INNOCENT III, POPE; JOHN XXII, POPE; LYONS, COUNCILS OF; MEDIEVAL CHRISTIANITY (IN THE WEST); MEDIEVAL CHURCH; ORDERS (RELIGIOUS); POVERTY (RELIGIOUS VOW); SPIRITUAL FRANCISCANS.

FRANCIS OF ASSISI (1182?–1226)

Giovanni di Bernadone was the son of a cloth merchant of Assisi and remains best known by his nickname, "Francesco" or "little Frenchman." As a young man, Francis underwent a gradual conversion process in which he disassociated himself from his family and his friends and gradually came to adopt the life of poverty and preaching to which he felt he was called by the command of Jesus in the Gospel of Matthew. He quickly formed a group of followers around him dedicated to the same principles. In 1210 this band appealed to Pope Innocent III for formal approval of their way of life, an approval that was attained after some initial hesitation on the part of the Pope. This marks the beginning of the Order of the Friars Minor or, as they are usually known, the Franciscans. In 1212 Clare of Assisi wished to join Francis's group. A sort of compromise was reached when Francis supported Clare in the formation of a religious order for women, the Poor Clares. Francis's movement, driven by his own remarkable sanctity and charismatic personality, grew rapidly. In 1219 Francis led a band of friars to Egypt where he hoped to convert the Muslims. During his absence, the strict rules on poverty began to be loosened, a move Francis opposed upon his return. This disagreement would mark the first of many disagreements within the Franciscan Order on the role of poverty. Although Francis wrote a new order for the Franciscans in 1221, he slowly relinquished actual leadership of the Franciscans. In 1223, as the culmination of a mystical experience, Francis received the stigmata, an event that only accelerated his rapidly deteriorating health. Francis died in 1226 in the little church of the Portiuncula near Assisi. Francis was canonized less than two years later. He remains the most popular of medieval saints.

Gary Macy

See also FRANCISCANS; FRIARS; INNOCENT III, POPE; MEDIEVAL CHRISTIANITY (IN THE WEST); POVERTY (RELIGIOUS VOW); SPIRITUAL FRANCISCANS.

FRAZER, SIR JAMES G. (1854–1941)

Born in Glasgow, Scotland. Trinity College fellow, 1879. Professor of anthropology at the University of Liverpool, 1907; knighted in 1914. Frazer is best known as the author of the twelve-volume *Golden Bough*, a survey of "primitive" religions around the world published in 1890. His theories, based on reports of missionaries, anthropologists, and classical thinkers, proposed that humans experience an evolutionary development in their understanding of the spirit world. First, people try to control the world through magic. When this proves ineffective, people then turn to religion, seeking to induce the natural world to cooperate with human desires. Once religion fails, people turn to science to rationally control and explain natural phenomena. Frazer's theory assumes an evolutionary framework for cultural development, and that all human societies will progress through the same stages. Accordingly, Europe's scientific and technological achievements were hallmarks of an "advanced" or superior society. His view of religion, like that of E. B. Tylor, was a rationalist one. All beliefs and institutions, including religion, were seen as products of human reason. In the *Golden Bough*, one of the most widely circulated, popular, and best-known ethnological works of the time, he suggested that people use magic as an early form of science to control the natural and supernatural world around them. His work contributed to theoretical discussions of imitative and contagious magic and the development of religion.

Christine Greenway

See also MAGIC; MYTH; RATIONALISM.

FREE CATHOLIC CHURCH

See OLD CATHOLICS.

FREE CHURCH TRADITION

A free church is a Christian church to which one belongs by choice and supports through donations, freely given contributions, as opposed to a state church to which all citizens nominally belong and that is supported by public tax monies. The free church tradition is especially important in Europe, with a tradition of state churches in France, Germany, England, and the Netherlands, among others. In the eighteenth and nineteenth centuries, political and economic revolution weakened state establishments and gave rise to free churches. The separation of church and state increased, and laws enforcing religious uniformity were abolished. In the twentieth century, even in countries like England, where a nominal establishment still exists, free churches among the Methodists and Baptists flourish.

In the United States, where there were colonial establishments, but the explicit separation of church and state in the Constitution, all churches are free churches. The free church tradition is the custom of the country. Religious freedom has also spawned voluntarism, the voluntary participation in and support of religious communities, and competition, rivalry between denominations for adherents. Most importantly, from the free church tradition in the United States emerged denominationalism, the development of religious communities on an equal footing with one another with only slight variations in theology and liturgy. Baptists, Methodists, Presbyterians, Lutherans, even Catholics and Jews, were effectively denominationalized. Denominationalism has created a religious mainstream and margin, minimizing theological differences between denominations and magnifying them between denominations and peripheral groups known as sects and cults.

Evelyn A. Kirkley

See also RELIGION, FREEDOM OF.

FREEDOM
Freedom is a central value in the Western liberal democratic tradition that has been promoted to secure individual liberty, not public justice. The dominant ethical tradition in the West has appropriated the assumption of liberalism that the individual moral agent is free and self-directing.

This assumption that freedom and liberty is part of the human condition is challenged by moral agents who struggle to avoid the constraints and devastating effects of structural oppression. They recognize that such structures as social class, white supremacy, gender, and heterosexism, for example, work to give some a wider range of choices, while they restrict the choices of others. The struggle for survival and liberation of self, family, and community, not freedom to make a wide range of autonomous choices, is the major ethical category for those dominated by structural oppression.

Beyond survival, many view freedom or liberation as the achievement of shared resources and shared power. That is, those who struggle for liberation from oppression view freedom not only as self-direction and the ability to impact others. Rather, freedom also includes the security and openness to be profoundly influenced and changed by another, thereby enlarging the freedom of all to both give and receive. Freedom is sharing power and mutually reshaping society in the context of human/earth interdependence and community.

Mary E. Hobgood

See also DIGNITY; FAMILY; JUSTICE; RACISM; SEXISM; SOLIDARITY.

FREE WILL
Free will refers to the human faculty or capacity for free choice or free decision, that is, freely choosing or not choosing particular goods. As a translation of the Latin term *liberum arbitrium*, it is usually distinguished from related concepts like freedom, voluntariness, and deliberation.

The meaning of the phenomenon (and reference of the term) of free will has been fiercely debated in Western philosophy and theology particularly around the issue of the relationship between free will and God's action (grace or providence).

For classical Greek philosophers, the issue centered on the relationship between human choices (and actions) and providence or cosmic order. For Christian thinkers, most notably Augustine of Hippo, the problem was reconciling salvation as God's free gift with the human person's responsibility for sin. How can human beings be held accountable for sin if they do not have free will? But how can God's freedom as the cause of salvation and holiness be maintained if the human person could simply choose the supreme good as an act of free will (cf. Pelagius)?

Thomas Aquinas sought to resolve the matter by distinguishing the objects of free will to be finite (limited) goods, and that the human being is not free with respect to an infinite good (that would compel choice). With this in mind, a person does not enjoy genuine or complete freedom unless he or she is directed toward the actual supreme good.

Reformers emphasized the grace of God in salvation and thus flirted with theories suggesting that some people are predestined for grace and others not. The Reformers were reacting to tendencies in the Roman Catholic tradition toward assigning salvational merit to specific kinds of religious acts.

Several modern philosophers have sought to illustrate the strict determinism of human choices by identifying preceding feelings and emotions as compelling choice.

Michael J. Hartwig

See also ELECTION (DOCTRINE OF); GRACE; JUSTIFICATION; PREDESTINATION (IN CHRISTIANITY); TRADITION.

FREIRE, PAULO (1921–97)

Born in Recife, Brazil, Paulo Freire experienced as a boy the effects of extreme poverty and sociopolitical oppression and came to see how the educational system of his country prevented the oppressed from raising their voices against injustice. Through formal study of the history and philosophy of education (he received a doctorate in 1959) and, even more important, years of practical experience teaching literacy in Recife, he developed a "pedagogy of the oppressed" through which illiterate adults both learned to read and to understand the structural causes of the oppression they suffered. Considered a threat to the established order by Brazil's military government, Freire was jailed in 1964 and then exiled from his country. He then took his educational method to Chile, Harvard University in the United States, and to the Office of Education of the World Council of Churches in Geneva. At the heart of Freire's approach is the conviction that all human beings—no matter how submerged in the "culture of silence"—are capable of becoming Subjects who determine their own future. Early proponents of liberation theology and Latin America's "basic ecclesial communities" made creative use of his ideas. Freire developed these ideas most completely in *Pedagogy of the Oppressed* (1968) and *Education for Critical Consciousness* (1973).

James B. Nickoloff

FREUD, SIGMUND (1856–1939)

Often called the "Father of Psychoanalysis," Sigmund Freud was the first to examine scientifically the unconscious mind. For most of his life, Freud lived and worked in Vienna, Austria, where he began a career in biological research, but turned to clinical practice in order to support his family. In 1900 he presented a comprehensive exposition of the new science of psychoanalysis in *The Interpretation of Dreams.*

Freud wrote four influential books on religion: *Totem and Taboo* (1913), *The Future of an Illusion* (1927), *Civilization and Its Discontents* (1930), and *Moses and Monotheism* (1939). He believed that religious beliefs are "nothing but psychology projected into the external world," and are rooted in "the longing for the father" who protected the child in infancy. Since Freud understood religious beliefs to be based not on reality but on unconscious wishes and guilt, he judged religion to be dangerous to society and harmful to individuals.

Helen deLaurentis

See also ERIKSON, ERIK H.; FROMM, ERICH; JUNG, CARL GUSTAV.

FRIARS

The word "friar" comes from the Latin word *frater*, meaning brother, and refers to those religious orders that sprang up in the thirteenth century dedicated to personal and corporate poverty, to membership in a universal religious organization, and to a life in the world. Friars are also referred to as "mendicants" or beggers, since they were meant to beg for their livelihood. In the early years of the friars, this was taken quite literally, but later practice defined begging in the larger sense of what now might be called "fundraising." The friars started as lay folk who took private vows of poverty and started to wander the countryside preaching. This was an entirely new experiment in Christian living, although the people themselves would have understood their lives as an imitation of the life of Christ and his disciples. Quite soon, orders were written for most of these groups, and some gained approval. Others, like the Waldensians, split off from ecclesiastical authority and were considered heretical. This way of life was very attractive, and the number of groups of friars grew tremendously in the thirteenth century. Friars are to be distinguished from monks. Monks take a vow of personal poverty, but the monastery to which they belong does not. The monastery can own land or other wealth. The monk's allegience is to his individual monastery, rather than to a worldwide order. Monks in general also stay within the monastery walls rather than preaching in the world, as friars are likely to do. There were at least nine orders of friars in 1274 when the Second Council of Lyons ruled that no new medicant orders were to be formed. Full approval was finally attained for four orders of friars, the Franciscans, the Dominicans, the Carmelites, and the Augustinian Friars. All four orders are still active today, and still treasure their adherence to the ideals of poverty, universal mission, and preaching in the world.

Gary Macy

See also CARMELITES; DOMINICANS; FRANCISCANS; MEDIEVAL CHRISTIANITY (IN THE WEST); MEDIEVAL CHURCH; MONASTICISM IN WESTERN CHRISTIANITY; ORDERS (RELIGIOUS); POVERTY (RELIGIOUS VOW); WALDENSIANS.

FRIES, HEINRICH (1911–98)

German Catholic theologian. Fries was professor of fundamental theology at Tübingen and later at Munich. His interests in the philosophy of religion, in the theology of revelation, in ecumenism, and ecclesiology have made him a dominant figure in the post–Vatican II renewal of theology in Germany. His works, such as *Bultmann, Barth and Catholic Theology*

(1967) and *Unity of the Church: An Actual Possibility*, show a sensitivity to ecumenical thought. He was an astute observer of the internal struggle for renewal after Vatican Council II as in *Suffering from the Church: Renewal or Restoration?* (1985). Fries' work can be found in the theological encyclopedias for which he served as collaborator and editor, for instance, *Lexikon für Kirche and Theologie* and *Sacramentum Mundi*.

Patricia Plovanich

FROMM, ERICH (1900–80)

Erich Fromm grew up in an orthodox Jewish family in Frankfurt, Germany, and moved from Nazi Germany to New York City in 1934. He was a psychoanalyst, philosopher, and anthropologist who emphasized the role of culture in the formation of personality. Fromm defines religion broadly, as "any system of thought and action shared by a group." He distinguishes two types of religion: the humanistic and the authoritarian. The prevailing mood of humanistic religion is one of joy, and it emphasizes the believer's capacities for thinking and feeling. It understands God to be a symbol of the person's higher self, of what a person ought to become. Authoritarian religion emphasizes surrender in obedience to a power that transcends humankind, regardless of that power's moral qualities.

Helen deLaurentis

See also ERIKSON, ERIK H.; FEUERBACH, LUDWIG; FREUD, SIGMUND; MARX, KARL.

FRUITS OF THE SPIRIT

The phrase "fruits of the Spirit" refers to a passage in Paul's letter to the Galatians in the New Testament. In Galatians 5:19-23, Paul contrasts the "works of the flesh," impurity, idolatry, jealousy, anger, envy, fornication, and drunkenness, among others, with the "fruits of the spirit": love, joy, peace, patience, kindness, generosity, faithfulness, gentleness, and self-control. According to Paul, the lives of those who live in Jesus the Christ and guided by the Holy Spirit reap this fruit.

Among Pentecostal Christians, fruits of the Spirit also refer to the manifestations of the Holy Spirit. Pentecostals believe that the new apostolic age has dawned, the New Testament church restored, and the second coming of Christ imminent. Church history between the first and the twentieth centuries is effectively erased. Therefore, following Acts 2, Pentecostals believe that Christians undergo two baptisms. The first is the baptism in Jesus Christ and acknowledges receipt of the gift of salvation. The second is baptism in the Holy Spirit that manifests in "entire sanctification," or perfectionism in the believer. After the second baptism, the believer is not flawless, but has a will so completely aligned with God's that he or she no longer engages in intentional sin. Pentecostals further believe that sanctification results in all the gifts, or fruits, of the Holy Spirit as listed in Galatians 5 and 1 Corinthians 12 and 14. In addition to the fruits listed above, these gifts include healing, prophesying, preaching, and most importantly, speaking in and interpreting tongues.

Speaking in tongues, or glossolalia, is the hallmark of Pentecostalism and the most distinctive fruit of the Holy Spirit. Glossolalia recalls the experience of Christ's disciples in Acts 2 when they heard the sound of rushing wind, felt sparks of fire touch them, and suddenly, filled with the power of the Holy Spirit, had the ability to speak in unknown tongues. Pentecostals believe that through the Holy Spirit, Christians once again receive the gift of tongues in the context of worship through a trance-like state. Since tongues is an unrecognizable language, another person in the worship service is given the gift of interpreting the message. The fruits of the Spirit are the basis of numerous Pentecostal denominations, including the Church of God in Christ, the Pentecostal Holiness Church, the Church of the Foursquare Gospel, and the Assemblies of God. Moreover, they have influenced Protestant and Catholic Churches through charismatic renewal.

Evelyn A. Kirkley

See also ASSEMBLIES OF GOD; GLOSSOLALIA; PENTECOSTALISM.

FUCHS, ERNST (1903–83)

This German New Testament scholar, a student of Rudolf Bultmann, taught New Testament first in Berlin (1955) and then in Marburg (1961–70). In the 1950s, together with Gerhard Ebeling, another student of Bultmann's, Fuchs became the initiator of a movement that came to be called the "New Hermeneutic." Influenced both by Bultmann and by the philosophy of Martin Heidegger, this "New Hermeneutic" of Fuchs and Ebeling paid close attention to the functions of language. Grounded in being itself, and not only in thought, language communicates reality. The language of biblical texts, as the Word of God, challenges readers to acquire a new level of insight, to arrive at a new understanding of their existence. In this way, Fuchs argued, the text functions as a "language event" (Sprachereignis).

Fuchs is also known for his contribution to the post-Bultmannian "New Quest" for the historical Jesus (see his Studies of the Historical Jesus [London: SCM Press,

1964]), emphasizing the significance of Jesus' conduct as the key to his self-understanding as God's eschatological representative. Fuchs found in Jesus' table fellowship with marginalized members of society the lived expression of God's redemptive will in action.

Jean-Pierre Ruiz

See also BULTMANN, RUDOLF; EBELING, GERHARD; HEIDEGGER, MARTIN; HERMENEUTICS; JESUS OF HISTORY.

FUCHS, JOSEF (1912–2005)

A German moral theologian and a member of the Society of Jesus (Jesuits). Fuchs' influence was most notable while he taught at the Pontifical Gregorian University in Rome from the 1950s on. Fuchs elaborated a more historical understanding of natural law, a theory of compromise in moral decision making, and a concept of fundamental option. He laid important foundations for much of the reform of moral theology represented in Vatican Council II and consequent pastoral pronouncements.

Michael J. Hartwig

FUNDAMENTALISM (ATTITUDE)

Fundamentalism is a mindset that manifests itself in a variety of movements within Christianity, Islam, Judaism, and other religions. It is a ideology founded on the presupposition that modernity is a threat to selected "fundamental" principles, social structures, and values presumed to be divinely established and disclosed in a literal reading of selected sacred texts. By avoiding the ambiguities that stem from the critical methods of interpretation that emerged since the Enlightenment, fundamentalism provides an alternative vision that fortifies its adherents against the profound moral, social, economic, and political dilemmas of the contemporary pluralistic world. It often manifests as an aggressive commitment to reshaping the religious, social, and political orders to conform to the selected "fundamentals" that have been retrieved and refined from the past, and are linked together with unprecedented truth claims and even doctrinal innovations.

Regina A. Boisclair

FUNDAMENTALISM (CHRISTIAN HISTORICAL MOVEMENT)

Fundamentalism has been defined by historian George Marsden as "militantly anti-modernist Protestant evangelicalism"; he has also called a fundamentalist "an evangelical who is angry about something." While one definition is slightly more precise than the other, both express fundamentalism's core: it is oppositional Evangelicalism. Fundamentalism emerged in the United States in the late nineteenth century among Protestant evangelicals troubled by contemporary social and intellectual developments. Urbanization, immigration, industrialization, and modern technology challenged evangelical control of U.S. institutions and indicated creeping secularization. More significantly, Darwinism and higher criticism of the Bible questioned evangelical assumptions of creation by divine fiat in seven twenty-four-hour days and the reliability and truthfulness of the Scriptures.

While some evangelicals believed Christianity could accommodate these developments, some believed they could not accept these changes without violating the essentials of the faith. They rejected Darwinism and biblical criticism as incompatible with true Christianity, and asserted the inerrant, literal truth of the Scriptures. In making this assertion, they were not anti-intellectual rubes, but were grounded in an Enlightenment philosophy called Scottish Commonsense Realism. Fundamentalists were among the most educated and erudite evangelicals, including theologians and seminary professors like Charles Hodge and J. Gresham Machen. Fundamentalism was popularized, however, by revivalist Dwight Moody and through Bible study conferences.

Fundamentalism had three distinctive theological features: premillennial dispensationalism, holiness, and propositional understanding of the faith. First, fundamentalists viewed human history as divided into seven chronological dispensations, each characterized by a covenant relationship between humanity and God. In each dispensation, humans failed the covenant, and God was forced to punish them and start again with a new dispensation. Believing in the literal fulfillment of biblical prophecy, fundamentalists preach that humanity is currently living in the sixth dispensation that will end with the second coming of Christ, the rapture, and the cosmic battle between Christ and the forces of evil at Armageddon. After the second coming, Jesus will establish the kingdom of God on earth, inaugurating the millennium, a thousand years of peace and prosperity. Premillennial dispensationalism was promulgated in *The Scofield Bible* (1909).

Second, fundamentalists believed in holiness, the purification of the will through the mediation of the Holy Spirit. Fundamentalists believed in original sin, that humans could only overcome sin through supernatural means. After conversion assured the individual of salvation, a second conversion was necessary to free him or her from sin's power. This "second blessing" aligned the believer's will with God's and purged the urge to sin. Subsequently, the believer was perfect, not flawless, but perfectly sinless. Belief in holiness led to Pentecostalism, the practice of glossolalia or speaking tongues, which resulted from a second baptism in the Holy Spirit and the restoration of New Testament church norms. While not all fundamentalists were Pentecostalists, all Pentecostalists were fundamentalists.

Third, fundamentalists believed that the Christian faith was encapsulated in certain doctrinal propositions. One was a Christian through intellectual assent to these propositions, or fundamentals. The movement got its name after the 1910–5 publication of *The Fundamentals*, a twelve-volume series of pamphlets that outlined the irrefutable core of the faith, without which it was not Christian. Among these propositions were the virgin birth of Jesus, the reality of miracles, the substitutionary atonement, physical resurrection of Jesus from the dead, and the inerrancy of the Bible.

Fundamentalism led to heresy trials in Protestant seminaries and denominational divisions. Successfully expelling professors who did not teach the inerrancy of Scripture, fundamentalists appeared to maintain their strength until 1925 and the Scopes "monkey" trial in Dayton, Tennessee. State law prohibited teaching Darwinian evolution in public schools; John Scopes, a high school science teacher, was arrested and tried for violating the ordinance. The trial attracted national attention since the prosecuting attorney was four-time presidential candidate William Jennings Bryan, and counsel for the defense, well-known agnostic Clarence Darrow. The culmination of the trial was when Bryan allowed himself to be placed on the stand as an expert witness on the Bible, and Darrow humiliated him with questions on biblical contradictions and inconsistencies. Although Scopes was found guilty, the trial discredited fundamentalism as the belief system of uneducated, hayseed-chewing, Southern hicks.

For the next fifty years, fundamentalists faded from public view, organizing and strengthening the movement internally. Many departed mainline Protestant denominations to form their own, including the Presbyterian Church of America, Orthodox Presbyterian Church, and General Association of Regular Baptist Churches. They established strong seminaries and Bible institutes, the most important being Moody Bible Institute in Chicago, Fuller Theological Seminary in Pasadena, California, Westminster Theological Seminary in Philadelphia, and Dallas Theological Seminary. Seizing the possibilities of mass media, they bought radio and television stations. In 1941 they formed the American Council of Christian Churches. Yet, despite their cooperation, fundamentalists experienced internal conflicts over premillennial dispensationalism, Pentecostalism, ecumenism, and separatism. Without an external threat, they were constantly in danger of fragmentation.

In the 1970s, fundamentalism burst on the public scene with new vigor. Hal Lindsey's 1970 bestseller *The Late Great Planet Earth* utilized premillennial dispensationalism to predict the end of the world through the fulfillment of biblical prophecy in the Soviet Union and Eastern Europe. With the election of Jimmy Carter to the presidency, *Newsweek* magazine proclaimed 1976 the "Year of the Evangelical." The "electronic church," also known as televangelism, brought fundamentalism and Evangelicalism into homes through the ministries of Oral Roberts,

Jim Bakker, Jimmy Swaggart, and Pat Robertson. In 1979 fundamentalists seized control of the largest Protestant denomination in the United States, the Southern Baptist Convention.

More importantly, in the same year, Jerry Falwell, a Baptist pastor in Lynchburg, Virginia, founded the Moral Majority to harness fundamentalist political power. Believing that the United States had strayed from God's will, the Moral Majority urged a return to traditional, "family values." It advocated nuclear heterosexual families, stay-at-home mothers, school prayer, and teaching scientific creationism in public schools. It opposed abortion, feminism, and lesbian/ gay rights. The Moral Majority was the germ of the Religious Right of the 1980s and 1990s.

In the 1990s, fundamentalism showed no sign of abating, despite setbacks with sex scandals of televangelists Jim Bakker and Jimmy Swaggart in the 1980s. Expanding beyond Protestantism to attract charismatic and pro-life Catholics, fundamentalism has focused on its political agenda through the Christian Coalition and other organizations collectively known as the Religious Right. Their methods may have changed, but their original impulse remains the same: vehement opposition to what they perceive as modern, secular incursions on the authentic Christian Gospel.

Evelyn A. Kirkley

See also DISPENSATIONALISM; EVANGELICALS; EVANGELICAL THEOLOGY; GLOSSOLALIA; MILLENARIANISM; PENTECOSTALISM; RAPTURE (IN AMERICAN PROTESTANTISM).

FUNDAMENTAL OPTION

This theory refers to the human person's basic disposition for or against God. Most often associated with Karl Rahner's theology of the human person, it presupposes the existence of a radical freedom for self-disposition before God distinct from (although not independent of) concrete freedom of choice. This exercise of basic freedom before God is not entirely accessible to conscious reflection; nonetheless, it is a decision mediated by any concrete, moral choice.

Fundamental option theory has important implications for Roman Catholic understandings of sin and the possibility of intrinsically evil actions. This theory suggests that a transgression is mortal, or a serious offense against God, insofar as it engages the agent's core freedom rather than equating mortal sin primarily with the seriousness of the action. If core freedom is not engaged, or is compromised in some way, an objectively immoral action would not affect the subject's fundamental option in a definitive way. Fundamental option theory, then, emphasizes the priority of the goodness or badness of the moral agent over the goodness or badness of particular actions. This theory has been criticized in the encyclical *Veritatis Splendor* for unduly separating the moral agent's concrete actions in history and his or her ultimate relationship with God. The accuracy of this criticism has been challenged by those who point out that the fundamental option can only be determined by concrete actions, actions that genuinely engage the agent's freedom.

Brian F. Linnane, S.J.

See also MORAL THEOLOGY/CHRISTIAN ETHICS; PROPORTIONALISM; SIN, PERSONAL; VERITATIS SPLENDOR.

FUNDAMENTAL THEOLOGY

Also sometimes referred to as "foundational theology," fundamental theology is the term given to the successor of "apologetics" in some contemporary schemas of the theological sciences. As a prolegomenon to historical and systematic theology that focuses on a specific religious tradition, fundamental theology addresses those questions about God and/or religion that in principle transcend each specific religious tradition; for example, the condition of the possibility of religion and religious belief, through the use of evidence and warrants relatively independent of the scriptural or dogmatic tradition of a specific religion. In this task, fundamental theology serves to establish the terms, relations, and axioms that set the parameters for systematic theology.

Substantively, the agenda of questions of fundamental theology usually differs little from that of "philosophy of God" or "philosophy of religion." (Whether fundamental theology converges with one or the other varies in a given case according to whether the horizon of relevant data is restricted to the Semitic religious traditions or includes these together with the Indian and Chinese religions.) Functionally, fundamental theology differs from philosophy of God or philosophy of religion in that it is an enterprise subordinate to the overall *telos* of theological science, for example, the explication of the contemporary intellectual and practical meaning of a specific religious tradition.

J. A. Colombo

See also METHOD IN THEOLOGY; PHILOSOPHICAL THEOLOGY; PHILOSOPHY OF RELIGION.

G

GADAMER, HANS-GEORG (1900–2002)

German philosopher. A seminal figure in contemporary hermeneutics, Gadamer's work is a response to the historicist trend of eighteenth- and nineteenth-century hermeneutics, that is, the understanding of hermeneutics as the "method" of the human sciences that seeks to reconstruct the past through the suppression of the interpreter's present subjectivity. Building on Martin Heidegger's fundamental ontology and Edmund Husserl's work on the "life-world," Gadamer reformulates hermeneutics to denote the pre-reflective "understanding" of human beings-in-the-world that is the condition of the possibility of explicit, reflective, methodical interpretation of texts, and so on, and rearticluates the task of the latter in light of the former. Among the basic themes of Gadamer's hermeneutics, delineated in his magnum opus *Wahrheit und Methode* (*Truth and Method*) are the linguistic character of understanding and existence, the importance of "prejudice" as defining both the historicity and possibility of understanding, the goal of hermeneutics as a achieving a "fusion of horizons" between the past and present, and the autonomy of meaning from its authorial intention.

Gadamer's hermeneutics has been criticized both by those who object to the social conservatism and elitism of its claim to universality, for example, Jürgen Habermas, as well as by those who argue that the meaning of texts is governed by their authors' intentions, for example, E. D. Hirsch.

J. A. Colombo

See also HERMENEUTICS.

GALILEA, SEGUNDO (1928–)

Chilean Catholic theologian, ordained a priest in 1956, Galilea has been very active and influential in training hundreds of Latin American pastoral agents in theology and ministry, and in reflecting on Christian themes from the perspective of pastoral reality. He has lived and taught in his native Chile, and in Ecuador, Colombia, Mexico, and Cuba. In the United States, he has worked in the theological and pastoral formation of Latinos in the northeast. Influenced by liberation theology, his theological writings show his interest in ministry to the poor and in a spirituality that responds to their needs. He was among the first contemporary Latin American theologians to reflect on popular Catholicism. From among his many books a few stand out: *Para una pastoral latinoamericana* (1968), *Evangelización en América Latina* (1970), and especially *Religiosidad popular y pastoral* (1979).

Orlando Espín

See also CULTURE; EVANGELIZATION; INCULTURATION; LATIN AMERICAN CATHOLICISM; LATIN AMERICAN THEOLOGIES; LATINO/A; LATINO CATHOLICISM; LIBERATION THEOLOGIES; MINISTRY/MINISTERIAL; POPULAR CATHOLICISM; SPIRITUALITY.

GALLICAN ARTICLES

In 1682 an assembly of the French clergy adopted four articles, composed principally by Bishop Jacques Bossuet, in which the autonomy of the French church was affirmed in several ways. These "Gallican" articles asserted: (1) the pope does not have dominion have over temporal affairs; subjects may not be dispensed by the pope from allegiance to a sovereign; (2) a council of bishops, not the pope, is the highest authority in the church; (3) traditional Gallican (= French) liberties may not be taken away; (4) papal decisions are not definitive unless approved by a council.

There was both a specific and a more general context for this declaration of the French clergy. In the 1680s, King Louis XIV was engaged in a dispute with the papacy concerning the revenues of dioceses awaiting appointment of new bishops. Both the monarchy and the papacy coveted such revenues, for the gain could be considerable in the case of a long vacancy in a wealthy diocese. The less immediate setting for the Gallican Articles was ongoing debate about the relationship between pope and council. Since the early fifteenth century, when the Council of Constance (1414–8) affirmed its superiority to the papacy, this question had been actively debated in the church. The Council of Trent (1545–63) avoided taking a

position on the question and the debate continued in the church after Trent.

In the 1690s, however, Pope Alexander VIII was successful in forcing both Louis XIV and the French clergy to withdraw the four articles. Despite this victory for papal power, the French church, in the eighteenth century and beyond, continued to affirm its national traditions, independence, and liberty.

Thomas Worcester, s.j.

See also BOSSUET, JACQUES BÉNIGNE; CONCILIARISM; ECCLESIOLOGY; GALLICANISM; TRENT, COUNCIL OF.

GALLICANISM

Opposite of Ultramontanism, this tendency in the French church emphasizes national autonomy rather than subordination of the local church to papal authority. The Gallican Articles of 1682 are a good example of Gallican perspectives, but the inclination of the church in France to highlight its particularity and autonomy was already pronounced in earlier periods. Distinction is often made between royal and episcopal Gallicanism: the former provided for control of the French church by the king; the latter affirmed the dignity and authority of bishops apart from the papacy.

With the sixteenth century, a new agreement governed the relationship of the French church to Rome. In 1516 King Francis I and Pope Leo X signed the Concordat of Bologna. This provided for royal nomination and papal confirmation of appointments of bishops and abbots in France. As long as the monarchy respected certain criteria, it could expect papal sanction for its choices. Those appointed as bishops of dioceses or abbots of monasteries tended to come from prominent families allied with the sovereign.

The king thus had considerable control of the church through jurisdiction over appointments.

Controversy with Rome continued, however, with resistance to formal reception of the canons and decrees of the Council of Trent. Whereas in many Catholic states Trent was given the force of civil law, in France only the clergy, not the monarchy or the state, accepted Trent. Resistance to Rome was also an important part of the Jansenist movement.

After the French Revolution had nearly destroyed the church, Napoleon made peace with the papacy in 1801. Napoleon, however, made of the French clergy state bureaucrats, paid by the government, but also under state control. As the nineteenth century progressed, Ultramontanist voices gained strength in France and elsewhere, with Gallicanism fighting a losing battle to preserve traditional autonomy or liberty. The First Vatican Council of 1869–70, with its affirmation of papal infallibility under certain circumstances, rejected outright many Gallican principles. The Second Vatican Council of 1962–5, through its promotion of episcopal collegiality, may have pointed the way to a renewal of local autonomy in the church.

Thomas Worcester, s.j.

See also CONCILIARISM; D'AILLY, PIERRE; ECCLESIOLOGY; FEBRONIANISM; GALLICAN ARTICLES; GERSON, JOHN; JANSENISM; ULTRAMONTANISM; VATICAN, FIRST COUNCIL OF THE; VATICAN, SECOND COUNCIL OF THE.

GALUT
See DIASPORA.

GAMALIEL
The name of a number of important rabbinic authorities in the first centuries C.E.

Gamaliel I, known as Gamaliel haZaqen ("the elder"), was a grandson of Hillel and patriarch of the Jewish community in the land of Israel at the beginning of the first century C.E. His grandson, Gamaliel II, also known as Gamaliel of Yavneh, succeeded to the patriarchate in about 80 C.E. He was one of the greatest authorities of his generation and is a frequently cited, central authority in the Mishnah. Later bearers of the name Gamaliel, active through early Talmudic times, were not as influential as these two. The name Gamaliel without further elaboration normally refers to Gamaliel II. The Gamaliel at Acts 5:24 and 22:3 is apparently Gamaliel I, although the historical veracity of the New Testament accounts is debatable.

Alan J. Avery-Peck

GANDHI, MOHANDAS K. (1869–1948)
Perhaps the most important figure behind India's struggle to gain independence from British colonial rule, Mohandas Karamchand Gandhi was at the same time a spiritual leader and a social reformer. Better known by the title Mahatma (Sanskrit, Great Soul), Gandhi combined in his life and thought the spirituality and ascetic ethos of Hinduism, the non-violence (*ahimsa*) of Jainism, and Western ethical concerns for social justice, to forge his method of peaceful political and social change, which he called *satyagraha*.

First working out his ideas of non-violent resistance while fighting for the rights of the Indian population in South Africa, Gandhi returned to India and took up the struggle for his country's independence. At the same time, he fought for the removal of the injustices of the Hindu caste system and championed the rights of the untouchables. Much of his power to influence India's masses came from the fact that he identified himself with them in his simple manner of dress and diet, and his otherwise frugal lifestyle. He became recognized in the popular mind as a saint who embraced Hinduism, Islam, Christianity, and other religions with equal respect. Gandhi is also known for his defense of the rights of women and his concern—as an alternative to the destructive industrialism that he saw overtaking the West—for reviving India's localized, village economic structure. The latter dimension of his thinking became graphically manifest in his adoption of the traditional handheld spinning wheel as the symbol of his movement. Gandhi was much distressed by the violence that followed India's independence in 1947. He was assassinated in 1948 by a right-wing Hindu who, it seems, thought he was too sympathetic to Muslims. Although India has thought it expedient not to follow Gandhi's principles of nonviolence, Gandhi remains a much revered figure. His influence on movements for peace and social justice worldwide has been profound.

Lance E. Nelson

See also AHIMSA; CASTE; CASTES, SCHEDULED; HINDUISM; JAINISM; SATYAGRAHA.

GANESHA

An extremely popular Hindu deity, Ganesha is known especially for his elephant's head and large potbelly. The son of Shiva and Parvati, Ganesha is revered by Hindus as the god of successful beginnings, who removes obstacles in the way of any undertaking. Thus, Ganesha's image will often be the first one encounters when entering a Hindu temple, and many Hindu rituals begin with an invocation to Ganesha, asking for his blessings to ensure the success of the rite. Hindus who are moving into a new house, starting a business, or undertaking any similar project, will typically ask for Ganesha's help to ensure the success of the new venture.

Lance E. Nelson

See also DEVA/DEVI; HINDUISM; PARVATI; SHIVA.

GARDEN OF EDEN

(Hebrew, *Gan Eden*). In Genesis 2:8–3:24, this is the original place created by God for human habitation. Here Adam and Eve were created and lived until they disobeyed God's command not to eat the fruit of the tree of the knowledge of good and evil that led to their being banished. The utopian setting of the Garden of Eden thus is contrasted with the current, hostile human world, in which people toil, endure pain in childbirth, and experience death. In later Jewish tradition, the term Garden of Eden is synonymous with paradise.

Alan J. Avery-Peck

See also SIN, ORIGINAL.

GATHAS

A collection of seventeen hymns attributed to Zoroaster, the *Gathas* are the most sacred portion of the Avesta, the scripture of Zoroastrianism. Arranged in five groups, the *Gathas* are composed in an archaic dialect of Old Iranian and reflect a personal relationship with God (Ahura Mazda), a strong ethical concern, and a conspicuous eschatological orientation, all of which distinguish them from the remaining texts of the Avesta that tend to evoke a sacrificial, polytheistic religious ethos similar to that of the *Rig Veda*, to which they are closely related.

Lance E. Nelson

See also AHURA MAZDA; ARYAN; AVESTA; VEDAS; ZOROASTER; ZOROASTRIANISM.

GAUDIUM ET SPES

This Vatican II document, The Pastoral Constitution on the Church in the Modern World, the last document promulgated by the Second Vatican Council on December 7, 1965, is usually referred to by the first two words of the Latin text, *Gaudium et Spes* ("The joys and hopes"). In the Introduction to this "pastoral constitution," the council recognizes the church's duty to scrutinize the "signs of the times" (a phrase found in Matt 16:3, frequently used by Pope John XXIII, and a byword in the postconciliar Catholic Church) and to interpret them in the light of the Gospel. Such "signs" include the intellectual, psychological, moral, and religious changes contemporary people are experiencing and the hope and anguish such changes cause. Part I of the document sets forth the church's teaching on the meaning of human existence in the contemporary world and the role of the church and of Catholics in that world, both grounded in the fundamental dignity of the human person. In Part II, *Gaudium et Spes* takes up "some problems of special urgency" such as marriage and the family, the development of culture, socioeconomic life, modern politics, and the establishment of peace in the world. Though not a "dogmatic constitution" that defines immutable doctrine (such as *Lumen Gentium* on the nature of the church, or *Dei Verbum* on divine revelation), *Gaudium et Spes* does offer an authoritative summary of the tradition of Catholic social teaching. It also provided the springboard for further developments of social teaching by Popes Paul VI and John Paul II, by regional and national conferences of bishops (such as those of Latin America and the United States), and by theologians in the years following Vatican II. In its attention to concrete problems faced by contemporary people and in its hopeful tone, *Gaudium et Spes* represents a unique document in the history of ecumenical councils of the Catholic Church. For the first time, such a council issued no anathemas (formal excommunications) against those who reject its positions. Instead, "inspired by no earthly ambition, the church seeks but a solitary goal: to carry forward the work of Christ himself under the lead of the befriending Spirit. And Christ entered this world to give witness to the truth, to rescue and not to sit in judgment, to serve and not to be served" (GS 3). If *aggiornamento* (Italian for "updating" or "modernization") defines the goal of the Second Vatican Council as a whole, *Gaudium et Spes* is perhaps the council's most characteristic statement.

James B. Nickoloff

See also COUNCIL, ECUMENICAL; JOHN XXIII, POPE; VATICAN, SECOND COUNCIL OF THE.

GAYATRI

The Gayatri is among the most revered *mantras*, or prayer formulas, of Hinduism. For many Hindus, it is the most sacred and most potent. Initiation as a twiceborn Hindu centers around a boy's introduction to this mantra in the *upanayana* rite, and males in the three higher caste categories are traditionally required to recite it daily during ritual prayer. In contemporary Hinduism, the Gayatri is revered and recited by women as well as men. A verse from the *Rig Veda* (3.62.10), the Gayatri is addressed to the Vedic sun god, Surya or Savitri. Hence it is also referred to as the Savitri. A prayer for inspiration (*dhi*) and illumination, the Gayatri translates roughly as follows: "We meditate on the effulgence of the god Savitri. May he enliven and enlighten our minds." In post-Vedic Hinduism, Gayatri came to be regarded as a goddess.

Lance E. Nelson

See also CASTE; HINDUISM; MANTRA; RIG VEDA; SAMSKARA (RITUALS); VEDAS.

GAY THEOLOGY

While the term "gay theology" may broadly be construed as encompassing a variety of biblical, historical, philosophical, ethical, and systematic theological studies that embody a positive valuation of same-sex desire, actions, persons and / or relations, the term more narrowly denotes a species of liberation theology, that is, a reflection on the meaning of the Christian tradition from the social location of a specific community of the oppressed —gay men and lesbians. Distinctive of such theologies are their immediate opposition to the present negative judgment of most Christian communities on same-sex desire, actions, and relations. Thus, familiar themes and motifs of liberation theology appear—the return to the historical (biblical) Jesus, emphasis on the praxis of doing-justice, base Christian communities as the leaven for a renewal and reform of the church, the hermeneutic privilege of the oppressed, and so forth—refracted through the experience of a community that is still the object of condemnation by the Christian churches.

J. A. Colombo

See also LIBERATION THEOLOGIES.

GEBARA, IVONE (1944–)

Brazilian liberation theologian and woman religious, Gebara is one of the most significant voices in contemporary ecofeminist movements. She is perhaps best known for the Vatican inquiry into her scholarship in the early 1990s, after her public favoring legalized abortion in Brazil. She was eventually silenced by the Vatican and forced to undergo two years of theological "re-education" in France. Gebara's theological reflection emerges from a commitment to the struggles of poor women. She links humanity's objectification and exploitation of nature with that of women, who are symbolically identified with nature. Undermining an anthropomorphic understanding of creation, Gebara argues for an inclusive vision of the cosmos as the center of Christian theology. Through her work with poor women in Brazilian slums, Gebara has developed an urban ecofeminist perspective that intertwines the concrete issues of urban daily life with ecofeminist concerns. Among her more important publications are *Longing for Running Water: Ecofeminism and Liberation* (1999) and *Out of the Depths: Women's Experience of Evil and Salvation* (2002).

Michelle González

See also ECOLOGY; FEMINISM; FEMINIST THEOLOGIES; LATIN AMERICAN THEOLOGIES; LIBERATION THEOLOGIES.

GEFFRÉ, CLAUDE (1931–)

French Catholic theologian, and member of the Dominican Order. His fundamental concern has been theological methodology and its philosophical justification. This has led him to study the effect of modern hermeneutics on theology and doctrine, as well as the complex relationship between faith, theology, and culture. His work has been very important for theologians of culture and hermeneutics, especially in Europe and in the Third World. Geffré has a long list of publications, but arguably his most influential ones have been *Humanisme et foi chrétienne* (1976), *Le christianisme au risque de l'interprétation* (1983), and *Théologie et choc des cultures* (1984).

Orlando Espín

See also CULTURE; DEVELOPMENT OF DOGMA/OF DOCTRINE; DOCTRINE; DOGMA; EPISTEMOLOGY; FAITH; HERME-NEUTICS; HISTORICAL CRITIQUE; INCUL-TURATION; METHOD IN THEOLOGY; MODERNITY; POSTMODERNITY.

GEHENNA

Originally, this term referred to a valley surrounding parts of Jerusalem (the Valley of Hinnom). In antiquity it was a place of human sacrifices, and consequently it was considered (by the Hebrews) a polluted place, associated with blood and punishment. Because of this history, Gehenna later came to be associated with a place of divine punishment of public sinners and of betrayers of Israel. In the New Testament it is used as a symbol for the place of final punishment of sinners, following later Jewish thought.

Orlando Espín

See also HELL; SALVATION.

GELASIUS I OF ROME (?–496)

Gelasius became pope around 492 and died in office in 496. In these few short years, Gelasius wrote several important letters setting forth the power of the patriarchs and especially the patriarch of Rome over against the claims of the emperor. Gelasius argued for the superiority of the sacerdotal realm over that of the secular in matters of faith and discipline.

Gelasius also took a strong stand against the remnants of Pelagianism, Manchaeism, and paganism in the Western church. Six theological treatises of Gelasius survive along with his many decretal letters.

Gary Macy

See also DECRETALS; MANCHAEISM; PATRIARCH; PELAGIANISM; POPE.

GEMARA
See TALMUD.

GEMILUT HASADIM
(Hebrew, acts of righteousness). In Judaism, the responsibility to act ethically, sympathetically, and kindly toward one's fellow human. Gemilut Hasadim normally are understood to encompass special acts of kindness, ranging from kindness to strangers and visiting the sick to giving charity. Mishnah Avot 1:2 designates Gemilut Hasadim one of the three pillars of Judaism, along with observing the Torah and fulfilling the obligations of the worship of God.

Alan J. Avery-Peck

GENDER
All people would agree that men and women are fundamentally, physically differentiated; and further, that these differences, in part, respond to God's command to "Be fruitful and multiply" (Gen 1:28), that is, to procreate and propagate humanity. People disagree, however, concerning the personal, interpersonal, and communal implications of sexual differentiation. Questions of gender derive primarily from the psychological, emotional, and sociological manifestations of sexual differentiation. It is from these considerations that gender attempts to respond to the question: What does it

mean to be male or female from the point of view of Christian tradition, Scripture, and contemporary society? Within the Christian tradition, the recognition and scientific investigation of the gender question is a relatively recent phenomenon that gives it both a positive and negative aspect. That the gender question is recognized as a legitimate subject of inquiry not only marks a dramatic break with "traditional," accepted views of men's and women's roles, but also makes possible new analysis and investigation. In this strength, however, lies its weakness. Since investigation and analysis are still in the early stages, there is a great deal of ambiguity in discerning the implications such studies have for understanding gender. Speculation and the accumulation of data from the empirical sciences such as psychology, sociology, and anthropology must be analyzed and interpreted not only in themselves, but in relation to Scripture and tradition to derive the implications of such studies for our understanding of what it means to be male or female.

The far-reaching implications of the investigation into the gender question can be seen in the issue of women's ordination as ministers/priests. Until quite recently, it was argued on the basis of Scripture and tradition that only males could be ordained. An argument ran as follows: All of Jesus' disciples were males; therefore, only males can be legitimate leaders within the Christian community. While the tradition of an exclusively male priesthood continues in the Greek Orthodox and Roman Catholic traditions, most Protestant religions recognize the validity of the ordination of women. And while Scripture and tradition derived from, and in the context of, a patriarchal society support the argument limiting ordination to males, it is highly debatable whether such an argument remains valid when removed from that context. Issues such as this highlight the importance of further investigating how gender differentiation will, or should, impact the (re)formation of doctrines, moral teachings, and perspectives within contemporary Christian communities.

Todd A. Salzman

See also ETHICS, SOCIAL; FEMINISM; FEMINIST THEOLOGIES; PATRIARCHY; WOMEN, ORDINATION OF.

GENEALOGY

A listing of ancestors and their descendents. Such a listing establishes the relationship and often the legitimacy of people separated by long periods of time. Most of the genealogies in the Pentateuch are ascribed to the Priestly source and function to connect the vignettes recorded about more central characters. Genesis 5, for example, connects the generations from Adam to Noah; Genesis 10 enumerates the descendants of Noah's sons after the Flood and asserts that it was from these groupings that the "nations of the earth branched out after the flood" (v. 32). Numbers 1 records a census purported to have been taken by Moses and Aaron of those men fit for military duty who came out of the land of Egypt (cf. Numbers 26).

The most obvious example of a genealogy in the New Testament occurs in Matthew 1. The chapter traces human history from Abraham to David, from David to the Exile, and from the Exile to the advent of Jesus. The genealogy serves to legitimize Jesus as a descendent of David and allows him therefore to have attributed to him the identity of the promised Messiah.

Alice L. Laffey

GENEALOGY OF JESUS

Genealogies, listings of ancestors of Jesus, are found in two of the four canonical Gospels, Matthew and Luke. There are more differences than similarities between them. For example, Matthew's goes back to Abraham, Luke's to Adam. Also, there is significant variation in the names included. Luke, for instance, has thirty-six names not mentioned in Matthew or the Old Testament. It is not the purpose of either genealogy to provide a historically accurate family record, but to underscore the unique importance of Jesus in God's salvific plan.

Matthew begins his Gospel with the genealogy of Jesus, tracing it, in ascending order, from Abraham to Joseph (Matt 1:1-17). This is a literary way to introduce Jesus, the central figure of the book, and to underscore his significance. To the reader, the genealogy says that if you want to understand Jesus, it is essential to know the story of the Old Testament as represented by the people mentioned. Structurally, the genealogy, divided into three parts of fourteen generations each, is not completely accurate historically since, for instance, five names have been omitted in the second part to arrive at the number fourteen.

The monotonous father-son pattern of the genealogy is broken up by the mention of David's title (king), by the mention of the Babylonian exile, and by the inclusion of five women (Tamar, Rahab, Ruth, Bathsheba the wife of Uriah, and Mary, Joseph's wife). The women are included either because there was something irregular, if not scandalous in their marital union, or they showed initiative in the role they played in God's plan. Notable, too, is the way Jesus is included, not as the son of Joseph, but as the child of Mary (Matt 1:16).

In Luke's Gospel the genealogy (Luke 3:23-38) comes at the end of the infancy narratives, the appearance of the Baptist, and the baptism of Jesus. Unlike Matthew, Luke follows a descending order, beginning with Jesus and going all the way back to "Adam, son of God." In all, there are seven (a sacred biblical number) times eleven names. Chronologically, Jesus begins the twelfth and last series, indicating that he is the culmination and fulfillment of a divine plan beginning with the creation of the first human being. Luke also utilizes the literary form of genealogy to show that Jesus is a descendant of David.

In Luke, in contrast with Matthew, Jesus is linked closely to Joseph, "He was the son (as was thought) of Joseph" (Luke 3:23).

John Gillman

See also ANNUNCIATION; INFANCY NARRATIVES; MARY OF NAZARETH.

GENTILES

Non-Jews, defined in Judaism as members of the nations of the earth with whom God did not initiate a covenant; who, therefore, are exempt from the commandments of Judaism. According to Judaism, Gentiles are, however, subject to God's rule and, depending upon their actions and behavior, receive salvation equally with Jews. While exempt from the Jewish *mitzvoth*, Gentiles are viewed by Judaism as subject to seven laws given by God to Noah. These require the creation of a legal system and prohibit idolatry, bloodshed, sexual sin, stealing, blasphemy, and eating a limb torn from a living animal. Especially in contemporary times, Jews recognize a category of people known as "righteous Gentiles" (*Hasidei Ummot HaOlam*), applied to non-Jews who, at great risk to their own lives, saved Jews from Nazi persecution during World War II.

Alan J. Avery-Peck

See also CONVERSION; ISRAEL, PEOPLE OF.

GENUFLECTION

The act of lowering oneself on one knee. The word comes from two Latin words: *genu* (knee) and *flectare* (to bend). In current Roman Catholic practice, one genuflects when passing before the eucharistic Bread or Wine, as a sign of reverence for the presence of Christ in the sacrament. The *General Instruction on the Roman Missal* notes three other times when the presider genuflects during Mass: after the elevation of the Host; after the elevation of the chalice; and before Communion (no. 233). Genuflecting, at first on two knees, did not originate as a sign of reverence for the eucharistic Presence, but as a tenth-century gesture for venerating the wood of the cross on Good Friday. "It was a short step from veneration of the cross to adoration of Christ present in the eucharist" (Leonard and Mitchell, 38). By the fourteenth century, this shift had begun to take hold.

Patrick L. Malloy

See also EUCHARISTIC PRAYER; TRANSUBSTANTIATION.

GERSON, JOHN (1363–1429)

John entered the University of Paris in 1377, earning his doctorate in theology in 1392. In 1395 John became chancellor of the university. As chancellor, he worked assiduously to bring an end to the Western Schism while also fostering a stronger spiritual life to counter the effects of the schism. He advocated conciliarism as a solution to the schism and supported the Council of Pisa in 1409. An important leader at the Council of Constance (1415–7), Gerson not only helped to end the schism through the election of the new pope, Martin V, but was also instrumental in the heresy trial of John Hus. Unable to return to Paris for political reasons, John retired to Lyons where he continued his interest in mysticism. One of his last acts was a written defense of Joan of Arc.

Gary Macy

See also BASLE-FLORENCE-FERRARA (COUNCILS OF); CONCILIARISM; HUS, JOHN; MEDIEVAL CHRISTIANITY (IN THE WEST); SCHISM, GREAT WESTERN.

GERUSHIN

In Judaism, the formal dissolution of matrimony through divorce. The husband alone has the legal right of divorce and, according to Talmudic law, can dissolve the marriage for any cause whatsoever, without the wife's needing to consent. Later Judaism restricted the husband's ability to a divorce his wife, holding by the eleventh century that a divorce could be finalized only with the wife's consent. Similarly, the right of the wife to force her husband to grant her a divorce increasingly was recognized.

Judaism does not view divorce as a sin but, rather, as an agreement made by the involved parties concerning their personal status. Accordingly, Judaism sees no need to establish guilt, and the parties themselves must agree to the terms of the settlement that only in the most extreme cases can be imposed by a religious court (*beit din*).

In Jewish law, the husband is explicitly granted the right to sue for divorce in a case in which the wife committed adultery or apostasy, acted immorally, refused sexual relations, was barren, had an incurable disease, or refused to live where he desired. Similarly, the wife's right to petition for divorce is recognized in cases in which the husband behaves immorally or cruelly, has a disease or disgusting occupation, is sterile, refuses to have sexual relations, becomes an apostate, fails to support the wife, or engages in crime. The court itself may impose a divorce when the partners are found to comprise a forbidden (for example, incestuous) relationship, when the wife engaged in adultery and the husband refused to sue for divorce, or when health reasons make cohabitation dangerous. In contemporary Judaism, these lists of reasons are largely irrelevant; a Jewish divorce generally is carried out as a consequence of the completion of a civil divorce.

The divorce itself is effected through a bill of divorce, called a "get" or "sefer keritot" ("document of separation"). In light of the serious nature of divorce, forms of this document may not be mass produced or prepared ahead of time. Rather, each *get* must be individually prepared by a scribe at the request of the husband and for the particular woman he wishes to divorce.

In contemporary Judaism, the religious divorce ceremony normally is conducted only after a civil divorce has been completed. In the Conservative and Orthodox movements, a Jew who has not received a Jewish divorce is not permitted to remarry in a religious ceremony, even if a civil divorce has been obtained. The Reform movement has dispensed with the process of *gerushin*, accepting the civil divorce as determinative of the status of the individuals.

Alan J. Avery-Peck

See also BEIT DIN; KETUBAH; MARRIAGE (IN JUDAISM).

GERUT
(Hebrew, "conversion"). The process through which a non-Jew becomes a member of the Jewish people and a practitioner of Judaism. Conversion to Judaism requires an appearance before a rabbinic court (*beit din*) that evaluates the potential proselyte's sincerity and questions him or her on knowledge of Jewish history, religious belief, and ritual. The conversion is finalized through circumcision (for men) and immersion.

In the Greco-Roman world, conversion of pagans to Judaism was commonplace. By contrast, under Christianity, conversion was outlawed and thus ceased almost entirely. Perhaps as a result, the Talmudic literature is divided on conversion: some authorities see proselytes as not truly Jewish and as potentially damaging to the integrity of the Jewish people; others view proselytes as especially loved by God, having come to Judaism through a personal decision rather than birth.

In contemporary times, especially in the United States, a marked increase in conversions to Judaism has occurred, frequently by non-Jews engaged to be married to Jews. Negative attitudes toward converts, referred to now as "Jews by choice," have declined. In the face of high rates of intermarriage and Jewish assimilation, the Reform and Conservative movements have developed programs to enhance the Jewish experience of converts and to encourage the non-Jewish spouses of Jews to consider conversion.

Alan J. Avery-Peck

See also BEIT DIN; CIRCUMCISION; CONVERSION; IMMERSION.

GHOSE, AUROBINDO (1872–1950)
More commonly known as Sri Aurobindo, Aurobindo Ghose was a Bengali Hindu who was educated in England and, after returning to India, spent time as a militant revolutionary fighting for the cause of India's independence from British rule. While serving time in a British prison as a result of his revolutionary activities,

Aurobindo took up the practice of yoga, which led to a profound religious experience. He eventually became one of twentieth-century India's most important religious leaders. Like many other Hindu spiritual teachers, he was regarded by his followers as a powerful guru and even an *avatara*. What especially distinguished Aurobindo from traditional Hindu thinkers, however, was his evolutionary conception of the cosmos, somewhat reminiscent of that of Teilhard de Chardin. He taught that human beings, and indeed matter and the very cosmos itself, were being progressively spiritualized, and that the practice of yoga could facilitate that process. Aurobindo wrote voluminously, earning a reputation for his mystic poetry as well as for his philosophical and exegetical works. In keeping with his vision of cosmic evolution toward a "life divine" on earth, he founded a utopian, international spiritual community, known as Auroville, in the French enclave of Pondicherry in South India.

Lance E. Nelson

See also AVATARA/AVATAR; GURU; TEILHARD DE CHARDIN, PIERRE.

GHOST DANCE

This ritual arose in the period following the defeat and removal to reservations of the Western Indians. It is most known for its connection with the tragedy that occurred at Wounded Knee Creek in 1890 among the Dakota. But, in fact, its origin can be traced to a series of visions received among the Paiute, beginning in the 1860s. There, a medicine man, Tavibo, and his son, Wovoka after him, saw visions of redemption coming from the Great Spirit. The essence of these centered on the emptying of Indian lands of the whites, and their return to the original inhabitants who could then resume their traditional life. It specifically preached a doctrine of nonviolence, adding that the transformation would take place in response to a new religion and the ritual that expressed its hope. The message was truly pathetic in light of the large numbers of people who had been lost in the Plains wars as the army worked to sequester the native peoples and avert danger to the increasing hordes of settlers. With the loss of their lands and the diminishment of their peoples (among whom should be noted the heavy loss of spiritual and military leaders), the very survival of the native Indians was at stake.

In a manner reminiscent of biblical history, the response to this urgent need was the prophetic voice. Consistent with their traditional ways, the word of prophecy was received in a vision—in this case, a vision that occurred in the form of a trance. Wovoka's description adheres to the time-honored initiation of a shaman, and he was received as such by those who came to find in him a word of healing and hope. So it was that spiritual leaders came from many points in the Plains, united by the plight that afflicted their people. Not all who came were convinced, but the Dakota believed and carried back to their people the requirements that the prophet assured would alleviate their misery.

The doctrine recommended a return to traditional ways, a putting away of all the material and cultural aspects of the whites, and an attempt to regain the high moral practice that had been the hallmark of traditional religious life. Along with these stipulations, the people were to celebrate a ritual honoring the dead and affirming their continued presence to the people. Inherent in this ritual act was the belief that it would hasten the return of the departed to rejoin their relatives upon a regenerated earth. Response to this was swift, to the dismay of the Indian agent at Pine Ridge, who misread the gathering of many Indians as a sign of preparation for war. The conditions on the reservation were so bad that a revolt would have been reasonable. His alertness drew the army to the reservation, and seeing this martial demonstration, many fled to the Badlands. This situation was intolerable to their military keepers, who tried to negotiate with them to return. History records the sad story of the interception of Big Foot's band at dawn on Wounded Knee Creek, the frightened skirmish that followed, and the indefensible massacre that ensued.

The Ghost Dance perished for the Dakota and many others at that point, though it continued in a much-diminished form elsewhere for a while. Because it is linked with the continuing travesty of treatment of Native Americans, it survived as tragic symbol, and has recently been revived by the Lakota medicine man Leonard Crow Dog. It is, in its present form, a statement of resistance to continuing injustice.

Kathleen Dugan

See also PROPHECY.

GIFTS OF THE SPIRIT

In speaking about the "branch" that will grow from the roots of Jesse, Isaiah describes a person endowed with the "spirit of the Lord." He then lists seven characteristics of that spirit (11:2-3). These have been taken to refer to the characteristics either of the Messiah, or of the whole remnant people of Israel, personified here.

Christian reflection has traditionally taken this passage to refer to the action of the Holy Spirit in Jesus, and then the gifts of the Holy Spirit for each believer. Thomas Aquinas, in considering these gifts, points out that these seven are sufficient for the complete sanctification of the person since four (wisdom, understanding, counsel, knowledge) apply to the intellective, and three (fortitude, piety, fear of the Lord) to the appetitive (will, desires, senses) dimension of the human person. Modern ethicists such as Paul Wadell, C.P., have recovered the Thomistic sense of the spiritual gifts as completions of the virtues.

We should also mention the "charismatic" gifts of the Spirit found throughout the Acts of the Apostles and the Epistles of Paul, but especially see 1 Corinthians 12 and 14. These include speaking in tongues, interpretation of tongues, healing, prophecy (sometimes called "the external gifts"), and discernment, knowledge, wisdom, and so on (sometimes called the "internal gifts").

G. Simon Harak, S.J.

See also FEAR OF GOD; FORTITUDE; HOLY SPIRIT; PIETY; WISDOM.

GILGAMESH, EPIC OF

Gilgamesh was one of the kings of ancient Erech, a city of Sumer (in southern Mesopotamia), and the hero of a complex of stories which range in date from the early dynastic period of Sumer to the time of the fall of Assyria. The Epic of Gilgamesh is made up of multiple episodes joined together into a collection that could cover up to twelve tablets. Copies and fragments of Gilagamesh are preserved from numerous sites from the ancient Near East in Sumerian, Akkadian, Hittite, and Hurrian. The epic is a composition that skillfully weaves together these originally separate episodes into a whole that explores the limits to which human beings are subject, such as death. The epic was widely known in the ancient Near East.

Russell Fuller

GILKEY, LANGDON (1919–2004)

Influential American Protestant theologian. Gilkey studied at Harvard and Columbia universities, and at Union Theological Seminary in New York. He taught at Vassar College and at Vanderbilt University before becoming a professor at the University of Chicago Divinity School (retiring in 1989). Gilkey's theological work dealt with the sciences, myth, and philosophical questions. Among his many important publications are *Maker of Heaven and Earth* (1959), the influential *Naming the Whirlwind: The Renewal of God Language* (1969), *Religion and the Scientific Future* (1970), and *Catholicism Confronts Modernity* (1975).

Orlando Espín

See also CULTURE; LIBERAL THEOLOGY; NIEBUHR, H. RICHARD; NIEBUHR, REINHOLD; SOCIAL GOSPEL.

GILSON, ETIENNE (1884–1978)

French philosopher and medievalist. Gilson studied with Lévy-Bruhl, Durkheim, and Bergson, and developed his interest in the Middle Ages through the study of Cartesian thought's medieval roots. His broad grasp of the era is evident in his studies of leading medieval thinkers, as in *The Philosophy of St. Bonaventure* (1938) and *The Christian Philosophy of St. Thomas Aquinas* (1956). He illuminated the era's root concepts in studies such as *Reason and Revelation in the Middle Ages* (1938) and *The Spirit of Mediaeval Philosophy* (1938). Gilson is credited with the discovery of the

dynamic character of Thomas Aquinas's concept of *esse* and of his existential interpretation of Aristotelian philosophy. He also considered the problem of philosophy's relationship to metaphysics and religion in *God and Philosophy* (1941) and *Being and Some Philosophers* (1949). He was a founder of the Institute of Medieval Studies in Toronto, Canada, the leading center of medieval studies in North America.

Patricia Plovanich

GLORY/GLORIFICATION

Glory is an important theological term derived from the Hebrew word *kabod*, meaning "importance" or "weight." The Bible uses the word glory to indicate that importance is a characteristic of oneself, another, or something. Old Testament texts most often associate "glory" with God. While glory is used in an active sense as a synonym for praise, worship, and adoration, the texts often use the term "glory" in a symbolic way to indicate a direct or intermediary form of God's visible manifestation to humans (Num 16:19, 42; Ps 102:16; Ezra 10:4). For example, on Mt. Sinai God's glory appears as a cloud and as fire (Exod 16:10; 24:16-17); glory is also the term associated with God's abiding presence in the tabernacle or the Temple (Exod 40:34; Num 20:6; Ps 24:7-20).

The New Testament continues to use the word glory in similar ways, especially for reference to visible manifestations of God (Luke 2:9; John 11:40; Acts 7:55; Rev 15:8). However, the term "glory" is also applied to Jesus in Luke's account of his transfiguration (9:32) in speaking of or alluding to the risen Christ (John 7:39; 12:16; Acts 3:13; 2 Cor 2:8; Heb 2:7, 9; 1 Pet 1:11; Rev 5:12-13) and in accounts of his Second Coming as Son of Man (Matt 24:30; 25:31; Mark 8:38; Luke 9:26; 21:27; Titus 2:13).

In the Gospel of John the word "glory" is a prominent term as one of the unifying themes of this Gospel. In the prologue, the fact that the Word became flesh is attested by the words "we have beheld his glory, glory as the only Son" (John 1:14; see also 17:24). Jesus' human existence is a manifestation of God's glory (John 13:31). He is glorified by God (12:28), as God is glorified in him (13:32; 14:13; 15:8), and by him (17:4). The glory of Jesus is manifested in his miracles (2:11; 11:14), but ultimately it is his death that John considers his hour of glorification (12:23; 17:1; see also 7:39).

After the experiences of the risen Lord ended, his followers came to sense that he had entered into the presence of God where he was exalted by God (Phil 2:9), and that he would remain with God until he came again in glory. Paul and John also spoke of the eschatological expectation that those who believe in Christ will ultimately participate in his glorification (John 17:22; Rom 5:2; 8:17, 30).

Regina A. Boisclair

GLOSSA ORDINARIA

Glossa ordinaria is Latin for "the ordinary commentary." The phrase can refer to any standard commentary on a set text, but usually refers to the commentary on the Vulgate version of the Bible compiled during the twelfth century. Although earlier material was used, the compilation seems to have begun in the cathedral school at Laon under the leadership of the theologians Anselm and Ralph of Laon and their students. The text of the glossa was written in the spaces between the lines of the biblical text (interlinear glosses), or along the margins of the page with the biblical text on it (marginal glosses). The glossa ordinaria had a core

text, but different authors added or subtracted from the commentary as they needed for teaching. It might be best to think of the gloss as lecture notes in the margins of the textbook to help the professor out in class. The glossa ordinaria on the Bible continued to be printed into the sixteenth century. There was also a "glossa ordinaria" on the Decretum of Gratian, the standard textbook for teaching canon law.

Gary Macy

See also GRATIAN; MEDIEVAL CHRISTIANITY (IN THE WEST); SCHOLASTICISM; VULGATE.

GLOSSOLALIA

From the Greek word for "chatter," glossolalia is the Christian practice of speaking in a mystical language known as tongues. It is the most distinctive characteristic of the Pentecostal movement that preaches the dawning of a new apostolic age in which the New Testament church and manifestations of the Holy Spirit are restored as on the day of Pentecost in Acts 2. As the disciples gathered in Jerusalem, a mighty wind rushed through the house, and sparks of fire rested on them. They were filled with the power of the Holy Spirit, and suddenly began preaching in languages they did not know, converting many from other regions and countries who heard the Gospel in their own native tongues. Pentecostals interpret this passage to mean that tongues is a spiritual language different from any known language.

The first modern manifestation of glossolalia occurred in 1901 in Topeka, Kansas, among students and faculty at a Bible institute founded by Charles Fox Parham. It spread across the country after the phenomenal success of the Pentecostal revival at the Apostolic Faith Gospel Mission on Azusa Street in Los Angeles led by William Seymour from 1906–9. In addition to glossolalia, Pentecostalism stresses faith healing, the fulfillment of prophecy, a literal reading of the Bible, and strict ethical and moral standards. Pentecostal denominations include the Church of God in Christ, the Pentecostal Holiness Church, the Church of the Foursquare Gospel, and the Assemblies of God. Moreover, glossolalia spread through Protestant and Catholic churches as part of charismatic renewal.

To most hearers, glossolalia sounds like mumbled gibberish or baby talk. It is usually spoken in the context of worship when a believer falls into a kind of trance. When one is given the gift of tongues, another present is given the gift of interpreting them for the edification of all present. Glossolalia is not intended to be solely a private, individual experience. Scholars have debated the phenomenon of glossolalia. Some claim it is an automatic motor response to external stimuli, while others describe it as a self-induced hypnotic state. Skeptics have claimed to effect glossolalia under ordinary circumstances. Persons experiencing glossolalia report heightened awareness and transformed consciousness. For them it is a mystical spiritual experience, impossible to analyze or explain.

Evelyn A. Kirkley

See also ASSEMBLIES OF GOD; FRUITS OF THE SPIRIT; PENTECOSTALISM.

GNOSIS/GNOSTICISM

Within the collection of movements that made up ancient Gnosticism, the Greek word *gnosis* was used to refer to "hidden" knowledge not accessible to most human beings. As used in biblical studies and the study of early Christianity, Gnosis refers to a religious and/or philosophical movement in the early centuries of the common era that came to rival Judaism and Christianity, and that eventually came to be viewed as heretical by church leaders. This movement or complex of movements is labeled by scholars Gnosticism. Gnosis refers to secret knowledge that, when fully assimilated, allowed each individual to realize his or her true self that Gnostics thought of as a "spark of the divine" imprisoned in the body. All varieties of Gnostics seem to have shared the following points in common.

(1) There is a true God, a transcendent being who is unknowable and utterly different and removed from the visible universe. The world was created by a lesser being usually called a demiurge, and in some varieties of Gnosticism is identified with the God of the Hebrew Scriptures.

(2) Each person's true self or identity is a "spark of the divine" that is immortal but trapped in the body and the world by the powers of this world.

(3) The self can only gain release and return to the divine, its true home, by receiving the gnosis and a divine call that awakes it to its true nature.

(4) This return to the divine may occur at the end of an individual's life or at the end of the world.

In Christianized Gnostic systems, gnosis and the divine call come from a Redeemer (= Christ) who has descended from heaven and delivered the gnosis and then returned to heaven. There seem to have been numerous Gnostic systems, many of which were referred to by the name of their founder by church fathers such as Irenaeus, Hippolytus, and Origen who argued against them. Most of our information about Gnostic beliefs and practices came from church fathers who wrote against them until the discovery in 1945–6 of a collection of Gnostic writings near the town of Nag Hammadi in Egypt. Since that discovery, our knowledge of Gnosticism has become more and more detailed, and these primary texts allow us to recognize the biases in our secondary sources.

Gnosticism had some influence on some of the writings of early Judaism and Christianity. Such ideas as the descent and ascent of the Redeemer, the revelation of gnosis, and the dualism of flesh and spirit are all ideas found in second-century Gnosticism and in the New Testament.

Russell Fuller

See also NAG HAMMADI.

GOD

Ultimately, every topic or question in Christian theology resolves itself into some form of a question about God, because God alone constitutes the proper subject matter of theology. Nonetheless, discourse about God in contemporary theology (and philosophy) is bounded by five distinct but often overlapping trajectories of questions or reflections: the plausibility of religion's claim to truth; the implications of the pluralism of religions; the coherence of classical (Christian) theism; the recovery of a specifically trinitarian Christian understanding of God; and the recognition of the "social location" of all discourse about God.

Plausibility of religion. Increasingly in the West since the Enlightenment, the question of God is inseparable from the question of whether or not the most adequate and appropriate interpretation of reality includes reference to a divine being. Historically, this question has taken the form of challenges to religion's claim to speak truthfully about the divine (God)

and attacks charging that the classical task of metaphysics—the elaboration of an ontotheology—is logical "nonsense" and therefore without meaning regarding states of affairs in the world. Both these challenges and responses to them have immediate relevance to the trio of questions, "Does God exist?" "What can be known about God?" and "What is the manner and epistemic status of 'talk about God.'"

Pluralism of religions. Increasingly in the twentieth century, Christian theologians have come to recognize that the "other" religions are not simply "false religions," "superstitions," "manifestations of idolatry," and so forth. The manifest difference, however, in the material content of the world religions' talk about the divine—Hinayana Buddhism's understanding of nirvana, the impersonal Tao in Taoism, the multitude of gods and goddesses in Hinduism—has thrown into stark relief both the historicality and cultural relativity of traditional Christian discourse about "God" and consequently Christianity's traditional claim to be the "absolute" religion or final revelation. Indeed, such a trajectory of questions calls into question the self-evidence that talk about the divine is necessarily talk about a personal divine being at all.

Coherence of classical theism. The synthesis of Greek philosophy and biblical traditions called "classical theism" still remains the fullest, dominant explication of the Christian worldview, that is, explication of the relation between God and the world through the traditional understanding of the divine attributes. Especially with the elaboration of a neoclassical or process theism and the theology of Jürgen Moltmann, however, the internal coherence of this synthesis, its consistency with other knowledge and beliefs commonly held about the world, and its adequacy as a representation of the biblical message, have been subject to vigorous critique, leading to a radical reconceptualization of what constitutes divine perfection.

Recovery of trinitarian theism. The twentieth century witnessed a renaissance of reflection on the Trinity largely effected by the work of Karl Barth and Karl Rahner, who criticized theology's tendency to reduce the Trinity to a logical puzzle or mere appendix of theology, thus aiding popular Christianity's identification of its doctrine of God with a simple "monotheism." In distinctive ways, both theologians maintained that the Christian doctrine of God is inherently trinitarian, and a doctrine of God that was not so was not Christian. The legacy of these two men has been to inspire a "second generation" of twentieth-century theologians, for example, Jürgen Moltmann, Walter Kaspar, and Wolfhart Pannenberg, to a Christian doctrine of God and its relation to the world in an explicitly trinitarian manner.

Social location of "God-talk." The cumulative effect of decades of contributions by Latin American, black, and feminist liberation theologians has widely forced the recognition among Christian theologians that all discourse about God is constructed by humans who occupy a specific "social location" of relative power or powerlessness along the axes of class, race, gender, sexual orientation, national identity, and so forth. Laden in such locations are interests that inevitably enter into talk about God, either implicitly or explicitly. The formulation of such an awareness in, for example, the concept of the "hermeneutical privilege of the oppressed," has not only challenged the ideal of a "timeless" discourse about God, but also forced Christian theologians to confront the question, "From whose perspective does one speak of a trinitarian God in and of history?"

J. A. Colombo

See also THEOLOGY.

GODDESS RELIGION

Worship of goddesses flowered in the Neolithic age and continues in many cultures even to the present day. In the ancient Mediterranean and Near Eastern worlds, goddesses with various names represented the creative power of nature, the periodic renewal of the world, and, especially, the regeneration of life after death. Nut, worshiped in Egypt from about 3000 B.C.E., is the creator goddess who, with the sun god, gave birth to other deities of the Egyptian pantheon. The Egyptian goddess Isis was mother of the god-kings of Egypt. Her myth tells that she rescued her husband–brother Osiris from his enemies and restored him to life. Eventually, Isis became the most honored goddess of the ancient world, incorporating other Greek and Roman goddesses. The Romans named her *Stella Maris* (star of the sea). The cult of Isis persisted during the first five centuries of the Christian era, until persecution halted cult activities. Ishtar was the goddess whom Babylonians and Assyrians worshiped as the compassionate mother of all life who brought fertility to the earth, human offspring, and relief from sickness. Known by the Sumerians as Inanna and by the Phoenicians as Astarte, Ishtar was also the goddess of sexual love and war. Her myth tells of her imprisonment by the queen of the underworld, where Ishtar had gone to visit her lover Tammuz, the god of vegetation. The union of Ishtar and Tammuz represents the reawakening of life in the spring. Cybele, the mother goddess of ancient Anatolia, was the Semitic counterpart of Ishtar, and was worshiped for her control over fertility and untamed nature. She was associated in myth with a young consort, Attis, who, out of devotion to her, castrated himself and died beneath a pine tree. Because violets sprang from drops of his blood, he was considered a symbol of immortality, promising everlasting life to other devotees of Cybele. In about 200 B.C.E., her symbol was carried from Anatolia to Rome where she was installed on the Palatine as Cybele Magna Mater (Great Mother Cybele). All of these mothergoddesses died as their cultures died, or as patriarchal societies displaced them.

In Mesoamerica, goddesses flourished from early in the Common Era until about 1500 C.E. when the area became subject to Christian influence. Coatlicue was the Aztec creator-goddess of the earth. Her statue in Mexico City displays her face and her skirt made of snakes, a familiar natural symbol in goddess iconography. Chalchiuhtlicue was the Aztec vegetation goddess—particularly a corn goddess—who is responsible for crops and other natural events. She is the guardian goddess of young women.

Goddesses of the East (India, China, Japan) differ from those of the Western world in two ways: first, worship of them has not been interrupted or halted, but their roles have changed over the centuries; second, they typically promise present help to their devotees rather than regeneration after death. Prthivi is a Hindu mother goddess of earth, the female aspect of the creator god Dyaus Pitar. Known from about 1500 B.C.E., she is the source of plant life and is worshiped today by farmers and herders. Laksmi is a major Hindu goddess who probably originated as a fertility goddess around 300 B.C.E., but who now represents wealth and prosperity. She is the consort of Visnu and changes forms as Visnu changes incarnations. She epitomizes the Brahmanical idea of the active female principle in a male deity. Often depicted as a beautiful woman with four or two arms, she usually stands or rests on a lotus. Sarasvati has been worshiped from prehistoric times through the present. She is a mother goddess who brings fertility and good harvests; in a more general sense, she offers prosperity. Her legend says that she invented Sanskrit and, perhaps because of this, is honored as goddess of wisdom and of the arts. Parvati and Sati are goddesses of fertility and consorts of the god Siva. Both are exemplars of the Hindu wife's devotion and steadfastness.

Kuan-yin (hearer of cries) is the pure and benevolent bodhisattva of Chinese Buddho-Taoism whose cult gradually rose to prominence during the fifth century C.E. and continues to the present. In the literature of Pure Land Buddhism, she is portrayed as friend and protector in life and death. Amaterasu-O-Mi-Kami is the Shinto sun goddess venerated from about 600 C.E. until the present. Her shrine in Japan is visited by about five million devotees a year. Worshiped from prehistoric times through the present, Hsi Wang Mu is the Chinese goddess of longevity and is associated with autumn, the season of old age. Her sign is the crane, Chinese symbol of longevity.

Helen deLaurentis

See also BUDDHISM; GRECO-ROMAN RELIGION; HINDUISM; MYSTERY RELIGIONS; SHINTO.

GOGARTEN, FRIEDRICH (1887–1967)

German theologian, professor of systematic theology at Jena and then Göttingen, and authority on the work of Luther. After WWI, Gogarten joined Barth and Bultmann in challenging modern liberal Protestant theology. Gogarten used modern existentialist thought to critique the post-Reformation Protestant orthodoxy that he felt had obscured Luther's rescue of Christian theology from the grip of medieval metaphysics. Breaking the medieval doctrinal view of history as simply mirroring a static metaphysical scheme gives new depth to the role of human choices, and places metaphysical systems themselves under historical scrutiny. Christianity emerges as no mere metaphysical system, but a divine summons through Christ to take direct ownership for our actions in history under God's word. For Gogarten, modern existentialism supports Luther's central insight. In stripping both the world and the Christian Gospel of any mythical, suprahistorical halo, we are forced to face our responsibility as heirs of God's creation.

Francis D. Connolly-Weinert

GOIZUETA, ROBERTO (1954–)

Roberto Goizueta is a prominent Cuban-American theologian. He is widely respected for his grasp of theological method and Latino theology. Goizueta was born December 8, 1954, in Havana, Cuba. He completed his doctoral studies in 1984 at Marquette University. His dissertation was published as *Liberation, Method, and Dialogue: Enrique Dussel and North American Theological Discourse*. He has been codirector of the Aquinas Center of Theology at Emory University and president of the Academy of Catholic Hispanic Theologians in the United States. Goizueta has written extensively on theological method and Latino theology. His current interests concern the role of aesthetics in

a Latino understanding of praxis, a theme most fully developed in his book *Caminemos con Jesús: Toward a Hispanic/Latino Theology of Accompaniment* (1995).

Alex García-Rivera

See also AESTHETICS; LATINO THEOLOGY (-IES).

GONZÁLEZ, JUSTO L. (1937–)

Born in La Habana, Cuba, Justo L. González is a renowned church historian and U.S. Latino theologian. A Cuban American Methodist, he is the author of over fifty books and three hundred articles in the areas of church history, historical theology, and U.S. Latino theology. His multivolume *A History of Christian Thought* is widely regarded as the preeminent work in the field. Likewise, his book *Mañana: Christian Theology from a Hispanic Perspective* is a seminal work in U.S. Latino theology. He is editor of *Apuntes*, the first journal of Hispanic theology in the United States, and general editor of *Obras de Wesley*.

After receiving his Ph.D. from Yale University in 1961, González held teaching positions at the Evangelical Seminary of Puerto Rico, Emory University, Interdenominational Theological Center, and Columbia Theological Seminary. He has also lectured and taught in various capacities at schools throughout the United States and Latin America.

González has had a profound influence on theological education in the Americas. Currently president of the *Asociación para la Educación Teológica Hispana* and director of the Hispanic Summer Program, he has also served as a consultant to numerous national and international organizations. Among the many honors he has received are an honorary doctorate from the Evangelical Seminary of Puerto Rico, the Gold Medallion Book Award from the Evangelical Christian Publishers Association, and the Virgilio Elizondo Award from the Academy of Catholic Hispanic Theologians of the United States.

Roberto S. Goizueta

See also LATIN AMERICAN PROTESTANTISM; LATINO PROTESTANTISM; LATINO THEOLOGY (-IES).

GONZÁLEZ-FAUS, JOSÉ IGNACIO (1933–)

Spanish Catholic theologian and member of the Society of Jesus, González-Faus' theology was informed and shaped by the atrocities of the Jewish Holocaust, Spain during the Franco regime, the civil war in El Salvador, the Pinochet regime in Chile, and the Rwandan genocide. His theology focuses on the poor and oppressed as a central christological question. His two major works—a volume on christology and a volume on Christian anthropology—speak to the radical unity of Christ's humanity and divinity as well as the relational nature of the human being that corresponds to such a vision of Christ and salvation. Therefore, he posits the human project as an unfolding process of becoming sons and daughters of God and brothers and sisters to each other—a relational identity that is broken and impeded by sin and that finds concrete expression in relationships damaged by injustice and structural oppression. González-Faus is the founder of the Jesuit study center Cristianisme i Justicia in Barcelona where noted theologians contribute to the ongoing analysis of culture (politics, economics, religion, media, etc.) through the lenses of liberation and political theologies. Through the center he continues to publish prolifically on such topics as the sins of the Enlightenment, sacramental ethics and justice, the idolatry of the West, the myths of capitalism, and the negative effects of globalization. He has also published critiques on the topic of the priesthood and ordination, and on the selection of bishops. Among González-Faus' main publications are La humanidad nueva. Ensayo de cristología (1984), Proyecto de hermano. Visión creyente del hombre (1987), and Where the Spirit Breathes: Prophetic Dissent in the Church (1989).

María Teresa Dávila

See also CHRISTOLOGY; LIBERATION THEOLOGIES; ORDINATION; POLITICAL THEOLOGY (-IES); PRIESTHOOD; SIN (SOCIAL, STRUCTURAL); SOCIETY OF JESUS; THEOLOGICAL ANTHROPOLOGY.

GOOD WORKS

The role of "good" works in salvation was one of the most controversial issues in the Reformation. For Luther, as for many other Reformers, the Roman Catholic Church had erred in teaching that such works are necessary in order to be saved. According to these Reformers, the sole good work necessary for salvation was the work accomplished by Christ on the cross.

The medieval church, as well as the Council of Trent (1545–63), taught that faith formed by charity was necessary in order to be saved. Charity was understood not simply as an inclination or attitude, but as something expressed in active works done for the sake of one's neighbor. The Roman Catholic Church after Trent was especially concerned to promote "good works" such as care for the poor and the sick, and education of the ignorant.

Thomas Worcester, S.J.

See also CHARITY; COUNTER-REFORMATION/CATHOLIC REFORMATION; JUSTIFICATION; LUTHER, MARTIN; MERIT; REFORMATION; SALVATION; SOLA GRATIA; TRENT, COUNCIL OF.

GOPI

The *gopis* (Sanskrit, "cowherd girls") play an important role in the biography of the Hindu deity Krishna. They were young women of the cow-herding community of Vrindavana, the village in which Krishna grew up. They fell hopelessly in love with the youthful Krishna, whose divine beauty captivated and overwhelmed them. The stories of amorous liaisons between Krishna and the *gopis* are central to Krishnaite spirituality. They are celebrated endlessly in Vaishnava literature, especially in the tenth book of the *Bhagavata Purana*, as symbolic evocations of the intense longing and overwhelming joy that energizes the soul's quest for God. Radha, Krishna's favorite among the gopis, becomes identified theologically as Krishna's highest power (*shakti*). She is thereby granted status as an inseparable part of the deity, who is then often addressed, in hyphenated form, as Radha-Krishna.

Lance E. Nelson

See also BHAGAVATA PURANA; BHAKTI; BHAKTI-YOGA; HINDUISM; KRISHNA; SHAKTA; SHAKTI; VAISHNAVA.

GORE, CHARLES (1853–1932)

An Anglican bishop and theologian, Charles Gore was born in Wimbledon, Surrey, England, and educated at Balliol College, Oxford. After his ordination in 1878, he served in several parishes and a theological college before being named bishop of Worcester in 1902. He later served as bishop of Birmingham and Oxford, and as dean of theology at Kings College, London. As a church leader, Gore was noted for his concern for social issues, prompted by a visit to the Oxford Mission in Calcutta, India. He was active in the Christian Social Union, and in 1892 founded an Anglican religious order, the

Community of the Resurrection, over which he presided until 1901. As a theologian, he combined Anglo-Catholicism with Modernism, to the dismay of more conservative clergy. His writings include *The Ministry of the Christian Church* (1888, 1919), *The Incarnation of the Son of God* (1891), *The Body of Christ* (1901), and *The Reconstruction of Belief* (1926). At the same time, he vigorously opposed Roman Catholicism and the Lambeth Conference of Bishops' plans for union with the church of South India.

Evelyn A. Kirkley

See also MODERNISM.

GOSPEL

The English translation of the Greek word *euangellion* literally means "good news." In the Greco-Roman world, the term *euangellion* most frequently designated announcements of military victories or proclamations of important events in the lives of emperors. While the early Christians may have recognized an affinity between their beliefs, sentiments, and feelings with the connotations associated with this term among the general population, it is more likely that the early church drew the term from Isaiah 40:9; 52:7; 60:6; and 61:1 in the Septuagint where it identifies Israel's liberation from Exile as glad tidings.

The Jesus movement reshaped this word into a technical term to summarize what God did for humanity in Jesus or to refer in a general way to the message Jesus proclaimed announcing the advent of the reign of God. While it is not possible to establish when the early church first used the word "gospel" it was a technical Christian word very early. Paul, the first extant Christian author, used this word in a way that would only make sense if he could assume that even Christians who were not familiar with his own teachings were familiar with its technical Christian meaning (Rom 10:16; 11:28. See also 1 Cor 4:15; 9:14, 18). Later the term would be applied to a form of Christian literature that recounts the story of the life, ministry, death, and resurrection of Jesus. This usage appears to have been derived from Mark 1:1 who begins his account with the words: "The beginning of the gospel of Jesus Christ."

Regina A. Boisclair

GOSPELS (TEXTS)

Since the word "gospel" was used by the earliest church as a summary term referring to Jesus,' life, death, and resurrection, it is not surprising that it was later applied to written accounts about Jesus. The first four books of the New Testament are Gospels. They are not biographies in the modern sense of the term, where the explicit intention of a contemporary biographer is to report an accurate, objective historical account of someone's life and the development of his or her personality. The Gospels are biographies in the Hellenistic sense of the term, where the explicit intention of an ancient biographer was to relate someone's importance as a model of social and moral values validated by accounts of discrete illustrative episodes that often included a tragic death.

The Gospels are interpretations of who Jesus was in narratives that should not be mistaken for reports of what Jesus actually said or did on specific occasions in history. The Gospels are presented in a loosely connected series of episodes in Jesus' ministry that focus on his behavior and teachings and rarely mention his feelings or show any development of his personality. Each of the four Gospels was based on memories of the historical Jesus that were shaped from the perspective of resurrection faith and theological reflections pertaining to his religious significance within the context of a specific community. The Gospels were written by believers for believers to clarify the understanding of Jesus and to identify the ideal attitudes, behavior, and values of his followers. The Gospels have been called passion narratives with an extended prologue. The death of Jesus is the climax of all four accounts, and resurrection narratives serve as epilogues that confirm his religious significance. For Christians, the four Gospels are not only the most important books in the New Testament, they are the most important books in the Bible.

The canonical Gospels were written between 70–100 C.E. Their authors are called evangelists. While scholars have been able to learn many things about each evangelist from internal evidence in their respective texts, their names are not known. Matthew, Mark, Luke, and John are names derived from second-century traditions and remain a convenient way to identify each of these works and their anonymous authors. While it has been impossible to determine if any of the evangelists knew or were companions of any of the apostles, it has been possible to discern that none of the evangelists was an eyewitness to the events related in his Gospel.

In the early church, the memories of Jesus were first shaped by oral preaching. Some of these traditions were set into written form and clusters of traditions began to come together. The evangelists not only drew from written and possibly oral traditions, but each reshaped his sources to provide what he considered to be the most appropriate and powerful message for his community.

Matthew, Mark, and Luke are called Synoptic Gospels. At first glance, they appear to present their accounts of Jesus from the same perspective ("synoptic" means "one eye"). Upon closer inspection, each of the Synoptic Gospels is very different from the other two. The Gospel of John is unique among the four Gospels and is sometimes identified as the Fourth Gospel. John makes use of different traditions, provides a different chronology, and presents a much higher christology than that of Matthew, Mark, or Luke.

There are some extant anonymous or pseudepigraphical texts from the second and third centuries that are also called "gospels." The existence of others that did not survive is known from patristic sources. Those that survived, in whole or in part, have been collected and published in English in *The Other Gospels. Non-Canonical Gospel Texts*, Ron Cameron, ed. (Philadelphia: Westminster, 1982). These accounts provide stories of Jesus' childhood, report postresurrection instructions to his followers, recount stories about Jesus, or introduce secret teachings. Among these gospels, the most important is a collection of sayings called the Gospel of Thomas. Many of the sayings in Thomas are also found in the canonical Gospels; many believe that some of the sayings in Thomas more closely preserve some of the words of the historical Jesus than the version(s) of these sayings in the canonical texts.

Regina A. Boisclair

GOTHIC

The Gothic style in art and architecture was a prominent one from the late twelfth century to, in some places, the beginning of the sixteenth century. Three distinct periods can be defined: Early Gothic, beginning around 1140; High Gothic, beginning around 1200; and Late Gothic, beginning around 1300. A Gothic cathedral was characterized by a number of features: high external spires; sculptural "programs" or elaborate designs over (for example, the *tympanum*) and around (for example, the *jambs*) the exterior doorways (or *portals*); the rib vault and the pointed arch; and the *flying buttresses*, or external support arches providing additional support to the external stone walls. On the inside, columns setting off the side aisles from the nave were much thinner than in the earlier Romanesque style, but like that earlier style, ambulatories and side chapels could be found. The emphasis throughout the building was on height (verticality) and light. Light, in particular, was understood to be a key element expressing the presence of God. The elaborate and vivid stained-glass windows were the most striking examples of this concern; Gothic architects were often said to have tried to construct "walls of glass" instead of stone.

Many scholars have made strong connections between the faith experience of thirteenth-century Christian European society and Gothic architecture. The expense, time, and effort in human resources devoted to the construction of these churches all over Europe has often been compared that to the space program of the twentieth century. The Gothic style, for instance, an arch or a window, is often the first pictorial image that comes to the mind of many Westerners when they think of a Christian church building. Indeed, the architectural style enjoyed a rebirth in the nineteenth century as *Gothic revival*, or *Neo-Gothic*, especially in the United States and England.

Joanne M. Pierce

See also BAROQUE; BASILICA; CATHEDRAL; CHAPEL; ROMANESQUE.

GRACE

A Christian theological term (from the Latin *gratia*) that refers both to the gratuitous, loving manner in which God relates with humankind, and to the favors and gifts God bestows on the human family and its individual members. Certainly not a "thing" or a "substance," grace can be thought of as the manner of God's being and acting toward us, and of our inner transformation in the likeness of God.

With evident roots in the Hebrew Scriptures, and with occasional parallels in some of the world's other major religions (for instance, the notion and experience of *ashé* in Candomblé/Santería), the theological reflection on grace among Christians owes its start to the thought of the apostle Paul. Other New Testament authors certainly reflected on some of the general themes and intuitions commonly associated with a theology of grace, but it was Paul who first thematized and named the experience and consequences of encountering God's loving care and gifts. Through the life and ministry of Jesus, but especially through his Cross and Resurrection, God opened wide the divine mercy and took the initiative to extend compassion to the entire human family. This divine initiative was absolutely free, motivated only by love, and definitively irrevocable. Paul affirms both divine and human freedoms, but elaborates little on their relationship. For Paul, the Greek term *charis*, or *gratia* among Latin-speaking Christians, seemed adequate enough to speak of God's free offer of salvation and love to humankind. *Charis* and *gratia*, in everyday speech, indicated gratuity and beauty for Paul's contemporaries.

As the history of Christianity progressed, so did theological reflection on grace. It is no exaggeration to see in that ongoing reflection the developing Christian doctrines on God, the world, the human person, sin, salvation, and so on. The theology of grace implicates all of Christian belief, spirituality, worship, and public and private ethics.

Parallel to the theologians' reflections (that became more scholarly with the passing of time), there was, and still is, another important reflection on grace—the one done by pastoral agents and by the laity in contexts of their daily struggles. This other reflection is just as crucial and indispensable as the one developed by theologians.

The scholarly approach to, discussions about, and reflections on grace are necessary and must not be considered irrelevant to Christian life—the New Testament, the church's tradition, history, and common sense do not allow us the naive and wrong conclusion that scholarly theology is not important in Christianity. However, it would also be wrong and naive to conclude that only this type of theology has seriously spoken on grace. Indeed, implicated in church ministry and in popular Christian spirituality are very profound, true, and important insights on grace. No Christian life would be conceivable without some implied theology of grace.

This parallel, nonscholarly, and "unofficial" reflection on grace has always been found (for example) in Christian liturgy and other forms of prayer, in pilgrimages and other devotional practices, in public or private conversations among Christians, in homilies and sermons, in moral decision-making, in pastoral counseling, in Christian family living, in popular religious education, in correspondence, and in music, hymns, church architecture, and art. These varied means to reflect on grace are certainly not external or secondary to Christian life or to Christian theology. Unfortunately, since it is frequently difficult to historically research a "theology" that has not been transmitted in writing, the study of developments in the (Western) Christian reflection on grace is often limited to written scholarly works. Contemporary studies on the theologies implicit in popular Christianity (and on a number of other related disciplines) will open new and substantive doors to a more accurate understanding of the church's (and not just the theologians' and clergy's) reflection on grace. For now, however (and, consequently, in this entry), we do not have the means of fully tracing the history of this development (for significant periods of the church's long life) beyond the written evidence.

Among early Christians, soon after the apostolic generation, grace seems to have been associated with communion with God in and through Christ (for example, Ignatius of Antioch, d. 107). Amazement at and gratitude for God's immense compassion (bestowed in and through Christ) was the most important motive behind early Christian reflections on grace.

Early Hellenic (Eastern) Christian reflection conceived of grace as the divine gift that leads to and accomplishes human "divinization." Now, these thinkers were clearly not suggesting that humans were to become gods, but rather that they could be made (by God's grace) to share in immortality—which belongs to God alone. This "divinization" is like being shaped into the image of the risen Christ. Irenaeus of Lyons (d. 200), Clement of Alexandria (d. 215), and Origen (d. 254) are among those who developed the theology of grace along these lines. Later Hellenic

(Eastern) Christian thought was to further reflect on the notion of human "divinization," seeing it as the ultimate aim of Christ's mission and offer of salvation (for example, Basil of Caesarea [d. 379], Gregory Nazianzus [d. 389], Gregory of Nyssa [d. 395], Didymus the Blind [d. 398], and especially Cyril of Alexandria [d. 444]). The Holy Spirit was understood by these theologians as the one ultimately responsible for human "divinization," transforming Christians (beginning at baptism) into the likeness of Christ.

In early Latin (Western) Christian reflection, Tertullian (d. 225) thought of grace as God's power or energy working within individuals. But there is little doubt that in the Latin West the theology of grace owes much (perhaps too much) to the fifth-century controversy between Augustine of Hippo and Pelagius. This controversy and its aftermath actually led to the first real differentiation between Hellenic (Eastern) and Latin (Western) theologies of grace.

A respected spiritual writer, Pelagius had taught that although God's compassionate grace was given to humankind in and through Christ, this did not imply that humans were incapable of doing what was right without God's grace. Were this true, he argued, God could not conceivably hold humans responsible for their sinful failures—how could a loving and fair God hold us morally responsible for what we could not avoid doing? Pelagius theorized that we could indeed do what was right and good without God's help, although divine grace was important as an aid in knowing and doing what was morally right better and with more ease. Pelagius believed that after Christ opened for humankind the doors of salvation, it was up to individual humans to strive toward it, reaching it (or not) depending on their sincere efforts, and not on God's grace. Pelagius was very optimistic in his understanding of the potential and goodness of human nature. Some of Pelagius's views were condemned several times as heretical by church councils and synods during the course of his dispute with Augustine.

Augustine of Hippo fiercely opposed Pelagius's teaching. Augustine believed that humans could do nothing good without Christ and Christ's grace. Humankind is utterly sinful, he argued, and this sinfulness is universal and comes from the very origins of the human family (that is, the "sin of Adam," or "original sin"). Humanity had "fallen" from what God had intended, and it could not lift itself up without God's explicit help. Humanity's fall had so profoundly degraded and wounded humankind that it had lost the ability to know and do what is good. Without God's initiative and help ("grace"), humankind's destination is eternal damnation. On the other hand, God's grace in and through Christ heals and restores degraded human nature, making it only then possible for humans to know and do what is good in the eyes of God.

Augustine was quite pessimistic in his understanding of human nature without God's grace. He believed that God's alone was the initiative to lead us to goodness, as well as the aid necessary to actually live by and do what is good. This double-thrust of divine activity is totally free and unmerited—we could do nothing to deserve it. Somehow Augustine realized that his reflections on human freedom and its cooperation with God's grace were not clear at all, so he went on to theorize on human responsibility and free will, too. His insufficient reflections on these points proved to be cause for nasty con-

troversies. Indeed, the later theological doctrine called semi-Pelagianism, in its attempt to mediate between Augustine's and Pelagius's followers, created more confusion when it raised questions regarding predestination.

A middle ground on the relationship between divine grace and human freedom was found at the Second Council of Orange (in the year 529), and it has remained the core of the mainstream Christian answer. The importance of this council's doctrinal decisions cannot be overestimated in the history of the Western theology of grace. Orange taught that "prevenient grace" (Augustine's term for God's free initiative and help that precedes conversion and makes it possible) was indeed necessary but not irresistible, although it was indispensable as the first step toward justification. Human free choice could accept or reject prevenient grace. Orange also taught, again following Augustine in this, that human cooperation with grace remained necessary after conversion. This council explicitly rejected as heretical the theory that humankind and/or individual humans were predestined by God to damnation, and hence that nothing these humans could do would change their final destiny. Orange believed that the implications about God's being and about God's motives (in this heretical theory of predestination) directly contradicted the witness of the New Testament and of the church's tradition.

Later on, in the ninth century, a theologian named Gottschalk again denied that Christ had died for all because some are predestined to damnation, and the church again condemned this teaching as heretical. For several centuries after Gottschalk (and certainly beyond), the questions remained the same: if humans need God's help to do anything right and good, how then can humans be free, or morally responsible when they choose not to do what is right and good? It is quite interesting to note that many medieval theologians (of the twelfth and thirteenth centuries) discussed grace within the context of their reflections on love and compassion.

The incorporation of Aristotelian philosophical terminology into theology, in the later Middle Ages, opened the door for new issues, theoretical developments, and controversies about grace. With Thomas Aquinas (d. 1274), Duns Scotus (d. 1308), and Bonaventure (d. 1274), among others, the theology of grace took a turn to center stage. Grace came to be understood and explained in various ways; for example, as a "supernatural state of the human soul" (Aquinas), or as "the virtue of love" (Duns Scotus). New terminology was coined to refer to and explain the action of grace within human life, its effects, its effectiveness, its role in sacramental celebrations, and so on. And, as can be expected, no consensus was reached on the age-old question of the relationship between human freedom and the necessity of God's grace.

Thomas Aquinas's thought on grace was arguably one of the most creative reflections on the subject, and since his theology of grace was part of his broader system, it can only be fully understood within that system. Unfortunately, Thomas was not as influential during the Middle Ages as he became after the Council of Trent. Aquinas taught that a life lived toward God and goodness was the only possible way of attaining humankind's ultimate goal: union with God. He also taught that this type of life could be freely chosen by humans, but only as a response to God's absolutely free initiative, and only if humans understood this life to be

good (since no one may morally choose what one understands to be evil). Furthermore, Aquinas insisted that even after the first choice toward God (itself a response to God's grace made possible by grace), humans still needed God's assistance and support (that is, again, God's grace) in order to be faithful and do what is good and right. Thomas believed that all humans are born into a world dominated by sin, and that all humans are collectively and individually dominated by sin without the gift of God's grace.

For Aquinas, "justification" is an act of God through which individuals are transformed from "sinner" to "just" (a person whose life is directed toward God and goodness). When a person is "justified," one is converted, forgiven, and graced. To the degree that grace could then be spoken of as the life-orientation of the converted individual, Aquinas spoke of "habitual" grace. And to the degree that grace could be referred to as healing and empowering the converted individual, Thomas spoke of "sanctifying" grace. But since God's help is also necessary for doing what is right and good in real daily living, the motions or suggestions from God within an individual's conscience (that prepare for, help carry out, and preserve what is good and right in daily living) could be called "actual" graces. Aquinas thought that God could command and expect a good life from us because God was committing the necessary divine assistance (grace) to make possible humankind's free response to God. Thomas's views on the relationship between human freedom and the need for divine grace were based on philosophical and anthropological considerations and categories; he did not see this relationship as a theological problem, but more as an expression and consequence of the inherent (and unavoidable) limitation of human freedom as essentially created, social, and finite.

The doctrinal middle ground of the Council of Orange seemed to hold during most of the Middle Ages, until the school of thought called Nominalism showed the first signs of departure from the mainstream. Nominalists came to teach that grace was a "name" for God's arbitrary will, power, and action upon (but not really "within") humankind, and therefore grace had little effect or significance intrinsic to human life. It seemed that Nominalism was proposing that salvation (insofar as it is not merely extrinsic to human life) was dependent on human activity and choices. God simply entered the picture as ultimate enforcer of the consequences of human choice. These views on grace were clearly a debasement of typical medieval reflection; but they were somewhat popular in the period that immediately preceded the Reformation. The medieval church's practice of offering indulgences, and the more frequent explanations of these at the end of the Middle Ages, were further degradation of the earlier notions of grace.

Martin Luther (d. 1546) reacted against these (and other) deteriorating trends in theology and in pastoral practice. Luther returned to Augustine's notions, but without much of the balance that had been achieved at the Council of Orange. Apparently not familiar with Thomas Aquinas or with the best medieval reflection on grace, and based on his own study of Scripture, Luther came to the conviction that God's grace is exclusively responsible for the call to conversion and for every good human action thereafter. Faith (understood as "utter trust") in God's invitation to conversion, and faith in the power of Christ's Cross, is all that God wants from humans. "Justification," therefore, is by faith alone because there is absolutely nothing that humans could really do for conversion or in their subsequent Christian lives that God has not already promised to do for them. They only need to trust God's faithfulness—this complete trust is the assurance of their having been justified. At least in his earlier teaching, Luther also promoted the notion of absolute predestination and the absolute debasement of human freedom after Adam's sin. For Luther, justification makes us "acceptable to God" by covering our sinfulness with Christ's merits.

John Calvin (d. 1564) adopted and adapted much of what Luther taught on grace, and added his own reflection. Equally unfamiliar with the best medieval theology, Calvin also based his thought on his interpretation of Scripture. He believed that Adam's sin (and thus, humanity's "fall") was willed by God, and that after this first sin, human nature became so degraded and debased that there is nothing humans can do on their own but sin. Hence, there is truly no human freedom left, and humankind inevitably follows either the attractions of sin or of grace. No human action is good in itself— not even the good actions of Christians. Complete trust ("faith") in God's power and compassion is the only condition for justification. God alone calls whom God alone chooses for conversion and justification, and so predestination is absolute; there being nothing that those destined to damnation could do to change their fate. On the other hand, certainty of salvation is possible to those predestined to glory.

Later generations of Lutherans and Calvinists continued these two theological reflections, and further developed or modified Luther's and Calvin's foundational doctrines.

The churches of the Anglican Communion, during the sixteenth century and thereafter, have remained (with minor variations and a few attempts to the contrary) within the mainstream position advocated by the early Council of Orange. And so did the Roman Catholic Church at the Council of Trent (1545–63). In this long and very important gathering of bishops and experts, "original sin" was reaffirmed as Catholic doctrine, and interpreted to mean the cause whereby human nature was degraded and wounded beyond humanity's own self-healing ability. This state of decadence, the council said, was against God's will and intention. Baptism erases original sin but not some of its consequences (especially, it does not wipe away the inclination to sin). Avoiding what it understood to be Luther's pronounced pessimism regarding the human condition, Trent equally avoided Pelagian-style optimism. Degraded by sin and profoundly wounded, and in complete need of God's grace, human nature nevertheless remained "foundationally" good. Trent's decree on justification, in a language that owed much to spirituality, tried to frame its doctrine in a way that was not apologetic or mainly anti-Lutheran. The council taught the necessity of God's grace for and throughout the entire process of justification, including human cooperation with grace. Trent indeed taught the importance and need of human cooperation with God, and the need for the will's indispensable acceptance of grace for justification; but the council was clear in teaching that this necessary human contribution to justification (through faith, and love, and hope) was itself made possible and guided by grace. Justification, therefore, comes through faith, but not without love and hope. Against Luther and Calvin, then, Trent emphasized the need for human cooperation; and it also taught that justification actually wipes away sin (and hence, not just "covers" it) as well as it sanctifies and heals the person. Contrary to Calvin and Luther, Trent taught that knowledge or certainty of one's own eternal destination ("predestination") is not possible, because it is known by God alone, and because eternal life is not a reward but a gift. Ultimately, Trent sided with Orange and the historical mainstream.

After the sixteenth century, the development of the Western theology of grace has mostly walked down the roads opened by Orange, the great medieval thinkers, and Trent, and by Luther and Calvin. There were (for example) the teachings of Arminius and of the Jansenists, as well as the controversy called *de auxiliis* between Dominican and Jesuit theologians within the Catholic Church. But all too frequently the same issues of the Reformation period were revived by one or all sides, or new angles discovered within the same discussion. Never settled to everyone's satisfaction has been the age-old question of the relationship between the need for God's grace and the autonomy of human freedom.

Since the 1960s there have been new and very significant turns in the Western theology of grace, with the consolidation of the ecumenical spirit among most Christian theologians, with the increase of interdisciplinary approaches, and with a greater awareness and use of patristic and historical sources. The advance of biblical hermeneutics has made appeals to Scripture less simplistic and much more nuanced. The social sciences, cultural studies, and contemporary tools of social analysis no longer permit a naive reflection on grace that is unaware of the categories of gender, culture, and class, or that is conceived apart from real-life issues of real-life peoples. Furthermore, the growing ecumenicity and complexity of Christian scholarly thought on grace has finally begun to pay serious attention to the traditions of popular spirituality and liturgy and to the reflections on grace that these bear witness to.

One very crucial contribution from the social sciences is the realization that there is no human experience outside cultural contexts, or not shaped by these, and that these contexts are themselves quite distinct and diverse. Although grace is not a cultural product, the human experience of grace is undeniably cultural (or it would not be human). It is still too early to know what might be the long-term implications and consequences of this insight on the theology of grace. It is hoped that the next few decades will see the theological and pastoral fruits of current research and ecumenical dialogues.

The importance of the theology of grace in Christianity, as well as its impact on the world beyond Christianity, cannot be exaggerated. Even contemporary capitalism and democracy, if sociologist Max Weber and many others are right, find their modern roots in the Christian debates over God's grace.

Orlando Espín

See also AQUINAS, THOMAS, ST.; ARMINIANISM; AUGUSTINE OF HIPPO; CALVIN, JOHN; CALVINISM; COUNTER-REFORMATION/CATHOLIC REFORMATION; DEVELOPMENT OF DOGMA/OF DOCTRINE; DIVINIZATION; DOCTRINE; DOGMA; ELECTION (DOCTRINE OF); FAITH; FATHERS OF THE CHURCH; FRANÇA MIRANDA, MÁRIO DE; FREEDOM; FREE WILL; GOD; HUMAN BEING; JANSENISM; JUSTICE; JUSTIFICATION; LITURGY (IN CHRISTIANITY); LUTHER, MARTIN; LUTHERANISM; MEDIEVAL CHURCH; MISSIOLOGY; MOLINA, LUIS DE; NATURE, HUMAN; NOMINALISM; ORANGE, COUNCILS OF; ORIGINAL JUSTICE; PELAGIANISM; PELAGIUS; PREDESTINATION (IN CHRISTIANITY); PROTESTANTISM; RAHNER, KARL; REFORMATION; SACRAMENT; SALVATION; SCHOLASTICISM; SEMI-PELAGIANISM; SIN, ORIGINAL; SOTERIOLOGY; THEOLOGICAL ANTHROPOLOGY; THOMISM/TRANSCENDENTAL THOMISM; TRENT, COUNCIL OF; TRIDENTINISM.

GRAMSCI, ANTONIO (1891–1937)

Italian philosopher. Gramsci has been called the main theoretician of the philosophy of praxis. Marxist by conviction, he was very active in the Italian labor movement and in anti-Fascist struggles. Gramsci suffered much for his ideals and commitments, dying in prison after spending the last nine years of his life there. His writings display a broad concern with and awareness of the cultural, social, and political issues of his day. His analyses of praxis, hegemony, culture, the role of popular religion, "organic" intellectuals, and the like, became (and have remained) very influential both in Europe and in Latin America. It is difficult to study liberation theologies without discovering there some of Gramsci's contributions and concerns. He wrote mostly in difficult prison circumstances, so his thought on any subject is actually spread throughout his writings from prison. One important collection of these texts appeared as *Lettere dal carcere* (*Letters from Prison*, 1947 and 1965), and the numerous and crucial *Quaderni del carcere* (*Notebooks from Prison*) published separately under several titles between 1948 and 1951 and finally edited together in 1975.

Orlando Espín

See also CULTURE; ETHICS, SOCIAL; HISTORICAL CRITIQUE; IDEOLOGY

(IDEOLOGIES); LIBERATION THEOLOGIES; MADURO, OTTO; MARX, KARL; MARXISM; POPULAR CATHOLICISM; POPULAR RELIGIONS; PRAXIS; RIBEIRO DE OLIVEIRA, PEDRO; SOCIALISM.

GRANADA, LUIS DE (1504–88)

Spanish theologian, writer, and member of the Dominican Order. Disciple and close friend of Juan de Ávila (John of Avila), his main interest was spirituality and the theological schools of thought that discussed it. Carefully avoiding what was considered heresy in his days, Luis de Granada developed a modern theology of prayer and a "mystical theology" that was to have great influence in Spain and in the Spanish-speaking countries of the Americas. His publications were very numerous, and his intention was consistently catechetical. His writings are considered classics of the Spanish language. Among his main books are *Introducción al símbolo de la fe* (1583), *Libro de oración y meditación* (1554), *Guía de pecadores* (1574), and *Memorial de la vida cristiana* (1565).

Orlando Espín

See also CATECHESIS / CATECHETICAL; COUNTER-REFORMATION / CATHOLIC REFORMATION; DOMINICANS; JOHN (JUAN) OF AVILA; SPIRITUALITY; TRENT, COUNCIL OF.

GRATIAN (TWELFTH CENTURY)

Very little is know of Gratian's life, apart from the fact that he taught canon law in Bologna from about 1130 to 1140. His major work, however, the *Concordia discordantium canonum* (*Concord of Discordant Canons*) became the most famous lawbook in church history, although it is almost always called simply the *Decretum*. Using earlier collections of church laws, Gratian compiled a massive collection of church laws organized by topic. As the title of

the book indicates, Gratian worked out methods for reconciling laws that appear to contradict themselves. The book was so thorough and so useable that it became the standard text for teaching canon law for centuries. The *Decretum* was also used as the standard book of church law, and together with collections of papal letters (called decretals) made up the *Body of Canon Law* (*Corpus juris canonici*) that remained the official collection of church law in Western Christianity until the Reformation and the standard book of church law for Roman Catholics until 1917.

Gary Macy

See also CANON LAW; DECRETALS; MEDIEVAL CHRISTIANITY (IN THE WEST).

GRAVISSIMUM EDUCATIONIS

Declaration on Christian Education, issued by the Second Vatican Council on October 28, 1965. This conciliar document acknowledges and applauds contemporary progress in education, clearly reaffirming the Catholic Church's right and obligation to be involved in education (through its own institutions and through the work of its members in non-Catholic institutions) because education is a significant contributor to the welfare and development of humankind. The council also clearly teaches that all persons, regardless of race, nationality, gender, social class, or age, have a God-given right to education. All Christians also have a right to Christian religious education. In the case of children, parents have the right to determine the type of education their children will receive, although parents also have the obligation to seek assistance (from their communities and from civil society) in the educational process of their children. The family, says Vatican II, is the first and foremost educator of children and of all other persons. The church, as part of society, is also capable of assisting parents and communities by offering quality education through Catholic educational institutions. Catholic institutions (from elementary schools to universities) must seek academic excellence, and must also see to the religious and moral education of students.

Although *Gravissimum Educationis* is not one of Vatican II's better known or more innovative documents, it is a clear and good summary of the church's basic views on education and a restatement of its right to participate in education. As with all conciliar documents, this declaration on Christian education should be read within the context of Vatican II's overall teaching, and especially in light of the council's constitutions on the church (*Lumen Gentium*) and on the church in the modern world (*Gaudium et Spes*).

Orlando Espín

See also GAUDIUM ET SPES; LUMEN GENTIUM; MISSION OF THE CHURCH; RELIGIOUS EDUCATION; UNIVERSITY, CATHOLIC; VATICAN, SECOND COUNCIL OF THE.

GREAT AWAKENING(S) (EURO-AMERICAN RELIGIOUS HISTORY)

Great Awakenings are waves of Christian revivalism that have periodically swept the United States. They are vehicles for the evangelization of U.S. citizens and one of the reasons why the United States is known as a Christian nation. The First Great Awakening occurred in the 1730s–1740s: a transdenominational explosion of religious fervor fueled by European pietism. Its leaders included Jonathan Edwards (Congregationalist), George Whitefield (Anglican), John Wesley (founder of Methodists), Theodore Frelinghuysen (Dutch Reformed), and Gilbert and William Tennent (Presbyterian). Throughout the thirteen colonies, these preachers exhorted their hearers to repent and turn their lives over to Jesus the Christ. The First Great Awakening had several implications: it unified the colonies through a message of God's divine mission for the country; it led to the development of improved transportation and communication, thus preparing for the Revolutionary War; it increased dissension by weakening Anglican and Puritan establishments; and it stimulated interest in higher education.

The Second Great Awakening occurred in the first two decades of the nineteenth century in two primary venues: the urban northeast and the southern and western frontiers. In New England, especially Connecticut, Jonathan Edwards' followers Asahel Nettleton and Timothy Dwight sought to reconcile Calvinist Puritanism with revivalism. In the cities of the brand-new Erie Canal and in Boston, New York, Philadelphia, and London, Charles G. Finney, the "father of modern revivalism," pioneered his "New Measures," a series of enormously successful techniques to win souls to Christ. Notably in Cane Ridge, Kentucky, the then-western frontier was swept by camp meetings, revivals led by teams of itinerant preachers in temporary settlements similar to tent cities. Camp meetings were characterized by simple, lively presentations of the Gospel message and by dramatic manifestations of the Holy Spirit including fainting, dancing, jerking, and barking. Consequences of the Second Awakening included the expansion and stabilization of frontier communities; multiplication of Baptists, Methodists, Presbyterians, and Disciples of Christ; promulgation of evangelical theology; organization of social reform around abolition, temperance, and woman's rights; and the evangelization of African and Native Americans.

Most historians of U.S. religion recognize the First and Second Great Awakenings; however, they disagree on subsequent ones. Some have argued for as many as five distinct additional periods of revival in the nineteenth and twentieth centuries. Others state that because revivalism has been a continuous feature of U.S. Christianity, identifying separate periods of Awakening is impossible. Still others declare that, with the increasing pluralism of the United States, calling some revivals "Great" and implying their universal influence is inaccurate. Despite these interpretive differences, two conclusions are clear: the First and Second Great Awakenings had a profound impact on the United States, and through them, revivalism became a defining feature of the U.S. religious landscape.

Evelyn A. Kirkley

See also EDWARDS, JONATHAN; EVANGELICAL THEOLOGY; PIETISM; REVIVALISM; WESLEY, JOHN.

GRECO-ROMAN RELIGION

"Greco-Roman" religion is called such because Greek civilization preceded the establishment of the Roman Republic by at least three hundred years and, while the Romans were great engineers and organizers, they borrowed many of their cultural forms—art, architecture, drama, poetry, religious ideas—from the Greeks. Moreover, many colonies of Greek emigrants had established independent city-states on the Italian mainland and islands as early as 750 B.C.E.; thus Greek influence on Roman cultural forms—including religious forms—was notable.

Neolithic Period (7000 B.C.E.–3000 B.C.E.)

People have lived on the Greek mainland and islands for forty thousand years, and evidence of religious practice there stretches back to the seventh millennium B.C.E. Images of Bird and Snake Goddesses are found in Thessaly, Macedonia, and Crete from the sixth millennium. The Bird Goddess is sometimes a crane or a goose; at other times, a duck, an owl, or a bird-woman hybrid with beaked face, high, cylindrical neck, and arms supporting breasts. She is goddess of air and water, able to transcend the limits of earthbound mortals. Her ideograms (picture symbols) include the "V"—the same "V" used by children to signify birds in their drawings—the chevron, the egg and ovoid forms that became standard decorative motifs in later Greek pottery and on Greek temples. The Snake Goddess is displayed on bird-shaped figurines, or as a woman's head on a snake's body. Ideograms of the Bird Goddess include enormous eyes, spirals, and coils.

Bronze Age (3000–1100 B.C.E.)

During the Aegean Bronze Age, two very different cultures dominated the Greek mainland and islands. The first centered on the island of Crete, and has been named "Minoan" by twentieth-century archeologists. Minoan religious ceremonies centered on nature, dancing, and sports; caves were the principal places of worship, but some high religious ceremonies were held in the elegant Minoan palaces. Religious themes popular during the Neolithic Age persist in Minoan pottery but are brought to a high level of artistic competence: jugs with beaks, wings, or nipples for spouts; ewers shaped like winding snakes; pottery and architecture embellished with egg shapes, zigzags, enormous eyes. In Crete, moreover, the goddess (or her priestess) takes actual human form, appearing on gold seals, signet rings, and sculptures as a female figure elegantly skirted, bare-breasted, standing between lions and holding snakes; or as winged females with snakes or birds atop their heads. A series of immigrations throughout the second millennium B.C.E. introduced into the Aegean area an Indo-European people who have come to be known as Mycenaeans. From their homeland beyond the Black Sea and the Danube, they brought with them horses, chariots, and their own gods and goddesses. By about 1500 B.C.E., the Mycenaeans had entered Crete, and a fusion of Minoan and Mycenaean deities occurred. Most of the later classical Greek deities—Zeus, Hera, Poseidon, Athena, Hermes, Dionysus—are mentioned on clay tablets from the time, but unfamiliar names are also found. In the thirteenth and twelfth centuries B.C.E. much of the Mycenaean world was destroyed (although exactly who or what destroyed it is unknown). Population plummeted, the art of writing was lost, and many Mycenaeans fled to the coast of Anatolia that came to be called Ionia. A "Dark Age" lasting for about three hundred years settled over much of Greece.

The Archaic Age (800 B.C.E.–479 B.C.E.)

Greeks of the Archaic Age were a robust, creative people who lived in relatively small communities called *poleis* (sing. *polis*) in which they made their lives and from which they took their identities. They called themselves not "Greeks" but "Athenians" or "Corinthians" or "Spartans," according to the geographic communities in which they lived. Each *polis* had its own style of government and each had at least one protecting deity. The magnificently simple Greek temples were not, like our churches, places of worship, but homes for the gods and goddesses who lived among the people of the *polis*. Besides the gods who favored each *polis*, there were deities shared by all archaic Greeks. Demeter and Dionysos were gods of grain and grape, respectively, for all the Greeks, and were responsible for good crops that gave the people bread and wine.

There never was a Greek "scripture" that told of the actions of the gods in relation to the people. There were only stories, passed in song from generation to generation, and paintings and sculptures that illustrated the stories; and ritual sacrifices. Hesiod and Homer, poets who lived during this age, supply the principal sources from which Greeks drew their religious stories. Homer's *Iliad* tells of the involvement of the Olympian divinities in the Greek war with the Trojans. The Olympians include the following: Zeus and his wife, Hera; the brothers of Zeus, Poseidon and Hades; the twins Apollo and Artemis; Athena; Ares; Aphrodite; Hephaestus; Hermes and Hestia. Hesiod's work is quite different; he set out to write a *Theogony*, a word meaning "the origin of the gods." Hesiod tells of a great war between the Olympians and the pre-Greek gods and goddesses who had gone before them. The triumph of the Olympians symbolizes for Hesiod the coming of a just and moral order both in the universe and in Greek society. It was principally the Olympian gods whom Archaic Greeks honored as their civic deities, but they honored other deities as well. The chthonian deities (Greek, *chthon* = earth) were earth gods and goddesses, responsible for good harvests. At first worshiped by the classes who did agricultural work, they eventually were honored by all Greeks in secret ceremonies called "mysteries." Demeter and Dionysos were centers of mystery cults.

Classical Greece (479 B.C.E.–323 B.C.E.)

A new stage of Greek history begins in 479 B.C.E. when, vastly outnumbered, the Greeks under Athenian leadership fought off an attempted invasion by the mighty nation of Persia. As victory was celebrated, the Athenians organized many of the city-states into a league of states to whom Athens promised protection in the event of future invasions, and from whom Athens collected tribute. New Athenian wealth led to an outpouring of creativity, especially in drama, and allowed the city to adorn itself with public buildings of unsurpassable beauty, such as the Parthenon, the temple to Athena on the Acropolis and, on the same hill, the temple of Athena Nike (Victory) that was a gift to Athena for granting victory over the Persians. Within the Parthenon stood a huge statue of Athena, adorned with a snake and a bird, remnants of the goddess worship of old. Greek theater rose in conjunction with the worship of Dionysos, and throughout this age, playwrights competed in dramatic competitions held at the spring festival called the Greater Dionysia. This period is the Golden Age of Greece, but it could not last because the city-states, fiercely independent and jealous of Athenian power, soon engaged in a war among themselves that weakened them all. Their weakness led to the conquest of the Greeks first by Philip of Macedon and his son, Alexander the Great (d. 323 B.C.E.), and then, in 146 B.C.E., by the Romans.

The Hellenistic and Roman Periods (322 B.C.E.–284 C.E.)

The period between the death (323 B.C.E.) of Alexander the Great, king of Macedonia, and the beginning of the Roman Empire (30 B.C.E.) is usually called the Hellenistic Age.

The name *Hellenistic* refers to the civilization that developed from the interaction between Greek culture and the non-Greek societies of the old Persian empire; and to the cultural fusion of Western (Greek) and Eastern (Persian) motifs and styles. The religion of the self-contained polis vanished as new large cities sprang up. Belief in Fate, already present in fifth-century Greece, came more and more to grip the minds of Hellenistic peoples. Fate was seen as a nonmoral, predestined force against which magic, astrology, and the practices of mystery cults were invoked. In addition to the chthonic religions already practiced in Greece, new religions imported from Persia and Egypt entered the Hellenistic world: the cults of Isis from Egypt, Cybele from Anatolia, and Mithra from Persia. Hellenistic culture became the foundation of Roman civilization. In Rome, early Etruscan deities had by this time been assimilated with the Greek Olympians who were renamed in the following ways: Zeus becomes Jupiter; Hera is Juno; Poseidon is Neptune; Hades is Pluto; Artemis is Diana; Ares is Mars; Aphrodite is Venus; Hephaestus is Vulcan; Athena is Minerva; Hermes is Mercury; and Hestia is Vesta. Romans worshiped these civic gods from ca. 400 B.C.E. to ca. 400 C.E., but the mystery deities of the Hellenistic world gradually came to dominate Roman religious practice. Another significant innovation brought to Rome on the chariot of Hellenistic culture was the worship of rulers as gods. Persian rulers and then Hellenistic kings had routinely seen themselves as divine and demanded worship from their subjects. Certain Roman emperors adopted the same stance, and the number of Roman "gods" increased. With gods multiplying from all sides, religion was soon enough left to the uneducated. Thus, even as Roman civic religion was losing ground to the mystery religions, religion of any kind was gradually losing ground to philosophy.

Helen deLaurentis

See also GODDESS RELIGION; MITHRA; MITHRAISM; MYSTERY RELIGIONS.

GREED
Also called avarice or covetousness, greed is an excessive desire for money or possessions. Religions tend to look negatively upon attachments to material things due to the effects both upon one's spiritual life, since love of things can replace love of God, and upon the well-being of the poor, whom the greedy deprive of needed goods. Some religious movements, such as Christian and Buddhist monasticism, promote detachment from possessions as a spiritual discipline; accordingly, monastic communities hold most property in common. Other traditions are less suspicious of possessions, and warn only against material desires that are deemed excessive. Greed is condemned in the Old Testament, where it is seen as a vice of the wicked that leads to personal ruin (Job 20:20; Prov 1:19; 15:27; 28:25) and a grave injustice against the poor and vulnerable (Amos 8:4-14; Mic 2:1-13). Most significantly, covetousness is a violation of the Ten Commandments (Exod 20:17). The same attitudes and practices are denounced in the New Testament (Luke 12:15; 1 Cor 5:11; Jas 5:1-6) and in the scriptures of many faiths, including Hinduism (*Isa Upanishad* 1), Taoism (*Tao Te Ching* 44), and Buddhism (*Dhammapada* 355). In the Roman Catholic tradition, greed is listed as one of the seven deadly sins. These condemnations of greed are rooted in corresponding affirmations: first, that the goods of the earth were created for all and are meant to be shared fairly; and second, that to love and know God (or to attain spiritual enlightenment) are the only things that bring one true happiness.

Brian Stiltner

See also MATERIALISM; POVERTY; SINS, SEVEN DEADLY.

GREEK CATHOLIC CHURCH
A small church in full communion with Rome since 1860. It separated from the Greek Orthodox Church.

Orlando Espín

See also CATHOLIC TRADITION; COMMUNION (ECCLESIOLOGICAL); EASTERN CATHOLIC CHURCHES; GREEK ORTHODOX CHURCH; ORTHODOX CHURCHES; ROME, SEE OF.

GREEK ORTHODOX CHURCH
The Greek Orthodox Church is directly descendant of the early communities of Christians established in the first century C.E. by the apostle Paul and others. Its importance increased with the establishment of the new imperial capital at Constantinople, on the site of the old city of Byzantium. During the Iconoclastic controversy (about 725–842), Greek Christians sided with those who supported the continued veneration of images ("icons"). The church managed to survive the Turkish occupation of Greece (from 1453) until independence in the nineteenth century. The Greek Orthodox clergy were significantly involved in that struggle for independence. The archbishop of Athens is the presiding bishop of the church that includes most of Greece's population and

another few million members worldwide. The Greek Orthodox Church is in full communion with the see of Constantinople and with the other Orthodox Churches.

Orlando Espín

See also BYZANTIUM/BYZANTINE; CATHOLIC TRADITION; CONSTANTINOPLE, SEE OF; EASTERN CATHOLIC CHURCHES; GREEK CATHOLIC CHURCH; ICON; ICONOCLASTIC CONTROVERSY; MOUNT ATHOS; ORIENTAL CHURCHES; ORTHODOX CHURCHES; PATRISTICS/ PATROLOGY.

GREGORIAN CHANT

The form of chant traditionally used in the Roman Rite for liturgical purposes is attributed to Pope St. Gregory the Great (590–604). However, it is generally agreed upon that while Gregory exerted strong musical and liturgical influence on the development of the Roman Rite, there is no clear evidence that this style of chant can be attributed to him. Gregorian chant is to be distinguished from the Old-Roman chant that was more ornate and melismatic. The origins of these two chant styles and their relationship are disputed.

Chant began to recede in the West with the rise of polyphony that began in the Carolingian renaissance of the ninth century with a simpler form of counterpoint known as organum. In subsequent centuries, chant was all but replaced by the later elaborations of polyphony. At the Council of Trent there was an unsuccessful reaction to limit liturgical music to monophony, although some curtailing of the more obvious abuses of the theatrical were achieved for a time. The nineteenth century revival of monasticism led to a more serious interest in Gregorian chant and its restoration. Much of this work was carried out at the Benedictine abbey of Solesmes (France). Musicologists in recent years have accomplished much in the accurate replication and performance of earlier forms of Western chant forms. However, the regular use of chant, while officially encouraged in Roman Catholic practice, is minimal in post–Vatican II parishes; only a few prosaic pieces survive in the repertory of most Christian communities.

Dennis W. Krouse

See also CHANT (IN CHRISTIANITY); EUCHARIST; LITURGY (IN CHRISTIANITY); LITURGY OF THE HOURS; MASS.

GREGORIAN REFORMS

The Gregorian reforms refer to a movement for the renewal of the church starting in the tenth century and continuing into the twelfth century. The impetus for reform originally came from the monasteries of Cluny and Gorze with the support of the Holy Roman Emperors. The movement's overall goal was the reform of the spiritual/moral life of the clergy. Specifically, this took the form of reducing lay control over clerical life through the implementation of clerical celibacy and the prohibition of lay interference in clerical appointments. Although the movement is named after its most energetic proponent, Pope Gregory VII, the movement started much earlier. The first effective papal advocate of reform was Pope Leo IX who invigorated the papal administration and began holding councils to enforce clerical celibacy and to forbid simony in ecclesiastical appointments. Clerical celibacy was advocated for two reasons. First, it was considered a holier way of life than marriage; and second, it removed church lands from the political entanglements of inheritance. Simony, the selling of spiritual offices, had long been a considered a serious sin. The reformers, however, were particularly interested in the practice of lay appointment of clergy. This practice was customarily accompanied by a fee paid by the office-holder to the lord who appointed him. By condemning this practice as simony, the reformers could move toward eliminating all lay control over clerical appointments. The final stage of this process was the particularly bitter battle between the papacy and the secular lords over the practice of lay investiture. Gregory VII was involved in a protracted dispute with Emperor Henry IV over this thorny question. Although Gregory died in exile, seemingly defeated by Henry, his successor, Urban II, managed to secure agreements first with the kings of England and France, and later with the emperor, in which they renounced the practice of lay investiture. This compromise was formalized in the Concordat of Worms in 1122. The Gregorian reforms are important as the foundation of the strong papal government of the following centuries, and as one of the first reform movements in Christianity that involved large-scale participation of both clergy and laity. As such, the Gregorian reforms were part of a much larger revival of cultural and religious life that swept Europe in the twelfth and thirteenth centuries.

Gary Macy

See also CALLISTUS II OF ROME; CELIBACY; CHRISTIANITY; GREGORY VII, POPE; INVESTITURE CONTROVERSY; LATERAN (COUNCILS OF THE); MEDIEVAL CHRISTIANITY (IN THE WEST); SIMONY; WORMS, CONCORDAT OF.

GREGORY I THE GREAT, POPE (540?–604)

Gregory was the son of a Roman senator and became prefect of the city of Rome around 572. In 574–5, Gregory became a monk, turning his family home into the monastery of St. Andrew. Gregory served as embassy of the pope to Constantinople from 579 to 585/6. Gregory reluctantly accepted the papacy in 590, and during his fourteen-year reign initiated several important projects, including a reform of the papal administration and the mission to evangelize England. Gregory annunciated the important principle that missionaries should change as little of a culture as possible in introducing Christianity. He strongly upheld papal prerogatives while using his vast wealth to support charitable efforts. Gregory's writings are vast, the most important being the *Moralia on Job*, the *Pastoral Rule*, and the *Dialogues*, all works widely read and very influential in the Middle Ages. Gregory was also a powerful supporter of monasticism, and Benedict of Nursia was one of the heroes of his *Dialogues*. He fostered liturgical reform and is linked so closely to plainchant that this form of singing is often referred to as "Gregorian chant." Energetic, pastoral, and politically astute, Gregory seems deserving of his name, "the Great."

Gary Macy

See also AUGUSTINE OF CANTERBURY; BENEDICT OF NURSIA; GREGORIAN CHANT; LITURGY (IN CHRISTIANITY); MISSIONARIES; MONASTICISM IN WESTERN CHRISTIANITY; PAPACY/PAPAL.

GREGORY NAZIANZUS (330–90?)

Gregory Nazianzus was a poet, orator, and theologian, and with Gregory of Nyssa and Basil of Caesarea, one of the Cappadocian fathers of the church. Gregory was born at his parents' country estate at Arianzum in Cappadocia. His father, bishop of Nazianzus, provided an excellent education for his son. During his school years at Caesarea in Cappadocia, he met his lifelong friend Basil who later became bishop of Caesarea. Gregory continued his studies at Caesarea in Palestine and Alexandria and joined Basil at Athens where the two friends completed their education. Gregory was baptized around 358 and lived with Basil in monastic retirement where Gregory helped Basil compile an anthology of Origen's works and Basil's *Monastic Rules*. Despite Gregory's reluctance, in 362, his father ordained him priest to help him in the Diocese of Nazianzus. In 371 Emperor Valens divided the province of Cappadocia. Basil, bishop of Cappadocia's capital, ordained his friend Gregory bishop of Sasima in the territory the Emperor had removed from Basil's province. Gregory was never installed in his see. However, now a bishop, he continued helping his father, and after his death in 374, took over the administration of the Diocese of Nazianzus. From 375 to 379, Gregory took up the monastic life again, this time in Seleucia. In 379, after the death of the Arian emperor Valens, Gregory accepted the plea of the Nicene Christians at Constantinople to become their leader. Here Gregory preached in the summer and fall of 380 the *Five Orations on the Divinity of the Logos*. This work provided the final theological groundwork for the Council of Constantinople in 381 to define the doctrine of the Trinity. It also won for Gregory the name by which he is known in the Greek-speaking world—The Theologian. When the new emperor of the East, Theodosius, entered his capital city on December 24, 380, he recognized Gregory as bishop of Constantinople, an act that the Council of Constantinople formally approved in May 381. Soon thereafter, Gregory resigned the see of Constantinople, returned to Nazianzus, and then

in 384, resigned his father's see. He retired to his family's estate at Arianzum where he lived a monastic life and devoted himself to writing until his death in the winter of 389–90.

Herbert J. Ryan, s.j.

See also ARIANISM; BASIL THE GREAT; CAPPADOCIANS; CONSTANTINOPLE, FIRST COUNCIL OF; GREGORY OF NYSSA; MONASTICISM IN EASTERN CHRISTIANITY; TRINITY/TRINITARIAN THEOLOGY/TRINITARIAN PROCESSIONS.

GREGORY OF NYSSA (335–94?)

Gregory of Nyssa was the younger brother of Basil the Great and Macrina, the head of a convent of nuns, who won her older brother Basil to the ascetic life. Basil and Macrina educated their younger brother who became a teacher of rhetoric and married. After the death of his wife, he entered a monastery his brother Basil had founded. In the autumn of 371, Basil consecrated his brother bishop of Nyssa. Gregory met with great opposition from the Arians of his diocese who trumped up a charge of misappropriation of church funds, and Gregory was deposed from his see in 376. On the death of the Arian emperor Valens in 378, the charges against Gregory were shown to be false and he triumphantly returned to his see. In 381 he played a prominent role in the ecumenical Council of Constantinople. He was so famous as a preacher that he gave the funeral oration at Constantinople for both the princess Pulcheria in 385 and for her mother, the empress Flaccilla. He wrote a major refutation of Eunomius in which, with great subtlety, he elaborated what would become the church's teaching on the unity of God in three Persons, Father, Son, and Holy Spirit. The exposition of trinitarian doctrine is the major theme of works against the Pneumatomachi and a famous work addressed to Ablabius. Gregory created a theological anthropology and wrote many treatises on the life of prayer and the union of the soul with God. He wrote an influential essay on virginity and a much-admired life of his sister Macrina. His most important work is his large *Catechesis* composed about the year 385. It represents, in the Greek patristic tradition, a remarkable systematic theology on a scale to rival that of Origen. Gregory believes, with Origen, in the universal restoration of all things (*apocatastasis*) at the end of time and the complete victory of good over evil. Gregory clearly distinguishes between the generation of the Son and the procession of the Holy Spirit in the Trinity. Likewise, Gregory clearly enunciates a language system about the incarnate Logos in which attributes of the human nature can be said of the divine Person (*communicatio idiomatum*). In current theology, Gregory of Nyssa is considered the deepest and most subtle theologian of the three Cappadocian Fathers.

Herbert J. Ryan, s.j.

See also APOCATASTASIS; BASIL THE GREAT; COMMUNICATIO IDIOMATUM; CONSTANTINOPLE, FIRST COUNCIL OF; EUNOMIANISM; GREGORY NAZIANZUS.

GREGORY OF TOURS (538?–94)

Born Georgius Florentius, Gregory was bishop of Tours from 573 until his death. Gregory is best known for his popularly titled *History of the Franks* (Gregory's title was *Ten Books of History*), a universal history of the world that in fact concentrates on the immediate problems of the Merovingian nation. The book provides historians with a wealth of detail on the cultural and political life of sixth-century France. Gregory also wrote a series of lives of the saints noted for their fascination with the miraculous.

Gary Macy

See also HISTORY; MEDIEVAL CHRISTIANITY (IN THE WEST); SAINTS (CHRISTIAN), DEVOTION TO.

GREGORY PALAMAS (1296?–1359)

Gregory, his brothers, sisters, and mother all embraced the spiritual life. Both Gregory and his brother joined the monastic community on Mount Athos where Gregory was trained in the Hesychast tradition. A method of contemplation making use of constant repetitions of the Jesus Prayer, the advocates of this tradition believed the gifted would, through meditation, be able to see the Divine Light, the same light that surrounded Jesus at the Transfiguration. When the tradition came under attack from the monk Barlaam of Calabria as superstitious and heretical, Gregory became its most ardent defender. Gregory's position was upheld at several councils, and Gregory himself became archbishop of Thessalonica in 1347. Gregory was canonized in 1368.

Gary Macy

See also HESYCHASM; MONASTICISM IN EASTERN CHRISTIANITY.

GREGORY THAUMATURGUS (213?–70?)

Gregory Thaumaturgus was a nobleman of Neocaesarea in Pontus who was converted to Christianity by Origen about 233 and under whom he studied for five years. Upon his return to Neocaesarea in 238, Gregory became the bishop of the city, and was so successful in evangelizing the city and the province that both soon accepted Christianity. The numerous legends about his working miracles account for his surname of Thaumaturgus or "Wonder Worker." His writings provide valuable information about Origen's life and teaching and the pastoral life of the third-century church, especially concerning its penitential discipline. His *Exposition of the Faith* contains the first written record of an apparition of the Blessed Virgin Mary.

Herbert J. Ryan, s.j.

See also MARIOLOGY; MIRACLE; ORIGEN; RECONCILIATION, SACRAMENT OF.

GREGORY VII, POPE (1020?–85)

Born in Tuscany, Hildebrand moved to Rome, and by 1046 was working for Pope Gregory VI. Hildebrand joined Gregory in exile between 1047 and 1049, returning to Rome with Pope Leo IX after the latter's succession to Gregory. Hildebrand held several important posts under Leo and his successors, Victor II, Stephen X, Nicholas II, and Alexander II, aiding them in their attempts to reform the church. This reform movement, however, received both its name, "the Gregorian reforms" and its greatest champion when Hildegard himself was chosen Pope Gregory VII in 1073. Gregory felt strongly that the papacy was the Vicar of Peter on earth, and as such had the duty and the power to ensure that a just society prevailed. He demanded that ecclesiastical offices be freed from control by secular lords, that no ecclesiastical offices be purchased (the sin of simony), and that all priests practice celibacy. While earlier popes, particularly Leo IX, had urged the same reforms, Gregory was unbending and uncompromising in his enforcement of the decrees of his predecessors. Gregory laid out his understanding of the powers of the papacy in his *Dictatus papae* that declared, among other things, that the pope alone can depose emperors, that the pope alone can be judged by no one, and that the pope alone can absolve subjects from obedience to their lords. Although Gregory and his predecessors, in fact, wielded no such powers, the *Dictatus papae* strongly influenced the agenda of later popes. In compliance with these principles, Gregory strongly opposed the attempt by Emperor Henry IV of Germany to influence the appointment of the archbishop of Milan in 1075. Henry responded by calling a council of German bishops that deposed Gregory in 1076. Gregory, in turn, excommunicated Henry and removed Henry's subjects from obedience to him. When the German lords threatened to choose a new emperor if the excommunication was not lifted, Henry crossed the Alps in the middle of winter and begged forgiveness of the Pope at the castle of Canossa. As soon as Gregory lifted the excommunication, however, Henry abondoned the promises made at Canossa and crushed the remaining rival lords in a civil war in 1080. Gregory excommunicated Henry a second time in 1080, and Henry responded by not only naming his own pope, but by attacking Rome itself in 1084. Gregory called on the help of the Normans of southern Italy, who drove off Henry's troops but also sacked the city of Rome. Gregory was forced to leave Rome with the Normans and spent his last year in exile in Salerno. Although Gregory and his principles seemed to have been defeated by Henry, the moral victory was Gregory's, and succeeding popes were eventually succeessful in enacting Gregory's reform program.

Gary Macy

See also CELIBACY; GREGORIAN REFORMS; INVESTITURE CONTROVERSY; MEDIEVAL

CHRISTIANITY (IN THE WEST); PAPACY/
PAPAL; VICAR OF PETER.

GRIFFITHS, BEDE (1906–93)

An English Benedictine priest and Christian missionary in India, Fr. Bede Griffiths
was an advocate of greater Christian appreciation of the riches of Hindu spirituality. An associate of the French monks
Jules Monchanin and Henri Le Saux
(a.k.a. Swami Abhishiktananda), Griffiths
adopted, like Le Saux, the monastic robes
and lifestyle of a Hindu *sannyasin* and
lived in an *ashram* that, though Christian,
borrowed much in its design and routine
from Hindu ashrams, even in the architecture of its place of worship, modeled
after a Hindu temple. Although Griffiths
saw this aspect of his work as an effort to
"inculturate" the Gospel in an Indian cultural context, he was much criticized by
Hindu spiritual leaders for appropriating
their symbols and practices for what was
ultimately a missionary purpose. Nevertheless, Griffiths is much appreciated by
Christians who are interested in Hindu
meditative practices and interreligious
understanding, both for his deep spirituality and his valuable writings on subjects that bear upon Hindu-Christian
dialogue.

Lance E. Nelson

See also ABHISHIKTANANDA, SWAMI;
ASHRAMA/ASHRAM; COMPARATIVE
RELIGION; HINDUISM; INCULTURATION;
SANNYASA.

GROTIUS, HUGO (1583–1645)

A child genius, Huig de Groot attended
the University of Leyden at twelve, and at
eighteen became historian of the Estates
General. Grotius's support of Arminianism and his call for reconciliation among
Christians led to a sentence of lifelong
imprisonment. Smuggled out of Holland
in a box of books, Grotius settled in Paris
in 1621. After an unsuccessful attempt
to return to Holland, Grotius became
ambassador to France from Sweden. He
died in 1642 after suffering a shipwreck.
The most famous of his many works are
the theological treatise *On the Truth of the
Christian Religions* and the legal classic *On
the Law of Wars and Peace*. The first book,
written for missionaries, argues from
natural theology for the superiority of
Christianity over other religions. The
second text introduced the idea that law
should be founded on the unchangeable
laws of nature rather than on divine law.
Because of the influence of *On the Law of
Wars and Peace*, Grotius is considered the
Father of International Law.

Gary Macy

See also ARMINIANISM; MISSIONARIES.

GROUND PAINTING
(IN AFRICAN AND
AFRO-LATIN RELIGIONS)

Some African and Afro-Latin religions use
ground painting as part of ritual, or as a
preparation for it. A specially designated
minister (usually a priest or priestess)
draws the sacred designs on the bare floor
of the place of worship. The line drawings are made with a mixture of ground
eggshells, ashes, and coffee powder (or
powdered kola nuts). In some communities, cornmeal is substituted for the ground
eggshells. The paintings are usually very
elaborate, displaying the symbols of the
divinities or spirits to be venerated by the
community on a given day. By the end of
the ritual celebration, the painting has
been erased by the movement of the
participants. Haitian and Dominican
Vodoun, as well as the Fon traditional
religion in Africa, are renowned for their

beautifully elaborate ground paintings they call *vévé*.

Orlando Espín

See also AFRICAN TRADITIONAL RELIGIONS; AFRO-LATIN RELIGIONS; CULTURE; DIVINATION; VODOUN.

GROUND PAINTING (IN NATIVE AMERICAN TRADITIONS)

The art of designing religious patterns on the earth is a special aspect of Native American rituals. The most familiar, due to their representation in art, are the sand paintings of the Navajo, but in reality, many peoples, from the Hopi to the Luiseno, practiced their ritual art in this form. However they are named, the term "ground painting" most accurately reflects their reality, for many organic and mineral substances are used in addition to sand. Moreover, they are earth-oriented and make a statement because of this. Their purpose is representational and functional. The artist who directs their making aims to reproduce a visible image of a portion of a myth intrinsic to the peoples' origins, sense of identity, and relatedness to the sacred. The blueprint for such an image is kept entirely in the memory of the ritual leader, and may vary in its secondary details from person to person. The second function of the painting is to serve as the reservoir of power from which the leader can draw to heal and strengthen the person for whom the ritual is being held.

Thus, these paintings are cosmic in their scope, and are regarded as highly sacred ritual space. It is the privilege of the patient to enter this space and to sit or lie upon it. In so doing, he or she has unique access to the spiritual forms that are present, and a special perspective that derives from living within, for the time

of the ritual, a sacred cosmos. The healer heightens the potential of this advantage by knowing how to summon the spirits and evoke their powers for healing. This is done by perfect incantation of the myth that the painting represents, and by bringing the grains of sand, color, seeds, and the like, to the patient's body with the healer's hands. Though only the patient seems directly involved, in reality the complexity of this form of ritual would not be possible without the generous assistance of family. The goal of the ritual is to bring a person back into harmony with all the powers of the creation, and the visible presence of the Holy People is an effective means to that end.

Kathleen Dugan

See also HOZHO.

GUADALUPE, VIRGIN OF

The name of arguably the holiest religious (and national) symbol among Mexicans and Mexican Americans. The veneration of the Virgin of Guadalupe is also known in other Latin American nations, and it is spreading among other U.S. Latino and Euro-American groups. Historical data show that the devotion to Guadalupe has centered around a painting of Mary. The painting has been housed in a church (today a large basilica) on the hill called Tepeyac (originally outside Mexico City). The devotion began quite early in the colonial period—by 1556, at the latest. In 1648 and 1649, the first written accounts of the Guadalupe apparition stories were published in Mexico City. The *Nican Mopohua* (the 1649 Nahuatl-language account of the apparitions) claims to reproduce older native sources, but there are no earlier historical records for what the *Nican Mopohua* claims to have occurred over a century before, in 1531, to a poor Nahua native named Juan Diego. Nevertheless, this account of the apparitions was accepted by church and people as historically correct, and the influence Guadalupe has exerted since is simply extraordinary. Gathering in itself the Christian and the Nahua, the painting of the Virgin of Guadalupe is a clear example of what today we call inculturation. It is naive (and factually incorrect) to speak of Guadalupe as simply replacing or covering over the pre-Christian Nahua worship of the goddess Tonantzin (whose sacred ground had indeed been on the same hill of Tepeyac); but it would be equally simplistic to just identify Guadalupe with Mary of Nazareth, in typical Catholic fashion. Much has been written on Guadalupe, and much more still needs to be researched; but the Virgin's importance in the development of Mexican and Mexican American national, cultural, and religious identities cannot be overestimated. The present-day basilica of Guadalupe, in Mexico City, is the most visited Catholic shrine in the world.

Orlando Espín

See also ALEGRE, FRANCISCO XAVIER; APPARITIONS; CLAVIGERO, FRANCISCO XAVIER; CULTURE; DEVOTIONS; ELIZONDO, VIRGILIO; INCULTURATION; LATIN AMERICAN CATHOLICISM; LATIN AMERICAN THEOLOGIES; LATINO/A; LATINO CATHOLICISM; LATINO THEOLOGY (-IES); MARIAN DEVOTIONS; MARIOLOGY; NAHUA TRADITIONAL RELIGION; POPULAR CATHOLICISM; POPULAR RELIGIONS; SAINTS (CHRISTIAN), DEVOTION TO; SYMBOL; TEPEYAC.

GUARDIAN ANGELS

A guardian angel is a spiritual being assigned by God to watch over a particular person. Especially in Roman Catholic thought, it is believed that each person has his or her own guardian angel.

Gary Macy

See also ANGEL.

GUARDIAN SPIRIT

Ruth Benedict stated in a monograph published in 1930 that the quest for a Guardian Spirit was the most universal religious fact in North America. Her opinion was based on wide research of customs and on the trusted word of those Native Americans who engaged in dialogue with her. Since that time, that judgment has received support, especially in the testimonies that medicine men and women have given to change the unfavorable or incorrect views held by the mainstream. This has done much more; it has revealed a tradition that deserves to be considered with the "great" traditions of the world.

The practice of seeking a spirit ally in the difficult struggle of life may well go back to the beginnings of culture. In North America, it emerged from the studies done by early anthropologists of the last remaining aboriginal cultures of the Plains. Here, it was discovered to be the goal of a ritual that served to initiate a person to the adult state in tribal society: the *vision quest*. This practice exists in the broader context of belief in the omnipresent nearness of spiritual powers who, in the plan of creation, were accessible as helpers. As possessors of great powers, they would also share it with humans if approached in the proper way. That way was marked by reverence, sacrifice, and humble prayer, and when it was correctly done, it conjoined with the benevolence of the spirits to produce gifts for life.

The guardian spirit was the path to success in the roles of life, and, for some, it gave unique gifts such as the power to heal, to see prophetic visions, and to be invulnerable in war. Such gifts distinguished those who were leaders, but in traditional societies these gifts were seen as given for the sake of the whole community. Nonetheless, every person understood that such a guardian was necessary. The gift of a spirit guardian was signified by the accouterments that placed a person in a new state, and especially by the taking of a new name linking the person to the spirit forever. From that time on, the recipient had the right to wear some item symbolizing that relationship. Thus, the guardian spirit was the treasured companion of a person's life, and a communal blessing.

The outward form of the guardian spirit was taken from the animal life native to the people's territory. Different animals possessed different powers; for example, the elk was believed to convey success in love, the eagle, in wisdom and courage, and so on. Each animal was associated with qualities that resembled its actual strengths in reality. Joseph Brown has done a fine description of the relations of the spirit animals (not to be confused with their earthly counterparts) in his work *Animals of the Soul*. A fundamental principle of primal religions evident in this concept is that we are all relatives, and that, as sharers in the web of life, harmony and cooperation should prevail among us.

Kathleen Dugan

See also TOTEM/TOTEMISM; VISIONS (IN CHRISTIAN MYSTICISM).

GUARDINI, ROMANO (1885–1968)

German theologian, philosopher of religion, and pastoral leader in the German church. Guardini was the first professor for Catholic theology at Berlin (1923), later taught at Tübingen (1945), and was appointed to Munich's Chair for Catholic Studies and the Philosophy of Religion in 1948. His theology is cognizant of the era's renewal movements (liturgical reform, the New Theology, and the German youth movement). His analyses of faith and reality use both theological and anthropological categories to communicate faith's truth and significance for the modern problem of the meaning of existence. A popular theologian whose work succeeded with a broad German and international audience, Guardini's exposition of dogmatic topics has a pastoral emphasis as well, as seen in *Faith and the Modern Man* (1952) and his classic, *The Lord* (1954). His theology prepared a generation for the renewals of Vatican Council II.

Patricia Plovanich

GUILT

Guilt can refer to the breaking of a law, moral rule, or some standard of conduct, or it can refer to the feeling that accompanies an individual who believes he or she has violated some moral or legal norm. The Catholic moral tradition has distinguished between formal guilt (the intentional breaking of a moral norm) and material guilt (unintentional breaking of a moral norm). Thus individuals may feel no guilt in situations where they have actually performed wrongful actions. And since some legal and moral norms change (or are unfounded), some individuals may feel guilt when there is no real transgression of a moral (or legal) good.

Some individuals suffer from a pathological obsession with moral guilt, a condition called scrupulosity. Sociobiologists are now developing theories to account for the genesis of feelings of guilt and shame. They attempt to understand what evolutionary or adaptational role guilt may have played in primitive human and prehuman contexts.

Michael J. Hartwig

See also CONSCIENCE; SCRUPULOSITY; SIN, PERSONAL.

GUNA

The term *guna* (Sanskrit, strand, quality) is commonly used in Hindu theology and philosophy to designate one of three forces that come together as *prakriti*, the basic "stuff" of which the manifest universe is formed, mental as well as physical. The three gunas are: (1) *sattva*, the force of creativity and illumination; (2) *rajas*, the factor of activity and passion; and (3) *tamas*, identified with inertia and darkness. Everything, then, other than the highest spiritual reality (*brahman, atman, purusha*) and—in some Hindu schools—the bodies and the heavenly realms of deities, is composed of these three factors. For example, both food and the human mind are so constituted. Since sattva-guna is thought to promote a person's spiritual awareness, the desire to enhance the sattva qualities of the mind through proper diet (especially vegetarianism) is an important aspect of Hindu spirituality.

Lance E. Nelson

See also HINDUISM; PRAKRITI; SANKHYA; YOGA.

GUNKEL, HERMANN (1862–1932)

This German biblical scholar, a founding member of the Göttingen "history of religions school," is best known as the father of form criticism. Born May 23, 1862, at Springe (Hannover), in 1888 Gunkel became *Privatdozent* in biblical theology and exegesis at Göttingen; in 1889, *Privatdozent*

in Old Testament at Halle; and in 1895, associate professor in Berlin. In 1907 Gunkel became professor at Giessen, and in 1920 he returned to Halle, a post from which he retired in 1927. Gunkel died there on March 11, 1932.

In 1895 Gunkel published *Schöpfung und Chaos in Urzeit und Endzeit. Eine religionsgeschichtliche Untersuchung über Genesis 1 und Apokalypse Johannis 12* (Creation and Chaos in Primordial Time and at the End of Time: A History of Religions Investigation of Genesis 1 and Revelation 12), a work in which he set out to explain the biblical accounts of Creation and of the end of the world in the context of ancient Babylonian mythology. Going well beyond previous efforts that had largely been limited to simple comparison of the biblical and Mesopotamian materials, Gunkel did not downplay either the originality or the distinctiveness of the biblical reworkings of these materials.

Gunkel's work in Old Testament form criticism—a method he labeled *Gattungsforschung*, genre analysis—involved both the recovery of the various preliterary and oral traditional units of which the biblical documents are composed, and the effort to locate the life situation (*Sitz im Leben*) within which these underlying literary forms (such as, hymns, laments, proverbs, curses, tales) functioned in Israelite society. Regarding Genesis, Gunkel noted that once we have reconstructed the life situations in which the individual stories arose, it then becomes possible to trace the various stages through which these stories have developed. Regarding the psalms, Gunkel's form-critical approach was crucial in clarifying their cultic context and their classification according to various literary types (such as thanksgiving, lament, praise).

Gunkel's major published contributions to Old Testament form criticism include his commentaries on Genesis (*Genesis* [Göttingen: Vandenhoeck and Ruprecht, 1901]) and on the psalms (*Psalmen* [Göttingen: Vandenhoeck and Ruprecht, 1926); together with his introduction to the psalms (*Einleitung in die Psalmen* [Göttingen: Vandenhoeck and Ruprecht, 1933]) that was completed after Gunkel's death by his student Joachim Begrich.

Jean-Pierre Ruiz

See also FORM CRITICISM; PSALMS/ PSALTER; SITZ IM LEBEN.

GURU

Guru is the Sanskrit word for "teacher." Although any teacher in India—whether a school teacher or the teacher of an art or craft—can be referred to as a guru, the term is especially associated with the idea of the spiritual preceptor in Hinduism. Many Hindus believe that it is not possible to gain *moksha* without the aid and guidance of a teacher who has him- or herself directly experienced the full reality of the spiritual goal. Often regarded as a living saint, and sometimes as an *avatara*, the guru aids the disciple, not only by example and verbal guidance, but also by his or her spiritual power that can be transferred to the disciple as a potent and spiritually helpful blessing. Many gurus are believed to possess psychic powers (*siddhis*), having a shamanistic quality about them, so that devotees approach them seeking worldly as well as purely spiritual benefits. The concept of the guru (*lama* in Tibetan) is also important in Tantric Buddhism.

Lance E. Nelson

See also AVATARA/AVATAR; HINDUISM; TANTRA; TANTRIC BUDDHISM; VAJRAYANA BUDDHISM.

GUSTAFSON, JAMES M. (1926–)

Theologian, ethicist, and professor at the Divinity Schools of Yale and the University of Chicago, as well as university professor at Emory, Gustafson was highly influential for his work on the methodology of Christian ethics, the integration of Protestant and Roman Catholic ethics, Christian reflection on medical ethics, and for his theocentric theological ethic.

Brian F. Linnane, S.J.

See also MORAL THEOLOGY/CHRISTIAN ETHICS.

GUTIÉRREZ, GUSTAVO (1928–)

Born in Lima, Peru, Gustavo Gutiérrez Merino is widely recognized as the "father of liberation theology." After studying psychology, philosophy, and theology in Europe (1950–9), he returned to Peru where, in the course of his pastoral ministry as a priest of the Archdiocese of Lima, professor of theology at the Pontifical Catholic University of Peru, and advisor to the National Catholic University Students Association, he reconsidered the theology he had learned in light of the massive reality of poverty and oppression in Latin America. In a 1968 address he spoke of developing a "theology of liberation"; in 1971 he published *A Theology of Liberation*, recognized as a classic restatement of Christian faith. His book soon became a stimulus to countless subsequent theological efforts in Latin America and around the world. Other important works include *We Drink from Our Own Wells* (1983), *The God of Life* (1989) and *Las Casas: In Search of the Poor of Jesus Christ* (1992). He served as an important theological advisor at the Medellín conference (1968) at which the Latin American bishops called the church to authentic solidarity with the poor. Gutiérrez played a key role in formulating the principle of God's, and thus the church's, "preferential option for the poor," a formula officially sanctioned by the Catholic Church's magisterium since the Latin American bishops' conference at Puebla (1979).

James B. Nickoloff

See also LIBERATION THEOLOGIES; MEDELLÍN DOCUMENTS; OPTION FOR THE POOR; PUEBLA DOCUMENT.

H

HABERMAS, JÜRGEN (1929–)

German "critical" philosopher. Member of the Frankfurt School, Habermas has been very influential in the elaboration and spread of the school's "critical theory of society." Habermas, however, has developed his own thought beyond the Marxist premises of the Frankfurt School's earlier members. He is committed to what could be called "radical reform," in pursuit of which he has analyzed the relationship between theory and praxis in several contexts, especially in the interplay among science, politics, and public opinion in contemporary capitalism. Habermas has also reflected, as part of his overall project, on the connections between knowledge and (social, class) interest, and has developed a social theory. His work has had significant influence on European and European-American philosophers and theologians. Among his publications are *Knowledge and Human Interest* (1968), and *Theory and Practice* (1971).

Orlando Espín

See also CLASSISM; CRITICAL
THEORY; EPISTEMOLOGY; MARXISM;
METHOD IN THEOLOGY; MODERNITY;
POSTMODERNITY; PRAXIS;
SOCIALISM; SOCIAL JUSTICE;
THEORY.

HABIT (CLOTHING)

The religious habit refers to the particular manner of dress adopted by individual communities. The wearing of a tunic or scapular and cincture, or the wearing of a veil in the case of women, is common to many groups. Where a community's legislation does not specify a particular mode of dress or habit, male religious are usually required to adopt the same clothing as secular clergy. The idea of a distinctive manner of attire dates from the fourth century, when virgins took veils as a sign of their dedication to Christ. Putting on the religious habit symbolizes a person's commitment to the way of life of a particular community. Some religious have questioned the appropriateness of a form of dress that separates them from the rest of the Christian community, since all Christians pledge through baptism to clothe themselves with Christ. Others regard the habit as a significant counter-cultural sign.

William Reiser, S.J.

See also CONGREGATIONS/ORDERS
(RELIGIOUS); CONVENT/CONVENTUAL;
NUN; RELIGIOUS (VOWED).

HABIT (ETHICAL)

The theological concept of "habit" was borrowed, during the Middle Ages, from the philosophy of Aristotle. A habit is a disposition leading an individual to act in a certain way. A habit may be acquired (through repetition) or infused by God (as in the case of "habitual" grace). During the Middle Ages many theologians centered their reflections on Christian ethics on questions of "habits," since these were thought to be the direct cause of morally good or bad actions.

Orlando Espín

See also AQUINAS, THOMAS, ST.; GRACE; MORAL THEOLOGY/CHRISTIAN ETHICS; THOMISM; TRANSCENDENTAL THOMISM; VIRTUE.

HADES

Hades ('ades) is the usual translation of Hebrew Sheol in the Septuagint. It is also used ten times in the New Testament to refer to the Abode of the Dead, but not necessarily the place of the punishment of the wicked dead. In Greek thought, Hades was the name of the god of the underworld and his realm was originally called the house of Hades, later simply Hades. In English Bibles, Hades is sometimes erroneously translated as hell. Like Sheol, Hades was originally a place of darkness and gloom where all the dead dwelt, the underworld. Over time, in some traditions, Hades becomes the place where some punishment of the dead occurred, and in those traditions fire also becomes part of Hades to torment the dead; see for example Luke 16:27-31.

Russell Fuller

HADITH

Literally, a report of something the Prophet Muhammad (570–632) said or did that has become the foundation for Islamic *sunna* or custom. Though not considered divine revelation, the *hadith* are used as one of the elements in the establishment of Islamic law. The validity of reported hadith depends upon the reliability of the one who reported it. Two famous collections of "sound" or valid hadith, called *Sahih*, were compiled by al-Bukhari (d. 870 C.E.) and Husayn Muslim (d. 875 C.E.).

Ronald A. Pachence

See also SHARIA/SHARIʾA; SUNNA/SUNNI/SUNNISM.

HAFTARAH

Hebrew meaning "dismiss," or from the Greek meaning "addition."

The *haftarah* is a specially selected passage from the biblical books of the Prophets that is chanted immediately following the reading of the Torah at Sabbath and festival morning Jewish worship services. The particular selection was chosen by the rabbinic sages for its thematic connection to the Torah portion, in order to add depth of meaning and understanding. The chanting of the haftarah is preceded and followed by the recitation of special blessings.

The *haftarah* was added to the Jewish worship service during the Greek and Roman occupation of the land of Israel, leading up to the destruction and the exile in 70 C.E. Some scholars contend that the prophetic reading was added because the Torah reading was being censored by the foreign oppressors, and that a selected reading from the Prophets maintained a scriptural reading as part of the worship service. These scholars contend that the word *haftarah* comes from Greek and means "addition"—for the "addition" to the service. Other scholars contend that the prophetic reading was added to the end of the service as an inspirational conclusion to the worship. These scholars contend that the word *haftarah* comes from Hebrew and means "dismiss"—for the reading constituted the "dismissal" from the service.

Much later, when the weekly Torah reading was formally fixed by chapters, verses, and portions, specific sections from the Prophets were selected and assigned for each Torah reading, based on thematic connection. These are the *haftarah* selections that are still chanted today.

Most often the Bar/Bat Mitzvah boy/girl chants the *haftarah*, so these prophetic selections have become closely associated with the Jewish coming of age ceremony.

Wayne Dosick

See also BAR/BAT MITZVAH; KERIAT HATORAH; SHABBAT.

HAGGADAH

A Jewish liturgical book containing the ritual for the Seder held on Passover eve. The Haggadah contains a narration of the story of the Exodus from Egypt, illustrated through symbolic foods and embellished through a line-by-line interpretation of Deuteronomy 26:5-9.

The ritual found in the Haggadah is first referred to at Mishnah Pesahim Chapter 10 describing a festival meal marked by a set order of foods and a required liturgy. At the heart of the meal is an explanation of the significance of three foods (unleavened bread, bitter herbs, and the Passover offering) and the recitation of psalms. In Talmudic times, this ceremony was expanded through the addition of a discussion of Israelite history leading up to and including captivity in Egypt. In later developments, continuing to the present, liturgical poems and other homilies have

been added to the basic format set in the Talmudic period.

The body of the Haggadah begins by associating unleavened bread with "the bread of affliction" consumed by the Israelites in Egypt. This passage expresses the hope that all who participate in the Passover will, in the coming year, enjoy freedom in the land of Israel. Next comes a set of questions regarding the ways in which the night of the Passover Seder differs from all other nights ("Mah Nishtanah," "The Four Questions," traditionally recited by the youngest child present). The answer to these questions, beginning in the passage Avadim Hayinu ("We were enslaved by Pharaoh"), introduces several stories regarding the obligation to recount the story of the Exodus and the recitation of that story itself. This recitation is introduced by Deuteronomy 26:5-9, interpreted in the Haggadah to mean "An Aramean would have destroyed my father" and embellished by homilies that focus upon the inability of the Egyptians to break the spirit of their Israelite captives. These passages expand as well upon the plagues and the dividing of the sea that allowed the Israelites to escape the pursuing Egyptians.

The actual Passover meal is introduced by a passage cited in the name of Gamaliel, who explains that during the meal one must explain the significance of the Passover sacrifice, the bitter herbs, and the unleavened bread (see Exod 12:8). The meal is followed by the usual grace and then by a medieval compilation, Shefok Chamatkha ("Pour out your wrath"), comprised of scriptural verses that urge God to take vengeance on nations that oppress the people of Israel and to bring Elijah the prophet, the precursor of the messiah. Recitation of psalms follows, and the Haggadah is concluded by a number of passages that praise God as the source of all life.

Alan J. Avery-Peck

See also PASSOVER; SEDER.

HAGIOGRAPHY

Technically, hagiography (*hagios* means "holy" or "saint" in Greek) is the study of saints, not only their lives, but also the legends associated with them and cults attached to them. Since lives of the saints are often written to emphasize their sanctity and miracles that result from that sanctity, the term "hagiography" is sometimes used in a derogatory sense to describe a biography that is overly praiseworth and/or historically inaccurate.

Gary Macy

See also SAINTS (CHRISTIAN), DEVOTION TO; VITA.

HAIGHT, ROGER (1936–)

Catholic theologian and Jesuit priest. Haight earned his doctorate in theology from the University of Chicago Divinity School (in 1973). He has taught at theological institutions in the Philippines, Peru, Canada, France, Kenya, and in the U.S. at the Weston School of Theology (in Cambridge, Massachusetts) and at Union Theological Seminary (in New York City). He has written extensively on christology, grace, and ecclesiology. In ecclesiology he is currently attempting an understanding of "church" that transcends most Christian ecclesiological traditions while remaining faithful to the necessary elements of those same traditions. He is a past president of the Catholic Theological Society of America. Among his best-known works are *Experience and Language of Grace* (1979); *Jesus: Symbol of God* (2000); *Dynamics of Theology* (2001); *Christian Community in History,* two of three vols. published (2004–5); and *The Future of Christology* (2005).

Orlando Espín

See also CHRISTOLOGY; ECCLESIOLOGY.

HAIL MARY

The "Hail Mary" is the title in English of a prayer text used by some Christian traditions addressed to the Blessed Virgin Mary; it is most often used in Roman Catholic devotion during the recitation of the rosary. The title comes from the first two words of the text: "Hail Mary, full of grace, the Lord is with you." This part of the prayer is also called the "angelic salutation," since it is taken from the greeting given to Mary by the angel at the Annunciation (Luke 1:28). In the Middle Ages, the prayer was recited in Latin, and was referred to by the first two words of the text in Latin, *Ave Maria;* one was expected to say a certain number of *"Aves"* for a specific intention or as a penance. The Latin text has also been set to music by a number of noted composers in the history of Western music.

Joanne M. Pierce

See also ANNUNCIATION; HYPERDULIA; MARY OF NAZARETH; ROSARY; VIRGINITY (OF MARY).

HAJJ

In Islam, the fifth pillar (foundational belief or practice): pilgrimage to the holiest city of Islam, Mecca in Saudi Arabia. If one's health and financial status permit, every Muslim should make the *hajj* at least one time, preferably during the twelfth month of the Islamic year called *Dhu-l-Hajjah.* During the hajj, pilgrims observe a number of rituals intended to strengthen their faith in God, help them experience a sense of solidarity with fellow Muslims, and recall God's mercy and majesty. Mecca is the site designated for pilgrimage by the Qur'an (3:97) because the Ka'ba is located there. This ancient structure, according to Islamic tradition, was built by Adam and rebuilt by Abraham. Muslims all over the world face toward the Ka'ba when offering daily prayers (*Salat*). Mecca is also sacred to Muslims because the Prophet Muhammad (570–632) was born there.

Ronald A. Pachence

See also FIVE PILLARS (IN ISLAM); KA'BA/KAABA; MUHAMMAD; SALAT.

HAKO
Celebrated among many tribes on the prairie (for example, the Pawnee and the Omaha), this ceremony made a relative of a person from another tribe. The frequent background was a situation of skirmishes or warfare that occupied the time and drained the resources of a people. This beautiful ceremony is the embodiment of the desire for peace. In this ceremony, a tribe invited a member of another to enter into a covenant that would create a permanent bond of friendship between the person and the host. The bond was expected to be honored by both sides and include the extended communities of both sides. This rite, in form a type of adoption, was actually a most sacred transaction that altered the biological kinship and broadened it into a spiritual relationship transcending tribal boundaries.

Kathleen Dugan

See also RITUAL.

HAL
In Sufi spirituality, a "state" or transitional "condition" one experiences when passing from one of the many "stations" of spiritual wisdom to the next. Each of these prescribed stations or levels of attainment must be achieved in ascending order through intense personal effort, and once each is achieved, it is considered permanent (*maqam*). *Hal*, however, is a passing state, given freely by God as a kind of gift to Sufis after they have exerted the effort to attain a lower level of knowledge and before they ascend to the next higher one. The hal experience has been described as a "lightning flash," or "illumination." Examples of reported hal include joy and exaltation on the one hand, and on the other, sorrow and even depression.

Ronald A. Pachence

See also SUFI/SUFISM.

HALAKHAH
(Hebrew, path). In Judaism, the legal content of the Talmudic, Midrashic, and later rabbinic literature, as distinguished from the Aggadah, or exegetical and homiletical materials. In common parlance, the term Halakhah denotes the sum total of Jewish law, defining thereby the Jewish way of life and encompassing matters ranging from religious ritual and ethics to rules regulating social interactions and business practices.

Alan J. Avery-Peck

See also MITZVAH.

HALEVI, SOLOMON
See KABBALAT SHABBAT.

HALLEL PSALMS
A group of psalms from the biblical Psalter so named because of the occurrence of the Hebrew expression *hallel*, "praise." Specifically psalms 113–118 are sometimes called the "Egyptian Hallel" and were and are used in the observance of

Passover. At the Passover, psalms 113–114 are sung before the meal and psalms 115–118 are sung after the meal.

Russell Fuller

HAMAS

A militant Palestinian Muslim movement formed in 1987 by Ahmad Yasin and associated historically with the (Sunni) Muslim Brotherhood founded in Egypt by Hassan al-Banna in 1928. An acronym for *Harakat al-Muqawama al-Islamiyya* ("Islamic Resistance Movement" in Arabic), Hamas describes itself in its Charter or "Covenant" of 1988 as an organization "whose allegiance is to Allah and whose way of life is Islam" (Article 6). Hamas claims that "every inch of Palestine" is the sacred trust (*waqf*) of Islam and because it is, the State of Israel has no right to exist. It must, therefore, be eliminated by force of arms. As Article 13 of the Charter puts it: "There is no solution for the Palestinian question except through jihad" (which, according to this usage, means a war sanctioned by God). This belligerent position caused significant diplomatic problems for Hamas, both within and outside the Islamic world, when its leader Mahmoud al-Zahar became the elected leader of Palestine in 2006 and refused to repudiate the Hamas position on Israel.

Ronald A. Pachence

See also ISLAMIC RADICALISM (FUNDA-MENTALISM); JIHAD; MUSLIM BROTHER-HOOD; SUNNA/SUNNI/SUNNISM.

HAMATSA

The figure of the Hamatsa belongs to the peoples of the Northwest Coast of America, but can also be traced to a lingering nightmare of the human psyche. Among any people for whom starvation is a real issue, the dread of cannibalism rises from the dark side of the soul. In imagining ways to conquer its dreadful effects, these people personified the temptation in the form of a ravenous spirit (the Hamatsa) that could overtake and possess an unwary and vulnerable person. Such a condition was believed to manifest itself in tendencies recognizable in persons diseased and antisocial. A person thus afflicted was a danger to the community, and had to be controlled and, if possible, healed.

The means for this was an elaborate ceremony that led a person through the steps of a symbolic and effective release. One of the signs of genius of this ritual was its wisdom in creating a visible image of a possessed person in the throes of madness, and then showing a release capable of breaking the hold of the Hamatsa. The healed person was simultaneously initiated into the Hamatsa society and regarded as the keeper of great power that served as a reservoir for the people. In so dealing with a persistent dilemma of human society, these peoples showed a remarkable acuity about how best to transform the demonic within us.

Kathleen Dugan

See also RITUAL; SHAMAN.

HAMETZ

(Hebrew, leavened dough). In Judaism, any food prohibited for consumption on Passover because it actually contains leaven or because it in any other way was not prepared in conformity with the restrictions prohibiting consumption of leavened foods on that festival. Even dishes or utensils used with leavened products during the rest of the year may not be used on Passover and so are referred to as *hametz*.

Exodus 12:15 prohibits Israelites even from possessing hametz during Passover. Prior to the start of the holiday, therefore, all hametz is physically removed from the Jew's home or put in a storage area and sold to a non-Jew, who becomes its legal owner for the duration of the festival. After Passover, the original Jewish owner may buy it back. Hametz that remains in the possession of a Jew over Passover becomes forbidden for use forever.

Alan J. Avery-Peck

See also MATZAH; PASSOVER; SEDER.

HANAFITE

Also referred to as the Hanafi or Hanafiya School of Law in Sunni Islam. Named for its founder, Abu Hanifa (700–67), it is one of the four Sunni *madhabib* (schools of law, each with its distinctive approach to jurisprudence). The Hanafite School, popular today in Turkey, Afghanistan, North Egypt, and India, is known for its flexibility and more liberal interpretations of the law. Hanifa, for example, was one of the first jurists to use the principle of *qiyas* or analogy in settling complex legal issues.

Ronald A. Pachence

See also FIQH; QIYAS; SHARIAH/SHARI'A; SUNNA/SUNNI/SUNNISM.

HANBALITE

(Also Hanbali or Hanbaliya). One of the four schools of Islamic jurisprudence in Sunni Islam named for its founder Ahmad Ibn Hanbal (780-855) who grounded his approach to Islamic law in his extensive knowledge of the *hadith*. In Islam, hadith are extra-Qur'anic teachings or deeds of the Prophet Muhammad (570–632) that establish Islamic custom and are one of the criteria for Islamic law. Hanbal is said

to have memorized and published a million hadiths. The Hanbalites, like their founder, were fiercely apposed to the rationalist philosophy of the Mu'tazilites who were popular in ninth-century C.E. Baghdad where Hanbal lived. The Hanabalites believed that God's law, not human reason, should guide believers in their faith.

Ronald A. Pachence

See also FIQH; HADITH; MUHAMMAD; MU'TAZILITES; QUR'AN; SHARIA/SHARI'A; SUNNA/SUNNI/SUNNISM.

HANDSOME LAKE

In one of the remarkable stories of regeneration made necessary by defeat of the indigenous peoples of North America, the Iroquois recall a man who rose from the pathetic condition of a drunkard to become a religious reformer among a depressed people. In the early nineteenth century, the Iroquois were trying to recover from the brutal treatment they had received from their enemies and conquerors, the Americans. As one who had felt its bitter effects in a thoroughgoing way, Handsome Lake received a vision in which he was called to reform his own life and work to achieve a regeneration among his people.

He was eventually received as a successor of Deganawidah, and his teaching took root among his people. Specifically, he told them that the Creator wanted them to put away the vices they had learned from the whites, and to return to the strong ethics of their traditional past. They were urged to avoid the dangers of whiskey and to lead lives that were exemplary in their industriousness. Thus he advised them to accommodate in the way of clothing and work ethic of the whites, but to strengthen the religious foundations of their rich past. Implicit in this way was the refusal to surrender any land, for it was their home, given to them by the Creator, and from it they had received formative gifts. The teachings of Deganawidah were eventually written down in scrolls sacred to the Iroquois. Underlying all its precepts is a counsel to seek peace and to follow the traditional ways of the Longhouse tradition. It continues today to inspire and support the people of the Iroquois nation.

Kathleen Dugan

See also DEGANAWIDAH; PROPHECY.

HAN FEI TZU (?–233 B.C.E.)

(Chinese, *Han Fei Zi*). One of the primary Chinese exponents of the Legalist School during the Warring States Period (450–221) in China and author of the Han Fei Tzu text of statecraft used by Ch'in emperors (221–206 B.C.E.). Seen as the culminating theorist of the Legalist School, he believed that "man" (the human being) was inherently self-centered and all of his actions and relations were permeated by a desire for advantage. He advocated a tough system of law to maintain order and harmony.

G. D. DeAngelis

See also LEGALISM (CHINESE); ZHOU DYNASTY.

HANIF

An Arabic adjective, used frequently in the Qur'an (sacred scripture of Islam), for believers in the one true God professed by Muslims. According to this usage, Abraham was *hanif*; so was Jesus Christ. Indeed, all monotheists would be described by this term.

Ronald A. Pachence

See also ABRAHAM; ISLAM; JESUS (AS PROPHET OF ISLAM); MUSLIM; QUR'AN.

HANNAH

The mother of Samuel, according to the biblical book of 1 Samuel. Hannah's conception of Samuel is similar to that of many of the matriarchs. She was barren, and only an act of God could overcome the obstacle to her conception. Hannah is not the only wife of Elkanah; his other wife Peninnah is fertile. Hannah is like Rachel (Gen 29:31-32), insofar as her co-wife Leah is fertile.

Hannah prays to God for a child and God does intervene. Her prayer of praise and thanksgiving, after the priest Eli indicates to her that God has heard her petition, appears in 1 Samuel 2:1-10. It is the only prayer in the Hebrew Scriptures uttered directly to God by a woman. (Esther's prayer, considered canonical by Roman Catholics and Greek Orthodox, is in Aramaic, not Hebrew.) Hannah's prayer is often compared to Mary's *Magnificat* (Luke 1:46-55) since much of its vocabulary and its themes are similar. Most likely the author of Luke's Gospel used Hannah's prayer as a model for Mary's hymn of praise.

The Targum of Jonathan considers Hannah a prophet, and the rabbis use the vignette of Hannah to derive the four characteristics of appropriate prayer: (1) in a low voice; (2) with lips moving; (3) with concentration; and (4) not when drunk.

Alice L. Laffey

See also TARGUM.

HANUKKAH

(Hebrew, dedication). The Jewish eight-day festival commemorating the victory of Judah Macabbee and his followers over the Syrians, who, in 168 B.C.E., had outlawed the practice of Judaism, insisting instead that Jews assimilate into Hellenistic culture and pagan religious practices. In 164 B.C.E., Judah recaptured Jerusalem, purified the Jewish Temple, and relit the eternal light that miraculously remained lit for eight days fueled by a single day's supply of holy oil. Accordingly, Jews observe the festival, known also as the "Feast of Lights," by kindling an eight branched candelabra (*Menorah* or *Hannukiah*), adding an additional candle each night until, on the final night of the festival, all eight branches as well as a ninth, which holds a candle used to light the others, are lit. This festive holiday also is marked by the giving of gifts, eating of fried foods (reminiscent of the oil), and playing of games, especially with a top (*Dreidle* or *Sevivon*) marked with the Hebrew acronym for the slogan, "A great miracle happened there."

A minor holiday in early rabbinic and medieval times, Hanukkah has become extremely popular in the contemporary period. This is explained by the appropriateness in modern thinking of Hanukkah's message, which focuses upon religious freedom, by the parallel between the Macabbean victory over the much more powerful Syrian army and the plight of modern-day Israel in its conflict with its Arab neighbors, and by the extent to which this joyous festival provides an opportunity for family activity and celebration. Especially in the United States, Jewish celebration of Hanukkah is spurred as well by the fact that Hanukkah falls in the same season as Christmas and so provides Jews with a superficially parallel seasonal holiday.

Alan J. Avery-Peck

HANUMAN

In Hinduism, Hanuman is a much-beloved deity. Envisioned in myth and devotion as having the body of a monkey, Hanuman is the devoted companion and loyal servant of Rama in the *Ramayana*. Because of this, he emerges as a paradigmatic devotee (*bhakta*) of God in Vaishnava devotional spirituality. Possessed of tremendous strength and the ability to leap great distances and change his size and shape, Hanuman remains a popular figure in folklore in Indonesia and other parts of Southeast Asia as well as in India.

Lance E. Nelson

See also BHAKTI; BHAKTI-YOGA; HINDUISM; RAMA; RAMAYANA; VAISHNAVA.

HAPPINESS

All philosophies and theologies consider the nature of happiness, but under different descriptions. Jeremy Bentham and John Stuart Mill, for example, taught that human good consisted in the happiness of the whole. Kant considered happiness as a good, but not as important as doing one's moral duty. Sartre and other existentialists considered happiness to be created by the individual out of her freedom. Hobbes, Hume, and others considered happiness to be entirely subjective, determined by the person herself and no one else. The predominant Christian thinking on happiness, however, comes from Thomas Aquinas through his use of Aristotle.

Aristotle taught that happiness (*eudaimonia*) is what all people seek. Aristotle meant that happiness is an "end" (*telos*) in the sense of a final goal toward which we tend, the pursuit of which influences and characterizes all our actions and passions. Any *telos*, or final goal, constituted a thing to be what it was. So for example, for a human being to be happy, she had to engage those dimensions that make one distinctively human, namely, intellective powers (wonder, contemplation of the truth, choice, and so on), and practical (moral) powers (courage, generosity, and so forth). Modern use of the word "happiness" tends to carry the connotation of a kind of passive state. Aristotle's concept was much closer to the modern use of the word "flow," as, for example, when we watch a competitor fully exercising her natural and practiced powers in an athletic contest.

For Aristotle, one could not decide not to be happy, since that desire defined what it meant to be human. Thus, Aristotle thought of happiness as having objective, discernible content. He acknowledged, however, that one could be mistaken in what brought happiness. He also acknowledged that different people had different ideas of happiness, but that they were somehow responsible for what appeared to them to be good, and that their moral (human) duty was to attain to fully human happiness.

Aristotle's thinking on happiness was brought into Christian theology by Thomas Aquinas, who stated that the defining *telos* and happiness for human beings was union with God. That happy union could take place in various ways on earth through delight in creation, pursuit of truth, practice of the virtues, prayer, and the sacraments, for example, and fully in heaven. For Aquinas, too, happiness had an objective content, discernible in part by reason, and found especially in the teachings of Scripture and the Catholic Church. One important dimension of Aquinas's understanding of happiness as distinct from Aristotle's was its essentially *relational* quality.

In some discussions, the purely subjective understanding of happiness is being challenged epistemologically and by the postmodern "linguistic turn." That is, a person claiming to be happy can be shown to be epistemologically mistaken on her own terms. That requires a historical perspective: looking back on her life and forward into the future to see if the course of her life has satisfied or is likely to satisfy her own express description of happiness. The postmodern linguistic turn takes note of the fact that language is essentially relational and that therefore concepts like happiness must be considered relationally—that is, how my own happiness must relate to that of others.

G. Simon Harak, s.j.

HARAE

(Japanese, ritual purity). The act of ritual purification has traditionally been an integral part of Shinto shrine practice. This ritual act enables the individual to purify oneself both externally and internally. It is only through purification, both internally and externally, that one is able to stand in the presence of a *kami*. The O-Harai is the great purification ceremony performed at Ise by the emperor to absolve the nation of guilt.

G. D. DeAngelis

See also AMATERASU; ISE; KAMI; SHINTO; SHRINE.

HARAM

Literally, "prohibited" or "forbidden" by Islamic law. The eating of pork, drinking alcoholic beverages, and gambling are examples of *haram*, or prohibited practices. The English word harem, from the Arabic *harem* refers specifically to the household quarters reserved for women. Like *haram*, harem suggests something "off limits," in this case parts of the house that are forbidden to unauthorized men.

Ronald A. Pachence

See also SHARIA/SHARI'A.

HARE KRISHNA MOVEMENT

The so-called Hare Krishnas are a Hindu-based movement, more formally known as the International Society for Krishna Consciousness (ISKCON). This organization was founded in the mid-1960s by Swami Bhaktivedanta Prabhupada (1896–1977), who transplanted to the West a traditional form of Krishnaite Hinduism, known as Gaudiya or Bengal Vaishnavism, inspired by the medieval saint Caitanya.

Although this *bhakti* tradition refers to itself as Vaishnava, acknowledging its roots in the stream of Hindu spirituality devoted to Vishnu as the highest deity, its theology elevates Krishna, regarded by other Vaishnava sects as an *avatara* of Vishnu, to the status of supreme Divinity and source of all avataras. Its primary scriptural authority is the *Bhagavata Purana*. Following this text, Bengal Vaishnavism —and the Hare Krishna movement— advocates an emotional devotion (*bhakti*) to the Deity as the most efficacious form of spiritual practice. This devotion is most typically evoked and intensified through the chanting of the now famous Hare Krishna mantra: *hare krishna, hare krishna, krishna krishna hare hare; hare rama hare rama, rama rama hare hare* (*hare* and *rama* being interpreted as alternate names of Krishna).

Followers—most of whom are not from traditionally Hindu backgrounds—adopt a frugal, disciplined rule of life that involves early rising for worship, daily rounds of mantra recitation, a purely vegetarian diet, and a strict sexual ethic. Hare Krishna temples are approximations of traditional Hindu temples, and especially when worshiping, many devotees wear Indian-style clothing. Their highest goal is the bliss of communion with Krishna. Although its membership has not been expanding in recent years, ISKCON retains an important international presence with a worldwide network of temples.

Lance E. Nelson

See also AVATARA/AVATAR; BHAGAVATA PURANA; BHAKTI; BHAKTI-YOGA; CAITANYA; HINDUISM; KRISHNA; MANTRA; VAISHNAVA; VISHNU.

HARI-HARA

A syncretistic image of the Supreme Being in Hindu iconography, the Hari-Hara icon is divided vertically, one half displaying the characteristic features of Hari (that is, Vishnu) and the other the features of Hara (that is, Shiva). It is intended to suggest the possibility of reconciliation between the two major sects of Hinduism, the Vaishnava and the Shiva, as also the idea, important to many (but not all) Hindus, that the ultimate reality, Brahman, transcends identification with any particular deity.

Lance E. Nelson

See also ADVAITA VEDANTA; HINDUISM; NIRGUNA BRAHMAN; SHAIVA; SHIVA; VAISHNAVA; VISHNU.

HÄRING, BERNARD (1912–98)

A German moral theologian and member of the Redemptorist Order who taught at the Alfonsian Academy in Rome. Häring is noted for his landmark book, *The Law of Christ* (1954), which initiated extensive reform of Roman Catholic moral theology, notably a more biblical, liturgical, and pastoral approach to moral teaching. His reform had profound influence on

Vatican Council II and subsequent moral pastoral changes in Catholic life.

Michael J. Hartwig

HARNACK, ADOLF VON
(1851–1930)

A German Lutheran and liberal Protestant theologian and historian who proposed a provocative theory of the development, or in this case the decline, of doctrine and the church. Building on the rise of modern historical consciousness, Harnack studied the increasing intermingling of early Christianity and Greek philosophy that in his view led to the development of christological and trinitarian dogmas in the fourth and fifth centuries that fundamentally obscured and/or outright corrupted what he took to be the essence of the Christian message. In one of his most well-renowned works, *What is Christianity?* Harnack sought to redress what he considered an excessive intellectualization, Hellenization, and legalization of Christianity by using a historical-critical method to separate the essence of Christianity from its historically conditioned forms. Harnack aimed to identify a normative essence of Christianity, that is, an eternal essence or "kernel" that influenced all its later historical forms and that could be critically retrieved from all its "husks" or changeable historical forms. The goal of Harnack's historical-critical interpretation of Christianity was to highlight the timeless, permanent, and ahistorical validity of this essence and thus prove the universal authority and relevance of Christianity to all historical times and places. Harnack associated the immutable essence of Christianity with the manifestation of the Gospel in the person and preaching of Jesus Christ (and not in a body of dogmatic creeds or institutional teachings), and elaborated on that essence through three main themes, namely, the fatherhood of God and the infinite worth of the human soul; the inner coming kingdom of God; and a Gospel-based morality of love.

Other German Protestant theologians like Ernst Troeltsch (1865–1923) rightly pointed out that the attempt to define an abstract essence of Christianity through historical-critical studies was not consistent with principles of historical inquiry, and therefore not tenable, given that (1) early Christianity was situated in specific historical contexts and shaped in a syncretic way by a variety of religious traditions, and that (2) Christianity in its subsequent history is constituted by and not merely conditioned by a rich matrix of different historical forms across different times and places. Using a historical approach to Christianity to abstract an essence of Christian faith from its history is fundamentally misguided; faith and history in Troeltsch's view cannot be separated, because the essence of Christian faith is always already situated in specific sociohistorical contexts, and thus is inextricably linked to those contexts. In a way, debates in nineteenth- and early twentieth-century German Protestant theology between the timeless universality and the actual historicity of Christianity presage the turn to contextual theologies and to postcolonial criticisms of Western Christianity in the mid-to-later twentieth century. Similar to Troeltsch, local or contextual theologies insist that Christianity is situated in and fundamentally shaped by particular social locations, while postcolonial theologies reject the appeal to the finality of Western European definitions and forms of Christianity for all global Christianities.

Rosemary P. Carbine

See also LIBERAL THEOLOGY; TROELTSCH,
ERNST.

HARTSHORNE, CHARLES
(1897–2000)

American process philosopher/theologian. Hartshorne was influenced by the philosophy of Alfred North Whitehead, and, in accord with Whitehead, he interprets reality as consisting of experiential events that succeed one another through time. Objects that endure, such as molecules, cells, stones, and planets, are taken to be four-dimensional societies of these experiential events. The unity of these societies results from patterns of order that later events receive from earlier ones through a process called prehension. However, Hartshorne's position differs from Whitehead's in that a dominant event spatially overlaps its associated subservient events. Thus, the event that represents a molecule at a certain instant of time overlaps the events that represent its constituent atoms.

Hartshorne carries this distinctive feature into his theory of the human soul and God. The human soul is a society of experiential events that overlaps (at least) the society of events that is the brain, and God is a society of events that overlaps the vast number of societies that constitute the physical universe. The relationship between God and the world is analogous to the relationship between the human soul and the body, so that God may properly be conceived as the soul of the universe. Furthermore, just as the human soul is constantly interacting with the body, God is constantly interacting with the universe.

Hartshorne's writings about God are extensive, and they feature well-argued criticisms of the theory of God developed by the Christian theologians of the Middle Ages. According to that theory, God is an omniscient, omnipotent, omnibenevolent, and essentially changeless being who creates the physical universe ex nihilo (out of nothing), governs it through providence, and is unaffected by contingent happenings within it. Hartshorne claims that this theory is internally incoherent and is largely responsible for the atheism of the modern day.

Any God who is omniscient, in the strict sense, sees the outcome of human actions sub specie aeternitate (under the image of eternity, or in an eternal present), which means that these outcomes are determined to occur as God sees them—which renders human freedom an illusion. Furthermore, any God who can anticipate future evil, and who has the power to prevent it, participates in that evil—which conflicts with omnibenevolence. Further, because the relationship between a knowing mind and a known object is essentially one of dependence, with the mind changing in accord with the object, the intrinsic immutability of God renders any knowledge (or love) of the world impossible. Further, the idea that God created the universe ex nihilo implies that time had a beginning—which makes no sense. Finally, human choices count for nothing in the face of a divine providence that rules the world in accord with an eternal, unchanging vision.

In place of this theory, Hartshorne recommends one that depicts God as a sequence of experiential events eternally related to the world and affected by the changes that occur within it. In accord with the metaphysical requirements that govern all experiential events, God is dipolar, comprising a physical pole and an abstract, mental pole. In virtue of his mental pole, God provides loving guidance to the universe, and in virtue of his physical pole, God receives into God's own being the joys, sorrows, failures, and accomplishments of finite creatures. Only a God that is conceived in this way, Hartshorne argues, can be adequate to the requirements of modern religion.

Among several arguments Hartshorne advanced in support of the existence of God is the ontological argument, first formulated by Anselm of Canterbury in the eleventh century. This argument begins with the concept of a being than which nothing greater can be conceived and concludes that such a being exists of necessity. If it did not exist, then it would not be that than which nothing greater can be conceived. Now most philosophers who have advanced this argument have concluded that a changeless being that lacks any attachment to the world is superior to one that changes and is so attached. Thus, God must be of the former sort. However, Hartshorne argues that this alleged superiority is illusory in that a God who lacks the accidental qualities reflecting an attachment to the world is inferior to one that possesses these accidents. Thus, he concludes that the ontological argument really proves the existence of a God as conceived by his own philosophy.

Hartshorne's more important writings include *Beyond Humanism: Essays in the Philosophy of Nature* (1937), *The Divine Relativity: A Social Conception of God* (1947), *Reality as Social Process: Studies in Metaphysics and Religion* (1953), *The Logic of Perfection* (1962), *Creative Synthesis and Philosophic Method* (1983), *Insights and Oversights of Great Thinkers: An Evaluation of Western Philosophy* (1983), and *Omnipotence and Other Theological Mistakes* (1984).

Patrick J. Hurley

See also ANSELM OF CANTERBURY; ONTOLOGICAL ARGUMENT; WHITEHEAD, ALFRED NORTH.

HASIDISM

A movement in Judaism originating early in the eighteenth century; Rabbi Israel Baal Shem Tov (about 1700–60) is generally regarded as its founder. While Hasidism calls for strict adherence to biblical and rabbinic law, especially in the period of its inception it placed less emphasis on intellectual pursuits and more upon the joyous expression of religion in song and dance and fellowship. In addition, Hasidism emphasizes the role of the rabbi, called in Hasidism "rebbe" or "zaddik" ("righteous one"), who is leader, teacher, guide, counselor, and confidant of his disciples. These divergences from traditional rabbinic Judaism—in particular early Hasidism's rejection of the study of Torah as Judaism's central activity and its embrace of Jewish mystical thinking (Kabbalah)—led to serious confrontations with the mainstream Judaism of the eighteenth century and brought schism to the Jewish communities of Poland, the Ukraine, and White Russia. Today, Hasidism generally is viewed as a type of ultraorthodox Judaism.

A number of Hasidic movements, each of which regards a particular "rebbe" and his descendants as its leader, are found in the U.S.A., Israel, and in Europe today. There are significant differences between these Hasidic groups. While, in the early twentieth century, Hasidism appeared to be on the wane, recent times have witnessed a significant resurgence of the movement. This is evident especially in the movement known as Habad or Lubovich Hasidism.

Alan J. Avery-Peck

See also ELIJAH BEN SOLOMON; KABBALAH; ORTHODOX JUDAISM.

HASMONEANS

See MACCABEES.

HAVDALAH

Hebrew meaning "separation." *Havdalah* is the service that marks the separation between the Jewish Sabbath—which ends at sundown on Saturday evening—and the rest of the week.

The holy Sabbath is not permitted to just fade away into another week, but it is bid farewell with this brief but beautiful service that takes place both at the synagogue and at home. Prayers and blessings are recited over a cup of wine, a symbol of joy; sweet-smelling spices are sniffed to keep the sweetness of the Sabbath for a few moments longer; and a burning multiwicked candle, symbolically indicating that activities prohibited on the Sabbath because they constitute "work" are now permitted again. The final blessing praises God who "separates the holy from the ordinary."

A modified havdalah service is recited at the end of each major festival, to mark the conlcusion of that festival.

Wayne Dosick

See also SHABBAT.

HAYES, DIANA L. (1947–)

Roman Catholic systematic theologian. The first African American Catholic laywoman to receive the doctoral degree in systematic theology (1989) from the Catholic University of Louivain (Belgium), Hayes is tenured associate professor of theology at Georgetown University, Washington, D.C., and a member of the faculty of the Institute for Black Catholic Studies of Xavier University of Louisiana. Prior to her theological studies, Hayes was an attorney. The author of two books, one monograph, and over thirty book chapters and journal articles, Hayes' theological research focuses on interpreting black theology and

formulating a womanist theology. Hayes has worked closely with the National Black Catholic Congress to prepare, analyze, and theologically interpret the national pastoral plan for black Catholics. Hayes is a member of the Black Catholic Theological Symposium, an elected member of the Society for the Study of Black Religion, and a former board member of the Catholic Theological Society of America.

M. Shawn Copeland

See also BLACK THEOLOGY; WOMANIST THEOLOGY.

HEAVEN

Heaven is a metaphor for the condition of personal community with God after death, also described as the fullness of salvation, union with God, or participation in God's life achieved through personal responsiveness to faith and grace during life. Hebrew Scriptures give the word a cosmological reference, a location where God dwells, sometimes suggesting divine transcendence and at other times the mystical experience of God. The reference to mystical experience occurs in the New Testament that reinterprets heaven in light of the Resurrection. The word then describes the transformation of humanity and earth in the end time (eschaton), an eschatological meaning. In Christianity the term connotes the completed transformation of persons through the relationship with God begun during their earthly lives, communion with God that involves the fuller encounter of the beatific vision. Heaven often has suggested a location, God's dwelling place with the faithful and with the angelic hosts. The collective meaning suggests an appreciation of human solidarity, of the present communal dimension of life that is part of the fullness of life with God.

Patricia Plovanich

See also ESCHATON.

HEBREW (LANGUAGE)

Hebrew is the language of most of the Old Testament. It is a member of the Semitic family of languages that includes Arabic, Aramaic, Phoenician, and Akkadian, among others. In the Old Testament, the language spoken by the Israelites is not called Hebrew, but rather, "the language of Canaan" (Isa 19:18). Like many languages, Hebrew may be divided into both historical phases and dialects. The earliest phases of the language are accessible only through comparative study of other Semitic languages and the earliest written materials, both biblical and nonbiblical. One of the better-known phases of the language is that of "classical" Hebrew, the language of much of the narrative in the Hebrew Scriptures. This phase of the language runs from the ninth through the sixth centuries B.C.E. During this period, there is a northern dialect and a southern dialect of Hebrew we may differentiate on the basis of orthographic evidence. The Hebrew language did not disappear with the close of the biblical period, but continued to develop and to be used both as a liturgical language and the language of everyday life for some groups. It is true that, beginning in the fifth century B.C.E., Aramaic became one of the dominant languages in those areas where the Persians ruled, including ancient Palestine. Nevertheless, Hebrew did not become either a forgotten language or an esoteric one as the epigraphic evidence shows. The next phase of the Hebrew language is called Mishnaic Hebrew, since it is represented primarily in the collection of halakhic writings known as the Mishna that together with the Gemara make up the Talmud. Modern Hebrew, the latest phase of the language, is a creation of the nineteenth and twentieth centuries that was formed on the basis of older forms of the language as well as the influence of other modern languages. It is the official language of the modern state of Israel.

Russell Fuller

HEBREW SCRIPTURES

The sections of the Bible accepted by Jews as authoritative, including the books of Genesis through Malachi, but excluding the New Testament. Use of the designation "Hebrew Scriptures" avoids the Christian perspective inherent in the title "Old Testament" that assumes the authority of the New Testament. "Hebrew" refers either to the language in which almost the entirety of the Hebrew Scriptures were written or, alternatively, to the Hebrew nation, whose story these books relate.

Alan J. Avery-Peck

See also TANAK.

HEBREW SCRIPTURES, BOOKS AND THE CANON OF
General

A name reveals some of the perspective and the preunderstanding of the observer. The names Hebrew Scriptures/ Hebrew Bible are mostly used in the academic study of the "Old Testament" and were introduced by Christian scholars who were sensitive to the theological implications of the term *"Old* Testament" and wished to avoid them. Within Judaism, other names are frequent such as the acronym Tanak which is based on the first letter of the Hebrew name of the three divisions of the Jewish canon: Torah, Neviʾim (= Prophets); Ketuvim (= Writings). There are twenty-four books in the Hebrew Bible or Tanak. The content is identical to that of the Old Testament of the Protestant Canon, but the material is arranged differently.

Torah

The first division is the Torah of Moses also known as the Five Books of Moses or Chumash. The Torah is the center of the Tanak in Judaism. It contains the most sacred material and the foundational concepts of the religion of ancient Israel and Judaism. The heart of the Torah is the Exodus from Egypt and the subsequent covenant between Yahweh and the people. It is in covenant that humans learn of their obligation to be loyal followers of Yahweh. The books of Exodus, Leviticus, and Deuteronomy also contain important and ancient collections of legislation that are eclectic in nature. They may concern social, economic, or religious issues. The Five Books of the Pentateuch took shape gradually over many centuries, although according to tradition the Torah was received by Moses on Mt. Sinai. At least four traditions of different time periods, and from different factions of the society were combined perhaps beginning in the Babylonian exile (587–538 B.C.E.) to produce this first division of the Jewish canon. The Torah apparently became the law of the Persian province of Yehud (= Judah) under the leadership of Ezra in the fifth century B.C.E.

Neviʾim

The Neviʾim or the prophets, the second division of the Tanak, is further divided into two sections, (1) the Former Prophets, and (2) the Latter Prophets. The first section, the Former Prophets, includes the books of Joshua, Judges, 1 and 2 Samuel, and 1 and 2 Kings. These books consist of a variety of traditions woven together in ancient times, perhaps as early as the seventh century B.C.E. They present the story of Israel from the time they take the Land of Palestine under the leadership of Joshua until the time they are exiled from the land by the Babylonians. Many scholars are convinced that the Former Prophets were first edited together in the seventh century B.C.E. and combined with the book of Deuteronomy that served as the introduction to what has been called the "Deuteronomistic History." Later in the Babylonian exile, this Deuteronomistic History was edited and expanded and reached the form of the books which we know today. Whatever their editorial history, the Former Prophets are made up of materials from very different time periods and of various types. There are royal archival material, songs, laments, folk tales, and rituals. The editors even cited their sources occasionally.

The Latter Prophets include the books of such figures as Isaiah, Jeremiah, Ezekiel, and the Twelve "minor " Prophets. The prophets are linked to the narrative of Israel's history contained in the Former Prophets by chronological headings and titles that introduce eleven of the fifteen books. Many of these prophetic compositions have been important influences on both Judaism and Christianity in thinking about how to serve God, the Messiah of God, and proper social and economic ethics. The prophets whose oracles are contained in the Latter Prophets range in date from the early eighth to the fifth century B.C.E.

Ketuvim

The Ketuvim or the Writings form the last division of the Hebrew Scriptures or

Tanak. The Writings are an eclectic collection of materials of different types or genres. There is poetry, such as the book of Psalms, also called the Psalter; there are wisdom writings like the book of Proverbs or Job and Ecclesiastes; there are historiographical writings like Ezra, Nehemiah, and 1 and 2 Chronicles. These last four books together retell the history of Israel from the first humans down to the time of the writer, probably in the fourth century B.C.E. The books of Samuel and Kings served as sources for the writer(s).

Russell Fuller

See also CANON, BIBLICAL; KETUVIM; OLD TESTAMENT; PENTATEUCH; PROPHETS.

HECKER, ISAAC (1819–88)

Catholic convert, founder of the Paulist Order, author. Son of New York German immigrants, Hecker entertained the religious views of the American transcendentalists before converting to Catholicism (1844). He became priest and missionary in the Redemptorist Society, then founded the Congregation of St. Paul (the Paulists) to attract Protestants to the Catholic Church (1858). To further their mission, the order sponsored the Catholic Publication Society, and Hecker himself published two journals, *The Young Catholic* and *The Catholic World*, publications disseminating Hecker's theological views. Hecker and his friend, Orestes Brownson, believed America and the Catholic Church to be in Providence's plan for the future. He advocated an indigenous spirituality to renew the American Catholic Church and society and proposed devotion to the Holy Spirit to effect this renewal. His views interested the Americanist bishops but were investigated by Roman authorities when a French biography distorted his teachings. A mistaken version of his teaching was indicated in the papal condemnation of Americanism.

Patricia Plovanich

See also AMERICANISM; BROWNSON, ORESTES.

HEGEL, G.W.F. (1770–1831)

German philosopher. One of the most influential modern European philosophers, Hegel's writings encompass virtually every significant philosophical topic. The hallmark of his system of Absolute Idealism, however, is the affirmation of the identity of reason and reality. Above all, reality is "history," the sphere within which the Idea or Spirit comes to realize and to know itself, culminating in Hegel's philosophy. The mechanism for the realization of Absolute Spirit in history is "change," understood through the dialectic of thesis, antithesis, and synthesis by which Spirit posits an "other" to come to itself, again and again, in synthesis. Hegel's reflections on the history of philosophy, art, and religion continue to be significant for subsequent generations (even when explicitly rejected), even though his synthesis—the identity of reason and reality and the theological character of the former—was almost immediately rejected by critics such as Ludwig Feuerbach, Karl Marx, and Bruno Bauer.

J. A. Colombo

See also ABSOLUTE; BAUER, BRUNO; FEUERBACH, LUDWIG; MARX, KARL.

HEGESIPPUS

Writing in Rome during the second century, Hegesippus was a Christian, probably of Jewish origin. He wrote a book of "memories" of the apostolic preaching that is now preserved only by the quotations contained in Eusebius's *Ecclesiastical History*. The remaining fragments are an invaluable witness to the early years of Christianity.

Gary Macy

See also EUSEBIUS OF CAESAREA; HISTORY.

HEIDEGGER, MARTIN (1889–1976)

German existentialist philosopher, and arguably one of the most influential European thinkers of the twentieth century. His impact on Catholic, Anglican, and Protestant theologians cannot be exaggerated. Educated by the Jesuits and at the University of Freiburg, he specialized in medieval philosophy. He was then deeply influenced by the writings of Franz Brentano and Edmund Husserl, and began gravitating toward what has come to be known as existentialism. In 1923 he became professor at the University of Marburg, where his colleagues included Paul Tillich and Rudolf Bultmann. In 1929 he returned to Freiburg, where he had studied, to succeed Husserl as professor. Heidegger was indeed indebted to Husserl's phenomenological method, but thought that phenomenology was only a first step toward what should be contemporary philosophy's true concern: the nature of "being." Ambivalent toward Nazism, Heidegger spent most of his adult life away from the university world. He often created his own terminology, and was difficult in his conceptual constructions. Heidegger developed a "metaphysic" of the human person, and tried to understand what it meant to "be" and "exist." Focusing on the existing human being as the only being capable of reflecting upon and questioning his or her existence, Heidegger analyzed human existence as either "authentic" (that is, real existence, with and within all the consequences of historical, free, vulnerable, and concrete existence) or "inauthentic" (that is, mere survival as a domesticated being in domesticating society). The conscious acceptance of death as part of real existence is an important sign of authenticity. In his later works, Heidegger emphasized his reflection on the relationship between language and being. One may find neither atheism nor theism in Heidegger: his starting premises never allowed him full clarity on these questions, although he is usually credited with having opened philosophical spaces that would permit a more contemporary understanding of (and even encounter with) God. Among his most important publications are *Being and Time* (1927), and *Existence and Being* (1949).

Orlando Espín

See also BULTMANN, RUDOLF; EXISTENCE; EXISTENTIALISM; LEVINAS, EMMANUEL; METAPHYSICS; METHOD IN THEOLOGY; MODERNITY; PHENOMENOLOGY; POSTMODERNITY; SALVATION; SARTRE, JEAN PAUL; SIN; TILLICH, PAUL; ZUBIRI, XAVIER.

HEILSGESCHICHTE

A German term meaning "salvation history." It denotes an approach where history is seen as a series of redemptive epochs. For example, when *Heilsgeschichte* is seen as a major key in understanding the New Testament, as found especially in the work of O. Cullman, the Christ-event functions as the fulcrum or midpoint of a time line that extends from a previous period of preparation for Christ, through the present stage of the church and on into the eschatological future. In this approach to biblical history, a tension exists between promise and fulfillment, between the past and present, and between the past/present and the future, that is, "the already and the not yet." In the New Testament it is especially the theologies of Luke and of Paul that have been given a *heilsgeschichtlich* interpretation by many.

F. M. Gillman

See also CULLMAN, OSCAR; LUKE/LUKAN; PAULINE THEOLOGY.

HELL

Hell is a popular term of a person's estrangement from God after death. The word from the old German *hel* is a concept similar to *Gehenna* or *Sheol*, the place of the dead. The concept lacks clear roots in the biblical tradition, but conveys three theological convictions. In Christianity, it is linked to the conviction about Christ's resurrection and, contingent on that, the personal resurrection of the faithful. It affirms human freedom and the permanent significance of human choices. Finally, it suggests a sense of God's justice and of the ethical dimension of life that stems from the covenant relationship with God, particularly with reference to one's fellow humans. Thus the concept, hell, expresses the opposite of resurrection, heaven and beatific vision. It is the symbol for the human choice to refuse covenant with God and humanity. Through popular preaching, hell has acquired the sense of location, a place of damnation and of punishment filled with pain and terror. This imagery, intended as an ethical deterrent for Christian behavior, has no roots in Scripture. Thus, modern reflection queries whether hell exists and whether extinction is not a better penalty for turning against God. The sense of the historical consequences of evil actions

and the need for an accounting for those affecting others, aids the survival of the concept that is usually described as a condition of complete isolation, of entrapment in the concerns of the self.

Patricia Plovanich

See also BEATIFIC VISION; DAMNATION; HEAVEN.

HELLENISM/HELLENISTIC

(From *'ellas*, Greece). Hellenism refers to the spread of Greek thought, language, and culture beginning with the conquests of Alexander the Great (336–23 B.C.E.) and continuing under his Hellenistic successors and some Roman emperors. Alexander and his successors made a regular practice of founding Greek cities in all the areas they conquered. Alexander founded approximately seventy cities, the most famous of which was ancient Alexandria in Egypt.

Russell Fuller

See also ALEXANDER THE GREAT.

HELOISE (1100?–63?)

Heloise was the niece of Fulbert, a canon of the cathedral of Notre Dame in Paris. Around the year 1117 she became the student of the theologian Peter Abelard. The two fell passionately in love and, when Heloise became pregnant, they were secretly married. Heloise returned to Abelard's home in Brittany to bear their son, Peter Astralabe. Fulbert, furious with Abelard, hired thugs to castrate him. As a result, Abelard entered the monastery of St. Denis and ordered Heloise to join the convent of Argenteuil. When the nuns of Argenteuil were expelled by Suger, the abbot of St. Denis, Abelard offered them his now deserted oratory, the Paraclete, as a refuge. First as prioress and then as abbess, Heloise emerged as a successful administrator. The Paraclete grew to house sixty nuns, and six sister convents were founded under Heloise's direction. Heloise was renowned by popes and abbots for her learning, piety, and organizational skills. When she died, she was buried alongside her husband at the Paraclete. The two famous lovers are now interred at Père LaChaise Cemetery in Paris.

Gary Macy

See also ABELARD, PETER; MEDIEVAL CHRISTIANITY (IN THE WEST); MONASTICISM IN WESTERN CHRISTIANITY.

HELVETIC CONFESSIONS

These two confessions of faith helped to solidify and institutionalize the Swiss Reformation. The first Helvetic Confession was produced in 1536 by Johann Heinrich Bullinger (1504–75) and several other Reformers. Bullinger had played an important role in the Zurich Reformation since the death of Zwingli in 1531. Whereas the Confession of 1536 was affirmed solely in Switzerland, the second Helvetic Confession, also composed in large part by Bullinger, was published in 1566 at the request of Frederick III, Elector of the Palatinate in Germany. Frederick had recently made public his Calvinism and sought the support of a renewed doctrinal summary. The second Helvetic Confession, longer than the first, was accepted by Swiss Protestants as well as by Calvinists in other countries.

Both Helvetic Confessions point to a growing proliferation of confessions of faith, creeds, and catechisms, in the Reformation and the Counter-Reformation. Some historians speak of the late sixteenth and seventeenth centuries as an age of confessionalization.

Thomas Worcester, S.J.

See also CALVIN, JOHN; CALVINISM; REFORMATION; REFORMED CHURCH; REFORMED THEOLOGY; ZWINGLI, ULRICH.

HENGEL, MARTIN (1926–)

German biblical scholar and professor of New Testament at Erlangen and then Tübingen, who is widely known for his careful study of the Jewish historical setting of the New Testament (*Judaism and Hellenism*). Hengel warns against distinguishing too sharply between Palestinian and Hellenistic features in the New Testament, arguing that by Jesus' time Judaism already was quite Hellenized, innovative, and interpreted its Hebrew Scriptures in widely varied ways. Hengel's ongoing study of the New Testament sociocultural world emerges in his best-known book *The Charismatic Leader and His Followers*; as well as *Property and Riches in the Early Church: Aspects of the Hellenization of Judaism in the Pre-Christian Period; The Son of God; Crucifixion in the Ancient World and the Folly of the Message of the Cross; Jews, Greeks and Barbarians; Between Jesus and Paul; The "Hellenization" of Judaea in the First Century after Christ; The Pre-Christian Paul; Studies in Early Christology; The Zealots;* and *The Septuagint as Christian Scripture.*

Francis D. Connolly-Weinert

HENOTHEISM

A term that refers to a person's (or a community's) commitment to the worship and service of only one god while admitting the existence of other gods. It is different from monotheism because the latter term expressly assumes the existence of only one god.

Orlando Espín

See also MONOTHEISM; POLYTHEISM.

HENOTICON, THE

The name of a theological document put forward by the Byzantine emperor in 482 C.E. as a means of finding a reconciliation formula acceptable to those who accepted the Chalcedonian definitions (Jesus has both human and divine natures) and to the supporters of Monophysitism in the East (Jesus has solely divine nature). The document avoided the question of how many "natures" there are in Christ, and instead emphasized the Nicene-Constantinopolitan Creed as the sure criterion of orthodox faith. It was widely accepted by the Eastern Churches, but not so by the Western Churches.

Orlando Espín

See also BYZANTIUM/BYZANTINE; CATHOLIC TRADITION; CHALCEDON, COUNCIL OF; CHRISTOLOGY; CREED; FATHERS OF THE CHURCH; HYPOSTASIS; HYPOSTATIC UNION; MONOPHYSITISM; NESTORIANISM; NESTORIUS; NICAEA, FIRST COUNCIL OF; ORTHODOX CHURCHES; PATRISTICS/PATROLOGY; RULE OF FAITH.

HERDER, JOHANN G. (1744–1803)

German theologian, philosopher, historian, and Lutheran pastor, Herder combined a life of pastoral service with a career as distinguished scholar whose insights shaped biblical studies in the late eighteenth and nineteenth centuries. Influenced by the Enlightenment and Romantic philosophical movements, Herder opposed the strictly epistemological approach to truth and language proposed by Kantian philosophy. He opposed the dogmatic approach to biblical exegesis as well, and advocated the use of literary methods to illuminate Scripture's human significance. Herder grasped the historical and cultural character of language and so proposed the quest for truth and meaning, even of biblical texts, to mandate a progressive search for the historical development of themes. The theories and methods pioneered in his work influenced the study of history and anticipated many modern approaches to the scientific and literary study of Scripture.

Patricia Plovanich

HERESIARCH

Literally, from the Greek, a "promoter of heresies." Thus a *heresiarch* is someone who stands at the head of a heresy, like the leader of a school of thought.

William Reiser, S.J.

See also ARIUS; BASILIDES; HERESY; HERETIC/HERETICAL; NESTORIUS; NOVATIAN OF ROME; ORTHODOXY; PELAGIUS.

HERESY

The term heresy comes from a Greek word meaning "choice." In Christian tradition heresy refers to false teaching; to embrace false teaching is to separate oneself from what the tradition holds to be true. Heresy generally implies that one has intentionally separated oneself from the universal communion of faith and practice, and has either formed or joined a sect. As unsound and unacceptable teaching or opinion, heresy can only be defined with respect to what the community understands to be orthodox, that is, "right" or "correct" teaching. Teaching is right when it is in conformity with (1) Scripture, (2) the apostolic tradition as it has come down through the bishops and through the "sense of the faithful," and (3) the church's faith as expressed in its prayer and worship.

While heresy usually refers to false or dangerous teaching, the term has sometimes been used too loosely. Not every theological opinion that falls outside the mainstream is necessarily erroneous and harmful. In addition to the categories of orthodoxy and heresy, there is theological pluralism, an idea which has been "canonized" by contemporary biblical and historical scholarship. Views may be different, yet still be biblically sound and within the bounds of apostolic tradition. Theological diversity is clearly present in the New Testament. The inability to recognize and deal with the reality of pluralism has caused considerable suffering and disunity over the centuries. The church's creeds were developed in order to provide local churches with a rule of faith and to protect the people against false teaching or exaggerations of the Gospel message. Yet not everyone whose views were eventually labeled "heretical" was in bad faith. Often such people were earnestly looking for the truth and their lives were truly exemplary.

Today, theologians attach as much importance to "right practice" as to "right belief," for verbal orthodoxy alone is no guarantee that a person or a community is actually standing in the truth. In other words, heresy can also take the form of false or sinful practice. Thus Christians need to exercise caution and humility when they invoke the term "heresy" to characterize the teaching or practice of other believers. Interestingly, the notion of heresy does not appear in the documents of Vatican II.

William Reiser, s.j.

See also DEVELOPMENT OF DOGMA/OF DOCTRINE; DOGMA; HERETIC/HERETI-CAL; HETERODOX/HETERODOXY; HIERARCHY OF TRUTHS; ORTHODOXY (IN CHRISTIANITY); ORTHOPRAXIS; PLURALISM.

HERETIC/HERETICAL

A heretic is, by definition, someone who has embraced a heresy, that is (according to canon law), "the obstinate postbaptismal denial of some truth which must be believed with divine and catholic faith, or it is likewise an obstinate doubt concerning the same" (Can. 751). A heretic is not an apostate, for the heretic does not renounce Christian faith altogether. Heretical normally refers to false teaching. While it would be rather simple to list those whom the church has formally judged to be heretics over the centuries, such a record would most likely be very unfair. First, history is usually written by the winners, not the losers. Many of the accounts we have do not accurately portray the theological positions of those who advanced minority views or whose opinions were rejected on political or cultural, rather than strictly religious grounds. Second, the church has been slow in recognizing and respecting the reality of theological pluralism. The effort to impose uniformity in the understanding of belief does a great disservice to those who have a different insight into Christian faith. Early church writers, as well as later theologians, were often perplexed by the New Testament writings because theological pluralism or diversity was not one of their categories. Their attempts to harmonize the message of the various New Testament writers were bound to fail.

Consequently, the term "heretic" is not very illuminating. Some of the classical "heresiarchs" like Arius and Nestorius were vilified by their enemies. Modern research into ancient controversies has shed considerable light on those whom the tradition labeled heretics. The title was frequently undeserved, especially when it implied bad faith. Origen, the eminent third-century biblical scholar, is a good example of someone whose theological positions were eventually judged heretical and who was vilified by his adversaries, but who really ranks with Augustine as one of the two foremost thinkers in the early church, and whose holiness was well attested. Similarly, one would be ill-advised to refer to the Protestant Reformers of the sixteenth century as heretics. Unless the label heretic merely designates someone who disagrees with us, then Christians need to acknowledge that the circle of understanding can be very wide, certainly as wide as the diversity within the New Testament itself. This is not to say that there are no boundaries to what can be proposed for belief, only that the circle should not be drawn too narrowly.

William Reiser, s.j.

See also APOSTASY; CANON LAW; DOGMA; HERESIARCH; HERESY; ORIGEN.

HERMAS
Known only by the autobiographical sketch in his only work, The Shepherd, Hermas was a first-century Roman Christian strongly influenced by Jewish thought. Freed from slavery, he committed a serious sin against the community, but was allowed to do penance and return to the church. In fact, The Shepherd itself is a sustained argument in favor of accepting back into the church those who repent. Set in the form of an apocalyptic vision, the book argues that sinners have one last chance to repent and rejoin the church before Christ returns. There is a scholarly debate whether the entire book, or only the first section, dates from the first century and hence was written by Hermas. There is little question, however, of its influence. Some early Christians even treated The Shepherd as Scripture, while modern scholars find the book an invaluable source for understanding the Roman Christian community of the first century.

Gary Macy

See also APOCALYPTIC; REPENTANCE (IN CHRISTIAN PERSPECTIVE).

HERMENEUTICAL CIRCLE
First articulated by Friedrich Ast and Friedrich Schleiermacher, the term refers to the dialectical relation between "part" and "whole" that constitutes understanding the meaning of cultural phenomena and texts. For example, the meaning of an individual word ("part") is achieved through an anticipatory and hypothetical understanding of the meaning of the entire sentence ("whole"), but understanding the meaning of the entire sentence is only achieved by understanding its specific words. Thus, the understanding of the one ("part" or "whole") is corrected in the process of understanding the other ("part" or "whole") and vice versa. In the work of Martin Heidegger and Hans-Georg Gadamer, the meaning of the term was broadened to describe the work of human understanding per se.

J. A. Colombo

See also GADAMER, HANS-GEORG; HEIDEGGER, MARTIN; HERMENEUTICS; SCHLEIERMACHER, FRIEDRICH.

HERMENEUTICAL SUSPICION
Hermeneutics is the study of interpretation, that is, of the methods and approaches used in determining the meaning of a text or event. The term "hermeneutical suspicion" derives from the 1970 study Freud and Philosophy by Paul Ricoeur in which Ricoeur referred to "masters of suspicion," specifically Karl Marx, Friedrich Nietzsche, and Sigmund Freud. What

joins these three "masters" (who analyzed human reality in very different ways) is their starting point: as Ricoeur showed, each assumed that the literal or conventional meaning of a text or event often hides political interests served by the false but widely accepted interpretation. Thus these "masters" have taught succeeding generations to be suspicious of what "meets the eye" and to attempt to uncover the real purpose of a particular interpretation. Hermeneutical suspicion may be applied to any field, but because Marx, Nietzsche, and Freud all analyzed the ways in which religion hides reality, it is not surprising that it has been widely used in religious studies and theology. The theologies of liberation (which include feminist theology) have, in particular, employed hermeneutical suspicion in their approaches to the interpretation of Scripture and tradition. Indeed, they have rejected the very possibility of objectivity or neutrality in interpretation and have attempted to pay careful attention to the social location of the author(s) of religious texts and doctrines. For example, liberation theologians have demonstrated that while certain biblical texts are in fact oppressive, the Bible also contains a liberating message that has too often been hidden from the oppressed of the world. In both cases inadequate or false interpretations have served to protect the privilege of the powerful while making such privilege relatively invisible to the oppressed.

James B. Nickoloff

See also FREUD, SIGMUND; LIBERATION THEOLOGIES; MARX, KARL; NIETZSCHE, FRIEDRICH; RICOEUR, PAUL.

HERMENEUTICS

Hermeneutics is the art of interpreting the meaning of texts and, more generally, the phenomena of human culture. In its development from the late eighteenth century to our own (from Friedrich Ast and Friedrich Schleiermacher through Wilhelm Dilthey and Martin Heidegger to Hans-Georg Gadamer and Paul Ricoeur), various abiding tensions have marked this discipline. In general and despite notable exceptions such as Emilio Betti and E. D. Hirsch, the trend in hermeneutics has been its development from a collection of methods for the interpretation of texts when understanding reaches an impasse, to a description of the mode of understanding appropriate and specific to the *Geisteswissenschaften* ("human sciences"), to a form of fundamental ontology, that is, a reflection on the nature of understanding per se and the conditions of its possibility in the life-world that is itself a condition of all second-order reflective activity.

At the heart of contemporary hermeneutics is a debate over the nature of "meaning": is meaning governed by the intentionality of the author/speaker or is meaning quasi-independent of that intention, residing in the autonomy and play of language itself? To the extent that positions tend to the former, hermeneutics as a discrete discipline directed toward the reconstruction or divination of authorial intention is emphasized; to the extent that positions tend toward the latter, hermeneutics becomes a form of fundamental ontology. Further, in the last two decades, significant debates have arisen about the claims of hermeneutics as a form of fundamental ontology from the positions of "ideology-critique," for instance, Jürgen Habermas, and "deconstructionism," for example, Jacques Derrida.

J. A. Colombo

See also GADAMER, HANS-GEORG; HEIDEGGER, MARTIN; HERMENEUTICAL CIRCLE; RICOEUR, PAUL.

HERMETIC BOOKS

Also known as the *Corpus Hermeticum*, this collection of texts from the second and third centuries C.E., mostly preserved in Greek, probably originated in Egypt. The documents purport to be proclamations of "Thrice Great Hermes," (*Hermes Trismegistos*), the Greek god Hermes, whose name is a later designation for the Egyptian god of Wisdom, Thoth, the father and protector of all knowledge. Hermes appears in the texts not just as a messenger, however, but as revealer, father, personified reason (*nous*), and especially as mystagogue. This collection represents a syncretistic pagan philosophy of religion, drawing religious concepts from very diverse sectors of Greek religion, with Jewish influences as well.

Among the more than two dozen books, some have a Gnostic character, especially the first, "Shepherd of Men" (*Poimandres*). This writing, in its cosmological and astronomical teaching, describes the soul's return to God through the seven spheres of the planets. Others of the writings, written more from a perspective of a moderated dualism and a pantheistic worldview, are in controversy with Gnosticism.

The existence of these documents has caused an ongoing debate concerning whether there was a pagan Gnostic mystery religion *independent* of Christianity.

F. M. Gillman

See also GNOSIS/GNOSTICISM; MYSTERY RELIGIONS; PAGANISM/PAGANS.

HERMIT (IN CHRISTIANITY)

A Christian who has chosen to live a solitary life, seeking God through penance and prayer. Christian hermits first appeared in Egypt (by the third century C.E.), and in the following centuries spread throughout Eastern and Western Christendom. Rare now in Western Christianity (although hermits are still found in religious orders such as the Carthusians and the Camaldolese), in Eastern Christianity they have always been an ecclesial presence. Hermits generally follow the eremitical monastic model in one of its two variations: solitary hermits, or a loosely bound community of hermits.

Orlando Espín

See also ANCHORITES; ANTONY OF EGYPT; ASCETICISM/ASCETICAL; CARTHUSIANS; CONTEMPLATIVES; MONASTICISM IN EASTERN CHRISTIANITY; MONASTICISM IN WESTERN CHRISTIANITY; NUN; PACHOMIUS.

HEROD

A family of Idumean origin, collaborators with the Roman occupation of Palestine who participated in governing Palestine and some surrounding regions under a variety of titles from the mid-second century B.C.E. until the end of the first century C.E. Since the Idumeans had been forcibly converted to Judaism by John Hyrcanus (ruled 134–104 B.C.E.), the Herods were technically Jewish.

The family dynasty can be traced to Antipater who became military commander of Idumea under the Hasmonean rule of Alexander Janneus and Salome Alexandra. His son, also named Antipater, known as well by the shorter name, Antipas, had five children, one of whom became the best known of the Herods, Herod the Great (about 73–4 B.C.E.). Appointed king of Judea by the Roman Senate in 40 B.C.E., Herod the Great's rule until his death in 4 B.C.E. was characterized by loyalty to Rome, grandiose building projects, and brutally harsh repression of any opposition or challenge to his power.

According to Matthew 2:1-18, the birth of Jesus took place while Herod was king, thus no later than 4 B.C.E. Herod's brutality toward suspected opposition from his family members forms the backdrop for the story in Matthew 2:16-17 concerning the slaying of children in Bethlehem. Numerous descendants of Herod the Great, members of the Jewish ruling aristocracy of the first century C.E., are also mentioned in the New Testament documents. These include Herod Antipas, Herodias, Agrippa I, Agrippa II, Bernice, and Drusilla.

F. M. Gillman

See also HERODIANS; INFANCY NARRATIVES.

HERODIANS
A term literally meaning adherents of Herod, or of the dynasty of the Herods. The word occurs three times in the Gospels of Mark and Matthew (Mark 3:6; 12:13 = Matt 22:16) to designate a group who, along with the Pharisees, opposed Jesus. While many theories exist concerning precisely what distinguished the Herodians from others groups, no consensus has been reached, although most suppose the name to indicate support for the rule and policies of Herod Antipas (tetrarch of Galilee and Perea 4 B.C.E.–39 C.E.).

F. M. Gillman

See also HEROD.

HESCHEL, ABRAHAM JOSHUA (1907–72)
A foremost scholar and philosopher of Judaism known for his theology of modern Judaism and his leading role in humanitarian causes, especially the civil rights campaigns in the United States of the 1960s. Heschel received his doctorate at the *Hochschule für die Wissenschaft des Judentums* in Berlin, where he taught until 1938 when the Nazis deported him to Poland. He went to London in 1940 and after the war accepted a professorship in ethics and mysticism at the Jewish Theological Seminary in New York, where he taught beginning in 1945.

Heschel argued that the divine–human encounter takes place at a deeper level than is attainable by the rational mind. Stressing the interdependence of God and humanity, he reached out to skeptical Jews, trying to make Judaism accessible and meaningful in the modern world. Heschel held that God supports ethical human action, such that people express their faith through humanitarianism. He lived according to this theology, playing an active role in social change. His theological writing draws upon the mystical thinking of neo-Hasidism. His *God in Search of Man* is the paramount statement of Judaic theology of the mid-twentieth century.

Alan J. Avery-Peck

HESIOD
Writing around 730–700 B.C.E., Hesiod is one of the earliest of the Greek poets. His poem *Theogony* explains the origin and relationships between the different Greek divinities. The poem lists some three hundred Greek gods and goddesses and has remained one of the major sources for Greek mythology.

Gary Macy

HESYCHASM
The name of an Orthodox Christian spiritual tradition that emphasizes inner, mystical prayer, especially seeking union of mind and heart. It is believed that this

manner of praying (usually focused on the monastic "Jesus Prayer") might lead some, by God's gift, to contemplate God's own light. Hesychasm was promoted by the monks of Mount Athos and staunchly defended by Gregory Palamas and others, and became an acceptable form of prayer in the East.

Orlando Espín

See also GREGORY PALAMAS; JOHN CLIMACUS; MONASTICISM IN EASTERN CHRISTIANITY; MOUNT ATHOS; MYSTICISM/MYSTICS (IN CHRISTIANITY); ORTHODOX CHURCHES; PRAYER; SPIRITUALITY.

HETERODOX/HETERODOXY

This is the term used to characterize suspect (or literally, from the Greek, "different" in the sense of "strange") teaching. A teaching is considered suspect or doubtful because it does not conform to what the church holds to be orthodox or in keeping with the rule of faith as found in the ancient creeds, conciliar teaching, apostolic tradition, or Scripture. While it can refer to a view that might eventually be declared heretical, heterodox connotes a degree of ambiguity about a position in relationship to what is considered normative.

Although heterodoxy and heresy have occasionally been used interchangeably, heresy denotes a definitive negative judgment by the church. Not infrequently, however, theological opinions or ideas that were considered heterodox or questionable at one period were later acknowledged as sound. Theological understanding develops as the church finds itself in new cultural and geopolitical situations; theological understanding also grows with advances in the natural and human sciences.

William Reiser, s.j.

See also DEVELOPMENT OF DOGMA/OF DOCTRINE; HERESY; HERMENEUTICAL SUSPICION; HERMENEUTICS; ORTHODOXY (IN CHRISTIANITY).

HETERONOMY

A philosophical and theological term, originally coined by Immanuel Kant and more recently developed by Paul Tillich. By heteronomy Kant meant that the human will (or human feeling or interest) was not sufficient ground for moral judgment; rather, a law external to the human will must be the foundation for moral judgment. Tillich developed Kant's perspective and introduced the notion of "theonomy" as a way of understanding the foundations of moral judgment. Heteronomy assumes that humans are incapable of acting morally on their own, thereby requiring an external law to compel and guide their moral judgment. Theonomy assumes that this external law is, in fact, implanted in and as the innermost core of humanness, and that it is rooted in the divine law and image.

Orlando Espín

See also KANT, IMMANUEL; THEOLOGICAL ANTHROPOLOGY; THEONOMY; TILLICH, PAUL.

HEURISTIC

The term "heuristic" comes from the Greek *heuriskein*, "to discover," and means a study whose goal is to explore something presently unknown. A heuristic effort is not an unguided search but adopts methods, categories, and structures having the potential to produce knowledge about a subject. A heuristic approach always has an element of exploration, of trial and error, and it does not guarantee clear outcomes. One may speak about heuristic structures, categories, and so on, that designate their experimental character.

Patricia Plovanich

HIERARCHY OF TRUTHS

The hierarchy of truths is a theological principle proposed by the Catholic Church at Vatican Council II in *Unitatis Redintegratio* (1964) to promote and guide ecumenical dialogue, given the doctrinal differences that divided churches. The document proposed a hierarchy of a few central symbols or truths to be the foundation and sources of all other teachings. This schema promoted a *reductio* or concentration of faith in core Christian convictions about revelation, the trinitarian nature of God, and the Incarnation's significance for existence. The foundational symbols clarified the significance of the other doctrines and their relationship to the whole. It permitted a legitimate diversity of dogmatic expressions and a means of distinguishing the permanent and central from the peripheral and temporary. Finally, the concept of the hierarchy of truths restored to Catholics a sense of the symbolic character of dogma that expresses the mystery of divine presence in history.

Patricia Plovanich

HIEROPHANY

A manifestation of the Holy or Sacred. The manifestation could be in or through objects, events, or persons. The term is more frequent in religious studies (for example, history of religions, comparative religions) than in theology.

Orlando Espín

HIGH CHURCH/LOW CHURCH

Terms for contrasting styles of theology, liturgy, and church governance that were first used to describe conflicting positions and parties in the Church of England.

A High Church style is characterized by adherence to the full tradition of the undivided Catholic Church, to the authority of the episcopate, to celebration of the sacraments by ordained priests, and to a relatively elaborate liturgical ceremonial, sometimes jokingly called "smells (incense) and bells."

A Low Church style is characterized by its stress on certain elements of the tradition, such as the Bible alone as normative of church life, and being "born again." These are held to be the essentials of the Gospel; all the other elements of religion are deemed unnecessary and sometimes even dangerous, insofar as they might distract people from the essentials. Low Church worship services are quite spare in their ceremonies.

Jon Nilson

HIGH GOD/SUPREME GOD

Many religions assume and believe in the existence of a high or supreme god. However, not all religions hold this belief (because, surprisingly perhaps, not all religions believe in a god or in many gods). Some monotheistic religions (Christianity, Judaism, Islam, Baha'i, for example) hold that there is only one god, and that this one god is not accompanied by other beings who might share in the one god's divinity or activity. Other religions (for example, Santería) hold that there is only one god, but because this god is absent from the daily world of humans, all concerns for daily life have been delegated by the one god to sacred beings who are responsible for responding to humankind's needs and for running the world—these sacred beings, however, are not "gods" or really divine as the only god is fully divine.

There are other religions that believe in two equally important and equally divine gods (for example, Zoroastrianism), while other religions hold that many gods do exist, but all somehow under the authority of a supreme god (ancient Roman and Greek religion, for example). Finally, some religions believe in the existence of many gods, holding that these gods are ultimately only manifestations of the divinity of the one supreme god (for example, Hinduism, Nahua religion).

Orlando Espín

See also CHRISTIANITY; DEUS ABSCONDITUS; DEUS OTIOSUS; GOD; HENOTHEISM; HINDUISM; INDIGENOUS RELIGIOUS TRADITIONS; ISLAM; JUDAISM; MONOTHEISM (IN CHRISTIANITY AND ISLAM); MONOTHEISM (IN JUDAISM); NAHUA TRADITIONAL RELIGION; POLYTHEISM; RELIGION; SANTERÍA; ZOROASTRIANISM.

HIGH PRIEST (IN JUDAISM)
(Hebrew, *Cohen Gadol*). In Judaism, the head of the cult in the Jerusalem Temple, an ancestral office conferred on Aaron and his descendants (Exod 27:21). In the Solomonic Temple, destroyed in 586 B.C.E., the high priest was responsible primarily for cultic activities, including consulting the divine oracle (Urim and Thummim, Exod 28:30). In the Second Temple, built in the early fifth century B.C.E. and destroyed in 70 C.E., the high priest had broad administrative authority, including power over the secular policy of the Jewish state and responsibility for the conduct of foreign diplomacy. Following the Maccabean uprising of 164 B.C.E., the high priesthood was controlled by the Hasmonean dynasty. At the end of the Second Temple period, high priests were appointed by the Roman rulers.

Alan J. Avery-Peck

HIJRA (IN ISLAM)
The migration of the Prophet Muhammad (570–632) from the city of Mecca to Yathrib (now called Medina) in Arabia on September 17, 622 C.E. *Hijra* is sometimes translated as "flight," but the word more properly means breaking off relations with one's own family or tribe, and in the case of the Prophet Muhammad, this is the more accurate understanding of the term. After facing fierce opposition to the message of Islam that he attempted to preach among his own people in Mecca, the Prophet left his ancestral city to join a small group of loyal followers in Yathrib where he established the first Islamic *umma* (political-religious community). The hijra, therefore, marks the beginning of the religious tradition we call Islam today. For this reason, 622 C.E. became the first year of the Islamic calendar.

Ronald A. Pachence

See also ISLAM; MECCA; MEDINA; MUHAMMAD; UMMA.

HILARY OF POITIERS (?–367)
Possibly a convert from Neoplatonism, Hilary was elected bishop of Poitiers in southern France about 353. He was exiled by the emperor for four years (356–60) for his defense of orthodoxy against the Arians. While in exile in Asia, he was in contact with the other leaders in the struggle against Arianism. Hilary worked hard to unite in opposition to Arianism both those theologians who defended the *homoousios* ("of the same substance") of the Nicene Creed and those who preferred the milder *homoiousios* ("like in substance to"). Most of Hilary's works were written against the Arians, although some of his scriptural commentaries and three hymns also survive.

Gary Macy

See also ARIANISM; HOMOIOUSIOS; HOMOOUSIOS; PLATONISM.

HILDEGARD OF BINGEN
(1098–1179)

Abbess of the monastery of Disebodenburg, Hildegard was one of the most learned people of her age. She corresponded with emperors, popes, and other high officials, and authored many works in addition to her letters: accounts of her visions, prophecies, songs, a morality play, and a handbook on medicine. Her best-known work is the *Scivias*, an autobiography that emphasizes the content of her many visions and for which she ordered and supervised a series of illustrations. In that work, her visions are not so intensely personal that they focus on an isolated element of Christian teaching, but lead her to genuinely theological reflection upon the divine nature, the mystery of the Trinity, the humanity of Christ, and the nature of the human person who is *imago dei*. All of her writings bring together scientific knowledge, philosophic reflection, and mystical imagery in a fusion that still intrigues both scholars and poets.

Marie Anne Mayeski

See also MEDIEVAL CHRISTIANITY (IN THE WEST); MYSTICISM/MYSTICS (IN CHRISTIANITY); NUN.

HILLEL

A Jewish scholar in Jerusalem at the time of Herod the Great, viewed by later Judaism as the main force in the creation of rabbinic Judaism. Born in Babylonia, Hillel studied biblical exposition in the Land of Israel and is credited with developing the system of hermeneutics central to later rabbinic interpretation of Scripture.

In the earliest materials ascribed to Hillel, found in the Mishnah and Tosefta, he has four areas of concern: (1) cultic cleanness, (2) agricultural tithes, (3) animal offerings, and (4) economic rules, especially his method of circumventing Scripture's Sabbatical remission of debts (Deut 15:1-4). Moral sayings are attributed to Hillel primarily in a later period, represented by Mishnah Avot and the Midrashic and Talmudic literatures. In Avot, Hillel preaches conformity to the mores and rules of the community, condemns gossip, and impugns unfair judging of others. While praising study, piety, and patience, he maligns the body and things of this world. In many of these later sources, Shammai, with whom Hillel often is found in debate, functions as a foil, personalizing negative traits, just as Hillel represents the good. In all, Hillel is presented as a pious individual who, for instance, studied Torah every day even as a poor man, giving half of the little he earned to the doorkeeper at the house of study.

A number of stories epitomize Hillel's wisdom and approach to universal issues regarding the nature of God and humanity. Emblematic is his statement at Mishnah Avot 1:12, enjoining all Israelites to "Be disciples of Aaron, loving peace and pursuing peace, loving people and drawing them near to the Torah." His broader understanding of the significance of Jewish thought and practice is revealed in the story found at Babylonian Talmud Shabbat 31a that recounts his response to a potential proselyte. Hillel tells him, "What is hateful to you, to your fellow do not do. That is the entirety of the Torah; everything else is elaboration. So go, study."

Alan J. Avery-Peck

See also SHAMMAI.

HINAYANA

A term designating the earliest eighteen Buddhist monastic schools of the "Lesser Vehicle," as it was coined and used polemically by early Mahayana ("Great Vehicle") exponents. (There are many examples in the history of religions in which the labels of opponents eventually find acceptance.) This outcome is also ironic with reference to the history of Buddhism in South Asia, where, through the first millennium of the faith's successful expansion, Hinayana institutions were in the great majority, and monks loyal to each were recorded as occupying the same monasteries.

Although only the Theravada among these schools endures in modern Thailand, Burma, Cambodia, Laos, and Sri Lanka, Theravada and Hinayana cannot be used properly as synonyms. Modern Theravadins naturally dislike the term "Hinayana," and this term should not be used for the modern tradition; but it is also problematic to substitute "Theravada" for the eighteen Indic Sthavira schools, as the Theravadins were very limited in their geographic scope (southern India and Sri Lanka) and in adherents, especially in comparison to the largest school, the Sarvastivadins. Although only their canon (the Pali Canon) survives in its entirety, Theravada traditions cannot be regarded as entirely representative of the Sthavira historically, especially in terms of monastic norms, ritual practice, and in certain areas of doctrinal interpretation.

Noting these historical complexities and that these designations refer to (and had meaning only for) the small minority of Buddhists who became monks and nuns of the sangha, several general features of Hinayana or Sthavira Buddhism can be discussed.

All schools emphasized the ethos of the individual striving for enlightenment, whether one was at the beginning stage of moral observance or at an advanced stage in one's meditative pursuits. There was also a strong emphasis on developing the Buddhist community, with donations to the sangha and Buddhist shrines promoted as meritorious to the laity; this and reciprocal service to the laity by the sangha (medical, ritual, educational, exhortative, and so forth) was the basis of Buddhist civilization. Inscriptions record a great concern at Hinayana sites expressed by laity *and* sangha members for finding perpetual proximity to the Buddha's relics and for making meritorious donations aimed to improve the well-being of their parents.

The enlightened *Arahant* was celebrated as the exemplary ideal in the Sthavira schools. Their cosmology focused upon the earth-centered frame of reference, and the historical primacy of Shakyamuni as the only guide in this world era, with the next Buddha Maitreya anticipated as the vehicle for the faith's revival. For the small circles of scholastic philosophers, the fine points and extensions of the doctrine were worked out in the various *Abhidharmas* and commentaries.

Todd T. Lewis

See also ABHIDHARMA/ABHIDHAMMA PITAKA; SARVASTIVADIN SCHOOL; THERAVADA BUDDHISM.

HINCMAR OF REIMS (806?–82)

Hincmar was educated in Paris, where he was introduced to the court of Louis the Pious, the son of Charlemagne. Hincmar worked closely with Louis's son, Charles the Bald, throughout most of his career. Hincmar became archbishop of Reims in 845, and as archbishop worked to assert the rights of bishops as the supreme authority in the church. Hincmar not only wrote in favor of these rights, but also produced works of history, pastoral care, and canon law.

Gary Macy

See also CHARLEMAGNE; MEDIEVAL CHRISTIANITY (IN THE WEST); SCOTTUS ERIUGENA, JOHN.

HINDUISM

What the West refers to as "Hinduism" is in reality a complex family of religious traditions. Indeed, whether one should properly think of it as a single religious tradition or a collection of closely related traditions has been a matter of debate. Hindus share, for the most part, a common belief in a multiplicity of deities, reincarnation, and especially the sanctity and authority of the Vedas, the tradition's holiest scriptures. They draw selectively from a common store of ritual practices and mythology (especially that contained in the *Mahabharata*), and participate in a common, religiously defined social structure, the caste system. At the same time, however, the many Hindu subtraditions display wide divergences in theologies and have strong disagreements about practice.

The advent of Islam in the subcontinent around the end of the first millennium C.E. introduced South Asians to the idea of a monolithic religious community with clearly defined boundaries. In the late nineteenth century, Western-educated Hindus began using the term "Hinduism"—coined by, and borrowed from, Western orientalists—to refer to their religion, now conceived as one of several world religions. Prior to these and other related developments, it is not clear that Hindus thought of themselves as belonging to a single religion. Rather, they may well have identified themselves, at least

primarily, as members of divergent religious denominations or "lineages" (*sampradayas, paramparas*). Despite the fact that these numerous subtraditions or denominations have been well established for centuries, they are typically (and misleadingly) referred to as "sects" or "sectarian traditions" by Western scholars.

In addition to its diversity, there are other reasons that the Hindu tradition has been and continues to be something of a puzzle to Western students. For example, Hindus recognize the existence of many gods (*devas*), but any given Hindu will commonly regard only one as the Supreme Being. Because of the diversity of subtraditions, however, there is no universal agreement as to which deity ought to be so recognized. Hinduism, moreover, has no central authority to decide this or any other issue. Hindus have tolerated a wide variety of beliefs and practices, but at the same time have insisted upon the unifying norms of a fixed and hierarchical social structure, the caste system.

Historically speaking, Hinduism has no single founder. Orthodox Hindus, in fact, regard their tradition as the "eternal way" (*sanatana dharma*). It is initiated—at the beginning of each cycle in the beginningless and endless series of cycles that the universe goes through—by sages or seers (*rishis*), to whom the most sacred scriptures, the Vedas, are revealed. Modern scholarship sees the origins of Hinduism in the confluence of the religion of the Sanskrit-speaking Aryans, who entered the subcontinent from the northwest around the middle of the second millennium B.C.E., and indigenous, so-called pre-Aryan religious cultures. The latter are represented in part by the Indus Valley Civilization (around 3,000–1600 B.C.E.). The rishis, in this view, were the priests of the Aryans and the poets who composed the Vedas. The Aryans brought with them, and developed as they settled down and inculturated, a religion Western scholars call Vedism or Brahmanism, the latter term derived from the name of the priestly caste category *brahmana* (brahmin in English). The Vedic religion focused on a multiplicity of deities, many regarded as powers of nature, to whom ritual sacrifices (*yajna*) were offered, along with prayers for material well-being and visionary inspiration. It appears that this religion gradually blended with indigenous traditions, which were even more ancient than the advent of Vedism in India, to produce what we know now as classical Hinduism. The transition between Brahmanism and classical Hinduism is generally marked by the redaction of the *Bhagavad Gita*, somewhere between 200 B.C.E. and 200 C.E. If then one wants an answer to the question of when Hinduism began, one might look to the Aryan migration into South Asia and the beginnings of the composition of the Vedas, around 1500 B.C.E., or to the composition of the *Bhagavad Gita*, toward the end of the first millennium B.C.E., or—with considerable justification—to the origins of pre-Aryan religion that are suggested, perhaps, in the Indus Valley Civilization, but are finally lost in prehistory.

The Hindu tradition looks to a number of sacred books as authoritative. Most important for many Hindus (though few actually read them) are the Vedas, regarded, as indicated above, as eternal truths revealed to the rishis. Attached to, and considered a part of, the Vedas are the Upanishads, which contain theological meditations that are the basis of Hindu theology, or Vedanta. Also important are the *Mahabharata* and *Ramayana* (the two great epics of India), the *Bhagavad Gita* (which forms a part of the *Mahabharata*), the Puranas (storehouses of myth and theistic devotion), the Tantras or Agamas (manuals of theology, ritual, and meditation), and several collections of hymns composed by saints.

For purposes of simplification, the denominations (*sampradayas*) that make up medieval Hinduism can be divided roughly into four main traditions: (1) the Vaishnava, (2) the Shaiva, (3) the Shakta, and (4) the Smarta. These traditions and their offshoots continue to the present day, though some schools have lost their vitality under the impact of modernity or are even in danger of disappearing altogether as lived spiritualities. In addition to these "sectarian" traditions, scholars identify an additional movement that is extremely important in modern Hinduism and to the face that Hinduism presents to the outside world. Usually termed "Neo-Hinduism," it can be thought of as a fifth tradition, but of a recent type that draws its following from more or less well-educated, modernized Hindus.

The Vaishava *sampradayas* are so called because most focus on Vishnu as the supreme Deity (the Krishnaite sects are an exception). Vaishnavas tend to stress devotion (*bhakti*) as the most efficacious spiritual path and look forward to loving communion with the deity in a heavenly paradise as the highest spiritual goal. For Shaivas, on the other hand, Shiva is the Supreme Being. While many Shaivas stress a bhakti-oriented spirituality that resembles that of the Vaishnavas, others stress yogic practice and seek a radically nondualist divinization of both self and world. Shaktas stress the feminine aspect of the divine, worshiping Shakti (literally, "divine power"), the Great Goddess, as supreme. Like Shaivas, Shaktas may be divided into those that stress bhakti—in this case, a loving relationship with the Goddess as Mother—and those that adopt a more strenuous, yogic approach to liberation. Since Shakti, Durga, Parvati, Kala, and the other forms under with the Goddess is typically worshiped are identified mythologically as the spouse of Shiva, Shaktas are often considered to be a branch of Shaivism. Vaishnavas, Shaivas, and Shaktas may be described as theistic in their orientation, since they all believe that the Supreme Being is more or less personal in nature.

Smartas—literally, "those who follow the traditional texts" (*smritis*)—are different. Since they are theologically aligned with the nondualist Vedanta of Shankara, and thus believe that the supreme reality, Brahman, transcends all of the various forms of personal divinity, their outlook may be described as transtheistic. Smarta monks or *sannyasins* traditionally follow the yoga of knowledge (*jnana-yoga*), while Smarta laity generally adopt some form of bhakti practice. The particular deity worshiped by the latter, however, may be a matter of personal preference, according to the doctrine of "chosen deity" (*ishta–devata*). In either case, however, their ultimate goal is complete abandonment of individual selfhood in blissful identity with the transpersonal (*nirguna*) Brahman. Because of their conservative emphasis on the social norms articulated in the Dharma Shastras, their theological focus on Vedic revelation (as opposed to Tantras, Agamas, Puranas, or vernacular texts), and their consequent longstanding prestige in the tradition, the Smarta denomination is often taken as a touchstone of brahminical orthodoxy.

Several points should be noticed about all of these Hindu denominations. First, although they may regard one Deity (or Absolute) as supreme, they do not deny the existence of, or demonize, other Hindu deities. They simply relegate the other gods to lower levels in the divine hierarchy. Vaishnavas, for example, regard other Hindu deities, such as Shiva, as lesser gods, and—while usually tolerant toward other belief systems—typically hold that any yogic realizations, gifts of grace, or states of liberation (*moksha*) attained by a devotee of Shiva or the Goddess will be less perfect than those obtained by a Vaishnava. Second, while Yoga as a separately identifiable school of thought, classically associated with the *Yoga Sutras* of Patanjali, has ceased to be important, yoga has always been a pan-Hindu phenomenon, with numerous schools emerging, flourishing, and falling into oblivion throughout Hindu history. All the major traditions within Hinduism so far discussed have adopted as an essential part of their spirituality some forms of yogic discipline. Third, they have all been deeply influenced, in their yogic and ritual practice and sometimes their official theology, by the esoteric, ritualistic practices of Tantra, a trans-Indian spiritual movement that also transformed aspects of Buddhism.

Beginning in the late eighteenth and early nineteenth centuries (continuing to the present), there has emerged, in response to the colonial experience in India and the impact of modernity, a new mode of being Hindu, one that explicitly acknowledges itself as being part (or, indeed, the essence) of Hinduism, conceived as one among the several world religions. This movement is associated with the so-called Hindu renaissance, a movement that began in the nineteenth century. It enabled Hindus to revitalize their tradition and their pride therein after its vitality had ebbed during a period of social ossification and religious conservatism that had been compounded by centuries of foreign rule. Among the leaders of this movement were, most notably, Ram Mohan Roy, Swami Dayananda, Sri Ramakrishna, Swami Vivekanada, Mahatma Gandhi, and S. Radhakrishnan. They and others were concerned in particular to respond to the Christian and liberal-humanitarian critique leveled by Europeans at what the latter decried as evidence of the "backwardness" of Hinduism. Singled out in particular for criticism by Christian missionaries were Hindu polytheism and its supposed "idolatry," neither of which were well understood, and Hindu social practices, especially the caste system and the treatment of women, which were offensive to Western concepts of social justice. In response, leaders of the Hindu reform movement agitated vigorously against social evils such as child-marriage, restrictions on the education of women, the poor treatment of widows, and untouchability. On a theological level, they counterattacked, comparing the narrowness, intolerance, and dogmatism of Christianity as they had experienced it with a modernized form of Advaita Vedanta said to be tolerant and profoundly spiritual. Proponents of this reformed Hinduism taught that all religions—including the traditional denominations within Hinduism—offer valid approaches to knowledge of the one supreme reality (although they implied that the latter is understood most correctly by Advaita Vedanta). They advocated what they saw as a universal, experiential form of spirituality based on yogic meditation. Referred to by Western scholars as Neo-Vedanta or Neo-Hinduism, this religious vision was articulated forcefully around the world in the late nineteenth century by Swami Vivekananda, but received its most polished presentation in the work of the twentieth-century scholar and philosopher S. Radhakrishnan.

Lance E. Nelson

See also ADVAITA VEDANTA; BHAGAVAD GITA; BHAGAVATA PURANA; BHAKTI; BHAKTI-YOGA; BRAHMANA/BRAHMIN; CASTE; CASTES, SCHEDULED; DEVA/DEVI; ISHTA-DEVATA; KARMA-YOGA; PATANJALI; RADHAKRISHNAN, SARVEPALLI; RAJA-YOGA; RISHI; SHAIVA; SHAKTA; SHAKTI; SHIVA; TANTRA; TANTRIC HINDUISM; VAISHNAVA; VEDANTA; VEDAS; VISHNU; VIVEKANANDA, SWAMI; YOGA.

HIPPOLYTUS OF ROME (170?–236?)

Hippolytus was an important *presbyteros* in the church of Rome. He strongly opposed the teaching of Sabellius. He also disagreed with Zephrinus, the *episkopos* of Rome, over the Sabellian question. When Callistus was chosen to succeed Zepherinus as the leader of the Roman Church, Hippolytus rejected Callistus as a heretic both for supporting Sabellius and for allowing those who sinned after being baptized back into the church. Hippolytus may even have set himself up as a rival *episkopos* to Callistus. When he was exiled together with the new leader of the Roman community, Pontian, Hippolytus was reconciled with the Roman leadership. He was given a martyr's burial. A statue of Hippolytus dating from his lifetime was found in the sixteenth century with a list of his works carved on the side. The two most important works attributed to Hippolytus are the *Apostolic Traditions* that describes the liturgy of that period, and the *Refutation of All Heresies*.

Gary Macy

See also EPISKOPOS; PRESBYTEROS (IN
THE NEW TESTAMENT); SABELLIANISM/
SABELLIUS.

HISPANIC

This term refers to things and persons pertaining to Spain, its culture, or its language. In the United States it became,
since the later 1960s, a generic term frequently applied to all persons and groups
perceived to have roots in the former
Spanish colonial empire in the Americas.
However, this use of the term began by
initiative of *non*-"Hispanics" and mostly
for non-"Hispanic" use in gathering under
one label a wide variety of cultures and
groups. Some "Hispanics" use the term
for themselves. Although there are some
evident reasons for its legitimate use, most
of the groups and persons who were to be
identified by it are increasingly turning to
the name "Latino" as preferable.

Orlando Espín

See also CULTURE; LATINO/A; LATINO
CATHOLICISM; LATINO PROTESTANTISM;
LATINO THEOLOGY (-IES).

HISTORICAL CONSCIOUSNESS

Ultimately grounded on the historicity of
humanity, that is, on humanity's inevitable contextualization in time and (thus)
in history. And because of this, historical
consciousness is also grounded on the
inescapable possibility and reality of
change that occurs over time.

In Christian theology, history is in God's
hands, and it follows God's mysterious
will and plan. Because of human freedom
(sin, response to grace, and so on) history
is not a single unambiguous and ever-
positive development; although Christian theology holds that at the ultimate
end of human history there will follow
the perfect and good establishment of the
reign of God. But before the establishment of the reign, history will remain
ambiguous and thus in need of discernment and real-life commitments on the
part of Christians (and of all persons of
good will).

Within the overall and inevitable
context of human historicity one may
theologically speak of "historical consciousness" as a more recent development (in Christian theology as well as in
most of the world's cultures). Historical
consciousness in theology is dependent
on the historical character of all theologies and of all doctrines, as these are
heard, received, believed, and formulated
by humans in this inescapably historical
world. Historical consciousness further
depends on the very mission of the
church to proclaim the Gospel (and the
complex of doctrines, moral requirements, and community life forms that
have historically developed from it) in
and to ever-changing cultural and social
human contexts. The very condition and
possibility of change and of ambiguity
inevitably intertwined with humanity's
(and thus, with the church's) evident contextualization in time have not always
been fully appreciated by lay Christians,
by theologians (and theologies), and by
the ordained ministers of the church. It
might be possible to say that, beginning
in the eighteenth century, a process of
historical awareness has been developing
that is contributing to a change in our cultures' consciousness—a change toward a
historical consciousness.

This development, itself the product
of history, has made Christian theologians (and theologies) increasingly aware
of the historicity of all humanity (including, of course, Christian humanity—that
is, the church), of the inescapable historical (and other) conditioning of all human

knowledge and acts (including doctrines and theological knowledge, and all forms of Christian life and ecclesial formations). This developing historical consciousness has had, and will continue to have, an impact on theologies and doctrines, and on church life in general.

Historical consciousness, however, neither implies nor requires the denial of constants in the church or in the church's proclamation (doctrinal, and so forth)—but it does increasingly assume that the church does not exist and has never existed outside history or human historicity, and therefore its interpretation (and the interpretation of its doctrines, institutional forms, pastoral approaches, and so on) requires a historical, theological discernment that adequately accounts for continuity as well as for change.

A number of Catholic theological disciplines over the past century or two tried to take human and ecclesial historicity seriously (the history of dogmas, and the theology of history, for example). Today, all theological disciplines seem clearly aware of the developing historical consciousness and do not hesitate to interpret and understand human and ecclesial historicity as typical and necessary context for their respective disciplinary constructs, further understanding these, too, as always historical, at times ambiguous, and inevitably open to change.

Orlando Espín

See also CHURCH; CONTEXTUALIZATION; CRITICAL THEORY; CULTURE; DEVELOPMENT OF DOGMA/OF DOCTRINE; HISTORICAL CRITICISM; HISTORICAL CRITIQUE; HISTORY; REIGN OF GOD.

HISTORICAL CRITICISM

Broadly understood, historical criticism is a synonym for what is often called the "historical-critical method" that subsumes a collection of powerful methodologies taking a "diachronic" approach to a biblical text. By moving backward through (*dia*) time (*chronos*), these critical methods trace a canonical text through every discernible layer of its written and oral formulations that shaped, interpreted, and preserved the memories of the event(s) presented in a text. Thus understood, the protocols of historical criticism are the composite exercises of text, source, form, tradio-historical, composition, and redaction criticism. Individually and collectively, these methods have the capacity to cast enormous light on the prehistory and history of a text. At every level, historical criticism seeks to establish the discrete life situations that influenced precisely how and why traditions were shaped. Thus considered, a biblical text may be considered the window to the multilayered history that lies behind each unit of the text.

Narrowly defined, historical criticism is the study of the history of a biblical document that identifies what can be known about the time and place it was written, as well as establishes what can be known from internal and external evidence about the events, dates, individuals, and places mentioned in a text. Today the social history of every relevant era is claiming much attention, especially in the study of Christian origins. In both its broad and narrow understandings, the conventions and goals of historical criticism use historical reasearch as its paradigm, and are distinguished from literary criticism that explores the literary characteristics of biblical texts by adapting the conventions and goals of literary research.

The broad understanding of historical criticism has its roots in the Enlightenment when a few scholars recognized that many biblical accounts were incompatible with new understandings of science and history. While most overlooked the implications of this insight for a time, by the end of the nineteenth century, ignoring this issue was no longer possible. As historical religions, Judaism and Christianity had an enormous investment in the historical validity of their insights and were forced either to make fundamental changes to some long-standing presuppositions or to reject modern history and science. The adjustments were not without controversy. Furor over biblical historicity catalyzed the splintering of many North American Evangelical denominations in the early twentieth century. Both the premises and methods of historical criticism were viewed with suspicion by most Catholic authorities until the publication of the encyclical Divino *Afflante Spiritu* by Pope Pius XII in 1943. Although Reformed Jews accepted historical criticism, Conservative Jewry refused to apply them to the Torah until relatively recently, and few orthodox Jewish scholars have any interest in modern critical methods. Despite these and other controversies within believing communities, historical criticism dominated the academic study of the Bible throughout the twentieth century.

Historical criticism, as it is broadly understood, transformed the assumption that biblical texts provide an accurate account of history into the more sophisticated appreciation of the fact that ancient believing communities shaped and preserved their fundamental religious insights in stories of truths that were developed over time and are not to be confused with true stories. These stories became the vehicles to articulate understandings of God and God's benevolence to humanity. Many of the stories also established paradigmatic themes that were later applied to interpret new circumstances in new generations. These insights enable belief without the necessity of either disconnecting religious convictions from the knowledge of history and science or denying the validity of modern scientific and historical research. Today Catholics, mainline Protestants, as well as Conservative, Reconstructionist, and Reformed Jewish scholars accept the premises of historical criticism. All but the most conservative Protestant and Orthodox Jewish biblical scholars are trained to use its approaches and methods.

Admittedly, there have been and continue to be abuses. Some sensationalize their research in publications that are designed to shock those without a foundation to recognize how critical insights are compatible with faith. Others, albeit often inadvertently, turn the Bible into an archeological tell (an ancient mound in the Middle East composed of remains of successive settlements) and invest the greatest authority in the most primitive layer of a tradition. Since historical criticism exclusively focused on historical questions, it actually provides limited contributions to the life of believing communities. Many scholars have begun to adopt new literary methods that have a greater capacity to draw out the religious dimensions of biblical texts.

Regina A. Boisclair

See also CANONICAL CRITICISM; FORM CRITICISM; LITERARY CRITICISM; REDACTION CRITICISM; SOURCE CRITICISM; TEXT CRITICISM; TRADITIO-HISTORICAL CRITICISM.

HISTORICAL JESUS
See JESUS OF HISTORY.

HISTORICAL THEOLOGY

Historical theology is a branch of theology used primarily by Christians that investigated the traditions, structures, and beliefs of a particular church or churches. It is usually paired with biblical theology, moral theology, and dogmatic theology, although these categories vary greatly. Historical theology covers a range of different but related fields. Church history studies the ecclesiastical structure, political setting, devotions, and liturgy of Christianity. "History of Christian thought" studies all forms of Christian reflection while "history of theology" investigates the narrower realm of theological expression. "History of Christian doctrine" limits its focus to a study of those issues considered important to Christians while "history of dogma" is reserved for the study of those doctrines that have been declared essential for Christian belief.

Since the essential truths of Christianity have traditionally been held to be unchanging, there is an inherent contradiction in the practice of historical theology. History implies a change, but dogmas are held to be the same for all historical periods. This problem was recognized by earlier Christian writers, but became particularly acute in the early modern period when historians began to challenge the continuity of Christian beliefs. Some Christians have responded by arguing that the essential insights of Christian doctrine do not change but are expressed differently in different times and places, or that the full understanding of a particular dogma only becomes clear over time. Most recently, some postmodern theologians have suggested that Christian beliefs are completely historically conditioned and therefore do change over time. According to these writers, each age must recreate for itself an understanding of the Christian message based on traditions it has inherited.

Gary Macy

See also DEVELOPMENT OF DOGMA/ OF DOCTRINE; DOCTRINE; DOGMA; HEILSGESCHICHTE; HISTORY; POSTMODERNITY.

HISTORY

History plays an important role in any tradition, at least insofar as traditions retain memories of their founders (whether divine or human) and of important moments in the development of the tradition. Most also preserve important ancient texts. For Judaism, Christianity, and Islam, however, history itself plays a role as revelatory of God's interaction with humans. History is a form of sacred time in which God works to reveal both God's plan and God's nature. God's promises in the past are seen to have been fulfilled in later events or expected to be fulfilled in future events. Human history reveals and indeed performs divine purposes. For Judaism, God's promise to provide a land for the people of Israel and to send to Israel a Messiah makes possible a history of the fulfillment of that plan. Christianity reinterpreted this history to proclaim Jesus as the Messiah and to understand Jesus' kingdom (however that might be understood) as the Promised Land of Israel. Islam understands Muhammad as the culmination of the prophets of both Judaism and of Christianity.

A prophetic interpretation of history can claim that events destructive of a church or people were the result of the infidelity of that church or people to God. Present infidelity or immorality can be interpreted to predict future punishment by God. Apocalyptic interpretations of history see past and present events as signs of a coming end time. History can also be read as providing "signs of the times" to which churches and groups are being called by God to respond. Overarching "salvation histories" (*Heilsgeschichte*) have also been written to explain all of human history as the gradual working out of God's plan for the redemption of humankind.

Although many churches and traditions continue to understand God as working in history, especially in the modern period, serious challenges have been advanced against the claims that God's purpose can be discerned in history. Obviously, the histories advanced by Judaism, Christianity and Islam cannot all be correct. Furthermore, claims that Christianity supplanted Judaism or that Islam supplanted both Judaism and Christianity can and have led to a dangerous triumphalism resulting in the marginalization and persecution of the "supplanted" tradition. Thus there would seem to be more than one "salvation history," and, even within the same tradition, different histories have been written interpreting the same events as supporting very different interpretations of God's purpose in those events. Secondly, secular historians have challenged the presuppositions and the accuracy of religious histories by providing an alternative reading of historical events. Rather than seeing God as the moving force of history, secular historians either understand human history as the result of some sort of progress of the human spirit or as the result of random events. These historians would look for social, economic, and political forces as the final causes for historical change. Finally, religious histories have been challenged from within their own traditions. If God is truly ineffable and unknowable, then ultimately God's

purposes in history cannot be known, or at best, can only be known when the entire historical process is at an end. Identifying God's will in history, this objection argues, has too often been used as a rationalization to justify the ends of a particular political or social movement.

Most recently, postmodern theologians have questioned the assumption of religious history that another divine realm exists outside that of human history into which God breaks or from which God controls human activity. These theologians suggest that no such realm exists, and that God should be understood as part of human history itself. This objection flows from the postmodern assumption that all history is a product of the present, shaped by the concerns and historical conditioning of those writing the history. Since the concerns and social setting of historians differ, there exists a plurality of histories of the same periods and events, thus making it difficult to determine which might be "God's history."

History and tradition will remain essential in religious tradition despite the many problems raised concerning the interpretation and creation of that history. The continued attempt to proclaim a God who works in history, while responding critically to the challenges presented to that view, promises to continue to be one of the central concerns of contemporary theology.

Gary Macy

See also APOCALYPTIC; CHRISTIANITY; HEILSGESCHICHTE; ISLAM; JUDAISM; MESSIAH; PROPHECY; SALVATION; TRADITION.

HISTORY OF RELIGIONS
A field of modern scholarship dedicated to the scientific and comparative study

of the religions of the world. The discipline is dedicated to the pursuit of understanding religion(s) using methodologies avoiding a priori theological, faith, or hermeneutical commitments; it also draws upon the whole range of data available via textual, archeological, and social scientific research. A product of the Enlightenment, particularly liberating intellectuals to investigate all phenomena free from church interference, the field of the history of religions seeks unbiased assessments and scientifically rigorous accounts of the universal appearance of religion in human history.

The field had its origins in nineteenth-century Germany where it was called *Religionswissenschaft*. The field itself traces its roots to Schleiermacher and has been associated since the mid-twentieth century with faculty at the University of Chicago, particularly Joachim Wach (1898–1955), Joseph Kitagawa (1915–92), and Mircea Eliade (1907–86).

The history of religions values and evaluates religions via the doctrinal and ritual traditions through which all faiths have been transmitted; it also employs any other extratradition data to shed light on its subject matter. The field does not confine its object of study to elites or texts, but typically seeks to analyze the holistic presence that "religion" has occupied in human societies and how there has been continuity and change within systems of doctrine, belief, and practice through time.

One particular methodology that has developed in the field is the use of ideal typologies or archetypes derived from various fields. These include "animism," "charisma," "legitimation," "shamanism," "sacred versus profane," "the center." These ideal phenomenological constructs are developed to assist in the comparative enterprises of the field: as heuristic devices to help pose useful research queries or guide analytical inquiries to discover "family resemblances" between case studies. Critics have pointed out how, when the field has failed to go beyond the early categories, the history of religions has reified a new set of a priori assumptions.

Todd T. Lewis

See also COMPARATIVE RELIGION; RELIGION, THEORIES OF.

HIZBULLAH
(Also spelled *Hizb Allah,* Hizbollah, Hizballah, Hezbollah). Literally, the "Party of God"—a contemporary organization of militant Muslims identified with Shiʿite Islam. The term is found in the Qurʾan (58:22) where it refers to true believers, as opposed to "the Party of the Evil One" (58:19) whose allegiance to Satan will doom them to eternal damnation. The modern *Hizbullah* was founded after the Iranian revolution (1978–9), led by the Ayatollah Khomeini. It supported Khomeini's socioreligious reforms and attempted to export his interpretation of Islam throughout the Middle East mostly through armed conflict that its members considered a *jihad* (a holy war of self-defense). Its targets are "imperialist" Western nations and their allies, particularly Israel, as well as any institution deemed hostile toward what it understands to be the authentic practice of Islam. Hizbullah is active in Lebanon and continues to be closely associated with the Iranian revolutionary government and its agenda.

Ronald A. Pachence

See also AYATOLLAH; ISLAMIC RADICALISM (FUNDAMENTALISM); JIHAD; SHIʿA/SHIʿI/SHIʿITE/SHIʿISM.

HOBBES, THOMAS (1588–1679)

The first prominent philosopher to write in the English language. Hobbes interpreted all reality in terms of a mechanistic materialism, and although he claimed to believe in the existence of God, a consistent rendering of his position suggests that he was really an atheist.

As a thoroughgoing materialist, Hobbes reacted strongly against the philosophies of the Middle Ages. He interpreted all phenomena in terms of bodies in motion, and he defined philosophy as the knowledge of the causes of those motions. All physical change was attributed to motion in the parts of bodies; sensation was the result of particles moving from the sense object which, upon striking the organ of sense, cause motions in the particles of the nerves and brain, and all feelings (passions) and even ideas were identified with subtle particles in motion. The brain was the seat of the thinking process that rendered any appeal to a nonmaterial mind or soul superfluous, and the region around the heart was the seat of the passions. Of course, without a soul, any form of human immortality was thought to be impossible.

Hobbes also reduced the activity of human choice to the motion of particles in the body. As a result, given that all motion is governed by strict causal laws, he claimed that all human choices are strictly determined. However, a person is said to have "liberty" to the extent that his actions are free of external constraints.

Hobbes identified good with pleasure and evil with pain, and these he equated with various passions. Happiness consists in the maximization of pleasure and the minimization of pain. Since the passions are nothing but various motions of particles, and since the cause of all motion is power, it follows that happiness requires power. This fact makes human life a never-ending struggle for power. As he wrote in *Leviathan*, his masterwork, "I put for a general inclination of all mankind a perpetual and relentless desire of power after power, that ceaseth only in death" (I, 11). Besides power, the only other requirement for happiness is knowledge of how the various passions are caused, and this knowledge Hobbes equated with ethics. In *Leviathan* Hobbes presented an extensive sketch of how the various passions are linked to one another. This sketch was intended to serve as a kind of road map to happiness.

The perpetual quest for power, Hobbes thought, is the condition of humanity in the state of nature: "In such condition there is no place for industry, because the fruit thereof is uncertain: and consequently no culture of the earth; no navigation, nor use of the commodities that may be imported by sea; no commodious building; no instruments of moving and removing such things as require much force; no knowledge of the face of the earth; no account of time; no arts; no letters; no society; and which is worst of all, continual fear, and danger of violent death; and the life of man, solitary, poor, nasty, brutish, and short" (*Leviathan*, I, 13). The state of nature inevitably leads to a condition of war of all against all, and to avoid this condition, humans have created that great Leviathan, or "mortal god," known as the state.

The sovereign is the person, or group of persons, in charge of the state, and to preserve the peace the sovereign must have absolute power. Laws are the free creations of the will of the sovereign, and their validity is not dependent on their conforming to some "higher law," as the Christian philosophers of the Middle Ages had held. The sovereign has the right to enforce its laws under penalty of death, and citizens have no right ever to object to the actions of the sovereign.

Hobbes' attitude toward God is that the nature of God is unknowable because it is impossible for a finite mind to comprehend an infinite being. However, in one place Hobbes wrote that God is "a most pure and most simple corporeal spirit." Such a description is consistent with Hobbes' commitment to materialism, and it seems to reduce God to some kind of mist or fog. Religion, Hobbes thought, results from the incapacity of common people to attain a knowledge of the causes of things. The fear of unknown causes (such as the cause of plagues and other calamities) leads people to invent religion and indulge in prayers and forms of worship. This being the case, religion is essentially identical with superstition.

Given the general popularity of religion and the power it has over the minds of common people, it is essential that there be only one church and that the sovereign be the head of it. Public prayers and forms of worship are, in the hands of the sovereign, indispensable tools for acquiring complete control over the citizens.

Hobbes' rejection of any explanatory appeals to God and other immaterial entities was instrumental in dissolving the marriage between religion and philosophy that had endured for fifteen hundred years. Also, his depiction of the human condition in the state of nature laid the foundation for the theory of "realpolitic" that has survived to this day.

Hobbes's more important writings include *Elements of Law* (circulated in 1640, published in 1650), *De Cive* (1642), *De Corpore* (1665), *Leviathan* (1651), and *Of Liberty and Necessity* (1654).

Patrick J. Hurley

HOLINESS

("Note" of the church). Since the adoption of the Nicene Creed at the Council of Constantinople in 381 c.e., Christians have professed faith in "one, holy, catholic, and apostolic church." Holiness is thus an essential mark of the church of Christ. This affirmation refers, in the first place, to *God's* fidelity to the church, which means that God guarantees the holiness and efficacy of the means through which the church is constituted as God's saving instrument in history (sacraments, preaching, pastoral activity, witness). The indwelling of the Holy Spirit in the church also gives rise to individual holy men and women. Yet because individual Christians *do* sin when they are not faithful to the gift of God's love, the Roman Catholic bishops said at the Second Vatican Council (1962–5) that the church as a whole is "at once holy and in need of purification" and is called to take "the path of penance and renewal" (*Lumen Gentium* 8). Because sin results from personal decision, modern Catholic teaching holds that sinfulness cannot be regarded as characteristic of the church's very being. At the same time, theologians speak of the *ecclesia sempre reformanda* ("the church always being reformed"). In early and medieval Christianity, theologians called the church the "unfaithful bride" of Christ. When leaders of the Protestant Reformation of the sixteenth century one-sidedly pointed to the church's sinfulness, Catholic apologists responded by one-sidedly stressing the church's holiness. In light of the church's checkered history, today some theologians have begun to speak of the church itself (and not just its members) as at once "holy and sinful."

James B. Nickoloff

See also APOSTOLICITY; CATHOLICITY; NOTES OF THE CHURCH; UNITY.

HOLINESS/SANCTITY (IN CHRISTIANITY)

The two terms are virtually synonymous, except that sanctity is ordinarily used in reference to human beings; holiness applies primarily to God, and secondarily to human beings as a result of their association with the divine mystery. Holiness often refers to the "otherness," the sacred, "numinous" and awesome nature, the perfection and the mystery of God. Human beings are said to be holy to the degree that they are of God, or, in Christian theology, insofar as they partake of the divine nature (which is called "divinization" by grace).

The way human beings envision the holiness of God affects how they understand their own call to perfection. Thus, when holiness is construed in terms of apartness, human beings in search of God are inclined to withdraw from the world. Our sense of where God is to be found, or of the sacred, can lead to a dichotomy between the sphere of the holy and that of the everyday or profane. Contemporary spiritual writing would underline God's presence within the world, particularly in the historical experience of the poor. As a result, the model or phenomenological form of sanctity today is going to include a prominent social dimension. For the holiness and justice of God cannot be separated.

William Reiser, s.j.

See also GOD; GRACE; NUMINOUS;
OPTION FOR THE POOR; PERFECTION;
SACRED/SACRAL/SACRALIZED.

HOLINESS/SANCTITY (IN JUDAISM)

Judaism holds that sanctity is a property of God that pertains as well to people or acts dedicated to the performance of God's will as described in the Torah. The most holy ritual object in Judaism is the Torah scroll that records God's revelation, followed by the ark (*Aron HaKodesh*) in which Torah scrolls are kept in the synagogue. Other objects used in prayer also are deemed dedicated to the service of God and so to require special treatment, in particular, prayer books, prayer shawls, and Tephilim.

Alongside ritual objects, Judaism conceives holidays and Sabbaths, designated by God as periods of respite from the workaday world, as holy time. During holy time, people are commanded to cease all forms of creative activity ("work"), through which they normally express control over the world. Instead, they engage in prayer and reflection upon God's actual ownership of the world and on God's role in providing the conditions under which humans exist.

While the concept of sanctification is expressed most clearly in areas of ritual, Judaism conceives of the entire system of social and ethical laws that comprises the Torah as describing a holy way of life. By leading all aspects of life in accordance with the precepts established by God, the Jew understands him- or herself to be leading a holy life and to be contributing to the sanctification of the world. Holiness thus is seen to emerge from the Jewish commitment to social justice.

While Judaism finds holiness in many everyday human actions, it is not a sacramental religion. None of its rites is understood directly to convey to a person or object a status of sanctification, and its leadership, in the person of the rabbi, has no special cultic powers or standing. Indeed, the rabbi is distinguished from other Jews only through his or her knowledge and position as a teacher. All Jewish rituals may be carried out by lay leaders; a rabbi is not required for any of them. In Judaism, sanctification thus emerges from people's adherence to God's will and from their actions in setting certain objects aside for ritual use. But Judaism has neither a cultic locus (for example, an altar) nor a religious figurehead (for instance, a priest) with the power to impose a status of sanctification outside the people's intention to use an object as holy.

Alan J. Avery-Peck

See also ARON HAKODESH; RABBI; SYNAGOGUE; TEPHILIM; TORAH.

HOLLENBACH, DAVID (1942–)
American Catholic theologian. A native of Philadelphia, Hollenbach studied physics and philosophy before earning his doctorate in religious ethics at Yale University in 1975. He is a member of the Society of Jesus. Currently a professor of theology at Boston College, Hollenbach's research has focused on the foundations of Christian social ethics, on theories of justice and human rights, and on the role of religion in social and political life. Hollenbach's work has interwoven the traditions and contributions of Catholic social doctrine with contributions from the social and economic sciences, thereby developing an interdisciplinary social ethic that can and does dialogue with Christian and non-Christian alike. He is considered one of the best and most influential social ethicists in the country, and one of the Catholic Church's top theologians in the area of social ethics. Among his best publications, from an impressive list of contributions, are *Justice, Peace, and Human Rights: American Catholic Social Ethics in a Pluralistic World* (1990), *Nuclear Ethics: A Christian Moral Argument* (1983),

and *Claims in Conflict: Retrieving and Renewing the Catholic Human Rights Tradition* (1979).

Orlando Espín

See also CATHOLIC SOCIAL TEACHING; ETHICS; ETHICS, SOCIAL; HUMAN RIGHTS; MORAL THEOLOGY/CHRISTIAN ETHICS; SOCIAL JUSTICE; SOCIETY OF JESUS.

HOLY DAY OF OBLIGATION
Feast days on which Catholics are required by church law to celebrate the Eucharist and observe other customs that foster worship, joy, and relaxation (Canon 1247). Sunday is the foremost holy day of obligation (Canon 1246). Canon law mandates ten others, but allows the bishops in a given conference to abolish or transfer some of them to Sunday. In the United States, the days of Christmas (December 25); Ascension (Thursday in the Sixth Week of Easter); Mary, Mother of God (January 1); Immaculate Conception (December 8); Assumption (August 15); and All Saints' (November 1) are retained as holy days of obligation, while Epiphany (January 6) and Corpus Christi (Thursday after Trinity Sunday) are celebrated on nearby Sundays. The U.S. bishops have removed the obligation from the feasts of SS. Peter and Paul, and St. Joseph.

Patrick L. Malloy

See also COMMANDMENTS OF THE CHURCH; EPISCOPAL CONFERENCES.

HOLY LAND
Holy Land is a term widely used and poorly, if ever, defined. In general, it is used to refer to the area of ancient Syria-Palestine in the biblical period and may be interchangeable with the expression, "Land of the Bible." In terms of modern

boundaries it would have included Israel, Lebanon, part of Syria, Jordan, and the Sinai Peninsula.

Russell Fuller

HOLY OFFICE

A former name of the current Sacred Congregation for the Doctrine of the Faith, a department of the Vatican whose official charge is "to promote and safeguard the doctrine on the faith and morals throughout the Catholic world." The congregation came into existence in 1542 as the Sacred Congregation of the Roman and Universal Inquisition that was to oppose heretical teaching as part of the papacy's response to the growing influence of the Protestant Reformation. (It was not directly connected to the more infamous Spanish Inquisition, whose particular goals and methods were the product of local church collaboration with government officials within the Spanish Empire.) After reforms early in the twentieth century, the Roman Inquisition was officially called the Sacred Congregation of the Holy Office, and following the Second Vatican Council in 1965 it was renamed the Sacred Congregation for the Doctrine of the Faith. Currently consisting of twenty-five bishops, archbishops, and cardinals, with a number of theological and legal consultants, the congregation reviews published works on Catholic faith or morals, makes rulings on controversial teaching or writing, and issues documents that seek to emphasize or clarify particular points of Catholic doctrine.

William A. Clark, s.j.

HOLY OF HOLIES

(Hebrew, *qodesh haq-qedoshim*). A Hebrew expression referring to the innermost room of the Temple of YHWH in Jerusalem. Like many temples in ancient Canaan and Syria, the Temple in Jerusalem was rectangular in shape, divided laterally into three rooms inside. The entrance was on the short side that faced East. The Holy of Holies or *devir* as it is also called in Hebrew, was the westernmost of the three rooms. According to 1 Kings 5–8, in Solomon's Temple the Holy of Holies contained statues of two cherubim with wings outstretched. Under the wings of the cherubim was the ark of the covenant that contained the two tablets of stone Moses had placed there. YHWH was thought to appear or to be invisibly present in the Holy of Holies.

Russell Fuller

HOLY PEOPLE

In the Navajo story of Emergence, the present-day humans travel through four lower worlds to enter the Fifth World. In their journey, they are accompanied by sacred beings who are collectively called the Holy People. These divine beings preexist humans (Earth Surface people) and assist them in coming into being after preparing the present world as a home for them. They do this by creating the inner forms of all the natural phenomena. Named in the myth are sacred persons such as First Man, First Woman, Talking God, Black God, and so on. Most important is Changing Woman, who creates humans from her own skin.

The Holy People are not holy in the sense of spiritual holiness, but rather in terms of the abundance of power they possess. This power is not good or evil in the moral sense, but of a magnitude that outruns the human ability to fully understand it. Thus it is usually regarded as ambivalent in itself, and it is up to the Navajo to approach them in the prescribed manner, with all due formality and respect. It is this principle that directs Navajo ritual practice. They are capable of bestowing power that can assist in all the crises of life and return human life to full harmony. There is a special relation between the Navajo and the Holy People that has been profoundly learned over all the generations of their shared history. In essence, this is the truth that both the humans and the gods are of the same reality, breathed into life by the generative principle of the universe, focused by the Navajo in the sacred Wind. Each Navajo is therefore called to grow into closer likeness to his or her guardians and mentors, and if all ritual obligations are honorably fulfilled, each will share the same destiny —life forever in union with the Power that calls all things into being.

Kathleen Dugan

See also CHANGING WOMAN; MYTH.

HOLY SEE

A term for the office, authority, and administrative apparatus of the Papacy, frequently used by Catholics. From early in the church's history, the authority of a bishop was symbolized by the chair from which he presided over church assemblies. By derivation from the Latin word for "seat"—*sedes*—the place where a bishop lived came to be called his "see." The special designation of the See of Rome as the "*Holy* See" arose because of Rome's special distinction as the only see in the western Roman Empire to claim a direct connection to apostles of Jesus, specifically the apostles Peter and Paul, who were both martyred in Rome. In particular, the connection to Peter (who appears in parts of the New Testament as the "chief of the apostles") helped to give the Bishops of Rome an elevated prestige

in the early church, leading to the development of the Papacy as the preeminent authority in Roman Catholicism.

William A. Clark, s.j.

HOLY SPIRIT

The expression "Spirit of God" (*ruach*) appears in the Old Testament, but it does not have the same the meaning as the Christian expression "Holy Spirit"—in the Old Testament it refers primarily to the mysterious power of God present (or inferred) in God's actions and in the life of the people (and especially the prophets). The New Testament refers to the "Paraclete" (the "Advocate" or "Counselor"), and to the "Holy Spirit" and the "Spirit of God," but not with the same (trinitarian) doctrinal meaning that these expressions came to have among later Christians. In the New Testament period, Christians believed that Jesus had been anointed by the Spirit of God, and that it was the Spirit of God who empowered the church to announce the Gospel and to spread throughout the world. The newly baptized received the Spirit and were thus empowered themselves to continue the mission of the church as members thereof. Paul taught that there is a reciprocity between "being in" Christ and "being in" the Holy Spirit. Paul saw Christ as giving specificity to the actions of the Holy Spirit, while the Holy Spirit makes present and extends the presence of Christ in history.

The trinitarian doctrines regarding the Holy Spirit became accepted and standard among most Christians during the patristic period, especially after the doctrinal definitions of the Council of Constantinople (381 C.E.). However, it must be emphasized that (as in many other doctrinal situations) the liturgical and the personal/

communal experience of the Holy Spirit not only preceded but acted as context for the development of the standard trinitarian doctrines regarding the Holy Spirit. Consequently, many theologians remind us that without these liturgical and personal/communal experiences, Christians would not fully understand the richness of the pneumatological doctrines nor the relationship of these with other doctrines and (more importantly) with the life of the church.

Today Christians hold that the Holy Spirit is the Third Person of the Trinity that is God. The Holy Spirit is co-eternal, co-equal, and consubstantial with the other two Persons of the Trinity. The expression "Holy Spirit" is employed by Christians to name that eternal manner of God's being that is the outpouring of God's being and life as limitless love, in God's eternal mystery and in God's self-communication to humanity. The Spirit of God, some contemporary theologians have argued, can also be understood as the "maternal face" of God.

The creed of Nicaea Constantinople (that most Christians repeat in the Sunday liturgies) teaches that the Holy Spirit "proceeds" from the Father. In Western Christianity, apparently because of the great influence of Augustine of Hippo's pneumatology, there developed the understanding that the Holy Spirit "proceeds" from the Father *and* the Son— thereby attempting to emphasize the intimate connection between the Holy Spirit and Christ. This doctrinal development led Western Christians to add the expression "and from the Son" (*Filioque*, in Latin) to the Nicaea–Constantinople Creed. Eastern Orthodox Christians have never accepted this unilateral addition to the ancient conciliar creed shared by most Christians, further insisting that this Western doctrinal development subordinates the Holy Spirit to Christ.

The Holy Spirit makes present and "detectable" (through discernment), and unfolds, the will of God in human history in the myriad manners that lead this history forward toward the fullness of the reign of God. All humans are involved in this Spirit-led historical process because all humans are made in the "image of God" and are beloved of God. Human freedom permits human beings to positively participate, or not, in the unfolding of history; and faith (as response to God's grace) permits human beings to specifically name the "reason for their hope" in Christian terms. Nevertheless, it is possible for humans who for honorable reasons do not share in the Christian faith, and therefore who do not name their hope and life in Christian terms, to continue to participate in the Spirit-led unfolding of history "anonymously" by lives and hearts committed to love, compassion, justice, and truth.

Orlando Espín

See also ANONYMOUS CHRISTIANS; CONSTANTINOPLE, FIRST COUNCIL OF; CONSTANTINOPLE, SECOND COUNCIL OF; CONSTANTINOPLE, THIRD COUNCIL OF; CREEDS; CULTURE; FAITH; FILIOQUE; GOD; GRACE; HISTORY; NICAEA, FIRST COUNCIL OF; NICAEA, SECOND COUNCIL OF; ORTHODOX CHURCHES; PERSON/ PROSOPON; PNEUMATOLOGY; REIGN OF GOD; TRINITY/TRINITARIAN THEOLOGY/ TRINITARIAN PROCESSIONS.

HOLY WATER

Ordinary water blessed by a priest. In the liturgy, it is used principally as a reminder of baptism (for example, when it is sprinkled on an assembly during the *Asperges* or upon a coffin at the beginning of the Mass of Christian Burial). It is also used liturgically as a symbol of purification or consecration (for instance, when it is sprinkled on items that are being set apart for a special purpose, like ashes on Ash Wednesday). Holy water is also a common element in personal devotional customs (for example, when a person touches holy water at the door of a church before making the sign of the cross). As in the liturgy, when holy water is used devotionally, it generally suggests baptism or purification.

Patrick L. Malloy

See also ASPERGES; BLESSING (CHRISTI-ANITY).

HOLY WEEK

Known as Great Week in most Eastern churches, Holy Week is in a sense a non-liturgical expression that bridges the Lenten and Easter seasons. Holy Week begins on Passion (Palm) Sunday and continues through Holy Saturday, thus including part of the special period known as the Easter Triduum that begins Holy Thursday evening with the Mass of the Lord's Supper and concludes with evening prayer of Easter Sunday.

The earliest observances of Holy Week were associated with prayer and fasting in preparation for the celebration of baptism at the Easter Vigil. In the first two centuries, this preparation was for one or two days (*Didache*, Irenaeus of Lyons), and by the third century was a week long in some places (*Didascalia Apostolorum*). The practices of fourth-century Jerusalem are the singular most significant influence on the development of the liturgical services of Holy Week. These are first recorded for us by Egeria, a Spanish nun on pilgrimage to Jerusalem in the late fourth century, and whose descriptions are confirmed by the list of readings given in the *Armenian Lectionary* of the same period. In Jerusalem the unitive feast of the Pasch tends to be broken down and historicized by shaping daily liturgical services to the historical events and places of the last week of Jesus' life. This was possible with the legalization of Christianity by Constantine (313), his building of shrines on the holy places, and the large influx of pilgrims and ascetics who searched to follow in the footsteps of Jesus. Consequently, most of the ceremonies we associate with Holy Week, for example, Palm Sunday procession, readings of the passion, commemoration of the Last Supper, Good Friday observances with the veneration of the cross, and the lighting of the Easter lamp/candle (*lucernarium*), have their origins in fourth-century Jerusalem. As pilgrims returned home, these practices spread to other churches and were adapted to fit local liturgical customs and spaces.

Dennis W. Krouse

See also CALENDAR (LITURGICAL); DIDACHE, THE; DIDASCALIA APOSTOLO-RUM, THE; EASTER TRIDUUM; IRENAEUS OF LYONS; PASCHAL; PASCHAL MYSTERY; PASSOVER; RESURRECTION (IN CHRISTIANITY); RESURRECTION OF CHRIST; RESURRECTION OF THE BODY.

HOMA

In the Vedic rituals (*yajna*) of Hinduism, brahmin priests offered *homa*, oblations of clarified butter and other substances, into a sacrificial fire.

Lance E. Nelson

See also BRAHMANA; HINDUISM; VEDAS; YAJNA.

HOMER

The ancient Greeks believed that a blind poet named Homer had composed humankind's earliest epics, the *Iliad* and the *Odyssey*. Homer probably lived in the ninth or eighth century B.C.E. on one of the islands of the Aegean. According to tradition, he traveled among the Greek states and islands, making his living as a storyteller and court singer. Since the ancient Greeks had no sacred scriptures, works such as Homer's supplied the data of religious tradition. The *Iliad* offers a rich story of gods and goddesses, their relationships, their loyalties, their relative powers and spheres of influence. In addition, the *Iliad* recounts the burial customs, beliefs in an afterlife, and styles of worship of the ancient Greeks. The *Odyssey* contains less religious content than the *Iliad*, but it offers a detailed picture of the relationship between one goddess, Athena, and the hero, Odysseus. Another religious book, the *Homeric Hymns*, is not attributed to Homer.

Helen deLaurentis

See also GRECO-ROMAN RELIGION.

HOMILY

A term referring to a form of liturgical preaching given after the proclamation of the Gospel during the Liturgy of the Word. In the patristic era, this was primarily conceived as a commentary on the Scripture reading(s) of the day, often line by line, usually with practical applications for Christian living. During the Middle Ages, regular preaching declined in many places, and where it did occur it was reduced to the so-called sermon, which was usually a catechetical instruction, often on a subject unrelated to the biblical readings of the liturgy or to the celebration itself. The reforms of the Second Vatican Council restored the homily as integral to the liturgy itself and normative, required at all Sunday and holyday eucharistic celebrations, at public celebrations of the other

sacraments, and encouraged at weekday Masses and other liturgical services. The Constitution on the Sacred Liturgy (52) directs that the homily is to explain the mysteries of the faith and the guiding principles of the Christian life based on the liturgical texts of the day. Subsequent ecclesiastical instructions and liturgical commentators view the homily as a vehicle to connect the particular celebration with the practical life of the community. It should be suited to the capacity of the community and relevant to the concrete circumstances of people's lives. In a sense, the homily is to be a catalyst that unites the members of the assembly with the actual mystery being celebrated, and calls forth from them a response in faith leading to the transformation of life and the world in which they live. It is the principal way of manifesting the unity of the one bread of the table of the Word and the table of the Eucharist. The homily's primary function is not education (this belongs to catechesis); rather, it is celebration, a reliving of and an integration into the mystery proclaimed in this particular liturgy by this particular community.

Canon law (Can. 766) allows a layperson to preach when delegated by the local ordinary, or for pastoral reasons qualified adults may preach after the Gospel in Masses with children (*Directory for Masses with Children* 24). Nevertheless, the homily as such is reserved for a presbyter or deacon (Can. 767).

Dennis W. Krouse

See also EUCHARIST; LITURGY OF THE WORD; MASS; PREACHING (IN CATHOLICISM); WORD OF GOD.

HOMOIOUSIOS TO PATRI

Homoiousios to Patri ("like in substance to the Father") was the term used by the followers of the theology of Origen to express the relation of the Father and the Son within the Godhead. This term was used by Basil, bishop of Ancyra (336–60), in reaction to the synod of Constantinople in 360 that proposed to settle the Arian controversy with the formula that "the Son is like the Father." Basil of Ancyra saw that this formula championed by the emperor Constantius did not exclude the original doctrine of Arius himself. In opposition to Constantius' minimizing formula that the Logos is "like" the Father, proponents of the *homoiousios* insisted that the Logos/Son is "like in respect of substance" to the Father. This development among the followers of Origen contributed to the theological acceptance of the *homoousios* and the definition of the doctrine of the Trinity at the Council of Constantinople in 381.

Herbert J. Ryan, s.j.

See also ARIANISM; BASIL THE GREAT; CONSTANTINOPLE, FIRST COUNCIL OF; HOMOOUSIOS TO PATRI; NICAEA, FIRST COUNCIL OF; ORIGEN; OUSIA; TRINITY/ TRINITARIAN THEOLOGY/TRINITARIAN PROCESSIONS.

HOMOOUSIOS TO PATRI

Homoousios to Patri ("of the same substance as the Father, of one nature with the Father") was the term used in the Creed of Nicaea (325) to express the relations of the Father and the Son within the Godhead. This technical term affirmed that the Father and the Son are of the same nature (are of *one* nature) or "substance." This term excluded Arianism. The term is nonbiblical. Though used from the second century onward, the word had a controversial history the opponents of Nicaea utilized to attack the council. In common usage the word meant "made of the same stuff." As a theological term, it expressed

an overall unity despite existing diversity. Paul of Samosata, a Monarchian theologian, used the term to assert that the Father and the Son are one and the same Person. In 267, at Antioch, a synod of bishops condemned Paul of Samosata and the meaning he gave the term. Nicaea's use of the term excludes any imperfection from the Son and stresses the Son's full equality with the Father. The Council of Constantinople I avoids the term when it defines the full and equal divinity of the Holy Spirit. The Council of Chalcedon teaches that the Lord Jesus Christ, the Son Incarnate, is of the same substance *homoousios* (consubstantial) as the Father regarding the Son's divine nature, and *homoousios* (consubstantial) with us in regard to his human nature.

Herbert J. Ryan, s.j.

See also ARIANISM; CHALCEDON, COUNCIL OF; CONSTANTINOPLE, FIRST COUNCIL OF; HOMOIOUSIOS TO PATRI; MONARCHIANISM; NICAEA, FIRST COUNCIL OF; OUSIA; PAUL OF SAMOSATA; TRINITY/TRINITARIAN THEOLOGY/ TRINITARIAN PROCESSIONS.

HOMOPHOBIA

An irrational fear of homosexuals and homosexuality that leads one to avoid gay people and to hold prejudiced opinions about them. Homophobia is an attitude held by individuals, though the term can also denote a cultural revulsion to homosexuality. Closely related is the term *heterosexism*, discrimination by heterosexuals against homosexuals. Until quite recently, religious traditions did not identify homophobia as a reality, let alone an ethical problem. Many have changed their stance due to changes in social attitudes: gay people have become more vocal for their civil rights, and most doctors have stopped considering homosexuality an illness or a perversion. Many religious bodies in the last twenty to thirty years have officially decried homophobia and heterosexism, particularly the more "liberal" churches in the U.S. and Europe. Some churches that pioneered tolerance for gay persons in the U.S. are the Society of Friends, the Moravian Church, the Lutheran Church in America, the Unitarian Universalist Association, and Reform Judaism. Even so, at the level of the membership, the practice of tolerance sometimes falls short of a church's policy.

"Homophobia" is an emotionally charged word that, judiciously used, points out instances of unloving and unjust attitudes toward gay persons. It can also be improperly used as a dismissive label for every moral qualm about homosexuality; thus it can cut short the legitimate debate each religion must have about whether it should morally and liturgically sanction homosexual partnerships. A view that enjoys increasing support is to distinguish homosexual activity from a homosexual orientation. The Roman Catholic Church and various Protestant denominations use this distinction to maintain that even though homosexual activity is wrong, gay persons still deserve love and respect. Thus they make common cause with the liberal churches in condemning homophobia and heterosexism, even as the debate rages about the morality of homosexuality itself.

Brian Stiltner

See also DISCRIMINATION; HOMOSEXUALITY (CHRISTIAN PERSPECTIVES); PREJUDICE; TOLERANCE.

HOMOSEXUALITY (CHRISTIAN PERSPECTIVES)

The current understanding of homosexuality is conditioned by the therapeutic and life sciences where it is variously understood as a type of sexual orientation (and hence one component of "sexual identity"), as a stable inclination of an individual's desire, affections, and imagination, and as sexual acts between persons of the same sex. The consensus of the therapeutic sciences is that an individual's sexual orientation is a natural variation, largely settled by adolescence, and in 1973 the American Psychiatric Association dropped homosexuality as a mental illness from its *Diagnostic and Statistical Manual*. Research in the biological sciences since the mid-1980s (for example, twin-studies, genetic, brain, and hormone studies) supports the hypothesis that there is some significant biological component in the determination of sexual orientation, although conclusions remain tentative at this time. These developments in the sciences overlap with the growing social visibility ("coming out") and institutional organization of gay men and lesbians in professional, social, legal, political, and religious groups. These broader social trends are often dated to the Stonewall Riots in New York City in 1969 and were catalyzed by the AIDS crisis that began in 1982.

The current state of the question for the Christian churches and Christian theology regarding homosexuality can be described as occurring within the space defined by the developments noted above and the virtually universal negative stigma attached to homosexual acts in the Christian tradition. At stake are the answers to normative questions concerning the practical life of the churches: "Under what conditions, if any, should a homosexual person be regarded as a member of the church?" "Under what conditions, if any, should same-sex unions be recognized by the church?" "Under what conditions, if any, can a homosexual person serve in ordained ministry?" "To what extent, if any, should churches intervene (positively or negatively) in current (secular) political and legal debates regarding the criminalization of homosexual conduct, marriage and adoption rights, nondiscrimination in employment, benefits, housing?" and so on.

The negative stigma attached to homosexual acts in the Christian tradition is variously warranted through appeal to Scripture (for example, Gen 19:4-11; Lev 18:22; 20:13; Deut 23:17; Rom 1:27; 1 Cor 6:9-10; 1 Tim 1:9-10), the order of creation (for example, Gen 1:28; 2:21-24; Mark 10:2-11 and par.), and/or the natural law. Although these three warrants (that is, appeal to biblical texts, to the order of creation, and to natural law) are not mutually exclusive, appeal to the first two tends to be more common in Protestant churches while appeal to the third tends to be more common in Roman Catholicism. Both the visibility of "faithful" gay men and lesbians in the churches today and intellectual developments associated with modernity—historical biblical criticism, the demise of final causality as understood in Aristotelian philosophy—have rendered immediate appeal to these three warrants problematic today. Consequently, defense and criticism of these warrants, the assumptions behind them, and their consistency with the current investigations of the various therapeutic, social, and biological sciences accordingly engages biblical, historical, systematic, moral, and pastoral theologians today. The current teaching of the Roman Catholic Church can be stated in three theses. First, the homosexual *person* is fully a person in the theological sense (that is, a creature made in the image and likeness of God and hence endowed with an inalienable dignity and rights that must be respected by other persons). Second, the *inclination* toward homosexual acts is, by the standard of the natural law, "objectively disordered" (that is, not in accord with the objective purpose of the sexual act: procreation). This inclination is not sin per se. Third, homosexual *acts* are sin per se.

J. A. Colombo

See also MORAL THEOLOGY/CHRISTIAN ETHICS; SEXUALITY.

HOMOSEXUALITY IN NON-CHRISTIAN RELIGIONS

Considering religious understandings of homosexuality presents a number of analytic difficulties. First, there is an enormous amount of cultural variation in what is included within the rubric of homosexuality. For example, in many cultures same-sex friendship has a number of physical expressions, such as handholding and sleeping together, which are not sexual in nature although they might appear to be so from a conventional Western perspective. Second, there is a distinction between homosexual orientation and sexual acts normally associated with homosexual practice. Most religious traditions, however, elide this distinction and focus their attention on proscribing particular "homosexual" acts.

The Genesis story of Sodom provides a dominant biblical trope that speaks of God's anger toward "unnatural" sexual practices. Indeed, homosexual rape is one of the practices of the "Sodomites" as reflected in their demand that Lot's angelic guests be sent out so that "they may know them" (Gen 19:5). The book of Leviticus explicitly establishes death as the penalty for a man who lies with another man "as with a woman" (Lev 20:13).

The Jewish legal tradition (*halakah*) has generally maintained this position against homosexual acts, although the supporting reasoning behind the prohibition has been a matter of conjecture: some commentators consider homosexuality unnatural in and of itself while others argue that homosexual liaisons threaten the family. The Jewish orthodox tradition has posited a particularly strong position against homosexual anal intercourse, considering it an act that should be avoided even at the cost of death. While the conservative tradition has upheld this prohibition against anal intercourse, it has recently adopted a resolution that allowed the possibility of accepting gay rabbis and same-sex relationships. The reformed and Reconstructionist arms of the Jewish tradition have sanctioned monogamous homosexual relationships. Homosexuality has also been a matter of reflection in the Jewish mystical tradition. For example, as Laurence Fine records in his study of Isaac Luria, Kabbalah prescribes lengthy expiatory acts for the commission of homosexual intercourse on the grounds that anal intercourse prevents the proper distribution of the ten qualities of the divine (*serifot*) within the human person.

Islamic tradition also draws upon the trope of Sodom. For example, "The Heights" and "The Poets," respectively the seventh and twenty-sixth chapters of the Qur'an, explicitly label the residents of Sodom as those who have sinned most grievously for their practice of lusting after men in preference to women. Within Islamic law (*shariah*), homosexuality is generally considered as a subset of prohibitions against adultery (*zina*), and there are a number of sayings (*hadiths*) attributed to the Prophet Muhammad that explicitly prohibit anal intercourse. In Islamic law, there is also a specific concept of "sodomy" (*liwat*) although there are debates concerning whether *liwat* specifically and exclusively refers to anal intercourse or might be applied to other forms of unlawful penetration. In *Before Homosexuality in the Arab World: 1500–1800*, Khaled El-Rouayheb argues that "homosexuality" is far too general a term to encompass the variety of attitudes toward same-sex relations in the Arab Islamic world. For example, El-Rouayheb outlines a complex taxonomy in the Arab world that distinguished between the penetrator and the penetrated as well as between lustful and chaste same-sex love. The point is that modern understandings of homosexuality often distort the complex frames of reference in which same-sex relationships were viewed in Arab society and culture.

Hinduism would generally prohibit sexual practices associated with homosexuality. For example, anal and oral sex would be classified as *ayoni*, or nonvaginal, and thus prohibited not only as unnatural but also as highly polluting. *The Laws of Manu* prescribes the loss of caste as the penalty for homosexual activity unless the transgressor performs what is described as "The Painful Vow" in expiation. While *The Laws of Manu* is a medieval text, and not necessarily normative for all Hindus, it nonetheless exemplifies general religious attitudes toward homosexuality. Often in explicit challenge to such attitudes, some scholars of Hinduism have attempted to retrieve or unmask strong currents of homoeroticism within Hindu spirituality. Most controversially, Jeffrey Kripal has argued in *Kali's Child* that Ramakrishna, the nineteenth-century Bengali mystic, was motivated by strong same-sex attraction that shaped his devotion to the goddess Kali. Other scholars have challenged Kripal for misunderstanding Bengali texts and for applying Western psycho-analytic categories to a cultural and religious context where their applicability is very limited. While debate continues over the supposed homoerotic or homosexual themes in Hindu mysticism, it is undeniable that many Hindu myths understand gender identity as fluid or malleable. For example, the figure Bhagirath, who brings down the Ganges from heaven, was born from the union of two women.

Sexuality in Buddhism is often understood within the framework of craving since sexuality and desire are often quite intimately linked. Accordingly, any kind of sexual activity can have potentially dangerous karmic effects by increasing craving and deepening egoism. The Buddha himself did not mention homosexuality per se and, for this reason, some commentators have understood Buddhism to be essentially neutral on the issue of whether homosexuality or heterosexuality is more permissible. Certainly, within the diverse cultures shaped by the Buddhist tradition, same-sex relationships have quite often been celebrated. For example, in Japanese Buddhism, there is the *chingo monogatari*, a tradition of homoerotic tales about acolytes and their teachers. Recently the Dalai Lama has spoken about homosexuality and observed that some specific homosexual practices are "unnatural" because they use organs not intended for procreation or sexual activity. In spite of this, the Dalai Lama also observed that same-sex orientation or attraction is not something that should be condemned.

Mathew N. Schmalz

See also HOMOPHOBIA; HOMOSEXUALITY (CHRISTIAN PERSPECTIVES); KABBALAH; SEXUALITY.

HONEN (1133–1212)

Japanese founder of the Jodo Shu Sect (Pure Land) within the Tendai School of Japanese Buddhism. He challenged the prevailing Tendai belief that a strenuous life of works was necessary for salvation, claiming that one could attain rebirth in the Pure Land through the saving grace of Amida Buddha and by merely invoking Amida's name. It is said that Honen attained enlightenment while repeating the formula *namu amida butsu* (hail Amida Buddha). The repetition of the formula, called *nembutsu*, became the focus of practice in the Pure Land School of Honen.

G. D. DeAngelis

See also AMITABHA/AMIDA; JODO SHIN SHU; JODO SHU; PURE LAND BUDDHISM; TENDAI.

HONORIUS I OF ROME

Pope from 625 to 638, Honorius was known in his lifetime for his extensive building projects as well as for his pastoral work. He is best known now, however, for his problematic theology. Honorius wrote two letters to Sergius, the patriarch of Constantinople, on the Monothelite question that later caused Honorius to be condemned for heresy at the Second Council of Constantinople in 680/1. The condemnation was upheld by Pope Leo II. The condemnation of Honorius has generated heated discussions concerning the whole question of whether a pope can be validly condemned for heresy.

Gary Macy

See also CONSTANTINOPLE, SECOND COUNCIL OF; MONOTHELITISM; POPE.

HOOKER, RICHARD (1553?–1600)

Arguably the greatest theologian of Anglicanism, whose *Laws of Ecclesiastical Polity*

(Books I–IV, 1594; Book V, 1597; Books VI, VIII, 1648; Book VII, 1662) provided it with a coherent rationale and form. The *Laws* grew out of his debates with the Puritans, who held that all doctrines and institutions of the church had to be contained in Scripture. For Hooker, Scripture was authoritative but not necessarily sufficient. Influenced by Aquinas, he held reason to be God's gift and necessary to interpret Scripture accurately and decide issues Scripture does not resolve. He held that the English Reformation did not create a new church, but a renewed one in continuity with the traditions and purity of the ancient, undivided church. He argued for episcopacy and the Book of Common Prayer against those who thought the English Reformation was not radical enough. The Episcopal Church commemorates him on November 3.

Jon Nilson

HOPE (IN CHRISTIANITY)

In his *Treatise on the Passions*, Thomas Aquinas calls hope an "irascible passion," that is, a passion that pursues a good that is difficult to obtain, or an evil that is difficult to avoid. Although it is true of all the passions, hope especially is possible "through the power of another."

Hope is also one of the three theological virtues named by Paul in 1 Corinthians 13. Christian hope has past, present, and future dimensions. It rests on the already accomplished resurrection of Jesus. Jesus' resurrection is understood as the "first fruits" of the action of the Spirit. That is, Jesus' resurrection power is active in the life of each Christian now, empowering Christians to live as Jesus lived, and to share his struggle to establish the reign of God on earth. The gift of the Spirit is the guarantor of that hope. For the future,

each Christian hopes that the promised bodily resurrection will be hers, when she will be raised up as Jesus was raised. Further, in the return of Jesus on the "last day," the reign of God will be fully established on earth and in heaven.

In *Images of Hope*, a marvelous work of spirituality/psychology, William F. Lynch describes hope as a healer of the helpless, an empowering of the imagination. Some forty years ago, Jürgen Moltmann published *A Theology of Hope* (1967), part of a trilogy of works (with *The Crucified God* [1974], and *The Church in the Power of the Spirit* [1977]), that led to a renewal of theological interest in eschatology. Liberation theologians especially focus on the importance of hope to sustain the community's struggle for justice.

G. Simon Harak, s.j.

See also CHARITY; FAITH; LOVE (IN GENERAL); THEOLOGICAL VIRTUES.

HORMISDAS (?–523?)

Of Persian or Eastern origin, Hormisdas was archdeacon of Rome when, on July 20, 514, he succeeded Symmachus as Pope. Twenty-two years later, Hormisdas's son, Silverius, became Pope on the death of Agapetus I. Roman Catholics venerate both Hormisdas and Silverius as saints. In 515 the rebel general Vitalian forced Emperor Anastasius I to request Pope Hormisdas to summon a council of bishops to restore canonical communion between Rome and Constantinople. In July 484 Pope Felix III had excommunicated Acacius, the patriarch of Constantinople, for recognizing Peter Mongus, a Monophysite, as patriarch of Alexandria. Acacius and Peter Mongus had jointly composed the *Henoticon* (*Decree of Union*) for the emperor Zeno who was attempting to assuage the Egyptian church's anger over the condemnation of Monophysitism at the Council of Chalcedon. Four years of delicate negotiation between Hormisdas and the emperors at Constantinople bore fruit when the emperor Justin I in 519 agreed to the *Formula of Hormisdas* as the basis to restore canonical communion between Rome and Constantinople. Hormisdas had drafted this document in 517 and the bishops of Spain subscribed to it that same year. The document holds that orthodox doctrine is what the Roman See has defined as such. In addition, the *Formula of Hormisdas* equates churches in communion with the Roman See with the Catholic Church. Quotes from the *Formula of Hormisdas* begin the dogmatic constitution *Pastor Aeternus (Eternal Shepherd)* of Vatican Council I of 1870 on the infallible magisterium of the Roman Pontiff.

Herbert J. Ryan, s.j.

See also CHALCEDON, DEFINITION OF THE COUNCIL OF; HENOTICON; INFALLIBILITY; JUSTINIAN; LEO I THE GREAT, POPE; MONOPHYSITISM; PASTOR AETERNUS.

HOSIUS OF CORDOVA (257?–357)

Hosius was chosen bishop of Cordova around 296 and became theological advisor to Constantine early in the emperor's reign. Hosius was sent by Constantine to investigate the dispute between the patriarch, Alexander of Alexanderia, and the presbyter, Arius. Hosius played a leading role in the Council of Nicaea, but in 355 he was banished by the emperor for his support of Athanasius of Alexandria. Hosius was allowed to return to his diocese when he signed the Arian creed of Sirmium, an act he reputed before his death.

Gary Macy

See also ALEXANDER OF ALEXANDRIA; ARIANISM; ARIUS; ATHANASIUS, PATRI-ARCH OF ALEXANDRIA; CONSTANTINE; NICAEA, FIRST COUNCIL OF; NICAEA, SECOND COUNCIL OF; PATRIARCH.

HOST

The word "host" comes from the Latin word *hostia* and usually refers to the wafer of unleavened bread consecrated at Mass. The Latin word means "victim" or "sacrifice," and the word was applied to the bread used at Mass because once consecrated, the bread was identified with the risen Christ who had died to save humans. The Mass, or Eucharist, has been understood by Christians as memorial of the death and resurrection of Jesus. This use of the word started in the Middle Ages when the use of wafers, rather than loaves of bread, became common. The word "host" is also used in some translations of Scripture to indicate an army, as in the phrase, "a host of angels." This English word actually comes from a different Latin word, *hostis*, that meant "enemy" and is, for example, the root of the English word, "hostile."

Gary Macy

See also COMMUNION (LITURGICAL); EUCHARIST; MASS.

HOZHO

This word refers to the central, guiding principle in Navajo life. It is a term extremely rich and almost impossible to define. Thus, even in Navajo descriptions, it is not so much defined as indicated by images that convey its centrality and dominance. However, some related words can introduce us to its meaning. The basic cause of evil and suffering in human life is believed to be in falling out of harmony with the rest of creation. In a worldview in which all forms of life are inseparably linked, certain actions or failures to act wrench the bonds that unite us to all things. The remedy is seen in those actions that seek to repair the breach, and these are always connected to ritual. Ritual's essential role is, therefore, to restore harmony, order, and balance. When this is done, life returns to a blessed state in which we can experience happiness and serenity. This state of perfect harmony, within and without, in the meaning of Hozho.

Kathleen Dugan

See also CHANTWAY.

HROSWITHA

A tenth-century nun of the monastery at Gandersheim, Hroswitha (considered by many Germany's first significant poet and playwright) published six Christian Latin comedies in imitation of Terence. In one of the prefaces to her plays, she justified her literary work by saying that the plays of Terence and other pagans depicted women behaving in such a way as "to bring a blush to [her] cheek." It is not her modesty that is to be noted here but her careful reading of Latin classics; Hroswitha is good evidence of the level of education in early medieval monasteries for women. Ignored for centuries, Hroswitha became popular during the Renaissance when many of her works were translated into the vernacular. Undoubtedly, Renaissance scholars found her interest in the classics a foretaste of their own.

Marie Anne Mayeski

See also MEDIEVAL CHRISTIANITY (IN THE WEST); NUN.

HSIEN

(Chinese, *xian*, immortal). These were mysterious and capricious figures in reli-gious (popular) Taoism who were thought to have achieved immortality through a combination of alchemy, asceticism, and meditation. As Immortals who could either remain invisible to ordinary humans or manifest themselves in mortal form, they were believed to possess magic powers and would reward and guide the virtuous while punishing the wicked. While belief in immortality by the Chinese goes back to the early Zhou Period (around the eighth century B.C.E.), the formalized Cult of the Immortals in religious Taoism didn't appear as a popular movement until the Han Dynasty (206 B.C.E.–220 C.E.).

G. D. DeAngelis

See also DAOISM.

HSIN

(Chinese, lit. mind-heart). According to classical Confucian theory, each individual possesses an inner organ with the same moral qualities as heaven. This organ, intellectual as well as moral, is the heavenly source within the individual of correct moral and social behavior, and is the seat of wisdom, intelligence, and emotion.

G. D. DeAngelis

See also CHUN-TZU; CONFUCIANISM; CONFUCIUS; JEN; LI; TE.

HSI WANG-MU

(Chinese, *Xi Wang-mu*, Queen Mother of the West). Goddess of the Western Paradise whose abode was the Chinese mythical mountain K'un Lun, she was a mythological figure from the period of prehistory when the Tao was the mother of chaotic wholeness. She became popular in China during the Han Dynasty (206 B.C.E.–220 C.E.) as the goddess of death and immortality. Her romantic relationship with the Emperor Mu was detailed in the Mu T'ien-Tzu Chuan (account of Emperor Mu, about 300 B.C.E.).

G. D. DeAngelis

HSUN-TZU (298?–238? B.C.E.)

(Chinese, *Xun-zi*). Prominent Confucian philosopher of the Warring States Period (third century B.C.E.) who helped define and defend Confucius' teachings. Popularly referred to as the "heterodox champion" of Confucianism, he was a hard-headed realist who was greatly influenced by the Legalists and Taoists. He departed from the view of Mencius and earlier Confucians that "man" (the human being) was innately good in asserting that man was, by nature, bad, and his goodness was only acquired by training. He also denied the existence of supernatural agencies and the belief that heaven watches over man with any kind of personal concern. In addition, he rejected the Confucian idealization of the past and argued for a completely rational and naturalistic vision of man and the universe in which harmony and order could only be achieved by the virtuous but exacting efforts of the state. In time it was Mencius' more optimistic view of man and life that served as the orthodox interpretation of Confucius' teachings.

G. D. DeAngelis

See also CHU HSI; CHUNG YUNG; CONFUCIANISM; CONFUCIUS; MENCIUS; NEO-CONFUCIANISM; WANG YANG-MING.

HUA-YEN BUDDHIST SCHOOL

A distinctive school of Chinese Mahayana Buddhism that cohered by the early seventh century and was derived from the *Avatamsaka Sutra* (Flower Garland Text) in both name, pantheon, and doctrine. It emphasizes: (1) the universality of Buddhahood and its magical intervention in human experience beyond description; and (2) the true nature of the cosmos as the *dharmadhatu*, a realm in radiant flux in total interdependence that can be perceived only via meditation. One of the most well-known analogies of this interpenetration of reality is that of Indra's Net: just as a mirror affixed to every joint of the net reflects all other points *ad infinitum*, so does every point in the universe reflect a totality and mystery, the Buddha nature. Some scholars have suggested that the Hua-yen School is in reality an attempt to explain Ch'an/Zen meditation. The popularity of the school in China was evidenced by figures derived from the Avatamsaka text: monumental images of Vairocana Buddha dominated at early cave sites, and it was this text's focal bodhisattva Samantabhadra who inspired recitations of vows and stories by early Chinese lay societies. Although the separate Chinese Hua-yen lineage declined during the Sung dynasty (960–1278), Hua-yen was introduced to Japan in the eighth century where it is called the Kegon, and there it endures to the present with temples numbering over 170.

Todd T. Lewis

See also DHARMADHATU; TATHAGATAGARBHA DOCTRINE.

HUGH OF ST. VICTOR (?–1142)

Very little is known about Hugh's early life. He became a canon at the abbey of St. Victor in Paris in 1125. There he established a distinctive and influential school of theology whose teachers are known as the Victorines. Hugh's teaching integrated scriptural study, theology, and mysticism in a manner rarely achieved in Christian writing. His book *De sacramentis christianae fidei* (On the Symbols of the Christian Faith) was one of the first theological "summas" (complete collections) of the Middle Ages, and certainly one of the most influential. Hugh was a great and gentle teacher who influenced the theologians well into the fifteenth and even sixteenth century.

Gary Macy

See also MEDIEVAL CHRISTIANITY (IN THE WEST); MYSTICISM/MYSTICS (IN CHRISTIANITY); SCHOLASTICISM.

HUGUENOTS

Of disputed origin, this term refers to French Protestants. Strongly influenced by Calvin's reforms in Geneva, the Reformation in France was formalized in 1559, when the Protestant Synod of Paris gave an organization to a French Reformed Church.

Catholic reaction to the growth and institutionalization of the French Reformation was not slow to develop. In 1561 the Colloquy of Poissy failed in its attempt to conciliate Catholics and Calvinists. The following year, civil war between Catholic and Protestant princes broke out and lasted, with some interruptions, for more than thirty years. The most infamous event was the Saint Batholomew's Day Massacre of August 24, 1572. Several thousand Huguenots, in Paris and the provinces, were slaughtered in mob violence.

From 1589 the Protestant Henry of Navarre claimed the French throne. His 1593 conversion to Catholicism helped to bring the civil wars to an end; five years later, in the Edict of Nantes, Henry decreed religious toleration, though with some restrictions, for Protestants in France.

Under King Louis XIV, religious and other minorities did not fare well in France. In 1685 Louis revoked the Edict of Nantes.

Many Huguenots left France in the following years for places better disposed to the Reformed Church, such as Holland, England, and parts of Germany. Some eventually made their way to British North America. In 1702 a Huguenot revolt in southern France arose, but it was brutally put down by the royal armies.

Only on the eve of the French Revolution was the Revocation of 1685 itself revoked by Louis XVI, and toleration once again offered to Huguenots. French Protestants were, for the most part, supporters of the Revolution and of the creation of a republic. In the nineteenth and twentieth centuries, though small in numbers, French Protestants were leaders in the political, intellectual, and economic life of France.

Thomas Worcester, S.J.

See also CALVIN, JOHN; CALVINISM; COUNTER-REFORMATION/CATHOLIC REFORMATION; PROTESTANTISM; REFORMATION; REFORMED CHURCH; TOLERATION.

HUMAN BEING

In a biological perspective, a human being is designated as *Homo sapiens* and is a mammalian bipedal primate distinguished from other animals not only by its erect body mobility, but also by characteristics that include its superior mental development, speech and thought capacities, and profound interest in and need for socialization and understanding. (In the beginning of his *Metaphysics*, Aristotle writes, "All human beings desire by nature to know.") Contemporary advances in genetic science, most notably comparative results drawn from the human genome project and the chimpanzee genome project, have the potential to yield even greater insight into the particularity and uniqueness of the human being since humans and chimps genetically differ from each other by only 1 percent. Any offspring of human beings, by virtue of the fact that it is offspring and displays qualities or attributes proper to or distinctive of humans, regardless of whether or not these capacities are or even can be exercised (for example, in the case of extreme mental and/or physical disability), is a human being.

In a Christian theological framework, what a human being is must be understood in and through its relationship to God. The biblical tradition beginning with the first Genesis creation narrative, but especially Genesis 1:26-28, upholds that human beings, both female and male, were created in God's image as part of God's good creation, a mode of being not earned or deserved by human beings, but rather indelibly bestowed by God. While generations of theologians and philosophers have explored the complexities of what exactly "God's image" or *imago Dei* might be or mean, what can be understood very basically is that the human being reflects, and thus shows forth, God. As such, *all* human beings, in that they have been created by and reflect God, have inherent dignity and worth, and thus are deserving of treatment appropriate to their status as children of God made in God's image. Consequently, to recognize the humanity of an individual is to recognize her or his relatedness to God and the divinely endowed rights that attend this designation. The same requirement of recognition holds true when considering humankind as the collective of human beings; social structures as well as individual actions must acknowledge and foster the *imago Dei* status of individual human beings and humankind generally. All too often, however, human beings, whether as individuals or in groups, have been *dehumanized* purposefully in order to protect the privileges of the powerful; if human beings are considered to be subhuman or inhuman, then there are modified or even no perceived obligations to them. Such dehumanization is a deep and sinful affront not only to the dignity of a human being and humankind, but also to God, who created and whose image the human being is.

Meghan T. Sweeney

See also HUMAN RIGHTS; IMAGO DEI/ IMAGE OF GOD; PATRIARCHY; THEO- LOGICAL ANTHROPOLOGY.

HUMAN RIGHTS

Human rights are rights belonging to a human being simply by virtue of being a human being. Unlike political rights that are conferred by a particular governmental authority (and that consequently can be taken away), no human power awards human rights because the claim to them is inherent in and fundamental to every human being. Thus, human rights extend to *all* humans, regardless of, for example, an individual's sex, gender, race, religion, nationality, age, health, political affiliation, or sexual orientation.

Responding to the heinous atrocities of the Second World War, chief among them Nazi attempts to create a "purified" race by extreme measures to eradicate through systematic murder Jews, disabled people, homosexuals, Jehovah's Witnesses, and Romani people, the newly formed United Nations in 1948 adopted the Universal Declaration of Human Rights. Although this particular explication of human rights is fairly recent, many different religious texts and various civilizations from multiple eras have given attention to the inherent rights and responsibilities of human beings. In the

Christian theological framework, the foundational basis for human rights is every human being's creation in the *imago Dei* (image of God). To violate an individual's human rights is to sin against God.

Meghan T. Sweeney

See also DISCRIMINATION; HOMOPHOBIA; HUMAN BEING; IMAGO DEI/IMAGE OF GOD; OPTION FOR THE POOR; SOCIAL JUSTICE; THEOLOGICAL ANTHROPOLOGY.

HUMANAE VITAE

("On Human Life"). An encyclical letter issued by Pope Paul VI in 1968 on the subject of birth control. He affirmed the traditional Roman Catholic prohibition of artificial contraception while acknowledging that the demands of responsible parenthood may legitimate limiting the size of families. Pope Paul's rejection of artificial birth control, while consistent with the natural law tradition, is based on the claim that there are two equally fundamental and interrelated goods or purposes to marital sexuality: the procreation and education of children, and the enhancement of the love shared by the couple. Any artificial separation of these two goods—engaging in sexual relations as an expression of marital love while simultaneously frustrating its procreative power by artificial means, for example—undermines and contradicts God's purposes for human sexuality. Pope Paul feared that widespread use of artificial contraceptives would increase marital infidelity and promiscuity among the young, would objectify women as objects of male sexual gratification, and would undermine the choice to procreate in the face of governmental pressure to limit growing populations. Any legitimate regulation or limitation of births must be the result of "natural" methods that take advantage of cycles of fertility or by sexual abstinence.

This encyclical plays an important role in the history of Roman Catholicism following the Second Vatican Council. When issued, it was met with dissent from both theologians and the faithful. This has raised questions about the limits to theological dissent in the church and the authoritative status of encyclical teaching on human sexuality. Some conservative theologians claim that the teaching in *Humanae Vitae* is infallible, while most others argue it is an authoritative teaching of the ordinary magisterium and so—theoretically—subject to revision. In any case, the reception of *Humanae Vitae* marked the start of a decline in the ability of the church to teach persuasively in the area of sexual morality.

Brian F. Linnane, s.j.

See also CONTRACEPTION/BIRTH CONTROL; ETHICS, SEXUAL; EVANGELIUM VITAE; MARRIAGE; MORAL THEOLOGY/CHRISTIAN ETHICS; NATURAL LAW; SEXUALITY.

HUMANI GENERIS

Humani Generis was a major encyclical issued by Pope Pius XII on August 12, 1950. In this encyclical, Pius XII sought to condemn a number of modern tendencies considered threatening to the foundations of Catholic teaching. His condemnations include nontheistic theories about the origin of the cosmos and the evolution of species (including the human species), historical criticism of dogmas of the church, historical and textual criticism of Scripture, and the idea that human beings originated from human beings other than Adam and Eve (polygenism). He emphasized the perennial value and truth of Scholastic (Thomistic) philosophy, the authoritative nature of papal encyclicals such that the matters to which they refer are not a matter for free debate among theologians, and a nonsymbolic interpretation of the doctrine of transubstantiation. Many of the points made in *Humani Generis* were reversed or at least differently nuanced by Vatican Council II.

Michael J. Hartwig

See also VATICAN, SECOND COUNCIL OF THE.

HUMANISM

Any intellectual, social, or religious movement that supports and seeks the full dignity of humanity as well as interrelates the achievement of full human dignity with the renewal of culture, society, and/ or religion. In the history of Western Christian thought, humanism is mainly associated with the fourteenth- through the sixteenth-century European Renaissance that involved the study and recovery of intellectual and cultural resources from biblical, classical Greco-Roman, and early Christian worlds for the purpose of faithful yet critical reform of European Christianities and cultures. In reaction to medieval Christian theology in both monastic and Scholastic settings, Renaissance humanists focused on the intrinsic links between intellectual study, inward piety, and church reform. Recent historical studies of Renaissance humanism argue that the craft of writing among men and women of letters not only helped cultivate an interior relationship with God but also helped signify right relationships with others and society that in turn advanced wider societal and church reform.

One leading figure in Renaissance humanism was Erasmus of Rotterdam (d. 1536). Erasmus helped to lay the foundations for modern biblical and patristic studies through his linguistic and textual studies of biblical and theological texts that led him to publish critical editions of early Christian patristic writings and of the New Testament Scriptures. Renaissance humanism deeply impacted and influenced the sixteenth-century Catholic and Protestant Reformers, for example, in producing biblical translations, such as Martin Luther's translation as well as the King James Bible. Another leading figure in the sixteenth century, Ignatius of Loyola (d. 1556) founded the Society of Jesus (Jesuits) that undertook an educational ministry alongside a global missionary ministry. The Jesuits formulated a program of education, the *ratio studiorum*, that emerged in part from the intellectual efforts of Renaissance humanism.

More contemporary Catholic humanism is illustrated in the Vatican II (1962–5) document *Gaudium et Spes* that grounds the dignity of all humanity (1) in a theological claim regarding the creation of humanity in the image and likeness of God and (2) in our responsibilities to one another. This document also critically applies theological resources to oppose all offenses against human dignity in personal, family, social, cultural, economic, and political life, and to likewise support human flourishing in the same arenas of life.

Contemporary feminist and liberationist theologies also reflect a new kind of Christian humanism based on right and responsible relations with God and with one another. In 1983, Catholic feminist theologian Rosemary Radford Ruether coined the "critical principle of feminist theology" that articulates a theological rationale for the full humanity of women and men, already rooted in creation but not yet fully realized in the church or society. And, in the 1960s and 1970s, Peruvian Catholic priest and Latin American liberation theologian Gustavo Gutiérrez placed liberation at the center of theological praxis (of engaged theological reflection), a liberation in which our full humanity includes and intertwines personal, social, and religious transformation. Both feminist and liberationist theologies critically recover an array of biblical, patristic, and theological resources for the purpose of reconstructing theological claims, Christian practices, and everyday living that support full human dignity, especially but not exclusively for the poor, the oppressed, and the marginalized.

Rosemary P. Carbine

See also ERASMUS OF ROTTERDAM; FEMINIST THEOLOGIES; GAUDIUM ET SPES; GUTIÉRREZ, GUSTAVO; LIBERATION THEOLOGIES; RUETHER, ROSEMARY RADFORD.

HUME, DAVID (1711–76)

British philosopher. Together with John Locke, David Hume is regarded as one of the founders of British empiricism in philosophy. His major contributions to the philosophy of religion include: *The Natural History of Religion* (1756), arguing against the hypothesis of a primordial monotheism and religion as divine revelation; the essay; "On Miracles" (1758), arguing that testimonies to miraculous events are not sufficient evidence for the claim to truth of religion; and *Dialogues Concerning Natural Religion* (1779), arguing that the teleological argument is insufficient as a foundation for a religion of reason. Cumulatively, the effect of these works called into question the reasonableness of religious belief and the rational foundation of religion, seemingly leaving subsequent generations with the dilemma of skeptical

agnosticism or fideism as fundamental standpoints regarding religion.

J. A. Colombo

See also AGNOSTICISM; FIDEISM.

HUMILITY (IN CHRISTIANITY)

From the Latin root "earth" (*humus*), humility is taken to mean that one is "grounded," and therefore not overestimating oneself or one's accomplishments. In a modern reflection, Norvin Richards states that humility is an accurate sense of oneself, whose virtue lies in its power to resist incorrect evaluations of oneself. Here, Richards is offering a corrective to the popular notion of humility, expressed for example by Henry Sidgwick as humility prescribing "a low opinion of our merits."

Classical ethics did not take humility to be a virtue, but the humility of Jesus (cf. Phil 2:5-11) made humility an important Christian consideration. Christian Scholastic ethics, borrowing the form of Greek virtue ethics, took humility to be a virtue characterized by the orderly subjection of the inferior (in excellence) to the superior. That did not, however, account for the humility of Jesus that was subjection of the superior to the inferior (cf. John 14:28b). Thus, Christian humility is more accurately seen as imitation of Christ in an attitude and activity of ongoing and completely self-sacrificial service, especially of the poor and oppressed.

In the *Spiritual Exercises*, Ignatius Loyola focuses on humility as characteristic of our *relationship* to God in Jesus. He distinguishes three degrees. The first, necessary for salvation, is "in all things to obey the law of God our Lord," never breaking a commandment that binds under mortal sin. The second, more perfect, is what is often called by the technical spiritual term, "indifference." That is: "that I do not desire, nor feel myself attached to, riches more than poverty, honor more than dishonor, a long life more than a short one," as long as the service of God our Lord and the salvation of one's soul is unaffected. Also, "not for all created things, nor should my life be endangered, would I even think about committing a venial sin." Finally, if one has attained to the first and second degrees, "in order better to imitate Christ our Lord and to become actually more like to Him, I desire and choose poverty with Christ poor, rather than riches; insults with Christ burdened with them, I desire to be accounted as worthless and a fool for Christ, who was first held to be such, rather than wise and prudent in this world." This last is a truly Christian virtue and more, the *desire* for such humility is a uniquely Christian *passion*.

Simon Harak, s.j.

HUN

(Chinese, spiritual soul). This term is related to early Chinese belief in the existence of multiple souls within the individual. During the development of religious cosmology in the Han Period (206 B.C.E.–220 C.E.), the individual was believed to have two souls, *hun* and *p'o*, that were connected with *yin* and *yang*. Hun, the yang soul, was conceived as the spiritual entity believed to ascend to heaven after death and send down blessings to the family. The physical soul was the p'o, the material or yin component. This soul would reside in the grave, entering the earth with the body, and could turn into a *kuei* (evil spirit) if not placated by suitable burial and sacrifices.

G. D. DeAngelis

See also KUEI; SHEN; YIN AND YANG.

HUS, JOHN (1373?–1415)

John was born in Husinec in Bohemia, and it is from this village that he takes his name. He studied at the University of Prague, receiving his bachelor's degree in 1393. In 1396 Hus began to teach in the arts faculty, but changed to the study of theology around the year 1400. In 1402 he was chosen by his colleagues as preacher of the Bethlehem chapel. Extremely popular as a preacher, Hus spent the next ten years in teaching, preaching, and spiritual direction. Hus's teaching combined aspects of John Wycliff's thought with Czech nationalism. Not only did Hus attack clerical abuse and the papacy, he also argued that the Czech church and the University of Prague should be free of its present domination by German clergy. The German contingent responded by accusing Hus and his followers of being heretics for teaching the ideas of the officially condemned Wycliff. In 1409, however, the Czechs gained control of the university from the Germans and Hus was elected rector of the university. That same year, the archbishop of Prague appealed to Rome for support against Hus and was granted a bull forbidding preaching in Bethlehem chapel. Copies of Wycliff's books were burnt by the archbishop, while Hus defended Wycliff's books and continued to preach. Angry crowds denounced the archbishop as the Antichrist, and Hus was excommunicated first by the archbishop and then by the pope. In 1412 Hus preached against the selling of indulgences, resulting in a further papal excommunication, and Prague was placed under interdict. Hus retired from the city so the interdict could be lifted and spent the next two years writing. In 1414 the emperor invited Hus to present his case before the Council of Constance, offering an escort of knights and a letter of safe conduct. At Constance,

Hus was almost immediately imprisoned and charged with heresy for teaching Wycliff's ideas. Hus was denied the chance to defend himself, but instead was presented with a list of teachings he was asked to condemn. Hus refused to recant the teachings listed since, as he staunchly claimed, he never held them in the first place. On July 6, 1415, Hus was condemned as a heretic and turned over to the secular authorities. Hus continued to confidently proclaim his innocence as he was led out of town to be burned at the stake. Hus was immediately hailed as a martyr by the Czechs, who continued to push for national self-rule and for ecclesiastical reform. The followers of Hus, commonly called "Hussites," continued his struggle, and at least one group of Hussites, now called the Moravian Brethren, continue as a separate church to the present day.

Gary Macy

See also BULL; CLERGY; CONSTANCE, COUNCIL OF; EXCOMMUNICATION; HERESY; HUSSITES; INTERDICT; MEDIEVAL CHRISTIANITY (IN THE WEST); WYCLIFF, JOHN.

HUSAYN (624–80)

Grandson of the Prophet Muhammad (570–632), son of Ali, the fourth caliph of Islam, and the Prophet's daughter Fatima. Husayn, who died at the Battle of Karbala (Iraq) in an armed conflict over succession to the caliphate (Islamic leadership), is considered a martyr by the party that supported his father and him for the leadership of Islam. This party, the Shi'ites, claimed that Ali (d. 661) was the only legitimate caliph of the first four, and they wanted to restore his family's leadership after the death of Ali's successor, Mu'awiya in 680 and the seizure of power by yet another rival, Yazid. The battlefield death of Husayn at the hands of Yazid's forces is commemorated to this day by Twelver Shi'ites, and Husayn's tomb at Karbala remains an important shrine for them.

Ronald A. Pachence

See also ALI; CALIPH (KALIPHA)/ CALIPHATE; KARBALA; SHI'A/SHI'I/ SHI'ITE/SHI'ISM; TWELVERS (IN ISLAM); UMAYYADS.

HUSSERL, EDMUND (1859–1938)

German philosopher and founder of phenomenology. Born in Moravia of Jewish parents, Husserl studied in Leipzig, Berlin, and Vienna. He was professor of philosophy at the universities of Halle, Göttingen, and Freiburg. His studies in the philosophy of mathematics moved him to create what he called phenomenology—a philosophical school of thought that developed further and has had significant influence on Western philosophy and theology. Husserl converted to Christianity in 1887. He is also known for the important disciples who followed his philosophical lead. Among his more important publications are *Investigations in Logic* and *Experience and Judgment*.

Orlando Espín

See also PHENOMENOLOGY; STEIN, EDITH.

HUSSITES

The term used by their enemies for those followers of Jan Hus who continued his teaching after his death at the Council of Constance in 1415. The Hussites' most distinguishing characteristic was their practice of reception of both the wine and the bread at the Communion service. Almost from the start, the Hussites were divided into two groups. The more moderate group, often labeled "Utraquists" from the Latin meaning "both [bread and wine]," sought acceptance from Rome for the practice of reception under both bread and wine as well as recognition of the Czech supremacy at the university and in the government. The more radical wing, called "Taborites" after the biblical Mount Tabor, introduced an entirely new liturgy in Czech, rather than in Latin, and began dismantling many of the medieval devotions. In 1419 the new emperor Sigismund required full political submission from the Czechs in return for his toleration of reception under both species. The moderates agreed, but the radicals did not. The radicals, under persecution by both Catholics and moderates, formed a large communal settlement where they hoped to establish the kingdom of God on earth. The two groups merged again for mutual defense when faced with an anti-Hussite crusade led by Sigismund, whose policy had changed from negotiation to conquest. The crusading forces were defeated in 1420. The two groups split almost immediately after defeating the crusade, and the radicals formally broke with Rome by the end of 1420. The moderates attempted to negotiate a settlement with Rome at the Council of Basle in 1433, but this initially failed. Relations between the radicals and moderates worsened, and in 1434 the radicals received a crushing defeat in battle at the hands of the moderates. An agreement was then reached with the Council of Basle in 1434–7 allowing the moderate Hussites to keep Communion in both bread and wine while remaining in the Catholic Church. A few radicals remained active, and in the 1450s they founded the Bohemian Brethren, later known as the Moravian Brethren, a group that remains active to the present day.

Gary Macy

See also BASLE-FLORENCE-FERRARA, COUNCILS OF; CONSTANCE, COUNCIL OF; CRUSADES; HUS, JAN; MEDIEVAL CHRISTIANITY (IN THE WEST).

HYBRIS (OR HUBRIS)
Human arrogance, pride, or sense of self-importance. It comes from the Greek word for insolence. This term is frequently used in the Christian theology of grace, although it is not an exclusively theological concept.

Orlando Espín

See also GRACE; HUMILITY (IN CHRISTIANITY).

HYLOMORPHISM
According to hylomorphic theory, the ultimate metaphysical constituents or most basic principles of being of any substance are matter and form. The ancient Greek philosopher Aristotle (384–322 B.C.E.) and the medieval theologian and philosopher St. Thomas Aquinas (about 1224–74 C.E.) are among the most famous proponents of hylomorphism. Aristotle and Aquinas held that all animals and plants, as well as all natural inanimate beings, are subject to hylomorphic composition. In his *Physics*, Book II, Aristotle uses the following analogy to illustrate the distinction between form and matter. A statue can be regarded as having two most basic components—the "stuff" of which it is made (for example, bronze) and its shape or organizational structure. The bronze of the statue is its matter and the shape is its form. In animate or living beings, such as a cat or cactus, the form or most basic organizational structure is called the "soul." The soul is responsible for the life of the substance and is what enables it to have the sort of structure required for the performance of activities characteristic of its species. The matter, in such substances, is just the "stuff" that gets organized by, and

is given life through the form. St. Thomas Aquinas held that, of all the animate substances on earth, only human beings have a form or soul capable of surviving separation from matter.

Linda L. Peterson

See also AQUINAS, THOMAS, ST.; ARISTOTELIANISM; ARISTOTLE; SOUL.

HYMNAL
A book for each member of a liturgical assembly, containing hymns (metrical poems set to music) and other music for use during religious services. Some hymnals also include nonmusical material, such as outlines of services and the texts of readings, psalms, and prayers. Some denominations, for example, the Episcopal Church and the Lutheran Church, have official national hymnals. The Catholic Church in the U.S., however, has no official hymnal. Parishes are free to choose from among a number of hymnals of various musical styles. These hymnals are generally produced by independent publishers, although a few are church-related.

Patrick L. Malloy

HYPERDULIA
Hyperdulia refers to the special degree of *dulia* (or veneration) which, according to some Christian traditions, is properly reserved for the Blessed Virgin Mary, above that due to the saints. This veneration is different from the *latria*, or adoration and worship that is understood to be rendered only to God.

Joanne M. Pierce

See also ADORATION; DULIA; LATRIA.

HYPOSTASIS
Hypostasis is a Greek term used in trinitarian theology to indicate the distinctions of Father, Son, and Spirit in the one divine existence. In christology, it indicates the union of Christ's divine and human natures (hypostatic union). The Greek word, originally meaning "support" or "substratum," came to denote reality or objectivity. Origen (d. 254) adapted it to denote the distinctions in trinitarian life in the third century. Although the word resembles *ousia* (essential nature of being), in time *ousia* meant the common divine existence; *hypostasis* referred to the three Persons. This usage prevailed in the Eastern Church that questioned the Western designation of distinction by *prosopon* (person). Similarly, the Western Church was wary of the tritheist connotation of *hypostasis*. The matter resolved when the regions retained their familiar terms but accepted the orthodoxy of the other, and two trinitarian traditions continued using different categories to convey one reality: *hypostasis* in the East; "person" in the West. Cyril of Alexandria (d. 444) adapted the term for christological use a century later when he affirmed the real union of Christ's two natures as a hypostatic union against those who questioned the reality of Jesus' human soul. This designation was accepted by Pope Leo I and the Council of Chalcedon, confirming the custom of describing the unity of natures in the one person, Christ, as a hypostatic union.

Patricia Plovanich

See also CHALCEDON, COUNCIL OF; CHALCEDONIAN DEFINITION; HYPOSTATIC UNION; TRINITY/TRINITARIAN THEOLOGY/TRINITARIAN PROCESSIONS.

HYPOSTATIC UNION
The doctrine that Jesus Christ is one divine Person with two natures is known as the hypostatic union. This teaching was

affirmed by the Council of Chalcedon in 451. The main point here is that Jesus Christ, the Word made flesh, is both one with God and one with us: "one in Being with the Father" ("consubstantial" with the Father), and at the same time "consubstantial" with us, fully sharing our humanity—except its sinfulness. As the adjectival form of the Greek word *hypostasis*, the word "hypostatic" became part of a technical expression that states, but does not (because it cannot) explain, the union of the divine and human in Christ. The word's intent is that Jesus Christ is fully and really God, and fully and really human. Divinity and humanity come together without bleeding into one another. The result is "a single person and a single subsistent being [*hypostasis*]." At stake here is whether it can be said that God is truly one with us and that human beings have the possibility of being joined to God. The divine motive for the Word's becoming flesh was that human beings might become children of God (John 1:12), possess the fullness of life (John 10:10), and be one with the Father in Christ (John 17:23)—that is, their salvation. Salvation would not be possible if Jesus were only human (for in being joined to him we would not be joined with God), or if Jesus were only divine (since our humanity would have remained untouched).

William Reiser, s.j.

See also CHALCEDON, COUNCIL OF; CHALCEDONIAN DEFINITION; CHRISTOLOGY; FILIOQUE; HYPOSTASIS; INCARNATION.

I

IAMBLICHUS (250?–330?)

Neoplatonist philosopher. Probably from Syria, he spent many years there as a teacher. He wrote and taught about Plato's and Plotinus's systems, and about Pythagorean philosophy. Inclined to combine philosophy with mythologies and to delve in symbolic numerology, he described the superstitions of his day. Iamblichus was read and followed by many opponents of Christianity in the early Constantinian period (especially by emperor Julian the Apostate). He was also translated and widely read during the later European Renaissance.

Orlando Espín

See also ASTROLOGY; GRECO-ROMAN RELIGIONS; HUMANISM; JULIAN THE APOSTATE; NEOPLATONISM; PLATONISM; RENAISSANCE.

IBADAT

(Sometimes *ibadah*). From the Arabic word meaning "to offer service," the Islamic term for ritual worship. *Ibadat*, however, is not confined to *salat* or prayer. It also includes three other pillars or fundamental practices in Islam: *zakat* (almsgiving); *sawm* (fasting during the month of Ramadan); and *hajj* (pilgrimage to Mecca); as well as the laws of ritual purity (*tahara*). This indicates that in Islam, worship involves a wide range of activity and commitment to God in one's daily life.

Ronald A. Pachence

See also DIN; FIVE PILLARS (IN ISLAM); HAJJ; RAMADAN; SALAT; ZAKAT.

IBLIS

From the Greek word *diabolos*, the devil. In Islam, Iblis is Satan (*Shaytan*), the fallen angel who refused to "bow down to Adam" (Qur'an 7:11) because he considered himself superior to Adam (2:34; 7:12; 15:33). The Qur'an says God consigned Iblis to hell along with all his followers (38:85). The Qur'an also teaches that Iblis tempted Adam and his wife to eat the fruit of the forbidden tree in the Garden (20:120-121).

Ronald A. Pachence

See also ADAM (AS PROPHET OF ISLAM); DEVIL; QUR'AN.

I-CHING

(Chinese, *yi-jing*, Book of Changes). A very early Chinese text dealing with the metaphysical structure of the universe and the practice of divination that became one of the most influential books in Chinese history. In time, it became the most important and influential of the Confucian Classics. Originally, this text was neither Confucian nor Taoist, but a divination manual analogous to a fortune teller's guide. However, this text grew and developed over the centuries, reaching its present form near the end of the Han Dynasty (206 B.C.E.–220 C.E.). It ultimately developed into a book comprised of two sections: one containing symbolic diagrams (hexagrams) and answers to divinatory questions; and another, consisting of general philosophical writings, including commentaries ascribed to Confucius. This text became a uniquely Chinese combination of philosophy, practical wisdom, and esoteric lore with the Confucian commentaries providing a profound revelation about the principles of the cosmos. The system of symbols or diagrams, used for divining purposes, was seen as both a conceptualization of the universe and as a code for deciphering the patterns of cosmic change as it affects human affairs. The Confucian commentaries included the theories of *yin* and *yang* and the five elemental phases (*wu-hsing*) in conceptualizing the universe as a functioning organism where man [humanity], earth, and heaven are organically related rather than as a static object or mechanism.

What makes the *I-Ching* extraordinary is its combination of cosmology and divination where not only is the nature of the universe explained, but the symbolic diagrams have the operational power to bring about changes that would enable humans to live life in harmony with the natural operation of the cosmos.

G. D. DeAngelis

See also CH'I; CONFUCIANISM; FENG-SHUI; HSIN; T'AI CHI; WU-HSING; YIN AND YANG.

ICON

From Greek, *eikon*, an image. A two-dimensional painted image prominent in the public worship and personal piety of Eastern Christians. Increasingly, icons are making their way into the churches and homes of Western Christians as well. The significance of icons in Eastern theology, however, is radically different from the theological meaning of statues and religious paintings in the West. Whereas Western Christians look upon the religious image as a snapshot of a holy reality, Eastern Christians view the icon as a window, through which believers on earth gain actual access to the things of heaven. Icons, furthermore, are seen as vehicles through which the authentic Christian tradition is passed along. Icons are, in a sense, parallel to the Scripture, functioning as visual, rather than written, words. Two periods of iconoclasm (movements against the use of icons) erupted in the eighth and ninth centuries, but the use and veneration of icons was upheld by the Council of Nicaea II (787). Because the Eastern Church holds icons in such high regard, it views icon painters as ministers in the church. They are expected to observe discipline and devotion in their lives, and their paintings must follow ancient stylistic and iconographic guidelines. The goal of such personal and artistic discipline is to allow the Holy Spirit, rather than false doctrine or the personality of the iconographer, to gain expression through the icon.

Patrick L. Malloy

See also CULT, LITURGICAL; ICONOSTASIS; IMAGES, VENERATION OF; NICAEA, FIRST COUNCIL OF; NICAEA, SECOND COUNCIL OF.

ICONOCLASTIC CONTROVERSY

The iconoclast controversy rocked the Eastern Church from 725 until 843. The controversy revolved around the question of whether Jesus, Mary, or the saints could be portrayed as images (icons), and venerated in those images. As a result of the Monophysite controversy, and perhaps influenced by the iconoclasm of Islam, the iconoclasts argued that veneration of icons of Mary and the saints was idol worship, while veneration of icons of Jesus were heretical for venerating only his human substance so represented. Emperor Leo III (the Isaurian) in 725 openly opposed the use of relics, forbade the cult of icons, and ordered the destruction of all sacred images. Popes Gregory II (pope, 715–31) and Gregory III (pope, 731–41) both objected to this policy and theology. Gregory II held two synods in Rome condemning Leo's supporters. In the East, the patriarch of Constantinople, Germanus, was deposed for opposing the emperor, and the famous theologian John Damascene wrote a defense of the veneration of icons. Leo III's son, Constantine V (Copyronymus), continued and extended the persecution of all those who supported the use of relics. The Council of Hiereia in 752 decreed the destruction of all images found in churches. After the death of Constantine in 775, his son Leo IV and his wife, Empress Irene, pursued a more moderate policy. When Leo IV died in 780, the empress, acting as regent, restored the cult of images, and called a council in 787 at Nicaea, the seventh ecumenical council in Christian history (and the last recognized by both the East and the West). The council justified the venereation of icons and reversed the decrees of the Council of Hiereia. The acts of Nicaea were accepted by Pope Hadrian I (pope, 772–95) but opposed by the court of Charlemagne that based its opinion on the faulty translation of the acts of the council. The conflict was renewed under Leo V (the Armeian) (pope,

813–20) who annulled the decisions of Nicaea and renewed the persecution of the iconodules. The emperors Michael II and Theophilus continued the iconoclast policy. When Theophilus died in 842, his widow, Theodora, acting as regent, once again restored the cult of images in 843 with a feast in honor of the icons. This feast is now kept in the Eastern Church as the "Feast of Orthodoxy."

Gary Macy

See also CHARLEMAGNE; COUNCIL, ECUMENICAL; DAMASCENE, JOHN; ICONOCLASTS; ICONODULES; MONOPHYSITISM.

ICONOCLASTS

Literally, an "icon smasher," an iconoclast referred originally to those who objected to the use of painting or sculpture in Christian art during the iconoclastic controversy. The word was also used to describe those who were similarly opposed to statues and paintings during the Protestant reformation. The term now refers to anyone who attacks established custom, laws, or ideas.

Gary Macy

See also ICONOCLASTIC CONTROVERSY; ICONODULES; REFORMATION.

ICONODULES

Literally, an "icon lover," an iconodule referred to those who defended the use of painting or sculpture in Christian art during the iconoclastic controversy.

Gary Macy

See also ICONOCLASTS; ICONOCLASTIC CONTROVERSY.

ICONOGRAPHY

A system linking ideas, groups, or persons to specific symbols that then become a standard way of representing them. One might say that in American iconography, Uncle Sam represents the United States. In the Christian iconographic tradition, for instance, an image of Jesus' heart suggests God's love for humanity; loaves and fishes symbolize the eucharistic banquet. Many saints also have traditional symbols by which they are represented in Christian iconography. St. Joseph, for example, is often represented by a lily, symbol of purity.

Patrick L. Malloy

See also ICON; IMAGES, VENERATION OF.

ICONOSTASIS

An icon-covered screen separating nave and sanctuary in Byzantine churches. Three doors allow passage: the central Royal Doors, and the deacon's doors on each side. The iconostasis evolved in three stages. (1) Low, open barriers separated the body of the church from the altar area (fourth century). (2) These grew higher and were decorated with icons (ninth century) and (3) finally became opaque with icons (fourteenth–fifteenth centuries). The icons are arranged on the iconostasis in five rows according to a traditional yet flexible pattern. In the rows, from top to bottom, are the Hebrew patriarchs, then the prophets, then icons of the twelve principal annual feasts. Then, in the fourth row, Christ the Judge sits in the center with the Blessed Virgin, John the Baptist, and other saints to the sides. On the lowest tier, the Annunciation covers the Royal Doors, flanked by Christ Pantocrator, and the Virgin and Child.

Patrick L. Malloy

See also ICON; IMAGES, VENERATION OF.

IDEALISM, CLASSICAL GERMAN

While the term "idealism" broadly describes a family resemblance among those philosophies that maintain the knowing subject is the key to the nature of reality, "classical German Idealism" names a specific movement in eighteenth-century philosophy, usually including the (disparate) positions of Friedrich Schelling, Johann Fichte, Georg Hegel, and Immanuel Kant.

J. A. Colombo

See also FICHTE, JOHANN GOTTLIEB; HEGEL, G.F.W.; KANT, IMMANUEL; SCHELLING, FRIEDRICH WILHELM VON.

IDEOLOGY (IDEOLOGIES)

The wide range of uses of the term "ideology," in everyday discourse as well as among theologians, makes it difficult to define it with precision. In common usage, the term refers to (a) deliberately propagated untruth and (b) nonempirical knowledge. Drawing on Karl Marx's analysis of society, some theologians use it to refer to (c) the uncritically held ideas that govern the consciousness of a social group, (d) the universalization and absolutization of those ideas, or (e) the manipulation of those ideas by the dominant group in a society to advance its own interests at the expense of less powerful sectors. Still others use ideology in a neutral sense to refer to (f) a system of ideas that mediates Christian faith in history. In this last view, Christian faith cannot have an impact in history without "going through" those political ideas which (imperfectly, it is true) give it concreteness. Marx's claim that religion (and Christianity in particular) functions as an ideology in society— that is, as a system of thought serving the interests of the bourgeois class in capitalist societies—has been disputed by Christians since the nineteenth century. In late twentieth-century theology, especially among the various liberation theologies (for example, Latin American, feminist, or black), the Marxist indictment has been addressed rather than simply rejected. Many liberation theologians agree that systems of religious belief—Christianity or other world religions—have functioned in history as ideologies in senses (c), (d), and (e) above. Yet they deny that Christianity is *necessarily* ideological. On the contrary, they hold that, when rooted both in a historical praxis of liberation and in eschatological hope, Christian faith serves to unmask ideological elements in political as well as religious theories and practices. Still, even liberation theologians themselves do not all use the term "ideology" in the same way. Gustavo Gutiérrez, for example, writes about the exploitative power of ideology [sense (e)] while Juan Luis Segundo accepts the inevitable relationship between faith and ideologies [sense (f)].

James B. Nickoloff

See also LIBERATION THEOLOGIES; MARX, KARL.

IDOLATRY

Few (if any) of humanity's religions engage in idolatry understood as the actual worship of human-made images or objects. Many traditional religions, however, do worship the divine beings or spirits that may make themselves known through human-made images or objects, or who may dwell or be somehow present therein. In other words, it is the divine being or spirit who is worshiped, and not the image or object itself. Idolatry, in the popular sense, is very rarely found.

But there is another kind of idolatry, and that is the type of relationship that humans often have with economic or political systems, parties, ideologies, rituals, persons, attitudes, and the like, and that endows

these with excessive ("God"-like) powers and control over humankind. This idolatry is practiced when individual human beings and/or whole peoples are sacrificed, disposed of, or otherwise have their rights violated because of the demands of the said systems, ideologies, rituals, persons, and so on. This sort of idolatry is more attitudinal, but in history it has proven to be the most pervasive and perverse type. Idolatry, thus understood, is morally and doctrinally repugnant to the religious worship of God(s).

Orlando Espín

See also CULTURE; ETHICS, SOCIAL; IDEOLOGY (IDEOLOGIES); IMAGES, WORSHIP OF; INDIGENOUS RELIGIOUS TRADITIONS; MISSIOLOGY; RELIGION.

IGNATIUS LOYOLA (1491–1556)

The Spanish saint credited with founding the Society of Jesus (the Jesuits), Ignatius was born in the Basque province of Guipuzcoa and died in Rome on July 31, 1556. Ignatius' legendary conversion occurred while he was recuperating from a battle wound. As he was making his way through a medieval Lives of the Saints, he was stunned by a form of heroism that radically challenged his values and ideals. At thirty-one, he suddenly needed to devote himself to an extended period of prayer, penance, and reflection. Ignatius retreated to the town of Manresa, where he really started to learn about discernment and the way of the Spirit. Eventually, Ignatius wound up studying theology at the University of Paris, where he gathered around himself a number of companions to whom he had given the *Spiritual Exercises* and who thereby came to share his enthusiasm for the kingdom of God; these would become the nucleus of the future "*compañia de Jesús.*" They had initially intended to spend their lives in the Holy Land, working for the conversion of the Muslims; but the plan had to be abandoned. Instead, the companions placed themselves at the disposition of the pope.

Ignatius bequeathed to the church an insight into religious life in which action and contemplation were combined for the sake of mission. Once the young Society was formally approved by Paul III, Ignatius, as its first superior general, oversaw its growth and development and composed its *Constitutions*, the document that more than anything else reveals the Ignatian charism. A very determined individual, Ignatius was also a man of the church. He balanced commitment, drive, and singleness of purpose with a profound sense of providence and grace, "finding God in all things." He was declared a saint on March 12, 1622, together with Francis Xavier (one of his first companions), Teresa of Avila, and Isidore of Seville.

William Reiser, s.j.

See also SOCIETY OF JESUS; SPIRITUAL EXERCISES.

IGNATIUS OF ANTIOCH

Ignatius was the *episkopos* in Antioch when, sometime between 110 and 130 C.E., he was taken under guard of ten soldiers from Antioch to Rome after being arrested as a Christian. While on the journey, Ignatius wrote seven very moving letters to other churches. When he arrived in Smyrna, the overseer, Polycarp, received Ignatius with great honor. The letters of Ignatius are a very important early witness to the problems of the church in Antioch. Ignatius pleaded for unity under the headship of the *episkopos* and attacked the teaching of the Docetists. Ignatius under-stood his own martyrdom as uniting him intimately with Christ, a position he outlines in his letter to the Roman church begging them not to prevent his impending death.

Gary Macy

See also DOCETISM; EPISKOPOS; POLYCARP.

IHRAM/MUHRIM

From the Arabic *haram*, "forbidden"—a technical term for someone who has rejected some otherwise legitimate activities and entered *muhrim*, a state of ritual purity. This may apply to a person who is fasting, to a pilgrim performing *hajj* (pilgrimage to Mecca), or to worshipers who have cleansed themselves and have begun *salat* (prayer). *Ihram* is also used to describe the simple white garment people wear when they go to Mecca for the hajj.

Ronald A. Pachence

See also HAJJ; HARAM; SALAT.

IJMA

In Sunni Islamic law, the principle of "consensus" reached by religious authorities on a particular legal or religious issue not treated explicitly in the Qur'an or the *hadith* (tradition of the Prophet Muhammad, 570–632). *Ijma* developed along with and includes the major features of three other legal principles: *ra'y* (a personal legal opinion), *qiyas* (a legal opinion based upon an analogous situation), and *ijtihad* (the legal reasoning of an individual *mujtahid*, that is, a recognized legal authority).

Ronald A. Pachence

See also HADITH; IJTIHAD; MUJTAHID; QIYAS; SUNNA/SUNNI/SUNNISM.

IJTIHAD

One of the four principles of Sunni Islamic law that has been employed when the Qur'an or the *hadith* (tradition of the Prophet Muhammad, 570–632) is not explicit regarding the resolution of a particular religious or legal question. Specifically, *ijtihad* is the "effort" exerted by an individual legal authority called a *mujtahid* to settle a question for which there is no clear precedent or analogous situation. Since the knowledge of virtually every facet of Islamic law is required of one who would be recognized as a bonafide *mujtahid*, this principle has fallen into disuse today.

Ronald A. Pachence

See also HADITH; IJMA; MUJTAHID; QIYAS; SUNNA/SUNNI/SUNNISM.

ILDEFONSUS OF TOLEDO
(607–67)

Spanish theologian, Benedictine abbot, archbishop of Toledo, and one of the "fathers" of the church. He actively participated in three of the councils of Toledo, and was renowned in his day for his pastoral work, his intellectual acumen, and his devotion to Mary. Most of his works have been lost, but the four that have survived show him to have been familiar with the theological thinking of Augustine of Hippo, Isidore of Seville (whom some believe was his teacher), and of Pope Gregory the Great. Ildefonsus is especially important for our knowledge of the practice of the catechumenate in Spain, as well as for the early history of the influential Visigothic-Mozarabic Church. He was an important source for many medieval theologians in France and Italy, as well as in his own Spain.

Orlando Espín

See also ABBOT; ARCHBISHOP; BENEDICTINES; CATECHUMENATE; FATHERS OF THE CHURCH; ISIDORE OF SEVILLE; LEANDER OF SEVILLE; MARIAN DEVOTIONS; MARIOLOGY; MEDIEVAL CHRISTIANITY (IN THE WEST); MEDIEVAL CHURCH; MOZARABIC CATHOLIC CHURCH; TOLEDO, COUNCILS OF.

IMAGES, VENERATION OF

The Decalogue prohibits the worship of images (Exod 20:4-5). Yet, second-century Christian catacombs, and churches as early as the third century contained religious wall paintings. The Council of Nicaea II (787) defended creating and venerating icons, but not worshiping them. Veneration means honoring a thing because of what it represents, such as the photograph of a friend. Worship, by contrast, means honoring something because of what it is *in itself*. Only God merits worship. In Christian tradition icons of Jesus are acceptable since in him God assumed a human form. The *Catechism of the Catholic Church* reiterates the decree of Nicaea. "The veneration of sacred images is based on the mystery of the Incarnation of the Word of God. It is not contrary to the first commandment" (2141; see also 1159–1162).

Patrick L. Malloy

See also DECALOGUE; IMAGES, WORSHIP OF; LATRIA; NICAEA, FIRST COUNCIL OF; NICAEA, SECOND COUNCIL OF.

IMAGES, WORSHIP OF

In the monotheistic religions originating in West Asia (Judaism, Christianity, Islam), worship of images is strongly discouraged, since it is thought to compromise the oneness and the transcendence of the deity. In other traditions, however, it can be recognized as forming an important part of practical spirituality. Since, however, the

West (along with the Muslim world) has a long-standing, historically rooted bias against what is branded pejoratively as "idolatry," the nature of image worship must be carefully understood.

It would perhaps be better to describe this phenomenon, common enough in the history of religion, as the sacramental *use* of images, rather than as image *worship*. In almost all cases, religious images—ranging from natural objects such as rocks or bones that have been painted or carved, to highly refined paintings and sculptures—undergo some process of sacralization or consecration before they become objects of worship. This sacralization can occur spontaneously, as when an individual encounters the manifestation of a spirit or deity (an experience known as a hierophany) or otherwise comes to sense that the sacred is powerfully present in a particular object. On the other hand, many religious traditions possess carefully articulated rituals of consecration, often carried out by priests who have themselves been consecrated to the task. Such rites formally invoke or invite the power and presence of a spirit or deity into images—be they paintings or sculptures—or objects. In this case, the ritual sacralization is in function comparable to the consecration of the bread and wine in the Christian Eucharist. Certain ritual words and actions evoke what is felt to be the "real presence" of the divine in the image that thereafter becomes a focus of sacramental power. Thus for example, in the Vaishnava theology of Hinduism, the deity is said to consent, when invited, to become present in a sacred image in the form of an *arca–avatara*, an "incarnation for the purposes of worship." This is understood to be an act of grace by which Vishnu allows his devotees (*bhaktas*) to have easy, intimate access to him, so that his blessings may more readily fill their lives. Similar rituals are found in Buddhism and other traditions. Among other issues, this sacramental use of images raises the question of the extent to which matter can be used as a vehicle of spirit, as also the issue—important in contemporary spirituality—of whether and to what extent the dualism of spirit and matter can actually be overcome in sacramental experience.

In all these cases, it is important to note that, however closely the two may be identified in the mind of the devotee, it is not the image itself that is being worshiped, but the presence of the divine therein. To use a Hindu example again, even the simplest villagers are well aware that their festival images of gods and goddesses are made locally, by people they know. The presence of the deity is invoked in the image in a special consecration ceremony (*abhisheka*) that all may attend. And, most important, at the end of the festival the image is ritually "deconsecrated," the deity being politely asked to leave, and then the image (often made of a special unfired clay that dissolves in water) is ceremonially dumped into a river or the ocean.

It is also of significance that some religious images, although they may be consecrated, and while the faithful may in practice assume an attitude of worship toward them, are created more as reminders than as a means of actually approaching a deity or other holy being. Theravada Buddhist images of Gautama Buddha or Jain images of Tirthankaras are instructive examples of this kind of image, since the beings represented are explicitly held to be no longer active or accessible within the phenomenal realm. While it may be thought possible for those who revere the image to tap into the same power that the enlightened being left behind before departing, religious leaders will often assert that the images are no more than vehicles for meditation or symbols for the mental uplift of the faithful.

Finally, it should be noted that, despite their official condemnation of idolatry, the monotheistic religious have not remained totally aniconic. Religious images often play an important part in popular spirituality of these traditions. Examples would be the icons or statues of Christ and the saints in Orthodox Christianity and Roman Catholicism and practices surrounding the cults of Sufi saints in Islam. The theologians of these traditions—representing the orthodox, learned elite—have typically found such use of images problematic, since it creates the danger of compromising the official monotheism of the traditions. They have solved this problem, in part, by articulating a distinction between the *worship* of images (or saints), which would be idolatry, and the *veneration* of them, which would not. It is not clear, however, to what extent this distinction is borne in mind by the masses of ordinary worshipers who are not theologically educated. In any event, as has already been established, it is rare indeed that the actual image itself is worshiped. So again, the phenomenon being addressed would be better understood as the sacramental use of images, not image worship.

Lance E. Nelson

See also ABHISHEKA; BUDDHA; DARSHANA/DARSHAN; HIEROPHANY; ICON; ICONOCLASTS; IDOLATRY; IMAGES, VENERATION OF; JAINISM; MONOTHEISM (IN CHRISTIANITY AND ISLAM); MONOTHEISM (IN JUDAISM); SACRAMENT; SACRAMENTAL THEOLOGY; SHIRK; SUFI; THERAVADA BUDDHISM; VAISHNAVA.

IMAGO DEI/IMAGE OF GOD

"*Imago dei*" is Latin for "image of God" and refers to the belief that human beings some-

how mirror God in their very being. In the Hebrew Bible/Old Testament, the image of God is mentioned several times in texts usually attributed to the Priestly Source or Tradition. The term first occurs in Genesis 1:26 and 27 in connection with the creation of humans (compare also Gen 5:1 and 9:6, all P texts). "Then God said, 'Let us make humankind in our image, according to our likeness . . .'"; "So God created humankind in his image, in the image of God he created them; male and female he created them" (NRSV). There seems to be no warrant for assuming that the phrase "image of God" here referred to anything other than both the physical and the spiritual or intellectual components of humans. The texts in Genesis seem to mean that humans are similar to God in appearance as well as perhaps their intellectual attributes. In this assumption, the Priestly Tradition in Genesis was no different than other traditions in the ancient Near East.

Christians, starting with St. Paul, have held that the image of God was restored by Christ after having been lost in the Fall. Theologians have identified the image of God as reason, or the intellectual nature, or free will or simply human superiority over other creatures. The concept has been heavily influenced by Platonic thought that understands all being to be dependent upon the divine being for its existence. In several mystical traditions of Judaism, Christianity, and Islam, it is the image of God in each person that makes it possible for humans to enter into a kind of unity with God whether through meditation or ecstatic devotion or purity of heart.

Russell Fuller and Gary Macy

See also CHRISTIANITY; HEBREW SCRIPTURES; ISLAM; JUDAISM; MYSTICISM/MYSTICS (IN CHRISTIANITY); PLATO; PLATONISM; PRIESTLY SOURCE.

IMAM

In Islam, a religious leader. The term, however, has two distinct meanings: the one as *imam* is used by Sunni Muslims (about 85 percent of the Islamic world); the other as used by the Shi'ites (about 10 percent of Muslims). In Sunni Islam, an imam is prayer leader in the mosque, chosen for this role because of his evident knowledge of the Qur'an and the Islamic tradition. He may also function as the director of a local Islamic center, though not necessarily so. Sunnis do not claim that their imams have any special divine guidance or inspiration, nor are they thought to be divinely appointed. If a mosque has only one imam and he is absent, any acceptable male could function as imam and lead the prayers.

In Shi'ite Islam, an imam is far more than a leader of prayer. He earns this title when he gains recognition as a religious authority sent by God and endowed with special knowledge and divine legitimation. In effect, the Shi'ite imam functions as a mediator between believers and God and is thought to be a link in the chain of spiritual leadership that extends back to the fourth caliph (and the only one considered legitimate by Shi'ites), Ali (598–661). At any given time, there can be only one authentic imam.

Yet a third usage of the term imam in Islam is found in Islamic jurisprudence where it is an honorary title for the founders of schools of law.

Ronald A. Pachence

See also CALIPH (KHALIPH)/CALIPHATE; MOSQUE/MASJID; MUSLIM; QUR'AN; SHI'A/SHI'I/SHI'ITE/SHI'ISM; SUNNA/SUNNI/SUNNISM.

IMAM (THE HIDDEN IMAM)

In Shi'ite Islam, a divinely appointed leader or *imam* who is believed to be in hiding until his reappearance at the end of time. According to Shi'ite belief, the Hidden Imam did not die. He simply disappeared until, by God's will, he returns to establish an Islamic age of justice and peace. In "Twelver" Shi'ite Islam, sometimes called the Imamis, the Hidden Imam is Muhammad (d. 940?) who disappeared when he was four years old and was "represented" by four vicegerents in succession until the death of the last one in 940. Twelvers refer to Muhammad as *al-Muntazar*, "the awaited one." In "Sevener" Shi'ite Islam, also known as the Isma'ilis, Isma'il (d. 768), the seventh imam is recognized as the one who is to come.

Closely associated with the tradition of the Hidden Imam, which is unique to Shi'ite Islam, is belief in an eschatological figure embraced by many Muslims, both Sunnis and Shi'ites alike. This figure is known as *al-Mahdi*, "the guided one." The *Mahdi* is a savior personality who will come just before the Day of Judgment at the end of the world. He will reign for a brief period during which he will restore righteousness to the world. Shi'ites tend to identify the *Mahdi* with the Hidden Imam, while Sunnis think of him as Jesus in his second coming or as a Messianic figure who will come before Jesus Christ.

Ronald A. Pachence

See also DAY OF JUDGMENT (IN ISLAM); IMAM; JESUS (AS PROPHET OF ISLAM); MAHDI; SEVENERS (IN ISLAM); SHI'A/SHI'I/SHI'ITE/SHI'ISM; TWELVERS (IN ISLAM).

IMITATION OF CHRIST (BOOK, CONCEPT)

As a concept, the imitation of the life of Jesus has been the goal of devout Christians since earliest times. The actual living out of this goal has, however, taken quite different forms at different times. The mendicant movement in particular was a conscious effort to imitate the life of Jesus through an active life of voluntary poverty and wandering preaching. The book *Imitation of Christ* is a handbook for the spiritual life arising from the *Devotio moderna* movement. It was printed for the first time anonymously in 1418, but is commonly attributed to Thomas à Kempis. In the *Imitation of Christ*, stress is placed on the interior life, on liberation from the world, and on a strong devotion to the Eucharist. Its interior following of Christ focuses on withdrawal from the world, as opposed, for instance, to the active imitation of Christ of the friars. The book *Imitation of Christ* has been for centuries a very popular spiritual manual for Christians from many different communities.

Gary Macy

See also DEVOTIO MODERNA; FRIARS; MENDICANTS.

IMMACULATE CONCEPTION

A Roman Catholic dogma that affirms that Mary, the mother of Jesus, was free of original sin from the first moment of her conception. This dogma was defined by Pope Pius IX on December 8, 1854. The main justification for this doctrine is that *because* Mary was to become the mother of the Savior (hence, the Mother of God in Catholic belief), she was given by God the unique privilege of being free from original sin.

The doctrine of the Immaculate Conception of Mary developed slowly in Christian piety and theology before the papal definition of 1854. During the church's first eight centuries some biblical texts were often cited in reference to Mary's sinlessness (Gen 3:15 and Luke 1:28, for example), but the patristic church's reflections on Mary's sinlessness owe more to the thought of such theologians as Justin Martyr, Irenaeus of Lyons, Andrew of Crete, and John of Damascus, and to the conciliar definition of Mary as Mother of God (Council of Ephesus). The feast of Mary's "conception" was a popular liturgical celebration, becoming increasingly so in western Europe after the seventh century. Nevertheless, some of the great medieval theologians raised important objections to any belief on Mary's immaculate conception (Thomas Aquinas, Albert the Great, Bonaventure), while others defended it (Duns Scotus). The medieval Council of Basle (1439) accepted the belief but only as a "pious opinion," while the Council of Trent (1545–63) made sure to exclude Mary from its decree on original sin. Modern popes and several important religious orders promoted the feast and the doctrine until, in 1854, Pius IX solemnly declared it a dogma of Catholic faith.

Because of Mary's traditional role in theology as model of the church, and following the Second Vatican Council (for example, *Lumen Gentium*, the Dogmatic Constitution on the Church), some contemporary theologians have suggested that this doctrine must be linked to Christ and to the church, and must be placed and contextualized within the broader theological fields of christology, ecclesiology, and Mariology.

Orlando Espín

See also CHRISTOLOGY; CHURCH; DEFINITION (OF DOCTRINES); DEPOSIT OF FAITH; DEVELOPMENT OF DOGMA/OF DOCTRINE; DOGMA; ECCLESIOLOGY; INFALLIBILITY; LUMEN GENTIUM; MARIOLOGY; METHOD IN THEOLOGY; MOTHER OF GOD/THEOTOKOS.

IMMACULATE HEART OF MARY

A patronal title of Mary linked with devotion to the Sacred Heart of Jesus. This devotion stresses the affective nature of Mary's love and concern for all who call upon her. It was made popular in the seventeenth century by John Eudes, who linked it to devotion to the Sacred Heart of Jesus. In 1942 Pius XII (1939–58) consecrated the world to the Immaculate Heart of Mary. The title is used by a number of religious orders of women and is a popular name for Catholic parishes.

Mary Ann Hinsdale

See also SACRED HEART OF JESUS.

IMMANENCE

Often linked with the term, transcendence, "immanence" refers to one aspect of God's relation to the world: the manner in which God is present to and in the world. In addition to process theology, those contemporary Christian theologies with a "strong" doctrine of the Holy Spirit, for instance, Jürgen Moltmann, Karl Barth, and Yves Congar, tend to emphasize the immanence of God in the world.

J. A. Colombo

See also PROCESS THEOLOGY.

IMMANUEL

(Hebrew, ʿimmanu ʾel). Immanuel is a Hebrew personal name meaning "God is with us." Immanuel is mentioned in Isaiah 7:14 by the prophet Isaiah (eighth century B.C.E.) as part of the sign to Ahaz, the king of Judah, that YHWH will intervene to save the land. The sign seems intended in this context to give the king an idea of how long it will be before the problem he faces will be resolved. The name also occurs in Isaiah 8:8, and the phrase ʿimmanu ʾel in Isaiah 8:10 is perhaps used as a means to link the intervening oracles together. The identity of Immanuel in Isaiah 7:14 was probably intended to be Hezekiah, the son and heir of Ahaz. The mother of Immanuel in Isaiah 7:14 is described in the Hebrew text as an ʿalmah, or "young woman."

There would probably not have been much attention devoted to this verse in Isaiah except that it is cited in Matthew 1:23 in connection with the birth story of Jesus. The writer of Matthew's Gospel cites the Greek translation of Isaiah found in the Septuagint translation. In this form of the text, the mother of Immanuel is described as being a parthenos, or "virgin." For the Gospel writer and many early Christian communities, this made a perfect fit between Mary, the virgin mother of Jesus, and this oracle from Isaiah. For early Christians, Immanuel in Isaiah 7:14 clearly referred to Jesus. Early Christians and Jews naturally disagreed about the identity of Immanuel in Isaiah 7:14. The difference in wording used to describe the mother of Immanuel in the Hebrew text, used by many Jews, and the Greek Septuagint, used by many Christians, became a source of dispute and accusation between Jews and Christians, and as early as the early second century C.E., this passage is mentioned already in the Dialogue of Justin Martyr.

Although the Greek word parthenos could mean simply "young woman" or "maiden," which would make it an accurate translation of the Hebrew word ʿalmah, when it came to be applied to the mother of Jesus in the early church, it took on the modern connotations of the word "virgin," designating a woman who has never engaged in sexual intercourse.

Russell Fuller

IMMERSION

In Christianity, immersion in water is one ancient method of conferring baptism. Jesus Christ himself was said to have been baptized by John the Baptist in the river Jordan, as the Gospels attest (Mark 1:4-11; Matt 3:1-17; Luke 3:1-22; cf. John 1:19-34). In the earliest Christian practice, converts would be baptized in any kind of "living" or flowing water, either indoors or outdoors, for example, in a river or a stream (see Acts 8:36-39). Later, the use of an indoor *font* (the size of a tub or shallow pool) became common, generally placed in an inner room (called a *baptistry*) of a house-church (for example, Dura Europos, about 250 C.E.). Finally, beginning in the fourth century, a large, free-standing font (often circular or eight-sided) would be situated in a small building separate from the main church building (or *basilica*), also called a *baptistery*. These fonts were quite large, easily big enough for a deacon to immerse candidates by lowering or dipping them completely under the water level. As Christian baptismal practice shifted from adult baptism to infant baptism, fonts became smaller and smaller; large enough to lean a baby's head over, or, at most, to sit a baby in while water was poured over the head.

During the time of the Reformation, some Protestant groups (for example, Anabaptists) advocated a return to adult (or *believer's*) baptism. Later denominations also insisted on immersion as the correct form for baptism for scriptural reasons (for example, the modern Baptist churches). Even in other, more traditional churches, the liturgical practice of immersion is gaining modified acceptance; baptismal architecture, especially in the construction of larger baptismal fonts or pools, has changed in the later twentieth century.

Joanne M. Pierce

See also BAPTISM/CONFIRMATION; BASILICA; EASTER.

IMMORTALITY

Most broadly, immortality refers to the existence without end after death of a subjective center of consciousness. In the West, the concept of immortality as "immortality of the soul" is generally attributed to Socrates and Plato. While hope for immortality appears to be basic to Christianity in the biblical witness, its precise nature remains elusive and is controversial for two reasons. First, there is little clarity about what happens to the individual immediately upon death and, further, the relationship of this to the broader eschatological hope for the kingdom of God as the future of the world and history. Second, there is little clarity regarding the relation between hope for a "resurrection of the body"—associated with the coming of the kingdom—and the extent to which the biblical sources implicitly affirm an immortality of the soul. Recent historical work has shown that there was a great deal of unsettledness and development in the entire field of Christian eschatology through the thirteenth and fourteenth centuries.

Most recently, process philosophy (and theology) has argued that the idea of "subjective immortality" is incoherent and thus should be replaced by the affirmation of "objective immortality," that is, the values realized in space and time by individual actual entities exist eternally in, and as a constituent element of, the divine life.

J. A. Colombo

See also ESCHATOLOGY (IN CHRISTIANITY); ETERNAL LIFE; ETERNITY.

IMMORTALS, THE

See HSIEN.

IMMUTABILITY

From the Latin *immutabilis*, meaning "not subject to change." Within classical theism, the term is a divine attribute arising from the identification, by means of the idea of "perfection," of the biblical portrait of God with the Greek understanding of Being as broadly understood in classical—especially Platonic and Neoplatonic—philosophy. For the latter, the mutability of a being is a mark of its imperfection because change is either an achievement of or departure from perfection and neither is consistent with the affirmation that God is perfect.

Neoclassical or process theism challenges this axiom by elaborating a metaphysics, cosmology, and theology where "becoming" and therefore change is a more basic ontological category than "being." Within this paradigm, God exists in time because God is internally related to the world and thus is subject to change. The divine perfection lies in God's perfect—regarding both scope and adequacy—concrete internal relations to all creatures. Considered abstractly, it may be said that God is immutable in that the perfection of God's relationality to the world is constant; considered concretely, God is not immutable because the content of the divine experience is dependent on and internally related to change in creatures.

J. A. Colombo

See also IMPASSABILITY; PROCESS THEOLOGY.

IMPASSABILITY

From the Latin *impassibilis*, the term means "incapable of suffering" or, more broadly, incapable of being moved or acted upon by another. It is a divine attribute that follows from classical theism's understanding of divine perfection insofar as to be moved or acted upon by another is a form of "change" and thus incompatible with the affirmation of divine immutability. Medieval theology codified this attribute in the axiom that "God is externally, not internally, related to the world," that is, God's relation to things other than God is such as to introduce no change in God's being. In this sense, one might describe the divine being so understood as literally "apathetic" and "monarchial," that is, God acts upon the world while not being acted upon by the world.

There is a tension between the affirmation of divine impassibility and the prima facie biblical statements that speak of God's joy, anger, longing, love, and the like, and thus appear to affirm that God is internally related to things other than God. This tension became an explicit theme under the rubric of the "suffering God" in the so-called "kenotic" theologies of the late nineteenth and early twentieth centuries associated with Gottfried Thomasius (d. 1873) in Germany and Charles Gore (d. 1932) in Britain. Today, process theology (as well as the theology of Jürgen Moltmann, albeit in a different manner) represents a clear attempt to reverse the monarchial description of the divine being through its axiom that God is internally related to the world.

J. A. Colombo

See also IMMUTABILITY; PROCESS THEOLOGY.

IMPRIMATUR

A Latin term that literally means "let it be printed." It is the official certification, granted by a Catholic bishop or his delegate, that a given book or pamphlet is free of doctrinal or moral error. It is not to be construed as agreement with the contents of the publication. The *imprimatur* is frequently preceded by an official reviewer's certification of *nihil obstat* (literally, "nothing prevents," that is, there is nothing in the contents of the book or pamphlet that might be an impediment to the granting of the *imprimatur*). The publications that require an *imprimatur* are: new translations of the Bible, catechisms and other religious education textbooks, and liturgical books.

Orlando Espín

See also BISHOP (EPISCOPACY); CANON LAW; DEVELOPMENT OF DOGMA/OF DOCTRINE; DOCTRINE; DOGMA; HERESY; INDEX OF FORBIDDEN BOOKS; ROMAN CATHOLIC CHURCH; TRIDENTINISM; VICAR.

IMPUTATION

A key term in Luther's theology, the "imputation" in question refers to imputation of the righteousness of Christ to a sinner. For Luther, when the merit or righteousness of Christ is "imputed" to sinners, they are considered as righteous persons, even though righteousness belongs to Christ alone. The sinner can in no way whatsoever claim any credit for this merit or righteousness. For Luther and for many other Protestant Reformers, the Roman Catholic Church had obscured the righteousness of Christ by affirming righteousness elsewhere, in good works other than the work of Christ alone.

Imputed righteousness is contrasted with "inherent" righteousness. For the Council of Trent (1545–63), the righteousness of Christ is inherent, that is, it dwells within the baptized or forgiven sinner, transforming that sinner into a truly righteous person. Whereas Luther insists on righteousness as external to the sinner, Trent understands such righteousness as

a grace poured into the heart by the Holy Spirit, a grace one may freely choose to accept or reject.

Thomas Worcester, S.J.

See also COUNTER-REFORMATION/ CATHOLIC REFORMATION; GOOD WORKS; JUSTIFICATION; LUTHER, MARTIN; REFORMATION; RIGHTEOUSNESS (IN CHRISTIAN PERSPECTIVE); SIMUL IUSTUS ET PECCATOR; SOLA GRATIA; TRENT, COUNCIL OF.

INCARNATION

The term comes from the Latin translation of John 1:14, *"Et Verbum caro factum est,"* that is, "and the Word became flesh." The notion of the "enfleshment" of the divine Word (who came to be identified with the Son as the Second Person of the Trinity) is most likely derived from Jewish ideas about divine wisdom entering the human world (see Proverbs 8:22ff.). For the Fourth Gospel, the story of Jesus is nothing less than the story of divine wisdom "in the flesh." Writers have pointed out that the Incarnation encompasses the entire mystery of Jesus, from conception to resurrection; the opening verses or prologue to the Fourth Gospel are not about the birth of Jesus but a reflection on his whole life and its meaning. Indeed, the genealogies given in the first chapter of Matthew and Luke 3:23-38 suggest that the enfleshment of the Word also has a prehistory or ancestry that dates back to Abraham (Matt 1:2) and even to Adam (Luke 3:38).

The church's teaching about the Incarnation is perhaps the richest of Christian mysteries. Belief in God's oneness with the human condition in Jesus has indelibly marked Catholic imagination. Works of literature, art, architecture, and music; liturgy and sacraments; Christian prayer and practice; the Gospel's call to live justly and in solidarity: all of this and more finds its religious coherence and compelling beauty in Christ as the Word made flesh, that is, as the Word become fully human and historical.

The doctrine of the Incarnation is intimately connected to God's having raised Jesus from the dead. Without the resurrection, it is hard to see how the reflective process that gave rise to the text "and the Word became flesh" could have taken place. But more importantly, the resurrection revealed Jesus' abiding oneness with his community (see Matt 28:20) and gave visible expression to the words "with you I am well pleased" (Mark 1:11)—words that make most sense after Jesus completed his mission.

The Incarnation profoundly affects how the church understands what it means to be human (theological anthropology). Some early Christian writers would say that we have been created in the divine image, but it takes a lifetime to put on the divine likeness, where Christ is the likeness—"the new self" (Eph 4:24)—with which we are meant to be clothed. Christ thus represents human nature's deepest potential. Incarnation reveals, therefore, the human being's mysterious possibility of sharing the divine life, the creature's openness to divinization. To make clear the difference between Jesus and us, the church employed Paul's language of our being God's children by adoption (for example, Rom 8:15; Gal 4:5; Eph 1:5). The human potential for becoming fully God's daughters and sons was perhaps most vividly expressed in the words of an ancient prayer preserved in the liturgy: "By the mystery of this water and wine may we come to share in the divinity of Christ, who humbled himself to share in our humanity."

The church held firmly to its belief in the Incarnation because of the bearing this truth has on salvation itself. The Creed makes clear that the divine motive for the Word's becoming flesh is human salvation ("For us men and for our salvation he came down from heaven"). In other words, salvation (from one point of view) consists of our putting on the divine likeness, something impossible without the help of the Spirit. If any part of us or our nature were untouched by God's creative, merciful, and saving love, then our salvation would be incomplete. In the Word made flesh, divine solidarity with the human condition was revealed to be total, real, and concrete. Unless this were true, following Jesus would be impossible, because we could never become like him in his compassion, faith, and obedience.

William Reiser, s.j.

See also CHRIST OF FAITH; CHRISTOLOGY; INCULTURATION; JESUS OF HISTORY; RESURRECTION (IN CHRISTIANITY).

INCENSE

Incense (from the Latin *incendere*, "to burn") is a mixture of aromatic herbs, spices, and resins which, when scattered as powder or "grains" over burning coals, gives off a strong, pleasant fragrance and a thick, white smoke. The burning of incense had been taken as a sign of offering, prayer, worship, or adoration in many ancient traditions. The use of incense in the Christian tradition stems from its use and mention in early Judaism (and the Old Testament), and its use in worship and court ceremonial in Greco-Roman tradition. It is still used today in many of the more "liturgical" Christian traditions as a sign of blessing, sanctification, and adoration, especially when used at the Eucharist or other prayer services involving adoration of the Blessed Sacrament (or consecrated Host).

Joanne M. Pierce

See also ADORATION; EUCHARIST; MASS; MONSTRANCE; PASCHAL CANDLE.

INCULTURATION

A Christian (initially Catholic) theological term first employed by Jesuit missiologist Arij Roest Crollius. "Inculturation" (not to be confused with the social scientific notions of "acculturation" or "enculturation") entered official church usage by way of the World Synod of Bishops of 1977 (in speeches by Cardinal Jaime Sin of Manila, and by Jesuit superior general Pedro Arrupe). Pope Paul VI explained the principle of inculturation (but not the term) in his important 1975 apostolic exhortation *Evangelii Nuntiandi*, and Pope John Paul II used the term in his 1979 exhortation *Catechesi Tradendae*. As a theological principle, however, inculturation is rooted in the fundamental Christian belief in the Incarnation.

Christians believe that God definitively revealed Godself in the person and ministry of Jesus of Nazareth. Jesus, in Christian faith, is the historical and personal outpouring and self-donation of God in human history. In the words of the New Testament, Jesus is "the (visible) image of the invisible God" (Col 1:15). Being God's definitive revelation, however, did not diminish or compromise Jesus' humanness. He was fully human in all things but sin, as Christians believe. The personal reality of Jesus, consequently, is the paradigm for the church's own mission and reality: bearer and witness of God's message of salvation, the church is at the same time a human community. This implies, among other things, that the church is impacted (as any human community is) by cultural, political, linguistic, economic, historical, and other social circumstances and contexts. Indeed, it is impossible for Christians (individually or communally) to understand and transmit the Word of God through means other than those available to them within their cultural, social, historical, linguistic, and political milieus. God's revelation is God's, but once it is received and witnessed to by human beings, it also becomes a human message. Consequently, Christianity is and has always been the multiform inculturation of the Word of God.

The theological principle of inculturation attempts to justify and explain that the Christian message can and, indeed, must be announced through culturally authentic and culturally respectful means in order for it to be correctly understood and lived by the incredibly diverse peoples of the world. Christians cannot legitimately engage in cultural colonization in the name of the Gospel. The Word of God, therefore, must be "inculturated" ("take on the flesh of culture") in order for evangelization to be authentic and fruitful. The theological reflection on inculturation, however, has not been sufficient when it comes to explaining *how* the Word of God can be known and somehow distinguished from the cultures in which and through which it is witnessed to and lived. In other words, Christians (and those evangelized by Christians) never have access to the Gospel in a pure state. The Gospel is always and has always been mediated by cultures. So, if the Christian message must be announced in an inculturated manner (and this now seems beyond discussion), "where" is this message to be found, and "what" are its constitutive components, *before* the message is culturally announced in a new context? Given that the Christian message is *already* inculturated in the evangelizers' own cultures, how can they distinguish the message from the cultural mediations through which it came to be known to them? Might not questions of idolatry of (dominant) culture be legitimately raised if the inculturation of the Gospel is judged to be only a "missionary" concern?

Theological discussions on the principle of inculturation seem to point toward other, equally foundational questions. What is the relationship between culture and doctrinal development and expression? What is the relationship between grace and culture? What function does culture have in the ministry and mission of the church? What role does culture play in the act and life of faith? What effect does or should the Gospel have upon a newly evangelized culture, and upon the cultures of the evangelizers? The theology of inculturation has led to extraordinary advances in missiology and in practical theology, and it has opened a new field of theological inquiry on culture.

Some authors, in fact, no longer refer to inculturation but to the "transculturation" of the Gospel. There is today serious critique of inculturation from the growing field of intercultural theology and philosophy (especially Raúl Fornet-Betancourt's work). The main criticism is focused on inculturation's assumption that there is or could ever be an "a-cultural" content that can be transferred to cultures other than the one where the content originated. Interculturalists suggest that inculturation exposes itself to charges of ideological colonialism, further suggesting that what happens (and can only happen) in inculturation, in fact, is "transculturation," because the Gospel

and all missionaries are inevitably and always "cultured."

Orlando Espín

See also CULTURE; DEVELOPMENT OF DOGMA/OF DOCTRINE; DOCTRINE; DOGMA; ECCLESIOLOGY; EVANGELII NUNTIANDI; EVANGELIZATION; FORNET-BETANCOURT, RAÚL; INCARNATION; INTERCULTURAL THOUGHT; METHOD IN THEOLOGY; MISSIOLOGY; MISSION OF THE CHURCH; MISSIONS; ROEST CROLLIUS, ARIJ.

INDEX OF FORBIDDEN BOOKS

Often referred to simply as the "Index," it was an official list of books that members of the Roman Catholic Church were forbidden to read or own. Originally established in 1557, as part of Catholicism's Counter-Reformation efforts, the Index was revised many times thereafter. The purpose of establishing such a list of forbidden books was to prevent Catholics from reading materials that could threaten their faith or morals. Evidently, the Index was founded on the assumption that lay Catholics were mostly incapable of discerning truth from error, besides being theologically untrained. In today's Catholic Church, with increasing lay participation and leadership, and with a more theologically aware laity, the Index lost whatever importance it might have had in the past. The contemporary global cultural context has also made the Index theologically and philosophically untenable and canonically unenforceable. After 1966 Catholics were no longer bound by the Index's prohibitions.

Orlando Espín

See also CANON LAW; COUNTER-REFORMATION/CATHOLIC REFORMATION; IMPRIMATUR; LAITY; VATICAN, SECOND COUNCIL OF THE.

INDIFFERENTISM

The Catholic Church's negative word for the nineteenth-century belief that the particularity of the church (or any faith community) and the uniqueness of its teaching (dogma), could be dismissed as unimportant. In its stead, one could accept general principles, supposedly common to all (or any) faith, of living the "good life." The binding force of such principles need not come from divine command or from the teaching authority of the faith community. Pius IX explicitly condemned Indifferentism in his 1864 *Syllabus of Errors* (*Syllabus Errorum*, DS 2915-18).

The Christian church has always claimed to be both particular (in the life and teaching of Jesus), and universal (in its claim that Jesus is the Savior of the world). "Indifferentism" does away with this fruitful tension. Further, it sets up its own especially exclusive particularity, based, for example, on the superiority of reason or science.

G. Simon Harak, s.j.

See also PIUS IX, POPE; SYLLABUS OF ERRORS.

INDIGENOUS RELIGIOUS TRADITIONS

Indigenous religious traditions are the religions of small, land-centered communities that do not use writing. Based on subsistence economies, being either hunter-gatherers or small-scale agriculturalists, these peoples existed in relative isolation from, or on the periphery of, the great historical religious cultures of Eurasia, at least until the colonial era. Individual groups within this category identify themselves as separate people, different from other peoples of which they are aware. The terms "indigenous peoples" and "indigenous religions" originated in the West; until recently members of these groups had no conception of their belonging to some common category. Indeed, it must be pointed out that the very concept of "religion," as a separately identifiable sphere of human life, is foreign to these cultures that uniformly have no word for the aspect of life the West has identified as religion. For them, everything they do is religious, or has some connection to what we would call the "spiritual." Religion is not segmented out as a separate part of life, but is rather diffused throughout culture.

While sharing certain features in common with religious expressions stretching back as much as one hundred thousand years or more, the religions of indigenous people remain a vital, contributing part of the human situation today. This is true despite the fact that the traditional societies involved have been so profoundly impacted by the encounter with dominant outside cultures, especially the Christian West, that many have become radically destabilized or, all too often, extinct.

Terminology

In recent years there has been much debate about the proper designation of this type of religious culture. Terms used by previous generations of Western scholars—such as "primitive" or "savage"—have been abandoned as conveying obvious bias. We will not get very far in understanding these traditions if we see them as uncivilized and inherently inferior. Even if the best reading of these terms is taken as implying, perhaps, an archaic, pristine simplicity, the terms are misleading. We should be very cautious about regarding contemporary indigenous traditions as living museums containing relics of humanity's (or even their own) past. One only has to consider the centrality of the horse in the culture and religion of the Native Americans of the Southwest and the Great Plains, the horse being introduced to the region by the Spanish only in the seventeenth century. Similar problems may be discerned in the term "primal," for some time popular as a substitute for "primitive." Again, we should be wary of, and critically examine, any suggestions that these traditions represent what we, as moderns, once were, as well as romantic ideas that these traditions have retained sensibilities that we, suffering from the psychic stress of our technological success, have lost and need somehow to recapture. Some have sought to avoid such problems by calling these traditions *tribal*, since they are most commonly practiced among small, closely knit groups. This, however, would eliminate some indigenous peoples who are not organized tribally. Recently, the term *loc-oral* has been proposed, referring (if awkwardly) to the fact that these religions occur in localized, nonliterate societies. Currently, the American Academy of Religion, the largest association of religion scholars in North America, promotes discussion of this aspect of human religion under a program unit titled "Indigenous Religions."

Variety

Despite the devastating results of confrontation with outsiders, there remain in existence thousands of small-scale indigenous cultural groups scattered throughout the world, each typically speaking its own language. The religious beliefs and practices of these peoples vary widely, and so it is not possible in an article such as this to do anything more than describe certain features that are common to most of these traditions. The reader will understand, however, that not

all the features presented will apply to all the traditions encompassed.

Defining Features

Two features of the indigenous religious traditions are taken as defining. First, they are geographically restricted, each being localized in a particular area. Second, their cultures are preserved and transmitted orally. We will begin by considering these defining features in order.

Being limited geographically, indigenous religions are, one could say, not available for export. Not only are they not transferable cross-culturally (the religion and the culture are inseparable); they are equally difficult to transfer geographically (the religion and the land are inextricably interrelated). These traditions are, therefore, emphatically not missionary in spirit. Their land is part of their religion, being for them the sacred center of the world, often regarded as having been given to them by the Supreme Being (see High God, below) to care for. There is a sacred topography of the land. It is marked by sacred landmarks hallowed by mythic associations with an ancient past. Mountains, rivers, trees, and other features of the land are holy, some more so than others, and may themselves be regarded as powerful spirit beings, hallowing particular places by their presence.

The religious cultures we consider here have, in addition, not traditionally written their language or used any form of written communication aside from occasional use by certain groups of pictographs and other devices as memory aids. Their culture is transmitted orally, and through other unwritten means such as ritual and art. This means, obviously, that they have not produced any scriptures, theological writings, or other texts. For this reason, earlier generations of scholars of religion, who habitually focused on such written materials in their studies, tended to leave the study of these traditions to anthropologists. Lately, however, historians of religion have let go of their bias in favor of written artifacts, and have become more aware of the vital importance of the aural, the visual, and especially the performative elements of religion.

Of course, to be nonliterate is not the same as being ignorant. One can be learned and highly cultured in a nonliterate society. Since they must rely on memory, nonliterate peoples—especially their religious leaders—must in fact memorize a prodigious amount of material. Individual members of the community become repositories of the cultural tradition that —as long as the tradition is intact—remains vital as a living part of each person. Nor does nonliterate mean lacking in intellectual power. Oral cultures have sophisticated religious teachings and intellectual traditions, but these are carried in the memory of their living members, especially the elders, both men and women.

In nonliterate cultures, the spoken word has creative, spiritually potent, even magical dimensions. Storytelling is central to life experience. Stories, songs, even simple names, have spiritual power when intoned. There is a proliferation of festivals, all-night ceremonies, and other gatherings that create ritually charged opportunities for the sacred songs to be sung and stories to be heard. Such events combine education with entertainment and associate cultural transmission with spiritual renewal.

Other Typical Features

From within these traditions, as in the great religions of Asia, the world is experienced predominantly in terms of cyclic time, time that repeats, not going anywhere in particular. Like the cycles of the day, the moon, and the seasons, time revolves again and again, the world remaining much the same. This produces an orientation profoundly different from the Western sense of linear time, according to which time has a definite beginning and is progressing forward toward a final state of perfection. While the great historical religions typically look forward to the possibility, either for the individual or the world as a whole, of a complete transcendence of the ambiguities of ordinary life, indigenous religions typically do not. Life will always be more or less the same, sometimes better, sometimes worse, but still basically good just as it is.

Of course, such visions did not take into account the radically disruptive nature of colonial domination. Interesting exceptions to this generally cyclic vision, as well as examples of change in these so-called traditional societies, are the outbreaks of millenarian movements among various indigenous peoples. These occurred in reaction to the extreme cultural stress brought on by the encounter with European and American colonists and missionaries. In the Ghost Dance movement in North America, the cargo cults of Melanesia, and other similar movements, indigenous peoples incorporated into their view of life images of apocalyptic struggle and hope for future redemption—and even an earthly paradise—ironically inspired by the scriptures and eschatological myths of the very culture that had dispossessed them of their way of life.

Indigenous peoples have a vivid sense that the visible, surface aspect of the world is not the only dimension in which they live. The spiritual realm, though invisible to normal perception, is experienced as being at least as real, and often more real, than the visible, physical dimension. Curiously, at the same time, there may be no strict dichotomy between the immaterial "spiritual" and the "physical." On occasion, spirit beings can be seen, spoken with, even touched. The spiritual is the depth dimension of the physical, but as such is not necessarily opposed to it.

While they are vividly aware of the existence of the spiritual world in the present, indigenous peoples often understand it as being, at the same time, a *past* paradise, a perfect time before, or outside, time when "we lived in close contact with the spirit world." It was—and somehow still is—a time of order and happiness, when human beings were perhaps deathless, parallel to the biblical Eden. This paradisal past/present realm is often called, after the practice of the indigenous people of Australia, the Dreamtime (*Alcheringa*). It is the domain of powerful spirits and the great ancestors. Especially important are the "culture heroes" who instituted the group's patterns of living, hunting, eating, love-making, fighting, resolving disputes, and so on, through paradigmatic acts in this time of beginnings. Since time (being cyclic) is not passing away in linear fashion, this sacred realm of the Beginnings is always available, even in the present. Its "pastness" signifies logical priority rather than remoteness in time. The line between the powerful time of origins and the present is thin, permeable. It is possible to reenter, re-actualize, and, to an extent, constantly relive that sacred dimension through ritual and vision.

A related feature of these traditions is an interest in altered states of consciousness. Through ritual, time can be collapsed back into its source. Rituals that induce

visions and trance states, especially, allow participants to see beyond the surface of things into the invisible realm of spirit. Spiritual visions, therefore, are sought and taken very seriously—as are dreams that are also regarded as bearing revelations from the sacred world. Psychotropic substances, such as peyote or datura, are sometimes used; more commonly, techniques of trance induction, spirit possession, and vision seeking are employed.

Indigenous cultures typically support individuals who specialize in altered states of consciousness, gifted visionaries who are recognized to a greater or lesser extent as the religious leaders of the community. Such persons, whether male or female, are termed shamans. A shaman is someone who is understood to be able to communicate readily with the spirit world and serve as a channel of sacred power for the benefit of others. Shamans are the custodians of the cultural, ritual, and spiritual lore of the tribe, but differ from priests in that they must have direct, experiential access to the spirit world. Women as well as men may be called to this kind of spiritual–cultural leadership. Among a shaman's expected roles, that of healer is typically prominent. The shamanic healing process almost always involves ritual trance. Other features, such as the removal of a foreign object, a journey through the spirit realm to recover the soul of the subject, or a struggle to exorcize evil spirits possessing the subject, may play a role. Often a cure is effected simply by identifying a particular spirit the subject has offended or a taboo the subject has broken, along with a prescription of measures to rectify the situation.

In larger, more complex indigenous cultures, religious leadership includes persons who may be termed priests. Unlike shamans, priests are not necessarily expected to have visionary or healing abilities. Rather, they are individuals who have gone through extensive training in the complex public rituals and religious dramas of the ceremonial calendar. In some cultures, elders belong to secret societies, typically separated by gender into men's and women's groups, sometimes organized into multiple levels of initiation.

Indigenous peoples are typically keenly aware of evil spirits and the possibility that human beings can use spiritual power for evil purposes. Sorcery and black magic are part of the assumed fabric of life, and people take measures to protect themselves against spells and the like through the use of amulets, talismans, and other protective devices. They also enlist the services of shamans who can exorcize or otherwise counteract malevolent influences. When things go inexplicably wrong, or when one is afflicted with illness with no obvious cause, a ready explanation may be found in the assumption that such calamities are the result of evil spirits or black magic. In such cases, the shaman may resort to divination, through trance or possession by a good spirit, to determine the source of the evil and the means of counteracting it. Of course, it may be discovered that the disturbance was not caused by an evil spirit at all, but rather by an ordinarily good spirit or ancestor whose rituals have been neglected. One should note that evil spirits in this context are relatively minor powers that have gone awry; there is no concept here of any cosmic power of primal evil, such as Satan, that stands in irrevocable opposition to the Supreme Being or human welfare.

In part because of the emphasis they place on the sacredness of geography and place, indigenous traditions see a religious value in nature. Often the distinction be-tween the sacred and nature is blurred or effaced altogether; everything in the world has a sacred dimension, and just about anything in nature can have religious significance. Nature is not divorced from the sacred. Holy power is present everywhere, informing everything.

Another distinction that gets blurred in these cultures is that between persons and things. The indigenous religious mind has a much wider concept of personhood than entertained in the West; all (or almost all) "things" may be experienced as "persons," spiritual beings endowed with intelligence and worthy of respect. Not only are animals and plants living, intelligent beings from whom humans may learn; even rocks and other "inanimate" objects may be so regarded.

This idea of expanded personhood leads us back to the concepts of spirit powers in indigenous traditions. We have already mentioned the holy beings that inhabit the sacred realms visited by shamans. Indigenous peoples are, in fact, aware of the world as being filled with spirit powers, supernatural beings variously termed spirits or gods, sometimes hard to distinguish from the spirits of ancestors. This outlook has by academics traditionally been called *animism* (from Latin *anima*, "soul"). The idea is that everything (or nearly everything) has, perhaps not exactly a soul, but some intelligent being or spirit associated with it. All things, having personhood, are alive. These spirit beings are, of course, not ordinarily visible. Still, they are very real and very much a part of life. They may manifest themselves and even speak to human beings through natural phenomena, such as wind, rain, and animals, with which they are often identified. Manifestations of spirit beings in animal form are of particular importance in hunting and gathering cultures. Some spirits are to be feared and have to be placated; others are benevolent.

Researchers have found that almost every known small-scale oral society acknowledges, in addition to a multitude of spirit powers, the existence of a single Supreme Being that is the creator of, and final power behind, the whole world. This deity may be visualized as male (for example, as Father or Grandfather), female (often Mother), or androgynous. The Supreme Being of indigenous peoples is most often what scholars refer to as a "High God" or "Hidden God" (*deus otiosus*), because he or she or it is typically aloof, not readily accessible. The High God is no longer active in the world, content, rather, to leave everyday affairs in the hands of subordinate spirit beings. Hence, the High God does not commonly play an important role in the ordinary religious life of the people, who are concerned with crops, rain, success in hunting, and so on. These practical aspects of life are the sphere of lesser, local spirits. The High God is not worshiped in usual ritual practice, only in extraordinary need, in crisis situations when "all else fails."

Concepts of the human self in indigenous religions vary widely and can get fairly complicated. The idea of some type of spiritual self or soul is almost universally recognized, but the soul may consist of multiple parts, or single individuals may be understood to have multiple souls. For example, indigenous African religions typically recognize three types of souls. There may be a vital soul, containing the energies of life and the physical body. This may pass away at death. A personal soul, embodying the will and personality of the individual, may survive after death in the world of the ancestors.

Finally, there may be a spiritual or transcendent soul that determines a person's destiny and returns to the Supreme Being after death. In some cultures, certain ancestors are understood to be incorporated into the self as souls. Alternately, various souls, or aspects of the self, may be located in different parts of the body. Furthermore, there is always the possibility of soul-loss (leading to sickness or death) or possession of the self by some external soul (of an ancestor, for example) or spirit, whether the possessing spirit be good or evil.

Concepts of the afterlife in indigenous religions are as varied as the cultures themselves. Some indigenous peoples have only vague ideas about the afterlife; others, more detailed conceptions. Generally speaking, one's spirit travels to an afterworld, the world of the ancestors, or the world of the spirit powers more generally conceived. In this realm, one becomes an ancestor/spirit power. This realm may be an underworld, in the sky or clouds, or in a remote location on earth—for example, on a mountain or island, in a canyon, or just an indefinite distance off in a particular direction. During the transitional state between death and the final rituals that convey the soul to the world of the ancestors, the spirit of the deceased may be regarded as dangerous to the living, but once it is properly installed in the other world, the danger passes. The afterlife is generally not an unhappy state, but it is not glorified as a blissful state of salvation from the pain and ambiguity of human existence. It is preferable to be alive rather than dead, even as a happy ancestral spirit. The religious goals of indigenous peoples have, in fact, a marked tendency to be "this-worldly" rather than otherworldly. The spirit powers, the ancestors, human beings, and the Supreme Being as well—all are understood to be working to maintain the harmony and vitality of this present world. The self attains fulfillment through living the good life in this world, not by escaping it. This is done by being happily embedded in, and supported by, a web of reciprocal interactions between self, family, society, spirit powers, ancestors, and the Supreme Deity, all working together for the health, preservation, and smooth functioning of the whole. Souls in the afterlife are not distant from their descendants, but take a continuing interest in their affairs. In some cultures, souls temporarily revisit the world of the living, in a ritual context, to bestow blessings. Not uncommon is the idea that individuals may reincarnate in their former families to participate in the ongoing process of life. In short, there is an unreservedly life-affirming emphasis on existence in this world as the focus of the religious life.

The idea of mutual interdependence between human beings and the spirit powers applies especially to the relationship between the living and the dead. Ancestor veneration is, in fact, a common feature of indigenous religion. Through ritual, the living nourish and sustain the dead, who in turn work in the spirit world to ensure the prosperity of the living. Some ancestors, such as the great culture-creating heroes and heroines of the past, benefit the entire society. Others, of less renown, work on behalf of their own living family. In either case, however, they must be honored, for they can be offended by neglect, and their anger can bring disaster: drought, famine, infertility, and sickness. Good relations with the ancestors, on the other hand, assures the well-being of the family and society, adequate rainfall, and abundance.

Another typical feature of these traditions is a religious concern for fertility and a perception of its connection with the sacred. Fertility has to do, of course, with an abundance of animals and/or crops, on one hand, and plentiful human offspring, on the other. Indigenous oral peoples, typically living on subsistence economies, close to and dependent upon nature, are concerned with survival, flourishing—and food. They have not, however, commonly been concerned with overpopulation. For them, therefore, fertility is the basis of abundance, prosperity, and the good life. Hunting and harvest rituals are often fertility rites, designed to assure an abundance of both children and food. The world itself may be seen as a product of the sacred interplay of male and female, heaven and earth. Sexuality is seen as part of the cosmic order, indeed, as representing the holy mystery of life. There is a world-affirming celebration and sacralization of the basic processes of existence.

Ceremonies great and small are the very fabric of life in indigenous oral cultures, ensuring that no aspect of existence is lived in isolation from the sacred. Ritual life, usually regulated by a liturgical calendar attuned to rhythms of hunting and planting, aims at fostering positive relationships between human beings and the spirit world. Combining song, dance, music, masks, and costumes, ritual provides opportunities for storytellers to recount the foundational myths of the culture. A skilled storyteller, recounting the sacred stories of the tribe in a public, ritual context, is able to make the sacred and the sacred powers present and alive through the power of language and symbol. Ritual in indigenous societies typically involves sacrifice as an offering to the spirit or ancestral powers. This may involve self-sacrifice, as in the Native American sun dance, animal sacrifice, or—in some cultures in the past—human sacrifice. Sacrifice is a demonstration of one's earnestness in approaching the spirit world, and there is a sense that new life and vitality arises from sacrificial death and the ritual spilling of blood.

Perhaps the most significant type of ritual identified by scholars of religion, one found commonly in the great historical religions as well as in indigenous communities, is the rite of passage. Rites of passage are rituals to mark the important transitions in the life of individuals, for example birth, adulthood ("coming of age"), religious membership, marriage, death, also any significant change in social status. Often, they are equivalent to initiation rites. For example, the vision quest of the indigenous peoples of the North American Great Plains involves going apart from the tribe—typically to a mountain top—for a period of solitary prayer and fasting, to seek direct contact with, and guidance from, the spirit world. It follows the typical initiatory pattern of separation, a transformative ordeal, and then a return to the community with new power and status. The vision gives the individual a sense of purpose or vocation and the spiritual power to accomplish that purpose. One who has had a vision seeks subsequently to live his or her life in relation to what was revealed in the vision. While often functioning as an initiation into adulthood, the vision quest may be repeated later on in life, especially in times of crisis.

Another typical ritual of indigenous peoples is the ritual of cosmic renewal. Concern for fertility in this context extends to a concern for rejuvenating the energies of the cosmos and nature. Indigenous peoples typically feel that human beings have a responsibility to cooperate with the forces of nature and the spirit world for the maintenance of cosmic well-being. Fertility rites may thus become rites of world renewal, periodically working to reactivate and revitalize the creative energies of nature. An example of such a rite, again from the Native Americans of the Great Plains, is the sun dance, a yearly gathering of the clans for a ritual renewal of all life. Those who are called by a vision to participate are tethered to the sacred center pole of the medicine lodge by thongs attached to skewers piercing the muscles of their chests. They dance until the flesh rips open and they are freed. Through their suffering, they confirm and reactivate the law of sacrifice that is the fundamental dynamic of life and its renewal. Associated with the sun dance are symbols of fertility, especially connected to the buffalo, the primary source of food for these peoples.

Other important rituals are connected with hunting and the planting and harvesting of crops. Hunting is regarded as an act of interplay with spiritual forces. Life demands sacrifice, in this case, animals offering themselves in sacrifice for their human brothers and sisters. Hunting, killing, utilizing the animal, disposal of its remains—all are ritual acts. The hunters must seek the consent of animals and atone for any wrong done to them. They must respectfully use—or ritually dispose of—every part of the animals killed. Sometimes the hunter aims for a kind of mystical union with the guardian spirit of the animals he hunts. Such a being is referred to as the "master of the animals," for example, Caribou Man. Or the hunter in his quest may mystically identify himself with the archetypal First Hunter, a culture hero of the Dreamtime. Often there are rituals for the recirculation or "recycling" of animal souls: those that are honored with proper ceremony return to offer themselves again.

Lance E. Nelson

See also DIVINATION; FETISH; MANA; MIL-LENARIANISM; OMEN; REVELATION (IN OTHER RELIGIONS); SACRIFICE; SHAMAN; TABOO OR TABU; TOTEM/TOTEMISM.

INDISSOLUBILITY

Indissolubility is the doctrine of the Roman Catholic Church stating that a sacramental marriage (one between two baptized persons) that is consummated is a permanent union for life and excludes divorce and remarriage. Separation or civil divorce without remarriage is permitted for a serious reason. The biblical roots of the doctrine are found in Matthew 5:31-32; 19:3-12; Mark 10:2-12; Luke 16:18; and 1 Corinthians 7:10-11. However, the Matthean texts admit of an exception in the case of *porneia*, variously translated as lewd conduct, prostitution, incest (see 1 Cor 5:1 and possibly Acts 15:20, 29) and adultery. Until recent biblical scholarship, the exception of *porneia* in Matthew's accounts was consistently identified with adultery. Since the second century, the West interpreted the texts as a reason to allow separation in the case of adultery, but not remarriage. In the East they were viewed as the basis for the toleration of a second marriage in the case of adultery, after penance was undertaken. The Protestant Reformers invoked the texts to support an even more liberal approach to subsequent marriages in the case of adultery (and eventually for other serious reasons). Today most biblical scholars identify *porneia* with lewd conduct, such as an incestuous marriage, or marriage to a prostitute, both not uncommon in the ancient Hellenistic world. Thus Matthew's texts would require that, in these cases,

the Christian (probably a convert) would have to leave such a marriage because it is unchristian and sinful at its root (in today's vocabulary, "invalid"). Matthew's so-called exception is, then, a support for indissolubility. Thus the New Testament represents a radical departure from the contemporary Jewish practice that allowed easy divorce as a right only of the husband in the case of adultery or, according to another school of thought, for any significant reason. The New Testament texts call both husband and wife to an equal commitment to the permanency of Christian marriage. Whether these texts are to be interpreted as absolute, or as an important ideal, is the difference between the Roman Catholic position and those of Orthodoxy and Protestantism. However, it must be said that when the Council of Trent defined indissolubility, requiring it even in the case of adultery, it did so in a way that did not condemn the Orthodox position. In 1980 the Synod of Bishops proposed to the pope that the Orthodox practice be considered carefully for what it could offer Roman Catholic pastoral care for divorced and remarried Catholics.

Dennis W. Krouse

See also ANNULMENT; CANONICAL FORM (OF MARRIAGE); DIVORCE (IN CHRISTIANITY); MARRIAGE IN CATHOLIC PERSPECTIVE; PAULINE PRIVILEGE; PETRINE PRIVILEGE.

INDRA

One of the most important deities in the *Rig Veda*, Indra is associated with the sky, thunder, and the rain. He is the leader of the gods in war, and is invoked to help worshipers conquer their enemies. In later, post-Vedic Hinduism, his importance is diminished. Although he remains as the king of the *devas* (gods), he is far less important than the great Gods Vishnu and Shiva, and the Goddess (Shakti, Devi). Although Buddhism denies the existence of a supreme creator God, Indra appears in the literature of Indian Buddhism as the king of the lesser gods, who are just as much in need of the Buddha's teachings as human beings.

Lance E. Nelson

See also BUDDHISM; DEVA/DEVI; HINDUISM; SHAKTI; SHIVA; VEDAS; VISHNU.

INDULGENCE

An indulgence is the forgiveness of temporal punishment due to sin. Since this canonical definition is often misunderstood, it would be best first to describe what indulgences are not. Indulgences do not forgive sin and they cannot remove or alleviate the eternal punishment of damnation. The concept of indulgences depends on several interconnected beliefs. First, one must assume that each sin carries with it a form of penance, or temporal punishment. This approach to penance seems to have developed first among the Celtic monks of the early Middle Ages. Each sin was assigned a penance that needed to be performed by the penitent or by the penitent's delegate after the forgiveness of sins. A further related belief was that this penance would need to be fulfilled in the afterlife if it were not completed before death. The place of this cleansing was purgatory. The final step in the development of indulgences was the notion of a "treasury of merits," that is, an overflowing abundance of penance already completed by Jesus, Mary, and the saints, that the church could substitute for penance due in purgatory.

The first widespread use of indulgences was during the Crusades when those who died in battle were granted a full remission of all temporal punishment due to their sins. Soon indulgences of all kinds were granted for pilgrimages, prayers, good works, and almsgiving. The presumption was always that the sins for which the punishment was remitted had already been forgiven and repentance had taken place. By the late Middle Ages, however, abuses had crept in, and some indulgence salesmen (called in English, "pardoners") were suggesting to their audiences that cash donations could free one's soul from purgatory even before sins were committed, much less forgiven. Far more powerful was the appeal of the pardoners to relatives of the deceased to "buy" indulgences to free their loved ones from the pains of purgatory. It was against this kind of abuse that Martin Luther directed his Ninety-Five Theses in 1517. The Council of Trent (1545–63) upheld the use of indulgences, but forbade many of their abuses and abolished the office of pardoner. Pope Paul VI in his constitution *Indulgentiarum doctrina* greatly reduced the number of plenary indulgences and urged the faithful to understand indulgences as part of the entire penitential process through which the faithful can develop a greater desire for charity and for a total renunciation of sin.

Gary Macy

See also LUTHER, MARTIN; PAUL VI, POPE; PURGATORY; RECONCILIATION, SACRAMENT OF; SIN, PERSONAL; TRENT, COUNCIL OF.

INDULT

In Roman Catholicism, special permission for a permanent exemption from some provision of church law. As opposed to a *dispensation*, an indult applies to a particular *type* of situation, not to a single case. The word is most properly used of exemptions from general canon law, granted by the Holy See (the pope or one of his administrative offices). One of the most discussed indults in recent times has been that granted to bishops to allow the celebration of Mass according to the old Tridentine (Latin) Rite that was officially replaced by the revised rite in 1970 after the Second Vatican Council.

William A. Clark, s.j.

INERRANCY

Inerrant means freedom from error. It is a characteristic attributed to the Bible that flows from the belief that biblical texts originated under the inspiration of God. Thus the texts are by nature the self-revelation of God. While conservative evangelical and fundamentalist Christians are committed to the premise that every aspect of the Bible is without error, Catholics and most mainline Protestants nuance their understanding of inerrancy.

The Second Vatican Council states, "the books of Scripture firmly, faithfully and without error teach that truth which God for the sake of our salvation, wished to see confided to the sacred Scriptures" (*Dei Verbum* 11). Thus, while affirming that the books of the Bible are reliable guides to salvation, the council implicitly recognized that biblical texts introduce premises and events that are no longer plausible in light of contemporary scientific and historical knowledge. While the council's statement would be considered inadequate by Christians who insist that John 10:36, "The scripture cannot be broken," establishes the biblical authority of inerrant texts, radical interpreters consider inspiration and inerrancy impossible for intelligent people today.

Since Christian tradition also affirms that God's revelation is disclosed in creation, history, persons, society, and reason, it is the task of the believing community in every age to discern the core truths within the biblical texts that pertain to God's salvific fidelity and have the capacity to lead people into a union with God. Such an interpretive process recognizes that some of the social premises assumed or advocated by the inspired authors are presuppositions that were common to their times. They are not a divine plan for all people of all times. Issues that are called into question reflect the progress of knowledge and social reflection of each era. For example, despite the early nineteenth-century appeal by some made to the Bible to reject slavery, others found passages to claim divine approval of slavery as a social institution. While no one appeals to the Bible to advocate slavery today, it is somewhat astonishing that some use the very same passages to assert that the subordination of wives to their husbands is a social construct designed by God.

While it is essential for believers to recognize that "all Scripture is inspired by God, and profitable for teaching, for reproof, for correction" (2 Tim 3:16-17), it is also essential to acknowledge with Paul, "at present we see indistinctly as in a mirror . . . at present I know partially" (1 Cor 13:12).

Regina A. Boisclair

See also CANON; INSPIRATION; REVELATION.

INFALLIBILITY

The doctrine of the infallibility of the Catholic Church's magisterium, or official teaching authority, asserts that the pope alone, or an ecumenical council (the pope and bishops gathered together in general council), or the college of bishops dispersed throughout the world are, under certain conditions, protected by the Holy Spirit from teaching erroneous doctrine in matters of faith and morals. Infallibility is not considered one of the classical notes (essential attributes) of the church (one, holy, catholic, and apostolic) and is rooted in God's fidelity to the church, not a presumed perfection inherent in the church. The doctrine of papal infallibility was proclaimed explicitly at Vatican I; at Vatican II the bishops stated that "the whole body of the faithful who have an anointing that comes from the holy one cannot err in matters of belief" (LG 12). In other words, the infallibility of the pope and the bishops is rooted in their relationship to the whole church and does not belong to them apart from that relationship. Vatican II also highlighted the relationship of collegiality that ought to exist between the pope (Bishop of Rome) and the other members of the worldwide college of bishops who are joined together "in a bond of unity, charity, and peace" (LG 22).

The doctrine of infallibility is widely misunderstood both inside and outside the Catholic Church, usually because it is understood too broadly and applied to all Catholic teaching equally. However, as Vatican II made clear, "there exists an order or 'hierarchy' of truths [which] vary in their relation to the foundation of the Christian faith" (UR 11). This means that while Catholics must respect all church teaching, only "definitive" or "irreversible" dogmas concerning faith and morals require "allegiance of mind" and "submission of will" (LG 25). Thus not all teachings are seen as infallible.

Various conditions must all be met before a teaching may be considered infallible: (1) the teaching must be addressed to the whole church; (2) the pope, when acting alone, must speak *ex cathedra*, that is, as universal pastor of the church; (3) the teaching must concern matters of faith and morals, that is, eternal salvation and nothing more; (4) the teaching must be clearly recognizable as infallible (for example, it might be preceded by phrases such as "we teach and define as divinely revealed dogma"); and (5) the teaching cannot be new but must belong to the apostolic tradition. While individual bishops do not teach infallibly, they do so as a body when joined in communion with the pope, when teaching about faith and morals, and when they are "in agreement that a particular teaching is to be held definitively and absolutely" (LG 25). Catholic theologians do not agree on the precise number of dogmas infallibly proclaimed by a pope speaking *ex cathedra*, but there is agreement that the solemn definitions of the Immaculate Conception (1854) and the Assumption of Mary (1950) fall into this category. No recent popes have defined a dogma infallibly despite the authoritative character they have claimed for their teachings.

While some scholars find little direct support in Scripture for the doctrine of infallibility as this is understood in the Catholic Church today, the doctrine may be grounded in Jesus' promises to be with the disciples to the end of time (Matt 20:28) and to send them the Holy Spirit as guide to the complete truth (John 16:13). Historically, the doctrine of infallibility emerged over time with the gradual recognition by other local churches of the importance and, then, the orthodoxy of the faith of the church of Rome, traditionally believed to have been founded by the apostle Peter. Nevertheless, overly broad understandings of infallibility and unacceptable exercises of papal and episcopal authority have been challenged constantly in the history of the church, by Catholics themselves and especially by Eastern Christians and the Protestant Reformation.

The doctrine of infallibility should be distinguished from the notions of inerrancy, indefectibility, and impeccability. *Inerrancy* refers to the church's understanding of the trustworthiness of the Bible as mediating the Word of God. As the bishops said at the Second Vatican Council, "[t]he books of Scripture firmly, faithfully, and without error teach that truth which God, for the sake of our salvation, wished to see confided to the sacred Scriptures" (DV 11). *Indefectibility* refers to the belief that the Holy Spirit will remain with the church throughout its historical journey; the presence of the Holy Spirit will protect the church as a whole from straying from the truth of the Gospel. *Impeccability* refers to the belief that Jesus not only did not sin but was incapable of sinning.

James B. Nickoloff

See also ECCLESIOLOGY; INERRANCY; SENSUS FIDELIUM/SENSUS FIDEI; SYNODS.

INFANCY NARRATIVES

These are sections of the Gospels in the New Testament about the events surrounding the birth of Jesus. Infancy narratives are found only in Matthew and Luke, constituting the first two chapters of each work. In light of the dependence of those Gospels on Mark, which had no traditions concerning Jesus' earliest years, both Matthew and Luke clearly felt a need to include such material in their redactions of Mark. Probably they wanted to prevent the interpretation, theoretically possible

for the beginning of the Gospel of Mark, that Jesus' identity as Savior and as God's Son is derived from his baptism seen as an adoption.

A comparison of the infancy narratives reflects both significant agreements as well as differences. While this suggests that Matthew and Luke probably did not get their material from an identical source, either oral or written, it remains very difficult for scholars to assess both evangelists' pre-Gospel sources as well as their own free composition.

The dissemination of these canonical infancy narratives of Matthew and Luke contributed to the emergence of various later infancy Gospels such as the Infancy Gospel of Thomas (not to be confused with the Gospel of Thomas). The desire for answers to questions about the early life of Jesus not supplied by the Matthean and Lukan infancy narratives formed the impetus to create and transmit the additional stories about Jesus found in such documents.

F. M. Gillman

See also SYNOPTIC GOSPELS; SYNOPTIC PROBLEM.

INFANT BAPTISM

Infant baptism is the practice of baptizing infants or children before they reach the age of consent or reason. There is some dispute over how early Christians began to baptize infants, but the custom existed at least from the second century and maybe even earlier. Infant baptism continued to be practiced in both Eastern and Western Christianity, although customs in the two areas differed. In the West, the final anointing was separated from the ritual ablution and performed by the bishop when the infant reached adolescence. This ceremony became the sacrament of confirmation. Communion, too, was withheld until the child reached the age of reason. In the East, all three ceremonies continued to be enacted as part of infant baptism. In the West, the custom of infant baptism became particularly urgent since, following the teaching of Augustine, it was believed that infants inherited original sin from their parents and therefore could not be saved without baptism, even if they had committed no sins of their own. The Council of Florence in 1442 urged parents to have their children baptized as soon as possible.

The great controversy over infant baptism began in the early sixteenth century when different groups whom their opponents dubbed "Anabaptists" rejected infant baptism on the grounds that it was not found in Scripture and that accepting Jesus must be a conscious choice. Starting in Zurich in 1525, Anabaptists began the practice of rebaptizing those who had been baptized as infants. Anabaptist groups such as the Hutterites and the Mennonites continue this practice. The largest group of Christians who insist on adult baptism, however, are the Baptists. In the sixteenth century, under the influence of the Mennonites, John Smyth organized the first Baptist communities. For Baptists, the ceremony is an outward sign of being chosen by Christ as a member of the community of the saved. The emphasis is on the action of God, rather than any action on the part of the adult, since Baptists generally hold to the Calvinistic principle of predestination.

Infant baptism continued to be practiced by most other Christian groups; however, in recent times, more emphasis has been placed on infant baptism as a sign of faith and acceptance by the community of the faithful through which the infant gradually will grow into a recogni-tion and acceptance of the commitment made at baptism.

Gary Macy

See also ANABAPTISTS; AUGUSTINE OF HIPPO; BAPTISM/CONFIRMATION; BAPTIST THEOLOGY; MENNONITES.

INFIDELS

In general, a term used for unbelievers—from the Latin *infidelis* ("not faithful"). In particular, it has been used by Christians to describe non-Christians or enemies of Christianity including Muslims. The term is also used by Muslims (*al-Kufr* in Arabic) for those who do not believe in the one God. This would include atheists and polytheists, but not Christians. According to Islamic belief, Christians, as well as Jews are believers ("People of the Book"). Hence they cannot be called infidels, though today some Muslim extremists apply the term infidel to all non-Muslims, especially those living in the Western world. In recent years, Christian thought has avoided the use of this term, especially in reference to Muslims and Jews.

Ronald A. Pachence

See also ALLAH (ISLAM); ISLAM; KAFIR; PEOPLE OF THE BOOK; SHIRK.

INFINITE

Not finite; without boundary or limit. Two distinct notions of infinite can be traced in the Hellenistic and medieval traditions. On the one hand, in the pre-Socratic notion of the *apeiron* and the Aristotelian-Thomist analysis of "prime matter," the infinite is conceived negatively, that is, as utterly without form or as the pure potentiality for act (form). On the other hand, in Plato's *Timaeus*, where the forms and demiurge have an infinity of completeness and perfection, and in

Thomas's identification of "God" with the "act of being itself," the notion of a positive infinity emerges, that is, all positive predicates belong to the act of being itself. With Descartes, continuing through the work of the so-called transcendental Thomists and Wolfhart Pannenberg, a further theme regarding the infinite has emerged within the broader context of a philosophical "turn to the subject": the intuition or preconception of positive infinity is a condition of the possibility of knowledge of the finite world and the foundation for religious belief.

J. A. Colombo

INFRALAPSARIANISM

A frequent Calvinist teaching on predestination (since 1618) that holds that God decreed ("elected") who is and who is not to be saved only after Adam's fall. This doctrine is also known as "sublapsarianism" and as "postlapsarianism." It contrasts with "supralapsarianism," the rigid (and also Calvinist) view that predestination or election for salvation occurred even before the first human sin.

Orlando Espín

See also CALVIN, JOHN; CALVINISM; ELECTION (DOCTRINE OF); GRACE; JUSTIFICATION; ORIGINAL JUSTICE; PREDESTINATION (CALVANIST); SIN, ORIGINAL.

INITIATION (NON-CHRISTIAN)

A ceremonial transition from one social status to another or induction into an age sect, secret society, religious office, or community. It is a rite of passage that may involve rituals, tests, ordeals, seclusion, and other features to mark the transition from one state to another. Initiations can be associated with the life cycle; for example,

they may represent the move from adolescence to adulthood. Nearly all cultures have a form of rite of passage to demarcate different stages of life or movement to a different social status or identity. Initiations also serve to signify membership in particular groups, such as religious orders, or attainment of status as a religious practitioner such as a shaman. Vision quests among certain Native American groups, for example, may offer both a transition to adult status as well as acquisition of a guardian spirit and the ability to heal. Initiation rites help individuals through crucial life crises—birth, puberty, marriage, parenthood, death, or change of class or occupational status. Examples of initiation rituals are found in South America, Australia, Melanesia, and New Guinea, and are linked with life cycle and age status transitions.

Arnold van Gennep, a Belgian anthropologist, wrote a classic study of different rites of passage throughout the world. He found similarities in life transition rituals such as births, initiations, confirmations, weddings, and funerals. As a result, he identified three characteristic stages that all such rituals possess: separation, margin or limin, and aggregation or incorporation. The first phase, separation, removes initiates from society. They leave behind the symbols, roles, and norms associated with their former position. In the second phase, marginality or liminality, people are in a state of transition or temporary period of ambiguity while they are between statuses. During this phase, while they are separate from the larger society or their former activities, they undergo traditional ordeals, indoctrination, or instruction. In the final ritual phase, aggregation, individuals return to the group with a new status and new duties and obligations. They are treated differently by other members of the group as a result of their transformation.

To illustrate his model, van Gennep described the male initiation rituals of Australian Aborigines. The elders decide when young boys are ready to be initiated. They remove the boys from their families while the women cry and try to resist. At a site distant from camp, groups of male representatives of many groups gather. While the elders sing and dance, the boys are considered symbolically dead to ordinary life. During their seclusion, they undergo a bodily operation—either circumcision or the knocking out of a tooth. They are shown secret ceremonies and instructed about tribal lore. Victor Turner, in work on the rites of passage of the Ndembu of Africa, elaborated on the theory of liminality and argued that the sharing of the building blocks of culture, the *sacra*, is so powerful because of the shared feeling of unity (*communitas*) between the neophytes. The lessons the boys are taught take on such meaning because of the connection between the tests and ordeals to underlying sacred truths. Often the lessons are linked to the morals and values shared by the society. The virtues that are conveyed reflect the standards and values associated with the particular culture. The ordeals associated with the liminal phase assure that the initiates remember everything; the seriousness of the subject matter and one's retention of it is underscored by the drama and deprivation associated with the liminal phase. This is particularly important in nonliterate cultures that depend on oral traditions for maintaining mythology, religious knowledge, and ritual practices. At the last phase, the incorporation, the aboriginal boys are treated as if they are returning from the dead. In some societies, this phase is

associated with birth symbolism or with the mothers acting as if they no longer recognize their own sons and grieving for the loss of their boys. The newly made men have new rights and responsibilities. The boys are prepared for adulthood and manhood.

In contrast to Australian aboriginal preparation for manhood, Mende girls of West Africa were prepared for womanhood. After their first menstruation, they are removed from society to spend weeks or months in seclusion. At the first ritual stage, their girlhood clothing is removed. The initiates dress in beads and skirts, and smear their bodies with white clay. During the liminal phase, they undergo surgery to remove the clitoris and part of the labia minor; this is believed to enhance their procreative potential. Once the surgery is done, they know they are women. When they return to their homes, they have been trained in the moral and practical responsibilities of potential childbearers. During the initiation rite, they also receive training in singing, dancing, and storytelling. At the final phase, incorporation, they make a medicine to wash off the magical protections of the liminal phase. When they emerge from their seclusion, they are women, not girls, and are knowledgeable about sexuality and eligible to marry and rear children. The pain and danger associated with the circumcision is symbolically linked to that of childbirth. The pain is endured in the company of women and with their strong social support. The ritual reinforces the bonding between the women and initiates girls into the Sande Association, an organization of women.

Initiation rites transform the individual from one status to another and provide membership in a new group of adults, or believers, or married people, or other status. The initiations often include tests for worthiness and important knowledge and instructions regarding new responsibilities, secrets, and tribal lore. Initiates may be given marks, insignia, or other symbolic indications of their completion of the rite. At the completion, they behave differently and are given new social roles.

Christine Greenway

See also INDIGENOUS RELIGIOUS TRADITIONS; LIMINAL/ LIMINALITY; RITUAL.

INITIATION (RITES OF CHRISTIAN)

See RITES OF CHRISTIAN INITIATION (RCIA).

INNOCENT I, POPE

Innocent was pope from 402 until 417. Coming from a papal family himself, Innocent did not hesitate to assert patriarchal authority in several important causes. He insisted on disciplinary conformity on the part of the bishops of Gaul (France), rallied the North African bishops against Pelagianism, and sided with John Chrysostom against the patriarchs of Alexandria and Antioch. Based on the thirty-six letters of Innocent that survive, scholars consider him one of the important early advocates of papal authority.

Gary Macy

See also JOHN CHRYSOSTOM; PATRIARCH; PELAGIANISM; POPE.

INNOCENT III, POPE (1160/1–1216)

The son of Trasimund, the count of Segni, Lothario dei Segni received his theological training in Paris and his legal training at Bologna. He was appointed cardinal by Pope Clement III in 1189/90. Lothario published two very popular works while cardinal, one a commentary on the liturgy, and the second a treatise on contempt for the world. Lothario was chosen pope at the age of thirty-seven in 1198, taking the name Innocent III. A brilliant, zealous, and energetic pope, Innocent brought the medieval papacy to the height of its power. According to Innocent, the pope was "placed between God and man, lower than God but higher than man, the judge of all men who can be judged by none." Innocent almost immediately reorganized the papal government and the Papal States. Frequently embroiled in secular affairs, he excommunicated both King John of England and King Philip II of France. Innocent wished to win back the Holy Land through crusade, but in this he was not successful, as both the Fourth and Fifth Crusades failed to attain their purpose. Innocent also moved decisively against the Cathars and other heretical groups. At first, peaceful conversion was attempted, a method successful with some groups, although not with the Cathars. When a papal legate was murdered by the Cathars, Innocent supported a crusade against them, the notorious Albigensian Crusade. Later, at the Fourth Lateran Council, Innocent established laws for suppressing heresy that were the basis for later inquisitions. Innnocent approved the communities of both Francis of Assisi and Dominic de Guzmán, the founders respectively of the Franciscans and the Dominicans, thus encouraging a revival of preaching and teaching. Innocent's crowning achievement, however, was the Fourth Lateran Council held in 1215. The council reformed much of Christian life, establishing, for instance, the practice of yearly confession and Communion for all Western Christians. Innocent died unexpectedly at the young age of fifty-seven, but not without leaving a legacy that would affect Western Christianity down to the present day.

Gary Macy

See also CATHARS; CRUSADES; DOMINIC DE GUZMÁN; EXCOMMUNICATION; FRANCIS OF ASSISI; HERESY; INQUISITION; LATERAN (COUNCILS OF THE); MEDIEVAL CHRISTIANITY (IN THE WEST); PAPACY/PAPAL; VICAR OF CHRIST.

INQUISITION

In its original meaning, an *inquisitio* in Latin means an "inquest" or "investigation." In this sense, an "inquisition" means any investigation into a crime. In modern parlance, however, the phrase always refers to an inquest into heresy. Contrary to popular opinion, there was no centralized Inquisition in the Middle Ages, but rather many inquisitions into heresy in different periods at different times. England, for instance, never had an inquisition. The inquisition was particularly used against the Cathars and the Waldensians, although other heretical groups were also targeted. In 1215 Pope Innocent III repeated earlier appeals for the secular authorities to aid in the eradication of heresy, but it was Pope Gregory IX who in 1231 established procedures for independent judges to concentrate specifically on interrogating suspects of heresy. In 1252 Pope Innocent IV allowed for the use of torture to extract information from suspects. Wandering tribunals, usually headed by Dominicans or Franciscans, were most active from the mid-thirteenth century through the end of the fourteenth century when the inquisitions virtually cease. The punishments of the inquisition ranged from fines and penances to life imprisonment. The inquisition itself did not impose capital punishment, but since heresy was a capital crime in many states, the turning over of a convicted heretic to the secular authorities was a certain death sentence, usually by burning.

The Spanish Inquisition was a completely separate, secular court established by Ferdinand and Isabella of Spain in 1481, although with the approval of the pope. The Spanish Inquisition particularly targeted converted Jews (in Spanish, *Marranos*) and Muslims (in Spanish, *Moriscos*) who were suspected of retaining their former beliefs and practices. The Spanish Inquisition was suspended in 1808 and abolished in 1843.

The Roman Congregation of the Inquisition was established by Pope Paul III in 1542 to combat the Protestant Reformation. One of its duties was to maintain the Index of Forbidden Books, a list of books that Roman Catholics could read only with special permission. The Congregation of the Inquisition was renamed by Pope Paul VI in 1965 the Congregation for the Doctrine of the Faith, and the Index of Forbidden Books was withdrawn in 1966.

Although the persistent, popular image of the inquisition as a cruel and bloodthirsty institution has been shown to be false by modern historical studies, still the methods and punishments of the inquisition remain a disgrace to the history of Christianity.

Gary Macy

See also CATHARS; DOMINICANS; FRANCISCANS; INNOCENT III, POPE; MEDIEVAL CHRISTIANITY (IN THE WEST); PAPACY/PAPAL; PAUL VI, POPE; REFORMATION; TORQUEMADA, TOMÁS; WALDENSIANS.

INSPIRATION

Inspiration refers to the influence of spirit on someone or something. In the Bible, it first appears as a way of characterizing certain forms of discourse and behaviors, particularly those pronounced and/or performed by prophets. For example, in Numbers 24:2 the spirit of God comes upon Balaam, who is then able to pronounce the oracle that follows in 24:3-9. In 1 Samuel 10:6 the prophet Samuel explains the effects of the spirit's influence to Saul: "the spirit of the LORD will possess you and you will be in a prophetic frenzy . . . and be turned into a different person." Spirit lifts the prophet Ezekiel up (Ezek 2:2; 3:12, 14, 24), bringing him to the Temple in Jerusalem (8:11; 11:1), back to Babylon (11:24); to the valley full of dry bones (37:1) into which spirit enters so that they come to life; and finally to the restored Temple (43:5).

In the New Testament, Acts 2 cites Joel 2:28-32 to indicate that the Pentecost event, in which a diverse crowd hears the apostolic speech "in other languages, as the Spirit gave them ability" (2:4), represented the eschatological gift of the spirit of God: "In the last days it will be, God declares, that I will pour out my Spirit upon all flesh, and your sons and daughters shall prophesy" (Acts 2:17). Early Christians shared with contemporary Jewish tradition the understanding that the Scriptures spoke with divine authority, to the extent that "it is written" in Acts 13:33 (introducing a citation of Ps 2:7) is synonymous with "he [God] has spoken" in Acts 13:34 (introducing a citation of Isa 55:3) and "he [God] has also said" in Acts 13:35 (introducing a citation of Ps 16:10).

It is especially on the basis of texts from two New Testament documents, 2 Timothy and 2 Peter, that Christians have come to understand the Bible as inspired, that is, composed under the influence of the spirit of God. According to 2 Peter 1:20-21, "First of all, you must understand this, that no prophecy of scripture is a matter of one's own interpretation, because no prophecy ever came by human will, but men and women moved by the Holy Spirit spoke from God." By "scripture" (*graphē*), the author of 2 Peter may be referring to the prophetic books of the Hebrew Bible, or perhaps even to New Testament prophecies. The emphasis of the affirmation is not on the writings as such, but on the solidly grounded character of prophecy as a matter of divine inspiration and not of human initiative.

In 2 Timothy, framed as instruction by the senior Paul to a disciple entrusted with pastoral care of a first century Christian community, we read that "All scripture is inspired by God and is useful for teaching, for reproof, for correction, and for training in righteousness, so that everyone who belongs to God may be proficient, equipped for every good work" (2 Tim 3:16-17). "All scripture" (*pasa graphē*) is an ambiguous phrase, but reference in the preceding verse to "the sacred writings" (*ta hiera grammata*) that Timothy is said to have known from his youth (2 Tim 3:15) makes it likely that the expression refers to the Hebrew Scriptures. As for "inspired by God," this phrase renders the Greek term *theopneustos*, a rare expression found only here in the New Testament. It literally means "God-breathed," or "God-inspired," which accounts for its usual translation. Thus the Pauline author of 2 Timothy here asserts that the value of the Scriptures for teaching and so forth is based on their divine inspiration.

Over the centuries it has been far easier for Christians to affirm *that* the Bible is inspired by God than it has been to seek to explain *how* the Bible is inspired and exactly what biblical inspiration involves. Sandra Schneiders (*The Revelatory Text,*

46) succinctly details the complexity of the theological issues involving biblical inspiration, matters that include: the meaning and nature of inspiration; its location (in the author, the text, the reader, and/or reading); its extent (whether all Scripture or only certain parts are inspired and whether there are degrees of inspiration); its effects (whether inspiration makes the Bible revelatory, invests it with divine authority, renders it inerrant); its uniqueness (whether biblical inspiration differs essentially from the inspiration of other religious or artistic classics); and the mode of its occurrence (prophetic ecstasy, dictation, illumination, social or historical processes within the community).

Efforts to understand biblical inspiration have sought to find an appropriate balance between the elements of divine influence and human responsibility, of the simultaneous divine and human authorship of the Scriptures. In the patristic period, the discussion focused mainly on whether inspiration should be understood according to the prophetic model, where God influenced the writers of the biblical texts (Augustine's position), or whether inspiration described the divinely influenced text itself (Origen's position). In the Middle Ages, Thomas Aquinas used Aristotelian philosophical language to explain that God was the true author of Scripture as its primary, efficient cause, while human writers were responsible according to secondary, instrumental causality. A number of Reformation and Counter-Reformation thinkers espoused the notion of plenary verbal inspiration, an understanding that continues to be held by many people to this day, especially more conservative Christians. According to this view, each word of Sacred Scripture, down to the last letter, is divinely inspired. Plenary verbal inspiration works on the understanding that because all of Scripture is the word of God, and because God is entirely truthful, therefore every word of the Scriptures must be true. This notion of biblical inerrancy received particular emphasis with the rise of historical criticism in the nineteenth century, since many Protestants and Catholics saw the historical-critical approach to the Bible as a serious threat to an integral notion of biblical inspiration. Other models of biblical inspiration, besides strict or plenary verbal inspiration, include limited verbal inspiration (which restricts the inerrancy of Scripture to its religious teaching, not to scientific or historical data), nontextual inspiration (of ideas and/or individuals), and social inspiration (according to which the believing community is understood to be the recipient of inspiration).

The current Roman Catholic magisterial understanding of inspiration is described in the Dogmatic Constitution on Divine Revelation (*Dei Verbum*) of the Second Vatican Council, promulgated in 1965:

> The divinely revealed realities, which are contained and presented in the text of sacred Scripture, have been written down under the inspiration of the Holy Spirit. For Holy Mother Church relying on the faith of the apostolic age, accepts as sacred and canonical the books of the Old and New Testaments, whole and entire, with all their parts, on the grounds that, written under the inspiration of the Holy Spirit, they have God as their author, and have been handed on as such to the Church herself (*Dei Verbum* 11).

Underlining the important place of the inspired Scriptures in the church, the council also addressed the notion of biblical inerrancy that can be understood as a consequence of the divine inspiration of the Scriptures: "Since, therefore, all that the inspired authors, or sacred writers, affirm should be regarded as affirmed by the Holy Spirit, we must acknowledge that the books of Scripture, firmly, faithfully and without error, teach that truth which God, for the sake of our salvation, wished to see confided to the sacred Scriptures" (*Dei Verbum* 11). By not specifying precisely what "that truth which God, for the sake of our salvation, wished to see confided to the sacred Scriptures" might or might not be, the council sought to maintain a careful balance between the divine and human authorship of the Bible, while also remaining silent as to *how* the process of inspiration operates.

In *The Revelatory Text*, Sandra M. Schneiders presents a theological understanding of biblical inspiration as an affirmation of faith, maintaining of Scripture that "To affirm that this book is divinely inspired is to profess to have experienced it as uniquely disclosive of the divine" (50). Recognizing the close relationship between revelation and inspiration, she points out that inspiration is

> the subject of a faith affirmation about the revelatory character of sacred scripture. Inspiration is not strictly identical with revelation, because inspiration refers primarily to the divine influence in virtue of which scripture is revelatory rather than to the revelatory character itself. . . . Scripture is disclosive (revelatory) because of the divine influence upon it (inspiration); we recognize it as inspired (divinely influenced) because we experience it as revelatory (disclosive). Inspiration focuses our attention on the divine influence at work in the text and reader while revelation focuses our attention on the disclosive potential of the text as it comes to actualization (*The Revelatory Text*, 51).

This view balances the elements of divine initiative (insofar as Scripture is maintained as uniquely disclosive of God) and of human response, the reception of this revelation in faith.

Jean-Pierre Ruiz

See also AQUINAS, THOMAS, ST.; DEI VERBUM; FUNDAMENTALISM; HISTORICAL CRITICISM; INERRANCY; PROPHETS/NEVI'IM (IN ISRAEL); REVELATION; SCRIPTURES (GENERIC).

INSTITUTES OF THE CHRISTIAN RELIGION

John Calvin's collected works include sermons, Scripture commentaries, and other writings; the *Institutes* constitute his most influential work. Calvin published the first edition in 1536 in Latin, and dedicated it to King Francis I of France. A native Frenchman, in some ways in exile in Geneva, Calvin hoped to gain the support or at least tolerance of the French monarchy for the Reformation. If Francis I's attitude toward the Reformation proved disappointing for Calvin, the *Institutes* were to be very successful as an authoritative summary of the doctrine of the Reformed Church. An enlarged, second edition appeared in 1539; later editions Calvin published in both Latin and in his own French version; the definitive versions of the *Institutes* were published in 1559 (Latin) and 1560 (French).

The four books of the *Institutes* treat: the Creator; the Redeemer; the Holy Spirit; the church. Calvin begins by examining what reason can demonstrate about God, and moves from there to exposition of Scripture and the church fathers. If Calvin affirms, like Luther, a principle of "Scripture alone" as the source and norm for church doctrine, he also relies heavily on reason and on earlier theologians in his presentation of Christian doctrine. The absolute sovereignty of God and the justification of the sinner by faith alone are central doctrines. Predestination is a subject included in the *Institutes*, but it does not preoccupy Calvin to the degree that it would some later generations of Calvinists.

Thomas Worcester, s.j.

See also CALVIN, JOHN; CALVINISM; JUSTIFICATION; PREDESTINATIONISM (CALVINIST); REFORMATION; REFORMED CHURCH; REFORMED THEOLOGY; SOLA SCRIPTURA.

INSTRUCTION (DOCUMENT)

In the Roman Catholic Church, a document that discusses the application of church law or doctrine to a specific situation. Instructions are frequently issued by the congregations (departments) of the Vatican to clarify the church's official stance on current questions and problems. They are not intended to represent any new or changed doctrine, but do give notice of the way in which certain teachings will be interpreted and emphasized in the face of a particular issue. In 1984 and 1986, for example, the Congregation for the Doctrine of the Faith issued two instructions concerning liberation theology, the first using traditional Catholic doctrine to point out perceived problems with certain forms of this theology, and the second discussing the ways in which traditional Catholic doctrine actually supports fundamental tenets of this theology.

William A. Clark, s.j.

INTEGRALISM

An attitude that has pervaded a number of reform movements throughout the world, leading them to link the beliefs, symbols, and demands of a religion with the specific kind of society they seek to create through their reforms. Integralism seeks power in order to force the creation of a new society, legitimizing itself on religious grounds. Integralism is most frequently linked to religiously conservative groups. It is often confused with "fundamentalism" in the United States.

Orlando Espín

See also FUNDAMENTALISM; IDEOLOGY (IDEOLOGIES); TRIDENTINISM.

INTERCESSION

Most commonly, this term refers to petitionary prayer in which the believer asks God to intercede on someone's behalf. Most Christian worship includes such prayer in some form. In Christian *theology*, intercession refers to one of the "offices," or functions, of Christ, namely, his role as the high priest of the people of God (besides priest, Christ is seen as prophet and ruler). Many Christians have held that in his own death, Christ offered a single, perfectly effective, and unrepeatable sacrifice for all sins (see Heb 3:1–10:18). Risen from the dead and "seated at the right hand of God," Christ pleads the cause of humanity before God the father (Heb 7:25; Rom 8:34). This affirmation does not imply, however, that without the intercession of Christ, God would wish us harm. Christ's own saving work demonstrates God's prior love for sinful human beings. Thus, genuine Christian worship explicitly or implicitly links intercessory prayer (for present needs) to the prayer of thanksgiving (for past gifts).

James B. Nickoloff

See also PRAYER.

INTERCOMMUNION

Intercommunion is the term applied primarily to the reception of the Eucharist in Roman Catholic Churches by members of other Christian denominational churches. Specific guidelines have been established, notably in a 1972 Pastoral Instruction from Pope Paul VI, which mandate the circumstances under which such reception would be possible. These include the requirement that recipients manifest the belief in the "Real Presence of Christ" in the Eucharist, that they experience a real spiritual need, and that they are unable, for some period of time, to have access to ministers of their own denominational community. On the other hand, in the 1983 revision of the Code of Canon Law, Canon 844 permits Catholics without access to a Catholic priest to receive not only Eucharist, but also penance and anointing of the sick "from non-Catholic ministers in whose churches these sacraments are valid."

Robert D. McCleary

See also ECUMENISM; EUCHARIST; SACRAMENT.

INTERCULTURAL THOUGHT

The theories that today we may gather under the rubric "intercultural thought," with a number of allied fields, seem to have coalesced in the late 1980s and early 1990s. Scholars (mostly philosophers) from Europe, India, and Latin America have been at the forefront of this movement. The work of intercultural philosopher Raúl Fornet-Betancourt is particularly insightful and rich as dialogue partner for theology (and religious studies), and is regarded as one of the most articulate presentations of today's intercultural thought. This entry describes intercultural thought from Fornet-Betancourt's contributions and perspective. It is a somewhat long entry because intercultural thought is fast becoming a crucial philosophical and methodological challenge for all Christian theology (as well as for the discipline of religious studies).

1. Inculturation and interculturality.

It is important to understand that interculturality is not inculturation. The latter supposes a "necessary something" that exists independent of a culture and that can be "poured" or "transmitted" into other cultures. The "necessary something" supposed by inculturation assumes, furthermore, an interpretation or understanding possible only within, and from within, a dominant culture, because the "necessary something" does not interpret itself, and, therefore, does not understand or proclaim itself (or by itself) as "necessary." A frequent example of a "necessary something," appealed to and mentioned by those who promote inculturation, is the Christian Gospel.

For something in inculturation to be considered "necessary" implies that someone, in and from a specific cultural horizon, determined (and thus, because of a set of interests proper to the cultural horizon of the one doing the determining) that this "something" exists, and that it is definitively "necessary." Inculturation, consequently, includes the possibility (and perhaps the reality) of colonization. Inculturation thus understood has little to do with the truth that is discovered and that convinces, but rather it has to do with the acceptance of someone else's proclamation (inevitably constructed from within the proclaimer's cultural perspective) that the truth being "brought" to me should or must convince me.

Instead of inculturation we should perhaps speak of "inter-transculturation," whereby another "witnesses" to me, in an open dialogue, what he or she understands and lives as truth; and I, within and from within my own cultural perspective, will contrast and perhaps assume that truth, because I have discovered it as truth (within and from within my cultural horizon). And I, in turn, upon my discovery of truth (possible within and from within my cultural perspective), will "witness" to the other, again in an open dialogue, what I have come to understand and live as truth, inviting the other to question and/or grow in what he or she understands and lives as truth —thereby moving the process into an ever-deepening and continuing dialogue where truth is discovered and affirmed, over and over, through mutual witnessing, open dialogue, and noncolonizing reflection.

The discovery of truth, then, results from "inter-cultural" dialogue, and not from arguments and concepts born within a cultural horizon foreign to me and designed to convince me by pulling me away from my own cultural horizon. The argument that truth (including the Gospel's truth) must critique cultures cannot be made to imply or provoke colonization, and such would be the implication if the understanding of truth (including the Gospel's truth), which is offered for acceptance by another, proceeds from a dominant culture (or a hegemonic group within a dominant culture) that has access to my culture precisely because of their hegemony or dominance, or when the critique of culture is not the historically possible fruit of the receiving culture's own possibilities.

Convivir (which in Spanish means "to live-with," and comes from the Latin *convivire*) is the necessary assumption or precondition for interculturality. "To live-with" implies, among other things, that those who *conviven* are actually present with and to one another for a sufficiently prolonged period of time and, further, that their presence with and to one another engages them with and in one another's daily lives in ways that *each* considers sufficiently meaningful and sufficiently mutually respectful.

2. *Truth: universally "valid" or universally "relevant."*

Truth is a cultural and an intercultural process. No culture, and no cultural situation, may be considered as the definitive locus of truth, or as the best vehicle for the expression of truth. Cultures only offer us the possibilities and instruments for seeking after truth. Truth will only unveil itself to us if we are willing (in intercultural dialogue) to risk "contrasting" *our* truth with the truth claims and/or truth expressions originating in other cultures. As anthropology and other social sciences have demonstrated, reality (and thus truth) is not "monochrome" or judged the same everywhere by everyone; rather, reality (and thus truth) is "plurichrome" or judged variously in many places and by many peoples.

It would be nonsense to assume, in today's globalized and globalizing world, that the truth claims of one religious or national group are "universally valid" *just because* this one group has (through its own cultural categories and assessment) discovered or affirmed something to be true. By "universal validity" is meant that a truth claim, from within a specific culture, is presented to and is possibly imposed on the potential recipients because the claim's birthing culture assumes its particular perspectives (that is, its questions and themes, its answers and solutions, its practices and approaches) to be applicable to and correct for all other cultures. The claim to universal validity has usually accompanied the history of power and colonization, and has been all too frequently legitimized by these. Unless a group acknowledges to itself and others that there are indeed other claims to truth, just as evidently true within and through other equally legitimate cultural categories, the group's claims to universal validity may be regarded either as an indication of human hubris or as a violation of other people's right to cultural self-determination.

Only in intercultural dialogue, "contrasting" truth claims with one another, can there begin to appear what may be said to be a "universally relevant" truth claim. By "universal relevance" is meant that a truth claim may be offered, from within a specific culture or group, to others who may find the claim to be useful, suggestive, or even true, thereby opening for and within the recipients perspectives (for example, questions and themes, answers and solutions, practices and approaches) that had hitherto remained closed, confused, or ignored. It might be possible to discover common threads and denominators among the truth claims with universal relevance, but the original claim does *not* present itself as *necessarily* applicable or correct for *all* possible recipients and in *all* possible cultural contexts. The recipients must consent to the relevance of the claim offered to them. Only in the "contrasting" intercultural dialogue necessary for the discovery of universally relevant claims can truth be acknowledged, and only then can truth unveil itself without the trappings of empire, imposition, or idolatry.

It might be important to pluck our understanding of truth from the prison of concepts, seeking it instead in our open dialogue with others' lives, with others' historical realities, and so on. It might be important to let others, and to let truth itself, be "un-defined" for us (within our own cultural perspective), letting their distinctiveness communicate with us as distinct or different and, therefore, without necessarily cleanly "fitting" within our categories. This "in-definition" has nothing to do with relativism—on the contrary, it is the humble acceptance of our own cultural limitation and a critique to our own cultural inclination to self-idolatry. If only God is absolute truth, then only *after encountering and relating with* God could humans claim to have received truths from God—and then only as humans can, given their condition as creatures, understand (or claim they understand) a divine truth.

3. *First World postmodern thought and particular universalities.*

One important intercultural concern is how to integrate the diversity of the world into each cultural particularity (opposed to and different from the attempt to integrate the culturally particular into some sort of evident human universality). The postmodern emphasis on cultural particularity seems to have little future in the world of globalization because cultural particularities, seen from many postmodern perspectives, appear in fact to close themselves off to the world's diversity, instead of seeking to integrate diversity into the cultural particularities. Some postmodern perspectives presume that diversities *need not* dialogue in mutually challenging, critiquing, and/or enriching ways. Confronted with the contemporary difficulty of making universally valid claims, many postmodern philosophical views on particularities have practically chosen to enclose themselves within their particular cultural worlds, giving up on the *need* for intercultural dialogue (which might unveil universally relevant truth), while philosophically legitimizing this closing-off as the intellectually honest and best option. There sometimes seems to be an implied universally valid truth claim made on behalf of postmodernism's denial of universally valid claims!

It seems that First World postmodernism can become an attempt at ethically justifying self-sufficiency and the silencing of the voices of the others, especially when the others might either challenge our self-sufficiency, our particular cultural hubris, our silence in situations of injustice, or the asymmetric and unfair power structures of globalization (which clearly benefit many of the First World proponents of postmodernity). It also seems that many First World postmodern proposals are mostly lacking in the analyses of their ethical responsibilities in today's globalized and globalizing world. Many postmodern views on particularity can become an enclosed circle, risking ultimate sterility. What is ethically needed is a radical critique of each cultural particularity's self-sufficiency, as well as a radical and critical openness to the others who question and challenge our cultural particularity toward solidarity with them (even, and especially, when there is no benefit to be obtained for *our* particularity in and through that solidarity). This seems to be the ethical way to avoid drowning in our First World cultural specificity as well as avoiding moral deafness at the crucifixion of the majority of humans in the globalized world. Contemporary First World postmodernism, by arguing that its views are the best philosophical explanations for and in today's globalized world, is but refashioning and preserving

the same First World colonial mentality that in past centuries set itself up as the world's standard and silenced most alternative voices.

The alternative to First World postmodern approaches is *not* the return to what has been called "foundationalism." The alternative proposed is intercultural dialogue, which can acknowledge and accept much of postmodernism's critique of foundationalism while refusing to share postmodernism's inclination to sterile particularisms or its uncritical and ideological legitimation (by omission) of the First World's interests.

4. *Particular universalities.*

There is no one evident human universality; rather, there are multiple historical and cultural human particular universalities that can encounter one another, challenge one another, and which, through intercultural dialogue, might engage in the process of unveiling universally relevant truth. Each one of the many particular universalities acts as the platform from which a way of thought is opened and launched in the world—opening and launching each particular universality to dialogue with other particular universalities and with other truth processes. Our own particular historical, cultural universality is but the first point of reference from which to know and say what is ours, insofar as it is our concrete life and thought universe. But it is also our first point of reference in learning and perceiving the contingency of our knowing and saying. This discovery of self-contingency is a *sine qua non* condition for self-critiquing our particular historical, cultural universality, thereby avoiding the self-idolatry of our historical, cultural universe. By acknowledging the contingency of our particular universality (and of its knowing, living, and saying), we open our universality to the possibility, indeed to the *need*, for dialogue, for learning from other particular historical and cultural universalities, and for allowing our universality to be called to solidarity with others.

Dialogue with others and self-critique are not and cannot *merely* be options or possibilities (although they most certainly are). Dialogue and self-critique should be recognized as life *needs*, without which any particular cultural, historical universality simply withers into self-idolatry and ultimate meaninglessness.

Consequently, intercultural dialogue is the opposite of the First World's dominant provincialism, whereby the dominant Western cultures decree and define their own universality as the only "universally valid" universality.

Intercultural dialogue does not assume or propose any culture, any particular universality, or any philosophical or theological current as the best way (in any sense) for the world. Indeed, intercultural dialogue assumes itself to be also in need of critique, as it too acknowledges itself contingent. It holds (radically open to correction) that the process of "contrasting" conversation, where all is risked in and for the sake of truth-searching dialogue, is capable of determining or clarifying what the intercultural dialogue should be and how it should be carried out.

5. *Broadening the sources.*

There seems to be a need in theology and religious studies (and in philosophy and in the social sciences) to multiply and broaden the sources. This does not simply mean that we have to add to the list of sources the names and contributions of other "objects of study" we might have set aside in the past—although this addition might prove itself important too. By multiplying and broadening the sources of theology is meant that the voices of other, previously unheard or silenced "theologizing subjects" must be heard and considered on an *equal* basis as the voices of the "theologizing subjects" of Europe and European America. In other words, the "theologizing subjects" from nondominant communities must be positively and actively acknowledged as *being* also at the theological table (at the *con-vivencia*), and *as always having been there*, even if mostly unheard and disregarded, as bearers of perspectives, alternatives, universalities, logic, and truth, *and* as "theologizing subjects" who might challenge and critique what First World theology assumed to be self-evident.

Intercultural thought requires that we learn to think in new ways. In other words, interculturality invites us to go beyond attempts at "enriching" *our* First World perspectives by somehow incorporating the contributions of others, because this "enrichment" approach would ultimately leave our assumptions and methods untouched and uncritiqued, since it would be through them that we "enrich" what already is. What is new in the way of intercultural thinking is found in risking our assumptions and methods by "contrasting" them with the assumptions and methods of others—and through this contrasting dialogue be willing to give up (some or many of our) assumptions and methods and to acquire new ones in and through the intercultural contrasting dialogue. We are thus called to learn to see ourselves, our cultural particular universalities, our histories, and our lives, as well as our theological (and religious studies) assumptions and methods, under the new light offered us by those who are culturally different from us. The new way of intercultural thinking is thus "polyphonic," as it would ultimately lead us to see our theology (and religious studies), as well as our cultures and history, as bound and related to and with others, thereby negating the temptation to self-enclosing idolatry and culturally feared relativism.

6. Conditions for intercultural dialogue.

It should be apparent that any serious intercultural dialogue relies on there being conditions for dialogue. This should be obvious from what has been discussed above. The conditions for dialogue to which we are referring include the political, economic, social, gendered, and other dimensions that contextualize any intercultural exchange today. Therefore, before any serious conversation may occur, the "theologizing subjects" must acknowledge and face the issues and consequences provoked by these dimensions among and for the "theologizing subjects," as well as the conditions for or against equality these may imply for intercultural dialogue. Once again we must recall that theology (indeed, all Christianity) occurs only in this world as this world exists. Today a de-contextualized dialogue (or one that does not begin by acknowledging and facing the dimensions impinging on its credibility as honest search for truth) would be an ideological exercise only benefiting those favored by globalization.

7. Meaning, meaningfulness, and conflict in cultures.

One last and important note on cultures. All human cultures are primarily the historically and ecologically possible means and ways through which a people construct and unveil themselves (to themselves, and secondarily to others) as meaningfully human, constructing the meaning of "human" too in this same process. The values, meanings, and goals of cultures, which define the human communities that construct them, have effective incidence on the social organization of the contextual-material universes these communities affirm as their own because they *are* in them. Even the most marginalized cultures are still meaningful vehicles of meaningful interpretations of life and reality for the communities that construct and claim them. And it is within, and from within, this meaningfulness that human communities create and speak their logic, their perspectives, their sense of life, and engage in the quest for truth. It is within and from within this meaningfulness too that human communities universalize their interpretive universes. True universality, thus, is not the de-contextualization of thought or concepts (as globalization and modernity might lead some to believe), but the dialogue that engages the human communities' meaningful vehicles of meaningful interpretations of themselves and their worlds (that is, their particular cultural universes), acknowledging each one of them as human and potentially relevant—thereby suggesting that there is a "human condition" which, although constructed and defined in and by every particular universality, can (by contrasting dialogue) be effectively acknowledged as possessing universally relevant elements or description.

Furthermore, because the intercultural view of culture is historical, it presupposes that no culture is a monolithic block—as if a culture were the naive or simple development of a single tradition that grew without conflict or contradiction. Rather, every culture bears witness to an *internal history of conflict* and struggle for the determination and control of its values, meanings, logic, and overall contour. The internal history of struggle for inner cultural hegemony is also part of the global intercultural dialogue, as that internal history reminds us of other silenced traditions and marginalized life experiences. Each human culture could have turned out differently, but if cultures exhibit their current values, meanings, logic, and so forth, it is because of the struggles for internal hegemony that they historically endured and that provided for the present outcomes.

8. *Intercultural thought and theology.*

This, in turn, leads to the conclusion that intercultural dialogue (because it engages human cultures) *is not and can never be the goal of theology*, but rather a *necessary* avenue for the joint discovery of viable and universally relevant truth in our globalized and globalizing world. The sacralization of cultures (given every culture's internal history) would itself contradict intercultural dialogue.

Intercultural thought has much to offer theology, religious studies, and philosophy. Nevertheless, and specifically within the field of theology, questions must be raised and sufficiently answered (even through an intercultural perspective and "contrasting" dialogue) regarding some fundamental (Christian) faith assumptions. One example, among several: Can there be a truly intercultural understanding of revelation (respectful of the Christian belief that revelation in Christ is God's definitive self-donation to humankind)? Can revelation be considered radically open to or in need of human critique, as intercultural dialogue appears to demand? Although, is not revelation—to the degree it is perceived and understood by humans—also human and thus cultural? Many issues remain before inter-

cultural thought becomes fully integrated as an authentically theological perspective or method, but the growth of the intercultural thought movement in philosophy and in the social and educational sciences seems to suggest that soon it will also become a methodological imperative in Christian theology.

Orlando Espín

See also CULTURE; FORNET-BETANCOURT, RAÚL; INCULTURATION; METHOD IN THEOLOGY; MODERNITY; POSTMODERNITY.

INTERDICT

An ecclesiastical type of punishment whereby an individual person or group (for example, parish, town, convent, region) may be denied the celebration of sacraments and other pastoral care in order to encourage repentance, but without going as far as excommunication. In the Catholic Church, interdicts have been attested since the sixth century. Today interdicts are very rare, and imposed in only the most extreme cases of public denial or disregard of faith or morals.

Orlando Espín

See also BISHOP (EPISCOPACY); CANON LAW; EXCOMMUNICATION; ROMAN CATHOLIC CHURCH; SACRAMENTS.

INTER MIRIFICA

This Vatican II document, The Decree on the Instruments of Social Communication [commonly known as *Inter Mirifica*, the first two words of the Latin text, which mean "among the marvelous (inventions)"] was overwhelmingly approved by the bishops of the Second Vatican Council and promulgated on December 4, 1963. Because this document treats a practical issue, it is called a "decree" rather than a "constitution" (which deals with larger theological problems) or a "declaration" (which states particular principles that should guide practical considerations). Typical of a council convened to "update" the Catholic Church is its concern with modern technological advances and, in particular, with the field of mass communications. The fundamental reason for the church's interest is the effect the media have on the human spirit —for good or for ill—and, for the first time in a document addressed to the whole church, the council asserts the church's right and obligation to make use of the media. In chapter 1, the council sets forth principles for the use of the media that should promote the good of Christians and the whole human family. These include the norms of morality (to be observed by professionals, civil authority, and parents); the dignity of the human person; the right of people to information; and the duty of the young to learn self-control in using the media. Chapter 2 takes up the use of the media in the church's pastoral activity; the training of Catholics, lay and clerical, in the use of the media; and the establishment of Catholic offices for the promotion of the proper use of the media. In *Inter Mirifica* the council sought to avoid both an overly negative view of the media and an exaggeration of the church's right to oversee the media. The stress on the special competence of the laity in the area of social communications, independent of control by the clergy, is noteworthy.

James B. Nickoloff

See also VATICAN, SECOND COUNCIL OF THE.

INTERNATIONAL SOCIETY FOR KRISHNA CONSCIOUSNESS

See HARE KRISHNA MOVEMENT.

INTINCTION
The term "intinction" is used for the Christian practice of distributing Communion by the priest or minister dipping a piece of the consecrated bread (sometimes called a *Host*) into the consecrated wine, then putting it directly on the tongue of the recipient. The practice is more commonly used in some Eastern churches: the priest places pieces of the consecrated bread into a large Communion chalice, and distributes it to the faithful on a spoon.

Intinction had been condemned in the Western church in the eleventh century. Since the liturgical reforms of Vatican II, Roman Catholics may receive Communion from the cup in one of four ways: drinking directly from the chalice; intinction; the use of a special straw or tube; and the use of a spoon, in the Eastern fashion. However, the practice of self-intinction by laypeople is forbidden.

Joanne M. Pierce

See also CHALICE; COMMUNION (LITURGICAL).

INVESTITURE CONTROVERSY
Technically, investiture is the handing over to an abbot or a bishop-elect the signs of their office, that is, the ring and the staff, before they are ordained or placed into their new offices. A custom had grown up in the early Middle Ages by which investiture was performed by the secular lord at which time the person chosen to be abbot or bishop did homage to the lord. The custom arose as part of a much larger institution, that of the proprietal churches. Under this system, individual churches or monasteries belonged to the lord who built and financed them. Thus a lord had the right to appoint whomever he wished as parish priest of the church or abbot of the monastery he had founded. The lord

even had the right to use the church buildings as he chose. Soon, the more powerful lords, such as the kings of England and France and particularly the Holy Roman Emperors in Germany, thought it their right to appoint bishops and, in the case of the emperor, even the pope. The lords looked back to the caesaropapism of the Roman emperors for precedent in this practice. A further custom was that of paying the lords for the privilege of being appointed priest, bishop, or abbot. This was not necessarily seen as "buying" the position, but more as a gesture of gratitude and a recognition of overlordship, although the system was certainly open to both misuse and abuse.

The investiture controversy arose as part of the larger Gregorian reform movement of the eleventh and twelfth centuries. The Gregorian reform movement opposed the selling of ecclesiastical offices (simony) and began to enforce clerical celibacy. Both these moves were meant not only to improve the moral life of the clergy, but also to free the clergy from lay control. The Holy Roman Emperor, Henry III, not only supported these reforms but actually appointed the first reforming popes. The changes introduced, particularly by Pope Leo IX, began to shake the foundations of the proprietal system. Bishops, priests, or abbots who had paid a fee to the local lord for their positions could find themselves deposed, or at least subject to confession and penance. Inevitably, however, the practice of appointing and investing bishops and abbots came under attack. The reformers argued that a true reform of the clergy could not take place as long as the secular lords still controlled the loyalty of the clergy they appointed.

Investiture by lay lords was condemned by Pope Nicholas II in 1059 and the decree was repeated by Pope Alexander II in 1063. The issue came to a head, however, in 1075 when the emperor Henry IV and Pope Gregory VII began a protracted battle over the appointment and investiture of the archbishop of Milan. Gregory died in 1085, exiled from Rome; Henry, it seemed, was clearly victorious. Gregory's successors, especially Pope Urban II (1088–99), however, managed to turn public opinion in favor of the papacy and of the reform movement. In England, the archbishop of Canterbury, Anselm, refused to do homage before the king, Henry I, in 1100 and threatened with excommunication all who gave or received lay investiture. By 1105, a compromise was reached with the English king by which the king renounced all rights of lay investiture in return for receiving homage from the bishop or abbot-elect for the lands the bishop owned but over which the king was lord. A similar deal was struck with the French king in 1107. The emperors held out against the papacy until a formal settlement was reached through the Concordat of Worms in 1122. Again, the emperor retained control over the lands the bishop or abbot held in fief from the lord, but all rights to lay investiture were renounced. The provisions of the concordat were promulgated by the First Lateran Council in 1123.

The investiture controversy was an important part in the long struggle to free the clergy from lay control in the Middle Ages. To speak of this controversy in modern terms of "church" versus "state," however, can be misleading. No one doubted that the secular rulers were part of the church and indeed an important part of the church. They continued to have input and influence over important ecclesiastical posts. The Gregorian reform movement and the investiture controversy were more accurately a debate about the respective roles of clergy and laity in the church. The papal victory in this debate made possible a relative freedom of the clergy from lay control that, in part, made possible the lively revival of learning, art, literature, architecture, and law that occurred in the twelfth and thirteenth centuries.

Gary Macy

See also ABBOT/ABBESS; ANSELM OF CANTERBURY; BISHOP (EPISCOPACY); CALLISTUS II OF ROME; CELIBACY; CLERGY; GREGORIAN REFORMS; GREGORY VII, POPE; LATERAN (COUNCILS OF THE); MEDIEVAL CHRISTIANITY (IN THE WEST); SIMONY; WORMS, CONCORDAT OF.

IPSISSIMA VERBA IESU

A Latin expression meaning "the very words of Jesus." In New Testament studies, this phrase describes those sayings or words in the New Testament that are held to have been actually said by Jesus. This category excludes all sayings or words placed in the mouth of Jesus, yet edited or created by, for example, early Christian oral tradition or the Gospel writers.

Since the New Testament documents are written in Greek, and since Jesus is not known to have spoken Greek, those words or phrases termed *ipsissima verba Iesu* assume an accurate translation into Greek, unless they have been retained in Aramaic within the Greek text. The term *abba* is an example of the latter. There is very little agreement in biblical scholarship concerning which New Testament passages may be defined as having come verbatim (albeit, almost all later put into Greek) from Jesus himself.

F. M. Gillman

See also ABBA; FORM CRITICISM; REDACTION CRITICISM.

IRENAEUS OF LYONS (130/140–98?)

Born in Asia Minor, Irenaeus heard Polycarp preach. He may have studied in Rome, and eventually became a *presbyteros* in the city of Lyons in southern France. When the *episkopos* was martyred in 177 C.E., Irenaeus took over. Irenaeus wrote to Victor, the *episkopos* of Rome, around 189–98, but this is the last reliable historical witness to his life. Two works of Irenaeus survive, the influential *Against the Heretics* and the shorter catechism, the *Demonstration of the Apostolic Preaching*. In opposition to the Gnostics, Irenaeus was one of the first Christian writers to develop a complete history of salvation and christiology to prove that Jesus Christ not only was but had to be a real human being. Irenaeus also laid down criteria by which one could discern the true tradition of the teaching of Jesus from the more recently conceived teaching of the Gnostics.

Gary Macy

See also EPISKOPOS; GNOSIS/GNOSTICISM; HISTORY; POLYCARP.

ISAAC

(Hebrew, *Yitzhak*). In the Hebrew Bible, the son of Abraham and Sarah in their old age; the first Israelite to be circumcised at the age of eight days; husband of Rebecca and father of Jacob and Esau. According to Genesis 22:1-14, Isaac was almost sacrificed by his father, the result of a divinely ordered test of Abraham's faith. Late in Isaac's life, he was deceived into giving Jacob, his younger son, the blessing of the firstborn, thus assuring that the Israelite patriarchal line would continue through Jacob and not Esau (Gen 27:1-40; see Gen 21:12). Isaac died at the age of 180 (Gen 35:28).

Alan J. Avery-Peck

ISAIAH

The prophet Isaiah was active in the southern kingdom of Judah and its capital Jerusalem from approximately 742 B.C.E. until 687 B.C.E. This was the period in which the power of Assyria grew to dominate most of the ancient Near East. Israel was destroyed in 721 B.C.E., and Judah became an Assyrian vassal during Isaiah's lifetime. We know little to nothing about the prophet himself; some scholars speculate he may have been a priest. The book of Isaiah is usually divided by scholars into three sections based on the date of each section. Only chapters 1–39 may be assigned to the prophet Isaiah who was active in the eighth century B.C.E. during the time of Assyrian domination. Chapters 40–55 are attributed to an anonymous prophet who was active at the end of the Babylonian Exile in the sixth century, called by scholars Second Isaiah or Deutero-Isaiah. He mentions Cyrus of Persia by name several times. Chapters 56–66 are probably from the fifth century, although there is no consensus on this date. The author or authors are called simply Third Isaiah or Trito-Isaiah. The first section of Isaiah begins with Isaiah's memoirs (1:1–12:6), followed by a collection of oracles against foreign nations (13:1–23:18). Chapters 24–27 are called by scholars the "Isaiah Apocalypse" (24:1–27:13), since the focus is on the future intervention of Yahweh in history or perhaps at the end of history. The next section (28:1–32:20) contains oracles concerning Judah and its infidelity to Yahweh. This is followed (33:1–35:10) by a collection of oracles many scholars assign to the postexilic period and oracles that are eschatological in nature. The final section of First Isaiah (36:1–39:8) contains a sort of historical appendix that largely overlaps with 2 Kings 18:13–20:19.

Russell Fuller

ISASI-DÍAZ, ADA MARÍA (1943–)

Born in Cuba, Ada María Isasi-Díaz graduated from a private American high school, Merici Academy, in Havana, Cuba. She received her B.A. from the College of New Rochelle, New York, a master's in medieval history from the New York State University at Brockport, and the M.Div., M.Phil., and Ph.D. degrees from the Union Theological Seminary in New York City. For eight years she lived as an Ursuline sister, and in the 1990s she joined the faculty at Drew University as a professor of ethics.

Although she has written extensively on solidarity, Hispanic women, and feminism, Isasi-Díaz has also made significant contributions in *Mujerista* theology by pursuing justice and peace, particularly within the community of U.S. Hispanic women as they struggle for self-determination.

Throughout her life, Isasi-Díaz recognizes several formative communities, events, and ideas. The greatest influence in her life has been her family, whose home was disrupted by the political climate of Cuba. Since 1960, she has lived in the United States, and yet she has always felt, in her own words, "politically exiled." She credits her family and religious affiliation as influencing her character development to include a commitment to service, honor, and the dignity of the person.

Isasi-Díaz' theology has also been shaped by her experience of having worked with the poor in Lima, Peru. She credits the poor of Lima with teaching her what it means to be a Christian, learning from them the value of popular religion, and becoming involved, on their behalf, in action to promote justice.

A third formative influence in her life has been feminism. The oppression of women in the church and the oppression of women by the church made her a feminist.

In her interaction with participants in the Anglo feminist scholarly community, Isasi-Díaz calls them to hear the voices of their Mujerista sisters, as well as the voices and experiences of all other "different" women, and to allow these voices and experiences to change them.

Isasi-Díaz identifies her work as Hispanic women's liberation theology. She looks at the experience of the Hispanic woman through a liberative lens that she honed and focused during her time in Latin America. Reflecting upon the lived experience of Hispanic women within the dominant culture of North America, Isasi-Díaz searches for themes of liberation: as women, as women of a particular culture, and as women of faith within a patriarchal church.

One of Isasi-Díaz' distinct contributions is that she connects the academic and the Latina worlds. A professionally trained theologian whose experience includes university teaching, Isasi-Díaz insists on the validity and importance of Latinas' religious understanding and practices for the academic theological world and for churches themselves. In doing her theology, Isasi-Díaz searches for the life-giving elements of religious understanding that people carry in their hearts and minds in order to survive. Pointing to the long-standing tradition of the *sensus fidelium*, which acknowledges that persons comprising the large body of the faithful can understand God's action in their lives through their anointing by the Holy Spirit in baptism, Isasi-Díaz repeatedly urges theologians and the church in general to listen to the voices of those who are not usually heard within theological circles, and to gain from them a privileged and unique interpretive perspective in theology.

The methodology that Isasi-Díaz highlights is twofold: doing ethnography, or gathering information by interviewing women about their lived-out experience; and providing meta-ethnography, or analyzing information and weaving together the common scenes that emerge.

A key element of their experience is their ethnicity, which, in general, is the multiplicity and complexity of beliefs and traditions held in common by a group of people of a particular linguistic, historical, religious, racial, and/or cultural origin.

Isasi-Díaz pointedly discusses the fact that the survival of Hispanic women is directly related to the fate of the Hispanic culture that includes the symbolic system for generating, expressing, and maintaining meaning and values.

Isasi-Díaz does not reduce survival to a socioeconomic function; she asserts, instead, that the struggle to survive is also cultural: "the cultural struggle is a struggle for life" (*En la Lucha*, 27). For Isasi-Díaz, culture, which guides relationships, provides social structures, and gives one a sense of rootedness in life, is a social reality involving thoughts, feelings, and religious understandings and practices formed in each member of the community since birth.

Jeanette Rodríguez

See also JUSTICE; MUJERISTA THEOLOGY.

ISE

A Japanese term pointing to the earthly residence of Amaterasu (Sun Goddess) and the seat of the Great Imperial Shrine located on the Japanese Island of Honshu about two hundred miles southwest of Tokyo. It is believed that this spot was chosen by Amaterasu and was where she first descended from heaven. The beauty of the spot enhances its heavenly aura. Ise is the most honored of all shrines and the most popular pilgrimage spot in Japan. It is actually comprised of two shrines: the Naigu—inner shrine to Amaterasu, built in the third century C.E.; and the Gegu—outer shrine to Toyo-Uke-Hime (Goddess of Agriculture) built in the fifth century C.E. Traditionally, a representative of the Imperial Court (a princess) would reside at Ise year-round with the emperor visiting annually for the Festival of Prayer for the yearly harvest. Even today, each new emperor goes to Ise for the accession to the throne ceremony. The shrine is rebuilt and rededicated every twenty years.

G. D. DeAngelis

See also AMATERASU; IZANAGI; IZANAMI; KAMI; MATSURI; NIHONGI; SHINTO; SHRINE.

ISHTA-DEVATA

A Sanskrit term meaning "chosen deity," the concept of *ishta–devata* (or *ishta–deva*) is important in the practical spirituality of Advaita Vedanta and related modern schools of Hinduism. The idea is that, since the ultimate reality, Brahman, transcends all personal forms of deity, it is not critical which particular form of god that one might choose to worship or meditate upon. With the advice of the guru, who is responsible for initiating the disciple into spiritual practice, the student may elect to focus his or her devotional life upon any of the major deities or incarnations (Vishnu, Rama, Krishna, Shiva, or a form of the Goddess) as a support for the earlier stages of spiritual practice. Typically, a mantra that evokes the power of the chosen deity will be imparted by the guru for use in meditation. In some cases, the guru him- or herself, as an em-

bodiment of divinity, can be taken as one's *ishta–devata*. In practice, the "choice" of deity may be influenced by the guru's predilections or the family traditions of the disciple. Still, the idea is important to modern Hindus as a symbol of the perceived tolerance and lack of dogmatism in their tradition.

Lance E. Nelson

See also ADVAITA VEDANTA; AVATARA/ AVATAR; DEVA/DEVI; GURU; HINDUISM; KRISHNA; MANTRA; RAMA; SHAKTI; SHIVA.

ISHVARA

Ishvara (Sanskrit, Lord) is a generic term for the Supreme Being in Hinduism, especially in Advaita Vedanta. Both Vishnu and Shiva may be invoked as Ishvara, as the Goddess in any of her aspects may be designated by the feminine form, Ishvari.

Lance E. Nelson

ISIDORE OF SEVILLE (?–636)

The last child of a noble Roman family, Isidore followed his brothers and sister into the religious life. Isidore is most famous for his *Etymologies*, a vast encyclopedia of both Greco-Roman and Christian knowledge. This work provided the following generations with a single, simply arranged guide to ancient learning. Equally important, however, were Isidore's theological works, especially his *Sentences*, a dogmatic and moral guide for the Visigothic society of Isidore's time. Isidore was more than a scholar, however, and as bishop of Seville he called two important councils for his diocese and maintained a literary friendship with the Visigothic king, Sisebut. Isidore, in both his writings and his work, sought to provide a guide to ancient literature and practice for the newly emerging Gothic kingdoms that would form the basis for the early Middle Ages in western Europe.

Gary Macy

See also LEANDER OF SEVILLE; MEDIEVAL CHRISTIANITY (IN THE WEST).

ISKCON

See HARE KRISHNA MOVEMENT.

ISLAM

A monotheistic religion that understands itself as the recipient of the final and inerrant revelation of God's will for all humankind. Islam is based upon a series of divinely inspired revelations Muslims say were "recited" between 610 and 632 C.E. by the Prophet Muhammad (570–632), an Arab who lived in Mecca. Islam is the youngest of the three major Semitic religions (Judaism, Christianity, and Islam), and, according to Islamic belief, its scripture (the Qur'an) corrects and completes the two testaments of the Bible.

The followers of this tradition are called Muslims (who should never be referred to as "Muhammadans"). This is because the religion, according to believing Muslims, was not really *founded* by Muhammad. Muhammad was simply God's Prophet (*Nabi*) and Messenger (*rasul*)—an ordinary human being in every respect except for the great honor God bestowed upon him by raising him up to be the final Prophet. Muslims would say that *God* "founded" Islam, and from the beginning of human history He (Muslims always refer to God with the masculine pronoun) began to reveal the religion through a long line of prophets beginning with Adam. Other messengers of God accepted in Islam include Noah, Abraham, Moses, and Jesus.

The term Islam means "submission" to God, whom the Muslims call Allah (*the* God). It also connotes the "peace" one enjoys once he or she surrenders to the will of God and lives according to God's eternal law. The term Muslim means "one who has submitted." Submission or obedience to God is demonstrated by Muslims in three ways: first, through a genuine act of faith in the unity of God and God's Messenger, Muhammad; second, through the daily practice of the religion as stipulated by custom and law; and third, through the effort it takes to live a virtuous life. Muslims note that Islam is, therefore, a comprehensive religion in the sense that it involves the whole person in every facet of life all the time. No distinction is made between secular and sacred spheres of life. Every human activity, whether it involves politics, family, relationships, dining, praying, sexual practices, or the pursuit of knowledge is governed by the religion and its tenets.

Islamic faith and practice are summarized by what are called the Five Pillars (foundations) of Islam: profession of faith that there is no god but Allah and that Muhammad is God's Messenger; prayer, five times a day; the giving of alms; fasting from dawn to sunset every day during the Islamic month of Ramadan; and pilgrimage to the holy city of Mecca in Saudi Arabia (city of Muhammad's birth and first revelations) at least once in a person's lifetime if it can be afforded.

Theologically, Islam differs from Judaism and Christianity, primarily in the claim that it perfects revealed religion, and that its Prophet, Muhammad, is the "Seal of the Prophets," that is, the last of the authentic messengers of God. Its similarities to Judaism and Christianity, however, are far more numerous than the differences. Islam shares with both religions a belief in one creator God, angels, prophets, the event of divine revelation, caring for the needs of others, and the importance of living a virtuous life. With Christianity, Islam professes life after death—either in paradise (heaven) where the just shall abide forever with God, or in hell, the abode of those whose evil deeds lead to eternal condemnation. In recognition of these similarities, Muslims call Jews and Christians *ahl al-Kitab*, "People of the Book," that is to say, believers in the one true God.

One of the major features of Islam is its belief in the equality of all Muslim people. To emphasize the importance of this concept, Islam refers to the places where Islam is practiced as the *dar-al-Islam*, the "abode" of Islam, suggesting the image of a "family" of believers. Unlike Arabian society before the coming of the Prophet Muhammad, Islam is an association of people bonded by the faith—not by ties of blood or tribe or devotion to family deities. This understanding has allowed Islam to become a truly international, cross-cultural tradition. Though its Prophet is an Arab, and though its scripture is (and must always remain) written and recited in Arabic, it is incorrect to call Islam an "Arab religion." It is a universal religion, with no favor shown to Arab Muslims over Muslims from other cultures. In fact, the vast majority of the world's 1.3 billion Muslims do not live in the Arab world.

There are two major groups of Muslims: the Sunnis and the Shi'ites. It is estimated that about 85 percent of the Islamic population professes Sunni Islam and about 10 percent practice Shi'ite Islam. While the two groups are identical in most respects, the Shi'ites disagree with the Sunnis over the legitimacy of the early leadership of the Islamic community (the caliphate), and they have a different understanding of how the message of the Prophet Muhammad has been preserved and communicated throughout the centuries.

After the death of the Prophet in 632 C.E., Islam quickly spread throughout the Middle East, Persia (Iran), and North Africa; and later, it extended as far west as Spain and eventually eastward to northern India, central, and then eastern Asia. Wherever it was accepted, Islam brought with it the great achievements of Islamic law, as well as the cultural heritage of its artisans and scholars, particularly in the fields of theology, medicine, mathematics, and architecture. Islam also exported a way of life that prizes devotion to family and dedication to the community, as well as strict prohibitions against alcohol and drugs, usury, gambling, theft, and sexual immorality. Many Muslims believe that it is this way of life that accounts for Islam's attractiveness today and for the fact that it is one of the fastest growing religions in the world.

Ronald A. Pachence

See also AHL AL-KITAB; ALLAH (ISLAM); CALIPH (KALIPHA)/CALIPHATE; DAR AL-ISLAM; FIVE PILLARS (IN ISLAM); IMAM; JESUS (AS PROPHET OF ISLAM); MUHAMMAD; MUSLIM; NABI (IN ISLAM); QUR'AN; RASUL; REVELATION (IN ISLAM); SHI'A/SHI'I/SHI'ITE/SHI'ISM; SUNNA/SUNNI/SUNNISM.

ISLAMIC RADICALISM (FUNDAMENTALISM)

In common parlance, religious radicals are extremists in the cause of their faith traditions who often express their views and beliefs through social or political confrontation with existing institutions. In this sense, the term "radical" connotes a fanatical minority group whose objectives frequently constitute a threat to the majority who do not share their ideology. When applied to Islam, radicalism is generally understood as the position of ultraconservative Muslims who reject all non-Islamic influences on their religion, particularly the social, political, and cultural influences coming from the West. Militant radicals, according to this use of the term, would be willing to combat such influences through revolution, armed conflict, and even suicide attacks, in the belief that their cause represents a defense of Islam and the will of God. Examples of militant radicals (sometimes called jihadists in the West) include Osama bin Laden, founder of al-Qaeda ("the camp") and mastermind of the September 11, 2001, attacks on U.S. targets, as well as the Taliban in Afghanistan, and any one of a number of loosely affiliated terrorist groups whose stated intent is to wage war on the West and/or on the State of Israel.

It should be noted, however, that "radicalism" is a term often freely applied to certain Islamic groups (for example, the Shiʿite Muslims of Iran) by people outside those groups, particularly Western media commentators or even representatives of other Muslim institutions. As defined above, therefore, it normally implies a negative judgment of the radicals' agenda or methods. For their part, "radicals" believe that they stand for the revival and survival of Islam.

Fundamentalism is often used in the West as a synonym for radicalism, but both Muslims and non-Muslims agree that "fundamentalism" does not necessarily imply radicalism at all. In fact, the word should not even be applied to Islam. Historically, when the term came into use in the early twentieth century, it referred to very conservative American Protestant Christians whose goal it was to return to the fundamentals of biblical religion by absolute adherence to the Scriptures as the revealed Word of God. By definition, all Muslims believe that their scripture, the Qurʾan, is the literal Word of God, and they would say that Islam is founded on the practice of religious and social "fundamentals" revealed in the Qurʾan by God through the Prophet Muhammad (570–632). This would make all Muslims fundamentalists in the strict sense of the word, but it certainly does not define them as "radicals" any more than fundamentalist Christians can be called radicals. The expression "Islamic fundamentalism," therefore, should be avoided.

Ronald A. Pachence

See also FUNDAMENTALISM (CHRISTIAN HISTORICAL MOVEMENT); HIZBULLAH; ISLAM; MUHAMMAD; QURʾAN; SHIʿA/SHIʿI/SHIʿITE/SHIʿISM; WAHHABIYA.

ISMAʾILIS (SEVENERS)
See SEVENERS (IN ISLAM).

ISRAEL
The people who, according to the Hebrew Bible, were chosen by God for a special covenant and revelation; the descendants of Abraham, Isaac, and, in particular, Jacob, who, in Genesis 32:24-28, struggles with a messenger of God and as a result is given the name Israel (which means "struggles with God"). Denoting a nation and its distinctive culture, the adjective Israel can apply to that people's land and religion as well: "Land of Israel" suggests the territory promised by God to the Israelite nation and is distinguished from "State of Israel," the modern homeland of the Jews. "Religion of Israel" similarly denotes the theology and cultic practices described in the Hebrew Bible and is dis-

tinguished from the later evolution of that religion, which is called Judaism. In modern secular usage, the term Israel without qualification refers to the State of Israel. In Jewish liturgical usage, as in the Hebrew Bible, the term refers by contrast to the entire community of the people of Israel, past, present, and future, understood to be the recipients of God's revelation and thus a holy nation especially subject to God's protection and grace.

Alan J. Avery-Peck

ISRAEL, STATE OF
(Hebrew, Medinat Yisrael). The Modern Jewish homeland, founded in Palestine on May 14, 1948. Citizens of the State of Israel are called Israelis. While the State of Israel is ruled as a secular democracy, it is seen by many Jews as a sign of God's salvific actions in history, in particular as a redemptive response to the Holocaust. Accordingly, in contemporary Jewish liturgy the State of Israel often is referred to as "the beginning of the dawn of our redemption."

Alan J. Avery-Peck

IVO OF CHARTRES (1040?–1115)
Ivo studied in Paris and with Lanfranc at the monastery of Bec. In 1090 he became bishop of Chartres in France. As bishop, Ivo strongly supported the pope in the Investiture Controversy and encouraged the important episcopal school at Chartres.

He is most famous for his three books of canon law that were an important source for Gratian's *Decretum*.

Gary Macy

See also GRATIAN; INVESTITURE CONTROVERSY; MEDIEVAL CHRISTIANITY (IN THE WEST).

IZANAGI
(Japanese, he who invites).

See IZANAMI.

IZANAMI
(Japanese, she who is invited). In Japanese mythology (Nihongi and Kojiki), she is the female member of the heavenly primordial couple. Along with her partner Izanagi, she created the Japanese Islands and descended there to produce other *kami* to inhabit these Islands. It is said that Izanami was fatally burned by one of her offspring and retreated to the underworld land of death. She was followed by the inconsolable Izanagi, who, upon seeing her decayed form, fled to the upper world and bathed in the ocean to purify himself. During his purification, three offspring were produced: from his left eye the Sun Goddess Amaterasu; from his right eye the Moon Goddess Tsuki-Yomi; from his nostrils the Storm God Susa-No-Wo.

G. D. DeAngelis

See also AMATERASU; ISE; KAMI; KOJIKI; NIHONGI; SHINTO.

J

JACA, FRANCISCO JOSÉ DE (1645–88?)

Catholic missionary in Cuba and Venezuela, and member of the Capuchin Order. Born in Spain, Jaca was sent as missionary to Venezuela first. His courageous defense of African slaves and his anti-slavery preaching led the authorities to send him to Cuba. There he met fellow Capuchin Epifanio de Moirans, also in serious trouble for the same reasons, and both deeply influenced each other's reflections on the immorality of slavery. He paid a heavy price for his fight against slavery, suffering imprisonment and exile. He and Moirans are among the earliest abolitionists. His brief *Resolución sobre la libertad de los negros* (1684) is adamant in its denunciation of slavery and clear in its theological arguments based on principles of Catholic morality.

Orlando Espín

See also AFRO-LATIN RELIGIONS; LATIN AMERICAN CATHOLICISM; LIBERATION THEOLOGIES; MISSIONS; MOIRANS, EPIFANIO DE; SLAVERY.

JACOB

The biblical patriarch, son of Isaac and Rebecca, grandson of Abraham. His life was marked by conflict with his older twin brother Esau, whose patrimony and blessing Jacob stole so as to become a progenitor of the people of Israel. The name Israel derives from Jacob's own second name, given to him by God (Gen 32:28).

Within Judaism, Jacob's life is viewed as symbolic of later Jewish history. Insofar as he was called Israel, Jacob represents the nation as a whole, while his chief antagonists, Esau and his father-in-law Laban, are equated with Rome. In this interpretation, the conflict between the Israelite nation and Rome was predestined, represented in the struggle that took place in Rebecca's womb even before Jacob and Esau's birth (Gen 25:22; Gensis Rabbah 63:6). At the heart of the Jewish treatment of Jacob is an explanation of the apparent deviousness by which Jacob acquired the birthright and blessing of the firstborn. Jewish tradition explains that Jacob did not act out of selfishness, but wished only to acquire from the spiritually unworthy Esau the right to offer family sacrifices, a right at that time given to the firstborn (Genesis Rabbah 63:13). Comparably, Jacob did not intend to deceive his father by telling him, "I am Esau, your firstborn" (Gen 27:19). The sentence is properly understood as laconic and actually included the following bracketed

657

words: "I am [the one who will receive the Ten Commandments, which begin with the word 'I'], [but] Esau [is indeed] your first born" (Genesis Rabbah 65:14).

While generally a model of correct behavior, Jacob is not above criticism. The calamitous result of Jacob's preferential treatment of his own son Joseph proves the importance of a parent's treating all of his children equally (Babylonian Talmud Shabbat 10b). Jacob also is denounced for not interceding with God and preventing the Israelites' enslavement in Egypt (Babylonian Talmud Shabbat 89b). Overall, however, Jacob is viewed very positively. Along with Abraham and Isaac, Judaism understands him to be one of only three people to whom God gave a foretaste of the world to come. He was one of six people over whom the angel of death had no power (Babylonian Talmud Baba Batra 17a). According to one source, like the immortal Jewish people, Jacob never died at all (Babylonian Talmud Taanit 5b).

Alan J. Avery-Peck

JACOBITE CATHOLIC CHURCH
See SYRIAN CATHOLIC CHURCH.

JADE EMPEROR
(Chinese, *Yu-Wang Shang-Ti, Yu-Ti*). In the pantheon of Religious Taoism, he is considered the celestial ruler and most powerful deity who serves as the supreme lord of the physical world, the savior of men [humanity] and the marshal of supernatural beings. It is believed that the universe is governed by a great divine-human bureaucracy headed by the Jade Emperor and nobles and officials of his heavenly court. He is considered the creator of heaven, of physical laws, the controller of time, embodiment of the Way (Tao) and of good, and the controller of divination.

In Religious Taoism, he became one of the official Taoist Trinity (Three Purities) along with Lao-Tzu and Ling Pao. He became particularly prominent in the ninth century C.E. when emperors began to declare direct relationship to the Jade Emperor. He is still a popular figure today in Taoist temples in Taiwan.

G. D. DeAngelis

See also DAOISM; LAO-TZU; TAO.

JAFARI
The school of law accepted by Twelver Shiʿite Islam, named after its founder, Jafar as-Sadiq (699–765). Jafar was the sixth imam who is accepted by the Shiʿites as one of the specially designated teachers of spiritual wisdom passed on from the Prophet Muhammad (570–632). He is also recognized as a scholar and mystic who was endowed with secret knowledge that allowed him to mediate God's will to Muslims.

Ronald A. Pachence

See also IMAM; MUHAMMAD; MUSLIM; SHIʿA/SHIʿI/SHIʿITE/SHIʿISM; TWELVERS (IN ISLAM).

JAHILIYYA
(Also *Jahiliya*). From the Arabic word *jahil* meaning "ignorant." In Islamic thought, *al-Jahiliyya* describes the "era of ignorance" in pre-Islamic Arabia. This period, Muslims say, was characterized by the practice of polytheistic religions, immorality, and pagan rituals. Compared with the dawn of Islam which replaced it, *al-Jahiliyya* is considered an age of spiritual darkness by Muslims. With the advent of Islam, the competing tribal religions of Arabia gave way to a faith whose believers were united, not by ties of blood, but by their submission to the one true God.

It is important to note that for Muslims, Christians, and Jews who lived during the *Jahiliyya* are not considered infidels. They were monotheists who, like the Muslims who were to come, believed in the truth revealed by the one God and God's prophets.

Ronald A. Pachence

See also AHL AL-KITAB; INFIDELS; ISLAM; MUSLIM.

JAINISM

Jainism is a religious tradition that has roots deep in the prehistory of ancient India. Like Buddhism, Jainism is nontheistic, denying the existence of a supreme, creator God. However, Jainism is distinguished from Buddhism by, among other things, its teachings regarding the soul, its understanding of karma, and its emphasis on radical asceticism.

Western scholarship identifies Mahavira (sixth century B.C.E.) and his predecessor Parshvanatha (ninth century B.C.E.) as the founders of the tradition, understanding Jainism as a product of the same period of religious ferment in North India that produced Buddhism. Jainism and Buddhism became, in this view, the most successful of the many reformist, antibrahminical sects of the era. But the Jain tradition itself traces its origins back into mythic time, stating that Mahavira was only the last of twenty-four Tirthankaras, or Crossing-Makers, sages who pointed the way across the vast river of existence, that is, samsara. The Tirthankaras are also honored as Jinas (Conquerors). Hence, their followers are called Jainas or—in modern Indian languages—Jains, meaning "the disciples of the Jinas." The earliest of these world-conquering Crossing-Makers is said to have been Rshaba, who lived an inconceivably long time ago. While there is obviously no historical evidence for the existence of this most ancient of the Tirthankaras, there is some evidence (largely in Buddhist texts) for the historicity of Parshvanatha, the twenty-third Crossing-Maker, and there is no doubt about the historicity of Mahavira. In any event, it is clear that the Jain tradition draws upon an ancient store of religious concepts, certainly much that predates the two historical Tirthankaras, such that scholarship is inclined to recognize in its ethos our best evidence of at least one aspect of the prehistoric spirituality of South Asia.

The followers of Jainism are nowadays few (fewer than one percent of the population of India). Still, their influence, both in India and in the rest of the world, has been disproportional to their number. This is in part because the Jains are very influential in modern India's business community. A more important (but curiously related) reason is that, although Hindus and Buddhists have advocated nonviolence as part of their ethical systems, it is the Jains especially who have articulated the idea most forcefully and radically, making the practice of *ahimsa* (nonharming) incumbent on all followers. Mahatma Gandhi, though a Hindu, was born and grew up in Gujarat, a part of India in which there remains a high concentration of Jains. Through him, the ideal of ahimsa came to be part of the global ethical vocabulary, important now for environmental ethics as well as discussions of conflict and conflict resolution.

The ideal of ahimsa is anchored in two basic aspects of the Jain view of the world. First is the idea that all beings have souls (*jivas*). Like the other religions originating in India, Jainism assumes the doctrine of reincarnation, but it is perhaps even more inclusive than the others in the levels of creation that are believed to participate in the process. Jains count just about everything as having a transmigrating soul: from the basic elements, through rocks, plants and animals, up to human beings and the gods. (As in Buddhism, there are gods—*devas*—but no God.) Therefore, for Jains, who differ from Buddhists in their recognition of an eternal, substantial self or soul (jiva) as the core reality of each being, there are souls everywhere, in all of nature. So there is what approaches a hylozoistic view of the world, with many opportunities, for those who are not sensitive and careful, to injure living beings. Second, the Jains accept what is apparently an archaic version of the pan-Indian doctrine of karma. In the Jain view, karma is a quasi-material substance that sticks to, or even mingles with, the soul. Good karma is lighter in quality, bad karma heavier, but in either case, whenever we act, there is an influx (*ashrava*) of karmic matter that encumbers the jiva, so that the jiva becomes heavily burdened with karmic substance. This karmic substance creates further bondage to the cycles of reincarnation, since its nature is to generate further experience and, thus, further embodiment. Now, since killing or causing pain to other beings causes the very worst kind of karma to adhere to the soul, violence (*himsa*) must be scrupulously avoided, out of compassion, to be sure, but also out of self-interest. Injuring other beings is the surest and most drastic way of setting back one's progress toward happiness within, and eventually final release from, the mundane world. And, to make the Jain doctrine even more radical in its day-to-day practice, the quasi-material understanding of karma means that the karmic influx accrues irrespective of the actor's intentions. Hence, if one kills an insect unintention-

ally as one walks, or unconsciously destroys a microbe by drinking water in which it dwells, one is committing a kind of violence and will reap the karmic consequences. This is why Jain monks observe such disciplines as sweeping the ground gently with a whisk broom before sitting and filtering their water before drinking. Jain laypeople avoid farming, which, because of the necessity of breaking the soil, involves injury to a great number of beings. Hence their prominence in the business community of India, to which they have gravitated.

As in Theravada Buddhism, the life of Jain laypeople revolves around the monastic community that provides religious instruction to, and is in turn supported by, the laity. Faithful Jain laypeople take upon themselves a modified, less stringent version of the monastic vows, and live a life committed to strict vegetarianism, regular meditation, twice-monthly fasting, occasional sexual abstinence, and the obligation to support monks by giving alms. Jain practice includes visits to temples where images of Tirthankaras are venerated with offerings of fruit and flowers. There are several famous Jain temple sites in India, among them the complex at Mt. Abu in Rajasthan, known for its astoundingly beautiful marble carving. Unlike Buddhism, Jainism has continued to be a vital part of Indian society; this may be due in part to the Jain acceptance of the Hindu caste system.

The overall aim of lay Jain spirituality, divided into a scheme of eleven stages of increasing rigor, is to gradually reduce the karmic burden of the soul so that it can be slowly liberated from samsara and the sufferings thereof. This is done, in the beginning stages, through an ethical discipline of performing only actions that are positive or at least neutral, and avoiding those that have negative karmic implications. This ensures that the bad karma burdening the soul is gradually exhausted and replaced by good karma, which, though still a form of bondage, is lighter and more conducive to happiness and the religious life. Meditation also is an aid in the dissolving of the soul's karmic accretions. When, after a good number of lifetimes of spiritual practice, one's karmic burden has been considerably lightened, one begins gradually withdrawing from all unnecessary actions, even positive ones, so that the relatively lighter coating of good karma still encrusting the soul can be worn away. This eventually requires monasticism, of which Jainism has an ancient and still strong tradition, for both monks and nuns. Jain ascetics engage in meditation and ascetic penance, gradually reducing their activity. They abstain completely from sex, eat little, fast frequently, and meditate, until their karmic residues are almost completely worn away and they have attained an exalted stage of awareness.

At a certain point, when a number of carefully defined spiritual conditions have been met, ensuring that the proper state of mind and purity of motivation has been attained, a monk or nun may take the *sallekhana* vow involving a fast unto death. The practice is essentially a religious suicide; its purpose is to consume the final remaining karma and lead, at death, to total liberation. If they have the proper motivation, advanced Jain laypeople may also take this vow (under the supervision of a monastic), when it becomes certain that their death, from other causes, is both imminent and inevitable.

As the jiva is gradually freed by spiritual practice from its karmic burden, its consciousness begins to expand and it starts to regain its innate state of blissful omniscience. Thus, advanced Jain monastics are expected to have certain spiritual powers, though they seldom display them. When the karma is completely consumed, one's body is discarded, and the jiva ascends to a kind of heavenly paradise, located above the realm of the gods at the pinnacle of the cosmos, where the perfected soul (*siddha*) enjoys a blissful eternity of disembodied but fully expanded awareness.

The Jain community was, by the first century C.E., divided into two groups, the Shvetambara (white-clad) and the Digambara (sky-clad, naked). The monastics of the former division wear a simple white garment. Even that much covering is rejected by the latter, who believe clothing to be a sign of attachment to the body. Although Mahavira himself is said to have had thirty-six thousand female monastic disciples, the Digambaras do not allow women to become nuns. The Shvetambaras and Digambaras preserve separate canons of scripture (referred to as *agama*, "tradition"), written mostly in Prakrit, which (like the Pali of the Buddhist texts) is a vernacular language related to Sanskrit. The oldest Jain texts belong to the Shvetambara school. They are the eleven *Angas* (limbs), which record the teachings of Mahavira. While the two schools differ on matters of practice and monastic rule, they have few doctrinal disagreements.

Jain scholars of both traditions have contributed a great deal to the intellectual and literary life of India. They are noted especially for their perspectival, relativistic system of logic that seems to carry the ethic of nonviolence even into the arena of debate. Formalized in the *anekanta–vada*, the "doctrine of many-sidedness," and the *syad–vada*, the "doctrine of 'perhaps,'" this way of thinking is epitomized in the well-known Jain story of the blind men whose "truth" about an elephant depends upon which part each one happens to be grasping. Truth, at least within this realm of life, depends upon the point of view from which we approach it.

Jainism flourished in northwest, central, and south India from the third century B.C.E. onward, but it began to lose influence toward the end of the first millennium C.E. with the rise of Hindu *bhakti* movements.

Lance E. Nelson

See also AHIMSA; BHAKTI; BUDDHISM; GANDHI, MOHANDAS K.; HINDUISM; IMAGES, WORSHIP OF; KARMA; PALI; SAMSARA; SATYAGRAHA.

JAMES, WILLIAM (1842–1910)

Born in New York, James was a pioneer of pragmatic philosophy and experimental psychology. He inherited his interest in religion from his father, theologian Henry James Sr., who was reared in a Presbyterian home but drifted to Swedenborgianism as an adult. William James was raised without affiliation to a religious community. He yearned all his life for a spiritual home and suffered from anxiety and depression. A man of wide-ranging academic interests, he taught at Harvard from 1872–1907, first in physiology, then psychology, and finally philosophy. His writings impacted all three fields and include *Principles of Psychology* (1890), *The Will to Believe* (1897), *The Varieties of Religious Experience* (1902), and *Pragmatism* (1907).

James made three significant contributions to religious thought in the United States: empiricism, pragmatism, and the importance of faith. First, he applied an empirical methodology to the study of religion, investigating its psychological and social motivators through such categories as mysticism, saintliness, intuition, and healthy-mindedness. He challenged Christianity's claim to exclusive truth, declaring that the value of religion was not the scientific verifiability of theological claims, but the verifiable goodness it did in the world. He was part of a broader scholarly movement to analyze religion from the perspectives of psychology, sociology, and anthropology. Religion and science were not mutually exclusive, but supportive of one another.

Second, James stressed the practical benefits of religious belief. Reacting against Hegelian idealism, he had little use for abstract religious dogma; he was more interested in the experiential benefits of religious belief and practice. To James, religion had positive individual and societal benefits in this world rather than the next. It helps individuals and groups orient themselves, create meaning, and live moral lives. People become religious because religion alleviates human suffering. Although James' work was distorted by later interpreters to mean that whatever religion makes one feel good is right, he did not have that intention. To him, religion was a source of strength, not compensation for weakness. He affirmed the value of religion, but was not uncritical of it.

Third, and most significant, James asserted the necessity of faith in the modern world. He sought to validate religion in the modern world against those who claimed that it had outlived its usefulness. Defining faith as the force that prevents humanity from destroying itself, he argued that it provided a means of coping with the fragmentation and chaos of contemporary U.S. culture. Religion offered wholeness in place of the brokenness of modern life. The search for truth and "will to believe" were necessary for survival amidst pluralism. Emphasizing individualism over organized religion, he affirmed a human religious impulse that steered clear of nihilism, dogmatism, and authoritarianism. At its best, faith is therapeutic, a source of peacefulness and serenity.

Evelyn A. Kirkley

See also PRAGMATISM.

JANSEN, CORNELIUS (1585–1638)

Theologian at the University of Louvain (in present-day Belgium), Jansen devoted much of his work to the study of Saint Augustine, especially Augustine's theology of grace. In 1636 Jansen was made bishop of Ypres. Only two years after his death, in 1640 in Louvain, and the following year in Paris, was his major work, *Augustinus*, published; it was immediately the source of vigorous controversy.

For Jansen, many theologians in the Catholic Church of his day, Jesuits in particular, were Pelagian rather than Augustinian. "Pelagians," in Jansen's view, were those who taught that human beings could freely choose to work out their salvation by following God's commandments; "Augustinians," however, stressed the inability of fallen humanity to be saved but through the grace given to those whom God freely chose without regard for their merits. Jansen's *Augustinus* provoked the greatest strife in France, where "Jansenism" became for at least a century a major movement in the church. By the eighteenth century, if not before, the term "Jansenism" included some ideas with which Jansen would most likely have disagreed.

Thomas Worcester, S.J.

See also AUGUSTINE OF HIPPO; AUGUS- TINIANISM; BAIUS; JANSENISM; MERIT; MOLINA, LUIS DE; PASCAL, BLAISE; PELAGIANISM; SAINT-CYRAN, ABBOT OF; SIN, ORIGINAL; SOLA GRATIA.

JANSENISM

This term designates, at its origin, a theological movement initiated in 1640 by publication of Bishop Cornelius Jansen's *Augustinus*. Jansenism inspired and divided the Roman Catholic Church for nearly a century and a half. Especially prominent in France, Jansenism gained adherents elsewhere as well, particularly in Jansen's own southern Netherlands and in Italy. Jansen himself had died in 1638. The movement that bore his name was at first an effort to promote an alternative form of Catholic Reformation to that advanced by the Jesuits, an alternative rooted in a return to Saint Augustine's theology of sin and grace. By the end of the seventeenth century, "Jansenists" opposed not only the Jesuits but also the French monarchy. Eighteenth-century Jansenism was often more concerned with politics than with the theological questions that had preoccupied earlier generations.

Jansenist Theology

In continuity with the optimistic assessment of human potential that had animated much of the Renaissance, seventeenth-century Jesuits taught and preached a theology and spirituality that emphasized human freedom and possibility. The Catholic Reformation, as pursued by the Society of Jesus, aimed to use that freedom for the greater glory of God, a glory that could be magnified by the free choice to cooperate with God's grace. Original sin had damaged human freedom, but it had not abolished it. The world was a world of beauty and order, a world where nature and grace worked together in harmony.

Jansen and his disciples found such a theology far too optimistic; for them, Jesuits were guilty of reviving the Pelagian heresy that had been so appropriately and thoroughly condemned by Augustine. In France, the convent of Port-Royal became the center of Jansenist sympathy and influence. Under the spiritual direction of Saint-Cyran, and under the authority of Abbess Angélique Arnauld, the spirituality of Port-Royal was a penitential and austere one, a spirituality suited to those who saw the world as damned and themselves as sojourning in a vale of tears. Mère Angélique's brother, Antoine Arnauld, took up the task of castigating Jesuit sacramental practice. For Antoine Arnauld, Jesuits were altogether too ready to absolve sins and too inclined to promote the practice of frequent reception of the Eucharist. In a lengthy work published in 1643, Arnauld argued for the necessity of a period of penitential preparation between confession and Communion. Communion was to be approached neither lightly nor very often; confessors were not to absolve quickly or easily. For Arnauld, denial or a least delay of absolution was far too infrequent in the practice of Jesuit confessors.

According to the Jesuits, Jansenists were crypto-Calvinists, guilty of teaching what had already been condemned by the Council of Trent (1545–63). Jesuits sought and obtained from the papacy repudiation of five propositions said to be contained in Jansen's *Augustinus*. The five propositions condemned in Pope Innocent X's bull *Cum Occasione* of 1653 affirmed, among other things, that grace was irresistible. Articulating the Jansenist response, Antoine Arnauld argued that though the five propositions were indeed heretical, they were in fact not to be found in the *Augustinus*. Thus controversy continued.

Blaise Pascal's *Provincial Letters*, of 1656–7, contained both a defense of Arnauld and especially a mockery of Jesuit casuistry. Casuistry was the art of determining the morality or immorality of a particular act according to its circumstances. Pascal led his readers to conclude that Jesuits were shameless "laxists," willing to excuse and justify any act, murder included. The *Provincial Letters*, cleverly composed in an elegant French, were a great literary success, and gave Jansenism its most enduring expression.

Jansenist Politics

King of France from 1643 to 1715, Louis XIV grew ever less tolerant of sources of division in his kingdom. Such intolerance eventually led to revocation of the freedom of religion that had been granted to Protestants in France in 1598; it also led to persecution of the Jansenists.

To continued debate about the five propositions were added other sources of tension in late seventeenth-century and early eighteenth-century France. Jansenists were skeptical of the monarchy's growing pretensions to absolute power; Jansenists were numerous among those hostile to centralized authority in general, civil or ecclesial. In 1709 Louis XIV expelled the nuns from Port-Royal and soon after had the buildings destroyed. In 1713, with encouragement from Louis XIV and from the Jesuits, Pope Clement XI issued *Unigenitus*, a bull that condemned propositions from a book of "moral reflections" by Jansenist Pasquier Quesnel. Those hostile to *Unigenitus* included the archbishop of Paris; though he eventually submitted to papal and royal pressure, Jansenists appealed for suspension of the bull until a council could be called. Thus Jansenism evolved into a kind of Gallicanism, seeking to place a council of bishops above the pope. Jansenists also promoted the local church by some instances of translation of the liturgy into the vernacular.

Jansenist influence continued into the late eighteenth century. The papal suppression of the Jesuits in 1773 would perhaps not have taken place without Jansenism. The 1786 Synod of Pistoia, with its affirmation of Jansenist principles, testifies to the strength of Italian Jansenism. Many historians have seen in Jansenist opposition to centralized authority a preparation for the French Revolution.

Thomas Worcester, s.j.

See also ARNAULD, ANGÉLIQUE AND ANTOINE; AUGUSTINE OF HIPPO; AUGUSTINIANISM; CALVINISM; CASUISTRY; COUNTER-REFORMATION / CATHOLIC REFORMATION; GALLICANISM; GRACE; JANSEN, CORNELIUS; PASCAL, BLAISE; RENAISSANCE; SAINT-CYRAN, ABBOT OF; SIN, ORIGINAL; SOCIETY OF JESUS; TRENT, COUNCIL OF.

JAPA
A Sanskrit word meaning "murmuring" or "whispering," *japa* refers to the practice in Hinduism and the other Indic religions of reciting a mantra or prayer formula in a low voice, or silently, as a spiritual practice. Such continuous, devout repetition, often done a set number of times and counted with the help of a rosary (*japa–mala*), is said to purify and elevate the mind, preparing it for spiritual experience.

Lance E. Nelson

See also HARE KRISHNA; HINDUISM; MANTRA.

JASPERS, KARL (1883–1969)
German philosopher. After an early and brief career in medicine and psychology, he turned to philosophy and taught at universities in Heidelberg and Basle. His thought places him in the existentialist tradition. Jaspers understood philosophy as alternative to religion, and attempted to show the limits of science. He theorized on the cultural and philosophical role of myths as signs of transcendence, and on history as the sum of millions of individual decisions. His more important books are *The Perennial Scope of Philosophy* (1950), *The Origin and Goal of History* (1953), and *Philosophical Faith and Revelation* (1967).

Orlando Espín

See also CULTURE; EXISTENTIALISM; MARCEL, GABRIEL; METHOD IN THEOLOGY; MYTH; RICOEUR, PAUL.

JASSY, SYNOD OF
One of the most important gatherings of bishops in the history of the eastern Orthodox Churches, after the ecumenical councils. Held in 1642 in the city of Jassy, in Rumania, it included representatives from the Orthodox Churches under Slavic (Christian) control as well as from those then within the Ottoman (Muslim) Empire. The Synod of Jassy condemned Calvinism, and accepted the *Orthodox Confession* drafted by Archbishop Peter Mogila and modified somewhat at the Jassy meeting. This document, accepted by all the Orthodox patriarchs and churches, was first published in 1645 and is still regarded as one of the great theological works of the Orthodox tradition.

Orlando Espín

See also CALVINISM; JERUSALEM, SYNOD OF; MOGILA, PETER; ORTHODOX CHURCHES; PATRIARCH; SYNODS; TRADITION (IN CHRISTIANITY).

JATAKA
A birth story recounting an incarnation of the bodhisattva ("future Buddha"). A

typical *jataka* contains a frame narrative in which an audience elicits the story "from the past" by the Buddha; the story proper in which the bodhisattva can be a human, animal, or spirit; and the identification of the characters, often with prominent disciples and/or enemies of Shakyamuni involved. Jatakas, like Buddhist *avadanas* ("stories"), synthesize popular narratives from South Asia, redacting them to illustrate an essential Buddhist moral teaching, the power of merit (*punya*), the value of asceticism, or a point of worldly wisdom. There were collections made by monks writing in every major school and language. Jatakas were used by all Buddhists, both to explain the origins of monastic customs and as material for sermons and popular lay observances.

Todd T. Lewis

See also BODHISATTVA; MERIT (PUNYA); PALI CANON.

JATI

In the Hindu social system, a *jati* is a caste, properly speaking, that is, an endogamous, hereditary social group that is classified, with other jatis, as belonging to one of the four classically recognized caste categories (*varna*) of Hinduism: brahmin, *kshatriya*, *vaishya*, *shudra*.

Lance E. Nelson

See also CASTE; CASTE, SCHEDULED; HINDUISM; VARNA.

JEHOVAH

See YHWH.

JEHOVAH'S WITNESSES

The Jehovah's Witnesses originated in the United States from the Adventist movement, Christians anticipating the immi-

nent return of Jesus Christ. After William Miller's predictions of 1843–4 failed, the Adventists split into a number of smaller groups. The Jehovah's Witnesses emerged from this fragmentation, Bible students looking for signs of the Second Coming led by Charles Taze Russell (1852–1916). From his study of the Bible, Russell denied the existence of the Trinity, declared that Jesus Christ had returned in 1874, not as a visible entity but as an invisible presence, and announced that the end of the world would occur in 1914. To publicize his theology, he began to publish *The Watch Tower and Herald of Christ's Presence* in 1879, and in 1884 incorporated the Watch Tower Bible and Tract Society.

Although the outbreak of World War I sparked anticipation that the world was ending, Russell's prediction did not come true, and in the midst of the resulting confusion, he died in 1916. He was succeeded as president of the Society by J. F. Rutherford (1869–1942). Rutherford united the far-flung Society congregations into a centralized organization, and he initiated the controversial practice of members distributing tracts door to door. He preached less about the Second Coming and instead attacked the Satanic institutions of church and state. Rutherford also preached that God's true name was Jehovah, and in 1931, members adopted the name Jehovah's Witnesses (although the Society retained its official title).

Leaders since Rutherford have continued his vision of a hierarchical and authoritarian organization, defending its beliefs against a hostile society. Witnesses see themselves as a theocracy, obedient to no church or government but solely to God. Allegiance to God makes loyalty to earthly institutions idolatrous. Failed predictions that the Second Coming would occur in 1975 shook the Society, but it continued to grow in the 1980s through North and South America, Africa, Asia, and Europe. The international headquarters are in Brooklyn, New York.

Although the Witnesses consider themselves authentic Christians, most other Christians do not. Denying the divinity of Christ, the Witnesses believe he was God's first creation, similar to Arianism, a belief condemned by the Council of Nicaea in the fourth century C.E. Humans are saved through faith and obedience to Jehovah rather than through Christ's death and resurrection. Although the Witnesses now hesitate to set precise timetables, they believe the end of the world is coming and that Christians must prepare for the end of Satan's rule on earth. After the Battle of Armageddon, Jehovah will reign supreme on earth with most Christians, while a select 144,000 will live in heaven with Christ. To testify to their obedience, Witnesses are expected to attend worship at least once a week, distribute magazines, pamphlets, and books, and witness to their faith. Every member is considered a minister. Due to their message of spiritual empowerment and detachment from earthly institutions, the Witnesses have been especially attractive to women, ethnic and racial minorities, the poor, and other socially marginalized people.

The Witnesses have been embroiled in controversy from early in their history. They have encountered persecution from national governments, the surrounding community, and other religious bodies. In part this opposition has been initiated by the Witnesses' refusal to compromise their absolute loyalty to God. They refuse to serve in the military, vote, or salute the flag; however, they do pay taxes. During World War I, J. F. Rutherford was imprisoned for his pacifism. In the United States, the Witnesses have won several Supreme Court battles to exercise their religious freedom. In Germany, they were deported to concentration camps during the Holocaust along with Jews, homosexuals, and gypsies, and many died there.

Due to their perceived lack of patriotism, door-to-door evangelism, and distinctive beliefs, the Witnesses have provoked popular prejudice. Based on biblical prohibitions against drinking blood, they refuse to receive blood transfusions, creating conflict with the medical establishment and additional court cases that upheld their right to refuse conventional medical treatment. Witnesses abstain from alcohol, caffeine, and tobacco. A number of ex-Witnesses have attacked their beliefs and practices, as have numerous evangelical and fundamentalist Christians who consider them a cult. In recent years, the Witnesses have made inroads in traditionally Roman Catholic countries, arousing the church's opposition.

Evelyn A. Kirkley

See also ADVENTISM; ARIANISM; MILLENARIANISM; RELIGION, FREEDOM OF.

JEN

(Chinese, *ren*, lit., being humane). This is one of the cardinal virtues of Confucianism, found in the Analects (*Lun Yu*), meaning compassion, love, human-heartedness. It was considered the moral ideal of human relations and combined with proper ritual action (*li*) it characterized the expected behavior of the Ideal Man (*chun-tzu*). Many scholars believe that this ideal is at the heart of the Confucian view of life.

G. D. DeAngelis

See also ANALECTS; CHUN-TZU; CONFUCIANISM; CONFUCIUS; LI; MENCIUS; TE.

JEREMIAH

A prophet active in the seventh century B.C.E. (ca. 627–580 B.C.E.?) in the kingdom of Judah. According to the dates given in Jeremiah 1:1-3, his activity stretched from the reign of Josiah until after the fall of Jerusalem in 587 B.C.E. He died in Egypt sometime after 587. Jeremiah was the son of Hilkiah, a priest from the town of Anathoth. He may well have been a descendant of Abiathar, one of the high priests of David who was exiled to Anathoth by Solomon after he took power. The book of Jeremiah contains a collection of Jeremiah's oracles concerning Judah and Jerusalem that Jeremiah is said to have dictated to his scribe Baruch. The oracles are not in chronological order and are supplemented by third-person narratives about Jeremiah, Baruch's memoirs, a collection of oracles against foreign nations, an introduction, and a historical appendix. Jeremiah was concerned about the relationship between Yahweh and Judah that he thought had reached a low point because of the people's worship of other gods. Jeremiah repeatedly warned of Yahweh's impending punishment. He predicted exile for the people with eventual restoration.

Russell Fuller

JEREMIAS, JOACHIM (1900–79)

This German Lutheran New Testament scholar taught first at Greifswald (1929) and then at Göttingen (1935). According to Robert Morgan and John Barton, Jeremias pursued the quest of the historical Jesus, employing "history of traditions methods to peel off the layers of Gospel tradition in pursuit of the historical Jesus behind them" (*Biblical Interpretation* [Oxford: Oxford University Press, 1988] 123).

Jeremias was the author of *Eucharistic Words of Jesus* (German 1935, English trans-

lation 1966); *The Parables of Jesus* (German 1947, English translation 1954). In both of these works, he sought to recover the *ipsissima verba Jesu*, the words of Jesus himself, by reconstructing the original Aramaic spoken by Jesus on the basis of the Greek accounts found in the New Testament. His book *The Parables of Jesus* was the most influential work of its time on the parables, for in it Jeremias drew on his prodigious knowledge of first-century Palestine to explain the details of everyday life on which the parables drew. In addition, Jeremias pointed out that the parables underwent changes as they moved from Jesus himself to the oral teaching of the early church and then to their final incorporation into the text of the New Testament Gospels. Jeremias also wrote *Jerusalem in the Time of Jesus* (German 1962, English translation 1969); and *Theology of the New Testament* (German 1971, English translation 1971).

A key contribution of Jeremias to the understanding of New Testament theology was his preference for the notion of "realizing eschatology" in place of the exclusively future eschatology of Albert Schweitzer and Rudolf Bultmann on the one hand, and C. H. Dodd's notion of "realized eschatology" on the other. Jeremias held that, for Jesus, the reign of God was both a present reality and a reality yet to come.

Jean-Pierre Ruiz

See also ABBA; ARAMAIC; BULTMANN, RUDOLF; DODD, CHARLES H.; ESCHATOLOGY; JESUS OF HISTORY; PARABLE; SCHWEITZER, ALBERT; TRADITIO-HISTORICAL CRITICISM.

JEROME (347?–419)

Eusebius Hieronymus was born in Dalmatia and educated in Rome. He gave up a career in the Roman government to form a monastic community with several of his friends, including Rufinus of Aquileia. This friendship ended when the two monks split over the Origenist controversy. Jerome moved to Syria to practice a stricter monasticism, and there he learned Hebrew, perfected his Greek, and studied biblical exegesis. Involved in the church politics of Antioch, Jerome moved first to Constantinople and then to Rome. In Rome, he became friends with the wealthy Marcella and Paula of Rome. Throughout his life, Jerome's work was supported and funded by these women and their families. After a long journey with Paula, Jerome settled in Bethlehem where he lived out the rest of his life. Jerome is best known for his translation of the Bible into Latin, the so-called Vulgate that became the standard text of the medieval Western church. However, he produced many other important translations, commentaries on Scripture, and theologicial tracts. A passionate, sometimes excessive, but certainly brilliant person, Jerome was one the most influential of the early church writers.

Gary Macy

See also EXEGESIS/EISEGESIS; MARCELLA; ORIGENISM; PAULA OF ROME; RUFINUS OF AQUILEIA; VULGATE.

JERUSALEM (FOR CHRISTIANS)

The New Testament records that Jerusalem was the site of the final days of Jesus' ministry, passion, death, and burial. Some experienced the risen Christ in Jerusalem (Matt 28:9-10; Mark 16:9, 14; Luke 24:34-49; John 20:11-29). Acts recounts that the Spirit descended on those followers of Jesus who were gathered in a room in the city; the earliest Jesus movement was centered in and spread out from Jerusalem.

Rome destroyed the Temple and razed Jerusalem in 70 C.E., and razed it again during the Bar Kochba rebellion in 135 C.E. Hadrian, the emperor, then renamed Jerusalem Aelia Capitolina (135–326), expelled all Jews from the city, and transformed it into a pagan center. Since Christians in the area were Jewish converts, it is unlikely that any Christians remained in the city.

Constantine renamed the city Jerusalem, transformed the city into a Christian center, and sponsored an effort to locate the sites associated with Jesus. Since that time, Jerusalem and its immediate surroundings have been a destination for Christian pilgrims. Most of these sites are verified only by legends of miraculous events associated with their identification. It is impossible to determine if any Christians in the surrounding areas were consulted or knew many of the actual locations.

Hadrian had constructed a major temple on the site on which the Church of the Holy Sepulchre (also known as the *Anastasis*) is now situated. The present church that dates from the Crusader period contains some of the columns that adorned the shrines built by Constantine. Within the walls of the church are the traditional sites of Jesus' crucifixion and burial. Many believe that it would have been unlikely that even Constantine would have razed a temple to construct a church without a powerful tradition associated with that particular place. While the evidence is and will remain inconclusive, this traditional site of Jesus' death and burial has a good claim to authenticity.

Recently, archeologists from the École Biblique et Archéologique Française de Jérusalem explored a site that has an enormous claim to being where John situated his account of the miracle by the

Sheep Gate (John 5:1-9). The historical location of any other of the events situated in Jerusalem in the New Testament cannot be identified with virtual certainty. However, all the traditional sites presently identified with specific events are consecrated by the prayers of Christians over the centuries.

When Islam swept through the Middle East, Jerusalem fell into Muslim control. Various Crusades were led by European nobles. Sovereignty over the city moved back and forth between Christians and Muslims until it stabilized with the Ottoman Empire. However, Christian pilgrims were allowed access to their holy sites. Today, as the capital of the State of Israel, Jerusalem welcomes Christian pilgrims from around the world.

Christians have not only considered Jerusalem as a historical location, but have applied Jerusalem as a metaphor for the church, the human soul, and for heaven. John Cassian (d. about 435) illustrated the four senses of Scripture (literal, allegorical, moral, and eschatological) that dominated medieval exegesis with these four meanings of Jerusalem. Such applications appear to be expansions of Old Testament references to the city of Zion to speak of God's special presence that was uniquely associated with the Temple. Christians adopted this metaphorical use very early. In addition, the book of Revelation identifies the site of eschatological existence as Jerusalem. While a metaphorical use of Jerusalem is not prominent today, the image continues to function in Christian hymns and popular piety.

Regina A. Boisclair

JERUSALEM (FOR JEWS)
Judaism's holy city since the construction there of the First Temple by Solomon in about 950 B.C.E. As the site of the Temple and sacrificial cult, to which all Israelite males were obligated to make a pilgrimage three times a year (Deut 16:16), Jerusalem remained the center of Jewish worship until the Romans' destruction of the Second Temple in 70 C.E. In the aftermath of the cessation of the cult and the end of the position of Jerusalem as the capital of the Jewish theocratic state, the city assumed a symbolic role in Jewish theology and messianic yearning. In Jewish liturgy and thought, the city's past was glorified and its future rebuilding viewed as a principal sign of the arrival of the messianic age. For many Jews, the renewed Jewish presence in Jerusalem since the formation of the State of Israel in 1948 along with the reunification of the city following the Israeli–Arab war of 1967 symbolize the beginning of God's redemption and of the fulfillment of the Jews' covenant with God. In Jerusalem, the Western Wall, also called the Wailing Wall, is the one remaining section of the destroyed Temple and is the holiest site in Judaism, a place of pilgrimage for Jews from around the world.

Alan J. Avery-Peck

JERUSALEM (FOR MUSLIMS)
The third holiest city in Islam (after Mecca and Medina). Muslims call Jerusalem *al-Quds* in Arabic, meaning "the Holy." The prominence of Jerusalem stems in part from its place of honor in the Bible. Because Muslims believe that Islam completes and, where necessary, corrects Judaism and Christianity, they revere Jerusalem as the home of great Jewish prophets and of Jesus. More importantly, however, it was the city where the Prophet's famous *mi'raj* (Night Journey) began. According to the Qur'an (17:1), Muhammad (570–632) was miraculously

transported by the power of God from the Ka'ba in Mecca to the Dome of the Rock on the Temple Mount in Jerusalem. Tradition has it that the angel Gabriel ascended with the Prophet from the Dome of the Rock to see the heavens. The Muslim armies captured Jerusalem in 638, and except for a relatively brief period of time (1095–1187), the ancient part of the city remained under Islamic control until the Six-Day War in 1967.

Ronald A. Pachence

See also DOME OF THE ROCK; ISLAM; JESUS (AS PROPHET OF ISLAM); KA'BA/KAABA; MECCA; MEDINA; MIRAJ/MI'RAJ; MUHAMMAD.

JERUSALEM, SYNOD OF

Also known as the Synod of Bethlehem, it is the most important gathering of bishops in the history of the Eastern Orthodox Churches, after the ecumenical councils. Held in 1672 in Bethlehem (not in Jerusalem!) and brought together by the Orthodox patriarch of Jerusalem, this synod (as Jassy had done thirty years before) condemned Calvinism. The decrees of the Synod of Jerusalem actually brought Western Catholicism and Eastern Orthodoxy doctrinally closer to each other. This synod defined (among many other things) that the ancient traditions of the church are as infallible as the Scriptures, that one may not separate faith and works, that there are seven sacraments ("mysteries," as they are called), and so forth. The Synod of Jerusalem, as the one of Jassy had done, accepted the *Orthodox Confession* of Archbishop Peter Mogila. The doctrinal decrees of the synod are regarded as obligatory among the Orthodox Churches.

Orlando Espín

See also CALVINISM; CATHOLIC TRADITION; FAITH; JASSY, SYNOD OF; MOGILA, PETER; ORTHODOX CHURCHES; PATRIARCH; SYNODS; TRADITION (IN CHRISTIANITY).

JESUS (AS PROPHET OF ISLAM)

Muslims call Jesus Isa ibn Maryam, or Isa, son of Mary. They also refer to him as *masih* or messiah (Christ), though according to Islamic thought, he is the messiah in the sense that he is God's special messenger sent only to "the Children of Israel" (Qur'an 3:49). Muslims, therefore, do not accept Jesus as the savior of the world, nor do they believe he is divine, or the Son of God (5:17). These claims, Muslims say, were made by the followers of Jesus—not by Jesus himself (9:30). In fact, the Qur'an, the sacred scripture of Islam, teaches (61:6) that Jesus thought of himself as a prophetic messenger of God, and in this capacity he predicted the coming "Ahmad" (Muhammad). This belief gives Jesus the status of a great prophet in the Islamic tradition and a precursor of the Prophet of Islam, Muhammad (570–632).

Though his divine nature and universal salvific mission are rejected, the Qur'an affirms several biblical teachings about Jesus. These include his virginal conception (3:45-47), his miracles, referred to as "signs" or "clear signs" in the Qur'an (3:49), and his proclamation of the Gospel (5:46). Because, however, the evangelists did not accurately record the "Glad Tidings" of Jesus, Muslims hold that the scriptures Christians call the Gospel contain errors and misinformation that are corrected by the Qur'an.

Besides the mistaken doctrine of Jesus' divinity, the Qur'an denies that Jesus was crucified, and by implication, if he was not crucified, he could not have been raised from the dead on the third day. According to the Qur'an, Jesus only "appeared" to be crucified (4:157), though in a manner not fully understood, God "raised him up unto Himself" (4:158), perhaps in the sense of giving him great honor.

A more accurate understanding of Jesus and his mission, Muslims say, is found in the testimony of his disciples, recorded in the Qur'an: "They said, 'We have faith, and do thou bear witness that we bow to Allah as Muslims'" (5:111). Muslims would, therefore, say that Jesus proclaimed the message of Islam and for this reason he is respected as one of Islam's greatest Prophets.

Ronald A. Pachence

See also ISLAM; MUHAMMAD; QUR'AN; REVELATION (IN ISLAM).

JESUS OF HISTORY

New Testament scholars and theologians have found it methodologically helpful to distinguish the "Jesus of history" from "the Christ of faith." The Jesus of history represents what can be known about Jesus from the available historical avenues: biblical and a number of nonbiblical texts from the time of Jesus, archeological research, and cross-cultural studies of life in the ancient Mediterranean world. Forming a picture of the historical Jesus is not simple, since the primary documents (the four canonical Gospels in their present form) were probably not composed by eyewitnesses. Historians of the Gospels have not always acknowledged the limitations of their search for Jesus. Nevertheless, scholars can move carefully through the Gospel texts and recover, through the various layers of tradition, a fairly reliable portrait of the ministry and teaching of Jesus as he was remembered by his followers. We have no direct access, however, into his psyche. Whatever we know

about the historical figure Jesus of Nazareth, we know principally through the eyes and ears of those who were close to him.

Of course, those who initially followed Jesus eventually confessed him to be the Son of God; they believed and bore witness that God had raised Jesus from the dead. Even before the Resurrection, the disciples responded to his message about the kingdom of God and entrusted themselves to Jesus as their teacher or rabbi. The Jesus of the early apostolic witness and preaching is known as the Christ of faith, where "Christ" means God's anointed one or messiah. The Jesus who is preached is thus known as "the Christ." What we know about Jesus as the Christ or Messiah of God comes to us from the New Testament writings and the subsequent history of Christian worship and practice. The Christ of faith is the Jesus of the church's experience, the risen or "real" Jesus who is known in faith and through prayer. The Jesus of history and the Christ of faith are continuous with each other. The Jesus to whom the Christian community relates in faith has a history, and that history constantly informs Christian imagination.

William Reiser, S.J.

See also CHRIST OF FAITH; CHRISTOLOGY.

JEWISH AGENCY, THE

The international, nongovernmental body, centered in Jerusalem that is the executive body and representative of the World Zionist Organization. It encourages and assists Jews throughout the world to aid in the settlement and development of the Land of Israel.

Founded in 1929, the Agency was recognized by the British Mandate over Palestine as the political body representing

Zionism in Palestine. With the establishment of the State of Israel in 1948, many of the functions of the Agency became governmental. However, the Agency maintained many activities, including responsibility for immigration and absorption, land settlement, and work in agricultural settlements. It continues to engage in many activities outside Israel, including encouragement of immigration, youth involvement with Israel, and encouragement of investment in Israel. It is the chief vehicle for support of world Jewry for the State of Israel, as it collects and distributes funds for social service programs within Israel.

Wayne Dosick

See also ERETZ YISRAEL; MEDINAT YISRAEL.

JEWISH RENEWAL MOVEMENT

A contemporary Jewish religious movement characterized by Jews seeking a deep spiritual connection to God, to the higher self, and to a community of friends through fully participatory, egalitarian worship—often combined with ancient meditative practices—intense study, and joyous celebration.

While the Jewish Renewal Movement does not have the number of adherents, or the same organizational structure as the main movements within Judaism—Orthodox, Conservative, Reform, and Reconstructionist—it is growing in numbers and enthusiasm.

The founder and "grandfather" of the Jewish Renewal Movement is Rabbi Zalman Schachter-Shalomi.

Wayne Dosick

See also JUDAISM; RABBINIC JUDAISM; RECONSTRUCTIONIST JUDAISM; REFORM JUDAISM.

JIHAD

Considered by some Muslims to be the sixth pillar (foundational belief or practice) of Islam, *jihad* literally means "striving" or "exerting effort" in the cause of God and God's religion, Islam. Frequently interpreted by Western journalists and used by Muslim extremist groups to mean "holy war," it is important to note the theological nuances of this word in order to understand it properly.

Actually, Muslims speak of two kinds of jihad: the greater and the lesser. The greater jihad has nothing to do with armed conflict. It is rather the spiritual struggle all Muslims must engage in to combat the forces of evil within themselves. When Muslims face challenges to their faith, or have doubts about their commitment to Islam, or have temptations of any kind, their confrontation of these threats to their fidelity is jihad. The lesser jihad, however, may indeed involve armed conflict, but even here non-Muslims should take great care to understand what Islam says on the subject.

Most Muslims, for example, would include as part of the lesser jihad efforts to overcome ignorance of Islam and social injustice. This would include providing correct information about the faith, helping the needy, and working to overcome economic inequities. It is only when, as a last resort, Islam must defend itself by force of arms or when Muslims living in non-Muslim countries are prohibited from practicing their faith unless they fight for this right, that jihad in the sense of "war" is permitted. It is further required that an armed conflict should not begin unless there is a reasonable prospect of success and that once the danger has subsided, jihad should cease immediately. Under no circumstances can a war among Muslims be called jihad.

A proper appreciation of the lesser jihad is somewhat complicated by the Islamic understanding of the *dar a-harb* (the "abode of war") that technically includes any territory inhabited by unbelievers and that, according to the Qur'an (8:60), is an enemy of Islam. It is further complicated by the claim of militant radicals ("jihadists") that God sanctions—indeed commands—unconditional war against dar a-harb "infidels." But even here, the Qur'an (the sacred scripture of Islam) does not call for indiscriminate armed conflict with perceived adversaries. This is clearly stated in 8:61 of the Qur'an: "If the enemy incline toward peace, do thou also incline towards peace, and trust in Allah . . ."

Ronald A. Pachence

See also DAR AL-HARB; FIVE PILLARS (IN ISLAM); INFIDELS; ISLAM; ISLAMIC RADICALISM (FUNDAMENTALISM); KAFIR; QUR'AN.

JIMÉNEZ DE CISNEROS, FRANCISCO (1436–1517)

Spanish reformer, statesman, humanist, and cardinal archbishop of Toledo. After a brief career in minor diocesan administrative posts, he became a friar, leading a very austere life. In 1492 he reluctantly became confessor to Queen Isabel of Castile, and soon thereafter his advice was sought on all sorts of matters by the queen. He successfully carried out a thorough and difficult reform of the conventual Franciscans in Spain, and was thereafter appointed archbishop of Toledo, primate of Spain, and later cardinal of the church. He also became the royal chancellor of Castile (similar to a prime minister), but in spite of the honors and dignities, Jiménez de Cisneros continued his life of austerity. Due to a number of circum-stances, he became regent first of Castile, then of Aragon, and later of unified Spain. He founded the famous university at Alcalá, and was notorious for his lavish support of the arts and sciences. Jiménez de Cisneros did much to further the conversion of Spanish Muslims to Christianity, and was responsible for reviving the nearly dead Mozarabic Church. His most lasting contribution to scholarship was the important translation of the Bible commonly called *Complutensian Polyglot*.

Orlando Espín

See also ARCHBISHOP; CARDINAL; HUMANISM; MEDIEVAL CHRISTIANITY (IN THE WEST); MEDIEVAL CHURCH; MOZARABIC CATHOLIC CHURCH; PRIMATE/PRIMATIAL SEE.

JINA

An Indic word meaning "victor" or "conqueror," *Jina* is an honorific title in Jainism for the renowned saints of the tradition, especially its twenty-four most revered teachers, the Tirthankaras. It suggests a being who has conquered the world in a spiritual sense, that is, one who has achieved victory over karma, ignorance, desire, and the other obstacles to liberation. The word is also used in Buddhist literature as a title for the Buddha.

Lance E. Nelson

See also BUDDHISM; JAINISM.

JINN

Plural Arabic noun (singular: *jinni*) for a species of spiritual beings said to have been created "from fire free of smoke" (Qur'an 55:15). While the Qur'an, the sacred scripture of Islam, identifies Iblis (the devil) with the *jinn* (18:50), it also speaks of them as spirits capable of belief or unbelief (72:1-15). Some Islamic commentators have identified the jinn with the good and evil qualities of the human personality. Besides these religious understandings of the term, the jinn are also the subject of Middle Eastern folklore where they are described as magical beings capable of helping humans or causing mischief, usually the latter. They appear unexpectedly from their hiding places, do their work, and then vanish again, as in stories about the "genie" who comes out of the bottle.

Ronald A. Pachence

See also IBLIS; ISLAM; QUR'AN.

JIVA

A Sanskrit word that means, roughly, "soul," *jiva* is used in Indic religious traditions (other than Buddhism) to designate the entity that transmigrates from life to life in the process of reincarnation. In systems like Hindu Vaishnavism and Jainism that recognize a plurality of souls, the jiva is an individual entity or substance whose primary characteristics are consciousness, bliss, and eternal being. The infinite number of jivas that populate the universe are quantitatively distinct but qualitatively the same. (Dvaita Vedanta is an exception; it recognizes a *qualitative* difference among jivas.) In any case, the jiva in these systems is the true, eternal essence of spiritual selfhood, to be distinguished from the mental and physical self. The concept of the jiva in Advaita Vedanta, however, is rather different. In this influential nondualist system, only one authentic Self, termed Atman, is recognized. The term jiva is still used to refer to the individual transmigrating "souls," but these are understood as temporary products of the reflection of the one Atman in the many individual minds. The jiva is therefore said in Advaita to be a product of igno-rance (*avidya*), a false superimposition of limited, individual selfhood on the one infinite Self, and as such destined to dissolve when true knowledge of the Atman is attained.

Lance E. Nelson

See also ADVAITA VEDANTA; DVAITA VEDANTA; JAINISM; SOUL; VAISHNAVA; VEDANTA; VISHISTADVAITA VEDANTA.

JIZO

(Japanese, *Ksitigarbha*). A Buddhist bodhisattva (saint) of benevolence and mercy, called Ti-Tsang in China, who, on behalf of grieving relatives, stands between this world and the next to save those on their way to hell. In Japan he has filled numerous roles, including an intermediary between the living and the dead, special protector of children, an aide to women in the ordeal of childbirth, a guide to those in danger of going astray, and at times has been identified with the Shinto war god Hachiman and consequently a favorite of Japanese soldiers. Along with Kannon and Amida, he is the most popular of the bodhisattvas in Japanese Buddhism.

G. D. DeAngelis

See also AMITABHA/AMIDA; BODHISATTVA; BUDDHISM; KUAN-YIN.

JNANA

The Sanskrit word for knowledge, *jnana* refers in Indic religions to contemplative or supersensory knowledge, especially (in Hinduism) to the direct knowledge of Brahman, the Absolute. In pronunciation, as in the case of its Greek and English cognates (*gnōsis*, knowledge), the first consonant is generally silent.

Lance E. Nelson

See also ADVAITA VEDANTA; HINDUISM; JNANA-YOGA.

JNANA-YOGA

In Hinduism, *jnana-yoga* is the yoga, or spiritual discipline, of knowledge. As a yoga, it is a method of attaining direct awareness of Brahman, the Absolute, in this case through a kind of intellectual mysticism, involving (1) study of scripture (especially the Upanishads) and related commentarial literature, (2) careful reasoning about the teachings expressed therein, and (3) deep meditative reflection. The chief object of this intellectual contemplation is the identity of one's inner Self (Atman) with Brahman. To make this truth a direct, vivid realization, one must practice a kind of intellectual discrimination, rejecting all that is other than the Atman—including world, body, and mind—as false projections of *maya*, the mysterious power that conjures up the world appearance. The yoga of knowledge, to be effective, is said to require the direct supervision of an enlightened guru, whose verbal instruction catalyzes one's final realization. Associated especially with Advaita Vedanta, *jnana-yoga* was traditionally a path open only to *sannyasins*, world renouncers, although in modern Hinduism it is being taken up also by the laity.

Lance E. Nelson

See also ADVAITA VEDANTA; ATMAN; BRAHMAN; GURU; SANNYASA; UPANISHADS; YOGA.

JOACHIM OF FIORE (1135?–1202)

The early years of Joachim's life are not known. He was a monk at the Cistercian monastery of Casamari before becoming abbot of his own monastery at Corazzo. Joachim later founded his own order, the Florensians, at the monastery of San Giovanni in Fiore. Joachim was famous during the later years of his life for his writings on Scripture that divided all time into three ages: the age of the Father, dominated by the laity; the age of the Son, dominated by the clergy; and the final age of the Spirit, dominated by monks. In reading Scripture in a historical sense, Joachim revived the apocalyptic tradition and soon after his death, several different groups claimed that they represented the third age of Joachim's predictions. The two Spiritual Franciscans, Gerard of Borgo San Donnino and Peter John Olivi, relied heavily on the teaching of Joachim to demonstrate that the Franciscans were the monks predicted by Joachim to dominate the third age. In an important sense, Joachim is the forerunner of the many writers since his time who have tried to tie present political events to Scripture in order to predict the end of the world. Joachim probably never intended such a result, and his orthodoxy was approved by the pope in 1220.

Gary Macy

See also APOCALYPTIC; MEDIEVAL CHRISTIANITY (IN THE WEST); SPIRITUAL FRANCISCANS.

JOAN OF ARC (1412?–31)

Also known as "La Pucelle" or as the "Maid of Orléans," Joan was born into a peasant family in the village of Domremy during the Hundred Years War between France and England. France was in the midst of a civil war when King Henry V of England invaded French territory in 1415, claiming to be the rightful heir to the throne of France. Henry won an important battle at Agincourt and soon gained the support of the Burgundian faction of the civil war. England and Burgundy controlled most of France when they attacked the city of Orléans in 1428. Although Joan claimed to have visions of saints from an early age, in 1428 she said that visions of

St. Catherine, St. Margaret, and St. Michael urged her to lead an army against the English and the Burgundians in defense of Charles of Ponthieu, the last heir of the Valois dynasty of France. After three unsuccessful attempts, Joan met Charles, impressing him with her ability to recognize him despite a disguise and by a secret sign that Charles never revealed. After three weeks of examination by theologians, Joan was approved by the court and given titular command of the army. Joan donned armor and carried a white banner with the words "Jesus–Mary." Encouraged and led by Joan, the French army took the city of Orléans back from the English, and a series of other French victories (also led by Joan) culminated in the consecration of Charles as king of France (Charles VII) on July 17, 1429. Joan gradually lost influence at court, and by 1430 only had command over a small band of soldiers. While leading this reduced army, Joan was captured by the Burgundians on May 23, 1430. They turned her over to the English who tried her in the city of Rouen for heresy and witchcraft. The transcripts of the trial show Joan to be an intelligent and even witty adversary. Condemned, among other things, for wearing men's clothes, Joan was burned at the stake on May 30, 1431. An appellate court appointed by Pope Callistus III overturned the verdict of Joan's trial in 1456. She was canonized by the Catholic Church in 1920 and is the second patron saint of France. Her story has inspired many writers, musicians, and filmmakers.

Gary Macy

See also CATHERINE OF SIENA; HERESY; SAINTS (CHRISTIAN), DEVOTION TO.

JOAN (STORY OF THE POPESS)
Starting in the thirteenth century, a story was told of a learned woman scholar, disguised as a man, who was elected pope sometime around the year 1000, or in some versions, after the pontificate of Leo IV who died in 855. According to the legend, the deception was discovered two years into the papacy when the pope gave birth to a child during a procession. There is no historical evidence that any such "Pope Joan" ever existed, but the story may have its basis in the reign of Pope John XII, whose grandmother, Marozia, had considerable influence over the papacy.

Gary Macy

See also JOHN XII, POPE; MEDIEVAL CHRISTIANITY (IN THE WEST).

JOCHANAN BEN ZAKKAI
Living in the first century C.E., this was a teacher and sage who survived the destruction of the Holy Temple in Jerusalem in 70 C.E. and founded the Academy at Yavneh.

According to legend, Ben Zakkai's students smuggled him out of Jerusalem in a coffin. He appealed to the Roman general for a parcel of land on which to live, and was granted the small town of Yavneh. There, he is credited with saving Judaism.

With the destruction of the Holy Temple, the priests were no longer able to officiate at the sacrificial rites, and sacrifice as the chief form of worship ceased. Yavneh became the new center of Jewish life, and Ben Zakkai led the development of Judaism in new directions. The synagogue took the place of the Holy Temple; prayer took the place of sacrifices; and scholarly rabbis and sages took the place of the priests. Ben Zakkai insisted that God could be worshiped anywhere—not just in the Holy Temple—and that Judaism could survive wherever there were Jews committed to God and Torah.

Under Ben Zakkai's leadership, Judaism—which could have ceased to exist because its institutions lay in ruins—was revived and renewed, and continued to flourish in a new form.

Wayne Dosick

See also BEIT HAMIKDASH; KOHEN.

JODO SHIN SHU

(Japanese, True Pure Land School). School established by the Buddhist monk Shinran Shonin (1173–1262), who was a disciple of Honen, founder of the Jodo School. Like his teacher Honen, Shinran also proclaimed the saving grace of Amida Buddha, but he took an even more radical departure than Honen from prevailing Tendai doctrine in claiming that the compassion and mercy of Amida, which was his gift to all beings, was enough to guarantee salvation. Not only were good works and faith not required but neither was *nembutsu* practice (Buddha name recitation). In addition, Shinran challenged centuries-old Buddhist tradition by claiming that the requirements for a Buddhist life and salvation could be fulfilled outside monastic life. In effect, he established a new model for Buddhist religious life by taking on a family and showing devotion to Buddhist practice and thought while immersed in lay life as well. This feature of monks engaging in family life became a distinctive aspect of Japanese Buddhism. Jodo Shin Shu, because of its inclusiveness and guarantee of salvation, has become the most popular form of Buddhism in Japan.

G. D. DeAngelis

See also AMITABHA/AMIDA; BUDDHISM; HONEN; JODO SHU; KAMAKURA PERIOD; NEMBUTSU; PURE LAND BUDDHISM; SHINRAN; TENDAI.

JODO SHU

(Japanese, Pure Land School). Japanese Buddhist school founded by the monk Honen (1133–1212) during the Kamakura Period (1185–1333). This sect developed out of the Tendai School and opposed the Tendai belief that a strenuous life of good works was necessary for salvation. Honen claimed that during the degenerate age (*mappo*) of the Dharma (Buddha's teaching), all that was needed for salvation was faith in the saving grace of Amida Buddha, and that a life of good works was unnecessary. The focus of practice in the Jodo School was the repetition of the formula praise to Amida Buddha (*nembutsu*). The nembutsu and faith in Amida Buddha were enough to deliver one after death, through the infinite compassion and mercy of Amida Buddha, to the Pure Land.

G. D. DeAngelis

See also AMITABHA/AMIDA; BUDDHISM; HONEN; JODO SHIN SHU; KAMAKURA PERIOD; NEMBUTSU; PURE LAND BUDDHISM; SHINRAN; TENDAI.

JOHANNINE CORPUS

A group of five New Testament books, also known as the Johannine literature, which, because of various similarities, some have assumed were written by one and the same author, John the apostle of Jesus and son of Zebedee. Of these five books, namely the Gospel of John, the epistles 1, 2, and 3 John, and the book of Revelation, only Revelation actually contains the name of its author in the text (1:4). The Johannine authorship of the other four is an attribution coming from post-New Testament tradition.

According to John 21:24, the traditions upon which the Gospel are based came from the "Beloved Disciple." While this person is not named in the Gospel, he has traditionally, but perhaps inaccurately, been equated with John the son of Zebedee, who was held to have lived in Ephesus after the death of Jesus and to have written the Gospel there. There are many problems in these links, however. For example, John 21:23 suggests that actually the Beloved Disciple did not live very long. Also, it is doubtful that any immediate follower of Jesus actually wrote the whole Gospel since it reflects the hand of a number of redactors and a highly developed theology most likely coming from late in the first century C.E. This leads to the final form of the text generally being dated between 90–100 C.E. Many therefore suggest that the Gospel is most likely the product of a Johannine school of Christianity, which perhaps began with a group linked to the Beloved Disciple and his teachings and may even have been written in Ephesus, although Syria, perhaps Antioch, and Alexandria, have been suggested as well.

The theory of a Johannine school further explains the similarities between the Gospel and the three epistles of John that are widely judged as coming from authors other than those who wrote the Gospel, yet evidently being products of the same school or group. While 1 John gives no name for its author, 2 and 3 John are identified as being written by "the Elder."

In the book of Revelation, also called the Apocalypse, the author, obviously writing during a time of persecution, is said to be a certain John who was exiled because of his faith on the Aegean island of Patmos, off the coast of Asia Minor. Nothing in the text, however, connects him with either John the son of Zebedee or with the Elder who wrote 2 and 3 John.

F. M. Gillman

See also JOHN THE EVANGELIST; NEW TESTAMENT LETTERS.

JOHN (JUAN) OF AVILA (1499–1569)

Spanish Catholic reformer and teacher. From a Jewish family newly converted to Catholicism, John studied at Salamanca and at Alcalá. He was ordained to the priesthood and started leading a life of great pastoral activity. Falsely accused of heresy, he was imprisoned. There he wrote his masterpiece, *Audi filia* (1531). Once freed of all charges, he went to southern Spain's Andalusía region and became a tireless preacher and teacher. Although he once thought of joining the newly founded Society of Jesus, he decided to support it by sending it his best followers. He had an immense impact on several generations of important Spanish Christians (for example, Francis Borgia, Teresa of Avila, John of the Cross, John of God), who in turn influenced the whole church. John of Avila was canonized by the Catholic Church in 1970.

Orlando Espín

See also CANONIZATION; COUNTER-REFORMATION/CATHOLIC REFORMATION; INQUISITION; SOCIETY OF JESUS; SPIRITUALITY; TRENT, COUNCIL OF.

JOHN CHRYSOSTOM (345/355?–407)

Born into a wealthy family in Antioch, John was trained for a career in the imperial service. He gave up his career first to study Scripture at Antioch and then to move to a more severe form of life as a hermit. His health damaged by ascetic practice, he moved back to Antioch where he became famous for sermons, earning the nickname "Golden Mouth" (in Greek, *Chrysostom*). Against his wishes, John was made patriarch of Constantinople in 398 where he made powerful enemies, particularly the empress, Eudoxia, by his preaching against the corruption of the imperial court. His enemies first framed him on heresy charges, and when this strategy failed, they had him banished. He finally died in 407 when, despite poor health, he was forced to travel during inclement weather. Although John wrote several works, he is best known for his powerful, but sometimes overly passionate and even intolerant sermons.

Gary Macy

See also ANTIOCHENE THEOLOGY; EUDOXIA; HERESY; PATRIARCH.

JOHN CLIMACUS (570?–680?)
Eastern Christian monk and spiritual writer. His best-known work is the *Ladder of Paradise*, in which he discusses the monastic life and mysticism as an ascension to paradise. This book had an enormous impact on monasticism during the church's patristic period. ("Ladder," in Greek, is *klimax* that became the nickname history gave John.) He became abbot of a monastery on Mount Sinai and is considered the father of hesychasm (an Orthodox Christian spiritual tradition).

Orlando Espín

See also ABBOT; HESYCHASM; MONASTICISM IN EASTERN CHRISTIANITY; MYSTICISM/MYSTICS (IN CHRISTIANITY); ORTHODOX CHURCHES; ORTHODOX THEOLOGY.

JOHN DAMASCENE
See JOHN OF DAMASCUS.

JOHN OF DAMASCUS (650?–750?)
An Arab Christian, Yanah ibn Masur, better known as John of Damascus, was a member of a distinguished family and as a young man held a ministerial position under Caliph ʿAbd al-Malik. He resigned his position sometime after the year 700, was ordained a priest by the patriarch of Jerusalem, and retired to the monastery of Mar Sabas outside Jerusalem. John wrote in defense of the veneration of icons during the iconoclastic controversy. Of John's extensive theological and exegetical writings, his most famous is the *Font of Knowledge*. This work itself is divided into three parts: a philosophical introduction, a guide to heresies, and an exposition of the faith. John's work was a personal synthesis of the best of the traditions of the early church and became influential not only in the Eastern Church, but also in the Western Church after the translation of the *Font of Knowledge* into Latin in the twelfth century.

Gary Macy

See also HERESY; ICONOCLASTIC CONTROVERSY; ORTHODOX THEOLOGY.

JOHN OF THE CROSS (1542–91)
Born Juan de Yepes et Alvarez, this deeply religious man eventually joined the Carmelite Order and was chosen by Teresa of Avila to assist her in reforming the Ancient Order of Carmel. He did not live in quiet times, but rather in the throes of the Reformation and the Inquisition that rose to counter it. He took the religious name of Juan de la Cruz, and it is as such that he is most known. In the space of a life dedicated to love of God and of the church, he established a unique reputation as a spiritual guide. This was considerably enhanced when Teresa found that only he had the experience to direct her exceptional path in the spiritual life.

Though he would have preferred to avoid the political turmoils of his time, his own order (the members of which had made him the head) fell prey to inner dissension, and he was imprisoned for about a year in wretched conditions. Even under such duress, his own spiritual journey continued to develop, and the fruit of this was evident in his classic treatise, *The Dark Night of the Soul*. Along with other major works that have become established sources of the spiritual life (for example, *The Ascent of Mount Carmel*, *The Spiritual Canticle*, and *The Living Flame of Love*), he was early recognized as one of the true masters of the spiritual life. He died as he had lived, in great poverty and luminous suffering. He was canonized in 1725 by Benedict XIII, and named a Doctor of the Universal Church in 1926 by Pius XI.

Kathleen Dugan

See also INQUISITION; MYSTICISM/
MYSTICS (IN CHRISTIANITY);
REFORMATION; TRENT, COUNCIL OF.

JOHN PAUL II, POPE (1920–2005)

The first Polish pope. Born in Wadowice, Poland (1920), Karol Wojtyla was a student during World War II. Ordained in 1946, awarded the doctorate in theology (1948), and another in philosophy (1960), Wojtyla taught the existential philosophies of Buber, Marcel, and Scheler as professor of ethics at Lublin. Appointed bishop in 1958, he rose rapidly to archbishop of Kraków (1964) and cardinal (1967). He defended the rights of the Polish Catholic Church under communism, attended Vatican Council II and four synods, and was elected pope in 1978. He is renowned for the activist character of his papacy (frequent international pilgrimages, meetings with Catholic youth, the sick, and poor), and by his unrelenting advocacy for social justice. John Paul has reiterated conservative papal teaching on divorce, contraception, abortion, homosexuality, priestly celibacy, and women's ordination. His encyclicals include *Redemptor Hominis*

(1979), *Dives in Misericordia* (1980) and *Laborem Exercens* (1981).

Patricia Plovanich

JOHNSON, ELIZABETH A. (1941–)

Contemporary U.S. Catholic feminist theologian, Elizabeth Johnson holds the position of Distinguished Professor, Systematic Theology, at Fordham University, and belongs to a congregation of women religious, the Sisters of Saint Joseph. She received her doctoral degree from The Catholic University of America in 1981 with a dissertation focused on christology in the theology of Wolfhart Pannenberg. She served as president of the Catholic Theological Society of America, one of the largest associations of Catholic theologians in the United States, and continues to serve on editorial boards of scholarly theological journals, such as *Theological Studies* and *Horizons*.

Johnson is widely known in the United States and around the globe for her constructive theological projects regarding the Trinity, christology, pneumatology, ecclesiology, and Mariology, all elaborated from a critical feminist theological perspective solidly grounded in Catholic theological traditions and in women's experiences in a patriarchal church and society. Johnson's most innovative contributions to contemporary theology demonstrate the "effective history" of the emphasis on the maleness of Jesus, which raises significant questions about women's ability to identify with and image the divine, to imitate Christ, and to be saved. In other words, the maleness of Jesus has been construed to legitimate androcentric rather than inclusive language for God, to justify the christomorphic character of men and prohibit women from acting *in persona Christi* or representing Christ in ordained priestly ministry, and to possibly challenge the salvation of women by a male savior if, according to classical christology, "what is not assumed is not redeemed." Moreover, Johnson's most constructive contributions to contemporary theology reread the mystery of God and christology from the perspective of the Wisdom literature, or a collection of books in the Old Testament and Apocrypha (such as Proverbs, Sirach, Wisdom of Solomon) that describe a female personification of the divine. In the book of Proverbs, Wisdom plays the roles of prophetic street preacher, creator, and banquet hostess of justice and peace. In intertestamental texts like the Wisdom of Solomon, Wisdom participates in creating, redeeming, and sustaining everyday life. For Johnson, the figure of Wisdom is God, revealed, active, and relationally present in the world. Moreover, portraying Jesus as Wisdom and/or as a prophet of Wisdom supports a retelling of the story of the person and work of Jesus that counteracts the "effective history" of an androcentric christology and God-talk, of women's inability to image both God and Jesus and to be saved.

Her major books include: *Consider Jesus: Waves of Renewal in Christology* (1990); *She Who Is: The Mystery of God in Feminist Theological Discourse* (1992); *Women, Earth, and Creator Spirit* (1993); *Friends of God and Prophets* (1998); *The Church Women Want* (2002); and *Truly Our Sister: A Theology of Mary in the Communion of Saints* (2003).

Rosemary P. Carbine

JOHNSON, SAMUEL (1696–1772)

Born in Guilford, Connecticut, Johnson was a theologian, pastor, and first president of King's College (later Columbia University). He became well known in 1722 when, as a Congregational pastor in West Haven, Connecticut, he joined other pastors and Yale College faculty in defecting from the Congregational Church (then the established church in the colony) to seek ordination within the Church of England. Influenced by Bishop Berkeley's idealistic philosophy, Johnson was persuaded by the validity of episcopacy and the rationalism of Anglican theology. He became a moderate Arminian and staunch Tory, advocating natural morality and the appointment of an Anglican bishop to the colonies. Along with Jonathan Edwards, Johnson sought to resolve the tensions inherent in Puritanism, although his resolution radically differed from that of Edwards.

Evelyn A. Kirkley

See also ANGLICAN COMMUNION; ARMINIANISM; CONGREGATIONAL THEOLOGIES; EDWARDS, JONATHAN; IDEALISM, CLASSICAL GERMAN; PURITANISM.

JOHN THE BAPTIST

Named in all four canonical Gospels and in Josephus as a mentor for, a precursor to, and the one who baptized Jesus. He was a prophet who lived in the wilderness and practiced asceticism. He preached "a baptism of repentance for the forgiveness of sins" (Mark 1:4). Rejected and harshly attacked by the Pharisees, Sadducees, and the unrepentant powerful, he was ultimately put to death by order of the ruler, Herod Antipas. According to the Gospel of Mark, the Baptist's death came about through the instigation of the wife of Antipas, Herodias, and her daughter, and was due to Herodias' revenge for John's preaching about the immorality of her marriage to Antipas. The historian Josephus, in his *Antiquities* 18.116-119, attributes John's death to the fear Antipas had of his political power over crowds.

In his preaching, John proclaimed an imminent day of wrath for the unrepentant. Those who did believe in his message, including, for example, outcasts such as tax collectors and harlots, were baptized. One of those who went out to the desert to hear him, and who may have been one of his followers initially, was Jesus. Like many others, Jesus was baptized by John.

John Gillman

See also HEROD; INFANCY NARRATIVES; JOSEPHUS (FLAVIUS).

JOHN THE EVANGELIST

One of the twelve apostles who, according to tradition, was the author of the Gospel of John, the three epistles of John, and the book of Revelation. John was the son of Zebedee and the brother of James. Probably due to the impetuous character of the two brothers, both of whom were fishermen like their father, Mark 3:17 indicates that Jesus called them *Boanerges,* which Mark translates as "sons of thunder." The Gospels portray John as one of the first followers of the itinerant Jesus during his Galilean ministry and as one of the Twelve called apostles. Throughout Matthew, Mark, and Luke, John plays a consistent role in the events of Jesus' life and ministry. According to Acts, following the death of Jesus, he was a member of the Jerusalem community of believers and one of the leaders of the assembly, since Paul in Galatians 2:9-10 mentions him along with James and Cephas as one of the "pillars" of that group of Christians.

Ecclesiastical tradition, now widely debated in scholarship, has equated this John the son of Zebedee with the Beloved Disciple, who presumed to have written the Gospel of John. Tradition also held that, following upon his leadership role in the Jerusalem church, John moved to Ephesus (taking Mary, the mother of Jesus, with him) and that he died there at an old age. During his Ephesian period, John was held to have been banished for a time to the island of Patmos, as witnessed by his assumed authorship of the book of Revelation.

In addition to the Gospel of John and the book of Revelation, tradition also attributed the epistles 1, 2, and 3 John to this apostle. Historical criticism, however, has demonstrated that all five books, the so-called Johannine Corpus, cannot be by the same author, and that, furthermore, it is unlikely that John the son of Zebedee was the author of any of them. That he might nevertheless be at the origins of a Johannine school of Christianity, whose members produced the corpus, is a possibility widely considered.

F. M. Gillman

See also JOHANNINE CORPUS; NEW TESTAMENT LETTERS; TWELVE, THE (IN SCRIPTURE).

JOHN XII, POPE (?–964)

With Pope John XII, the papacy reached one of its lowest points. John XII, who was born Octavian, came from a family that had controlled Rome and the papacy for several generations. His great-grandfather, Theophylact, his grandmother, Marozia, and his father, Alberic, had all tried to make the papacy family property. John became pope because his father had the Romans swear to elect his son, Octavian, as the next pope. When Pope Agapitus II died in 955, the eighteen-year-old Octavian became Pope John XII. When John was faced with invasion by his enemies, he appealed to Emperor

Otto I. Otto saved John, but only after John had sworn allegiance to Otto. When John broke his promise, Otto returned to Italy, deposed John, and demanded that henceforth all papal elections had to be approved by the emperor. At this stage, the papacy passed from control of the noble Roman families to control by the emperors. The stage was set for renewal of the papacy and the beginning of the Investiture Controversy.

Gary Macy

See also INVESTITURE CONTROVERSY; JOAN (STORY OF THE POPESS); MEDIEVAL CHRISTIANITY (IN THE WEST); POPE.

JOHN XXII, POPE (1244–1334)
John was one of the important popes during the time the papal court was in Avignon rather than in Rome. Born Jacques Duése, John was trained in canon law in Paris and Orléans. In 1311 he was ordained bishop of Avignon and in 1312 he was made a cardinal. When John was chosen pope after a two-year vacancy, he immediately began a reform and reorganization of the papal bureaucracy. In doing so, he developed more effective control over the appointment of offices and over taxation of those offices. This did not make him popular, although his reforms did much to improve papal government. John also strongly disagreed with the Spiritual Franciscans and declared their teaching heretical. For this stand, he earned the enmity of William of Ockam, among others. In 1331 John developed a rather idiosyncratic idea about how the deceased might see God in the afterlife. Many theologians were opposed to John's ideas and he changed his mind on this deathbed.

Gary Macy

See also AVIGNON (PAPACY AT); FRANCISCANS; MEDIEVAL CHRISTIAN-ITY (IN THE WEST); OCKHAM, WILLIAM OF; POPE; SPIRITUAL FRANCISCANS.

JOHN XXIII, POPE (1881–1963)
The first person in church history to be called John XXIII was one of the three men claiming to be Pope during the fifteenth century's Great Western Schism. His election is considered invalid, and he is not listed in the official list of popes. The second person to be called John XXIII was born Angelo Giuseppe Roncalli, who was Pope from 1958 until his death in 1963. This is the John XXIII most Catholics remember as one of the twentieth century's most important and beloved pontiffs (and the one this entry refers to).

John XXIII was born to a poor peasant family in a village near Bergamo, Italy. After seminary studies in Bergamo, he was ordained a priest in 1904. He served as an army chaplain during the First World War, and later as head of Italy's official Catholic missionary agency. He became a bishop in 1925 and then began a long and distinguished career as a Vatican diplomat (in Bulgaria, Turkey, Greece, and France). During his time in Turkey he established enduring friendships with the patriarch of Constantinople and others in the Eastern Orthodox Churches. He organized relief efforts during the Second World War and was of significant help to the Jewish community of Istanbul. During the closing months of the war (1944) he was sent as nuncio to France. In 1953 he was made a cardinal of the church by Pope Pius XII, and appointed archbishop of Venice where he displayed great pastoral sensitivity and creativity. Five years later (in 1958) he was unexpectedly elected Pope.

During his years as a seminary student, he had begun writing a spiritual diary he continued throughout his life, and that was published (in 1964) after his death under the title *Journal of a Soul*. He had also published, during his years in Bergamo, a few scholarly works on Italian church history.

The greatest and most enduring achievement of John XXIII's pontificate was the convocation of the Second Vatican Council (which began in 1962). John XXIII hoped that Vatican II would internally renew the church (*aggiornamento*), as well as open it to dialogue with other Christian churches, with Judaism, and with the modern world. The council, continued by his successor, Paul VI, did live up to John XXIII's expectations.

Apart from Vatican II, John XXIII was a promoter of Christian unity, especially with the Orthodox and the Anglican Churches. He significantly expanded the social teachings of Catholicism in his encyclicals *Mater et Magistra* (1961) and *Pacem in Terris* (1963), through which he pleaded for an end to the arms race, for an end to colonialism, and for the establishment of peace based on foundations of justice. He also argued in favor of the dignity of women and ethnic minorities.

When he died in 1963, John XXIII was mourned by Catholics throughout the world. His years as Pope had opened many doors in and for the church, and had given Catholicism a renewed sense of hope, confidence, and enthusiasm. Perhaps no other twentieth-century pope has had a more enduring legacy than he. His immediate successor, Paul VI, began the official proceedings for John XXIII's eventual beatification. He was beatified by John Paul II in 2000.

Orlando Espín

See also AGGIORNAMENTO; ANGLICAN COMMUNION; BEATIFICATION; CARDINAL; CONSTANTINOPLE, SEE OF; MATER ET MAGISTRA; NUNCIO; ORTHODOX CHURCHES; PACEM IN TERRIS; PAUL VI, POPE; POPE; ROMAN CATHOLIC CHURCH; SCHISM, GREAT WESTERN; VATICAN, SECOND COUNCIL OF THE.

JOSEPHINISM

Joseph II, Austrian emperor from 1765 to 1790, implemented a controversial reform of church/state relations. On the one hand, toleration of diverse religions was implemented; on the other hand, interference by the state in religious affairs increased. Some religious orders were suppressed; monasteries lost their independence and were placed under supervision by bishops; papal decrees could be published only if and when authorized by civil sanction.

Josephinism should be viewed in the context of the Enlightenment of the eighteenth century. The measures adopted by Joseph II, sometimes termed "enlightened despotism," were not unlike those adopted elsewhere in Europe at that time. Yet, after the death of Emperor Joseph, many of the reforms he had pursued were repudiated by his successors.

Thomas Worcester, S.J.

See also ENLIGHTENMENT IN WESTERN HISTORY; FEBRONIANISM; GALLICANISM; TOLERATION.

JOSEPHUS (FLAVIUS)
(CA. 37–100 C.E.)

Josephus ben Matthias or Flavius Josephus was a Jewish historian. Born into a priestly family, and also claiming descent from the Hasmoneans, he led the Jewish forces in Galilee at the start of the Jewish revolt against Rome (66–70) until he was captured in 67 at Jotapata by forces of the Roman general Vespasian. He then became an interpreter for the Romans and went with them to Rome at the war's end.

He spent the rest of his life there engaged in writing, supported by the imperial patronage of the Flavians, as is reflected in the additional name he adopted.

Four of his works are extant: *The Jewish War*, an account in seven books that surveys the Jewish revolt, prefaced by an overview of Jewish history from the second century B.C.E.; *The Antiquities of the Jews*, twenty volumes that paraphrase the Jewish Scriptures and also contain the postbiblical history of the Jews; *Against Apion*, a two-part work refuting slander against Jews; and *The Life*, an autobiographical appendix to *The Antiquities*.

The general goals of the works of Josephus were to explain his own Jewish people, their history, and traditions to the Romans, and to elicit sympathy for the Jews. In his view, the Jewish War had been caused by only a small fanatical group of Jews.

F. M. Gillman

See also HEROD; HERODIANS.

JOY

Great happiness and satisfaction, especially as the fruit of prayer, worship, and a faithful relationship to God. Each of the world's major religions says that happiness will result for those who follow its tenets. This happiness is understood as true contentment, the satisfaction of possessing, knowing, or becoming what is most real and true—be it God, Brahman, nirvana, or something similar. Seeking these goals may well occasion difficulties and hardships, but believers are consoled by seeing these tribulations in a new light, perhaps by not seeing them as real at all. In religions that posit an afterlife, believers are also consoled by knowing that their joy will be completed after their earthly existence.

For Judaism and Christianity, joy is available to believers now, though that which will give complete joy, the establishment of God's kingdom, is yet to come. "Eschatological joy" is the glad anticipation of that fulfillment that will by marked for Jews by the restoration of Israel (Isa 66:10-14), and for Christians by the return of Jesus (Rev 19:1-10). Joy is not only a state, but an act. The Old and New Testaments frequently exhort believers to rejoice in God: "Sing joyfully to the Lord, all you lands, serve the Lord with gladness; come before him with joyful singing" (Ps 100:1-2). Particular traditions within these faiths are noted for particularly exuberant worship and joyful celebration, for instance, the Hasidim within Judaism, and Pentecostals within Christianity.

Brian Stiltner

See also CELEBRATION; ECSTASY; HAPPINESS.

JUAN DE SANTO TOMÁS
(1589–1644)

Portuguese Dominican philosopher and theologian. Born in Lisbon, Juan studied philosophy and theology at the universities of Coimbra and Louvain. He earned doctorates in 1633. Juan became a Dominican friar in Spain, and taught for many years at the University of Alcalá. He became one of the most important interpreters of Thomas Aquinas during the early post–Reformation period, and his philosophical influence was important on both Protestant and Catholic thinkers during the seventeenth century. His influence is also evident in Jacques Maritain and other twentieth-century philosophers, as well as in the school of thought known as "transcendental Thomism." The *Cursus philosophicus* (1631–5) and the *Cursus theologicus*

(1637–67) are his best-known works, along with his *Tratado sobre los dones del Espíritu Santo* (1643).

Orlando Espín

See also AQUINAS, THOMAS, ST.; DOMINI-CANS; MARITAIN, JACQUES; THOMISM/TRANSCENDENTAL THOMISM.

JUBILEES, BOOK OF

The *Book of Jubilees* was probably composed between 170 and 140 B.C.E. in Hebrew and was later translated into Greek and possibly Syriac, and later still from Greek into Latin and Ethiopic. Complete copies of *Jubilees* exist only in Ethiopic, while fragments of the original Hebrew have been found among the Dead Sea Scrolls dating from approximately 100 B.C.E. The name of this composition is taken from its division of time into forty-nine-year periods, jubilees. It presents itself as a revelation to Moses on Mt. Sinai in which Moses is told of all the future sins of the people of Israel and their eventual salvation. Following an introductory section addressed to Moses, an "angel of the presence" delivers a first-person narration that is basically an edited retelling of the biblical narrative from Genesis 1 to Exodus 20. Not all of the biblical material is included, and sometimes new material is added. History is divided into jubilees. The focus of interest in the book seems to be priestly. There is great interest in redating to the patriarchal period the important feasts and laws of Israel. Levi is a central figure as the ancestor of Israel's priests, and ritual purity and sacrifice are stressed. There is no expectation of a messiah in *Jubilees* nor is the idea of resurrection in evidence. Although this work probably predates the founding of the community at Qumran that many scholars think was an Essene center, the writer of *Jubilees* may well have been a member of the movement that later settled there.

Russell Fuller

JUBILEE YEARS (IN CHRISTIANITY)

Also known as holy years, Christian use of jubilee years are an adaptation from the practice of preexilic Judaism to keep every fiftieth year as a year of restoring alienated lands, liberating slaves, and abstaining from sowing and harvesting (Lev 25:8-55). The Christian jubilee year is a celebration of the Christian's liberation from the slavery of death and of restoration in Christ, a time of spiritual renewal, prayer, and works of mercy. The first Christian holy year was 1300, decreed by Pope Boniface VIII, who also decreed that every subsequent hundredth year should be celebrated as a holy year. In 1343 Pope Clement VI changed the period to every fiftieth year, making 1350 the second holy year. In 1389 Pope Urban VI changed it to the thirty-third year in honor of Christ's earthly lifespan. In 1470 Pope Paul II reduced the period to every twenty-five years, the period that has been kept since, with only minor exceptions. Each holy year is proclaimed through the issuance of a special papal bull that lays down the conditions (usually worthy reception of the sacraments and church visitation), special benefits (confessors are given faculties to absolve reserved sins), and indulgences (normally plenary) that can be gained by visitors to Rome. Originally, pilgrimage visits to the Basilicas of St. Peter and St. Paul's Outside the Walls were required. Pope Urban VI added visits to two more basilicas, St. John Lateran and St. Mary Major.

In 1500 Pope Alexander VI prescribed the prayers and ceremonial to be followed;

in essence, these are still used today. The holy year begins when the pope opens the walled up Holy Door of St. Peter's before First Vespers of Christmas (the evening of December 24), while assigned cardinals do the same at the other three basilicas. Pilgrims visiting these churches pass through the holy doors as one of the conditions for the spiritual benefits of the jubilee. The holy year ends when the pope and cardinals wall up the holy doors of the respective basilicas the following Christmas Eve. In the twentieth century, holy years were celebrated in 1900, 1925, 1933 (proclaimed as a special celebration of the anniversary of Christ's death and resurrection), 1950, and 1975. Recent popes have extended the privileges of the holy year to dioceses throughout the world. Local bishops can establish pilgrim churches to be visited with the same conditions and benefits as in Rome.

Pope John Paul II called the preparation for the great jubilee of the year 2000 the "hermeneutical key for my pontificate." His first encyclical (*Redemptor Hominis*, March 4, 1979) opened with a statement that the church is already in preparation for this great holy year that marks Christianity's entry into the third millennium. In nearly every subsequent encyclical, and frequently in his public addresses, the Pope alluded to the coming millennial jubilee. In the apostolic letter *Tertio Millennio Adveniente* (Nov. 19, 1994), he outlined an elaborate plan of preparation for the celebration of the year 2000 that involved an emphasis on evangelization, ecumenism, interreligious dialogue, religious and human freedom, secular commitment to justice and peace, sorrow for the church's sins of the past, and a renewal of Christian faith. The Pope envisioned a worldwide celebration both religious and secular, ecumenical and interreligious, an occasion for joy and thanksgiving, but also repentance and renewal as humankind entered the third millenium.

Dennis W. Krouse

See also INDULGENCE; MILLENARIANISM; REPENTANCE (IN CHRISTIAN PERSPECTIVE).

JUBILEE YEARS (IN JUDAISM)

In the Hebrew Scriptures/Old Testament, the institution known as the jubilee year was supposed to occur every forty-nine years. Scholars are divided over whether the jubilee, as described in Leviticus 25, was an ancient institution that was simply not mentioned in any other sources, or a utopian ideal that was developed in the postexilic period. The jubilee combined the Sabbatical Year regulations concerning the freeing of Hebrew slaves who had been enslaved for debt (Exod 21:2-11 and Deut 15:12-17) with the reversion of property to its original owners. The ideal enshrined in this legislation in Leviticus 25 is that Yahweh is the actual owner of the land the Israelites have received as a gift. The land is not to be alienated in perpetuity, but must revert to the owner or their family who held it originally from Yahweh. The name jubilee (Hebrew *yobel*) is derived from the Hebrew word for trumpets that were blown to announce the beginning of the jubilee year.

Russell Fuller

JUDAH

According to the book of Genesis, the fourth son of Jacob's twelve sons, a son by Leah. According to Genesis 49:9-12, his brothers shall praise him and bow down to him; he is compared to a lion; "the scepter shall not depart from his house." Such claims, though associated with a person, are really descriptive of his tribe and the later southern kingdom. By eponomy, each of Jacob's sons really represents a tribe. The narrative suggests that each had large families, and that these families together made up the people of Israel. Historical scholars assume that the history has been inverted. A group of people or a tribe is symbolized by one man, in this case, Judah.

In approximately 922 B.C.E. the kingdom of Israel split in two. According to the account preserved in 1 Kings 11–12, this division of a united Israel came about both because of the unfaithfulness of Solomon (in exacting forced labor from his own people but especially because he loved foreign women who led him to support the worship of foreign gods) and because of the stupidity or political naiveté of his son Rehoboam. When Rehoboam succeeded his father, he proceeded to exact more from his citizenry than even his father had done. As a result, the people revolted and most of them became part of a northern kingdom, Israel, ruled by a former military leader under Solomon, that is, Jeroboam. One tribe, however, remained loyal to David's dynasty, to David's grandson, Rehoboam. This tribe became its own kingdom, the southern kingdom, Judah. Judah was eventually destroyed by the Babylonians in 586 B.C.E., but hope for restoration remained alive.

Alice L. Laffey

JUDAH HALEVI (1075?–1141?)

Jewish poet, philosopher, and physician, who left a large volume of writings. Spanish born, at the end of his life, he set out for Jerusalem, reaching Egypt in 1140, where he died. One of the best-known medieval Hebrew poets, he introduced forms of Arab poetry into Hebrew verse, writing frequently of his longing for Zion. Alongside his more than eight hundred extant poems, he is best known for his major philosophic work, The *Kuzari*, that takes the form of a dialogue with a pagan king of the Khazars seeking spiritual direction. In this work, Judah HaLevi asserts that Judaism is superior to Christianity and Islam, since the God of Israel is known through the received tradition and not through philosophy, with its syllogisms and mathematical reasoning.

Alan J. Avery-Peck

JUDAH HANASI

Jewish patriarch, Roman appointed leader of the Jewish community of Judea in the second to third centuries C.E.; successor of his father, Simeon ben Gamaliel. Jewish tradition recognizes him as the final redactor of the Mishnah. Judah lived in Bet Shearim and Sephoris in Galilee. Jewish tradition remembers him for his piety and humility as well as his wisdom.

Alan J. Avery-Peck

See also MISHNAH.

JUDAISM

A way of life, worldview, and theology that recognizes the Pentateuch to be the complete account of God's manifestation to humanity; a religion promulgated by a people that calls itself "Israel," understood to be the group to which the Pentateuch and other parts of the Hebrew Bible refer. Through time, many such systems of religion have existed, so that the term Judaism encompasses a complex religious world. Additionally, the adherents of these traditions, the Jews, form one of humanity's oldest groups, and their history is represented in diverse cultures and societies throughout Europe, Asia, North and South Africa, North and Latin America, and Australia. While the Jews in all these cultures share their appeal to the Hebrew Bible and the traditions spawned by that document, no single history describes all their histories. Jews, rather, have formed a variety of Judaic religious systems responding to their distinctive needs in diverse areas of settlement and cultural, social, and economic settings. In speaking about Judaism, we therefore demarcate both the form of Judaism under consideration—Essene, Pharisaic, rabbinic, Contemporary, Reform—and the geographical setting in which that distinctive Judaism has its particular expression—the rabbinic Judaism practiced by Jews of Sephardic or North African descent by contrast to that practiced by the Jews of Western Europe; Reform Judaism in the U.S.A. in contrast to that practiced in England or Western Europe.

While expressed through diverse languages, cultural norms, and modes of religious ritual and belief, these forms of Judaism are united by their common appeal to the Hebrew Bible that states that the one God made a covenant with the Israelite people, demanding that this nation adhere to a detailed system of law and grant exclusive fealty to God. In exchange, God offered the Israelite people special protections and the promise that it would become a great and mighty nation dwelling in its own land (referred to as the land of Israel or Zion). The diverse traditions that fall under the designation "Judaism" share this understanding of the relationship between God and the people of Israel. Through interpretations of the Hebrew Bible, each works out its own particular codification of the laws and theologies presented in Scripture, and each works to assure that the law and

ethic that emerges from the biblical canon comprises the foundation of its communal life. In this way, all forms of Judaism share the desire to create a human society modeled on the will of God, as expressed in the revelation given to Moses at Sinai and recorded in the Hebrew Bible. They further identify as the goal of Judaism and the mission of the Jews to teach the other peoples of the world to recognize the sovereignty of the one God and to practice the moral precepts that are at the heart of all forms of Judaism.

Alan J. Avery-Peck

See also CONSERVATIVE JUDAISM; COVENANT IN JUDAISM; DIASPORA; ISRAEL; MISSION (IN JUDAISM); MITZVAH; ORTHODOX JUDAISM; RABBINIC JUDAISM; RECONSTRUCTIONIST JUDAISM; REFORM JUDAISM; TORAH; ZION.

JUDAIZERS

Those who urge non-Jews, that is, Gentiles, to take on Jewish customs; hence, to Judaize. In most frequent usage, this does not imply full conversion. In the examples of this practice in ancient sources, the reasons Gentiles Judaized vary from attraction to Jewish practices to fear for the political or social consequences of not Judaizing in some situations. In the same texts, those who suggested that others should Judaize might be Jews, Jewish Christians, or other Gentiles.

Judaizing was a major issue in early Christianity as the movement worked out the integration of Gentiles into the proclamation that the Jewish Messiah had come (see Gal 2). Debates concerning the degree to which Gentiles were to be required to observe the Law of Moses, especially the requirement of male circumcision (see Acts 15), led to various levels of Judaizing that in turn caused heated controversy.

This is sharply evident, for example, in Paul's letter to the Galatians, the whole backdrop of which is tension created in his Galatian churches by Judaizers.

F. M. Gillman

See also GENTILES; PAUL.

JUDAS

The Hellenistic form of the Hebrew name *Yehuda* (Judah), Judas is the first name of twelve biblical characters. They include: (1) A brother of Jesus (Mark 6:3 and Matt 13:35); (2) one of the twelve called "the son of James" (Luke 6:16, Acts 1:13, and John 14:22), who is probably the same individual as Thaddaeus in Matthew 10:3 and Mark 3:18; (3) Judas Maccabeus, one of the Maccabean leaders of the Judaean revolt against the religious persecution imposed by the Seleucid, Antichus IV Epiphanes (1–2 Macc); (4) one of the men in Jesus' inner circle who likely served as treasurer who is distinguished from "the son of James" by being identified as "Iscariot" (Matt 10:4; 26:14; Mark 3:19; 14:10; Luke 6:16; 22:3; John 6:71; John 12:4-6; 13:2, 26, 29).

While Judas Maccabeus is remembered for liberating and cleansing the Temple Mount before its rededication that Jews commemorate to this day at *Chanukah*, Judas Iscariot is the most significant Judas to Christians. He is remembered for having handed Jesus over to Judaean religious authorities. However, without harmonizing conflicting accounts, it is impossible to establish why Judas handed Jesus over, or how he did so. The earliest layer of the tradition has no record that Judas was a paid informant who committed suicide. His act of "handing over" (*paradidomai*) came to be understood as "betrayal," and Judas' role as villain was heightened as time passed (compare Mark 14:10; Matt 26:15a; Luke 22:3; John 6:70). Thus, just as Judas is identified by the act of betrayal in Mark 14:21, one who betrays another is called a "Judas."

Historical and theological problems associated with this elusive, tragic figure have been recognized since the time of Origen. It is possible that the culpability associated with Judas stems from a memory that, although Judas was only the first among Jesus' inner circle of male followers who all eventually abandoned their master before his crucifixion, he was the only one who never returned.

Regina A. Boisclair

JULIAN OF NORWICH (CA. 1342/43–CA. 1416/20)

English woman mystic, visionary, writer, and anchoress, who lived in religious solitude in a cell attached to the Church of St. Julian in Norwich. During a near fatal illness around 1372/73, Julian experienced a series of sixteen mystical visions. Upon recovering from her illness, she described these visions in her spiritual writings titled *Showings* (also titled *Revelations of Divine Love*); here, Julian explained that she prayed for this visionary experience and illness, as well as for "three wounds" of contrition, compassion, and longing for God. She authored two versions of *Showings*, one short, descriptive account and one longer, more theologically sophisticated account about fifteen to twenty years later that interrelate her visions with Christian Scriptures and teachings regarding the love of God, among other theological themes. By 1394, Julian practiced an anchoritic religious life devoted to living apart from the world and to daily activities of prayer, contemplation, and giving spiritual counsel to visitors.

In reflecting on her visions, Julian offered a theology of consolation centered on the phrase "all shall be well," and a rich set of theological reflections on God, the Trinity, the Incarnation, the suffering and death of Jesus, sin, and redemption. A striking vision of the suffering and death of Jesus, with a particular emphasis on blood piety, constitutes the first showing; overall, several of Julian's visions or showings are preoccupied with the passion and death of Christ. Of more contemporary interest, Julian developed a range of theological images for the Trinity, referring to God the Creator in paternal and maternal images, to Jesus as savior, mother, and brother, and to the Spirit as spouse. As historian Carolyn Walker Bynum has observed, medieval European monastics commonly used female images of Jesus for a variety of complex reasons related to self-identity, devotional practices, and theological claims.

Nonetheless, more contemporary feminist theologians seek to critically recover and appropriate such alternative but overlooked female images for God from Christian Scriptures and traditions in order (1) to offset predominantly androcentric (male-dominated) images of God that forge what feminist theologian Elizabeth Johnson calls a spurious "ontological connection" between maleness and God, and (2) to open up theological space for women to identify with and image God. And yet, paternal and maternal images of God carry potentially dangerous implications for theological constructions of the self and for ethics. As feminist theologians Anne Carr and Dorothee Sölle argued, parental and maternal imagery for God can theologically justify traditional gender stereotypes for men and women as well as infantilize contemporary Christians from taking responsibility for our actions and for the world.

Rosemary P. Carbine

JULIAN THE APOSTATE (331–63)
Flavius Julianus Augustus was the nephew of Constantine the Great. Julian and his brother Gallus were the survivers of the murder of all his male relatives by Constantine in 337–8. Despite a Christian education and an early interest in orders, Julian turned violently against Christianity after his brother was beheaded, and Julian himself was exiled to Athens. After a successful military career, Julian became emperor in 361. He attempted to restore the ancient Roman religion to the empire through reorganization and sponsorship of the ancient rites. He died fighting the Persians in 363. His reign was the last attempt to remove Christianity from its favored position in the Roman Empire.

Gary Macy

See also CONSTANTINE I THE GREAT.

JUNG, CARL GUSTAV (1875–1961)
Carl Gustav Jung was a Swiss psychiatrist and early follower of Freud. Jung's work on religion centered on the affinity between symbols rising from the personal lives of individuals and the symbolic images underlying mythological and religious systems of many cultures and eras. Jung explained the correspondence between personal symbols and cultural symbols by positing the existence of two layers of the unconscious psyche: the personal and the collective. The personal unconscious comprises mental contents acquired during the individual's life that have been forgotten or repressed, whereas the collective unconscious is an inherited structure common to all humankind and composed of the archetypes—innate

predispositions to experience and to symbolize universal human situations in distinctively human ways. Many of the great religious symbols of the world—the Christ figure, for example—are understood by Jung to symbolize the psychic process of the death of the inflated ego in order that the integrated self—the Son of God—may become incarnate within the psyche.

Helen deLaurentis

See also FREUD, SIGMUND; FROMM, ERICH.

JÜNGEL, EBERHARD (1934–)

German Lutheran theologian. After studies in Naumburg, Berlin, Zürich, and Basle, he became professor of New Testament studies and systematic theology in Berlin and in Zürich. In 1969 he moved to the University of Tübingen, where he taught systematic theology and philosophy. Jüngel has been especially influenced by Hegel, Barth, and Ebeling. He has tried to understand the ultimate foundations for asserting that faith in the God of Jesus is reasonably possible in the modern world, and that God (as the God who is love) is the basic "mystery of the world." Indeed, because humans can think and understand "love," they must also be capable of thinking and understanding "God." Jüngel has argued from the Christian experience of God (especially from God as "crucified") to what he considers a universally valid concept of God. His thought is very much part of the modern European discussion about belief and unbelief. Among Jüngel's more than seven books, *God as Mystery of the World* (1976) is considered his best and most influential.

Orlando Espín

See also ATHEISM; BARTH, KARL; EBELING, GERHARD; FAITH; GOD; HEGEL, G.W.F.; LUTHERAN THEOLOGY; MODERNITY; MYSTERY; POSTMODERNITY; TÜBINGEN SCHOOL.

JUNGMANN, JOSEF ANDREAS (1899–1975)

Josef (or Joseph) A. Jungmann was an Austrian Jesuit who became one of the most important catechetical and liturgical scholars of the twentieth century. Jungmann taught at the University of Innsbruck from 1925 to 1963; however, during World War II, the department was shut down (1938–45), and Jungmann spent some of those years as chaplain to a community of nuns at Hainstetten. It was during that time that his most influential work, the two-volume history of the Roman Mass (*Missarum Sollemnia*, or *Mass of the Roman Rite*, in English translation) was completed.

Jungmann was an important figure in the liturgical reforms that took place in the Catholic Church after Vatican II (1962–5). His work on the history of the Eucharist and Christian prayer is still widely used today by students and scholars. His most important liturgical publications in English are *The Mass of the Roman Rite* (1955); *The Early Liturgy* (1959); *Pastoral Liturgy* (1962); *The Place of Christ in Liturgical Prayer* (1965); an abridged one-volume revision, *The Mass: An Historical, Theological, and Pastoral Survey* (1976); and *Christian Prayer through the Centuries* (1978).

Joanne M. Pierce

See also CATECHESIS/CATECHETICAL; EUCHARIST; LITURGICAL MOVEMENT; MASS; VATICAN, SECOND COUNCIL OF THE.

JUST

In the Christian theology of grace, any person who has been "justified" ("declared righteous") by God is called "just." In social ethics, "just" is the person who lives by and practices justice.

Orlando Espín

See also ELECTION (DOCTRINE OF); ETHICS, SOCIAL; FAITH; FREE WILL; GRACE; JUSTICE; JUSTIFICATION.

JUSTICE

In Christian theological ethics, justice is not "treating like cases alike" or establishing "fair procedures" within present social arrangements, as in philosophical ethics. The Christian notion of justice emanates from the notion that the people of God are to establish right relationships and that these are to be discerned by attention to how the society deals with the economically exploited, the politically oppressed, and the culturally marginalized.

Biblical justice focuses particularly on the obligation to address concrete human need. The teachings of the Christian churches on issues related to justice strive to identify and transform structures of privilege and oppression to serve the process of human liberation. They focus on the structural inequalities that define life in contemporary society, distort every dimension of human activity, and shape much of the suffering that humans, other earth creatures, and the planet itself, endure.

It is this attention to concrete human and ecological needs and to the inequalities and unjust relations perpetrated by larger political, economic, and cultural institutions, that defines the Christian theory and praxis of justice. The 1971 World Synod of Catholic Bishops stated that "action on behalf of justice and participation in the transformation of the world fully appear to us as a constitutive dimension of the preaching of the

Gospel." Justice theories in Christian theological ethics continue to develop.

Mary E. Hobgood

See also ETHICS, SOCIAL; FREEDOM; JUSTICE IN THE WORLD; MATERIALISM; SOLIDARITY.

JUSTICE IN THE WORLD

(Synod document). At the Third International Synod of Bishops in 1971, representatives of the worldwide Catholic episcopate took up "the mission of the People of God to further justice in the world" and concluded that acting for justice in an unjust world is a "constitutive dimension of the preaching of the Gospel." The synod's final document, called "Justice in the World," was issued on November 30, 1971. This document reaffirms the teaching of the Second Vatican Council (especially as found in *Gaudium et Spes*) on social justice, but it also incorporates postconciliar developments in Catholic thinking arising from the experience of Christians involved in struggles for justice around the world. Some of these ideas had already been discussed at regional bishops' conferences such as the one in Medellín, Colombia, in 1968.

The theological linchpin of "Justice in the World" is found in its introduction, which affirms the church's conviction that the Gospel "through the power of the Holy Spirit, frees [people] from personal sin and from its consequences in social life." The Gospel thus challenges an unjust world that "by its perversity contradicts the plan of its Creator." The document comprises four sections.

Part I, "Justice and World Society," examines the reality of injustice, including social and economic oppression, religious persecution, violation of the rights of individuals (and in particular political prisoners), legalized abortion, and social manipulation by the media. The bishops criticize a deterministic understanding of evolution that sees future progress as automatic. They affirm the notion (without using the phrase itself) of a "preferential option for the poor" in asserting that the goal of "a more human society" must be approached by acting first on behalf of those who are the "silent, indeed voiceless, victims of injustice."

Part II, "The Gospel Message and the Mission of the Church," acknowledges that we human beings are both responsible for the grave sin of injustice, yet unable to overcome it by our own strength. The church's proclamation of the Gospel message will only be credible if Christians also act for justice in the world. Love of neighbor alone makes love for God visible. The work of creating a just world does not fall to the church alone, nor should the church "offer concrete solutions in the social, economic, and political spheres." Yet the Christian community does have a "proper and specific responsibility," namely, to "give witness" to love and justice by promoting the "dignity and fundamental rights of the human person."

Part III, "The Practice of Justice," turns to the behavior, possessions, and lifestyle found within the church itself. The bishops call for the recognition in the church of the rights of laypeople and women, dialogue, and due process. They warn against allowing material possessions to obscure its witness to the Gospel. Religious education means education for justice. The liturgy, too, serves to educate Catholics for justice; since giving thanks to God makes visible our brother- and sisterhood, the readings remind us of what earlier believers taught about justice, and the Eucharist "forms the community and places it at the service of humanity."

In Part IV, "A Word of Hope," the bishops conclude that the "radical transformation of the world" demanded by the Gospel will take place through the power of the Holy Spirit and the generosity of human beings (especially the young) who choose to collaborate with God.

James B. Nickoloff

See also BISHOP (EPISCOPACY); GAUDIUM ET SPES; SYNODS.

JUSTIFICATION

A Christian theological term that refers, first of all, to God's merciful "declaration of righteousness" in favor of human beings. The term also names the proper relationship between God and humans that results from God's merciful "declaration of righteousness."

There are serious doubts as to whether the historical Jesus of Nazareth ever taught something resembling the current Christian notion of justification. However, the New Testament, and especially the apostle Paul, did teach that Jesus' sufferings, death, and resurrection have made it possible for God to declare some humans "righteous," "just." Indeed, New Testament writers teach that God so designates any human being who has faith in Jesus and lives accordingly. The New Testament witness, however, nowhere makes justification the crucial or most important Christian doctrine. Later church history simply followed the New Testament lead, discussing justification only as one element within the theologies of grace and salvation. The Protestant Reformation changed this attitude by bringing justification to center stage, giving it a doctrinal importance that it did not have before.

Luther taught that faith alone can make a human "just." For him, justification by faith alone was the cornerstone of the

Christian Gospel. Luther further taught that justification occurs exclusively as a result of God's mercy and grace, without human merit, and only as a consequence of God's acceptance of Jesus' Cross as substitute for human sinners. In this sense, the "declaration of righteousness" is never based on human works but on Jesus' self-sacrifice, and consequently only implies that God treats humans *as if* they were righteous. Hence, justification is really extrinsic, juridical. Calvin's views, for the most part, follow Luther's.

The Council of Trent reacted to Luther's teaching by reform legislation designed to "clean up" Catholic practices, and, more importantly, by its doctrinal statements on the subject. Trent taught that Catholicism believed that justification was exclusively a result of God's mercy and grace, because of Jesus' self-sacrifice on the cross. The council insisted that faith was necessary for human acceptance of justification, but that without love and hope that faith would be dead and useless. Hence, Trent's doctrine on justification included the requirement of faith, as well as the requirement of human response in love and hope. The council further taught that justification actually heals a human being's sinful condition (although not some existential consequences of that condition); therefore, justification is intrinsic, although still viewed somewhat juridically.

Contemporary Catholic and Protestant theologians now understand that the doctrines of justification they inherited from the sixteenth-century Reformations (Lutheran, Anglican, and Tridentine, specifically), do not exclude each other. Current New Testament scholarship has done much to clarify what Paul, James, and the four evangelists really held. The official consultations between Lutherans and Roman Catholics have decided that there are no substantive reasons, based on the New Testament witness, to conclude that the Lutheran and Catholic positions on justification cannot be both acceptable. The two views complement and balance each other. The Roman Catholic Church and the World Lutheran Federation signed an official "Joint Declaration on the Doctrine of Justification" in 1999. The World Methodist Council announced in 2006 that it too will sign the Joint Declaration.

It is very important to a contemporary, biblically based theology of justification that the evident social dimensions of justification not be pushed aside in the theological reflection. Jesus of Nazareth did not preach from the perspective of individualism (that would have been unknown in his day), and New Testament Christians would not have agreed with a teaching that denied normative weight to effective love and compassion. It seems that any sound explanation of justification must not avoid the social, and even political, implications and consequences of being "righteous" according to the will of God. This in no way supports impossible attempts at establishing a theocratic order, but does promote necessary Christian involvement in the search for a just and reconciled world.

Orlando Espín

See also CALVIN, JOHN; CALVINISM; ELECTION (DOCTRINE OF); FREE WILL; GRACE; INFRALAPSARIANISM; JUST; LUTHER, MARTIN; LUTHERANISM; NATURE, HUMAN; ORIGINAL JUSTICE; PREDESTINATION (IN CHRISTIANITY); PROTESTANTISM; SALVATION; SIN, ORIGINAL; THEOLOGICAL ANTHROPOLOGY; TRENT, COUNCIL OF.

JUSTINIAN (482–565)

Falvius Petrus Sabbatius Iustinianus was Roman Emperor in Constantinople from

527 until his death. Justinian began his political career as advisor to his uncle, the Emperor Justin. In 525 he married the former actress Theodora who, from that point on, exerted considerable influence on imperial affairs. Justinian succeeded in uniting the former Roman Empire by a series of conquests of the western territories that had fallen to the invading Gothic tribes. Under the leadership of the generals Belisarius and Narses, the Roman armies reconquered North Africa, Italy, and southeast Spain. Justinian considered himself the head of the orthodox Christian Church and strongly opposed any form of heresy, himself authoring several theological tracts. He embodied this view of rulership in his famous code of Roman law, the *Codex Justinianus*, that had considerable influence on later jurists. Justinian also built many beautiful new churches, the most famous being the Hagia Sophia (Holy Wisdom) church in Constantinople. Justinian's impressive achievements did not last, however; the Western Empire quickly regained its independence, and the Eastern Empire was unable to maintain the internal unity for which Justinian had so long labored.

Gary Macy

See also ANTIOCHENE THEOLOGY; CAESAROPAPISM; ORIGENISM; PELEGIUS I OF ROME; SEVERUS OF ANTIOCH; THEODORA; THEODORE OF MOPSUESTIA; THEODORET, BISHOP OF CYRRHUS; THE THREE CHAPTERS; VIGILIUS OF ROME.

JUSTIN MARTYR (?–165)
Justin was born in the city of Flavia Neopolis (now Nablus) in Samaria of Greek parents. He spend his life in pursuit of wisdom, studying all the different philosophies of his day. He was finally convinced around the year 130 that Christianity was the greatest philosophy. He taught Christianity as a philosophy first in Ephesus, and then in Rome. He wrote two versions of an apology for Christianity as well as a dialogue with the Jew, Trypho. He was martyred in Rome around 165. Justin was the first Christian to attempt a thoroughgoing reconciliation of Christian belief with of the philosophy of the time, which in Justin's case was Middle Platonism. Justin's work greatly influenced other early Christian writers.

Gary Macy

See also APOLOGISTS; CHRISTIANITY; MARTYR/MARTYRDOM; PLATONISM.

JUST WAR THEORY
This theory is not an exclusively Christian theory, but developed out of Greek and Roman thought that was concerned to limit war. The theory was Christianized by Augustine and Aquinas and is still developing, especially within the Catholic tradition.

The theory holds that, because war overrides the fundamental moral obligation not to harm or kill others, it demands weighty or significant reasons. Criteria that frequently appear in exposition of the theory are the following: (1) the war must be declared by legitimate or competent authority; (2) it must be waged for a just cause like protecting the innocent, or restoring rights wrongfully denied; (3) it can be waged only as a last resort after all other possible nonviolent means have been exhausted and sufficient warnings have been given; (4) there must be reasonable hope that the war can be successful; (5) the war must be waged in a just manner, including protecting the lives of noncombatants.

In recent history, the just war theory has been seen as increasingly problematic due to such factors as the existence of competing theories of the nature of justice, and due to the exigencies of technological warfare that, for example, make it impossible to protect civilians. The major challenge to just war theory, however, lies in the changing character of global violence that increasingly no longer resembles traditional war. Since Vatican II, there has been a growing debate within Catholicism between the just war theory and pacifism.

Mary E. Hobgood

See also CHALLENGE OF PEACE; JUSTICE; PEACE; WAR.

K

KAʾBA/KAABA

An Arabic word literally meaning "cube," a Muslim shrine. Located in the city of Mecca in Saudi Arabia, the Kaʾba is a structure made of stone and draped with a black cloth. Its four walls measure fifty feet in height and vary in length from some thirty-five to forty feet, roughly forming the shape of a cube. Situated in the center of the Grand Mosque of Mecca, the Kaʾba is the most sacred site in Islam. It marks the direction (*kibla*) toward which Muslims all over the world face when they pray five times each day, and it is the focus of the annual *hajj* or pilgrimage to Mecca. Muslims revere the Kaʾba because, according to Islamic tradition, it was originally established by Adam and built by Abraham. Rebuilt several times over the centuries, Muslims believe that it represents God's divine presence, and that it served as a shrine for believers in the one true God long before the coming of the Prophet Muhammad (570–632). In pre-Islamic Arabia, the Kaʾba became a center of worship and pilgrim shrine for tribal religions the Muslims regarded as pagan cults.

Set in the southeast corner of the structure, there is a Black Stone that, according to Islamic belief, was placed there by Adam, perhaps to symbolize God's eternity. During the *hajj*, pilgrims circumambulate (walk around) the Kaʾba seven times, and those close enough to the Black Stone pause to kiss it. Others make gestures of reverence toward the stone as they pass by.

When the armies of Islam entered Mecca as conquerors in 630 C.E., Muhammad ordered the destruction of the 360 "pagan" idols that had been placed around the Kaʾba. The number of these statues suggests that the Kaʾba may have served some astronomical function in pre-Islamic religion. It is said that there were also images of Jesus and Mary on the structure, but these were not destroyed by the victorious Muslims. Just before his death in 632, Muhammad made a final pilgrimage to the Kaʾba, and, at that time, established the *hajj* rituals much as they are observed today, including veneration of the Black Stone. Muslims point out that, while the Kaʾba is an important Islamic shrine, neither the structure itself nor the Black Stone are objects of worship. Worship, they say, belongs to God alone.

Ronald A. Pachence

See also ADAM (AS PROPHET OF ISLAM); HAJJ; ISLAM; JESUS (AS PROPHET OF ISLAM); KIBLA; MECCA; MOSQUE/ MASJID; MUHAMMAD; MUSLIM.

KABBALAH

(Hebrew, received [knowledge]). A form of Jewish mysticism emerging in southern France (Provence) in the twelfth century and northern Spain in the thirteenth; an important movement in the medieval period, with continued significance within Hasidic Judaism today. The Kabbalah developed from systematic speculations about God's relationship to humanity and developed through new forms of commentary on Scripture that found hidden levels of meaning in the sacred text. Unique to Kabbalah is its theory of the existence of ten divine emanations—called *Sefirot*—which the Kabbalists see as spanning the void between the infinite God and the finite world.

The central document of Kabbalah, the *Zohar*, was written by Moses DeLeon in around 1280 C.E. but attributed to the Mishnaic authority Yohanan ben Zakkai. DeLeon described God as both transcendent and immanent. God, that is, was a creator, separate from the created world and not subject to the forces of nature. At the same time, DeLeon saw God as everywhere present and accessible in the form of the Shekinah, a feminine, worldly manifestation of God. The Kabbalah thus rejected central tenets of medieval Jewish philosophy that defined God as unitary and radically other. By contrast, the Kabbalists envisioned God as comprised of two distinct parts, one of them, the Ein Sof ("infinite"), an unknowable, unreachable, concealed aspect, and the other, the Shekinah, a personification of God directly experienced by human beings.

The Kabbalah saw these two aspects of God as connected through the Sefirot, spiritual realities distinct from the Ein Sof but illuminated by the divine radiance that flows from the concealed part of God. Through these emanations, the essence and being of the Ein Sof becomes manifest in the world in which humans dwell. Since the earthly world thus is a visible representation of the upper world, worldly phenomena reveal the nature of the divine. In keeping with this thinking, the Kabbalah goes beyond the biblical conception that humans were created in God's image, recognizing an actual identification between the human and the divine. This identification is represented by the *Neshamah* (Hebrew, spirit), the highest part of the soul, which the Kabbalists understand to be derived directly from God and to be made up in part of the same stuff as God.

In Kabbalistic theory, prior to Adam's sin described at the beginning of the book of Genesis, there was no material world at all. Then the Sefirot interacted in perfect harmony. Only after the first sin did Adam take physical form and were the distinct male and female aspects of the Sefirot created. According to the Kabbalah, it has henceforth been people's task to restore the harmony in which the world was created. People accomplish this through ritual and moral activity. According to the Kabbalah, every proper deed contributes to the well-being of God, reversing the impact of Adam's sin by (1) reuniting the aspects of God represented at the highest level of the Sefirot and (2) reestablishing the relationship between individual people and the Sefirot as a whole. The Kabbalah thus brought an entirely new function to the religious observances central in rabbinic Judaism. According to the Kabbalah, such observances do not simply lead to a good and moral life or respond to God's command. Rather, they have cosmic repercussions, helping to reunite God and the Shekinah and so to return the world to the perfect state in which God originally created it.

Alan J. Avery-Peck

See also HASIDISM; LURIA, ISAAC; SHEKINAH; ZOHAR.

KABBALAT SHABBAT

(Hebrew, Reception of the Sabbath). Jewish worship service traditionally held immediately after sundown on Friday evening, marking the beginning of the Sabbath. Kabbalat Shabbat is followed by the regular evening prayer service. It consists of the recitation of Psalm 29 (and, in the practice of some communities, Pss 95–99), the chanting of the hymn *Lekhah Dodi*, and, finally, Psalms 92–93. *Lekhah Dodi* (Hebrew, "Come, my friend") was written in the sixteenth century by the mystic Solomon HaLevi and sets the tone for the service as a whole. It reflects the Jewish mystical practice of greeting the Sabbath as a queen who represents the Shekinah, the mystical, female personification of God.

Alan J. Avery-Peck

See also SABBATH; SHEKINAH.

KACHINAS

The word is Hopi—meaning "respected spirit"—but the reality to which it points is universal in Native America. These are the inner forms of all life, in a sense covering more than the simply organic. In the cosmology, the kachinas accompanied the Hopi on their journey of emergence, and in the present Fourth World watch over them still. This continuing presence draws very close each year as the growing season is prepared for and the Hopi acknowledge their need for spiritual help in a very arid climate. In the traditional sequence of events, the ritual year begins in November and extends throughout the growing season, ending with Niman Kachina in August. In the winter solstice ceremony of Soyal, the kachinas come from their mountain homes to dwell with the Hopi and help them; they depart during Niman (the Going-Home Dance of the kachinas) and take with them the petitions of the Hopi for the rest of the year. In an exceptional way, this visit of their spiritual allies is made visible for all to see. The men of the village, those who have accepted the call and responsibility to host a kachina for the rituals, enter in a marvelous procession, each beating out its own unique rhythm in dance steps. They are clothed in costumes that have gained recognizable form over the centuries, but the major aspect of this costume is the mask. Each mask represents a specific kachina, and there have been at different times three hundred known. Some can depart, and new kachinas emerge. The constant element is the profound discipline that accompanies their representation and their reverent reception by the Hopi. The bearer of the mask usually accepts that role for life, and his mask is buried with him. The mask is considered absolutely sacred, and any act of disrespect is regarded as a sacrilegious violation.

The kachinas also represent the sanctified dead ancestors. In the Hopi model of life, human destiny aims so perfectly to follow the strict prescriptions of the Hopi Way as to break free of rebirth into the cycle of life and attain the state of the kachinas. In a way that is thoroughly consonant with their material culture, such a state is usually manifest as clouds that gift the people with life-giving rain. It is necessary to note that the Hopi do not think they are the sole possessors of the kachinas, and so designate some as representing various tribes. This is matched by a similar recognition by other Southwestern peoples of these powerful sources of life.

Kathleen Dugan

See also LIMINAL/LIMINALITY; REINCARNATION; RITUAL; SPIRIT.

KADDISH

(Aramaic, holy). In Jewish liturgy, a doxology recited in Aramaic (except for its final clause, in Hebrew), used to mark the close of individual sections of public worship services and on occasions when praise of God is appropriate. The Kaddish appears in four main forms: the full and half Kaddish, used as dividers within the liturgy; the mourners' Kaddish, recited by mourners to express their continued praise of God despite the loss they have experienced; and the scholars' Kaddish, recited after the study of Jewish texts, in recognition of the greatness of God's revelation and to bring blessing upon those who study it.

In light of its use by mourners, in contemporary times, the Kaddish is perhaps the best known and most evocative of Jewish prayers. The recognition of the power of this doxology is not, however, only modern. The Talmud expresses the notion that the recitation of the Kaddish by a son or grandson exerts a redeeming influence on behalf of the soul of a departed father or grandfather (Babylonian Talmud Sanhedrin 104a). Accordingly, it became the custom for the mourner to recite the Kaddish at each daily prayer service during the first year (in more recent times, eleven months) after death, during which time Judaism understands the soul of the departed to be subject to judgment. The Kaddish is again recited on behalf of the deceased on each subsequent anniversary of the death.

The text of the Kaddish is as follows:

Leader: Magnified and sanctified be his great name in the world he has created according to his will. And may he establish his kingdom during your life and during your days and during the life of the whole household of Israel, speedily and in a near time! So say, "Amen!"

Response: Let his great name be blessed forever and unto all eternity!

Leader: Blessed, praised, and glorified, exalted, extolled, and honored, uplifted and lauded by the name of the holy one, blessed be he, above all the blessings and hymns, the praises and consolations, which are uttered in the world. So say, "Amen!" May the prayers and supplications of all Israel be accepted by their father, who is in Heaven! So say "Amen."

Alan J. Avery-Peck

See also DOXOLOGY.

KAFIR

An Arabic term used in Islam to describe one who refuses to accept God's divine revelation disclosed through the Prophet Muhammad (570–632). Literally, *kafir* connotes the action of a person who "covers" in the sense of hiding something away. As applied to the unbeliever, the word suggests rejection of and lack of gratitude for the gift of the truth offered to people by God's revealed Word. Kafir is applied most frequently to atheists and infidels.

Ronald A. Pachence

See also INFIDELS; REVELATION (IN ISLAM); SHIRK.

KAGURA

(Japanese, *kami-no kura*, seat of the *kami*). An ancient practice of dance and music used in classical Shinto ritual for the entertainment and enjoyment of the kami. It is usually performed at night to symbolize the mythical ritual performance, found in the Nihongi, used to lure Amaterasu (Sun Goddess) from her cave and restore light to the world. More generally, it is believed that through this ritual performance a kami will be brought forward to renew purity, goodness, and creativity to benefit the world.

G. D. DeAngelis

See also AMATERASU; KAMI; NIHONGI; SHINTO; SHRINE.

KÄHLER, MARTIN (1835–1912)
German conservative Lutheran theologian and professor of New Testament and systematic theology at Halle. His thought, exemplified in his small book *The So-Called Historical Jesus and the Historic Biblical Christ* (1892; ET 1964), stresses the theological nature of the Gospels and Jesus' enduring, transhistorical meaning. Reversing the argument of his liberal colleagues about the historical Jesus and the Christ of faith, Kähler held that the real Christ is actually the "preached" Christ of the whole Bible, not some speculative historical reconstruction. Kähler vigorously attacked their efforts as futile, asking how Jesus can be the real object of faith for all Christians if his true identity and teaching are accessible only through the sophisticated methods of a modern scholarly elite. Foreshadowing the dialectical theology of Barth and Bultmann, as well as his student Paul Tillich and later work by Brunner, Kähler's work was reclaimed by New Testament scholars in the 1950s as part of their "New Quest" for the historical Jesus, and has remained a benchmark for such discussion since then.

Francis D. Connolly-Weinert

KAIROS
In Greek antiquity, this term referred to a moment of crisis in which a person was confronted with and called to make very crucial decisions. In the New Testament, *kairós* refers to the time of salvation, the fullness of time, and the moment of God's final offer of grace, thereby requiring the most crucial decisions.

Orlando Espín

See also GRACE; REVELATION; SALVATION.

KALAM
An Arabic term literally meaning "word." In Islamic thought, *kalam* refers to "words" about the Word of God, that is, the study of divine revelation. The most precise English translation of kalam would be "theology." The Islamic expression for Muslim scholars involved in kalam is *ahl al-kalam* ("people of kalam"), or in English, "theologians." Islamic theologians, like their counterparts in Christianity, use the faculty of human reasoning to gain a deeper understanding of the revealed Word of God and the faith of the believing community. In Islam, however, while systematic, logical thinking is employed in the discipline, theologians may never conclude to positions that contradict the teachings of the Qurʾan (the sacred scripture of Islam) or any doctrine considered part of divine revelation. Such conclusions would amount to unorthodox *bidʾa* or "innovation," and would be rejected as false no matter how logically coherent they appeared to be.

Ronald A. Pachence

See also FIQH; QURʾAN; REVELATION (IN ISLAM).

KALI
In Hinduism, Kali is a form of the Great Goddess. Horrific in appearance, she

embodies all in the world that is frightening and chaotic. Artists and poets depict her as haunting cremation grounds, where she dances wildly with disheveled hair, naked save for a garland of skulls, a waistband made of severed human arms, and other gruesome ornaments. As such, she invites her devotees to confront, come to terms with, and go beyond their fears and limitations, along with all the dualities (good and bad, pure and impure, beautiful and ugly) that keep humans bound to samsara (the cosmos). In approaching the religious meaning of Kali, it is important to bear in mind that Hinduism does not understand the world in terms of a "good versus evil" conflict dualism. Indeed, the theology behind the Kali image is thoroughly nondualist in outlook. Kali is not, therefore, a personification of evil, but rather a reminder that the divine encompasses the bad and the good, and ultimately transcends both.

Lance E. Nelson

See also HINDUISM; SHAKTA; SHAKTI; TANTRA; TANTRIC HINDUISM.

KALPA

A measure of cosmic time in Hindu myth, a *kalpa* represents one complete cycle in the beginningless and endless series of cycles through which the cosmos (samsara) is passing. Lasting some 311 trillion years, according to calculations in the Puranas, a kalpa starts with the re-creation of the universe and ends with its (temporary) dissolution. Kalpas are divided into smaller cycles, known as *yugas*.

Lance E. Nelson

See also HINDUISM; PURANA; YUGA.

KAMA

A Sanskrit word meaning "desire" and, by extension, "sensual pleasure," *kama* is one of the four goals of life (*purusarthas*) recognized in Hinduism as legitimate pursuits of human existence. The other three are *dharma* (religious duty), *artha* (material prosperity), and *moksha* (liberation). While Hindus thus accept that the fulfillment of one's desires for pleasure—in sex, art, food, and other aspects of life—is a necessary stage in human development, they do not do so uncritically. Pleasure must, of course, be sought within the limitations of morality (dharma). More importantly, Hindus recognize that desire in the final analysis is one of the chief psychological forces that perpetuate karmic bondage and keep the soul tied to perpetual rebirths in samsara (the cosmos). Thus the *Bhagavad Gita* teaches that, while desire leads to bondage, action without desire (*nishkama–karma*) is conducive to liberation. In this, it may be echoing the teaching of the Buddha, who identified desire or "thirst" (*trisna*) as the cause of all suffering. Nevertheless, while most Indic religions identify desire as something that is in the end best abandoned by spiritual seekers, Tantric Hinduism and Buddhism seek to harness the strong psychological power of desire to catalyze the process of attaining enlightenment.

Lance E. Nelson

See also BHAGAVAD GITA; BUDDHISM; DHARMA (IN BUDDHISM); DHARMA (IN HINDUISM); HINDUISM; KARMA-YOGA; TANTRA; TANTRIC BUDDHISM; TANTRIC HINDUISM; TRUTHS, FOUR NOBLE.

KAMAKURA PERIOD (1185–1333)

An era of great change in Japanese society characterized by new directions in politics, social order, culture, and religion. The seat of government moved form Heian to Kamakura, and a new governance structure saw the emergence of political dominance by the Bushi (warrior) military class. Following a period of disorder and uncertainty, new Buddhist movements, better suited to the times, emerged during this era, for example, Zen, Nichirenism, and Pure Land. These schools represent the development of a more Japanese form of Buddhism. In addition, this era was marked by an increasing nationalistic tone that encouraged attempts to purify Shinto of Buddhist influence.

G. D. DeAngelis

See also DOGEN; HONEN; JODO SHIN SHU; JODO SHU; NICHIREN; PURE LAND BUDDHISM; SHINRAN; SHINTO; ZEN.

KAMI

(Japanese, sacred, divine). This is a rather ambiguous term, found in Shinto and Japanese folk religion, with numerous etymological interpretations regarding its meaning; for example, above, special, powerful, lifted up, mysterious, and so on. It is most commonly translated as god, spirit, sacred, divine, or anything that commands awe and reverence from humans. Not only are there a large number of *kami* throughout the world and cosmos, but they take on numerous forms such as natural objects, animals, human beings, gods, spirits, and so forth. While kami take many forms, it is more a quality of that form than the specific form itself, that is, a person can be a kami or a river can be kami—what makes either kami is that it manifests a kind of sacred, mysterious, awesome power. Many kami have become specific objects of worship in Shinto practice (Mt. Fuji, for example), while others have their presence invoked at Shinto shrines through the use of ritual practice. While most kami have been perceived as protective spirits, evil kami exist as well. A great deal of Shinto practice, in both shrines and the home (*kamidana*—

home shrine), deals with calling upon and honoring kami.

G. D. DeAngelis

See also AMATERASU; IZANAGI; IZANAMI; KAGURA; KAMIDANA; KOJIKI; MATSURI; NIHONJI; NORITO; SHINTO; SHRINE; TORII.

KAMIDANA

(Japanese, god shelf). In Shinto practice, a small household shrine that contains objects of veneration such as memorial tablets of ancestors or patron deities, *emma* and talismans collected from visits to different shrines, and generally any object of special significance to the family. Not only does it serve as the center for daily prayers, but it symbolizes the central religious function of the home.

G. D. DeAngelis

See also BUTSUDAN; KAMI; SHINTO.

KANNON

See KUAN-YIN.

KANT, IMMANUEL (1724–1804)

German philosopher. Immanuel Kant is often credited with having effected a "Copernican revolution" in philosophy through his "turn to the subject." In effect, this turn reversed the methodological order of classical (Greek) philosophy by maintaining that the investigation on how humans "know" precedes and limits what humans can know, that is, metaphysics. In the *Critique of Pure Reason* (1781; 1787), Kant deprived religion of its foundation in pure (speculative) reason by arguing that the classical "proofs" of the existence of God exceeded the limits of possible human knowing and thus led to metaphysical contradictions. In his writings on ethics, including the *Critique of Practical*

Reason (1788), he argued that the foundation of religion lay in practical reason, that is, belief in the existence of God and a future life were "postulates" necessary for the consistency of the moral life. From this perspective, Kant offered a commentary on Christian doctrine in *Religion Within the Limits of Reason Alone* (1792), a text that functioned as a source of the Ritschelian strand of liberal theology.

J. A. Colombo

See also LIBERAL THEOLOGY; RITSCHL, ALBRECHT.

KARAITES

A Jewish movement that began in the eighth century C.E. under the leadership of Anan ben David that maintained that the Bible alone was binding for religious behavior. The Karaites rejected the Talmud and the legal interpretation of the Torah preserved in the Mishnah and the Gemara, the two sections of the Talmud. They rejected rabbinic authority and sometimes even their interpretive rules. Anan maintained the necessity for the constant study of the Hebrew Scriptures in order to interpret them properly and arrive at rules for daily life. Each Karaite was to study the Bible personally in order to arrive at his or her own understanding. Karaism seems to have been in part a revolt against authority. Later leaders were not quite so fanatical and even adopted some rabbinic legal rulings as well as rabbinic interpretive methods. After the first generation, a literature developed among the Karaites in both Aramaic and Hebrew. Karaism reached its peak in the eleventh and twelfth centuries when rabbinic authorities declared it heretical and forbade intermarriage with Karaites.

Russell Fuller

KARBALA

City in Iraq where, on October 10, 680, Husayn, grandson of the Prophet Muhammad (570–632), was killed by the forces of the Ummayad Caliphate (Islamic leadership). Two of Husayn's sons, as well as some seventy others who accompanied Husayn, also lost their lives in the confrontation. The Ummayads had gained control of the caliphate after the assassination of Husayn's father, Ali. The dispute between the Ummayads and Ali's family over the caliphate led to a division in Islam that continues until this day. After Husayn's death, the partisans of Ali and Husayn established their own Islamic movement called Shi'ism, distinguishing themselves from the majority group of Muslims, the Sunnis. Shi'ites consider Husayn's death a martyrdom they commemorate each year at Karbala by reenacting the event in what is sometimes described as a "passion play."

Ronald A. Pachence

See also ALI; CALIPH (KALIPHA)/CALIPHATE; SHI'A/SHI'I/SHI'ITE/SHI'ISM; SUNNA/SUNNI/SUNNISM; TWELVERS (IN ISLAM); UMMAYADS.

KARMA

Karma (sometimes written *karman*) is a Sanskrit word meaning "action." It is used in this simple sense in the compound *karma-yoga*, the yoga of action. Most typically, however, especially when it is used alone, it refers to a somewhat more complex idea: the notion that the actions we perform produce inevitable moral consequences. Accepted, with variations, by all of the Indic religions (Hinduism, Buddhism, Jainism, Sikhism), the doctrine of karma teaches that every action creates effects that eventually, whether in this or another life, will generate further experience for its author. The moral effects of action, which lead to good or bad future consequences in perfect measure with the quality of the actions that produced them, are called karma. The course of our repeated births in samsara (the cosmos), and the quality of our experience in those births, are determined, on this theory, by our accumulated karma. Those who accept the doctrine of karma see in it a scheme of universal justice and an answer to the problem of evil. Still, it is believed that karma can be dissipated by asceticism, yogic practice, and spiritual knowledge (*jnana*). In theistic Hinduism, it is believed that devotees (*bhaktas*) can be freed of their karmic burdens by the grace of a great deity such as Shiva or Vishnu.

Lance E. Nelson

See also BHAKTI; BUDDHISM; CASTE; EVIL; HINDUISM; JAINISM; KARMA-YOGA; SIKHISM; THEODICY.

KARMA-YOGA

One of the four *yogas* in Hinduism, *karma-yoga* (Sanskrit, "action–discipline") is the yoga, or spiritual discipline, of action. Taught especially in the *Bhagavad Gita*, karma-yoga is designed to make the everyday duties of a person's life a means to liberation rather than a source of bondage. The secret, according to the *Gita*, is to perform one's actions in a selfless way, without desire (*niskama*). If one performs the actions enjoined by one's dharma (religious duty) without attachment and personal desire, solely because it is one's destiny and sacred obligation to do so, they will not generate karmic bondage. Rather, they will purify the mind and bring one closer to moksha (liberation). Like *bhakti-yoga*, karma-yoga is a discipline that is open to laypeople, and forms an important component of the spirituality of active Hindus. Mahatma Gandhi is perhaps the best modern example of a practitioner of karma-yoga. Note that the word karma in this context means simply "action," not—as when speaking of the theory of karma—the moral consequences of one's action.

Lance E. Nelson

See also BHAGAVAD GITA; BHAKTI-YOGA; HINDUISM; YOGA.

KARUNA

A Sanskrit term meaning "compassion," a spiritual quality perfectly embodied by a Buddha and an ideal for all Buddhists. According to accounts of Shakyamuni's life, after enlightenment he was initially not convinced that others would understand his doctrine, but was moved to help them grasp it, out of compassion for humanity. It is compassion, not pessimism, that is the outcome of Buddhism's emphasis on life's inevitable suffering (*duhkha*). The texts directed to the laity emphasize various ways a Buddhist society should be marked by reciprocal concerns among students and teachers, husbands and wives, children and parents, even gods and humans. In Mahayana Buddhism, *karuna* was also emphasized strongly: bodhisattvas are instructed to balance attempts to see all phenomena as absent of independent existence with commitment to serve deluded, suffering human beings. The bodhisattva vows state that only when all beings have been compassionately enlightened will any truly reach nirvana.

Todd T. Lewis

See also BODHISATTVA; BUDDHA.

KÄSEMANN, ERNST (1906–98)

Born July 12, 1906, in Bochum-Dahlhausen, this German Lutheran New Testament scholar began his theological studies in 1925 and received his licentiate in 1931. In 1933 he became pastor of the Lutheran church in Gelsenkirchen-Rotthausen; because of his anti-Nazi preaching there Käsemann was arrested and imprisoned for four weeks in 1937. During these weeks he worked on *Das wandernde Gottesvolk: Eine Untersuchung zum Hebräerbrief* (*The Wandering People of God: An Investigation of the Letter to the Hebrews*), a work written with the Confessing Church in mind. In 1942 he was drafted into the army, serving in Paris and in Greece during the Second World War. Käsemann became associate professor at the University of Mainz in 1946, receiving his doctorate the following year from the University of Marburg, where he studied under Rudolf Bultmann. In 1951 he went as full professor to the University of Göttingen, and then in 1959 to the University of Tübingen, from which he retired in 1971.

With his 1953 article entitled, "The Problem of the Historical Jesus," Käsemann launched what came to be known as the "New Quest for the Historical Jesus," a reaction against Bultmann by scholars who had been his own students, challenging Bultmann's claim that there was no connection between the Jesus of history and the Christ of faith. In that article, Käsemann wrote of Jesus that "if he can be placed at all, it must be in terms of historical particularity. . . . For to his particularity there corresponds the particularity of faith, for which the real history of Jesus is always happening afresh; it is now the history of the exalted Lord, but it does not cease to be the earthly history it once was, in which the call and the claim of the Gospel are encountered" (*Essays on New Testament Themes*, 46–7).

In addition to his contributions to historical Jesus research, it was Käsemann

who argued that apocalyptic is the "mother of Christian theology." In his study of the letters of Paul, particularly of Romans, Käsemann devoted much attention to the significance of the "righteousness of God."

Works by Käsemann available in English include *The Testament of Jesus: A Study of the Gospel of John in the Light of Chapter 17* (1968); *New Testament Questions of Today* (1969); *Jesus Means Freedom* (1970); *Perspectives on Paul* (1971); and *Commentary on Romans* (1980).

Jean-Pierre Ruiz

See also APOCALYPTIC; BULTMANN, RUDOLF; CONFESSING CHURCH; JESUS OF HISTORY; RIGHTEOUSNESS (IN CHRISTIAN PERSPECTIVE).

KASHRUT

In Judaism, biblical and rabbinic regulations delimiting permitted and prohibited foods and describing acceptable methods of food preparation. The foundation of the Jewish dietary system derives from Scripture, which distinguishes animals that are forbidden or permitted for consumption, defines basic requirements for slaughter of animals for meat, and indicates how food must be prepared in order to be permitted for consumption. Rabbinic writings dramatically expand the legislation in each of these areas.

To be permitted for consumption, animals must chew the cud and have cloven hooves; fowl must have an extra toe and a gizzard the sac of which can be peeled; and fish must have fins and scales that can be removed without tearing the skin. Insects and reptiles are uniformly forbidden except, according to the Talmud, for certain locusts that have four legs and wings. So long as they derive from permitted animals and are prepared without any meat additives, dairy products are permitted, as are all fruits and vegetables, which are subject to no special requirements. Wine, a special category, is permitted only if prepared under Jewish jurisdiction. This regulation resulted from the fear in classical Judaism that a non-Jew might pour some wine out as a libation and thereby dedicate the entire vat to a pagan deity.

Of particular concern in the preparation of foods is the slaughter of animals for meat, a procedure subject to intricate regulations designed to assure that the animal is killed quickly and painlessly, that it has no internal defects, and that no blood is consumed. The slaughter must sever the animal's esophagus and trachea in one swift cut without chopping or tearing the flesh. After slaughter, the cut and all of the animal's organs are examined for defects such as perforations, blisters, cysts, swelling, and other blemishes. Such defects, which the Talmud understands as likely to have led to the animal's death within a year (Babylonian Talmud Hullin 11a-b), render the meat impermissible for consumption by Jews.

Finally, all blood must be removed, in compliance with Scripture's prohibition against consuming blood, the symbol of the animal's life belonging to God (Lev 7:26-27; Lev 17:10-14). To accomplish this, certain veins are removed, and the meat is soaked and salted. The lungs, liver, and other parts of the carcass that contain significant amounts of blood must be perforated or sliced open to allow all blood to drain. Meat that is not salted and drained of blood within seventy-two hours of slaughter may be consumed only if it is roasted over an open flame, deemed an effective method of removing blood.

The preparation of other foods is governed by the principle that meat and dairy products may not be cooked together or even prepared in or served on the same utensils. The rules of kashrut accordingly require the use of separate cooking utensils, serving dishes, plates, and cutlery for meat and dairy foods. This prevents the actual mixing of the food or even the imparting of a dairy taste to meat or vice versa. To further prevent the mixing of meat and dairy foods, these different categories are not eaten together at the same meal, and it is customary to wait a period of time, ranging from an hour to several hours, between eating one category of food and the other. Fruits, vegetables, and eggs are deemed a separate category of their own (*pareve*), and may be consumed with meat or dairy products.

Jews generally understand the food taboos to promote moral conduct, but do not attempt to explain them philosophically. The Talmudic literature states that it is of no concern to God how an animal is killed, and recognizes instead the human significance of observing divine edicts for their own sake (Genesis Rabbah 44:1; Leviticus Rabbah 13:3; Sifra 11:22). In later periods, the dietary restrictions have variously been explained as a system of health and disease prevention, as methods of assuring the humane treatment of animals, as a system of social differentiation, or, in line with the Talmudic view, as an aspect of adherence to the divine will that requires no philosophical or social explanation.

Alan J. Avery-Peck

KASPER, WALTER (1933–)

German Catholic theologian, bishop, and cardinal. Professor of dogmatic theology at Münster (1964–70), then at Tübingen (1970–89), Kasper's work features a contemporary application of the Catholic Tübingen School's theological approach. This means considering the problem of faith and theology to history, and exploring the historical development of theological themes in service of contemporary speculation and proclamation. Kasper's theology advocates theological reflection rooted in Scripture and the study of tradition. This approach is described in *The Methods of Dogmatic Theology* (1969); its results are seen in his two dogmatic treatises, *Jesus the Christ* (1976) and *The God of Jesus Christ* (1988). These works focus less on the contemporary explication of topics and more on the methodological issues and tradition history that bear on the subject. Kasper was named bishop of Rottenburg-Stuttgart in 1989 and named as a cardinal in 2001 when he was also appointed as President of the Pontifical Council for Promoting Christian Unity. Kasper's interest remains in exploring the unrealized potential of Vatican Council II for the church and for contemporary faith and theology.

Patricia Plovanich

KEBLE, JOHN (1792–1866)
Priest and pastor in the Church of England; Oxford professor of poetry (1831–41). Newman and others considered him as the founder of the Oxford Movement by virtue of his sermon "National Apostasy" in July 1833, in which he attacked the extreme Erastianism of the Church of England. He and his allies in the Oxford Movement sought to invigorate the authority of tradition and to ground the authority of bishops not in the nation, Crown, or Parliament, but in apostolic succession. He wrote seven of the movement's "Tracts for the Times," as well as an extraordinarily popular devotional work, *The Christian Year* (published anonymously), and edited the first modern version of the works of Hooker (1836). He also collaborated with Newman and Pusey on *The Library of the Fathers*. Keble was renowned for his holiness. The Episcopal Church commemorates him on March 29.

Jon Nilson

See also ERASTIANISM; NEWMAN, JOHN HENRY; OXFORD MOVEMENT; PUSEY, EDWARD B.

KEDUSHAH
(Hebrew, sanctification). In Judaism, the third of the Eighteen Benedictions, the central liturgical formulation that stands at the heart of all the Jewish morning, additional, and afternoon worship services. In the Kedushah, the congregation stands and imagines itself as the earthly embodiment of the heavenly host described in Ezekiel, chapter 1. The text of the Kedushah for weekday mornings is as follows:

Leader: We proclaim Your holiness on earth as it is proclaimed in the heavens above. As it is written in your prophet's vision, they called one to the other and said:

Response: Holy, holy, holy is the Lord of hosts, the whole world is filled with his glory (Isa 6:3).

Leader: Heavenly voices respond with praise:

Response: Praised is the glory of the Lord from his place (Ezek 3:12).

Leader: And in Your holy psalms it is written:

Response: The Lord shall reign through all generations; your God, Zion, shall reign forever and ever. Halleluiah (Ps 146:10).

Leader: We declare Your greatness through all generations, hallow your holiness to all eternity. Your praise will never leave your lips, for you are God and ruler, great and holy.

The Kedushah is recited only in a quorum of ten Jews. While its basic structure is always as recited on weekday mornings, on Sabbaths and festivals it is expanded to include two additional responses of the congregation, a declaration of the Shema (Deut 6:4), and a citation of God's statement, "I am the Lord your God" (Isa 43:4 and elsewhere).

Alan J. Avery-Peck

See also SHEMA; SHEMONAH ESREH.

KENOSIS

From the Greek term *kenos*, meaning "empty." *Kenosis* is an aspect of Pauline christology derived from Paul's statement in Philippians 2:6-7 that Christ Jesus, "though he was in the form of God, did not regard equality with God as something to be exploited, but emptied himself, taking the form of a slave, being born in human likeness." Kenosis, understood theologically as a process of deliberate self-emptying, refers to the extreme limit of self-denial that characterized Christ Jesus, a self-emptying even to death. According to the rest of the hymn quoted in Philippians 2:6-11, because of this kenosis Christ was given by God the name "Lord," that is above every name. It is debated whether the self-emptying of Jesus "in the form of God" implies his preexistence or refers rather solely to his earthly existence.

Kenosis is an important concept in Christian reflection not only about the meaning of Christ but also about what discipleship concretely entails. The example Christ gave in his selfless death reminds believers of the necessity of their own obedience to God's will. Likewise, Christ's self-emptying service to others is the inspiration for what should similarly be a characteristic of believers' lives.

F. M. Gillman

See also CHRISTOLOGY; INCARNATION; LORD/LORDSHIP; PAULINE THEOLOGY; RESURRECTION (IN CHRISTIANITY).

KENRICK, FRANCIS P. (1797–1863)

American Catholic bishop, archbishop, and theologian. Prelate in the mid-nineteenth century, Kenrick served as bishop of Philadelphia (1842–50), then as archbishop of Baltimore (1851–63), and engaged many issues facing the fledgling church. His protest to the Philadelphia School Board for forcing Catholic students to use the Protestant Bible stirred up anti-Catholic riots in 1844. He remained preoccupied with problems stemming from the rapid growth of the American church. His passivity toward the violence was criticized by Bishop John Hughes of New York. Archbishop of Baltimore during the Civil War, Kenrick remained silent about the war and slavery. He was an opponent of lay involvement in ecclesial affairs and presided over the First Plenary Council of Baltimore (1852) to address the new problems. A scholar educated in Rome, Kenrick published a volume of moral theology for seminary use, studies of the Old Testament, and English translations of the Gospels and psalms. He criticized Pius IX's definition of the dogma of the Immaculate Conception (1864) for its imprecise use of Scripture and tradition and its insensitivity to ecumenical reaction.

Patricia Plovanich

See also BALTIMORE, COUNCILS OF; IMMACULATE CONCEPTION.

KEPAH

Also known as *yarmulka*, this is a head-covering worn by Jews.

Judaism was born and grew up in the Eastern world where a sign of respect to other people and surely to God was—and still is—a covered head. Though Judaism moved to the Western world—where the sign of respect is to uncover the head—it has maintained its original custom of the covered head as a sign of respect to God, through the wearing of a *kepah*.

Reasoning that they are always in the presence of God, Orthodox Jews wear a kepah all the time. More liberal Jews wear a kepah for worship, study, and eating. Reform Judaism adopted the Western custom of showing respect with an uncovered head, and eliminated the use of a kepah. However, in recent times, many Reform Jews have returned to wearing a kepah for worship.

In addition to being a sign of respect for God, the wearing of the kepah today is a symbol and a statement of Jewish identity.

Until recent times, it was only men who wore a kepah. Now many women choose to wear a kepah also.

Wayne Dosick

See also YARMULKA.

KERI'AH

(Hebrew, tearing). A Jewish ritual in which, immediately preceding the funeral, near relatives of the deceased rip a part of their clothing as a sign of grief. In current prac-tice, the tear commonly is made in a piece of black ribbon pinned to the mourners' attire.

Alan J. Avery-Peck

KERIAT HATORAH

Hebrew meaning, "reading of the Torah." The centerpiece of certain Jewish worship services during the course of each week is the reading of the Torah.

The Torah—the Five Books of Moses—has been divided into fifty-four separate sections or portions. One portion is read each week (sometimes two are combined) so that the entire Torah is read from beginning to end in the course of one year.

The Torah is read four times each week. The first part of the weekly portion is read for the first time on Saturday afternoon at the Shabbat *minchah* service, and is repeated at the *shacharit* service on Monday morning and on Thursday morning. The entire weekly portion is read at the Shabbat morning service. The Torah is also read on all holiday and festival mornings, including Hanukah, Rosh Hodesh, and on fast days. The Torah reading for each festival was specially selected by the sages for its thematic connection and relevance to the holiday being celebrated.

Wayne Dosick

See also HANUKKAH; MINCHAH; ROSH HODESH; SHABBAT; SHACHARIT.

KERULLARIOS, MICHAEL (?–1058)

Michael originally intended to go into politics, but when his brother committed suicide, he gave himself over to the monastic life. Michael became patriarch of Constantinople in 1043 when he became involved in a fierce controversy with the Western Christians over the *Filioque* clause and over the use of unleavened bread in the Eucharist. The pope sent a delegation to Constantinople to work out an agreement, but negotiations went very badly. Finally, in 1054 the Western delegation slapped a writ of excommunication on the altar of the cathedral of Constantinople and left. As patriarch, Michael Kerullarios responded by excommunicating the Western Church. Although eventually the excommunications were lifted, the Great Schism between Eastern and Western Christianity is usually dated from this time.

Gary Macy

See also EUCHARIST; EXCOMMUNICATION; FILIOQUE; PATRIARCH; PHOTIUS; SCHISM, GREAT EASTERN.

KERYGMA

In Christian discourse the term "kerygma" incorporates the meaning of the Greek verb *kerysso* (to announce or to make an authoritative proclamation) and noun *kerygma* (proclamation) to speak of both the content and the act of preaching the Christian message. At the most fundamental level, the content of the kerygma is the death (1 Cor 1:23) and resurrection of Christ (1 Cor 15:12). However, the term incorporates all the memories of Jesus and their implications as they were interpreted by his earliest followers. The act of proclamation is not only understood as preaching the Christian understanding of what God accomplished in the life, death, and resurrection of Jesus, but it also conveys that the very act of proclamation actualizes the salvific significance of the kerygma in the life of believers (1 Cor 1:21; 2:4-5). While the early Christians also used words such as "the Gospel," or "the tradition" (*paradosis*) as technical terms to summarize the content of the kerygma, as well as words such as "to evangelize," or "to witness" when speaking of the act

of preaching, the word "kerygma" incorporates the two and so nuances both a historical and an eschatological understanding of God's past, present, and ongoing redemptive activity.

Many passages in the New Testament provide summaries of the content of the kerygma (for example, Acts 2:14-36; 3:12-26; 4:8-12; 10:34-42; 13:16-41; Rom 1:3-4; Phil 2:6-11, and the like). These passages shape biographical details of Jesus according to early Christian interpretations of the religious traditions of Israel read from the perspective of the Resurrection experience. The New Testament understands this proclamation to be in continuity with the preaching of Jesus as well as that of John the Baptist, although while Jesus proclaimed the reign of God, his followers proclaimed Jesus.

In some patristic writings the word "kerygma" consisted of the apostolic preaching, or the "rule of faith," that is, belief in God as Creator, Jesus as Son of God, and the Spirit as sanctifier in addition to the "economics" of salvation: the Incarnation, virginal conception, Passion, Resurrection, and the expectation of Christ's second coming in glory as universal judge of humanity (Irenaeus, *Haer.* 1.10.1). Others understood the term in its larger sense of preaching the truth of the reign of God as manifested by the salvific activities of Christ that were actualized by the missionary activity of the apostles and continues in the church, especially by the Bishops of Rome (Eusebius, *Hist. eccl.* I.10.1, 7; II.1.13, 9.4, 22.4; III.24.7, 32.8; IV.14.8; V.6.5, 28.3). These applications of the term were shaped as responses to various interpretations of Jesus that were rejected by the larger church.

Between 1950–60 there was a strong trend to reintroduce kerygmatic elements in the study and teaching of Christianity.

It centered on the idea that catechetical instruction should be an invitation to faith and commitment.

Regina A. Boisclair

See also KERYGMATIC THEOLOGY.

KERYGMATIC THEOLOGY

An approach to the study and teaching of Christianity that emphasized the core contents of the Christian faith. It had a meteoric rise and dominance in North American catechetics during the middle of the twentieth century (1955–70). Although kerygmatic theology has been displaced by other theological approaches and educational premises, many of its presuppositions were revived in *The Catechism of the Catholic Church* promulgated in 1992.

Taking its name from the Greek term *kerygma*, translated as "preaching" or "proclamation," kerygmatic theology was an outgrowth of the biblical theology and liturgical movements that began in Europe during the late nineteenth century. Both movements stressed "salvation history" (*Heilsgeschichte*) that assumes that Christ is the center of God's progressive Self-revelation in history. Thus, it assumed that the New Testament fulfills and completes the Old.

By stressing salvation history as the "economy of salvation," the kerygmatic approach emphasized God's salvific plan fulfilled in Jesus Christ and shaped by the proclamation of the early church. In Protestant churches it transformed Christian nurture from teachings stressing how to be Christian into a presentation of the Gospel that stressed what it means to be Christian by using biblical characters and stories as prototypes. Among Catholics, the kerygmatic approach sought to transform the Scholastic tendency to emphasize dogmatic concepts and to isolate ancillary pieces of knowledge with a question-and-answer catechism. Catholic catechesis was reshaped into a proclamation of their biblical heritage.

The kerygmatic approach was useful to introduce Catholics to biblical texts that they were just beginning to feel encouraged to read. However, developments in biblical studies rightfully challenged the premise that salvation history unified the biblical message. In addition, Jewish-Christian dialogues made it increasingly apparent that the foundational presuppositions of kerygmatic theology promoted a supersessionist understanding of Israel and Judaism. The kerygmatic approach did not recognize that a promise-fulfillment approach is a secondary reading of the Old Testament from a christological perspective. While this secondary reading is in fact introduced in New Testament texts and may yield important insights for Christians, it is not the only possible interpretation of Old Testament texts, and it can lead to important misunderstandings.

Regina A. Boisclair

KETUBAH

In Judaism, a marriage contract outlining the financial and personal obligations of the husband to the wife within the context of the marriage, and setting out the sum of money to be paid by the husband or his estate to the wife in the event of a divorce or of his death. The Ketubah is signed by witnesses who attest that the groom has formally accepted the responsibilities toward the bride described in the document; traditionally the Ketubah is not signed by the bride and groom themselves.

By defining the husband's financial obligation to the wife, the Ketubah limited his otherwise free right of divorce (in Judaism, divorce does not require the consent of the woman). If a high enough figure is stipulated, the husband may find it impossible to effect a divorce at all. The serious legal and financial ramifications of the Ketubah are clear by the fact that, in classical Jewish practice, the Ketubah represented a lien against the husband's property. While the wife could in no circumstance release her husband from the obligations of the Ketubah, she did have the right to sell this lien to another who would, in the event of the husband's death or of a divorce, collect the stipulated amount in place of the wife.

The Ketubah originated in the first centuries C.E. and is written in Aramaic, the Jewish vernacular of the Greco-Roman period. Its reading comprises a central part of the traditional Jewish wedding ceremony. In modern times, many Conservative and Reform Jews use an altered text that speaks as well of the obligations of the wife to the husband. Those in the Reform movement in particular use a document that refers to spiritual and personal, rather than financial, obligations.

The Ketubah is a popular Jewish art form, prepared with a text and illuminations illustrating themes important to the bride and groom, and often depicting above the text an image of Jerusalem.

Alan J. Avery-Peck

See also GET; MARRIAGE (IN JUDAISM).

KETUBAH KIDDUSHIN

See MARRIAGE (IN JUDAISM).

KHADIJA (555?–619)

In the Islamic tradition, this was the Prophet Muhammad's (570–632) first wife whom he married when he was twenty-five and she was forty. By all accounts, Khadija was a prosperous widow and trader before she married the Prophet. After the marriage, Muhammad managed her caravans. The couple had two sons who died in their infancy, and four daughters.

Ronald A. Pachence

See also ISLAM; MUHAMMAD.

KHARIJITES

An Islamic sect whose name means "seceders." The Kharijites took this name because it describes their rejection of an arbitrated settlement between Ali, the fourth caliph (leader) of Islam, and Ali's rival Mu'awiya. At issue were some disputes that lingered after the murder of the third caliph, Uthman. The Kharijites, who had originally sided with Ali, believed that Ali's cause was compromised when Ali accepted Mu'awiya's proposal for arbitration of their differences during the Battle of Suffin (657 C.E.). God's will, they said, not arbitration should guide Islam. As it turned out, it was a Kharijite named Ibn Muljam who assassinated Ali in 661 C.E., thus setting the stage for Mu'awiya and his family to seize control of the caliphate. Theologically, the Kharijites developed a controversial doctrine of salvation that holds that some grave sins, like theft and adultery, deprive people of salvation no matter how much their faith prompts them to call on God's divine mercy. They also advocated that serious sinners should be executed.

Ronald A. Pachence

See also ALI; CALIPH (KALIPHA)/CALIPHATE; SHI'A/SHI'I/SHI'ITE/SHI'ISM; UMMAYADS; UTHMAN.

KIBLA

Also written *qibla*, an Arabic word meaning "direction." In Islam, *kibla* is the direction of Mecca from any given location in the world. Determining this direction is important for Muslims who offer their prayers five times each day facing the holy city of Mecca. In every mosque, kibla is indicated by a niche (*mihrab*) usually located in the front of the structure.

Ronald A. Pachence

See also MECCA; MIHRAB; MOSQUE/
MASJID; MUSLIM; SALAT.

KIDDUSH

(Hebrew, sanctification). In Judaism, the liturgical formulation recited over a cup of wine in the home before the evening meal or in the synagogue during evening prayers to mark the beginning of the Sabbath or other festival. A benediction over wine ("Blessed are you, Lord our God, Ruler over the universe, who has brought forth the fruit of the vine") is followed by other benedictions that reflect the particular theme of the Sabbath or festival being marked. These benedictions thank God for making a covenant with the people of Israel and for providing the particular occasion for celebration. An abbreviated form of the Kiddush is recited prior to the midday meal on the Sabbath or festival itself.

The use of the Kiddush to mark the beginning of Sabbaths and festivals is known in the Mishnah, where the specifics of this liturgy are disputed by the Houses of Hillel and Shammai (first century C.E.). While there is no proof for this claim, Babylonian Talmud Berakhot 33a states that the ceremony's origins are hundreds of years earlier.

Alan J. Avery-Peck

KIERKEGAARD, SØREN (1813–55)

Danish Lutheran philosopher and theologian. Kierkegaard's works on literature, philosophy, theology, and ethics are distinguished by a severe criticism of the romantic interpretations of Christianity popularized by Hegel, Schelling, and others. Dedicated to the Protestant scriptural principle, Kierkegaard believed the Bible to reveal Christianity's essential opposition to human culture. His dialectical method featured antitheses to express the infinite qualitative difference between God and humanity and to criticize the Christian philosophies of his era and the religious practice of his milieu. His works emphasize the import of human freedom in the quest for meaning, contrast natural life with the life of faith, and propose faith alone to disclose ultimate meaning. In essence, Kierkegaard's works are an existential reflection on the conflicted themes of his life and era. He is considered the founder of existentialism, and his dialectical method influenced the later work of neo-orthodox theologians such as Karl Barth.

Patricia Plovanich

See also BARTH, KARL; EXISTENTIALISM.

KING, MARTIN LUTHER, JR. (1929–68)

The civil rights movement of the 1950s and 1960s is linked intimately to the name of a young Baptist minister and theologian, the Reverend Martin Luther King Jr. King was born January 15, 1929, in Atlanta, Georgia, the son and grandson of Baptist ministers. He attended segregated public schools in Atlanta and graduated from Morehouse College in 1948 at the age of nineteen. King earned a graduate degree from Crozier Theological Seminary and a doctoral degree in systematic theology from Boston University in 1955. In 1953 he married Coretta Scott and the couple moved to Montgomery, Alabama, where King took up duties as full-time pastor of Dexter Avenue Baptist Church. Four children were born into their family.

The refusal of Rosa Parks to yield her seat to a white bus patron on December 1, 1955, and her subsequent arrest sparked Montgomery's black community to action. King's prayerful and thoughtful leadership galvanized the black community and awakened the moral conscience of America. Despite white intimidation of local blacks, the bombing of King's home and threats against him, the boycott of the bus system lasted 381 days. On November 13, 1956, the Supreme Court of the United States declared Alabama's state and local laws enforcing segregation on buses to be unconstitutional.

From 1957 through 1968, King led the Southern Christian Leadership Conference, an organization that provided leadership for the civil rights movement in the struggle against segregation and discrimination. King joined Gandhian tactics of nonviolence to a Christian vision of justice through neighbor-love. At the age of thirty-five, King became the youngest recipient of the Nobel Peace Prize. Following the passage of civil rights legislation by the U.S. Congress in the mid-1960s, King turned his attention to two issues that he saw as closely related to racial justice: economic justice and the war in Vietnam. His solidarity with the poor of all races and his outspoken opposition to the war won him both praise and harsh criticism. He was gunned down on April 4, 1968, in Memphis, Tennessee, where he had gone to support a strike by garbage workers of that city.

M. Shawn Copeland

KITTEL, GERHARD (1888–1948)

German biblical scholar, son of Rudolf Kittel, and professor of New Testament at Tübingen. Gerhard Kittel specialized in the study of first- and second-century Christianity and Judaism. He is best known for his series of nine volumes called *Theologisches Wörterbuch zum Neuen Testament* (*TWzNT*, 1933–73), or in its English translation, *Theological Dictionary of the New Testament* (*TDNT*, 1964–74). *TWzNT* enlisted major German scholars to discuss selected New Testament words against the background of their Greek, Hebrew, and Hellenistic roots. Then it studies their use in first-century Christian and non-Christian writings, and in the early church fathers. Despite grave questions about its linguistic and theological presumptions, *TWzNT* remains a basic reference work for modern New Testament scholarship.

Francis D. Connolly-Weinert

KITTEL, RUDOLF (1853–1929)

German biblical scholar and professor at Leipzig who supervised production of a critical edition of the Hebrew text of the Old Testament called the *Biblia Hebraica*. Kittel sought to produce a comprehensive work based mainly on the Leningrad manuscript, one of the oldest surviving copies of the complete Hebrew Bible. In keeping with his aim, to correct inconsistencies and also to incorporate recent manuscript discoveries from Qumran, Kittel's work has been revised in updated editions supervised by K. Elliger and W. Rudolf (1967), G. Weil (1977), as well as H. Rüger and A. Schenker (1997).

Francis D. Connolly-Weinert

KNIGHTS OF COLUMBUS

The Knights of Columbus is a Catholic fraternal society founded by Fr. Michael

McGivney in Connecticut in 1882. From its inception, it provided Catholic men opportunities for social life, for financial assistance (an insurance program), for spiritual development and church service, and for education about Catholic culture and faith. As many early members were Irish immigrants, their commitment to the patron, Columbus, attested their conviction about the compatibility of Catholicism and American citizenship, and they promised to work for the civil and social rights of all Americans. The society developed a large international membership and a national administration that even today provides economic support for church projects and an educational program that promotes the use of the print as well as the television media.

Patricia Plovanich

KNITTER, PAUL F. (1939–)

American Catholic theologian. A native of Chicago, Knitter earned his doctorate in theology at the University of Marburg, Germany. He has taught at the Catholic Theological Union and, since 1975, at Cincinnati's Xavier University. Knitter has made significant contributions to the Christian theological reflection on the salvific meaning and importance of non-Christian religions and to interreligious dialogue. Within American Catholicism he was among the first to open new avenues of discourse and thought on the possibility of interreligious theology. Among his more important books are *No Other Name? A Critical Survey of Christian Attitudes toward the World's Religions* (1985), *The Myth of Christian Uniqueness* (1987), and *One Earth, Many Religions: Multifaith Dialogue and Global Responsibility* (1995).

Orlando Espín

See also CULTURE; INCULTURATION; MISSIOLOGY; RELIGION; THEOLOGY OF RELIGIONS.

KNOX, JOHN (1513?–72)

Scottish Reformer Knox played a central role in the definitive establishment of Calvinism in Scotland. A chaplain at the court of King Edward VI of England, Knox fled to the Continent when the Catholic Queen Mary became the English sovereign. In Geneva, Knox gained greater familiarity with Calvin's approach to reform of the church. Knox wrote, in 1558, *First Blast of the Trumpet against the Monstrous Regiment of Women*, a work in which he insists that women have no right to rule. Knox also produced various theological works on subjects such as predestination. Returning to Scotland in 1559, Knox soon became one of the principal opponents of Mary, Queen of Scots, a Catholic. After Mary abdicated as sovereign, her young son was crowned as James VI; he was raised as a Protestant. Knox was active in the early years of the reign of James VI in securing Protestant control of Scotland.

Thomas Worcester, S.J.

See also CALVIN, JOHN; CALVINISM; PREDESTINATIONISM (CALVINIST); REFORMATION; REFORMED CHURCH; REFORMED THEOLOGY (-IES).

KOAN

(Japanese, lit., public theme; Chinese, *kung-an*). A tool used in Zen (Rinzai) practice to help overcome dualistic thinking. The *koan* generally takes the form of an enigmatic riddle or problem the disciple is asked to solve that cannot be solved by the discursive mind and logical reasoning. In effect, it stops the discursive mind in its tracks and forces the mind to go beyond intellect to intuition and a deeper level of awareness, where one will see life as it actually is. Two of the more popular koans are: What is the sound of one hand clapping? Does a dog have Buddha nature?

G. D. DeAngelis

See also BODHI; RINZAI; SANZEN; SATORI; SESSHIN; ZAZEN; ZEN.

KOBO DAISHI (774–835)

(Japanese, Kukai, master teacher of the dharma). This was the honorific name bestowed posthumously upon the ninth-century Japanese Buddhist monk and founder of the Shingon sect, Kukai. He was widely recognized as a saint, poet, teacher, and calligrapher who made numerous contributions to the religious and cultural life of Japan, where he is still greatly revered today. He was originally trained for government service but, in time, developed an interest in spiritual and religious matters. He became a Buddhist monk, but quickly became disenchanted with the prevailing Buddhist practice and teaching in Nara. In 804 he traveled to China in search of "true" Buddhism and spent two years with the Chen Yen (True Word) School. Chen Yen was a form of esoteric Buddhism with its roots in the Tantric Buddhism of India. It taught that all the varied phenomena of the universe were but a manifestation of the single, all-inclusive Buddha manifested in the form of Vairocana—the Great Sun Buddha known as Dainichi. The goal of one's life was to experience the unity of all being in becoming one with the Buddha. This could be accomplished through complex and esoteric ritual and meditative practice.

Kobo Daishi brought this new form of Buddhism back to Japan and founded the Shingon (True Word) School. He established a monastery and Buddhist Center at Mt. Koya (east of the old Buddhist capital of Nara) emphasizing the need to make Buddhism native to Japan. His identification of Vairocana (Dainichi) with the Sun Goddess (Amaterasu) certainly assisted in the widespread acceptance of the Shingon School. It became common to Shingon belief that not only was Kukai a great teacher but, in fact, he had acquired the secret teaching (true word) of the Buddha and did not really die but continues to walk around in various parts of Japan offering his blessings to those in need. One of the more popular pilgrimages in Japan today is the Kobo Daishi pilgrimage to Mt. Koya and the Island of Shokoku (where he was born), and is referred to as walking with Kobo Daishi.

G. D. DeAngelis

See also BUDDHISM; SHINGON; TENDAI.

KOHANIM

See KOHEN.

KOHEN

(Hebrew, priest; pl., kohanim). In Judaism, a male descendent of the line of Aaron, brother of Moses, designated by God to be a functionary in the divine service of the ancient Israelite people (Exod 28:1). According to Scripture, the priestly caste received no portion of land within the people, but was supported instead by tithes and portions of the sacrifices the priests offered upon the altar of the wilderness tabernacle and, later, of the Jerusalem Temple. After the destruction of the Temple in 70 C.E., the priests' actual cultic function ceased. Judaism recalls their special status by giving them precedence in reciting a benediction before the reading of the Torah in worship services. Additionally, on festivals (and, in Israel, daily), members of the priestly caste in Orthodox and some conservative congregations bless the people using the priestly blessing formula found at Numbers 6:24-26. Priests further serve in the ritual redemption of the firstborn (*Pidyon HaBen*).

Alan J. Avery-Peck

See also PIDYON HABEN.

KOINĒ GREEK

Greek is one of the languages making up the Indo-European family. Due to the conquests of Alexander the Great, different dialects were absorbed into Attic Greek producing a widespread dialect called Hellenistic or *Koinē* Greek, literally, "common Greek." This *lingua franca* of the Hellenistic world, in common use in the countries of the Mediterranean region in the first century C.E., is the language in which the books of the New Testament were written.

F. M. Gillman

See also HELLENISM / HELLENIC.

KOINONIA

From the Greek *koinos*, meaning "common." *Koinonia* is an abstract term that denotes "participation," "fellowship," and implies a close bond. In the New Testament, for example, in Acts 2:42 Luke employs this term to refer to the earliest Christians in Jerusalem who "devoted themselves to the apostles' teaching and fellowship, to the breaking of bread and prayers." Since these Christians had not yet separated from their Jewish matrix, koinonia here denotes, not exclusively the society of Christians themselves, but a circle of very close fellowship experienced within their broader context.

In Pauline theology in the New Testament, for example, Paul sometimes uses the term quite specifically for the reli-

gious fellowship and participation of believers in Christ as well as for the mutual fellowship among believers. This koinonia is founded upon the believers' faith in Christ.

In Paul's view, those who partake in the Lord's Supper participate in a koinonia with his Body and Blood (1 Cor 10:21); the bread and the wine, as understood by Paul, are vehicles of the presence of Christ; to partake is to experience union with Christ. In their common union with Christ, there is also koinonia among the participants; Christ is as one loaf of bread (10:17).

For Paul, koinonia with Christ means that believers participate in the various phases of the Lord's life. Thus he speaks of believers suffering, dying, and rising with Christ. He sees this not merely in an individual sense, however. The whole community of believers experiences a spiritual koinonia in their sufferings with Christ.

F. M. Gillman

See also KENOSIS; PAULINE THEOLOGY; RESURRECTION (IN CHRISTIANITY).

KOJIKI

(Japanese, Chronicle of Ancient Events). One of the first and most important written records in Japan, completed around 712 C.E. It was intended as a history of Japan from the creation of the world to the middle of the seventh century C.E. It is basically a mixture of cosmology, myth, and chronicle. It contains the earliest recorded forms of Shinto, and it is considered a watershed of myth from which all later Japanese religion, particularly Shinto, is derived. Like the Nihongi, the other major classical text of this period, the Kojiki, in all probability, was compiled by the literati of the imperial court to create a sense of national unity in the face of Chinese social, political, and religious encroachment in Japan. What, in effect, was created was a national myth supporting an imperial line of divine origin by weaving together stories and myths into a unified sequence. Over time the Kojiki became a semisacred text for most Japanese.

G. D. DeAngelis

See also AMATERASU; IZANAGI; IZANAMI; KAMI; NIHONGI; SHINTO.

KOKORO

(Japanese, mind-heart). Shinto belief that there is an organ within human beings that is the locus of feelings, consciousness, and emotional sensitivity. This organ can be used to perceive truth (*makoto*). It is also used in a philosophical sense to refer to the soul or substance that combines the intellect and spiritual nature.

G. D. DeAngelis

See also MAKOTO; SHINTO.

KORAN

See QUR'AN.

KOTEL HAMA'ARAVI

The Western Wall, the last remaining remnant of the Holy Temple in Jerusalem.

When the Romans destroyed the Holy Temple in 70 C.E., they utterly devastated the building and almost all its surrounding structures. The only remnant of the Temple left standing was a wall—not part of the Temple itself, but a portion of the western retaining wall surrounding the Temple Mount. It became known as the Kotel HaMa'aravi, the Western Wall, or simply, the Kotel.

The Kotel became an important symbol for the Jewish people. It achieved a holy status because it was the last vestige of the spot where the Holy Temple once stood. It also became a place for mourning and

weeping over the destruction and the exile. That is why the Western Wall became known as the "Wailing Wall." It also served as a symbol of the hope and promise of return and restoration.

Throughout the centuries, Jews who lived in the Land of Israel, and those who could make pilgrimage there, always came to the Kotel to pray. A Jewish legend says that if a person places a letter or a note of prayer directly into one of the cracks between the stones of the Kotel, the prayer will go straight to God.

With the establishment of the modern State of Israel in 1948, Jewish access to the Kotel was still cut off by the Arab nations that controlled East Jerusalem. In 1967 Israel captured all Jerusalem, and since that time, Jews—as well as people of all faiths and nations—have been able to come to the Kotel.

Wayne Dosick

See also ERETZ YISRAEL; JERUSALEM; MEDINAT YISRAEL.

KOYAMA, KOSUKE (1929–)

Born into a Japanese Christian family (United Church of Christ) and raised during the period of Japan's preparations for World War II, Koyama was partly educated in the West and lived in the United States for many years. As a theologian and missionary, he has also lived in Thailand (eight years), Singapore (six years), and New Zealand (six years). As a missionary to both Asian and Western countries, he has focused his theological attention on the encounter of Asia and the West and has contributed to the development of an inculturated Christian theology, which he sees as the future of Christianity.

James B. Nickoloff

See also CULTURE; INCULTURATION.

KRISHNA

Among the most popular deities in Hinduism, Krishna is regarded by some Hindus as an *avatara* (incarnation) of Vishnu, by others as the source of all avataras and gods, including Vishnu. In either case, he is worshiped by his devotees as the Supreme Being, the creator and sustainer of the universe. The mythic accounts of Krishna's earthly career as avatara, said to have occurred some four thousand years ago, are contained in a number of scriptures, especially the *Mahabharata* and the *Bhagavata Purana*. As recounted in these and other texts, Krishna's life may be divided into two periods: his childhood and youth in the vicinity of Vrindavana (now a sacred city in North India), and his mature life as teacher, warrior, and statesman. In Vrindavana, his childhood was marked by mischievous play, and his youth by intense amorous relations with the young women of the area, the *gopis*. These episodes introduce the themes of God's activity as divine play (*lila*) and of God himself as divine lover. The latter motif is of particular importance to Vaishnava *bhakti* movements, many of which thematize the bliss of human love as a metaphor for the all-consuming joy of the highest states of religious devotion. In his later career, Krishna was intimately involved as warrior and statesman in the great war of the *Mahabharata* and the events preceding it, and he became Hinduism's most famous teacher as the voice of the divine in the *Bhagavad Gita*. The death of Krishna soon after the end of the *Mahabharata* war is said to have marked the beginning of the present dark age, the Kali Yuga. As to the historicity of Krishna, there is some textual evidence for the existence of such a person, perhaps in the first half of the first millennium B.C.E., but it is at best scant and inconclusive.

Lance E. Nelson

See also BHAGAVAD GITA; BHAGAVATA PURANA; BHAKTI; BHAKTI-YOGA; GOPI; LILA; MAHABHARATA; VAISHNAVA; VISHNU; YUGA.

KRISHNAMURTI, JIDDU (1895–1989)

An internationally known spiritual teacher and thinker, Jiddu Krishnamurti was born in India as a Hindu. From the age of twelve, he was raised and educated in Theosophical circles. The Theosophists, whose movement at the time was centered at Adyar, near Madras in South India, believed that they had discovered in Krishnamurti their next World Teacher, whom they identified as Lord Maitreya. In 1929, however, after much excitement over his advent had been generated by Theosophists worldwide, Krishnamurti renounced this role and split with his mentors. He spent the rest of his life traveling internationally, presenting eloquently to large audiences his iconoclastic views on religion and the authentic spiritual life. He taught his followers to eschew gurus or spiritual guides and discover the truth in their own "choiceless awareness." Although he wrote little, many of his talks and interviews have been transcribed and published.

Lance E. Nelson

See also GURU.

KSHATRIYA

In the Hindu caste system, the *kshatriyas* form, after the brahmins, the second of the four pan-Indian caste categories known as *varnas*. The *kshatriya varna* has traditionally been associated with military and governmental occupations. Classified within the kshatriya varna are many kshatriya castes (*jatis*), which are often further divided into smaller groups. Below the kshatriyas in the social hierarchy are the *vaishyas, shudras,* and untouchables.

Lance E. Nelson

See also BRAHMANA/BRAHMIN; CASTE; CASTES, SCHEDULED; HINDUISM; SHUDRA; VAISHYA.

KUAN-YIN

(Chinese, *Guan-yin;* Japanese, Kannon, lit., The Great Compassionate One). Chinese and Japanese form of the great bodhisattva originally known in India and Central Asia as Avalokiteshvara. This deity was initially introduced into China around the fifth century C.E. as a male entity representing the compassion of the Buddha. By the second millennium C.E., Kuan-Shih-Yin had become the focus of a widespread cult and was commonly portrayed as a female figure embodying loving-kindness, a giver of male children to childless wives, and a source of help in time of need. While Kuan-Yin has been perceived primarily as an *avatar* (incarnation) of Amida Buddha's infinite compassion, she also has been recognized as a Taoist deity analogous to the Queen of Heaven and embraced in popular folk religion as a compassionate mother figure. In whatever form Kuan-Yin has taken, she continues to be perceived as a divine being of all-embracing love and benevolence and a great compassionate savior.

G. D. DeAngelis

See also AMITABHA/AMIDA; AVALOKITESHVARA; AVATARA/AVATAR; BODHISATTVA; BUDDHA; BUDDHISM.

KUEI

(Chinese, *gui,* lit., ghosts, demons). In Chinese folk religion, the belief that two classes of spirits inhabit the universe: *kuei*—malevolent *yin* spirits; and *shen*—benevolent *yang* spirits. These kuei are believed to exist in every conceivable variety, are infinite in number, and inhabit every environment. They usually appear as sinister apparitions, sometimes seen as vultures or vampires, and associated with illnesses, suicides, and general misfortune. The actions of the kuei have, at times, been perceived as retributive justice or karma. One of the most widely observed festivals in the Chinese calendar is the Ghost Festival or All Souls' Day, when the kuei are offered propitiation and comfort to insure that the resentment of these neglected spirits would not bring misfortune to the living. In most instances they are feared and guarded against.

G. D. DeAngelis

See also ANCESTORS, CHINESE; HUN; SHEN.

KULTURKAMPF

Kulturkampf is a German word meaning "cultural struggle" or "battle over culture." The *Kulturkampf* was a dispute about church–state relations in Germany in the 1870s, and, in particular, the campaign waged by the Prussian government (1874–8) under Bismarck to establish state control over German Catholic life. Stirred in part by reactions to Pius IX's promulgation of the *Syllabus of Errors* (1864) and the Vatican I declaration of papal infallibility (1870), the antichurch, anticlerical campaign pitted the Prussian government against the German Catholic hierarchy for control of Catholic education, marriage, and church authority over clerical education and parish appointments. The most virulent era saw the expulsion of many religious orders from Germany, the imprisonment of bishops, and unstaffed parishes due to the shortage of priests. Bismarck abandoned the program because of strong resistance from German

Catholics and the diplomatic efforts of Pope Leo XIII after Pius IX's death. However, Catholic–Protestant relations were soured and German–Catholic suspicion of the government prevailed for decades.

Patricia Plovanich

See also INFALLIBILITY; LEO XIII, POPE; PIUS IX, POPE; SYLLABUS OF ERRORS; VATICAN, FIRST COUNCIL OF THE.

KUNDALINI

In Tantric Hinduism, *kundalini* is a spiritual energy (*shakti*) that is said to lie dormant at the base of the spine. When enlivened through spiritual practice, especially yogic meditation, it rises through a subtle spiritual channel along the spine, awakening spiritual centers known as *chakras*. As the kundalini moves upward, it activates chakras associated with progressively higher levels of spiritual consciousness. When the kundalini reaches the uppermost chakra at the crown of the head, union with the deity (often Shiva) or complete enlightenment is said to occur.

Lance E. Nelson

See also CAKRA/CHAKRA; HINDUISM; TANTRA; TANTRIC HINDUISM; YOGA.

KÜNG, HANS (1928–)

A Swiss theologian, ordained priest, and professor emeritus at the University of Tübingen, who along with German Jesuit theologian Karl Rahner (1904–84) and Belgian Dominican priest and theologian Edward Schillebeeckx (b. 1914), is considered among the most influential figures in twentieth-century European Roman Catholic theology. Küng was ordained in 1954, matriculated at the Institut Catholique at the Sorbonne in Paris for his doctoral studies, and taught at Tübin-

gen from 1960 to 1996. At the invitation of Pope John XXIII, he served as a *peritus* (Lat., "expert") or appointed theological expert at Vatican II (1962–5). After Vatican II, Küng authored some of his most controversial works, *The Church* (1967) and *Infallible? An Enquiry* (1970; rev. ed. 1994), suggesting a series of reforms to resolve the crises of ecclesiology and authority in the Catholic Church based on a critical reexamination of the papacy on both scriptural and theological grounds. After repeated investigations and censures of Küng's works, in 1979 the Congregation for the Doctrine of the Faith (CDF) revoked his licentiate to teach Catholic theology. However, Küng continued to teach and write at Tübingen in the Institute for Ecumenical Research. Küng published a memoir of these investigations, censures, and ongoing struggles in *My Struggle for Freedom* (2003).

In addition to ecclesiology, or theological reflection on the nature, mission, models, and marks of the church, Küng has significantly contributed to critical theological reflection on the mutual interrelationship of church and world, interreligious dialogue among Christianity and other world religions, and global religious ethics. His many books include *Justification: The Doctrine of Karl Barth and a Catholic Reflection* (1964, 2004); *On Being a Christian* (1976); *Does God Exist?* (1980); *Christianity and the World Religions* (1986; rev. ed. 1993); *Theology for the Third Millennium* (1988); *Global Responsibility: In Search of a New World Ethic* (1991). In his more recent writings, Küng addresses theological issues related to death and dying, a global ethic of politics and economics, and the roles of women in Christianity.

Rosemary P. Carbine

L

LABOREM EXERCENS

On September 14, 1981, Pope John Paul II issued the document *Laborem Exercens* to commemorate the ninetieth anniversary of Pope Leo XIII's 1891 encyclical *Rerum Novarum* ("The Condition of Labor"). Like his predecessor, John Paul II addresses a "basic dimension of human existence"—namely, work which allows humankind to survive and even flourish. In the late twentieth century, the Pope's consideration of human work necessarily involves a discussion of both creativity and suffering, human rights and injustice, technological wonders and environmental pollution. At the heart of the letter stands John Paul II's reiteration of a fundamental principle of Catholic social teaching: "the basis for determining the value of human work is not primarily the kind of work being done, but the fact that the one who is doing it is a person" (par. 6). This means that primacy belongs to human beings in the production process, not to the things they produce; this in turn leads to the conclusion that labor always has priority over capital (par. 12). The Pope also highlights why the church is firmly committed to justice for the workers of the world: such a commitment, he says, is "a proof of her fidelity to Christ" and is what allows the church to "truly be the church of the poor" (par. 8).

Following the statement of basic principles in Parts I and II, John Paul II turns to concrete issues. In Part III, called "The Conflict between Labor and Capital in the Present Phase of History," the Pope critiques both Marxist collectivism, which denies the right to private property, and liberal capitalism, which views this right as absolute and untouchable (par. 14). By contrast, Catholic teaching "has always understood this right within the broader context of the right common to all to use the goods of the whole of creation." Thus, "the right to private property is subordinated to the right to common use, to the fact that goods are meant for everyone" (par. 14). Likewise, "each person is fully entitled to consider himself or herself a part-owner of the great workbench at which he or she is working with everyone else" (par. 14).

In Part IV, called "The Rights of Workers," the pope affirms that "[w]hile work, in all its many senses, is an obligation, that is to say a duty, it is also a source of rights on the part of the worker" (par. 16). Indeed, a just wage is the concrete means —even the key means—of determining the justice or injustice of any socioeconomic

725

system in the world today (par. 19). Other basic rights of workers include the rights to rest, to receive a pension and retirement insurance, and to organize labor unions (pars. 19–20).

In Part V, the encyclical's conclusion, called "Elements for a Spirituality of Work," John Paul II offers a theological analysis of work in which he attempts to discover "the meaning which [work] has in the eyes of God" and to understand how work enters into the process of human salvation (par. 24). He also analyzes work as a pastoral challenge for the church whose duty it is to "form a spirituality of work which will help all people to come closer, through work, to God, the creator and redeemer" (par. 24). In the final analysis, says the Pope, the key to understanding the full meaning of human labor is Jesus Christ, "the man of work," who invites all people to collaborate with the Son of God for the redemption of humanity (par. 27).

James B. Nickoloff

See also ENCYCLICAL; RERUM NOVARUM.

LACORDAIRE, JEAN-BAPTISTE HENRI DOMINIQUE (1802–61)

French theologian, member of the Dominican Order, and famous preacher. A successful Parisian lawyer without any particular religious faith, Lacordaire was converted to Catholicism, and in 1827 was ordained to the priesthood. Influenced by Lammenais, he soon broke with the latter. Theologically Ultramontane but politically very progressive, he joined the Dominicans and did much to revive the order in France. His most influential publication was the collection of his *Conférences de Nôtre-Dame de Paris* (1844–51), directed especially at atheists and agnostics.

Orlando Espín

See also AGNOSTICISM; ATHEISM; DOMINICANS; LAMENNAIS, FÉLICITÉ ROBERT DE; MODERNISM; MODERNITY; POSTMODERNITY; ROMAN CATHOLICISM; ULTRAMONTANISM.

LACTANTIUS (260?–330?)

Lucius Caecilius Firmianus Lactantius was born in North Africa and studied under the famous rhetor, Arnobius. Converted to Christianity as a young man, Lactantius taught rhetoric in Nicomedia until he was forced to abandon his profession during the persecution of Diocletian. When Constantine became emperor, he hired Lactantius to teach Constantine's son, Crispus. According to Jerome, Lactantius was a prolific writer, but only four of his works survive, the most famous being a defense of Christianity entitled the *Divine Institutions*. Although Lactantius's theology leaves much to be desired, and his style of writing is sometimes overblown, the *Divine Institutions* was very influential. The book reached out for the first time in Latin to the cultured and literate Roman world in an attempt to convince it that Christianity was a way of life compatible with that world.

Gary Macy

See also APOLOGISTS; CONSTANTINE; DIOCLETIAN; JEROME; PERSECUTION (IN CHRISTIANITY).

LADINO

A term of contempt (originally from the Spanish dialect spoken by Sephardic Jews) for anyone who was considered racially or religiously impure or undesirable. It came to be used for Jews who converted to Christianity, and in Latin America for descendants of natives who joined the dominant European way of life.

Orlando Espín

See also LATIN AMERICAN CATHOLICISM; SEPHARDIM.

LAINEZ, DIEGO (1512–65)

Spanish theologian, and second superior general of the Society of Jesus (Jesuits). Lainez studied at the universities of Alcalá and Paris; while a student at Paris, he met Ignatius Loyola and his group of friends, and in 1546 (under Loyola's leadership) joined in founding the Society of Jesus. He participated as theologian at the Council of Trent (1545–63), where he proved to be a persuasive defender of the pope's authority and universal ministry, as well as a decisive opponent of Calvinism's teachings on justification and predestination. He was one of the key writers of Trent's final decree on justification. Lainez succeeded Loyola as superior general of the Jesuits in 1556, and guided them as they successfully expanded throughout Europe, the Americas, and Asia.

Orlando Espín

See also IGNATIUS LOYOLA; JUSTIFICA-TION; PREDESTINATION (CALVINIST); SOCIETY OF JESUS; TRENT, COUNCIL OF.

LAITY

(Greek, laos tou theou, the people of God). In the Septuagint, laos represented the people of Israel as a nation, chosen and set apart. The earliest Christian church was primarily a lay movement, with lay (non-ordained) members in leadership positions, presiding, preaching, and celebrating at worship. By the beginning of the second century, with the rise of a fixed hierarchy and priesthood in the church, laity came to refer to the common people (viz. Clement of Rome, Letter to Corinth, 40), the ecclesia docens, or "learning church." Other early Christian writers, such as Origen and Clement of Alexandria, used the rather pejorative form, laikos, to suggest the ignorance of the masses and their required deference to their leaders in mat-ters of faith and morals. The late twentieth century saw a renewed appreciation of the specific vocational role of the laity and of lay spirituality, with an emphasis on the "universal call to holiness." The Roman Catholic Church's Second Vatican Council advanced these notions, especially in the document Lumen Gentium, where each layperson is described as a "living instrument of the mission of the church herself" (LG 33) with a special mission in the area of family life. The document Apostolicam Actuositatem, also promulgated by the Second Vatican Council, further describes the nature of the laity's participation in the mission of the church and the spirituality specific to this calling. The World Synod on the Laity, held in 1987, saw the vocation of the laity in terms of ministry to the world in the ordinary circumstances of daily life, with a view toward establishing the kingdom of God in civil society. Today, the laity comprises over 98 percent of the Catholic Church.

Robert D. McCleary

See also APOSTOLICAM ACTUOSITATEM; LAY MINISTRY; LUMEN GENTIUM; SEPTUAGINT.

LAKSHMI

Also known as Shri, Lakshmi is the Hindu goddess of beauty and abundance, and the consort of Vishnu. Most Hindu homes display an image of Lakshmi as a sign and anticipation of the goddess's presence in the house. Hindu wives are often said to be incarnations of Lakshmi, since they are in many ways regarded as the source of the family's good luck and prosperity.

Lance E. Nelson

See also DEVA/DEVI; HINDUISM; SHAKTI; VRATA.

LAMA

A Tibetan term for the equivalent Sanskrit term "guru" used in Tibetan Buddhism and Bon to mean tantric teachers. In Buddhism, the *lama* is not necessarily an ordained monk (Tibetan, *gelong*) who has taken on vows of celibacy or renounced the householder's life. The lama in traditional Tibet, unlike the *bhikkhu* in Theravada societies, was called upon to perform pragmatic rituals designed to influence gods and spirits. He was also expected to adapt the teachings according to each disciple's spiritual state and potential.

Since 1100, the most significant lamas in Tibet have usually been located in reincarnating lineages; these individuals, called *tulku*, had their own enduring households (Tibetan, *labrang*) that perpetuated their role within monasteries. The Dalai Lama is the most famous in this category.

Todd T. Lewis

See also BHIKSHU/BHIKSHUNI; DALAI LAMA; TANTRIC BUDDHISM.

LAMB (IN CHRISTIANITY)

In John's Gospel, John the Baptizer refers to Jesus as "the Lamb of God who takes away the sins of the world" (John 1:29). The image of Jesus as Lamb is echoed later in the Gospel, during the account of Jesus' death. According to John's Gospel, Jesus died on the Day of Preparation, the same day when the Jews slaughtered the lambs for the Passover meal. In this way, John suggests a parallel between Jesus and the Passover lambs. The imagery of Jesus as Lamb comes to a climax in the book of Revelation. In Revelation, Jesus is again imaged as a slaughtered Lamb (Rev 5:6). In this book, however, the Lamb has been glorified and participates with the Father in judging the world. Revelation includes a number of hymns to the Lamb such as, "Worthy is the Lamb that was slain / to receive all power and wealth / wisdom and might / honor and glory and praise!" (Rev 5:12). These hymns may have been used in actual first-century Christian liturgies. In the modern Roman Liturgy, the image of the Lamb continues to hold a central place. In the Eucharist, for example, a hymn to the Lamb (*Agnus Dei*) is sung while the Bread is broken and the Wine is poured. The rites of Protestant and Anglican churches incorporate similar texts in which Jesus is referred to as the Lamb of God. Christians of the Eastern Rites, in addition to using texts echoing this image, refer to the leavened bread they use in the Eucharist as the "lamb." Before the "lambs" are baked, they are stamped with various patterns and images, by means of a round wooden die. In preparation for the Divine Liturgy, a deacon or priest cuts the "lamb" into pieces, following the patterns stamped on it.

Patrick L. Malloy

See also ORTHODOXY.

LAMB (IN JUDAISM)

While important in the sacrificial cult (Exod 29:38-40) and central in the rite of Passover (Exod 12:3-5), the lamb has no theological significance in Judaism. Especially since the destruction of the Second Temple in Jerusalem in 70 C.E. that led to the cessation of animal sacrifices and the paschal offering, the lamb has had little even symbolic value. At the Passover Seder, it serves as a remembrance of the particular way in which God rescued the Israelites from Egyptian bondage, that is, by having them put the blood of a lamb on the doorposts of their homes (Exod 12:3-7). But, unlike in Christianity, in Judaism the sacrifice of a lamb does not serve as a paradigm for future redemption or salvation from sin.

Alan J. Avery-Peck

LAMBETH CONFERENCES

Meetings of the bishops of the Anglican Communion that have been held approximately every ten years since 1867, interrupted only by the two world wars. They are so called because they were originally held at Lambeth Palace, the archbishop of Canterbury's London residence. The archbishop convokes and presides over the conference. Together with the Anglican Consultative Council and the Primates' Meeting, the conference is an important means of maintaining the cohesiveness of the worldwide, diverse, and independent churches of the Communion.

In 1865 the Synod of the Province of Canada was troubled by the refusal of Bishop John Colenso in Africa to step down from his post on the grounds of heresy. The synod urged the Convocation of Canterbury to ask the archbishop to summon all the Anglican bishops to a meeting. It was felt that the Communion could profit by the opportunity to discuss problems that many churches might share. Archbishop Longley agreed with the suggestion and invited the bishops to Lambeth. Seventy-six responded positively. The first Lambeth Conference was held in 1867.

Longley had cautioned, however, that the conference was to be deliberative, not legislative: "Such a meeting would not be competent to make declarations or lay down definitions on points of doctrine. But united worship and common counsels would greatly tend to maintain practically the unity of faith. . . ." Lambeth has never evolved into a synod or council. Until and unless an autonomous province of the Communion formally adopts a Lambeth action as its own, the conference's resolutions and decisions are not binding on any bishop or church. Lambeth has only a persuasive or moral authority. Proposals to give the conference more power than this have not yet been passed.

Nonetheless, certain Lambeth Conferences have significantly influenced Christianity in the twentieth century. The first conference in 1867 acclerated the process for involving laypeople in the governance of the church. The Chicago-Lambeth Quadrilateral, adopted in 1888, remains the authoritative text for Anglican ecumenical efforts. The conference of 1930 broke new ground with its limited acceptance of the morality of contraception. Pius XI responded with an encyclical, *Casti Connubii*, also in 1930, that opened the way for theologians to develop the new understanding of marriage that emerged at Vatican II.

Jon Nilson

See also ANGLICAN COMMUNION; CONVOCATIONS OF CANTERBURY; LAMBETH QUADRILATERAL.

LAMBETH QUADRILATERAL

The authoritative text of the Anglican Communion on the fundamentals of the faith, first approved by 145 bishops at the Lambeth Conference of 1888. The Lambeth Conference of 1920 approved a reformulation of the Quadrilateral, but the 1888 version has remained the standard. Other committees of Lambeth have proposed further reformulations and explications, but the conference has not approved them.

The text proposes four points as the basis for approaching the reunion of the Christian churches: the Scriptures of the Old and New Testaments as "containing all things necessary to salvation" and as the "ultimate standard of faith"; the Apostles' and Nicene Creeds; the sacraments of baptism and the Lord's Supper "ordained by Christ himself"; and the historic episcopate "locally adapted." This fourfold basis is sufficient for an approach to reunion, not for reunion itself. Thus the Quadrilateral is not, as sometimes alleged, an effort to minimize the content of the Christian faith.

The text is also known as the Chicago-Lambeth Quadrilateral, since an earlier version was adopted by the House of Bishops of the Episcopal Church that met at St. James Cathedral in Chicago in 1886. Their prefatory statement describes the four points as "principles of unity exemplified by the undivided Catholic Church during the first ages of its existence." This version speaks of the Scripture simply as "the revealed Word of God" and omits the Apostles' Creed and the words "ordained by Christ Himself." The text was revised by Lambeth in 1888 to harmonize it more closely with the wording of VI, VIII, and XXV of the Thirty-Nine Articles.

The Quadrilateral was developed chiefly from the initiative of William Reed Huntington, an Episcopal priest and a leader in the church's House of Deputies, who founded an ecumenical clergy fellowship with a Roman Catholic priest friend. The fullest statement of Huntington's vision is his book *The Church-Idea: An Essay Towards Unity* (1870). The Episcopal Church commemorates him on July 27.

The text remains an authoritative guide for the participation of the Episcopal Church in the ecumenical movement. Thus, it appears in its Book of Common Prayer.

Jon Nilson

See also ANGLICAN COMMUNION; EPISCOPAL CHURCH; THIRTY-NINE ARTICLES.

LAMENNAIS, FÉLICITÉ ROBERT DE (1782–1854)

French cleric, author of works on politics and religion, associated with the French movements of traditionalism, Ultramontanism and liberalism. Lamennais' early work embraced the traditionalist theologies of de Maistre and Bonald, supported the theory that faith's certitude stems from positive revelation and, therefore, from tradition, not from natural (unaided) reason, and consequently advocated the separation of religion from civil affairs. He espoused Ultramontanism and supported the authority of the papacy in theological and church affairs in opposition to the Gallican convictions of the French episcopacy. An early supporter of the French restorationist movement, he abandoned it when the monarchy disappointed his expectations. He then became an advocate for French Catholic liberalism, defending the movement and its themes of common consent in his publication, *L'avenir* (1820). He left the Catholic Church bitter and disillusioned after Gregory XVI condemned his ideas in 1834.

Patricia Plovanich

See also GALLICANISM; ULTRAMONTANISM.

LANFRANC (1010?–89)

Lanfranc, born in Italy, became a famous scholar and prior at the monastery of Bec in Normandy. In 1163 Lanfranc became abbot of St. Stephen's Monastery in Caen, and in 1070 he was made archbishop of Canterbury under the auspices of William (the Conqueror) of Normandy. Lanfranc was a brilliant teacher and writer whose students included Anselm of Canterbury and Ivo of Chartres. Lanfranc's best-known work is his *De corpore et sanguine domini* (*On the Body and Blood of the Lord*) written against the teachings of Berengar of Tours. Lanfranc was equally well known in his own time as an administrator. He not only established Bec as an important monastery and educational center, but helped to introduce the Gregorian reforms into England.

Gary Macy

See also ANSELM OF CANTERBURY; BERENGAR OF TOURS; EUCHARIST; GREGORIAN REFORMS; IVO OF CHARTRES; MEDIEVAL CHRISTIANITY (IN THE WEST); MONASTICISM IN WESTERN CHRISTIANITY; SCHOLASTICISM.

LANKAVATARA SUTRA

An influential early Indic Mahayana text that defines, albeit unsystematically, the basic Yogachara doctrines. This text had particular importance in the Ch'an/Zen schools of East Asia. The *Lankavatara Sutra* begins as Shakyamuni Buddha descends to Lanka (modern Sri Lanka), and most of it is addressed to the celestial bodhisattva Manjushri and to the deity Ravana, who here is a devout Buddhist layman (not, as in the Hindu *Ramayana*, an evil demon). The oldest portion of the text takes issue with Hindu doctrines. Later strata embrace the *tathagatagarbha* doctrine, identifying the *alaya vijnana* as the Buddha nature within all beings. This underlying "store consciousness" is said to have seven forms of awareness related to it as waves are perturbations of the great ocean but do not disturb its depths.

Todd T. Lewis

See also CITTAMATRA; MAHAYANA BUDDHISM; TATHAGATAGARBHA DOCTRINE.

LAO-TZU (604 B.C.E.–?)

(Chinese, *Lao-zi*, lit., Old Master). He is regarded as one of China's great sages, the nominal founder of Taoism, and supposed author of the *Tao Te Ching*. Very little is known about his actual life or even if he existed at all. According to the second-century B.C.E. historian Su-Ma Chien, his real name was Li Erh and he was born around 604 B.C.E. He also recorded that Lao-Tzu worked at the Zhou Court as an archivist, but became disenchanted with the decline of Zhou culture and ultimately left China. Before leaving China for good, it is said that he set down his thoughts and insights about the nature of life that later became the Taoist classic *Tao Te Ching*. The *Tao Te Ching* is a brief, enigmatic explication of humans' relationship to nature and the universe and the guiding principles of life based on natural patterns. His emphasis was on humans and nature rather than humans and society.

G. D. DeAngelis

See also CHUANG TZU; DAOISM; TAO; TAO TE CHING; ZHOU DYNASTY.

LAPSED

Literally meaning "the fallen," this is a term used for Christians who have denied their faith under persecution. During the first few centuries of the church (especially after the persecution during the reign of Decius (250–1 C.E.), the "lapsed" were the cause of a serious doctrinal and pastoral problem. Some rigorist Christian groups were adamant in never accepting the "lapsed" back into the church, but a more forgiving attitude prevailed in most of the church whereby the "lapsed" were accepted back if they did penance and underwent a period of probation. The arguments over the "lapsed" continued and were finally settled (for most Christians) in the fourth century.

Orlando Espín

See also APOSTASY; AUGUSTINE OF HIPPO; DONATISM; PERSECUTION (IN CHRISTIANITY); RIGORISM.

LAPSI

A Latin term that means the same as "lapsed."

See LAPSED.

LAS CASAS, BARTOLOMÉ DE (1484–1566)

Born in Seville, Spain, Bartolomé de Las Casas arrived in the West Indies in 1502 where he witnessed firsthand the effects of the Spanish Conquest on the indigenous population. Believing himself called by God to challenge the church's cooperation with injustice, Las Casas used his influence as a priest, as a member of the missionary Dominican Order, and later as the bishop of Chiapa (Mexico) to awaken the consciences of both ecclesiastical and political authorities. By allowing real-life experience to challenge his views, he came to reject the colonial society being established by Spain (for example, his earlier unquestioning acceptance of Indian and African enslavement) as well as commonly accepted theological positions (for example, that the lack of baptism assures eternal damnation). By the end of his life, Las Casas rejected both the right of the Spanish Crown to hold power in the Americas and the legitimacy of forced conversion to Christianity. His principal weapon in attempting to defend the rights, and even the lives, of the Indians was the pen he wielded until his death in 1566. Writings such as *Historia de las Indias* (begun in 1527), *De unico vocationis modo* (1533?),

and *Brevísima relación de la destrucción de las Indias* (1542) demonstrate the evolution, originality, and profundity of his political and theological views.

James B. Nickoloff

See also LATIN AMERICAN CATHOLICISM; MONTESINOS, ANTONIO.

LAST JUDGMENT (IN CHRISTIANITY)

The Last Judgment is an eschatological concept that indicates two ways in which God assesses human life or human history at its end. The collective or general judgment affirms the Christian conviction that Christ will judge humanity's deeds at the Second Coming. This adaptation of the Old Testament's Day of the Lord notes the significance of human freedom, the collective responsibility of social entities, and the retributive character of divine justice. In the second century of Christianity, the Last Judgment acquired a more immediate application, the proposal of a divine assessment of the individual's life and her or his relationship to God at the time of death. The teaching affirmed the enduring significance of one's acceptance or rejection of community with God. This meaning is often discussed as one of the Last Things (or events at life's end): death, judgment, heaven, or hell. The portrayal of this judgment and the Last Things has been greatly embellished in popular pious images that portray God as judge.

Patricia Plovanich

See also ESCHATOLOGY (IN CHRISTIANITY); ETERNAL LIFE; HEAVEN; HELL; PURGATORY.

LAST JUDGMENT (IN JUDAISM)
See ESCHATOLOGY (IN JUDAISM).

LAST SUPPER

Commonly, in Christianity, this expression refers to Jesus' last supper with his closest disciples before his arrest, trial, and crucifixion. The supper was a Jewish Passover *Seder*, and Christians have regarded it as the occasion (and "institution") of the first Eucharist. The four canonical Gospels include accounts of the Last Supper, and there are references to it in Paul's First Letter to the Corinthians.

Orlando Espín

See also EUCHARIST; GOSPELS (TEXTS); LITURGY (IN CHRISTIANITY).

LATERAN (COUNCILS OF THE)

There were five councils considered ecumenical by the Roman Catholic Church that met at the Lateran Palace in Rome. The First Lateran Council was called by Pope Calixtus II in 1123 and is most noteworthy for its ratification of the Concordat of Worms, thus effectively ending the investiture controversy. The condemnations of simony, of lay investiture, and of clerical marriage comprising the Gregorian reform movement were repeated. The Second Lateran Council was called by Pope Innocent II in 1139 to end the brief schism resulting from the election of the rival pope, Anacletus II. The decrees of the Gregorian reform were again promulgated and tournaments were forbidden, as well as the use of crossbows against Christians. The Third Lateran Council was called by Pope Alexander III in 1179. The council established that a two-thirds majority of the cardinals would be necessary for the election of a pope as well as condemning the Cathar heresy. A series of reforms of the clerical life was enacted in addition to regulations defining relations between Christians and Jews. Further, each cathedral church was to endow a master to teach both clergy and indigent students free of charge. The Fourth Lateran Council was called by Pope Innocent III in 1215 and remains one of the great disciplinary and reforming councils in Western Christianity. Two dogmatic constitutions and sixty-eight disciplinary decrees were issued. In the opening creed directed against the Cathars and Waldensians, the term "transubstantiation" was used for the first time in an official church document. The beginnings of the Inquisition against these heretics can be traced to these decrees as well. The council made annual confession and Communion mandatory for all Western Christians. It required more careful scrutiny of clergy to ensure they were properly caring for souls and established more stringent restrictions on Jews. The Fifth Lateran Council was called by Pope Julius II in 1512–7 mainly to invalidate the decrees of a council called by the French king, Louis XII.

Gary Macy

See also CATHARS; COUNCIL, ECUMENICAL; EUCHARIST; GREGORIAN REFORMS; INNOCENT III, POPE; INVESTITURE CONTROVERSY; MEDIEVAL CHRISTIANITY (IN THE WEST); RECONCILIATION, SACRAMENT OF; TRANSUBSTANTIATION; WORMS, CONCORDAT OF.

LATERAN (TREATY OF THE)

An agreement signed on February 11, 1929, it brought an end to territorial and jurisdictional conflict between Italy and the papacy. Since 1870, when Italy had been unified as a kingdom and the Papal States included in it, the status of Rome had been a disputed issue. The Lateran Treaty recognized Vatican City as a sovereign state, but also brought an end to papal claims to other territories. A concordat attached to the treaty concerned the rights and duties of the Catholic Church in Italy. While the church was allowed great authority in areas such as education and marriage, bishops were to swear an oath of loyalty to the Italian state.

Thomas Worcester, s.j.

See also CONCORDAT; PIUS IX, POPE; PIUS XI, POPE; VATICAN, FIRST COUNCIL OF THE.

LATIMER, HUGH (1485?–1555)

Scholar whose preaching abilities, zeal for church reform, and support of Henry VIII's divorce from Catherine and marriage to Anne Boleyn made him bishop of Worcester in 1535 and one of the leaders of the English Reformation. He was accused of heresy during Henry's reign and imprisoned until the accession of Edward VI. When Queen Mary Tudor began the Catholic restoration, he was arrested along with Cranmer and Ridley. He refused to accept the Catholic notions of transubstantiation and the Mass as a sacrifice and so was excommunicated and burned at the stake with Bishop Nicholas Ridley. Latimer is renowned for his last words: "Be of good comfort, Master Ridley, and play the man; we shall this day light such a candle by God's grace in England as I trust shall never be put out." The Episcopal Church commemorates him on October 16.

Jon Nilson

See also CRANMER, THOMAS.

LATIN AMERICAN CATHOLICISM

While people commonly view Latin America as an almost entirely Catholic continent, religious pluralism marks every country, with some likely to have Evangelical (or Protestant) majorities in the near future. Yet, as the Argentinian Methodist theologian José Míguez Bonino has correctly noted, because of its dominance in Latin America since the arrival of the first Europeans in the fifteenth century, Catholicism has left its mark on all Latin American life. At the same time, Catholicism itself represents an exceedingly diverse phenomenon in Latin America. Thus, at the beginning of the twenty-first century, Latin America is less Catholic and its Catholicism is less monolithic than many think.

The violent nature of the conquest of indigenous peoples by Spanish and Portuguese soldiers of fortune in the first century of European occupation shaped the religious development of Latin America as well as its socioeconomic and political history. From the beginning, intense efforts by Catholic missionaries to suppress native religious practice and beliefs and replace these with Iberian Catholicism resulted in a complex religious situation in many places. Though outright Indian resistance allowed pre-Columbian traditions to survive in some regions, on the whole, the conquered peoples adopted the Catholic beliefs and practices of their conquerors. Still, Indian creativity resulted in a colonial Catholicism in Latin America that allowed the religious practices of the common people to exist side by side with those of the institutional church that was supported by the Spanish and Portuguese Crowns.

After achieving independence in the nineteenth century, most Latin American countries maintained Catholicism as the official religion of the state. Though a uniquely powerful institution in most Latin American societies up to the present, the infrastructure of the Catholic Church nevertheless did not penetrate the world of the masses of poor rural and urban Latin Americans until after the Second Vatican Council (1962–5) and the Second General Conference of Latin American Bishops held in Medellín, Colombia, in 1968. The "preferential option for the poor" elaborated at the Third General Conference in 1979 at Puebla, Mexico, signals both the Catholic Church's new awareness of the poor and, at the same time, the standing achieved by the poor in the church. Since Medellín, then, the poor have come to see the institutional church as an ally in the fight for social justice and ethno-cultural survival, and at least part of the church has come to see the poor as the heart of the church's mission and the key to the church's fidelity to the message of the Gospel. Not surprisingly, the new pastoral practices of the institutional church— such as the establishment of Base Christian Communities among the poor—have provoked resistance among some members of the clergy and some laypeople.

James B. Nickoloff

See also "BASIC" ECCLESIAL COMMUNITIES; CATHOLICISM/CATHOLIC TRADITION; LAS CASAS, BARTOLOMÉ DE; LATINO CATHOLICISM; MEDELLÍN CONCLUSIONS; PUEBLA DOCUMENT; TÚPAC AMARU, JOSÉ GABRIEL; VATICAN, SECOND COUNCIL OF THE.

LATIN AMERICAN PROTESTANTISM

The first Protestants in what is now Latin America were generally British and German travelers, traders, and adventurers who visited the Spanish and Portuguese colonies in the Western Hemisphere. However, since they did not establish ongoing communities, the historical origins of present-day Protestantism in Latin America came immediately after independence.

Between 1810 and 1825, partly as a result of the French and American Revolutions and of the Napoleonic Wars, Spain and Portugal lost almost all their colonies in the Americas—the main exceptions were Cuba and Puerto Rico that remained under Spanish rule until 1898. Since the movement for independence was fostered in part by the modern liberal ideas of democracy, freedom of thought, and the like, and since in general the Roman Catholic hierarchy had opposed both those ideas and their political consequences in the colonies, many of the leaders of the newly founded nations, while remaining Roman Catholic, sought to limit the political power of the hierarchy. With that end in mind, they fostered emmigration from Protestant nations in Europe, and some even lent support to the early Protestant missionaries.

This means that Protestant churches in Latin America stem mostly from three sources: immigration, missionary work, and the rise of autochthonous churches in Latin America itself.

Already before independence, there were in some regions of Latin America small enclaves of Protestant immigrants. However, the number of immigrants grew rapidly during the first two decades after independence, when the new nations still feared Spain's attempts at restoration, and their leaders felt that immigrants from Protestant Europe would help consolidate independence and the liberal ideals of democracy and free trade. After that time, immigration continued, so that to this day there are many Protestants in Latin America who are descendants of Scottish, English, German, and Dutch settlers. Although freedom of worship was not granted by most of the early constitutions of Latin America, the desire to foster immigration, as well as the pressure of liberal ideas, slowly but inexorably moved in that direction.

Profiting from the new circumstances, Protestant missionaries traveled to Latin America. The first was James Thomson, from Scotland, who arrived in Argentina in 1818, and subsequently traveled to Uruguay, Chile, Peru, Ecuador, Colombia, Mexico, Cuba, and Puerto Rico. He went both as a missionary and as a proponent of what was then an advanced method of education, thus illustrating the early connection between Protestant missions in Latin America and the liberal ideas of progress and freedom that at that time went hand in hand with Protestantism. Throughout the rest of the century, and well into the next, Methodists, Presbyterians, Baptists, and others usually associated their missionary work with the promotion of education, democracy, freedom of thought, and the like. It was not until the late nineteenth century, with the development of fundamentalism in the U.S., that more conservative missionaries began developing a different sort of Protestantism in Latin America.

Early in the twentieth century, Pentecostal ideas and practices began entering Latin America, mostly through people connected with the Azusa Street revival in California. There was resistance in the older Protestant Churches, and schism was often the result. This is the origin of some of the largest Pentecostal churches in Latin America that were not founded directly by Pentecostal missionaries from abroad, but rather by people in Latin America who were already Protestants, and who either left their churches or were expelled from them for their charismatic teaching and practices. Typical of this history is the origin of the Methodist Pentecostal Church of Chile. Charismatic manifestations had begun to take place among the Methodists in Chile in 1902, and were later reinforced by contacts with the Azusa Street revival movement. By 1910 the Methodist Church in Chile condemned the movement, whose leaders and members left to form the Methodist Pentecostal Church. Very soon this newly formed denomination outstripped its mother in membership.

Soon Pentecostal churches from the United States such as the Assemblies of God and the Church of God, and eventually many smaller denominations and splinter groups, began sending missionaries to Latin America, with the result that now there are in every country in Latin America dozens of Pentecostal denominations and often hundreds of independent churches.

The early ecumenical movement in Europe and the United States excluded Latin American Protestantism for fear of offending those who felt that missions to Catholic countries should not be encouraged. Slowly, however, Latin American Protestantism has become more ecumenical. Today there is a Latin American Council of Churches (CLAI) that includes most major Protestant Churches, and a vast majority of whose membership is Pentecostal.

It is impossible to ascertain the exact number of Protestants in Latin America. In some countries, such as Guatemala, Chile, Brazil, and Haiti, their numbers are quite large. In most others they are at least 5 percent of the population.

Justo L. González

LATIN AMERICAN THEOLOGIES
Today many believe that Latin American theology began during the second half of the twentieth century, with the theological movement called "liberation theol-

ogy," but historically Christian theology entered Latin America in the sixteenth century with Spanish missionaries, and it soon found itself at home in the continent. Indeed, it is even possible to argue (as it has been argued by historians) that the roots and many themes of Latin America's theologies today can be detected in and directly traced back to the Iberian peninsula's late patristic period, in the centuries of the Iberian *convivencia* and *reconquista*, as well as (and especially) in the Latin American conquest, colonial, and national periods.

In some important ways, U.S. Latino/a theologies today are also heirs to this long history and to the Latin American liberation theology movement of the last four decades.

Of course, we must remember that by "theology" is usually meant "faith in search of understanding." And this, more specifically, implies and requires that theology be a reasoned and disciplined discourse, grounded in and developed from specific sources, and elaborated with and through the highest possible standards of intellectual rigor. In other words, not all religious reflection qualifies as "theology." That having been said, it is also important to note that Latin American theology has shown a wide variety of possibilities and limitations in its self-understanding, methods, topics, and so on, over the past five centuries—deeply impacted by the history and sociocultural processes of each Latin American nation and of the entire region.

Furthermore, because all theologies and theologians are always contextual and contextualized, it is very important for the reader to consider carefully what is explained in the entry on "Method in Theology" to appreciate the history and development of Latin American theology.

1. *Period of the conquest (1492–1553)*

After Columbus' first trip to the Americas in 1492, the Spanish and Portuguese conquest of the continent took place rather quickly. The first Christian theology of the Americas, clearly born as response to the European conquest, was crafted by theologically trained missionaries, some of whom were bishops. These first works in theology were composed almost exclusively to serve the prophetic defense of native populations against the atrocities committed by European Christians. The early Latin American theologians often discussed human rights and dignity, freedom and justice, evangelization and soteriology, and at times created their reflections in or after dialogue with theologians of the native religions. Bartolomé de Las Casas (1474–1566) is perhaps the best-known example of the early Latin American bishop-theologian, but there were other theologians who also engaged and crafted the prophetic theology of the Latin American conquest period: for example, Antonio de Montesinos (d. 1545), Bernardino de Sahagún (d. 1590), Vasco de Quiroga (d. 1565), and Alonso de la Vera Cruz (d. 1584). It is well known that some of these early theologians had an impact on others working in Europe at the time; Las Casas and Montesinos, for example, were very important to Francisco de Vitoria in Salamanca.

2. *Period of the colony (1553–1808)*

In 1538 the University of Santo Domingo (in present-day Dominican Republic) opened its doors as the first institution of higher education in the Americas. Dominican friars began teaching theology there, but none of their works or lessons have been preserved. In 1553 the University of Mexico was established, and Francisco Cervantes de Salazar became its first theology professor, soon to be followed by Alonso de la Vera Cruz and Pedro de la Peña. In 1558 the University of San Marcos opened in Lima, Peru. But with rare exceptions, during most of the colonial period, academic theology at these three universities and in most other institutions of (theological) higher education typically followed the European model of what has been called "second Scholasticism." Spain's and Portugal's colonial legislation made it increasingly difficult for nonwhites to attend universities, *colegios mayores*, or seminaries, and thus the interests and questions of the non-Europeans in the Americas were mostly lost to theology in Latin America, while European concerns became identified as the important issues for the continent's theologians.

Beginning in 1622, *colegios mayores* (free-standing undergraduate and graduate schools of philosophy and theology) were founded in Cuba, throughout Mexico, and also in Guatemala, Panama, Venezuela, Colombia, Chile, Ecuador, Peru, and Argentina. And after 1640 a handful of academically outstanding seminaries were established in Mexico, Cuba, Peru, and Colombia. Most of the teaching methods and theological contents in *colegios mayores* still followed the European models of the seventeenth and eighteenth centuries, while very large and important theological libraries appeared in Chile, Peru, and Mexico (for example), and many works—often in substantive dialogue with the best and latest in Europe—were written by theologians in Latin America: Bartolomé de Ledesma (d. 1604), Pedro de Ortisoga (d. 1626), Andrés de Valencia (d. 1645), and Domingo Muriel (d. 1795). Without universities, but with a handful of seminaries, Brazilian colonial theology can boast

of Antonio Vieira (d. 1698). The expulsion of the Jesuits from all Spanish and Portuguese territories by 1767 seriously harmed Latin American theology and theological institutions toward the end of the colonial period and during the struggles for independence—precisely when it was about to escape from the long colonial period of merely reflecting on European models.

3. *Period of independence and national consolidation (1808–1959)*

Some Latin American theologians became deeply committed to the cause of independence and constructed theological justifications for their countries' separation(s) from Spain. Juan Germán Roscío (in Venezuela) is a good and typical example; but we should also remember Juan Fernández de Sotomayor (in Colombia) and Félix Varela (in Cuba): independence, freedom, democracy, and justice were justified *theologically*. But Latin American theology still continued to mirror European theology, even if with an increasing degree of sophistication. After independence, the cause of democracy, justice, and the like, remained outside Latin American academic theology again.

The official church's repeated stance against independence led to profound crises in church and theology once independence was achieved. Most of the new Latin American nations had come to be led by elites hostile to the church (and also hostile to theology). Institutions of theological education suffered greatly at the hands of inimical educational authorities, or due to the collapse of (colonial) state support for church and theology. Nevertheless, as new generations of theologians grew and supported their national states, new questions and concerns began to be raised in and for theology in

Latin America. By the middle of the nineteenth century a noninstitutional "nationalist" theology began to appear (Mariano Soler, in Uruguay, for example) that supported Catholicism's acknowledgment of and participation in the national life of the respective Latin American nations, but this was a "nationalist" theology that appeared conservative, elitist, mistrustful of modernity, and (after Vatican I) increasingly "Romanized." After 1850 Protestant churches were established in Latin America but, at the time, without their own theological production—still mirroring U.S. or European Protestant methods, contents, and interests.

Nevertheless, after the 1930s, new theological approaches began to coalesce and take shape in several Latin American countries. Still influenced by European methods and concerns, these new theological approaches could be variously labeled as "developmentalist," "reformist," "burgeois," "elitist," and so on. Rome's Gregorian University and Belgium's University of Louvain had enormous impact on Latin American theology and theologians during the first half of the twentieth century. These two European institutions inspired and became models for the Xaveriana University (Bogotá, founded in 1937), the Catholic University of Lima (founded in 1942), the Catholic University of Rio de Janeiro (founded in 1947), and several others.

The preceding centuries of theological education, reflections, and difficulties finally led to the growing quality and resources of institutions of higher education offering doctoral studies in theology, and these became the context for the new post-1930s approach to theology in Latin America. During the second half of the twentieth century, with the birth of Latin America's theology of liberation, a new movement began that would profoundly impact worldwide theology.

4. Period of liberation theology (1959 to the present)

Preparations for (and expectations of) the Second Vatican Council began when it was first announced by Pope John XXIII in 1959, but the council actually held its sessions in Rome (at the Vatican) from 1962 through 1965. Latin American bishops actively participated in the council, and the Latin American Catholic Church was impacted by the reforming conciliar decrees as much as other parts of the world.

The Latin American Episcopal Council (CELAM) and its leader at the time (bishop Manuel Larraín, of Talca, Chile) led the Latin American Catholic Church to the important Medellín Conference of 1968 (so called because it was held in the Colombian city of Medellín). This conference of bishops from all the Latin American countries "grounded" the reforms of the Vatican Council II in Latin America's reality and profoundly reshaped and relaunched the Catholic Church in the continent in directions unimaginable two decades before. Vatican Council II and Medellín (building on the preceding four and a half centuries of theological groundwork) made possible the transformation of Latin American theology. It is also important to recognize the impact (on Latin American theology) of two documents published by Pope Paul VI after Vatican Council II: the encyclical *Populorum Progressio* (1967) and the exhortation *Evangelii Nuntiandi* (1975).

In the immediate aftermath of Vatican Council II, and even at the Medellín Conference itself, Latin American theology remained "developmentalist" at heart, but the effervescence of the *post*-Medellín period contributed to the permanent end of this earlier approach. With Medellín, Latin American theology became truly and indisputably *Latin American*. After Medellín, Latin American theologies and theologians began to take their place at the worldwide theological table, no longer as mirrors of Europe but as significant, necessary, and original contributors to worldwide theology.

From Medellín in 1968 to 1979 (when the Puebla Conference took place— named after the Mexican city where bishops gathered from all over Latin America), theology in the continent came into its own. Leading bishops depended on and contributed to it: Helder Câmara of Brazil, Manuel Larraín of Chile, Oscar Romero of El Salvador, and Sergio Méndez Arceo of Mexico are a few examples. Numerous scholarly theological journals were established, new theological educational institutions and research centers were founded (or older ones deeply renewed), and publishing houses began to distribute throughout the world the works of eminent Latin American theological thinkers. Catholic universities throughout the continent began to educate professional theologians. And a handful of Protestant institutions of theological education (for example, ISEDET in Buenos Aires, and the Seminario Bíblico in San José, Costa Rica) came to be recognized as important centers of theological production.

Latin American theology of liberation was born more as a distinct theological method and hermeneutic than as a specific content—although this method has been employed in order to more fully understand and reflect on the "typical" topics of theology. Latin American theology of liberation wanted (and wants) to theologize from the reality and context of the people of God in Latin America—as the people of God *exist in Latin America* (which necessarily implies realities of poverty, marginalization, oppression and powerlessness, economic injustice, and so on). The Latin American theology of liberation has been very explicitly committed to liberation and justice. It has been prophetic, academically rigorous, in dialogue with social reality, increasingly ecumenical, and very much on the side of the poor and powerless among God's people. In some important ways, the theology of liberation has retrieved and again highlighted the best of the earliest Latin American theology (that of the period of the conquest, for example).

In 1972, and for the first time, many of the Latin American theologians who had been crafting the theology of liberation met in El Escorial (outside Madrid, in Spain), thereby giving their respective theological contributions the characteristics of a continental movement. Among the Latin American theologians who need to be mentioned in connection with the theology of liberation are: Gustavo Gutiérrez (Peru), who is most often regarded as the first among equals; and then Juan Luis Segundo (Uruguay); José Comblin (Brazil); Lucio Gera (Argentina); Jon Sobrino (El Salvador); Ignacio Ellacuría (El Salvador); Hugo Assmann (Brazil); Leonardo Boff (Brazil); Carlos Mesters (Brazil); Carlos Bravo (Mexico); Luis del Valle (Mexico); José Míguez Bonino (Argentina); Juan Carlos Scannone (Argentina); Virgilio Elizondo (U.S.); Enrique Dússel (Argentina); to name a few. If asked who wrote the first works that sparked the birth of liberation theology in Latin America, most scholars today would name Gustavo Gutiérrez and perhaps Juan Luis Segundo —although given Latin American reality and ecclesial reflections in, on, and from that reality, it would be very simplistic and historically inaccurate to assume that one or two authors (no matter how brilliant and courageous) alone could have created the liberation theology movement.

In 1979, at the Puebla Conference, the Medellín spirit (which had profoundly marked the theology of liberation) was again confirmed and officially supported by the Latin American bishops. But other winds were beginning to blow in the worldwide Catholic Church, and a new pope (John Paul II, elected in 1978) became increasingly opposed to a distinctively Latin American theology and, more specifically, to a Latin American theology of liberation. John Paul II espoused the return to the "developmentalist" theologies typical in the Latin American Church of 1930–60, mostly in renewed imitation of Europe. During John Paul II's early pontificate, an *Instruction* on Latin American liberation theology was issued that seriously questioned some issues said to be part of liberation theology. It seems, however, that the *Instruction* factually misrepresented liberation theology. Under increasing pressure from Rome, local bishops became more "prudent" in their public support of liberation theology, and, in time, few new bishops would accept any connection with the theology of liberation. However, many among the poor and many of those who pastorally work with them still support the vision and contributions of the Latin American theology of liberation.

In part as a response to Roman pressures, but in part also because of the history of Latin American theology, after 1959 there were attempts (with varying degrees of success or quality) at creating theological constructs not just within the movement of liberation theology. For example, some tried a "theology of reconciliation."

Very important for the future of Latin American theology in general were (and are) the new theological approaches created from within Latin American realities often ignored by the liberation theology mainstream. These other new approaches never came to center stage within the theology of liberation, although they clearly shared the latter's fundamental vision, purpose, and method—for example, Latin American Black theologies, native theologies, feminist theologies, and the like.

5. *A new period?*

It is probable that today's Latin American theology is entering a new period that will likely be defined as both a reaffirmation of the fundamental intuitions and vision of Medellín and Puebla and as a stage beyond these. This new period will likely affirm the value, vision, fundamental intuitions, and methodological approaches of the theology of liberation. But it will possibly move beyond some limits of the historical (theological) stage now ending. For example, there will be greater and deeper emphasis on popular Catholicism and on popular religions in general; there will be a clearer focus on globalization and its consequences (not only on the social, economic justice issues raised by globalization but especially and more emphatically on the cultural problems posed by it); there will possibly be growing awareness of and reflection on the continent's migrations and immigrations, and the theological significance of these for theology and for the Americas. Intercultural concerns also appear to be growing in Latin American theology today. The new (theological) period may openly and emphatically deal with questions not emphasized by liberation theology in the past: gender, race, ethnicity, and sexual orientation. Evidently, there will be other defining topics in this probable new period of Latin American theology (as yet without a period name).

It is difficult to say yet if U.S. and Canadian theologies (and theologians) will ever join their Latin American peers in creating a truly continental theology—the fascination with Europe in U.S. and Canadian theologies (among several other important reasons) remains a strong "provincializing" factor.

Orlando Espín

See also BOFF, LEONARDO; CELAM; CULTURE; DEVELOPMENT OF DOGMA/OF DOCTRINE; ELLACURÍA, IGNACIO; ENCYCLICAL; EVANGELII NUNTIANDI; GUTIÉRREZ, GUSTAVO; INCULTURATION; INTERCULTURAL THOUGHT; LAS CASAS, BARTOLOMÉ DE; LATIN AMERICAN CATHOLICISM; LATINO THEOLOGY (-IES); LIBERATION THEOLOGIES; MEDELLIN CONCLUSIONS; METHOD IN THEOLOGY; POPULAR CATHOLICISM; POPULORUM PROGRESSIO; PUEBLA DOCUMENT; ROMERO, OSCAR ARNULFO; ROSCÍO, JUAN GERMÁN; SCHOLASTICISM; SEGUNDO, JUAN LUIS; VATICAN, SECOND COUNCIL OF THE; VIEIRA, ANTONIO; VITORIA, FRANCISCO DE.

LATINO/A
A Spanish term that simply means "Latin." However, in the United States it is increasingly preferred as an accurate self-identifying term shared by Mexican Americans, Puerto Ricans, Cuban Americans, and the like. Indeed, the term "Latino/a" is used exclusively for U.S. populations, and does not refer to Latin Americans. As the term "Hispanic" attempted to identify these communities and cultures by what they received from the Spanish colonial period, the term

"Latino" (and its feminine form "Latina") identifies them by what they share—historically, socially, ethnically, and culturally—with Latin America. "Latino/a," therefore, does not narrowly depend on what is Spanish to establish a defining identity, but on the actual mixture (*mestizaje*) of experiences, classes, races, and so on, that is at the core of the Latino/a and Latin American identities. Not denying the Spanish contribution at all, the use of "Latino/a" establishes a more accurate (and less colonizing) term for self-identity. However, "Latino/a" is still fundamentally a term used in non-Latino/a contexts and for non-Latino/a publics in the U.S., because the Latino/a communities still prefer the more culturally specific labels for internal self-identification (for instance, Mexican American/Chicano, Puerto Rican, Cuban American, and so on).

Orlando Espín

See also CULTURE; HISPANIC; LATINO CATHOLICISM; LATINO PROTESTANTISM; LATINO THEOLOGY (-IES); MESTIZAJE.

LATINO CATHOLICISM
The expression refers to a vast and diverse tradition within the Catholic Church *in the U.S.*, with evident roots and plentiful parallels in Latin America. Most demographic projections foresee that in a few years Latinos/as will be at least half of all Catholics in the U.S. They already are, when added to their Latin American counterparts, the largest cultural group within the world's entire Catholic population. Latino Catholicism, however, is quite different from European and European-American Catholicism.

There is no doubt that the most frequent religion among U.S. Latinos is "popular Catholicism." This is the case among all the different cultural communities (Mexican and Mexican-American, Puerto Rican, Cuban-American, and so on). Certainly, many Latinos participate in the "official" type of Catholicism, but both numerically and culturally the symbolic universe of the popular version of the religion is by far the more widespread and commanding of the two. It can be argued that, first of all, *popular Catholicism is the manner in and through which most Latinos/as are Catholic;* and secondly, that this *popular Catholicism is a key matrix of all Latino cultures.*

If forced to attempt a nearly impossible description of such a diverse phenomenon as Latino Catholicism, we might say that it incorporates at least the following elements: (1) it focuses and centers on Christ, and especially his humanness; (2) it has great admiration for and devotion to Mary (and secondarily the saints); (3) it emphasizes the laity (especially of older women) and lay leadership, although it respects the church and its ordained ministers; (4) it is family-centered (hence, not parish-centered, or individualist); (5) it is symbolic, affective, and public in its expressions of the sacred; (6) it "performs" (rather than "explains") its beliefs and doctrines; (7) it greatly appreciates wisdom, and the role of the *sensus fidelium;* (8) it seems to mistrust authoritarian, "clericalized," or "institutionalized" approaches to Christianity; and (9) it distinguishes communal solidarity and compassion (especially with the poor) as the two most important Christian virtues. With significant consequences for the interpretation of the religion, the socioculturally marginalized are by far the vast majority of Latino Catholics.

Latino Catholicism cannot be properly understood apart from its history. Its beliefs and practices developed not only as a result of general inner-Catholic or intra-Christian events, although it certainly shares in worldwide Christian history and overall doctrine. Latino Catholicism's shape and contents are especially the consequence of historical confrontations with the realities of conquest, annexation, and religio-cultural invasions.

This history encompasses the pre–Tridentine Christianity of what today is Spain. This earlier Christianity was the one brought to the Americas after 1492, the one preached to the natives and the slaves, and the one that really survived among the vast majority of people even after Trent. Spanish politics (for example, the "royal patronage" over the church, and the like) kept most of Trent's reforms away from most natives, slaves, and mestizos. The legal prohibitions against nonwhite clergy and religious furthered the distance between the reformed Catholicism of Trent (that has come to be identified with modern Roman Catholicism) and the people's Catholicism (that preceded Trent to the Americas, and brought with it fifteen hundred years of earlier Christian tradition).

The religion taken to be "normative" Christianity, in the early colonial period, was Catholicism as *traditio* (in its medieval, Iberian, pre–Tridentine version). It was this religion that was reinterpreted by the native and slave populations (and later by mestizos) in their attempt to make cultural and religious sense out of their conquest and vanquishment.

This "interpreted" Catholicism was perceived, late in colonial times, to be in need of reevangelization. Mestizos were by then fast becoming the majority of the population, and it was through and to them that the new catechetical efforts were channeled. This allowed for some elements of reevangelization to reach

Amerindians and Africans, but the latter groups' religion remained basically as it had been.

The late colonial reevangelization mainly reached the mestizos. This allowed them to interpret the new messages being presented through the prism of their inherited popular, medieval Catholicism (still seen by them as "normative"). This latest reinterpretation slowly became the Catholic norm for the mixed-race majority. It was this religion, for all practical purposes, that was the only Catholicism acceptable to most people during the period of the independence movements.

A split can be clearly detected at the start of the nineteenth century, bound to widen thereafter. The "official" (Tridentine) Christianity of the bishops and of the social elites, presenting itself as the sole valid norm, was quite distinct from the Christianity (pre–Tridentine) of the vast majority of the population. This "popular" religion also claimed to be the valid norm, though acknowledging the existence of the "clerical" version.

By the time pro-independence movements broke out, the bearers of "official" Catholicism had usually become the main pillars of Spain's colonial rule (and therefore, inimical to the anticolonial forces). The other strand of Catholicism, the "popular" version that the ecclesiastical and social elites so deplored, was the religion of the independentists (or at least openly allied with them).

It became commonplace to find the symbols of popular Catholicism used as gathering banners for the people against Spain. The people (and some of the parish clergy) fighting Spain appealed to God, to the Virgin, to the faith, and to religious symbols of the majority in order to demonstrate that God was indeed on their side. After independence (or after the American occupation in the case of Puerto Rico), what had been official colonial Catholicism soon identified itself with *criollo*, elite interests, while most mestizos still claimed popular religion as theirs. Therefore, even after Spain's defeat, the "dual-level" Catholicism of the late colonial period was preserved. And the link between the two versions of the religion was maintained thanks to the mestizos' gift for cultural reinterpretation. Some mestizos had finally entered the clergy and risen through its ranks, allowing popular Catholicism to receive partial acceptability from the post-independence ecclesiastical hierarchy. This belated acceptability, however, had its price.

During most of the post-independence period in Mexico, and during the colonial nineteenth century in Puerto Rico and in Cuba, the church hierarchy started participating in some key rites of popular Catholicism. Whether the bishops (and other clergy) suspected these rites of syncretic, superstitious, or other elements did not seem as important as the fact that these rituals were "Catholic." They were a sacred, public link between the hierarchy and the people, recognized as such by all.

The maintenance of this sacred and public link became very important during the nineteenth century. The institutions of the church came increasingly under attack by a growing intellectual elite, *criolla* and mestiza, that were influenced by the European currents of modern thought. The Enlightenment had arrived in the Americas with an anti-church zeal. The ecclesiastical hierarchy, apparently sensing the danger, saw in popular Catholicism an ally and tool in the church's defense strategy. The natives, slaves, and mestizos, for centuries marginalized from the official institutions of Catholicism, were now courted and their religion blest.

On the other hand, the intellectual elites—in typical nineteenth-century rationalist style—had no use for the church and its economic and political power, while also condemning popular Catholicism as obscurantist ignorance. They thought popular religion prevented the people from achieving higher levels of educational and material development. Intellectuals of the last century, in Mexico and the Antilles, in their disdain for church and ignorance, actually fomented a strategic alliance (necessarily clothed in acceptable theological and pastoral language) between the ecclesiastical hierarchy and the masses of people.

Nineteenth-century official and popular Catholicisms confronted the same enemy in Mexico and the Antilles, and they joined forces. But by then the "official" brand of the religion was itself far too imbued with the mentality of the post–Reformation and the Enlightenment. It was only a matter of time before the rationalist intellectuals and the church establishment would discover a sufficiently comfortable dialogue, and then turn their sights and disdain to popular Catholicism.

The intellectual elites of the nineteenth century have—over a century later—either lost their influence or have (most probably) transformed themselves into other ideological or political shapes and adopted new names. Much of modern-day education, business, politics, and so on, in Mexico and in the Antilles, as well as among U.S. Latinos, depend on the new versions of the rationalist mentality. Curiously enough, the powerful elites of the Right as well as many of the Left share the same basic worldview that sees the people's religion as an unfortunate (or at best, folkloric) vestige of the past.

In their common view, the best use of popular religious symbol is its instrumentalization.

The nineteenth century is the time of the American purchase of Florida and of the U.S. military conquest and annexation of Mexico's northern half. Florida's Latino Catholics, mostly gathered in the cities of St. Augustine and Pensacola, chose either of two paths when their purchase from Spain occurred—a few decided to stay in the new American territory, while most elected to leave Florida and settle in Spanish Cuba. It would not be until several decades later (in the mid-nineteenth century) when large communities of Latino Catholics settled again in the peninsula, fleeing the increasingly repressive Spanish colonial authorities in Cuba. The new settlers, however, established themselves in Tampa and Key West. Smaller groups of Cubans went to Philadelphia and New York. There are indications that in Tampa and Key West there were some forms of Latino popular religion during the last decades of the nineteenth century; but one must be very careful on this point, because of the religious apathy that accompanied much of the Cuban nineteenth century.

The story of the Southwest, however, was different from that of Florida. The lands from Texas to California were annexed by the United States after military intervention, and the many Mexican towns and villages were occupied. Some of these had been founded three centuries before, and the presence of Catholicism in them was as old.

The "dual-level" Christianity of Mexico had also become part of the religious life of the Southwest (these lands were still, after all, part of Mexico). Here, however, popular Catholicism seems to have had so heavy an influence that even the local ecclesiastical establishment—too weak to claim power on its own—had to actively promote it, thereby publicly linking it to the clergy. The same fundamental reasons of defense and buffer, evident in the rest of Mexico at the time, were operative in the northern frontier as the clergy allied itself here with the symbols of popular religion. The new American Southwest had been Mexico's remote northern border. Not many of the Mexican progressive elites of the period would have chosen to leave the big cities in the south and come to settle the frontier. Even the few residents who pretended to belong to these elites were numerically insignificant and ultimately powerless.

Popular Catholicism remained the de facto religion of the vast majority of the population. Its shape, functions, and socio-doctrinal developmental process paralleled the rest of Mexico. In other words, the popular Christianity that preceded the American annexations was at its core the pre–Tridentine *traditio*. It was mestizo, but in this case because mestizos were the ones who mainly settled here. This religion assumed as normative the Catholicism that had been interpreted by earlier "popular" generations in southern Mexico. However, the reevangelization efforts, so important during much of the late colonial period, had barely any effect in the lands from Texas to California.

But then came the American military conquest and subsequent annexations. For the first time, Latino Catholicism faced the Reformation and a type of Christianity that was not Catholic. The confrontation happened between, on one side, a militant Protestant nation, increasingly aware of its military might and apparently convinced of its moral superiority (its "Manifest Destiny"). On the other side there was a conquered people, suddenly and violently deprived of rights and land, whose religion had long roots in the medieval past the new conquerors loathed. The Catholicism of the people was not the post–Tridentine version, by now common enough in Catholic Europe and in the eastern American states. It had assumed as self-evident that truth was "Catholic." It seemed to be no intellectual match for the Protestantism of the occupiers. The religion of the people, furthermore, was also going to face another confrontation—the arrival, with the annexation, of post–Tridentine Catholics.

Latino Catholicism in the U.S. is now displaying the effects and consequences of its first one hundred years of confrontation with post–Tridentine Roman Christianity, with the heirs of the Protestant Reformation, and with the modern world (initiated and disseminated mainly by the Calvinist and Roman theological traditions).

The implementation of the decrees and doctrines of the Council of Trent had been very selective in Spanish America. Tridentine Catholicism, arriving at least a century after the conquest, became identified mostly with the Spaniards and *criollos*, and limited to their social circles. There were so few Protestants in Spain's colonies that the European urgency for reform seemed foreign here. One result, as we have seen, was the preservation of pre–Tridentine Christianity in the Western Hemisphere. The "reevangelization" of the late colonial period attempted to bring Tridentine Catholicism to the people, but only with very limited success. By then even the official religion was undergoing a profound change that would eventually lead to the centralizing Romanization started by Pius IX.

Latinos were forced to deal with the church of Trent immediately after the American annexation. Their Catholicism, fundamentally untouched by the Tridentine reforms, suddenly confronted a new type of church that seemed always on the defensive, that emphasized doctrinal knowledge (and guilt) over experience and affect, and that devalued lay participation. Worst of all, this new church supported the American conquest of the Southwest.

Today we can understand why the Catholicism of the American eastern states appeared to be on the defensive: it faced Protestant dominance. And perhaps this in turn led to American Catholics' perceiving public, popular Latino Catholicism as superstition in need of correction and catechesis. Compounding this perception, however, was the growing influence and control of the Irish in the U.S. church, among whom the Irish became racially motivated opponents of the Mexicans in the annexed lands. The American (specifically Irish) Catholics' need for acceptance and respect in the wider U.S. society led many to conceive of Latino religion as an added weight they did not want to carry, and as a source of embarrassment to their reformed, Tridentine church.

Some of the public, social celebrations of popular Catholicism were soon transformed into more private, family expressions. The new church organized itself basically according to the ecclesiastical patterns developed in the eastern states. Although most Catholics in the Southwest were Latino, their participation and leadership in the institutions of religion were drastically diminished and often avoided. The people's alternative seems to have been withdrawal into the universe of popular Catholicism—it was *theirs*, and it made familiar sense of God and Christianity. By taking refuge in this religious world, Latinos were also preserving one of the most important roots of their cultural identity as well as their very ancient type of Christianity.

However, for the new European-American ecclesiastical establishment in the Southwest, Latino flight into traditional religion implied that the new, "white" Catholic elites could ignore Latino Christianity and further emphasize, to the Protestant majority, that Latino Catholicism was not really "Catholic"—only a marginal anachronism from the past in need of instruction. European-American Catholics had, thereby, assumed as true and valid the Protestant Reformation's premise that pre–Tridentine Christianity was deviant.

As long as the church in the Southwest doctrinally and pastorally ignored Latinos, and as long as the latter maintained the ritual link with the Roman clergy (thereby identifying themselves as Catholics), Latinos could keep their popular Catholicism with only occasional hierarchical interference. Some local Latinos joined the ranks of the clergy, but their meager numbers and lack of real institutional influence did not alter the fundamentally ritual ("devotional") relationship that existed between priests and people since the colonial days. But this uneasy truce between the official European-American (mostly Irish) church and Latino popular Catholicism started to unravel in the middle of the twentieth century, and more specifically after Vatican II.

Several elements of the contemporary world came together to force the current confrontation. There is, for example, the influence that decades of access to European-American mass media have had on the sacral worldview underlying and sustaining much of Latino Catholicism. There, too, are the efforts of public education in communicating the values and worldview of modernity. It is difficult to imagine how the long exposure to European-American society (heir to the Calvinist religious tradition, imbued of individualism, and increasingly secularized) could *not* have affected the very foundations and premises of the Latino religious and communal universe. The growth of urbanization and of a city-based job market after World War II began to deeply impact the stable, traditional family and community relationships so fundamental to Latino religion. Finally, the upsurge of immigration (to American cities) from Mexico and the Antilles added huge concentrations of Latinos. This immigrant wave (which has not ended) brings to the U.S. people who are not accustomed to being treated as foreigners in their societies or church.

Finally, and more importantly, the poverty and discrimination (and consequences thereof) suffered by so many Latinos seem to have socially justified, in the eyes of the larger society, the perpetuation of the marginal role of the Latino populations. The dominant ideology has long attempted to explain and "prove" the supposed reasons for this marginal status. Needless to say, precisely as a symptom of their social vulnerability, many Latinos have internalized the "proofs" put forth by the dominant ideology. Unfortunately, the European-American Catholic Church frequently and uncritically assumed these ideological justifications, thereby reaffirming the "validity" of the arguments of prejudice within its ecclesiastical milieu. It also became an active accomplice in the Latino internalization of the dominant ideology.

Nevertheless, demographics (and probably not the longstanding pastoral need) finally made the European-American Church take notice, although it is also true that many were moved to action by the new vision of Vatican II. But whatever the motive, the alternatives offered by official Catholicism ("progressive" or "conservative") to U.S. Latinos seem clear and are certainly not new: either leave the pre–Tridentine style of Catholicism behind by becoming religiously "Americanized," or face the continued onslaught of accusations of ignorance and superstition, followed by pastoral activity geared to "correctly" educate in "real" Roman Christianity. The American church's attempts at understanding Latino Catholicism have frequently seemed to be motivated by the hope of the latter's early and definitive demise.

The current trend at "multiculturalizing" the American church perhaps conceals the obvious (and not surprising) fact that those who *really* set the pastoral agendas, determine the doctrinal parameters, and direct the implementation strategies for the so-called multicultural dioceses and parishes of the future, are still the European-American Catholics. Therefore, even this well-intentioned effort at cultural diversity does not question the unspoken premise that U.S. Latino Catholicism (to the degree that it is distinctly Latino) must be left behind.

The U.S. Latino responses to the alternatives offered by the European-American Church have been creative attempts at religious and cultural survival. There is still, for example, the learned pattern of flight into the traditional religious universe. Some Latinos (perhaps the majority among a certain age group, and among many recent immigrants) do choose to perpetuate the forms and vision of pre–Tridentine Catholicism. They are probably not aware of its having been the "official" religion up to a few centuries ago, nor are they familiar with the long history of

Christianity that preceded the Reformation. For them, simply, this is *their* Catholicism, *their* way of being Christian, and that reason suffices.

But there have been other responses to the official church's alternatives. These alternatives have been, in different ways and to varying degrees, culturally optimizing paths for preserving traditional religion and its sustaining worldview vis-à-vis the always encroaching world of modernity and post–Tridentine Catholicism. These newer responses are compromises with a European-American reality perceived as (at best) overwhelming or (at worst) dangerously invasive.

It may be argued that nonparochial lay movements and associations, such as the Cursillos de Cristiandad or even the more traditional *cofradías*, have allowed for the formation of an alternative Latino church within the broader community of Catholicism. This Latino church has acted, for all practical purposes, as parallel parish and diocese, permitting a high degree of participation and leadership to Latinos otherwise marginalized from the European-American controlled parishes and dioceses. Through the acceptance of varying degrees of (preferably nonintrusive) institutional links to the hierarchy, Latinos managed to preserve a considerable degree of autonomy within the lay movements.

A close examination of the latter would show how deep, indeed, is the influence of the symbols and the worldview of popular Catholicism on the movements. Acts of public piety, for example, are consistently encouraged, praised, and performed. Some of the associations have been specifically established for the purpose of preserving traditional forms of devotion and communal prayer. Through this lay-led, parallel Catholicism, Latinos

have managed to preserve and reinterpret significant elements of their shared worldview, together with their emphasis on family and community. The movements have also served as important vehicles for the dissemination of many of the doctrinal contents of popular Catholicism, though sufficiently adapted (*and* concealed) in forms acceptable to the modern ecclesiastical realities.

The European-American Church's reaction to the Latino lay movements and associations has been frequently adverse, demanding that local (European-American) parishes and dioceses exercise control over the people's alternative Catholic "spaces." Increasingly perceived by many Latinos as the institution's sociological need to control, the church's reactions have often been understood by the people as one more battle in the European-American clergy's relentless struggle to dismantle Latino religion.

It is important to note that as Latino popular religion attempts to survive by adapting to post–Tridentine Roman Catholicism, it has begun to modify and reinterpret the doctrinal contents and symbols that have traditionally distinguished it. For example, the connection between the Virgin of Guadalupe and the Mary of Catholic devotion is (apparently) progressing. There is also a growing sense of social protagonism as part of the discerned will of God, thereby beginning the transformation of the mostly fatalistic past image of divine providence. Symbols of popular Catholicism have prominently appeared in and been associated with some important social and political movements among U.S. Latinos.

The most telling example of the contemporary reinterpretation of symbols and contents refers to the Bible. It is highly inaccurate (indeed arrogant) to think that

Western Christianity did not know the Bible before Trent and the Reformation. In the Iberian villages, where people did not usually know how to read and where medieval culture was still very much alive, the Bible's contents were presented graphically through art, *autos sacramentales*, storytelling, and preaching. The same, as we saw, held true of pre–Tridentine colonial Christianity in the Americas. The Bible was known at the popular level, but through performed or visual symbol and the spoken word, not through reading the printed page (in others words, as in early Christianity).

Currently, however, with the ever-increasing literacy rate, the direct reading of the text of the Bible has become widespread. There is no doubt that, after Vatican II, the official Roman Catholic insistence on biblical reading was heeded by Latinos. The growing numbers of Latino Protestants have also been a strong influence. Whatever the reasons for this scriptural awakening, there is no question that the written text of the Bible has been taken out of the hands (and potential control) of the ecclesiastical institution and is now being interpreted by the people themselves. Interestingly, this increase in familiarity with the sacred texts of Christians does not seem to have decidedly contributed to the exodus of so many Latino Catholics from the Roman Church. It seems, in fact, to be strengthening the symbols and fundamental worldview of popular Catholicism through another process of reinterpretation, this time biblical.

There is another common response to the either/or alternatives offered to Latino Catholicism. This is Pentecostalism. Latino Pentecostalism has shown itself as an important, culturally acceptable vehicle for the preservation of the pre–Tridentine (and premodern) religious worldview. Though obviously (and consciously) rejecting many medieval and colonial Catholic symbols and practices, Pentecostalism has managed to hold on to the very "sacramental," symbolic ethos and worldview that made pre–Reformation Christianity possible. Many symbols have been "reformed" and some modern ones added, but the fundamental structures and premises of the traditionally religious Latino worldview have basically remained. One cannot understand the current popularity of the Catholic charismatic movement among Latinos, or the ever increasing number of Protestant Pentecostal churches in the *barrios*, without realizing the seemingly crucial role of cultural and religious preservation that the Pentecostal movement (in its Catholic or Protestant versions) is playing. It is well documented that the growth of the charismatic, Pentecostal communities is in direct relation to people's perceived sense of threat or invasion at the hands of modernity. In these studies, the Christian churches (of any denomination) that appear allied to the modern worldview and against the traditional religious and communal relations will suffer considerable numerical losses. It is, therefore, highly ironic that the Roman Catholic Church that engaged in the ideological battles following the Reformation on the side of tradition should now be an uncritical bearer of the Reformation's and modernity's own theological premises vis-à-vis pre–Tridentine Latino Catholicism. It almost seems that the contemporary confrontation of Latino Catholicism with the European-American Roman Catholic Church is the modern version of the sixteenth-century Reformation that Latino religion never had to face. This time, however, it is official Roman Catholicism that has taken the side of the Protestant Reformers, arguing through similar logic and with surprisingly similar doctrinal assumptions. Unfortunately, Latino Catholicism had been robbed (by the consequences of annexation, prejudice, and poverty) of most theological and institutional means of defense and self-affirmation needed in this new Reformation.

There are, evidently, many Latino individuals across the country who participate in the life of the official Roman Catholic (European-American) Church, who are well educated in theology, who are successful in ministry (ordained or not), and who are respected leaders of their faith communities. There are even a few Latino diocesan bishops, and a few more auxiliary bishops. But these individuals, so far, do not alter the reality that popular Catholicism remains the manner in and through which most Latinos are Catholic. Arguably, however, the day will come when a majority of U.S. Latinos will be more "official" and less "popular" in their Catholicism. Will this transformation imply that their Latino cultural and religious specificity will be lost? Will the future mean that the European-American "religious invasion" will finally succeed? The answer to both questions is probably no, if present trends continue. The demographic growth of Latinos will make it impossible for the European-American Church to remain what it is. It too will be changed. In other words, what the future will probably bring is a profound and thorough religious *mestizaje*, and a new style of American Catholicism will develop.

It is important to note that there already are clear (although only local) early indications of what this future Catholic *mestizaje* might look like. There are also signs that Latinos are beginning to take ownership of the "official" Roman Catholic Church, as well as to exert pressure and demand changes. New organizations have been established that, in the short and especially in the long runs, will have a deep impact on mainstream American Catholicism: the National Catholic Council on Hispanic Ministry, the Academy of Catholic Hispanic Theologians of the U.S., the *Instituto de Liturgia Hispana*, and the *Asociación de Sacerdotes Hispanos*, among others.

Orlando Espín

See also AUTO SACRAMENTAL; CULTURE; GRAMSCI, ANTONIO; HISPANIC; INCULTURATION; LATINO/A; LATINO PROTESTANTISM; LATINO THEOLOGY (-IES); MESTIZAJE; MODERNITY; POPULAR CATHOLICISM; POSTMODERNITY; ROMAN CATHOLIC CHURCH; SENSUS FIDELIUM/SENSUS FIDEI; TRADITION AND TRADITIONS; TRENT, COUNCIL OF; TRIDENTINE; TRIDENTINISM.

LATINO PROTESTANTISM

The origins of Latino Protestantism are to be found in the Mexican-American War and the ensuing annexation by the U.S. of what had been approximately half the land of Mexico. Particularly in New Mexico, there was resistance among Mexican Catholics to the Americanization of their church. The leader of this resistance was Fr. Antonio José Martínez, who clashed repeatedly with the bishop sent to Santa Fe from Baltimore. Although Martínez never became a Protestant, one of his sons was the first Latino to be ordained a Presbyterian minister, and many of the first Latino Protestants in New Mexico were former followers of Martínez.

In other regions of the country, as Euro-American Protestants encountered Latinos, a few among them became interested in missionizing their Latino neighbors. Quite often, in those early stages, Latinos were lumped together with Italians and Portuguese, and attempts were made to provide them with common churches, or at least to apply the same strategies for all three groups. Since Italians and Portuguese tended to assimilate, but Latinos tended to retain their cultural identity, these common policies most often failed, or at best produced meager results. Slowly, however, Latino Protestant congregations—and in some cases Latino Protestant judicatories such as Methodist annual conferences or Presbyterian presbyteries—were formed in areas such as Texas, California, New York, and Miami.

For many years, none of the major Protestant denominations had a concerted strategy for the development of Latino parishes or congregations. In fact, it is only during the last decades that such strategies have begun to emerge, with several major denominations developing national plans for Latinos, or at least appointing staff to take major responsibility for the Latino membership of the denomination.

Given these circumstances, most of the growth of Latino Protestantism has been the result of the work of Latino Protestants themselves. Some of these have been members of Latino congregations in the U.S. Others have come to this country from Latin America, where they were already Protestants. Thus, for instance, although there were Latino Protestant churches in Miami prior to the Cuban Revolution, these were few and small. It has been after that revolution, with vast numbers of Cuban Protestants seeking exile in South Florida (and later with exiles and immigrants from other countries) that South Florida Latino Protestantism has really grown. Likewise, much of the strength of Protestantism among Latinos in New York and environs is due to Puerto Rican and Dominican Protestants settling in the area. The same is true of Texas and Southern California, although in this case the immigration has come mostly from Mexico and Central America.

As in Latin America, the vast majority of Protestant Latinos are Pentecostal. Among the "mainline" denominations, the Southern Baptists have the largest number of Latino members, with United Methodists a distant second. The United Methodist Church has three Latino bishops and one Latino annual conference. And some Pentecostal denominations— notably the Assemblies of God and the Church of God—have Latino districts. Several denominations publish books and curriculum materials in Spanish, as well as magazines for their Latino constituencies.

Two developments in recent years are worthy of note. The first is the development and growing self-consciousness of Latino Protestant Hispanic theology. The roots of this theology are to be found in the work of Orlando Costas and others, some of it published as adult Sunday school materials and in the journal *Apuntes*. This relatively recent Latino Protestant theology is widely ecumenical, including "mainline" Protestants as well as Pentecostals, and in friendly dialogue with Roman Catholic Latinos and Latinas.

The second significant development is the birth of a number of agencies and organizations run by Latinos and Latinas, whose purpose is to serve the Latino community. The Hispanic Association of Bilingual Bicultural Ministries (HABBIM) seeks to help the churches face the challenges of second- and third-generation Latinos. The Alianza de Ministerios Evangélicos Nacionales (AMEN) brings together Protestant leaders in a variety of ministries. The Asociación para la Educación Teológica Hispana (AETH) is an association of persons (some of them Roman Catholic) who are committed to theological education at various levels and in different settings. For a time, AETH also managed the Hispanic Summer Program, a widely ecumenical program that provides Latinas and Latinos with experiences in theological education that are particularly relevant to their settings and interests.

Justo L. González

LATINO THEOLOGY (-IES)

The name used to refer not merely (or mainly) to the theology produced by U.S. Latino professional theologians, but to the specific *type* of theology they produce. Because of its growing diversity, it is possible to refer to this type of theology in the plural.

Latino theology is *not* Latin American theology. Although similar in many ways, the two are distinct schools of thought. Latino theology was/is born from the faith experience and sociocultural realities of *United States'* populations that identify themselves as Latino/a. Nevertheless, it is nearly impossible to explain the birth of Latino theology without recognizing the foundational influence of such Latin Americans as Gustavo Gutiérrez, Jon Sobrino, Juan Luis Segundo, Juan Carlos Scannone, Ignacio Ellacuría, Leonardo Boff, José Míguez Bonino, Orlando Costas, and Enrique Dussel, among others. The heritage of European scholarship has also left its mark on Latino theology through the works of contemporary scholars like Karl Rahner, Jürgen Moltmann, Antonio Gramsci, and Johann B. Metz. Then there is the evident impact of such Catholic

ecclesial texts as the documents of the Second Vatican Council, and of the Latin American bishops' conferences at Medellín, Puebla, and Santo Domingo.

Latino theology may be described as exhibiting (in diverse ways and degrees) the following characteristics: (1) it is part of the overall methodology of liberation theologies (hence, consciously choosing to be on the side of the marginalized Latino populations, it theologizes from within the "soil" of Latino reality and daily struggles); (2) it sees in "popular" Catholicism an indispensable and privileged methodological, epistemological, and thematic source; (3) it is sensitive to the contributions of the social sciences and social analyses, and is in open dialogue with them; (4) it incorporates the history of the people in the interpretation of the faith of that people; (5) it methodologically acknowledges and values daily, familial, and communal life; (6) it is increasingly aware of the indispensable contributions of feminist epistemologies and theologies; (7) it continues to develop or critique the (theological/social/historical/cultural) category of "mestizaje"; (8) it firmly rejects European and European-American "universalizing" thought; (9) consequently, it is also a severe critic of post-Enlightenment "modernity," and of its inclusion in mainstream Catholic and Protestant Christianity; (10) it is pastorally sensitive, and consciously interested in reflecting pastoral and social realities; and (11) it is ecumenically aware and respectful. The future of U. S. Latino theology will probably bring it into closer contact with a growing number of Third World (especially Latin American) theologies of culture.

U.S. Latino theologians are more frequently Catholic, but an increasing number of Protestants are making significant contributions to the field. The relations among Catholic and Protestant Latino theologians have always been respectful and supportive, both personally and professionally. Fortunately, the acrimony often found among (Protestant and Catholic) Latino ministers and laity is absent among theologians.

Most Latino theologians are laypeople, although there is still a greater number of men than of women. Two organizations have been crucial to the development of U.S. Latino theology: the Academy of Catholic Hispanic Theologians of the U.S. (ACHTUS), founded in 1988, and La Comunidad of Hispanic American Scholars of Theology and Religion, founded in 1990. La Comunidad, unfortunately, has not proven as successful as ACHTUS. Two periodical publications have been indispensable to Latino theology's growth, diversification, and diffusion: ACHTUS' *Journal of Hispanic/Latino Theology*, and the Protestant journal *Apuntes* (published at Perkins School of Theology).

In the opinion of most specialists, Virgilio Elizondo (a Catholic) and Justo González (a Methodist) have been the two most influential Latino theologians. Elizondo is acknowledged as the first to have produced a self-consciously Latino theological work (in 1968); and his reflections on mestizaje have been widely used. González' historical scholarship is universally recognized, as well as his masterful ability at bringing the breadth of his knowledge of history to bear on theological issues. Both Elizondo and González have contributed to the ecumenical goodwill evident among Latino theologians.

Other theologians often mentioned as representative of this movement are (among many others): Roberto Goizueta, María Pilar Aquino, Orlando Espín, Ada María Isasi-Díaz, Jeanette Rodríguez, Alex García-Rivera, Samuel Soliván, Eldin Villafañe, Harold Recinos, Miguel Díaz, Michelle González, Arturo Bañuelas, and Allan Figueroa Deck. A number of European-American authors (for example, James Nickoloff, Timothy Matovina) have joined the Latino theological perspective. Respected Latino biblical scholars (for instance, Jean-Pierre Ruiz, Fernando Segovia, and Francisco Lozada) have contributed their expertise to the field.

Orlando Espín

See also AQUINO, MARÍA PILAR; CULTURE; ELIZONDO, VIRGILIO; EPISTEMOLOGY; ESPÍN, ORLANDO; EURO-AMERICAN THEOLOGIES; GOIZUETA, ROBERTO; GONZÁLEZ, JUSTO L.; HISPANIC; IDEOLOGY (IDEOLOGIES); INCULTURATION; ISASI-DÍAZ, ADA MARÍA; LATIN AMERICAN THEOLOGIES; LATINO/A; LATINO CATHOLICISM; LATINO PROTESTANTISM; LIBERATION THEOLOGIES; MESTIZAJE; METHOD IN THEOLOGY; MODERNITY; ORTHOPRAXIS; POPULAR CATHOLICISM; POSTMODERNITY; PRAXIS; PUEBLA, DOCUMENT; SANTO DOMINGO DOCUMENT; THEOLOGICAL ANTHROPOLOGY; VATICAN, SECOND COUNCIL OF THE.

LATOURELLE, RENÉ (1918–)

Twentieth-century Roman Catholic theologian. Latourelle was born in Montreal, Canada. He was ordained a priest in the Society of Jesus (Jesuits), and spent many years as a professor of fundamental theology at the Gregorian University in Rome. Following the Second Vatican Council (1962–5), Latourelle took up the challenge of reexamining the foundations of Catholic Christian faith in the light of the council's concern for the church's pastoral mission to the whole world, and with the aid of tools of modern scholarship that, before the council, had been looked on with suspicion. Latourelle thus built a case for the credibility of Christian belief in the contemporary world, putting at the service of his theology such tools as historical-critical study, biblical hermeneutics (the science of interpretation of texts), and anthropology. At the same time, he clung to the council's heightened awareness of the *mystical* and *sacramental* dimensions of Christian faith. Latourelle's works include *Theology of Revelation*, a survey of centuries of Catholic theology about how human beings come to know God that incorporated Vatican II's focus on a Christ-centered (and therefore *interpersonal* and *biblical*) understanding of this doctrine. In *Theology: Science of Salvation*, he described Catholic theological study, contrary to the isolation in which it had operated for centuries, as needing to make the value of Christian doctrine clear and vibrant for the lives of modern persons. A series of three later books, *Finding Jesus Through the Gospels*, *Man and His Problems in the Light of Jesus Christ*, and *The Miracles of Jesus and the Theology of Miracles*, sought to demonstrate how Christ can be known truly and credibly through the Gospels. In addition to a number of other major works on these and similar themes, Latourelle also edited a *Dictionary of Fundamental Theology* and an evaluation of the ongoing impact of the council entitled *Vatican II: Assessment and Perspectives Twenty-Five Years After* (1962–1987). He has also contributed to historical research on the lives and work of early Jesuit missionaries in North America.

William Clark, S.J.

LATRIA

This word refers to the worship human beings should rightly render only to God as the Creator of all. It is distinct in degree and kind from the veneration (*dulia*) used by many Christians to honor the saints, and the especially intense degree of veneration (*hyperdulia*) some Christians reserve for the Blessed Virgin Mary, Mother of Jesus Christ.

Joanne M. Pierce

See also ADORATION; DULIA; HYPERDULIA; ICONOCLASTIC CONTROVERSY.

LAUD, WILLIAM (1573–1645)

Archbishop of Canterbury (1633–40) who promoted vigorously and sometimes forcibly the liturgical traditions, teaching, and discipline of the undivided church within the Church of England. Thus, while he explored possibilities for reunion with the Orthodox and fostered relationships with leaders of the Continental Reformation, he refused to permit intercommunion with churches that had abolished the episcopacy. He was convinced that ecclesiastical uniformity would engender a true unity of spirit within the Church of England. His strategy for promoting uniformity involved both persuasive scholarship and coercive power. His intolerance and authoritarian temperament, as well as his close association with Charles I, made him enemies, especially with the Puritans. He was impeached by the Long Parliament (1640–60), tried, and executed for treason. He died rejecting the charge that he had tried to import popery back into the English church. The Episcopal Church commemorates him on January 10.

Jon Nilson

LAWS OF MANU

See MANU SMRITI.

LAYING ON OF HANDS

A liturgical gesture in which a minister places his or her open palms upon the head of another person. Both the Old and New Testaments attest to the use of this rite and to its multiple meanings. It can signify empowerment, healing, reconciliation, or commissioning. In each case, it symbolizes a bond between the two people, and a bestowal from one to the other. The Laying on of Hands is used in the rites of the catechumenate and baptism, confirmation, reconciliation, ordination, and the sacrament of the sick. It also accompanies many blessings. The General Introduction to the Catholic *Book of Blessings* says that "the laying on of hands holds a special place among gestures of blessing. Christ often used this sign of blessing, spoke of it to his disciples, saying: 'They will lay hands on the sick and these will recover' (Mark 16:18), and continues to use it in and through the Church" (no. 26b). A related gesture is the stretching of the hands or arms over a person in blessing, over an assembly, or even over an object. The gesture made over the bread and wine at the epiclesis of the eucharistic prayer, for example, in which the presider extends his hands over them, is a modification of the laying on of hands.

Patrick L. Malloy

See also ANOINTING OF THE SICK (SACRAMENT OF); EPICLESIS; ORDINATION.

LAY MINISTRY

(Latin, *laicus*; Greek, *laikos*, of the people; *Laos Theou*, chosen people of God). (Latin, *minister*; Greek, *diakonoi*, servant). A nonordained person who provides public service or leadership within the Catholic Church is considered a lay minister. A lay minister is one of many laypeople whose roles vary according to the many existing ministries and may be titled according to diocesan or local policies and practices. In many cases, laypeople (both men and women) serve in roles formerly assumed only by ordained men or by religious. Because religious brothers and sisters (nuns) do not receive clerical orders, they are considered laity within the legal categories of the church.

Originally, all disciples of Jesus were the "people of God" and all were considered as equals. Likewise, as needs arose, Christian communities developed ministries to handle them. As these communities grew, leadership developed, as did the distinction of roles and a hierarchy of leadership and authority. The "chosen people" often took part in missionary work, preaching, leadership, sacraments, and presiding at the Eucharist. In time, official positions developed. Besides bishops, there were presbyters, both men and women deacons, teachers, prophets, widows, confessors, doorkeepers, lectors, acolytes, and gravediggers. Even as the distinctions developed, the ministries varied from place to place and were not so clearly defined as today.

By the end of the first century the word "laity" was used for the common people. By the end of the second century, the church had an established hierarchy. By the early fourth century, the church had become a state institution of the Roman Empire. The clergy became the educated scholars and "princes" of the church with fairly well-defined roles while the laity became the second-class citizens who were to serve the clergy. Only the ordained performed those services deemed as "ministry." With the development of the monastic movement and mendicant orders, many of the ministries or services were absorbed by both the monastic and mendicant communities of men and women.

Problems arose between diocesan and religious institutions concerning the jurisdiction of the ministries. Much of the reform of the Protestant Reformation (sixteenth century) concerned the hold of the hierarchy over the ministries and the separation between the clergy and laity. The response of the Council of Trent (1545–63) was to solidify that separation by determining that sacramental ministry was based on the power of orders. Preaching, teaching, and ministries of government were based on the power of jurisdiction, thereby restricting the ministries to the ordained.

Despite this restriction, many new ministries developed as new needs arose, especially in the areas of education, health care, social work, spiritual direction, pastoral counseling, and the like. These ministries often involved the laity in those services. In general, though, either religious or diocesan clergy directed or supervised the ministries.

For many years, especially after the Reformation, the term "ministry" within the Catholic Church referred to the role of the priest or deacon in conjunction with administering the sacraments. Most of the other services were called apostolic works. The priest was the *ordinary minister* of most of the sacraments. Only Protestant clergy used "minister" as a title, while Catholic clergy were called priests or deacons.

Vatican II changed the emphasis when it declared that baptism is a call to all the chosen people of God to minister in their rightful places in the world, but also within the church (LG 35). The full membership of the laity was stressed in three documents: Dogmatic Constitution on the Church, the Pastoral Constitution on the Church in the Modern World, and the Decree on the Apostolate of Lay People. These documents stressed the value of the work of the laity in the family, work-place, and the political and social life of the community. However, even these documents referred to the services of the laity within the institutional church structures as "works of the Apostolate" and to laypeople as helpers in the ministry of the bishop. Gradually, since Vatican II, the laity have begun to take leadership roles in education, in parochial schools, the formation of pastoral councils, hospitals, and social services. The laity also entered more visibly into the special area of liturgical ministries. No longer serving just as musicians, sacristans, gatekeepers, and cleaners, the laity, first men and then women, began to proclaim the Scriptures in the vernacular, assist in the distribution of the Eucharist, in serving at the altar, and taking part in liturgical gesture and dance to enhance a Scripture reading, a hymn, a procession.

As houses of theological studies joined into "unions" and consortiums, many women entered into the study of theology to be professionally qualified for the pastoral roles they were called upon to take. As priests and theologians left seminary faculty positions for university faculties, the extent of theological and pastoral studies expanded and soon included many laypeople. In the meantime, the term "minister" became a title of changing definition. At first, only the ordained could be rightly called minister, then those laypeople officially appointed by a bishop. As administrators of parishes, directors of education, and other services, besides teaching, liturgical functions, and spiritual direction were served by the laity, the definition grew in breadth. At one point, ministry, in common usage, referred to anything done for another with the intention of service. Because of the rights of jurisdiction, the understanding of the title of lay minister continues to vary from place to place.

M. Jane Gorman

See also LAITY; MINISTRY/MINISTERIAL; TRENT, COUNCIL OF.

LAYNEZ, JAMES OR DIEGO
See LAINEZ, DIEGO.

LEAH
The elder daughter of Laban, Rebecca's brother (Gen 29:16). Because Rebecca, who was married to Isaac, wished that her son Jacob be married from within the family, Jacob was sent to Laban's household to procure a wife. Jacob chose Laban's more beautiful younger daughter, Rachel, but Laban successfully deceived Jacob, disguising his elder daughter Leah as his younger daughter, so that in fact Jacob did marry Leah.

Jacob worked for Laban for seven more years in order to earn Laban's younger daughter Rachel. Thus one man married two sisters, the one more beautiful and more truly loved by her husband. Leah, however, proved to be the more fertile of the two, in a culture where women's value derived from the number and status of the sons they bore. Leah is herself credited as being the mother of six of Jacob's twelve sons, including Judah, and mother of his only daughter, Dinah.

Alice L. Laffey

LEANDER OF SEVILLE (545?–600?)
The older brother of Isidore of Seville, Leander undertook the leadership of the family and the education of his younger brother upon the death of their father. Leander spent the greater part of his career in the church in a successful attempt to convert the Visigothic rulers from Arian to orthodox Christianity. His first success came when he converted one of the royal princes. The king, however, killed his son in 582 and banished Leander to Constantinople where Leander befriended Leo the Great. Recalled by the king, Leander became archbishop of Seville in 584 and undertook the education and conversion of another prince, Recared. When Recared later became king, the work of conversion begun under Leander quickly gained momentum. Most of Leander's writings are lost, although one surviving work, a monastic rule dedicated to his sister, reveals a warm and spiritual person.

Gary Macy

See also CONVERSION; GREGORY I THE GREAT, POPE; ISIDORE OF SEVILLE; MEDIEVAL CHRISTIANITY (IN THE WEST).

LEAVENED BREAD
See HAMETZ.

LECTIO DIVINA
Meaning literally "divine reading," this phrase refers to the monastic practice of slowly and carefully reading the biblical text with the purpose of allowing the meaning of that text to seep, as it were, into both the mind and the heart. *Lectio divina* included the extended reflection on the text that later came to be called by the terms "meditation" and "contemplation." Indeed, *lectio divina* and oral prayer are the two most ancient and traditional prayer forms.

It is important to understand that, throughout medieval times, reading meant reading aloud (at least in a low tone), and books were large—sometimes, very large—and bulky items. The entire process of reading, therefore, was considered a physical activity, making incarnate once again the Word of God. Spiritual writers, using the words of God to the prophet Ezekiel (Ezek 3:1-3), compared *lectio divina* to "eating" the word of God, and used all sorts of synonyms such as "chew" and "savor" to stress the way the devout person was to work the text so that all possible meaning and devotion could be extracted from it. Those who followed the Benedictine Rule (even in its later reformed traditions) did sacred reading on a daily basis; this complemented the oral proclamation of the Bible in the Liturgy of the Hours, what Benedictines called the *opus Dei* (work of God).

Both of these central monastic activities required, obviously, that the monks be literate, and training young monks to read, if they did not already possess that skill, was one of the tasks implemented during the probationary period called the novitiate. Monastic schools, originally intended for the novices and then extended to others, became a central service supplied by the monasteries and convents to the general Christian population. Monastic scriptoria were developed to copy the books needed for *lectio divina* and the schoolbooks needed to prepare monks and others to grasp the literary and theological riches of the biblical text. Both schools and scriptoria were, ultimately, crucial to the preservation and extension, not only of Christian faith, but of the culture of classical antiquity as well. The monastic obligation of divine reading had far-reaching consequences indeed.

Marie Anne Mayeski

See also BENEDICTINE RULE (RULE OF ST. BENEDICT); CONTEMPLATION; LITURGY (IN CHRISTIANITY); LITURGY OF THE HOURS; MEDITATION (CHRISTIAN).

LECTIONARY

(1) A table (or *ordo*) of preselected passages from sacred texts assigned to a specific occasion on religious calendars for proclamation in public worship. (2) Books that provide the full text of the biblical readings in the order in which they are assigned by the ordo. Lectionaries are used by all Jews, most Christians, and some Muslims.

The practice of following a fixed cycle of readings from the Torah was introduced in the synagogues by the first century B.C.E. A selection of Prophetic passages thematically related to the Torah portions was inaugurated by the first century C.E. Until the tenth century C.E., some Jews followed a three-year lectionary that stemmed from Palestine when the one-year lectionary devised in Babylon became the standard of world Jewry. Both lectionaries provided for the proclamation of the whole Torah in canonical order, although special festivals were assigned passages especially suited to these occasions. Thus, most selections from the Torah follow the principle of "continuous readings" (*lectio continua*); all portions from the Prophets (*Haftorah*) follow the principle of "selected readings" (*lectio electa*).

Although the earliest Christian communities had a variety of different practices, by the second century, many communities were reading from the Scriptures of Israel as well as Christian writings during worship. Later, one of the criteria used to establish the New Testament canon was the liturgical use by the vast majority of communities.

Justin Martyr states that, in second-century Rome, readings were proclaimed "as long as time allows." The fourth-century *Apostolic Constitutions* identifies a sequence of five readings "of law and the prophets, of our epistles and Acts, as well as the Gospels." Between the fourth and seventh centuries, the liturgical centers of the East and West devised a variety of one-year lectionaries. Fifth-century Rome and Constantinople reduced the readings to three lessons and most other rites followed. Rome and Constantinople later reduced the reading to two, although some other rites retained three readings. Eastern Orthodox Churches and Eastern-rite Catholics follow their ancient one-year lectionaries that were devised in the first Christian millennium.

In the West, Charlemagne commissioned Alcuin to devise liturgical texts to solidify his empire with uniform liturgical practices. Alcuin's lectionary was based on the seventh-century Roman practices. Changes introduced in Northern Europe were subsequently adopted in Rome in the tenth century, but variations devised for local practices coexisted in Europe until the sixteenth century. The lectionary used in Rome became the basis of a uniform lectionary mandated by the Council of Trent and introduced in 1570. Although a few subsequent changes were introduced, the Tridentine lectionary was used by Latin-rite Catholics until 1970.

Guided by the principle that whatever was not contrary to the Gospel should be retained, Luther made no changes to the lectionary he adopted. Cranmer introduced a few changes to the lectionary of the *Sarum Missal* as the basis of his Book of Common Prayer. Many Reformed and all Free Church denominations rejected the use of lectionaries. Over the centuries changes and alternative lectionaries were introduced by Anglicans, Lutherans, and Reformed, but the tables were almost identical to the Roman lectionary.

In *Sacrosanctum Concilium* (35.1; 51) the Second Vatican Council called for a new lectionary to provide a more extensive system of readings designed for more than one year. The Lectionary for Sundays and Solemnities introduced in 1969 became mandatory in the Roman Rite in 1971. The new Lectionary (a) replaced an annual table of readings with a three-year cycle; (b) provided for three biblical readings together with a psalm or canticle in place of a gospel that had usually been preceded by a brief segment from an epistle; and (c) appointed regular readings from the Old Testament that were rarely included in the 1570 ordo.

This Lectionary selected readings to suit the important feasts and seasons. It also adopted semicontinuous selections from the gospels and epistles for the remaining Sundays. All the Old Testament portions were designed to correspond to one or both of the other readings, most frequently to the Gospel passage. A slight revision was introduced in 1981. The 1981 revision was introduced in 1992 in Canada; it was introduced in the United States in 1998. In addition, a two-year, two-reading daily Lectionary was introduced in 1969 along with lectionaries for sacramental usage.

The 1969 Catholic Lectionary captured the imagination of many other churches in North America. Episcopal, Lutheran, Methodist, and Presbyterian variants of the Catholic Sunday Lectionary were quickly introduced. In 1986 the Consultation of Common Texts devised the Common Lectionary designed as a consensus lectionary that was adopted by many Anglican and Protestant churches throughout the world. The Common Lectionary was replaced in 1994 by the Revised Common Lectionary and has been approved for trial use by the Episcopal Church of the U.S.A. as an alternative lectionary. On the first Sunday of Advent 1995, the Evangelical Lutheran Church of North

America began to use the Revised Common Lectionary.

In Islam all gatherings for public worship among Shi'a and Sunni Muslims begin with the first *sura* of the Qu'ran. The five compulsory prayers that follow include at least three *ayat* from the Qu'ran that are appointed over the year. Although the use of a lectionary of extended readings from the Qu'ran is followed in some Islamic countries, most Muslims frown on this practice.

Regina A. Boisclair

See also BOOK OF COMMON PRAYER; CRANMER, THOMAS; LUTHER, MARTIN; VATICAN, SECOND COUNCIL OF THE.

LECTOR

Before Vatican II the term "lector" was a title given exclusively to those who received the second of the four "minor orders" (doorkeeper, lector, exorcist, alcolyte) that were conferred on those preparing for the ministerial priesthood. A lector read selections from the church fathers during the Liturgy of the Hours and sang the epistle in solemn celebrations of Mass. Cyprian notes that individuals were ordained to this office in the third century (Epistles 20:4).

Since Vatican II the term "lector" has been used to designate the role of the qualified layperson who exercises the Ministry of the Word in a liturgical celebration by reading the Old Testament selection and/or the New Testament lesson established by the Lectionary. The 1983 Code of Canon Law reserves to men the right to be installed in the stable office as Lector (Canon 230:1), but it also stipulates that all laypeople (men and women) may exercise this role in liturgical celebrations (Canon 230:2).

Regina A. Boisclair

LEFÈVRE D'ÉTAPLES, JACQUES (1455?–1536)

French humanist and priest, Lefèvre d'Étaples was a leading Scripture scholar in Renaissance France. In 1512 he published an important commentary on St. Paul; his French translations of the New Testament (1523) and the Old Testament (1528) helped to establish the authority of the French Bible.

Lefèvre was a prominent figure in the humanist circle associated with Guillaume Briçonnet, bishop of Meaux. A critic of pious traditions that had conflated several stories about various women in the New Testament with Mary Magdalene, Lefèvre was eventually condemned by the theology faculty of the University of Paris. Though he remained a Roman Catholic, Lefèvre has often been seen as a forerunner to Protestant Reformers in France.

Thomas Worcester, S.J.

See also COUNTER-REFORMATION/ CATHOLIC REFORMATION; HUMANISM; MARY MAGDALEN; REFORMATION; RENAISSANCE.

LEGALISM (CHINESE)

(Chinese, *Fa-Chia*, School of Laws). Politico- philosophical school that emerged in China during the Warring States Period (450–221 B.C.E.) in opposition to the Confucians. This was a loosely organized and diverse group of thinkers who agreed that the answer to social disorder was tough, all-embracing laws and a system of rewards and punishments. The group laid the foundation for the ruthless and autocratic Shi Huang Di, the "First Emperor," who unified China during the Chin Dynasty (221–206 B.C.E.) under the Legalist ideology of might makes right. While the direct influence of the Legalists was short-lived, Legalist ideology linked with Taoist and Confucian thought had a lasting impact on Imperial China.

G. D. DeAngelis

See also HAN FEI TZU; ZHOU DYNASTY.

LEGALISM (JUDEO-CHRISTIAN)

A type of ethic that prescribes, often in minute detail, rules or laws applicable to any situation. Legalism also designates a certain mental disposition toward an ethical code that entails a scrupulous conscience focusing on the letter of the law rather than the spirit of the law. This mentality frequently results in minimalism, that is, the belief that a person is morally justified by following the minimum the law requires, even if the supreme law (for example, the law of charity), demands more. Throughout Christian tradition, and what will be addressed here, this legalistic mentality is criticized more than a legalistic ethic. Whereas the Old Testament reveals a positive understanding of legalism, the roots for legalism in its contemporary pejorative sense are in the New Testament.

Within the Old Testament, legalism is a virtue. The law (torah) was sacred to Israel; it was a manifestation of the Jewish people's relationship with Yahweh expressed in the form of covenant. When the Israelite people followed the law, they were responding to, and fulfilling, this covenantal relationship. Within this context, legalism designates this love relationship and how it was lived out between, and among, God and God's people.

Jesus' harsh words toward the "scribes and Pharisees" throughout the Gospels foreshadow the contemporary usage of the term legalism. For example, when the Pharisees criticize Jesus for allowing his disciples to pick grain on the Sabbath, thereby violating the prohibition to work, Jesus retorts that the Sabbath was made for human beings, not human beings for the Sabbath (Mark 2:23-28; Matt 12:1-8; Luke 6:1-5). What Jesus condemned was neither the Sabbath nor the law of the Old Testament, for in other Gospel passages he strictly upholds the law and its demands (for example, Matt 5:17-20); he condemns the Pharisees' legalistic mentality that places the external conformity to the law above the internal disposition of the person and the demands of the situation. In fact, we frequently find the two words used interchangeably: legalistic and pharasaical. The law of charity was absent in the legalism of the Pharisees and resulted in Jesus' harsh words toward them.

While rules and laws are necessary and essential to a code of ethics, such rules and laws must be applied prudently under the guise of charity. A legalistic mentality fails to take into account the ambiguity of reality and the need for flexibility when applying rules or laws to particular ethical situations.

Todd A. Salzman

See also CASUISTRY; DEONTOLOGICAL; MANUALS, THEOLOGY OF THE; NATURAL LAW.

LEGION OF MARY

A Catholic lay organization, founded in Ireland (1921), and at one point very widespread throughout U.S. Catholic parishes. It works for conversions to the church, and for the retention of those already Catholic. It also promotes devotion to Mary at the parish level.

Orlando Espín

See also ECCLESIOLOGY; LAITY; MARIOLOGY; MARY OF NAZARETH; PARISH; ROMAN CATHOLIC CHURCH.

LEIBNIZ, GOTTFRIED WILHELM (1646–1716)

German philosopher and mathematician, and co-inventor (with Isaac Newton) of the Calculus.

Leibniz's later philosophical position, as presented in the *Monadology* (1714), can be interpreted as a grand attempt to solve Descartes' mind–body problem. In place of Descartes' two substances, one material, the other immaterial, Leibniz postulated a single kind of immaterial substance he called a monad. Monads are defined as simple substances, meaning they have no parts. Since anything material has parts, it immediately follows that monads are immaterial. Also, since they have no parts, once created, monads cannot come a-part, so it follows that they are everlasting. All monads are endowed with both appetition and perception, and they can be graded in terms of their level of perception. Those with bare perception are the least sophisticated. These are followed by monads with perception and memory, and these in turn are followed by monads with apperception—conscious perception.

Since monads are independently existing things, it follows that no genuine causal interaction is possible between any two of them. (Causal interaction implies mutual dependence.) As a result, nothing ever leaves any monad or enters into any monad. In other words, monads are "windowless." Every monad is created with all of the perceptions it will ever have, and the flow of perception is driven forward by internal appetition.

Everything that exists is either a monad, a composite of monads, or an idea in a monad. Human souls are individual monads, bodies are composites of monads, and God is the supreme monad who continually creates finite monads through "fulgurations" from the divine substance.

In the process of creating finite monads, God attunes each one to every other monad in the universe. This attunement is called preestablished harmony, and it amounts to a kind of internal programming that regulates the perception of monads. For example, the monads constituting a physical object, such as a brown table, are all attuned to one another, and are all perceiving brown. Any sophisticated monad that perceives the table as a whole is attuned to the monads in the table, and it perceives the table as brown because the monads constituting the table are perceiving brown.

The principle of fitness, or principle of the best, requires that God, in creating the world, selects the best of all possible worlds for actual existence. However, none of these possible worlds is completely without evil. This is because a world without any evil at all would be absolutely perfect and would therefore be indistinguishable from God. By the principle of the identity of indiscernables, such a world would be identical with God. Thus, in creating a world that is genuinely distinct from himself, God necessarily creates a world containing evil.

Leibniz claimed to have solved the mind–body problem through an appeal to preestablished harmony. As an illustration of this solution, suppose that a certain high-grade monad constituting the soul of a human being is perceiving a tree off in the distance. The eye monads of the perceiver are attuned to the tree monads, the optic nerve monads are attuned to the eye monads, the brain monads are attuned to the optic nerve monads, and the single monad constituting the soul is attuned to the brain monads. Thus, the activity of perception involves the appearance of causal transmission without there being any genuine transmission. In the same way, two clocks sitting next to each another can read the same time without there being any causal transmission between them.

Since all monads are immortal, it follows that the souls of human beings are immortal. The possibility of a heavenly reward for a soul monad hinges on whether God has programmed that monad to enjoy high-grade perceptions following its separation from the body at death. As a result, it appears that Leibniz's theory involves some form of predestination. In fact, most commentators interpret preestablished harmony as entailing the most rigid determinism that excludes any shred of human freedom. However, in response to this interpretation, Leibniz might argue that God, in God's omniscience, anticipated the outcome of every free human choice and then programmed every high-grade monad (soul) to make that choice.

Preestablished harmony is the divine glue that holds Leibniz's later metaphysical system together, and at first glance it may appear to be an outlandish hypothesis. However, it is quite consistent with the philosophical tradition of the Middle Ages in that it amounts to little more than an elaboration of the doctrine of divine providence as developed by Thomas Aquinas and other theologians.

Leibniz's more important writings include *Discourse on Metaphysics* (1686), *Theodicy* (1710), *The Monadology* (1714), and *Leibniz-Clarke Correspondence* (1717).

Patrick J. Hurley

LEKHAH DODI

See KABBALAT SHABBAT.

LENT

Lent is the forty-day period of prayer and penitential preparation for the Christian celebration of Easter (in March or April). The word comes from an Anglo-Saxon root referring to spring (literally, the lengthening of the days in the late winter and early spring). Since the date of Easter depends on the date of the first full moon of spring (that is, after the spring equinox on March 21), the beginning of Lent is also variable (mid-late February or early March).

In early Roman Christianity, Lent began as a brief period of fasting during the week immediately before the celebration of Easter; gradually, the period of preparation was extended to three weeks; then, by the mid-fourth century, to the six-week length still observed by some churches today. The extension of Lent was also intertwined with other influences: the final preparation period for those advanced catechumens readying themselves for baptism, and the later parallel development of a penitential period of preparation for those in the order of penitents, in advance of their formal reconciliation with the church before Easter (on Holy Thursday).

The number of fast days in Lent was eventually set at forty, an echo of the Gospel references to the forty days Jesus spent fasting in the desert (for example, Matt 4:1-2); hence the Latin name for the season, *Quadragesima*. However, since fasting was prohibited on Sunday (the weekly Christian feast day), in the sixth century the start of Lent was pushed back to the Wednesday before the first Sunday of Lent, to fill out the exact number of forty weekdays of fasting. By the eleventh century, this day became known as Ash Wednesday, from the custom of receiving ashes on the forehead during the liturgy of the day as a sign of penitence and sorrow for sin.

The day before Ash Wednesday was therefore the last "ordinary" day before the general period of fast and abstinence; in many areas, it became customary to feast on that day, as a final celebration before Easter. The contemporary *Mardi Gras* (or "Fat Tuesday") celebrations in many areas of the world stem from this practice. The strictness of the seasonal fast also varied according to century: for the early church, fasting usually meant taking only one meal, usually in the evening; however, in the early medieval period, abstaining from eating certain foods also became an element (such as wine, meat, dairy products). Pancakes were often served on this day to use up the eggs, butter, and milk that would not be served again until Easter.

The penitential nature of Lent is expressed in a number of different ways. The custom in some Christian traditions of "giving up something for Lent," usually something pleasurable like a specific kind of food (for example, chocolate) or drink (for instance, alcohol) or a recreational activity (for example, television), traces back to the fasting and abstinence of antiquity and the medieval period. Fridays in Lent continue to be days of communal abstinence from meat in some Christian churches (Roman Catholic, for example).

In some traditions, the liturgical color assigned to Lent is violet or purple, a color that expresses the subdued, penitential nature of the season; for example, some of the vestments of the presider (or other ministers) at liturgy will be made from fabric of this color (for example, the stole). In Roman Catholic churches before Vatican II, the statues and crucifix in the building would also have been draped in violet cloth during Lent. In the Roman Catholic tradition, the liturgical mood is lightened midway during Lent in anticipation of the feast and rejoicing to come:

this fourth Sunday of Lent, called *Laetare* Sunday (from the Latin word meaning "to rejoice"), carries this theme through in the readings and prayer texts, and expresses it through the use of the liturgical color of rose (a kind of purple-pink).

Joanne M. Pierce

See also ASH WEDNESDAY; BAPTISM/ CONFIRMATION; EASTER; FASTS/FASTING (IN CHRISTIANITY); FEAST; LITURGICAL YEAR; RECONCILIATION, SACRAMENT OF; VESTMENTS, LITURGICAL.

LEO, TOME OF

The Tome of Leo is a small treatise or book (*Tomus* in Latin) that Pope Leo I wrote in 449. In the Ballerini edition of Leo's works the Tome is Letter XXVIII and entitled *Ad Flavianum* (To Flavian) because Pope Leo wrote the work to send it to Flavian the patriarch of Constantinople to refute the christological position of Eutyches known as Monophysitism. It is the most famous of Pope Leo's many writings and a classical expression of the Latin church's christology. Dioscorus, bishop of Alexandria, prohibited the public reading of the Tome to the Synod of Ephesus in 449. Pope Leo subsequently sent the Tome to church leaders throughout the empire. In 451 at the Council of Chalcedon it was publicly read and its teaching acclaimed as the traditional faith of the church. Leo's Tome insists that the dual birth of Christ from both God and Mary shows that there are two natures in Christ, each with its respective properties and activities, although they are united in one single subject (Person) to whom they are attributed.

Herbert J. Ryan, S.J.

See also CHALCEDON, COUNCIL OF; CHALCEDONIAN DEFINITION; CHRISTOLOGY; EUTYCHES; HYPOSTATIC UNION;

LEO I THE GREAT, POPE; MONOPHYSIT-
ISM; MOTHER OF GOD/THEOTOKOS.

LEO I THE GREAT, POPE (?–461)

Leo was a deacon of the church of Rome
before he became Pope in 440. As Pope,
Leo forcefully advanced and defended the
prestige of the Roman church, rejecting
the claim of the Council of Chalcedon in
451 that the church of Constantinople was
equal in dignity to the church of Rome.
Leo's contribution to the christological
controversies of the fifth century, called
Leo's *Tome*, was accepted as one touchstone of faith by the same council. Leo met
with the advancing army of Attila the Hun
and managed to convince Attila to withdraw beyond the Danube rather than attack Rome. When the sack of Rome under
the Vandals was unavoidable, Leo negotiated concessions to protect as many people
as he could. Numerous letters and nearly
one hundred of Leo's sermons survive.

Gary Macy

See also CHALCEDON, COUNCIL OF;
CONSTANTINOPLE, SEE OF; LEO, TOME
OF; PAPACY/PAPAL; POPE.

LEO XIII, POPE (1810–1903)

Born Gioacchino Pecci, his entire life after
ordination (1810) was devoted to church
service. After his election as pope (1879),
he resolved some of the church–state conflicts that marked the papacy of Pius IX,
negotiating an end to the German *Kulturkampf*. His most famous encyclical, *Rerum
Novarum*, that supported workers' rights
and trade unions, established the tradition of the Catholic concern about social
justice. Leo was wary of the recently
secularized states and culture of late
nineteenth-century Europe and proposed
the development of Catholic scholarship
as a means of defending faith in this new
situation. Encyclicals and letters addressing this task are *Aeterni Patris* (1879) that
mandated the use of Thomist philosophy
in seminary and universities; *Providentissimus Deus* (1893), a cautious acknowledgment of historical methods of biblical
exegesis; and *Testamentum Benevolentiae*
(1899), the censure of the so-called heresy
of Americanism. Leo also founded the
Pontifical Biblical Commission (1902) and
initiated some cautious steps toward
church reunion, ordering the exploration
of the issue of Anglican Orders (1895).

Patricia Plovanich

LEVINAS, EMMANUEL (1905–95)

Lithuanian-born Jewish philosopher. He
was educated in France and taught there
most of his life. A survivor of Nazi anti-
Semitic persecution, Levinas has been very
important for Latin American liberation
theologians and philosophers, especially
the Brazilians. Coming from the existentialist school of thought, he was influenced
by Husserl, by Heidegger, and especially
by Buber. Levinas has reflected philosophically on the encounter and fundamental
relationship between humans. Among his
best books are *Totalité et infini* (1961) and
L'humanisme de l'autre homme (1972).

Orlando Espín

See also BUBER, MARTIN; EXISTENTIAL-
ISM; HEIDEGGER, MARTIN; HUSSERL,
EDMUND; LATIN AMERICAN THEOLO-
GIES; LATINO THEOLOGY (-IES); LIBERA-
TION THEOLOGIES; PERSONALISM;
RICOEUR, PAUL; THEOLOGICAL ANTHRO-
POLOGY.

LEVITE

In Judaism, a descendant of the tribe of
Levite (Hebrew, *Levi*; plural, *Leviʾim*), consecrated to serve God and excluded from
receiving a portion of land in the Prom-

ised Land (Exod 32:26-29; Deut 10:8-9; Josh 13:14). Later, the other tribes assigned the Levites forty-eight cities out of their own tribal portions (Josh 21). In the wilderness Tabernacle and First and Second Temples in Jerusalem, the Levites served various cultic functions under the priests (Num 3:6). The rabbinic literature remembers them in particular as Temple singers and musicians. Later Judaism recalls their special cultic function by calling a Levi second, after a Kohen, to recite the benediction that accompanies the public reading of the Torah in worship services. In recognition of their previous role in the Temple, they also wash the hands of the Kohanim prior to the recitation of the priestly blessing.

Alan J. Avery-Peck

LÉVI-STRAUSS, CLAUDE (1908–)

Belgian-born French anthropologist who studied in Paris, and was university professor in Brazil, returning to France only after World War II. He is one of the key figures in "Structuralism." He studied the relationship between culture, nature, and language, and was concerned with methodology. His importance for theology lies also in his work on myths, which he understands as means used by human communities to solve problems of existence and societal living. Among his best books are *The Elementary Structures of Kinship* (1969) and his four-volume *Introduction to the Science of Mythology* (1964–72).

Orlando Espín

See also AFRICAN TRADITIONAL RELIGIONS; CULTURE; METHOD IN THEOLOGY; MYTH; SOCIETY.

LÉVY-BRUHL, LUCIEN (1857–1939)

French philosopher. A professor at the Sorbonne in Paris, his work was focused mostly on primitive societies. He developed a theory to explain that "natives" think prerationally and can therefore accept contradictions that would be unthinkable in European societies. Because of the potentially racist implications and misuse of his theories, and because of mounting factual evidence to the contrary, Lévy-Bruhl revised much of his thought later in his life. His more important books are *How Natives Think* (1910), and *Primitive Mentality* (1922).

Orlando Espín

See also CULTURE; EPISTEMOLOGY; RACISM.

LEX ORANDI, LEX CREDENDI

Literally, "Law of praying, law of believing." This is a shortened form of Prosper of Aquitaine's (about 390–463) dictum, *Lex orandi statuat legem credendi*, ("The law of praying establishes the law of believing"). Prosper used this idea to answer a theological question troubling the church: Does God initiate the process of saving a person, or must the person begin the process by moving toward God first? Prosper noted that in the liturgy, Christians pray for people who have had no experience of God, even those who have no interest in seeking God. He reasoned that by asking God to touch such persons, the church was indicating that God has to make the first move. The way we pray (*lex orandi*) indicates what we believe (*lex credendi*). In other words, Prosper believed that theologians can learn a great deal about God and the church by studying how the church prays. Modern liturgical theologians, following Prosper's lead, attempt to understand the church's faith by studying what it says and does in worship. Some theologians, however, while accepting the accuracy of Prosper's dictum, argue that patterns of Christian worship can sometimes go off track. In such cases, they suggest, the law of praying must be altered to bring it back in line with the law of believing.

Patrick L. Malloy

See also PROSPER OF AQUITAINE.

LI

(Chinese, propriety, ritual, ideal standard of conduct). One of the primary ethical principles of Confucius. While it is a word that has a variety of definitions, for example, rites, ritual, social ceremony, and the like, it seems to imply that there is an ideal standard of social and religious conduct that leads to order and harmony in society. According to Confucius in the *Li-Ching* (Book of Ritual), it is the regulating principle of human behavior embodying the laws of heaven. While the practice of *li* appears to be a rather formalistic governing of human lives, from a Confucian perspective there is an implied naturalism in li. First, the original meaning of this term was "the pattern in jade" or "grain in wood," suggesting the natural way for things to go. Second, correct ritual or social form had to be combined with sincerity and humaneness (*jen*) to be effective. Confucius believed that the practice of li was essential in bringing about a harmonious, courteous, and just society.

G. D. DeAngelis

See also CHU HSI; CHUNG YUNG; CHUN-TZU; CONFUCIANISM; CONFUCIUS; HSUN-TZU; JEN; MENCIUS; NEO-CONFUCIANISM; TE; WANG YANG-MING.

LIBÂNIO, JOÃO BATISTA (1932–)

Brazilian Catholic theologian, and member of the Society of Jesus (Jesuits). Educated in Brazil and Europe, Libânio has taught in Rio de Janeiro and is currently at the Jesuits' school of theology in Belo Horizonte. A prolific and influential theological writer, Libânio has also gained a solid reputation as teacher. Well in the mainstream of liberation theology, he has studied the meaning and formation of conscience in society, and lately has focused on eschatology and its social implications. Among his many works, some of his more influential books have been *A formação da consciência crítica* (1979), *Discernimento e política* (1977), *A volta à grande disciplina* (1983) and, with Maria Clara Bingemer, *Escatologia cristã* (1985).

Orlando Espín

See also CONSCIENCE; CULTURE; DISCERNMENT; ESCHATOLOGY (IN CHRISTIANITY); LATIN AMERICAN CATHOLICISM; LATIN AMERICAN THEOLOGIES; LIBERATION THEOLOGIES; PRIVATIZATION OF RELIGION; SOCIETY; SOCIETY OF JESUS.

LIBERAL CATHOLIC CHURCH
See OLD CATHOLICS.

LIBERAL THEOLOGY

The term refers to the dominant theological movement of the nineteenth and early twentieth centuries that included, for example, Friedrich Schleiermacher, Alois Biedermann, Albrecht Ritsch, Walter Rauschenbusch, Adolph von Harnack, Ernst Troeltsch (Protestants); and Maurice Blondel, Alfred Loisy, Auguste Sabatier, Ernst Renan, and George Tyrrell (Roman Catholics). Roman Catholic liberal theology is often referred to as "Modernism."

At the heart of liberal theology was the project of establishing a synthesis between Christian faith and modernity, that is, the epistemological revolution of the "turn to the subject" of the Enlightenment period, the cognitive challenges of the emerging natural and historical sciences, and the social and political exigencies attending the rise of modern nation-states and the industrial revolution. In general, liberal theology sought to secure the foundation and intelligibility of Christian faith by elaborating a theological anthropology utilizing the philosophical resources of Kant, Hegel, or Schleiermacher. Further, it confronted the exigencies of modern historical knowledge by elaborating the tools of biblical criticism and subjecting affirmations of the dogmatic tradition to historical scrutiny.

Liberal theology's abiding achievement lay both in its readiness to reflect on the condition of the possibility of Christian faith and to revise the Christian tradition in the light of modern—especially historical—knowledge and its worldview. Its weakness lay in its optimism about enlightenment in modernity, its intellectualistic focus on the individual, and its naiveté about the perfectibility of human beings and society. These weaknesses were made manifest, following the First World War, by the neoorthodox critiques of liberal theology.

J. A. Colombo

See also BLONDEL, MAURICE; HARNACK, ADOLF VON; LOISY, ALFRED; MODERNISM; RAUSCHENBUSCH, WALTER; RITSCHL, ALBRECHT; SCHLEIERMACHER, FRIEDRICH; TROELTSCH, ERNST; TYRRELL, GEORGE.

LIBERATION THEOLOGIES
The term "liberation theologies" refers to the multiple efforts to reformulate the Christian message in relation to the various struggles against oppression, and for full human liberation underway in the last third of the twentieth century. Examples include Latin American liberation theology, African American or Black theology, feminist theology, womanist theology, U.S. Hispanic theology, *mujerista* theology, gay and lesbian liberation theology, and many Third World theologies. (Theologies of liberation have also been developed in religious traditions beyond Christianity, for example, by Jews and Muslims.) All theologies, liberation or otherwise, are contextual in the sense that a theology (that is, a particular understanding of God) can only arise within and in response to a concrete socioeconomic, political, and cultural context. Nevertheless, liberation theologians have been more aware of this than some others and have consciously attempted to keep their theological reflection rooted in particular social contexts. This means that these theologies for the most part share a common methodology: they attempt to correlate human reality (often understood with the help of the social sciences) and faith, allowing each to challenge and enrich the other. (Some have described this method as "doing theology with the Bible in one hand and the newspaper in the other.") But in analyzing their social contexts and rethinking their faith traditions, liberation theologians typically make an "option for the poor," which means that they view both social reality and the claims of faith from the vantage point of the marginalized. Such an approach has led liberation theologians to call into question important elements of their respective theological traditions (for example, the exclusively eschatological nature of salvation, the neutrality of God in the face of oppression, or the saving power of the Cross of Jesus) which, in turn, has caused

defenders of the traditions to censure liberation theologies as unorthodox. At the same time, liberation theologies have been deepened by self-criticism, by mutual critique, and by cross-fertilization. From their first appearance in the 1960s, then, liberation theologies have aroused opposition, especially in those who fear the loss of power and privileges based on class, gender, race, ethnicity, or sexual orientation. For many others, however, liberation theologies have renewed their hope, strengthened their faith, and prompted them to love God and neighbor *in* the struggle for social justice.

James B. Nickoloff

See also ARIANISM; ATHANASIUS, PATRIARCH OF ALEXANDRIA; HILARY; NICAEA, FIRST COUNCIL OF; NICAEA, SECOND COUNCIL OF; POPE.

LI-CHING

(Chinese, *Li-jing*, Book of Rites). Confucian text describing and commenting on ritual as well as other aspects of religious and social behavior. Considered one of China's Five Classics, it is actually composed of three separate texts with the Li Chi becoming the most prominent. It was compiled during the first century B.C.E. but reflected the religious beliefs and ritual observances of the Zhou Dynasty (1050–256 B.C.E.). Its combination of Confucian, Taoist, and Legalist influences reflect the syncretism of the Han Dynasty (206 B.C.E.–220 C.E.).

G. D. DeAngelis

See also AFRICAN AMERICAN THEOLOGY; AFRICAN THEOLOGIES; BLACK THEOLOGY; CONTEXTUALIZATION; FEMINIST THEOLOGIES; GAY THEOLOGY; LATIN AMERICAN THEOLOGIES; MUJERISTA THEOLOGY; THIRD WORLD THEOLOGIES; WOMANIST THEOLOGY.

See also CHUN-TZU; CONFUCIANISM; DAOISM; JEN; LEGALISM (CHINESE); LI; TE.

LIBERIUS OF ROME

Pope from 352 to 366, Liberius is most famous for his role in the Arian controversy. A supporter of the Council of Nicaea, he refused to support the condemnation of Athanasius engineered by the Emperor Constantius in 353 and again in 355. In an attempt to force Liberius to accept his radical Arianism, Constantius had Liberius banished. Under pressure from the emperor, Liberius finally agreed to support the Arian cause and was allowed to return to Rome. Despite the forced nature of his agreement, Athanasius and Hilary considered Liberius to have abadoned his theological principles. After Constantius' death, Liberius once again asserted his support of the Council of Nicaea.

Gary Macy

LIFE

Life refers to those organisms that have protoplasm, a cellular enclosed system of functions and structures that make it possible to take in food, derive energy, grow, adapt to an environment, and reproduce. A living entity is distinguished from inert or inorganic matter that does not perform any of the above. Complex living organisms carry out the above functions with multicellular organs. To integrate various living functions, complex organisms need increasingly sophisticated centers of control and response. These centers of mental activity are the foundation for a sense of self and may account for the experience of being alive.

In human beings, organic functions are necessary for sustaining mental life (consciousness), and mental life is critical for the overall integration and preservation of organic life. Due to the cellular makeup of life, it is irreducibly individual. An entity experiences itself as alive in an individual sense.

Organic and mental life are subject to irreversible loss and injury. Human beings are aware of the fragility of life and thus tend to regard their own life and that of others as precious. The view that one did not initiate one's own life and that, once lost, it cannot be retrieved, has led many religious and philosophical systems to posit the notion that life is a gift over which human beings have been given the responsibility of stewardship, not dominion. Thus, individual life, particularly individual human life, is frequently regarded as sacred and of incomparable value. Individual human life is thus not to be intentionally harmed or terminated, even for apparently important reasons.

Contemporary ethical questions persist about whether embryonic or early fetal human life possesses sufficient individuality or self-awareness to warrant the same moral respect (and right to life) given to human persons. Bioethicists have generally reached consensus that when brain life has been irreversibly lost (compare definitions of "brain death"), an individual is no longer alive even if vital functions can be sustained artificially. Those who have irreversibly lost cerebral cortex function but not brainstem function can sustain organic function but not consciousness. In what sense are they alive? New ethical questions are being raised about the moral respect due to nonhuman life forms. This regards the problems associated with research using animals and the general decrease in the biodiversity of the planet due to human activity. Artificial creation of new life forms through recombinant DNA also poses new ethical dilemmas regarding life.

Michael J. Hartwig

LILA

A Sanskrit word meaning "play," "drama," or "sport," *lila* encapsulates an important theme of Hindu myth and theology. Evoking the motiveless play of the self-sufficient deity, lila is the primary metaphor for God's cosmic activity and the primary reason given for creation. Like a child who frolics with no particular aim other than the sheer joy of it, God plays the universe. In Sanskrit and Indian vernaculars, lila also refers to actual religious dramas, acted out on temporary stages during festivals, during which the gods themselves are held to be sacramentally present in the actors.

Lance E. Nelson

See also HINDUISM; KRISHNA.

LIMBO

Limbo is a theory or theologoumenon that describes the condition of persons who died sinless but unbaptized, whose lives continue in a natural state of happiness but not that of communion with God and of the beatific vision. The teaching is a theological construct that developed from the Augustinian and Pelagian debates about salvation. Against Augustine's insistence on an explicit decision for faith expressed in baptism as required for salvation, Pelagius advocated the survival of the innocent, such as infants who died before baptism, some intermediary condition, since they were incapable of a decision for or against God. Limbo was never defined as a dogma of the Catholic Church (though many did not know this). In 2007 the Vatican's International Theological Commission declared that a growing awareness of God's mercy leads the church to believe that there is a good reason to hope that infants who die without being baptized will go to heaven.

Patricia Plovanich

See also AUGUSTINE OF HIPPO; BEATIFIC VISION; PELAGIANISM.

LIMINAL/LIMINALITY

The use of this word in religion derives from Latin, meaning "boundary," and appeared initially in sociologist Arnold van Gennep (*Les rites de passage*, 1909), and then in the extensive studies of anthropologist Victor Turner in the field of rituals. Turner redefined it to refer to that special experience attained in the ritual process. More specifically, this experience appeared to him to include a feeling of being lifted outside ordinary space and time. The ritual does this by suspending ordinary space/time and allowing the participants to reach new dimensions of awareness, for example, in ecstasy achieved in prayer, and in sense of relatedness—a different way of relating to others and to God. Thus the word "liminal" refers to this specialized experience and the word "liminality" refers to the state itself.

Kathleen Dugan

See also ELIADE, MIRCEA; RITUAL.

LINDBECK, GEORGE A. (1923–)

An American scholar of historical theology who represented the Lutheran World Federation as an observer at the Second Vatican Council. Lindbeck also served on several national and international Lutheran-Roman Catholic Dialogues and was a signatory to their agreements.

Born in China in 1923, Lindbeck was educated at Gustavus Adolphus College (B.A., 1943) and Yale University (B.D., 1946; Ph.D., 1955). He served on the faculty of Yale University and Yale Divinity School as Pitkin Professor of Historical Theology until 1993. His most significant work to date, *The Nature of Doctrine. Religion in a Postliberal Age*, proposes what he calls a "cultural-linguistic" approach to creeds, doctrines, and dogmas. Lindbeck distinguishes (1) Christian beliefs that inform Christians and Christian culture from (2) the way beliefs are formulated in creeds, doctrines, and dogmas. He recognizes that creeds, doctrines, and dogmas are classical rules formulated in and for a particular time and culture. Lindbeck is convinced that many of the polarities, seemingly inherent in contradictory, church-dividing formulations, are more apparent than real, and will be diffused once their original cultural contexts are clarified and their insights reformulated in and for contemporary contexts. This study provided a comprehensible key to postmodern theological enterprises.

Regina A. Boisclair

LINGA

A Sanskrit term meaning both "mark" and "phallus," the *linga* is the most common icon representing Shiva in Hindu temples. Indeed, it is an aniconic icon, for—being in recent centuries little more than a pillar of stone resting in a circular receptacle—it has no anthropomorphic features. Modern Hindus see it as a representation of the formless, abstract energy of the Supreme Deity. The earliest known linga, however, are clearly representative of the male organ, and the circular base surrounding the image (called the *yoni*, Sanskrit for womb or vulva) clearly suggests the female. Scholars are therefore inclined to see in the combined image a symbol of the basic powers of creation. It is at once earthy and sublime, for in Shaiva theology, the universe is the interplay of Shiva and Shakti, the divine male and female principles, and the ultimate reality is the perfect union of the two (*shiva–shakti–samarasa*).

Lance E. Nelson

See also HINDUISM; NATARAJA; SHAIVA; SHAKTA; SHAKTI; SHIVA.

LINGAYAT
Also known as Virashaivas (the heroic Shiva worshipers), the Lingayats are a South Indian denomination of Shaivism. Founded by the twelfth-century saint Basava, the Lingayats practice a spirituality centered on ardent *bhakti* (devotion) to Shiva, as expressed in the well-known poems (*vacanas*) of their founder. They are recognized for their practice of wearing small stone linga, as a symbol of Shiva, on a string around their necks, and for their rejection of the Hindu caste system. In practice, however, they have become a caste unto themselves.

Lance E. Nelson

See also BHAKTI; BHAKTI-YOGA; HINDUISM; LINGA; SHAIVA; SHIVA.

LINGUISTIC ANALYSIS
A term denoting a broad trend in twentieth-century philosophy based on the axiom that language is the key to reality. Thus, philosophical problems are linguistic problems, and linguistic analysis focuses on the rules and uses of language. Positions cover a broad spectrum from the logical atomism of Bertrand Russell and the "early" Wittgenstein, that is, there is a one-to-one mirroring relation between language and what it signifies, to the exploration of the uses of language in "language games" in the later Wittgenstein and the hermeneutics of Paul Ricoeur. The term, however, is more commonly used to describe positions tending to the former rather than the latter. A subset of this trend has been especially important for Christian theology: the debate over the verification and falsification of religious or theological statements. Prominent contemporary figures in linguistic analysis are Noam Chomsky, John Austin, and John Searle.

J. A. Colombo

See also VERIFICATION/FALSIFICATION AND THEOLOGY; WITTGENSTEIN, LUDWIG.

LITANY
A prayer form in which each of the petitions or acclamations in a service is followed by an invariable response. Litanies are to be found in nearly every religious tradition. Judaism, for example, includes litanies among its psalms and other biblical songs (for example, Ps 136; Dan 3:52-56, 57-90). The Jewish use of litanies would have influenced Christians to adopt this prayer form. Other religions Christianity encountered as it spread beyond Israel may also have contributed to the popularity of litanies among Christians. By at least the fourth century, litanies with the invariable response "Lord, have mercy" (Greek, *Kyrie eleison*) were used widely in Christian liturgy. In today's eucharistic rite, the first and third forms of the penitential rite incorporate a litany that uses this response. The general intercessions are also a litany, alternating between lector and assembly. The *Lamb of God* is also increasingly being enacted as a litany, with a cantor singing a number of verses and the assembly responding with an invariable conclusion. This litany can

continue as long as necessary to accompany the breaking of the Bread and pouring of the Wine for Communion. The most well known of all the liturgical litanies is the Litany of the Saints sung at baptisms, ordinations, religious professions, blessings of abbots and abbesses, and the dedication of churches and altars.

Patrick L. Malloy

LITERALISM

An approach to biblical interpretation that affirms that the Bible is the actual, direct word of God. This view is based on the doctrine of inerrancy developed after the Reformation by a movement called Protestant Scholasticism. Inerrancy holds that the Bible was dictated by God to writers in such a way as to override their human characteristics and deficiencies.

F. M. Gillman

See also FUNDAMENTALISM (ATTITUDE); FUNDAMENTALISM (CHRISTIAN HISTORICAL MOVEMENT); INERRANCY.

LITERARY CRITICISM

In the first half of the twentieth century, the study of what could be known about the biblical authors and the sources that they used was called literary criticism. It replaced the term "higher criticism" after the development of form criticism carried the study of written sources to the earlier stages of oral formulations. In the 1950s it incorporated redaction criticism that examined the theological contributions of the authors who shaped the canonical texts. Some European scholars continue to use the term "literary criticism" as a collective designation for all the approaches associated with the historical-critical method: source, form, and redaction criticism.

In the late 1960s a number of English-speaking scholars realized that important dimensions of the text were lost when the Bible was studied only as a window to the events and stages of oral and written transmission that lie behind the received texts. These scholars began to appropriate the premises and approaches developed by the New Critics for studying literature in the 1940s. These biblical scholars began to recognize that a biblical text could be considered as a mirror to establish what the author communicates to a reader who encounters the text at any time. This new understanding of literary criticism takes two approaches and includes a variety of critical methods. Structuralism and narrative criticism are text-centered approaches, while rhetorical criticism and reader-response criticism are reader-centered. While all these literary methods share a number of presuppositions, each begins with different premises and asks different kinds of questions.

Regina A. Boisclair

See also DECONSTRUCTION; LÉVI-STRAUSS, CLAUDE; NARRATIVE CRITICISM.

LITURGICAL MOVEMENT

An ongoing movement begun in the mid-nineteenth century to restore liturgical worship to a central place in church life. Proponents of the movement seek to accomplish this renewal through a process of historical research, pastoral education, artistic excellence, and active participation. Prosper Guérenger (1805–75), the founder of the Benedictine monastery of Solesmes, France, is generally recognized as the father of the movement. The European liturgical movement focused on renewing liturgy within monasteries so as to provide models for the rest of the church. The ideals of the liturgical movement were brought to the United States by Virgil Michel, a priest and monk of St. John's Abbey, Collegeville, Minnesota. Michel, joined by many other American reformers, quickly moved the liturgical movement out of the monasteries and into the parishes. Michel founded Liturgical Press (today one of the world's foremost publishers of theological and liturgical material) and inaugurated the journal *Worship*, an important source for scholarly research on the liturgy. Another American milestone was the creation of a program in liturgical studies at the University of Notre Dame under the direction of Michael Mathis, c.s.c. Notre Dame's summer school of liturgy brought Europe's foremost liturgical scholars to the United States as guest lecturers, and created a forum for an emerging body of American scholars. As the effects of the liturgical movement began to spread, annual "Liturgical Weeks" were held in various American cities. These weeks brought together interested Catholics from across the country. The movement is rooted in the conviction that by celebrating the liturgy in unity and harmony, Christians can learn how to live in harmony. As the founders of the movement would say, in the liturgy, the participants act as the unified Body of Christ and thereby learn to live as the Body of Christ. The aims of the liturgical movement were applauded by Pope Pius XII in his encyclical *Mediator Dei* (1947) and by Vatican II's Constitution on the Sacred Liturgy (1963). Today, the work of implementing the vision of the liturgical movement goes on in parishes and among pastoral and scholarly leaders. The liturgical movement is by no means a strictly Roman Catholic phenomenon. The Oxford and Cambridge Movements in the Church of England marked the beginning of a similar renewal in the Anglican Communion, and the rediscovery of classical Lutheranism among some Evangelical churches encouraged a heightened regard for liturgy among Protestants. Today, nearly every Christian tradition has been deeply affected by the vision of the liturgical movement.

Patrick L. Malloy

See also ANGLICAN COMMUNION; OXFORD MOVEMENT; PIUS X, POPE; PIUS XII, POPE; SOLESMES, ABBEY OF.

LITURGICAL YEAR

The Christian churches divide the year into several liturgical seasons punctuated by liturgical feasts. The *liturgical* aspect of these seasons is expressed through the texts, music, and structures of various public worship services (the *liturgy*); for example, the Eucharist (or Mass), or the Liturgy of the Hours (or Divine Office).

The first (and earliest) division of time begins with the week, centered around the celebration of the Eucharist (or Mass) on Sunday. Gradually, some Sunday celebrations began to take on more specific theological themes: the earliest was the celebration of Easter (generally on the first Sunday after the spring equinox), followed fifty days later by the feast of Pentecost. These major feasts came to be followed by weeks, or *seasons*, of celebration (for example, the fifty days after Easter, known as the Easter season), and were preceded by periods or seasons of preparation (for example, Lent for Easter; Advent for Christmas). In modern times, weeks (and Sundays) that do not fall in a specific season are (in some traditions) said to belong to *Ordinary Time*.

Other days of the week also came to be marked by liturgical celebrations. In antiquity, Wednesdays and Fridays became days of fast (abstaining from all food until sundown); the Roman Catholic Church still observes the practice of abstaining from meat on Fridays in Lent. Early Christians also marked certain times, or hours, of each day with brief periods of private (or domestic) prayer. After Constantine, these private "hours" came to be observed publicly in churches; the services (like the Eucharist) were presided over by the clergy. Chief among these were Morning and Evening Prayer. Due to the influence of communal (or cenobitic) monasticism on the secular (or non-monastic) clergy, other "hours" of prayer were added; by the sixth century, this *Divine Office* was observed in the West by monks and increasingly in cathedral churches by secular clergy.

The celebration of the Eucharist (or Mass) on days of the week other than Sunday also became the custom in the early centuries; by the early eighth century, every day of the week in every liturgical season had specific eucharistic texts and readings assigned to it (a *Mass formulary*).

The structure of the liturgical year continued to evolve over the course of time. The two main elements of the liturgical year were the *temporal* cycle (larger seasons and major feasts of the Lord, such as Christmas and Easter), and the *sanctoral* cycle (individual feasts, largely those of Mary and the saints). In addition, parts of the temporal (or seasonal) cycle are tied to the lunar calendar, and so are not observed on the same dates each year. Easter is generally celebrated on the first Sunday after the first full moon of spring, the exact date of which changes from year to year; therefore, all feasts and seasons that depend on the date of Easter are also variable (such as Ash Wednesday, Ascension Thursday, Pentecost Sunday). However, other feasts are assigned a specific calendar date: Christmas, for example, is always observed on December 25, regardless of the day of the week on which that date may fall.

In general, then, feast days were appointed for a number of persons, events, or themes: certain events in the life of Jesus Christ (feasts of the Lord, such as Ascension Thursday, or the Transfiguration) or the Blessed Virgin Mary (Marian feasts; for example, the Annunciation on March 25, the Assumption on August 15, and the Immaculate Conception on December 8); to commemorate various saints (like St. Patrick on March 17, or St. Nicholas on December 6) or events (for example, the Triumph of the Cross on September 14); or, finally, to celebrate certain more abstract theological concepts (such as Trinity Sunday, the feast of Corpus Christi, and the feast of Christ the King). In some Christian churches, the calendar is still flexible. In the Roman Catholic tradition, for example, the structure of the liturgical calendar was revised after the Second Vatican Council, giving local (or national) churches more freedom to add liturgical celebrations relevant to their own communities. In the United States, special Masses can be used on Thanksgiving Day or Independence Day. And, as new saints are canonized, their feast days are also added to the calendar, like that of the American St. Elizabeth Ann Seton (canonized in 1975, feast day January 4).

Various feasts or seasons in the liturgical year are commemorated in the liturgy through the biblical texts (readings), prayer texts, music, and sometimes special liturgical actions or rites (like the rite of sprinkling the congregation with holy water, or *Asperges*, during the Easter season, as a reminder of baptism). Liturgical colors (in some Western Christian traditions) are also assigned to certain seasons, or feasts: green for Ordinary Time; violet (purple) for Lent and Advent (or other celebrations with a penitential theme; rose, or dark pink, is occasionally used during these seasons as an anticipation of the feast to come); white (sometimes gold) for festive celebrations or rejoicing, like Easter or Christmas; and red, for martyrs, or feasts of the Holy Spirit (for example, Pentecost). Some traditions also use blue for Advent or for Marian feasts.

Joanne M. Pierce

See also ADVENT; ASH WEDNESDAY; CHRISTMAS; CHRIST THE KING; EASTER; EUCHARIST; FASTS/FASTING (IN CHRISTIANITY); FEAST; LENT; LITURGY (IN CHRISTIANITY); MASS; VESTMENTS, LITURGICAL.

LITURGY (IN CHRISTIANITY)

The word liturgy is derived from the Greek, *leitourgia*, meaning public service or public work. In Hellenistic usage it could refer to such communal/public enterprises as taxation, education, waging war, road-building, public sacrifices/worship in pagan Hellenism (not because they were acts of worship, but because they were public and official, offered by priests on the payroll of the state). The term even extended to legalized prostitution. The word is found in the Septuagint (the Greek translation of the Old Testament) where it is used for the public worship of Israel inasmuch as it is an act of the corporate reality of the whole people or done on behalf of others, or for something done on behalf of the state. From there it was incorporated into the New Testament where it is used with a variety of meanings and takes various forms: six times as a noun: Zachary's offering of public sacrifice in the Temple (Luke 1:23); a collection for the poor (2 Cor 9:12); sacrificial service for others and services ren-

dered to Paul as a public missionary (Phil 2:17, 30); the heavenly worship/ministry of Jesus (Heb 8:6); Mosaic worship (Heb 9:21); three times as a verb: to do communal prayer in preparation for missionary ministry (Acts 13:2); to take up a collection for the poor (Rom. 15:27); to offer the sacrifices of the Mosaic Law (Heb 10:11). The term *leitourgos* is also found, meaning variously public minister, public servant, cultic priest (Rom 13:6; 15:16; Phil 2:25; Heb 1:7; 8:2).

While early Christian writers applied the term to worship, it is more commonly used to denote the public work of the Christian community such as catechesis, missionary efforts, and care for the poor. In the East the term gradually is restricted to the celebration of the Eucharist, for example, the Liturgy of St. James, and the Liturgy of St. John Chrysostom. In the West, with the rise of Latin for ecclesiastical use in the fourth century, other Latin terms are preferred: *officium sanctum, officium divinum, ministerium, servitus*. In the sixteenth century the Greek word is rediscovered in the West, Latinized, and used in various studies of Christian worship.

In 1947, Pope Pius XII, in *Mediator Dei*, an encyclical known as the magna charta of the liturgical movement, defined liturgy as "the integral public worship of the Mystical Body of Jesus Christ, head and members" (MD 20). The Second Vatican Council subsumed that definition but also broadened it considerably, in a sense returning to the earlier Christian understanding of liturgy as the public work of the church, with *sacred* liturgy denoting the public worship of the church. The Constitution on the Sacred Liturgy (*Sacrosanctum Concilium*, Dec. 4, 1963) does not precisely define liturgy, but rather describes it in broad terms: the carrying out of the work of redemption, especially in the paschal mystery (SC 2, 6); the exercise of the priestly office of Christ (SC 7); a sacred action beyond all others because it is the action of Christ the priest and of his Body the Church (SC 7); a foretaste of the heavenly liturgy (SC 8); "the summit toward which the activity of the Church is directed" and "the fount from which all her power flows" (SC 10). From such an approach to liturgy it follows that "full, active, conscious participation" is "demanded by the very nature of the liturgy" and to which the Christian people "have a right and obligation by reason of their baptism," for the liturgy is not the only, but the "primary and indispensable source" of the true Christian spirit (SC 14). Liturgy is to be distinguished from private prayer and popular devotions that nevertheless are to be imbued with the spirit of the liturgy (SC 12, 13); see also the *Directory on Popular Piety and the Liturgy: Principles and Guidelines* (Congregation for Divine Worship and Discipline of the Sacraments, 2001).

Liturgy is composed of the public, communal ritual activities the church recognizes as embodying its purpose of human sanctification and the glorification of God, presented "under the guise of signs perceptible by the senses" (SC 7). The council undertook a reform of the liturgy so that these signs (texts and rites) would "express more clearly the holy things which they signify," for the "Christian people, as far as possible, should be able to understand them with ease and take part in them fully, actively, and as a community" (SC 21). Two documents of the Bishops' Committee on the Liturgy, *Environment and Art in Catholic Worship* (1978) and *Music in Catholic Worship* (1972; revised 1983), emphasize that the proper celebration of the liturgical rites demands quality and authenticity in its use of texts, music, gesture, vesture, environment, and various ritual objects.

Liturgy extends to the seven sacraments: Christian initiation—baptism, confirmation, Eucharist; sacraments of healing—reconciliation, anointing of the sick; sacraments of vocation—marriage and holy orders. Liturgy also includes the feasts and seasons of the church's year, the rites of installation of liturgical ministers, rites for the dying (Viaticum and commendation of the dying), rites of Christian burial, rites for the dedication of a church, for religious profession and for the consecration of virgins, various blessings, and the liturgy of the hours.

Dennis W. Krouse

See also CALENDAR (LITURGICAL); LITURGY OF THE EUCHARIST; LITURGY OF THE HOURS; LITURGY OF THE WORD; SACRAMENT; SACRAMENTALS; SACROSANCTUM CONCILIUM.

LITURGY (IN JUDAISM)

Judaism requires the recitation of a fixed liturgy at three set times each day, *shacharit* (morning worship), *minchah* (afternoon worship), and *maariv* (evening worship), with the latter two services normally recited consecutively, for convenience. On Sabbaths and holidays, morning worship is followed by *musaf* (additional worship) that takes the place of the additional sacrifice once offered on Sabbaths and festivals in the Jerusalem Temple. While Judaism obligates individuals to recite the statutory liturgy wherever they may find themselves, worship primarily occurs in the synagogue, within a community of Jews. The holiest prayers of Judaism may be recited only in the presence of a quorum of ten adults (in Orthodox Judaism, males only), called a minyan; the reading of Scripture—the central focus of Sabbath and festival worship as well as of morning prayers on Monday and Thursday—also may be carried out only in such a community.

Hebrew, the traditional language of Jewish prayer, is maintained in Orthodox and Conservative Judaism; Reform Jews, by contrast, use the vernacular for much of the liturgy. While the musical tradition of Judaism once consisted primarily of the chanting of liturgical texts by a cantor, Reform Judaism in particular has created a modern form of worship through the addition of choirs, organs, and other musical instruments. The Reform and Conservative movements also have published contemporary revisions of the Jewish prayer book, intended to make both the language and content of prayer more accessible to the modern Jew. In keeping with this interest, many Reform synagogues have abandoned traditional prayer garb—yarmulka, tallit and tephilim—seen as unnecessary vestiges of an earlier period of Jewish ritual practice.

Since the Jewish liturgy may be recited anywhere, the synagogue is special primarily in that it is outfitted for worship and that the Torah scrolls are kept there. Alongside the synagogue, however, the home, and, in particular, the table, where family meals are shared, is a locus for prayer, especially the blessings that precede meals, the grace that follows, and the Kiddush liturgy that introduces Sabbaths and festivals. Other liturgies that occur in the home are the Havdalah ceremony that concludes Sabbaths and festivals and a number of special festival liturgies, such as the Passover Seder.

Alan J. Avery-Peck

See also ALIYAH; BAR/BAT MITZVAH; BLESSING (JUDAISM); CANTOR (IN JUDAISM); HAFTARAH; HAVDALAH; KIDDUSH; MAARIV; MACHZOR; MINCHAH; MINYAN; MUSAF; SEDER; SHACHARIT; SHEMONAH ESREH; SIDDUR; SYNAGOGUE; TALLIT; TEPHILIM; YARMULKA.

LITURGY OF THE EUCHARIST

The Liturgy of the Eucharist is one of the four major units—along with introductory rites, the Liturgy of the Word, and concluding rites—that together make up the Mass. The Liturgy of the Eucharist begins with the preparation of the gifts, includes the eucharistic prayer and Communion rite, and concludes with the prayer after Communion. The basic format of the Liturgy of the Eucharist follows Jesus' practice at the Last Supper. Since then, it has remained essentially consistent. Dom Gregory Dix, whose monumental work, *The Shape of the Liturgy*, has greatly influenced modern liturgical studies, discerned a fourfold pattern in the liturgy of the Eucharist: taking bread and wine, blessing God for them, breaking the bread, and sharing the bread and wine. In its earliest form, this fourfold action was part of a complete meal. At the Last Supper, following the usual Jewish meal custom, Jesus took bread, blessed it, broke it, and gave it to his companions to share. A meal ensued. At the end of it, Jesus repeated the four gestures, but now with the cup of wine (see Luke 22:19-20; 1 Cor 11:23-25). Before the end of the first century, this pattern appears to have been changing. The ceremonies of bread and wine now came together before the meal. Perhaps Christians were even performing the rites of bread and wine without a meal. Justin Martyr's description of how the Eucharist was celebrated in 150 makes no mention of a full meal, but the essential four-part process of taking, blessing/thanking God, breaking, and sharing, continued to structure the Eucharist.

During the ensuing centuries, a number of changes obscured this basic fourfold shape. Prayers of petition were gradually inserted into the prayer of blessing and thanksgiving, shifting the focus away from God's gifts to the community's needs. The sharing of bread and cup was deemphasized, as increasingly fewer members of the liturgical assembly received Communion. A sense that ordinary Christians were unworthy was largely to blame. By 1215, so few were receiving Communion that Lateran Council IV required every Christian to receive Communion at least once a year, during Lent or Easter. The acts of breaking and pouring that were a central reminder for early Christians of the death of Christ and the unity of the church were also downplayed, as tiny wafers replaced loaves of bread, and as laypeople stopped receiving the eucharistic Wine. Christians of the time were so fearful of spilling the Lord's sacramental Blood that the chalice was never moved from the altar. During this era, people discovered new ways to relate to the Eucharist. While the priests prayed the Liturgy of the Eucharist (by now entirely in Latin, a language most people did not understand), the people said prayers of their own. In some cases, these echoed the words of the priest, but usually did not. Another way believers compensated for not receiving the eucharistic food in their hands and mouths was to internalize it through their eyes. Hence, the elevation of the eucharistic bread and (eventually) the eucharistic cup so the people could see them became the climax of the Liturgy of the Eucharist.

Throughout history, movements arose to restore the emphasis of the early church on the fourfold shape of the eucharistic liturgy. The reformer John Hus (about 1369–1415), for example, insisted upon the return of the chalice to the laity. Such renewal movements reached their zenith in the Protestant Reformation. Nearly all of the major theologians and reforming pastors of the Reformation worked toward the restoration of the Liturgy of the Eucharist, and urged especially that the laity receive Communion every week under the forms of both bread and wine. Generally, the reformers met with very little success. Similar plans to encourage frequent Communion in the Roman Catholic Church also generally failed. All these attempts to restore the Liturgy of the Eucharist began to take hold only in the nineteenth century, thanks to the efforts of the liturgical movement. In the Catholic Church, the efforts of Pius X (1835–1914) to make the reception of Communion a regular part of Christian life were highly successful. At the Second Vatican Council, a number of ritual changes worked together to highlight the Liturgy of the Eucharist. For example, the procession with the gifts of bread and wine just before the eucharistic prayer emphasized anew the *taking* aspect of the eucharistic act. New eucharistic prayers focused on *thanksgiving and the blessing of God* and less on petition. The rubrics or directions for celebrating the Mass suggested that bread that looks and tastes like bread should replace tiny Communion wafers to allow for a fuller *breaking of the bread*. Finally, the people were encouraged to *share* in Communion as frequently as possible. Under many circumstances, they are allowed to partake of the forms of both bread and wine, once again restoring a fuller expression of the Liturgy of the Eucharist.

Patrick L. Malloy

See also BREAKING OF BREAD (IN CHRISTIANITY); HUS, JOHN; LAST SUPPER; OFFERTORY; ORDINARY, LITURGICAL.

LITURGY OF THE HOURS

The Liturgy of the Hours, also known as the Divine Office, is the pattern of non-sacramental liturgies celebrated (more often privately recited by many Christians) at specified intervals during the day. In the ante-Nicene church, regular, daily prayer at fixed times was enjoined on all Christians as a way of fulfilling Paul's admonition to "pray without ceasing" (1 Thess 5:17). This was fulfilled in various ways in various churches. Tertullian and Cyprian recommended prayer five times a day, around 9:00 A.M., noon, 3:00 P.M., evening, and again in the middle of the night, with other prayer at meal times. This was somewhat supported by Hippolytus' *Apostolic Tradition* (ca. 215), although he mentioned no Evening Prayer. The *Didache* called for prayer three times a day, morning, afternoon and evening; to this the Egyptian practice (Clement of Alexandria and Origen) added prayer in the night.

What was prayed is unclear, although the *Didache* and Tertullian speak of the Lord's Prayer. Available evidence indicates that praise and thanksgiving moving into intercession was the usual pattern, although the more devout added psalms (Tertullian); these, however, were more normative at meals, especially the agape, and during services of the word at community assemblies on Sundays during Eucharist, on Wednesdays and Fridays, and at times of catechetical instruction. There is no clear evidence of communal prayer on a daily basis in the sense of the later Office, other than that done at home with family and/or friends. Until recently, since the 1944 work of C. W. Dugmore

(*The Influence of the Synagogue on the Divine Office*), it was thought that the Christian Office was derived directly from what was presumed to be daily synagogue prayer, in terms of both time of prayer and content. It is now generally accepted that the Divine Office as such, that is, daily, formal communal prayer at fixed hours, emerged only in the fourth century with the legalization of Christianity.

Two forms of the Office, monastic and cathedral, and various combinations of the same, have served as the major influences in the exceedingly complicated development of the Office. The monastic forms, in actuality a formalized, communal continuation of the earlier domestic, devotional forms of daily prayer, were typified by a recitation of the whole Psalter in its biblical order, without regard for the fittingness of a given psalm for the actual occasion or time of prayer, distributed over a day, a week, or a month. This form of prayer was undertaken as an ascetic practice, a disciplinary tool to assist in personal meditative prayer, and ultimately became clericalized, even though the monastic movement was originally entirely lay. It was eventually divided into eight Offices, one during the night and the others throughout the day. The various forms of cathedral Office were all characterized as popular services of praise and intercession, by their use of symbols and ritual actions, such as lighting and blessing of evening light, incensations, and processions; by diversity of ministries, for example, bishop, deacon, cantors, and lectors; by their select use of psalms or parts of psalms appropriate for the hour or service; and by their use of various forms of chants, such as antiphons, responsories, and hymns. In nearly all rites of the church, the cathedral Office was superseded by the monastic, but especially in the West, where even traces of the cathedral Office all but disappeared.

Over the centuries, numerous reforms of the Office have been undertaken, none entirely successful, including that mandated by the Second Vatican Council (*Sacrosanctum Concilium* 83–101). While the council and the General Instruction of the Liturgy of the Hours made efforts toward simplification and inclusion of lay participation, especially at the principal hours of Morning and Evening Prayer, the Liturgy of the Hours remains largely a clerical asceticism, monastic in form and privatized in practice. In some places where unofficial, more cathedral-like forms of the Office have been adopted and adapted, they have proved to be popular.

Dennis W. Krouse

See also LITURGY (IN CHRISTIANITY); MONASTICISM IN WESTERN CHRISTIANITY; PRAYER.

LITURGY OF THE WORD

A service centered on the reading of Scripture. In modern liturgies, its general format is: opening song, greeting between the presider and the assembly, penitential rite, opening prayer, readings and psalmody, preaching, intercessions, and concluding rites. Nearly every sacramental or liturgical act of the church can or must begin with a Liturgy of the Word. The Eucharist begins with a Liturgy of the Word sometimes called the Mass of the Catechumens, since historically it was the only segment of the Eucharist to which catechumens (those preparing to be baptized) were admitted. Only after they were dismissed did the community begin the Liturgy of the Eucharist. The basic format of the Liturgy of the Word comes from Jewish synagogue worship. Christians of the first generations would have continued

to assemble with other Jews for these Word services. In addition, they probably conducted similar services of reading and preaching in conjunction with their weekly celebration of the Lord's Supper as early as the New Testament era.

Justin Martyr leaves us with an outline of what the liturgy of the Word was like in the middle of the second century. He writes that the Christians assembled on Sunday for readings from the prophets (in what we now call the Old Testament) and from the memoirs of the apostles (the forerunner of the Christian Scriptures). These readings, he says, continued as long as time permitted. A person whom Justin called the president—the one recognized as the community's leader—then preached. Prayers for all people followed, then the community exchanged the sign of peace and the Liturgy of the Eucharist began. The basic format of the Christian Liturgy of the Word was thus established at least eighteen hundred years ago.

As with all other aspects of liturgy, time brought increasing regulation and complexity. The Liturgy of the Word, however, changed far less than some other aspects of liturgy. The most noteworthy development was the evolution of various systems according to which the Bible was to be parceled out for reading. From early systems of *lectio continua*, that is, beginning each day's reading from exactly where the community left off when it had last assembled, more complex lectionary systems developed. In these systems, specific passages from the Bible were assigned to each day in the liturgical year. When it became the custom to celebrate the liturgy in Latin, even though the people no longer spoke or understood it, the readings gradually lost their importance in the religious life of most believers and the Liturgy of the Word was overshadowed by the Liturgy of the Eucharist. One of the aims of the sixteenth-century Protestant Reformation was to make the Bible, including the biblical readings in church, accessible to common people again. This meant translating them into languages the people understood. The Second Vatican Council not only accepted the use of vernacular translations of the Bible for Liturgies of the Word, it also constructed a new lectionary system so that more of the Bible would be proclaimed at the liturgy. In this system, key passages of Scripture are proclaimed on Sundays and feast days in a three-year cycle. On weekdays, other passages are spread over two years. Similar systems have been implemented by all the major Christian churches. Some Protestant churches, however, leave the selection of the week's scriptural passages to the pastor. From a Catholic point of view, this system is questionable, since it does not assure that the church will hear the entire Bible proclaimed.

The church understands the Liturgy of the Word to be a real encounter between the church and God. As the Bible is read and its meaning for contemporary life is explored in the homily, God speaks anew to the church. "God speaks to his people, revealing the mystery of their redemption and salvation and offering them spiritual nourishment. Through his word, Christ himself is present in the assembly of his people" (*General Instruction on the Roman Missal*, no. 33). The Liturgy of the Word, then, is not a liturgy in which the church only hears the words of God, but one in which it comes into contact with Jesus, the Word of God, who speaks anew.

Patrick L. Malloy

See also LECTIONARY; LITURGY OF THE EUCHARIST.

LLULL, RAMÓN (1233?–1315?)

Born into a wealthy family in Majorca, Ramón became a knight, married, and had two children. At thirty years of age, he recieved a vision calling him to a life of serving Christ through the conversion of Muslims. Under the advice of Raymond of Peñafort, he spent the next nine years studying Arabic and Christian thought. In 1276 he persuaded James II of Majorca to set up a Franciscan school for the study of oriental languages, a proposal that was taken up by the Council of Vienne (1311–2) which, in turn, established departments of oriental languages at five universities. Ramón's theology used Sufi and Islamic elements in his rather obscure method of combining theological terms. His methods were quite unlike the Scholastic theology of his day and had few followers. Ramón's mystical poetry, however, influenced such great figures as Teresa of Avila and John of the Cross.

Gary Macy

See also ISLAM; JOHN OF THE CROSS; MEDIEVAL CHRISTIANITY (IN THE WEST); MYSTICISM/MYSTIC (IN CHRISTIANITY); SCHOLASTICISM.

LOCAL CHURCH

Roman Catholic ecclesiology (that is, theology dealing with the mission and structure of the church) uses this term to designate the church as it exists in a particular place, rather than as a universal phenomenon or a more abstract concept. In the documents of the Second Vatican Council, the term is generally used for a *diocese* (the region presided over by a bishop), but it is also used to indicate the individual *parish* or other congregation. Vatican II understood the local churches as concrete manifestations of the overall, universal church (see, for example, the documents *Sacrosanctum Concilium* 41, or *Lumen Gentium* 23), rather than as "branch offices" of the church overshadowed by its central administration. In the decades following the council, several approaches to an "ecclesiology of communion" have been developed as a way of further discussing the nature of the vital relationship between the local churches and the universal church.

William A. Clark, s.j.

LOCKE, JOHN (1632–1704)

British philosopher. Together with David Hume, John Locke is regarded as one of the founders of British empiricism in philosophy. Sometimes regarded (debatably) as a deist, John Locke's writings on religion are characterized by a twin commitment to a recognition of the limitations of reason together with fidelity to accessible evidence and to individual rights and freedom. These hallmarks are clearly evident in his *Letter Concerning Toleration* (1689) that urged respect for liberty of conscience in matters religious, and the distinction between the "church" and the "commonwealth" concerned with the public good of all its subjects. Locke's *The Reasonableness of Christianity* (1695) sought to defend a middle position between deist rationalism and orthodox supernaturalism by arguing (sometimes obscurely) for the possibility of truths above reason through revelation, but not contrary to the canons of reason.

J. A. Colombo

See also HUME, DAVID.

LOCUS THEOLOGICUS

The term *theological locus* means literally seat or place, and indicates the sources theologians consult as authorities on theological topics, sources yielding perennial insight into faith. The idea of these authorities had developed by the Middle Ages, but the use as known today was delineated by the Spanish Dominican Melchior Cano, a baroque theologian in Salamanca, in his treatise *De loci theologicis* (1563). The work gives a precise and systematic description of the authorities, arranged in a hierarchical order according to their proximity to revelation. Scripture and tradition are primary loci. Five other loci are honored as privileged interpretations of these sources: the church's faith (as a whole), ecumenical councils, the pope, the fathers of the church, and the Scholastics. Cano proposed five other sources, termed alien or foreign, supplementary sources for the purposes of theological exposition: natural reason, philosophy, the work of jurists, history, and human tradition. Cano's schema influenced theological exposition for several centuries, but contemporary theology has reevaluated the hierarchical arrangement. In the modern appraisal of the inherent historicity of human knowledge, contemporary cultural and social works are held by many theologians to be a primary locus for theological reflection.

Patricia Plovanich

LOGOS (PATRISTIC TIMES)

Following St. John's Gospel, Ignatius of Antioch views the Logos (Greek for "word") as God's Son manifesting himself through Jesus Christ (*Magnesians* 8). The apologists of the second century use the notion of Logos as a means to make Christ and Christian teaching acceptable to those with some knowledge of the Greek philosophical tradition. For Justin

Martyr, the Logos is the very principle of the intelligibility of the created world. Christ as the incarnate Logos sums up all knowledge in himself, and thus whoever knows anything grasps in that knowledge some aspect of the Logos who is Christ. Justin is unclear whether the Logos is fully divine. Theophilus of Antioch's distinction between the Logos immanent in God before the creation and the Logos as the instrument of creation typifies the ambiguity of the fully divine status of the Logos in the writings of the apologists. Clement of Alexandria holds that the Logos has always been the teacher of humankind, and that Jesus is the Logos who is the proper guide of all humanity. Origen believed that the Logos was generated from the Father and thus begotten by God. The Logos was subordinate to the Father. Arius so stressed the subordination of the Logos to the Father that he denied the divinity of the Logos and maintained the Logos is a creature. At the Council of Nicaea in 325, Arius' position was condemned. The council taught that the Logos was God, a position strongly defended in the theological writings of St. Athanasius during the fourth century.

Herbert J. Ryan, s.j.

See also APOLOGISTS; ARIANISM; ATHANASIUS, PATRIARCH OF ALEXANDRIA; CLEMENT OF ALEXANDRIA; HOMOOUSIOS TO PATRI; IGNATIUS OF ANTIOCH; JUSTIN MARTYR; LOGOS/WORD; NICAEA, FIRST COUNCIL OF; ORIGEN; SUBORDINATIONISM; TRINITY/TRINITARIAN THEOLOGY/TRINITARIAN PROCESSIONS.

LOGOS SPERMATIKOS

Logos spermatikos (*logoi spermatikoi* in the plural) in Greek or *rationes seminalis* in Latin is difficult to translate into English but means something like "seminal reasons" or "seeds of the Mind" where Mind refers to the World Mind or Soul. The term was first used by the Stoic philosophers to explain how the Logos (God) was active in individual things. The *logoi spermatikoi* were "parts of God" that developed into the forms of individuals; to put it crudely, they were the part of God that is in everything. The idea was picked up by Plotinus to explain how the transcendent, unchanging God could possibly be connected to a changing universe. According to Plotinus, the *logoi spermatikoi* were reflections of the divine ideas contained in the World Soul. The World Soul, in turn, connects individual souls to God through contemplation.

Augustine found the term in Plotinus and used it to explain how God could have both created everything at once and yet different creatures appear at different times (plants before animals, for instance). Augustine reasoned that God created the potential for all things that Augustine called the *rationes seminales*, all at once. These "seeds of reason" or "seminal reasons" are invisible and intangible, more pure potency than anything we would think of as physical. They gradually unfold on their own, and over time become what they were meant to become. Since Augustine did not understand the days of Creation in any literal sense, this could be a long period of time. The *rationes seminales*, therefore, of animals were created long before any animals actually appeared. It is the Augustinian sense of *rationes seminales* that influenced later Western Christian thought. Bonaventure, for instance, accepted Augustine's idea, while Thomas Aquinas rejected it. The use of this term by Augustine did, however, make it much easier for Christians in this tradition to accept the idea that

Creation was gradual, and that therefore evolution was not a contradiction of Scripture.

Gary Macy

See also AQUINAS, THOMAS, ST.; AUGUSTINE OF HIPPO; BONAVENTURE; CREATIONISM; LOGOS/WORD; PLOTINUS; STOICISM.

LOGOS/WORD

From the Greek word *logos*, meaning "word," this is a title given to Christ in the Gospel according to John (1:1-14) and in the First Letter of John (1:1). According to these Johannine texts, the Logos is pre-existent, is with God, and is God. Everything was created through the Logos, who became human flesh in history. The Johannine notion of Logos has a parallel in the Hebrew notion of Wisdom, but the two are not identical. During the first few centuries of Christianity, there was a significant development of a theology of the Logos, with important consequences for christology and trinitarian doctrines.

In Christian theologies and doctrinal formulations, the Logos is the Second Person of the Trinity that is God, as the (eternally and in history) self-pronounced utterance of God's being and life. When this utterance of God's being and life is communicated in human words and history, it is the "Word of God" (and this is a reason for referring to the Scriptures as the Word of God too—although Jesus Christ is, before and above the written words of the Bible, *the* Word of God because *Christ* is the Word that is God, a claim that cannot be made for the Bible).

Orlando Espín

See also CHRISTOLOGY; PERSON/ PROSOPON; TRINITY/TRINITARIAN THEOLOGY/TRINITARIAN PROCESSIONS; WISDOM.

LOHAN

See ARAHANT.

LOISY, ALFRED (1857–1940)

French biblical scholar and Modernist. Loisy is distinguished by his advocacy of historical-critical method in biblical studies long before its acceptance in Catholicism as a legitimate exegetical tool. Professor of Hebrew and Biblical Studies at the Institut Catholique in Paris, Loisy intended to study the Bible as a literary and historical document distinct from its theological and dogmatic interpretations, a conviction rooted in his suspicion about the religious significance of dogma and his interest in apologetics. His ideas explained in *Gospel and Church* caused the loss of his university position in 1892. His works were placed on the *Index of Errors* in 1903, and apparently included among the Modernist errors listed in Pius X's 1907 encyclical, *Pascendi.* When Loisy continued to teach and publish, he was excommunicated (1908). Most of his views on biblical interpretation have since been accepted in Catholic biblical circles.

Patricia Plovanich

LOLLARDS

The word "lollard" or "loller" comes from the Dutch word meaning "to mumble" and was a derogatory name for the followers of the teachings of John Wycliff, the Oxford theologian who died in 1384. Already in Wycliff's lifetime, his students began writing down and disseminating his teaching. At first, the Lollards had support in all levels of society, but most importantly in the court of Richard II. Despite episcopal opposition, the Lollards established thriving communities and produced a venacular translation of the Bible as well as other treatises. In 1401, however, the death penalty for heresy was introduced into England and ecclesiastical officials moved more aggressively against the Lollards as heretics. Trials were held, some Lollards were burned, and strict laws governing preaching and especially the reading of the vernacular Bible were introduced. In 1413 the Lollards were struck a serious blow when Sir John Oldcastle, a wealthy and influential knight, was convicted of Lollard beliefs. He was condemned to death, but escaped and organized a revolt against the government by the Lollards. The revolt failed and though Oldcastle escaped, the Lollards had earned the enmity of the government and never recovered as a political force. The Lollards continued, but were confined mostly to the lower classes. The Lollards, despite persistent persecution, continued to preach and proselytize until they joined with the Lutheran movement in the sixteenth century. Their basic beliefs were similar to those originally espoused by Wycliff. They rejected transubstantiation and sacraments in general. They argued for the free use of a vernacular Scripture. They strongly attacked the abuses of the clergy and especially the papacy, opposed religious orders, and condemned the worship of images and the making of pilgrimages.

Gary Macy

See also HERESY; HUS, JOHN; LUTHERANISM; MEDIEVAL CHRISTIANITY (IN THE WEST); SACRAMENTS; TRANSUBSTANTIATION; WYCLIFF, JOHN.

LONERGAN, BERNARD (1904–84)

One of the seminal thinkers in the twentieth-century English-speaking theological world, Bernard J. F. Lonergan was born in Buckingham, Quebec, and entered the Jesuits in 1922. He was a professor of systematic theology first at the Jesuit schools of philosophy and theology in Montreal and Toronto (1940–53), and then at the Gregorian University in Rome (1953–65). Later he held distinguished professorships at Harvard Divinity School (1971–2) and Boston College (1975–83), where the Lonergan Institute was established. He died in Pickering, Ontario, the same year as Karl Rahner. Lonergan is perhaps best known for his pioneering study *Insight: A Study of Human Understanding*, which represented a creative retrieval of Thomas Aquinas's theory of knowledge. His interest in human consciousness, hermeneutics, and the nature of conversion, especially as evidenced in *Method in Theology*, sparked numerous studies by other scholars. Later in his life he resumed his earlier study of economics.

William Reiser, S.J.

See also METHOD IN THEOLOGY; RAHNER, KARL.

LORD/LORDSHIP

A lord is a person who has great power and authority over others, as that of a superior over inferiors. The term is used as a title to acknowledge dignity and express respect. While this general, or secular, sense of the term is applied to masters or owners throughout the Bible, both the Old and the New Testaments very specifically also use "Lord" to speak of God and Jesus.

In the Old Testament, the English term "Lord" translates the Hebrew word *adôn*, frequently used as a title of God. In other instances in the Old Testament, God is often given the name Yahweh. Interestingly, in Judaism in the years after the Old Testament was completed, it became the custom to avoid using God's name and instead to substitute for it with the title of "Lord," or more specifically, "my Lord," *adonai*. This had the result of associating the title of "Lord" with God even more closely than the Old Testament text itself does in its use of *adôn*.

In the New Testament, "Lord" is a common title for Jesus. It is judged quite probable, in view of the Gospel traditions, that Jesus was actually called "Lord" during his historical life by his followers and others, that is, especially by those who asked for his help. For the early Christians who believed Jesus was the Messiah, that is, the eschatological king descended from David, "Lord" became an important title in proclaiming his identity, resurrection, exaltation, and saving power to the Gentiles.

The early Christian naming of Jesus as Lord (*kyrios* in Greek) grew to bear a meaning beyond the proclamation that Jesus was Messiah. The title "Lord" came to reflect the conviction that Jesus rules all of heaven and earth at God's right hand, and that he was with God from the beginning.

F. M. Gillman

See also CHRISTOLOGY; MESSIAH (IN JUDAISM); PAULINE THEOLOGY; RESURRECTION (IN CHRISTIANITY).

LORD'S PRAYER

The "Our Father." A prayer of Jesus recorded in Matthew (6:9-13) and Luke (11:2-4). Matthew's text and Luke's, however, are quite different. This suggests that they are probably examples of how Jesus prayed rather than exact quotations. The English translation used in Catholic liturgies is a revised form of a translation made by Thomas Cranmer for the 1549 Book of Common Prayer. Many Christian churches conclude the Lord's Prayer with the dox-

ology, "for thine is the kingdom, and the power, and the glory, forever and ever." Scholars agree that this phrase was not in the most ancient biblical manuscripts. Jews and Christians of the biblical and postbiblical era often ended their prayers this way, however, and so some scribes added it to Matthew's version when they were copying the Gospel, to reflect the way the people actually prayed.

Patrick L. Malloy

See also BOOK OF COMMON PRAYER; CRANMER, THOMAS; DOXOLOGY.

LORD'S SUPPER

See EUCHARIST.

LOSSKY, VLADIMIR (1903–58)

Russian Orthodox lay theologian. Son of a respected philosopher, he was expelled from Russia in 1922 by the Soviet government. After some years in Europe, he migrated to the United States. There he dedicated his life and career to explaining Orthodox thought to North American and Western European audiences. He also opposed Sergei Bulgakov's theories on the wisdom (sophia) of God. His most important book is *Essay on the Mystical Theology of the Eastern Church* (1944).

Orlando Espín

See also BULGAKOV, SERGEI; ORTHODOX CHURCHES; RUSSIAN ORTHODOX CHURCH.

LOTUS SUTRA

Perhaps the most influential text in Northern Buddhism, the *Lotus Sutra* (Sanskrit, *Saddharmapundarika*, "Lotus of the True Law") attempts to unify all Buddhist schools while establishing the superiority of the Mahayana. Employing popular parables and dramatic theatrical turns, the *Lotus* seeks to explode the Sthavira-Hinayana notion of Buddhahood limited to rare figures like the historical Shakyamuni; instead, it has Shakyamuni appear to instruct Arhants in the true nature of Buddhahood as a cosmic reality unrestricted by time or space. Basic doctrines of early Mahayana are set forth, with Hinayana teachings explained as preliminary and selfish; instead, the myriad doctrines ascribed to the Buddha are said to lead all on a single path, the *ekayana*, and that has every disciple eventually become bodhisattvas destined to also reach the level of Buddhahood. The text also introduces a pantheon of celestial bodhisattvas, most notably Avalokiteshvara.

This text inspired the early successful East Asian schools—the Chinese T'ien T'ai and Japanese Tendai—that saw the *Lotus* as the Buddha's highest teaching. In later Japanese Buddhism, the monk Nichiren (1222–82) established a separate school whose central practices were chanting the name of the text (in translation)—*Nam Myoho Renge Kyo*—and gazing at a diagram of his design with faith showing that the Dharma, the Buddha, and all beings are one.

Todd T. Lewis

See also AVALOKITESHVARA; BUDDHA; MAHAYANA BUDDHISM; UPAYA.

LOVE (IN GENERAL)

Anders Nygren noted the broad distinction in early Christian writings between *eros* (natural human attraction) and *agapē*, the love of God. Popular theologian C. S. Lewis offered a more defined taxonomy. After discussing "liking" (which we often call "loving," as in "I love ice cream!"), Lewis distinguishes "four loves" characteristic of the human. The first he calls "affection," his translation of the Greek *storgē*

(principally referring to parent-child interaction). The second is friendship (in Greek, "philios"). Aristotle calls this the "form" of all the virtues, meaning that the true place for the exercise of all moral virtues is within a friendship. Lewis calls friendship the least jealous of the loves, and relies on the discovery that the other shares a treasure that the one had previously thought entirely unique to himself. The third is eros, which Lewis calls "that kind of love which lovers are 'in.'" Eros has sexuality as an ingredient, and makes a person really want not just anyone, but this particular one. In its truest form, eros wants the other as a someone "admirable in [its own] self," with an importance beyond one's own wanting. The last is Christian love, called agape.

Christian Love: Mistaken Notions

Agapē was translated into Latin as *caritas*, and then into English as "charity." The word "charity," however, often has negative connotations in present U.S. English usage. Though sometimes we praise "giving to charity," we often say, "I don't want your charity," or "I'm not doing you a charity," afraid that it means humiliation of some sort. That is because "charity" often means "giving a needy person something without empowering that person, and/or without attending to the larger issues of social injustice by which the person is oppressed." Of course, the full notion of *agapē* must include justice, since this is a feature of God's love. With such a strongly negative connotation, most refer to *agapē* not as "charity," but as "love," and to distinguish it from the other kinds of love, usually call *agapē* "unconditional love."

Though it is popular, it is nevertheless mistaken to translate *agapē* as "unconditional love." This generally is taken to mean that, because God loves us always, and everyone the same, we can do whatever we want (or at least not really terrible things), and it does not really matter. At the end of John's Gospel, however, Jesus asks Simon Peter if he loves ("agapeis") him "more than these others do" (John 21:15), indicating that *agapē* admits of degrees. In general, God's own preference for the poor and oppressed argue against such a notion. And no one who has read the conditions following Jesus in the Gospels (including, of course, a preference for the poor and oppressed) could ever settle for such a vacuous translation as "unconditional love."

In fact, the Christians took the word *agapē* and gave it a new content, and so the best way to translate the word is, "the way Jesus loved us." First Corinthians 13 gives us a brief, but by no means adequate, description of *agapē*.

We might mention here that love of *enemies* has a privileged place in the denoting of *agapē*. Unique among the monotheistic religions, this dimension of *agapē* is evinced by Jesus throughout his ministry, and especially in his words of forgiveness on the cross. Jesus commands his followers to love their enemies in the same way.

Love as Jesus Loved

The command to love (*agapein*) as Jesus loved (John 13:34) would be impossible without the Holy Spirit, who *is* the love of God poured out on us, empowering us to love and act as Jesus did (1 John 2:6). In fact, the whole of Acts can be read as the Holy Spirit refashioning persons and the community into the presence of Christ. Note especially that the first Christian martyr, Stephen, dies as Jesus died: forgiving those who killed him and

commending his spirit to divine safe-keeping (Acts 7:59-60. Of course Stephen commits his spirit to *Jesus*). Thus to call Jesus' commands and way of life an "ideal" is to seriously mistake *agapē* and the granting of the Holy Spirit to Christians. Even to regard Jesus as a "model," as we might, for example, regard Dorothy Day or Mohandas Gandhi, is a mistake. Christians are empowered by the Holy Spirit, who is *agapē*, to live as Christ in the world. Another way to say this is to say that the Gospels are the story of *our* life.

Development

The development of the understanding of *agapē* (Latin, *caritas*) in postscriptural Christian thought is variegated and rich. Sometimes the development is a deformation, as when Ambrose and Augustine tried to explain how a Christian fighting in a war could "love their enemy" and kill them at the same time. Here we will only consider the understanding of charity as a *virtue*.

Pope Gregory the Great stated that the three "theological virtues," faith, hope, and *agapē*/*caritas*, were necessary for salvation in Catholic understanding. As the highest of the theological virtues, love was considered to be higher even than the "cardinal (*cardo*, "hinge") virtues." As such, and importantly, *agapē* was not ruled by "prudence" as were all the other virtues. This explains why the church has always admired and canonized the extravagant acts and sufferings done in love by the saints in response to the extravagant gift of God in Christ. In that sense, Duns Scotus was right in saying that Christian love was more of an ec-static (from the Greek, "ek-stasis," "standing outside [oneself]") reality for Christians, since the practice of God's love was unfathomable and unattainable to natural human activity.

In another sense, because God is the Creator, even the virtue of *agapē* was looked upon as complementary and even perfecting of created human nature. In that way, love was the fulfillment of all the human virtues. *Agapē* was thought to inform the other virtues, such as prudence. This was the line of thought taken by the Scholastics, most notably Thomas Aquinas. Borrowing from Aristotle, who said that *friendship* was the moral *environ* for the practice of the virtues, Thomas Aquinas said that the *environ* for the practice of *Christian* virtues was friendship with *God*, which is how he defined *caritas* (charity). Charity is the "form" of all the virtues in Thomas (*ST* I–II q. 62, a. 4). That is, it gives specific identity, character, origin, development, and goal to all the virtues.

G. Simon Harak, s.j.

See also FAITH; HOPE (IN CHRISTIANITY); THEOLOGICAL VIRTUES; VIRTUE.

LUCIFER
Beginning in the early centuries of the Common Era, this term was used by Christian exegetes as one of the names of Satan. The term *lucifer* is Latin and means literally "light bearer." It was used to refer to the planet Venus when it was visible as the "morning star." In the Latin Vulgate of Isaiah 14:12, *lucifer* translates the Hebrew word *helel*, translated as "Day Star" or "Morning Star," and also refers to the planet Venus.

Russell Fuller

LUCKMANN, THOMAS (1927–)
American sociologist. Educated in Europe, he taught at American institutions and then at a Swiss university. He focused his research on the modern privatization of ethical and religious values away from the institutional churches. He has also studied religious-like ideologies present in modern societies that compete with the churches. His more important books are *The Invisible Religion* (1967) and, with Peter L. Berger, the very influential *The Social Construction of Reality* (1966).

Orlando Espín

See also BERGER, PETER L.; CIVIL RELIGION; ETHICS, SOCIAL; IDEOLOGY (IDEOLOGIES); MODERNITY; POST-MODERNITY; PRIVATIZATION OF RELIGION; SECULARIZATION/SECULAR/SECULARIZED; VALUES.

LUKE/LUKAN
The Gospel of Luke and the Acts of the Apostles form a two-part work that has traditionally been attributed to Luke the physician and occasional collaborator with Paul. While it is certain both documents are by the same author, some doubts surround the attribution of Lukan authorship since Luke in Acts shows little acquaintance with Paul's theology. On the other hand, since there is no reason why the early church would have attributed this Gospel to such an obscure figure, the tradition of Lukan authorship may be valid.

Luke's Gospel is a compilation of the Gospel of Mark, Q, and other material known to Luke. Thus it must be dated after Mark (late 60s) and after the destruction of Jerusalem in 70 that it presupposes had happened. Since it does not reflect the controversy between churches and synagogues following the developments at Jamnia in 85–90, a date of 80–85 is widely proposed. Given the primarily Gentile audience with well-to-do members whom Luke addresses, the place of the Gospel's composition may have been Syrian Antioch, Luke's home city according to various ancient sources.

Luke was an immensely talented author, a master of Greek with the ability to write in elegant, even Septuagintal, phrasing. The Gospel text is very carefully structured, especially through the use of parallelism. A geographical scheme is also evident: Jesus journeys from Galilee to Jerusalem and to God; from Jerusalem the church, led by the Spirit, journeys to the ends of the earth.

F. M. Gillman

See also ACTS OF THE APOSTLES; GENE-ALOGY OF JESUS; INFANCY NARRATIVES; MARK/MARKAN; Q SOURCE; SYNOPTIC GOSPELS; SYNOPTIC PROBLEM.

LUKUMI
See SANTERÍA.

LULAV

In Judaism, a palm branch. Together with a citron (etrog), and branches of willow and myrtle, it is used on the festival of Tabernacles to fulfill the requirements of Leviticus 23:40: "And you shall take on the first day the fruit of goodly trees, branches of palm trees, and boughs of leafy trees, and willows of the brook; and you shall rejoice before the LORD your God seven days." Scripture views these species as representing the bounty of the land and so as appropriately used in a celebration of the harvest season.

Alan J. Avery-Peck

See also ETROG; TABERNACLES, FEAST OF.

LUMEN GENTIUM

(Document of Vatican II). The Dogmatic Constitution on the Church, approved overwhelmingly by the bishops of the Second Vatican Council (2,152 to 5) on November 21, 1964, after much controversy, is considered by some to be the most important document of the council. Commonly known as *Lumen Gentium*, the first two words of the Latin text ("Light of the peoples"), the dogmatic constitution represents the culmination of a long process of doctrinal development and stands today as the church's most authoritative statement of its own self-understanding. As a "dogmatic constitution" (and not merely a "decree" or "declaration"), *Lumen Gentium* carries for Catholics the highest degree of doctrinal authority. It also provides the theological foundation for most of the other pronouncements of the council.

Lumen Gentium attempts, "for the benefit of the faithful and of the whole world, to set forth, as clearly as possible, and in the tradition laid down by earlier Councils, [the church's] own nature and universal mission" (LG 1). The council is thus speaking to both Catholics and non-Catholics when it says that in Christ the church is meant to be "a sign and instrument . . . of communion with God and of unity among all people" (LG 1). *Lumen Gentium* consists of eight chapters whose titles and order are significant. They are as follows: (1) "The Mystery of the Church"; (2) "The People of God"; (3) "The Church Is Hierarchical"; (4) "The Laity"; (5) "The Call to Holiness"; (6) "Religious"; (7) "The Pilgrim Church"; (8) "Our Lady (the Virgin Mary)." The order and the content of these chapters reveal significant theological breakthroughs in twentieth-century Catholic thinking about the church; they also highlight some of the tensions in the church's understanding of its nature and mission in the world. By employing the term "mystery" (from *mystērion*, the Greek equivalent of the Latin *sacramentum*) in reference to the church, the council not only indicates the church's mysterious divine origin and alludes to the Catholic tradition of seven sacraments; it also advances Catholic ecclesiology by conceiving the whole of the church itself as "in the nature of sacrament," that is, as both a sign and an instrument of God's grace that seeks to establish communion between God and humanity and unity among human beings. This fundamental sacramental nature thus provides the framework for understanding all other statements about the church made in the following chapters. The placement of the second and third chapters marks a significant shift in many Catholics' understanding of the church. By treating the church as a whole (employing the biblical term "people of God") before considering its "hierarchy" (bishops, priests, and deacons), the council affirmed the common vocation of all believers, laity and clergy alike, to act as priests and prophets in the world. (The constant use of biblical terms and images to express its views is characteristic of Vatican II in general and somewhat novel in the history of conciliar documents.) The fifth chapter of *Lumen Gentium* deals with the call to holiness central to the life and activity of all Christians. The sixth chapter treats the form of Christian discipleship known in the Catholic Church as "religious life" in which lay men and women or clerics seek holiness and apostolic effectiveness through membership in communities that live according to the "evangelical counsels"— that is, poverty, chastity, and obedience. The seventh chapter recalls with humility the church's historical imperfection and relates its present reality to God's "promised and hoped for restoration" at the end of time (LG 48). This marks a significant shift away from an earlier, triumphalistic

Catholic ecclesiology that one-sidedly emphasized the church's holiness. The final chapter on the Virgin Mary affirms the Catholic view of Mary's role in the mystery of Christ and the church. At the same time, by including this section in *Lumen Gentium* instead of issuing a separate document on Mary, the council avoided treating Mariology in isolation, a longstanding concern of many Protestant Christians.

Taken as a whole, the significance of the Dogmatic Constitution on the Church for Catholic theology, for church practice, for the lives of individual Catholics, and for dialogue among Christian churches cannot be overestimated.

James B. Nickoloff

See also ECCLESIOLOGY; VATICAN, SECOND COUNCIL OF THE.

LUNAR CALENDAR

Most world religions fixed the regular celebration of yearly festivals according to the most easily observed natural phenomenon of the moon's phases. Although different cultural understandings define the exact choices of both auspicious and inauspicious points according to the moon's waxing and waning phases, the lunar reference point is common. In Asia, the full moon (Sanskrit, *purnima*) was regarded as the most propitious day for religious observances from antiquity as the early Vedic era's day of sacrifice. It was adopted by the Buddhists for monastic assemblies and lay ritualism. The eighth and eleventh days are also regarded as auspicious by both Hindus and Buddhists.

In East Asia, the lunar cycle was integrated with other divination factors (elements, year, cycle of imperial rule) to reckon the best days for ritual activity.

Todd T. Lewis

LURIA, ISAAC BEN SOLOMON ASHKENAZI (1534–72)

One of the greatest Jewish mystical thinkers, known in Hebrew as *HaAri*. Born in Jerusalem, he was brought up in Egypt, moving in 1570 to Safed, which became the center of Jewish mystical thought. Luria was renowned for his saintliness and ascetic character. His oral teachings were transmitted by his students, in particular Chaim Vital, and the mystical system he launched, known as Lurianic Kabbalah, deeply influenced all later Jewish life. At the heart of his system are the notions that, in order to make room for the world, God had withdrawn into Godself (*Zimzum*); that the void between God and the world is filled with ten spheres (*sefirot*) representing intermediate agents of God; and that it is the task of individual Jews, through proper ritual observance and piety, to restore the world into the perfect order in which God originally created it (*Tikkun Olam*). A large number of works, published between 1596 and 1839, were attributed to Luria by his disciples. Chief among these is the six-volume *Etz Chaim* ("Tree of Life"), which includes, among a wide range of topics, mystical interpretations of the Bible and the liturgy, a study of the commandments, and a treatise on metempsychosis.

Alan J. Avery-Peck

See also KABBALAH.

LUTHER, MARTIN (1483–1546)

Reformer, Scripture scholar and prolific theologian, Luther initiated the Reformation in Germany. Luther's life and work are the subjects of an enormous quantity of studies in many languages. It is customary to distinguish three periods in his life: 1483 to 1517; 1517 to 1530; 1530 to 1546.

Young Luther (1483–1517)

Born in the German town of Eisleben, Luther studied at the University of Erfurt from 1501. In 1505, in the middle of a thunderstorm, he made a vow to Saint Ann that he would enter a monastery if he survived the storm. Later that year Luther kept his word and became an Augustinian friar in Erfurt. Ordained a priest in 1507, Luther began the following year to lecture at the University of Wittenberg. In 1510 Luther traveled to Rome on business for the Augustinians; he returned to Wittenberg scandalized by the decadence and corruption he had seen in Rome. The next year he became a doctor of theology and a professor of Scripture in Wittenberg. Luther's lectures and commentaries on Scripture in the following years are where he began to develop a theology different from what he had been taught as a student. Sometime during these years, he had an experience he would later describe as similar to entrance into paradise: a sudden experience or insight in which he saw for the first time that salvation came not through human works but through the undeserved grace of God. Justification of the sinner came through faith alone, not through works.

Mature Luther (1517–30)

On October 31, 1517, Luther posted ninety-five "theses" on the door of the castle church in Wittenberg. These theses challenged the sale of indulgences, a practice common at the time. An "indulgence" was a remission of the punishment due for the sins of the living or the dead; obtaining an indulgence was thus seen as a way of hastening entrance of an individual to heaven. It could be obtained for oneself or for others, including those believed to be in purgatory. Luther's theses challenged not only the financial abuses involved in the sale of indulgences, but also the theological sanction for them. For Luther, indulgences led people to believe that salvation came through human merit and human works; they led people to believe that they had to earn their way to redemption. This belief, in Luther's view, contradicted the Gospel and made the work of Christ superfluous.

From 1517 on Luther's ideas spread rapidly, gaining for him many disciples and colleagues, and also many enemies. Support from various princes gave him the political support needed to continue in the face of hostility from the papacy and from Charles V, emperor of the Holy Roman Empire, an empire that included Germany.

In 1520 Luther produced three important treatises. *The Freedom of a Christian* expounded freedom from anxiety about salvation and about one's standing before God, a freedom that comes from placing one's faith or trust in Christ alone. Such freedom also meant the service of one's neighbor without concern about recompense or reward from God. In *The Babylonian Captivity of the Church* Luther discussed the sacraments, applying the principle of "Scripture alone" as the norm for Christian belief and practice. Luther thus rejected the seven sacraments of the Roman Catholic Church, retaining only baptism and Eucharist. In 1520 he was not yet ready to reject penance altogether, for in the words of absolution he found a comfort for the penitent sinner. Luther found, however, that the practice of the sacrament of penance tended to increase anxiety about salvation rather than to comfort consciences. For this reason, Luther would later repudiate penance as a sacrament. In *An Address to the Christian Nobility*, Luther appealed for the German princes to assist him in reforming the church and in freeing Germany from exploitation by Rome. This treatise helped to link the Reformation with national aspirations in sixteenth-century Europe.

Early in 1521 Luther was excommunicated by Pope Leo X. Later that year, after refusing to recant his opinions, Luther was declared an outlaw in the Holy Roman Empire. Protected by princes, Luther went into seclusion for a while at Wartburg castle, where he produced a German edition of the New Testament.

In 1525 Luther married Catherine von Bora. From then on he became an articulate advocate of marriage for the clergy.

The year 1525 also saw Luther condemn both the views of Erasmus on free will and the actions of the peasants of Germany engaged in a war for greater political and economic freedom. For Luther, if Erasmus was wrong to attribute any part to human free will or choice in what belongs to God's grace alone, that is, salvation, the peasants had misinterpreted the true meaning of the "freedom" of a Christian. Luther insisted that the freedom proclaimed by the Gospel had nothing to do with economic or political freedom for peasants, but solely with the freedom from anxiety about salvation.

By the late 1520s, Zwingli's reform of the church in Zurich had become a rival model of church reform. At the Colloquy of Marburg in 1529, Luther and Zwingli were unable to reconcile their differences. The principal source of dispute was the Eucharist, with Zwingli insisting on a symbolic presence only of the Body of Christ, and with Luther maintaining a doctrine of Real Presence.

Older Luther (1530–46)

In the 1530s and 1540s Luther's influence continued to spread, inside and outside Germany. If Zwingli and other Reformers challenged Luther on various matters, many, such as Philip Melanchthon, supported Luther even as they established their own credentials as Reformers. The *Augsburg Confession* of 1530, a summary of doctrine written by Melanchthon and other "Lutheran" Reformers, helped to systematize Luther's teaching and make it normative for "Lutheran" churches. The older Luther continued, however, to produce theological works as well as more informal writings. His complete works, in the original Latin and German, cover some one hundred volumes.

Thomas Worcester, S.J.

See also AUGSBURG CONFESSION; DEUS PRO NOBIS; FIDES FIDUCIALIS; GOOD WORKS; IMPUTATION; JUSTIFICATION; LUTHERANISM; LUTHERAN THEOLOGY; MELANCHTHON, PHILIP; NINETY-FIVE THESES; REAL PRESENCE; REFORMATION; SIMUL IUSTUS ET PECCATOR; SOLA FIDE; SOLA GRATIA; SOLA SCRIPTURA; UBIQUITARIANISM; WITTENBERG.

LUTHERANISM
Origin and Spread

The label "Lutheranism" was originally a derogatory term, first used by the papal theologian John Eck in his debate with Martin Luther (who was then still an Augustinian friar) at Leipzig in July 1519. (The debate concerned issues of church authority that arose out of the "Ninety-Five Theses" Luther had posted at Wittenberg on October 31, 1517, condemning the selling of indulgences as contrary to the Gospel.) Luther himself always disliked the terms "Lutheran" and "Lutheranism"; he did not want his movement to bear his name but rather to be called "Evangelical" (from the Greek word *evangelion*, meaning "good news" or

"gospel"). By either name, Luther's movement spread like wildfire. Following his excommunication in December 1520, it spread all through central and northern Germany; following the excommunication of these "Lutheranized" populations (due to papal rejection of the *Augsburg Confession* of June 1530), it spread all through Scandinavia. By 1555, in the Religious Peace of Augsburg, the Holy Roman Empire was forced to grant Lutheranism equal status with the Roman Catholic Church, thus formally ending the religious unity of Western Europe. By 1600, a little more than half a century after Luther's death in February 1546, Lutheranism was the established "state church" not only in Germany but also in Denmark, Iceland, Norway, Sweden, Finland, Latvia, Estonia, and parts of Bohemia and Hungary.

To be sure, in each country Lutheranism was always shaped by national politics and culture, even regarding forms of worship (in the Mass and popular hymnody) and church leadership (in the episcopate and control by the state). Nevertheless, it did amount to a whole new "Third Christendom," an Evangelical (Lutheran) Christendom of the North now separated and distinct from both the (Greek) Orthodox Christendom of the East and the (Latin) Catholic Christendom of the West. And yet, ironically, in this very success it failed in its original mission: not to create yet another Christian community but to renew the ancient, already existing church according to the Gospel.

A "Confessional Movement"

It is in this connection that a very valuable study of Lutheranism describes it as follows:

"If the Lutheran proposals had been ecumenically accepted, there would be no Lutheranism. As it is, Lutheranism is a *confessional movement* within the Church catholic. . . . Whether this movement is organized as a 'church' or not is secondary to its purpose. . . . 'The Lutheran Church' is, indeed, an ecumenical movement of its own: it is a fellowship of territorial churches, denominations, and sects that contains within itself nearly every possible kind of church life and organization, and is held together only by common dedication to the Lutheran theological movement.

The Lutheran proposal of dogma has one great theme: justification by faith alone, apart from works of law. This is the heart of the matter . . ." (Eric W. Gritsch and Robert W. Jenson, *Lutheranism: The Theological Movement and Its Confessional Writings*, Philadelphia: Fortress Press, 1976, 5–6).

Lutheranism since 1600

The past four hundred years have seen European Lutheranism go through many convulsive changes: from a scholastic *Orthodoxy* (that was devastated by the horrors of the Thirty Year War, 1618–48), to an intensely personalized *Pietism* (with its world missions and social ministry), to a *Rationalism* that reflected the eighteenth-century Enlightenment, to a gradual revival of confessional, liturgical, and pastoral theology beginning in the nineteenth century and continuing in the present.

European Lutherans began coming to North America in colonial times and, especially in the nineteenth century, created a bewildering plethora of separate denominations based on ethnic and doctrinal differences. With no common structure whatever, it has taken the (roughly) nine million Lutherans in the United States many laborious mergers to reach the point

where the vast majority now belong to one of two denominations: The Evangelical Lutheran Church in America or the Lutheran Church—Missouri Synod (generally characterized as "more liberal" or "more conservative," respectively).

However, Lutheranism is today a vastly international and multicultural movement, from Norway to Namibia and from Texas to Taiwan, with some sixty million adherents, the majority of whom belong to churches affiliated with the Lutheran World Federation (headquartered in Geneva, Switzerland).

Perhaps the most important Lutheran figure in the twentieth century, both as a theologian and as a symbol, was Dietrich Bonhoeffer, the German pastor who led the underground "Confessing Church" against Nazism during the Third Reich, and who was finally hanged by the Gestapo at Flossenberg on April 9, 1945, for involvement in the conspiracy to assassinate Adolph Hitler. In Bonhoeffer, Lutherans see confessional integrity struggling to find its way through moral dilemmas in resistance to the evils of modern totalitarianism.

And what of the future of Lutheranism? Lutherans themselves disagree: some would have it continue as a denomination in its own right; others would dissolve it into nondenominational "community church" Protestantism; and still others, impressed by the reforms flowing from the Second Vatican Council, would have it seek some form of reunion with Rome.

Whatever happens, it was surely the sign of a new day when, on December 11, 1983, in commemoration of the five hundredth anniversary of Martin Luther's birth (November 10, 1483), Pope John Paul II paid the first-ever papal visit to the Lutheran church in Rome and said: "We seem to see rise in the distance like the dawn the restoration of our unity and of our community" (*L'Osservatore Romano* 9 January 1984, 13).

Jack E. Lindquist

See also AUGSBURG CONFESSION; BONHOEFFER, DIETRICH; INDULGENCE; LUTHER, MARTIN; LUTHERAN THEOLOGY; NINETY-FIVE THESES; PROTESTANTISM/PROTESTANT; REFORMATION; WITTENBERG; WORMS, DISPUTATION OF.

LUTHERAN THEOLOGY

The official theology of Lutheranism is set forth in *The Book of Concord* of 1580, a collection of confessions of faith written by Martin Luther himself (1483–1546), his colleague Philip Melanchthon (1497–1560), and others, following their deaths. From this "confessional theology," it is clear that the Lutheran Reformation did not intend to start a new and separate Christian church, but rather to be an evangelical and catholic movement for the renewal of the faith, ministry, and worship of the universal church according to the Gospel. Rearranged in chronological order, the Lutheran confessions show the following theological development.

The Apostles', Nicene, and Athanasian Creeds. Lutheran theology claimed to be grounded on the doctrine of the Ancient Church.

1529: The Small Catechism and the Large Catechism of Martin Luther. Lutheran theology centered on pastoral exposition of Law and Gospel in the essentials of the Ten Commandments, the Apostles' Creed, the Lord's Prayer, the Sacrament of Holy Baptism, Confession and Absolution, and the Sacrament of the Altar. The incarnational emphasis was very strong: Jesus Christ is both "true God" and "true man"; salvation is truly given through the water of baptism; sins are truly forgiven through the human words of absolution; the Body and Blood of Christ are truly present "in and under the bread and wine" in Holy Communion.

1530: The Augsburg Confession (Melanchthon). Lutheran theology made a very irenic presentation of itself as an "evangelical catholicism," offering to remain as a reform movement within the Roman Catholic Church on the "Lutheranized" territories of the Holy Roman Empire of Charles V.

1531: The Apology of the Augsburg Confession (Melanchthon). Lutheran theology defended itself against condemnations by Roman Catholic authorities, refused to submit to Rome, and thus became the theology of a separate and distinct Christian community, after all.

1537: The Smalcald Articles (Luther). Lutheran theology hardened into a list of non-negotiable beliefs and reforms for possible presentation at a Roman Catholic council summoned by Pope Paul III. (The council, held at Trent, did not finally convene until 1545, the year before Luther's death, and the Lutherans were not invited.)

1537: Treatise on the Power and Primacy of the Pope (Melanchthon). In an addendum to the Augsburg Confession of seven years before that avoided any mention of the papacy, Lutheran theology now explicitly rejected the claim of the popes to rule "by divine right," as well as many practices stemming from that claim: indulgencies, obligatory celibacy, supremacy over the civil power, and so on.

1577: Formula of Concord (Jacob Andreae, Martin Chemnitz, and others). In its final official confession, Lutheran theology endeavored to define itself over against certain teachings of the Council of Trent (1545–63) and various Protestant movements (Calvinist, Zwinglian, Anabaptist, and so forth), and also to settle several serious doctrinal disputes that had divided Lutherans for a generation.

However, Lutheran theology has always continued to suffer from serious internal differences, even while its relations with other theologies (Roman Catholic, Reformed, and so on) have improved dramatically due to the modern ecumenical movements.

According to Carl Braaten in *Principles of Lutheran Theology* (Philadelphia: Fortress Press, 1983), truly authentic Lutheran theology is grounded on seven principles:

The Canonical Principle: "Authority in matters of faith rests on the Gospel of Scripture. . . . The Word of Scripture alone (*sola scriptura*) is to be believed and accepted as finally valid with respect to the concerns of faith and salvation" (4).

The Confessional Principle: In all the confessions mentioned above, Lutheran theology finds its identity and integrity, and its continuity with the Ancient Church.

The Ecumenical Principle: As a movement for the universal church, Lutherans must unite with other Christians when agreement is reached on the Gospel and the sacraments.

The Christocentric Principle: In its teaching of the Gospel of Christ, Lutheran theology must "equip the Church to proclaim a message that is absolutely unique, universal, decisive, and definitive of salvation for all humanity and the world" (65).

The Sacramental Principle: The God of the Gospel is only known "deep in the flesh": of Jesus, the Word Incarnate; of the proclaiming and absolving in Jesus' name; of the baptismal water and the eucharistic bread and wine, through which Jesus is present and active today; of those who are Jesus' "needy members."

The Law/Gospel Principle: "The law is God's controversy with his people. The law terrifies, accuses, condemns, denounces, punishes, and kills. If this is not true, then the Gospel cannot comfort, strengthen, forgive, liberate, and renew. In the religious life, law and Gospel are correlative. . . . The law tells us what we ought to do, the Gospel declares what God does" (111–2).

The Two-Kingdoms Principle: "The Christian message in its totality, therefore, speaks of two things that God is doing in the world. God is pressing for the historical liberation of human beings through a host of secular media, and for Christ's sake he promises eternal salvation through the preaching of the Word and the administration of the sacraments" (134).

Jack E. Lindquist

See also AUGSBURG CONFESSION; LUTHER, MARTIN; LUTHERANISM; MELANCHTHON, PHILIP; NYGREN, ANDERS; PANNENBERG, WOLFHART; PELIKAN, JAROSLAV; PRIESTHOOD; SIMUL IUSTUS ET PECCATOR; SOLA FIDE; SOLA GRATIA; SOLA SCRIPTURA; THIELICKE, HELMUT; UBIQUITARIANISM.

LYONS, COUNCILS OF

In Roman Catholic reckoning, two councils held in Lyons rank as ecumenical councils. The Council of Lyons in 1245 (the thirteenth ecumenical council) was called by Pope Innocent IV to promote moral reform of the clergy, to call for a Crusade and, most imporantly, to reply to the persecution of the Papacy by the Emperor Fredrick II. The main achievement of the council was to declare Fredrick deposed as emperor. The Council of Lyons in 1274 (the fourteenth ecumenical council) was called by Pope Gregory X in order to promote moral reform of the church, to call for a Crusade, and to restore unity to the Eastern and Western Churches. Among the notables in attendance were Albert the Great, Bonaventure, and Peter of Tarentaise, the future Pope Innocent V. Thomas Aquinas died while on his way to the council. Under fear of attack from the armies of Charles of Anjou, the representatives of the Greek emperor declared their assent to Roman authority and faith. This union that constituted the major achievement of the council, however, was never accepted in the East, and the union proved short-lived.

Gary Macy

See also ALBERT THE GREAT; AQUINAS, THOMAS, ST.; BONAVENTURE; COUNCIL, ECUMENICAL; CRUSADES; MEDIEVAL CHRISTIANITY (IN THE WEST); SCHISM, GREAT EASTERN.

M

MA'ARIV

Hebrew meaning "evening," is the evening Jewish worship service.

A traditional Jew prays three times a day. The *ma'ariv* service is the evening service, and since a Jewish day begins and ends at sundown, ma'ariv is the first service of a Jewish day. It is recited every day. On the Sabbath and festivals there are certain changes and additions that reflect the special nature of the day.

The ma'ariv service can be recited any time after the sun has set, up until midnight.

Wayne Dosick

See also MINCHAH; SHACHARIT.

MAASAWU

In the Hopi story of Emergence, Maasawu is the guardian of the Fourth (or present). He is portrayed as a skeleton who bears the welfare of the Hopi close to his heart. A sacred being, he was the one who met their scout as they worried about whether it was safe to enter the world above. His message was one of welcome, but equally one of warning. They had had many diminishments in the worlds below, because they had not been able to carry out the Creator's command to live in harmony and to remember to be grateful. Yet his message was that they would have to learn to live with great restraint and discipline upon the earth. The Hopi understood his words, and found them wise and truthful. So they accepted the challenge and submitted to his guidance. Ever since that time, he has been their guardian and helper, first, in giving them instructions for their migrations through which they were to consecrate the earth and eventually find their own home in it. Then, for all the time to come in this Fourth World, they are assured that he will continue to teach and protect them.

Kathleen Dugan

MACCABEES

Maccabee means "hammer" and comes from a nickname given to Judas, the son of Matthias, the founder of the Maccabean or Hasmonean dynasty (1 Maccabees 2:4; 3:1). The term "Maccabees" refers to both the apocryphal books of 1 and 2 Maccabees as well as to the dynasty begun by Matthias, a priest (d. 166 B.C.E.), and his sons Judas, John, Simon, Eleazar, and Jonathan. The family of Matthias helped to lead a revolt against the Seleucid ruler Antiochus Epiphanes who had made the practice of Judaism illegal. The story of the revolt and the successes and failures of the family are found in the book of 1 Maccabees, and to some extent also in 2 Maccabees. The conflict, begun by Matthias in 167 B.C.E., was continued by his son Judas (d. 160 B.C.E.) who was succeeded by his brother Jonathan (160–142 B.C.E.). It is under Jonathan that a lasting agreement was reached with the Seleucids which allowed for an autonomous Jewish state ruled by the Maccabees. This independent state lasted from approximately 160 to 63 B.C.E. when the Romans intervened directly in Palestine.

Russell Fuller

MACHZOR

(Hebrew, cycle). In Judaism, a prayer book containing the liturgy for the Jewish High Holidays and, sometimes, other festivals. It is contrasted to a "siddur," which primarily contains only daily and Sabbath prayers.

Alan J. Avery-Peck

MACRINA

The name of two learned Christians of the same family in the fourth century. The elder Macrina was a student of the theologian Gregory the Thaumaturge (Wonderworker). Her famous grandson, Basil the Great, credited her for his own strong faith. The younger Macrina was the granddaughter of the elder Macrina and sister of Basil the Great and Gregory of Nyssa. Gregory wrote the story of his sister's life, praising her learning and spiritual insights. She was the author of dialogue on the Resurrection.

Gary Macy

See also BASIL THE GREAT; CAPPODO-CIANS; GREGORY OF NYSSA.

MACUMBA

See UMBANDA.

MADHVA

See DVAITA VEDANTA.

MADHYAMAKA/MADHYAMIKA SCHOOL

One of the four great schools of Indic Buddhism transmitted to China (*San-lun Tsung*), Japan (*Sanron-shu*), and Tibet (*Dbuma-pa*). Its name means "Middle Way follower," a term used by Nagarjuna (150–250 C.E.), the monk-philosopher and school's founder, to indicate his view that the Buddha's essential doctrine—characterized in the earliest texts as "The Middle Way"—held that all things exist in dependence upon other things. Nagarjuna in his commentaries on the *Prajnaparamita sutras* and in his own treatises (*Madhyamakakarika*) supports this by emphasizing the core formulation of dependent co-origination (*pratityasamutpada*), interpreting it to mean that reality is empty (*shunya*) of independent, eternal existence (*svabhava*). Thus, the Madhyamaka view is that things neither exist nor do they not exist absolutely.

As articulated by successors such as Aryadeva (170–270 C.E.), Candrakirti (600–50 C.E.), and Sthiramati (510–70 C.E.), this school's dialectic methods had religious importance: the negation method was used to break down all dualisms in religious interpretation, fearlessly critiquing any attachment to merely verbal constructions of doctrine or experience (for example, nirvana vs. samsara). It also emphasized the utter impossibility of finding religious truth in any moment but the present moment, valorizing experiences transcending linguistic categories via meditation.

Todd T. Lewis

See also CANDRAKIRTI; MAHAYANA BUDDHISM; NAGARJUNA; NIRVANA;

PRAJNAPARAMITA LITERATURE;
PRATITYASAMUTPADA.

MADRASAH/MADRASA

An institution of higher learning in the Islamic world. Though the *madrasah* is thought to be the forerunner of the medieval European universities, it was more like a house of studies than a place where instruction took place. Typically, students went to an adjacent mosque for their classes in Islamic law, history, literature, grammar, logic, and Qur'anic studies (Islamic scripture). The madrasah was their residence. A course of study at the madrasah earned students a certificate from their teachers. Some of the earliest madrasahs date from the ninth century C.E. and were located all over the Islamic world.

Ronald A. Pachence

See also MOSQUE/MASJID; QUR'AN.

MADURO, OTTO (1945–)

Venezuelan sociologist and philosopher of religion. Maduro was educated in Venezuela and Europe. He has taught at several Latin American universities, and is currently professor at Drew University in New Jersey. He is arguably one of the best sociologists of religion in the Americas, having had a significant impact on many Latin American liberation theologians. He masterfully showed how Marxist analysis of religion, if employed critically, can aid Christian theology's tasks. He has more recently focused on questions of social epistemology. Among his best books are *Religión y conflicto social* (1977), and *Mapas para la fiesta: Reflexiones sobre la crisis y el conocimiento* (1992).

Orlando Espín

See also CONFLICT; CULTURE; EPISTE-MOLOGY; GRAMSCI, ANTONIO; IDEOLOGY (IDEOLOGIES); LATIN AMERICAN CATHOLICISM; LATINO THEOLOGY (-IES); LIBERATION THEOLOGIES; MARXISM; PRAXIS; PRIVATIZATION OF RELIGION; RIBEIRO DE OLIVEIRA, PEDRO; SECULARIZATION/SECULAR/SECULARIZED.

MAGI

The Magi (from the Greek root meaning "magic"), or Wise Men, are mentioned in the infancy narrative of Matthew 2:1-18. They were sages like many others within a widespread wisdom movement found, for example, in Israel, Egypt, Persia, and Babylon. In Israel, groups of the wise had developed along with priests and prophets (see Jer 18:18). Some references specifically mention wise women (see 2 Sam 14:2; 20:16). Various wisdom books like Proverbs, Job, Ecclesiasticus, Ecclesiastes, and the Wisdom of Solomon may have been composed by professional wise people.

The Magi mentioned by Matthew, said to have been guided by a rising star, are "from the East" (2:1), which he could have envisioned as Arabia, Mesopotamia, or elsewhere. They are cast as Gentile astrologers since they were concerned with the star, and also did not know where the Scriptures prophesied the Messiah would be born. Matthew does not give their number, but since he says they left three gifts, popular tradition as first seen in Origen concluded there were three wise men. That they were kings, and that their names were Caspar, Melchior, and Balthasar, are also ideas from postbiblical periods. Epiphany (January 6), is the annual commemoration of the visit of the Magi as the manifestation of Jesus to the first Gentiles to pay him homage.

The Magi were held to be saints in the Middle Ages, and the Milanese claimed to possess their relics that had been brought from Constantinople in the fifth century. In the twelfth century, these were taken to the Cologne cathedral where they have remained. The adoration of the Magi has found much representation in art; the earliest extant example, dating from the second century, comes from the Catacomb of Priscilla.

F. M. Gillman

See also INFANCY NARRATIVES; WISDOM; WISDOM LITERATURE; ZOROASTRIANISM.

MAGIC
The term magic is used to refer to a number of related practices or attitudes, and it is sometimes opposed to "religion." In general, magic is an attempt at controlling or manipulating natural or human events through ritual or spells. Magic can attempt to control or manipulate these events by ritually influencing the divine or spiritual realms. The usual goals of magic are health, desirable solutions to an individual life's problems, or to national or international conflicts. But "black" magic can also be used to cause harm or death to others; this is sometimes referred to as sorcery. As an attitude, magic assumes that human actions (rituals) can influence or change the decisions of God (or of the gods, spirits, and so forth) and bend them to the outcomes desired by humans. All religions have either incorporated magic into their ritual lives, or rejected it; but no religion seems to have been completely free from the human inclination to engage in magic. Whether or not magic rituals are regarded as positive, usually effective means of impacting events will depend on the individual person's (and communities') belief system and cultural assumptions.

Orlando Espín

See also AMULET; ASTROLOGY; CHARM OR SPELL; CULTURE; IDOLATRY; INDIGENOUS RELIGIOUS TRADITIONS; INTERCULTURAL THOUGHT; POPULAR RELIGIONS; RITUAL.

MAGISTERIUM, EXTRAORDINARY
The pope and the bishops comprise the official teaching office, or magisterium (Latin, *magister*, teacher), of the Catholic Church. The term "extraordinary" magisterium refers to the instances whereby either the pope alone (acting *ex cathedra*) or the bishops gathered in ecumenical council (together with the pope) define dogma. An exercise of teaching authority by the extraordinary magisterium is considered infallible.

Mary Ann Hinsdale

See also BISHOP (EPISCOPACY); EX CATHEDRA; INFALLIBILITY; MAGISTERIUM, MINISTRY OF THE; MAGISTERIUM, ORDINARY; PAPACY/ PAPAL.

MAGISTERIUM, MINISTRY OF THE
The ministry of the "teaching office" (magisterium) of the pope and bishops in the Catholic Church is both pastoral and juridical. As teachers, the pope and bishops are to confirm (strengthen) the faith and exhort the members of their flock to true Christian living. The ministry of teaching belongs to the threefold charism (gift) of teaching, governing, and sanctifying, that the bishops share with Christ.

Mary Ann Hinsdale

See also BISHOP (EPISCOPACY); CHARISM; MAGISTERIUM, EXTRAORDINARY; MAGISTERIUM, ORDINARY; PAPACY/ PAPAL.

MAGISTERIUM, ORDINARY

Magisterium (Latin, *magister*, teacher) refers to the teaching authority of the church. Broadly speaking, the entire people of God participates in this authority through the sacrament of baptism in which persons share the threefold mission of Christ as prophet, priest, and king. In a more restricted sense, teaching authority belongs to the hierarchy, the bishops, and the pope. In the Middle Ages, Thomas Aquinas distinguished between the magisterium of the bishop and the magisterium of the theologian, who possessed a special competence by reason of study and teaching, either in the monastery or at the university. After the Reformation, the pastoral duty of preserving the unity of the faith was reserved to the pope and bishops.

The ordinary magisterium concerns the day-to-day teaching function of the pope and bishops. The pope's ordinary way of teaching is through encyclicals. Bishops exercise their teaching authority in pastoral letters, in synods, in declarations of Vatican congregations (with the approval of the pope), and in ecumenical councils.

Mary Ann Hinsdale

See also MAGISTERIUM, EXTRAORDINARY; MAGISTERIUM, MINISTRY OF THE.

MAHABHARATA

The *Mahabharata* is one of the two great Hindu epics, the other being the *Ramayana*. The longest poem in the world, the *Mahabharata* comprises nearly one hundred thousand Sanskrit verses. It was probably compiled between around 300 B.C.E. and 300 C.E., though the core story is thought to be much older. With many digressions that lead through all the complex byways of ancient Hindu mores and mythic lore, the *Mahabharata* tells the story of a great battle that consumed all of North India some four thousand years ago, according to tradition. The heroes of the story are the five Pandava brothers and their one wife, Draupadi. The villains are the Pandavas' cousins, the Kaurava brothers, who conspire to take the Pandavas' rightful kingdom from them. Krishna appears as a statesman who tries to prevent the inevitable catastrophe and as the charioteer of the great warrior Arjuna, one of the Pandavas. He also figures as Arjuna's teacher in the *Bhagavad Gita*, which forms a portion of the epic. At the end of the story, almost all the kings and princes of North India are dead, and Krishna himself dies. His departure ushers in the beginning of the present world-eon, the Kali Yuga, or Age of Darkness. This story is still tremendously popular in India, a recent television version drawing rapt audiences of millions.

Lance E. Nelson

See also ARJUNA; BHAGAVAD GITA; HINDUISM; KRISHNA; RAMAYANA; YUGA.

MAHARISHI MAHESH YOGI
See MAHESH YOGI, MAHARISHI.

MAHAVARA
See JAINISM.

MAHAVIRA
See JAINISM.

MAHAYANA BUDDHISM

The "Great Vehicle," one of the two separate streams of the Buddhist faith. In South Asia, where the earliest of its texts were composed, Mahayana adherents were a minority, with the possible exception of the northeast (Bengal and Bihar) in the Pala era (eighth–twelfth centuries). In Sri Lanka and Southeast Asia, the Mahayana existed alongside other schools until "reforms" of the last six hundred years or Islamic conversion (in the case of Insular S.E. Asia) ended support for the tradition. It was in northwest India and Central Asia where the Mahayana first gained strong community allegiance; from these sites via the Silk Route, monks brought the Great Vehicle's texts and teachings to China (by 200 c.e.). In China, the Mahayana became the dominant form of Buddhism and organized into numerous "schools" that saw the highest teaching in different texts. From China, Buddhism later spread to Korea, Japan, and Tibet. Tibetan Buddhism is also strongly Mahayana, although its contacts with Northern India and Nepal continued to admit additional later Indic Mahayana developments, including the Vajrayana or tantric forms of meditation and ritual. Tibetan missionaries later spread the faith to Mongolia and other steppe peoples.

The Mahayana distinguishes itself from the other form of Buddhism that it labels "Hinayana" ("Little Vehicle") by a starkly different cosmic vision and in its emphasis on the bodhisattva as a universal spiritual ideal. For this school, Buddhahood is the one true reality in the universe, having human, divine, and ultimate presence (the "*Trikaya* theory"); the cosmos is therefore defined by uncountable Buddha fields where the doctrine is taught by embodiments of the Dharma (Buddhas) and supramundane bodhisattvas ("future Buddhas"). Mahayana societies have been distinguished by temples and rituals established to venerate these figures (who number in the hundreds). Human disciples seek their compassionate assistance in mundane matters and as part of their enlightenment practices.

Another corollary to the Mahayana cosmological vision is that all beings and all material elements have the "Buddha nature or presence" (*Tathagatagarba*) and hence the capacity for enlightenment. The human ideal upheld by the Mahayana is the bodhisattva who acknowledges the interpenetration of all reality and sees his own salvation inseparable from that of all others, and so works selflessly for his own and all others' enlightenment.

There was also a strong philosophical lineage with the Mahayana (represented by Nagarjuna, Candrakirti, and the *Prajnaparamita* text writers) that argued strongly against the Hinayana schools' notions of phenomenal impermanence (especially the *dharma* theory in their *Abhidharmas*), interdependence, and nirvana by emphasizing the central teaching of *shunyata* ("emptiness" or "no-thingness") and the limitations of discursive theorizing. This position, developed by the Madhyamaka school, was extended further by philosophers of the Cittamatra school who argued, as their name indicates, that only consciousness is real and that meditative experience is the only true path to liberation.

The Mahayana coalesced in various major schools in northern and highland Asia. The most popular was that of "Pure Land Buddhism" in which disciples focused their karmic aspirations and ritual practices on reaching *Sukhavati*, the "Pure Land" of Amitabha Buddha (Chinese, *Amitofo*; Japanese, *Amida*) where enlightenment was eventually assured. The T'ien T'ai School that dominated in the early assimilation of the faith in China and Japan (where it is called Tendai) was centered upon the *Lotus Sutra*. This is one of the earliest and most dramatic Mahayana texts that reveal via parable and drama the true nature of the cosmos and the profundity of the teachings. Another school that focused upon meditation and strict monastic discipline is called the Ch'an in China and Zen in Japan.

A belief and practice that all schools encouraged was the repetition of *mantras* or *dharanis*, short strings of sounds revealed by enlightened beings that benefited individuals and their communities.

Although some scholars (and exponents) argue for it being a third school of Buddhism, the Vajrayana can be seen as a movement within the Mahayana. It emphasized these mantra recitations, visualization meditations on the celestial Buddhas and Bodhisattvas (including their fierce forms), and ritual practices including sexual union designed to eliminate attachment to mundane categories and experience.

Todd T. Lewis

See also AMITABHA/AMIDA;
AVALOKITESHVARA; CITTAMATRA;
DHARANI; DHARMADHATU;
DHARMAKAYA; MANJUSHRI;
NAGARJUNA; NORTHERN BUDDHISM;
PARAMITA; PRAJNAPARAMITA
LITERATURE; PURE LAND BUDDHISM;
SHANTIDEVA; SHUNYATA/SUNYA/
SHUNYA; SIDDHA; TANTRIC BUDDHISM;
TATHAGATAGARBHA DOCTRINE;
TRIKAYA (DOCTRINE OF).

MAHDI

Sometimes written *al-Mahdi*, this is an Arabic word that means "the one who is guided." According to Islamic belief, the *Mahdi* is a leader, or as some Muslims would say, a messianic figure, who will come right before the end of the world (the Day of Judgment) to establish a golden age of Islam. Within Islam, however, there is a wide variety of opinion about the nature and function of the Mahdi. Some say he will be a descendent of the Prophet Muhammad (570–632). Others believe that he will come before Jesus returns. Still others identify the Mahdi with Jesus at his second coming. Twelver Shi'ites call the Mahdi *al-Muntazar*, "the awaited one." They also refer to him as the Hidden Imam.

Ronald A. Pachence

See also DAY OF JUDGMENT (IN ISLAM);
IMAM (THE HIDDEN IMAM); ISLAM;
JESUS (AS PROPHET OF ISLAM); SHI'A/
SHI'I/SHI'ITE/SHI'ISM; TWELVERS (IN
ISLAM).

MAHEO

Maheo is the Creator God in the origin myth of the Cheyenne. In reference to the persistent discussion about the forms of divinity in primal religions, this symbol is a close approximation to the image at the heart of monotheism. Yet there is one interesting difference: the myth tells that Maheo draws some of his creatures into a final step of creation. This also means that, as the myth states, his power is limited. This dimension corresponds to suggestions in the history of Christianity, notably process theology in the present, that the concept of an omniscient God is vulnerable to critique, considering the counter-evidence. However, that debate is foreign to the ancient symbol of the Cheyenne, and so the meaning of this detail must lie elsewhere. It seems likely that Maheo's invitation relates to a recurring aspect of Native American religious traditions, that is, that all creation is interdependent. As Maheo's name indicates, he is the All-Father, and is always teaching his children.

Kathleen Dugan

MAHESH YOGI, MAHARISHI (1911–)

Maharishi Mahesh Yogi is the founder of the Hindu-based Transcendental Meditation movement. Also known as TM, Transcendental Meditation is a simple form of mantra meditation. Beginning in the mid-1960s, the Maharishi (Sanskrit, "Great Sage") offered it to the West as a purportedly religion-free technique of stress reduction and spiritual enhancement. Having gained fame as the guru of the Beatles and for his claim that twenty minutes of TM morning and evening could usher in world peace, the Maharishi more than anyone else has been responsible for making meditation a household word in the West. In recent years, however, his movement has turned inward, offering advanced instruction to its existing membership, but gaining few new followers.

Lance E. Nelson

See also GURU; HINDUISM; MANTRA; YOGA.

MAIMONIDES (1135–1204)

(Hebrew, Moses ben Maimon). An outstanding Jewish philosopher, rabbinic authority, and codifier of Jewish law. Born in Cordoba, Spain, Maimonides spent his most productive years in Cairo, where he served as a royal physician and where the Arabic cultural environment brought him into contact with classical Greek philosophy. Maimonides fused neo-Aristotelian thinking with the Jewish legal tradition to create a systemic whole. His main philosophic work, *The Guide for the Perplexed (Moreh Nevukim)*, is an apologetic appeal to rationalists troubled by the corporeality of God in the biblical accounts. Maimonides proposes a philosophical interpretation of the Bible that emphasizes abstract and spiritual meaning over literal interpretation. In the context of a commentary on the Mishnah, Maimonides formulated thirteen principles of faith that later Jews have accepted as representing the irreducible core of Judaism. Alongside his philosophical work, Maimonides is recognized for his Mishneh Torah ("Repetition of the Law"), also called the Yad ha Hazakah ("Mighty Hand," or "Mighty Fourteen"), in which he codified under fourteen topical divisions the law found in the Mishnah. This work, as well as his philosophical studies, were highly controversial in Maimonides' own day, and Maimonides himself became a central figure in the dispute between philosophical rationalists and conservative traditionalists. From shortly after his own day, however, Maimonides has been embraced as one of the greatest thinkers and legal scholars of Jewish history.

Alan J. Avery-Peck

See also MISHNEH TORAH.

MAITREYA

The next Buddha who will be born on earth. Consistent with the early belief that there is a Buddha for every age, and that Buddhas existed before Shakyamuni Buddha (560–480 B.C.E.), Buddhists have anticipated the coming of another enlightened one for at least 1500 years. *Maitreya* is regarded as inspiring individuals in meditation and through providing scholarly teachings and spiritual insights. He was also a patron of Buddhist missionaries.

Some texts state that the future Maitreya (Pali, *Metteyya*) currently resides as a bodhisattva in the Tushita heaven awaiting human birth. This realm, thought accessible to advanced Buddhist meditators, provided another avenue of contact between devotees and the great bodhisattva.

Maitreya's coming will reverse the decline in human spiritual capacity. Some modern Buddhists in Southeast Asia accept that their religious goal is only to find favorable human rebirth until Maitreya's appearance, when by hearing his discourses they will realize nirvana. In fat and happy images of Mi-lo Fo, Chinese brought their own figure of Maitreya, the future Buddha, into popular awareness.

Todd T. Lewis

See also BUDDHA; MAPPO; THERAVADA BUDDHISM.

MAJOR ARCHBISHOP

An archbishop who has all the prerogatives, duties, and responsibilities of a patriarch of an Eastern Catholic Church, except the title. There are currently two Eastern Catholic Churches led by major archbishops: the Ukrainian Church and the Malabar Church.

Orlando Espín

See also BISHOP (EPISCOPACY); DIOCESE/ ARCHDIOCESE; EASTERN CATHOLIC CHURCHES; MALABAR CATHOLIC CHURCH; ORTHODOX CHURCHES; PATRIARCH; UKRAINIAN CATHOLIC CHURCH.

MAKOTO

(Japanese, true sincerity). In Shinto belief, the divine nature or essence of *kami* found within humans. It is perceived as a state of the mind-heart (*kokuro*) where truth is lived and experienced intuitively and characterized by deep sincerity, purity, and emotional sensitivity. During the Shinto revival of the eighteenth century C.E., it was promoted as the ideal human state.

G. D. DeAngelis

See also KOKORO; MONO-NO-AWARE; NAKA IMA; SHINTO; YUGEN.

MALABAR CATHOLIC CHURCH

Descendants of the "Thomas Christians" of southwestern India, they trace their particular history to at least the fourth century. They had been Monophysites when in 1599 their church established full communion with Rome. A schism occurred later and a group broke away from Rome and formed the Mar Thoma Church. Most "Thomas Christians," however, are members of the Malabar Catholic Church that has some four million members under the overall jurisdiction of a major archbishop (who functions as a patriarch).

Orlando Espín

See also COMMUNION (ECCLESIOLOGICAL); EASTERN CATHOLIC CHURCHES; MAJOR ARCHBISHOP; MALANKARESE CATHOLIC CHURCH; MONOPHYSITISM; ROME, SEE OF; SCHISM; THOMAS CHRISTIANS.

MALANKARESE CATHOLIC CHURCH

A Catholic church in India, descendant of the "Thomas Christians." After establishing full communion with Rome in 1599, a group broke away (mostly because of Roman administrative and liturgical intransigence) and formed the Mar Thoma Church. But in 1930 a new schism occurred in this church that led some communities to reestablish communion with Rome. These communities are collectively known and recognized as the Malankarese Catholic Church.

Orlando Espín

See also COMMUNION (ECCLESIOLOGICAL); EASTERN CATHOLIC CHURCHES; MALABAR CATHOLIC CHURCH; ROME, SEE OF; SCHISM; THOMAS CHRISTIANS.

MALCOLM X (1925–65)

An eloquent and charismatic U.S. Black Muslim leader during the Civil Rights Movement from about 1956–65, whose spiritual quest and political activism for racial justice is chronicled in *The Autobiography of Malcolm X*, with Alex Haley. While imprisoned for burglary between 1946 and 1952, Malcolm converted to the Nation of Islam (NOI), an Islamic militant group that stressed both the recovery of the African American heritage through the practice of Islam and a religiously based black separatist nationalism. Upon release from jail in 1952, Malcolm met with Elijah Muhammad, the leader of the NOI, in Chicago and adopted the last name X, signifying the rejection of the effective history of slavery, the lack of an authentic African name, and the renunciation of his former ways of life: "Ex-smoker. Ex-drinker. Ex-Christian. Ex-slave." In 1958 he married Betty (Sanders) X (later Betty Shabazz, d. 1997); they had six daughters, with the last two daughters, a set of twins, born after he was assassinated on February 21, 1965, by three NOI members while giving a speech at the Audobon Ballroom in Harlem. The assassins allegedly worked for either Elijah Muhammad or Louis Farrakhan, the present NOI leader.

After his conversion, Malcolm quickly became a major NOI spokesperson, founding major mosques around the U.S. to forge a black religious nationalism, and was eventually appointed minister of the NOI's prominent Mosque no. 7 in Harlem, New York. He also campaigned for the NOI on the global stage by undertaking a major trip to Africa in 1959. Several debates within the NOI about Muhammad's sexual improprieties and about Malcolm's comments regarding the assassination of U.S. President John F. Kennedy (d. 1963) led to a very public break between Malcolm and Muhammad in 1964. The break allowed Malcolm the opportunity to form an alternative religious organization, Muslim Mosque, Inc., and to pursue a religious practice of orthodox Sunni Islam that included making the *hajj*, or the pilgrimage to Mecca, Saudi Arabia, required of all financially able and able-bodied Muslims. On a speaking tour subsequent to the pilgrimage, he received the name Omowale (Yoruba, "the son returns home") from a Muslim student group at the University of Ibadan, Nigeria.

In the struggles for African American civil rights, he advocated a black militant separatist nationalism, mainly on political and economic grounds, rather than on solely religious grounds of the NOI. His speeches stressed black pride, a self-love that led to potentially violent acts of self-defense, and a self-determination "by any means necessary," including a potentially violent revolution against an ideologically white racist society. After he returned from the pilgrimage to Mecca in 1964, Malcolm (now with the Muslim name *El-Hajj* Malik El-Shabazz) rejected black nationalism, embraced racial equality, and explicitly linked African American and African struggles to the construction of a universal brotherhood. In 1965 he established the Organization for Afro-American Unity to situate African American civil rights within the broader goal of global human rights.

The views of Malcolm X about racial justice "by any means necessary" contrasted sharply with black preacher and civil rights activist Martin Luther King Jr. (1929–68), who promoted racial reconciliation based on a Christian theological platform of justice, love, hope, redemptive suffering, and nonviolent direct mass action. In his speeches and writings collected in *I Have a Dream: Writings and*

Speeches That Changed the World, edited by James M. Washington (1992), King offered a sustained apologetic for nonviolent direct action against more militant black nationalist and black power groups, who, building on Malcolm's ideas, advocated potentially retaliatory measures of self-defense and of revolutionary riots to overthrow an intrinsically racist U.S. government and society. For King, the purpose of nonviolent direct action is to educate, that is to "dramatize" the racism of U.S. socioeconomic and political structures, to "arouse the conscience" of the society and of the churches, and thus to bring about radical social, political, and religious change. King rejected pure nonviolence, violence in the service of self-defense, or revolutionary violence, and instead articulated moral reasons for pursuing nonviolent mass action. Nonviolent mass action protected and advanced the well-being of the African American community, not just the individual; it also coincided with rather than contradicted the religious and moral commitments of the Civil Rights Movement itself.

However, as argued by black theologian James Cone in his landmark study, *Martin, Malcolm, and America* (1991), Malcolm and Martin gradually converged in their views, especially about a universal brotherhood and notions of power. For example, rather than define power as political dominance, King proposed that nonviolent action carried moral rather than political power. Moral power is expressed in marches, boycotts, and social organizations (political, economic, workers, interest groups). It is expressed creatively in boycotts, sit-in and sit-down demonstrations, strikes, mass meetings, marches, and the like. King situated this moral power among the "powerful weapons" of mass action. Later in his life and writings, King, more similar to Malcolm, defined power in social terms, especially as a "social force" rooted in African American solidarity and in building interracial coalitions or what he called "alliance politics." Building coalitions among minority and majority groups was absolutely central to achieving social and political rights as well as to building the beloved community. Beyond moral power, African Americans in King's view wielded other kinds of power, namely, ideological power to redefine democracy, economic power to unionize, boycott, and strike on behalf of workers' rights, and political power to vote and to mobilize community-based organizations. In one of his later writings, titled "Where Do We Go From Here?" (1967), King, similar to Malcolm, pointed out that, in terms of politics, the self-worth of blacks must be proclaimed, and only secondarily protected by politics, and that, in terms of power, the definition of power should demonstrate "the ability to achieve purpose . . . to bring about social, political, and economic change" for African Americans and for all people living under the triple oppressions of racism, poverty, and war. Both Martin and Malcolm gradually developed a similar agenda that would interpret African American struggles for racial justice in the context of larger global structures of poverty, globalization, and in King's case, militarism.

Rosemary P. Carbine

See also KING, MARTIN LUTHER, JR.; NATION OF ISLAM.

MALDONADO, JUAN (1533–83)

Spanish Catholic theologian, biblical scholar, and member of the Society of Jesus

(Jesuits). He was educated at Salamanca, and in 1564 became a professor at the Jesuit college in Paris. He was arguably the best interpreter of the Bible in France in the early stages of the Reformation there, and did much to rescue Catholic biblical scholarship from sterility. His best work is the two-volume *Commentaries on the Gospels* (1596–7) published after his death.

Orlando Espín

See also COUNTER-REFORMATION/ CATHOLIC REFORMATION; HUMANISM; REFORMATION; SOCIETY OF JESUS.

MALIKITE

Also known as Maliki, one of the four recognized schools of Sunni Islamic law. Named for its founder, Malik ibn Anas, who lived in Medina Arabia from 716 to 795, this approach to jurisprudence is based largely on the *hadiths* (traditions) of the Prophet Muhammad (570–632). In fact, Malik established legal precedent at this early stage of Islamic history by publishing one of the earliest collections of hadiths in a book called *al-Muwatta* (*The Beaten Path*). This "traditionalist" approach to the law distinguishes Maliki teaching from other schools, which rely more on the judicial principles of consensus and scholarly opinion. The Maliki School is popular today in southern Egypt and northern Africa.

Ronald A. Pachence

See also FIQH; HADITH; HANAFITE; IJMA; SHARIA/SHARI'A; SUNNA/ SUNNI/SUNNISM.

MANA

A term that refers to a (supernatural) impersonal force or power that is believed to be pervasive (throughout the cosmos, for example) or to exist within all things (or sometimes only within living things). The word *mana* is of Polynesian origin, and it entered modern anthropology as a way of naming the belief, widespread among many religions and cultures (including Polynesian religions and cultures), that all that is, or all that lives, has a (supernatural) power or force within. It is in some important ways similar to (but not identical with) the notion of *ashé* found in Santería Lukumí and in Candomblé.

Orlando Espín

See also CANDOMBLÉ; SANTERÍA.

MANDAENISM

A small Christian sect defined by ethnic descent traced to John the Baptist with apparent early connections to Gnostic Christianity. The Mandeans claim to have settled in settlements in the upper Tigris-Euphrates River Valley after the fall of the Jerusalem Temple in 70 C.E. and endured into the modern period in Iraq and Iran. Their belief in salvation is inflected with Gnostic terminology, that is, that the spiritual soul is imprisoned in the evil material world and that life itself entails a struggle between the forces of dark and light. Mandeans find the final salvation of each soul only possible through the intervention of the future savior, Manda d'Hayye, from which the sect derives its name.

Todd T. Lewis

MANDALA

A Sanskrit term literally meaning "circle" used in all Indic religions to indicate complex geometric diagrams for organizing sacred space in temple design, ritual performance, and meditation. The origins of the *mandala* derive from the Vedic sacrifice, where exacting standards for the placement of deities and ritualists had to be insured. For the construction of Hindu temples, a square *vatsumandala* was commonly used to design the plan and placement of deities. Another temple form is the directional *padmamandala*, that has nine (*nava*) squares with lotuses (*padma*) at the center and that serve as the homes of all the gods. In Jainism as well as Mahayana Buddhism, every divinity has its own mandala form to depict its ideal celestial abode.

Mandalas were used in tantric initiations in which a blindfolded initiate is led by the teacher to throw a flower upon a mandala, its landing point indicating the appropriate divinities for meditation. In tantric Hinduism and Buddhism, mandalas developed as mnemonic devices to aid the meditator in constructing via visualization three-dimensional spaces in which the yogin located, worshiped, and identified with a deity and his or her retinue. One form of mandala, a *yantra*, is a simple geometric design used for concentrating on the spiritual essence of a deity or deities.

Todd T. Lewis

See also SHUNYATA/SUNYA/SHUNYA; TANTRIC BUDDHISM; TANTRIC HINDUISM; VEDANTA; YOGA.

MANDATE OF HEAVEN

See T'IEN MING.

MANICHAEISM

Manes (born 216, died 274 or 277), the founder of Manichaeism, was the son of a Persian prince and a Judeo-Christian mother. At an earlier age, Manes felt called by the Spirit and at the age of twenty-four proclaimed himself an apostle of salvation. At first, Manes was supported by the Persian court and traveled extensively studying other beliefs, including Buddhism, and also expounding his own religion. A change in government led to his torture and death, by which time Manichaeism was already spreading rapidly throughout the Roman Empire. Manichees teach that there is a radical dualism in the world. All matter is evil, and all spirit is good. The purpose of life is to remove the spiritual part of ourselves (the Light) from the matter (the Darkness) in which it is trapped. The Manichees were divided into two groups, the Elect and the Hearers. The Elect followed an ascetic regime, while the Hearers gained merit through prayer and almsgiving. Eventually the effects of creation (a great cosmic mistake) would be reversed, and all spirit would be finally separated from matter. Manichaeism was very popular in the fourth century, including such noted converts as Augustine. It continued in China until the thirteenth century. The similarities between Manichaeism and the Cathars of medieval Europe caused contemporaries to identify the two religions, although scholars have yet to find a firm historical link between the two groups.

Gary Macy

See also AUGUSTINE OF HIPPO; BUDDHISM; CATHARS; DUALISM/DUALISTIC.

MANITOS

The *manitos* are the spiritual sources of Ojibwe life. They were seen as constituting the web of power that connects all things and gives energy and vitality. As such, they were essential allies in the struggle of a hunting people to survive, often through harsh winters that caused famine. Though spirits, they are recognizable as living persons, and they are approached as such in ritual. Their form as persons links them with humans in that they share desires and movements of will. Thus they are not always benevolent. Yet they are strikingly different by virtue of the incomparable power they possess.

Their power places them at the center of Ojibwe religion, where they are acknowledged and propitiated in sincere humility. One among them, the culture hero Nanabozho, serves as the exemplar of their life. Others fill more specific functions. Turtle, for example, is the bringer of knowledge in the Shaking Tent ceremony, and the Great Owl drives the game to hunters. Perhaps their most important role is to serve individual Ojibwe as a guardian. The vision quest held at puberty sought that gift, and if successful, won for the person a richly blessed life.

Kathleen Dugan

See also GUARDIAN SPIRIT; INITIATION (NON-CHRISTIAN).

MANJUSHRI

A most advanced celestial bodhisattva who is the embodiment of insight or wisdom (*prajna*). In Buddhist texts and art, Manjushri is depicted as a youthful crowned prince who is ever wise in discerning reality and in expressing it aptly. It is in the *Vimalakirtinirdesha Sutra* where he most famously discusses emptiness in terms of the Madhyamaka school's understanding.

Depicted holding a text signifying wisdom and a sword symbolic of his prajna cutting through delusion, Manjushri is the bodhisattva most often associated with scholars. He is often invoked as a source of inspired guidance by Buddhist monks such as the Ch'an monk Hsu-yun or the Tibetan sage Tsong-kha-pa. Manjushri is also identified with geographic centers of Buddhism: early in Chinese Buddhist history, he was thought to dwell on Mt. Wu T'ai, and by 800 C.E., Buddhists across Asia, including India, went on pilgrimage there in search of a vision of him. Newar Buddhists of Nepal identify Manjushri as the divine teacher who drained the former lake to create their land in the Katmandu Valley and taught their ancestors agriculture and the arts of civilization.

Todd T. Lewis

See also BODHISATTVA; MADHYAMAKA/ MADHYAMIKA SCHOOL; MAHAYANA BUDDHISM; PRAJNA; VIMALAKIRTI.

MANNA

(Hebrew, *man*; Greek, *man/manna*). The sweet, bread-like substance given to the Israelites as recorded in the book of Exodus during their wanderings in the wilderness. The manna is first mentioned in Exodus 16, before the Israelites reach Sinai/Horeb, and was given daily, except Sabbaths, until they entered the land and ate the first produce of the land (Joshua 5:11-12). Manna is mentioned primarily in connection with the wandering of the Israelites in the wilderness. It is not mentioned in connection with the Sinai traditions.

Russell Fuller

MANNHEIM, KARL (1893–1947)

Hungarian sociologist. Mannheim studied and taught in Germany, but after the Nazi takeover he moved to England. His work focused mainly on what is now called the "sociology of knowledge." Mannheim showed how human thought and thought processes are deeply conditioned by social class. He came to the conclusion that all thought was "ideological," and consequently that there could be no such thing as "objective" thought. His key work is *Ideology and Utopia* (1929).

Orlando Espín

See also CLASSISM; CULTURE; EPISTE-MOLOGY; ETHICS, SOCIAL; IDEOLOGY (IDEOLOGIES).

MANTRA

A *mantra* is a sacred verbal formula that is repeated as a focus for meditation or as part of a ritual in the Indic religious traditions, including Hinduism and Tantric Buddhism. Mantras are usually in Sanskrit or composed of a more or less meaningless combination of Sanskritic phonemes. Even if they have a meaning, the syllables of a mantra are typically more important for their acoustic (sometimes called "mantric") quality, rather than their semantic value. The sound of the mantra is said to embody, in vibrational form, the very essence of the deity to which the mantra is addressed. Its chanting or silent repetition, therefore, brings the mind into direct contact with the power of the deity, thus purifying it and preparing it for mystical experience. To be most efficacious, it is believed, mantras should be imparted personally to a receptive disciple by an enlightened guru. The most famous of these formulas are the sacred syllable *om* and the Hare Krishna mantra. Others are the Shaiva mantra, *om namah shivaya* (Om, homage to Shiva), and the Buddhist mantra, *om mani padme hum* (Om, the jewel is in the lotus), the latter evoking the Bodhisattva Avalokiteshvara. The hymns of the *Rig Veda* are also referred to as mantras.

Lance E. Nelson

See also HINDUISM; JAPA; MANTRA; OM; TANTRA; TANTRIC BUDDHISM.

MANU, LAWS OF
See MANU SMRITI.

MANU SMRITI
The *Manu Smriti* (Laws of Manu), also known as the *Manava Dharma Shastra* (Manu's Treatise on Dharma), is perhaps the most important of the Hindu Law Books. As its title indicates, the subject of this text is *dharma*, a term that encompasses the range of the English words *law, ethics, custom, social obligations*, and *religious duty*. The *Manu Smriti*, then, is concerned with the ideals of proper behavior in classical Hindu society on all levels. In addition to the principles of civil and criminal law and the punishment of crimes, this encyclopedic work describes the duties of kings, the four great caste categories (*varnas*) that are the basis of the caste system, and the four stages of life (*ashramas*). Other topics covered include rules of diet and hospitality, the rites of marriage, issues of religious pollution and purification, and the mutual obligations of husbands and wives, parents and children, students and teachers. The author sets his prescriptions within their wider religious context, speaking authoritatively for the tradition not only on legal matters, but on such theological issues as the creation of the world, the doctrine of karma, and the punishments that await evildoers in the various hells. The Manu to whom this text is attributed is, in fact, a mythic being, the primordial ancestor of the human family. The *Manu Smriti* as we have it was probably composed between 200 B.C.E. and 200 C.E.

Lance E. Nelson

See also ASHRAMA (LIFE STAGES); CASTE; DHARMA (IN HINDUISM); HINDUISM; KARMA.

MANUALS, THEOLOGY OF THE

During the period that followed the Council of Trent (after 1563), there developed a need for handbooks or textbooks (the "manuals") that would give sufficient and adequate theological education to students in the newly established seminaries. The majority of seminary students did not need (and would find little use for) the more elaborate theological literature required by university theology students and professors. As Catholic theology came to be more centered on seminaries and, consequently, on the needs of seminary students preparing for the priesthood, the quest for more of these manuals increased, and more theologians produced these volumes to assist professors in the theological education of seminarians. This became clearly evident during the second half of the nineteenth century and the first half of the twentieth. There always remained university faculties of theology, of course, but at the time most theological production came to revolve around seminaries, reflecting the concerns of the clergy and of its pastoral roles in the church. It was not until the second half of the twentieth century, and especially with and after the Second Vatican Council (ended in 1965), that theology and most theologians moved back to university settings (although seminaries remain).

The manuals of theology had developed a way of presenting issues and conclusions, and of arguing topics, that was deductive, often in an argumentative form inspired on (but not identical with) the medieval Scholastic method. The theology of the manuals sought accuracy and precision in formulation and in argumentation (sometimes with great sophistication), believing that a theological discipline could be thoroughly discussed in a single textbook. The nineteenth-century reinterpretation of medieval Scholasticism became the frequent philosophical underpinning for the theology of the textbooks, providing them with terms and definitions. But the manuals gave insufficient and often inadequate consideration to historical contexts and developments in doctrine, spirituality, and church life, and paid little attention to cultural and social concerns and contexts needed to understand any theological or doctrinal construct. The terminology and concepts employed in the manuals no longer reflected the pastoral and cultural world in which most seminary candidates would serve as priests. Therefore, the manuals, originally intended to be useful tools in the education of future priests, in time came to be regarded by many as an obstacle to that goal. Today it is very difficult to find, even in seminaries, manuals that would pretend to exhaust a theological discipline in a single textbook or argue theologically without regard to culture or society.

Orlando Espín

See also CULTURE; DOGMATIC THEOLOGY; SCHOLASTICISM.

MANUSCRIPT

A manuscript is any document written by hand. Since this was the most common way of preserving writing before the invention of printing, the oldest copies of most works of religious literature produced before printing exist in manuscripts. Since before the invention of printing, manuscript books and scrolls could only be reproduced painstakingly by hand, and preservation of documents was an expensive and time-consuming undertaking. Because of this, few copies were made, and if these manuscripts were destroyed, the texts they contained were lost forever. When scholars want to read the earliest versions of most ancient texts, they have to consult these precious early handwritten copies.

Gary Macy

MAPPO

Japanese term (Chinese, *ma-fo*) for a declining spiritual state of the Buddhist teachings in the world, often translated as "Latter-Day *Dharma*." Most early Buddhist schools report predictions made by Shakyamuni that the tradition would decline over time, until the coming of the next Buddha Maitreya. This idea was doubtless influenced by the Indic notion of cyclical world eras (*yugas*) and the current millennia being in the lowest phase (*kali yuga*). By 300 C.E., there were further interpretations, and up to the present era disputations as to the exact reckoning of this period and its implications for the nature of practice continue into the present day. Pure Land School followers, the Japanese teacher Nichiren, and tantric exponents found in the Mappo doctrine legitimating rationale for their admittedly innovative approaches. Modern Theravadins have also explained the dearth of Arhants as due to the decline of the faith, a point modernists often contest. The Ch'an/Zen tradition, however, rejected the doctrine of Mappo.

Todd T. Lewis

See also BUDDHISM; NICHIREN; PURE LAND BUDDHISM; ZEN.

MARA

"The Evil One," a supernatural being thought to deter the Buddha and his disciples in their efforts to lead a spiritual life. In Shakyamuni biography, it is Mara who tries to obstruct Buddhism's success; for example, he discourages Gautama's final efforts toward nirvana realization and seeks to tempt the Buddha with lust for his sensuous "daughters" and with fear for his armed hordes. Mara then discourages Shakyamuni to preach to humanity.

In early Buddhism, when monks and nuns were blocked in their practice, this is often blamed on Mara's evil influences. Mara is described in the Pali Canon as the dominating force in the *kamadhatu*, the "realm of desire"; in the Abhidharma, he is said to stand for everything that abides bound by the "three characteristics of existence": suffering, impermanence, nonsoul.

Todd T. Lewis

See also BUDDHA; DEMON (IN WORLD RELIGIONS).

MARCEL, GABRIEL (1869–1973)

French existentialist philosopher. Educated in Paris, Marcel was a journalist, university professor, and playwright. He converted to Roman Catholicism and thereafter attempted to find a way for a "believing" existentialism, although he often claimed that he was not an existentialist (given the atheistic convictions of many existentialists at the time). Marcel often preferred to be called "neo-Socratic." His reflections centered on the deeper distinctions between human life as mystery and/or as problem, and between being and having. He also discussed some fundamental human attitudes like creativity, hope, commitment, and availability. Marcel influenced a generation of Catholic theologians and philosophers in France and in the United States. Some of his best books are *Being and Having* (1935), and the two-volume *The Mystery of Being* (1950–1).

Orlando Espín

See also EXISTENTIALISM; HOPE (IN CHRISTIANITY); MYSTERY; PERSONALISM;

RICOEUR, PAUL; THEOLOGICAL ANTHROPOLOGY.

MARCELLA (?–410)

A Christian Roman noblewomen, Marcella lost her husband after only six months of marriage and refused to ever marry again. When Athanasius visited Rome while in exile from Alexandria, Marcella learned from him of the monks of Egypt. Influenced by their example and joined by her own mother and other noblewomen, she established a monastery of her own on the Aventine Hill in Rome. During his stay in Rome, Jerome became the spiritual consultant of the group, and it is from Jerome's letters that our knowledge of Marcella's life comes. Jerome, among others, recognized and appreciated Marcella's own learning, especially her expertise in scriptural studies. When the Goths sacked Rome in 410, Marcella was tortured by the invaders and died a few days later.

Gary Macy

See also ATHANASIUS, PATRIARCH OF ALEXANDRIA; JEROME; MONASTICISM IN WESTERN CHRISTIANITY.

MARCELLINUS OF ROME (?–304/5)

Little is known for certain about Marcellinus except that he was Bishop of Rome from 296 until his death in 304/5. In the fourth century, the Donatists charged Marcellinus with handing over the sacred books to the Roman government during the persecution of Diocletian. This was denied by Augustine, but by the fifth century Marcellinus was believed to have weakened during the persecution but to have later confessed and, as Pope, condemned himself. This story was later used to establish the principle that the

Pope can be judged by no one except himself.

Gary Macy

See also AUGUSTINE OF HIPPO; DIOCLETIAN; DONATISM; PERSECUTION (IN CHRISTIANITY); POPE.

MARCELLUS I OF ROME (?–309)

Marcellus was Bishop of Rome for one year, from 308 to 309. After the Diocletian persecution, the Roman church was torn by the dispute concerning the fate of the *lapsi*, those who had given up the faith during the persecution, but who wished now to repent and rejoin the church. For four years after the death of Marcellinus, the Roman church was unable to decide upon a successor. Marcellus was finally chosen and quickly moved to organize the chaotic Roman community. When fighting broke out over the question of the *lapsi*, however, Marcellus was banished by the Emperor Maxentius and Marcellus soon died in exile.

Gary Macy

See also DIOCLETIAN; DONATISM; LAPSED; PERSECUTION (IN CHRISTIANITY); POPE.

MARCELLUS OF ANCYRA (?–375?)

One of the staunchest opponents of Arius, Marcellus was bishop of Ancyra when he attended the Council of Nicaea in 325. Marcellus was deposed by Constantine in 336 and joined Athanasius in Rome when he was unable to return to his see upon the death of Constantine in 338. Accused of Sabellianism by the Eastern bishops, Marcellus appealed to the Roman church that found him orthodox. Condemned on numerous occasions by the Eastern church, Rome and Athanasius continued to defend him against charges of heresy. When one of Marcellus's students, Photinus, pushed his doctrine to its extremes, the West, too, began to withdraw support from Marcellus, although he himself was not condemned. Only fragments of Marcellus's anti-Arian writing remain, as well as a tract *On the Holy Church*.

Gary Macy

See also ARIANISM; ARIUS; ATHANASIUS, PATRIARCH OF ALEXANDRIA; SABELLIANISM/SABELLIUS.

MARCIONISM

Marcion of Pontus was a second-century theologian and exegete who argued that the God portrayed in the Old Testament cannot be the same as the God proclaimed by Jesus. Marcion constrasted the cruelty, jealousy, and harsh justice of the God of the Old Testament with the God of pure mercy proclaimed by Jesus. Based on this understanding of Scripture, Marcion posited that the God of the Old Testament was the Creator God, but inferior and different from the God of mercy proclaimed by Jesus. The God of Jesus, acting out of pure mercy, sent the spirit Jesus to save those creatures of the Old Testament God who would believe in him. These believers would then live without fear of punishment for sin; a life which in turn would automatically be virtuous in thanksgiving to God for such a great gift. To support this theology, Marcion created his own canon of Scripture, the first in Christian history. He rejected all the Old Testament, and accepted only Paul and Luke as genuine, but even these he modified by deleting certain passages. Marcion believed that the original teachings of Jesus had been modified and corrupted by the followers of the Old Testament God, and that this tampering was

apparent in Christian Scripture as it then existed. Marcionism is Docetic, and rejects the resurrection of the body. Marcionists do not believe in procreation, since this would further the work of the Creator God. While not, strictly speaking, Gnostics, the Marcionists do have some teachings in common and may have had contacts with Gnostic groups.

Gary Macy

See also DOCETISM; GNOSIS/GNOSTICISM; HERESY; MARCION OF PONTUS; NEW TESTAMENT CANON.

MARCION OF PONTUS (?–160?)

All we know about this second-century teacher comes from writers antagonistic to him. According to these sources, he became rich as a ship builder in the city of Sinope, then moved to Rome where he donated a great deal of money to the Roman church. In 144 he was expelled from the church and his donations were returned. Marcion then founded his own church that spread rapidly. Although Marcion died around 160, the church he founded persisted in the West until the end of the third century, and in the East until the middle of the fifth century.

Gary Macy

See also HERESY; MARCIONISM.

MARÉCHAL, JOSEPH (1878–44)

Belgian Jesuit, a founder of Transcendental Thomism. Maréchal sought to demonstrate the modernity of St. Thomas's thought by demonstrating the validity of ontological epistemology in opposition to Kant's critique of metaphysics. Against the Kantian analysis restricting objective thought to phenomena, Maréchal proposed human intellection to perceive objects through a dynamic intuition of a greater horizon of being which horizon was the condition for every objective judgment. Proposing this analysis as Thomas's own epistemology, Maréchal argued for the validity of metaphysics and the possibility of the natural knowledge of God, albeit in the mode of the ontological argument. Maréchal's studies in his five-volume work *Le point de départ de la métaphysique* (1944–9) spurred the dynamic approach to Thomist philosophy found in the works of Karl Rahner and Bernard Lonergan. He is known also for his interest in mysticism, discussed in his work *Studies in the Psychology of the Mystics* (1927).

Patricia Plovanich

See also LONERGAN, BERNARD; RAHNER, KARL; THOMISM/TRANSCENDENTAL THOMISM.

MARGA

A Sanskrit term meaning "way" or "road," *marga* is used in Hinduism to designate the various spiritual paths thought to be suitable to different personality types. There are four classically recognized margas, which are in fact the same as the four yogas, namely, those of knowledge, psychophysical discipline, action, and devotion (*jnana, raja, karma, bhakti*).

Lance E. Nelson

See also BHAKTI-YOGA; KARMA-YOGA; RAJA-YOGA; YOGA.

MARIANA, JUAN DE (1536–1623)

Spanish theologian and member of the Society of Jesus (Jesuits). After becoming a Jesuit in 1554, Mariana taught at universities in Rome, Paris, and Toledo. He is well known for his important histories of Spain, but is best remembered for his book *De rege et regis institutione* (1559) in which he morally justified the killing of cruel and unfair rulers. This book, and his fellow Jesuits, were subsequently blamed for the assassination of King Henry IV of France, and for attempts on the lives of other European kings and princes. The Jesuit superiors emphatically (and correctly) denied any connection between the order and Mariana's teaching.

Orlando Espín

See also ETHICS, SOCIAL; JUSTICE; SOCIETY OF JESUS.

MARIAN DEVOTIONS

Devotion to Mary, the mother of Jesus of Nazareth, is frequent in the Catholic and Orthodox churches, as well as among many Anglicans.

Marian devotions, and their claims and external symbols, must not be confused with the churches' official doctrines about Mary. Sometimes devotional practices fundamentally coincide with these doctrines or flow from them, but historically there have also been devotional exaggerations that cannot be interpreted as being part of Catholic and/or Orthodox official belief.

The admiration for Mary, as her son's first disciple and as symbol of the church, is very ancient in Christianity. This admiration, added to her evident role as the mother of the Redeemer, are the root of legitimate Christian Marian devotion. The development of Marian doctrines contributed to enhance the legitimacy of devotion. Marian devotion, especially after the Second Vatican Council (1962–5), views her as model of Christian discipleship and community, and as instrument for the empowerment of the poor.

Since at least the third century there were prayers directed to Mary, asking for her intercession with God. Devotion to her among Christians was widespread by the time of the Council of Ephesus (431 C.E.) and its teaching that Mary was indeed the *Theotokos* (the "Mother of God"). It seems that popular Marian devotion was a significant element in this council's doctrinal discussions. After Ephesus there was an extraordinary increase in references to Mary in the church's official liturgy and in popular prayers. In Western Christianity, the devotion to Mary spread through the liturgy. The feast of the Assumption of Mary (the "Dormition," as it is called in Eastern Christianity), although not defined as official Catholic doctrine until 1950, was by far the most popular Marian liturgical celebration during much of the Catholic Church's history. This liturgical feast developed from an earlier, more general celebration of Mary during the Christmas season.

During the Middle Ages there was a significant increase in Marian pious practices after the eleventh century, with claims of miracles and apparitions increasing as well. There had been references to apparitions of Mary since the third century, but the second half of the Middle Ages saw the growth in the number of such claims. Miracles attributed to Mary, or miraculous discoveries of her images, seemed to abound after the eleventh century. Arguably, a number of sociocultural, and even economic reasons played an important role in this development. Religious reasons alone do not seem sufficient explanation, although these too played their part, as well as credulity and insufficient catechesis. Exaggerated claims, fabulous stories, and impossible miracles were common enough during this historical period. Although the sixteenth-century Protestant Reformers opposed all forms of Marian devotions, the Council of Trent managed to begin the process of purification of Marian piety that was very much needed at the time. Although it took longer than most council participants expected, Marian devotional practices were "cleaned up" in most places, and the exaggerated claims contained. But at the popular level, many fabulous stories and expectations continued until the present century.

During the period that immediately preceded the Catholic and Protestant Reformations, and paralleling them, European Catholics discovered and conquered the Americas. With and after the conquest came the missionaries, and with them the usual Marian devotions from Europe. Which specific practices came to this side of the Atlantic often depended on the origins (which home village, or region) of the missionaries and colonizers. However, the most important Marian devotions in the Americas began here: *Guadalupe* in Mexico, *Caridad* in Cuba, and so on. It is well documented that Mary became quite popular and well accepted among the native populations and the African slaves during the centuries of Spanish and Portuguese rule. It is also clear that Marian devotional practices were instrumental in expanding colonial Christianity in the Americas. These devotions are still popular in Latin America and among U.S. Latinos, and have become increasingly important to serious theological reflection on the *sensus fidelium*, on tradition, and on the poor's image of themselves and of God. Mary has become a symbol and instrument of empowerment for the poor in many places of Latin America and among U.S. Latinos. Indeed, in many contexts Mary is deeply tied to issues of cultural identity and dignity.

Although Marian piety and symbols have also been used and abused by both church authorities and governments with serious alienating results, Mary does not seem to have lost a certain subversive character and role among the poor or disenfranchised. She has been and is, for the poor, a bearer of their culture and identity. Marian devotion is still helping the expansion of contemporary Catholicism. Modern Latin American and U.S. Latino Protestant denominations remain opposed to most forms of Marian piety, although a few of these churches have begun to question if there might not be some value in a qualified devotion.

Claims of apparitions have continued in Catholic contexts throughout the world. Among the more recent ones are those that have centered on events at Fatima (in Portugal), Lourdes (in France), La Salette (also in France), and Medjugorje (in Croatia). However, apparitions or claims of apparitions occur in all continents. They have never been (and could never be) understood in Catholicism as necessary. There is no obligation to believe in apparitions, even when church authorities may have accepted the resulting devotional practices.

When Catholics refer to devotional Marian titles or names ("Our Lady of . . ."), they are usually referring to devotions established either because of a claimed apparition or miracle (Fatima, Guadalupe), or because of a certain Christian virtue that Mary is said to exemplify (charity, mercy), or because of a specific devotional practice (for example, the rosary).

Orlando Espín

See also APPARITIONS; ASSUMPTION OF MARY; DEVOTIONS; EPHESUS, COUNCIL OF; GUADALUPE, VIRGIN OF; HYPERDULIA; IMMACULATE HEART OF MARY; LUMEN GENTIUM; MARIOLOGY; MARY OF NAZARETH; MOTHER OF GOD/ THEOTOKOS; ROSARY; SAINTS (CHRISTIAN), DEVOTION TO; SENSUS FIDELIUM/ SENSUS FIDEI; TRADITION (IN CHRISTIANITY); VIRGIN BIRTH; VIRGINITY OF MARY.

MARIÁTEGUI, JOSÉ CARLOS (1894–1930)

Peruvian journalist and social scientist Mariátegui is best known as a socialist essayist. From 1919 to 1923 he lived in Europe where he was deeply influenced by Marxism and organized a Peruvian communist group in Rome. However, back in Peru he modified his views and worked for what he called an "Ibero-Indian-American socialism." In Lima he edited the radical journal *Amauta* and in 1928 published his most influential work, *Seven Essays on the Interpretation of Peruvian Reality*. In his essay on the religious factor in Peruvian history he demonstrated his appreciation of popular religion's revolutionary potential. His work profoundly influenced the thought of Peruvian theologian Gustavo Gutiérrez.

James B. Nickoloff

See also GUTIÉRREZ, GUSTAVO; LATIN AMERICAN THEOLOGIES; LIBERATION THEOLOGIES; MARX, KARL; MARXISM; SOCIALISM.

MARIOLOGY

The theological discipline that systematically studies the Christian doctrines referring to Mary, the mother of Jesus of Nazareth. It is important to keep in mind that *devotional* claims about Mary are *not* frequently paralleled by, or are necessary to, *doctrinal*, *dogmatic* statements on Mary. Doctrines about Mary can be ultimately traced back to specific theological, dogmatic needs to defend or clarify doctrines about Christ or the church.

Mary is important in the Catholic and Orthodox (and perhaps in the Anglican) theological traditions because she is the mother of Jesus the Christ. In other words, it is Christ (and Christ alone) who gives Mary a place in Christian doctrine and devotion. Marian doctrines never claim for her a role in salvation like Christ's. Mary is indeed the mother of the Redeemer, and the most eminent of the saints, but she is only a human creature of God and not equal to her son. Then how has she become so theologically important in the history of Christianity?

The New Testament mentions Mary in the infancy narratives of the Gospels of Matthew and Luke, as well as in a few other Synoptic (Matthew, Mark, Luke) narratives of Jesus' ministry. She is again mentioned in John's account of the wedding at Cana, and in the passion story. According to Acts, she was present at Pentecost. The book of Revelation's reference to a woman surrounded by stars does not really refer to Mary, although later Christian devotional writers might have thought so.

The earliest Christian references to Mary, after the New Testament, tended to contrast her to Eve (for example, Justin Martyr, before 165 C.E.). The apocryphal Book of James, written sometime before 150 C.E., is the first source to mention Mary's perpetual virginity; but this teaching was also proposed by Irenaeus of Lyons (d. 202). This doctrine was increasingly accepted by the early theologians, and it became standard Christian belief certainly by the fifth century. The Ecumenical Council of Ephesus (431) declared that Mary was, and can be legitimately called, the *Theotokos* ("God-bearer," "Mother of God").

In Western Christianity, the devotion to and doctrines about Mary developed more slowly than in Eastern Christianity, but the beliefs in her perpetual virginity and in her being the *Theotokos* were certainly accepted quite early, as in the East. In the West there was a particular emphasis on Mary as symbol of the church (for example, Ambrose of Milan). The doctrine of the Assumption (called "Dormition" in the East) was commonly believed from the fifth or sixth century. However, the teaching on Mary's immaculate conception did encounter resistance throughout most of the church's history.

As a consequence of the Catholic theological tradition's reflection on Mary, only these four doctrines are officially taught (as necessary) by the church: (1) her perpetual virginity; (2) that she is indeed the *Theotokos* ("Mother of God"); (3) her assumption to heaven; and (4) her immaculate conception.

The Second Vatican Council (1962–5) included its teaching on Mary within the constitution *Lumen Gentium* on the church, thereby following the earliest Western theological tradition. The Orthodox Churches believe about Mary what Catholics believe (even if the theological explanations and terms might occasionally differ); but the Orthodox have never made a decision on the dogmatic status of the doctrine of the "Dormition" (Assumption) of Mary. The only Catholic doctrine that the Orthodox do not share is the Immaculate Conception.

Sixteenth-century Protestant Reformers were strongly opposed to any devotion to Mary, and to what they perceived as Catholic glorification of her. They emphatically denied the Catholic–Orthodox doctrines on Mary. But Luther, for example, taught that she was a model of humility and faith. The Anglican Communion at first joined the Protestants in their rejection, but in the last century or so most Anglicans have rediscovered Mary doctrinally and devotionally. Even European Protestant theologians have begun to reflect on her.

Many contemporary Catholic theologians discuss Mary in ways that either follow the theological insights of the Second Vatican Council (for example, Mary as symbol of the Christian Church, and/or as the model disciple of her son, and the like), or in ways that attempt to thematize and interpret Mary's unique role in popular Catholicism. These two approaches have also been influenced by concerns raised by feminist theologies. There seems to be a growing ecumenical, scholarly interest in Mariology, but no longer focused on devotional justifications or on the exaggerated glorification of Mary. Some recent authors have also attempted to associate Mary to renewed trinitarian studies (especially on the Holy Spirit).

Orlando Espín

See also APPARITIONS; ASSUMPTION OF MARY; CATHOLIC TRADITION; EPHESUS, COUNCIL OF; HYPERDULIA; LUMEN GENTIUM; MARIAN DEVOTIONS; MARY OF NAZARETH; MOTHER OF GOD/ THEOTOKOS; SENSUS FIDELIUM/SENSUS FIDEI; TRADITION (IN CHRISTIANITY); VIRGIN BIRTH; VIRGINITY OF MARY.

MARITAIN, JACQUES (1882–1973)

French philosopher and Thomist. Maritain, a former student of Henri Bergson, embraced Catholicism (with Raissa, his wife) in 1906, then pursued the study of classical Thomism (the Cajetan School). His early preoccupation with the Enlightenment critique of faith (the possibility of knowledge of God) is found in several volumes on epistemology and metaphysics, including *The Degrees of Knowledge*. His interest in the application of Thomist

thought to other aspects of life (shared with Etienne Gilson), is found in his works on ethics, art, and culture, for instance, *Art and Scholasticism*. Maritain taught at the Institut Catholique in Paris, the Institute for Mediaeval Studies in Toronto, and at Princeton University in the U.S. He was visiting professor at Columbia University, the University of Chicago, and at Notre Dame. Maritain's writings gained a following in the popular neo-Thomist revival among mid-twentieth-century Catholic intellectuals. His autobiography, *The Peasant of the Garonne*, chronicles his life and expresses his concern about the Catholic Church after Vatican Council II.

Patricia Plovanich

See also BERGSON, HENRI; ENLIGHTENMENT IN WESTERN HISTORY; GILSON, ETIENNE; THOMISM/TRANSCENDENTAL THOMISM.

MARK/MARKAN

According to Papias of Hierapolis (early second century), as quoted in Eusebius, *Hist. eccl.* 3.39.15, "Mark, having become Peter's interpreter, wrote down accurately whatever he remembered of what was said or done by the Lord, however not in order." On this basis, the Gospel of Mark has traditionally been ascribed to John Mark who was Peter's coworker (1 Pet 5:13) and is held to have been written in Rome after Peter's death around 64–7.

Nothing in the text of the Gospel itself, however, identifies its author by name, and uncertainty exists. Rome, as the place of composition, is supported not only by the inference of Papias' statement, but also by various Latin loanwords used in the Greek text and a sense of impending persecution throughout the Gospel. Since the apocalyptic passage of Mark 13, with its heavy use of imagery from the Jewish

War (66–70), does not assume the destruction of the Temple in Jerusalem (70), the Gospel was probably written just before 70.

Structurally, the narrative of the Gospel moves geographically from Galilee to Jerusalem. Following the prologue (1:1-15), the first half of the text describes Jesus' activities in the region of Galilee (1:16–8:21). The second half centers on Jerusalem, describing first the journey from Galilee to Jerusalem (8:22–10:52), followed by the events of passion week in Jerusalem (11:1–16:8). Theologically, the Gospel text also reflects careful structuring. After Jesus is identified (1:1-15), his authority is revealed (1:16–3:6), only to be rejected by his own people (3:7–6:6a) and misunderstood by his followers (6:6b–8:21). On the journey to Jerusalem (8:22–10:52) Jesus teaches the true nature of his authority and what that entails for his followers. In Jerusalem his teaching is not accepted (11:1–13:37) and those who reject his authority put him to death (14:1–16:8).

The term *evangelion*, "gospel," was used prior to Mark's Gospel in the writings of Paul, where it denotes that "good news" of the kerygma Paul was preaching. It is Mark, however, who seems to have used the term first to refer to his literary genre of writing an orderly account of Jesus' life and mission, a genre other Gospel writers then adopted from him.

Markan theology is centered upon Jesus' announcement of the kingdom of God, as summarized in 1:15. Mark describes the teaching of Jesus, especially his parables, as preparing his followers for the kingdom; and his healing miracles anticipate how life will be in God's kingdom. For Mark, however, Jesus' teaching and miracles can only be understood against the backdrop of his passion and death. This relates to a striking feature of Markan christology, "the messianic secret," a phrase referring to those numerous instances in the Gospel where Jesus tells people not to speak about his actions or identity. Among the Gospel's complex reasons for portraying Jesus on occasion as commanding silence about himself, it is widely held that in Markan theology the full comprehension of Jesus as Messiah could become clear to his followers only with his death and resurrection.

F. M. Gillman

See also LUKE/LUKAN; MATTHEW/MATTHEAN; MESSIANIC SECRET (IN MARK); PARABLE; PETER; SYNOPTIC PROBLEM; TWO-SOURCE THEORY (OF SYNOPTICS).

MARKS OF THE CHURCH
See NOTES OF THE CHURCH.

MARONITE CATHOLIC CHURCH
The full title of the Maronite Church as it is used today is the Antiochene Syriac Maronite Church. It is called Antiochene because its leader holds the title of patriarch of Antioch and its liturgy borrows much from the Liturgy of St. James, originally of Jerusalem provenance, but adopted by the West Syrian liturgical tradition centered in Antioch. It is called Syriac because it uses the ancient language of Syriac (Aramaic) and also connects the rite with the East Syrian tradition of Edessa (later known as Nestorian/Chaldean) through use of Edessan hymns and prayers, especially those of St. Ephrem the Syrian, of eucharistic prayers of East Syrian origin, especially *Sharar*, that shows strong influence from the anaphora of Addai and Mari, and other structural elements of the liturgy. The East Syrian tradition also uses the Syriac language

liturgically as opposed to the Greek of the non-Maronite West Syrians. According to some scholars, the church is called Maronite because of St. John Maron, considered the first patriarch of the Maronites (seventh century). However, long-standing tradition attributes the name to the church's early fifth-century spiritual founder, St. Maron (Maro, Maroon), a hermit of the region of Apamea in Syria Secunda on the Orontes River, a known confidant of St. John Chrysostom. Maron was renowned as an especially gifted spiritual guide and worker of miracles. After his death sometime before 423, a church was built over his tomb. Later a monastery was established that grew to considerable influence. Eventually its monks, known as followers of Maron, Maronites, traveled about the villages preaching repentance and offering spiritual guidance. A strong tie developed between these monks and the rural people of the area, partly because the monks used Syriac in their liturgy, the language of the local people, as opposed to the Greek of the larger cities, and partly because the monks and these locals were strong supporters of Chalcedonian doctrine against the Monophysites (those who maintained only one nature in Christ, a divine one), who were in religious and civil control in Syria and who persecuted the Chalcedonians, including the Maronites. This, along with other persecutions by Melchites and Muslims, fostered the formation of a strong bond among Maronites. Sometime during the early eighth century, the Maronites began migrating with their clergy to the mountains of Lebanon that provided them with safety and relative peace. In this isolation, the patriarch seems to have been both a religious and civil ruler assisted by bishops and nobility, and no doubt was a significant factor in fostering the cohesiveness of Maronites that continues to this day.

The Maronite Church is also Catholic in that it is in union with the Bishop of Rome and the Roman Catholic Church. It is disputed as to how long this union has been in effect. Maronites themselves maintain an unbroken union with the West. However, some historians accuse the Maronites of Monothelitism (a doctrine maintaining only one will in Christ, condemned at the Third Council of Constantinople, 681). The actual history is shrouded in legend and will perhaps never be known. It is significant, however, that there is no non-Catholic counterpart to the Maronites, a situation that would tend to support the Maronite claim to orthodoxy, since it is virtually unknown in other Eastern churches for the total membership to return to union with Rome without leaving dissidents.

The Maronite liturgy is strongly influenced by its monastic origins and expresses an almost constant theme of a call to conversion. It is highly Christocentric, even addressing parts of its many eucharistic prayers directly to Christ, who in turn carries the prayer to the Father. There is also a strong trinitarian emphasis, including the traditional Eastern emphasis on a pneumatic epiclesis (invocation of the Holy Spirit), for example, for the consecration of the Eucharist and for the blessing of the font. The rite possesses an exceedingly rich hymnic tradition that continues to be deeply imbedded in Maronite culture and practice. Contact with the Crusaders in the twelfth century brought clearer union with Rome as well as the beginnings of a process of liturgical Latinization that climaxed in the sixteenth century and was codified in the eighteenth during various synods. This included the Roman imposition of Western vestments and eucharistic vessels (ones made only of gold, silver, or tin, in place of the simpler monastic custom of using glass or wood); use of unleavened bread; Roman formulas for some of the sacraments, including the words of institution that had varied with each anaphora; alteration of prayer texts, including truncation of the eucharistic epiclesis; and the imposition of many aspects of Roman canon law, especially for marriage and church polity. In recent years a liturgical reform has removed many of the Latinizations and restored a significant number of traditional forms and texts to the Maronite liturgy. The liturgy is generally celebrated in the vernacular; in Lebanon, Arabic, but also maintains the use of Syriac, especially for the words of institution, the Trisagion, and certain hymns.

Today Maronites number close to four million members worldwide. The patriarch currently resides in Bkerkè, Lebanon. North America has three Maronite dioceses (eparchies); one for Canada, see city, Montreal; one for the western U.S., see city, Los Angeles; and one for the eastern U.S., see city, Brooklyn.

Dennis W. Krouse

See also ANTIOCHENE THEOLOGY; CATHOLIC TRADITION; CHALCEDON, COUNCIL OF; CHALCEDONIAN CHRISTIANS; COMMUNION (ECCLESIOLOGICAL); CONSTANTINOPLE, FIRST COUNCIL OF; CONSTANTINOPLE, SECOND COUNCIL OF; CONSTANTINOPLE, THIRD COUNCIL OF; EASTERN CATHOLIC CHURCHES; MONOPHYSITISM; MONOTHELITISM; ORTHODOX CHURCHES; PATRIARCH; ROME, SEE OF; TRADITION.

MARRIAGE (IN JUDAISM)

Judaism refers to the marriage ceremony as "Kiddushin," meaning "sanctification." This expresses the classical Jewish conception that, through marriage, a woman becomes the sacrosanct possession of her husband. The ceremony consists of the signing of a document outlining the financial obligations of the husband and rights of the wife (Ketubah), the presentation by the groom to the bride of an object of value, normally a ring, and the recitation of seven blessings ("Sheva Berakhot") that reflect upon the national and religious significance of the creation of a new household within the people of Israel. The ceremony is followed by a brief period in which the bride and groom are alone together, a symbolic consummation of the marriage ("Yihud").

Alan J. Avery-Peck

See also GERUSHIN.

MARRIAGE IN CATHOLIC PERSPECTIVE

The contemporary Roman Catholic view of marriage is set forth by the Second Vatican Council when it described marriage as an intimate, equal partnership of life and love, established by the Creator and governed by its own laws; marriage is rooted in the covenant made by the spouses through their irrevocable personal consent. Thus, in the human act by which spouses mutually hand themselves over to and receive each other, a relationship arises that by divine will and in the eyes of society is a permanent one; this sacred bond, in view of the good of the spouses, of their children, and of society, does not depend on human decision alone; God is its author and has given it many purposes and values (*Gaudium et Spes* 48).

The council's deliberations on marriage and on other related aspects of Christian life resulted in some significant shifts of thinking and practice regarding marriage.

The first shift of special note is the council's return to the biblical notion of covenant as an apt description of the marriage relationship that replaced the legalistic notion of contract that had dominated since the twelfth century. Contracts negotiate services rendered, goods received, rights and duties; covenants effect the most solemn of bonds between persons made in the sight of God and have life–death implications. This shift has opened the door to a richer appreciation of marriage from biblical and personalist perspectives and as a sacrament modeled on and making concretely present the covenant of Christ and the church.

Secondly, the council moved to reorder the traditional primary end of marriage, procreation, and secondary end, the unitive dimension of mutual love and fidelity, as equal (GS 50), with later papal teaching asserting their inseparability, both in the relationship as a whole and in every sexual act. This position of the magisterium is at the foundation of its teaching against artificial contraception and birth control, and against homosexual relationships and acts, since they cannot be procreative. Many theologians suggest that the procreative and unitive purposes of marriage and sexuality should be viewed as belonging to the relationship as a whole, and not reduced to a biological consideration of each sexual act; furthermore, the procreative purpose of the relationship can be fulfilled by a fruitfulness derived from ministry, career, and volunteer work, in addition to or even in place of offspring.

Third, the council emphasized that the foundation of marriage as a sacrament is the mutual surrender in love the couple makes to each other; this love is taken up into divine love and is ruled and enriched by the redemptive power of Christ and the salvific work of the church (GS 48). In other words the sacrament is not added to human love and commitment, but grows out of it, a view contradicting what prevailed theologically at the time of the Council of Trent and that tended to separate marriage as a contract under the jurisdiction of the state, and marriage as a sacrament under the jurisdiction of the church. This dualistic view tended to portray human love as intrinsically tainted and in need of the sacrament to exorcize it. Vatican II sees the sacrament of marriage founded in a human love already blessed by God and intrinsically good. As sacrament this love must continue to grow and move beyond itself in love of children and in commitment to the well-being of others as a manifestation of Christ's love of the church.

A fourth emphasis of the council was the need for a genuine faith commitment for the celebration of any sacrament (*Sacrosanctum Concilium* 59). Thus, the mere fact of having been baptized is insufficient for an effective sacramental marriage, unfortunately an all too frequent practice in the past. Grace, the transforming presence of God, is never automatic, whether in marriage or any other sacrament. The external ritual of a sacrament (in marriage the commitment to live together in love) must be matched by an interior disposition of a personal faith commitment. Thus, a genuine Christian marriage is a living out of one's baptismal faith as a particular calling from God.

Since the Middle Ages, the church has seen the biological consummation of marriage after the exchange of consent as necessary for marriage to be indissoluble. In a fifth shift of thinking, the council moved beyond such a narrow view and asserted that the consummation of marriage must be on all levels of the persons in a commitment of love that involves the good of the whole person (GS 49). Thus authentic consummation involves a continued growth in an intimate communion of life that is spiritual, intellectual, psychological, social, physical, and genital. As a result of this shift in thinking, when such communion of persons does not take place, and a marriage fails, the church is more readily able to grant an annulment. Changes in the Code of Canon Law (1983) reflect this shift in its procedures for dissolution of the marriage bond and decrees of nullity. Much of this canonical reform was anticipated in earlier decrees issued after the council. The Code provides a much more personalist and less legalistic approach in most of its considerations of marriage.

A sixth emphasis of the council was to assert that the exercise of the acts of marriage, including sexual ones, are "noble and honorable," and their truly human performance "fosters the self-giving they signify and enriches the spouses in joy and gratitude" (GS 49). This disabuses us of the Augustinian view, repeated in papal teaching as late as the seventeenth century, that even in marriage, sexual acts, including those for procreation, are always tainted with at least venial sin, tolerated by God for the sake of procreation and because they are a remedy for concupiscence, enabling the couple to remain faithful. The council supported a wholesome regard for human sexuality as a gift from God, in need of development and discipline, but also a means of joyful response to another. A negative, suspicious view of human sexuality would be a contradiction of the council's perspective.

A seventh significant shift in thinking about marriage is rooted in the council's deliberations on the nature of the church. This gave a broader ecclesial/communal emphasis to marriage in that Christian spouses signify and share in the mystery of that union and fruitful love that exists between Christ and the church (see Ephesians 5:32); further, the council stated that Christian spouses "by reason of their own state in life and their order [in suo vitae statu et ordine] . . . have their own gifts in the People of God" (Lumen Gentium 11). In using the word "order" for marriage, the council returned to a patristic notion of church as composed of various orders or ranks of persons grouped ministerially, not unlike religious orders or the holy orders of ordination that offer various services to the church and the world. One can also say, as did John Chrysostom, that marriage is a "little church," and must therefore function minsterially, the couple first to each other, next to their children, and then beyond to the church and society at large. Moreover, fostering marriage and family life is a responsibility for the membership of the whole church; however, married persons and family associations have a primary responsibility here (GS 52). This emphasis of the council has found great fruit in the involvement of married couples in marriage preparation programs such as Engaged Encounter and Pre-Cana Conferences. Married couples have also contributed greatly to the many and varied marriage and family-enrichment programs and movements that have emerged since the time of the council.

An eighth shift affecting marriage is derived from the council's inauguration of a renewed liturgy for the church. The council's emphasis on "full, active, conscious participation" in worship requires that the wedding ceremony be a true experience of community prayer (SC 14). The marriage rite is to be celebrated in

Mass after the reading and homily (prior to the reform it was a very brief ceremony celebrated before Mass), or, if outside of Mass, after a full Liturgy of the Word and homily. The nuptial blessing, used only for sacramental marriages, is now given to both bride and groom, rather than to the bride alone. There are also many choices of prayer texts and lections to be made by the couple in planning their wedding ceremony. New rituals are to be composed, taking into account local customs and ceremonies that appropriately signify the meaning of Christian married life (SC 77). Currently, a revised ritual for marriage in the English-speaking world is being prepared by the International Committee on English in the Liturgy. This ritual, with more choices of prayer and biblical texts, a revision of translations of existing texts, especially regarding horizontally inclusive language, and variations in the ceremony itself, must first be approved by the English-speaking episcopal conferences of the world and then confirmed by the Holy See.

Finally, shifts derived from the council's deliberations on religious freedom and the primacy of conscience and on ecumenism permit that a Catholic, when marrying a non-Catholic, out of respect for this person's conscience, family situation, or other serious reason, can be married outside the canonical form of marriage (a priest with appropriate faculties and two witnesses, required for validity since the decree *Tametsi* of the Council of Trent) with the permission of one's ordinary. Ecumenical weddings can also be celebrated with ministers from both churches or religions, provided that only one minister receive the vows of the couple and there be an integrated ritual. Any semblance of two separate ceremonies is to be avoided. Furthermore, the council's reforms place the responsibility for the baptism and Catholic religious education of children on the Catholic spouse. The non-Catholic is no longer required to promise to undertake this responsibility.

Some recent theological reflection with a more personalist view emphasizes the inner communal life of the Trinity as a model for Christian marriage. God in Christian understanding is, as it were, a "family," the three Persons totally involved in each other through harmonious acts of knowing, loving, and self-donation. Spouses, through their mutual acts of growing in knowledge and love of each other, and through their mutual self-donation, manifest and concretely render present the Trinity in our world. Thus the Christian family is called to reflect, model, and be a sacrament of the greatest of mysteries, the Holy Trinity.

Dennis W. Krouse

See also ANNULMENT; CANONICAL FORM (OF MARRIAGE); DIVORCE (IN CHRISTIANITY); INDISSOLUBILITY; PAULINE PRIVILEGE; PETRINE PRIVILEGE.

MARSIGLIO OF PADUA (1275?–1342)

Marsiglio studied medicine at Paris around 1311 and was made rector of the university in 1312. From 1320, he practiced medicine in Paris, writing his famous *Defender of the Peace* anonymously in 1324. When the authorship of this treatise was discovered, Marsiglio fled to the protection of Emperor Louis of Bavaria. In 1327 Pope John XXII excommunicated Marsiglio and condemned the *Defender*. From 1327 to 1329, Marsiglio served as imperial vicar for the emperor in Rome. He spent the rest of his life at the court of Louis in Munich. The *Defender* argues that the church should be subservient to the state that in turn derives its authority from the people. The hierarchy of the church, according to Marsiglio, has no basis in Scripture, and all power and property of the church comes from the state. The highest authority of the church should be a general council composed both of clerics and laity. The *Defender* was a revolutionary book and had much influence in later centuries.

Gary Macy

See also CONCILIARISM; EXCOMMUNICATION; JOHN XXII, POPE; MEDIEVAL CHRISTIANITY (IN THE WEST).

MARTIN OF TOURS (316/17–97)

A native of Pannonia (now part of Hungary), Martin's first career was that of a soldier. In 356 he joined the entourage of Hilary of Poitier, and in 361 Martin founded the monastery at Ligugé, one of the first in Europe. Reluctantly, he was also made bishop of Tours. As bishop and monk, Martin worked ceaselessly to convert the Gallo-Roman population. A protector of the poor and the persecuted, Martin was highly esteemed even during his lifetime. The life of Martin, written by Sulpicius Severus, increased Martin's popularity, particularly in France.

Gary Macy

See also CONVERSION; HILARY OF POITIER; MONASTICISM IN WESTERN CHRISTIANITY; SULPICIUS SEVERUS.

MARTY, MARTIN E. (1928–)

American theologian and historian. A native of Nebraska, Marty studied at Concordia Seminary, at Chicago's Lutheran School of Theology, and finally at the University of Chicago. After some years as a Lutheran pastor, he became (in 1963) a professor at the University of Chicago's Divinity School. He has been editor of the journals *Christian Century* and *Christian History*. Marty has specialized in the study of the American religious experience, and is considered one of the world's authorities in this field. His writings and research, as well as his impact on a generation of religion scholars, have had profound influence on American ecumenism and scholarship. Marty has also been involved with social issues, especially as these relate to public health and medical ethics. Among his list of distinguished publications are *The New Shape of American Religion* (1959), *Protestantism in the United States* (1985), and *An Invitation to American Catholic History* (1986). He is currently working on a collaborative multivolume study of fundamentalism.

Orlando Espín

See also ECUMENICAL MOVEMENT/ECUMENISM; FUNDAMENTALISM; HISTORY.

MARTYR/MARTYRDOM

A martyr is a person who willingly suffers death in defense of his or her beliefs. Martyrdom is the actual death of such a person. The New Testament records the death of Stephen as the first Christian martyrdom (Acts 7:57-60). Many believers died for the faith during the first Christian centuries, but martyrdoms were generally sporadic. In the middle of the third century, however, the Emperor Decius undertook an aggressive campaign against the church, including the widespread and systematic martyring of believers. The Roman government charged these Christians with refusing to worship the Roman state deities. This was considered to be an act of treason. The most severe period of persecution came under the Emperor Diocletian, beginning in 304, less than a decade before

Christianity was decriminalized by the Emperor Constantine. From the beginning, Christians held their martyrs in great respect, and cherished their bodies. The bodies of the martyrs were signs that the Spirit of Christ continued to live in the church. Occasionally, such a high regard for the martyrs actually led some Christians to look for ways to be martyred, a quest actively discouraged by many leaders and teachers in the church. Believers concluded that the fate of the martyrs was certain: they entered into the presence of God immediately after death. Hence, it was common to try to speak to those who were about to be martyred, to ask them to remember one's needs and intentions before the throne of God. After the legalization of Christianity, the martyrdom of Christians quickly ceased in the Roman Empire. That, however, was not the end of Christian martyrdom. After the fall of the Empire, and as Christianity expanded into new regions, isolated instances of persecution and large-scale martyrdom occurred. No age has been without Christian martyrs. The only American martyrs who have been officially recognized as saints are Isaac Jogues, Jean de Brébeuf, and their companions. These Jesuits worked among Native Americans in the seventeenth century and were killed between 1642 and 1649. Their memorial in the liturgical calendar is October 19. America has had other Christian martyrs who have not been officially canonized, that is, declared saints. Most notable are the North American missionary women, the Jesuits with their associates, and Archbishop Oscar Romero of Mexico, all martyred in El Salvador.

Patrick L. Malloy

See also CANONIZATION; CONSTANTINE I THE GREAT; MARTYROLOGY; RELIC (IN CHRISTIANITY).

MARTYROLOGY

A record of the lives of the saints, organized by date of death. Originally, calendars kept by local churches listed the names of martyrs on the date of death. Each year, on the anniversary of their death, these martyrs were remembered by the church at the Eucharist. As the systematic martyring of Christians ceased in the fourth century, communities began to record on their calendars the deaths of exemplary Christians who had not been forced to die for their faith, but who had suffered persecution. These were called confessors, since they had publicly confessed their faith despite the threat of martyrdom. In time, even these confessors had all died, and the church began to commemorate the deaths of others who had lived exemplary Christian lives. The earliest known example is Martin of Tours who died in 397. Key events in the life of Christ (such as his nativity) were eventually listed in the calendars as well. Scholars have shown, however, that the dates associated with the life of Christ are conjectures, since the actual dates are unknown. The earliest such calendars were local documents that recorded only the saints who had been a part of a specific church and whose bodies were buried nearby. Eventually, local churches began to freely borrow the anniversaries observed by other communities. This was the beginning of the martyrology, that is, a list of feast days observed by Christians everywhere. By the eighth-ninth centuries, martyrologies were constructed that included not only the names of the saints, but also their biographies. Records of other historical events significant in the life of the church, such as the date when important local churches had been dedicated, were noted as well. The Roman Catholic Church arrived at an official martyrology in 1584 as part of the reforms of the Council of Trent. Since then, the martyrology has seen numerous editions, each of which added more recent saints and corrected older entries according to newly gained historical information. A key supplement to the Roman Martyrology is the Acta Sanctorum, an ongoing work of a group of Belgian Jesuits called the Bollandists. The Bollandists were founded in the seventh century to carry out careful historical research into the lives of the saints, thereby providing accurate information and weeding out legends that have no historical basis.

Patrick L. Malloy

See also ACTA SANCTORUM; CALENDAR (LITURGICAL); MARTIN OF TOURS; MARTYR/MARTYRDOM.

MARX, KARL (1818–83)

German philosopher. Although not very well known during his lifetime, Marx became an extraordinarily influential thinker after his death, especially (but certainly not only) because of the Bolshevik victory during the Russian revolution that brought Lenin and other Marxists to power. It is impossible to understand the twentieth century, politically and in the history of ideas, without encountering Marx's thought and influence. Born to a Prussian Jewish family, Marx's father (and family) converted to Lutheranism in order to avoid further anti-Semitic pressures. After earlier studies in Trier, Marx attended the University of Berlin but earned his doctorate in philosophy (1841) at the University of Jena. By then he had already earned a reputation as one of the "Young Hegelian" radicals (young scholars who followed Ludwig Feuerbach and Bruno Bauer against Hegel, although they used the latter's dialectical method). In 1843,

in Paris, he met Friedrich Engels who enkindled in Marx a lasting interest in the proletariat or working class. While in Paris, Marx finally broke with the Young Hegelians. His intellectual partnership with Engels, however, remained fruitful until Marx's death, and in time allowed Marx to write his most influential works. After the failure of the French uprising of 1848, Marx moved to London where he stayed the rest of his life. In 1848, with Engels, he wrote his best-known pamphlet, the *Communist Manifesto*. While in Paris and especially during his London years, Marx devoted considerable time and energy to organizing and supporting the First International (originally named the "International Workingmen's Association"). In London he wrote the *Grundisse* (only published in 1941)—a major work on capital, property, labor, the state, and the market economy. In 1859 he published *Contribution to the Critique of Political Economy*. During the 1860s he wrote *Theories of Surplus Value* and also his better-known work, *Capital*—a major theoretical study on the capitalist means of production, and on labor and surplus value, while projecting the demise of industrial capitalism. These and other works authored by Marx, over the several intellectual and political stages of his life, are still the object of intense scrutiny and debate among scholars, and have impacted many other theorists (and many other theories) since Marx's death.

Orlando Espín

See also ALTHUSSER, LOUIS PIERRE; ASSMANN, HUGO; CRITICAL THEORY; FEUERBACH, LUDWIG; GRAMSCI, ANTONIO; HABERMAS, JÜRGEN; HEGEL, G.W.F.; IDEOLOGY (IDEOLOGIES); LATIN AMERICAN THEOLOGIES; LIBERATION THEOLOGIES; MADURO, OTTO; MARXISM; PRAXIS; SOCIALISM.

MARXISM

A name given to a broad group of social theorists and theories that have their genesis in (or at least have been deeply influenced by) Karl Marx's thought. This intellectual movement, in turn, had immense impact on political and other forces in world society during most of the twentieth century, and deeply marked most areas of human learning during that same period. Today, during the early years of the twenty-first century, Marxism's influence is not as pronounced but it remains a powerful force in some national (China, and others), social (politics, and political parties and movements), and intellectual (social sciences, philosophy, and so forth) contexts.

There is no (and probably there has never been a) *single* strand of social thought one could strictly call "Marxist" with a clearly understood and universally accepted meaning. Both supporters and enemies of "Marxism" have tried to appeal to this term as if it were concisely defined, but in fact the thought that developed from Marx's influential writings has not followed a single strand or developed into universally supported or agreed-upon categories. Perhaps only Karl Marx's own works and thought can be strictly called Marxist, although most scholars today agree that even Marx's intellectual development defies the easy classification of his own contributions. Unfortunately and incorrectly, the term "Marxist" has often come to be identified as synonymous with "Communism." Perhaps the more correct term, potentially broader and less open to political misuse, is "Marxian." But given the better-known term employed as this entry's heading, we will use it here, in spite of the reservations just mentioned.

Influenced by earlier western European radical thought, the movement called Marxism identifiably began with the collaborative work of Friedrich Engels and Karl Marx, who jointly authored (in 1848) the *Communist Manifesto*—a political pamphlet designed to synthetically present the ideals of what the authors understood as the new Communist movement. Not all who called themselves "Communist" were supported by Engels and Marx, and in fact many "Communists" were often criticized by both Engels and Marx for adulterating or misunderstanding the serious thought and analysis they believed was required of true Communism. Nevertheless, both Marx and Engels devoted considerable energy and time to the development of the movement, as they understood it. After Marx's death in 1883, Engels dedicated the rest of his life to publishing and translating his friend's writings (although Engels himself continued his reflections and writing on issues that would later surface, for example, in contemporary feminist theory).

Marxist thought, as it can be reconstructed from the writings of Marx and Engels, can be said to (at least) focus on seven key areas of reflection and analysis. Very briefly and synthetically presented, these seven areas are:

1. *Mode (or manner) of production* (the combination of the productive forces in an economy, indispensably including labor and the means of production; together with the social relations governing and resulting from production, including class and personal relations, laws, and the relations of workers with their work).

2. *Means of production* (the combination of the means and subjects of labor: tools, industrial plants, infrastructure, and so on, together with raw materials. It should be understood that, for Marx, the means of production require labor in order to actually "produce" something).

3. *Infra- and superstructure* (the infrastructure refers to the means of production in society, while the superstructure —"built" on top of the infrastructure and determined by the latter in a "dialectic" relationship—includes ideologies, legal and political systems, religions, artistic and intellectual productions, and so forth).

4. *Social classes* ("classes" are social groups formed by and derived from their *relationship* with the *means of production*, and therefore not grounded mainly or solely on possession of wealth. Any capitalist society has several social classes, but according to Marx there are two main groups: the proletariat, or those who sell their labor because they do not own the means of production [but who, by selling their labor, add "value" to the products their labor creates]; and the bourgeoisie, or those who own the means of production, and who buy and benefit from the labor of the proletariat [although the wealthy bourgeoisie and the "small" or petit bourgeoisie should be distinguished, because the latter also sell their labor besides purchasing the labor of the proletariat]).

5. *Class consciousness* (the self-awareness of the members of a social class as members of that social class, as well as their ability to act [somewhat together] in order to pursue their shared class interests).

6. *Ideology* (the self-understanding, worldview, and so forth, of a society is determined by the infrastructure, that is, by the society's means of production. Because the wealthy bourgeoisie own and/or control the means of production, the ideology of society [and all else in the superstructure] will be created and sustained according to the interests of the ruling class and not according to the interests of the majority or the factual relationships of social life).

7. *Historical materialism* (although this expression was never used by Marx himself, it refers to the study of human historical development, with a clear focus on the economy and society's relationships with the infra- and superstructures. It attempts to understand and explain a society by way of economic analysis).

After Marx and Engels, their thought (especially Marx's thought) began to spread in two major directions: as the "official" ideology of parties; and, later, of governments and states that claimed to be implementing Marx's (and Engels') contributions as guides in the struggle toward "communist" societies, and as methodological approaches to philosophical, historical, and social scientific constructs that would result in more accurate theoretical explanations of today's world (economies, political and legal systems, religions, and so on). In this latter direction, one could mention French Marxist "structuralism" of the 1960s and 1970s, as well as a variety of "neo-Marxian" theories and intellectual movements (like The Frankfurt School, "cultural" and "humanist" Marxism, and so forth).

The "Frankfurt School" has been one such important and influential "neo-Marxian" intellectual movement that coalesced around Frankfurt's Institute of Social Research. Very critical of capitalism, the movement's members were also as critical of "typical" Marxists whom the movement considered to be adulterating or simplifying the real, complex Marx. After World War II, the Frankfurt School began using Marx's thought in creative combination with other theories of social analysis in order to interpret new world situations that Marx could never have contemplated in his day. The Frankfurt School's "critical theory" has done much to enlighten areas of Marx's complex thought and their potential contributions to today's world, while enriching Marx with the thought of other theorists.

Among Marxism's more influential thinkers (after Marx and Engels themselves) we could mention Georg Lukács (1885–1971), Antonio Gramsci (1891–1937), Louis Althusser (1918–90), and Herbert Marcuse (1898–1979). Many other important authors (Jürgen Habermas, José Carlos Mariátegui, and others) have been deeply influenced by Marxism, but either never identified as Marxists or have carefully nuanced Marxism's influence on their work.

Orlando Espín

See also ALTHUSSER, LOUIS PIERRE; CRITICAL THEORY; GRAMSCI, ANTONIO; HABERMAS, JÜRGEN; HEGEL, G.W.F.; IDEOLOGY (IDEOLOGIES); MARIÁTEGUI, JOSÉ CARLOS; MARX, KARL; PRAXIS; SOCIALISM.

MARXSEN, WILLI (1919–93)

This German Lutheran New Testament scholar who was professor of New Testament in the Protestant Theological Faculty of the Westphalian Wilhelms University in Münster, Germany, earned his doctorate in 1954 from the University of Kiel with a dissertation that was published two years later as *Der Evangelist Markus: Studien zur Redaktionsgeschichte des Evangeliums* (1956). By the time of its appearance in English translation in 1969 as *Mark the Evangelist: Studies on the Redaction History of the Gospel* (1969), this study's subtitle had already helped to bring the term *Redaktionsgeschichte*, redaction criticism, into common usage in New Testament scholarship. Focusing on four topics, namely, John the

Baptist, the geographical outline of Mark, *euaggelion* ("gospel"), and Mark 13, Marxsen established the specifically Markan point of view. He did so by distinguishing among three life situations reflected in the text: first, the activity of Jesus himself; second, the situation of the early church; third, the situation of the evangelists and the circumstances involved at the time each of the Gospels was set in writing.

Marxsen's *The Resurrection of Jesus of Nazareth* (German original 1968; English translation 1970) generated significant attention and controversy by suggesting that it is of primary importance that the "cause of Jesus" lives on to address and challenge present-day believers, whatever else may be known about the historicity of the resurrection of Jesus on the basis of the evidence available. In October 1988 Marxsen presented a series of lectures in the U.S. in which he continued to address the issue of the resurrection of the historical Jesus, lectures subsequently published as *Jesus and Easter: Did God Raise the Historical Jesus from the Dead?* (1990). In one of those lectures, Marxsen writes of those who formulated the statement about the resurrection of Jesus, "There are two or three gathered in the name of Jesus, and they encourage each other to live the faith into which Jesus had invited them. So they live this faith and in the living of it they become certain that he (truly, *he*) is among them. . . . Subsequently, one of *these* people expresses it in this way: 'He whose faith we live, him God has raised from the dead'" (p. 77).

English versions of other works by Marxsen, originally published in German, include: *Introduction to the New Testament: An Approach to its Problems* (1968); *The Significance of the Message of* the Resurrection for Faith in Jesus (1968); The Beginnings of Christology, a Study in Its Problems (1969); The Resurrection of Jesus of Nazareth (1970); The New Testament as the Church's Book (1972); Jesus and the Church: The Beginnings of Christianity (1992); and New Testament Foundations for Christian Ethics (1993).

Jean-Pierre Ruiz

See also EVANGELIST; GOSPEL; JESUS OF HISTORY; REDACTION CRITICISM; RESURRECTION OF CHRIST.

MARYKNOLL

The Catholic Foreign Mission Society of America, commonly called Maryknoll, was organized in 1911 by two priests, James Walsh and Thomas Price, as a missionary organization of priests and brothers based in the United States. In 1912 Mary Josephine Rogers and other laywomen offered to help the Maryknoll Fathers with their publication Field Afar, and in 1920 these women organized the Maryknoll Sisters of St. Dominic. The earliest Maryknoll missions were in China, but after the 1949 communist victory in that country, Maryknoll fathers, brothers, and sisters turned their attention to Latin America and Africa. Since Vatican II, Maryknollers have led the way in redefining the missionary vocation within the Catholic Church. At its heart, they see (1) the integration of faith in God and work for justice and (2) the inculturation of Christianity in non-Western regions. In recent years, the incorporation of priest, religious, and lay associate members, including married couples with children, into the work of Maryknoll has revitalized both the men's and women's branches of Maryknoll. Maryknoll's strong commitment to justice for the poor of the world has resulted in persecution and even martyr-

dom for some missioners, particularly in Latin America.

James B. Nickoloff

See also INCULTURATION; MARTYR/ MARTYRDOM; MISSIONARIES; MISSIONS.

MARY MAGDALEN

In the Gospels, several women named Mary are followers of Jesus; Mary Magdalen is the most prominent. She is presumed to have come from Magdala, a fishing center on the western shore of the Sea of Galilee five miles north of Capernaum. She appears in all four Gospels as a witness to Jesus' death, burial, and the empty tomb. She is consistently identified first in every synoptic list of women, some named, others unnamed, who were part of Jesus' inner circle and who accompanied him from Galilee to Jerusalem (Matt 27:55-56; 28:1; Mark 15:40-41, 47; 16:1; Luke 8:1-3; 25:10). In John and the canonical ending of Mark, she is the very first to witness the risen Christ (Mark 16:9; John 20:13-16); in Matthew, she is among the women who were the very first to see the risen Lord (Matt 26).

There are indications that Mary Magdalen was a prominent leader in the early church. Gnostic texts suggest that this memory was retained in heterodox groups where her importance rivaled that of Peter. Although the Catholic Church calls her, "The Apostle to the Apostles," she is chiefly remembered from a legend that claims she was a repentant prostitute. Scholars now recognize that the legend is a fabrication without basis in the New Testament. However, the legend has dominated her image in art, literature, and popular piety. Some have surmised that the legend emerged to support the patriarchal interests of the hierarchy and have suggested reconstructions of how this may have happened. Nevertheless, Mary Magdalen's image has proved flexible enough to model the prominent concerns of many different eras, including the efforts of many Christian women in the late twentieth century, to claim their rightful equality in the church.

Regina A. Boisclair

MARY OF NAZARETH

The tradition that Jesus was the son of a woman named Mary is very strong; the tradition that Jesus was from Nazareth is beyond question. Mary of Nazareth is an apt way to refer to the historical mother of Jesus as well as to the mother of Jesus as she is portrayed in the New Testament. There are important differences between what can be said with virtual certainty about the Mary of history and what is said about her in the New Testament. There are striking differences between Mary of Nazareth and the various Marian doctrines, legends, devotions, and apparitions that have been prominent in Catholic piety as well as those aspects of Mariology that emphasize Mary's special privileges (for example, the Immaculate Conception) or titles (like Mother of God).

When critically considered, the New Testament provides reliable evidence that the historical mother of Jesus was a Jewish woman (Gal 4:4; Matt 1:1-16), named Mary (Mark 6:3; Luke 1:27; Acts 1:14, and others), who married a carpenter named Joseph (Matt 1:16, 18; Luke 2:5; John 1:45, and others), and raised Jesus in Nazareth, where the family came to live after Jesus was born (Matt 2:23; Luke 2:39; 4:16, and others; see also, Matt 2:23; Mark 1:9; Luke 2:39; John 1:46, and others; and Matt 26:71; Mark 1:24; Luke 4:34; John 1:45, and others). These points not only conform to what is known about the Jesus of history, but are also attested by more than one source. They neither contradict information provided elsewhere nor suggest themselves as traditions devised to promote christological insights.

The New Testament adds other details in its presentation of Mary that provide glimpses of Mary before Jesus' birth (Matt 1:18-26; Luke 1:26-56), at his birth and infancy (Matt 2:11-15, 19-23; Luke 2:1-40), during his early life (Luke 2:41-52) and ministry (Mark 3:32-35 and parallels; John 2:1-11), as well as at his death (John 19:25-27) and after the Resurrection (Acts 1:14). Many are designed either to make a theological point (John 2:1-11; 19:25-27) or provide a circumstance that enhances the impact of Jesus' words (Mark 3:31-35; 6:1-6 and parallels).

Of major significance are Matthew 1:26-38 and Luke 1:18-25 that indicate that Mary conceived Jesus by the Holy Spirit. These passages are part of the highly symbolic, theologically charged infancy narratives in the first two chapters of Matthew and Luke that were designed to establish christological insights. While a literal belief in Mary's virginal conception of Jesus has been dominant throughout Christian history, contemporary Scripture scholars recognize the evidence for historicity is fragile. However, it does not really matter whether these biblical accounts are considered historical or symbolic. In either case, they serve as a sign that in Mary of Nazareth God intervened in human history. As she is presented in the New Testament, Mary of Nazareth is best understood in light of the Gospels of Luke and John. In both these Gospels she is portrayed as a woman of faith and the prototype of the ideal disciple.

Regina A. Boisclair

See also MARIAN DEVOTIONS; MARIOLOGY; VIRGINITY OF MARY.

MASKS/FALSE FACES

The masked rituals of North America are stunning examples of the dramatic power of ritual. In the history of religions, the use of masks is widely present, and where it occurs, it marks a high achievement of ritual art. In the native peoples of North America, masks can be seen in all the culture areas. By the twentieth century, they have emerged to public awareness for their artistry and otherworldly beauty, as demonstrated by the great False Face Masks of the Iroquois, the wonderful headdresses of the Apache Mountain Spirits, the Kachinas of the Hopi and others, and the Deer mask of the Yaqui, to name just a few.

The mask is intended both to reveal and conceal the real presence of the spirits in native life. This reality is certain, and the great function of the masks is to allow the invisible to become visible, and at the same time, to preserve the sheer qualitative difference between them and us. They are, from the moment of their consecration, entirely sacred, and careful rubrics surround them with reverence. They are considered to have awesome power, and they are normally buried with their owners.

The False Faces are a perfect example of the meaning of the mask. They are chosen from living trees and cut in such a way that the tree is not harmed. Since the myth of the Iroquois places them in the primeval forest that is the traditional home of the Iroquois, they are encountered by chosen ones who dream of their presence. They are also identified as the relatives of a being so powerful and so ancient that the Creator left them this territory on the condition that they would help the Iroquois. Thus they continue to serve the people in their quest for food and health. Significantly, those who dream of them endure a shamanic initiation, and when healed, become members of the society of healers who have all been empowered by the False Faces. Their link with the natural environment is very significant.

Kathleen Dugan

See also INITIATION (NON-CHRISTIAN); MEDICINE; RITUAL.

MASS

The word *Mass* is taken from the Latin (*missarum sollemnia*), referring to the series of ritual dismissals that took place at the Eucharist (for example, catechumens, those preparing for baptism, would be dismissed at the end of the Liturgy of the Word). While the usual liturgical (and theological) language in the West during the earliest centuries of Christianity was Greek, by the fourth century, Latin was in wide use. The Greek name for the breaking of the bread, *Eucharist*, was the earliest in use in Christianity, and continued to be used to refer not only to the service, but to the consecrated bread and wine themselves. However, in the early medieval period, the term *missa* came to be used in the West to refer to the celebration of the Eucharist in its entirety; the Anglicized form, *Mass*, continues to be used in some traditions, especially Roman Catholicism. In addition, the English names of certain holidays and feasts reflect the fact that the Mass would have been celebrated on those days, such as Christmas and Candlemas.

During the time of the Reformation, the term *Mass* was dropped by many of the Protestant traditions, since it seemed to carry with it many of the meanings and practices the Reformers had rejected as being nonscriptural or "popish" inventions (for example, the idea of the Mass as a sacrifice offered by a priest to God, or the application of the "fruits" of a Mass to help a deceased relative be freed from purgatory). Many Protestant churches referred to their reformed services with simpler, more scriptural terms, such as "the Holy Communion," or the celebration of "the Lord's Supper."

In the twentieth century, the Roman Catholic Church has also used the term *Eucharist* more widely to refer to the service as a whole, although the word *Mass* (and some of its parallels in other languages, for example, *Messe* in German, *mis* in Dutch, *mässa* in Swedish, *msza* in Polish, *misa* in Spanish, or *messe* in French) continues in popular use as well.

Joanne M. Pierce

See also COMMUNION (LITURGICAL); EUCHARIST; LITURGY OF THE EUCHARIST; LITURGY OF THE WORD; MISSAL; SACRIFICE OF THE MASS.

MASS MEDIA

Although the mass media can trace their origin to the invention of the printing press and the wide distribution of the first mechanically reproduced texts, modern forms consist of electronically reproduced and distributed audio and visual, as well as printed, materials. Therefore, mass media today include television (video), radio, and other wireless audio communication, motion pictures, as well as magazines, newspapers, books, and the Internet. The media, then, can be seen as interrelated modes of distributing ideas, news, and information as well as various forms of entertainment.

Today religious groups may see the mass media as presenting opportunities for the distribution and promulgation of religious ideas or as a threat to the existence of those ideas. Because the media

convey, instill, and enforce social norms, moral "truths," ethical values, and concepts of the public good in ways similar to those historically associated with religious institutions, they are being subjected to theological as well as sociological, psychological, and economic analysis.

Robert D. McCleary

MATER ET MAGISTRA

On May 15, 1961, Pope John XXIII, who had been elected Pope in 1958 and had called for the Second Vatican Council to begin in 1962, issued his first encyclical letter called "Christianity and Social Progress." The letter making up this document is commonly known by the first two words of the Latin text, *Mater et Magistra* ("Mother and Teacher," referring to the role of the church in the world). To mark the seventieth anniversary of Pope Leo XIII's letter on "The Condition of Labor" (*Rerum Novarum*, 1891), generally seen as the starting point of modern Catholic social teaching, John XXIII sought to strengthen that teaching by applying Catholic principles to contemporary social issues. Among them he took up the growing economic, social, and cultural imbalance within and among the nations of the world and, at the same time, the increasing interdependence of peoples. He called for wages that are not only just and equitable but "sufficient to lead a life worthy of a human being" (no. 71). He reaffirmed the Catholic view of private property as a natural human right, but he also noted that societies have the duty of extending this right to all their citizens. Furthermore, he recalled the "social function of property," meaning that material wealth as well as personal gifts are given to human beings by God for the dual purpose of "their own perfection and . . .

for the benefit of others" (no. 119). He affirmed labor unions and the right of workers to be "partners in enterprises . . . wherein they work" (no. 91). The Pope also gave special attention to the problems of agriculture and rural life, population increase, especially in poor nations (calling for greater productivity rather than population control), and the need for international cooperation in solving basic problems. In calling Catholics to apply the church's social teaching to temporal affairs (nos. 226–57), the Pope urged them to follow the threefold method of "look, judge, act," which means examining the actual situation, evaluating it in terms of the church's social teaching, and then acting in accord with that evaluation (no. 236). With *Mater et Magistra* Pope John XXIII thus not only made an important contribution to Catholic social thought but also influenced the direction taken by the Second Vatican Council (1962–5) as the footnotes to the council's Pastoral Constitution on the Church in the Modern World (1965) demonstrate.

James B. Nickoloff

See also JOHN XXIII, POPE; VATICAN, SECOND COUNCIL OF THE.

MATERIALISM

A term in Marxism that attempts to uncover the nature of human relationships in capitalist societies. The theory of materialism holds that people's consciousness and understanding of the world is largely shaped by their economic situations. This is so because engagement in sensuous human labor involves the greatest parts of one's waking efforts and largely governs people's well-being or lack thereof.

In Marxist versions of materialism, capitalist economic structures produce a small class that owns and controls the means of production and directs the political economy. Capitalism also produces subordinate classes that comprise the majority and are subject to varying degrees of political oppression, economic exploitation, and cultural domination by the capitalist class. The Marxist doctrine of materialism is historical because it claims that the economic structures of any society continue to develop, while those who primarily benefit from these structures fight to preserve the status quo, despite its growing irrationality. This sustains ongoing class struggle and social change.

The Catholic Church has traditionally critiqued Marxism as a philosophy that promoted "atheistic materialism" and violence. More recent popes, however, like John XXIII and Paul VI, have had positive things to say about Marxists, if not Marxism. Some religious ethicists have found historical materialism useful in that it views capitalist political economy as creating an environment that reproduces nonmutual (unjust) relations at all levels of society. They find illuminating Marxism's understanding that socially mediated action with the material relations of production shapes and limits humans and their theories of knowledge. This is in contrast to the body and matter denying spiritualism of much of the Christian tradition that does not acknowledge that labor and access to material resources are even more important to the spiritual life than is prayer.

These religious ethicists have also criticized materialism because it needs to be supplemented by other experiences and theories of oppression and privilege that also shape knowledge and behavior. Domination and subordination are about more than control of labor power, and the transformation of knowledge and society depends also on liberation from other experiences of oppression like racism, male dominance, heterosexism, authoritarianism, naturism, and other cultural dynamics.

Mary E. Hobgood

See also CLASSISM; ETHICS, SOCIAL; JUSTICE; RACISM; SEXISM.

MA-TSU

(Chinese, Ma-zu, lit., Mother of Heaven). Popular national deity in China, also referred to as the "Empress of Heaven" and "Consort of Heaven." Originally, she was recognized as a patron deity of seafarers in South China during the Sung Period (960–1279) for her filial efforts in saving her father and brothers during a storm. In addition to this heroic episode, she also became famous for telling fortunes as a young girl on Meichou Island. These stories, plus an untimely death, led to the emergence of a cult honoring her as a divine being among villagers and seamen. After her death, her popularity spread, further enhanced by many miracles attributed to her. Over a long period of time, her status was elevated as legends grew regarding her protection of military leaders as well as seamen. During the Ching Dynasty (1644–1911) she was honored by imperial decree with the title of "Queen of Heaven" (T'ien Mou). Ma-Tsu worship continues today in Taiwan and Hong Kong.

G. D. DeAngelis

MATSURI

(Japanese, festival). Traditionally, these have been religious ceremonies, rituals, and rites associated with Shinto shrines. The term refers to a wide variety of religious ceremonies as well as festivities, for example, dance, music, and drama, associated with religious ceremonies held annually at a Shinto shrine as a public festival of communal worship and celebration. These festivals have traditionally been held to renew the bond between the local kami and the community to insure a good harvest and general well-being for the community. In contemporary Japan, while the presence of kami is still invoked at these festivals, many matsuri have lost their religious significance.

G. D. DeAngelis

See also KAGURA; KAMI; NORITO; SHINTO; SHRINE.

MATTHEW/MATTHEAN

The Gospel of Matthew is a synthesis of the Gospel of Mark, a collection of the sayings of Jesus (the so-called Logien-Quelle, Sayings Source, or Q), and other material known to the author. Traditionally, the author has been held to be the apostle Matthew, based on a statement from Papias of Hierapolis (early second century) as quoted in Eusebius Hist eccl. 3.39.16: "Matthew compiled the Sayings in the Aramaic language, and everyone translated them as well as he could." The apostle Matthew may have been at the start of this Gospel's tradition if he compiled sayings of Jesus in a collection similar to Q. But, Papias' statement offers no help in ascertaining who wrote the Greek text of the Gospel, widely agreed not to be a translation from an earlier Aramaic version. It is improbable that the author was an eyewitness apostle, since an eyewitness would hardly copy from the text of someone (for example, Mark) who was not. Matthew's Gospel itself reflects that the author was a Christian church leader and teacher, perhaps a converted scribe.

The Gospel has a predominantly Jewish-Christian outlook, with an openness to the Gentile mission. It must have been composed after Mark (late 60s), yet before 110, since it is known to Ignatius of Antioch. Some indications within the text that the evangelist was in dialogue with the rabbinic academy at Jamnia help narrow the dating to between 80 and 90. Many locales have been suggested as the place of composition, including Antioch, various Phoenician cities, and Caesarea Maritima.

As to content, the Gospel is a combination of both narrative and discourse material. Five great discourses can be recognized, leading some to view the Gospel as divided into five books, suggesting a Matthean Pentateuch, although numerous other structurings of the text have been widely proposed. Theologically, the Gospel has two major points of focus, Jesus as the Messiah, and the imminence of the kingdom of God he proclaims. Special Matthean emphasis is placed upon justice or righteousness that in Matthew's usage refers to a person's response in obedience to God's will. In Matthew's view, the Law of Moses is generally affirmed, but it is Jesus' interpretation rather than the Pharisaic approach that is valid. Matthew's Gospel is also characterized by being the only Gospel to mention the church (16:18; 18:18), and by its many allusions to and quotations of the Old Testament.

F. M. Gillman

See also ARAMAIC MATTHEW; Q SOURCE; SYNOPTIC GOSPELS; SYNOPTIC PROBLEM; TWO-SOURCE THEORY (OF SYNOPTICS).

MATZAH

In Judaism, unleavened bread, the only food containing flour that may be consumed on Passover, following the prescription of Exodus 12:15: "Seven days you shall eat unleavened bread; on the first day you shall put away leaven out of your houses, for if any one eats what is leavened, from the first day until the seventh day, that person shall be cut off from Israel."

Matzah is made from flour and water, kneaded together without yeast or any other additive. (Some authorities allow the elderly or ill people to eat "enriched" matzah, prepared according to the rules given here but containing egg and apple juice in place of water.) The dough is shaped into flat squares or circles, and, to keep it from swelling during baking, it is perforated with a toothed rolling pin. Further, to prevent the dough from beginning in any way to ferment and become leavened, it is prepared quickly, with the entire procedure from the initial mixing through placement in the oven taking no more than a few minutes.

Jewish law deems eating matzah to be obligatory only on the first night (in the Diaspora, the first two nights) of Passover. During the rest of the festival, the individual must refrain from eating leavened bread or other foods containing flour or leaven, but may choose as well not to eat matzah.

While eating matzah on the first night of Passover fulfills a religious obligation, the matzah itself has no status of sanctification and throughout the year may be prepared and eaten like any other food.

Alan J. Avery-Peck

See also HAMETZ; PASSOVER.

MAXIMUS THE CONFESSOR
(579/80–662)

At ten years of age, Moshion was given to the care of Abbot Pantaleon of the monastery of St. Charito. Pantaleon renamed the boy "Maximus," and began to teach him the theology of Origen. In 626 Maximus fled from the invasion of the Persians to Constantinople and from there to Africa where he wrote against the Monothelitism of the patriarchs of Constantinople, Sergius, and Pyrrhus. Maximus attended the Council of Rome in 647 where he successfully helped Pope Martin I defend the teaching that Christ had two wills, human and divine. When he returned to Constantinople in 653, he was tried and condemned to exile for his opposition to the patriarchs. Without the protection of Martin I, who died in 655, Maximus was again tried in 662. He was not only once again exiled, but his right hand and tongue were mutilated as punishment for his writing and teaching. Maximus died shortly after this torture.

Gary Macy

See also MONASTICISM IN EASTERN CHRISTIANITY; MONOTHELITISM; ORIGEN; PATRIARCH.

MAYA

A Sanskrit word whose meaning ranges from "artistic creation" through "magic" to "deception" or even "illusion," *maya* is used in Hindu myth and theology to designate the mysterious power of the divine that projects the world appearance. It also sometimes indicates the appearance itself, as in the statement, "The world is Vishnu's maya," that is, his mysterious creation. The concept of maya and its interpretation are of immense importance to Hindu theology, for it is at once the primary cosmogonic principle and the fundamental cause of human spiritual bondage. Although it is frequently translated simply as "illusion," it does not often mean that. In Advaita Vedanta,

the world produced by maya is a false appearance, but not a bare illusion, since it is experienced intersubjectively and is eternal in duration. In Vaishnava Vedanta, maya is God's mysterious, magical, creative power, but the world it creates—though it may obscure the highest spiritual verities—is fully real.

Lance E. Nelson

See also ADVAITA VEDANTA; DVAITA VEDANTA; VISHISHTADVAITA VEDANTA.

MAYA TRADITIONAL RELIGION

The Maya peoples developed their distinct cultures and societies in the Mesoamerican region east of the Isthmus of Tehuantepec. Centuries before the Spanish conquest, the Maya had developed highly sophisticated kingdoms (ruled by dominant city-states) and cultures. Their decline, probably due to climatic changes and internal warfare, had occurred well before the arrival of the Spanish—but the Maya people never disappeared, being today the majority population in significant regions of southern Mexico and northern Central America. Within the Maya religious universe (past and present) it is possible to discover a variety of beliefs and practices that, nevertheless, can yield some common elements. Transmitted over the centuries mainly by oral tradition, the crucially important religious text known as the *Popol Vuh* was written by a Quiché Maya scribe (of western Guatemala) around 1555, using the Roman alphabet and, therefore, at the time of the Spanish conquest. The *Popol Vuh* and older inscriptions, murals, and archeological artifacts and monuments are the sources for the modern reconstruction of the ancient Maya traditional religion.

Maya traditional religion is both syncretic and synthetic. With roots not only in their own cultural and social experience, the religion of the Maya borrowed from the earlier Olmec and Toltec and from other ancient Mesoamerican peoples. The religion synthesized much of Maya reflection on life in a complex set of interlocking segments. Combining sophisticated philosophical ideas (for example, "nothingness" and the mathematical zero that do not exclude but assume the existence of one primordial god who was alone and in the heart of heaven) with profound theological reflections (for example, the ultimate divine is and has always been one, even after this god multiplied godself into numerous but lesser divinities who are only aspects of the one, ultimate divine being). It seems highly inaccurate, from the Maya perspective, to speak of their traditional religion as polytheistic, given their belief in the oneness of the ultimate divine being. All other divinities were regarded as "aspects" of the ultimate divine.

Time and calendars for the measurement of time were very important to and in the Mayan traditional religion. Their astronomic, cosmological observations and theories (highly advanced by any standard) all led to considerations of time as a religious category, the measurement of which (calendars) was necessary to guarantee understanding of the universe and the divinities, and to guarantee cosmic order. The whole cosmos (heaven, hell, and earth) was explained through calendric, mathematical metaphors. The Maya also believed that there had been four distinct and subsequent creations (the present being the fourth). The first three creations had failed because of the unworthiness of the creatures who had populated each of them, and because they had all refused to gratefully bear the burden of time. Humankind (who came to be in the fourth creation) was made from corn and, in that way, somehow participates in the divine reality because corn is divine. Humans will survive as long as they show gratitude for their creation by responsibly bearing the burden and consequences of time (of their personal and collective destinies).

Despite their emphatic belief in the oneness of the ultimate divine being, the Maya traditional religion was also deeply dualistic. The one primordial god was addressed as both Father and Mother, and it was this one god's sexual act with him- or herself that began the process of creation. And after this one creative sexual act, all reality (and all resulting beings, divine and human) is related to itself dualistically.

The Maya traditional religion held responsibility in high esteem. All that is and happens has been brought about by the acts and/or behavior of gods and persons; and thus, what is ethically good resulted from responsible actions or behavior, and what is ethically bad came about because of irresponsible acts or behavior. Duty was enforced by guilt and shame, and all signs of individualism were to be repressed. One's "face" was the external expression of one's real, inner self; and thus honor, reputation, and "saving face" were very important to the Maya. The spoken word, and names, all had religious significance as well as the observance (and maintenance) of one's rank and position in society.

Maya rituals seem to have been present at every moment and stage of personal and social life. Their rituals were very elaborate and time-consuming. Many of the Maya rituals would today be judged as cruel or, at the very least, gory. For the Maya, however, these ritual actions were expected and unavoidable. These included self-mutilation, bloodletting, and human sacrifices, as well as long vigils, fasts, long periods of sexual abstinence, and so forth. Offerings were frequently made, in sacred places, to the gods. Omens, prophecies, and dreams were also important in the Maya religious life, as well as the many symbols that conveyed to them the meaning of and relation among the different dimensions of the cosmos and of daily life.

Today's Maya preserve some of the traditional religion, but rarely in its ancient form. Catholicism, and more recently evangelical and Pentecostal Protestantism, have impacted modern Maya religious life. Most Maya now claim membership in one or another branch of Christianity, although many of the old rituals and religious beliefs (and worldviews) remain in syncretized forms under apparently Christian façades. But there is no necessary connection between those who are Maya today and their ancestors' religion, except (perhaps) for historical and/or cultural links.

Orlando Espín

See also CULTURE; NAHUA TRADITIONAL RELIGION; RELIGION; RELIGION, THEORIES OF; RITUAL; SYNCRETISM.

MAZEL TOV

Hebrew, meaning "good luck" or "congratulations."

This is one of Judaism's most well-known phrases and popular expressions. It is used to offer good wishes and congratulations at the time of life-cycle events or joyous occasions such as a Bar Mitzvah, wedding, graduation, birthday, or anniversary, or for any accomplishment or life-triumph.

Wayne Dosick

MBITI, JOHN S. (1931–)

Kenyan philosopher and theologian. Mbiti studied in Kenya, Uganda, and the United States, before going to England's Cambridge University. Moving from an African Christian denomination to the Anglican Church, he is now a member of the Swiss Reformed Church. He has been very active in the ecumenical movement through the World Council of Churches. Mbiti's theological and philosophical works have challenged many European and North American theologians' superficial notions about African traditional religions and their understanding of revelation. Mbiti argues that the God of Jesus may be found in African traditional religions. His most important books are *African Religions and Philosophy* (1961), and *Bible and Theology in African Christianity* (1986).

Orlando Espín

See also AFRICAN CHRISTIANITY; AFRICAN TRADITIONAL RELIGIONS; CULTURE; INCULTURATION.

McCORMICK, RICHARD A. (1922–2000)

In a career spanning over fifty years of teaching and nearly twenty volumes and numerous articles, Richard McCormick has served the field of moral theology in a number of significant ways. Principal among those were his "Notes on Moral Theology" published in the journal *Theological Studies* and then collected in several books. In his "Notes," year by year, McCormick kept the community of ethicists current with every major development in the field. His evaluation of each author's thought was concise, brilliant, always respectful, yet incisive and exemplary in its logical analysis. He demonstrated not only his vast knowledge of the field of ethics, but also his ability to see connections between the work of various authors.

Besides coauthoring or coediting works with Charles E. Curran, McCormick authored his own texts. There, he used a "natural law" approach to reflect principally on bioethics and sexual ethics. His work held great currency in the medical and scientific professions because it relied more on scientific discovery and logic than on explicit applications of faith-based truth claims. A Jesuit priest, McCormick held a number of prestigious posts, including the Rose F. Kennedy professor of Christian ethics at Georgetown University's Kennedy Center for Bioethics, and the John A. O'Brien professor of Christian ethics at the University of Notre Dame in Indiana.

G. Simon Harak, s.j.

See also CURRAN, CHARLES E.

McFAGUE, SALLIE (1934–)

Sallie McFague, among the leading eco-feminist theologians of the United States, was educated at Smith College and Yale University and spent most of her career teaching at Vanderbilt University. Among her most important contributions has been her argument for the expansion of Christians' religious imagination to include images of God beyond the symbols of "father" and "king." While traditional, these two images are also dangerous in her view, especially when taken in isolation, because they legitimate both the oppression of women and the unchecked exploitation of the earth. In her groundbreaking book *Metaphorical Theology: Models of God in Religious Language* (1982), she argued that all religious language is metaphorical and therefore not fixed but open to new images. In *Models of God:*

Theology for an Ecological, Nuclear Age (1987), McFague proposed three additional and corrective ways of understanding God—namely, as mother, lover, and friend. In another major work, *The Body of God: An Ecological Theology* (1993), she tackled the clash between scientific and faith claims. Here she argued that if Christians can see the cosmos as in some sense the "body of God," then a scientific understanding of the cosmos ought to enrich, rather than damage, their theology—that is, their language for speaking about God. She has also published *Super, Natural Christians: How We Should Love Nature* (1997) and *Life Abundant: Rethinking Theology and Economy for a Planet in Peril* (2000).

James B. Nickoloff

McNEILL, JOHN J. (1925–)

Best known for his writings on homosexuality, the church, and gay spirituality, McNeill received a doctorate in philosophy from Louvain, concentrating on the work of Maurice Blondel. Entering the Jesuits in 1948, McNeill began a ministry to gay and lesbian Catholics in the early 1970s, publishing *The Church and the Homosexual* (1976), in which he judged the church's attitude toward homosexuality as an example of "structured social injustice," and called for a reappraisal of the church's teaching and pastoral response to the gay community. Following orders from the Vatican's Congregation for the Doctrine of the Faith, McNeill's Jesuit superiors instructed him to discontinue speaking and writing on the questions of homosexuality and sexual ethics, eventually extending their prohibition to include any and all ministry to homosexual persons. Obedient for nearly ten years, he was finally expelled from the Society of Jesus in 1987 when he issued a critical public response to a Vatican document, "Letter to the Bishops of the Catholic Church on the Pastoral Care of Homosexual Persons." He continues to minister to the gay community privately as a counselor and psychotherapist, writing extensively on gay spirituality (*Taking a Chance on God*, 1988, and *Freedom, Glorious Freedom*, 1995), and publishing his autobiography, *Both Feet Firmly Planted in Midair* in 1998.

Robert D. McCleary

See also HOMOSEXUALITY (CHRISTIAN PERSPECTIVES); SOCIETY OF JESUS.

MECCA/MAKKAH
Holiest city in Islam. Located in Saudi Arabia at the crossroads of several ancient trading routes, Mecca's prominence is due to many factors. It is the city of the Prophet Muhammad's birth in 570 C.E., and it was there that he received his first revelations in 610 C.E. The most sacred shrine of Islam, the Ka'ba, is located in Mecca. When Muslims all over the world offer their prayers five times each day, they face the direction of the Ka'ba. In addition, Mecca is the site of the *hajj* or pilgrimage all Muslims are supposed to make at least once during their lifetimes if they can afford it. The sanctity of this city is illustrated by the restriction that only Muslims may enter it. Because of its importance, Mecca is also referred to by Muslims as "Mecca the Blessed," and "Mother of Cities."

Ronald A. Pachence

See also HAJJ; KA'BA/KAABA; KIBLA; MUHAMMAD.

MEDELLÍN DOCUMENTS
Between August 24 and September 6, 1968, the Catholic bishops of Latin America met in Medellín, Colombia, to consider the theme of "The Church in the Present-Day Transformation of Latin America in the Light of the Council" (that is, the Second Vatican Council of 1962–5). Opened by Pope Paul VI, the Medellín conference (formally called the Second General Conference of the Latin American Episcopate; the first had been held in Rio de Janeiro in 1955) followed a threefold method in approaching the sixteen topics it considered. This method, first developed in the 1930s by the Catholic Action movement in Europe, consists of three steps, commonly called "see," "judge," and "act." Thus each of the sixteen documents begins with a sociohistorical analysis of a real-life situation ("seeing" reality) followed by an analysis based on relevant doctrinal (theological) principles ("judging" or evaluating the reality from the standpoint of faith). These two steps set the stage for the conclusion of each document, which proposes pastoral guidelines or recommendations for concrete actions to be taken by the church and its members.

The sixteen documents produced at Medellín were divided into three areas of concern. Part One, called "Human Promotion," included treatments of justice, peace, family and demography, education, and youth; Part Two, called "Evangelization and Growth in the Faith," addressed the pastoral care of the masses, pastoral concern for the elites, catechesis, and liturgy; and Part Three, called "The Visible Church and Its Structures," took up the themes of lay movements, priests, religious, formation of the clergy, poverty of the church, joint pastoral planning, and the mass media.

Perhaps the term that best sums up the Medellín conference and its final documents is its call for "solidarity with the poor" ("Poverty" 10). This mandate reflected radically new thinking and practice in the Latin American Catholic Church and led the bishops to place the church's resources and personnel in service of the urban and rural poor who for almost five centuries had largely been neglected by the institutional church. In the decade following Medellín, countless lay Catholics, priests, and religious, and even bishops actively sought to "come closer to the poor" ("Poverty" 9), often by actually moving into poor and marginalized regions.

Some have noted that in the end Medellín reversed its original aim—that is, instead of "applying" Vatican II to the realities of Latin America, the conference amounted to a rereading of Vatican II in light of Latin American realities, especially the fact of massive and unjust poverty. Because of this, the Medellín conference may be seen as a significant step in the coming of age of the institutional church in Latin America, which until this time had not found its own voice but had largely taken its cues from church authorities in Spain, Portugal, and Rome. Medellín's call for justice for the poor and for institutional solidarity with those struggling for liberation provoked strong reactions, pro and con, in Latin America and elsewhere. It also provided the impetus for the development of liberation theology. Medellín marks a turning point in Christian history, not only in Latin America but around the world.

James B. Nickoloff

See also LATIN AMERICAN THEOLOGIES; LIBERATION THEOLOGIES; OPTION FOR THE POOR; PROPHETS (IN CHRISTIANITY); PUEBLA DOCUMENT; SANTO DOMINGO DOCUMENT; SOCIAL JUSTICE; THIRD WORLD THEOLOGIES.

MEDIATOR (IN CHRISTIANITY)

In a social context, the mediator serves as one who stands in the middle between disputing parties and attempts to effect an agreement, compromise, or reconciliation. Christians have seen Jesus Christ, as Son of God and Son of Man, sent by God to save his people, as the unique and ultimate mediator between God and humankind. "For there is one God, and there is one mediator between God and human beings, the man Christ Jesus, who gave himself as a ransom for all" (1 Tim 2:5-6). The church itself continues the act of mediation between God and humankind. The role of mediator (or mediatrix in the feminine form) has also been assigned to Mary, Jude, or any other saint or personage to whom Christians pray in the hope of having their needs presented to God in the saint's own name.

Robert D. McCleary

See also CHRISTOLOGY; ECCLESIOLOGY.

MEDICINE

The word "medicine" has quite a different content in native religious traditions in the Americas. Its primary meaning is "power," that type of power that comes from the sacred and is the cause of life itself. Power belongs first to the sacred, but it has been shared with creatures at the moment of creation, and continues to permeate that creation in all its aspects. As the ambiance of our existence, it is accessible to those who know how to seek it properly—that is, with generous sacrifice and reverent humility. Once obtained, it can be directed to many uses. One of the central uses touches closely upon the common English meaning: it is used to heal those who suffer illnesses of body and soul. In this area, it is the special property of the shaman or medicine person. But it is the universal belief that every person needs a share of medicine power in order to live a full life.

Kathleen Dugan

See also GRACE; RITUAL.

MEDIEVAL CHRISTIANITY (IN THE WEST)

The term "medieval" is problematic since it is an arbitrary and often derogatory term for the period of time that runs roughly from the movement of the Teutonic tribes into the western Roman Empire until the Protestant Reformation. This long historical span covers such diversity that it is difficult to speak of "medieval Christianity" as any kind of unity. It may be more accurate to speak of "medieval Christianities" to describe the different forms Western Christianity took during this period. Acknowledging that other schemas are possible and that different geographical areas developed important differences, it may be useful to speak of three major forms of "medieval Christianity." If there is a unity to this period, it comes from the self-understanding of Western Christians that they were, or at least should be, an institution combining church and state over against the church-state institution of Eastern Christianity.

The conversion and evangelization of the Teutonic tribes during the sixth through tenth centuries resulted in a form of Christianity with characteristics quite distinct from that of the earlier western Roman Empire. Ecclesiastical authority was vested in powerful bishops and in lay rulers. In fact, lay rulers often owned churches and monasteries and appointed the clergy who served in them. This is often referred to as the "proprietal church" system. Monasticism played an extremely important role in both evangelization and education. Celtic practices of private confession with the resultant penance system slowly spread throughout Europe. Penitential prayers were added to the liturgy that, as the Latin of the Mass become incomprehensible to the laity, came to be seen as a dramatic representation of the life and death of Jesus. Devotion to local saints and shrines played an important role in the lives of the faithful insofar as they understood Christianity and distinguished it from early Germanic religious practices.

Starting with the introduction of the Gregorian reforms, Christianity changed dramatically. Power shifted from the lay lords and bishops more and more to the papacy. Canon law developed its own courts whose ruling could be appealed to Rome. Learning shifted from the monasteries to the cathedral schools and finally to the universities, a Christian invention of the late twelfth and early thirteenth centuries. This meant that a separate class of scholars, apart from the pope and bishops, had an important voice in determining Christian beliefs and opinions. Devotional life shifted dramatically as well, when interest in the human Jesus and the human Mary intensified. New forms of Christian life flourished, the most novel being the introduction of the friars. Along with experimentation came heresy, and the line between heretic and saint was often thin indeed. This was an extremely optimistic period in European history that saw important contributions in scholarship, architecture, literature, art, and law. Christianity determined that marriage was constituted by the consent of the couple, a revolutionary idea whose impact is still being felt today. Christianity expanded in territory, establishing kingdoms by force of arms in Byzantium and in the Holy Land. Growing bureaucracy also led to greater intolerance of diversity with the introduction of inquisitions for heresy in many parts of Europe.

With the devastation of the Black Death in the second half of the fourteenth century, Europe seemed to lose the optimism of the early period. The papacy suffered a loss of esteem due to the Avignon papacy and the Great Western Schism. The religious orders, especially the friars, were satirized for their loss of devotion. Learning flourished and diversified, however, as different schools of Scholastic thought vied with the new humanist learning. New universities were founded throughout Europe, but particularly in eastern Europe. Religious life turned inward, and this is a period of the great mystical writers of the interior life. Lush extraliturgical and popular devotions focused on purgatory and the need to redeem the temporal punishment performed there both for the living and the dead. Reform of the church was advocated by many groups from the orthodox Conciliarists and Humanists to the heterodox Lollards and Hussites. This movement for reform led eventually to the Protestant Reformation when the unity of Western Christianity was shattered and "medieval Christianity" can be said to have come to an end.

Gary Macy

See also ALBIGENSIANS; AVIGNON (PAPACY AT); BENEDICTINES; BYZANTIUM/BYZANTINE; CATHARS; CONCILIARISM; DEVOTIO MODERNA; DOMINICANS; FRANCISCANS; FRIARS; GREGORIAN REFORMS; HISTORY; INDULGENCE; INVESTITURE CONTROVERSY; LOLLARDS; MEDIEVAL CHURCH; NOMINALISM; ORDERS, RELIGIOUS; PAPACY/PAPAL; PENITENTIALS; PURGATORY; RELIC (IN CHRISTIANITY); SCHISM, GREAT WESTERN; WALDESIANS.

MEDIEVAL CHURCH

The period of time that runs roughly from the movement of the Teutonic tribes into the western Roman Empire until the Protestant Reformation is so complex that it is difficult to speak of "the medieval church" as any kind of unity. First of all, contemporaries did not use the term "church" in the same way modern writers might. Throughout most of the "Middle Ages" the term "church" could refer to the local community and/or its leadership or the international community and/or its leadership or to the entire "Body of Christ," that is, all those who have been or will be saved. Most theologians defined "the church" in the last-mentioned sense. Only in the mid-fourteenth century did definitions of the church begin to appear that identified it with the institution. When modern writers do study the medieval church as an institution, therefore, they need to be aware that they are using a definition of the church different from that used by the people they are studying.

Secondly, even as an institution, the church changed, sometimes dramatically, during the Middle Ages. In the early centuries, control of the institution of the church lay primarily in the hands of powerful bishops, abbots, and lay rulers. After the Gregorian reforms, power began to shift in favor of the papacy that developed a growing bureaucracy to deal with this shift in power. During the late Middle Ages, the structure of the institutional church was much disputed and no clear resolution to this issue was reached before the Protestant Reformation; indeed, the Reformation was in part a result of such disputes.

Writers often refer to the church in the Middle Ages as Catholic, or even Roman Catholic. There is a sense in which referring to late medieval Christianity as "Roman" and "Catholic" is quite correct. Western Christianity was focused upon Rome as a source of unity, and the papacy did claim a growing authority in later centuries of the Middle Ages. The term "Catholic" also applies, if used in its original Greek sense of "universal" as opposed to a local or national church. If, however, this implies that the church was the same as the Roman Catholic Church that emerged from the Council of Trent, then serious reservations must be raised. There are more differences than continuities between the late medieval church and the post-Tridentine Roman church and even less continuity between the early medieval church and post-Tridentine Roman church.

Gary Macy

See also BODY OF CHRIST (IN CHURCH USE); COMMUNION OF SAINTS; CONCILIARISM; GREGORIAN REFORMS; HISTORY; INVESTITURE CONTROVERSY; MEDIEVAL CHRISTIANITY (IN THE WEST); PAPACY/PAPAL; SCHISM, GREAT WESTERN.

MEDINA

Sometimes written Madina or al-Madina. In Arabic, Medina means "city," and for Muslims who regard this city as sacred, it is more properly referred to as Madinat an-Nabi, "City of the Prophet (Muhammad)." Known as Yathrib before 622 C.E., Medina is located some three hundred miles north of Mecca. The name of the city was changed permanently after the Prophet Muhammad (570–632) emigrated there from hostile Mecca in a journey called the *hijra* in 622. This journey marked the beginning of the first Islamic society or *umma* Muhammad established upon his arrival in Medina. Though the Islamic armies eventually subdued Mecca in 630, Medina remained Muhammad's home until his death in 632. Many pilgrims on their *hajj* (pilgrimage) to Mecca also visit the tomb of the Prophet in Medina.

Ronald A. Pachence

See also HAJJ; HIJRA (IN ISLAM); MECCA; MUHAMMAD; UMMA.

MEDINAT YISRAEL
See ISRAEL, STATE OF.

MEDITATION (CHRISTIAN)
Meditation has customarily been called a form of mental prayer, that is, a praying with the mind rather than with the imagination or the heart. This analysis may be somewhat artificial, however, since mental activity cannot be so neatly segmented. Nevertheless, meditation draws attention to the role of thinking, considering, questioning, weighing evidence, teasing out insight, interpreting, and so forth. In meditation, the mind is certainly active. Sometimes, after arriving at an idea or insight, the mind rests and the individual simply relishes the insight or fresh comprehension. Since meditation is basically an exercise, it is learned by doing, ideally under the direction of a spiritual mentor.

A meditative reading of biblical texts, for example, would consist of an unrushed effort to appreciate the weight of each word in a passage, almost to "taste" its meaning. The medieval monks called this *lectio divina*. Modern biblical scholarship has shown that a reader needs some introduction to the nature of biblical writing in order to avoid doing those ancient texts a disservice. The study of Scripture, then, as a preparation for meditation upon ancient texts, can be seen as part of the process of mental prayer. What distinguishes meditation as prayer from the activity of thinking in general is the conscious orientation of one's reason and intelligence toward God. The world itself can be viewed as a giant text upon which the believing mind can meditate, and thus all human knowing can be ordered toward prayer.

William Reiser, S.J.

See also CONTEMPLATION; LECTIO DIVINA; PRAYER.

MEDIUM

This term refers to a person who claims to have the ability either to communicate with spirits or "channel" their presence. Some of the world's religions have known and approved of mediums, while others reject all such claims as impossible and as nonsense. There is no scientific proof or validation for the ability claimed by mediums.

Orlando Espín

MEGILLAH

(Hebrew, scroll). In Judaism, the biblical books of Esther (read on Purim), Ruth (read on Pentecost), Lamentations (read on Tisha B'Av), Ecclesiastes (read on the Sabbath of Tabernacles), and Song of Songs (read on the Sabbath of Passover). While referred to as "the five scrolls" (Chamesh Megillot), only Esther is actually read from the scroll written out on parchment by a scribe in the same manner as a scroll of the Pentateuch (Torah). The other books are read from printed texts. In light of the scroll of Esther's special preparation, the term Megillah used without further specification refers to it.

Alan J. Avery-Peck

MELANCHTHON, PHILIP
(1497–1560)

Professor of Greek at the University of Wittenberg from 1518, Melanchthon was a humanist and a younger colleague of Martin Luther, also professor at Wittenberg. In 1521, while Luther took refuge in the Wartburg castle from possible persecution, Melanchthon assumed leadership of the Reformation begun in Wittenberg. Unlike Luther, Melanchthon was more inclined to moderate rather than to accentuate theological controversy. It was Melanchthon who was chosen to preside over composition of the *Augsburg Confession* of 1530, a summary of faith intended less to provoke than to conciliate Roman Catholic sensibilities. Later, Melanchthon played an important role in creating an organizational structure for the "Lutheran" church in Saxony.

Thomas Worcester, S.J.

See also AUGSBURG CONFESSION; HUMANISM; LUTHER, MARTIN; LUTHERANISM; LUTHERAN THEOLOGY; REFORMATION; WITTENBERG; WORMS, DISPUTATION OF.

MELAND, BERNARD E.
(1899–1993)

Theologian, theological educator, and Presbyterian minister. After attending Park College, University of Illinois, McCormick Theological Seminary, and the University of Chicago, he taught at Central College in Missouri, Pomona College in California, and the University of Chicago Divinity School. During his twenty years in Chicago, he pioneered "empirical theology," the analysis of social sciences, natural sciences, and the humanities for their contributions to Christian theology. Meland believed that disciplines other than theology provided key theological insights; he wrote in 1957, "Life in all its complexity and its ultimacy commands the Christian theologian's attention." His books include *Faith and Culture* (1953), *The Secularization of Modern Culture* (1966), *Fallible Forms and Symbols* (1976), and an edited volume, *The Future of Empirical Theology* (1969).

Evelyn A. Kirkley

MELKITE CATHOLIC CHURCH

A church in full communion with Rome since 1684. It descends from Christian communities in the Middle East that refused to follow Monophysitism and accepted the definitions of the Council of Chalcedon (in 451 C.E.). These same communities later remained loyal to the see of Constantinople even after the Muslim invasions. They follow the Byzantine Rite. There are over one million Melkite Catholics worldwide, under the overall jurisdiction of the patriarch of Antioch (in Damascus). The term "Melkite" comes from the Syriac term *malko*, "king"— originally a reference to the "king's people" who had accepted the Council of Chalcedon.

Orlando Espín

See also ANTIOCHENE THEOLOGY; BYZANTIUM/BYZANTINE; CATHOLIC TRADITION; CHALCEDON, COUNCIL OF; COMMUNION (ECCLESIOLOGICAL); CONSTANTINOPLE, SEE OF; EASTERN CATHOLIC CHURCHES; MONOPHYSITISM; ORTHODOX CHURCHES; ROME, SEE OF.

MENCIUS (372–289 B.C.E.)

(Chinese, *Meng-tzu/Meng-zi*, Master Meng). Born in the state of T'sou about two hundred years after the death of Confucius, he is generally recognized as both the orthodox interpreter of Confucianism and the greatest writer of the Confucian School. Like Confucius, he traveled from state to state exhorting rulers to follow the Confucian way and emphasizing the importance of moral leadership. True to basic Confucian principles, Mencius stressed the innate goodness of man [humanity] and, in the face of social chaos, the adequacy of the feudal system to develop and maintain man's [human] goodness. His ethical and political ideals were based on this belief in man's [humanity's] essential goodness that he felt was bestowed by heaven. Education and government should promote and nurture this goodness for the well-being of humankind under the leadership of a philosopher-king who would embody the principles of *li* (correct behavior) and *jen* (human-heartedness). His synthesis of Confucian teaching became authoritative, and the book bearing his name became one of the Confucian Classics.

G. D. DeAngelis

See also CHU HSI; CHUNG YUNG; CONFUCIANISM; CONFUCIUS; FILIAL PIETY; HSUN-TZU; JEN; LI; NEO-CONFUCIANISM; TE; WANG YANG-MING.

MENDELSSOHN, MOSES (1729–86)

German Jewish philosopher known as the "father" of the Jewish Enlightenment.

Mendelssohn was given a traditional Jewish education in his hometown of Dessau. In 1743 he followed his teacher to Berlin where he was exposed to secular literature and philosophy. He became a leading proponent of the Jewish Enlightenment, attempting to balance traditional Jewish belief and practice with life in the Western secular, cultural world.

Mendelssohn authored the *Biur*, a German translation and commentary of the Bible. He also wrote *Phaedon*, a philosophical discussion of the immortality of the soul; and *Jerusalem*, an argument for the separation of church and state.

Although Mendelssohn remained a traditional Jew throughout his lifetime, and although he was one of the leading Jewish figures of eighteenth-century Judaism, he is suspect in some Jewish quarters because all his grandchildren became baptized Christians. Nevertheless, Mendelssohn is credited with the pioneering work in reconciling traditional Judaism with the modern age, and his influence remains dominant and strong in contemporary times.

Wayne Dosick

See also ENLIGHTENMENT IN WESTERN HISTORY.

MENDICANTS

The word "mendicant" comes from the Latin *mendicare*, that is, "to beg," and refers to those religious orders that take vows renouncing all ownership, both personal and corporate. The ideal of apostolic poverty gained popularity in the late twelfth and thirteenth centuries in Western Christianity and numerous groups espousing radical poverty appeared. Some, like the Waldensians, were considered heretical, while others, especially the Franciscans, Dominicans, Carmelites, and Augustinians, led an important spiritual renewal through their experiments in living this new form of Christian life. Francis and Dominic originally intended that their followers would beg each day for their food and lodging, possessing nothing of their own. Over time this demand was greatly modified, but the ideal of the freedom that voluntary and radical poverty brings still drives the mendicant tradition.

Gary Macy

See also CARMELITES; DOMINICANS; DOMINIC DE GUZMÁN; FRANCISCANS; FRANCIS OF ASSISI; FRIARS; MEDIEVAL CHRISTIANITY (IN THE WEST); POVERTY (RELIGIOUS VOW); WALDENSIANS.

MENNONITES

Mennonites are a Christian movement descended from the Anabaptists, the radical wing of the Protestant Reformation. They were founded by Menno Simons (1496–1551), a Dutch Catholic priest who became an Anabaptist in 1536 and began preaching in the Netherlands, Switzerland, and Northern Germany. His message reflected Anabaptist beliefs in believer's baptism, pietism, the literal truth of Scripture, and the complete separation of church and state. Like other Anabaptists, Mennonites refused to serve in the military, hold public office, or take oaths.

However, they differed from Anabaptists by rejecting violence in any form. Simons stressed pacifism and strict adherence to the ethics of the Sermon on the Mount. Moreover, he emphasized cooperation between his followers and civil authorities as long as it did not conflict with Scripture. Mennonites aspired to inner perfection and lived according to strict rules of behavior; members who violated them were shunned. Although they did not practice communal ownership of property, they possessed a strong sense of community and created a tightly knit family ethos based on spirituality and ethnicity. They practiced adult baptism by pouring and a ritual of foot-washing.

Due to their higher degree of cooperation with local governments, Mennonites experienced less persecution than other Anabaptists. However, they were still considered subversive to civil and ecclesiastical authorities, and they dispersed throughout eastern Europe. In the seventeenth and eighteenth centuries, many Mennonites emigrated to the North American British colonies where they found toleration in Pennsylvania. Mennonites settled in Germantown, Pennsylvania, as early as 1683; Lancaster County became a Mennonite center. Communities also formed in Virginia, the Carolinas, Ohio, and Indiana. During the American Revolution, the Mennonites' pacifism gained them the reputation as British sympathizers. Emigration to the United States slowed, and Mennonite communities grew in Canada, Russia, and the Ukraine. In the nineteenth and twentieth centuries, many Mennonites moved to South America.

Away from the unity created by pressure and persecution, the Mennonites experienced internal conflict and schism, primarily over the degree of accommodation to "worldly" standards. How separate should faithful Mennonites be from the modern world? They split into numerous smaller groups, from traditionalists who rejected modern technology such as cars, telephones, and computers, to assimilated Mennonites virtually indistinguishable from other Protestants. Mennonites have also established colleges, a seminary, and a publishing house in the United States. They continue to stress strict moral norms; many disapprove of public athletic events and bikini beaches. In cooperation with other "peace churches," the Amish, Brethren, and Quakers, Mennonites were instrumental in establishing conscientious objector status for those who refused military service on religious grounds.

Evelyn A. Kirkley

See also ANABAPTISTS; BOHEMIAN BRETHREN/MORAVIANS; PIETISM.

MENORAH
(Hebrew, candelabra). In Judaism, the seven-branched oil lamp used in the wilderness Tabernacle (see Exod 25) and in Solomon's Temple (see 1 Kings 7:49). In contemporary parlance, the term also refers to the eight-branched candelabra used on Hanukkah, known as well as a Hanukkiah. The seven-branched menorah is the symbol of the modern state of Israel.

Alan J. Avery-Peck

See also HANUKKAH.

MERCY
Understood best as one of a constellation of attitudes and practices such as contrition, forgiveness, and reconciliation, mercy differs from forgiveness in that it is always unilateral, not mutual. In addition, it always seems to be unidirectional, from a superior person or position to an inferior. Finally, in contrast to forgiveness that seems to be a characteristic of a subject (or of intersubjectivity, if forgiveness is received or shared), mercy proceeds from a subject to an object/other and is determined by its effect on that other.

Mercy seems to have two facets. The first is as an aspect of judgment. That is, judgment has been made of wrongdoing, and punishment assigned. Then the judge releases the wrongdoer from the punishment, so exercising "mercy." The second aspect is more theological, referring to the mercy of God. Whereas we can acknowledge God as exercising mercy in the first sense, theologians are also aware of the great disparity between the perfection of God and the imperfection of God's creatures, especially of the human being. Thus, even without specific reference to their sin, God must have mercy toward creatures so that they can continue to live in God's presence. In short, "What God has created, God's mercy sustains."

G. Simon Harak, s.j.

See also CONTRITION; FORGIVENESS; RECONCILIATION.

MERICI, ANGELA (1474?–1540)

As a member of the Third Order of St. Francis, Angela Merici of Brescia, Italy, spent more than twenty-five years serving the poor and needy, working for church reform in the period immediately preceding the Council of Trent, and acting as spiritual guide to many. In 1535 she founded the Company of St. Ursula (often called the Ursulines), a group of laywomen who were to engage in various good works, especially catechizing children, and meet regularly for prayer and spiritual companionship, but remain living with their families. Thus, according to the original rule Angela wrote, they were not "religious" as Trent defined that term. After Angela's death, however, when members of the Company moved to Milan, they were urged to begin living together; later, in France, they became cloistered religious. They did retain the aim of education, however, by means of a special vow of instruction and by modifications in their cloister to permit poor girls to attend day school in the monastery.

Mary Anne Foley, C.N.D.

See also CLOISTER; CONGREGATIONS (ORDERS); COUNTER-REFORMATION/ CATHOLIC REFORMATION; RELIGIOUS (VOWED); THIRD ORDERS; TRENT, COUNCIL OF.

MERIT

In its technical, theological meaning, "merit" indicates the human claim to a reward from God for a virtuous action done according to God's will or command-ment. In both the Old and New Testaments there are frequent promises of rewards to those who keep the commandments, who follow the will of God, who live virtuously, who love their neighbors, and the like (for example, see Exod 23:20-22; Deut 5:28-33; Matt 5:3-12; 6:4, 19ff.). Since Tertullian and Cyprian of Carthage, there have been theological elaborations on merit among Christians.

Medieval theologians developed the reflection on merit, and made a distinction between what they called *merit de condigno* and *merit de congruo. De condigno* implied that a reward was due on grounds of justice because a specific action was performed ("God, you *owe* me this"). *De congruo,* on the other hand, implied that the reward was possible only if the person who received it was already trying to live according to God's will ("God, I *trust and know* that you will keep *your* promised reward"). Today we must remember that juridical ("justice") terminology and categories were frequently used by earlier generations of Christian scholars in their reflections on salvation (and, hence, on merit). Medieval theologians thought that, under certain conditions, both types of merit were possible to Christians and non-Christians alike, but *de congruo* only to persons living in Christian faith, hope, and love. Sixteenth-century Protestant Reformers strongly rejected the whole idea of merit, believing that it was against the very notion of justification by faith. The Council of Trent also taught that no human merit could effect or initiate the process of salvation without God's grace —that is, no human merit could in any way "earn" or "purchase" salvation from God or substitute for faith; but Trent also reminded Christians that God does reward (according to God's own promises) good, loving, human actions.

Currently, there is little explicit theological discussion on merit (although in the past the controversies were numerous and frequent). Today the reflection has begun to shift, as it had to, to questions of salvation and grace, and to the relationship between human actions in the service of social justice (and the like) and salvation.

Orlando Espín

See also COUNTER-REFORMATION/ CATHOLIC REFORMATION; ELECTION (DOCTRINE OF); ETHICS, SOCIAL; GRACE; JUST; JUSTICE; JUSTIFICATION; REFORMATION; SALVATION; TRENT, COUNCIL OF.

MERIT (PUNYA)

Good karma, the accumulation of which is the goal of most Hindus and Buddhists as it leads to better destiny, both in this life and in future incarnations. In Buddhism, individuals are thought to accumulate karma by actions of body, speech, and mind. The preaching of the tradition instructs individuals to make as much merit as they can, and to avoid demerit (*apunya* or *papa*) in their everyday conduct. An early listing of ways of making *punya* begins with *dana* ("giving") to support the monks, nuns, and Buddhist institutions; the need to make merit thus underlies the exchanges essential to the perpetuation of the faith. Meditation and the cultivation of insight (*prajna*) increase one's store of merit; some philosophers even assert that these practices "burn up" bad karma. Other forms of merit-making include respect for elders, service to a superior, instruction, listening, and changing one's mind for the right. It is also meritorious to transfer merit to others, a practice that connected social groups and linked humans to nonhuman beings also subject to karmic law.

Todd T. Lewis

See also BODHISATTVA; JATAKA; KARMA; SHILA; UPAYA.

MERLEAU-PONTY, MAURICE (1905–61)

French existentialist philosopher. Influenced by Edmund Husserl and phenomenology, Merleau-Ponty moved closer to existentialism, emphasizing the indispensable role of "meaning" in human life. He thought that if there were an Absolute (that is, "God"), all possible meaning would have been achieved already, but without human contribution or effort. For Merleau-Ponty this would imply, as a consequence, that no human action could be done for meaningful purposes (because no human act or life could add anything to the totality of meaning already attained in the Absolute). Merleau-Ponty decided that the only possible and reasonable way of discovering and safeguarding meaning in human action and life, and of avoiding utter absurdity, would be to deny that there is an Absolute (hence, deny "God"). Not all existentialists (not even those who were atheists) agreed with him. Among Merleau-Ponty's publications are his *Lectures at the College de France* (1960), *Sense and Non-Sense* (1964), and *The Structure of Behavior* (1963).

Orlando Espín

See also ABSOLUTE; EXISTENTIALISM; GOD; HEIDEGGER, MARTIN; JASPERS, KARL; MARCEL, GABRIEL; MODERNITY; PHENOMENOLOGY; POSTMODERNITY; SARTRE, JEAN PAUL.

MERTON, THOMAS (1915–68)

Born in France, raised in Britain and the United States, and educated at Cambridge and Columbia Universities, Thomas Merton converted to Catholicism and entered the Trappist monastery of Our Lady of Gethsemani (Kentucky) in 1941. Never able to overcome his desire to write, he published his autobiography, *The Seven Storey Mountain*, in 1948, and almost overnight became the best-known figure in Western monasticism in the twentieth century. From an early focus on Christian contemplation and prayer, his concerns expanded to embrace contemporary sociopolitical questions (civil rights, nuclear war, poverty). He also became deeply engrossed in the study of Eastern methods of meditation, especially as practiced in Buddhism. He died in 1968 while in Thailand to attend a conference on monasticism. Other important works include *New Seeds of Contemplation* (1961) and *The Asian Journal* (1975).

James B. Nickoloff

See also CONTEMPLATION; CONTEMPLATIVES; MONASTICISM IN WESTERN CHRISTIANITY; TRAPPISTS.

MESSIAH (IN JUDAISM)

(Hebrew, *Meshiah*, anointed one). In classical Jewish thought, the redeemer of the Jewish people, who brings an end to exile and returns the Jews to the land of Israel; this redeemer's arrival marks the conclusion of the current order ("this world") and the beginning of the messianic age ("the world to come"). The Hebrew Bible understands the term "anointed one" to refer to an earthly king, in particular, David or one of his descendants. The eschatological understanding of the messiah found in later Judaism developed in the last several centuries B.C.E., when, under oppressive Roman rule, the Jewish longing for a temporal savior evolved into a hope for a miraculous figure who would fulfill God's promises found in the Hebrew Bible. While Talmudic teachings about the messiah are unsystematic, by the medieval period, a more uniform eschatology emerged in which, especially in mystical circles, contemporary events were interpreted as signs of the messiah's arrival. Rabbinic leaders cautioned against such predictions, but the period in all events saw the emergence of a number of messianic pretenders, foremost among them Shabbatai Tzvi and Jacob Frank.

With the exception of some Hasidic groups, modern Jewish movements have deemphasized messianic thinking and the notion of a messianic figure. Reform Judaism in particular has replaced the traditional longing for a messiah with the hope for a messianic age, an era of peace and wholeness for all people.

Alan J. Avery-Peck

See also ESCHATOLOGY (IN JUDAISM); RESURRECTION (IN JUDAISM); SHABBATAI TZVI.

MESSIANIC JUDAISM

A Christian missionary movement, first organized in San Francisco in 1973 under the name Jews for Jesus, intended to convert Jews to Christianity. Holding that Jesus was the Jewish messiah, the movement believes that Jews' acceptance of him is an essential element of proper Jewish theology and is compatible with continuing Jewish self-identity and religious practice. This is a Christian theology, distinct from any Jewish belief from the early second century and up to today.

Alan J. Avery-Peck

MESSIANIC MOVEMENTS

A sociological, anthropological term to describe a group movement, begun by and centered around the leadership of a "divinely appointed messenger." Evidently borrowing the term "messiah" from the Judeo-Christian tradition, messianic movements have historically occurred in most "prophetic" religions (Judaism, Christianity, Islam, and the like). Most millenarian groups would not classify as messianic movements; to qualify, a millenarian group needs to be led by a single person, appointed by God, and whose sole purpose is the establishment of a perfect society for the elect in the midst of this world. There seem to be three preconditions, within the context of millenarian expectations, for the birth of a messianic movement: (a) there must be a group that perceives itself to be marginalized or oppressed by a dominant society (and religion) that the group interprets as somehow decadent; (b) there must be some distinct hope in divine intervention, in favor of the oppressed group (a hope that usually centers around the arrival of a divinely appointed leader who will be the group's liberator); and (c) the group must believe that there can be a perfect place for them on earth, to which the leader will take them. Within these general parameters, it is possible to identify messianic movements and their leaders. Examples from the recent past: "Father Divine" and his Harlem congregations (in the U.S., in the 1930s); Antonio Conselheiro and the town of Canudos (in Brazil, in the 1890s); the Ghost Dance movement among Native Americans (in the 1870s–1890s); and even more recent ones like the Branch Davidian group of David Koresh (in Texas, in the 1990s) and Jim Jones and Jonestown (in Guyana, in the 1970s). The list of examples could be quite long.

Orlando Espín

See also CULTURE; ELECTION (DOCTRINE OF); GRACE; JUSTICE; MESSIAH (IN JUDAISM); MILLENARIANISM; PROPHETISM (IN WORLD RELIGIONS); SALVATION.

MESSIANIC SECRET (IN MARK)

An unusual feature of Markan christology that relates to those instances when Jesus tells people to be silent about his actions or identity (see Mark 1:33, 44; 3:12; 5:43; 7:36; 8:26, 30; 9:9). While some have defended the historicity of these commands by Jesus, W. Wrede in his 1901 classic, *Das Messiasgeheimnis in den Evangelien* (= *The Messianic Secret* [Cambridge, 1971]), explained this as Mark's way to show that Jesus neither claimed to be nor was recognized in his lifetime as the Messiah. The messianic secret was rather a tradition coming from the early Christians that they had read into Jesus' life and that Mark had taken over. His Gospel was thus more a theological statement about Jesus' identity than an objective account of his life.

As the discussion has developed in this century, the reasons given for Mark's use of the technique have proliferated. Many scholars agree that Wrede identified an important, even key, element of Markan christology, that is, that the secrecy theme is an important element in Mark's christology. Further, there is much concurrence that the secrecy concerns the identity of Jesus, that cannot be understood apart from the Cross/Resurrection events. But precisely why Mark, or his tradition, introduced this motif, and exactly how it functions literarily and theologically, seem yet to be fully explained.

F. M. Gillman

See also CHRISTOLOGY; MARK/MARKAN; MESSIAH (IN JUDAISM); MESSIANIC JUDAISM.

MESTIZAJE

The name of a long sociohistorical *process* of integration and mutual reinterpretation by two or more distinct cultural groups that have been brought together by historical events and forced to share the same space and the same society. History shows that the cultural groups that engage in *mestizaje* usually do so unwillingly, and frequently as the result of one group conquering or unduly influencing the other(s). Although there might be extensive racial mixing as part of the mestizaje process, the cultural mingling is by far the most important element and result of mestizaje. The terms *mestizo* (in the masculine) and *mestiza* (in the feminine) refer to the individuals, groups, religions, cultures, and so on, that result from mestizaje. All human groups in the modern world, whether they are aware of it or not, are *mestizos*— at least culturally.

The notion of mestizaje, as theological category, has been of critical importance in U.S. Latino theology and in Latin American thought. Philosophers José Vasconcelos, Leopoldo Zea, and José Carlos Mariátegui, as well as a number of social scientists, have impacted the theological interpretation and use of mestizaje. In U.S. Latino theology, Virgilio Elizondo stands out as the first author who systematically pointed to the richness and potential of the term. Others have followed his lead and intuitions (for example, Roberto Goizueta, Alex García-Rivera, and Jeanette Rodríguez).

Mestizaje has also become crucial for understanding Latin Americans and U.S. Latinos (and their cultures, societies, and religions), from the social scientific and historical perspectives.

The term mestizaje was introduced during the Latin American colonial period, and it explicitly referred to the mingling (cultural, racial) of Spanish and native. Mestizos were considered socially and racially inferior by both the native populations and European colonizers. As their numbers grew, the mestizos turned against the natives in their attempt to be admitted into white colonial society. And as mestizos became the demographic majority, in the second half of the nineteenth century, they began to present themselves as the desirable and authentic synthesis of the Latin American peoples.

Today, however, the term mestizaje is frequently used for cultural and/or racial mixing, regardless of the specific groups involved, and with little regard for the historical roots of the term. It should also be noted that, since the colonial period as well, the terms *mulataje, mulato* and *mulata* continue to be used specifically where mestizaje occurred between/among European and African groups in the Americas. Today there is a growing awareness of the limitations and difficulties inherent in the category of mestizaje. Consequently (and especially among younger theologians: cf. Néstor Medina) there is increased criticism of mestizaje as a theological category.

Orlando Espín

See also CULTURE; ELIZONDO, VIRGILIO; ESPÍN, ORLANDO; GOIZUETA, ROBERTO S.; INCULTURATION; LATINO/A; LATINO CATHOLICISM; LATINO PROTESTANTISM; LATINO THEOLOGY (-IES); LIBERATION THEOLOGIES; THEOLOGICAL ANTHROPOLOGY.

MESTIZO/A

See MESTIZAJE.

METANOIA

In Christian discourse, the word "metanoia" (from Greek for "change of mind or heart") is a technical term that melds the concepts of repentance and conversion. Thus understood, the term coalesces four separable considerations: (1) a recognition of the inadequacy of one's past attitude to God; (2) an acknowledgment that this deficient attitude has been manifested by sinful conduct; (3) a sincere internal regret for both the attitude and the behavior; and (4) an unconditional commitment to a complete internal reorientation as well as the manifestation of this redirection in external conduct. The term is found in the New Testament and is especially prominent in the writings of the apostolic fathers.

There are places in late postexilic apocalyptic and pseudepigraphical literature as well as in the works of Philo in which the term "metanoia" includes the concepts of repentance and conversion. They are the first examples of the use of this Greek word to express one of the major concerns of the prophets of Israel. In the Hellenistic world, metanoia conveyed the concept of "change" in feelings, will, and thought that may or may not include the idea of regret. In the prophets of Israel, there is a consistent call to return (*sub*, that is, to turn back to God) *and* to transform behavior accordingly. The preexilic prophets stressed a communal "about-face"; the exilic and postexilic prophets also called individuals. While the prophets did not reject the penitential practices of the cult (like fasting, wearing sackcloth and ashes), they insisted that when external behavior was not accompanied by a complete internal change of heart, external practices were useless.

In the New Testament, forms of "metanoia" are included in accounts of the preaching and baptizing ministry of John the Baptist (Matt 3:2, 8, 11; Mark 1:4; Luke 3:3, 8; Acts 13:24; 19:4). In these instances,

the term reflects John's role as the forerunner who anticipates Jesus as the Elijah that Malachi predicted would come as a messenger to prepare the way for God's eschatological inbreak into history (see Mal 3:1, 23; Matt 11:11-15; 17:10-13; Mark 9:11-13).

The Gospels are designed to demonstrate that the call to repentance and conversion was the goal of Jesus' life and ministry. The Synoptics include forms of "metanoia" in the preaching of Jesus (Matt 4:17; 11:20, 21; 12:41; Mark 1:15; Luke 5:31; 10:13; 11:3, 5, 32; 15:7, 10, 15; 16:30; 17:3, 4). His inner circle of followers also preach "metanoia" to others during Jesus' ministry (Mark 6:12). The risen Christ commissions his followers to understand that by his suffering and death all the nations are called to "metanoia" (repentance and conversion) and thus, to the forgiveness of sins (Luke 24:47).

The word is at the heart of the accounts of the apostolic preaching (Acts 2:38; 3:19; 5:31; 8:22; 11:18; 17:30; 20:21; 26:20) where it is understood as both a gift of God and a human response (Acts 2:38; 5:31), founded on Christ's salvific role (Acts 5:31), made possible by the gifts of the Spirit (Acts 11:18), affecting and effecting every aspect of life (Acts 3:19). Belief in the imminence of the parousia lent an urgency to this message (Rev 2:5, 16, 21, 22; 3:3, 19), although the delay of the parousia came to be understood as the Lord's desire for all to experience metanoia (2 Pet 3:9). Paul presupposes repentance and conversion in his understanding of faith; however, he uses the term to specify the need for a radical break from the past (2 Cor 12:21; see also Heb 6:1), remorse (2 Cor 7:9-10), and to stress God's benevolence (Rom 2:4; see also 2 Tim 2:25).

Regina A. Boisclair

See also CONVERSION.

METEMPSYCHOSIS

See REINCARNATION.

METHOD IN THEOLOGY

All theological constructs, whether they consciously reflect on it or not, imply (and result from) certain social and cultural contextualizations. Furthermore, theological works follow methods that are always dependent on those contextualizations and on the (non-innocent) methodological assumptions and choices of the theologians. All the different branches of theology—systematic, moral/ethical, pastoral, fundamental, and others—have their distinctive methods, without there being one *single* method possible within each discipline, but a wide variety of them. There are some common traits, historically speaking, in most theological methods—all scholarly attempts at developing (theological) understanding.

1. A commonly used (but certainly not the only) description or definition of theology, as an academic discipline, was coined by Anselm of Canterbury in the eleventh century (paraphrasing Augustine of Hippo). *Fides quaerens intellectum* ("faith seeking understanding") is the Anselmian phrase—simple and accurate enough to describe what theology is, but deceptively lacking in contextual specifics. However, for all its success in describing theology for the next one thousand years, an eleventh-century phrase, no matter how descriptively correct, cannot be naively assumed to be sufficient in the twenty-first century. Anselm's phrase must be interpreted today in more complex ways, because theology has continued reflecting on "faith" and on "understanding," as well as on the means and purposes of "seeking" understanding, throughout the ten centuries since Anselm's time.

Today, in the early years of the twenty-first century, theology's self-description (even as "faith seeking understanding") leads it to reflect on Christian faith, and on its various expressions and elements, in rigorous dialogue with our discipline's long history and contributions, as well as with the church's pastoral reality and needs. For instance, the last one hundred years of biblical research render it impossible for us today to make claims and statements on the nature and workings of faith in the manner employed by Anselm in his day. His definitions of faith would be very seriously challenged by modern-day biblical scholarship. And biblical scholarship embraces but a fraction of other contemporary academic disciplines that have an impact on current understandings of Christian faith and of Christian faith's presence in the world. Psychology, philosophy, sociology and the social sciences, economics, history, and so on, have all led theology to acknowledge (among other things) the developmental and contextual character of all Christian faith and of all Christian faith statements.

Anselm's phrase does not indicate, by itself, what he thought faith was meant to understand theologically, or what he thought Christians engaged in theology should do, in this world, with this acquired understanding. Anselm's phrase only indicates that theology involves a "search," a continuous seeking for understanding. Because theologians and theology have never ceased searching and questioning, we might ask today: What is the purpose of understanding in theology at the dawn of the Third Millennium? And what should Christians do with that understanding in this conflictual world of increased globalization and increased cultural and religious tensions?

Not irrelevantly, Anselm's eleventh-century description of theology assumed that a typical theologian was a male cleric, working in the western European social and ecclesiastical context of his day. Ten centuries after Anselm, Christian theology cannot and does not assume such geographical and social contexts, or the male and clerical status of most of its practitioners. The contexts of professional theology have dramatically changed over the last millennium, as well as the identity of theologians. Today's theology is increasingly crafted by nonordained persons, women and men, with decidedly international and intercultural perspectives. Consequently, many other questions arise now that would have never occurred to Anselm and his contemporaries: Whose faith seeks understanding? How do those who nowadays professionally train in theology impact the Christian communities' understanding of faith? What impact do cultural, historical, social, linguistic, gender, and other studies have on theology as an academic discipline and as a socially responsible task, and on those who practice it? Why should faith seek understanding in a world that seems increasingly secularized and uninterested in rigorous reflection within Christianity? What is it today, in a globalized and globalizing world, that faith should try to comprehend? How should theologians reflect on faith and on faith expressions, given the great cultural and ethnic diversity of humankind and of church membership?

These and numerous other questions stand before twenty-first-century theologians, demand their disciplined attention, and require their careful analyses and consideration. Anselm would be baffled, for sure, but he would also be proud of his successors in theology, because faith is still seeking understanding, and because theology is still as alive and lively as it was in the eleventh century. Theology remains as rigorous, disciplined, and committed as in Anselm's day, albeit transformed in a myriad of methodological and contextual ways over the centuries in order to reflect and satisfy the increasing demands of theological scholarship.

One trait of Anselm of Canterbury's scholarly production, as well as that of many theologians who have followed down the centuries, has been the ability to dialogue with other disciplines. In the Middle Ages, philosophy was the great dialogue partner (perhaps the only one possible at the time), and it remains a privileged partner still. But as newer sciences developed with and since the Enlightenment, theology learned to engage and talk with many other voices and many other perspectives. Consequently, contemporary theologians are often familiar with the social, behavioral, and natural sciences, and with the several branches of the humanities, as well as with economic theory, and with interdisciplinary scholarship (for example, feminist hermeneutics, cultural studies, postcolonial theories, and the like). Dialogue is a historical trademark of the best Christian theology. But theology is more than just "a dialogue" with other sciences.

2. Theology, as its name might suggest, "studies God." Yet sound theologies, precisely because they take God seriously, recognize that no human effort could ever "study" God directly, because God cannot be an "object of study." Consequently, theology studies *what Christians (and others) believe about God, and what Christians (and others) claim God has said about God and about humankind* (that is, revelation).

If there is a God—and theology obviously believes there is—then God must be "the Reality which determines all reality" (Pannenberg). Theology, then, does not study God as an "object" among many other "objects of study." Rather, theology methodologically approaches and tries to understand those dimensions or horizons of human life, of human societies, and of the whole world, that persons and communities of (Christian) faith regard as ultimately grounding and determining meaning and life. Furthermore, theology studies human life, human societies, and the whole world because these are both loci and protagonists in revelation (which is *the* grounding "theological" relationship).

Theology is still "faith seeking understanding" to the degree that faith is the grounding *perspective* from and through which the revealed God and the whole world are "studied" and made understandable. This perspective (faith) and this process (theology), in turn, require interdisciplinary approaches (at least) because no human learning (theology included) could exhaustively name or comprehend life's ultimate meaning.

However, it would seem woefully inadequate to consider theology's task today as exclusively a matter of naming, knowing, or understanding even something as profound and arguably crucial as ultimate meaning. There is no question, of course, that theology does attempt to know and understand—and no apologies are made for this—but this "noetic" dimension is far from exhausting what theology's task is in the contemporary world.

Christian theology is not exclusively or mainly a theoretical, hermeneutic exercise, no matter how satisfying, important, or attractive. Christian theology

is disciplined reflection on reality, within reality's dynamics and social configurations, *for* reality's transformation, from the perspective of faith in the reign of God and in the God of the reign as announced by Jesus the Christ.

Therefore and conversely, if the intimate connections with reality (as locus and aim of the theologian's craft) were not present in a theology, or if the ultimate goal of reality's transformation were absent from a theological construct, then that theology would be deeply flawed as Christian theology—regardless of its otherwise impressive academic apparatus. And yet again conversely, if the scholarly theoretical tools were absent in, or were merely incidental to, what is presented as theology, that work too would be profoundly flawed as Christian theology, because theology must make use of the best theoretical tools for the purpose of enlightening and informing action.

It is precisely this understanding of theology today that leads theologians to affirm their discipline's interdisciplinary character and dialogical vocation. Therefore, it is not the latest academic fad, or some need to appear still relevant, that presses Christian theology into conversation with philosophy, with the social or natural sciences, or with any other scholarly discipline. It is the very *self*-definition of theology that marks it as interdisciplinary.

It must be emphasized, however, that by "interdisciplinary" is not meant, in any way or form, some sort of academic "syncretic smorgasbord." On the contrary, the starting point (human reality under the call of revelation), perspective (faith), and aims of theology (the transformation of all human reality according to God's revelation), are all clearly its own. The interdisciplinary character of the discipline *pertains to its methods*—and this is no less important in theology than its starting point, perspective, and aims. But since theology's methods make possible theology's understanding of reality, of revelation, of faith, and of the many processes, conditions, and contexts impacting the aforementioned, then inter-disciplinarity shapes and conditions theology's work and constructs in a manner not extrinsic to theology itself.

3. All theological constructs assume the existence of method in theology—although it would be more accurate to use the plural "methods." The diversity of cultures and social locations, personal and communal faith experiences, personal commitments and modes of ecclesial participation, and so forth that must all be taken seriously into consideration by any theologian, make it difficult to summarize the diversity of theological methods, and yet there are some basic methodological *operations* that seem to cut across theological disciplines and across distinctions and differences in methodological approaches. These common methodological operations are not necessarily explicit or conscious (for the theologian, or in a theological work), but they appear in all theological constructs. Although these operations might appear to be assumptions, they are not conceptual but dynamically operative in all theology:

a. All theologies are contextual and contextualized. Theologians are human beings. And, therefore, they are and have been shaped (and are members of) their respective cultures, social locations, genders, and so on; and reflect in their lives and work (because the latter is inescapably part of the former) the positives and the negatives of their respective and varied contexts. Theologians, therefore,

reflect (again, in life and work) the biases and prejudices, as well as the humanizing possibilities, of their respective, varied contexts. Because human beings (and thus, theologians) perceive reality and truth, elaborate theories, and apply them, all within and from within their respective, varied contexts, it is impossible to conceive of theology (as the "product" of human beings whose "work" is theology) except as a specifically contextualized construction. Hence, there is no (and there can never be a) universally valid, perennial theology.

b. All theologies serve a social and cultural legitimizing or de-legitimizing purpose. As members of cultures and societies, theologians construct knowledge ("seek understanding") within and thanks to their respective, varied cultural and social contexts. And because all human beings have and assume their locations in culture and society (that is, their social locations), theologians do too. Furthermore, location both opens and limits the epistemological vision of every member of every society and culture—thereby impacting (among other things) their perception and understanding of truth and the truth claims they can make. This, in turn, aids in every human being's assumptions of reality, of one's ethical conduct in reality, and of one's truth claims about reality. That is why no knowledge (including theological knowledge) is ethically innocent; knowledge serves a social, cultural purpose. Knowledge (including theological knowledge) will help either to endorse or legitimize society and culture in their current formations; or it will help to critique and de-legitimize the current forms of society and culture; or it will attempt to navigate between endorsing and critiquing (and thus between legitimizing and de-legitimizing) society and culture by choosing to legitimize (by assuming it as either inevitable, evident, or best) the more general social and cultural formation while promoting adjustments or betterment of specific (but secondary) elements within the social and cultural formation. The choice of theological topics on which to do research and write is directly dependent on this operation.

c. Depending on where a given theologian contextually stands, and for which cultural, social purpose he or she ethically opts, the theologian will look for and select the data he or she considers real, evident, or necessary. And based on the selected data (the selection of which, again, is not socially and culturally innocent, and always occurs contextually), the theologian will assume or conclude that these documents and authors, human experiences and historical periods, truths, perspectives, and so on, and not others, are the ones mainly or exclusively relevant for one's theological reflection and work.

d. Then, based on this last operation, the theologian will choose the methodological approach that will help him or her further research, enlighten and focus, fine-tune, understand, critique, expand, and so forth, the already chosen theological topic. The selected method might accomplish all these expected tasks, thereby serving to "seek understanding," but this search and its resulting understanding are made possible by the contextualized social and cultural location of the theologian and by her or his supportive or critical perspective of the social, cultural formations within which the theologian lives and works. It is important to remember that all serious theologians will consciously choose methods that display intellectual rigor and that will produce a scholarly work.

e. Granting and assuming the preceding four operations, then (and *only* then) can it be said that most theologians have historically selected methods that allowed them to research, reflect, and construct theological works through the study of Scripture, church history (including the patristic period and its writings), church documents (conciliar, papal, synodal, and so on), and the works of other (preceding and contemporary) theologians. Depending on historical periods and specific contextualizations, philosophy, the social and/or natural sciences, and other scholarly disciplines will have been methodologically engaged. In earliest Christian theology, as well as more recently, there has been a dialogue with the perspectives and contributions of non-Christian religions. Perhaps after the eleventh century but certainly after the sixteenth, most Christian theologies have been aware of the existing (and often conflicting) diversity of theological perspectives among separated Christians, although today a more irenic ("ecumenical") perspective predominates among most Catholic, Protestant, Anglican, and Orthodox theologians.

Orlando Espín

See also ANSELM OF CANTERBURY; CONTEXTUALIZATION; CULTURE; THEOLOGY.

METHODIST CHURCHES

The name given to those churches tracing their origins to the Methodist revival, led in England in the eighteenth century by the brothers John and Charles Wesley.

The Wesleys had no intention of founding a new denomination or of breaking away from the Church of England. Most of the members of the early Methodist Societies were Anglican, as were the Wesleys themselves. Although there was mounting tension between the Methodist leaders and the hierarchy of the Church of England, John Wesley sought to lessen those tensions in a number of ways—for instance, his societies were not to meet on Sundays, for on that day their members were expected to attend services in their parish churches, and the places where Methodists met were not called "churches," but rather "chapels," again to show that they were not intended to take the place of the parish church.

The break between Methodism and the Church of England came as a direct result of U.S. independence. As a result of that event, it soon became clear that most Methodists in the U.S. were no longer Anglican, and that the Church of England was unable to minister to them. Wesley repeatedly and unsuccessfully asked the church to ordain ministers for his flock across the Atlantic. Finally, driven by the need to provide leadership for the growing Methodist membership in the New World, Wesley decided to ordain such leaders himself. He based his decision on historical scholarship that had recently been published, and that argued that in the early church there were only two orders: deacon and elder/bishop. Since he was ordained an elder (priest) in the Church of England, he took this to mean that, under extraordinary circumstances, he had the power of ordination. He then proceeded to ordain leadership for the Methodists in the United States. Although at the time of his death the break with the Church of England had not become official, it was clear that the differences were now such that Methodism would become a separate denomination.

In the United States, Methodism grew rapidly. This was partly due to its use of lay preachers and of an itinerant ordained ministry that could move with the advancing Western frontier. The tensions surrounding slavery and the eventual Civil War led to the breakup of the Methodist Church into three branches that were not reunited until 1939, forming the Methodist Church.

Much earlier, in the eighteenth century, and among German Reformed immigrants in Pennsylvania and elsewhere, Philip William Otterbein had founded a movement, deeply influenced by Methodism, known as the United Brethren in Christ. At about the same time, Jacob Albright founded a similar organization, the Evangelical Association. These two joined in 1922 to form the Evangelical United Brethren. And these in turn joined with the Methodist Church to form the present United Methodist Church. In the United States, this church now has approximately ten million members.

The emphasis on sanctification has led to repeated schism within the Methodist movement, for at various times some have felt that the main body had given up on crucial matters having to do with the life of holiness. Thus, around 1830, the Wesleyan Church separated from the rest of Methodism, which they felt did not take a sufficiently strong stance on sanctification and against slavery. Likewise, some thirty years later, the Free Methodists arose as a protest against the practice of renting church pews to particular families within the church. The Church of the Nazarene, which took that name in 1919, had been formed two decades earlier out of a similar emphasis on holy living. After that time, other holiness groups have separated from the main Methodist Church as well as from other churches of the same tradition. At present there are more than twenty major Methodist bodies in the United States. Of these the largest are, besides The United

Methodist Church, the African Methodist Episcopal (AME) Church, the African Methodist Episcopal Zion (AME Zion) Church, and the Christian Methodist Episcopal (CME) Church. In Great Britain, the most important movement separating itself from the Methodist Church was the Salvation Army, now an international organization.

Each of these various branches of Methodism has carried on extensive missionary work, so that today there are strong Methodist churches throughout the world. Many of those originally related to The United Methodist Church are now autonomous churches. In Latin America, there are such autonomous churches among other countries, in Mexico, Brazil, Argentina, Chile, Bolivia, Uruguay, Cuba, and Puerto Rico, although by far the most numerous Wesleyan bodies are Pentecostal churches such as the Iglesia Metodista Pentecostal de Chile, and others in various countries. In Africa, there are approximately three million members of various Methodist Churches, and five million in Asia. In Great Britain, there are approximately half a million Methodists, and slightly fewer in the rest of Europe.

Justo L. González

See also ANGLICAN COMMUNION; WESLEY, CHARLES; WESLEY, JOHN.

METHODIST THEOLOGY

The theology of those churches tracing their origins to the revival that took place in Great Britain in the eighteenth century under the leadership of John Wesley and his brother Charles.

In order to understand the polarities in Methodist theology (or rather, in Methodist theolog*ies*), one has to take into account the polarities in Wesley as well as in the situation in which he found himself.

First of all, Wesley was a man of deep convictions who also exhibited an exceptionally open mind. While he was convinced of his beliefs, and was willing to argue many a detail of Christian doctrine, he always insisted on the distinction between such details and the essentials of the Christian faith. He would say to anyone who held to such essentials, and differed on other matters: "Keep you your opinion, I mine; and that as steadily as ever. You need not even endeavour to come over to me, or bring me over to you. . . . Let all opinions alone on one side and the other. Only give me thy hand" (Sermon 39, "On a Catholic Spirit"). At the same time, however, he would argue fiercely against what he took to be error or immorality—including such matters as Sabbath-breaking, excessive riches, or immodest dress. Thus, some among his heirs have leaned more in the direction of strict orthodoxy, and others more toward leniency.

Likewise, Wesley was at once a fiery preacher whose sermons often elicited emotional responses, and a serious scholar who sought to ground his preaching on tradition and on careful preparation. This in turn has resulted in a tradition in which some insist on one of these two poles, and some on the other.

Finally, Wesley did not believe that he was founding a new church. The meetings of the Methodist Societies were to serve, among other things, as preparation for Sunday worship that was to take place in the Anglican Church, centering on Communion and using the rituals of the Book of Common Prayer. When the Societies broke away from the Anglican church, the result was that some Methodists tended to emphasize the activities that had always taken place in such meetings—prayer, Bible study, testimonials, mutual support—while others tended to emphasize the Anglican rituals that had always been so important for Wesley himself. Again, the result is that some Methodists are highly liturgical, centering their worship on Communion and on a relatively set liturgy, and others follow the opposite direction, centering their worship almost exclusively on preaching, singing, and spontaneous prayers.

In spite of these divergences, Methodist theologies hold a number of characteristics in common. Some of these stem from the use of the Quadrilateral that holds that, besides Scripture and tradition, experience and reason provide guidance for Christian belief and life. In particular, the emphasis on personal experience has become a common mark in all varieties of Methodism. Although not all insist that one should be able to give the exact date and time of one's encounter with Christ, all do affirm the premise that such experience is central to the Christian life, and fundamental for proper Christian theology.

Another common characteristic of all Methodist theologies is their insistence on sanctification. Much of Protestantism has paid so much attention to justification —to the fact of being saved by faith in Christ—that little attention is given to the ongoing process of becoming what God desires us to be. Methodist theology— partly through the influence of Calvin on Wesley—has always insisted on sanctification, and even on the goal of Christian perfection (although whether such perfection can be attained in this life, and how it is known, has been another point of disagreement). This is one of the reasons why the Holiness Movement, and the churches stemming from it, drew its inspiration from Wesley and from Methodist theology.

Finally, it should be pointed out that, although Wesley was profoundly influenced by Calvin and Calvinism on the matter of sanctification, he strongly disagreed with orthodox Calvinism on the matter of predestination. In this regard, he was a proud Arminian. Thus, Methodist theology has always insisted that, no matter how one understands what Scripture says on predestination, this must not be such that it obliterates human freedom and responsibility.

Justo L. González

See also ARMINIANISM; QUADRILATERAL; WESLEY, CHARLES; WESLEY, JOHN.

METHOD OF CORRELATION
A phrase used by Paul Tillich to describe his theological method whereby an analysis of the questions of human/secular existence is correlated with the answers of the Christian tradition. Only by such a procedure, where the questions of the "world" heuristically act to frame the "answers" of the tradition, Tillich maintained, could the relevance and meaning of the Christian faith be vindicated.

J. A. Colombo

See also TILLICH, PAUL.

METROPOLITAN
Title given in the Roman Catholic Church to an archbishop who heads an ecclesiastical province. Part of the responsibilities of a metropolitan include calling and presiding at provincial synods and suggesting candidates for vacant dioceses within his province. The title itself was used officially for the first time by the Council of Nicaea (in 325 C.E.), and the duties expected of metropolitans have varied over time. Today, many of the churches of the Anglican Communion also employ the

title and ministry of metropolitans, as do most Orthodox Churches.

Orlando Espín

See also ANGLICAN COMMUNION; ARCHBISHOP; CATHOLIC TRADITION; DIOCESE/ARCHDIOCESE; EASTERN CATHOLIC CHURCHES; ECCLESIASTICAL PROVINCE; EPARCH; ORTHODOX CHURCHES; ROMAN CATHOLIC CHURCH; SYNODS.

METZ, JOHANN (1928–)

German theologian. Together with Jürgen Moltmann, Johann Metz was one of the major exponents of so-called political theology in Europe. Metz arrived at the position that Christian faith demands a constructive engagement with the realm of the "secular" through an immanent critique of the work of Karl Rahner, articulated in *Christliche Anthropozentrik* (1962). In his "middle period" of political theology, reflected in *Theology of the World* (1966), Metz emphasized the "world as history" and the eschatological orientation of Christianity toward the kingdom of God. His later elaboration in *Faith in History and Society* (1980) and *The Emergent Church* (1981) of a "practical fundamental theology," that is, a fundamental theology based in praxis rather than theory, has accentuated these themes and has been elaborated in a series of essays, fragments, meditations, and the like. In this later work, Metz has increasingly emphasized a cluster of basic themes such as the narrative memory of the crucified and risen Christ, the mystical and political dimensions of the discipleship of Christ, apocalyptic time, the emergence of the "church from below," as well as the distinction between theory and praxis.

J. A. Colombo

See also MOLTMANN, JÜRGEN.

MEZUZAH

Hebrew, literally meaning "doorpost," this term has come to mean the decorative container and the parchment inscribed with words from the Torah placed on the doorpost of a Jewish home.

The Torah commands, "You shall love the Lord your God with all your heart, all your soul and all your might" (Deut 6:5). It continues, "And these words (to love the Lord your God) . . . you shall write them on the *mezuzot* (plural) doorposts, of your house and on your gates" (Deut 6:6, 9).

There are three reasons for this commandment: First, there is a connection to the sign of blood Hebrew slaves were told to put on their doorposts in Egypt so that the Angel of Death would protect and pass over their houses. The words on the doorpost serve as an everlasting reminder of God's providential care. Next, the words on the doorpost serve as a constant reminder to love God. Finally, the words on the doorpost identify the home as a Jewish home where the commandments of God are practiced.

Originally, the words were written directly on the doorpost. Later they were written on parchment, placed in an artistically decorative container (now called the *mezuzah*), and placed on the doorpost.

This is one ritual most Jews still practice, so almost every Jewish home has a *mezuzah* on its doorpost as a sign of identity and commitment. Traditional Jews kiss their fingertips and then reach up to touch the *mezuzah* every time they enter or leave the house, as a sign of love for God.

Wayne Dosick

See also SHEMA.

MIDEWIWIN

This ritual belongs to a sacred society among the Ojibwe that arose as a new religious movement and as a means of revitalization in the eighteenth century. It is also known as the Grand Medicine Society, a name indicating the nature of its members, all of whom are shamans who have gone through a special initiation. Its modern quality is shown by the blending of Christian and native religious elements. For example, one of the requirements was that the initiate had to have been healed of an illness—a typical shamanic sign. And, while it retained prayers to Nanabozho and other manitos, it also recognized the Gitche Manito, clearly a concept influenced by Christianity. The members met in dramatic and complex rituals to retell the great myths of creation and to demonstrate their powers. One of the constants in the ritual was a symbolic slaying and rebirth of the initiate(s), an element that Christopher Vecsey identifies as a reaffirmation of the theme of the necessity of death for the prolonging of life in the Creation cycle.

Kathleen Dugan

See also NANABOZHO; SHAMAN.

MIDRASH

(Plural, *Midrashim*). *Midrash* is a noun based on the Hebrew verb *darash*, meaning "seek" or "interpret." Midrash refers to interpretations of Scripture, usually within Judaism, although some New Testament scholars use the term to describe interpretations of older Scripture found within the New Testament. Midrash frequently builds on details of the biblical text and may be interested in different aspects of the passage, such as moral, ethical, or legal points. Midrash may also add information the biblical passage under interpretation leaves out or left unclear. In this way midrash may border on a rewriting of Scripture. Some of the earliest midrashim

known are interpretations of biblical texts found among the Dead Sea Scrolls. These are usually known as *Pesharim* from the Hebrew term *pesher*, also meaning "interpretation" used in the compositions. Other examples include the Passover *Haggadah* and the Wisdom of Solomon.

Russell Fuller

MIDWINTER CEREMONY

In the Iroquois ceremonial cycle, the Midwinter Ceremony holds priority of place. It was a rite heralding the new year, and in a manner that is very sophisticated, the people were urged to clean out all that was old and no longer of use, both in the material realm and also in the psycho-spiritual area. The climax of this preparation occurs in a ritual event that has long been recognized as astonishing in its sharp perception. The Iroquois, as the early Jesuits had carefully noted, paid great attention to their dreams, and understood them to be of two kinds. The more common revealed the deep wishes of the soul by means of the dream, which they recognized as its language. The second was a form of revelation of the sacred, and belonged to the community, but the first were highly personal. Long before Freud, the Iroquois knew that the deep desires of the soul had to be expressed and satisfied in an appropriate manner. So in the Midwinter Ritual, all were encouraged to act out their dreams in pantomime, and the community was charged with recognizing the needs expressed and answering them. In a sacred event, and in a respectful way, the needs of the soul were thus acknowledged and compassionately treated. Only then could a new cycle of life and time begin.

Kathleen Dugan

See also DREAMS; RITUAL.

MIGNE, JACQUES PAUL (1800–75)

Jacques Paul Migne was ordained a priest in Orléans, France, in 1824, but moved to Paris to start a career in publishing in 1833. In 1836 he started his own publishing house so he could publish an inexpensive library of all Christian writers from the beginning down to his own time. While this might seem an impossible project, Migne nearly did it. His most famous collection of texts is called the *Patrologia*, and there is a series in Greek of 161 volumes and a series in Latin of 221 volumes. From Tertullian to Innocent III in Latin, and from the "letter of Barnabas" to the Council of Florence in 1438 in Greek, almost every important Christian writer appears in Migne's collection. It is one of the most amazing publishing feats in history, and still very valuable for scholars. A fire destroyed the printing presses in 1868, and a long legal battle over the insurance put an end to the publishing for years. Migne never really got his project going again.

Gary Macy

See also BARNABAS, LETTER OF; BASLE-FLORENCE-FERRARA (COUNCILS OF); INNOCENT III, POPE; TERTULLIAN.

MÍGUEZ BONINO, JOSÉ (1924–)

José Míguez Bonino was born in Santa Fe, Argentina, and is considered one of the leading liberation theologians of Latin America, particularly noteworthy because of his Protestant faith. He received a licentiate in theology in 1948 from the Facultad Evangélica de Teología (Argentina), a master's in theology in 1952 from Emory University (U.S.A.), and a doctorate in theology in 1960 from Union Theological Seminary (U.S.A.). An ordained Methodist minister, he has served on the Commission on Faith and Order of the World Council of Churches and as an of-ficial observer from the Methodist Church at the Second Vatican Council. Among Míguez Bonino's most important theological contributions are his articulation of a Christian political ethic for our time and his demonstration of the priority of orthopraxis over orthodoxy for a truly Christian theology. His attempts to defend the relevance of Marxist social analysis for Christians (as one instrument for understanding certain aspects of society) have been rejected by some Marxists and some Christians who see Marxism as offering a complete account of human reality. His major works include *Doing Theology in a Revolutionary Situation* (1975), *Christians and Marxists: The Mutual Challenge to Revolution* (1976), and *Toward a Christian Political Ethics* (1983).

James B. Nickoloff

See also LIBERATION THEOLOGIES; ORTHOPRAXIS.

MIHRAB

An Arabic word used for a niche or cave-like recess in a wall. Specifically, it refers to the niche built into one wall of every mosque indicating the *kibla* or direction of Mecca toward which worshipers face when offering their prayers five times each day. There is no sacred significance to the *mihrab* itself. Its importance lies rather in its function. This structural design for mosques has been used since the early eighth century C.E.

Ronald A. Pachence

See also KIBLA; MECCA; MOSQUE/MASJID; SALAT.

MIKI NAKAYAMA (1798–1887)

Japanese founder of Tenrikyo (Religion of Divine Wisdom), one of Japan's "New Religions" and the oldest and largest of the New Shinto Group. Miki grew up as a farm woman near Nara and was believed to be possessed by the creator high god Tenri-No-Mikoto (God of Heavenly Wisdom, God the Parent). She received her first divine contact while in a shamanic trance when God called on her to spread his message and live her life as a divine model. Her followers believed that she was possessed by Tenrishogun and nine other *kami* and that she offered a new revelation and a new understanding of the origins and meaning of the cosmos. These revelations came to serve as the scripture for the Tenrikyo Sect.

G. D. DeAngelis

See also KAMI; NEW RELIGIONS; SHINTO; TENRIKYO.

MIKVEH

Hebrew, meaning "collection" (of waters) as a ritual pool.

In Judaism, ritual impurity that can be caused by any number of factors renders a person ineligible for participation in certain ritual practices. The Torah enjoins that, in order to reenter a state of ritual purity, a person is to bathe—to immerse in natural, flowing water as a symbolic act of purification (Lev 14:8; 15:5, 9; 22:6; Deut 23:12). The waters are not used to remove any physical uncleanliness, but rather serve as a symbolic rebirth, an emergence from the purified, cleansing waters of new beginnings. The act of immersion is called *tevilah*.

The required place for ritual immersion is a natural body of water. However, when Jews live in a locale where there is no natural body of water, or in climates where the waters are frozen over for a part of the year, a *mikveh* is built. The mikveh is a pool-like structure built to collect natural waters from rain and melt-

ing snow. In places where there is never enough rain or melting snow for the mikveh, an adjoining pool is built and filled with regular water. A plug between the two pools is opened, the collected waters and the regular waters are permitted to merge, and declaration is made that all the water is naturally collected water. Over the pool, a building is constructed not only to protect the pooled waters from the elements, but to protect the modesty of the one immersing, because tevilah is always done completely unclothed so that the waters can touch every part of the body.

The mikveh is used before performing a sacred task such as writing a Torah Scroll. Many traditional men immerse in the mikveh each week before Shabbat. Many brides immerse in the *mikveh* before their weddings. But the main uses of the mikveh are for two rituals: women fulfilling the laws of *taharat hamispachah*, family purity, and for *gerut*, immersion as part of the rituals of conversion to Judaism.

Wayne Dosick

See also BEIT DIN; GERUT; TAHARAT HAMISPACHAH.

MILAN, EDICT OF

The traditional name given to a letter written in 313 in Milan to the provincial governors from Constantine I and Licinius, joint rulers of the Roman Empire. According to the document, Christians were allowed freedom of worship, and goods taken from Christian communities during the recent persecutions were to be restored. The decree ended the persecution of Diocletian and marked Rome's first official recognition of Christianity as a legitimate society.

Gary Macy

See also CONSTANTINE I THE GREAT;
DIOCLETIAN; PERSECUTION (IN CHRIS-
TIANITY).

MILAREPA (1040–1143)

Tantric yogin-sage of the Kagyu school
within Tibetan Buddhism. Following
his early years when he learned deadly
shamanic arts and punished those who
deprived him, his sister, and mother of all
their wealth, Milarepa became the disciple
of Marpa (1012–96) who subjected him to
many trials and humiliations before giving
him tantric initiations. Milarepa excelled
in meditation, including long periods of
cave meditation; he became one of the
great *siddhas* of Tibet and is regarded as
having achieved enlightenment. Milarepa
became much beloved across the Himala-
yan region for his dramatic life story and
his myriad song compositions expressing
Buddhist teachings.

Todd T. Lewis

See also LAMA; SIDDHA; TANTRIC
BUDDHISM.

MILITARY ORDERS

Of all the experiments in Christian living
attempted down through the centuries,
the military orders are certainly some of
the most interesting. Military orders
attempted to wed the devotional and
ascetic life of monasticism with the duties
of knighthood. Founded to defend the
newly conquered Holy Land, the first of
the military orders was that of the Order
of the Temple or "Knights Templars"
founded by Hugh of Payens around 1119
in Jerusalem. The Knights took the monastic vows of chastity, poverty, and obedience and recited the canonical Hours
just like other monks, but they also dedicated themselves to the protection of pilgrims and the defense of the Holy Land

by force of arms. Bernard of Clairvaux
sang the praises of what he called the
"new knighthood," and as a result, new
military orders sprang up in Spain and
Portugal modeled on the Templars and
dedicated to the reconquest of Spain from
the Muslims. These orders included the
Calatrava (the earliest order, founded in
1158), the Knights of Alcàntara, the Order
of Aviz, the Knights of Montesa, the
Order of Christ, and the Knights of
St. James. Meanwhile, in the Holy Land,
two other orders were founded. The
Order of the Hospital of St. John of Jerusalem or "Hospitallers" were already in
existence caring for the sick and pilgrims,
but now also took up the sword. The
"Hospitallers" were later to be known as
the Knights of Rhodes or the Knights of
Malta. The Teutonic Knights (the Order
of the Brothers of the Hospital of St. Mary
of the Germans in Jerusalem) were also
founded in the Holy Land, but soon
moved to Germany where they gained
notariety for their attacks on eastern Europe. Theoretically, their mission was to
conquer the pagan Prussians and Lithu-
anians, but they continued to expand
their kingdom even against the Christian
Poles and Russians.

The Templars were suppressed by
Pope Clement V in 1312 under pressure
by Philip the Fair, king of France, in a raw
grab for the Templars' vast wealth. When
the Holy Land was regained by Muslim
armies and the reconquest of Spain was
complete, the other military orders lost
their reason for being and many disappeared. The Teutonic Knights were
defeated by a Polish-Lithuanian army in
1410, and the last Grand Master secularized the kingdom of the Knights when he
espoused Lutheranism in 1525. The Hospitallers and the nursing branch of the
Teutonic Knights still survive, doing

charitable work, but otherwise the military orders survive only as honorary societies.

Gary Macy

See also BERNARD OF CLAIRVAUX; HOLY LAND; LUTHERANISM; MEDIEVAL CHRISTIANITY (IN THE WEST); MONASTICISM IN WESTERN CHRISTIANITY; ORDERS, RELIGIOUS; VOWS (RELIGIOUS).

MILLENARIANISM

Millenarianism is the belief of Christians in the millennium, a thousand-year reign of Jesus the Christ in peace and prosperity. Closely connected to adventism, millenarianism is based on literal interpretations of biblical prophecy, especially Daniel, Isaiah, and Revelation. The millennium is the kingdom of God on earth, a heavenly society in which the lion and lamb will lie down together led by a small child. In the United States, the idea of the millennium has been adopted by Millerites, Seventh-Day Adventists, Jehovah's Witnesses, the Church of Jesus Christ of Latter-Day Saints, and the Nation of Islam. However, it has had widest influence in Evangelical and fundamentalist theology.

While many Christians share a belief in the millennium, they differ on when and how it will occur. Most are either premillennialists or postmillennialists. Premillennialists believe that the Second Coming will occur before the millennium. They believe that the earth is declining, engulfed by sin, evidenced by war, pestilence, and increasing immorality. Jesus will halt this decline, and his advent will inaugurate the millennium, accompanied by the rapture, tribulation, Armageddon, and appearance of the Antichrist. Premillennialists look for signs that these

prophecies are being fulfilled. With a pessimistic view of human nature, most premillennialists are fundamentalists and believe in dispensationalism.

Postmillennialists believe that the Second Coming will occur after the millennium. They see the world as improving, gradually becoming more loving and compassionate in anticipation of the millennium. They have faith in human goodness and the capacity to overcome sin. As the world gets better, human society moves closer to the kingdom of God, and after the millennium, Jesus arrives. Postmillennialists are most often Protestant liberals.

Not all Christians are pre- or postmillennialists. Amillennialists believe the millennium is not a separate historical epoch, but that prophecies regarding the Second Coming and Antichrist are being fulfilled simultaneously. Other Christians do not believe in an actual millennium at all; they see the Bible as a metaphorical book that does not predict earthly events. They see the millennium as a poetic vision of what creation might be through the power of Christ.

In addition to Christian interpretations of the millennium, there is also a secular version particular to the United States. As early as the seventeenth and eighteenth centuries, Christian leaders such as John Winthrop and Jonathan Edwards speculated that the territory that would become the United States had a special role in ushering in the millennium. After the birth of the country, many U.S. citizens believed that the virtues of democracy and freedom made the United States uniquely suited as the site of the kingdom of God. The United States had a divinely ordained "manifest destiny" in God's plan for redeeming humanity. Millenarianism thus became an aspect of civil religion, creating pride, self-righteousness, and a sense of national responsibility.

Evelyn A. Kirkley

See also ADVENTISTS; CIVIL RELIGION; DISPENSATION; FUNDAMENTALISM (CHRISTIAN HISTORICAL MOVEMENT); RAPTURE (IN AMERICAN PROTESTANTISM); SOCIAL GOSPEL.

MIMAMSA

Mimamsa (Sanskrit, thoughtful inquiry) is the discipline of scriptural interpretation in Hinduism. In particular, mimamsa is the science of Vedic hermeneutics, which all serious Hindu scholars are required to master, since the Vedas are held to be revelations of an eternal, supersensory wisdom not available to human beings through any other channel. As an established tradition of thought, the Mimamsa is divided into two schools: the Purva Mimamsa (Earlier Inquiry) and the Uttara Mimamsa (Subsequent Inquiry). The Purva Mimamsa investigates the meaning of Vedic ritual texts, with a view to establishing correct ritual performance. It is therefore also known as the Karma Mimamsa, or Inquiry into (Ritual) Action. It presents rules for determining the correct sense of scriptural passages by reference to grammar, context, and other factors, so that disputed issues can be resolved, or at least systematically argued. Its teachings are given classical expression in the *Purva Mimamsa Sutra* of Jaimini. The Uttara Mimamsa, otherwise known as the Vedanta, examines the "knowledge portion" (*jnana–kanda*) of the Veda—the Upanishads. It endeavors to present a systematic interpretation thereof, with particular interest in the doctrine of Brahman, ultimate reality. The foundational text of this school is Badarayana's *Uttara Mimamsa Sutras*, more commonly known as the *Brahma Sutras* or the *Vedanta Sutras*. The most famous commentary on the *Brahma Sutras* is that of Shankara.

Lance E. Nelson

See also ADVAITA VEDANTA; HINDUISM; VEDANTA; VEDAS; YAJNA.

MINARET

See MOSQUE / MASJID; MUEZZIN / MU'ADHDHIN.

MINBAR

(Or *mimbar*). The pulpit that resembles a flight of stairs with a small landing at the top found in mosques (places of worship in Islam). The *minbar* is conspicuous since mosques contain no pews, kneelers, or other kinds of furniture. It is used during the Friday noon service by the preacher (*khatib*) who delivers the sermon (*khutba*) for the day.

Ronald A. Pachence

See also MOSQUE / MASJID.

MINCHAH

Hebrew, meaning "gift" or "offering," it is the afternoon Jewish worship service.

When sacrifices were brought to the Holy Temple, the afternoon sacrificial offering was of fine grain or meal. Since this offering was not as elaborate as the regular daily sacrifices made in the morning, the *minchah* was a much simpler ritual than the morning rites. Reflecting that simplicity, the minchah worship service is a much abbreviated form of the morning service.

A traditional Jew prays three times a day. Since a Jewish day begins and ends at sundown, the minchah service is the third and final service of a Jewish day. It is recited every day. On the Sabbath and festivals there are certain changes and additions reflecting the special nature of the day.

The minchah service can be recited anytime in the afternoon. Many Jews recite the minchah and the ma'ariv—evening—services separately—minchah anytime in the afternoon and ma'ariv much later, after dark. But for practical reasons, the minchah and ma'ariv services are often recited one following the other—minchah right before sunset, and ma'ariv just after sunset, so that the worshipers gather at the synagogue just once rather than twice over a short period of time.

Wayne Dosick

See also MA'ARIV; SHACHARIT.

MINDFULNESS
An English rendering for a distinctively Buddhist form of meditation.

See VIPASHYANA/VIPASSANA.

MINHAG
(Hebrew, custom). In Judaism, a traditional practice or way of doing things, not understood to be strictly required by Jewish law. A *minhag* thus is distinguished from a *mitzvah* or religious obligation. The term frequently is used to describe variations in liturgical or other everyday customs that developed over time among Jews living in diverse geographical or cultural settings.

Alan J. Avery-Peck

MINISTRY/MINISTERIAL
Term derived from the Latin translation of the Greek word *diakonia*, common in the New Testament. There, it is a reference to the service rendered by members of the Christian community toward one another and the world at large, in response to the example and Spirit of Christ. "Min-

istry" is thus *service* to the church and the world, and "ministerial" describes whatever pertains to that service. In the very early church, all these terms were applied to Christians in general, with a strong emphasis on the varied spiritual gifts and talents (charisms) the Holy Spirit was understood to give to persons for the benefit of the whole church. (See St. Paul's lists of the different gifts and ministries in the New Testament: Romans 12:6-8; 1 Corinthians 12:4-11, 28-31; Ephesians 4:11.) As early as the second century of the church's existence, however, more formalized practices of ordination to offices in the church began to create the now-familiar distinction between clergy and laity, and the gradual restriction of the term "ministry" to members of the clergy. In Roman Catholicism, the Second Vatican Council (1962–5), while reserving the use of the word "ministry" to formally ordained clergy, emphasized the essential role of laypeople in the work of the church, particularly in its relationships with the secular world. (See especially *Lumen Gentium* 4 and 5; *Gaudium et Spes* 4; and the Decree on the Apostolate of the Laity.) Following the council, during the pontificate of Paul VI, even many institutional church functions previously reserved to priests were opened to laypeople, and the term "lay ministry" became common. A reaction against this trend during the pontificate of John Paul II was evident in the apostolic exhortation *Christifideles Laici* (1988) and in a 1997 Vatican instruction on lay collaboration with clergy. These documents and others have sought to reemphasize the clergy–laity distinction and, with little immediate success, to curtail the use of the word "ministry" in reference to nonordained persons.

William A. Clark, s.j.

MINJUNG THEOLOGY

Minjung (from Korean *min*, or "people," and *jung*, or "common") theology, like Latin American liberation theology, feminist theology, and North American and South African black theologies, represents a rejection of a European monopoly on theology in the late twentieth century. Originating in South Korea in the 1970s, *minjung* theology begins with the question: "How have the poor and oppressed people of Korea believed in God while enduring unbearable suffering?" It answers this question by affirming that the very history and culture of those who have resisted oppression in Korea reveal God's activity in history. Such historical and cultural particularity is at the same time the key to *minjung* theology's universal claims.

James B. Nickoloff

See also CULTURE; INCULTURATION; LIBERATION THEOLOGIES; THIRD WORLD THEOLOGIES.

MINOR ORDERS

Formal but less prominent positions in the clerical hierarchies of both Eastern and Western Christianity and, before 1972, preliminary stages in the process of priestly ordination in the Roman Catholic Church. In the third and fourth centuries, many different types of official church ministry were developed and recognized by various local churches. Seven of these survived through medieval times to be formalized by the Council of Trent in 1563. Of these, three were considered "major orders" (conferred by the actual sacrament of holy orders): subdeacons (discontinued after 1972), deacons, and priests. The other four were considered "minor orders" (conferred by a "sacramental" commissioning): porters, lectors, exorcists, and acolytes. As the practical functions of these orders had largely disappeared, they were discontinued after the Second Vatican Council and replaced with the two official "ministries" of lector and acolyte. These ministries are still formally conferred only on men who are preparing for major orders (as deacons or priests), but lay men and women may now be commissioned to exercise their functions (reading the Scriptures, assisting at the altar, distributing Communion) in the absence of a formally installed lector or acolyte.

William A. Clark, s.j.

MINYAN

Hebrew, meaning "quorum," this is the minimum number of people necessary for public Jewish worship.

Private personal prayer can be recited by a Jew anywhere, at any time. But public worship takes place at certain specific times using the structured rubric of the prayer service.

The sages decided that it would take a minimum number—a quorum—of ten Jews to make up a "congregation" or a "community" for public worship—they called a *minyan*. They based their decision on the juxtaposition of two biblical verses, where the implication is that a "congregation" is made up of "ten" people (Psalm 8:21; Num 14:27).

To be counted toward making up a minyan, a Jew must be thirteen years of age or older (Bar Mitzvah). In Orthodox Judaism, only men count toward the number required for a minyan. In the liberal branches of Judaism, both men and women count.

Because the minyan-quorum is necessary for public worship, the word minyan has also taken on the connotation of the worship service itself. For example, "Are you going to the minyan (meaning, service) today?"

Wayne Dosick

MIRABAI

A woman saint of the sixteenth century known across India for her songs of devotion to Krishna in human form. Although married to a human husband from the Rajput caste, she would not compromise her sacred devotion to Krishna in conforming to the rituals or affections of human marriage. Eventually, after the husband's family tried to kill her by various means, she is said to have magically escaped with the help of Krishna, while her husband turned to stone. From this time onward, Mira lived in Brindhavan, the town of Krishna populated by his fervent devotees, where she composed many songs dedicated to "The Dark Lord." Mirabai most often addresses Krishna as her "Mountain Lifter," referring to his salvific action when he rescues cows and cowherds from Indra by shielding them with an upheld mountain. Mira's poems and life itself exemplify the *bhakti* ideal of putting one's Lord first before everything else.

Todd T. Lewis

See also BHAGAVAD GITA; BHAKTI; KRISHNA.

MIRACLE

A term traditionally interpreted to mean an extraordinary event that implies the temporary suspension by God(s) of the laws of nature. This interpretation of what a miracle is seems to be implied in all religions' explanations of the origins of the miraculous. Christianity is no exception.

Contemporary Christian theologians and biblical scholars seem to interpret miracles as means through which God communicates or reveals meaning, or through which God issues an invitation to conversion and faith. It is in this sense that the New Testament understood Jesus' "mighty deeds." In contemporary theology, the question about a miracle's "fact," therefore, is less important than the question about the "meaning" of the event.

Many individuals in modern secular society feel uncomfortable with talk about miracles, although some are inclined to credulous acceptance of every miraculous claim. There also seems to be an evident shyness in modern scholarship when it comes to miracles. Perhaps it has to do with the lingering and false assumption that there is some sort of inimical, mutually excluding tension between faith and reason, or between nature and "the spiritual." There is little doubt that many extraordinary events that believers sincerely identified as miracles can in fact be explained as the results of natural causes. Indeed, humankind cannot pretend to already know or understand all nature's laws and workings. But the natural origins of most extraordinary events do not imply the absolute impossibility of miracles.

The (Catholic) theological principle that "grace builds on nature" might offer interpretive insights when understanding miracles today, at least within the Christian tradition. The notion that miracles are whimsical, capricious acts of God, however, must be rejected. Furthermore, the Christian God cannot be portrayed as meanly using miracles against people.

Orlando Espín

See also CULTURE; GOD; GRACE; HERMENEUTICS; NATURE, HUMAN; OMNIBENEVOLENCE; OMNIPOTENCE; PROVIDENCE.

MIRAJ/MI'RAJ

In Arabic, the "ascent" of the Prophet Muhammad (570–632) from Jerusalem to heaven that Muslims believe took place before the *hijra* or the Prophet's emigration from Mecca to Medina in 622 C.E. The *mi'raj* is the second part of a single event usually referred to as the "Night Journey." The first part of this journey was Muhammad's miraculous transport (*isra*) from Mecca, where he was sleeping near the Ka'ba, to the Dome of the Rock in Jerusalem, the point of his actual mi'raj into the "seven heavens." Muslims call this event *"laylat al-isra wa-l mi'raj,"* the "night of the journey and the ascent (into heaven)." The Night Journey, which is mentioned in the sacred scripture of Islam, the Qur'an (17:1), is important in Islamic theology because it validates Muhammad's mission as a prophet of God. It is said that before he ascended to the Divine Presence in heaven, he first joined with other prophets, including Abraham, Moses, and Jesus, in offering prayers at the ruins of the old Temple of Solomon.

Ronald A. Pachence

See also DOME OF THE ROCK; HIJRA (IN ISLAM); ISLAM; KA'BA/KAABA; MUHAMMAD; QUR'AN; TEMPLE (OF JERUSALEM).

MIRIAM

A prophet who is also identified as a sister of Moses. According to Exodus 15, she led the people in a victory refrain, celebrating and thanking God for the Hebrews' successful crossing of the Red Sea. According to the account in Numbers 12, she, along with her brother Aaron, reprimanded their brother Moses for taking a Cushite woman in marriage. Although both Miriam and Aaron were reprimanded for challenging Moses' authority, Miriam is punished with leprosy while Aaron experienced no comparable punishment. Miriam was ostracized from the community and was only able to return after Moses' prayer on her behalf and her subsequent cleansing.

Although Miriam is never explicitly named as the sister of Moses who participates in his deliverance at the Nile (Exod 2), she is the only woman ever identified as his sister, and she is so named several times. That Miriam was remembered as a significant player in Israel's earliest memory is clear from her presence in the genealogies (Exod 6:20; Num 26:59; 1 Chr 5:29). It is most unusual that women appear in the genealogies at all, never mind three times. In Micah 6:4 she is identified alongside Moses and Aaron, and is seemingly of equal stature: "For I brought you up from the land of Egypt, from the place of slavery I released you; And I sent before you Moses, Aaron, and Miriam."

Alice L. Laffey

MISHNAH

The first document of rabbinic Judaism, a legal composition redacted early in the third century C.E. but containing statements attributed to rabbis who lived over the preceding approximately two hundred years. Referred to variously as a legal code, a transcript of scholastic debates, or a rabbinic study book, the *Mishnah* presents in a highly formalized language anonymous rules and discussions by named rabbis on a wide range of issues important to the implementation of rules only briefly sketched in the Hebrew Bible. While almost all of the Mishnah's topics and basic information are drawn from Scripture, in the Mishnah itself, Scripture itself is rarely quoted. Instead, the Mishnah presents the rabbis' own discussions of how the law is to be carried out.

The Mishnah is in six major topical sections, called Siddarim ("divisions"), each of which is divided into individual tractates, called Masekhtot. The divisions are: (1) Agriculture, concerning the payment to priests, Levites, and the poor of tithes from food growing on the land of Israel; (2) Appointed Times, on holiday observance; (3) Women, on family law, including the rules for marriage and divorce; (4) Damages, on civil and criminal law, the court system, and the theocratic governance of the Israelite nation; (5) Holy Things, on the cult of the Jerusalem Temple; and (6) Purities, on cultic impurity and the rules for attaining ritual cleanness.

In large part, the Mishnah provides a utopian picture of the way Jews should act in a perfect world. Accordingly, it refers to topics such as Temple-sacrifices, which, in the rabbis' own day, could not be offered, the Jerusalem Temple having been destroyed in 70 C.E. This utopian image stands at the foundation of the Palestinian and Babylonian Talmuds, the defining documents of the evolving rabbinic religion that are themselves commentaries on the Mishnah's laws and discussions. Judaism views the Mishnah as the central core of the Oral Law (*Torah She'B'Al Peh*), understood to have been transmitted by God to Moses at Mt. Sinai along with the written revelation, preserved in the Hebrew Scriptures. Accordingly, while the Mishnah's rules are cited in the names of specific rabbinic authorities, they are understood to have their ultimate legitimacy as aspects of the original revelation of God to the People of Israel.

Alan J. Avery-Peck

See also RABBINIC JUDAISM.

MISHNEH TORAH

(Hebrew, Repetition of the Torah). In the late twelfth century, the first complete systematic compilation of biblical and rabbinic law, produced by the great Jewish philosopher and legal scholar Moses Maimonides. Maimonides organized the commandments of Judaism in fourteen categories, leading his admirers to refer to the work as Yad haHazakah, that is, "The Mighty Fourteen" (in Hebrew, a play on the expression "the mighty hand"; see, for example, Deut 4:34). Maimonides' innovations in the Mishneh Torah were (1) his writing in Hebrew instead of Talmudic Aramaic; (2) his use of his own classificatory system instead of the one found in the prior Talmudic literature; (3) his willingness to decide the law on the basis of texts other than the Babylonian Talmud, heretofore considered solely authoritative; and (4) his decision to give his view of the law without presenting citations to the original sources or indicating dissenting opinions. Especially as a result of this final innovation, the Mishneh Torah was, upon its appearance, bitterly attacked. Even so, the work soon was accepted as authoritative, and it served as the foundation for all later Jewish legal codes. Despite this success, Maimonides' express purpose in writing the Mishneh Torah, to facilitate study of Jewish law without reference to the original Talmudic sources, was not accomplished. Rather, the Mishneh Torah itself became a prime subject of analysis and interpretation, with Maimonides' approach to and understanding of the Talmudic texts with which he worked being carefully and completely analyzed much as those texts themselves had previously been studied.

Alan J. Avery-Peck

See also MAIMONIDES.

MISSAL

A *missal* (or *Mass-book*) is a book containing the texts (prayers, readings, and some chants) necessary for the celebration of Mass. The term was used more widely in the Roman Catholic tradition before the liturgical reforms of Vatican II (1962–5). Increasingly through the medieval period, the priest was expected to read (or chant) all the texts assigned for the Mass of the day (whether or not there were others in attendance, like a choir). Earlier, these texts could be found in different books used by ministers taking various roles in the liturgical celebration (for example, the Lectionary, or book of readings, used by the lector, or reader). However, by the thirteenth century, all these texts had been collected into a single volume for the use of the priest (the *full missal* or *missale plenum*). The missal was revised and standardized for the use of Roman Catholics after the Council of Trent (1570); it remained essentially unchanged until the liturgical reforms mandated by Vatican II in the mid-twentieth century. The Roman Missal (or Sacramentary) was revised again in 1970, and the custom of using a number of different liturgical books was revived.

By the twentieth century, a missal for the use of the laity was also available; this contained the texts used at Masses throughout the year, most translated into the vernacular (or common spoken language of a region or country), and others provided in parallel columns with the Latin texts used by the priest (especially the Ordinary of the Mass, for example, the Canon, or eucharistic prayer, consisting of prayer texts that did not change or vary according to the feast or season of the year). Today, in many Roman Catholic churches, booklets are provided in church pews for those attending the Mass (or Eucharist) that contain the readings, possible hymns, and prayer texts for the season (such as Advent or Lent); these are often called missalettes, or "little missals."

Joanne M. Pierce

See also EUCHARIST; LECTIONARY; LITURGY OF THE EUCHARIST; LITURGY OF THE WORD; MASS; SACRAMENTARY.

MISSIOLOGY

A discipline within mainstream Christian theology that discusses the nature, purposes, methods, history, assumptions, and the like, of the missionary efforts of Christianity. Missiology is also in close dialogue with the cultural and social sciences.

Orlando Espín

See also AD GENTES; CULTURE; ECCLESIOLOGY; EVANGELII NUNTIANDI; INCULTURATION; ISLAM; MISSIONARIES; MISSIONS; NOSTRA AETATE.

MISSION (IN JUDAISM)

See DIASPORA; JUDAISM.

MISSIONARIES

The individuals who propagate a religion outside and beyond its usual geographic or ethnic contexts. Some religions (such as Christianity and Islam) view all their members, given the religions' self-understanding, as necessarily "missionary." Historically, however, the term "missionary" has been reserved for those individuals who are somehow officially recognized or commissioned with the task of propagating the religion.

In Christianity, missionary work occurs both by individual initiative and by church-sponsored projects. Many communities and organizations have been established with exclusive missionary purposes. It has been common (inaccurately) to identify missionary work mainly with developing lands or peoples.

Orlando Espín

See also AD GENTES; CULTURE; ECCLESIOLOGY; EVANGELII NUNTIANDI; INCULTURATION; ISLAM; MISSIOLOGY; MISSIONS; NOSTRA AETATE.

MISSION OF THE CHURCH

The Christian church owes its existence to Jesus and to the earliest apostolic community. From its very beginning Christianity has understood itself as being sent by God in order to announce the Good News to all who would listen. Therefore, and in general terms, the mission of the church is to announce to the world the message the church received from God in and through Jesus, and of which the early apostolic community was privileged witness. More specifically, the church's mission is a historical extension of the mission received by the apostolic generation.

The New Testament indicates that Jesus taught the impending dawn of the reign of God (Mark 1:15). Jesus taught about the reign of God through his statements, options, and actions on behalf of the most marginalized persons and groups of his day. The reign of God, however, is not to be understood mainly as an otherworldly, strictly spiritual reality. On the contrary, the reign of God begins now in history, in this world, although it will come to its fullest completion only beyond the end of history (at a time and in a manner only known to God). What would our world be like if God reigned? What would people (individually, and as families and communities) and nations (and economic and political systems) be like if God reigned? The answers to these questions might adequately begin to describe the reign of God as taught by Jesus and the early apostolic community. Evidently, the reign of God will be "good news" only if the God who would reign is understood (as Jesus did) as a compassionate and merciful God who really accepts and loves all persons and peoples, always and everywhere, without conditions and without exceptions. So, if the reign of God is dawning in human history, and if God is as Jesus said God is, then this is very good news. Our world, Christians believe, can change and is changing, thanks to God's initiative. This dawning presence of the reign of God, however, is made visible (by God through human cooperation) by options and actions that in multiple ways show how humans and the world can be (and are) when the compassionate God reigns.

Jesus suffered death for loyally holding on to this message. Christians believe that God raised Jesus from death as the definitive way of showing that Jesus had indeed spoken the truth. After Jesus' resurrection, and after the outpouring of God's confirming Spirit, Christians have no doubt that Jesus spoke in God's name and that the reign of God is dawning, as Jesus said. His resurrection, furthermore, became an integral part of the church's teaching (ever since the days of the earliest apostolic community) because it is the seal and guarantee of the credibility of Jesus' (and the church's) message. The preaching of the church, consequently, has no other authority than that of Jesus and God's confirming Spirit.

The mission of the church, therefore, is to announce to all who would listen, and to make visible in the world, the dawning reign of God and the compassionate mercy of the God of the reign, through words, options, and actions that loyally reflect and follow the options and actions of Jesus and of the early apostolic community, convinced that the risen Jesus and God's confirming Spirit will always guide and support the church's mission.

It must be added, however, that the actual words, options, and actions chosen by the church to carry out its mission throughout the world and across the centuries are not and cannot be carbon copies of Jesus' own words, options, and actions. The cultural and historical circumstances change, and thus the church must adapt to ("inculturate" in) its diverse contexts, and further understand and apply the message of Jesus in the world as the world exists. Christians believe that the Spirit of God, in various ways, keeps them faithful to the mission of the church in the midst of human and historical diversity.

Orlando Espín

See also APOSTLE; APOSTOLIC FATHERS; CHRIST; CHRIST OF FAITH; CHURCH; DEVELOPMENT OF DOGMA/OF DOCTRINE; ECCLESIOLOGY; GRACE; HOLY SPIRIT; INCULTURATION; JESUS OF HISTORY; MAGISTERIUM, ORDINARY; OPTION FOR THE POOR; REIGN OF GOD; RESURRECTION (IN CHRISTIANITY); SENSUS FIDELIUM/SENSUS FIDEI.

MISSIONS
The organized propagation of a religion outside and beyond its usual geographic or ethnic context. Some religions do not perceive themselves as "missionary" (such as Judaism or Hinduism), while others could not understand themselves without the missionary thrust (Christianity, Islam).

In Christian history, missionary expansion has occurred since the days of the apostles. Undivided Christianity spread the Gospel throughout Europe until about 1015. During the Middle Ages, Western Churches attempted to convert Muslims, and also sent unsuccessful missions to China and Mongolia. But the greatest expansion of Christianity began in the sixteenth century with Spain's and Portugal's conquest of new lands and peoples in the Americas, Asia, and Africa.

Most Christian missionary work has been historically carried out by the Catholic Church, although since the eighteenth and nineteenth centuries Protestant denominations have also contributed to the missionary effort. Unfortunately, competition with other Christians has been too important to many missionaries, leading some to attempt expansion among members of other churches instead of non-Christians.

The Second Vatican Council's decree *Ad Gentes* (1965), on the missionary activity of the Catholic Church, again emphasized the missionary nature of Christianity. However, it also required that the cultures and peoples be respected by missionaries, and that sincere respect be shown all non-Christian religions. Contemporary Catholicism's understanding of mission (as explained in *Ad Gentes* and in Paul VI's *Evangelii Nuntiandi*) must be understood within its broader reflection on non-Christian religions (cf. Vatican II's decree *Nostra Aetate*) and on grace and salvation.

Orlando Espín

See also AD GENTES; BAPTISM OF DESIRE; CONVERSION; ECCLESIOLOGY; EVANGELII NUNTIANDI; FAITH; GRACE; ISLAM; MISSIOLOGY; MISSIONARIES; NOSTRA AETATE; SALVATION.

MISSISSIPPIAN CULTURE
From its location in the Mississippi Valley, this term refers to the prehistoric culture that flourished between 700 and 1600 C.E. It represents a highly developed civilization that demonstrated its achievements

in well-crafted artifacts and in impressive cities that surrounded a temple mound (hence the name by which it is more well known—the Temple Mound Culture). Its greatest city, Cahokia, was the center of an extensive trade network, and had so many inhabitants that not until the nineteenth century was there an American city comparable to it. Its outstanding religious feature is the massive structure that served as the heart of the city and as its religious center. There is good archeological evidence that the ruler was revered as a god, and this links the Mississippian culture with the great city-states of Central America.

Kathleen Dugan

See also MONASTERY.

MITHRA

The god Mithra (Greek, Mithras) was the Indo-Iranian god worshiped from about 400 B.C.E. to 200 C.E. in Iran, and until the fourth century C.E. in Rome. Mithra originated in India as a god of light. According to the *Avesta*, he had ten thousand eyes and rode through the sky in a chariot drawn by white horses. Mithra was transferred to Persia and there became an attendant of the god Ahura Mazda. As such, he acted as intermediary—thus the name "Mithra" or "Middle"—between gods and men, responsible for oaths and contracts, representing truth. Mithra engaged in a struggle with Ahura Mazda's first creation, a wild bull, whom Mithra subdued and later killed by slitting its throat. Plant life on earth sprang from the spilled blood, and the ritual slaying of a bull became part of Mithraic worship.

Helen deLaurentis

See also MITHRAISM; MYSTERY RELIGIONS.

MITHRAISM

According to Plutarch, Mithraism was brought into the Greco-Roman Empire from Persia by pirates whom the Roman general Pompey suppressed but allowed to live. Another version tells that Mithraism was introduced into the West by Roman soldiers who had fought in Parthia, a province of ancient Persia. The focus of the cult was the Persian god Mithra; the cult centered on the eternal struggle between good and evil, life and death. Entrance to the cult was gained through seven ritual stages of initiation corresponding to the seven visible celestial bodies—Moon, Mercury, Venus, Sun, Mars, Jupiter, and Saturn—heavenly orbs thought to exist in enveloping spheres around the earth. The human soul was believed to have descended through each when coming to be born; each stage of initiation symbolically carried the initiate from earth back up to the next sphere. At each stage, the member lost one of the passions or limitations that sullied his life. Completion of the initiation was believed to confer immortality in a place of perfect purity and light.

Members of the cult met in small, secret groups in grottoes or caves where a bull sacrifice, the *taurobolium*, was performed, reenacting Mithra's killing of the cosmic bull of creation. The myth of Mithra tells the following story: the young god Mithra saw the primal bull grazing on a mountainside, mounted the animal, and rode it until it collapsed. Then Mithra hauled the live bull to his cave and waited until he was told by a raven sent by the sun to sacrifice the bull. Mithra plunged his blade into the bull, and from the bull's spine came wheat, from its blood flowed wine, and from its seed came the useful animals that serve men and women. The Mithric myth can thus be understood as a myth of death and regeneration: from the sacrificial death of the cosmic bull comes new life for the world.

When a bull was again slaughtered in the cult rituals, the theme of death and regeneration remained but was given a different focus. The bull was positioned above a pit in which the initiate lay. As the animal was killed, his blood drenched the initiate—a literal "baptism of blood." From immersion in the sacrificial blood of the bull came the guarantee of new, everlasting life to the initiate.

Caves in which the Mithric cult members met were adorned with depictions of Mithra the bull-killer and with others showing him feasting with Helios, the sun god. Mithra's followers celebrated each seventh day as Sun Day, and December 25, the winter solstice, as the birthday of Mithras. His strong connection with Helios reflects the origin of Mithras as an Indo-Iranian god of light, but it also emphasizes his salvific role in the symbolic pattern, death–rebirth. Each day the sun dies and rises; at each winter solstice the earth symbolically dies, only to be reborn as spring returns.

Since Mithraism exalted military virtues such as courage and loyalty, it gained great popularity among the Roman legions; its members also included merchants and officials of the Roman Empire. Women were excluded from the cult. By the first century C.E. sanctuaries to Mithra existed in Rome and also at far-flung Roman outposts. Some scholars suggest that Mithraism was a major rival to early Christianity. By the fourth century C.E. the cult was quite powerful, but it died out under persecution by the Christian emperor Constantine.

Helen deLaurentis

See also MITHRA; MYSTERY RELIGIONS.

MITZVAH

(Hebrew, commandment). In Judaism, a commandment, precept, or religious duty; the opposite of a sin (*averah*). In the plural (*mitzvoth*), the term is used to encompass biblical and rabbinic law as a whole and, hence, to refer to the complete system of Jewish religious, ethical, and social practices.

The Talmud stated that there are a total of 613 (Hebrew, *Taryag*) *mitzvot*. Two hundred and forty-eight of these, said to correspond to the number of limbs in the human body, are positive responsibilities, while 365, equaling the number of days in the year, are prohibitions (Babylonian Talmud Makkot 23b). While medieval and modern thinkers have catalogued the commandments in conformity with these numbers, no agreed-upon system has emerged.

Judaism demarcates commandments expressly stated in Scripture from those that have their source in rabbinic interpretation. Jews further distinguish important commandments from less significant ones (although Judaism in general demands that all mitzvoth be equally observed). Within these divisions, prohibitions banning a certain action are generally deemed the weightiest of the commandments. This is because transgressing a prohibition results from a physical action on the part of the individual, such that the individual can clearly be said to have sinned. This is unlike the failure to perform a positive responsibility that may not comprise a sin at all. One positive precept, for instance, states that Jews living in the Diaspora should make a pilgrimage to the Land of Israel. A Jew who fails to do so does not enjoy the spiritual benefit of having fulfilled that particular mitzvah. But this failure is in no way a sin.

The obligation to observe the commandments commences at the age of majority, calculated in premodern times as thirteen for boys and twelve for girls. In contemporary practice, by contrast, the age of thirteen generally is used for both. This is when the Bar or Bat Mitzvah celebration is held, marking the point at which the child becomes subject to the mitzvoth. Prior to reaching this age of majority, children are instructed in the observance of Jewish law, but their failure to do so is not considered a transgression.

While Judaism obligates men to follow all the commandments, it exempts women from positive precepts that must be performed at a fixed time; for example, statutory prayer, which must be recited at set times in the morning, afternoon, and night. The exemption of women from such obligations was on the theory that household responsibilities might preclude their fulfilling them at the required time. In Reform practice and increasingly in Conservative Judaism, this distinction between men and women has been abolished.

In contemporary parlance, Jews use the term *mitzvah* to refer simply to a good deed, whether or not the deed is required by religious law. The usage is presaged in the Talmud, where the term also on occasion is applied to meritorious acts that are not religious obligations.

Alan J. Avery-Peck

See also ATONEMENT, HEBREW;
BAR/BAT MITZVAH; SIN, PERSONAL.

MODALISM

Although the Christian doctrine of the Trinity is conceptually complex, the awareness of God as triune originates in the paschal experience of Jesus' first followers. They lived for God, in Christ, through the power of the Spirit. As Jews, Jesus and his disciples were monotheists. But as a result of Jesus' death and resurrection, his followers started to experience God in a way that proved distinctive enough to set them apart from mainstream Judaism and that would eventually lead to their belief in the divine mystery as Trinity. Some wondered, however, whether the three Persons of Father, Son, and Holy Spirit were not simply three aspects or modes of the divine being that was essentially one. The church concluded that the divine Persons were really distinct, but in a way that did not compromise the unity of the divine mystery.

The problem is that, while the Persons are distinct, the action often associated with each one is not. Typically, the Father is seen as creating, the Son as redeeming, and the Spirit as making holy. But in daily life, the creative action of God is at the same time forgiving and redeeming us, and the other side of our being redeemed is our being made holy—or being created fully into the image and likeness of God. Are the many ways we experience the mystery of God basically modes of the same divine outreach? The New Testament itself does not speak of Father, Christ, and Spirit in modalistic fashion. God (the Father) calls human beings into existence and calls them further to follow Jesus. Jesus teaches them the way to the Father—where Jesus himself is the way. Over the course of their lives, their imaginations, minds, and hearts move ever more deeply into the Gospel narratives to learn from Jesus and be transformed by closeness to him. The purifying and liberating power that Jesus' disciples experience in daily life is the same Spirit that came upon Jesus in the Jordan, driving him into the wilderness and empowering him for his mission. Perhaps the most effective way to resolve any tendency toward Modalism, therefore, is to appreciate the distinctiveness of Christian religious experience by participating in it.

William Reiser, S.J.

See also TRINITY/TRINITARIAN THEOLOGY/TRINITARIAN PROCESSIONS.

MODERNISM

The term Modernism can mean any theory that explains revelation as merely a human religious intuition and excludes the possibility of objective revelation or the objective formulation of religious beliefs. Theologians such as Karl Barth and Karl Rahner have criticized this view.

Modernism is also the name given to an early twentieth-century theological trend condemned by Pope Pius X in the papal decree *Lamentabili* (1907) and the encyclical *Pascendi Dominici Gregis* (1907). The decrees targeted a group of liberal thinkers whose work utilized modern methods of biblical and historical studies. It cited sixty-five erroneous positions in their writings, among them: an immanentist theory of religion and the rejection of metaphysics. It ascribed to the movement an intention to undermine Catholic faith, the church, and its authority.

The heart of the conflict was the Modernists' characterization of the historical character of revelation and faith, and by extension, the historicity of religious truth and dogma. The theologians in question did propose an experiential or intuitive view of revelation along with revelation's objective form. They recognized the distinction between the linguistic, historical expression of faith and its permanent truth, suggesting the symbolic and (potentially) changing character of dogma and forms of church life. Particular targets were the French biblical scholar, Alfred Loisy, whose book *The Gospel and the Church* demonstrated the dynamic relationship between Jesus' teaching and later tradition (in opposition to Harnack who argued for a dichotomy between them) and the English Jesuit George Tyrrell who proposed understanding the church and faith statements in a historically open way. The Modernists argued to no avail that their theories were misrepresented. Their works were condemned and major figures were excommunicated. The censure also affected social theorists in Italy and the seminary faculty at Dunwoodie in Yonkers, New York, whose professors had explored the exegetical potential of historical criticism in their journal *The New York Review* (1905–8).

The severe papal censure held extreme consequences for decades of Catholic scholarship. Papal action mandated an anti-Modernist oath for clergy before ordination. An investigational system designed to ferret out error before it could spread fostered a climate of suspicion in theological and seminary faculties and suppressed all efforts at modern thought. Pope Benedict XV abandoned the strictures, but the negative environment prevailed to the mid-twentieth century. The acceptance of modern forms of biblical and historical studies as well as for speculative theology was confirmed only at Vatican Council II.

Patricia Plovanich

MODERNITY

In its most literal sense, this term refers to the period of Western history stretching, roughly, from the fifteenth century to the present. The dates and events that constitute the beginning and end of this period remain, however, widely debated.

The advent of modernity is often associated with the Enlightenment, more specifically, with the philosopher René Descartes (1596–1650). Recently, some Third World scholars, such as Enrique Dussel (1934–), have suggested that the event that ushers in the modern period is the European conquest of the "New World." In the economic order, the development of mercantile capitalism in the sixteenth century marks the first stages of the modern period.

The term "modernity," however, is distinguished less by a specific time period than by a particular worldview; it is not so much a date as a mindset. What characterize the modern worldview are, above all: an unprecedented confidence in the power of unaided human reason, especially scientific, logical reason; an exaltation of the individual (and its corollary, individual freedom and rights); an assertion of the right and duty of the rational individual to control and subdue the environment; the reduction of all knowledge to empirical, technical knowledge, that is, knowledge useful for controlling and subduing the environment; a faith in the inevitability of historical and moral progress; and a suspicion of tradition as a threat to individual freedom and social progress. The belief that the starting point of all knowledge is the rational individual is perhaps best exemplified by Descartes' well-known axiom, *Cogito ergo sum* ("I think, therefore I am"). Here, human existence is defined as that of an autonomous individual, or *ego*, who is, in turn, defined by his or her capacity for rational thought, or cognition. This ego is autonomous, that is, it exists independently of any inherent relationship to its environment that is the object of the ego's actions. The ego thus exerts itself *over against* its environment. It is in this sense that Descartes' axiom implies an ego that imposes itself, as subject, upon the external world, as object; *Cogito, ergo sum* implies *Conquisto, ergo sum* ("I conquer, therefore I am"). This latter identification of the Western subject with the act of conquest initially manifests itself in the conquest of the indigenous peoples of the "New World," representing, according to Enrique Dussel, the birth of the modern age.

Modern rationalism and individualism have had important ramifications for religion and theology. The identification of the human person with his or her rational intellect and the reduction of all knowledge to empirical knowledge called into question the very basis of religious belief, where this is understood as a *trans-*rational (if not irrational) knowledge of a *non-*empirical reality, God. Likewise, the modern individualism and suspicion of tradition manifested most acutely in the French Revolution gave birth in the West to a widespread process of secularization, where religious faith would be relegated to the private sphere of the individual conscience and the public role of those religious institutions that passed on the religious traditions would be severely circumscribed.

Modernity's emphasis on reason has been accompanied, however, by various undercurrents of romanticism that, in extolling the value of human feelings and emotions over against that of reason, have reacted against the modern cult of reason. For example, the last half of the eighteenth century witnessed what has often been called the Age of Sentimentalism. In the nineteenth century, especially, the romantic cult of feelings, with its distrust of human reason, and the glorification of nature, with its attendant distrust of human "civilization," came to full flower throughout Europe.

The last decades of the twentieth century saw a rebirth of this romantic, anti-rational (if not irrational) sentiment, now in the form of artistic and philosophical movements that, in their disavowal of the modern worldview described above, have heralded the dawn of the "postmodern" age. These "postmodern" movements respond to a historical reality in which modern assumptions concerning the inevitability of progress and the liberative character of human reason are called into question by the destructive, irrational, and oppressive consequences of modern rationalism and individualism: for example, the Holocaust, nuclear weapons, ecological crises, economic inequality, social fragmentation, alienation, oppression of "irrational" and "uncivilized" cultures, and peoples. Given the connections and similarities between modern romanticism and the postmodern rejection of reason, however, postmodernity's claim to have superseded modernity remains an object of contention.

Roberto S. Goizueta

See also MODERNISM; POSTMODERNITY; RATIONALISM; SECULARISM; SECULAR-IZATION / SECULAR / SECULARIZED.

MOGILA, PETER (1597–1646)
Orthodox theologian. Mogila was educated in Paris, later became abbot of a monastery in Ukraine, and finally metropolitan archbishop of Kiev in 1632. He wrote Orthodox Confession, still considered one of the most important works in Orthodox theology. In it Mogila presented a thorough survey of the doctrines and practices of Eastern Orthodoxy. The Confession was accepted by the Synods of Jassy (1642) and Jerusalem (1672). Mogila

also wrote a Catechism that became quite popular.

Orlando Espín

See also ARCHBISHOP; JASSY, SYNOD OF; JERUSALEM, SYNOD OF; METROPOLITAN; ORTHODOX CHURCHES; SYNODS.

MOHISM
See MO-TZU.

MOIRANS, EPIFANIO DE (1644–89)
Catholic missionary in Latin America and member of the Capuchin Order. Born in France, he became a missionary in Cuba and in Venezuela. His defense of African slaves and his relentless denunciations of slavery as an illegitimate and morally unjustifiable system were explicitly argued by him from principles of Catholic moral theology. Moirans was one of the earliest abolitionists. He wrote a small and influential book, Servi liberi seu naturalis mancipiorum libertatis iusta defensio (1682) whose publication cost him imprisonment and exile. His life and thought were influenced by his friend and fellow Capuchin, Francisco de Jaca.

Orlando Espín

See also AFRICAN TRADITIONAL RELI-GIONS; AFRO-LATIN RELIGIONS; CULTURE; ETHICS, SOCIAL; JACA, FRANCISCO JOSE DE; JUSTICE; MISSIONS; SLAVERY.

MOKSHA
In many, but not all, schools of Hinduism, moksha is the ultimate goal of spiritual striving. A Sanskrit word meaning "liberation" or "release," moksha (or mukti) is the final liberation of the jiva (soul) from its rounds of reincarnation in samsara. This much all schools agree on, but there is disagreement as to what this release from samsara leads to. In Advaita Vedanta,

moksha is understood nondualistically as the dissolution of individuality in a blissful realization of complete identity with Brahman, the impersonal Infinite. In most other schools, liberation is not identity but rather intimate communion with a personally conceived deity, an experience enjoyed in the highest heavenly paradise. In this case, the soul (*jiva, atman*) retains some individuality. It should be noted that several important devotional schools within Hinduism say that *bhakti* (blissful love of God), not moksha, is the supreme goal of life, and indeed that they are willing to return again and again to samsara, provided they can enjoy the bliss of loving devotion to the Lord.

Lance E. Nelson

See also ADVAITA VEDANTA; BHAKTI; HINDUISM; SAMSARA; SHAIVA; VAISHNAVA.

MOLINA, LUIS DE (1535–1600)

Spanish Catholic theologian and member of the Society of Jesus (Jesuits). His writing on the relationship between divine grace and human free will ignited one of the most passionate scholarly debates in the history of Catholic theology. Opposed to what he perceived as the deterministic theologies of Luther and Calvin, Molina championed the fundamental ability of human freedom—under the influence and guidance of God's grace—to respond to grace and to choose to do good. His explanations on grace and free will that also theorized about God's foreknowledge of human free choices came to be challenged by Domingo Báñez and many other Dominican theologians. The latter suspected that Molina was advocating a new form of Pelagianism, thereby curtailing the efficacy and absolute necessity of God's grace as precondition for any good

human choice. The controversy began as European theologians were passionately involved in the various sides of the Reformation, and so mutual charges of heresy were hurled at both sides (Dominicans vs. Jesuits) of this particular intra-Catholic confrontation. As the debate (called *de auxiliis* by historians) between Báñez and Molina continued, many other Dominicans and Jesuits joined in, leading to such verbal violence between theologians of the two orders that a scholarly stalemate was imposed by Pope Paul V in 1611. The fundamental questions raised by the *de auxiliis* controversy have never been officially settled within Catholicism. Molina's book that started it all was called *Concordia liberi arbitrii cum gratiae donis* (1588).

Orlando Espín

See also BÁÑEZ, DOMINGO; DETERMINISM; DOMINICANS; FREEDOM; FREE WILL; GOD; GRACE; JUSTIFICATION; NATURE, HUMAN; OMNIPOTENCE; PELAGIANISM; SEMI-PELAGIANISM; SOCIETY OF JESUS; TRENT, COUNCIL OF.

MOLINOS, MIGUEL DE (1628–98)

Spanish Quietist teacher. One of Quietism's few representatives in Spain, although he was most influential in Italy, Molinos was a Catholic priest who had a successful and widespread ministry as spiritual director. He is a key figure in the history of Quietism in the seventeenth century. He taught a method of contemplative prayer that led to intimate union with God, and that suggested (to many of his followers) that the church (and its sacraments), the Bible, and even Jesus himself were no more than stages on the way to the ultimate goal of union with God. After several attempts failed to condemn him, Molinos was accused and convicted of heresy in 1685. He chose to remain within the Catholic Church, so he reformed his views enough to conform, but many of his Italian followers refused to imitate him on this. Molinos' most influential book was his *Guía espiritual* (1675).

Orlando Espín

See also CHURCH; CONTEMPLATION; COUNTER-REFORMATION/CATHOLIC REFORMATION; ECCLESIOLOGY; GRACE; PRAYER; QUIETISM; REFORMATION.

MOLTMANN, JÜRGEN (1926–)

German theologian. Together with Johann Metz, Jürgen Moltmann has been one of the major exponents of so-called political theology in Europe. A student of Karl Barth, Moltmann's *Theology of Hope* (1964) placed eschatology, through the central biblical categories of "promise" and "fulfillment," and the "kingdom of God," at the heart of Christian faith and theology. Because the eschatology of the kingdom was affirmed as the future of the world as history, political engagement with the "secular" became a hallmark of Moltmann's work. With the publication of *A Crucified God* (1973), Moltmann began to elaborate the specifically trinitarian foundation of his position through reflection on the significance of the Cross for understanding both the divine life and its relation to the world. Beginning in 1975, Moltmann has published a continuing series of "contributions to theology" on the Trinity, ecclesiology, christology, creation, and pneumatology that have been both in fundamental continuity with and elaborations of his position in *The Crucified God.*

J. A. Colombo

See also METZ, JOHANN; POLITICAL THEOLOGY (-IES).

MONARCHIANISM

During the second and third centuries C.E., many Christians were concerned with safeguarding monotheism and the unity of God, and in order to accomplish this some theologians proposed a number of doctrines that were later condemned as heretical. Monarchianism is the umbrella name given to this varied and internally diverse theological movement in early Christianity. One branch of the movement was called Adoptionism because it taught that Jesus was divine only in the sense that in him God's force was present, thereby "adopting" Jesus as divine. Another branch of the movement was called Modalism (or Sabellianism, after the name of one of its proponents) because it held that the only differentiation in God is a mere succession of "modes" or operations. Modalism is also referred to as Patripassianism because a consequence of its original teaching led its proponents to affirm that God the Father suffered as the Son.

Orlando Espín

See also ADOPTIONISM; CHRISTOLOGY; HERESY; MODALISM; PERSON/PROSOPON; TRINITY/TRINITARIAN THEOLOGY/ TRINITARIAN PROCESSIONS.

MONASTERY

From the Latin *monachos*, this word refers to the place in early Christianity where people lived in groups set apart from the ordinary life. It arose in response to a shared recognition that the synthesis of Roman civilization had decayed, and that restoration was only possible in leaving it behind. The dwellings of these early monks (often rude in their simplicity) were placed in remote areas where solitude could be found. They also cultivated asceticism so that the spiritual life could grow unfettered. The first recluses were hermits, but experience taught that the support of a community was necessary for most. Thus the monastery became the home of those who shared a desire to perfect their following of Christ.

Kathleen Dugan

See also MONASTICISM (OUTSIDE CHRISTIANITY); MONASTICISM IN EASTERN CHRISTIANITY; MONASTICISM IN WESTERN CHRISTIANITY.

MONASTICISM (OUTSIDE CHRISTIANITY)

Introduction

If the institution of monasticism is defined broadly as an organized collectivity dedicated to spiritual pursuits, then it has been a significant and central reason for the successful domestication and expansion of many world religions including Hinduism, Buddhism, Taoism, and Christianity. This entry reviews the non-Christian instances of monasticism, focusing predominantly on the history of Buddhist monasticism due to the fact that it significantly affected the other two Asian faiths. It should be noted that Islam found renunciation contrary to the Qur'anic revelation, although Sufi brotherhoods did tend to build institutions according to their *tariqas* that resembled monasteries.

Hindu Traditions

It is within early Hinduism that teachers (*gurus*) and disciples (*chelas*) formed institutions dedicated to the study of the Vedic rituals and the yoga practices revealed in the Upanishads. Not all holy men (*sadhus*) accepted disciples, but those who did often established communal residences, and such permanent settlements were called *matha* or *ashramas*. Until the reforms of Shankara (788–820 C.E.), Hindu monasteries likely had no panregional organization and rose and fell based on the tradition of teaching and initiation (*abhisheka*) passed down from teacher to teacher in ordination lineages (*parampara*). With Shankara, perhaps in imitation of the Buddhist *sangha* (see below), there began an organization of regional monasteries for ascetics in the Advaita Vedanta school and rules for ten suborders within (*dashanami*). Subsequent great Hindu teachers such as Ramanuja (active 1020 C.E.), Nimbarka (active 1162 C.E.), Madhava (1199–1278), Vallabha (active 1500), and Chaitanya (1485–1533) established monastic lineages and institutions across the subcontinent that organized their ascetic specialists and propagated their teachings. (In modern parlance, the *matha* often refers to a more complex institution.)

The Buddhist Sangha

Like many other heterodox *shramana* teachers of the sixth century B.C.E., Shakyamuni Buddha organized his ordained ascetic disciples into a community of monks and nuns who submitted to common and detailed rules of communal life (*Vinaya*). The Buddhist *sangha* is the oldest religious institution in the world that endures until the present day and its success in large part explains the global expansion of the faith.

After the first centuries, when monks and nuns wandered except for the monsoon rain retreat (*varsa*), the sangha adopted a predominantly settled existence in monasteries (*vihara*) utilizing rock-cut caves or buildings where monks (or nuns) would take their communal vows and recite the fortnightly *pratimoksha* code of conduct affirming their conformity to the rules. In these compounds, they could meditate and study; these institutions also supported individuals who practiced medicine, performed rituals essential to the Buddhist lifestyle of the locality, or managed the institution. Over time, a distinction developed within Buddhist monasticism: the forest monastery, where meditation and optional ascetic practices (*dhutanga*) could be undertaken (often under the leadership of a charismatic monk-teacher); and the village monastery, where compassionate service to the community (ritual, medical, educational) could be blended with individual cultivation and study. The typical career of a Buddhist monk or nun would find one moving between village and urban monasteries and then going out for periods "in the forest." In many areas, the leadership and inspiration for forest dwellers has been a charismatic monk possessing spiritual powers and exemplary teaching skill. The standard biography of such monks mirrors that of Shakyamuni in which they also experience disillusion, renunciation, and then retreat to the wilderness on the path to nirvana.

Successful Buddhist monasteries multiplied by sending out monks to establish satellite institutions, often in frontier zones. This network of "mother–daughter" monasteries shaped all sorts of alliances, religious and otherwise, providing Buddhism's distinctive pattern of institution building. In many contexts, Buddhist *viharas* did also function to break down ethnic and class boundaries, blurring divisions between peoples. At its peak (600–1000 C.E.), Buddhism's chain of monasteries extended from Japan across the seas to Southeast Asia and Sri Lanka, from India into the Himalayas and through Central Asia back into China. It is also noteworthy that the large celibate monastery was not Buddhism's only institutional form.

History has shown that states favoring Buddhism often placed controls on the Buddhist monastery's development. Along the frontiers of polities in which Buddhism developed, the "forest monastery" tied Buddhist institutions to a polity's outward expansion. Buddhist exponents invoked the memory of Ashoka (250 B.C.E.), as a legendary model of an ideal Buddhist ruler in subsequent eras. A just, generous king (governor, or official, or the like) could be called a *bodhisattva* ("future Buddha"), a *dharmaraja* ("just king"), or a *chakravartin* ("wheel-turning just ruler and zealous devotee"). Thus, the sangha could offer those wielding political power the highest terms of legitimation in the eyes of the faithful, and in this manner Buddhism evolved to be capable of unifying states politically as well as ideologically. This ancient and fundamental dynamic of institutional expansion, moral leadership, and ethnic integration has continued in modern Asia, as nations still struggle to integrate tribal peoples into their state's civil society.

When the faith thrived in both cities and villages, Buddhist monasteries evolved to be complex institutions that were much more than refuges for ascetics. The monastery was often the only local school and Buddhism served societies by spreading the rare premodern ability to read and write. In many important venues, monasteries also became lending institutions: appointed treasurers utilized the excess monies donated at shrines to reinvest them (usually as trade loans) back into the community. On the trade routes especially, this practice was combined with renting monastery-owned buildings to merchants for warehousing or retailing enterprises, a practice that added even further wealth. Such developments are attested by 200 c.e. in India and China, and explain the economic foundations for Buddhism traveling across the Asian landscape on the basis of trade, supported by traders, and in cities along the commercial routes.

Another component in vibrant Buddhist institutions across Asia was its accumulation of lands donated by individuals and the state as perpetual endowments. As it became a landlord, and since monks were forbidden to till the soil, the sangha (mostly through lay managers) would rent out its cultivated lands. The monastic institution derived the food or cash needed for the sangha's upkeep. Up until this century, the larger Buddhist institutions could also have indentured workers or even slaves (usually meaning entire families) donated and attached to them, making the management of the monastery holdings a demanding job administered by the monks/nuns or by a lay committee. In most times and places, governments would honor these holdings as tax-free. Buddhism's strength through concentrating wealth and human resources was also its historical weakness: monasteries were vulnerable to the vagaries of corruption, state patronage, and royal protection. Finally, shrines located within or adjacent to the monasteries—*stupas*, *caityas*, or in buildings with enshrined Buddha images —would also earn income for the sangha in the form of offerings. Thus, Buddhists attracted a following in societies across Asia with spiritual teachings but also with well-built, often remarkable monastic buildings, shrines, and image halls that complemented them. When tied to the productive base of society, Buddhist monasteries were ornamented with masterful art works; its libraries grew with manuscript production (primarily via copyists), and its leaders could develop an effective presentation of the teachings and spiritual practices. Many Buddhist monasteries also organized endowed charities that fed the poor and dispensed free medical care.

As might be expected, these developments led to certain historical patterns over the centuries: Buddhism was tied to trade and the agriculture of its locality; it was also dependent upon whatever governmental authority enforced its economic relationships (land tenure, loan agreements, indentured labor, slavery). Thus, natural disasters and civil disorder in dynastic transitions were precarious times for the faith. Charting the history of Buddhism therefore means following the fate of its institutions in each polity. The trend toward monastic autonomy and the lack of an overarching authoritative body that supervised conformity to monastic discipline in a sense made the integrity of Buddhism dependent upon political leaders who had to "purify the sangha" periodically.

Taoist Monastic Traditions

Taoist monasticism arose in response to the Chinese acceptance of the Buddhist sangha and in order to adapt to the state's early patronage and legal recognition of Buddhist monasteries. By 300 c.e., one segment among those adhering to Taoist traditions began to organize institutions to transmit the teachings and train those engaging in meditation and priestly rituals. Small communities of Taoist seekers of immortality via alchemy have endured for over two millennia, and the Ch'uanchen Chiao ("Sect of Total Perfection") developed this institutional tradition in more remote settings across China.

But it was the press toward the codification of texts and the systematization of rituals along with rules of conduct, all inspired by Buddhist examples, that helped Taoist tradition move beyond regionalism and small-scale, teacher–disciple modes of cultural transmission. The lineage established early in Szechwan by Chang Tao-Ling in the early post-Han era (after 220 C.E.) ordained men who mastered the early literature and trained in ritual performance. Their goal was to be designated *t'ien shih* ("Heaven-designated Master"), a prestigious title won by study with a master and textual comprehension, a rank that assured recognition and spiritual powers to those monks who, in most cases, later returned to serve as healers and temple ritualists back within village or town society. Eventually, many Taoist monasteries, temples, and distinguished monk-priests attracted patronage, offering an indigenous avenue for patronage in opposition to "foreign" Buddhists. The Chang lineage in southern China has passed on the leadership of the *T'ien Shih* line since Sung times, with its sixty-fifth incumbent now living in Taiwan. Although Taoist monasteries have been far fewer in number compared to Buddhist institutions, their priests have been more involved in popular Chinese religious practices than Buddhist monks.

Todd T. Lewis

See also ASCETICISM/ASCETIC; ASHRAMA/ASHRAM; DAOISM; REFUGE, THREEFOLD; SADHU; SANGHA; SHANKARA; VINAYA.

MONASTICISM IN EASTERN CHRISTIANITY

Christian monasticism was born within the context of Eastern Christianity. The earliest monks seem to have individually practiced various forms of asceticism, seeking God through penance and prayer. By the fourth century C.E. the monastic movement was clearly recognizable in Egypt. Antony and Pachomius are credited with being the forerunners of Christian monasticism's two basic models: eremitical (solitary) and cenobitical (communal). Monasticism spread very quickly throughout most of the Mediterranean world. Within the Byzantine Empire, monks became very influential in society and church, and members of monastic communities took part in the theological controversies of the patristic period and thereafter.

Monasticism never gave rise, in Eastern Christianity, to various religious orders (as it did in Western Christianity), but two main monastic styles did appear: (a) the *lavra* or *skete* style that gathered groups of hermits (living according to the eremitical model); and (b) the monastery that gathered monks according to the communal, cenobitical model (although some monasteries did allow individual monks the freedom to choose the model they wanted to follow). Both monastic styles have been followed by men and women, although no hermitage or monastery ever serves both genders. Most monks follow the doctrine and practice of some of Eastern monasticism's great teachers (for example, Basil the Great and Theodore of Studios). As Orthodox Christianity spread, the monastic movement spread with it, becoming very important in all the great Orthodox Churches of the East. Perhaps the most remarkable gathering of monks in Orthodoxy is the "monastic republic" of Mount Athos, in Greece.

Monasticism was (and still is) very important in all Eastern Christian Churches. Much of Orthodox theology is due to the reflection of great monastic teachers (for example, besides those already mentioned, Gregory of Nyssa, Gregory Nazianzus, Gregory Palamas, Maximus the Confessor, John Climacus, John of Damascus, and many others). Indeed, contemporary Christian doctrine owes much to the work of these great teachers and of countless other monks. Eastern monasticism has not been (and is not) only a quest for individual spiritual growth and development; monasticism has understood itself as a corporate body also responsible for preserving the faith of the church.

The monastic desire to find God through prayer and penance is rooted in the New Testament themes of Cross and Resurrection. Every monastic commits himself or herself to the exclusive following of Christ, to the exclusion of every other interest. It may be said that monasticism is, in the last analysis, a radicalization of the Christian baptismal commitment.

Orlando Espín

See also ANCHORITES; ANTONY OF EGYPT; ASCETICAL THEOLOGY; ASCETICISM / ASCETIC; BASIL THE GREAT; GREGORY NAZIANZUS; GREGORY OF NYSSA; HERMIT; JOHN CLIMACUS; JOHN OF DAMASCUS; MAXIMUS THE CONFESSOR; MONASTERY; MONASTICISM IN WESTERN CHRISTIANITY; MOUNT ATHOS; NUN; ORTHODOX CHURCHES; ORTHODOXY, THE FEAST OF; PACHOMIUS; RULE (MONASTIC/RELIGIOUS); THEODORE OF STUDIOS.

MONASTICISM IN WESTERN CHRISTIANITY

Monasticism in the West shares the same goals and methods as its sister institutions in the East. Members retire from the world to live together under a rule that hopes to train the body through ascetic practices and the mind through prayer.

Together these practices lead to a closer and closer union with God. Early monastic formulas for monks and nuns varied, but included the evangelical counsels of poverty, chastity, and obedience that became explicit vows in religious orders after the twelfth century.

While independent ascetical movements existed in the West, the desire for the monastic life was greatly enhanced when Athanasius of Alexandria was exiled to Trier in 336. His *Life of Antony* influenced Western Christians to adopt monastic practices. Further impetus came from Jerome, Rufinus, and others who translated Eastern monastic texts into Latin in the fourth century. Monastic houses were established by Martin of Tours (372) and several fourth-century bishops, including Augustine of Hippo and Ambrose of Milan, organized their diocesan clergy along monastic lines. John Cassian established two monasteries near Marseilles around 415 where he wrote his *Institutes*, containing a monastic rule that would have great influence in the West.

In the early years of monasticism, there were several monastic rules used in the West. Irish monasticism produced the *Rule of Columban*. In Italy, the works of John Cassian as well as the anonymous *Rule of the Master* influenced Benedict of Nursia who wrote the *Rule of Benedict* in the early sixth century. This rule, according to its author, wished "to establish a school for the service of the Lord. In founding it we hope to introduce nothing harsh or burdensome" (Prol. 45–6). Such leniency contrasted with the stark asceticism of other rules. Benedict's approach did not appeal to all, however. Monks in the south of Italy followed monastic rules from Eastern Christianity and several monasteries used some combination of these different rules.

Under the influence of Benedict of Aniane, Emperor Louis the Pious imposed the use of the *Rule of Benedict* on all Western monasteries in 816–7. While independent rules continued to be followed in Celtic countries and Visigothic Spain, Europe gradually came to adopt the *Rule of Benedict* as the standard monastic rule. By the tenth century, most monasteries belonged to the Benedictine Order.

During the ninth and tenth centuries, many monasteries were established by local lords as personal fiefs. The abbots were understood to be subject to these lords, and the monastic lands and buildings belonged to the lords. A reform movement to free the monasteries, and eventually the larger church, from control of the lords came with the establishment of the Benedictine monastery of Cluny in France in 909. Cluny was independent of any lord, and it became the center for over a thousand "Cluniac" monasteries by the end of the eleventh century. All these monasteries were free of outside politcal control and looked to Cluny for leadership as their founding abbey.

Stricter forms of the Benedictine life appeared in the twelfth century. The most important of these new orders were the Cistercians. Under the charismatic leadership of Bernard, abbot of Clairvaux, the order grew to 700 monasteries by 1300. Cistercians built monasteries devoid of any decoration in remote areas of Europe where they lived an austere life. Other reform movements included the Carthusian Order, an organized monastic life for hermits, as well as the austere orders of the Vallombrosians and Camaldolese. The popularity of the monastic life reached a peak in the twelfth century. Thereafter, the mendicant orders of the thirteenth century proved far more attractive than the monastic life, and monasteries suffered further decline during the Black Death.

Renewal of Benedictine life took place in seventeenth century in Italy, Austria, Germany, Portugal, and England. The reformed congregation of Valladolid established monasteries beyond Europe in Mexico and Peru. The Congregations of St. Vanne (1604) and St. Maur (1621) gained a reputation for their outstanding scholarship. Between 1600 and 1660 the number of Benedictine nuns nearly doubled to 18,000. Cistercian monasticism was reformed by Abbot Armand de Rancé whose movement was recognized as the Order of Cistercians of Strict Observance (Trappists) by the pope in 1712.

Monasticism declined markedly in the eighteenth century due to the suppressions of the French Revolution and the anticlericalism of the Enlightenment. The French government closed all monastic houses, while Emperor Joseph II of Austria suppressed many Benedictine houses in Austria, Bohemia, Hungary, and Poland. Monasteries in the Netherlands and Switzerland were forced to close in 1796, and under Napoleonic rule, monasteries were suppressed in Italy, Prussia, Germany, and Spain. By 1810 there were fewer monasteries in Europe than at any time since the early Middle Ages.

Monasticism began to revive during the nineteenth century in England, Bavaria, Italy, and particularly in France, at the ancient monastery of Solesmes. Benedictines from these newly founded houses went to Africa, Australia, South America, and Asia. By 1950 there were thriving Benedictine houses in Argentina, Mexico, Vietnam, India, Morocco, and Madagascar. Monasteries were also founded in North America at St. Vincent (1846), St. Meinrad

(1854), and Conception (1871) Abbeys. Pope Leo XIII established the monastery of St. Anselmo in Rome as the central house of Benedictine studies, and the new position of Abbot Primate was created to unify Benedictine monasteries worldwide. Despite this revival of monastic life, setbacks occurred. Some monks were expelled from Mexico in 1913; the monastery of Pueyo was attacked in Spain in 1936; and Benedictines were driven from mainland China after World War II. Monks from Eastern Europe and Asia were forced to leave their monasteries as communism extended its influence.

An intense renewal of monastic life occurred in the middle of the twentieth century. Benedictine scholars, notably Jean Leclercq, recovered the classic literature and history of the monastic movement. Centers of learning were established at the Benedictine Pontifical University of Sant' Anselmo in Rome, and at Saint John's Abbey in Collegeville, Minnesota. Benedictines assumed the leadership in the renewal of religious life, notably Rembert Weakland, abbot primate in 1967, and Basil Hume, archbishop of Westminster.

Further centralization and consolidation of Benedictine monasticism was achieved when the Vallombrosian, Camaldolese, Olivetan, and Sylvestine branches of Benedictinism joined the Benedictine Confederation. The Anglican and Lutheran Churches saw a renewed growth in non-Catholic Benedictine houses. Particularly under the leadership of the Trappist Thomas Merton, Christian monks began a dialogue with monks in other religious traditions. While the enthusiasm of the sixties has waned, and Benedictines saw a decline in numbers from 1965 to 2000, the monastic life continues to attract young men and women who desire to devote themselves to the discipline of work and prayer envisioned by the founders of Western monasticism.

Gary Macy

See also ABBEY; ABBOT / ABBESS; AMBROSE OF MILAN; ANGLICAN COMMUNION; ANTONY OF EGYPT; ATHANASIUS, PATRIARCH OF ALEXANDRIA; AUGUSTINE OF HIPPO; BENEDICTINE RULE (RULE OF ST. BENEDICT); BENEDICTINES; BENEDICT OF NURSIA; BERNARD OF CLAIRVAUX; CARTHUSIANS; CASSIAN, JOHN; CHASTITY; CISTERCIANS; CLUNY, ABBEY OF; JEROME; JOSEPHINISM; LEO XIII, POPE; LUTHERANISM; MARTIN OF TOURS; MERTON, THOMAS; MONASTERY; MONASTICISM IN EASTERN CHRISTIANITY; NUN; OBEDIENCE; ORDERS, RELIGIOUS; PONTIFICAL UNIVERSITY; POVERTY (RELIGIOUS VOW); RELIGIOUS (VOWED); RUFINUS OF AQUILEIA; RULE (MONASTIC / RELIGIOUS); SOLESMES, ABBEY OF; TRAPPISTS.

MONICA (331–87)

The mother of Augustine whose writings provide the only information on her life. Born into a Christian family, Monica married Patricius, a pagan and minor noble of Thagaste. She had three children: Augustine, his younger brother, Navigius, and a daughter whose name is lost to history. Monica dedicated her life to Augustine's education and conversion to Christianity, following him in his journey to Carthage, Rome, and finally Milan. Monica died in Ostia as she and Augustine were returning to North Africa.

Gary Macy

See also AUGUSTINE OF HIPPO.

MONOGAMY

In current usage, monogamy refers to an exclusive romantic or sexual relationship between two persons. Traditionally, it has referred to marriage and indicates that married persons are to have only one spouse at a time (or more accurately, a man may only be married to one woman at a time). It may be contrasted with polygyny in which a man may be married to more than one woman or polyandry in which a woman may be married to more than one man. In the Christian tradition, monogamy has been viewed as most conducive to marital harmony and a successful family life.

Brian F. Linnane, s.j.

See also ETHICS, SEXUAL; MARRIAGE IN CATHOLIC PERSPECTIVE.

MONOGENESIS

The thesis that humanity descends from a single pair of human progenitors identified as Adam and Eve in Genesis 2–3. Christian tradition has assumed that every person is not only biologically descendent from this original couple, but also shares the legacy of their original disobedience to God. Monogenesis (also called monogenism) is distinguished from the monophyletic theory that claims humanity evolved from a single species although it had many progenitors.

While some ancient myths do suggest that humanity stems from several progenitors, polygenism was rarely taken seriously until modern times. However, after the theory of evolution was introduced, many questioned the traditional belief that humanity descended from a single pair.

In his 1950 encyclical *Humani Generis*, Pope Pius XII affirmed the right of Catholics to accept the theory of evolution as a scientific opinion. However, he denounced polygenism by claiming that it was "not apparent" how it could be reconciled with the doctrine of original sin. Thus, his argument for monogenesis was an indirect deduction that harmonized human origins with the traditional premise that original sin proceeds from a sin actually committed by the first couple and passed on to all future generations.

Subsequently, the increasing sophistication in biblical studies made it more generally understood that the creation accounts in Genesis were etiological myths, and all other biblical references to human origins and what came to be called original sin were derived from the stories in Genesis. Most Christians recognize that these biblical accounts were founded on an ancient conceptual construct that conveys theological truths in images that were never intended to communicate scientific facts. Today, the issue is not a burning question for most Catholics or mainline Christians. However, a vocal minority of conservative and fundamentalist Christians holds a literal understanding of Genesis called creationism.

Regina A. Boisclair

See also AETIOLOGY / ETIOLOGY; CREATIONISM; POLYGENESIS; SIN, ORIGINAL.

MONOGENISM

See MONOGENESIS.

MONOLATRY

Monolatry may be defined as the worship of a single god while acknowledging that other deities exist. The religion of ancient Israel may be accurately described as monolatry for much of its history. The prologue of the Decalogue, "you shall have no other gods before me" (Exod 20:3) is usually understood to be a demand that the Israelites remain exclusively loyal to Yahweh and worship no other gods. It assumes that other gods exist.

Russell Fuller

MONO-NO-AWARE

(Japanese, sensitivity to things). A term representing one of the primary religio-aesthetic concepts of the Heian Period (794–1185), indicating a kind of gentle sadness in response to the transitory nature of life. Popularized in the Japanese classic "The Tale of Gengi," it reflects an emotional, aesthetic sensitivity to both the beauty of life and the pathos of life. Its focus on emotional response to perishability and impermanence reflects the strong Buddhist influence of this period.

G. D. DeAngelis

See also BUDDHISM; DUKKHA; NAKA IMA; YUGEN.

MONOPHYSITISM

From the Greek words *monos* ("only one") and *physis* ("nature"), Monophysitism is a doctrine that claims that in the Person of the incarnate Word (that is, in Jesus Christ) there was only one nature—the divine. This doctrine is in direct contradiction to the common Christian teaching that in the Person of the incarnate Word there are two natures—the human and the divine. The common Christian teaching was formally defined at the ecumenical Council of Chalcedon (in 451 C.E.). Monophysitism was condemned at Chalcedon, and is considered heretical by most Christians, although it became acceptable doctrine in the Armenian and Syrian–Jacobite churches, and among many Coptic Christians. With today's better understanding of the Chalcedonian doctrine, as well as with clearer insights into early Monophysitism, some substantial ecumenical dialogues promise to bridge the doctrinal divisions raised by this ancient controversy.

Orlando Espín

See also CHALCEDON, COUNCIL OF; CHRISTOLOGY; PERSON/PROSOPON; TRINITY/TRINITARIAN THEOLOGY/TRINITARIAN PROCESSIONS.

MONOTHEISM
(IN CHRISTIANITY AND ISLAM)

Belief in one (*mono*) God (*theos*). Both Christians and Muslims (those who practice Islam), as well as Jews, profess faith in the one God who is revealed in the first two books of the Bible as the creator of the universe and of humankind (Genesis 1 and 2). All three Middle Eastern religious traditions—Judaism, Christianity, and Islam—worship the same God. All three speak of God as personal, that is, a God who interacts with humans for their benefit. All three believe that this God is one and that there is no other God.

While Christians and Muslims share this monotheistic faith inherited from Judaism, they have each developed it in unique ways. Monotheism in Islam is actually quite similar to the theology of God found in Judaism. In fact, the only major theological difference between Islam and Judaism is Islam's acceptance of Muhammad (570–632) as a prophet of God who came with a revelation recorded in the Muslim scripture (the Qur'an) that Muslims say completes and perfects the biblical revelation. In most other respects, the Islamic and Jewish concepts of God are identical. The one God, both religions would affirm, created the world, sent prophets to disclose God's will, is lawgiver and judge, is kind and merciful, and directs humans to live justly as a sign of their fidelity to God.

Christians would also make these affirmations, but their understanding of God includes a belief that neither Muslims nor Jews can accept. For Christians, the one God is triune. This trinitarian doctrine is founded on the Christian belief that Jesus Christ is God's only begotten Son, one in "substance" with God the Father. Christians also believe that after Jesus was raised from the dead and ascended into heaven, the Father and the Son sent the Holy Spirit, a distinct "Person" of the Trinity but fully God, to guide the Christian community and lead it to truth. According to Christian theology, God is eternally triune, so that even before God sent the Son and the Spirit, there were "three Persons in one God."

It is this trinitarian understanding of the one God that distinguishes monotheism in Christianity from monotheism in Islam and Judaism. Islam, in particular, finds the Trinity objectionable. Muslims call God Allah, literally meaning *the* (one and only) God. For them, speaking of three persons in one amounts to "blasphemy." The Qur'an puts it this way:

They do blaspheme who say:
Allah is one of three
In a Trinity: for there is
No god except One God.
—5:73

Ronald A. Pachence

See also ALLAH (ISLAM); HOLY SPIRIT; JESUS (AS PROPHET OF ISLAM); MONOTHEISM (IN JUDAISM); QUR'AN; REVELATION IN ISLAM); TRINITY/TRINITARIAN THEOLOGY/TRINITARIAN PROCESSIONS.

MONOTHEISM (IN JUDAISM)

Monotheism may be simply defined as the belief or conviction that only one god exists, there are no others. This stands in contrast to monolatry which is the devotion to one god, while conceding that others exist and have power. In ancient Israel during the period of time that the Hebrew Bible was developing, monotheism, as defined above, developed slowly, coming to clear expression only by the end of the Babylonian Exile (587–538

B.C.E.) in the writings of Deutero-Isaiah (Isa 40–55). Before this, Israel's religion may be described as monolatrous, requiring exclusive loyalty to Yahweh on the part of the Israelites, but at the same time acknowledging that other deities not only exist, but also are the objects of devotion for other peoples.

Russell Fuller

MONOTHELITISM

From the Greek *monos* ("only one") and *thelein* ("to will"), Monothelitism was a seventh-century doctrine that claimed that in the incarnate Word (that is, in Jesus Christ) there was only one will. It was an attempt (political, more than theological) to heal the breach between Monophysitism and the majority Catholic/Orthodox view that supported the teaching of the Council of Chalcedon. Monothelitism was condemned as heretical at the Council of Constantinople in the year 680.

Orlando Espín

See also CHALCEDON, COUNCIL OF; CHRISTOLOGY; HERESY; TRINITY/TRINITARIAN THEOLOGY/TRINITARIAN PROCESSIONS.

MONSIGNOR

A title granted (usually by the pope at the recommendation of local bishops) to some members of the Roman Catholic clergy as a way of honoring them for their services to the church and/or society. There are no particular duties attached to the title. In many countries, it is also the proper term to use when referring to or addressing bishops.

Orlando Espín

See also BISHOP (EPISCOPACY); CLERGY; PRIESTHOOD; ROMAN CATHOLIC CHURCH.

MONSTRANCE

The word monstrance comes from the Latin word meaning "to show" or "point out" (*monstrare*). Essentially, a monstrance is a stand on which a consecrated Host can be placed to expose or display it publicly for a procession or for adoration. The Host (or disk of consecrated altar bread) is placed in the top part, called a *lunette;* this is basically an ornate small case (or *pyx*) with circular windows forming the front and back. The lunette is fixed to a metal stand with a stem and base that can be placed upright on an altar or carried in the hand. The use of such a liturgical vessel is confined to Christian churches that have a belief in the Real Presence, that is, that Christ is really present in the consecrated Host. *Exposition* of the Eucharist in this way began during the high Middle Ages; some scholars view the practice as especially characteristic of the Catholic Reformation, and thus Catholic piety in the Baroque period (the sixteenth and seventeenth centuries).

Joanne M. Pierce

See also ADORATION; BAROQUE; COMMUNION (LITURGICAL); CONSECRATION (CHRISTIAN); EUCHARIST; MASS; TABERNACLE (CHRISTIAN LITURGICAL).

MONTALEMBERT, CHARLES RENÉ (1810–70)

French politician, historian, and Catholic layman, Montalembert was a religious liberal who sought, among other things, to free the church from state control. With Robert de Lamennais and Henri-Dominique Lacordaire, he helped to edit *L'Avenir*, a Catholic newspaper condemned by Rome in 1831. A member of the French Chamber of Deputies from 1848 to 1857, Montalembert devoted many of his later years to publication of works on medieval monasticism.

Thomas Worcester, S.J.

See also LACORDAIRE, JEAN-BAPTISTE HENRI DOMINIQUE; LAMENNAIS, ROBERT DE.

MONTANISM

An early Christian movement claiming that Montanus, Maximilla, and Priscilla, prophets from Phrygia, were unique mediums for the Paraclete. Their ecstatic utterances were believed to be a new revelation supplementing that of the New Testament. Denying all other ecclesiastical authority, the prophets predicted that the end of the world was imminent, and indeed would take place upon the death of Maximilla when the new Jerusalem was expected to appear in Phrygia. In preparation for the end times, a strict asceticism was observed, marriage was forbidden, fasting and charity were encouraged, and martyrdom was seen as the ideal Christian act. The movement was well organized, enthusiastic, and spread rapidly, despite its condemnation by several churches in Asia Minor. Drawing on the tradition of enthusiasm in early Christianity and avoiding doctrinal issues, the movement was difficult for church leaders to counter. When Maximilla's death in 179 did not result in the second coming of Christ, Montanism lost some of its enthusiasm but found a rebirth in a renewed moral rigorism. The major spokesperson for this second phase of Montanism is Tertullian of Carthage, who joined the Montanists in 207. The movement slowly faded, but Montanist groups were still active in Phrygia in the fourth century.

Gary Macy

See also APOCALYPTICISM; ASCETICISM/ASCETIC; MONTANUS; PARACLETE; TERTULLIAN.

MONTANUS

The founder of Montanism. Little is actually known about Montanus. He started prophesying in Phrygia around 155–60, claiming to be the Paraclete promised in John. Not only Montanus, however, but also the prophetesses Maximilla and Priscilla were thought to be ecstatic prophets of a new revelation, going beyond that of the New Testament. The movement spread rapidly throughout Christianity, winning over Tertullian, the North African theologian, as its most famous convert.

Gary Macy

See also MONTANISM; TERTULLIAN.

MONTECASSINO, ABBEY OF

The abbey of Montecassino was founded by St. Benedict himself around 529, and so is considered the mother of all Benedictine monasteries. The monastery has a long and tumultuous history, but is still active today. The first problems came about 581 when the monastery was destroyed by the Lombards. The monks were taken in by Pope Gregory I (the Great), but the monastery was not restored until 717. For almost 170 years, Montecassino was again the model monastery for all Europe, the home of kings and scholars. In 883 the monastery was again destroyed, this time by Islamic armies. The monks fled and again rebuilt in the tenth century. The eleventh century was perhaps the abbey's greatest period, no less than three popes coming from the monks of Montecassino during that period. The high Middle Ages saw a decline in the fortunes of this great abbey, and an earthquake destroyed part of the monastery in 1349. A real revival for Montecassino took place in the sixteenth and seventeenth centuries, a period of building and renewed scholarship. In 1866 the monastery became a national monument, but under the care of the Benedictines. The last great tragedy to hit Montecassino came in 1945 when the Allied troops bombed and destroyed the monastery. Rebuilding began soon after the end of the Second World War, and Pope Paul VI reconsecrated the monastery in 1964.

Gary Macy

See also BENEDICTINES; BENEDICT OF NURSIA; GREGORY I THE GREAT, POPE; MONASTERY; MONASTICISM IN WESTERN CHRISTIANITY; PAUL VI, POPE.

MONTESINOS, ANTONIO (1486?–1530?)

Born in Spain, Antonio Montesinos arrived on the island of Española (Hispaniola) in the West Indies as a member of the missionary Order of Preachers (Dominicans) around 1510. He is best known for the two sermons he preached to Spanish colonists on the fourth Sunday of Advent and on the following Sunday (December 21 and 28) in 1511 in Santo Domingo. On behalf of his fellow missionaries, he deplored the enslavement of the native population by the Spanish conquerors and warned the latter that they were living, and would die, "in mortal sin." In response, Spanish colonists denounced the Dominicans and appealed to the king of Spain who considered the sermon subversive. Nevertheless, with other Dominican missionaries Montesinos worked for the protection of Indian rights and lives until he died, according to Dominican tradition, as a martyr.

James B. Nickoloff

See also LAS CASAS, BARTOLOMÉ DE; LATIN AMERICAN CATHOLICISM.

MONTSERRAT, MONASTERY OF

Famous Benedictine monastery, built on Mt. Serrat (hence the name), near Barcelona in Spain's Catalonia region. Although established in the eleventh century, Montserrat became one of the most popular symbols of Catalonian nationality only since the fifteenth century. The monastery has exercised important political and religious leadership since the Reformation, providing both scholarship and enlightenment to the Catalonian church. Montserrat has also been influential on French Catholicism and in Latin America. The monastery church houses the black statue of the "Virgin of Montserrat," the object of popular pilgrimages.

Orlando Espín

See also BENEDICTINES; MARIAN DEVOTIONS; MEDIEVAL CHRISTIANITY (IN THE WEST); MEDIEVAL CHURCH; MONASTERY; MONASTICISM IN WESTERN CHRISTIANITY; POPULAR CATHOLICISM.

MONTSERRAT, VIRGIN OF

So-called because a medieval statuette of a sitting Mary with Jesus on her knees is venerated in the Benedictine monastery of Montserrat (on the mountain bearing the same name) in Catalonia (northeast Spain). The dark color of the statuette is due to centuries of candles burning in its presence. The Virgin of Montserrat has historically been a symbol of Catalonian identity, while the Benedictine monastery has played a very important role in Catalonian history and learning. During most of the Middle Ages and throughout the Renaissance, the Virgin of Montserrat was the focus of intense devotion and pilgrimages (Ignatius Loyola, for example, went on pilgrimage there before the experiences that led to his Spiritual Exercises

and his founding of the Jesuits). In the Americas, this Marian devotion became well known from as early as the mid-sixteenth century. It is still counted among the most widespread and popular devotions to Mary anywhere in the (Catholic) world.

Orlando Espín

See also DEVOTIONS; MARIOLOGY; MARY OF NAZARETH; POPULAR CATHOLICISM; POPULAR RELIGIOSITY.

MORAL THEOLOGY/CHRISTIAN ETHICS

Although conceptually distinct, the terms moral theology and Christian ethics are used interchangeably, and generally refer to systematic Christian reflection on the sources, obligations, implications, and objectives of the moral life. Historically, the term moral theology is associated with the Roman Catholic and Anglican traditions. This reflects a tendency in Catholicism to relate free human behavior to salvation; thus ethics in this context is seen as a properly theological discipline probing the relationship between God and human persons. Protestants, who have traditionally understood salvation as a free gift from God independent of behavior or merit, have understood Christian ethics as the study of moral demands of divine revelation and of the general norms appropriate for followers of Christ.

Historical Roots

While the writings of both the Old and the New Testaments are rich in ethical content (for example, the Ten Commandments of Exodus, the laws of Leviticus, Jesus' love command in Matthew and Mark, Paul's injunctions against sexual immorality in Romans) and the early church fathers addressed questions of morality, most scholars see the origins of the discipline of Christian ethics in the sixth-century penitential manuals. These books arose in response to the development of the practice of a frequent confession of sins, a practice encouraged by Celtic monks and that became dominant in Western Christianity due to their missionary activity. The Penitentials were written to assist priest confessors in determining the appropriate penance for specific sins. This had the effect of focusing moral theology on sins to be avoided rather than on cultivating a good or virtuous life. This in turn encouraged a minimalistic attitude toward the moral life. Further, these manuals encouraged a sort of "works-righteousness," the idea that God's mercy and forgiveness depended on some type of human activity. The Penitentials also had a practical orientation; the sinful experiences considered were drawn from the lives of the penitents while the penalties imposed tended to reflect ascetical discipline of the monastic life (fasting from food, chanting psalms); thus they did not represent a theoretical advance to the discipline of Christian ethics. For such an advance, one must look to the great medieval theologian, Thomas Aquinas (1224–74).

Arguably the most significant theologian in the Roman Catholic tradition, Aquinas developed natural law and virtue theories that continue to influence the work of Roman Catholic and Protestant ethicists alike. Greatly influenced by the reintroduction of Aristotle's works on metaphysics, ethics, and psychology in the Christian West, Aquinas used Aristotelian categories as a philosophical basis for a systemic account of a Catholic theology informed by traditional theological sources such as the writings of Peter Lombard and Augustine. Regarding

ethics, the Aristotelian influence can be discerned in Aquinas's teleological (goal-oriented) understanding of human nature and human actions (human nature is oriented toward its happiness/perfection; a person acts to achieve some understanding of what is desirable or good), in his high regard for human rationality, and in his understanding of the virtues. Regarding persons, Aquinas claims that the natural law is the law of their being; it is human participation in God's Eternal Law. As such it is active within the human person and so is experienced not as an external obligation but as an internal call to human flourishing. His natural law theory incorporates emphases on rationality or "right reason" and the order of nature, emphases that some theorists find contradictory. The "right reason" dimension holds that because persons can come to know what is conducive for their flourishing, they encounter an obligation to act according to that knowledge. The "order of nature" dimension reflects on the physical or bodily dimension of reality and its laws. It holds that physical faculties have particular goals and what frustrates or circumvents those ends is a violation of the natural law. In this light, the goal of sexual faculties is procreation; any nonprocreative use of those faculties (same-sex relations, for example) is contrary to the natural law. This physicalistic perspective is found in official Roman Catholic teaching on sexual and medical ethics. It also has tended to reinforce a legalistic and act-centered moral theology.

While Aquinas's natural law theory has had the greater influence in Roman Catholic ethics, many experts argue that his virtue theory is at the heart of his ethical vision. In virtue theories, the evaluation of acts is subordinated to a consideration of character or the type of person the agent is becoming. In Aquinas's account, virtues are habits or dispositions for making good moral choices. They are character traits that promote consistent action conducive to the human *telos*, that is, human excellence or flourishing. The basic elements of Thomistic virtue theory are similar to the accounts of classical philosophers. It is the central role of the theological virtues that distinguishes Aquinas's account. For Aquinas, the theological virtues of faith, hope, and charity are "infused" virtues, given by means of divine assistance. It is these virtues that enable and direct moral virtues to the ultimate goal of persons—eternal salvation. Aquinas's understanding of the human person and his moral theory allow for a certain optimism; because the person is fundamentally rational, he or she is capable of knowing and doing what is right and good. Finally, Scripture did not play a large role in Aquinas's moral theory; indeed, it was often cited only as a proof-text. It is philosophical reflection shaped by theological tradition that is at the heart of the Thomistic account. It was in the ethics of the Reformation that the Sacred Scriptures are of central importance.

The Protestant Reformation of the sixteenth century was the source of enormous change for Christian theological ethics. While there are significant differences between the thought of Martin Luther and John Calvin, it is not possible to survey them here; rather, a general overview of Reformation themes will be presented. Both Martin Luther and John Calvin were influenced by Augustine's views on the profound effects of original sin. The Reformers, while confident there was a natural law, were deeply skeptical about the capacity of sin-affected human

persons to know this law and conform to it. Luther and Calvin vigorously resisted any suggestion of an act-centered morality, rejecting what has been referred to as "works righteousness." Individual salvation does not, in the Reformation account, depend upon performing certain actions or avoiding particular sins; rather, it results from faith bestowed on the individual by means of God's gracious and free action. What is significant in this is not that individual sinners stop sinning and so merit God's love; rather, it is that God's love is bestowed upon the sinner while he or she is still sinning. Thus the spirit of the Reformation is not essentially ethical although this movement in the history of Christianity had profound implications for ethics. Another important shift is the Reformation understanding of the relationship between law and Gospel. For the reformers, law is most often contrasted with Gospel. Luther saw that there were two uses for law: the civil use restraining human action and the moral use convicting persons of their sinfulness. Knowledge of sinfulness does not assist the agent in overcoming sin; only the Gospel —the revelation of Christ—can accomplish this.

In their break with papal authority, the Reformers rejected the claims of the Roman Catholic tradition of the church's ability to teach definitively on matters of faith and morals. In place of this universal, hierarchical teaching ministry (often referred to as the magisterium), the Protestant Reformation has tended to emphasize the sovereignty of the individual conscience and centrality of the Bible for ethical discernment. Indeed, James Gustafson has argued that it is this primacy of Sacred Scripture, or *sola scriptura*, that is the most distinctive contribution of the Reformation to Christian theology and ethics. This primacy suggests that any adequate Christian discernment or decision-making process must begin with an analysis of Scripture or relevant biblical themes. Special appeal is made to the life, ministry, and teachings of Jesus of Nazareth as well as to the letters of St. Paul.

The Modern Period

In Roman Catholic moral theology, the period between the Council of Trent (1545–63) and Vatican Council II (1962–5) can be characterized as the manualist tradition, referring to the manuals of moral theology that dominated the discipline. Manuals were the texts used in seminary classes to prepare future priests for the ministry of confession. These texts were generally based on a more or less adequate interpretation of Thomas Aquinas. Although traditional natural law theory continues to play a dominant role in official Roman Catholic teaching on sexual and bioethical teaching, moral theology after Vatican II tends to focus more on the person as a whole rather than on nature alone and therefore more on character than on actions.

Theoretical developments in Roman Catholic moral theology, like fundamental option and proportionalism, have undermined traditional views on personal sin and on intrinsic evil; that is, the understanding that some actions are always gravely evil and that no circumstance or intention can ever justify them. The negative reaction to the papal encyclical on birth control (*Humanae Vitae*, 1968) on the part of many moral theologians has served to raise questions about the limits of theological dissent and about the level of papal authority asserted in such teachings. Indeed, a minority of moral theologians has argued that the teachings

of *Humanae Vitae* are infallible. In the realm of social and political ethics, personalism has generated a body of official documents strongly supporting human rights and the cause of economic justice.

Protestant ethics in this century has been influenced both by the optimism of the Enlightenment (notably Kantianism) with its faith in the power of human reason and the Social Gospel and its faith in progress, as well as by the strong reaction against those influences of Karl Barth and Reinhold Niebuhr. Barth, a towering figure in twentieth-century Reformed theology in Europe, argues that God's will cannot be discerned from existing social orders, but rather confronts believers as a free command. Reinhold Niebuhr's theological training in the early twentieth century shaped him in the optimism of liberal American Protestantism. However, his liberalism was replaced by what came to be known as "Christian realism" as a result of experiencing the harsh realities of industrial life while a pastor in Detroit. His writings expressed skepticism about the ability of groups to do the work of love, and about the efficacy of nonviolence as a tactic against injustice. His brother, H. Richard Niebuhr, was also an important theological ethicist during the mid-twentieth century. The brothers' debate in *The Christian Century* on the proper response to aggressive wars remains influential. H. Richard's principal contribution is his understanding of ethics as relational. The task of the Christian is to be attentive to what God is doing in a given situation and to discern the proper response to God's activity.

James M. Gustafson, a prominent Protestant ethicist, has noted some convergence between recent Protestant and Roman Catholic ethics. Roman Catholics since Vatican II have been paying increased attention to the place of Scripture in ethics and to the important process of moral discernment, while some Protestants have been attentive to the role of right reason or rationality in morals. Both traditions have been influenced by the revival in virtue theory, concerns about environmental and medical ethics, and liberation and feminist theologies.

Brian F. Linnane, s.j.

See also CATHOLIC SOCIAL TEACHING; DOUBLE EFFECT; ETHICS; ETHICS, SEXUAL; ETHICS, SOCIAL; EVANGELIUM VITAE; FUNDAMENTAL OPTION; HUMANAE VITAE; NATURAL LAW; PERSONALISM; PROPORTIONALISM; SIN (SOCIAL, STRUCTURAL); SIN, PERSONAL; SOCIAL GOSPEL; THEOCENTRIC; VERITATIS SPLENDOR; VIRTUE.

MORE, THOMAS (1478–1535)

English humanist, friend of Erasmus and John Colet, More was Lord Chancellor of England under King Henry VIII. More married in 1505; he is often cited as a "Renaissance man" whose interests and competence included law, literature, politics, religion, and family life. Author of *Utopia* (1516), a brilliant work of political commentary and imagination, More came into conflict with Henry VIII when he refused to accept Henry's divorce and Henry's reform of the church. More resigned as chancellor in 1532 and was imprisoned in 1534. While awaiting his fate, he wrote a spiritual work, *Dialogue of Comfort against Tribulation*. Condemned as a traitor for refusal to accept the Act of Supremacy, by which Henry was declared head of the Church of England, More was beheaded in London on July 6, 1535. He was canonized as a saint four centuries later, in 1935.

Thomas Worcester, s.j.

See also COUNTER-REFORMATION/ CATHOLIC REFORMATION; ERASMUS OF ROTTERDAM; HUMANISM; REFORMATION; RENAISSANCE.

MORMON, BOOK OF

Along with the Bible, the Book of Mormon is the sacred scripture for the Church of Jesus Christ of Latter Day Saints, also known as the Mormons. Between 1823 and 1827, Joseph Smith Jr., founder and prophet of the church, received visions from the angel Moroni directing him to unearth golden tablets from a hill near his home in Palmyra, New York. Inscribed in ancient hieroglyphics, the plates were translated by Smith and published in 1830 as the Book of Mormon. It tells the story of the pre-Columbian inhabitants of North and Central America, whom the Book claims descended from the ancient Israelites. These peoples migrated to the Western Hemisphere and ultimately divided into two warring groups, the dark-skinned Lamanites and the light-skinned Nephites. Jesus made a postresurrection appearance to them and inaugurated a two-hundred-year era of peace. Conflict reerupted, and the Lamanites massacred the Nephites. Mormon and his son Moroni were the last Nephite survivors. Mormon wrote the history of his people, and Moroni buried the plates and guided Joseph Smith to find them. The Lamanites became the ancestors of the Native Americans.

The Book of Mormon has aroused intense controversy. Smith has been called a fraud who never found any golden plates and created the Book of Mormon from his own head. Despite these charges, the Book of Mormon is regarded as divine revelation by Mormons and is widely distributed. It can be found in every room in the Marriott hotel chain next to a Bible. In form, it resembles the Bible, divided into books, chapters, and verses; its language is similar to the King James (Authorized) Version. Besides its ancient history, it addresses pressing theological, social, and religious issues of Jacksonian America, including revivalism; the proliferation of Christian groups; conflicting Calvinist and Arminian theologies; and social issues such as the enslavement of African Americans and the treatment of Native Americans.

Evelyn A. Kirkley

See also CHURCH OF JESUS CHRIST OF LATTER-DAY SAINTS.

MORMONS
See CHURCH OF JESUS CHRIST OF LATTER-DAY SAINTS.

MORNING STAR
In a perception that is surely universal in religious cultures, Native Americans had great reverence for the first star to appear in the east in the morning. Harbinger of daylight, and thus of life, it appears in myths of those who show a marked attention to the skies (for example, the Cheyenne and the Pawnee), and is often represented in artistic form in ritual designs. In all Plains tribes who shared the Sun Dance, each day of the ritual opens with a salutation to the rising sun. This begins in darkness, as the Morning Star yields to the greater light. This direction is distinguished by its identification as a primary symbol of the generative power of creation, and is seen as wholly beneficent. The Morning Star symbol is also feminine, and among the Cheyenne this is related to a social system that highly values its women.

Kathleen Dugan

See also SUN DANCE.

MORTIFICATION
"Mortification" generally refers to the practice of "putting to death" those things in us that run counter to the life of the Spirit and would hinder our growth in virtue or our perfect following of Christ. When one notices a tendency within oneself toward pride or selfishness, for example, one learns how to act against that tendency by engaging in activities or works that will promote humility and generosity. Someone given to rash judgment might work at developing compassion, while someone given to greed might act against the tendency to hoard by regular almsgiving.

The redemption of human desiring does not happen without discipline and effort. Paul speaks of "the body of sin" being destroyed (Rom 6:6) and the need to "put to death" whatever is earthly (Col 3:5), while the Gospel teaches the necessity of denying oneself in order to follow Christ (Mark 8:34). The term mortification sometimes implies, however, a denigration of the body and a view of spiritual development as a basically negative process of self-denial, penance, shouldering one's Cross, and dying with Christ. But a truly "mortified" person is someone who has put on the mind of Christ and "emptied himself" (Phil 2:7); from a Christian perspective, a mortified man or woman is someone who is inwardly free and capable of being led by the Spirit.

William Reiser, S.J.

See also ABSTINENCE; ASCETICISM/ ASCETIC; DISCIPLINE; FASTS/FASTING (IN CHRISTIANITY); LENT.

MOSES
God's intermediary in delivering the Hebrew people from bondage into freedom.

According to Deuteronomy 34:10-12, Moses was a prophet, in fact, the greatest of Israel's prophets.

Special circumstances surround the birth of Moses: he is saved from death by the courageous actions of several women (Exod 2). Although raised in Pharaoh's court, he is outraged by the cruel treatment of Hebrew slaves by Egyptian overseers and takes sides on behalf of the oppressed people. Because he kills an Egyptian, he is forced to flee; in Midiam he marries Zipporah. He is called by God (Exod 3) to return to Egypt in order to deliver the Hebrews, a mission he reluctantly accepts. After the Hebrews leave Egypt, Moses leads them into the desert.

On Sinai, Moses meets with God face to face (Deut 5:4; cf. Exod 33:11) and receives the articulation of Israel's covenant with God in the form of "ten words." According to the biblical text, Moses continues to lead the people through the desert and to the brink of the land that God had promised them. On Mount Nebo in Moab, Moses dies, leaving the leadership of the Israelites' entrance into the land in the hands of his successor, Joshua.

In the New Testament, Moses is associated with the Law. At Jesus' Transfiguration, Moses (the lawgiver) appears on one side of Jesus, and Elijah (the prophet) on the other (Matt 17:1-8; Mark 9:2-8; Luke 9:28-36).

Moses' association with the Law is contrasted with "grace and truth" that come through Jesus Christ in the Gospel of John (1:17; cf. v. 45; 5:45-46). The letter to the Romans associates Moses with the righteousness that comes from the Law, distinguishing it from the righteousness that comes from faith in Christ, the end of the Law (10:4-7).

Alice L. Laffey

MOSES BEN MAIMON
See MAIMONIDES.

MOSES DE LEON
See ZOHAR.

MOSES THE BLACK (330–405)
Cited in a number of historical sources of the period, especially *The Lausiac History of Palladius*, we know Moses to be an Ethiopian, a former slave, and an outlaw. The leader of a band of outlaws in the Egyptian desert, Moses (a name probably taken after his conversion) was converted to Christianity and became a monk. Known for his asceticism and holiness, he was eventually ordained a priest, unusual for monks at that time. Abba Moses (a title given to monks who were spiritual teachers) became the spiritual leader of a group of hermits in the desert to the south of Alexandria and was martyred there in 405 C.E. His writings on monasticism and the monastic life mark him as one of the leading teachers of early monasticism and a foundational influence for the spirituality of the church and later spiritual writings.

The existence of Abba Moses is significant not only for the history of the early church, but for the history of African peoples' presence in the church. His presence, Cyprian Davis believes, is a "good indication that more than likely there were other Black Africans in the desert whose names have not been recorded."

Diana L. Hayes

See also DAVIS, CYPRIAN; MONASTICISM IN EASTERN CHRISTIANITY.

MOSLEM
See MUSLIM.

MOSQUE/MASJID

Place of worship for Muslims. The Arabic word for mosque, *masjid*, literally means "place of prostrations," indicating one of the postures of prayer (*salat*) in the Islamic tradition. Muslims are directed to offer prayers five times each day, though they do not have to pray in the mosque. Muslims, however, try to make their noon prayer on Fridays at a mosque since that is the prayer time dedicated specifically to community prayer and the preaching of a sermon. Women who attend the mosque offer their prayers in a separate gallery behind or above the men and obscured from them.

The design of the mosque is simple. There are no pews or kneelers, no statues or pictures, no altar. The structure is adorned only with carpets, lighting, and phrases from the Qur'an, often written on wall tiles. A recess in one wall called the *mihrab* indicates the *kibla* or direction of Mecca. Mosques also have a *minbar* (pulpit) used for the Friday sermon. Outside and towering above the mosque there is a *minaret*, a tall rocket-like appendage used to call the community to prayer. In addition, every mosque has a place, either inside the building or a fountain outside, for the prescribed washing before prayers.

Ronald A. Pachence

See also KIBLA; MIHRAB; MINBAR; SALAT.

MOTHER EARTH

In the native religious traditions of North America, a special reverence is accorded to the Earth viewed as a generative principle. As the partner of the Sky, the Earth is feminine in gender and described with all the maternal aspects that follow naturally. Yet, as Mother, the earth is also a spiritual presence, and the qualities of nurturing she exhibits are qualitatively enhanced. Though the Earth was always regarded as sacred, and ritual duties and taboos demonstrated this, a distinct change happened in the period when all native culture, especially the land, was threatened with removal. In those circumstances, Mother Earth emerges as the element of tradition most sacred and also most in peril. Thus, Chief Joseph, Tecumseh, and Smohalla (to name just a few), spoke eloquently of the consequences of violating the sanctity of the earth. As a spirit assisting the human beings and all creatures from the mythic origins of creation, the Earth has consistently been acknowledged as the source of continuing life, and in many cosmologies has been next to the Creator.

Kathleen Dugan

See also INDIGENOUS RELIGIOUS TRADITIONS, MYTH.

MOTHER OF GOD/THEOTOKOS

Theotokos is simply Greek for "Mother of God," or literally, "God-bearer," a title given to Mary, the mother of Jesus. Devotion to Mary as the Mother of God and the first uses of the term *theotokos* come from Alexandria in the late third and early fourth centuries. The aptness of this title was questioned by Nestorius of Constantinople who argued that it was absurd to call a human being the mother of the unbegotten God. Nestorius, schooled in Antioch, wished, as did other Antiochene theologians, to carefully separate the human from the divine in Jesus. At best, Nestorius argued, Mary might be called the "Mother of Christ," but to speak of her as the "Mother of God" was theologically inept at best and blasphemous at worst. This attack by Nestorius shocked both theologians in Alexandria and the many faithful devoted to Mary as "Mother of God." This conflict was one of the immediate causes of the Nestorian controversy.

By the end of the controversy, orthodox theologians generally agreed that the devotion to Mary as "Mother of God" was allowable because whatever is said of Christ as human may be said of Christ as God and vice versa—the so-called *communicatio idiomata*. Devotion to Mary as the Mother of God continued throughout the Middle Ages and into the present in both the East and West. It is still an important devotion for Eastern Christians and for Roman Catholics in the West.

Gary Macy

See also CYRIL OF ALEXANDRIA; JESUS OF HISTORY; MARIAN DEVOTIONS; MARIOLOGY; MARY OF NAZARETH; NESTORIANISM; NESTORIUS.

MOTU PROPRIO

A papal document issued by the direct authority of the pope (literally "on his own initiative"), rather than through one of the Vatican congregations (administrative departments), and with his personal signature. Decrees issued *motu proprio* usually deal with particular practical situations and can override more general church law. More expansive considerations of theological or moral subjects would ordinarily be presented in other types of papal documents, such as an encyclical letter.

William A. Clark, s.j.

See also DECLARATION (DOCUMENT); ENCYCLICAL.

MO-TZU (468?–390?)

(Chinese, *Mo-zi*). Moral philosopher originally known as Mo-ti, born in the state of Lu and founder of the Mohist School. Not a great deal is known about his personal life except that he was originally a Confucian who ultimately rejected Confucius' teachings and adopted a less formal and more broadly democratic attitude toward social reform. He promulgated a doctrine of universal love as the foundation of a classless society in which all would be devoted to the common good. This universal love and compassion was a gift and directive from Shang Ti (Heavenly Sovereign), and the restoration of harmony and order would result from following the will of heaven. In addition, he was very utilitarian in rejecting all forms of ritual and music in the belief that all human energy should be concentrated on achieving social goals such as feeding, clothing, and housing people. While Mo-Tzu and his school failed to have any widespread social or political impact in China, his philosophy of a life of service to others left an enduring legacy to the Chinese people.

G. D. DeAngelis

See also CONFUCIANISM; ZHOU DYNASTY.

MOUNT ATHOS

Literally, in Greek, "the holy mountain," this is the name of a Greek peninsula jutting into the Aegean Sea. There are about twenty Orthodox monasteries on Mount Athos, and together they form a nearly independent state within modern Greece. The monasteries hold an invaluable manuscript collection. They have been very important in the long history of Greek Orthodoxy.

Orlando Espín

See also CONSTANTINOPLE, SEE OF; GREEK ORTHODOX CHURCH; MONASTERY; MONASTICISM IN EASTERN CHRISTIANITY; ORTHODOX CHURCHES.

MOURNING IN JUDAISM

See SHIVAH.

MOZARABIC CHURCH AND RITE

The usual way of referring to the ancient Catholic Church and liturgical traditions ("rite") of Spain. The Mozarabic church was not founded from the patriarchate of Rome, and scholars prefer to indicate a North African source. Its very elaborate liturgical practices are different from those of the Roman Rite and bear the marks of early North African, Gallican, and Byzantine Rites.

The smallest of the Western Catholic Churches, its historical roots go back to the earliest patristic-period church of Roman and Visigothic Hispania. The Mozarabic church flourished before the centuries of Islamic rule in Spain (before 711 C.E.), and it continued its strong presence in southern Spain during most of the Islamic period. It has a proud and long history as a church that prized education and learning (for example, Isidore of Seville's work *The Etymologies* was very influential during most of the Middle Ages), and several of this church's councils and synods (at Elvira, at Toledo) have had lasting doctrinal and canonical importance in Western Catholicism. The Mozarabic liturgy was important to the development of early English and Irish ritual books.

Mozarabic decline began when the kings of Castile and León—for mostly political reasons, from 1080 onward—forced most Mozarabic Catholics (in the former Muslim lands "reconquered" by Christian armies) to change to the Roman Rite and jurisdiction that had been brought to Spain around 1050 by monks from the abbey of Cluny. After 1495 the Mozarabic church became (for all practical purposes) only a liturgical rite; and in that year,

Cardinal Jiménez de Cisneros decided to preserve its traditions by ordering that Mozarabic books and rituals be kept in print, and by allowing to continue its presence (although really insignificant) within the Archdiocese of Toledo. The Mozarabic church is today trying to recover from centuries of neglect and intolerance, slowly recuperating its own distinct traditions and autonomy. Mozarabic (medieval) Spanish is still the liturgical language, and Toledo has always been its primatial see.

Orlando Espín

See also CATHOLIC TRADITION; CLUNY, ABBEY OF; COMMUNION (ECCLESIOLOGICAL); EASTERN CATHOLIC CHURCHES; ELVIRA, COUNCIL OF; ILDEFONSUS OF TOLEDO; ISIDORE OF SEVILLE; JIMÉNEZ DE CISNEROS, FRANCISCO; LEANDER OF SEVILLE; MEDIEVAL CHRISTIANITY (IN THE WEST); MEDIEVAL CHURCH; PATRIARCH; PRIMATE/PRIMATIAL SEE; TOLEDO, COUNCILS OF; WESTERN CATHOLIC CHURCHES.

MUDRA

Symbolic hand gesture characteristic of the iconography of divinities and for humans in the practice of yoga and rituals. In both Hinduism and Buddhism, divinities are recognized based on the number of arms and heads, and by the *mudras* and implements held. In the rituals performed by both Brahman priests and Buddhist monks (especially the Mahayana monk-officiants, the *vajracaryas*), mudras may refer to historical incidents, doctrines, or the deities worshiped, constituting a kind of offering.

In Yoga practice, theories evolved to explain the psycho-spiritual effects of mudras on the practitioner. Several hundred have been codified. In tantric Hinduism and Buddhism, mudra gestures along with mantras chanted are designed to "seize the divine ego" of the visualized deity; in tantric Buddhist texts, mudra may also refer to the chants and even to one's yoga consort.

Todd T. Lewis

See also SIDDHA; TANTRIC BUDDHISM; TANTRIC HINDUISM.

MUENZER, THOMAS (1490?–1525)

German Reformer. Muenzer briefly embraced Luther's effort to reform the church before rejecting it in favor of a more radical approach. Claiming inspiration by the Holy Spirit, Muenzer preached a message of imminent divine judgment and called on the people to take up the sword to exterminate God's enemies. Rejecting infant baptism, Muenzer envisioned a church that would be restricted to an elect group of adults. He was thus one of the first "Anabaptist" Reformers in the sixteenth century.

Muenzer joined the Peasants' War in early 1525, a war in which German peasants and other common folk sought greater liberty. With Luther's approval and encouragement, German princes defeated the peasants. Muenzer himself was captured at the battle of Frankenhausen on May 15, 1525, and executed shortly thereafter.

Thomas Worcester, s.j.

See also ANABAPTISTS; LUTHER, MARTIN; REFORMATION.

MUEZZIN/MU'ADHDIN

The person who calls the Islamic community to prayer (*salat*) from the top of the minaret of the mosque five times each day. Traditionally, the *muezzin* made this call to prayer by climbing up a winding staircase inside the minaret and standing on a platform built into the top. As he faced in the direction of Mecca (*kibla*), he would chant the seven or eight lines of the call in a loud voice. In most Islamic countries today, however, speakers have been installed on the platform and the *muezzin* announces prayer times electronically.

Ronald A. Pachence

See also KIBLA; MOSQUE/MASJID; SALAT.

MUFTI

Arabic word used for an expert in Islamic law. Though he may or may not be a judge (*qadi*), the *mufti* is authorized to render a legal opinion called a *fatwa*. This opinion has the force of an official ruling, though parties dissatisfied with a mufti's ruling may seek a second opinion from some other expert.

Ronald A. Pachence

See also FATWA; SHARIA/SHARI'A; ULAMA/ULEMA.

MUHAMMAD (570–632)

The Prophet of Islam who is considered by Muslims to be the final prophet sent by God. He is also called Messenger (*rasul*) of God and "Seal of the Prophets." Muhammad's name literally means the "praised" or "glorified one," although Muslims are quick to point out that he was no more than a human being. They do not assign to him the divine status Christians claim for Jesus Christ.

Properly speaking, Muhammad is not considered the founder of Islam. Islam, Muslims say, is the religion God was revealing to the world through every prophet, from Adam to Jesus. Muhammad is understood as the Prophet of Islam—an honor that is evident in the special revelation that Allah (God) sent him to proclaim. This revelation, Muslims believe, was preserved word for word, in "recitations" Muhammad received and never forgot, and subsequently recorded in the inerrant scripture of Islam, the Qur'an.

For Muslims, the Qur'an is the only miracle or sign Muhammad performed. They call it a miracle because, according to tradition, the Prophet could not read or write; or if he could, he certainly did not have the kind of education to compose such a distinctly beautiful and sophisticated text as the Qur'an. For this reason, it is clear to Muslims that God spoke the words of the Qur'an and used Muhammad as the divine Messenger and Prophet. This assertion is found in the first of the Five Pillars (foundational beliefs and practices) of Islam: "There is no god but Allah (the God) and Muhammad is the Messenger (*rasul*) of God."

Like many of the Hebrew prophets before him, Muhammad did not seek his prophetic mission. In fact, until he received his first revelation in 610, there did not appear to be anything extraordinary about him. His father died before he was born, and his mother lived only until Muhammad was six. He was raised by his uncle, Abu Talib, in Mecca, a city in the country we now call Saudi Arabia. At the age of twenty-five, he married Khadija, a forty-year-old widow and his employer. He continued to manage her caravans, apparently content with his life as a businessman, husband, and father.

Then the unsolicited and unexpected revelations began, and with these revelations came the scorn and rejection of his fellow Qurayshi tribesmen. Believing he spoke for God, Muhammad condemned the polytheism and immoral practices of his people. The more he urged them to become Muslims (those who submit to the one God), the fiercer their opposition to his message became, but according to Qurayshi law, no one could harm him because he was under the protection of his Qurayshi uncle, Abu Talib. In 619, that protection ended with Abu Talib's death.

By 622, Muhammad's life was seriously threatened and he decided that it was time to separate himself from his tribal ties in Mecca and "emigrate" to the city of Yathrib (now called Medina) where a small group of Muslim converts awaited him and his close friend, Abu Bakr. This event, called the *hijra* ("emigration"), was the beginning of the first Islamic community (*umma*). Between the time of his arrival at Yathrib on September 17, 622, and his death on June 8, 632, Muhammad demonstrated that he was a statesman and a military leader as well as a prophet.

After a series of battles and negotiations, he subdued Mecca in 630, and before he died, he directed the expansion of Islam into much of the Arabian peninsula. He also laid a firm foundation for the practice of Islam by the traditions he established as leader of the Median *umma* (community). These traditions, called *sunna*, were later collected and published by various scholars in texts called *hadith*, and they remain an important criterion for the development of Islamic law to this day. Muhammad was buried in Medina and his tomb is a popular pilgrimage destination for Muslims from all over the world.

The religion Muhammad proclaimed is called Islam, literally meaning "surrender" or "submission" to God. Its triliteral root, SLM, also connotes "peace" and "reconciliation." Because followers of Islam believe their tradition comes *from* God *through* the prophecy of Muhammad, it is offensive to Muslims to be called "Muhammadans" or their religion "Muhammadanism." As the Qur'an explicitly says: "This day I (Allah) perfected your religion for you, completed My favor upon you, and have chosen for you Islam as your religion" (5:3).

Ronald A. Pachence

See also ADAM (AS PROPHET OF ISLAM); FIVE PILLARS (IN ISLAM); HIJRA (IN ISLAM); ISLAM; JESUS (AS PROPHET OF ISLAM); KHADIJA; MECCA; MEDINA; MONOTHEISM (IN CHRISTIANITY AND ISLAM); MUSLIM; QUR'AN; QURAYSH; REVELATION (IN ISLAM); UMMA.

MUHARRAM

According to the Islamic calendar, the first month of the year. Because the calendar used by Muslims is based upon the lunar cycle that has only 354 or 355 days a year, the Islamic new year does not fall at the same time of the 365-day cycle used by the solar calendar. In Sunni Islam, the first day of Muharram or New Year's Day (*ra's al-'am*) is a simple celebration. For Shi'ite Muslims, however, the first ten days of this month are dedicated to commemorating the martyrdom of their great saint, Husayn. This period of mourning includes the performance of the *ta'ziyah* or "passion play" during which mourners do physical penance for the suffering endured at Karbala by Husayn and his family.

Ronald A. Pachence

See also HUSAYN; ISLAM; KARBALA; SHI'A/SHI'I/SHI'ITE/SHI'ISM; SUNNA/SUNNI/SUNNISM.

MUJADDID

Arabic word meaning "reformer" or someone who "renews" Islamic faith and practice. According to one tradition of the Prophet Muhammad, a *mujaddid* would be born once every century. The Persian mystic, theologian, and philosopher al-Ghazali (1058–1111) is an example of someone who is considered to be a mujaddid.

Ronald A. Pachence

See also AL-GHAZALI; ISLAM; MUHAMMAD.

MUJERISTA THEOLOGY

Mujerista theology is an approach within Latina feminist liberation theology that places the voices and grassroots struggles of Latinas as the starting point and center of its work. This theology has been primarily articulated by Ada María Isasi-Díaz.

Mujerista theology emphasizes a multifaceted analysis of Latinas' lives and contexts, including how gender, race, ethnicity, and class shape Latina identity in the United States. Its methodology is marked by its use of ethnography and the inclusion of grassroots Latinas' voices within the discourse of academic theology. Rather than embracing the term "Latina feminist" or *feminista hispana, mujerista* theology claims that in naming itself as *mujerista* it is embracing a term that is more inclusive of Latinas, who often feel feminism is a European-American construction. Nonetheless, a feminist hermeneutic is fundamental to the *mujerista* position.

In addition to its ethnographic approach, *mujerista* theology is clearly dominated by ethical concerns. Nonetheless, especially through the work of Isasi-Díaz, a broader attention to traditional themes within systematic theology is now part of the *mujerista* theological reflection. Within its theological anthropology, *mujerista* theology emphasizes the importance of family/community, Latinas' struggles, and Latinas' historical agency. The themes of solidarity and concrete praxis saturate much of Isasi-Díaz's scholarship. Methodologically, *mujerista* theology's emphasis on daily life, *mestizaje/mulatez*, and liberating praxis are significant. Within discussions of *mestizaje/mulatez*, *mujerista* theology maintains a clear sense of the indigenous, Spanish, and African roots of Latino/a identity as marks of Latino/a hybridity, while arguing that the affirmation of one's racial/cultural identity is an ethical stance for Latino/as. This is framed by the larger question of the category of "difference" and its significance for contemporary theology. Ada M. Isasi-Díaz's own publications remain the most important (but not the only) works within *mujerista* theology.

Michelle González

See also FEMINISM; FEMINIST THEOLO-GIES; ISASI-DÍAZ, ADA MARÍA; LATINO THEOLOGY (-IES); MESTIZAJE; METHOD IN THEOLOGY; MULATAJE.

MUJTAHID

(Plural, *mujtahidun*). An Arabic term derived from the word *ijtihad* (effort). In Islam, a *mujtahid* is a legal scholar whose insight and "effort" result in a new interpretation or opinion regarding the law the community accepts as orthodox. In Sunni Islam, this term is generally reserved to the founders of the four Schools of Law, since Sunnis do not accept the possibility of any new orthodox approaches to religious law. This means that Sunni legal experts rely heavily upon precedent in their interpretations. In Shi'ite Islam, however, *mujtahidun* continue to play an important role in jurisprudence.

Ronald A. Pachence

See also IJTIHAD; SHI'A/SHI'I/SHI'ITE/ SHI'ISM; SUNNA/SUNNI/SUNNISM.

MULATAJE

A term, originally from the Spanish, used to refer to the social, historical processes through which cultures and persons of African origin are mixed with cultures and persons of European origin. *Mulataje*, therefore, correctly describes the peoples, cultures, and histories of many Spanish-, French-, and Portuguese-speaking nations in the Third World, as well as those of many minority populations in the First World. In some ways it is akin to *mestizaje*, but not coextensive with or identical to it. *Mulataje* made possible the survival, outside Africa, of great religions, artistic contributions, cultural patterns, social formations, languages, and so forth, but most importantly, *mulataje* made possible the continuation of African identities outside Africa—although all that survived was impacted by slavery and racism. *Mulataje* did not occur without the traumatic and violent imposition of slavery on millions of Africans and African descendants. The processes that are referred to by *mulataje*, therefore, were physically vicious and morally denigrating to millions of innocent humans, thereby making their attempts at survival in white racist societies (attempts included under the term *mulataje*) even more significant and, in the long run, remarkably successful. Often accompanying discussions of *mulataje*, there have been unspoken but continuing attempts at suppressing the African by proclaiming a "culture of *mulatez*" that, in real social life and history, is tantamount to subsuming the African into new national or cultural realities that emphasize the European much more than the African, and only recognize the latter in subservient, ancillary, or folkloric roles. *Mulato/a* is the individual (person or culture) that results from the processes of *mulataje*; and *mulatez* is the condition of being *mulato/a*. The English word "mulatto," sometimes used in a denigrating manner, does not convey all that the Spanish terms do.

Orlando Espín

See also CULTURE; INCULTURATION; INTERCULTURAL THOUGHT; MESTIZAJE; RACISM; SLAVERY.

MULATEZ
See MULATAJE.

MULATO/A
See MESTIZAJE.

MULLAH
From the Farsi (Persian) word *mawla*, meaning "master (of the law)." In Shiʿite Islam, the most renowned *mullahs* are also considered *mujtahids*, legal experts whose interpretations or opinions on legal matters are regarded as normative by the community. These *mullahs* serve as members of the *ulama*, the recognized body of legal authorities on religious matters.

Ronald A. Pachence

See also MUJTAHID; SHIʿA/SHIʿI/ SHIʿITE/SHIʿISM; ULAMA/ULEMA.

MURATORIAN CANON
First published in 1740 by Ludovico Antonio Muratori (hence the manuscript's name), the Muratorian Canon is the oldest surviving list (or "canon") of New Testament writings. It seems to have been written originally during the second century C.E. Because the manuscript's Latin is so faulty, some scholars suspect it might be a translation of a Greek original. This text is also known as the Muratorian Fragment because it is missing both a beginning and an end. Ludovico Muratori found the manuscript in the Ambrosian Library, in Milan, Italy.

Orlando Espín

See also CANON, BIBLICAL; NEW TESTAMENT CANON.

MURJIʾAH
Also written Murjiʾites or Murjiʾa. An Arabic word that suggests a "delay" of God's judgment upon sinners. The Murjiʾites were a sect that developed early in Islamic history as a reaction against the Kharijites who taught that grave sins like theft and adultery could not be forgiven by God or the community. For the Murjiʾites, this extreme view amounted to a denial of God's mercy, and their more tolerant theological opinion eventually became a part of the tradition in Sunni Islam.

Ronald A. Pachence

See also ALLAH (ISLAM); ISLAM; KHARIJITES; MUTAZILITES; SHIʿA/SHIʿI/SHIʿITE/SHIʿISM; SUNNA/SUNNI/SUNNISM.

MURRAY, JOHN COURTNEY (1904–67)
American Jesuit theologian. Professor of theology at Woodstock College, Murray engaged new theological trends in his own theology and in *Theological Studies*, the Jesuit journal he edited. Along with Gustave Weigel, Murray became interested in ecumenism and interfaith dialogue in the United States and featured reviews of Protestant theologians in his journal. He is best known for his reflec-

tions on the church–state relationship and the problem of religious tolerance, a problem for the American church after a return of anti-Catholic fever in the 1950s. Against both Protestant critics and Catholic conservatives, Murray argued that the Catholic tradition supported religious tolerance and the separation of church and state, aptly describing the delicate balance between the individual's religious freedom and the legitimate teaching authority of the church. Appointed expert advisor (*peritus*) to Vatican Council II, Murray played a major role in formulating one of its most significant documents, the Declaration on Religious Freedom (1964), known in Latin as *Dignitatis Humanae*.

Patricia Plovanich

MUSAF

Hebrew, meaning "additional," this is the additional service, added to the Jewish morning worship service on Sabbath, festivals, and the first day of each new month.

This service acknowledges the specialness of the Sabbath, the festivals, and the first day of the new month, and reflects the additional sacrificial offerings that were brought to the Holy Temple on these special days. Just as there was an additional offering on these days, there is now an additional service.

Since sacrificial worship has long passed into history, the Reform movement contends that there is no reason to continually invoke its memory and has eliminated the recitation of the *musaf* service.

Wayne Dosick

See also REFORM JUDAISM; ROSH HODESH; SHABBAT.

MUSHIN

(Japanese, *mu*, lit., no mind). In Zen and Buddhism in general, this is the "nothingness" mind or the empty mind beyond the ordinary discriminating mind. It is a state of nondualistic awareness where the knower and known are the same. In Zen it is also referred to as the natural mind apart from all delusion and desire—a state of egolessness—the clear mind that sees things as they actually are. Much of Buddhist practice is geared toward acquiring the *mu* mind.

G. D. DeAngelis

See also BODHI; KOAN; MINDFULNESS; SANZEN; SATORI; ZAZEN; ZEN.

MUSLIM

The proper term for people who profess Islam as their religion. "Muslim" is literally defined as, "someone who has submitted to the one true God." It also connotes one whose act of surrender to God brings peace. According to Islamic teaching, everyone is born a Muslim. One does not actually become a Muslim, however, until he or she makes the act of faith ("There is no god but God and Muhammad as the Messenger of God") and until the believer practices that faith by keeping God's law. Today there are about 1.3 billion Muslims who observe a religion that dates from the beginning of the seventh century C.E. Students of Islam should avoid using the term "Muhammadans" when referring to Muslims, or "Mohammadanism" to speak of Islam. These terms suggest that Islam derives from the words or actions of Muhammad (570–632) and for Muslims, this is offensive. They believe that Islam comes directly from God.

Ronald A. Pachence

See also ISLAM; MUHAMMAD.

MUSLIM BROTHERHOOD

In Arabic *al-Ikhwan al-Muslimun*. A political and religious organization established in 1928 by Hasan al-Banna in Egypt to combat such Western influences as materialism, secularism, and sexual license. Al-Banna and his followers feared that Islam would be seriously threatened if these excesses were not confronted through a concerted effort of renewal on the part of all Muslims. The Brotherhood attempted to accomplish its mission by enlisting the support of ordinary Muslims against national leaders in Egypt, Syria, and other Arab nations who were deemed too "secular." Though even some Muslims have accused the Brotherhood of terrorism and radicalism, particularly in Egypt during World War II and the postwar years, the organization asserts that it is a nonviolent reform movement, which involves itself in mainstream Egyptian politics and is dedicated to charitable works on behalf of the poor and disadvantaged throughout the Middle East.

Ronald A. Pachence

See also ISLAMIC RADICALISM (FUNDAMENTALISM).

MU'TAZILITES

From an Arabic word meaning, "to stand apart from," a "school" of philosophical theology in Islam whose origins are said to lie in the controversy between the Kharijites and the Murji'ites over the consequences of serious sin. The Mu'tazilites agreed with neither on the harsh position of the former who advocated death for the sinners, nor the more tolerant position of the latter. Hence their name. Though eventually rejected by the religious leadership because of its overly rationalistic approach to questions about God, the Qur'an (Islam's sacred scripture), free will, punishment for sin and morality, Mu'tazilite thought enjoyed considerable success during the Abbasid Caliphate, particularly in the eighth and ninth centuries C.E. One of the Mu'tazilite positions that led to its rejection by orthodox Sunni lawyers and scholars was the teaching that the Qur'an was created. Mu'tazilites reasoned that an eternal Qur'an would make the "Word" of God (recorded in the Qur'an) divine, resulting in a book that was "part" of God. This, they said, offends against the absolute unity of God. The problem with this position was not its logic, but its contradiction of a Qur'anic revelation that implies the Qur'an is coeternal with God (85:21-22). With the defection of some of its former proponents like al-Ash'ari (873–935), and with growing pressure from Islamic legal scholars in the tenth and eleventh centuries C.E., Mu'tazilite thought was repudiated and all but abandoned by the twelfth century C.E.

Ronald A. Pachence

See also ABBASIDS; AL-ASH'ARI / ASH'ARISM; KALAM; KHARIJITES; MURJI'AH; QUR'AN.

MYSTAGOGY

(Greek, *mystagogus, mystes*; to lead, to initiate, to study mystical doctrines). Also called Mystagogia, or postbaptismal period, Mystagogy is the fourth and final stage of the Rite of Christian Initiation of Adults. This stage begins with the celebration of the initiation sacraments of baptism, confirmation, and Eucharist at the Easter Vigil. The Easter season, especially Easter week, is designed to help the initiates (neophytes) and the community reflect on the paschal mystery they have just celebrated. Having experienced the "sacred mysteries," it is then possible to understand the teachings and symbolism of the paschal events. Mystagogy is an attempt to "break open" the awesomeness of God's love and care. It is a celebration of the "Sunday time of the year."

Originally, the Greek word for "mystery" meant a divine action in which humans participated through rites, experiencing God and having God touch them with a sense of "awe." By the fourth century, "mystery" referred to secret rituals used by exclusive groups or cults, such as the Mithras (a mystery religion quite common in the Roman Empire), for initiation or other ritual purposes.

Until the fourth century, Christians had no special words for mystagogy. Baptism marked a person's conversion and entrance into membership of the community. The system of integration and inclusion in the early communities continued to function after baptism. As the small communities began to disappear, institutional structures gradually replaced the functions of the small communities. Immediate preparation for baptism consisted of a few weeks of Lent. Baptism was often perceived as a magical ritual rather than the sign of a person of faith living a new lifestyle within the community. Since anyone could be baptized, it was necessary to see that adults were instructed about the rights of membership and the meaning of the Easter Vigil. During Easter week, the community gathered with the bishop each day for instruction concerning the sacraments. Remnants of these instructions were left in the homilies of St. Ambrose of Milan, Cyril of Jerusalem, and John Chrysostom.

Today, the community gathers to help neophytes on their journey into community life and ministry. The neophytes retain their special places among the faithful during Sunday liturgy until Pentecost, accompanied by their godparent or sponsor. Often, a mentor in ministry is also assigned to the neophytes as they enter into special training for specific parish or community ministries.

M. Jane Gorman

See also EASTER; NEOPHYTE; RITES OF CHRISTIAN INITIATION (RCIA).

MYSTERY

Word derived from the Greek *mysterion*, with its roots in the word for "to close." *Mysterion* was used in ancient Greek to designate the secret rites of certain religious cults, emphasizing that they were closed to all but the initiated. Early Christian uses of the word apply it to religious truths that had been "secrets" unknown to human beings until they were revealed by God in Christ. By analogy with the older pagan cults, *mysterion* also came to be used of Christian rites, especially the Eucharist. In Christian theology, therefore, a "mystery" is much more than "something that cannot be understood," but rather designates a truth that is revealed within a relationship of faith with God and grasped "from the inside" rather than by an external analysis.

William A. Clark, S.J.

MYSTERY RELIGIONS

The term "mystery religions" generally refers to certain religions of the ancient worlds of Greece and Rome. They were practiced alongside the official, public worship of the state or city-state, and were often more popular than civic religions. Mystery religions focused on the search for eternal life; members believed that by means of the performance of secret rituals they would gain knowledge not available to the uninitiated and thus effect a mystical union with the divine. The central figures were usually gods or goddesses who had died and were then reborn. Initiates sought spiritual rebirth and immortality for themselves by reenacting the death and rebirth of the divinity. Both the features of the initiation and the experiences of the initiates were generally kept secret. The most significant mystery cults were these: the mysteries of Eleusis, the Dionysiac (or Bacchic) mysteries, and those of Isis, Magna Mater, and Mithras.

The mysteries at Eleusis were dedicated to the grain goddess, Demeter, and her daughter, Persephone. According to myth, Persephone was captured by Hades, king of the underworld, who carried her down to his dark kingdom to be his bride. Her cries were heard by Demeter, who searched the earth for her daughter, finally arriving at Eleusis, a small city fourteen miles west of Athens. The people of Eleusis built a temple for Demeter, and there she stayed in mourning for a year during which the earth remained completely barren. Finally, Persephone was returned to Eleusis itself, and the earth bloomed again. Because Persephone had taken food in Hades's house, however, she had to return to him for the four winter months. Each autumn, the Athenians held ceremonies at Eleusis, thanking Demeter both for the grain of life and for the Mysteries which promised hope for a happy afterlife.

The cult of Dionysus (Bacchus in Rome) had no fixed sanctuary but was practiced throughout the Greek and later the Roman world. Dionysus was the ancient god of fertility, wine, ecstasy, and mysticism. Myth told that Dionysus had died at the hands of the Titans, who tore him apart, roasted the pieces, and began to eat them. Zeus saved some of the pieces and had Apollo bury them at Delphi where, it was believed, Dionysus arose from the dead each year and reigned during the winter months. The heart of the Dionysian mystery was union of the devotee with the god. As the priest of Dionysus played on his flute, devotees entered an ecstatic frenzy during which they dismembered an animal, ate its raw flesh, and drank its blood. Participants believed they were in fact partaking of the god's body and blood.

The Egyptian goddess Isis was wife and sister of the god Osiris, who was murdered by his brother, Seth. Isis searched for his body without ceasing, found it, impregnated herself with Osiris's seed, and bore their son, Horus. By the fourth century B.C.E. her cult had spread to the countries around the Mediterranean Sea; by about 300 B.C.E. it became also a mystery religion. Initiates fasted for ten days before the night of their initiation; other disciplines were also required. The Roman writer Apuleius tells something of the power of the experience of initiation, and the visions of "gods celestial and gods infernal" that were experienced. Despite periodic purges of the cult, worship of Isis continued well into the sixth century C.E.

The goddess Cybele was the form of the great mother goddess adopted by the Romans in 204 B.C.E. and worshiped in Rome as Magna Mater ("Great Mother") until about the fifth century C.E. The aristocrats of Rome literally brought her, in the form of a sacred black stone, from Anatolia (Asiatic Turkey) in order to quiet the fears of the people in the face of attacks by Hannibal, who was defeated by the Romans in 201. The myth of Cybele tells of a young Phrygian boy named Attis who loved the goddess with a great, chaste passion. She asked of him exclusive devotion forever; he agreed, but fell in love with a nymph. The jealous Cybele drove Attis mad and he castrated himself, mangling his body with a sharp stone and dying. The mother goddess mourned him so much that he returned to life and was reunited with her. The annual festival of Cybele became a national celebration held at public expense, with processions, banquets, and the sacrifice of bulls whose blood dripped down to bathe the initiate standing in a pit below. The intention was the rebirth of the initiate in the blood of the animal that represented the life of Attis. From the fourth century C.E. the celebration of Attis's triumph over death became an increasingly important part of the Magna Mater cult, with spring ceremonies commemorating his death, burial, and rebirth.

Helen deLaurentis

See also GODDESS RELIGION; GRECO-ROMAN RELIGION; MITHRA; MITHRAISM.

MYSTICAL BODY OF CHRIST

The Body of Christ carries a wide range of Christian theological meanings, including the historical human body of Jesus; the Body and Blood of Christ in the sacrament of the Eucharist; and, the risen body of Christ, transfigured by the resurrection, filled with the Holy Spirit, united in a universal way to all humanity, and representative of redeemed humanity as well as a new creation. The mystical body of Christ emerges in the context of ecclesiology, or the subdiscipline of Christian theology that addresses the nature, characteristics, and mission of the church in the world.

The New Testament treats a plurality of models or images of the church, such as people of God (Rom 9:25; 1 Pet 2:9-10), temple and community of the Holy Spirit (1 Cor 3:16; 6:19; Acts 1–2; 4:32-37), family or household of God (Eph 2:19-22), servant of God (Mark 10:45; Matt 16:24-26; 20:25-28; 25:31-46), and spouse of Christ (Eph 5:25-32). Multiple models of the church, including those models drawn from agriculture and nature, assist in critical and constructive theological reflection on the nature and mission of the church in the world. Many models of the church also attest to the historical and ongoing contextualization of the church, or the church's living witness to the Gospel in particular times and places and in the quest for social justice (which especially but not exclusively applies to Spirit and servant ecclesiologies).

In the context of ecclesiology, the Mystical Body of Christ signifies a model of the church that is primarily elaborated in the Pauline epistles to the Corinthians (1 Cor 12:12-27), Romans (Rom 12:4-5), and Ephesians (Eph 1:22-23). Christians are incorporated into and collectively create the Body of Christ through baptism in the Holy Spirit (1 Cor 12:13). Just as the different members of the human body are united into one body and cannot function properly apart from that unity, so also the church is characterized by an interdependent unity among its members. "[A]ll are members of one another" (Rom 12:5), that is, all members of the church are interrelated in their accountability to and care for one another, especially for the marginated and the suffering (1 Cor 12:25-26). The Eucharist can exemplify the unity, interdependence, and mutual care among Christians and for the suffering.

Models of the church as people of God and Body of Christ figure most prominently in Catholic theology, although since the 1985 Synod of Bishops the notion of communion has gained increasing attention in Euro-American Catholic ecclesiology and has attracted increasing criticism in liberationist theologies. Vatican II (1962–5) in the document *Lumen Gentium* articulated and further developed the model of the church as the people of God to decentralize the prevalent institutional model of the church that located the church in the hierarchical magisterium, an ecclesiology promoted at the Council of Trent (1545–63) and reaffirmed against the rise of modern rationalism and historical consciousness at Vatican I (1869–70). As liberation theologian Jose Comblin has observed, Vatican II identified the church with the whole people of God, comprised of the magisterium and the laity, in order to emphasize the fundamental equality of all baptized Christians and to resist the establishment of two orders or two classes of members in the church, ordained and nonordained. In keeping with Vatican II, Latin American liberation theologies also counteracted a predominantly institutional model of church by endorsing a more grassroots, populist model of the church, oriented to equality not only in the church but also in society. Brazilian liberation theologian and former Franciscan priest Leonardo Boff located base ecclesial (or base Christian) communities—or small lay-led groups oriented to prayer, biblical study, community fellowship, and a praxis of personal, social, and religious transformation—in the theological context of the people of God.

Contemporary feminist theologians critically retrieve the model of the church as the Body of Christ to articulate and advocate an egalitarian religious and social order, what some feminist theologians commonly call a "discipleship of equals." Unity, equality, and mutual accountability in the Mystical Body of Christ have significant implications for opposing ideologies of domination, especially patriarchy. In feminist theory and theology, patriarchy is an analytical concept that helps examine and problematize the social construction of some men's empowered status and most women's subordinate, marginal, disempowered status. It does not suggest a sex/gender

system of universal male dominance of all men over all women, but rather refers to hierarchically graded power relations along multiple interlinked axes of race, gender, class, sexuality, and culture that lead to and legitimate relative privilege and marginalization in religious, social, economic, and political life. Feminist theologians often take Galatians 3:28, an early Christian baptismal formula, as a theological starting point for an egalitarian rather than patriarchal church and society: "There is no longer Jew or Greek, there is no longer slave or free, there is no longer male or female; for all of you are one in Christ Jesus." Spiritual unity and equality in Christ cannot substitute for or obscure other inequalities in the church and society. Rather, spiritual equality in Christ, when combined with the equal creation of all humanity in the image and likeness of God (Gen 1:26-27), can form a critical prophetic theological basis to resist all violations of human dignity, equality, and rights. Ecclesiology, or the self-understanding of the church, is thus inextricably interconnected with social ethics and with public theology, or the intersection of the church and public/political life.

Nonetheless, the model of the church as the Mystical Body of Christ and its associated baptismal formulas may further legitimate rather than contest patriarchy. In the letter to the Ephesians, Christ is regarded as the "head" of the "body" of the church, subject to and saved by his rule (Eph 1:22-23). When placed in the context of first-century Greco-Roman households, this New Testament ecclesiology can reinscribe the subordination of most women, children, slaves, and other members of the household to the rule, headship, and superiority of some privileged men. As analyzed by feminist New

Testament scholar and theologian Elisabeth Schüssler Fiorenza, Greco-Roman democracy and family life created a complex system of dominant and subordinate relations that entitled only certain elite, propertied, free-born, educated men to household rule and to full citizenship. An idealized elite, white, male paradigm of personhood still predominates in contemporary Euro-American democratic and family life that prompted Fiorenza to redefine patriarchy as "kyriarchy," or "the rule of the master or lord." As demonstrated by such feminist analyses, ecclesiologies based on the Body of Christ can simultaneously underscore and undercut equality, if they are overly spiritualized, uncritically appropriated, and/or disconnected from a praxis of social justice.

Rosemary P. Carbine

MYSTICISM/MYSTICS (IN CHRISTIANITY)

Among Christians, in general, mysticism refers to the state of steady, pervasive, and intense oneness with God. That oneness can manifest itself in a variety of ways in a person's everyday actions and in a person's prayer, although frequently such people would never think of themselves as mystics, since mysticism probably sounds too esoteric for ordinary believers. The relationship with God implied by mysticism takes the form of the sort of knowing born only from love.

Although God is both the source and the goal of the heart's desiring, the heart of a mystic increasingly embraces the neighbor. Indeed, the mystic's way of knowing and loving God ordinarily starts with love of his or her sisters and brothers. "The mystical life is thus the ordinary condition of the Christian, the life which is hid with Christ in God. Mystical theol-

ogy is basic Christian theology, mysticism is a fundamental constituent of all Christian experience" (Kenneth Leech, *Experiencing God*, 334). If mysticism is the "ordinary condition" of the Christian, then everyday asceticism is the uncelebrated means of spiritual growth and purification by which a person arrives at wisdom, humility, compassion, and the facility of recognizing God in all things.

William Reiser, S.J.

See also ASCETICISM/ASCETIC; CONTEMPLATION; ECSTASY; HOLINESS; NIRVANA; PERFECTION; PRAYER; SANNYASA; SUFI; VIA UNITIVA.

MYSTICISM/MYSTICS (IN JUDAISM)

See KABBALAH.

MYSTICISM/MYSTICS (IN WORLD RELIGIONS)

In all world religions, there are traditions that direct humans to experience the immediacy of the sacred. In the Western monotheistic faiths, the mystics seeking to feel God's presence in their own embodied perception have often been suspected of heresy or insanity, especially by the priestly and scholastic elites. For them, God's transcendence and their own role as intermediaries are central to the orthodox, institutional representatives of these religions. Sufism in Islam and Kabala in Judaism continue to enjoy the most widespread support among Western adherents. In the Asian religions where sages and ascetics were founders of major faiths (Buddhism, Jainism, Hinduism, Taoism) and are respected as embodiments of the highest human revelation, individuals following the prescribed religious practices who entered into states of ecstatic union with the divine are regarded with reverence, awe, and respect. These faiths, as well as the shamanic traditions surviving among tribal peoples, see the sacred as immanent in the world and therefore see mysticism as a normative and desirable aspect of their traditions.

Todd T. Lewis

See also TRANCE.

MYTH

In daily use, "myth" is often employed as synonymous with legend, falsehood, untruth, or error. In early Greek *mythos* simply meant "story"; but when in later Greek the same term came to be used only for "stories about the gods," many (even in ancient times) came to understand myth as equal to imaginary tales with no relation to truth or fact. Some Greek philosophers proposed *logos* (as reason, the true and the reasonable) against *mythos* (as invented untruth and the false), and in this sense the New Testament used and understood *mythos*. Throughout most of Western history this connection between myth and falsehood remained unchallenged. During the twentieth century some scholarly disciplines (ethnology and anthropology, psychology and psychoanalysis, historiography and hermeneutics, biblical studies, and the like) began to challenge that connection. Rudolf Bultmann, within Christian theology and biblical studies, proposed the notion or process of "demythologizing" as a way of interpreting myths (and not as a way of eliminating them) in the biblical texts and in Christian doctrines. Myths exist (and seem always to have existed) in all religions known to humankind and in all human societies.

Today most scholars understand myth as a way of thinking that represents and conveys the most profound meaning(s) of human reality and existence. This meaning and this reality are represented and conveyed through narratives (stories) whose intention is, precisely, to direct attention and reflection toward the most fundamental meaning(s) of human reality.

Myths are not just or mainly stories about God or gods or other sacred beings, although many myths certainly present themselves as stories of divine actors. However, the stories themselves, their plots and their characters, are not the true, final intent or interest of the myths but, rather, the representation (often understood as "re-presentation") and conveyance of the deepest meaning(s) of human reality and existence.

In theistic religions myths will refer to divine actors because God or the gods are intimately implicated in and with the deepest meaning(s) of human existence, and because sometimes (always, in monotheistic religions) God or the gods are believed to be that most profound of meanings and the ultimate reality grounding human existence.

There can be stories of God or gods or other sacred beings that are not myths, strictly speaking. There are also social (even secular) myths that attempt to represent and convey the fundamental meaning(s) of a social reality or of a society through (for example) stories of founders, of patriotic actions, of heroes and villains, and such. But always the true meaning or message of a myth is to be sought in its representation and conveyance of the deepest meaning(s) of human reality and existence, not in the mythical story itself.

Orlando Espín

See also BULTMANN, RUDOLF; DEMYTHOLOGIZATION; WORLDVIEW.

N

NABI (IN ISLAM)

Prophet. In Islamic thought, a prophet is a person sent by God to bring good news and/or a warning to a particular religious community. In this, they are agents of God's mercy as well as God's judgment. Muslims believe that over the centuries God has sent prophets to every people—by some accounts one hundred and twenty-four thousand of them. The Qur'an (Islam's sacred scripture) mentions only a few prophets by name including Adam, Noah, Abraham, Jonah, Moses, Jesus, and of course, Muhammad whom Muslims regard as the "Seal of the Prophets" (the final prophet). The prophets in general are distinguished from a special category of prophets, *rasul Allah* (messenger of God), in that the former do not bring a new revelation while the latter do. John the Baptist, for example, is called *nabi* but not *rasul*, but Jesus (called *'Isa* in the Qur'an) and Muhammad are both *nabi* and *rasul*. So are Adam, Noah, Abraham, and Moses, among others.

Ronald A. Pachence

See also ADAM (AS PROPHET OF ISLAM); JESUS (AS PROPHET OF ISLAM); MUHAMMAD; RASUL.

NAFS

In Arabic, a word meaning "soul." In Islamic theology, *nafs* refers to what makes a particular human self a distinct individual. It is important to distinguish between this element of individualization, and the *ruh*, which Muslims say is the human "spirit." While the nafs can incline people toward ignorance and passion as well as wisdom and responsible moral decisions, the ruh of men and women is their God-given link to the Supreme Being, Allah. Some would describe nafs as the "lower soul" or the "individual soul," and ruh as that aspect of humanity giving human beings their intellects and raising them above all other creatures, including the angels.

Ronald A. Pachence

See also ALLAH (ISLAM); ISLAM; MUSLIM; RUH.

NAGARJUNA
(ACTIVE CA. 200–300 C.E.)

One of the pioneering and pivotal figures in the scholastic development of Buddhist thought, Nagarjuna established the terms of analysis and methods of debate for religious discourse in the Mahayana school.

The popular biography of Nagarjuna recounts his birth in a Brahmin family of

South India and his classical education in Sanskrit, the systematic thought of the main Hindu orthodox schools, and in logical argumentation. After his conversion and ordination as a Buddhist monk, legend explains his name arising due to his garnering teachings from the *nagas*, snake spirits, after a descent to their underground domain. Although over forty different works are attributed to him, including hymns, poetic verses, commentaries on several Prajnaparamita works, Nagarjuna's main philosophical compositions are the *Mula-Madhyamaka-karikas* and the *Vigraha-Vyavartani*. His treatises are centered on establishing two kinds of discourse about reality: the conventional and ultimate. Their chief goal is to demonstrate how all statements depend upon others, lacking in any potential for fixing certain spiritual truth. Through exposing concepts proposed about reality to such logical scrutiny—including those adopted by the early Buddhist schools (especially the Abhidharmists)—Nagarjuna advanced the Buddhist practice of discriminating the real from the unreal and disentangling oneself from subtle attachments based upon dualistic constructions.

Todd T. Lewis

See also MADHYAMAKA/MADHYAMIKA SCHOOL; MAHAYANA BUDDHISM; NIRVANA; SHUNYATA/SUNYA/SHUNYA; VIMALAKIRTI.

NAG HAMMADI

(The Nag Hammadi Codices). Nag Hammadi refers to a collection of Gnostic and other writings found near the modern town of Nag Hammadi in Egypt in 1945–6. The codices were found in an ancient tomb near the modern town located approximately forty miles northwest of Luxor. The codices date from the fourth century C.E. and consist of approximately fifty-seven compositions, some of which were already known. The value of the Nag Hammadi Codices for scholarship of early Christianity and to a lesser extent Judaism is inestimable since they are documents that speak firsthand of Gnostic belief and practice, a movement that rivaled Christianity and Judaism in the second and third centuries of the Common Era.

Russell Fuller

NAHUA TRADITIONAL RELIGION

The Nahuas of Mesoamerica are a group of peoples that migrated to the central valley of Mexico after the fall of the Toltec empire (that occurred with the destruction of Tula in 1170 C.E.). During the thirteenth and fourteenth centuries, the Chichimecs (a broad group of "tribes" or clans), the Alcohuas, the Tepanecs, and the Mexicas, all came from the northern region of present-day Mexico and occupied abandoned towns and lands in the central valley, or conquered the weakened resident populations. The name "Nahua" is commonly applied to these groups, especially because they shared Náhuatl as their language. They had much in common, culturally. And once settled in the Valley of Mexico, these groups proceeded to assimilate Toltec culture, and came to believe themselves to be the legitimate heirs of that highly respected civilization. The name "Aztec" is really applicable only to the Mexica, the last of the Nahua groups to migrate from the north (indeed, the name "Aztec" is derived from Aztlan, the name of their legendary land of origin to the north).

Few literate peoples have been so profoundly religious as the Nahuas. Religion was not just an integral part of their culture. Indeed, there was nothing as important (or as "real") as what could be called the "supernatural" or religious dimension of existence. They were passionately and sincerely pious, perhaps to an extreme. Nahuas held that since all of existence was held together, and then only barely, by the gods, it was their people's obligation and responsibility to make sure that reality was kept intact by their constant service of the divinities. Indeed, this sense of the precariousness of life seems to have led to a profound sense of existential anguish in Nahua culture, although balanced by much beauty, cultural pride, and philosophical depth.

As the Aztec city of Tenochtítlan (present-day Mexico City) became the capital and center of a large, sophisticated, and mighty empire, the Mexicas produced the most impressive literature of any people in the Americas before the Spanish conquest. Through their books and other written sources (inscriptions on walls, monuments, statues, and the like) we get considerable information on Nahua religion. We also have a significant body of literature describing the Nahuas written by natives themselves or by Spaniards after the conquest.

Nahua religion was a (somewhat modified) mirror of the Toltec one, at least until the Mexica reform led by Tlacaelel (who was like a prime minister to several Aztec kings between 1426–80). This reform changed the self-image the Mexicas had of themselves, made them empire-builders, and convinced them of the incessant need to "feed" the Sun in order to guarantee the continuation of reality and of human existence. Tlacaelel taught his people that they were *the* people of the Sun, and that by divine election their most crucial mission was to keep the Sun

alive—if they failed to do so, reality would collapse into utter chaos. The Mexica mission to "feed" the Sun, and so keep reality going, was the fundamental religious motive and legitimation of the Aztecs' empire-building wars and administrative genius. The capture of victims for human sacrifice (more specifically, for offering human hearts), needed to "feed" the Sun, became one of the most important and frequent reasons for warfare. Indeed, the so-called "flowery wars" were organized with the sole purpose of capturing sacrificial victims.

Nahua religion seems to have existed in an elite version, sanctioned and promoted by the state, and in a popular version that was the most likely religion of the majority of the people. The elite version, obviously, is the one we know best because it belonged to the educated and the powerful. Books, temples, and other monuments usually reflected this version. In no way implying that the two forms of Nahua religion were somehow inimical to each other, it is evident that the elites had developed a highly sophisticated theological and philosophical reflection on the meaning of divinity, of life, and so on, that was not easily accessible to the majority. The elite religion had a theological understanding of God and of the gods that did not reflect the working people's belief in the actual existence and daily activities of hundreds of gods.

Nahua traditional religion believed in one supreme god, Ometéotl—"god of the twos." This supreme deity was a dual god in whom the opposites were integrated (visible/invisible, matter/spirit, masculine/feminine, tangible/intangible, for example). The first and most original god, the source of all that exists, Ometéotl was the only uncreated god, and was known by many titles. For example, Tloque in

Nahuáque was the most excellent of those names ("the owner of the near and close") and it signified closeness, intimacy, interiority, as well as omnipresence. Ollintéotl ("the divine movement") suggested that the supreme god was the source or origin of all existence. Ipalnemohuáni ("the one because of whom we live") indicated that Ometéotl was also the source of all meaning—and meaning was the most fundamental quest of all Nahua religious thought. Moyocoyáni ("the one who created himself") pointed to Ometéotl as the uncreated, original god. And *In nelli in téotl* ("the true god") implied that this supreme god was truly and really divine, like no other. Ometéotl is the source of human thought and freedom. One of the supreme god's contributions to humanity is precisely the ability to doubt, because it leads to reflection and wisdom. Tezcatlipoca ("smoking mirror") might have been at one point, perhaps before the Toltec past, the most visible expression of Ometéotl, but by the time of the Nahuas Tezcatlipoca was fundamentally associated with royal power and with ruling dynasties—although many myths taught that there were four Tezcatlipocas.

In elite Nahua culture and religion, all the gods were somehow believed to be "manifestations" of Ometéotl, or "personifications" of Ometéotl's various attributes. In popular Nahua culture, however, the gods (with few exceptions) were considered to be distinct beings in themselves (although it was very frequent that the same god be known by several different names).

In the extraordinarily elaborate (and very confusing) mythology of the Nahuas, Ometecúhtli ("the lord, the one of dual divinity") is the masculine representation of the supreme divinity; in this guise it stands for the divine, creative force, the divine semen that enters Omecíhuatl; and its symbols are the stone and lightning. Omecíhuatl ("the lady, the one of dual divinity") is the feminine manifestation of Ometéotl, and consort of Ometecúhtli (with whom she forms the creating pair). Omecíhuatl represents the divine womb that makes development and growth possible. Her symbols are earth and serpents, and a skirt made of stars. Coatlícue ("the one with the skirt of serpents") is similar to the earth goddess and is really only the first title of Omecíhuatl. The mother of the gods, she is both creator and destroyer, a synthesis of life and death. Tonántzin ("our true mother") was one of the titles of Coatlícue.

The Mexica reforms promoted by Tlacáelel completed the exclusive identification of their particular tribal god, Huitzilopóchtli ("blue hummingbird of the left"), with the Sun. Coatlícue is said to have been his mother. His sister, Coyolxáuhqui ("the one with bells painted on her face"), killed their mother because Coatlícue got pregnant through an illicit union. Right before dying, Coatlícue gave birth to Huitzilopóchtli, who in turn killed the heavenly warriors (the stars) and decapitated Coyolxáuqui. There is a daily reenactment of the battle between Coyolxáuhqui (the Moon) and Huitzilopóchtli (the Sun), the latter always defeating his sister in order to make the days and light survive. Huitzilopóchtli, the Sun, must be "fed" by his people through human sacrifices.

Inherited from the Toltec past are two other important divinities: Tlaloc ("the juice of the earth"), who was god of rain and main guardian of all agriculture and of peasants; and Quetzalcóatl ("feathered serpent"). Quetzalcóatl was the god of self-sacrifice and abundance. Responsible for the existence of present reality ("the fifth Sun"), Quetzalcóatl created it by going to the underworld and stealing the bones of ancestors from earlier realities (that is, from the preceding "four Suns"), and then making himself bleed on them. Quetzalcóatl discovered corn and gave it to humans. He keeps the sky from collapsing onto earth, and unites the heavenly with the earthly, matter with spirit. It seems that there was, at least partially, a historical person behind some of the myths about Quetzalcóatl. Indeed, *Ce Acatl Topiltzin Quetzalcóatl* ("1 Reed, our prince, the reed of justice and feathered serpent") was an individual who had been divinized and associated with the god Quetzalcóatl. He was king (*tlatóani*) of the great Toltec city of Tula, who ruled from either 925 or 977 c.e. Under him, Tula entered the period of its greatest splendor, power, and wealth. Quetzalcóatl's fame and teaching became very widespread throughout most of Mesoamerica. He was against ritual human sacrifices, but encouraged self-sacrifice, self-discipline, and severe punishment against those who would break the moral code. The priests of Yayáuhqui (a god later associated with evil and bad luck) managed to trick him into breaking his own moral code, forcing him to flee in shame. Quetzalcóatl abandoned Tula in 999 c.e. Some Toltecs followed him and spread his fame throughout much of Mesoamerica. A later legend says that he reached the Atlantic coast and built a boat in order to reach Tlíllan Tlapállan ("the place of wisdom"). His flight from Tula led to the creation and spread of many legends about him, and to his divinization and association with the god Quetzalcóatl. The king of Tula became a symbol of wisdom, of self-sacrifice, and of virtuous living. After his association with the god, Quetzalcóatl became one of the most im-

portant and beloved divinities among the Nahuas (and Mayas). A legend, abused by Spanish conquerors in the sixteenth century, promised Quetzalcóatl's return from the sea.

Teotihuácan ("where the gods are made") was the most sacred city in Mesoamerican history. The legendary place where two ancient deities sacrificed themselves, thereby becoming the Sun and the Moon, Teotihuácan was first settled around 400 b.c.e. Several groups arrived later (from the Gulf of Mexico coast) bringing with them the traditions and rituals that in time would become the cults of Tlaloc and Quetzalcóatl. The city had been very important as a cultural and religious center even before the Toltecs, and much before the Nahuas. Teotihuácan was built around broad processional boulevards and the two monumental pyramids dedicated to the Sun and to the Moon (in honor of the deities that sacrificed themselves there). Not surprisingly, Tenochtítlan (the Mexica capital) was rebuilt to parallel the grandeur and sanctity of Teotihuácan. Tenochtítlan's majestic processional boulevards that crossed at the large ceremonial center where the main temples were, impressed all visitors (including the conquering Spaniards, who praised the Mexica capital for its beauty, magnificence, and size). All Nahua cities seem to have been built thinking of their important ceremonial role.

Worship services were presided over by priests who were usually celibate and of unkempt appearance. These men had attended school (like most other men and women in Nahua cities and towns), and were specifically trained for a life dedicated to ritual and prayer. Besides the solemn and very public rites that involved human sacrifice, all Nahuas participated in many other religious ceremonies dictated by the exact calculations of their calendar, and by the daily estimates of their priests. There were daily rituals and weekly ones; some were held during the daytime hours and others at night; every month witnessed city-wide ceremonies; and every number of months and of years there were further rites. Every fifty-two years Nahuas feared that the Sun could collapse, so the most solemn and anguished religious services were held on that occasion, to make sure that the Sun would continue shining and the world would not end. Nahua (and specifically Mexica) liturgies were extraordinarily elaborate, no matter what the occasion might have been.

Nahua traditional religion believed in an afterlife—a sort of earthly paradise in the Sun. Warriors fallen in battle and women who died at childbirth received the highest reward from the gods and were immediately taken to paradise. Daily life was not considered as desirable as an honorable death.

After Spain discovered (in 1519) and conquered Tenochtítlan (in 1521) and the Mexica empire, the Nahuas and their religion did not go away or disappear. Their elaborate religious tradition and sophisticated theology were confronted by European Christianity, and, through the long process called *mestizaje*, the descendants of the Nahuas became Christian *mestizos*. It is highly inaccurate to think that the resulting Christianity is simply a syncretic mixture of the native and Spanish religions. A "re-reading" or reinterpretation of Christianity, still within the latter's parameters of orthodoxy, is the more accurate understanding of what occurred. The story of and devotion to the Virgin of Guadalupe are clear examples of this reinterpretation. The Nahua traditional religion acted as prism through which the native populations heard and understood the Christian religion. Millions of present-day U.S. Latinos and Mexicans are mestizo heirs to the Nahua religious traditions. Even today, in the central valley of Mexico, some Nahua villages and towns still survive—as does their traditional religion, even if often surreptitiously.

Orlando Espín

See also CULTURE; EPISTEMOLOGY; GOD; GUADALUPE, VIRGIN OF; HERMENEUTICS; INCULTURATION; LATIN AMERICAN CATHOLICISM; LATINO/A; LATINO CATHOLICISM; MESTIZAJE; MISSIOLOGY; MISSIONS; POPULAR CATHOLICISM; POPULAR RELIGIONS; RELIGION; RELIGION, THEORIES OF.

NAKA IMA

(Japanese, lit., middle now). A Shinto religio-aesthetic ideal, popularized during the Heian Period (794–1185), indicating a state of mind and being in the present moment between the past and the future. The emphasis is on the appreciation of the beauty of life through the direct immediate experience as opposed to understanding through ideas. This notion helped to promote aesthetic experience as crucial to religious life.

G. D. DeAngelis

See also MONO-NO-AWARE; SHINTO; YUGEN.

NAME/NAMING (IN ISRAEL)

Names in ancient Israel as well as elsewhere in the ancient Near East were meaningful and reflected something of the bearers' essence and identity. Names also naturally reflected the language of the family group and sometimes something of their situation. Frequently, in the narratives in the book of Genesis, a name given to a child or a place will reflect the recent experience of the parents or an event connected to the place. That the name of an individual reflects something of their identity or essence is shown in the story of Jacob in Genesis 32 when he wrestles with a divine being. His name is changed to reflect the fact of this experience that has changed his essence; he is no longer just Jacob, he is Israel, understood to mean "he who strives with God." If the patriarchal narratives reflect actual practice at some time in Israel's history, then the naming of children seems to have been in the hands of the mother or the women of the household (see Genesis 30 and Ruth 4). Hebrew names, as many in the ancient Near East, were meaningful, and frequently abbreviated sentences that might include a name of God as one of their elements. Examples of this type of name include, "Shemiah"—"Yahweh has heard," and "Elijah"—"Yahweh is my god." The element yah/jah on names of this type are abbreviated forms of the complete divine name Yahweh.

Russell Fuller

NAMES OF GOD (IN JUDAISM)
The names of God found in the Hebrew Scriptures are used frequently in Jewish liturgical and ritual contexts. These include *Elohim*, normally rendered as "God," and the four-letter divine name (tetragrammaton), YHWH, normally translated as "the Lord." Since Jewish law prohibits pronunciation of the tetragrammaton, Jews replace it with the term *Adonai*, meaning "my Lord." The common non-Jewish transcription of the tetragrammaton, Jehovah, has no foundation in biblical or postbiblical Jewish sources. It derives from a reading of the consonants YHWH with the vowels of the word *Adonai*.

Outside liturgical and ritual contexts, traditional Jews most commonly refer to God as HaShem ("the Name"). The Hebrew Bible and later Jewish literatures, however, include many other names for God that may be used in nonsacred contexts, including "the omnipresent," "the holy one, blessed be he," "the merciful one," and "master of the universe." Because of the taboo against destroying any object on which the name of God is written, traditional Jews avoid spelling out God's name, writing instead "G–d" or "L–rd." Similarly, the prohibition against taking God's name in vain leads Orthodox Jews who, outside a liturgical context, are reading sacred literature out loud to use slight variations of the correct pronunciation of the divine names, for example, *Elokim* instead of *Elohim*.

Alan J. Avery-Peck

NANABOZHO
He is the major character in the creation cycle of the Ojibwe. His adventures and the lessons learned in their context are the traditional text in which the Ojibwe learn how best to live their lives. His identity falls within the category of both the Culture Hero and the Trickster, for he is a sacred person whose destiny and duty are to make civilization possible. Yet he is also capable of trickery. In form he is variously described, but one of the most common is that of the large northern hare. In that guise, he has a particular advantage that makes him an efficient hunter in the winter. His large feet serve as snowshoes, and the Ojibwe credit their invention to him.

As their example, Nanabozho demonstrates the abilities most needed for

Ojibwe survival. He is a superb hunter, not by nature, but by training. From the wolves he gained a wolf–brother who taught him the skills and joined him to make an efficient hunting pair. In the myth, the Ojibwe see the advantage of this cooperation and are also counseled to exercise restraint. It was too great a success that caused the animal guardians to plot to kill the wolf–brother. Thus the Ojibwe learned that overhunting led to a break of the natural covenant between the hunter and the animals. Diminishment of Ojibwe traditional culture has affected the high esteem that once surrounded Nanabozho, and his presence is a shadow of its former self. This is considered a great loss.

Kathleen Dugan

See also CULTURE HERO; TRICKSTER.

NANAK (1469–1539)

Nanak, more properly referred to as "Guru" (spiritual teacher) Nanak, was the founder of Sikhism. The religion derives its name from the word *sikh* or "disciple" in the Punjabi language. Guru Nanak was born in the area of northwestern India called the Punjab, part of modern-day Pakistan, where Hindus and Muslims were often in conflict with one another. Sikhs consider Guru Nanak the first in a line of ten gurus.

A Hindu by birth, Guru Nanak was a married man with two children and an accountant. According to tradition, he was never prone to earthly pleasures or treasures. When he was thirty, something happened to him that changed his life. After completing a customary Hindu purification ritual in the river, he disappeared into the forest for three days where he experienced actually being drawn into the presence of God. This experience convinced him that God had called him to announce that neither the Hindu nor the Muslim understanding of the divine adequately expresses the mystery of God. Far less could either or any religion claim that its teachings about God are superior to those of other faith traditions. God is one and all who worship God worship the same and only God.

This revelation prompted Guru Nanak to embark on a missionary journey, along with his Muslim friend Mardana, to carry Sikhism to every direction of the compass, including visits south to the rest of India as well as to Persia, Sri Lanka, and the Arabian peninsula. Everywhere they went, Guru Nanak and Mardana spread a message that critiqued some practices of both Hinduism and Islam and promoted elements of both, though Sikhs today insist that Guru Nanak proclaimed a new religion—not a synthesis of Hinduism and Islam.

At the age of fifty, Guru Nanak returned to the Punjab where, after naming a successor, he died twenty years later.

Ronald A. Pachence

See also SIKHISM.

NARRATIVE CRITICISM

A story is an account of the interactions of characters, events, and settings that form a plot. Any work of literature that tells a story is a narrative. Every narrative communicates a story in a particular way. How a story is told is called discourse. Narrative criticism studies a story as discourse. It is a text-centered approach that considers what is being communicated by an author to a reader by the way the story is told. Narrative criticism has been especially prominent in studies of the Gospels; it is increasingly applied to the stories in both testaments.

Narrative critics presuppose that communication consists of a sender (author) who conveys a message (text) to a receiver (reader). They recognize that the message conveyed by the discourse of a text shapes the story. They distinguish the real author from a hypothetical implied author, the text from the narrative, real readers from a hypothetical implied reader. They also recognize that a narrative is told by a narrator, to a narratee. The relationships among these distinctions are diagramed as follows:

Sender ➔   Message ➔ Receiver

Real author ➔   Text ➔   Real reader

Implied author ➔ Narrative ➔ Implied reader

Narrator ➔   Story ➔   Narratee

The terms "implied author" and "implied reader" are constructs that critics draw from within the narrative to clarify discourse. These constructs presuppose: (1) The sentiments, the understanding of the world, and the values found in a narrative introduce an evaluative point of view that shapes the discourse. Since no text discloses all the opinions and insights of a real author, the point of view disclosed by a narrative is that of the implied author, implied within the narrative, often in the voice of the narrator. (2) Although the actual responses of the real readers of a text are unpredictable, the discourse of every narrative fosters specific responses of one who would be an ideal reader. The ideal reader is implied in the narrative as the narratee to whom the story is being told. In biblical stories the narrator is usually the inconspicuous voice of the implied author who tells the story, offers explanations, and provides occasional comments. The narratee is usually the implied reader who can be constructed from what the text assumes an ideal reader does or does not know by what is or is not explained.

Narrative critics seek to read the story as the implied reader. These critics try to avoid asking questions or considering issues that would not concern the implied reader. They do consider how the narrator shapes and evaluates the characters, events, and settings in the plot; they examine how such rhetorical devices as symbolism, irony, and narrative patterns (for example, repetition, comparison, contrast, chiasm, and so on) underscore the evaluative point of view of the implied author in order to foster specific responses in the ideal, implied reader.

Since it focuses on the text rather than issues about the text, many find narrative criticism a refreshing change in biblical studies. It provides insights into biblical passages that are as accessible to the average adult reader as they are to scholars. It is also capable of drawing out the religious dimensions of biblical stories and of offering a new way to understand how the bible engages its readers. Because narrative criticism enters the text at any point in time and is not interested in reconstructing the development of traditions or evaluating the historicity of the events reported in the text, it is considered a synchronic (*syn* = one; *chronos* = time) form of analysis.

Narrative criticism is one of the new methods of literary criticism in biblical scholarship. It is an important addition that enhances an appreciation of the biblical texts without displacing the significance of considerations that are proper to other methods. It has been closely associated with structural criticism, deconstruction criticism, and reader-response criticism, although there are important differences among these methods and between these methods and narrative criticism proper.

Regina A. Boisclair

See also DECONSTRUCTION.

NARRATIVE THEOLOGY

The term names a trend in recent Christian theology and can be taken in both a "weak" and "strong" sense. In its "weak" sense, narrative theology refers to a renewed appreciation that the primary form of the expression of the intelligibility of Christian faith lies in "narrative"—especially the biblical witness—and, further, that the subject matter of those narratives cannot be translated without remainder into any conceptual system of theology or metaphysics. In its "strong" sense, narrative theology includes the foregoing but adds an explicit antifoundationalist stance, that is, a stance against grounding the possibility and intelligibility of Christian faith in a more general analysis of human experience or the world. Narrative theology in its strong sense maintains that narratives carry and create the conditions of their own intelligibility. Thus, judging the meaning and truth of narratives from a standpoint outside the narrative universe is both inappropriate and a betrayal of the narrative itself. Exponents of strong narrative theology include George Lindbeck, Hans Frei, Ronald Thiemann, and Stanley Hauerwas.

J. A. Colombo

NATARAJA

The Hindu god Shiva is often addressed by his devotees and portrayed in iconography as Nataraja, the Lord of the Dance. Dating from the fifth century C.E., the Nataraja image—typically cast in bronze—depicts, under a ring of flame, a four-armed, four-legged deity in a dynamic but gracefully balanced dance pose. The gestures displayed symbolize Shiva's five functions: the manifestation, maintenance, and dissolution of the universe, the concealment of reality, and liberating grace. Suggesting the power and freedom that underlies Shiva's activity as cosmic Lord, the image reminds the worshiper that the extraordinary power of the deity includes the aspect of divine protection and grace. While the linga is the most common representation of Shiva, the Nataraja icon is popular, especially in South India, where it has been so for centuries. It has also become recognized as one of the most profound images of divinity in world art.

Lance E. Nelson

See also HINDUISM; IMAGES, WORSHIP OF; LINGA; SHAIVA; SHIVA.

NATION OF ISLAM

A religio-political militant movement that stressed both the recovery of the African American heritage through the practice of Islam and a religiously based black separatist nationalism. The Nation of Islam (NOI) was started by W. D. Fard (Master Fard Muhammad; 1891–1934) in Detroit, Michigan, to resist racial discrimination and to promote the personal, spiritual, cultural, socioeconomic, and political dignity of black men and women.

After the disappearance or death of Master Fard, the NOI was popularized by one of his closest disciples and ministers, Elijah Muhammad (born Elijah Poole, 1897–1975). Being a member of the NOI involved an intellectual assent to the religious teachings of Elijah Muhammad, regular attendance at NOI meetings, and a petition for membership, including a request for a new name to signify the putting off of a former, exploited, enslaved identity and the putting on of a new, independent black identity. Muhammad taught the incarnation of Allah in Master Fard and proclaimed himself the messenger of God. Also, he espoused a controversial doctrine of creation that professed the superiority of blacks and the creation of whites, in this case devils, not by God but by a certain mad scientist, Yakub. Finally, he imagined an apocalyptic vision of the eschaton or the end times in which whites would be judged and condemned, the earth would be consumed in a purgative fire, and the black faithful would construct a new earth, a more just and egalitarian society. The membership of the NOI increased from about five hundred in 1952 to roughly thirty thousand in 1963 as a result of the charismatic leadership of one of the NOI's most prominent ministers, Malcolm X (d. 1965).

The death of Elijah Muhammad sparked a variety of splinter sects of the NOI. One particular sect, called the American Muslim Mission and headed by Muhammad's son Warith Deen Muhammad (b. 1933), emphasized the five pillars of orthodox Islamic practice and worked toward the reconciliation of the NOI with other traditional beliefs and practices of Sunni Islam. Another sect under the name NOI continued at the headquarters in Chicago, Illinois, in Mosque Maryam and is presently headed by Louis Farrakhan. Farrakhan, formerly Louis Eugene Walcott, joined the NOI in 1955 and took over as the minister of Mosque no.7 in Harlem, New York, after the assassination of Malcolm X (d. 1965). Farrakhan restored Elijah Muhammad's teachings to the center of the NOI, although Farrakhan encouraged the NOI to slightly alter or outright reject Muhammad's original teachings about not fasting during Rama-

dan and not engaging in political activism. Under the leadership of Farrakhan, the NOI has publicly decried Christianity for its role in providing theological justifications for slavery and racism, as well as promoting anti-Semitic rhetoric and inciting hostility among blacks and Jews, for example, by positing in the 1990s a spurious connection between Jews and the slave trade.

Rosemary P. Carbine

NATIVE AMERICAN CHURCH

This new religion arose in the mid-nineteenth century to counter the great demoralization that followed the defeat and removal to reservations of many native tribes. The cult is based upon the ritual use of peyote and it is believed to be derived from the ancient use of this substance in Mexico. In North America, it is seen first among the Oklahoma peoples who had collectively suffered the great trauma of removal from their former homelands and had been settled in Oklahoma Territory. The ritual is complex and is focused on the ceremonial taking of peyote in the context of a communion ritual. The resulting hallucinatory state yields visions that give strength for life. It is credited by the Native Americans and external scholars with providing a valuable support and means of personal transformation to countless people.

There was immediate negative reaction to this movement from the mainstream. This reaction linked the use of peyote to the catalogue of vices that had alcohol abuse at its center. This was a completely erroneous perception; in fact, it can be argued that this ritual is highly regenerative, morally and spiritually. Among its teaching is a complete proscription of alcohol, and a command to become moral members of society. The Indians stress that this ritual belongs to the native peoples, and whites are discouraged from attempting to enter it. This early and continuing controversy led Quanah Parker, one of the early Peyote chiefs, to seek protection under the First Amendment. Thus, in 1918, he succeeded in getting it incorporated as a religious body, under the above title, to receive protection from unsympathetic attacks. It remains a source of controversy under state interpretation of the First Amendment at the beginning of the twenty-first century.

Kathleen Dugan

See also CULTS; FREEDOM.

NATURALISM

A form of philosophical monism that maintains reality is solely constituted by the set of objects and events in principle accessible through the canons of human knowing as exemplified in science. As such, naturalism is distinct from "materialism" because, unlike the latter, it admits the possibility that ideational elements are part of reality. While naturalism flourished in the middle decades of the past century in the United States, John Dewey's *Experience and Nature* (1925) remains the most noteworthy exponent of this position.

J. A. Colombo

See also DEWEY, JOHN.

NATURAL LAW

The term natural law refers to those diverse theories that generate systems of ethics or social philosophy based on realism, that is, an account of the way things are perceived actually to be. Usually, such realism proposes a self-evident account of human nature from which basic human rights and/or duties are deduced. From a Christian perspective, natural law theory is significant because it continues to play a significant role in Roman Catholic official ethical teaching and in moral theology.

Origins in Classical Thought

Some of the earliest systematic reflection on natural law is found among the ancient Greeks, who asked whether law was simply based on human custom or whether there was a deeper foundation to law and therefore of society. While Aristotle did not develop a full account of natural law, he maintains that there are universally binding moral obligations based upon human nature and that are accessible by means of human rationality. This relationship between natural law and rationality is developed further in the Greco-Roman philosophy of the Stoics. It is this philosophy that most influenced Christian versions of natural law. The Stoic philosopher Cicero argued for the divine origin of genuine law and defined such law in the following terms: "[t]rue law is right reason in agreement with nature, it is of universal application, unchanging and everlasting . . ." (*De re publica*). Genuine law, then, is rational and in accord with the purposes of nature, and so with the purposes of the Creator of nature.

Thomas Aquinas on Law

Aquinas discusses four major types of law in his treatise on law: eternal law, divine law, natural law, and human law. He understands that the eternal law is the source of all other genuine law. The eternal law is the principle of creation and of the universe's governance. The other types of law participate or share in the eternal law to some degree, but in no way do they fully coincide with it. Natural law, for Aquinas, is that aspect of the eternal law accessible to human persons by means of their reason. It is in this reasonableness of natural law that we see the influence of Aristotle on Aquinas.

In Aquinas's account, it is self-evident that everything in being is inclined toward its own perfection or, in his terms, its "good." Thus he articulates the first principle of natural law as "good is to be done and pursued and evil avoided" (*Summa Theologiae* I–II, q. 94, a. 2c). Insofar as persons rationally encounter perfective inclinations, they have an obligatory character. While the first principle of natural law is "formal," in that it does not specify these goods or evils, Thomas does offer some examples of these self-evident, perfective inclinations. In common with all that is in being, human beings are inclined toward self-preservation; commonality with animals demonstrates an inclination for procreation and nurturing the young; commonality with rational being points to a desire to know the truth about God and social existence. Exactly how these examples generate moral norms or rules—as well as the stringency of such rules—continues to be a matter of debate.

In addition to the Stoic and Aristotelian views, Aquinas's account of natural law is also influenced by Roman law—notably by the Roman legal theorist Ulpian and his account of *jus naturale*. Ulpian claims that our physical faculties themselves have specific purposes that generate ethical obligation. For example, the physical faculty of speech has the natural purpose of expressing the truth; thus lying is contrary to natural law. Similarly, the genital organs function for procreation, and so any sexual use of the genitals that precludes procreation is a violation of the natural law. This results in a certain "physicalist" tendency, or a view that the physical dimension alone captures the moral meaning, in Thomistic and Roman Catholic sexual ethics. As Josef Fuchs has pointed out, it is also this strand of Aquinas's natural law theory that makes it vulnerable to the "naturalist fallacy" criticism in a way that the "right reason" strand is not. The naturalist fallacy reminds us that descriptions alone cannot generate moral obligation; that "is" does not necessarily imply "ought."

Contemporary Implications

The distinction between the Aristotelian "right reason" tradition of natural law and the more physicalist interpretation continues to be felt in contemporary Roman Catholic moral theology and official church teaching. For example, Roman Catholic teachings on social and economic justice tend to appeal to the right reason tradition, suggesting broad principles to be implemented by persons of good will in ways appropriate to their particular society and tradition. Official Roman Catholic teaching on sexual and biomedical ethics, on the other hand, tends to follow the *jus naturale* tradition and so generates specific, inviolable moral norms that are universally applicable. Many Roman Catholic moral theologians in western Europe and North America, influenced by personalist approaches to ethics, tend to favor an Aristotelian approach to natural law without denying the capacity of the physical to generate norms, or at least play a significant role in their generation. Others argue that human natural inclinations yield a number of self-evident basic human goods, such as life, procreation, knowledge, and friendship, that may never be directly acted against even to promote another basic good. These inviolable basic goods then generate stringent moral norms. The basic value of life, for example, forbids the use of all artificial birth control and any recourse to direct abortion.

Natural law theory has had a significant role in the history of Christian ethics. Some forms of the theory continue to be influential, particularly at a time when the very possibility of epistemological foundations and objectivity in morals is questioned.

Brian F. Linnane, s.j.

See also BIOETHICS; ETHICS; ETHICS, SEXUAL; ETHICS, SOCIAL; MORAL THEOLOGY/CHRISTIAN ETHICS; PERSONALISM; SEXUALITY.

NATURE, HUMAN

Human nature has had a wide array of meanings in theology's long history. The concept of a "nature" (generally) has been used to refer to God and Trinity, to Christ, to humankind, to creation as a whole, and even to angels. In the history of theology, "*human* nature" (specifically) has more frequently meant: either (1) the "essence of being," understood as that without which humanness could not be what it is; and/or (2) what essentially underlies and ultimately makes possible history and culture, but is in fact prior to and beyond them. In either case, "human nature" is a reality shared by all humans, not individually forged. It is a reality that foundationally underlies and makes possible all human beings' "humanness"— however this "humanness" is explained.

The list of elements considered to be intrinsic parts of human nature, as indicated by the many attempted descriptions or definitions, has greatly depended on the theoretical and social perspectives of the authors. Many contemporary theologians propose that human nature is what could be called or identified as "the humanness of our being" (individually, socially)—an essential quality or dimension that distinguishes humankind from all other beings and is humanity's created foundation. Other contemporary theologians suggest that human nature is the sum total of the complex and inherited biological, cultural, and social (and other) conditions into which humans are born and that really shape them as human, but over which there is little individual control. Human nature, in any case, is historical.

The notion of human nature has been very important in the history of Western thought (theological, philosophical, juridical, political). In Christian theology, it is very important in discussions on grace, salvation, justification, free will, social and personal ethics, natural law, and the like.

Orlando Espín

See also CREATION; ETHICS, SEXUAL; ETHICS, SOCIAL; FREE WILL; GRACE; JUSTIFICATION; MORAL THEOLOGY/ CHRISTIAN ETHICS; ORIGINAL JUSTICE; SALVATION; SIN, ORIGINAL; THEOLOGICAL ANTHROPOLOGY.

NEMBUTSU

(Japanese, lit., calling on Buddha). The practice in Pure Land Buddhism of repeating the formula *Namu Amida Butsu* ("hail Amida Buddha") to elicit his saving grace and leading, after death, to rebirth in the Pure Land. It was claimed by the monk Honen, founder of the Jodo School, that he attained enlightenment by merely repeating the *nembutsu* and that was enough to deliver one to the Pure Land. Neither a strenuous life of good works nor meditation was necessary. This ritual became an integral part of Pure Land practice.

G. D. DeAngelis

See also AMITABHA / AMIDA; BUDDHISM; HONEN; JODO SHIN SHU; JODO SHU; PURE LAND BUDDHISM; TENDAI.

NEO-CONFUCIANISM

One of the dominant philosophical developments of premodern China marking a significant Confucian revival during the Sung Dynasty (960–1276). After the fall of the Tang Dynasty (618–907) and its state sponsorship of Buddhism and Taoism and the corruption of Confucianism by both of these traditions, the Sung rulers returned to Confucianism to bring stability to the government. The early founders of the Neo-Confucian movement, Ch'eng I and Shao Yung, promoted a return to the traditional teachings of Confucius and Mencius. However, the influence of Buddhism and Taoism was significant and forced the Confucian revivalists to concentrate more on metaphysical and mystical elements in response to the needs of a new age.

Historically, the Neo-Confucian movement divided itself into two contrasting schools: School of Principle (Li-Hsueh) and School of Mind (Hsin Hsueh), both developing a system of moral philosophy to explain Confucian ethics in metaphysical terms. The major proponents of these two schools were Chu Hsi and Wang Yang-Ming. While the philosophical basics of each differed significantly, they both advocated a way of ultimate transformation that was primarily ethical. While the detailed teachings of this movement were too elevated for most people, its integration of Taoist and Buddhist principles with Confucian ideology proved to have a significant and lasting impact on China as well as other areas of East Asia, such as, Japan, Korea, Vietnam, and others.

G. D. DeAngelis

See also CHU HSI; CONFUCIANISM; CONFUCIUS; DAOISM; HSUN-TZU; MENCIUS; WANG YANG-MING.

NEO-ORTHODOX THEOLOGY

Sometimes also referred to as "Dialectical Theology" or "Theology of Crisis," the term refers to a dominant theological—and largely Protestant—movement in the twentieth century that included, for example, Karl Barth, Rudolph Bultmann, Friedrich Gogarten, Emil Brunner, Paul Tillich, Rheinhold Niebuhr, H. Richard Niebuhr, as well as Roman Catholics Eduard Schillebeeckx and Karl Rahner.

Although they differed and disagreed on specific theological issues, each implicitly or explicitly rejected the synthesis between Christianity and modernity characteristic of liberal theology. H. Richard Niebuhr's famous description of the lacunae of that synthesis—"a God without wrath, brought men without sin, into a Kingdom without judgment, through the ministrations of a Christ without a cross"—summarizes the neo-orthodox theologians' negative estimate that liberal theology compromised the radical promise and demand of the Gospel as God's revelation, in order to establish and secure a new Christendom. In the cognitive, moral, and political correlation between Christianity and modernity, the naiveté of liberal theology was its concession to the latter to dictate terms regarding how the former was to be understood.

This negative judgment of neo-orthodoxy is inseparable from a positive, constructive task: the project of "retrieval." First, retrieval meant a rediscovery of the "strange, new world of the Bible," and thus both the autonomy of the Word of God and the oppositional element between God's revelation and both modern culture and human religion. Second, it signified an attempt to explicate and defend the existential relevance and meaning of traditional doctrinal and theological formulations regarding, for example, revelation and sin and forgiveness, that liberal theology was all too ready to reject as relics of a premodern age.

In this constructive task, however, neo-orthodoxy was not simply a return to "premodern" orthodoxy. To various degrees—most clearly in Bultmann's program of "demythologization"—the neo-orthodox theologians utilized the resources of modernity, such as modern biblical criticism, existential philosophy, depth psychology, and transcendental Thomism, to accomplish their constructive task. Nonetheless, as the subsequent movements of political and liberation theology have argued, the success of the neo-orthodox project was also its weakness, that is, in neo-orthodoxy's focus on the meaning of the Gospel for the private realm of the individual person, it more often than not simply ignored the public realm of political, economic, and social structures. In this, neo-orthodoxy often accepted both the political and economic status quo and, ironically, the quintessentially modern separation of the "private" from the "public" realm with the restriction of religion to the former. It should be borne in mind, however, that some commentators, like David Tracy, have maintained that political and liberation theology still remain fundamentally within a neo-orthodox model.

J. A. Colombo

See also BARTH, KARL; BRUNNER, EMIL; BULTMANN, RUDOLPH; GOGARTEN, FRIEDRICH; LIBERAL THEOLOGY; NEIBUHR, H. RICHARD; NIEBUHR, REINHOLD; RAHNER, KARL; SCHILLEBEECKX, EDUARD; TILLICH, PAUL.

NEOPHYTE (IN CHRISTIANITY)

(Greek, *neophytos*, new growth, new convert). A person in the postbaptismal or fourth stage of the Rite of Christian Initiation of Adults (*Mystagogy*). Having celebrated the initiation sacraments at the Easter Vigil, the neophyte enters a period of reflection and prayer on the Easter experience that lasts at least until Pentecost. Neophytes continue to be sponsored and supported as they enter more deeply into the sacramental life of the church, discern personal charisms for ministry, and prepare to enter more thoroughly into the church community. Some parishes continue a structured Mystagogy for a year after initiation or place neophytes in small faith communities. Research shows that such support makes much stronger, more involved members of the community.

Taken from the language of third and fourth centuries, parishes seldom use the word "neophyte." Many parishes do not provide a special period of Mystagogy. Others simply call neophytes "newly received members."

M. Jane Gorman

See also CATECHUMENATE; MYSTAGOGY; RITES OF CHRISTIAN INITIATION (RCIA).

NEOPLATONISM

Any Neoplatonic system of thought is characterized by its debt to the work of the ancient Greek philosopher Plato (428/7–348/7 B.C.E.). Plotinus would surely rank as one of the greatest of the Neoplatonists. In the area of Christian theology, St. Augustine (354–430 C.E.) of Tagaste in Northern Africa and the Roman philosopher Boethius were heavily influenced by Neoplatonism. The "new Platonism" received its expression in Augustine's thought through his attempt to synthesize Platonic metaphysics (theory of the ultimate nature of reality) and epistemology (theory of the nature and foundations of knowledge) with the basic elements of Christian doctrine. Boethius, who studied philosophy in Athens, was similarly able to incorporate many aspects of Platonism into his own theorizing about the nature of God, the nature of human beings, and the character and quality of the moral life. The work of both philosophers had a profound impact on theological and philosophical theorizing throughout the Middle Ages and into the modern era.

St. Augustine followed Plato in holding that the ultimate principles of reality are eternal, immutable, and immaterial "Forms." According to Plato, particular objects in the world derive their existence and the characteristics that account for their being included in their respective categories or kinds from the Forms. Thus, a tiger derives its being qua tiger from the Form "Tigerness," and similarly with all creatures. For St. Augustine, the idea that there is a multiplicity of eternal, unchanging, creative principles entailed the existence of a multiplicity of gods—a conclusion incompatible with Christian monotheism and one that Augustine was, therefore, compelled to reject. In order to render the Platonic account of Forms consistent with the Christian view that there is but one eternal God, Augustine held that the Forms or eternal exemplars exist as ideas or thoughts in the divine mind,

thus subsuming all these eternal principles under a single ontological category or mode of being—divine thought.

Augustine further followed Plato in holding that a human being is essentially a soul which is housed in a body during the mortal life of the individual. Yet, owing to his adherence to Christian doctrine, he could not endorse Plato's theory that the soul undergoes a succession of reincarnations. Plato held that the soul, in a previous life, encountered the Forms in an immaterial realm of being transcending the physical universe and that, in learning about the ultimate natures of things, the soul has to recall what it learned in its prior mode of existence. For Augustine, the soul has no life prior to its life on earth. Still, he agreed with Plato's position that the process of understanding the true natures of things involves having direct intuitional access to the Forms or Divine Ideas.

Accordingly, he modified the Platonic view, holding, instead, that an individual human being can encounter the "archetypal forms" or "stable and immutable essences of things" through contemplation and meditation. On Augustine's account, God dwells within the human soul and, by looking within and directing one's spiritual gaze toward God, one can behold the divine exemplars and understand the true natures of all things.

In keeping with his position that human beings are essentially spiritual beings, St. Augustine held that virtue comes from having a well-ordered soul—a soul whose will is directed toward the eternal, the immutable, and the necessarily existent, that is, God. A soul becomes vice-ridden when it turns from its source of being and illumination toward objects in the changing, contingent, physical realm. Augustine's moral theorizing was thus heavily influenced by his Platonist antimaterialism.

Boethius' view of the soul/body relation was the same as Augustine's. The body is nothing more than the temporary house of the soul that it abandons at death. What happens to the body is of relatively little importance. This Platonic antimaterialism played a significant role in the development of Boethius' moral philosophy as expressed in his treatise *The Consolation of Philosophy.* This treatise was written while Boethius was in prison awaiting execution after having been accused of treason. Though the accusation and punishment were politically motivated and unjust, Boethius' view of his apparent misfortune was that he was not really being harmed after all. His position was that, since one's personhood is located in the soul, an immaterial principle, what happens to the body cannot harm the individual qua spirit. According to Boethius, to suffer evil is to have something of true value taken from you against your will. Yet the person whose soul is rightly ordered values only spiritual, immaterial goods. These are the goods constitutive of the divine principle within the soul and these can never be taken from a person unwillingly.

Both Augustine and Boethius held that there are gradations of reality or levels of reality with God at the pinnacle of the ontological hierarchy or scale of being. God, the source of goodness and existence, is also supremely powerful. Objects lower down on the ontological scale are more or less powerful relative to their proximity to the divine source of power. Hence, on this view, corrupt spirits, which are far removed from God, are less powerful than virtuous spirits. A person whose rightly ordered will is focused on the eternal and immutable spiritual goods is more powerful than any vicious spirit and cannot be negatively influenced by such a spirit.

In general, any theological system that posits a creative principle transcending the world of sensory experience and that holds that the material world exists less fully than the spiritual world owes a debt to Neoplatonic thought. Further, any theology that emphasizes the importance of contemplation and meditation in knowledge acquisition is similarly indebted.

Linda L. Peterson

See also AUGUSTINE OF HIPPO; BOETHIUS; PLATO; PLATONISM; PLOTINUS.

NEO-SCHOLASTICISM

A theological movement that prevailed in late nineteenth- and early twentieth-century Catholicism that sought a return to the Scholasticism of the Middle Ages. Scholasticism was an approach to learning, flourishing between the eleventh and thirteenth centuries, that applied principles of logic to the reading of authoritative texts (such as the Bible or the writings of the early "church fathers") in order to resolve apparent contradictions among them and arrive at the truth that was assumed to lie at the root of all of them. It had been gradually superseded after the fourteenth century by a more humanistic approach that emphasized literature and history. Nineteenth-century Catholic theologians, challenged by the Enlightenment philosophy of the eighteenth and early nineteenth centuries, chose to return to what they considered a "genuinely Catholic" mode of thinking. This Neo-Scholastic movement was officially sanctioned by Pope Leo XIII in his 1879 encyclical *Aeterni Patris* that held up the work of Thomas Aquinas (1225–74) as a model for Catholic scholarship, with appropriate updating made necessary by the progress of human thought over six hundred years. The complications of this updating, as well as questions and disagreements about the original intentions and methods of the Scholastic philosophers, contributed to a variety of competing types of Neo-Scholastic thought among Catholic theologians up to the time of the Second Vatican Council (1962–5). In the meantime, standard theological texts ("manuals") for the training of priests in seminaries often presented oversimplified forms of basic Scholastic arguments and conclusions, without regard for the more subtle questions over which the theologians were disagreeing. Following Vatican II, a new appreciation for the possibility of a fruitful relationship between Catholic tradition and modern scholarship introduced a host of new questions and methods into Catholic theology, and brought the prevalence of Neo-Scholasticism to a close.

William A. Clark, s.j.

See also SCHOLASTICISM.

NER TAMID

(Hebrew, Eternal Lamp). In the synagogue, this is a light burning perpetually before the ark in which the Torah-scrolls are kept. The *Ner Tamid* symbolizes the candelabra that burned continually in the wilderness tabernacle and later in the Jerusalem Temple (see Exod 27:20; Lev 24:2). In synagogues today, the Ner Tamid is normally an electric bulb placed in a decorative housing and suspended before the ark. Oil lamps and candles may also be used.

Alan J. Avery-Peck

See also ARON HAKODESH; SYNAGOGUE; TORAH.

NESTLE, EBEHARD (1851–1913)

German scholar and professor of Old Testament and Semitic languages at Ulm and Tübingen, whose study of Syriac and the Septuagint Greek translation of the Old Testament inspired him to produce a comprehensive, critical edition of the New Testament Greek text. Nestle combined earlier works by Tischendorff, Wescott-Hort, Weymouth, and B. Weiss, favoring the text supported by the majority. In cases of serious doubt, he offered a "mean" reading, giving special weight to the "Western" family of New Testament manuscript copies. The "Nestle" Greek text first appeared in 1898. In 1904 the British and Foreign Bible Society in London used it to replace the "Received Text" as the basis for English missionary translations throughout the world. His son, Erwin Nestle, supervised the tenth to twenty-first revisions of his father's work (1914–52), and the twenty-second to twenty-fifth editions (1956–63) along with Kurt Aland.

Francis D. Connolly-Weinert

NESTORIANISM

Nestorianism is the teaching that there are two persons and two natures in Christ in opposition to the more widely held Christian belief, upheld at the Council of Chalcedon in 451, that there are two natures but only one Person in Christ. The human person and the divine Person in Nestorianism form a conjunction of mind and will rather than hypostatic union of the human and divine nature affirmed by Chalcedon. This theology attempts to safeguard the existence of a true human being, Jesus, with his own mind, will, and soul. The opposite tendency in theology, called Monophysitism, asserts the oneness of the person of the Christ, denying there is any separate human person in

Jesus. When a compromise was reached at the Council of Chalcedon, these two groups refused to accept it and established their own separate Christian churches. The two groups remain separate from the main body of Christians to this day.

The name Nestorianism stems from Nestorius, patriarch of Constantinople from 428 to 431. After Nestorius, a student of the Antiochene school of theology, publically and forcefully upheld the teaching that there are two separate natures in Christ, an extended and sometimes politically unsavory struggle took place between the representatives of the Alexandrian school of theology, led by the patriarch of Alexandria, Cyril, and the bishops and theologians of the Antiochene school of thought. The more radical of this second group refused to accept the compromise reached in 433 between Cyril and John, the patriarch of Antioch, and under the leadership of Ibas, bishop of Edessa from 435 to 457, began to see themselves as a separate church.

After the Council of Chalcedon, the Nestorians regrouped in Persia and established a flourishing theological center in Nisibis as well as their own patriarchate at Seleucia–Ctesiphon. Nestorian missionaries established churches in Arabia, India, and East Asia. The Church of the East, as the Nestorians called themselves, continued to thrive under Islamic rulers in the seventh through ninth centuries, resisting all attempts from Constantinople to reunite the churches. Only in the fourteenth century did they meet with serious persecution by the Mongols. The Assyrian Church, as the Nestorians are commonly known, continues to exist in the Middle East. They retain their ancient Syriac liturgy and distinct theological traditions.

Gary Macy

See also CHALCEDON, COUNCIL OF; CHRIST; CYRIL OF ALEXANDRIA; EUTYCHES; HYPOSTATIC UNION; MONOPHYSITISM; NESTORIUS; PATRIARCH; PERSON/PROSOPON.

NESTORIUS (381–451?)

Patriarch of Constantinople from 428 to 431, Nestorius was a monk and priest from Antioch famous for his preaching. In an attempt to reform the church of Constantinople, Nestorius attacked the popular devotion to Mary as "Mother of God (*Theotokos*) as inaccurate and even impious. A student of the school at Antioch, Nestorius was concerned to preserve the separation between the divine and human natures in Christ. Cyril, patriarch of Alexandria, immediately responded by accusing Nestorius of teaching that there were two separate persons in Christ, a human person and a divine Person. When both patriarchs appealed to Rome for support, Celestine of Rome instructed Cyril to ask Nestorius to confess his errors. Cyril embroidered quite a bit on Celestine's request and sent Nestorius a letter including twelve anathemas that would be completely unacceptable to anyone trained in Antioch. The emperor Theodosius II called a council that met in Ephesus in 431. Cyril, who arrived first, rallied his supporters and condemned and deposed Nestorius before he and his followers could arrive. When Nestorius did arrive, he and his supporters condemned and deposed Cyril. This confusion, and the emperor's own indecision, led Theodosius to accept both depositions as valid. Cyril's deposition never went into effect, but Nestorius voluntarily retired to the monastery in Antioch. Although the Nestorian controversy continued, Nestorius himself took no further role in the discussion, despite his protest late in life that he accepted orthodox teaching. He was exiled from Antioch and died sometime after the Council of Chalcedon in 451.

Gary Macy

See also CHALCEDON, COUNCIL OF; CYRIL OF ALEXANDRIA; EPHESUS, COUNCIL OF; NESTORIANISM; PATRIARCH.

NEUSNER, J. (1932–)

Scholar of the history of Judaism, central in bringing the study of Judaism into the contemporary, secular academy. Neusner was the first to apply contemporary norms of historical analysis to the texts of rabbinic Judaism. While these texts derive from widely divergent historical and social settings, they previously had been interpreted as representing a single, monolithic Judaic tradition. Neusner, by contrast, introduced the now generally accepted notion that each text must be interpreted first and foremost as an independent statement of its own authors, who responded to the distinctive needs and circumstances of their own day. In the course of his interpretation of Judaic systems in late antiquity, Neusner has almost single-handedly produced translations and interpretations of the entire Talmudic literature. Alongside this work, he has written widely on contemporary Jewish culture and religion, on Judaism and Zionism, and on the relationship between Judaism and Christianity.

Alan J. Avery-Peck

NEW AGE MOVEMENT

A religious movement of eclectic doctrines and vague boundaries, begun in the 1970s by proponents of Eastern mysticism and philosophies (but also with roots going back to the cultural revolution of the previous decade).

The focus and core of the movement has been the promotion of a new age and a new consciousness for humankind, brought about by individuals through meditation and mystical experience, "psychic journeys," "metaphysical" healing, "natural" lifestyles, ecological awareness, astrological alignments, and the like. Participants believe there is a "universal energy" that permeates and underlies all existence. Tapping into this energy flow, and becoming increasingly sensitive to it, is an apparent requirement for movement members. New Age emphasizes self-knowledge and "inner exploration" in the hope of connecting with the universal energy, seeking constant internal transformation. The movement, therefore, proposes a vision and a hope, but is extraordinarily diverse in its doctrinal and practical expressions. Doctrinal explanations, although present, are not considered important or necessary.

The influence of some Eastern religions is apparent in New Age's teaching on reincarnation, karma, sadhana, and similar topics. There is a pantheist belief in (one) God as the ultimate unifying principle of all that exists. The great religious teachers of the past (Jesus, Buddha, and others) are regarded as extraordinary expressions of God and of the universal energy that flows from God. Individual believers are "channels" of that same divine and universal energy; although some individuals might be more advanced in their "channeling" than others. These more "advanced" persons may become teachers or guides ("gurus") to others. Places and objects (for example, crystals) can also be "channels" for the universal energy.

Among the first national exponents of New Age thought was Baba Ram Dass (formerly known as Richard Alpert, a Harvard professor); but others have also written and taught within the movement—for example: Kirpal Singh, Swami Muktananda, Marilyn Ferguson, David Spangler, and Judith Skutch. The movement has organized itself as networks of communes, meditation schools and teachers, alternative health care centers, "metaphysical" bookstores, and the like.

The hope that the new age of humankind could happen within the near future seems to have been progressively abandoned, and the appeal to the name ("New Age") has declined. However, it is evident that millions of people still share in practices and beliefs associated with and popularized by the New Age movement, even when not associating themselves with the name ("New Age") itself. Under a variety of different labels, New Age continues to thrive and to religiously influence U.S. society. The movement's doctrinal and ritual eclecticism and its emphasis on inner religious experience added to its lack of "church-like" institutionalization, provide New Age with the ability to attract a wide and growing public, often tired of denominational rigidity and in search of a fulfilling spiritual life.

Orlando Espín

See also ASTROLOGY; CULTURE; GOD; GURU; KARMA; MEDITATION (CHRISTIAN); MYSTICISM/MYSTICS (IN CHRISTIANITY); PANTHEISM; POPULAR RELIGIONS; REINCARNATION; SADHANA; THEOLOGICAL ANTHROPOLOGY.

NEW ISRAEL

While Israel is both an ethnic and political term in the Old Testament, it is a fundamental theological idea as well. Central to that idea is the concept of election that understands Israel as God's chosen people, as chosen to live in covenant relationship with God, as chosen by God to receive the Torah, and as chosen to live in the land promised by God to Israel's ancestors.

In apocalyptic Judaism this was combined with the expectation of the inbreaking of God's universal rule. It was believed, however, that only when Israel was truly observing the precepts of the Torah could the kingdom of God arrive. This led to distinctions made within the Jewish community based on law observance as to who was a true Israelite. The Qumran sectarians are an example of a group who regarded themselves as the true Israel.

In the New Testament the same tendency to make these distinctions can be noted, for example, when Paul points out that there is a difference between those who are Jews by physical descent and those who are Jews by faith in Christ (Rom 2:28-29; 9:6). This reflects that in the New Testament, while the term Israel in numerous instances continues to refer to the historic people of God, it is also spiritualized as in the Pauline example to refer to the believers in Jesus. This transition in meaning was rooted in the preaching of Jesus that it was he who was announcing and establishing the reign of God. Those who followed him understood that they were thus the legitimate heirs of ancient Israel (see, for example, Gal 6:16; Jas 1:1; 1 Pet 2:9). In their understanding, through faith and through adoption in Jesus, they had become not only part of the covenant people but were in fact the true descendants of Abraham (Gal 3:7). The Christians therefore saw themselves as the new Israel of God who inherited the privileges of ancient Israel.

The Christians' interpretation of themselves as the new Israel raises many fundamental questions concerning, for example, how they viewed God's faithfulness to the covenant with Israel and how they interpreted the rejection of Jesus as Messiah by most Jews. Romans 9–11 is one of the most sustained reflections on these issues in the New Testament.

F. M. Gillman

See also COVENANT IN JUDAISM; ISRAEL, STATE OF; QUMRAN; REIGN OF GOD.

NEWMAN, JOHN HENRY (1801–90)

English priest, theologian, and Roman Catholic cardinal. Raised and educated in the Church of England, he became a popular and important member of the Oxford Movement. Some of his Anglican writings and sermons were very influential. After 1839 he started moving toward Roman Catholicism, and in 1845 joined the Roman Catholic Church (appointed cardinal by pope Leo XIII in 1879). Newman continued his writing and preaching, but had constant difficulties with Rome. His most durable and important theological contributions have been his theories on the development of doctrine, and on how and why humans assent to faith. His theological works have had a significant influence on Roman Catholic scholars in the English-speaking world. Among his best books are *Parochial and Plain Sermons* (1834–42), *Essay on the Development of Doctrine* (1845), and *A Grammar of Assent* (1870).

Orlando Espín

See also ANGLICAN COMMUNION; CANTERBURY, SEE OF; CARDINAL; CATHOLIC TRADITION; DEVELOPMENT OF DOGMA/OF DOCTRINE; ECCLESIOLOGY; EPISTEMOLOGY; FAITH; GRACE; METHOD IN THEOLOGY; OXFORD MOVEMENT; ROMAN CATHOLIC CHURCH; WESTERN CATHOLIC CHURCHES.

NEW RELIGIONS

(Japanese, *Shin Shukyo*). This term covers a wide variety of religious movements and expressions in Japan during the nineteenth and twentieth centuries. While these traditions tend to be quite diverse, there is some commonality in intent and in maintaining a certain continuity with the past. The major periods of development of these traditions were: first, during the Meiji Era (1868–1911), when the traditional feudal structure began to break down and Western influence became prominent, giving rise to such traditions as Tenrikyo, Konkokyo, and Kurozumikyo; second, during the post–World War I period with the emergence of religions such as Soka Gakkai and Reiyukai; third, the post–World War II period witnessed the most extensive development of new religions with increased industrialization, urbanization, and secularization.

While many of these new religions have some link with the traditional religions of Shinto, Buddhism, and Confucianism, most of them share the common characteristic of reshaping traditional religious expression into distinctive ways to meet the changing religious needs of a changing world. In particular, post–World War II Japan has had to deal with issues of national identity, increased secularization, the breakdown of traditional family structures, and loss of continuity with the past. The new religions, for the most part, have responded to this vacuum of religious meaning, need for communal structures, and increasing interest in practical and immediate benefits in such areas as happiness, purification, health, and wealth by reinterpreting the basic values and patterns consistent with Shinto, Buddhist, and Confucian morality and practice. They have also responded by applying these to contemporary issues and a this-worldly orientation, and by guiding their adherents in contemporary techniques of self-transformation.

G. D. DeAngelis

See also MIKI NAKAYAMA; SHINTO; SOKA GAKKAI; TENRIKYO.

NEW TESTAMENT

The story of the life, death, and resurrection of Jesus, as well as his teachings, were communicated, preserved, and shaped by preachers who traveled spreading the Gospel. After time and distance separated communities from living eyewitnesses, Christians began to write, collect, and preserve their own literature. These writings transformed the medium of the Gospel from oral proclamation to written texts. By the fourth century C.E., there was a general acceptance of a twenty-seven-book New Testament containing four Gospels, one history, twenty-one letters (some are actually sermons or treatises), and one apocalypse.

The books in the New Testament present the efforts of some first-century Christians to identify who Jesus was; to explain his significance in God's redemptive care for humanity; to recount the memories of Jesus' life, teachings, death, and resurrection; to authenticate these memories by identifying witnesses; to disclose the expectations of those who believe; and to clarify the implications of what it means to live a life of faith in Jesus.

The authors of most New Testament texts are anonymous. While Paul's identity is assured, he is considered the author of only seven "undisputed" letters (Romans, 1 and 2 Corinthians, Galatians, Philippians, 1 Thessalonians, and Philemon). The "disputed" Pauline letters (Ephesians, Colossians, 2 Thessalonians, 1 and 2 Timothy, and Titus) are pseudonymous as are James, 1 and 2 Peter, and Jude. While there is no reason to question that a man named John, a visionary at Patmos, wrote the book of Revelation, apart from what he said about himself in Revelation 1:9, nothing is known about him. The author of 2 and 3 John identifies himself only as "the Elder." It is certain the author of Luke also wrote Acts (see Acts 1:1). Most assume the author of the prologue in John's Gospel (John 1:1-18) also wrote 1 John.

Although there is evidence of the influence of various aspects of Hellenistic culture in the New Testament, the religious presuppositions of the early Christians were formed and informed by the Scriptures of Israel and Jewish postbiblical literature. The New Testament is filled with language, content, perspectives, and categories taken from these texts. Like all early Christians, the New Testament authors read and interpreted the religious literature of Israel in light of their faith in Jesus and used citations, typology, and allusions to underscore and validate particular insights. Their methods of interpretation were already prominent in postexilic Israel. Thus, when they appealed to events and prophecies in Israel's past to explain Jesus or his significance in God's eschatological redemption of all, they continued an interpretive process found in the Old Testament itself. Some New Testament passages apply a promise–fulfillment scheme drawn from a Christian reading of God's promises to Israel. However, the message of the cross and resurrection of Jesus is more than an eschatological redemptive event in continuity with the Old Testament. Nothing in the religious texts of Israel makes the Christian fulfillment scheme obvious or necessary. There is discontinuity as well as continuity between the testaments. The Old Testament has meaning for both Jews and Christians apart from Christian interpretations. However, the New Testament cannot be fully understood without an understanding of the Old.

One distinctive feature of the New Testament is that these texts bear witness to the diversity in the early church. This diversity points to struggles within and among communities in developing an understanding of what is authentically Christian. However, within the contingencies there is significant coherence. While their coherence points to the fact that unity within diversity has always coexisted in the church, by establishing a canon, the church set limits on acceptable contingencies.

Regina A. Boisclair

NEW TESTAMENT CANON

The list of twenty-seven books by Christian authors that the church considers revelation, inspired by God, having a regulating value for faith and morals.

Before the end of the fourth century C.E., when the term "canon" came to be commonly used to designate both the list and the sacred qualities of texts on the list, most churches of the East and West accepted a twenty-seven-book New Testament. These twenty-seven books include four Gospels, one history, twenty-one "epistles" (although some are actually sermons or treatises), and one apocalypse. From patristic writings it is clear that these texts were chosen because: (1) they were considered of apostolic origins, (2) they had been preserved, (3) they were used throughout the church, and (4) their teachings conformed to the rule of faith. However, some extant variant lists and a few ancient texts of the Bible have more or less than twenty-seven books, indicating that the New Testament canon was not fully stabilized until the seventh century. The canons of either testament were not officially defined as such until the Council of Trent. The Roman Catholic, Orthodox, and Protestant Churches all follow the same New Testament canon.

The lists of canonical books served to establish the order in which the twenty-seven New Testament books are introduced in all Bibles. The canonical order is: Matthew, Mark, Luke, John, Acts of the Apostles, Romans, 1 Corinthians, 2 Corinthians, Galatians, Ephesians, Philippians, Colossians, 1 Thessalonians, 2 Thessalonians, 1 Timothy, 2 Timothy, Titus, Philemon, Hebrews, James, 1 Peter, 2 Peter, 1 John, 2 John, 3 John, Jude, and the book of Revelation.

The canonical texts are a selection among early Christian texts. Some that were not chosen belonged to heterodox groups that may have continued practices and social structures that were closer to the teachings of the historical Jesus or the primal communities than those that were accepted in the larger church. Some are writings of the apostolic fathers that were likely excluded only because they were either not known or used in a significant number of communities. All the early extant Christian writings, whether orthodox or heterodox, are of enormous significance to New Testament studies. They provide valuable clues to how traditions developed and changed as well as the varieties of early Christian insights.

Today, Scripture scholars recognize that usage was probably the most prominent factor in the selection of most of these particular texts. Chance, also very likely, had a role in the preservation of some less important letters like Philemon and Jude. Although these minor works were probably included because of their claim to apostolicity, it must be acknowledged that, apart from the undisputed letters of Paul (Romans, 1–2 Corinthians, Galatians, Philippians, 1 Thessalonians, Philemon), none of the remaining texts were written by an apostle. It is impossible to state that any texts were written by a companion of one of the apostles as had once been assumed of Mark and Luke. Today, apostolic origin can only be understood in the broad sense of teachings consistent with that of the apostles. Apostolic origins has become another way to speak of the core traditions known as the rule of faith.

Regina A. Boisclair

NEW TESTAMENT LETTERS

Of the twenty-seven documents comprising the canon of the New Testament, the twenty-one found between Acts and Revelation have the form of letters or epistles. Most of these are true letters, but Hebrews and 1 John are more like treatises made to seem like letters.

A standard format is found on the whole within the letters corresponding to the conventional letter writing of the time, although with some variations and modifications made due to the purposes of the Christian writers. The letters usually begin with a greeting that identifies the sender(s) and recipient(s). Then follows a prayer, most often in the form of a thanksgiving. Next, usually due to situations within the community being addressed, the body of the letter will discuss relevant aspects of Christian teaching or practice and may also comment on moral behavior. Details concerning practical matters, such as the sender's travel plans, are often mentioned as well. The letters conclude with advice and farewells.

The New Testament letters fall into two large groupings, with various sub-groupings. Fourteen of the twenty-one letters have traditionally been attributed to Paul and comprise the Pauline Corpus (although authorship of seven of these fourteen is called into question by many scholars). They are arranged in an order of more or less decreasing length from Romans to Philemon, with Hebrews added at the end. Four of these letters (Ephesians, Philippians, Colossians, and Philemon) are called the Captivity Letters since each indicates the author is in prison while writing. Three others (1 and 2 Timothy and Titus) are known as the Pastoral Epistles because they offer advice to pastors of Christian communities.

The other seven letters in the New Testament (James, 1 and 2 Peter, 1, 2, and 3 John, and Jude) that are found after the Pauline Corpus, as a group are known as the Catholic Epistles. Catholic, meaning "universal," refers in this context to the fact that most of these letters are addressed not to a single church or individual or the churches of one city or region, as the letters of the Pauline Corpus generally are, but rather are intended for the wider audience of the universal church.

Three of these letters, those attributed to John and closely related to the Gospel of John, belong to the Johannine Corpus. Like the letters of the Pauline Corpus, the Catholic epistles are also arranged in somewhat of a descending order of length, although the Johannine letters are grouped together and the epistle of Jude is placed at the end.

F. M. Gillman

See also JOHANNINE CORPUS; PAULINE CORPUS.

NICAEA, FIRST COUNCIL OF

In 325 Constantine summoned to Nicaea, the imperial capital, located in modern-day Turkey, the Christian bishops of the Roman Empire to settle doctrinal questions about the Son that the priest Arius had raised in his native Diocese of Alexandria. Arius held that both Scripture and reason required one to hold that the Son who became incarnate in Jesus was not God. For Arius the Logos/Son was the first creature created out of nothing by the Father. Thus, there was a moment when the Father existed in which the Logos/Son did not. Hence, the Logos/Son was not coeternal with the Father. Moreover, the Logos/Son could not share the divine, unbegotten nature of the Father since the Logos/Son was begotten by the Father. Arius believed the Father's begetting the Logos/Son was the same as creating the Logos/Son from nothing.

As a result, the council decreed that the Christian faith rightly stated that the Son was of the same substance (*homoousios*) as the Father, begotten, not created, and consubstantial with the Father. The council denied the Son was made from nothing, another *hypostasis* or *ousia* (essence). At this stage of the development of theological terminology, hypostasis and ousia are synonyms. By the time of the Second Council of Constantinople in 553, these terms will be differentiated: ousia will mean nature or essence and hypostasis will mean subsistence or person.

Herbert J. Ryan, S.J.

See also ARIANISM; CONSTANTINE I THE GREAT; CONSTANTINOPLE, SECOND COUNCIL OF; HOMOOUSIOS TO PATRI; HYPOSTASIS; LOGOS/WORD; OUSIA.

NICAEA, SECOND COUNCIL OF

Empress Irene convoked the last of the seven ecumenical councils of the early church on August 29, 784. The council was summoned to deal with the issue of iconoclasm. It met for the first time on August 1, 786, at Constantinople, in the presence of Emperor Constantine VI and his mother, Empress Irene. The proceedings were interrupted on August 17 by the violent entry of iconoclast soldiers into the Church of the Holy Apostles, and the council was adjourned until the arrival of reliable troops. It assembled again at Nicaea in the Church of Saint Sophia on September 24, 787, where the patriarch Tarasius of Constantinople presided at the sessions. In the seventh session of the council, the doctrinal definition approving the veneration of images was promulgated. The question at issue was whether it was proper for Christians to depict God, Jesus, and the saints in art works, and then to reverence these works of art. Some Christians in the Empire thought such activity superstitious at best and idolatrous at worst. The council decreed, however, that Christians may indeed venerate images, agreeing with the position Pope Hadrian I had outlined in his letter to Empress Irene. The council maintained that images are honored with a relative love, whereas absolute adoration (*latria*) is reserved to God alone. In veneration (*proskunesis*), the honor given to the image passes on to its prototype. Pope Hadrian I was informed about the council, and though he did not write a reply to Tarasius, he defended the council in 794 in correspondence with Charlemagne.

Herbert J. Ryan, S.J.

See also COUNCIL, ECUMENICAL; DULIA; HYPERDULIA; ICONOCLASTIC CONTROVERSY; LATRIA.

NICENE CREED

The text of the creedal formula popularly known as the Nicene Creed is actually the formula of faith adopted by the Council of Constantinople in 381. This Creed follows the outline of a statement of faith Christian communities clustered around Jerusalem or Antioch used in their baptismal liturgy. Two additions were made at the council to this original baptismal Creed. The term *homoousion* (consubstantial) was incorporated into the Creed to designate the relationship of the Son to the Father as the Council of Nicaea I in 325 taught. Moreover, further phrases were inserted into the Creed to express the Council of Constantinople's teaching regarding the full deity and consubstantiality of the Holy Spirit with the Father and Son.

In the fifth century, local churches throughout the Eastern Roman Empire incorporated the recitation of this Nicene-Constantinopolitan Creed into their baptismal and eucharistic liturgies. In the following century, the Latin-speaking churches of the West did the same. However, the Western churches, beginning with those of Spain and quickly followed by the local churches of France, Northern Italy, and Germany, added the phrase *Filioque* (and the Son) to this Creed. The Eastern churches protested this change in the Creed, and the church at Rome voiced serious objection to any alteration of the Creed. Only after several centuries did Rome accept the *Filioque* into the Creed. *Filioque* states the position of St. Augustine that the Holy Spirit "proceeds from the Father and the Son" (*Filioque*). The churches of the East did not follow St. Augustine's teaching on the Trinity. Since the original Greek text of the Creed was written decades before St. Augustine developed his trinitarian doctrine, the Greek text of this Creed makes no mention of the procession of the Holy Spirit from the Father and the Son (*Filioque*).

Herbert J. Ryan, s.j.

See also AUGUSTINE OF HIPPO; CONSTANTINOPLE, FIRST COUNCIL OF; CREED (SYMBOL OF FAITH); FILIOQUE; HOLY SPIRIT; HOMOOUSIOS TO PATRI; NICAEA, FIRST COUNCIL OF; PNEUMATOMACHIANS; TRINITY/ TRINITARIAN THEOLOGY/TRINITARIAN PROCESSIONS.

NICHIREN (1222–82)

Japanese Tendai Buddhist monk and founder of the Nichiren School (Nichiren Shoshu) that was based on the teachings of the *Lotus Sutra*. Nichiren was a major figure in the religious ferment of the Kamakura Period (1185–1333), claiming that the prevailing Buddhist schools of the period had lost sight of the true message of the Buddha as found in the *Lotus Sutra* and consequently were following false paths. Empowered by a vision in which he saw himself as the bodhisattva called to restore the dharma (truth) to the world during this degenerate age, his aim was to restore original Buddhism by launching a crusade to call the Japanese people back to the *Lotus Sutra*. He promoted an eschatological vision in which Japan, under the cosmic Buddha, "would usher in a new Buddhist age and be the home of a new historical Buddha"—it was the destiny of Japan to serve as a beacon for the rest of the world.

Nichiren Shoshu reflected a characteristically Japanese Buddhist sociopolitical orientation, and in time spawned a number of sects with a strong evangelical and nationalistic orientation. The most prominent of these in contemporary Japan is Soka Gakkai.

G. D. DeAngelis

See also BODHISATTVA; BUDDHISM; KAMAKURA PERIOD; LOTUS SUTRA; MAPPO; SOKA GAKKAI; TENDAI.

NICHOLAS OF CUSA (1401–64)

Niclas Krebs was born in the city of Kues (in Latin, *Cusa*) in Germany. He attended the universities of Heidelberg and Padua, graduating with a degree in canon law in 1423. Nicholas was teaching canon law in Cologne when he attended the Council of Basel on legal business in 1432. Nicholas, who had a reputation as a classical scholar, became a regular member of the council. He eventually disagreed with the Conciliarism of the council and became a papal envoy of Pope Eugene IV. Pope Nicholas V appointed Nicholas cardinal, and Nicholas became bishop of Brixen in 1450. Nicholas was instrumental in the short-lived reunion of the Eastern and Western Churches in 1437–8 and wrote numerous books on topics as diverse as church authority, geometry, geography, and mathematics. He is best known, however, for his book *De docta ignorantia* (*On Learned Ignorance*) where Nicholas argues that God is ultimately unknowable, and any ideas we have of God, no matter how necessary they may be, are certainly not descriptions of what God really is. Nicholas's theology continues to fascinate and influence theologians to the present day.

Gary Macy

See also APOPHATIC THEOLOGY; BASLE-FLORENCE-FERRARA (COUNCILS OF); CONCILIARISM; MEDIEVAL CHRISTIANITY (IN THE WEST); SCHISM, GREAT EASTERN.

NIEBUHR, H. RICHARD (1894–1962)

Son of a German Evangelical pastor, Missouri native H. Richard Niebuhr, like his brother Reinhold, was a strong critic and advocate of the connections between Christianity and modern culture in the United States. After graduating from Eden Theological Seminary and Yale, he became a professor of ethics, theology, and church history at Yale Divinity School in 1931. Through his writing, he articulated Barthian, neo-orthodox, and Christian realist theology in contrast to liberal Protestant thought. In *The Social Sources of Denominationalism* (1929), he argued that denominational divisions stemmed from the failure of Christianity to heal racial, ethnic, and class hatred. In *The Kingdom of God in America* (1937), he traced the development of the kingdom of God as a prophetic stance among Puritans and nineteenth-century evangelicals. In *Christ and Culture* (1951), he developed a typology through which to understand the relation of the church to its surrounding culture. Like his brother, H. Richard Niebuhr's greatest impact was in seminaries, where his work influenced generations of Protestant pastors.

Evelyn A. Kirkley

See also BARTH, KARL; EVANGELICAL THEOLOGY; NEO-ORTHODOX THEOLOGY; NIEBUHR, REINHOLD; PURITANISM.

NIEBUHR, REINHOLD (1892–1971)

Born in Missouri, son of a German Evangelical pastor, brother to H. Richard Niebuhr, Reinhold Niebuhr pioneered neo-orthodox theology in the United States. A graduate from Eden Theological Seminary and Yale, he began his career as a pastor in Detroit, where he confronted urban and immigrant poverty. In 1928 he joined the faculty at Union Theological Seminary in New York as professor of social ethics. In works such as *Moral Man and Immoral Society* (1932), *Reflections on the End of an Era* (1934), *The Nature and Destiny of Man* (1941–3), and *The Irony of American History* (1952), Niebuhr critiqued the overoptimism of liberal Protestant theology, reasserted the sovereignty of God, and argued for a new Christian realism by emphasizing sin, evil, and grace. Yet while he attacked liberalism and the Social Gospel, he was nonetheless shaped by it. Challenging American social, economic, and political institutions, he led a theological renewal in the seminaries by translating the neo-orthodox theology of Karl Barth for a U.S. context. While this new theology flourished in seminaries, it had little impact on people in the pew.

Evelyn A. Kirkley

See also BARTH, KARL; NEO-ORTHODOX THEOLOGY; NIEBUHR, H. RICHARD; SOCIAL GOSPEL.

NIETZSCHE, FRIEDRICH (1844–1900)

German philosopher. One of the most protean writers of the nineteenth century, Friedrich Nietzsche wrote on virtually every aspect of Western culture—the history of philosophy, ethics, aesthetics, democracy, music, tragedy, and religion —seeking to name and unmask the decay and sickness of both Western culture and European society. At the root of this decadence was a cultural Platonism that denigrated the world and change as inferior to eternity and changelessness. While having a relatively positive estimate of Jesus, in *The Antichrist* (1888) Nietzsche condemned Christianity as a "Platonism for the masses" that witnessed to a "slave morality" and was largely due to the "genius" of Paul the apostle. In the quasi-poetic *Thus Spake Zarathustra* (1883–5), he articulated a counterpoint to

the sick Platonism of the West (and Christianity) through the figure of Zarathustra and his full affirmation of the world ("a transvaluation of values"), culminating in Zarathustra's willing of "the eternal return of the same." Collapsing on a street in 1889, he died after eleven years of insanity. Nietzsche's work influenced both the existentialist movement and deconstructionism in the twentieth century.

J. A. Colombo

NIGHT CHANT
This beautiful ritual is frequently celebrated as part of the ceremonial system of the Navajo. As is the case with all the chantways, the aim of its presentation is for the healing and strengthening of an individual who has fallen out of harmony. It is patterned in its chant and sand painting on the story of Emergence and has the role of drawing the Holy People to assist in the ritual. It is a good example of the seriousness with which such chants are held, lasting nine days. During that time there is much going on; the patient is cleansed with emetics and ritual bathing, and constantly directed in prayerful attention to the powerful presence of the supernaturals who are sacramentally embodied in the painting. The goal is that of all Navajo life: restoration to beauty and harmony.

Kathleen Dugan

See also CHANT (NATIVE AMERICAN); HOLY PEOPLE; HOZHO.

NIHILISM
Originally, the term denoted a group of late nineteenth-century Russian anarchists that sought to topple the czarist regime through acts of terrorism and assassination without any proposal of what should replace that regime. More broadly, the term

has come to describe any philosophical position maintaining that reality, including the moral good, is unknowable. Given the radical cognitive and moral skepticism associated with nihilism, atheism is inevitably included within this concept. Schopenhauer, Nietzsche, Bakunin, and Camus are the most common figures (debatably) associated with nihilism.

J. A. Colombo

See also CAMUS, ALBERT; NIETZSCHE, FRIEDRICH; SCHOPENHAUER, ARTHUR.

NIHIL OBSTAT

See IMPRIMATUR.

NIHONGI

(Japanese, also *Nihon Shoki*, Chronicles of Japan). One of the two major classical texts (also *Kojiki*) of the Nara Period (710–84) completed around 720 C.E., containing myths, legends, and historical accounts centering on the Imperial Clan in Japan. It is very similar to the *Kojiki* in form and content, but in this text there is more of an emphasis on establishing the divine descent of Japan and her people and the proliferation of *kami* intimately related to the land and the people. In addition, the persistent theme of the characteristic Japanese love of nature as a combination of religious and aesthetic emotions is greatly nurtured. *Nihongi*, like the *Kojiki*, has also come to be considered a semi-sacred text.

G. D. DeAngelis

See also AMATERASU; IZANAGI; IZANAMI; KAMI; KOJIKI; SHINTO.

NIMAN KACHINA

This is the going-home dance that celebrates and bids farewell to the Hopi kachinas who have graciously dwelt with them during the growing season. At its end, in late July or August, the kachinas depart in a magnificent procession to return to their mountain home. The Hopi thank them and ask them to remember their intentions for the period in which they will be absent. It is a moving ritual that shows the close and loving relationship between the Hopi and their guardian spirits.

Kathleen Dugan

See also KACHINAS; RITUAL.

NINETY-FIVE THESES

Posted by Martin Luther on the door of the castle church in Wittenberg on October 31, 1517, these "theses" are considered by most historians to mark the beginning of the Reformation. Intended by Luther as theological theses or opinions to be debated and examined with other theologians, the principal topic they treated was the question of indulgences.

The practice of granting indulgences had developed in the medieval church in connection with the sacrament of penance. This sacrament was understood to include contrition or sorrow for sins, confession of sins, absolution of sins by a priest confessor, and satisfaction. "Satisfaction" meant some good work or action to be accomplished by the absolved sinner as a way of restoring a right relationship with God. Though in earlier centuries satisfaction had sometimes included long pilgrimages, severe fasts of bread and water, and other harsh or burdensome practices, by Luther's time such severity had been mitigated. An "indulgence" was a remission of satisfaction: the one to whom an indulgence was granted needed to perform little or no satisfaction.

Indulgences were authorized by the pope. By the end of the fifteenth century, both the pope and many theologians taught that indulgences were effective not only in this world but also for the souls in purgatory. Thus one could obtain an indulgence for the sake of one's mother or father or other family members and friends who, it was believed, were suffering in purgatory. Indulgences could be partial or plenary: a partial indulgence shortened the time a soul would otherwise need to spend in purgatory while a plenary indulgence allowed immediate access to heaven.

Indulgences were a significant source of revenue for the church. The present basilica of St. Peter in Rome was begun in the early sixteenth century; to help pay construction costs, the pope granted an indulgence to be preached in Germany. The Dominican friar Johann Tetzel took on this task and made the connection between payment and release from purgatory crude but unambiguous: "As the coin in the coffer clinks, so the soul from purgatory springs."

In his Ninety-Five Theses, Luther challenged not only the financial abuses that accompanied the granting of indulgences but also, indeed especially, the theological presuppositions that made indulgences possible.

Indulgences were inseparable from the late medieval cult of the saints. It was believed that the saints in heaven had gained more merit, while on earth, than was necessary for their own salvation. This superabundance of merit constituted a "treasury" upon which the church could draw, applying to needy sinners the merit of the saints in lieu of their own.

Luther challenged the very concept of merit that grounded the granting of indulgences; he also questioned the power and authority of the papacy. For Luther, the sole merit was the merit of Christ.

Salvation came through Christ alone, not some combination of Christ and supposed merit earned by individual Christians, be they considered saints or not. Moreover, the pope had erred when he presumed to govern purgatory or anything else beyond this world. Though in 1517 Luther had not yet altogether rejected papal authority, he argued that the papacy had gone too far in claiming for itself power over the dead.

If Luther's theological arguments were rejected by the Catholic Church of the sixteenth century, his criticism of financial abuses did not go entirely unheeded. Though the Council of Trent (1545–63) affirmed the practice of granting indulgences, it also condemned the methods of preachers such as Tetzel.

Thomas Worcester, S.J.

See also INDULGENCE; LUTHER, MARTIN; MERIT; PURGATORY; REFORMATION; SAINTS (CHRISTIAN), DEVOTION TO; SATISFACTION; TRENT, COUNCIL OF; WITTENBERG.

NIRGUNA BRAHMAN

In order to stress the utter transcendence of the ultimate reality, the Advaita Vedanta tradition of Hinduism distinguishes between two aspects of Brahman, the *nirguna* (unqualified, attributeless) and the *saguna* (qualified, with attributes). The attributes or qualities (*gunas*) denied in the nirguna concept include all the attributes typically associated with the Supreme Being, such as personhood, creative power, omniscience, love, grace, capacity to respond to prayer, and so on. Advaita Vedanta conceives all such qualities as limitations to the authentic transcendence and infinity of the Absolute, since they imply relativity and the exclusion of their opposites. Advaita therefore claims that the ultimate reality, the supreme or *para*-Brahman, is nirguna: beyond all limitation, utterly inconceivable by the human mind. The highest relative manifestation of that transcendent Absolute—the nirguna Brahman conditioned, as it were, by the power of maya—is the saguna, or qualified, Brahman. This, the penultimate reality, is the personal God, termed Ishvara (the Lord). Ishvara or the saguna Brahman, possessing all the attributes typically associated with a Supreme Being, is a loving, personal Deity in the fullest sense, except for being relegated to penultimacy. It is the latter feature of this conception of God that causes the saguna–nirguna distinction, as formulated by Advaita, to be stridently rejected by Vaishnava *bhakti* theologians such as Ramanuja, whose conception of deity is thoroughly personal.

Lance E. Nelson

See also ADVAITA VEDANTA; BHAKTI; GUNA; HINDUISM; MAYA; PRAKRITI; SHANKARA; VAISHNAVA; VISHISHTADVAITA VEDANTA.

NIRVANA

The state reached as the final goal of all Buddhists. The entire religion is oriented toward nirvana realization, as stated in an early text: "As the vast ocean, O monks, is impregnated with one flavor, the flavor of salt, so also, O monks, is my teaching and discipline impregnated with just one flavor, the flavor of emancipation."

The meaning of *nirvana* (Pali, *nibbana*) is based on the Sanskrit verb meaning "to cool by blowing" and refers to one who has "cooled" the feverish *kleshas* ("hindrances"; "poisons")—greed, hatred, delusion—that create karma and bind the individual in samsara, the world of rebirth and suffering. Arahants and Buddhas share this common state that both men and women can attain.

Buddhists can reach nirvana through the cultivation of *prajna* ("insight") via moral practice and meditation; the person thus lives on in the state referred to, in Pali as the irreversible *kilesa–nibbana* ("nirvana in principle"). (Buddhist salvation is also referred to as "Enlightenment" because this fullness of prajna eliminates ignorance and clears the mind to see reality clearly.) The state an Arahant or Buddha achieves at death, referred to as *Parinirvana* ("Complete nirvana"), although said, strictly speaking, to be beyond conception, has been described in negative and positive terms in the early texts: a realm where there is neither sun nor moon, coming or going; but also to be a realm that is tranquil, pure, and deathless. Most of the early Abhidharma schools identified nirvana as the only permanent reality in the cosmos. It is not, as with early Western interpreters, seen as "annihilation," an extreme position rejected by the Buddha.

In the Mahayana philosophical schools, nirvana remains as the highest goal, and meditation remained the essential practice, although its definition was brought "down the earth" in the famous dictum of Madhyamaka sage Nagarjuna: "There is not the merest difference between samsara and nirvana." Ultimately, nirvana is beyond all conditions, including "otherness." It is through the understanding of reality as constructed with no-thing-ness (*shunyata*) that one is released from all rebirth bondage. The emphasis on interdependence in Mahayana thought led their analysts to view the Sthavira schools' emphasis on the individual pursuit of nirvana as "selfish" and based upon ignorance of the Buddha's complete teaching. The bodhisattva replaces the

Arahant as the Mahayana ideal in recognizing the inseparability of personal and universal enlightenment; it also has held that the laity as well as monks could attain nirvana.

Todd T. Lewis

See also ARAHANT; BODHI; BUDDHA; PRAJNA.

NOBLE EIGHTFOLD PATH

Among the many doctrinal lists compiled to describe the Buddhist path, "The Eightfold Path" has been the most widely disseminated early summary compilation reputedly expounded by the Buddha in his first sermon. The Eightfold Path is in fact the fourth element in the "Four Noble Truths," the formula that sets forth the human responses to the natural truths of human existence: life as suffering and unsatisfactory (TRUTH ONE); the cause of suffering is craving (*trishna*; Pali, *tanha*) for sensual existence, becoming, and non-becoming (TRUTH TWO); that cessation from this state of craving and nirvana is possible (TRUTH THREE); and that the Eightfold Path is the means of achieving this cessation in the realization of nirvana.

The usual order of the Eightfold Path is: 1. Right Views, especially of the Noble Truths; 2. Right Thought that is shaped by detachment from hatred, cruelty; 3. Right Speech that refrains from falsehood, gossip, frivolity; 4. Right Action, defined negatively as action free of killing, stealing, harming; 5. Right Livelihood that does not involve earning a living via astrology, magic spells, or careers that involve killing; 6. Right Effort to clear and calm the mind; 7. Right Mindfulness refers to the distinctive form of Buddhist meditation that observes dispassionately the mind and body to cultivate detach-

ment; and 8. Right Concentration, another form of meditation that cultivates the mastery of trance states.

An early and important arrangement of the Eightfold Path was made according to another ancient schema, the three central categories of Buddhist practice:

Shila ("Morality") entails Speech, Action, Morality.

Dhyana ("Meditation") entails Effort, Mindfulness, Concentration.

Prajna ("Insight" or "Wisdom") entails Understanding and Thought.

The Theravadin commentator Buddhaghosa organized his entire summary of Buddhism based upon this schema; he refers to the two legs of practice as Morality and Meditation, upon which the body of salvific Insight stands. Another interpretation of the Eightfold Path universally accepted in the Buddhist schools emphasizes that moral progress is the essential foundation for successful meditation and that the measure of successful meditation is the awakening and deepening of prajna.

In the Mahayana schools, the Eightfold Path schema was reshaped into the six or (later) ten *paramitas* ("perfections") that are more specific benchmarks guiding the bodhisattva's progress.

Todd T. Lewis

See also ARAHANT; BODHI; BODHISATTVA; BUDDHAGHOSA; MERIT (PUNYA); PARAMITA; PRAJNA; SHILA; TRUTHS, FOUR NOBLE; VIPASHYANA/VIPASSANA.

NOMBRE DE DIOS MISSION

Name of the oldest permanent Christian (Roman Catholic) church and mission in what is now the United States. It was established just outside the colonial city limits of St. Augustine (Florida), although today the mission is within the city itself. St. Augustine and its mission were established in 1565 by Pedro Menéndez de Avilés, as well as the city's first parish—the oldest, permanent parish in the United States. The parish's first pastor was Fr. Martín López de Mendoza y Grajales.

Orlando Espín

See also LATINO CATHOLICISM; MISSIONARIES; MISSIONS; PARISH; VARELA, FELIX.

NOMINALISM

Nominalism is the philosophical position that holds that only individuals really exist and that universal concepts are mental constructs. The name first arose in the late twelfth and early thirteenth centuries to refer to those, like Abelard and his teacher Roscelin, who opposed the Platonic position that universals were real (that is,"realism"). A stronger form of nominalism appeared in writing of the Franciscan philosopher and theologian William of Ockham (about 1285–1347). Although few theologians followed Ockham's theology completely, a modified nominalism continued to find support among theologians in both Oxford and Paris. With the revival of the modified realism of earlier thirteenth-century theologians like Thomas Aquinas, theological faculties were split between the *via antiqua* (old way) of the realists and the *via moderna* (new way) of the nominalists. Since nominalists would deny that universal concepts exist per se, then they would also tend to deny that there is a universal basis for morality or that a natural theology is possible. One result of nominalism, then, can be a reliance on faith alone rather than on reason as well in theological issues.

Gary Macy

See also ABELARD, PETER; AQUINAS, THOMAS, ST.; MEDIEVAL CHRISTIANITY (IN THE WEST); OCKHAM, WILLIAM OF; SCHOLASTICISM.

NON-CHALCEDONIAN CHURCHES

General name applicable to the Eastern Churches that do not accept key doctrinal decisions of the Council of Chalcedon, of 451 C.E., especially those conciliar teachings that refer to the person and natures of the Christ. Doctrinally, these churches would be considered Monophysite and Nestorian. Furthermore, these churches do not accept some other doctrines of the first seven ecumenical councils of undivided Christianity. Many non-Chalcedonian Christians are members of the Ancient Churches of the East. There are approximately eleven million Christians throughout the world who belong to these Eastern Churches. Among the Western Christian Churches, a number of reformed, fundamentalist, and Pentecostal communities are non-Chalcedonian.

Orlando Espín

See also ANCIENT CHURCHES OF THE EAST; APOSTOLIC FATHERS; CATHOLIC TRADITION; CHALCEDON, COUNCIL OF; CHALCEDONIAN CHRISTIANS; CHRISTOLOGY; COUNCIL, ECUMENICAL; EASTERN CATHOLIC CHURCHES; EPHESUS, COUNCIL OF; FATHERS OF THE CHURCH; MONOPHYSITISM; NESTORIANISM; NESTORIUS; ORIENTAL CHURCHES; ORTHODOX CHURCHES; ROMAN CATHOLIC CHURCH.

NONDUALISM/NONDUALISTIC

A mode of thought characteristic especially of certain schools of Hinduism, Buddhism, and Taoism, nondualism (Sanskrit, *advaita*, *advaya*) teaches that the multiplicity of the universe is reducible to one essential reality.

Sanskrit does have a term (*aikya*) that suggests the absolute oneness of monism, so the negative form nondualism (*a-dvaita*) would seem to be preferred, at least by some Indian thinkers, in order to evoke the mystery of a practically experienced duality that is at the same time somehow, in truth, "not-dual." The nonduality inheres between subject (the self) and its object (the world), and also between the ultimate reality (Brahman, the Buddha-nature, and so forth) and the self, between the ultimate reality and the world (as in the famous Buddhist identification of nirvana and samsara), between selves, and between the multiple entities of the world. This is not merely speculative philosophy, however; Hindus, Buddhists, and Taoists have forms of practical spirituality (yoga, zazen, and so on) that are said to lead to an experiential overcoming of dualistic awareness. This can entail the vivid realization that the things of the world are false projections, not really there, or that they are there, but are somehow not separate from the self. Alternately, both "self" and "things" can be experienced as not other than the ultimate reality. Sometimes the realization is expressed in terms of utter loss of the self in the great mystery of the world. There are thus several kinds of nondualism. Some, like Advaita Vedanta, aim at complete transcendence of any experience of multiplicity; others, like certain Hindu and Buddhist Tantric schools, would rather transform our vision of reality, teaching that it is not the "things" of the world, or the world itself, that are false, but just our way of perceiving them. The Kashmir Shaivism of Abhinavagupta (eleventh century) is an interesting example, within Hinduism, of a dynamic, explicitly *theistic* form of nondualism.

Lance E. Nelson

See also ADVAITA; ADVAITA VEDANTA; BUDDHISM; MADHYAMAKA/MADYAMIKA SCHOOL; MAHAYANA BUDDHISM; SHAIVA; SHUNYATA/SUNYA/SHUNYA; TANTRA; TANTRIC BUDDHISM; TANTRIC HINDUISM; YOGACARA; ZEN.

NORITO

(Japanese, ritual prayer). A form of prayer used in Shinto services. These are liturgical prayers addressed to *kami* consisting of words of praise, petition, and thanksgiving, to be recited by the priest (*guji*). Norito originally referred to the human words addressed to the kami as well as the kamis' words spoken to humans, and were collected in the tenth-century C.E. ritual text *Engi-Shiki* (compilation of Shinto traditions). These norito found in the *Engi-Shiki* served for centuries as the models of prayers in all Shinto shrines. While still used today by Shinto priests, there is some flexibility in developing new prayers.

G. D. DeAngelis

See also KAGURA; KAMI; SHINTO; SHRINE.

NORMATIVE (IN CHRISTIANITY)

Beliefs, texts, practices, and various traditions that form an integral and constitutive part of a particular religion. Essential Christian beliefs are elaborated in, but not reduced to, the apostolic preaching contained in the New Testament; in the Nicene-Constantinopolitan Creed, regularly recited in the context of worship in many Christian communities; and in the teachings of ecumenical councils, especially the first seven councils between the fourth to eighth centuries C.E. that are recognized by both Catholic and Eastern Orthodox Christians. Catholic Christianity would also include infallible papal teachings, papal encyclicals, bishops' pastoral letters, and the pronouncements of the ordinary magisterium or teaching office of the church.

Vatican II (1962–5) in the document *Unitatis Redintegratio* developed the theological principle of the "hierarchy of truths" to interpret the order of Christian teachings that are of central and relative importance to the normative foundations of Christian faith (for example, Trinity, christology, salvation). All truths are to be believed, but all truths do not carry the same theological importance for the central Gospel message of salvation offered by God in Christ through the Holy Spirit—a claim which thereby promotes ecumenical dialogues and movements among the diversity of Christian churches. Taking a more postmodern approach, more contemporary U.S. Catholic and Protestant theologians contend that the claim "Jesus saves" signifies a norm of Christian identity, but that there is a wide range of Christian diversity about who Jesus is, how he saves, and what is involved in salvation, as evidenced in the history of global Christian thought and practice.

In outlining a method for doing theology or ongoing critical and faith-based inquiry into ultimate questions about God and about human life in reference to God, theologians often distinguish between sources and norms of theological claims. A Christian theological claim is articulated based on certain sources (revelation, Scriptures, traditions, experiences) and is adjudicated in light of certain norms or central criteria drawn from those sources. Modern and contemporary Christian theology varies widely in its use and identification of theological sources and norms. For example, neoorthodox theology represented by the German Protestant Reformed theologian

Karl Barth (d. 1968) considered theology primarily a matter of and for the whole church, and thus drew on the Gospel, sacraments, preaching, and other pastoral sources that attest to the Word of God. For Barth, theology investigates the consistency of the church's beliefs and practices with the Word of God. Thus, the Word of God, revealed primarily but not only in Scripture and in Christ, functions as both the source and norm of theological claims. By contrast, liberal Protestant theology and later twentieth-century Catholic theology, represented respectively by German Protestant theologian Paul Tillich (d. 1965) and Catholic theologian and philosopher David Tracy (b. 1939), use a method of correlation that formulates theological claims in light of Scripture, tradition, and experience. Tillich argued that theology correlated major existential questions of human experience (anxiety, finitude, death) with the answers to those questions in the Christian message. While a correlational theology attempts to explain Christian faith in light of existential questions, and thus make Christian claims tenable for modern times and peoples, it still privileges as a norm the Christian message over against the sources of existential questions drawn from human experience. Tracy suggests critical correlation as an alternative method that enables the mutual critical interrelation of questions and answers found in Scripture and tradition on the one hand and in everyday human experience on the other. In sum, more contemporary Catholic theology together with a growing body of global scholarship on contextual theologies emphasize human experience as both a source and norm of theological reflection.

Liberationist and feminist theologians continue this emphasis on experience alongside Scripture and tradition as a source and norm of theological reflection, but focus on the particularities rather than on the alleged existential universalities of human experience that have often been shaped by androcentric, patriarchal Euro-American theologies that assimilated human experience under one uniform, universal ideal. For example, liberationist theologies stress praxis as a theological source and norm, or the daily lived struggles for justice, for survival, for well-being, that take place "from below," that is, from particular social locations of oppressed peoples and from solidarity with oppressed peoples. Feminist theologies, broadly conceived, privilege a wide range of women's experiences (of race, gender, class, sexuality, ability, and age as mediated through bodily, social, economic, political, cultural, personal, communal, psychological, spiritual, aesthetic, and so on, realities) as a source and norm for critical and constructive theological reflection. The appeal to critical reflection on Scripture, tradition, and experience as sources and norms of theological claims has led to the formulation of at least two concurrent criteria for making and defending theological claims, namely appropriateness, or whether a claim fits with inherited Christian Scriptures, teachings, and traditions, and adequacy, or whether a claim is intelligible for our time and is applicable especially but not exclusively to oppressed, marginated, and suffering peoples.

Rosemary P. Carbine

NORTHERN BUDDHISM

A term usually used to make modern geographic reference to Mahayana Buddhism in contrast to Theravada as "Southern Buddhism." Northern Buddhism includes the countries and regions known as Tibet, Central Asia, Nepal, China, Mongolia, Korea, and Japan. While this designation is true in relating the overall layout of Asia in the early modern period, it can mislead on two fronts: Theravada Buddhism was introduced into Central Asia, China, and Japan, and enjoyed many centuries of development "in the north" even though in the eventual minority; Mahayana Buddhism likewise was found in every region of the Buddhist world in earlier historical periods in Sri Lanka and Southeast Asia.

Todd T. Lewis

See also BUDDHISM; MAHAYANA BUDDHISM; TANTRIC BUDDHISM.

NOSTRA AETATE

This document, The Declaration on the Relationship of the Church to Non-Christian Religions, commonly known as Nostra Aetate (from the first two words of the Latin text meaning "In this age of ours"), was approved by the bishops of the Second Vatican Council on October 28, 1965. It represents a major step in the development of Catholic teaching about other religions. Prior to Vatican II, the church had made a clear distinction between Christianity and other faiths, finding the latter inadequate vehicles for eternal salvation. Furthermore, the idea that Jews are a "deicide people" (having put Christ to death) had taken hold among some Catholics over the centuries. The church itself had not spoken clearly against anti-Semitism. In this relatively short declaration, the council dealt with specific questions omitted from its earlier Decree on Ecumenism, Redingratio Unitatis, approved in 1964. Now the council declared that all peoples form "but one community" and "stem from the one stock which

God created to people the entire earth" (no. 1). They also share "a common destiny, namely God" (no. 1). On this basis, then, the church "rejects nothing of what is true and holy" in other religions (no. 2). In treating (in this order) Hinduism, Islam, and Judaism in particular, the council urges Christians to "witness to their own faith and way of life" but also to "acknowledge, preserve, and encourage the spiritual and moral truths found among non-Christians" as well as the values in their society and culture (no. 2). The church explicitly "deplores all hatreds, persecutions, and displays of anti-semitism leveled at any time or from any source against the Jews" (no. 4). Such pronouncements reflect the history of the twentieth-century (the Holocaust in particular), theological developments prior to the council (especially in the area of salvation theory), and the plea of Pope John XXIII to all peoples to "forget the past" and to make a sincere effort to achieve mutual understanding. *Nostra Aetate* does not spell out the practical steps that may lead to such understanding, nor does it resolve important theoretical questions (such as the unique role of Christ in salvation history). Still, the declaration represents a genuine call for interreligious dialogue unprecedented in Catholic history.

James B. Nickoloff

See also REDINGRATIO UNITATIS; VATICAN, SECOND COUNCIL OF THE.

NOTES OF THE CHURCH

In the Nicene Creed, adopted by the Council of Constantinople in 381 C.E., Christians profess their faith in "one, holy, Catholic, and apostolic church." These four "notes," or marks, of the church were reaffirmed at the Councils of Ephesus (431 C.E.) and Chalcedon (451 C.E.). When disputes about the church's identity and mission have divided Christians, or even caused schism, the notes have served as means of identifying the true church of Christ. The church's oneness (its fundamental unity), holiness (derived from God's promise of fidelity to the church), catholicity (the universality of God's offer of salvation through the church), and apostolicity (the continuity of the church's ministry and/or teaching with those of the original apostles) are believed to preserve its identity.

James B. Nickoloff

See also APOSTOLICITY; CATHOLICITY; HOLINESS; UNITY.

NOTH, MARTIN (1902–68)

Noth was one of the most influential biblical scholars of the twentieth century. He taught at the Universities of Leipzig, Königsberg, and Bonn. From 1965 until his death, he directed the Institute for Holy Land Studies in Jerusalem. Noth is best known for two of his books: (1) *The History of Israel* (German 1950; English 1958) and (2) *A History of Pentateuchal Traditions* (German 1948; English 1971), and two of his theories. He argued that "Israel came into being as an amphictyony of tribes which followed the invasion of ancient Palestine by some of the tribes"; he thought that reliable historical information concerning the prehistory of Israel before that point did not exist; he developed the hypothesis of the Deuteronomistic History that states that the book of Deuteronomy served as the introduction to a unified history of Israel in the land composed during the Babylonian Exile by a single writer using pre-existing material. The Deuteronomistic History (Dtr) is made up of Deuteronomy,

Joshua, Judges, 1 and 2 Samuel, and 1 and 2 Kings. He further argued that the narratives found in Joshua concerning the conquest of the land had replaced J and E accounts of the entry into the land. Revisions of this theory are used today by most scholars in the field.

Russell Fuller

See also DEUTERONOMIC HISTORY; DEUTERONOMIC THEOLOGY.

NOVATIANISM

The teachings of the schismatic community founded by Novatian of Rome. Novatian and his followers desired a pure church of martyrs and prophets under the guidance of the Holy Spirit. Salvation was obtained through faith, but also through austerity of life. The Novatianists separated to form their own church rather than accept back into the community those members who had given up the faith during the Decian persecutions. They required rebaptism of anyone who entered their church from the orthodox community. In many ways, the Novatianists resembled the later Donatist communities. The movement spread from Rome to Carthage and hence to the rest of North Africa and beyond. There is evidence that Novatianist communities existed into the seventh century.

Gary Macy

See also CORNELIUS OF ROME; CYPRIAN OF CARTHAGE; DONATISM; NOVATIAN OF ROME; PERSECUTION (IN CHRISTIANITY).

NOVATIAN OF ROME

The facts of Novatian's life are uncertain, but it seems he was a learned Roman who was baptized during a grave illness. Upon recovery, he lived as a hermit until the middle of the third century, when he was ordained a presbyter of the Roman church. In 251, when he was bypassed for the office of *episkopos* of Rome, Novatian found three Italian bishops who would ordain him to this office, and, based on this ordination, Novatian started his own rival community in Rome. Novatian refused to allow those who had fallen away during the Decian persecution any forgiveness or reentry into the community. Novatian called for a pure church of the saved and sent his follower Maximus to Carthage to spread his views. From there, the Novatian church spread rapidly. The Roman community lasted at least into the fourth century when Celestine I expelled them from the city. Novatian was a skilled theologian and several of writings survive, the best known being his treatise *On the Trinity*.

Gary Macy

See also CORNELIUS OF ROME; CYPRIAN OF CARTHAGE; NOVATIANISM; PERSECUTION (IN CHRISTIANITY).

NOVENA

In Western Catholic tradition, this term refers to a period of nine consecutive days (or weeks) dedicated to either public or private prayer. The practice was first associated with the nine days of prayer immediately following someone's death, as it is still done in many places. However, the term "novena" is more frequently used in reference to a more modern custom that began in the seventeenth century, usually involving a set prayer (perhaps accompanied by other devotional practices) repeated once for each of nine consecutive days, seeking a specific favor from God. Quite often the nine daily prayers are addressed to Mary or one of the saints, asking these to beg God for the favor.

Orlando Espín

See also CATHOLIC TRADITION;
DEVOTIONS; MARIAN DEVOTIONS;
MARIOLOGY; POPULAR CATHOLICISM;
PRAYER; SAINTS (CHRISTIAN), DEVO-
TION TO.

NOVICE

Literally, a "novice" is a person who is new to something, or inexperienced. In religious life, a novice is someone who has been formally accepted as a candidate for admission to a religious community. The novice ordinarily wears the garb of the community (if there is a habit), but it is understood that a novice is someone whose religious calling is being tested to make sure (1) that the desire to be a religious comes from the Spirit and (2) that the individual possesses the necessary maturity and emotional stability to undertake the commitment involved in religious profession. The novice, then, is on probation (normally for a period of one year) and may freely leave the community (or be asked to leave) should it become clear that God is not calling the individual to religious life.

William Reiser, S.J.

See also FORMATION; NOVITIATE;
VOWS (RELIGIOUS).

NOVITIATE

The term used to designate the program or process through which individuals are introduced to the fundamentals of religious life and to the spirit and history of a particular religious community, under the direction of a master or mistress of novices. The novitiate ordinarily lasts a year, although in the case of Jesuits it lasts two years, and with the Trappists it lasts two years after a six-month period as a "postulant." (A postulant is someone awaiting admission to the novitiate program, during which time the person is screened for psychological health and emotional maturity, helped with spiritual direction, and prepared for the lifestyle of a religious). Each religious community designs its novitiate program in accordance with the spirit and overall aims of its institute or constitutions. Thus the novitiate training of a community that is strictly contemplative will be different from a community engaged in various works such as education, parishes, preaching, writing, foreign missions, care of the sick, and so forth.

William Reiser, S.J.

See also NOVICE; ORDERS, RELIGIOUS.

NUMINOUS

A term coined by Rudolf Otto (see his *The Idea of the Holy*, 1917), referring to the "totally Other." Otto claimed that it points to the one foundation of all religious and spiritual beliefs, realities, and experiences. He explained the Numinous as the *mysterium tremendum et fascinans* (the Mystery both awesome and fascinating).

Orlando Espín

See also GOD; MYSTERY; OTTO, RUDOLF.

NUN

A nun is a woman religious, that is, someone living under the vows of poverty, chastity, and obedience, and residing in a convent or monastery. The church's 1983 Code of Canon Law does not define the term more precisely, as the previous Code had done. Formerly, nuns were often distinguished from sisters in terms of solemn and simple vows. Among those communities whose constitutions continue to define their members as nuns, rules of cloister apply (Can. 667, par. 3). Writers today frequently employ the term "women religious" in place of nun and sister.

William Reiser, s.j.

See also CLOISTER; CONVENT/CONVENTUAL.

NUNCIO

A diplomatic representative of the Vatican, equivalent to an ambassador in rank and function, accredited to civil governments with which the Vatican has diplomatic relations. A nuncio also acts as liaison between the See of Rome and the bishops of the nation where the nuncio is accredited. Traditionally, nuncios were considered the honorary heads (the "deans") of the corps of diplomatic representatives in a nation's capital, but where this precedence was not recognized, they were called "pro-nuncios." An "apostolic delegate" is similar to a nuncio, except that his status is ecclesiastical, and is not formally recognized as a diplomat by the government of the nation to which he is accredited. The Vatican diplomatic corps is the oldest in western Europe.

Orlando Espín

See also VATICAN.

NYGREN, ANDERS (1890–1978)

A systematic theologian and major representative of the (Lutheran) Lundensian School that sought to establish a scientific method for theological discourse. Born in Gothenburg, Sweden, and educated at the University of Lund (Teol. Kand., 1912; Teol. lic., 1921; Teol. Dr., 1923), Nygren served on the faculty of the same university until 1948 when he became bishop of the (Lutheran) Diocese of Lund, 1948–58. Between 1947–52, Nygren was president of the Lutheran World Federation. He served on the Central Committee of the World Council of Churches (1948–54) and chaired its Faith and Order Commission (1953–63).

Nygren was one of the major proponents of "motif research" that examines how meaning changes in different contexts. His major work, *Agape and Eros*, contrasts the human search for love in Hellenism and Judaism (*eros*) with the love God wills for humanity as understood in early Christianity (*agapē*), and the medieval synthesis (*caritas*), which he credits to Augustine. Although his work is now considered a Lutheran apologetic that often distorts classical, Jewish, and Catholic thought, his recognition that "context" has a significant hermeneutical impact on ideas, continues to have enormous influence. He was most read during the mid-twentieth century, when he laid an important foundation for Protestant entrance into intra-Christian and interreligious dialogue.

Regina A. Boisclair

See also CONTEXTUAL THEOLOGY; METHOD IN THEOLOGY.

O

OBEDIENCE

The third of the three evangelical counsels, obedience refers to the vow taken by religious to follow the will of a superior. Among the desert Christians of the third, fourth, and fifth centuries, obedience was highly esteemed because of its connection with humility, and without humility there could be no growth in the life of the spirit. Indeed, the stories and legends from the desert reveal countless examples of individuals being asked by one holier and wiser (though not necessarily "smarter") to perform obviously foolish actions, with astonishing results when orders were carried out! The deeper issue always involved pride, the traps of self-deception, lack of trust, or the need to learn that God's foolishness is wiser than human wisdom (1 Cor 1:25). Voluntary obedience to a religious superior or one's community also enables coordination of apostolic effort and the tranquil arrangement of common life. Sometimes religious obedience is presented in cultic imagery as a kind of sacrifice, as in the letter to the Hebrews (see Heb 5:8; 10:5-10).

But evangelical obedience is modeled after the practice of Jesus, as revealed in the Gospels. For Jesus, the will of God was to be honored and followed at all times, as we see in the Lord's Prayer (Matt 6:10) and again in Gethsemani (Mark 14:36). In this regard, Jesus' attitude was that of a true son of Israel (see Deut 6:4-9). What is significant about Jesus' obedience is not his unquestioning submission to God's will (we do not know whether God's will was always clear to him, or whether Jesus ever "questioned" God), but his complete and unswerving dedication to what he referred to as the kingdom of God. Obedience literally means a radical listening: in this case, a desire to be as attentive as possible to the word of God and a readiness to put that word into practice. That Jesus obeyed God goes without saying, for he was a man of faith. What distinguished his obedience, however, was his willingness to put himself completely at the service of the kingdom.

William Reiser, S.J.

See also CHASTITY; COUNSELS (OF PERFECTION); POVERTY; VOWS (RELIGIOUS).

OBEDIENTIAL POTENCY

Obediential potency is a term used in fundamental theology to explain the human person's inherent openness to revelation and to relationship with God. The word "potency" or "potential" indicates the receptive or passive character of the disposition for a relationship humanity cannot initiate. The word "obediential" notes the supernatural and gratuitous character of revelation and grace that human beings receive as a gift. The assertion of the obediential potency is a Catholic explanation of the human disposition for a relationship with God. Already recognized in the writings of the fathers of the church, the phrase was coined by Thomas Aquinas. The conviction it expresses about the inherent human orientation to God grounds the Catholic commitment to the possibility of natural knowledge of God and of the theological use of the *analogia entis*. In contrast to this view, Reformed theology generally asserts a greater rift between Creator and creature and emphasizes the divine initiative in revelation over the human disposition for it.

Patricia Plovanich

See also ANALOGIA ENTIS (ANALOGY OF BEING); ANALOGIA FIDEI (ANALOGY OF FAITH).

OCHINO, BERNARDINO (1487–1564)

Born in Siena, Italy, Ochino was perhaps the most spectacular example of an Italian clergyman who rejected the Roman Catholic Church and adopted the Protestant Reformation. By the sixteenth century, the Franciscan Order was divided into several branches. Ochino first joined one branch of the order, then left it to join the newest branch, the Capuchins. The Capuchins were devoted to restoration of the original ideals of St. Francis of Assisi and to active ministry, preaching in particular. Vicar general of the Capuchins from 1538, Ochino came in contact with the ideas of Peter Martyr Vermigli, an Italian Augustinian friar favorable to the Reformation in Zurich and Strasbourg. Ochino left the Capuchins and Italy in 1541; he went to Geneva, and then spent the rest of his life working for the Reformation in various countries, England and Poland among them.

Thomas Worcester, S.J.

See also FRANCISCANS; PETER MARTYR (REFORMER); REFORMATION.

OCKHAM, WILLIAM OF (1285?–1347)

William entered the Franciscan Order at an early age and studied in London before going to Oxford around 1317. From about 1320 to 1324, William taught in a Franciscan school, probably in London. During this period, he wrote most of his philosophical and theological works. In 1324 he was called to the papal court at Avignon in order to answer charges of heresy. He was there four years while his case was being investigated. In the end, the charges were dropped, but while in Avignon, William became convinced, along with the minister general of the Franciscans, Michael Cesena, that the Pope, John XXII, was a heretic for his views on the poverty of Jesus and his disciples. When the Pope found out, William and Michael had to flee for safety to the Emperor, Louis IV. William spent the rest of life under the protection of the emperor and wrote vehemently against the Pope and in favor of a reform of the church. William was one of the most brilliant and influential medieval thinkers. His philosophy is considered to be the most important example of late medieval nominalism, and had a great influence on later thinkers. William's theology built on that of his predecessor, the Franciscan, Duns Scotus.

Gary Macy

See also DUNS SCOTUS, JOHN; FRANCIS-
CANS; HERESY; JOHN XXII, POPE;
MARSIGLIO OF PADUA; MEDIEVAL CHRIS-
TIANITY (IN THE WEST); SPIRITUAL
FRANCISCANS.

OCTAVE, LITURGICAL

From the Latin *octavus*, "eighth." The prolonging of a liturgical feast for eight days,
beginning with and including the feast
itself. The final day of the festival period
is also called the "octave" or the "octave
day." Prior to the revision of the liturgical
calendar in 1970, a number of feasts had
octaves. Now, only Easter and Christmas
have them. The liturgy during the Easter
Octave focuses on Christ's movement
from life through death to glory, and on
those who were initiated at the Easter
Vigil. This octave originated in the fourth
century as a period called mystagogy,
during which the newly baptized were
instructed further in the Christian life
and given an explanation of the initiatory
ceremonies they had undergone. The
Octave of Christmas does not have such
a uniform focus, and even includes the
diverse feasts of St. Stephen, St. John, and
the Holy Innocents.

Patrick L. Malloy

See also CHRISTMAS; EASTER.

OCTOGESIMA ADVENIENS

On May 14, 1971, Pope Paul VI issued the
document "A Call to Action," more commonly known by the first two words of
the Latin text, *Octogesima Adveniens* ("The
eightieth anniversary"), on the anniversary of Pope Leo XIII's encyclical on "The
Condition of Labor" (*Rerum Novarum*,
1891). Addressed to the whole church,
Paul VI's apostolic letter recalls concerns
treated in earlier papal letters (such as the
condition of workers, social and economic

inequities, and the destitution of millions
of poor people) and takes up new issues
raised for humanity—and thus for the
church that seeks to be of service in the
quest for human fulfillment—by massive
urbanization, the alienation of youth, the
demands by women for equality, environmental destruction, emigration, the power
of the mass media, uncritically accepted
political ideologies, and the complexities
of political responsibility. The Pope affirms
the legitimacy of the twin aspirations of
human beings to equality and to participation in society. The Pope also asserts
the Gospel requirement of "preferential
respect due to the poor and the special
attention they have in society" (no. 23).
Thus *Octogesima Adveniens* provides one
of the earliest papal references to what
later became known as the church's
"preferential option for the poor." Within
the threefold framework of concern for
equality and participation and priority
for the poor, the Pope examines the two
leading ideologies of the day, Marxism
and liberalism, and the socioeconomic
systems to which they give rise (socialism
and capitalism), and finds both lacking
from the perspective of Christian faith.
Though he distinguishes (a) the unselfish
aspiration of socialists for a just society
from (b) Marxist political movements in
history and (c) a Marxist ideology claiming to give a complete picture of human
beings, the Pope warns Christians attracted to socialism to exercise careful
judgment in order to avoid totalitarian
thinking and violent action. At the same
time he criticizes the very root of philosophical liberalism, namely, the "erroneous affirmation of the autonomy of the
individual" (no. 35) without concern for
the common good (no. 23). The Pope also
notes the ambiguity of the modern
sciences, natural and human: while they

provide hitherto unavailable knowledge about human beings and the means to build a new society, they also bring about ambiguous changes for humanity. Furthermore, the sciences do not—and cannot—answer the question about "what sort of persons" we wish to be (nos. 39–40). Faced with these momentous challenges, and acknowledging the pluralism of legitimate options, the Pope urges Christians to become involved in society by "spread[ing] . . . the energies of the gospel" (no. 48).

James B. Nickoloff

See also PAUL VI, POPE.

ODES OF SOLOMON

The Odes of Solomon have been described as an early Jewish Christian hymn book especially concerned to celebrate the eternal life and love achieved by Jesus Christ through the incarnation, crucifixion, descent into hell, and the resurrection. The Odes are dated around the end of the first century C.E. There are many points of contact with the sectarian literature of the Dead Sea Scrolls and the Johannine literature. The Odes are extant in Syriac, possibly the original language of composition.

Russell Fuller

ODO OF CLUNY (879?–944)

As second abbot of the monastery of Cluny from 927 until his death, Odo made Cluny an important center of monastic reform. The son of a knight, Odo was brought up in the household of William, the Duke of Aquitaine, who later founded the abbey of Cluny. Odo worked closely with Berno, the first abbot of Cluny, and upon succeeding Berno, Odo worked to make Cluny both independent of secular interests and a model for reformed monas-

ticism in Europe. By the twelfth century, some one thousand Cluniac monasteries were established.

Gary Macy

See also GREGORIAN REFORMS; MEDIEVAL CHRISTIANITY (IN THE WEST); MONASTICISM IN WESTERN CHRISTIANITY.

ODUYOYE, MERCY AMBA (1934–)

Ghanaian Protestant theologian, frequently regarded as the foremost African woman theologian. Oduyoye has served as deputy general secretary of the World Council of Churches in Geneva, and was a founder of the Circle of Concerned African Women Theologians. She is presently on the faculty of Trinity Theological Seminary in Accra, Ghana, where she also serves as director of the Talitha Qumi Centre—an institute on women, religion, and culture. Oduyoye has focused her work on the cultural and social roles of women in Africa and on the liberation of African women. In her theology, Oduyoye highlights the future of African women, given the realities of patriarchy in Africa (so negatively reinforced by Western colonialism). She is as critical of Euro-American feminism as she is of African patriarchy because, in her view, North American and European feminisms have focused too narrowly on gender analysis, leaving issues of class, race, and colonialism on the side. Oduyoye understands African women and men as victims of First World imperialism and neocolonialism, and so their liberation requires their partnership. For Oduyoye, Jesus means freedom and equality for women as well as men—because Jesus announces another way of being human, a way different from that of the patriarchal societies. In spite of the many negative factors associated with Christianity in Africa, Oduyoye still sees the continued appeal of Christianity in its response to the African cry for salvation. Among Professor Oduyoye's books are *Daughters of Anowa: African Women and Patriarchy* (1995); *One Gospel—Many Cultures: Case Studies and Reflections on Cross-Cultural Theology* (2003); *Beads and Strands: Reflections of an African Woman on Christianity in Africa* (2002); and *Introducing African Women's Theology* (2001).

Orlando Espín

See also AFRICAN CHRISTIANITY; AFRICAN THEOLOGIES; FEMINIST THEOLOGIES.

OFFERTORY

The word *offertory* comes from a Latin verb (*offerre*), meaning "to bring in," "present," or "offer." In Christian liturgical use, the offertory is a section of the celebration of the Eucharist (or Mass) during which the gifts or offerings (the bread and wine to be used) are brought to the altar in preparation for the beginning of the Liturgy of the Eucharist. In antiquity, other offerings might also have been brought up (such as oil, olives, cheese), but this custom fell into disuse. Later, offerings of money would be collected at this time as well.

In the Roman Catholic tradition, the offertory is now referred to as the preparation of the gifts, according to the liturgical reforms of Vatican II. In addition, the practice of having a procession at this time (the *offertory procession*), once a feature of early Christian worship, has also been revived. The procession can be more or less formally structured, but in essence the action involves a small number of participants at the Eucharist (usually from the general congregation or assembly)

bringing up the chalice, a flask or smaller cruets of wine, and the unconsecrated altar breads (often in the form of small, flat disks called *hosts*) that have been placed in a basket or on a metal dish or plate (a *paten*).

Theologically, the idea of making an offering is tied to the concept of sacrifice: one offers, or gives, something to be set aside for sacred use. Using sacrificial language, a victim of some kind is offered by being hallowed and slain; Christian theology identifies this "saving victim" with Christ. The Eucharist becomes the sacramental event in which the assembled Christian community enters into the paschal mystery of Christ, his once-and-for-all sacrifice of life and self to God. Christians unite themselves in Christ with this act of self-offering, bringing to God their lives, prayer, and praise.

Joanne M. Pierce

See also COMMUNION (LITURGICAL); EUCHARIST; LITURGY OF THE EUCHARIST; MASS; SACRIFICE OF THE MASS.

OHRMAZD

See AHURA MAZDA.

OLD CATHOLICS

The name usually given to a group of churches that separated from the Roman Catholic Church at various times since 1724. The more significant among these are the following: (1) the "Church of Utrecht" that separated in 1724 over doctrinal questions raised by Jansenism and by Rome's condemnation of this movement. It is found especially in the Netherlands. (2) National Churches in Germany, Austria, and Switzerland that separated between 1874 and 1875 mainly because of their refusal to accept the First Vatican Council's doctrines on papal infallibility and universal ordinary jurisdiction. (3) The Polish National Catholic Church that separated from Rome toward the end of the nineteenth century mainly over pastoral and theological difficulties confronted by Polish immigrants in the U.S., and that the American Roman Catholic Church was unwilling to attend to at the time. The Polish National Catholic Church is currently in dialogue with the Roman Catholic Church, hoping that a reunion of the two churches might be possible in the near future. (4) There are other tiny churches that gather themselves under the Old Catholic label, and are variously called Free Catholics, Liberal Catholics, and the like, and that may follow somewhat extravagant interpretations of the Old Catholic tradition.

The Old Catholic Churches have preserved the "apostolic succession." The common doctrinal statement is the "Declaration of Utrecht" (1889) that recognizes the first seven ecumenical councils of undivided Christianity, as well as all the doctrines agreed upon by Orthodox and Catholics before their separation in 1054. Most Old Catholics, in fact, also accept most of the teachings of the Council of Trent (except those they identify as too specifically Roman), and reject the teachings of the First Vatican Council, as well as two Marian dogmas. The main Old Catholic Churches are in full communion with most Anglican Churches. The archbishop of Utrecht (in the Netherlands) holds a first place of respect among many Old Catholics, but not as primate or patriarch.

Orlando Espín

See also ANGLICAN COMMUNION; APOSTOLIC SUCCESSION; ARCHBISHOP; CATHOLIC TRADITION; COMMUNION (ECCLESIOLOGICAL); ECCLESIOLOGY; INFALLIBILITY; JANSENISM; ORTHODOX CHURCHES; PATRIARCH; POPE; PRIMATE/PRIMATIAL SEE; ROMAN CATHOLIC CHURCH; TRENT, COUNCIL OF; UTRECHT, SEE OF; VATICAN, FIRST COUNCIL OF THE; WESTERN CATHOLIC CHURCHES.

OLD TESTAMENT

"Old Testament" is a Christian term that seems to have originated as early as the second century C.E. and was used by such early figures as Melito of Sardis (170–90 C.E.) and later by Clement of Alexandria and Tertullian. Not only is Old Testament a Christian expression, but it is also an expression that could only exist once there was a "New Testament" with which it stood in contrast or opposition. This term is used by Christians to refer to the Scriptures inherited from Judaism that have become the first section of the Christian Scriptures. The term carries with it not only a contrast with the New Testament, referring to the second section of the Christian Bible, but also an implicit theological supersessionism. In the second century C.E., the Gnostic Marcion argued that the God reflected in the Old Testament had nothing to do with Jesus, and so the Old Testament was of no use for Christians. His view was rejected by the early church that maintained the sacredness of the inherited Scriptures. Marcion's attitude has often surfaced in the history of Christianity since that time; most recently, in the thinking of Adolph von Harnack, an expert on Marcion, who thought that Martin Luther should have rejected the Old Testament as Scripture. The overwhelming view within Christianity has maintained the evident and essential continuity between the two collections, recognizing in both the word of the one God of both "Testaments."

Russell Fuller

See also HEBREW SCRIPTURES; PENTA-
TEUCH; WRITINGS/KETUVIM (IN HEBREW
SCRIPTURES).

OLÓDÙMARÈ

The holiest name of the supreme (and only)
God in the Yoruba traditional religion, as
well as in Santería and Candomblé. The
name can be translated as either "The
One who holds the future in his hands,"
or as "The One who has all absolute perfections." The same supreme God is also
known as Olófin ("The One who owns
all power"), and as Olórùn ("The One
who owns the skies"). Olódùmarè may
be described as a *deus absconditus*.

Orlando Espín

See also AFRICAN TRADITIONAL RELI-
GIONS; AFRO-LATIN RELIGIONS;
CANDOMBLÉ; DEUS ABSCONDITUS; GOD;
SANTERÍA.

OM

The most important Hindu mantra, Om
(sometimes written Aum) is said to encompass all states of being, all states of
consciousness. As such, it is the primary
symbol of the Infinite in Hinduism, the
veritable sound form of Brahman (*nada–
brahman*). It is used as a focus for meditation, in ritual chanting, and at the
beginning and end of recited prayers, to
elevate consciousness of the reciter and
evoke the felt presence of the Ultimate.
The nature and structure of this holy syllable receives its classical exposition in
the *Mandukya Upanishad*. Om is also used
as part of Tantric Buddhist mantras.

Lance E. Nelson

See also BRAHMAN; HINDUISM; MANTRA;
TANTRIC BUDDHISM; UPANISHADS.

OMAR

See UMAR.

OMEN

A phenomenon supposed to indicate
forthcoming good or evil, a sign of something about to happen. In indigenous
religions especially, the world is seen as
magically interconnected, full of syn-
chronicities. The sight of a particular bird,
a visit from a particular person, or other
similar, seemingly ordinary, events may
become omens if thought to portend
good or evil.

Lance E. Nelson

See also DIVINATION; INDIGENOUS
RELIGIOUS TRADITIONS.

OMNIBENEVOLENCE

From the Latin *omnis* and *benevolentia*, the
term is a divine attribute meaning "all-
benevolent" both regarding the scope
and perfect quality of God's benevolence
toward the world. While this attribute is
ultimately grounded in the biblical witness to God's salvific will culminating in
the Christ, the affirmation of God's omnibenevolence in classical theism, together
with the affirmation of God's omnipotence, has posed at least two significant
and recurring questions for Christian theology: "Why was the Christ permitted to
die?" and "Why does genuine evil continue to exist in the world?"

J. A. Colombo

See also EVIL; EVIL, PROBLEM OF;
OMNIPOTENCE.

OMNIPOTENCE

From the Latin *omnis* and *potentia*, the
term is a divine attribute meaning "all-
powerful" found in the earliest Christian
creeds as an attribute of the Father, that
is, the "Almighty" (Pantocrator). Particularly in the context of classical theism and
the doctrine of *creatio ex nihilo* ("creation

out of nothing"), the term has been understood to mean that divine power is essentially unlimited, that is, not limited by any other actuality or actualities. Divine power in relation to the world is thus unilateral or coercive. Traditionally, this understanding of God's power does not preclude (1) the possibility of a voluntary divine self-limitation, for example, noninterference with the "laws of nature" or the kenosis implied in the Incarnation —codified in the late medieval distinction between God's *potentia absoluta* and *potentia ordinata*—or (2) a limitation of divine power by logical impossibilities.

More recently, neoclassical or process theism has challenged this understanding of omnipotence. Arguing that the divine creative process is best understood as "bringing order out of chaos" and not "creation out of nothing," neoclassical theism maintains that some actualities with (partial) power of self-determination and power to influence others have always existed alongside God. God's power is therefore essentially limited by the power possessed by these actualities. Nonetheless, God's power is the greatest conceivable power relative to the existence of these actualities and therefore is absolute with respect to both scope and constancy. Divine power in relation to the world is thus also essentially shared and persuasive and not coercive.

J. A. Colombo

See also PROCESS THEOLOGY.

OMNIPRESENCE

From the Latin *omnis* and *praesens*, the term means "present everywhere" or "present to all." A divine attribute, omnipresence refers to God's immanence in and to the world. Specific understandings of the manner of God's omnipresence is insepa-

rable from how God's omnipotence is understood, and discussions of the former are usually subordinated to the latter.

J. A. Colombo

See also IMMANENCE; OMNIPOTENCE; PROCESS THEOLOGY.

OMNISCIENCE

From the Latin *omnis* and *scire*, the term is a divine attribute of perfection meaning "all-knowing." In classical theism, divine knowledge extends to all events— what is perceived in time as past, present, and future—in the modality of eternity where what is dispersed through time actually exists as it were in a single present. The manner of the divine knowledge of contingent future events especially preoccupied the great medieval theologians, for example, Albertus Magnus, Aquinas, and Duns Scotus.

In neoclassical or process theism, because God exists in time and not "above" it, that is, in eternity, and because the future is not actual but solely the realm of the possible, divine knowledge of what is actually the case extends only to all past and present events. Contingent future events as those events that have not yet become actual also remain contingent for God. In sum, God knows past and present events as actualities and the future solely as possibilities. The perfection of the divine knowledge lies in both the extension and fullness of God's knowledge of actualities, not that possibilities are known as actualities.

J. A. Colombo

See also PROCESS THEOLOGY.

ONTOLOGICAL ARGUMENT

First attributed to Anselm of Canterbury (d. 1109), the ontological argument seeks to demonstrate that analysis of the idea of God as a perfect being entails that being's necessary existence. Because the ontological argument deduces existence from concepts, it is called an *a priori* argument. Rejected by Aquinas, the argument was used by Descartes and Spinoza and is vigorously defended today in the work of Charles Hartshorne.

J. A. Colombo

OPTION FOR THE POOR

Among the most significant developments in Catholic theology since the Second Vatican Council (1962–5) has been the formulation and widespread endorsement of the principle of God's "option for the poor." In one sense, the notion is not new: in both the Hebrew Bible and the Christian New Testament God is often portrayed as having intense concern for, and even taking the side of, those who are politically or economically oppressed and/or socially shunned (see, for example, Deut 26:5-10 and Luke 4:18). The consequence of God's stance for the Christian church's own practice was stated clearly by Pope John XXIII: the church "is and wants to be . . . the church of all and in particular the church of the poor." Vatican II called attention to the Lord's close identification with the poor, noting that "in the poor and the suffering the church recognizes the face of its poor and suffering founder" (LG 8). In response to the council and to the stark reality of massive, unjust poverty and marginalization in their countries, the Catholic bishops of Latin America in 1968 called on the church to enter into genuine solidarity with "the poorest and . . . those segregated for any cause whatsoever" (Medellín Document, "Poverty of the Church," nos. 9–10). In 1979 at Puebla, Mexico, the Latin American bishops acknowledged that the church had learned much about the Gospel itself through its growing solidarity with the poor, and they promulgated what has become a classic formulation of the "preferential option for the poor." Because the image of God in which all human beings are made is "dimmed and even defiled" by the poverty inflicted on the poor, "God takes on their defense and loves them. That is why the poor are the first ones to whom Jesus' mission is directed." In other words, God's option— and thus the church's—has nothing to do with romanticized notions of the moral purity or deep faith of the poor; they merit priority simply because they are poor. The church thus rejects the distinction between the "deserving" and "undeserving" poor common to much political discourse (Puebla Document, nos. 1134–1165). For his part Pope John Paul II forcefully affirmed "the *option* or *love of preference* for the poor . . . to which the whole tradition of the church bears witness" (*Sollicitudo Rei Socialis* 42). Conferences of Catholic bishops around the world, including those of the United States, and the leaders of other Christian churches have followed the lead of the Latin American church and endorsed the option for the poor, which has also been the subject of widespread analysis by theologians in recent years.

The option for the poor involves more than the church's social teaching (social ethics); at its core it concerns the church's deepest understanding of who God is (theology). The term "option" signifies choice or commitment—in the first place, God's choice to stand with the poor against their poverty and against the attitudes and practices of those responsible for their poverty. But this stance is, in fact, an option *for all people* since it represents an invitation to the powerful and privileged to undergo conversion. Thus, in the second place, "option" refers to the choice made by Jesus' disciples to do the same as God does. In no way does "option" refer to something "optional" or dispensable; for Christians the option for the poor is binding. This includes poor Christians themselves who frequently face the temptation of escaping from their misery through the exploitation of other poor persons. In practice, "opting" for (choosing to stand with) the poor means (1) analyzing reality from their vantage point (which is not the same as agreeing with their views); (2) taking action for their well-being—and thus for the well-being of all; and (3) evaluating actions taken by how they affect the poor. Because God in Christ has chosen solidarity with the poor (seen explicitly, for example, the parable of the Last Judgment, Matt 25:31-46), those who choose to live in solidarity with the poor choose to stand with Christ. Perhaps a common practice of Jesus best elucidates the inner logic of the preferential option for the poor. While Jesus was pleased to dine with anyone, he was known to prefer the company of those considered outcasts or sinners (Mark 2:15-17, for example). All others who wished to join Jesus had to share the meal with his "favorites" (as Pope John Paul II called them). This means that to join the banquet of Christ, oppressors must be willing to cease oppressing and to break bread in friendship with those they once ignored, scorned, or oppressed.

James B. Nickoloff

See also CELAM; JOHN PAUL II, POPE; JOHN XXIII, POPE; MEDELLÍN DOCUMENTS; PUEBLA DOCUMENT; SOLLICITUDO REI SOCIALIS; VATICAN, SECOND COUNCIL OF THE.

OPUS DEI (INSTITUTION)

(Latin, *opus*, work; *Dei*, of God). First used as a designation for the Liturgy of the Hours in monastic communities, the expression in this case refers to a religious movement founded in Spain for the laity by Monsignor Josemaría Escrivá de Balaguer (1902–75). The group stressed the holiness of one's life found in ordinary work and the need to spread that holiness throughout society. Priests were recruited to serve as directors of the laity's rigorous spiritual life and to coordinate the "Work." The clergy formed a parallel group, the Priestly Society of the Holy Cross, who remained under the local bishop but recruited for Opus through parochial contacts and other work. The movement passed through several stages of development. Declared a Pious Union in 1941 and a secular institute in 1947, with final approbation in 1950, Pope John Paul II granted Opus the status of "personal prelature" in 1982. This canonical term means that Opus's jurisdiction covers Opus Dei members rather than a specific geographic region. Although mostly Spanish, Opus Dei has become a multinational organization.

Opus Dei has many levels of membership and commitment. The *Head* (prelate), surrounded by an inner circle of priests called *inscripti* (leaders), forms the center of its hierarchical structure of concentric circles. The next circle is composed of *numeraries* who are priests or lay celibates with baccalaureate, graduate, or professional degrees, and who live together in a *House.* This group works solely for Opus, running the business of the Houses. *Aggregates* (associates) are pledged totally to Opus but live and recruit outside the Houses of the Work. They have no university degrees, social class, or professions. All of the above categories are limited to men.

The *numerary assistants* are celibate women recruited as teenagers and trained in "catering" (cooking and housekeeping) schools to serve in the Houses of the Work. The women are housed separately and do not fraternize with the college-graduate *numerary* members. The *Super numerarii* circle consists of both single and married people who work part-time for Opus and whose main obligation is to pursue sanctity according to Opus Dei direction and seek suitable recruits from friends, family, and professional associates. The final circle includes the *cooperators* who are friends, sympathizers, and fellow workers who may attend Opus functions. The circles are not interchangeable. Each circle receives only enough information to fulfill its specific duties.

The dictums of Escriva's *The Way* (1935–9) that contains 999 spiritual maxims, provides the basis for Opus's spirituality. Often accused of being a secret society with a medieval monastic spirituality, Opus tends to be theologically conservative. It has become an object of controversy within the church, especially concerning its perceived secrecy and its methods of proselytism on college campuses. The latter practice has raised many questions, especially from diocesan clergy, campus ministers, and parents of present and former members. Despite the controversy and opposition, Pope John Paul II not only endorsed the organization, but he beatified Escrevía de Balaguer in 1992 only eighteen years after his death.

M. Jane Gorman

See also PROSELYTISM.

ORACLE

A term that refers to a person, an institution, an object, or a location that (it is claimed) has the ability to interpret signs of the present or foretell the future (usually accomplished during or after a ritual). Oracles, and the belief in oracles, were common in most religions of the ancient world (regardless of continent).

Orlando Espín

ORAIBI

One of the oldest remaining inhabited villages of North America, this Hopi pueblo has occupied a central place in traditional life. It is considered the parent and home of ceremonial life, and was the focus of ritual organization. Both the Hopi and archeologists agree that settlement there happened nearly 2,000 years ago. In the early twentieth century a dispute over the degree to which tradition was being properly maintained led to a split and the founding of Hotevilla that since then has also claimed to share the original Knowledge of the Hopi Covenant.

Kathleen Dugan

See also RITUAL.

ORANGE, COUNCILS OF

Two councils were held in the city of Orange during the early centuries of Christianity. The first in 441, over which Hilary of Arles presided, dealt mostly with pastoral problems. The second and more important council was held in 529 to settle the semi-Pelagian controversy. Among the bishops present was Caesarius of Arles. The council upheld the Augustinian teaching that the baptized are able to fulfill the duties necessary for salvation with the assistance of God's grace. The decisions of the council were approved by Pope Boniface II in 531.

Gary Macy

See also AUGUSTINIANISM; HILARY OF ARLES; SEMI-PELAGIANISM.

ORATORY/ORATORIANS

An oratory is a private or semiprivate place of worship as opposed to a church that is open to everyone. It is, in effect, a private chapel where Mass is permitted to be celebrated. The Oratory refers to the Institute of the Oratory of St. Philip Neri. Founded by Philip Neri in 1575 in order to revive the spiritual life of secular priests, the group derives its name from the oratory in Rome where they met. The Oratorians have an interesting organization. They are all priests and lay brothers who take no vows; in fact, all vows, oaths, or promises to the Institute are forbidden. They live a communal life, but each member is expected to support himself to the best of his ability, and the leadership is democratically elected. Each oratory is independent of the others. A second group of Oratorians was founded in 1611 by Pierre de Bérulle in Paris. The French Oratorians differ only in that they have centralized organizations with a Superior-General of the Institute. Several famous scholars have belonged to the Oratorians, including John Henry Newman. The musical form, the oratorio, developed out of the songs used by the Oratorians in their services.

Gary Macy

See also NEWMAN, JOHN HENRY; ORDERS, RELIGIOUS; VOWS (RELIGIOUS).

ORDAINED MINISTRIES, SACRAMENT OF

Imperial Roman society had two primary divisions: governors and the governed. The governing authorities were said to be in "orders," that is, *ranks*, of leadership. The New Testament Christian community seems to have known no such rigid distinctions. The Scriptures describe it as essentially a society of equals bound together by God's Spirit. This Spirit produced, not divisions of rank, but numerous ministries for the community's life and service (1 Cor 12:4-11). Especially high standards fell upon those who possessed gifts of leadership (1 Tim 3:1-13; 5:17-22), but the New Testament does not suggest that they formed a distinct class. At least some communities commissioned key ministers through the laying on of hands (Acts 6:6; 13:3; 1 Tim 4:14; 2 Tim 1:6). It is unclear, however, whether all the communities followed this procedure, and whether each community used it consistently.

In the second century, this fluidity yielded to more consistent patterns. First, the ministries of *episcopos* (overseer, bishop), *presbyteros* (bishop's advisor, elder), and *diakonos* (bishop's assistant, servant) became key in every community. Second, these three ministries were instituted by the laying on of hands by those already in the ministry or by the board of presbyters. Third, these ministers began to be spoken of as belonging to a distinct *order* within the church. Their commissioning, therefore, could be called an *ordination*. Tertullian of Carthage (about 155–220) is often credited as the first major Christian writer to use the vocabulary of order/ordination to describe church leadership.

These changes served two valuable functions. First, they stabilized the community's life. Second, they provided a chain through which the authentic message of Jesus could be passed. This was a time before the New Testament was finalized, and so the ministers of the church formed an "apostolic succession" or human chain back to Jesus himself. A third-century Roman document, the *Apostolic Tradition* of Hippolytus (215), gives concrete evidence that the ministries of episcopos, presbyteros, and diaconos were ritualized by the imposition of a bishop's hands and the invocation of the Holy Spirit. This pattern has endured.

It was the bishop who pastored the congregation, assisted by his deacons, and was advised by the community's presbyters, the elders. As the church grew and it became impossible for all the people in a city and its environs to come to the bishop's church for Sunday Eucharist, bishops delegated elders to celebrate with the people in distant regions. As this pattern became increasingly common, people began to think of these presbyters as the basic Christian ministers, and to consider the bishops as presbyters of a higher rank. Deacons became less and less important in the church's life and eventually became only presbyters-in-training.

Perhaps the most important change to effect the ordained ministry was the Carolingian tendency to liken it to the Jewish priesthood. As history has shown, the first Christian ministers were understood as community leaders, not as priests who stood as intermediaries between the community and God. As eighth- and ninth-century Christians began to liken presbyters to Jewish sacrificing priests, and bishops to high priests, the idea of ordained ministers as a distinct and elevated "order" became further solidified. Late medieval Scholastic theologians taught that what distinguished ordained ministers from other Christians was a permanent "character," a sort of spiritual branding they received at ordination. The character aligned them with Christ in such a way that they could speak and offer sacrifice in his place.

The sixteenth-century Protestant Reformers challenged what had evolved. First, they claimed the New Testament did not indicate that Jesus has instituted an ordained ministry, or at least not the sort that had evolved. Second, they said Christian ministry was one of service, not of offering sacrifice or mediating between humans and God. Third, they questioned the strict division between "ordained" and "lay," and emphasized instead what was common to all Christians by baptism. The Council of Trent responded by defending the patterns and theology that had evolved, saying that it was an authentic development of the will of Jesus. At the same time, Trent sought to assure that those who exercised ordained ministry would do so intelligently and would live disciplined and moral lives.

The Second Vatican Council reaffirmed the teaching of Trent. It did, however, balance those teachings by emphasizing forgotten elements of the earlier tradition: the bishop is the chief pastor; the church is primarily a society of equals, and only secondarily a society of distinct groups; deacons are a distinct order, not just a stepping stone to priesthood; and, perhaps most important, ordained ministry is only one of the ministries in the church. All baptized persons have been given gifts for the sake of the church and the good of its mission.

Patrick L. Malloy

See also ORDINATION; SEMINARY; TRENT, COUNCIL OF.

ORDER OF CHRISTIAN INITIATION OF ADULTS

See RITES OF CHRISTIAN INITIATION (RCIA).

ORDERS, RELIGIOUS

The word *ordo* in Latin means, among other things, "rule," and in its simple meaning a religious order is a congregation of Christian men or women, or rarely men and women together, who share a common "rule" of life. Christians early in their history began experimenting with different ways of living out the Christian message and some of these experimenters wrote down the rules by which their members lived. These experiments were all attempts to find the most perfect and challenging form of Christian life. Pachomius of Egypt, for instance, formed a rule for the hermits living in the desert. Basil of Caesaria also wrote a famous rule of life for his monks in the fourth century, while Benedict of Nursia wrote the influential *Rule of St. Benedict* in the early sixth century. Groups of Christian women organized themselves under the title of Virgins or Widows, and laws were written that regulated those forms of life as well. At first, all these movements were only meant to help organize already existing communities of Christians who needed a handbook for their way of life. As time passed, the term "religious order" became more precise, referring to those who took vows of chastity, poverty, and obedience, and who lived a communal life. Some of the rules resulted in large, international organizations like the Order of St. Benedict (Benedictines) or the Order of the Friars Minor (the Franciscans). Other orders attracted only a few individuals. In Western Christianity, several attempts have been made to stop the proliferation of new "orders" in the church, but the result of this has been simply to proliferate the names by which the new groups are designated. Instead of orders, they are called congregations or institutes or societies. These groups may officially take one of the existing rules, but then they modify it to fit their needs. There are also "third orders," organizations of laity living in the world who take private vows to live a simple,

holy, and chaste life. The rules of the various groups can be quite different, depending on the purpose for which the organization was founded. Benedictines, for instance, are monks. They generally stay in their monasteries and devote themselves to work and prayer. The Order of Preachers or Dominicans, on the other hand, devote themselves to study and then to preaching. Their work takes them out into the world. All orders, however, follow a particular set of rules approved for their form of life by the appropriate ecclesiastical authority. Although most religious orders now are Catholic, there are also Protestant and Anglican religious orders.

Gary Macy

See also BASIL THE GREAT; BENEDICTINE RULE (RULE OF ST. BENEDICT); BENEDICTINES; BENEDICT OF NURSIA; DOMINICANS; FRANCISCANS; FRIARS; MONASTICISM IN EASTERN CHRISTIANITY; MONASTICISM IN WESTERN CHRISTIANITY; PACHOMIUS; THIRD ORDERS; VOWS (RELIGIOUS); WIDOWS (IN THE EARLY CHURCH).

ORDINARY (CANONICAL)

In Roman Catholic "canon" (that is, ecclesiastical) law, an "ordinary" is someone who has legal jurisdiction within the church, either over a territory and the Catholics who live within it (the case of bishops, for example), or over a specific group of Catholics (the case of superiors of religious congregations or orders of priests, brothers, and nuns). The term "ordinary" is also used, with similar meaning, in the churches of the Anglican Communion.

Orlando Espín

See also ANGLICAN COMMUNION; BISHOP (EPISCOPACY); CANON LAW;

CONGREGATIONS (ORDERS); RELIGIOUS (VOWED); ROMAN CATHOLIC CHURCH.

ORDINARY, LITURGICAL

From the Latin *ordo*, meaning "order." In liturgical services, certain elements change from day to day and season to season, such as the readings. Other elements, however, do not vary. These are called the "ordinary." In the Eucharist, the ordinary is made up of the *Lord, Have Mercy, Glory to God*, Creed, *Holy*, memorial acclamation, Amen, and *Lamb of God*. The word ordinary applies especially to a musical setting of these invariable hymns and acclamations. Some modern composers and publishers do not use the word "ordinary" but instead call these musical compositions "Mass settings."

Patrick L. Malloy

See also LITURGY OF THE EUCHARIST; LITURGY OF THE WORD.

ORDINATION

In the Roman Catholic Church, one of the seven sacraments. By ordination, a man is permanently made a deacon, priest, or bishop. The central gesture is the laying of the bishop's hands upon the head of the candidate. Only a bishop can ordain. The church traces ordination to Jesus, who commissioned certain of his disciples as preachers, ministers of the sacraments, servants of the needy, and so forth. The gesture of imposing hands is described in the Bible, where it had many meanings, including commissioning for service. Biblical scholars caution, however, that there is no evidence that Jesus himself ever used that gesture to designate any of his disciples as ministers, or that Jesus divided his disciples into the groups we would call "lay" and "ordained." The Catholic position is that Jesus intended only men to receive ordination, but many other Christian churches now ordain women as well.

Patrick L. Malloy

See also LAYING ON OF HANDS; ORDAINED MINISTRIES, SACRAMENT OF.

ORENDA

This Algonquian word for sacred power indicates an awareness of the omnipresence of spiritual beings, and indeed the entire web of energy that embraces all living things. With all traditional peoples, this power takes face and form and appears to human beings. This can take place in spontaneous encounters at the will of the sacred, or be the result of a ritual quest for such a meeting. It is believed that all success in life depends on personal sharing in this power; this is gained by prayer and fasting.

Kathleen Dugan

See also FASTS/FASTING (IN CHRISTIANITY).

ORICHA

See SANTERÍA.

ORIENTAL CHURCHES

A generic term (from the Latin word *orientalis*, meaning "eastern") applicable to all Eastern Churches whether Orthodox, Catholic, or others.

Orlando Espín

See also ANCIENT CHURCHES OF THE EAST; EASTERN CATHOLIC CHURCHES; ORTHODOX CHURCHES.

ORIENTALIUM ECCLESIARUM

Name of a document (a "decree") issued by the Second Vatican Council, on November 21, 1964. This decree covers a wide range of issues (such as ecclesial traditions, patriarchs, liturgy, synods, and the like), all dealing with Eastern Churches that are in full communion with Rome. The basic thrust of the document is to defend, protect, and support the distinctive identities, autonomy, and ancient traditions of each of the Eastern Catholic Churches.

Orlando Espín

See also COMMUNION (ECCLESIOLOGICAL); EASTERN CATHOLIC CHURCHES; VATICAN, SECOND COUNCIL OF THE.

ORIGEN (185?–254)

The oldest of seven children, Origen received a thoroughly Christian education in his home in Alexandria. In 202 his father, Leonides, was martyred. In order to support his family, Origen opened a secular school, but also began teaching in the catechetical school of Alexandria. Origen lived a life of strict asceticism and scholarship, drawing many students to the catechetical school that eventually became his full-time occupation. When Origen was ordained priest by the bishop of Palestine, the bishop of Alexandria, Demetrius, had Origen banished from Egypt for being ordained without his permission. Origen established a new school in Caesaria that quickly became an important center of learning. In 250 C.E. he was imprisoned and tortured by the Roman government in hopes that such a famous Christian would retract his religion. Despite prolonged punishment, Origen never denied his faith. When he was finally freed from prison, however, Origen's health was broken, and he died a few years later at the age of sixty-nine.

Origen was one of the most prolific authors in antiquity, but unfortunately, not all of his work has survived. His greatest work was perhaps in scriptural studies, and he is justly considered one of the greatest Scripture scholars of all time. Despite the loss of many of his works due to the Origenist controversies, Origen's thought has remained an abiding influence on later Christian thinkers.

Gary Macy

See also ALEXANDRIAN THEOLOGY; EXEGESIS/EISEGESIS; ORIGENISM; PERSECUTION (IN CHRISTIANITY).

ORIGENISM

In its most general terms, Origenism refers to the teaching and influence of the third-century theologian, Origen. While Origen's theology has had both fervent advocates and ardent detractors in its long history, there have been two serious attempts to discredit Origen's theology during the early centuries of Christianity, and it is to these movements that the word "Origenism" most frequently applies.

The first sustained attack upon Origen's theology occurred in the late fourth and early fifth centuries. Epiphanius of Cyprus included Origen's teaching as one of many heresies he listed in his collections of errors, and on this basis a petition began to circulate calling for the condemnation of Origen. A literary war erupted between the defenders of Origen, led by Rufinus of Aquileia, and opponents of Origen, lead by Rufinus's friend, Jerome. Called upon to settle the issue, the patriarch of Alexandria, Theophilus, condemned the teaching of Origen in a local synod held in 400.

Despite this condemnation, Origen's support remained strong, and another attempt was made to condemn his theology in the sixth century. In this case, monks living in Palestine, basing themselves on Origen's theology, taught a form of pantheism in which all minds, including that of Christ, have been and will be again, one. The emperor Justinian, in response to this teaching, listed Origen as a heretic in the Acts of the Second Council of Constantinople. Due to this condemnation, many of Origen's works were destroyed.

Opponents of Origen's theology objected to Origen's speculation that all souls were originally created equal and existed before bodies, that all (even the devil) might eventually be saved, and that the Logos was of lesser divinity than the Father.

Gary Macy

See also HERESY; JEROME; JUSTINIAN; ORIGEN; RUFINUS OF AQUILEIA.

ORIGINAL JUSTICE

A Christian theological term (more frequent in some Roman Catholic theologies of grace and justification) referring to the supposed condition or state of humankind before Adam's sin. It has been described as a situation wherein humans enjoyed freedom, happiness, justice, and even bodily immortality—since these gifts were lost with original sin. The theoretical concept of original justice has been useful, in the history of theology, to better understand the consequences of human sinfulness. Evidently, there is no archeological or historical evidence for such a perfect pre-Fall situation; the concept is a theoretical construct.

Orlando Espín

See also FREE WILL; GRACE; INFRALAPSARIANISM; JUSTIFICATION; NATURE, HUMAN; SIN, ORIGINAL; THEOLOGICAL ANTHROPOLOGY; TRENT, COUNCIL OF.

ORISHA

See SANTERÍA.

ORTEGA Y GASSET, JOSÉ (1883–1955)

Spanish philosopher. Brilliant student and professor, Ortega y Gasset founded the periodical *Revista de Occidente* in 1923, and through its pages influenced Spanish and Latin American philosophies for several decades. He was part of a philosophical movement called both "vitalism" and "philosophy of life" that flourished in Europe during the first few decades of the twentieth century. This movement cast doubts on the pretended universal validity and foundations of all systems of thought. It believed, in a nuanced manner, that the only critically valid philosophy was one based on fundamental human experience. "Vitalism" fiercely critiqued all that it interpreted as rigid (in the sciences, in philosophy, and in theology and the religions), and eagerly supported human freedom of conscience, intuitiveness, and creativity. In many ways, "vitalism" prepared the way for existentialism. Ortega y Gasset kept nuancing and reforming "vitalist" philosophy throughout his own life. He also contributed to social philosophy. Ortega's ideas clashed with many of the conservative theological theories frequent in the Spanish church during his lifetime, leading to many public confrontations with theologians and bishops. Among his more important books are *Meditaciones del Quijote* (1914), and *La rebelión de las masas* (1930).

Orlando Espín

See also EPISTEMOLOGY; ETHICS, SOCIAL; EXISTENTIALISM; METHOD IN THEOLOGY; PERSONALISM; ZUBIRI, XAVIER.

ORTHODOX CHURCHES

The generic name applied to a significant number of churches, mostly from eastern

Europe and the Middle East, that accept the honorary primacy of the patriarch of Constantinople, and share among them the same faith, the same basic doctrines, the same sacraments, and the apostolic succession. All Orthodox Churches are in full communion with each other, although each church is "autocephalous," that is, administratively independent of the others.

Orthodox Churches of today are the heirs of the ancient patriarchal sees of the Eastern Roman (or Byzantine) Empire. After some churches that chose to follow Monophysitism separated from the rest of undivided Christianity, the Orthodox found themselves in a situation of increasing tension with the Western European ("Catholic") churches. The two great halves of Christianity, after a series of incidents and circumstances that took place over a period of three centuries, finally and unfortunately broke with each other (in the so-called Great Schism) in the year 1054.

The main points of doctrinal contention (in 1054 and thereafter) between the Orthodox and the Catholics were the claims to effective universal primacy made by the popes (that is, the patriarchs of Rome), and the Western churches' unilateral addition of the phrase *Filioque* to the Nicene-Constantinopolitan Creed of undivided Christianity. There were some liturgical customs, on both sides, that contributed to the ambience of mistrust. Several attempts at reconciliation between Orthodox and Catholics (especially in the thirteenth and fifteenth centuries) were not successful.

The Orthodox Churches have historically suffered greatly for their faith, especially after the Middle East and parts of eastern Europe fell to Muslim conquest (gradually, since the seventh century), and more recently under Soviet communism.

Orthodox Christians accept as fundamental the doctrinal definitions of the first seven ecumenical councils of undivided Christianity, and regard these ecumenical councils as having the highest importance and relevance. Some later councils of Orthodox bishops have also contributed to doctrinal clarification and development, and are held in high esteem by the Orthodox (but not in the same category of importance as the first seven ecumenical councils). Although not in full communion with Rome because of (among other issues) papal claims to effective universal jurisdiction, the Orthodox would accept the pope—since he is the patriarch of Rome—as honorary "first among equals" (among all the bishops of the church).

Orthodox Christianity has carefully preserved the "apostolic succession" of its bishops. It accepts that there are seven sacraments (called "mysteries"), and fundamentally believes about the sacraments the same as Catholics believe. Indeed, on just about everything else Orthodox and Catholics believe alike, although the "theological" expressions or explanations often differ, and the liturgies are celebrated following various rites.

The liturgy, and especially the eucharistic liturgy, is central to all Orthodox Churches. Music is constant in worship services, as well as community participation. Orthodox liturgy is majestic and complex, engaging the entire person in the communal celebration. Icons play an important part in public liturgy and private devotion. Most Orthodox liturgies today are derived from the ancient Byzantine patriarchal liturgy. The two more frequent liturgical orders followed today are those of St. Basil and of St. John Chrysostom.

Monastic life has been very influential in Orthodox history, and bishops are usually monks. Parish priests are typically married (before ordination).

The "autocephalous" churches that are part of the Orthodox Communion are: (1) the four ancient patriarchal churches of Constantinople, Alexandria, Antioch, and Jerusalem; (2) the other—and "newer" —patriarchal churches of Russia, Serbia, Rumania, Bulgaria, and Georgia; (3) the Orthodox Churches of Greece, Albania, Cyprus, China, the Czech and Slovak republics, Hungary, Finland, Latvia, Lithuania, Estonia, Ukraine, and the United States (the "Orthodox Church of America"), and other smaller national groups. A significant number of Orthodox Churches have members spread throughout much of the modern world. There are about two hundred million Orthodox Christians worldwide.

Orlando Espín

See also APOSTOLIC FATHERS; APOSTOLIC SUCCESSION; AUTOCEPHALOUS CHURCHES; BYZANTIUM/BYZANTINE; CATHOLIC TRADITION; CHALCEDONIAN CHRISTIANS; COMMUNION (ECCLESIO-LOGICAL); CONSTANTINOPLE, SEE OF; COUNCIL, ECUMENICAL; DIVINIZATION; EASTERN CATHOLIC CHURCHES; ECUMENICAL PATRIARCH; EPARCH; EXARCH; FATHERS/MOTHERS OF THE DESERT; FATHERS OF THE CHURCH; FILIOQUE; GREEK ORTHODOX CHURCH; ICON; ICONOCLASTIC CONTROVERSY; LITURGY (IN CHRISTIANITY); MONASTI-CISM IN EASTERN CHRISTIANITY; MOUNT ATHOS; ORTHODOXY, THE FEAST OF; PATRIARCH; PATRISTICS/PATROLOGY; RUSSIAN ORTHODOX CHURCH; SYNODS; UNIATES.

ORTHODOX CONFESSION

See JASSY, SYNOD OF; MOGILA, PETER.

ORTHODOX JUDAISM

A general name for a number of contemporary approaches to Jewish theology and practice affirming the revealed character of the oral and written Torah and insisting that, to be authentic, Jews must observe all of the practices set out in the Talmudic and post-Talmudic rabbinic literatures. While Orthodox Jews see themselves as continuing the rabbinic Judaism of the premodern world, Orthodox movements are in fact modern, based upon ideologies that are self-consciously traditional and explicitly formulated to stem the tide of assimilation and religious reform that occurred beginning with the Enlightenment and Jewish emancipation in the eighteenth century.

Modern varieties of Orthodox Judaism share a belief in the divine origin of the law and in the obligation that Jews follow all aspects of this law, as it is interpreted by Orthodox rabbinic authorities. These movements uniformly deny the validity of contemporary forms of Judaism— Reform, Conservative, and Reconstructionist—that see the law as an evolving, human creation with, at most, a divine core. Beyond these shared ideas, Orthodox Judaism is marked by a great diversity of specific theologies and modes of practice. This diversity is most easily grasped through an evaluation of the two main branches of Orthodoxy: the most traditionalist groups, often referred to as "ultra-Orthodox," on the one side, and the centrist groups, usually known as "neo-Orthodox," on the other.

The ultra-Orthodox withdraw from all aspects of contemporary culture and life, seen as threats to Jewish authenticity. Even secular education, beyond what may be needed for employment, is frowned upon as potentially in conflict with the teachings of the Torah. Ultra-Orthodox groups often are recognized by distinctive Jewish styles of dress and the use of Yiddish, the traditional European Jewish language. Best known among the ultra-Orthodox groups are Hasidic Jews, members of movements that, despite their controversial origins within Judaism, are viewed today as the most traditional and authentic of contemporary Jewish groups.

Following the approach of Samson Raphael Hirsch (1808–88), who worked to revitalize the traditional Judaism of his day, the neo-Orthodox find value in modern culture and secular society, participation in which they believe can enhance one's fulfillment of God's will as defined in the Torah. Neo-Orthodoxy sees secular learning and the acquisition of a secular profession as avenues for deepening one's understanding of the world and of the God who created it. By locating religious value in secular activities, the neo-Orthodox seek to resolve the contradiction between modern life and traditional Jewish practice and theology, a contradiction that the ultra-Orthodox (not unlike the Reform, Conservative, and Reconstructionist movements) understand to be insurmountable. The main representative institution of neo-Orthodoxy in the United States is Yeshiva University in New York City. Yeshiva University's motto, "Torah and Scientific Knowledge" (Torah Umadda), highlights its goal of uniting secular study and traditional Jewish learning.

Alan J. Avery-Peck

See also CONSERVATIVE JUDAISM; HASIDIM; RABBINIC JUDAISM; RECONSTRUCTIONIST JUDAISM; REFORM JUDAISM; TORAH.

ORTHODOX THEOLOGY

The theology (-ies) of the autocephalous Eastern Orthodox Churches in communion with the ecumenical patriarch of Constantinople. These churches understand themselves to be direct descendants of the earliest apostolic and patristic Christian churches. Since 1054 C.E. the Eastern Orthodox Churches have been separated from the Western Catholic Churches. In most essential matters of doctrine, however, both groups of churches remain very close.

Orthodox theology holds that God has revealed Godself first to Israel and then, through Jesus the Christ, to the church and (through the church) to humankind. Indispensable witness to this revelation is the Bible. The Orthodox Churches hold the Bible to be the revealed word of God, but do not interpret the biblical text literally. Biblical interpretation occurs within the context of the church, the liturgy, and the tradition.

Eastern Orthodoxy holds in highest regard the doctrinal definitions of the first seven ecumenical councils (and does not consider "ecumenical" any council held after 787 C.E.). Orthodox Churches also grant importance to several other (local) synods that correctly expressed Orthodox doctrine and faith—two such synods, for example, were held at Jassy (in 1642) and at Jerusalem (in 1672). Nevertheless, much Orthodox doctrine has never been formally defined or formulated, although Orthodox Christians believe that the Bible, ecclesial tradition (especially as expressed through the ecumenical councils), and the liturgy correctly embody and express their faith and beliefs.

Eastern Orthodoxy has carefully preserved apostolic succession. The ecclesiology of these churches has been profoundly influenced by their trinitarian doctrine, thereby making collegiality (and conciliarity: sobornost) a trademark of their ecclesial life. Although respectful of their bishops and clergy, the Orthodox laity have traditionally been, and still are, very much involved in the life of their churches. Monasticism has also played a very important role in the life and doctrinal development of Eastern Orthodoxy. The liturgy holds a special place in these churches, as expression of faith and belief, and literally as "sacrament" of transcendence. The Orthodox acknowledge and celebrate the seven sacraments (they call them "mysteries"), although the notion of "sacrament" has never been clearly defined.

Associated with "sacrament" is the icon, very prominent in liturgy and popular piety. Icons are much more than religious art forms. They are visual expressions of doctrine—that is why icons are so venerated by the Orthodox and why they are used in the liturgy. Following strictly traditional (artistic and theological) styles, the images represented by the icons are intended to evoke and express truth, and to open a "window" to transcendence.

Orthodox theology has tended to be sensitive to divine transcendence as well as respectful of the (God-given) human ability to encounter God. However, Orthodox theology has also emphatically insisted on the unknowability of God ("apophatic" theology); consequently, reverence and awe (together with trust, belief, and obedience) must be the fundamental attitudes of humans who encounter God. Human reason cannot understand God or God's uncreated divine reality. Yet this same God has chosen to communicate Godself to humankind. Grace is, in Orthodox theology, God's free and loving self-giving to humanity, in order to make it possible for humans to encounter God and enter into relationship with God.

The affirmation that God is unknowable is accompanied in Orthodox theology by the equally important demand that theology, doctrine, and practice conform faithfully to revealed truth ("cataphatic" theology). Therefore, Eastern Orthodoxy achieves a doctrinal and theological middle ground between the subjectivism possible to apophatic thought when left to itself, and the objectivism possible to insistence on correct doctrinal formulations when also left to itself. Revealed truth is historically found, first and foremost, in the apostolic tradition. This apostolic tradition, however, is not just revealed truths and practices (although it is these too), but especially an ethos, an approach to life and reality, a frame of mind, a lifestyle. The apostolic tradition that the Orthodox believe to be inspired and guided by the Holy Spirit has unfolded and developed throughout history, and it has found necessary doctrinal (dogmatic) expression in the Bible, in the teachings of the ecumenical councils, and in the liturgy. Other important expressions of the developing apostolic tradition have been the fathers of the church and some doctrinally influential synods.

The Orthodox doctrine on God is clearly trinitarian: God has revealed Godself as Creator, Redeemer, and Sanctifier. There is only one God who is one divine essence, from all eternity, and who from all eternity is God in three "Persons" (*hypostases*). This belief, which was taught by the Council of Chalcedon (in 451 C.E.), does not explain the reality or nature of God in human rational terms, but it is a minimal dogmatic description to which all Orthodox theology must hold if it claims to present the revealed truth about God.

God created humans as God's image and likeness. The creation of humankind intended a perfect humanity, capable of correctly exercising free choice, and endowed with the possibility (if freedom were correctly exercised) of participating (as humans could have) in the nature of God. Sin, however, broke the possibility of this participation by profoundly distorting (although not destroying) the image and likeness of God within humankind.

Jesus the Christ is the incarnation of the Second "Person" of the Trinity. He is one person, completely divine and completely human (in all things, except sin). He came to the world in order to save humankind. Christ assumed human nature in order to redeem it; and by taking on himself the consequences of sin, he has destroyed their ultimate power over humankind. Christ, therefore, is the "victor"—as emphasized by the Holy Week liturgy and by many icons. Redemption restored humanity's potential for full communion and participation with God by restoring the image and likeness of God in humans. When Orthodox theology refers to "deification" or "divinization," it refers to the redeemed human possibility of becoming that which humans were created to be: the image and likeness of God. It is the Holy Spirit and God's grace that make this divinization possible, with human cooperation (also made possible by grace).

The church is sent by God, through the work and guidance of the Holy Spirit, to announce the "good news" to the world. Through baptism, confirmation ("chrismation"), and Eucharist, humans are incorporated into the church and participate in its life and mission. The church is believed to be one, holy, catholic, and apostolic. The church of Christ can be identified on earth by its adherence to the apostolic faith and tradition, by apostolic succession, and by the uninterrupted celebration of the eucharistic liturgy and the communion it establishes. The Eastern Orthodox Churches believe that only they can be identified today as the true church of Christ, although they also hold that other Christian communities have some share, to a greater or lesser degree, in the true church of Christ.

Orlando Espín

See also ALEXANDRIAN THEOLOGY; ANTIOCHENE THEOLOGY; APOPHATIC THEOLOGY; APOSTOLIC SUCCESSION; AUTOCEPHALOUS CHURCHES; CHALCEDONIAN CHRISTIANS; COMMUNION (ECCLESIOLOGICAL); CONSTANTINOPLE, SEE OF; COUNCIL, ECUMENICAL; EASTERN CATHOLIC CHURCHES; ECCLESIOLOGY; ECUMENICAL PATRIARCH; FATHERS OF THE CHURCH; GRACE; HESYCHASM; HYPOSTASIS; ICON; JASSY, SYNOD OF; JERUSALEM, SYNOD OF; MONASTICISM IN EASTERN CHRISTIANITY; ORTHODOX CHURCHES; PATRISTICS / PATROLOGY; RUSSIAN ORTHODOX CHURCH; SIN, ORIGINAL; SOBORNOST; STARETZ; SYNODAL POLITY; TRADITION (IN CHRISTIANITY); TRINITY / TRINITARIAN THEOLOGY / TRINITARIAN PROCESSIONS; TRULLO, SYNOD OF; WESTERN CATHOLIC CHURCHES.

ORTHODOXY (IN CHRISTIANITY)

Derived from two Greek words meaning "right, correct" and "opinion, teaching," or "praise," orthodoxy is the quality of being in agreement with the accepted basic teaching of the church. (Its opposite is "heterodoxy" or "heresy.") The word itself was used only rarely in ancient Greek, until it was taken up by Christian theologians during the third century. At that time, it became important among Christians to distinguish the religious doctrine held by the majority of Christian communities and taught by their bishops, from those held by a wide variety of smaller sects (especially the "Gnostic" sects) who rejected various aspects of mainstream Christian belief (such as the humanity of Jesus, the divine creation of the material world, the authority of the Old Testament, and the universal offer of salvation). Into the seventh century of Christian history, there were also important disagreements *within* the mainstream church about how orthodox teaching should be explained and understood, particularly regarding the doctrine of the Trinity and the relationship of humanity and divinity within the person of Jesus. The Eastern Christian churches (those with origins in the eastern part of the Roman Empire, centered on the patriarchal cities of Constantinople, Antioch, Jerusalem, and Alexandria) came to refer to themselves as Orthodox churches in contrast to the opposing parties in these controversies. (Even now, however, certain Orthodox churches—known as *"Oriental* Orthodox Churches"—differ from *Eastern* Orthodoxy in their theological understanding of Christ.) In recent times, the liberation theology movement has called attention to the complementary term "ortho*praxis,*" in order to emphasize the importance of a lived or "practiced" faith over the merely passive acceptance of teachings. Partly in response to this development, some conservative Roman Catholics have appropriated "orthodox" and "orthodoxy" in more or less partisan ways, to indicate strict adherence to current Vatican teaching and policy in certain areas. By contrast with this popular usage, theological movements that have used the term (the mid-twentieth-century "Neo-Orthodoxy" and the more recent "Radical Orthodoxy") have attempted complex and careful explanations of the relationship of traditional Christian doctrine to contemporary human experience and social theory.

William A. Clark, s.j.

See also HERESY; HERETIC/HERETICAL; HETERODOX/HETERODOXY; NEO-ORTHODOX THEOLOGY; ORTHOPRAXIS.

ORTHODOXY, THE FEAST OF

The celebration, in Orthodox and Eastern Catholic Churches, of the defeat of the iconoclasts and of the restoration of the veneration of icons. The feast was established in the year 843, and it is usually held on the first Sunday of Lent. In time this feast also came to celebrate the defeat of all heresies and the victory of correct and true doctrine (that is, "orthodoxy").

Orlando Espín

See also CATHOLIC TRADITION; CONSTANTINOPLE, SEE OF; EASTERN CATHOLIC CHURCHES; HERESY; ICON; ICONOCLASTIC CONTROVERSY; ICONO-CLASTS; ICONODULES; MARIOLOGY; ORTHODOX CHURCHES; ORTHODOXY; SAINTS (CHRISTIAN), DEVOTION TO.

ORTHOLALIA

A neologism ("new word") meaning "correct speech." It is used to indicate those verbal or written expressions of mere *external* acceptance of doctrine or authority, and/or the public behavior that would indicate such external acceptance. Ortholalia is the *appearance* of orthodoxy or of ethical and obedient living, but it does not implicate sincere internal commitment to either. Although it could possibly be a cover-up for hypocrisy, it is especially a defense mechanism whereby those persecuted by intransigent authority can gain some relief by appearing to submit to the persecutor.

Orlando Espín

See also AUTHORITY; DOCTRINE; EPISTEMOLOGY; ETHICS, SOCIAL; JUSTICE; ORTHODOXY (IN CHRISTIAN-ITY); ORTHOPRAXIS.

ORTHOPRAXIS

In the 1960s and 1970s both European "political theology" and Latin American "liberation theology" asserted the priority of *orthopraxis*, or "right action" (from the Greek *orthos*, meaning "correct," and *praxis*, meaning "conduct") over *orthodoxy*, or "right thinking" (from the Greek *doxa*, meaning "opinion"). Political and liberation theologians claim that putting faith into action should take precedence over confessing faith in words and base their claim on the Bible itself (see, for example, Matt 7:21, Matt 25:31-45, and the Letter of James). They do not, however, contend that orthodoxy—thinking correctly about God—is insignificant. On the contrary, they maintain that action prompts reflection and careful reflection informs new actions. Thus the two are dialectically related. Yet, because Christian theologies in the past often emphasized the importance of holding correct beliefs and neglected the practice of love and justice, political and liberation theologians address the imbalance. At bottom their understanding of the relationship between orthopraxis and orthodoxy reflects their view that a true knowledge of God is possible only by loving God (through concrete acts of love of human neighbors) and a genuine knowledge of Jesus is attained only through discipleship (following Jesus).

James B. Nickoloff

See also ORTHODOXY (IN CHRISTIANITY); PRAXIS.

OSAMA BIN LADEN

See ISLAMIC RADICALISM (FUNDAMENTALISM).

OTTO, RUDOLF (1869–1937)

Otto was a nineteenth-century scholar of the history of religion, and from his extensive research into the growing number of available primary sources, he created a classic study called *The Idea of the Holy*. In it he explored the dense concepts that have clustered around the human experience of the sacred. He incorporated some new dimensions, broadening the technical language to include the sense of feeling. Using personal accounts, he suggested that the experience of the Holy is one of numinous significance, and creates in us feelings of awe and attraction. From his work, the word "numinous" has entered religious language.

Kathleen Dugan

See also NUMINOUS.

OTTOMAN

Adjective describing the Turkish peoples who conquered and ruled much of the Muslim world between the middle of the fourteenth century to the early part of the twentieth century C.E. Descended from other Turkish peoples who came from Central Asia, the Ottomans gained a foothold in western Asia Minor, in the country now called Turkey, in the thirteenth century C.E., and from there they began a series of conquests that eventually led to the establishment of the Ottoman Empire. At its height in the sixteenth century, this Islamic superpower controlled territories from the coast of Arabia in the south to southern Russia in the north, and from Asia Minor westward to the Balkans, Hungary, and the gates of Vienna. The Ottomans also ruled Egypt and North Africa. Though the empire suffered setbacks at the naval Battle of Lepanto in 1571 and in a second failed attempt to conquer Vienna in 1683, it continued to exist until 1923 when Mustafa Kamal Atatürk (1881–1938) abolished it and became the first president of the

Turkish Republic. By this time, most of the old empire had been lost in the wake of the Ottoman Empire's disastrous alliance with the Germans in World War I.

As they ascended to power and celebrated their military victories, the most impressive of which was the conquest of Constantinople (now called Istanbul) in 1453, the Ottomans also attempted to establish themselves as legitimate heirs of the Islamic religious leadership. Very early in their history, the Turks had embraced Sunni Islam, and as they expanded their political and military influence over many parts of the Islamic world, they claimed that the Abbasid Caliphate had passed from the Egyptians to them. Many Muslims reject this claim, and it is a matter of historic record that the Ottoman sultans (rulers) were far more concerned with the details of running their empire than with providing spiritual and moral guidance for the Muslims under their control.

Despite whatever shortcomings they may have had, the Ottoman sultans presided over an energetic and dedicated population. Known after the sixteenth century as Saracens by the Europeans who feared them and misunderstood their religion, the Turks have always been a hospitable people who enjoy conversation and the exchange of ideas. Their architects and builders constructed many beautiful mosques and monuments, especially in the city of Istanbul, and their artisans are famous for their handwoven carpets, brass works, and tiles. Today, the heir of the Ottoman Empire is called the Turkish Republic, a democracy known for its openness to Western culture and thought.

Ronald A. Pachence

See also ABBASIDS; ATATÜRK, MUSTAFA; MOSQUE/MASJID; SULTAN; SUNNA/SUNNI/SUNNISM.

OUSIA

Ousia ("substance") was the term used in the Creed of Nicaea (325) to express what the Father and the Son share within the Godhead and what guarantees their unity. The Cappadocian Fathers will finally state trinitarian orthodoxy in the formula of one ousia and three hypostases, a formula the Second Council of Constantinople in 553 will promulgate in its first anathema as "the Father, Son, and Holy Spirit have one nature (*physin*) or substance (*ousian*), that they have one power and authority, that there is a consubstantial (*homoousion*) Trinity, one Deity to be adored in three subsistences (*hypostasesin*) or persons (*prosopois*)."

Herbert J. Ryan, S.J.

See also ARIANISM; CAPPADOCIANS; CONSTANTINOPLE, SECOND COUNCIL OF; HOMOIOUSIOS TO PATRI; HOMOOUSIOS TO PATRI; HYPOSTASIS; NICAEA, FIRST COUNCIL OF; TRINITY/TRINITARIAN THEOLOGY/TRINITARIAN PROCESSIONS.

OXFORD MOVEMENT

Also known as Tractarianism and Puseyism, the nineteenth-century efforts of Keble, Newman, Pusey, and others to reinvigorate the Catholic (but not Roman) character of the Church of England and to promote the ideals of its seventeenth-century spiritual leaders. Keble is considered to be its founder by reason of his sermon "National Apostasy" in July 1833, when the church acceded to Parliament's suppression of ten Irish bishoprics.

The Movement's agenda was advanced by the leaflets (or "tracts") its leaders addressed to the clergy of the Church of England to publicize and argue the cause of a church more independent of the state and more faithful to traditional Catholic teachings and practices. These appeared in a series called "Tracts for the Times" and became quite popular. In 1838 over sixty thousand Tracts were sold. The leaflets soon evolved into learned treatises with the contributions of Pusey on baptism.

The Movement's leaders stressed the Incarnation, not the Atonement, as did the Evangelicals. They held that the Church of England was a branch of the church founded by Jesus Christ, that its clergy stood in unbroken apostolic succession that validated its sacraments, and that the Book of Common Prayer constituted the church's rule of faith. They revived more elaborate rituals in the liturgy for their aesthetic value as well as their religious efficacy. Thus, according to Newman, the Church of England would become more truly what it was, the *via media* (the middle way) between the aberrations of Protestantism and the corruptions of Roman Catholicism. Debates over the character and identity of the Church of England that began then continue today.

The credibility of the Movement's leaders was enhanced by their personal holiness and their intellectual talents, demonstrated in their sermons and tracts. While they held bishops to be successors of the apostles, however, they opposed bishops they considered too Protestant or liberal (that is, inclusive). English Evangelicals resisted the Movement for fear that it would lead to reunion with Rome. Many Roman Catholics were not sympathetic either, for they saw the attempt to be Catholic without being Roman a hollow pretense.

The Movement failed to accomplish all its aims, but its reinvigoration of Catholic forms of worship continue to influence Anglican liturgical practice today.

Jon Nilson

See also BOOK OF COMMON PRAYER; KEBLE, JOHN; NEWMAN, JOHN HENRY; PUSEY, EDWARD.

P

PACEM IN TERRIS

In 1963 Pope John XXIII addressed the encyclical letter *Pacem in Terris* (meaning "Peace on Earth") to the entire church and to all people of good will. In the context of the threat of nuclear war, hanging over humanity since World War II, and of massive social injustice in the world, the Pope offered guidelines for establishing true peace based on Catholic principles. Necessary for such peace, he argued, are truth, justice, love, and liberty. The five parts of his letter deal with individual rights and duties; the authority of the state, and the relations between the individual and the state; relations between states based on the rights and duties of states; the relation between the universal common good and modern states; and finally, the duties of Catholics in public life. Especially noteworthy in this encyclical letter is the Pope's demand (in nos. 109–119) for an end to the arms race because of the fear it creates in people and because its economic cost impedes social progress, especially in the less developed countries. "It is contrary to reason," declares the Pope, "to hold that war is now a suitable way to restore rights which have been violated" (no. 127). This theme was taken up by the Second Vatican Council in 1965 in *Gaudium et Spes* (Pastoral Constitution on the Church in the Modern World).

James B. Nickoloff

See also JOHN XXIII, POPE.

PACHOMIUS (292?–347)

Pachomius was converted from paganism to Christianity in 313 and immediately felt drawn to the monastic life. After monastic training under the hermit Palamon, Pachomius formed his own community of monks. His was the first really successful experiment in the monastic common life, and therefore Pachomius is known as the founder of cenobitism (monks living in community). He organized several monasteries with thousands of monks and nuns, all living under his rule of strict poverty and rigid discipline. Athanasius of Alexander supported Pachomius, and Jerome translated his Rule into Latin.

Gary Macy

See also ATHANASIUS, PATRIARCH OF ALEXANDRIA; JEROME; MONASTICISM IN EASTERN CHRISTIANITY; RULE (MONASTIC/RELIGIOUS).

PACIFISM

See ETHICS, SOCIAL; PEACE; WAR.

PAGANISM/PAGANS

These terms are used mostly by Christians to refer pejoratively to non-monotheistic religions and their followers. Originally, *paganus* (in Latin) simply meant "country-side dweller" and, by extension, something like "rustic." But in time Christians began to employ *paganus* to refer first to those who continued practicing the old Greco-Roman religion and later to followers of any other non-monotheistic religion (Jews and Muslims, therefore, are not "pagans" in the Christian use of the term). Unfortunately, the term "paganism" has also been popularly and incorrectly used to refer to folk or popular religions. The modern survival or invention, in the West, of some practices associated with nature or with European pre-Christian religions has been labeled "paganism" or "neopaganism" by some of their practitioners, but this contemporary use of the term is so broad, encompassing such a great variety of practices and beliefs, that it is difficult to determine its meaning—although it seems that present-day "paganism" has little direct historical connection to pre-Christian European religions.

Orlando Espín

See also HIGH GOD/SUPREME GOD; GRECO-ROMAN RELIGION; INDIGENOUS RELIGIOUS TRADITIONS; MONOTHEISM (IN CHRISTIANITY AND ISLAM); MONOTHEISM (IN JUDAISM); POLYTHEISM; POPULAR RELIGIONS.

PAHO

From the Hopi, this literally means "something breathed upon," and refers to the ritual objects created of natural symbols and usually adorned with a wild bird's feather. Once made, they are used to convey blessings upon homes, persons, and natural places that are considered sacred. They are seen as bearers of prayer, and they are meant to be used in this way. For instance, left at a spring, they continue to express the prayer of the person who placed it there. Thus they are part of a universal family of ritual objects that act similarly, from Christian candles to Tibetan Buddhist prayer flags and wheels.

Kathleen Dugan

See also KACHINAS; PRAYER.

PALI

The language of the Theravada Buddhist canon, the earliest scriptures of Buddhism, Pali is a Prakrit language, that is, a vernacular related to Sanskrit. Important Pali and Sanskrit words are therefore often close in spelling and pronunciation, as evidenced in the following Pali/Sanskrit pairs: *nibbana/nirvana*, *dhamma/dharma*, *kamma/karma*.

Lance E. Nelson

See also BUDDHISM; SANSKRIT; THERAVADA BUDDHISM.

PALI CANON

The term refers to the entire Tripitaka ("Three Baskets") of the Theravadin school that was committed to writing in Sri Lanka during the reign of King Vattagamani (29–17 B.C.E.): the *Vinaya Pitaka* on monastic discipline; the *Sutta Pitaka* of Discourses by the Buddha and leading disciples; and the *Abhidhamma Pitaka* of advanced and systematic philosophical analysis. It was assumed closed at that time.

Pali refers to a Sanskrit-derived language of north India, one among a number of spoken and literary vernaculars (*prakrits*), that came into use for Indic literatures in antiquity. The entire Pali Canon has a full commentarial and subcommentarial literature to supplement it. After initial codification in Sri Lanka, this collection became authoritative for the Theravada school, and copies were preserved in the different scripts in Burma, Laos, Cambodia, and Thailand. The entire Pali Canon has been translated (along with major commentaries) into English by the Pali Text Society. Its length in printed form is roughly four times the size of the Bible.

Todd T. Lewis

See also BUDDHAGHOSHA; THERAVADA BUDDHISM; TRIPITAKA.

PALIMPSEST

A term that may refer to different types of material, parchment, papyrus, or the like, that have been inscribed more than once. The previous texts are still visible to a greater or lesser extent on a palimpsest since they have not been fully erased. Palimpsests exist because writing materials were reused, usually for a different type of material. Of the two hundred and fifty uncial manuscripts of the New Testament known today, fifty-two are palimpsests. Frequently it is only through the use of modern technology that the obliterated writing is able to be read.

Russell Fuller

PALO MAYOMBE

A complex of magical practices and beliefs of Kongo-Angolan origins preserved and subsequently developed among some Afro-Cuban descendants of former Kongo slaves. *Palo* is sometimes practiced by followers of Santería, but legitimate *santeros* strongly object to the rituals performed by *paleros*. Palo mayombe is commonly associated with magic performed for evil or harmful purposes, and is held by its practitioners to be very efficient in achieving results. Although far from the sophistication and popularity of Santería in the U.S. and in Latin America, Palo's presence and attraction are well documented.

Orlando Espín

See also AFRICAN TRADITIONAL RELIGIONS; AFRO-LATIN RELIGIONS; CANDOMBLÉ; MACUMBA; MAGIC; SANTERÍA; VODOUN.

PANENTHEISM

From the Greek *pan* and *theos* meaning "all in God," the term refers to those theological positions that maintain the world is distinct but not separate from God. Thus, panentheism is to be distinguished from pantheism that identifies God with the world. Broadly, the term is used as a synonym for process or neoclassical metaphysics.

J. A. Colombo

See also PANTHEISM; PROCESS THEOLOGY.

PANIKKAR, RAIMUNDO (1918–)

Dr. Panikkar has over a lifetime created an impressive body of theological works. His advantage of being born into a family that shared two cultures and two religions inclined him to study the encounter of the world's religions in a way that was new. His insight has deepened and grown to offer a most challenging approach to this new frontier. He has been at the forefront of interreligious dialogue for thirty years, but more important, he has the intellectual foundation to interpret its meaning as it develops in wider forums. His connection with the challenges raised by Vatican II is clear. He is a pioneer in many ways, helping to rethink the core beliefs of Christianity as it enters into dialogue with other religions.

Kathleen Dugan

See also VATICAN, SECOND COUNCIL OF THE.

PANNENBERG, WOLFHART
(1928–)

German Lutheran theologian. While writing on almost every topic in fundamental and systematic theology for the last thirty years, Wolfhart Pannenberg's corpus shows remarkable consistency in elaborating an eschatologically oriented Christian theology of universal history. Unlike his neo-orthodox contemporaries, Pannenberg's work—especially his works on anthropology, christology, and philosophy of science—embodies a constructive engagement with both the human and natural sciences that has earned him the label "rationalist" by some. His *Jesus— God and Man* (1968) remains one of the major works of christology in the twentieth century, distinguished by a tenacious defense of the historicity of the resurrection. In 1993, Pannenberg completed his *Systematic Theology*.

J. A. Colombo

PANTHEISM

A philosophical teaching claiming that all that exists is, ultimately, an expression or appearance of one single reality. The term "pantheism" was first used in 1709 by John Toland, but the idea goes back to the ancient Greeks and to classical Eastern religions. Philosophically, two strands of pantheism might be detected. One strand sees God as the one and only reality, thereby understanding all that exists as only an appearance or expression of God without any reality of its own. The second strand of pantheistic thought sees God as an immanent part of all that exists, thereby not denying the reality of what exists but never separating God and all else that exists. Pantheism is not equivalent to panentheism.

Orlando Espín

See also PANENTHEISM; THEISM/THEISTIC.

PAPACY/PAPAL

"Papacy," or the adjective, "papal," refers to the exercise of the Petrine ministry by the pope, the Bishop of Rome. The term "pope" in Italian ("papa") means "father." The duration of a pope's office (comprising the period from his election as pope until his death) is also referred to as his "papacy." For example, "John Paul II traveled more extensively during his papacy than any other pontiff."

Mary Ann Hinsdale

See also PETRINE MINISTRY; PONTIFF; POPE.

PAPYRUS

As early as the third millennium B.C.E. papyrus was used as a writing material in Egypt. It was also an important trade item. Papyrus was made from the papyrus plant, *cyperus papyrus*, that was abundant in lower Egypt in ancient times. The material was manufactured from strips of the inner pith of the plant that were placed one on top of the other in horizontal and vertical strips. A glue was then applied, and when dry the finished sheet would be smoothed and polished using shell or stone implements. Sheets could be glued together to make rolls. Papyrus was used to copy manuscripts of both the Old and the New Testaments. Some biblical manuscripts from Qumran written on papyrus have survived, although the majority of manuscripts were written on leather. Earlier in Israel's history papyrus may have been used more than leather.

Russell Fuller

PARABLE

A term from the Greek *parabolē*, the root of which means to place things side by side for comparison. In the LXX (Septuagint), *parabolē* usually translates the Hebrew *mashal* and covers various literary forms. Strictly speaking, a parable is a literary form, a short story with a double meaning that intends to point beyond its literal sense to another truth.

The use of parables is, for example, the most striking feature of the teaching of Jesus as it is recorded in the Synoptic Gospels (there are none in John). Over one-third of the teaching of Jesus as reflected in the Gospel traditions is in the form of parables. Similarly, in the early centuries of the Common Era, the Jewish rabbis extensively used parables as a major teaching device.

As can be observed in Jesus' teaching, a parable sets forth a comparison rooted in nature or common life experience, something illustrating a moral or religious point. While it is not easy to draw distinctions among parables, metaphors, and similes, since all involve comparisons, generally the parable is more extended. In other words, very often it is a developed simile or metaphor, as reflected in the introductory formula for numerous Gospel parables, "The kingdom of heaven is like . . ." In contrast to fables, which are also fictitious stories, a parable, though fictitious, always sounds plausible and true to life.

When someone such as Jesus begins to tell a parable, the listeners usually experience an abrupt change of subject. Parables seem to function as deviations from what the subject of dialogue had been up to the point the parable is told. This "irritant" causes listeners to ask what relevance the speaker sees in introducing the story. It is precisely in this way that a parable, functioning as a seeming intruder into a dialogue, has the power to make listeners think. Parables require that hearers figure out for themselves why the story is being told in the current context. As Jesus used them, they were intended to "shock" his hearers to undertake action and reform. Thus C. H. Dodd could state in his definition, now classic, that "at its simplest the parable is a metaphor or simile drawn from nature or common life, arresting the hearer by its vividness or strangeness, and leaving the mind in sufficient doubt about its precise application to tease it into active thought" (*The Parables of the Kingdom* [1961] 16).

F. M. Gillman

See also ALLEGORY IN JUDAISM; SEPTUAGINT; SYNOPTIC GOSPELS.

PARACLETE

This English term is the transliteration of a Greek word derived from legal terminology, meaning "called to the side of" in the sense of being an advocate or defense attorney. Its importance in biblical studies is due to its use in the Johannine writings.

In 1 John 2:1 Jesus himself is described as an Advocate with the Father on behalf of Christians who might sin. Here the image of a trial before God underlies the use of the term. In the Gospel of John, however, there are instances where the term is used in a broader and more general sense of "helper" for the Christians (see, for example, John 14:16-17, 26; 15:26; 16:7-15). Jesus promises his followers that after he leaves he will send them another Paraclete, variously translated as "Counselor," "Comforter," and "Advocate," who will remain with them. It is evident that the Paraclete in these instances is the Holy Spirit or the Spirit of Truth.

In John 14:16 Jesus describes the Spirit of truth as being *another* Advocate. Thus, in Johannine thought Jesus is seen as the first Advocate, the intercessor for the Christians in heaven, while the Paraclete spoken of in the Gospel, the helper of Christians, described as teacher, witness to Jesus, and prosecutor of the world, is the continued presence in the world of that Jesus who has returned to God.

F. M. Gillman

See also HOLY SPIRIT; JOHANNINE CORPUS; PNEUMA.

PARADISE (IN JUDAISM)

See GARDEN OF EDEN.

PARADOSIS

See TRADITION.

PARAMITA

A Buddhist Sanskrit term for a "per fection" needed for enlightenment. Although known in the early texts (Pali, *parami*) as general ideals, in the Mahayana they became more systematically expounded qualities to be cultivated by bodhisattvas. In these schools, the *paramitas* together combine the ideals of compassion for all beings with the spiritual insight into the interdependence of all existence and the ultimately empty nature (*shunyata*) of all things. In the early *Prajnaparamita Sutras*, there are six stages: *dana* ("giving"), *shila* ("morality"), *kshanti* ("patience"), *virya* ("energy"), *samadhi* ("trance"), and *prajna* ("insight"). Later texts, such as Asanga's *Bodhisattvabhumi*, expanded on the number of paramitas to ten with the addition of *pranidhana* ("vow resolution"), *upaya* ("skill in means"), *bala* ("power"), and finally *jhana* ("knowledge").

Todd T. Lewis

See also BODHISATTVA; MAHAYANA BUDDHISM.

PARENESIS

Taken from the Greek *parainesis*, meaning "counsel," or "exhortation." In the New Testament, only the verb appears (Acts 27:9, 22). The form critic Martin Dibelius coined this word for a series of moral sayings and warnings that lack specific reference to their source or situation. Parenetic texts offer friendly yet authoritative moral advice, citing broad maxims of standard ethical wisdom and heroic persons as models of virtue. Notice, for example, how 1 Thessalonians 5:1-11 moves from concrete issues about the timing of Jesus' final return to wider exhortation about living as children of light. Parenesis may strengthen uniquely Christian arguments, provide pastoral advice, enrich a moralizing sermon, or complement worship practice. New Testament parenesis often resembles typical Hellenistic lists of social virtues and vices, or Jewish "household codes" about suitable behavior between household members. Parenetic texts occur often in Paul's letters, James, 1 John, Jude, 1 and 2 Peter, the Pastoral Letters, and especially the Epistle to the Hebrews. Pre-Christian examples appear in Deuteronomy, Proverbs, and the prose of Jeremiah.

Francis D. Connolly-Weinert

See also WISDOM LITERATURE.

PARINIRVANA

The "complete nirvana" in Buddhism that involves the disintegration of the psychophysical being who has "blown out" the flame of karma and realized *bodhi* as a Buddha or Arahant. The *parinirvana* of Shakyamuni that occurred in his eightieth year, roughly forty-five years after his realization of enlightenment under the Bodhi Tree, became one of the four essential scenes in early Buddhist art; this site in Kushinagara was one of the eight essential pilgrimage places for Indian Buddhists.

After parinirvana, the enlightened "enters" a state beyond expressible metaphor, negative in the sense of being absent of all individual qualities, positive in the sense of being (to use textual terms) "immortal, blissful, pure." For the Theravada schools, the parinirvana state is the same for all; for the Mahayana schools, the Shakyamuni Buddha's parinirvana was a "mere show" to inspire disciples to strive hard and take the limitations of their mortality seriously.

Todd T. Lewis

See also BODHI; MAHAYANA BUDDHISM; NIRVANA; TATHAGATA; THERAVADA BUDDHISM.

PARISH

(Greek, *paroiki*; Latin, *parochia*, dwelling near). A group of Christian faithful, usually living within a specific geographic area within a diocese, form a parish. Traditionally, the bishop entrusts the pastoral care of this community to a priest called the pastor. It is within a parish that most Catholics live out the call of their baptism to minister to the needs of the world. The parish usually contains a specific building (church, parish hall) for gathering for worship, prayer, education, fellowship, and social outreach. The bishop may approve a recognizable group as a parish according to rite, nationality, language, ethnicity, or other religious needs, and it may contain no special territory. Canon law protects the stability of a parish, giving it a juridical identity. A bishop must consult with the presbyteral council (advisory group of priests) of the diocese before making major changes such as opening or closing a parish, and developing procedures for

removing or transferring pastors. When a pastor vacates his parish (death or other causes), the bishop or his representative is expected to consult the parish leadership in order to provide a parish profile before deciding on a successor (Can. 524).

Today, many changes are taking place in the structure of parishes. Some dioceses have a policy of keeping parishes small so that parishioners may maintain a sense of community. In some cases, the bishop designates a deacon or layperson as leader. In other areas, the numbers of Catholics make small parishes economically unfeasible. Small parishes merge into larger ones. Parishes struggle to find structures and sufficient personnel to care for their many ministries and still maintain the sense of community called for by the reforms of Vatican II. Many parishes facilitate the formation of small communities within the parish structure. Trained laypeople carry out leadership roles within these communities. These communities may gather around neighborhoods, specific ministries, small faith-sharing groups, or "microchurches" that perform the major ministries of the church, but do it within the confines of the community. Such groups promote the development of parish identity and unity and they prove to be great instruments of evangelization.

According to the research done by the parish study of the University of Notre Dame (1987), the most important character of a truly active parish is its hospitality, followed by active liturgy and education for *all* members. The parish becomes energized when it gives obvious witness to its mission by its commitment to areas of social concerns and outreach.

M. Jane Gorman

See also COMMUNION (ECCLESIOLOGICAL); ECCLESIOLOGY.

PARITTA

A term for a class of "protective chants" in the Theravada Buddhist tradition handed down by Shakyamuni Buddha. He taught monks and nuns to chant these verses to create auspiciousness in an environment, allay fear, expel spirits, and to cure specific forms of illness such as snakebite. This class of scripture is called *raksha* in Buddhist Sanskrit literature.

Paritta texts became one of the most popular recitations in all Buddhist societies, representing the pragmatic domain of Buddhism, a perspective that is often overlooked in historical assessments of the faith. In the Pali Canon there are at least five different *parittas*.

Todd T. Lewis

See also DEMON (IN WORLD RELIGIONS); EXORCISM; MARA.

PARKER, MATTHEW (1504–75)

Archbishop of Canterbury (1559–75). He was appointed chaplain first to Queen Anne Boleyn and then to King Henry VIII. During the Catholic Restoration under Mary Tudor, he went into hiding where he pursued private studies.

Preferring the scholar's life, he reluctantly accepted Elizabeth I's appointment as archbishop of Canterbury. The "Nag's Head Fable" recounts his supposedly irregular and irreverent consecration at the Nag's Head Tavern and was used by some Roman Catholics to deny the validity of Anglican orders. This was, however, a fabrication. Parker was prudent and moderate as archbishop. He was the chief author of the Thirty-Nine Articles finalized in 1571. He was also a major architect of the Elizabethan Settlement (1559) that created the Church of England as a state church claiming continuity with the ancient and undivided church and taking the middle way (*via media*) between Roman Catholicism and Puritanism.

Jon Nilson

See also ANGLICAN ORDERS, CONTROVERSY OVER; THIRTY-NINE ARTICLES.

PAROUSIA

In the Greco-Roman world, the term *parousia* was used to speak of the elaborate visits of state officials as well as of appearances or the invisible presence of the gods at cultic services. The early church applied this term, literally meaning "active presence," to express the expectation of the imminent second coming of Christ (1 Cor 15:23; 1 Thess 2:19; 3:13; 4:15; 5:23; 2 Thess 2:1, 8; Jas 5:7, 8; 2 Pet 1:16; 3:4; 1 John 2:28).

In the late postexilic era there was an expectation that God would break into history and establish a new heaven and new earth. Some believed that, at that time, the righteous dead would be raised, and many believed the new eschatological (final) age would be established by God's anointed agent, a Messiah, who would vanquish the forces of evil in a cataclysmic battle. The pseudepigraphal apocalyptic texts, 4 Ezra and 2 Baruch, stress the belief that the imminent end of the present age would be followed by the inbreaking of God's rule, inaugurating an age of peace and joy. Enoch 37–71 sketches the general nature of these prominent first-century eschatological expectations, although it does not appear that any particular eschatological beliefs had solidified into a consensus.

Since the reign of God was the central focus of his teachings, the Jesus of history drew upon the eschatological hopes of postexilic Israel. When, after experiencing his resurrection, his followers fully understood him as the Messiah, they came to believe that his advent in history and especially his death inaugurated the eschatological age. The early Christians anticipated that Christ would come again soon to fully establish the reign of God. Paul speculates on this event in 1 Thessalonians 4:13-17 and 1 Corinthians 15:22-57. There are several other passages that refer to this expectation in the Second Testament (for example, Matt 24:29-31; Mark 13:24-27; Luke 24:25-28; it is most developed in the book of Revelation 19:11–22:7). These passages explain that at the parousia Christ will come again, the dead will be raised, evil forces will be destroyed, all are judged by Christ, and some will be condemned to eternal punishment while others will enter eternal life with God.

Since the parousia did not occur within the first generation of the Resurrection, Christian authors began to put less emphasis on its imminence (for example, Matt 25:1-13; Mark 13:32-37; Luke 21:7-9; 2 Pet 3:1-13). While the belief that Christ will come again remains a feature of Christian expectation to this day, New Testament texts indicate that since the late first century there has been a tendency to modify eschatology from its exclusive association with the parousia by understandings associated with realized eschatology (such as Rom 6). Realized eschatology recognizes that Christ comes to those who have faith, and that the gift and grace of faith empowers Christians to transform their hearts and lives according to the ideals of God's reign within history while awaiting its fulfillment at some unknown time in the future (for example, John 14:18-23).

Regina A. Boisclair

See also ESCHATOLOGY (IN CHRISTIANITY).

PARVATI

In Hinduism, Parvati is a name of the Great Goddess, identified with Shakti, the supreme cosmic energy. Parvati is in myth the spouse of Shiva and the mother of Ganesha. Hindus typically regard Parvati, Sati, and Durga as forms of the same deity.

Lance E. Nelson

See also DURGA; KALI; SHAKTA; SHAKTI.

PASCAL, BLAISE (1623–62)

French scientist and mathematician, philosopher, and religious polemicist, Pascal not only invented the barometer, but also gave the Jansenists their most eloquent spokesperson. Pascal's own sister, Jacqueline, entered the convent of Port-Royal, the center of Jansenist sentiment; her brother Blaise was a frequent guest at the convent. In 1656–7 Pascal published a series of eighteen letters in which he defended Antoine Arnauld's sacramental theology and attacked the Jesuits for "laxity" in moral theology. Written in graceful, sophisticated French, the *Provincial Letters* defended a rigorous approach to the sacraments of penance and Eucharist, one in which absolution would be given sparingly and Communion approached infrequently. The Jesuits were mocked and reproached for allowing easy access to the Eucharist, for absolving all too readily, and for minimizing the gravity of sin. Pascal specifically attacked casuistry, that is, the methods of those moral theologians and confessors who evaluate the sinfulness of an act in relation to its particular context and circumstances.

In 1670, several years after Pascal's death, his *Pensées* were first published. These "thoughts" were fragments of an unfinished work designed as an apology for the Christian faith. Here, Pascal examined the misery and greatness of humanity and attempted to demonstrate the advantages of belief in God.

Thomas Worcester, s.j.

See also ARNAULD, ANGÉLIQUE AND ANTOINE; CASUISTRY; JANSENISM; SOCIETY OF JESUS.

PASCHAL

The word paschal is derived from the Greek word for Easter (*pascha*) that in turn comes from the Hebrew word for Passover (*pesah*). It is the adjectival form used for ideas, elements, or objects relating to the theological concept of Christ's suffering, death, and resurrection, or to the liturgical celebration of that event at Easter.

Joanne M. Pierce

See also EASTER; PASCHAL CANDLE; PASCHAL MYSTERY.

PASCHAL CANDLE

The paschal (or Easter) candle is a piece of liturgical furnishing used at the Easter Vigil, during the Easter season, and during baptismal liturgies in Christian denominations that have a rather "high" (or ceremonial) view of Christian worship. The candle itself is large and rather tall (in the Middle Ages the candle could often be very massive, weighing tens of pounds), and it is inscribed with five grains of incense in a cross-shaped pattern. These five grains of incense are ritually placed in the cross as the candle is blessed and ceremonially lighted at the beginning of the Easter Vigil on Holy Saturday evening. The candle is then carried in procession, and placed in a large, often ornate, stand in a prominent place near the altar and pulpit at the front of the church (in the sanctuary).

Joanne M. Pierce

See also EASTER; HOLY WEEK; LENT.

PASCHAL MYSTERY

The Christian term *paschal mystery* refers to the suffering (passion), death, and resurrection of Jesus Christ. The word *paschal* refers to Passover/Easter, the time when the *mystery* is understood to have take place at the end of Christ's life. In Christian theology, it is this paschal mystery, the death and resurrection of Christ, that is the core of both Christian faith (cf. 1 Cor 15:12-17), and the expression of that faith in liturgical celebration. For example, the liturgical year revolves around this theological theme, not just the Lent/Easter seasons (which are perhaps most obviously centered on the theme of the death and resurrection of Christ), but all the feasts and fasts of liturgical time (for instance, Advent/Christmas, with their emphases on the culmination of time in the First and Second Comings of Christ in the Incarnation).

All the liturgical rites of the church participate in the paschal mystery, and make it present in the here and now. This can be seen most intensively in the sacraments of baptism and Eucharist. In baptism, one can be said to die and rise with Christ, and thus become one with Christ. And at the celebration of the Eucharist (or Mass), the assembly affirms and realizes its unity as the Body of Christ by making memorial (*anamnesis*) of Christ's death and resurrection, and sacramentally "enter into" the paschal mystery by receiving together Christ's Body and Blood. Thus the paschal mystery can be said to lie at the heart of all Christian worship, and because of the central role worship plays in the reality of the church, it lies at the heart of the true Christian life as well.

Joanne M. Pierce

See also ADVENT; CHRISTMAS; EASTER; LENT; LITURGICAL YEAR; SACRAMENT; SACRAMENTAL THEOLOGY.

PASSION NARRATIVES

The accounts of the arrest, trial, crucifixion, and death of Jesus found in each of the four canonical Gospels. The term "passion" comes from the Latin verb *patior*, meaning "to bear," or "to suffer"; hence, in this context, "the suffering of Jesus." The Greek word is *paschō*, occurring only in Acts 1:3 with reference to the suffering of Jesus.

Each of the Gospels concludes with a well-formulated and detailed account of the last days of Jesus. More than in the rest of the Gospel sections, attention in the passion narratives is given to sequence of events, time, interaction of characters, and unified theme. Not only the events themselves but also the meaning they bear is unfolded. Although other New Testament authors do not present a passion narrative itself, they do summarize and assume this story in their theological interpretation.

Citing what may well have been one of the earliest Christian creeds in First Corinthians, Paul tells the community that he is handing on what he received: "that Christ died for our sins in accordance with the scriptures, and that he was buried, and that he was raised on the third day . . ." (1 Cor 15:3-4). In this statement Paul does three things: (1) names the event—the death of Christ, that is, his passion; (2) gives a theological interpretation—for our sins; and (3) offers the rationale for this meaning—according to the Scriptures. The Gospel writers accomplish a similar purpose in their more extended narratives.

In Mark, generally regarded as the earliest of the Gospels, the passion narrative is found in chapters 14 and 15; in Matthew, chapters 26–27; in Luke, 22–23; and finally, in John, 13–19. This extensive narrative, by far the longest in the Jesus story, is remarkably similar in all the Gospels. Of these, John offers the longest as well as the most distinctive account of the death of Jesus, thus indicating the more dominant role this story plays in the Fourth Gospel.

The historical causes for the death of Jesus remain a topic of continual debate. The manner of Jesus' death presented a significant challenge to the early Christian missionaries. Dying on a cross, called crucifixion, was a form of capital punishment used by the Roman authorities. Thus, on the surface, Jesus did not die a hero's or martyr's death like, for example, the Maccabean brothers two centuries earlier, or Gandhi, in the twentieth century. Several historical factors probably led to Jesus being condemned to death, including the religious charge of blasphemy and the political charge of claiming to be king of the Jews.

Faced with the task of explaining Christ crucified, "a stumbling block to Jews [for cursed is the one who dies on a tree], and foolishness to Gentiles" (1 Cor 1:23), Paul asserted that the Cross was indeed the "wisdom of God" (1 Cor 1:21). For their part, the four evangelists interpreted the scandal of the Cross in light of the Old Testament. A number of passages speak about the (divine) "necessity" for the Messiah to suffer and die (Mark 8:31; Luke 17:25; 24:26, 48).

The passion narratives make the point that although Jesus died a criminal's death, he was unjustly condemned. Indeed, he was innocent, and like the innocent faithful ones put to death before him in the tradition, God vindicated him. Jesus was vindicated by being raised to life. The motif of the Suffering Servant who died on behalf of many (Isaiah 53) and themes from the psalms of lament (like Psalm 22) were mined for their interpretative value.

As the psalmist suffers anguish, cries out to God for deliverance, and ultimately experiences triumph with God, so too does the suffering Jesus.

In Mark's Gospel, the imminent death of Jesus is indicated much before the passion narrative itself. Religious authorities plot how to destroy him (3:6); three times Jesus speaks about the suffering and death of the Son of man (8:31; 9:30-32; 10:33-34). Then, the passion story unfolds at Passover time, beginning with the account of a woman who comes to anoint him, followed by the Last Supper. At this meal Jesus speaks about "my blood . . . which is poured out for many" (14:24). Immediately following, Jesus is denied three times by Peter and betrayed by Judas, both of them among his chosen disciples.

His impending fate nears as religious leaders charge him with blasphemy, and lead him to Pilate, the Roman governor of Judea. Yielding to the demands of the frenzied crowd, Pilate had Jesus crucified. On the cross, as Jesus gave out a loud cry and expired, a Roman centurion came to believe, saying: "Truly this man was God's Son!" (15:39). None of Jesus' chosen disciples were there except a few women who looked on from a distance, and Joseph of Arimathea, who had gotten permission to take the body of Jesus and place it in a tomb. This Jesus who was crucified, died, and was buried, is then gloriously raised up by the living God in the climactic chapter of Mark's Gospel.

Matthew and Luke each narrate the Passion following Mark's version, yet with their own emphases. In Matthew, cosmic signs after the death of Jesus are expanded, the scriptural fulfillment motif is highlighted, and the vindicated Son of man charges the community to proclaim the Good News to all nations (28:16-20). For Luke, Jesus' death is the ultimate form of servant leadership as opposed to oppressive leadership. Jesus is portrayed as the faithful Israelite who suffers unjustly, who forgives his executioners and the repentant criminal, and whose last cry is: "Father, into your hands I commend my spirit" (23:46).

In John's Gospel, the passion narrative includes an extensive farewell discourse of Jesus addressing his disciples. Jesus instructs them about God's love and promises them the gift of the Spirit. Beginning with the arrest, Jesus the prisoner is presented as in charge of the events, giving commands and challenging accusers. In a scene unique to this Gospel, while on the cross, Jesus entrusts the disciple whom he loved to his mother, and then his mother to the disciple, a final act that creates a new community.

John Gillman

See also GOSPEL; RESURRECTION OF CHRIST; SYNOPTIC PROBLEM.

PASSOVER

(Hebrew, *Pesah*). With Tabernacles and Pentecost, one of Judaism's three pilgrimage festivals on which, in biblical times, all Israelite males were obligated to appear at the Temple in Jerusalem (Deut 16:16). Passover commemorates the Exodus from Egypt, described in the first fourteen chapters of the biblical book of Exodus. Particular emphasis is upon the unleavened bread eaten by the Israelites as a result of their hasty departure from Egypt (Exod 12). Passover is celebrated for seven (in the Diaspora, eight) days, the first and last day (in the Diaspora, two days) of which are holy days and the middle days of which are in the status of Chol HaMoed. On the first night (in the Diaspora, two nights), the events of the Exodus are relived through a ritual meal called a Seder, at which the text of the Haggadah is read. During the entire duration of the Passover, Jews are forbidden from consuming, or even possessing, leavened products.

Alan J. Avery-Peck

See also CHOL HAMOED; HAGGADAH; HAMETZ; MATZAH; SEDER.

PASTOR
This term originally referred to a shepherd or herdsman who fed his flock or herd. The title, pastor, designates the clergyperson serving as head of a local church or parish. Within the Catholic tradition, the pastor is a priest designated by the bishop of a diocese to direct and foster the life of a community within a specific geographic area or a specific group of people without a territory. The pastor is responsible for overseeing the pastoral ministries of the parish including all areas of education, liturgy, social justice, and outreach, hospitality, administration, and finances. The role also entails enabling the laity to participate in, and even lead, the many ministries open to their participation. Today, there are parishes or missions that have a deacon or layperson serving as parish coordinator and ministry enabler. An ordained priest visits regularly to celebrate those sacraments requiring the presence of an ordained minister, especially the Eucharist and the sacrament of reconciliation.

M. Jane Gorman

See also BISHOP (ORDINARY); CHURCH; DIOCESE/ARCHDIOCESE; MINISTRY/ MINISTERIAL; PARISH.

PASTOR AETERNUS
Literally, "eternal pastor," the first two words of the Dogmatic Constitution on the Church of Christ, issued by Vatican I on July 18, 1870. This document defined papal primacy and papal infallibility. The original intention of the council was to go much further in defining the nature of the church, but the council was forced to adjourn due to the outbreak of the Franco-Prussian War.

Mary Ann Hinsdale

See also CHURCH; INFALLIBILITY; PAPACY/PAPAL; PRIMACY; VATICAN, FIRST COUNCIL OF THE.

PASTORAL
Besides describing rural settings and works pertaining to shepherding or herding, "pastoral" describes the many works and activities of a Roman Catholic parish led by a pastor. Used as a noun, a pastoral refers to a letter from a pastor to his congregation or a letter addressed by a bishop to his diocese.

M. Jane Gorman

See also BISHOP (EPISCOPACY); PARISH; PASTOR; PASTORAL LETTER.

PASTORAL LETTER
In Roman Catholicism, an official communication of a bishop to the people of his diocese, or of a conference of bishops to their collective dioceses, regarding some issue deemed to be of spiritual and pastoral importance to the people. On the diocesan level, these might be thought of as the local equivalent of the pope's encyclical letters; the bishop's authority to teach in this way is secured by his position as the chief pastor of his diocese. At the level of regional or national conferences, the bishops exercise a feature of their *collegiality*—their cooperative responsibility for the whole church—by teaching together on a topic of importance

for their region. In the United States, outstanding examples of this approach include "The Challenge of Peace" in 1983, on the ethical aspects of national policy with regard to nuclear weapons, and with "Economic Justice for All" in 1986, on ethical questions arising from national economic policy.

William A. Clark, s.j.

See also CHALLENGE OF PEACE; ECONOMIC JUSTICE FOR ALL.

PASTORAL THEOLOGY

Theology—the academic discipline that investigates and seeks to understand God's self-revelation as that revelation is received in the Scriptures and traditions of Christianity. *Pastoral*—the brand of theology focusing on the ways in which Christian faith is expressed, communicated, and lived by believers. Specifically, pastoral theology addresses issues of concern to Christian ministers such as religious education, worship, preaching, pastoral counseling, and social justice. It is called "pastoral" in the sense that it involves the mission or ministry of the church; from the Latin *pastor* or shepherd —an ancient image for the caring concern Christ and his followers have for all God's people.

Ronald A. Pachence

See also MINISTRY/MINISTERIAL; PASTORAL; PRACTICAL THEOLOGY; REVELATION (IN CHRISTIAN PERSPECTIVE).

PATANJALI

See YOGA SUTRAS.

PATH

All world religions define a sacred cosmos, contain myths of the earth's and human origins, and specify what is sacred in the community's midst. Equally important for understanding the great traditions is how they prescribe a right way of life, the means to achieving the good, a way to achieve salvation: the religious path. Path (*marga*) is the fourth of Buddhism's Four Noble Truths, explicitly defining how moral living, energetic meditation, and existential discernment or insight are essential to complete the path to nirvana.

Todd T. Lewis

See also BUDDHISM; NIRVANA.

PATRIARCH

The title of the bishops of Rome, Constantinople, Alexandria, Antioch, and Jerusalem. These five were the most important and influential episcopal sees of undivided Christianity, and their bishops started using the title "patriarch" from at least the sixth century. The ecclesiastical jurisdiction and influence of these patriarchs extended over extensive territories. Today the title is still used by: (1) the Orthodox and Catholic bishops of the five ancient sees; (2) the bishops who preside over the more important autocephalous Orthodox Churches; and (3) most of the bishops who preside over Eastern Catholic Churches. Among Eastern Catholics, a patriarch has jurisdiction over all of the dioceses of his particular church in the entire world.

Orlando Espín

See also AUTOCEPHALOUS CHURCHES; BISHOP/EPISCOPACY; CONSTANTINOPLE, SEE OF; DIOCESE/ARCHDIOCESE; EASTERN CATHOLIC CHURCHES; ECUMENICAL PATRIARCH; ORTHODOX CHURCHES; POPE; ROMAN CATHOLIC CHURCH.

PATRIARCHY

Patriarchy is any kind of social system ruled by men, and/or a system in which men predominate and in which cultural values and norms favor men. In patriarchy, men are considered to be "subjects" and "normative" human beings, with the result that women are infantilized and treated as less-than-fully human objects who exist for the sake of benefiting men. Rooted in father-rule, patriarchy denotes all social systems in which one group oppresses and/or exploits another (for example, racist, sexist, or clan-based social systems). In this sense "patriarchy" is the overarching term while "sexism" is a subcategory of patriarchy.

In the Christian theological context, patriarchy is rampant. Despite practices and teachings of Jesus that challenged value distinctions based on sex, that embraced women as both disciples and church leaders, and that referred to God, the First Person of the Trinity, as both mother and father, the developing Christian church, capitulating to Greek and Roman social norms of father-rule, focused on the maleness of Jesus, the maleness of the disciples (thus discounting women as disciples *because* they were women), and, even trumping Jesus, defaulted to the apostle Paul's reification of male over female. Pioneering Catholic feminist theologian Mary Daly quite pointedly diagnosed the insidiousness of patriarchy in Christianity when she stated, "If God is male, then the male is God." The consequence of this focus on maleness has been the systematic exclusion and erasure of women through the pervasiveness and predominance of patriarchy in all dimensions of Christian life and belief, including theological doctrine, ecclesial structures, ecclesiological self-understanding, and liturgical speech and practices. The challenge of patriarchy is so enormous that some Christian feminists, most notably Rosemary Radford Ruether, have asked the very pointed question, "Can a male savior save women?"

Meghan T. Sweeney

See also DISCRIMINATION; ECOLOGY; FEMINIST THEOLOGIES; HUMAN BEING; HUMAN RIGHTS; LIBERATION THEOLOGIES; SEXISM; SOCIAL JUSTICE; THEOLOGICAL ANTHROPOLOGY.

PATRIPASSIANISM

A form of Modalist Monarchianism, it is also known as Sabellianism (after Sabellius, one of Modalism's third-century proponents). Patripassianism claimed that God the Father suffered as the Son. It is considered a heresy in most of Christianity today.

Orlando Espín

See also CHRISTOLOGY; HERESY; MODALISM; MONARCHIANISM; TRINITY / TRINITARIAN THEOLOGY / TRINITARIAN PROCESSIONS.

PATRISTICS/PATROLOGY

Derived from the Latin word *pater*, meaning "father," "patrology" was a word invented in the seventeenth century to refer to the study of the life and works of early Christian writers. The closely related term "patristics" originally referred to the study of patristic theology, that is, the study of the theology of the early Christian writers. Again, the term appears in the seventeeth century and was used to distinguish "patristic theology" from biblical, Scholastic, symbolic, and speculative approaches to theology. Although the terms are still in use, they are used less and less due to several shortcomings. Obviously, not all early

Christian writers or leaders were men, making the term "father" not only inexact, but sexist. Secondly, theology is no longer divided into the same categories that it was in the seventeenth century, and so the descriptive force of the term "patristics" has been lost. Finally, the artificial separation of the early church writers (as the only "Fathers") exists only from the seventeenth century and tends to exaggerate the importance of these writers in the Christian tradition. For these reasons, many historians prefer to speak simply of the early church and of the theology of early church writers when describing this particular period of history.

Gary Macy

See also FATHERS OF THE CHURCH.

PAUL

Paul, also known as Saul, was a Pharisaic Hebrew from the Hellenistic city of Tarsus in Cilicia. He was probably born in the first decade C.E. Acts 22:3 states that he was educated for a time in Jerusalem under the Pharisee Gamaliel. Nothing in his own letters or in Acts, the major primary and secondary sources, respectively, for information and traditions concerning his life, suggests that Paul ever met the historical Jesus.

A devout Jew and advanced in his observance of the Law of Moses, he opposed the earliest preaching of Jesus as resurrected and as the awaited Messiah of the Jews to the extent that he condoned the stoning of Stephen. When Stephen's martyrdom caused other believers in Jesus to flee Jerusalem for Damascus, Paul pursued them, intending to arrest them. In a profound religious experience on the road to Damascus that he knew to be an encounter with the risen Lord, Paul

was converted to belief in Jesus as Messiah. From then on he felt himself called to proclaim the Gospel of Christ, especially to the Gentiles.

For the rest of his life, some thirty years altogether, Paul preached the Gospel as he journeyed at length throughout the eastern Mediterranean as far as Rome. He founded numerous churches and, when situations demanded it, corresponded by letter with groups he had started as well as various others (for instance, the churches in Rome). At least seven of the epistles he wrote, as well as fragments of others, have survived, although none in original manuscript form.

The Pauline epistles and the traditions about Paul in Acts reflect that his was a brilliant theological mind coupled with a deep mysticism and a most forthright character. Theological and pastoral controversies were abundant in his ministry, many of which stemmed from Christianity's greatest initial issue, the integration of the Gentiles into a predominantly Jewish religious movement. The controversies in which Paul was embroiled resulted in numerous imprisonments, the last of which, according to Acts, placed him under the jurisdiction of the Romans in Judea. In the custody of a Roman centurion, Paul was sent by sea as a prisoner to Rome for trial under the imperial system. Various post-New Testament writings indicate that a few years later, Paul was martyred by beheading in Rome under Nero (ca. 67 C.E.). He is said to have been buried on the Via Ostiensis near the site of the modern basilica of *San Paolo fuori le Mura*.

F. M. Gillman

See also ACTS OF THE APOSTLES; NEW TESTAMENT LETTERS; PAULINE CORPUS; PAULINE THEOLOGY; PHARISEES.

PAULA OF ROME (?–404)

After the death of her husband, the Roman noblewoman Paula joined the group of ascetic women founded by Marcella, under the spiritual direction of Jerome. In 385 Paula and her daughter left Rome for Bethlehem where she founded a hospice for pilgrims, and both a male and female monastery.

Gary Macy

See also JEROME; MARCELLA; MONASTICISM IN WESTERN CHRISTIANITY.

PAULINE CORPUS

The fourteen books of the New Testament traditionally attributed to Paul: Romans, 1 and 2 Corinthians, Galatians, Ephesians, Philippians, Colossians, 1 and 2 Thessalonians, 1 and 2 Timothy, Titus, Philemon, and Hebrews. Hebrews itself is not technically an epistle, as are the other documents and, more significantly, does not claim to be by Paul. Nevertheless, when it was accepted into the canon it was placed at the end of the Pauline Corpus. The other thirteen, arranged roughly in descending order of length, each indicate in some way that Paul was their author.

In fact, however, biblical scholarship holds Paul responsible for only some of these documents. The seven widely agreed upon as authentically Pauline are Romans, 1 and 2 Corinthians, Galatians, Philippians, 1 Thessalonians, and Philemon. These authentic letters, generally regarded as written in the 50s and early 60s, all predate the New Testament Gospels.

Scholars are divided over the Pauline authorship of three additional letters, 2 Thessalonians, Colossians, and Ephesians. While many think 2 Thessalonians is indeed by Paul, fewer argue for his authorship of Colossians and even fewer think he wrote Ephesians. These three disputed letters are sometimes called Deutero-Pauline, that is, secondarily Pauline, implying that if they are not by Paul, they are nevertheless developments of Pauline thought and probably were written by his disciples.

There is generally a consensus that the rest of the Pauline Corpus is clearly not from Paul. First and Second Timothy and Titus, the Pastoral Letters, are considered post-Pauline (or Deutero-Pauline by some), coming from a generation who admired Paul and yet whose thought had moved quite far from Paul's. Hebrews, with a literary style and thought very unlike that of Paul, is regarded as non-Pauline.

F. M. Gillman

See also CANON; NEW TESTAMENT LETTERS; PAUL.

PAULINE PRIVILEGE

The so-called "Pauline privilege" is a historical and canonical elaboration based on 1 Corinthians 7:12-16, where Paul on his own authority ("I say, not the Lord") states that if an unbeliever is willing to live in peace with his or her spouse after this spouse has been baptized, it is permitted; if not, then it is permitted for them to separate. The more probable interpretation of the text is that it only allows separation in such cases, not remarriage. Since the fourth century, however, commentators have generally interpreted the text as allowing a second marriage, that is, as allowing a dissolution (breaking) of a natural bond of marriage, when a convert becomes baptized and the unbaptized spouse is unwilling to live in peace. Later theological development justified this by asserting that absolute indissolubility applied only to a sacramental (and consummated) marriage. Thus the Pauline privilege is in fact an instance of Catholic divorce (even though the term is never used), since a valid but in this case nonsacramental bond is actually broken.

Since the sixteenth century the application of the Pauline privilege has expanded in various ways and escalated due to the greater missionary enterprise of the church. Current legislation, found in Canons 1143–1150, the Code of Canon Law (1983), requires that ordinarily the unbaptized person be interpellated whether he or she is willing to be baptized and whether he or she is willing to live in peace with the baptized spouse. When the unbaptized spouse responds in the negative and/or departs, or in fact does not live in peace with the baptized spouse, the marriage is considered to be dissolved in favor of the faith of the baptized person by the very fact of a subsequent new marriage. Canons 1148 and 1149 are developments derived from and going beyond sixteenth-century applications of the privilege. Canon 1148 allows in polygamous or polyandrous marriages for the convert to choose any one of his or her spouses for a subsequent Christian marriage (even if that person remains unbaptized), if cohabitation with the first spouse is difficult; provisions in justice and charity are to be made for the dismissed spouses. Canon 1149 allows a second marriage after baptism for a convert when cohabitation with a first spouse cannot be restored due to captivity or persecution, even if the first spouse becomes baptized. All applications of the Pauline privilege require the adjudication of the local ordinary.

Dennis W. Krouse

See also ANNULMENT; DIVORCE (IN CHRISTIANITY); INDISSOLUBILITY; MARRIAGE IN CATHOLIC PERSPECTIVE; PETRINE PRIVILEGE.

PAULINE THEOLOGY

A systematization of the apostle Paul's theological thought, as reflected in his genuine letters. Since not all the letters traditionally included within the Pauline Corpus are regarded as authentically by Paul, compilations of Pauline theology are generally done on the basis of those seven letters widely agreed to have come from Paul himself: Romans, 1 and 2 Corinthians, Galatians, Philippians, 1 Thessalonians, and Philemon.

Any synthesis of Pauline thought must take into account the *nonsystematic* character of his writings that were themselves composed ad hoc, usually to address situations or issues in the Pauline churches and not as theological treatises. Paul's theology is one of several theologies in the New Testament and a part of biblical theology as a whole.

Particularly since the Reformation, many arguments have been set forth concerning what the key, core, or center of Pauline theology is, if indeed there is one, and how all other elements of Paul's thought relate to that center. For example, some have held justification by faith or eschatological Christ-mysticism or christological soteriology to be at the essence of Paul's theology.

The summary of Pauline theology that follows here, a very brief and extremely sketchy one due to space, is based on the fully elaborated, detailed analysis of Paul by one of the major Pauline scholars of the twentieth century, Joseph A. Fitzmyer, as found in his *Paul and His Theology. A Brief Sketch* (1989). In Fitzmyer's analysis, Paul's theology is centered above all on a christology oriented to soteriology, God's mode of salvation made known in a new way through the lordship of Christ, as evidenced in his resurrection. All else in Paul's teaching must be seen in the light of this Christocentric soteriology. In other words, Paul's theology is primarily a functional christology; his concern is to explain the significance of Christ, not in himself, but for humanity.

Paul describes what he had to say about the Christ-event as his "gospel," that is, "the good news of Jesus Christ." Fundamentally, the Good News Paul preached was that Jesus had been raised from the dead by God and had been given the title of "Lord." The glory the Father gave to Jesus as Lord became *his* power, power to bring about new life in those who believe in him. Thus Paul could believe and preach that the Risen Lord, possessed of power coming from the Father, is capable of bringing about the resurrection of Christians.

Paul saw his gospel as revealing the reality of the new age or *eschaton*, namely, that God's salvific activity has been made known in a new way through the Lordship of Jesus Christ in whom all humanity, both Jews and Gentiles, share in the salvific inheritance of Israel. Paul sees God offering a new mode of salvation for humanity in justification by grace through faith in Jesus Christ.

That Paul sees God making a new initiative toward humanity in Jesus reflects that he thought in terms of a divine plan of salvation history (*Heilsgeschichte*). His three-staged view, most probably derived from his thorough background in Judaism, sees a first period extending from Adam to Moses (the period before the Mosaic Law, a time when humans nevertheless did evil); a second period from the time of Moses to the Messiah (when the Law was added, humanity transgressed it, and was held in custody under the Law); and a third and final period beginning with the time of the Messiah, the Christ (when the end of the Law or its fulfillment has been reached and humans are justified by faith).

In Paul's view, Christians live in the last period. The eschaton has therefore been inaugurated, yet the "end" has nevertheless not yet come. Christ the Lord does not yet reign supreme, nor has he yet handed over the kingdom to the Father. The experience whereby a person begins to perceive (from hearing the Gospel preached) and accept the effects in human history of the Christ-event is for Paul called "faith." Faith, seen as an unmerited gift of God, is an awareness of the difference the Lordship of Christ makes in human history. Expressed in baptism, and lived out as obedience to Christ in all things, faith requires that the believer reject the ongoing attempt of evil to dominate his or her existence and continually re-acknowledge the Lordship of Christ. In Paul's view, the human being, under every aspect from which Paul chose to speak of persons—*sōma, sarx, psychē, pneuma, nous, kardia*—has died with Christ and now lives in Christ, in hope and expectation of living with him in resurrection.

F. M. Gillman

See also BIBLICAL THEOLOGY; CHRISTOLOGY; ESCHATON; FLESH/SARX; HEILSGESCHICHTE; LORD/LORDSHIP; NEW TESTAMENT LETTERS; PAUL; PAULINE CORPUS; PNEUMA; SOMA (GREEK); SOTERIOLOGY.

PAULINUS OF NOLA (355–431)

Paulinus was born into a wealthy and influential Roman family in Aquitaine. He rose rapidly in the Roman government, becoming a senator in 378 and attaining, soon afterwards, a Roman governorship. When Emperor Valentinian II began his support of the radical Arians, Paulinus retired from office, at which time he met Ambrose of Milan from whom Paulinus received baptismal instruction. In 389 Paulinus and his wife, Terasia, fled into Spain to avoid persecution. There Paulinus was converted to a more ascetic form of life, gave away his considerable possessions, and eventually retired to Nola where he lived under the spiritual guidance of St. Felix. In 409/10 Paulinus became bishop of Nola. Paulinus is best known for his poetry and for his extensive correspondence with many of the leading Christians of his day, including Augustine, Ambrose, Jerome, Rufinus, and Sulpicius Severus.

Gary Macy

See also AMBROSE OF MILAN; ARIANISM; AUGUSTINE OF HIPPO; JEROME; RUFINUS OF AQUILEIA; SULPICIUS SEVERUS.

PAULIST FATHERS

Common name for the members of the "Missionary Society of St. Paul the Apostle in the State of New York." The Paulists were founded by Isaac Hecker in 1858, and have become pastorally involved in modern mass media and campus ministries throughout the United States.

Orlando Espín

See also CONGREGATIONS (ORDERS); EVANGELIZATION; HECKER, ISAAC; PRIESTHOOD; RELIGIOUS (VOWED); ROMAN CATHOLIC CHURCH.

PAUL OF SAMOSATA

Paul was both bishop of Samosata and official of the Queen's treasury between 260 and 270. Both his conduct as bishop and his theology came under attack, and his theology was condemned at a council held in Antioch in 268. Paul was eventually removed from church buildings by secular forces. Paul taught an adoptionist form of Monarchianism. He believed that

the Logos was an impersonal faculty of God active in the world and had no separate existence. For Paul, the term "Son of God" refers only to the human Jesus, in whom the Logos dwelt. This indwelling gave Jesus a special status, but did not raise him above the level of human mortality. Paul's followers formed a separate community called the Paulicians that were still in evidence at the time of the Council of Nicaea in 325.

Gary Macy

See also CHRIST; MONARCHIANISM; NICAEA, FIRST COUNCIL OF; NICAEA, SECOND COUNCIL OF; SON OF GOD.

PAUL VI, POPE (1897–1978)

Pope from 1963 to 1978. Born Giovanni Battista Montini, he was ordained to the priesthood in 1920. Montini served in the Vatican Secretariat of State for over thirty years, working with Cardinal Eugenio Pacelli both before and after the Cardinal's election as Pope Pius XII. In 1954 Montini became archbishop of Milan, and although not yet a cardinal when the Pope died in 1958, Montini was considered a possible successor to Pius XII. Shortly after John XXIII was elected instead, Montini was made a cardinal, and in 1963 he succeeded John as Pope Paul VI. As pope, Paul presided over the successful conclusion of the Second Vatican Council that John had convoked, was the promulgator of all sixteen of the council's final documents, and oversaw the vast array of practical changes undertaken in response to the conciliar decrees. These tasks marked the remainder of his pontificate both with the vitality of ongoing reform and with the heightened tension between traditionalist and progressivist elements that the reforms exacerbated. His promulgation of the revised rite for the celebration of the Mass (1970), which brought about many of the most visible changes (prayers in the local language, rearrangement of altar furnishings, direct participation of the whole congregation, and so on), gained him strong opposition among conservatives, even within the hierarchy itself. On the other hand, his issuing of the encyclical *Humanae Vitae*, in which he maintained the church's ban on artificial contraception against the majority recommendation of a mixed lay–clergy commission, precipitated a major authority crisis among progressives. Particularly in the light of subsequent developments, however, Paul VI will be remembered as a moderate progressive who vigorously pursued far-reaching reforms in response to the council.

William A. Clark, S.J.

PAX CHRISTI

The Latin words literally mean "the peace of Christ." It is the name of an international Catholic organization, founded in 1948 in France (by French and German Catholics, after the end of World War II), in order to actively promote peace and justice.

Orlando Espín

See also ETHICS, SOCIAL; JUSTICE; JUSTICE IN THE WORLD; JUST WAR THEORY; PEACE; WAR.

PEACE

Rooted in the Hebrew tradition of "shalom," peace is more than the absence of war because peace necessitates prosperity and the full flourishing of all creation. Peace has to do with establishing right relationships between persons, nations, and the planet. Pope Paul VI reflected this understanding in his encyclical *Populorum Progressio* (1967) when he said that peace is a product of just cultural, political, and economic structures in which all people participate in the decisions that affect their lives.

Mary E. Hobgood

See also CHALLENGE OF PEACE; CLASSISM; JUST WAR THEORY; POPULORUM PROGRESSIO; WAR.

PÉGUY, CHARLES (1873–1914)

French patriot and prolific writer, Péguy turned from socialism in his youth to a militant nationalism and Catholicism. He was among those who helped to develop the cult of Joan of Arc and thus to prepare the way for her canonization as a saint in 1920. Joan was a fifteenth-century French woman and warrior who had helped to revive France's fortunes in the Hundred Years' War against England. Péguy saw in her a model for the French who had lost the Franco-Prussian War of 1870 but looked forward to a resurgent France. In an age when many rejected the church as irrelevant to the modern era, Péguy looked back with nostalgia to the role the church had played in making France great. His own patriotism was put to the test early in World War I: he was killed in battle in September 1914.

Thomas Worcester, S.J.

See also GALLICANISM.

PELAGIANISM

A Christian heresy, usually associated with the English-born monk Pelagius (d. 410?), although the term has been used to cover a broader set of doctrines not necessarily taught by Pelagius himself. Pelagianism, however, did begin with the man whose name it bears. While living in Rome, he became alarmed at the declining moral standards of Western European societies, and so he began to insist on personal moral responsibility. Pelagius taught that humans were no more inclined by nature to do evil than to do good. He held that God had given humans the possibility of moral free choice, and therefore it was human responsibility to exercise that free choice for good; unfortunately, his views left little if any room for God's grace or initiative.

Pelagius's disciples (especially one named Celestius) further developed their teacher's insights, and later taught that human beings alone can take the necessary steps toward salvation on their own (hence, God's grace is not absolutely necessary for salvation but only an aid toward it). Pelagians insisted that humans were free to choose to be saved (and thereby effect their salvation) because of their God-given nature. Christ, they said, was the exemplar of the right, moral life. Furthermore, Celestius taught that "original sin" was only Adam's sin, and in no way affected any other human generation or individual; and so baptism was ultimately unnecessary.

Pelagian doctrines were considered heretical by most contemporary theologians and church leaders, condemning them in a series of synods and regional councils. Pelagians tended to be laypeople, affluent, optimistic about humankind's future, but quite ascetic in lifestyles. Their movement became involved in all kinds of political and ecclesiastical intrigues, and found their greatest opponent in Augustine of Hippo. Because of his fierce attack on Pelagianism (or on what he understood to be Pelagius's ideas), Augustine developed a theology of grace and sin that has had an enormous impact on Western Christian theology. The great defender of Pelagianism's doctrines, after Pelagius and Celestius, was a bishop

named Julian of the Italian town of Eclanum. Pelagianism never had much influence in the Eastern Christian Churches, but in western Europe it did, surviving in places into the sixth century until the Council of Orange (529 C.E.) finally put an end to it. A later development called semi-Pelagianism is not to be confused with the earlier movement.

Orlando Espín

See also ASCETICISM/ASCETIC; AUGUSTINE OF HIPPO; BAPTISM/CONFIRMATION; FREE WILL; GRACE; HERESY; JUSTIFICATION; NATURE, HUMAN; ORANGE, COUNCILS OF; ORIGINAL JUSTICE; ORTHODOXY (IN CHRISTIANITY); PELAGIUS; PREDESTINATION (IN CHRISTIANITY); SALVATION; SEMI-PELAGIANISM; SIN, ORIGINAL; SIN, PERSONAL; THEOLOGICAL ANTHROPOLOGY; WESTERN THEOLOGY.

PELAGIUS (?–410?)

English-born theologian involved in the origins of Pelagianism. Living in Rome at the end of the fourth century, Pelagius was apparently disgusted by what he considered moral laxity. He began to teach that humans were no more inclined to do evil than to do good. He held that God had given humans the possibility of moral free choice. He later moved to Northern Africa and Palestine and there continued his teaching. Although it is far from certain whether Pelagius personally stepped over the line of doctrinal orthodoxy, he was accused of heresy (especially by Augustine of Hippo and his allies). He successfully cleared his name several times, but was ultimately condemned for heresy. Pelagius was not involved in the later doctrinal controversies and heresy promoted by his disciples and that came to be (inaccurately) associated with his name.

Orlando Espín

See also ASCETICISM/ASCETIC; AUGUSTINE OF HIPPO; FREE WILL; GRACE; HERESY; JUSTIFICATION; ORTHODOXY (IN CHRISTIANITY); PELAGIANISM; SALVATION; SEMI-PELAGIANISM; SIN, ORIGINAL; SIN, PERSONAL.

PELAGIUS I OF ROME (D. 561)

Pelagius was a deacon of the Roman church and the formal representative of Pope Vigilius. When Vigilius was called to Rome by Emperor Justinian because of his refusal to accept the so-called "Three Chapters," Pelagius took over the church of Rome while supporting Vigilius's opposition to the condemnation. When Vigilius gave way under the pressure of the emperor, Pelagius at first rebuked him, but then also agreed to the condemnation despite strong opposition from the Western bishops. Pelagius was appointed pope by the emperor upon the death of Vigilius over the protests of the Roman clergy and people. The churches of Aquileia refused to accept Pelagius or the condemnation of the Three Chapters, and a lengthy schism resulted. After Pelagius, popes were required to ask for approval of their election by the emperor and thus, for a time, the papacy became a functionary of the emperor.

Gary Macy

See also CAESAROPAPISM; JUSTINIAN; POPE; THE THREE CHAPTERS; VIGILIUS OF ROME.

PELIKAN, JAROSLAV (1923–2006)

Born in Akron, Ohio, Pelikan was a church historian and minister in the Lutheran Church, Missouri Synod. He attended Concordia Junior College, Concordia Theological Seminary, and the University of Chicago Divinity School, where he received a Ph.D. in 1946. He began his teaching career at Valparaiso University, Concordia Seminary, and the University of Chicago. In 1962 he moved to Yale University where he taught ecclesiastical history for more than thirty years, and from 1975–8 served as acting dean of the Graduate School. Pelikan made lasting contributions to church history through his studies of the early church and the Protestant Reformation, including works on Augustine and Martin Luther. He specialized in historical theology and doctrinal studies such as *Historical Theology: Continuity and Change in Christian Doctrine* (1971), *The Christian Tradition: A History of the Development of Doctrine* (1971–89), and *Jesus Through the Centuries* (1985).

Evelyn A. Kirkley

See also HISTORICAL THEOLOGY; HISTORY.

PEÑAFORT (OR PENYAFORT), RAMÓN DE (1185–1275)

Spanish (Catalonian) theologian. One of the most influential theologians and churchmen of his day, Ramón de Peñafort was a distinguished member of the Dominican Order and its third superior general. A respected canon lawyer too, he compiled and edited the *Liber extra* (1234) that became part of the core canonical legislation of Roman Catholicism until the early twentieth century. Peñafort was advisor to kings and popes over a wide array of issues. He promoted Christian missionary work in Muslim lands, establishing educational institutions for that purpose. Thomas Aquinas wrote the *Summa Contra Gentiles* at Peñafort's request. Peñafort had a profound influence on other great theologians of his day, especially and more directly on Ramón Llull. He is considered one of the great medieval teachers, and his *Summa de casibus poenitentiae* (1225) became a standard theological text.

Orlando Espín

See also AQUINAS, THOMAS, ST.; CANON LAW; DOMINICANS; LLUL, RAMÓN; MEDIEVAL CHRISTIANITY (IN THE WEST); MEDIEVAL CHURCH; MISSIONS; ROMAN CATHOLIC CHURCH.

PENITENTIALS

Penitentials are handbooks for confessors consisting mainly of a lengthy list of sins and their corresponding penances. The handbooks were used for the practice of private confession. Private confession, in turn, developed from the Celtic practice of spiritual guidance by monks. The earliest penitentials date from the sixth century and come from Ireland, but they soon appear in England as well. The first penitential to reach continental Europe was that of the Irish missionary monk Columbanus. The penitentials were very popular in Europe during the seventh and eighth centuries as the practice of private confession was gradually introduced to the European continent from Ireland and England. A reaction set in against the penitentials during the ninth century, but penitentials continued to be used until they were replaced by the penitential manuals of the late twelfth and thirteenth centuries. The penitentials contained harsh and lengthy penances, and at least in the manuals produced in continental Europe, substitutions for the penance were incorporated into the text. A person could commute the sentence with alms or recitation of prayers or even by having someone else perform the penance for them. These commutations could easily lead to abuses, and certainly the legalistic view of penance the penitentials suggested was one of the factors leading

eventually to the development of both the notion of purgatory and the practice of indulgences.

Gary Macy

See also INDULGENCE; MEDIEVAL CHRISTIANITY (IN THE WEST); PURGATORY; RECONCILIATION, SACRAMENT OF.

PENTATEUCH

(Greek, *penta*, five + *teuchos*, scroll). Pentateuch refers to the first five books of the Hebrew Scriptures also known as the Five Books of Moses: Genesis, Exodus, Leviticus, Numbers, and Deuteronomy. The term *Pentateuch* in reference to these books has been mostly used by Christian biblical scholars as opposed to the terms used within Judaism that include Torah and Chumash. Within Judaism, the Pentateuch/Torah is the most sacred part of the Bible. According to ancient Jewish tradition, Moses received the Torah from Yahweh on Mount Sinai and brought it to the people. The Pentateuch/Torah represents the terms of the covenant between God and the people; it is the foundational document of Judaism.

The Pentateuch/Torah contains some of the most important religious concepts shared by Jews, Christians, and Muslims. These include foundational concepts such as Exodus, "covenant," loyalty, and love of God. These concepts undergo enormous development in all three traditions. The Pentateuch/Torah also tells the story of the prehistory of the people of Israel. The story begins with two creation stories, one of the entire universe and all living creatures, and then one that focuses on the creation of humans and human society. Genesis in particular is filled with etiologies, stories telling of the origin of human customs and behaviors, as well as religious institutions such as the Sabbath. The Pentateuch/Torah tells of the ancestors of Israel, the patriarchs and matriarchs from whom the twelve tribes of later Israel were thought to descend; it tells of the origin of the twelve tribes, their servitude in Egypt, and the mighty acts with which God freed them. The central point of the Pentateuch/Torah is the story of the Exodus from Egypt that leads to the formation of the covenant at Mount Sinai. It is at Sinai that the people who came out of Egypt become Israel, the people of God. It is at Sinai that Moses receives the Torah or the Law. And it is at Sinai that the people learn how to worship God properly. The remainder of the Pentateuch/Torah tells of the people's journey to Palestine.

Russell Fuller

PENTECOST (IN CHRISTIANITY)

In the Christian calendar, the final day of the fifty-day Easter Season is Pentecost Sunday. The Christian fifty-day Easter observance reproduces the fifty-day Jewish Omer period that begins two days after Passover and concludes with *Shavuot* (also called Pentecost or the Feast of Weeks). On Pentecost, Christians commemorate the descent and indwelling of the Holy Spirit upon the men and women who were Jesus' disciples. The Spirit empowered these disciples for their mission to proclaim the Gospel to all peoples and to baptize those who believed. Pentecost is considered the birthday of the church. It is one of the most important feasts in the Christian calendar, ranking only after Easter and Christmas.

Paul mentions Pentecost in 1 Corinthians 16:8. However, it is impossible to determine if he is speaking about a first-century Christian observance. It is likely that Paul's observation is based on the Jewish calendar, since this reference would have been understood by some if not all the Christians in Corinth. In the second century, some Christian communities had a fifty-day observance of Easter that concluded with Pentecost. By the fourth century, Pentecost was observed throughout the church.

The feast of Pentecost memorializes an episode that is only reported in Acts 1:1–2:41. There are several reasons to suspect that Luke deliberately structured his chronology to allow the Jewish calendar to underscore the theological insight he invests in this narrative. In specifying that the appearances of the risen Christ took place over a forty-day interval, there is an inherent allusion to several intervals of forty in the Scriptures of Israel, the most significant being the detail that Moses spent forty days on Mt. Sinai (Exod 24:18) before receiving the Law. On Shavuot (also known as Pentecost) Jews celebrate the giving of the revelation and the Law that established them as the people of God. There is an inherent symmetry between the giving of the Law and the giving of the Spirit that empowered the establishment of the church.

Shavuot was originally an agricultural festival, and a number of authorities believe the idea of celebrating the Law on this feast originated after 70 C.E. to give the Jewish community something to celebrate on a feast prescribed in the Bible that made no sense after the destruction of the Temple. However, other authorities concede that this idea of celebrating the giving of the Law on Shavuot could have originated during Exile or in the Diaspora before the Temple was destroyed. The account in Acts would be a major piece of evidence for the latter. The inherent similarities between the giving of the Law and the giving of the Spirit make it inconceivable that the Jewish community would devise a feast that had affinities with how Christians appropriated it. It is far more plausible that Luke seized an idea that was already developing in Judaism and used it to underscore his account.

Christian Scripture scholars are convinced that while the experience of the Risen One and that of the Spirit were always recognized to be different, separable experiences, they were more simultaneous than Acts leads one to believe. While the evidence for this is only clearly stated in John 20:22, both the commissioning in Matthew (28:18-20) and the longer ending in Mark (16:15-18), and even the opening of the disciples' minds to understand the Scripture in Luke (24:45-47) lend support to this critical insight.

Regina A. Boisclair

See also FEAST OF WEEKS.

PENTECOSTALISM

Pentecostalism is a movement within evangelical Christianity to restore the belief and practice of the New Testament church. Radically ahistorical, it holds that a new apostolic age has dawned, an age heralded by manifestations of the Holy Spirit as on the day of Pentecost. As recorded in Acts 2, after Jesus' death, resurrection, and ascension, his disciples had gathered in Jerusalem when gusts of wind swept through the house and tongues of fire rested on each of them. Filled with the Holy Spirit, they left the house and began preaching in languages they did not know. A crowd gathered, marveling that those from different regions and countries could understand the Gospel preached in their native languages. When questions were raised about this miraculous occurrence, Peter explained that the disciples were not drunk, but were filled with the Holy Spirit, fulfilling the prophecies of Joel 2:23.

Pentecostals believe that these miracles are not limited to the early church, but occur in the present. Pentecostalism emerged in the early twentieth century in the United States, shaped by the Holiness and fundamentalist movements. An outgrowth of Methodism and the teachings of John Wesley, the Holiness movement stressed the entire sanctification of the believer through the second blessing of the Holy Spirit, subsequent to the first blessing of salvation. The second blessing, an instantaneous, immediate, and dramatic experience, purified the believer's will and transported him or her to a state of holiness. This experience aligned the believer's will with God's, so that he or she was subsequently free of sinful impulses, a condition maintained through prayer, discipline, and vigilance. The movement produced leaders such as Phoebe Palmer, Hannah Whitall Smith, and Asa Mahan, and spawned a number of denominations, including the Church of the Nazarene, Wesleyan Church, Church of God (Anderson, Indiana), and the Salvation Army.

Pentecostalism was also influenced by fundamentalism, a movement of evangelical Christians who resisted modern intellectual and social developments, especially Darwinism and higher criticism of the Bible. Refusing to compromise traditional evangelical theology, they adopted a view of the Bible as literally true and inerrant and a series of dogmatic propositions as critical to the Christian faith. These "fundamentals" included the virgin birth of Jesus of Nazareth, miracles, the substitutionary atonement, and the physical resurrection of Jesus from the dead. Moreover, fundamentalists believed in the fulfillment of biblical prophecy through premillennial dispensationalism. This theory stated that human history was divided into seven dispensations, in which God had made a covenant with humanity for its salvation. Humanity failed its end of the covenant, God punished it with a dramatic cataclysm, and started again with a new dispensation. Key to premillennial dispensationalism was an interpretation of the eschaton, including the rapture, tribulation, emergence of the Antichrist, Armageddon, and the Second Coming.

From Holiness, Pentecostals borrowed the second blessing of entire sanctification, and from fundamentalism, biblical literalism and premillennial dispensationalism. Yet Pentecostals took both movements further. Unlike fundamentalists, they privileged enthusiastic experience over doctrine, and unlike Holiness adherents, they believed the second blessing resulted not only in entire sanctification, but in all charisms, or gifts, of the Holy Spirit as enumerated in 1 Corinthians 12 and 14, including healing, prophecy, and speaking in tongues. In the Appalachian Mountains, smaller Pentecostal groups have expanded this list to include handling poisonous snakes and ingesting toxic substances. Moreover, Pentecostals profess a strict code of morality, including abstention from alcohol, smoking, sexual sin, dancing, card-playing, and among some, the avoidance of jewelry and cosmetics for women.

The most distinctive Pentecostal trait is speaking in tongues or glossolalia, defined not as in Acts, as foreign languages, but as a mystical language unrelated to any known language. The first recorded modern manifestation of glossolalia occurred on January 1, 1901, in Topeka, Kansas, at a Bible institute founded by Charles Fox Parham, a Holiness evangelist. Agnes Ozman, a student at the institute, was reportedly the first to receive the gift of tongues, followed by other students and faculty. A revival flared in the region, died out, and was reinspired in 1903 when Parham began a career as a faith healer. In 1905 Parham's teachings about glossolalia and the new apostolic age attracted African American Holiness preacher William J. Seymour. He introduced Parham's teachings to his congregation, the Apostolic Faith Gospel Mission on Azusa Street in Los Angeles. There Pentecostalism exploded from 1906–9, converting Euro-, African, Asian, and Latino/a Americans, a wide swath of Los Angeles's diverse community. The three-year Azusa Street revival grabbed national attention, and Pentecostalism spread eastward, especially among Holiness and Baptist groups.

A popular, charismatic, and non-hierarchical movement, Pentecostalism struggled to organize. It flourished in urban storefront churches among the socially and economically marginalized, especially the poor, women, and persons of color. The initially interracial and interdenominational movement soon fractured along racial lines. Among African Americans, the Church of God in Christ is the largest Pentecostal denomination. As well, numerous smaller African American Pentecostal denominations formed, including Christ's Sanctified Holy Church, the Apostolic Overcoming Holy Church of God, the Fire-Baptized Holiness Church of God, and the Church of Our Lord Jesus Christ of the Apostolic Faith. The largest Euro-American Pentecostal denominations are the Pentecostal Holiness Church, founded in 1911, and the Assemblies of God, formed in 1914. Other predominantly white groups include the Church of God (Cleveland, Tennessee) and the Church of God of

Prophecy. Flamboyant revivalist Aimee Semple McPherson started the Church of the Foursquare Gospel in Los Angeles in 1927, stressing Christ as Savior, Healer, Baptizer, and Soon-Coming King.

In the 1960s, the charismatic movement spread beyond Pentecostal denominations to middle-class Protestant and Catholic churches. In 1960, an Episcopal priest announced to his congregation in Van Nuys, California, that he had experienced rebirth in the Holy Spirit. Although he resigned from that church due to the hostile response he received, Pentecostalism spread through mainline Protestantism, from Lutherans in Minnesota to students at Yale Divinity School in Connecticut. Those who became involved saw it as a renewal movement stressing prayer, piety, and a sense of belonging to God, as well as speaking in tongues. Opponents declared those involved believed themselves superior to other Christians by virtue of their charismatic experience. Although Pentecostalism forged transdenominational bonds between Protestants, most remained in their original denominations and formed small charismatic fellowships.

Pentecostalism began among Catholics in 1967 at Duchesne University in Pittsburgh, Pennsylvania, among faculty members who had experienced Protestant Pentecostalism and the intense spirituality of a Cursillo renewal retreat. Within a few months, the movement spread to the University of Notre Dame and University of Michigan. In 1969 the Catholic hierarchy gave cautious permission to the new movement, and it spread to universities and churches across the country. It manifested in glossolalia, faith healing, prayer groups, and the creation of covenant communities, in which members pooled their financial resources and covenanted with one another for a common spiritual and worship life. As in Protestantism, Pentecostal Catholicism was characterized by intense emotionalism and commitment to renewal; as well, it received criticism for hyperemotionalism, fundamentalism, privatism, lack of social consciousness, and the attitude of being a superior form of Christianity. It has been charged with exploiting young people, women, and ethnic minorities.

Despite these criticisms, Pentecostalism was one of the most powerful renewal movements in twentieth-century Catholicism. Some Pentecostal Catholics remained loyal to the church, and their presence has brought renewed attention to enthusiasm, individual piety, and literal interpretation of the Bible. However, the Catholic Church has been alarmed by the aggressiveness of Pentecostal missionaries, who have converted large numbers of Catholics in Central and South America, as well as Latinos/as in the United States. Many Latino/a Catholics left the church to form their own churches and hire charismatic clergy. It has been estimated that by 1989, 20 percent of Hispanic Catholics had converted to conservative Protestantism.

In recent decades, prominent U.S. Pentecostals have included Oral Roberts, pioneer of televangelism, founder of Oral Roberts University, and a Pentecostal Holiness minister who became a Methodist in 1965; Jimmy Swaggart, popular televangelist, revivalist, and Assemblies of God minister; and Jim Bakker, Assemblies of God minister and head of the "PTL Club," a popular television ministry with his wife Tammy Faye. In the 1980s all three were discredited by public scandal; Bakker went to prison for financial mismanagement and Swaggart was stripped of his ministerial credentials for consorting with a prostitute. Despite these setbacks, Pentecostal churches grew enormously from the 1970s–1990s and have staunchly supported the Moral Majority and the Religious Right, movements to legislate conservative "family values."

Evelyn A. Kirkley

See also ASSEMBLIES OF GOD; CHARISMATIC MOVEMENT; DISPENSATION; ENTHUSIASM/ENTHUSIASTIC; FRUITS OF THE SPIRIT; GLOSSOLALIA; HOLINESS/SANCTITY (IN CHRISTIANITY); RAPTURE (IN AMERICAN PROTESTANTISM).

PENTHEKTE COUNCIL, OR SYNOD

See TRULLO, SYNOD OF.

PEOPLE OF GOD

Throughout the Hebrew Scriptures, Israel's self-understanding is depicted as being God's people, an understanding that came about through God's own call: "I will take you as my people, and I will be your God" (Exod 6:7). This understanding was adopted by the early Christian community that emerged from Judaism and applied to the church itself: "Once you were not a people, but now you are God's people; once you had not received mercy, but now you have received mercy" (1 Pet 2:10). However, this community is always understood eschatologically, that is, the church is ever "on the way" to becoming God's people. The final realization of this relationship awaits the fullness of the reign of God.

At the Second Vatican Council, the Roman Catholic Church made a significant shift in its ecclesiology. It moved away from a triumphalistic understanding of church as an exclusive "perfect society" to an inclusive understanding of church as people of God. For example, after much debate, the council fathers placed the chapter on the church as "The People of God" (Chapter 2) before the chapter on "The Hierarchical Structure of the Church" (Chapter 3) in its Dogmatic Constitution on the Church (*Lumen Gentium*) in order to emphasize the human and communal aspects of the church, rather than the institutional and hierarchical aspects that had been overstressed in the past. In Vatican II's understanding, the church is both community and institution; however, its use of the biblical notion "people of God" projects an inclusive view of the church that includes both clergy and laity and, potentially, all believers.

Mary Ann Hinsdale

See also ECCLESIOLOGY; LUMEN GENTIUM.

PEOPLE OF THE BOOK

See AHL AL-KITAB.

PERFECTAE CARITATIS

This is the Latin name [literally, "of perfect charity"] of the document from the Second Vatican Council (1962–5) entitled Decree on the Appropriate Renewal of the Religious Life. This renewal, according to the decree, involves "a continuous return to the sources of all Christian life and to the original inspiration behind a given community" and "an adjustment of the community to the changed conditions of the times" (no. 2). Renewal and adaptation are the key words. General renewal is sketched in terms of the traditional principles governing religious life, while the recovery of charism (or founding inspiration) is necessarily left to each community to undertake. Adaptation presupposes a sound understanding of contemporary social and cultural life, but the decree's recommendations tend once again to be more general than specific. Having given the impulse for renewal, the council left it to individual communities to update themselves, reminding them that exterior changes without interior renewal would lead to failure (no. 2e).

Noteworthy is the council's teaching that religious life is rooted in baptism and indeed can be viewed as a radical living out of the baptismal consecration (no. 5). Thus religious life is situated in the context of the whole church as a people together called to holiness and perfection: "all the faithful of Christ of whatever rank or status are called to the fullness of the Christian life and to the perfection of charity" (Dogmatic Constitution on the Church, no. 40).

William Reiser, s.j.

See also BAPTISM / CONFIRMATION; CHARITY; PERFECTION; RELIGIOUS (VOWED).

PERFECTION

The traditional and best answer as to what perfection consists of is charity. Human beings are said to become perfect the more they resemble God, and since the chief divine attribute is love, whoever is of God is someone who loves. The greater one's love for one's brothers and sisters, the closer one comes to being like God. The spiritual and moral challenge facing Christians, therefore, becomes one of defining what exactly love means or calls for here and now. The church teaches that all of us are called to perfection, meaning that all of us are capable of becoming like God. The fullest human expression of what being like God means is given to us in Christ. Christ represents the complete realization of the human

potential for God. Following Christ faithfully, meditating regularly on the Gospels, is our path to perfection. If being perfect means becoming like God, then perfection is tantamount to divinization; to the degree that one participates in the mystery of Christ, one shares the divine nature. This is the mystery of grace: the transformation of human beings, their adoption as God's own children, their sharing in the Holy Spirit, their becoming divine, their being made perfect or "whole" as God is perfect or "holy." Perfection is not achieved on the basis of human effort alone; we need the Spirit's assistance.

Yet Christian spiritual writers have long recognized that the pursuit of perfection cannot be an end in itself, for this too easily leads to self-absorption and the most subtle forms of pride and self-deception. The pursuit of perfection for its own sake could be compared to spiritual bodybuilding; narcissism is a perennial trap even in the realm of the spirit. Furthermore, perfection cannot simply be equated with the moral ideals of a given age and culture. To be civically and religiously law-abiding, for example, may be an important social quality; but it hardly sums up perfection, as we see in the writing of St. Paul. Among some early church writers, the portrait of a virtuous person embodied more of the human and moral ideals of Stoic thought than those of the Gospel, while the attitudes of obedience, resignation, and submission to the will of God were especially prized by spiritual writers of the seventeenth and eighteenth centuries (such as Francis de Sales in his *Introduction to the Devout Life* and Jean Pierre de Caussade in *Abandonment to Divine Providence*). For some, the outstanding Christian virtue might be humility, or service of the poor, or passion for justice. Some believe that the path to perfection requires separation from the world, while others would urge that perfection presupposes immersion within the world and its everyday concerns.

In short, there are numerous ways of modeling or depicting holiness. Thus, the shorthand formula that identifies Christian perfection with the capacity for loving is the most trustworthy answer to the nature of perfection. Spelling out what it means to love within the concrete historical and social circumstances of our time will enable us to see both how perfection is to be embodied and the path one must take to become perfect, as our heavenly Father is perfect.

William Reiser, S.J.

See also COUNSELS (OF PERFECTION); HOLINESS/SANCTITY (IN CHRISTIANITY); IMITATION OF CHRIST (BOOK, CONCEPT); PELAGIANISM.

PERFECTION OF WISDOM SUTRAS

Common English translation given to the texts known as the *Prajnaparamita* literature. Their style and scope vary widely from the lengthy 100,000-line version (*Shatasahasrika Prajnaparamita-sutra*), an 8,000-line recension (*Astasahasrika Prajnaparamita-sutra*), down to the popular shorter works such as the *Diamond Sutra* (*Vajracchedika Prajnaparamita-sutra*) and the *Heart Sutra* (*Hridaya Prajnaparamitasutra*).

Todd T. Lewis

See also MAHAYANA BUDDHISM; NAGARJUNA; PRAJNA; PRAJNAPARAMITA LITERATURE; SHUNYATA/SUNYA/SHUNYA.

PERICHORESIS

This Greek term means "penetration." It is equivalent to the Latin word *circumin-*

cessio. In Christian trinitarian theology the term is used to mean the necessary being-in-one-another of the three Persons of the Trinity. There being only one God and thus only one divine essence, the Father, the Son, and the Spirit are distinguishable only by the relations between them. It is important *not* to understand perichoresis in spatial or temporal terms.

Orlando Espín

See also CHRISTOLOGY; HYPOSTATIC UNION; PERSON/PROSOPON; PNEUMATOLOGY; TRINITY/TRINITARIAN THEOLOGY/TRINITARIAN PROCESSIONS.

PERICOPE

From the Greek *peri*, "about," and *koptein*, "to cut." A pericope is a short part of a larger work, such as a section of narrative or discourse. It is the task of form criticism to take such smaller units, for example, stories, sayings, hymns, and to analyze them in isolation from their biblical literary contexts and to compare them with similar units known elsewhere in the ancient world. Redaction criticism studies the same small units from the perspective of how the biblical author(s) situated them in their biblical contexts.

F. M. Gillman

See also FORM CRITICISM; REDACTION CRITICISM; SITZ IM LEBEN.

PERPETUA (D. 202)

A young Roman matron and Christian neophyte, Perpetua was the leader of a group of Christians executed in Carthage in 202. An account of their martyrdom, formerly thought to have been edited by Tertullian, is remarkable for its inclusion of an extended diary entry by Perpetua, describing her dreams and visions. She appears throughout the text as one whose zeal for martyrdom caused her to move beyond the roles considered appropriate for a woman such as submission to her father, and care for her child; in fact, in one dream she envisions herself as a warrior struggling against the devil.

Mary Anne Foley, C.N.D.

See also MARTYR/MARTYRDOM; TERTULLIAN.

PERRIN, NORMAN (1920–76)

Born November 29, 1920, in Wellingborough, Northhamptonshire, England, New Testament scholar Norman Perrin received a bachelor of arts degree from Manchester University in 1949, bachelor of divinity (1952) and master of theology degrees from London University. In 1949 Perrin was ordained in the Baptist Union of Great Britain and Northern Ireland, serving as pastor at Westbourne Park Baptist Church in London (1949–52) and at Sketty Baptist Church in Swansea, South Wales (1952–6). From 1956 to 1959 he studied under Joachim Jeremias at the University of Göttingen, earning the doctorate with a dissertation that was eventually published as The Kingdom of God in the Teaching of Jesus (1963). From 1959 to 1964 Perrin taught New Testament at the Candler School of Theology of Emory University and then, from 1964 until his death on November 25, 1976, at the Divinity School of the University of Chicago.

The author of thirty scholarly articles and eight books, Perrin's first book was the revision of his doctoral dissertation. This was followed by Rediscovering the Teaching of Jesus (1967); The Promise of Bultmann: The Promise of Theology (1969); What is Redaction Criticism? (1969); A Modern Pilgrimage in New Testament Christology (1974); The New Testament: An Introduction—Proclamation and Parenesis, Myth and History (1974); Jesus and the Language of the Kingdom: Symbol and Metaphor in New Testament Interpretation (1976); The Resurrection According to Matthew, Mark, and Luke (1977).

Perrin was influenced early on by T. W. Manson's conservative approach to the historicity of the Synoptic Gospel tradition and by Manson's confidence in the accessibility of the historical Jesus. This perspective was reinforced during Perrin's studies at Göttingen under Jeremias. Subsequently though, Perrin became increasingly familiar with and favorable toward the perspective of Rudolf Bultmann, eventually embracing Bultmann's radical form-critical approach. Later in his career, Perrin was the scholar largely responsible for familiarizing United States audiences with redaction criticism with his contribution to the Fortress Press Guides to Biblical Scholarship Series, What is Redaction Criticism? Perrin's later work reflects an increasing interest in hermeneutical issues (through the influence of his University of Chicago colleague Paul Ricoeur) and in myth (through the influence of his University of Chicago colleague Mircea Eliade) as well as the increasing influence of the movement in United States literary criticism known as the "New Criticism."

Jean-Pierre Ruiz

See also BULTMANN, RUDOLF; ELIADE, MIRCEA; HERMENEUTICS; JEREMIAS, JOACHIM; JESUS OF HISTORY; REDACTION CRITICISM; REIGN OF GOD; RICOEUR, PAUL.

PERSECUTION (IN CHRISTIANITY)

Persecution is an act of oppression or harrassment, and certainly many people have been persecuted throughout history for their beliefs. However, most commonly, when Christians speak of persecution with no other qualifications, they are speaking of the persecutions of Christianity from its beginning until the Edict of Milan in 313 C.E. The first persecution from this period came when the Christians were excluded from the Jewish synagogues, sometimes violently. Early martyrs from this period include Stephen the deacon (Acts 6 and 7), James, the brother of John (Acts 12:1-4), and James, the brother of the Lord.

At first the Roman government did not distinguish between Jews and Christians, and since the Romans tolerated national religions like Judaism, Christians were not persecuted by the Romans. Romans were fairly tolerant of religious groups, but Christians were suspect in the popular imagination for their antisocial behavior. They were accused of atheism, since they did not worship the Roman gods. Further, possibly deliberate misunderstandings of their "love feasts" and "eating of the Body and Blood" led some to accuse the Christians of incest and cannibalism. Sometime in the first century laws were passed, now lost, against being a Christian. The laws seemed to have been sporadically enforced at first. Persecutions took place under Nero in Rome in 64 C.E., when Christians were blamed for the burning of the city. Correspondence between Pliny, governor of Bythnia, and the emperor Trajan around 111-2 reveals that by then Christianity was a capital offense, but that Roman officials were not to seek the Christians out. Persecutions at this time seem to have been local. Ignatius, *episkopos* of Antioch, for example, was executed about 107.

The situation worsened under Emperor Marcus Aurelius (around 161-81). The Christian teacher Justin was martyred in Rome about 165, and Polycarp, the aged *episkopos* of Smyrna, in 167. A serious persecution also broke out in Lyons in 177 where some fifty Christians were executed. Septimus Severus (193-211) forbade the conversion to either Christianity or Judaism, and a number of catechumens were executed. Maximian (235-8) attempted to decapitate Christianity by banishing or executing its leadership. Again, both these attempts were limited in their effectiveness.

The first serious and widespread persecution took place under the emperors Decius (249-51) and Valerian (253-60). Decius believed that the declining fortunes of the Empire were due to a widespread lack of respect for the Roman gods, and so, in 250, he ordered all citizens to obtain a certificate, called a *libellus*, proving that they had sacrificed to the Roman gods. The Christian community was particularly hard hit. Some Christians purchased or obtained *libelli* illegally, actions that horrified those who risked their lives by refusing to sacrifice. The communities of Rome and Carthage were seriously split over the question of what to do with these "lapsed" Christians. Valerian continued the persecutions of Decius and further forbade meeting for worship, targeting *episkopoi* and other leaders for execution. When Valerian died in battle in 261, the new Emperor Gallienus issued an edict of toleration. For forty years, Christianity was left in peace to spread rapidly throughout the Roman Empire.

The last great persecution came under the Emperor Diocletian (284-305), lasting in the eastern half of the Empire until 313. In 303, when the oracles of Miletus failed to provide the emperor with a suitable answer, the silence of the gods was blamed on Christians present who had blessed themselves. Diocletian, like Decius before him, felt that a religious restoration was in order, and the desecration at Miletus was clear evidence that the Christians had offended the gods. All Christian churches were to be destroyed, all Bibles and liturgical books turned over to the Romans, all liturgical vessels confiscated, and all meetings for worship forbidden. In the eastern part of the Empire, the persecution was particularly severe. All clergy were supposed to be arrested, but the prisons simply could not hold so many. In 304 it became a capital crime not to sacrifice to the Roman gods. The persecution finally ended with the signing of the Edict of Milan in 313. The persecution had been much worse in the eastern Empire than in the western Empire, but once again the legacy of persecution was schism. Particularly in North Africa, deep disputes arose over how those who had lapsed in their faith should be treated. The controversies over these questions lasted for centuries. The most lasting legacy of the persecutions, however, were the witness of the martyrs and the inspiration their faith instilled in the Christian community. Cults grew up around many of the martyrs who continue to be venerated in the Christian liturgy until the present day.

Gary Macy

See also ALEXANDER OF ALEXANDRIA; CLEMENT OF ALEXANDRIA; CONSTANTINE THE GREAT; CORNELIUS OF ROME; CYPRIAN OF CARTHAGE; DIOCLETIAN; DONATISM; EPISKOPOS; EUSEBIUS OF CAESAREA; HIPPOLYTUS OF ROME; IGNATIUS OF ANTIOCH; JUDAISM; JUSTIN MARTYR; LACTANTIUS; MARCELLINUS OF ROME; MARCELLUS I OF ROME; MARTYR/MARTYRDOM; MILAN, EDICT OF; NOVATIAN OF ROME; ORIGEN; PAULINUS OF NOLA; POLYCARP OF SMYRNA; STEPHEN I OF ROME.

PERSON

In a Western philosophical framework, a person is understood as a conscious or rational human being who exercises agency and self-determination, the capacity for which depends on the cultivation of personhood. While there is contemporary philosophical debate regarding the origins of personhood, in a Christian theological framework the predominant view is that the seed of one's personhood, what makes an individual essentially particular or unique, is a component part of a human being's ontological core. Thus, a person *qua* person manifests the confluence of soul and self. To become or grow into a person is seen as an ongoing, lifelong process and achievement, a kind of self-discovery, the successful development of which requires a continuous process of action and introspective reflection. Especially in strands of twentieth- and twenty-first-century theologies that have been influenced by the European philosophical movement known as phenomenology, the importance of developing one's personhood in the context of everyday being-in-the-world cannot be underestimated, because, through acting in the world, individuals achieve and reveal their personhood, and thus can better understand themselves and who they are as persons.

Because becoming a person is an achievement marked by agency and self-determination, its realization requires worldly living conditions. Attention thus must be paid to the role of education, housing, healthcare, the arts, and other structures that influence the development of personhood. Unfortunately, marginalized individuals have tended to have even the possibility of their subjective personhood discounted by those in power, a profound discrimination that objectifies and denies marginalized individuals' agency and self-determination. This erasure can be reflected in usually subpar educational, housing, political, and health-care access. However, within recent decades, marginalized individuals, through such means as writing and political mobilization, have begun to assert and insist upon their personhood. No longer determined and characterized by group membership by belonging, for example, to a particular race, sex, or class, the particular uniqueness of the individual person is increasingly acknowledged and respected.

Meghan T. Sweeney

See also HUMAN BEING; HUMAN RIGHTS; THEOLOGICAL ANTHROPOLOGY.

PERSONALISM

Personalism is a school of contemporary Roman Catholic moral theology holding that the human person, considered in fullness, is the necessary starting point for an adequate Christian ethic. It represents a significant departure from traditional Roman Catholic ethics with its emphasis on natural law that was perceived to give priority to the physical dimension of human experience and that was act- rather than character-centered.

Proponents find the theory's theological warrant in the official commentary on Vatican II's Pastoral Constitution on the Church in the Modern World that suggests that "human activity must be judged insofar as it refers to the human person integrally and adequately considered." It is generally understood that an adequate consideration of the person includes an account of the person as an embodied subject (rational and free), relational (to persons, communities, environment, and ultimately to God), historical, and unique

but fundamentally equal. An action, then, is morally right if it is beneficial to the person in her or his totality and to the person's relationships. Personalism, then, is concerned with the type of character being developed by means of choice and action rather than an isolated evaluation of acts.

Brian F. Linnane, S.J.

See also ETHICS, SEXUAL; FUNDAMENTAL OPTION; GAUDIUM ET SPES; MORAL THEOLOGY/CHRISTIAN ETHICS; PROPORTIONALISM; THEOCENTRIC; VIRTUE.

PERSON/PROSOPON

The Greek term *prosopon* originally meant an actor's mask (in the Greek theater). The Latin word *persona* intended to translate the original Greek meaning. Today "person" is not used in this sense in Christian trinitarian theology.

God's self-communication to humanity (by the Incarnation and by grace) has allowed theology to understand that the threefold manner of this divine self-communication must be the way God is in and for Godself in eternity: the unoriginated origin of being and life, the self-pronounced utterance of that being and life, and the outpouring of this being and life as limitless love. Each of these three manners of divine self-communication is inseparable from the others, and is in the others, distinguishable only by its relation to the others. There being only one God, and thus one divine essence, God's three manners of self-communication are all equally divine, being-one-in-another, not separable temporally or spatially.

In Christian theology the terms *prosopon* and *persona* have been used to name each of the three manners of divine self-communication, but these terms cannot be made to imply separation among the "persons," or any form of tritheism (belief in three gods), or any suggestion of "superiority" of one manner over another. The three "persons" of the Trinity are not three "subjects" but the threefold manner of the one God's self-communication to humanity.

Orlando Espín

See also CHRISTOLOGY; HYPOSTATIC UNION; PERICHORESIS; PNEUMATOLOGY; TRINITY/TRINITARIAN THEOLOGY/ TRINITARIAN PROCESSIONS.

PERUSHIM
See PHARISEES.

PESACH
See PASSOVER.

PESHITTA
The Syriac translation of the Old and New Testaments, probably completed in Edessa sometime in the first four centuries C.E. This is the accepted Bible of the Syrian Church.

Alan J. Avery-Peck

PETER
Among the first of the Twelve chosen by Jesus. Originally called Simon, he was given the nickname "rock" (*petra* in Greek; *Cepha'* in Aramaic) by Jesus. Peter was a fisherman from Galilee, the son of a man named John and brother of Andrew, another of the twelve disciples. The brothers, who came from Bethsaida, were followers of John the Baptist before they met Jesus. Peter was married and had a house in Capernaum where Jesus stayed and once healed his mother-in-law.

Peter is portrayed in the New Testament texts as a leader and often spokesperson among Jesus' disciples during his ministry. Against that setting, Peter's threefold denial during Jesus' passion of having known and been his disciple is dramatically heightened. In an encounter with the resurrected Jesus, Peter's repentance for his great sin was resolved in a threefold declaration of love Jesus elicited from him.

In the earliest days of the Christian preaching, Peter was one of the leaders of the Jerusalem community. Acts 10 portrays him as the first to have converted a Gentile, and Acts 15 shows that he supported a mission to the Gentiles that did not demand male circumcision. At the same time, Peter came into conflict with Paul over some aspects of Jewish and Gentile believers associating together at meals.

The few sketchy details that can be related to Peter's missionary career connect him especially with the churches of Corinth and Rome. He is reported as having died a martyr in Rome (*1 Clem.* 5.1–6.1), perhaps during the Neronian persecution (around 64–7). Excavations of the traditional place of his burial, under St. Peter's Basilica in Vatican City, have been conducted and may be visited, but archeologists are not convinced that the remains of Peter himself have been found.

F. M. Gillman

See also APOSTLE; TWELVE, THE (IN SCRIPTURE).

PETER CHRYSOLOGUS (400?–450?)
Peter was bishop of Ravenna in Italy from around 431 until his death. At the time, Ravenna was the capital of the Western Roman Empire, so Peter's post was important. He was a friend of both Pope Sixtus III and Pope Leo I (the Great). Peter is mostly known through his sermons that earned him the title "Chrysologus"

or "Golden Word" in the seventh century. The sermons speak often of everyday problems, and so give insight into Christian life in Ravenna in the fifth century.

Gary Macy

See also BISHOP (EPISCOPACY); LEO I THE GREAT, POPE; SERMON.

PETER DAMIAN (1007–72)

Peter entered the monastery of Fonte Avellana in 1035 after a brief career as teacher in Ravenna. He became abbot of that monastery by 1043 and introduced a strict variation of the Benedictine Rule. Peter was one of the strongest and most active supporters of the Gregorian reforms. Peter emphatically rejected simony and very much favored celibacy for all priests. He was appointed cardinal by Pope Stephen IX and worked ceaselessly to support the papacy through writing and diplomatic missions. Indeed, Peter wrote almost continuously, producing numerous tracts, sermons, letters, and prayers. He is considered a "Doctor (Teacher) of the Church" by Roman Catholics.

Gary Macy

See also CELIBACY; DOCTORS OF THE CHURCH; GREGORIAN REFORMS; INVESTITURE CONTROVERSY; MEDIEVAL CHRISTIANITY (IN THE WEST); SIMONY.

PETER LOMBARD (1095?–1160)

A native of Lombardy in northern Italy, Peter studied theology in Italy and at Reims and then at the Abbey of St. Victor in Paris. By 1144, Peter was a canon of the cathedral of Paris and teaching theology at the cathedral school. He taught at the cathedral school until 1159 when he was chosen bishop of Paris. Peter was famous both as an exegete and as the author of the *Sentences*, a book of short theological discussions divided by topic. He wrote two commentaries on the letters of Paul as well as a commentary on the Psalms. More influential, however, was his *Sentences*. Scholars started using Peter's book as a basic text in theology by the end of the twelfth century, and by the early thirteenth century, every new professor of theology was expected to give a series of lectures on the *Sentences*. This practice continued through the sixteenth century, making the *Sentences* one of the most popular university textbooks of all time. This also gave Peter's book tremendous influence. It is probably the *Sentences'* description of seven basic rituals or sacraments in Christianity that greatly influenced the choice of that number in late medieval and Roman Catholic thought.

Gary Macy

See also EXEGESIS/EISEGESIS; HUGH OF ST. VICTOR; MEDIEVAL CHRISTIANITY (IN THE WEST); SACRAMENT; SCHOLASTICISM.

PETER MARTYR (REFORMER) (1500–62)

Not to be confused with Peter Martyr (1205–52), Dominican friar and saint, Peter Martyr Vermigli was an Augustinian friar who left Italy and his order to join the Reformation. While superior of the Augustinians in Spoleto and then Naples, Vermigli studied Scripture and works by Reformers such as Zwingli and Bucer. Leaving Italy in 1542, Peter Martyr Vermigli taught theology for a time in Strasbourg and, from 1548, was Regius Professor of Divinity at Oxford. Imprisoned when the Catholic Queen Mary became sovereign of England, he was eventually able to leave her realm for Strasbourg. From 1556 he taught Hebrew in Zurich. Peter Martyr Vermigli provides an excellent example of the international extension of the Reformation begun in Switzerland.

Thomas Worcester, S.J.

See also BUCER, MARTIN; CALVIN, JOHN; CALVINISM; OCHINO, BERNARDINO; REFORMATION; REFORMED CHURCHES; REFORMED THEOLOGY (-IES); ZWINGLI, ULRICH.

PETER OF ALCÁNTARA (1499–1562)

Born Peter Garavita in Alcántara, Spain, Peter entered the Franciscan Order in 1515. He became an important leader of the discalced ("without shoes") reform of the Franciscan Order in Spain. Under his guidance, the reform movement spread to Portugal, Italy, Central and South America, and even to the Far East. In his later years, he advised and encouraged Teresa of Avila. Peter was canonized in 1699 and in 1826 made the patron saint of Brazil.

Gary Macy

See also FRANCISCANS; SAINT.

PETER OF SPAIN (1205–77)

Also known as Peter or Petrus Hispanus, he was in fact born in Lisbon. After studying theology in Paris and medicine in Siena, and some years as university professor, he became archbishop of Braga and then cardinal of the church, and in 1276 he was elected pope as John XXI. Peter of Spain was a respected and influential intellectual in his own right. His *Tractatus* (1232), also known as *Summulae logicales*, was perhaps the most important text on logic to be produced during the Middle Ages, with editions published as late as the eighteenth century. The impact of his writings on logic was still felt in the theology manuals of the nineteenth and twentieth centuries, and in more recent authors such as J. Maritain and R. Garrigou-Lagrange. Peter was also known for his early commentaries on Aristotle and for his medical texts. Although he seems to have begun a process of inquiry that ultimately led to the condemnation (for Averroism) of several University of Paris theologians (Thomas Aquinas among them), Peter died before any canonical or doctrinal decision had been reached.

Orlando Espín

See also AQUINAS, THOMAS, ST.; ARISTOTELIANISM; AVERROISM; MANUALS, THEOLOGY OF THE; MARITAIN, JACQUES; SCHOLASTICISM; THOMISM/TRANSCENDENTAL THOMISM.

PETER THE CHANTER (?–1197)

Peter studied in Rheims in France before becoming a teacher of theology in Paris where he was teaching by 1173. He was called the Chanter because he was the "chanter" of the church of Notre Dame, that is, he was responsible for training the choir, along with teaching theology. Peter had many famous students, including Stephen Langton, the archbishop of Canterbury, and probably Pope Innocent III. He was one of the first theologians to teach the whole of Scripture, and his lectures, or commentaries, on the books of the Bible had a great deal of influence on later theologians. Peter was most concerned with practical, everyday questions of morality, and urged reforms that would make for a moral society.

Gary Macy

See also EXEGESIS/EISEGESIS; INNOCENT III, POPE; MEDIEVAL CHRISTIANITY (IN THE WEST); SCHOLASTICISM.

PETRINE MINISTRY

The ministry of Peter the apostle and of his successors in that ministry (that is, the Bishops of Rome). In Catholic belief, Peter and his successors have a special mission within the church, but this mission or ministry is not conceived of or exercised in isolation from the rest of the church but, rather, within the overall ecclesial vocation, mission, and context of discipleship. A number of biblical texts are commonly cited as justification for the Petrine ministry (Matt 16:17-19; Luke 23:31ff., for example). It does seem that the New Testament recognized a leadership role for Peter—a role given him by Jesus and acknowledged by the rest of the first Christian communities. The earlier Bishops of Rome (Clement, for example) already claimed to have a ministry that extended beyond their local church, a claim that has continued throughout the centuries. Some of the early ecumenical councils of undivided Christianity also acknowledged a first place of honor for the church of Rome and its bishops.

As the centuries passed, the primacy of Peter's successors was accepted in Western Christianity while Eastern Christianity, out of respect for the conciliar decisions in this regard, recognized in Rome's bishops only a primacy of honor. After the schism of 1054 that divided Western and Eastern Christians, the Western Church continued the development of the idea of Peter's ministry—was it just a primacy of honor ("first among equals") or was this ministry also one of jurisdiction over other local churches? Cultural and political contexts intervened, historically, to shape the ministry of the Bishops of Rome in ways that, on the one hand, developed a better understanding of the place and role of Peter's successors in the wider church while, on the other hand, conditioned expressions of that ministry in ways that were not always beneficial to the overall church or to the pastoral credibility of the Bishops of Rome. Among the many consequences deriving from the Reformations of the sixteenth century, Western Catholics rallied around the Bishops of Rome, increasing the claims concerning their primacy and jurisdiction in the overall church. In the nineteenth century, the First Vatican Council, for the first time in church history, defined the dogma of papal infallibility and the official understanding of both primacy and jurisdiction (finally deciding that the successors of Peter have both primacy and jurisdiction over the entire church).

According to the doctrine of the First Vatican Council, the unity of the church is the crucial and indispensable reason for, and the context of, any Catholic understanding of the Petrine ministry. In the twentieth century the Second Vatican Council further refined the church's understanding of the Petrine ministry by emphasizing that it must be understood with the entire context of the church (and of ecclesiology), both universal and local, and more specifically within the context of the whole episcopate. Today the doctrines of these two councils are standard among Catholics worldwide.

Orlando Espín

See also CHURCH; DEFINITION (OF DOCTRINES); DEVELOPMENT OF DOGMA/OF DOCTRINE; ECCLESIOLOGY; EPISCOPATE; INFALLIBILITY; LUMEN GENTIUM; MAGISTERIUM, ORDINARY; PASTOR AETERNUS; PETER; POPE; PRIMACY; ROMAN CATHOLIC CHURCH; ROME, SEE OF; VATICAN, FIRST COUNCIL OF THE; VATICAN, SECOND COUNCIL OF THE.

PETRINE PRIVILEGE

The so-called "Petrine privilege," now generally considered by canonists to be an inappropriate term, is better known as the privilege or favor of the faith (*in favorem fidei*), the application of which dissolves a presumably consummated, but nonsacramental, valid marriage bond between a baptized person and a non-baptized person. Unlike the Pauline privilege as traditionally understood, it does not involve a convert whose unbaptized spouse is unwilling to live in peace after the baptism. The practice of the privilege of the faith developed in the 1930s from cases presented to the Holy See from the United States. Initially, it was viewed as an exercise of papal authority (hence "Petrine") that dissolved a "natural," nonsacramental marriage bond, when the marriage was in fact dead (and civil divorce had taken place when appropriate). It was permitted for the sake of a higher good, that is, the spiritual welfare of one of the persons involved and the validation of a subsequent marriage. Although the 1980 draft of the new Code proposed a specific canon for this privilege as an act reserved to the Roman pontiff to dissolve a nonsacramental marriage, it was not promulgated in the Code of Canon Law (1983). Nevertheless, norms issued in 1973 and affirmed again in 1983 remain in effect under the exclusive jurisdiction of the Holy See. Roman Catholic jurisprudence, after much heated debate, and now the Vatican, see the privilege of the faith as an extension of the Pauline privilege in that the dissolution of the valid bond according to recent norms (*Canon Law Digest* 9, 678) states that the dissolution occurs not by papal declaration but with the consent made in the new marriage. The privilege of the faith is one of three instances in which the Roman Catholic Church dissolves (gives a divorce for) what it considers to be a valid bond of matrimony, the other two being nonbiological consummation, even in a sacramental union (Can. 1142) and the traditional Pauline privilege (Cans. 1143–50).

Dennis W. Krouse

See also DIVORCE (IN CHRISTIANITY); INDISSOLUBILITY; MARRIAGE IN CATHOLIC PERSPECTIVE; PAULINE PRIVILEGE.

PEYOTE

This is the substance used in the communion ritual of the Native American Church. It is found in nature as a cactus whose buttons when eaten produce a mild hallucinatory state in which concentration and introspection are deepened. Thus, it is used as an aid to meditation, the point of which is moral and spiritual regeneration. It is not addictive; in fact, it produces distinctly unpleasant effects. It is regarded as a sacred gift that bears with it the presence of the spirits. These range from the traditional sacred persons to Jesus, for there is a clear influence of Christianity in the peyote religion. The partaking of it results in a unitive experience that includes both the sacred and the ritual community.

Kathleen Dugan

See also COMMUNION (LITURGICAL); NATIVE AMERICAN CHURCH.

PHAN, PETER C. (1946–)

Asian American Catholic theologian and priest. Peter Cho Phan holds the Ellacuría Chair in Catholic Social Thought at Georgetown University (Washington, D.C.). Born in Vietnam, he emigrated to the U.S. in 1975. He earned doctorates in theology (Rome) and in philosophy and divinity

(London). Before joining the Georgetown faculty, Phan taught at the University of Dallas and at The Catholic University of America. He is a past president of the Catholic Theological Society of America (the first non-European American elected to that position). In his work Phan has focused on patristic theology, missiology, culture, and liberation. He is regarded as the most important Asian American theologian today. Phan has published over twenty books and hundreds of scholarly articles. Among his more influential works are *Christianity with an Asian Face: Asian American Theology in the Making* (2003); *In Our Own Tongues: Perspectives from Asia on Mission and Inculturation* (2003); *Grace and the Human Condition* (1988); and *Culture and Eschatology* (1985).

Orlando Espín

See also CULTURE; INCULTURATION; LIBERATION THEOLOGIES; METHOD IN THEOLOGY.

PHARAOH

An Egyptian head of state in the ancient Near East. The pharaoh or king of Egypt at the time of the Exodus is believed to have been Rameses II, though the biblical text does not name the pharaoh of the Exodus and there are no extant Egyptian texts that corroborate the Exodus as having occurred.

Five pharaohs are identified by name in the Hebrew Scriptures. These include: (1) Shishak, who gave asylum to Jeroboam (1 Kgs 11:40) and later invaded Israel (1 Kgs 14:25-26; 2 Chr 12:1-9); (2) Tirhakah, identified as the king of Ethiopia in 2 Kings 19:9 and Isaiah 37:9; (3) Neco, who defeated and killed Josiah, king of Judah, who removed Jehoahaz from the throne and replaced him with Jehoiakim (2 Kgs 23:29-35; 2 Chr 35:20–36:4), and

who lost territories under Egyptian control to Nebuchadnezzar, king of Babylon (2 Kgs 24:7); (4) Hophra, against whom Jeremiah prophesied (Jer 44:30); and (5) So, identified as the king of Egypt to whom King Hoshea of Judah sent messengers (2 Kgs 17:4).

Alice L. Laffey

PHARISEES

A group of especially observant, scholarly, and influential Jews found mainly in Palestine from the second century B.C.E. through the first century C.E. The origin of their name in Hebrew is uncertain. It may mean "the separated ones," alluding to their strict observances of ritual purity and tithing. The Pharisees are mentioned in the New Testament, Josephus, and in rabbinic sources, with each body of literature giving differing perspectives on them. Modern descriptions thus differ as well, depending upon the sources accepted or emphasized and how conflicting perceptions in the sources are resolved.

On the basis of the references as a whole, it is evident that the Pharisees had their own traditions concerning observance of the Jewish Law, with an emphasis on ritual purity, food tithes, and observance of the Sabbath. They had the sympathy of the people, and at some times were felt as a sociopolitical force over against foreign and Hellenized Jewish leaders (for instance, the Sadducees). At least some Pharisees were learned in the Law, and some were politically powerful.

In more recent biblical scholarship, caution is advised in assessing the New Testament data on the Pharisees. Therein they are portrayed almost always negatively, usually in opposition to Jesus and his interpretation of the Law. Many point out, however, that Jesus' close argumentation with them may stem in fact from an affinity on many levels. The New Testament negative view of the Pharisees is now recognized as primarily an early Christian polemic against the rabbinic leadership of the latter first century.

The New Testament emphasizes the contrast between the Pharisees, with their belief in resurrection, over against the Sadducees, who did not hold a belief in a life after death. That Pharisees in particular among the numerous groups in first-century Judaism may have been especially interested in the preaching of the resurrection of Jesus seems evident in the story of the Pharisee Nicodemus (John 3). The apostle Paul, outstanding among the earliest Christian missionaries, states explicitly that he had been a Pharisee (Phil 3:5).

F. M. Gillman

See also ESSENES; PAUL; RESURRECTION (IN CHRISTIANITY); RESURRECTION (IN JUDAISM); RESURRECTION OF THE BODY; SADDUCEES; SANHEDRIN.

PHELPS, JAMIE T.
Roman Catholic sister (Adrian Dominican) and systematic theologian, Phelps is the first African American to receive the doctorate in systematic theology from The Catholic University of America (1989). Phelps is a tenured associate professor of doctrinal and mission theology and founding director of the Augustus Tolton Pastoral Ministry Program at the Catholic Theological Union in Chicago. She is also associate director of the Theology of Ministry Degree Program, the Institute for Black Catholic Studies of Xavier University of Louisiana.

Phelps' theological studies were preceded by more than a decade of full-time work as a pastoral associate and a graduate degree in psychiatric social work along with extensive clinical experience. The author of more than thirty book chapters and journal articles, her current research focuses on ecclesiology (communio) and trinitarian theology. Phelps is convener of the Black Catholic Theological Symposium, an elected member of the Society for the Study of Black Religion, and former member of the Board of the Catholic Theological Society of America.

M. Shawn Copeland

See also BLACK THEOLOGY; WOMANIST THEOLOGY.

PHENOMENOLOGY
The name of a philosophical movement associated with the teachings of Edmund Husserl (1859–1938) and his followers. Although the term "phenomenology" had been employed earlier by Kant and Hegel (indeed, Hegel's first major work was called Phenomenology of the Spirit), the term generally refers today to Husserl's thought and to that of his disciples. Phenomenology understands itself as a rigorous search for and analysis of foundational meanings and essences. It wants to seek out and understand the "essences" intuited in all thought. Methodologically, it also wants to exclude metaphysical considerations, although this has proven to be very difficult. Husserl himself first tended toward a kind of Platonism (later developed along Augustinian lines by some of his disciples, especially Max Scheler and Johannes Hessen). Husserl also moved toward a "subjective" Idealism. Phenomenology was very influential in Germany in the thirty years that preceded the Nazi takeover, but Husserl's Jewish ancestry made him and his movement targets of Nazi attacks. Edith Stein

was among the best phenomenologists, but perhaps the existentialist Martin Heidegger did more to spread the movement's influence beyond Germany. After World War II there was renewed interest in phenomenology, often in connection with existentialism.

Orlando Espín

See also AUGUSTINE OF HIPPO; AUGUSTINIANISM; EXISTENTIALISM; HEGEL, G.W.F.; HEIDEGGER, MARTIN; IDEALISM, CLASSICAL GERMAN; KANT, IMMANUEL; MODERNITY; PHILOSOPHICAL THEOLOGY; POSTMODERNITY; SCHELER, MAX; STEIN, EDITH.

PHILARET, DROZDOV (1782–1867)
Russian Orthodox theologian. Educated in Moscow, he taught theology there and in St. Petersburg. Made bishop of Jaroslav and patriarch of Moscow, he was a good preacher and administrator, much admired by his people. He was also influential in the wider Russian church and state. Although at times suspected of Lutheran doctrinal sympathies, his *Christian Catechism of the Orthodox Catholic Eastern Greco-Russian Church* (1823) became very important in nineteenth-century Russian theological thought.

Orlando Espín

See also ORTHODOX CHURCHES; RUSSIAN ORTHODOX CHURCH; SOBORNOST.

PHILARET, THEODORE NIKITICH ROMANOV (1553–1633)
Father of the first Russian czar of the Romanov dynasty, Philaret had been active in public civil and ecclesiastical life when he was elected patriarch of Moscow and, therefore, head of the Russian Orthodox Church in 1619. Involved in politics until the end of his life, Philaret was also an avid reformer of his church, especially in the promotion of theological studies.

Orlando Espín

See also ORTHODOX CHURCHES; PATRIARCH; RUSSIAN ORTHODOX CHURCH.

PHILO OF ALEXANDRIA (20/15 B.C.E.–50 C.E.?)
Philo of Alexandria was a Hellenistic Jewish philosopher of first-century Alexandria. Alexandria was the location of the largest Jewish community outside of Palestine in the first century. Philo was a member of a prominent family in this community. The date of his birth is uncertain, and he died probably approximately a decade after leading a delegation of Alexandrian Jews to meet the emperor, Gaius Caligula, in Rome to petition for full citizenship rights and protections for the Jews of Alexandria. Philo is known primarily for his philosophical writings in which he presented the Law of Moses and Jewish tradition melded with elements of Greek philosophy. Philo is also known for his use of the allegorical method of biblical interpretation.

Russell Fuller

PHILOSOPHICAL THEOLOGY
There is considerable ambiguity with this term because it is often used interchangeably with a variety of other terms, for example, apologetics, natural theology, fundamental theology, and (less frequently) philosophy of religion. Insofar as the term approaches apologetics and natural theology, philosophical theology investigates the extent to which claims and concepts derived from a specific religious tradition and whose truth is secured in advance by the authority of a specific religious tradition, can be known by "reason alone" or are consistent with natural

reason. Insofar as the term approaches fundamental theology and philosophy of religion, philosophical theology becomes a second-order analysis of the claims and arguments of religion and theology, whose truth is not regarded as secured in advance by the authority of a specific religious tradition.

J. A. Colombo

See also FUNDAMENTAL THEOLOGY; PHILOSOPHY OF RELIGION.

PHILOSOPHY OF RELIGION

Historically, philosophy of religion emerged as a distinct discipline during the period of the Enlightenment as a second-order discourse of reflection on and analysis of the claims of religion—religion's beliefs, practices, experience, or consciousness—and the arguments of theology. This includes both the claims and arguments of religion and theology, respectively, to speak truthfully of the holy, God(s), divine, and the like. As such, philosophy of religion is not a part of the domain of religion and theology insofar as its canons (for example, procedures, concepts, and warrants) are in principle derived independently of the claims of religion and the arguments of theology.

J. A. Colombo

See also FUNDAMENTAL THEOLOGY; PHILOSOPHICAL THEOLOGY.

PHOTIUS OF CONSTANTINOPLE (820?–91)

Born in Constantinople of noble parents, Photius received an excellent education. Already head of the imperial chancellery and a member of the senate, he was appointed patriarch of Constantinople in 858 while still a layman upon the deposition of the former patriarch, Ignatius, by

Emperor Michael III. Pope Nicholas I refused to accept the deposition and declared Photius deposed as he was by the new emperor Basil in 867. Before his deposition, however, Photius excommunicated the Pope and attacked the Western church as heretical for adding the *Filioque* to the Creed. The split between East and West was short-lived, however. When Photius was restored to the patriarchate in 877, his position seems to have been accepted by Rome. Photius was again removed from office in 886.

Gary Macy

See also EXCOMMUNICATION; HERESY; PATRIARCH; POPE; SCHISM, GREAT EASTERN.

PHYSIS

Greek word deriving from the process of production and birth that gradually focused on patterns within changing events that revealed their stable, nonderivative roots. *Physis* stressed the inner reliability and self-direction that marked both worldly and divine affairs with wise, orderly purpose, unlike law or custom (*nomos*) that shapes events from outside. Hellenistic thought either identified such universal cosmic order as divine, or else saw it as deriving from a higher, invisible, ideal realm. There is no Hebrew equivalent for *physis*, and the word seldom occurs in early Jewish Greek writings. First-century Hellenistic Jewish writers like Philo (30 B.C.E.–45 C.E.) and Josephus (37–100 C.E.), however, use it often. Philo notably joins Greek and Jewish thought by combining *physis* with Mosaic Law as the norm by which the invisible God, known only by reason, created and cares for the world. In the New Testament, *physis* terminology never appears in the Gospels, and most of the nineteen examples are Pauline. Paul uses *physis* for countering Jewish claims to inherent superiority over Gentiles based on possessing Mosaic Law, or to portray life apart from Christ as bondage to the worldly scheme of things subject to God's just wrath. Later New Testament and early patristic examples largely reflect Hellenistic Jewish piety, while early Gnostic writing betrays a creeping determinism, pessimism, and personalization of the physical world as demonic. Later Western medieval and modern thought tends to distinguish things of nature from those of the mind, speculating on their respective inclusiveness, independence, and primacy.

Francis D. Connolly-Weinert

PICO DELLA MIRANDOLA, GIOVANNI (1463–94)

Giovanni was born into the ruling family of Mirandola in Italy and was himself the Count of Concordia. At fourteen, he began studying canon law in Bologna, then moved on to Florence where he studied philosophy. At the University of Padua, Giovanni picked up an interest in Hebrew and Arabic. In 1482 he returned to Florence to study Greek, then moved to Paris to study philosophy and theology. By the age of twenty-three, Giovanni felt ready to take on all challengers in the area of philosophy, which he did in 1486 by offering to defend nine hundred statements against anyone. Unfortunately, some of the statements were considered heretical and were condemned in 1487. The debates never took place. Giovanni settled in Florence where he worked to reconcile all the philosophies he knew into a single system. He died at thirty-one, his work incomplete. His nephew, who had the same name, published Giovanni's work after his death and his fame spread. Considered one of the Renaissance humanists, Giovanni believed that humans were capable, through philosophic contemplation, of raising themselves to the level of the angels.

Gary Macy

See also HERESY; HUMANISM; RENAISSANCE.

PIDYON HABEN

(Hebrew, redemption of the firstborn). In Judaism, the ceremony through which the firstborn son of an ordinary Israelite (that is, a Jew not of the lineage of the Temple-priests or Levites) is released from his status of being dedicated to God (see Num 18:16). This is accomplished through the payment to a person of priestly lineage (Kohen) of a sum of money as a substitute for the child. The ceremony takes place on the thirty-first day after birth. In contemporary practice, it is observed as a recognition of people's debt to God and of the continuing validity of God's claim to ownership of the firstborn of humans and animals. The rite also recognizes the special status of the Kohen, whose ancestors officiated in the Jerusalem Temple.

Alan J. Avery-Peck

See also KOHEN.

PIETISM

A Christian renewal movement in Germany in the late seventeenth century, Pietism originated among Protestants who believed that Reformed theology had become stale and lifeless. A Lutheran pastor in Frankfurt, Phillipp Spener (1635–1705), conducted Bible studies in his home that he called "colleges of piety." These groups stressed singing, prayer, and the application of the Gospel to daily life. In 1675 Spener published *Pia Desideria*, a program for the development of piety among Christians.

Spener de-emphasized the differences between laity and clergy and focused on the responsibility of all Christians to nurture their spiritual lives and a deep personal faith. Preachers should focus less on intellectual understandings of doctrine and more on the actual practice of discipleship. Calling for a reformation in spirituality, Spener stressed the experience of devotion over theological speculation, heart over head, deed over Creed. Moreover, he insisted on the contrast between Christian and human ethics; he claimed that Christians were called to a higher and deeper morality than non-Christians.

Spener's Pietism provoked opposition among Lutheran leaders for three reasons. First, they feared he emphasized experience to the neglect of necessary doctrinal training. Second, he focused on sanctification more than Luther, that is, the grace that enables Christians to live a holy and perfect life; orthodox Lutherans accused Spener of being a Calvinist. Third, Spener preached that the prophecies in Revelation were being fulfilled and that the end of the world was imminent. His apocalypticism heightened tension between his followers and the Lutheran Church.

Despite accusations of heresy, the Pietist movement grew. Among Spener's most important followers was a professor at the University of Halle, August H. Francke (1663–1727). Under his leadership, the university became a center for Pietism. He stressed the ineffable joy of the Christian life and the need for Christians to praise God for the gift of faith. Thousands were attracted to Pietism's stress on a dynamic, living faith. Most remained within Lutheran and Reformed Churches, invigorating them with spirit-filled hymns, intercessory prayer, and Protestant missionary endeavors. One of the earliest missions was established in 1707 in India, led by two of Francke's students and underwritten by the king of Denmark, a Pietist sympathizer.

Although Pietism (with a capital P) refers to the seventeenth-century movement in Germany, Christians since Spener and Francke can justifiably be called pietist by emphasizing personal piety. The Moravians, led by Count Nicholas von Zinzendorf in the 1730s and 1740s, established missions, communities, and schools, and focused on empathy with Christ's suffering on the cross. Founded by John Wesley in the eighteenth century, the Methodists were a renewal movement within the Church of England that articulated a "method" for nurturing spiritual enthusiasm. In the nineteenth century, Phoebe Palmer led a movement within the U.S. Methodist Church that stressed the achievement of perfect holiness, spawning Holiness denominations such as the Church of the Nazarene. Eighteenth- and nineteenth-century revivalism, such as the Great Awakenings in the United States, also reflect the spirit of Pietism.

Evelyn A. Kirkley

See also ANABAPTISTS; BOHEMIAN BRETHREN/MORAVIANS; MENNONITES.

PIETY

As a classical virtue, piety was more favored by Roman than by Greek philosophy. When Virgil referred to his hero as "pius Aeneas," he meant that Aeneas had the proper relationship to God, his family, and to others. Christians saw piety as one of the seven gifts of the Holy Spirit. In Thomas Aquinas, piety is similar to the virtue of religion in that it deals with the whole matter of justice of the will (desires, passions) with respect to God. It differs from the virtue of religion in that piety sees God not as simply Creator and Lord, but as Father (*ST* II–II, q. 121, a. 1; cf. Rom 8:15). As such, it is the expression of a more intimate than formal relationship with God. As a gift of the Holy Spirit, piety empowers one to love God for no other reason than that God *is* God. That is, one loves God irrespective of one's own suffering or lot in life, even without regard to one's own salvation. A classic expression of that dimension of piety is St. Francis Xavier's *"O Jesu ego amo te."* Finally, piety, according to John of St. Thomas, extends a fraternal/sororal love to *all* creatures, because they are in the family of God. A classic expression of that dimension of piety is St. Francis of Assisi's "Canticle to the Sun."

In the Catholic Church, "popular piety" includes an extremely broad range of devotional practices not commanded by the faith, but that help the person or community engage on a more personal, intimate, even physical level with the mysteries, teachings, and holiness of the faith. They may include acts like going on a pilgrimage to a holy shrine, praying the rosary, placing flowers or lighting candles before a statue of the Sacred Heart, kissing a picture or statue of a saint, saying the *Angelus*, or having special family gatherings for prayer. Sometimes, cultural practices are taken up into local church worship and become exercises of "folk piety." These may include processions with images of the city or national "patron saint," dances, or community song incorporated into the church liturgies.

G. Simon Harak, S.J.

See also HOLY SPIRIT.

PILATE, PONTIUS

The Roman prefect of Judea from 26–36 C.E. His time in office included the periods of the activity of John the Baptist and the public ministry of Jesus. Pilate played a central role in the trial and crucifixion of Jesus (Matt 27:1-2, 11-26; Mark 15:1-15; Luke 23:1-25; John 18:28–19:22; Acts 3:13; 4:27; 13:28; 1 Tim 6:13). His wife, who is not named in the New Testament, warned Pilate against ordering the death of Jesus due to a dream that had disturbed her (Matt 27:19), a message that went unheeded.

Outside the New Testament, information about Pilate can be found in the writings of Philo and Josephus. In 1961 a dedicatory inscription was found in Caesarea indicating Pilate's title was prefect, not procurator as had previously been held.

F. M. Gillman

See also HEROD; JOHN THE BAPTIST; JOSEPHUS (FLAVIUS); PASSION NARRATIVES.

PILGRIMAGE

This is a trip taken, for religious and devotional reasons (for instance, to seek divine assistance, or to show repentance, or to reinforce the pilgrim's faith commitment), to a holy place or shrine. Most religions of the world know the practice of pilgrimages. The manner of traveling to the holy place, besides the trip itself (which can be to a faraway place, or to a local shrine), is considered an important part of the pilgrimage. After arrival, there frequently are prescribed visits and practices that are followed by the pilgrims.

Orlando Espín

See also APPARITIONS; DEVOTIONS; FAITH; GUADALUPE, VIRGIN OF; LATIN

AMERICAN CATHOLICISM; LATINO
CATHOLICISM; MARIAN DEVOTIONS;
MARIOLOGY; MEDIEVAL CHRISTIANITY
(IN THE WEST); MEDIEVAL CHURCH;
POPULAR CATHOLICISM; POPULAR
RELIGIONS; RELIC (OUTSIDE CHRIS-
TIANITY); SAINTS (CHRISTIAN), DEVO-
TION TO; SANCTUARY (PLACE); SHRINE.

PILLARS OF ISLAM

See FIVE PILLARS (IN ISLAM).

PIR

The term used by Iranian and Indian
Muslims for a master or spiritual guide
in Sufism. In other parts of the Islamic
world, a *pir* is called *shaykh*.

Ronald A. Pachence

See also SHAYKH; SUFI/SUFISM.

PIRKE AVOT

See ETHICS OF THE FATHERS.

PISA, COUNCIL OF

In an attempt to heal the Western Schism
caused by the dual papacies of Avignon
and Rome, a group of twenty-four cardinals called for a general council to be held
at Pisa. The council was extremely well
attended, including over eighty bishops
and archbishops, more than one hundred
abbots, and representatives from most of
the European princes. In 1409 the assembly declared itself to have authority to
judge the two reigning popes based on
the conciliar theory then popular with
many theologians and canonists. The
council declared both popes schismatics
and heretics and henceforth deposed.
The cardinals present unanimously chose
Peter of Candia, the Franciscan cardinal
of Milan, as the new Pope Alexander V.
Although Alexander had a large following, the popes in Avignon and in Rome

refused to step down, and Europe was
faced with the prospect of three popes.
The successor of Alexander V, John XXIII,
called for another council to meet at Constance, and it was at this conference that
the Western Schism was finally ended.
Roman Catholics do not consider Pisa an
ecumenical council nor do they recognize
either Alexander V or John XXIII as legitimate popes.

Gary Macy

See also CONCILIARISM; CONSTANCE,
COUNCIL OF; COUNCIL, ECUMENICAL;
FRANCISCANS; MEDIEVAL CHRISTIANITY
(IN THE WEST); POPE; SCHISM, GREAT
WESTERN.

PIUS V, POPE (1504–72)

Roman Catholic pope. His original name
was Michele Ghislieri. He became a
member of the Dominican Order, and
was ordained to the priesthood in 1528.
Ghislieri had been professor of theology
and held several administrative posts
within his order when he was elected
bishop of Nepi and Sutri, and cardinal of
the church in 1556. He was also appointed
Inquisitor General. Ghislieri had a reputation as an austere and holy man throughout his entire life, and in 1566 he was
unanimously elected pope (Bishop of
Rome), taking then the name Pius. He was
a tireless advocate of thorough internal
reform of the Catholic Church. He insisted
that the reform legislation of the Council
of Trent be diligently implemented throughout the church; he also reformed the
liturgy, straightened out the Diocese of
Rome and papal administration, and
completed the so-called Roman Catechism. He tried to stop the spread of the
Protestant Reformation in Europe, but
mistakenly confused the Anglican reform
with Protestantism. During his reign as

Pope, the Turkish threat to Europe was definitively stopped by Catholic armies. He was canonized in 1712.

Orlando Espín

See also ANGLICAN COMMUNION; CANONIZATION; CARDINAL; CATECHISM; COUNTER-REFORMATION / CATHOLIC REFORMATION; DOMINICANS; INQUISITION; LITURGY (IN CHRISTIANITY); POPE; PROTESTANTISM; REFORMATION; ROMAN CATHOLIC CHURCH; ROSARY; SOCIETY OF JESUS; TRENT, COUNCIL OF; TRIDENTINISM.

PIUS IX, POPE (1791–1878)

Pope (1846–78). Pius's career as churchman exemplified two responses to modernity. In his early years as bishop and pope, he favored the liberal philosophies and reform movements of the day. He became a staunch opponent of these ideologies when Italian political movements effected the loss of the Italian papal territories (except Vatican City), initiating an era of church resistance to modernity. His encyclical *Quanta Cura* condemned many modern liberal doctrines as did the *Syllabus of Errors*, a short listing of the same (1864). His concern to defend the church's spiritual and moral authority took an Ultramontanist turn as he promoted papal authority and called Vatican Council I (1869–70) to defend the possibility of faith (*Dei Filius*), the church's teaching authority and infallible teaching authority of the papacy (*Pastor Aeternus*). Pius also worked to support the spirituality of the faithful by promoting Marian and other devotions and proclaimed the dogma of the Immaculate Conception on December 8, 1854.

Patricia Plovanich

See also IMMACULATE CONCEPTION; SYLLABUS OF ERRORS; ULTRAMONIANISM.

PIUS X, POPE (1835–1914)

Pastor, bishop, pope (1903–14). Born Giuseppe Sarto in Riese, Italy, Pius's papacy was shaped by his early experiences as pastor and seminary professor. Later bishop (1884), then cardinal / patriarch in Venice (1893), Pius remained interested in Catholic spiritual life, even after election to the papacy. He promoted the accessibility of the sacraments, advocating frequent Communion and early First Communion, advocated reforms in catechetics, church music, and in seminary spirituality, and encouraged lay participation in the church's work (Catholic Action). A revision of canon law and reorganization of the Vatican Curia were effected at his direction. Always suspicious of the modern separation of church and state and modernity, in general, he condemned various modern philosophies in the decree *Lamentabili*, new approaches to theological and biblical studies in the encyclical *Pascendi Dominici Gregis* (1907), mandated an oath ejecting Modernism for clergy, and maintained a careful watch over theological faculties. These actions prevented Catholic scholars from adopting theological innovations for several decades.

Patricia Plovanich

See also MODERNISM.

PIUS XI, POPE (1857–1939)

Born A. Ratti, Pius was seminary professor, archbishop-cardinal of Milan in 1921, then elected pope the next year (1922). He worked to maintain European equilibrium in the time between the world wars, signing treaties (concordats) with Mussolini and Hitler. These agreements secured some independence for the Vatican but rendered the church unable to criticize later actions of the regimes. In internal affairs, Pius advocated spiritual renewal, lay participation in church affairs through the Catholic Action movement, and promoted Catholic education and missionary activity. His social commentaries reiterate earlier papal teachings, for instance, support of workers in *Quadragesimo Anno* (1931).

This was the first Pope to make use of new communication media, setting up a Vatican radio station. The establishment of pontifical institutes for the study of archeology (1925) and science (1936) promoted Catholic scholarship in those fields.

Patricia Plovanich

PIUS XII, POPE (1876–1958)

Vatican diplomat, pope (1938–58). Born Eugenio Pacelli, Pius began his career in the Vatican diplomatic service after ordination (1899). Lengthy service in the Germanic states (Bavaria in 1917, the German Republic in 1930) engaged his admiration for German culture. As papal Secretary of State from 1930, he faced the rise of communist and of fascist states and used the politics of concordats to influence European affairs. His papacy began when World War II broke out (1939), and he is often criticized for not confronting the crisis directly. Many encyclicals decried the war, however, and Pius's efforts on behalf of refugees are well documented. His influence as teacher was seen in many encyclicals and reforms. *Divino Afflante Spiritu* sanctioned the use of the historical-critical method in biblical studies; *Mediator Dei* promoted liturgical reform. *Mystici Corporis Christi* explains the church with the popular ecclesial image of the era, mystical and incarnational reality. Pius advocated popular devotion, particularly Marian devotion, as a tool for spiritual renewal and declared the dogma of Mary's Assumption in 1950.

Patricia Plovanich

PLATO (428/7–348/7 B.C.E.)

The ancient Greek philosopher Plato is one of the greatest philosophers of all time. Plato and his student Aristotle had a profound influence on the development of theology in the Middle Ages. Plato is best known for his Theory of Forms and his Doctrine of Knowledge by Recollection. According to Plato, the fact that objects in the world of our experience fall into certain classes or kinds is due to their sharing some kind-making characteristic each individual member of the class possesses to a greater or lesser degree. What accounts for the possession of the kind-making characteristic is a Form—an object that does not exist in this physical world but exists, instead, in the realm of ultimate reality or being. Individual objects possessing the relevant characteristic are said to "imitate" or "participate in" the correlative Form. For example, individuals are more or less just insofar as they participate more or less fully in the Form Justice. Plato held that humans now alive once existed in the world of Forms where they were able to "behold" the Forms—that is, have direct, unmediated access to knowledge of the ultimate natures of things. When a human being is born, the person forgets what was learned while in the realm of Forms. Hence, on Plato's view, learning is a process by which one comes to recollect what they knew in a previous life. According to Plato, the study of philosophy is the best way to bring us to the recollection of our previous knowledge of the Forms.

Linda L. Peterson

See also ARISTOTELIANISM; ARISTOTLE; NEOPLATONISM; PLATONISM.

PLATONISM

The term "Platonism" is used to characterize any system of thought deriving from the teachings of the ancient Greek philosopher Plato (428/7–348/7 B.C.E.). The following are elements that tend to be present in any basically Platonic system of thought: (1) emphasis on gradations or levels of reality and the transcendent nature of ultimate reality; (2) opposition to materialism and to empiricist or sense-based theories of knowledge acquisition; (3) emphasis on the immortality of the soul and the ability of the human intellect to grasp the nature of transcendent reality.

In holding that reality admits of degrees, Platonists reject the commonsensical notion that any existing thing *exists* just as fully as any other. For example, it seems reasonable to think that a human being exists in the way a table or chair exists—by being an observable constituent of the physical universe. Yet, if one holds that a human being is essentially a soul or spiritual being that can exist in a realm transcending the limits of physical reality, then there is room for thinking that a human being exists to a higher degree than a merely physical object such as a table or chair. Platonists hold that the physical world, in general, exists less fully than objects that exist immaterially. Objects in the physical world are only shadows of reality. The ultimately real objects on a Platonic hierarchy of being (or ontological scale) are Forms. The Forms are the natures or essences of all that exists. The highest Form, the Form of the Good or Goodness-in-Itself, has often been associated with God. This Form has the highest possible level of reality. It is that through which all other

Forms or essences have their being. Platonists hold that there is an immaterial Form corresponding to every type or category of being in the world of our experience. Something is a tiger, for example, because it exemplifies "tiger-ness"—the correlative Form. The Form Tiger is the nonmaterial essence that characterizes the entire species. Individual members of the species depend for their existence on the Form that defines their category and the Form Tiger, in turn, depends for its existence on the ultimate Form from which the being of all things derives.

In conjunction with its antimaterialism, Platonism also stresses the nonsensory character of knowledge. What is known must be permanent and changeless, according to this tradition. Since all that is in the physical world is constantly changing, it is not possible to have genuine knowledge of physical objects. One can form opinions about objects and conditions in the realm of change and impermanence, but such opinions do not count as knowledge. The view that the only genuine objects of knowledge are perfectly stable and unchanging is linked to the thesis that, if one really knows something, one cannot be mistaken about it. The five senses are, by their very nature, fallible vehicles of ascertaining what is going on in mind-independent reality. For example, we often fall prey to sensory illusions when we rely on sense organs that are functioning suboptimally, or when the object sensed is remote. Further, given that the physical world is in constant flux, one can never be absolutely certain that what one observes at any given time still holds true at some subsequent time. Eternal truths, timeless and immutable, are within the grasp of our intellects, according to Platonism and, when properly grasped, it is impossible to be mistaken about them. When the intellect grasps the ultimate nature of reality—the Forms—it has genuine knowledge.

Since the Forms are transcendent, existing apart from the physical world, our knowledge of the Forms is not purely a function of experiences had in this life. Platonists reject empiricist theories of knowledge acquisition that hold that the intellect, at birth, is a *tabula rasa* or "blank slate" requiring sensory impressions to facilitate concept acquisition. Instead, Platonists tend to hold that concepts corresponding to the transcendent essences are innately present in the intellect. Plato held that we acquired such concepts in a previous life when the soul existed in the realm of the Forms and had direct, immediate, intuitional access to them. When the soul is re-embodied or reincarnated and returns to dwell in the physical world, it tends to forget what it learned in its previous existence in the realm of Forms. Accordingly, the soul needs to be brought to an awareness or recollection of what it, in some sense, already knows. The process whereby the recollection of the Forms is accomplished is a philosophical process. In Plato's dialogue *Meno*, a young Greek slave is initially unaware that he "knows" the Pythagorean theorem and is brought to an awareness of this latent knowledge through a series of questions posed to him by Socrates (Plato's teacher and the principal interlocutor in all of Plato's dialogues). Though adherence to the idea of the soul undergoing successive incarnations is not universal among Platonists, there has remained, throughout the centuries of Platonist thought, a tendency to endorse the doctrine of innate concepts. There has also remained a tendency to espouse the doctrine of the soul's immortality.

Plato held that the soul has three parts or elements—the rational part, the spirited element, and the appetitive element. The appetitive element, concerned with the satisfaction of baser desires, is the lowest part of the soul. The spirited element is what accounts for an individual's being more or less courageous. A well-ordered soul, on Plato's view, is one in which the highest part—the rational element—dominates. Platonist moral theory, following Plato's account of the soul's nature, emphasizes rationalism. The virtuous person is the individual whose soul is governed by reason. The rational element holds the inferior elements in check. No one, on this view, knowingly desires to be evil or vicious since such a desire would be incompatible with the natural desire for happiness and fulfillment. Evil objects of desire are held to be due to ignorance. An individual who desires something bad does so only because he or she mistakenly believes it to be good.

Linda L. Peterson

See also NEOPLATONISM; PLATO; PLOTINUS.

PLOTINUS (204?–70)

The great Neoplatonic philosopher Plotinus was born in Lyco (also known as Lycopolis) in Egypt. What is known of his life comes down to us through his biographer, Porphyry. He studied philosophy under Ammonius Saccas and began to write philosophical treatises at approximately fifty years of age. His literary works were collected together by Porphyry in a magnum opus known as *The Enneads*. Plotinus's thought was heavily influenced by the ancient Greek philosopher, Plato. At one point in his life, Plotinus wanted to found a city "Platonopolis" that would exemplify the ideal state as characterized in Plato's *Republic*. Owing to opposition from the Roman emperor, he was prevented from realizing this dream.

Plotinus's philosophical system encompasses all of the following areas of study: psychology (in his day, the study of the nature of the soul); metaphysics (the study of the ultimate principles of reality or being); cosmology (theory of the nature of the universe); aesthetics (study of the ultimate principles of beauty); and ethics (study of the nature of morality and the moral life). Plotinus followed Plato in construing the body to be the "prison house" of the soul. His theory is anti-materialistic. Embodiment debases the soul, and the soul is further debased by focusing on the objects of sensory experience. Yet, apart from its "descent" in which it is preoccupied with bodily states and ignores its true nature and calling, the soul is also capable of an "ascent" through contemplation in which it comes into contact with the ultimate realm of being and intelligibility (what really exists and really can be known). It is the "divine" part of the soul that can accomplish the ascent. In the fifth *Ennead*, Plotinus refers to the ascent up Diotima's Ladder as characterized in Plato's book *The Symposium*. Having canvassed a number of theories of the nature of love and attachment, Plato, as is typical in his dialogues, puts the truth in the mouth of his teacher, Socrates, who is one of the principal characters. Socrates credits a wise woman, Diotima of Mantinea, as the source of his own view. According to Diotima, the soul initially focuses on the beauty of material objects, but its attention must not rest there. Instead, it must be drawn to what beautifies bodies, that is, the soul. Plotinus's rendition of the ascent up the ladder begins, as does Plato's, with the contemplation of bodily beauty leading to reflections on psychology that, in turn, direct the soul's attention to "Intelligence" or the Platonic "Ideas"—the ultimately real exemplars from which all else derives beauty and goodness by imitation or participation. At the top (or it would be more appropriate to say "surpassing" the top) of the Plotinian ontological hierarchy (or scale of being) is The One. The One is that from which all else emanates or proceeds. It is what is prior to all existing things.

God, for Plotinus, is transcendent, that is, completely other than and beyond the realm of sensory experience. God cannot be described by language or even by thought. Ultimately, God, on Plotinus's view, is ineffable and incomprehensible. No properties can be predicated of God. In particular, it is impossible to describe God's nature or essence, nor can The One be described as having life or even being. Yet God is not nonbeing, but is rather, for Plotinus, the very foundation of being.

Though Plotinus was not a Christian, his philosophical system had a profound influence on subsequent Christian theorizing about the relation between God and human souls and, in particular, on the role of contemplation and meditation in the acquisition of knowledge.

Linda L. Peterson

See also NEOPLATONISM; PLATONISM.

PLURALISM

Religious pluralism, or religious diversity, is a constitutive feature of an increasingly global, postcolonial, postmodern world. In Christian theology, pluralism is distinguished from religious plurality. In a Euro-American theology of religions, pluralism represents one particular

Christian theological approach to the interrelationship among different religions, including and going beyond major world religions, such as Christianity, Judaism, Islam, Buddhism, and Hinduism.

Exclusivism (or particularism), inclusivism, and pluralism represent three distinct approaches to a Christian theology of religions. Exclusivism has been the predominant Christian approach to other religions throughout most of its history. Early Christians considered Jesus the only Son of God (John 1:1-18) and the only Savior of the world (John 14:6-7; Acts 4:12), two major christological claims that were reaffirmed at the Councils of Nicaea in 325 and Chalcedon in 451 and that are repeated regularly in contemporary Christian churches in the Nicene Creed. Second- to third-century Christian theologians like Cyprian of Carthage and Origen of Alexandria coined a theological claim "outside the church, there is no salvation" that aptly describes an exclusivist approach. This claim had profound sociopolitical implications on late medieval European church-state relations; for example, Pope Boniface VIII (d. 1303) explicitly used this claim as a theological basis to argue for papal primacy over secular political powers and institutions in his papal bull Unam Sanctam (1302). Modern formulations of exclusivism regard Jesus as the absolute revelation of God and Christianity as the one true religion. In 2000, the Vatican, through the Congregation for the Doctrine of the Faith, issued Dominus Iesus, which affirms that Jesus is the "definitive and complete" revelation of God as well as "the mediator and universal redeemer" of the world. Christianity, because it is centered on Christ, is not "parallel or complementary" to other religions. The "uniqueness" of Jesus and the "absoluteness" of Christianity promoted in a particularist theology of religions raise important theological questions about the possibility of truth and of salvation in other non-Christian religions.

Inclusivism recognizes the possibility of knowledge of God in other religions and attempts to reconcile the uniqueness of Jesus with the possibility of salvation in other religions. This second Christian approach to religious diversity is illustrated by the Second Vatican Council (1962–5). The Vatican II document Nostra Aetate recognizes a "ray of truth" found in other religions, since, according to the council fathers, all people share in creation in the image of God and all religions are theocentric or ultimately oriented to God. Some kinds of inclusivism also propose that the truth found in other religions is preparatory to accepting Christianity; in other words, other religions may reflect an implicit acceptance of Christ and Christianity. For example, the Catechism of the Catholic Church issued in 1992 cited Vatican II's claim that all people share a common origin and destiny, namely God, but went on to argue that the truth found in other religions is preparation for evangelization to Christianity.

Inclusivism encourages interreligious dialogue for the purpose of clarifying and enriching Christian beliefs and practices; often, the theological basis for such dialogue is soteriological. The twentieth-century German Jesuit theologian Karl Rahner (d. 1984) argued that the grace of Christ available in Christianity is mediated by other religions as well, thereby characterizing adherents of other religions as "anonymous Christians." On the one hand, inclusivism safeguards the absoluteness of Christianity as the one true legitimate religion and the fullest self-revelation of God in Christ; thus, Rahner still supported the church's mission to evangelize the world because it represents the most "explicit expression" of the truth or the "hidden reality" in other religions. On the other hand, inclusivism affirms the basic validity of non-Christian religions and opens up the possibility of salvation in other religions. Nevertheless, it may indirectly reinforce Western Christian theological imperialism by interpreting salvation in other religions on Christian terms, rather than enabling a give-and-take dialogue to mutually clarify and challenge Christian and non-Christian beliefs, practices, and ways of life related to salvation.

Pluralism, a third and more recent Christian theological approach to religious diversity, emphasizes the uniqueness of Jesus for Christians, but does not rule out God's self-revelation to other peoples in other particular historical contexts and settings. The twentieth-century British philosophical theologian John Hick is a leading representative of pluralism in his proposal for a theocentric rather than Christocentric theology of religions. Using a scientific metaphor, Hick urges a "Copernican revolution" in Christian theology, in which all religions revolve around God, not around Christ or Christianity. Using a visual metaphor, Hick claims that all religions are "different lenses" that reflect on and respond to God, or what he calls "the divine Reality." Pluralism is often charged with relativism, or an uncritical celebration of religious diversity, and with downplaying theological differences among religions. To address the charge of relativism, U.S. Catholic theologian Paul Knitter has formulated a liberation theology of religions, in which a hermeneutic of suspicion is directed at all religions to uncover potential ideologies, and in which a preferential option for the poor, or a commitment to the poor, can help distinct religious adherents find common ground. For Knitter, a pluralist theology of religions centers not on Christ or even on God but on soteriology, or the relationship of different religions to a praxis of a this-worldly salvation. Praxis or active religious and sociopolitical engagement on behalf of human and ecological well-being is used to evaluate the salvific efficacy of religions.

Rosemary P. Carbine

See also HERMENEUTICAL SUSPICION; SOTERIOLOGY.

PNEUMA

A Greek term meaning "spirit," used in the Bible to refer to the human spirit or to the Spirit of God (Holy Spirit). *Pneuma* is the Greek translation for the Hebrew *ruah*, a term meaning wind and breath. *Ruah* is the "breath of life" by which all living beings, humans and animals, exist.

In the second creation story of Genesis, the human person becomes a living being because God "breathed into his nostrils the breath of life" (Gen 2:7). God's breath, rather than the human soul, is the life-giving principle of humans. When it is withdrawn by God, death occurs (Gen 6:3). Also in the Old Testament, spirit is associated with emotions such as anger (Exod 6:9), subjective attitudes such as arrogance (Dan 5:20) or jealousy (Num 5:14). Further, spirit indicates intellectual traits such as "enlightenment, understanding, and excellent wisdom" (Dan 5:14; see Wis 7:7). In late Judaism, under the influence of Hellenistic thinking, the concept emerges of human spirit being the immaterial dimension of humans (cf. Wis 7:22).

In the New Testament, spirit signifies the principle of human life that departs at death (Luke 1:47; 8:55; Acts 7:59) and survives death ("spirits in prison," 1 Pet 3:19; cf. Heb 12:23). Spirit, the source of good tendencies, is opposed to flesh (*sarx*), from which comes evil impulses. Spirit connotes power, flesh weakness. On the Day of the Lord (Judgment Day), the spirit can be saved but the flesh is handed over for destruction (1 Cor 5:5).

In the Gospels, spirit can refer to good, or—much more frequently—to evil immaterial beings. Much of Jesus' ministry is focused on confronting and defeating evil spirits, also called demons.

The expression "Spirit of God," occurring frequently in the Old Testament, creates and sustains all life. By God's Spirit, Israel's leaders are inspired and empowered (Num 11:17); judges are raised up (Judg 3:10; 6:34), and kings are chosen and empowered (1 Sam 11:6; 16:13). Anointed and possessed by the Spirit of God, the prophets proclaim the divine word: "The Spirit of the Lord God is upon me, because the Lord has anointed me" (Isa 61:1; cf. Luke 4:18). An outpouring of the Spirit on the whole people is promised in the messianic age (Joel 3:1-2; cf. Acts 2:16-21).

In the New Testament Jesus is conceived by the Holy Spirit (Matt 1:18, 20; Luke 1:35), sees the Spirit of God coming down upon him at his baptism (Matt 3:16), and continually acts in the power of God's Spirit. Jesus heals under the impulse of the Holy Spirit (Mark 1:23-27) and drives out demons by the Spirit (Matt 12:28). The role of the Holy Spirit is especially prominent in Luke–Acts, where the phrase occurs fifty-six times. Using Isaiah 61:1-2 and 58:2, Luke interprets the descent of the Holy Spirit on Jesus as meaning that he is the Servant of Yahweh. The disciples are promised an outpouring of the Holy Spirit whom they receive at Pentecost (Acts 2:16-21). Through baptism, believers receive the Holy Spirit (Acts 2:38). The work of the apostles Peter and Paul is guided by the Spirit (Acts 10:19), and sometimes even hinders their movements (Acts 8:29; 13:4).

According to Paul, the Spirit is received from faith, not from works of the law (Gal 3:2). The Spirit of God dwells in believers (1 Cor 3:16) and makes them one "in Christ," a frequent Pauline phrase. Also, the variety of gifts needed for ministry all come from the one and same Spirit of God (1 Cor 12:4-11).

In the post–New Testament era, the rich presentation of the Spirit of God and Spirit of Jesus is articulated in the doctrine of the Trinity.

John Gillman

See also FLESH/SARX; HOLY SPIRIT; PNEUMATOLOGY; SOMA (GREEK); TRINITY/TRINITARIAN THEOLOGY/ TRINITARIAN PROCESSIONS.

PNEUMATOLOGY

From the Greek word *pneuma*, meaning spirit or breath, pneumatology is the branch of theology that studies the Holy Spirit. Pneumatology historically developed under the influence of christology and broader trinitarian studies. Much of pneumatology has been concerned with the soteriological (salvific) role of the Holy Spirit, as well as with the Spirit's relationship to the Father and the Son (for example, as the "love" that eternally binds and is expressed between Father and Son). Other typical topics within pneumatology are the distinct actions of the Holy Spirit, the gifts or charisms bestowed by the Spirit, the role of the Spirit in christology and ecclesiology, and so on. Much has been written on the relationship(s) between pneumatology and the theology of grace, liturgy, and spirituality. After the theological renewal brought about by the Second Vatican Council among Catholics, pneumatological reflection has developed beyond the typical theological topics (without disregarding them) into considerations of the role of the Holy Spirit in public life and society, in ethics, in non-Christian religions, and so on.

Orlando Espín

See also CHRISTOLOGY; DOGMATIC THEOLOGY; ECCLESIOLOGY; GRACE; HOLY SPIRIT; METHOD IN THEOLOGY; PNEUMA; PRAYER; SALVATION; SOTERIOLOGY; SPIRITUALITY; TRINITY/TRINITARIAN THEOLOGY/TRINITARIAN PROCESSIONS.

PNEUMATOMACHIANS

Derived from the Greek meaning "fighters of the Spirit," a fourth-century Christian group that denied the divinity of the Holy Spirit. The Council of Nicaea in 325 articulated the full divinity of the Son of God, incarnate in Jesus, against the Arians by borrowing the philosophical language of *ousia* (Greek, meaning "substance") to demonstrate that the Son was begotten, not made, "of the same substance" (Greek, *homoousios*) with the Father. The Council of Constantinople in 381 grounded the divinity of the Holy Spirit in scriptural terms, and, building on the theological precedent of consubstantiality in Nicaea, expanded the language of *ousia* to claim that the Father, Son, and Spirit all shared the same substance, thereby securing the equal divinity of all three Persons in one triune God. A scriptural and theological defense of the divinity of the Holy Spirit was mounted, in part, on the theological reflections of the fourth-century Eastern Christian Cappadocian fathers, namely Basil of Caesarea (d. 379), Gregory

Nazianzus (d. 389/390), and Gregory of Nyssa (d. 395). For example, Basil affirmed the divinity of the Spirit because the Spirit possesses divine attributes and plays divine roles; he thus forged a theological link between the attributes, activities, and the divinity of the Spirit. As Basil argued, the Holy Spirit shares the attributes of the one substance—indivisible, immaterial, infinite, immutable, all-knowing, all-powerful, transcendent and immanent, giver of all good gifts—that unites all three Persons in the Trinity. The Spirit also plays an important role in grace, in the sanctification or the full perfection of all life—personal, communal, earthly—according to the image and likeness of God. Grace is imbued in humanity by God, a process that takes place through a real communion with Christ and is given gratuitously to humanity by God for the purpose of renewal in the Holy Spirit.

Rosemary P. Carbine

See also PNEUMA; PNEUMATOLOGY.

P'O

See HUN.

POIESIS

The Greek term *poiesis* refers to the human activity of production. Aristotle used the term to distinguish between the act of production that derives its value from the results or products produced, and human activity that is its own end, whose value is intrinsic to the activity itself (*praxis*). The difference between these two types of human activity is analogous to the difference between building a house and creating a home. The value of the former is derived primarily from the result of the action, that product (the house) left over after the activity itself has ceased. The value of the latter, on the other hand, is derived from the interaction among the family members who live in the house; the common life of the family that constitutes a "home" has no purpose or end other than the family's enjoyment of and participation in that life itself. Thus, what characterizes the activity of production, or *poiesis*, is that its value is extrinsic to the activity itself; the value we attach to it is dependent on the results of the activity and the usefulness of the activity in bringing about the desired results. If the construction project did not yield a house, the activity would be deemed a failure.

According to Aristotle, *poiesis* corresponds to a particular type of knowledge, or rationality, he calls *techne* (as in technology). As opposed to *phronesis*, the type of knowledge or rationality that generally corresponds to praxis, *techne* generally implies a technical understanding of the act of production and the object to be produced that contributes to the efficacy and productivity of the action. Thus, the value of technical knowledge is predicated on its functional, or instrumental, efficacy.

In the wake of the modern technological and scientific revolutions, *poiesis* and *techne* have become increasingly important categories for understanding and evaluating human action in the world. As the value of human action is increasingly predicated upon the human person's productivity, so is human knowledge increasingly reduced to that type of knowledge ("skills") necessary to be an effective producer or worker. The human person is then defined by his or her productivity. When this happens, the value of human life as an end in itself (*praxis*) is reduced to its value as an instrument of production (*poiesis*).

Roberto S. Goizueta

See also PRAXIS.

POLISH NATIONAL CATHOLIC CHURCH

See OLD CATHOLICS.

POLITICAL THEOLOGY (-IES)

The problem of the proper relationship between Christian faith and the political activity of Christians arose in early Christianity and remains in dispute after two millennia. Some Christians have identified particular political systems (such as the Holy Roman Empire, European monarchies after the French Revolution, twentieth-century fascist states, or modern democracies) with the reign of God, that is, as embodiments of God's will. Others have attempted to keep Christian faith separate from political choices, political activity, and political systems, maintaining the essentially personal and private character of faith. Yet, nineteenth-century German philosophers G.W.F. Hegel and Karl Marx have convinced many Christians that faith cannot be politically irrelevant, despite personal intentions, since inaction amounts to tacit support for the political status quo.

Following the Second Vatican Council (1962–5), German Catholic theologian Johannes B. Metz proposed a "new political theology" that would avoid the pitfalls of both uncritical accommodation to the status quo and naive withdrawal from the political process by Christians. In Metz's view, the church is called by God to exercise a prophetic function in society—that is, to question openly all unjust political and social arrangements. This does not mean, however, that the church possesses a blueprint for establishing the reign of God on earth. Rather, political theology challenges Christians to be aware of their sometimes-unconscious place in the political process and to take a stand in favor of social justice. Two principles proposed by Metz unmask the twin dangers of ingenuous privatization and unwarranted politicization of faith. First, by remembering the massive reality of unjust suffering in history and acting in favor of those today who suffer unjustly, Christians will reject the temptation to withdraw from political activity into privatized religion. Second, in recalling the eschatological character of God's reign (that is, its final completion will come only beyond history), Christians must question every political arrangement in history and note that none represents the definitive incarnation of God's reign. Metz's political theology, then, urges Christians (indeed the church itself) to examine continually their political alignments, denounce arrangements of power that produce unjust suffering, work to create a just social order, and remember that the results of even sincere efforts will always be imperfect. The tension between the last two requirements—to strive wholeheartedly to build a world that can only be partially realized in history—is, in Metz's view, at the heart of Christian faith.

James B. Nickoloff

See also METZ, JOHANN.

POLITICS

In Christian ethics, politics is action for the purpose of social transformation. There is much agreement on the need for increasing attention to what constitutes revolutionary praxis and the economic and political transformation envisioned by liberation theology and ethics.

The politics of social transformation emanates from authentic self-love that finds its fulfillment in solidarity. When persons can identify suffering in their own lives and the lives of others, and they possess a social analysis that enables them to link this self/other suffering with larger public structures, they may be impelled to act collectively for social change.

The politics of social transformation is also enabled by a theological/biblical vision that nourishes the imagination of new social possibilities and the hope that the present order does not have to remain as it is. The politics of social transformation explores questions related to social conflict, social movements, and the dynamics of revolutionary change. It has been particularly exhibited, for example, by Christian base communities in the Two-thirds World, by groups of religious women, and by particular black churches in the United States.

Mary E. Hobgood

See also JUSTICE; SOLIDARITY.

POLYCARP OF SMYRNA (81?–167)

The *episkopos* of Smyrna, Polycarp taught Irenaeus of Lyons who mentions that Polycarp himself heard "John" preach. This may not have been John the apostle, but nonetheless, Polycarp is one of the few representatives of the second generation of Christians to leave a written witness. When persecution broke out in Smyrna, Polycarp was executed at the age of eighty-six. Polycarp defended the Eastern custom of celebrating Easter over against the Roman practice. A letter to the Philippians survives which is attributed to Polycarp, as well as the account of his martyrdom, the earliest such account, and the first to use the word "martyr" to designate one who dies for one's faith.

Gary Macy

See also EASTER; IRENAEUS OF LYONS; JOHN THE EVANGELIST; MARTYR/MARTYRDOM.

POLYGENESIS

The thesis that humanity has many more progenitors than a single pair. Polygenesis (also call polygenism) may be either monophyletic or polyphyletic depending on whether one believes only one or many species of animals evolved to human status.

In the 1950 encyclical *Humani Generis*, Pope Pius XII stated that it was "not apparent" how polygenism could be reconciled with the doctrine of original sin. Despite the fact that *Humani Generis* rejected the idea that Catholics could accept polygenesis, it is noteworthy it was neither called false nor heretical. The same encyclical affirmed the right for Catholics to accept the theory of evolution as a scientific opinion. It is paradoxical, however, that the same encyclical that implies that it is acceptable to understand the story of Creation in Genesis 2 as an etiological myth rather than a historical report also suggests that it is not acceptable to question the historicity of the account of the disobedience of Adam and Eve in Genesis 3.

Regina A. Boisclair

See also CREATIONISM; HUMANI GENERIS; MONOGENESIS; SIN, ORIGINAL.

POLYTHEISM

The English term meaning "belief in or worship of multiple gods." Since "polytheism" has a long history of variegated, polemical, and imprecise use in religious discourse, it is not favored in the history of religions. Theology and doctrine in all the world's religions hold that there are a multitude of supernatural deities that impinge on human existence. This includes the prophetic monotheisms that recognize angels, devils, spirits, Satan, and even saints in the category of "supra-mundane beings." The analysis of the pantheon in any religious tradition more exactingly concerns the "divine hierarchy," that is, the relations between the divine beings and humanity. In the history of religions, every monotheism emphasizes the preeminence of its chief deity in potency and ritual service. Their theological dogma insisting on a strict monopoly in reverence for its own one "true god" has often misrepresented their opponents' theological understandings of "multiple gods."

Defined by their pantheons in which deities divide the task of creating world order and maintaining the cosmos, with different figures contending for superiority, "polytheistic religions" have been found principally in the history of religions among the urban "high cultures" of antiquity (for example, Egypt, Babylon, Iran) and among the still-extant traditions of South and East Asia. In these instances, the cosmos is conceived as having a bureaucratic organization, with the myths and rituals associated with each deity serving the larger goal of maintaining cosmic harmony and human prosperity. The merging of ethnic peoples in the urban centers may well have been mirrored in the pantheon; often, over time, efforts of priestly castes and ritualists have attempted to systematize, merge, or reinterpret this pluralism.

Early modern historical scholarship attempted to trace grand theories of religious evolution from polytheism to monotheism. Although later scholars have shown no universal pathway of religious transformation, it is clear that the great monotheisms (Judaism, Christianity, Islam) all struggled against the more inclusive religious attitude of those inclined to polytheism. In fact, to Muslims especially, even the Trinity doctrine of

Christianity has been regarded as an unfortunate reversion to "polytheism."

The history of these religions evidences many instances in which polytheistic peoples have been subject to spiritual conquest by monotheistic traditions that have denied the reality of other gods (while often adopting their festivals) and made worship of nonsanctioned deities a serious moral offense subject to violent persecution. (See, for example, the book of Deuteronomy.) In other instances, polytheistic cultures have fostered new tendencies toward pantheism, henotheism, and monism. The former typically entails a theory in which one god comes to be regarded as containing all others, as in the Greek Orphic poem, "Zeus is the beginning, Zeus is the middle, from Zeus all things came into existence." Henotheism, a term coined by Max Müller to describe Vedic religion in ancient India, involves a serial focus among the greatest deities: as the next high god is worshiped, that god is regarded for that moment as supremely real and absolute. An example of monism is the later Hindu Vedanta school that accepts the 330 million gods as only provisionally real, with the universal spirit (*Brahman*) the ultimate reality from which they all emerge.

Todd T. Lewis

See also HENOTHEISM; MONOTHEISM (IN CHRISTIANITY AND ISLAM); MONOTHEISM (IN JUDAISM); PANTHEISM; VEDANTA.

PONTIFF

The English translation of the Latin term *pontifex* (probably meaning "bridge builder"). The term was originally used for the chief priest of Rome before Christianity, but during the Middle Ages it came to be used by the popes as Bishops of Rome and by other diocesan bishops. After the fifteenth century, the term has been confined to the popes. It is often used in titles such as "sovereign pontiff," or "supreme pontiff."

Orlando Espín

See also MEDIEVAL CHRISTIANITY (IN THE WEST); MEDIEVAL CHURCH; PONTIFICAL; POPE; PRIMACY.

PONTIFICAL

This term has two meanings. (1) In Western Catholic and Anglican usage, the "pontifical" is the name of a book used only in liturgies presided over by bishops (for example, rites of confirmation and of ordination). (2) It is the adjective corresponding to the noun "pontiff," thereby indicating a juridical or charter connection to the Bishop of Rome as "supreme pontiff."

Orlando Espín

See also LITURGY (IN CHRISTIANITY); PONTIFF; PONTIFICAL UNIVERSITY; POPE; ROMAN CATHOLIC CHURCH.

PONTIFICAL UNIVERSITY

Any Catholic university, anywhere in the world, that has been legally chartered and authorized by the Vatican to award graduate degrees in some specific disciplines (usually including theology and philosophy). The vast majority of Catholic universities throughout the world, however, are not pontifical.

Orlando Espín

See also CURIA, CONGREGATIONS OF THE (ROMAN); PONTIFF; PONTIFICAL; UNIVERSITY; UNIVERSITY, CATHOLIC.

PONTIUS PILATE

See PILATE, PONTIUS.

POPE

(Latin, *papa*, father). The pope is the Bishop of Rome and the earthly head of the Roman Catholic Church. Each pope is considered to be a successor of Saint Peter, who, according to Scripture, was named first head of the church by Jesus (Matt 16:18-19) and whom tradition holds was martyred in the imperial city of Rome. Therefore the pope possesses the additional titles of Vicar of Jesus Christ and Successor of the Chief of the Apostles. Additional titles for the pope include Servant of the Servants of God and Sovereign of the Vatican City State. As Supreme Pontiff (*pontifex maximus*, Latin, supreme bridge-builder), the pope is seen as bridging the gap between the divine and the human, heaven and earth. Papal hegemony over all other bishops and the churches they serve, while a reality in the Roman church, has proven a major obstacle to ecumenical reunification of all Christian churches, especially for the schismatic churches of the East. Popes serve for life and are elected by ballot(s) taken at a meeting of the College of Cardinals that convenes in the Vatican upon the death of the reigning pope.

Robert D. McCleary

See also ECCLESIOLOGY; PAPACY/PAPAL; PETRINE MINISTRY; PONTIFF; ROME, SEE OF.

POPULAR CATHOLICISM

The "people's" version of the Catholic tradition ("popular" is the adjective corresponding to the noun "people").

Groups of religious "experts" seem to have developed in most religions, thereby becoming responsible for defining what is and what is not normative within the religions. Most believers, however, either do not or cannot have access to the training required for understanding the doctrinal arguments proposed by the "experts," and hence the majority are placed in the role of following the symbolic production and doctrinal decisions of the specialists.

History shows, nevertheless, that among the majority of believers alternative paths are created to circumvent the exclusive definitional power of the "experts." Catholicism is an example. It is evident that its "experts" are the theologians and the clergy (especially bishops and popes). It is the role of these specialists to define and set the limits as to what is or is not acceptable and normative in the church. For most people, however, theological work and episcopal/papal ministry are not the common ways of participating in the religion. Most Catholics play the role of recipients of the doctrinal and liturgical production of the specialists. Nevertheless, the long history of Catholicism (in many culturally shaped ways) has witnessed the birth of parallel paths that attempt to bring the religion close to the people's needs and circumstances. Often enough these paths have reread "official" Catholicism in the ways indicated above, and thereby produced the people's own version of the religion. This is "popular" Catholicism. It claims to be authentically Catholic, and yet it has reinterpreted the normative as set forth by the church's "experts."

Apparently, popular Catholicism came into being very early in the history of the religion. The reactions to it, on the part of the specialists, have historically run the gamut from co-optation to outright persecution. The widely varying official reactions throughout the centuries seem to have depended on how far the popular rereading of the normative had gone, and on how the "experts" perceived the importance of maintaining links to popular religion in each historical context. All too often, political and other social reasons determined the official reactions to popular Catholicism more than strictly doctrinal considerations. Although popular Catholicism exists in every social class and ethnic group where the church has made itself present, the popular strand seems to be most frequent among the economically, politically, and culturally marginalized.

Orlando Espín

See also APPARITIONS; CLERICALISM; DEVELOPMENT OF DOGMA/OF DOCTRINE; DEVOTIONS; DOCTRINE; ECCLESIOLOGY; EPISTEMOLOGY; FAITH; GRACE; GUADALUPE, VIRGIN OF; IDEOLOGY (IDEOLOGIES); LAITY; LATIN AMERICAN CATHOLICISM; LATINO CATHOLICISM; LATINO THEOLOGY (-IES); MARIAN DEVOTIONS; METHOD IN THEOLOGY; NOVENA; PILGRIMAGE; POPULAR RELIGIONS; POPULAR RELIGIOSITY; PRAXIS; SAINTS (CHRISTIAN), DEVOTION TO; SCAPULAR; SENSUS FIDELIUM/SENSUS FIDEI; TRADITION (IN CHRISTIANITY).

POPULAR RELIGIONS

Some religions are called "popular" not because they are widespread (although they might be too), but because the adjective "popular" refers to the noun "people." In other words, a religion is "popular" if the people, especially the poorer segments of a society, are its source and the majority of its followers.

Groups of religious "experts" seem to have developed in most religions, thereby becoming responsible for defining what is and what is not normative within the religions. Most believers, however, either do not have or cannot have access to the training required for understanding the doctrinal arguments proposed by the "experts," and hence the majority are placed in the role of following the symbolic production and doctrinal decisions of the specialists.

History shows, however, that among the majority of believers alternative paths are created to circumvent the exclusive definitional power of the "experts." These paths can and do lead to the formation of what could be called a "popular" version of the religion, somehow still connected with the normative version of the religion, and yet parallel to the pretended "official" doctrinal and liturgical norms set up and controlled by the specialists.

The "popular" religion's connection with the "official" version appears to be one of selectively shared symbols and ethos, and an appeal to common foundational figures or events. Similarly, there is a rereading of the doctrines and rites of the "official" religion whereby a set of different emphases is given to them. Furthermore, this rereading can interpret the religion to the point of altogether disregarding some elements the "experts" might consider essential, while inversely considering fundamental certain beliefs, rites, or behaviors that the specialists would not emphasize or accept at all.

All the major world religions have a popular parallel to their "official" or "elite" core of doctrines and rituals. The elite and popular versions of the same religion need not be in opposition to each other. In fact, they usually coexist within the same religious context.

A popular religion can also be understood as the sum of experiences, beliefs, and rituals that socioculturally peripheral groups create and follow in order to relate with God (or the gods, and so on) and find salvation (or immortality, or perfect union with the sacred source of all life, and so on). In the name of the deeper meaning of the religion, the popular variation acts as a critique of those with power to determine the ingredients of the official version. These peripheral groups perceive themselves to have been marginalized by the religious and social institutions (and leadership) of their societies. Most often, these groups are not only culturally peripheral but also economically poor and politically powerless.

There seems to be a distinct epistemology typical of popular religion that is not available to the followers of official religion. This epistemology appears to be more dependent on the marginal status of the popular religion's participants than on the foundational message or events of the overall religious tradition; however, this distinct, popular epistemology enriches the overall interpretation of the foundational elements of the religion.

Orlando Espín

See also IDEOLOGY (IDEOLOGIES); POPULAR CATHOLICISM; POPULAR RELIGIOSITY; PRAXIS; RELIGION.

POPULAR RELIGIOSITY

A phrase first used in Latin American pastoral circles to refer to popular religion or, more frequently, to popular Catholicism. The term "religiosity," however, implied a dismissal of the people's religion as a "real religion." For this reason, most Latin American authors have been turning away from it, choosing "popular religion" instead. In the U.S., one might still find occasional use of the phrase.

Orlando Espín

See also IDEOLOGY (IDEOLOGIES); LATIN AMERICAN CATHOLICISM; POPULAR CATHOLICISM; POPULAR RELIGIONS; RELIGION.

POPULORUM PROGRESSIO

On March 26, 1967, Pope Paul VI issued his encyclical letter "On the Development of Peoples" known as *Populorum Progressio* (from the first two words of the Latin text). The encyclical (meaning "intended for wide distribution") is addressed to all Catholics and to all people of good will in the world and seeks to alert the church and the entire world both to the increasingly grave situation of poverty and social injustice in the world and, conversely, to the realistic hope for the creation of a different kind of world in the future. Heeding the calls of his predecessor John XXIII and of the Second Vatican Council (1962–5) for greater attention to the "cry of anguish" rising from the poor of the world, Paul VI takes up themes about which he had spoken before the General Assembly of the United Nations in 1965. The Pope is convinced that the wide, and widening, gap between rich and poor nations not only threatens world peace, but also poses a challenge to the Christian, indeed, the human, conscience. What is at stake in the question of economic justice, says the Pope, is the survival of millions and the souls of all. For this reason, he outlines a broad understanding of "development." Real progress for humanity, he believes, must not only be measured in material terms, though the lives of the destitute and the futures of poor nations demand fundamental shifts in the economic systems prevailing in the world today. (In this regard, he is critical both of forms of capitalism based on the profit motive alone and forms of socialism that deny individual rights and, especially, the ultimate openness of the human being to God.) The welfare of the human spirit— the primary concern of the church— cannot be separated from the material conditions in which people live. Both destitution and affluence pose threats to moral, psychological, and spiritual well-being. Thus Pope Paul calls for an "integral" (or complete) development of the human person and of all persons. By this he means advancing, as he writes in numbers 20–21, from "less human conditions" (the material poverty of some and the moral deficiency—selfishness—of others) to "more human conditions" (the "possession of necessities" by the poor and "increased esteem for the dignity of others" by the affluent). The Pope reminds affluent readers of the words of St. Ambrose: "You are not making a gift of your possessions to the poor person. You are handing over to him what is his" (no. 23). But "more human conditions" also include the growth of knowledge, the acquisition of culture, cooperation for the common good, and the acknowledgment of God as the origin of supreme values. Above all else, faith in God and unity among all peoples will make life "more human." Such progress, the Pope believes, is what following Christ demands.

James B. Nickoloff

See also PAUL VI, POPE.

PORPHYRY (232/3–305?)

Malchus, called Porphyry, was a Syrian and probably the most famous student of the Neoplatonic philosopher Plotinus. Porphyry took over Plotinus's school of philosophy in Rome after the death of Plotinus in 270. The teaching of both Plotinus and Porphyry influenced Ambrose and Augustine. Porphyry, however, was violently opposed to Christianity and attacked it in his *Against the Christians*. Although this work is lost, large parts can be reconstructed from the many Christian responses it engendered.

Gary Macy

See also AMBROSE OF MILAN; AUGUSTINE OF HIPPO; NEOPLATONISM; PLOTINUS.

POSITIVE THEOLOGY

An approach to Christian theology that methodologically emphasizes the importance of facts and history. It attempts to avoid speculations regarding religious laws or intuitions of universal validity. Today it seems to be a perspective frequently found incorporated (but not to the necessary exclusion of other perspectives) in the methodological approaches of several branches of mainstream Christian theology.

Orlando Espín

See also METHOD IN THEOLOGY.

POSITIVISM

A term first used by Claude-Henri Saint-Simon and Auguste Comte in the eighteenth and nineteenth centuries to name their vision for a rational reconstruction of society (for example, philosophy, state, culture, religion) under the aegis of science. More commonly, the term is used today to refer to the program of logical positivism of the so-called Vienna Circle and their followers, such as Rudolf Carnap, Moritz Schlick, the early work of Ludwig Wittgenstein, and such figures as Bertrand Russell, G. E. Moore and A. J. Ayer in England. Negatively, logical positivism sought to unmask the meaninglessness of metaphysics and to dispel the same. Positively, it was characterized by the conviction that formal logic is the primary organon for philosophic method.

J. A. Colombo

See also WITTGENSTEIN, LUDWIG.

POSSESSION

Some religions have a belief in possession. In the histories of Christianity, Judaism, and others, possession has been frequently interpreted as an evil, and has been said to occur as the result of a demonic attack on the individual victim (often, but not always, adolescent girls and older women are the targets of such attack). The possessed would display behavior and capabilities otherwise impossible to them. They, in turn, become a source of temptation and dismay for those who surround them. The histories of other religions (for example, Candomblé/Santería, and the like) explain possessions as divine gifts and as welcome visits from the spiritual realm. Indeed, the highest point of these religions' liturgical life is possession.

It would be naive and unwarranted to judge the positive understanding of possession as incorrect merely because it does not fit, or is repulsive to, the socially dominant view of possession as evil. Indeed, Christianity is also aware of the Holy Spirit's taking hold of a believer's life and of the behavior changes that subsequently occur in that individual's life. The term "possession" is not used in this case, but this does not mean that it is not a possession.

Most religions that have a belief in possessions also insist on the need for what has been called "discernment of spirits," that is, the proper evaluation of each specific case in order to ascertain its origin, development, and consequences. In the same way, the fact that most stories of possession seem to be associated with women, with the poor, or with those who are somehow socially or religiously marginalized, cannot be judged irrelevant at the time of discerning claims of possession.

Much of contemporary Christian theology, as well as most modern sciences, would have serious difficulty in even granting the possibility of possession in the strict sense. Although admitting the reality of the behavioral changes in the afflicted individual, today's theologians and scientists would probably point to the mind and to social conditions as the more frequent sources of so-called "possessions."

Orlando Espín

See also AFRICAN TRADITIONAL RELIGIONS; AFRO-LATIN RELIGIONS; CATHOLIC TRADITION; DEMON (IN THE BIBLE); DEMON (IN WORLD RELIGIONS); DEVIL; DISCERNMENT; EVIL; EXORCISM; FAITH; FREE WILL; HINDUISM; ISLAM; JUDAISM; SANTERÍA; SATAN; SPIRIT; THEOLOGICAL ANTHROPOLOGY; VODOUN.

POSTCOLONIALISM

While well known in academic circles today, postcolonial theory is not an established method, governed by programmatic procedures, nor is its theoretical foundation accompanied by standardized principles and assumptions. Rather, postcolonial theory represents a fluid approach that aims to de-ideologize "colonial" interpretations that universalize or totalize history, tradition, and/or what is considered "other" by dominant cultures, countries, and persons.

In the 1980s, diasporic intellectuals from "third world" countries with a long history of political, economic, military, and cultural colonization by the United States and/or European countries began to focus on the intellectual consequences of colonization. What sparked this new inquiry can be attributed to three interrelated geopolitical events: first, the Soviet Union collapsed as one of the most powerful empires of the twentieth century, no longer politically, militarily, or economically controlling and supporting its client states throughout Eastern Europe and other places around the globe; second, as a result, the United States became the world's sole empire, thus extending its domination politically, economically, and militarily; and third, the phenomenon of globalization promoted by the United States and Western Europe began to disrupt local economies and cultural identities worldwide, making them newly dependent upon U.S. and Western European interests. These more or less simultaneous events led intellectuals like Edward Said (*Orientalism*), Gayatri Chakravorty Spivak (*In Other Worlds*), and Homi Bhabha (*The Location of Culture*) to open a debate on the ramifications of colonialism and neocolonialism, thus inspiring other diasporic intellectual communities (for example, ethnic and racial minorities in the United States) to begin to examine the colonial configurations of their own textual canons and interpretative traditions.

The term "postcolonial" is sometimes understood to refer to the historical period following the independence of a colony from its colonizer. However, among postcolonial theorists the term refers to various political phases and sociopsychological effects of colonization. For instance, postcolonial theorists study the phase leading up to colonization (precolonization), the phase after colonization (postcolonization), and the phase after postcolonization (neocolonization). The last of these phases concerns those countries formally independent but in fact often dependent upon former colonizers politically, economically, and militarily. Postcolonial theorists also examine the sociopsychological ramifications of colonization, that is, the frame of mind of individuals and communities whose memories and identities are still colonized and seen as "other" (that is, different from the norm).

The application of postcolonial theory, particularly to the field of religious studies, does not seek to create new knowledge (as the new field of "empire studies" does in biblical studies or constructive Christian theology), but rather examines and critiques existing knowledge embedded within colonial formulations of the Christian tradition. Thus it analyzes the notions of superior/inferior, center/margin, and civilized/savage embedded in the very language of the New Testament and Christian theological tradition and repudiates the notions that "true" theology only emanates from "the European West," and that all other theologies, particularly from the "third world" or from ethnic and racial groups within "the West," have nothing to teach the world. It also analyzes anticolonial texts and traditions of resistance to colonization in order to understand how they may contribute to liberation. Finally, it rejects interpretations that support Christian superiority over other religions. It is clear, then, that postcolonial theory questions the fixed boundaries of knowledge.

Francisco Lozada

See also AFRICAN THEOLOGIES; ASIAN (CHRISTIAN) THEOLOGIES; CULTURE; EPISTEMOLOGY; FEMINIST THEOLOGIES; HERMENEUTICAL SUSPICION; INTERCULTURAL THOUGHT; LATIN AMERICAN THEOLOGIES; LIBERATION THEOLOGIES; METHOD IN THEOLOGY.

POSTLAPSARIANISM
See INFRALAPSARIANISM.

POSTMODERNITY
By definition, "postmodernity" is a relative term that can only be understood in relation to "modernity." In its historical, temporal sense, postmodernity refers to

the contemporary period in Western societies insofar as the various social, political, cultural, and religious features of these societies may be understood as differing from and superseding the features that characterized modernity in the West. More than a merely temporal reality, then, postmodernity refers to this entire complex of social, political, cultural, and religious characteristics, and to the worldview they reflect.

If modernity is defined by a confident affirmation of the autonomous, rational individual as the foundation of society, postmodernity radically calls into question the very possibility of autonomy and rationality and, thus, the claim of the modern individual to a historical existence as a substantive, coherent self, or subject. The self is, instead, conceived as an artificial construct. What defines "me" is the entire constellation of relationships, communities, cultures, languages, and so on within which I live and that, in their conjunction and interaction, define who "I" am. This "I," then, remains forever ambiguous, indeterminate, and in flux from one moment to the next. The self is, in fact, a plurality of "selves" defined by this complex web of interrelationships. Human society is characterized more by infinite difference, plurality, and fluidity than by coherence and givenness.

If postmodernity calls into question the autonomous self-sufficiency of the modern individual, so too does it challenge his or her claim to a rationality that, in its ability to reach universally valid conclusions and judgments, can arrive at some "objective" truth. If I am defined by my "social location," that is, by the many ongoing relationships, communities, and the like, in which I am immersed, then all my knowledge is necessarily particular (to my social location), perspectival, and

partial. All worldviews are thus human constructs; there is no possibility of arriving at a coherent, universally valid worldview. Human knowledge is not monolithic and coherent, but plural and ambiguous.

The postmodern critique of modernity does not emerge from merely abstract, philosophical differences but from a confrontation with the "underside of modernity," the destructive and, indeed, barbaric elements in modernity. The many technological and social advances of the modern world have often had unintended, detrimental consequences. Modern rationality has created not only cures for many diseases but also concentration camps, environmental pollution, nuclear weapons, and so on. Modernity's emphasis on the individual has not only secured greater individual freedom for some individuals but, by generating greater competition and inequality among individuals, has also exacerbated social divisions. The postmodern view of knowledge as always partial and ambiguous is thus a reaction to the destructive consequences of a modern Western rationality that, claiming to be objective and universal, has often ignored its own social location and, hence, its own limitations. And the postmodern deconstruction of the "self" is a reaction to the alienating and socially divisive consequences of modern individualism, with its view of society as a collection of isolated, autonomous individuals.

The postmodern emphasis on ambiguity, social location, difference, and particularity has had important ramifications for theology and the study of religion. Theologians and scholars of religion have become increasingly aware of how their own social location influences their understanding and interpretation of religious phenomena; one's knowledge (whether its object is God or Hinduism) is always partial, perspectival, and limited. This appreciation of particularity and difference can also lead, then, to a greater openness to religious differences; as we become more aware of the limitations of our own theological and religious perspectives, we become increasingly open to other perspectives. Thus, increased attention is paid to those religions and forms of religion that, in modern Western Christianity, had been ignored and marginalized because they had been deemed false in relation to the "universal truth" of Western, European Christianity.

With its appreciation of ambiguity, the postmodern worldview has also tended to value forms of religious knowledge and expression that, because they are not "logical" and conceptual, have been marginalized in modern Western cultures. Whereas modernity tended to identify religion with the private beliefs of the autonomous rational individual, postmodernity stresses the communal, nonconceptual dimensions of religious experience. Thus, postmodernity has been characterized by a renewed appreciation of the centrality of communal ritual, narrative, symbol, spirituality, and affect in the religious life.

Roberto S. Goizueta

See also AESTHETICS; MODERNITY; RATIONALISM.

POTLATCH

In traditional regions of the Northwest Coast of America, the potlatch was the major communal festival of the peoples. It is essentially a giveaway in which those who are wealthy distribute that wealth to those who do not have it. In the highly structured social organization of the coastal peoples, it was also aligned with status. In the impressive distribution of wealth that won prestige and pride of place, the giver literally made himself poor. It was understood that he would be on the receiving end at a future gathering, since every receiver became obligated to return the gesture. Not surprisingly, the government misunderstood this ritual, which included many other aspects reaffirming traditional life, and forbade it. The restoration of this ritual has been a priority among the Northwest peoples.

Kathleen Dugan

See also RITUAL.

POVERTY

A situation of economic suffering often accompanied by spiritual impoverishment. Poverty, always a concern of the churches, is escalating in the United States and worldwide according to U.S. government statistics and United Nations reports on social development.

While the Christian churches do not agree on the root cause(s) of poverty, they do point to the need to examine social structures such as capitalism, science, and technology, that give unearned power and advantage to some and keep others in social, political, and economic marginalization. These structures diminish the ability of increasing numbers to participate in the political economy in a dignified way, by eroding their sense of responsibility and accountability, and depriving them of the energy that comes with economic security and meaningful participation in community. These structures often drain the poor, as well as the affluent, psychologically and spiritually.

In over a century of modern teaching about Christian responsibility regarding poverty, the Roman Catholic Church has promoted norms that address poverty,

such as universal dignified social participation, the accountability of property to
the commonweal, the priority of labor
over capital, and a preferential option for
poor people who exhibit human dignity
by struggling against injustice.

Mary E. Hobgood

See also CLASSISM; DIGNITY; ECONOMIC
JUSTICE FOR ALL; ECONOMY; JUSTICE;
OPTION FOR THE POOR; POLITICS;
WORK/EMPLOYMENT.

POVERTY (RELIGIOUS VOW)

The first of the classical vows of religious
life, or evangelical counsels, poverty is
probably the most important. In religious
communities, poverty refers to a renunciation of ownership of material goods;
but what is the motive for this practice?
Voluntary poverty is not unknown in
non-Christian forms of monasticism; it
calls attention to the fact that all human
beings must die and thus ultimately are
forced to let go of everything, and it is an
ascetical practice assisting the mind and
heart to concentrate on what is essential
to the life of the spirit by stripping away
what is nonessential.

Evangelical poverty is different for at
least two reasons. First, it is modeled after
the life of Jesus as the Gospels portray
him. And second, evangelical poverty is
a deliberate choice to enter into solidarity
with the poor of history on the basis of
Jesus' example of self-emptying (see
2 Cor 8:9; Phil 2:7). The vow of poverty,
therefore, is basically positive, not negative. In recent years, a considerable
amount of writing has been devoted to
the preferential option for the poor, an
idea that lies at the heart of evangelical
poverty within religious life, but is by no
means restricted to religious communities.
The first of the Beatitudes in Matthew's

Gospel sums up a major Christian ideal
(Matt 5:3), while the first in Luke's account
underlines divine partisanship: God has
taken the side of the poor in the long
struggle throughout history for justice
(Luke 6:20). Jesus' advice to the rich man
indicates that the poor were always on
his mind (Mark 10:21); their condition
was not just a momentary observation on
Jesus' part. In short, while religious pronounce a vow of poverty, its spirit and
practice (in terms of solidarity with the
poor) appear to be central to Jesus' message for all his followers.

William Reiser, S.J.

See also OPTION FOR THE POOR; POVERTY;
RELIGIOUS (VOWED).

PRABHUPADA

See BHAKTIVEDANTA, SWAMI.

PRACTICAL THEOLOGY

A branch of theology considered by some
theologians to be synonymous with pastoral theology. According to this usage,
practical or pastoral theology interprets
the insights of theological investigation
(academic theology) and applies them to
the multiple concerns of hands-on
Christian ministry (preaching, education,
sacramental celebration, and Christian
counseling). Another approach to practical theology sees its relationship to the
academic study of theology as more fluid
and interactive. Rather than simply applying theological discourse to the concerns of the ministry, this other approach
defines practical theology as a critical
investigation of issues that emerge when
Christian tradition confronts the perspectives and problems of contemporary life.
In this, it explores ways one can be faithful both to the demands of biblical religion and to the challenges of participation

in a pluralistic society. According to this usage, the "data" the pastoral theologian relies upon for reflection and study are not just the work of academic theologians in various fields (ethics, Scripture, systematics), but also—and very importantly—the lived experience of Christian people.

Ronald A. Pachence

See also DOGMATIC THEOLOGY; MINISTRY/MINISTERIAL; PASTORAL; PASTORAL THEOLOGY.

PRAGMATISM

Pragmatism is a philosophy founded in the United States and uniquely expressive of the U.S. character. Pioneered by Harvard philosopher and psychologist William James in works such as *Pragmatism* (1907) and *The Meaning of Truth* (1909), pragmatism posits that truth should not be determined by abstract ideals, but by its usefulness to people confronting everyday life. Influenced by English philosopher John Stuart Mill, James defined pragmatism as both a method and a theory. As a method, it is an *"attitude of looking away from first things, principles, 'categories,' supposed necessities; and of looking towards last things, fruits, consequences, facts"* (italics in text). As a theory, it means *"that ideas (which themselves are but parts of our experience) become true just in so far as they help us to get into satisfactory relations with other parts of our experience"* (italics in text). As both method and theory, pragmatism opposes dogma, artificiality, and final answers. James exhorted his readers to test truth for its "practical cash-value, set it at work within the stream of your experience."

In *The Varieties of Religious Experience* (1902), James applied pragmatism to religion. He defined religion as *"the feelings, acts, and experiences of individual men [sic]*

in their solitude, so far as they apprehend themselves to stand in relation to whatever they may consider the divine" (italics in text). Religion was primarily an intense, emotional experience of individual self-transcendence. However, according to James, religion also had collective implications. It should have ameliorative effects for individuals and societies, alleviating suffering and generating tolerance, compassion, and unselfishness. In short, to James, the value of religion was in this world rather than the next.

James was not alone in preaching religion's practical benefits. In *A Common Faith* (1934), John Dewey, philosopher and secular humanist, stressed religion's importance in formulating ethical and social values, in furthering democracy, freedom, and the public good. Later interpreters have distorted James' and Dewey's pragmatic approach to justify an "anything goes, if it feels good, do it" religion. This relativism was not their intention. They advocated a coherent set of values that would be strengthened by religion: justice, compassion, empathy, freedom. These benefits did not vary from individual to individual, but applied to everyone; neither James nor Dewey addressed the possible conflicts between these values in a society.

Pragmatism's instrumental and utilitarian understanding of truth has strongly influenced U.S. religious life. Among Protestant Christians in the early twentieth century, pragmatism was a significant element of the Social Gospel. In effect, the Social Gospel was pragmatic Christianity, evaluating Christian truth claims by their applicability to social issues. True Christianity resulted in justice and compassion to the poor and disenfranchised. Christianity's value was demonstrated not by adherence to dogma, but by its fruits. In general, pragmatism was more compatible with liberalism than fundamentalism. Along with pragmatists, liberals believed that the truth of ideas must be tested by their relation to life. An empirical and experiential belief system, liberalism promoted tolerance of others' beliefs and undermined any religion's claims to exclusive truth.

In contrast, fundamentalism opposed pragmatism. For fundamentalists, truth was objective, propositional, and dogmatic. Belief was not validated by action, but necessary due to the self-evident truth of Christianity. Yet pragmatic concerns nonetheless affected fundamentalism in at least two ways. First, fundamentalists believed the truth of their beliefs was confirmed by the fulfillment of biblical prophecy. Second, although they argued for the self-evident truth of Christianity, numbers of conversions empirically verified their understanding of the Gospel.

Evelyn A. Kirkley

See also DEWEY, JOHN; FUNDAMENTALISM; JAMES, WILLIAM; SOCIAL GOSPEL.

PRAJNA

The quality, when fully developed, necessary for the realization of nirvana. Often translated as "wisdom," *prajna* (Pali, *Panna*) is better rendered as "insight," as it refers to the capacity for active spiritual discernment into the nature of reality as it truly is: suffering, impermanent, soul-less (in terms of the three marks of existence).

All schools of Buddhism recognize the development of prajna as essential to salvation. The Theravada school emphasizes *vipassana* meditation as the most important means of cultivation. The Mahayana develops the path of the bodhisattva in reference to prajna, with it as the culminating level of the *paramitas* ("perfec-

tions"), and they agree that meditation is essential. Each Buddhist doctrinal school has defined the exact awareness through prajna cultivation consistent with its view of the ultimate reality: the Madhyamakas as the understanding of *shunya* ("emptiness") and the Yogacharins as the recognition of pure consciousness.

Todd T. Lewis

See also BODHISATTVA; MAHAYANA BUDDHISM; PARAMITA; PRAJNAPARAMITA LITERATURE; THERAVADA BUDDHISM; VIPASHYANA/VIPASSANA.

PRAJNAPARAMITA LITERATURE

A class of Mahayana Buddhist texts that elaborates the progress of a bodhisattva through different stages of perfection (*paramita*), culminating in the realization of enlightenment (*bodhi*) through the attainment of insight (*prajna*). All follow the format of dialogue between the Buddha and different disciples, with shallow and deeper levels of understanding critiqued. The texts also are sectarian in their dismissal of Shariputra, an honored figure in the *Nikayas* of the early Pali Canon and in the *Agamas* of the early Sanskrit canons. He has trouble comprehending the Mahayana doctrines of emptiness, universal compassion, the unreality of dharmas in Abhidharma analysis, and typifies the insufficient spiritual aspiration of the Arahant in Mahayana reckoning.

Todd T. Lewis

See also BODHISATTVA; MAHAYANA BUDDHISM; PARAMITA; PERFECTION OF WISDOM SUTRAS; PRAJNA.

PRAKRIT

A class of "natural" languages derived from Sanskrit but much simpler in grammar and pronunciation. *Prakrits* were once spoken in provinces across ancient India and they were used for religious literatures of heterodox Indic religions. Early Buddhists of the Sthaviravada school (modern Theravada) used Pali; the Jains used Ardha-Magadhi. The edicts of Ashoka were inscribed in Magadhi. By the Gupta era (320–467 C.E.), the Prakrits were standardized (as was Sanskrit) as the spoken languages continued to evolve beyond them.

Todd T. Lewis

See also JAINISM; PALI CANON; SANSKRIT.

PRAKRITI

In Hindu thought, *prakriti* is the basic substance of which the entire manifest universe—mental as well as physical—is formed. Often translated as "Nature," *prakriti* is said to be composed of three factors or qualities, the three *gunas*. *Prakriti*, as the feminine (in symbolism and grammatical gender) principle of manifestation, is paired in the Sankhya system of thought with *purusha*, the male principle of pure spirit. As the creative principle, it is often identified with *maya* and *shakti*.

Lance E. Nelson

See also GUNA; HINDUISM; MAYA; SHAKTI.

PRANA

In Hindu thought, *prana* is the vital breath. The concept is similar to the idea of *ch'i/qi* in Taoism.

Lance E. Nelson

See also CH'I; DAOISM; HINDUISM.

PRASADA

The Sanskrit word for "grace," *prasada* in Hinduism can mean one of two things.

In theology, it refers to a phenomenon analogous to the Christian concept of grace: the favor, mercy, or blessing that God may bestow upon a devotee. In ritual, prasada (often *prasad* in modern Indian languages) is the food or flowers that have been consecrated by offering to a deity at the altar in a temple or home. Having been offered, and thus mingled with the substance of the deity, the items become grace-laden and are returned to the worshiper to be eaten or otherwise cherished, as a sacramental vehicle of divine blessings.

Lance E. Nelson

See also HINDUISM; IMAGES, WORSHIP OF; SACRAMENT.

PRATITYASAMUTPADA

A Buddhist formula (Pali, *Paticcasamuppada*) that expresses the fundamental doctrine that antecedent psychic and bodily states condition their future evolution; it underlies the definition of reality as an ongoing, impermanent, and interdependent flux, giving the human instance of this truth. The twelve links (envisioned as a circle) are: ignorance (*avidya*) → karmic habits (*samskaras*) → consciousness (*vijñana*) → name and form (*namarupa*) → six sense bases (*sadayatana*, including "mind") → contact (*sparsha*) → feeling (*vedana*) → craving (*trishna*) → grasping acts (*upadana*) → becoming (*bhava*) → birth (*jati*) → old age-death (*jaramarana*).

Most often translated as "The Chain of Causality" or "Dependent Origination," *pratityasamutpada* came to be regarded as a circle: whatever point of entry chosen would be diagnostic of cause and effect analysis and connected to other core doctrinal concepts such as craving as the core cause of suffering (Noble Truths, no. 2), ignorance as creating certain bondage in the cycle of karma-determined birth and death, and the breakdown of the human being into five main, changing units (*skandhas*). The Mahayana philosophers relied on this universally accepted formula to argue that all reality lacks essential self-existence (*svabhava*) and is inherently empty (*shunya*). This teaching of causal interdependence also discounts theological notions of creation by God or gods, and rejects atomistic theories of reality or fatalism. It is intended as a practical guide on how to break the pattern of bondage to re-death, rebirth, and suffering.

Todd T. Lewis

See also MADHYAMAKA/MADHYMIKA SCHOOL; NAGARJUNA; SKANDHA; TRUTHS, FOUR NOBLE; VIPASHYANA/ VIPASSANA.

PRATYEKABUDDHA

In pan-Buddhist thought, a being (Pali, *Paccekabuddha*) who wins full enlightenment in isolation from a teacher or disciples. In the non-Mahayana schools, this doctrinal possibility indicates the universality of the enlightenment (*bodhi*) experience. In the Mahayana schools, the *Pratyekabuddha* does not understand the highest teaching of emptiness (*shunya*) and has therefore not had complete enlightenment.

Todd T. Lewis

See also BUDDHA; MAHAYANA BUDDHISM.

PRAXIS

Though this Greek term can be literally translated as "practice," its connotations are much broader than what is conveyed by the English word. For Aristotle, the term praxis referred to that human action, or activity, that is its own end. Praxis is human action whose value is intrinsic rather than extrinsic, that is, activity that has no ulterior purpose other than its very performance. He thus distinguished praxis from *poiesis*, human action whose value is extrinsic in that it derives from the results, or product, of the action rather than from the action itself. The paradigm of praxis is the relationship between human persons in the *polis*, where the interaction, or participation is its own end; the interaction among friends has intrinsic value, apart from anything that might result from or be produced by that interaction. The paradigm of *poiesis*, on the other hand, is the act of production, where the action is not an end in itself; its end is the achievement of a prescribed result, or product. The value of *poiesis* is thus derived, not from the action itself, but from the results, or product, of the action. Thus, the construction of a house is *poiesis*, but the family's home life is praxis.

In modernity, this distinction between praxis and *poiesis* becomes attenuated. Whereas, for Aristotle, what primarily defines human action as human is precisely its intrinsic value, its character as praxis, in modernity human action comes to be defined primarily as instrumental, as action whose value derives from its results. In the wake of the industrial, scientific, and technological revolutions, an increased emphasis is placed on the productive, or utilitarian character of human activity: to be human is to achieve, to produce, to make. In capitalism, human life itself (as praxis) becomes reduced to "*making* a living" (*poiesis*); to be unemployed is thus to be literally a nobody. In socialism, human life becomes reduced to "making a classless society"; to be a counter-revolutionary is to be a nobody.

For Karl Marx, praxis became associated with social transformation; the struggle for social change is the highest form of human activity.

In modernity, moreover, praxis becomes increasingly separated from theory, or reflection. Whereas, for Aristotle, reflection was a dimension of praxis, in modernity praxis becomes increasingly identified with "practice," understood as the opposite of theory; what is "theoretical" is not "practical," and vice versa. Thus, Aristotle's more holistic understanding of human action as involving not only the body, but also the intellect and affect (as in human relationships, which involve the whole person) becomes reduced to the technical, physical manipulation of the external world to achieve a desired result: for example, a finished house, a financial profit, a classless society, a successful career. What then defines human action as human is its "practicality" in achieving that result; its meaning and value derive from its utility, or usefulness, not from a quality intrinsic to the action itself.

Praxis has played a central methodological role, especially, in Latin American liberation theology and other theologies articulated and developed by historically marginalized groups. Insofar as Western European theologians have understood their task as an exclusively intellectual, theoretical task unrelated to their actual participation in society (praxis), their theologies have legitimated the oppression of marginalized groups. This legitimation can be either explicit, as when Christian theology legitimated the praxis of slavery in the U.S. South, or implicit, as when the silence and inaction of theologians (or any Christian) in the face of social injustice effectively and implicitly functions as silent consent and complicity in that injustice. In reaction to the Latin American experience of this disjunction between the God of Life taught and proclaimed by Western Christians and the oppression so often experienced by the Latin American poor at the hands of those same Christians, liberation theologians have thus emphasized the fundamental importance of praxis in the theological enterprise. The validity, or truth, of theological arguments is dependent more on the praxis in which they are based than on purely "rational" criteria. Knowledge of God is defined less by theoretical understanding than by the *doing* of God's will: to know God is to do justice. An authentically Christian theology must thus be grounded in a "preferential option for the poor," an active identification with the poor in their everyday lives, their lived religious faith, and their struggle for justice. If Jesus Christ is himself identified with the hungry person, the thirsty person, the naked person, and the stranger (Matt 25:31-46), then, in order to know that Christ, the Christian must likewise identify himself or herself with the poor (preferentially, not exclusively). Correct belief, or orthodoxy, must be grounded in an active life of discipleship, or orthopraxis.

Roberto S. Goizueta

See also DISCIPLESHIP; ORTHODOXY; ORTHOPRAXIS; POIESIS.

PRAYER

Essentially, prayer is addressing oneself to God. Praying presupposes that one believes that God exists and that one is attempting to lead one's life in a conscious acknowledgment of God's sovereignty and love. Prayer thus expresses the multiple ways human beings relate to God as the one who creates them and ever remains the source and goal of their life. To think of prayer, then, is to think of what human beings do according to their nature, the more they realize that they cannot adequately define who they are without appealing to the God who made them: they give thanks and praise, they seek forgiveness and strength, they express love and hope. Of course, the act of praying would be meaningless apart from the belief that God wants to be in relation to us, a conviction that lies at the heart of the Judeo-Christian tradition.

While people often pray unseen (Matt 6:6), there is nothing private or secret about prayer itself. Liturgical prayer is intrinsically communal, but even prayer in solitude embraces the world. Whenever one prays in the Spirit of Christ, the entire body of believers is present, for a purely private relationship with God is not possible. Although the social or communal nature of the Christian religious experience has not always been fully attended to, the fact remains that the risen Christ dwells among his sisters and brothers. To encounter them is to encounter him, and to encounter him in the Spirit is to encounter all who belong to him.

William Reiser, s.j.

See also CONTEMPLATION; MEDITATION (CHRISTIAN).

PREACHING (IN CATHOLICISM)

In 1982 the U.S. bishops issued the document *Fulfilled in Your Hearing: The Homily in the Sunday Assembly*. The title refers to Luke 4:21. Luke tells of Jesus going to the synagogue in Nazareth on the Sabbath. He was given the charge of reading the day's Scripture and preaching. He read from Isaiah, concerning one who would free the people from oppression (Isa 61:1-2). He then began to preach, saying, "Today, this passage is fulfilled in your hearing." Here is a model of good preaching.

(1) Scriptural. Good preaching springs from the texts just proclaimed. The preacher therefore must understand Scripture, know how the Bible has been understood throughout Christian history, and be skilled at using modern scientific and literary tools.

The Lectionary, not the whim of the preacher, governs the homily's topic. Over the course of three years, most of the New Testament and significant parts of the Old Testament are read at Sunday Eucharist. This provides both assembly and preacher with many "lenses" through which to explore themselves and Jesus.

(2) Contemporary. Although Jesus rooted his preaching in the biblical text, it was not about the Bible. "Today," he began, not "back then." Good preaching uses biblical texts to shed light upon what Jesus is doing and saying here and now. By no means does this mean that the Bible is secondary. It focuses, colors, and clarifies everything the preacher sees and says.

(3) Liturgical. In the Catholic tradition, preaching generally occurs within the liturgy, an event in which Jesus makes himself present. Catholics recognize Jesus in the eucharistic Food and Drink. They are less likely to recognize that when the Word is proclaimed and preached, Jesus himself speaks. At Nazareth, Jesus proclaimed that the Messiah was not only *spoken of* in the Bible but was actually *speaking*. Preaching, then, is not an insertion or intermission in Jesus' action in the liturgy, but part of it.

Since preaching is liturgical, the liturgical presider normally preaches: the bishop, priest, or the assisting deacon. In some circumstances others may preach. The *Directory for Masses with Children* (no. 24), for example, allows the priest to delegate a layperson to preach who can better address the children. In parishes without a resident priest, the bishop can authorize a layperson to preach. Outside the liturgy, all Christians have an obligation and right to preach by word and example (Canon 759).

Patrick L. Malloy

See also BOSSUET, JACQUES BENIGNE; EXEGESIS/EISEGESIS; LECTIONARY; LITURGY OF THE WORD; SERMON; SIGNS OF THE TIMES.

PRECEPTS (BUDDHIST)

The basic early formulae for defining the Buddhist's ideal moral practice, comprising the foundation of the Buddhist path toward nirvana. Buddhist ethics build upon various doctrinal emphases: the ideology of merit, in which making good karma and avoiding bad is the only intelligent approach to life; seeing that through the vast number of transmigrations, all beings have been one's parents and children; and the emphasis of an ethos that cultivates detachment, discernment, and compassion (*karuna*). The lists of precepts across the Buddhist world derived from these teachings reflect the different doctrinal and praxis emphases in the different schools.

The Five Precepts

The Five Precepts are likely the earliest that developed in ancient India and are found in the early scriptures. The five precepts are as follows, with the corresponding positive traits emphasized to counteract the chance of transgression: 1. Not to destroy life intentionally (kindness and compassion); 2. Not to steal (generosity and renunciation); 3. Not to engage in sexual misconduct (seeking "joyous satisfaction with one's wife"); 4. Not to lie (loving the truth, seeking it,

pursuing discernment and insight); 5. No intoxication (mindfulness, contentment, awareness via meditation). In South and Southeast Asia, the Five Precepts are chanted regularly in modern Theravada rituals by both monks and laity; in these communities, they are regarded as general ideals. In East Asia, the precepts have tended to be regarded as vows that should be taken only if one intends to follow them completely. (One can therefore omit a precept if one cannot expect to observe it fully.)

The Eight Precepts

Both main schools of Buddhism also recognize the Eight Precepts that entail more strict interpretations of the original five, and three additional renunciations. Precept Three becomes strict chastity, and there are further abstentions: 6. Not to eat [solid] food after noon; 7. No participation in shows, dancing, singing; or wearing garlands, perfumes, jewelry; and 8. No sleeping on high or wide beds. The Eight Precepts are usually taken for the twenty-four-hour "fast days," on the new and full moon days, and/or on the two eighth lunar days. Observing the Eight Precepts on these days, usually marked by ritual chanting before the sangha, is one mark of being an *upasaka/upasika* ("devout lay man/woman").

The Ten Precepts

These precepts are observed by novice Theravada monks and taken as long-term commitments. The Ten Precepts are constructed from the eight, with no. 7 split into two and a final prohibition—Not to touch gold or silver—a rule designed to insure that begging is at the center of the Buddha's rule of asceticism and basis of the mutual exchanges that bind the Buddhist community. It is important to note that the moral duty of the laity to give generously is also a central Buddhist theme and universal community emphasis: only by the householders giving food and clothing can the more devout monks and nuns keep the precepts.

In the Soto Zen tradition, there are "The Three Great Precepts" ("Cease from evil, do only good, do good for others") as well as a slightly different "Ten Great Precepts": the first four as above, plus 5. No taking or selling drugs or alcohol; 6. No speaking against others; 7. No praising oneself or abusing others; 8. Not being mean in giving the Dharma or wealth; 9. Not being angry; and 10. Not defaming the Three Refuges.

Todd T. Lewis

See also MERIT (PUNYA); NOBLE EIGHT-FOLD PATH; REFUGE, THREEFOLD; VINAYA.

PREDESTINATIONISM (CALVINIST)

Though God's predestination of some persons for salvation and of others for damnation was one of the doctrines taught by John Calvin, later generations of Calvinists gave such a doctrine more prominence than it had for Calvin himself. By the early seventeenth century, what came to be known as Calvinist "orthodoxy" emphasized this "double" predestination of the elect and nonelect. God was thus asserted to have determined, by an eternal and irreformable decree, who would or would not be saved; this determination had taken place without regard for any foreseen merit on the part of the predestined.

Among theologians responsible for articulation and defense of such orthodoxy was the Dutchman Francis Gomar (1563–1641). Professor of theology at Leiden, at Saumur, and at Groningen, he was a leader of those who opposed Arminianism, a movement within the Reformed Church that rejected the doctrine of predestination. Gomar was victorious at the Synod of Dort (1618–9), an assembly of Calvinist theologians that reaffirmed the doctrine of divine election and nonelection without reference to merit of any kind on the part of those predestined.

Among those affirming the doctrine of predestination there was, however, a difference of opinion concerning the relationship between the sin of Adam and Eve and God's decree. For "supralapsarians" God's decree of predestination, for all of humanity, occurred even before original sin. For "sublapsarians" this decree was pronounced only after that sin. The supralapsarian doctrine placed God's selection of the saved and the (more numerous) damned at the very creation of humanity, even before there was any sin. Calvin had not articulated a clear position on this matter, and many Calvinists supported a sublapsarian interpretation of predestination.

For Calvin, the doctrine of divine predestination was a comforting doctrine, one that relieved Christians of anxiety about an imagined need to earn salvation. This doctrine promised for the elect the (unearned) grace of perseverance; the free gift of election could not be lost for the divine decree was irrevocable. Placing their trust in God alone for their eternal salvation, Christians could give their energies to praise of God, to family, and to civic duties, and to hard work in the world. Yet, at times, Calvinists were preoccupied by a desire for proof of election, a proof often sought in holiness of life. If some members of the Reformed Church remained anxious about their own election or nonelection, others found in "predestinationism" a source of strength and assurance. The confidence and zeal of the Calvinists who founded New England in America give eloquent witness to such assurance.

Thomas Worcester, s.j.

See also ARMINIANISM; AUGUSTINE OF HIPPO; AUGUSTINIANISM; CALVIN, JOHN; CALVINISM; GRACE; INFRALAPSARIAN; INSTITUTES OF THE CHRISTIAN RELIGION; MERIT; PREDESTINATION (IN CHRISTIANITY); PURITANISM; REFORMATION; REFORMED THEOLOGY (-IES); SIN, ORIGINAL.

PREDESTINATION (IN CHRISTIANITY)

A belief, among some Christians, according to which the eternal destiny of individuals has been "pre-ordained" (or "pre-determined") by a divine decree. In this view, some individuals are being infallibly guided by God to salvation, while most are being allowed to continue their march to eternal damnation. The use of this term, however, has more frequently been associated with those who are being brought to salvation. Although there is no clearly discernable doctrine of predestination in the Old Testament, there are New Testament texts that do seem to teach it (for example, Matt 20:23; John 10:29; Rom 8:28-30; Eph 1:3-14; and 2 Tim 1:9). Since the days of the early church, Christian theologians have discussed the meaning and extension of the concept of predestination, and many doctrinal controversies have centered on this issue (especially in Western Christianity). With the theological reflections on grace and salvation that developed as a result of the Pelagian and semi-Pelagian disputes (fourth, fifth, and sixth centuries), discussions on predestination remained basically Augustinian but with significant variations (mostly intended to soften Augustine's rigidity on the subject). Calvin rejected the universal saving will of God, and emphasized predestination in the strictest terms, but some of his followers have since softened the original Calvinist position. The post-Tridentine, Catholic controversy called *de auxiliis* had its roots in the concept of predestination. Some smaller Christian denominations have spent much time attempting (unsuccessfully) to determine the number of those predestined for salvation. The whole notion of predestination, however, cannot be properly understood without the results of solid biblical interpretation (including studies on Jesus' teaching on the reign of God), and of cultural studies. Furthermore, predestination must be considered only in its original context within the framework of the theologies of grace and salvation, and within the overall Christian belief in God's merciful compassion.

Orlando Espín

See also AUGUSTINE OF HIPPO; CALVIN, JOHN; CALVINISM; DETERMINISM; ELECTION (DOCTRINE OF); FAITH; FREE WILL; GOD; GRACE; JUSTIFICATION; MERCY; MOLINA, LUIS DE; OMNIPOTENCE; ORANGE, COUNCILS OF; ORIGINAL JUSTICE; PELAGIANISM; PREDESTINATION (CALVINIST); REIGN OF GOD; SALVATION; SEMI-PELAGIANISM; SIN, ORIGINAL; THEOLOGICAL ANTHROPOLOGY; TRENT, COUNCIL OF.

PREDESTINATION (IN ISLAM)

The belief that God has determined in advance ("pre") the fate of every individual in this life and the next. This teaching, based upon Qur'anic revelation (God's revealed Word in Islam's sacred scripture, the Qur'an) and upon traditions of the Prophet Muhammad (570–632), intends to preserve the sovereignty of God, especially

God's divine knowledge of all things. One Qur'anic passage in particular appears to support the doctrine of predestination: "Whom Allah guides, he is on the right path; whom He rejects from this guidance, such are the persons who perish" (7:178). This scripture is supported by a *hadith* (a tradition handed down by Muhammad) which says that even before creation, God had already recorded the destiny of every person who would live.

There are, however, other Islamic teachings that seem to contradict predestination, especially the belief in God's mercy and the free will God has given human beings. Every sura or chapter in the Qur'an begins with the words: "In the name of Allah, most Gracious, most Merciful"; and there are no fewer than five references to free will found in the Qur'an as well. One of these texts (10:99) says that there should be no compulsion in religion, that is, the will of humans must be free in determining which religion to follow. Yet, the next verse goes on to say that "no soul can believe, except by the Will of Allah, and He will place doubt . . . on those who will not understand." This suggests that there is a tension in Islam between predestination and free will.

Some scholars note that while both doctrines exist in the tradition, the Prophet Muhammad appeared to emphasize predestination, especially toward the end of his life. An extreme interpretation of this view was subsequently reflected in the teachings of the Jabariyya school of theology that maintained a radically fatalistic approach to human destiny. Everything that happens to us, these theologians said, is determined by God. On the other side of the question of predestination and free will were the Qadarites and the Mu'tazilites who were steadfast champions of free will.

Orthodox Muslim opinion today accepts the divine origin of both teachings. It maintains that if people have problems reconciling these apparently antithetical doctrines, they should recognize that the human mind can never fully comprehend the mind of God. The problem, therefore, is the limited intellectual capacity of humans, not the Qur'anic teachings.

Ronald A. Pachence

See also HADITH; ISLAM; MUSLIM; MU'TAZILITES; QUR'AN; REVELATION (IN ISLAM).

PREFECTURE, APOSTOLIC
See PRELATURE.

PREJUDICE
An attitude about a person or thing that is not based on reason and personal investigation, but reflects prejudgment. To be prejudiced is "to make one's mind up ahead of time" and to be unduly influenced by what others have said. This prejudgment can be positive or negative. As an ethical term, prejudice refers to negative ideas that lead to discrimination against a class of people; it issues in anti-Semitism, sexism, racism, heterosexism, and so on. Discriminatory practices, by keeping people of different backgrounds separate and inimical, reinforce old prejudices and create new ones. Therefore, prejudice is a serious obstacle to the good of community sought by religions.

Prejudices have particular social locations, so religious groups are implicated in them in various ways. There is no doubting that religions have frequently contributed to prejudice and discrimination. Examples include white Christians in the U.S. who condoned slavery and resisted equal rights for blacks; the mutual distrust among Jews, Christians, and

Muslims that has expressed itself in the Middle East throughout the ages; the conflicts between Protestants and Catholics in Northern Ireland; and the civil war in the former Yugoslavia that involved Orthodox Christians, Roman Catholics, and Muslims. Each of these (and any other example) must be investigated carefully, for while religion undoubtedly plays a role in each conflict, that role may be primary or secondary. It should also be noted that no religious group is homogenous in thought and action, and that the acts of religious adherents are not necessarily to be taken as representative of the religion.

In such examples we can also identify religious figures who act in exemplary ways, drawing upon their beliefs to raise an ethical critique of the prejudice from which they suffer, or which their coreligionists practice on others. Some of the most notable opponents of prejudice around the globe in this century have been religious leaders and organizations, including the Rev. Martin Luther King Jr. in the U.S.; Mohandas K. Gandhi in India; Archbishop Desmond Tutu in South Africa; the Anti-Defamation League of B'nai Brith, a Jewish anti-Semitic organization founded in 1913; and the American Friends Service Committee, a Quaker organization.

Brian Stiltner

See also ANTI-SEMITISM; DISCRIMINATION; HOMOPHOBIA; RACISM; SEXISM; TOLERANCE.

PRELATE
See PRELATURE.

PRELATURE
According to the Roman Catholic Church's Code of Canon Law, there can be "personal" and "territorial" prelates. The latter ("territorial prelature") functions, for all practical purposes, as a diocese. The "ordinary" of a territorial prelature is usually a bishop, but another member of the clergy who is not a bishop may be appointed the prelature's ordinary. Territorial prelatures are created by a papal decree, and usually (but not necessarily) in mission territories. They are often subsidized by mission funds, missionary societies, and/or the Vatican.

"Personal prelatures" can also be established by papal decree (a novelty added to the 1983 Roman Catholic Code of Canon Law). These personal prelatures are not dioceses, nor may they function as such. As in territorial prelatures, the ordinary need not be a bishop. In both cases (that is, in territorial and personal prelatures) the ordinary is called a "prelate."

Orlando Espín

See also BISHOP (ORDINARY); CANON LAW; DIOCESE/ARCHDIOCESE; MISSIONARIES; MISSIONS; OPUS DEI; ORDINARY (CANONICAL).

PRESBYTERAL COUNCIL
(Greek, *presbyteros*, elder). An advisory council or senate is mandated by Catholic canon law to advise the bishop on important matters. The bishop must take some areas of diocesan life to this council of priests for consultation and validation. Such areas concern the erection, suppression, division, or merger of parishes, as well as the remuneration for diocesan clergy. The Conference of Bishops sets the standards for the councils. About half are elected by the priests. Some members serve *ex officio*, some by appointment. Most members are diocesan priests, although order priests, priests living in the

diocese who may or may not serve the diocese, may be eligible for membership. The bishop both calls and presides over the council and proposes the agenda, although any member may make suggestions for discussion or action. The bishop is encouraged to consult regularly with the council on all important governmental matters.

M. Jane Gorman

See also PRESBYTEROS (IN THE NEW TESTAMENT).

PRESBYTERIAN CHURCHES

A presbyterian church is a Protestant Christian congregation that practices presbyterian polity. The word "presbyter" derives from a Greek word translated "priest" or "elder" and designated leaders of Christian churches in the first centuries of their existence. Followed by Presbyterian and many Reformed churches, presbyterian polity is a form of church government in which congregations cooperate with each other to establish policy, ordain individuals to the ministry, and settle disputes. Individual congregations are governed by the session, a group of elders and ministerial staff. Congregations in a region unite to form a presbytery, similar to a diocese or association, but not headed by a bishop; the presbytery is composed of elected lay and clerical representatives of member churches. Elected delegates also compose synods that represent groups of presbyteries and the General Assembly that legislates issues of national importance. Crucial to presbyterian polity is fair representation of clergy and laity, the democratic process of election, and uniformity of governance, liturgy, and theology.

As an independent denomination, Presbyterianism originated in Scotland during the sixteenth century. A follower of John Calvin and a charismatic leader, John Knox sought to recreate Calvin's Geneva in Scotland and established the Church of Scotland in 1560 on presbyterian principles. Scottish Presbyterians discovered allies among English Puritans and tensions with the English monarchy that sought to impose an episcopal ecclesiastical system. These tensions exploded in the 1640s with the English Civil War and the execution of King Charles I. The Church of Scotland was not stabilized until the 1688 "Glorious Revolution" that restored a more tolerant monarchy to the British throne. A key theological development during this period was the Westminster Confession of 1646, an exposition of Christian theology from a Calvinist perspective, including double predestination and strict observance of the Sabbath.

In the seventeenth and eighteenth centuries, Presbyterians emigrated to the North American British colonies. English Puritans settled in Connecticut and formed "consociations," groups of congregations similar to presbyteries, a polity affirmed by the Saybrook Platform of 1708. Scottish Presbyterians settled in New York, New Jersey, and Pennsylvania and, organized by Francis Makemie, formed the first North American presbytery in Philadelphia in 1706. So-called Scotch-Irish Presbyterians, a group formed by forced colonization of Scots to Ireland by the English government, emigrated to Pennsylvania, then westward and southward to the Shenandoah Valley of Virginia, the Appalachian mountains of West Virginia and North Carolina, and across the Cumberland Gap into Tennessee and Kentucky. Poor, independent, and fiercely resistant to authority, they were the backbone of the frontier.

In the mid-eighteenth century, like other religious groups, Presbyterians encountered growth and dissension as a result of the First Great Awakening. Supported primarily by English Presbyterians, the pro-revival faction or "New Side" was led by the Tennent family of preachers, father William and son Gilbert. New Side Presbyterians formed the New Brunswick Presbytery in 1741, the Synod of New York in 1745, and the College of New Jersey in 1746, later known as Princeton College. "Old Side" Presbyterians, composed mostly of Scotch-Irish, supported doctrinal rigor and opposed the emotional preaching of the revivals. New and Old Sides reconciled in 1758 after revival fires had cooled, but tensions remained that would reignite after the American Revolution, in which Presbyterians overwhelmingly supported the cause of independence. The only clergyperson to sign the Declaration of Independence was Presbyterian John Witherspoon.

As the nineteenth century dawned, Presbyterianism encompassed countervailing tendencies in its predominant English and Scotch-Irish constituencies. English Presbyterians, centered in urban areas of the eastern seaboard, stressed educational achievement, upward social mobility, and order in theology and polity. Scotch-Irish Presbyterians on the frontier placed a premium on enthusiasm, discounted worldly status, and vociferously defended individual liberty. In 1837 these tendencies exploded in conflict between traditionalists and innovators over Evangelicalism, resulting in schism between "Old School" and "New School" Presbyterians. Slavery further split both groups, the New School dividing into northern and southern branches in 1857 and the Old in 1861. After the Civil War, Presbyterians regrouped along regional lines, forming northern and southern denominations.

Despite these internal conflicts, Presbyterians prospered in the nineteenth century. Presbyterians James McGready, Barton Stone, and Alexander Campbell were among the leaders of the Second Great Awakening on the Kentucky frontier, although Stone and Campbell left the Presbyterians to form the Christian Church/Disciples of Christ. Presbyterians and Congregationalists cooperated in the 1801 Plan of Union that sponsored home missions, church planting, and revivals, including the work of Charles G. Finney. Moreover, both Old and New School, pro- and anti-slavery Presbyterians supported missions and social reform. By the late nineteenth century, Presbyterians were predominantly Euro-American, middle class, and well educated: the epitome of the status quo.

In the late nineteenth and early twentieth centuries, however, liberalism and fundamentalism caused dissension among Presbyterians, as in other mainline Protestant denominations. In 1893, Charles Briggs, a professor of Old Testament at the Presbyterian Union Theological Seminary in New York City, was convicted of teaching contrary to Presbyterian (and biblical) orthodoxy and stripped of his ministerial credentials. In an unusual move, the seminary supported him, and instead of forcing him to resign, left the denomination and became an independent, liberal seminary. Liberal Presbyterians like Charles Stelzle, head of the Federal Council of Churches' Commission on Church and Social Service, also supported the ecumenical movement and the Social Gospel.

Princeton Theological Seminary became the center of fundamentalist Presbyterianism. Theology professor Charles Hodge argued that Darwinism was incompatible with Christian belief, while New Testament professor J. Gresham Machen defended authentic Christianity against the belief called liberalism, with which it had nothing in common. For some fundamentalist Presbyterians, these efforts did not go far enough; schism among northern Presbyterians spawned the Presbyterian Church of America (PCA) in 1936, the Bible Presbyterian Church in 1937, and Orthodox Presbyterian Church in 1939 from a PCA schism. Even Machen departed Princeton in 1929 to teach at the more conservative Westminster Theological Seminary in Philadelphia, was expelled from the northern Presbyterians, and helped found the PCA. While the northern Presbyterians divided over liberalism and fundamentalism, southern Presbyterians remained consistently fundamentalist.

In the later twentieth century, Presbyterians turned from schism to merger. In 1958 the United Presbyterian Church in the U.S.A. (UPCUSA) united the northern Presbyterians with the United Presbyterian Church in North America, a smaller group of Scottish origins. The Presbyterian Church in the United States (PCUS) had previously merged the southern Presbyterians, Cumberland Presbyterian Church, and Welsh Calvinist Methodists. In 1983, after lengthy negotiation, the UPCUSA and PCUS merged to form a national body called the Presbyterian Church (U.S.A.). Theologically, it is moderately evangelical, with vocal left and right wings. In the 1970s and 1980s, the ordination of women and inclusive language aroused dissension. In the 1990s, the ordination of gay men and lesbians to the ministry caused national controversy in the newly formed denomination; in 1996, over vigorous objection, the General Assembly officially prohibited the ordination of "practicing" homosexuals.

Evelyn A. Kirkley

See also CALVIN, JOHN; CALVINISM; ELDER (IN CHRISTIANITY); EVANGELICALS; EVANGELICAL THEOLOGY; FUNDAMENTALISM (CHRISTIAN HISTORICAL MOVEMENT); GREAT AWAKENING(S) (EURO-AMERICAN RELIGIOUS HISTORY); PRESBYTERIAN THEOLOGY; REFORMED CHURCHES; REFORMED THEOLOGY (-IES); REVIVALISM.

PRESBYTERIAN THEOLOGY

Presbyterian theology was first codified in the Westminster Confession of 1646, created by order of the English Parliament during the period of civil war. It reflected the collaboration of Scottish Presbyterians and English Puritans to expound Calvinist theology. It claimed the authority of Scripture as "Supreme Judge" in any theological controversy and stated that "the infallible rule of interpretation of Scripture is the Scripture itself." Like the canons of the Synod of Dort, it affirmed the total depravity of humanity and the absolute sovereignty of God. Although all humans deserved to be damned, God, in mercy, had chosen some to be saved. Christ died only to save those whom God had elected. The elect were justified and sanctified through the power of the Holy Spirit. Along with double predestination and limited atonement, the Westminster Confession declared that grace was irresistible, that the elect can never fall out of a state of grace. A reification of Calvin's theology, the Westminster Confession became the standard for Presbyterian orthodoxy in Europe and the United States.

From the mid-eighteenth to mid-nineteenth centuries, Presbyterians in the

United States were among the leaders of and those strongly influenced by revivalism and Evangelicalism. Contrary to Baptists and Methodists, who stressed the emotional aspect of conversion, Presbyterians sought to balance emotional experience with reason and use of the intellect. In the 1740s, revivalist Gilbert Tennent attracted supporters and inflamed opponents with his sermon "The Danger of an Unconverted Ministry," in which he argued that clergy must experience a true revival of the heart along with preaching doctrinal truth, creating suspicion among laypeople that their pastors might not be true Christians. In 1746 Presbyterians founded the College of New Jersey, later Princeton College, that became the bastion of Calvinist orthodoxy, advocate of Enlightenment Scottish Commonsense philosophy, and later center of fundamentalism. During the 1820s and 1830s, Charles Grandison Finney, a Presbyterian evangelist who never felt restricted by Presbyterian orthodoxy, pioneered "New Measures" of revivalism, including advance publicity, protracted meetings, mourner's bench, and women praying in public. Finney's New Measures revolutionized evangelism.

In the late nineteenth and early twentieth centuries, Presbyterian theologians divided into liberal and fundamentalist camps. The 1893 heresy trial of New York City's Union Theological Seminary professor Charles Briggs threw down the gauntlet. Although Briggs was convicted by northern Presbyterians of teaching doctrine contrary to Scripture and stripped of his clerical standing, many Presbyterians supported him, including Union Seminary, which abandoned its status as a Presbyterian institution and became interdenominational as a result

of the trial. Princeton Theological Seminary professors Charles Hodge and J. Gresham Machen became primary defenders of Presbyterian orthodoxy. In his three-volume *Systematic Theology* (1872–5), Hodge elaborated Presbyterian orthodoxy as adherence to historic Christian creeds and the Westminster Confession. In *Christianity and Liberalism* (1923), Machen sharply distinguished true Christianity founded on the Bible from relativistic, immoral liberalism founded on secular humanism. Based on the Enlightenment philosophy of Scottish Commonsense Realism, the fundamentalism of Hodge and Machen rejected doctrinal innovation and stressed intellectual rigor.

Presbyterian theology has continued to diversify through the twentieth century, influenced not only by liberalism and fundamentalism, but also by neoorthodoxy, and process, liberation, black, and feminist theologies. What unites these varieties of Presbyterian theology are commitments to order, rationalism, and the heritage of Calvinism.

Evelyn A. Kirkley

See also CALVIN, JOHN; CALVINISM; EVANGELICALS; EVANGELICAL THEOLOGY; FUNDAMENTALISM; PREDESTINATION (IN CHRISTIANITY); PRESBYTERIAN CHURCHES; REFORMED THEOLOGY (-IES); REVIVALISM.

PRESBYTERORUM ORDINIS

This document, The Decree on the Ministry and Life of Priests, was adopted by the Second Vatican Council on December 7, 1965, at the end of its fourth and final session. The decree is meant to complement treatments of the priesthood made in several previous documents (especially *Sacrosanctum Concilium*, on the liturgy, and

Lumen Gentium, on the church), and is aimed particularly at priests in direct pastoral ministry ("the care of souls"— no. 1). In describing the nature and functions of the priesthood, the document details the relationships of priests to Christ (from whom they receive the threefold ministry of word, sacrament, and leadership), to bishops (with whom, in a subordinate degree, they share a common priesthood), to other priests (with whom they share a communal bond), and to laypeople (with whom they are "members of the same Body of Christ which all are commanded to build up"—no. 9). In exhorting priests to exemplary ministry, the decree urges availability, holiness, unity and harmony, humility and obedience, and the interior life of prayer and study. The decree extols priestly celibacy as a gift from God, although it also explicitly acknowledges the existence of married priests in the Eastern Churches and concludes that celibacy "is not demanded of the priesthood by its nature" (no. 16). (The question of women in the priesthood is not touched upon.) Priests are urged to be concerned for fostering priestly vocations among the young. The necessity of providing "just remuneration" (no. 20) and "social security" (no. 21) for priests is also discussed, but on the other hand, frugal living and even voluntary poverty are highly recommended for both their pastoral and their personal spiritual benefits. The decree concludes by acknowledging the "obstacles," "fruitlessness," and "bitter loneliness" (no. 22) that many priests face in the modern world, but urges them to recall that this world that they serve "is the world God has so loved as to give his only-begotten Son for it" (no. 22).

William A. Clark, s.j.

PRESBYTEROS
(IN THE NEW TESTAMENT)

A Greek term meaning "elder" or "presbyter." In the New Testament the masculine plural form, *presbyteroi*, is used to speak of older men (Acts 2:17; 1 Tim 5:1) and, probably inclusively, to refer to both elder men and women. In 1 Timothy 5:2 the feminine plural form, *presbyterai*, refers to older women only.

In some instances the *presbyteroi* are Jewish officials, such as members of local councils and synagogues and lay members of the Sanhedrin (for example, Matt 15:2; Mark 14:43; Luke 7:3; Acts 4:8). Their role seems to have been primarily judicial.

The New Testament also contains numerous references to "elders," using the term to designate specific members of the emerging Christian communities (Acts 11:30; 14:23; 15:2), a designation that evidences the influence of Jewish structures on those of nascent Christianity. It is striking to observe that, while Luke in Acts 14:23 states that Paul and Barnabas "appointed elders . . . in each church," in fact Paul's own letters do not refer to elders. Some suggest this indicates a later emergence of those designated as elders from the earlier charismatic and diaconal roles as seen in 1 Corinthians 12:4-5.

Within Acts the elders have various administrative and decision-making functions. The Letter of James states that the elders of the church should be called when anyone was sick, reflecting a liturgical role for them as well (5:14). In the Pastoral Letters, coming from late in the New Testament period, the references to elders reflect some development of administrative and leadership roles within the churches. Titus 1:5-6 reflects a move to appoint elders in every town in Crete, whose necessary qualities are said to be "blameless, married only once, whose children are believers, not accused of debauchery and not rebellious." Immediately following this text, the requisite qualities for bishops are listed, raising the question of the relationship between the roles of elder and bishop. Some interpret the passage as reflecting that the bishops were a select group from among the elders. Because one of the most important functions of the presbyter/bishops was to rule and teach (1 Tim 5:17-18), and because no woman was permitted to have authority over or to teach men (1 Tim 2:12), it is not clear if there were still women presbyters in the churches as known to the Pastorals.

The very restrictiveness applied by the Pastorals on the ministerial roles of women, when taken in comparison with the generally gender-inclusive use of the term *presbyteroi* in Greek texts, as well as when compared with the evidence of female elders within councils of Jewish Diaspora communities, suggests that probably there had in fact been women among the presbyters in the earlier Christian communities. This supposition is undergirded by the evidence of the widely held Christian leadership roles of women as, for example, teachers (Acts 18:26), leaders of house churches (Rom 16:3-5), deacons (Rom 16:1-2), and apostles (Rom 16:7).

F. M. Gillman

See also DIAKONIA; EPISKOPOS; NEW TESTAMENT LETTERS; SANHEDRIN.

PRETERNATURAL GIFTS
See ORIGINAL JUSTICE.

PRIESTHOOD
In Christian tradition, priesthood can be looked at from the viewpoint of ministry

and function, and from the viewpoint of life in the Spirit that begins with baptism. Among Catholics, bishops and priests are consecrated to preach and proclaim the Gospel, to be pastors for the people of God, to offer the eucharistic sacrifice with their people, to forgive sins in the name of Christ, and to anoint the sick. Priesthood, when viewed in terms of ministerial function, is usually associated with the hierarchical structure of the church, although ministry is broader than priesthood. Not every ministry or form of service in the church requires ordination. Traditionally, ordained ministry has been understood in terms of three roles—bishop, priest, and deacon; but priesthood embraces only the "order" of bishops and the "order" of priests. The New Testament distinguishes the roles of overseer (bishop), elder (presbyter), and deacon in the day-to-day life of the Christian community. By the end of the second century, the basically pastoral functions of teaching and leadership exercised by bishops and presbyters were being combined with the cultic notion of priesthood drawn from the Old Testament.

Nevertheless, as Vatican II teaches, the whole people of God are priestly by virtue of their insertion into the mystery of Christ through baptism. Each Christian—ordained and lay alike—shares in the priesthood of Christ by offering "spiritual sacrifice" to God in worship (1 Pet 2:5, 9). One's entire life, rooted in faith and grounded in love, becomes a sacrifice that the believer offers to God, just as Jesus did (see *Lumen Gentium*, Dogmatic Constitution on the Church, no. 34). In the sixteenth century, Protestant Reformers stressed "the priesthood of all believers." They picked up on New Testament texts such as 1 Peter 2:5, 9 and Revelation 1:6 in order to downplay any sacramental, essential difference between those who have been baptized and those who have been ordained. A Catholic understanding of priesthood, however, presupposes a theology of church, sacraments, and ministry that balances office and function within the Christian community with the holiness to which all believers are called.

The concept of priesthood is found in many religious cultures. Egypt, for example, had its priests (Gen 47:22); so did the Greeks (Acts 14:13), not to mention the indigenous peoples of Central and South America, and Hinduism. Among the Jewish people, an established priesthood begins with Aaron and his sons (Exod 28:1). The priest exercised the role of mediator between the holiness of God and the people. For the Jews, the priest both prayed for his people and offered sacrifice on their behalf in order to praise and thank God, and to win forgiveness for their sins. According to the letter to the Hebrews, the Old Testament priesthood has been definitively replaced by Christ, who is the eternal High Priest. For the church, therefore, the priest shares in, and is a sign of, the priesthood of Christ, who is the one mediator between God and humanity (1 Tim 2:5).

William Reiser, s.j.

See also BAPTISM/CONFIRMATION; EUCHARIST; KOHEN; MINISTRY/ MINISTERIAL; ORDAINED MINISTRIES, SACRAMENT OF; SACRIFICE.

PRIEST IN JUDAISM
See KOHEN.

PRIESTLY SOURCE
Known also as "P," one of the sources used in the creation of the Pentateuch and book of Joshua; distinguished from the Yahwistic source (J), Elohistic source (E), and Deuteronomistic source (D). Reflecting the interests of the Temple priesthood in particular, the Priestly source is believed to stand behind much of the pentateuchal materials on the Temple cult, rules for the priesthood, and cultic purity.

Alan J. Avery-Peck

PRIMACY
A Christian theological term used to refer to the ecclesial role and dignity of a bishop who holds (normally because of his or her see) a leadership role among other bishops in a church. In the Anglican Communion, primacy belongs to the presiding bishop of each Province or national church and (but only in an honorary manner) to the archbishop of Canterbury. This is also the case with the patriarchs of the Eastern Orthodox churches and in reference to the ecumenical patriarch of Constantinople. Although in the Catholic Church it is possible to speak of primacy in relation to the patriarchs of the Eastern Catholic churches as well as in reference to the primates of churches of the Latin Rite, within Catholicism primacy usually refers to the Bishops of Rome (that is, the popes). Papal primacy includes, in the Catholic understanding, not only a dignity of honor. Primacy, in this case, implies and means the leadership role inherent in the ministry of Peter and his successors, as guarantor of the church's unity of faith and apostolic continuity, and as "visible head" of the church. Furthermore, primacy also requires that the Petrine ministry be recognized as bearing authority (jurisdiction) within the church. The exercise of primacy, within Catholicism and other Christian churches, has developed, changed, and varied throughout history, indicating that although primacy is nec-

essary (at least for Catholics), the specific manners through which it has been carried out in history might not be.

Orlando Espín

See also ANGLICAN COMMUNION; BISHOP (ORDINARY); ECCLESIOLOGY; JURISDICTION; ORTHODOX CHURCHES; PAPACY/PAPAL; PATRIARCH; PETRINE MINISTRY; PRIMATE/PRIMATIAL SEE; ROMAN CATHOLIC CHURCH.

PRIMAL RELIGIONS
See INDIGENOUS RELIGIOUS TRADITIONS.

PRIMATE/PRIMATIAL SEE
The title "Primate," in Catholic and Anglican usage, is currently given to the first bishop within a country or region. This bishop could be "first" because his or her see (the "Primatial See") was historically established before all others in the country or region, or because it later became the first in prestige and importance. Not all countries have an officially recognized Primate. The terms "primate" and "primatial" derive from the Latin words *primus* (in the masculine) or *prima* (in the feminine), both meaning "first."

Orlando Espín

See also ANGLICAN COMMUNION; ARCHBISHOP; BISHOP (EPISCOPACY); CANTERBURY, SEE OF; DIOCESE/ARCH-DIOCESE; METROPOLITAN; ROMAN CATHOLIC CHURCH; SEE; UTRECHT, SEE OF.

PRIMITIVE RELIGIONS
See INDIGENOUS RELIGIOUS TRADITIONS.

PRISCILLIANISM
The teachings of Priscillian of Avila, a fourth-century Spanish theologian. It is difficult to reconstruct Priscillian's actual teaching even from the few works from his circle that have survived. Priscillian and his followers were accused of teaching Gnosticism, Docetism, magic, and astrology. More likely, Priscillian taught a severe form of asceticism, denying the value of marriage and indeed of material creation itself. Priscillianists also appeared to hold a form of Monarchianism, stressing the unity of the Godhead.

Gary Macy

See also ASCETICISM/ASCETIC; DOCETISM; GNOSIS/GNOSTICISM; HERESY; MONAR-CHIANISM; PRISCILLIAN OF AVILA.

PRISCILLIAN OF AVILA
Around 370–5, Priscillian, then a layman, began to preach a rigid form of asceticism in Spain. His teaching met with popular success, but earned the emnity of Idatius, bishop of Mérida, and Ithacius, bishop of Ossonuba. In 380 the Council of Sarragosa condemned Priscillian's teaching. However, by then Priscillian had won the support of the bishops Instantius and Salvianus. These two bishops ordained Priscillian himself bishop of Avila. When Idatius and Ithacius convinced the Emperor Gratian to include Priscillian's teaching in the condemnation of Manichaeism, Priscillian journeyed to Rome to gain the support of Ambrose of Milan and of Damasus of Rome. He failed to win their support, but did manage to get the imperial condemnation reversed. Condemned at the Council of Bordeaux in 384, Priscillian appealed directly to the new emperor, Maximus. The influence of Idatius and Ithacius on Maximus prevailed, and the emperor ordered Priscillian and one of his followers to be beheaded, despite the protests of Martin of Tours. The first execution for heresy in Christian history, the act was roundly condemned,

resulting in Ithacius's deposition and Idatius's resignation.

Gary Macy

See also AMBROSE OF MILAN; DAMASUS OF ROME; HERESY; MARTIN OF TOURS; PRISCILLIANISM.

PRIVATIZATION OF RELIGION

The attempt, typical of the post-Enlightenment and of individualist "modernity," to make religious belief and commitment a matter of "private" (that is, individual) choice and, consequently, to consider all expressions of religious belief and commitment as proper to the "private sphere." The result, evidently, is the disappearance of religious belief and commitment from public life and from public debate. The premise on which the privatization of religion is based is that religious belief and commitment are indeed, and of their nature, private. This premise, of course, is not proven, and (as in the case of mainstream Christianity) it is diametrically opposed to the essentially public, social nature and message of most world religions. It is important to distinguish between privatization of religion, on one hand, and the constitutional separation between religious institutions and civil institutions and governments, on the other hand. The alternative to privatization of religion is not the breakdown of this constitutional separation, but the inclusion of religious belief and commitment in the public debate on such fundamental moral issues that affect the fabric and well-being of society. At the Second Vatican Council (for instance, in *Gaudium et Spes*), the Catholic Church explicitly emphasized the social, public nature of the church's mission and message, thereby challenging the premise of the privatization of religion. The social teaching of the Catholic Church strongly opposes privatization.

Orlando Espín

See also AGNOSTICISM; ATHEISM; BELLAH, ROBERT; BERGER, PETER L.; CIVIL RELIGION; ECONOMY; ENLIGHTENMENT IN WESTERN HISTORY; EPISTEMOLOGY; ETHICS, SOCIAL; EURO-AMERICAN THEOLOGIES; FAITH; FREEDOM; HABERMAS, JÜRGEN; IDEOLOGY (IDEOLOGIES); LUCKMANN, THOMAS; METZ, JOHANN; MODERNITY; POSTMODERNITY; RELIGION; SECULARISM; SECULARIZATION/ SECULAR/SECULARIZED; THEOLOGICAL ANTHROPOLOGY.

PROBABILIORISM

Probabiliorism is a method of moral reasoning developed in reaction to probabilism. This system holds that when the rightness or wrongness of an action is in doubt, one must abide by the relevant law unless the opinion in favor of liberty from the law is clearly more probable. In the event that opinions for both law and liberty are equally probable, the opinion for law must be followed.

Brian F. Linnane, s.j.

See also CASUISTRY; PROBABILISM.

PROBABILISM

Probabilism is a method of moral reasoning found in traditional Roman Catholic moral theology that holds that when the rightness or wrongness of a course of action is in doubt, a probable opinion in favor of liberty may be lawfully pursued. The option for liberty depends upon a reasonable and sincere opinion in favor of the action, even though the stronger evidence may favor a more stringent view. It is based upon the traditional reflex principle, "A doubtful law does not bind." Probabilism has been criticized for promoting moral laxity.

Brian F. Linnane, s.j.

See also CASUISTRY; PROBABILIORISM.

PROCESSIONS (DEVOTIONAL)

In Catholic usage, processions occur either as part of the official liturgy of the church, or as devotional practices. Devotional processions can be held to celebrate an event or a saint's feast day, or they can be held to ask God for mercy or for a specific favor. In either case, processions are always public, organized, and ritual manifestations of a community's faith. Indeed, they can be very important cultural, religious expressions in some Catholic communities, at times more culturally authentic than some official liturgical rites. Not frequent in modern Euro-American contexts, processions are readily found in many European, Latin American, Filipino, and U.S. Latino Catholic contexts.

Orlando Espín

See also CULTURE; DEVOTIONS; FAITH; INCULTURATION; LATIN AMERICAN CATHOLICISM; LATINO CATHOLICISM; LITURGY (IN CHRISTIANITY); MARIAN DEVOTIONS; POPULAR CATHOLICISM; RITUAL; SAINTS (CHRISTIAN), DEVOTION TO; SHRINE.

PROCESS THEOLOGY

Process theology—exemplified in the work of John Cobb, Lewis Ford, David Ray Griffin, Schubert Ogden, Marjorie Suchocki, and Daniel Day Williams—is an attempt to utilize the philosophies of Alfred North Whitehead and Charles Hartshorne for the presentation of Christian faith. Unlike much twentieth-century theology, process theology maintains that the most adequate presentation of Christian faith demands a conceptual expression that is explicitly metaphysical and cosmological in scope. Unlike traditional Christian theology, process theology rejects as incoherent the presuppositions of classical (Greek) metaphysics, that is, that "being" is ontologically more fundamental than "becoming," and thus classical theism. From this follows a wholesale reformulation of the doctrine of God and the understanding of the divine attributes—sometimes referred to as "panentheism"—through the position that the world is distinct but not separate from the being of God, and thus that God is internally related to the world. Such a fundamental shift has led process theologians to radical revisions of the traditional understanding of the doctrines of creation, sin, and evil, Christ and anthropology, and eschatology.

J. A. Colombo

See also IMMORTALITY; IMMUTABILITY; IMPASSIBILITY; OMNIPOTENCE; OMNISCIENCE; PANENTHEISM.

PROFESSED

According to the Catholic Church's Code of Canon Law, religious profession means that "members [of a religious community] assume by public vow the observance of the three evangelical counsels, are consecrated to God through the ministry of the Church, and are incorporated into the institute [that is, the religious community] with rights and duties defined by law" (Can. 654). Religious profession, therefore, is a promise, made in the presence of a believing community representing the entire church, to follow Christ poor, chaste, and obedient. "First profession," made at the conclusion of one's novitiate, is usually temporary and anticipates periodic renewal of vows; "final" profession, occurring at the end of one's program of formation, is perpetual. However, the expression "the professed" often designates those who have pronounced their final, solemn vows in a religious community.

Religious profession may be viewed as directing and intensifying one's baptismal commitment to embrace the Gospel with one's heart, mind, and soul. Religious life does not constitute a parallel church. On the contrary, through its public profession and in response to an impulse from the Spirit, a religious community seeks to embody in a way almost sacramental the spirit of faith, prayer, service, and zeal for the kingdom that characterizes the church as people of God. Similarly, the marriage profession embodies and sacramentalizes divine passion, love, and fidelity. Thus these two "professions" or public commitments complement one another for the upbuilding of the church.

William Reiser, S.J.

See also FORMATION; NOVICE; RELIGIOUS (VOWED); VOWS.

PROFESSION OF FAITH

A Profession of Faith is a public recitation of a creed, a short confession of faith, or a doxology that signals commitment to a group's religious vision, or is an act of worship, expressing praise or thanksgiving. The baptismal creeds of the early church, the Nicene-Constantinople and Apostles' Creeds, are examples of faith formulas used for public profession of faith. The Trisagion is a profession of faith used for worship in the liturgy of Eastern Churches. There are several kinds of profession formulas: creeds, doxologies, and faith confessions (short formulas of faith).

Patricia Plovanich

See also CONFESSION OF FAITH.

PROLEPSIS/PROLEPTIC

In rhetoric, the term refers to a speaker's anticipation of possible objections to an argument. Theologically, the term is usually associated with Wolfhart Pannenberg's theology as an event in the present that anticipates and instantiates the yet-to-be-realized future. For Pannenberg, the term is especially applied to Jesus Christ—and more specifically his resurrection—as a past event that anticipates the "end of history" and thus the full revelation of the being of God in relation to the world.

J. A. Colombo

See also PANNENBERG, WOLFHART.

PROMISE

In the Old Testament, promise came to be associated with God's part of covenant faithfulness. God promised Abraham: (a) that he would become a great nation; (b) that his name would be great; and (c) that he would be a blessing. God further promised that God would (d) bless those who blessed Abraham; (e) curse those who cursed him; and that (f) all the communities of the earth would find blessing in him (Gen 12:2-3).

Further, God made a covenant with Abraham promising that he would be the recipient of land "from the Wadi of Egypt to the Great River (the Euphrates), the land of the Kenites, the Kenizzites, the Kadmonites, the Hittites, the Perizzites, the Rephaim, the Amorites, the Canaanites, the Girgashites, and the Jebusites" (Gen 15:18-19). The land is often identified in the biblical text as "flowing with milk and honey" (for example, Exod 3:8), "the land which the Lord . . . promised" (for example, Exod 12:25). Promises God made to Abraham are reiterated as promises to Isaac (Gen 24:7) and Jacob (Gen 28:13-15) also.

While in many passages God's covenant—as promises—can be counted on for their fulfillment with no strings attached, the text also includes assertions that the fulfillment of the promises is conditional. Thus in Genesis 17:3-14, God's promises to Abraham—that he would become the father of a host of nations, that he would be exceedingly fertile, that kings would stem from him, and that the whole land of Canaan would be his permanent possession—are reiterated as future gifts, the fulfillment and reception of which are conditioned by the requirement that Abraham and his descendents be circumcised.

The New Testament contains several references to the promise made by God to Abraham (for example, Acts 7:17). God's promise includes a savior, who has come, Jesus (Acts 13:23; cf. 26:6-7). Paul stresses the unconditional character of God's promise to Abraham (Rom 4:13-20; 9:8-9).

Alice L. Laffey

PROPHECY

(Greek, *propheteia*). In the Bible, prophecy is the speech of a prophet that may be either oral or written in form. It may be poetic or nonpoetic. In ancient Israel, the prophet was a man or a woman who, at least as early as the seventh century B.C.E., was understood to be one who spoke for Yahweh. Deuteronomy 18:9-22 gives this seventh-century understanding of the origin and function of prophecy and prophets. The origin is understood to go back to the beginning of the relationship between Yahweh and Israel at Sinai/Horeb when the people were too frightened to stay close to the mountain and requested Moses to act as a "go between." According to Deuteronomy, from that time Yahweh

periodically raised up prophets to act as Moses did, that is, to bring the words of Yahweh to the people, especially at important points in their history. There is, however, an important distinction between Moses and all other prophets according to this text. Moses brought to Israel the Torah of Yahweh by which Israel was to live, and Moses spoke with God face to face. No other prophet was so favored, and no other prophet brought Torah to Israel. In addition to this reason for there being prophets and prophecy in Israel, Deuteronomy 18 also forbids the Israelites to seek information from the spirit world by any other means. They are forbidden to use necromancy, to consult the dead, or to use any means to consult the spirit world.

Prophecy may either be written or oral. In the Old Testament, most prophecy seems to be presented orally so that the assumption grew among scholars that most prophecy in ancient Israel was oral. However, this seems not always to have been the case, as is indicated by such passages as Isaiah 8:1, 16, and Jeremiah 36. These passages are clear evidence that at least some prophecy in the preexilic period was written. During the Babylonian Exile (587–538 B.C.E.) and afterwards, prophecy in written form probably became more and more the norm.

The word prophet is the translation equivalent of the Hebrew word *nabi*', meaning approximately "one called." The English word *prophet* is taken from the Greek *prophetes*, literally "one who speaks for another." Since the word of Yahweh that the prophet delivered frequently had to do with the "near future" consequences of an action or decision, prophecy came to be identified with foretelling the future. In ancient Israel, prophecy was not understood to announce an unalterable, predetermined future, but rather the probable consequences of past and present actions by individuals and/or the nation as a whole.

Although Deuteronomy 18 traces the beginning of prophecy to the time of Moses and makes him the great example of a prophet, prophecy in ancient Israel probably began much earlier. That this was the case may be indicated by evidence within the Bible as well as from the nations and cultures surrounding ancient Israel. In the book of Amos, the core of which probably dates from the middle of the eighth century B.C.E., prophets are equated with Nazirites, early examples of which were the judge Samson (Judges 13–16) and the judge and prophet Samuel. Samuel is also called a "seer," another early name for figures who are later called prophets. In the surrounding cultures, there were also figures who functioned as prophets of Yahweh did in ancient Israel, so that prophecy was not unique to Israel.

In early Christianity prophecy was a widespread phenomenon and is well attested in the New Testament. Both Jesus and John the Baptist are called prophets. In the writings of Paul, prophecy is listed as one of the gifts of the Spirit (1 Cor 14:23) and prophets are named alongside teachers and apostles as ministers with a divine calling. Prophecy continued in early Christianity, only slowly becoming unpopular.

Russell Fuller

PROPHET DANCE

About 1855, a prophet named Smohalla began to preach about visions he had received. This moment was one of the great struggles for the native peoples of the Plateau area, for they were caught between the settlers and the missionaries. In response to his teaching, a set of ceremonies developed, based on an already existing ritual called the Prophet Dance. Smohalla preached that, if the new ritual was followed, it would result in the elimination of the whites. The values of the white culture, especially agriculture, were condemned. The fault with agriculture was that it defiled Mother Earth. His teaching was also negative toward Christianity. It was thus a fully nativistic doctrine, and hostile in theory, if not in action. It became famous in the saga of Chief Joseph and the Nez Perce, for Joseph had clearly been influenced by Smohalla. It is thus a part of the tragedy of Native American life in the nineteenth century.

Kathleen Dugan

See also PROPHECY.

PROPHETIC BOOKS (IN THE OLD TESTAMENT)

The expression, "The Prophets" reflects the Hebrew word *han-nebiʾim* that refers to the third division of the Hebrew Scriptures in Jewish tradition. This third division of the Old Testament contains the "Former Prophets": Joshua, Judges, 1 and 2 Samuel, 1 and 2 Kings; and the "Latter Prophets": Isaiah, Jeremiah, Ezekiel; Hosea, Joel, Amos, Obadiah, Jonah, Micah, Nahum, Habakkuk, Zephaniah, Haggai, Zechariah, Malachi. The Former Prophets are considered to be historical books in Christian Bibles. The prophetic books proper in the Hebrew Scriptures include the following books in this order: *The Three:* Isaiah, Jeremiah, Ezekiel; *The Twelve:* Hosea, Joel, Amos, Obadiah, Jonah, Micah, Nahum, Habakkuk, Zephaniah, Haggai, Zechariah, Malachi.

The order is identical in the Protestant canon with the exception that Lamentations follows Jeremiah, who was traditionally understood to be the author, and the book of Daniel follows Ezekiel. In the Catholic canon, in addition, Baruch follows Lamentations. In the Hebrew Scriptures, this large group is further divided into two groups, the Three and the Twelve. It is evident there were several factors involved in the ordering of these compositions. One concern seems to have been the apparent date of activity. Isaiah was active in the eighth century B.C.E. and so precedes Jeremiah and Ezekiel who were active in the seventh century B.C.E. Why the Three precede the Twelve is uncertain except that this order is attested already in the early second century B.C.E. (Sirach 48–49). It is possible that a factor in the relative ordering of the Three and the Twelve had to do with the practice of copying the Twelve on a single scroll; this is attested as early as the middle of the second century B.C.E. (4QXII^b) in manuscript evidence and may be implied by Sirach 49:10 that mentions "the bones of the Twelve Prophets." The Three may also have been copied on a single scroll, of about the same length as the scroll of the Twelve. Jewish tradition is unanimous in placing the Three before the Twelve, although the order of the Three is not always that given above.

The present collection of prophetic books as it exists in Jewish and Christian traditions developed slowly over many centuries. One of the considerations that motivated the preservation and continuous interpretation of the prophetic books was the understanding that they contained the words of Yahweh to Israel. In Deuteronomy 18, the only way to determine whether or not a prophet's words were truly the words of Yahweh was to wait to see if they came to pass. If they did, then they were Yahweh's words, if they did not, then they were not Yahweh's words. This idea would have necessitated the copying and continuous study and interpretation of the oracles delivered by prophets. This would have led naturally to the growth of collections of prophetic oracles attributed to specific prophets. As the word of Yahweh, these collections of oracles would have been considered sacred very early on.

Russell Fuller

PROPHETISM (IN WORLD RELIGIONS)

Historically speaking, the prophetic role had its origins in the ancient Near Eastern monotheism of Judaism and was also central in forming the doctrines of revelation, divinity, and moral life in Christianity and Islam. However, aspects of prophetism have been observed globally in certain eras and communities, particularly in cases of human mediumship of communications between divinity and humankind and in calls for moral or ritual reform based upon divine instigation.

In the phenomenological sense, one could see the various traditions associated with shamans, oracles, and mediums as being in the same realm as prophets. Or, conversely, one could interpret the monotheistic prophetic role arising out of or as a special case of mediumship, an association most clearly indicated in the case of Muhammad's early reception in Arabia, where his behavior reminded audiences of the Arab shamans called *kahin*.

Indeed, there are recorded instances of shamans or oracles making divine pronouncements that have been regarded as politically volatile for their message's incitement to new moral or ritual reforms. The most well-known example of this in early modern times was the Paiute Native American shaman Wovoka who led Plains Indians in the late nineteenth century to dance and chant in response to his visions, with the promise that the ghosts of ancestors would return to install the oppressed people to their proper status. The widespread cargo cults of Polynesia that began as a response to the incursions of Western peoples and their technologies were often led by similar mediums; they typically reported visions that proclaimed means by which communities could bring back their ancestors who would return with the technological cargo that would restore the people to equal status with the intruders.

In Asia, where the ideal of the sage dominated the religious imagination, shaping a very different sense of the sacred as realizable within the individual's experience, there were individual teachers who at times stood up to "speak truth to power" and challenge prevailing norms based upon divine inspiration. In India, there were *bhakti* saints such as Kabir and Ravidas who in the fifteenth century challenged the norms of the caste system based upon divine revelations. In medieval Japan, the Buddhist reformers Nichiren (1222–82) and Shinran (1173–1263) challenged their societies (and other Buddhist schools) based upon revelations from Buddhist divinities, incurring the wrath of the imperial court. Other Buddhist monks, including modern reformers, may adopt aspects of the prophetic role.

One final aspect of prophetism in comparative perspective concerns its prevalence in popular religions, particularly movements originating in the lower classes of society and aimed against the abuses, injustices, and hypocrisies of the ruling-class elite. Prophets have arisen who connect the local struggle with the perennial truths of the tradition, often offering new interpretations of doctrine.

Todd T. Lewis

PROPHETS (IN CHRISTIANITY)

Inheriting the long-standing Hebrew tradition of prophecy, Christianity has from its beginning seen the prophet as one who is called by God to speak for God. In some branches of Christianity the term "prophet" has come to designate a person who is, thanks to special revelations from God, able to foretell the future. In other Christian traditions, however, the broader biblical meaning of the term has been retained; in this case, the prophet is the one who is called by God to proclaim divine judgment on sinful personal or social behavior. In this way, the prophet invites a person or the people as a whole to repentance and conversion. In the New Testament, Jesus is called "prophet" (for example, John 9:17) and calls himself a prophet (Luke 4:24). John the Baptist plays the role of prophet (Luke 3:2-18), responding to God's word by calling the people to repentance. As Jesus made clear, taking others to task for their failings usually brings rejection and even persecution to the prophet (Luke 4:24). Indeed, the deaths by execution of both Jesus and John illustrate the all-too-common price to be paid by those who dare to raise prophetic voices. Nevertheless, from the first to the twenty-first century, Christian prophets have come forward to call society and the church itself to change direction and to take up the task of building the reign of God on earth. Twentieth-century examples of Christian prophets include Dorothy Day and Martin Luther King Jr. of the United States, and Oscar Arnulfo Romero of El Salvador.

James B. Nickoloff

See also PROPHECY.

PROPHETS/NEVI'IM (IN ISRAEL)

See PROPHECY.

PROPITIATION

A term generally meaning the appeasement or placation of the wrath of God by prayer or sacrifice when an offense against God has been committed. The wrath of God is not understood to be a divine emotion, that is, God's angry frame of mind, but rather God's righteous reaction to evil and sin.

Propitiation is often confused with, and must be distinguished from expiation, denoting the means by which sin is obliterated. Expiation wipes away human sin, while propitiation, from the human perspective, is seen to end the wrath of God. Put another way, these nonsynonymous terms speak of two dimensions in looking at the sinful situation of humanity and the need for atonement (reconciliation, peace, harmony with God): expiation relates to the sin that causes humanity's alienation from God, thus the transgression violating God's covenant, and the issue of how it is to be blotted out; propitiation, in contrast, focuses on God's justifiable anger with transgressors, an anger God presumably maintains until appeasement or placation takes place. Propitiation is thus concerned with warding off or mollifying God's divine wrath.

F. M. Gillman

See also ATONEMENT, CHRISTIAN; SACRIFICE; WRATH OF GOD.

PROPORTIONALISM

Proportionalism is a method, popular among Roman Catholic moral theologians in the U.S.A. and in Western Europe, for determining whether individual actions are morally right or wrong. Specifically, it challenges the notion that a physical description of the action itself, without some account of the circumstances surrounding the action and intentions of the agent, can reveal the moral status of the action. A physical description of the action and its goal can only reveal physical (premoral, ontic) evil or good. While there is a basic obligation to avoid physical evil, some physical evil may be tolerated or justified in the face of a *proportionate* reason. Proportionate reason indicates that the physical evil is tolerated in the service of a greater good. A proportionate reason does not render physical evil good or even morally neutral; it simply justifies it in this case. An example of premoral or physical evil is killing; killing is always to be avoided and never a good; however, in cases of a just war or reasonable self-defense, it may be tolerated.

Proportionalism is most often confused with *consequentialism* (the idea that a [potentially] good outcome provides a moral justification for any action). No proportionalist, however, would suggest that a good intention or dire circumstances can justify an action judged to be morally evil. When an action is understood as morally evil, nothing can justify it. Thus if a killing is understood as murder (immoral killing), no good intention can justify it. Critics of this approach argue that it is not practical because the calculation of physical evils and goods in a given action is beyond the ability of the average moral agent. This is particularly problematic, in their view, because they understand any comparison among diverse physical goods or evils to be impossible. Finally, it is argued that proportionalism undermines the possibility that some actions can be characterized as intrinsically evil; that is, that they are always grievously wrong regardless of circumstance or intention.

Brian F. Linnane, s.j.

See also DOUBLE EFFECT; EVIL; FUCHS, JOSEF; MCCORMICK, RICHARD A.;

MORAL THEOLOGY/CHRISTIAN ETHICS; SIN, PERSONAL; VERITATIS SPLENDOR.

PROSELYTISM

The meaning of the word proselytism has changed over the centuries. Proselytism originally referred to converting outsiders or foreigners to the practice of Judaic law. People who have experienced a conversion desire that others share the same beliefs and feelings. As early Christianity developed from Judaism, the disciples set out to spread the Good News of salvation (Acts). Not only did they feel that the "end time" was near and the need for salvation was urgent; they believed that Jesus demanded it. In general, proselytism was the missionary process of bringing the Gospel and its way of life to non-Christians. However, as Europe became Christian, proselytism lost its energy.

Discoveries of the New World rekindled missionary activity. Catholic missionary activities flourished, sometimes to the detriment of the peoples being converted. Political and cultural factors in the colonization process often demeaned and oppressed the people while attempting to destroy their culture in the name of religion. In Europe, the Protestant Reformation grew and new forms of Christianity appeared, demanding a different belief system and lifestyle. Proselytism became essential to their mission. Some groups became very exclusive and countercultural in lifestyle, publicly preaching and stressing their new way of life. In their fervor, some Evangelical and fundamentalist denominations set about trying to convert Catholics and Christians of other denominations as well as the unchurched. In the latter part of this century, many Christian sects and cults developed that used very deceptive and coercive methods to attract vulnerable young people.

In the ecumenical spirit of today, most Protestant denominations frown upon subversive proselytism, while not denying the need for missionary activity. The mainline churches look for what they have in common and often collaborate in issues of social concerns and ministries, sharing facilities and personnel. Their missionary activities reach out to the unchurched. Their efforts concentrate on humanizing the world in preparation for the reign of God rather than simply preaching and demanding strict adherence to older ways of life.

For Roman Catholics, Vatican II, in its affirmation of a more scriptural vision of the nature of the Catholic Church, used images like people of God and pilgrim people to describe Catholics. In this self-awareness, Roman Catholics changed their missionary emphasis. Missionaries became more aware of the extensive length of time conversion takes. The Popes, especially Pius XII, John XXIII, Paul VI, and John Paul II, have taught that missionary activity must continue, but it must be a way of life, not just a preaching of sermons and formal teaching. In Catholic vocabulary, the word *evangelization* took on the positive, missionary meaning of proselytism. Evangelization must respect different cultures. It rejects all forms of coercion or use of hidden enticement of any kind. Conversion has to be a freely chosen process.

Since the fall of the Iron Curtain in Eastern Europe and the emigration movements in Africa and Latin America, fundamentalist groups have made inroads into the Catholic population. In a time of chaos, uncertainty, emigration, and proliferation of ideologies and religions, such single-mindedness can be very attractive. Many of the new groups have made a point of filling ordinary human needs of people in transition and this has proven very effective. In the Catholic Church, theological and pastoral discussions are underway concerning the balance needed in the missionary/teaching aspects of the church and provision of human services in its missionary activities. Within the Catholic Church, the word *proselytism* now generally means using enticement or forms of coercion in attempting to make converts, while in some Protestant circles the word continues to be synonymous with missionary activity.

M. Jane Gorman

See also EVANGELICALS; EVANGELISM; EVANGELIZATION; FUNDAMENTALISM; MISSIOLOGY; MISSIONARIES; MISSIONS.

PROSPER OF AQUITAINE (?–455?)

Born end of the fourth century, died after 455. Prosper was a classically trained layman who strongly defended Augustine's theology during the semi-Pelagian controversy in southern France in the first half of the fifth century. Prosper spent his last years in the service of Pope Leo I. Besides his theological tracts, Prosper also wrote a history of the world that he carried up to the year 455.

Gary Macy

See also AUGUSTINE OF HIPPO; LEO I THE GREAT, POPE; SEMI-PELAGIANISM.

PROTESTANTISM/PROTESTANT

A movement originating in the Protestant Reformation of the sixteenth century and, along with Roman Catholicism and Eastern Orthodoxy, one of the three main branches of Christianity. Although it had a number of antecedents in the Middle Ages, its beginning is usually counted from the year 1517, when Luther's protest against the sale of indulgences drew attention to his theology. In its classical expression, as it developed in the sixteenth century, Protestantism takes four main forms: Lutheranism, Calvinism, Anabaptism, and Anglicanism.

Lutheranism stems directly from Martin Luther. Its original strongholds are in Germany and Scandinavia. It holds fast to Luther's doctrines of justification by faith alone, of the final authority of Scripture above tradition, of the priesthood of all believers, and of the sanctity of the common (that is, not monastic) life. Doctrinally, it is distinguished from other branches of Protestantism by its insistence on the real and physical presence of Christ in the Eucharist. Its main doctrinal statements, uniting the various national and regional Lutheran churches, are the *Augsburg Confession*, and the Formula of Concord.

Calvinism is the name usually given to the theology shared by the Reformed Churches, most of which is derived from Calvin and Zwingli. Essentially, the Reformed Churches hold to the same basic Protestant doctrines as do Lutherans. However, rather than affirming the physical presence of Christ in Communion, Calvin and his followers hold that Christ is really, although spiritually, present in the sacrament. Also, going beyond Luther's insistence on justification, Calvinism tends to emphasize sanctification as the necessary corollary of justification, and as the goal of human existence.

In the seventeenth century, Calvinists in the Netherlands split over issues having to do with predestination. While the stricter Calvinists insisted on absolute, unconditional predestination—the total depravity of all humankind apart from grace, limited atonement (that is, Christ died only for the elect), irresistible grace, and the perseverance of the saints (that is, the elect cannot fall from grace)—their opponents, the Arminians, rejected those doctrines. At the Synod of Dort in 1619, the position of the Arminians was rejected, and ever since "Calvinism" has come to mean, not only what Calvin actually held, but also the shape this tradition took in response to the Arminian challenge. Besides the Canons of Dort, the Reformed Churches hold to other creeds and confessions—most notably, the Westminster Confession.

Anabaptism seems to have arisen independently in various places at about the same time. In general, Anabaptists held that the church should seek to be as close to the New Testament church as possible. Since that was a church one entered by conversion and a profession of faith, the Anabaptists rejected infant baptism and insisted that those who had received that rite must be baptized again. Hence the name "Anabaptists," given to them by their enemies, and meaning "re-baptizers." At first some Anabaptists were quite revolutionary, and some even sought to bring about God's reign by force. Eventually, however, the pacifist wing of the movement won out, and to this day most Anabaptists are pacifists.

The Anglican Communion stems from the Reformation in England. Henry VIII's marital troubles led him to declare himself head of the Church of England, and this provided the opportunity for those who wished to reform the church along lines parallel to what was happening on the Continent. It was under the reigns of Edward VI and Elizabeth I that Anglicanism took its definitive shape. While generally holding to Protestant doctrine (usually a moderate form of Calvinism), the Church of England kept many of the traditional rites and structures of Roman Catholicism—so much so, that many Anglicans prefer not to be classified as Protestants. Its main doctrinal statement is the Thirty-Nine Articles promulgated in 1562. However, Anglicanism's most distinctive trait is the Book of Common Prayer that sets the ceremonial practices of the church.

During the seventeenth and eighteenth centuries, "Protestant Orthodoxy" gained hold of most Protestant churches. This was a movement that sought to define every theological issue, with the result that there were major controversies over minute points of doctrine.

Partly as a reaction to Protestant Orthodoxy, and partly as a reaction against the rationalism of the times, the eighteenth century saw the rise of a number of movements that emphasized personal piety and Christian experience over strict rational orthodoxy. Among Lutherans in Germany, this took the form of Pietism. Among Husites from Moravia who sought refuge in the German estates of Count Zinzendorf, the followers of the movement were called "Moravians." In Great Britain, it took the form of Methodism. And in the British colonies in the Western Hemisphere, it gave rise to the Great Awakening. One of the traits of these various movements was their interest in missionary work. Thus, the German Pietists began a school devoted to the training of missionaries at the University of Halle, the Moravians soon spread throughout the world, and the Methodists did likewise.

The two most important developments within Protestantism in the nineteenth century had to do with theology and with missions. In the field of theology, many Protestant theologians saw the promises of the modern age with great optimism, and sought to adapt their understanding of the Gospel to modernity. This gave rise to Protestant liberalism that gave great credence to modern historical studies of the Bible and of the Christian tradition, and that sought to demonstrate that Christianity—and Protestantism within it—was the form of religion best suited for the modern world. (Since, at the same time, popes such as Pius IX were rejecting and condemning much of modernity, it may well be said that Protestantism and Roman Catholicism were further apart in the nineteenth century than they had been in the sixteenth.) As a reaction to liberalism, some of the more conservative elements in the United States began stressing the "fundamentals" of the Christian faith—the inerrancy of Scripture, miracles, the virgin birth, the substitutionary atonement, and the second coming of Jesus—thus giving rise to fundamentalism.

It was in its missionary enterprise that nineteenth-century Protestantism made enormous strides. This was the time of the great advance of the British Empire, and of other Protestant colonial powers such as the Netherlands, Denmark, and Germany. Sometimes supported by colonial interests, and sometimes diametrically opposed to them, Protestant missionaries established churches in almost every country in the world. By the end of the century, these churches had begun to develop their own indigenous leadership, and many had undertaken the task of preaching to their own nations. Thus, it was the nineteenth century that made Protestantism a worldwide movement.

One of the most important developments within Protestantism in the twentieth century was the growth of the ecumenical movement. Much of this stemmed from the need for unity that missionaries had discovered abroad. Thus, the World Missionary Conference that gathered at Edinburgh in 1910 is often seen as the beginning point of the modern ecumenical movement. Soon there were significant reunions whereby various denominations in the mission field merged into one—the most famous of which is the Church of South India. By 1948, a series of conferences and organizations stemming from the meeting at Edinburgh gave rise to the World Council of Churches, which also included a number of Orthodox churches. With the pontificate of John XXIII and the Second Vatican Council, Roman Catholicism officially became part of this quest after Christian unity.

Another important development within Protestantism in the twentieth century was the growth of Pentecostalism. Originally a relatively isolated phenomenon that appeared sporadically in various places, in the twentieth century Pentecostalism became a powerful force, to the point that in many countries its membership far surpassed that of the more traditional Protestant denominations.

Finally, it should be noted that the twentieth century was also a period of great theological activity among Protestants. The various currents of the nineteenth century continued well into the twentieth. During the second quarter of the century, neo-orthodoxy, led by Karl Barth, became a powerful theological force, and put an end to the supremacy of liberalism. During the second half of the century, various contextual theologies emerged, each with its own significant contribution to the whole—black theologies, feminist theologies, Latino theologies, and so on. In general, these various contexts provided bridges to their Roman

Catholic counterparts, and thus toward the end of the twentieth century Protestant theology was becoming more ecumenical than ever.

Justo L. González

See also ANABAPTISTS; ANGLICAN COMMUNION; ARMINIANISM; ATONEMENT, CHRISTIAN; AUGSBURG CONFESSION; BARTH, KARL; CALVIN, JOHN; CONCORD, FORMULA AND BOOK OF; EUCHARIST; FUNDAMENTALISM; HUS, JOHN; JOHN XXIII, POPE; LUTHER, MARTIN; METHODIST CHURCHES; PIETISM; REFORMED CHURCHES; VATICAN, SECOND COUNCIL OF THE; ZWINGLI, ULRICH.

PROVIDENCE

As a Christian term, it generally refers to God's loving care and wise guidance of the world. Contemporary theologies differ in their interpretation and explanation of the meaning of providence. Most of the differences are based on the various (and prior) understandings of "God," grace, salvation, human freedom, autonomy of nature, and so forth. The term itself preceded Christianity, referring (in Greek Stoic philosophy) to the power and knowledge of God in the direction of the world. During the first three or four centuries of the church, Christian authors emphasized the loving and merciful motives of God's providence. With Augustine of Hippo (fifth century), and his theology of grace and salvation, there began a shift backwards to a Stoic-like understanding of providence (that is, emphases on divine power and knowledge). The Christian controversies on grace and salvation have been mostly responsible for the varying meanings providence has had in Christian history.

Orlando Espín

See also FREEDOM; GOD; GRACE; JUSTIFICATION; MERCY; NATURE, HUMAN; OMNIBENEVOLENCE; OMNIPOTENCE; REIGN OF GOD; SALVATION.

PROVINCE

This term has two meanings in current Western Catholic and Anglican usage. (1) The name of a group of dioceses that together form an ecclesiastical jurisdiction. (2) The name of a territory under the jurisdiction of a superior within a religious order or congregation. This administrative territory includes a number of the local houses of the religious order or congregation.

Orlando Espín

See also CANON LAW; CONGREGATIONS (ORDERS); ECCLESIASTICAL PROVINCE; ORDINARY (CANONICAL).

PRUDENCE

Aristotle's *phronesis*, a virtue that sought the mean of right action through experience, deliberation, and counsel, was translated into Latin by the word *prudentia*, prudence. With justice, courage, and temperance, it was considered by traditional Catholic theology to be one of the four cardinal (*cardo*, "hinge") virtues, and the principal among those, governing all other moral virtues (*ST* I–II, q. 61). For Thomas Aquinas, prudence was the human correspondent of divine providence, in that it looked to the future and to the final end (happiness), and to the common, rather than the individual good (II–II, q. 47, a. 10).

Beginning with Thomas Hobbes, prudence has not fared so well among modern thinkers. For Hobbes, prudence was merely a memory of a succession of events in time past that gave some insight into future efforts (*Leviathan*, ch. 46). Kant thought prudence was another name for "self-interest" and so disparaged it, teaching that morality is the self-disinterested pursuit of moral duty (*Fundamental Principles of the Metaphysics of Morals*, II, 33). Aladsair MacIntyre has an extended study of prudence in chapters 12–16 of *Whose Justice? Which Rationality?* and submits what is perhaps the best summary of the modern understanding: "a cautious habit of consideration and forethought discerning what may be advantageous or hurtful in life" (278).

G. Simon Harak, s.j.

See also HAPPINESS.

PRUDENTIUS (348–410?)

Aurelius Clemens Prudentius was a Spaniard by birth. After a distinguished career in civil administration, he spent his retirement writing a series of lengthy Christian poems. The three important collections of his poems include the *Hymns for Every Day*, the *Martyrs' Crowns*, and *Spiritual Combat*. His poems influenced many later Christian poets, and extracts from his poetry are used in the daily Office.

Gary Macy

PRZYWARA, ERICH (1889–1972)

German Jesuit theologian who wrote for the German Jesuit theological journal *Stimmen der Zeit*. Przywara is renowned for his masterful explication of the *analogia entis* against Barth's criticism of analogical reflection. Przywara argued that symbolization was an intrinsic mode of human understanding, indispensable for thought. He defended the theological propriety of analogy as rooted in the Creator–creature relationship that does not dissolve the distinction between God and the world. Przywara proposed to understand the God–world relationship in the mode of a polarity in tension such that each pole's independence is preserved, yet the divine mystery remains transcendent. The dynamic relationship is conveyed in symbols, but the divine mystery remains greater than symbols can express. His work has influenced the theologies of von Balthasar, Joseph Ratzinger, and Walter Kasper, among others.

Patricia Plovanich

See also SYMBOL.

PSALM(S)/PSALTER

The word psalm comes from the Greek *psalmos* meaning "song of praise." Psalter is derived from the same form and usually refers to the canonical collection of psalms in the Bible. Psalter may also refer to a separately printed volume of the biblical psalms to be used for liturgical purposes or private devotion. The term psalm translates the Hebrew word *tehillah* that also refers to a song of praise. Tehillah refers to all of the psalms in the canonical collection, even those that are not strictly speaking songs of praise. The biblical psalms are traditionally associated with David, Israel's greatest king, because he was known already in his time as a musician or at least a patron of music. Scholars think the biblical psalms range in date from the early history of Israel until the postexilic period. Many of the psalms have introductory titles that were composed in ancient times in attempts to associate some of the psalms with David or even with a specific event in his life. Scholars think the psalms were used in the worship of God and were part of formal liturgies. They seem to have been performed to music, as some elements of the titles and other terms in the psalms indicate (see Psalm 150). The Psalter of the Jewish and Protestant canons has five sections or books with a total of one hundred and fifty psalms. The divisions are: Book 1: 1–41; Book 2: 42–72; Book 3: 73–89; Book 4: 90–106; Book 5: 107–150. The division and numbering of the psalms in the Hebrew Old Testament is not identical to that in the Greek Septuagint:

Hebrew Old Testament	Septuagint
1–8	1–8
9/10	9
11–113	10–112
114–115	113
116:1-9	114
116:10-19	115
117–146	116–145
147:1-11	146
147:12-20	147
148–150	148–150

There are different types of psalms, perhaps originally for different types of liturgies. The most frequent type of psalm is the hymn—a psalm of praise. A good example of a hymn is Psalm 8. Another type of psalm is the lament. A lament is a composition describing the terrible situation of the psalmist and implores God to intervene to right the situation. There are laments that were composed for an individual, and there are laments that are clearly for the nation or community as a whole. There are also psalms that have at their center the person of the king. Good examples are Psalm 2 and Psalm 110; these are known as royal psalms. There are also psalms that seem to have a great interest in wisdom, such as Psalm 119. The biblical psalms have been used both for formal communal prayer as well as individual devotion for millennia.

Russell Fuller

PSALTER (CHRISTIAN)

In Christian usage, the term Psalter, derived from the Greek word for a stringed instrument that in ancient and medieval times accompanied singing, refers to the collection of the one hundred fifty psalms of the Old Testament viewed as a prayer-book for both private and liturgical use. The New Testament has various references to the book of Psalms (for example, Matt 22:43-45; Luke 20:42; 24:44) and references to incorporation of psalms into communal prayer (for example, 1 Cor 14:26; Eph 5:19; Col 3:16), although these latter references may be alluding to free and personal compositions of a more charismatic nature. In its own original compositions of psalms, especially in Luke 1–2 and in the hymns of Revelation, the New Testament quotes or alludes to many of the Hebrew psalms. Early Christian writers interpreted many of the psalms as messianic and specifically christological, especially Psalms 2, 22, 69, 110, and 118. Until recent years, the prevailing scholarly opinion was that early Christians simply adopted the Hebrew Psalter as their own and that the Christian use of the psalms grew directly out of Jewish synagogue practice (Dugmore). This position has been rejected as unnuanced by many modern scholars (Beckwith, Bradshaw, Taft). More likely, Christians adopted the universal practice of praying daily at fixed times, one also found in Judaism. As for the structure of the service or the precise selection of psalms, there seems to be no clear evidence to support a direct influence from Jewish practice, one that varied greatly during the early Christian era.

The development of the Psalter as a separate liturgical book has its roots in the fourth century with the general development of ritual patterns after the practices of major Christian centers and the adoption of fixed liturgical texts. In the West, the Latin Psalters were translated from the Septuagint. Such books were used for the processional chants and for the responsory between readings during Eucharist, and for the Divine Office. Thus they often included additional biblical canticles, collections of concluding collects to individual psalms (psalm prayers), and antiphons. The oldest complete text is the Old Latin Psalter of North African origin, preserved in the manuscript of the Verona Psalter (sixth–seventh centuries). In general usage, this was replaced by the Gallican Psalter, translated by Jerome in 392, so-called because of its use in Gallican liturgy. In Italy another translation, long attributed to Jerome, but now disputed, known as the Roman Psalter, was used until Pope Pius V (1566–72) when it was replaced by the Gallican Psalter due to the reforms of the Council of Trent. Another translation made by Jerome around 400 based on the Hebrew book of Psalms, while sometimes included in a parallel column with the other translations, was never widely used.

Many devotional Psalters for nonliturgical use, often with elaborate illuminations, some demonstrating a very high level of artistry, survive from both East (Greek) and West (Latin). The oldest extant manuscripts date from the ninth–tenth centuries and continue in abundance until the fifteenth century, attesting to their popularity among the laity as well as clergy. These illuminated Psalters changed with the advent of the printing press, but continued to be popular. Since that time, among Roman Catholics, various forms of prayerbooks, some including psalm selections, have been widely used.

Since the sixteenth century, the Reformation, with its insistence on vernacular and biblical prayer, has led to the development of multiple translations and versions of metrical Psalters that allow for the popular singing of the psalms. The notable exception is in Lutheran Germany with its emphasis on the use of the chorale.

The liturgical reforms of the Second Vatican Council and those of the more liturgical Protestant churches have led to a fuller, richer, and more varied use of the psalms in the churches of the West. In the Roman Rite, this is demonstrated by the use of the whole or at least larger sections of a sung responsorial psalm (in place of the more truncated gradual), the attempts at the popular restoration of the Liturgy of the Hours, especially Morning and Evening Prayer, and the emphasis on the psalms as a basis for the composition of modern liturgical hymnody.

Dennis W. Krouse

See also EUCHARIST; GREGORIAN CHANT; LITURGY (IN CHRISTIANITY); LITURGY OF THE HOURS; LITURGY OF THE WORD; MASS; PSALM; RESPONSORIAL PSALM.

PSEUDO-DIONYSIUS

See DIONYSIUS THE AREOPAGITE (PSEUDO).

PSYCHOLOGY OF RELIGION

Augustine of Hippo is sometimes described as the first psychologist for his probing into the depths of his "restless heart" in the fifth century C.E., but psychology in the modern sense grew out of the nineteenth century's focus on subjectivity and feelings. The discussion of religious subjectivity (as opposed to objectivity) ranged from the atheism of Ludwig Feuerbach to the theism of Søren Kierkegaard. Feelings (as opposed to beliefs) were the basis of Friedrich Schleiermacher's definition of religion. Then came efforts to understand human behavior, including religious behavior, in scientific terms. In England, Sir Francis Galton published his "Statistical Inquiries into the Efficacy of Prayer" in 1872. In the United States, William James' monumental *Varieties of Religious Experience* appeared in 1902, and G. Stanley Hall established the *Journal of Religious Psychology* in 1904. Within the next few years, Germans began to study mythology and folk religion. The French turned to studies of the physiology and psychology of ecstatic experiences, some of which considered these states to be pathological. However, psychological studies of religion are not always sympathetic to religion.

Sigmund Freud, the founder of twentieth-century psychoanalysis, declared that religion is neurotic, originating in a fixation of infantile desires to be protected by an omnipotent father. The Heavenly Father is a projected illusion that is then supported by a delusional belief system and threats of divine retribution for those who dare to rebel. In the next generation of psychoanalysts, Carl Jung, whom Freud at one time intended to be his successor, described religion in more positive terms. To him, the archetypes that arise from the "collective unconscious" lead to the myths and rituals of religion that are basic to the process of "individuation." In the generation after that, Erik Erickson likewise found positive correlations between maturity and religion. Recent psychodynamic developments include the Object Relations school that focuses on the infant's fragmented world of "split objects" (good mother/bad mother, and so forth), sometimes describing the therapist's role in quasi-

religious terms, as a "priest of wholeness," for example. Such descriptions are common in psychological literature.

Twentieth-century biological and chemical studies of religion begin with G. Stanley Hall's "genetic" psychology of religion, and a view of Jesus as the product of creative evolution. Beginning in the 1920s, studies of "temperament" (physical/emotional typologies) examined religious figures like Martin Luther (pyknic) and John Calvin (leptomorphic). Beginning in the 1930s, "heliotropic" theories relate the religious imagery of light to what has come to be known as "seasonal affective disorder." Studies of the psychophysiology of meditation practices began in the 1940s. The relation of hallucinatory drugs to religious experience was examined in the famous "miracle of Marsh chapel" experiments of Walter Pahnke in the 1960s. More recently, Julian Jaynes relates religious experience to theories of the bilaterality of the brain developed by William Penfield and others, claiming that until about 1,000 C.E. the main function of the gods was to guide people in novel situations by means of audible voices originating in the right hemisphere of the brain.

Behavioral theories led from reflex arc and stimulus-response theories early in the century to B. F. Skinner, who claims that inquiries into the subjective mind are a waste of time and energy, that religion is a fiction used to rationalize behavior by "adventitious reinforcement" and "miracle working" rather than operant conditioning and positive reinforcement. This point of view has been modified recently by cognitive behaviorism that accepts the importance of thinking and strives to change behavior by transforming "dysfunctional attitudes" in a way reminiscent of the religious positive thinking of Norman Vincent Peale.

"Descriptive" theories began with William James' *Varieties of Religious Experience*. In religious experience, he argues, people's lives are transformed emotionally in dramatic and positive ways. These transformations are accountable only as shifts in attitude that go beyond rationality. James' work anticipates the "phenomenological" description of religious experience as the experience of awe in Rudolf Otto's *The Idea of the Holy* (1917). Phenomenology then mixes with Existentialism in ways that are often sympathetic to religion later in the century, as in Victor Frankl and Rollo May. From early in the century, Martin Buber and other "personalists" have had a sizable effect on psychotherapy, helping to create the "humanistic" school of psychotherapy, including Abraham Maslow's description of "peak experiences."

Psychology of religion continues to reexamine its roots as well as to branch out in new directions. Paul Ricoeur, for example, acknowledges the validity of much of Freud's criticism of religion, but he insists that, properly understood and practiced, religion can be a transformer of narcissism rather than a sign of neurosis. Psychology of religion is forever growing and changing.

Jesse Thomas

See also BUBER, MARTIN; FREUD, SIGMUND; JAMES, WILLIAM; JUNG, CARL; OTTO, RUDOLF; RICOEUR, PAUL.

PUBLICAN

A collector of taxes or tolls in the Roman Empire. The Romans distributed contracts for tax collection to wealthy people who in turn hired locals in each region to do the actual collection. An example of a person working within this system is Zacchaeus in Luke 19:1, the chief publican in Jericho.

The publicans were responsible for turning over the taxes to the government, and they were free to assess and extort additional taxes as profit for themselves. Due to the corruption pervading their ranks, tax collectors were widely despised in the Roman Empire. This is reflected, for example, in the New Testament where in Matthew 9:11 "tax collectors and sinners" are grouped as undesirables. Jesus was criticized for associating with such people, one of whom was the apostle Matthew himself (Matt 9:9). Jews rejected publicans not only for their widespread fraudulent practices in lining their own pockets, and their cooperation with the Roman occupiers, but also because they had contact with the ritually unclean Gentiles.

F. M. Gillman

See also LUKE/LUKAN; MATTHEW/ MATTHEAN.

PUEBLA DOCUMENT

A decade after their historic conference at Medellín, Colombia (1968), at which they linked Christian faith and "solidarity with the poor," the Catholic bishops of Latin America met from January 27 to February 13, 1979, in Puebla, Mexico, to evaluate the church's commitment to God, to those in whom God's image is defiled by unjust poverty, and to the church's own ongoing conversion. Between Medellín and Puebla, Latin America saw poverty worsen, right-wing military dictatorships established, and civil wars break out. At the same time, the church witnessed the rise of countless grassroots Christian communities dedicated to the creation of just societies. Corresponding to this was the impressive development of liberation theology, or the theology of the poor. Because of Medellín, the weight of the institutional church in Latin American societies, and the importance of Latin America in the wider Catholic Church, the eyes of the world were focused on the Puebla conference, officially known as the Third General Conference of Latin American Bishops.

Unlike the Medellín conference, Puebla produced only one (rather lengthy) document called "Evangelization in Latin America's Present and Future." The title indicates that the main focus is the mission of the church in Latin American societies—specifically, the proclamation of the Gospel. But such a task requires a sound knowledge of the real-life situation of the people to whom the Good News is to be preached. Thus, the bishops followed the same threefold approach at Puebla as they had at Medellín: (1) a sociohistorical analysis of the actual situation confronting the church; (2) a theological consideration of the meaning of evangelization in light of the reality of Latin America; and (3) a description of concrete ecclesial commitments that follow from the two previous steps.

The heart of the document is found in its best-known declaration—the "preferential option for the poor" (nos. 1134–65). Here the bishops moved beyond the simple call for "solidarity with the poor" enunciated at Medellín. Now they elaborated the theological basis for the church's commitment to justice for the poor: because the poor are made in the image and likeness of God and because this image is "dimmed and even defiled" by poverty, "God takes on their defense and loves them" (no. 1142). Likewise, no matter what their moral or personal standing, "the poor merit [the church's] preferen-

tial attention" (no. 1142). Thus there is no distinction made between the "deserving" and "undeserving" poor. Furthermore, as the bishops reflected on the experiences of countless pastoral agents, lay and clerical alike, who had committed themselves to solidarity with the poor over the previous decade, they came to recognize what they called "the evangelizing potential of the poor" who "challenge the Church constantly, summoning it to conversion" (no. 1146). And while Puebla also speaks of a "preferential option for young people" (nos. 1166–1205), this is not really a second, or separate, commitment since it calls for a pastoral approach to youth that takes "due account of the social reality of young people on our continent" and that offers them "resources for becoming factors for change and also . . . for participating actively in the Church and in the transformation of society" (no. 1187).

While liberation theology is not mentioned explicitly in the final document of Puebla, the conference did call for "the true and integral liberation of each and all of the human beings who make up our people" (no. 189). Using one of liberation theology's well-known formulas, the bishops said that real freedom is embodied "on three inseparable planes": our relationships to the world, to other persons, and to God (no. 322). It was Puebla's unequivocal response to "the cry of a suffering people who demand justice, freedom, and respect" (no. 87) that caused joy in some quarters and dismay in others.

James B. Nickoloff

See also LATIN AMERICAN THEOLOGIES; MEDELLÍN DOCUMENTS; OPTION FOR THE POOR; SANTO DOMINGO DOCUMENT; SOCIAL JUSTICE.

PUJA

Fundamentally, a hospitality ritual. The deity is invited to be present using verbal prayers and invocations. Ritual gestures of welcome—such as offerings of food, flowers, oil lamps, and incense—are presented before the image on an altar. The food that is offered is thereby consecrated and is consumed as a kind of blessing. Often a family ritual in a home shrine, simple forms of *puja* do not necessarily require the assistance of a trained priest. Puja can also be offered, in Hinduism and Tantric Buddhism, to a living saint, usually one's guru, who is considered to be an embodiment of one's chosen form of the divine. Theravada Buddhists use the word puja for devotional offerings to Buddha-images and monks, but the sense is (at least officially) more honorific than sacramental.

Lance E. Nelson

See also BUDDHISM; HINDUISM; IMAGES, WORSHIP OF; PRASADA; TANTRA; TANTRIC BUDDHISM; THERAVADA BUDDHISM.

PULCHERIA (399–453)

Aelia Pulcheria Augusta was the daughter of Emperor Arcadius and his wife, Eudoxia. Pulcheria was a virgin in the church of Constantinople. In 414 she was named "Augusta" and as such had control of her younger brother's education. Upon his ascent to the throne in 408 as Theodosius II, Pulcheria continued to exercise great control over him. Upon his death in 450, Pulcheria took over as empress and married the Roman general Marcion who became emperor. Well versed in theology, Pulcheria organized the Council of Chalcedon in 451. She left her vast fortune for the poor and for other worthy causes upon her death.

Gary Macy

See also CHALCEDON, COUNCIL OF; EUDOXIA; VIRGINITY.

PULPIT

A reading stand. In most churches, the pulpit stands to the left of the altar. Often, all the Scripture readings are proclaimed and the homily is preached from it, but in some churches it is used only for the gospel and the homily. Another stand or "lectern" is then set up for the other readings and the general intercessions. Since Vatican II, the Catholic Church has placed a strong emphasis on Scripture and preaching, making the pulpit an increasingly important aspect of church architecture. The pulpit is the descendent of the "ambo," a large reading platform, often many steps above floor level, found in early Christian churches. It was used almost exclusively for the reading of the gospel, since the bishop usually preached from his chair.

Patrick L. Malloy

See also PREACHING (IN CATHOLICISM); SERMON.

PURANA

The Puranas (literally, "ancient lore") are a class of Hindu sacred texts, written in Sanskrit, that cover a wide range of topics including myth, history, theology, ritual, morality, and spiritual practice. Composed during an age in which Hinduism was becoming increasingly dominated by *bhakti*-oriented spirituality, the Puranas are generally devotional in tone. Individual texts are biased toward, and extol the superiority of, one or another of the major deities, especially Vishnu (or Krishna), Shiva, or Devi, the Great Goddess. Most of the eighteen major Puranas (listed variously in different sources) were composed between about 300 and 1300 C.E., but some are later. Among the most important are the *Shiva Purana*, the *Vishnu Purana*, and the *Bhagavata Purana*. There are also numerous minor Puranas, many of which were composed to legitimate the sanctity of, and to glorify, particular temples or pilgrimage sites. The Puranas are not typically regarded by brahminical orthodoxy as possessing the same authoritativeness as the Vedic revelation (*shruti*), but they are often more important in the religious life of the people and the theology of certain bhakti traditions.

Lance E. Nelson

See also BHAKTI; HINDUISM; SHRUTI; VAISHNAVA; VEDAS.

PURDAH

From the Hindu word *parda*, meaning screen or veil. *Purdah* is the practice, observed by some Muslims and Hindus, of secluding women from the view of the public. Among Muslims, the practice is popular in Iran and is linked to the Qur'anic command that women dress modestly (24:31) and cover their bodies when they appear in public (33:59). Modified purdah is also found in Islam; that is, covering the body and wearing a scarf over one's head but leaving the face and hands uncovered.

Ronald A. Pachence

See also CHADOR; MUSLIM; QUR'AN.

PURE LAND BUDDHISM

A distinct school of Mahayana Buddhism that formed in China and was perhaps the most popular in the East Asian history of the faith. In the early Indic period of the Mahayana's emergence, a few texts describe a series of different rebirth paradises created solely for the salvation practices of those wishing to be born in them. In each case, an advanced bodhisattva

vows to create his own realm upon his becoming a Buddha. Among these is Abhirati Paradise created by Akshobhya located in the eastern direction and the Vaiduryanirbhasa Paradise created by Bhaisajyaguru, the Medicine Buddha. In the Mahayana text called the *Karuna-pundarika*, even the earth is called Shakyamuni's "Buddha Land." Advanced celestial bodhisattvas are also designated in each instance as helpers who assist Buddhist practitioners achieve rebirth in the Pure Land after death; others act within the paradise to help individuals reborn there to achieve nirvana.

The most popular among the Pure Land lineages was yet another connected with the advanced bodhisattva named Dharmakara: in a series of vows (forty-eight in the main text) associated with his Buddhahood as Amitabha (Chinese, *Amito-fo*; Japanese, *Amida*), he created in the western direction *Sukhavati* ("Realm of Bliss"), a paradise where salvation practice would be guaranteed successful. In India, where the foundation texts of this school all were first recorded, rebirth in a "pure land" was never more than a generalized goal; in East Asia, however, focus on specific practices associated with this paradise coalesced in a very popular lineage of Mahayana Buddhism that developed in China and then was transmitted to Japan, where it then evolved further on distinct sectarian lines.

Theorists in the East Asian schools drew strongly upon the widely accepted doctrine predicting the decline of Buddhism (Japanese, *mappo*) and the concomitant belief in later humanity's inability to practice strict meditation. Hence, Buddhist practice in these schools was directed not toward the realization of nirvana, but on attaining Pure Land rebirth, relying on the "other power" of the compassionate Buddha of the West. (Other Buddhist schools such as Ch'an/Zen disagreed with this entire regime, asserting the continuing efficacy of "self power.")

Pure Land practice still involved the observance of traditional moral strictures; more distinctive was the honorific repetition of Amitabha Buddha's name (Chinese, *Namo Amito-fo*; Japanese, *Namo Amida Butsu*), with these recitations ideally numbering in the many hundred thousands. More advanced practice involved detailed visualizations of Sukhavati and preparations for death, the time when Amitabha with his retinue would appear to calm and accompany the worthy to paradise.

In Japan, the innovative Pure Land leader Shinran (1173–1263) pushed elements of the school's thought to their furthest possible extensions and past that of his popular teacher Honen (1133–1212, of the Jodo Shu School). Shinran's views were similar to developments in early Protestant theology: salvation is possible only via Amida's grace, with even the number of repetitions (Japanese, *nembutsu*) irrelevant in the face of the omnipotent power of this Buddha to save whom he will, even the least worthy. Shinran, while supporting traditional morality, also argued that monastic discipline was a hopeless vanity; his school that became known as the Jodo Shin Shu continued largely along the lineages of his married disciples.

Todd T. Lewis

See also AMITABHA/AMIDA; HONEN; MAPPO; SHINRAN; SUKHAVATI.

PURGATORY

The teaching about purgatory asserts the necessity of an intermediate stage or condition between a person's death and the union with God that characterizes the resurrected life. This stage purifies persons from those conditions that prevent their union with God. Purgatory is sometimes described as a location, as in Dante Alighieri's *Purgatorio*. The teaching lacks clear roots in Scripture but stems from the piety of the early church's practice of praying for the dead. The activity implied a sense of the deceased's imperfection or unreadiness for God that could be remedied by prayer. The concept was greatly elaborated in the Middle Ages and linked to an elaborate system of calculating penalties for sin and equivalent reparational remedies. The juridical character of these reflections suggests the church's preoccupation with ecclesial jurisdiction, not only in matters of life, but of death as well. Abuses tied to this understanding were a factor in Luther's criticism of the church.

The doctrine of purgatory was affirmed in several church councils, Second Lyons (1276), Florence (1429), and Trent (1563). The greatest elaboration of the doctrine has occurred in popular piety and preaching that has often portrayed it as a place of compensatory pain and suffering, similar to the pains of hell but lacking hell's finality. The core concept of the doctrine is the recognition of the reality of sin that inhibits the person's capacity for relationship with God. Contemporary theology declines to speculate about the character of purgatory, but simply observes the importance of the individual's complete surrender to God.

Patricia Plovanich

PURIM

A minor Jewish festival, falling in the late winter, marking the Jews' deliverance from Haman's plot to destroy them, recorded in the book of Esther. Purim is celebrated through a reading of the Scroll of Esther (Megillah), the use of noise makers (Grogger) to drown out the name of the enemy Haman, by the exchange of gifts (Shelah Manot), and through the giving of charity. The celebratory atmosphere is enhanced by children's and adults' wearing of costumes and, especially in the modern period, by synagogues' or other Jewish institutions' hosting of carnivals. Despite the merriment, the holiday presents a serious theological message. By recalling the potential danger of Diaspora life to the Jews, Purim reflects upon the evil of complacency. At the same time, it declares that, because of the ever watchful God who works quietly to make the right thing happen, the Jewish nation will outlive history.

Alan J. Avery-Peck

See also GROGGER; MEGILLAH.

PURITANISM

Puritanism was a renewal movement within the Church of England in the sixteenth and seventeenth centuries; it had a major impact on the development of religious life in Britain and the British colonies in North America. Calvinists who believed in double predestination, limited atonement, and irresistible grace, they wanted to purify the Church of England of "popishness" (thus their name). Instituting simpler worship, they rejected priestly vestments, ostentatious iconography, and using an altar to celebrate Eucharist. Seeking a Christian life guided solely by the Scriptures, they opposed the theater, drunkenness, and sexual immorality, and they insisted on strict observance of the Sabbath. Most Puritans rejected episcopal church government and advocated a congregational or pres-byterian system; some practiced infant baptism and others, adult. What they agreed on was that the Church of England needed more thoroughgoing reformation.

Puritan tensions simmered during Elizabeth I's attempts (1558–1603) to find a "middle way" and broke out openly during the reign of her successor, James I (James VI of Scotland, 1603–25). The son of a Catholic, suspicious of Protestant power in Scotland, James opposed Puritanism. When James' son Charles I (1625–49) married a Catholic and granted concessions to Catholics, Puritans feared the restoration of what they considered idolatry. Hostilities between Puritans and the Crown ultimately led to civil war. In 1649 Charles I was beheaded, and Oliver Cromwell led England as "Lord Protector." However, Puritans were divided among themselves and could not sustain the government. Peace was not restored until 1688 with the ascension of William and Mary to the throne and the granting of limited religious toleration. By then Puritanism had faded as a political movement, but it lingered in works such as John Bunyan's *Pilgrim's Progress* and John Milton's *Paradise Lost*.

Puritanism impacted the North American British colonies in New England; in 1620 a group of Separatist Pilgrims settled at Plymouth Plantation, and in 1630 a larger group of Puritans founded Massachusetts Bay Colony. Led by governor John Winthrop, the latter group stressed they were not separating from the Church of England, but establishing a "city on a hill" that would serve as example to Old England. Emulating Calvin's Geneva, they created a Christian commonwealth, with a state church and moral regulations enforced by civil authority. They sought to gather a church of visible saints.

Although church attendance was mandatory, only those women and men who could testify to their experience of saving grace to the satisfaction of the other saints could become members. Church members could take Communion, vote on church affairs, and only male church members could participate in civil government. Potential saints prepared themselves for the possible infusion of God's grace by living a holy life, and after conversion, saints were likewise expected to live a sanctified life.

Seeing themselves as a chosen people like the children of Israel, the Puritans believed themselves in a special covenant relationship with God and with one another. Hence, they applied the Christian Gospel to every area of life: ecclesiastical, political, social, and familial. A covenant existed between husbands and wives, parents and children, God and community, with each party owing certain responsibilities to the other. If they did not uphold their end of the covenant, God would punish them. Thus, Puritans constantly examined themselves for signs of God's favor or disfavor. Natural disasters, illness, and Native American revolts were perceived as signs of God's displeasure. All life was directed toward God's glory.

Although the New England Puritans had a remarkable unity of purpose, there were early challenges to their Christian commonwealth. In 1631 Roger Williams arrived in Massachusetts Bay. A pastor and Puritan's Puritan, he urged the complete separation of church and state and withdrawal of New England churches from the Church of England. Anything less was hypocritical. After her 1634 emigration, Anne Hutchinson also accused the Puritans of hypocrisy. She declared that since only God chose the elect, living an ethical life was no evidence of justification thus the Puritans were laboring under a doctrine of works. Williams and Hutchinson were tried for heresy, excommunicated, and banished from the colony. In 1692 witchcraft hysteria in Salem revealed deep divisions in the "New England way." More serious was the waning of enthusiasm. Second- and third-generation Puritans lacked the fervor of the first settlers who survived a transatlantic voyage, starvation, and wilderness; moreover, economic prosperity distracted many from more pious pursuits. Church membership waned, especially among men. This decline had serious political repercussions, since only male church members could vote. As early as 1662, church leaders instituted modifications to church membership standards. In sermons called *jeremiads* (after the prophet Jeremiah), ministers called the faithful to repent and return to the Puritan mission.

Although the church was not disestablished in Massachusetts until 1833, Puritanism as an organized system faded by the mid-eighteenth century. Its last great theologian was Jonathan Edwards, revivalist in the First Great Awakening. Most descendants of Puritan congregations are today affiliated with either the United Church of Christ or the Unitarian–Universalist Association. However, Puritanism left a significant legacy to the United States. Although Puritans did not permit universal suffrage, they did extend the franchise compared to Old England and provided a model for later U.S. democracy. They promoted thrift and hard work, leading to the "Puritan work ethic." They encouraged education and universal literacy, and they founded Harvard and Yale Colleges. Their understanding of themselves as a chosen nation with a special mission was translated into the ideology of America's manifest destiny. Their self-righteousness became part of the U.S. ethos as well.

Evelyn A. Kirkley

See also ANGLICAN COMMUNION; CALVINISM; CONGREGATIONAL CHURCHES; EDWARDS, JONATHAN; PRESBYTERIAN CHURCHES.

PURUSHA

In Hindu scripture and theology, *purusha* (Sanskrit, "person," "male") typically refers to the spiritual self, but it can also designate the personal deity. In the Sankhya and Yoga systems, it is the technical term for the core, transpersonal self, consisting of pure consciousness, which lies behind and supports the empirical, psychophysical self. As such, the concept is similar to the idea of *atman*, or *jiva*, as conceived in the theistic Vedanta systems and Jainism, in that all beings are thought to have their own individual purushas, there being a plurality of the same, each qualitatively identical though quantitatively distinct. The term purusha is also sometimes used for the one universal Self or Atman that is said to be identical with Brahman in the Advaita (nondualist) Vedanta tradition. As a designation of the personal deity, the term is found in the famous "Hymn to the Cosmic Person," *Rig Veda* 10.90. It is also used elsewhere, especially in Vaishnava literature, to refer to the supreme God, typically in compound form, for example, *Purusha–uttama*

and *Parama–purusha*, both terms meaning "Supreme Person."

Lance E. Nelson

See also ADVAITA VEDANTA; DVAITA VEDANTA; HINDUISM; SANKHYA; VAISHNAVA; VISHISHTADVAITA VEDANTA; YOGA.

PUSEY, EDWARD BOUVERIE (1800–82)

Scholar and church reformer. In 1833 he became associated with Keble and Newman by signing Tract 18, thereby committing his prestige to the Oxford Movement and demonstrating its potential for influence in the Church of England. His *Scriptural Views of Holy Baptism* (1835) elevated the Tracts from pamphlets to theological contributions. With Newman and Keble, he edited the *Library of the Fathers* that eventually reached forty-five volumes. He defended the Real Presence of Christ in the Eucharist and the reality of priestly absolution. He helped to reestablish religious communities of women in the church. He was spiritual director to many and renowned for his concern for social justice and promotion of Catholic ceremonial elements in the Anglican liturgy. When Newman became a Roman Catholic in 1845, Pusey became the main leader of the Movement; thus, it is also known as Puseyism. The Episcopal Church commemorates him on September 18.

Jon Nilson

See also KEBLE, JOHN; NEWMAN, JOHN HENRY; OXFORD MOVEMENT.

Q

QI

See CH'I.

QIBLA

See KIBLA.

QIYAS

In Islamic law, the principle of analogical reasoning developed by the jurist Ash-Shafi-i (767–820 C.E.) to guide religious lawyers and judges in cases that cannot be resolved by reference to the Qur'an (Islam's sacred scripture) or to *sunna* (tradition). Over time, *qiyas* became accepted in Sunni Islam as a third source of Islamic law. According to this principle, when the Qur'an or the sunna is silent about a particular legal issue, it is permissible to render a decision based upon a similar though different case for which a precedent exists.

Ronald A. Pachence

See also QUR'AN; SHAFI'TE; SHARIA/SHARI'A; SUNNA/SUNNI/SUNNISM.

Q SOURCE

The name for the hypothetical sayings source utilized, according to the Two-Source Theory, by Matthew and Luke for the non-Markan material they have in common. The letter "Q" is popularly thought to come from the German word *Quelle*, "source." The Q Source is called hypothetical because there are no extant ancient manuscripts containing this source, nor are there any references or allusions to the existence of such a source in early Christian literature. Rather, the supposed content of this source is derived by extracting the non-Markan material Matthew and Luke have in common. (The expression "non-Markan" means simply that the material is found in one or more of the other Gospels, but does not appear in Mark.)

The Q hypothesis was conceived in connection with the hypothesis of the priority of Mark in the early nineteenth century. The priority of Mark means that the Gospel of Mark is thought to be the first of the Synoptic Gospels to be composed, and that it was a source utilized by Matthew and Luke. The two sources, Mark and Q, constitute the basis of the Two-Source Theory.

Three observations led to the assumption of a second source in addition to Mark that was utilized by Matthew and Luke: (1) a similarity in content in much of non-Markan material in Matthew and Luke; (2) a common order in Matthew and Luke in some of their non-Markan material; and (3) the presence of doublets, namely, the same saying found in a Markan form and again in a Q form.

Although there is ongoing debate about the exact content of the Q source, there is a general consensus regarding double tradition passages (non-Markan texts common to Matthew and Luke) that are part of Q. These double tradition passages are easily recognized through the use of a resource for Gospel studies called a *Synopsis*, a book which presents the texts in their narrative order in Matthew, Mark, and Luke in parallel columns.

The double tradition passages (and thus the major content of Q) in the order of Luke are: 3:7-9, 16-17; 4:2-13; 6:20-23, 27-49; 7:1-10, 18-35; 9:57-60; 10:2-16, 21-24; 11:2-4, 9-26, 29-35, 39-44, 46-52; 12:2-12, 22-31, 33-34, 39-40, 42-46, 51-56, 58-59; 13:18-21, 24-30, 34-35; 14:16-23, 26-27, 34-35; 15:4-7; 16:13, 16-18; 17:1, 3-4, 6, 23-24, 26, 27, 30, 33, 34-35, 37; 19:12-27; 22:18-30 (list from F. Neirynck). It is generally thought that the original order of material in the Q source is more faithfully represented by Luke than it is by Matthew.

Approaching the Q material from its presentation in the Gospel of Matthew, one finds a substantial similarity in the order of passages when compared to that of Luke. There are, however, some inversions that may be attributed to Matthew's editorial activity.

In recent years there has been considerable effort to reconstruct the actual Greek text of the Q Source. This is a fairly easy task for those passages that have almost identical wording in Matthew and Luke (for example, Luke 10:13-15, 21-22, 24-25). Where there are substantial differences in wording, the task of reconstruction is more challenging, resulting in differing opinions by biblical scholars. Nonethe-less, the varying reconstructions are not reason to doubt the existence of a written Q Source. The differences in wording or in order are attributed to the editorial activity of the evangelists Matthew and Luke.

To what literary genre (or type) does the Q source belong? It does not belong to the genre of Gospel, since, unlike the four canonical Gospels, the Q Source does not contain a passion narrative. Some have called it a "sayings source" because of the collection of sayings, whether prophetic or wisdom, that it contains. Others prefer to call it a "discourse source," since it is more than a mere sayings collection.

Attention has also been given to the theology, specifically the christology, of the Q Source. A further question is its place of origin, for which three proposals can be mentioned: (1) a Palestinian community of Christians; (2) a Hellenistic community that presented the teaching of Jesus in the form of eschatological judgment; and (3) a missionary community.

John Gillman

See also FOUR-SOURCE THEORY (OF SYNOPTICS); SYNOPTIC GOSPELS; SYNOPTIC PROBLEM; TWO-SOURCE THEORY (OF SYNOPTICS).

QUADRAGESIMO ANNO

The encyclical issued by Pope Pius XI in 1931 on the fortieth anniversary of *Rerum Novarum* (1891). The purpose of this letter was to apply the economic teaching of *Rerum Novarum* to the situation of worldwide depression and massive unemployment in the 1930s. Even though Pius XI, like Leo XIII before him, spoke out against the threat of socialism, he was not as anxious as Leo to align the church with the liberal forces of capitalism.

As a middle way between capitalism and socialism, Pius XI proposed restructuring the social order along lines that had prevailed in medieval Christianity. This corporative system would maintain class hierarchy, while it linked the ownership of the means of production with social responsibility.

Quadragesimo Anno criticized the interstructuring of wealth, government, and power in the capitalist system, but it did not intend a rejection of capitalism. While Pius XI taught that it was important that ownership be socially accountable, he, like Leo XIII before him, believed that ownership was part of the natural law, and that the right to ownership, including the right to inheritance, is more fundamental than the responsibility for the social use of that property. Like *Rerum Novarum*, this encyclical also assumed the patriarchal family.

Nevertheless, this encyclical also contributed to a social vision beyond the status quo. While supporting the justice of the wage contract, *Quadragesimo Anno* also advocated the partnership of capital and labor in ownership, management, and profit sharing "when possible." The encyclical was also clear that charity cannot substitute for justice. A well-known teaching from this encyclical is the claim that "charity cannot take the place of justice unfairly withheld" (QA 137).

Mary E. Hobgood

See also CATHOLIC SOCIAL TEACHING; ECONOMIC JUSTICE FOR ALL; RERUM NOVARUM; WORK/EMPLOYMENT.

QUADRILATERAL (IN METHODIST/WESLEYAN THEOLOGY)

The name usually given to the four elements on which traditional Wesleyan theology claims to base itself: Scripture, reason, tradition, and experience. Although John Wesley did not use the term "quadrilateral," or list these four and discuss them systematically, most Wesley scholars are agreed that they represent a fair portrayal of Wesley's basic principles. (Where there is some disagreement is as to whether these are all to be used equally as "sources" of theology, or whether Scripture holds a special place.)

Wesley believed that Scripture is divinely inspired, and thus the rule of all truth and conduct. He was a careful scholar of the Bible, as may be seen in his *Explanatory Notes on the New Testament*, where he repeatedly improves on the authorized version commonly used at the time. Yet, he was also acutely aware of the many innovative and even peculiar interpretations that were being offered by persons with great respect for the Bible, but little for the tradition of the church or even for common sense.

It was for this reason that he repeatedly put forth tradition and reason (by which he often meant common sense) as important guides in biblical interpretation. (At this point, it should be noted that he was also a careful student of Christian tradition, especially of patristic theology.) Tradition and reason should then serve as guards against privatistic or idiosyncratic scriptural interpretation.

Finally, experience (by which he often meant Christian experience) was important for Wesley, because his own interpretation of Scripture had been greatly enriched by his own encounter with the forgiving grace of God. He was therefore convinced that a proper interpretation of Scripture requires not only the use of reason and proper regard for tradition but also that the interpreter be a person of Christian experience.

Justo L. González

See also WESLEY, JOHN.

QUAKERS

The Quakers, whose official name is the Religious Society of Friends, began in England in the seventeenth century as a Christian renewal movement. Founder George Fox (1624–91) was a seeker discouraged by the shallowness of Christianity. In 1646 he had a revelation that humans were endowed by God with an "Inner Light." The spiritual manifestation of God's presence in every individual, the Inner Light was divine truth discovered by sincere listening, an authority higher than church or Scriptures. It meant that revelation was not restricted to the Bible.

Since every person was a source of Inner Light, Fox preached, there was no need for ordained clergy or formal worship. Hymns, sermons, sacraments, and creeds were unnecessary hindrances to the movement of God's spirit. Friends worshiped in silence, broken only by those moved by the Inner Light to speak. Meetings were conducted in spartan meetinghouses. While Quakers had no clergy, elders oversaw administrative matters and community discipline. Meetings emphasized community solidarity; decisions were made only by unanimous consent. Business meetings were conducted monthly, and as the movement grew and developed, delegates from local meetings met quarterly and annually.

According to Fox, God calls all Christians to live a holy and consecrated life. Calling one another "Friends," Quakers did not recognize earthly distinctions of birth, wealth, or education; they treated all people alike, refusing to swear oaths, use titles, or remove their hats in court. Women and men were considered equal in God's sight. They emphasized simple living, hard work, and thrift. Moreover, according to Fox, humans could not morally engage in armed conflict or military service.

Aided by his wife, Margaret Fell, Fox attracted many followers, especially among the Puritans, who gravitated toward the movement's earnestness, individualism, and mysticism. The first Quaker meeting was founded in northern England by 1652; within two years, it was established in London and other British cities. Missionaries spread the movement across western Europe, the West Indies, and the North American British colonies. Quakers arrived in New England in 1656, where they were systematically persecuted by the Puritan establishment. Quaker William Penn chartered the colony of Pennsylvania and founded Philadelphia in 1682. Like Massachusetts Bay, Pennsylvania was established as a model Christian community, a "holy experiment" in religious freedom, but unlike it, there was no state church. The colony became a haven for Moravians, Amish, Mennonites, and Brethren, as well as Quakers. In the mid-eighteenth century, Quakers relinquished control of the government rather than pay taxes to the British government for military efforts.

The Quakers also attracted enemies. They were first called "Quakers" by their detractors for their "quaking," physical trembling generated by intense enthusiasm. Aggressive evangelists, they often interrupted other Christians' worship services with messages from the Spirit and were called blasphemous fanatics. They repeatedly defied edicts ordering them to pay taxes to the state church and forbidding them to meet publicly. Their pacifism, egalitarianism, and rejection of civil authority threatened the established social order. Fox and many Friends were imprisoned; many were even executed for their beliefs. Quakers were not granted religious freedom in England until 1689, and in the North American British colonies they were widely regarded with suspicion during the Revolutionary War as Tories.

Despite persecution, the movement was well established by the time of Fox's death, numbering in the tens of thousands. In the United States, Quakers were among the earliest advocates of human rights. John Woolman traveled the eastern seaboard in the 1750s exhorting Friends to manumit captive Africans. During the Civil War, Quakers actively opposed chattel slavery and supported the Underground Railroad. Susan B. Anthony, suffragist and advocate of equal rights for women, was also a Quaker. Along with other "peace churches," such as the Mennonites and Bohemian Brethren, Quakers pioneered conscientious objector status for those refusing military service on religious grounds. In 1917 they founded the American Friends Service Committee to help conscientious objectors find alternate wartime service and support philanthropic activities. They founded Earlham, Swarthmore, and Haverford Colleges, and two U.S. presidents, Herbert Hoover and Richard Nixon, had Quaker backgrounds.

The Friends have struggled with internal divisions. In 1827 they split into two factions, Hicksite and Orthodox. The former regarded themselves as restorationists, seeking to return the Friends to their original Inner Light tradition. The latter were accommodationists who had adapted more churchly worship and greater emphasis on the Bible and Jesus.

A second schism occurred in 1847. By the late twentieth century, there were three major groups of Friends in the United States. Some meetings resemble conservative evangelical Protestantism in theology, organization, and worship, while others maintain historic Quaker stances of civil resistance and silent meeting. Friends continue to wrestle with their political, social, and theological identity.

Evelyn A. Kirkley

See also BOHEMIAN BRETHREN/
MORAVIANS; FOX, GEORGE; MENNONITES;
PURITANISM.

QUALIFIED NONDUALISM
See VISHISHTADVAITA VEDANTA.

QUIETISM
Broadly speaking, quietism is a mystical teaching in which spiritual perfection is attained through annihilation of the will and passive submergence in contemplation of the divine. In this sense, quietism is a persistent theme in Christianity, Buddhism, and sectarian movements such as Spiritualism and Transcendental Meditation. Quietism also refers to a specific seventeenth-century devotional movement in the Catholic Church in France and Italy led by Spanish priest Miguel de Molinos (1628–96). After settling in Rome in 1663, he developed a new teaching of contemplation outlined in his *Spiritual Guide*, published simultaneously in Spanish and Italian in 1685. Although initially supported by the church, Molinos was attacked by Jesuits who felt his teachings disregarded meditation, vocal prayer, asceticism, and devotions to Jesus and Mary. He was arrested, tried, and condemned in 1687, and spent the remainder of his life in prison charged with heresy and sexual improprieties.

Dubbed "Quietism" in the 1680s by his enemies, Molinos' central premise was that through divine grace, Christians can achieve complete union with God. This union requires passive contemplation of God, emptying the self, and evisceration of the individual will. It results in God filling one's soul, purging all desires, and becoming sovereign over the body and all animal instincts. Prayer, confession, concern for salvation, and devotion to Jesus, Mary, and the saints are unnecessary and even detrimental, insofar as they sustain the illusion of a separate will. Union with God is available to any Christian regardless of birth, gender, wealth, or education, and once attained, is permanent. After this transformation, the soul is effectively separated from the body, and the body can be forced by the devil to sin, especially sexual sin, or directed by God to do good works.

Quietism was unacceptable to the church because it eroded traditional morality and exonerated people from responsibility for their actions. Moreover, it eliminated the role of the church as mediator between the believer and God, as well as ritual, discipline, and intellectual endeavor. Although Molinos saw himself as a reformer within the church, his teachings effectively rendered it dispensable. Molinos' followers included François Salignac de Fénelon and Jeanne Marie de la Mothe Guyon (1648–1717), a French woman who expounded a metaphysical version of Quietism in which the transformed soul was undifferentiated from God, like a river flowing into the ocean. Individual selfhood was intrinsically evil. Guyon was imprisoned in 1688 and from 1695 to 1702 for propagating heresy. In 1699 Pope Innocent XI formally condemned Quietism based on writings of Fénelon. Although Quietism clearly contradicted church teachings, its condemnation stifled the development of Catholic mysticism for decades.

Evelyn A. Kirkley

See also FÉNELON, FRANÇOIS; MOLINOS, MIGUEL DE.

QUIMBANDA
See UMBANDA.

QUIÑONES, FRANCISCO DE (?–1540)
Spanish liturgist and cardinal of the church. He was a Franciscan friar who was elected superior general of his order, and also bishop of Coria, and cardinal. A renowned liturgist, he composed a new book for the Liturgy of the Hours that became very popular among both friars and laity. It was suppressed by the liturgical reforms promoted by the Council of Trent and by Pius V, but it deeply influenced Anglican liturgical reforms and the first Book of Common Prayer.

Orlando Espín

See also ANGLICAN COMMUNION; BOOK OF COMMON PRAYER; CARDINAL; COUNTER-REFORMATION/CATHOLIC REFORMATION; FRANCISCANS; FRIARS; LAITY; LITURGY (IN CHRISTIANITY); LITURGY OF THE HOURS; PIUS V, POPE; TRENT, COUNCIL OF.

QUIROGA, VASCO DE (1470–1565)
Spanish Franciscan missionary in Mexico. First bishop of Michoacán, he is considered one of the first theologians of colonial Latin America. A contemporary of Bartolomé de Las Casas, Quiroga arrived in Mexico as a layman and as judge in the court system Spain was establishing in the newly conquered lands. Trained as a lawyer, Quiroga took up the defense of the natives against colonial atrocities, and

ultimately left the courts and joined the Franciscans. After he was appointed bishop in 1538, Quiroga committed himself to the evangelization and defense of the native populations of central Mexico. He was renowned for his personal poverty and for his dedication to those abused by the colonial system. His theological thought, also in defense of the natives and influenced by contemporary utopian expectations, was mainly expressed in his *Información en Derecho* (1535), and in the *De debellandis Indis* (1542). Quiroga's theological method and insights were remarkable for the period: he believed that all theological reflection must be preceded by careful examination of economic, social, and cultural reality; he also thought that no one could be truly Christian without an "option for the poor," and that theology's aim was to assist in the promotion of justice for the poor.

Orlando Espín

See also CULTURE; EVANGELIZATION; FRANCISCANS; INCULTURATION; JUSTICE; LAS CASAS, BARTOLOMÉ DE; LATIN AMERICAN CATHOLICISM; LATINO CATHOLICISM; LIBERATION THEOLOGIES; MISSIONS; OPTION FOR THE POOR.

QUMRAN

(Khirbet Qumran). Qumran is the modern name of the site on the northwest shore of the Dead Sea near where the Dead Sea Scrolls were found beginning in 1947. Excavations at this site, approximately nine miles south of Jericho, revealed that it had been settled from around the middle of the second century B.C.E. until the First Jewish Revolt (66–73 C.E.). The settlement seems to have been communal in nature and is thought by many scholars to be the remains of a settlement of Essenes who may have preserved and written the scrolls found in the nearby caves.

Russell Fuller

See also ESSENES.

QUR'AN

In Arabic, "recitation." The Qur'an is the sacred scripture of Islam. It is called "recitation" because, according to Islamic belief, the Qur'an is the literal word of God disclosed to, and then recited in every detail by, the Prophet Muhammad (570–632). As such, the Qur'an is considered the inerrant revelation of God, "sent down" (*tanzil*) verbatim in Arabic and recorded without error in the sacred text. For Muslims, the Qur'an is God's final revelation that corrects and expands upon the Bible. The holy words of this text are referred to as *Kalam Allah* (the "speech of God"). While Muslims accept the divine origin of biblical revelation, they say that both the Old and the New Testaments contain errors caused by inaccurate recording of the Word of God after it was faithfully transmitted by the prophets, the apostles, and Jesus.

Muslims believe that the Prophet Muhammad received the first revelation while at prayer in the year 610 and that the revelations continued off and on throughout his life. It is said that Muhammad never forgot a single word disclosed to him, and because he could not read or write, he dictated the revelations to a scribe. In this way, he was able to verify that the written text of the Qur'an as recited back to him was precisely what God had disclosed to him.

The Qur'an, about the same length as the New Testament, is divided into one hundred fourteen *suras* or chapters arranged from the longest to the shortest (except Sura 1, a brief revelation called "The Opening"). Each sura is comprised of verses or *ayas*, much like the arrangement of the passages in the Bible. The material found in the Qur'an varies widely. The earlier revelations, received in Mecca before 622, contain revelations about God and God's relation to humankind, divine judgment, and matters of Islamic doctrine. The later suras are called Median, because they were received in Medina after the Prophet's emigration from Mecca (*hijra*) in 622. These later revelations deal more with social and juridical concerns that would naturally have arisen as the prophet established the first Islamic *umma* or community.

The canonical (authorized) edition of the Qur'anic text was compiled not long after the Prophet's death, during the caliphate (leadership) of Uthman (d. 656), thus assuring the authenticity of the text as it was transmitted to future generations. Muslims, therefore, believe that the Arabic words they have in the Qur'an today are the very words God spoke to Muhammad and that Muhammad recited. This revelation is regarded as eternal and uncreated; unaltered and unalterable; perfect and final. In fact, a translation of the Qur'an from its original Arabic into another language is not accepted as the authentic Qur'an by Muslims. It would be called an "interpretation" or given a title like "*The Meaning of the Holy Qur'an.*"

Ronald A. Pachence

See also AYA; HIJRA (IN ISLAM); ISLAM; JESUS (AS PROPHET OF ISLAM); KALAM; MUHAMMAD; MUSLIM; REVELATION (IN ISLAM); SURA; UMMA; UTHMAN.

QURAYSH

A prominent Arab tribe in and around the city of Mecca, located in western Arabia. The Prophet of Islam, Muhammad (570–632), belonged to the Hashimite clan of the Quraysh tribe. So, too, did the fourth Islamic leader (caliph), Ali (598–661). The other three early caliphs who preceded Ali as leaders of the growing Islamic community were members of the Quraysh tribe, but not Hashimites. Because Mecca was situated on an important trading route, the Quraysh were able to profit from the city's commerce, and as a result, they enjoyed prosperity and the power that derives from wealth. When the Prophet began preaching the new religion called Islam, the Quraysh bitterly opposed him. They continued to resist accepting Islam until Muhammad, who had left Mecca in 622, returned as conqueror of the city in 630.

Ronald A. Pachence

See also ALI; CALIPH (KALIPHA)/ CALIPHATE; ISLAM; MUHAMMAD.

R

RABANUS MAURUS (780?–856)

Rabanus (the raven) was a monk of the monastery of Fulda (Germany) who studied under Alcuin in 801–2. Alcuin gave him the name "Maurus" after one of Benedict's favorite monks. Rabanus became abbot of the Benedictine monastery of Fulda in 822. In 842 Rabanus had to resign as abbot for political reasons but continued his attempts to reform the church as archbishop of Mainz, a post he held from 847 until his death. Rabanus was very concerned to preserve learning during a time of chaotic government. His major works include an encyclopedia and a book for educating priests, both intended to help produce a learned clergy. Rabanus also wrote extensive commentaries on Scripture and a large number of poems.

Gary Macy

See also ALCUIN; BENEDICT OF NURSIA; MEDIEVAL CHRISTIANITY (IN THE WEST).

RABBI

A Jewish spiritual leader and guide, a trained scholar in Judaica, a teacher of Jewish texts and traditions, and an interpreter and decider of Jewish law.

In modern times, the role of the rabbi has been expanded to include being a pastor-counselor, community organizer and leader, and a professionally trained leader of Jewish institutions. The contemporary rabbi also acts as the officiant at life cycle ceremonies such as circumcisions, baby namings, Bar/Bat Mitzvahs, weddings, and funerals.

The most visible role of the rabbi is as the leader of synagogue worship, although any learned and capable Jew can serve in that capacity.

Despite the rabbi's great visibility and authority, he or she has no special powers or relationship with God. The rabbi learns and transmits God's word and will, attempting to inspire Jews to a relationship with God, to living a life committed to Jewish values and ethics, to observance of Jewish rituals, and to participation in the life of the Jewish community.

In Orthodox Judaism, only men are ordained as rabbis. In all other denominations, both men and women are ordained as rabbis.

The Hebrew word for rabbi is *rav*, but in modern times, calling a rabbi a rav usually implies that rabbi's status as an outstanding scholar and expert in matters of Jewish law. Calling a rabbi a *rebbe* usually implies that the rabbi has status as a beloved and often charismatic spiritual guide.

Wayne Dosick

RABBINIC JUDAISM

The form of Judaism developed by Jewish sages, called rabbis, in the aftermath of the Roman destruction of the Jerusalem Temple in 70 C.E. Articulated in the Mishnah, Midrashic literature, and in the Talmuds of the land of Israel and Babylonia, this form of Judaism is the basis for all later forms of Judaism that are direct descendants of rabbinic theology and practice and that grow out of contemporary interpretations of rabbinic documents.

Rabbinic Judaism emerged in a period in which Jews found their inherited religious ideologies—no less than themselves—under attack. Rome ruled over the land of Israel, challenging the Bible's notion that the people of Israel would be sovereign in its own land; the destruction of the Jerusalem Temple meant the end of animal sacrifices, previously understood to be the only way the people could atone for their sins; and the disastrous Bar Kochba revolt of 133–5 C.E. ended any live expectation for the Temple's being rebuilt and Jewish life's return to the way it had been throughout the Second Temple period.

Judaism's rabbis responded to this situation by presenting a system of belief and practice that took into account the reality of their day. They developed a form of Judaism that could operate independent of the Temple and Temple priesthood, a Judaism that proclaimed that what mattered most to God was the commitment of each individual Jew, in his or her own home and at his or her own table, to observe the terms of the Sinaitic covenant. By following the divine will in matters of ethics and home ritual, the nation would encourage God to bring about redemption. Salvation in this view would come when each person correctly observed the Sabbath and the other laws of Judaism, not as the result of a messianic revolt, as had been attempted under Bar Kochba.

The rabbis' delineation of the laws the people were to follow was based upon their idea that God's revelation to Moses at Sinai, described in the book of Exodus, contained two distinct parts. One component was the Written Torah, embodied in the text of the Pentateuch that had always been transmitted in writing and that had been made accessible to all of the people of Israel. The other part was the Oral Torah, formulated for memorization and transmitted orally by successive generations of sages, ultimately passing into the hands of rabbinic authorities (Mishnah Abot 1:1). In the Oral Torah, the rabbis claimed to possess an otherwise unknown component of God's revelation and so to be direct successors to Moses, whom they called "our Rabbi," thus designating him the first rabbinic sage. According to this view, only under rabbinic guidance could the Jewish people correctly observe God's will, since the written Scriptures alone do not provide all the information needed to follow the law properly.

By the sixth century C.E., with the completion of the Babylonian Talmud, Rabbinic Judaism became the dominant form of Jewish practice and belief. It achieved this stature because of its compelling message, especially in the period of the ascent of Christianity, which claimed to embody a new covenant that replaced the one Jews understood to exist between themselves and God. Rabbinic ideology refocused the people's concerns from the events of political history that are, after all, beyond the control of the individual, to events within the life and control of each person and family. Under the rabbis, what came to matter were the everyday details of life, the recurring actions that, day in and day out, defined who the people were and that demarcated what was truly important to them: the way in which they related to family and community; the ethic by which they carried out their business dealings; the way in which they acknowledged their debt to God for the food they ate and for the wonders of nature. By making such aspects of life the central focus of Judaism, the rabbis assured that, as Scripture had proposed, the people would live as a nation of priests: eating their common food as though it were a sacrifice on the Temple's altar, seeing in their personal daily prayers and in their shared deeds of loving kindness a replacement for the sacrifices no longer offered.

Rabbinic Judaism remained messianic insofar as the people understood their religious observances to cause God to act on their behalf. But the rabbinic system led them to expect no quick, spectacular response. A messiah would come, but only in some distant future. In the meantime, the observance of the law and rituals of Judaism was its own reward. Creating a community based on the model defined by God through the Torah offered a taste of redemption and of a perfected world. This could be accomplished even though, within the bounds of real history, the Jews frequently had no control over their own destiny.

Those who created rabbinic Judaism thus responded to the critical theological problem of their day. God's presence and love of the people had always been seen in the military victories that were understood to reflect God's protection of his people. Beginning in the first centuries, it appeared as though such protection no longer could be expected, let alone depended upon. The rabbis accordingly identified a new proof for the existence

of God and a new explanation for how the people could be assured of God's support. It found this explanation in a new attitude toward God that said that the people must create communities and lead their daily lives according to the exacting precepts expressed by God in the Torah. They would experience the presence of God through the perfection of their communities while at the same time laying the foundation for the moment when God would fulfill the messianic promise expressed in Scripture, ingathering the Jewish exiles and reestablishing the Israelite nation within its ancestral homeland, where it would be ruled by God through a messianic scion of the house of David.

Alan J. Avery-Peck

See also BAR KOCHBA; COVENANT IN JUDAISM; DIASPORA; ESCHATOLOGY (IN JUDAISM); MESSIAH (IN JUDAISM); MIDRASH; MISHNAH; MITZVAH; RABBI; TALMUD; TORAH.

RACHEL

Beautiful younger daughter of Laban who was chosen by Jacob to become his wife (Gen 29:16-18). Due to a trick by her father, Jacob was not able to marry Rachel until after he had married her older and less attractive sister Leah. After the marriage, Rachel continued to be the favored of Jacob. She bore him two sons, Joseph and Benjamin. Most of the text of Genesis 37–50 describes the adventures of Joseph, the older of Rachel's sons, Jacob's firstborn of Rachel. Because of Joseph, the descendents of Abraham find themselves in Egypt positioned for the Exodus.

Rachel's solidarity with her husband Jacob against the wiles of Laban, her father, is evident in the narrative when she takes her father's household idols while he is out shearing sheep, hides them, and brings them along with her when they leave Laban for Jacob's home (Gen 31:19-35).

Rachel dies giving birth to her second son, whom she names Benoni, that is, son of my affliction. Jacob renames the child Benjamin, that is "son of" my "right hand." Perhaps Rachel's name for her son combined with her role as the beloved wife of Jacob, father of the tribes, accounts for the reference to Rachel's grieving in Jeremiah 31. The prophet describes Rachel moaning and weeping bitterly, mourning for her children and refusing to be comforted because her children are no more. The text was probably produced at the time of Judah's exile and refers to the many dead and the end of the kingdom. However, the prophet continues: "Cease your cries of mourning, wipe the tears from your eyes . . . they shall return from the enemy's land" (vv. 15-16).

There is only one reference to Rachel in the New Testament. It occurs in Matthew 2, as an interpretation of the text of Jeremiah. The Gospel writer uses the Jeremiah passage to refer to the "massacre of the infants." The New Testament passage, however, provides no reason why Rachel should not grieve.

Alice L. Laffey

RACISM

A pattern of contempt embedded in ideology and social structures that (in most cases) gives whites and Gentiles power and privileges in society denied to people of color and Jews.

Since Europeans first classified people by "race" in the latter part of the seventeenth century, racism has played an integral role in the psychological structures and economic and cultural institutions of Western societies. Racism both supports and is reinforced by such structures as gender, heterosexism, and class oppression.

Racism as a psychological structure is sustained by such cultural institutions and practices as the use of language in white supremacist discourse, the shaping of psychosexual identities, notions of "scientific" rationality, the suppression of diversity, and aesthetic values that assume the superiority of whiteness and the inferiority of people of color.

Racism functions in the political economy by promoting persistent forms of class exploitation and political repression of non-European peoples. For example, Christian anti-Semitism in the Middle Ages, anti-Indian racism in colonialism, and anti-blackism in the slave trade provided much of the economic base for the rise and success of industrial capitalism. Scholars document how this economic exploitation, political oppression, and cultural marginalization of non-European peoples has continued during the periods of monopoly capitalism and global corporate capitalism. In their 1979 pastoral letter on racism, *Brothers and Sisters to Us*, the U.S. Catholic bishops said that "racism is an evil that endures in our society and the Church."

Mary E. Hobgood

See also CLASSISM; FAMILY; FREEDOM; MATERIALISM; POLITICS; SLAVERY; SOLIDARITY; VICTIM.

RADHA

See GOPI; SHAKTA; SHAKTI.

RADHAKRISHNAN, SARVEPALLI (1888–1975)

An important twentieth-century Hindu philosopher, Sarvepalli Radhakrishnan was a prominent spokesperson for a modernized version of Advaita Vedanta, sometimes referred to as Neo-Vedanta, which he presented eloquently as a universal, tolerant, and inclusive spirituality. In his many books, he argued that the nondualistic Vedanta was the clearest expression of the single truth that underlies all of humankind's religions. Well educated in Western philosophy, he taught at Oxford University, later becoming the vice-chancellor of Banaras Hindu University. He also distinguished himself as a diplomat and statesman, serving as the second president of India (1962–7).

Lance E. Nelson

See also ADVAITA VEDANTA; HINDUISM.

RAHNER, KARL (1904–84)
German Jesuit theologian, professor at Innsbruck, Munich, and Münster. From his studies of Maréchal and Heidegger, Rahner developed a dynamic explanation of central problems in fundamental theology, the human potential for knowledge of God and the relationship of nature to grace. His account of the dynamic orientation of human spirit to revelation (the supernatural existential) in *Spirit in the World* (1968) and *Hearers of the Word* (1969) established foundational concepts in his theological vision. His articles on symbol and mystery create other categories for examining the experience of revelation. From these starting points, Rahner addressed various problems in dogmatic theology in the articles published in his *Theological Investigations.* Besides teaching and writing, Rahner directed the publication of several theological encyclopedias, among them *Sacramentum Mundi* (1975). The originality and force of his theological vision attracted an international following, and he can be described as the leading

Catholic theological thinker in the twentieth century. A synthesis of his theological vision is found in *Foundations of Christian Faith* (1978).

Patricia Plovanich

RAJA-YOGA
The "royal" (*raja*) discipline, *raja-yoga* is one of the four classically recognized spiritual paths of Hinduism, along with the yogas of knowledge (*jnana*), action (*karma*), and loving devotion (*bhakti*). Best described as a comprehensive program of ethical, physical, and spiritual practice, *raja-yoga* is given its authoritative exposition in the *Yoga Sutras* (*Aphorisms on Yoga*, about the third century C.E.). This text, attributed to the sage Patanjali, forms the basis of Yoga as one of the six orthodox systems of Hindu thought. In the *Yoga Sutras*, raja-yoga is divided into eight fields of practice termed "limbs" (*anga*). Hence it is also known as the *ashtanga*, or eight-limbed, *yoga*. The eight limbs described by Patanjali are: (1–2) ethical restraints (*yama*) and disciplines (*niyama*), (3) yogic posture (*asana*), (4) breathing exercises (*pranayama*), (5) sense withdrawal (*pratyahara*), (6) concentration (*dharana*), (7) meditation (*dhyana*), and spiritual absorption (*samadhi*). In the deepest levels of samadhi, the yoga (practitioner) realizes the transcendent self (*purusha, atman*), an experience that leads to liberation (*moksha*). In lower levels of samadhi, the yoga is said to have access to supernormal powers (*siddhis*). These are, however, regarded cautiously as potential causes of ego-inflation. Traditionally, raja-yoga was a discipline for monastics, to be practiced under the intimate supervision of a guru. In modern Hinduism, elements of the discipline are practiced by Hindu laity. The *Yoga Sutras* do not insist on belief in

God, and Hindu teachers in the West have presented this form of yoga as a spiritual method that can be practiced independently of any belief system. For this reason and others, disciplines related to raja-yoga have gained adherents among non-Hindus interested in a more experiential approach to religion.

Lance E. Nelson

See also BHAKTI-YOGA; DARSHANA/ DARSHAN; HINDUISM; JNANA-YOGA; KARMA-YOGA; PATANJALI; YOGA.

RAMA

An important Hindu deity, Rama is generally regarded as an incarnation (*avatara*) of Vishnu. He is the divine hero of the *Ramayana*, and has been adored by *bhakti*-oriented Hindus for centuries. Rama continues to be an immensely popular object of devotion for Hindus today. His name, often shortened to Ram in Indian vernaculars, is used by many Hindus, especially in North India, as a non-sectarian synonym for "God." The concept of *Rama–rajya* (the rule of Rama), borrowed from the *Ramayana* as a symbol of the ideal Hindu state, has been used by modern Hindu nationalists as a potent political metaphor.

Lance E. Nelson

See also AVATARA/AVATAR; HINDUISM; RAMAYANA; VAISHNAVA; VISHNU.

RAMADAN

Ninth month of the year according to the lunar calendar used by Muslims. During Ramadan, practicing Muslims fast from dawn until sunset. The fast, called *sawm*, involves abstinence from food or drink, including water; from sexual intercourse; and from any kind of enjoyment that would detract from the spirit of prayer

that surrounds this holy season. Children, women who are pregnant or nursing, the elderly and sick, and people on long journeys are exempt from observing the fast. Considered one of the Five Pillars (foundational beliefs or practices) of Islam, the Ramadan fast commemorates the month in which the Qur'an was first revealed. It is also understood as a time of spiritual cleansing and renewal when believers reaffirm their submission to God. The month ends with a joyous festival called *id al-fitr*, the Feast of Fast Breaking.

Ronald A. Pachence

See also FIVE PILLARS (IN ISLAM); ISLAM; MUSLIM; QUR'AN.

RAMAKRISHNA, SRI (1836–86)

A saint who had an incalculable influence on modern Hinduism, Sri Ramakrishna was a village brahmin who became as a youth a priest in a small temple dedicated to the Goddess Kali on the outskirts of Calcutta. There he lived for the rest of his spiritually eventful life. A great devotee of Kali, Ramakrishna was also an extraordinary mystic and visionary who came to be regarded by his followers as an *avatara*. In his spiritual life he is understood to have replicated experientially the truths that were later (largely under his inspiration) to become the basis of the modern, Neo-Hindu view of religion and religions, namely, that all religions point to the same core reality. After undergoing an intense mystical awakening, as the result of which he could enter into visionary awareness of Kali seemingly at will, Ramakrishna was drawn to experience the divine, in similarly vivid fashion, through the other paths of Hinduism. He became, for example, a devotee in succession of Rama, Krishna, and Shiva—

following spiritual paths associated with each to their conclusion in mystic awareness of the deity involved. He then was initiated into the meditational disciplines of Advaita Vedanta and quickly attained a profound realization of the *nirguna* Brahman. He also studied with a Sufi *shaykh* and went through a period of devotion to Jesus and Mary, achieving, we are told, visionary awareness of the divine as Allah and Jesus. As a result of this spiritual journey, he was able to articulate forcefully, and with the authority of his own yogic realizations, the idea that all religious were valid approaches to the one supreme reality. This Ultimate he identified with the nirguna Brahman, the nature of which, his followers were to claim, was articulated most clearly by the Hindu Advaita Vedanta. This understanding helped Hindus comprehend the diversity of their own tradition, as well as its place in the world of religions.

It should be noted that a good deal of Ramakrishna's influence over the vast numbers of Hindus stems from the fact that, unlike Ram Mohan Roy, Dayananda, and several other reformers, Ramakrishna did not deny the value of such things as image worship, polytheism, and the exuberant "popular" religion of the Puranas, which had proved so offensive to Western critics of the day. Indeed, his spiritual journey validated the whole gamut of traditional Hindu religious teaching and experience as various approaches, suitable to different temperaments, to the one Divine.

Ramakrishna's name is often preceded, in writing and oral discourse, with the title "Sri" (Sanskrit, *shri*, illustrious), an honorific often attached to the names of holy men and deities. He himself was only semiliterate, and so far as we know, wrote noting. His teachings were carried to India and the world by his well-educated, articulate disciple Swami Vivekananda, who founded the Ramakrishna Mission and the Ramakrishna Order in India and the Vedanta Society in the West.

Lance E. Nelson

See also ADVAITA VEDANTA; DAYANANDA, SWAMI; KALI; NIRGUNA BRAHMAN; ROY, RAM MOHAN; VIVEKANANDA, SWAMI.

RAMANA MAHARSHI (1879–1951)

An important twentieth-century Hindu saint and religious teacher, Ramana Maharshi, remains for millions of followers a forceful exemplar of the truth of *advaita*, or nondualism. Although he had never studied the teachings of Advaita Vedanta, he is said to have validated their truth in his own extraordinary spiritual experiences that began in his seventeenth year. Leaving his boyhood home, he settled and lived the remainder of his life in the vicinity of Arunachala, a sacred mountain in South India, focusing on spiritual practice and teaching, and displaying little interest in wider movements of human thought and history. While he spoke little, often telling his disciples, "Find out who you are, and all your questions will be answered," he gained an international following and reputation. Advocating the practice of "self-inquiry" as his core spiritual method, he is probably the most important example, for contemporary Hindus, of a jnana-yogi, a saint who followed the yoga of knowledge.

Lance E. Nelson

See also ADVAITA; ADVAITA VEDANTA; HINDUISM; JNANA-YOGA.

RAMANUJA
See VISHISHNADVAITA VEDANTA.

RAMAYANA

The *Ramayana*, traditionally attributed to the sage Valmiki, is one of the two great Hindu epics, the other being the *Mahabharata*. Considered the first and paradigmatic example of *kavya*, the ornate stylized Sanskrit poetry of the classical era, the *Ramayana* was probably composed in stages between about 200 B.C.E. and 200 C.E. It tells the story of Rama, regarded by tradition as an *avatara* of Vishnu, and his loyal wife, Sita, also regarded as a divine incarnation. To fulfill a vow foolishly made by his father, King Dasharatha of Ayodhya, Prince Rama and his wife underwent a voluntary fourteen-year exile in the forest. The couple undergo many adventures, accompanied by Rama's devoted brother Lakshmana. The most important followed upon the abduction of Sita by the ten-headed demon Ravana, ruler of Lanka, the island kingdom. In order to rescue Sita from the clutches of Ravana, Rama raises an army and, with the aid especially of Hanuman, the monkey god, defeats and slays the demon. Upon their return to Ayodhya, Rama and Sita are welcomed with joy.

The heroes of the *Ramayana*, especially Rama and Sita, are taken as ideal exemplars of dharma, or virtuous conduct. As devotion to Rama increased with the popularity of Vaishnava bhakti movements in the medieval period, the epic was translated repeatedly into vernacular versions of high poetic value, but with the devotional elements further embellished, examples being the Hindi *Ramacaritamanas* of Tulsidas and the Tamil *Ramayana* of Kamban. These texts are of immense importance in the devotional life of Hindus. The *Ramayana* story was carried by Indian traders through Southeast Asia, where it remains an important source for classical dance and drama.

Lance E. Nelson

See also BHAKTI; HINDUISM; MAHABHARATA; RAMA; VAISHNAVA; VISHNU.

RAMOS, SAMUEL (1897–1959)

Mexican philosopher. Ramos was educated in his native country and in Europe, held several important governmental posts, and was a professor of philosophy at the Autonomous National University of Mexico for many years. He is considered one of his country's important thinkers. Ramos's work analyzes the relationship between cultural particularity and universal values and truths. He attempted to reconcile the tension between materialism and "spiritualism" by developing a humanism that owes much to Ortega y Gasset. Ramos continued Vasconcelos' philosophical project (for example, on *mestizaje*), and was one of the main influences on Zea's later work. Among Ramos's many books are *Profile of Man and Culture in Mexico* (1934 and 1962), and *Hacia un nuevo humanismo* (1940).

Orlando Espín

See also CULTURE; HERMENEUTICS; IDEOLOGY (IDEOLOGIES); MATERIALISM; ORTEGA Y GASSET, JOSÉ; THEOLOGICAL ANTHROPOLOGY; UNIVERSALS; VASCONCELOS, JOSÉ C.; ZEA, LEOPOLDO.

RAMSEY, ARTHUR MICHAEL (1904–88)

Priest, theologian, bishop of Durham, archbishop of York, and archbishop of Canterbury (1961–74). He considered the vocation of the Anglican Communion to be that of reconciling Protestantism and Roman Catholicism. During his official visit to Rome in 1966, he and Pope Paul VI established the first Anglican–Roman Catholic Commission (ARCIC) as "a serious dialogue which . . . may lead to that unity in truth for which Christ prayed." He also strongly supported the Anglican–Methodist Scheme of Unity that, however, failed to receive the required number of votes of the General Synod in 1972. During his tenure, the General Synod was established in the Church of England with its three houses of bishops, clergy, and laity, and the archbishop of Canterbury as its president. He wrote, among other books, *The Gospel and the Catholic Church* (1936) and *God, Christ and the World* (1969). He resigned in 1974.

Jon Nilson

See also ANGLICAN COMMUNION; CANTERBURY, SEE OF.

RAMSEY, PAUL (1913–88)

An American Methodist, Ramsey was an eminent Christian ethicist of the twentieth century who significantly shaped the current generation of professional religious ethicists. He was notable for his writings on medical ethics, of which *The Patient as Person* (1970) is the most well known. His first book, *Basic Christian Ethics* (1950), provides a biblically-grounded account of Christian morality around the central principle of "obedient love." In several writings, Ramsey explained that Christian love (agape), though not restricted by laws or rules, generates rules and principles and must work through them. He criticized the "situation ethics" popularized in the 1960s by Joseph Fletcher, who held that Christians should do whatever appears "most loving" in a given situation. Ramsey responded that such a principle is far removed from the agape by which God enters into covenant with the human family. Ramsey's understanding of love, covenant, and rules guided his influential applications to medical ethics —where he argued against euthanasia and medical experimentation with children—and political ethics— where he used just war theory to defend the United States' war in Vietnam and its possession of nuclear weapons. Though some of these views were controversial, it is not doubted that Ramsey based them on an unerring respect for the human being as a creature of God.

Brian Stiltner

RANKE, LEOPOLD VON (1795–1886)

German Lutheran historian. Educated in classics, history, and theology at Leipzig, Ranke began a long tenure as professor of history at Berlin (1825–71). A critic of progressivist theories of history, Ranke proposed the construction of history through the use of original sources, particularly of archival materials. He is regarded as a pioneer in the application of scientific methodology to historical research, and his work is distinguished by its objective approach to subjects. A prolific writer, Ranke is noted for his studies of German history. Of special interest to the study of theology are his series *The History of Germany in the Reformation* and his studies of the modern papacy.

Patricia Plovanich

RAPTURE (IN AMERICAN PROTESTANTISM)

Belief in the rapture is a variant on the belief in Adventism shared by the earliest Christians, Seventh-Day Adventists, and Jehovah's Witnesses, and is characteristic of Christian fundamentalism. Biblical literalists and inerrantists, most fundamentalists promulgate a theory of history called premillennial dispensationalism. Dispensationalism posits that human history is divided into epochs called dispensations, each initiated by a covenant between God and humanity. Humanity fails to uphold its end of the covenant, and God terminates the dispensation, usually with a cataclysmic event. The rapture is a future occurrence, prophesied in Daniel and Revelation, part of an eschatological chain of events that will end the present dispensation and prepare the way for Christ's second coming.

Although fundamentalists disagree on the precise chronology, they agree that the end times will include certain events. The Antichrist, a false prophet, will appear, backed by apostate churches (some fundamentalists consider the pope the Antichrist). A political leader called the "Beast" will reunite the nations of the Roman Empire. The Jews will return to Palestine. Christians and Jews will be intensely persecuted during the "great tribulation." Christ will return and, with an army of the faithful, will battle the Antichrist, the Beast, and the forces of evil at a site in the Middle East called Armageddon. After Armageddon, Christ will initiate his millennial kingdom, a thousand-year reign of peace and justice. True Christian believers will be assumed into heaven in a dramatic rapture.

During the rapture, true Christians will magically disappear in the blink of an eye from homes, workplaces, and schools. Transportation will be snarled, and offices and factories will be forced to close. Panic and confusion will ensue among nonbelievers and those false believers who thought they would be raptured.

Fundamentalists disagree on whether the rapture will occur prior to the great tribulation or subsequent to it, and in 1901 the movement divided between pre- and post-tribulationists. The division halted international fundamentalist biblical conferences from 1901 to 1914, the most influential group being the pre-tribulationists led by C. I. Scofield, creator of *The Scofield Bible* (1909), an important fundamentalist biblical translation. Fundamentalists are still divided on this issue.

Evelyn A. Kirkley

See also ADVENTISTS; DISPENSATIONAL-ISM; FUNDAMENTALISM; INERRANCY; MILLENARIANISM.

RASHI (R. SHLOMO BEN YITZCHAK)

See SOLOMON BEN ISAAC.

RAS SHAMRA TABLETS

Ras Shamra is the modern name of a site on the Mediterranean coast that was the location of the ancient Canaanite city of Ugarit. Ras Shamra, meaning "Fennel's Head," is located in modern Syria. The site was discovered in 1929 and was found to contain hundreds of tablets written in an ancient Semitic language closely related to biblical Hebrew, but written in an alphabetic cuneiform script. The Ras Shamra Tablets are of great importance because they provide us with Canaanite religious and mythological texts that greatly increase our knowledge of Canaanite religious beliefs and practices that are similar to those of ancient Israel. They thus provide us with essential background information that allows us to understand the religious thought world of ancient Israel better. Ugaritic, the language of most of the Ras Shamra Tablets, has been helpful in understanding rare and obscure vocabulary in ancient Hebrew as well as some grammatical and syntactic features of the language. The mythological texts from Ugarit have increased our understanding of such deities as Baal, Anat, El, Asherah, and Mot or Death.

Russell Fuller

RASUL

Arabic word meaning "messenger" of God. In Islam, a *rasul* is understood as a prophetic personality to whom God has given the special mission of revealing something new. In this sense, the rasul not only calls believers back to a more faithful practice of religion, but he also discloses a genuinely new understanding of God and the divine will. Muslims speak of Adam as rasul Allah (messenger of God). Other messengers accepted by Islamic tradition include Noah, Abraham, Moses, and Jesus, among others. For Muslims, however, the greatest rasul was Muhammad (570–632) whom God chose as the Prophet of Islam. Muslims call Muhammad the "Seal of the Prophets" because they believe he was the last and most important rasul entrusted by God with the final revelation. This last revelation is considered by Muslims to be God's own "speech" (*Kalam Allah*), preserved in the scripture called the Qur᾽an.

Ronald A. Pachence

See also ADAM (AS PROPHET OF ISLAM); ISLAM; JESUS (AS PROPHET OF ISLAM); KALAM; MUHAMMAD; NABI (IN ISLAM); QUR᾽AN; REVELATION (IN ISLAM).

RATIONALISM

This term refers to the philosophical outlook or theory that emphasizes the role of reason as the sole way of apprehending reality, to the exclusion of other ways of apprehending reality, such as sensory experience, faith, imagination, or tradition. Generally speaking, the various forms of rationalism are dualistic, that is, they view the world as divided into two realms: the realm of ideas—eternal, universal, and disembodied; and the realm of matter—limited, partial, and physical. It is in the higher realm of eternal, abstract ideas that eternal truths are to be found, since the material realm is inherently time-bound and limited.

Rationalism is often identified with the Enlightenment in Western Europe, especially with certain philosophers of the seventeenth and eighteenth centuries, such as Descartes, Leibniz, and Spinoza. Descartes' famous axiom, "I think, therefore I am," reflects a rationalistic anthropology, in which human existence itself is identified with the exercise of the rational intellect; it is only through the exercise of the rational faculty that we can apprehend reality. For rationalists, the "real" world is the world of abstract, disembodied, clear, precise, and distinct ideas, unencumbered by the many limitations of material existence. The highest form of knowledge, therefore, is the most abstract, disembodied, precise, and universal, namely, mathematics.

This dualistic worldview is accompanied by an instrumental approach to the material world, including bodily existence. Separated from the external environment, including the individual's own physical body, the rational intellect exists *over against* that environment that, as an external object, is now manipulated to the ends prescribed by the rational intellect. The goal of the rational ego thus becomes that of achieving total control of this external world, including the individual's own physical body, feelings, passions, instincts, and so on.

The implications of modern rationalism for religious faith are, of course, quite profound. The exaltation of the rational intellect, or logical reason, as the sole source of truth calls into question the epistemological claims of religious faith, especially the authoritative claims of religious beliefs and tradition. As "external" to the rational intellect, these are perceived as irrational impediments to the individual's free exercise of his or her rational faculties. This distrust of and, indeed, hostility toward the authority of religious tradition is exemplified in the eighteenth century, for example, by the widespread sacking and razing of monasteries and churches that took place during the French Revolution. Perhaps the most powerful symbol of the French rationalists' hostility to religious faith was the conversion of the Cathedral of Notre Dame in Paris into the "Temple of Reason," where the Virgin Mary was replaced by the Goddess of Reason. This rejection of religion as irrational found expression, later, in the various forms of modern atheism espoused by, among others, Feuerbach, Marx, Nietzsche, Freud, Camus, and Sartre.

However, the relationship between Christianity and rationalism has, by no means, been exclusively antagonistic. Rationalist ideas have been integrated into and adapted by Christian theology, such as in the various forms of Christian humanism. Some Western philosophers, like Leibniz, Voltaire, and Locke, have developed rational arguments for the existence of God while, nevertheless, rejecting Christian arguments based on faith and tradition. In the nineteenth century, the emphasis on logical, rational argumentation also was reflected in an increasingly detailed and overwrought Catholic Scholasticism; Aquinas's insistence on the relationship between reason and faith thus became displaced in an ever more rationalistic direction.

The increased rationalization of Christian faith engendered, in turn, several reactions in the twentieth century. Neoorthodox theology, as represented above all by the writings of Karl Barth, emphasized the absolute supremacy of Divine Revelation as the sole source of truth. The World Wars, the Holocaust, the nuclear arms race, and other twentieth-century human crises have called into question the earlier confidence placed in the power of human reason to overcome social problems. Liberation theologies reject the primacy of reason, instead emphasizing the practical ground and end of human reason: the form of knowledge (of God) represented by Christian faith is thus not primarily a rational knowledge but a knowledge that comes through an active participation in the world, especially in the struggle for human liberation. Postmodern theologies emphasize the unknowability, otherness, silence, or absence of God as the ways in which God is "known." All these represent reactions to the perceived failures of rationalistic theologies to provide adequate responses to the unprecedented human and ecological crises of the twentieth century. Indeed, insofar as concentration camps, nuclear weapons, ecological destruction, and the like, are the consequences of an efficient and unimpeded development of human rational capacities, rationalism has come to be seen by many as a principal cause of human suffering today.

Roberto S. Goizueta

See also MODERNISM; MODERNITY; POSTMODERNITY.

RATZINGER, JOSEPH

See BENEDICT XVI, POPE.

RAUSCHENBUSCH, WALTER (1861–1918)

Born in Rochester, New York, Rauschenbusch was the preeminent theologian of the Social Gospel. He began his career as a Baptist pastor in New York City, where he encountered poverty, hunger, and unemployment at close range. In 1897 he joined the faculty at Rochester Baptist Seminary and developed his vision of the Social Gospel. In *Christianity and the Social Crisis* (1907), *Christianizing the Social Order* (1912), and *A Theology for the Social Gospel* (1917), Rauschenbusch argued that Jesus' redemption did not apply solely to individuals but also to society. The goal of Christianity was to realize the kingdom of God on earth, and the responsibility of Christians was to work toward societal justice and equality rather than merely to save souls. With passion and clarity, he applied the Gospel to poverty, labor unrest, crime, and industrial exploitation. Although early in his career he tended toward over-optimism that the earthly kingdom of God was possible, he took a more sober view as he grew older and witnessed the outbreak of world war. Rauschenbusch provided a critical theoretical foundation for the Social Gospel, and thus for settlement houses, fair labor laws, church social outreach programs, and ecumenical efforts at addressing social problems.

Evelyn A. Kirkley

See also SOCIAL GOSPEL.

RAV

See RABBI.

RAVANA

See RAMAYANA.

RCIA

See RITES OF CHRISTIAN INITIATION (RCIA).

REAL PRESENCE

In Christian theology, the phrase "real presence" refers to the presence of the risen Christ experienced in the celebration of the Christian ritual meal, the Eucharist. From the very beginning of Christianity, one of the ways Christians experienced Christ as risen has been in the communal celebration of the ritual meal. In the Gospel of Luke, the disciples returning to Emmaus recognized the risen Christ in the breaking of the bread. Writing in the second century, Justin Martyr and Irenaeus of Lyons explained that the Christian community understood the bread and wine blessed at the ritual meal to be the flesh and blood of Christ. Augustine of Hippo, Hilary of Poitiers, Ambrose of Milan, and many others would assert this same understanding of the presence of the risen Christ in the fourth century. Given the underlying Platonism of the majority of these writers, the presence of Christ they described in the Eucharist was real, but certainly not available to the senses (what most modern people would think of as physical). The presence was dynamic, transforming the entire community into the Body of Christ active in the world.

In the ninth century, the monk Paschasius Radbertus introduced a new explanation of the presence of the Christ in the Eucharist into Western Christian theology. Paschasius understood the Body and Blood of Christ in the Eucharist as identical to those of Jesus when he was on earth. This identification sparked off a controversy some two hundred years later when Berengar of Tours denied that such an identification was possible. The discussion became particularly important when the Cathars denied any value to the Eucharist in the twelfth century. An elaborate theology grew up in the newly founded universities that not only insisted on the Real Presence of Christ, but also sought to explain how that presence could come about. Scholars used the philosophy of

Aristotle to explain that the Real Presence was caused by a "transubstantiation" of the bread and wine into the Body and Blood of Christ. Writers continued to insist that the dynamic and transforming experience of the risen Christ active in the community was far more important than how one might explain that change, but more and more, popular devotion in the later Middle Ages focused on the consecrated bread and wine as relics, even placing them in reliquaries to be adored. The feast of Corpus Christi was founded to celebrate that presence.

In the Reformation, there was a strong reaction against these devotions as well as against the complicated explanations of transubstantiation. Martin Luther, while unhappy with the Scholastic theories of how the Real Presence could occur, insisted very strongly that consecrated bread and wine contained the Body and Blood of Christ. Ulrich Zwingli, the Swiss Reformer, denied that the Body and Blood of Christ were present in the ritual, but that this memorial meal celebrated Christ already active in the life of the community. Despite attempts to mediate these differences, especially by John Calvin, the Reformers split on this issue. Calvinist communities tended to adopt a form of Zwinglian theology, denying the presence of the Body and Blood, while Lutherans insisted on such a presence. Roman Catholics upheld the value of transubstantiation as an explanation of how Christ was present. Until the twentieth century, these divisions sharply separated Western Christians. More recently, attempts have been made in all the different communities to stress the dynamic experience of Christ in the community and to understand the presence of Christ in the Eucharist as part of that larger experience. Roman Catholic theologians have also attempted to explain that presence in more modern philosophical terms, thus translating the Aristotelian categories of transubstantiation. These movements have brought the Christian churches much closer together in their understanding of their shared experience of the risen Christ in their communities.

Gary Macy

See also AMBROSE OF MILAN; ARISTOTE-LIANISM; AUGUSTINE OF HIPPO; BERENGAR OF TOURS; BODY OF CHRIST (IN CHURCH USE); BREAKING OF BREAD (IN CHRISTIANITY); CALVIN, JOHN; CHRIST; COMMUNION (LITURGICAL); CONSUBSTANTIATION; CORPUS CHRISTI; EUCHARIST; HILARY OF POITIERS; JUSTIN MARTYR; LITURGY (IN CHRISTIANITY); LUKE/LUKAN; LUTHER, MARTIN; REFORMATION; RELIC (IN CHRISTIAN-ITY); TRANSIGNIFICATION; TRANSUB-STANTIATION; TRENT, COUNCIL OF; ZWINGLI, ULRICH.

REBBE
See RABBI.

REBECCA
The second of Israel's matriarchs in the Hebrew Scriptures (Gen 24:67). She is the daughter of Bethuel, the sister of Laban, the wife of Isaac, and the mother of the twins, Esau and Jacob.

Rebecca is first mentioned in Genesis 22, though Genesis 24–27 are the chapters in which her character emerges. Chapter 24 narrates Abraham's concern that his son Isaac not have a Canaanite wife and his consequent efforts to secure a wife for his son from among his own relatives. He sends a servant to his homeland and, en route, the servant encounters Rebecca at a well. She impresses him favorably, and when he learns her lineage, he knows that she is the right wife for Isaac. Rebecca agrees to go with Abraham's servant in order to become Isaac's wife.

Chapter 25 records Rebecca's marriage and the birth of her twin sons. Because they were jostling in her womb, Rebecca consulted the Lord about her pregnancy. God answered, "Two nations are in your womb, two peoples are quarreling while still within you; But one shall surpass the other, and the older shall serve the younger" (v. 23). Rebecca preferred her younger son, Jacob, and when it was time for her husband to die, she helped Jacob secure his father's blessing (Gen 27:5-29).

There is only one reference to Rebecca in the New Testament (Rom 9:10-13). It quotes Genesis 25:23 where Rebecca is told about her twin sons, "the older shall serve the younger." Paul uses this quote to support his assertion of God's free choice, that God's mercy does not depend on a person's will or exertion but upon God's showing mercy, indiscriminately, to whomever God chooses. While Esau and Jacob were still in Rebecca's womb, God chose Jacob over Esau.

Alice L. Laffey

RECEPTION OF DOCTRINE

Reception of doctrine, generally speaking, is the process through which a conciliar, papal, or ecclesial teaching is "received" (or assented to) by the church because the teaching is "sensed" to be in conformity with the Scripture and earlier tradition. Reception of a doctrine does not create the doctrine, but merely affirms that it is in fundamental accord with Scripture and tradition.

More importantly, reception of doctrine points to a constitutive dimension of Christianity, since Christianity exists because the apostolic preaching was and is accepted (that is, *received*, assented to) by all who become members of the church. Theologically speaking, the reception of a doctrine or teaching occurs as a consequence of the guiding action of the Holy Spirit, who preserves the entire church from error. Today some theologians use the expression "reception of doctrine" to also refer to the acceptance of a doctrine that originated in one Christian church (or denomination), by another Christian church (or denomination).

The reception of a conciliar or papal doctrine is not historically guaranteed. There have been cases of doctrines officially proposed by a council (for example, the conciliarist teaching of the Council of Constance) or by a pope (for example, Boniface VIII's teaching that salvation requires submission to papal authority) that were not received by the members of the church. The specific manner or procedure through which a doctrine is received in and by the church has never been established because it has greatly varied throughout history. Any contemporary attempt at describing the process of reception will also have to contend with the very serious questions raised by inculturation.

The idea that doctrine has to be received by the members of the church emerged during the first centuries of Christianity, when the prevalent ecclesiological model understood the universal church to be a community of communities. After the (Roman Catholic) Council of Trent (1546–63), and especially after the First Vatican Council (1869–70), the idea of reception of doctrine was transformed in Western Catholicism to mean obligatory assent to the doctrinal decisions of the magisterium. However, after the Second Vatican Council (1962–5), Catholic theology began to reflect again on the nature, importance, and need of reception of doctrines, on the role the *sensus fidelium* plays in that reception, and on how reception occurs in contemporary Catholicism's ecclesiological model. This newer reflection is important because reception of doctrine is a process that involves the entire church, and it cannot be reduced to assent to a juridical determination. Furthermore, reception of doctrine must not be confused with contemporary democratic processes because what is sought by reception is not doctrinal agreement among the members of the church but agreement with and assent to apostolic preaching and tradition.

Orlando Espín

See also BONIFACE VIII, POPE; CHURCH; CONCILIARISM; DEPOSIT OF FAITH; DEVELOPMENT OF DOGMA / OF DOCTRINE; DOCTRINE; DOGMA; ECCLESIOLOGY; INDEFECTIBILITY; INFALLIBILITY; MAGISTERIUM, ORDINARY; SENSUS FIDELIUM; TRADITION (IN CHRISTIANITY); VATICAN, SECOND COUNCIL OF THE.

RECONCILIATION

Understood best as one of a constellation of attitudes and practices such as contrition, forgiveness, and mercy, reconciliation's chief feature is that it must be mutual: both the wrongdoer and the wronged must accede to and practice the restoration of a relationship. Further, reconciliation can take place after the wrongdoer has suffered punishment, in contrast to the exercise of mercy.

After Vatican II, the Catholic Church reconceived the sacrament of reconciliation, formerly known as penance or "confession." The reforms shifted the sacrament from the predominantly casuistic approach to sin (with assigned penances) to a more pastoral approach. Emphasis was placed on reconciliation with God and with the community, for which the priest was the spokesperson.

G. Simon Harak, s.j.

See also CONTRITION; FORGIVENESS; MERCY.

RECONCILIATION, SACRAMENT OF

Also called "penance" or "confession." In the Roman Catholic Church, one of the seven sacraments, and one way the church carries on Christ's mission of reconciling the world to God. In the first Christian centuries, an explicit liturgical act of reconciliation was required only for those who had committed the gravest of sins: murder, idolatry, apostasy, or adultery. After acknowledging their failure, these sinners were grouped with others in an order of penitents. Much like those who were preparing for baptism (catechumens), the penitents followed an intense discipline of prayer, fasting, and penance, often lasting for years. When the community determined that the penitent had truly reformed, it readmitted the sinner to the regular life of the community and to eucharistic Communion. The usual sign of reconciliation was the laying on of hands by the bishop/pastor. Christians could undergo this process, called canonical penance, only once in a lifetime. In some churches, those who had completed canonical penance were expected to continue some form of self-denial, such as sexual abstinence, until death. To avoid such restrictions, many Christians waited until they were dying to seek reconciliation.

Beginning in the seventh century, Irish monks introduced an alternative form of penance. Penitents confessed privately to a monk who assigned an act of penance. The monk, although wise in the spiritual life, was often not a priest. Since he was not an ordained minister of the community, the rite was not seen as an act of the church but as a sort of private spiritual counseling session. The purpose of the penance was to correct the personal flaw that led to the sin and to give the sinner a way to make restitution to God. The perceived need to compensate God led to the creation of books called Penitentials that listed what penances were appropriate for which sins. The notion of penance as a sort of fine or repayment reached its zenith with the creation of tables indicating how a penitent could actually pay another person to do a penance, or substitute one penance for another. This system of payments and equivalencies is called tariff penance. Unlike canonical penance, tariff penance could be repeated as often as necessary in a person's life. Also, whereas canonical penance emphasized the social nature of sin and reconciliation, tariff penance envisioned reconciliation as a transaction essentially between God and the penitent, with little involvement of the community.

Beginning in the late ninth century, priests began to take the roles formerly held by monks in penance. While the church was still not as actively involved as it had been in canonical penance, it was at least represented by its official minister, the priest. Unlike canonical penance, however, that placed the moment of reconciliation at the end of the period of penance, this new system had the minister pronounce the absolution (declaration of forgiveness) immediately after the confession of sins, even before the penance was begun. This de-emphasized the importance of the penance as a vehicle for personal conversion and even led to the theory that it was the very humiliation of confession that paid the price for the sin.

The Protestant Reformers of the sixteenth century challenged the form of reconciliation that had evolved. The Council of Trent, however, while correcting some of the abuses that had arisen, upheld auricular confession—the telling of one's sins to a priest—as the method of reconciliation established by the Lord himself. In 1963 the Vatican II Constitution on the Sacred Liturgy mandated a reform of the rites of reconciliation so that they more clearly express both the nature and effect of the sacrament (no. 72), namely, reconciliation with God and with the church (see *Lumen Gentium* 11). The new rite, issued in 1973, has three possible forms. The first is an encounter between priest and penitent for prayer, Scripture reading, confession of sins, counsel, absolution, and praise of God's mercy. The second is like the first, but it envisions a public liturgy of prayer, Scripture reading, and song, during which penitents may approach a priest for private confession. In the third form, often called general absolution, a group of penitents recites a declaration of sinfulness and receives absolution from the priest without private confession. This form is to be used only in emergencies (danger of death) or practical difficulties (too many penitents for the number of priests present).

Many commentators have suggested that the sacrament of reconciliation is in crisis. Studies indicate that Catholics are celebrating the sacrament far less frequently than they were even a generation ago. Some parishes, however, have established an order of penitents as in the days of canonical penance for those who wish to return to the church after years of being away.

Patrick L. Malloy

See also CATECHUMENATE; CONTRITION; LUTHERAN THEOLOGY; MONASTICISM IN

WESTERN CHRISTIANITY; REPENTANCE (IN CHRISTIAN PERSPECTIVE); SIN, PERSONAL; SIN (SOCIAL, STRUCTURAL); SPIRITUAL DIRECTION.

RECONSTRUCTIONIST JUDAISM

A twentieth-century North American Jewish movement inspired by the teaching of Mordechai Kaplan (1881–1983), an Orthodox ordained rabbi who taught from 1909–63 at the Conservative movement's Jewish Theological Seminary. Reconstructionism was formally organized in 1940 on the foundation of the Society for the Advancement of Judaism that itself had been created in 1922. Its seminary, the Reconstructionist Rabbinical College, was founded in Philadelphia in 1968. By far the smallest of North America's several Jewish movements, approximately one hundred congregations now are affiliated with the Federation of Reconstructionist Congregations and Havurot. About two hundred rabbis are members of the Reconstructionist Rabbinical Association.

Reconstructionism advances Kaplan's view that Judaism is a social rather than spiritual phenomenon. It rejects traditional theistic claims and notions of the supernatural, viewing God, rather, as a force promoting justice, goodness, and truth. In line with this disavowal of the traditional notion of God, Reconstructionism also denies the concept of chosenness, so central in traditional Jewish theology. In the place of concepts of God and chosenness, Reconstructionism focuses upon community as the center of Jewish life. It holds that all Jewish activity, including adherence to the law, affirmed by Kaplan, should be designed to promote the community of Judaism that Kaplan referred to as a civilization, the people of which are the source of authority and of their own salvation.

Rejecting the concept of God as a sovereign Creator, Reconstructionism adjures contemporary Jews to follow the practices of Jewish tradition for reasons that make sense now. Jewish practice, that is, is to be "reconstructed" so as to express values and meanings appropriate within the lives of Jews today. Prayer and ritual in particular are to be rethought in order to maximize the impact they have on the individual, not because they affect God. In light of Kaplan's understanding of the sociological nature of Judaism, he imagined the synagogue not just as a place of worship but as a community center where study, art, drama, physical exercise, and a range of social activities could take their proper place as central aspects of the Jewish experience.

Alan J. Avery-Peck

RECTIFICATION OF NAMES

(Chinese, *Cheng Ming*, correct use of terminology). Known popularly as the rectification of names, this is a central concept in Confucius' plan for the restoration of order and harmony in society. It is based on the belief that intellectual disorder results in moral perversity. Confucius suggested that names (terms) must correspond to actualities; that is, only when society knows, and there is consensus on, what a particular term such as justice means and then acts in accord with that definition, will there be true social order. It is said that Confucius considered this the linchpin of his system.

G. D. DeAngelis

See also ANALECTS; CONFUCIANISM; CONFUCIUS; LI; TE.

RECTOR

A title that has several meanings. (1) In the Roman Catholic Church, it is given to the priests who serve as acting pastors of cathedral churches. (2) In some Catholic religious orders (especially the Jesuits) it is the title of the superior of a local community or house of the order. (3) In most countries, it is the title of the presidents of universities and colleges. (4) In the churches of the Anglican Communion, it is the title of some more important local pastors.

Orlando Espín

See also CATHEDRAL; CONGREGATIONS (ORDERS); DIOCESE/ARCHDIOCESE; PARISH; PASTOR; RELIGIOUS (VOWED); ROMAN CATHOLIC CHURCH; SOCIETY OF JESUS; UNIVERSITY.

RECTORY

In the Roman Catholic Church, the rectory is a residence for priests who serve a parish or church institution. It is also called a presbytery. Usually, the rectory is on church property, or quite close by, so that the priests may have access to their places of ministry and be available to the people. The rectory also provides for some sense of community living when there is more than one priest in a parish or area. Today, many parishes have only one priest and find that maintaining a large rectory is no longer affordable. In some dioceses, a parish priest lives in an apartment or at a residence some distance from the church building in order to have more privacy. Former rectories often serve as parish offices or meeting space and may still be called by this title. In the Protestant Episcopal Church the rectory is the residence of the rector, the clergyperson in charge of a parish.

M. Jane Gorman

See also PARISH; RECTOR.

REDACTION CRITICISM

A redactor is someone who shapes existing oral traditions and written materials into a single composition by arranging, revising, and editing earlier sources to promote particular perspectives. There is no doubt that the canonical Gospels reached their present form because of the work of their final redactors. Redactional activity is present in all the books in the Bible.

Redaction criticism seeks to establish the theological perspectives found in the canonical text by the way disparate material has been put into its final form. While the study of the creative contributions of the final redactor to a text has also been called composition criticism, redaction criticism and composition criticism are used synonymously. They represent two parts of a single enterprise.

The early source and form critics were interested in reconstructing the developments that preceded the final text and neglected the creative activity of the final redactors. Redaction criticism presupposes and builds on the results of source criticism and form criticism. It is the third stage of the enterprise known as the historical-critical method. However, in Old Testament studies, the preferred term is tradition criticism, since there are many more layers of redactional activity to be considered.

Redaction criticism was introduced in studies of the Synoptic Gospels. Günther Bornkamm (1948), Hans Conzelmann (1954), and Willi Marxsen (1954) are credited with introducing the method. It was quickly adopted by other scholars. Many consider it the most important aspect of the historical-critical method.

Regina A. Boisclair

See also FORM CRITICISM; HISTORICAL CRITICISM; SOURCE CRITICISM.

REDEMPTION, CHRISTIAN

The experience of being alienated from other human beings and even one's true or authentic self can be read as a sign and a consequence of a still deeper estrangement from our origins in God—the estrangement of creatures from their Creator as depicted in the opening chapters of Genesis. The tragic "fall" of Adam and Eve, humanity's first parents, gives rise to a need of and desire for reconciliation, reunion, or homecoming. Redemption is the story of God reaching out to estranged, wandering, and confused humanity in order to rejoin men and women with their Creator. The result of reunion with God will be the creation of lasting community among all God's people, a communion really, albeit imperfectly, made present by the church. The Bible can be read as the history of God's saving outreach to fallen humanity represented by the people of Israel, and the climax of that outreach is the crucified Jesus, the definitive sign of God's love for the world (John 3:16). In Jesus, God demonstrates vividly what it means to be humanity's neighbor (see Luke 10:36-37).

The word "redemption" is a metaphor. As such, it suffers from a number of limitations. To redeem means to purchase or to buy back; but from whom or from what is God or Christ buying humanity back? It makes no sense to suggest that, through the death of Jesus, God was buying human beings back from Satan. What the term "redemption" stands for, consequently, is the experience—sometimes joyful, sometimes painful, but always liberating—of having been made whole or even created anew by the Father, in Jesus, through the power of the Spirit. It is characteristic of God to rescue human beings from themselves, that is, from their own self-destructive capacities. The

autonomy that we tried to buy or "grasp" (Phil 2:6) through pride and disobedience turns out to be an illusion; God, we might say, redeemed us from ourselves. Jesus represents the human being that each of us is intended to be—the fullest expression of the divine image and likeness. By joining oneself to Jesus in faith, we allow the Spirit of Jesus to reshape our hearts and minds so completely that we too can know and address God intimately as "Abba, Father" (Rom 8:15). Thus redemption is a way of naming the ongoing, ever deeper insertion of the human being into God's own life. The believer feels that he or she has been "ransomed," that someone has purchased her or his freedom. Yet the price for our freedom is not so much the death of Jesus as the unimaginable richness of God's love that alone can put an end to our poverty.

Christian theology usually locates the "moment" of redemption in the death of Jesus, that is, we have been redeemed through his Blood (see, for example, Rom 3:25; Eph 1:7; Col 1:20; Rev 1:5). But we should not freeze that moment and lift it away from history and daily life as if it were a timeless, spaceless event. Objectively, perhaps, redemption occurred with the death of Jesus; but subjectively every human being must come to terms with his or her own sinfulness, and allow herself or himself to be confronted by the mystery of divine compassion. While there is a sense in which humanity has been redeemed even though many human beings are hardly conscious of the fact that "God so loved the world," people will not be challenged and transformed by God's love unless they realize, as Paul did, that the Son of God "loved *me* and gave himself *for me*" (Gal 2:20). In short, we cannot think about redemption without thinking about conversion.

William Reiser, s.j.

See also ATONEMENT, CHRISTIAN; CONVERSION; CREATION; CROSS, THEOLOGY OF THE; GRACE; SALVATION; SIN, ORIGINAL.

REFORMATION

Calls for reform of the church, including its doctrine, its practices, its head and members, from pope to common people, and its relationship to the state and to society, were frequent throughout the late Middle Ages and the Renaissance. If such appeals for reform went largely unheeded in the fourteenth and fifteenth centuries, in the sixteenth century, Martin Luther, John Calvin, and other Reformers, were successful in carrying out what each of them considered to be a return to the church as instituted by Christ. These Reformers, who argued that the Roman Catholic Church had deviated from the teaching of Scripture, later came to be known as Protestants and their work as the "Protestant Reformation," or simply the "Reformation." The Reformation is critically important for the history of Christian theology, for the history of politics and religion, and for an understanding of relations between the church and society in the modern world.

Theology and Reform

The Renaissance was an intellectual and literary movement that found its ideals in antiquity, both pagan and Christian. Renaissance scholars looked to the Greek and Roman past as a golden age of eloquent language and literature; they also looked to early Christianity, especially to Scripture in its original Hebrew and Greek, and to the teaching and life of the first Christians as normative for the church of any age. With the invention of the printing press around 1450, the ancient texts so highly valued by the Renaissance could be made far more widely available. Erasmus (about 1469–1536) stands out among Renaissance scholars as one who sought reform of the church through such propagation of the Bible and other ancient texts.

Erasmus, however, like many other "humanists," sought a moral reform of the church rather than a theological or doctrinal one. For Martin Luther (1483–1546), the principal error of the Roman Church was in doctrine; Rome, through its false teaching, was leading Christians away from Christ and toward damnation. An Augustinian friar trained in exposition of Scripture, and a professor at the University of Wittenberg in Germany, Luther used the printing presses of his day very effectively to spread his message. Beginning with his Ninety-Five Theses of 1517, a polemical manifesto in which he denounced the sale of indulgences, Luther relentlessly exposed shameful and self-serving ways in which Rome was teaching people to place their hope of salvation somewhere other than in Christ alone.

In dozens of treatises in German and Latin, Luther articulated a theology of justification by faith alone. He juxtaposed this to an anxious search for salvation engendered by Rome's teaching. For Luther, Christians led astray by the pope and his theologians looked to the merit of the saints, or to their own merit through "good" works, as means to salvation or justification before God. Luther, relying heavily on the letters of Paul and on the Gospel of John, asserted that salvation came through grace alone, through God's unmerited gift of grace in Christ, and not through anything else. The sole way in which salvation had been "merited" was through the death of Christ, of Christ in whom Christians had but to place a trusting faith. To pulpit oratory and to printed treatises, Luther added hymns as a means of making known the Gospel of justification by faith. "A Mighty Fortress is our God" is the best known of his hymns.

Relying on a principle of "Scripture alone" as source of Christian doctrine, Luther set aside the Roman teaching on seven sacraments, retaining eventually only baptism and Eucharist. Regarding the latter, Luther affirmed a doctrine of the Real Presence of Christ in the Eucharist, but rejected the Roman Catholic doctrine of transubstantiation, for it relied on philosophical categories and language not found in Scripture.

The church, for Luther, was to be the place where true doctrine would be preached without ambiguity and in a language all could understand. Yet Luther did not focus his energies on a reform of church structures; doctrine, not institutional structures, remained his passion. Luther, like other Protestant Reformers, did not see himself as founding a separate or new church, but as restoring the old, original church.

Ulrich Zwingli (1484–1531) in Zurich, and later John Calvin (1509–64) in Geneva, echoed Luther's teachings on grace and justification by faith alone. Calvin's doctrine of predestination is but a logical development of a doctrine of salvation by grace alone. Like Luther, Zwingli and Calvin made Scripture the norm for doctrine. Yet they rejected the doctrine of the Real Presence as defended by Luther; for Zwingli especially, the Body of Christ was now in heaven and could be present in but a symbolic way in the Eucharist.

Unlike Luther, Zwingli and Calvin made reform of church practices and structures a priority as important as doctrinal reform. They found the practice of adorning churches with images to be idolatry; the destruction of images, especially images of miracle-working saints, was carried out in most places where the Zwinglian or Calvinist model of reform was adopted, in Switzerland and beyond. Calvin especially, in his *Institutes of the Christian Religion* and his own reforming work in Geneva, replaced a church structure based on bishops with a less hierarchical model of the church in which the laity played a major role. In the office of "elder," members of the laity were to collaborate with clergy in the governance of the church, including participation in the policing and preservation of moral standards by the members of the church.

Diversity of reform priorities grew as the Reformation progressed. Moral reform was of the highest urgency for "Anabaptist" Reformers; their reform of the church is sometimes referred to as the "radical" or "left wing" of the Reformation. It was a reform that sought to restore the church in the image of that portrayed in the Acts of the Apostles, where goods were held in common and all had according to their needs. Sanctification was to be pursued by living apart from the evil world, in community, and in imitation of Jesus who was poor, humble, and persecuted.

Anabaptists rejected the practice of infant baptism, arguing that this sacrament of initiation should be reserved for adults who are believers and who are committed to living exemplary lives. Some Anabaptists, such as those who controlled the city of Muenster in 1534–5, believed that the kingdom of God was about to be established on earth. They sought to hasten this event, not only through rebaptism of true believers, but through violence, cleansing the city of unbelievers by use of the sword as needed. Most Anabaptists, however, such as the

Dutchman Menno Simons (1496–1561), were pacifists, unwilling to take up arms even to defend themselves. The events at Muenster unfairly gave all Anabaptists a negative reputation, one that led to their savage persecution by Protestants and Catholics alike.

Politics

Whatever their differences on other matters, all Protestant Reformers rejected the papacy and its international pretensions. Most Reformers relied on state support to carry out their reform of the church; the Reformation was often warmly embraced by those civil leaders who sought to promote national or local power and autonomy in place of imperial, papal, or other centralized authority. As Reformation Churches were organized on a local or national basis, and celebrated their liturgies in the language of the local people rather than in Latin, they served to promote national consciousness and identity in early modern Europe.

Theology often had a direct impact on politics. The "freedom" of a Christian that Luther had explained as the freedom from anxiety about salvation enjoyed by those who placed their faith in Christ alone, was interpreted by some in Germany to mean a new political and economic freedom for the peasants and other poorer classes. The Peasants' War of 1524–5 sought to make such freedom a reality. With the encouragement of Luther, however, the princes defeated the peasants and with them the possibility of the Reformation in Germany engendering a political or economic revolution.

England provides perhaps the best example of the close association of church reform and politics. King Henry VIII (reign 1509–47) was declared head of the Church of England by the Act of Supremacy of 1534. Thus the papacy was eliminated from church life in England and a national church established. In its theology of sin and salvation, the English Reformation was strongly influenced by developments in Calvin's Geneva; in church structures and ceremonies, however, the English church retained an episcopate as well as more elements of Catholic ritual than most Protestant Churches. It was Queen Elizabeth I (reign 1558–1603) who firmly instituted such a "middle way" for England, a way that was difficult to maintain against those who found it too Catholic or too Calvinist.

Society

If Elizabeth played a key role in establishing the Church of England, the Reformation's impact on women is a controversial issue among Reformation historians today. Some, such as Steven Ozment, point to the marriage of clergy as a reform that changed for the better the status of women. Women were no longer viewed as temptresses of the clergy, and family life was no longer seen as inferior to celibacy. Other historians, such as R. W. Scribner, suggest that the Reformation's elimination of devotion to the saints, including many female saints, made religion more male than ever. If medieval Catholicism was patriarchal, was Protestantism even more so?

The Reformation is also important for the history of education. Along with its focus on the reading of Scripture and its reliance on the printing press for propagation of its message, the Reformation founded or reformed schools of all levels. Rates of literacy rose substantially in those parts of Europe where the Reformation was adopted. Those who learned to read were trained especially to read the Bible and the catechism. Printed catechisms were published in abundance and sought to eliminate doctrinal ignorance or error and to guide the reading of Scripture. If literacy had appeared as optional for Catholic devotion, it was necessary for Protestant piety.

Protestantism may also have played a role in the development of modern capitalist society. Max Weber's thesis, on a link between, on the one hand, a Protestant ethic of hard work, individualism, and thrift, and, on the other hand, the growth of capitalism, is seen by some as particularly evident in the history of the United States.

Thomas Worcester, s.j.

See also ANABAPTISTS; AUGSBURG CONFESSION; BUCER, MARTIN; CALVIN, JOHN; CALVINISM; COUNTER-REFORMA-TION/CATHOLIC REFORMATION; ERASMUS OF ROTTERDAM; FIDES FIDUCIALIS; IMPUTATION; JUSTIFICA-TION; LUTHER, MARTIN; LUTHERANISM; MELANCHTHON, PHILIP; MENNONITES; MUENZER, THOMAS; NINETY-FIVE THESES; PROTESTANTISM; REFORMED CHURCHES; REFORMED THEOLOGY (-IES); SIMUL IUSTUS ET PECCATOR; SOLA FIDE; SOLA GRATIA; SOLA SCRIPTURA; WITTENBERG; ZWINGLI, ULRICH.

REFORMED CHURCHES

In the broadest sense, a Reformed church is any one emerging from the Protestant Reformation of the sixteenth century in Europe, including Lutherans, Presbyterians, Congregationalists, Baptists, and Anabaptists. However, the term has come to refer specifically to churches following John Calvin and Calvinism in opposition to Martin Luther and the Lutherans. In the sixteenth and seventeenth centuries, Reformed churches formed in the Netherlands, Switzerland, France, and areas of contemporary Germany and Hungary.

Early on, what distinguished Reformed from Lutheran churches was their different understanding of Communion. Lutherans believed that Christ's actual presence was manifest in the elements of Communion, while Calvinists affirmed Christ's presence as spiritual rather than physical. As time passed, differences between Lutheran and Reformed churches widened, especially the doctrine of double predestination. Reformed churches also practiced presbyterian polity.

Dutch Reformed emigrants arrived in the North American colonies as early as the 1610s. They settled in Albany and New Amsterdam, later New York City. The first Dutch Reformed Church was formed in New Amsterdam in 1628. They also established communities on Long Island and northern New Jersey. Even after the takeover of New York by the English in 1664, the Dutch Reformed retained their privileged status as the state church. An early leader of the First Great Awakening was a Dutch Reformed pastor in New Jersey, Theodore Frelinghuysen. In 1747 he and his followers established a coetus, an association of churches analogous to a presbytery. Prior to that time, Reformed churches were under the authority of the classis of Amsterdam. In New Brunswick, New Jersey, the Dutch Reformed founded Queen's College in 1766, now known as Rutgers University, and a seminary in 1784, New Brunswick Theological Seminary.

The Reformed Protestant Dutch Church became an independent denomination in 1792, changing its name to the Reformed Church of America (RCA) in 1867. Besides New York and New Jersey, the Dutch Reformed settled in Iowa, Michigan, and parts of California. Primarily from political reasons, the RCA experienced schism in 1856, leading eventually to the formation of the Christian Reformed Church (CRC). Although the RCA and CRC shared Calvinist theology and Dutch heritage, they differed in their adaptation to the United States. The RCA is more Americanized and is virtually indistinguishable from the mainstream of Protestantism, while the CRC maintained the use of Dutch into the twentieth century and objected to what they saw as liberal accommodationism of the RCA. The CRC founded Calvin College and Calvin Seminary in Grand Rapids, Michigan. Two well-known Dutch Reformed ministers in the twentieth century were Norman Vincent Peale of Marble Collegiate Church in New York City and Robert Schuller of the Crystal Cathedral in Garden Grove, California, purveyors of positive thinking and mass-market religion.

German Reformed emigrants settled in Pennsylvania beginning in the 1720s and 1730s and were mistakenly called "Pennsylvania Dutch," a corruption of Deutsch or German. Possessing a stronger ethnic than religious identity, they cooperated with other Germans regardless of theological predilection, especially German Lutherans. Without a strong central organization, the first German Reformed synod did not form until 1793 in Lancaster, Pennsylvania. As the German Reformed Church became more Americanized, it dropped "German" from its name in 1869 and in the twentieth century embarked on a series of mergers with other Reformed groups. In 1924, it absorbed the Hungarian Reformed Church, and in 1934, united with the Evangelical Synod of North America, itself a union of German Lutherans and Reformed for political rather than theological reasons.

The resulting denomination, the Evangelical and Reformed Church, existed until 1957, when it merged with the Congregational Christian Churches to form the United Church of Christ. Leaders in the German Reformed tradition include John W. Nevin and Philip Schaff, exponents of the so-called "Mercersburg theology," professors at the German Reformed Seminary in Mercersburg, Pennsylvania, later relocated in Lancaster; and brothers H. Richard and Reinhold Niebuhr, professors at Yale Divinity School and Union Theological Seminary respectively, leaders of neo-orthodox theology in the United States.

Evelyn A. Kirkley

See also CALVIN, JOHN; CALVINISM; PRESBYTERIAN CHURCHES; PRESBYTERIAN THEOLOGY; REFORMED THEOLOGY (-IES).

REFORMED THEOLOGY (-IES)

Like Presbyterian theology, the predominant influence on Reformed theology is Calvinism, articulated in the Heidelberg Catechism (1563), canons of the Synod of Dort (1618–9) and the Westminster Confession (1646). Calvinism's key tenet is divine sovereignty: God is all-powerful, wise, and loving. Humanity, by contrast, is utterly sinful, doomed by original sin and total depravity to yearn to do good yet be unable to do so. Although humanity deserves to be condemned to hell, God in mercy has determined that some will be spared that fate. God has unconditionally elected some to be saved and others to be damned, not based on their own merit, wealth, birth, or education, but solely on God's inscrutable will. Christ died and was resurrected to save these elect. God's grace bestowed through the power of the Holy Spirit is irresistible; one cannot reject, jeopardize, or lose it. Likewise, one can do nothing to change one's fate if damned. Although to later

Christians Calvinism would appear fatalistic, to Calvin and his followers, it was a joyful, democratic, and liberating gospel, one that trusted God's wisdom instead of earthly standards. Reformed theology was also scholarly and rationalistic.

In the United States, several theologians have applied Reformed theology to the U.S. religious landscape. In the mid-nineteenth century, John W. Nevin (1803–66) and Philip Schaff (1819–93), professors at the German Reformed seminary in Mercersburg, Pennsylvania, articulated what came to be known as the "Mercersburg Theology." Characterized as a "High Church" or "catholicizing" movement, the Mercersburg Theology stressed the historic traditions of the church and its creeds against the restorationist, primitivist tendencies of evangelical Protestantism.

Nevin sought to recover the spirit of Reformed theology in *The History and Genius of the Heidelberg Catechism* (1841–2), and he critiqued the emotional excesses and lack of intellectual rigor of revivalism in *The Anxious Bench* (1843). In *The Mystical Presence; or a Vindication of the Reformed or Calvinistic Doctrine of the Holy Eucharist* (1846), he affirmed the importance of sacramentalism and argued that it had been all but lost in U.S. Protestantism. In *The Principle of Protestantism* (1845), Schaff affirmed the Incarnation as the beginning point of Christian theology and the person of Christ as its central focus. In *What Is Church History? A Vindication of the Idea of Historical Development* (1846), he traced interpretations of church history since the sixteenth century, concluding that the richness of church history reveals God's purposes and must be examined for what it teaches contemporary Christians.

In the twentieth century, two brothers, sons of a German Reformed pastor in Missouri, were astute interpreters of neo-orthodox theology in the United States. Reinhold (1892–1970) and H. Richard (1894–1962) attended Eden Theological Seminary in St. Louis and pursued academic careers. Reinhold became a professor of social ethics at Union Theological Seminary in New York, and H. Richard, at Yale Divinity School in New Haven, Connecticut. Their prolific writings affirmed Reformed themes of humanity's fallenness and finitude, God's power and profundity, and the dangers of optimism and Christian accommodation to prevailing culture. However, their thought was not identical. In *Leaves from the Notebook of a Tamed Cynic* (1929), *Moral Man and Immoral Society* (1932), and *The Nature and Destiny of Man* (1941–3), Reinhold Niebuhr attacked unjust U.S. social, economic, and political institutions. He lambasted liberal Christian attempts to reform society and declared that institutions by their very nature are unable to act ethically. Social ethics cannot be absolute but must be applied to particular contexts. In *The Social Sources of Denominationalism* (1929), *The Kingdom of God in America* (1937), and *Christ and Culture* (1951), H. Richard Niebuhr analyzed the reasons why Christian institutions had failed and in a few cases fulfilled their potential. He argued that racial, ethnic, and economic oppression divided Christians from one another and prevented them from realizing a transformative kingdom of God in the United States.

The Reformed themes that unite Schaff, Nevin, and the Niebuhrs are a commitment to the church, respect for Christian history, and an intellectual rather than emotional approach to theology. All affirm the limitations of human nature and the depth of sinfulness; they are suspicious of placing too much trust in human capability. Yet all celebrate the glory and love of God and the necessity of faith.

Evelyn A. Kirkley

See also CALVIN, JOHN; CALVINISM; NIEBUHR, H. RICHARD; NIEBUHR, REINHOLD; PRESBYTERIAN CHURCHES; PRESBYTERIAN THEOLOGY; REFORMED CHURCHES.

REFORM JUDAISM

Emerging in eighteenth-century Europe, this was a movement that adjusted classical Jewish practice and beliefs to the changes brought about by the Enlightenment and Jewish emancipation. Reform thus responded to the increased social and cultural integration of Jews and non-Jews and to the increased secularity of modern culture. At the heart of Reform Judaism is the rejection of the claim of traditional Judaism that the biblical and rabbinic writings contain the revealed, and hence unchanging, will of God. Reform instead holds that revelation is progressive, that each age must determine which practices and theologies are appropriate and valid. According to Reform, Judaism thus is an evolving faith that does not contradict the results of modern scientific or philosophical inquiry and does not preclude full Jewish participation in contemporary society.

As early as the beginning of the nineteenth century, some German Jews rejected the encompassing system of law and ritual that defined rabbinic Judaism. They held that, like the Christianity practiced by their neighbors, Judaism has an essence, expressed in core beliefs and articulated by only a small number of rituals that heighten the moral character and enhance the spiritual fulfillment of the Jew. Early reformers worked in particular to restructure synagogue practice so as to create a worship service analogous to that of Protestant Christianity. They shortened the Jewish service, abolished the use of traditional prayer-garments (Tallit and Yarmulke), and eliminated the chanting of prayers that was seen as an inappropriate oriental element. They used the vernacular as the primary language of prayer, and added to the service contemporary hymns sung by a choir and accompanied by an organ. The focus of the service became the rabbi's sermon, delivered in German.

German Reform was brought to America by the German immigrants of the early decades of the nineteenth century, and the first successful reform synagogue was established in Baltimore in 1842. The Pittsburgh Platform of 1885, the classical statement of American Reform, defined Judaism as an evolutionary and progressive faith that contains an essential core of moral laws and ideas and that promotes social justice. Customs and ceremonies that do not promote this end were seen as vestiges of an unscientific age and were to be abolished. The Jews were defined not as a people or nation but as a religious confession. Early American Reform thus rejected Zionism as an appropriate outlet for American Jewish self-identity.

The arrival in America of approximately two million less assimilated eastern European Jewish immigrants between 1881 and 1914 coupled with a growing concern in the America Jewish community about the potential for the survival of Judaism here, led Reform Judaism to take an increasingly more positive view of previously rejected practices and traditions. The Columbus Platform of 1937 encouraged the use of Hebrew and other traditional symbols. It also supported

Zionism, a first within the Reform movement, and the central reason that this platform was widely rejected by practitioners of Reform. Still, in the period since the Columbus Platform, and particularly in the past thirty years, the Reform movement has firmly expressed its support for Israel and for the concept of Jewish peoplehood. Indeed, while retaining its commitment to social justice and ethics, Reform has experienced a significant reawakening of interest in previously discarded traditions, ranging from the wearing of prayer-garb to the observance of dietary laws. These developments are particularly evident in the "Statement of Principles of Reform Judaism" adopted at the May 1999, Pittsburgh meeting of the Central Conference of American Rabbis. In this way, the movement has adjusted to the needs and interests of the more ethnically self-conscious Jewish population of the contemporary United States.

Reform is the dominant Jewish movement in North America and has significant representation as well in other Western countries with Jewish populations. Reform is not recognized by the Israeli Rabbinate and, like other non-Orthodox Judaisms, is represented by only a small movement in Israel today.

Alan J. Avery-Peck

See also JUDAISM; RABBINIC JUDAISM; RECONSTRUCTIONIST JUDAISM.

REFUGE, THREEFOLD

The basic, beginning, and universally accepted focus of devotion in Buddhism. "Taking Threefold Refuge" in the Buddha (Shakyamuni and others), Dharma ("Teachings"), and Sangha ("The Devout Community") is the early self-definition of the core tradition and repeated by all Buddhists regularly.

Repeating the refuge formula three times: *Buddha/Dharma/Sangha saranam gacchami* ("I go for refuge in the Buddha/Dharma/Sangha") defines conversion to Buddhism and marks the beginning of any communal or individual ritual event. Taking refuge in the Buddha often is done with reference to an image or *stupa;* devotees, including monks and nuns, connect with the Dharma through written texts or memorized recitations; the Sangha, narrowly defined as monks and nuns or extended to include dedicated lay brothers (*upasakas*) and sisters (*upasikas*), is found connected with monasteries and temples. The Mahayana school added the refuge with the bodhisattvas to the list; Vajrayana adherents added the tantric guru.

Todd T. Lewis

See also BUDDHA; DHARMA (IN BUDDHISM); MAHAYANA BUDDHISM; SANGHA; TANTRIC BUDDHISM.

REGULA FIDEI

See RULE OF FAITH; TRADITION (IN CHRISTIANITY).

REIGN OF GOD

Also commonly referred to as the kingdom of God, this is a central theme in the preaching of Jesus. The concept "reign of God" is deeply rooted in the Old Testament, prominent in the New Testament, particularly the Synoptic Gospels, and, through Christian history, has been variously related to the church as well as to secular society.

Each of the two expressions, "reign of God" and "kingdom of God," carries with it distinctive, though not mutually exclusive nuances. "Reign of God" points more to the personal, authoritative activity of ruling by a king; this is the king's reign. "Kingdom of God" refers more to a spatial entity, a geographical territory where the king rules.

Although the phrase "kingdom of God" does not occur in the Old Testament, and only once in the deuterocanonical literature (Wisdom of Solomon 10:10), the theme of God as a ruling king is prevalent. Numerous traditions acclaim God as king of all history, specifically of the people Israel. Throughout the story of the Hebrew people God is the sovereign one, having freed them from the slavery of Egypt, then claiming them as God's people in the covenant on Mt. Sinai, giving them the Promised Land as an inheritance, chastising them during the Exile, and restoring them again to the land of Israel. No human monarchy, no group of prophets or priests controls the destiny of the people, for God alone is the one who rules over the history of Israel.

A number of the Enthronement Psalms proclaim God as reigning over the nations, indeed over all creation (93; 95–99). As the divine king, God establishes and maintains order in the universe and blesses or punishes Israel or Israel's enemies. Beginning with the postexilic period and extending into the apocalyptic climate of the intertestamental period, God's kingly rule becomes increasingly connected with the hope that God would bring to an end the present rebellious state of the world and usher in a new age of justice, peace, and goodness.

Into this climate, Jesus appears announcing the imminence of God's kingdom: "The time is fulfilled, and the kingdom of God has come near; repent, and believe in the good news" (Mark 1:15). Jesus may well have been the first to employ regularly the "kingdom of God" motif to announce what he was about. Richly and diversely manifested through his words and deeds, the kingdom of God functions as a symbol that cannot be exhausted by any one action or saying.

Jesus understood this central symbol as being *already*, though *not yet* fully present. The kingdom of God, Jesus proclaimed, is coming definitively in the near future marked by an end to the present stage of things and the dawn of God's absolute rule over all peoples, Israel in particular. While the kingdom is imminent, Jesus did not set any timetable for its appearance. He did teach his disciples to pray for its coming: "your kingdom come, your will be done, on earth as in heaven" (Matt 6:10).

For Jesus, the kingdom of God is also already present, radically altering what is. "The kingdom of God is in your midst" (Luke 17:21); "Happy the eyes that see what you see" (Luke 10:23). One needed to look no further than the person of Jesus, who embodied the kingdom. To encounter him was to encounter God's kingdom of love, justice, and mercy already come. The presence of the kingdom is manifested in the reversal of fortunes for the rich and the poor, the hungry being fed, the satisfied going hungry (Beatitudes), demons being cast out, and the joyful participation of believers in the heavenly banquet with Israel's patriarchs (Matt 8:11-12). Participation in the Eucharist is an anticipation of eating and drinking at the Lord's table in the kingdom (cf. Luke 22:30; Mark 14:25).

Matthew's Gospel speaks more about the kingdom than any other. The most characteristic expression is "kingdom of heaven," a phrase with the same meaning as "kingdom of God." "Heaven" is used instead of "God" out of respect for the divine name that in Jewish religious tradition is too sacred to be uttered. Many parables portray the kingdom, beginning, "The kingdom of heaven is like . . ."

Notable is the parable of the Great Judgment when the king comes to separate the sheep from the goats (Matt 25:31-46).

In Paul the kingdom functions as the basis of ethical exhortation: evildoers are excluded from inheriting the kingdom (1 Cor 6:9-10; Gal 5:21; cf. Eph 5:5). One of the best brief definitions of the kingdom is given by Paul in Romans: "For the kingdom of God is . . . righteousness, peace, and joy in the holy Spirit" (Rom 14:17).

Throughout Christian history, the expression "kingdom of God" has received many interpretations from the mystical, equating it with inner experiences of the soul, to the political, equating it with a particular political regime or form of government, such as the Holy Roman Empire. Up until Vatican II, following Augustine, the church has been regularly identified with the kingdom of God. In one of its most significant statements, the council defined the church as subordinate to the kingdom of God, "always in need of being purified, and incessantly [pursuing] the path of penance and renewal" (*Lumen Gentium* 8).

John Gillman

See also APOCALYPTIC; CHURCH; ECCLESIOLOGY; ESCHATOLOGY (IN CHRISTIANITY); ESCHATOLOGY (IN JUDAISM); NEW ISRAEL.

REINCARNATION

Also referred to as transmigration or metempsychosis, reincarnation is the idea that the soul or psychic self of a being that has died returns and takes up another body to experience another lifetime. It is a doctrine common to the religions of India, certain schools of ancient Greek religion, Manichaeism, mystical Judaism, and a number of nonliterate indigenous traditions, as well as sectarian movements within other religious traditions. A number of modern religious movements, such as Theosophy, also believe in reincarnation.

The Indic religions, which include animals and other "lower" forms of life in the transmigratory process, regard the world in which one experiences reincarnation (*samsara*) as a place of suffering (*duhkha*). Reincarnation (in Sanskrit, *punar–janman* or *punar–bhava*, "rebirth") is therefore seen as an ultimately undesirable phenomenon, and the spiritual goal of most Indic traditions is formulated, at least initially, in terms of liberation (*moksha, mukti, nirvana*) from the process. Since Buddhism's *anatta/anatman* (nosoul) doctrine denies the existence of any substantial self, it is sometimes argued that the reincarnation doctrine is incompatible with Buddhist psychology. But this is no more the case than in the Hindu Advaita Vedanta, which teaches that the only true Self is the one universal atman, identical with the *nirguna* Brahman, which is no more capable of traveling from life to life than the nonexistent Buddhist self. In both cases, it is the insubstantial, ever-fluctuating psychic self—termed in Hinduism the "subtle body" (*linga–sharira*) and in Buddhism the "stream of consciousness" (*vinnana–sota*)—that goes from one body to the next, a process propelled and giving continuity by desire and karmic momentum. The quality of the life one is reborn into is determined, in the Indic traditions, by the quality of one's karma, the accumulated moral residue of one's past actions. Good karma can lead to rebirth in a better human life, or even life as a god. Evil karma leads to a life of suffering, whether as a human being or as an animal or other form of life. One can avoid reincarnation by nullifying one's accumulated karma through ascetic practice (*tapas*) or spiritual knowledge (*jnana*), or by relying upon the grace of God (*prasada*).

In the ancient West, the Orphic mystery cults and certain Greek philosophers, including Pythagoras, Plato, and Plotinus, accepted the doctrine of reincarnation, along with the idea of an eternal soul. Plato, for example, taught that the soul would reincarnate until, through the discipline of philosophy, it could attain full contemplation of the idea of the Good. Among Jews, Christians, and Muslims, the orthodox have consistently rejected the doctrine of reincarnation; among other reasons, it is difficult to reconcile with the traditionally accepted eschatology of those traditions, especially the ideas of postmortem punishment in hell and of the final resurrection. However, in the Kabbalist tradition of Judaism, the idea of reincarnation (Hebrew, *gilgul*) was introduced in the *Sefer Bahir*, a twelfth-century text. While early Kabbalists thought that gilgul was a punishment for grievous sin, and an opportunity for evildoers to correct and purify their souls, it later came to be understood as a universal phenomenon, including non-Jews and allowing the possibility of reincarnation in animal and other life forms. There was also debate as to whether souls were reincarnated three times, as many as one thousand, or whether, like the Bodhisattvas of Mahayana Buddhism, righteous souls reincarnate repeatedly, until the resurrection, as benefactors of the world. As for reconciling reincarnation with the doctrine of resurrection, some Kabbalists taught that the soul would divide itself between its various bodies, others that only the last body in the series would be resurrected. Although it is not found in the Bible, the Talmud, or the teachings of the ancient rabbis, and was vigorously opposed by medieval Jewish philosophers, the doctrine of reincarnation was and continues to be important to Jews interested in the mystical aspects of the tradition, especially in the Hasidic community.

Nonliterate indigenous peoples that accept reincarnation (not all do), generally view it as a positive opportunity to extend one's life. In these cultures, reincarnation tends to be associated with ancestor veneration: the belief is typically that some or all children are reincarnations of particular ancestors of the kinship group. The Aborigines of Australia accept that human souls regularly reincarnate, not only in animals and plants, but also in inanimate forms, such as rocks and water, or in celestial bodies, such as the stars.

Lance E. Nelson

See also BUDDHISM; GRECO-ROMAN RELIGION; HASIDISM; HINDUISM; INDIGENOUS RELIGIOUS TRADITIONS; JAINISM; JUDAISM; KABBALAH; PLATONISM; SIKHISM.

RELIC (IN CHRISTIANITY)

The body, or part of a body of a saint, as well as objects that may have contacted the body of saints, are considered relics. Early in the history of Christianity, the remains of holy people and particularly of the martyrs were accorded great honor. Although the veneration (in Greek, *dulia*) of relics is carefully distinguished in theological thought from the worship (in Greek, *latria*) owed to God, popular devotion, especially in Western medieval Christianity, accorded great power to relics. They were understood to be a source of contact between the holy person now in heaven and the community here on earth. The saint was to be honored in his or her relics by the community, who then expected to be protected and promoted by the holy patron. Excesses in the devotion to relics caused the Reformers of the sixteenth century to reject relics entirely. Roman Catholics, however, continued the veneration of relics, and this practice still plays an important role in popular devotion for many Roman Catholic communities.

Gary Macy

See also COMMUNION OF SAINTS; MARTYR/MARTYRDOM; SAINT.

RELIC (OUTSIDE CHRISTIANITY)

In Islam and Buddhism, a corpse or cremated remains is considered unclean or impure, and so must be discarded through burial or immersion in flowing water to prevent close proximity to the human community. The exception to this generalization is for those regarded as saints. Devotees have used the "sacred traces," the bodily remains of holy persons as media that, when enshrined, allow continued connection and blessing. Muslims go to the tombs of saints to experience their grace (*baraka*) and pray for assistance and intervention at the last judgment. Buddhists followed the Buddha's own instruction to place his own cremation remains and other items associated with him (bowl, robe, and so on) in mounds called *stupas*, where they should remember him, make offerings, play music, and expect extraordinary, meritorious impact on them. Jains also have a similar tradition.

Todd T. Lewis

See also STUPA.

RELIGION

Religion is clearly a difficult and complex phenomenon to define. One key split in such an endeavor occurs between those who are believers in a particular religious tradition versus those who are "scientists of religion" who strive to attain a definition applicable to the vast variety of beliefs and practices found in different societies around the world. It has been defined by Anthony Wallace as "a set of rituals, rationalized by myth, which mobilizes supernatural powers for the purpose of achieving or preventing transformations of state in man and nature." E. B. Tylor more succinctly stated that it is a "belief in spirits." And Clifford Geertz offered the following: "(1) a system of symbols which acts to (2) establish powerful, pervasive and long-lasting moods and motivations in men [sic] by (3) formulating conceptions of a general order of existence and (4) clothing these conceptions with such an aura of factuality that (5) the moods and motivations seem uniquely realistic."

Broadly, religion consists of "a system of beliefs and practices that are linked to superhuman beings" or supernatural forces. Such beings are capable of acts that humans cannot do. They can be male, female, or androgynous. They may be gods, goddesses, ancestors, spirits, or impersonal powers that can cause evil or good to people or groups. The beings may be alone or in various combinations or hierarchies. The system of beliefs is also linked to practices, myths, and rituals associated with the supernatural that may include ceremonies, prayers, songs, dances, offerings, sacrifices, and other behaviors and paraphernalia. Through these activities people try to manipulate the supernatural beings and powers in humans' favor. In all societies there are certain individuals with skills at dealing with the superhuman beings and powers. Religious practitioners, such as shamans, may be part-time intermediaries between the human and supernatural realms who work to influence the supernatural to do the will of the shamans' clients, such as bringing about physical or material well-being. In other societies, full-time religious practitioners, priests or priestesses, receive formalized training and education in the sacred, and sometimes secret, ritual lore and practice. Full-time religious figures tend to relay the will of the supernatural to humans and to encourage appropriate and moral human behavior in order to bring about the desired response on the part of the supernatural entity or powers. Typically, in religious systems there is a body of myths that rationalizes or explains the system in a way that is consistent with people's experiences and worldview. The mythology may provide an explanation for the culture's origins and often provides a charter for appropriate behavior.

Religion is a universal phenomenon; no human society has been identified that does not have some form of religion, and it has been present in human societies for at least one hundred thousand years. Earliest evidence of some form of belief system or ritual activity is found in Neanderthal cave burials. One explanation for its universality is that all religions offer explanations and solutions for individual and community problems along social, psychological, and cultural dimensions. Some of the important psychological functions of religious beliefs and practices are that they reduce anxiety by explaining the unknown and making it understandable by providing comfort in times of crisis, and by providing a sense of belonging to a group. Another important function is that religions sanction a range of human conduct and behavior. Additionally, often the burden of decision-making is given to the supernatural. Religions also encompass and foster the creation of oral traditions. Many important kinds of information necessary to group survival—such as ecological, social, or historical material—may be symbolically encoded in religious stories and songs. Religion promotes solidarity among a group of people. People gain identity through mythological links of community or group origin to cosmological understanding. Rituals that mark transformations of status or life events—such as birth, adulthood, or death—help move individuals through times of life crisis and provide instruction in new roles and statuses. Religious beliefs and activities give meaning to life for humans and offer spiritual identity to groups. People receive moral sanctions, values, and a common purpose through their identification with a particular religion or cosmological understanding of the world. As Geertz has noted, religion provides both a "model of" and a "model for" human behavior. Each religion embodies culturally understood truths about humans, society, and cosmos.

The continuing appeal and growth of religion in the face of Western rationalism testifies to its power as a dynamic force in society. It addresses universal human questions of meaning and fulfills social, cultural, and psychological functions in such a powerful way that it is not likely to diminish as a fundamental aspect of human culture regardless of future social and cultural change.

Christine Greenway

RELIGION, CRITIQUE OF

Criticism of religion is probably as old and diverse as religion itself. Prior to the eighteenth-century Enlightenment in the

West, however, critiques of religion took the form of criticizing "corruptions" in one's own religion or criticizing religions other than one's own as "barbaric," "pagan," "superstitious," "idolatrous," and so on. Even the classical critique of religion by Lucretius (d. 55 B.C.E.) in *On the Nature of the Universe* was arguably more directed at specific positive religions than religion per se.

Enlightenment and post-Enlightenment atheistic critiques of religion differ from the preceding in that they are in principle applicable to all religions and are often a variation on the "projection theory of religion." In its three theses, the projection theory treats the cognitive status of religious ideas as well as the motivation behind, and consequences of, religious belief. First, religion is *nothing but* the product of the human imagination, and thus what it speaks of does not exist, apart from the mind, in the coordinates of reality. Second, religion is *nothing but* an ersatz compensation for some real social or psychological need unsatisfied by reality itself. Third, religious belief is *nothing but* an impediment or obstacle to achievement of intellectual and moral autonomy. In diverse ways, Ludwig Feuerbach, Sigmund Freud, Karl Marx, and Jean Paul Sartre are exemplars of this position.

A variation is found in those critics of religion who hold the first two theses and reject the third if religion is "correctly" understood in a nonrealist manner. For exemplars of this position, for example, Emile Durkheim, R. B. Braithwaite, and Don Cupitt, religion has some individual or collective utility if and only if taken in a nonrealist manner.

Within the Christian religious tradition, criticism of religion has often taken the form of denouncing both "other" (idolatrous) religions and "idolatry" within the Christian religion. Neo-orthodox theology—sometimes utilizing the insights of atheistic critics—made the latter a central theological motif, especially in the theologies of Karl Barth, Dietrich Bonhoeffer, Paul Tillich, and Reinhold Niebuhr. For neo-orthodoxy, "religion" was viewed as the revolt of humans against divine revelation. The Christian religion, in particular, was viewed as an often successful and sinful attempt to compromise the radical demands and promise of the Gospel. Thus, the dialectical tension between "religion" and "revelation" demands the rigorous criticism and continuous reformation of the former—especially the Christian religion—in the name of the latter, even though the latter is only available through the former.

J. A. Colombo

See also AGNOSTICISM; ATHEISM; ENLIGHTENMENT IN WESTERN HISTORY; FEUERBACH, LUDWIG; FREUD, SIGMUND; IDOLATRY; MARX, KARL; NEO-ORTHODOXY; PAGANISM/PAGANS; PHILOSOPHY OF RELIGION; SARTRE, JEAN PAUL.

RELIGION, FREEDOM OF

Freedom of religion has played a significant role in the United States in two ways. First, it was a primary impetus for emigration. From the seventeenth century to the twentieth, persons from all over the world have come to this country to practice their religious beliefs free of interference. In the early 1600s, Anglicans, Pilgrims, and Puritans sought freedom of religion as well as commercial success in Virginia and New England, although they did not extend that freedom to others, notably Native Americans, Africans, and Quakers. Three of the first thirteen colonies explicitly extended religious tolerance: Rhode Island, founded by dissident

Puritan Roger Williams; Pennsylvania, founded by Quaker William Penn; and Maryland, founded by the Roman Catholic Calvert family. All three advocated tolerance on the grounds of religious freedom as well as practical expediency to attract settlers.

Second, freedom of religion is a crucial part of the U.S. Constitution in the First Amendment to the Bill of Rights: "Congress shall make no law respecting an establishment of religion, or prohibiting the free exercise thereof." The separation of church and state has two facets: no religious group will be supported or privileged by the state, and all residents of the United States are free to practice religion as they choose. The separation of church and state has had three implications for U.S. religious culture. First, religious affiliation is completely voluntary; there is no state coercion to join a community of faith. Second, since voluntarism means that all religious groups are on equal footing, they must compete with one another for members and financial support. They are rivals in the free religious market, forced to use whatever means necessary to survive. Third, voluntarism and competition led to denominationalism, the development of religious communities with only slight variations in theology and liturgy. To attract adherents, often "stealing" them from other communities of faith, denominations minimize their differences with one another. At the same time, they magnify the difference between themselves and peripheral groups called cults and sects.

Religious freedom has contributed to religious innovation and pluralism in the United States. Yet despite the rhetoric, the reality has been slow in coming. Although no formal establishment exists, groups not conforming to the norms of dominant Euro-American Protestantism have experienced oppression. In the nineteenth century, Jews, Mormons, and Roman Catholics were persecuted for beliefs and practices thought contrary to the "American" way of life. In the twentieth, Christian Scientists, Jehovah's Witnesses, and pacifist churches waged battles in court for free exercise, including the right to refuse conventional medical treatment, saluting the flag and saying the Pledge of Allegiance, and bearing arms. In 1990 members of the Native American church fought unsuccessfully for the right to use peyote, a hallucinogenic substance, in their worship services. Courts have overturned laws legalizing prayer in public schools or teaching creation science as violating the separation of church and state. More remains to be done before true freedom of religion is realized in the United States.

Evelyn A. Kirkley

See also CIVIL RELIGION; FREE CHURCH TRADITION.

RELIGION, THEORIES OF

Theoretical approaches to religion strive to address fundamental questions concerning its origins and functions through systematic and critical analysis. Examples of the kinds of questions theorists have posed include: Why is religion universal? How and when did it originate? What individual and societal needs are fulfilled by religion? Such questions provoked a variety of responses by thinkers such as Freud, Durkheim, Marx, Tylor, Geertz, and others. The theoretical approaches to explaining religion include psychological, sociological, functionalist, rationalist, and interpretive.

Some early theories about the origins of religion included those of J. G. Frazer and E. B. Tylor. Both offered intellectualist or rationalist explanations. Tylor, in his work *Primitive Culture*, explored animism, the belief that all things, living or inanimate, contain a spiritual essence. He was interested in investigating the prehistoric origins of religious beliefs. Tylor proposed a notion of intellectual evolution and a principle of psychic unity. He argued that different people may discover the same ideas or invent the same customs independently of one another. In his view, such independent invention was not coincidental; rather, it was evidence that the human mind is fundamentally uniform and human beings are the same regarding mental capacity and logical ability. Although his evolutionary view is ethnocentric, his stress that all humans in all places and times have the same cognitive capacity was a significant contribution to cross-culturally comparative and relativistic studies. When he applied his notions of intellectual evolution to religion, he asserted that all human groups will go through a similar developmental process, and the earlier stages of religion will become explanations for later or higher stages. In other words, animism, in his view the earliest and simplest form of religion, will ultimately in all human groups develop into polytheistic and then monotheistic forms. He further postulated that religion originally derives from the human capacity to reason intellectually about puzzling phenomena, such as death, unconsciousness, and dream states. Early human groups observed such mysterious things and theorized that humans are animated by a soul or spiritual principle that can separate from the body during death, unconsciousness, or sleep states. From that notion, early religious beliefs about spirits and supernatural beings emerged, and these

ideas continue to develop and change. In this view, early humans are considered philosophers engaged in solving intellectual problems, and religion is defined as a set of ideas that answer such questions; and while it is false, it is not irrational. Both Frazer and Tylor can be viewed as scientific theorists of religion. They collected observations and compared and classified them in order to formulate a general theory that would account for the cross-cultural variations that had been documented. One drawback of their work is that they compared various examples without attention to their social and historical context.

Sociological theories of religion are based on Durkheim's contributions. Sociological theories focus on the importance of society and social structure in understanding human thought and behavior. Religion is viewed in terms of its social dimensions and functions. In *The Elementary Forms of the Religious Life*, he rejected Tylor's theories about animism and argued that society itself is sacred and is the root of religious belief. According to Durkheim, Tylor's theory did not explain how the idea of a soul evolves into notions of a sacred ancestor or ancestral cult. He posits, instead, the view that religious beliefs are symbolic projections of the collective life and are symbolic of social facts. The object of religion is a collective reality; as groups gather together, they experience a collective "effervescence" that gives rise to their ideas about the sacred. The totemic god is the representation of the clan itself. Religion further provides behavioral rules regarding sacred objects.

Freud provided a psychological perspective to theories regarding the origins and functions of religion. He agreed with Durkheim that totemism is the source of the origin of religion. Its origin, he hypothesized, derived from a specific act. He thought the earliest humans lived in a primal horde. Young males were restricted by the oldest, most powerful male from mating with the females. In order to gain access to the females, they kill the male, the "father." Feeling guilt over their deed, they create a commemorative feast with the corpse as the meal. Periodic ritual practices symbolically reenact the original deed. His theory also attempts to explain how taboos cause guilt and pain which, in turn, are lessened by adherence to religious practices. For Freud, religion derives from psychological repression based on illusions, projections, and desires. He correlated the images, stories, and themes that recur in mythology, art, folklore, and religion with the subjects and images of dreams. He argued that the similarities demonstrate the power of the unconscious. He viewed religious beliefs as erroneous and superstitious but interesting because they raise questions about human nature. If religion is not rational, he wanted to know how and why people acquire it. He was also interested in the ways religious behavior resembles mental illness and viewed religion as rooted in obsessional neurosis. Religion has psychological functions and arises in response to emotional conflict and weaknesses that are unconscious and rooted in the events of early childhood. In this view, when psychoanalysis has solved such individual neuroses, religion will become irrelevant and disappear. In contrast, for Jung, another psychological theorist, religion draws on resources of the collective unconscious and is not viewed as a form of neurosis, but as a healthy expression of human nature.

Functionalist approaches address what religion does for people psychologically or for a group socially or in terms of social structure and why, once it originated, it exists universally. A. R. Radcliffe Brown explained that cultures are integrated systems, and all parts of a culture perform a specific function. The function of religious belief and ritual is to express and maintain sentiments necessary for social cohesion. Malinowski proposed that the basic needs religion satisfies are biological, while Durkheim argued the elementary needs are social. Homans asserted that both were correct: individual biological as well as group needs for the reduction of anxiety are solved by religion. Other functionalists argued that rituals and beliefs are either expressive, or else cognitive, rational explanations for empirical observations. Victor Turner unifies these theories with his analysis of religious symbols as multivocal with cognitive, physical, and emotional value. Generally, functional theories state that religious beliefs in particular social contexts satisfy real social needs.

Phenomenological approaches to the study of religion, exemplified by the work of Rudolf Otto and Mircea Eliade, view the history of religion as the history of the manifestation of the sacred. The sacred is defined as "ultimate reality" and is viewed as transcendent. Such approaches are associated with the construction of typologies of religion that demonstrate various ways the sacred has been manifested throughout history. This approach rejects the sociological, psychological, sociobiological, and political/economic theories as reductionistic. The phenomenological or history of religions approach leads to an understanding of religion based in theology or faith.

Karl Marx viewed religion as alienation. The primary role of religion, in his view, is to justify and uphold society's economic and political structures. He argued that economic exploitation and oppression underlie all previous and existing societies, and religion serves to glorify and reproduce oppressive social orders in symbolic form. Marx believed religion would vanish once social oppression was eliminated by communism.

A recent development in theorizing about religion is found in the work of Clifford Geertz and others. Geertz defines religion as a cultural system and opposes the reductionism of functionalist approaches. He argues that it is necessary to grasp the system of meanings conveyed by a religion. Religion is a worldview and an ethos; it consists of ideas and beliefs about the world and feelings and behaviors that are in accordance with those ideas. In other words, religion is both a "model of" and a "model for" behavior. Thus, Geertz's theory encompasses the sociological, emotional, symbolic, and rational aspects of religion. According to Geertz, following Weber, all humans are confronted by problems of meaning that result from unpredictable, random, and unjust events. The problems faced by humans include bafflement, suffering, and evil. Religion provides an explanation for the source and meaning of these problems and offers intellectual, emotional, and behavioral solutions to such crises of meaning. Intellectually, religions contain ideas that move, motivate, and inspire people. People believe religious ideas are true and valuable and are ideas that should be followed. Approaches such as that of Geertz are interpretive and aim at deciphering the meaning that religious beliefs and practices have for their adherents.

The variety of theoretical approaches to the study of religion have spurred debate, prompted data collection and analysis, and led to the development of academic disciplines. All strive to make sense of, in a scientific way, the existence and persistence of religious ritual and belief.

Christine Greenway

RELIGIOUS (VOWED)

Men and women who formally and publicly embrace the three evangelical counsels of poverty, chastity, and obedience within a religious community approved by the church are referred to as religious. The word religious here functions as a noun, not an adjective. A religious promises or "vows" to observe the traditional marks of evangelical living by being poor, chaste, and obedient in imitation of Christ. These vows may be simple or solemn, temporary or perpetual. In communities where temporary vows are taken, it is normally understood that they will be renewed at specified intervals. Thus religious vows envision a lifelong commitment. A particular community might add a fourth vow, or additional promises, to the basic three. The Benedictines, for instance, take a vow of stability, that is, they promise to remain affiliated for life with the monastery wherein they pronounce their vows. The Jesuits pronounce a fourth vow of obedience to the pope regarding missions. But poverty, chastity, and obedience are elements that have constituted religious life at least since the time of St. Benedict in the sixth century.

William Reiser, s.j.

See also CHASTITY; OBEDIENCE; POVERTY (RELIGIOUS VOW); PROFESSED; VOWS.

RELIGIOUS EDUCATION

The noun *education*, in its broadest sense, refers to the human examination of life. When it is modified by the adjective *religious*, it has been applied in the following ways: first, to an inquiry into the classic religious traditions of the world; second, to the general investigation of a religious dimension to human life; third, to the human quest for a transcendent ground of being; finally, to the education carried on among members of a religious denomination. From about the turn of the twentieth century, use of the terms *religious education*, *Christian education*, and *catechesis* has revealed an ongoing tension in the United States about the ends and means of education in religion. Those who favor the term religious education claim that only this term is broad enough to encompass the whole body of practice and theory that rightly ensues from the conjunction of religion and education; namely, investigation of and dialogue with the world's religious traditions, philosophic criticism of the claims of various religious traditions, and religious criticism of the social, political, economic, and educational patterns of a society. Those who favor the terms Christian education and catechesis claim that religious education is limited to "teaching about" religion, while Christian education and catechesis aim at introducing learners to the very realities proclaimed in the Scriptures, symbols, rituals, and doctrines of the Christian tradition. Proponents of the term *catechesis* point to its use in Christian Scripture and throughout the history of the church as the word used to identify the educational activities of the church. They maintain that catechesis is not limited to oral instruction but refers to a process whereby individuals are initiated into and socialized within the church community. Instruction under the rubric *religious education* is generally carried on in public schools and universities, while the terms *Christian education* and *catechesis* are more frequently used to describe reli-

gious instruction in religious schools and Sunday schools.

Helen deLaurentis

See also CATECHESIS/CATECHETICAL.

RELIGIOUS STUDIES

A term employed to designate the study of religion as distinct from theology and independent from a particular dogmatic theological position. "Religious studies" also owes its wide use to the reluctance of public institutions of higher learning, particularly in the United States (with its constitutional commitment to the separation of church and state), to organize their academic offerings to give explicit support to, or even the appearance of favoring, any religion or any denomination of Christianity.

Religious studies implies acceptance of an interdisciplinary methodology, including within its domain the philosophy of religion, literary studies of sacred scripture (usually including the Bible), social scientific approaches, the study of ethics, and theology. It also often assumes a serious commitment to articulating nuanced comparisons between world religions; "religious studies" as a designation also tends to be adopted by individuals and institutions with a liberal, nontriumphal religious orientation.

Todd T. Lewis

See also COMPARATIVE RELIGION; HISTORY OF RELIGIONS; RELIGION, THEORIES OF.

RENAISSANCE

A French word signifying rebirth, the "Renaissance" refers to a period in the history of Western Europe and, more specifically, to a cultural movement that began in Italy and spread from there to other parts of Europe. As a period of time, the Renaissance includes the three centuries from about 1300 to around 1600: it thus overlaps with the late Middle Ages as well as the Reformation and Counter- or Catholic Reformation. As a cultural event or movement, the Renaissance sought to revive or rekindle antiquity: Greek, Roman, and Christian antiquity. This effort of revival concerned language, literature, and the arts; it integrated an optimistic anthropological perspective; it promoted religious reform through a return to Christian origins.

Arts and Letters

In Renaissance Italy, architecture, sculpture, and painting enjoyed the often lavish patronage of civil and ecclesiastical patrons. Architects and sculptors sought to emulate classical precedents in the harmony and order of forms. Painters left behind the relative flatness of medieval painting and developed the depth of perspective; Giotto's early fourteenth-century wall-paintings in Assisi and Florence are some of the first examples of the new style. Later Renaissance artists include Fra Angelico, Leonardo da Vinci, Michelangelo, and Vasari. Though much of Renaissance art was religious, with great attention given to depiction of lives of the saints and stories from Scripture, secular subjects also received attention. Portrait painting developed, with attention given to the particular traits of each individual subject.

Meanwhile, classical Latin and Greek were given the place of honor in Renaissance schools, and ancient history was seen as providing examples of heroic and virtuous lives to imitate. At the same time, however, vernacular languages such as Italian and French were promoted not only as spoken tongues but as elegant, literary languages. In the case of Italy,

Dante's *Divine Comedy*, composed in Italian in the first two decades of the fourteenth century, helped to establish the dignity of the vernacular. The Renaissance was a period in European history when national consciousness grew more important; development of national languages aided such growth.

The printing press was invented around 1450 in Germany. It gave a new impetus to the literary aspirations of the Renaissance; it also changed the way Christians thought about the Bible. Scholars such as Erasmus produced editions of the New Testament in its original Greek; others published the Old Testament in its original Hebrew; translations of the Bible into various vernacular languages were proliferating by the early sixteenth century. From a text available to but a few and in manuscript form, the Bible became accessible to all who could read.

Anthropology

The term "humanists" is often given to those Renaissance scholars who devoted themselves to ancient Hebrew, Greek, and Latin. In this sense, the term is related to the "humanities," a nomenclature familiar to colleges and universities in the United States. The term "humanism" may also refer to a philosophy or anthropology that privileges the freedom and dignity of the human being. In this way, the "humanism" of the Renaissance concerns an optimism and enthusiasm about human potential and human accomplishments. For example, Pico della Mirandola, a fifteenth-century philosopher, produced an *Oration on Human Dignity* in which he located that dignity in the freedom of the individual to choose good or evil, in the freedom of the individual to imitate the angels or the demons.

Many historians have emphasized the development of individual consciousness in the Renaissance. For Jacob Burckhardt, medieval Europeans had placed belonging to a group far ahead of any individual identity. Burckhardt saw the beginnings of "modernity" in the Renaissance sense of individuality; some historians of the Reformation see in such a sense or consciousness preparation for, or anticipation of, Protestantism.

Religion and Reform

If there is continuity between the values of the Renaissance and those of the Reformation, there is also discontinuity. A new focus on Scripture, and dramatically improved availability of Scripture to potential readers, surely helped to make the Reformation possible. Reformers called for reform through return to the religion of biblical times. Also, development of national languages and national identities prepared the way for political conflict with the papacy and its international profession.

Yet, Renaissance optimism about the individual's ability to freely choose good or evil was rejected by Luther and other major Reformers. For Luther, original sin had left all human beings in a state of bondage to evil, a bondage from which only God could free them. More optimistic about human freedom, even after original sin, the Counter-Reformation rejected Luther's teaching on bondage of the will and affirmed that the individual Christian, with the help of grace, could choose good rather than evil. The Counter-Reformation (or Catholic Reformation) was, however, unwilling to endorse the reading of Scripture by all and in the vernacular; the authority of tradition and of the papacy was given priority over individual interpretations of Scripture, as

well as over the aspirations of national churches.

Thomas Worcester, s.j.

See also COUNTER-REFORMATION / CATHOLIC REFORMATION; DEVOTIO MODERNA; ERASMUS OF ROTTERDAM; FICINO, MARSILIO; FREE WILL; HUMANISM; IMITATION OF CHRIST (BOOK, CONCEPT); MORE, THOMAS; PICO DELLA MIRANDOLA, GIOVANI; REFORMATION; SIN, ORIGINAL; TRENT, COUNCIL OF.

RENEWAL MOVEMENT
See JEWISH RENEWAL MOVEMENT.

REPARATION
Reparation has to do with making amends for wrongdoings, offenses, and sins (committed after baptism) against God and others; it brings about reconciliation with God and others. Reparation takes place mainly through a combination of prayers, ascetic practices (like abstinence and fasting), almsgiving, and good works. It is sometimes associated with participating in the work of Christ for the redemption of the world from sin. In Catholic Christian faith and life, it follows the sacrament of reconciliation, one of the seven sacraments defined and further developed during the sixteenth-century European Reformation by the Council of Trent (1545–63). In this sacrament, a penitent confesses personal sins as well as expresses a real contrition for sins and an intent not to sin again; consequently, a priest absolves sins as well as assigns a penance, or acts of reparation, that enables a penitent to convert from sin to right relations with God and the community.

When connected to participating in the work of Christ for the sake of salvation, the notion of reparation for sin emerges in the context of atonement theology, or theological reflection on the means of reconciling all humanity with God. Atonement theology is illustrated in Jewish theological reflection on ritual and other practices associated with Yom Kippur, and in Christian theological reflection on the significance of Jesus' death and resurrection. A brief survey of early and medieval Christian theology suggests several theological interpretations of Jesus' death for the remission of sin and the reconciliation of sinners with God, namely ransom, recapitulation, battle, satisfaction, and moral example—all of which are grounded in scriptural texts and influenced by the particular social location of theologians. For example, one prominent medieval Christian atonement theology, articulated by Anselm of Canterbury (d. 1109) and defended by Thomas Aquinas (d. 1274), claimed that the obedience of Christ unto death makes satisfaction to (or appeases) God for the infinite offense of humanity's original sin of disobedience. This satisfaction model of the atonement is analogous to a kenotic (Greek, *kenosis*, "emptying") christology expressed in Philippians 2:5-11, and was shaped according to medieval European understandings of restoring honor, or making reparations for dishonor in a feudal system.

In traditional Christian theologies, Jesus atones for the sin of humanity through a self-sacrificial, substitutionary death. United States feminist and womanist theologians as well as Asian American feminist theologians have pointed out that atonement theology often truncates the reconciling work of Jesus Christ to his death and resurrection, thereby neglecting the theological significance of his life and ministry—of forgiveness, of healing, and of table fellowship with marginated peoples, as described, for example, in the majority of the Gospel of Mark—for the purpose of reconciling humanity with God and with one another. Moreover, as argued by womanist theologian Delores Williams, traditional Christian atonement theologies tend to glorify surrogate suffering in the work of reconciliation and thereby perpetuate African American women's surrogacy experiences, that is, substitutionary manual, domestic, and sexual labor that denies the full integrity and dignity of black women's self-identity. Global feminist theologies continue to focus on the articulation of a theology of the suffering and death of Jesus—considered a reparation for original sin, or the universal sinful human condition—that can be critically appropriated to challenge rather than support such theological and social scapegoating.

Rosemary P. Carbine

See also ATONEMENT, CHRISTIAN.

REPENTANCE
(IN CHRISTIAN PERSPECTIVE)

Throughout Scripture men and women are regularly summoned to repentance through the word of a prophet or by God speaking through the events and circumstances of history. In the Gospel, repentance and conversion are the same thing. Repentance implies moral reform, since repenting means turning away from the evil actions, thoughts, fantasies, desires, and so forth, that have marked a person's life. John the Baptist preached a baptism of repentance as a prelude to receiving God's forgiveness (Mark 1:4), and Jesus continued that theme (Mark 1:15). But Christians understand that repentance is an enduring feature of their lives, because the victory over personal sinfulness will never be fully complete until we are joined to the mystery of God through death and resurrection.

The fact that human beings need to repent points to what might be described as a structural weakness of the human being. While biblical writers are certainly familiar with the waywardness of the human heart, they do not speculate about its causes. Sometimes, God is presented as disgusted with his creatures because they fail; at other times, God is portrayed as longsuffering and compassionate. The tradition seems to be telling us, however, that perfection does not come to the human being all at once; indeed, maybe it cannot. Repentance is thus a sign of human fallenness, but how we read or account for that fallenness is bound to affect our view of repentance. Those who regularly fail and repent, believing that God always expects moral perfection of us, are likely to be victims of lifelong guilt; they can never measure up to God's standards. If repentance is viewed as a sign of the human being on pilgrimage, or in the process of being created, then repentance is actually something positive, because it centers on the love that calls, guides, and creates us rather than on the sin that keeps telling us how much we have failed. In the Gospel, repentance is a response to the word preached, and it always entails a humble, grateful turning toward God.

The other side of repentance, therefore, is the Christian experience of God as ever merciful, patient, and forgiving. Yet the closer one draws to God, the more one can be seized by the extent of God's love for the world, even with its sinfulness. When the native poverty of the human spirit comes into contact with the unfathomable richness of divine love, there is generated a profound interior reform (distinct from moral reform) such that the human spirit itself is gradually created

anew or set free. This fact may help to explain why some Christians continue to "repent" even though they have not committed any evil actions. Their sense of inadequacy before God leaves them feeling spiritually raw and in constant need of God's healing, liberating love.

William Reiser, s.j.

See also BAPTISM/CONFIRMATION; CONTRITION; CONVERSION; FASTS/ FASTING (IN CHRISTIANITY); FORGIVENESS; VIA PURGATIVA.

REPENTANCE (IN JUDAISM)

See ATONEMENT, HEBREW.

RERUM NOVARUM

An encyclical issued in 1891 by Leo XIII as a response to three major factors: the Roman Catholic Church's loss of political power with the demise of the feudal order; the economic suffering of the working masses under the Industrial Revolution; and the ensuing threat of socialist revolution.

Leo XIII delivered this encyclical to show the civil authorities that the church could be useful in the emerging capitalist order because it could protect private property, discipline workers, and encourage employers to better treat their workers. *Rerum Novarum* endeavored to educate the public conscience against what it believed to be the tyranny of socialism and the anarchy of liberal capitalism. Leo believed the church could generate moral action by teaching moral ideas. In this way the church would function to "keep down the pride of those who are well off and to cheer the spirit of the afflicted; to incline the former to generosity and the latter to tranquil resignation" (RN 20).

Rerum Novarum criticized the tremendous power disparity between the social classes and the clear relationship between economic ownership and political control. But it also assumed the potential harmony of class interests, state intervention on behalf of the working poor, and the effectiveness of a disciplined and subordinate trade union movement. While *Rerum Novarum* was viewed in the United States as primarily an antisocialist document, in Europe it was interpreted as a call to massive social reform.

Later popes marked the importance of this document by attempting to update its teaching on economic justice on the anniversaries of its publication: *Quadragesimo Anno*, Pius XI, (1931); *Mater et Magistra*, John XXIII, (1961); *Octogesima Adveniens*, Paul VI, (1971); *Laborem Exercens*, John Paul II, (1981); and *Centesimus Annus*, John Paul II, (1991).

Mary E. Hobgood

See also CATHOLIC SOCIAL TEACHING; CLASSISM; ECONOMIC JUSTICE FOR ALL; QUADRAGESIMO ANNO; WORK/EMPLOYMENT.

RESPONSA LITERATURE

(Hebrew, *Sheelot veTeshuvot*; questions and answers). In Judaism, these are replies of rabbinic legal authorities to questions posed in writing concerning proper Jewish ritual and ethical practice and religious belief. They were particularly important in the medieval period, when rabbinic responses circulated from community to community. This method of addressing issues in Jewish law has been the primary mode of development of Jewish legal thinking since the early medieval period.

Alan J. Avery-Peck

RESPONSORIAL PSALM

A method of singing or reciting a psalm in which a set response is acclaimed by an assembly after each verse of the psalm is proclaimed by a cantor, reader, or choir. After the first reading at Mass and at other liturgical services, a psalm or portion of a psalm is prayed responsorially. The psalm echoes the images in the preceding reading or ideas suggested by the feast day. The response the assembly sings, often taken from the psalm itself, is generally chosen to highlight this key image. The responsorial method is not the only way of praying the psalms. For example, in the Liturgy of the Hours the psalms are usually prayed antiphonally, that is, with two groups alternating the recitation verse by verse. The *General Instruction on the Liturgy of the Hours* suggests that even in the Hours, however, the psalms can be prayed responsorially. Christians borrowed this method of singing psalms from Judaism. Some psalms and other Jewish hymns were composed with a built-in refrain (for example, Ps 136; Dan 3:52-56, 57-90) and some may have included an Alleluia response after each verse (Pss 146–150). In a culture where books and scrolls were rare and most people were illiterate, this method had great advantages. Even if the cantor were the only one with a copy of the text or the only one who could read, the responsorial method allowed the entire assembly to take part by repeating over and over the refrain they had learned. In Christianity, the music used to sing the psalms became increasingly complex, and professional liturgical singers began to proclaim the psalms without giving any part to the rest of the assembly. The music grew in such detail and length that eventually the response and just one verse from the psalm replaced the entire psalm. This very brief passage was called the "Gradual," from the Latin *gradus*, or step, since the cantors generally stood on the steps of the ambo/pulpit while they sang these verses. The liturgical reforms of Vatican II restored the responsorial psalm to its fuller form. Many modern composers have written music for the psalms to make them once again an accessible form of liturgical prayer.

Patrick L. Malloy

See also ALLELUIA (IN CHRISTIANITY); HALLEL PSALMS; LITURGY OF THE HOURS; LITURGY OF THE WORD; PSALMS/PSALTER.

RESURRECTION (IN CHRISTIANITY)

The resurrection of Jesus, as well as the resurrection of those who believe in him, constitutes the core of Christian faith. The proclamation of the resurrection has been the major element in Christian belief and teaching for the two millennia of Christianity's existence.

In the Jewish milieu of Jesus, the Sadducees and Pharisees represented opposing viewpoints concerning whether God raised the dead. The Sadducees held there is no resurrection, while the approach of the Pharisees was essentially that God indeed vindicates the righteous by raising them from the dead.

The New Testament reflects the belief that, according to the earliest Christian proclamation or kerygma, God raised the crucified Jesus from the dead (for example, 1 Cor 15:3-5; Acts 2:30-33; 3:15). It was the realization of the resurrection of Jesus that empowered his followers to preach, erasing the fear and defeat they had felt in the events surrounding his death. Their proclamation, however, while in continuity with the Pharisaic approach that resurrection was essentially a reward to the just in the face of their sufferings, also went beyond that belief.

In the view of the New Testament, while the resurrection of Jesus is certainly a vindication by God of his faithfulness, Jesus was also understood as having been exalted to the right hand of God (Rom 4:24-25), invested with the name of God, "Lord" (see Phil 2:6-11), and "made Son of God in power according to the spirit of holiness" (Rom 1:3-4). So empowered, Jesus therefore participates in God's rule, including the final judgment when evil is once and for all overcome and God's rule is fully established.

Because Jesus' resurrection involved his exaltation to a new and unique status with God, Christians conceivably could have believed that while Jesus himself was raised, no conclusions could be drawn from that about the fate of believers themselves. That there was skepticism concerning the resurrection of believers is evident in 1 Thessalonians 4:13-14 and 1 Corinthians 15:12.

The response to such skepticism, as given by Paul, for example, is that the resurrection and exaltation places Christ in a new relationship with believers. The power given him in his exaltation is precisely the power to bring about new life in those who believe in him, that is, are incorporated into him. At his resurrection the Lord thus because the "last Adam," a life-giving Spirit (1 Cor 15:45). For this reason, Paul, as any believer, could also say that it is not he but the risen Christ who lives in him (Gal 2:20). Likewise, he could write that all who through baptism enter into union with Christ in his death will likewise in union with him also be raised from the dead (Rom 6:3-5). Paul speaks of longing "to know Christ and the power of his resurrection" (Phil 3:10), reflecting his understanding that the exalted Lord possesses the power, coming from the Father, that can bring about the resurrection of those who unite their lives to his. This he speaks of as both a process of conformation to Jesus (Phil 3:10) and a transformation into the same image as the Lord (2 Cor 3:18), that is, the new life or existence of resurrection.

Throughout the history of Christianity, the central affirmation of the resurrection of believers has been variously linked to and explained with respect to questions concerning the parousia of the Lord, the death of individuals, individual and general judgment, and various other religious or philosophical doctrines such as the immortality of the soul.

F. M. Gillman

See also CRUCIFIXION; DEATH (CHRISTIAN); IMMORTALITY; KERYGMA; PAROUSIA; PHARISEES; RESURRECTION (IN JUDAISM); RESURRECTION (OUTSIDE JUDEO-CHRISTIAN TRADITIONS); RESURRECTION OF CHRIST; RESURRECTION OF THE BODY; SADDUCEES; SOUL.

RESURRECTION (IN JUDAISM)
See ESCHATOLOGY (IN JUDAISM).

RESURRECTION (OUTSIDE JUDEO-CHRISTIAN TRADITIONS)
The idea of resurrection, in the sense of the revival of a dead individual, is an important belief in Islam: at the time of the Last Judgment, all humanity will be judged. Those already dead will arise from their graves and face Allah as their deeds are measured to determine whether there will be eternal damnation or residence in paradise. The assumption of resurrection underlies Islamic law prescribing burial as the only method for disposing of the dead.

In Asian religions, the idea of resurrection is found only rarely and is usually associated with ascetics, sages, or magicians. In Chinese Taoism, sages pursuing forms of meditation and alchemy aimed toward immortality are thought capable of reviving themselves after their "normal" biological death, resurrecting their divine essence to dwell between heaven and earth. In esoteric Tibetan Buddhist tantric practice, an advanced siddha yogin is thought capable of transferring consciousness (his own or that of another human being) into a recently dead body and resurrecting it.

Todd T. Lewis

See also DAOISM; IMMORTALITY; TANTRIC BUDDHISM.

RESURRECTION OF CHRIST
That Jesus of Nazareth was raised bodily from the dead on the third day after being crucified has been central to the Christian message from the church's beginning (for example, Acts 2:22-24; 3:15; 4:10). Furthermore, Jesus did not raise himself—God did (Gal 1:1). As a result, the resurrection of Jesus reveals in a spectacular way what the God of Israel is like; the raising of the dead is thematically continuous with creating the heavens and the earth (Gen 1:1).

The various Gospel accounts make it clear that Jesus' risen body is continuous with yet different from his mortal body. The risen body does not lose the marks of crucifixion (John 20:27), but neither is it immediately recognizable (Luke 24:16; John 20:14). The empty tomb may be taken as a sign of Jesus' having been raised, but it does not necessarily prove resurrection (Matt 28:12-13). The fact that Jesus never appears to his enemies but only to his disciples suggests that the Resurrection was not meant to be merely a confirmation of his divine status or God's way of approving his ministry and mission. The Resurrection has much to do with the religious experience of the disciples. They came to see not only that the God of Israel was a God of life and that death does not have the final say, but they also found themselves liberated, saved, redeemed, created anew—and summoned to share Jesus' ministry and mission.

The resurrection of Christ goes beyond resuscitation, such as the raising of the daughter of Jairus (Mark 5:41-42) and of Lazarus (John 11:43-44). For Jesus' contemporaries, the raising of the dead would have signaled that the final age had begun, leading Jesus' earliest followers to conclude, mistakenly, that a general resurrection was soon to follow. Since Jesus, like the Pharisees and many other (though not all) Jews already believed in an afterlife, it seems unlikely that in raising Jesus the divine intention was simply to affirm the truthfulness of this belief. From a theological perspective, therefore, the Resurrection seems to be about the abiding presence of Jesus among his followers, empowering them to bear witness to him by proclaiming and living the kingdom of God. Above all, the Resurrection reveals the depth of divine solidarity with humanity, especially with victims. As a consequence of the Resurrection, the mystery of the Incarnation becomes thinkable. Resurrection forced the earliest communities to ponder carefully who and what Jesus was.

William Reiser, S.J.

See also CHRISTOLOGY; INCARNATION.

RESURRECTION OF THE BODY

This phrase (or phrases such as resurrection of the flesh and of the dead) is an article of faith in some ancient creeds. The Christian concept is not related to the body–spirit dichotomy in the Greek proposal of the soul's immortality, but is rooted in the conviction about God's salvific will for the faithful, the transformation and perfection of persons who embrace God, a condition exemplified in Jesus' resurrection. The emphasis on the bodily or enfleshed dimension reflects the broader dimension of the biblical *sarx* that expresses the general condition of embodiment. Emphasis on embodiment and on the historical and communitarian dimensions of life are affirmed against all overly spiritualist interpretations of salvation, particularly Gnostic views. Contemporary theological analysis of the concept does not dwell on discussion of what is resurrected. Against rationalist descriptions of persons, it emphasizes the integrity of the body/spirit relation and the body's role as symbolic medium for spirit. It interprets the bodily resurrection to imply the continuance and perfection of the entire historical and communitarian dimension of human life in the communion with God that occurs after death.

Patricia Plovanich

REVELATION

Revelation (from the Latin *revelare* meaning to uncover or unveil) in Christianity means, in general, the event of God's self-disclosure to humanity; in particular, it means God's self-disclosure through Jesus Christ, the supreme moment of revelation history. The Christian community has used many models to understand revelation. One line of thought emphasizes the propositional character or objective content of the encounter (what is revealed). Some models emphasize the personal and interpersonal character of revelation, describing it as God's self-communication or as a divine–human encounter. Recent revelation theologies have considered the historical character of God's presence in history. Whatever the theory, Christian theology emphasizes God revealed as absolutely gracious and merciful mystery. It acknowledges the continuing efforts to understand the divine presence in revelation history (including revelation in Hebrew Scripture), and affirms both the significance of the community's reception of revelation and the objective testimony that interprets that experience for each era of Christian history.

Ronald A. Pachence

See also TORAH.

REVELATION (IN BAHA'I)

In general, revelation in Baha'i is the one truth disclosed progressively and continuously by the one God to prophets and sages of all the world religions throughout the centuries. In this sense, all religions have a common origin since they are bearers of what Baha'i founder Baha'u'llah (d. 1892) called the primal Word of God. Speaking of the prophets of the great religions, Baha'u'llah wrote: "From their knowledge, the knowledge of God is revealed, and from the light of their countenance, the splendor of the Face of God is made manifest." In particular, Baha'is identify revelation with the teachings of Baha'u'llah that are believed to be correct and unify the diverse doctrines of the many "Manifestations of God" (the religions of the world). His writings, particularly the *Kitab-I-Iqan* (*The Book of Certitude*), represent the clearest expression of the one evolving truth for Baha'is because these sources of revelation show humankind how to create universal harmony through the elimination of nationalism, racism, warfare, and religious sectarianism. The designated successors of Baha'u'llah are also accepted as divinely appointed authorities who can correctly interpret the revelation of God.

An apocalyptic element can be identified in the message of Baha'i. As expressed in the teachings of the great grandson of Baha'u'llah, Shoghi Effendi (d. 1957), the modern world is witnessing the final stage of human evolution. In this stage, God is calling humans to accept the message of Baha'i and move toward a world government that will inaugurate the "Most Great Peace," a new era of history in which everyone will live in accordance with the law of God. Revelation in the Baha'i tradition has been referred to as an example of syncretism in that it utilizes selected elements of many different religions and philosophical systems to create a new faith and way of life. For followers of Baha'u'llah, however, the revelation of Baha'i represents the fullest expression of God's eternal will for all people.

Ronald A. Pachence

See also BAHA'I.

REVELATION (IN CHRISTIAN PERSPECTIVE)

Related to the Greek term *apocalypses* and Latin term *revelare*, both meaning "to unveil," revelation in Christian theology involves the ongoing self-disclosure of God to humanity and the ongoing human response to that divine disclosure regarding the nature, attributes, and will of God as well as God's relationship to the world in salvation. Revelation takes place through a variety of media in the Hebrew and Christian scriptures, for example in nature, in wisdom that comes with experience, in prophesies and visions, in the giving of laws, but mostly in deeds and in historical events.

Medieval and Reformation theology distinguished between natural and revealed theology, or knowledge of God available to reason, and knowledge of God available through revelation in Scripture and tradition. There is a common distinction in modern Christian theology between general and special revelation. General revelation, also known as natural knowledge of God, has to do with what can be known about God through reasoned reflection on creation, human history, and ordinary human experience. Reason is a primary but not the only ground for knowledge of God. Special revelation pertains to what can be known about God through specific sources, namely, Jesus Christ as well as Christian Scriptures (including the Old and New Testaments), official doctrines and teachings, and traditions. An appeal to revelation does not yield a total comprehensive knowledge of God because the self-disclosure of God takes place within the limits of human reason and history as well as in humanly produced texts, teachings, and traditions, albeit under the guidance and inspiration of the Holy Spirit. God is an ultimate and inexhaustible mystery; thus, special revelation still partly reveals and partly conceals the character of God because it takes place in historical peoples, places, and events that cannot fully contain the reality of God. God is revealed and yet partly concealed in revelation; this point is illustrated in the work of Blaise Pascal, mid-seventeenth-century French philosopher, who argued that God is partly concealed in revelation to stress the limits of human knowledge and human nature.

Revelation represents a kind of practical knowledge of God that reorients human relations with God, with the world, and with others. Special revelation is not simply additional or supplemental knowledge of God; rather, it may challenge and completely change prevalent images and ideas of God that in turn may challenge and change ways of interpreting and acting in the world. Both Protestant and Catholic theology emphasize special revelation for more certain and deeper knowledge of God, paying particular attention to what they regard as the full and complete self-revelation of God in Jesus Christ. Sixteenth-century European Protestant Reformers like Martin Luther and John Calvin distinguished between a general or natural knowledge of God based on reason that God exists and created the world, and a special knowledge of God rooted in Scripture and in Christ that reveals God's will, especially for salvation. Special revelation does not trump general revelation, but builds on, clarifies, and completes general revelation.

Twentieth-century official Catholic theology illustrated by the document *Dei Verbum* from Vatican II (1962–5) also argued that divine revelation takes place primarily through divine words and deeds in particular historical events, especially in the total Christ event, and secondarily through the sacramentality of the created world, imprinted with the image and likeness of God. Christ represents the definitive divine revelation because the Christ-event comprises the agent, the process, and the content of God's self-communication. Nonetheless, because of the Incarnation, of God taking on the reality of human life in Jesus, revelation is situated in specific historical and ecological contexts. The Incarnation upholds the sacramentality of all life, or the presence of God in all human and earthly life; thus, theologians take seriously all facets and features of human and earthly life for religious reflection on God. Of particular interest is the argument in *Dei Verbum* that revelation is not restricted to the past; rather, God continues to self-communicate to the world, but in Christian perspective does not add anything substantially new to the Christ-event. In keeping with this argument about an ongoing revelation that fundamentally depends on Christ, *Gaudium et Spes*, the Pastoral Constitution on the Church in the Modern World from Vatican II, highlighted the significant role of human experience and history for mediating the presence of God, a claim summarized in the phrase "reading the signs of the times in light of the Gospel." Also of particular interest is the Vatican II document *Nostra Aetate* that recognized the possibility of divine self-revelation in other non-Christian religions, while still affirming the finality of Jesus Christ for knowledge of God and salvation.

Both Protestant and Catholic theology are Christocentric in their approach to special revelation. However, Protestant theologies of revelation mainly focus on Scripture (summarized in the phrase *sola scriptura*) as it refers to the Word of God in Christ, whereas in Catholic theology illustrated by Vatican II, Scripture and tradition constitute "a single sacred deposit of the word of God" or a "sole deposit of faith." Scripture and tradition are equally revered sources of special revelation because of their common theocentric origin and their shared attention to the total mystery of Christ. God's self-revelation in Scripture and tradition has to do first with a divine self-disclosure to humanity that invites a response of faith, and second with a divine communication of religious truths about God and salvation that warrants intellectual assent, as opposed to nineteenth-century official Catholic teaching that described this single deposit in propositional terms as a set of official doctrines.

Contemporary papal theology, especially the theology of Pope John Paul II (d. 2005), regards human experience, especially suffering, as a theologically significant site of revelation, or as a theological locus alongside Scripture and tradition for mediating the salvific presence and will of God. Contemporary theologies based on women's experiences, especially Euro-American feminist, African American womanist, and Latina feminist/*mujerista* theologies, contend that suffering in and of itself is not revelatory. Asian feminist theologians and African American womanist theologians have rightly pointed out that some theologies of suffering can glorify rather than resist the suffering of women and other victims of all sorts of race, class, gender, and sexual oppression.

While the Christ-event described in Christian Scriptures, teachings, and traditions remains the primary site of revelation, contemporary Catholic theology offers a theological aesthetics of revelation by focusing on the revelatory power of symbols. The symbol of God as one of the central organizing symbols of Christian faith not only influences other doctrines but also shapes larger religious and sociocultural ways of life. As demonstrated in Christian feminist and ecofeminist theologies, major Christian symbols for God that rely on mainly male terms and images —such as the trinitarian names of Father, Son, and Spirit or the monarchical image of God as a transcendent king and ruler over the world—function to legitimate a mistaken literal belief in the androcentric nature of God as well as to reinforce the patriarchal domination of women, nondominant peoples, and the earth. Alternative symbols for God—when critically retrieved from the patriarchal content and context of Scripture and tradition—stress the analogical, metaphorical, and indirect nature of God-language, thereby refuting any idolatrous images and concepts of God. For example, Rosemary Radford Ruether critically applied the prophetic-liberating tradition of the Exodus story and of the Christ-event to construct the term "God/ess," and Elisabeth Schüssler Fiorenza critically reflected on the Wisdom literature and tradition to propose the terms "Sophia–God" or in her more recent work "G*d." Rooted in Scripture and tradition and transformed by women's experiences of struggle in religio-cultural patriarchies, these symbols emphasize the fundamentally inclusive, incomprehensible mystery of God. Also, alternative symbols for the divine include women's experiences in the reality of God as well as enable women to claim and realize their full human dignity as equally created in the image and likeness of God. For example, a number of feminist theologians, most notably Schüssler Fiorenza and Elizabeth Johnson, recovered long-overlooked female images and personifications of God found in the Wisdom literature to reconstruct more egalitarian, more just theological symbols of God and of Christian community. Finally, alternative symbols for the divine provide a theological means to undermine any form of religiously backed ideological domination of other human beings or of the earth. For example, African American womanist theologians like Delores Williams and Diana Hayes reflected on the Genesis story of Hagar, the Egyptian slave, victim–survivor of rape, and poor, homeless, single mother, to offer an understanding of God as friend and companion in women's struggles to survive and create a better quality of life amid the interrelated dynamics of race, class, gender, and sexual oppression. Eco-feminist theologians like Sallie McFague innovatively applied the central Christian belief in the incarnation of God as a fully human being in Jesus Christ to formulate the symbol of the world as the body of God. This new theological symbol promotes the sacramentality of all bodies, lays a theological foundation for an ecological ethic of justice for all human and earthly bodies, and opposes the exploitation of the earth's resources on theological grounds.

As illustrated in these few examples of a growing body of theological scholarship in feminist, womanist, and ecofeminist theologies, contemporary constructive theologies of God point the way toward a theology of revelation that transforms the kind of knowledge of God available in revelation. Beyond general knowledge of the existence and attributes of God and beyond special knowledge of the salvific will of God, contemporary theological symbols of God attest not only to the reality and will of God but also to the goal of common life not yet fully realized in the world.

Rosemary P. Carbine

See also BIBLE; CALVIN, JOHN; CHRIST OF FAITH; CHRISTOLOGY; DEI VERBUM; GAUDIUM ET SPES; LUTHER, MARTIN; REFORMED THEOLOGY (-IES); RUETHER, ROSEMARY RADFORD; SYMBOL.

REVELATION (IN ISLAM)

For Muslims, revelation is God's Word, "sent down" (*tanzil*) by God through a divinely appointed messenger (*rasul*). Revelation refers both to the content of the message (God's self-disclosure and will for all God's creatures) and to the process by which the message is communicated (*tanzil*). From the beginning of time, God ("Allah" in Arabic) has been revealing the divine Word, first through Adam and subsequently through a long list of great messengers or prophets including Noah, Abraham, Ishmael, Moses, Jesus, and finally Muhammad (570–632), the "seal" of the prophets. After the revelation received by the Prophet Muhammad, recorded accurately in the holy scripture of Islam (the Qur'an), Muslims believe that God's Word has been disclosed in its entirety and that no new or different revelation will follow.

According to Islamic belief, the Qur'an completes and corrects the two testaments of the Bible. While Muslims agree that the Bible contains revelation, they say it also includes mistakes in the transmission of God's Word. These errors are corrected in the Qur'an, and the new revelation received through God's last prophet, Muhammad, is included there as well.

Muslim theologians also use the Arabic word for "inspiration from God" (*al-wahy*) to describe the concept of the English word *revelation*. In this sense, revelation is understood in terms of its source—the transcendent creator God. This suggests that while divine revelation has been given to God's creatures in a genre they can understand, a book of the prophetic recitation of God's Word (the Qur'an), no one will ever be able to fathom the God of revelation. What is more, since God is the source of the revealed Word, Qur'anic doctrines that appear to contradict one another (for example, predestination and free will) illustrate the inability of the human mind to understand God completely. Such apparent contradictions, therefore, do not compromise the reliability of the revealed Word or its divine author.

Ronald A. Pachence

See also ADAM (AS PROPHET OF ISLAM); ALLAH (ISLAM); ISLAM; JESUS (AS PROPHET OF ISLAM); MUHAMMAD; NABI (IN ISLAM); PREDESTINATION (IN ISLAM); QUR'AN; RASUL.

REVELATION (IN JUDAISM)
See TORAH.

REVELATION (IN OTHER RELIGIONS)
Revelation, defined broadly as the communication of knowledge from the transcendent to human beings, is an almost universal phenomenon in the history of religions. People in traditional cultures, facing the uncertainties of life, have nearly always sought security and certitude in wisdom regarded as having come from a source higher than the human, wisdom that human beings would not have access to using their normal faculties (the senses, reason, and so on). It has been thought better, in most cultures, not to base ways of life—and especially ways to salvation— on mere human artifice, but instead to anchor them in a vision that is sure because it arises from the very heart of reality. In many cases, as in Hinduism and Mahayana Buddhism, it is explicitly recognized that, without such revelation, humankind would remain forever in ignorance and bondage.

The source of this knowledge has, of course, been variously understood. Depending upon the worldview of the culture in which it occurs, revelation may be experienced as coming from a supreme deity, lesser gods or spirits, ancestors, other supernatural beings, or a more abstract ultimate reality or Absolute. The knowledge conveyed has also been, correspondingly, of various types: it may pertain to the nature and/or the mode of action of the sacred source of revelation itself, or the nature of other realities both supernatural and mundane. Alternately, it may announce the will or commandments of a supernatural being, or give insight into mundane affairs and advice on how to deal with them. Processes by which the revelations are conveyed include visions, dreams, ecstasy, prophecy, inspiration, possession, divination, and omens. Revelations intended for a wider community may be received by founders of religions, shamans, prophets, oracles, priests, sages, religious teachers, and others in leadership roles, whether they are already religious specialists, or whether they become so by virtue of the revelation received. Such public revelations tend to be codified in scripture or oral tradition. Private revelations, providing individual inspiration, guidance, and empowerment, are also common.

To what extent revelation can be regarded as an ongoing, universal activity of the divine, so that any religious experience is to some extent revelatory, is a matter of debate. However, it is usually held that revelation, while it may be solicited, implies the free intent of the transcendent, revealing agent. Even truths of a religious nature would not be counted as revelation if they are arrived at by human reason alone (since they are not gifts from a transcendent source). Similarly, knowledge obtained through magic would not be so counted by most scholars, since magic (as ordinarily defined) seeks to exert some degree of coercion over the sacred realm. Also problematic on this count are mystical states of awareness, visions, and related experiences of the transcendent, if they appear to be attained by means of human effort; for example, through ascetic disciplines such as fasting, contemplative prayer, or yoga. Unless some concept of

supernatural grace (divine aid or a calling from the spirit world, for example) is understood to be operative in the experience, many scholars would be inclined to exclude knowledge gained through such means from the category of revelation.

Despite such qualifications, there are many examples of religious phenomena outside the Jewish, Christian, and Islamic traditions that can clearly be classified as revelatory, using the broad definition given above. Perhaps the most famous example in the nonliterate, indigenous traditions of the world is the great vision that came as an unsought calling to the Lakota shaman Black Elk when he was a young boy. Through this vision, he was given a life mission and a ritual that would help him carry it out. Tribal religious traditions, of course, provide numerous other examples of revelation—in dreams, divination, omens, states of possession, and oracles—through which the spirit world is felt to communicate with humankind.

Hinduism has a particularly strong conception of revelation. Its holiest scriptures, the Vedas, are traditionally regarded as *shruti* (literally, "that which was heard"). They are said to embody the eternal Speech or Word (*vak*), which descends into the realm of mortals anew at the beginning of every cosmic cycle. Vak chooses to reveal herself as infallible wisdom to seers (*rishis*), who engage in austerity to make themselves receptive. As the eternal Word, the Vedas are regarded by some Hindu schools to be authored by God, but by others to be impersonal (*aparusheya*), that is, authored by no one, either human or divine. They convey knowledge that is essential for both correct ritual performance and final liberation (*moksha*), knowledge that can be obtained from no other source. The most sacred Vedic mantra, the Gayatri (*Rig Veda* 3.62.10), is essentially a prayer for revelatory inspiration (*dhi*). Also in Hinduism, the concept of the avatara or gracious decent of God into the human realm affords ample instances of revelatory contact between the humans and the divine (see *Bhagavad Gita*, ch. 11), as does the Hindu experience of the guru, who—purified of ego— is regarded as an embodiment of the transcendent and often, indeed, as an avatara.

The case of Buddhism, especially Theravada, is much more problematic, since the tradition explicitly denies the existence of a supreme creator deity, acknowledges that Gautama Buddha's enlightenment was achieved solely by dint of ascetic discipline, and maintains through most of its history an undercurrent of skepticism toward the value of all external authority, especially that of words and texts. The knowledge of Truth (the Dharma) that was disclosed in Gautama's enlightenment experience did not come, then, at the initiative of the divine, nor was his enlightenment attributable to the operation of the grace of any deity. Nor was it unique, for there were Buddhas in previous ages, and there will be more in ages to come. It is clear, however, that the tradition regards Gautama as having obtained infallible, supernatural knowledge available only to the rarest and most extraordinary of human beings (the world cannot bear the virtue of more than one Buddha in any given eon, *Milindapanho* 4.6.5). It is also apparent that the words of the Buddha (*buddha–vacana*) function as revelation for the Buddhist community. If revelation, as the communication of transcendent knowledge to humankind, is present here, it is the Buddha himself who must be counted the revealer. In Mahayana Buddhism, the presence of grace and supernatural initiative, and therefore of revelation, is more easily recognizable. Gautama is regarded as a being who had attained fully enlightened, omniscient Buddhahood innumerable eons before his appearance in history as the Buddha of this age, and who had become by that time thoroughly supramundane in nature and power. He manifested earthly form voluntarily out of compassion for the world. The vision of Mahayana Buddhism, moreover, also includes numerous other Buddhas, Bodhisattvas, and other beings—many of whom are purely mythical (and, hence, supernatural)—that engage in countless revelatory exchanges with humans and other creatures, motivated by their compassionate vow to bring enlightenment and freedom from suffering to "all sentient beings."

In Chinese religion, the practice of divination is attested from the time of the Shang dynasty (around 1766–1122 B.C.E.). The will of divinized ancestral spirits was thought to be made manifest in cracks formed by heating oracle bones or turtle shells, or in the random patterns of tossed yarrow stalks (later formalized as the method of consulting the *I-Ching*, the oracular *Book of Changes*). In Chinese popular religion, the use of spirit mediums to consult deities and ancestor spirits has always been common. The humanism of the Confucian tradition, however, removes its foundational wisdom further than even the *buddha–vacana* of Theravada Buddhism from any traditional concept of revelation. The knowledge of reality that is embodied in the Classics (*Ching*) and the Four Books (*Ssu-shu*) of Confucianism is derived from the penetrating understanding of human sages (*sheng*), including Confucius, who were thereby empowered to show the ways of heaven to humankind. But their wisdom is not typically endowed with any supernatural aura. In many ways the authority of Confucian texts rests more upon the belief that they are the most effective mediators for the present generation of the ethos of a past golden age, rather than on any claim that their authors had absolute knowledge. Associated with the Confucian tradition, however, is at least one clear recognition of the kind of divine-human communication we are looking for, one that is an exception to the fact that —outside the religions of Semitic origin— the historical process is rarely taken as a vehicle of revelation. The doctrine of the Mandate of Heaven (*t'ien-ming*) has been used throughout Chinese history to interpret astrological and earthly portents, and social unrest, as signs that heaven has withdrawn its sanction from an evil regime and is intervening to work its downfall. Turning to Taoism, we find further and even more striking examples of revelation. Not only is nature in general taken as revelatory of the mysterious workings of the Tao, but there is a clear concept of scriptural revelation. Certain scriptures within the enormous compass of the Tao Tsang, the canon of religious Taoism, are said to have originated in the vital energy (*ch'i*) of deities or the primordial ether. Some texts are held to have preexisted the creation of the world only to be revealed at the right moment in history. The mechanism of revelation, in Taoism and Chinese popular religion, varies. In some cases, scriptures are thought to have been announced personally by the Jade Emperor, the deified Lao-tzu, or other deities. Others were hidden in caves by divine beings, to be uncovered and promulgated by sages of later generations. Still others were, and continue to be, transmitted mediumisti-

cally by automatic "spirit-writing" (*fuluan*). Indeed, there are spirit-writing temples dedicated to receiving, cherishing, and propagating such contemporary instances of revelation.

Were space not limited, examples of revelation in other traditions could also be cited (for example, in Zoroastrianism, which teaches that the Avesta in its entirety was given to Zoroaster by Ahura Mazda). It is important to mention, however, that the concept of revelation as we know it in Western discourse was articulated in a biblical, largely Christian context, where it has often been defined more narrowly than it has been here. Historians of religion have extended it, as in the present article, to encompass parallel phenomena in other religious traditions. Whether or not Christian (or Jewish) theologians accept such usage will depend on the particular definitions that the individual scholars are working with.

Lance E. Nelson

See also AFRO-LATIN RELIGIONS; AVATARA/AVATAR; AVESTA; BHAGAVAD GITA; BUDDHISM; CONFUCIANISM; DAOISM; DIVINATION; GURU; HINDUISM; I-CHING; INSPIRATION; JUDAISM; MAHAYANA BUDDHISM; MANU SMRITI; OMEN; POSSESSION; REVELATION (IN BAHA'I); REVELATION (IN CHRISTIAN PERSPECTIVE); REVELATION (IN ISLAM); SCRIPTURES (GENERIC); SHAMAN; SHRUTI; TAO; THERAVADA BUDDHISM; ZOROASTRIANISM.

REVIVALISM

Fueled by freedom of religion, revivalism is a method of Christian evangelism unique to the United States. It is the dominant mode whereby Protestantism spread across the country and the world in the eighteenth through twentieth centuries. Particularly suited to Evangelical theology, revivalism's purpose is to prepare individuals for conversion, to convince them of the depth of sin, the need for repentance, and the reality of justification. It seeks to persuade people to accept God's gift of grace offered through Jesus Christ and be born again as Christ's disciples.

Revivalism began during the First Great Awakening of the 1730s–1740s with the preaching of Congregationalist Jonathan Edwards and Anglican George Whitefield, among others. Influenced by pietism, it was an outbreak of religious enthusiasm accompanied by intense fervor and numerous conversions. A pastor in western Massachusetts and a Calvinist, Edwards sought to induce a change of consciousness in his hearers, to prepare them for the infusion of God's grace. His vivid sermonic imagery and emphasis on "religious affections," holy emotions stimulated by the Holy Spirit, provoked conversions in his congregation that Edwards interpreted as spontaneous outpourings of God's grace. Known as the "Grand Itinerant," British priest Whitefield traveled the colonies on popular preaching tours, speaking in open fields to huge crowds, exhorting them to repent. He was so charismatic that he could reportedly reduce an audience to tears by speaking the word "Mesopotamia."

During the Second Great Awakening of the early nineteenth century, revivalism became systematized by Presbyterian evangelist Charles G. Finney, known as the "father of modern revivalism." In his *Lectures on Revivals of Religion* (1835), he outlined his "New Measures," sure-fire techniques for organizing revivals to win souls. First, he encouraged advance publicity through newspapers, word of mouth, and prayer groups, especially of women, in the town where the revival would occur, to pray for its success. Second, he advocated protracted meetings, services that lasted for hours over days, designed to break down the individual's will. Third, he developed the "mourner's bench" or "anxious bench," a special pew placed in front of the pulpit where people sat when they felt the stirrings of the Holy Spirit, where the revivalist addressed them directly. Fourth, Finney articulated a new role for women, to pray and even testify before mixed groups of men and women during the revival. Although he opposed women preaching, he believed they were special channels of grace.

Finney's New Measures moved revivalism from spontaneous outpourings of the Holy Spirit to foolproof steps engineered by the revivalist. They were wildly successful. Finney worked primarily in urban areas of the Northeast and Great Britain, but his methods were adopted by frontier evangelists in camp meetings and tent revivals. By the Civil War, Methodists, Baptists, Presbyterians, and Disciples of Christ had burgeoned as a result of revivals. Revivalism was even utilized by liturgical traditions such as Episcopalians and Roman Catholics.

With few innovations, Finney's techniques became the norm for nineteenth- and twentieth-century evangelists. The best-known revivalists were Dwight Moody, founder of Moody Bible Institute in Chicago; Billy Sunday, whose theatrical tactics included jumping on the pulpit and waving an American flag; and Billy Graham, who conducted mass crusades in the 1950s and 1960s. Revivalism was so popular that Sinclair Lewis satirized it in *Elmer Gantry* (1927) with some justification as self-serving manipulation. Later innovations included the prominent place of music, both instrumental and hymnal, and the increased use of mass media. In the second half of the twentieth century, revivals were frequently communicated through television, a practice dubbed televangelism.

Evelyn A. Kirkley

See also EDWARDS, JONATHAN; ENTHU-SIASM/ENTHUSIASTIC; EVANGELICAL THEOLOGY; GREAT AWAKENING(S) (EURO-AMERICAN RELIGIOUS HISTORY); PIETISM.

RHETORIC

This term refers to a genre of human discourse in which the intellectual content, or message, communicated is understood to be intrinsically linked to the form and context of the communication. Oral rhetorical communication always takes place in a particular place, between particular interlocutors, through particular modes of expression that include vocal inflections, tone of voice, facial expressions, and physical gestures. Rhetoric is as concerned with *what* is said as with *how* it is said; its goal is not only to inform but to persuade. Rhetoric is thus a holistic form of discourse, with both verbal and physical dimensions, that considers the physical, concrete, sociohistorical mediation a key element of the communication process.

The historical roots of rhetoric can be traced to the Greek world of the fifth century B.C.E. In that society, the political and military leaders used rhetoric as a means of persuading the populace to support their political policies and military campaigns. The first major philosophical school to give a central role to rhetorical discourse was that of the Greek Sophists, represented especially by Protagoras (b. about 486 B.C.E.) and Gorgias (about 483–374 B.C.E.). The epistemological skep-ticism of the Sophists, for whom "truth" did not exist except in the intersubjective act of communication, accorded a special prominence to the art of persuasion and argumentation.

Another major figure who gave important impetus to the development of the art of rhetoric was Plato (428–348 B.C.E.). Yet Plato's role in that development was essentially negative: he insisted on the superiority of *episteme* (knowledge, truth) to mere *doxa* (opinion, argument). Plato was especially concerned about the power of rhetorical speech to seduce, or "bewitch" people, leading them astray of the truth. In Plato's dialogues, the Sophists' attempts to seduce and convince through the power of argumentation is repeatedly subverted by the questions Socrates repeatedly interjects. This attitude of *questioning* the speaker, forcing him or her to interrupt the line of argumentation in order to clarify and explain, is a form of dialogue Plato called "dialectic," and that he considers superior to rhetoric. In his groundbreaking work *Rhetoric*, Aristotle (384–322 B.C.E.) was influenced by Plato's suspicions of rhetoric but synthesized the Platonic emphasis on dialectics with a renewed appreciation of the role of rhetoric in the *polis*: Aristotle describes rhetoric as "the counterpart of dialectics."

In modernity, as exemplified above all in the thought of René Descartes (1596–1650), knowledge was reduced to what is universal, abstract, clear, and precise, the paradigm for which is mathematical knowledge. Thus, a sharp separation developed between rational knowledge—universal and abstract—and "mere" rhetoric, rooted in the particularity and concreteness of historical context. Postmodern philosophers, however, are today giving renewed attention to rhetoric. The postmodern suspicion of all putatively universal discourses, and the concomitant emphasis on the significance of particular historical context or "social location," have once again brought rhetoric to the fore as an important form of communication.

Roberto S. Goizueta

See also POSTMODERNITY; TRUTH.

RIBEIRO DE OLIVEIRA, PEDRO (1941–)

Brazilian sociologist of religion. Educated in Brazil and Belgium, Ribeiro de Oliveira has been professor at several Brazilian universities and research centers. His analyses of nineteenth-century Latin American Catholicism on the so-called "Romanization" of the church since Pius IX, and especially his theories on popular religion, have influenced the thinking of many Latin American theologians. Familiar with Gramsci's thought, Ribeiro de Oliveira adapted and shaped the latter, combining it with perspectives from sociologists François Houtart and Pierre Bourdieu to create a more thorough examination and theoretical explanation of popular Catholicism and of the current Latin American Church. Among his books are *Evangelização e comportamento religioso popular* (1978), *Religiosidade popular na América Latina* (1972), and *Catolicismo popular e hegemonia burguesa no Brasil* (1979).

Orlando Espín

See also ESPÍN, ORLANDO; GRAMSCI, ANTONIO; IDEOLOGY (IDEOLOGIES); LATIN AMERICAN CATHOLICISM; LATIN AMERICAN THEOLOGIES; LATINO THEOLOGY (-IES); LIBERATION THEOLOGIES; MADURO, OTTO; PIUS IX, POPE; POPULAR CATHOLICISM; POPULAR RELIGIONS; PRIVATIZATION OF RELIGION.

RICCI, MATTEO (1552–1610)

Matteo Ricci, born in Macerata, Italy, became the outstanding Jesuit missionary to China thanks to his intellectual genius, Christian commitment, and unorthodox method of evangelization. Arriving in the Portuguese colony of Macao in 1582, Ricci and his fellow Jesuits moved into the heart of a China hostile to Christianity. In response, Ricci followed the guidelines of the Jesuit superior in Asia, Alessandro Valignano, which called for the conversion of the Chinese elite and, through them, the masses. By embracing the ways of a Chinese scholar and impressing the Chinese nobility with his knowledge of their literature and of Western science, Ricci was able to win a hearing for Christianity as well. Appreciated as a conduit for the exchange of Eastern and Western knowledge, he was admitted to the imperial city of Beijing in 1601. After his death, his method of adapting Christianity to Chinese culture gave rise in Europe to the so-called "Chinese Rites Controversy," which ended in the official condemnation of his approach by the Catholic Church until Vatican II (1962–5).

James B. Nickoloff

RICOEUR, PAUL (1913–2005)

French philosopher. Educated at the Sorbonne, and classmate of existentialist Gabriel Marcel, Ricoeur was a combatant in World War II and a prisoner of war. He later became professor at several French universities and in the United States. First interested in phenomenology, he attempted to harmonize the philosophies of Marcel and Jaspers, but soon the reality and experience of evil led him to reflect on hermeneutics and symbol. Because of his work on hermeneutics, he has had a profound impact on many European as well as on North and Latin American theologians. Among his books are *The Symbolism of Evil* (1960), *Conflit des interprétations* (1969), and *Histoire et verité* (1955).

Orlando Espín

See also EVIL; EXISTENTIALISM; HERMENEUTICS; JASPERS, KARL; MARCEL, GABRIEL; MODERNITY; PHENOMENOLOGY; POSTMODERNITY; THEOLOGICAL ANTHROPOLOGY; SYMBOL.

RIGHTEOUS GENTILES
See GENTILES.

RIGHTEOUSNESS (IN CHRISTIAN PERSPECTIVE)
See JUSTIFICATION.

RIGHTEOUSNESS (IN JUDAISM)
See GEMILUT HASADIM.

RIGORISM
Rigorism refers to a strict following of moral law or moral precepts. According to rigorism, one should not deviate from a moral law even when there are doubts about its validity. Technically referred to as "tutiorism" (*opinio tutior* = "the safer opinion"), this approach to moral decision making was rejected by the church as inconsistent with the development of moral conscience and the capacity to apply moral principles to complex situations. It fails to appreciate the inexactness of some moral precepts as well as those situations where moral values may be in conflict or tension.

Michael J. Hartwig

See also PROBABILISM.

RIG VEDA
See VEDAS.

RINZAI
One of the two major Zen Buddhist schools in Japan (also Soto) that developed during the Kamakura Period (1185–1333). This form of Zen, based on the Chinese Li-Chi School, was brought to Japan from China in 1191 by the Japanese monk Eisai (1141–1215). While Rinzai was initially embraced by the warrior class, its teachings and practice ultimately spread to the general population. It is based on the simple notion that every person can attain enlightenment by insight into his or her own experience and the surrounding world. The practice itself is an attempt to empty the mind completely so that one can experience reality directly. This is done through the use of enigmatic puzzles or riddles (koans) designed to bring the mind to the limits of ordinary rational thought where it will then let go and move to deeper levels of consciousness and insight. This school of Zen was made popular in the West through the writings of D. T. Suzuki.

G. D. DeAngelis

See also BODHI; KOAN; MUSHIN; ROHATSU; ROSHI; SANZEN; SATORI; SHUNYATA / SUNYA / SHUNYA; SOTO; SUZUKI, DAISETSU TEITARO; ZAZEN; ZEN.

RIPALDA, JUAN MARTÍNEZ DE (1594–1648)
Spanish theologian, and member of the Society of Jesus (Jesuits). One of the great theologians of his day, Ripalda was professor at several prestigious universities in Spain. He wrote on a number of issues, but his main works were the three volumes of *De ente supernaturali* (1634–48) on grace and the supernatural. This Ripalda is not to be confused with Jerónimo Ripalda, another Spaniard, who wrote (in 1547) a very popular and enduring *Catecismo*.

Orlando Espín

See also CATECHISM; COUNTER-REFORMATION / CATHOLIC REFORMATION; FREE WILL; GRACE;

REFORMATION; SOCIETY OF JESUS;
SUPERNATURAL.

RISHI

The *rishis* (Sanskrit, those who see) are the
sages or seers of Hindu myth, sometimes
regarded as semidivine beings. The most
important of the rishis are understood as
the receivers of the Vedic revelation at the
beginning of each of the great world cycles.
As such, the rishis are the closest analog,
in Hindu thinking, to the single "founders" of religions such as Buddhism, Christianity, and Islam. Historically, the rishis
seem to have been the priests of the Indo-
Aryans. The *Rig Veda* itself identifies
them as the divinely inspired poets who
gave utterance to its hymns.

Lance E. Nelson

See also HINDUISM; KALPA; REVELATION
(IN OTHER RELIGIONS); VEDAS; YUGA.

RITA

The Sanskrit word *rita* figures in the religion of the Vedas as a designation for the
cosmic order or moral design of the universe, of which the god Varuna is the
guardian. In later Hinduism, the allied
concept of dharma largely replaces rita
in this cosmic sense, although rita continues to be used in its root meaning of
"truth."

Lance E. Nelson

See also DHARMA (IN HINDUISM);
HINDUISM; VARUNA; VEDAS.

RITES OF CHRISTIAN INITIATION
(RCIA)

The liturgical and formational process of
initiation into the Catholic Church fell
into general disuse by the sixth century.
The practice of infant baptisms and the
indiscriminate baptism of "barbarian"
invaders caused the catechumenate to
disappear. Remnants of the process
remained in North Africa and in the rites
for infant baptism. Vatican II mandated
the restoration of the catechumenate (Rite
of Christian Initiation) in the Constitution
on the Sacred Liturgy (art. 64), followed
by a decree by Pope Paul VI. The mandate
called for a reformation of infant baptism
that emphasized parental formation and
the community's role. Later directives
called for special formation for children
old enough to be catechized and who
would receive the sacraments of baptism,
confirmation, and Eucharist.

The restored process of initiation distinguishes the unbaptized (catechumens)
from the baptized, but not catechized,
and from those baptized in other Christian traditions who wish to seek full
communion with the Catholic Church
(candidates). This distinction preserves
the dignity of baptism.

The RCIA is divided into four stages
or periods of formation. (1) *Evangelization
and Precatechumenate*. This stage provides
a time for questions, introduction to the
Gospel, life of the community, and faith
development. The "inquiry," as it is often
called, consists of no fixed duration or
structure, but must convey an openness
to the needs of the individual and a lack
of coercion on the part of the church.
(2) *Catechumenate*. Begins with the rite of
welcoming/acceptance. The liturgy includes a public declaration of intention
and its acceptance by the community. The
catechumenate nurtures the person's
conversion and faith growth through
celebrations of the Word, basic, adult-
appropriate catechetical instruction, and
community experiences. The duration of
this stage depends upon the readiness of
the catechumen and dates of the liturgical
season of Easter or Epiphany. (3) *Election/*

Enlightenment. Catechumens enter the third stage upon the celebration of the liturgical rite of election when the church formally recognizes their readiness for the initiation sacraments and enrolls them by name. The bishop usually celebrates this rite on the first Sunday of Lent. (4) *Postbaptismal Catechesis or Mystagogy.* The rites of initiation sacraments at the Easter Vigil begin the last stage of the process. This final stage, lasting until Pentecost or longer, assists the community and the neophytes in deepening their understanding of the paschal mystery, making it a part of their lives, joining in the Eucharist and ministries of the parish.

M. Jane Gorman

See also BAPTISM/CONFIRMATION; CATECHUMENATE; CONVERSION; EASTER; HOLY WEEK; LENT; MYSTAGOGY.

RITSCHL, ALBRECHT (1822–89)

German theologian. One of the most influential exponents of liberal theology, Albrecht Ritschl responded to the Enlightenment critique of the rationality of religious faith through a distinctive appropriation of Kant's work. Ritschl contended that religious knowledge ("faith") consists in the "value-judgments" of practical reason and thus is distinct and separate from both "science" and "metaphysics." In his major work, *The Christian Doctrine of Justification and Reconciliation* (1874), Ritschl argued that Christianity is a teleological (ethical) religion whereby, through justification and reconciliation mediated by Christ through the church— the core of his dogmatics—humans are elevated over the natural nexus of the world to participation in the will of God, the kingdom of God. By the end of the nineteenth century, Ritschl's students or those heavily influenced by him, such as Adolph von Harnack, Wilhelm Herrmann, and Julius Kaftan, dominated the (Protestant) theological faculties in German universities.

J. A. Colombo

See also LIBERAL THEOLOGY.

RITUAL

Ritual is a term that frequently refers to symbolic behavior shaped by rules, and repeated, always in the same pattern. Rituals are performed by one or more persons, and are common in human cultures, frequently marking the important moments of a (small or large) community's shared life (many of these are called calendrical rituals). Individuals also perform rituals to mark the key moments of their lives (often referred to as critical rituals, or rites of transition). Consequently, rituals could be performed in and by the smallest units of society (even by individuals) as well as jointly by large numbers of people. Although many rituals have direct connections to religion (mostly because rituals are an indispensable part of religions), some rituals have connections mainly to (apparently) nonreligious moments (like sport or political events) in social or personal life. For religious persons, some rituals are solemn and necessary while others might be more optative and informal. The forms and meanings of rituals vary greatly—from culture to culture, from religion to religion, and throughout history. This is why some rituals seem to imitate real life while others act out great social or religious myths; some rituals attempt to balance nature and/or life while others seem to assault them; some rituals seem to enhance harmonious social behavior while others pretend to subvert social harmony.

But all rituals (religious or not) are repetitive and rule-determined. Rituals are also privileged means by which societies and religions educate their members in the societies' and the religions' belief systems, thereby (also) encouraging increased commitment to and participation in those systems.

Orlando Espín

See also DEVOTIONS; DHIKR; GHOST DANCE; HAJJ; MYTH; PUJA; SACRAMENT; SALAT; SAMSKARA (RITUALS); SANTERÍA; SYMBOL.

ROBINSON, J.A.T. (1919–83)

A British Anglican bishop, John A. T. Robinson specialized in New Testament studies and published extensively on topics such as eschatology, the body in Pauline theology, liturgy, and ethics, in addition to landmark textual studies of Romans and the Gospel of John. Robinson also presaged one of the central themes at the Second Vatican Council (1962–5), namely, the role of the church in the modern world, in his similarly titled book, *On Being the Church in the World* (1960). While bishop of Woolwich between 1959 and 1969, he wrote a number of controversial works, including *Honest to God* (1963), widely translated and discussed as a result of its main thesis concerning the inadequacy of traditional Christian images of, language for, and claims about God in modern and postmodern times. After he was appointed lecturer in theology at Trinity College in Cambridge, England, in 1969, Robinson published a major book, *Redating the New Testament* (1976), supporting an earlier date for the writing of the four Gospels than commonly accepted by most New Testament scholars of his time.

Rosemary P. Carbine

ROEST CROLLIUS, ARIJ (1933–)

This Dutch Jesuit, born in Tilburg, has left his mark on theological and religious studies in four main areas. His studies and formation in such diverse countries as Holland, Lebanon, Egypt, India, Italy, Israel, and Japan, have allowed him to posit a more descriptive, analogical understanding of human reality, as opposed to a more deductive, philosophical perception. His approach reveals a theology in continual dialogue with cultural anthropology, sociology, and ethnology.

In the area of fundamental theology, his comparative studies of the experience of revelation in both Islam and Hinduism have attempted to demonstrate the originality and universal significance of the Christian revelation. Second, he has been one of the leading figures in studies on inculturation. In this area, he has worked toward a clarification of the concepts of culture and inculturation to facilitate a theological discourse on these realities. Third, his works on interreligious and intercultural studies have focused on the relationship between the Catholic Church and major world religions, more specifically, Judaism and Islam. Finally, he has lectured and written about spiritual experience and growth. It is because of his personal familiarity with the spiritual traditions of different religions that he has been able to highlight some of the many points of convergence.

Eduardo C. Fernández, s.j.

See also CULTURE; ECUMENICAL MOVEMENT/ECUMENISM; INCULTURATION; MISSIOLOGY.

ROHATSU

(Japanese, *rohatsu dai sesshin*, intense meditative session). The most intense and difficult of all meditation sessions within Zen practice, with the hope for enlightenment.

It is generally undertaken between the first and eighth of December, and is based on the belief that the Buddha attained enlightenment on December eighth.

G. D. DeAngelis

See also BODHI; MUSHIN; SANZEN; SATORI; SESSHIN; SHUNYATA/SUNYA/SHUNYA; ZAZEN; ZEN.

ROIG, ARTURO ANDRÉS (1922–)

Argentine philosopher. Educated in his native country and at Paris's Sorbonne, Roig was for many years professor of philosophy at the University of Cuyo, Argentina. He was also visiting professor at several European, U.S., and Latin American universities. He has developed a historical empiricism that attempts to supersede some of the dichotomies he finds in most Western thought: subject–object, spirit–matter, signified–signifying, and so on. Roig places the human within society, while birthing, individuating, and contextualizing the person only in community. He proposes an epistemology only possible within this communal, social matrix. His impact on Latin American liberation thought (especially on Segundo, Dussel, and Scannone) is evident. Among his many books are *La filosofía de las luces en la ciudad agrícola* (1964), *Platón o la filosofía como libertad y expectativa* (1972), and *Bolivarismo y filosofía latinoamericana* (1984).

Orlando Espín

See also DUSSEL, ENRIQUE; EPISTEMOLOGY; HERMENEUTICS; LATIN AMERICAN THEOLOGIES; LIBERATION THEOLOGIES; SCANNONE, JUAN CARLOS; SEGUNDO, JUAN LUIS; SOCIETY; SYMBOL; THEOLOGICAL ANTHROPOLOGY.

ROMAN CATHOLIC CHURCH

This term encompasses a worldwide community of some one billion Christians unified under the Bishop of Rome, and centered in Jesus Christ as the fullness of the revelation of God and God's Son ever present through the Holy Spirit. It is "Roman" to make specific the unique authority of the Bishop of Rome which, in the eleventh century in relation to the Eastern churches, and in the sixteenth century with regard to the Reformation, was under attack. It is "Catholic" as Ignatius of Antioch (d. ca. 115 C.E.) first used the term to distinguish the whole church from local churches. In terms of *beliefs*, the basis of the teachings and life of the church comes from the Old and New Testaments, with the beginnings of the church understood to be when Jesus gathered his disciples after his resurrection and commissioned them to proclaim the Gospel everywhere, and designated Peter as the head and foundation of the community (Matt 28:18-20; 16:13-19; Luke 22:31-32). The *tradition* of the church, its reflections on Scripture, its teachings, rituals, councils, and sacramental life, together with Scripture, form the ongoing sources from which the church draws its understanding of the mystery of the way God saves us through the life, death, and resurrection of Jesus Christ in the Holy Spirit. God is a Trinity of Persons, Father, Son, and Holy Spirit, respectively and functionally designated as Creator, Redeemer, and Sanctifier. The Virgin Mary, mother of Jesus, is Mother of God and mother of the church, conceived without sin and assumed into heaven. The church, the Body of Christ's sacramental presence in the world, continues the mission of Christ by offering salvation to all through the ministry of the seven sacraments, which welcome people into and celebrate the paschal mystery of Christ's dying and rising. As the Body of Christ in the world, the church offers the reign of God as the reconciling grace to transform and orient humankind toward its proper goal, life with God. It calls itself and others to a moral life based on the Scriptures and tradition, whose purpose and end is union with God. Hell would be the complete absence of God, reserved for those who reject completely God's offer of salvation, while purgatory is understood as a purifying preparation for entrance to the complete presence of God. The pope, Bishop of Rome, is the head of the church, infallible when speaking on faith or morals, and governs in union with the bishops, heads of churches throughout the world.

Thomas McElligott

See also APOSTOLICITY; CATHOLICITY; PAPACY/PAPAL; PETRINE MINISTRY; PRIMACY; POPE; ROME, SEE OF.

ROMANESQUE

The Romanesque style of church architecture dates from the mid-tenth through mid-twelfth centuries, when it is eventually succeeded by the Gothic style. Romanesque churches can be larger than the earlier basilica-style buildings; many of them served as gathering points for large groups of Christian pilgrims on pilgrimage at this time. One important example is the church of La Madeleine at Vézelay in France, starting point of a pilgrimage route to the shrine of St. James in Spain (Santiago de Compostela). Romanesque churches do preserve in many ways a layout or plan similar to the earlier basilica (narthex, nave, side aisles, transepts, and apse); some show architectural elaboration for the needs of the faithful, for example, the addition of a kind of corridor, or *ambulatory* along the edge of the apse, with side chapels radiating into the exterior walls. Stone is the primary building material; the interior of the church is dominated by rounded arches, barrel vaults, and massive stone pillars. Color is provided by stained-glass windows, more than by paint or mosaics on the interior walls. The exterior of the churches are decorated with sculptures, especially over (the *lintel* and *tympanum*) and alongside (the *jambs*) the doors (*portals*) to the building. In Europe, some churches show evidence of both the Romanesque and Gothic styles, having been begun in one century and finished in another, for example, Durham cathedral in England.

Joanne M. Pierce

See also BAROQUE; BASILICA; CATHEDRAL; CHAPEL; GOTHIC.

ROMANTICISM

A late eighteenth-century and nineteenth-century European as well as global intellectual and sociocultural movement that shifted attention away *from* Enlightenment analytic rationalism (grounded in philosophy, metaphysics, and so forth) *to* organic intuition, founded on individualism, aesthetics (imagination, emotion, mysticism), historicity, and nature in literature, music, art, and religion. In terms of religion, German philosopher Friedrich von Schelling (1775–1854) introduced in the early nineteenth century what is called "a philosophy of identity" or an understanding of the absolute manifesting itself in human history that he later further developed into a trinitarian theology. In distinction from Schelling, Georg Hegel (1770–1831) developed in his many works a dialectical synthesis of absolute Spirit moving from a lack of self-consciousness to absolute self-consciousness within art (the senses), religion (symbols), and philosophy (concepts).

Both Protestant and Catholic theologies in Germany reflected the turn to Romanticism. There is an ongoing scholarly debate about whether Friedrich Schleiermacher (d. 1834), a pioneer of modern liberal Protestant theology, self-identified as a Romantic, but his *Speeches on Religion* (1799) bespeak the influence of Romanticism: "True religion is sense and taste for the infinite." Similar to other Romantics, Schleiermacher supported a spiritual intuition of the divine and of an underlying organic unity of all reality; religion has less to do with pure metaphysical reason or practical moral reason and more to do with the perception of the infinite and the feeling of totality in the world that in turn help to shape personal identity and action. Often resistant to Enlightenment rationalism and secularism, Catholic theologies of the time illustrated by Johann Sebastian Drey and Johann Adam Möhler of the University of Tübingen embraced Romanticism and its emphasis on the immanence of the divine and personal piety by bringing, among other things, the Incarnation, the sacramentality of all reality, and an organic model of the church as a community of believers to the forefront of Christian theology.

Rosemary P. Carbine

ROME, SEE OF

A Christian community existed in the city of Rome by the year 58 C.E. (the approximate date of Paul's letter to the Romans). From the time of Emperor Nero (ca. 64 C.E.) on, Christians in Rome suffered almost three centuries of persecutions and misunderstandings from the general population of the city and from the imperial governments. An ancient tradition (with some archeological substantiation) places the apostle Peter in Rome at around 42 C.E.; thus Roman Catholics hold Peter to have been the city's first bishop. From at least the end of the first century C.E., the Bishops of Rome began making claims to a pastoral ministry encompassing the wider church, beyond the limits of their local Roman church. The apostolic presence and possible foundation of the Roman Christian community, as well as its location in the capital of the empire and its reputation for holding on to the apostolic preaching, earned the church of Rome great respect and unquestioned leadership throughout the first several centuries of Christian history. Thereafter the see of Rome had a long history of leadership among the churches, and several ancient Christian councils recognized its preeminence as the first among the patriarchal churches. However, after 1054 and the schism between Western and Eastern churches, Rome remained only the undisputed presiding see in the West. After the sixteenth-century Reformations, only "Roman" Catholics remained in communion with the see of Rome (although in more recent times several Eastern churches have established full communion with Rome). The primacy of the Roman see and its bishop remains one of the great stumbling blocks in the ecumenical movement.

Orlando Espín

See also ECCLESIOLOGY; PAPACY/PAPAL; PRIMACY; ROMAN CATHOLIC CHURCH; TRADITION (IN CHRISTIANITY).

ROMERO, OSCAR ARNULFO (1917–80)

Archbishop of San Salvador, martyred on March 24, 1980, while celebrating the Eucharist. Born into a poor family in Ciudad Barrios, El Salvador, he studied for the priesthood in his native country and in

Rome, and was ordained in 1942. As a priest and later as seminary rector, Romero was publicly known to oppose many of the reforms of the Second Vatican Council as well as Latin American liberation theology. In 1974 he became bishop of Santiago de María where he exercised his episcopal ministry as a staunch conservative. Probably because of this conservatism, in 1977 he was appointed archbishop of San Salvador. However, the murder of Rutilio Grande, a Jesuit priest and personal friend, as well as the increasing number of atrocities committed by the Salvadoran Armed Forces and by right-wing political groups, led Romero to a dramatic change: he became an ardent defender of the poor, an outspoken critic of the military and of political conservatism, and a supporter of liberation theology. He saw his episcopal ministry as the voice of the voiceless. He soon became, as archbishop, the leading figure struggling (always by peaceful means) for justice in El Salvador. He also became a supporter of the theological and philosophical work being developed at the time at the Jesuit university in San Salvador (especially the work of Ignacio Ellacuría). Romero's sermons (transmitted by radio to the entire country) were heard by most of the population, and his pastoral letters were read by many of his fellow Salvadorans. The sermons and pastoral letters were relentless appeals for justice and compassion. Romero became a symbol for many Christians across Latin America who were in similar situations. The right-wing ordered his assassination because of Romero's unwavering ministry on behalf of the poor and his support of the Gospel. His grave, in the cathedral in San Salvador, is today a place of pilgrimage for very many from El Salvador and from across Latin America and the world. The pro-

cess for his beatification and eventual canonization as martyr has begun.

Orlando Espín

See also BISHOP (EPISCOPACY); ELLACURÍA, IGNACIO; JUSTICE; LATIN AMERICAN THEOLOGIES; LIBERATION THEOLOGIES; MAGISTERIUM, ORDINARY; MARTYR/MARTYRDOM.

ROSARY

A Catholic devotion that centers on fifteen "mysteries" ("scenes" or moments) in the lives of Jesus and Mary. The purpose of the rosary is to bring the individual to meditate on the meaning of each of the "mysteries" (on the Incarnation, the Birth of Jesus, the Crucifixion, and so on). In order to achieve this, a set of ten "Hail Marys" is prayed per mystery. Each set of ten is preceded in turn by the recitation of the Lord's Prayer, and followed by the brief doxology called the *Gloria Patri.* Common practice has grouped the fifteen mysteries in three cycles of five mysteries each, so that only five mysteries are prayed at a time. To help keep track, the prayers are counted on beads set on a string or chain also called a "rosary." A tradition from the fifteenth century associates the creation of the rosary with Dominic of Guzmán and the early Dominicans.

Orlando Espín

See also APPARITIONS; DEVOTIONS; DOMINIC OF GUZMAN; HAIL MARY; JESUS; LORD'S PRAYER; MARIAN DEVOTIONS; MARIOLOGY; MARY OF NAZARETH; MEDITATION (CHRISTIAN); POPULAR CATHOLICISM; PRAYER; SAINTS (CHRISTIAN), DEVOTION TO.

ROSCÍO, JUAN GERMÁN (1763–1821)

Venezuelan Catholic lay theologian. With doctorates in canon and civil law, Roscío was a distinguished member of colonial society when, in 1809, he actively embraced the cause of independence against Spain. He always remained publicly committed to Catholicism, but had to suffer much for opposing his church's position on the issue of loyalty to Spain. He was afterwards elected vice president of his newly independent country. In 1811 he published a book called *El patriotismo de Nirgua y el abuso de los reyes*, and in 1815 his better-known *El triunfo de la libertad sobre el despotismo*. In both, but especially in the latter, Roscío theologically defends the cause of independence against the royalist clergy, and justifies Catholics who struggle against authorities who act unjustly and who violate the rights of the people. His thought is counted among the precursors of contemporary liberation theology.

Orlando Espín

See also CANON LAW; CLERICALISM; FREEDOM; IDEOLOGY (IDEOLOGIES); LAITY; LATIN AMERICAN THEOLOGIES; LIBERATION THEOLOGIES; PRAXIS; THEOLOGICAL ANTHROPOLOGY.

ROSH HASHANAH

Hebrew, literally meaning "head of the year," this is the Jewish New Year. It occurs on the first and second days of the Hebrew month of Tishri, the first month of the Jewish year, corresponding to September or early October.

Unlike some cultures and societies that celebrate the coming of a new year with raucous behavior, Judaism greets its new year with serious introspection, self-evaluation, and prayer—an annual personal and collective "soul inventory." In this way, the future can be shaped by assessing the failures and the successes of the past.

Rosh HaShanah begins a ten-day period called *Aseret Y'may T'shuvah*, the Ten Days of Repentance, culminating in Yom Kippur, the Day of Atonement. Together, Rosh HaShanah and Yom Kippur are called in Hebrew, *Yamim No'raim*, the Days of Awe. In English, they are known as the High Holidays. The prayers for these days revolve around evaluation of personal conduct, repentance for mistakes and transgressions, and seeking forgiveness from fellow human beings and from God. On the Saturday evening before Rosh HaShanah, the *Selichot* service—penitential prayers for forgiveness—is held, setting the tone and mood for the season.

Rosh HaShanah begins with a home meal, where it is customary to eat apples dipped in honey, symbolic of a sweet new year. At the synagogue, all the ritual objects are dressed in white, symbolic of the quest for ethical purity. The synagogue services for the holiday are rather lengthy, and are chanted from the *machzor*, the special High Holiday prayer book, in a distinct prayer melody that evokes the special character of the day. Special poem-prayers called *piyyutim* are added to embellish and enhance the worship. Many of the prayers are elaborate metaphors picturing God as king, sitting on the Throne of Judgment, writing the fate of each individual in a Book of Life. Because of these themes, Rosh HaShanah is also called *Yom HaDin*, the Day of Judgment, and *Yom HaZikaron*, the Day of Remembrance, where God is asked to remember each person for good. The central ritual of the Rosh HaShanah service is the sounding of the *shofar*, the ram's horn. Its plaintive, wailing sound moves worshipers toward introspection and repentance.

On Rosh HaShanah afternoon (on the afternoon of the second day, if the first days falls on the Sabbath) the *Tashlich* service is held. Worshipers go to a body of flowing water to symbolically "cast" their transgressions into the water to be carried away by the currents.

While Rosh HaShanah prayers are solemn and serious, they are also filled with joy and with hope, for Judaism teaches that God is ready and willing to forgive the transgressions of those who come in sincere repentance.

The greeting for Rosh HaShanah is *"Shanah Tovah,"* "May it be a good year" for you and those you love.

Wayne Dosick

See also MACHZOR; SHOFAR; YOM KIPPUR.

ROSH HODESH

Hebrew, literally meaning "head of the month," is the first day of a Jewish month.

There are twelve months in the Hebrew or Jewish calendar—a soli-lunar calendar.

A soli-lunar calendar, based on the revolution of the moon around the sun, has twenty-nine and a half days each month. Since a month cannot have a half day, each year, six Hebrew months alternatingly have twenty-nine days, and six have thirty days—the twelve half days counting as a full day every other month.

In the months that have thirty days, the thiritieth day is designated as Rosh Hodesh along with the first day of the new month. Since half of the thiritieth day technically belongs to the new month, it is considered an honorary part of the new month.

Judaism recognizes and celebrates the sanctity of time, so each new Jewish month is greeted with prayers and blessings. On the Sabbath preceding the week in which the new month will begin, a Blessing of the New Month is recited in the synagogue to remind the worshipers that the new month is coming, and to ask God for a multitude of blessings in the month ahead. On the day of Rosh Hodesh, special prayers are added to the synagogue service, and a short portion is read from the Torah at the morning service, in honor of the day.

Rosh Hodesh is considered a "half-holiday." Traditionally it has been known as a "women's holiday," because on Rosh Hodesh, women would stop their work early in the day and come together to study and celebrate. Today, many Jewish women have reclaimed the spirit of Rosh Hodesh as a celebration of and for women by writing new prayers and liturgies, and by gathering together in prayer and study groups to mark the monthly observance.

Wayne Dosick

See also KERIAT HATORAH; SHABBAT.

ROSHI

(Japanese, lit., venerable teacher). Honorific title within the Zen tradition meaning "great teacher." Traditionally, it is used to refer to one who has mastered and embodied the dharma (truth) and is thus able to guide others by example. The function of the *roshi* is to guide and inspire his disciples along the path to self-realization.

G. D. DeAngelis

See also BODHI; DHARMA; MUSHIN; RINZAI; SATORI; SOTO; ZEN.

ROY, RAM MOHAN (1772–1833)

One of the earliest leaders of the nineteenth-century Hindu reform movement, Ram Mohan Roy was called by those who admired him the "Father of Modern

Hinduism." He is known especially for his founding, in 1828, of the Brahmo Samaj (Society of God), a Calcutta-based movement dedicated to religious and social reform. Championing what he conceived to be the original monotheism of the Upanishads, Roy sought to reform Hinduism by purging it of image worship, polytheism, doctrines of transmigration and divine incarnation (*avatara*), and other elements of the medieval tradition that he, responding to the harsh critiques of Christian missionaries, had decided were objectionable. Roy and many of his followers were great admirers of Jesus and his teachings, though they rejected the traditional Christian understanding of him. Roy was also influenced by Islam and Unitarianism. At their weekly meetings, the Samajists sat in pews, sang hymns, and heard sermons, all on the Christian model. Roy and members of the Samaj undertook important efforts toward social reform within Hinduism, especially in relation to the treatment of women. The Samaj never gained a wide following, appealing mostly to educated, Westernized Hindu intellectuals. In the end, the Brahmos' most important legacy is probably their work against such abuses as widow burning (*sati*), child-marriage, and laws against widow remarriage, and their introduction into Hindu discourse of a clear theoretical distinction between social practice and religion. The latter had the important long-term effect of allowing social reform to proceed without appearing to be a threat to the religious life of Hindus.

Lance E. Nelson

See also DAYANANDA, SWAMI; HINDUISM; SEN, KESHAB CHANDRA; UPANISHADS.

RUAH

Ruah is a Hebrew word meaning breath, wind, or spirit. In the latter sense, it may refer to human disposition or emotion. *Ruah* may also be used to refer to the non-material aspect of human beings, and thus *ruah* may sometimes parallel *nephesh* in usage. Generally, *ruah* is translated by *pneuma* in the Septuagint and by *spiritus* in the Vulgate.

Russell Fuller

RUETHER, ROSEMARY RADFORD (1936–)

A pioneer in feminist theology and a historian by training, Ruether, who was born to a Roman Catholic mother and an Episcopalian father, received a B.A. in philosophy from Scripps College (1958), and an M.A. in ancient history (1960) and a Ph.D. in classics and patristics (1965) from Claremont Graduate School in Claremont, California. Rooted in a prophetic-liberating hermeneutic of Christian Scriptures, Ruether's groundbreaking 1983 *Sexism and God-Talk: Toward a Feminist Theology* boldly asserts that the critical principle necessary for sound theology is the promotion of the full humanity of women, a fullness determined by a feminist epistemology, with the consequence that only what promotes the full humanity of women can be considered divine or of the Holy. The upshot of her claim is that the preponderance of Christian theology, because it is patriarchal, is unholy, thus necessitating feminist theology's rehabilitation of Christian themes, an example of which is her 1998 *Women and Redemption: A Theological History*. Ruether has also been highly influential in the development of feminist spirituality and liturgical movements, as well as ecofeminist theology, through her well-known and important books *Women-Church: Theology and Practice of Feminist Liturgical Communities* (1985) and *Gaia and God: An*

Ecofeminist Theology of Earth Healing (1992). She is a highly sought-after speaker and continues to teach at Claremont Graduate University. Her most recent books include *Integrating Ecofeminism, Globalization, and World Religions* (2005), *Goddesses and the Divine Feminine: A Western Religious History* (2005), and *Interpreting the Postmodern: Responses to "Radical Orthodoxy"* (2006).

Meghan T. Sweeney

See also FEMINIST THEOLOGIES; LIBERATION THEOLOGIES; PATRIARCHY; SEXISM.

RUFINUS OF AQUILEIA (345?–410)

While a student at Rome, Rufinus befriended Jerome. Together they were part of a monastic group formed in Concordia, Rufinus's hometown. From 373 until 380, Rufinus lived in Egypt, after which he settled in a monastery in Jerusalem. In 397 he returned to Rome, finally moving to Sicily to escape the invading Goths. Rufinus was a Christian scholar best known for his translations of Origen and of Basil the Great. Rufinius's admiration and support for Origen caused him to quarrel with his old friend, Jerome. It is thanks to Rufinus that many of Origen's works survived the purges of the Origenist controversy, albeit in altered translation.

Gary Macy

See also BASIL THE GREAT; JEROME; MONASTICISM IN WESTERN CHRISTIANITY; ORIGEN; ORIGENISM.

RUH

In Islam, *ruh* is the spiritual dimension of humans and their unique, God-given link to the Supreme Being. The term is usually translated as "spirit," but it should not be confused with another aspect of the human person, the *nafs* or soul. Nafs refers to the individuality of people with all the proclivities toward sin and ignorance that characterize the human condition. The ruh, by contrast, raises humankind to a higher realm of being and places humans above the angels and all other creatures in the hierarchy of creation. It is the ruh that gives humanity its special dignity. The sacred scripture of Islam, the Qur'an, refers to Jesus Christ, whom Muslims regard as a revered prophet, as the *ruh* Allah, the "Spirit of God" (4:171).

Ronald A. Pachence

See also ISLAM; JESUS (AS PROPHET OF ISLAM); NAFS; QUR'AN.

RULE (MONASTIC/RELIGIOUS)

Since the third century, efforts have been made by church authorities to regulate the lives of those looking for a "more perfect way" to follow Christ. The reason was to prevent pastoral and spiritual chaos in the absence of a program or plan for those who had chosen an alternative religious lifestyle. Eventually, religious communities would form, and each community would design its "rule of life" in order to facilitate common life and to protect individuals against excessive zeal. The need for guidance, prudence, spiritual direction, and some generally recognized pattern of religious observance became increasingly necessary as Christians were drawn to monastic life. Each religious institute thus developed its own manner of proceeding or "rule" of life.

William Reiser, S.J.

See also BENEDICTINE RULE (RULE OF ST. BENEDICT); CONGREGATIONS (ORDERS); COUNSELS (OF PERFECTION); RELIGIOUS (VOWED).

RULE OF FAITH

Also known by the Latin equivalent *regula fidei*. An early theological term among

Christians used to indicate the parameters within which authentic Christian beliefs *and* practices could be found. The Rules of Faith were useful to theologians and church ministers as the Rules indicated the acceptable outer boundaries of doctrinal research and of pastoral (often liturgical) practice. To cross these boundaries implied either heresy or inauthenticity. Irenaeus of Lyons (d. 200 C.E.) suggested that the best Rule was the consensus among the Christian communities that were founded by the apostles. Tertullian (d. 225), Origen (d. 254), and others, also offered their versions and criteria for determining adequate Rules of Faith. Vincent of Lérins' (d. 450?) Rule of Faith became better known and more widespread in western Europe— "what has been believed and/or practiced always, everywhere, and by all." The use of and insistence on Rules of Faith contributed to the early Christian efforts to safeguard and transmit the essential core of Christianity.

Orlando Espín

See also CATHOLIC TRADITION; DEVELOPMENT OF DOGMA/OF DOCTRINE; DOCTRINE; DOGMA; HERESY; IDEOLOGY (IDEOLOGIES); IRENAEUS OF LYONS; LITURGY (IN CHRISTIANITY); MAGISTERIUM, ORDINARY; MINISTRY/ MINISTERIAL; ORIGEN; ORTHODOXY (IN CHRISTIANITY); ORTHOPRAXIS; POPULAR CATHOLICISM; PRAXIS; SENSUS FIDELIUM/SENSUS FIDEI; TERTULLIAN; TRADITION (IN CHRISTIANITY); TRADITION AND TRADITIONS; VINCENT OF LÉRINS.

RUMI, JALAL AL-DIN (1207–73)

Also written Jalal al-Din ar-Rumi, he was an Islamic poet and mystic, referred to as *Mawlana*, "our master," for his role in founding the famous Sufi religious order in Konya, Turkey, frequently called the "Whirling Dervishes" by Westerners. The order is more properly known as "Mevlevi" from the Turkish translation of *Mawlana* (*Mevlana*). Born in Afghanistan, Rumi was attracted to Sufism, a mystical spirituality in Islam, when he was twenty-five, and within ten years he had already earned recognition as a Sufi spiritual guide (*shaykh*). It was about this time that Rumi met Shams al-Din al Tabrizi, a fellow mystic, who became his admired and revered companion. While the intensity of this relationship eventually caused problems between Rumi and his disciples, who murdered Shams in 1247, Shams inspired Rumi to develop a spirituality emphasizing a deep longing for and personal love of God. This spirituality is eloquently expressed, not only in the Persian words of Rumi's extensive corpus of religious poetry, but also in the ecstatic, whirling dance he introduced to his followers after Sham's death. It has been suggested that the somber tone and sense of longing in the music used to accompany this religious dance reflect Rumi's persistent grief over Sham's death, as well as the desire all believers have to be with God. Although disbanded by the first president of the Turkish Republic, Mustafa Kamal Atatürk (1881–1938), the Whirling Dervishes of the Mevlevi order continue to dance in Konya and elsewhere in what is officially described today by the Turkish government as an exhibition of Turkish folklore.

Ronald A. Pachence

See also ATATÜRK, MUSTAFA; ISLAM; SHAYKH; SUFI/SUFISM; WHIRLING DERVISHES.

RUSSIAN ORTHODOX CHURCH

The origins of this church can be traced back to ninth- and tenth-century missionaries, and to the conversion to Christianity by prince Vladimir (tenth century), who made it the official religion within his domains. Under the direct influence of the Greek church during its early period, the Russian church soon developed its own clergy and its own ecclesial and liturgical identity. In the Great Schism of 1054 (that separated Catholics and Orthodox), the Russians took the side of Constantinople against Rome. Monasticism flourished, and the monasteries' staunch defense of people and national identity during the long periods of invasion and instability made the Russian Orthodox Church a symbol of the national spirit. In 1589 the Patriarchate of Moscow was established, being recognized by the other Orthodox Churches, including Constantinople. Allied with the czars, and often controlled by them, the Russian church had begun a reform process when the 1917 revolution deposed the czar and brought the communists to power. Persecution soon followed, and although the church was never officially suppressed, it was seriously wounded and hindered by communist rule. After the Soviet collapse, the Russian Orthodox Church began its recovery. It still commands the allegiance of millions of Russians. The church is currently spread throughout Europe and the Americas.

Orlando Espín

See also ANCIENT CHURCHES OF THE EAST; AUTOCEPHALOUS CHURCHES; BULGAKOV, SERGEI; BYZANTIUM/ BYZANTINE; CHALCEDONIAN CHRISTIANS; COMMUNION (ECCLESIOLOGICAL); CONSTANTINOPLE, SEE OF; DOSTOYEVSKY, FEODOR; EASTERN CATHOLIC CHURCHES; ECCLESIOLOGY; FILIOQUE; GREEK ORTHODOX CHURCH; ICON; LITURGY (IN CHRISTIANITY); LOSSKY, VLADIMIR; MARIOLOGY; MARXISM; MONASTERY; MONASTICISM IN EASTERN CHRISTIANITY; ORTHODOX CHURCHES; PATRIARCH; PHILARET, DROZDOV; PHILARET, THEODORE NIKITICH ROMANOV; RUTHENIAN CATHOLIC CHURCH; SCHISM, GREAT EASTERN; SERGEI OF RADONEZH; SOBORNOST; UKRAINIAN CATHOLIC CHURCH.

RUTHENIAN CATHOLIC CHURCH

Name of several Christian communities in full communion with Rome. These communities descend from the Russian Orthodox Church, but separated from it at various times (1596 and 1646) and formed different ecclesiastical jurisdictions. There are some seven hundred thousand Ruthenian Catholics worldwide, spread throughout Europe, the Americas, and Australia.

Orlando Espín

See also COMMUNION (ECCLESIOLOGICAL); EASTERN CATHOLIC CHURCHES; ORTHODOX CHURCHES; RUSSIAN ORTHODOX CHURCH.

RUYSBROECK (RUUSBROEC), JAN VAN (1293–1381)

Jan van Ruysbroeck is best known for his mystical treatises, particularly *The Spiritual Espousals*. After serving for a number of years as parish priest in Brussels, he joined with a small number of like-minded priests in the more secluded setting of Groenendaal to reflect and write on spiritual life.

Like so many spiritual writers, he envisioned a three-stage progression he called the active life, the "interior, exalted life of desire," and the "superessential, contemplative life." In all three stages, however, he considered the essence of the spiritual life to be the same—participation in the twofold movement of rest and "going out," participation, that is, in the very life of God. For in Ruysbroeck's view, at the heart of the life of the Trinity is the twofold movement of resting in Unity and moving outward to generate the Son and breathe forth the Spirit.

Mary Anne Foley, C.N.D.

See also MYSTICISM/MYSTICS (IN CHRISTIANITY); TRINITY/TRINITARIAN THEOLOGY/TRINITARIAN PROCESSIONS.

RYOBU

(Japanese, *Ryobu-Shugo* Shinto, lit., unification of both sides). Sometimes referred to as "mixed" or "dual" Shinto. It is a syncretic form of Shinto that was primarily a synthesis of Buddhism and the indigenous religious tradition (Shinto). This merger began during the Heian Period (794–1185) through the efforts of two Buddhist monks, Saicho and Kukai, and emerged as a unified tradition during the Kamakura Period (1192–1336). Ryobu was basically an attempt to interpret Shinto in accord with the doctrines of the Shingon School of Buddhism, establishing a direct relationship between Japanese *kami* and Buddhist divinities. Ryobu Shinto persisted until the nineteenth century when Shinto was instituted as the state religion and purged of any foreign elements, including Buddhism. In more general terms, it can also be perceived as a pattern of coexistence between Buddhism and Shinto.

G. D. DeAngelis

See also BUDDHISM; KAMAKURA PERIOD; KOBO DAISHI; SHINGON; SHINTO.

S

SAADYA GAON (882–942)

(Hebrew, Saadya ben Joseph Alfayumi). Born in Egypt, Saadya became the leader or "Gaon" of the Babylonian Jewish community. He issued virulent attacks against the powerful Karaite movement that rejected the authority of rabbinic Judaism. Saadya is reputed to be the first medieval philosopher to write monographs on topics of Jewish law and the first to write in Arabic. Saadya was also the first Jew to elaborate systematic and formal proofs of the existence of God. He took an interest in liturgy, grammar, and astrology. His theological and mystical writings on the *Shekinah* (divine presence) and the *Ruah haKodesh* (spirit of God) influenced medieval Hasidism and Kabbalah. He is best known for his major philosophical work *The Book of Beliefs and Opinions*, for his systematic compilation of the prayer book, and for his liturgical poems.

Alan J. Avery-Peck

SABAOTH

Term meaning "hosts" or "armies." In the Old Testament, the term is used to refer to the "God of Sabaoth," that is, the God of armies, the most powerful God at whose command are all of the forces throughout all creation. When God is depicted as a divine warrior who fights for Israel, then the armies of Israel are the Lord's armies; the Lord is the God of armies, in this case, Israel's army.

There are a few occurrences of the term in 1–2 Samuel and in 1–2 Kings as a name for God, a title of honor that assumes God's power, including the power to achieve victory over enemies, whether those enemies be the Philistines or the Baals. The most frequent references to God as the God of hosts occur in First Isaiah and in Jeremiah, where clearly the intention is an affirmation of God's power.

The New Testament names God as "God of Hosts" only twice, and both references are drawn from the Old Testament. Romans 9:29 is a quotation from Isaiah 1:9, and James 5:4 is dependent on Malachi 3:5.

Alice L. Laffey

SABATIER, (LOUIS) AUGUSTE (1839–1901)

French Protestant theologian. After studies in France, Switzerland and Germany, Sabatier taught at universities in Strasbourg and Paris. He was impacted by the thought of Schleiermacher and Ritschl, and did much to make them known in

1193

France. A very religious person, he was enthusiastic about the application of the methods of historical criticism to biblical interpretation and to the interpretation of Christian dogmas. Sabatier was one of the key influences on the early stages of the theological movement called "Modernism" in the Catholic Church. Among his books are *La vie intime des dogmes* (1890) and his posthumous *The Religion of Authority and the Religion of Spirit* (1903).

Orlando Espín

See also BIBLICAL CRITICISM; DEVELOPMENT OF DOGMA/OF DOCTRINE; DOGMA; HERMENEUTICS; HISTORICAL CRITICISM; MODERNISM; MODERNITY; POSTMODERNITY; RITSCHL, ALBRECHT; SCHLEIERMACHER, FRIEDRICH.

SABBATH (IN CHRISTIANITY)

As in Judaism, the Sabbath in Christianity is the Lord's Day, a day of rest that commemorates the day God rested after the labors of creation as recorded in Genesis. Jews and Christians believe that Sabbath-keeping was mandated by God in the fourth of the Ten Commandments. However, due to a different calculation of time, Christians celebrate the Sabbath on Sunday rather than sundown Friday to sundown Saturday. With the exception of a few Christian groups that follow the Jewish practice and hold the Sabbath on Saturday, including Seventh-Day Adventists and Seventh-Day Baptists, Christians have honored Sunday as the Sabbath day.

The earliest Christians gathered on Sundays to commemorate the resurrection of Jesus the Christ, celebrating the new age inaugurated by the Messiah. By the Middle Ages in Europe, Sunday was a day for relaxation as well as worship and often included games and dancing. During the Protestant Reformation, John Calvin and his followers believed this laxness profaned the Sabbath and urged its strict observance in prayer and scriptural study. This strictness flourished among Calvinists in the sixteenth and seventeenth centuries in Switzerland, Scotland, the Netherlands, and the English colonies. In colonial New England, Puritans endured two two-hour worship services each Sunday and abstained from all labor and recreation.

In the nineteenth century, Sabbath-keeping was a social and moral reform of evangelical Protestants in the United States. Methodists, Baptists, Presbyterians, Disciples of Christ, Congregationalists, and many Lutherans saw keeping the Sabbath as a means not only of demonstrating discipleship, but also of Christianizing the country and transforming society toward godliness. Honoring the Sabbath meant attendance at worship, Bible study and prayer, quiet conversation with friends and family, and above all, no boisterousness or frivolity. Groups like the General Union for Promoting the Observance of the Christian Sabbath worked to pass laws prohibiting the operation of businesses and the delivery of mail on Sunday. Enacted before labor unions and fair labor laws, during a time when workers routinely toiled sixty hours a week or more, these laws declaring Sunday as a day of rest were significant labor legislation. However, evangelical Protestants also used Sabbatarianism to assert their superiority. Along with temperance, it was a rallying cry of nativism. Catholic immigrants were disparaged for relaxing and playing on the Sabbath.

By the end of the nineteenth century, Sabbatarianism lost popularity. Evangelical efforts to close the 1876 Centennial

Exposition in Philadelphia and 1893 Columbian Exhibition in Chicago on Sundays failed due to financial pressures. Commercial considerations, the desire for profit and expanding leisure industries, eventually doomed the Sabbath-keeping movement. Moreover, many Protestants themselves resisted it, remembering gloomy, solemn Sundays of their youth. By the late twentieth century, despite evangelicals' dire prediction that church attendance would inevitably decline, most Sabbath-keeping laws were overturned or disregarded. Protestants' fears were not unfounded; church attendance has declined between 1955–95.

Evelyn A. Kirkley

See also EVANGELICALS; EVANGELICAL THEOLOGY; FUNDAMENTALISM.

SABELLIANISM/SABELLIUS

Little is known of the Christian teacher Sabellius, apart from his condemnation by Callistus, the Bishop of Rome, around 220. Sabellius and his followers taught a form of Monarchianism, that is, they argued that God was a single entity or Person, manifested in the Old Testament as the Father, in the incarnation as the Christ, and at Pentecost as the Holy Spirit. Sabellius's theology was opposed by Hippolytus of Rome, who taught that the Father, the Son, and the Spirit must be separate Persons, or else one is forced to say that it was the eternal Father who suffered on the cross. Sabellianism is, then, the heresy that teaches that there is only one Person or entity in God, making no real distinction between the Father, the Son, and the Spirit. Since the term was applied liberally and often inappropriately as an accusation against the supporters of Nicaea during the Arian controversy, it is difficult to ascertain how

widespread this understanding was during early centuries of Christianity.

Gary Macy

See also ARIANISM; HIPPOLYTUS OF ROME; MODALISM; MONARCHIANISM; PATRIPASSIANISM.

SACCIDANANDA
See SAT-CHIT-ANANDA.

SACRAMENT

Historically, the word *sacrament* comes from a Latin word (*sacramentum*) that originally referred to an "oath" or "pledge" (or even a deposit of money) that, in ancient Roman practice, one might make in a temple. The word was used to translate a Greek word (*mysterion*, something "hidden, concealed, or secret"), used in the New Testament (originally written in Greek) to refer to a number of complex theological issues, such as marriage. Early Christian theologians used the word not only to refer to liturgical celebrations, but also of theological issues or ideas that were ultimately beyond human comprehension, for example, the Trinity.

In the medieval period, the Christian theologians in the West attempted to number and list the chief liturgical rituals of the church. The theologian Peter Lombard (about 1180) compiled a list of seven: baptism, confirmation, Eucharist, penance, marriage, orders (ordination), and anointing of the sick (or extreme unction). These seven rites became known in the Western Catholic Church as the seven sacraments. Another concern for medieval theologians was when and how these sacraments could be said to be valid (that is, to be real and effectual, to "count"). The liturgical structures and texts of the sacraments were analyzed to find the key, or core, elements: the matter (the actual physical sign) and the form (the words that "made" the sacrament). For example, the matter of baptism was held to be water (and no other fluid or substance), and the form the trinitarian formula "I baptize you in the name of the Father, Son, and Holy Spirit." Intention was also a key element in determining validity: the person "performing" the sacrament had to do so with the correct intention, in agreement with the intention of the church. For example, a three-year-old child who sprinkled his baby sister's head with water and blurted out the words of baptism could not be said to have performed a baptism, because he would be incapable of intending to do what the church intends in baptism. Sacraments could not, therefore, be performed "by accident," or for heretical reasons.

During the time of the Reformation, one of the issues on which the Protestants challenged the Roman church was the nature and number of the sacraments. In light of the Reformation emphasis on the sovereignty of God and the primary importance of the Scriptures, they insisted that only those sacraments that could be explicitly found in the New Testament were truly of divine, not human, invention, and were real sacraments. Most found only two: baptism and Eucharist. Others of the seven were either dropped completely (for example, anointing of the sick), or celebrated for the sake of good order (for example, marriage or ordination). The Roman Catholic Church at the Council of Trent (1545–63) reaffirmed the traditional list of the seven sacraments, and declared many of the Protestant theological ideas about the sacraments to be *anathema*, or heretical.

Theologically, the concepts of sacrament and sacramentality refer to the relationship between the divine (or the transcendent) and the human (or the material). A sacrament communicates and makes real, in an "incomplete" way, the presence of God in Christ through the church. Important ideas in understanding sacramental reality are those of sign and symbol. A sign is a physical or tangible element that "stands for" something else. It can do so in a simple way, like a price tag or a stop sign, communicating only one specific and arbitrary (static) meaning or message, or it can do so in a more complex way, as a symbol. A symbol (from the Greek word *symbolon*, "that which is thrown or placed together") communicates a deeper meaning or reality in a way that is dynamic (symbols can change meanings, like the swastika), polyvalent (or has multiple layers of meaning, like the American flag), and intrinsic (a symbol participates in some way in the reality that it signifies). Symbols can function not just as isolated words, objects, or gestures, but as more organized systems of communicating meaning, such as *myth* and *ritual*. Certain Christian rituals are said to be sacraments (as discussed above). Therefore, Christian sacraments function as real symbolic activity, that is, they actually participate in a dynamic, polyvalent way in the reality that they signify.

In Christian theology, the holy is understood to be *mediated* by the material world, or creation, but only partially. God reveals Self in creation, since God is the source and author of creation; creation is, in a way, God's Self-expression, in the same way that an artist might reveal himself or herself in a painting or sculpture. But for Christians, God's revelation of Self can be experienced even more deeply in the Incarnation, since Christians believe that Jesus Christ was both divine and human. Divinity and creation are joined together uniquely in Christ; therefore, as some have suggested, Jesus Christ in his humanity can be understood to be the "primordial" sacrament of God in the world. But Christian faith also holds that Christ no longer walks in the world in the same way he did before his death and resurrection, but is now "at the right hand of the Father." Christ is present today in the world through his church, the Body of Christ; therefore, some theologians note that the church can be understood to be the "basic" sacrament of Christ in the world. Thus, all actions of the church that are in keeping with the Gospel can be said to be "sacramental." Some of these actions, the public, corporate worship of God in the church's liturgy, make real the presence of Christ in the world more intensively. Some of these ritual actions historically have been given special priority in some Christian traditions (see above), and are themselves called sacraments.

Joanne M. Pierce

See also ANOINTING OF THE SICK (SACRAMENT OF); BAPTISM / CONFIRMATION; EUCHARIST; LITURGY (IN CHRISTIANITY); MARRIAGE IN CATHOLIC PERSPECTIVE; MASS; ORDAINED MINISTRIES, SACRAMENT OF; RECONCILIATION, SACRAMENT OF; SACRAMENTAL THEOLOGY.

SACRAMENTALS

Certain acts of religious devotion or piety, common in Catholic Church history. The sacramentals are not sacraments, and do not have the same importance or effect. However, sacramentals were once popularly thought to be close to the sacraments (hence the name), and during part of the Middle Ages some sacramentals were even listed as real sacraments. After the council of Trent (1545–63) there is no doctrinal confusion possible between the two, but cultural issues still raise ques-

tions as to the real-life distinction (and possibility thereof) between sacramentals and sacraments in popular Catholicism. Among the more frequent sacramentals are the praying of the rosary, blessings, novenas, prayerful lighting of candles, and so on. There is no set number of sacramentals.

Orlando Espín

See also BLESSING (CHRISTIAN); CANDLES, LIGHTING OF; CATECHESIS / CATECHETICAL; CULTURE; DEVOTIONS; EVANGELIZATION; GRACE; HOLY WATER; INCULTURATION; LATIN AMERICAN CATHOLICISM; LATINO CATHOLICISM; LITURGY (IN CHRISTIANITY); MARIAN DEVOTIONS; MEDIEVAL CHRISTIANITY (IN THE WEST); MEDIEVAL CHURCH; NOVENA; POPULAR CATHOLICISM; PRAYER; PRIVATIZATION OF RELIGION; ROSARY; SACRAMENT; SAINTS (CHRISTIAN), DEVOTION TO; SCAPULAR; SYMBOL; TRENT, COUNCIL OF.

SACRAMENTAL THEOLOGY

Sacramental theology is the branch of Christian theological thought dealing with the sacraments, and more broadly, the sacramentality of the church. Sacramental theology is rooted in the fundamentals of Christianity: Creation, Incarnation, the triune nature of the one God, the nature of the church itself. God Self-reveals through created reality; the Father is revealed most fully in the world through the incarnation of the Son in Jesus Christ (so Jesus Christ is "sacrament" of the Father); the church is now the Body of Christ that reveals Christ and is the presence of Christ in the world (so the church is "sacrament" of Christ). All those acts of the church in which Christ is revealed can be said to be "sacramental"; and the church realizes itself most fully as the Body of Christ in the celebration of the liturgy. Christian tradition singles out some of the church's primary liturgical rites to be called sacraments (the Roman Catholic Church, for example, holds that there are seven sacraments).

Sacramental theology can be studied in a number of different ways. One can focus on the systematic thought of a particular theologian, and the understanding of sacrament (and the sacraments) that is part of that system; one can also broaden that approach, and study the theological view of a specific Christian church or denomination. A comparative approach is also possible, by which the similarities and differences among individual theologians or various Christian traditions are highlighted and/or other disciplines are used, for example, anthropology, sociology, or philosophy. A historical approach allows one to examine the cultures and thought of a particular century or other time period, and compare one period with another. Finally, one can also take a textual approach, and examine specific prayer texts and ritual structures in order to determine the underlying theological themes.

Joanne M. Pierce

See also DOXOLOGY; LITURGY (IN CHRISTIANITY); SACRAMENT; WORSHIP.

SACRAMENTARY

The Sacramentary is the Western Christian liturgical book used by the presider (either a priest or a bishop) for the celebration of the Eucharist (or Mass). The Sacramentary evolved in the early medieval period from the practice of composing and collecting small written booklets (called *libelli*) that contained the prayer texts to be used for the celebration of Mass on various days (called *Mass formularies*). As these booklets were collected, they were arranged in chronological order according to the liturgical year and sanctoral cycle. Early sacramentaries also contained the presider's prayer texts for other liturgical services. Later in the medieval period, the Sacramentary was combined with other liturgical books that had earlier contained texts for the use of other ministers at the Mass, for example, the *Lectionary*, which contained the series of Scripture readings to be used at Mass during the year, to be read by the *lector*, or reader. This larger volume was called the full Missal (*missale plenum*); its use spread as the presider (either a priest or a bishop) eventually became the one person responsible for reciting all the texts and chants during the Mass. Thus, a priest could be said to "say Mass," "read Mass," or "sing Mass," and could do so with minimal assistance and no congregation present. The Missal continued in use into the twentieth century by the Roman Catholic Church, until the liturgical reforms of Vatican II in the mid-twentieth century. The liturgical books were then revised (the first appeared in 1970), and the earlier medieval practice of dividing the texts, readings, and music for the celebration of the Eucharist into individual volumes for the use of several liturgical ministers was revived.

Joanne M. Pierce

See also EUCHARIST; LECTIONARY; MASS; MISSAL; PRIESTHOOD.

SACRED HEART OF JESUS

A popular Roman Catholic devotion to the heart of Jesus as symbol and center of his life and compassion. With roots in medieval mysticism (for example, Julian of Norwich, Bonaventure, and the Carthusians) and in the medieval popular devotion to the wounds of the crucified

Jesus, it is only in the sixteenth and seventeenth centuries that the modern devotion to the Sacred Heart took its current shape. The Jesuits (for example, Claude de la Colombiere), and the nuns of the order of the Visitation (for example, Margaret Mary de Alacoque), were mainly responsible for the devotion's spread and acceptance throughout the Catholic world.

Orlando Espín

See also BONAVENTURE; CHRISTOLOGY; DEVOTIONS; JESUS OF HISTORY; JULIAN OF NORWICH; LITURGY (IN CHRISTIANITY); MEDIEVAL CHRISTIANITY (IN THE WEST); MEDIEVAL CHURCH; MYSTICISM/MYSTICS (IN CHRISTIANITY); POPULAR CATHOLICISM; PRAYER; ROMAN CATHOLIC CHURCH; SOCIETY OF JESUS.

SACRED/SACRAL/SACRALIZED

Common categories in the analysis of religious traditions. To say that a phenomenon is "sacred" is to separate certain geographic places, architectural spaces, or intervals of time aside from the routine, everyday, or "profane." The realm of the sacred that intrinsically conveys a "wholly other" status to objects, experiences, and individuals associated with it, supplies distinctive regard for them. The related terms sacral or sacralize imply an integral process.

The roles religious traditions play in shaping human life are manifested clearly in the recurring movement between these dual poles of distinct experience; through this oscillation, the sacred comes to define the relative reality and parameters of the profane realm. This analysis applies on the macro level of societies and on the micro level of individuals. It is ritual that regularly separates these two realms.

Todd T. Lewis

See also COMPARATIVE RELIGION; ELIADE, MIRCEA; HISTORY OF RELIGIONS; RELIGION, THEORIES OF.

SACRIFICE

A common motif in religious rituals expressing the core idea that an individual or community must offer up something to a deity, many gods, or spirits in order to win their blessings. The core notion builds upon the universal idea that human presence on the earth and actions necessary for survival depend upon the divine; this dependence has evolved in religious traditions through ritual exchanges from humanity to the supernatural realm. Sacrifice is the human response and it seeks to maintain cosmic order.

In some cases specific offerings are intermittently or lovingly made; in others, they must be made coercively to ward off dire punishments. Items for sacrifice span all that is natural (food grains, living wild animals) and cultural (human-made items, distilled intoxicants, domesticated animals). The sacrifice may simply involve placing the item in a special place; in others, fire may be thought essential to convey the item to the gods via the upward-rising smoke. Often, the divinities are thought to consume the "essence" of the sacrifice, after which the community consumes the remainder.

In many tribal societies, when animals are killed in the hunt, a portion of the body—symbolic of the soul's return to the spirit realm for reembodiment—must be returned via ritual before the flesh is consumed. This act insures balance and fairness in the cosmos, as well as the future supply of the animals.

Todd T. Lewis

See also RELIGION, THEORIES OF; RITUAL.

SACRIFICE OF THE MASS

A sacrifice is fundamentally the offering to God of a gift, especially a gift of great value. The earliest Christians understood the death of Jesus of Nazareth to be a sacrifice of his own life to God, a sacrifice they eventually saw as replacing the sacrifices of the Jewish Temple. When Christians celebrated their ritual meal in memory of Jesus, they understood this meal to be a call to share in the sacrifice of Jesus by sacrificing their own lives either through persecution and martyrdom or through a life of faith and love. This understanding of the Eucharist, the Christian memorial meal, as a call to share in and imitate the sacrificial life of Jesus as the Christ stands at the heart of the notion of a "sacrifice of the Mass." Without ever losing sight of the personal commitment involved in participation in the liturgy of the meal, called "Mass" in the medieval West, the meal was also seen as a reenactment of the death and sacrifice of Jesus. By the late Middle Ages, the further practice developed of allowing the priest to determine for whom the merits of the sacrifice of the Mass should be designated. The practice of designating large numbers of Masses, particularly for those in purgatory, became an important part of late medieval devotion. The Reformers of the sixteenth century saw this practice as an abuse on the grounds that the sacrifice of Christ was a once-and-for-all event that could not be repeated in the Mass. They further objected to the practice of making a monetary offering for celebrating these Masses. The Roman Catholic and Protestant Churches disagreed on this issue, the Protestants rejecting the idea that there was "another" sacrifice of the Mass different from that of Christ. The Roman Catholics, on the other hand, followed the decree of the Council of Trent that taught that the Mass contained an unbloody sacrifice of Christ as opposed to the physical sacrifice of Christ at his death. In recent years, a recovery of the biblical notion of sacrifice as well as a renewed emphasis on the personal sacrifice to which each Christian pledges herself or himself has brought the different Christian groups closer in their understanding of the role played by sacrifice in the Christian ritual meal.

Gary Macy

See also CHRIST; CRUCIFIXION; EUCHARIST; HOST; JESUS OF HISTORY; LITURGY (IN CHRISTIANITY); MASS; PRIESTHOOD; REFORMATION; ROMAN CATHOLIC CHURCH; SACRIFICE; TRENT, COUNCIL OF.

SACRILEGE

An act violating the norms of appropriate ritual behavior in human relations with the sacred. This transgression can span the wide definitions of what constitutes the sacred and where it is located. Most religious traditions recognize times, places, persons, animals, and symbols that are directly connected with the sacred and typically require special, if not extraordinary, treatment by the human community. For orthodox high-caste Hindus, the cow symbolizes the pantheon, and so cows are not molested or eaten; for Jews and Muslims, pork is prohibited in their scripture and so must be avoided. Almost every culture has the notion of pollution and purity; typically, all "polluting" items must be kept apart from sacred spaces.

Many world religions also have strong linguistic norms about uttering the name(s) of the gods and specify behaviors (such as incest) that violate divine law. Since breaking the rules regarding the sacred may endanger the relationship between the community and the sacred, even—in extreme cases—threatening divine disaster and/or the fate of individuals (for example, with eternal damnation), sacrilege often invokes strong sanctions to those who commit the offense. Religious elites, whose authority can be threatened by sacrilege and whose livelihood may depend upon a society's strict maintenance of the sacred traditions, are often zealous guardians of orthodoxy.

Todd T. Lewis

See also COMPARATIVE RELIGION; RELIGION, THEORIES OF; SACRED/SACRAL/SACRALIZED.

SACROSANCTUM CONCILIUM

This Vatican II document, whose title is taken from its first words, "The sacred council," is also known as the Constitution on the Sacred Liturgy. It was promulgated on December 4, 1963, as the first decree of the Second Vatican Council. In the practical life of the church it is the most significant decree of the council in that it has touched the lives of the majority of Roman Catholics more directly and consistently than any other. This was achieved primarily through its permission for the use of vernacular languages in liturgical celebration (no. 35) and through its mandate for full, active, conscious participation of all the faithful in the liturgy (no. 36). The document itself consists of an introduction, seven chapters, and an appendix.

The introduction (no. 1) announces the underlying, fourfold purpose of the council: (1) to impart an increasing vigor to the Christian life of the faithful; (2) to adapt those institutions of the church capable of change more closely to the needs of the modern age; (3) to foster Christian unity; and (4) to strengthen whatever will help

to bring people into the fold of the church. To achieve these ends, the council sees especially cogent reasons for undertaking the reform and promotion of the liturgy. The second paragraph, in outlining these reasons, emphasizes the importance of the theological assertion that the liturgy is coextensive with the work of redemption, the mystery of Christ, and the mystery of the church. Thus, by tending to the liturgical life of the church, these mysteries of faith are made real and effective in the lives of Christians, empower them to preach Christ to all, and provide for the church to be a sign and a means of unity for all of God's children. In its two concluding paragraphs, the introduction states that while the practical norms of the document apply only to the Roman Rite, its basic principles apply to all rites (ritual families) of the church that are recognized as equal in right and dignity, but where necessary should also be revised to meet modern circumstances and needs.

Chapter one deals with the general principles for the restoration and promotion of the liturgy. It lays the foundation for the liturgical renewal and therefore is the most important section of the document. It briefly outlines salvation history and then shows how the work of salvation, present in Christ, is made available to the church through the liturgy, especially in the celebration of the sacraments, particularly the Eucharist (nos. 5, 6). The document insists on a much broader sense of the ecclesial and sacramental sense of the presence of Christ (no. 7), describes the liturgy as a many-faceted experience that goes beyond the narrower juridical definition of officially approved rites contained in the approved liturgical books that prevailed earlier (nos. 8, 9). It claims the liturgy as the "source" and "summit" of the entire life of the church (no. 10), requiring more than valid and lawful celebration on the part of pastors (no. 11); rather, insisting on the interiority necessary for "full, active, conscious participation" that is the right and duty of every Christian by reason of baptism and the "primary and indispensable source of the true Christian spirit" (no. 14). Private prayer and popular devotions are important but must be imbued with the spirit of the liturgy (nos. 12, 13). The document calls for effective liturgical training of the clergy so that all may understand and fruitfully celebrate the liturgy (nos. 15–20). The remainder of the chapter deals with specific principles for the restoration of the liturgy to remove intrusive or less suitable elements that were added due to various historical circumstances, and then to adapt the liturgy for the needs of the modern world. It gives special emphasis to the role of Scripture (no. 24), the public nature of celebration (nos. 26, 27), the need for a full complement of properly trained liturgical ministers (presiders, lectors, servers, musicians, and the like), each fulfilling one's appropriate ministry (as opposed to earlier practice that focused on the function of the priest who had taken over most other liturgical ministries), and the special role of the community's participation through song, responses, gesture, actions, bodily attitudes, and reflective silence (nos. 28–32). While the liturgical act is essentially the worship of God, it necessitates effective communication; numbers 33–35, deal with the instructional, dialogical nature of liturgy, use of vernacular, more abundant inclusion of Scripture, rites distinguished by "noble simplicity," short, clear, and within people's capacity for comprehension. The document calls for adaptation of the Roman Rite to various cultures and peoples (nos. 37–40), a process that only began to occur in the later revisions of liturgical texts. Numbers 42 and 43 discuss the roles of the bishop and clergy, the importance of the local parish, and above all the common celebration of the Sunday Mass. The chapter concludes with an emphasis on the need for continued promotion and restoration of pastoral liturgical activity, calling it a sign of the Holy Spirit and a distinguishing mark of the church. To this end, competent authorities are to establish liturgical commissions and institutes, and commissions of sacred art and music with properly trained personnel, including laity, to regulate the liturgical renewal, promote studies, and undertake necessary experimentation of new liturgical forms (nos. 43–46).

Subsequent chapters are relatively short and deal with specific rites to be renewed. Chapter two deals with the restoration of the eucharistic rite so that it will involve the community with full devotion and collaboration in its celebration, especially on Sunday and feasts. The Mass is to be simplified so that its various parts are clearer and more unified; the biblical readings are to be enriched; the homily is to be an intrinsic part of the celebration; the prayer of the faithful is to be restored; both vernacular and simple Latin parts are to be encouraged; frequent Communion is urged; Communion under the forms of both bread and wine and concelebration are restored.

Chapter three deals with other sacraments and the sacramentals of the church. The purpose of the sacraments is to sanctify, to build up the Body of Christ, and give worship to God; as signs, sacraments also instruct. In the past, sacraments had often been viewed as almost automatically giving grace, only presupposing the presence of an active faith life. Now, emphasis is given to sacraments as signs and expressions of faith, saying that they should be easily understood so that the faith they express is nourished (no. 59).

Sacramentals are holy signs resembling sacraments derived from church practice and assist in helping people celebrate the sacraments and sanctify various occasions in life (no. 60). They include blessings, consecration of virgins, religious profession, renewal of religious vows, and funeral rites, all of which are to be appropriately revised, with an emphasis on active participation and the needs of the modern world (nos. 79–82). The chapter calls for the revision of all the sacraments, leaving the details to the postconciliar commission. However, some important points are made (nos. 64–78). The catechumenate is to be restored as a period of spiritual preparation and instruction with distinct rites to mark advancement toward baptism and may include appropriate elements indigenous to various cultures; there are to be separate rites for baptism of adults and infants and a special rite for welcoming baptized converts. Confirmation is to be more closely connected to baptism and, when separate, may also be celebrated within Mass. Extreme unction is now to be known as anointing of the sick and is to be celebrated in any serious illness or in advanced age, not only in the proximate danger of death, as had been the custom. The marriage rite is to reflect the meaning and duties of spousal life and may be celebrated within Mass after the homily (instead of before the nuptial Mass, as was the custom); when celebrated outside Mass, a Liturgy of the Word is to be included; rites suited to specific cultures are encouraged.

Chapter four (nos. 83–100) deals with the Divine Office or Liturgy of the Hours, seeing it as the priestly work of Jesus Christ continued in the church through the praise of God and intercession for the salvation of the world. Although this section has been criticized as excessively clerical, it nevertheless restores daily prayer, especially Lauds (Morning Prayer) and Vespers (Evening Prayer) to the whole church. Of particular note is the encouragement of the use of the vernacular and the celebration of Sunday Vespers in parish churches.

Chapter five deals with the reform of the liturgical year, that is, the celebration of feasts and seasons and the keeping of fasts, so that it more clearly unfolds and emphasizes the whole mystery of Christ, especially its paschal nature, and the subordinate role of Mary, the martyrs, and saints in that mystery. It restores Sunday, the Lord's Day, as the original feast day, a day of joy and freedom from work in order to celebrate the paschal mystery, calling Christ's faithful to come together to listen to God's Word and to share in the Eucharist, (nos. 102, 106). Customs and practices of the various seasons are to be reformed appropriately and adapted to local and modern needs (nos. 107, 108). Lent is to reflect more clearly its baptismal character, that is, the renewal of preparation for Christian initiation; its penitential character and observance is not only to be internal and individual but also external and social (nos. 109, 110). Due to the excesses of the past that distorted the balance of the liturgical year, the sanctoral cycle is to be limited (no. 111).

Chapter six deals with liturgical music, its place in the life of the church, its preservation, and expansion. The document states that while Gregorian chant is specially suited to the Roman Rite, other forms of music are to be included so long as they accord with the spirit of the liturgical action (no. 116). Similarly, while the pipe organ has pride of place in the liturgical tradition of the Roman Rite, other suitable instruments can also be used (no. 120). Composers are encouraged to develop compositions for the active participation of the worshiping community (no. 121).

Chapter seven treats liturgical art and furnishings, emphasizing the role of the church as a patron of the fine arts. It points out that the church has not adopted any particular style of art, but has admitted all suitable styles from every period of history (nos. 122–123). Bishops are to consult experts when passing judgment on the artistic and liturgical suitability of church buildings, art forms, furnishings, and vestments (nos. 126–128).

An appendix of the constitution states that the council is open to establishing a fixed Sunday of the year for the date of Easter, provided churches separated from the Apostolic See give their assent. The appendix also declares no opposition to the establishment of a perpetual calendar in civil society, provided the seven-day week with Sunday is preserved.

Dennis W. Krouse

SADDUCEES

A leadership group in Palestinian Judaism during the late Hellenistic and early Roman periods; in Jerusalem they probably were part of the wealthy power elite and leaders there among the aristocratic levels of society. Their name may come from the Hebrew *tsaddîqîm*, "righteous ones," although it is more likely based on the name of the high priest, Zadok. References to Sadducees are found in Josephus, the New Testament, and the rabbinic corpus. Since there is conflicting data in these sources, and none of them is sympathetic to the Sadducees, clarity has not been achieved about their social status, beliefs, and practices, as well as regarding the extent to which they and the priesthood interpenetrated. On the whole, however, the sources reflect that while the Sadducees followed various of the Pharisaic legal rulings, on some issues the two groups came into conflict, especially concerning laws of purity. Thus the Sadducees are said to have rejected the Pharisees' oral law, that is, their interpretation of the Mosaic revelation. The New Testament places much emphasis on the Sadducees' rejection of the doctrine of the resurrection in contrast to a strong Pharisaic belief in it.

Sadducees seem to have dominated the Sanhedrin, and, as political leaders, many appear to have been Hellenized and cooperative to a great extent with Roman occupation. Prior to the Jewish War, they unsuccessfully attempted some mediation. It has often been held that the Sadducees disappeared with the destruction of the Second Temple in 70 C.E., but this was premised on the now-challenged assumption that they were heavily coextensive with the Temple priesthood. Their disappearance in history may have more to do with the Pharisaic/rabbinic ascendance after 70 C.E., leaving merely a minor role for the Sadducees in the documents surviving from that period.

F. M. Gillman

See also ESCHATOLOGY (IN JUDAISM); PHARISEES; SANHEDRIN.

SADHANA

In Indic religions, *sadhana* (Sanskrit, performance) can designate a particular spiritual practice, or spiritual practice in general. Any number of disciplines—ranging from meditation, through ritual activity or repetition of mantras, to ethical observance—may be referred to as sadhanas. Thus a Hindu might ask what sadhana one is doing, or whether one is doing any sadhana at all. Various sadhanas are connected with each of the four yogas in classical Hinduism, and also with various courses of discipline in Hindu and Buddhist Tantra. Their object is spiritual perfection, understood variously as, for example, *moksha* (liberation) in Hinduism or *sambodhi* (enlightenment) in Buddhism.

Lance E. Nelson

See also BODHI; HINDUISM; MOKSHA; TANTRA; TANTRIC BUDDHISM; TANTRIC HINDUISM; YOGA.

SADHU

In Indic religions, a *sadhu* (Sanskrit, "good," "righteous") is a holy man or an ascetic, typically itinerant. Devout laypeople have great respect for sadhus, toward whose support they are expected to contribute by the giving of alms, especially food. The great majority of such ascetics are male, but not all. The feminine form is *sadhvi*.

Lance E. Nelson

See also HINDUISM; JAINISM; SANNYASA.

SAGUNA/SAGUNA BRAHMAN

See NIRGUNA BRAHMAN.

SAINT

This term has three meanings in Christian history. (1) A baptized member of the Christian church (a use of the term that is clear in several New Testament writings). (2) An admirable Christian who has been canonized by the church. (3) Any Christian who is already enjoying eternal life with God. Other world religions (for example, Buddhism) have saints too, although evidently defined according to their own traditions.

Orlando Espín

See also ANGLICAN COMMUNION; BEATIFICATION; BUDDHISM; CANONIZATION; CATHOLIC TRADITION; DEVOTIONS; EASTERN CATHOLIC CHURCHES; ORTHODOX CHURCHES; POPULAR CATHOLICISM; ROMAN CATHOLIC CHURCH; SAINTS (CHRISTIAN), DEVOTION TO; WESTERN CATHOLIC CHURCHES.

SAINT-CYRAN, ABBOT OF

Fellow student and friend of Cornelius Jansen, Jean Duvergier de Hauranne (1581–1643) was named abbot of the abbey of Saint-Cyran in 1620. Known henceforth as Saint-Cyran, this French theologian was one of the founders of Jansenism. Associated with the Arnauld family from the 1620s, Saint-Cyran was, from 1633, spiritual director of the abbey of Port-Royal, the abbey reformed by Angélique Arnauld.

Saint-Cyran dared to oppose various policies of Cardinal Richelieu, the prime minister of France, from 1624 until his death in 1642. On orders of the cardinal, Saint-Cyran was imprisoned in 1638; he was not released until after Richelieu's death, and he himself died shortly thereafter. Later in the seventeenth century Saint-Cyran was seen as a martyr for the Jansenist movement.

Thomas Worcester, s.j.

See also ARNAULD, ANGÉLIQUE AND ANTOINE; AUGUSTINIANISM; JANSEN, CORNELIUS; JANSENISM.

SAINTS (CHRISTIAN), DEVOTION TO

A practice common in Catholic, Anglican, and Orthodox Churches. Veneration or devotion to "saints" is also known in other world religions (for example, Buddhism), but according to norms and customs deemed authentic in their own particular traditions.

Christian veneration of saints has roots in Jewish practices described in the books of the Maccabees. The apostle Paul's doctrine of the "Body of Christ" is the main (but not only) New Testament foundation for the Christian practice. The veneration of saints is seen as an authentic and obvious development of this teaching of Paul. In any case, as early as 150 C.E. (and probably before) there is unmistakable evidence of Christians' celebrating feast days of saints and of invoking their assistance.

The notion of "saint" implied in their veneration points to the belief that the saints are with God, enjoying eternal life. The saints have been blest (with eternal life) by God because on earth they led admirable, heroic, and holy lives as Christians. In other words, the saints are living, immortal proof that God keeps God's promises to the church. And since the saints are Christians now in glory, they are still members of the "Body of Christ" (that is, the church, or "communion of saints") and, consequently, may be asked by other Christians (members of the same "communion of saints" on earth) to pray for them and to seek God's help on behalf of those struggling in daily life. Because God has blessed them after death, and because of the admirable and holy lives they led, the saints are also seen as role models or examples for other Christians. The official doctrines of the Catholic, Anglican, and Orthodox Churches do not allow any deviation from the basic understanding of the veneration or devotion to saints.

Historically, the veneration of saints developed from the admiration of early Christians for their martyrs, and with the respect shown their bodily remains and personal belongings (what later came to be called "relics"). The early Christians believed that to die a martyr's death implied immediate entrance into heaven's glory. Soon, also those who had been tortured or suffered in other ways during the Roman persecutions, but had died from other causes, began to be honored as the martyrs were. It was only a matter of time before the honor was extended to other (dead) Christians who had lived exemplary and heroic lives. Origen (d. 254) seems to have been the first Christian author to theologically justify the veneration of the saints.

After the emperor Constantine the Great ended the Roman persecutions against Christianity (early fourth century), the practice of devotion to the saints became very widespread. There was occasional opposition, however, but the veneration of saints had become too popular to be stopped. Because of abuses, patristic theologians (fifth to seventh centuries) made a distinction between what they called *latria* (the worship due to God alone) and *dulia* (the admiration and honor shown to the saints). Saints, under no circumstance, could be venerated in a manner that indicated *latria*. This theological distinction is still found in contemporary Catholic, Anglican, and Orthodox theology. In the early fourth century (as indicated by Augustine of Hippo), names of saints were already included in the official liturgy of the church, and their feast days were observed liturgically. By the Middle Ages, the veneration of saints had reached such widespread popularity that church authorities and (more frequently) theologians and some medieval Reformers, had to offer correctives to excesses. Superstitious practices, stories, and explanations were not rare. The sixteenth-century Reformers varied in the intensity of their repudiation of the devotion to saints; in their view, there was no biblical foundation for this practice. The Catholic and Orthodox Churches, however, have never rejected it, although they have frequently insisted that their members be educated on the real meaning and purpose of the veneration of saints, on its relationship to the worship of God, and on the need to avoid abuses and exaggerations. After an initial period of repudiation and hesitation, the churches of the Anglican Communion have returned (especially after the Oxford Movement, and with studied moderation) to this ancient Christian practice.

Orlando Espín

See also BODY OF CHRIST (IN CHURCH USE); CATHOLIC TRADITION; COMMUNION OF SAINTS; DEVOTIONS; DULIA; EASTERN CATHOLIC CHURCHES; ECCLESIOLOGY; MARTYR/MARTYRDOM; MEDIEVAL CHRISTIANITY (IN THE WEST); MEDIEVAL CHURCH; ORTHODOX CHURCHES; POPULAR CATHOLICISM; RELIC (IN CHRISTIANITY); ROMAN CATHOLIC CHURCH; SAINT; WESTERN CATHOLIC CHURCHES.

SALAT

Sometimes written *salah*. In Islam, this is the required prayer believers offer five times each day. Prayer made at other times (*du'a*) is encouraged, but in order to satisfy the demands of *salat*, one must pray at the prescribed times in the prescribed way. In Islamic countries, prayer times are announced by a designated member of the community (*muezzin*) who calls people to prayer from the *minaret* of the local mosque (Islamic place of worship), but in the absence of this helpful reminder, Muslims can consult timetables

readily available to them. In general, the five salat times are: dawn, noon, late afternoon, sunset, and night. The prescribed way of prayer includes three elements. First, prayer must be offered facing the direction of Mecca (*kibla*). It is not necessary to go to a mosque, though Muslims try to attend the Friday noon prayer there. Second, worshipers must be clean (all mosques have fountains for this purpose), and they must offer their prayers in a clean place, usually on a mat or carpet. Since shoes are considered dirty, Muslims always pray in bare or stocking feet. Third, each time Muslims pray, they are required to complete the appropriate *rak'as*—"cycles" of prayer—that include words, gestures, postures, and the stipulation regarding whether the designated cycle is to be said aloud or silently. During salat, men are not supposed to be distracted by women. For this reason, mosques have special enclosed galleries for women, usually in the back of the structure or in a balcony.

Ronald A. Pachence

See also FIVE PILLARS (IN ISLAM); ISLAM; KIBLA; MOSQUE/MASJID; MUEZZIN/MU'ADHDIN.

SALESIANS

"Salesians" is the popular name for the order of priests properly known as the Society of St. Francis de Sales. The Society was founded in Turin by St. John Bosco in 1859 with the purpose of helping poor boys. A similar Society was established by St. Mary Mazzarello for the aid of young girls, and in 1872 they formally took the name Daughters of Our Lady Help of Christians. The two congregations are active worldwide.

Gary Macy

See also CONGREGATIONS (ORDERS).

SALVATION

A fundamental concept in Christian theology. This concept includes dimensions and issues (for example, redemption, sin, grace, immortality, and so on) also discussed by other theological disciplines.

Many Western philosophers and writers, even those who do not claim any religious connection or interest whatsoever, have tended to reflect on themes of interest to a Christian theology of salvation. Existentialists (for example, Marcel, Jaspers, Heidegger, Camus) and socialists (for example, Marx, Mariátegui, Gramsci, Luxemburg, Saint-Simon) are examples of modern philosophers who, in their own ways and using their particular terminologies and methods, have attempted to deal with some fundamental "salvation" issues. Vaclav Havel, Eduardo Galeano, Flannery O'Connor, and William Faulkner, among many others, are writers who have reflected on salvation through literary means.

The Christian idea of salvation is not necessarily paralleled in other religions. The notions of nirvana (Buddhism), moksha (Hinduism), and Dar al-Salam and "Day of Judgment" (in Islam), for example, are not equivalent or similar concepts, nor do they point to the same belief.

Theologically, for the concept of salvation to be possible, there needs to be a prior sense of or belief in some "original sin" or in a "sinful human nature." The very term "salvation," after all (derived from the Latin *salus*, "health"), implies "healing."

It seems clear that Jesus of Nazareth preached the imminent dawn of the reign of God. This reign was not to be just a spiritual or simply moral reality, but rather a radical transformation of all human reality according to the merciful will of God. The reign would, therefore, profoundly transform the structures of human society as well as the hearts of human individuals. Consequently, it may be said that the message of the reign is "salvific."

The reign of God started dawning with and through Jesus' own ministry (according to the Gospels' witness) but was far from being fully here—hence, the reign is both present and future. The God of the reign has particular predilection for sinners, outcasts, and the poor; therefore, the marginalized were the first to hear the "Good News." Jesus' faithfulness to his God and his mission, as well as his solidarity with the religious and social outcasts of his day, brought him to the cross. It is doubtful, historically, that Jesus of Nazareth ever understood his own death "salvifically," although later Christian generations (starting with the apostles' own generation) have unhesitatingly interpreted it that way. The Easter events (however scholars might explain the Resurrection) became the crucial confirmation, for Christians, that Jesus' teaching and life were indeed according to God's will. Hence, the Resurrection proved that Jesus had spoken the truth and, therefore, that the message of the dawning reign of God was also true.

The apostle Paul, a few years after Jesus, stands at the beginning of the long (and still not ended) process of Christian reflection on the meaning of Jesus' message, life, death, and resurrection for the entire world (and not just for members of the church). Indeed, the impact of Paul's reflection has been enormous on succeeding generations of Christians. Paul expressed his own thought on salvation in different ways. For example, he said that Jesus' death was "expiation" for human sins (that is, Jesus' death "takes away," or "washes away" human sin). Implied in this thought, of course, is the existence of prior human sinfulness that requires healing or salvation. According to Paul, human nature is enslaved to sin and its consequences, and there is nothing humans can do to free themselves from this condition without facing new and utter failure. God has accepted Jesus' death as *the* means and price for freeing humankind from slavery to sin. According to Paul, faith in Jesus will make it possible for humans to be finally free of enslavement to sin. It is interesting to note that only once (in the authentically Pauline letters) does Paul call Jesus by the title "savior" (Phil 3:20). Furthermore, it seems that in Paul's theology, salvation is fundamentally a future event. Probably because of his own belief in the imminent return of Christ in glory, Paul emphasizes the future dimension of salvation in most of his reflections on it. However, the "deutero-Pauline" and "Pastoral" Letters do speak of salvation as a present and even past event ("we have been saved"), and Jesus is more frequently called "savior" in these texts.

After the New Testament period, the history of the theology of salvation, as well as the history of the term itself, show that Christians have had little difficulty in creatively understanding, in the most diverse ways, their belief in Jesus as Savior of humankind and in the reality of God's offer of salvation through Jesus. It seems that one determining factor in the varied understanding of salvation has been what each generation (or group) of Christians has considered to be "sinful" and, consequently, in need of salvation. Evidently, if human experience (individually and socially) were just fine, there would be no need for a savior or for salvation. Consequently, there has been

some cultural and sociological "projection" of the contents and meaning of salvation throughout history; as well as frequent Christian efforts designed to make other humans (and other Christians) discover how terrible humankind's fundamental condition is. As far as Christians are concerned, they are speaking the truth to a world enslaved by social injustices and human sin.

Christians in the first five centuries of the church often thought of salvation as knowledge (truth) and light, brought to us by Christ, to free us from ignorance and darkness, leading us to recognize God's glory and mercy toward us (for example, *Letter of Barnabas*, Clement of Rome, *Didache*). Salvation is thus the new doctrine or "education" (*paideia*) that Christ offers us. Early Christian theologians also considered Christ as the *logos* (that is, the ultimate meaning) of the world, and, consequently, salvation involved human acceptance and understanding of this definitive *logos* sent by God (for example, Justin Martyr, Irenaeus of Lyons, Clement of Alexandria). Another concept frequently used to explain salvation, during the first few centuries, was immortality (for example, *Didache*, Hippolytus of Rome, Clement of Alexandria)—immortal life is the paramount gift brought by Jesus and the most fundamental consequence of faith in him. The idea of the divinization of humankind, as the primary purpose and content of God's offer of salvation, is also present in early Christian writers (Origen, Athanasius). Lastly, another explanation of salvation, that will become more important in later Western Christian history, is the notion that to be saved is to be freed from Satan's enslavement because Jesus' blood has paid the ransom price (Tertullian, Augustine of Hippo). Indeed, in Western theology there was, from Tertullian on, a certain tendency to understand salvation in almost juridical terms.

The doctrine of original sin, so typical of Western Christian theology, became a fundamental cornerstone in the theology of salvation. Based on this doctrine, and greatly influenced by the thought of Augustine of Hippo, a frequent Western explanation of salvation developed along the following lines. Since all humans are born sinners (because of original sin), and since their humanness (or "nature") has been profoundly wounded by this inherited sinful condition, there is nothing humans can do (except through God's grace) that would not further their reality as sinners and their eternal damnation. The only way humankind can find salvation from this self-perpetuating situation, somehow breaking free from this enslavement, is by God's extraordinary and free offer of salvation. This offer was made known to humans, definitively and for all ages, through Jesus the Christ. For humans to avail themselves of this merciful offer they must believe it has in fact been offered by God through Jesus, and behave (and believe) thereafter according to Jesus' teaching. The first necessary step is to seek baptism and incorporation into the Christian church. However, to reject Jesus and baptism is, consequently, to reject the only possible hope for salvation and to choose eternal condemnation.

Mainstream Christian reflection added to this overall explanation; still, during the first few centuries, to reject the church (as visible community) was also to reject salvation.

Medieval theology continued developing the various explanations of salvation of the earlier centuries. The Eastern churches, for example, emphasized the idea of divinization much more than the Western churches. In the West, the more frequent explanations were those influenced by Augustine's thought. Anselm of Canterbury (1033–1109), for example, became very important in establishing the terms and orientation of Western medieval reflection on salvation. Anselm took earlier Augustinian notions, added to the increased understanding of salvation in juridical terms, and from there developed a theology of salvation as satisfaction (that is, humans need to "pay" for their sins, "satisfy" or cancel the "debt" they contracted with God because of sin). According to Anselm, the only way humankind could "satisfy" God for sin is Jesus' self-sacrifice, because only Jesus is without sin. And because Jesus is also divine, his self-sacrifice on the cross has infinite value and therefore can pay the debt incurred by humankind (because Jesus is also human). Anselm's views, obviously, wholly depend on what is called "high christology," possible only to Christian theology after sophisticated philosophical (Aristotelian, Platonic) and doctrinal (Nicean, Chalcedonian) developments had been reached. Anselm of Canterbury's theories became so widely accepted that it may be argued that later inter-Christian disagreement on salvation was due partly to Anselm. His emphasis on juridical, legal categories (although popular in his day) seriously hindered a healthier development of the theology of salvation in the West.

There certainly were other medieval views on salvation that were not Anselm's. Abelard, for example, held that salvation was a consequence of the incarnate Christ's love and faithfulness. Because Christ's love is God's love, and because divine love has (in Christ's incarnation) assumed human nature, humankind is consequently offered salvation. Humans accept or reject the offer insofar as they accept or reject God's love in Christ. Although Abelard's views may seem attractive to us today, they were not so to his medieval contemporaries.

Thomas Aquinas, on the other hand, followed Anselm of Canterbury's thought on salvation while somewhat modifying and softening it. For example, Aquinas was less emphatic on the "exchange" (or "payment") element of Anselm's concept of satisfaction. While preserving the centrality of the notion of satisfaction in his theology of salvation, Aquinas expanded Anselm's ideas so as to make the "payment" be not of equal value as the offense, but of much greater worth—namely, Christ's own love that infinitely surpasses all human sin, no matter how immense the latter might be or have been. The human will and love of Christ were presented by Thomas as the instruments (or "sacraments," in today's language) of God's work of salvation on behalf of humankind. Aquinas's thought on salvation remained fundamentally Anselmian and, consequently, became very widespread within Catholicism after the Reformation.

It may yet be argued that Luther's and Calvin's views on salvation, so distinctly Augustinian, were further developments of Anselm of Canterbury's thought. The main emphasis of the Reformers' theologies of salvation seem to be the substitutional role of Christ in salvation—that is, Jesus was the sinless representative of sinful humankind, and substituted his own death and suffering for what we really deserved. By taking on himself what was human guilt and deserved punishment, Christ did a "happy exchange" (Luther): he bore our sin and we share in his merits and righteousness. Although humans could never really "satisfy" for

their sinfulness, Christ's Cross made it possible for God to show mercy as if they had. Calvin's views on salvation are the most rigorist interpretation possible within the Reformation's substitutional model. And yet, neither Calvin nor Luther avoid the juridical language Western European Christians had inherited from Anselm of Canterbury. On the contrary, some Reformers seem to have carried this sort of terminology to further extremes (for example, Calvin).

The theology of the council of Trent (1545–63), although still fundamentally Anselmian, apparently interpreted salvation through the eyes of Thomas Aquinas (as the latter was understood in the sixteenth century). Within Roman Catholicism, changes in the theology of salvation began to occur as a result of pastoral and missionary realities. The European discoveries and conquests of the sixteenth century (mostly by Catholic Spain and Portugal) forced onto Catholic theology a long series of questions to which medieval (or Tridentine, or Protestant) authors could not provide answers. Slowly, the debate on salvation within Catholicism (also on related issues, like the nature of humanness) resulted in the opening of the Catholic position on salvation beyond the Protestant–Catholic controversies. Doctrinal confrontations led to further clarification.

Questions arising from the teachings of Jansenism (sixteenth and seventeenth centuries) became one of the first moments, within Catholicism, for official decisions on the possibility of salvation outside the church. Even Popes Pius IX (nineteenth century) and Pius XII (in 1949) taught that salvation was possible to those outside Christianity under certain conditions. The Second Vatican Council, in 1964, in its constitution *Lumen*

Gentium (16), very clearly stated the church's contemporary view: all humans who follow their consciences and try to lead good lives, and who, through no fault of their own, have not heard the Gospel message, or have not come to believe in God, may still be saved by God's grace. Vatican II's teaching was based on a variety of theological developments of the last four centuries, among which Catholicism's own growing awareness of the magnitude and legitimacy of human diversity, as well as deeper understandings of God's universal mercy and of the church's role as "sacrament" of salvation. Catholic theologians after Vatican II (for example, Rahner, Metz, Segundo, L. Boff, Gelabert, and many others), have continued developing the reflection on salvation following a few basic notions: the being of God as mercy, the church as "sacrament," the presence and action of God's grace in non-Christian religions, the continued existence and revival of non-Christian religions (and the evident signs of holiness in them), and so on. Interreligious dialogue, as well as ecumenical conversations among Christians, plus more recent developments in historical and cultural studies, will only benefit overall reflection on salvation and its related issues.

One very important contemporary development in the theology of salvation has been the rediscovery of the essential political and social (hence public) consequences of Jesus' preaching on the reign of God. Liberation theologies, especially those from Latin America, have been very clear on the political, social dimensions of the central Christian message, and on the absolute necessity for Christianity to reexamine (and "re-form") itself in the light of Jesus' teaching on the reign and its public consequences. Salvation is not simply an individual's experience, but the ultimate hope and need of all humankind (and of humankind's societies, cultures, and institutions, and even of the entire cosmos). Salvation, therefore, is irrevocably involved with the promotion and future of justice and goodness in this world.

Orlando Espín

See also CALVINISM; CATHOLIC TRADITION; CULTURE; DAR AL-SALAM; DAY OF JUDGMENT (IN ISLAM); DEVELOPMENT OF DOGMA/OF DOCTRINE; ELECTION (DOCTRINE OF); EXISTENTIALISM; GARDEN OF EDEN; GRACE; IMMORTALITY; JANSENISM; JUSTIFICATION; LIBERATION THEOLOGIES; LUTHERANISM; MOKSHA; NIRVANA; ORIGINAL JUSTICE; PELAGIANISM; PREDESTINATION (IN CHRISTIANITY); PROVIDENCE; REDEMPTION, CHRISTIAN; REIGN OF GOD; SEMI-PELAGIANISM; SIN, ORIGINAL; SOCIALISM; SOTERIOLOGY; THEOLOGICAL ANTHROPOLOGY; TRENT, COUNCIL OF.

SAMADHI

A Sanskrit word meaning "collectedness" or "absorption," *samadhi* is used in Indic religions to designate states of complete meditative introversion. In Hindu yoga, samadhi is the highest stage of practice, following on *dhyana* (meditation), in which the mind is either totally identified with the object of meditation or has ceased activity altogether in a nondualistic realization of pure spirit (*purusha, atman*). In Buddhist meditative practice, samadhi is an intermediate stage in the meditative practice that gives one access to the higher states of absorption—termed, in Pali, the *jhanas* (Sanskrit, dhyana).

Lance E. Nelson

See also RAJA-YOGA; VIPASHYANA/VIPASSANA; YOGA.

SAMARITANS

Religious group claiming descent from the pre-Davidic northern Israelite tribes. Few scholars accept this, or the bitter critique of Samaritan origins found in Jewish sources. Assyria destroyed the region in 722 B.C.E. and brought in foreign settlers who intermarried with the survivors. About five hundred Samaritans now remain. Most live near Nablus, a city in central Israel close to their ancestral holy mountain, Mt. Gerizim. Samaritans today are best known for their annual traditional spring sacrifice of Passover lambs at Mt. Gerizim, and for their writings (including the Samaritan Pentateuch, biblical commentaries in Aramaic, liturgical, historical, and inspirational books) that offer ancient and intriguing contrasts to traditional Jewish biblical texts.

In the Old Testament, the Hebrew word *shomeronim* occurs only in 2 Kings 17, describing the foreign settlement of Samaria and fusion with native religious custom fostered by Assyrian policy. Judean Yahwist revivals under the Davidic kings Hezekiah (724–655 B.C.E.) and Josiah (642–609 B.C.E.) failed to heal their rift with the Samaritans. Rooted in northern Israel's secession from Judea in 922, this feud went on even after Babylon razed Jerusalem and deported its nobility in 586. When postexilic Judean reformers under Nehemiah and Ezra harshly rejected them, the Samaritans built their own temple at Mt. Gerizim. Samaria became a magnet for Judean dissidents, and a scornful term for renegade Jews (cf. John 8:48). Long after the Judean ruler John Hyrcanus destroyed their sanctuary in 128 B.C.E., Samaritans retaliated by secretly defiling the Jerusalem Temple at Passover. Deep bitterness, lasting well beyond Rome's destruction of the Jerusalem Temple in 70 C.E., has slowly yielded to limited reconciliation with modern rabbinic Judaism. Almost all the New Testament references to Samaritans occur in John's Gospel or Luke–Acts. These early Christian traditions view Samaritan belief as inferior to Judaism, but see Samaria as a suitable bridge for spreading the Gospel to the Gentile world.

Francis D. Connolly-Weinert

SAMA VEDA

See VEDAS.

SAMSARA

The Sanskrit term *samsara*, in accordance with its literal meaning, "flowing together," refers to the beginningless succession of births and rebirths through which, in the religions of India, the self is understood to go. It is thus frequently translated as "transmigratory existence," "the chain of rebirth," or even simply, if imprecisely, "reincarnation." By extension, samsara refers to the sphere in which one experiences this procession of lives. In this usage, it connotes the universe in its broadest sense, with its beginningless and endless cosmic cycles (*yugas, kalpas*), involving an infinite number of temporary dissolutions (*pralaya*) and re-manifestations (*srishti*). Thus samsara may often also be translated as "world," "the mundane universe," or even "worldly life." In Buddhism, samsara consists of the "six realms" in which it is possible to be reborn: the spheres of human beings, titans, gods, animals, hungry ghosts, and hell. In the vernacular languages of South India, samsara also means "family" or "family life." Almost always, the word carries a negative connotation, evoking a state of recurring bondage from which it is difficult to extricate oneself. Salvation in Hinduism, Buddhism, and the other Indic religions is typically understood as liberation from samsara.

Lance E. Nelson

See also BUDDHISM; HINDUISM; JAINISM; MOKSHA; REINCARNATION; SIKHISM.

SAMSKARA (DISPOSITIONS)

In the yogic psychology of Hinduism, a *samskara* is a mental trace or impression, laid down in the unconscious by previous experiences, that conditions our present state of mind, creating a predisposition to act in certain ways. One's samskaras working collectively form one's character. Yogic practice is thought to purify the mind by uprooting these dispositions, thus preparing the way for final liberation (*moksha*). In Buddhism, samskara—understood in roughly the same sense—is the second link in the chain of dependent origination (*pratityasamutpada*).

Lance E. Nelson

See also BUDDHISM; PRATIYASAMUTPADA; RAJA-YOGA; YOGA.

SAMSKARA (RITUALS)

The *samskaras* (Sanskrit, "making perfect, consecration") are the life-cycle rituals observed by traditional Hindu householders of the three higher caste categories (brahmins, *kshatriyas*, *vaishyas*). The samskaras, often described as Hindu sacraments, vary in number from twelve to forty or more, depending upon the authority consulted. They include such rites as the naming of a newborn child (*nama–karana*), a child's first feeding of solid food (*anna–prashana*), the investiture with the sacred thread and beginning of Vedic study (*upanayana*, for males only), the marriage ceremony (*vivaha*), and the funeral (*antyeshti*).

Lance E. Nelson

See also CASTE; HINDUISM; RITUAL; SACRAMENT.

SAMSON RAPHAEL HIRSCH

See ORTHODOX JUDAISM.

SAMURAI

See BUSHIDO.

SANCTIFICATION (IN CHRISTIANITY)

See GRACE.

SANCTIFICATION (IN JUDAISM)

See HOLINESS/SANCTITY (IN JUDAISM).

SANCTUARY (PLACE)

From the Latin, meaning "holy place." In Catholic church buildings, "sanctuary" refers to the area surrounding the altar, pulpit, and so forth. Often, this area is elevated, emphasizing the actions that take place there and allowing greater visibility. In some buildings, particularly modern constructions and renovations, the altar, pulpit, and so forth, are not all gathered in one place but are placed throughout the room. In such spaces, the word "sanctuary" cannot be easily applied. Likewise, as modern liturgical theology emphasizes that the liturgy is an action of all those who gather, it seems inaccurate to refer to only one part of the room as "the holy place." Many modern floor plans, therefore, speak of the "altar platform" rather than the "sanctuary." Protestants generally use the word "sanctuary" to refer to the entire worship space, and the word "church" to mean the larger complex (including offices, classrooms, and so on).

Patrick L. Malloy

See also PROTESTANTISM/PROTESTANT; PULPIT.

SANCTUARY MOVEMENT

In Roman and English law, sanctuary was a place of refuge in churches or other sacred places where fugitives from the law were immune from arrest. The Sanctuary Movement of the 1980s built on this ancient tradition, as well as the Underground Railroad for the escape of slaves in the nineteenth century.

The Sanctuary Movement was a network of over four hundred Christian and Jewish congregations, as well as many cities, that extended from the Mexican border to the northwest, Midwest, and northeast U.S. and Canada. The Sanctuary Movement involved at least fifty thousand Americans who risked jail sentences in order to give refuge to thousands of Central Americans. These refugees were fleeing government sponsored terror and were threatened with expulsion under U.S. immigration law. Quaker Jim Corbett said of the movement: "Only in community can we do justice."

Mary E. Hobgood

See also DIGNITY; JUSTICE; POLITICS; SOLIDARITY.

SANDOVAL, ALONSO DE (?–1652)

Spanish-born Jesuit missionary, raised in Peru and Chile. He was pastorally active especially in the area of Cartagena, Colombia. He dedicated himself to the care and defense of the African slaves, writing on their behalf (in 1627) one of the most important works on African slavery in the Americas, the De instauranda aethiopum salute. This historical and ethnographic study includes a theological treatment of slavery in the Americas. Sandoval influenced many young Jesuits in Cartagena, especially Pedro Claver.

Orlando Espín

See also AFRICAN TRADITIONAL RELIGIONS; AFRO-LATIN RELIGIONS; ETHICS, SOCIAL; FREEDOM; JACA, FRANCISCO JOSÉ DE; JUSTICE; MISSIONS; MOIRANS, EPIFANIO DE; SLAVERY; SOCIETY OF JESUS.

SANGHA

The community especially dedicated to Buddhist practice; one of the three refuges for Buddhists. The most common of sangha's several meanings designates the monks (bhikshus) and nuns (bhikshunis) who take vows to follow the Vinaya rule book and its over two hundred rules governing celibacy, possessions, food consumption, and communal living. A broader definition extends to include devout laymen (upasakas) and laywomen (upasikas) who take the threefold refuge and vows to observe moral precepts. (The norms for the latter vary regionally.)

The sangha does not act primarily in a "priestly" role for the wider community, but it does remain involved with it through doctrinal instruction and receiving alms. The sangha ideal is to be a refuge for those individuals wishing to renounce the householder life and seek nirvana by asceticism and meditation. But one of the sangha's primary roles in Buddhist history was also to serve as a "field of merit" for the householders, allowing the latter to improve their destiny in samsara by meritorious donations.

In Mahayana Buddhism, some members of the sangha developed more elaborate rituals to chant the texts, serve in monastery temples for celestial bodhisattvas, and to seek the best possible destiny for the dying and dead.

Todd T. Lewis

See also BHIKSHU/BHIKSHUNI; PRECEPTS (BUDDHIST); REFUGE, THREEFOLD; VINAYA.

SANHEDRIN

A term coming from the Greek *synedrion* meaning "a council of leaders." The New Testament, Josephus, and rabbinic literature mention various Jewish bodies identified as sanhedrins from the second century B.C.E. through the second century C.E.

With respect to the Sanhedrin in Jerusalem, due to the diverse data the above sources offer, it is difficult to harmonize the information into one clear-cut description covering its membership and functions throughout that whole period. What is obvious is that there were a series of councils spread over the centuries, with a membership made up of the powerful and influential of the time who exercised various powers at different times. Suggestions that there were concurrent Jerusalem Sanhedrins, for example, one political and one religious as some propose for the time of Jesus, seem unacceptable due to the interpenetration of religion and politics in Jewish society.

In the New Testament literature the Jerusalem Sanhedrin is mentioned but without giving its specific composition and powers. Among those clearly associated with it are the high priest, the chief priests, elders, and scribes (Mark 14:54-55; 15:1), the chief priests and Pharisees (John 11:47), the high priest, the high priestly class, leaders, elders, scribes, Pharisees, and Sadducees (Acts 4:5-6; 5:34; 23:6). As reflected in the interplay in those texts between the Sanhedrin and Jesus, Peter, John, and Paul, it functioned essentially as a senate and high court.

F. M. Gillman

See also PHARISEES; SADDUCEES.

SANKHYA

Allied with Patanjali's Yoga system, Sankhya (or Samkhya) is recognized as one of the six orthodox schools (*darshanas*) of Hindu thought. Its classical formulation is in a text known as the *Sankhyakarika* (around 300–400 C.E.), attributed to Ishvarakrishna, but its origins are said to go back into mythic antiquity to the sage Kapila. Sankhya envisions a dualism of spirit and matter, postulating a multiplicity of spiritual selves known as *purushas*, whose nature is pure, inactive witness consciousness. The purusha has become entangled with *prakriti* (matter, nature) because of an epistemological error understood as a kind of primordial ignorance or unawareness (*avidya*). This error or confusion causes purusha to be identified with prakriti and its evolutes. The evolutes of prakriti include twenty-five material principles, ranging from intellect (*buddhi*), ego (*ahamkara*), and mind (*manas*) through the senses to the gross material elements. As long as it remains identified with the body-mind complex produced by prakriti, the purusha remains in bondage. By attaining discriminative wisdom (*viveka*), it gains liberation. Although most other forms of Hindu theology strove to avoid or overcome this system's dualism, almost all have borrowed, with certain modification, Sankhya's list (or "enumeration," the literal meaning of *sankhya* in Sanskrit) of the material elements. Its doctrine of prakriti and prakriti's constituent elements, the three *gunas*, became almost universally accepted. Despite, or perhaps because of, its wide-ranging influence, Sankhya has now largely ceased to exist in India as an independent school of thought.

Lance E. Nelson

See also DARSHANA (PHILOSOPHY); DUALISM/DUALISTIC; GUNA; HINDUISM; YOGA; YOGA SUTRAS.

SAN MIGUEL DE GUADALUPE

Name of the first proven European settlement and Catholic mission in what is now the United States (in the present-day state of Virginia). Established in 1526 by Spaniards, it was later abandoned. There are indications that this was also the site (in 1570?) of another Spanish mission, established by the Jesuits. However, the Roman Catholic parish community at St. Augustine, in Florida, remains the oldest uninterrupted (since 1565) Christian presence in the United States.

Orlando Espín

See also LATINO CATHOLICISM; MISSIONS; NOMBRE DE DIOS MISSION.

SANNYASA

Sannyasa (Sanskrit, renunciation) is the state of complete abandonment of worldly involvement for the sake of dedication to the quest for liberation (*moksha*). A person undertakes sannyasa through a solemn ritual involving unbreakable vows. One who has done so is referred to as a *sannyasi* or *sannyasin* (renouncer) and is typically addressed by the title *svami* (English, Swami), meaning "master." Some orthodox authorities (particularly those of the Advaita Vedanta tradition) held that only male brahmins were eligible for sannyasa; others allowed male *kshatriyas* and *vaishyas* to take the vows. A few even allowed women, under exceptional circumstances. Although sannyasa is counted as the fourth of the four Hindu stages of life (*ashramas*), to be entered only after one's children had grown and one had retired from active life, young men who were strongly motivated have long been allowed to enter directly from the first ashrama, that of student life (*brahmacarya*), thus bypassing marriage and family responsibilities. It has also been possible for relatively young men to abandon their wives and families for sannyasa, though Hindu religious leaders have generally discouraged this option. Traditionally, sannyasins were required to live an itinerant lifestyle, begging for their food. Some still do so today, at least periodically, but many live relatively settled lives in monasteries (*mathas*) or religious communities (*ashrams*). Sannyasins have generally belonged to organized monastic orders, associated with particular theological outlooks. Nowadays, a number of Hindu reform movements have established orders for women who wish to take vows of sannyasa.

Lance E. Nelson

See also ADVAITA VEDANTA; ASHRAMA (LIFE STAGES); ASHRAMA/ASHRAM; HINDUISM.

SANNYASI

See SANNYASA.

SANNYASIN

See SANNYASA.

SANSKRIT

An Indo-European language, Sanskrit is the sacred, liturgical language of India. The Vedas, the most sacred of Hindu scriptures, were written in an archaic form of Sanskrit, usually referred to as Vedic, a language closely related to Avestan. Indeed, the vast majority of Hinduism's sacred texts were written in Sanskrit—including the Upanishads, the *Mahabharata* and *Ramayana*, the *Bhagavad Gita*, the Puranas, the Agamas, and the Tantras. Since Sanskrit served in India, like Latin in Europe, as the language of scholarship and scholarly communication, most of the numerous commentaries and other works of classical Hindu theology are also in Sanskrit. Again, most of the priestly worship in Hindu temples is conducted in Sanskrit, and devout Hindus, even if they have not studied the language, typically memorize a good number of Sanskrit sacred verses for use in their private devotions. Although the early canonical works of Buddhism were written in Pali, an Indic vernacular related to Sanskrit, most of the sacred texts and commentaries of Indian Mahayana Buddhism were eventually written in Sanskrit, though a good number are available now only in Tibetan or Chinese versions.

Orthodox Hindus regard Sanskrit as the "language of the gods" (*deva–bhasha*), holding that Sanskrit words have a perfect and intrinsic connection with the objects, actions, and relationships they denote. Many would assert that Sanskrit is the source of all other languages. The English word *Sanskrit* is an anglicization of *sanskrita*, which means "refined" or "purified."

Lance E. Nelson

See also AVESTA; HINDUISM; MAHAYANA BUDDHISM; MANTRA; VEDAS.

SANTERÍA

Also called Lukumí, this is a Cuban religion of African roots. It is a direct descendant of the Yoruba traditional religion of colonial Nigeria, but somewhat modified and simplified due to the experience and forced limitations of slavery. Santería has spread throughout most of the Spanish-speaking Caribbean, South and Central America, Mexico, and the United States. Brazilian Candomblé is its sister religion that has in turn spread throughout Brazil (especially the state of Bahia) and into other South American countries. The differences between Santería and Candomblé are minimal and quite superficial.

Although it is difficult to know with certainty, the religion (Santería/Candomblé) seems to have some twenty-five million followers in the Western Hemisphere. What is said below, therefore, is applicable to Candomblé too. These two religions are very different, however, from Umbanda and Vodoun.

Santería believes that there is only one God. This God has several names, each capable of describing a dimension of the Supreme Being, whom they believe to be beyond all understanding. The holy names of God are Olòdúmaré ("the one who has the future in his hands"), Olòrún ("the owner of the heavens") and Olòfín ("owner of the past," but it can also mean "mighty king"). These three divine names are composed of different (masculine) words in the Yoruba language (remaining sacred in Santería liturgy), and some variations might be obtained, depending on which are the original words that were combined to form the names.

The only God is so perfect and holy that he is far above normal human beings. God is never offered a sacrifice, because he doesn't need it. God is not usually part of the liturgy or of the divination rites. These are too imperfect for him to be involved with. More than a faraway *Deus otiosus*, as in some religions, in Santería, God is more a *Deus absconditus*. But be that as it may, God is the source of all that exists, the goal toward which all is progressing, and the final judge of all creatures.

God's very essence and life is *ashé*, a word that has no equivalent in any Western language. *Ashé* might be best "approximated" as Life—both physical and spiritual. It is also grace (in the theological sense), and strength, and virtue, and the principle of life, and the substance of all that lives, and what we all share with every living thing (human, divine, animal, vegetable, and so on). So, everything and everyone has *ashé*, lives by it and because of it, and needs it to survive. The whole of Santería is the quest for *ashé*: to receive it, to protect it, to live it and by it, to share it, to increase it, and so forth. This religion, in its most orthodox and solid communities, is a sacred way of being dedicated to Life, in all its forms. Santería can be understood as a never-ending and ritualized "quest for Life."

The essence of Santería, then, is the concern for *ashé*. This *ashé* is the essence and "substance" of God. It is what makes God be "divine." Only Olòdúmaré has this *ashé* in its perfection. Only God is this *ashé*, and thus, only God has a right to *ashé*. But, according to the myths, God gave out part of this infinite *ashé* and created Obatalá and Odudúwa, respectively the male and female creators. Especially Obatalá is remembered as creator of all that exists. Yet, though the myths speak of a male and a female "creator *orishá*," there is no mention ever of creation being the result of a sexual activity between the two. Rather, Obatalá made the forms of all that is created, including the human form, and presented these to Olòdúmaré who then gave each form part of his *ashé*, and thus they all came into existence. Till this day, that is how people and plants, animals and things come into being, according to Santería.

As the world was being created by the first *orishá* couple (although Odudúwa's role in creation is seldom mentioned anymore), God continued sharing his *ashé*, thereby bringing forth more *orishás* and placing them in charge of every imaginable dimension of human, animal, and material life. They, in turn, parceled creation among themselves even further. They came to live here on earth, as well as in *orún* ("heaven," where they all gather with God every so often). The daily affairs of people are solved, made troublesome, and so forth, by the *orishás*. God willed it this way. That is why they must be respected and venerated. They are, in fact, the center of Santería's prayer, worship, and mythology.

The *orishás* are not "gods"; Santería only recognizes Olòdúmaré as "God" in the strict sense. None of the *orishás* are "gods" because all have been created and owe their existence to the *ashé* of the one God. And just as they came into existence, they can disappear (though some "santeros" fear saying this out of respect for the *orishás*; but they all know of *orishás* that have been forgotten and that no longer exist in the religion). Sacrifices, offerings, and prayers keep the *orishás* alive, because they "eat" the *ashé* found in the sacrificed and/or offered things.

Historically, it seems that *orishás* originated in three ways. (1) There were some individuals in ancient Yoruba history who somehow became *orishás* through their "incarnating" attributes of God's *ashé* to a remarkable degree (for example, Shangó was actually a king of the important city of Oyó, and apparently his military accomplishments, as well as his procreation of numerous children, contributed to his being remembered long after his death, and he was eventually venerated as *orishá* of war and virility). (2) Some qualities of *ashé* (or, arguably, of Olòdúmaré) have been perceived or understood by traditional wisdom as being of crucial importance for human life and/or for understanding God. Hence, "beauty," "truth," and the like, become personified as *orishás* with "a name and a face" in mythology (for example, Ifá, Irokó, and so on). (3) There are also natural forces (for example, sea, rivers, sky) or natural events beyond human control (death, growth, illness) that communicate powers or mysteries associated with God, and are also personified as *orishás* because they too have much to do with human life (for example, Babalú-Ayé, Iyondó, Yemanyá, Oshún, Oyá). Fundamentally, then, *orishás* seem to be personifications of attributes of *ashé* that is in turn the very being of Olòdúmaré, the one God.

All *orishás* seem to display a very human type of behavior, both good and bad. They are very close to the believers, making their presence felt in many daily ways. Any self-respecting "santero" (an initiated member of the religion) will have the symbols of the *orishás* he or she venerates somewhere in a sacred space in his or her home. Not every "santero" venerates the same *orishás,* but rather must discover which *orishá* has chosen him or her as "son" or "daughter."

Santería believes we are all born with a certain life pattern spelled out for us by God. God also determines which *orishás* will be our main protectors. One can discover who these are by observation of the person's character and/or by divination ("throwing" the coconut, or the *dilogún*). We each have the obligation to find out, and then the further obligation to become initiated "children" of the appointed *orishás.* There are several ways of doing this, but they all involve some kind of ritual cycle. The first and most common one is the "washing of the head." The crown of a person's head is the most sacred part of the human body. There the soul sits, and through there one's *orishá* will enter the body. There are some ceremonies for the "washing" of the head in order to make it accessible to the holy beings.

The liturgy of "possession" is the advent and/or incarnation of the *orishás* in the bodies of the believers. Through the "prepared" crown of the head, the *orishás* enter the human bodies of the believers, always in a communal liturgical context under the supervision of priests, and dance with their people, talk with them, chastise them when they have been unfaithful, admonish, advise, make jokes, and in general just act very casually and normally in the midst of the believing community. The faithful act toward the possessed person and address him or her as if he or she were, in fact, the *orishá* he or she incarnated (because believers believe that it is literally so). Nothing "devilish" happens during a liturgy of possession, except that once in a while it might become a bit too gross for a Westerner's culturally determined taste (but our Western cultural biases are not universal standards).

The first thing that strikes the outsider is Santería's very elaborate liturgy, there being liturgical acts for almost every imaginable human situation. A few rituals have to do with animal sacrifice, but very often there are simply offerings of food and other objects. The most important liturgical functions, however, always include the sacrifice of animals. These are of several different species, depending on the type of ritual being performed and on the *orishá* that will receive it. The animals sacrificed are, as a norm, consumed by the faithful after the ritual is completed. However, some smaller animals (always birds or chickens) can be left in the open for the *orishás* to "nourish" themselves with it. Sacrifice, in Santería, is always an offering made so that the *orishás* may "nourish" themselves with the *ashé* ("Life") of that which is offered, and then in turn come to the assistance of the offerer. God never receives a sacrifice because God does not need to be "nourished" by *ashé*, since God is *ashé*. Sometimes, however, sacrifice is an act of thanksgiving for a favor received from an *orishá*.

Santería also has many prayers that accompany the ritual actions, explaining them, thereby making them "religious" and not "magical" acts. Believers are asked to have faith before engaging in liturgy, so that it might not be magic. All the day's activities start with the holiest of prayers (because it is the only prayer ever addressed to God): "Ashé Olòdúmaré!" ("Give me Life, you who have my future in your hand!").

Santería has a very long and beautiful collection of myths, used at different circumstances in the average believer's life. Some of these myths (collectively called *patakís* or *appatakís*) are used on an almost daily basis. These are like vignettes of popular wisdom, explaining daily episodes, questions, and so on, by appealing to sacred stories wherein the *orishás* encountered a similar situation, or taught someone about it. Some other myths are used as sources or tools for discernment of the divine will (when employed in one or another [or both] of the sacred methods allowed for the discovery of the divine will: the *dilogún* of Ifá, and the coconut).

The *dilogún* is a method whereby the specialized priest called *babalâwo* throws a number of shells and kola nuts and tiny bones (usually bound together in a chain called the *ékwéle*) onto a straw mat. The divine will is expressed by the way the shells, nuts, and bones have arranged themselves after falling. There are hundreds of possibilities, of course, and a good *babalâwo* will know myths for each of these possibilities. The training of these priests, who are at the top of the prestige ladder, is very long and intense. The *dilogún* is said to belong to Ifá, because Ifá (also called Orúnmila or Orúla) is the

orishá assigned the task of speaking about the future in God's name. The second method of divination is through the coconut (called *orí*). A normal coconut is cut into four equal pieces and thrown onto the floor or mat. There are sixteen possible combinations. Each possibility is called an *odú* or "letter of future," that, in turn, prescribes several myths that are then told in order to give the person the tools necessary to interpret the divine will. Any male or female priest (called *babalorishá* or "father of the orishá," or *iyalorishá* or "mother of the orishá") can preside at this simpler divination method; but only *babalâwos*, who are the priests of Ifá, may preside at the "throwing of the *dilogún*." Ritual offerings usually precede or follow either method of divination. The objects used for divination, in either method, have been previously consecrated.

Many Santería myths (*patakís*) are told to more deeply explain other theological questions: the origin of the world, the origin of evil, the meaning of life, and so on. These are the oldest, the most sacred, and the most beautiful of all the Santería myths. These fundamental myths are usually those directly inherited from the Yoruba ancestors. Oral tradition is of utmost importance in Santería. But, as generations pass, variations are creeping into some fundamental *patakís* (surprisingly few, however). A few new myths have been created in the Western Hemisphere, usually of the type that tries to understand slavery, injustices against the slaves and/or their descendants, prejudice against their religion, and so forth. All myths, regardless of place of origin, portray the *orishás* doing or saying something seen as paradigmatic for humans. The literary beauty and the wisdom of some of these myths are great.

Because of Spain's and the Catholic Church's prohibition of non-Christian religions during the colonial period in Cuba, and because of the racial and religious prejudices that endure till today, Santería has had to "cover up" its African reality. (Do remember that Cuba, the birthplace of Santería, was a colony of Spain until 1898, and then it was an American protectorate till 1902, when the island became independent. Slavery was legal until 1878.) The practitioners of Santería were forced to modify their inherited Yoruba religion by simplifying it. The slave system did not allow enough room for all that was possible in Africa, nor did it allow for the priesthood schools that existed there. So, priesthood was prepared for through an apprenticeship system. Many myths were combined and shortened (for quick memorization). The many dozens of *orishás* known in the Yoruba land of Nigeria were reduced to no more than twenty, some increasing and some decreasing in importance as this process went on. The prerogatives and the functions of different *orishás* were often combined with those of another. The end result is a religion that is undoubtedly African in its core, doctrine, liturgy, and the like, but no longer a replica of the Yoruba traditional religion. It is the same religion in many ways, but in some significant ways it is not. What came from Yoruba lands was transformed into Santería in Cuba, and in the past thirty or so years has been spreading rapidly across the Caribbean basin and into the U.S., growing well outside the confines of the Cuban communities.

The Yoruba were also brought to Brazil during exactly the same period (most of the nineteenth century), and there faced almost identical circumstances as other Yorubas faced in Cuba. The same ances-tral religion underwent very, very similar changes in Brazil, producing the religion called Candomblé (which is so close to Santería that all specialists and believers call it the same religion).

The persecutions of the Catholic Church, and the racism of society and church this century, made Santería "cover" itself up, for defensive purposes, with some of the symbols of the Catholic Church. It is an utter disregard for the truth to say that Santería is the "sum" of an African religion with Catholicism, just as it is equally false to say that it is the "result" of some kind of doctrinal or liturgical mixture of the two. There has been no mixture, at least not among legitimate communities of believers. Santería found itself, in nineteenth-century Cuba, to be surrounded by a Catholicism that: (1) emphasized the veneration of saints, (2) was very "visual/iconographic" in its expression, (3) was very much dependent on popular religiosity for its outreach to people, and (4) was incredibly lacking in its evangelization of the slaves (besides the very fact that it blessed and justified slavery in the name of the Christian God). As it happened, "santeros" realized that there were a number of similarities between some stories about Catholic saints and the *orishás*, and other similarities between symbols identified with saints and with *orishás*. They also soon discovered that to openly venerate their *orishás* was against the law and severely punished. And since they could not believe in a Catholicism that made them slaves and justified their slavery and subsequent racism in the name of God, they "covered" the *orishás* with images and symbols of the Catholic saints. Under the guise of venerating saints, they continued to venerate their own *orishás*. They knew, and still know, what they were doing, because the Catholic statues were emptied, and holes made in them, so as to keep inside them the sacred symbols of the *orishás* venerated under the "appearance" of the Catholic saints. The Spaniards were happy, because they thought they had finally converted the slaves, and so, left in peace, "Santería" (hence, the name) continued to grow and develop.

An example might help in understanding why they seem to venerate a Catholic saint while believing that it is not the saint but the *orishá* hidden by the Catholic image. Catholics believe in the "real presence" of Christ in the Eucharist. Now, for an unbeliever, what Catholics seem to be doing is worshiping a piece of bread. They must be, the non-Catholic could say, committing idolatry since they are worshiping a piece of bread. But for Catholics, there is no bread here. They are adoring God, not a thing, because the thing is merely an external form and not the "real presence" that only faith can see and understand. The same basic explanation can be applied to Santería's use of Catholic symbols and images. In other words, the contributions of Catholicism to Santería have been at the peripheral level where symbols might be shared externally, but not in their meanings—a few symbols at that, since we are not talking about massive borrowings.

There are some holy symbols of Santería in which the *orishás* reside and can be really found. There are different symbols for each *orishá*, but the most sacred of all is the "stone" (the *otán*). Each *orishá* has a stone, found somewhere by divine guidance, that has been properly consecrated and made to be the real presence of that particular *orishá*. These stones are much more sacred than the Catholic statues that might contain them. The stones were often placed, during the persecution periods, inside Catholic saints' statues (depending on which saint was related to which *orishá*). But after persecution ended, and certainly with more and more frequency today, the stones are placed in the same containers as they were both in Africa and in the earlier colonial period: in big, nice-looking soup tureens (called *soperas* in Spanish). The faithful, once they have been initiated into the religion (weeks are required for these ceremonies of initiation), bring the *soperas* home with them, where they are placed in a reserved area, and prayers and offerings are made there every day thereafter.

Other holy symbols include the necklaces the faithful wear as they are committed to the *orishás*. The necklaces are long, rosary-like, and varied in color and pattern according to the *orishá* they are meant to represent.

The Yoruba language (especially of the mid- and late-nineteenth century) is still regarded as the only legitimate liturgical language by the practitioners of Santería. A well-educated Santería priest or priestess will be fluent enough in Yoruba, or at least will know the meaning and words of all liturgical texts. Many loose phrases and words, still in nineteenth-century Yoruba, sprinkle the daily religious language of a believer.

Some *santeros* have used the Spanish word *santo* to improperly and inaccurately translate the word *orishá*. In Yoruba, the latter term literally means "the holy life (or "holy one") who rests on the head" (from *orí*, "head," and *ashé*, "life"). Santería has also been traditionally known as Regla de Osha (that is, *de orishá*), and as the Lukumí religion.

Orlando Espín

See also AFRICAN TRADITIONAL RELIGIONS; AFRO-LATIN RELIGIONS;

CANDOMBLÉ; COMPARATIVE RELIGIONS; CULTURE; DEUS ABSCONDITUS; DEUS OTIOSUS; GRACE; LATIN AMERICAN CATHOLICISM; MYTH; OLÓDÙMARÉ; ORTHOLALIA; PALO MAYOMBE; RELIGION; RITUAL; SAINTS (CHRISTIAN), DEVOTION TO; SALVATION; SYMBOL; SYNCRETISM; TRICKSTER; UMBANDA; VODOUN.

SANTIAGO DE COMPOSTELA

See COMPOSTELA.

SANTIDEVA/SHANTIDEVA
(685–763 C.E.)

One of the greatest scholars and exponents of Mahayana Buddhism in India. His collection, the *Shikshasamuccaya* ("Collection of Teachings"), records excerpts from over one hundred texts known in his era; his masterwork, the *Bodhicaryavatara* ("Introduction to the Conduct That Leads to Enlightenment") traces in very down-to-earth and emotional terms the career of the human seeking to be an enlightened bodhisattva, from acts of charity and moral practices to meditative practices and ultimate expressions of the highest truth.

Todd T. Lewis

See also BUDDHISM; MAHAYANA BUDDHISM.

SANTO DOMINGO DOCUMENT

Following groundbreaking meetings at Medellín, Colombia (1968), and Puebla, Mexico (1979), the Fourth General Conference of the Latin American Episcopate took place at Santo Domingo, Dominican Republic, between October 12 and 28, 1992. The conference date (the 500th anniversary of Columbus' voyage) and site (the first permanent European settlement in the Americas) pointed to a complicated historical fact: the Gospel of Jesus Christ arrived in the Western Hemisphere together with the imperialist ambitions of Spanish and Portuguese conquerors. Besides reiterating the church's option for the poor articulated at Puebla (nos. 178–81), the bishops joined Pope John Paul II in asking God's forgiveness for the abuse of Latin America's indigenous population by Catholic colonists and for their involvement in the African slave trade (no. 20). The bishops also paid special attention to the dignity and rights of women (nos. 104–10). Nevertheless, the final document produced at Santo Domingo, called "New Evangelization, Human Development, Christian Culture," does not display the theological or pastoral creativity found at Medellín and Puebla. This was mainly due to a methodological shift: instead of beginning with the actual reality of Latin America and then examining the church's doctrine and pastoral commitments in light of that reality (as they had done at the two previous conferences), at Santo Domingo the bishops began with dogma (in particular the church's teaching about Jesus Christ) and then attempted to apply that teaching to the three main tasks facing the church: the proclamation of the Gospel, the promotion of human development, and the creation of a Christian culture in Latin America.

James B. Nickoloff

See also LATIN AMERICAN THEOLOGIES; LIBERATION THEOLOGIES; MEDELLÍN DOCUMENTS; OPTION FOR THE POOR; PUEBLA DOCUMENT; SOCIAL JUSTICE.

SANZEN

(Japanese, *dokusan*, lit., sitting with a master). An important component of Zen practice, particularly in the Rinzai tradition, where a disciple will sit privately with his teacher to discuss what he has learned. Dokusan is a more specific type of *sanzen* in which the master provides guidance and eventually sanction to the student's understanding of a particular koan (riddle).

G. D. DeAngelis

See also KOAN; RINZAI; ROSHI; SATORI; SESSHIN; ZAZEN; ZEN.

SARAH

Israel's first matriarch and Abraham's "sister–wife." Sarah is the barren wife of Abraham who eventually becomes the mother of Isaac. Originally, her name is Sarai (Gen 11:29–17:4) until God, when speaking his promise to Abraham, tells him no longer to call her Sarai but Sarah. The *-ah* ending may indicate that she is one of the Lord's, that is, Ya*h*weh's, people.

God makes a promise to Abraham regarding Sarah as follows: "I will bless her and I will give you a son by her . . . your wife Sarah is to bear you a son, and you shall call him Isaac" (Gen 17:16-19). Much of chapter 18 relates the confirmation of this promise, while chapter 21 details its fulfillment. Sarah's barrenness and her age as obstacles to motherhood are overcome.

In the New Testament, God's freedom of choice is expressed in the promise that Sarah will have a son (Rom 9:9). In Romans 4:19 and Hebrews 11:11, Abraham's faith is championed; he believes God's promise that his aged wife Sarah will bear a son.

Alice L. Laffey

SARASVATI

The Hindu goddess of learning and art, Sarasvati is identified with Vak, the goddess of speech, and said to be the spouse of the god Brahma. She is connected with a river of the same name that is important in the Vedas and later Hindu myth and ritual, though its historical location is uncertain.

Lance E. Nelson

See also BRAHMA; HINDUISM; SHAKTA; SHAKTI.

SARTRE, JEAN PAUL (1905–80)

French existentialist philosopher. Educated in France and Germany, he participated in the French underground resistance against Nazi occupation during World War II. Influenced by Hegel, Heidegger, and Husserl, Sartre became an atheist and active promoter of radical politics. He wrote both novels and plays as well as strictly philosophical works. During the two and a half decades that followed the last World War, he was a very important thinker in Europe and North America. His thought on individual human freedom, on the apparent meaninglessness of existence, and on individual responsibility had a significant impact on both philosophy and theology. Among his major works are *Being and Nothingness* (1943), *Nausea* (1938), and *Critique de la raison dialectique* (1960).

Orlando Espín

See also AGNOSTICISM; ATHEISM; ETHICS, SOCIAL; EXISTENTIALISM; FREEDOM; HEGEL, G.W.F.; HEIDEGGER, MARTIN; JUSTICE; MARCEL, GABRIEL; THEOLOGICAL ANTHROPOLOGY.

SARVASTIVADIN SCHOOL

The most influential Hinayana school in ancient North India. The Sarvastivadin name can be translated as "Holders of the Doctrine that All Exists," since they maintained that experience can be analyzed into seventy-five discrete "dharmas" (here: "reality instants"), each with its own distinct "self-nature" (*svabhava*). These dharmas fell into regular patterns, despite their ever-changing manifestations, a continuity maintained through past, present, and future. This doctrine was promulgated to explain how deeds in the past, through the accumulation of karma, must be conveyed in the future in keeping with the doctrine of impermanence.

It was against this school's *Abhidharma* analyses and its Sanskrit commentaries, with their imputed rejection of the teaching of impermanence, that the early Mahayana scholastics fashioned their arguments. Despite this, Sarvastivadin *Vinayas* still became the guiding disciplinary texts for communities in predominantly Mahayana Tibet and East Asia.

Todd T. Lewis

See also ASANGA; HINAYANA; THERAVADA BUDDHISM; VASUBANDHU.

SATAN

A Hebrew noun that literally means "accuser" or "adversary." In Greek translation, "the devil."

In the Old Testament, the term is applied to (a) humans (1 Sam 29:4; 2 Sam 19:22; 1 Kgs 5:4; Ps 109:6); (b) an angel sent by God to oppose Balaam (Num 22:22, 32); (c) a member of the heavenly court who accuses human beings before God (Job 1–2; Zech 3:1-2); (d) what is said to have incited David to take a census (1 Chr 21:1).

In the postexilic period, Satan became the most popular name for a malevolent celestial figure who led an army of demons against God in a cosmic struggle that perverted the earth. The tradition appears to have developed from a coalescing of elements from Canaanite mythology, Zoroastrian cosmology, and Israelite traditions. Satan personified those polluting influences that inhibited Israel from realizing the cultic or national ideals envisioned as God's will. Intertestamental works provide various accounts of Satan's origins and identify Satan with "the serpent" in Genesis 3.

During the time of Jesus, belief in Satan and the demonic world was assumed as a convenient way to resolve human failure and fragility, including historical disappointments and disasters. The New Testament presumes that the opponents of Jesus and those of the early church were influenced by Satan, and insists that Christians are not immune to the designs of this temptor. However, both Jewish and Christian sources consistently recognize that God is more powerful and will ultimately vanquish Satan and will vindicate the faithful.

Traditionally, Christianity considered Satan a rebellious angel, who, after being cast out of heaven with a legion of followers, seduces human beings to oppose God. In the past, Christians identified the gods of others as demons in Satan's legion. The tendency to consider real or imagined opponents under the influence of Satan has marked much of Christian history. Today, some Christians question the reality of a being who embodies evil, but most continue to use the term as an image to acknowledge the reality of evil. Many Christians remain convinced of the reality of Satan and the demonic world.

Regina A. Boisclair

SAT-CHIT-ANANDA

A compound of three Sanskrit words, *sat-chit-ananda* is said in Hindu Vedanta to indicate the essential nature of Brahman, the Absolute. *Sat* is infinite being, *chit* is pure consciousness, and *ananda* is absolute bliss. The compound is also, and more correctly, transliterated as *saccidananda*.

Lance E. Nelson

See also BRAHMAN; HINDUISM; VEDANTA.

SATI

Sati (in English, suttee) was the practice, among some uppercaste Hindu groups in certain parts of India, of widows immolating themselves on their husbands' funeral pyres. In theory voluntary, but in actuality not always so, sati was considered the supreme act of wifely dedication to her husband. Because widows were not allowed to remarry, sati was an alternative to the severely restricted life of a traditional Hindu widow. Sati was outlawed in 1829 by the British, in part as a result of agitation against it by Hindu reformers. Since then, its practice has become rare, though from time to time incidences have been reported.

Lance E. Nelson

See also DAYANANDA, SWAMI; HINDUISM; ROY, RAM MOHAN.

SATISFACTION

See ATONEMENT, CHRISTIAN; SALVATION.

SATORI

(Japanese, *kensho*, insight, understanding). A term generally used for enlightenment in Zen practice. It is actually the moment of awakening, a flash of insight, a moment of radical realization, following upon Zen practice, where all things become clear. This realization is said to be the direct experience of the unitary quality of life and a sudden awakening to one's true nature, based on the belief that the ultimate truth of life cannot be grasped con-ceptually or intellectually but intuitively through direct experience. This "awakening" or "realization" generally follows years of rigorous meditative practice (zazen), and for some, koan practice, to overcome the limits of conceptual thought. It is said that without *satori* there is no Zen.

G. D. DeAngelis

See also BODHI; KOAN; MUSHIN; SHUNYATA/SUNYA/SHUNYA; ZEN.

SATURNALIA

An ancient Roman (and very popular) celebration in honor of the god Saturn. At the main temple of Saturn in the city of Rome, sacrifices were offered to the god, and the symbolic ropes that tied (the statue of) Saturn during most of the year were ceremoniously untied for the festivities in his honor. The popular celebrations collectively called the Saturnalia lasted several days, involved the exchange of gifts among relatives and friends, banquets and drinking parties, and special dinners were served for the slaves. During Saturnalia slaves were not punished and often ridiculed their masters without fear of reprisals.

Orlando Espín

See also GRECO-ROMAN RELIGION.

SATYAGRAHA

Translating literally as "grasping the truth," *satyagraha* is the name given by Mahatma Gandhi to his method of nonviolent resistance and political change. Most typically, it involved mass demonstrations by followers of Gandhi who had taken strict vows not to resist or even defend themselves against violence inflicted upon them by the authorities. Gandhi called on his followers to be willing to endure physical injury for the sake of overcoming evil. Satyagraha, which was inspired by a combination of Christian pacifism, Jain and Hindu doctrines of nonviolence (*ahimsa*), and H. D. Thoreau's concept of civil disobedience, was an important element in the Indian nationalist struggle to gain independence from colonial rule. Martin Luther King Jr., who wrote his doctoral dissertation on Gandhi, introduced elements of satyagraha into the American Civil Rights Movement.

Lance E. Nelson

See also AHIMSA; ETHICS, SOCIAL; GANDHI, MOHANDAS K.; HINDUISM; JAINISM; KING, MARTIN LUTHER, JR.; PACIFISM.

SAUL

Saul, the son of Kish of the tribe of Benjamin, was the first king (Hebrew, *melek*) of Israel (1 Sam 9–2 Sam 1). According to the biblical narratives found in the books of Samuel, Saul was anointed as Israel's first king by the judge and prophet Samuel. The account in 1 Samuel 8 in which the people approach Samuel and demand a human king to lead the army presents kingship as an institution foreign to ancient Israel, an idea copied from the surrounding nations. Since this material is a part of the Deuteronomistic History (Deuteronomy through 2 Kings), it is necessary to use this account carefully to reconstruct the rise of Saul and the development of kingship in ancient Israel. Saul was apparently instrumental in leading the Israelite struggle against the Philistines. He and his oldest son and heir, Jonathan, were killed fighting against the Philistines in the battle of Gilboa (1 Sam 31). Saul was succeeded by his son Ishbaal.

Russell Fuller

SAVITA
See GAYATRA.

SAVONAROLA, GIROLAMO (1452–98)

Savonarola originally studied to be a physician, like his grandfather, but while at school suddenly joined the Dominican Order in 1475. Beginning in 1482, Savonarola would spend most of his career teaching and especially preaching in Florence. His sermons were famous and very moving. Savonarola felt the world and church were corrupt and that God would soon chastise Italy for its immorality. When a French army invaded Italy and the government of Florence fled the city, Savonarola took this as a sign that God had begun to punish Italy. He became virtual dictator of Florence and established a regime of strict moral reform. Pope Alexander VI, concerned with Savonarola's politics as well as his preaching, summoned the Dominican to Rome. Savonarola refused to go, and the Pope suspended him from preaching in 1495. At first, Savonarola agreed, but soon began to preach again, and in 1497 the Pope excommunicated him. Savonarola called for a general council to depose Alexander VI and reform the church, and when popular support for Savonarola began to fade, the government of Florence arrested him. Savonarola was tortured, tried, convicted, hanged, and then burned. Many people in Florence considered him a martyr.

Gary Macy

See also DOMINICANS; EXCOMMUNICATION; MEDIEVAL CHRISTIANITY (IN THE WEST); SERMON.

SAWM
See RAMADAN.

SCANNONE, JUAN CARLOS
(1931–)

Argentine philosopher and theologian, and member of the Society of Jesus (Jesuits). Educated in Argentina, Germany, and Austria, Scannone has been editor of the prestigious journal *Stromata*, and professor at the Jesuit university in Buenos Aires. He has researched and written extensively on the complex relationship between culture—especially popular culture—and theology. Consequently, he has philosophically and theologically discussed subjects like inculturation, evangelization, and popular Catholicism. His philosophical work on culture and cultural identity is highly respected on both sides of the Atlantic. Scannone's influence continues to grow as Latin American and U.S. Latino theologies deepen their reflections on culture and its epistemological consequences. Among his more important books are *Hacia una filosofía de la liberación latinoamericana* (1973), *Teología de la liberación y praxis popular* (1976), *Evangelización, cultura y teología* (1990), and *Nuevo punto de partida en la filosofía latinoamericana* (1991).

Orlando Espín

See also CULTURE; EPISTEMOLOGY; EVANGELIZATION; HERMENEUTICS; IDEOLOGY (IDEOLOGIES); INCULTURATION; JUSTICE; LATIN AMERICAN CATHOLICISM; LATIN AMERICAN THEOLOGIES; LATINO CATHOLICISM; LIBERATION THEOLOGIES; POPULAR CATHOLICISM; PRAXIS; SOCIETY OF JESUS.

SCAPULAR

Originally, a piece of cloth that medieval monks wore (as part of the monastic habit) over their shoulders, hanging down in front and in back. It became a popular religious clothing item, still worn in the monastic style, during the late Middle Ages and thereafter, by people who made penitential promises or who somehow wanted to express their renewed commitment to religion or to a practice thereof. Today the scapular is frequently made up of two small pieces of cloth, tied by cords, worn over the shoulders hanging in front and in back. It is more commonly used by Roman Catholics who have become affiliated with lay branches of religious orders.

Orlando Espín

See also DEVOTIONS; FRIARS; MARIAN DEVOTIONS; MARIOLOGY; MEDIEVAL CHRISTIANITY (IN THE WEST); MONASTICISM IN WESTERN CHRISTIANITY; POPULAR CATHOLICISM; PRAYER; RELIGIOUS (VOWED).

SCHEEBEN, MATHIAS JOSEPH
(1835–88)

German Catholic theologian. Educated in Rome, Scheeben taught in Cologne for most of his life. During the controversies surrounding the First Vatican Council, he was one of the most eloquent defenders of the doctrine of papal infallibility. Among other works, Scheeben attempted a complete explanation of Catholic doctrine in a systematic and erudite work named *Handbook of Catholic Dogmatics* (1873–87), in which he emphasized the supernatural character of faith, as opposed to the frequent rationalist tendencies of his day. He was an enthusiast of Thomist thought and of patristic studies.

Orlando Espín

See also COUNCIL, ECUMENICAL; FAITH; INFALLIBILITY; NEO-SCHOLASTICISM; PATRISTICS/PATROLOGY; PIUS IX, POPE; POPE; PRIMACY; ROME, SEE OF; THOMISM/TRANSCENDENTAL THOMISM;

ULTRAMONTANISM; VATICAN, FIRST COUNCIL OF THE.

SCHELER, MAX (1874–1928)

A German theologian, Scheler's work could be divided into two epochs. In the first epoch, represented by his *Formalism* (1913), Scheler did much to rescue emotions and passions from their Enlightenment disparagement as second-order processes that had to be ruled by the intellect (or will—Kant) in order to attain moral status. He insisted that human beings had *value* and that their experience of "felt values" was prior to perception and knowledge. The highest value was the "holy"—how each person related to the absolute. In the region of the absolute, the only satisfactory relationship was with God as a person, with God who *loves*. Thus, the felt value that defined the human being was love; the human was a being of love corresponding to the personal God of love. In that, Scheler is often regarded as the forerunner of the phenomenology of religion.

In the second epoch of his work (after 1921, represented principally by his *On the Eternal in Man*), Scheler used his reflections on human experience of the divine, and especially on the human experience of longing, to postulate that the deity itself was unperfected. The deity was itself composed of an "urge to become" (*Drang*) and Spirit (*Geist*). That "becoming" of God was not only evidenced in the longing of human heart but also in the theater of human history. Scheler combined his metaphysical reflections with his knowledge of sociology to envision a unity between Eastern and Western civilizations.

G. Simon Harak, s.j.

See also VALUE.

SCHELLING, FRIEDRICH WILHELM VON (1775–1854)

German "Idealist" philosopher. He was the son of a Lutheran pastor. Schelling was a contemporary of Hegel while both were university students at Tübingen. He was professor at several German schools (Jena, Würzburg, Munich, Erlangen) until his appointment to the University of Berlin in 1841. Early in his career, Schelling had been involved with the so-called "Romantic Movement," but he is more frequently associated with German Idealist philosophy. His thought was influenced by Fichte, Spinoza, Boehme, and by some of the scientific theories popular in his day. Schelling reflected on nature, the relationship of nature and spirit, and of idea and matter. In his later years he tried to reconcile his (often changing) philosophy with Christian theology, reflecting on the trinitarian nature and inner relations of God. Among his publications were *Philosophie und Religion* (1804), and his *Berlin Lectures* (published after his death, 1856–8).

Orlando Espín

See also FICHTE, JOHANN GOTTLIEB; HEGEL, G.W.F.; IDEALISM, CLASSICAL GERMAN; LUTHERAN THEOLOGY; MODERNITY; PANTHEISM; POSTMODERNITY; SPINOZA, BENEDICT; TRINITY/TRINITARIAN THEOLOGY/ TRINITARIAN PROCESSIONS; TÜBINGEN SCHOOL.

SCHILLEBEECKX, EDWARD (1914–)

Born in Antwerp, Belgium, Edward Schillebeeckx entered the Order of Preachers, or Dominicans, in 1934, was ordained a priest in 1941, earned a doctorate in theology from the Dominican faculty of Le Saulchoir (France) in 1951, and taught theology from 1957 to 1983 at the University of Nijmegen (Netherlands). Among the most influential Catholic theologians of the post-Vatican II period, Schillebeeckx focused his work on ecclesiology and christology. Examining the church's relation to the world, he concluded that Christians owe loyalty to both the church and the world, and that the church's ministry and sacramental life must be carried out in relation to, and not completely apart from, the secular world. He conceives of God fundamentally as mystery—that is, as both beyond rational concepts and as close to humanity, especially in its suffering. In presenting Jesus Christ, he points to the link between the Christ proclaimed by the early church and the Jesus who prompted that proclamation. Schillebeeckx's most influential works include *Christ the Sacrament of the Encounter with God* (1963), *Ministry: Leadership in the Community of Jesus Christ* (1980), and his trilogy *Jesus* (1979), *Christ* (1980), and *Church* (1989).

James B. Nickoloff

SCHISM

A formal and willful separation from the visible unity of the church, or a break in the visible unity of the church, not due to disagreement over fundamental beliefs. Schism is not the same as heresy.

Orlando Espín

See also COMMUNION (ECCLESIOLOGICAL); ECCLESIOLOGY; HERESY; SCHISM, GREAT EASTERN; SCHISM, GREAT WESTERN.

SCHISM, GREAT EASTERN

The separation between Eastern Christians and Western Christians was a gradual process that was caused as much by differences in culture and customs as it was driven by doctrinal disputes. With the triumph of Islam in the Near East, the two remaining strongholds of orthodox Christianity were Rome and Constantinople. Nestorian and Monophysite Christians did continue to function and even flourish under Muslim rule, but they had long considered themselves separate churches. The first serious friction between Rome and Constantinople arose over the Iconoclast Controversy, when Popes Gregory II and Gregory III refused to cooperate with imperial policy. A much more serious break occurred with the East when, against the commands of the emperor in Constantinople, the Popes negotiated a settlement with the Frankish leaders for protection against the Lombards. In the year 800, during the Christmas liturgy, the Pope crowned the greatest of the Frankish leaders, Charlemagne, as Roman emperor. This could not but infuriate the current empress. This was tantamount to treason, and marked the end of the political unity of the Eastern and Western Empires.

Ecclesiastical unity had been restored by the mutual condemnation of iconoclasm at the Second Council of Nicaea in 787, but a new schism broke out under the patriarch, Photius, in 867. Pope Nicholas I (858–67) intervened in Byzantine politics by opposing Photius as a usurper to the patriarchate. Photius in turn excommunicated Nicholas and condemned several Western practices, including the addition to the Creed of the words "and the Son" (*Filioque* in Latin). This brief liturgical addition would become one of the most serious of the doctrinal disputes between East and West. Once again, however, the schism was healed at the council of union held at Constantinople in 879/80.

The ninth and tenth centuries saw no further breaks in East–West relations, but serious hostility broke out again in the eleventh century. When a council in southern Italy condemned the Greek practices used there, the patriarch, Michael Kerullarios, responded by ordering the Latin churches to use Greek liturgies and by attacking the use of the *Filioque* by the West. This time, however, a new issue arose. The Byzantine theologians also attacked the West for using unleavened rather than leavened bread for Communion. A delegation was sent from Rome to discuss these issues, but negotiations went very wrong when the head of the Western delegation not only accused the patriarch of heresy, but laid a writ of excommunication on the altar of the Church of Hagia Sophia in Constantinople. The patriarch responded with his own excommunication. Many scholars date the final break between Constantinople and Rome to this mutual excommunication in 1054. Matters were only exacerbated when the Crusaders conquered Constantinople in 1204 and imposed a Western, Latin government.

Several attempts were made to heal the schism. An agreement was reached between the representatives of the Greek emperor and the Western Church at the Council of Lyons in 1274, but was rejected by the East upon the death of the emperor. A second agreement on unity was accomplished at the Council of Florence in 1439, but this was formally rejected by the Synod of Constantinople in 1472. Since the Second Vatican Council, relations between the Eastern Orthodox Churches and the Roman Catholics are closer, but important theological differences remain, the greatest being the role of the pope in the governance of the church. The Eastern Orthodox are willing to regard the pope as first among equals of the patriarchs, while Roman Catholics understand the pope as the sole head of the Christian community. The question of the *Filioque* still remains of theological concern, but no longer holds the central place it did in earlier disputes.

Gary Macy

See also BASLE-FLORENCE-FERRARA (COUNCILS OF); BYZANTIUM/BYZANTINE; FILIOQUE; KERULLARIOS, MICHAEL; LYONS, COUNCILS OF; MONOPHYSITISM; NESTORIANISM; ORIENTAL CHURCHES; ORTHODOX CHURCHES; PAPACY/PAPAL; PHOTIUS OF CONSTANTINOPLE; UNIATES; VATICAN, SECOND COUNCIL OF THE.

SCHISM, GREAT WESTERN

The Greast Western Schism refers to the period between 1378 and 1415 when there were two and later three claimants to the papal throne. The schism had its beginnings when Pope Gregory XI returned the papacy to Rome from Avignon in 1377. Already in poor health, Gregory died in 1378. The Romans, long deprived of the papacy, urged and even threatened the cardinals to insure the election of an Italian as pope. The cardinals in the end did choose an Italian, Barolomeo Prignano, as Pope Urban VI. Urban immediately embarked on a reform of the church, starting with the cardinals—in the process of which he became more and more abusive until the cardinals gradually left Rome, met in Fondi, and declared Urban's election invalid because of the intimidation of the Romans. They went on to elect another cardinal, Robert of Geneva, as Pope Clement VII. When Clement could not expel Gregory from Rome, he moved back to the papal palace in Avignon. Both men claimed to be the properly elected pope. At first, little was done to end the schism as the secular princes saw the advantages of a weakened papacy. Europe, however, was badly divided. France, much of Spain, Scotland, and Sicily recognized the legitimacy of the pope in Avignon, while England, Ireland, Poland, Hungary, most of the Holy Roman Empire, and the Scandinavian countries recognized the Roman pope. Only when both popes died and successors were chosen did a strong movement to end the schism receive widespread support. The preferred way of ending the schism was through mutual abdication by both popes. This met with little success. A second solution came from the university professors and canonists in the form of the conciliar theory. Conciliarism argued that a council of the church had jurisdiction even over the papacy and could therefore depose both popes if they were unwilling to resign. A version of the theory held that the cardinals held the power to call a council for this purpose and this is, in fact, what happened in March of 1409. A joint commission of cardinals from both Rome and Avignon met in Pisa to end the schism. The Council of Pisa deposed both popes and elected a new pope, Alexander V, to unite the Western church once again. Although much weakened, both the popes of Rome and of Avignon managed to hang onto their power, thus creating the even more untenable position of having three popes in Europe. The issue was finally settled at the Council of Constance in 1415 when the Roman pope resigned and the two others were deposed. The pope chosen at the council, Martin V, did manage to reunite Europe under one pope again. The cost of the schism, however, was a tremendous loss of respect for the papacy as an institution in Europe.

Gary Macy

See also AVIGNON (PAPACY AT); CONCILIARISM; CONSTANCE, COUNCIL OF; MEDIEVAL CHRISTIANITY (IN THE WEST); PAPACY/PAPAL; PISA, COUNCIL OF; POPE.

SCHLEIERMACHER, FRIEDRICH (1768–1834)

German theologian. Often recognized as "the father of modern theology," Friedrich Schleiermacher anticipated twentieth-century existential analysis by placing the foundation of religion in *Gefuhl* ("feeling") as distinct from both Kantian practical reason or Hegelian speculative reason. In *Speeches to the Cultured Despisers of Religion* (1800), Schleiermacher sought both to vindicate religion against its "cultured despisers" by showing the continuity between religion and culture, and to supply a foundation for a Christian dogmatics. The latter came to fruition with the publication of his *Glaubenslehre* (*The Christian Faith*) in 1821/22. Eschewing the standpoints of a supernaturalistic theism and deism, Schleiermacher interpreted (and often revised) the doctrines of the Christian faith soteriologically, that is, focusing on the opposition to and emergence of "God-consciousness" mediated through the Christ and the church. Regarded as one of the "founders" of liberal theology, Schleiermacher's influence on nineteenth- and twentieth-century theology through his work in philosophical theology and theological method, biblical historical criticism, hermeneutics, ethics, and systematic theology cannot be overestimated.

J. A. Colombo

See also LIBERAL THEOLOGY.

SCHMAUS, MICHAEL (1897–1993)

German Catholic dogmatic theologian. Professor at Prague (1929), Münster (1933), and director of the Grabmann-Institut in Munich (1946). Schmaus championed dogmatic theology's turn from the ahistorical exposition of official doctrine to a dynamic reflection on dogma, rooted in Scripture and tradition, and concerned about faith's significance for contemporary life. His multivolume work *Church Dogmatics* chronicles the shift in method, starting point, and philosophical categories occurring in mid-twentieth-century Continental theology. Schmaus's activity on behalf of the liturgical, youth, and Catholic renewal movements in Germany abetted the sense of theology as a lively enterprise, and Munich attracted both foreign and lay students (the first to earn theological degrees in Germany) to study under his tutelage. An expert (*peritus*) at Vatican Council II, Schmaus expressed apprehension about newer theological positions, and his popularity declined thereafter. He should be remembered as one of the original craftsmen of the theological methods used today.

Patricia Plovanich

SCHMEMANN, ALEXANDER (1921–83)

Distinguished Russian Orthodox theologian and priest. Born in Estonia of Russian parents, Schmemann was educated at the Orthodox Theological Institute of St. Sergius in Paris. He was ordained a priest in 1946. After ordination he taught theology in Paris, and since 1951 he was on the faculty at St. Vladimir's Orthodox Theological Seminary in New York. He soon became dean at St. Vladimir's—a post he held until his death. He also taught as adjunct faculty at Columbia University, New York University, Union Theological Seminary, and General Theological Seminary. Schmemann was an official observer at the Second Vatican Council, and was active in the establishment of the Orthodox Church in America and in securing its recognition as an autocephalous church. Much of Schmemann's best work was on liturgical theology; and among his most influential publications are *For the Life of the World: Sacraments and Orthodoxy* (1970), *Liturgy and Life: Christian Development Through Liturgical Experience* (1974), *The Historical Road of Eastern Orthodoxy* (1977), and *The Eucharist: Sacrament of the Kingdom* (1988).

Orlando Espín

See also AUTOCEPHALOUS CHURCHES; LITURGY (IN CHRISTIANITY); ORTHODOX CHURCHES; ORTHODOX THEOLOGY; RUSSIAN ORTHODOX CHURCH.

SCHNACKENBURG, RUDOLF (1914–)

This Roman Catholic German New Testament scholar, now professor emeritus of New Testament exegesis at the University of Würzburg, earned his doctorate at the University of Munich with a dissertation entitled *Das Heilsgeschehen bei der Taufe nach dem Apostel Paulus: eine Studie zur paulinischen Theologie* (English trans., *Baptism in the Thought of St. Paul: A Study in Pauline Theology*, 1964). Among Schnackenburg's many exegetical publications are his monumental commentary on the Fourth Gospel (*Das Johannesevangelium* [1965–84]; English trans., *The Gospel according to St. John*, 1968–82), and a major commentary on the Johannine epistles (first German ed., 1953; [English trans., *The Johannine Epistles: Introduction and Commentary*, 1992]). He is also the author of a commentary on Ephesians (1982; English trans., *Ephesians: A Commentary* [1991]). In the area of New Testament theology, he is the author of *Die Kirche im Neuen Testament: ihre Wirklichkeit und theologische Deutung; ihr Wesen und*

Geheimnis (1961; English trans., *The Church in the New Testament* [1965]) and *Die Sittliche Botschaft des Neuen Testaments* (1962; 1986–8; English trans., *The Moral Teaching of the New Testament* [1965]). Most recently, he published *Die Person Jesu Christi im Spiegel der Vier Evangelien* (1993; English trans., *Jesus in the Gospels: A Biblical Christology* [1995]).

Jean-Pierre Ruiz

See also JOHANNINE CORPUS.

SCHNEIDERS, SANDRA (1937–)

Sandra M. Schneiders, I.H.M., is professor of New Testament and Spirituality at the Jesuit School of Theology at Berkeley (JSTB). She received her B.A. from Marygrove College (Detroit), an M.A. in philosophy from St. Louis University, an S.T.L. from the Institut Catholique in Paris, and her S.T.D. from the Gregorian University in Rome. A member of the Sisters, Servants of the Immaculate Heart of Mary, she is the author of numerous articles and books on biblical spirituality, the theology of religious life, and feminist theology. Among her most recent works are *Women and the Word* (1986), *Beyond Patching* (1991), *The Revelatory Text* (1991), *Finding the Treasure* (2000), *Selling All* (2001), and *Written That You May Believe: Encountering Jesus in the Fourth Gospel* (2003).

Mary Ann Hinsdale

See also FEMINIST THEOLOGIES; RELIGIOUS (VOWED); SPIRITUALITY.

SCHOLASTICISM

The Scholastic style of teaching and writing had its genesis with the founding of the first universities in Europe during the twelfth century. At that time, these medieval universities or schools initiated a systematic program of study emphasizing theology and philosophy. The term "Scholasticism" derives from the word "scola" (school).

There is no single amalgam of tenets, doctrines, or theories that characterizes Scholasticism in its entirety. Among Scholastic theologians and philosophers are thinkers as diverse as St. Bonaventure, St. Thomas Aquinas, Duns Scotus, and William of Ockham. Though there is a common adherence to the basic elements of Christian doctrine, Scholastics differ markedly in their treatment of particular issues and problems.

What they tend to share in common is methodology. The Scholastic method has its basis in the pedagogical style employed in the universities. Teaching centered on the reading ("lectio") of certain texts regarded as essential prerequisites to the systematic study of theology and philosophy. Readings were followed by disputations focusing on particular questions that asked, for example, whether the existence of God can be demonstrated by reason, whether the soul is immortal, and so on. The questions addressed number in the thousands and encompass all areas of theology and philosophy.

A dialectical approach was adopted in considering the various questions. Students were required to examine all issues from both the affirmative and negative perspectives. This teaching style is reflected in the writings of the Scholastics. There is always the presentation of a question followed by the assertion of a hypothetical answer that is evaluated by considering objections, reasons for the position advanced, and responses to the objections.

The Scriptures and the *Libra Quattuor Sententiarum* of Peter Lombard were regarded as indispensable texts and were universally required. Peter Lombard's four books of "sentences" presented the teachings of the church fathers in their entirety. Most Scholastics wrote "sentence commentaries" on Lombard's work, and such commentaries were the medieval equivalents of present-day doctoral dissertations. The Scholastics had available to them Latin translations of a host of Greek, Islamic, and Jewish thinkers. The teachings of the ancient Greek philosophers Plato and Aristotle were given primary emphasis. In the thirteenth century, St. Thomas Aquinas undertook a systematic synthesis of Aristotelian metaphysics (theory of the ultimate nature of reality) and epistemology (theory of knowledge) with the basic elements of Christian doctrine. In accomplishing this synthesis, St. Thomas was careful always to give priority to Christian doctrine that was not always easy to combine with Greek thought. His most well-known works, the *Summa Theologiae* and the *Summa Contra Gentiles* are magnificent examples of this synthesis.

Contemporary thinkers sometimes criticize the Scholastics for their tendency to appeal to authority. While it is true that the Scholastic method required posing questions within the context of traditionally held positions on the issue being addressed, it is unfair to see the Scholastics as mindlessly submitting to the dictates of authority. The Scholastics were certainly not prone to unreflective assimilation of the teachings of the church fathers and the views of ancient philosophers. The fact that they employed a dialectical approach to the examination of every question constitutes a clear challenge to the notion that they simply reiterated the legacy of tradition.

The relation between reason and faith was an important issue for all the Scho-

lastics. The twelfth-century theologian and philosopher St. Anselm of Canterbury followed St. Augustine in giving primacy to faith. "Credo, ut intelligam" ("I believe in order that I might understand") implies that understanding follows belief. Yet the belief that is prior to understanding, on St. Anselm's account, is not irrational belief or mere superstition. St. Anselm distinguished between two modes of understanding. One mode of understanding is what comes with the preliminary grasp of the meaning of a term or concept, such as when one is initially introduced to the term or concept through a dictionary definition. Another mode of understanding involves having a full-fledged grasp of the nature or essence of what is understood. According to St. Anselm, the nonbeliever is capable only of a minimal or preliminary understanding of what is communicated through revelation. Faith is required as a vehicle toward the acquisition of a full and complete understanding of the elements of faith. Faith, on this account, opens the mind to a view of the truth, and it is then possible for reason to cooperate with faith in facilitating a more complete understanding of what has been revealed.

"Faith seeking understanding" is an apt characterization of Scholastic thought in general. The Scholastics held that unaided human reason is inadequate as a means of knowing the truth about God and the relation between God and creatures. Revelation is essential. It is the role of reason to expound on and clarify the dictates of revelation, but reason must never be used to supplant or undermine revelation. Philosophy, for the Scholastics, must always be regarded as the servant of theology, never as its master.

Linda L. Peterson

See also AQUINAS, THOMAS, ST.;
ARISTOTELIANISM; NEOPLATONISM;
PLATONISM.

SCHOONENBERG, PIET (1911–99)

Dutch Jesuit theologian. A significant figure in post–Vatican II renewal of dogmatic theology, Schoonenberg's efforts to rethink the dogmatic treatises have two concerns. First is capturing a sense of the root theological insights of Scripture and patristic theology. Next is to translate this intuition using the personalist and existential categories of modern philosophy to convey a sense of God's dynamic presence in history. While at Nimegen, Schoonenberg published studies on the doctrines of creation (*Creation and Covenant: God's World in the Making*), and on the christological doctrine of Chalcedon (*Christ: A Study of the God–Man Relation*). Later he worked to reinterpret the trinitarian doctrine by examining the economic Trinity (God in history) in order to understand the immanent Trinity (God's internal life), and these efforts have spurred others to engage trinitarian theology as a timely and lively subject. Roman objections to his positions have prevented him from teaching and publishing in recent years.

Patricia Plovanich

SCHREITER, ROBERT (1947–)

American Catholic theologian. Schreiter was educated in the U.S., England, and the Netherlands. Since 1974 he has been a professor at Chicago's Catholic Theological Union. Schreiter is considered one of the world's authorities on questions of inculturation, mission, and culturally contextualized theologies. His teaching and publications have given his thought considerable weight in contemporary theology and missionary activity. His two most important books are *Constructing Local Theologies* (1985) and *The New Catholicity* (1995).

Orlando Espín

See also CONTEXTUALIZATION; CULTURE; EPISTEMOLOGY; HERMENEUTICS; IDEOLOGY (IDEOLOGIES); INCULTURATION; LIBERATION THEOLOGIES; MISSIOLOGY; MISSIONS; ORTHOPRAXIS; PRAXIS.

SCHÜSSLER FIORENZA, ELISABETH (1938–)

As the most significant feminist biblical scholar of her generation, Elisabeth Schüssler Fiorenza challenged the prevailing premise that "value neutral," or "objective" study is even possible. She recognized that scholars bring presuppositions and loyalties to their questions and conclusions, and that none have been as pervasive as the androcentric biases of the academy and the churches. Schüssler Fiorenza has worked out a cohesive method for a feminist reconstruction of Christian origins and illustrates her approach in exegetical studies of various texts. She acknowledges that she incorporates an explicit feminist perspective in solidarity with women who have been oppressed in every age and culture. By focusing on the women characters, female imagery, and those issues that directly impact women's lives, she seeks to establish liberating insights that coexist within the inherently patriarchical presuppositions of the Bible.

Born in Germany, Schüssler Fiorenza studied at the University of Würzberg (M. Div., 1962; Lic. Theol., 1963) and at the University of Münster (Dr. Theol., 1970). She served on the faculties of Notre Dame University, the Episcopal Divinity School in Cambridge, Massachusetts, and currently is the Krister Stendahl Professor of

Scripture and Interpretation at Harvard University Divinity School. In 1987 she became the first woman president of the Society of Biblical Literature. Her major publications include: *In Memory of Her. A Feminist Theological Reconstruction of Christian Origins* (1983); *Bread Not Stone. The Challenge of Feminist Biblical Interpretation* (1984); *But She Said. Feminist Practices of Biblical Interpretation* (1992); *Jesus Miriam's Child. Sophia's Prophet. Critical Issues in Feminist Christology* (1994); *Rhetoric and Ethic. The Politics of Biblical Studies* (1999); *Jesus and the Politics of Interpretation* (2000); and *Wisdom Ways. Introducing Feminist Biblical Interpretation* (2001).

Regina A. Boisclair

SCHWEITZER, ALBERT (1875–1965)

German New Testament scholar, expert musician, medical missionary in Africa (1913–7; 1924–65), and noted humanitarian. Schweitzer won the Nobel Peace Prize in 1952. His most famous work, *The Quest of the Historical Jesus* (1906; ET 1910), brilliantly unmasked most nineteenth-century studies on the life of Christ, setting a pessimistic tone for such inquiry in the twentieth century. His theory about a turning point in Jesus' aims based on Matthew 10:23 suffers from the same flaw Schweitzer exposed in others. But by showing the key role of the coming Son of Man and the imminent end of the world in Jesus' teaching, Schweitzer's "thoroughgoing" eschatology moved such apocalyptic issues to the center of modern biblical study. Schweitzer's other works include *Paul and His Interpreters* (1911; ET 1912), *The Psychiatric Study of Jesus* (1913; ET 1948), and *The Mysticism of Paul the Apostle* (ET 1930).

Francis D. Connolly-Weinert

SCHWEIZER, EDUARD (1913–)

This German New Testament scholar studied under Rudolf Bultmann and Karl Barth, earned his doctorate in 1938 with a dissertation on the Gospel of John, and was professor at the University of Zurich from 1949 to 1978. Much of Schweizer's academic research has focused on the christologies of the New Testament. He is the author of commentaries on Mark (1967; ET 1970), Matthew (1973; ET 1975), Luke (1982; ET 1984), Colossians (1976; ET 1982) and 1 Peter (1972). Other books by Schweizer available in English include *Lordship and Discipleship* (1955; ET 1960), *Church Order in the New Testament* (1959; ET 1961), *The Church as the Body of Christ* (1964), *Jesus* (1968; ET 1971), *The Holy Spirit* (1980), and *Luke: A Challenge to Present Theology* (1982).

Jean-Pierre Ruiz

See also BARTH, KARL; BULTMANN, RUDOLF; CHRISTOLOGY.

SCIENCE, AUTONOMY OF

The term may be taken in a twofold manner. First, it may refer to the historical episodes—sometimes treated under the rubric of the "conflict between science and religion"—whereby the natural sciences freed themselves from the authority of both classical science/philosophy and the biblical worldview. The conflicts over heliocentrism, the age of the world, "the Flood," and evolution are the most noted episodes in the fields of physics, geology, and biology, respectively. Derivatively, the term may also refer to the debates in the twentieth century over the application of the historical-critical method to the New Testament in general and the historical Jesus in particular.

Second, the term may also refer to those positions in philosophy of science and philosophy of religion that argue for a complementarity between the discourses of science and religion. In general, such positions assert that science and religion talk about reality in distinct and separate ways so that, properly understood, there can be no conflict in principle between the two. Thus, both science and religion are autonomous from one another.

J. A. Colombo

SCIENCE AND THEOLOGY

The history of the modern natural sciences and their relation to the Christian religion and theology has, on the whole, not been a harmonious one. The emergence and consolidation of disciplinary matrices for astronomy, geology, biology, and physics have led to a variety of conclusions—heliocentrism, estimates of the age of the earth, and theories on the origins of human beings and the cosmos, for example—that appear to be incompatible with the traditional Christian worldview. Four models identified by theologian-physicist Ian Barbour in his 1990 Gifford Lectures help sketch the possible relations between science and theology: models of conflict, independence, dialogue, and integration.

The source of the conflict model lies not only in the difference in content between the conclusions of science and the affirmations of theology, but in a specific self-understanding of each enterprise (scientific materialism or biblical literalism, for example) where the claim to truth of the one enterprise is regarded as necessarily excluding the claim to truth of the other. The independence model exhibited in various liberal and neo-orthodox theologies is distinguished by its claim that science and theology are essentially complementary to one another. In principle, a conflict between the conclusions of science and the affirmations of theology is not possible because their unique methods and languages reflect the distinct aspects of reality that constitute each endeavor's proper subject matter.

The model of dialogue (for example, Ernan McMullin, Karl Rahner, and Ian Barbour) represents a correction to the independence model: while the relative autonomy of science and theology is maintained, there is a recognition and emphasis of an indirect relation between the two. The strategy for uncovering this relation is twofold. First, there are boundary questions by which theology examines the self-sufficiency of the presuppositions of science, seeking to establish a consonance between the conclusions of science and theology. Second, drawing on the work of contemporary philosophers of science such as Thomas Kuhn, theologians have examined and articulated methodological parallels between science and religion/theology; for example, the existence of paradigms and models within each.

Finally, the model of integration embodied in contemporary natural theologies, theologies of nature, and process theology maintains the possibility of an integration between the content of science and theology.

J. A. Colombo

See also LIBERAL THEOLOGY; NEO-ORTHODOX THEOLOGY; PROCESS THEOLOGY; SCIENCE, AUTONOMY OF.

SCIENTOLOGY, CHURCH OF

The Church of Scientology was founded by science fiction writer L. Ron Hubbard (1911–86). While recovering from wounds he sustained during World War II, he developed a new way of achieving mental and emotional health that he published in 1950 as *Dianetics, the Modern Science of Mental Health*. In 1952 he founded the Hubbard Association of Scientologists International, and the following year incorporated the Church of Scientology. Congregations quickly spread across the United States and in fifty countries across the world. In 1966 Hubbard retired from public view, devoting the remainder of his life to developing the system of Scientology and training advanced students. In the 1970s and 1980s, the church established organizations to apply Scientological insights to business, education, drug rehabilitation, and prison reform.

Scientology rests on the proposition that human beings are inherently good, and that they possess an immortal essence Hubbard called the Thetan. Thetanhood has been distorted by conflicts and traumas carried from lifetime to lifetime. These negative impressions lead to self-destructive behaviors and can be removed through work with an auditor, a trained Scientological counselor. Through exercises and the use of an electric device called an E-meter, auditors help individuals to become "clear," to realize their inner potential. Individuals move through levels of clarity and progress toward recovery of their full Thetanhood.

Although individual work with an auditor takes precedence over community worship, weekly services are held at Scientology churches, holidays are celebrated (such as Hubbard's birthday), and members have a strong loyalty to the church and one another. The atmosphere is a warm, loving family. Scientology is especially popular among artists, musicians, and entertainers; its international headquarters are in Hollywood, California.

The church has faced controversy almost from its inception. It has been widely considered a cult and accused by secular and Christian anticult groups of brainwashing its members. Strong opposition has come from the Internal Revenue Service, Food and Drug Administration, Federal Bureau of Investigation, and the psychiatric profession. In 1958 the IRS revoked the church's tax-exempt status, and in the early 1980s, Hubbard and other church leaders were accused of tax evasion. In 1963 the FDA seized E-meters as illegal devices for medical treatment. In 1977 the FBI raided Los Angeles and Washington, D.C., churches and seized official records. Although the raid was declared illegal, the documents were retained and made available to the public. Psychiatrists have long attacked Scientology as fraudulent therapy.

The church has responded aggressively to these attacks. It has filed lawsuits charging libel and mounted extensive public relations campaigns to divert criticism. It claims that it has been unfairly persecuted by an anti-Scientology conspiracy threatened by its effectiveness. Its confrontational approach to criticism has brought additional negative publicity. It continues to promote a positive image against widespread public suspicion.

Evelyn A. Kirkley

See also CULTS.

SCOTTUS ERIUGENA, JOHN (?–877/79?)

John's name is actually redundant, since "Scottus" is Latin for "from Ireland" and "Eriugena" is Greek for "one from the island of Erin." Not much is known of his life except that he moved from his homeland to Carolingian France and taught and wrote theology there in the mid-ninth century. John, like his contemporary, Hincmar of Reims, worked under the patronage of the emperor Charles the Bald, grandson of Charlemagne. John was one of the few scholars of his period who knew Greek, and John's translation of the works of the Pseudo-Dionysius was an important contribution to later medieval thought. John also wrote influential scriptural commentaries and original theological treatises, the most famous being his *Periphyseon*.

Gary Macy

See also CHARLEMAGNE; DIONYSIUS THE AREOPAGITE (PSEUDO); HINCMAR OF REIMS; MEDIEVAL CHRISTIANITY (IN THE WEST).

SCRIPTURES (GENERIC)

Scriptures (from Latin, *scriptura*, writing) are religious texts that have been invested with an aura of authority, sacrality, and special power. All the major religious traditions have some form of scripture. Typically, they are thought to be passed down from the founders of the tradition, often from hoary antiquity, or are even regarded as being eternal. Almost always, scriptures are said to have been revealed by a transcendent source. They may be taken as the exact words of a deity or deities, a record of the visions of seers, the teachings of an enlightened being, the inspired witness of saints, or the profound wisdom of ancient sages. However their origin is conceived, scriptures play a central role in the faith and practice of religious communities, providing the foundational symbols through which faith is expressed. They are a primary source of myth, doctrine, ritual, and moral guidelines. They formulate the highest spiritual ideals of the tradition and give instruction as to how religious goals may

be attained. They exert a profound influence on the language, literature, and arts of the civilizations they inspire and mold.

It is only recently, however, that private reading of printed editions of scripture has become commonplace. For most of history, the vast majority of the faithful in all religious traditions experienced scripture solely, or at least primarily, through oral presentation in a ritual context. Indeed, a number of texts—most notably the Hindu Vedas—remained unwritten for centuries, transmitted by more or less elaborate systems of memorization and oral recitation. Even today, among nonliterate indigenous peoples, there remain "texts" that function effectively as scripture but have been preserved exclusively by oral methods. Indeed, in some religious traditions, it is the sound of the words of scripture rather than their meaning that is most important. When chanted, the holy power of the sounds is released, having a beneficial impact on all who hear, even if the words are not understood. Scriptures are revered as sacramental objects, enclosed in talismans and curative charms, used in rites of divination, and recited to bring good fortune and ward off evil. They are treated with the respect due to deities, powerful spirits, and gurus.

It is to be noted that the category of scripture in some religious traditions—for example, in Hinduism, Buddhism, and Taoism—often embraces an extraordinarily large and unwieldy number of texts of disparate origins. This is confusing for Westerners accustomed to a single, readily circumscribable holy book such as the Bible. Furthermore, while such traditions often officially distinguish certain scriptures that are regarded as more sacred or authoritative than others, this distinction often breaks down in practice, since the texts important to certain denominations or sects are frequently elevated in practice to the highest grade of authority within those particular religious circles.

Lance E. Nelson

See also INSPIRATION; PALI; QUR'AN; REVELATION; VEDAS.

SCRUPLES

The Latin word *scrupulus* means "a small sharp stone or pebble," probably lodged in one's footgear. By analogy, scruples are an ongoing oversensitivity of conscience, condemning oneself severely for slight or imagined faults.

G. Simon Harak, s.j.

See also SCRUPULOSITY.

SCRUPULOSITY

The state of one who has scruples. Usually scrupulosity manifests itself as a fear that one may have possibly yielded to "impure thoughts," or has inadvertently violated a divine command or inadvertently been irreverent, such as stepping on two pieces of straw that happen to resemble a cross. St. Ignatius of Loyola suffered greatly from scruples after his conversion, to the point of considering suicide. Thereafter he wrote that, at the beginning of the spiritual life, scruples could be useful as a goad to greater perfection, but that later in the spiritual life, they become an obstacle to deeper relationship with God. Ignatius himself seemed to have a great gift for freeing people from scrupulosity. Until recently, it was thought that the best strategy for scrupulosity was for the sufferer to surrender his will and conscience entirely to his confessor. Now, scrupulosity is seen

more as a psychological disorder, and prayerful care is required to lead the scrupulous person to a more robust sense of self in relationship to the divine.

G. Simon Harak, s.j.

SCRUTINY

Rituals that solemnly celebrate the third stage (purification and enlightenment) of the preparation for reception of the sacraments of baptism, confirmation, and Eucharist. This stage is introduced by the rite of election that takes place with the bishop of the diocese during which the elect sign their names in the Book of the Elect. Usually, the scrutinies are celebrated on the third, fourth, and fifth Sundays of Lent to coincide with the readings of John's Gospel. These rites provide prayerful moments for the elect and the community to search their lives and souls and repent of past deeds. The spiritual purpose of the scrutinies is to gradually introduce the mystery of sin, to uncover and heal what is weak or sinful while strengthening that which is strong and good.

During each of the rites that take place during the Mass after the readings and the homily, the elect come forward and kneel to pray in silence. Everyone stands for the general intercessions. A prayer of exorcism is said, and the presider lays his hands on the head of each person. Upon completion of the rite, the elect leave the assembly to discuss the readings and the experience of the ritual.

The first rite includes an exorcism pronounced to deliver the elect from the power of sin, temptation, and Satan, and in order to strengthen them to follow Christ (Gospel: John 4, the Samaritan woman). The rite is followed by the presentation of the Creed for study and reflection. The second rite invites reflection upon one's past life and, consequently, repentance (Gospel: John 9, the man born blind). The third rite includes a final exorcism with reflection upon death and resurrection (Gospel: John 11, raising of Lazarus). This rite is followed with the presentation of the Lord's Prayer.

The scrutinies can give powerful witness not only to the elect, but also to the whole community when they are expanded to allow for testimonies by the elect or by their sponsors. Stories of conversion in their lives compel all to examine the state of their lives and their relationship to God, family, and church.

M. Jane Gorman

See also HOMILY; LORD'S PRAYER; RITES OF CHRISTIAN INITIATION (RCIA); SATAN.

SEABURY, SAMUEL (1729–96)
Connecticut native, Seabury was the first Anglican bishop in the United States. A Yale College graduate and Anglican missionary to New York, he was instrumental in the survival of the Church of England in the United States after the American Revolution. During the war, the church, never strongly established as the state church, declined precipitously; its support from the British Crown evaporated, many clergy departed the colonies, and it was widely distrusted as Loyalist. A Loyalist and chaplain for the British army (therefore, unpopular in many quarters), Seabury was nonetheless selected by a group of Connecticut clergy to seek episcopal ordination. He was consecrated in Aberdeen, Scotland, in 1784. His ordination strengthened the Protestant Episcopal Church in the U.S. that had been organized in 1783 from the remains of the Church of England. In 1789 he worked to effect a compromise between High Church Loyalist and Low Church Patriot factions on liturgical and polity issues. This compromise enabled the Protestant Episcopal Church to thrive in the United States in a democratic rather than a monarchical environment: it had a strong hierarchy cooperating with lay leadership at the local vestry level.

Evelyn A. Kirkley

See also ANGLICAN COMMUNION; EPISCOPALIAN CHURCH.

SEAL OF CONFESSION
An expression used, in Catholic and Anglican Churches, for the obligation to complete secrecy imposed on the priest who hears a confession (but only within the context of the sacrament of reconciliation). The obligation is absolute, without any exception or attenuating circumstance whatsoever. Under the seal of confession, the priest may not repeat, use, or hint at the contents of any confession heard by him, ever. Church law severely punishes any breach in secrecy.

Orlando Espín

See also ANGLICAN COMMUNION; CANON LAW; CONFESSOR; EASTERN CATHOLIC CHURCHES; MINISTRY/MINISTERIAL; PRIESTHOOD; RECONCILIATION, SACRAMENT OF; ROMAN CATHOLIC CHURCH; SACRAMENT.

SECULAR CLERGY
An expression, first used in the Middle Ages, for Catholic priests whose ordinary is a diocesan bishop, and who are not members of any religious order or congregation. They are called "secular" because in medieval Latin *saeculum* also meant the daily world. They are distinct from the "regular clergy" who are members of

religious orders or congregations, living under their rules (*regula* in Latin).

Orlando Espín

See also CLERGY; CONGREGATIONS (ORDERS); DIOCESE/ARCHDIOCESE; FRIARS; MEDIEVAL CHRISTIANITY (IN THE WEST); MEDIEVAL CHURCH; ORDINARY (CANONICAL); PRIESTHOOD; RELIGIOUS (VOWED); ROMAN CATHOLIC CHURCH.

SECULAR INSTITUTES

These are recognized organizations in the Roman Catholic Church, formed by lay-people and/or members of the clergy. There is an immense variety of styles and aims among secular institutes, but they are not religious communities with vows. The members can usually continue to live as either married or single persons, alone or in community, working or not as full-time ministers of the church. The fundamental intuition behind the secular institutes is, precisely, that they are "secular"—that (in the church) implies that they live their Christian commitment "in the world." Most secular institutes started as local associations of Catholics and slowly grew into international organizations, officially recognized by church law. There are dozens of secular institutes in the world, and they are usually part of the World Conference of Secular Institutes that has a U.S. branch.

Orlando Espín

See also BAPTISM/CONFIRMATION; CHURCH; LAITY; MISSION OF THE CHURCH; RELIGIOUS (VOWED); VOCATION; VOWS.

SECULARISM

This term refers to the modern ideology emphasizing the autonomy of the human order, thereby denying the existence of a supernatural dimension in human history. This leads to a suspicion of and, indeed, an antipathy toward religion. Religious belief is perceived as a threat to the affirmation of human autonomy and the ability of human beings to accept full responsibility for the course of history; dependence on God to solve social problems prevents humanity from fully realizing its potential for self-liberation. At best, religious faith is privatized, relegated to the realm of the individual person's private conscience, but effectively excluded from the public sphere (for example, politics, economics) and precluded from having any explicit, overt impact in the public, social order.

The public, secularized, social order is perceived as organized around rational principles, while religion is perceived as based on "irrational" faith. Consequently, the ideology of secularism is closely linked to the equally modern ideology of rationalism. If religious belief impedes human liberation in history, religion is an "irrational" response to human problems that can only be solved through the unimpeded exercise of our human rational capacities. Likewise, once the possibility of a supernatural or spiritual dimension of history is rejected, so too is the possibility of divine revelation as a source of human knowledge. A further corollary of secularism is, thus, an empiricism that reduces knowledge to what can be ascertained through the senses, through empirical analysis. Spiritual, religious, and ethical criteria are excluded as measures of social advancement and human happiness since these assumed to be purely "subjective" matters of private conscience or individual taste. Consequently, the theocentric worldview of medieval Christianity gives way, in secularist ideology, to a thoroughly anthropocentric worldview, where the human being is the center of his or her universe. History is not the unfolding of a divine, providential plan, but a purely human achievement, and that achievement is measured by empirical criteria (such as per capita income). In secularism, the human person truly becomes "the measure of all things."

Roberto S. Goizueta

See also MODERNITY; SECULARIZATION/ SECULAR/SECULARIZED.

SECULARIZATION/SECULAR/ SECULARIZED

These terms refer to the process by which human persons have come to see themselves as rational and autonomous historical agents. The process of secularization is one of the defining features of modern Western cultures, wherein an increased attention is paid to the rational human subject as the source of knowledge and the agent of historical change. While, in its most extreme form, secularization can lead to an ideological secularism that denies the supernatural or spiritual dimension of history altogether, the process of secularization has influenced the development of Christianity itself.

It may, indeed, be argued that the Christian doctrine of the Incarnation already bears within it the seeds of secularity. In affirming the value of concrete, historical existence, that doctrine affirms the value of secular life (for example, culture, politics, economics). Likewise, the strong sense of history found in Judaism leads to a special appreciation of this world and an affirmation of the value of human social-historical existence. Covenantal religion leads to an increased consciousness of human subjectivity and historical responsibility. Having been de-

sacralized, or denuminized, the cosmos is now viewed as the creation of a supernatural God. As creatures, human beings thus have a relative autonomy vis-à-vis their Creator.

Thus, the process of secularization implies more than the valuing of secular life; it also implies the relative autonomy of social-historical existence vis-à-vis the supernatural order. This autonomy increases in the modern West, in reaction to the corruption resulting from the alliance between religious and secular institutions in medieval Western Christendom. As religious institutions are forced to surrender their social and political influence in Western societies under the authority of secular state governments, the exercise of political authority becomes increasingly autonomous, governed by the humanistic principles of the social sciences rather than by the theological principles of the church. While, in the extreme, this process could theoretically lead to the absolute separation of the religious and the secular advocated by secularist ideologies, what, in fact, has developed in most Western societies is not a separation but a differentiation of religious and secular orders, with each retaining relative autonomy, but also interrelating with the other, even if only in informal ways.

Roberto S. Goizueta

See also MODERNITY; SECULARISM.

SEDER

Hebrew, meaning "order," this is the ritual meal held on the Jewish festival of Passover that recalls the story of the exodus from Egypt.

The major observance of Passover, held in the home on the first night of the holiday (and on the second night also in the Diaspora) is the festive, ritual meal called the Seder. With words, songs, special foods, and prayers of praise, the story of the exodus from Egypt is told, reenacted, and explained.

The *haggadah*, the book used to tell the story and guide the rituals, is filled with biblical quotations and rabbinic interpretations about the Exodus. It outlines the fourteen separate rituals of the Seder, and explains the meaning of the symbols, objects, and foods used during the Seder to tell the story of slavery and freedom.

The Seder table contains a Seder plate with five foods, each helping to symbolically tell the story of Passover. A separate plate holds *matzah*, the flat, unleavened bread that the Israelites ate on their sojourn out of Egypt. During the Seder, four cups of wine are drunk, corresponding to the four statements of redemption made by God and recorded in the Torah. The Seder table also contains the wine cup of Elijah the prophet, who will foretell the messianic era of world peace—the ultimate redemption.

By participating in the Seder, by telling the story, singing the songs, ingesting the foods, and performing the rituals, Jews fulfill the command that "in every generation each person is to consider himself or herself as if he or she personally went out from Egypt."

The Passover Seder is the most popular of all Jewish observances because it links family, community, history, and the hope and promise of freedom for all human beings.

Wayne Dosick

See also ELIJAH; HAGGADAH; HAMETZ; MATZAH; PASSOVER.

SEE

An English derivation of the Latin word *sedes* (seat). It is a term used for the city,

and by implication the diocese, where a bishop has his *sedes*. The actual "seat" of the bishop is the presidential chair near the main altar in Catholic, Anglican, and Orthodox cathedral churches.

Orlando Espín

See also ANGLICAN COMMUNION; ARCHBISHOP; BISHOP (EPISCOPACY); CATHEDRAL; DIOCESE/ARCHDIOCESE; EASTERN CATHOLIC CHURCHES; METROPOLITAN; ORTHODOX CHURCHES; PATRIARCH; ROMAN CATHOLIC CHURCH.

SEFER TORAH

Hebrew, literally meaning "book of the Torah" or "book of the Law," this is the Torah Scroll, the handwritten parchment containing the text of the Torah, the Five Books of Moses—Genesis, Exodus, Leviticus, Numbers, and Deuteronomy.

The Sefer Torah is the primary and most sacred ritual object of Jewish life—indispensable for Jewish worship, and essential in establishing and maintaining a synagogue. It is kept in a place of honor, the Holy Ark, in the synagogue, and is read on specific occasions during worship services.

The Sefer Torah is handwritten by a highly trained scribe.

In Ashkenazic synagogues, the Sefer Torah is dressed in a beautiful velvet or silk covering, and is often decorated with a breastplate and a crown of silver or gold. In Sephardic synagogues, the Sefer Torah is often kept in a decorative silver or gold cylindrical container.

Wayne Dosick

See also ARON HAKODESH.

SEFIRAT HAOMER

Hebrew, meaning "counting of the omer" —a measure of grain—this is the process and the period of marking forty-nine days, seven complete weeks, between the Jewish festivals of Passover and Shavuot.

As an agricultural festival, Passover marks the spring barley harvest. Seven weeks later, in the late spring or very early summer, newly ripened wheat is ready for harvest. At the same time, the first fruits ripen on the vines and trees and are ready for picking.

The Torah enjoins a very careful counting from harvest to harvest, most likely in order to assure that the crops would be well tended, and that the harvest would take place at exactly the right time.

While there is little evidence of how the counting took place in ancient times, speculation is that each day a measure of grain—called an *omer*—was added to a container that held precisely forty-nine measures. When the container was filled, the counting of the seven weeks was complete and the harvest began. Now, the counting is marked by the recitation of a prayer as part of the evening service.

From the Rabbinic Period on (beginning about 200 B.C.E.), Sefirat HaOmer has been treated as a period of mourning. Some suggest this is a reflection of pagan and Roman notions about the spirits of the dead returning to earth at this time of year. Others contend that it is because of a number of misfortunes that befell the Jewish people at this time of year. Whatever the original reason, these seven weeks embody a number of mourning practices for traditional Jews. Some refrain from shaving and cutting hair, and celebrations are not held—with the most practical result being that weddings do not take place during this time period.

Mourning practices are suspended on certain days during the period, including Lag B'Omer, the thirty-third day of the Sefirat HaOmer period.

The seven-week period of Sefirat HaOmer concludes with the festival of Shavuot, the spring harvest festival.

Wayne Dosick

See also PASSOVER; SHAVUOT.

SEGOVIA, FERNANDO F. (1948–)

U.S. Latino Catholic biblical scholar, currently the Oberlin Professor of New Testament and Early Christianity at the Divinity School, Vanderbilt University. Born in Cuba, Segovia immigrated to the U.S. in his early teens. He earned a doctorate in biblical studies at the University of Notre Dame (1978), and taught at Marquette University before joining the Vanderbilt faculty in 1984. Segovia's scholarship has focused on Johannine studies, ideological and cultural criticism, and postcolonial theory. His work on postcolonial hermeneutics is widely admired. Segovia has worked on numerous editorial and professional association boards, and is a past president of the Academy of Catholic Hispanic Theologians of the U.S. Among his most influential books are *Reading from This Place*, with Mary Ann Tolbert (two volumes, 1995); *Hispanic/Latino Theology: Challenge and Promise*, with Ada M. Isasi-Díaz (1996); *Farewell of the Word: The Johannine Call to Abide* (1991); *Decolonizing Biblical Studies* (2000); and *Post-Colonial Biblical Criticism: Interdisciplinary Intersections*, with Stephen D. Moore (2005).

Orlando Espín

See also CULTURE; HERMENEUTICS; INCULTURATION; LATINO THEOLOGY (-IES); POSTCOLONIALISM; POSTMODERNITY.

SEGUNDO, JUAN LUIS (1925–96)

Born in Montevideo, Uruguay, Juan Luis Segundo studied theology in Argentina,

Belgium, and France, was ordained a Jesuit priest in 1955, and founded the Peter Faber Center in Montevideo in 1965 (and was director from 1965 to 1971). Among the most prolific Latin American liberation theologians, Segundo focused his attention on questions of theological methodology (he developed the notion of the "hermeneutical circle" as a dialogue between Scripture and experience) and ecclesiology (he saw the church as called to be a leaven in human history, and not a mass organization). As chaplain to lay communities in Uruguay, he sought to overcome the separation of faith and everyday life experienced by many Christians. Theologically, he rejected a dualistic separation of the sacred and the secular, proposed a dialectical and necessary relationship between faith and ideologies, and saw Christian doctrine as the fruit of a process of learning through trial and error. These views placed Segundo in tension with authorities of the Roman Catholic Church. His principal writings include two multivolume works, *A Theology for Artisans of a New Humanity* (1968–72) and *Jesus of Nazareth, Yesterday and Today* (1982), as well as his influential books *The Liberation of Theology* (1976) and *The Liberation of Dogma* (1989).

James B. Nickoloff

See also LIBERATION THEOLOGIES.

SEMANTICS

Semantics derives from the Greek *sēmantikos*, "significant." Semantics involves itself with the study of meaning that has a long history beginning with the Stoics. The "meaning of meaning," however, is elusive. Odgen and Richards assigned no less than twenty-three meanings to *meaning*. These twenty-three senses to *meaning*, however, derive from the relationships among three major terms, *meaning, sense*, and *reference*. These relationships see meaning as a general term encompassing sense and reference. Sense and reference are terms derived from the brilliant work of the philosopher of language Gottlob Frege. Frege's famous example is the difference between the sense (*Sinn*) and reference (*Bedeutung*) of the two terms "morning star" and "evening star." Both terms have the same reference but they are not synonymous. Morning star is the name of the planet Venus "when seen in the morning before sunrise" and evening star is the name of the planet Venus "when it appears in the heavens after sunset." Frege's famous distinction has led to two major schools of semantic theory: monists and dualists. Monist semantic theories explain the nature of meaning using only sense or reference or use. These semantic theories favor the dyadic model of sign developed by Charles de Saussure. Dualist semantic theories explain the nature of meaning by taking into account both sense and reference. These semantic theories favor the triadic model of sign developed by Charles Peirce.

Perhaps the most influential of semantic theories derives from the work of Charles William Morris (1901–79). Morris recognized the triadic nature of *semiosis* and distinguished its three basic dimensions in terms of the relationships inherent in *semiosis*. As such, meaning becomes one of three dimensions of a social process that generates relationships between signs, what signs refer to, and the interpreters of those signs. Thus, Morris distinguished those aspects of *semiosis* that relate signs to other signs as *syntactics*, those that relate signs to their interpreters as *pragmatics*, and those that relate signs to what they refer to as *semantics*. Semantics, then, is one of three principal branches of the field of semiotics and studies the nature of the relationship between a sign or word and what it refers to.

Alex García-Rivera

See also SEMIOTICS; SIGN; SYMBOL; SYMBOLICS.

SEMI-ARIANISM

Semi-Arianism is the name for an alleged fourth-century christological heresy. The group designated and more properly called Homoiousions were theological moderates who espoused neither the Nicene nor Arian interpretations of Christ after the Council of Nicaea (325). They proposed the less rigorous term *homoiousios* (of like substance with the Father) in place of the *homoousios* (of the same substance as the Father) as consistent with the tradition of Origen. The group eventually accepted the *homoousios* formula at the Council of Constantinople (381). Epiphanius, a bishop from Cyprus and avid supporter of the Nicene formula, gave the group the pejorative name "Semi-Arian" in his work *Panarion* (or *Haeresis*), a treatise on the heresies of the period.

Patricia Plovanich

SEMINARY

A type of school, often a graduate-level school, for the training of candidates for the ministry. The term originated in the Roman Catholic Church as one of the reforms mandated by the Council of Trent. The Catholic seminaries have undergone many changes since their establishment in the sixteenth century. Other Christian churches (and even other religions) later began to use the name to refer to their own ministry-training institutions.

Orlando Espín

See also COUNTER-REFORMATION/ CATHOLIC REFORMATION; MINISTRY/ MINISTERIAL; PRESBYTERORUM ORDINIS; PRIESTHOOD; TRENT, COUNCIL OF; VINCENTIAN FATHERS.

SEMIOTICS

Semiotics derives from the Greek *semeion* (sign) and *sema* (signal) and designates the discipline that studies signs and sign relations. Semiotics began as an ancient branch of medical science. Galen of Pergamum (139–99) referred to diagnosis as a process of *semeiosis*. The Hellenic philosophers also espoused the study of signs, especially in the analysis of language. Christian philosophy amplified the study of signs with its attempt to understand the symbolic nature of sacraments and to explain the apparent contradictions found in scriptural texts. The study of signs, however, was not identified as a separate discipline until the beginning of the modern age. Semiotics as an independent field of study was first suggested in 1690 by the philosopher John Locke. In his *Essay Concerning Human Understanding*, Locke proposed the term *semeiotike* as the "doctrine of signs." Locke, unfortunately, did not use his new term systematically. The field of semiotics lay dormant until Charles Peirce suggested the term anew in the late nineteenth century.

Charles S. Peirce concerned himself with the relationship the mind has to some object. Does the mind receive passively information about the object (a realist position), or does the mind play an active part in determining the nature of the object (an idealist position)? Peirce's concern was to give both sides of these truths equal weight and come out as a moderate realist. His solution was to concentrate not so much on the object per se but on the relationships between objects. Such a strategy can go to one of two extremes. One extreme assumes a position that says that meaning flows from the difference between objects. Such a strategy is contextual in character and intent. The other assumes the opposite: meaning is carried in the difference of the object itself. Such a strategy can be characterized as contextless in character. What Peirce recognized was that both understandings of meaning were needed for a strategy that proposed a moderate realism. Peirce's own strategy to give the intellect and the world its due consisted of connecting logic (the action of the mind) and ontology (the action of the world) through phenomenology (the suspension of mind so as to perceive directly the structure of reality). Such a system calls for a logic of relations Peirce called *semiotics*. Peirce called his phenomenological categories Firstness, Secondness, and Thirdness. Firstness carries the idea of originality, of freedom, of potentiality. Secondness, on the other hand, is the "brute actions of one subject or substance on another." In a word, Secondness is essentially "otherness." Finally, Thirdness involves the idea of "composition," or combination. "A combination is something which is what it is owing to the parts which it brings into mutual relationship." Peirce used these categories to understand the nature of sign.

Peirce approached an understanding of sign through his famous example of the thermometer. The rise in mercury in a thermometer occurs through Secondness, that is, "in a purely brute and dyadic way" through an increase of "ambient warmth" (a Firstness). This rise, however, "on being perceived by someone familiar with thermometers, also produces the idea of increasing warmth in the environment" (a Thirdness). Thus, the thermometer, as the subject of dyadic, physical forces, is a "thing." The thermometer, on being seen, however, is not so much recognized as it is cognized or "known," that is, it becomes an element of experience. On being read, a third factor enters —interpretation. In other words, if the thermometer is both seen and recognized as a thermometer, it is not only a thing become an element of experience, but also an element of experience become sign. As a thing, it merely exists. Moreover, it also exists for someone as an element of experience. As a sign, however, it stands not only as an element of experience and as a "thing" in the world but also for something besides itself. Said differently, it not only exists (thing), it not only stands to someone (an element of experience), it also stands to someone for something else (sign). Thus Peirce defined the sign as "something which stands to somebody for something in some respect or capacity."

Peirce's definition of sign lends itself to amazing generalization into a comprehensive logic of signs, the modern science of semiotics. Peirce's semiotics has been applied to verbal and nonverbal language, mathematics, medicine, biology, zoology, sociology, and cultural anthropology. The field of semiotics revived by Peirce offers theology and religious studies an important tool. Signs and symbols are important notions for the theologian. More recently, semiotics has been applied to theology through the work of Robert Schreiter and Alex García-Rivera. Schreiter and García-Rivera developed the *semiotics of culture* in which signs and symbols make up a cultural "text" that can be "read." García-Rivera applied this notion to the beatification process of St. Martin de Porres, revealing a theology of the human being. As such, the semiotics of culture promises to be an important application of semiotics for theology and religious studies.

Alex García-Rivera

See also SEMANTICS; SIGN; SYMBOL; SYMBOLICS.

SEMI-PELAGIANISM

This term is a rather recent one, having been coined at the end of the sixteenth century as part of the controversy called *de auxiliis*, between Dominicans and Jesuits. However, the term is no longer used in reference to this original context, having instead become exclusively identified with a heretical movement of the fifth and sixth centuries.

While not denying the necessity of God's grace for salvation (as Pelagianism seems to have done), semi-Pelagians taught that the initiative (the first necessary steps toward salvation) could be taken by human beings on their own. God's grace was then offered in order to guarantee that human initiative would in fact result in salvation. Semi-Pelagianism was frequent in monastic circles of southern France, and it seems that its doctrines were developed in order to counterbalance Augustine of Hippo's extreme views (espoused late in his life) on predestination and sinful human nature. Cassian of Marseilles (d. 420?) and Vincent of Lérins (d. 450?) seem to have promoted semi-Pelagian teaching, while Fulgentius of Ruspe (d. 533) and Caesarius of Arles (d. 542) actively opposed these views. Semi-Pelagianism was finally condemned at the Council of Orange in 529. Together with Pelagianism, this movement's insights and questions have continued reappearing in Christian theologies of grace and salvation, under various terminologies, throughout the centuries.

Orlando Espín

See also AUGUSTINE OF HIPPO; CAESARIUS OF ARLES; DOMINICANS; FAITH; FREE WILL; GRACE; JANSENISM; JUSTIFICATION; MOLINA, LUIS DE; MONASTICISM IN WESTERN CHRISTIANITY; NATURE, HUMAN; ORANGE, COUNCIL OF; PELAGIANISM; PELAGIUS; PREDESTINATION (IN CHRISTIANITY); SALVATION; SIN, ORIGINAL; SIN, PERSONAL; SOCIETY OF JESUS; TRENT, COUNCIL OF; VINCENT OF LÉRINS.

SEMITIC

An adjective referring to the peoples who speak Akkadian, Hebrew, Phoenician, Aramaic, or Arabic, known collectively as the Semitic languages. Surviving among these peoples today are Arabs and Jews. When used in the construct "anti-Semitism," the term Semitic refers specifically to hatred of Jews or the Jewish religion.

Alan J. Avery-Peck

SEN, KESHAB CHANDRA (1838–84)

An important leader of nineteenth-century Hinduism, Keshab Chandra Sen was a leader of the Brahmo Samaj, a religious reform movement founded by Ram Mohan Roy. He caused controversy, and more than one split in the Samaj, because of his status as a nonbrahmin, his emphasis on devotion to Christ, and his general idiosyncratic, eclectic approach to religion. Sen encouraged much valuable social service and reform work, however, and was instrumental in making the important Bengali saint Sri Ramakrishna known to a wider public.

Lance E. Nelson

See also HINDUISM; RAMAKRISHNA, SRI; ROY, RAM MOHAN.

SENSES OF SCRIPTURE

The "senses of Scripture" refer in Christian thought to the different levels of meaning available to the reader in the text of the Bible. Since Christians believe that the Bible is inspired by God, and that the texts of Hebrew Scripture refer, however obliquely, to Jesus as the Christ, they understand the "real" or "spiritual" or "deeper" meaning of Scripture to lay behind the literal meaning of the text. In the third and fourth centuries, the Christian scholars of Alexandria tended to stress the spiritual meaning of Scripture over the literal meaning, while the Christian scholars of Antioch placed more importance on the literal meaning of the text. Based on Augustine and John Cassian, medieval scholars looked for four meanings in the Scripture. The literal meaning was the historical sense of the text, that is, what the author originally intended. The allegorical sense of Scripture uncovered the doctrinal or spiritual sense of the text usually as it related to Christ or to the church. The moral sense of Scripture revealed the pastoral or ethical meaning and the anagogical sense of the text referred to eschatology, that is, it prefigured the end times. While most scholars preferred the allegorical or moral meaning of Scriptures, others such as Andrew of St. Victor in the twelfth century or Hugh of St. Cher in the thirteenth century placed great value on discovering the literal meaning of the text. Some scholars, like Hugh of St. Cher and Nicholas of Lyra, would write two commentaries on Scripture, one literal and one moral, the moral commentaries being used to teach preaching.

Gary Macy

See also AUGUSTINE OF HIPPO; BIBLE; CASSIAN, JOHN; ESCHATOLOGY (IN CHRISTIANITY); ESCHATON; EXEGESIS/ EISEGESIS; SCRIPTURES (GENERIC).

SENSUS FIDELIUM/SENSUS FIDEI

Technical terms, in Catholic theology and doctrine, that (in Latin) literally and respectively mean "the sense of the faithful," and "the sense of the faith." They are usually studied within the theology of revelation and tradition, and in ecclesiology.

Within the overall theological discussion of revelation and the development of doctrine, with many ramifications into other theological areas, there lies the study of tradition. In the past, some Catholic authors used to consider tradition, together with but distinct from the Scriptures, as a "source" of revelation. This "two-fonts theory," however, was discarded as the theology of revelation correctly came to emphasize that Jesus Christ is the revelation of God, and that this revelation is not primarily the communication of doctrinal truths but rather the outpouring of God's love and self in human history.

The two-fonts theory also failed when the relation between the biblical text and tradition was carefully examined. It is evident that the Scriptures have a privileged position as the inspired and normative witness to God's revelation. Tradition is correctly valued as the context within which the biblical texts came to be written and within which the very canon of the Scriptures came to be fixed and accepted as inspired. Tradition is also the ecclesial (and sometimes normative) interpretation of the Scriptures. The fixed texts of the Bible are proclaimed, explained, applied to life, and interpreted by tradition for every Christian generation. This role of tradition (in Catholic and Orthodox belief) is guided and protected from error by the Spirit of God who also inspired the biblical texts.

Scripture is the normative, written expression of a preceding tradition that proclaims and witnesses to the revelation of God to Israel and in Christ, and from him through the apostolic community for the universal, postapostolic church. Scripture, therefore, communicates all the essential contents (gathered in the biblical canon and received by the church) necessary for complete, true, and saving faith. Scripture, which must always be interpreted in the light of the tradition that precedes and accompanies it, is the norm for the church's preaching and faith.

Postapostolic tradition, on the other hand, is essentially interpretation and reception of the one Gospel of God that has found its concrete, written expression in Scripture. The common content of Scripture and tradition is, simply put, their normative witness to the God revealed in Jesus Christ. The Bible and tradition share the same content in the sense that tradition, through postapostolic expressions, symbols, and language, recognizes and confesses (Creed), refines correct meaning against falsehood (dogmas), and witnesses to that same truth Scripture communicates through the language, expressions, and symbols of Israel and the apostolic church. Scripture has been received and its canon fixed forever, while tradition is necessarily living in and through history.

One could speak of tradition as exemplified in the definitions of the great ecumenical councils of Christian antiquity, as expounded by the fathers of the church, and as communicated and witnessed to by the ecclesial magisterium and by the theologians throughout history. Tradition is certainly expressed in and through all these means. Theologians studying tradition usually concentrate on written conciliar documents, patristic texts, episcopal or papal declarations, and so on. Quite correctly, this written material (as also the text of Scripture) is very carefully examined and the methods of textual interpretation applied to it. Most theologians are aware of the need to properly understand a written document within its linguistic, cultural, political, historical, and doctrinal contexts. Without this careful study, the interpretation of the text could be prejudiced or inaccurate and, as a consequence, yield wrong conclusions that could mislead other theological research dependent on the proper interpretation of tradition's texts.

However, just as important as the written texts of tradition (or, in fact, more important) is the *living witness and faith* of the Christian people. However, they do not seem to be taken as seriously by those who study tradition. It is evident that it is difficult to limit the object of one's study when the latter is supposed to be found mainly at the experiential level in every community of the faithful. Cultural differences, diversity of languages, and all sorts of other variations make the actual theological study and interpretation of the life and faith of real Christian people a very difficult task indeed. And to complicate things even further, the object of the study (though expressed through cultural categories, languages, and the like, that run the full gamut of human diversity) is to be found at the level of intuition. It is this "faith-full" intuition that makes real Christian people sense that something is true or not vis-à-vis the Gospel, or that someone is acting in accordance with the Christian Gospel or not, or that something important for Christianity is not being heard.

This intuition in turn allows for and encourages a belief and a style of life and prayer that express and witness to the fundamental Christian message: God as revealed in Jesus Christ. This "faith-full" intuition is technically called the *sensus fidelium* or *sensus fidei* (in Latin, "sense of the faithful," and "sense of the faith," respectively).

The whole church has received the revelation of God and accepted it in faith. And, as a consequence, the whole church is charged with proclaiming, living, and transmitting the fullness of revelation. Therefore, the necessary task of expressing the contents of Scripture and tradition is not and cannot be limited to the ordained ministers of the church. The whole church has this mission, and the Spirit was promised to the whole church for this task. Christian laity, consequently, are indispensable witnesses and bearers of the Gospel—as indispensable as the magisterium of the church. Furthermore, because the foundational origin of the *sensus fidelium* is the Holy Spirit, it can be said that this "sense of the faithful" is infallible, preserved by the Spirit from error in matters necessary to revelation. In other words, the "faith-full" intuition (*sensus fidei*) of real Christian laypeople infallibly transmits the contents of tradition and thus infallibly senses the proper interpretation and application of Scripture.

The main problem with the study of the *sensus fidelium* as a necessary component in any adequate reflection on tradition is, precisely, its being a "sense," an intuition. This sense is never discovered in some kind of pure state. The *sensus fidelium* is always expressed through the symbols, language, and culture of the faithful and, therefore, it is in need of intense, constant, interpretive processes and methods similar to those called for by the written texts of tradition and Scripture. Without this careful examination and interpretation of its means of expression, the true "faith-full" intuition of the Christian people could be inadequately understood or even falsified. This is where theology and the magisterium must play their indispensable hermeneutic roles, though this process is not without its own limitations and problems.

The means through which the *sensus fidelium* expresses itself are extremely varied, showing the cultural wealth of the Christian people. Given the global demographics of today's church, the means tend to be more like they have been throughout most of Christian history: *oral, experiential, and symbolic.* These expressions also show (because of their origin in human culture) the wound of sinfulness capable of obscuring (but never destroying) the "faith-full" and infallible intuitions of the Christian people. The interpretation and discernment needed in the study of the *sensus fidelium* must, therefore, try to ascertain the authenticity of the intuitions (their coherence and fundamental agreement with the other witnesses of revelation) and the appropriateness of the expressions (their validity as vehicles for the communication of revelation, realizing that no human expression is ever totally transparent to God and the Gospel). This process calls for at least three confrontations.

The first of these confrontations must be with the Bible, because what claims to be a necessary component of Christian revelation must prove itself to be in fundamental coherence with the Scriptures. Although not everything most Christians hold to be truly revealed is expressedly stated in the text of Scripture, nothing held to be revealed can ever be against Scripture or incapable of showing its authentic development from a legitimate interpretation of Scripture.

The second confrontation must be with the written texts of the tradition. By these we mean conciliar definitions of doctrine (dogmas), the teachings of the fathers of the church, the documents of the magisterium of the church, the history of the development of doctrines, the various theological traditions and authors, and so on. Throughout twenty centuries of Christian history, the church has reflected on God's revelation and has come to a number of fundamental decisions on the proper understanding of some dimensions or elements of that revelation, and has made these decisions normative for itself and for all following generations of Christians. As a consequence, all intuitions that claim to be "faith-full" (as well as all means of expression of those intuitions) must be in basic agreement with those normative decisions of the church, and must also show some degree of coherence with the general doctrinal and spiritual thrust of the history of the church.

The third confrontation must be with the historical and sociological contexts within which these "faith-full" intuitions and their means of expression appear. If a "sense" of the faith is to be discerned as true or false bearer of tradition, it must be capable of promoting the *results expected* of the Christian message and of Christian living. In the same way, the vehicles through which the intuition of faith expresses itself (given the fact that all these means are cultural, historical, and sociological) must somehow be coherent with Christianity's necessary proclamation and practice of justice, peace, liberation, reconciliation, and so on, as indispensable dimensions of a world according to God's will. The expressions of the *sensus fidelium* must facilitate and not hinder the people's participation in the construction of the reign of God. This third confrontation, evidently, will demand of theologians an awareness of culture and of economic and political reality, as well as awareness of their hidden (but certainly present) class and ethno-cultural biases and interests that may blind them to dimensions of revelation present precisely in the "faith-full" intuitions they are studying. This latter danger seems most evident among many theologians trained in the North Atlantic presupposition that European or Euro-American theologies are "the" truly profound, systematic, real, and normative theologies, the ones—they claim—that effectively dialogue with the truest and most fundamental issues of human existence. Of course, these North Atlantic theologies assume (very often implicitly) that their cultural, political, and economic contexts define what is truest and most fundamental for humanity, while considering that definitions from other contexts are either inconsequential or merely tangential to the tasks of their pretended "real" theologies. This third confrontation, obviously, calls on the theologian to become aware of the cultural and ideological limitedness and bias of the very theological tools he or she is employing in the study of the *sensus fidelium*. North Atlantic theologies (European or Euro-American) seem most in need of this third confrontation and exercise of profound hermeneutic humility.

If the infallible, "faith-full" intuitions of the Christian people can only be expressed through culturally given means, then it is possible that the same intuition could be communicated by different Christian communities through different cultural means. It is in this context, and as a consequence of the preceding discussion, that popular Catholicism may be considered a culturally possible and authentic expression of some fundamental intuitions of the Christian faith. Popular Catholicism is arguably a means for the communication of many Christian communities' *sensus fidei*.

Orlando Espín

See also BISHOP (EPISCOPACY); CHURCH; CULTURE; DEVELOPMENT OF DOGMA/ OF DOCTRINE; DOCTRINE; DOGMA; ECCLESIOLOGY; EPISTEMOLOGY; HERMENEUTICS; HOLY SPIRIT; IDEOLOGY (IDEOLOGIES); INCULTURATION; INFALLIBILITY; LAITY; LATIN AMERICAN THEOLOGIES; LATINO THEOLOGY (-IES); LITURGY (IN CHRISTIANITY); MAGISTERIUM, ORDINARY; ORTHOPRAXIS; POPE; POPULAR CATHOLICISM; RECEPTION OF DOCTRINE; REIGN OF GOD; REVELATION (IN CHRISTIAN PERSPECTIVE); TRADITION (IN CHRISTIANITY); TRADITION AND TRADITIONS; TRENT, COUNCIL OF.

SEPHARDIM

Since the Middle Ages, there have been three groups of the Jewish people, designated by the geographical area from which they come: Sephardim, Ashkenazim, and Edot HaMizrach.

The word "Sepharad" means "Spain." It is used to designate Jews who are descendants of the Jews of Spain, those who fled from Spain in the expulsion of 1492 to Mediterranean, Arab, and Asian countries, and some eventually to countries in South America, Central America, and North America.

All Jews share basic beliefs and practices. The differences revolve around custom, usually stemming from cultural influences—food, dress, music, dance—of the countries and communities of origin.

The first Jews who immigrated to what was to become the United States in 1654 were Sephardic Jews from Brazil. Until the early 1800s, the majority of the Jewish

population of the United States was Sephardic. With the vast immigration from Germany and then Eastern Europe, the Sephardic population of America became the minority. For most of the existence of the modern State of Israel, the Sephardic population was the minority. In the late 1970s, it became the majority, but, with the large Russian immigration of the 1990s, the Sephardic population is again the minority in Israel. For a long time, Sephardic Jews considered themselves—and were treated—as the "lower class" of Israeli society. But in recent years, with universal army service and so many marriages taking place between Sephardic and Ashkenazic Jews, there is a merging and blending of cultures, with the best and most enriching of each culture combining in newly forming families.

Wayne Dosick

See also ASHKENAZIM; EDOT HAMIZRACH.

SEPTUAGINT

Greek translation of the Old Testament, dated to the third century B.C.E. and probably produced in Alexandria in Egypt. While it is most likely not an accurate historical record, *The Letter of Aristeas* records that seventy-two Jewish scholars were brought to Alexandria to translate the Old Testament into Greek.

The Septuagint translation of the Bible, rendered LXX, differs in places from the most common Hebrew text, the Masoretic text. Some of the books are arranged in a different order within the books (Psalms and Proverbs, for example); some of the books contain both additions and omissions (for example, Joshua); some of the books are shorter (Jeremiah, for example). Discovery of Hebrew manuscripts at Qumran verifies the existence of other Hebrew versions of the Scriptures that predated the Masoretic text and to which the Septuagint more closely conforms.

Alice L. Laffey

SERGEI OF RADONEZH (1314–92)

Russian Orthodox reformer and monk. Born in Rostov, but raised in Radonezh, he was responsible for reestablishing monasticism in Russia. A man of deep faith and courage, Sergei had a great influence on the religious and civil life of his country. He inspired Russian resistance against Tartar invasions. He was canonized by the Russian Orthodox Church and is arguably one of the most venerated saints of that church.

Orlando Espín

See also CANONIZATION; MONASTICISM IN EASTERN CHRISTIANITY; ORTHODOX CHURCHES; RUSSIAN ORTHODOX CHURCH.

SERIPANDO, GIROLAMO (1493–1563)

Italian Catholic theologian and humanist. Seripando was an Augustinian friar and a cardinal of the church. He became archbishop of Salerno after serving many years as superior general of the Augustinian Order. He was very influential at the Council of Trent (1545–63). Indeed, Seripando was one of the pope's legates at the council. True to his order's theological traditions, he promoted a doctrine of justification that appeared close to Luther's own (Martin Luther had been an Augustinian friar himself). Seripando helped write Trent's final decrees on justification and original sin. He successfully argued against the council's adoption of a proposed definition of transubstantiation as dogma. Seripando was eloquent in his defense of the superiority of Scripture over tradition. As cardinal-archbishop of

Salerno, he was committed to the Tridentine reform program.

Orlando Espín

See also ARCHBISHOP; AUGUSTINIANISM; CARDINAL; COUNTER-REFORMATION/ CATHOLIC REFORMATION; DOGMA; FRIARS; JUSTIFICATION; LUTHER, MARTIN; SIN, ORIGINAL; TRADITION; TRADITION AND TRADITIONS; TRANSUBSTANTIATION; TRENT, COUNCIL OF.

SERMON

From Latin sermo, "speech." Contemporary Roman Catholics tend to use the word sermon to designate a form of preaching not necessarily connected to the biblical readings and heard outside the context of the liturgy. Preaching directly linked to Scripture and occurring within the liturgy, seeking to relate the day's texts to the community's life, is now commonly called a homily. The distinction, however, is a matter of convention rather than strict definition.

Patrick L. Malloy

SESSHIN

A Japanese term (usually associated with the Zen schools) meaning "collecting the mind," most often used to indicate a period of intensive meditative training in a Buddhist monastery. Although the duration may vary, sesshin focuses upon sitting and walking meditation, silent, simple meals, daily group instruction by the abbot, as well as one or more daily individual interviews. In the Rinzai school, this involves immersion in koan answer-responses with the master (sanzen); in the Soto school, the master guides intensive cultivation of breathing meditation (shikantaza). Sesshin periods in most monasteries limit the inmates' sleep; physical encouragement through wacks of the *keisaku* stick on the shoulders by the meditation hall disciplinarian urge the practitioners toward the breakthrough enlightenment experience (*satori*).

Todd T. Lewis

See also BODHI; SANGHA; VINAYA; ZEN.

SETON, ELIZABETH ANN (1774–1821)

Her canonization in 1975 made Elizabeth Bayley Seton the first person born in the United States to be officially declared a saint. Raised an Episcopalian, Seton was received into the Roman Catholic Church after the death of her husband. From 1807 until her death she opened boarding schools and then a day school, the first in the United States, thus helping to lay the foundations for the Catholic parochial school system in the United States. With the women who joined her as educators, and with the assistance of Sulpician priests and Bishop John Carroll of Baltimore, she founded the Sisters of Charity, the first native United States religious congregation. Their rule of life was based on that established by Vincent de Paul for the French Daughters of Charity during the seventeenth century. Elizabeth Seton's influence can be seen in the tradition of teacher training she began, in her treatises on the spiritual life, and in the North American religious congregations of Sisters of Charity and Daughters of Charity.

Mary Anne Foley, C.N.D.

See also DE PAUL, VINCENT; RELIGIOUS (VOWED).

SEVENERS (IN ISLAM)

Also known as the Isma'ilis, this is a branch of Shi'ite Islam named after Isma'il who died in 760 (762?). Isma'il is regarded as the seventh *imam* (divinely guided Shi'ite leader and infallible source of special religious knowledge) in the hereditary line of Ali (598–661), the fourth caliph or successor of the Prophet Muhammad (570–632). The Isma'ilis split from the larger Shi'ite group, now called the Twelvers or Imamis, in a dispute over whether Isma'il's father, Ja'far al-Sadiq (d. 765), who outlived Isma'il, was an authentic imam. The Twelvers rejected Ja'far's claim to the title, and hence the legitimacy of his son, Isma'il, and they went on to develop their own understanding of succession that they say ended with the mysterious disappearance of the twelfth imam, Muhammad al-Muntazar, in 873.

Over the centuries, the Seveners splintered into numerous subgroups whose religious and political influence extended from Egypt to northern India. In spite of their obvious differences, both Twelver and Sevener Shi'ites agree that the leadership of Islam belongs to a man appointed and divinely guided by God—someone who cannot err in his transmission of some secret truth and wisdom known only to him. By contrast, the majority branch of Islam, the Sunnis, hold that God guides Islam by the informed consensus (*ijma*) of Muslim lawyers, scholars, and judges.

Ronald A. Pachence

See also ALI; CALIPH (KALIPHA)/ CALIPHATE; IJMA; IMAM (THE HIDDEN IMAM); MAHDI; MUHAMMAD; SHI'A/ SHI'I/SHI'ITE/SHI'ISM; TWELVERS (IN ISLAM).

SEVENTH-DAY ADVENTISTS

Like the Jehovah's Witnesses, the Seventh-Day Adventists emerged out of dashed hopes for the second coming of Jesus

Christ as predicted by William Miller in 1843–4 in the northeastern United States. While many caught up in the fervor were disillusioned and embittered, others remained and splintered into a number of smaller Adventist groups. One was led by Ellen Gould White (1827–1915), a follower of Miller and wife of an Adventist minister. She and her followers organized the Seventh-Day Adventist Church in 1860. White was a sickly woman who sought faith healing and a prophet who received more than two thousand visions. She reinterpreted Miller's message in light of the 1843–4 "Great Disappointment" and added her own distinctive emphases. She claimed that the Second Coming had occurred in heaven, but had been delayed on earth until an unspecified date.

However, according to White, Christians were nonetheless to prepare themselves for Jesus' return in two ways. First, they were to observe the Sabbath on Saturday, the seventh day of the week like the Jews, rather than on Sunday. Second, White had a vision that Christians were to live a healthy life, abstaining from alcohol, meat, and tobacco; avoiding doctors and drugs whenever possible; and getting adequate exercise, sunshine, and rest. She also forbade masturbation as a form of sexual uncleanliness. Seventh-Day Adventists became leaders of health reform, advocating hydropathic and homeopathic cures. At their home in Battle Creek, Michigan, the Whites and their followers experimented with diets rich in fruits, vegetables, and grains. One Seventh-Day Adventist, John Kellogg, developed the cornflake and turned it into a popular cold breakfast cereal; due to conflict with White, he later left the church, and it never received financial benefit from his products.

The church grew steadily in the first half of the twentieth century, not only in the United States, but throughout the world through successful mission efforts. By the 1970s, three-quarters of church members lived outside the United States. The church has also established numerous hospitals, sanitariums, elementary schools, colleges, a theological seminary, and dental and medical schools. This network of charitable and educational institutions is ironic for a group dedicated to the expectation of the imminent end of the world. Church members believe they have restored the true first-century Christian church, but they are not considered Christians by all others. Like Christian fundamentalists, they tend toward dogmatism and legalism. Their worship services are virtually indistinguishable from mainstream Protestants. At the same time, their beliefs about the Sabbath, health, and their reverence for White's teachings distinguish them from other Christians. Their headquarters are in Takoma Park, Maryland, outside Washington, D.C.

Evelyn A. Kirkley

See also ADVENTISTS; JEHOVAH'S WITNESSES.

SEVERUS OF ANTIOCH (?–538)

After studying in Alexandria and Beirut, Severus entered a monastery near Gaza in 488. He became the leading representative of a moderate Monophysitism and, as such, went to Constantinople in 509 to uphold this position. In 512 Severus was consecrated bishop of Antioch, but he was compelled to return to Egypt by the anti-Monophysite emperor Justin. In 535 Severus returned briefly to Constantinople to consult with Justinian, who wished, unsuccessfully, to end the

Monophysite controversy. Many of Severus's works were lost due to Justinian's decree in 536 that Severus's works be destroyed. However, some Syrian translations exist of the many polemical works Severus wrote in defense of the Monophysite cause.

Gary Macy

See also JUSTINIAN; MONOPHYSITISM.

SEXISM

The fear and hatred of women and the social, political, and economic control of their productive and reproductive labor. Sexism has its origin in patriarchal consciousness that strove to separate itself from community, nature, and the material world. These areas were relegated to women and made invisible in Western dominant consciousness characterized by anthropocentric dualism and philosophical idealism. Sexist gender assumptions pervade all dimensions of human experience including language, culture, work, politics, and the family.

Ancient gender oppression has been actively interstructured historically with systems of racism, economic exploitation, and political and cultural (including religious) marginalization. Since the experience of sexism is radically qualified by other systems of oppression and privilege, sexism is not the same in the experiences of women in diverse social locations.

A specifically Christian feminist theological agenda includes the assertion that the Gospel will never be truly revealed until sexism is fully recognized as having deformed Christianity's own structure, theology, and praxis from the very beginning to the present.

Mary E. Hobgood

See also CLASSISM; FAMILY; RACISM; SOLIDARITY; VICTIM.

SEXUALITY

Sexuality is that dimension of human existence that encompasses experiences of embodiment, gender role, erotic attraction, and sensual pleasure. It is frequently related to human reproduction, as well as to power relationships within particular cultures. At first glance, it might appear that a rudimentary interpretation of Sigmund Freud's assertion, "anatomy is destiny," would clarify human sexuality. In other words, sexual roles (and so gender and sociocultural roles) are directly and intrinsically related to genital-anatomical structure. However, anatomy can be deceptive or ambiguous, and the variety of human sexual response and attraction indicates that a consideration of anatomy alone is inadequate. A full treatment of human sexuality would, then, necessarily involve consideration of genetic, hormonal, anatomical, psychological, and sociocultural factors.

Naturalist or Essentialist Understandings of Sexuality

In the Western, Christian tradition, human sexuality has been understood as naturally given; that is, that certain patterns of sexual interaction are part of the unchanging essence of what it is to be a human person, or more specifically, what it is to be a male or a female. This tradition has emphasized a primary and fundamental relationship between sexuality and reproduction. In this light, only male–female or heterosexual intercourse within marriage is understood to conform to the nature and purpose of sexuality, and so it is viewed as the normative expression of human sexuality. Other sexual expressions (same-sex relations or masturbation, for example) are traditionally viewed as "unnatural" and so as deviant. This perspective is often referred to as *essentialism*.

Since the nineteenth century, questions of sexuality have been understood to be most adequately addressed from the perspective of science and medicine. In this view, sexuality was best examined in the neutral framework of health and disease or pathology, free from the cultural and religious biases. The introduction of psychoanalysis by Sigmund Freud (1856–1939) was instrumental in this development of a more clinical approach. Other physicians and scientific researchers (Kräft-Ebbing, Kinsey, Masters and Johnson) have offered empirical analyses of human sexuality, often comparing it with the sexual activity of nonhuman mammals in order to ascertain what is "natural" and "healthy." The medical model has, however, been criticized by contemporary theorists who argue that science is not in fact free from cultural bias. Further, they claim that the medical model perpetuates essentialist evaluations of human sexuality.

The medical model is essentialist in that it focuses upon physical sexual response without regard to the psychological dimensions or power relationships implicit in such responses. Thus, empirical research that demonstrates men are more sexually aggressive than women can result in the labeling of that phenomenon as natural without considering differences in the role patriarchy plays in the socialization of women and men across diverse cultures. Criticisms of this sort are often generated by philosophers and social theorists of the *social constructivist* school.

Sexuality, Power, and Control:
Constructivist Interpretations

Social constructivism is the direct opposite of essentialism. Unlike essentialism, which relates moral and/or scientific value to a fundamental and universal human essence or nature, social constructivists argue that all systems of value and judgment are reflections of the power arrangements in particular, historical periods and cultures. Appeals to universal foundations such as human nature actually work to obscure the contingent, constructed and relative nature of morals and all human judgment. Regarding sexuality, then, what is considered to be normal or healthy (or similarly, deviant or sick) reflects the distribution of power in a given culture so as to benefit those with the greater power. For most cultures, certainly every culture in the West, this power arrangement is understood to favor (Euro-American) men and so is referred to as patriarchal. Any sexual arrangement or practice perceived to threaten the social and economic dominance of men is negatively evaluated and so subject to control, according to social constructivists. The sexuality of women and homosexual (same-sex attracted) men are often offered as examples of this phenomenon. Regarding the sexuality of women, commentators point to a long tradition of viewing it as potentially unsettling and distracting to men, who are perceived to be vulnerable to the control of women by means of sex. Thus, female sexuality must be controlled by means of carefully channeling it into marriage and procreation or virginity. The experience of women in general and their sexual experience in particular is devalued. Sexual relations between men are viewed as threatening because those who presumably have access to status accorded by power over women appear to reject and subvert that relationship.

Further, the hierarchical nature of patriarchy has been linked to sexual abuse in that those of a lesser power status are viewed as sexually available to those of a greater power status. In fact, historical evidence suggests that behaviors presently considered abusive were morally and legally acceptable in earlier periods. For example, the notion of marital rape—illegitimately forcing sexual contact from one's spouse—is a relatively new concept that replaces the notion of a spouse's (most particularly the wife's) obligation to provide sexual favors on demand. Further, a man's prerogative to physically discipline his wife was widely accepted prior to the 1970s, when the feminist movement brought attention to the phenomenon known as spousal abuse or wife beating. Of course, many persons have always considered a man striking a woman (or child) to be ungentlemanly or undignified; nonetheless, public authorities implicitly and explicitly sanctioned the right of a man to do so until recent times. Social constructivism helps us to see that in both examples the behavior in question has a long history; it is the moral and legal evaluation of that behavior that has changed.

Interactionist Approaches

Just as social constructivists have shown that essentialist theories of sexuality ignore the role of social and cultural forces at their peril, they too perhaps need to be more attentive to the role of genetics, hormones, and physiology in human sexuality. Thus some theorists have suggested that an adequate account of human sexuality requires an understanding of the interactive, dynamic relationship between biology and sociocultural forces. An interactionist approach would acknowledge the role of physiology in human sexual response as well as the individual forces of erotic attraction that are themselves subject to cultural and socioeconomic determination and interpretation. Such an interactionist methodology would

avoid any suggestion that the physiological dimension of gender and sexuality is unambiguous or not the subject of sociocultural interpretation.

Brian F. Linnane, s.j.

See also BODY; ETHICS, SEXUAL; FEMINISM; NATURAL LAW.

SHABBAT

Also known as Shabbas, this term is Hebrew for the Sabbath, the Jewish day of rest occurring each week from sundown on Friday until sundown on Saturday.

According to the Torah, God finished the work of creation in six days, and on the seventh day, God ceased from work and rested—establishing Shabbat, a day of physical rest and spiritual rejuvenation (Gen 2:1-3). Since God rested on the seventh day, human beings—created in the image of God—are to imitate God, and cease from work to rest each seventh day.

On Shabbat, all manner of work is prohibited. Shabbat is to be a twenty-four-hour period of complete rest and relaxation—physical, mental, and spiritual—and of refreshment of psyche and soul.

Shabbat is the core celebration of Jewish life because it is the weekly reminder of the creation of the universe and of humankind, and of the creation of the covenant between God and the Jewish people. In a fast-paced, often frenetic world, it is the time each week that permits each Jew to connect with God, family, community, and self. Shabbat is the weekly time not "to do," but "to be."

The first ritual of Shabbat that occurs just as the sun sets on Friday evening is the lighting of Shabbat candles. The main Friday evening observance is Shabbat dinner, where family and friends gather to celebrate the festive day.

Synagogue prayer is central to Shabbat observance. On Friday evening, the traditional evening service is preceded by *Kabbalat Shabbat*, a series of psalms and prayers welcoming the Sabbath. The Saturday morning service is rather lengthy, with the reading of the weekly Torah portion as its centerpiece. The Saturday afternoon service includes a Torah reading, the opening verses of the following week's portion. At the conclusion of Shabbat, a short service called *havdalah* separates the holy Sabbath from the rest of the week.

During the Shabbat day, in addition to the synagogue services and family meals, there is time for rest and quiet leisure.

Wherever Jews have gone, they have observed Shabbat, and it has kept them—individually and collectively—unified and strong, committed to God and each other. The modern Hebrew poet Achad Ha-Am taught, "More than Israel has kept (observed) the Sabbath, the Sabbath has kept (preserved) Israel."

The Shabbat greeting is "Shabbat Shalom," "May it be a Sabbath of peace" for you, the ones you love, the Jewish people, and all the inhabitants of the world.

Wayne Dosick

See also HAVDALAH; KABBALAT SHABBAT; KERIAT HATORAH.

SHABBATAI TZVI (1626–76)

A false messiah, leader of a significant Jewish messianic movement. The product of a traditional Jewish education in Turkey, Shabbatai Tzvi had a propensity to perform "strange acts" that violated Jewish law; he was encouraged by his contemporary, Nathan of Gaza, known for his prophetic abilities, to declare himself to be the messiah. Sabbateanism, the ensuing movement, spread through many communities in Europe, North Africa, and in particular the Middle East, wreaking havoc upon the Jewish community as a result of Shabbatai's use of his power to depose current rabbinical authorities and to declare aspects of the ritual law null. In 1666, having been arrested by the sultan and forced to choose between conversion to Islam and execution, Shabbatai Tzvi chose conversion. This led to terrible disillusionment, confusion, and humiliation among Sabbateanism's followers, who included many leading rabbis. At the same time, certain people continued to accept Shabbatai Tzvi as messiah, and a new branch of Jewish mysticism subsequently emerged, focused upon explaining the mystery of the messiah's apostasy.

Alan J. Avery-Peck

See also KABBALAH; MYSTICISM / MYSTICS (IN JUDAISM).

SHACHARIT

Hebrew, meaning "dawn" or "morning," this is the morning Jewish worship service.

A traditional Jew prays three times a day. The *shacharit* service is the morning service, and since a Jewish day begins and ends at sundown, shacharit is the second service of a Jewish day. It is recited every day. On the Sabbath and festivals, there are certain changes and additions that reflect the special nature of the day.

Shacharit begins with a set of introductory prayers called *Birchot HaShachar*, the Morning Blessings, and *P'sukay D'zimrah*, the Verses of Song. These blessings and prayers of praise to God—many taken from the biblical book of Psalms—set the tone and mood for worship, and serve as the transition from the "outside world" to the sanctuary and the purpose of the worship service.

The shacharit service can be recited anytime after dawn until about ten o'clock in the morning.

Wayne Dosick

See also MA'ARIV; MINCHAH.

SHAFI'TE

Sometimes written Shafi'i, this is one of the four principal schools of law (*Sharia*) in Sunni Islam. Like the other three schools (Hanafite, Malikite, and Hanbalite), this juridical system is called *madhhab* in Arabic (plural, *madhahib*)—a word literally meaning "way" or "procedure." The Shafi'te "procedure," named after its inspiration, Muhammad ibn Idris ash-Shafi'i (767–820), is distinguished by its preference for *hadith*, recorded Islamic traditions based on the life and teachings of the Prophet Muhammad (570–632). This approach to Islamic jurisprudence relies more upon precedents established by reflection on what the Prophet said and did than upon the more fluid analogical method pioneered by the earlier Hanafite School. The madhhab of ash-Shafi'i is popular today in northern Egypt, the eastern part of Africa, and in south Arabia.

Ronald A. Pachence

See also HADITH; HANAFITE; HANBALITE; MALIKITE; SHARIA/SHARI'A; SUNNA/SUNNI/SUNNISM.

SHAHADAH

The first of the Five Pillars (foundational beliefs and practices) of Islam, the profession of faith. *Shahadah* literally means to "witness" or "testify" to something because one has observed that it is true. The shahadah, therefore, is as much an affir-mation of God's reliability and the validity of God's prophets as it is a statement about what one believes. In English, the shahadah states: "I bear witness that there is no god but the God (Allah) and that Muhammad is the Messenger (*rasul*) of God." In order to become a Muslim (follower of Islam), it is necessary to recite this creed with sincerity, but even the most genuine recitation of the shahadah does not make people Muslims unless they also demonstrate their faith commitment by their strict observance of Islamic law.

Ronald A. Pachence

See also ALLAH (ISLAM); FIVE PILLARS (IN ISLAM); ISLAM; MUHAMMAD; MUSLIM; RASUL.

SHAIVA

In Hinduism, a Shaiva is a person devoted to Shiva, the deity he or she will regard as the Supreme Being. There are many denominations (usually referred to by Indologists as "sects") within the Hindu tradition that are Shaiva in orientation. The general movement, which has roots in the prehistory of the Indian subcontinent, is referred to in English as Shaivism. Scriptures important to Shaivism include the *Mahabharata* and the Puranas that celebrate the myths associated with Shiva; the *Shvetashvatara Upanishad*, perhaps the earliest text to identify Shiva with Brahman, the ultimate reality of the Vedanta traditions; numerous devotional hymns composed by saints; and various theological treatises and commentaries written by important Shaiva masters. For many Shaivas, however, the most revered scriptures are the *Agamas*, Sanskrit texts believed to be directly revealed by Shiva and to be at least as authoritative as the Vedas. The two most important Shaiva traditions theologically are the Shaiva Siddhanta, centered in the Tamil-speaking region of South India, and the Trika Shaivism of Kashmir, which articulates an interesting example of theistic nondualism.

Lance E. Nelson

See also BRAHMAN; HINDUISM; LINGA; LINGAYAT; REVELATION; SHAKTA; SHAKTI; UPANISHADS; VAISHNAVA; VISHNU.

SHAKTA

In Hinduism, a Shakta is a person devoted to Shakti, the Great Goddess, the deity he or she will worship as the Supreme Being. Although the deity may be referred to generically as Shakti (Power) or Devi (the Goddess), she is typically worshiped in individual forms—such as Durga, Kali, and Parvati—with distinct personalities and theological attributes. Shakti is typically envisioned as the feminine, active, immanent pole of a bipolar Ultimate, the other pole being a static, transcendent principle, construed as masculine. Since this masculine principle is typically identified with Shiva, Shakta traditions are sometimes classified as being a part of Shaivism. Shaktas, however, may be distinguished from Shaivas by their subordination—in myth and worship especially—of the masculine principle to the feminine. There are several denominations (usually referred to by Indologists as "sects") within the Hindu tradition that are Shakta in orientation. The general movement, which—like the worship of Shiva—has roots in the prehistory of the Indian subcontinent, is referred in English as Shaktism. Shaktism is closely associated with the Tantric movement, which typically exalts the feminine aspect of the divine above the masculine and

extols the sacrality and even the spirituality superiority of women, at least in principle. Scriptures important to Shaktism include various texts from the Puranas, such as the *Devi Bhagavata* and the *Devi Mahatmya*, and numerous Tantras, such as the *Mahanirvana Tantra*. In recent times, Shaktism has been adopted as a generic term for any form of goddess worship in India, and both Indian and Western feminists have turned to Shakta literature as a source of images for female empowerment.

Lance E. Nelson

See also DURGA; HINDUISM; KALI; SHAIVA; SHAKTI; SHIVA; TANTRA; TANTRIC HINDUISM.

SHAKTI

A Sanskrit word meaning "energy" or "power," *Shakti* is an important concept in Indic religions, especially in Hinduism, where it refers to the universal creative power of the supreme deity. As the creative principle, Shakti is sometimes used as a synonym of *maya* or *prakriti* (all three terms being grammatically feminine). Thus, in Vaishnava theology, the universe is said to be a manifestation of Vishnu's shakti or, sometimes, his *maya–shakti*. A deity's shakti or creative power is typically personified as his spouse. Thus Shri is the shakti and consort of Vishnu, and Radha of Krishna, among Vaishnavas. Durga, Parvati, and Kali—often addressed simply as Shakti—are different forms under which Shiva's shakti is personified, again as his spouse, among Shaivas and Shaktas. In Shaivism (and certain Vaishnava schools) the feminine principle of immanent creativity is regarded as ontologically equal to the transcendent, masculine principle, both existing in bipolar unity. This results in a "hyphenated" deity, conceived by Shaivas as *shiva–shakti–samarasa* (the indissoluble union of Shiva and Shakti) and addressed by Vaishnavas as Radha–Krishna (with, interestingly, the feminine element named first). Shaktism adopts this concept of bipolar deity, but gives Shakti preeminence—in myth, ritual, and devotion—over Shiva, the male principle.

Lance E. Nelson

See also DURGA; GOPI; HINDUISM; KRISHNA; MAYA; PRAKRITI; SHAIVA; SHAKTA; SHIVA; TANTRA; TANTRIC HINDUISM; VAISHNAVA; VISHNU.

SHALOM

(Hebrew, peace, wholeness, perfection). The Hebrew word for "peace," in both contemporary and classical Hebrew, used also as a greeting and salutation. The centrality of the concept of peace in Judaism is suggested by its rank as the greatest possible blessing, understood to encompass all other blessings (Leviticus Rabbah 9:9; Mishnah Uqsin 3:12). Babylonian Talmud Gittin 59b states that achieving peace is the goal of the entirety of the Jewish religion and way of life. This notion is expressed succinctly in one of the most famous statements of Hillel, a founder of rabbinic Judaism, who says that at the heart of Judaism is the precept "Love peace and pursue it" (Mishnah Avot 1:12). All other Jewish laws and practices, he says, are ancillary to this obligation.

Alan J. Avery-Peck

SHAMAN

The shaman is the key religious specialist in tribal societies, a medium connecting humanity to the spirit world. The term "shaman" (pronounced SHAY-man, SHAH-man, or shah-MAN) comes from the Evenk, a group of hunters and reindeer herders in Siberia. The term was adopted for all similar practitioners because early scholars thought the Siberian shaman tradition had spread across Eurasia and into the Americas. Although this is a disputed theory today, it is likely that prehistoric cave paintings indicate that the shaman was the first religious practitioner of our species; the shaman endures in the modern world despite the many transformations in human life and in spite of many instances of persecution by the major world religions and modern states.

Referred to variously as, for example, "medicine man," "folk healer," "spirit medium," "witch doctor," or "mystic," these terms taken together point out the various traits that shamans possess. These include healing (both literal and metaphorical), though among some peoples shamans can also act to injure or kill enemies. Shamans are ritual specialists who act as intermediaries to connect the human world to others; some serve the role of social worker, helping to knit together the community in the face of the chaos of disease, death, and discord; and they are in a sense mystics who teach that the daily, ordinary world is not all there is, and that a deeper spiritual order enfolds it.

If the living community and the dead sacred ancestors form one community in the primal traditions unconnected to the great world religions, it is the shaman who is the bridge that ties the two parts of the community together by his or her ability to visit both worlds and communicate the needs of each to the other. For many peoples, only the shaman can bring them back into harmony again.

Exactly how the shaman in a particular region of the world performs this role varies, and there are over a thousand known societies where shamans have been found. Based upon commonly held animistic conceptions, sickness can be caused by an individual losing his soul by accident or theft by another; illness can also be induced by an enemy inserting a harmful object (a piece of bone or an insect, for example) into a person's body. The defining characteristic of the shaman's intervention is that he or she enters an altered state of consciousness or trance to communicate with the unseen spirits or see the inner reality of a situation. In many traditions, the shaman is thought to be able to leave the physical body, freeing his or her soul to fly to the heavens, beneath the earth, or under the sea. These "soul flights" locate another person's soul, usually due to its wandering off in this world or after it has passed on into the afterlife. The shaman can bring back a "lost soul" or, while in trance, remove a venomous object from a patient.

Through initiation, shamans find connection with and then draw upon the help of a protective tutelary spirit to perform heroic soul flights, negotiate with evil spirits, compel a soul to return, and to increase the healing power. Shamans risk injury to their bodies when engaging in soul travel as well as insanity from spirits or the spirit-infused herbs they ingest.

The shamanic world is one in which spirits coexist with humans in a layered cosmos, with humans occupying the earth between an upper and lower world. The spirits reside in many objects and places, and are particularly accessible to humans in a special location called an *axis mundi* ("center of the world"). Most commonly, these are actual or symbolic sacred mountains or sacred trees, revered for their being places of original revelations and numinous presence, or springs that give access to the lower realms.

Individuals who become shamans must train through long apprenticeships. But in most groups it is common for shamans to feel that it was a tutelary spirit that chose them, often in spite of their own resistance. In many societies, shamans must finally prove their ability by surviving an initiatory ordeal that entails going into trance, showing the grace of a tutelary spirit, and providing evidence of superhuman powers. Many shamans feel they wear out their bodies by repeatedly undergoing near-death experiences. To be initiated as shaman and to achieve such ability, an individual must memorize chants, rhythms, struts, then attract the support of his ancestral spirits. In some parts of the world, predominantly in the tropical New World, the shaman must also master the use of psychoactive plants that his teacher repeatedly blows into his nostrils using a bamboo tube. One example is found among the Yanomami tribe of the Amazon. Here shamans utilize *ebene* snuff as a powerful spirit ally essential for opening the shaman's body to see and contact the world's spirits. The Yanomami shaman also has the power to conduct the spirits into the human circle, and allow assistants to question them through the medium of his own body. The spirits can then be induced to respond to questions about matters of concern, small or great. At times and without invitation, they also deliver sermons about groups' origins, life's meaning, or the hidden facts behind recent events. Other peoples utilize the cactus peyote, the vine extract *ayahuasca*, and plants such as *jimson* and *datura*. What is universal for shamans across the world, even among shamans utilizing psychoactive drugs, is reliance on the impact of fast, rhythmic drumming, dancing, chanting, and fasting to induce trance experiences. Thus, it is the drum or the rattle that is the universal symbol representing the shaman's religious practice.

Among North American native peoples we find one of the few premodern examples of shamans in the same tribe forming alliances, or medicine societies. The Ojibwe, Pueblo, and Navajo each developed more elaborate and standardized shamanic rituals, creating a more complex organization of religious life. In most places across the world, however, shamanism has been a tradition sustained by independent, individual practitioners who serve and pass on their abilities to apprentices.

Shamanism is still widespread in the world today. Even where one or more of the great world religions has been adopted by a population, shamanic traditions continue to find adherents. In some cases, shamans confirm the doctrines of the now dominant world religion (for example, existence of the soul, of hell, or the force of karma). In other instances, the shamanic cosmos exists side by side with that of the world religion. In today's world, shaman traditions in some places remain underground due to persecution, or they can be tolerated or integrated with the dominant world religion.

Todd T. Lewis

See also ANIMISM; MEDIUM; NUMINOUS; ORACLE; TRANCE.

SHAMMAI

A Jewish sage and leader of the Sanhedrin, active in the first century B.C.E. He often appears in debate with Hillel, in comparison to whom he seems harsh and unyielding in matters of law and practice. Shammai's followers appear frequently in the rabbinic literature, where they are referred to as the "House of Shammai."

Alan J. Avery-Peck

See also HILLEL.

SHANG DYNASTY
(CA. 1750–1050 B.C.E.)

The second Chinese dynasty founded by King T'ang and the first recognizable state in China. Along with the Zhou, this was one of the first early periods in Chinese history where the foundation was established for later classical culture. The Shang people were located in north-central China, about five hundred miles southwest of present Beijing; they were primarily agrarian and possessed a fairly advanced sociopolitical culture for their time. Two significant religious developments emerged during this period that would greatly impact Chinese culture: first, devotion to ancestors became a central religious practice that led to the development of the ancestor cult in China; second, the Shang established a theocracy led by rulers who held power by virtue of their special relationship with divine beings and in particular with Shang-Ti (Supreme Lord). The kings were responsible, through ritual offerings, to maintain good relationships with the gods and Shang-Ti to bring blessings upon the people. Also during this period, divination became an important practice in governing, natural powers (wind, rain, and the like) were personified and honored, and a divine political hierarchy in the spirit world was established. According to archeological evidence, the Shang kings, who were wise and benevolent, enjoying the sanction and blessings of heaven, eventually became corrupt and cruel. As a result, heaven called upon the Zhou leaders to overthrow the Shang and institute a new dynasty, putting into practice the mandate of heaven (*t'ien ming*) to rule.

G. D. DeAngelis

See also ANCESTORS, CHINESE; SHANG-TI; T'IEN; T'IEN MING; ZHOU DYNASTY.

SHANG-TI

(Chinese, *Shang Di*; lit., Supreme Lord, Highest Divine Ruler). Popular during the Shang Dynasty (1750–1050 B.C.E.), he was the ruler of heaven and ruler of the spiritual world where he presided over an elaborate hierarchy of spirits. While he had no clearly defined character, he was perceived as a divine ancestor of the ruling family (Shang), and the divine ruler who watches over human society and regulates the working of the universe. His popularity began to fade during the Zhou Dynasty (around 1050–256 B.C.E.) as heaven began to take on a more impersonal status with an emphasis on the heavenly sphere (*t'ien*) rather than on a divine being.

G. D. DeAngelis

See also ANCESTORS, CHINESE; SHANG DYNASTY; T'IEN; ZHOU DYNASTY.

SHANKARA

See ADVAITA VEDANTA.

SHANTI

A Sanskrit term literally meaning "peace," frequently chanted in both Hindu and Buddhist recitations. (The classical example is the Upanishads' invocation and benediction "*Om Shanti Shanti Shanti.*") Shanti implies a host of associations and a religious ideal on both the cosmic and individual levels. World peace and harmony would be the proper realization of all beings if they recognized their interrelatedness in the world of rebirth (*samsara*) and acted accordingly to make good karma by not harming others (*ahimsa*). In both traditions as well, shanti implies an existential tranquility that comes through faith or meditation. Influenced by these notions, Mahatma Gandhi linked the attainment of world peace to justice, and taught that this was only attainable by cultivating the citizenry's religious faith, meditation, and the discipline of non-violence.

Todd T. Lewis

See also GANDHI, MOHANDAS K.; YOGA.

SHANTIDEVA

See SANTIDEVA/SHANTIDEVA.

SHARIA/SHARIᵖA

An Arabic word which literally means "the way to the watering hole." In Islam, *shariᵖa* is the "way" in the sense that it designates the correct path one must follow to learn God's will. It is normally translated as "law," though for Muslims, the "law of God" is far more than a set of rules or a statement of conventional behaviors. Because sharia is grounded in the very words God disclosed to the Prophet Muhammad (570–632) in the Qurᵖan, and because submitting in obedience to God is the obligation of all creatures, the law is understood as a way *to* life ("watering hole") and a way *of* life for all who believe in the one God. Sharia, therefore, is considered eternal and unchangeable because it comes from God—not from humans. It is also appreciated as a gift of God.

Besides giving humankind the Qurᵖan as the inerrant source of law, Muslims say that God directs believers through the words and deeds of the Prophet Muhammad. This second foundation of Islamic sharia is called *hadith*. Together with divine revelation in the Qur'an, the collections of "sound" or authentic hadith, compiled very early in Islamic history, establish additional moral norms that cannot be changed. The hadith are believed to convey a particular tradition (*sunna*) from the Prophet demonstrating how to fulfill one's duties toward God and other people.

Islamic theology differentiates between sharia, the law itself with its twin sources of the Qur'an and hadith, and *fiqh*, the attempt of human beings to interpret, understand, and apply the law. Fiqh may be understood as the science or discipline of jurisprudence whose task it is to determine what Muslims call "the straight path" (Qur'an 1:6) in situations not explicitly addressed in either the Qur'an or in the hadith of the Prophet. Traditionally, four sources of fiqh have been practiced and accepted to one extent or another by the major schools of law in Sunni Islam: *ra'y* (a ruling based on the opinion of a legal expert); *qiyas* (the use of an analytical case to render a decision); *ijtihad* (developing an understanding of a particular point of law when there is no clear precedent or analogy available); and *ijma* (consensus of legal opinion). Unlike the Shi'ites, who rely on an infallible *imam* (teacher) to guide the community by his personal, God-given authority, Sunnis invest no single person with such power. For them, it is the responsibility of the scholarly community to investigate carefully the teachings of the Qur'an and Islamic tradition in order to discern God's will for people. Four major *madhahib*, or schools of law, developed in Sunni Islam to provide systematic approaches to inter-

preting the will of God, and all four of these schools continue to influence Islamic jurisprudence to this day. They are known as Hanafite, Hanabalite, Malikite and Shafi'ite legal schools.

Islamic sharia recognizes five principles or categories of the law. They are: (1) mandatory and obligatory acts (for example, observing the Five Pillars); (2) recommended but not obligatory acts (for example, saying extra prayers each day beyond the *salat*); (3) acts toward which the law is indifferent (for example, flying an airplane); (4) acts that are discouraged (for example, remaining single and not raising a family); and (5) forbidden acts (for example, eating pork or drinking alcohol).

Ronald A. Pachence

See also FIQH; FIVE PILLARS (IN ISLAM); HADITH; HANAFITE; HANBALITE; IJMA; IJTIHAD; IMAM; MALIKITE; MUHAMMAD; QIYAS; QUR'AN; SALAT; SHAFI'TE; SHI'A/SHI'I/SHI'ITE/SHI'ISM; SUNNA/SUNNI/SUNNISM.

SHAVUOT

Hebrew, meaning "weeks," this is the Jewish Feast of Weeks or Pentecost.

Shavuot is a one-day or (in the Diaspora) two-day festival that occurs on the sixth (and seventh) day of the Hebrew month of Sivan, the ninth month of the Jewish calendar, corresponding to late May or early June.

Shavuot was originally an agricultural festival, marking the conclusion of the barley harvest that had begun at Passover and the beginning of the spring wheat harvest. That is why the holiday is called Shavuot, for forty-nine days, seven complete weeks, were carefully counted between Passover and Shavuot to make sure the spring harvest would take place at the correct time. Another name for Shavuot is *Chag HaKatzir*, the Festival of Harvesting or Reaping.

Later, the rabbis and sages infused Shavuot with another meaning. It became the commemoration of the giving of Torah at Mt. Sinai, for the sages concluded that it was exactly forty-nine days, seven complete weeks, from the exodus from Egypt until the Israelites stood at Sinai to receive the Law.

The major celebrations of Shavuot take place at the synagogue with worship services, including special prayers for the festival. To commemorate the giving of Torah on Shavuot, since the time of the Jewish mystics beginning in the sixteenth century, it has been custom to stay up all night on Shavuot studying Torah and other sacred literature. This custom is called *Tikkun Layel Shavuot*, literally "the prepared (texts) of the night of Shavuot."

Another Shavuot custom was established in the twentieth century in the United States by the Reform Movement. On Shavuot, many Reform (and some Conservative) synagogues hold Confirmation ceremonies, when the high school age students of the religious school mark the conclusion of their formal studies by "confirming" their beliefs in God and Torah.

On Shavuot it is customary to decorate the home and synagogue with flowers and greens, marking the spring harvest, and it is customary to eat dairy foods because the Children of Israel were "like babies" when they received Torah.

The festival of Shavuot affirms the centrality of Torah in Jewish life.

Wayne Dosick

See also PASSOVER; SEFIRAT HAOMER; SINAI; TORAH.

SHAWNEE PROPHET

During the difficult times when the eastern tribes were struggling to hold their own against the colonizing forces of the early nineteenth century, two Shawnee brothers arose to lead their embattled people. The older, Tecumseh, is well known for his military prowess. His younger brother, Tenskwatawa, born in 1775, emerged from a youth lost to alcoholism to speak from a transforming vision a message that would challenge his people to return to the traditional ways and reject the false morals they had picked up from the alien culture. He was heard as a prophet and became the spiritual leader of the resistance, alongside his brother.

Together they mounted the valiant but doomed resistance to Harrison and the Americans, uniting the Delawares and other similarly afflicted tribes in a pan-Indian vision that mobilized a concerted effort. Military efforts, even alliance with the British, and Tecumseh's powers of oration failed to forestall for long the inevitable end. In the Battle of Fallen Timbers, Tecumseh died, and the fight for the western border lands of Ohio and the sacred lands from there to the Great Lakes was lost forever. It was October 5, 1813. The Prophet was discredited and faded from sight.

Kathleen Dugan

See also PROPHECY; REVELATION.

SHAYKH

An Arabic word literally meaning "elder" in the sense of "old man." In Muslim societies, the word connotes leadership in religious matters or respectability because of one's personal holiness or scholarship. In the Ottoman Empire, the term became part of a title (*Shaykh al-Islam*) bestowed upon a religious leader who had specific religious duties in the government. In Sufism, a mystical spirituality in Islam, the *shaykh* was the "master" and spiritual guide of a particular group or order of Sufis. In Iran and India a shaykh is called *pir*.

Ronald A. Pachence

See also OTTOMAN; PIR; SUFI/SUFISM.

SHAYTAN
See IBLIS.

SHEKINAH
In Judaism, the worldly manifestation of God, as the deity is experienced by humankind, especially in contexts of revelation or in the perceived sanctification of specific objects, people, or locations. Derived from the Hebrew root signifying "to dwell," the Shekinah is often described as God's indwelling presence, that is, the aspect of God experienced as residing in earthly contexts.

First appearing in early postbiblical texts, the term Shekinah corresponds roughly to the "Logos" or "Holy Spirit" of early Christian thought. In Aramaic translations of the Hebrew Bible, the term translates expressions such as "face of God" and "glory of God." The Targums thus avoid attributing blatantly anthropomorphic features directly to God. In rabbinic texts, Shekinah is used more broadly, both to designate the physical manifestation of God and, on occasion, simply as another word for God.

Talmudic rabbis understood the term Shekinah metaphorically and did not view the Shekinah as a real, physical aspect of God. The talmudic literature presents descriptions of conversations between God and the Shekinah and images of the Shekinah's presence within this world, especially in the form of light

(for example, Exodus Rabbah 32:4). But such passages often are introduced with the caveat "as if it could be," making explicit their metaphorical sense.

Medieval Jewish philosophers avoided all possibility of anthropomorphism by describing the Shekinah not as a physical representation of God or as an aspect of God's essence but as an independent entity created by God. Saadiah Gaon (882–942) followed by Maimonides (1135–1204) describes the Shekinah as the intermediary between God and humans that accounts for prophetic visions. Following this same view, Judah HaLevi (about 1075–1141) holds that the Shekinah and not God appeared in prophetic visions. According to HaLevi, this same visible aspect of the Shekinah dwelled in the Temple in Jerusalem. A different, unseen, spiritual Shekinah dwells with every righteous Israelite.

Kabbalists defined the Shekinah as the sphere closest to the empirical world, of which it is the sustaining force. Representing the feminine principle, the Shekinah has no light of its own, but receives divine light from the other spheres. In the mystics' view, through prayer and following the commandments, Jews assist in reuniting the Shekinah with the heavenly masculine principle. They thus work to restore the original unity of God that had been destroyed by the people's sins, by evil powers, and as a result of the Jews' exile.

Alan J. Avery-Peck

See also KABBALAH; MAIMONIDES; SAADYA GAON.

SHEMA
Hebrew, meaning "listen" or "hear," this is the first word of the biblical verse known as Judaism's declaration of faith.

The Bible proclaims, "Hear O Israel, the Lord is our God, the Lord is One" (Deut

6:4). Because the belief in one, unique, singular, indivisible God is the centerpiece of Jewish theology, this verse, with its insistence of the oneness of God, is known as the Jewish "declaration of faith."

The verse has become one of the central prayers of the morning and evening Jewish worship service, and it is recited when going to bed each night. The Shema declaration/prayer is so quintessential to Jewish belief and practice that its words are to be recited with the dying breath of every Jew.

Wayne Dosick

SHEMINI ATZERET

(Hebrew, eighth day of convocation). In Judaism, the eighth and final day of the festival of Tabernacles (Lev 23:34-36), understood within postbiblical Judaism as a separate festival unto itself. On Shemini Atzeret, in the synagogue a special prayer that abundant rain will fall in the Land of Israel is said, and, as on the final day of all festivals, memorial prayers are recited. In the land of Israel, Shemini Atzeret coincides with the festival of Simhat Torah.

Alan J. Avery-Peck

See also SIMHAT TORAH; TABERNACLES, FEAST OF.

SHEMONAH ESREH

(Hebrew, eighteen). "The Eighteen Benedictions," the central prayer of the Jewish liturgy, known also as the Amidah ("Standing Prayer," since it is recited while standing) and, in the Talmudic literature, simply as HaTefillah ("The Prayer" par excellence). The Shemonah Esreh occurs in all Jewish worship services in a variety of formulations appropriate to the specific weekday, Sabbath, or holiday.

Originally comprised of eighteen benedictions, in Talmudic times a nineteenth was introduced, a malediction against heretics. These nineteen, recited during all daily worship services, include statements of God's power and prayers requesting that God grant to people understanding, forgiveness of sin, healing of the sick, ingathering of the Jewish people, humbling of the arrogant, the rebuilding of Jerusalem, and bringing the messiah. On Sabbaths and festivals, the Shemonah Esreh contains a smaller number of benedictions, with the requests found in the daily prayers replaced with a section that concerns the specific themes of the Sabbath or festival.

During daytime prayer services, the Shemonah Esreh is first recited silently by the congregation and then repeated by the prayer leader. During this repetition, the congregation joins with the leader in reciting the Kedushah. If an individual prays along, or if the required quorum of ten is not present, the Shemonah Esreh is not repeated aloud, and the Kedushah is not recited at all.

Alan J. Avery-Peck

See also BIRKAT HAMINIM; KEDUSHAH; LITURGY (IN JUDAISM).

SHEN

(Chinese, lit., gods, spirits). In Chinese folk religion, this is the generic term for kindly or beneficent spiritual beings: for example, deities or ancestors and protectors against kuei (ghosts). It is also used, at times, to refer to the spiritual essence of the yang soul (hun) or one's spiritual nature.

G. D. DeAngelis

See also ANCESTORS, CHINESE; HUN; KUEI.

SHEOL

The most frequently occurring name for the underworld, the abode of the dead in the Old Testament. Sheol may also designate death personified and all that is associated with Death. It is a place of gloom and darkness to which, originally, all of the dead go. It is not first and foremost a place of punishment for the wicked dead. Sheol was located in the subterranean regions of the earth, although some passages treat the grave and Sheol as identical. Water imagery is sometimes associated with Sheol (cf. Jonah 2:3-6). The gates of Sheol are mentioned several times in the Old Testament. The gates were intended to keep the dead in. As in Mesopotamian thinking, Sheol was the "land of no return," at least normally. Sometimes the spirits of the dead could be summoned by the living as Samuel was summoned by the woman of Endor for Saul (1 Sam 28). The dead in Sheol are called rephaim, a term known also from the texts of Ugarit where they are mentioned frequently.

Russell Fuller

SHEPHERD OF HERMAS

See HERMAS.

SHEVA BERAKHOT

See MARRIAGE (IN JUDAISM).

SHI'A/SHI'I/SHI'ITE/SHI'ISM

All four of these terms are derived from the Arabic expression, shi'at Ali, the "party" or "partisans" of a man named Ali ibn Abi Talib (598–661) who was the fourth caliph (successor of the Prophet Muhammad and Muslim leader). The terms are used interchangeably to refer to a sect of Islam that takes its name from Ali and his cause. Members of this sect are most commonly called Shi'ites.

Throughout its history, Islam has split into several branches or sects, but two are most prominent in the tradition: the Sunnis who compromise about 85 percent of the approximately 1.3 billion Muslims in the world, and the Shi'ites who make up about 10 percent of the Islamic population. This minority Islamic sect is further divided into several smaller groups, the three largest of which are the Imamis (or "Twelvers"), the Zaydis (or "Fivers"), and the Isma'ilis (or "Seveners"). Shi'ites belonging to one or more of these three groups are found today primarily in Iran, Iraq, Syria, Lebanon, Pakistan, Central Asia, and some of the Gulf States.

Shi'ite and Sunni Muslims agree on the basics of Islam. Both groups accept the validity of Muhammad's (570–632) prophecy and the legitimacy of the Qur'an as God's revealed and final Word to humankind. Both acknowledge the Five Pillars as the foundation of Islamic belief and practice. Both believe in the one God who rewards the just with eternal happiness and punishes evildoers forever in hell. Their differences, however, which are significant, are grounded in a dispute over who should have succeeded the Prophet Muhammad as caliph (Islamic leader). Over time, this difference of opinion developed into a further disagreement over the nature and function of authority itself within Islam.

The Issue of Succession

Sunni Muslims say that the Prophet Muhammad left no instructions regarding the selection of a successor (a claim disputed by the Shi'ites), so after the Prophet's death in 632, a few of his closest companions selected as the first caliph (leader) Abu Bakr (573–634), one of the earliest converts to Islam and the Prophet's father-in-law. The partisans of Ali objected on the grounds that Ali was the Prophet's cousin and son-in-law, and that the Prophet had intended him to assume the position of leadership. They were not convinced by arguments that Abu Bakr was twenty-five years older than Ali and much better suited for the office.

Though Ali had earned a reputation for being a fierce fighter for Islam, he was passed over for caliph twice more; in 634 when Umar was elected and in 644, when Uthman was chosen. It is said that Ali was actually offered the position after Umar's death if he agreed to carry out all his predecessor's policies. Ali refused and Uthman became the third caliph.

Finally, Ali was selected caliph in 656 after Uthman was murdered in what seems to have been an ongoing drama of political intrigue and insurrection that plagued the early Islamic community. In fact, his first task as caliph was to put down a revolt supported by one of the widows of the Prophet. Though successful in that effort, Ali faced further opposition from within his ranks (the Kharijites who abandoned him) and from pretenders to the caliphate under the leadership of a man named Muʾawiya who would soon found the Umayyad Dynasty after Ali's death and a brief period of rule by Ali's son, Hasan. In 661 Ali was assassinated by a Kharijite. His son, Hasan, the fifth caliph, capitulated to Muʾawiya and Husayn; his other son by Fatima (the Prophet's daughter) was killed by the forces of Muʾawiya in 680 at Karbala.

This saga of frustrated ambition and personal tragedy is the background for the development of Shiʿism. Partisans of Ali believe their leader was robbed of his right to lead the Islamic community, and

after the events of 680, they effectively split from the rest of Islam. The death of Husayn is commemorated by the Shiʿites each year in a manner reminiscent of how Christians mourn the execution of Jesus Christ.

Shiʿite Understanding of Authority

In the wake of their turbulent confrontation with those they claimed usurped Ali's prerogative to govern the Islamic community, the Shiʿites proceeded to develop their own theology of leadership— a theology they say is founded on the wishes of the Prophet Muhammad.

For them, the authority to lead Islam after the Prophet's death was given to the descendants of Ali, just as it had been given to Ali, by none other than God. Once identified as this divinely appointed leader, called an *imam*, Shiʿites accept the imam as God's infallible spokesman on earth. What is more, they hold that these imams are the only ones who can interpret the hidden meaning concealed in the Qurʾan. As such, they and they alone can communicate the secret wisdom revealed by God to Muhammad and disclosed by him to Ali, and subsequently to all other legitimate imams throughout history. From the time of Ali—even, as some Shiʿites would say, up until the present day—God has provided for an unbroken chain of inerrant leadership. The Shiʿites also say that one day in the future God will allow one of the early imams who has been "in hiding" to return and inaugurate a new golden age of Islamic justice. This "Hidden Imam," also called *al-Mahdi* ("the guided one"), will appear shortly before the end of the world, though not all Shiʿites agree on precisely which imam will fulfill this role. The Imami Shiʿites say it will be the twelfth imam; the Ismaʾilis claim that it will be the seventh; and the

Zaydis hold that the fifth imam will reappear as al-Mahdi.

Ronald A. Pachence

See also ABU BAKR; ALI; CALIPH (KHALIFA)/CALIPHATE; FIVE PILLARS (IN ISLAM); HUSAYN; IMAM; IMAM (THE HIDDEN IMAM); ISLAM; KARBALA; KHARIJITES; MAHDI; MUHAMMAD; MUSLIM; QUR'AN; SEVENERS (IN ISLAM); SUNNA/SUNNI/SUNNISM; TWELVERS (IN ISLAM); UMAR; UMAYYADS; UTHMAN.

SHILA

A Sanskrit term used in Buddhism glossed as "moral cultivation" or "virtue." *Shila* is one of the three divisions in the Buddhist spiritual path; it is the foundation necessary for successful *samadhi* (meditative concentration), and both are essential for the cultivation of salvific *prajna* (insight). These three can be used to divide the Noble Eightfold Path, with *shila* encompassing Right Speech, Right Action, and Right Livelihood. Moral perfection in Buddhism is defined in terms of the adhering to the eight or ten precepts.

Todd T. Lewis

See also NOBLE EIGHTFOLD PATH; PRECEPTS (BUDDHIST).

SHINGON

(Japanese, True Word School). This sect of Japanese Buddhism, which developed from the Chinese Chen Yen School, was founded in the ninth century C.E. by Kukai (774–835), one of the great figures of Japanese religious history. In recognition of his stature, Kukai was posthumously renamed Kobo Daishi or "master teacher of the Dharma." Kukai presented a ritual and doctrinal synthesis of Buddhist practice and teaching that made Shingon accessible to common people as well as monks and the nobility. In addition, his recogni-

tion of Dainichi (Great Sun Buddha; Sanskrit, Mahavairocana), the central deity and personification of the essence of the universe (Sanskrit, Dharmakaya or "truth body"), and Dainichi's connection with Amaterasu (Sun Goddess) made Shingon universally popular throughout Japan.

For Kukai, the Dai-Nichi Kyo (Great Sun Sutra) was the crown of Buddhist teaching and the key to higher knowledge from which all other teachings should be interpreted. He asserted that by teachings through mystical means, using tantric practices of hand gestures, chanting, meditation, and other rituals, one could become one with the essence of the universe and achieve Buddhahood in this lifetime. He also claimed two types of knowledge, lower and higher, for those at different levels of consciousness, with ultimately the lower leading to the higher.

The elaborate use of ritual and symbol, the claim of Buddhahood for all in this lifetime, and the charismatic figure of Kukai (Kobo Daishi), are all a part of the ongoing popularity of this school in Japan.

G. D. DeAngelis

See also AMATERASU; BODHI; BUDDHA; BUDDHISM; DHARMA (IN BUDDHISM); KOBO DAISHI.

SHINRAN (1173–1263)

One of the great saints in Japanese Pure Land Buddhism who shaped the subsequent development of a distinctive school bearing his name (Jodo Shin Shu). Like his teacher Honen (1133–1212), Shinran came to believe in the doctrine of *mappo* (age of spiritual decadence) and the uniquely effective force of the cosmic Buddha Amitabha's (Japanese, Amida's) vow to save humanity. Shinran traveled the countryside to preach on the need to take refuge in Amida, but unlike Honen he even abandoned the constant repetition of Amida's name (*nembutsu*) and other acts of spiritual "self power," since he felt humanity is helpless and completely dependent upon Amida's "other power" to avoid rebirth in purgatory. Shinran also gave up celibacy as a requirement of the Jodo Shin Shu sangha.

Todd T. Lewis

See also MAHAYANA BUDDHISM; MAPPO; PURE LAND BUDDHISM.

SHINTO

(Japanese, Way of the spirits/*kami*). The popular name for the Japanese religious tradition Kami-No-Michi. It is sometimes referred to as the national religion of Japan, but it is more a collective term referring to a complex of religious and national beliefs and practices, including ritual observances, folklore, nationalism, worship of *kami*, love of nature, myths, and so on. In a sense, it is more a celebration of the land, people, and culture of Japan than a systematically developed religion.

Shinto's roots are in the worship of kami (divine presences), a type of animistic practice that over time incorporated ancient beliefs, observances, rituals, and ceremonies. In response to Buddhist and Confucian influences around the seventh–eighth century C.E., Shinto began to take on the character of a state or national religion, developing a cosmology and worldview based on mythological tales found in the Japanese classics *Nihongi* and *Kojiki*. In these texts a vision of the world emerged where humans and nature were intimately related through the presence of kami. This was a reinforcement of the agrarian animistic tradition that already existed at the local level. In addition, a broader and more developed cosmological scheme emerged, depicting Japan as a place created by heavenly spirits and the emperor being a descendant of Amaterasu (Sun Goddess), the patron deity of Japan, and the Japanese people as descendents from other kami. In time, these myths led to a later Shinto view of the emperor as a divine being, Japan as a sacred land, and the Japanese people as a chosen people.

At different points in Japanese history efforts were made to organize these beliefs and practices into a national religion fostered by developments in social/political life and in reaction to the popularity of Buddhism, Confucianism, and Neo-Confucianism. While there have, at times, been institutionalized developments and divisions in Shinto—Sectarian (Kyoha), Shrine (Jinja, formerly State Shinto), Folk (Minkan) and the Imperial House (Koshitsu)—it remains primarily a collective term referring to various Japanese religious beliefs and practices, national observances, and Japanese patterns of social convention. There has never been any ethical development in the form of some binding moral code or commandments and very little theological speculation. Shinto is now one among many religious options for the Japanese but, in many ways, it is still a vital part of what it means to be Japanese.

G. D. DeAngelis

See also AMATERASU; DO; ISE; IZANAGI; IZANAMI; KAGURA; KAMI; KAMIDANA; KOJIKI; KOKORO; MAKOTO; MATSURI; NORITO; RYOBU.

SHIRK

Arabic word meaning "association" in the sense of "associating" something or someone of finite value with the infinite

God. In Islamic theology, *shirk* is the sin of idolatry or of atheism. The Qur'an, the sacred scripture of Islam, says that "to set up partners with Allah (God) is to devise a sin most heinous indeed" (4:48). In that same passage, it is suggested that God can forgive all sins except shirk. The concept of shirk is based upon Islamic faith in the radical unity and sovereignty of God who has no partners or equals.

Ronald A. Pachence

See also ISLAM; KAFIR; QUR'AN.

SHIVA

One of the two great Gods of classical Hinduism, along with Vishnu, Shiva is a relatively minor deity in the Vedas, emerging as an important image of the Supreme Being only the late *Shvetashvatara Upanishad*, the *Mahabharata*, and the Puranas. Shiva is important especially to several South Indian *bhakti* movements, a number of Tantric schools, and various sectarian ascetic movements. His devotees regard him as the Supreme Being and ultimate reality. Among Shiva's most common epithets are Mahadeva, "Great God," and Parameshvara, "Supreme Lord." He is depicted in myth and iconography as the primordial ascetic and yogi, meditating eternally on Mt. Kailas in the far reaches of the Himalayas, and also as the cosmic dancer, who manifests, sustains, and dissolves the universe with the dynamic but graceful gestures of his body. His most typical icon, however, is the linga, regarded as a symbol of cosmic creative energy. Shiva, unlike Vishnu, is not commonly thought to descend earth in the form of avataras.

Lance E. Nelson

See also AVATARA/AVATAR; HINDUISM; LINGA; LINGAYAT; NATARAJA; SHAIVA; VAISHNAVA; VISHNU.

SHIVAH

(Hebrew, seven). In Judaism, this is the period of mourning that lasts for seven days after the funeral. During this period, close relatives of the deceased are expected to remain at home, where daily prayer services are held and where visitors are received to offer condolences. Jews refer to the observance of this ritual as "sitting Shivah."

Traditionally, in the home in which Shivah is observed, mirrors are covered, a symbol of turning away from human vanity and a recognition that in the end all people face death. A candle is kept burning, the light serving as a symbol of the soul. Observing an ancient sign of mourning, the mourners themselves sit on low stools or the floor. Except under the constraint of severe financial loss, mourners are prohibited from conducting business and similarly do not engage in housework or other temporal matters. During Shivah they refrain from luxuries, including the donning of leather shoes and bathing or engaging in other activities solely for pleasure. In contemporary practice, members of the Conservative and especially the Reform movements do not invariably observe all these traditions and frequently sit Shivah for fewer than the traditionally mandated seven days.

Alan J. Avery-Peck

SHLOMO BEN YITZHAK

See SOLOMON BEN ISAAC.

SHOFAR

Hebrew, meaning "ram's horn." The *shofar*, a horn-like musical instrument made of a ram's horn, is used during Jewish worship on Rosh HaShanah, the Jewish New Year, and at the very end of the worship services on Yom Kippur, the Day of Atonement.

In biblical times, the shofar was used to call people together or to give warning if danger were near. On Rosh HaShanah the shofar is sounded to produce three different sounds: *teki'ah*, one long blast; *shevarim*, three short blasts; and *teru'ah*, nine short staccato blasts. Hearing the shofar sounded on Rosh HaShanah serves many purposes: it acclaims God as King; it recalls the giving of Torah at Mt. Sinai, where the sound of the shofar was heard as the commandments were given (Exod 19:19); it serves as a warning to worshipers to scrutinize their deeds and improve their conduct; it serves as a prelude to the announcement of God's judgment; and it serves as a reminder that one day the kingdom of God will be announced to the whole world. On Rosh HaShanah, when each worshiper honestly and sincerely comes humbly seeking forgiveness for transgression, the heart-piercing sound of the shofar is the perfect sound to lead the way to deep introspection and reflection, and the direct path to God.

Wayne Dosick

See also ROSH HASHANAH; SINAI; YOM KIPPUR.

SHOTOKU (574–622)

Among the most brilliant and influential rulers of Japan, he is often referred to by scholars as the founder of Japanese civilization due to the extraordinary developments in Japan during his reign. He played a major role in both establishing Buddhism in Japan and importing Chinese culture. Traditionally honored as the founder of Buddhism in Japan, he built the first large temple complex at Nara and also wrote commentaries on the Buddhist scriptures. In the teachings of the Buddha he saw both a profound philosophy of life and a sound foundation for the state, and was able to use Buddhism as a national religion and unifying ideology in order to transcend individual clan differences and interests.

G. D. DeAngelis

See also BUDDHA; BUDDHISM; DHARMA (IN BUDDHISM).

SHRADDHA

In Hinduism, the *shraddha* is a ritual offering to the ancestors involving balls of rice, sesame seeds, and water. As in Chinese religion, there is thought to be a reciprocal relationship between the dead and the living. Sustained by the shraddha offerings—performed, traditionally, by the eldest son—the ancestors in turn are able to promote the interests of their living descendants. The shraddha is the most important Vedic ritual still widely practiced.

Lance E. Nelson

See also ANCESTORS, CHINESE; HINDUISM; VEDAS.

SHRAMANA

A term for an individual ascetic or ascetic groups in ancient India who challenged the authority of the Vedas and the spiritual superiority of the Brahman caste. *Shramanas* were part of North India's axial age, an era of searching for spiritual principles to solve the new situation of urban life in the early states (800–300 B.C.E.). Most of these "heterodox" communities (sanghas) lived collectively, practiced some form of asceticism, engaged in public debates, and competed for the support of kings and householders. Among the shramanas were the well-known Buddhists and Jains, whose traditions survive to the present. There were also countless other groups at the time of the Buddha and Mahavira whose teachings did not endure: the Lokayata argued for materialist analysis of reality and strict empirical standards of ascertaining truth; led by their teacher Gosala, the colorful Ajivika school articulated a doctrine of cosmic fatalism and ascetic nudity that endured for over one thousand years. The Buddhists adopted the term to designate novice monks under probationary vows.

Todd T. Lewis

See also ASCETICISM/ASCETIC; SANGHA; YOGA.

SHRINE

A sacred place. Typically, shrines commemorate a holy person or an ancestor by housing relics or covering the tomb of the person. In some cases, shrines honor a spirit or spiritual force associated with the location itself. Shrines are important in Korean, Japanese, Islamic, and Christian traditions. Shrines are often considered places of spiritual power where sufferers of mental and physical ailments can be cured. The reasons pilgrims have for visiting a shrine may vary. Some explanations include: to heal illness, to attain worldly gains, to cure infertility, to fulfill a vow, to acquire a particular religious status, or to be possessed or blessed by the shrine's deity or spiritual force. Shrines may be attended by descendants of the individual, by religious experts or organizations, or the government civil servants. Shrines are often sources of revenue and political influence. They may also draw tourists or other nonreligious visitors.

In Islam, shrines are usually centered around tombs and graves of sacred individuals. One important exception (not a grave) is the principal shrine of Islam—the holy Kaaba at Mecca. This shrine orients the direction of prayer for Muslims. It is the main goal of the annual Hajj (pilgrimage). Muslims spend eight days to complete their visitation cycle of the significant shrines, including the tomb of the prophet Mohammed. In many religions, shrines that develop around tombs are associated with vows that pilgrims make. At Islamic shrines, pilgrims tie strings to the latticework of the shrine or nearby trees and donate gifts to the shrine.

In Japanese religious belief, *kami* are deities who are worshiped in natural settings. A specific location is set aside as sacred. Historically, these sites were marked by thatched buildings. The kami were invoked ritually with sacred objects and then sent away; they did not reside permanently in the shrine. Only rarely do Shinto shrines house paintings, sculpture, or other objects that would attract or house the kami. In the Shinto religion, shrines vary in size, style, and associated traditions. Usually they include an archway. This is passed through to a site of running water used for rinsing hands and mouth to purify; then the worshiper progresses along steps to the hall of worship. One must ring a bell, place money in the offering box, clap hands, bow, and pray silently.

Korean shrines are national; they include all the dynastic shrines of various ruling houses. Additionally, the Shrine to Culture is maintained at the National Academy in Seoul; altars to heaven and earth, the altar to god of land and grain, and government sponsored temples, such as the memorial to the Korean War dead and to a seventeenth-century general, all exemplify Korean shrines. At one time each shrine had scheduled ceremonies, carried out at government expense. Today, however, they are maintained as cultural property by voluntary or private associations.

Christian shrines include ones dedicated to the Virgin Mary, Christ, or various saints. They are often associated with pilgrimages, healing, and local and regional identity. Examples include the Shrine of Fatima, the Shrine of Guadalupe, and the Shrine of Lourdes. In the Americas, such shrines often combine indigenous and Christian beliefs and traditions.

Christine Greenway

See also HAJJ; ISLAM; MECCA; PILGRIMAGE; RELIC (OUTSIDE CHRISTIANITY); SAINT; STUPA; VOWS.

SHRUTI

In Hinduism, *shruti* (Sanskrit, "that which is heard") designates a class of scripture, the Vedas, as revelation. In the orthodox view, the Vedas are the eternal Speech (*nitya vak*) "heard" (not authored) by the seers (*rishis*) at the beginning of each of the endless cosmic cycles that the universe goes through. The shruti is also "heard" in the sense of being passed down orally over the generations from teacher to pupil, using elaborate techniques of memorization, being until relatively recently considered too sacred to commit to writing. The whole of the Veda —the Brahmanas, the Aranyakas, and the Upanishads as well as the Samhita—is considered shruti. As revelation, the shruti is distinguished from another class of scripture, the *smriti* (what is remembered), which is admitted to be of human authorship and is in theory regarded as less authoritative. The smriti literature includes the Dharma Sutras and Dharma Shastras (law books), the *Mahabharata* and the *Ramayana*, the Puranas, and other texts and commentaries. Although this is changing in modern Hinduism, only males of the twice-born caste categories were traditionally permitted to hear the shruti, whereas all Hindus were given access to the smriti texts. In certain Hindu denominations, favored smriti texts are given authority functionally equal to that of the Vedas. A notable example of this phenomenon is found in the Krishnaite schools of Vaishnavism, which—though they pay due homage to shruti—take the *Bhagavata Purana* in practice as their highest authority.

Lance E. Nelson

See also BHAGAVATA PURANA; HINDUISM; KALPA; MAHABHARATA; MANU SMRITI; RAMAYANA; REVELATION (IN OTHER RELIGIONS); YUGA.

SHUDRA

In the Hindu caste system, the *shudras* form—after the brahmins, the *kshatriyas*, and the *vaishyas*—the fourth of the four pan-Indian caste categories known as *varnas*. The shudra varna has traditionally been associated with manual labor and related occupations. Classified within this varna are many shudra castes (*jatis*), which are often further divided into smaller groups. Below the shudras in the social hierarchy are the untouchables or *dalits*.

Lance E. Nelson

See also BRAHMANA/BRAHMIN; CASTE; CASTES, SCHEDULED; HINDUISM; KSHATRIYA; VAISHYA.

SHULCHAN ARUCH

Hebrew, meaning "Prepared Table," this is a compilation of Jewish law written by Joseph Karo, about 1567, in the town of Safed in northern Israel.

Karo yearned for every Jew to follow God's law with precision and devotion, as a prelude to the coming of the messiah and the ultimate redemption of the world.

The *Shulchan Aruch* was his attempt to make the law clear and accessible to every Jew. It is written in a very concise, straightforward manner; the laws are simply listed without much reason or explanation given. The four volumes of the *Shulchan Aruch* are identical in structure, titles and subject division to the *Arba'ah Turim* written by Jacob ben Asher in Spain in 1475: *Orach Chayim*, "The Path of Life," dealing with laws and liturgy of prayer and the festivals; *Yoreh De'ah*, "The Teachings of Knowledge," dealing with ritual laws of everyday life; *Eben HaEzer*, "The Stone of Help," dealing with the laws of marriage and divorce; and *Choshen Hamishpat*, "The Breastplate of Judgment," dealing with Jewish civil law.

Karo was a Sephardic Jew who brought the influence of Sephardic custom to the writing of the *Shulchan Aruch*. Rabbi Moses Isserles of Poland, an Ashkenazic Jew, wrote commentary and dissenting opinion to the *Shulchan Aruch* based on Ashkenazic custom. With the addition of the commentary of Isserles—known as the *Mapat HaShulchan*, literally, "The Tablecloth of the Table"—the *Shulchan Aruch* became acceptable to and accepted by every segment of the Jewish community. It is the last formal compilation of Jewish law, and remains to this day the guide to all matters of Jewish law.

Wayne Dosick

See also ARBA'AH TURIM; HALACHAH.

SHUNYATA/SUNYA/SHUNYA

The doctrine of "emptiness" or "voidness" central to the analysis of the ultimate reality in many Mahayana Buddhist texts. It is the monk-philosopher Nagarjuna who first systematically discusses *shunyata*, making it one of the central notions in Mahayana philosophy throughout its subsequent scholastic history. This same theme is also found in the *Prajnaparamita* literature and is discussed most extensively in treatises by philosophers of the Madhyamaka school, who direct their arguments against the use of *dharma* analysis in the early *Abhidharmas*.

This doctrine that all domains of reality —physical, psychological, linguistic—are empty of self-sustaining or self-established existence is argued to be the logical extension of two early Buddhist doctrines: the *anatman* ("no soul") teaching and *pratitya-samutpada* ("dependent co-origination"). Like them, shunyata doctrine seeks to demonstrate that the world is an interconnected web of fluxing, interdependent phenomena; it shows that all assertions assuming the real, enduring existence of any entity ends up under scrutiny showing its inevitable dependence upon other entities to ascribe any meaning to it. The purpose of developing discourse on shunyata is ultimately religious: for an individual to apply this deconstruction process is to remove any grounds for attachment, gross or subtle, in one's experience. This dissolution of desire and attachment is a common goal of all Buddhist schools.

Language provides a good example of the shunyata analysis: the system of sounds and words that speakers of a given language use to express all manner of identifications, intentions, actions, and abstract meanings, are built upon a vast, interconnected set of arbitrary correspondences. Even though among speakers, words are mutually recognized and seemingly real, they are void of any "ultimate reality" and depend totally upon other words for their meaning. The discoveries of modern physics also provide another analogy: while we may be convinced of the reality of stainless steel and solid glass, under scrutiny these hard realities turn out to be constructed by our senses very erroneously and are moving, interdependent particles in flux.

The teaching of shunyata analysis was also employed for the religious goal of breaking beyond the superficial religious refuge of words and dogmas to experience oneself and the world without the mediation of linguistic constructs—through meditation. Most Mahayana Buddhist interpreters were careful to point out that shunyata was not an ontological state but a method to destroy false constructions of reality.

Todd T. Lewis

See also ABHIDHARMA/ABHIDHAMMA PITAKA; ANATMAN DOCTRINE; MADHYAMAKA/MADHYAMIKA SCHOOL; MAHAYANA BUDDHISM; NAGARJUNA; PRAJNAPARAMITA LITERATURE; PRATITYASAMUTPADA.

SIBYLLINE ORACLES

A collection of oracles purporting in its prose prologue to be utterances of Greek Sibyls, female ecstatics, of various periods. In actuality, the writings were done over many centuries, with some being of Jewish origin, others adapted by or composed by Christians. The dates of the Jewish sections of the material range from approximately the Maccabean period to the rule of Hadrian; the Christian parts seem to date from the late second century onward. This compilation, imitating the older pagan "Sibylline Books" written in Greek hexameters and characterized by the use of acrostics, consists of fifteen books. The flavor of the writings is monotheistic and messianic, their pagan format apparently having been chosen to attract pagan readers to Jewish or Christian teachings.

Some early Christian writers (for example, Theophilus of Antioch and Clement of Alexandria) who accepted the claim of pagan sibyllic origins, thought these texts gave pagan testimony to the truth of Christ and Christianity. Such assumptions paved the way for the preservation of the *Sibyllines* by early Christianity.

F. M. Gillman

See also APOCRYPHA.

SIDDHA

A Sanskrit term applied to accomplished yogins in both the Hindu and Buddhist traditions who have developed supernormal powers (*siddhi-s*). In Buddhism, coming into possession of these powers is not necessarily a sign of enlightenment, and monks are not to boast about them. In Hinduism, *siddhas* were assumed to have reached advanced spiritual accomplishment and some can use their powers to overcome death and aid disciples in extraordinary ways. The true siddha as *guru* (teacher), for example, is assumed capable of discerning a disciple's spiritual state using these powers. To Shaivas, Shiva as Adi-Natha is the "Supreme Siddha," the divine progenitor of perfection of whom all human adepts are incarnations.

Sages in the tantric yogin traditions were commonly referred to as siddhas; Buddhist tantric tradition developed a list of "The Eighty-four Siddhas."

Todd T. Lewis

See also GURU; TANTRIC BUDDHISM; TANTRIC HINDUISM; YOGA.

SIDDUR

Hebrew, meaning "order," this is the Jewish prayer book. The *siddur* is the structured, organized collection of Jewish prayers recited on weekdays and the Sabbath.

When prayers with words began to replace sacrifices of animals and agricultural products as the main method of Jewish worship, a regular structure of prayer times and prayer modes began to develop. As an agreed-upon order of prayer began to be fixed, the repository of the order of prayer, the prayer book came to be called siddur—order.

The first systematic siddur was outlined by Rabbi Amram ben Sheshna Gaon in the Babylonian Academy of Sura in about 870 c.e. Less than a century later, Rabbi Saadya Gaon compiled a more complete siddur that to this day still serves as the basic format of Jewish prayer.

The siddur is in Hebrew, but its words have been translated into every language of every country in which Jews have lived. It is the most flexible and fluid of all Jewish books, for some of its prayers were taken from the Bible; some were written by the rabbis and sages throughout the centuries; some are contemporary and have just been added to the siddur in the modern era. The siddur's fixed structure has given format to prayer, but its openness to accepting evolving ideas and words has permitted new inspiration for approaching God to come from each generation of Jews.

Wayne Dosick

See also AMRAM BEN SHESHNA GAON; MACHZOR; SAADYA GAON.

SIGHTS, FOUR PASSING

According to all accounts of the future Buddha Siddhartha's life as a householder, his spiritual maturity was hastened when he ventured out into the world for an encounter face to face with four realities. The Buddha's biographies describe his birth as a king's son and upbringing in a royal household, including the intricate arrangements made by his father to shelter him in isolation from life's harsh features and from knowing any alternative to taking over as heir apparent and member of the *kshatriya* (warrior) caste.

Eventually, Gautama chafes at these restrictions and insists on his charioteer's venturing out with him into the city where they encounter in successive incidents the four passing sights: a sick man, an old man, a dead man, and an ascetic. According to the texts, the future Buddha had not been exposed to the sick, the old, or to death. Seeing them destroyed his rosy projections of the good life lived without limitations; they caused both a strong feeling of compassion and tremendous turmoil. The effect of these three sights was Gautama's firm commitment to find a means to overcome these inevitable afflictions that conquer all humanity.

The fourth sight also directed him to a solution: toward renouncing the householder's life soon afterwards through his escape to the forest. This dramatic step was taken despite the objections of his father and wife, and despite that it meant abandoning his infant son. The texts also emphasize that the future Buddha's drive to conquer suffering and death was not for himself or his kin alone, but for the good of all. Thus, the four passing sights were the causes that led to the Buddha's awakening of universal compassion, emphasis on suffering, and his ardent and successful search for nirvana.

Todd T. Lewis

See also BODHISATTVA; BUDDHA; KARUNA; NIRVANA.

SIGN

The Western concept of sign attempts to articulate a deeply felt conviction that there is an intrinsic connection between the body, the mind, and other minds. This intrinsic connection makes up what is known as *sign*. The word "sign" can be traced to the Greek word *sema* that means "mark sign" and is the root for the related term *semantics*. Semantics concerns itself with the nature of "meaning." Indeed, a sign, above all, "perceives" meaning. It does this through the human process of *semiosis* (the work of many minds) in which a *sign* (a representative image or notion in a mind) and a *referent* (the object referred to) are brought together to produce a particular *meaning*. Augustine put it this way in his *De Doctrina Cristiana*: "a sign is a thing which, over and above the impression it makes on the senses, causes something else to come into the mind as a consequence of itself." The most general characterization of a sign, however, is given in the medieval formula, *aliquid stat pro aliquo:* "that which stands for another."

Both the medieval and Augustinian definitions of sign leave ambiguous the relationship between the mind and the referent. Does the sign simply allow the mind to recognize the sign's referent or does the mind also play a role in the nature of the sign? This question basically turns on the distinction between sense and reference. The sense of a sign implies a social process (other minds) through which a sign gains a "sense" to some mind. As such, the mind plays a great role in the signification process. The reference of a sign, on the other hand, implies a simple recognition by some mind of the sign's referent. As such, the mind plays little role in the signification process. Those definitions of the signs that give the mind a great role to play are called *triadic* because they involve three elements—the sign, its referent, and the mind. Those definitions of the sign that give the mind

a lesser role to play are called *dyadic* because they primarily involve only two elements—the sign and its referent. Charles de Saussure's definition of sign is perhaps the most influential dyadic notion of sign in contemporary times. According to Saussure, a sign is a "two-sided psychological entity," that is, an arbitrary relationship between a *concept* (the signified) and a *sound-image* (the signified). Saussure's definition has become the basis for a generalized theory of linguistics and the most influential understanding of sign in Europe. Charles Peirce's definition of sign, on the other hand, corresponds to a triadic definition of sign. According to Peirce, "a sign, or representamen, is something which stands to somebody for something in some respect or capacity." Peirce's definition of sign has become the basis for a general science of signs and the most influential understanding of sign in America.

Alex García-Rivera

See also SEMANTICS; SEMIOTICS; SYMBOL; SYMBOLICS.

SIGNS OF THE TIMES

This expression came to be frequently used in Catholic theological and pastoral writings during and after the Second Vatican Council, and it is sometimes used today. The Second Vatican Council (especially in the constitutions *Lumen Gentium* and *Gaudium et Spes*) employed the phrase as a way of indicating the trends and elements of contemporary cultures and societies the church (in its theology and its pastoral practices) had to take seriously into consideration. The council understood that the providential will of God was also expressed through the signs of the times; therefore, the signs of the times require serious discernment on the part of Christians. Today the same intuition is more often expressed in theology through various other concepts and means.

Orlando Espín

See also CULTURE; DISCERNMENT; GAUD-IUM ET SPES; LUMEN GENTIUM; THEOL-OGY; VATICAN, SECOND COUNCIL OF THE.

SIKHISM

A reform, devotional movement originating in the fifteenth-century Punjab (India) that drew strongly upon religious elements of both *bhakti* Hinduism and Islam. Sikhism owes its origin to a charismatic teacher, Guru Nanak (1469–1539), whose spiritual experience at age thirty was summarized by the pronouncement, "There is neither Hindu nor Muslim, so whose path shall I follow? I shall follow God's [lit., *"Niranjan's"*] path. God is neither Hindu nor Muslim and so the path I follow is God's."

For the next thirty years, Nanak drew disciples through his wide-ranging wanderings, reputedly including Tibet, Sri Lanka, and even Mecca; when he returned to the Punjab and settled into an *ashram*, he built the first community of Sikhs based upon his teachings. ("Sikh" simply means "disciple.") The community life he began was based upon the singing of hymns at the beginning and end of the day, and with fulfilling one's duties to family and fellow disciple, considered a sacred duty.

Nanak designated a successor to lead the Sikh community, and the next nine Gurus are respected equally as carriers of revelation's "divine light." From the fourth Guru onward, all are from the same lineage, acceding to Guruship hereditarily.

The City of Amritsar, begun by the Fourth Guru, and its Golden Temple, built by Arjan, the Fifth Guru, later became the center of the faith. The latter

Guru also began the definitive compilation of the *Adi Granth* ("Original Book"), the collection of hymns that would unite and guide the growing number of Sikh communities spreading across the Punjab.

The Tenth Guru, Gobind Singh, founded an important Sikh subgroup, the Khalsa Panch. Members who swore utter loyalty to the Guru were initiated and took vows to adopt the "5 K-s" (all beginning with "k" in Punjabi): unshorn hair, a comb, a sword, steel wristlet, and short trousers. He encouraged all Sikh men of the Khalsa to wear a turban (like the Gurus) and adopt the same last name (Singh, "lion"); women likewise were to use the same last name, Kaur ("princess"). These changes reflected the religious ideal of ending caste practices and distinctions as against Hindu members of society. The Tenth Guru also designated the now closed and codified *Adi Granth* as "The Guru" for all future generations. The Khalsa was central in defending the Sikh community against later repression by Mughal rulers after Akbar.

Sikh doctrines draw upon *nirguna bhakti*, the Hindu theology that sees the divine as beyond human conception. Sikhs rejected the doctrine of divine incarnations (*avataras*), the practice of worshiping idols, asceticism, pilgrimage, and all forms of caste pollution observance. It also rejected the authority of the Vedas and the role of the Brahman priest as intermediary. All castes could convert to Sikhism. While these teachings were compatible with Islamic theology, Sikh theology does differ strongly with Islam in accepting the reality of karma and rebirth, with liberation from rebirth coming only to one who admits God as inner Guru and responds to that voice by obedient living. The most important expression of this obedience, the opposite of self-centered living, is adopting the practice of *nam simran*, permeating one's life with God-awareness primarily by individual and corporate hymn singing. It is only by the grace of the divine that salvation comes.

Todd T. Lewis

See also NANAK; SAINT.

SILA/SHILLA

A term for Buddhist moral practice, the first of three basic stages on the path to enlightenment.

Todd T. Lewis

See also PARAMITA.

SIMEON STYLITES (390–459)

A shepherd, Simeon entered the monastery of Eusebonas where he was renowned for his austerities. In order to escape the large number of pilgrims he attracted, Simeon began to live atop a column that gradually increased in height, reaching some sixteen meters before his death. A large church and monastery where built around Simeon and his tower and tourists flocked to the holy site. Simeon thus became the first of the "Stylite" or pillar saints. A second Simeon took to a pillar in 541 near Antioch, and he is sometimes referred to as Simeon the Stylite the Younger to distinguish him from his more famous predecessor.

Gary Macy

See also MONASTICISM IN EASTERN CHRISTIANITY.

SIMHAT TORAH

(Hebrew, "rejoicing of the Torah"). In Judaism, the final day of Tabernacles on which, in the synagogue, the annual cycle of weekly readings of the Torah is completed and begun anew. To celebrate, Torah scrolls are carried around the synagogue in seven processions, and each person is given the opportunity to recite the benediction that accompanies the reading of the Torah. The one who recites the benediction over the final passage in the book of Deuteronomy is called "bridegroom of the Torah," and the one who says the benediction immediately following, for the beginning of the Torah, is called "bridegroom of Genesis."

In Diaspora synagogues in which festivals are celebrated on two days instead of the single day prescribed by Scripture, Simhat Torah is an independent day, following Shemini Atzeret. In the land of Israel and in Reform congregations, where only one festival day is celebrated, Shemini Atzeret and Simhat Torah coincide.

Alan J. Avery-Peck

See also SHEMINI ATZERET; TABERNACLES, FEAST OF.

SIMONY

Derived from the story (and name) of Simon Magus in Acts 8, the term "simony" refers to the sale or purchase (for money or other benefits) of religious objects, spiritual benefits, or ecclesiastical positions. It has always been strictly forbidden in Christian tradition and church legislation, but it has been a frequent temptation in the history of most Christian denominations.

Orlando Espín

See also CANON LAW; ECCLESIOLOGY; ETHICS; SIN, PERSONAL.

SIMUL IUSTUS ET PECCATOR

A Latin phrase meaning "at once righteous and a sinner," the concept is central to Luther's theology. According to Luther,

Roman Catholic theology had promoted the anxiety of sinners, even forgiven sinners, who were made to see themselves as on an uncertain path toward righteousness. Sinners making progress toward righteousness and away from sin had always to fear a reversal of direction, and could never be certain of their status before God. In Luther's theology, forgiven sinners, pardoned by grace alone and in no way through their own merits, are simultaneously righteous in the sight of God on account of the righteousness of Christ imputed to them, *and* still sinners on account of their sin. Christians, placing their trust in Christ alone, can thus put aside fear and anxiety about their standing before God.

Thomas Worcester, s.j.

See also FIDES FIDUCIALIS; GOOD WORKS; IMPUTATION; JUSTIFICATION; LUTHER, MARTIN; REFORMATION; RIGHTEOUSNESS; SOLA FIDE; SOLA GRATIA.

SIN (IN JUDAISM)

In Judaism, an act that transgresses the provisions of the covenant with God, delineated in Jewish law. Scripture uses a number of terms to refer to sin, including "het" (a failure to carry out a duty), "pesha" (a breach of covenantal responsibility), and "avon" (crookedness or transgression). Postbiblical Judaism most commonly uses the term "averah," from a root meaning "to go beyond." The term connotes the idea of transgression of God's will. Rabbinic interpretation additionally plays upon its relationship to the concepts of passing forth or making public, stating that though a person might sin in private, God will reveal the matter in public (Babylonian Talmud Sotah 3a).

Judaism distinguishes sins of omission, in which the individual fails to do what he should, from sins of commission, in which he does what is expressly prohibited. Sins of commission generally are considered more serious, since they involve a conscious act on the part of the individual. The most severe sins are murder, idolatry, and sexual impropriety, the only sins that one must not commit even under duress, to prevent being killed him- or herself (Babylonian Talmud Sanhedrin 74a).

Judaism holds that people have an inclination to engage in wrong actions ("yetser ha-ra"; see Gen 8:21), but the concept of this inclination is not equivalent to the Christian idea of original sin. According to Judaism, people do not have an inherited, corrupt nature; rather, they are subject to temptation, a monstrous force that must constantly be fought. Judaism recognizes that the reason for the existence of death is Adam's sin, so that all people suffer for that first misdeed. But it sees each person's own actions as the proximate cause of his or her death. While death was instituted with Adam, people die as a consequence of their own sins (Tanhuma Genesis 29; Tanhuma Hukkat 39).

Though Judaism recognizes the temptation toward sin as a force to be consistently fought, some early rabbis also saw in temptation one of life's motivating powers. Babylonian Talmud Yoma 69b relates that, when the men of the great synagogue succeeded in capturing the yetser ha-ra for three days, they discovered that, during that time, no productive activity took place. Similarly, Genesis Rabbah 9:7 states that, were it not for the yetser ha-ra, people would not be motivated to engage in business, marry, raise a family, or construct a house. Human productivity thus is viewed as a positive result of people's need constantly to rise above their tendency toward evil. This occurs when people recognize the ever present eyes and ears of God (Mishnah Abot 2:1) and when they study Torah and practice Judaism's religious law (Babylonian Talmud Sotah 21a).

Alan J. Avery-Peck

See also MITZVOT; REPENTANCE (IN JUDAISM).

SIN (SOCIAL, STRUCTURAL)

Broadly defined, sin in the Christian perspective is whatever prevents humanity's attainment of the fullness of relationship with God. In the Western theological tradition, sin prevents beatitude; in the Eastern tradition, sin prevents deification or *theosis*. In Christianity, because Jesus commanded his followers to love both God and neighbor, loving God and seeking full relationship with God are inextricably interconnected with loving neighbor and seeking full relationship with neighbor. Scriptural commandments to either do or not do certain acts must be understood and appropriately interpreted as either promoting or rupturing this foundational divine-human-neighbor relationship, all the parties to which are negatively impacted by sin.

Although Christianity has spilled much ink and blood attempting to understand and regulate perceived sexual sin, the scandal of the larger category of social sin (of which sexual sin is one component) has gone largely unnoticed, and has often been (and continues to be) perpetuated by Christianity itself. Instead of recognizing an individual (or oneself) as a brother or sister in Christ, or as a child of God made good in God's image and likeness, with all the dignity and worth that attend these statuses, social sins are those sins that involve the dehumanizing and un-dignified disregard for others (or oneself) who are treated as objects and used as means to pursue one's own ends, whether tangible or intangible. Social sins are especially heinous when committed against disadvantaged and/or vulnerable individuals. Examples of social sin include stealing, exploitation, fraud, deception and lying, malice and maliciousness, abuse, rape, human trafficking, bigotry, discrimination, and extortion. Individuals who wield social influence and power are able to transfer their personal social sins into the foundational, everyday, and often legal structures of society. Inasmuch as social sin becomes structural sin through this transference, social sin can—paradoxically and deceptively—be both avoided and routinely committed. For example, individuals may not directly exploit or steal from other people, but the energy company that provides their utilities may exploit and steal from its poorly paid and uninsured workers who log unpaid overtime in unsafe energy plants. Likewise, individuals may claim that they are not bigots while nevertheless participating in social institutions and cultural scripts that are deeply racist and/or sexist. While it is difficult enough to cease committing personal social sins, in an era of rampant globalization the uprooting of structural sin is an intimidating and formidable Christian obligation.

Rooted in the Christian social tradition and as a response to the industrial revolution, Christian theology in the late nineteenth century began to address explicitly the import of Jesus and the Gospels for society, especially economic and labor conditions. Notable breakthroughs occurred in the Protestant world with Walter Rauschenbusch's *A Theology for the Social Gospel*, and in the Roman Catholic world with the issuance of the papal encyclical *Rerum Novarum*. Twentieth- and twenty-first-century liberationist theologies have picked up on social Gospel impulses, and have extended considerations of social and structural sin beyond exclusively economic concerns to include race, sex, gender, sexual orientation, colonialization, globalization, environmental exploitation, and the various ways in which social sins have been structurally codified in society and even in Christian theology itself.

Meghan T. Sweeney

See also DISCRIMINATION; ECOLOGY; FEMINIST THEOLOGIES; HOMOPHOBIA; LATIN AMERICAN THEOLOGIES; PATRIARCHY; SEXISM.

SIN, ORIGINAL

A Christian theological term, "original sin" is used to refer to the fall of humankind, as narrated in Genesis 3:1-24. The story of the Fall is not mentioned anywhere else in the Old Testament (except as a passing remark in Ezek 28:11-16). The New Testament mentions it in Romans 5:12-21, and again in 1 Corinthians 15:21-22 and in 1 Timothy 2:13-14. Evidently, the biblical teaching on original sin is a Christian development (Paul's) based on one Hebrew text whose correct interpretation would probably not allow for most Christian theological elaborations on original sin. Be that as it may, original sin is a very crucial concept in Christianity.

The concept itself does not really focus on Adam's sin itself but on the serious damage done to human nature by that first human sin. Obviously, the very notion of a sin that has so damaged human nature assumes that all humans have thereafter descended from that first sinful human being, and that the first human being somehow communicated this "original" sin's consequences to all succeeding generations (thereby damaging all other humans' inherited nature).

The first developments of the doctrine of original sin, after the New Testament, seem to have come from the controversies against Gnosticism during the second century. The concept soon developed into a key component in most christological and soteriological discussions. Western Christian theologians (Tertullian, Cyprian of Carthage, Ambrose of Milan, Augustine of Hippo) gave original sin more attention than their Eastern counterparts. By the Council of Orange (in 529), the doctrine of original sin was firmly established and widely accepted in Western theological thought. Augustine of Hippo's teaching on the subject became the norm for mainstream Christian theology during the Middle Ages. With the Reformations in the sixteenth century, all sides attempted to interpret Augustine and the biblical witness. Trent, Luther, and Calvin all assumed the existence and reality of original sin, although they differed as to its consequences and the depth of the damage done to human nature. Trent was the more optimistic (or perhaps, less pessimistic), while Calvin was the most pessimistic.

A mainstream contemporary understanding of original sin usually avoids the scientifically impossible ideas of so-called "creationism" and of the single individual as parent of the entire human species. These ideas are not necessary for a theological concept of original sin. Rather, what is emphasized is the reality of sinfulness, and of the unavoidable human inclination to sin. This sinfulness is understood as universal (historically and geographically) as well as individual; it is not extrinsic to humanness (to human "nature"), having seriously wounded it beyond self-healing. Therefore, this human sinfulness makes salvation impossible without God's grace and loving intervention. Since this condition of sinfulness is not the result of individual human beings' sins (rather, these are a consequence of the former), and since this sinfulness has been suffered by all human generations, it can be referred to as the "original sin." Furthermore, a contemporary theological understanding will take seriously the contributions and insights of the cultural and social sciences, and will indeed see structural sin, social injustices, and the like as consequences, too, of original sin, and equally in need of and involved in the process of salvation.

There is no equivalent to "original sin" in any of the other world religions.

Orlando Espín

See also AUGUSTINE OF HIPPO; CALVINISM; CATHOLIC TRADITION; CONCUPISCENCE; COUNTER-REFORMATION/CATHOLIC REFORMATION; FAITH; GNOSIS/GNOSTICISM; GRACE; JUSTIFICATION; LUTHERANISM; NATURE, HUMAN; ORANGE, COUNCIL OF; ORIGINAL JUSTICE; PELAGIANISM; PREDESTINATION (IN CHRISTIANITY); PROVIDENCE; REFORMATION; SALVATION; SEMI-PELAGIANISM; SIN, PERSONAL; THEOLOGICAL ANTHROPOLOGY; TRADITION (IN CHRISTIANITY); TRENT, COUNCIL OF.

SIN, PERSONAL

In Christian theology, the concept of personal sin indicates the capacity of the human person (as rational and free) to reject God by means of evil action. Sins are committed when an agent recognizes an action is evil and freely chooses to do it. In the Roman Catholic tradition, personal sins are often referred to as *mortal*

and *venial*, a distinction that customarily indicates the seriousness of the evil act. A mortal, or deadly, sin involves grave matter, like premeditated murder, and breaks the human–divine relationship completely. Without sacramental absolution a mortal sin precludes the possibility of eternal salvation. Venial sins involve lesser values, but if part of a pattern, can be seen to undermine the agent's relationship with God.

Recent developments in Roman Catholic moral theology, like the concept of fundamental option, challenge this traditional distinction, suggesting that it is not the seriousness of the action that causes the break with God as much as it is the level of freedom engaged by the action. This view suggests that any action— whether grave or not—that violates the command to love God and neighbor *and* engages the human capacity for ultimate determination can reflect the agent's definitive rejection of God.

Brian F. Linnane, s.j.

See also CONCUPISCENCE; CONTRITION; FORGIVENESS; FREE WILL; FUNDAMENTAL OPTION; GUILT; MORAL THEOLOGY/CHRISTIAN ETHICS; PERSONALISM; RECONCILIATION, SACRAMENT OF; SCRUPLES; SCRUPULOSITY; SIN, ORIGINAL; SIN (SOCIAL, STRUCTURAL); VERITATIS SPLENDOR; VICE.

SINAI

The name of the Mountain of God in the Sinai desert, were Yahweh affirmed the covenant with the Israelites by giving the Ten Commandments (Exod 18–24).

Sinai is used in both the Yahwist Tradition and the Priestly Tradition in the Pentateuch, while the name Horeb is used in Deuteronomy and other materials to refer to the Mountain of the Lord. In the oldest biblical traditions, Sinai seems to have been the dwelling place of Yahweh, hence the Israelites are led to Sinai after Yahweh freed them from Egypt. Gradually the place of Sinai is taken by Zion that, as the location of God's Temple, also became the place of God's dwelling.

The actual location of the biblical Sinai is unknown; speculation revolves around a number of mountains in the Sinai desert.

Russell Fuller and Wayne Dosick

SINS, SEVEN DEADLY

A list of the roots or sources of all sins, that is, thoughts, words, or actions (or lack of actions) that disobey the central Christian command to love God and neighbor as oneself and thereby break right relations with God, with others, and with the earth. The list basically consists of (in alphabetical order) anger, envy, gluttony, greed, lust, pride, and sloth, although over the history of Christian thought theologians have differed about the order, number, and kinds of sinful dispositions in the list of deadly, major, or (sometimes called) capital sins.

Augustine, the fourth- to fifth-century bishop of Hippo in North Africa, interpreted Genesis 3 (the Fall) to argue that sin, especially original sin, results from the root sin of pride, from a free, voluntary, deliberate choice to reject God and to turn the human will away from a healthy dependence on God, as well as from an interdependent relationship with others and the earth. A prideful turning away of the human will from God is the origin of sin, and this original turning away from God has affected all human beings, leading to a universal sinful human condition as well as to actual sins or individual sinful acts that follow from this condition. The fourth-century Egyptian

monk Evagrius Ponticus delineated a list of eight dispositions that endangered monastic life and that encouraged other sins. In the sixth century, Pope Gregory the Great extended the list of capital sins to include vainglory (as separate from pride), and applied it beyond monastic life to explain certain tendencies in human nature that prevented cultivating a good Christian life. The thirteenth-century Scholastic theologian Thomas Aquinas recombined pride and vainglory, as well as retitled the list as capital sins, in order to stress their ability to generate other sins, capital being derived from the Latin *caput* meaning "head." As historians of Christian thought have demonstrated, the list of capital sins significantly impacted medieval European Catholic sacramental life; in the thirteenth century, it was used together with the Ten Commandments to assist in the examination of conscience and in confession.

More contemporary theologians have engaged in constructive theological reflection on the capital or major sins in light of gender, class, race, and sexuality; they critically deconstruct traditional theologies of sin in order to articulate a more adequate theology of sin based on everyday human experiences in different historical and sociopolitical contexts. U.S. feminist theologians, such as Valerie Saiving, Judith Plaskow, and Serene Jones, have proposed gendered accounts of sin. In pervasively patriarchal societies, the sin of pride (self-aggrandizement and social domination) may more properly apply to some men, whereas some women in such societies may lack a strong sense of self and thereby lose or diffuse themselves in relationships; thus, women may tend toward the sin of self-abnegation or apathy about self-actualization. While Western Christian theology often focuses on the individual reality of sin that follows from a sinful human nature, Latin American liberation theologians have called attention to both the personal and social dimensions of sin, especially the sin of greed (avarice, acquisitiveness) as it is embodied and embedded in personal acts and social structures that reinforce gross inequities of material wealth and poverty. African American womanist theologians have deepened theological reflection on the personal and social nature of sin by analyzing the complex interrelations of race, class, and gender to distinguish the specific expressions of sins of oppressors and of victim-survivors of oppression. For Delores Williams, the broad range of social structures associated with racism stem from the sin of pride, of white Western male supremacy, while victims of those structures, and especially women, commit the sin of self-loathing by internalizing the prevailing rhetorics of racism, sexism, and classism. The point of feminist, liberationist, and womanist theologies of sin is that personal sins, or an individual's sinful acts, impact larger sociocultural, economic, and political structures in ways that reinforce structural sins or social dimensions of sin, like racism, sexism, and poverty. While personal and structural sins are mutually reinforcing, structural sin in no way grants absolution from responsibility for personal (or sometimes called actual) sins, whether committed by oppressors or victims in those structures. Contemporary contextual theologies take issue with the notion that certain dispositions lead to or engender sin.

Finally, theologians who work with victim-survivors of domestic and sexual abuse like Mary Potter Engel and Marie M. Fortune have innovatively argued that traditional Christian theology often associates sin (that is, anger, pride) with the necessary, healthy strategies that enable physical and psychological recovery of victims from such abuse. Rather than classified as capital or deadly sins, some of their human tendencies or dispositions are vital to reclaiming and maintaining a healthy self-identity in the context of trauma, violence, and recovery.

Rosemary P. Carbine

SITZ IM LEBEN

A German phrase meaning "setting in life." It is used in form criticism in a technical sense to denote the socioreligious context—preaching, teaching, moral exhortation, worship—in which the smaller units of the biblical texts functioned before authors placed them in their literary contexts.

F. M. Gillman

See also FORM CRITICISM; PERICOPE.

SIX SYSTEMS OF HINDU PHILOSOPHY

See DARSHANA (PHILOSOPHY).

SKANDHA

Literally "heaps" or "aggregates" in Sanskrit and Pali, a Buddhist term indicating the most elementary division of the phenomena defining "the human being." The five *skandhas* are: *rupa*, the physical body that is made of combinations of the four elements (earth, water, fire, air); feelings (*vedana*) that arise from sensory contact; perceptions (*samjna*) that attach categories good, evil, neutral to sensory input; habitual mental dispositions (*samskara-s*) that inject karma-producing will to mental action; and consciousness (*vijnana*) that arises when mental and physical organs come in contact with the external world.

Buddhism recognizes six consciousness types based upon the five senses and mind. Most Buddhist analysts understood Buddhism's soulless rebirth process as the migration of the *vijnana* skandha to a new womb.

Todd T. Lewis

See also ANITYA; BUDDHISM.

SKHAK

See TABERNACLES, FEAST OF.

SLAVERY

In the United States, an economic institution of capitalism, built on racism and sexism, for the systematic attempted brutalization and the super-exploitation of kidnapped Africans, and the reproduction (through white men's rape of slave women) of chattel slaves. From the seventeenth to the nineteenth centuries, enslaved Africans, numbering in the millions, had no rights over their bodies, including their sexuality and their work, and no right to maintain family bonds.

But slavery in its modern versions consists of various forms of U.S. economic apartheid, and exists on a continuum determined by the needs of the developing capitalist system. For example, while chattel slavery was useful for the early accumulation of capital, it was too rigid for later industrial development. Two and a half centuries of legal slavery have given way to other enslaved forms of existence for African Americans like sharecropping, prison labor, the lowest rungs of wage labor, and the highest rates of unemployment that are most beneficial for generating profits for the owners and controllers of capital.

Technological capitalism continues to build itself on the ongoing economic exploitation and political repression of non-dominant peoples, including the white working class. For example, white mill-workers in nineteenth-century New England textile factories thought of themselves as enslaved, and marched and sang in protest against their "slavery." Contemporary versions of slavery include the fact that in the U.S., the low-wage, low-benefit, dead-end jobs of the secondary labor market sector, and the sweatshop jobs of the underground economy of unregulated capitalism are monopolized by poor whites, and people from diverse communities of color and their children.

Mary E. Hobgood

See also CLASSISM; RACISM; VICTIM; WORK/EMPLOYMENT.

SMARTA

See HINDUISM.

SMITH, WILFRED CANTWELL (1916–2000)

A minister in the United Church of Canada and a pioneering historian of religion, Wilfred Cantwell Smith specialized in Islamic Studies and in comparative religion. In 1948, he received his doctorate in Islamic Studies from Princeton University, and immediately thereafter in 1999 taught at McGill University in Montreal, Canada, where he founded the Institute of Islamic Studies and published a major work, *Islam in Modern History* (1957). From 1964 to 1973, he directed the Center for the Study of World Religions at Harvard University; he returned to teach at Harvard from 1978–84. While chairing the undergraduate and graduate programs in religious studies in the faculty of arts and sciences at Harvard, Smith turned his scholarly interests more principally toward the articulation of a Christian theology of world religions, published in his book *Towards A World Theology* (1981).

Smith emphasized a practical, dialogical, and interdisciplinary approach to the study of religion that examined religion as a lived way of life expressed in texts, practices, symbols, rituals, and personal encounters across religions, rather than as purely privatized beliefs or institutionalized beliefs. In *The Meaning and End of Religion* (1963), Smith traced the history of the term "religion" and different Western academic approaches to the study of religion; he also carved out his own academic approach to religious studies that abandoned the term "religion" altogether and instead distinguished between subjective and objective categories of faith and tradition, with a particular emphasis on the former subjective, lived experiences of actual persons of faith. In later works, Smith further developed the category of faith to include faith in the transcendent, and proposed that religious studies has to do with the exploration of varied human responses to the transcendent. Critics of Smith disagree with the apparent application of Christian terms and categories to the study of non-Christian religions, as well as object to an opposition between insiders and outsiders that is implicit in the distinction between faith and tradition.

Rosemary P. Carbine

SNAKE-HANDLING

See PENTECOSTALISM.

SOBORNOST

A Russian term roughly equivalent to the English terms "catholicity" and "conciliarity." It is used in Russian Orthodox theology to indicate that all persons in the church retain their individual autonomy and freedom while at the same time sharing in the fullness of the ecclesial community's life.

Orlando Espín

See also CATHOLICITY; COMMUNION (ECCLESIOLOGICAL); ECCLESIOLOGY; FREEDOM; LAITY; ORTHODOX CHURCHES; RUSSIAN ORTHODOX CHURCH; TRADITION (IN CHRISTIANITY).

SOBRINO, JON (1934–)

Jon Sobrino was born in Bilbao, Spain, of Basque parents and, because of the Spanish Civil War, knew firsthand the suffering caused by war, poverty, and oppression. He entered the Society of Jesus in 1957, was ordained a Jesuit priest, and received his doctorate in theology from the Hochsuchle Sankt Georgen (Frankfurt, 1975). He is now a citizen of El Salvador and is professor of philosophy and theology at the Universidad José Simeón Cañas (San Salvador). Among the best-known Latin American liberation theologians, Sobrino has focused his work on christology, ecclesiology, and spirituality. In each area he brings together Catholic teaching and the actual reality of Latin America, consciously carrying out his analyses of both theology and society from the standpoint of the poor. The murder of six Jesuit colleagues, their cook, and her daughter in 1989 by Salvadoran security forces deeply affected Sobrino and his work, especially in spirituality. His most influential works include *Christology at the Crossroads* (1978), *The True Church and the Poor* (1984), *Companions of Jesus* (1991), *Jesus the Liberator* (1993), and *Christ the Liberator* (2001).

James B. Nickoloff

See also LIBERATION THEOLOGIES.

SOCIAL GOSPEL

The Social Gospel was a movement within U.S. Protestant Christianity in the late nineteenth and early twentieth centuries that sought to apply liberal Christianity to contemporary social problems. Toward the end of the nineteenth century, the United States experienced considerable social upheaval due to industrialization, urbanization, and immigration. The chasm between rich and poor was increasing. There was no legislation regulating wages, working hours, or child labor. Social Gospellers addressed this situation. They viewed the Gospel as having societal implications; they tried to practice the parenthood of God and community of humanity. Optimists and postmillennialists, they hoped to usher in the kingdom of God.

The Social Gospel had four expressions: theological, activist, academic, and institutional. The primary theologian of the movement was Walter Rauschenbusch, professor at Rochester Baptist Theological Seminary. After a pastorate in New York's Hell's Kitchen showed him that poverty was not the fault of the poor, in books such as *A Theology for the Social Gospel* (1917) he argued that Jesus came to redeem society as well as individuals. He envisioned the realization of the kingdom of God on earth through social justice and equality.

Social Gospel activism was expressed in Washington Gladden, a Congregationalist pastor in Springfield, Massachusetts, and Columbus, Ohio. He preached on social issues, supported the growing labor movement, encouraged cooperation between workers and management, and advocated ecumenical, interfaith, and interracial dialogue. Through his and others' efforts, Social Gospellers supported minimum wages, prohibition, and humane working conditions for women and children.

Social Gospellers also advocated the application of academic theory to social issues; they developed the study of sociology, economics, and politics from an empirical, scientific perspective. Sociologists Vida Scudder at Wellesley College, Richard Ely of Johns Hopkins, and Albion Small of Colby College and the University of Chicago critiqued the excesses of capitalism and analyzed the complexity of social issues. Social Gospel academics also founded the new field of social ethics.

Finally, Social Gospellers established programs. Churches created clothing closets, soup kitchens, and shelters for the homeless. Some congregations, such as St. Bartholomew's or Judson Memorial, both in New York, went even further and became "institutional churches." Institutional churches not only conducted worship and Christian education, but established a network of social outreach programs, including daycare centers, camps for youth, job training for the unemployed, and community aid organizations for the poor. Institutional churches were closely affiliated with the settlement house movement, such as Jane Addams' Hull House in Chicago. Beyond the congregational level, denominations created offices to address poverty, labor, and unemployment. Ecumenical organizations, such as the Federal (later National) Council of Churches founded in 1908, promoted social outreach programs on a national level.

The Social Gospel was part of the larger context of social Christianity. To its left were Marxist and socialist Christians, while on the right were more conservative Christian groups like the Salvation Army and the Young Men's and Young Women's Christian Associations. Despite the sincerity of their aims, Social Gospellers had their limitations. Few were sympathetic to racial injustice or feminism, and many were guilty of paternalism and ethnocentrism. Their solutions to social problems were often vague and did not address the systemic origins of economic injustice. However, the Social Gospel did make human suffering a central concern of mainstream Protestantism. They raised the consciousness of middle-class Americans to an oppressive social order and created a basis of popular support for secular reforms of the Progressive Era and New Deal.

Evelyn A. Kirkley

See also MILLENARIANISM;
RAUSCHENBUSCH, WALTER.

SOCIALISM

This term refers to a broad variety of sociopolitical theories and movements that began emerging during the nineteenth century, first in Europe and later throughout much of the world. Socialism, as an umbrella term, gathers under it the theories and movements that defend or have defended the establishment of a political, economic system grounded on the interests of the working class, usually (but not always) involving the social ownership of the means of production or of significant segments thereof, and a just redistribution of wealth. The means proposed for achieving these goals, however, have been diverse (and sometimes contradictory) throughout the history of socialism.

Socialist ideas began appearing in Europe (from the early nineteenth century) as a consequence of the dislocations and injustices brought about by the Industrial Revolution, but there never was a common "socialist" doctrine or vision shared by all or most of those who would identify themselves as socialists, except perhaps the few ideas presented in the preceding paragraph. The history of the socialist movement is a history of opposing visions seeking justice for the working class.

Although building on the work of earlier social critics (Jean-Jacques Rousseau and François Noël Babeuf, for example), socialism first made its appearance in England and France among thinkers who severely criticized the terrible injustices they saw as inevitable consequences of early industrial capitalism. These authors proposed deep social reforms that would include a just and fair redistribution of wealth and the transformation of the capitalist state into a community of egalitarian communities where private property would be unnecessary and even prejudicial; however, there was little agreement among them as to how society should achieve these goals. Among these early socialist thinkers we can mention Robert Owen, Charles Fourier, Pierre Joseph Proudhon, and Henri Saint-Simon.

It should be noted that the terms "socialism" and "communism," during most of the nineteenth century, were used almost as synonyms. It was toward the end of the nineteenth century and throughout the twentieth that the two terms began to be applied to different social proposals (especially after communism came to be identified with the thought of Marx and Engels). Communism, for its proponents, came to be viewed as the inevitable, final historical outcome of the class struggles between the proletariat and the bourgeoisie, implying the dissolution of all social classes and of the state. Communists also came to regard socialism as a transitory stage toward communism. Nevertheless, no one can deny the influence of Marx and Engels on most (noncommunist) strands of socialism.

Most socialists, however, became involved in state politics, organizing parties that participated in the political arena. "Social democratic" (or "moderate") socialism, in fact, became the option for most socialists. Perhaps the main area of socialist influence was the new trade or labor unions. Through the unions and the parties, socialism became a significant force in western Europe and in the Americas. As a result of socialist pressures, mobilizations, and political savvy, laws were increasingly passed in nation after nation protecting workers, establishing the weekend rest and limiting the number of days of the typical workweek, prohibiting child labor, providing for minimum wages, safety nets for health and retirement, and so forth. As the twentieth century progressed, especially after World War II, most socialists in western Europe clearly opted for the "social democratic" version of their movement and not for the communist strand propagated by the Soviet Union and its allies. In most of the Third World, socialists also came to the "social democratic" option by the 1980s. Today's labor laws (in most countries across the world) owe a great deal to socialism's involvement in the political process (through unions and parties) and to its repeated emphasis on the interests of the working class. Nevertheless, political influence and success, although unquestionably fruitful for workers, have also impacted "social democratic" socialism by diminishing its social vision and compromising its goals with present-day capitalist globalization.

The history of the overall socialist movement has also included such strands as anarchism, agrarianism, cooperativism, and so on. Mikhail Bakunin (1814–76) was perhaps the best-known theorist of anarchism, but he and other anarchists were viewed by most socialists as extremists. On the other hand, many groups that were founded with explicit socialist or even revolutionary ideals and agendas in time became purely "reformist" parties (for example, the Section Française de l'Internationale Ouvrière under Jean Jaurès and León Blum, or the Alianza Popular Revolucionaria Americana under Víctor R. Haya de la Torre).

The Socialist Labor Party of America was founded in 1877, and it merged with the Social Democratic Party in 1901. For a number of reasons (especially the U.S.'s various reactions to the Soviet Union, before and after World War II) socialist political parties have never been successful in the U.S.—not even as "social democracy." However, ideals originally socialist have entered the U.S. political and social mainstream, and are now regarded as important gains by most Americans.

During the 1970s and 1980s, the evident excesses of the Soviet Union and its communist allies, despite their successes, led increasing numbers of western European and Third World communists to gravitate toward the already existing "social democratic" parties and movements, or to transform the old communist parties in the social democratic image. Interestingly, during the same period, many of the successful social democratic parties and institutions of the past began adopting neoliberal (free market, globalizing) recipes in the economy and politics. With the collapse of the Soviet Union and its allies in eastern Europe during 1989–92, the communist strand of socialism has all but disappeared as an international force (officially remaining, but profoundly reformed, in China and perhaps Vietnam; and with increasing irrelevance in North Korea and Cuba. The recent emergence of "Bolivarian socialism" in Venezuela has yet to practically demonstrate, beyond rhetoric, its vision and its ability to "deliver" on its promises).

In the fields of philosophy, social sciences, history, and even theology and religious studies, the direct or indirect contributions of socialists and of socialist ideas cannot be denied. However, much of what originally came to these disciplines from the socialist camp is now so "acceptable" that few scholars remember the genesis of methods, approaches, and established principles so frequent today in their work. Even scholars who politically or socially would today regard themselves as opposed to socialism do not hesitate to assume or employ what their respective disciplines gained from socialist-inspired earlier (or contemporary) scholarship.

Orlando Espín

See also ASSMANN, HUGO; CRITICAL THEORY; GRAMSCI, ANTONIO; HABERMAS, JÜRGEN; IDEOLOGY (IDEOLOGIES); LATIN AMERICAN THEOLOGIES; LIBERATION THEOLOGIES; MARIÁTEGUI, JOSÉ CARLOS; MARX, KARL; MARXISM; METHOD IN THEOLOGY; PRAXIS.

SOCIALIZATION

The process of adapting something to a social context. The more specific meaning of the term varies according to the context. In psychological and sociological contexts, socialization is the lifelong process by which one develops interpersonal skills, learns to relate to others, and acquires the beliefs, values, and practices of one's social group(s). The family is the earliest and most crucial agent of socialization in a child's life. As a child ages, many other institutions play a role—schools, daycare settings, peer groups, and the media, especially television. The family's religious affiliation is an impor-

tant factor in socialization, providing a sense of heritage and group identity. Religious beliefs shape one's morals, attitudes, and life goals; each of these in turn affects how one comports himself or herself in social contexts.

In political and economic contexts, socialization is the process by which a society organizes its use of resources and coordinates them through governmental institutions. The term is often, but not solely, associated with socialist and Marxist economics, where it refers to a government's taking control of the means of production, such as industries and natural resources.

Taking off from the political/economic meaning, the term receives a specialized definition in Roman Catholic social thought. Pope John XXIII used the term in his 1961 encyclical letter *Mater et Magistra* (nos. 59–67) to denote "the multiplication of social relationships, that is, a daily more complex interdependence of citizens, introducing into their lives and activities many and varied forms of association." A "symptom and cause" of this phenomenon is "the growing intervention of public authorities" into many social and personal affairs. John XXIII is generally positive about socialization, for it gives persons more access to social goods, greater acknowledgment of their human rights, and increased powers of participation in society. Yet the Pope points out a corresponding danger: that government will exceed its proper powers, encroaching upon the freedoms of individuals and groups. The key is to maximize the advantages of socialization and minimize the dangers; this can be accomplished by safeguarding human rights and maintaining a firm commitment to the common good. By using the word socialization, John XXIII was not condoning socialism (something many readers initially feared), but was acknowledging that the government has an important role in coordinating the economy and ensuring economic justice.

Brian Stiltner

See also ECONOMY; FAMILY; MATER ET MAGISTRA; SOCIALISM; SOCIAL JUSTICE; SOCIETY.

SOCIAL JUSTICE

In a Christian context, justice enacts and reflects God's reign, an understanding derived from the practices and teachings of Jesus, who advocated on behalf of the poor and preached liberation and embrace to the oppressed, thus revealing that God's justice is essentially concerned with the social. Christians, both as individuals and as members of societies, who are called to a life of *imitatio Christi* (to follow and be like Jesus) are thus called to envision and enact social justice in *this* world. Nevertheless, too often efforts to undertake social justice have been thwarted in favor of, at best, charitable acts and, at worst, private, individual piety and deferred eschatological hope and liberation.

To enact and reflect God's reign, social justice seeks to dismantle social and structural sin. This involves analyzing interlocking systems of oppression that give rise to dehumanizing conditions and treatment. For example, instead of only charitably feeding the hungry, social justice also requires understanding and dismantling structures that give rise to and perpetuate the sinful condition of systemic hunger. Martin Luther King Jr. stated, "Philanthropy is commendable, but it must not cause the philanthropist to overlook the circumstances of economic injustice which make philanthropy neces-

sary." In an era of unchecked globalization, a pervasive threat to achieving social justice is overwhelming despair that leaves people thinking and feeling that no matter what efforts are undertaken and what advances are made, social sin is not and cannot be eradicated. However, to reject hopelessness and instead respond to the challenge and demand of social justice through participating in ushering in the fullness of God's reign is a profound act of faith.

Meghan T. Sweeney

See also HUMAN BEING; HUMAN RIGHTS; LIBERATION THEOLOGIES; OPTION FOR THE POOR; SIN (SOCIAL, STRUCTURAL); THEOLOGICAL ANTHROPOLOGY; THIRD WORLD THEOLOGIES.

SOCIETY

A large group of persons who are united by shared bonds—which may include language, ethnicity, religion, and history —and who interact through institutions of culture, economics, and politics. No one of these bonds or activities is essential for a group to be a society, but a group that recognizes itself as such will be linked by several of them. In addition to the people themselves, a society includes all the institutions that maintain their bonds and enable their cooperative activities. These institutions range from the large and bureaucratic (such as government and corporations) to the intermediate (churches, schools, and neighborhoods) to the most intimate (families).

Society should be distinguished from two other entities. First, it differs from a nation, the political entity in which a society exists. Often the two are coextensive, but sometimes separate or partially separate societies exist within a nation (such as Native American/Indian nations within the U.S. and the French-speaking Quebecois within Canada), and sometimes a society is divided by national boundaries (such as the Palestinians, who have been divided among various countries in the Middle East). Second, society may be distinguished from community. The German sociologist Ferdinand Tönnies (1855–1936) contrasted community (*Gemeinschaft*) as a small, intimate, traditional form of social organization with society (*Gesellschaft*) as a large, impersonal, modern form. Though most religious scholars do not follow Tönnies's exact usage, they typically apply "community" to groups that are small, voluntary, or homogenous (like churches, clubs, and ethnic groups), and "society" to the large system of institutions that comprises many communities. Note that society is generally a descriptive term, while community can take on a prescriptive use; thus authors may speak of promoting a sense of "community" throughout society.

Religion and society

Religion is a social phenomenon, meaning that every religion influences and is influenced by the society it inhabits. Religions seek to bring social life into harmony with their systems of beliefs and values. They exert influence through their adherents. For instance, religions mandate and condemn certain behaviors for their members, and religious values inspire a wide array of behaviors. These teachings and values reach into every facet of life, including cultural, political, and economic practices. Religions can also exert direct influence on social systems when their authorities possess political, legal, or economic powers. By the same token, social institutions influence religion. They too approve and sanction certain behaviors, even those reaching into the religious sphere. They provide motivations and values that may support or undermine religious ones. They too wield power, and may cooperate with religious bodies or try to control them. Such interactions must be taken into account in order to understand how religions and societies change over time, and why the same religion can express itself variously in different societies.

There are two general approaches to studying the relations of religion and society. The first and earlier of these is the religious analysis of society. All religions need to define the proper relation of the sacred and the profane, the type and amount of interaction their institutions will have with others, and how members are to comport themselves in their social lives. How a religion answers these questions is guided by its fundamental theological and anthropological claims, as well as by various practical needs as it secures its place in society. In this approach, religious leaders and scholars make normative claims about how a given faith should relate to society. One of the first and greatest systematic studies of society in Christianity was Augustine's *The City of God*, completed in 426.

Starting with Auguste Comte in the nineteenth century, a second approach emerged: the scholarly analysis of religion as a social/cultural phenomenon. This approach emerged in the disciplines of sociology, psychology, anthropology, and philosophy. Some theorists—such as Feuerbach, Marx, and Freud—have held that the object of religion is illusory and that human beings' need for religion will fade when their other material or psychological needs are met. Others—such as Durkheim, Weber, and Jung—have argued that religion serves some basic human needs, both individual and social, and thus that religion is an enduring, even essential, facet of human culture. The religious analysis of society and the sociological study of religion are not mutually exclusive. Indeed, there has been tremendous cross-fertilization between the approaches, as seen in the development of the field of religious studies itself as well as in the work of constructive theologians and ethicists such as Adolf von Harnack, Rudolf Otto, H. Richard Niebuhr, Reinhold Niebuhr, Paul Ricoeur, Jacques Ellul, and David Tracy.

Brian Stiltner

See also CIVIL RELIGION; COMPARATIVE RELIGION; PLURALISM; POLITICS; RELIGION; RELIGION, CRITIQUE OF; RELIGIOUS STUDIES; SECULARISM; SOCIALIZATION; SYNCRETISM.

SOCIETY OF JESUS

The religious order known as the Society of Jesus (or the Jesuits; their initials are S.J.) was founded by Ignatius Loyola and his companions and solemnly approved by Pope Paul III on September 27, 1540. Its purpose was "to strive especially for the defense and propagation of the faith and for the progress of souls in Christian life and doctrine, by means of public preaching, lectures, and any other ministration whatsoever of the word of God, and further by means of the Spiritual Exercises, the education of children and unlettered persons in Christianity, and the spiritual consolation of Christ's faithful through hearing confessions and administering the other sacraments" (from The Formula of the Institute). In the tumultuous sixteenth century, the Society served the church well in helping to stem the tide of the Protestant Reformation and

in carrying the faith to remote corners of the globe. While the Society is probably best known for its educational institutions and retreat work, its members have traditionally been engaged in a wide variety of missionary, pastoral, and scholarly activities.

By the time Ignatius died, the Society had expanded considerably. But by the middle of the eighteenth century, the Society fell victim to fiercely hostile political and religious interests, and by 1773 it was suppressed everywhere, except in Russia, where Catherine the Great refused to promulgate the papal decree. In 1814 the Society was restored throughout the world by Pius VII. Responding to the Second Vatican Council's call to religious communities to recover their founding charisms, the Society, under the leadership of Pedro Arrupe, its twenty-eighth superior general (and, like Ignatius, a Basque), began to define its mission today in terms of faith and justice, and the preferential option for the poor. Fr. Arrupe has sometimes been called the Society's second founder.

William Reiser, S.J.

See also IGNATIUS LOYOLA; SPIRITUAL EXERCISES.

SOCINIANISM

A Unitarianism associated with Fausto Paolo Sozzini (1539–1604), this movement was especially active in late sixteenth- and early seventeenth-century Poland. Unitarians deny the divinity of Christ and the doctrine of the Trinity; they affirm the existence of God as one person.

Sozzini was not the first Unitarian in Reformation Europe. Michael Servetus (1511–53) had already paid with his life, in Geneva, for his antitrinitarian teaching. Unitarians found somewhat greater freedom in Eastern Europe, Hungary, and Poland especially. However, by the mid-seventeenth century, Catholics secured expulsion of the Socinians from Poland, and the disciples of Sozzini found few other places of freedom.

Unitarianism did not exert great influence in the English-speaking world until the late eighteenth century. In Enlightenment England and America, many Calvinists adopted a Socinian theology. Since the early nineteenth century, Boston, Massachusetts, and especially the Divinity School at Harvard University, have been active centers of Unitarianism.

Thomas Worcester, s.j.

See also CALVINISM; REFORMATION; SOCINUS, FAUSTO; TRINITY/TRINITARIAN THEOLOGY/TRINITARIAN PROCESSIONS; UNITARIANISM.

SOCINUS, FAUSTO (1539–1604)
Italian Reformer. Fausto Paolo Sozzini (his name Latinized as Socinus) published a work in 1562 that denied the divinity of Christ. He later denied the doctrine of the Trinity and is considered one of the founders of Unitarianism. Sozzini spent some time in Switzerland, but soon sought refuge in Transylvania and then Poland. In 1598 his views led to his departure from Cracow, but he remained in Poland until his death. Fausto Sozzini was influenced in this theology by his uncle, Lelio Francesco Maria Sozini (one z).

Thomas Worcester, s.j.

See also REFORMATION; SOCINIANISM; TRINITY/TRINITARIAN THEOLOGY/TRINITARIAN PROCESSIONS; UNITARIANISM.

SOKA GAKKAI
(Japanese, lit., value-creating society). One of the "New Religions" of Japan, founded in 1937 by Makiguchi Tsunesaburo (1871–1944), this is primarily a lay Buddhist organization associated with Nichiren Shoshu. Like Nichiren Shoshu it is a militant and evangelical form of Buddhism whose adherents and advocates claim that a more aggressive form of Buddhism is needed for a new age. This is the most popular of Japan's New Religions and appeals to those looking for a sense of meaning, purpose, and community in what they find to be an increasingly meaningless secular society. Rather than focusing on the self-transformation and search for enlightenment of traditional Buddhism, Soka Gakkai, influenced by Western pragmatism and scientific materialism, reinterprets the theme of becoming a Buddha to mean the achievement of health, benefit, and happiness in this life. Tsunesaburo felt that absolute truth cannot be known, so one should seek what is pragmatically helpful in order to live fuller, happier lives here and now. The emphasis is on concrete, immediate benefits, and it is seen by its adherents as a modern version of an ancient faith better adapted to an urban, industrial, material society.

G. D. DeAngelis

See also BUDDHA; BUDDHISM; LOTUS SUTRA; NEW RELIGIONS; NICHIREN.

SOLA FIDE
Like sola gratia and sola scriptura, sola fide (Latin for "faith alone") was one of several sola slogans used by the sixteenth-century Lutheran Reformation to set forth its central message that may be summarized as follows: it is not our own good works but God who justifies us (makes us acceptable) to God, by grace alone, through faith alone, which trusts in Christ alone, as proclaimed in Scripture alone.

Martin Luther claimed that this teaching of "justification by faith alone, apart from works of law," is the central message of the Scriptures, reveals the gracious and loving heart of God toward sinners, and is very powerfully asserted in the writings of Saint Paul, especially in this passage from the letter to the Romans: "But now apart from law, the righteousness of God has been disclosed, and is attested by the law and the prophets, the righteousness of God through faith in Jesus Christ for all who believe. . . . For we hold that a person is justified by faith apart from works prescribed by the law" (Rom 3:21-28, NRSV).

Such justifying faith is not mere intellectual assent, or belief *that* God exists, or beliefs *about* Christ; "even the demons believe" in this purely propositional sense, according to James 2:19. No, true faith *in* Christ involves a surrender of the will.

Further, justifying faith is not divorced from one's daily life and behavior. As Martin Luther put it in his *Preface to Romans*: "Faith is a divine work in us which changes us and births us anew out of God (John 1:13). . . . Oh it is a living, busy, active, mighty thing, this faith, so it is impossible that it should not do good. It does not ask if good works should be done, but before one asks, has done them and is already active" (quoted in Gerhard O. Forde, *Justification By Faith—A Matter of Death and Life*. Philadelphia: Fortress Press, 1982, 55).

Finally, justifying faith is not some "private relationship with Jesus" apart from the Christian community and the official ministry of the church. On the contrary, it is precisely through this ministry that God creates faith. As the Lutheran Reformers stated in their *Augsburg Confession*, Article V: "To obtain such faith God instituted the office of the ministry, that is, provided the Gospel and the sacraments. Through these, as through means, he gives the Holy Spirit, who works faith, when and where he pleases, in those who hear the Gospel."

For Lutherans, justifying faith is always "faith alone" because it is the receiving of an unmerited, life-transforming *gift*: salvation in Jesus Christ.

Jack E. Lindquist

See also AUGSBURG CONFESSION; LUTHER, MARTIN; LUTHERAN THEOLOGY; SIMUL IUSTUS ET PECCATOR; SOLA GRATIA; SOLA SCRIPTURA.

SOLA GRATIA

The Lutheran Reformation exploded in late medieval Europe as an announcement of "good news" or "Gospel": It is *God* who restores and reconciles sinful human beings to God, through the saving work of Jesus Christ. Indeed, declared Martin Luther, every aspect of salvation, including the believer's own faith in Christ, is God's undeserving gift, so that all of it may be summed up in the slogan *sola gratia* (Latin for "grace alone"). The response of the believer is to be a life of gratitude expressed in loving service to God and the neighbor.

In preaching salvation "by grace alone," Luther believed he was being faithful to the teaching of the church father Augustine of Hippo. (Luther himself was an Augustinian friar for fifteen years, from 1505 until his excommunication by Pope Leo X in 1520.) In the fifth century, Augustine contended (against Pelagius) that human nature was radically fallen and that, apart from the working of God's grace, human beings were incapable of either true faith or holiness.

More importantly, Luther believed that the Gospel of "grace alone" was the "original Gospel" of the Scriptures, as spelled out in the letter to the Ephesians: "For by grace you have been saved through faith, and this is not your own doing; it is the gift of God—not the result of works, so that no one may boast. For we are what he made us, created in Christ Jesus for good works, which God prepared beforehand to be our way of life" (Eph 2:8-10, NRSV).

Thus, for Luther, the church is "the workshop of the Holy Spirit" in which sinners are worked on by God's grace in Word and Sacrament until they leave this life. Christian life is a matter of "grace alone" from baptism to burial.

To Luther's Roman Catholic opponents, however, "grace alone" left no place for the free, decisional cooperation of believers with God's grace, even as "faith alone" seemed to eliminate any role or requirement for accompanying works of love.

In recent times, the theologians involved in the official Lutheran–Roman Catholic dialogues have reached agreement on "grace alone" in a common statement, as follows: "*Our entire hope of justification and salvation rests on Christ Jesus and on the Gospel whereby the good news of God's merciful action in Christ is made known; we do not place our ultimate trust in anything other than God's promise and saving work in Christ.* This excludes ultimate reliance on our faith, virtues, or merits, even though we acknowledge God working in these by grace alone (*sola gratia*). In brief, hope and trust for salvation are gifts of the Holy Spirit and finally rest solely on God in Christ" (*Lutherans and Catholics in Dialogue VII: Justification by Faith*. Minneapolis: Augsburg Publishing House, 1985).

Jack E. Lindquist

See also AUGUSTINIANISM; LUTHER, MARTIN; LUTHERAN THEOLOGY; PELAGIANISM; SIMUL IUSTUS ET PECCATOR; SOLA FIDE; SOLA SCRIPTURA.

SOLA SCRIPTURA

The Lutheran slogan *sola scriptura* (Latin for "Scripture alone") did not mean for Lutheranism itself what it came to mean in later, more radical forms of sixteenth-century Protestantism: the complete rejection of all tradition outside of Scripture, and of church tradition in scriptural interpretation in favor of private interpretation "from scratch." On the contrary, even though Luther's own polemics could at times vehemently pit the Word in Scripture against "the authority of popes and councils," both he and his followers strongly affirmed tradition that serves Scripture; that is, tradition that truly confesses, teaches, and celebrates the scriptural Gospel.

A prime example is the *Augsburg Confession* of 1530, the chief Lutheran confession of faith. In its Article I ("God") that subscribes to the Nicene Creed, tradition is normative in doctrine when it upholds the Gospel. In Article XV ("Church Usages") that refers to liturgical practice, tradition has a rightful role in worship as long as it is not "contrary to the Gospel." In Article XXVIII ("The Power of Bishops") that affirms the divine institution of an episcopal teaching office, tradition is to be followed in church order as long as the bishops teach "according to the Gospel."

In the Lutheran view, the Gospel in Scripture is the judge of tradition; but tradition is also necessary and unavoidable. It is, once again, concretely how the church confesses, teaches, and celebrates the Gospel; and "Scripture alone" must always be set within that. How, then, should this slogan be understood? In the view of Carl Braaten, "not as a battle cry *against* the Church and its tradition. Rather, *sola scriptura* means that everything essential in the original apostolic preaching which founded the Church is written down in Scripture, and that no later tradition can negate or supersede it" (*Principles of Lutheran Theology*, Philadelphia: Fortress Press, 1983, 24).

In a 1995 common statement on "The Word God: Scripture and Tradition," (*Lutherans and Catholics in Dialogue IX.* Minneapolis: Augsburg Fortress, 1995, 50), the official Lutheran–Roman Catholic dialogue group made this encouraging comment: "We have found that the Lutheran *sola scriptura*, when taken in conjunction with other Reformation principles, such as *sola fide, sola gratia*, and *solus Christus*, gives rise to a dynamic understanding of the Word of God that approximates what Catholics often understand as tradition in the active sense: the Spirit-assisted 'handing on' of God's revelation in Christ. We also found that Catholics no longer speak of tradition as a separate source but see it, together with Scripture, as the Word of God for the life of the Church."

Jack E. Lindquist

See also AUGSBURG CONFESSION; LUTHER, MARTIN; LUTHERAN THEOLOGY; SOLA FIDE; SOLA GRATIA.

SOLESMES, ABBEY OF

Though most well known for its impact on the modern liturgical movement, the Benedictine abbey of Solesmes was founded in 1010 in France. Its modern history begins with Dom Prosper Guéranger who purchased what had been monastery land and refounded the monastery in 1833 (after its destruction during the French Revolution). Guéranger, who became abbot in 1837, was a scholar influenced by the great developments in historical studies marking nineteenth-century Christian theology. Under his leadership, scholars of the abbey avidly pursued the history of monastic liturgy, using the oldest manuscripts available (from the eleventh and twelfth centuries); the community began to implement the results of its study, especially in the area of Gregorian chant, making Solesmes not just a center of research but a laboratory for experiments in retrieval and adaptation. After the death of Guéranger, the historical research continued under Josepht Pothier, and in 1883 he published the *Liber Gradualis*. The Solemes style of change, based on the conclusions of these nineteenth-century scholars, was not universally accepted. Debates over the authentic way to determine tempo and other musical measurements in the chant continued for many decades. Closed for a brief period early in the twentieth century by civil anticlerical legislation, Solesmes was reopened in 1922 and remains an important center for liturgical research. The scholars of Solesmes have been responsible for reliable modern editions of the works of SS. Gertrude and Mechtild, William of St. Thierry, John of the Cross, and the English mystics.

Marie Anne Mayeski

See also ABBEY; BENEDICTINE RULE (RULE OF ST. BENEDICT); HISTORICAL THEOLOGY; LITURGY OF THE HOURS.

SOLIDARITY

Not simply a matter of agreeing with, or identifying with, or being inspired by the cause of a particular people, solidarity means being accountable to those engaged in struggle for liberation. Solidarity is grounded in the reality that all human beings, their welfare, and the social structures in which they live, are interrelated. Solidarity is engagement in concrete sociopolitical struggle that responds to the analysis of interstructured oppression as understood by liberation theology and ethics.

Solidarity is shared resistance to oppression and mutual accountability and fidelity to different others in the struggle for social transformation over the long haul. It is impelled by the understanding that *all persons* in society are damaged by interstructured oppression, including the privileged, and that alleviating the conditions of the most oppressed in society, working for justice, is necessary for one to achieve one's *own* liberation.

Solidarity stands in contrast to the notion of altruism in liberal theological ethics that sees the individual as solitary and unrelated to larger social systems, and maintains the self/other split according to the worldview of Western dualism.

Mary E. Hobgood

See also DIGNITY; FREEDOM; JUSTICE; POLITICS.

SOLIPSISM

The term solipsism designates the view also termed extreme subjectivist Idealism. The theory asserts that a subject knows only itself with certitude. The conviction about other existents is affirmed only as a matter of faith, and awareness of such existents occurs only through some modifications of the self. The nineteenth-century German philosopher, Kasper Schmidt (1806–56), who wrote under the pseudonym Max Stirner, was a proponent of the theory.

Patricia Plovanich

SOLLICITUDO REI SOCIALIS

On December 30, 1987, Pope John Paul II addressed the encyclical letter "On Social Concern," known officially as *Sollicitudo Rei Socialis* (from the first three words of the Latin text that mean "concern for social things"), to all Catholics and to all people of good will. Commemorating the twentieth anniversary of Pope Paul VI's influential encyclical *Populorum Progressio*, John Paul II notes with dismay the situation in the late 1980s of worsening poverty, oppression, ideological division, and war in the world—despite sincere efforts by many people to follow Paul VI's invitation to create "more human" conditions on earth. John Paul II now urges individuals, societies, and the whole community of nations to recognize that true progress must include, but also go beyond, economic and technological advances. Respect for the dignity of the human person requires the dismantling of "structures of sin" that thwart God's plan for humanity. The Pope restates three principles of Catholic social teaching that ought to guide an authentically human process of development: (1) the right of all people to a share of the goods of the world; (2) the preferential option, or love of preference, for the poor; and (3) the fundamental interdependence of human beings and the solidarity among them it requires. He is convinced that fidelity to these guidelines and a decision by individuals and nations to turn away from the "modern idols" of "profit and power at any price" (no. 37) will permit humanity to overcome the destructive deadlock caused by the two opposed ideological blocs prevailing at present, namely, Marxist collectivism and liberal capitalism. He also believes that such personal and social conversion is the only path to genuine peace. Despite many reasons for discouragement at present, despair is inappropriate because of the fundamental goodness of humanity given and sustained by the triune God (no. 47). The Pope sees justification for his hope in humanity in the new consciousness of interdependence and a growing willingness to "lay down one's life for others" among people around the world. Hope for "true liberation," he concludes, rests on the fact that "our present history does not remain closed in upon itself but is open to the Kingdom of God" (no. 47).

James B. Nickoloff

See also JOHN PAUL II, POPE; OPTION FOR THE POOR; POPULORUM PROGRESSIO.

SOLOMON

Solomon was the second son of David and Bath-Sheba; the first son of this union died as a part of David's punishment for the affair with Bath-Sheba and the murder of her husband Uriah (2 Sam 11–12). Solomon ruled from approximately 960 to 920 B.C.E., beating out his half brother Adonijah for the throne when David was old and apparently senile. After Solomon was crowned king of Judah and Israel, he is said to have had a dream in which Yahweh appeared to him and offered him whatever he should ask. Solomon asked for wisdom in order to govern properly (1 Kgs 3). This is the beginning of the tradition linking Solomon with wisdom in Israel and with the Wisdom writings such as the book of Proverbs and Ecclesiastes. Solomon was responsible for building the Temple to house the ark of the covenant in Jerusalem, and for many other building projects throughout Israelite territory. His reign is generally presented as nearly ideal by early Israelite historians, although they also foreshadow the division of the kingdom after his death (1 Kgs 11)

and attribute it to his infidelity to Yahweh caused by his marriage to foreign women.

Russell Fuller

SOLOMON BEN ISAAC (1040–1105)

Jewish medieval exegete and legal authority, known as Rashi from the acronym for his full name, *Rabbi Shlomo ben Isaac*, of Troyes, France; author of the most famous medieval commentaries to the Hebrew Bible and Babylonian Talmud. Writing in a simple, lucid, and uniform style, he explained the Bible by providing a synthesis of Talmudic interpretation and adding his own insightful comments. He utilized the so-called *peshat* method of exegesis, interpreting the Bible in terms of the world of ancient Israel instead of offering fanciful explanations that reflected primarily the circumstances and environment of his own day. He explained complex and ambiguous passages by adducing details from the biblical world and by analyzing the Hebrew language. Rashi also produced the most influential commentary to the Babylonian Talmud, printed alongside the Talmudic text itself in every standard edition of the Talmud.

Alan J. Avery-Peck

SOMA (DRINK)
See YAJNA.

SOMA (GREEK)

The Greek work for "body," *Soma* is an important anthropological and theological term in the New Testament, especially the Pauline Corpus. In harmony with the Old Testament understanding and in contrast with its use in the Hellenistic world, *soma* in the New Testament is used in a holistic sense. It names the whole person, with reference to the body, not as something possessed (for example, "I have a body") but as what a person is, a corporeal being.

For the most part, the Old Testament is not concerned with distinguishing the "body" as one component of the human person in contrast to the rest of one's personality, the "soul" or "spirit." The human being does not possess component parts of body and soul; rather he or she is flesh and soul, full of life, yet mortal, subject to illness, decay, and death. The Old Testament has no single word for (physical) body, although it does have names for various parts of the body, such as belly or flesh.

In the Hellenistic world, the term *soma* is used by Homer as primarily a corpse. Later, it came to mean a living human or animal body. Plato's view was that the body was a tomb (*sema*; note the pun on *soma*), or shell that imprisons the immortal soul. With death comes the liberation of the soul from its bondage to the material world, the body.

By contrast, in the New Testament *soma* is a key anthropological term employed by Paul to name the resurrected, spiritual body (*soma pneumatikon*, 1 Cor 15:44) of Christians. It is precisely the *soma*, the body, that will be raised, having been transformed from a "physical body" (*soma psychikon*) into a "spiritual body" (v. 44). Or, as Paul puts it later in this passage: "Flesh and blood cannot inherit the kingdom of God . . . we will all be changed" (vv. 50-51).

In other Pauline uses it is the body that is to be offered as a living sacrifice (Rom 12:1); it is the body, not the soul, that is the temple of the Holy Spirit (1 Cor 6:19-20); and it is in the body that the death of Jesus is manifested so that, paradoxically,

"the life of Jesus may also be visible in our bodies" (1 Cor 4:10).

The term *soma* is used consistently in the narratives of the Lord's Supper with reference to Jesus: "This is my body" (1 Cor 11:24; Mark 14:22). *Soma* also has a corporate sense: individual believers are all members of the one "Body of Christ" (1 Cor 12:27), because they are all baptized into one body (v. 13). Developing the imagery in a different direction, Colossians and Ephesians speak about Christ as "the head of the body, the church" (Col 1:18; cf. Eph 1:22-23).

John Gillman

See also FLESH/SARX; PNEUMA; RESURRECTION OF CHRIST; RESURRECTION OF THE BODY.

SON OF GOD

In ancient Judah, the southern kingdom, the king was called the "son of God," that is, the son of Yahweh. This seems to have been true of all the kings in Jerusalem during the period of the Divided Monarchy (around 920–720 B.C.E.) and beyond the end of the kingdom and the Babylonian Exile. Psalm 2 preserves a ritual from the coronation of the king in Jerusalem. Verse 7, spoken by the newly crowned king, seems to imply that, as part of the coronation ritual, the king became the adopted son of God. Other royal psalms also imply this relationship between the king and Yahweh. The background of this understanding, that the ruler was closely related to the patron deity, is also seen in ancient Canaan at the city of Ugarit. In the Kirta/Keret epic the king is frequently called the son or the darling of El, the head of the Ugaritic pantheon and the king of the gods. A striking aspect of this conception is also illustrated by the Kirta/Keret epic. When the king becomes ill and is close to death, his family is shocked, seemingly not aware that the king as the son of El can die. The king could and did die, of course. Being the son of the god did not mean that the king was not mortal. The language of kinship, that is, father/son, was used to describe the close relationship between the god and the god's chosen agent on earth among humans. The king was chosen by the god, his rule was established by the god and supported by the god in times of trouble or war—if the king had been loyal. Similar concepts are evident in ancient Israel as well. In 2 Samuel 7, David receives promises, in effect a divine grant of kingship, from Yahweh. One of the promises is that Yahweh will establish the throne of David, and his son on the throne. Yahweh would be a father to the king and he would be a son to Yahweh, his chosen one, his anointed one. Yahweh also promises an eternal grant of kingship to David's dynasty. This is one of the primary texts concerning the concept in ancient Israel that the anointed king in Jerusalem was the son of Yahweh. From this point, the language of father and son is used to describe the relationship between Yahweh and the king. This language becomes part of the royal ideology. In the period of the Babylonian Exile and afterwards, when there is no longer a king in Israel, but there is still an expectation of one, the expected and hoped-for future king is also described as the son of God as well as "the anointed one." This is the concept and the language that becomes mixed in with ideas about other future agents of Yahweh, some of whom, such as the "son of man" in the book of Daniel, are not human, but rather, divine beings. In early Christian thinking, this title of the anointed king of God, who is also "son of God" and "son of man," blends with the idea of the divine or semidivine savior figure of Hellenistic thinking so that, as applied to Jesus, the title "son of God" rapidly becomes an indication of divinity rather than his royal heritage, especially in communities such as the Johannine community.

Russell Fuller

SON OF MAN

"Son of Man" is used in the Synoptic Gospels—Matthew, Mark, and Luke—by Jesus to refer to himself, especially to the Passion. No other character uses the expression. In early Christianity, it rapidly became simply one of the titles of Jesus and almost equivalent to "son of God." The phrase "son of man" is found in the book of Ezekiel, a prophet active before and after the fall of Jerusalem in 587 B.C.E. It is a Hebrew phrase used to refer to the prophet and simply means "mortal." The expression also occurs in the book of Daniel, chapter 13, where it is used to describe the appearance or the form of the divine being who is God's chosen agent to whom God has granted complete authority over the earth. This "one like a son of man," as the Aramaic text describes him, comes on the clouds, like a latter-day storm god. The figure in question may have been the angel Michael, who is elsewhere described as the Prince of Israel in the book of Daniel. This piece moves us from the time of the Babylonian Exile, Ezekiel, to the Hellenistic period, the time of the Seleucid ruler Antiochus IV Epiphanes. Shortly before the middle of the second century B.C.E. the expression "son of man" has moved from referring to a mortal prophet to a heavenly being who is Yahweh's chosen agent to save Israel and rule the earth. A similar usage is found in the pseudepigraphic work called the Book of Enoch. Enoch was a popular figure in the Persian and Hellenistic periods as is attested by the many writings attributed to him and their widespread use in different Jewish communities. The Book of Enoch also has a heavenly son of man figure. These three writings make up the Jewish background of the expression "son of man" as it comes to be used in the Synoptic Gospels and elsewhere in early Christianity. Jesus is the mortal "son of man" who is God's chosen servant and who will suffer and die. He is also or he becomes the heavenly "son of man" who will return on the clouds and judge the earth and rule as God's designated agent. This usage of the expression and its background is especially clear in the Gospel of Mark that cites the book of Daniel, chapter 13, and applies it to Jesus after the crucifixion. Especially, given the heavenly nature of the "son of man" who comes on the clouds, and the development in the understanding of the expression "son of God," these two titles probably become almost synonymous within early Christianity.

Russell Fuller

SOTERIOLOGY

The discipline or branch, within Christian theology, that studies "salvation" and most issues related to it. Consequently, it also contributes (with other theological disciplines) to the reflection on sin, atonement, human nature, grace, eschatology, and the like. The term "soteriology" is derived from the Greek word *soteria*, meaning "salvation."

Orlando Espín

See also ATONEMENT, CHRISTIAN; CHRISTOLOGY; ECCLESIOLOGY; ESCHATOLOGY (IN CHRISTIANITY); FAITH; FREE WILL; GRACE; JUSTIFICATION; NATURE, HUMAN; PREDESTINATION (IN CHRISTIANITY); PROVIDENCE; SALVATION; SIN, PERSONAL.

SOTO

One of the major schools of Zen Buddhism in Japan that developed during the Kamakura Period (1185–1333). It was founded by the monk Dogen (1200–53) who traveled to China to receive training from the Ts'ao-tung Sect. Upon his return to Japan, he spread this new version of Zen, pronounced Soto in Japanese. Unlike Rinzai, the other major school of Zen, the Soto School emphasized a more gradual path to enlightenment through the study of scripture and zazen (seated meditation) practice. In addition, Dogen put more emphasis on the way to enlightenment rather than on enlightenment itself. The Soto tradition tended to identify more with the common people, and became one of the most popular Buddhist schools in Japan.

G. D. DeAngelis

See also BODHI; DOGEN; MUSHIN; RINZAI; ROHATSU; ROSHI; SANZEN; SATORI; SESSHIN; SUZUKI, SHUNRYU; ZAZEN; ZEN.

SOTO, DOMINGO DE (1494–1560)

Spanish Catholic theologian and member of the Dominican Order. Educated at the universities of Alcalá and Paris, Soto was chosen as imperial theologian at the Council of Trent. He was an expert on the theologies of grace, justification, and original sin, defending a Thomist view of them at Trent. He succeeded Melchor Cano as principal theologian in Salamanca, where he became very influential and a close collaborator of the famed Francisco de Vitoria. Soto greatly contributed to the Catholic theological renaissance that followed Trent (especially in Spain). He wrote a number of books, among which are his *De natura et gratia* (1547), *De iustitia et iure* (1553), and *Tratado del amor de Dios* (1555).

Orlando Espín

See also COUNTER-REFORMATION/CATHOLIC REFORMATION; DOMINICANS; GRACE; JUSTIFICATION; REFORMATION; SIN, ORIGINAL; THOMISM/TRANSCENDENTAL THOMISM; TRENT, COUNCIL OF; VITORIA, FRANCISCO DE.

SOUL

The term "soul" has a long and varied history in human thought and escapes easy definition or identification. According to Aristotle, the soul is an intrinsic force or principle of movement by which living things live (*De Anima*, 413a 20-21). The human soul is said to differ from vegetative and animal souls in that it is the internal principle by which humans live, perceive, and think (*De Anima*, 414a 12-13). One might conclude from this that the human soul is rational. This belief gave way to the idea that the soul is an immaterial substance or principle that ordered the so-called material and irrational body. Many thinkers have followed a largely Platonic notion that the soul preexists its present incarnate life and will continue to exist after the death of the body (the immortality of the soul). Others have argued that the soul is created at conception (or shortly thereafter) and will continue to exist after the death of the body. Both these approaches tend to suggest that the soul has a perfection and reality independent of its bodily existence.

Existentialist philosophers (cf. Heidegger, Jaspers, Sartre) have been critical of this notion of a preexistent soul and have elaborated various notions of soul that derive from embodied existential experiences. In this sense, soul is created or constituted by the individual in and through choices and actions. Soul, here, would refer to the depth, interiority, or inwardness that emerges as the human person matures in life.

Michael J. Hartwig

See also DUALISM/DUALISTIC; PLATONISM.

SOUL (IN JUDAISM)

In the Hebrew Bible and later Jewish writings, the soul is associated primarily with respiration, narrowly signifying the life force. It is thus signified by Hebrew words that refer specifically to breath: *nefesh* ("life force"), *neshamah* ("respiration"), and *ruah* ("wind, breath"). Judaism thus differs from other Near Eastern cultures, in which the soul was more broadly associated with power, destiny, and appearance, concepts that do not appear in this connection in Judaism.

In the Talmud a close relationship is described between the body and the soul. The soul's immortality is not envisioned as separate from that of the body; nor does the concept of the transmigration of the soul from one body to another occur. Body and soul, rather, are described as separate only in origin, the body deriving from human parents and the soul originating with God, to whom it returns when the body dies. Later, at the time of the resurrection of the dead, the soul will be restored to that same body (see Jerusalem Talmud Kilaim 8:4, 31c, and Babylonian Talmud Berakhot 60a).

The Talmud states that all human souls were formed at the time of creation, when they derived from the breath (*ruah*) of

God referred to in Genesis 1:2. The messiah will come either when all these souls have been used or, alternatively, when God has finished creating all the souls he intended to create from the beginning (see, for example, Babylonian Talmud Abodah Zarah 5a).

The soul enters the womb at the time of conception, conscious of its origins and accompanied by divine messengers (Babylonian Talmud Berakhot 60b). During sleep, it ascends to heaven, in the morning returning renewed to the body (Genesis Rabbah 14:9). Although the soul objects to its birth into the world, it also protests the body's death and lingers near the body for three days, hoping that it will return to life (Tanhuma, Miqetz 4; Pequdei 3). After this period, it returns to God to await the time of the messianic resurrection (Babylonian Talmud Sanhedrin 90b-91a). During the first year after death, however, the soul remains in contact with the disintegrating body (Babylonian Talmud Shabbat 152b-153a). After this, the souls of the righteous go to paradise (*Gan Eden*, the Garden of Eden) and the souls of the wicked go to hell (*gehinnom*).

Medieval Jewish philosophers deemed all living things to have souls, including animals and plants as well as humans. They disagreed, however, about the nature of the association between the soul and the physical body. Those who followed Plato (for example, Solomon Ibn Gabirol, 1021–58) generally treated the soul as a distinct entity conjoined with the body. Those who followed Aristotle (Abraham Ibn Daud, 1110–80, for example), treated the soul as an aspect of the body, responsible for the body's ability to engage in independent activity. In this latter view, unlike in the earlier perspective, body and soul can have no existence independent of each other.

Like the earlier rabbinic view, medieval Jewish philosophers renounced any belief in the transmigration of souls, which they saw as incompatible with the more fundamental doctrine of the messianic resurrection of the dead. In this, the Jewish medieval philosophical tradition differed from Kabbalistic mysticism, in which the doctrine of transmigration is central.

Alan J. Avery-Peck

See also ESCHATOLOGY (IN JUDAISM); GARDEN OF EDEN; KABBALAH; REINCARNATION.

SOURCE CRITICISM

Source criticism seeks to identify the material a biblical author used. In antiquity, authors freely transcribed existing material into their work. Although they altered and added to their sources, they also copied large sections word for word. Their accounts, presented without citations, did not identify what had been appropriated. While such practices would now be considered plagiarism, it was an accepted literary convention in the Greco-Roman world. Many books in the Bible are composites of units of oral traditions put together in written form before they were incorporated into the received texts. There is often enough evidence to identify and date the various pieces of earlier materials that were the sources for the author of the canonical text.

To separate and identify these sources, critics look for: inconsistent sequence of events (for example, Num 22:20-22), incompatible points of view (for example, 1 Sam 9:15-16; 10:1 vs. 1 Sam 8:1-22; 10:17-19), repetitions (for example, Gen 1:1–2:4a and 2:4b-25), interwoven accounts (for example, Gen 6–7), duplicate details (for example, Exod 24:9, 13, 18), contorted episodes (for example, Josh 3:14–4:18), or doublets (for example, Gen 37:21-22 and Gen 37:26-27). They also consider stylistic differences (vocabulary, tone of presentation, and perspective) in adjoining segments of the text, indicating the presence of separate sources (for example, Exod 14:1-31; 15:22-27 with Exod 15:1-21), as well as stylistic similarities in separated passages identifying different parts of the same source (for example, Exod 1:6-7, 13-14, 23b-24). Source critics also identify "link passages," attributed to the final editor (Gen 25:12), since these passages frequently bridge different sources.

Source criticism originated in the nineteenth century. It was originally called "higher criticism" and then "literary criticism." Higher criticism was considered more ambitious than "lower criticism" (text criticism) since it sought to resolve questions about the origin of the material, the interrelationship of literary complexes, authorship, and dating, while lower criticism focused on establishing what was the most likely original reading. After form and redaction criticism were introduced, what had been called higher criticism was called literary criticism for a time. While this is still true in Europe, in English-speaking countries the term literary criticism has taken on different functions in biblical studies.

Source criticism has made important contributions to the study of both testaments. In Old Testament research, source critical studies of the Pentateuch produced the "documentary hypothesis" that proved to be an important key to the door of recognizing the validity of historical criticism. In New Testament research, source studies of the Synoptic Gospels have produced the "two-source hypothesis," that is considered of comparable significance. While corrections

and modifications continue to be made to these classical theories, they have achieved the general acceptance of most scholars.

Regina A. Boisclair

See also SYNOPTIC PROBLEM; TWO-SOURCE THEORY (OF SYNOPTICS).

SOUTHERN BUDDHISM

A geographic designation referring to the South and Southeast Asian lineages of Theravada Buddhism in Burma, Thailand, Laos, Cambodia, and Sri Lanka as against the Mahayana Buddhist schools found in Northern Asia, principally Tibet, Mongolia, China, Japan, Korea. This usage attempts to employ neutral terms to distinguish the main division between Buddhist schools, thereby avoiding adopting the Mahayana ("Great Vehicle") vs. Hinayana ("Lesser Vehicle") categories coined by the former, implying obvious denigration of the latter.

The "Southern–Northern" axis, however, invites other problems. While this designation is true in relating the overall layout of Asia in the early modern period, it can mislead in three senses:

(1) Hinayana/Theravada Buddhism was introduced into Central Asia, China, and Japan and enjoyed many centuries of development "in the north" even though in the minority; modern reform Theravada organizations have been reintroduced in many of these "northern" countries in the post-World War II era.

(2) Mahayana Buddhism likewise was found in every region of the Buddhist world in earlier historical periods, including Burma, Sri Lanka, Cambodia, Vietnam, and Insular Southeast Asia; it has also been reintroduced in the "south" through the Chinese diaspora and modern global missions of certain Mahayana groups,

primarily from Japanese and Korean schools.

(3) The "Hinayana" books specifying the rules of monastic discipline (*Vinaya*), particularly those of the Sarvastivadin schools, have been authoritative for almost all Mahayana monks and nuns, past and present. This indicates the actual interpenetration of both schools in both practice and history.

Todd T. Lewis

See also HINAYANA; MAHAYANA BUD-DHISM; NORTHERN BUDDHISM; TANTRIC BUDDHISM.

SPINOZA, BENEDICT (BARUCH) (1632–77)

Dutch Jewish philosopher. Influenced by Descartes' ideal of a deductive system of necessary truths and Aristotle's concepts of substance and essential property, Benedict Spinoza elaborated in his *Ethics* (published posthumously) a monistic system treating God, the world, and human beings that equally could be named "God" or "Nature," thus earning him simultaneously the epithets of "atheist" and "pantheist." His *Theologico-Political Treatise* (1670) was influential both for its articulation of principles of biblical criticism and for its defense of freedom of thought within the state.

J. A. Colombo

SPIRIT

Disembodied essence or any soul-like being. It is often the animus of some place, such as a mountain or other location. Spirits are often anthropomorphized, but may also include animals or supernatural creatures. Spirits are distinct from souls in that they may not necessarily be associated with a particular individual or linked to a particular body. In some socie-ties such as Native American and Andean cultures, however, souls and spirits are associated with individuals. The soul and spirit are distinct from one another, and humans may possess a soul as well as spirits that animate the body or parts of the body. In some African belief systems, spirits are believed to cause illness, death, infertility, and other misfortunes. They are capable of attacking humans as well as more generally causing harm or bene-fit. Spirits are capable of doing good or evil; the kinds of activities they engage in differ according to cultural context. Often, spirits are supplicated as a way of con-trolling supernatural forces or the fate of individuals and groups. Communication with spirits is a primary aim of shamanic ritual, prayer, and other forms of religious worship or practice. Often spirits have to be supplicated by humans with offerings, prayers, animal sacrifice, or other gifts to maintain harmony, balance, and well-being for individuals and groups.

"A belief in spirits" was the crux of E. B. Tylor's concise definition of religion. He investigated animism, a belief that all things (rocks, earth, air, water) contain a spiritual essence and postulated that animistic beliefs were the origin of other forms of religious ideas. The idea that a spiritual essence or force pervades all living beings and inanimate entities is a feature of numerous traditional religions.

In shamanic traditions, possession or selection by a divinity or spirit invests religious practitioners with powers and knowledge not possessed by others in the group. In some instances (in India, for example) shamans derive their powers from intimate connection with a specific god or spirit. In other words, they must marry a spirit husband or wife. The spirit spouse visits in dreams. Female shamans give birth to spirit children and shamans will become spirits themselves after death.

Possession by spirits is a way of attaining religious status, being cured, or communicating with the divine. Spirit possession also offers proof for believers of the reality of their religious worldview, as the spirit may be the tangible manifestation of the divine or the supernatural that confirms a group's shared cosmological vision.

Spirits are often associated with the dead and may be referred to as ghosts. The prevalence of a fear of the spirits of the dead exists in many cultures. This fear is predicated on the belief that after death the individual's spirit continues to exist, but becomes malevolent, and potentially dangerous to the living. Other cultures that conceive of spirits as linked to the dead do not necessarily view them as evil or harmful. Such spirits can remain as members of the kin group or community. They have increased helpful powers to improve the lives of the living. Groups that practice ancestor worship revere the spirits of the dead and propitiate them with offerings and pleas for assistance in return.

Christine Greenway

See also ANCESTORS, CHINESE; ANIMISM; SOUL.

SPIRITISM

A system of doctrines and practices based on the premise that communication with the dead is possible through a specially sensitive human "medium." Probably originating from the teaching and experiences of New England's Fox family in 1848, the modern version of Spiritism has spread throughout much of the Western world. It has contributed to the contemporary New Age Movement. Alain Kardec, a nineteenth-century Frenchman who attempted to systematize Spiritist doctrine and harmonize it with scientific discoveries, has had significant influence on the development of twentieth-century Spiritism.

Orlando Espín

See also NEW AGE MOVEMENT; SPIRIT; SYNCRETISM; UMBANDA.

SPIRITUAL DIRECTION

The notion of a religious guide to mentor someone through the process of becoming more familiar with God is ancient. Among the communities of desert Christians of late antiquity, the *abba* (father) figure of a wise and holy monk played an important role in moderating penance, offering suggestions for prayer, giving practical counsel for dealing with the traps and delusions inherent to life in the wilderness, sharing psychological and spiritual insight into human nature, and helping to discern the Spirit of God. In the same way that the priest Eli helped the young Samuel to recognize and respond to the Lord's voice (see 1 Sam 3), the spiritual director cooperates with God in the ministry of spiritual direction by helping the one who comes for direction to attend to the active presence of God in her or his life.

While many people used to frequent the sacrament of confession for the sake of receiving spiritual direction, not every confessor was equally skilled at giving direction. Today, spiritual direction has emerged as an important ministry requiring both psychological training and listening skills, as well as prudence, faith, and supervision. While many directors come from the ranks of religious communities, increasingly, lay men and women are being drawn to this ministry.

William Reiser, S.J.

See also DISCERNMENT.

SPIRITUAL EXERCISES

This short book has probably been the best-known retreat text in the church for over four hundred years. Originally written in Spanish, it consists of meditations, practical directions for prayer, and assorted recommendations for Christian living. The book is essentially a manual, not a piece of devotional literature. It represents the fruit of Ignatius of Loyola's religious experience over a number of months in the year 1522, following his conversion. He continued to refine the text until its final revision in 1541.

The *Exercises* are divided into four "Weeks," each of which is dedicated to a specific set of meditations. The First Week is devoted to the mystery of sin and forgiveness, the Second to meditations on scenes from the life of Christ, the Third to the passion and death of Christ, and the Fourth Week to the resurrection appearances. Framed against the background of the sixteenth-century Catholic Counter-Reformation, Ignatius intended the *Exercises* to be made by men and women, religious and lay, who occupied positions of influence, or whose native abilities showed great promise, since much good could come to the church through the renewal of such gifted people. The *Spiritual Exercises* may be looked upon as a school of seeking and finding God through inner conversion and being drawn into an affective relationship with Jesus in order to render concrete service to the poor of this world. Ignatius envisioned the *Exercises* as a means of clearing the heart and attaining a high degree of interior freedom so that a person could make an option for the kingdom of God.

William Reiser, s.j.

See also IGNATIUS LOYOLA; MEDITATION (CHRISTIAN); SOCIETY OF JESUS.

SPIRITUAL FRANCISCANS

The Spiritual Franciscans were those Franciscans, including some of Francis of Assisi's original followers, who objected to the relaxation of the strict embrace of poverty Francis wished for his followers. The Spirituals first appear as a force at the general chapter meeting the Franciscans held in 1244. The Spirituals refused to live in convents and some, inspired by the writings of Joachim of Fiore, claimed to be the harbingers of the new age of the Holy Spirit. The minister generals of the Franciscans tried to force the Spirituals to observe the Rule of St. Francis as the ministers interpreted it, but to no avail. The apocalyptic views of some of the Spirituals were expressed in a controversial book, *The Introduction to the Eternal Gospel*, written by a Franciscan at the University of Paris. The book was condemned, and the Spirituals became more suspect. At the Second Council of Lyons in 1274, the leaders of the Spiritual Franciscans were condemned to life imprisonment. The Spirituals found a new champion, however, in the French Franciscan theologian Peter John Olivi. Olivi, while rejecting the more radical apocalypticism of the Spirituals, was certainly supportive of their views. He died in 1298, but became one of the heroes of the Spirituals when the general chapter ordered all his books burned in 1299. One of Peter's students, Ubertino of Casale, became an important new leader for the Spirituals. The Spiritual Franciscans found more than a hero, but a supporter, in Pope Celestine V, who in 1294 allowed them to leave the Franciscans and found a new order, the Poor Hermits of Pope Celestine. Unfortunately, Celestine was Pope only a few short months, and his successor, Boniface VIII, suppressed the newly founded order. In 1310 Pope Clement V attempted to heal the division between the Spirituals and the rest of the Franciscans, known commonly as the "Conventuals." He agreed that the Conventuals were not living up to Francis's ideals, but urged the Spirituals to join the regular Conventual convents. This victory was short-lived, however, as Pope John XXII virtually declared war on the Spirituals in 1317. Four Spirituals were burned at the papal court in Avignon. Other Spirituals were driven underground or into different religious orders. The Spirituals seemed to have been successfully suppressed. Their ideals lived on, however, both in their writings and by word of mouth, and the Spiritual's devotion to Francis's original vision of the embrace of poverty was revived some fifty years later by the Observant movement, a form of reformed Franciscans life that survives to the present day.

Gary Macy

See also BONIFACE VIII, POPE; FRANCIS-CANS; FRANCIS OF ASSISI; FRIARS; JOHN XXII, POPE; LYONS, COUNCILS OF; MEDIEVAL CHRISTIANITY (IN THE WEST); MEDIEVAL CHURCH; ORDERS, RELIGIOUS; POVERTY (RELIGIOUS VOW).

SPIRITUALITY

This has become the term most widely used to designate whatever pertains to the interior life. Some writers have had reservations with the term because it suggests a body–soul dualism with an emphasis being placed on spirit at the expense of our physical nature. This dualism originated with the influence of Neoplatonism on early Christian thought, although it enlisted some conceptual support from Paul's sharp distinction between flesh and spirit (see Rom 7–8). Paul, however, reflected a very different

thought world. His elementary categories were biblical ones: life/death, spirit/flesh, slavery/freedom, Adam/Christ, and what he was attempting to portray was the newness of life according to the Spirit of the risen Jesus; eventually the body too would be redeemed (Rom 8:23). Pauline "spirituality," therefore, does not fit with the negative view of matter and bodiliness that emerged several centuries later.

Indeed, the tendency to regard the body as a prison from which the soul or spirit needs to free itself through meditation and other ascetical practices has been evident in both Christian and non-Christian spiritualities from time to time; the body with its needs and desires thus becomes inimical to the life of the soul. But spirit can also refer to what is most distinctive about human beings. As such, it would subsume all we are physically and mentally: our minds, imaginations, hearts and wills, our very selves, that would be inconceivable apart from bodiliness. Spirit is shorthand for referring to what is of God in us. Spirituality, therefore, is concerned with the development of the human potential for God. That development entails the purification and growth of human freedom, and the highest exercise or expression of that freedom is love.

Spirituality also embraces the means by which human beings grow in holiness, namely, prayer and action (or practice) motivated by faith. But not everyone approaches the pursuit of holiness the same way. Throughout history, some individuals have been blessed with a particular insight into the interior life, and they have been able to communicate that insight to others. Thus we can speak of spiritualities, such as desert or early monastic spirituality, Franciscan spirituality, Jesuit spirituality, Carmelite spirituality, and so on. Today, what might be called "regional spiritualities" have been appearing, that is, ways of understanding and living Christian faith in response to a particular set of social and cultural circumstances. Liberation spirituality reflects a background of political and economic oppression; feminist spirituality reflects the cultural and anthropological realities of women's experience; ecumenical spirituality reflects the increasing openness of men and women to the presence of the Spirit both in other Christian churches and in other world faiths, and so forth.

William Reiser, s.j.

See also ASCETICAL THEOLOGY; ASCETICISM/ASCETIC; CONTEMPLATIVES; MYSTICISM/MYSTICS (IN CHRISTIANITY); PERFECTION; PRAYER.

SPIRITUALS, AFRICAN AMERICAN

The spirituals are the singular religio-cultural gift of the enslaved Africans to their descendants in the United States, and, indeed, to all humanity. These sacred songs were forged in the violent encounter between ritual retentions of traditional African religio-cultural life and Christianity. The creation and performance of the spirituals was nourished by a West African aesthetic attitude—*the beautiful is to be done* in dance, in song, in poetry making, in instrumentalizing—and selected material, heard or picked up rather than read, from the Hebrew and Christian Scriptures. The spirituals are the fountainhead of all African American sacred music.

Through the themes, stories, characters, and places about which they sing, the spirituals open a window on the religious, social, aesthetic, emotional, and psychological worldview of the enslaved peoples. John Lovell, the foremost student of African American spirituals, identifies three central themes in these sacred songs: (1) a desire for freedom; (2) a desire for God's just judgment on oppressors; and (3) resistance to all limitations imposed under white supremacy. These themes are explored through biblical personages, including Noah, Abraham, Jacob, Moses and the Israelites, Pharaoh, Joshua, Ezekiel, Jonah, and Daniel; Jesus, Mary, the mother of Jesus, John the Baptist, the apostles John, Peter, Thomas, and Paul; Mary and Martha of Bethany, Mary Magdalen, Lazarus, Dives, and Pilate; and biblical places such as the River Jordan, Egypt, Canaan, and Galilee.

In a very real sense, the spirituals are the *songs of the people.* The tunes and harmonies are derived from traditional African melodies; the words voice the common experience of enslavement and oppression, common values and hopes and dreams; the first person pronoun is frequent, but the "I" is always communal; the pattern of *call–response* allowed not only for rhythmic manipulation of time, text, and pitch, but participation of the whole community. Finally, the spirituals are linked most intimately to a form of ecstatic danced worship called the ring-shout; the song is danced with the whole body—hands, feet, shoulders, hips. When the spiritual begins, the dancers form a circle and move counterclockwise in a ring, first walking slowly, then shuffling —the foot just slightly lifted from the floor—with increasing intensity and emotion.

M. Shawn Copeland

See also AFRICAN RELIGIOUS TRADITIONS; AFRICAN AMERICAN THEOLOGY.

STANTON, ELIZABETH CADY
(1815–1902)

Elizabeth Cady Stanton was a major advocate for women's rights and women's suffrage throughout the nineteenth century. After some six decades of struggling for justice for women, she concluded that *misuse and misinterpretation* of the Bible gives the greatest support to the ongoing subordination of women to men. Thus, in 1893 and 1895 she and her Revising Committee published a two-volume feminist commentary on the Bible, *The Woman's Bible*. This work has contributed some impetus, symbolically more so than in terms of its content, to the development of feminist biblical hermeneutics since the 1960s.

F. M. Gillman

See also FEMINIST THEOLOGIES.

STARETZ

From the Russian, originally meaning "old man." In the Russian Orthodox tradition, a *staretz* is a person (man or woman, lay or ordained) regarded as endowed by God with the gift of counsel. Like a spiritual director in the Western church, the staretz serves as advisor and guide in Christian living. The staretz's personal holiness and competence as counselor are his or her only necessary credentials.

Orlando Espín

See also CATHOLIC TRADITION; LAITY; ORTHODOX CHURCHES; RUSSIAN ORTHODOX CHURCH; SPIRITUAL DIRECTION.

STAR OF DAVID

The six-pointed star that is the best-known and most popular modern symbol of Judaism.

Known in Hebrew as *Magen David*, the "Shield of David," the Star of David is also known as the Jewish Star.

The six-points star was not created by Jews, but was a common and often used design in the ancient world. Some attribute "magical powers" to it because its shape points to and encompasses the entire universe.

According to legend, the star was on the shield of King David's warriors and soldiers because they wanted their armaments marked with this powerful symbol of protection.

The first documented use of the six-pointed star in Jewish life is on a cemetery tombstone from the third century C.E. in southern Italy. *Magen David*, the shield of David, is mentioned in the Talmud (Pesachim 117b) as part of a liturgical formula. A twelfth-century manuscript indicates that the star is to be placed on the doorpost of a house as a sign of God's protection. The star has been used to symbolize the Jewish community: on the flag of the Jewish community of Prague in the fourteenth century; as a seal of the Viennese Jewish community in the seventeenth century; and on the coat of arms of the Rothschild family in France in the nineteenth century.

The six-pointed star is so well known as a Jewish symbol that during the Nazi Holocaust, European Jews were forced to wear stars made of yellow cloth as identification. Since 1948, the Star of David has been the symbol on the flag of the State of Israel. Today, it is used throughout the world as a clear and unique identifying symbol of Jews and Judaism.

Wayne Dosick

STATIONS OF THE CROSS

A series of fourteen crosses, very frequently accompanied by paintings or carvings, arranged around the interior walls of many Catholic and Anglican churches. The Stations of the Cross (also known as *via crucis*, "way of the cross") are a popular Lenten devotion that depicts the "stations" or "stops" of Jesus on his way from Pilate's house to the cross, and then his being taken down from the cross and buried. Based on the actual practice of pilgrims in Jerusalem, this devotion was popularized in the Middle Ages by the Franciscans. The number fourteen has no particular significance, and a few of the traditional "stations" are not based on any biblical reference. There have been several recent attempts to make all the "stations" conform to the biblical narrative.

Orlando Espín

See also CHRISTOLOGY; CROSS, VENERATION OF THE; CRUCIFIXION; DEVOTIONS; FRANCISCANS; JESUS OF HISTORY; LENT; MEDIEVAL CHRISTIANITY (IN THE WEST); MEDIEVAL CHURCH; PASCHAL MYSTERY; PASSION NARRATIVES; PILGRIMAGE; POPULAR CATHOLICISM; SENSUS FIDELIUM/SENSUS FIDEI.

ST. AUGUSTINE, FLORIDA
See NOMBRE DE DIOS MISSION.

STEIN, EDITH (1891–1942)
German philosopher and mystic. She was a student of Edmund Husserl's, earning her doctorate from the University of Freiburg *summa cum laude*. Unable to pursue the *Habilitation* necessary for an academic position within the university, she spent her life teaching, writing, and serving the poor in Speyer and Münster. Her studies and writing were consistently concerned with a quest to understand the true being of the human person—through psychology, philosophy, and theology.

She lectured internationally, advocating equal access for women to the educational process, and underscoring the responsibility of Catholics for the creation of a just society. In 1933 she entered the Carmelite monastery in Cologne, and in 1942 she was arrested and taken to Westerbork and then killed in Auschwitz. Her work and life show an integration of love for her Jewish people with her devotion to the Cross.

Elizabeth Esther Mikova Carr

STEPHEN I OF ROME
Episkopos in Rome from 254 to 257, Stephen is best remembered for his disagreement with Cyprian of Carthage over rebaptism. Stephen firmly insisted that baptism by heretics was valid and rejected Cyprian's position in favor of rebaptism. Stephen also intervened in dogmatic disputes in Gaul and in Spain.

Gary Macy

See also BAPTISM/CONFIRMATION; CYPRIAN OF CARTHAGE; EPISKOPOS; NOVATIONISM; POPE.

STEWARDSHIP
The Scriptures use the image of *steward* for one who supervises the provision and distribution of food, drink, and other necessities within an institution. The story of Joseph delineates the duties of steward (Genesis). Jesus also uses the image to demonstrate the manner in which the goods of the kingdom should be managed well and distributed justly (Luke 12:42). Many Christian churches use a board of stewards or hire a steward to manage their property and money. The Catholic Church, as an institution, also has the obligation to manage the contributions given by the faithful in an orderly and just manner.

Stewardship is considered the individual's responsibility to manage one's life and goods with proper regard to justice and the rights of others. Stewardship refers to the money and service a person or family gives to their church as a form of "tithing." The command to tithe (to give 10 percent of one's total income) can be found in the books of Numbers, Leviticus, and Deuteronomy.

Stewardship is a way of life based on each person's call to mission and communion. As every baptized person is initiated into community and called to ministry and service, each shares the responsibility to pray, study, reflect and determine the talents, the amount of time, and the amount of money one is able to give to church and community. Stewardship is based on the understanding that everything one has comes from God. Sharing what one has with others shows gratitude to God. Stewardship is a decision and commitment freely made to give of one's time, talent, and treasure, on a regular basis, not from surplus but from one's sustenance.

Catholic dioceses use the term in development campaigns to raise money for the many ministries a diocese must maintain to carry out the mission Jesus entrusted to the church. Many parishes also use the term for their annual fundraising activities. Some parishes call the process of conversion and action "sacrificial giving," a parish process whereby every member gives what he or she is able on a regular basis. The parish, in turn, budgets and manages that money, including an institutional tithing for services to the poor. In turn, the parish does not charge any tuition or fees for parish programs and services. More than that, stewardship is an acknowledgment of one's human need to give of oneself to others and provides a process whereby more needs of the community can be met.

M. Jane Gorman

See also DIOCESE/ARCHDIOCESE; TITHES/TITHING.

STIGMATA

The reproduction on a person's body of the wounds of Jesus suffered during his passion—the nail wounds on hands and feet, and the crown of thorns around the head (and occasionally the lance wound on the side of the abdomen). The actual location of these wounds, as they might have been inflicted on Jesus' body, do not correspond to the traditional ones of the stigmata. The latter usually reflect the artistic and popular depictions most common in crucifixes and other church art forms. Claims of stigmata—always a rare occurrence—began about the thirteenth century as a consequence of the growing popular devotion to the suffering Christ. In no case have church authorities officially judged stigmata to be the real wounds of Jesus on another person's body, nor is belief in this phenomenon held by the church to be important or necessary. Natural and psychological causes usually tend to be responsible for the appearance of stigmata.

Orlando Espín

See also CHRISTOLOGY; CROSS, THEOLOGY OF THE; CRUCIFIXION; DEVOTIONS; FRANCIS OF ASSISI; JESUS OF HISTORY; POPULAR CATHOLICISM.

STOICISM

The Stoic philosophers span a roughly five-hundred-year period beginning in Athens with Zeno of Cyprus (336/5–264/3 B.C.E.). Their influence began to be felt in Rome around 156 B.C.E. Stoic philosophy and theology continued to underwrite Roman thought for centuries thereafter, particularly through the work of the late Stoa, among whom feature most prominently Seneca (d. 65 C.E.), Epictetus (50–138 C.E.), and the emperor, Marcus Aurelius (161–80 C.E.).

The Stoics were *monists* in that they held that all that exists can be accounted for in terms of a single ultimate principle of being—matter in its various aspects. According to their view, matter has both an active and a passive character. In its active aspect, matter is seen as a rational principle imposing order on matter viewed as receptive or passive.

Stoic theology is pantheistic. God permeates and exists through all that is present in the world order. God, a material principle, is nonetheless held to be conscious. The consciousness that is God is that primal source from which all of the elements (fire, air, water, earth) proceed. God, then, is both the creative and generative source of the corporeal world, while being, at the same time, identical with the world.

The Stoics set forth the doctrine of the Eternal Recurrence that, in modern philosophy, was emphasized in the nineteenth-century German philosopher Nietzsche's thought.

The world, according to this doctrine, had its origin when fire, the primary element, generates the cosmos and initiates the process of change whereby the other elements are produced. The induction of order into the cosmos continues for a span of time the Stoics termed a "period." Near the end of the period, the tendency toward disorder or entropy becomes predominant, and ultimately the world ends in a fiery conflagration. Then things begin again, exactly as before. The Stoics held that each successive period contains exactly the same objects and events as before. So, for example, each individual person lives the same life over and over again without variation. Each individual action will be repeated, without fail, in each successive lifetime. The idea that each person is predestined to perform the same actions over an infinite number of lifetimes is a sobering thought, to say the least. This thought played a profound role in the development of Stoic moral theory.

The Doctrine of the Eternal Recurrence leaves practically no room for freedom of choice. Yet the Stoics held that there is one area of human life in which an individual's choice can make a difference. While accepting that one's actions and circumstances are governed by fate, one can still choose inwardly to accept one's lot in life or to rebel against it. An attitude of submission and resignation was considered virtuous by the Stoics. This component of Stoic moral philosophy is mirrored in our present-day use of the word "stoical" to describe someone who is resigned to or accepting of their position or state.

In assessing the relative praiseworthiness or blameworthiness of any human action, the Stoics maintained that one must regard the action as having two components—a physical component and an intentional component. The physical component is just the movement of the body, as in raising one's arm. The intentional component has to do with the person's state of mind in performing the action. Accordingly, the agent's desires, motives, attitudes, ambitions, beliefs, and so on, are all included in the intentional component. For the Stoics, only the intentional component has any moral significance. They held this position based on the consideration that two actions having a similar physical component can differ in moral status based on the intentional component. For example, the action of kicking can be morally innocuous if performed as part of an exercise routine, but morally reprehensible if performed in order to injure someone. The moral difference has to do with the agent's intention in performing the action.

While emphasizing the social necessity of punishing wrongdoing, the Stoics tended to oppose retributivist theories of the justification of punishment. Retributivists hold that punishment is justified because the victim is entitled to be avenged. Anti-retributivists, such as the Stoics, tend to see punishment as justified only when some benefit can be derived from it, such as the social benefit of deterrence of further crimes.

The Stoics held that the existence of a providential ordering principle, God, could be demonstrated by attending to manifestations of design in the cosmos. The world order, from their point of view, provides evidence that it is the artifact or creation of an intelligent being as opposed to being the product of a random confluence of natural events. Beauty, in the world, was taken to be further evidence of a providential creator.

According to the Stoics, all humans have an innate tendency to believe in God. This innate disposition toward belief in a providential God can be undermined when one observes the amount of evil or innocent suffering present in our world. The question then arises about why an intelligent and providential divine principle would allow such evil. The Stoics felt they could answer this question through what has come to be known as the "Counterpart Theodicy." A theodicy is any attempt to demonstrate how the existence of God is compatible with the presence of evil in the world. The Counterpart Theodicy maintains that good and evil are "correlatives" in the sense that their existence is mutually interdependent. "Genuine" and "counterfeit," for example, are correlatives. The idea of something's being counterfeit is parasitic on the existence of similar items that are genuine. One cannot imagine a monetary system in which all the money is counterfeit. Similarly, the idea of light does not make sense without darkness as its correlative, and the existence of pain is prerequisite for the recognition of what it means for something to be pleasurable. Hence, in order to make goodness manifest in our world, a providential God must include evil as a correlative component.

Linda L. Peterson

See also NEOPLATONISM; THEODICY.

STRUCTURALISM
See LÉVI-STRAUSS, CLAUDE.

ST. THOMAS CHRISTIANS
See THOMAS CHRISTIANS.

STUPA
From antiquity, *stupa* and *caitya* were often used as synonyms in Buddhist inscriptions and literature. But definitions on usage varied, with some early sources suggesting the existence of a technical distinction between shrines with relics (*stupa*) and shrines without relics (*caitya*).

Chinese pilgrim I-Tsing in 700 indicated the diverse media used in India to shape these shrines: gold, silver, copper, iron, earth, lacquer, bricks, and stone, or sand are used. Inside are placed the Buddha's "remains" in the form of bodily relics, his clothing, or other objects used (begging bowl, for example), or even his words.

Early texts and epigraphs link stupa worship with Shakyamuni Buddha's life, and especially the key venues in his religious career. The tradition eventually recognized a standard "Eight Great Caityas" for pilgrimage and veneration. Stupa or caitya worship thus became the chief focus of Buddhist ritual activity, linking veneration of the Buddha's "sacred traces" to an individual's attention to managing karma destiny and mundane well-being.

Throughout history, Buddhist writers have advanced many explanations of stupa veneration. First, a stupa site marks supernatural celestial events associated with a Buddha and for remembering him through joyful devotional celebration. The Pali Canon's *Mahaparinibbana Sutta* describes the origins of the first veneration directed to Shakyamuni's relics. Celestial wonders are also made visible at caityas. As Nagasena explains in the *Milindapanha* (IV.8.51): "Some woman or some man of believing heart, able, intelligent, wise, endowed with insight, may deliberately take perfumes, or a garland, or a cloth, and place it on a caitya, making the resolve: 'May such and such a wonder take place!'"

The subsequent elaborations on stupa ritualism in Buddhist history are extensive: a "power place" tapping the relic's Buddha presence and healing power; a site to earn merit through veneration; a monument marking the conversion and control of indigenous deities or demons. The archeological record shows that stupas were frequently built in the center of monastery courtyards, often by monks themselves, and their worship was central in the sangha's communal life.

In the Mahayana schools, the stupa came to symbolize yet other ideas: of Buddhahood's omnipresence; a center of

textual revelation; a place of worship guaranteeing rebirth in a Pure Land; and an ideal prototypical form showing the unity of the five basic elements with Buddha nature. Later Buddhists also identified the stupa as the physical representation of the *Dharmakaya* ("Dharma Body") in the "Three Bodies of the Buddha" schema. One ritual dimension to stupa veneration was a votive/mortuary aspect: certain Buddhists, and especially monks, apparently had their own ashes deposited in small votive caityas, often arranged close to a Buddha relic stupa. These structures perhaps established a means for perpetual merit-generation for the deceased.

Finally, the Vajrayana tradition also utilized the stupa as a mandala and a model for visualization meditation. In the Nepalese-Tibetan Vajrayana traditions, these directional points also have esoteric correlates in the human body itself.

Thus, it is with these myriad understandings that Buddhist virtuosi as well as others at all levels of aspiration have circumambulated stupas. For this reason, these shrines became the centers and symbols of Buddhism, the ritual meeting places for those of varying spiritual orientations.

Todd T. Lewis

See also BUDDHA; CAITYA; PURE LAND BUDDHISM; RELIC (OUTSIDE CHRISTIANITY); TATHAGATA; TRIKAYA (DOCTRINE OF).

SUÁREZ, FRANCISCO
(1548–1617)

Spanish theologian and philosopher, and member of the Society of Jesus (Jesuits). After graduate studies at the university in Salamanca, he taught in Rome, Alcalá, and Coimbra. One of the great minds of his day, Suárez was renowned for his commentaries on Thomas Aquinas, and for his encyclopedic learning. He is regarded as one of the first thinkers to systematically reflect on individuality. His work *Disputationes metaphysicae* (1597), very influential among Catholic and Protestant philosophers, interpreted Aristotle and Aquinas for a "modern" audience in "real-life" situations. The sixteenth-century Spanish conquest of the Americas had a profound impact on his thought, providing Suárez with many philosophical, theological, and ethical questions, some of which he dealt with in his *De legibus* (1612). He also became involved in the *de auxiliis* controversy between Dominicans and Jesuits, and subsequently wrote several books on the theology of grace.

Orlando Espín

See also AQUINAS, THOMAS, ST.; BELLARMINE, ROBERT; COUNTER-REFORMATION / CATHOLIC REFORMATION; DOMINICANS; GRACE; MODERNITY; MOLINA, LUIS DE; REFORMATION; SOCIAL JUSTICE; SOCIETY OF JESUS; THOMISM / TRANSCENDENTAL THOMISM; VITORIA, FRANCISCO DE.

SUBLAPSARIANISM
See INFRALAPSARIANISM.

SUBORDINATIONISM
Given Jewish belief in the oneness of God, and that only the LORD is God, one understands why some early Christians tended to view Jesus as subordinate to the Father. This view was at odds with the developing Christian perception that God was triune and that the three Persons, while distinct, were equally divine. There are many New Testament texts depicting Jesus as standing in a faith relationship with God (Jesus prays, for instance). Clearly, as a human being, Jesus had to depend upon God in all things, just as every other man and woman does. A few New Testament texts can be read as suggesting that Jesus was "adopted" by God as the beloved son. As a way of getting a handle on such texts, the church distinguished two natures in Christ, human and divine. He is one "person" with two natures, although the way the early church used the word "person" is not the way we use the word today. Thus, in his human nature, Jesus manifested dependence upon God; in one sense, he was subordinate to God as all human beings are. From this perspective, one learns how to interpret passages where Jesus says the Father is greater than he is (John 14:28), or that there are some things the Son does not know (Mark 13:32), or where it is stated that Jesus learned obedience through suffering (Heb 5:8). One sees on what grounds Arius and his followers could believe that Jesus was an exalted creature. Arianism was condemned by the Council of Nicaea in 325, while subordinationism was condemned by the First Council of Constantinople in 381. Neither the Arians nor the subordinationists grasped the full dimensions of the Word's becoming flesh, and this failure led them to misread Scripture.

William Reiser, s.j.

See also ARIANISM; INCARNATION.

SUBSIDIARITY
A principle in Catholic social teaching that has as its purpose the maximum participation of all in the decisions affecting their lives. Subsidiarity supports the notion that "small is beautiful," that is, a larger structure should not do work or make decisions that can be better done by those smaller structures closer to the grassroots.

Pope John XXIII, however, modified the principle of subsidiarity, "small is beautiful," to include "but big whenever necessary." Pius XI and Pius XII had used the principle of subsidiarity to deny the right of civil authorities to interfere in the operations of organizations closer to the grassroots. But in the encyclicals *Mater et Magistra* (nos. 53–4, 58, 116–7) and *Pacem in Terris* (nos. 56–7), John was also concerned about the need for public authorities to intervene when power was too great to be left in private hands without damage to the common good, especially poor people.

What subsidiarity means is that each higher level of the society must be accountable to those levels below it.

Mary E. Hobgood

See also CATHOLIC SOCIAL TEACHING.

SUBSTANCE

"Substance" in English is a transliteration of the Latin word *substantia*, itself a translation of the Greek word *ousia*. The word was used by Plato to refer to the unchanging essence of the Forms in which all things shared. Each human being, for instance, shares in the Form "humanity" that would exist, for Plato, independently of any particular human being. Aristotle, Plato's student, disagreed that this essence or *ousia* existed apart from individual entities, and therefore changed the meaning of *ousia* to refer to that part of any particular entity that is its essence. Since something can change into something else, *ousia* can change, for Aristotle, into something; this is impossible in Plato's understanding of *ousia*. Basic to both these philosophers, however, is the notion that there is something essential about each entity that makes it what it is, despite outward changes in color or texture or shape or weight. That something is its *ousia* or substance.

Since Judaism, Christianity, and Islam all inherited and, to a greater or lesser degree, integrated Platonism and Aristotelianism into their thought worlds, it is not surprising that the notion of "substance," too, can be found in the writings of Jews, Christians, and Muslims. After a long and bitter battle, for instance, Christians incorporated the concept into their classical statements of faith, declaring the Son to be "one in substance" (*homoousios*) with the Father. The term "substance" also played an important role in medieval Christian discussions of the presence of the risen Lord in the Eucharist.

Gary Macy

See also ARIANISM; ARISTOTELIANISM; ARISTOTLE; CHRISTIANITY; CHRISTOLOGY; CREED (SYMBOL OF FAITH); HOMOOUSIOS TO PATRI; ISLAM; JUDAISM; OUSIA; PLATO; PLATONISM; TRANSUBSTANTIATION.

SUCCAH

Hebrew, meaning "booth" or "hut" or "tabernacle," this is the fragile booth built by Jews in observance of the festival of *Succot*.

To celebrate the festival of *Succot*, the fall harvest festival, Jews construct a temporary hut-like dwelling, a *succah*. The building of the succah recalls how, first during their trek in the desert and later at harvest time each year, Jews would live in fragile huts in the desert or in the fields.

The succah must be strong enough to last the entire seven (or eight) days of the festival, but it must be delicate enough to indicate that it is not a permanent dwelling place. It is built with a roof made of branches and leaves so the sun by day and the moon and stars by night are visible through the roof. The succah is often decorated with fruits, vegetables, and other products of the harvest, and decorations made by the children.

During the festival, it is customary to eat and entertain in the succah; some sleep there each night.

Wayne Dosick

See also SUCCOT; TABERNACLES, FEAST OF.

SUCCOT

Hebrew, meaning "booths" or "huts," this is the Jewish Festival of Tabernacles.

Succot occurs on the fifteenth day of the Hebrew month of Tishri, the first month of the Jewish year, corresponding to late September or early October. It is a seven-day holiday (eight in the Diaspora) with full festival celebrations on the first (and second) and the seventh (and eighth) days, with the middle days being designated as *Chol HaMoed*, the "intermediate days" of the festival, when the celebrations and rituals are lessened, but the holiday is still in full effect.

Succot is an agricultural festival, celebrating the fall harvest. Therefore, it is also known as *Chag HaAsif*, the Festival of Ingathering. It recalls how, first during their trek through the desert and then later at harvest time each year, Jews would live in small, fragile booths or huts (tabernacles) built in the desert or in the fields.

To remember the lives of the ancestors, to identify with their journeys, and to acknowledge harvest time, in celebration of the festival, Jews build a *succah*, a small, fragile booth/hut. During the festival, it is customary to eat meals in the succah and to entertain guests there. Some sleep in the succah each night.

Two ritual objects that are used during Succot are the *lulav*, a palm branch with willow and myrtle leaves attached, and the *etrog*, a lemon-like citron. At a certain point in the Succot morning worship services, the lulav and etrog are held together and pointed in all directions—a reminder that God, provider of all blessings, is everywhere in the natural world. Throughout the festival, both at home and at the synagogue, many special rituals are performed and many special prayers are recited, reflecting the theme of the observance.

The final day of Succot is called Shemini Atzeret, the Eighth Day of Assembly. An additional observance has been added at the end of Succot—Simchat Torah, the Rejoicing of the Torah, the day when the yearly Torah reading cycle is completed through the reading of the concluding words of Deuteronomy, and begun again through the reading of the opening words of Genesis.

The festival of Succot celebrates connection to Creation and the Creator, and to the meaning and purpose of existence.

Wayne Dosick

See also ETROG; LULAV; SHEMINI ATZERET; SIMCHAT TORAH; SUCCAH.

SUFFERING

By definition, suffering is the pain human beings endure, no matter what the cause or source of that pain, and no matter whether it is considered "just" (deserved) or "unjust" (undeserved). The Christian effort to account for unjust suffering arises from our belief in the goodness and fairness of God; the question of theodicy —God's relationship to the world—is driven by the ongoing need to wrestle with the "problem of evil." Ultimately, the Christian resolves the problem through faith and prayer. Suffering can be regarded as a mystery pure and simple for which there is no satisfactory explanation or justification, as in the book of Job. It can be viewed as part of the process of spiritual purification, as instructive, as therapeutic, as liberating, as a testing of faith, as atoning for sin, as a manifestation of creation's incompleteness, as a participation in the suffering of Christ, and as meritorious. Suffering can also be regarded as a penalty for sin and disobedience. Each of these ways of interpreting the reality of human suffering is an expression of faith seeking understanding. The fact that, in Jesus, God has also become part of the history of human suffering does not explain suffering, but it does help us deal with and accept it. God as co-sufferer, above all under the sign of the Cross, has enabled many people to find peace, and sometimes even joy, in the midst of their diminishment.

Any account of suffering, however, has to make it clear that God does not enjoy our pain. While it is doubtlessly true that from our limited perspective we cannot always easily see what purpose is served by the suffering of individuals or even of entire nations, the Christian lives out of the conviction that for those who love God all things ultimately work together for good (Rom 8:28). Finally, however, every speculative effort to understand suffering must give way to prayer, since only in the context of a relationship with God can a person either endure suffering without succumbing to anger and despair, or find the strength to fight against suffering inflicted on us unjustly by others without succumbing to hatred and violence.

William Reiser, s.j.

See also ATONEMENT, CHRISTIAN; CROSS, THEOLOGY OF THE; EVIL; OPTION FOR THE POOR; PENANCE; SALVATION; THEODICY; VIA PURGATIVA.

SUFFERING SERVANT OF YAHWEH

The figure of the Suffering Servant of Yahweh is derived from the book of Isaiah, from the so-called "Servant Songs" found in Second Isaiah (Isa 40–55). There are four Servant Songs: Isaiah 42:1-4; 49:1-6; 50:4-11; 52:13–53:12. The fourth Servant Song, Isaiah 52:13–53:12, is the central source for the idea that the servant suffers. It is quite clear in this last poem that the servant not only suffers, but is innocent, and his suffering is vicarious, that is, it is in place of the deserved suffering of others. This poem expresses the idea that the servant is a sort of sacrifice that can atone for the sin of others. (Compare this with the ritual of the scapegoat in the Day of Atonement ritual in Leviticus 16.) From the early centuries of the Common Era, Jews and Christians have disagreed over the interpretation of these passages in the book of Isaiah. Christians, from the time of the Gospels if not earlier, have seen in the songs prophecies of Jesus and especially his suffering and atoning death. Jews naturally have disagreed with this understanding, and have pointed out that, in Second Isaiah, Israel is clearly called the Servant of Yahweh many times. It is also unclear within the songs themselves who the servant is. Modern critical scholars have devoted much time and effort to this question of the identity of the servant in the sixth century B.C.E. when the Second Isaiah was writing. One of the strong possibilities is that the songs do refer to Israel, or at least part of Israel, perhaps the exiles in Babylon themselves who have suffered in exile for all the people. It is extremely unlikely that the anonymous prophet who wrote Isaiah 40–55 was thinking of a single, suffering individual who redeemed the entire community.

Russell Fuller

SUFFRAGAN BISHOP/DIOCESE

A suffragan bishop, in the Catholic Churches, is a bishop who heads a diocese that is not the metropolitan see (that is, not an archdiocese) in an ecclesiastical province. The suffragan bishop's diocese is then, by extension, called a suffragan diocese. In the Anglican Churches, a suffragan bishop can also be an assistant or auxiliary bishop.

Orlando Espín

See also ANGLICAN COMMUNION; BISHOP (AUXILIARY, SUFFRAGAN); BISHOP (EPISCOPACY); BISHOP (ORDINARY); DIOCESE/ARCHDIOCESE; EASTERN CATHOLIC CHURCHES; ECCLESIASTICAL PROVINCE; METROPOLITAN; ROMAN CATHOLIC CHURCH; SEE.

SUFI/SUFISM

A Sufi is a Muslim who follows the spiritual path known as Sufism. The term is thought to be derived from the Arabic word *suf* (wool), the material used for making clothing that many of the first Sufis wore as a sign of their dedication to a simple life and self-denial. Some have suggested that the term *sufi* came from the word *safa*, (purity in Arabic).

Sufis trace their spirituality back to the earliest caliphs (leaders of Islam), particularly Abu Bakr (d. 634) and Umar (d. 644), and through them, to the Prophet Muhammad (d. 632) himself. One of the first proponents of Sufi spirituality was Hasan al-Basri (642–728), a recognized theologian in his day. Al-Basri saw the need for a more interior experience of Islam—one that transcends the external practice of the religion and seeks a deeper communion with God in this world. It is this craving for a personal and immediate sense of the divine presence that has characterized Sufism throughout its history. Because of their tendency to renounce worldly pursuits and luxury (asceticism), and their belief that special—sometimes even secret—knowledge of God is hidden in the sacred text of Islam, the Qur'an, Sufis are sometimes referred to as Islamic mystics. Like all mystics, they profess that absolutely nothing is more important in this life than devotion and surrender to God.

Sometimes referred to as *faqir* (from the Arabic word for poverty, *faqr*), Sufis attempt to embrace the ultimate state of detachment, the extinction of their own sense of self. This goal, called *fana*, prompts them to let God take complete control of their lives so that none other than God exists in and for them. Once this happens, Sufis believe they have complied with the ultimate demand of Islam: total surrender to and obedience of God.

One of the religious practices that helps Sufis "die" to themselves through fana is *dhikr*, the constant remembrance of God and repetition of God's Holy Names. In fact, contemporary Sufis would say that they do not have to belong to special religious orders and live apart from society as was often the case in the past. All one has to do to be a good Sufi is to practice dhikr during every waking moment of every day. In this way, God becomes everything to the believer, and nothing but God has a claim on him or her. Sufis have also fostered devotion to God through expressions of spiritual ecstasy that are not typical of Islamic piety, most notably poetry, music, song, and, in the case of Turkish Sufism (The Whirling Dervishes), dance. These unconventional devotions, coupled with the dedication Sufis frequently showed to their spiritual guides called *shaykhs* or *pirs*, sometimes resulted in severe criticism of Sufism voiced by the more mainstream Islamic leadership. In the case of one Sufi, al-Hallaj (857–922), this criticism led to execution. So convinced was al-Hallaj that none other than God existed in him that he proclaimed, *"Ana al-Haqq,"* meaning "I am the truth." Because this was tantamount to saying that "I am God," al-Hallaj was crucified.

Yet, whether they have lived in the world or apart from it in religious communities where they studied a particular Sufi system (*tariqa*), most Sufis throughout history have attempted to integrate their unique spirituality with the orthodox practice of Islam. As a result, many scholars agree that Sufis have contributed to Islamic spirituality by giving the tradition new insights into the importance of fostering a deep personal relationship with God and a spirit of detachment from the lures of the world.

Ronald A. Pachence

See also AL-HALLAJ; CALIPH (KALIPHA)/CALIPHATE; DHIKR; FANA; FAQIR; ISLAM; MUSLIM; PIR; SHAYKH; WHIRLING DERVISHES.

SUICIDE

The act of taking one's own life. In general, suicide is forbidden by the monotheistic religions, either because one's own life is considered a gift from God, and it would be wrong to take it in one's own hands (predominantly Jewish), or because one's life on earth is a preparation for heaven (Christianity and Islam), and one's deeds or sufferings (the latter especially Christian) on earth determine the degree of one's happiness in heaven. St. Thomas Aquinas says that if we take our own lives, we will still have the problems that we had while we were in the flesh, but now the soul does not have the body to work its problems out with. It lacks "traction," as it were. Up until about fifty years ago, it was thought that suicide was an "unpardonable sin" because one died in the very act of sin, condemning the soul automatically to hell. Thus suicide victims were not buried in "holy ground" (cf. the burial of Ophelia in *Hamlet*).

Christian theology especially, however, has always taught that certain values supersede the value of one's life. For example, if one throws oneself out of a high building because that is the only way to avoid being part of a group committing a grave injustice, it would not be considered suicide in the strict sense. It would be defensible under the principle of "double effect," by which the evil (death) is a secondary and indirectly intended effect of the first intent and effect (avoiding doing the grave injustice).

Recently, we have witnessed controversy over "euthanasia," or "doctor-assisted suicide," centering on the activities of Dr. Jack Kevorkian. Essentially, patients in chronic pain with no hope of recovery may seek (or be encouraged to seek) death as an escape from pain, as a refusal to accept diminution of their "quality of life," or as a removal of themselves as a "burden to others." Theologically, such dispositions point to a decreasing sense of connection in our society between the self and others (community), and between this life and eternal life, as well as to a loss of the sense of life as divine gift. We should note that ethically, the Catholic Church has never required that "extraordinary means" be employed to keep a dying patient alive. A Christian pastoral response to such physical and community struggles of the dying patient is the offer of "hospice," a growing movement attending to the physical, psychological, and spiritual needs of the dying.

G. Simon Harak, s.j.

SUKHAVATI

The "Land of Happiness" or "Pure Land" in the west created and presided over by Amitabha or Amitayus (Chinese, *Amit'o*; Japanese, *Amida*), one of a number of Buddhist rebirth realms where there is no suffering and where complete enlightenment is certain for individuals born there. The early Indic texts, the *Larger and Smaller Sukhavativyuha Sutras*, emphasize the large stock of merit needed for rebirth there, the efficacy of chanting the names of Amitabha, and the death-time visions that appear to the devout who direct their merit and minds to rebirth in the Pure Land. The *Larger* tells how many eons ago a monk named Dharmakara made a series of vows to create this realm as a product of his extraordinary merit, having heard of other Pure Lands in the cosmos. A later text, the *Amitayurdhyana Sutra*, describes sixteen meditations necessary to perceive *Sukhavati*.

Todd T. Lewis

See also AMITABHA/AMIDA; MAHAYANA BUDDHISM; PURE LAND BUDDHISM.

SUKKAH

See TABERNACLES, FEAST OF.

SUKKOT

See TABERNACLES, FEAST OF.

SULPICIUS SEVERUS (360?–420?)

Sulpicius Severus was born into a noble Roman family of Aquitaine and was a rhetor by profession. He was converted to an ascetic and monastic way of life by Martin of Tours. Sulpicius is best known for his *Life of Martin*, a work that greatly influenced medieval hagiography. Attached to the *Life*, Sulpicius included as well three letters addressed to Martin and a set of dialogues. Sulpicius also wrote a history of the world from crea-

tion up until his own times. Renowned during his lifetime for his skill as a writer, Sulpicius helped to spread the ascetic ideals and the fame of Martin of Tours. Sulpicius's history also provides a valuable insight into the Arian, Pelagian, and Priscillianist heresies in Gaul.

Gary Macy

See also ARIANISM; HAGIOGRAPHY; MARTIN OF TOURS; PELAGIANISM; PRISCILLIANISM; VITA.

SULTAN

A title, no longer in use today, which meant "ruler" in some Islamic societies. The history of this Arabic word can be traced to the latter period of the Abbasid Dynasty that effectively lasted from 750 until the Mongols conquered its capital, Baghdad, in 1258. With the destruction of Baghdad, both the Abbasid caliphs (recognized religious and social leaders of Islam) and the office of the caliphate ceased to exist, though the honor of caliph was claimed for a while by Abbasid survivors in Egypt. After 1258, Islamic rulers were sometimes referred to as *sultans* who functioned mostly as heads of state and monarchs without any real religious authority. The title is most popularly associated with the sovereigns of the Ottoman Turkish Empire that was the dominant Islamic power in the Middle East, North Africa, and parts of Europe from the fourteenth to the early twentieth century.

Ronald A. Pachence

See also ABBASIDS; CALIPH (KALIPHA)/ CALIPHATE; OTTOMAN.

SUMMA CONTRA GENTILES

This great work of St. Thomas Aquinas (1224–74) was, reportedly, initiated at the request of Raymond of Penyafort, a Catalan Dominican who died shortly after the death of Aquinas. Penyafort was concerned about the influence of Islam in Spain, and hoped to be able to use Aquinas's treatise as a "proof text" for missionary purposes. Aquinas began writing the *Summa Contra Gentiles* in 1258, and the composition of the work continued for over five years.

While the treatise (consisting of four parts) is clearly a theological work intended for the education of non-Christians in the basic elements of the Christian faith, scholars are divided on the issue of the intended referent of "Gentiles" from Aquinas's point of view. Some Aquinas scholars hold that, given Penyafort's missionary intentions and his role in motivating the production of the work, its primary goal is to convert members of other faiths (Islam and Judaism, for example) to Catholicism. Others speculate that the work was really directed toward a group of theology professors at the University of Paris who had been, from Aquinas's point of view, subverted by the work of the twelfth-century Islamic philosopher and Aristotelian scholar Averroes. Averroes held that the soul, as Aristotle taught, is the substantial form or basic organizational principle of the human body, but that the intellect, as immaterial, is not a constituent of the human soul. Following Averroes' rendition of Aristotle's theory, there is but one immaterial intellect for the entire human species. On this view, there is no post-mortem survival of the soul and hence no life after death for the individual human being. Clearly, adherence to Averroes' teaching conflicts with belief in Christian doctrines concerning the immortality of the soul, the ultimate end of human existence as union with God, the Resurrection, and so forth. It is well known that St. Thomas was, indeed, concerned about the impact of Averroes' views on theol-

ogy students at the University of Paris. Whether the *Summa Contra Gentiles* was specifically directed toward undermining that impact is unclear. What is clear is that Aquinas, in this treatise, employs a method of defending Christian doctrine that uses argumentation based solely on reason, as opposed to arguments requiring adherence to certain articles of faith as a presuppositional backdrop. Accordingly, his intended audience is clearly composed of thinkers who would not be inclined to accept the basic tenets of Christian doctrine independently of their being convinced, by rational demonstration, to do so.

The work consists of four books. The first book treats of the existence and nature of God. The second book concerns the created order, while the third book focuses on the moral life. The overall schema or pattern of the *Summa Contra Gentiles* is thus similar to that of the *Summa Theologiae*. Creatures are seen as emanating or being brought forth from God, and then are assessed in terms of what (in the case of rational creatures) is necessary for a return to God. The final book concerns the incarnation of Christ and the sacraments, and defends a specifically Catholic account of the means by which humans can fulfill the ultimate goal of union with their Creator.

Linda L. Peterson

See also AQUINAS, THOMAS, ST.; ARISTO-TELIANISM; SUMMA THEOLOGIAE.

SUMMA THEOLOGIAE

St. Thomas Aquinas's *Summa Theologiae* is one of the most significant theological and philosophical works of all time. It is certainly the most famous of all the works included in St. Thomas's enormous literary output. Aquinas lived from 1224–74 and wrote during the time when European universities were still relatively young, and Scholasticism, as a methodology, was beginning to take hold across Europe. The *Summa Theologiae* was written in the Scholastic style, and was intended primarily as a text to teach theology students the basic elements of Christian doctrine and Catholic thought.

A "summa" is a summation, organization, and synthesis of a body of knowledge. Aquinas's summation of theology puts reason to work in the service of faith. He provides rational demonstrations of those articles of faith amenable to rational defense, and defends those for which a rational defense is impossible against objections raised against them. As a theological work, the *Summa Theologiae* considers all issues and problems as they relate to God. Hence, topics falling under the heading "natural philosophy," for example, the nature and ultimate metaphysical constitution of substances in the world—human beings and purely corporeal objects—are all treated in terms of the relation of the created order back to God, the Creator.

The *Summa Theologiae* has three parts. Part I treats of the existence and nature of God, of the Trinity, the procession of the Persons of the Trinity and the relations among the Persons. It also delineates the production of creatures by God. Angels are held to be purely spiritual creatures that can be divided into hierarchies or genera but are only one per species. Gabriel, for example, is taken to be the only possible member of the species "Gabrielhood." Human beings are assessed as being creatures who exist on a borderline between the spiritual and corporeal realms. The human soul is naturally intended to exist in matter as the substantial form of the human body, but is also capable of subsistence independently of matter during the postmortem life of the individual. The nature of creatures whose existence is exclusively corporeal (nonhuman animals, vegetative substances) is also treated in the First Part.

The Second Part is further divided into two parts. The first part of the Second Part considers the teleology of human life. Human life is goal-directed, with the ultimate end of human existence, on Aquinas's account, being a right relationship with God. In this part, St. Thomas assesses how human life can be directed toward that end, and also considers ways in which human actions and choices sometimes depart from their appointed path to God. The second part of the Second Part provides a comprehensive definition and analysis of the virtues. This part treats of the "theological virtues"—faith, hope, and charity, as well as of the "cardinal virtues"—prudence, justice, fortitude, and temperance. Accordingly, while the First Part can be viewed as an account of the emanation of creatures from God, the Second Part can be viewed as an account of the return of creatures to God.

The Third Part concerns the ways in which Christianity directs the return of humans to their Creator. This part treats of the incarnation of Christ and of the various sacraments (baptism, the Holy Eucharist, confirmation, and so on) as specifically Christian means by which humans may attain their ultimate goal of union with God.

Linda L. Peterson

See also AQUINAS, THOMAS, ST.; ARISTOTELIANISM; HYLOMORPHISM; SCHOLASTICISM.

SUN DANCE

A ceremony practiced among many (but not all) North American native peoples. Each people has its distinct variations of the dance, but there are some common features: dancing, singing, praying, drumming, the experience of visions, fasting, and piercing the flesh. Today women are allowed to participate in the Sun Dance ceremony but are not encouraged to pierce their skin (while some of the men who have so pledged are required to do so). A "sun dancer" makes a commitment to dance for four consecutive years—one year for each of the four cardinal points. The Sun Dance was the most important religious ceremony of the Plains Indians of North America, ordinarily held by each nation once a year, during eight days, at the time of the summer solstice. The Sun Dance was (and is) a ritual of regeneration and rebirth, emphasizing continuity and harmony among all living beings.

Orlando Espín

See also GHOST DANCE; NATIVE AMERICAN CHURCH.

SUNDAY

Sunday is the day of worship common to most Christian churches. The New Testament refers at least once to Christians gathering for the "breaking of the bread" on "the first day of the week" (Acts 20:7; cf. 1 Cor 16:1-2), although scholars are divided over the questions of how frequently early Christian communities celebrated the Eucharist, whether it was weekly on this "first day," and exactly what time (early morning or evening) the celebration would take place. References are also made to "the Lord's day" (Rev 1:10), and, in other early Christian writings, to "the eighth day" (that is, a day that foreshadows or anticipates the eternity of the new age or new creation).

By the second century, this regular day of Christian eucharistic worship is said to be "the first day of the week" in the Jewish calendar, or Sunday (the day of the Sun or *dies solis*) in the Roman calendar, reinforced by the reference in the Gospels to Christ's resurrection on "the first day of the week" (Matt 28:1; Mark 16:1; Luke 24:1; John 20:1). Thus, Sunday became the earliest Christian feast day, carrying many of the theological themes that would somewhat later be settled on certain yearly feasts (such as Easter and the Resurrection; Christmas and the Incarnation).

Before the legalization of Christianity, Sunday was an ordinary workday; Christians would gather before dawn for the eucharistic celebration. After the legalization of Christianity at the beginning of the fourth century, the emperor Constantine established Sunday ("the day of the sun") as a day of rest from work, because it was a day of worship in both Christianity and other cults of the sun (321 C.E.). With this development, the Christian Sunday takes on some of the characteristics of the Jewish Sabbath, as a day of worship, prayer, festivity, and rest from manual labor. This practice was continued for centuries in many areas; after the settling of the Americas, for example, in many parts of the United States, stores and other businesses were closed on Sundays by law. Sunday continues to be the weekly Christian feast day, although some Protestant churches do not celebrate the Eucharist every week. A few other Christian churches (e.g., the Seventh-Day Adventists) keep Saturday, not Sunday, as the day of rest and worship.

Joanne M. Pierce

See also CHRISTMAS; EASTER; EUCHARIST; FEAST; LITURGICAL YEAR; MASS; PASCHAL MYSTERY.

SUNNA/SUNNI/SUNNISM

In Arabic, *sunna* means "custom" or "traditional way" of living one's faith as a Muslim. It can be used as a legal term referring to the practices that are suggested or recommended, but it is more frequently applied to the *sunna* of the Prophet of Islam, Muhammad (570–632), as recorded in one of the collections of the Prophet's words and deeds called *hadith* (account or report). Along with the revealed and inerrant text of the Qur'an, Islam's sacred scripture, sunna provides the foundation for Islamic law, *sharia*.

The term Sunni Islam (sometimes referred to as Sunnism) takes its name from the concept of sunna. People who practice Sunnism are called Sunnis. This majority branch of Islam (about 85 percent of the Islamic population in the world) is officially known as *ahl as-sunna wa-l-ijma* which is translated, "people of the custom and consensus." As suggested by their name, Sunni Muslims hold that their interpretation of Islam is based upon the traditions of the Prophet Muhammad and upon the collective consensus of religious experts whose knowledge of the Qur'an and the sunna guide the Islamic community on what Muslims call the "straight path" to God. By contrast, the other major branch of Islam, the Shiʿites (about 10 percent of the Islamic population), accept the sunna of the Prophet, but reject the principle of *ijma* (consensus). For Shiʿites, God provides leadership for Islam, not through consensus, but by sending divinely guided leaders called *imams* who are thought to be descended from the fourth caliph (successor of Muhammad), Ali. This means that while both Sunnis and Shiʿites have developed complex and comprehensive legal systems, the Sunnis rely more on a legal process for determining what God deems right and wrong, and the Shiʿites rely more upon a legitimate and "infallible" imam (religious leader) to articulate God's will for the community. Sunnis also have imams, but in their tradition, they are simply leaders of community prayer in the mosque.

Ronald A. Pachence

See also ALI; CALIPH (KALIPHA)/ CALIPHATE; HADITH; IJMA; IMAM; MOSQUE/MASJID; MUHAMMAD; QUR'AN; SHARIA/SHARI'A; SHIʿA/SHIʿI/SHIʿITE/SHIʿISM.

SUPERNATURAL

This term usually has two basic meanings: (1) a reality (but not a place) that lies beyond this natural world; and (2) a quality of actions, communications, or gifts from God. The term is not equivalent to "spiritual," or "religious."

Orlando Espín

See also GRACE; IMMORTALITY; NATURAL LAW; SALVATION.

SUPERNATURAL EXISTENTIAL

Karl Rahner developed the phrase "supernatural existential" to explain human being's dynamic orientation toward an encounter with God. The concept is a dynamic interpretation of the traditional doctrine of the nature–grace relationship (the obediential potency). Rahner's interpretation of the relationship uses dynamic and existential concepts from Heidegger's philosophy. Rahner proposes human beings to have an inherent dynamic disposition (or orientation) in thought and will for being, existence (as such), although in an unthematic, nonconceptual way. This grasp of being is the horizon or background of every act of knowledge (concept) and freedom (choice). The intuition of being is not extraneous to human being; it is an ontological structure in human existence, an existential. The disposition grounds the human potential for the eventual acceptance of the Word of God, or the explicit encounter with God that comes as grace. The term "supernatural" notes the gratuitous character of revelation, of the realized relationship with God that comes always from the divine, not human initiative.

Patricia Plovanich

See also FREE WILL; GRACE; REVELATION.

SUPRALAPSARIANISM

See INFRALAPSARIANISM.

SURA

Sometimes written surah, the Arabic word for "row," used to designate one of the one hundred fourteen "chapters" of the Qur'an, the sacred scripture of Islam. Each sura is divided into ayas or "verses," much like the arrangement of texts in the Bible. For example, the citation of a particular passage of the Qur'an would look like this: 76:5. The number 76 refers to Sura 76, and 5, to the fifth aya of that sura. The suras of the Qur'an are arranged beginning with the longest (except Sura 1, called "The Opening," al-Fatihah in Arabic, which has only seven ayas), and ending with the shortest.

Ronald A. Pachence

See also AL-FATIHAH; AYA; QUR'AN.

SUTRA

A "thread" (Pali, Sutta) of connected sermons spoken by the Buddha. In Buddhist literature, these are distinct from Shastra, treatises composed by later philosophers that interpret the teachings. In the Sthavira schools, all the sermons thought authoritative were collected in one of the three collections of the early canon, the Sutra Pitaka (Pali, Sutta Pitaka). In the Mahayana schools there is no closed canon, and the standards for "authoritative" texts were extended to match the doctrinal acceptance of Buddhas as supramundane beings capable of supernatural forms of preaching after the human death of the Buddha Gautama.

Todd T. Lewis

See also BUDDHISM; SUTRA PITAKA.

SUTRA PITAKA

One of three divisions (pitaka = lit., "basket"), along with the Vinaya and Abhidharma Pitakas, that define the early Indic Buddhist canons. (The Theravadin Pali Canon's term is "Sutta Pitaka.") It contains almost every sermon of the Buddha of accepted authenticity, each of which begins with the testimony "thus I have heard," implying the community's verbatim memory of the occasion. This conventional opening reflects the practice over the tradition's first several centuries when all discourses were passed down orally by the monks.

The sermons are divided into five parts called Agamas (Pali, Nikayas), arranged according to the length of the remembered discourse.

Todd T. Lewis

See also ABHIDHARMA/ABHIDHAMMA PITAKA; HINAYANA; PALI; VINAYA.

SUZUKI, DAISETSU TEITARO (1870–1966)

One of Japan's foremost authorities on Zen Buddhism and popularizer of Zen in the West. He practiced, taught, and wrote about Zen in Japan for most of his life. In his later years he traveled to the West, teaching, lecturing, and writing about Zen and Japanese culture. He is generally viewed as the primary figure in the spread of Zen from Japan to the West with his focus, for the most part, on the Rinzai tradition. His many books include: *Introduction to Zen Buddhism*, *Zen and Japanese Culture*, and *The Essence of Buddhist Studies in Zen Buddhism*.

G. D. DeAngelis

See also ZEN.

SUZUKI, SHUNRYU (1905–71)

Well-known Japanese Zen master who helped to popularize Soto Zen practice in the United States. He is believed to be a direct spiritual descendant of the thirteenth-century Zen master Dogen. He visited the U.S. in 1958 and stayed on to found the San Francisco Zen Center and the Zen Mountain Center, the first Soto Zen training monastery outside of Asia. His book, *Zen Mind, Beginner's Mind*, has become a classic in the Western Zen tradition.

G. D. DeAngelis

See also DOGEN; ROHATSU; SANZEN; SATORI; SESSHIN; SOTO; ZAZEN; ZEN.

SWEDENBORG, EMANUEL (1688–1772)

Swedish visionary Emanuel Swedenborg significantly influenced the Western mystical, metaphysical, and occult traditions through his writings. He began his career as a scientist, but in his fifties turned to religious study after a series of visions. He developed a spiritualist approach to interpreting the Scriptures, arguing that the visible world reflects an invisible one. Everything material corresponds to aspects of the spiritual. Thus, the Bible can only be interpreted from a spiritual per-

spective; for example, Swedenborg proclaimed the Second Coming had occurred spiritually in 1757 through his revelation of its meaning. Rejecting Calvinism, Swedenborg preached millenarianism, universalism, and perfectionism. He did not establish a church, but his followers organized the Church of the New Jerusalem in 1784. Although he did not reach a wide audience during his lifetime, after his death, his ideas and especially his hermeneutical principles were adopted by a variety of religious groups, including Transcendentalists, Spiritualism, Theosophy, and mental healing.

Evelyn A. Kirkley

See also CHRISTIAN SCIENCE CHURCH; MILLENARIANISM; TRANSCENDENTALISM.

SYLLABUS OF ERRORS

This papal document (*Syllabus Errorum*) was issued with Pope Pius IX's encyclical *Quanta Cura* (1864) that condemned many nineteenth-century philosophical, political, and theological theories as erroneous. Among views condemned were pantheism and rationalism, the sociopolitical movements, communism, and socialism. Both documents condemned any theory proposing separation of church authority from that of the state and any challenge to papal primacy. The *Syllabus*, an addition to the letter, listed some eighty errors suggested in the encyclical in thesis form.

The encyclical and the *Syllabus* established the church's defensive and negative posture toward the modern world and anticipated the Vatican I defense of papal primacy and infallible authority and the condemnation of Modernism. However, it reiterated treasured Catholic convictions about the human potential for God and reason's capacity for the natural knowledge of God, although it did this in a negative way. The positions of Vatican Council II have generally displaced the positions espoused in this document and describe the church's situation in the modern world in a positive way.

Patricia Plovanich

SYMBOL

Winfried Nöth describes *symbol* in his *Handbook of Semiotics* as "perhaps the most overburdened term in the field of humanities." The burden arises not only with its near-synonymy with the term *sign* but also from three major connotations various disciplines have given the word. The first major connotation comes from the field of philosophy. Charles Peirce, the great American philosopher, defined the symbol as a conventional sign, that is, a sign whose meaning is agreed upon by convention. The notion of the conventionality of the symbol was applied to understanding the nature of human being by Ernst Cassirer. In *The Philosophy of Symbolic Forms*, Cassirer portrayed the human being as *animal symbolicum*. Human beings bridged the world of the senses and the world of the spirit by creating symbols. Human beings, then, know reality through the use of symbols. This insight by Cassirer has been influential in the anthropology of religion and the study of myth.

The second connotation of the word *symbol* comes from the field of aesthetics and was influenced greatly through the work of Charles de Saussure. This second connotation emphasizes the iconic nature of symbol, that is, its likeness to the object signified. Kant, for example, defined the symbol in his *Critique of Judgment* as "indirect representations of the concept through the medium of analogy." Saussure saw the symbol as "never wholly arbitrary; it is not empty, for there is the rudiment of a natural bond between the signifier and the signified. The symbol of justice, a pair of scales, could not be replaced by just any other symbol, such as the chariot."

The most influential understanding of symbol in theology, however, comes from its third connotation. This understanding sees symbol as a complex sign carrying a "surplus" of meaning. Tzevetan Todorov gave a classical definition of symbols as "defined by that excess of meaning with which the signified overflows the signifier." Paul Ricoeur has been the most influential writer on symbols for theology. According to Ricoeur, "there is a symbol where language produces compound signs whose meaning, not contented with designating one thing, designates another meaning that can only be realized by and from its own internal organization." In other words, the literal sense of a symbol has to be replaced by its figurative sense. As such, Ricoeur's understanding of symbol closely approximates the notion of metaphor. Ricoeur's "symbol" connotes a certain participation by the receiver of the symbol in the figurative reality denoted through the analogical or metaphorical nature of the symbol itself. "Symbol," then, does not designate a well-defined reality. Rather, it articulates a subtle reality associated with a fundamentally human process that creates complex signs in order to know reality—a conventionality whose members participate in a surplus of meaning.

Alex García-Rivera

See also SEMANTICS; SEMIOTICS; SIGN; SYMBOLICS.

SYMBOLICS

Symbolics as a term was first used in 1923 by the philosopher Ernst Cassirer in *The Philosophy of Symbolic Forms* and designates the study of symbols. The study of symbols, however, antedates Cassirer by hundreds of years. St. Augustine is believed by many to be one of the most influential students of symbols. St. Augustine developed his understanding of symbols in an attempt to explain the apparent contradictions found in the Scriptures. Augustine saw these contradictions vanish if they were given a symbolic rather than a literal interpretation. This symbolic interpretation of the Scriptures was known as an allegory. Allegory connoted a parallel but deeper meaning found alongside the literal meaning of a particular scriptural text. Augustine applied this understanding of symbols to the received liturgical tradition known as sacraments. Sacraments, for Augustine, became *sacrum signa*, visible signs of an invisible sacred reality.

Augustine's notion of symbols as manifestations of an invisible sacred reality has been tremendously influential ever since. The modern study of religion has carried implicitly this notion of symbols, joining it with an understanding of the nature of human being as fundamentally symbolic. Ernst Cassirer, for example, saw the human being as essentially *animal symbolicum*, that is, the animal who uses signs. Human being comes to know reality by uniting the perceptible world of the senses with the imperceptible world of the mind in the symbol. Thus, the human being creates a world of symbolic forms, giving meaning to human existence reflected in language, myth, art, religion, and science. Indeed, the world of symbolic forms does not merely imitate but creates the reality of the human being.

Mircea Eliade believed such worlds of symbolic forms were at the heart of human nature and, thus, could be compared across different human cultural groupings. Along a similar vein, the modern study of psychology has also joined the Augustinian notion of symbol to a dimension of human nature. The study of the human mind has seen symbols as perceptible manifestations (dreams, inappropriate behavior, emotions, and so on) of an invisible reality (the unconscious, collective archetypes).

Alex García-Rivera

See also SEMANTICS; SEMIOTICS; SIGN; SYMBOL.

SYNAGOGUE

(Hebrew, *Beit HaKnesset*). A place set aside for Jewish communal worship. Unlike a temple, conceived as a residence of God and administered by a priesthood, the synagogue is a community institution, a place of meeting and prayer, administered by a nonpriestly leadership, in particular, the rabbi and cantor. In modern times, synagogues are built and maintained by groups of Jews who voluntarily band together to create such institutions. While in the United States synagogues frequently are affiliated with, and pay dues to, the Orthodox, Conservative, or Reform movements, they are financially and administratively independent, hiring and firing personnel and determining the content and nature of their programs according to the needs and desires of their particular membership.

Following the destruction of the Jerusalem Temple in 70 C.E., the synagogue became the preeminent institutional center of Jewish religion and culture. The growth of the synagogue in the medieval period led to the creation of specific administrative posts; the cantor, responsible for leading worship; and the sexton, charged with maintenance of the building. Only in the nineteenth century, in Western Europe, did the rabbi, previously an employee of the Jewish community and primarily responsible for adjudicating matters of law, become a synagogue employee, charged with synagogue administration, leadership of worship, and pastoral duties. Since that time, especially in the United States, synagogues have increasingly become large, multipurpose institutions, housing not only sanctuaries for worship but also schools, social halls, and other meeting facilities.

Judaism has few set rules for synagogue architecture, so that synagogues normally are built according to the aesthetic demands of the community. In the Western Hemisphere, the sanctuary almost always faces east, toward Jerusalem, and it has as its focal point the ark where the Torah scrolls are kept. In traditional sanctuaries, women have a separate seating area, either behind a partition (*Mehitzah*) or in a balcony.

In modern times, especially in Reform Judaism, the synagogue often is referred to as a temple. This reflects the Reform movement's break from the traditional Jewish yearning for the rebuilding of the Jerusalem Temple and the reinstitution of the sacrificial cult that took place there. Early reformers in the U.S.A. took the name temple for their places of worship, arguing that their sanctuaries were comparable to the original Temple and that they had no desire for a return either to the Jewish ancestral homeland or for the re-creation of the earlier, priest-centered form of divine worship.

Alan J. Avery-Peck

See also ARON HAKODESH; BEIT HAMIKDASH; CANTOR (IN JUDAISM); EZRAT NASHIM; NER TAMID; RABBI.

SYNCRETISM

The combining and reinterpreting of various cultural and religious forms. Religious elements of diverse origins are brought together to form a new religion.

In Japanese culture, syncretism is favored and is the major feature of Japanese religion. If religious persecution occurs in Japan, it typically involves problems with devotion to a single religion. Buddhism, Shinto, Confucianism, Taoism, folk religion, and Christianity are all represented by mutual influence and borrowing. For example, Shinto borrowed magic and divination from Taoism, and Buddhism adapted to beliefs about the dead and the sacred mountains. Different traditions are assigned to different areas of life; for example, one may have a Shinto wedding and a Buddhist funeral, or different social groups may be associated with different religious obligations. Different religious practices are used on an ad hoc basis by individuals and groups to address their religious needs.

In the Americas, examples of syncretism are evident in the blending of Christianity with African and Native American religions. For example, Catholic saints are identified with African deities in many New World traditions. In Brazil, Cuba, Haiti, and Trinidad, there is a long tradition of borrowing, altering, and blending traditions. The vodoun religion combines elements of West African and Catholic religious beliefs and practices. The presence of Catholicism is apparent in vodoun ritual vocabulary, deities, iconography, and ritual practice. Vodoun practitioners who serve the spirits are Catholic and attend Mass, baptism, confession, and Communion, in part because they are directed to do so by the vodoun spirits. Catholic prayers, rites, images, and saints' names are integrated in the rituals in vodoun temples and cult houses. The characteristics of the bush priest exemplify the active force that Catholicism plays in vodoun. The religious leader knows the proper, Latin form of Catholic prayers and other aspects of Catholic ritual. Further, the Catholic liturgical calendar is an important aspect of vodoun ritual schedules. The religious system included parallels between Catholic saints and vodoun spirits. The use of Catholic saints is not to hide a sustained belief in West African deities. Rather, both traditions are blended.

In Latin America, a similar process of combining indigenous beliefs and practices with Christianity occurred. Christian practices of sacrifice, certain rituals, the variety of saints, and other features were assimilated into indigenous cosmologies. The merging of the various traditions in the syncretic process gives rise to powerful symbolic images and rituals that differ from the original sources. The rituals and images are also a way of sustaining prior indigenous worldviews and religious practices in the face of culture change. The new systems of belief may also provide a way of coping with rapid and disturbing culture change, as in the case of cargo cults and other revivalistic cults. Some of the new symbols, personages, and rituals that emerge from the process of syncretism become important representations of ethnic or national identity. The Virgin of Guadalupe in Mexico, for example, is a potent symbol of Mexican identity in that she represents the merging of pre-Columbian and Spanish deities in the same way the modern Mexican republic was forged with the linking of indigenous peoples and Spanish colonists.

Christine Greenway

See also AFRICAN TRADITIONAL RELIGIONS; AFRO-LATIN RELIGIONS; CARGO CULTS; VODOUN.

SYNODAL POLITY
A system of internal church government that grants highest authority to the synod. This system has been applied quite differently in several Christian denominations that follow the synodal form. In some cases, the synod is considered to be a meeting only of the bishops of the church, while in other cases it is the meeting of bishops, plus other clergy and representatives of the laity; the proportions of each group's representation in the synod also varies. Some denominations refer to the synod as the "general conference." The synodal polity is followed in churches of Calvinist and Baptist traditions, as well as in many Eastern Catholic, Anglican, and Orthodox Churches.

Orlando Espín

See also ANGLICAN COMMUNION; BAPTIST CHURCHES/BAPTIST CONVENTIONS; BAPTIST THEOLOGY; CALVINISM; CANON LAW; CONGREGATIONAL CHURCHES; CONGREGATIONAL THEOLOGIES; EASTERN CATHOLIC CHURCHES; ECCLESIOLOGY; METHODIST CHURCHES; METHODIST THEOLOGY; ORTHODOX CHURCHES; PRESBYTERIAN CHURCHES; PRESBYTERIAN THEOLOGY; REFORMED CHURCHES; REFORMED THEOLOGY (-IES); SYNODS.

SYNODS
Councils of bishops or other church leaders, meeting for deliberation on common

issues in the church. The term "synod" (from the Greek for "travel together") has several applications in modern Christian churches. The Second Vatican Council (1962–5), an authoritative gathering of Catholic bishops from all over the world otherwise called an *ecumenical council*, sometimes referred to itself as a "sacred synod." Occasional consultative gatherings of representative clergy and laity within a Roman Catholic diocese are referred to as *"diocesan* synods." In certain other Christian denominations, such representative bodies play essential roles in the overall governance of the church.

The custom of Christian leaders coming together to discuss matters of shared teaching and practice (particularly when a disagreement or a challenge had arisen) is as old as the New Testament. From time to time in the ancient and medieval church, certain *regional* synods of bishops produced statements later recognized as fundamental doctrine for the whole church. Although the importance of such localized gatherings of bishops diminished in Western Christianity as the influence of the Papacy increased, they continued to occur in a variety of places and circumstances. The ancient custom was revived and modernized by Vatican II in two forms. Permanent national or regional "conferences" of bishops meet periodically in their own regions all over the world for mutual support, consultation, and deliberation on common goals and problems. The World Synod of Bishops, a semi-regular gathering at the Vatican of selected bishops from all over the world, usually meets once every three or four years to share views and advise the pope on a single, prearranged topic.

William Clark, s.j.

SYNOPTIC GOSPELS

A term that refers collectively to the first three of the four written narratives of the Jesus story in the New Testament. These three accounts, Matthew, Mark, and Luke, are called the Synoptic Gospels because they present a similar view of Jesus' life and message. They "see" or "view" their subject "together." The term *synoptic* derives from two Greek terms: *opsis* (view) and *syn* (together). Because of their common narrative framework, these Gospels can be distinguished from the Fourth Gospel, the Gospel of John, that is unique in several aspects.

Before focusing more closely on the Synoptic Gospels, it is to be noted that all four Gospels in the New Testament share some general resemblance. For example, they agree in beginning their story of Jesus' public ministry with the activity of John the Baptist and culminate in recounting Jesus' suffering, death, and resurrection. Between the Baptist story and the passion narrative there are accounts of the sayings and mighty deeds of Jesus.

What then is the "similar view" that the Synoptic Gospels share with one another, in a way that distinguishes them from the Fourth Gospel? A similar pattern exists in that many of the same individual events are reported in the same order in all three Synoptics. Because of this, a useful tool for comparing these Gospel texts has been devised. This book, called a Synopsis, prints the texts of Matthew, Mark, and Luke in a parallel format that readily shows agreements (as well as variations) in order, wording, and meaning.

A close reading of the Synoptic Gospels gives the impression of agreements so striking that one is confronted with the question of how to understand these agreements. The consensus among biblical scholars is that they are best explained in terms of a literary relationship. To maintain that different documents have a literary relationship means that one has used the other as a source or that they have used a common source.

A literary relationship also means more than an author having some general knowledge of the same stories or that some coincidence in the arrangement of material has occurred. It is minimally required that a significant number of passages have the same basic content, given in generally the same sequence, with a high incidence of nearly identical words and phrases. This requirement is met, most would agree, by a comparison of the Gospels of Matthew, Mark, and Luke, thus affording a more precise meaning to the term "synoptic" used in the expression Synoptic Gospels. The explanation of this literary relationship between the three Synoptic Gospels is called the Synoptic Problem.

John Gillman

See also FOUR-SOURCE THEORY (OF SYNOPTICS); Q SOURCE; SYNOPTIC PROBLEM; TWO-SOURCE THEORY (OF SYNOPTICS).

SYNOPTIC PROBLEM

An expression used to name the questions arising when a literary comparison is made of the three Synoptic Gospels, Matthew, Mark, and Luke. A close comparison of these texts yields notable agreements as well as occasional divergences in three areas: (1) the order of narrative material, (2) the content of individual passages, and (3) the wording of the texts. How to explain satisfactorily the similarities and differences in the Synoptic Gospels is the challenge of the Synoptic Problem.

The same relative order of many narrative sections is found in all three Synoptics. There are, however, some variations. Using Mark as the common denominator, as is commonly done in Synoptic studies, there are times when the order in Matthew or in Luke diverges from that in Mark. To call Mark the common denominator means that the most logical way to speak of agreements and disagreements among the Synoptic Gospels is to do so with Mark as the reference. Two observations support making Mark the reference point: (1) where Matthew diverges from Mark, Mark's order is supported by Luke; and (2) where Luke diverges from Mark, Mark's order is attested by Matthew. Explaining the similarities and divergences in order is part of the Synoptic Problem.

A literary analysis of the content shows that some passages, such as the activity of John the Baptist, appear in all Gospels. These passages are referred to collectively as the "Triple Tradition." Other passages, such as the Sermon on the Mount/Plain, appear in only two of the Gospels, namely, Matthew and Luke, and not in Mark. These texts are called the "Double Tradition," a tradition that figures prominently in the discussion of the Q Source. A third group are those passages recounted in only one Gospel, and not in the others. Matthew, for instance, has a notable body of material, for example, the parable of the Sheep and the Goats (Matt 25:31-46), found only in his narrative. The same is true for the Gospel of Luke, who alone tells the parable of the Good Samaritan (Luke 10:29-37). The passages unique to any particular Gospel are often referred to as the "Special Tradition." Finding a way to explain the origin and interrelationship of the Triple Tradition, Double Tradition, and Special Tradition is an important part of the Synoptic Problem.

A third area of consideration for the literary relationship among the Synoptics involves a comparison of vocabulary, phrases, and syntax. For some passages of the Triple Tradition and the Double Tradition, there is remarkable agreement. How is this to be explained? At the same time, how does one account for the variations? Is it, for example, a matter of difference in style, the author's point of view, the intended audience, or the cultural context?

A particular type of data, called Minor Agreements, occurs in material from the Triple Tradition. There are a number of instances when Matthew and Luke agree with each other against Mark. Are these agreements coincidental or intentional? If the latter, do they come from some other source common to Matthew and Luke or are they the result of direct dependence between these two? These data are also grist for the mill of the Synoptic Problem.

The Two-Source Theory (from which developed the Four-Source Theory) is the most widely accepted explanation of the Synoptic Problem.

John Gillman

See also FOUR-SOURCE THEORY (OF SYNOPTICS); Q SOURCE; SYNOPTIC GOSPELS; TWO-SOURCE THEORY (OF SYNOPTICS).

SYRIAC VERSIONS OF THE BIBLE
Syriac is the best-known dialect of Eastern Aramaic, a language related to Hebrew and other Semitic languages. Syriac is well known because it became the language of the lectionary and the liturgy of much of Eastern Christianity in the second century C.E. Many Bible translations, com-

mentaries, and other writings survive in Syriac, and it continues as the liturgical language of Syriac Christianity today. Biblical translations in Syriac, both of the Old Testament and the New Testament, are of great importance for the textual criticism and textual history of the Bible. There are/were numerous Syriac versions of the Bible. The principal Syriac translation of the Old Testament is called the Peshitta, meaning, "the simple [version]." The name refers to the translation being easy to understand. It apparently stood in contrast to other Syriac versions that were more complicated and/or scholarly in nature. The Peshitta seems to have been a revision of older Syriac translations, not a new translation. It shows influence both from the Greek Septuagint and the Aramaic Targumim. It is uncertain how and when the Peshitta was created. Some scholars argue for a Jewish origin and link the translation to the conversion of the kingdom of Adiabene; other scholars argue for a Christian origin. There were other translations of the Old Testament into Syriac. One of the more important is the Syro-Hexaplar, a very careful, slavish translation of the Septuagint of Origen's Hexapla into Syriac that included the diacritical signs used to indicate the divergence between the Septuagint and the Hebrew text. This version, existing only in fragments, is of great importance for the history of the Septuagint. Of the many important Syriac translations of the New Testament, the best known is probably Tatian's *Diatessaron*. Tatian was a native of the Euphrates Valley who, in the middle of the second century C.E., created a compilation of the four Gospels in Syriac. The resulting *Diatessaron*, meaning, "through the four [Gospels]," was a work with great literary merit as well as fidelity to the Greek texts of the Gospels. Tatian apparently left out very little. The *Diatessaron* was used in the liturgy of Syriac Christian communities at least until the fourth century C.E.

Russell Fuller

SYRIAN CATHOLIC CHURCH

Also known as Jacobite Catholic, it is a church in full communion with Rome. Syrian Catholics descend from the Monophysite Syrian Church, often called "Jacobite." In the seventeenth century there was a group of Jacobites in communion with Rome, but they disappeared. Then in 1781 another community of Jacobites again established communion with Rome. They suffered terribly under Turkish persecution during World War I. Today there are about 120,000 Syrian Catholics spread throughout most of the world, under the overall jurisdiction of the patriarch of Antioch (in Damascus).

Orlando Espín

See also ANCIENT CHURCHES OF THE EAST; ANTIOCHENE THEOLOGY; COMMUNION (ECCLESIOLOGICAL); EASTERN CATHOLIC CHURCHES; MONOPHYSITISM; ORTHODOX CHURCHES; PATRIARCH.

SYRO-MALABAR CATHOLIC CHURCH
See MALABAR CATHOLIC CHURCH.

SYSTEMATICS/SYSTEMATIC THEOLOGY
See DOGMATIC THEOLOGY.

T

TABERNACLE (CHRISTIAN LITURGICAL)

The word *tabernacle* (from the Latin *tabernaculum*, a hut or tent, a location used for religious purposes) refers most commonly in modern Christian use to the small locked box, often made out of metal, in which consecrated Hosts left over from the celebration of the Eucharist (or Mass) are kept, or reserved. Some Christian churches continue the practice of reserving some previously consecrated Hosts in a special location in the church building. In earlier centuries, the reserved sacrament might be kept in the sacristy or in the main body of the church, in a small metal container suspended from the ceiling by a chain (often in the shape of a bird, called a *eucharistic dove*), or in an ornate pillar-like structure called a *sacrament tower*.

Consecrated Hosts were reserved for use as Viaticum for the sick and the dying; later, the practice of quiet prayer in the presence of the reserved sacrament developed, until often a reserved Host might be deliberately taken out and "exposed" in a transparent protective stand (a monstrance) for more formal blessings of the faithful (Benediction). In Roman Catholicism, the Council of Trent (1545–63) mandated the use of a secure location for the reserved sacrament, and so the tabernacle came into wide use. The tabernacle is often decorated, or covered with a veil, and can be placed on the central axis of the church (usually on what is called the high altar against the back wall) or on a side altar. This side altar may be located in the main church or in a separate chapel set aside for prayer and adoration.

Joanne M. Pierce

See also ADORATION; COMMUNION (LITURGICAL); CONSECRATION (CHRISTIAN); EUCHARIST; MONSTRANCE; VIATICUM.

TABERNACLES, FEAST OF

(Hebrew, Sukkot). With Passover and Pentecost, one of Judaism's three pilgrimage festivals, on which, in biblical times, all Israelites males were obligated to appear at the Temple in Jerusalem (Deut 16:16). Tabernacles commemorates the Israelites' dwelling in the wilderness in booths following the Exodus from Egypt (Lev 23:43). It also has an agricultural significance, marking the fall harvest in the Land of Israel (Deut 16:13).

In Jewish theology, Tabernacles commemorates of the rootless wandering of the Israelites in the wilderness following the receiving of the revelation at Sinai. Through observance of Tabernacles, Jews experience the delight of union with God, the splendor of the journey to the Promised Land, and the great bounty God provides. Tabernacles thus is a festival of commitment to God, with the image of the temporary booth leading to a renewed recognition that people are primarily dependent upon God for security and fulfillment of their needs. Tabernacles thus promotes dedication to God's law and way of life.

Tabernacles lasts seven days. The first (and, in the Diaspora, second) day is a holy day, on which work is prohibited. The eighth (and, in the Diaspora, ninth) day is Shemini Atzeret (and Simhat Torah), again a holy convocation on which work is prohibited (Lev 23:39). The intermediate days are called Chol HaMoed. The holiday is celebrated through worship services in the synagogue and, at home, through the construction of a booth ("Sukkah"), roofed with foliage ("Skhak"), through which the sky can be seen. The tradition is actually to dwell in this structure during the duration of the festival (Lev 23:42) or, at least, to eat meals there. Additionally, following the prescription of Leviticus 23:40, during Tabernacles, Jews say a benediction over the Lulav and Etrog, comprised of species of vegetation representing the bounty of the Land of Israel. In synagogue worship, these items are carried in processionals.

Alan J. Avery-Peck

See also CHOL HAMOED; ETROG; LULAV; SIMHAT TORAH.

TABOO OR TABU
A prohibition against approaching a certain person or place, handling a special object, performing a particular action, or saying a specific word that is regarded as sacred, dangerous, or otherwise forbidden. Often, the taboo object is dangerous precisely because it is sacred, that is, charged with spirit power or mana. Breaking a taboo, even unknowingly, may bring about misfortune or even death. At the least, some ritual of purification or atonement will be required. The word—coming into English through the writings of the eighteenth-century explorer of Polynesia James Cook—has, of course, come to have wider, but related, meanings in modern discourse.

Lance E. Nelson

See also INDIGENOUS RELIGIOUS TRADITIONS; MANA.

TABU
See TABOO OR TABU.

TACHRICHIN
In Judaism, these are the simple shrouds in which a deceased person is dressed for burial, normally constructed of plain linen cloth. The use of similar burial garb for rich and poor alike expresses Judaism's recognition that in death all people are equal. Thus the poor are saved from embarrassment, and the funeral is prevented from becoming an occasion on which wealth can be shown off.

Alan J. Avery-Peck

TAHARAH
(Hebrew, purification). In Judaism, this is the procedure by which a corpse is washed in preparation for burial, seen as a final sign of respect and honor for the dead. This ritual is not connected to the rituals of cultic purity that apply to the living (see Taharat Hamishpachah). In-

stead, the washing of the corpse is a continuation of the norms of hygiene that apply in life and an opportunity for the individuals performing the rite to honor the deceased in a totally selfless manner, insofar, as their actions cannot be repaid by the recipient.

Alan J. Avery-Peck

See also CHEVRA KADDISHA.

TAHARAT HAMISHPACHAH

(Hebrew, family purity). In Judaism, these are the religious laws defining periods of required sexual abstinence during and immediately following the wife's menstruation. These laws include regulations regarding the wife's monthly immersion in a ritual bath (Mikveh) to be cleansed of the cultic impurity understood to derive from menstrual blood. A basic aspect of the Orthodox Jewish way of life, Taharat Hamishpachah is rarely practiced among Conservative and Reform Jews.

Alan J. Avery-Peck

T'AI CHI

(Chinese, *tai ji*, The Supreme Ultimate). This is the early philosophical concept found in the *I-Ching* (Book of Changes) symbolizing the First Principle from which all being derives. Without engaging in activity it impels the vital force (*ch'i*) to generate movement and change within matter and thereby produces two energy modes (*yang* and *yin*) and the five elements (*wu-hsing*), leading to the creation of all phenomena. According to the *I-Ching*, "with reference to the entire universe, there is in it one Great Ultimate. With reference to the myriad things, there is a Great Ultimate in each of them."

G. D. DeAngelis

See also CH'I; CHU HSI; I-CHING; WU-HSING; YIN AND YANG.

TAIZÉ

Taizé is the town in France where, in 1940, Roger Schutz founded an interdenominational monastic order known as the Taizé Community, or simply "Taizé." This religious community has been especially concerned to promote Christian unity as well as to reinvigorate the practice of prayer and contemplation among Protestants. Composed of Catholic and Protestant members, the community is a living sign of reconciliation. They are committed to simplicity of life and live alongside the poor. A man of deep peace and compassion, Brother Roger was killed in 2005. The spirit of Taizé suggests a comparison with the ecumenical ashram founded by Bede Griffiths in India.

William Reiser, S.J.

See also ASHRAMA/ASHRAM; COUNSELS (OF PERFECTION); ECUMENICAL MOVEMENT/ECUMENISM; GRIFFITHS, BEDE; PROTESTANTISM/PROTESTANT.

TALAQ

The Islamic term for divorce, or more properly, the "repudiation" of one's wife by her husband. Though scholars are quick to point out that Muslim women today may exercise many more prerogatives in divorce proceedings than they have had in the past, including the initiation of a divorce or mutually agreeing with her husband to a permanent separation, *talaq* has traditionally referred to the husband's right to free himself from the marriage bond by stating this intention three times and observing the complex divorce protocols prescribed by the law. Students of Islam, however, should be careful to avoid the conclusion that divorce is treated lightly in Islam. Both Islamic law and tradition strongly discourage the dissolution of a marriage. Though permitted by the Qur'an, the sacred text of Islam (2:228-232; 65:1-7), the Prophet Muhammad (570–632) reportedly said that God hates divorce. The Qur'an itself counsels arbitration before a divorce is considered (4:35).

Ronald A. Pachence

See also ISLAM; MUHAMMAD; QUR'AN.

TALLIT

In Judaism, this is a rectangular garment with a fringe (Tzitzit) at each corner, worn as a shawl. The custom of wearing the tallit derives from Numbers 15:38, where God commands Israelites to place fringes on the corners of their garments. The Tallit normally serves as a prayer shawl and is worn by men (and, today, increasingly, women) during morning worship. Strictly orthodox Jews also wear a Tallit Qatan ("small Tallit") under their shirt throughout the day. In the contemporary Reform movement, the practice of wearing a Tallit during prayer has been largely abrogated.

Alan J. Avery-Peck

TALMUD

Either of two vast commentaries to the Mishnah, one created in the Land of Israel (around 400 C.E.) and called the Talmud of the Land of Israel or Palestinian Talmud (Hebrew, Yerushalmi, "Jerusalem" Talmud), and the other composed in Babylonia (around 600 C.E.), called the Talmud of Babylonia (Hebrew, Bavli). The Talmuds are comprised of two separate parts: the Mishnah, the underlying text subject to analysis; and the Gemara, comprising the rabbinic commentary on the Mishnah.

Generally, when the term Talmud is used, reference is to the Gemara, that is, to the Talmudic interpretation of the Mishnah.

The Babylonian Talmud contains explanations of thirty-seven of the Mishnah's sixty-three tractates. Excluded are the tractates devoted to agricultural tithes that are not paid from produce grown outside of the land of Israel, and Temple sacrifices that were no longer offered in the period of the Talmud's formulation. The Talmud of the land of Israel comments on thirty-nine of the Mishnah's tractates, including those on tithing, a topic pertinent to the rabbis of the land of Israel who created this document.

The Bavli is the larger Talmud, containing a significant amount of Midrashic material as well as commentary on the Mishnah. Because of its size and later date of composition, Judaism holds the Talmud of Babylonia to be the consummate text of rabbinic Judaism, melding together the various prior strains of material into one conclusive statement. The Babylonian Talmud therefore has stood at the foundation of all later theological and legal developments within Judaism from the time of its completion and until the present day.

Alan J. Avery-Peck

See also MISHNAH; RABBINIC JUDAISM.

TAMA

(Japanese, spirit). A somewhat obscure concept in Shinto referring to the soul or spirit of things that can be found in *kami* and humans. Various rituals are used to address and manipulate this spirit. It is believed to predate the notion of kami.

G. D. DeAngelis

See also KAMI; SHINTO.

TAMAYO ACOSTA, JUAN JOSÉ (1946–)

Spanish Catholic theologian. Tamayo received the licentiate in theology at the University of Comillas, Madrid, and then (in 1976) the doctorate in theology at the Pontifical University of Salamanca. He later (1990) earned a doctorate in philosophy at the University of Madrid. Tamayo has taught at several institutions and is currently professor of religious and human rights studies at the Carlos III University in Madrid. He was one of the founders of (and remains active in) Spain's respected John XXIII Theological Association. Tamayo is a frequent speaker at European and Latin American theological congresses, and has been actively involved in the development of progressive Catholic theology in Spain and Latin America. A friend and supporter of Latin American theologies and theologians, Tamayo has written extensively on topics related to progressive thought, human rights, liberation theology, and lay participation in the church. He was a frequent collaborator of Casiano Floristán. Among Tamayo's most influential works are *Por una Iglesia del pueblo* (1976); *Conceptos fundamentales del cristianismo* (1993); *Dios y Jesús. El horizonte religioso de Jesús de Nazaret* (2000); and *Nuevo paradigma teológico* (2003).

Orlando Espín

See also FLORISTÁN, CASIANO; LAITY; LATIN AMERICAN THEOLOGIES; LIBERATION THEOLOGIES; METHOD IN THEOLOGY; OPTION FOR THE POOR.

TAMEZ, ELSA (1950–)

Mexican feminist biblical scholar Elsa Tamez is one of the most prominent voices in contemporary Latin American feminism. Her method is characterized by the dual hermeneutic of reading the Bible from the perspective of the poor while infused with a feminist consciousness. Tamez is considered a foremother in Latin American feminist theology, as one of the first feminists to directly challenge male Latin American liberation theologians on the patriarchal presuppositions of their theology. A Methodist scholar, she has worked hard to create a forum for both grassroots and Latin American women scholars within the theological academy. Among her more important publications are *Against Machismo: Rubem Alves, Leonardo Boff, Gustavo Gutiérrez, José Míguez Bonino, Juan Luis Segundo and Others Talk about the Struggle of Women: Interviews* (1987); *The Scandalous Message of James: Faith without Works Is Dead* (2002); and *Struggles for Power in Early Christianity: A Study of the First Letter of Timothy* (2007).

Michelle González

See also BIBLICAL CRITICISM; FEMINISM; FEMINIST THEOLOGIES; LATIN AMERICAN THEOLOGIES; LIBERATION THEOLOGIES.

TANAK

In Judaism, an acronym connoting the Hebrew Scriptures, standing for Torah (Pentateuch), Neviim (Prophetic books), and Ketuvim (Hagiographa).

Alan J. Avery-Peck

See also HEBREW SCRIPTURES.

TANG DYNASTY (618–907 C.E.)

Often referred to as China's Golden Age, the Tang Dynasty was marked by a period of political unity, artistic and literary development, and a general flourishing of Chinese culture stimulated by foreign influences. This period also witnessed the increasing influence of foreign religions such as Buddhism, Christianity, Judaism, and Islam that were able to coexist with Confucianism, Taoism, and the native folk practices for a period of time. Buddhism even received state support that was eventually withdrawn when it was perceived as a political threat. However, the development of the Buddhist schools and truly Chinese forms of Buddhism enabled it to secure both a spiritual and intellectual foothold in China that would continue to the present day. This was a period in which Confucianism and Taoism flourished as well.

G. D. DeAngelis

See also BUDDHISM; CONFUCIANISM; DAOISM.

TANTRA

A pan-Indian religious movement, Tantra developed important Hindu and Buddhist schools, exerted a profound influence on the whole spectrum of Hindu practice, inspired certain developments in Jainism, and migrated to Tibet, East Asia, and Southeast Asia. Tantra first appears in history in texts dating from the sixth century C.E., although it undoubtedly has roots that are much more ancient. Tantra offered India a non-Vedic but still elaborately ritualistic approach to religious life, spiritual practice, and the quest for liberation. The rituals and worldview of this movement are expressed in scriptures known as Tantras and Agamas, which are, for Hindu tantrics, equal in authority to the Vedas and, for Buddhist adherents, equivalent to the word of the Buddha (*buddha–vacana*).

Tantric spirituality is characterized by the use of a kind of meditative ritual technology, often esoteric in nature. It emphasizes yogic practice rather than scholarship, employing such devices as *mantras, mudras* (ritual gestures), *mandalas* and *yantras* (mystical diagrams), and elaborate visualization exercises in which the practitioners identify themselves with deities through ritual meditations. Tantric practitioners rely heavily on initiatory empowerment and instruction by gurus, who themselves often became objects of worship. Although tantric schools came to include among their goals high states of mystical realization and the quest for moksha, elements with the tantric tradition, especially those that resisted assimilation into established orthodoxies, displayed as well a keen interest in the accumulation of spiritual and psychic powers (*siddhis*). Tantrism is typically associated in the popular mind with magical practices designed to secure worldly benefits, including sometimes black magic. The realized tantric adept is often called a *siddha* (accomplished one) and as such is expected to possess, and display more often than the saints of orthodoxy, magical powers or *siddhis*. Such emphases perhaps betray Tantra's early links to shamanism.

Another important feature of tantric spirituality is its religious valorization of the physical body and sensual experience. Tantra saw the body as a microcosm of the universe and the abode of spiritual forces that could be awakened and directed toward enlightenment. Tantrics also believed that the powerful energies associated with what were normally considered irreligious impulses, such as anger and the desire for sensual pleasure, including the erotic, could be harnessed to spiritual ends. Thus a small but significant portion of tantric practice involves, for certain qualified adepts, a kind of ritual sexual yoga, in which the yogi engages in prolonged meditative intercourse with a partner of the opposite sex, attempting to direct the energies thus released to a spiritual purpose. This utilization of experiences normally forbidden to spiritual aspirants in the more ascetically oriented schools is, in Hindu and Buddhist Tantra, justified in part by a thoroughly nondualistic theology. This way of thinking sees the world as a reflex of the ultimate reality, so that—as tantrics like to put it—the pure can be realized in the heart of the impure, thus overcoming the duality between the sacred and the profane. To demonstrate this radically nondualistic awareness, tantrics have been known to celebrate the repulsive and the offensive as well as indulge in the pleasurable. Thus human skulls, thigh bones, and corpses, along with the eating of meat and the drinking of liquor, have all played a part at times in tantric ritual.

Since such practices obviously offend the morality of the conventionally religious, who have typically regarded Tantrism with suspicion, tantrics have tended to keep their methods secret. This is another reason for the practitioner's extensive dependence on a guru, for the latter (who could be female as well as male) is expected to be in possession of oral traditions of knowledge that can unlock that which is hidden. A related feature of Tantra is the use in written texts of a kind of secretive code language, so that no one but initiates can have access to the details or real meaning of the most important rituals.

Lance E. Nelson

See also GURU; MANDALA; MANTRA; TANTRIC BUDDHISM; TANTRIC HINDUISM; VAJRAYANA BUDDHISM.

TANTRIC BUDDHISM

Also called *Vajrayana* ("Thunderbolt Vehicle") or *Mantrayana* ("Mantra Vehicle"), this term indicates the esoteric spiritual traditions that developed principally within later Mahayana Buddhism and as part of the pan-Indic yoga movement that sought quick enlightenment via unorthoprax means under the guidance of an accomplished teacher (*siddha*). Tantric Buddhism arose in continuity with the philosophical trends within Mahayana philosophy that equated *samsara* and *nirvana*, concluded that all beings partake of the buddha nature (*Tathagatagarba* doctrine), and found the essence of the Buddha's teaching the experience of unshakable diamond-like (hence, "*vajra*") insight (*prajna*) by whatever means necessary. It also arose to some extent in rejection of the established monastic Buddhism of post-Gupta India (after 500 C.E.) and especially in contrast to the path of the Mahayana bodhisattva who postponed the seeking of final enlightenment until a future lifetime.

There are in fact many recognized paths to enlightenment within tantric Buddhism, as it was comprised of dozens of traditions that cohered around separate texts (called *tantras*) that specified interrelated forms of initiation, ritual practice, medicine, *mantra* recitation, and visualization meditation, each focusing on a specific Buddhist deity surrounded by a *mandala* attendant deities. The central experience of tantric Buddhism is *sadhana*, communion with a celestial Buddha or bodhisattva through the experience of identification with his (or her) body, speech, and mind. Based on the assumption that the siddha who discovered each path had experienced the deity as the embodiment of enlightenment, an initiate is taught to place the deity (with entourage) in her mind's eye, repeat mantras that resonate with that form (or an entire *mandala*), and build an existential connection with it. Initiates perform *mudras* (hand gestures) and other rituals daily for the remainder of their lives that help to seal and deepen the identification. When the identification is complete, one's communion ultimately implies the attainment of coequal enlightenment with the divine form.

Some tantric traditions consciously break the norms of polite society, as men and women (who are often spouses) assume identities as divine, enlightened consorts. All their actions are thereby consecrated and seen symbolically, including sexual union, as embodying the unifying experience of *prajna* (the feminine, "insight") and *upaya* (the masculine, "apt practice"). Some of these tantric *yoga* traditions also involve the visualization and experience of transformative bodily energy, as the enlightenment force (called *bodhicitta* and identified as transformed semen) is made to move upward through a central bodily channel to reach visualized *cakras* (lotus-enclosed "wheels"); the highest cakra at the top of the skull, if suffused with bodhicitta, is identified with the experience of complete enlightenment. While sexual consort yoga was doubtless once an element in some tantric traditions, as these were developed in literary form and systematized within the monastic elite, the requirement of literal practice was often reinterpreted to be as merely visualized.

The tantric tradition traveled across Asia as a small monastic lineage within part of Mahayana Buddhism's north Asian diaspora to China (the Zhenyan school), Korea (Milgyo), and Japan (Shingon); in Nepal and Tibet, by 1000 C.E. it achieved dominance in monasteries and among the laity, as it was recognized as the most effective among the various Buddhist paths for humanity to reach enlighten-

ment today given humanity's declining spiritual capacity.

Todd T. Lewis

See also DHARANI; MAHAYANA BUDDHISM; MANTRA; SHUNYATA/SUNYA/SHUNYA; YOGA.

TANTRIC HINDUISM

Hindu Tantra is characterized, in its origins and in peripheral movements that have not been assimilated to orthodoxy, by an antibrahminical, anti-Vedic ethos, which has included the acceptance of low-caste and female practitioners, even in roles of leadership. Indeed, in the popular mind, any ritual that is not Vedic, or is performed by women, may be loosely classified as tantric. At the same time, however, aspects of brahminical orthodoxy have embraced Tantra and further extended its theology and ritual practice to highly sophisticated levels.

Hindu tantric theology centers on a theistically conceived bipolar Ultimate in which Shiva is the static, masculine principle of consciousness and knowledge and Shakti is the active, feminine principle of action and creativity. (Note that in Buddhist Tantra, the attributes of the masculine and feminine poles are reversed.) Most Tantrism is Shaiva or Shakta in orientation, but there are Vaishnava forms of Tantrism, in which Krishna and Radha take the place of Shiva and Shakti. This theology tends toward a thoroughgoing nondualism, in which the Ultimate is conceived to be the indissoluble union of the masculine and feminine principles, typically Shiva and Shakti. It is this unity that the advance adept seeks to replicate in consciousness and perceive vividly in every aspect of everyday life, and which is the theological support for Tantra's efforts to accept and spiritualize the sensual side of the personality. Since the world is Shakti, ultimately nondifferent from Shiva, then nothing of ordinary life needs to be excluded as profane.

A significant, if over-sensationalized, aspect of Hindu tantric practice is the ritual of the "Five Ms" (panca–makara), named after the five elements it uses sacramentally, the Sanskrit names of which all begin with the letter m. The five are: meat (mansa), fish (matsya), aphrodisiacs (mudra), liquor (mada), and sexual intercourse (maithuna). The qualified adept in this ritual aims at transcending conventional religious distinctions and, in meditative sexual congress, attaining —in awareness as well as act—the archetypal union of Shiva and Shakti.

A typical feature of Hindu Tantrism, and one that has had a wide influence on all yogic practice in India, is its interest in a spiritual energy known as kundalini, regarded as a manifestation of Shakti in the human body. This energy lies dormant at the base of the spine until it is awakened by spiritual practice, when it rises along the spine through psychospiritual centers known as chakras until it reaches the top of the skull, at which point the union of Shiva and Shakti is said to be experienced.

Two types of Hindu Tantra are generally distinguished: the "left-handed" practice (vamacara) and the "right-handed" (dakshinacara). The former, existing on the periphery of Hindu society, uses conventionally objectionable elements, such as the Five Ms, in its rituals. The latter eschews the actual use of such "sacraments," sometimes—but not always—replacing them by symbolic representations. Especially through its influence on the ubiquitous temple and home worship known as puja, this more socially acceptable form of Tantra has become, in its public forms, difficult to distinguish from mainstream Hindu ritual practice, excepting the relatively small segment of the latter that involves rites still identifiable as having their origins in the Vedic tradition.

Lance E. Nelson

See also CAKRA/CHAKRA; HINDUISM; KUNDALINI; PUJA; SHAIVA; SHAKTA; SHAKTI; SHIVA; TANTRA.

TAO

(Chinese, dao, lit., "Way"). An elusive but central concept in Chinese thought indicating that there is a natural way or pattern of movement and being for all things—the standard procedure of things. In a philosophical sense, there is an eternal "Way" of the universe or ultimate reality that is the ground of all being both transcendent and immanent and the regularity of operation of all things. For Confucians, the Tao is a sociopolitical concept implying that there is a correct standard of moral human conduct leading to harmony and order, integration and cooperation, and happiness. For Taoists, the Tao is conceived in metaphysical terms as the ultimate truth, the totality of all things, the reality behind or within appearances, and the ineffable power by which the universe exists in harmony. It is the primordial unity from which all things evolve and to which all things ultimately return. Its basic nature is obscure, elusive, mysterious, silent, formless, and ungraspable, and can only be known through direct experience of it.

G. D. DeAngelis

See also CH'I; CONFUCIANISM; CONFUCIUS; DAOISM; JEN; LAO-TZU; LI; T'AI CHI; WU-WEI; YIN AND YANG.

TAOISM

See DAOISM.

TAO SHIH

(Chinese, master of the Tao). In Religious Taoism, this is an ordained priest involved in the liturgical performances and magical rites. He engages in both communal liturgy as well as private ritual meditation. He is believed to serve as the intermediary between the divine and human worlds through his use of liturgy, ritual, and connection to the mystical body of Lao-Tzu. He is also believed to be capable of suppressing demonic forces.

G. D. DeAngelis

See also DAOISM; JADE EMPEROR; TAO.

TAO TE CHING

(Chinese, "The Scripture of the Way and its Power"). One of the great Chinese classics, believed to be the earliest work of Taoist philosophy. Popularly attributed to the Taoist sage Lao-Tzu, it is generally agreed that it is a compilation of insights and aphorisms from a number of early Taoist philosophers set down around 250 B.C.E. The text itself, written in a poetic and cryptic style, is a combination of old adages, enigmatic statements, poetry, prose, commentary, and the like. In one sense, it is a mystical and metaphysical text with its emphasis on quietism and spiritual union, and with a fondness for paradox. However, it is also a practical and political text written in a period of social chaos and intellectual ferment (Warring States Period, 441–205). While there is a clear political statement in the *Tao Te Ching* of laissez faire (minimal government), its primary impact has been religious and philosophical with its emphasis on the underlying principle of all life, the Tao, and the necessity for discovering and attuning oneself to the Tao. Its primary claim is that the Tao is the basic undivided unity in which all the contradictions and distinctions of existence are ultimately resolved. Not only has this text had an enormous impact on Chinese society and culture, but it is by far the most widely translated and most popular of the Chinese classics outside China.

G. D. DeAngelis

See also DAOISM; LAO-TZU; T'AI CHI; TAO; WU-WEI; YIN AND YANG.

TAPAS

A Sanskrit word meaning "heat," *tapas* in Indic religions refers to religious austerity and ascetic practices, such as meditation, fasting, and other more severe disciplines that are thought to generate spiritual power and "burn" accumulated karma. The word also refers to the power derived from austerity, which can be accumulated and used for spiritual or, sometimes, worldly ends. The ancient sages (*rishis*) of Hinduism especially were known for their tapas that enabled them, it is said, to become open to the Vedic revelation.

Lance E. Nelson

See also ASCETICISM/ASCETIC; REVELATION; RISHI; YOGA.

TARA

The great feminine celestial bodhisattva of Northern Buddhism who achieved particularly great popularity in Tibet and Nepal. Tara's genesis in popular narratives is said to be from a lotus growing from Avalokiteshvara's compassionate tears when he regarded the immeasurable suffering of beings. Assuming myriad forms, Tara works to save humanity in her vow: "There are many who desire Enlightenment in a man's body, but none who works for the benefits of sentient beings in the body of a woman." Twenty-one manifestations of the bodhisattva goddess eventually were identified for worship. In the Himalayas, Tara is particularly associated with long-life rituals; in her usual White or Green forms, she is the subject of visualization meditations as the ever-youthful, beautiful embodiment of compassion.

Todd T. Lewis

See also AVALOKITESHVARA; BODHISATTVA; BUDDHISM; MAHAYANA BUDDHISM.

TARGUM

A translation of the Hebrew Bible into Aramaic (in the first centuries B.C.E. and C.E.), the vernacular language of Jews in the land of Israel, Syria, and lands east. The best-known targums, preserved by Jewish scholars down through the centuries, are Targum Onkelos, the so-called Fragmentary Targums, and Targum (Pseudo-) Jonathan. All these are translations of the Pentateuch; Targum Jonathan contains the Prophets and the Hagiographa as well. These targums, along with Targum Neofiti to the Pentateuch, appear to have been completed between 300 and 700 C.E., although they are believed to contain some material that reflects the thinking of earlier periods.

In general, targums present a fairly literal rendering of the Hebrew text into Aramaic, although the translators often add to the literal rendition short interpolated comments. In addition, the targums occasionally contain sizable augmentations. These materials, and to a lesser extent the literal translations, reveal in-

formation concerning the use of Scripture by the translators. This information is important to modern scholars, in particular New Testament scholars, who hope to discover the way Scripture was understood by the Jews in the land of Israel in the first centuries C.E.

Alan J. Avery-Peck

TARYAG MITZVOT
See MITSVAH.

TATHAGATA

A term used to designate a Buddha, with its dual Sanskrit etymology indicating the term's multivalence for Buddhist devotees. Tathagata translates: "One who has come thus," that is, into the world of suffering to lead others; or "One who has gone thus," that is, into the transformative realization of nirvana in life and into parinirvana beyond death. In the Pali Canon, a Tathagata came to be regarded as possessing ten powers (*bala*) of knowing: what is possible or impossible; the ripening of his karma; where all paths of conduct lead; elements and factors of the world; intentions of individuals; faculties of other beings; the impurities and purities of various meditations; his former existences; a divine eye that sees beings going to their destinies according to their karma; and enlightenment. The Mahayana tradition goes even further, as quintessentially expressed in the *Lotus Sutra*, in which the extent of a Tathagata's powers is described as "inconceivable" to humans. They can assume whatever form desired anywhere in the cosmos.

Todd T. Lewis

See also BUDDHA; NIRVANA; PARANIRVANA.

TATHAGATAGARBHA DOCTRINE

The distinctively Mahayana Buddhist view that all beings have within them the potential for enlightenment. While the terms employ feminine imagery (lit., "Buddha-womb Doctrine"), this teaching follows from the Madhyamaka conclusion that nirvana and samsara completely interpenetrate, implicating all domains, environments, and experiences as potential existential venues for seeing the truth. It can surely, thus, abide with all beings and be translated, "Buddha potential," that is, as an ultimate, pure reality. In the *Lankavatara Sutra*, the *tathagatagarbha* is described as, "hidden in the body of every being like a gem of great value . . . eternal, permanent." Buddhist spiritual practice, in light of this understanding, can be seen, then, as the quest to eliminate the defilements that obscure the *tathagatagarbha*. For the Cittamatra school, this "Buddha potential" is located in the pure consciousness (*alaya vijnana*). Early Chinese Buddhists thought of the *tathagatagarbha* texts as defining a third school of Indian Mahayana Buddhism. More broadly, this view affected all East Asian Buddhist traditions.

Todd T. Lewis

See also CITTAMATRA; LANKAVATARA SUTRA; MAHAYANA BUDDHISM; ZEN.

TAT TVAM ASI

A Sanskrit phrase from the Hindu *Chandogya Upanishad* (6.8.7), *tat tvam asi* means, "That (*tat*) you are." The Advaita Vedanta tradition regards this statement as one of the "great declarations" (*mahavakya*) of scripture, since it reveals the truth of the identity of the inner Self or atman (the ultimate referent of the word "you") with the Absolute Brahman ("That"). Vaish-nava theologians such as Ramanuja and Madhva, who recognize a distinction between the individual soul and God, interpret this phrase as a compound, meaning "You are a part of That" or "You belong to That."

Lance E. Nelson

See also ADVAITA VEDANTA; DVAITA VEDANTA; UPANISHADS; VEDANTA; VISHISHTADVAITA VEDANTA.

TAWHID

From the Arabic verb *wahhada*, meaning, "to profess unity or oneness." In Islam, the *tawhid* is the testimony one gives to the unity of God. This testimony of divine sovereignty represents the most basic of all Islamic teachings, and it is emphasized in the first of the Five Pillars (foundational beliefs and practices) of Islam, the *shahada* (profession of faith): "I bear witness that there is no god but Allah (the one God) and that Muhammad is God's Messenger." Islam takes tawhid so seriously that associating anything or anyone with God as an equal to God (*shirk*) is considered the only unforgivable sin.

Ronald A. Pachence

See also FIVE PILLARS (IN ISLAM); SHAHADAH; SHIRK.

TE

(Chinese, *de*, lit., moral force, virtue, power). A force or power within individuals similar to what we would call character. For Confucius, this was seen as the heavenly conferred power by which men are ruled, and one of the five key concepts essential for harmony and social order. From a Confucian perspective, the true ruler (sage king) rules by the power of moral force (*te*) and thus inspires his subjects to act accordingly. While bestowed by heaven, this power had to be nurtured and cultivated by each ruler. In Taoism there is no separation between Tao and Te. Te is the active power in all existent things and, in effect, is the power of the manifested Tao. Wherever there is Tao there is Te.

G. D. DeAngelis

See also ANALECTS; CHUNG YUNG; CHUN-TZU; CONFUCIANISM; CONFUCIUS; DAOISM; TAO; TAO TE CHING.

TE DEUM

A fourth-century Latin hymn that begins, "*Te Deum Laudamus*," "You, God, we praise." It is sung or recited after the second reading of the Office of Readings on Sundays outside Lent, throughout the octaves of Easter and Christmas, and on solemnities and feasts. Writers once thought the *Te Deum* was the work of St. Ambrose and St. Augustine, but many scholars now believe that Bishop Nicetas of Remesiana, in modern Yugoslavia, was its author. That hypothesis, however, cannot be proved. The *Te Deum* begins with a number of stanzas praising God the Father, goes on to a section glorifying the Son, and ends with a series of petitions taken from the Psalms. Because of its strong elements of praise and its antiquity, it has been set to music by many composers, and it is often sung to mark occasions of great festivity and victory.

Patrick L. Malloy

See also AMBROSE OF MILAN; AUGUSTINE OF HIPPO; LITURGY OF THE HOURS.

TEILHARD DE CHARDIN, PIERRE (1881–1955)

French paleontologist and Catholic priest. At an early age he joined the Jesuit Order, and after service with the French army during World War I, Teilhard de Chardin went to work in China as a paleontologist. A series of remarkable discoveries (for example, he was part of the team that unearthed the specimen called "Peking Man") made him one of the world's most highly regarded scientists in his field. Teilhard de Chardin also wrote more theological texts inspired by and based on his scientific discoveries, and although he never contradicted his deeply held Catholic faith, he employed a language that made him suspect of heresy in the minds of church authorities—but was never formally accused or convicted of heresy. However, he was forbidden, by the same church authorities, from accepting an academic appointment at the prestigious Collège de France, and was not allowed to publish (during his lifetime) any of his theological writings. After World War II he moved to the United States. His theological texts were all finally published after his death, further enhancing his international prestige. During the twenty years after his death, his thought was deeply influential and very popular among educated Catholics throughout the world. His best-known theological writings are *The Phenomenon of Man* (1959) and *The Divine Milieu* (1960).

Orlando Espín

TELEOLOGICAL ARGUMENT

The teleological argument seeks to demonstrate that the existence of God is necessary to explain the order, harmony, and regularity observed in the physical, non-animate world. Thomas Aquinas's fifth argument and William Paley's *Natural Theology* are classic formulations of this argument. Contemporary versions often appeal to probability theory (for example, Richard Swinburne) or to strong (or weak) versions of the "anthropic principle" (for example, John Barrow and Frank Tipler).

J. A. Colombo

TEMPERANCE

The Latin *temperantia* is a translation of the Greek *sçphrosun²*. It is one of the four cardinal (*cardo*, "hinge") virtues, governing all the other virtues. As a virtue, it seeks the mean regarding all matters requiring restraint. A modern translation may well be "sobriety," in its particular (regarding to alcohol and drugs) and general sense. It is interesting to note that Thomas Aquinas says that one of the results of *temperantia* is "serenity of spirit," and that one of the constant prayers of those seeking sobriety in modern twelve-step programs is for serenity. In the understanding of Christian virtue, a temperate person acts and feels the right way not so much out of filial devotion to God, but out of love of his or her own integrity.

G. Simon Harak, s.j.

See also FORTITUDE; JUSTICE; PRUDENCE; VIRTUE.

TEMPLE

A sanctuary, building, or specially marked space for the worship or presence of a god, gods, ancestors, or spirits. It is the site of ritual practices such as offerings and sacrifice and may house priests and priestesses and sacred ritual paraphernalia. "The Temple" refers to three successive buildings constructed for the worshiping of Jehovah in Judaism. Temples in Babylonia, China, Mesoamerica, and South America were frequently built and maintained by corporate groups of worshipers, often a legally recognized group who owned the land, buildings, and other resources related to the temple. Mayan temples played a role in state formation

as centralized sites that served religious, political, and economic functions. They were the site of centralization of a religious elite, the reception of tribute payments, and the redistribution of goods to the broader populace. In various locales and traditions, temples may serve as the locus of charitable, educational, or medical activities. In some societies, secular and sacred architecture differs dramatically, and temple structures may be larger, more elaborate, and more luxurious than other buildings.

Christine Greenway

See also SACRIFICE; SANCTUARY (PLACE); WORSHIP.

TEMPLE (IN JUDAISM)

See SYNAGOGUE.

TEMPLE (OF JERUSALEM)

The Temple in Jerusalem was one of the most important sites for the worship of Yahweh in ancient Israel.

Solomon's Temple: The first Temple was built by Solomon, the son of David, to house the ark of the covenant, held sacred by all the tribes of Israel. David had brought the ark to Jerusalem during the establishment of his rule. The Temple was located on the eastern hill north of the city of David, where the Dome of the Rock is located today. This is the location of "the threshing floor of Araunah the Jebusite" (2 Samuel 24:18), "Mount Moriah" (2 Chr 3:1), and likely the "Zion" of the Psalms. The plan of the Temple was probably similar to that of the Tabernacle. A detailed description of Solomon's Temple is given in 1 Kings 6. It was rectangular with a porch or vestibule facing east, a nave, and a sanctuary or holy of holies where the ark was kept. This was the holiest part of the Temple.

The interior of the Temple was lined with cedar wood and gold. Besides the ark, the sanctuary also contained two figures of cherubim fashioned from olive wood and covered in gold. The nave contained a golden altar for incense, a golden lamp stand, and a golden table for the bread of the Presence. The Temple was surrounded by two courtyards. The inner courtyard contained the bronze altar for sacrifices, the ten bronze basins on either side of the Temple structure, and the great bronze sea. The Temple of Solomon was plundered several times in the history of Judah and was finally destroyed by Nebuchadnezzar of Babylon in 587 B.C.E.

Ezekiel: In chapters 40–48 of the book of Ezekiel, the prophet has a vision of a rebuilt Temple in Jerusalem. The vision does not exactly correspond to the Temple of Solomon but probably reflects other temples located in Judah.

Zerubbabel's Temple: The Babylonian exile ended in 538 B.C.E. with the decree of Cyrus of Persia that those Jews who wished could return to Jerusalem. The Temple was not immediately rebuilt and it was not until the urging of the prophets Haggai and Zechariah in 520 B.C.E. that the work to rebuild the Temple was taken up by Zerubbabel and Joshua the high priest. The Temple was finished in the year 515 B.C.E. and sacrifices resumed. In plan and size, the Second Temple was probably very similar to the Temple of Solomon.

Herod's Temple: Herod extensively renovated and expanded the Second Temple during the twentieth year of his rule. He did not tear the Second Temple down, but rather rebuilt it by sections using priests and Levites as workers in the sacred areas. Herod extended the size of the platform on which the Temple rested, using massive worked stones (ashlars) one to three meters in length. The remains of these retaining walls are visible today, and include the well-known "Western Wall." Herod's Temple was quite elaborate and was well known in antiquity as a masterpiece. The wonder this structure could evoke is recorded in the Synoptic Gospels. Herod's Temple was destroyed in 70 C.E. during the first Jewish revolt against Rome. Titus carried off the Menorah or lamp stand to Rome as part of the booty. This is pictured on the arch of Titus in the Roman forum.

Russell Fuller

TEMPTATION

Literally, temptation means being tested. Experientially, temptation refers to the tension that occurs when we are pulled in the direction of things we know or perceive to be bad for us. Temptation itself is hardly sinful; after all, Jesus was tempted in the desert (Mark 1:13), as the letter to the Hebrews reminds us (Heb 4:15); and it is not unlikely that Jesus was tempted on other occasions, as when Peter tried to dissuade him from his course and Jesus called Peter a "satan" (Mark 8:31-33). In the wilderness episode as drawn by Matthew (4:1-11) and Luke (4:1-13), Satan appears as the tester, the instrument by which Jesus' faith in God and his obedience to God's word were stretched, tried, and proven true. The Christian ascent to perfection would be inconceivable apart from the experience of temptation; virtue is not achieved without effort, and it cannot be maintained without practice. The best-known temptation story is probably that of Adam and Eve in the Garden (see Genesis 3), but we should not overlook God's testing the people in the wilderness (the Exodus story), or the testing of Job, or the many other instances in Scripture where an individual's faith and trust are "proven" or refined through a testing of some kind.

Temptation is thus not necessarily a sign of human brokenness, alienation, or moral weakness; sin is. But temptation does point to our incompleteness and the fact that we are still in the process of being created. Furthermore, human beings are not usually tempted by evil as such, but by things that in their own way are good, although they might not be good for us under a given set of circumstances. Learning to tell the difference between what is good and what is not good for us here and now constitutes elementary moral discernment. Yet not every mistake made along the way is automatically a sin. Existentially, it would be hard to learn the difference between life and death without ever having chosen wrongly and suffered the consequence. An individual who never endured any temptation would be spiritually feeble and bloodless, as Pierre Teilhard de Chardin observed (*Hymn of the Universe*, 88).

William Reiser, s.j.

See also CONSCIENCE; DISCERNMENT; FREE WILL; SIN, PERSONAL.

TEN COMMANDMENTS
See DECALOGUE.

TENDAI
The Japanese form of the Chinese Buddhist T'ien Tai (Heavenly Terrace) School brought to Japan in 805 C.E. by the Japanese monk Saicho (767–822), known posthumously by the honorific title of Dengyo Daishi. Saicho traveled to China around the same time (804) as his contemporary Kukai (Kobo Daishi), founder of the Shingon Sect. While Kukai immersed himself in the esoteric Chen Yen tradition in China, Saicho studied and practiced the more all-encompassing Mahayana T'ien Tai form of Buddhism.

Turning to the *Lotus Sutra* as the culmination of Buddha's teaching, Saicho attempted to synthesize all previous Buddhist teaching and practice into one great system. Like Kukai, he asserted that all beings have the potential for enlightenment and that "all forms of life stand on an equal basis in attaining Buddhahood." Unlike Kukai, Saicho's emphasis was less on esoteric ritual and more on meditative practice, scriptural study, and monastic living accompanied by faith in Amida Buddha.

With the support of the emperor, Saicho was able to establish the Tendai Sect and a new center at Mt. Hiei, outside of Kyoto, that became the new center of Buddhist studies in Japan. Not only did Tendai attempt to be a school inclusive of different types of Buddhism, nurturing the development of the Pure Land, Zen, and Nichiren traditions, but it also attempted to harmonize all religious views in Japan—Shinto, Buddhist, Confucian, popular/folk, and so on. While the practice of Tendai was ultimately too difficult for most people, it did play an integral role in making Buddhism Japanese.

G. D. DeAngelis

See also BUDDHISM; KOBO DAISHI; SHINGON; T'IEN TAI.

TENRIKYO
(Japanese, Religion of Divine Wisdom). One of Japan's "New Religions" and the oldest and largest of the New Shinto Group. It was founded by Miki Nakayama (1798–1887) after receiving a divine revelation from Tenri-No-Mikoto (God of Heavenly Wisdom) during a shamanic

trance. Her ongoing revelations provided the scriptural basis for practice and belief in this new movement. While Tenrikyo carried over many features of folk religion and popular and pluralistic shamanism, it is also taught that God, the Parent, who had created humanity, was attempting to call his people back to the original relationship between humans and God through his mediator, Miki Nakayama. Followers were called to Tenri City, the home of Miki and spiritual center of the world, where the Kandrodai (sacred pillar) stood, marking the spot of the creation of the world, to perform the sacred healing rites revealed by God. Tenrikyo is firmly rooted in traditional Japanese religion, but it is centered on a charismatic leader and developed its own ritual and scriptural forms, and, like many of the New Religions, nurtures a strong sense of community and a life of service to others.

G. D. DeAngelis

See also KAMI; MIKI NAKAYAMA; NEW RELIGIONS; SHINTO.

TEPEYAC
The name of a hill on the outskirts of Tenochtítlan (present-day Mexico City) on which there was a sanctuary to the Nahua goddess Tonántzin. A 1649 document called *Nican Mopohua* (written in the Nahua language) claims that in 1531 the Virgin of Guadalupe appeared on Tepeyac to a poor Nahua peasant named Juan Diego. There are serious historical difficulties with this claim. The church (today a magnificent basilica) on Tepeyac houses the painting of Guadalupe said by the *Nican Mopohua* to have appeared on Juan Diego's cloak. The basilica is the most-visited Catholic shrine in the world.

Orlando Espín

See also APPARITIONS; GUADALUPE, VIRGIN OF; INCULTURATION; LATINO CATHOLICISM; MARIAN DEVOTIONS; MARIOLOGY; NAHUA TRADITIONAL RELIGION; POPULAR CATHOLICISM.

TEPHILLIN
Hebrew, meaning "phylacteries," a ritual object for Jewish prayer. The Bible commands, "You shall bind them (these words which I command you this day—to love the Lord your God) as a sign upon your hand, and they shall be frontlets between your eyes" (Deut 6:8, and in variation: Exod 13:9, 16; and Deut 11:18).

The sages interpreted this command to mean that the words of God's commandment were to be written and attached to the heads and hands of pious Jews. They accomplished this by writing the words of the commandment on small parchment scrolls, and by placing the scrolls in small leather boxes, which, with leather straps, they placed on the arm and the head. These boxes with the parchment scrolls are called *tephillin*.

Tephillin are worn by traditional Jews at weekday morning worship services. They are considered a sign of love between God and the Jewish people, and they provide a vivid and dramatic connection to God and the commandments.

Wayne Dosick

TERTIAN
See TERTIARY.

TERTIARY
A member of a "third order." Usually a layperson associated with or committed to the ideals and spirit of a Catholic religious order (most frequently the Franciscans, the Dominicans, and the Carmelites). Less frequently, a "tertiary" could be a vowed member of a religious congregation

associated with the spirit or rule of one of the major orders. "Third orders" are so called, since their first canonical creation in the thirteenth century, because they gathered the laity associated with the "first" order (usually of friars) and the "second" order (usually of contemplative nuns).

Orlando Espín

See also CANON LAW; CARMELITES; CONGREGATIONS (ORDERS); CONTEM-PLATIVES; DOMINICANS; FRANCISCANS; FRIARS; LAITY; RELIGIOUS (VOWED); THIRD ORDERS.

TERTULLIAN

Born a pagan in North Africa, Tertullian received an excellent classical education. He converted to Christianity sometime before 197. By 212–3, he had joined an heretical Christian group called the Montanists, a puritanical and apocalyptic movement that expected a great outpouring of the Spirit followed by the end of the world. Tertullian died sometime after 222. By his own admission, Tertullian was an impatient and irritable man, and he tended to take extreme stands. Yet Tertullian was also a brilliant writer in his native tongue of Latin, and is one of the first Latin Christian writers. Tertullian was, for instance, the first to speak of three "Persons" in the Trinity in his opposition to Monarchianism. Tertullian has left an impressive number of treatises on topics ranging from proper dress to remarriage. He had a great deal of influence on later Latin Christian writers.

Gary Macy

See also APOCALYPTIC; HERESY; MONAR-CHIANISM; MONTANISM; PERSON/ PROSOPON; TRINITY/TRINITARIAN THEOLOGY/TRINITARIAN PROCESSIONS.

TESTAMENT

Literally, a legacy, the term is derived from the Latin *testamentum* to render the Greek *diatheke*, covenant.

Tertullian (ca. 160–230 C.E.) and Origen (185?–254? C.E.) introduced the terms "Old Testament" and "New Testament" to distinguish pre-Christian Scriptures from Christian writings that were invested with a similar sacred authority. By the fourth century, these designations were commonly used for the two major parts of the Christian Bible.

Recently, many English-speaking scholars have recognized that the English word "old," especially when juxtaposed with "new," carries negative connotations and may lend itself to the anti-Judaic replacement ideology that has dominated much of Christian history. However, popular alternatives, such as "Hebrew Bible," which excludes the deuterocanonical texts in Catholic and Orthodox Bibles, and the designation "Apostolic Writings," are inaccurate and inadequate. In the 1990s "First Testament" and "Second Testament" were considered the best alternatives. (See James A. Sanders, "First Testament and Second," *Biblical Theology Bulletin* 17 [1987] 47–9.) More recently, a number of scholars have returned to the traditional terms: "Old and New Testaments" while being very clear that these Christian designations speak of the Christian Bible that is to be distinguished from the Tanak that is to be honored as the Bible of Judaism.

Regina A. Boisclair

TESTAMENTS OF THE TWELVE PATRIARCHS

The *Testaments of the Twelve Patriarchs* (*T. 12 Patr.*) present themselves to be the final words of the twelve sons of Jacob.

They are clearly modeled on the last words of Jacob in Genesis 49. In each of the *Testaments*, the son gathers his offspring around him prior to his death and reflects on his life and his sins, and exhorts them to live a life of virtue. Each of the *Testaments* concludes with predictions about the future of Israel, and all of them give special attention to the tribes of Judah and Levi that produced the kings and the priests of Israel. Each of the *Testaments* recounts the burial of the patriarch of the tribe. The text of the *T. 12 Patr.* have come down to us in Greek, Armenian, and Slavonic. Fragments of testament have been found in Hebrew and Aramaic, but these do not seem to be directly related to the *T. 12 Patr.* The original language of the *Testaments* is uncertain; some scholars maintain a Semitic original, others argue for a Greek original. Although there are some Christian interpolations in the Testaments that probably originated in the second century C.E., it is likely that the *T. 12 Patr.* originated in the second century B.C.E. as is shown by the language, Greek, with use of the Septuagint and lack of historical allusions beyond the middle of the second century B.C.E. The *T. 12 Patr.* are important because they are part of a record of the diversity of perspective within Judaism in the last centuries B.C.E. and the first century C.E. This material also allows to see how the perspectives and beliefs, such as dyarchic (priest and king) messianism and devotion to the Law of Moses were taken over and developed by other groups within Judaism and early Christianity.

Russell Fuller

TESTEM BENEVOLENTIAE
An apostolic letter of Pope Leo XIII (January 22, 1899) to Cardinal James Gibbons

that condemned a series of opinions thought to be held by American bishops and theologians. Although it mentions the term only once, the letter is best known for its condemnation of "Americanism." The Pope warned against positions that claimed that the church's adaptation to the modern world demanded changes in doctrine. Some of the ideas condemned were attributed by Europeans to Isaac Hecker, the founder of the Paulist Order. These included key principles of the liberal secular state, such as the acceptance of religious pluralism and the denial of the political authority of the church. Whether any American Catholic thinker actually held such positions has continued to be debated by historians and theologians.

Mary Ann Hinsdale

See also AMERICANISM; HECKER, ISAAC.

TETRAGRAMMATON
A technical term that refers to the four-lettered holy name of God in Hebrew. The rendering of the name, in Roman characters, would be YHWH or JHVH. Because the name of God is held in such high reverence, it was seldom if ever pronounced. In time knowledge of the exact pronunciation of the name was lost. The devout Hebrews avoided pronouncing the holy name of God by simply substituting it with *Adonai* (which means "Lord"). The name "Jehovah," used by some Christians, is based on a sixteenth-century misinterpretation and misreading of the *Tetragrammaton* by combining the vowels of *Adonai* and the consonants YHWH.

Orlando Espín

See also ADONAI; EXODUS; HEBREW (LANGUAGE); JEHOVAH; JEHOVAH'S

WITNESSES; JUDAISM; LORD/LORDSHIP; YHWH.

TEXT CRITICISM

No copy of the authors' original manuscript—the "autograph"—of any book in the Bible survived antiquity. There are differences among the ancient manuscripts that have survived. Text criticism has two objectives: (1) To determine the most likely original reading by discerning why and how variant readings may have been introduced; and (2) to provide a history of the transmission of the texts through the centuries. To achieve these objectives, text critics consider all the existing ancient manuscripts and early fragments in the original languages. They also examine ancient translations, early lectionaries, and citations in patristic writings, since these sources may be based on texts that were more ancient than the extant manuscripts.

Variations among the manuscripts are classified as intentional or unintentional changes. Clearly, physical damages, caused by accident or decay that left holes in a manuscript, are unintentional changes. Those instances in which one or more lines or one or more letters are skipped, a homonym introduced, Hebrew vowels mispointed, or Greek letters misdivided, are presumed to be unconscious, unintentional scribal errors. When it is apparent that a scribe corrected the grammar to smooth out the style, introduced a more familiar reading from another biblical book, based the transcription on more than one manuscript, or expanded the text with personal comments, these differences are intentional. While some of these conditions are obvious, it is not always easy to determine how to classify some variant readings.

Text critics tend to prefer the shorter and/or the more difficult readings, since it is more plausible that someone would expand rather than abbreviate a text and/or simplify the grammar rather than introduce a more difficult reading. However, there are instances in which longer or smoother readings are considered more authentic, since the overall literary practices of each author must be taken into consideration.

Text criticism was once called "lower criticism" and was distinguished from "higher criticism." These nineteenth-century designations differentiated text criticism from what is now called "source criticism" that concerned more speculative issues considered to be of a "higher" order (that is, the origins of the material, the relationships of large complexes of materials, authorship, and dating). Since "lower" or text criticism is tied to the transmission of the texts, it is accepted by conservative Christians who reject all or some of the the historical-critical method (source, form, redaction, and canonical criticism).

Text critics have produced critical editions of the Greek New Testament that are reconstructions based on the ancient manuscripts. In these critical editions, footnotes are provided that list the variant readings and the manuscript(s) in which each appears. The Nestle-Aland Novum Testamentum Graece 27th edition of 1981 is the current critical edition of the new Testament.

Although there have been attempts to produce a critical edition of the Hebrew Bible, none have been accepted by a general community of scholars. The *Biblica Hebraica*, the most popular edition of the Hebrew Bible, reproduces a manuscript that dates from the eleventh century C.E. Until the discovery of the Dead Sea Scrolls at Qumran, Old Testament text criticism consisted of examining the differences between the Septuagint with the variants in the Masoretic Texts, with some consideration of the Samaritan Pentateuch and the Peshitta. Text-critical studies of the Hebrew Bible have taken on a new life because the Dead Sea Scrolls include manuscripts one thousand years older than the manuscript reproduced in the *Biblica Hebraica*.

Regina A. Boisclair

THEISM/THEISTIC

Derived from the Greek *theos*, meaning "God," theism consists of a philosophical system or movement, initially introduced during the European Enlightenment in seventeenth-century Britain and redefined by the eighteenth-century German philosopher Immanuel Kant (d. 1804), that characterizes a belief in and a portrait of the divine shared by some religions, such as Christianity, Judaism, and Islam. All three religions are theistic, in that they profess a transcendent and personal God who differs from the world but is immanently present and providentially active in it, especially in creating and sustaining the world, as well as in revelation, that is, divine self-disclosure. Theism defends the ongoing involvement of God in the world, in contrast to deism that in some forms describes God as a distant, detached, disengaged creator or cause of the world. Theism does not offer one explanation for how the origin of the world took place but only that God freely created it and continues to freely self-communicate to the world in revelation as well as in providential acts. Thus, theism professes the existence of God (as opposed to atheism), and is further specified in terms of monotheism, or the acceptance of one God. Thus, it is often contrasted with polytheism that postulates many gods, and with pantheism that borders on blurring the distinction between God and the world, thereby eclipsing divine transcendence. Panentheism, elaborated by U.S. ecofeminist theologians such as Sallie McFague, offers a theological middle ground between theism and pantheism; in describing a theological metaphor of the world as the body of God, McFague presents a panentheistic argument for an immanent transcendence, that is, God is immanently present in the world but not identical with it.

Rosemary P. Carbine

THEOCENTRIC

Theocentrism is often associated with the theology of the Reformed tradition; it stresses the absolute the sovereignty of God, implying the appropriate human response to the divine is one of awe, praise, and radical obedience. God—as radically Other—is the center of all value. It is often contrasted with theological anthropocentrism, that tendency in Christian theology to assume that God's purposes are identical to human well-being as it is construed by humans.

Brian F. Linnane, s.j.

See also CALVIN, JOHN; CALVINISM; EDWARDS, JONATHAN; GUSTAFSON, JAMES M.; NIEBUHR, H. RICHARD.

THEOCRACY

A political form of state organization in which state and religious functions and administration are combined. The head of state is believed to be a god or has a divine right to rule and act as an intermediary between human society and the divine. Examples of such systems include the Aztec and Inca empires, Hawaiian chiefdoms, and traditional Chinese society. In these cases, people rule because of their place in the moral and sacred order and not because of wealth or power. In the case of the Inca empire, for example, the Inca male ruler was identified with the sun god (similar to Rome and Japan). The Inca female ruler was considered the moon deity. The religious and ideological system reinforced the social and political power of these rulers. Divine leaders are able to call upon their status as deities to regulate tribute payments, social interaction, political power, and in some cases, conquest of other groups.

Christine Greenway

See also NAHUA TRADITIONAL RELIGION.

THEODICY

An attempt to answer the question, "Why does an omnipotent and omnibenevolent God permit genuine evil?" As distinct from a "defense" where the reason for God's permitting evil must only be *possibly* true, in theodicy, the reason must be *actually* true. Theodicies usually proceed by qualifying God's omnipotence (for example, process theism) or God's omnibenevolence (John Roth or Jeffrey Burton Russell's adaptation of the Jungian concept of "the shadow," for example), or, most frequently, by denying that genuine evil exists (for example, Augustine and John Hick). Most recently, some theologians (Terence Tilley, and Kenneth Surin, for example) have argued that the very practice of constructing a theodicy is an inappropriate or illegitimate theological endeavor.

J. A. Colombo

See also DEFENSE; EVIL; EVIL, PROBLEM OF.

THEODORA (497–548)

Theodora was the wife of Emperor Justinian. The daughter of a hippodrome guard, she pursued a career as an actress and courtesan before reforming her life and moving to Constantinople. There Theodora met and married Justinian. A brilliant and energetic women, she played a major role in governing the empire as "Augusta" and co-ruler with Justinian from 527 on. Theologically, she supported the Monophysites while encouraging humanitarian intiatives on the part of the church. The contemporary historian Procopius attacked Theodora's character because of her humble background, and his biased portrait of Theodora has unfortunately greatly influenced both historians and popular writers.

Gary Macy

See also JUSTINIAN; MONOPHYSITISM.

THEODORE OF MOPSUESTIA (350?–428)

One of the leading figures in Antiochean theology, Theodore studied under the theologian Diodore of Tarsus in Antioch. A monk and fellow student with John Chrysostom, Theodore became a priest in 383 and bishop of Mopsuestia in 392. Theodore's numerous writings were, for the most part, destroyed due to the condemnation of his theology by Justinian in the Three Chapters controversy. Some works have survived in translation, and fragments of others are quoted by contemporaries, allowing at least a partial insight into Theodore's work as a theology. Theodore commented extensively on Scripture, stressing a literal interpretation of the text. He is best remembered, however, for his christology in which he insisted on the full humanity of Jesus in the incarnate Christ.

Gary Macy

See also ANTIOCHENE THEOLOGY;
CHRISTOLOGY; JOHN CHRYSOSTOM;
JUSTINIAN; MONASTICISM IN EASTERN
CHRISTIANITY; THEODORET, BISHOP OF
CYRRHUS; THE THREE CHAPTERS.

THEODORE OF STUDIOS
(759–826)

Provided with an excellent education by
his parents, Theodore became a monk
under the direction of his uncle, Abbot
Plato, of the monastery of Symbola.
Theodore took over as abbot of Symbola
in 794. In 799 Theodore and his monks
moved to Constantinople where they
restored the abandoned monastery of
Studios. Theodore led the opposition to
the iconoclasm of Emperor Leo V, resulting in banishment for Theodore who died
in exile in 826. Theodore is remembered
not only for his strong stand against
iconoclasm, but also for his organization
of the monastery of Studios that became
a model for Eastern monasticism.

Gary Macy

See also ICONOCLAST CONTROVERSY;
MONASTICISM IN EASTERN CHRIS-
TIANITY.

THEODORET, BISHOP OF
CYRRHUS (393?–466?)

Theodoret distributed his wealth to the
poor and entered the monastery at about
the age of twenty. In 423 he was consecrated bishop of Cyrrhus in Syria. A friend
and defender of Nestorius, the patriarch
of Constantinople, Theodoret was the
leading representative of Antiochene theology during the Nestorian controversy.
In opposition to Cyril of Alexandria,
Theodoret defended the full humanity of
Jesus in the incarnate Christ. The formula
of reconciliation that temporarily ended
the Nestorian controversy in 433 was

probably written by Theodoret. At the
Council of Ephesus in 449, Theodoret
was deposed and exiled. Restored to his
see and to orthodoxy, Theodoret ruled his
diocese in peace until his death around
466. Theodoret's teaching, along with
that of Theodore of Mopusuestia, was
condemned by the emperor Justinian
about 544 during the Three Chapters controversy. Despite this condemnation,
many of Theodoret's works survive, including three important histories.

Gary Macy

See also ANTIOCHENE THEOLOGY;
CHRISTOLOGY; CYRIL OF ALEXANDRIA;
JOHN CHRYSOSTOM; JUSTINIAN;
NESTORIANISM; NESTORIUS;
PATRIARCH; THEODORE OF
MOPSUESTIA; THE THREE CHAPTERS.

THEOLOGICAL
ANTHROPOLOGY

A branch of Christian theology that studies the meaning of our "humanness" after
Christ and because of Christ. The question that has typically driven theological
anthropology has been "What is the
human person?"—a question that has
sought answers not merely philosophical
but explicitly theological, assuming (as
Christian theology must) that Jesus the
Christ has profoundly and forever
affected what we can understand as
humanness. The answer to "What is the
human person?" has frequently been
attempted through analytical, relational,
or phenomenological categories, but
these attempts have often led to generic
answers that, in turn, paint a generic
human that might exist—if such were
existence—in theory but not in real life.
Today theological anthropology's typical
driving question needs reconsideration.
Perhaps instead of "*What* is the human

person?" we should be asking *"Who* are human persons?" The latter question discloses real life, real persons and real communities, while the former question (at best) discloses theories. Theological anthropology is intimately bound to christology and soteriology, as well as to other branches of Christian theology.

Orlando Espín

See also CHRISTOLOGY; GRACE; HUMAN BEING; METHOD IN THEOLOGY; RAHNER, KARL; SALVATION; SOTERIOLOGY.

THEOLOGICAL VIRTUES

Christians have taken the three "theological virtues" to be described by Paul at the end of 1 Corinthians 13 as faith, hope, and love. They are the three virtues that "last," according to Paul, even in heaven. The idea that faith and love "last," even in heaven, can lead us to understand that heaven is a place of continuous dynamic growth (but without toil) for the human being—with love giving birth to hope and greater trust, and love in turn fulfilling the faith and hope it engendered.

Thought on each of these virtues individually is long and rich in Christian tradition. By the time of Pope Gregory the Great, it was agreed that these were uniquely and characteristically Christian in nature, and were "infused." That is, they could not be attained to by human reason or effort, but had to be given by God. They were the foundation of Christian spiritual life and necessary to salvation.

Later Scholastic thought saw the "theological virtues" as *above* all the other—even the "cardinal"—virtues. They were not seen as alien to human nature, though, but as fulfillments of human nature, adapting human nature to its spiritual nature and destiny as created in the

image and likeness of God. In this, they were the fulfillment of human nature and all the virtues. The Scholastic term for this was "connatural"—complementary to our nature. Because these virtues were "infused" at baptism, however, they were different from the other virtues acquired as habits through practice. The theological virtues were seen to be undeveloped powers, potentials for supernatural activity. Even in their earliest and most inchoate states, however, they nevertheless retained some characteristics in that they were principles of action and passion.

G. Simon Harak, s.j.

See also CHARITY; FAITH; HOPE (IN CHRISTIANITY); LOVE (IN GENERAL).

THEOLOGOUMENON

A theologoumenon is a theological statement that lacks the status of official doctrine (a teaching formally proclaimed by the church). This type of teaching is generally a theological construction that clarifies or develops the consequences of defined truths. Theologoumenon also suggest relationships among the doctrines of faith. These teachings do not require the assent of faith and are honored because of their merit in illuminating other doctrines. The doctrine of Mary's perpetual virginity is an example of a theologoumenon.

Patricia Plovanich

THEOLOGY

See ALEXANDRIAN THEOLOGY; ANTIOCHENE THEOLOGY; APOPHATIC THEOLOGY; ASCETICAL THEOLOGY; ASIAN (CHRISTIAN) THEOLOGIES; BIBLICAL THEOLOGY; CONSTRUCTIVE THEOLOGY; DEUTERONOMIC THEOLOGY; DOGMATIC THEOLOGY; EVANGELICAL THEOLOGY; FUNDAMENTAL THEOLOGY;

GAY THEOLOGY; HISTORICAL THEOLOGY; KERYGMATIC THEOLOGY; LIBERATION THEOLOGIES; MINJUNG THEOLOGY; NEO-ORTHODOX THEOLOGY; PASTORAL THEOLOGY; POLITICAL THEOLOGY (-IES); POSITIVE THEOLOGY; PRACTICAL THEOLOGY; PROCESS THEOLOGY; REFORMED THEOLOGY (-IES); SACRAMENTAL THEOLOGY.

THEOLOGY OF RELIGIONS

The theology of religions refers to Christian (theological) reflection on non-Christian religions in the light of biblical revelation and subsequent tradition, and especially on their possible relationship to Christian salvation.

The first minimal attempt at what might be called an incipient theology of religions appears in the Old Testament's recognition that other nations do worship other gods, although Israel may only worship the one God of Abraham, Isaac, and Jacob. This first reflection was expanded, also within the biblical period, in the Wisdom literature's polemic against and yet recognition of non-Israelite wisdom. Although the Hebrew Scriptures recognize that there are "Gentiles" who may act with sincere piety and reverence toward God, the biblical text is often emphatically polemical against all non-Israelite religion.

The early Christian church began (no later than the second century C.E.) to seriously question itself over the soteriological value of Greco-Roman wisdom and the relationship of this religious wisdom with Christian salvation. The Christian apologists seem to have led the way in this early theological reflection on non-Christian religions. And although it would be inappropriate to say that the patristic period had elaborated a theology of religions, it would nevertheless be historically inaccurate to suggest that there was

no serious and sustained reflection on the subject. In fact, during the patristic period, there seems to have developed two schools of thought on the question of non-Christian religions and their possible relationship to Christian salvation. These two schools of thought represent the two main attitudes toward non-Christian religions throughout later Christian history: (1) an antagonistic approach that radically opposed any concession to or dialogue with non-Christian religions (Tatian, Hermas, Theophilus of Antioch, for example), and (2) a more conciliatory approach, more open to dialogue, and that valued elements of non-Christian religions as "seeds of the Word" (*semina Verbi*, as for example, Justin Martyr) or even as God's pedagogy, early prophecy, and seminal inspiration (for example, Clement of Alexandria).

After Christianity became the dominant religion in the Greco-Roman world (by the fifth century C.E.), explicit reflection on non-Christian religions slowly waned from theological debate. Christianity, however, did engage at this time in a real but somewhat implicit dialogue with the non-Christian religions that had historically preceded it, because Christians appropriated philosophies and cultural values that had developed in the earlier Greco-Roman world. The arrival of Germanic religions in Christian Europe continued this implicit dialogue, even if explicitly the barbarian tribes were being evangelized away from their traditional religions.

During the long period known as the Middle Ages, there was little sustained theological reflection on non-Christians religions, except occasionally in reference to Islam and Judaism. Abelard, Ramón Llul, and Thomas Aquinas are among the authors who did attempt theological understandings of these two monotheistic religions. Medieval Spain's circumstances, as a great place of learning and as the privileged location for Muslim, Jewish, and Christian daily interaction, made it unique in western Europe at the time: sustained theological dialogue among the three religions was a frequent occurrence, as in the case of the thirteenth-century conversations of Toledo (sponsored by the primate archbishops of Spain).

The theology of religions entered a new phase during the fifteenth and sixteenth centuries. The theoretical foundations for the more systematic theological reflection developed in later centuries were laid during this period, roughly coinciding with the fall of Constantinople to the Muslims and with the conquest of the Americas by Europeans. In 1453 Nicholas of Cusa published his *De Pace Fidei*, and thereby established the modern theology of religions. Cusa insisted that the One God reflects Godself through a multiplicity of expressions, and so it is possible to find a presence of God in all of the world's religions. Christianity, Cusa argued, is the most perfect of these religions because it is the only one to have received and be founded on God's revelation. The other religions, nevertheless, share (even if imperfectly) some of the truths taught by Christianity. In the last part of his *Utopia*, Thomas More arrived (some decades after Cusa) at a similar conclusion. But the intra-Christian controversies raised by the Reformation, followed by the birth of the modern social sciences in the nineteenth century, practically put a stop to this theology of religions, only to be taken up again in the twentieth century.

Some Catholic and Protestant authors returned to the theology of religions in the first half of the twentieth century. Catholic theologian Garrigou-Lagrange wrote about Islam and Buddhism within the context of a theology of revelation, but ultimately dismissed both religious traditions as "merely human creations." It was Anglican missiologist J. N. Farquhar who again understood non-Christian religions (more specifically, Hinduism) as "seeds of the Word" come to fulfillment in Christianity. Liberal (Protestant) theology, under Hegel's influence, tried to discover the presence of God and true revelation in all the world's religions; but the neo-Orthodox reaction led by Karl Barth declared an abysmal incommensurability between Christianity and the other religions. Barth and his followers understood non-Christian religions to be the product of human hybris, and therefore in no way could "religion" be identified with revealed truth as the latter is present in Christianity. The critique of religion, so important during the second half of the twentieth century, made a serious Christian theology of religions nearly impossible among Protestants. However, among Catholics two authors reopened the reflection: Jean Daniélou (who spoke of a "cosmic revelation" that objectified itself variously in the world's religions), and Karl Rahner (who elaborated an incipient theology of religions based on his notions of the "supernatural existential" —the latter being socially "objectified" in the world religions—and of "anonymous Christianity"). Other Catholics followed Daniélou's and Rahner's lead, and through their own specific elaborations furthered the reflection of a contemporary theology of religions (for example, Schlette, Pannikar, Hillmann, Röper, Knitter).

The Second Vatican Council (especially in *Nostra Aetate* and in *Ad Gentes*) was careful when it came to explicit statements about the salvific value of non-Christian religions. Nevertheless, Vatican II (1962–5) was open to dialogue with and to a positive theological evaluation of the world's religions. The council claimed that non-Christian religions are "seeds of the Word," "wealth of the peoples," "contain elements of truth and grace," "can aid in the salvation of their members," and "are not against the (Christian) gospel." Pope Paul VI insisted (in a 1974 speech) that Catholics should no longer view non-Christian religions as "rivals or obstacles to evangelization, but as communities we accord respectful interest, and with whom we have established a growing friendship." Indeed, as early as 1954, Pope Pius XII (referring to the need of church membership for salvation) had explicitly taught that membership in the church is not an absolute condition for salvation for those who have, through no fault of their own, not heard or understood the Gospel as the message of salvation addressed to them.

There are, at least, a handful of themes that seem to be recurring in the contemporary Christian theology of religions, and that are variously discussed among theologians: (1) The foundational human religious experience that seems evident as the root of every religion of humankind. What can theologians say (theologically) about this experience? Is God not the ultimate source of this experience? And if so, how can Christian theology understand the divine presence and action in other religions? (2) The impact of grace and sin on humanity and on all religions. What has this impact been on non-Christian religions, and what effect has human sin played on the doctrinal and historical development of these religions? Can Christianity itself ever claim not to have also been impacted by sin? Has God's grace, which Christians believe God has definitively bestowed through Jesus, not

been also bestowed through other religious figures, and, if so, how? What would the possible bestowal of grace in other religions mean for Christianity's own universal claims? (3) Is Christian revelation the only revelation of God? And if other religions have received God's revelation, how do Christians theologically evaluate these religions and revelations? How does this affect Christianity's own claims as the definitive revelation of God to humankind?

Orlando Espín

See also AD GENTES; ANONYMOUS CHRISTIANITY; BARTH, KARL; CLEMENT OF ALEXANDRIA; DANIÉLOU, JEAN; GRACE; JUSTIN MARTYR; KNITTER, PAUL F.; LIBERAL THEOLOGY; LLUL, RAMÓN; LOGOS/WORD; NEO-ORTHODOX THEOLOGY; NICHOLAS OF CUSA; NOSTRA AETATE; PANNIKAR, RAIMON; PAUL VI, POPE; RAHNER, KARL; RELIGION; RELIGION, CRITIQUE OF; RELIGION, THEORIES OF; REVELATION; SALVATION; SIN, ORIGINAL; SOTERIOLOGY; SUPERNATURAL EXISTENTIAL; VATICAN, SECOND COUNCIL OF THE.

THEONOMY

Theonomy refers to a situation of identity or accord with God or divine nature. It is occasionally claimed by religious or political groups that regard their own life and moral norms to reflect God's very being and will. It is contrasted with heteronomy that refers to a situation or state of being untrue or discordant with God. From time to time, religious groups, while regarding themselves as theonomous, regard other religions as heteronomous. Such a self-regard often masks serious discrepancies between God and one's own tradition and is generally considered today to be presumptuous.

Michael J. Hartwig

THEOPASCHITES

From the Greek expression, "those who hold that God suffered." A term that refers to a group of sixth-century Eastern theologians (mostly Monophysites) who held that "one of the Trinity suffered." Although at first their expression of belief seemed acceptable, they were finally condemned because of the expression's imprecision (which allowed for the possibility that either the Father or the Holy Spirit could have suffered crucifixion).

Orlando Espín

See also CHALCEDON, COUNCIL OF; MONOPHYSITISM; TRINITY/TRINITARIAN THEOLOGY/TRINITARIAN PROCESSIONS.

THEOPHANY

A visible appearance of a god to a human. Examples of this phenomenon include the appearance of Christ to Quechua Indians in Peru in the late nineteenth century. These apparitions and their manifestation in the form of images of Christ in rocks have led to a series of annual pilgrimages that attract thousands of pilgrims to shrines located at these sites throughout the Peruvian Andes. In other societies, the appearance of deities may occur during religious rituals, ecstatic trances, and other activities in which religious practitioners seek out the presence of the god for the purposes of healing or the redressing of other misfortunes or problems. In ancient China, there were many incidents of gods appearing before travelers as poor beggars. In contemporary Christianity, visions of Christ on billboards, tortillas, trees, and other locations are continuing manifestations of this phenomenon. Interestingly, from a historical perspective, such appearances frequently occur to individuals who are powerless in economic, political, and social arenas. Their religious experience serves to help them interpret their circumstances in a meaningful way and may provide a means or motivation to engage in social and religious change.

Christine Greenway

See also APPARITIONS.

THEORY

This term refers to a particular type of knowledge. Plato distinguished between commonsense, an everyday, superficial kind of knowledge, and theoretical knowledge, the only true knowledge of reality. Aristotle distinguished among three types of knowledge: practical (phronesis), productive (techne), and theoretical (episteme). Like Plato, Aristotle accords a special place to theoretical knowledge in that it alone can put us in touch with eternal reality. The culmination of theoretical knowledge is wisdom (sophia), the highest form of knowledge, a contemplative knowledge of eternal reality. This contemplative knowledge is a way of life or type of existence having no ulterior motive or purpose; contemplative knowledge is to be loved for its own sake. As opposed to practical and productive knowledge, then, theory is, by definition, a useless form of knowledge.

Contemporary scholars, such as the German philosopher Jürgen Habermas, have suggested that, in the modern world, the Aristotelian distinctions among different kinds of knowledge no longer hold. In Habermas's view, the scientific revolution has generated a new epistemological paradigm in which all knowledge is effectively reduced to technical knowledge. In this view, all knowledge comes to derive its value from its usefulness, as technique, in manipulating the empirical world. What defines scientific knowledge is precisely its *usefulness* in helping the scientist reproduce natural processes in the laboratory. When scientific knowledge becomes the paradigm of *all* knowledge, the Aristotelian notion of theory, as knowledge that is its own end, is eclipsed by an understanding of theory as knowledge whose end, the technical control of the environment, is external to the knowledge itself. Thus, in modernity, the Aristotelian notion of productive knowledge, or *techne*, subsumes all other types of knowledge. Education and, indeed, human life itself comes to be seen as a process of acquiring the technical skills that will allow us to be more effective manipulators of our environment.

In contemporary theologies, "theory" is often used in a broader sense as denoting the process of theological reflection on praxis. Arguing against a separation of the theological task (theory) from the theologian's active participation in society and history (praxis), liberation theologies, for instance, insist that theory is never completely divorced from praxis but emerges from reflection on lived experience. Consequently, the theologies elaborated within historically marginalized communities (for example, Latin American liberation theologies, African American theologies, feminist theologies, U.S. Latino/a theologies) insist that the validity of any theologian's theoretical claims is fundamentally dependent on—even if not absolutely determined by—the character of the theologian's life, as the practical source of those claims.

Since the theoretical task of the theologian, or the Christian, is never a disembodied, ahistorical enterprise undertaken in isolation from the theologian's lived experience, and thus always involves a reflection *on* that experience, the cognitive claims of his or her theology can themselves never be judged in isolation from the character of their "object," the praxis of the theologian. The criteria for judging the accuracy and adequacy of theory, then, are not only rational (whether the theory is internally coherent, for example) but fundamentally practical (for example, whether the theory issues from good, or right action). In the words of the Peruvian liberation theologian Gustavo Gutiérrez, theology is a "second step," that "follows" praxis. If theological reflection claims to be a reflection on the Christian God, then that reflection must issue, more specifically, from a practical, social, historical solidarity with the struggles of the poor—from a preferential option for the poor.

These praxis-based, "contextual theologies" call into question the Aristotelian notion of theoretical knowledge (*episteme*) as separate from practical knowledge. They also reject the modern Western reduction of theory to technical knowledge (*techne*), where theory is defined in terms of usefulness or applicability. Instead, they stress the intrinsic connection between theory and praxis and the practical ground of theoretical knowledge, thereby subordinating theoretical knowledge to practical knowledge (*phronesis*). In these theologies, the modern, rationalist, and instrumentalist understanding of theory has thus given way to a more "postmodern" understanding that rejects any attempt to dislodge theoretical knowledge from its intrinsic connection to praxis.

Roberto S. Goizueta

See also MODERNITY; PRAXIS; RATIONALISM.

THERAVADA BUDDHISM

"Those who hold the doctrine of the elders (*thera*)," a term designating the sole surviving school among the eighteen original groups within early Buddhism. The Theravada owes its survival to development of the Sthavira tradition in Sri Lanka, where island accounts relate that King Ashoka (around 250 B.C.E.) sent a Buddhist mission led by his son, Mahinda. Although Mahayana adherents and other schools also existed on the isle for over a millennium, Sri Lanka's Theravada lineage exerted a strong influence on Buddhist schools in Southeast Asia, especially after the decline of the faith in its holy land of origin. At different times, Sri Lankan monks provided copies of its carefully maintained and commented-upon textual corpus, the Pali Canon, to distant schools while also transmitting respected ordination lineages, both in aid of efforts led by indigenous Burmese or Thai kings to "purify the faith." Theravadins from Southeast Asia also returned this service in the early modern era when European colonial invasion weakened the faith in Sri Lanka. Today, the Theravada is nearly the only Buddhist school extant there and in Laos, Thailand, and Cambodia.

Premodern Theravada Buddhist tradition is known for its conservative tendencies: leadership in the community was allotted to senior monks; ritual practices were very few in number and doctrinal interpretations remained close to a literal interpretation of the canonical texts and the monk Buddhaghosa's commentaries (500 C.E.); the lay majority was expected to earn merit and not expected to seek enlightenment by meditation. This expectation is based on the Theravada emphasis on the religious ideal of the Arahant, a very rare man or woman who wins enlightenment by dint of isolated and ascetic individual effort.

Sri Lankan exponents of the Theravada from the early centuries have argued that their school represents the original and only true teaching of the Buddha. With the decline of the faith and the arising of reformed Theravada Buddhism in Sri Lanka due to its colonization by the British, Theravadin modernists there were an important force leading in the movements of Buddhist reinterpretation and revival, an effect felt not only in Southeast Asia, but back into India, Nepal, and in the faith's global diaspora.

Todd T. Lewis

See also BUDDHISM; HINAYANA; SOUTHERN BUDDHISM.

THE THREE CHAPTERS

Technically, the phrase refers to the condemnation by the emperor Justinian in 543/4 of the person and writings of Theodore of Mopsuestia, the writings of Theodoret of Cyrrhus against Cyril of Alexandria, and the letter of Ibas of Edessa to Maris. The phrase, however, also came to refer to the three theologians in question. As the leading representatives of Antiochene theology, Theodore, Theodoret, and Ibas were considered by the Monophysites to be Nestorians. Justinian hoped that the condemnations would ease relations with the Monophysites, and the Eastern bishops accepted the decree. The Western Church, however, strongly objected, considering the decree an attack on the Council of Chalcedon, and Pope Vigilius refused to accept the condemnation. Vigilius was called to Constantinople and eventually accepted the decrees of the Second Council of Constantinople that included the condemnation of the Three Chapters.

Vigilius's successor, Pelagius I, also accepted the decree, but most of the Western bishops objected, and the bishop of Aquilea even withdrew from communion with Rome.

Gary Macy

See also ANTIOCHENE THEOLOGY; CHALCEDON, COUNCIL OF; CONSTANTINOPLE, FIRST COUNCIL OF; CONSTANTINOPLE, SECOND COUNCIL OF; CONSTANTINOPLE, THIRD COUNCIL OF; JUSTINIAN; MONOPHYSITISM; NESTORIANISM; PELAGIUS I OF ROME; THEODORE OF MOPSUESTIA; VIGILIUS OF ROME.

THIELICKE, HELMUT (1908–86)

Lutheran theologian, ethician, and church leader. Thielicke was professor of theology at Heidelberg, Tübingen, and Hamburg, where he served as rector and dean, combining his scholarly career with church service. As a theologian, Thielicke was committed to the neo-orthodox view of Karl Barth and others, explaining theology as an encounter with the Word of God in service of proclamation and ministry. His concern for the dynamic and transformative character of faith directed his thought to the ethical significance of Christian life in a fallen world. Best known for his ethics, his reflections on this dimension of Christianity are found in works such as *The Evangelical Faith* (3 vols., 1947–55) and *Theological Ethics* (2 vols., 1968, 1969).

Patricia Plovanich

THIRD ORDERS

Third orders are organizations of Christian laity who take private vows according to a particular religious order. They live in the world, but pledge themselves to live simply in regard to wealth, clothing, food, and drink; to live chastely; to contribute to charity; to do penance; to participate frequently in the sacraments of penance and the Eucharist; and to be obedient to authority. They are obliged to wear a scapular and a cord under their ordinary clothes. They are called "third orders" to distinguish them from the orders of religious men (the first orders) and that of religious women (the second orders). Although some third orders decided to live a communal life and eventually became religious congregations taking permanent vows, this was not the original purpose of the third orders. St. Francis of Assisi was the first to write a rule for those laypeople who wished to share in the ideals of his order, but could not leave their secular lives. A rule written by Francis for the third order was approved by Pope Honorius III in 1221. A similar order was approved by the Dominicans in 1285 and received papal approval in 1406. Several other third orders have been approved in more modern times, including a Third Order of Carmelites, a Third Order of Benedictines, and a Third Order of Augustinians.

Gary Macy

See also CARMELITES; DOMINICANS; FRANCISCANS; FRANCIS OF ASSISI; ORDERS (RELIGIOUS); SCAPULAR; VOWS (RELIGIOUS).

THIRD WORLD

Originally a term invented by the so-called First World in a political debate that carved up the world in terms of economic status—the highly industrialized and affluent nations in contrast to the less industrialized and impoverished nations. The "First World" consisted of Western Europe, the U.S., Canada, Japan, and Australia. The "Third World" were the "less developed" countries in Latin America, Asia, Africa, and the Middle East.

From the perspective of the so-called Third World nations, this term is racist and imperialistic. It fails to identify the unjust relationship between development and underdevelopment, robs individuals and societies of their particularity, and implies that there is something "third-rate" about them. It also disguises the fact that pockets of extraordinary affluence exist in the so-called Third World, while sectors of the so-called First World suffer from impoverishment and structural unemployment.

More recently, the term "Two-thirds World" is used in theology and ethics to denote the fact that the nations of Asia, Africa, and Latin America contain more than two-thirds of the world's people.

Mary E. Hobgood

See also USURY.

THIRD WORLD THEOLOGIES
See AFRICAN THEOLOGIES;
ASIAN (CHRISTIAN) THEOLOGIES;
LATIN AMERICAN THEOLOGIES.

THIRTY-NINE ARTICLES
The authoritative series of statements or "articles" expressing the Church of England's positions on certain controversies of the sixteenth-century Reformation and manifesting its ideal of a reformed catholicity. Chiefly the work of the archbishop of Canterbury, Matthew Parker, they were approved by the Convocation of Canterbury in final form in 1571. They are not a complete statement of the church's teachings nor an obligatory rule of faith, like the Augsburg Confession.

Taken apart from their historical context, the Articles are susceptible of a variety of interpretations. In his Tract 90 of 1841, Newman argued that they were written to provide space for both Protestant and Catholic tendencies in the church. Since his argument seemed to deny the Protesant character of the church, Newman found himself at the center of a storm of controversy. He became a Catholic in 1845.

Articles I–V concern the substance of faith. Articles VI–VIII concern the rule of faith, and IX–XVIII the life of faith. Articles XIX–XXII deal with the church, and XXIII–XXIV with its ministry. Articles XXVI–XXXI discuss the sacraments of baptism and the Lord's Supper, XXXII–XXXVI church discipline, and XXXVII–XXXIX, the role of the state.

The Thirty-Nine Articles were adapted to an American context in 1801. This version is titled the "Articles of Religion" and published as a historical document in the Episcopal Church's Book of Common Prayer.

Articles I–V declare the church's faith in the Trinity. Articles VI and VII concern the role and authority of the Scriptures. Article VIII recommends the Apostles' and Nicene Creeds. Articles IX–XVIII deal with justification, reflecting their Reformation origins. Articles XIX–XXI concern the church and its authority. Article XXII denies the reality of purgatory. Article XXIII provides the ordering of ministry, and XXIV stipulates use of the vernacular in the liturgy. Articles XXV–XXXI are devoted to the sacraments. Article XXXII permits clergy to marry. Article XXXIII tells how to treat persons excommunicated. Article XXXIV calls for legitimate diversity in the church. Article XXXV mandates reading of the Second Book of Homilies, once a suitable American version is prepared. Article XXXVI stipulates ordinations by the American ordinal, rather than the ordinal of Edward VI. Article XXXVII denies any authority in things spiritual to state officials, in contrast to the British version that subjects the church to the Crown. Article XXXVIII affirms a Christian's right to private property against the Anabaptists, and XXXIX sets forth the conditions for a Christian to swear an oath.

Jon Nilson

See also BOOK OF COMMON PRAYER; PARKER, MATTHEW.

THOMAS, GOSPEL OF

A collection of one hundred fourteen sayings, without an overall narrative structure. This document was purportedly dictated by Jesus to Didymus Judas Thomas, who recorded the sayings in writing. The text is not a gospel in the genre of the canonical Gospels, since no narrative is included about Jesus' birth, ministry, or passion. Rather, it is similar to Q, the collection of sayings incorporated into Matthew and Luke.

The work was discovered in 1945 as part of the Nag Hammadi library; the version found was a translation from Greek to Coptic. Three Greek fragments had been found earlier at the garbage heap of the ancient Egyptian town of Oxyrhynchus in 1898 and 1903. These had not been realized to be parts of the gospel, however, until the Coptic version came to light. Due to an early third-century dating for the earliest of the Greek fragments, the Gospel of Thomas must have been composed before 200 C.E. Some suggest even a first-century date, although it is most probably a second-century composition, due to the evident Gnostic intent of the redactor. It is likely to have been written in Syria where traditions about the apostle Judas Thomas, identifying him as the twin brother of Jesus, were common.

While this writing has an overarching Gnostic character, it also contains material that is not Gnostic in origin, reflecting that the collection must have passed through various editings that added different theological perspectives to it. Some of the material parallels sayings attributed to Jesus in the Synoptics, some parallels material in other New Testament apocrypha, and some was unknown before the manuscript discoveries. At issue is whether some sayings are as likely as those in the canonical Gospels to be authentically from Jesus. The debate on this is vigorous and has not reached consensus.

F. M. Gillman

See also APOCRYPHA; GNOSIS/GNOSTICISM; NAG HAMMADI; Q SOURCE.

THOMAS AQUINAS, ST.

See AQUINAS, THOMAS, ST.

THOMAS CHRISTIANS

Name given to the earliest Christian communities in India. It seems a historical fact that Christianity came to India before the fourth century. These Christians believed their church was established by the apostle Thomas (an unproven tradition). They were first under the jurisdiction of the Nestorian patriarchate of Baghdad and then of the Jacobite Syrian patriarchate. In 1599 a significant number of Thomas Christians formed the Malabar Catholic Church that established full communion with Rome. Those who did not join Rome became known as the Mar Thoma Church, and are mostly located in southwestern India. Another group broke away, entered full communion with Rome in 1930, and formed the Malankarese Catholic Church.

Orlando Espín

See also ANCIENT CHURCHES OF THE EAST; COMMUNION (ECCLESIOLOGICAL); EASTERN CATHOLIC CHURCHES; MALABAR CATHOLIC CHURCH; MALANKARESE CATHOLIC CHURCH; MONOPHYSITISM; NESTORIANISM; PATRIARCH.

THOMISM/TRANSCENDENTAL THOMISM

Philosophical and theological approaches based on the work of the medieval Scholastic thinker St. Thomas Aquinas (1225–74). Thomas's life work was the attempt to reconcile traditional Christian teaching with the newly received influences of the ancient Greek philosopher Aristotle and a host of Muslim and Jewish scholars and philosophers (including Avicena, Averroes, and Maimonides), whose works gradually became available in Western Europe during the twelfth century. Using Aristotle's philosophy, Thomas taught a unified human nature—the rational soul joined essentially to the material body—over against the more common notion at the time (influenced by the theology of St. Augustine and the philosophy of Plato) in which the spiritual soul and the material body were almost opposed to one another. In keeping with Aristotelian notions of how human beings know, Thomas understood physical sense impressions as the first source of knowledge that can be abstracted to form more general ideas. From such foundations, Thomas's writings present a strong emphasis on the *unity of truth*, that all sources of knowledge, whether based on human reason or on divine revelation, lead to a single source of Truth, and so cannot ultimately

contradict one another. Firmly convinced that human nature mirrors the intelligence and goodness of God, he further emphasized that many basic Christian doctrines found in divine revelation are also in principle discoverable by human reason.

Though subject to a variety of internal debates, and challenged by other forms of Scholastic philosophy (such as that of the followers of Duns Scotus), Thomism maintained a central place in Catholic philosophical and theological thinking into the seventeenth century. With the rise of rationalism and natural science after that time, however, and the subsequent development of Enlightenment philosophy with its intense focus on the subjective aspects of human knowing, Thomism found itself unable to address the most prevalent philosophical questions of the day. Only after the mid-nineteenth century did the approach of St. Thomas and other Scholastic philosophers begin to appear attractive once again, this time as part of a distinctive Catholic response to the problems of human dignity and the common good in the burgeoning scientific and industrial age. In 1879, in his encyclical *Aeterni Patris*, Pope Leo XIII held up the work of St. Thomas as a model for Catholic scholarship.

Leo's encyclical called for the appropriate updating of Thomas's thought, in light of six hundred years of further human experience. While much of the Thomism subsequently taught in seminary manuals was later judged to lack the serious depth that the study deserves, many other scholars actively tried to bring Thomism into dialogue with more modern philosophical schools. "Transcendental Thomism," initially associated with the work of such figures as Belgian Jesuit Joseph Maréchal (1878–1944), attempted to incorporate the "transcendental method" of the Enlightenment philosopher Immanuel Kant. Later developments extended the dialogue into philosophical trends such as phenomenology and existentialism. Philosophically, the aim of this form of Thomism was to focus on the human knower (the "subject") without relinquishing the objective reality of the things the knower grasps (the "object"). Theologically, this approach allowed for positions such as Karl Rahner's (1904–84) "supernatural existential": even though the natural (human) and the supernatural (divine) are objectively completely distinct from one another, human beings are still naturally capable of a kind of intuition of the divine that makes them natural seekers of God even before encountering explicit divine revelation.

William Clark, s.j.

THRONE OF GOD

The biblical psalms and prophetic writings perceive God, like a king ruling over and judging the earth, to sit on a heavenly throne. This image is often associated with the idea that the earth, and in particular, the Jerusalem Temple, is God's footstool (see, for example, Isa 66:1). By the end of the Talmudic period, Jewish speculation about the nature of God's throne and heavenly habitat led to the emergence of Merkaba (heavenly throne or chariot) and hekhalot (heavenly palace) mysticism. The writings associated with these types of mysticism depict mystical ascents to and offer descriptions of God's dwelling place.

Alan J. Avery-Peck

See also KABBALAH.

T'IEN

(Chinese, *tian*, lit., heaven, sky). This term appeared initially during the early Zhou Dynasty (about 1122–723 B.C.E.) and originally meant "the abode of the great spirits." During this early period, it was used, at times, synonymously with Shang-Ti (Supreme Lord) and ascribed certain anthropomorphic qualities. However, in time it came to mean the impersonal supreme power or principle in the universe representing a cosmic moral order that impartially guided the destinies of humans. This idea of heaven has played a significant role in Chinese religion right down to the twentieth century as part of a cosmological conception of an interrelated trinity of heaven, earth, and man [humanity]. During the classical period, the emperor (perceived as the Son of Heaven) had a central role as the intermediary responsible for favorable relations between heaven and earth, making offerings annually at the Temple of Heaven (T'ien Tan) in Beijing.

G. D. DeAngelis

See also SHANG DYNASTY; SHANG-TI; T'IEN MING; ZHOU DYNASTY.

T'IEN MING

(Chinese, *tian ming*, lit., mandate of heaven). Early Chinese governing principle that an individual or line of rulers has a right to rule by virtue of support from heaven that could also be withdrawn at any time if the rulers did not behave virtuously. This concept is very similar to the European notion of the divine right of kings. This concept was first used in China by the Zhous (1123–221 B.C.E.) in legitimating their overthrow of the Shang Dynasty (1766–1122 B.C.E.). From this period down to the twentieth century, this divinely directed process of changing dynasties, in which a new group of virtuous leaders would replace ones who had become corrupt, was how the Chinese have interpreted their political history. Confucian support of this theory helped make it an integral part of the religio-political orthodoxy of the state.

G. D. DeAngelis

See also CONFUCIANISM; SHANG DYNASTY; SHANG-TI; T'IEN; ZHOU DYNASTY.

T'IEN TAI

(Chinese, lit., heavenly terrace). A school of Chinese Buddhism founded by the monk Chih I (538–597) and established at Mt. T'ien Tai from which it took its name. This school represented one of the more significant efforts by Chinese Buddhists to harmonize the variety of Buddhist teachings represented by the numerous Indian Buddhist schools coming into China during the first six centuries C.E. Chih I claimed that the disparity in the Buddha's teachings in different texts was understandable in light of the differing needs of different people at different times. From Chih I's perspective, the Buddha revealed more as his followers reached higher levels of awareness and were thus able to understand more. In effect, the T'ien Tai School accepted all forms of Buddhism as part of an eclectic "super school" and ordered all the scriptures in relation to an increasing unfolding of the truth (dharma). At the top of this ranking, Chih I placed the *Lotus Sutra* as the most complete expression of the dharma, where it is revealed that the Buddha is a manifestation of a cosmic principle (Buddha nature) existent in all things.

The eclecticism and universality of salvation in the T'ien Tai School was quite appealing to the Chinese, but their rationalist intellectual approach was too impractical for the masses. In time, the T'ien Tai School disappeared, replaced by the more accessible and popular Ching-T'u or Pure Land School. T'ien Tai was carried to Japan in the eighth century by the Japanese Buddhist monk Saicho and became the popular Tendai School that still exists today.

G. D. DeAngelis

See also BODHI; BUDDHISM; LOTUS SUTRA; TENDAI.

TIKKUN OLAM

Hebrew, meaning "repairing/healing the world" is the Jewish concept of "perfecting the world under the kingdom of God."

A central Jewish mission is to heal the world of all its ills and evils, and to bring it to transformation and perfection—to the time when the messianic era of peace and good will infuses all existence.

Tikkun Olam is not only a goal, but also a process. So Jews are committed to the prophetic sense of social justice, to working each day to feed the hungry, clothe the naked, educate the illiterate, lift up the downtrodden, and bring hope where there is despair.

Tikkun Olam—both the ultimate goal and the daily process—is at the heart of Jewish life and lifestyle; it is the sacred calling of every Jew.

Wayne Dosick

TILLICH, PAUL (1886–1965)

German theologian who emigrated to the United States in 1933. One of the most influential neo-orthodox theologians in the twentieth century, Paul Tillich's theology is distinguished by his creative appropriation of existentialism, the ontology of classical German idealism and Martin Heidegger, and depth psychology as a vehicle for the articulation of Christian faith, for example, in utilizing the distinction between "Being itself" and finite Being to formulate the relation between "God" and the world. A prolific writer, Tillich's corpus includes works on art and religion, the pluralism of religions, sermons, ethics, biblical criticism, and politics—although his writings on the last declined after his forced emigration to the United States in 1933—in addition to his *Systematic Theology* (1951–63) and his more "popular" works, *The Courage to Be* (1952) and *The Dynamics of Faith* (1957). Through nearly three decades of teaching in the United States, Tillich influenced an entire generation of Christian theologians such as Langdon Gilkey and James Luther Adams.

J. A. Colombo

See also HEIDEGGER, MARTIN; NEO-ORTHODOX THEOLOGY.

TIME (SACRED)

In the description and analysis of the role of religious traditions in human life, researchers have noted that individuals and their communities alternate between two poles of existential experience as they move through the year and through their lifetimes. The majority of time is that spent meeting subsistence, familial, and social needs; although essential, such periods are characterized as "mundane" or "profane" time. But periodically interrupting the unfolding of profane time is sacred time, periods when "normal" activities are suspended or give way to other actions and distinctive experiences.

Sacred time is useful for understanding the role of religion in the individual and collective realms. Every ritual performed usually has a structure that marks it from the normal flow of events, and this period of suspended ordinariness is sacred time. Examples would be the arrival of the *Sabbath* for Jews; the moment of the Eucharist's transubstantiation for Christians; the beginning of the *salat* prayer ritual for Muslims; the point in which one establishes eye contact with the icon (*darshan*) in Hinduism.

As persons move through the life cycle, most societies have rituals to mark their passage from one existential state to another; for example, from infancy to childhood, from a child to an adult, from single to married status, from anonymity to clan elder, and so on. The rituals that establish the individual's new status usually involve activities done at no other time (confinement, dress, eating certain foods, and so on) and that involve a typical ritual enactment of separation, liminality, and reintegration, to use Victor Turner's well-known paradigm. Such times are sacred, carrying with them the common religious traits of being potentially both dangerous and transformative. Such times of passage may also be periods marked by deeper (even revolutionary) revelations or spiritual intuitions, as in initiations into religious orders or secret societies.

For communities, the same pattern emerges in the round of yearly holy days marking the celebration of a common faith or national civil religion. For the collectivity, normal time is interrupted, usual activities are suspended, and the existential "feel" of the day(s) or night(s) is strongly punctuated as different, as the predominance of the routine or subsistence-related matters gives way to other concerns. This oscillation between sacred and profane time, once a common and frequent fact of life in the yearly festival cycle of traditional societies, has become a fading awareness among more modernized peoples. In the Christian West, the existential shift to sacred time perhaps endures most clearly still in the unique experience of Christmas morning: businesses are closed, special foods are eaten (eggnog, and the like), and rituals unique to the day (opening stocking presents, for example) are performed.

In traditional societies, a common motif of the dramatic shift from sacred to profane time is the saturnalia festival, a period of role reversals when behaviors normally taboo are acceptable. These include taking intoxicants, freeing low-caste members or women to act boldly in public against authority figures, permitting cross-dressing, or sexual promiscuity. From within every religious tradition, the focal referents made in the midst of sacred time are the essentials of the faith: creation, revelation, group history, or ethical center. Scholars of religion have pointed out that the oscillation between the two forms of existential time constitutes an important aspect of religion's contribution to humanity's adaptation and to the individual's need for psychological integration.

Todd T. Lewis

See also RELIGION, THEORIES OF; SACRED / SACRAL / SACRALIZED; SATURNALIA.

TIRTHANKARA

Literally a "ford finder," the term for a saint commonly used in Jainism. The "ford" in this terminology draws upon the image of the river as the troubled world of suffering and rebirth (samsara), the sage who finds the way to the "other shore" or nirvana. As a ford is a shallow point of crossing, a *tirthankara* is one who teaches others how to follow in his wake, the crossing made easier due to his own successful striving.

Todd T. Lewis

See also JAINISM.

TISHAH B'AV

(Hebrew, Ninth of [the month of] Av). This is the saddest day in the Jewish calendar, a fast day that falls in the summer months and commemorates the destruction of the Second Temple in 70 C.E., the failed Bar Kokhba revolt of 133–5 C.E., and, by extension, all the calamities of Jewish history. Tishah B'Av facilitates acceptance of such tragedies by providing a set time and context for mourning, so that mourning and withdrawal from the world need not to be continual.

Tishah B'Av is marked by a full day's fast, the reciting of the book of Lamentations, and by other practices usually associated with mourning, for example, sitting on the floor or low stools and not wearing leather. The three weeks preceding Tishah B'Av are somber in mood, and during this period weddings and other joyous celebrations do not take place. The prophetic portions on the Sabbaths of these weeks speak of impending doom, the result of the people's sin. The weeks following Tishah B'Av, by contrast, comprise an appropriate introduction to the Jewish New Year and Day of Atonement that follow. These seven Sabbaths, referred to as the Sabbaths of Consolation, reflect upon God's reconciliation with the people of Israel, the future fulfillment of Scripture's messianic promise, and the eventual restoration of Zion.

Alan J. Avery-Peck

TITHES/TITHING

A tithe is 10 percent of possessions or produce given as an offering to God. To tithe is to make such an offering. The book of Deuteronomy (probably sixth century B.C.E.) records that Hebrews of the time annually tithed the harvest of the fields. The offering was made to God by partaking of the produce in the context of a sacred meal, held at a shrine (Deut 14:22-27). This sacred meal was shared with the Levites, members of the priestly tribe who, unlike the other Hebrew tribes, did not have land of their own on which to grow crops. Each third year, a person was to give not just a portion of the tithe but all of it to the those who had no land: the Levites, the resident aliens, widows, and the orphans. In this way, poverty and hunger was to be prevented in Israel. In time, the tithe came to include, not only the harvest of the field, but the yield of fruit trees and domesticated animals as well (Lev 27:30-33). Systems of equivalences evolved whereby money or possessions of approximately equal value could be substituted for the actual tithe. Jesus, while not condemning the practice of tithing, did insist that it could not substitute for the more essential acts of justice and mercy required by God (Matt 23:23). Early Christians understood tithing, along with other aspects of Jewish law, to have been rendered obsolete by Jesus. As the needs of the church increased, however, the ideal of the tithe was restored. Christians were expected to contribute a tenth of their income to the support of the community's life and its clergy. Charlemagne, at the end of the eighth century, made the payment of a tithe to the church a matter of civil law. Even as late as the sixteenth century, the Council of Trent mandated that all Catholics should pay a tithe of all their possessions to the church. This ruling had little effect, however, and in America the practice of tithing among Catholics was hardly ever recommended or observed. The most recent Code of Canon Law insists that Catholics must financially support the life, missionary activity, and charitable work of the church (Canon 222 §1), but it does not specify the tithe or any other percentage of giving.

Patrick L. Malloy

See also CHARLEMAGNE.

TOKUGAWA PERIOD (1600–1868)

An era characterized by order, unity, and stability that set the stage for Japan's development as a modern nation-state. This period was marked by an increasingly antiforeign attitude and a subsequent shift in interest from Buddhism to Shinto, Neo-Confucianism, and secularism. This shift was marked by an increased emphasis on order and stability in an ordered and just society, promoting values of loyalty, sincerity, and moral obligation. It also witnessed the resurgence of Shinto nationalism.

G. D. DeAngelis

See also BUDDHISM; NEO-CONFUCIANISM; SHINTO.

TOLEDO, COUNCILS OF

Although some thirty councils have been held in the city of Toledo between the fifth and the sixteenth centuries, the most famous of these councils were the sixteen councils called by the Visogothic kings of Spain and held between 589 and 702. The first of these councils (the Third Council of Toledo), held under the leadership of Leander of Seville, was the occasion of King Recared formally renouncing Arian beliefs. The Fourth Council of Toledo in 633 issued a number of important liturgical regulations under the leadership of Isidore of Seville.

Gary Macy

See also ISIDORE OF SEVILLE; LEANDER OF SEVILLE; MEDIEVAL CHRISTIANITY (IN THE WEST).

TOLERANCE (VIRTUE)

The virtue of tolerance consists of the ability to live amicably with differences of opinion, lifestyle, religious belief, and even of moral views when such differences do not infringe on the common good. In other words, tolerance has its limits. Christians might not agree with the moral stance of a nonbeliever and may have to tolerate what they believe to be morally wrong. But if something is gravely wrong, then the Christian has an obligation to protest, resist, and work for change. This obligation arises from the prophetic nature of life according to the Spirit. In any event, tolerance must be situated within a cluster of virtues: patience, courage, prudence, perseverance, charity, and humility. Tolerance may have been what Paul had in mind when he wrote: "Love is patient; love is kind . . . it does not insist on its own way. . . . It bears all things" (1 Cor 13:4-5, 7). Yet tolerance can never be an excuse for passivity, either, as Paul's correspondence amply demonstrates.

William Reiser, s.j.

See also PRUDENCE; VIRTUE.

TOLERATION

The principle of religious tolerance is a political and theological concept with roots in Judeo-Christian history, but it developed as an effective political and religious theory only in the modern era. The political principal of religious tolerance indicates the society or government that mandates or permits the religious liberty of its citizens. The principle may hold the constitutional status of church–state separation (the United States' model) or a customary tolerance toward all religions in those nations sponsoring a state church (the British model). The practical consequences of religious tolerance are a diversity of religious communities that coexist by recognizing that the religious liberty of each depends on accepting that of all other persons and groups.

The acceptance of the principle of religious tolerance is a recent development in church history, a recognition rooted in the reality of modern secular states in which religious groups would thrive or fail apart from their ability to control state affairs. This recognition is rooted in another principle, that of religious liberty. This principle recognizes the freedom of the individual's faith response to God, and, contingent on that, the freedom of individual conscience, even of one's choice of religions. The theological principle of religious freedom implicitly affirms the principle of religious tolerance.

The churches' official acceptance of religious tolerance is a recent achievement due to the new situation of religious faith in modern secular states. The principles guiding this acceptance are articulated well in the Second Vatican Council's Declaration on Religious Liberty (*Dignitatis Humanae*, 1965), a document crafted for the free nations and for those governments that restricted the practice of religion. The declaration summarizes the traditional principles grounding religious freedom. It acknowledges the individual's freedom that grounds the free act of faith as well as one's moral choices and moral responsibility. It insists that the social orientation of life does not negate, but requires, religious freedom for persons, families, and social groups. Finally, it argues that religious freedom does not hinder but abets the social good that is best served by persons fulfilled through their religious freedom.

The practical consequence of the recognition of religious freedom is the acceptance of religious tolerance as that theological and political principle that best achieves the individual's religious liberty. The various churches' acceptance of the principle has opened, not closed discussion of these principles as individuals, churches, and nations learn their meaning through living them.

Patricia Plovanich

TOME OF LEO
See LEO, TOME OF.

TONSURE
From the Latin "tondere," to shear or shave. (1) A ceremony in which a man's hair is cut to indicate that he is a vowed religious or a cleric; (2) the resulting haircut. The tonsure can be so severe that only a ring of hair remains, or quite modest, so that only a small circle is shaved on the crown of the head. It developed from the ancient Eastern custom of shaving the heads of slaves. It first appeared as a Christian rite in the eighth century, and eventually became universal. Some few religious communities still wear the tonsure, or at least give it to new members when they join. It was, however, officially suppressed for secular clergy by Paul VI in 1973. Before that time, American diocesan priests received the tonsure

only once, as seminarians, to signify their entrance into the clerical state.

Patrick L. Malloy

See also SECULAR CLERGY; SEMINARY.

TORAH
Derived from the Hebrew root meaning "instruction," in Judaism, Torah refers to the sum total of the revelation of God to humankind, encompassing the written (Torah Shebichtav) and oral (Torah Shebal'peh) laws. The former includes the books of the Hebrew Bible, said to have been transmitted by God to Moses in writing; the latter is represented in the Talmudic literature, understood to comprise teachings with which God orally instructed Moses and that were handed down through the generations, until, beginning in the first centuries C.E., they were written down to prevent their being lost. Having the sense of "revelation" and understood to define exactly what God expects of the Jews, the concept of Torah is central in Jewish practice and belief.

When used with the definite article ("The Torah"), the word signifies the Pentateuch alone, often referring in particular to the handwritten scroll containing the Five Books of Moses used in the Jewish synagogue.

Alan J. Avery-Peck

See also ARON HAQODESH; TALMUD; TANAK.

TORAH SHEBAL'PEH
See TORAH.

TORAH SHEBICHTAV
See TORAH.

TORII

(Japanese, lit., bird perch). At Shinto shrines, this is the arch or gateway marking the entrance to a sacred area and symbolizing the separation of the sacred and the profane. In its simplest and oldest form, it is constructed of three smooth tree trunks, two forming uprights and one lying horizontally across their tops. Traditionally, *torii* are found at Shinto shrines, but generally they mark any area that is inhabited by a *kami* (divine presence). According to Shinto mythology, the torii was originally a perch on which sacred birds landed outside the cave where Amaterasu (Sun Goddess) had retreated, leaving the world in darkness. The birds were sent by the kami to lure Amaterasu back into the world by their sacred songs, and subsequently the torii was used to mark the entrance to any sacred area.

G. D. DeAngelis

See also AMATERASU; KOJIKI; SHRINE.

TORQUEMADA, JUAN DE
(1388–1468)

Spanish theologian, canon lawyer, and member of the Dominican Order. He was papal theologian at the Council of Basle (1433), was active in (failed) reunification negotiations with the Greek Orthodox Church, and with Hus and his followers. He was appointed cardinal, and until the end of his life remained at the service of the papacy in several policymaking roles. His two main books were published after his death—a legal treatise, *Commentarii in decretum Gratiani* (1519), and an ecclesiological work that defended papal infallibility, *Summa de Ecclesia* (1489). His nephew, Tomás, was the notorious inquisitor.

Orlando Espín

See also CANON LAW; DOMINICANS; GREEK ORTHODOX CHURCH; HUS, JOHN; CARDINAL; CURIA, ROMAN; PAPACY/PAPAL.

TORQUEMADA, TOMÁS DE
(1420–98)

Spanish canon lawyer, Grand Inquisitor, and member of the Dominican Order. He was the nephew of Cardinal Juan de Torquemada. He was confessor to both King Ferdinand of Aragón and Queen Isabel of Castile. With the frequent Christian victories over Muslim armies in the last third of the fifteenth century, the continuing presence of non-Christians was a religious and political concern to Ferdinand and Isabel. Torquemada was appointed head of the newly established Inquisition. Although his name has been frequently associated with extreme cruelty, his methods were in fact typical of the judicial systems of the age and equally practiced in the rest of Europe. He was mainly responsible for the expulsion of most Jews in 1492 from unified Spain.

Orlando Espín

See also CANON LAW; DOMINICANS; INQUISITION; SEPHARDIM.

TOSEFTA

(Hebrew, supplement). A rabbinic supplement to and commentary on the Mishnah. Redacted at the beginning of the third century C.E., the Tosefta, like the Mishnah, contains material presumably preserved from the preceding centuries. In general, the Tosefta is less tightly reasoned and composed than the Mishnah and, since it is understood within the circles of traditional Judaism to contain materials purposely excluded from the Mishnah itself, it does not have a significant place in the determination of Jewish law. It accordingly has been the least studied legal document of early rabbinic Judaism.

Alan J. Avery-Peck

TOTEM/TOTEMISM

Although the word is from the Ojibwe (Native American) language, the beliefs associated with the term are widespread among many Native American nations and peoples (and beyond). The term itself refers to a (supernatural) being or (natural or supernatural) animal, plant, or phenomenon standing as originating ancestor and guardian of a clan (or other social unit) or of an entire people. By extension, the totem is also the emblem or symbol of the clan or people.

Orlando Espín

TRACTARIANISM

See OXFORD MOVEMENT.

TRACY, DAVID (1939–)

American theologian. David Tracy has had a significant effect on theology in the United States through his works, *A Blessed Rage for Order* (1975) and *The Analogical Imagination* (1981)—methodological reflections on fundamental and systematic theology, respectively. In the former, he argued for a "revisionist" theological model that sought to sublate the exigencies of previous theological models—orthodox, liberal, neo-orthodox, and radical theology. While process theology and the new quest for the historical Jesus were significant resources in his first work, contemporary hermeneutics in the form of the work of Hans Georg Gadamer and Paul Ricoeur were primary in the second as he explored the foundation of systematic theology in the plurality and ambiguity of interpretation of the "classic."

J. A. Colombo

TRADITIO-HISTORICAL CRITICISM

The Latin word *traditio* refers to the process of transmission. Traditio-historical criticism is the study of the history of the transmission of traditions found in biblical texts. This method seeks to reconstruct developments from the first oral formulation through all subsequent oral and written stages. Each development reflects the contributions of new individuals, communities, and generations who reinterpreted and reapplied the ancient material to themselves. The process also seeks to establish how a tradition came to be stabilized shortly before a text took on the religious authority that led to its canonical status.

Traditio-historical criticism is an integral process of the historical-critical method that follows after text, source, and form criticism. It constructs a plausible hypothesis about the probable course of alteration, expansion, omission, and combination with other traditions through which each tradition passed. Such reconstructions are grounded on details incorporated into the text that betray the evidence of different eras and circumstances within the communities responsible for preservation and transmission. It has had its greatest impact on Old Testament studies, although it has applications in the New. The Gospels rework the oral traditions and written sources. In the Pauline letters there are hymns (Phil 2:6-11) and creeds (Rom 1:3-4) that betray any number of levels of modifications.

Regina A. Boisclair

TRADITION (IN CHRISTIANITY)

The term "tradition" referred originally to the secular Greek concept of *paradosis* and to the (also secular) Latin notion of *traditio*. These two words (*paradosis, traditio*) are nouns that basically mean the same thing—"handing down" or "handing over." *Paradosis* in turn comes from the Greek verb *paradidomi* (more graphically) meaning "to turn over," "to entrust," "to commit (to another's care)." *Traditio* comes from the Latin verb *tradere*, meaning the same as its Greek counterpart, but further implies "instruction (for proper living or understanding)."

All religions known to humankind are "traditional," in the sense that all religions only exist in time and are, necessarily, situated in history and are heirs of history (whether they perceive/explain themselves historically or not). Religions survive and prolong their existence in time because they have managed to create the means of transmitting (*paradosis, traditio*) their beliefs, holy stories, rituals, and the like, from one generation to the next. Human beings, too, are necessarily "traditional" (in the sense meant here) and cannot be otherwise. From preceding generations, and by varied means of transmission, human beings are "entrusted" with language, customs, values, thought patterns, and so on; and while "in their trust" these cultural elements are shaped, reinterpreted, and made to grow. It is no exaggeration to say that human beings receive their self-understanding, and the tools for it, through and from "tradition."

Christians started using the terms *paradosis/traditio* already in the New Testament period. Their main guides were the experience and history of the people of Israel for whom the transgenerational transmission of peoplehood, and of its foundational elements and memories, was/is considered essential. Christians first referred the term and idea of "tradition" to the core kerygma (the most primitive preaching), and soon to the explanations and understandings of that kerygma as they developed in the first two Christian generations. When the "second coming of Christ" that had been expected immediately did not materialize as hoped, Christianity shifted from being a mainly "apocalyptic" religion to a more "historical" one—thereby granting its origins an even greater normative and defining character for later generations. The story of Jesus and the first generation's explanations and understandings of that story became the standard on which all authenticity rested and against which all developments were tested. Christians, therefore, granted hermeneutic primacy to the "apostolic church" and its witness. The early Christian *paradosis* was made up of stories (of Jesus and of the earliest Christians), doctrines, customs, rites, ethical expectations, and so on, that *collectively* attempted to transmit, "to hand over," the meaning and experience of Christianity as God's revelation to newer Christians (to converts, as well as to the children of older Christians). Those who received what was "entrusted" to them were expected to guard it, to understand and apply it, and in turn "to commit it" to the care of the following generation, having first "instructed" them in it. This entire process, and its "contents," was the Christian *paradosis*. "Tradition," therefore, is the Christian church's continued existence in history, and may be identified with both the substance and the meaning of that existence.

During the so-called "patristic" period of the church's history (roughly, from 110 to 700 C.E.), Christians needed assurance that what they held to be a part of Tradition was truly so. For this purpose, two extraordinarily important and mutually necessary developments occurred: the accepted list of books that together form the New Testament (the "canon") was determined mostly by consensus among the church's communities, and a "rule" (*regula fidei*, or "rule of faith," suggested by Vincent of Lérins and others) was established in order to determine the authenticity of what was held as important or necessary but was not contained in the New Testament—namely, that authentic Christian *paradosis* was what could be shown to have been believed/practiced always, everywhere, and by all. The influential Irenaeus of Lyons (d. 200 C.E.) had also insisted that the best "rule" of authenticity was the consensus among those Christian communities known to have been founded by the original apostles. In his view, since the church of Rome could prove its apostolic origins, it was especially important in setting the standards of Christian authenticity.

A crucially important and necessary dimension of all *regulae fidei* of the patristic period was the Christian people's "reception" of the elements of the Tradition. By "reception" was meant the people's acceptance and recognition of a belief or practice as "believed/practiced always, everywhere, and by all"—consequently, a part of authentic Christianity.

Doctrinal controversies, starting in the fourth century, led to the formal meetings of bishops that came to be called "ecumenical councils." The first seven eventually became extraordinarily important for subsequent generations of Christians, since these councils defined and shaped the fundamental christological and trinitarian doctrines still held by most

Christians. Two of these gatherings were emphatic on the importance of Tradition—the Second Council of Constantinople (in 553 C.E.), and the Second Council of Nicaea (in 787 C.E.). They both taught that doctrines and practices transmitted by Scripture, the "holy fathers" (the apostles and their more eminent successors), as well as the earlier ecumenical councils, were to be believed and followed. Indeed, Nicaea II formally declared that anyone who rejected the church's Tradition, "written or unwritten," was to be considered a heretic.

During the Middle Ages, in western Europe, there was a growing inclination to use legal means to enforce adherence to Christian tradition. The development of ecclesiastical canon law owes much to this western European trend, although it would be wrong to think that law became the more important means of transmitting the Tradition during this historical period. Indeed, liturgy and popular Catholicism were, since at least the second century C.E., much more crucial in transmitting Christian beliefs and practices than all canonical legislations ever were. In Western Christianity, another trend started to develop during the Middle Ages, but with roots in earlier periods of church history—the claim of the Bishops of Rome to be the final interpreters of the Tradition.

It is factually difficult, if not outright impossible, to talk about "the" church during the Middle Ages. There was so much diversity within Western Christianity that the so-called "medieval church" is perhaps more a modern invention than a historical reality. The creeds of Christian antiquity, regional liturgies, and local customs and traditions, were immensely more important than papal or even episcopal statements or definitions when it came to transmitting and preserving Christian Tradition.

With the Reformation's dismissal of Tradition as necessary, and with the Reformers' doctrine of *sola Scriptura* ("only the Scripture"), Protestants seemed to be rejecting the manner in which Christianity had transmitted and understood itself for fifteen centuries, thereby creating for the Reformation's descendants a number of difficult theological, historical, and doctrinal questions. The Reformers, however, were rightly reacting (among other issues) against the exaggerated claims and interpretations of the Tradition made by some individuals and communities during the second half of the medieval period. Most Reformers were not, however, rejecting or dismissing the role of the church and of Christian history. Among Lutherans, Tradition has not been ultimately challenged or ignored, although Lutheran theology has been (for understandable reasons) much more inclined to avoid certain theological terms that might appear to compromise Martin Luther's fundamental intuitions on the subject. The retention of the episcopate and of the liturgy had much to do with Lutheranism's moderate stance on the role of Tradition. Anglicans, who are not "Protestants," have stayed within the overall Catholic/Orthodox mainstream on Tradition. The Calvinist communities and their theological descendants (especially in the U.S.) are the ones who have actually attempted to fashion a Christianity without some sort of normative role for Tradition. A consequence of the sixteenth-century Protestant (especially Calvinist) emphasis on the exclusive normative role of the written text of Scripture, as opposed (by them) to the unwritten elements of Tradition, is the modern world's difficulty with the historical, "traditional," dimen-

sion of humanness, and its frequent disdain for orally and symbolically transmitted cultures (that has also fed some modern forms of racism). This has, in turn, contributed to the upsurge in integralism (popularly called "fundamentalism") among some Protestant communities.

The Council of Trent (1545–63) that spearheaded the Catholic Church's response to Protestantism as well as Catholicism's own internal reform, perceived itself as preserving and repeating the ancient understanding on the important, normative role of Tradition. In fact, Trent did preserve and deeply *reformed* what the Catholic Church believed about Tradition. Since theological uncertainty was quite typical of the world of Trent, the council needed to determine what had to be considered part of the so-called "deposit of faith" and what was theological or ecclesiastical opinion and practice, in order to be able to state the Catholic position on issues raised by the Protestant Reformers (themselves as varied as the medieval theological traditions they inherited). In discerning and determining what it considered to be part of the "deposit of faith," Trent not only validated the existence of the latter (quite a doctrinal and theological novelty at the time!), but also opened the door to a practical if unwanted divorce between doctrinal accuracy and daily Christian life and spirituality. The council's insistence on discovering what was part of "Tradition" actually led to a redefinition and reduction of the latter to doctrinal, categorial terms. The wealth of approaches and the methodological creativity implied in medieval theological diversity was lost in Trent. This council gave Catholicism a degree of doctrinal clarity, but it also deeply changed fifteen hundred years of Christian theological and doctrinal traditions. When coupled with what was happening in the Protestant contexts of the sixteenth century, what Trent did was but one side in the multisided demand for clarity and definition that created a strident world of colliding "certainties." Trent reaffirmed Catholic belief in the authority and revealed character of Scripture, also stating which books are believed to be part of the biblical canon. It acknowledged the normative role of Scripture, and saw in Tradition (as distinct from church "traditions") the normative interpreter of Scripture and an equally necessary witness to revelation and apostolic teaching. By proposing Bible and Tradition as witnesses to revelation, a notion inherited from patristic theology, Trent succeeded in preserving much of what it understood to be the living faith of the Catholic people; but it also unintentionally opened the possibility for a later development that identified the papacy's understanding of the Tradition with the Tradition itself.

In the past, some Catholic authors (misunderstanding the teaching of the Council of Trent) used to consider Tradition, together with but distinct from the Scriptures, as a "source" of revelation. This "two-fonts theory," however, was discarded as the Catholic theology of revelation (especially in and after the Second Vatican Council [1962–5]) correctly came to emphasize that Jesus Christ *is* the revelation of God, and that this revelation is not primarily the communication of doctrinal truths, but rather the outpouring of God's love and self in human history.

The two-fonts theory failed when the relation between the biblical text and Tradition was carefully examined. It is evident that the Scriptures have a privileged position as the inspired and norma-

tive witness to God's revelation. Tradition is correctly valued as the context within which the biblical texts came to be written and within which the very canon of the Scriptures came to be fixed and accepted as inspired. Tradition is also the ecclesial (and sometimes normative) interpretation of the Scriptures. The fixed texts of the Bible are proclaimed, explained, applied to life, and correctly interpreted by Tradition for every Christian generation. This role of Tradition is guided and protected from error by the Spirit of God who also inspired the biblical texts.

Scripture is the normative, written expression of a preceding tradition that proclaims and witnesses to the revelation of God to Israel and in Christ, and from him through the apostolic community for the universal, postapostolic church. Scripture, therefore, communicates all the essential contents (gathered in the biblical canon and received by the church) necessary for complete, true, and saving faith. Scripture, which must always be interpreted in the light of the Tradition that precedes and accompanies it, is the norm for the church's preaching and faith.

Postapostolic Tradition, on the other hand, is essentially interpretation and reception of the one Gospel of God that has found its concrete, written expression in Scripture. The common content of Scripture and Tradition is, simply put, their normative witness to the God revealed in Jesus Christ. The Bible and Tradition share the same content in the sense that tradition, *through postapostolic expressions, symbols, and language*, recognizes and confesses (Creed), refines correct meaning against falsehood (dogmas), and witnesses to that same truth Scripture communicates *through the language, expressions, and symbols of Israel and the apostolic church*. Scripture has been received and its canon fixed forever, while Tradition is necessarily living in and through history.

One could speak of Tradition as exemplified in the definitions of the great ecumenical councils of Christian antiquity, as expounded by the fathers of the church, and as communicated and witnessed to by the ecclesial magisterium and by the theologians throughout history. Tradition is certainly expressed in and through all these means. Theologians studying Tradition usually concentrate on written conciliar documents, patristic texts, episcopal or papal declarations, and the like. Quite correctly, this written material (as also the text of Scripture) is very carefully examined, and the methods of textual interpretation applied to it. Most theologians are aware of the need to properly understand a written document within its linguistic, cultural, political, historical, and doctrinal contexts. Without this careful study, the interpretation of the text could be prejudiced or inaccurate and, as a consequence, yield wrong conclusions that could mislead other theological research dependent on the proper interpretation of Tradition's texts.

However, just as important as the written texts of Tradition (or, in fact, more important) is the *living witness and faith of the Christian people*. This witness and faith have always been held (as official doctrine) to be an indispensable part of the Catholic understanding of Tradition. And yet, the witness and faith of the Christian people do not seem to be taken seriously by those who study tradition, although lay, real-life Christians are the primary subjects of tradition and of its very possibility. It is evident that it is difficult to limit the object of one's study when the latter is supposed to be found mainly at the experiential level in every community of the faithful. Cultural differences, diversity of languages, and all sorts of other variations make the actual theological study and interpretation of the life and faith of real Christian people a very difficult task indeed. And to complicate things even further, the object of the study (though expressed through cultural categories, languages, and so on, that run the full gamut of human diversity) is to be found at the level of intuition. It is this "faith-full" intuition that makes real Christian people sense that something is true or not vis-à-vis the Gospel, or that someone is acting in accordance with the Christian Gospel or not, or that something important for Christianity is not being heard. This intuition in turn allows for and encourages a belief and a style of life and prayer that express and witness to the fundamental Christian message: God as revealed in Jesus Christ. This "faith-full" intuition is technically called the *sensus fidelium* or *sensus fidei* (in Latin, "sense of the faithful," and "sense of the faith," respectively).

The whole church has received the revelation of God and accepted it in faith. And, as a consequence, the whole church is charged with proclaiming, living, and transmitting the fullness of revelation. Therefore, the necessary task of expressing the contents of Scripture and Tradition is not and cannot be limited to the ordained ministers of the church. The whole church has this mission, and the Spirit was promised to the whole church for this task. Christian laity, consequently, are indispensable witnesses and bearers of the Gospel—as indispensable as the magisterium of the church. Furthermore, because the foundational origin of the *sensus fidelium* is the Holy Spirit, it can be said (as it is said in Catholicism) that this "sense of the faithful" is infallible, preserved by the Spirit from error in matters necessary to revelation. In other words, the "faith-full" intuition (*sensus fidei*) of real Christian laypeople infallibly transmits the contents of Tradition and thus infallibly senses the proper interpretation and application of Scripture.

Orlando Espín

See also BIBLE; CANON, BIBLICAL; CATHOLIC TRADITION; CHURCH; COUNTER-REFORMATION/CATHOLIC REFORMATION; ECCLESIOLOGY; FAITH; GRACE; HOLY SPIRIT; INFALLIBILITY; LAITY; LATINO THEOLOGY (-IES); LITURGY (IN CHRISTIANITY); MAGISTERIUM, ORDINARY; PATRISTICS/PATROLOGY; POPULAR CATHOLICISM; RECEPTION OF DOCTRINE; REFORMATION; REVELATION; RULE OF FAITH; SENSUS FIDELIUM/ SENSUS FIDEI; TRADITION AND TRADITIONS; TRENT, COUNCIL OF; TRIDENTINISM.

TRADITION AND TRADITIONS
In Roman Catholicism, especially after the Council of Trent (1545–63), a distinction has been commonly made between "Tradition" (usually capitalized) and "traditions" (not capitalized). By "Tradition" is meant the written and unwritten contents of Christian faith and experience, regarded by Catholics as necessary elements of (or developments from) revelation, transmitted from one generation to another, especially guarded and proclaimed by the church's magisterium and the people's *sensus fidei*. By "traditions" are meant the customs, practices, institutional expressions, disciplinary decisions, doctrines, theological explanations, and so forth, that the church might endorse or propose during different periods of its history but are *not* considered to be part of revelation, developments thereof, or (consequently) irreformable. The distinction, if properly understood and applied,

can be quite useful to pastoral, theological, and doctrinal reflection. After Trent, however, and without any official statement to this effect, it seemed that liturgy, spirituality and holiness, piety, evangelization, and all pastoral work, much of moral/ethical teaching, and so on, came to be treated as "traditions." On the other hand, "Tradition" became increasingly and officially identified with doctrinal contents, and associated almost exclusively with papal understanding of doctrines. Although the Council of Trent (and especially the Jesuit theologians who participated in it) did make the distinction between Tradition and traditions (thereby profoundly changing much of what was commonly held before the sixteenth century on this matter), it *cannot* be said that the council meant to lead toward these later developments and consequences. So-called Tridentinism, the rigorist and often unwarranted interpretation of Trent that came after the council and seriously impacted subsequent Roman Catholicism, is to be held responsible for the later consequences of the original Tridentine distinction.

Orlando Espín

See also ECCLESIOLOGY; RECEPTION OF DOCTRINE; REVELATION; SENSUS FIDELIUM/SENSUS FIDEI; TRADITION (IN CHRISTIANITY); TRENT, COUNCIL OF; TRIDENTINISM.

TRADITION CRITICISM
See TRADITIO-HISTORICAL CRITICISM.

TRANCE
In many religions some individuals undergo experiences that can be described as trance-like. By "trance" is meant a temporary state of being (therefore affecting a person's entire behavior and perceptions

of what is real and true) that implies extraordinarily increased sensitivity and suggestibility. A trance experience can deeply affect and transform a person's life and even entire communities. Religious trances can be induced through rituals and/or chemicals, or they can come about by contact with a sacred person, symbol, or location. While in a state of trance, a person might (1) experience God, saints, ancestors, spirits, or other sacred beings; (2) spiritually travel to a sacred time or place; (3) encounter profound inner peace and meaning; (5) undergo "spiritual struggles"; or any combination of these. It seems clear that the person's prior religious beliefs will likely determine the contents and manner of the trance experience, and will make the experience itself possible, credible, and understandable (at least among believers). Some researchers include trance among a more general category of altered states of consciousness (ASC).

Orlando Espín

See also CONTEMPLATION; POSSESSION; RELIGION.

TRANSCENDENTALISM

Transcendentalism was a philosophical and religious movement in the early nineteenth century in the United States. In 1836 wealthy intellectuals in Boston formed the Transcendentalist Club, a discussion group focusing on contemporary ideas, especially the Romanticism of Goethe, Coleridge, and Wordsworth, and Eastern religions. Most members were dissatisfied Unitarians; its leading figures were Ralph Waldo Emerson, Henry David Thoreau, Margaret Fuller, and Bronson Alcott. Emerson (1803–82), a former Unitarian minister, shocked the orthodox religious community with his 1838 address at Harvard Divinity School, in which he proclaimed that eternal religious truth could not be encompassed by church, creed, or dogma. Emerson and other Transcendentalists affirmed that divinity permeated natural reality, and that an intense, mystical relationship with the holy was possible. Throwing off the shackles of organized religion, individuals should self-reliantly and fearlessly quest for sacred truth.

Although Transcendentalists resisted institutional development, they nonetheless pursued their ideals of Beauty, Reason, and Good in daily life. Emerson's friend Henry David Thoreau lived alone in a cabin to cultivate his relationship with nature and recorded his experiences in *Walden* (1854). In 1844 George and Sophia Ripley founded a Transcendentalist commune at Brook Farm in West Roxbury, Massachusetts. Intellectuals devoted to the nourishment of mind and heart were not well suited to the practical cultivation of agriculture, and the community disbanded in a few years. Transcendentalists also founded a journal, *The Dial*, edited by Emerson and Margaret Fuller, that provided a vehicle for young writers such as Nathaniel Hawthorne. While Boston was the center of the movement, smaller groups were founded in Louisville, Cincinnati, and St. Louis.

While Transcendentalism never became an independent denomination, it had four significant impacts on U.S. religious thought. First, it popularized European Romanticism, Buddhism, and Hinduism among an educated elite. It was a liberal rebellion against the arid intellectualism of Unitarianism. Second, it supported the development of a literary renaissance in New England. Third, it was a reaction to the alienation and impersonality of industrial capitalism, an early back-to-nature movement. Fourth, it influenced later theologians Horace Bushnell and Walter Rauschenbusch in developing metaphorical understandings of language and the Social Gospel, respectively. By the 1850s, Transcendentalism had faded as an organized movement. Some Transcendentalists drifted back to Unitarianism, while others became humanists or Freethinkers; two, Isaac Hecker and Orestes Brownson, became Catholic.

Evelyn A. Kirkley

See also BUSHNELL, HORACE; HECKER, ISAAC; RAUSCHENBUSCH, WALTER.

TRANSCENDENTAL MEDITATION

See MAHESH YOGI, MAHARISHI.

TRANSCENDENTALS

Transcendentals are philosophical concepts that have a universal reference and were used to discuss the possibilities and limits of knowledge by Scholastic philosophers and Immanuel Kant. The methodological use and meaning of the concept differs in each system. Transcendentals in Scholastic theology designated properties or attributes of being that were common to all existents (although not in the same degree) and were essential to the use of the analogy of being. Examples of transcendental categories are reality, being, truth, perfection, uniqueness, and identity. The Enlightenment philosopher Immanuel Kant distinguished between phenomenal knowledge rooted in objective reality and the a priori structures of intellect or intuitive categories, mental properties through which objects were known. For Kant the transcendentals had a necessary epistemological function but no link to objective reality. Modern

Thomists invoke both uses. Those scholars working in the classical or neo-Scholastic Thomist tradition have adapted the old Scholastic usage; the transcendental Thomists, particularly Bernard Lonergan, have amended the Kantian understanding to suggest an immanent intuition of the divine in every act of volition and intellection.

Patricia Plovanich

TRANSFIGURATION

An episode in the life of Jesus told, with variations, in the three Synoptic Gospels (Mark 9:2-10; Matt 17:1-9; Luke 9:28-36). These accounts relate that after Jesus led Peter, James, and John up a mountain to pray, his face was transformed, his clothing became white, and he talked with Moses and Elijah who appeared with him. After Peter asked if they should build three booths for Jesus, Moses, and Elijah, respectively, a cloud came over them and a voice was heard saying: "This is my beloved Son; listen to him." Then, Jesus was alone with the three disciples, and he instructed them not to speak of this experience until the Son of Man had risen from the dead.

The accounts of Jesus' transfiguration follow the general structure of rabbinic stories that report messages from heavenly voices. They also incorporate a sequence of events as well as several details that indicate the story was deliberately shaped to be reminiscent of the account of Moses on Mt. Sinai in Exodus 24. Matthew's account includes some redactional touches to that of Mark, some of which are suggestive of Daniel 10. Luke's account coalesced two sources. Luke derived the first half of his story from a primitive source that reported this event from the perspective of Jesus. The second half of

Luke's account follows the later account from Mark that recounts the episode from the perspective of the disciples.

This story has many difficulties. For example, how could Peter later deny Jesus if he had experienced such a theophany? Some exegetes believe that the story is a postresurrection account that was displaced by Mark or the tradition that he followed. However, in this story Moses and Elijah are the ones who appear, while Jesus was with his disciples from the start. In a relevant article, Jerome Murphy-O'Connor closely examined the various strata of the story in an attempt to establish a historical core of this incident. His reconstruction suggests that the account is indeed based on the memory of an incident during the ministry of Jesus. Murphy-O'Connor's hypothesis is that since Jesus was convinced that he had a mission from God, he was not sure why it was becoming increasingly clear that that he would very likely be executed. Then, when Jesus suddenly recognized that his mission would include death, his face changed, much like that of anyone who suddenly resolves a perplexing situation.

The three Gospels include this episode after the same sequence of events: Peter's confession of faith, Jesus' first prediction of his fate, and Jesus' instructions that those who follow them must deny themselves and take up their own crosses. Thus, whatever historical memory lies behind this episode, in the Gospels it is a christological climax that provides divine confirmation of Peter's confession of faith and authorizes Jesus' prediction of his own destiny, as well as his instructions concerning the destiny of his disciples (Matt 10:38f.; Mark 8:34; Luke 14:26f.).

Regina A. Boisclair

TRANSFINALIZATION
See TRANSIGNIFICATION; TRANSUB-STANTIATION.

TRANSIGNIFICATION
"Transignification" and "transfinalization" are terms introduced and developed by the Roman Catholic theologians Piet Schoonenberg and Edward Schillebeeckx to describe how the risen Christ is present in the bread and wine of the Eucharist. According to this theory, the presence of the risen Christ already present in the assembled Christian community is deepened by the designation by that community of the bread and wine as signs of the risen Lord. No physical change takes place in the bread and wine, but their designation as signs radically changes their significance for the community so that the final purpose of the bread and wine is to mediate the presence of the Lord to the community. The reason for this suggestion was to translate the theory of "transubstantiation," based on Aristotelian metaphysics, into the more modern philosophical approach of sign theory. In 1965, Pope Paul VI replied to these theories in the letter *Mysterium Fidei*, stating that the change of the bread and wine in the Eucharist is an ontological change, not just a change in meaning or purpose. Despite this caveat, contemporary Roman Catholic theologians continue to search for a suitable modern philosophical description of the Real Presence in the Eucharist.

Gary Macy

See also CHRIST; CONSUBSTANTIATION; EUCHARIST; PAUL VI, POPE; REAL PRESENCE; RESURRECTION OF CHRIST; SCHILLEBEECKX, EDWARD; SCHOONEN-BERG, PIET; TRANSUBSTANTIATION.

TRANSMIGRATION

See REINCARNATION.

TRANSUBSTANTIATION

A set of metaphysical theories that explains how the risen Christ becomes present in the bread and wine of the Eucharist. The theory is based on the Aristotelian distinction between substance (in Latin, *substantia*) and accidents (in Latin, *accidentia*). Substance, technically made up of matter and form, is roughly the essence of a thing, what makes it what it is. Accidents are, roughly, those things one can sense—color, weight, taste, and so on. Transubstantiation argues that the substance of the bread and wine are changed into, or replaced by, the substance of the Body and Blood of the risen Christ. The purpose of this theory is to explain how the risen Lord could be really present in the bread and wine, as Christians assert, and yet obviously there was no noticeable physical change in the bread and wine. Since substance can only be grasped by the mind, not the senses, this theory seemed to meet this need. Transubstantiation describes how a change can be real, but not sensed. The change in the bread and wine in the Eucharist was deemed be miraculous and the unique instance of this sort of change.

The term was first used in Western Christianity in the twelfth century and continued to be developed and modified throughout the Middle Ages. The verb "transubstantiated" was used to insist on the Real Presence in opposition to the Cathars in the creed written by the Fourth Lateran Council in 1215. Although contemporaries did not see this as giving the term any particular ecclesiastical approval, the idea that transubstantiation had been defined in 1215 as an article of belief was popularized by the Franciscan theologian John Duns Scotus in the early fourteenth century. Not all theologians, of course, agreed with Scotus, but many did. The theory of transubstantiation was attacked by John Wycliff in the late fourteenth century and during the Reformation became the focus of Roman Catholic and Protestant disagreements over the Eucharist. Roman Catholics defended transubstantiation, although the Council of Trent affirmed merely that "this change the holy Catholic Church properly and appropriately called transubstantiation." Protestants, on the other hand, denied that transubstantiation was a useful description of how the risen Christ could be present. Roman Catholics still often stoutly defend transubstantiation and Protestants often vehemently attack it, though few from either tradition could explain transubstantiation or the Aristotelian philosophy that lies behind it.

Gary Macy

See also ARISTOTELIANISM; ARISTOTLE; CHRIST; CONSUBSTANTIATION; DUNS SCOTUS, JOHN; EUCHARIST; LATERAN (COUNCILS OF THE); REAL PRESENCE; REFORMATION; RESURRECTION OF CHRIST; SUBSTANCE; TRANSIGNIFICATION; TRENT, COUNCIL OF; WYCLIFF, JOHN.

TRAPPISTS

"Trappist" is the popular name for the Order of the Cistercians of the Strict Observance. The order was founded in 1892 when several different groups of Cistercians who followed the strict observance were merged by Pope Leo XIII. All these groups find their roots in the Jansenist movement of the seventeenth century. A number of Cistercians at that time insisted on a strict observance of the Cistercian rule, including complete abstinence, hence their names, the "abstinents." The most famous of the leaders of this reformed group was Armand-Jean Bouthillier de Rancé, who was abbot of the monastery of La Trappe from 1664 to 1700. It is from this abbey that the movement still takes its name. In favor with the French nobility in the seventeenth century, the Trappists were dissolved during the French Revolution. Under the leadership of Augustin de Lestange, the last of the monks of La Trappe fled to Switzerland. The order continued to grow despite its continued wanderings. The monks returned to La Trappe in 1817. The order has always been noted for its austere practices of perpetual silence, total abstinence from meat, fish, and eggs, and self-support through manual labor. In recent times, there has been some relaxation of these rules, allowing for necessary speech; work outside the monastery and study have replaced some manual labor. In the United States, the Trappists are best known from the writings of the Trappist Thomas Merton.

Gary Macy

See also ABSTINENCE; CISTERCIANS; JANSENISM; MERTON, THOMAS; MONASTICISM IN WESTERN CHRISTIANITY.

TREF

In Judaism, any food or preparation of foods that does not conform to the Jewish dietary laws (kashrut). In contemporary parlance, the term also is used to refer to any behavior, belief, or object that has no appropriate place within Jewish life. The terms derives from the Hebrew root meaning "torn," referring originally to meat from an animal that was not slaughtered in conformity with the requirements of the Jewish dietary laws.

Alan J. Avery-Peck

See also KASHRUT.

TRENT, COUNCIL OF

Nineteenth ecumenical council in the reckoning of the Roman Catholic Church. It met in the northern Italian city of Trent, except for a very brief period at Bologna. After several frustrated attempts, many delays, and much political maneuvering, Pope Paul III agreed to open the council and send his delegates. The first session was poorly attended, and not all participants were interested in real reform. Pressure from Emperor Charles V (and later from Philip II of Spain) and from other Catholic kings and princes, as well as from some key bishops, theological faculties, and superiors of major religious orders, made the popes keep the Council of Trent in session. As political and religious events in Europe led to more crises and confrontations, the work of the Council of Trent was often interrupted and, more than once, seemed to presage the collapse of the entire conciliar reform effort. The intolerant Paul IV refused to call the council back into session while he was Pope, and only his successor (Pius IV) managed to bring Trent to conclusion, some twenty-three years after its opening. All hope of reconciliation with the Protestant Reformers was lost by the time the council formally ended.

There were twenty-five groups of meetings (called "sessions") held throughout the council's three periods: 1545–8, 1551–2, and 1562–3. Trent is arguably one of the most reforming councils in the history of the Catholic Church, and its impact is still felt today. Although it claimed to represent the entire Catholic Church, Trent included no representatives from Eastern Churches in full communion with Rome, or geographically from outside Europe at a time when Catholicism was rapidly expanding worldwide (indeed, the sole bishop of a Latin American diocese was in fact a Spaniard who had yet to travel to the Western Hemisphere). Protestants did not participate after 1548 (and only a handful had actually tried to participate between 1545 and 1548).

The popularized image of this council as reactionary and conservative is very misleading. Although Trent was indeed crucial to the Counter-Reformation ("Counter-Protestant") efforts of sixteenth-century European Catholicism, today it seems clear that the council's longest-lasting and most important result was its own profound reformation and transformation of medieval Catholicism. When the doctrinal decisions of Trent are understood within the context of the conversations and debates that actually occurred during the council's sessions (for which there are plentiful written sources), it becomes clear that the bishops and theologians gathered there cannot be simplistically labeled as reactionary or conservative. The council's participants often struggled with their consciences over long periods of time, and sought rigorous theological advice in order to determine which was the best formulation or answer to a debated theological or pastoral question. When understood historically and contextually, Trent seems to have been more inclined to nuance and tolerate in areas where there was no consensual certainty. And even in the areas of certainty it was less strict than later generations were led to believe. It was after 1590, with the passing of the conciliar generation, that a rigid interpretation of Trent gained the upper hand in the Catholic Church, and this perspective on the council's accomplishments became widespread. This rigid interpretation of Trent is known today as "Tridentinism" (arguably, Trent was not "Tridentinist" in this sense).

Clearly deferential to papal authority, Trent was not a papally controlled council (although its decrees were accepted and promulgated by the popes). Trent left to the popes the tasks of reforming the liturgy, of completing the official Latin translation of the Bible (known as the "Vulgate"), of establishing a list of forbidden books (the "Index"), and of reforming and revamping the Roman Curia, but the council did not seek and did not wait for papal approval for its more important doctrinal decisions and reforming legislation. Indeed, the tasks entrusted to the popes have all, in time, been changed or disregarded; but the doctrinal statements of Trent and most of its crucial reforming legislation are still very much part of modern Roman Catholicism. Trent's impact was so profound on the church that no other council gathered for another three centuries.

Most European and European-American historians of Trent focus on the Catholic militancy of the council, and yet what is in fact more amazing (and usually ignored by these historians) is that the bishops and experts at Trent seemed oblivious to the consequences and nature of the conquest of the Americas occurring as they met and that was actually funding their meetings. Catholic states were taking over most of the globe and consequently becoming very wealthy and powerful, rapidly expanding the frontiers of the church and adding millions of new converts to Catholicism. The city of Trent itself (while the council was in session) was a major trade route for gold and silver coming from the Western Hemisphere, and documents from the time of the council show that the bishops knew this important commerce was taking place as they met. Numerous ethical, pastoral, and doctrinal questions were being raised (especially in Spain, Portugal, and Italy), and significant controversies on these matters were raging in the most important Catholic universities of Europe. Yet the bishops at Trent seemed content with ignoring the conquests, the issues raised by these, as well as the birth of the modern world they ushered in. It is possible that the monarchies funding the council weighed heavily on the bishops' freedom to discuss these concerns, but it is also quite possible that a European council, lacking in cultural and confessional diversity overall, could not have been sensitive to questions raised by and on behalf of millions of human beings on the other side of the Atlantic. Perhaps this insensitivity, coupled with the implied assumption that European concerns were the only "really" important concerns for the Catholic Church, turned out to be Trent's major limitations (doctrinally and pastorally), with long-lasting and negative effects for the whole church's future. The council's disregard for the non-European seems to indicate that it shared in the attitudes of cultural and ethnic superiority that justified and demeaned what was happening in the Americas.

Prior to the start of the Lutheran Reformation there had been other recent attempts at reform. Some had been unsuccessful (the failed Fifth Lateran Council, 1512–7, for example), and some partially successful (for example, the movement gathered around the figure of Cardinal Jiménez de Cisneros in Spain). And yet, the first half of the sixteenth century seemed ripe for much deeper (and still needed) reform. Martin Luther not only hastened the reformations that led many to break full communion with the Church of Rome; he also made those who remained loyal to Rome come to grips with the unavoidable demands and need for reform. The bishops and theologians at the Council of Trent understood themselves, to a significant degree, as responding to Luther and, because of Luther, to crucial issues raised within the Catholic Church.

The fifteenth and early sixteenth centuries had inherited the long medieval tradition of theological diversity. On many important issues, the religious thought of Western Christianity had been far from unanimous, and yet this had not been usually interpreted as necessarily problematic. Indeed, the opposite view was probably more frequent. Luther's theology, therefore, was as much an heir to medieval doctrinal reflection as Trent's was. And since theological uncertainty was quite typical of the world of Trent, the council needed to determine what had to be considered part of the "deposit of faith" and what was theological or ecclesiastical opinion and practice, in order to be able to state the Catholic position on issues raised by the Protestant Reformers (themselves as varied as the medieval theological traditions they inherited). In discerning and determining what it considered to be part of the "deposit of faith," Trent not only validated the existence of the latter (quite a doctrinal and theological novelty at the time!), but also opened the door to a practical if unwanted divorce between doctrinal accuracy and daily Christian life and spirituality. The council's insistence on discovering what was part of "Tradition" actually led to a redefinition and reduction of the latter to doctrinal, categorical terms. The wealth of approaches and the methodological creativity implied in medieval theological diversity (no matter how flawed many of these may seem to us today) was lost in Trent. This council gave Catholicism a degree of doctrinal clarity, but it also deeply changed fifteen hundred years of Christian theological and doctrinal traditions. When coupled with what was happening in the Protestant contexts of the sixteenth century, what Trent did was but one side in the multisided demand for clarity and definition that created a strident world of colliding "certainties." These, in time, have led to the medieval-like plurality of views typical of our contemporary world, but now without the naive hope (still possible at the time of Trent) that new doctrinal statements could erase doubt and uncertainty.

The theological trends present at the Council of Trent were the ones current in European Catholic thought at the time—Thomism, Scotism, Nominalism, Augustinianism, and Humanism. Spanish Thomists were probably the most influential in the end, but others (especially Humanist theologians and churchmen) also had an important impact. Consensus was the aim, more than numerical majority, in the conciliar process of decision-making. So, when consensus was possible among the diverse schools of thought represented at the council, a doctrinal decree or definition was forthcoming. The absence of consensus also led to interesting silences: no Tridentine dogmatic declarations on papal primacy, on the ministry and nature of episcopacy, on the relationship between pope and bishops, on the relationship between divine grace and human free will, and so on. There were also numerous statements couched in carefully nuanced terms—for example, the declarations on the sacraments. In other words, it would be wrong to interpret all Tridentine doctrinal statements as having the same dogmatic weight, or the same doctrinal claims and consequences. The theological understanding

of Trent's teaching must try to be as nuanced and balanced as the council participants intended, avoiding the misuse of the texts of conciliar decrees in order to support and legitimize later developments in doctrine or church practice.

One important point to keep in mind when interpreting Trent's teaching is the meaning and use of the term *anathema* (a formal denunciation or excommunication). Many of the council's final doctrinal statements (called "canons") were phrased in a way that said that if a person held a certain condemned belief, he or she was in turn held to be *anathema* ("if anyone said that the sacraments of the New Dispensation were not instituted by our Lord Jesus Christ . . . let him be *anathema*," for example). In the official "Minutes" and other documents of the council, it is clearly indicated that this phrasing often meant to condemn those doctrines of Luther's (and later of Melanchton's and Calvin's) that Trent understood to be heretical (either not found in, or opposed to, the contents of the revealed "deposit of faith"). The use of *anathema*, in the conciliar understanding, was not always equal to implying that the doctrine opposite to the one condemned was held to be part of the "deposit of faith." This distinction is very important in order to avoid making Trent say what it in fact never said. Careful contextual analysis of the texts and their accompanying documents and explanations, therefore, is essential for an adequate interpretation of the council's doctrinal teaching.

Confronted with the church's lack of doctrinal clarity on many issues raised by the Protestant Reformers, Trent's participants chose to respond to these first. Significantly, Martin Luther (and to a lesser degree Philip Melanchton and John

Calvin) set much of the theological agenda for the Council of Trent. What the Protestant Reformers did not challenge, the council rarely defined. And yet, despite Protestant accusations and teaching, there were no Tridentine declarations on papal primacy, on the ministry and nature of episcopacy, on the relationship between pope and bishops, or on the relationship between divine grace and human free will.

The Council of Trent centered its theological, doctrinal contributions around four major areas. (1) It reaffirmed Catholic belief in the authority and revealed character of Scripture, also stating which books are believed to be part of the biblical canon. It acknowledged the normative role of Scripture. It also saw in Tradition (as distinct from church "traditions") the normative interpreter of Scripture and an equally necessary witness to revelation and apostolic teaching. By proposing Bible and Tradition as witnesses to revelation, a notion inherited from patristic theology, Trent succeeded in preserving much of what it understood to be the living faith of the Catholic people; but it also unintentionally opened the possibility for a later development that identified the papacy's understanding of the Tradition with the Tradition itself. The council's statement regarding the official character of the Latin translation of Scripture, known as the Vulgate, was certainly not intended as a doctrinal definition. (2) "Original sin" was reaffirmed as Catholic doctrine, and interpreted to mean the cause whereby human nature was degraded and wounded beyond humanity's sole healing ability. This state of decadence, the council said, was against God's will and intention. Baptism erases "original sin" but not some of its consequences (especially, it does not wipe away the

inclination to sin). Avoiding what it understood to be Luther's pronounced pessimism regarding the human condition, Trent equally avoided Pelagian-style optimism. Degraded by sin and profoundly wounded, and in complete need of God's grace, human nature is foundationally still good. (3) The decree on justification was the most theologically important decision, according to the council's participants. In a language that owed much to spirituality, Trent tried to frame its doctrine on justification in a way that was not basically apologetic or mainly anti-Lutheran. The council taught the necessity of God's grace for and throughout the entire process of justification, including human cooperation with grace. Trent indeed taught the importance and need of human cooperation with God, and the will's indispensable acceptance of grace for justification; but the council was clear in teaching that this necessary human contribution to justification (through faith, and love, and hope) was itself made possible and guided by grace. Justification, therefore, comes through faith, but not without love and hope. Against Luther, then, Trent emphasized the need for human cooperation, and it taught that justification not only wipes away sin but actually sanctifies the person. Furthermore, knowledge or certainty of one's own eternal destination ("election") is not possible, for it is known by God alone; because eternal life is not a reward but a gift. (4) Trent's teaching on the sacraments was not ultimately motivated by the questions raised by Protestants on these, but by the need (against what was taught by some Reformers) to doctrinally safeguard the belief in the visibility of the church. In other words, the council wanted to emphasize that the church of Christ can indeed be found on earth, that it is recognizable, and that there are some external (visible) signs of its presence and of membership in it. Consequently, Trent did not intend to settle or define all questions concerning the sacraments, nor was it interested in presenting a complete doctrinal statement on them. Trent's was not the final word on the meaning, significance, or nature of the sacraments. The council, however, did teach that since Christ is the origin of the church, he is therefore the origin (also) of the sacraments of the church. The sacraments are gifts from God, and their efficacy does not depend on human disposition alone, because the efficacy of the grace of God is not imprisoned by human dispositions. This is the intuition behind the sacramental doctrine known as *ex opere operato*. Trent also taught that the sacraments of the church were seven. On the specific doctrine of the "real presence" of Christ in the Eucharist, Trent opted for a nuanced, traditional Catholic "sacramental" definition (against Calvin and Zwingli). There were a number of other decisions regarding the doctrine of the sacraments: on the sacrificial character of the Mass, on the relation of penance to justification, and the like.

The Council of Trent did not just formulate doctrinal statements. The participants also arrived at administrative and pastoral decisions that have had a lasting effect on Roman Catholicism. Some of these decisions were left to the popes to carry out; for example, the final revision and publication of the Vulgate, the revamping of the central administration of the church (known as the Curia), and the establishment of a special office to assist in the implementation of the conciliar decrees and to officially interpret the meaning of conciliar texts. But among the tasks left to the popes to accomplish in

Trent's name, two stand out for their importance—the *Roman Catechism*, and the reform of the liturgy.

The council's participants had early on decided on the need for an official catechism, written explicitly for pastors, that would present a correct and full understanding of Catholic beliefs and ethical expectations, and that would assist the parish priests in preparation of homilies and in religious education in general. Experts at the council had tried to write the final text before adjournment, but it proved impossible; so they left the task to be accomplished by a papally appointed commission led by Charles Borromeo, the archbishop of Milan. The *Roman Catechism* was officially published in 1566 by Pius V. This manual became extraordinarily influential in that it led to the standardization of Catholic belief throughout the world. It became the source and point of reference of nearly all religious education texts published in the next four centuries. The *Roman Catechism* was translated into most modern European languages. The unexpected (and unwanted) negative effects of the catechism's widespread use were the impression given to many members of the church that Catholicism was a set of doctrines, and that Catholics would be considered well educated in their faith if they only mastered the meaning of a set of doctrines.

Another important task Trent left to the popes was the reform of the church's liturgy. The council had called for liturgical reform because of the number of very evident abuses that had been occurring for some time. However, during the church's long prior history, and certainly during the period in which Trent was in session, liturgical diversity had been the rule in Europe, and there had been a strong connection between liturgical practice and popular spirituality. Trent, it seems evident, did not intend to end either. It did insist, however, on stopping the abuses and exaggerations. And yet, while the liturgical reform carried out by Pius V did stop what was wrong, it also did away with what Trent had not seen in need of change. Pius V took the liturgical tradition, practices, and language of the Diocese of Rome (that had already spread, with variations, to much of Western Europe) and, with minor modifications, made them the only acceptable standard and sole rule for Western Catholicism's liturgy. Deviations from Rome's official liturgy were not to be permitted. Henceforth, Catholic liturgy literally became Roman liturgy. Gone were fifteen hundred years of diversity and the more significant links between liturgy and popular spirituality. Trent had not advocated this outcome, although it can be faulted for not having given the popes a definite set of criteria for liturgical reform.

Another decision made by Trent that began to be implemented even while the council was still in session (in 1563) was the establishment of seminaries for the education of the clergy. No other means proved as successful in ultimately transforming and reforming the Catholic Church in the image of Trent. Regardless of later shortcomings, the decision to establish these clergy schools was very wise. Before Trent, priests had been trained either as apprentices to older priests, or in monasteries, or at universities. With significant exceptions, the rank and file of pre-Tridentine priests were quite inadequately educated. Ill-trained clergy had become a serious source of moral abuse and doctrinal confusion before the Reformation. Cleaning up the priesthood was consequently very high on Trent's reform agenda, and the seminaries became one of the best means. Although it took two centuries for the worldwide (and very uneven) implementation of this conciliar decision, educational quality was never high except in some large-city seminaries. In most countries, and until recently, seminaries actually offered little more than basic education, with heavy dosages of religious practices and doctrinal formation. But regardless of quality, all seminaries became channels for Trent's doctrinal decrees and reforming legislation. One unintended and serious result of the Tridentine seminaries, however, was the development of a clericalized mentality within the church.

Although the council of Trent failed at reconciliation with Lutherans and other Protestant Reformers, and did not accomplish all it set itself to do, it nevertheless was a deeply reforming council. By creating unity and clarity within Catholicism, and by reinterpreting the shared Christian medieval inheritance (in some ways as substantially as Luther had), Trent allowed the Roman Catholic Church to regain its confidence as it entered a more pluralistic and often unfriendly world. Contemporary Catholicism owes most of its institutional, doctrinal, and liturgical shape to Trent.

Orlando Espín

See also ANGLICAN COMMUNION; AUGUSTINIANISM; BELLARMINE, ROBERT; BORROMEO, CHARLES; CALVIN, JOHN; CALVINISM; CATECHISM; CATHOLIC TRADITION; CHURCH; COUNTER-REFORMATION/CATHOLIC REFORMATION; CURIA, ROMAN; DEVELOPMENT OF DOGMA/OF DOCTRINE; DOCTRINE; DOGMA; DOMINICANS; DUNS SCOTUS, JOHN; ECCLESIOLOGY; FAITH; FRANCISCANS; GRACE; HUMANISM; IGNATIUS OF LOYOLA; JUSTIFICATION; LAINEZ, DIEGO;

LITURGY (IN CHRISTIANITY); LUTHER, MARTIN; LUTHERANISM; MEDIEVAL CHRISTIANITY (IN THE WEST); MEDIEVAL CHURCH; MODERNITY; NOMINALISM; PIUS V, POPE; POPE; PROTESTANTISM; REFORMATION; REVELATION; ROMAN CATHOLIC CHURCH; SEMINARY; SENSUS FIDELIUM/SENSUS FIDEI; SERIPANDO, GIROLAMO; SOCIETY OF JESUS; THOMISM/TRANSCENDENTAL THOMISM; TRADITION (IN CHRISTIANITY); TRADITION AND TRADITIONS; TRIDENTINE; TRIDENTINISM; VULGATE.

TRICKSTER

In some world religions, as well as in many ethnic religions, there is a (spiritual) personage whose main role is to trick individuals (human and/or sacred) into error, or to make their lives not always clear, orderly, and whole. The figure and role of the trickster often explains why something goes wrong in life, and why bad things happen to good people. The trickster can be harmful, devious and/or evil, or can also be playful and fun-loving. One contemporary example of the trickster in religion is Elegguá in Afro-Cuban Santería, but a trickster might also be at the origin of some Hebrew and later Christian notions of Satan or the devil. However, it would be inaccurate to simply equate the figure of the trickster in religions with Satan or the devil (as some Christian missionaries attempted to do in past centuries).

Orlando Espín

See also DEVIL; SANTERÍA; SATAN.

TRIDENTINE

An adjective that refers to the sessions, decrees, teachings, and the like, of the Council of Trent.

Orlando Espín

See also TRADITION AND TRADITIONS; TRENT, COUNCIL OF; TRIDENTINISM.

TRIDENTINISM

A rigorist interpretation of the meaning, teaching, and legislation of the Catholic Church's council of Trent (1545–63). Certainly not the only interpretation possible, Tridentinism promoted a literalist understanding of the texts of the council. It seems to have had little regard for the nuances, the struggles, and most other contextualizing conditions (very evident in Trent's historical records) that would have allowed for more comprehensive interpretations of the conciliar doctrinal and disciplinary decisions. Indeed, Tridentinism oversimplified the work of the council, and focused on the "canons" of Trent while disregarding the importance of the large number of other accompanying (and available) theological texts, minutes of meetings, notes, correspondence, and the like. Tridentinism became the norm in the Roman Catholic Church between the end of the sixteenth and the mid-twentieth centuries. With the passing of the generation that participated in the Council of Trent, the quest for and imposition of uniformity became ecclesiastical policy. Increasingly, most local and national ecclesial autonomy was lost in favor of growing papal centralization and control. Defensiveness and apologetics became typical in theological and doctrinal discussions, the Inquisition or Holy Office acquired enormous power over the members of the church, and the gap between a governing clergy and a passive laity widened. Biblical study became suspect, theological education was limited to the clergy, and lay piety was organized around numerous ecclesiastically sanctioned devotions. Unfortunately, other Christians often mistook Tridentinism as being the essence of Roman Catholicism. The birth of Tridentinism has been associated with the writings of Robert Bellarmine (d. 1621), and with the pontificates of Popes Sixtus V (d. 1590), and Paul V (d. 1621). With Popes John XXIII (d. 1963) and Paul VI (d. 1978), and certainly with the Second Vatican Council (1962–5), Tridentinism finally began to lose its hold on Roman Catholicism.

Orlando Espín

See also BELLARMINE, ROBERT; TRADITION AND TRADITIONS; TRENT, COUNCIL OF; ULTRAMONTANISM.

TRIKAYA (DOCTRINE OF)

"Three-bodies" referring to the doctrine that specifies the nature of cosmic Buddhahood and Buddha manifestations in Mahayana thought, particularly within the Yogachara school. It is in the *Lotus Sutra* (200 C.E.), however, where the supramundane interpretation of Buddhahood finds earliest and most dramatic expression, challenging the Sthavira understanding of limited historical appearances of enlightened human Buddhas. The *Lotus* reveals that Shakyamuni had been enlightened eons ago and taught in myriad other world systems; he assumed human form on earth out of compassion for humanity, undergoing apparent birth and death to encourage humans to make the most of their human rebirth. In fact, his preaching can still be heard on Vulture Peak, India, by advanced practitioners. Thus, Buddhas are omnipresent, all-knowing beings who can assume many bodily forms and act compassionately for humanity.

Later Mahayana texts systematized this teaching as the *Trikaya* and related it to the doctrine of celestial bodhisattvahood. The first bodily form is the *nirmanakaya*,

"manifestation body," that appears before humans and preaches the doctrine to them. Some texts describe the *nirmanakaya* as true incarnation in flesh and blood; others see it as mere manifestation. (Ecumenical modern Buddhist interpreters using this schema even have placed figures from other religions such as Jesus as "*nirmanakaya* forms.") Second, to teach advanced human and celestial bodhisattvas, Buddhas can appear in supramundane form, the *sambhogakaya*, the seeing of which gives rise to its name, the "enjoyment body." It is through the power of their own past vows and accomplishments as bodhisattvas that Buddhas can shape their *sambhogakaya* to aid these highly advanced practitioners. The later texts also note that each *sambhogakaya* manifestation also presides over his own realm (or "pure land") where he achieves enlightenment and often uses his merit to shape it for the benefit of other Buddhists.

The third body of the Buddha, the *dharmakaya*, is meant to suggest the ultimate nature of Buddhas and reality itself. Although this transcendent body of the Buddha can be perceived only by other enlightened beings, Buddhist iconography, by the tenth century, used the form of Vairocana, "the Resplendent," to indicate it.

In the Buddha nature theory schema, the *dharmakaya* is what permeates all reality, inclining beings toward nirvana-seeking; in the Yogachara school, the *dharmakaya* is also identified as the *bodhicitta*, "thought/mind of enlightenment," and located in the storehouse consciousness. From the highest perspective, the first two bodies can be termed both provisional, useful for leading others to the truth, but they are also ultimately empty.

Todd T. Lewis

See also BODHISATTVA; BUDDHA; MAHAYANA BUDDHISM; PURE LAND BUDDHISM; SHUNYATA/SUNYA/SHUNYA; TATHAGATAGARBHA DOCTRINE; YOGACHARA.

TRIMURTI

The *trimurti* (Sanskrit, "three-formed") is a syncretistic concept of deity in Hindu myth and iconography that was introduced in the later portions of the *Mahabharata* and developed in certain Puranas. Sometimes called the "Hindu Trinity," the trimurti doctrine seeks to encompass Brahma, Vishnu, and Shiva as three aspects of one supreme Godhead, functioning respectively as Creator, Preserver, and Destroyer (of the cosmos). While this idea is often evoked by modern Hindus seeking to explain the complexity of their tradition to outsiders, it has never played any significant role in actual Hindu worship. Brahma—who, though a deity, is typically regarded as a reincarnating being—has hardly any history of worship in India, and neither Shaivas nor Vaishnavas would be willing to place their supreme deity on an equal footing with the other two, though they sometimes recognize a similar triad of deities, with similar cosmic functions, as a lesser manifestation of their supreme God.

Lance E. Nelson

See also BRAHMA; HINDUISM; SHAIVA; VAISHNAVA.

TRINITY/TRINITARIAN THEOLOGY/TRINITARIAN PROCESSIONS

The central Christian doctrine of God states that there is one God in three eternal, equal, and distinct Persons, Father, Son, and Holy Spirit. The scriptural basis for this doctrine includes the account of the baptism of Jesus (Matthew 3:16-17), the liturgical formula used in the context of early Christian baptism (Matthew 28:19), and the confessions of God as triune in the context of early Christian prayer (Romans 8:15; Galatians 4:6).

The doctrine of the Trinity is not specifically revealed in the Christian Scriptures, but was further developed through external and internal Christian debates about God as well as through the teachings of ecumenical councils in response to these debates. The late second-century apologist Athenagoras of Athens responded to the pagan charge of atheism against Christianity by affirming one God in opposition to Roman polytheism and the imperial cult of emperor worship, as well as by acknowledging the Son of God and the Holy Spirit. The late second-century bishop Irenaeus of Lyons expressed an early trinitarian view of God in response to the Gnostics (Greek, meaning "knowledge"), a competing Christian group that believed in the efficacy of esoteric knowledge for salvation and in a Docetic christology, or the notion that Jesus only appeared human. In refuting the Gnostics, Irenaeus outlined three articles of faith about the distinctive roles of God the Father as Creator, the Son as co-Creator with the Father and fully incarnate Savior in Jesus Christ, and the Spirit as the source of inspiration for the prophets and of renewal of the world; he especially stressed the full incarnation of the Son as a human being. These articles of faith combined into a single rule of faith and thus constituted one of the earliest short creeds on the triune reality of God.

Two important ecumenical councils in the fourth century counteracted alternate, later-considered heterodox Christian beliefs about God, especially subordinationism, and adopted a theological language from Greek and Latin philosophy to more appropriately express orthodox Christian belief in one, triune God. Subordinationism ranks the Father, Son, and Spirit hierarchically; God the Father alone is divine and the Son and Spirit are created and therefore not equally divine. Subordinationism emphasizes the distinction among the Persons of the Father, Son, and Spirit, but denies full divinity to the Son and Spirit. In the early fourth century, Arius, a presbyter in Alexandria, Egypt, promoted a subordinationist understanding of the Trinity, by teaching that the Son had a beginning, was created but ranked the first among creatures, was not divine and consequently subordinate to the Father. The Council of Nicaea in 325 rejected Arianism, by claiming that the Son was begotten by the Father but not made like other creatures, and that the Son was of one substance or being (Greek, *homoousios*) with the Father. The language of substance (Greek, *ousia*) supported the full divinity of Jesus, and this language was expanded to defend the divinity of the Holy Spirit at the Council of Constantinople in 381. The Council of Constantinople also specified the relationships among Father, Son, and Spirit through the language of procession (Latin, *processio*, meaning "emanation"). God the Father is unoriginated and unbegotten, whereas there are two processions in the Trinity, begetting and spirating, to explain the origin of the Son and the Spirit. The Son proceeds or is begotten from the Father, while the Spirit proceeds or spirates from the Father and (or in some expressions through) the Son.

In keeping with longstanding local church liturgical practices, the Western Christian tradition in the sixth to the seventh centuries added the *filioque* clause (Latin, meaning "and the Son") into the Nicene-Constantinopolitan Creed to further explain the procession of the Spirit. The Second Council of Lyons in 1274 defended a doctrine of double procession, in which the Spirit proceeds from the Father and the Son. The Eastern Christian tradition rejected this insertion on ecclesiastical and theological grounds. The additional clause was not approved by an official church council (until six centuries later), thus raising political questions about a growing Roman primacy apart from a conciliar method of ecclesiastical governance. The clause also raised theological questions about the relations of the Persons within the Trinity; for the Eastern Christian tradition, the Spirit proceeds either from the Father alone or from the Father through the Son. The differences over the language of procession, among other political, ecclesiastical, and theological tensions, played a major role in the separation of Western and some Eastern Churches, usually dated 1054, and continue to serve as a major point of theological contention between Roman Catholic, Eastern Catholic, and Orthodox Churches.

Trinitarian theology begins from two inextricably linked loci, immanent Trinity or the intradivine life of God of one substance in three Persons, which is an ineffable mystery, and economic Trinity or the relation of God with the world, which is expressed in the distinct but not mutually exclusive salvific roles played by each Person of the Trinity in creation, redemption, and sanctification. The economic Trinity shows that salvation is offered by God through Jesus Christ in the power of the Holy Spirit.

Trinitarian theology also takes its starting point from what the thirteenth-century medieval Scholastic theologian Thomas Aquinas called the "analogy of being."

Analogical language for God begins with the created order and with everyday human experience because the created order is imprinted with the image and likeness of God (Gen 1:26-27). Analogical language is also metaphorical, to signify a likeness rather than equality between creatures and their creator. There are two prevailing analogies in historical and contemporary trinitarian theologies, namely psychological and social analogies. The fourth- to fifth-century North African bishop and theologian Augustine of Hippo articulated a psychological analogy of the Trinity in his theological treatise *De Trinitate*. For Augustine, a theology of the Trinity is grounded in vestiges or traces of it in the created world and in human experience, especially in the human mind and love. The relationship of mind, knowledge, and love signifies the Trinity; a mind loves and knows itself, and thus the three are inseparably united yet differentiated. The order of love also suggests the Trinity; the lover and the beloved generate and are unified by the love between them. The twelfth-century French monastic theologian Richard of St. Victor offered a social analogy of the Trinity, also based on human love relations. Sharing love and experiencing delight in sharing love imply the Trinity; if only one person existed, then no sharing would occur, and if only two persons existed, then no delight in sharing would take place. The order of love thus requires a sharing of love with another and a sharing of delight in that shared love. Both the psychological and the social analogies reflect on the Trinity through human love, but Richard's analogy emphasizes a social experience of sharing and of partnership. Augustine utilizes love to clarify the unity of the three Persons in one God, while Richard emphasizes love to account for the three Persons in one God. Both analogies help us gain a better if still imperfect understanding of Christian belief in a triune God.

The doctrine of the Trinity developed amid much theological controversy, and was clarified through a rather philosophically speculative language of substance, person, and procession. The doctrine itself—one substance in three Persons—resulted from a faith-based but abstract theology. More contemporary theologians attempt to reconnect the doctrine of the Trinity and its speculative, at times confusing, language to everyday human experience and earthly existence. A critical reappropriation of the notion of *perichoresis* (Greek, meaning "indwelling") provides a theological basis to challenge oppressive sociopolitical structures and at the same time to shape a theological vision and praxis of the good society. In a perichoretic dance of eternal life, mutual love, and communion within diversity, the three divine Persons represent differentiation and equality in community. Many voices in Euro-American, Latin American, and U.S. feminist theologies contend that the perichoresis within Trinity plays a critical role in identifying and promoting egalitarian rather than oppositional, hierarchical, or patriarchal relations. In addition, Latin American feminist theologian Ivone Gebara militates against the anthropocentrism of the traditional psychological and social analogies of the Trinity, and instead introduces a truly innovative theology of the Trinity that highlights relatedness rather than rugged individuality as ontologically basic to a human and earthly life that is fashioned in and fashioned to flourish within the image and likeness of a tripersonal and triune God.

Rosemary P. Carbine

TRIPITAKA

The "Three-Baskets (*Pitaka*)," a term designating the three-part division of the early Buddhist Canon: *Vinaya Pitaka*, the collection of monastic narratives governing the sangha; the *Sutra Pitaka*, the collection of sermons and some stories (*jatakas*, *apadanas*) told by the Buddha that begin "thus I have heard," implying verbatim reportage; and the *Abhidharma Pitaka*, the collected philosophical-psychological categories of advanced doctrinal analysis. The accepted historical emergence of the three is in the order given here, with the *Abhidharma* collection assembled last, no sooner than 100 C.E. Only in the Theravada tradition do these three *pitaka* remain as the total of accepted revealed scripture—in the Pali Canon. In the Mahayana schools, the *sutra* collection grew considerably, and the *Abhidharma Pitaka* was retained only as a study in preliminary or erroneous analysis, as other textual divisions and systematic doctrinal statements developed.

Todd T. Lewis

See also ABHIDHARMA/ADHIDHAMMA PITAKA; PALI CANON; SUTRA; SUTRA PITAKA; VINAYA.

TRISAGION

The Trisagion is a doxological refrain used since the fifth century in Eastern liturgies: Holy God, Holy Mighty, Holy Immortal, have mercy on us. The Trisagion became a subject of controversy during the trinitarian debates of the fifth and sixth centuries that pondered the possible interchange of properties between the divinity and humanity of Christ (*communicatio idiomatum*). Fifth-century Theopaschite Christians, who spoke of God's suffering, added the phrase, "who was crucified for us" to the refrain. The addition prompted a consideration of the doxology's reference, whether praise was directed to the Son alone or to the Father and Spirit as well. Western, Chaldean, and Byzantine Churches rejected the Theopaschite clause and retained the traditional simpler form. In time, the Western church abandoned the formula entirely except on Good Friday when it is recited in the Divine Office, and until recently, during the veneration of the Cross in the Good Friday liturgy.

Patricia Plovanich

TRITHEISM

Tritheism, meaning "three gods," is a misapprehension that the Christian trinitarian metaphor (Father, Son, and Spirit) indicates a plurality of divine principles (the position of non-Christian critics, particularly in the second century). In trinitarian theology, the term designates any theological exposition of the doctrine that emphasizes the distinctiveness of the trinitarian Persons to the detriment of the unitary divine principle. Thus, Arian christology, that proposed a subordinate relationship of Son and Spirit to the divine principle, Father, has been described as tritheist. Similarly, contemporary theologies that use the modern concept of persons (an individual center of self-awareness) to explain the trinitarian Persons run the risk of suggesting three divine principles. In theological practice, tritheism is not so much a clear position as an unsuccessful effort to craft an adequate trinitarian language that retains faith's intuition about the tri–unity of divine existence.

Patricia Plovanich

TROELTSCH, ERNST (1865–1923)

German theologian. One of the last great figures of liberal theology, Ernst Troeltsch is best known for his magisterial work in the sociology of religion, *The Social Teaching of the Christian Churches* (1911). Equally noteworthy, however, are both his methodological reflections on and his constructive work in Christian theology from a historicist perspective—a perspective that embraces both the exigencies of the historical-critical method and thus recognizes the historicity of all theological concepts. His wide-ranging books and essays, including his work on the relation between Christianity and "other" religions, came to fruition in his *Glaubenslehre* (*"The Christian Faith"*), published in 1925.

J. A. Colombo

See also LIBERAL THEOLOGY.

TRULLO, SYNOD OF

A meeting of Eastern bishops, held in 692 C.E., in the "domed hall" (*in trullo*, in Latin) of the imperial palace at Constantinople. This synod is also called *Penthekte* (Greek for "fifth–sixth") because it met after the fifth (533) and the sixth (680) ecumenical councils, and was convoked in order to pass ecclesiastical legislation the two councils had not been able to consider. The approved canons ("laws") dealt mostly with clerical marriage, requirements for ordination, impediments to marriage, and so on. This synod's legislation was never accepted by the Western Catholic Church, and this contributed to the further development of distinct practices in the Eastern and Western churches.

Orlando Espín

See also CANON LAW; CONSTANTINOPLE, FIRST COUNCIL OF; CONSTANTINOPLE, SECOND COUNCIL OF; CONSTANTINOPLE, SEE OF; COUNCIL, ECUMENICAL; ORTHODOX CHURCHES; SCHISM, GREAT EASTERN; SYNODS.

TRUSTEEISM

Trusteeism, or the lay trustee system, was a form of local church government, common in Europe since the Middle Ages and adopted for use in U.S. parishes during the first decades of U.S. Catholic history. Scarcity of clergy and problems of legal incorporation under the American system of church–state separation recommended the model for American use. Thus many parishes were established under lay administrators who collected pew rents, assumed financial and administrative responsibility for church property, directed the parish's charitable affairs, and through legal incorporation were often the owners of parish property and assets. The form of government was particularly apt for rural and frontier communities where Catholics often built a church and organized the community before petitioning the bishop for a pastor.

Disputes about jurisdiction, particularly about retention or appointment of pastors, brought some trustees and bishops into conflict. Some ethnic parishes refused the appointment of pastors from different nationalities; some parishes refused the transfer of popular pastors. In several cases, trustees declared independence from the bishop and functioned as schismatic churches. An extreme case in Buffalo, New York, captured public support and caused the passage of a state law prohibiting the incorporation of church property under the diocesan authority. The resolution of these conflicts and establishment of uniform diocesan and parish structures absorbed the energies of the United States' episcopacy for a half century. Almost all the Councils of Baltimore struggled with the issue. In time, parishes yielded quietly to episcopal authority or closed because of financial problems. However, the long struggle to establish episcopal control over parishes where the lay trustee system went awry eclipsed discussion of those churches where the model worked. Thus, lay trusteeism remained a specter haunting episcopal discussions of lay involvement in church affairs until Vatican Council II.

Patricia Plovanich

TRUTH

Each philosophy and theology is committed to the pursuit of truth. Its construal of truth distinguishes each kind of philosophy and theology. Broadly, truth is seen as subjective (depending on the knower) and objective (being independent of the knower), and most schools of thought combine the two aspects.

The Old Testament's understanding of "truth" lay closer to the concept of "faithfulness to the covenant." In the New Testament, Jesus himself was taken to be the Truth. Because Jesus was the Word of God, the Gospel was taken to be the truth—but a truth unavailable to ordinary human reasoning or insight that had to be revealed by God.

Led by Clement of Alexandria in the East and Augustine in the West, the church fathers began combining New Testament and Greek ideas of truth. What was most appealing about Plato and Aristotle was their idea that truth had an objective reality independent of human construction (though, of course, they believed it could be attained by right reason). That understanding of the truth was congenial to scriptural understanding, since God is beyond the human reason's power to grasp (and hence to construct). Greek (Western) reasoning was typically binary as seen, for example, in the statement that "a thing cannot be and not be at the same time." That, and its emphasis on logical deduction and

induction, sometimes foreclosed it to some dimensions of Eastern thought.

In modern times, Descartes, for example, responded to the Enlightenment by making truth the equivalent of [scientific] certitude—too reductionistic to encompass the truth-claims of faith. Kant defined truth as agreement with the laws of the intellect whose laws were first formed by truth itself. Currently, feminist thinkers in particular, and some African American theorists, have warned that claims of "objective truth" are often supportive of the status quo, particularly when the status quo is oppressive. They remind us that all truth-claims are "situated." From a biblical viewpoint, the truths of those who are poor and oppressed have a privileged and preferential claim on the attention of the faithful.

Some postmodern thinkers have been influenced by deconstructionism and poststructuralism, terms coined by Jacques Derrida (b. 1930) who criticized the hierarchical nature of traditional Western binary opposition. Poststructuralist thought ranges from claims that truth is multivocal (M. M. Bakhtin, 1895–1975), to claims that truth cannot be accessed (and may not exist), and that what we have been calling truth relies on intertextual connections that can be easily unraveled. Also characteristic of postmodern thought is the "linguistic turn" that observes that language, a characteristically human trait, is for communication. Hence, truth cannot be entirely subjective or (de-)constructed by the isolate subject, but must in some way be communal in nature. The theologian David Tracy has focused his recent work on the linguistic turn. John Thiel in *Nonfoundationalism* has shown how this idea of communal truth can be congenial to Christianity.

G. Simon Harak, s.j.

TRUTHS, FOUR NOBLE

Perhaps the earliest and most enduring formulation of Buddhist doctrine, the Four Noble Truths provide a Buddhist definition and analysis of the human condition as well as a diagnosis of the path toward liberation. Through this realization in his own experience, Gautama realized final enlightenment; for this reason they are labeled Aryan, "noble." The medical methodology of the Noble Truths' presentation also contributed to one of the epithets of the Buddha as "The Great Physician."

The first truth, "All life entails suffering" calls the Buddhist not to deny the inevitable experience of mortal existence: physical and mental disease, loss of loved ones, the bodily degeneration of old age, and final illness. The intention of this truth is to not to induce pessimism but to hold up clear, realistic observation. Even pleasure and good times have an unsatisfactory quality since they are temporary. The appropriate response to this truth is for the person to make the most of the spiritual opportunities of human birth and to act in all arenas of life by showing compassion (*karuna*) and loving-kindness (*maitri*) to alleviate suffering.

The second noble truth is, "The cause of suffering is desire." The term for "desire" (*trishna*) literally means "thirst" and entails all that human beings "thirst after" far beyond liquids: food and drink beyond biological need, possessions, power, and sex. (At the advanced stages of Buddhist practice, desire for doctrinal learning and even for one's own enlightenment must also be rejected as obstacles to spiritual progress.) The emphasis on desire in the second truth makes plain the need for renunciation, detachment, and asceticism in Buddhist tradition.

The third noble truth, "Removing desire removes suffering," provides a terse reference to the central Buddhist doctrine of causation: the same pattern of cyclical cause and effect, action and karma reaction that has attachment, lead to further rebirth, and suffering can also be reversed and stilled, with all karma-production eventually extinguished with nirvana realization. The twelvefold formula of dependent origination (*pratityasamutpada*) is the more extended treatment of this important and universal Buddhist conception. The emphasis on renunciation also signals the importance of the sangha as a refuge for individuals who wish to live the most complete approximation of the ideal.

The last truth, "The way to removing desire is to follow the Eightfold path," specifies the treatment needed to be "cured" of the human condition's continuous cycle of rebirth, suffering, and re-death. This involves eight practices in the progressive path to mastery of moral practice, meditation, and the cultivation of salvific *prajna* ("insight").

According to the Sanskrit *Mahapadesha Sutra*, the Four Noble Truths are the touchstone for judging the authenticity of a Buddhist text. All schools hold that, as the Buddhist progresses toward enlightenment, understanding of the Four Noble Truths deepens through meditation and reflection.

Todd T. Lewis

See also NOBLE EIGHTFOLD PATH; PRAJNA; PRATITYASAMUTPADA.

TSAO CHUN

(Chinese, *zao jun*, lit., lord of the stove). In Chinese folk religion, this is the god of the hearth or the kitchen whose worship dates back to the mid-second century B.C.E. This household spirit was seen not only as the guardian of the hearth (the center of family life), but also as the representative of the family interests in his annual visit to the supreme emperor Yu Huang Shang-ti, the celestial ruler in the Taoist pantheon and folk tradition. Upon his return home on New Year's Eve, a new picture is put up over the stove, symbolizing the renewal of his relationship with the family.

G. D. DeAngelis

See also CH'ENG HUANG; JADE EMPEROR; T'U TI KUNG.

TÜBINGEN SCHOOL

The term indicates either of two theological faculties at Eberhard–Karls University in Tübingen, a city in southwest Germany. The Protestant school is known for its famous alumni, Hegel, Schelling, and the poet, Hölderlin. The term, Tübingen School, referred first to two nineteenth-century biblical scholars on that faculty who used historical theories or methods in the discipline. F. C. Bauer (1792–1860) used Hegel's compelling concept of history to propose a dynamic and dialectical view of early church history. His student, David Straus (1808–74), wrote a *Life of Jesus* (1835), and argued for the mythical character of the Gospel accounts of Jesus' life. These positions are not generally held today, but the impetus to history spurred the development of historical methods in other New Testament circles. Noted members of the contemporary Protestant faculty are Ernst Käsemann, Jürgen Moltmann, and Eberhard Jungel. The Catholic Faculty, known as the Catholic Tübingen School, was founded by Johann Sebastian von Drey in 1817. Its famous faculty includes Johann Adam Mohler, Karl Adam, Josef Geiselmann, and most recently, Walter Kasper. The Catholic School is known for its interest in the historical character of faith and its study of theological history as a primary source for theology.

Patricia Plovanich

TU B'SHEVAT

(Hebrew, "the fifteenth of Shevat"). In Judaism, the New Year for trees, regarded for liturgical purposes as a minor-festival (see Mishnah Rosh Hashanah 1:1). In the modern state of Israel, Tu B'Shevat is celebrated as Arbor Day, marked by tree-planting ceremonies.

Alan J. Avery-Peck

TULKU

The Tibetan term for *nirmanakaya*, the first of the three bodies of the Buddha in Mahayana Buddhology, indicating his human (*nirmana-*) incarnation body (-*kaya*). The term *tulku* is used in two senses in Tibetan Buddhism: first, to refer to Shakyamuni, the Buddha born in 560 B.C.E. in the northern Gangetic plains; second, to refer to individuals regarded as reincarnations of great monk–saints of the various monasteries. The second usage builds on the Mahayana bodhisattva ideal and the vow to return to samsara again and again until all beings find salvation. This human institution was first known with the second Karmapa in the Kargyu school around 1200 C.E. Over two hundred tulkus are currently recognized, most of whom now exist in refugee communities.

The tulku reincarnation rediscovery process is a highly complex one. The determination may be based on: various indications by the aged lama before death; consultation with oracles and oracular lakes; and testing candidates as toddlers to identify with items from the previous lama's life. In Tibet, the tulku lines of major monasteries involve the institution of separate households, often with large endowments and political power. Both the Dalai Lama and the Panchen Lama are tulkus. Some identifications have been controversial, as the 1995–6 contestation between the Chinese government and the Dalai Lama on the recognition of the new Panchen Lama.

Todd T. Lewis

See also BODHISATTVA; DALAI LAMA; LAMA; TRIKAYA (DOCTRINE OF).

TÚPAC AMARU, JOSÉ GABRIEL (?–1781)

Leader of the most extensive Indian rebellion (1780–1) against European colonial authority in the Western Hemisphere, the Peruvian José Gabriel Túpac Amaru is noteworthy for his seemingly paradoxical commitments to the Inca past (he claimed to be a direct descendent of the last Inca emperor), a modern but non-European future for Peru, and Catholic Christianity. Yet, such beliefs are not inconsistent with each other. Educated by the Jesuits in Cusco, Túpac Amaru came to believe that the God of Moses and of Christians sided with the oppressed Indians against the cruelty of the Spaniards and had commissioned him to undertake the liberation of Peru. The rebellion resulted in over one hundred thousand deaths (mostly of Indians and their mestizo supporters) and ended after an intentionally brutal execution of its leaders, including José Gabriel, on May 18, 1781, aimed at intimidating the population. By linking Christianity and political liberation, Túpac Amaru stands as a significant religious, as well as political and military, figure of history.

James B. Nickoloff

TURNER, VICTOR (1920–83)

British anthropologist who taught mostly at American universities (for example, Cornell, Chicago, University of Virginia), while most of his field research work was in Zambia and Mexico. Turner's writings have been very influential because of his contributions to ritual and symbolic studies, and to the scholarly understanding of liminality and community. It seems impossible today to discuss any of these fields without direct reference to Turner's thought and categories, and much of the rich scholarly vocabulary he developed for his interpretive work is now part of religious studies and theological language across the world. Among his most important books are *The Forest of Symbols* (1967), *The Ritual Process: Structure and Anti-Structure* (1969), and *Dramas, Fields and Metaphors: Symbolic Action in Human Society* (1974).

Orlando Espín

See also LÉVI-STRAUSS, CLAUDE; LIMINAL/LIMINALITY; PROCESSIONS (DEVOTIONAL); RITUAL; SYMBOL.

T'U TI KUNG

(Chinese, local earth god). A generic term used in Chinese folk religion to refer to the local earth god. One of the oldest and most widespread of the patron deities in China, he is responsible for agricultural prosperity in a community; but his influence is generally limited to a small geographical area, and he can be dismissed by the community if they feel he is not doing his job.

G. D. DeAngelis

See also CH'ENG HUANG; JADE EMPEROR; TSAO CHUN.

TUTU, DESMOND (1931–)

Former Anglican archbishop of Cape Town, and winner of the Nobel Peace Prize in 1984. Educated in South Africa and Great Britain, Tutu has been a leading proponent of racial equality in his country, and a major foe of the racist *apartheid* system. His efforts, joined to those of many others, bore fruit in 1994 with the first-ever South African elections with the participation of peoples of all colors. His very public and courageous stand against racism and for equality was consistently based on Tutu's understanding of the Christian Gospel's message. He retired as archbishop in 1996, but has remained active in his country's public (civil and ecclesial) life.

Orlando Espín

See also AFRICAN CHRISTIANITY; ANGLICAN COMMUNION; CATHOLIC TRADITION; PROPHETS (IN CHRISTIANITY); SOCIAL JUSTICE.

TWELVE, THE (IN ECCLESIOLOGY)

The "Twelve" comprised the group of twelve disciples whom the New Testament regards as the foundational group of apostles. The term "the Twelve" is an eschatological symbol recalling the prophetic promise that the twelve tribes of Israel would be restored at the dawning of God's reign. In using this term to designate the core group of his disciples, Jesus was making a statement symbolic of the twelve patriarchs of Israel. Christian tradition, influenced by Luke's Gospel, refers to "the twelve apostles." However, the argument can be made that there were more than this number. St. Paul, for example, is considered an apostle; and, using the Greek meaning of "apostle" (*apostolos*, one sent out), one can include

Mary Magdalene who was "sent out" to tell the rest of the community about Jesus' resurrection.

Mary Ann Hinsdale

See also ECCLESIOLOGY.

TWELVE, THE (IN SCRIPTURE)

Disciples of Jesus whom he chose especially to accompany him and share his ministry. The three Synoptic narratives of the calling or commissioning of the Twelve (Matt 10:1-4; Mark 3:13-19; Luke 6:13-16) offer differing lists of their names (cf. also John 6:70; Acts 1:13). The number twelve refers to the twelve tribes of Israel and symbolizes their future restoration "at the renewal of all things, when the Son of Man is seated on the throne of his glory" (Matt 19:28; see also Luke 22:30; Rev 21:12-14). According to Matthew 10:5 and Luke 6:13, the Twelve were called apostles. The importance of their symbolic role is reflected in Acts 1:15-26 where their number must be maintained, and thus Matthias is chosen to replace Judas, who had died following his betrayal of Jesus. In numerous texts, Peter functions as the spokesperson of the Twelve, and he is generally accorded a certain primacy of place among the others.

F. M. Gillman

See also APOSTLE; DISCIPLE; NEW ISRAEL; PETER.

TWELVERS (IN ISLAM)

In Arabic, "*Ithna-ʾasharis*." The Twelvers are also known as the "Twelve Imam Shiʿites" and "Imamis." They take their name from a man named Muhammad (869–940?) whom the Twelvers regard as the twelfth *imam* (divinely appointed and infallible teacher) in the line of Ali (598–661), the fourth caliph or successor of the founding Prophet of Islam. (Islam's Prophet was also named Muhammad—570–632.) Twelvers believe that Ali was the privileged recipient of secret knowledge from the Prophet and that he, in turn, passed this religious wisdom on to the Shi'ite imams who succeeded him as God's designated emissaries in the world. According to Twelver tradition, Imam Muhammad went into hiding when he was four years old (873), and he was represented by four other holy men in succession until 940. Because the last of these representatives did not appoint someone to follow Muhammad, he is considered the final imam. Twelver Shi'ites call Muhammad *"al-Mahdi-l-Muntazar,"* the *"awaited" mahdi* or savior personality who will come out of hiding and inaugurate a golden age of Islamic justice shortly before the end of the world.

Ronald A. Pachence

See also ALI; IMAM; IMAM (THE HIDDEN IMAM); MAHDI; MUHAMMAD; SEVENERS (IN ISLAM); SHI'A/SHI'I/SHI'ITE/SHI'ISM.

TWICE BORN
See CASTE.

TWO-SOURCE THEORY (OF SYNOPTICS)
The name for a theory, widely accepted among biblical scholars, explaining the Synoptic Problem. According to this theory, the literary relationship among the three Synoptic Gospels (Matthew, Mark, Luke) can be best explained by maintaining that there are two main sources, namely Mark and "Q," used by Matthew and Luke in the composition of their respective Gospels.

According to this theory, Mark, the earliest of the Gospels, is used independently as a source by Matthew and Luke. This hypothesis goes a long way in explaining the similarity in content, wording, and sequence of passages in the three Synoptic Gospels. The other source, Q, is used independently by Matthew and Luke. This explains, in large part, the similarity of the non-Markan material in these two Gospels.

The material found only in Matthew is represented by the letter "M" (for Matthew's special source). Similarly, the material unique to Luke is represented by the symbol "L" (for Luke's special source). Related to the two-source theory is the four-source theory (Mark, "Q," "M," and "L"). The two-source theory is also sometimes called the Two-Document Hypothesis.

John Gillman

See also FOUR-SOURCE THEORY (OF SYNOPTICS); Q SOURCE; SYNOPTIC GOSPELS; SYNOPTIC PROBLEM.

TYNDALE, WILLIAM (1494–1536)
English humanist and Reformer, Tyndale was one of the founders of the Bible in modern English. Educated at Oxford and Cambridge, his sympathy for the Protestant Reformation led to his departure from England in 1524. Thereafter he worked in various places in Germany and the Netherlands, producing English translations of the New Testament and at least parts of the Old Testament. Condemned as a heretic, he was executed near Brussels, and has often been seen as a martyr for the Reformation.

Thomas Worcester, S.J.

See also HUMANISM; REFORMATION; RENAISSANCE; SOLA SCRIPTURA.

TYPE/TYPOLOGY

A type is a person, thing, or event that represents or symbolizes another, especially another that is to come. Typology is the study of types, symbols, and symbolism. Typology also refers to the symbolic meaning or representation a person, thing, or event suggests.

Within biblical studies, for example, typology is a form of biblical interpretation that deals with correspondences observed between persons, events, and institutions within the framework of salvation history. A renewed interest in typology in biblical studies has resulted from increased attention being given to the unity of the Bible as well as to the work of tradition criticism.

Some examples of biblical typology include the life of Moses as foreshadowing that of Christ (in Matthew's understanding) and the crucifixion of Jesus as analogous to the Passover sacrifice (in Paul's understanding).

Typology may involve the reuse of an older tradition or the fulfillment of prophecy. If the older is used to express a new act of God, the older is seen as the type that foreshadows the new, the antitype (as, for example, in Paul's view where Adam is the type and Christ the antitype). Where prophecy, however, is fulfilled, the original prophecy is the typological foreshadowing of the fulfillment (as, for example, David foreshadows Christ, in whom the promise to David reaches completion).

F. M. Gillman

See also ALLEGORY; HEILSGESCHICHTE; TRADITIO-HISTORICAL CRITICISM.

TYRRELL, GEORGE (1861–1909)

Tyrrell stood on the frontlines of modern Catholic theology in Ireland and England. Originally raised Anglican, Tyrrell entered the Catholic Church in 1879. He joined the Jesuits in 1880 and was ordained a priest in 1891. In his theological writings, he addressed the development of doctrine, ecclesiology (the nature, mission and marks or features of the church), and the central role of religious experience in Catholic thought and life. He attempted to combine Modernism and Catholic theology in a way that preserved the mystery of faith and defended modern rational inquiry. His writings, especially a public criticism of the 1907 papal encyclical *Pascendi Gregis* that condemned Modernism and laid the groundwork for the anti-Modernist oath in 1910, caused a widespread controversy. Tyrrell was expelled from the then anti-Modernist and pro-Scholastic Jesuits in 1906 and excommunicated from the Catholic Church in 1907.

Tyrrell is widely renowned for his attempt to adapt Catholicism to modern life, and for his strong opposition to the liberal Protestant theology of Adolf von Harnack as well as to the so-called nineteenth-century liberal Protestant "quest for the historical Jesus" that asserted the primacy of early Christianity against what they took to be considered its later, more corrupt historical forms. Much like his German contemporary Albert Schweitzer (1875–1965), Tyrrell observed that historical-critical inquiry allowed modern theologians and historians to project their present theological claims back onto the past historical Jesus; in other words, modern theologians reconstructed the historical Jesus in their own image and likeness, rather than in accord with the principles of historical inquiry. Tyrrell demonstrated this tension between modern historical-critical method and personal bias in *Christianity at the Cross-*

roads (1909): "The Christ that Harnack sees, looking back through nineteen centuries of Catholic darkness, is only the reflection of a liberal Protestant face, seen at the bottom of a deep well."

Rosemary P. Carbine

See also JESUS OF HISTORY; MODERNISM.

TZEDAKAH

Hebrew, meaning "justice" or "righteousness," this is the Jewish concept of charity—the right, the just, the responsible way human beings are to care for each other.

The Jewish idea of charity is not dependent on feelings of good-heartedness or on having ample financial resources. It is based in the sense of obligation, in the commandment of God, that human beings are responsible for each other's welfare.

Tzedakah is rooted in the Torah that teaches, "When you reap the harvest of your land, you shall not completely reap the corners of your field nor gather the gleanings of the vineyard, or gather the fallen fruit of your vineyard. You shall leave them for the poor and the stranger" (Lev 19:9-10). The poor, the hungry, the needing, do not have to depend on the generosity of the landowner because, according to the Torah, the corners and the gleanings already belong to them. The landowner is just the agent for providing what rightly belongs to those in need.

In practical terms, this means that people are not to give of their financial resources if or when they feel like it, but that they *must* give because it is their responsibility—that the "corners" of their money do not belong to them, but to the poor.

Giving tzedakah means giving directly to those in need or to the myriad causes and organizations that need help and assistance. It is an act of joining with God to provide for and preserve the dignity of every human being.

Wayne Dosick

U

UBIQUITARIANISM

This term arose out of the extremely heated and complex argument between two Protestant reformers, Martin Luther and Ulrich Zwingli, over whether or not the Body and Blood of Christ are truly present in the Lord's Supper. Lutheran theologian Carl Braaten provides the following summary of the debate:

Both Zwingli and Luther were literalists, but in different ways, and they both interpreted biblical texts symbolically, but at different places. When Luther read, "This *is* my body," he said the word "is" must be taken literally. But Zwingli took it symbolically; the *"est"* means "significant." When Zwingli read that Christ "ascended into heaven and sits at the right hand of the Father, "he took that literally to mean that the Lord's human body is located in heaven on God's right hand, as though he were sitting in a "golden chair" beside the Father; and, therefore, he cannot be bodily present in the Lord's Supper. Luther, however, interpreted the "right hand of God" symbolically to mean the omnipotent power of God by which he can be everywhere in all things, and that, therefore, Christ can also be present in his body in every Lord's Supper on earth no matter how many are taking place at the same time (Carl E. Braaten, *Principles of Lutheran Theology*. Philadelphia: Fortress Press, 1983, 90).

The Lutheran view came to be called "ubiquitarianism" because it asserted that Christ can now be "ubiquitous" (or "everywhere") wherever he wills to be, not only in his divine nature but also in his glorified humanity, his Body and Blood.

Jack E. Lindquist

See also CONSUBSTANTIATION; LUTHER, MARTIN; LUTHERAN THEOLOGY; ZWINGLI, ULRICH.

UKRAINIAN CATHOLIC CHURCH

A church in full communion with Rome. Descendant of the Russian Orthodox Church, the Ukrainians developed their distinct identity around the leadership of the metropolitans of Kiev. In 1595 Kiev and other dioceses of the Ukraine established communion with Rome, thereby separating from the Russian church. Other dioceses joined them during the following century. Together they formed the Ukrainian Catholic Church that today has about eight million members spread throughout Europe, the Americas, and Australia. This church was severely persecuted by

1423

Russian czarist and communist governments. Their major archbishop (who functions as a patriarch) resides in Lviv, in the Ukraine.

Orlando Espín

See also CATHOLIC TRADITION; COMMUNION (ECCLESIOLOGICAL); EASTERN CATHOLIC CHURCHES; MAJOR ARCHBISHOP; ORTHODOX CHURCHES; PATRIARCH; ROME, SEE OF; RUSSIAN ORTHODOX CHURCH.

ULAMA/ULEMA

From the Arabic word *alim*, meaning "a scholar"; also, "a servant." In Islam, the *ulama* (sometimes written *ulema*) are the recognized experts on Islamic law. The term designates a group or class of religious authorities who have distinguished themselves as judges, university professors, or leaders of local mosques. The role of the ulama is to make important spiritual, legal, and ethical decisions for the Muslim community. Since Islam no longer has a universally accepted, centralized system of governance, the selection process for this authoritative body varies from country to country depending on local custom, and whether Sunni or Shiʿite Islam is practiced. All Muslims, however, accept the same revealed sacred scripture (the Qurʾan) as the primary source of law, and because they do, this sacred text is the spiritual foundation for determining orthodox belief and practice throughout the Islamic world.

Ronald A. Pachence

See also MOSQUE/MASJID; QURʾAN; SHARIA/SHARIʾA; SHIʿA/SHIʿI/SHIʿITE/ SHIʿISM; SUNNA/SUNNI/SUNNISM.

ULPHILAS (311?–383)

Ulphilas (or Ulfila) was captured with his family by the Goths and grew up with the Gothic tribes. He was ordained a priest in Constantinople in 341 by Eusebius of Nicomedia. Ulphilas spend most of the rest of his life as a missionary among the Goths, even translating Scripture into Gothic. Ulphilas taught a form of Arianism, and for hundreds of years afterward, several of the Gothic tribes ascribed to an Arian understanding of Christianity.

Gary Macy

See also ARIANISM; MISSIONARIES.

ULTRAMONTANISM

A tendency within Roman Catholicism to centralize authority and decisions in the hands of the popes and Curia officials. The word itself makes reference to "beyond the mountains" (that is, beyond the Alps, in Italy), and it became popularized in and opposed by the writings and speeches of many eighteenth-century French theologians, bishops, and civil authorities who were becoming increasingly uncomfortable with what they perceived as papal and curial interference in the internal affairs of the Catholic Church in France. After the French Revolution and its aftermath, however, Ultramontanism gained momentum within European Catholicism because many of its earlier opponents had demonstrated their inability to critique the excesses of politicians or distance themselves from political tyranny. Although Roman centralization has brought some benefits to Catholicism, many question today whether earlier critiques of Ultramontanism might not be deserving of attention, especially since Ultramontane tendencies can in practice distort some of the most important ecclesiological teachings of the church.

Orlando Espín

See also CHURCH; CONCILIARISM; CURIA, ROMAN; ECCLESIOLOGY; GALLICANISM; POPE; ROMAN CATHOLIC CHURCH.

UMAR (?–644)

Second caliph or successor to the Prophet of Islam, Muhammad (570–632). Umar, who had a reputation for being strong-willed and austere, led the growing Islamic community from 634 to 644. It is said that Umar had been a staunch opponent of Islam before his conversion to Islam. At one point, he even tried to kill Muhammad, but after accepting Islam, he became one of its most ardent proponents. As caliph, he designated himself *Amir al-Mu'minin* or "Commander of the Faithful," a title that aptly describes his demand for strict discipline and severe punishment for lawbreakers in the Islamic community. All subsequent caliphates claimed this title until the abolition of the caliphate in 1258. Umar was assassinated in 644.

Ronald A. Pachence

See also CALIPH (KALIPHA)/CALIPHATE; ISLAM; MUHAMMAD.

UMAYYADS

In Islam, this is the first dynastic caliphate (dynasty that claimed to rule as successors of the Prophet Muhammad, 570–632). The Umayyads took control of the Islamic leadership after the assassination of the fourth and last of the so-called "Rightly Guided" (patriarchal) caliphs, Ali, in 661 and they ruled until 750 with their capital located in Damascus, Syria. Founded by an Arab named Mu'awiya, governor of Syria and opponent of Ali, the Umayyads have been accused of being repressive—even ruthless, although more recent stud-

ies suggest this may be a distorted view of their rule. They are credited with expanding Islam from Spain to China and with establishing stable, capable leadership for the growing Islamic Empire. One thing, however, is certain. The Umayyads were thoroughly Arab and they tended to treat the non-Arab peoples they conquered and converted to Islam as less than first-class members of the community. By the early part of the eighth century, disaffection for the Umayyads was mounting, and in 750 they were defeated by a rival ruling family, the Abbasids (from Abbas, uncle of the Prophet Muhammad). This ended Umayyad rule in the Middle East, although a few years later, in 756, Abd ar-Rathman established an Umayyad kingdom in Cordoba, Spain, that lasted until the eleventh century.

Ronald A. Pachence

See also ABBASIDS; ALI; CALIPH (KALIPHA)/CALIPHATE; MUHAMMAD.

UMBANDA

A deeply syncretic religion, created in and around the Brazilian city of Rio de Janeiro at the turn of the nineteenth to twentieth centuries. The name "Umbanda" (of uncertain meaning) was first used for the religion in the 1930s. Today there are Umbanda communities in most of Brazil, in the United States, and in several South American countries. Approximately ten million people practice the religion today.

Umbanda was formed by the creative combination of doctrinal and ritual elements taken from Candomblé, from Kongo–Angolese religions in Brazil, from native (indigenous) beliefs, from Portuguese Catholicism, and from Kardecian "Spiritism." There were also some borrowings from magic rituals commonly called *macumba* in Brazil—also named *quimbanda* when used for black magic purposes. Unfortunately, people unfamiliar with Afro-Brazilian religions have frequently and quite incorrectly extended the name *macumba* to all these religions.

There are two main branches of Umbanda—esoteric and popular. "Esoteric" Umbanda involves very complex and secretive initiation rites, and is inclined to elaborate and believe in difficult "hidden" doctrines. "Popular" Umbanda, on the other hand, has simpler doctrines and rituals (for Umbandist standards), and is consequently the more widespread of the two branches. Umbanda's houses of worship are independent of each other, and they are called either *terreiros*, *centros*, *tendas*, or *cabanas*.

Umbanda worships nine of Candomblé's *orishás*, but with significant mythological and ritual variations. They also venerate spirits of ancestors (*entidades*), spirits of the native peoples (*caboclos*), spirits of famous black slaves (*pretos velhos*), the spirits of children who were religiously endowed (*crianças*), and "spirits without light" (*Exús* or *Eshús*). The *orishás* hold the preeminent place among this vast array of worshiped beings. Umbanda rituals are elaborately complex and celebrated for numerous occasions. There is a type of Umbanda, called "white" (present in both the "esoteric" and "popular" branches of the religion), that has eradicated from its liturgy all ceremonies that might prove unacceptable to mainstream ("white") Brazilian society. Umbanda altars are typically filled with images and statues borrowed from Candomblé, Portuguese Catholicism, and Umbanda's own.

There is only one God, called Zâmbi, in Umbanda belief. But it is a *deus otiosus*, without worship, images, or symbols. Umbandists (the followers of the religion) usually believe in reincarnation. Perhaps the most famous and public Umbanda ritual is the one associated with Yemanjá; it takes place in Rio de Janeiro (and in many other coastline cities and towns throughout Brazil) on New Year's Eve.

Since the 1960s, Umbandists have become active in Brazilian politics, managing to elect a number of local, state, and federal officials. There have been some attempts at forming "federations" of houses of worship, but with uneven results.

Orlando Espín

See also CANDOMBLÉ; DEUS OTIOSUS; NEW AGE MOVEMENT; SANTERÍA; SPIRITISM; SYNCRETISM.

UMMA

According to Islamic usage, this is the people or community professing and bonded by a common faith in Islam. Theologically, the *umma* is intended to subordinate every other allegiance a person might have to family, tribe, clan, or nation. The first umma was established in 622 by the Prophet of Islam, Muhammad (570–632). After migrating from his tribal city of Mecca to the city of Yathrib (now called Medina) in what is known as the *hijra*, Muhammad founded the Medinan umma on the principle that spiritual kinship among believers supersedes all former ties of blood, and that the law of God, revealed in the sacred text of Islam, the Qur'an, replaces tribal law as the rule of life. Muslims still speak of the importance of the umma today, though rivalries among Islamic nation-states and their respective political and economic agendas have compromised the Prophet's vision of a single, unified Islamic community.

Ronald A. Pachence

See also HIJRAH (IN ISLAM); MECCA; MEDINA; MUHAMMAD; QUR'AN.

UNAM SANCTAM

Unam Sanctam is a papal bull issued by Pope Boniface VIII on November 18, 1302, during the controversy between Boniface and King Philip IV of France. This decree is the culmination of a series of ever sharper decrees issued against Philip by Boniface. The immediate cause for the bull was the arrest by Philip of the bishop of Palmier for treason. According to medieval law, clergy could not be tried by secular courts, but only by ecclesiastical courts, and so Boniface saw this as only one more in a series of affronts to papal and clerical authority by the French king. Scholarly opinion was still divided over the question of the nature of the church and the role of the Papacy within the church. Within that debate, *Unam Sanctam* embodies the strongest of those opinions favoring the sole leadership of the Papacy within the church. The decree is in fact a long treatise on the nature of the church, arguing that the church can have only one head, and that head must be the pope. Anyone, therefore, who resists the pope resists the government established by God. The bull ends with the dramatic definition, "We declare, state and define that it is absolutely necessary for salvation that every human creature be subject to the Roman Pontiff." While both Boniface himself and later Pope Clement V denied that this declaration implied that the pope was claiming temporal power for himself, *Unum Sanctam* has remained a controversial document and certainly one of the strongest statements of papal power.

Gary Macy

See also BONIFACE VIII, POPE; CHURCH; EXTRA ECCLESIAM NULLA SALUS; MEDIEVAL CHRISTIANITY (IN THE WEST); PAPACY/PAPAL; POPE; SALVATION; VICAR OF CHRIST.

UNAMUNO, MIGUEL DE (1864–1936)

Spanish philosopher. He studied in Madrid and became professor of philosophy in Salamanca, being exiled for his views. Deeply influenced by Kierkegaard and by liberal German theologians (and perhaps even by Karl Barth), Unamuno always managed to defy easy ideological categorization, although he seems perhaps more philosophically at home within the currents of Modernism, then popular in other European countries, or in later existentialism. Unamuno never pretended to be a theologian, and was often at odds with the Catholic Church. He championed individual freedom and the rights of the individual conscience, was against appeals to tradition as authority, and suspected reason and rationalism. And yet, he was often rationalistic in his method. Although he wrote of a desired reconciliation between faith and science, he is best remembered for his important reflections on the tragic dimension of life, on the inner contradictions of being, and on faith as the outcome of desperation, spiritual conflict, and doubt. Among his books are *La agonía del cristianismo* (1925), and *El sentido trágico de la vida* (1913).

Orlando Espín

See also AUTHORITY; BARTH, KARL; EXISTENTIALISM; FAITH; KIERKEGAARD, SØREN; LIBERAL THEOLOGY; MODERNISM;

MODERNITY; ORTEGA Y GASSET, JOSÉ; POSTMODERNITY; RATIONALISM.

UNCTION

The word "unction" is taken from the Latin word meaning anointing (*unctio*; *ungere*, to anoint). Thus, unction can be used to refer to liturgical anointing with some kind of blessed or consecrated oil. For example, in some Christian traditions (the Catholic, for example), anointing is part of the baptismal liturgy, a major element in the rites of confirmation and ordination, a part of the rites for the sick and dying, and can also be found in the rite for the dedication of a church. Before the liturgical reforms of Vatican II, the Catholic sacrament of the anointing of the sick was referred to as *Extreme Unction*, or the "last anointing." This anointing was reserved at that time for those who were in danger of death. Today, anointing of the sick is administered more generally to those who are sick or ill, whether the illness is life-threatening, acute, or chronic.

Joanne M. Pierce

See also ANOINTING OF THE SICK, SACRAMENT OF; BAPTISM/CONFIRMATION; BURIAL (IN CHRISTIANITY); CONSECRATION; DEATH (CHRISTIAN); ORDAINED MINISTRIES, SACRAMENT OF; RECONCILIATION, SACRAMENT OF; VIATICUM.

UNIATES

A term used in reference to the Eastern Catholic Churches in full communion with the See of Rome. The term "Uniate" was probably coined as an insult at the end of the sixteenth century by opponents of Eastern Catholic reunion with Rome. "Uniate" is an offensive term for the Eastern Catholic Churches, and is never used by them.

Orlando Espín

See also COMMUNION (ECCLESIOLOGICAL); EASTERN CATHOLIC CHURCHES; PREJUDICE; SEE.

UNIFICATION CHURCH

Pejoratively known as the Moonies, the official name of the Unification Church is the Holy Spirit Association for the Unification of World Christianity. It was founded in 1954 by Reverend Sun Myung Moon. Moon (1920–) was born in Korea and received a divine revelation at sixteen that God had chosen him to complete Jesus' unfulfilled mission. He became an independent preacher and businessman, was imprisoned for his beliefs, and published his convictions in 1957 as *The Divine Principle*. In 1972 he had a vision to move to the United States, where he established headquarters in New York City and missions throughout the world. He founded a seminary, political think tank, newspapers in New York City and Washington, D.C., and numerous organizations devoted to social issues such as intercultural dialogue, religious freedom, world peace, anti-Communism, and the elimination of poverty.

The central affirmation of the Unification Church is that Jesus Christ only partially fulfilled his mission as Messiah; he provided only spiritual salvation because he did not marry or have children. As a husband and father of twelve children, Reverend Moon completes the messianic mission and offers physical salvation. Through the combined work of Jesus and Moon, the kingdom of God is restored on earth. Church members prepare themselves for the restored kingdom through celibacy, until Reverend Moon (called "Father") finds them a suitable partner. Through the marriage ceremony conducted by Reverend and Mrs. Moon, the True Parents, church members reestablish the perfect human family across racial and national lines. Members commit themselves to evangelize the world and live according to kingdom values. While church members consider themselves authentic Christians, most other Christian groups do not.

The church has been vigorously engaged in controversy since 1972 when Moon relocated to the United States. It has been a primary target of both secular and Christian anticult groups and has been accused of brainwashing its members. A number of church-sponsored groups have been charged with hiding their connection to the church and recruiting members with deceptive tactics. Moon received negative publicity for his staunch support of Richard Nixon during the Watergate era, and he was convicted in 1982 for income tax evasion and jailed for more than a year. The church's family values, characterized by mass weddings, where hundreds of couples are married who have never before met one another, have also been highly criticized. The church has responded to these attacks by denying any involvement in illegal activity, defending their right to religious freedom, and seeking to generate a positive image through their newspapers, organizations, and academic conferences.

Evelyn A. Kirkley

See also CULTS.

UNIFORMITY, ACTS OF

Legislation enacted by Parliament in 1549, 1552, 1559, and 1662, that was intended to produce as much commonality as possible in the worship and administration of the sacraments in the Church of England. These Acts thus exemplified the medieval notion that it was the duty of the state to secure uniform doctrine and ritual throughout the realm.

The first Act in 1549 under Edward VI mandated usage of the first Book of Common Prayer throughout England. A second Act shortly thereafter imposed the revised Prayer Book and made it obligatory to attend public worship on Sundays and holy days. This Act was repealed during the Catholic Restoration under Queen Mary Tudor, but a new Act of 1559 under Elizabeth I imposed the 1552 Book of Common Prayer with formulations that allowed for a Catholic understanding of the Eucharist.

After the period of the Commonwealth (1645–60), the monarchy and the episcopacy was restored in England. Thus, in 1662, another Act mandated the usage of a revised and enlarged Book of Common Prayer. In 1791 exemptions from the penalties stipulated by the Acts were granted to Catholics, and gradually exceptions to their obligations have been given to other Christian churches and non-Christian religions.

By virtue of the 1662 Act, the 1662 Book of Common Prayer is still the official prayer book, but the Alternative Service Book has been widely used since 1980. Parliament no longer controls the church's worship.

Jon Nilson

See also BOOK OF COMMON PRAYER.

UNITARIANISM

Unitarianism is both a belief and an organized religious denomination in the United States. As opposed to Christians who believe in one God in three Persons, Unitarians believe in one God and reject the Trinity. While they believe Jesus of Nazareth was a great teacher, they believe he was human and not divine. The roots of Unitarianism stem from three sources. First, in the sixteenth century, Faustus Socinus and his followers in exile affirmed the oneness of God in Transylvania and Poland. Second, in seventeenth-century England, a small group of Christians declared that God was one and called themselves Unitarians.

Third and most significant, a group of Unitarian Congregationalists arose in Massachusetts in the mid-eighteenth century. During the First Great Awakening, Congregationalist clergy divided into two groups: "New Lights" like Jonathan Edwards who defended the revivals, and "Old Lights" who opposed their excessive emotionalism. Leaders of the latter group included Boston pastors Charles Chauncy, Jonathan Mayhew, and Ebenezer Gay. Besides attacking the revivals, they denied the Trinity, stressed the importance of rationalism, and criticized Calvinist doctrines of total depravity and predestination. They emphasized divine benevolence over judgment, immanence over transcendence, and human capability over sin.

The first public expression of Unitarianism occurred in 1785 at King's Chapel, an Anglican church in Boston, when the congregation adopted a prayer book from which references to the Trinity had been deleted. The movement caught on among a few Anglicans and many Congregationalists. A liberal movement in opposition to Puritanism, it grew among the educated and social elite of urban Boston. These early Unitarians sought to avoid open conflict with the more conservative faction of Congregationalists, but dissension was unavoidable. Harvard University, the primary educational institution for ministers, was a battleground, and a second victory for Unitarians came about when a Unitarian was appointed to the Hollis Professorship of Divinity in 1805. A third crucial event was an 1819 sermon of Boston pastor William Ellery Channing that established the movement's major emphases: the unity of God, divine benevolence, the human nature of Jesus, individual free will, and the commitment to Christian ethics.

In 1825 a group of liberal clergy in Boston formed an alliance to promote their interests. This organization, the American Unitarian Association, was the first institutional expression of Unitarian Christianity. The majority of churches in the Boston area left the Congregationalists and affiliated with the Unitarians. Through the nineteenth century, Unitarianism grew gradually among the wealthy and educated in the northeastern United States, and Boston remained its hub. Since Unitarians opposed revivalism, they did not grow in the antebellum evangelical explosion; in fact, evangelicals deplored them as heathens and infidels. Affirming human potential and progress through institutions, Unitarians supported progressive social and political reforms, including abolition, prison and sanitation reform, and women's rights. Suffragists Susan B. Anthony and Lucy Stone were Unitarians, and the denomination was among the first to ordain women to the ministry. Unitarians were also active in the Social Gospel.

Unitarians suffered a few defections over the years. Under the leadership of Ralph Waldo Emerson, the Transcendentalist movement of the 1830s–1840s grew out of Unitarianism, perceived as staid, dry, and overly intellectual. Transcendentalists affirmed the essential human ability to experience a deeper relationship with the divine eternal in nature. The Free Religious Association formed in 1867 and Ethical Culture Society in 1876, both with a substantial membership of disaffected Unitarians. Perceiving Unitarianism as too conservative, they departed in search of a less theistic faith. Those for whom Unitarianism was too liberal often became Episcopalians.

Despite denunciation by Protestant fundamentalists as a cult (or perhaps because of it), Unitarianism has experienced an upsurge of growth since the mid-twentieth century. In 1961 Unitarians merged with Universalists to form the Unitarian Universalist Association (UUA). The Universalist Church of America, although formed in 1833, had eighteenth-century New England roots like Unitarianism. Also, like Unitarians, they rejected the Trinity, adopted congregational polity, and opposed Puritan theology. However, unlike Unitarians, they lived in rural areas and small towns, were neither wealthy nor well educated, and believed that God saved all people, either in this world or the next. Due to God's love, salvation was universal.

Since the differences between Unitarians and Universalists were more sociological than theological, the merger was smooth. The UUA affirms the following beliefs: the freedom of religious expression; the conviction that all religions have intrinsic value; the authority of individual reason and conscience over church or Scripture; the quest for truth with an open heart and mind; justice, equality, and dignity for all persons; natural human ethics based in love; the unity of reality, the seamlessness between sacred and secular; the democratic decision-making process; the need for self-reflection; and the importance of religious community.

Although still headquartered in Boston, the UUA has active churches throughout the country, especially in urban areas, college and university communities, and centers for high-tech industries. Members generally have high income and education levels. Still a liberal, progressive denomination, the UUA is active in social causes such as gay/lesbian rights, homelessness, poverty, and multiculturalism. Theologically diverse, there are active groups of UU Pagans and UU Christians. The UUA remains a small denomination, with most members adult converts rather than those born and raised in the faith. Unitarian Universalists do not actively evangelize, but preach their beliefs, seeing spiritual growth and societal transformation as more important than institutional growth.

Evelyn A. Kirkley

See also GREAT AWAKENING(S) (EURO-AMERICAN RELIGIOUS HISTORY); PURITANISM; TRANSCENDENTALISM.

UNITATIS REDINTEGRATIO

This Vatican II document, The Decree on Ecumenism, was approved by the bishops of the Second Vatican Council (in a vote of 2,054 for to 64 against) on November 20, 1964. This did not come, however, without debate and controversy, some of which was overcome by removing the complex issues of religious freedom and non-Christian religions from the draft of this decree. (The deleted questions were taken up later in the two declarations *Dignitatis Humanae* and *Nostra Aetate* respectively.) Commonly known by the first two words of the Latin text, *Unitatis Redintegratio* ("The Restoration of Unity"), the decree marks a significant turning point in the difficult history of relations between the Catholic Church and all other Christian churches. Nearly two millennia of ruptures large and small, including the Eastern Schism fixed in 1054 and the Protestant Reformation erupting in 1517, had left the church—understood to be the Body of Christ—scandalously divided. Early in the twentieth century, Protestants began the process of dialogue among themselves that came to be known as the "ecumenical movement" (from the Greek word *oikoumenikos*, meaning "worldwide"). The Catholic Church maintained its distance from such conversations until Pope John XXIII, in convoking the Second Vatican Council in 1962, urged the assembled bishops to take up the question of the reunification of Christianity. (This was one of three issues proposed by the Pope for the council's consideration. The other two were the church's relation to the modern world and the scandal of world poverty.) In *Unitatis Redintegratio* the council first recognized that "many of the most significant elements" of the Christian life "can exist outside the visible boundaries of the Catholic Church. Thus the bishops affirm that the "separated Churches and communities as such" have been used by the Spirit of Christ as "means of salvation which derive their efficacy from the very fullness of grace and truth entrusted to the Catholic Church" (no. 3). Acknowledgment of the validity of other churches leads to the enumeration of guidelines for Catholic participation in the ecumenical movement being led by the Holy Spirit. These include a change of heart, prayer, study, care with language, and cooperation with other Christians in certain forms of prayer and in service to the world. The decree recognizes that the Eastern (Orthodox) Church already shares many things with the Catholic Church that Protestant Churches do not. However, the Bible, baptism, and a shared morality can become bases for unity in the West as well. While the Decree on Ecumenism represents a starting point for future discussions more than a goal

attained, centuries of discord and even religious wars among Christians mean that its very existence is significant.

James B. Nickoloff

See also VATICAN, SECOND COUNCIL OF THE.

UNITED CHURCH OF CHRIST

The United Church of Christ (UCC) is a Protestant Christian denomination in the United States formed in 1957 through the mergers of four groups: Reformed, Evangelical, Christian, and Congregational. The German Reformed Church originated in 1793 in Lancaster, Pennsylvania. They were a group of German Calvinists who had emigrated to Pennsylvania beginning in the 1720s and 1730s and became known as Pennsylvania Dutch (a corruption of "Deutsch," or German). By the nineteenth century, their ethnic identity had weakened to the point that they dropped "German" from their name in 1869, and in the twentieth century, embarked on a series of ecumenical unions. The Evangelical Synod of North America was a German Lutheran-Reformed denomination in which doctrinal differences had been submerged to ecclesiastical unity. The Reformed Church and the Evangelical Synod merged in 1934 to form the Evangelical and Reformed Church.

The Christian Churches was a restorationist Christian group that emerged between 1790 and 1810 and was related to the Campbellite–Stonite Disciples of Christ. It was composed of churches in New England that had broken away from Congregationalism, followers of dissident Methodist James O'Kelley in Virginia and North Carolina, and followers of Barton Stone who did not merge with the Campbellites. The Congregationalists descended from New England Puritans who advocated Calvinist theology and congregational polity. During the First Great Awakening, the Congregationalists divided over revivalism, leading to the Unitarian schism in 1825. In the nineteenth century, they were leaders of Evangelicalism, missions, and social reform. They were the first denomination to ordain a woman to the ministry, Antoinette Brown, in 1853. By the end of the century, they had adopted liberalism and the Social Gospel. In 1931 the Christian and Congregationalists merged to formed the Congregational Christian Churches. The Congregationalists have been the most dominant strand of the four forming the UCC.

Since the 1957 merger of the Evangelical and Reformed Church and the Congregational Churches, the United Church of Christ has become one of, if not the, most liberal Protestant denomination in the United States. Since polity is congregational, it is also one of the most diverse. Theology and worship vary from conservative Evangelical (although not fundamentalist) to virtually Unitarian (one joke goes that UCC stands for "Unitarians Considering Christ"). The most conservative churches are those from the Evangelical and Reformed tradition. Clergy are consistently liberal, and the denomination has issued statements favoring reproductive rights and opposition to nuclear warfare. The denomination also has special-interest caucuses for women, ethnic minorities, and charismatics. Congregations are loosely organized into associations and conferences for mutual support and shared programming. There is a national general synod that wields no authority over local congregations, but coordinates mission and reform activities.

Although its membership has declined from the 1960s to the 1990s, the UCC is strongest in the northeastern United States, including western New York and the lower Great Lakes area, the old stronghold of Congregationalism. It is also strong in the Midwest, where many Germans settled, in Pennsylvania, Ohio, and Missouri, bastion of the Evangelical and Reformed Church. They are also a strong presence in the Pacific Northwest and San Francisco Bay area of California. National headquarters are in Cleveland, Ohio. In the 1980s, they entered into a cooperative relationship (although not merger) with the Disciples of Christ.

Evelyn A. Kirkley

See also CONGREGATIONAL CHURCHES; CONGREGATIONAL THEOLOGIES; DISCIPLES OF CHRIST/CHURCHES OF CHRIST; PURITANISM.

UNITY

(As "Note" of the church.) In the second "Nicene" Creed (set forth at the Council of Constantinople in 381 C.E.), Christians confess their belief in "one, holy, catholic, and apostolic Church." Here the church claims an inner *oneness*, or unity, as the will of God. Nevertheless, diversity and pluralism, rooted to some degree in cultural differences, have marked Christianity from the beginning. Such diversity is inevitable given historical change. At some points in the church's history, it has been seen as compatible with the essential unity of the church, since it enriches that unity. This is the position of the Second Vatican Council of the Catholic Church (1962–5) (see *Gaudium et Spes* 58). However, deep divisions have also characterized the Christian church, leading to separation (schism) and the creation of new churches (examples include the separation of Eastern Orthodoxy and Roman Catholicism in the eleventh century and the breach in the Western Church between Rome and the Protestant Reformation in the sixteenth century). Unlike diversity, division contradicts the very identity bestowed upon the church by God.

Theologically, the church's unity derives from the doctrine of "one God" whose work of salvation in the "one crucified Lord" is made available to humanity in "one church." Likewise, the inner unity of the triune God grounds the unity of the church and the unity of humanity itself (see *Gaudium et Spes* 24). This belief binds local churches together, as does their common understanding of baptism, Eucharist, Gospel, and ministry—in short, their common faith (see Eph 4:1-6). A common faith, of course, demands a common discipleship, or way of life, modeled on Jesus.

In early Western theology (and invariably in Eastern theology), the unity of the church meant a communion of churches. After the East–West Schism, unity gradually came to mean uniformity in Roman Catholicism, and "communion with Rome" meant obedience to the pope whose office symbolized for Catholics the unity of the church. While the Catholic Church for centuries used the image of the "Body of Christ" almost exclusively to describe its unity, the Second Vatican Council added a variety of images from the New Testament such as "people of God," "temple of God," and "bride of Christ." In this way, the council helped to restore the early Christian understanding of the one church as a "communion of local churches." In the age of global Christianity, the requirements of inculturation today challenge Christians to probe anew

the meaning of the doctrine of church unity.

James B. Nickoloff

See also APOSTOLICITY; CATHOLICITY; HOLINESS; NOTES OF THE CHURCH.

UNIVERSALISM

The position that all men and women will be saved. Found in Origen's notion of *apokatastasis*, and put forward as a regulative idea in the work of Karl Barth, its strongest defense today can be found in the work of John Hick as an axiom essential to the resolution of the problem of evil.

J. A. Colombo

UNIVERSALS

The long-debated "problem of universals" arises out of the following set of considerations. We are able to group things into categories or classes on the basis of commonly shared characteristics or features. For example, a very small child who has not yet acquired a general understanding of what it is to be a cat may mistakenly identify all furry, four-legged creatures as cats. Eventually, the child somehow acquires an understanding of what is common and peculiar to all cats —what accounts for all individual cats being included in the relevant category and what accounts for animals of other sorts being excluded. What the child has been able to grasp is what is *universally* applicable to all members of the species and what differentiates this species from others. The problem arises when one asks what the common species-characterizing essence is. Does it exist apart from the individual members of the species? Is there a category, say, domestic felinity, existing independently of all individual cats? If there is such a category, does it exist in the world, in our minds, or in some abstract realm of being separate from the physical domain? Over the centuries, thinkers who have addressed these questions have come up with an array of strikingly different answers.

The ancient Greek philosopher Plato (428/7–348/7 B.C.E.) was one of the first to provide a theory of the nature of universals. Plato held that the ultimate natures of things (triangularity, felinity, humanity, justice, beauty, and so on) exist independently of the individual objects that exemplify those natures. Though these ultimate natures Plato called "Forms" are the primary objects of knowledge, their existence is independent of human thought processes. Since Plato held that universals are mind-independent beings, his view of universals falls under the heading "Realism." According to Plato, the Forms or universals exist in an immaterial realm separate from the physical world. Individual objects in our world derive their natures from these separately existing immaterial beings.

Plato, himself, recognized certain problems arising from his theory of universals. What, precisely, is the relation between the Forms and the particular objects deriving their kind-making characteristics from the Forms? Further, do the Forms possess these characteristics themselves? For example, is the Form "blueness" itself blue? If not, how can it convey that property to particular objects? If it is blue, then what accounts for its possession of that characteristic? Is there some superior Form that conveys the relevant property to the Form? If so, then the same set of questions will arise regarding that Form, and so on, leading to an infinite regress. Plato's student, Aristotle, attempted to solve this problem by denying that universals do not exist

in an immaterial, transcendent realm but are, instead, constituents of this world. Each individual substance, on Aristotle's view, has its own "substantial form" accounting for its possession of all of its species-characterizing features. Aristotle's theory of universals is also a realist theory, since he held that these forms are real, mind-independent features of the world and not simply functions of the ways in which we conceptualize objects.

The medieval theologian and philosopher St. Thomas Aquinas developed a theory of universals that is an instance of "moderate realism." According to St. Thomas, the mind forms concepts of the natures of physical objects by abstracting forms from sensory images or "phantasmata." The abstracted forms are known as "intelligible species." The universal exists, on this view, immaterially in the human intellect. Since the concept in the intellect is held to correspond to real, mind-independent features of the world, St. Thomas's theory still comes down on the side of realism.

Several modern and contemporary theories of universals are antirealist. Opponents of realism hold that universals are constructs of the human intellect and would not exist apart from human thought processes and linguistic conventions.

Linda L. Peterson

See also AQUINAS, THOMAS, ST.; ARISTOTLE; ESSENCE; PLATO.

UNIVERSITY

Fundamentally, this is a community of persons dedicated to the disciplined and reasoned discovery and discussion of truth and learning. In the modern world, these communities are organized and accredited in many ways, depending on each country's educational traditions and system. But however it might be institutionalized, the most basic reason for the existence of any university remains the quest for truth and learning, promoted by one generation for the benefit of another, within parameters of reason, disciplined method, and openness to newness. Freedom to seek, and to honestly share and critique whatever may be found, have always been understood to be essential requirements for the fulfillment of the university community's fundamental task.

Orlando Espín

See also FREEDOM; PONTIFICAL UNIVERSITY; TRUTH; UNIVERSITY, CATHOLIC.

UNIVERSITY, CATHOLIC

A Catholic university is, first of all, a university. As such, it is a community of persons dedicated to the disciplined and reasoned discovery and discussion of truth and learning. The "Catholic" dimension of a university is granted by its dedication to and promotion of serious, ongoing, and reasoned dialogue between the members of the university community—as seekers after truth and learning —the various scholarly disciplines present on campus, and the Catholic tradition, especially as articulated in Catholic theology. This dialogue should especially happen through recognized means of scholarship, and also in the context of campus ministry. The legal ("canonical") recognition of a university within the church is granted by either the Vatican (for "pontifical" universities only), by an episcopal conference or a local bishop, or by a religious congregation. A university can be recognized as Catholic and yet not be owned or directed by church authorities.

Orlando Espín

See also CATHOLIC TRADITION; FAITH; FREEDOM; PONTIFICAL UNIVERSITY; TRUTH; UNIVERSITY.

UNTOUCHABLES

See CASTE; CASTES, SCHEDULED.

UPANISHADS

Among the most influential scriptures of Hinduism, the Upanishads contain, most importantly, reflections on the nature of ultimate reality and the inner self, termed respectively Brahman and Atman. Much of the Upanishadic teaching is presented in the form of discussions between sages or dialogues between teachers and their disciples. The Upanishads themselves describe their wisdom as "secret" (*rahasya*), and the traditional derivation of the word is from a combination of a Sanskrit root (*sad*) with prefixes (*upa-ni*) meaning "sitting down near" and suggesting the image of pupils gathering around a preceptor for an intimate sharing of prized knowledge. Each of the four Vedas has several Upanishads attached to it. Some ten to fourteen are counted as the major Upanishads. They were composed, scholars believe, about 900–500 B.C.E. Orthodox Hindus, however, consider the Upanishads to be part of the Vedic revelation (*shruti*) and, as such, manifestations of eternal truths, not human compositions. The Upanishads are the primary scriptural sources of Vedanta, which—in its various schools—seeks to render a coherent interpretation of the meaning of these scriptures for the benefit of subsequent generations. The most important of the Upanishads, and probably the oldest, are the *Brihadaranyaka* and *Chandogya*.

Lance E. Nelson

See also ATMAN; BRAHMAN; HINDUISM; REVELATION (IN OTHER RELIGIONS); VEDANTA; VEDAS.

UPAYA

A Buddhist Sanskrit term meaning "skill in means," referring to the insightful communications and actions of enlightened Buddhas and advanced bodhisattvas to further the spiritual development of disciples. Based on the notion that a Buddha can discern the karma of other beings, it follows that his compassion motivates the Buddha to advise a disciple in a uniquely apt manner or preach to match an audience's level of spiritual understanding. The Buddha's *upaya* is used to explain the great diversity of Mahayana texts.

The Mahayana bodhisattva idea is stated to involve two avenues: the cultivation of insight (*prajna*) and the full expression of compassionate service informed by upaya, each incomplete without the perfection of the other. At points in Northern Buddhist history, the doctrine of upaya was used to legitimate Buddhist monks or laity acting in defiance of conventional morality (for example, "justifiable homicide") to serve their sense of wider morality or the reckoning of society's greater good.

Todd T. Lewis

See also BODHISATTVA; MAHAYANA BUDDHISM.

URIM AND THUMMIM

Objects, probably lots of some sort, used in ancient Israel for divination by the priests. The Urim and Thummim occur only during the early period of Israel's history; compare the stories of David in 1 Samuel where he inquires of Yahweh through a priest using the Urim and Thumim. Apparently only yes/no questions were possible with this system of divination (compare also Num 27:21).

Russell Fuller

See also DIVINATION.

U.S.C.C.B.

These initials stand for "United States Conference of Catholic Bishops," the administrative arm of the nation's bishops. Its headquarters are in Washington, D.C.

Orlando Espín

USURY

The interest that a lender of money charges to the borrower. In early Judaism, Christianity, and Islam, usury was forbidden. This is due in part to the fact that all three religious traditions make claims on their respective believers to take the poor more seriously than any other segment of the society.

In Christian tradition, most followers of Thomas Aquinas (1225–74) agreed that commercial trade was divinely ordained as long as it did not involve such overt evils as monopoly, fraud, or usury. The Catholic Church's opposition to usury was also rooted in Aristotle's notion that the proper function of money is a medium of exchange, not a means to acquire more money.

The main economic concern of the church in the seventeenth and eighteenth centuries was its opposition to usury. However, when the church drew close to the capitalist ethos by defending a stratified social model and a doctrine of property rights at the end of the nineteenth century, it no longer focused on the problem of usury. Recent teaching by Christian social ethicists, however, has found the interest owed by Two-thirds World countries on their debts to be unjust.

Mary E. Hobgood

See also QUADRAGESIMO ANNO; RERUM NOVARUM; THIRD WORLD.

UTHMAN (?–656)

In Islam, the third of four so-called "Rightly Guided" or patriarchal caliphs (successors of the Prophet of Islam, Muhammad, 570–632). Uthman's caliphate, lasting from 644–56, is not remembered kindly by historians. Unlike his predecessor, Umar, Uthman, though by all accounts a good and pious man, was not a strong leader. Moreover, he earned the resentment of many by appointing relatives from his Umayyad clan to high posts in the Islamic Empire, most notably his nephew, Muʾawiya, who was made governor of Syria, and who later (in 661, five years after Uthman's death) seized control of the caliphate and made it a dynastic institution. The one bright spot in Uthman's reign was his commissioning of an authorized edition of Islam's sacred scripture, the Qurʾan. He subsequently ordered that all other extant versions of the book be destroyed, thus assuring that no rival editions of the holy text would survive. It is widely believed that the Qurʾan Muslims have today is identical to the one promulgated by Uthman. The murder of the third caliph, however, reflects the suspicion and hostility his leadership created. Unguarded in his home at Medina, Uthman was assassinated in 656 by a group of disaffected Egyptian Muslims, and with his death and the election of Ali as, his successor, Islamic unity rapidly began to deteriorate.

Ronald A. Pachence

See also ALI; CALIPH (KALIPHA)/ CALIPHATE; MEDINA; MUHAMMAD; QURʾAN; UMAR; UMAYYADS.

UTILITARIANISM

A metaethical system most associated with nineteenth-century British philosophers Jeremy Bentham, James Mill, and John Stuart Mill. Utilitarianism maintains that the fundamental criterion of ethics is the amount of utility produced by the consequences of ethical decisions, for example, the greatest happiness for the greatest number. Frequently, a distinction is made between "act" and "rule" utilitarianism, depending on whether the basic subject matter of analysis is individual actions or rules (maxims) of action.

J. A. Colombo

UTOPIA

A future age of perfect (or near perfect) happiness, justice, and plenty. The great monotheistic religions, and some of the so-called "traditional" religions, believe (with variations and nuances, according to each religion) in the possibility of such a future age. Secular thought (Marx, for example) can also project a utopian future. Although the term "utopia" was popularized after Thomas More (d. 1535), it actually points to a widespread hope of humankind and a powerful source for the religious imagination and for religiously inspired social action. Utopia lies at the heart of the second-Temple Judaic notion of the "reign of God," and consequently appears again at the core of Jesus of Nazareth's teaching. Throughout the centuries, this utopic hope has acted as corrective to ecclesiastical complacency. Utopias have also been the founding hope for so-called "messianic movements," as well as for modern "integralist" or "fundamentalist" movements.

Orlando Espín

See also ESCHATOLOGY (IN CHRISTIANITY); ESCHATOLOGY (IN JUDAISM); ESCHATON; FUNDAMENTALISM; HOPE (IN CHRISTIANITY); INTEGRALISM;

JESUS OF HISTORY; LATIN AMERICAN THEOLOGIES; LIBERATION THEOLOGIES; MARXISM; MESSIANIC MOVEMENT; MILLENARIANISM; MORE, THOMAS; REIGN OF GOD; SOCIAL JUSTICE.

UTRECHT, SEE OF

The honorary "first see" among Old Catholic Churches. Utrecht (in the Netherlands) separated from Rome in 1724 over questions regarding the latteris condemnation of Jansenism. The "apostolic succession" of bishops in most Old Catholic Churches has been preserved, especially through the see of Utrecht. In 1889 an important doctrinal declaration of shared beliefs was written at Utrecht by a gathering of Old Catholic bishops from several countries.

Orlando Espín

See also APOSTOLIC SUCCESSION; BISHOP (EPISCOPACY); CATHOLIC TRADITION; COMMUNION (ECCLESIOLOGICAL); JANSENISM; OLD CATHOLICS; SEE.

V

VAISHNAVA

In Hinduism, a Vaishnava is a person devoted to Vishnu, the deity he or she will regard as the Supreme Being. There are many denominations (usually referred to by Indologists as "sects") within the Hindu tradition that are Vaishnava in orientation. The general movement, having roots in the Vedas, is referred to in English as Vaishnavism. Scriptures important to Vaishnavism include the *Ramayana*; portions of the *Mahabharata*, especially the *Bhagavad Gita*; a number of Puranas, the *Vishnu* and the *Bhagavata* in particular; the *Pancaratra Agamas*; certain collections of devotional hymns composed by saints; and various theological treatises and commentaries written by important Vaishnava masters. The theology of Vaishnavism is profoundly theistic, and its spirituality is strongly orientated toward devotion (*bhakti*). Among the most important Vaishnava denominations are the Shrivaishnavism of South India, whose most important theologian is Ramanuja, and the North Indian Krishnaite traditions, notably the Vallabha school and Bengal Vaishnavism (which gave rise to the Hare Krishna movement). It is important to note that the last two movements, though they call themselves Vaishnavas, subordinate Vishnu in their theology to Krishna, whom they regard as the Supreme Being.

Lance E. Nelson

See also BHAGAVAD GITA; BHAGAVATA PURANA; BHAKTI; BHAKTI-YOGA; CAITANYA/CHAITANYA; DVAITA VEDANTA; HARE KRISHNA MOVEMENT; HINDUISM; MAHABHARATA; PURANA; RAMAYANA; SHAKTA; VALLABHA; VISHISHTADVAITA VEDANTA; VISHNU.

VAISHYA

In the Hindu caste system, the *vaishyas* form, after the brahmins and *kshatriyas*, the third of the four pan-Indian caste categories known as *varnas*. The vaishya varna has traditionally been associated with the professions of merchant and farmer. Classified within this varna are many vaishya castes (*jatis*) that are often further divided into smaller groups. Below the vaishyas in the social hierarchy are the *shudras* and the untouchables.

Lance E. Nelson

See also BRAHMANA; CASTE; HINDUISM; KSHATRIYA; SHUDRA; UNTOUCHABLES.

VAJRAYANA BUDDHISM

See TANTRIC BUDDHISM.

VALDÉS, JUAN DE (1500–41)

Spanish humanist and theologian. After studies at the university of Alcalá, he moved to Italy in 1531, soon becoming the leader of a group of laypeople committed to ecclesiastical reform and spiritual revival. Although Valdés himself remained a Catholic, most of his followers became Protestants. His teaching stressed the centrality of individual religious feeling and frequently dismissed church tradition and authorities. His thought was very influential, especially because some of his followers became important Protestant Reformers (Peter Martyr and Bernardino Ochino, among others). Valdés' main works were *Diálogo de doctrina cristiana* (1529) and *Alfabeto cristiano* (1536). His brother, Alfonso de Valdés (1490–1532), was also a respected Catholic theologian and canon lawyer, an admirer of Erasmus, and a severe critic of the papacy.

Orlando Espín

See also CATHOLIC TRADITION; COUNTER-REFORMATION/CATHOLIC REFORMATION; ECCLESIOLOGY; HUMANISM; OCHINO, BERNARDINO; PETER MARTYR; PRAYER; PROTESTANTISM; REFORMATION; TRADITION (IN CHRISTIANITY).

VALENTINUS

A Gnostic Christian teacher of Egyptian origin, Valentinus taught in Rome around 140 and died shortly after 160. Most of our information about Valentinus's and his followers' teachings come to us from their opponents and so may not represent their original thought. Valentinus was said to have taught that original sin resulted in a separation of the unity of the divine Pleroma or fullness of God, originally consisting of thirty aeons, or divine beings. This unity can only be restored through the intervention of a number of the aeons, one of whom was Christ, whom the Valentinians understood as a pure spirit. Those humans who carry the divine spark of the spirit in them will be saved when the spiritual nature is separated from matter. Other psychic humans can attain a partial salvation through faith, while the remaining humans who carry no hint of the spiritual within them will simply return to the earth.

Gary Macy

See also CHRIST; DOCETISM; GNOSIS/GNOSTICISM; SALVATION.

VALIDITY, SACRAMENTAL

A sacrament is considered valid if certain minimal conditions are followed in its celebration. Validity rests on three factors: matter, form, and intention. In the Eucharist, for example, bread and wine are the necessary matter; the words of Christ ("This is my body . . . my blood") uttered by a priest are the necessary form; and the priest's desire to consecrate the Eucharist is the necessary intention. If cake and coffee, for example, replace bread and wine; if the words of Christ are not spoken, or not by a priest; or if the priest is merely demonstrating, rather than actually performing, the rite; there would be no valid sacrament. Related to the concept of validity is liceity or lawfulness. In the Catholic Church, for example, the law mandates unleavened bread for the Eucharist. The use of leavened bread, while not rendering the sacrament invalid, would effect its liceity. The question of sacramental validity is crucial in the process of marriage annulment. A valid sacramental marriage requires that both partners be baptized; commit themselves freely and permanently; are willing to have children; declare their intention in the presence of an ordained or licensed representative of the church; and subsequently engage in sexual intercourse. The absence of any of these renders the marriage sacramentally invalid. A marriage annulment, then, is not a divorce, but is a declaration that one of the requirements for sacramental validity was absent. For example, if one member of the couple was psychologically incapable of making a free choice to marry, there would be no sacramental validity. Because the church is a human organization, the establishment of minimal guidelines for sacramental validity is necessary for good order. These guidelines do not mean, however that: (1) the celebration of the sacraments requires only the absolute minimum (more is necessary if the sacraments are to achieve their full effect in the life of the church); (2) sacramental words and gestures are timeless or magic (they can change over time: they are merely how the church, in one time, in light of its best insights, regulates its life); (3) God is controlled by the church's guidelines. Because Jesus lives through the Christian community, when it acts in good faith, Jesus acts for and with it. Guidelines for sacramental validity set up boundaries in which the church, not God, can effectively operate.

Patrick L. Malloy

See also ANNULMENT; EFFICACY, SACRAMENTAL; EX OPERE OPERANTIS; EX OPERE OPERATO.

VALLABHA (1479–1531)

An important Hindu theologian, Vallabha was the founder of a Krishnaite Vaishnava movement popular in northern and western India. Vallabha taught a dynamic theistic nondualism known as Shuddhadvaita (Pure Nondualism), in which the world is fully real and the Supreme Being, Krisha, is *saguna*, qualified by rich attributes. The Vallabha tradition describes Shankara's Advaita Vedanta, by way of contrast, as Kevaladvaita, "exclusionistic nondualism," because of his emphasis on Brahman as *nirguna* (attributeless) and his illusionistic interpretation of *maya*, implying a radical world denial. All the major preceptors of Vallabha's lineage have been married, and his tradition stresses a kind of devotional (*bhakti*) spirituality that centers around household worship of Krishna and profound meditation on the story of Krishna's relations with the *gopis*, as recounted in the *Bhagavata Purana*. The core spirituality of the tradition is described as the Pushti Marga, the Path of Grace.

Lance E. Nelson

See also ADVAITA VEDANTA; BHAGAVATA PURANA; BHAKTI; DVAITA VEDANTA; GOPI; HINDUISM; VAISHNAVA; VISHISH-TADVAITA VEDANTA.

VALUES

It is a uniquely human trait to recognize values. In general, we can divide understandings of value into "objectivist" and "subjectivist" notions. The former holds that worth or value inheres in things themselves, the latter that things become valuable because of their worth to the person. Classical theology can be seen as combining the two. Value is essentially the same as "being," and virtuous persons would properly appreciate things of value, such as their God, their country, or even their own lives, and that proper appreciation of those things (and avoidance of what is inimical to them) in turn lends value to a person's life. This understanding is open to dialogue with Eastern notions such as *Tao*, or the *rta* of Hindu philosophy.

In post-Enlightenment thought, the question of values was articulated primarily because of scientific and mathematical claims of "valueless" research, and its superiority over other kinds of human seeking. Attention to values as a separate concern can be found in the work of F. W. Nietzsche at the end of the nineteenth century. In 1903 G. E. Moore (*Principia Ethica*) set the framework for most modern ethical discussion by posing the "fact/value" distinction. In the early twentieth century, Max Scheler focused attention on "intuited" values. In the United States, Ralph Barton Perry, John Dewey, and later, Elizabeth Flower contributed most to value theory. Current reflection, especially under the influence of the new "virtue ethicists," moves away from the strict fact/value distinction, preferring to consider the power of character to determine the nature of any perception.

For about a decade, beginning in the mid-seventies, value theory became popularized in certain circles, notably education, in the United States. Thus we heard of "values education" (Michael Silver, Norman Feather, Max Learner), "values clarification" (Gordon Hart), and "values in faith" (Roland and Doris Larson). One effect of this movement was to make clear how many different (and often conflicting) values were held, based on cultural, ethnic, religious, racial, and gender differences. For some, that realization meant a deploring of fragmentation in American society; for others, it meant a call for "multiculturalism" and greater tolerance; for still others, it meant a challenge to the values of the dominant society. Even with such fragmentation, the Rosen Publication Group from 1990–2, published a series of brief (sixty-four-page) popular pamphlets called *The Values Library*,

examining "commonly held" values such as citizenship, compassion, competitiveness, cooperation, courage, determination, persistence, honesty, self-control, sportsmanship, tolerance, and work ethic. For a more academic treatment, see the separate monographs of the "Values in Ethics Series" from Loyola University Press, such as, Elizabeth McGrath, *The Art of Ethics*, Mane Hajdin, *The Boundaries of Moral Discourse*, and Braulio Munoz, *Tensions in Social Theory*.

G. Simon Harak, s.j.

VARELA, FÉLIX (1788–1853)

Cuban Catholic philosopher and priest. Born in Cuba but raised since early childhood in Florida, he became a popular professor at the conciliar seminary in Havana, where he directly influenced many of the most important individuals in Cuba's late colonial history. His thought became foundational to the independence struggle. Elected to Spain's parliament, he had to flee to the United States because of his liberal views. First in Philadelphia and later in New York he became an ardent apologist for the church, for scholarship and learning, and a heroic pastor to poor Irish immigrants. Varela was the first Latino to receive a doctoral degree in theology at an American institution (1841). He was actively involved in the establishment of the Catholic press in the U.S., and for many years was also vicar general of the Diocese of New York, and participated in two of the councils of Baltimore. Because of ill health he returned to Florida, and there died. Varela's beatification is currently being considered in the Catholic Church. His thought was expressed and published in numerous newspaper articles, letters, and books. Among the more influential were his

Letters to Elpidio (1835–8), and the articles originally published in *El Habanero* since 1824 (first collected and published in book form in 1945).

Orlando Espín

See also APOLOGETICS (PATRISTIC PERIOD); APOLOGISTS; BALTIMORE, COUNCILS OF; BEATIFICATION; LATIN AMERICAN CATHOLICISM; LATINO/A; LATINO CATHOLICISM; LATINO THEOLOGY (-IES); NOMBRE DE DIOS MISSION; PASTOR; SOCIAL JUSTICE; THEOLOGY OF RELIGIONS; VICAR.

VARNA

See CASTE.

VARUNA

An important deity in the *Rig Veda*, Varuna is the guardian of *rita*, the moral and cosmic order. He snares with his noose those who violate rita, and prayers are offered to him for forgiveness of sin. In the later Hindu tradition, he is much diminished in importance, becoming the god of the sea and of waters in general.

Lance E. Nelson

See also VEDAS.

VASCONCELOS, JOSÉ C.
(1882–1959)

José Vasconcelos was an influential Mexican philosopher and political figure. His most famous work, *La Raza Cósmica* (1925), interprets the history of Mexico and Latin America as the emergence of a "cosmic race" that, as the product of the racial-cultural mixture of European and indigenous peoples, represents a historical drive toward racial-cultural inclusivity. This Latin American *mestizaje*, or racial-cultural mixture, thus represents a higher form of human community than those homogeneous communities (Anglo Saxon, for example) that, valuing racial-cultural "purity," define themselves over against other races and cultures. In other important works, such as *El monismo estético* (1918), he articulated an "aesthetic philosophy" grounded in the human experience of beauty. Vasconcelos was also active politically. In 1920 he became Mexico's Minister of Public Education and is widely considered the father of public education in Mexico. In 1929 he was an unsuccessful candidate for the presidency of Mexico.

Roberto S. Goizueta

See also AESTHETICS.

VASUBANDHU

One of the greatest Buddhist monk–scholars who lived in northwest India, likely Gandhara, around the second half of the fifth century C.E. In his early career, Vasubandhu was a commentator within the Sarvastivasdin school, with his main contribution the remarkable *Abhidharma-kosha*, a series of wide-ranging discussions about the varying hermeneutical approaches and doctrinal differences found in the different recensions of the *Abhidharma Pitakas* then extant.

According to legend, Vasubandhu's second career resulted when he was converted to the Cittamatra (or Yogachara) school of the Mahayana tradition by his brother, Asanga. His writings from the "Consciousness-Only" perspective became influential in Sanskrit and in their Tibetan and East Asian translations. In these, he argues to positively establish the doctrine by demonstrating that there is no other way to explain human experience than on the analogy of the dream.

Todd T. Lewis

See also ASANGA; CITTAMATRA; SARVASTIVADIN SCHOOL.

VATICAN

A sector of the city of Rome, across the Tiber River from the ancient center of the city, where well-attested tradition holds that the apostle Peter was both executed and buried. From ancient times, it has therefore been an important site for Christian worship. When the medieval Papacy returned to Rome after having been centered at Avignon in France for most of the fourteenth century, the Lateran palace that had previously been the residence of the Bishops of Rome was abandoned in favor of papal residences at the Vatican and elsewhere in the city. Renaissance popes greatly elaborated the architecture and decoration of the Vatican, and the current St. Peter's Basilica (replacing an ancient Roman construction) was completed in 1626. After that time, the Vatican became the primary location of the papal court, and the term "the Vatican" gradually came to be used as a reference to papal authority in the worldwide church.

Until 1870, the city of Rome and a varying amount of territory around it were ruled directly by the pope and were called the "Papal States." When, in that year, Italian nationalists, intent on the unification of Italy, captured the city and ended papal rule, Pope Pius IX remained in his palace at the Vatican and refused to accept the authority of the new Italian government. Pius and the next three popes were often then referred to as "Prisoner of the Vatican" (although they were not, in fact, being held against their will). In 1929 Pope Pius XI negotiated the Lateran Treaty with the government of Benito Mussolini, establishing the Vatican as an independent city-state within the city of Rome and ending the church's official rejection of Italian governmental authority.

William Clark, s.j.

VATICAN, FIRST COUNCIL OF THE

The twentieth ecumenical council meeting at Vatican City in Rome was convoked by Pope Pius IX in 1868 to deal with such issues as faith and reason, the infallibility of the pope, religious orders, and the relationship of church and state. The "Ultramontane" bishops (such as Ward, Veuillot, and Manning) who favored a centralized authority in the church and the definition of papal infallibility were in the majority. The minority bishops (like Newman, von Döllinger, and Dupanloup) sought a more nuanced definition of papal primacy and papal infallibility, locating the latter in the context of the infallibility of the church. In the end, the council's definition of infallibility stressed that papal definitions were "irreformable" in themselves (not because of the consent of the church), but only when the pope speaks *ex cathedra*. The constitution *Pastor Aeternus* was passed by 533 bishops. Two bishops voted against it, and sixty-one bishops left in protest before the final vote. Eventually the minority bishops accepted the council's decision on the condition of its reception by the church as a whole. As a result of this definition, some German-speaking Catholics split with the Roman church, calling themselves "Old Catholics."

Vatican I also issued a constitution on faith (*Dei Filius*) that defined the relationship between faith and reason and condemned rationalism, fideism, pantheism, and other errors of the "modern age." The definition of papal primacy and papal infallibility were intended to become part of a Constitution on the Church (*De Ecclesia*), but war broke out between France and Prussia in 1870 and the council was suspended. The council was never reconvened, and it would be almost one hundred years until the next ecumenical council, Vatican II (1962–5).

Mary Ann Hinsdale

See also COUNCIL, ECUMENICAL; INFALLIBILITY; PAPACY/PAPAL; PASTOR AETERNUS.

VATICAN, SECOND COUNCIL OF THE

The Second Vatican Council (1962–5) has to be considered the most significant event of the twentieth century in the life of the Catholic Church, if not of Christianity. In 1959, shortly after he was elected pope, John XXII called for an ecumenical council, the twenty-first such council in the history of the Catholic Church, to nearly everyone's surprise. The Pope formally opened the council on October 11, 1962, having asked the assembled bishops of the church to address three pressing issues: (1) updating the church (aggiornamento in Italian) in relation to the modern world; (2) overcoming the scandal of a seriously divided Christianity; and (3) addressing the global reality of poverty. While the first two matters received considerable attention in the sixteen constitutions, decrees, and declarations approved by the council and promulgated by Pope Paul VI (who assumed the leadership of the church and the council after John XXIII's death in 1963), the third topic is far less prominent in the council's documents.

Pastoral rather than dogmatic in nature, the council ushered in profound changes in the self-understanding of the church, its life, and its practice, not seen since the reforms of the Council of Trent (1543–65). Among its teachings, as the eminent American theologian Richard P. McBrian, has pointed out, are the following: the church is a mystery, a sacrament before it is an organization or institution, and

includes the whole people of God. As such, its mission is to preach the word of God and celebrate the sacraments in such a way that its action will foster justice and peace in the world. The term "church" refers to all Christians, not just Catholics; the church is a collegial gathering of local churches, an eschatological community on the way to the final reign of God. Laypeople have a direct role in the mission and life of the church, not simply derivative of the mission of the hierarchy. The truths of the Catholic faith do not all carry equal weight as to what is binding and essential; rather, there is a "hierarchy of truths." The encounter with God's saving action in the world cannot be restricted to membership in the Catholic Church. Other Christian churches, as well as non-Christian religions, also participate in God's offer of salvation. The freedom to exercise one's religious beliefs derives from the dignity and freedom of the person, and opposes the notion that "error has no rights." Most of these teachings may be found in the two longest, and perhaps most important, documents of the council, Lumen Gentium (The Dogmatic Constitution on the Church, 1964), and Gaudium et Spes (The Pastoral Constitution on the Church in the Modern World, 1965).

The consequences of the Second Vatican Council for the church and the societies in which the church exists have been enormous. While many Catholics and others have celebrated the breakthroughs of the council and have rejoiced in the new life it brought to Catholics and to the world, others have resisted the direction it set for the church. As with all great historical events, the final outcome of Vatican II will only be clear with the passage of time.

Thomas McElligott

See also AGGIORNAMENTO; COUNCIL, ECUMENICAL; DECLARATION (DOCU- MENT); ECUMENICAL MOVEMENT/ECU- MENISM; GAUDIUM ET SPES; JOHN XXIII, POPE; LAITY; LAY MINISTRY; LUMEN GENTIUM; PAPACY/PAPAL; PAUL VI, POPE; RELIGION, FREEDOM OF; VATICAN, FIRST COUNCIL OF THE.

VEDANTA

For centuries the most important of the six orthodox systems (*darshanas*) of Hindu thought, Vedanta is primarily an exegetical school, taking the Vedic revelation, particularly the Upanishads, as its supreme authority. Since the Upanishads make up the final books of each Veda, they themselves are termed the Vedanta, literally, the "end (*anta*) of the Veda." They are also said to be the "end of the Veda" in the sense of embodying its culminating truths about ultimate reality and the nature of the human self. By extension, the tradition of thought that articulates the meaning of the Upanishads is also termed Vedanta, and it is with this meaning that the term is, in fact, almost always used outside the primary texts.

The Upanishads, like scriptures in other religious traditions, contain diverse material that expresses apparently divergent visions of reality. At the same time, since they are regarded as revelations of absolute truth, it is assumed that they must have a single ultimate significance. The various schools of Vedanta, then, claim to arrive at the correct interpretation of the Upanishadic revelation using carefully reasoned arguments and, equally or more important, the systematic methods of scriptural exegesis that had been developed and refined by the Mimamsa system for the interpretation of the ritual portion of the Veda (the Brahmanas). The *Brahma Sutras*, also known as the *Vedanta Sutras*, is the earliest text representing the Vedanta as a system of theology (*darshana*). It is attributed to the sage Badarayana (about 400–200 B.C.E.). Shankara (seventh–eighth century C.E.), who wrote the earliest extant commentary on the *Brahma Sutras*, was the systematizer of the Advaita Vedanta tradition. Other schools of Vedanta include the Vishishtadvaita (Qualified Nondualism) of Ramanuja (1017–1137), the Dvaita (Dualism) of Madhva (1238–1317), and the Shuddhadvaita (Pure Nondualism) of Vallabha (1479–1531).

In recent Hindu discourse, the term "Vedanta" is often used without qualification to designate a version of Advaita Vedanta, modified to meet modern (mostly ethical) concerns, that was articulated by such figures as Swami Vivekananda and Sarvepalli Radhakrishnan. Presented as the highest vision and spiritual essence of Hinduism, and indeed of all religions, this mode of thought is commonly referred to by scholars as "Neo-Vedanta." It is for many modern, educated Hindus the preferred means of access to their traditional faith.

Lance E. Nelson

See also ADVAITA VEDANTA; DVAITA VEDANTA; HINDUISM; MIMAMSA; VALLABHA; VISHISHTADVAITA VEDANTA.

VEDAS

The most sacred scriptures of Hinduism, the Vedas are regarded by the tradition as expressions of eternal truth that are revealed to humankind through sages (*rishis*) at the beginning of every great cosmic cycle. Derived from the Sanskrit root *vid*, "to know," the word *veda* means "sacred knowledge" or "wisdom." Even though there are some Hindu groups that ignore or even diminish the importance of the Vedas, acceptance of their authority has been one of the few touchstones that Hindus have used to decide which religious groups in India could be counted as part of their tradition. Those who accepted Vedic authority were called *astikas* ("accepters," orthodox), and those that denied it, such as Buddhists and Jains, were called *nastikas* ("deniers," heterodox).

Scholars have generally held that the Vedic texts were composed by an Indo-European-speaking people known as the Aryans, who were moving into the Indian subcontinent from the northwest in the second millennium B.C.E. The date accepted by Western scholarship for the Aryan migration, and the beginning of the composition of the *Rig Veda*, has for years been around 1500 B.C.E., but discussion as to the accuracy of this date (and indeed the whole theory of Aryan migration) has recently been reopened, largely at the instigation of Hindu scholars, and is currently the subject of much heated debate in the field.

There are four Vedas: the *Rig Veda, Sama Veda, Yajur Veda*, and *Atharva Veda*. Each of these is further subdivided into four sections containing four types of text: the Samhita (the "collection" of hymns), the Brahmanas (containing commentary and ritual instructions), the Aranyakas ("forest texts," containing symbolic meditations on the ritual), and the Upanishads (containing reflections on Brahman, the ultimate reality). The most important of these texts is the samhita of the *Rig Veda*, which consists largely of hymns addressed to deities (*devas*), many associated with powers of nature. The hymns of the *Rig Veda*, composed in an archaic form of Sanskrit known as Vedic, are sophisticated metrically, and many are of great poetic value. With the exception of the Upanishads, the Vedas are largely litur-

gical texts, intended for chanting during the Vedic sacrifices (*yajna*), providing instructions or background for the rites, or suggesting symbolic meditations on their meaning. The Vedic texts were passed down in various schools (*shakas*), being preserved orally over the centuries using elaborate methods of rote memorization because, until relatively recently, they were considered too sacred to be written down. Since correct articulation was considered vital for success of the rituals (*yajnas*) at which the Vedic texts were chanted, scrupulous attention was given to preserving exact pronunciation, tone, and cadence.

Hindus today recite certain Vedic verses (especially the Gayatri) in their daily devotions, hear more extensive sections of the Vedas chanted in temple ritual (*puja*), and on special occasions witness abbreviated versions of ancient Vedic rituals, an integral part of which is Vedic recitation. The sound of the chanted hymns by itself (independent of the meaning of the words) is considered to be a potent means of spiritual uplift, and the Vedas are still much honored, indeed praised, as an unsurpassed fountainhead of wisdom. Still, with the exception of the Upanishads, the texts are rarely studied by any but scholars. The Upanishads—philosophical in tone, much more accessible to a modern audience, and widely available in translation—remain important, especially for educated Hindus who follow the reformed Hinduism generally known to scholars as Neo-Vedanta.

Lance E. Nelson

See also ARYAN; AVESTA; BRAHMANA; GAYATRI; HINDUISM; PUJA; REVELATION (IN OTHER RELIGIONS); RISHI; SCRIPTURES (GENERIC); YAJNA; ZOROASTRIANISM.

VEGETARIANISM (IN INDIA)

See AHIMSA; GUNA; JAINISM.

VENERATION

An attitude often present in religions, displaying admiration or high regard for a person, a place, or an object. Certainly not equal to adoration (= worship), the attitude of veneration is sometimes expressed through diverse ritual practices, according to the doctrinal or customary parameters of each religion.

Orlando Espín

See also ANCESTORS, CHINESE.

VERA CRUZ, ALONSO DE LA (1504–84)

Spanish missionary in colonial Mexico. A graduate of the universities of Alcalá and Salamanca, Alonso also taught in the latter. In 1536 he traveled to recently conquered Mexico and became an Augustinian friar in the city of Veracruz (hence the name by which he is commonly known). He spent the rest of his life in his adopted land, founding schools, and as professor of theology at the new royal and pontifical university in Mexico City. His philosophical and theological writings were the first ones, in those two disciplines, to be entirely written and published in the Western Hemisphere (in Mexico, 1554). Although clearly in line with the Thomist school of thought, Alonso was also deeply influenced by the humanist and reform currents so typical of the Spanish sixteenth century. He was well known in Mexico for his fierce defense of the natives' rights.

Orlando Espín

See also CULTURE; EVANGELIZATION; FRIARS; HUMANISM; HUMAN RIGHTS; INCULTURATION; LATIN AMERICAN CATHOLICISM; LATIN AMERICAN THEOLOGIES; LATINO THEOLOGY (-IES); MISSIONARIES; MISSIONS; THEOLOGY OF RELIGIONS; THOMISM/TRANSCENDENTAL THOMISM.

VERIFICATION/FALSIFICATION AND THEOLOGY

This debate, identified with the work of A. J. Ayer, Anthony Flew, and John Hick, arises from the axiom that to be meaningful as asserting a state of affairs in the world, a statement must either be analytic or make a difference in the structure of reality that is in principle accessible to human experience; otherwise, the statement is meaningless or nonsensical. This axiom was expressed in a variety of formulations regarding the conditions of the verifiability or falsifiability of statements. On the whole, theological statements (taken in a nonfundamentalist manner) were judged to be meaningless. This debate has often served as the context for a "broader" consideration of the status and functions of religious language—sometimes appealing to the work of the "later Wittgenstein"—in the work of other analytic philosophers such as Richard Hare, Basil Mitchell, D. Z. Phillips, I. M. Crombie, Donald Evans, and Alvin Plantinga.

J. A. Colombo

See also LINGUISTIC ANALYSIS; POSITIVISM; WITTGENSTEIN, LUDWIG.

VERITATIS SPLENDOR

(Latin, "The Splendor of Truth"). An encyclical letter on moral theology issued by Pope John Paul II in 1993. By means of this letter, the Pope attempts to correct some developments in post–Vatican II moral theology he sees as problematic. He criticizes those interpretations of fundamental option theory that claim mortal sin need not affect our essential relationship with God, asserting that mortal sin always severs the human divine-relationship. Against those interpretations of proportionalism claiming that a good intention or outcome justifies an evil action, he asserts that some actions are intrinsically evil, and thus nothing can justify performing them. Against those who claim that morals are relative, dependent on historical or cultural influences and particular circumstances, the Pope offers a ringing endorsement for the case of objective moral norms binding on all persons.

Some proponents of proportionalism and fundamental option have argued that the descriptions of those theories are somewhat distorted and so are not necessarily prone to the dangers the Pope points to. Even those moral theologians who do not share the Pope's assessment of proportionalism and fundamental option theory tend to agree with the Pope's call for some degree of objectivity in ethics in response to growing ethical relativism.

Brian F. Linnane, S.J.

See also EVIL; FREE WILL; FUCHS, JOSEPH; FUNDAMENTAL OPTION; MCCORMICK, RICHARD A.; MORAL THEOLOGY/CHRISTIAN ETHICS; NATURAL LAW; PERSONALISM; PROPORTIONALISM; SIN, PERSONAL; TRUTH; VICE; VIRTUE.

VERNACULAR

The language commonly spoken by the people. In the United States, English is the principal vernacular language, although Spanish is becoming increasingly common. Before Vatican II, most Roman Catholic worship was conducted in Latin and other liturgical languages. Now, nearly all Latin Rite Catholic liturgy is celebrated in the vernacular. The Vatican issues a Latin model of each liturgy, known as its "editio typica," which is then adapted and translated into the various vernacular languages. The English vernacular versions are prepared by ICEL (The International Commission on English in the Liturgy), a body of scholars, including liturgists, linguists, and poets, from all the major English-speaking nations of the world. A number of Eastern Churches, both Catholic and Orthodox, continue to worship in languages that are not vernacular, and even in some ancient languages, such as Church Slavonic, that are no longer spoken outside a liturgical context.

Patrick L. Malloy

VESTMENTS, LITURGICAL

Liturgical vestments in the Christian tradition refer to special clothing worn by presiders (usually ordained clergy) or other assisting ministers during worship services. Some of these specific articles of clothing may be worn only by clergy of a certain rank; others may be worn more generally by almost all assistants or servers.

Many of these particular articles of clothing have their origins in early Christianity. The use of garments other than the ordinary clothing of the time during liturgical celebrations (for example, the Eucharist) seems to have developed by the legalization of Christianity in the fourth century; because of imperial influence and other changes in everyday clothing, liturgical vesture seems to have become more formalized and ornate. This tendency became more pronounced during the medieval period; the actual doffing of the everyday clothes, accompanied by a ritual hand washing and followed by the ceremonial donning of each successive garment, becomes a part of a ritualized "preparation rite" before Mass. Each item of liturgical vesture was accompanied by a specific prayer (two, on occasion); these prayers were called *vesting prayers*. Clearly, the preparation for the celebration of the liturgy, especially the Mass, was an important moment in medieval spirituality; the sacredness of these celebrations was enhanced by the use of specialized clothing, or vestments.

The major vestments of medieval Western Christianity can be listed according to status. The *alb*, a long, white undertunic, the *amice*, a white linen neckpiece or kerchief, and the *cincture*, a linen cord used to belt the alb around the waist, were the liturgical undergarments common to most clerical ranks. The *stole*, a longer ornamented strip of cloth worn by priests around the neck as a scarf might be, was eventually reserved to those in priestly orders; those in deacon's orders also wore a stole, but draped over the left shoulder and across the chest, the ends tied together at the right hip.

Other vestments were then layered over these, especially for the celebration of the Eucharist (or Mass). The *tunicle* was an overtunic with sleeves, usually rather plain and often reserved for the subdeacon; the *dalmatic* was a more ornate overtunic, again with sleeves, worn by the deacon; and the *chasuble* was the vestment reserved for the priest (or bishop), more like a poncho than a coat, sleeveless, with an opening for the head. The folds of the garment would be draped over the arms; later, the girth of the chasuble would be reduced, and it would resemble a signboard worn front and back more than a poncho or rain cape. Finally came the *maniple*, a small loop of cloth worn over the left wrist, much as a waiter might drape a small napkin or towel over one arm.

Other vestments might be worn by the bishop: the *mitre* (or *miter*), a roughly triangular hat or headpiece of varying height or design; the *pallium*, a white, Y-shaped band of cloth draped across the shoulders; liturgical gloves; the episcopal ring; and in some cases, special liturgical shoes and stockings. Bishops would also wear other insignia of office, for example, a large cross on a chain hung around their necks, the pectoral cross, and carry a decorated staff of office originally shaped like a shepherd's crook, called a *crosier*.

Certain vestments were worn during liturgical celebrations outside the Mass: the *cope*, a kind of heavy decorated cape; the *surplice*, resembling a shorter version of the alb that came to be worn by servers and singers as well, over the long-sleeved gown or tunic (often, but not exclusively, black) known as the *cassock*; and, especially in England, the *tippet*, a kind of heavy woolen stole (usually black) worn by clergy during the Divine Office originally for warmth.

Some of the outer pieces of vesture, for example, the stole, the dalmatic, the chasuble, and the cope, were made of heavier materials than the linen alb and amice. They were also fabricated in various liturgical colors, often with decoration such as bands of fabric down the sides or middle, and later, pictorial representations (especially on the chasuble and cope) of religious persons or themes. Various colors came to be associated with (and later, standardized for) certain liturgical seasons or feasts, and the outer vestments would be made of these colors: violet or purple for penitential occasions or Lent (and Advent, in some places); white or gold for great feasts and their seasons (Easter or Christmas, for example); red for feasts of martyrs, the Cross, or the Holy Spirit (and so, for ordinations as well); green for ordinary days and seasons, known as *ferial* time. Other colors were used more rarely: rose was used twice a year, on the third Sunday of Advent and the fourth Sunday of Lent, to signify the anticipation of the festive joy to come; blue was used in some areas for Advent or feasts of the Blessed Virgin Mary; black was the color assigned for funerals and other Masses in memory of the dead.

In the Catholic tradition, these medieval vestments and their accompanying prayers were used until the reforms of Vatican II. A few of the liturgical vestments were dropped (for example, the maniple), while others have changed slightly (the thickness of the alb, or the fullness of the chasuble) or have been made optional (the amice). Some of the liturgical colors have also become optional (black, for example). By and large, however, most of these vestments are still used by Catholics and a few other Christian churches.

However, other Christian traditions dropped the use of certain liturgical vestments (and their accompanying prayers) much earlier, as part of the Protestant Reformation of the sixteenth century. Ministers in most of the Protestant churches (or denominations) preferred to wear the black gown of the academic teacher as a preaching gown, rejecting the "priestly/mediator" role of ministry emphasized by Catholics. Today, however, some Protestant churches are reviving the use of certain liturgical vestments, often the alb and the stole, for use during sacramental celebrations. Eastern churches use vestments similar to some of those of the Roman Catholic tradition, with a few exceptions; for example, the *epimanika*, or special decorated cuffs for the sleeves of the Eastern alb (or *sticharion*).

Joanne M. Pierce

See also ACOLYTE; BISHOP (ORDINARY); EUCHARIST; LITURGICAL YEAR; MASS; ORDAINED MINISTRIES, SACRAMENT OF; PRIESTHOOD.

VETUS LATINA (VERSION OF THE BIBLE)

The "Old Latin" version of the Bible, a Latin translation consisting of various Latin translations of the Old Greek or Septuagint. The Vetus Latina included the New Testament as well as the Old Testament. The Vetus Latina included various Latin translations of the Greek that varied from each other and that were produced in different parts of the western Roman Empire. Fragments of the Old Latin remain in existence and are important in the textual criticism of the Septuagint. Of the forms of the Vetus Latina known from antiquity, one of the more important for textual criticism is the Italian version known as the Itala; this is also the version favored by Augustine.

Russell Fuller

VÉVÉ

See GROUND PAINTING (IN AFRICAN AND AFRO-LATIN RELIGIONS).

VIA CRUCIS

See STATIONS OF THE CROSS.

VIA ILLUMINATIVA

The Latin expression for the second of the three classical stages or degrees of the interior life. The first is called the way of purgation ("via purgativa") and the third the way of union ("via unitiva"). During the "illuminative" stage, in which the individual demonstrates a growing proficiency in spiritual matters, prayer is increasingly marked by periods of silence in which the individual relishes spiritual insight without first having to engage in a great deal of mental exercise. At the same time, individuals begin to feel a certain estrangement from their customary way of relating to God, or of imagining the presence of Jesus; they experience a growing dissatisfaction with Gospel scenes that might once have proven very consoling. Like Mary Magdalene, they want to hold onto the familiar Jesus, but he seems to be withdrawing from them in order that he might be rediscovered in a new way (John 20:11-18). It is a time of testing for the imagination, although it can also be a time of inner tranquility and "enlightenment."

But the dynamics of the three stages concern more than prayer itself. Any development of the interior or spiritual life will have an impact on the other areas of our lives, and vice versa. Moral development, emotional maturity and human sexuality, interpersonal relationships, the life of the mind, self-knowledge, and prayer as a function of one's relatedness to God are all interconnected. Hence, the second stage remains an artificial construct unless it takes into account development in all the major areas of our lives. Conversely, "illumination" regarding prayer should translate into an ongoing transformation in the way we think, act, decide, and relate to others.

William Reiser, S.J.

See also ASCETICAL THEOLOGY; ASCETICISM/ASCETIC; CONTEMPLATION; MEDITATION (CHRISTIAN); PERFECTION; VIA PURGATIVA; VIA UNITIVA.

VIA NEGATIVA

The "negative way" or the "way of negation" is the term traditionally used to describe the experience of what God is not. One's awareness of divine transcen-

dence, or of God's unfathomable love, reveals the inadequacy of all human images and vocabulary to talk about God meaningfully. The individual who finds himself or herself along the "negative way" does not reject the need or the possibility of making statements about God, but realizes acutely the enormous differential between the holy mystery of God and all human concepts.

Although *via negativa* points to the limitations of human speech and thought and to our ignorance when it comes to the being of God, the spiritual impulse behind this "way" is basically positive. That is, the *via negativa* lands one in the inscrutability of Love itself, in that "unitive loving" that marks the summit of religious experience.

Some of the spiritual writers usually associated with the *via negativa* are Gregory of Nyssa, Dionysius the Areopagite, Julian of Norwich, and Meister Eckhart. The same "negative" reserve appears sometimes in the theological writing of Karl Rahner.

William Reiser, S.J.

See also APOPHATIC THEOLOGY; CONTEMPLATION; DARK NIGHT OF THE SOUL; DIONYSIUS THE AREOPAGITE (PSEUDO); ECKHART, J. (MEISTER); GREGORY OF NYSSA; JULIAN OF NORWICH; MEDITATION (CHRISTIAN); MYSTICISM/MYSTICS (IN CHRISTIANITY); PRAYER; VIA UNITIVA.

VIA PURGATIVA

The Latin expression for the way of purgation. Together with the illuminative way ("via illuminativa") and the unitive way ("via unitiva"), these "ways" mark traditionally recognized stages in the development of the interior life. The first and second stages can be of varying lengths of time, and even after the achievement of the unitive (or "perfective") stage, an individual may at times experience the dynamics of the early stages over again, although always from a different standpoint. While the stages relate primarily to the manner of one's prayer, they actually embrace the whole of one's interior life.

The purgative stage is characterized by the purification of heart, mind, and soul we normally associate with conversion and repentance. Life according to the Gospel requires many changes. Initially, despite the hard work of learning to think and act according to Gospel values, the individual is supported by a joy and excitement that make the new burden seem light (Matt 11:30). Prayer at this stage is heavily marked by the activity of thinking and considering, for the mind needs to discover and to trust the truth of God's word. A great deal of purification occurs as the old self dies and the new self is born. It must be stressed, however, that the three classical stages are descriptive rather than prescriptive. They provide ways of mapping religious experience, but they should not be regarded as universal laws of the spiritual life. Contemporary spiritual writing is less likely to draw on the classical "ways" and more inclined to take into account psychological approaches to faith development.

William Reiser, S.J.

See also ASCETICAL THEOLOGY; ASCETICISM/ASCETIC; CONTEMPLATION; MYSTICISM/MYSTICS (IN CHRISTIANITY); PERFECTION; PRAYER; VIA UNITIVA.

VIATICUM

Viaticum (from the Latin word referring to money or food for a journey) is the term in Christian liturgical use to refer to Communion administered to the dying.

In antiquity, it was considered important for those on the point of death (thus, seriously ill) to die with the Eucharist in their mouths (usually in the form of consecrated bread, sometimes dipped in consecrated wine, although consecrated wine could also be administered using a special Communion straw). In antiquity, the Viaticum was considered the most important element in the rites for the dying; anointing (and prayer for healing) was more generally administered to anyone who was ill. However, during the medieval period, the focus of the rites of the dying shifted from the reception of last Communion to confession of sins and absolution. The anointing of the sick also gradually came to be reserved for those who were seriously ill or in danger of death, and took on a more penitential theme. Viaticum was still administered if possible, but it was no longer considered the most important of the final rites. Today, in some Christian traditions (for example, Catholicism), Communion is generally brought to the sick either at home or in the hospital, and may be administered by a lay minister as well as by a priest or deacon.

Joanne M. Pierce

See also ANOINTING OF THE SICK (SACRAMENT OF); BURIAL (IN CHRISTIANITY); COMMUNION (LITURGICAL); DEATH (CHRISTIAN); EUCHARIST; MASS; UNCTION.

VIA UNITIVA

The Latin expression for the way of union or the unitive way, the third of the classical stages in the ascent to Christian perfection. In the unitive stage, individuals experience a deep, abiding and frequently wordless union with God. A sense of God's presence as love pervades the whole of their lives. They have an immediate, nondiscursive awareness of God's presence and action in the world. As a result of their contemplative oneness with the mystery of God, they become compassionate, as God is compassionate (Luke 6:36), and can even love their enemies (Matt 5:44). In short, they are capable of living the Gospel perfectly.

While the unitive stage might be described as being fully in love with God, one should not think of this union in romantic or emotional terms. To know oneself grasped by God is to experience a "harsh and dreadful love." The unitive way might also be seen as the way of humility and wisdom, for in this stage a person comprehends almost intuitively why Christ crucified is the power of God and the wisdom of God (1 Cor 1:24). Today, one would add that profound union with God in Christ is not possible apart from solidarity with the crucified peoples of the world.

William Reiser, s.j.

See also CHARITY; HOLINESS/SANCTITY (IN CHRISTIANITY); MYSTICISM/MYSTICS (IN CHRISTIANITY); PRAYER; VIA PURGATIVA.

VICAR

From a Latin word that literally means "substitute," the term is now used in several related senses. (1) It refers to parish priests in many Anglican Churches. (2) It also refers to officials in Catholic and Anglican dioceses who act as delegates of the bishops in certain jurisdictions within the dioceses. A "vicar general," consequently, is delegated to act in the entire diocese. (3) In the Catholic Church a "vicar apostolic" is a missionary bishop in territories where a local episcopate has not been established yet. (4) The popes have used the formal title "Vicars of Christ" since the thirteenth century, but before they were commonly known only as "Vicars of Peter."

Orlando Espín

See also ANGLICAN COMMUNION; BISHOP (EPISCOPACY); CLERGY; DIOCESE/ARCH-DIOCESE; MISSIONS; POPE; PRIESTHOOD; ROMAN CATHOLIC CHURCH; SECULAR CLERGY.

VICARIATE, APOSTOLIC
See PRELATURE.

VICARIOUS SUFFERING
Generally, refers to any suffering done by one person because of, or on behalf of another. In theology, it refers to the suffering of Jesus on behalf of sinners. Christian interpretation of the Garden of Eden story holds that suffering and death are not originally intended by God, but are the result of human sin (disobedience of God's will). On this understanding, the suffering of Jesus, who was sinless, is explained as suffering and death on behalf of, in the place of, sinful humankind. The principal New Testament image for this understanding is that of Jesus as the *lamb* (John 1:29; Mark 14:12 [note the parallel to the Passover lamb in John 19:33, 36]) who, though blameless (1 Pet 1:19), takes upon himself the sins of the people to heal and free them (Matt 8:17; 1 Pet 2:24-25).

Also in scriptural tradition is the notion that Christians themselves can suffer for other Christians, or for the world. This suffering is not just that of empathy or concern (2 Cor 11:28-29), but is actually liberating and redemptive (1 Cor 4:12, 15)—a sharing in the redemptive suffering of Christ (Col 1:24).

G. Simon Harak, s.j.

VICAR OF CHRIST

Since the thirteenth century, only the pope uses the title "Vicar of Christ" to indicate that responsibility for the care of the entire church that was given to the papacy when Jesus said to Peter, "Feed my lambs . . . Feed my sheep" (John 21:16-17). The title first appears in the third century, but at least through the eleventh century was used by bishops, by kings, and by emperors, as well as by the pope. Pope Innocent III (1198–1216) first claimed the title exclusively for the papacy, replacing the common earlier papal title of "Vicar of Peter."

Gary Macy

See also INNOCENT III, POPE; PAPACY/ PAPAL; VICAR OF PETER.

VICAR OF PETER

The importance in Christianity of keeping a record of the succession of leaders of the Christian community dates back at least to the second century. In this sense, the *episkopos* of Rome was considered to be the successor of Peter, considered along with Paul as the founder of the Roman community. The title became a common title for the Bishop of Rome as pope and some of the popes wrote as if they were the present embodiment of Peter. This title was particularly important to Leo I in the fourth century, Gregory I in the fifth and sixth centuries and, much later, to Gregory VII in the eleventh century. The title was replaced by the stronger title, "Vicar of Christ" in the thirteenth century by Innocent III.

Gary Macy

See also GREGORY I THE GREAT, POPE; GREGORY VII, POPE; INNOCENT III, POPE; LEO I THE GREAT, POPE; PAPACY/ PAPAL; PETER; PETRINE MINISTRY; VICAR OF CHRIST.

VICE

Simply put, vice is a bad habit, things one consistently and repeatedly does and/or feels that are morally bad. Thomas Aquinas suggests (*ST* I–II q. 71), that vice is the opposite of virtue. That has been mistakenly understood to mean that characteristics of virtue (rationality, intentionality, choice, purposefulness, and so on) are also present in vice; that is, that a person is rationally and purposefully choosing to act or feel in a particular, morally evil manner. In fact, however, the dynamics of vice are to remove rationality and choice. Rather, it seems that vice takes over the person's personality and character, and it is in *that* way that Thomas's statement on vice is best understood. If we can understand virtue as a growing spiral, always increasing the capacity of the Christian character to receive and minister the love of God, then vice is the opposite: human nature is ever-more constricted by vice, character is ever-more deformed, even the body is ever-more disfigured—all with the result that the light of God in the self is more and more obscured.

The anomaly of vice seems to be its compelling, yet involuntary nature. Often the person does not wish to do the vicious action, yet feels captured, compelled, forced by the vice. No matter how often the person "makes up his or her mind" to stop, he or she keeps returning to the vicious practice. The vice seems to "take over" the will of the person, at least at times, and so the person is less of a moral agent. The classic Scriptural text for that dynamic is found in Paul's letter to the Romans 7:15-25 that reads in part, "I cannot explain what is happening to me, because I do not do what I want, but on the contrary, the very things I hate. . . . I am not the one striving toward evil, but it is sin, living in me. . . . I can want to do what is right, but I am unable to do it. In fact I do not do the good I want, but the evil I hate. . . ." Classical Greek authors such as Aristotle also spoke about vice (*Eudemian Ethics*), usually in oblique conjunction with their discussions of virtue. In the *Nicomachean Ethics*, Aristotle stated the final classical position on vice: that it was possible to get into a vice, but not possible to get out of it. It was, he said, like throwing a stone in a pond. You had some control over the beginning of the action, but none once it was in progress. You could not be recalled from a vice any more than a stone could be recalled once it had been thrown.

An intriguing description of that struggle to emerge from vice is found in Augustine's *Confessions*. There Augustine describes his personal failure to muster the power to overcome his life of worldly attachments. At a certain point, however, he reports that God intervened and rescued him. The *Confessions* demonstrate, then, that one *can* emerge from vice, but only with the help of a greater-than-human power. It is exactly that power, however, that is made available to us by God in Jesus. Thus the Christians had a way to change the classical paradigm of vice as inescapable and, after Augustine, had a way to articulate that liberation.

This writer submits that the best modern analogue for classical category of vice is the notion of *addiction*. When one studies the dynamics of addiction to alcohol or drugs, to work or TV, to psychic states or to violence, one understands very well the characteristics of vice as described in this article. To understand, for example, the loss of agency (or choice) characteristic of vice, consider the common-language explanation of an active alcoholic's verbal attacks: "That was the drink talking." On the positive side, programs based on Alcoholics Anonymous (commonly called Twelve-Step Programs), such as Al-Anon (for families and/or friends caught in the alcoholic's disease), Coke-Anon, Overeaters Anonymous (for people fighting eating disorders), Parents Anonymous (for those who find themselves in "the hitting habit"), SLA (for those who struggle with sexual disorders), and so on, all rely on an admission that the addiction has got the better of the person, and that the only way to emerge is to rely on a higher power for rescue.

In the area of social justice, Judith Kay proposes an intriguing modern thesis, describing oppressive *systems* as vicious, studying their deformative impact on the character of those oppressed, and suggesting ways of emergence, based on Thomistic analysis.

G. Simon Harak, s.j.

See also VIRTUE.

VICO, GIOVANNI BATTISTA (1668–1744)

Italian philosopher and jurist, educated in Jesuit schools and at the University of Naples, where he became a professor in 1697. Vico is probably one of the first to reflect on a philosophy of history, defending historical thinking and study against Descartes' attacks. Vico tried to philosophically justify the methods of historical research and distinguish them from the methods of mathematics and natural sciences. He drew distinctions between knowledge and understanding, and between the ways of acting and thinking of ancient peoples and those of modern ones. His reflections on historical, juridical, and cultural development were clearly ahead of his time. Vico's theories became very influential and important during the nineteenth century, while the depth and accuracy of many of his insights still amaze today's scholars. Vico's fundamental publication was his *Principles of a New Science about the Common Nature of Nations* (1725; enlarged in 1730).

Orlando Espín

See also CULTURE; DESCARTES, RENÉ; ENLIGHTENMENT IN WESTERN HISTORY; HISTORICAL CONSCIOUSNESS; HISTORICAL CRITIQUE; HISTORY; MODERNISM; MODERNITY; POSTMODERNITY; RATIONALISM; SOCIETY OF JESUS.

VICTIM

In recent Christian ethics, those who are denied bodyright, the right of control over their bodies. For example, to name just a few instances: bodyright is denied children in relation to the so-called property rights of parents; it is denied women in terms of sexual and reproductive rights and the right to be free from abuse; and employees are denied bodyright in relation to the employer's temporary ownership of the bodyself as a worker. There is profound silence in traditional Christian ethics concerning these forms of violence and denial of bodyright.

Those who have survived severe violation of bodyright, especially regarding sexual abuse, are called survivors rather than victims in an effort to acknowledge persons as moral agents and active subjects in their own lives. Moving our culture toward more respect for bodyright will require fundamental social (including religious), political, and economic change.

Mary E. Hobgood

See also FREEDOM; SEXISM; SLAVERY; WORK/EMPLOYMENT.

VICTIM (BIBLICAL)

In the sacrificial system of ancient Israel as described in the Old Testament, both animals and produce could be sacrificed to God for various reasons. The animal so sacrificed is designated the "victim." This term is derived from Latin *victima* and thus does not reflect a Hebrew term or native category.

Russell Fuller

VIEIRA, ANTONIO (1608–97)

Portuguese missionary in Brazil, and member of the Society of Jesus (Jesuits). Vieira spent fifty-two years of his long life in Brazil, mostly in Bahia. He has been accused of compromising the independence of his pastoral work by his unquestioning acceptance of the morality of the colonial enterprise. In his defense it must be argued that during the seventeenth century there was little room allowed for ecclesiastical independence or questioning in colonial Brazil. Vieira went to his mission in the midst of general Portuguese euphoria at the restoration of the monarchy. The shadow of this event (and of the immensely popular, widespread, and grandiose claims about Portugal's role in God's plans) were to shape his thought and his work, as well as the whole of Brazilian colonial society. His theology, therefore, was nationalistic and "messianic." The driving principle of his thought was his belief in and commitment to the claim that God had indeed chosen Portugal as the means through which to finally establish God's reign on earth. His writings attempted to justify and prove this theologically and biblically. Vieira's well-known defense of the natives and of the African slaves must be placed in his theological and national contexts. He is very important in the construction of the history of Catholic Christianity's relationship to slavery. His more important theological works are *História do futuro* (1656) and *Clavis prophetarum* (1660).

Orlando Espín

See also LATIN AMERICAN CATHOLICISM; LATIN AMERICAN THEOLOGIES; MISSIONARIES; MISSIONS; REIGN OF GOD; SLAVERY; SOCIAL JUSTICE; SOCIETY OF JESUS; UTOPIA.

VIGIL

From the Latin *vigilia*, meaning "watch." A period of anticipation before a celebration, usually marked by asceticism and prayer. Vigils are usually celebrated after sundown on the preceding day. According to the Western way of viewing time, the vigil begins on the day before the actual celebration. In the Hebrew system, however, that reckons days from sunset to sunset (see Lev 23:32), the vigil occurs on the feast itself. The Roman Liturgy includes four types of vigils. (1) *Vigils of annual feasts.* The Easter Vigil, with its new fire, readings from the entire history of salvation, and rites of initiation, is often called the "Mother of All Vigils." This is because it ushers in the greatest of all feasts. Special liturgical texts are also provided for the Vigils of Christmas and Pentecost, in the Liturgy of the Hours, the Sacramentary, and the Lectionary. (2) *Vigils of Sunday.* A Mass celebrated on any Saturday evening, using the liturgical texts of the next day, constitutes a vigil of the Sunday. It is the first celebration of the day and satisfies the Sunday obligation (Can. 1248). (3) *Vigils celebrated in anticipation of special events in the life of a person or the entire church.* The prayer service in the presence of a body on the night before the funeral, for example, is called a "Vigil for the Deceased" (see the *Order of Christian Funerals,* nos. 51–97). The nature of vigils as a time of prayerful watching and waiting is summarized well in the funeral rite's description of the Vigil for the Deceased. "At the vigil the Christian community keeps watch with the family in prayer to the God of mercy and finds strength in Christ's presence" (no. 56). (4) *Vigils in the Liturgy of the Hours.* In some monastic communities, the first Office of a day is called "Vigils." It is celebrated in the night, well before sunrise. This service is also called Matins, and follows the pattern of the Office of Readings in the Roman Liturgy of the Hours. The Office of Readings, however, even though it can be celebrated in the night as a vigil, is equally suited for other times of the day.

Patrick L. Malloy

See also CANDLES, LIGHTING OF; EASTER TRIDUUM; LITURGY OF THE HOURS; RITES OF CHRISTIAN INITIATION (RCIA).

VIGILIUS OF ROME

Pope from 537 until 555. Vigilius was born of a noble Roman family and nominated as his successor by Pope Boniface II. The nomination, however, was declared uncanonical, and Vigilius took a position at the court in Constantinople. When Pope Sylverius was deposed by the Roman government in 537, Vigilius was appointed to take his place. Vigilius refused to support the emperor Justinian in the condemnation of the Three Chapters for which the Pope was called to Constantinople. There, Vigilius finally agreed to the uphold the condemnation. The Western bishops strongly objected to Vigilius's action, and the Pope was even excommunicated by a synod held in Carthage. Vigilius took back his condemnation of the Three Chapters and eventually fled Constantinople for Chalcedon. Vigilius refused to participate in or accept the decisions of the Council of Constantinople held in 553. When Justinian forbade the Pope to return to Rome unless he accept the council, Vigilius finally gave in but died on the return trip to Rome. The case of Vigilius was used as an argument against papal infallibillity during the First Vatican Council.

Gary Macy

See also INFALLIBILITY; JUSTINIAN; POPE; THE THREE CHAPTERS; VATICAN, FIRST COUNCIL OF THE.

VILNA GAON
See ELIJAH BEN SOLOMON.

VIMALAKIRTI
The Mahayana hero of the eponymous *Vimalakirti-Nirdesha Sutra* who demonstrates that the highest levels of spiritual accomplishment can be attained by a householder living in the world. In the text, Vimalakirti is identified as an advanced bodhisattva who humbles a succession of famous monks from the early Indic schools in doctrinal discussions. The text is written from the Madhyamaka perspective, and Vimalakirti is a master of dialectical argument; he wins a final argument with celestial bodhisattva Manjushri by maintaining silence, showing the "highest truth" of Buddhism to be empty (*shunya*) and quiescent.

As the embodiment of a married, well-traveled "man of the world" (described as having been merchant, physician, frequenter of bars and brothels), yet one who was still an advanced bodhisattva, Vimalakirti became a highly influential exemplar of "engaged Buddhists" who practiced while pursuing careers outside the monastery. This was an example that rang true, especially in the Ch'an/Zen

traditions. Vimalakirti and this text also found many sympathetic audiences in later eras due to his challenging the institutional monks' domination of the faith. It is also noteworthy that Vimalakirti rejects a common belief in innate female inferiority: in the text, a particularly patriarchal monk is humiliated after insulting a woman.

Todd T. Lewis

See also BODHISATTVA; MAHAYANA BUDDHISM.

VINAYA
The first collection of the early Buddhist canons that defined the rules of monastic life and their origins. All the early schools maintained their own *Vinayas*, although not all have survived. Each contains a version of the *pratimoksha*, a text recited each fortnight by every Buddhist sangha that summarizes all the rules to which monks and nuns vow obedience. The *Vinayas* also include rules that govern special assemblies of the community, and some provide additional material on their background, on Shakyamuni's biography, the great early monks, and the divisions between schools.

The *Vinayas* chart the development of a utopian, communal refuge offering the space and material support for the spiritual life. They also reveal the accommodations that made the Buddhist sangha the successful center of the Buddhist missions across Asia. The *Vinaya* enjoins democratic self-governing, autonomy to each sangha, including the resolution of disciplinary matters subject to interpretation; but it also recognizes the principle of seniority based on "time in the robes." The *Vinayas* also ordain patriarchal relations: Buddhist nuns (*bhikshunis*) also had a separate *Vinaya* that burdened them with additional rules, including the requirement of all nuns of whatever seniority deferring to every monk regardless of seniority. Although the Pali *Vinaya* is the only version fully translated into English, it should not be assumed as the normative recension for North India or Northern Buddhism, where the various Sarvastivadin versions were followed.

                                Todd T. Lewis

See also BUDDHISM; SANGHA; VINAYA PITAKA.

VINAYA PITAKA

A division in all the different versions of the earliest Buddhist canons that records the monastic rules as they evolved through cases presented to the Buddha and the stories he told to explain many circumstances.

                                Todd T. Lewis

See also BUDDHISM; VINAYA.

VINCENTIAN FATHERS

The Congregation of the Mission (C.M.) was founded in France by St. Vincent de Paul to evangelize the rural poor in 1625. Priests of that era provided for their own education and livelihood by means of obtaining benefices from wealthy families. Vincent served as chaplain and tutor to the family of Count de Gondi, general of the galleys. As Vincent ministered to the galley slaves and traveled the estates of the Gondis, he soon became aware of the appalling poverty, sickness, and ignorance of the rural and urban populations.

The dismal pastoral conditions spurred both Madame de Gondi and her husband to ask Vincent to give missions throughout their estates. He preached his first mission on January 25, 1617. He marked that sermon and mission as the beginning of his life's work.

By 1625, Vincent had gathered diocesan priests to assist him and established the base of his operations in Paris. By that time, Vincent had begun the establishment of "charities" wherever his priests preached missions. Vincent gathered the wealthy to assist in his efforts for the poor and sick, and recruited the widow Louise de Marillac le Gras to supervise the works of the ladies and the "charities."

As he expanded the role of Louise, Vincent turned to the formation of his "missioners" (secular priests who took simple vows). He collaborated with Pierre de Bérulle, his spiritual director, and Francis de Sales, in developing the Tuesday Conferences for clergy. These conferences proved pivotal in the ongoing education of diocesan clergy, since seminaries, as we know them today, did not exist. Vincent also gave ordination retreats to diocesan clergy as a form of education and spiritual formation for new priests.

Relocating to St. Lazare, the priests in France became known as Lazarists. In Vincent's lifetime, "Missioners" were already located throughout Europe, the British Isles, Africa, and preparing for work in the "New World." Father Felix De Andreis, of the Roman Province, brought the first Vincentians to the U.S. in 1815 to evangelize throughout the Louisiana Purchase. Vincentians soon established parishes among the poor and minority communities, as well as schools, seminaries, and colleges across the country. Of the remaining colleges and universities, De Paul University in Chicago, Niagara, in upper New York, and St. John's University, Long Island, maintain the Vincentian spirit of making academic and professional education attainable for all.

The American Vincentians have also opened missions in Panama, China, and Japan.

M. Jane Gorman

See also DE MARILLAC, LOUISE; DE PAUL, VINCENT; SEMINARY.

VINCENT OF LÉRINS

Died before 450. Very little is known of the life of the monk, Vincent. Originally a soldier, he became a monk at Lérins, where he was noted for his learning. Vincent is most famous for his *Memorial* (*Commonitorium*), a treatise that teaches how to distinguish between orthodoxy and heresy. Vincent's famous principle for determining orthodoxy states that what is to believed is what is held "everywhere, always and by everyone" (*Quod ubique, quod semper, quod ab omnibus*). This principle became particularly important during the Reformation, and has remained an important touchstone of orthodoxy since that time.

Gary Macy

See also HERESY; ORTHODOXY (IN CHRISTIANITY); REFORMATION.

VIPASHYANA/VIPASSANA

Term designating the uniquely Buddhist "mindfulness meditation" that focuses the mind on the essential nature of reality, personhood, and mortality. It is *vipashyana* (Pali, *vipassana*) meditation that is essential for an individual's cultivation of *prajna* ("insight"); since prajna is the capacity necessary for realizing enlightenment, vipashyana practice is at the heart of Buddhist spiritual culture oriented toward salvation.

Vipashyana practice includes a series of focal points: contemplation of the body (through breath, postures, body parts, four elements, and cemetery corpse contemplations), of feeling, mental states, and of mental contents. The meditation practice involves simple, careful noting of what appears ("bare attention"), then —when this is mastered—a calm assessment of the focal field ("clear comprehension") as impermanent, soul-less, and subject to suffering (according to the "three marks of existence"). Those who master vipashyana achieve an effortless concentration on these processes over long periods. The meditation makes good karma for the practitioner, ultimately making possible the ending of bondage to karma-producing actions, that is, realizing enlightenment.

Todd T. Lewis

See also BODHI; DHYANA; MEDITATION (CHRISTIAN); MERIT (PUNYA); NIRVANA; PRAJNA.

VIRGINAL CONCEPTION (BIBLICAL THEOLOGY)

"Virgin birth" is the most popular way to summarize the credal affirmation that Jesus was "conceived by the Holy Spirit and born of the Virgin Mary." "Virginal conception" more correctly conveys the essence of these beliefs.

In the New Testament, Matthew 2:18-25 and Luke 1:26-38 are the only passages suggesting that Jesus was not conceived by a human father. Attempts to identify implicit references to the virginal conception in verses such as Galatians 4:4-5, Mark 6:3, and others, impose a traditional belief into the silence of the texts. Matthew 1:23 cites Isaiah 7:14 from the Septuagint to claim that a virginal conception fulfilled prophecy. Although in the Septuagint the word *parthenos* literally means virgin, it is used to translate the Hebrew word *almah* that means a young woman of marriageable age. Nothing in the Old Testament or any other Jewish source suggests that the messiah would have a virginal conception. The belief originated before the modern understanding of chromosomes. Thus, while the idea of a virginal conception has always been paradoxical, the idea that Jesus could be fully human without having a human father was less challenging in the first century than it is today.

A close reading of the accounts in Matthew and Luke reveals conflicts between them. When these passages are juxtaposed to other passages in the Gospels, more questions surface. By focusing on particular parts of the narratives, some scholars suggest that historically, Jesus was the son of Joseph or that he was illegitimate, possibly conceived by rape. What must be recognized is that the biblical evidence is inconclusive (See Raymond E. Brown, *The Virginal Conception and Bodily Resurrection of Jesus* [Paulist, 1973]).

While Matthew and Luke certainly believed their traditions were historical, they were not really interested in Jesus' biological history. Their accounts were designed to establish that Jesus was God's Son from the very first moment of his existence. This insight represents a development of the more primitive ideas that Jesus was appointed Son of God after his resurrection and exultation (Rom 1:4) or that he was anointed Son of God at his baptism (Mark 1:9-11).

Regina A. Boisclair

See also VIRGINITY OF MARY (BIBLICAL THEOLOGY).

VIRGIN BIRTH

The virgin birth is a traditional teaching that proposes the conception and birth of Jesus to occur through the influence of the Holy Spirit without sexual intercourse. The theologoumenon originated in the patristic use of infancy narrative texts to clarify Jesus' relationship to the Logos. The teaching of the virgin birth served to emphasize the singular and miraculous character of the Incarnation. Two ideas, the virginal conception and painless birth that left Mary's biological virginity intact, emphasized the divine power in the Christ event. Assertions of Mary's lifelong virginity reinforced her role as Mother of God (*Theotokos*) emphasizing the divinity of Christ.

Theological speculation today has noted the problem of the ahistorical reading of Scripture and the theological anthropology that characterizes married life and birth in a negative light. Thus some analyses minimize the teaching or reinterpret it using modern human values. However, orthodox theologians such as Karl Barth insist on the veracity of the doctrine in order to uphold the divine character of revelation in history.

Patricia Plovanich

VIRGINITY

A virgin is someone who has never had sexual relations, and, according to some authors, has never consented to carnal desires in terms of thoughts and daydreams. Authors also distinguish the state of physical virginity from virginity in spirit or virginity of the heart: a virgin who is forcefully violated, they would argue, remains in the state of virginity because essentially we are dealing with a matter of spirit, affection, and will. While virginity can apply equally to men and women, the word "virgin" has more commonly referred to women.

Because the idea of virginity exalts a biological state, one sees in the background of its practice the influence of culture and society, as when single women are prized because they have never had sexual relations with a man, or when sexuality and the body itself are regarded as dangerous to the life of the soul. For that reason, virginity as a properly Christian state of life needs to be motivated by a desire for the kingdom of God (see Matt 19:10-12). As such, it is related to chastity and celibacy. Paul esteemed virginity over marriage, but that could be explained in terms of his expectation that the end of the age was at hand (1 Cor 7:25-40).

William Reiser, s.j.

See also CELIBACY; CHASTITY.

VIRGINITY OF MARY (BIBLICAL THEOLOGY)

Classical Christian creeds express the belief in Jesus' true humanity by stating he was: "born of the Virgin Mary." In the Catholic Church, this has been understood to mean that Mary remained a virgin throughout her life. Church formulations claim that the Mary was a virgin "before" (virginal conception), "during" (miraculous delivery), and "after" she gave birth to Jesus (perpetual virginity), although this doctrine has never been officially declared in a solemn, extraordinary way as an infallible truth. Among Protestants, the Mary's virginity is understood exclusively in terms of the virginal conception. Indeed, Matthew 1:25 seems to indicate that Mary and Joseph led a normal married life after his birth, and Luke 2:7 states that Jesus was Mary's "firstborn" son. Belief in Jesus' virginal conception is also a tenet of Islam.

Christians never questioned the virginal conception until biblical scholars recognized that the truth in the Gospels is not founded on their historical accuracy. Only Matthew 1:20-23 and Luke 1:26-38 suggest a virginal conception within infancy narratives (Matt 1–2; Luke 1–2) that are highly charged with symbolic imagery and have no impact on the rest of their respective Gospels. The ultimate intent of the idea of the virginal conception is to establish that Jesus was Son of God from the first moment of his human existence. However, the belief that Jesus is the Son of God has never been based on how he was conceived.

The New Testament states that Jesus was born (Matt 1:16, 18; 2:1; Luke 1:35; 2:7, 11; Gal 4:4; Phil 2:7). It assumes that there was nothing extraordinary about his birth. However, it was once believed that it was essential that Mary not have any physical effects from childbirth if her virginity were to remain unimpaired. Thus the idea that Mary remained a virgin "during" birth proposes that her womb was not opened by childbirth. Popular piety assumed that the birth was also a miraculous delivery and without pain. There is a significant christological problem with the idea that Jesus was not born in an ordinary manner since it calls into question his true humanity.

There is no biblical basis for the idea of Mary's perpetual virginity. "The Protevangelium of James," a noncanonical "gospel" from the mid-second to early third centuries, is the earliest extant evidence for the tradition of Mary's perpetual virginity. Since virginity was never an ideal in Israel, the legend that she made a vow of virginity as a child would have been inconceivable for a daughter of Israel even when Hellenistic influences were pervasive in the late postexilic period. In addition, it is impossible to ignore that there are references to Jesus' brothers and sisters (Matt 12:46; 13:55-6; Mark 3:31-32; 6:3; Luke 8:19-20; John 7:3, 5, 10;

Acts 1:14), or that Paul identifies James, one of the significant leaders of the early church in Jerusalem (Acts 12:17; 15:13; 21:18; 1 Cor 15:7; Gal 2:9), as "the brother of the Lord" (Gal 1:19). Catholics have considered these "brothers and sisters," cousins or the children of Joseph by a previous marriage. This interpretation stems from a need to accommodate the biblical texts to a nonbiblical tradition.

It is possible to consider the tradition of Mary's virginity in light of the prophetic idea of "Virgin Israel" (Jer 31:4; Amos 5:2, for example). Mary, thus becomes the embodiment of the ideal Israel within whose people Jesus was born as light to the nations. Such a typological interpretation is consistent with early Christian practices. It allows Mary as Virgin to remain a prototype for all Christians. It allows the advent of Jesus into human history as the incarnate Lord to reverberate within his kinship to the people of Israel. It also recognizes that the story of his biological origin are beyond confirmation. It also suggests that Mary is the incarnate "Virgin Israel," for no matter how Jesus was conceived, whether or not Mary had sexual relations, she is the daughter of Israel who gave birth to the Word made flesh.

Regina A. Boisclair

See also IMMACULATE CONCEPTION; MARIOLOGY; MARY OF NAZARETH; VIRGIN BIRTH; VIRGINAL CONCEPTION (BIBLICAL THEOLOGY).

VIRGINITY OF MARY (SYSTEMATIC THEOLOGY)

The virginity of Mary is a theologoumenon, a teaching that proposes Mary's virginal state at the time of Jesus' conception, during his birth and during Mary's entire life. The teaching that developed over several centuries of patristic speculation emphasizes the three stages of Mary's virginity or a lifelong virginity. Patristic speculation about the topic that emphasizes the Holy Spirit's creative role in Jesus' conception is linked to the affirmation of the Logos' divinity in the Incarnation. Later interest in the teaching seems to rest in the church's appraisal of the dedicated religious life, and of virginity and celibacy as choices for spiritual life that are superior to married life. Mary's virginity is then a symbol of the highest form of Christian life. Contemporary theology questions this tradition's reading of Scriptures and treats the topic within the framework of theological anthropology, not christology or spirituality. In this reflection, Mary's virginity can signify single-mindedness in God's service instead of affirming one form of Christian life over another.

Patricia Plovanich

VIRTUE

The word "virtue" comes to us through the Latin *virtus*, where it literally means "[manly] power." That Latin word was usually used to translate the Greek *aretē*, literally meaning "excellence," but has a long history of reflection behind it, from Socrates to Plato, Aristotle, and the Stoics. Hence the simple literal translation is not enough to convey the full meaning of the word. We can perhaps best define virtue as a habitual disposition to act and to be moved in the right way, at the right time, for the right reason, to the right extent, and toward the right person. Finding, defining, and practicing that "right way" is the subject of much investigation and debate.

Though the Scriptures have important notions like righteousness and covenant fidelity, neither the word "virtue," nor its philosophical implications are found in the Scripture, except after Greek thought has influenced the Testaments. The New Testament (which uses *aretē* only four times), especially in Paul, has lists of what we might call "virtues," (for example, in Gal 5:22-23; Rom 1:29-31, 2 Pet 1:5-7). It is important to note that these virtues were seen to be the effects of the action of the Holy Spirit upon the Christian's character, and not so much a result of the Christian's own effort. Beginning with the Apologists (Aristedes, Tertullian, Origen, and others), and especially with Lactantius, the early writers in the church began to employ the classical (Greek and Latin) category of virtue(s) to describe the characteristics of the Christian life. Especially congenial was the communitarian nature of virtue, because of the importance of the Christian community's self-understanding as the Body of Christ.

Classical thought considered two kinds of "excellences," intellective and moral. Intellective virtue were powers to excel at different pursuits, like academics, artistry, or crafts. This article, however, will concentrate more on moral virtue, since it figured much more prominently in Christian self-understanding.

The classical notion of moral virtue was involved with community/political life. A good community formed a virtuous man (the exclusionary term is intentional) whose character was that of a good citizen. One needed to be trained to choose the mean between two extremes as, for example, the virtue of courage was the mean between cowardice and foolhardiness. One did this by doing virtuous acts with the right intention (namely, to live a virtuous life), and in the way a virtuous man would do them. As one grew in virtue, one grew in empowerment, and

so was able to select or choose better and better actions and passions. The overall effect was a kind of a continuous positive moral feedback loop for the ethical man, an ever-growing spiral of empowerment and capability. The end ("telos"—a technical term) was to live, enjoy, and contemplate the virtuous life fully. Right actions and passions became "second nature" to the virtuous man. In his work, Paul Wadell, c.p., has reminded us that the ultimate *environ* for virtue in Aristotle was *friendship*.

When Augustine took over the classical notion of virtue, he insisted that Christians see their virtue as originating in the actions of God—hence his attention to "being moved," to *passions*, and to the empowerment of the *will* (this term, important to Christian thought, was very sparsely used in classical reflection). Also, the "telos" of virtue was eternal happiness with God in heaven. The governing virtue for the whole of Christian character was love. In both Lactantius and Augustine, it seems the ideal of classical virtue cannot be realized except in Christianity.

Gregory the Great stated that the "infused" virtues of faith, hope, and charity were necessary for salvation. By "infused," he meant they were unattainable by human effort (though of course they could, and must, be cooperated with), thus preserving the primacy of God's action in salvation. His work also stressed the four cardinal virtues (prudence, justice, fortitude (courage), and temperance), and the "unity of the virtues." His positions became accepted doctrine in the moral theology of the church.

The Scholastics were inheritors of two great traditions of reflection on the virtues: the church (mainly Augustine and Gregory), and the newly rediscovered texts of the Greek authors (especially Aristotle).

Hence their reflection on virtue was quite far-ranging and profound, epitomized in the writings of Thomas Aquinas.

In his *Summa Theologiae* (*ST*), Thomas built his consideration "Of Human Acts" around the notion of virtue. Thomas's reflection on virtue begins with his "Treatise on the Passions," the longest in the *ST* (I–II, q. 22-48). I submit that that is because Thomas wants to preserve the primacy of *receiving* God's grace (for which we are *in passion*), and because passions (like love), and the passion of Jesus, were so important in the Christian life. From there he moves to his discussion of *habit*. "Habit" is a very rich notion in Thomistic thought, meaning not only right dispositions gained by repetition, but also such things as perfections of capacities and choice, right ordering toward ends, and interrelationships in all their forms. After habit, Thomas discusses virtues, both acquired and infused. Once again, the effect of virtue in Thomas was an ever-increasing spiral of empowerment. But because of his grounding in passion, Thomas's spiral was an increasing of *capacity* as well. The "telos" of *that* growth was the capacity to be perfect friends of *God*. The name of that "friendship with God" was *caritas* (the Latin translation of the Greek *agapē*), and it was the form of all the virtues for Thomas.

In the late 1960s, Josef Pieper (*The Four Cardinal Virtues*), and Romano Guardini (*The Virtues: On Forms of Moral Life*), began reflecting again on the role of virtue in the Catholic tradition. The former relied on Thomas Aquinas to ground his reflections on virtue, the latter used a more phenomenological approach. For Karl Rahner, transcendental Thomist and one of the chief theologians of the twentieth century, Christian virtues were related to the grace of justification by God. They were moments of love, and "only distinguished from the grace which divinizes man's very being as its dynamic extension into his faculties" (*Sacramentum Mundi*, "Virtue," 337).

Beginning in the early 1970s with the writing of James Gustafson and Stanley Hauerwas, virtue ethics began enjoying a widespread revival in Christian ethics. The revival was helped by the enormous impact of Aladsair MacIntyre's *After Virtue* in the early 1980s. Though not a Christian work, *After Virtue* suggested that the classical category of virtue could not be practiced in our currently fractured world of moral discourse, but nevertheless was desperately needed. Since that time, many virtue ethicists like Diana F. Cates, Romanus Cessario, O.P., Judith Kay, Daniel M. Nelson, Jean Porter, Paul Wadell, C.P., and this writer, have all used Thomas Aquinas to frame their reflections on current issues.

G. Simon Harak, S.J.

See also CHARITY; FAITH; FORTITUDE; HOPE (IN CHRISTIANITY); HUMILITY (IN CHRISTIANITY); JUSTICE; PRUDENCE; TEMPERANCE; THEOLOGICAL VIRTUES.

VISHISHTADVAITA VEDANTA

A theistically oriented school of Hindu Vedanta, Vishishtadvaita (qualified nondualism) was systematized by the Vaishnava theologian Ramanuja (eleventh–twelfth centuries C.E.). This theologian was the first to successfully integrate Vaishnava devotionalism with the conservative, brahminical Vedanta tradition. Like other Vaishnavas, Ramanuja regards *bhakti* (devotion) as the surest path to God, but he identifies it with the Upanishadic concept of *upasana* (meditation) and, ultimately, with immediate knowledge (*jnana*) of Brahman. Brahman, the ultimate reality described in the Upanishads, he equates with Vishnu, the Supreme Being recognized by his tradition. Brahman thus is for him a loving personal deity, and he vehemently denies Advaita Vedanta's famous teaching that the Absolute is *nirguna*, attributeless. Ramanuja experiences God as thoroughly, and marvelously, *saguna*—possessed of innumerable auspicious attributes. Like Advaita Vedanta, Vishishtadvaita holds that nothing exists outside of Brahman, but Ramanuja's distinctive Qualified Nondualism is so called because, unlike the Advaita Vedanta, it accepts internal differences within Brahman, consisting especially of the world and the individual souls (*jivas*). The world is not merely an appearance supported by Brahman as its static ground, but rather a real transformation of Brahman. In a famous metaphor, Ramanuja declares that the world is the body of God and that God, in turn, is its soul. Alternately, he explains the world and the souls as qualifiers (*vishesha*) inseparably related to God, who is the qualified (*visheshya*), or as subordinate but inseparable parts or modes (*amsha, prakara*) of God, who is their center (*sheshin, prakarin*). In all of this, of course, God retains a transcendent dimension, so that Ramanuja's thought cannot be called pantheistic.

Ramanuja's most important work is the *Shribhashya*, his commentary on the *Brahma Sutras*. He is the leading *acharya* (preceptor) of the Shrivaishnava tradition of South Indian Vaishnavism. This denomination is distinctive in regarding the Tamil hymns of a series of twelve Vaishnava saints known as the Alvars, especially those of Nammalvar (a *shudra* by caste), as equal in authority to the Vedas.

Lance E. Nelson

See also ADVAITA VEDANTA; BHAKTI; DVAITA VEDANTA; HINDUISM; NIRGUNA BRAHMAN; UPANISHADS; VAISHNAVA; VALLABHA; VEDANTA; VEDAS; VISHNU.

VISHNU

One of the two great Gods of classical Hinduism, along with Shiva, Vishnu appears as a relatively unimportant deity in the *Rig Veda*, emerging as a major image of the Supreme Being only in the *Mahabharata* and the Puranas. Vishnu is known especially for his incarnations (*avataras*), of which the ten most important are listed as the *dashavatara* (ten incarnations). The most popular of these are Rama and Krishna, under which forms the deity is often worshiped, perhaps even more often than as Vishnu. Vishnu is depicted in myth and iconography as a divine monarch, seated regally and often accompanied by his consort, Shri or Lakshmi. Important Vaishnava (Vishnu-centered) movements include the South Indian Shrivaishnavas, the followers of Madhva in South and West India, and the Krishnaite Vallabha and Bengal Vaishnava traditions of North India. Vishnu is also commonly referred to as Narayana.

Lance E. Nelson

See also AVATARA/AVATAR; DVAITA VEDANTA; HARE KRISHNA MOVEMENT; HINDUISM; LINGA; SHAIVA; SHIVA; VAISHNAVA; VALLABHA.

VISION QUEST
See GUARDIAN SPIRIT.

VISIONS (IN CHRISTIAN MYSTICISM)
Spiritual writers have long noticed that certain interior events or experiences can accompany the development of a person's

prayer life or ascent to holiness. In the Christian contemplative tradition, visions have long been associated with the growth of the interior life as a type of spiritual illumination. The corresponding "audio form" of such an occurrence is called *locution*. Visions and locutions are probably best understood in terms of a doctrine of the "spiritual senses," as found, for instance, in the writing of Origen in the third century or Karl Rahner in the twentieth. Seeing and hearing, accordingly, would have both literal and metaphorical meanings.

Today, the study of such phenomena would have to be approached in terms of a psychology of religious experience, since one's experience of God can only occur within the limits and structures of the human psyche. People tend to distinguish visions from apparitions and private revelations. Visions refer to inner events, whereas apparitions have the semblance of being "out there." As its name implies, a private revelation is the disclosure of some truth to an individual, or to a group of individuals, the authenticity of which requires discernment in light of the Gospel. On the basis of Acts 2:17, we can probably posit a connection between vision and prophecy (see Paul's discussion of prophecy in 1 Cor 14 ["those who prophesy build up the church"]; the book of Revelation reflects a visionary experience that is also a prophetic message [Rev 1:1-3]). Whatever their origins in a believer's psyche, visions, at least within the New Testament, serve a church-building purpose. Theologically, a vision is a Spirit-prompted insight meant to guide Christian practice.

William Reiser, s.j.

See also APPARITIONS; ECSTASY; MYSTICISM/MYSTICS (IN CHRISTIANITY).

VITA

The word is Latin for "life," and refers to the story of a person's life, particularly a biography or autobiography. In the context of theological and religious study "vita" refers most often to the biography of a saint or other holy person. These biographies often have a particular literary form that concentrates more on miraculous happenings than on the historical facts of the subject's life.

Gary Macy

See also HAGIOGRAPHY.

VITORIA, FRANCISCO DE (1492–1546)

Spanish theologian, and member of the Dominican Order. Educated in Spain and France, Vitoria taught at the universities of Valladolid and Salamanca. The forerunner and founder of the very influential Salamanca school of theology, Vitoria's genius did much to make Salamanca one of Europe's best universities during the sixteenth century. Humanist, reformer, philosopher, eminent teacher, and theologian, Vitoria methodologically emphasized the study and interpretation of the Bible and of patristic literature in theology. He insisted that theological reflection had to focus on the burning issues of the day and not on sterile theoretical discussions. Familiar with the works of Peter Lombard and Thomas Aquinas, he was eloquent in his praise of Erasmus and in his defense of and admiration for Bartolomé de Las Casas. Vitoria's critique of and uneasiness with the Spanish conquest of the Americas (evidently influenced by Las Casas) made him reflect on the moral foundations of international relations, on the rights of native populations, and on the role of the natural law in the wider society of nations. He is frequently regarded as the "father" of international law. His theories on the possibilities of a just war were ahead of his time. Vitoria's many writings (usually revised and expanded versions of his university lectures) were published, in chaotic fashion, after his death. They have been gathered in three more orderly and recent collections, *Relecciones sobre indios, y sobre el derecho a la guerra* (1946), *Relecciones de Indias o libertad de los indios* (1967), and *Sentencias morales y sentencias de doctrina internacional* (1939–40).

Orlando Espín

See also AQUINAS, THOMAS, ST.; COUNTER-REFORMATION / CATHOLIC REFORMATION; DEVELOPMENT OF DOGMA / OF DOCTRINE; DOMINICANS; ERASMUS OF ROTTERDAM; ETHICS, SOCIAL; HUMANISM; JUSTICE; JUST WAR THEORY; LAS CASAS, BARTOLOMÉ DE; LATIN AMERICAN CATHOLICISM; MEDIEVAL CHURCH; MISSIONS; PATRISTICS / PATROLOGY; PETER LOMBARD; SOCIAL JUSTICE; THOMISM / TRANSCENDENTAL THOMISM.

VIVEKA

In the Vedanta school of Shankara (active around 800 C.E.), this is the power of discerning the real from the unreal in important soteriological domains: invisible spirit or Brahman from the visible world, the true self (*atman*) from the transient body, truth from falsity, and reality from illusion (*maya*). In his *Vivekachudamani*, Shankara describes developing this human faculty of discrimination as the central task in the spiritual life; he calls it the "crown jewel" of successful salvation practice. It is through the ascetic discipline of jnana yoga that this can be achieved.

Todd T. Lewis

See also JNANA; SHANKARA; YOGA.

VIVEKANANDA, SWAMI (1863–1902)

An important nineteenth-century Hindu spiritual leader and reformer, Swami Vivekananda was the leading disciple of Sri Ramakrishna. Unlike Ramakrishna, Vivekananda was well educated and articulate, and thus well qualified for what became his life's mission: to spread the message of his master to all of India and indeed the rest of the world. He became the first important Hindu teacher to visit the West, undertaking several visits to North America and Europe, the first as a delegate to the First World Parliament of Religions held in Chicago in 1893. In the West, he founded the Vedanta Society (1895) to propagate the teachings of Ramakrishna and his own activist interpretation of Advaita Vedanta. His success in the West gained him great respect in India, were he founded the Ramakrishna Order and Ramakrishna Mission (1897). Convinced of the spiritual superiority of Hinduism but impressed by the technical and social achievements of the West, Vivekananda was possibly the first to propagate the idea that the West needs India's deep spirituality while India needs the West's scientific prowess. In India, Vivekananda was responsible for introducing an active concern for social welfare work into the lives of Hindu monastics and devout laity; this was an aspect of the religious life on which Hinduism had previously placed little emphasis.

Lance E. Nelson

See also HINDUISM; RAMAKRISHNA, SRI.

VIVES, JUAN LUIS (1492–1540)

Spanish humanist, philosopher, and educator. Vives was born in Valencia of Jewish parents converted to Christianity, and educated in Spain and France. He lived in several European countries, especially England (where he taught Mary Tudor) and Belgium. A close friend of Erasmus, he shared the latter's mistrust of speculative theologies and support for biblical and patristic studies. Critical of much in the church of his day, Vives remained a Catholic layman. He struggled to promote European unity in a century of deep disunity by constantly proposing and defending the middle ground in most controversies. His friendship with Thomas More is well documented. Vives became increasingly disgusted with the relentlessly strident ambience of his day, and so he resigned his professorship in Belgium and retired to private life. His reflections centered on ethics, education, political philosophy, and spirituality. Among his many books are *De disciplinis* (1531), *De anima et vita* (1538), and *De veritate fidei christianae* (published in 1543, after his death).

Orlando Espín

See also COUNTER-REFORMATION/ CATHOLIC REFORMATION; ERASMUS OF ROTTERDAM; HUMANISM; LAITY; MORE, THOMAS; PATRISTICS/PATROLOGY; REFORMATION.

VOCATION

Vocation is the term often used to denote a calling by the Spirit to a specific way of life. While one may speak of a "vocation" to marriage or to a single way of life, ordinarily "vocation" refers to a person's being attracted to religious life or to ordained ministry. When a person responds to that attraction and embraces the life of the vows or ministry in the church, vocation (being "called") takes the form of mission (being sent). If vocation is the calling itself, then mission can be seen as the faithful living out of that calling or impulse from the Spirit.

Scripture contains many well-known call stories, such as God's calling of Abraham (Gen 12:1-3), Moses (Exod 3), and the various prophets (for example, Isa 6; Jer 1:4-10; Amos 7:14-15). Some writers regard Jesus' baptism in the Jordan as the moment of his calling, and the Gospels report the disciples' being called by Jesus to be his followers and companions, while Paul refers to his "vocation" to be an apostle (Rom 1:1; 1 Cor 1:1). The miraculous aspects of the call stories sometimes mislead people into expecting that every genuine vocation ought to be accompanied by special signs such as inner voices, revelations, dramatic confirmations, and so forth. In the Gospel call stories, for instance, these signs take the form of amazing catches of fish (Luke 5:1-11; John 21:1-8), or special illuminations (John 1:43-51); in Acts 9, the form is a heavenly voice.

But the mystery surrounding vocation is not a matter of miraculous confirmations. Rather, the mystery consists of the graced interaction of the Spirit's call and deep human desire for freedom and life. For men and women cannot be called to something they really do not want; call and desire are correlative. Thus, one can say that the heart's desire itself, taking shape from countless influences and experiences in our lives, is as much a grace as the actual events, people, or circumstances through which that desire is awakened and takes on clear definition. Ultimately, there is but one vocation all Christians share by virtue of their baptism, namely, the call to holiness or the fullness of life in the Spirit (see Eph 4:1-6).

William Reiser, s.j.

See also HOLINESS/SANCTITY (IN CHRISTIANITY); MINISTRY/MINISTERIAL; SPIRIT.

VODOUN

A Haitian religion of African roots, also present in the Dominican Republic, and in the United States. There are small Vodoun communities in Cuba, Brazil, and Jamaica. Vodoun (perhaps "Vodou" or "Vaudu," but certainly not "Voodoo") is a descendant of the traditional religion of the Fon people of ancient Dahomey (present-day Republic of Benin). Some ten to twelve million believers follow Vodoun today.

The magical rites present in New Orleans and other Gulf coast areas in the U.S., although claiming the religion's name for themselves, are not legitimately Vodoun. At most, these American practices are vestiges and ritual remnants of what might historically have been (during the French period) Vodoun roots. Furthermore, Vodoun is not to be confused with Umbanda, Palo Mayombe, Candomblé, or Santería.

The conditions of slavery forced significant modifications and simplifications of the ancestral Fon religion, ultimately leading to today's religion. There are some legends that place the birth of Vodoun in the early period of Haiti's struggle for abolition and independence from France; but in fact the religion was well on its way to its present form before the end of the eighteenth century.

There are at least two major types of Vodoun in Haiti—Radá and Petrô. In the Dominican Republic (that shares the island of Hispaniola with Haiti), both these types coexist with a simpler form native to this Spanish-speaking nation. Within Vodoun there are still smaller groupings, as well as communities that celebrate the Gagá during Lent and Holy Week. However, traditional, or "standard," Vodoun is usually associated with Haiti's Radá.

Voduists or Voduisants (both terms correctly refer to the followers of Vodoun) are usually baptized in the Catholic Church that has traditionally been the dominant religion in Haiti. But their membership in the Catholic Church has never proven to be an obstacle or difficulty to their equally sincere participation in Vodoun. The church, however, has been historically and theologically emphatic in its opposition to Vodoun.

Vodoun believes in only one God, whom it calls Bondyé (the Creole language rendering of the French words *"Bon Dieu"*— "good God"). Bondyé is omnipotent and all-knowing, dwells in the skies, and is pure spirit. Bondyé is the source and the goal of all that exists, and will ultimately make justice and goodness prevail. But, for now, Bondyé (also called "Great Teacher," "Gran Met") seems to have left the daily affairs of this world in the hands of the *loás* (literally, the "venerable ones").

The *loás* are spirits, manifestations of Bondyé. They are present everywhere, see all things, know all things, and direct the course of all things. Many are, in fact, the ancestral Fon divinities of Africa, but others are the result of Fon adaptations and creativity in Haiti (at times reflecting social formations and needs). There are numerous *loás*—the important ones are always remembered and worshiped, while some are simply forgotten and new ones discovered. All *loás* are grouped into four pantheons called *nanchóns* because of the characteristics they display when relating to the Voduisants. The *nanchóns* are named Radá, Petrô, Kongo, and Ibo— not to be identified with geographical or ethnic locations. Radá and Petrô are the two more important pantheons and, in very general and imprecise terms, they can be distinguished by their *loás'* inclination to do good (Radá) or to do evil (Petrô). All *nanchóns*, however, are ultimately subject (like all humanity is) to Bondyé's might, goodness, and justice.

The *loás* are a constant, daily presence in the life of every Voduisant. Nothing is done without their permission. The service of these spirits lies at the core of all worship, and in the liturgical celebrations they can inspire, advise, judge, and "possess" their followers. The *loás* are quite capable of kindness and generosity, as well as display baseness and violence. The veneration of the ancestors and the use of their power is frequent in Vodoun, because all human life is a dynamic continuation of the life of those who have gone before us. The attempt at magical interference with nature and daily life are well known in the religion.

An *oungán* ("priest") or a *mambó* ("priestess") is the usual leader of the worshiping community, although there are other lesser "ministers" in the religion. Liturgy is extraordinarily elaborate, and runs the full ritual gamut from the home-based veneration of the *loá rasin* (the ancestral protecting spirit of a family) to public celebrations in the *ounfó* (the place and community of worship). Ritual "possession" of the Voduisants by the *loás* is desired, expected, and encouraged. Indeed, possession is the climax of all liturgical services.

Vodoun is not inclined to engage in theological reflection. Although there is a mythology and a doctrine, ritual seems to be the main interest of the religion. Doctrine is never understood or proclaimed abstractly, but as graphically and concretely (and ritually!) as possible. Voduisants dance their faith and their beliefs. They meet their *loás* and the divine

attributes these manifest, in music, song, dance, and the drums. Vodoun is, above all else, a "performed" religion.

Orlando Espín

See also AFRICAN TRADITIONAL RELIGIONS; AFRO-LATIN RELIGIONS; CANDOMBLÉ; DEUS OTIOSUS; DRUMS (IN AFRICAN AND AFRO-LATIN RELIGIONS); GROUND PAINTING (IN AFRICAN AND AFRO-LATIN RELIGIONS); MACUMBA; MAGIC; PALO MAYOMBE; POSSESSION; RITUAL; SANTERÍA; UMBANDA.

VON BALTHASAR, HANS URS (1905–88)

Hans Urs von Balthasar was one of the foremost Catholic theologians of the twentieth century. Born in Switzerland, he was a member of the Society of Jesus until 1950, when he left the order to devote himself to the direction of a religious community he helped to found. He remained active as a priest in Basel until he died, shortly before he was to be made a cardinal. Keenly aware of the impoverishment of theologies that focus solely on the truth to be believed, or the good that is to be chosen, Balthasar called for a new starting point, beauty—the beauty of divine revelation that first engages our attention and demands our response. Jesus is not primarily a teacher of divine truths or giver of moral precepts, but the gracious expression of divine, self-giving love.

At the center of literally hundreds of books and articles stands a magisterial fifteen-volume trilogy: *Herrlichkeit* (ET: *Glory of the Lord*), *Theodramatik* (ET: *Theo-Drama*) and *Theologik* (ET: *Theo-Logic*). The first part is, perhaps, his most important and original contribution. It develops a theological aesthetics based on the conviction that the act of faith is structurally similar to aesthetic judgment. What convinces us of the beauty of a great work of art is both its perfect proportion and how it illumines reality in a deep, new way. Just as aesthetics reflects on worldly beauty, theological aesthetics reflects on the divine glory. It presents a theory of how faith perceives the integral whole or gestalt of Christ's person and mission as the concrete form of God's glory revealed in the world and how this form, in turn, has the power to inform and transform the lives of believers. The second part, the *Theo-Drama*, focuses on the drama of salvation history, the encounter between divine freedom and human freedom, as it reaches its climax in the Christ event. The mystery of his identity is intrinsically connected with his "role" or mission as the one sent by God. For the believer, too, suggests Balthasar, it is a particular "role" or vocation in this great drama that constitutes one's unique personal identity before God. Just how Christ, and the individual believer in Christ, act out that role is something that takes place in the freedom and imagination of the Holy Spirit. The final part of the trilogy, the *Theo-Logic*, is an extended reflection on the doctrine of the Trinity precisely as the underlying truth and logic of God's self-revelation in human flesh and history.

In addition, Balthasar is best known for his theology of Holy Saturday, the mystery of Christ's loving solidarity with sinners in the descent into hell, seen as God's refusal to abandon even those who reject God. This is the foundation for Balthasar's insistence upon the hope that we can and must have in universal salvation—that all men and women will be saved in the end. Key influences on him and his work were: *The Spiritual Exercises* of St. Ignatius Loyola, the understanding of the analogy of being in the philosophy of Erich Przywara, s.j. (1889–1972), the patristic theology and writings on nature and grace of Henri de Lubac, s.j. (1896–1991), his long friendship and dialogue with the Swiss Protestant Karl Barth (1886–1968), and his association with Adrienne von Speyer, a woman he believed to be a great mystic.

John R. Sachs, s.j.

See also AESTHETICS; APOCATASTASIS; BARTH, KARL; DE LUBAC, HENRI; PRZYWARA, ERICH; SPIRITUAL EXERCISES.

VON RAD, GERHARD (1901–71)

Von Rad was one of the most important of the German Old Testament biblical scholars and theologians in the twentieth century. He taught at the University of Heidelberg from 1949–67. He is known principally for his two-volume *Old Testament Theology* (English, 1962–4) in which he stressed the continuity of the biblical traditions through their reuse within the community. He emphasized the importance of the tradition of the interpretation of history as a part of God's plan for salvation as distinct from Israel's history as it might be reconstructed from biblical and extrabiblical evidence.

Russell Fuller

VOWS

A promise that commits one to the performance of a specific religious activity. Such promises can be private or public. A vow can also mark the adoption of a religious form of life, such as entry into a particular religious order. Making a vow is itself a religious act. In some cases, transitions between social states can be marked by such pledges. Marital status, political office, legal activity, and other secular acts are marked with a promise or pledge. The promise is made, in a religious sense, to carry out one's duties within a moral-religious framework. One's vows can refer to how one will live—vows of poverty, chastity, or how one will treat others—or how one will maintain a relationship with the supernatural. Vows may be performed at shrines, pilgrimage sites, temples, or other religious locations. They are frequently enacted with the aim of receiving favors, blessings, or well-being in return for the promise of worthy behavior.

Christine Greenway

See also PILGRIMAGE; VOWS (RELIGIOUS).

VOWS (RELIGIOUS)

The evangelical counsels of poverty, chastity, and obedience have comprised the formal vows of religious life since the twelfth century, although their actual practice dates much earlier. Vows are sometimes distinguished from promises in terms of the degree of consecration or commitment a person intends; the church accordingly recognizes the difference juridically. Occasionally, human beings make vows to one another, as in the case of the exchange of consent in marriage. But in general, vows are made to God and thus are considered acts or expressions of worship. It would be difficult to separate in practice a promise made to God from a vow. For that reason, the baptismal promises themselves could be designated as vows. Not only does baptism involve a consecration to the Lord through the pouring of water and the sealing or anointing with chrism; but baptism also looks to the future that belongs to the very essence of making a promise.

The religious vows, therefore, are oriented toward the future. They envision a lifelong effort at being faithful to the Gospel by embodying the teaching and example of Jesus. The three vows have become the classical way of abbreviating what is fundamentally a much more comprehensive commitment. Poverty without compassion and solidarity with suffering humanity would be meaningless, celibacy without selflessness would be destructive, obedience without humility and prayer would have no roots. The fact that something has not been vowed does not make its practice secondary or unessential. As acts of worship, the vows embrace the whole person.

William Reiser, s.j.

See also COUNSELS (OF PERFECTION); PERFECTION; PROFESSED; VOWS.

VRATA

The observance of *vratas* (Sanskrit, vow) is an important part of popular Hindu devotional practice. Involving a vow to undertake a particular religious austerity, perform certain rituals, or both, vratas are often, but not always, part of the spirituality of Hindu women, who typically perform them for the benefit of their husbands and family. A typical vrata might include a commitment to fast for a given number of hours or days, perhaps even maintaining a constant vigil, while repeatedly reciting a mantra or scriptural text related to the deity to whom the vrata is dedicated. Vratas are frequently undertaken at inauspicious times in the Hindu religious calendar, so as to ward off any potential evil influences.

Lance E. Nelson

See also HINDUISM; POPULAR RELIGIONS.

VULGATE

The Latin version of the Bible most widely used in Western Christianity. By the latter part of the fourth century, many differences were to be found in the accumulated early Latin translations of the Bible, those now called the Old Latin versions. In 382 Pope Damasus assigned the most competent biblical scholar then living, Eusebius Hieronymous (about 331–420), later known as Jerome, to revise the Latin text. He began his work in Rome and then later moved to Bethlehem. Although Jerome's Latin version was not immediately accepted, and for a long time coexisted with Old Latin versions, eventually his became the preferred translation and was given the name "Vulgate," that is, *editio vulgata*, "the common edition."

Over the centuries many errors in transmission crept into the Vulgate, leading to various attempts to standardize the text. A thirteenth-century revision by scholars at the University of Paris served as the basis for the first printed Bible published by Gutenberg in 1456. In 1546 the Council of Trent declared the Vulgate to be the only authentic Latin translation of the Scriptures. Instructions were given for the publication of an edition of the Vulgate to be printed as correctly as possible. This resulted in the Sixto-Clementine Vulgate of 1592 that effectively became the official Catholic Vulgate, although it, too, has undergone various revisions.

The oldest known manuscript containing the whole Vulgate is the Codex Amiatinus (Florence). Examples of other well-known Vulgate manuscripts include Codex Dublinensis (the Book of Armagh, Dublin) and the Lindisfarne Gospels (London, British Museum).

F. M. Gillman

See also JEROME; TRENT, COUNCIL OF.

W

WAHHABI

See WAHHABIYA.

WAHHABIYA

Also known as the Wahhabi (s), the Wahhabiya took their name from the movement's founder, Ibn Abd al-Wahhab (1703–92), a militant Muslim reformer from Arabia. For al-Wahhab and his followers, Islam must be anchored solely in the teachings of the revealed and inerrant Qur'an (the sacred scripture of Islam), and in the traditions handed down by Islam's Prophet, Muhammad (570–632). Wahhabis were—and remain—particularly suspicious of what they considered heretical innovations in Islam, especially rationalist philosophies, Sufi (mystical) spirituality, and the cult of saints, popular among Shi'ite Muslims. In their effort to restore Islam to an earlier, and for them a more authentic practice of religion, the Wahhabis organized themselves as a kind of doctrinal vigilante movement, empowered by God to administer physical punishment on all who strayed from their interpretation of orthodoxy. Their list of punishable offenses include not only major heresies ("unorthodox teachings") like the veneration of saints and pilgrimages to their shrines, but also shaving one's beard, enjoying music, and smoking. The most notorious example of Wahhabi extremism was their 1802 attack on the holy Shi'ite city of Karbala, site of Husayn's tomb. Shi'ites regard Husayn as a honored martyr and saint.

The austere and puritanical approach to Islam espoused by the Wahhabis continues to attract many zealous Muslims today, usually those who believe that Wahhabiya offers Islam the best opportunity to purge itself of dangerous foreign influences. As such, it is understood by them as the way to reform Islam from within and restore it to its pristine observance. Though far less fanatical than it was in the eighteenth and nineteenth centuries, the movement survives and has become an influential factor in the religion and politics of Saudi Arabia today.

Ronald A. Pachence

See also HUSAYN; ISLAM; ISLAMIC RADICALISM (FUNDAMENTALISM); KARBALA; MUHAMMAD; QUR'AN; SHI'A/SHI'I/SHI'ITE/SHI'ISM; SUFI.

WAILING WALL

See KOTEL HAMA'ARAVI.

1479

WALDENSIANS

The Waldensians are a Christian church that started as a heretical movement in the late twelfth century and continues to the present day. The movement began when a merchant in the city of Lyons named Waldes or Valdes underwent a radical conversion. After providing for his family, he sold his property and took up a life of voluntary poverty and preaching. In this respect, his life was much like that of the later preacher, Francis of Assisi. Unlike Francis, however, Valdes failed to win ecclesiastical approval for his new life. Pope Alexander III upheld the decree of the bishop of Lyons forbidding Valdes or his followers to preach or translate Christian writings into the vernacular. Valdes and the Waldensians continued to preach, however, and in 1182 they were excommunicated and expelled from Lyons. The movement spread rapidly, despite a second condemnation by Pope Lucius III in 1184.

The Waldensians began as a perfectly orthodox reform movement espousing voluntary poverty and preaching of the Gospel, especially against the Cathars. Once expelled from the orthodox church for disobedience, they began to develop their own particular, but decidely Christian, theology. Like the Donatists before them, the Waldensians claimed that merit, not ordination alone, was necessary for valid celebration of the sacraments. In their eyes, pious laymen and even laywomen could, by virtue of their lives, preach, hear confessions, and celebrate the Eucharist. The Waldensians also rejected the notion of purgatory. Upon death, all immediately entered either heaven or hell. This implied necessarily a rejection of indulgences. Waldensians embraced a strict moral code that disallowed all oaths or participation in law courts, rejected capital punishment, and embraced passivism.

Although the Waldensians were the object of the Inquisitions (papal and episcopal), they continued to exist in the mountains of southern France and northern Italy as well as in parts of Germany. During the sixteenth century, the remaining Waldensians joined the Reformation, retaining their identity as a separate Christian group, an identity they retain to the present day.

Gary Macy

See also ALBIGENSIANS; DONATISM; FRANCIS OF ASSISI; INQUISITION; MEDIEVAL CHRISTIANITY (IN THE WEST); PURGATORY.

WANG YANG-MING (1472–1529)

The leading Chinese Neo-Confucian philosopher of the Ming Period (1368–1644) and most famous proponent of the School of Mind (Hsin) or Lu-Wang School. He was a staunch opponent of the earlier Neo-Confucian Ch'eng-Chu School (principle) of Chu Hsi that perceived man [humanity] and the world as separate and held the belief that moral and spiritual cultivation could be developed through a process called the "investigation of things" (ko-wu), that is, discovering the basic principle in all things. While Wang Yang-Ming was also concerned with the moral and spiritual cultivation that would likewise lead to sagehood, he advocated looking within for this basic principle. In opposition to Chu Hsi, Wang emphasized innate knowledge, claiming that the guiding principle of the cosmos and of the individual were one and the same. This principle, that was moral, was equated with the mind and provided man [human beings] with an innate sense of right and wrong. However, man [human beings] has desires and passions that are ultimately self-destructive and must be purged if one's true self is to be identical with the heavenly principle that is the perfect good. Ultimately, this path to sage-hood is open to all and will lead to a ful-fillment of one's true nature in a unity of knowledge and action. As one knows and manifests the good, then one acts in accord with that knowledge. While the Lu-Wang School has had a lasting influ-ence on Confucian teaching and thinking, the Ch'eng-Chu School became the basis of Confucian orthodoxy in the state reli-gion of Imperial China.

G. D. DeAngelis

See also CHU HSI; CONFUCIANISM; CONFUCIUS; HSUN-TZU; MENCIUS; NEO-CONFUCIANISM.

WAR

The name given traditionally to the de-ploying of armed forces in substantial numbers to engage in direct and often prolonged hostilities with sustained gov-ernment and social attention to the con-flict. In the late twenty-first century, war had been transformed to reflect the crisis of late, advanced global capitalism that must silence any group's claims requir-ing reallocation of social power and material resources.

Methods of war now include various economic, political, and military measures that are combined to accomplish foreign policy goals having to do with maintain-ing and increasing present inequities in political power and economic control. Such measures are forms of violence that include foreign aid and debt management through "structural adjustment policies," nuclear proliferation and the arms trade, coercive diplomacy, low-intensity warfare, the use of surrogate forces, covert action, and forms of state terrorism as well as high intensity warfare.

In response to the changing character of global violence, the Catholic Church has adopted the cause of human rights as a prime focus of its ethical teaching and pastoral strategy. Commemorating the tenth anniversary of "The Challenge of Peace," the American bishops said: "An indispensable condition for a just and peaceful world is the promotion and defense of human rights . . . [including] the spectrum of civil, political, cultural and economic rights."

Mary E. Hobgood

See also CHALLENGE OF PEACE; DIGNITY; JUSTICE; JUST WAR THEORY; PEACE.

WARD, MARY (1585–1645)

English Catholic religious woman. Ward founded the "Institute of the English Ladies," a religious order directly pat-terned after the Society of Jesus (Jesuits). Her vision of religious life for women excluded the cloistered convents and the monastic choir and required freedom from episcopal jurisdiction and control. She ex-pected her religious to be actively involved in pastoral work of all kinds (especially in the education of women). Ward faced strong opposition from the clergy and especially from the papacy. Her order was disbanded by the pope in 1630, and she was imprisoned for a while in 1631. Ward finally gained official approval, but only after she agreed to modify her vision of women's religious life and place it under episcopal and papal jurisdictions, along more traditional conventual lines. She spent her last years in England.

Orlando Espín

See also CANON LAW; CATHOLIC TRADI-TION; CLOISTER; CONGREGATIONS

(ORDERS); CONVENT/CONVENTUAL; MONASTICISM IN EASTERN CHRISTIANITY; MONASTICISM IN WESTERN CHRISTIANITY; ORDINARY (CANONICAL); PAPACY; POPE; RELIGIOUS (VOWED); SOCIETY OF JESUS; TRIDENTINISM.

WEBER, (KARL EMIL MAXIMILIAN) MAX (1864–1920)

German sociologist. A famed professor of political economy at the universities of Freiburg and Heidelberg, ill health forced him to retire early. Weber was influenced by Ernst Troeltsch, who at one point lived in the same house with him. His theories on religion have been quite influential during the twentieth century, especially a collection of essays published after his death as *The Sociology of Religion* (1922), and his main book, *The Protestant Ethic and the Spirit of Capitalism* (1904–5). In this latter work, Weber argues that the Calvinist theology of predestination, and subsequent Calvinist spirituality, lie at the ideological root of capitalism.

Orlando Espín

See also CALVINISM; IDEOLOGY (IDEOLOGIES); PREDESTINATION (CALVINIST); RELIGION; RELIGION, CRITIQUE OF; TROELTSCH, ERNST.

WEIGEL, GUSTAVE (1906–64)

Jesuit theologian, ecumenist. Weigel entered the Jesuits in 1922, earned an S.T.D. at the Gregorian (1927), and taught at the University of Santiago, Chile, before joining the faculty of Woodstock College in Maryland where he taught fundamental theology and ecclesiology. As *Theological Studies'* specialist for Protestant theology, Weigel became acquainted with Protestant theology and its dominant thinkers (including Paul Tillich). He authored books on ecumenical topics such as *An American Dialogue: A Protestant Looks at Catholicism*

and a Catholic Looks at Protestantism (with R. McAfee Brown), and promoted ecumenical dialogue and the principle of religious tolerance. Appointed to the Secretariat for Promoting Christian Unity (1960), Weigel served as expert (*peritus*) at Vatican Council II, working out many of the council's ecumenical positions. He died before the council's close (1964).

Patricia Plovanich

WEIL, SIMONE (1909–43)

French writer, mystic. Weil, a French Jew, studied at the Ecole Normale Supérieure and taught philosophy until her Marxist convictions led her to active roles in the social issues of the 1930s. She showed solidarity with labor by joining workers in demonstrations and in factory and farm work and joined the Republican fight against Franco in the Spanish Civil War. Fleeing France before the Germans, she lived in the United States, then in England, chronicling her human and religious experiences in essays. Her writings received less attention during her life than after her death (1943). Then her existentialist reflections on the human condition and her accounts of the mystical experience of God's absence and presence, especially in the experience of suffering, attracted interest and established her reputation as a mystic. Weil was drawn to Christianity but remained unbaptized throughout her life. Her essays appear in collections such as *The Need for Roots* and *Waiting for God*.

Patricia Plovanich

WESLEY, CHARLES (1707–88)

Younger brother of John Wesley and, like his brother, an Anglican priest. He supported John in the leadership of nascent Methodism, and became particularly well know for his hundreds of hymns, many of which are now sung by all major Christian denominations.

Justo L. González

WESLEY, JOHN (1703–91)

Famous English preacher of the eighteenth century, and founder of Methodism. The son of an Anglican priest and a very devout mother, John Wesley studied at Oxford and was himself ordained a priest of the Church of England. In Oxford, he, his brother Charles, and several others formed a "Holy Club" devoted to holy living, prayer, the study of Scripture, visiting prisons, and other acts of charity. They were dubbed "methodist" in mockery at their orderly way of life. Years later, when he became the leader of a vast revival, Wesley took up the name of "Methodist" for his followers.

After many years of fairly frustrating work as an Anglican priest and missionary to Georgia, and of anguish over his own salvation, Wesley became convinced of his own salvation and began preaching with new zeal. The result was a revival that combined preaching to thousands— often in open fields—with small groups that met weekly for mutual support and guidance. These groups were called "Methodist Societies."

Wesley did not intend to found a new church, and until his death remained an Anglican. But when his movement needed pastoral leadership, seeing that the Anglican Church was not willing to provide it, he decided that, since in the very early church there was no difference between elders and bishops, and since he was an elder, he had the power to ordain such leadership. This marked the break between Methodism and the Church of England.

Justo L. González

See also METHODIST CHURCHES; METHODIST THEOLOGY.

WEST, CORNEL (1953–)

Black philosopher ranked among the most influential American philosophers. West has taught at Harvard University, Union Theological Seminary, and Yale University, and today is on the faculty at Princeton University (where he had earned, in 1980, his doctoral degree). He has been very publicly involved in struggles for civil and labor rights because he does not believe the work of an authentic scholar can be limited to the classroom and the library. He has had an enduring personal and scholarly interest in religion, having become an important contributor to Black theological developments. West's thought seems to have been influenced by his American Baptist religious background and the civil rights movement, and by pragmatism (especially Richard Rorty's pragmatism), transcendentalism, and Marxism. He has reflected on religion, race, class, democracy, and socialism, and almost always related them all into critical, creative, and powerful proposals. Among his more important publications are *Black Theology and Marxist Thought* (1979); *The American Evasion of Philosophy* (1989); *Beyond Eurocentrism and Multi-culturalism* (1993); *Race Matters* (1993); and *Democracy Matters* (2004).

Orlando Espín

See also AFRICAN AMERICAN THEOLOGY; BAPTIST THEOLOGY; BLACK THEOLOGY; CLASSISM; MARXISM; PRAGMATISM; RACISM.

WESTERN CATHOLIC CHURCHES

A term that refers to the Catholic Churches of western Europe, or with roots there, and to the ancient Christian tradition they embody. Frequently used for Roman Catholicism, the term is much broader. It must be applied also to the tiny Mozarabic Catholic Church (in full communion with Rome). The churches of the Anglican Communion and the main Old Catholic Churches are also, and legitimately, Western Catholic Churches. Therefore, the term is broader in meaning than any one denomination or group of churches.

Orlando Espín

See also ANGLICAN COMMUNION; CATHOLIC TRADITION; CHRISTIANITY; COMMUNION (ECCLESIOLOGICAL); EASTERN CATHOLIC CHURCHES; ECCLESIOLOGY; MEDIEVAL CHRISTIANITY (IN THE WEST); MEDIEVAL CHURCH; MOZARABIC CATHOLIC CHURCH; OLD CATHOLICS; ORTHODOX CHURCHES; ROMAN CATHOLIC CHURCH; TRADITION; WESTERN THEOLOGY.

WESTERN THEOLOGY

A general way of referring to the theological traditions and methods that have their roots within the long history of the western European churches. Going back to early theologians like Tertullian, Hippolytus of Rome, Cyprian of Carthage, and many others, Western theology was especially marked by the thought of Augustine of Hippo. After the collapse of the Western Roman Empire, this theological tradition grew and developed slowly under the impact and influence of the Germanic (cultural) invasions, the Muslim golden age in Spain, the rediscovery of Greek philosophical classics (through Muslim Spain), the spread and importance of monasticism, and the rise of medieval Scholasticism. It further expanded with the theological controversies over the European conquest of the Americas, and especially in the aftermath

of the Protestant, Anglican, and Catholic Reformations of the sixteenth century. The Enlightenment, rationalism, nationalism, the births of modern science and of modern historiography, the rise of capitalism and socialism, the growing awareness of the crucial roles of culture and economics, the awakening of Third World Christianity, and so on, have more recently given rise to important theological movements and methodologies that further develop, globalize, and hence diversify the Western theological tradition.

Orlando Espín

See also ANGLICAN COMMUNION; AUGUSTINE OF HIPPO; CALVINISM; CATHOLIC TRADITION; CHRISTIANITY; COUNTER-REFORMATION / CATHOLIC REFORMATION; CULTURE; HISTORICAL CONSCIOUSNESS; INCULTURATION; LIBERATION THEOLOGIES; LUTHERANISM; MEDIEVAL CHRISTIANITY (IN THE WEST); MEDIEVAL CHURCH; MODERNITY; POSTMODERNITY; PROTESTANTISM; RATIONALISM; REFORMATION; ROMAN CATHOLIC CHURCH; SOCIALISM; TRENT, COUNCIL OF; WESTERN CATHOLIC CHURCHES.

WHIRLING DERVISHES

Also known as the Mevlevi (or in Arabic, *Mawlawi*), the Whirling Dervishes are a religious order of Turkish Sufis (Islamic mystics) inspired by the teachings of Jalal ad-Din ar-Rumi (1207–73). The name of this spiritual community is derived from the unique kind of "whirling" dance performed by dervishes (Sufis who live a simple monastic life of meditation and prayer). Not all Sufis are Whirling Dervishes, but all Whirling Dervishes are Sufis—Muslims who seek to experience God's immediate and loving presence as the very core of their being through a spiritual path often referred to as mysticism. Like all Sufis, the Mevlevi (Whirling Dervishes) gain progress in their spiritual quest by learning from a master of their order, called a *shaykh* or a *pir*. As part of their initiation into and practice of Mevlevi spirituality, the Whirling Dervishes dress in floor-length skirts, circling around their shaykh while they whirl to the beat of drums and the music of the flutes. Throughout this dance, which takes about an hour to complete, the Dervishes tilt their heads to one side, while extending one arm upward to heaven as if to receive divine blessing, and the other, down toward the earth in a gesture that suggests a desire to share God's blessings with others. This dance is the most eloquent form of Mevlevi *dhikr* (or "remembrance" of God), which is a major ingredient of Sufi prayer. Though banned in Turkey by the first president of the Turkish Republic, Mustafa Kemal Atatürk (1881–1938), the Mevlevi remain active in Konya, their original home in Turkey, as well as in other cities throughout the world.

Ronald A. Pachence

See also ATATÜRK, MUSTAFA; DHIKR; PIR; RUMI, JALAL AL-DIN; SHAYKH; SUFI/SUFISM.

WHITEHEAD, ALFRED NORTH (1861–1947)

British-American philosopher and one of the founders of process philosophy/theology. In his metaphysical masterpiece, *Process and Reality*, Whitehead presents a theory of reality intended to replace the theory of substance, first introduced by Aristotle and modified by hundreds of other philosophers over a period of more than two thousand years. Traditionally, a substance was thought to be a relatively permanent entity that underwent changes through the addition and subtraction of accidents (attributes). Whitehead argued that the theory of substance could not account for the relationship of being to time, and it could not explain how being survives the passage of time. In place of substances, Whitehead recommends what he calls "actual entities," atomic units of experience that emerge from an earlier generation of "satisfied" actual entities, undergo a process of concrescence that adjusts and unifies the data received, and then perish, transmitting their achievements to the next generation.

Every actual entity has what is called a physical pole and a mental pole. Through its physical pole, an actual entity receives feelings from the past that are suffused with what Whitehead calls "eternal objects." These are forms of determiniteness not unlike Plato's Forms, but they have no existence apart from the actual entities they qualify. The eternal objects are then abstracted by the mental pole, giving enhanced emphasis to some and de-emphasis to others. The product of the mental pole is then integrated with the physical pole, and the process continues in this way until the concrescence reaches the final stage of "satisfaction." Thus, while substances are relatively permanent things that serve as the substrata for relatively impermanent accidental forms, actual entities are impermanent things that serve as the substrata for eternal forms.

Everything in the universe is either an actual entity, a component in an actual entity, or a composite of actual entities. Physical things are four-dimensional societies of actual entities; souls are (virtually) one-dimensional strings of actual entities through time; feelings are components of actual entities; abstract ideas are eternal objects in the mental poles of actual entities; and God is a single actual entity ever in process of concrescence and never reaching a final stage of satisfaction. At its moment of satisfaction, every actual entity occupies a determinate niche in space and time and exhibits spatial and temporal extensiveness, but because God never reaches this final stage, God is not in space or time properly speaking.

Whitehead's theory of God has had considerable influence on twentieth-century theology. Whitehead conceives God as endowed (chiefly) with two natures, primordial and consequent. In virtue of his primordial nature, God sustains in existence the reservoir of eternal objects and supplies them to the world. God is thus the originator of novelty in the world. Through his consequent nature, God receives the satisfied products of created actual entities and saves them from perishing. In this capacity, God is described as a "tender care that nothing be lost." Thus, God is continually involved in the creative advance of the world and participates in its adventure. In virtue of his primordial nature, God transcends the world; but God is also immanent in the world, and in virtue of the later function, Whitehead's God is susceptible to a pantheistic interpretation.

God, for Whitehead, is something vastly different from Aristotle's Prime Mover that exists as pure act. As a result, Whitehead's God cannot be said to be omniscient, omnipotent, or omnibenevolent in the sense envisioned by those philosophers of the Middle Ages who were inspired by Aristotle. While Whitehead's God might be said to be omniscient in the sense that his primordial nature comprehends the entire realm of eternal objects, God does not know the satisfied phases of actual entities before those phases actually occur. This is because all actual entities admit of at least the possibility of genuine freedom, and the souls of high-grade organisms exhibit considerable freedom. Thus, God does not literally "see" the future.

Also, God's power over the world is limited. God persuades the world toward rational forms of order and harmony in accord with Plato's image of reason persuading necessity. But God is not capable of forcing God's will on anything in the world in any complete sense. Thirdly, while God continually expresses an attitude of benevolence toward the world, God is not infinitely perfect in the sense of having every perfection—eliminating the possibility of any development or change. Evil is a factor genuinely present in the world, and God does God's best to ameliorate its effects, but God is not capable of eradicating it in an instant.

Every actual entity enjoys what Whitehead calls "objective immortality"—immortality as a kind of memory (as long as it lasts) in subsequent actual entities in the world, and in the consequent nature of God. However, the question of subjective immortality, as taught by the Christian philosophers of the Middle Ages, is a more difficult matter. Whitehead seems to suggest that objective immortality is the only kind of immortality that human souls can look forward to. However, subjective immortality as a prehension (feeling) in the everlasting divine concrescence as not completely ruled out.

Whitehead's more important works include (with Bertrand Russell) *Principia Mathematica* (1910–3), *The Concept of Nature* (1920), *Science and the Modern World* (1925), *Process and Reality* (1929), *Adventures of Ideas* (1933), and *Modes of Thought* (1938).

Patrick J. Hurley

See also PROCESS THEOLOGY.

WIDOWS (IN THE EARLY CHURCH)

Scattered references to widows in early church documents suggest they formed a distinct group and raise questions about their access to ecclesiastical function and ministry. The author of 1 Timothy (5:3-16) implies a special status for widows who are without family ties and who devote themselves to prayer and works of mercy; for these he gives rules of conduct comparable to those he draws up for other officials such as deacons (of both sexes) and bishops. In the subapostolic age, Polycarp, bishop of Smyrna, calls widows "the altar of God" who must be taught discretion regarding the faith (*Epistle to the Philippians*); his contemporary, Ignatius of Antioch, warns against neglecting widows (*Letter to Polycarp*). By the beginning of the third century, the discussion grows longer and more critical in tone. Hippolytus (around 230), in his *Apostolic Tradition*, writes against the possibility that widows be ordained; they are merely to be called by name and enrolled. By the late fourth century, the *Apostolic Constitutions*, while acknowledging and encouraging an "order of widows," prohibits their teaching or preaching and gives elaborate prescriptions for their behavior. Much is said about them staying at home, minding their own business, and cultivating enduring habits of silence and modesty. The very careful way in which these three later documents lay down a rationale for restricting the public ministry of widows and repeat the minute details of decorum expected suggests that the widows themselves had a different sense of their own position. There is no reason to think they were not adequately educated; they had the self-confidence of mature women and, possibly, the social position that administering their husbands' estates conferred; they may well have believed themselves capable of playing a significant role in church ministry. Failing objective and official descriptions of their positions, we are forced to extrapolate from the warnings given them and from the conclusions of social scientists about the possibilities of their social and economic condition. They seem, at the least, to have questioned the possibility of ordination and of teaching and preaching to the congregations in a public way; it is also possible that public ministries exercised by widows were accepted by Christians generally so that general prohibitions were thought necessary. This possibility is reinforced by the decrees and canons of church synods (both regional and general) from the fourth to the seventh century that repeat prohibitions against widows baptizing and preaching, and make even more elaborate restrictions on their activities and dress, ultimately enforcing the strictest enclosure.

Marie Anne Mayeski

See also APOSTOLIC CONSTITUTION; CLOISTER; DEACONESS; IGNATIUS OF ANTIOCH; POLYCARP OF SMYRNA; SYNODS; VIRGINITY.

WISDOM

(Hebrew, *hokmah*; Greek, *Sophia*). This is a term that occurs frequently in both the Hebrew Bible/Old Testament and in the New Testament. Wisdom refers to both an understanding of reality and a way of life reflective of that understanding. In the wisdom worldview, which is reflected especially in biblical Wisdom literature, God is understood to be creator and organizer of the world. The path of wisdom begins with the fear of God (Prov 1:7).

Wisdom is found in human experience and is also seen as the gift of God.

Russell Fuller

See also WISDOM LITERATURE.

WISDOM LITERATURE

Wisdom literature in the Old Testament includes the books of Proverbs, Job, and Ecclesiastes. This listing and order corresponds to both the Jewish and Protestant canons. In Roman Catholicism and Eastern Christian canons, the Wisdom literature includes in addition the Wisdom of Solomon and Ecclesiasticus or Ben Sirah. Wisdom was a concern and an area of study in ancient Israel just as it was elsewhere in the ancient Near East. Ancient Israelite wisdom frequently shows influence from neighboring wisdom traditions. Nevertheless, wisdom in Israel was distinctively Israelite, assuming an Israelite worldview. This included especially the centrality of Yahweh as the center of creation and its crafter. The wisdom writings of ancient Israel assume that since Yahweh is the creator of the cosmos, then it is possible to gain knowledge of the divine from the observation of nature. Some wisdom writings, such as Proverbs, also assume validity of the covenantal theology—briefly stated, that fidelity to Yahweh and the covenant leads to well being and material prosperity, while disloyalty to Yahweh leads to punishment and destruction. This understanding of how reality functions may also be seen in writings not associated with wisdom circles such as Deuteronomy. Not all the wise in ancient Israel were satisfied with this understanding, and thus we have compositions that critique this view of reality or radically disagree with it. The book of Job is the clearest example of this sort of "opposition" literature. Job seems to use as its basis an old story of a righteous man who suffered grievously, but persevered and was restored in the end. This may have been a widespread type of story since a composition as early as the story of Kirta/ Keret from Ugarit has the same basic plot. In Job, however, this story has the added element of a series of debates between the protagonist and his "friends" who support the traditional wisdom understanding of reality. In their view, if Job is suffering, then Job must have done something to deserve it. The book of Ecclesiastes or Koheleth is also a work that opposes or at least stands in obvious contrast to the mainstream view of the ancient sages. The author of Ecclesiastes adopts a pessimistic or a nihilistic view; he has no use for the Law of Moses or the covenant at the heart of Proverbs and the ancient wisdom view of reality. The ancient sages were also concerned with pragmatic issues and "worldly" success. They recorded and passed on to their male students their advice that was based on accumulated experience and observation of nature and human society. The ancient sages must also be credited with the creation of the idea that wisdom, *hokma* in Hebrew, a form that grammatically is a feminine form, was a woman, and although created by Yahweh at the beginning of time, was much more than a mere human being. Lady Wisdom is described in Proverbs 8:22-31 as the first of God's creations and even as a "master workman," suggesting that wisdom had a role in creation. This speculation about wisdom and her function continued and developed until finally wisdom is equated with the Torah or the word of God that is viewed as preexistent.

Russell Fuller

WITCHCRAFT

A set of practices that involve the magical manipulation of the environment or an individual with supernatural powers or forces. Both males and females can be practitioners. The distinction between sorcery and witchcraft is unclear; both may destructively impact others—in many settings, witches are blamed for death and injury. But witchcraft is not necessarily done to cause harm and its overall social functions may be positive. For example, cross-culturally, beliefs in witchcraft may discourage behavior that is considered immoral. People who engage in witchcraft are often believed to have the powers of divination, invulnerability, supernatural strength, transformation of self or others, invisibility, flight, animation of the inanimate, and ability to produce things at will. In some contexts, one's status as a practitioner may be inherited and in others the skills are learned. Variations in witchcraft beliefs and practices are found historically, in cross-cultural contexts, and in the contemporary setting.

Three distinct phenomena that are not necessarily similar or related have been identified as witchcraft. The first is simple sorcery, or the system of beliefs and practices whose purpose is to manipulate nature for the benefit of the witch or a client. This type is found worldwide, in all historical periods and many societies. References to witchcraft and association between humans and intermediary spirits date to the Greco-Roman era. A second type has been labeled "diabolical witchcraft." In medieval and early modern Europe, witchcraft was constructed as a Christian heresy. Witches were believed to have pacts with Satan and to engage in orgies, cannibalism, and infanticide; witches' rituals were held to be the inversion of those of Christians. Striking patterns emerge when one examines the kinds of individuals (often female, poor, or marginalized) and social context (shifting economic and political climates) of witchcraft accusations in Western culture. Waves of hysteria were often associated with witchcraft accusations. For example, in Salem, Massachusetts, in 1692, two hundred suspected witches were arrested and nineteen were executed. In 1957 the Massachusetts legislature exonerated the witches. Historians, psychologists, sociologists, anthropologists, and feminist scholars continue to provide interpretations of the complexity of social, economic, political, psychological, and gender issues that were manifested in the patterns of the accusations and convictions. Many scholars draw connections between their conclusions about the social and cultural functions of witchcraft accusations and some contemporary issues, referring, for example, to the McCarthy congressional hearings to identify communists in the 1950s or Satanic ritual abuse accusations as modern "witch hunts." The third type of witchcraft refers to the neopagan revival of the twentieth century.

In the cross-cultural context, witchcraft is associated with societies that have beliefs in the supernatural as detachable forces or as a power that is found in all things. As Western missionaries encountered non-Western, traditional religions, they often labeled the unfamiliar beliefs and practices as witchcraft. In some cases their assessment was ethnocentric and inaccurate. But witchcraft is found in a wide variety of societies and religions. Typically, witchcraft explains the unacceptable, evil, or unpredictable things that occur and provides an outlet for bringing social tensions to the surface and resolving them. Witchcraft beliefs and practices have not declined with contact between Western and non-Western cultures. For example, among the Ibibio of Nigeria researchers have documented an increased reliance on witchcraft as explanation for misfortune at the same time that more individuals have been involved in modern education and scientific training. Interestingly, younger people accuse older, more traditional members of society of bewitching them and causing their exam failures, unemployment, and other misfortunes. Among the Ibibio, witchcraft is a highly developed and long-standing system of explanation for misfortune. If a rat eats crops, or someone becomes ill, or dies, it is attributed to the work of a witch. Witchcraft explains why a particular individual, in a particular time and place suffers. The personalizing of evil removes the possibility of chance, explains why things happen, and proposes a means to remedy the situation. Ibibio witches are thought to be males or females who have a substance (threads, needles) inside them received from another witch and that gives psychic power to cause harm and death. When misfortune has been attributed to witchcraft, the search for the culprit in many African or other societies is a communal probe into social behavior. The investigation offers a public hearing into all relationships. Antisocial and hostile acts are discussed openly. People receive very public reminders of appropriate behavior and morality and is therefore a form of social control.

In the West, witchcraft was associated with reverence of nature, occultism, and other philosophies by the early twentieth century and has undergone a revival. Contemporary witchcraft, Wicca, is derived from the work of Michelet and other nineteenth-century writers who asserted that European witchcraft was a wide-spread pre-Christian fertility cult. A variety of intellectuals and poets developed the idea, and occultism became popular in that period. The occult tradition and the fertility-cult adherents merged in the 1940s and 1950s around the time Robert Graves wrote an imaginative book, *White Goddess*, about an alleged worldwide cult to the moon goddess, to produce a new form of witchcraft that has become a religious movement. This movement that has a variety of groups, includes, as its tenets, the worship of a fertility goddess, magic aimed at healing, or other positive ends, and various rituals. It blends a feminine principle, ideas of the variety and diversity of the godhead, rejection of the idea of the devil because the devil is a Christian construction, respect for nature, and other ideas.

The historical and cross-cultural variations on witchcraft clearly indicate widely divergent phenomena. In general, however, witchcraft, like any other system of religious beliefs, provides explanations for evil, disease, death, injustice, and other mysterious events. It offers not only a logical explanation, but remedies. The complexity of witchcraft beliefs, practices, and social implications is such that no single theoretical approach—historical, theological, sociological, psychological, or anthropological—provides an adequate explanation of the phenomena included under the rubric of witchcraft.

Christine Greenway

See also DIVINATION; MAGIC; PAGANISM/ PAGANS.

WITNESS/WITNESSING

In the Christian tradition, a witness is one who shares her or his faith in Jesus as the Christ, and witnessing is the act of sharing it. A form of evangelism, witnessing consists in telling others about Jesus' impact on one's life for the purpose of converting them to Christianity. By testifying to their own experience, they spread the Gospel. In the New Testament, the earliest witness was Mary Magdalene, who discovered the empty tomb, encountered the risen Christ, and related her experience to the other disciples. Another early witness was Paul, whose encounter with Jesus in a blinding light on the road to Damascus was the basis for his conversion. As early as the 1820s, U.S. Evangelist Charles G. Finney used witnesses, especially women, to stimulate conversions in revival meetings.

In contrast to catechetical or sacramental approaches to evangelism, witnessing is characteristic of Evangelical theology and often occurs in the context of revivalism. Witnessing fits well with a theology that emphasizes individuals being born again in a dramatic conversion experience. Witnesses testify to their own rebirth through Jesus' power and love, their life-changing experience of repentance, justification, and sanctification. They relate their personal encounter with Christ, often a dramatic story of the journey from sin to grace, ignorance to bliss, separation from God to commitment to become a disciple. Although it can be argumentative or exegetical, it is usually narrative, addressing specific questions. How did I come to know Christ? How did Jesus save me? Why do I believe Christianity is true? What difference has becoming a Christian made in my life?

Witnessing can occur formally or informally, in a sermon or in casual conversation. In some traditions, such as the Jehovah's Witnesses, the Church of Jesus Christ of Latter-Day Saints, and some fundamentalists, witnessing takes place through distributing tracts door-to-door or on street corners. Evangelicals also believe they testify to Christ's power through their actions, through living a devout and holy life. By living a righteous life, one witnesses to the lordship of Christ without uttering a word. And while some Evangelicals believe nature witnesses to God's glory, they agree that the Bible is the most powerful testimony to God's grace.

Evelyn A. Kirkley

See also EVANGELICAL; EVANGELICALS; EVANGELICAL THEOLOGY; GREAT AWAKENING(S) (EURO-AMERICAN RELIGIOUS HISTORY); REVIVALISM.

WITTENBERG

A city of some fifty thousand people in what is today northeastern Germany, Wittenberg was, in the sixteenth century, the place in which Martin Luther began his reform of the church. The University of Wittenberg had been founded in 1502, and Luther initiated his teaching career there in 1508. Luther's lectures on Scripture, especially those on the psalms and the letters of St. Paul, are where he first articulated a breach with the theology he had been taught as an Augustinian friar. On October 31, 1517, Luther posted his Ninety-Five Theses on the door of the castle church in Wittenberg. This event is often cited as the beginning of the Reformation. The University of Wittenberg was also the intellectual home of Luther's junior colleague, Philip Melanchthon. Wittenberg has at times been termed the Lutheran Rome.

Thomas Worcester, S.J.

See also LUTHERANISM; LUTHER, MARTIN; MELANCHTHON, PHILIP; NINETY-FIVE THESES; REFORMATION.

WITTGENSTEIN, LUDWIG (1889–1951)

An Austrian philosopher originally identified with the logical positivism of the Vienna Circle through his *Tractatus Logico-Philosophicus* (1921), Ludwig Wittgenstein later rejected the starting point of his early work—that the sole function of language is to "picture" the elementary facts that constitute the world and to state tautologies—in *The Blue and Brown Books* (1933–5). Here, as well as in his "journal" published posthumously, *Philosophical Investigations*, Wittgenstein explored the relative incommensurability of "language games" serving diverse purposes. These "language games" (picturing, cursing, praying, for example), in turn, mirror an intersubjective "form of life." Wittgenstein's late work was significant in reorienting analytic philosophy from the relatively narrow confines of logical positivism.

J. A. Colombo

See also POSITIVISM.

WOMANIST THEOLOGY

Womanist theology is a theology of, by, and for black (African) American women and other women of color. Yet, it is also a theology of liberation that seeks to be inclusive, holistic, and community-building. It celebrates and promotes the liberation, both physical and spiritual, of all, regardless of race, gender, class, or sexual orientation. Thus its emphasis is on the multiplicative oppressions of race, class, and gender as they impact all of humanity in myriad ways.

A womanist sees herself, both as individual and in community, but her individuality arises, in keeping with her holistic African heritage, from the black community in which she was born and

came to voice. She is grounded in the historical experience of black (African) American women in the United States who have persevered in their efforts to build a community of faith and love. Building on the original definition set forth by the writer and poet Alice Walker, black (African) American women have forged an understanding of themselves as strong, black women who have maintained a relationship with and faith in Jesus Christ against overwhelming odds. They have been the bearers of culture and the backbone of the black church and community.

Tracing themselves back to African women in Sacred Scripture, especially Hagar, the slave and concubine of Abraham, womanist theologians seek to uncover and recover the presence of women of color in feminist and black liberation theologies as well as in the Christian churches and the United States itself. Theirs is a "coming to voice" of women who have been the backbone of the black church and the black community in the United States in a way that lifts up the history of their struggle in a society, the United States, that has denied them both dignity and humanity.

Womanist theologians such as Katie Cannon, Delores Williams, Jacquelyn Grant, Kelly Brown Douglas, Emilie Townes, Toinette Eugene, and Diana L. Hayes, and others, are attempting to weave a new understanding of humanity in community. Their struggle is for the full liberation of all human beings from all forms of oppression. Many are ordained Protestant ministers and all seek, as well, to expose the contemporary weaknesses of the black church and all Christian churches in terms of their participation and affirmation of sexism. They also seek to challenge the church to fulfill its life-giving, liberating promise. Womanist theology is a challenge, as well, to theology itself, as it has historically been presented as a male Eurocentric theology, and contemporarily as male, black and white, but also Eurocentric female theology.

Diana L. Hayes

See also AFRICAN AMERICAN THEOLOGY.

WOMEN, ORDINATION OF

The concept of ordination in the first millennium of Christianity did not exclude important roles for women. Ordination during this period "signified the fact of being designated and consecrated to take up a certain place or better a certain function, *ordo*, in the community and at its service" according to the famous church historian Yves Congar. Therefore when women moved to new positions of service in the church, they underwent rites of ordination. Thus women were ordained as deaconesses, abbesses, canonesses, virgins, widows, nuns, empresses, and queens. Some references also survive for *presbyterae* (the feminine form in Latin for "priest"). Scholars debate what role these women served, some arguing that they functioned as priests, others suggesting that this was the designation of the wives of priests. The functions of the ministries undertaken by women varied, but they certainly heard confessions as abbesses and canonesses, and baptized as deaconesses. By the twelfth century, women had ceased to be ordained as deaconesses in both Eastern and Western Christianity. Western Christianity went further than Eastern Christianity, however, and redefined ordination to include only the ministries of priest, deacon, and subdeacon, that is, those ministries that served at the altar. No other ministries were any longer considered truly ordained. Women were judged to be unfit by their gender to fulfill any of these positions. It would not be until the late eighteenth and early twentieth century that certain Christian groups began to ordain women as ministers once again. The Society of Friends (Quakers) accepted women leaders from its beginnings in the seventeenth century. In 1853 Antoinette Brown was ordained by the Congregationalist Church, and in 1863 Olympia Brown was ordained by the Universalist denomination. The Salvation Army, founded in 1865, has always ordained both men and women. Methodists began ordaining women in 1880 and the Presbyterian Church in 1889. The Church of the Nazarene, Mennonites, Assemblies of God, and Baptists followed suit in the late nineteenth and early twentieth centuries. The Lutheran Church in American ordained the first women pastors in 1970, and the Anglican Communion witnessed the first regular ordination of women in 1971 in Hong Kong. The Greek Orthodox Church agreed to revive the ordination of deaconesses in 2005. Not all Christian denominations, however, ordain women to the ministry. The Catholic Church and The Church of Jesus Christ of Latter-Day Saints (Mormons) do not recognize the ordination of women, while the Southern Baptist Convention decided in 2000 that the ordination of women was unscriptural and would no longer be accepted.

Gary Macy

See also ABBOT/ABBESS; ANGLICAN COMMUNION; ASSEMBLIES OF GOD; BAPTISM/CONFIRMATION; BAPTIST CHURCHES/BAPTIST CONVENTIONS; CHURCH OF JESUS CHRIST OF LATTER-DAY SAINTS; CONFESSION OF FAITH; CONGREGATIONAL CHURCHES; DEACON;

WORD OF GOD

In systematic theology, Word of God is a metaphor for revelation that is used in several ways. The primary reference is to revelation in Jesus Christ, a usage that comes from the Johannine *logos* image, is furthered in the Logos christologies of the patristic era, and culminates in the identification of Logos and Son metaphors in the Nicene and Constantinople Creeds. The second reference in recent fundamental theology uses Word of God as a metaphor for revelation in its philosophical inquiries about the human potential for revelation or for the Word of God. The final usage inquires about the human recognition of revelation through the media of Scripture and proclamation; how these sources become revelation for the hearer of the Word. Protestant reflections on the image favor a dynamic interpersonal interpretation of the term. Catholic theology has generally adopted a doctrinal or propositional interpretation of Word of God.

Patricia Plovanich
and Jean-Pierre Ruiz

WORK/EMPLOYMENT

Like sexuality, work, or sensuous human labor, is a fundamental expression of one's human dignity and relationality. Good work is a necessary form of creative human self-expression that manifests our sociality and binds us to others in the common project of creating ourselves as a species.

However, for most people in economies shaped by global capitalism, work produces profits, not dignity and community, and is a source of suffering, endurance, boredom, and debilitation. Work is being restructured toward the extremes of a majority of menial, low-paying and non-union jobs at one end, and a minority of education-intensive, technical, managerial, and high-paying jobs at the other, with no ladder in between. Work at both ends of this spectrum is a source of economic insecurity and worry.

This is contrary to much teaching in the Christian churches, especially the social encyclicals of Pope John Paul II. In *Laborem Excercens* (1981), *Sollicitudo Rei Socialis* (1987) and *Centesimus Annus* (1991), the Pope gives clear priority to work and the needs of the worker for participation and dignity over capital and the desires for profit.

Mary E. Hobgood

See also CATHOLIC SOCIAL TEACHING; DIGNITY; FREEDOM; SEXUALITY; SLAVERY; VICTIM.

WORLD (IN THE NEW TESTAMENT)

Three Greek words are usually translated as "world" in English versions of the New Testament: *oikoumenē, aiōn* and *kosmos*. Each of the three has its own specific significance. *Oikoumenē*, a participle used as a noun, occurs fifteen times in the New Testament, referring to the inhabited world (*oikos* means "house"). In Luke 2:1, for example, we read, "In those days a decree went out from Emperor Augustus that all the world (*oikoumenē*) should be registered." The second term, *aiōn*, often translated as "aeon" or "age," has temporal connotations. For example, Ephesians 1:21 speaks of the exaltation of Christ "not only in this age (*aiōn*) but also in the age to come." *Aiōn* is occasionally translated as "world," as it is in Mark 4:19 and its Synoptic parallel, Matthew 13:22, that speak of "the cares of the world" that choke the word of God.

Kosmos occurs most frequently (one hundred eighty-six times) and is the most significant of the three terms for "world." C. R. North enumerates five distinct senses in which the New Testament uses *kosmos*: (1) as the universe; (2) as the earth and/or its inhabitants; (3) as the context of human activity; (4) in a pejorative sense, as an entity opposed to God; (5) as the object of Christ's salvific mission. In the first sense, *kosmos* refers to the universe as the well-ordered result of divine creative activity and as the object of transcendent divine sovereignty. This is the case, for instance, in Acts 17:24, "The God who made the world and everything that is in it, he who is Lord of heaven and earth, does not live in shrines made by human hands." The second sense, as a term that refers to the earth and/or those who inhabit it, is found in such New Testament texts as John 1:9, "The true light, which enlightens everyone, was coming into the world," and John 17:11, where the Johannine Jesus distinguishes between himself and the disciples, "now I am no longer in the world, but they are in the world." The third sense of *kosmos*, as the context of human activity, is found in such texts as 1 Corinthians 7:34 that mention anxiety about "the affairs of the world"; as well as in Mark 8:36 (and its Synoptic parallels Matt 16:26 and Luke 9:25), "For what will it profit them to gain the whole world and forfeit their life?"

The fourth sense of *kosmos*, as a pejorative reference to an entity that opposes and is at odds with God, is found most strongly in the Pauline and Johannine literature. In 1 Corinthians 3:19, Paul declares that "the wisdom of this world is foolishness with God," since worldly wisdom cannot comprehend the Cross. In Galatians 6:14, Paul exclaims, "May I never boast of the anything except the cross of our Lord Jesus Christ, by which the world has been crucified to me, and I to the world." This pessimistic sense of "world" is most intense in the Johannine literature where we read that "this is the judgment, that the light has come into the world, and people loved darkness rather than light because their deeds were evil" (John 3:19). According to John 12:31, "the world" is under the domination of the evil "ruler of this world," who is to be driven out of office by Jesus. The Johannine Jesus declares that his disciples can expect the same treatment from "the world" as he himself received: "If the world hates you, be aware that it hated me before it hated you" (John 15:18).

The fifth sense of *kosmos*, as the object of Christ's salvific mission, is also found in the Fourth Gospel: "For God so loved the world that he gave his only Son, so that everyone who believes in him may not perish but may have eternal life. Indeed, God did not send the Son into the world to condemn the world, but in order that the world might be saved through him" (John 3:16-17). In John 8:12, Jesus identifies himself as "the light of the world," who promises the light of life to those who follow him, while in John 9:5 he repeats this self-identification, adding "as long as I am in the world."

Jean-Pierre Ruiz

See also COSMOGONY; COSMOLOGY; JOHANNINE CORPUS.

WORLD COUNCIL OF CHURCHES (WCC)

The World Council of Churches (WCC) is a group of more than three hundred Christian church bodies from more than one hundred countries. Its members include most Protestant denominations and many Eastern Orthodox communions. It meets regularly to discuss theological, sacramental, and polity issues and to cooperate on mission and social reform efforts. Although it was founded in 1948, its antecedents date to the 1910 World Missionary Conference in Edinburgh, Scotland. Focusing on cooperative Christian missions to non-Christians, this conference purposefully excluded discussion of potentially divisive theological issues.

This omission led to the founding of the Faith and Order movement to discuss theology, ordination, sacraments, and polity. The first World Conference on Faith and Order gathered in Lausanne, Switzerland, in 1927 with Orthodox, Protestant, and Old Catholic (not Roman) representatives. Delegates agreed to report honestly on their discussions, stating the points on which they agreed and disagreed and why, rather than vague, meaningless statements. At the same time as the Faith and Order movement, the Life and Work movement organized for the practical work of applying Christianity to the modern world. The first Life and Work conference met in Stockholm, Sweden, in 1925 and addressed five issues: economics and industrialism, morality, international affairs, Christian education, and ways in which Christians could engage in future collaboration.

In 1937 the two movements called for a united World Council of Churches, but because of World War II, the first meeting was delayed until 1948. At the first meeting of the WCC in Amsterdam, more than one hundred churches from forty-four nations were represented, most from Europe and North America. Speakers included Karl Barth, Reinhold Niebuhr, and John Foster Dulles. The council did not merely absorb its parent organizations, but created Commissions on Faith and Order and on Life and Work. Subsequent meetings occurred in Evanston, Illinois, U.S.A. (1954); New Delhi, India (1961); Uppsala, Sweden (1968); Nairobi, Kenya (1975); and Vancouver, British Columbia, Canada (1983).

Since its formation, the WCC has not hesitated to take controversial stands on social issues. It has opposed Communism, free-market capitalism, imperialism, and industrial oppression. It has supported the rights of workers and labor justice. It rejected totalitarianism and war. Its positions have drawn attacks from conservative Christians, and the WCC includes few Evangelical or fundamentalist groups. Although the Catholic Church has never officially joined the WCC, since the Second Vatican Council, the church has cooperated with the WCC on joint ventures and holds observer status.

The WCC is a manifestation of the ecumenical impulse, the desire for a worldwide Christian church. Visible expression of Christian unity, it has fostered dialogue between Protestants, Orthodox, and Catholics. Symbol of the search for the meaning of Christian discipleship in the modern world, it has been instrumental in reflecting on the global church, affirming common beliefs and practices without ignoring theological, liturgical, or cultural differences.

Evelyn A. Kirkley

See also COUNCIL OF CHURCHES (WORLD, NATIONAL); ECUMENICAL MOVEMENT/ECUMENISM.

WORLD JEWISH CONGRESS

A voluntary association of representative Jewish bodies, communities, and organizations throughout the world, organized to "assure the survival, and to foster the unity of the Jewish people."

Founded in 1936, the first World Jewish Congress met in Geneva, Switzerland, with 280 delegates representing Jews in 32 countries. Today, Jewish institutions and organizations in more than 60 countries belong to the WJC.

The World Jewish Congress promotes and works toward the common interest of its members: to defend the rights and status of Jews, and the interests of Jews and Jewish communities; to encourage the creative development of Jewish religious, cultural, and social life; to come before governmental and intergovernmental organizations in matters of concern to the Jewish people; to fight anti-Semitism and danger to Jews and Jewish communities. Presently, the WJC maintains four branches of its executive offices—in North America, South America, Europe, and Israel. A plenary Assembly, consisting of delegates from all member organizations, is its ultimate governing body and authority.

Wayne Dosick

WORLDVIEW

A social vision, ideology, or way of perceiving the world that incorporates interlocking sets of beliefs about the nature of the world and how it works. A worldview reflects the basic interests, fears, ambitions, and activities of those who shape the worldview. Since they are created by agents in specific social, political, and economic locations, worldviews give rise to ideas and beliefs that are both particular and partial.

Worldviews shape the methods and theories ethicists incorporate into moral reflection. In social ethics, worldviews are more important than ethical principles or norms, because worldviews determine how norms and principles are understood and utilized.

Mary E. Hobgood

See also ETHICS, SOCIAL; JUSTICE.

WORMS, CONCORDAT OF

The agreement between Pope Callistus II and the emperor Henry V of 1122 that settled the Investiture controversy. The Emperor renounced all right to selection of bishops; the Pope conceded that the elections of bishops in the German kingdom were to take place in the Emperor's presence, and that the bishop-elect would receive his regalia from the Emperor.

Mary Ann Hinsdale

See also INVESTITURE CONTROVERSY.

WORMS, DISPUTATION OF

A conference was held in 1540–1 in Worms to reunite Catholics and Protestants in Germany. Johann Eck (for the Catholics) and Philip Melanchthon (for the Protestants) debated the doctrine of original sin. Such reunion was not, however, achieved.

Mary Ann Hinsdale

See also LUTHERAN THEOLOGY; MELANCHTHON, PHILIP; SIN, ORIGINAL.

WORSHIP

From Old English for *worthy-ship,* "worthiness." Worship is the human response to God's worthiness. It can be either an internal attitude or a set of external behaviors; spontaneous or planned; individual or communal; aiming to convey awe, gratitude, penitence, or pleading. Worship is both a reaction to God's presence and an activity that awakens one to, or makes one more aware of, that presence. Liturgy is a particular kind of worship: a set of words and acts passed from generation to generation by which an entire culture expresses its worship. In the Judaism of Jesus' time, liturgy centered in the Temple in Jerusalem and the synagogues in every Jewish settlement. The Temple housed the ark of the covenant, a symbol of God's presence among the people, and was a place of occasional pilgrimage more than a site for weekly worship. In the Temple, animals, food and drink, and incense were sacrificed in daily worship. In the synagogues, by contrast, prayer and praise—sacrifices of the lips—were offered morning, afternoon, and evening, replacing the material sacrifices of the Temple. Jesus, adhering to the Jewish pattern, worshiped alone, among his disciples, and in both synagogues and Temple. The first Christians followed a similar pattern (Acts 2:42-47). Christian worship was distinct from Jewish, however, in a least three ways. First, it introduced a new rite, the Eucharist, as central, and gave a heightened importance to the custom of baptism. Second, Christians emphasized that true worship is not a matter of rituals and sacrifices, but of giving oneself to God and God's work. Christians did not reject rituals, but insisted that ritual could not substitute for a life of self-sacrifice (1 Cor 11:17-34). Third, Christians believed that Jesus, not the Temple and its sacrifices, provided contact between God and humanity. This did not mean that the Christians rejected Temple worship, but that they accorded it a secondary significance. Periodic failures or apparent failures of the church to live up to these three ideals have given rise to reform movements, most notably the Protestant and Catholic Reformations of the sixteenth century.

Patrick L. Malloy

See also ARK OF THE COVENANT; COUNTER-REFORMATION/CATHOLIC REFORMATION; HOLY OF HOLIES; SYNAGOGUE.

WRATH OF GOD

A divine reaction to human unfaithfulness. In the Old Testament, the Lord becomes angry with individuals—Aaron and Miriam (Num 12:9); Aaron (Deut 9:20); Achan (Josh 7:15-26)—and with a host of others. He also becomes angry with the Israelites in general when they serve other gods (Judg 2:14, 20; 10:7). Finally, the Lord becomes angry with the other nations (for example, Isa 34:2).

In the New Testament, references to the wrath of God are few. Jesus becomes angry with those who in the synagogue on the Sabbath refuse to affirm Jesus' doing good—healing a man's withered hand (Mark 3:5). In the parable of the servant whose master forgave debts he could not possibly repay, but who then proceeded not to forgive a fellow servant for much smaller debts (Matt 18:21-35), the master became angry with the servant he had forgiven, and "handed him over to the torturers until he should pay back the whole debt" (v. 34). In Hebrews 3:16-17, the author uses Israel's unfaithfulness as a warning to his audience of the wrath of God. He recalls "those who came out of Egypt under Moses . . . who had sinned, whose corpses fell in the desert" (cf. Heb 3:11; 4:3).

Alice L. Laffey

WRITINGS/KETUVIM (IN HEBREW SCRIPTURES)

Ketuvim or Writings is the name of the third division/section of the in the Jewish canon. Within some Christian traditions, this material may be referred to as the Hagiographa. The material contained within the ketuvim are: Psalms, Job, Proverbs, Ruth, Song of Solomon, Ecclesiastes, Lamentations, Esther, Daniel, Ezra and Nehemiah, 1 and 2 Chronicles, in this order. This division of the Hebrew Bible corresponds more or less with the grouping of the poetry and wisdom writings in the Christian canons. The Ketuvim/Writings seems to have been the final section of the Hebrew Bible/Old Testament to be finalized. In the New Testament, there is mention of the books of Moses, referring to the Torah/Pentateuch and the Prophets, the second division of the Hebrew Bible, that scholars assume means that these sections were already complete and unchangeable. The third division is mentioned as either the Psalms, or simply "the other writings," suggesting that this section was not yet complete in the early part of the first century C.E.

Russell Fuller

See also CANON, BIBLICAL; HEBREW SCRIPTURES.

WU-HSING

(Chinese, *wu-xing*, lit., five elements, five phases). The theory in early Chinese cosmology that there are five elemental phases forming the basis of the cosmos. These phases are represented by earth, metal, wood, fire, and water, but they are really activities rather than elements that, impelled by *t'ai chi* and produced by the interaction of *yin* and *yang*, succeed one another in controlling human and natural events.

G. D. DeAngelis

See also CH'I; I-CHING; T'AI CHI; TAO; YIN AND YANG.

WU-WEI

(Chinese, lit., without action). Taoist ideal and central concept that, while translated as inaction, means spontaneous and natural action or movement that follows from attunement to the Tao. Such action is characterized by quietism, noninterference, simplicity, and suppleness. One who practices *wu-wei* acts, but in a natural, nonstraining, nonaggressive manner following the path of least resistance in which one's skill becomes instinctive and spontaneous—following the natural course of things. Confucianism also embraced this ideal as it applied to social relationships.

G. D. DeAngelis

See also CHUANG TZU; CONFUCIANISM; DAOISM; JEN; LAO-TZU; LI; TAO; TAO TE CHING.

WYCLIFF, JOHN (1335/8?–84)

John Wycliff's date and place of birth are uncertain. He lived and taught at Oxford from at least 1356 until 1382. He gained prominence as a professor of philosophy before he began to lecture on theology in 1371. In 1373 Pope Gregory XI issued a list of eighteen errors of which Wycliff was accused, but it was not until 1380 that Wycliff was condemned at Oxford for his teaching on the Eucharist. In 1382 a council in London condemned twenty-four of Wycliff's teachings. Wycliff was allowed to retire to Lutterworth where he continued to write, despite worsening health. He died in 1384, still in the good graces of the church. His teachings were frequently condemned after his death, most notably at the Council of Constance in 1415. In 1428 Wycliff's body was exhumed, burnt, and the ashes were thrown in the River Swift. Wycliff wrote several works in philosophy, but he is best remembered for his controversial theological opinions. Based partly on Marsilius of Padua, Wycliff argued that authority only resulted from righteousness; therefore, no one, not even the pope, had authority if they were not themselves righteous. Wycliff also argued for the predestination of the true church, and upheld Scripture as the ultimate criterion for Christian teaching. Anything that did not conform to Scripture should be condemned. In this category, Wycliff certainly included the wealth of the church as well as religious orders, indulgences, and prayers for the dead. Wycliff also rejected transubstantiation, the opinion that first got him into trouble. Wycliff's ideas were carried on by his followers who eventually came to be called the "Lollards." They translated the Bible into English, and despite persecution, continued to press for a more evangelical Christianity. Wycliff's teachings were further carried to Bohemia, where they greatly influenced John Hus and the Hussite movement.

Gary Macy

See also BIBLE; CONSTANCE, COUNCIL OF; EUCHARIST; HUS, JOHN; INDULGENCE; LOLLARDS; MARSILIUS OF PADUA; PREDESTINATION (IN CHRISTIANITY); ORDERS (RELIGIOUS); TRANSUBSTANTIATION.

X

XIMÉNEZ DE CISNEROS, FRANCISCO

See JIMÉNEZ DE CISNEROS, FRANCISCO.

Y

YAD HAHAZAKAH

See MISHNEH TORAH.

YAHRZEIT

Yiddish, meaning "a year's time," this is the anniversary of the death of a Jew.

In Jewish tradition, each year the anniversary of the death of a loved one—according to the Hebrew calendar—is commemorated. On the first anniversary following the death, the *yahrzeit* is commemorated on the day of the funeral. From then on, it is observed on the day of death.

The surviving relative lights a candle in the home, symbolic of the soul and the spirit of the deceased. The relative also attends synagogue services to recite the *kaddish*, the doxology recited by mourners. If possible, the grave is visited.

By commemorating the anniversary of the day of death, the life, words, and deeds of a beloved relative are remembered, and the deceased continues to live on in the memory of those commemorating the yahrzeit. Yahrzeit is a yearly tribute of remembrance and love.

Wayne Dosick

See also KADDISH; YIZKOR.

YAHWIST SOURCE

Historical-critical scholars believe this to be the earliest written source of the Pentateuch. The Yahwist source may have been developed in the south of Israel during the Davidic and Solomonic monarchies, that is, between 1000 B.C.E. and 932 B.C.E.

Characteristic of the Yahwist source is its name for God, Yahweh. Characteristic also is its narrative, dialogic style. The Yahwist source portrays God as anthropomorphic, as communicating directly with human beings rather than through messengers or angels or other types of intermediaries (for example, Gen 2:4b-3). It refers to the holy mountain of God as Sinai (not Horeb), and so forth. Often the Yahwist source is abbreviated as "J," the "J" (rather than "Y") deriving from the German "Jahvist." Scholars today believe that the bulk of the Old Epic tradition (JE) contained in the Pentateuch is from the hand of "J." Though the Elohist source has contributed to Israel's epic, the Yahwist source is considerably more extensive in the extant text.

Alice L. Laffey

YAJNA

The sacrificial ritual that was the center of Vedic religion, *yajna* consisted of offerings of grain, milk, clarified butter, and other substances, poured into a sacrificial fire to the accompaniment of chanted mantras (Vedic hymns). The yajnas were divided into two categories, the public (*shrauta*) rites and the domestic (*grihya*). The former could be exceedingly complex, involving three sacrificial fires, the ministrations of as many as sixteen or more brahmin priests, the construction of complex temporary altars, and the ritual slaughter for meat-offerings of domestic animals such as horses or goats. Although most lasted a period of several days, the public yajnas could last as long as two years. The most important yajnas involved also the offering of libations of *soma*, a juice pressed from a plant of the same name possessing psychoactive properties. The plant can no longer be identified with certainty. The sacrificer and the priests also drank soma, which had been valorized as a deity by the Vedic seers (*rishis*). The domestic rites involved a single fire, and could be conducted by the householders themselves, without the assistance of priests. Domestic ceremonies were conducted on a daily basis, with special rites scheduled, like the shrauta rituals, according to the lunar calendar. The most typical daily rites were the *panca–mahayajna*, the "five great sacrifices," relatively simple offerings to the gods, the elemental spirits, the ancestors, the sages (in the form of Vedic study and teaching), and humanity (as hospitality, charity, and so on).

By performing these sacrifices, human beings fulfilled their special responsibility to periodically reinvigorate the cosmic order (*rita*) and nourish the gods and ancestors. Nourished by the sacrifices, the gods and ancestors, in turn, bestowed blessings upon the sacrificers. The public (*shrauta*) rituals are nowadays only rarely performed, except in radically abbreviated forms. However, certain of the grihya rituals—most notably the *shraddha* and the *samskaras*—continue to be an impor-

tant part of life for observant Hindus of the higher caste categories.

Lance E. Nelson

See also HINDUISM; RITA; SACRIFICE; SAMSKARA (RITUALS); SHRADDHA; VEDAS.

YAJUR VEDA

See VEDAS.

YAMA (DEITY)

In Hindu myth from the Vedas onward, Yama (the Restrainer) is the god of death and the underworld. He is famous for his noose, with which he snares souls when their ordained time to depart has come. Although he presides over hells in which his servants torture those who have committed evil deeds on earth, Yama is not to be confused with Satan. Having the power to confer immortality, he is called Dharmaraja, the Lord of Justice. As such, he is the judge who sends the good to heavenly realms (where they are rewarded before being reborn) as well as sentencing the wicked to between-life punishments.

Lance E. Nelson

See also HINDUISM; VEDAS.

YAMA (PRACTICE)

Yama (Sanskrit, restraint) is first of eight fields of practice or "limbs" enumerated in the *Yoga Sutras* of Patanjali, the foundational text of Hindu yoga. It consists of five ethical disciplines: (1) nonviolence (*ahimsa*), (2) truthfulness, (3) nonstealing, (4) sexual abstinence (*brahmacarya*), and (5) nonpossession. The second of the eight limbs is *niyama* (Sanskrit, discipline), again fivefold, encompassing (1) cleanliness, (2) contentment, (3) austerity (*tapas*), (4) study, and (5) devotion to God (*Ishvara*). Taken together, yama and niyama constitute the fundamental ethical discipline that is considered indispensable to serious yogic practice.

Lance E. Nelson

See also AHIMSA; BRAHMACARIN; HINDUISM; RAJA-YOGA; YOGA.

YANTRA

A mystical diagram used in Hindu and Buddhist tantric ritual and meditation, a *yantra* is said to represent, and literally embody in visual form, the power and presence of a deity. Yantras are often understood as being translations into line and color of the sacred sounds of mantras and, like those sacred verbal formulas, to manifest for the initiated the essence of the god or goddess being worshiped.

Lance E. Nelson

See also TANTRA; TANTRIC BUDDHISM; TANTRIC HINDUISM; VAJRAYANA BUDDHISM.

YARLMULKA

See KEPAH.

YELLOW TURBANS

A term used to refer to the religiously inspired, messianic, and anti-imperial Chinese revolutionaries who united toward the end of the Han dynasty (205 B.C.E.–220 C.E.). Dedicated to the "Way of Great Peace" (*Tai-pingdao*), this movement, that began the downfall of the Han, was inspired largely by the religious Taoism of the *Daodejing* (*Tao Te Ching*) and various folk traditions of Shandong and Henan provinces. Named after the distinctive colored head kerchiefs they wore, the Yellow Turbans also cited the country's poverty and natural calamities (particularly flooding) to justify their mounting a series of highly organized armed rebellions begun in the east in 184 C.E., and in Szechwan in 189 C.E.

Todd T. Lewis

See also DAOISM.

YHWH

YHWH, the four consonants of the personal name of the God of Israel, is referred to as the "Tetragrammaton." A consensus exists among critical scholars that the name was spelled and pronounced approximately "Yahweh." In texts of the Old Testament vocalized for study, the vowels associated with the consonants of the name are those of the Hebrew word "adonai," a special form meaning "My Lord." Whenever the name occurs, the vowels for "adonai" are a guide and a reminder that the word "adonai" should be pronounced, not the divine name. This is known as a *qere* perpetuum, a "perpetual reading." Early attempts by scholars who were ignorant of this tradition to recover the original pronunciation of the name assumed that these vowels belonged with the consonants YHWH. This led to the creation of a form that never existed in ancient times, Jehovah, sometimes written Yehovah. Two early attempts to understand this name and to describe its origin are found in the book of Exodus. In Exodus 3:13-15 is found an early tradition associated with the Elohistic tradition in the Pentateuch/Torah. In this text, Moses is given the divine name, and the identification is made with the God of the ancestors of Israel. Likewise, in Exodus 6:2-9, the Priestly Tradition preserves another story of the revelation of the divine name to Moses. In this Priestly tradition, the identification of Yahweh with the God of the ancestors is made once again, but the point is also made that the ancestors had not known the name Yahweh revealed to Moses. The ancestors—Abraham, Isaac, and Jacob—knew Yahweh by the name El Shaddai, usually translated as God Almighty.

Russell Fuller

YIDDISH

A language associated with Jews and Judaism. Yiddish is a hybrid language—a combination of Hebrew and German, with a liberal sprinkling of Russian, Polish, and, in America, English, depending on the linguistic influences of the country of the speaker's residence. The origins of Yiddish may go back as far as 1000 C.E. to the beginnings of the Jewish sojourn in Eastern Europe. Its development and use permitted Jews to retain some of their native language of Hebrew while absorbing the language of the countries and cultures in which they lived. Yiddish is familiar to American Jews because so many of the Jewish immigrants to the United States in the late nineteenth and early twentieth centuries were Yiddish speakers from Eastern Europe.

Yiddish literature is vast, and many Yiddish stories—particularly those of Sholom Aleichem, Y. L. Peretz, and Nobel Prize winner Isaac Bashevis Singer—have been popularized in American theater and film. Many richly expressive Yiddish words have entered into the English language, and are used and understood by Jews and non-Jews alike.

Wayne Dosick

YIHUD

See MARRIAGE (IN JUDAISM).

YIN AND YANG

(Chinese, lit., shade and sunshine). This is the traditional Chinese cosmological conception pertaining to the bipolarity of nature, believed to have emerged in China as early as 1,000 B.C.E. It is based on the belief that underlying the entire cosmos is *ch'i* (vital energy). This vital energy is comprised of two opposite but complementary forces called *yin* (negative) and *yang* (positive). It is believed that not only are all existent things in the universe a combination of these two modes of energy, but, in fact, it is the interaction of these two forces that brings everything into existence. In the ceaseless flow of change, not only are these forces complementary and constantly interacting, but they invariably merge into each other and even become the other in the cyclical movement of life. Yin is primarily negative, fertile, dark, female, cold, wet, mysterious, slow keyed, and so on. Yang is male, active, bright, warm, procreative, and so forth.

G. D. DeAngelis

See also CH'I; DAOISM; FENG-SHUI; I-CHING; T'AI CHI; TAO; TAO TE CHING.

YISRAEL

See ISRAEL, PEOPLE OF.

YIZKOR

Hebrew, meaning "remember," this is a Jewish memorial service. Four times each year—on Yom Kippur, and on the last days of the festivals of Succot, Pesach, and Shavuot—the entire congregation joins together in reciting memorial prayers for all the deceased. The *yizkor* service includes both communal and individual prayers of memory, and is the public expression of both communal and private memory, tribute, and love. The central prayer calls on God to "remember" the souls of the deceased.

In modern times, prayers for those who perished in the Holocaust and for those who died defending the Land of Israel have been added to the yizkor services in many synagogues.

Wayne Dosick

YOGA

From the Sanskrit root *yuj*, to join or harness, *yoga* is a term used in all Indic religions. It refers to spiritual practice in the most general sense, as well as to specific patterns of spiritual practice, of which there are many. A practitioner of yoga is referred to as a *yogin* or *yogi*. The most important of these disciplines in Hinduism form a classically recognized set, the four yogas: the yoga of knowledge (*jnana-yoga*), the "royal" yoga of psychophysical discipline (*raja-yoga*), the yoga of loving devotion (*bhakti-yoga*), and the yoga of consecrated action (*karma-yoga*). The discipline of physical postures commonly taught in the West, known as *hatha-yoga*, is commonly classified as a preliminary form of raja-yoga, though it has votaries in India that have regarded it as an independent discipline. Although it no longer exists as such, Yoga was also identified as a particular school, one of the six orthodox systems (*darshanas*) of Hindu thought, the basic text of which was the *Yoga Sutras*. For purposes of understanding, yoga as spiritual practice may be described as a form of mysticism, since it aims at a gradual purification and elevation of consciousness, with the final goal of direct experience of the transcendent. As such, the term as been loosely applied by scholars to parallel forms of practice among Taoist adepts in China, although no historical connections have been proven.

Lance E. Nelson

See also BHAKTI-YOGA; JNANA-YOGA; KARMA-YOGA; RAJA-YOGA; YOGACHARA.

YOGACHARA

A philosophical school of Mahayana Buddhism whose name, "Yoga-Practitioner," points to its concern with reconciling the experiences of meditation with Buddhist doctrine, asserting that reality is centered in consciousness alone. For main discussion on this school, also called Vijnanavada ("Teaching on Consciousness"), see the Cittamatra entry.

Todd T. Lewis

See also CITTAMATRA; MAHAYANA BUDDHISM.

YOM HAATZMAUT

In Judaism, this is Israel independence day, marking the modern state of Israel's declaration of independence on May 14, 1948. In Jewish communities around the world, Yom HaAtzmaut is celebrated through joyous activities in a carnival atmosphere. In many synagogues, the day is marked by a special thanksgiving service.

Alan J. Avery-Peck

YOM HASHOAH

In Judaism, this marks Holocaust remembrance day, celebrated on the twenty-seventh of the Jewish month of Nisan, in the early spring. In synagogues, memorial services are held, and many Jewish organizations schedule appropriate commemorative events.

Alan J. Avery-Peck

YOM KIPPUR

(Hebrew, Day of Atonement). In Judaism, the most solemn holiday of the year, when God is understood to sit in judgment over people's deeds and to determine whether or not they deserve to live out the coming year (see Lev 16:29-31). Jews respond by repenting for past behaviors and committing themselves to return to the path of proper behavior set out by Judaism. In order to encourage such self-evaluation, on Yom Kippur, Judaism prohibits work as well as eating, drinking, washing, sexual intercourse, and other behaviors associated with pleasures of the body. The day is spent in the synagogue in prayer, with particular emphasis on communal and individual confession of sin, on recognizing the significance of repentance, and on portraying God's role as a judge who desires that people repent so as to be able to continue in life.

The Yom Kippur liturgy is best known for the service held the evening prior to the day of Yom Kippur, at which Kol Nidrei (Aramaic, "All Vows") is recited. This medieval formulation declares to be null all vows made unwittingly or rashly by an individual to God between that day and the following Yom Kippur. Yom Kippur ends the following evening with a service referred to as Neilah (Hebrew, "closing of the gates") that portrays the end of Yom Kippur as a time at which the gates of judgment are being locked, affording the individual just a few more moments to engage in true repentance. On Yom Kippur day itself, in addition to morning and afternoon worship, memorial prayers and martyrologies are recited, and the liturgy recalls the service of the high priest on the Day of Atonement, described at Leviticus 16:1-34.

The observance of Yom Kippur leads individuals to confront their failings in light of a recognition of human mortality and of God's role as judge over all. The individual accordingly rethinks priorities and emerges committed to a more moral and charitable lifestyle. While the mood of the holiday is solemn, it is also hopeful. The Yom Kippur liturgy focuses on God's desire not for the death of the sinner but to wipe away the stain of sin, if only the individual will turn from evil to good ways. Yom Kippur thus offers an opportunity for a fresh start at living life according to the teachings of Judaism. Occurring yearly, in Judaism this rebirth is an important aspect of life in this world. It reflects Judaism's comprehension of the relationship between people and God as a journey, during which, time and again, individuals must retrace their steps so as to find the right path. The self-evaluation and repentance that occur on Yom Kippur thus make each Jew a better, more honest, moral, and upright person in his or her life in this world, from one Day of Atonement to the next.

Alan J. Avery-Peck

See also ATONEMENT, HEBREW.

YUGA

In Hindu mythology, a *yuga* is a cosmic age, a measure of universal time. The Hindu concept of the universe (*samsara*), as articulated in the Puranas, envisions a beginningless and endless (infinite) series of cycles, involving vast stretches of time and repeated manifestations and dissolutions of the world. In this succession, the great cycles, between which the universe rests, are termed *kalpas*, which are said to last some 311 trillion years. Within these great cycles, the world goes through a repeated series of smaller cycles, each involving a succession of four ages. These four ages are termed yugas and, as in the corresponding conception in Greek mythology, are understood to be declining in terms of moral and spiritual value. From the viewpoint of the present cycle, the Kali Yuga, the first period, the golden age or Sat Yuga ("Age of Truth"), was a period in which the atmosphere was pure and utterly supportive of spirituality. It was in this age that the Vedas were revealed to the ancient sages, the *rishis*. In the Treta Yuga, the second age, things had declined to the extent that an *avatara* of Vishnu was necessary; Lord Vishnu descended as Rama to be for human beings the example of *dharma*. The third age, the Dvapara Yuga, was marked especially by the advent of the Krishna avatara, whose passing (some four thousand years ago) ushered in the last and darkest age, the Kali Yuga. The Kali Yuga—which will last 432,000 years and in the beginning of which we now live—will be marked by severe and increasing moral and spiritual decay, and eventually will be ended by Vishnu's final avatara, Kakin, who will destroy the forces of evil and preside over a conflagration that prepares the world for another Sat Yuga, the cycle of yugas thus beginning again.

Lance E. Nelson

See also HINDUISM; KALPA; PURANA; REVELATION; RISHI; VEDAS; ZOROASTRIANISM.

YUGEN

(Japanese, sublime beauty, obscurity, mystery). This is a central Shinto religio-aesthetic ideal of the Heian Period (794–1185) highlighting the mystery and beauty of the reality behind forms. It points one beyond external beauty to the beauty of mystery, remoteness, sublimity, and stillness, and it is based on the belief that this reality behind form cannot be understood by words or ideas but only intuitively.

G. D. DeAngelis

See also MONO-NO-AWARE; NAKA IMA; SHINTO; ZEN.

Z

ZAKAT

From an Arabic word suggesting "purification," this is one of the Five Pillars of Islam (foundational Islamic beliefs and practices). *Zakat* requires that Muslims who can afford to do so (those not in debt for, or in excess of, the amount due for zakat) give alms each year equaling 2½ percent of the liquid assets they have kept in their possession for one year. This formula indicates that the zakat intends to "purify" those with excess wealth in the sense that they are asked to share their bounty in support of charitable works. In Islamic countries, the zakat may be levied as a tax, but no matter where they live, Muslims are expected to make these funds available to the needy through appropriate channels in their local Islamic communities. In addition to zakat, believers are also encouraged to give the poor free-will offerings of food or money, called *sadaqah*, especially at the end of the annual month-long period of fasting, Ramadan.

Ronald A. Pachence

See also FIVE PILLARS (IN ISLAM); ISLAM; RAMADAN.

ZAZEN

(Japanese, seated meditation). The practice within the Zen tradition, particularly associated with the Soto School, of sitting in meditation. The intent of seated meditation is to empty and still the mind in order to see (experience) the world as it actually is. During this process—unlike Rinzai Zen practice that leads to a gradual awakening—the mind and body dichotomy disappear, and the enlightened mind experiences the immediate moment and realizes that the entire world is filled with the Buddha nature.

G. D. DeAngelis

See also BODHI; BUDDHA; BUDDHISM; DOGEN; SANZEN; SATORI; SESSHIN; SHUNYATA/SUNYA/SHUNYA; SOTO; ZEN.

ZEA, LEOPOLDO (1912–2004)

Mexican philosopher, diplomat, and university professor, Zea is one of the more important Latin American philosophers of the twentieth century. His reflections have centered on questions of cultural identity and autonomy, philosophy of history, liberation, and dependence, *mestizaje*, and Latin America as themes for philosophical inquiry. Although less influential than other philosophers during the earlier stages of liberation theology, Zea is increasingly read and critically interpreted by many Latin American and U.S. Latino theologians who reflect on culture, *mestizaje*, and identity. Among his many books are *El positivismo en México* (1968), *La filosofía americana como filosofía sin más* (1969), *Discurso desde la marginación y la barbarie* (1988), and *Descubrimiento e identidad latinoamericana* (1990).

Orlando Espín

See also CULTURE; HISTORICAL CONSCIOUSNESS; LATIN AMERICAN CATHOLICISM; LATIN AMERICAN THEOLOGIES; LATINO THEOLOGY (-IES); MESTIZAJE; METHOD IN THEOLOGY; MODERNITY; POSTMODERNITY.

ZEALOTS

In the oldest sense of the term, persons who were devoted to the Law of Moses, "zealous" for God (see, for example, Num 25:13; 1 Macc 2:58; 2 Kgs 10:16; Acts 22:3). This may be the sense to be read into the epithet "zealot" applied to Simon, one of the Twelve, in Luke 6:15 and Acts 1:13, a term used to distinguish him from Simon Peter. Perhaps he belonged to a group known for its zeal for the Law. Jesus is similarly characterized as having acted like a "zealot" when he drove the moneychangers out of the Temple: "Zeal for your house will consume me" (John 2:17).

Certain opponents of the Roman occupation of Palestine were also known as Zealots. The term designates the more radical and violence-prone rebels. There were various such groups, probably modeled on the Maccabean tradition of zeal for the Law, which constituted a significant part of the national resistance of Jews toward the Romans.

F. M. Gillman

See also MACCABEES.

ZEN

(Japanese, from Chinese, *Ch'an*; from Sanskrit, *Dhyana*, lit., meditation). A school of Chinese Buddhism (*Ch'an*) brought to Japan and propagated during the Kamakura Period (1185–1333) by the Japanese Buddhist monks Eisai (1141–1215) and Dogen (1200–53), focusing on the attainment of enlightenment (*satori*) by seeing directly into one's true nature (self-realization) and the nature of the world. While it has taken on institutional and sectarian forms, specifically, Rinzai (Chinese, *Lin-Chi*) and Soto (Chinese, *Ts'ao-Tung*), it is more a type of practice leading to enlightenment than a specific school of religion.

In China, Zen was introduced in the sixth century C.E. by the Indian Buddhist monk Bodhidharma, who popularized the practice of distinct forms of meditation and the mind-to-mind and oral transmission (outside of scriptures) of the Buddha's teachings from master to disciple. Based on the practice and teachings of Bodhidharma, a new form of Buddhism arose in China during the late seventh and early eighth centuries. This movement, referred to as Ch'an, was primarily a response to the scholasticism and formalism of the prevailing forms of Indian Buddhism in China at the time. The Ch'an School de-emphasized the use of scriptures, images, temples, and words, and concentrated on meditative practices leading directly to enlightenment. In addition, it offered a radical reinterpretation of Buddhist doctrine, claiming that one could attain instant enlightenment by seeing into (realizing) one's true nature— the true nature (Buddha nature) of all things. Thus, the emphasis in Ch'an was on enlightenment in this lifetime through self-realization and the existence of that possibility for all beings.

The divisions that developed within the Ch'an School were primarily along the lines of practice—how can enlightenment be attained?—rather than on doctrinal differences. Ultimately, two sects survived, the Lin-Chi (Rinzai) and Ts'ao-Tung (Soto), with the first advocating a strict discipline and the use of mental problems to wear down the mind, while the second promoted a more gradual path using scripture and texts along with meditation.

In some respects, the Ch'an movement represented a coming together of Buddhism and Taoism and thus carved out a niche for itself in China. However, the tradition that had begun in China found more fertile soil in Japan where it became one of the most popular forms of Japanese Buddhism. In Japan, where it was known as Zen, it became more than a sectarian expression of Buddhism or a personal experience of enlightenment; it became a pervasive aspect of Japanese culture at the religious, aesthetic, and, at times, political levels. Its stress on intuitiveness, quiet simplicity, aesthetic and religious appreciation of nature, self-reliance (*jiyu*), self-being (*jizai*), experiencing the immediacy of life, and enlightenment are all integral parts of the Japanese character.

G. D. DeAngelis

See also BODHI; BUDDHA; BUDDHISM; DHARMA (IN BUDDHISM); DOGEN; KAMAKURA PERIOD; KOAN; RINZAI; ROHATSU; ROSHI; SANZEN; SATORI; SESSHIN; SHUNYATA/SUNYA/SHUNYA; SOTO; SUZUKI, DAISETSU TEITARO; SUZUKI, SHUNRYU; YUGEN; ZAZEN.

ZHOU DYNASTY (1050–256 B.C.E.)

(Chinese, *Zhou*). The third and longest of ancient China's three dynasties (also Hsia and Shang). Three periods: Early or Western Zhou 1050–770 B.C.E.; Mid-Zhou (Spring and Autumn) 770–450 B.C.E.; and Warring States 450–221 B.C.E. It is one of

the great formative periods in Chinese history that laid the foundation for classical culture and the Chinese worldview plus the widespread development of folk religion. Specifically, this period saw the emergence of the notion of the ruling house being supported by a mandate from heaven (*T'ien-ming*) and the reigning king being recognized as the Son of Heaven (*T'ien Tzu*). In addition, the appearance of the Chinese classic text *I-Ching* (Book of Changes) represented a totally different cosmology from a universe controlled by anthropomorphic beings to one characterized by patterns of natural processes and cosmic change dictated by an ultimate ordering principle known as the Tao (Way).

The latter part of this era was marked by an extended period of social and political chaos that gave birth to new ways of thinking about life and society and humanity's place in the world and universe. Social philosophers such as Confucius, Lao-Tzu, Mencius, Chuang Tzu, Mo-Tzu, Han Fei Tzu, Hsun-Tzu, and other, emerged during this period to have a lasting impact on the development of Chinese society.

G. D. DeAngelis

See also CHUANG TZU; CONFUCIANISM; CONFUCIUS; DAOISM; HSUN-TZU; I-CHING; LAO-TZU; LEGALISM (CHINESE); MANDATE OF HEAVEN; MO-TZU; SHANG DYNASTY.

ZION

In biblical poetry, this is the name used for the city of Jerusalem and, sometimes, for the Temple-mount, a usage that became customary by the second century B.C.E. Zion originally referred to the Jebusite fortress southeast of Jerusalem. In modern times, the term has been taken up by organizations involved with the return of the Jews to the land of Israel, a movement known as Zionism.

Alan J. Avery-Peck

See also ISRAEL, STATE OF; ZIONISM.

ZIONISM

The modern belief that the Jews should have a homeland, made concrete in the nineteenth- and twentieth-century program of developing Palestine (the biblical Zion) as a Jewish state, called Israel. While the idea that the Jews will have Zion as their homeland goes back to the original promise of God to the patriarch Abraham, modern political Zionism dates only to the nineteenth century. In 1897 the Zionist Organization was organized in Basel, and European and American Jews began to work for the creation of a Jewish state in Palestine. The Zionist cause was boosted in 1917 when the British assumed control of Palestine and issued the Balfour Declaration that supported the establishment of a Jewish homeland in Palestine. Between 1917 and 1947 hundreds of thousands of Jews settled in Palestine. From 1933 to 1945, however, the Jews in Europe, facing the threat of murder by the German government under the Nazi party, were officially prohibited from entering the area in sizable numbers. In the aftermath of World War II, many of the Jews who had survived wanted to go to Palestine, and in 1947 the United Nations voted to create there a Jewish and an Arab state. In 1948 the Jewish state declared independence and survived a war by its Arab neighbors, thus fulfilling the dream of modern Zionism. Since then, Zionists have worked to assure the safety and stability of the Jewish state and to promote worldwide Jewish immigration to Israel. Today over five million Jews reside in the State of Israel, along with over a million Arabs.

Alan J. Avery-Peck

See also BALFOUR DECLARATION; ISRAEL, STATE OF.

ZOHAR

(Hebrew, "Splendor"). A thirteenth-century work of Jewish mysticism, written in Spain by Moses deLeon but containing some earlier materials attributed to Rabbi Simeon bar Yohai, who lived in the second century C.E. Taking the form of a commentary to the Pentateuch, the Zohar presents a symbolic interpretation of the inner life of God and God's relationship to humankind. The foundational book of the Jewish Kabbalah, alongside Scripture and the Talmudic literature, the Zohar is one of the most important books of Judaism.

Alan J. Avery-Peck

See also KABBALAH.

ZOMBI (OR ZOMBIE)

In Haitian Vodoun there is the belief that living persons may be punished by death and thereafter be "bought" by the living. The "dead" so acquired somehow survive as "living dead," employed as mindless slaves of those who punished them. Filmmakers and others have delighted in freely creating fantastic stories about zombies, without regard for accuracy or fact. In the 1970s, however, American and Haitian scientists confirmed that zombies do exist, although their supposed "death" turned out to be a scientifically explained state induced through the ingestion of substances obtained (among other sources) from a tropical fish frequent in Haitian waters. The antidote has been found, and has been successfully administered to victims of this terrible punishment. Many of the social and religious implications of the zombi phenomenon are still being studied.

Orlando Espín

See also AFRICAN TRADITIONAL RELIGIONS; AFRO-LATIN RELIGIONS; CANDOMBLÉ; DEATH (CHRISTIAN); PALO MAYOMBE; SANTERÍA; UMBANDA; VODOUN.

ZOROASTER

See ZOROASTRIANISM.

ZOROASTRIANISM

Zoroastrianism is the religious tradition inspired by a priestly seer and prophetic figure known in the West by his Greek name, Zoroaster (from the Avestan, Zarathushtra). Because of its apparent influence on other religious traditions, as well as its high ethical ideals, Zoroastrianism has had a significance far out of proportion to the present number of its adherents. Zoroastrians today number fewer than one hundred fifty thousand, most of them living in India in and around Mumbai and the neighboring state of Gujarat, where they are known as Parsis (Persians). The Parsis migrated to India after the Muslim conquest of Persia. A small Zoroastrian community remained in Persia, where they have been, since the advent of Islam, officially a protected minority but nevertheless subject to periodic persecution.

The date of Zoroaster, who is often spoken of as the earliest prophet, has proved difficult to establish. Scholars debate dates ranging from about 1400 B.C.E. through around 600 B.C.E. He is known only from passages in the Avesta, the Zoroastrian scripture, known as the *Gathas*. Indeed, historically speaking, he is *defined* as the author of the *Gathas*. The archaic language of these hymns makes it likely that their author lived no later that 1000 B.C.E., and probably somewhat earlier. The religion of Zoroaster's time seems to have been a polytheistic, ritual-centered faith, not unlike the religion of the *Rig Veda*, to which portions of the Avesta are closely related. It appears that Zoroaster sought to reorient the sacrificial religion of his contemporaries toward a faith with a strong ethical orientation that approached a genuine monotheism. Almost nothing is known with certainty about the details of Zoroaster's life, but according to pious tradition, Zoroaster had the first of seven visions at the age of thirty. Told to lay aside his body, he was led into the presence of Ahura Mazda (Lord Wisdom), the one creator God, from whom he received his revelation and into whose service he was called. Through this and his other visions, he was taught the principles of the "Good Religion of Mazda's followers" (*Daena Mazdayasni*), which he felt called by God to preach.

Zoroastrians regard Ahura Mazda as all-good and all-knowing. The power of this Wise Lord is, however, limited by the existence of another power, Angra Mainyu. This belief makes it difficult to classify Zoroastrianism as a true monotheism, especially as Angra Mainyu, like Ahura Mazda, is uncreated and, therefore, independent. Add to this the fact that Angra Mainyu is a being purely evil in nature and wholly malicious in intent, and it becomes apparent that the Zoroastrian vision is dualistic, embodying a profound ethical or conflict dualism of good versus evil.

As the "Wise Lord," Ahura Mazda is associated with the seven Amesha Spentas ("Holy Immortals"), personifications of his beneficent qualities: Good Mind, Truth, Power, Devotion, Wholeness, Immortality, and Holy Spirit. Also associated with

Ahura Mazda are the *yazatas* ("worshipful beings"), deities of the old Indo-Iranian pantheon, mentioned in the Avesta, who were incorporated into Zoroastrianism as the Wise Lord's celestial deputies. Angrya Maniyu is likewise in charge of a corresponding host of evil spirits.

It is said that Ahura Mazda created the world especially to serve as the arena—or battleground—upon which Angrya Mainyu and his forces of evil could be engaged and defeated. The Wise Lord created human beings, furthermore, to serve this cause; the ethical dimension of the religion rests on the idea, not only of punishment and reward after death, but on the more fundamental notion that by following the good we contribute to the eventual victory of Ahura Mazda, and by following evil we undermine the good and strengthen the power of Angra Mainyu. Along with concept of world as cosmic battleground, Zoroastrianism introduced, probably for the first time, ideas that have had, and continue to have, an incalculable effect on world culture. These center around the notion of linear time and the concept that history will have an end. In Zoroastrian myth, the Divine brings the world into existence in a unique act of creation, having a plan for the purposeful unfolding of the universe in the direction of a future goal that will be a final, nonrecurring state representing a vast improvement over present circumstances. The world progresses through, according to this vision, a succession of well-defined ages that culminate in the final defeat of Angra Mainyu. History moves from an initial paradise (the English word is derived from the Persian *pairidaēza*), through an attack and repeated assaults by Angra Mainyu and his forces, to a final battle between good and evil, all of which culminate in a healing of the world and the restoration of

paradise, a process known as the Renovation (*frasho–kereti*).

Related to this linear reading of mythic time is another important Zoroastrian innovation: the notion of cosmic eschatology. Zoroaster evokes, and the later tradition further articulates, what may be called an "eschatological scenario," an archetypal vision of the "last days," that is, the end of history. The developed myth involves: (1) the approaching end being signaled by widespread moral depravity and natural disasters; (2) the coming of a world savior, the Saoshyant, born of a virgin (impregnated by Zoroaster's own seed, miraculously preserved), to lead the forces of good; (3) the already mentioned final battle, in which evil is utterly defeated; (4) the resurrection of the dead; (5) the last judgment and the definitive separation of good and evil; and (5) the purification and restoration of the world to its paradisal state. The final state will differ from the original paradise, however, in that Angra Mainyu and his forces will have been completely destroyed. Thus it is called the Separation (of good and evil). The way is then cleared for Ahura Madza's power to become total and a state of timeless perfection to ensue. The ethical element of Zoroastrianism is heightened by the idea that the final outcome of the historical process is not predetermined. Although Ahura Mazda is believed to have a certain advantage, the final result depends, as specified above, to a considerable degree on the choices made by human beings, hopefully against evil and for the good.

Zoroastrians also have a concept of individual eschatology. After death, the soul must cross the Chinvat Bridge ("Bridge of the Separator") that is wide and comfortable for the righteous, who cross over easily to a heavenly reward, but that narrows to the dimensions of a knife's edge for the wicked who fall off into hell, a region of torment. Believing that cremating corpses would diminish the sacrality of fire, which they regard as sacred, and that decaying flesh would pollute the earth, Zoroastrians in Iran and India expose the bodies of their dead in walled structures known as *dakhmas*, often called "towers of silence." There the flesh is consumed by vultures, and eventually only the sun-bleached bones remain, to be piled in a central pit.

As indicated, the Zoroastrians regard fire as sacred. Formal worship is conducted in sacred precincts known as Fire Temples (*agiari*), from which non-Zoroastrians are excluded, around a fire that is kept perpetually burning. The image of a fire burning in an urn is an important symbol of the faith. Zoroastrianism's reverence for fire, along with its hereditary male priesthood and its practice of initiating youth around puberty with a sacred cord, are examples of elements it shares with Hinduism, elements that go back to the Indo-Iranian heritage of both traditions.

Despite the small number of its remaining adherents, Zoroastrianism is typically considered as one of the major world religions. This is not only because it once had numerous followers as the religion of three great Persian empires, the Achaemenian (559–642 B.C.E.), the Parthian (246 B.C.E.–226 C.E.), and the Sassanian (226–633 C.E.). Perhaps an even more important consideration is the possible influence that Zoroastrianism has had on other religious traditions. Readers familiar with Judaism, Christianity, or Islam will already have noted features that Zoroastrianism shares with those traditions. There is evidence, though it its not conclusive, that certain of these ideas were picked up from a cultural milieu much influenced by Zoroastrianism. Prior to the rise of the Achaemenian Empire, and the Babylo-

nian exile of the Jews, there is little evidence in Judaism, for example, of a satanic personification of evil (such as Angra Mainyu), angelic beings (such as the Amesha Spentas and *yazatas*), or developed concepts of life after death, resurrection, or cosmic eschatology (as in the Zoroastrian eschatological myth). Careful readers of the Christian New Testament will be aware that the doctrine of resurrection was a new and as yet not fully accepted idea in Judaism at the time of Jesus (as well as that the "wise men" who are said to have visited the infant Jesus may well have Zoroastrian priests, who were known as *magi*). To what extent the above ideas were the result of parallel developments in the great monotheistic traditions, and thus arrived at independently, and to what extent they represent Zoroastrian influence, is a matter of debate. Conservative Jewish, Christian, and Islamic scholars, for obvious reasons, tend to favor the former alternative. Given the paucity of data, especially concerning the development of Zoroastrianism prior to the Achaemenian period, these questions will probably never be settled with finality. Equally unsettled, and probably equally unlikely to be settled, is the question of the extent to which Zoroastrian eschatological concepts may have dispersed eastward. The possibility of Zoroastrian influence has been suggested for the Mahayana Buddhist conception of the future Buddha Maitreya and its millenarian myth of Shambhala, as well as for the Hindu mythology of Kalkin, the avatara to come, who ushers in the conflagration that marks the end of each cosmic cycle of yugas.

Lance E. Nelson

See also AHURA MAZDA; ANGEL; ANGRA MAINYU; AVATARA/AVATAR; AVESTA;

ESCHATOLOGY (IN CHRISTIANITY);
ESCHATOLOGY (IN JUDAISM); GATHAS;
RESURRECTION (IN CHRISTIANITY);
RESURRECTION (IN JUDAISM);
SAMSKARA (RITUALS); SHAMBHALA;
VEDAS; VISHNU; YUGA; ZOROASTER.

ZUBIRI, XAVIER (1898–1983)

Spanish philosopher. Spain's most eminent contemporary philosopher, Zubiri has been a major foundational influence on Latin American theology and theologians. In Rome and Madrid he earned doctorates in philosophy and theology, studied under Heidegger and Ortega, and eventually furthered his education with degrees in physics, mathematics, and cultural anthropology. Zubiri taught at Madrid's Universidad Complutense, and briefly in Barcelona; but most of his teaching was within the context of very well-attended off-campus courses. He attempted a dialogue between neo-Aristotelian thought and contemporary philosophy (mostly Husserl's, Heidegger's, and Ortega's). He was a proponent of a deeper and more systematic methodological conversation between philosophy and theology, on one side, and the natural and exact sciences, on the other. In Latin American theology he is better known for his reflections on existence and on the ontological structure of reality—indeed, it is difficult to understand the thought of such authors as Ellacuría and Sobrino without considering Zubiri's influence on them. Zubiri wrote numerous philosophical articles and essays, and among his major books are *Naturaleza, historia, dios* (1964), *Sobre la esencia* (1962), and *Cinco lecciones de filosofía* (1963).

Orlando Espín

See also ARISTOTELIANISM; CULTURE; ELLACURÍA, IGNACIO; EXISTENTIALISM; HEIDEGGER, MARTIN; HISTORICAL CONSCIOUSNESS; LATIN AMERICAN THEOLOGIES; LATINO THEOLOGY (-IES); LIBERATION THEOLOGIES; ORTEGA Y GASSET, JOSÉ; SCIENCE, AUTONOMY OF; SOBRINO, JON; SUÁREZ, FRANCISCO; VITORIA, FRANCISCO DE.

ZWINGLI, ULRICH (1484–1531)

Founder of the Reformation in German-speaking Switzerland, Zwingli was a diocesan priest who took issue with the Roman Catholic Church, with Anabaptist Reformers, and with some aspects of Luther's theology. Ordained in 1506, Zwingli was an admirer of Erasmus, and studied languages and Scripture as he served churches in various places near Zurich. He was also a chaplain to Swiss mercenaries fighting in Italy; the experience led him to call for an end to such mercenary activity. From 1518, Zwingli was pastor of the principal church in Zurich; by 1523, the Zurich city council gave its support to Zwingli's reform program. The Mass was suppressed in Zurich in 1525, and soon images were removed from churches. By the late 1520s, the cities of Basle and Berne had adopted a similar reform program. Zwingli supported repression of Anabaptists in Zurich. At the Colloquy of Marburg in 1529, Zwingli rejected Luther's doctrine of the Real Presence of Christ in the Eucharist. For Zwingli, the Body of Christ was now in heaven and could be present in the Eucharist only in a symbolic way. In 1531 Zwingli was killed in a battle between Zurich and Catholic regions of German-speaking Switzerland.

Thomas Worcester, S.J.

See also ANABAPTISTS; CALVIN, JOHN; ERASMUS OF ROTTERDAM; EUCHARIST; LUTHER, MARTIN; REAL PRESENCE; REFORMATION; REFORMED CHURCHES; REFORMED THEOLOGY (-IES).

Contributors

Alan J. Avery-Peck, College of the Holy Cross, Worcester, Massachusetts

Regina A. Boisclair, Alaska Pacific University, Anchorage, Alaska

Rosemary P. Carbine, College of the Holy Cross, Worcester, Massachusetts

William A. Clark, s.j., College of the Holy Cross, Worcester, Massachusetts

J. A. Colombo, University of San Diego, San Diego, California

M. Shawn Copeland, Boston College, Chestnut Hill, Massachusetts

Maria Teresa Dávila, Andover Newton Theological School, Newton, Massachusetts

Francis D. Connolly-Weinert, Saint John's University, Jamaica, New York

G. D. DeAngelis, College of the Holy Cross, Worcester, Massachusetts

Helen deLaurentis, University of San Diego, San Diego, California

Wayne Dosick, University of San Diego, San Diego, California

Kathleen Dugan, University of San Diego, San Diego, California

Orlando Espín, University of San Diego, San Diego, California

Eduardo C. Fernández, s.j., Jesuit School of Theology, Berkeley, California

Mary Anne Foley, c.n.d., University of Scranton, Scranton, Pennsylvania

Russell Fuller, University of San Diego, San Diego, California

Alejandro García-Rivera, Jesuit School of Theology, Berkeley, California

David Gardiner, Colorado College, Colorado Springs, Colorado

Florence M. Gillman, University of San Diego, San Diego, California

John Gillman, San Diego State University, San Diego, California

Roberto S. Goizueta, Boston College, Chestnut Hill, Massachusetts

Justo L. González, Decatur, Georgia

Michelle González, University of Miami, Coral Gables, Florida

M. Jane Gorman, University of San Diego, San Diego, California

Christine Greenway, Seattle, Washington

G. Simon Harak, s.j., Fairfield University, Fairfield, Connecticut

Michael J. Hartwig, Boston, Massachusetts

Diana L. Hayes, Georgetown University, Washington, D.C.

Mary Ann Hinsdale, Boston College, Chestnut Hill, Massachusetts

Mary E. Hobgood, College of the Holy Cross, Worcester, Massachusetts

Patrick J. Hurley, University of San Diego, San Diego, California

Evelyn A. Kirkley, University of San Diego, San Diego, California

Dennis W. Krouse, University of San Diego, San Diego, California

Alice L. Laffey, College of the Holy Cross, Worcester, Massachusetts

Francisco Lozada, Brite Divinity School, Fort Worth, Texas

Todd T. Lewis, College of the Holy Cross, Worcester, Massachusetts

Jack E. Lindquist, University of San Diego, San Diego, California

Brian F. Linnane, s.j., Loyola College of Maryland, Baltimore, Maryland

Gary Macy, Santa Clara University, Santa Clara, California

Patrick L. Malloy, Allentown, Pennsylvania

Marie Anne Mayeski, Loyola Marymount University, Los Angeles, California

Robert D. McCleary, Dorchester, Massachusetts

Thomas McElligott, St. Mary's College of California, Moraga, California

Elizabeth Esther Mikova Carr, Smith College, Northampton, Massachusetts

Lance E. Nelson, University of San Diego, San Diego, California

James B. Nickoloff, College of the Holy Cross, Worcester, Massachusetts

Jon Nilson, Loyola University, Chicago, Illinois

Ronald A. Pachence, University of San Diego, San Diego, California

Linda L. Peterson, University of San Diego, San Diego, California

Peter C. Phan, Georgetown University, Washington, D.C.

Gary A. Phillips, Wabash College, Crawfordsville, Indiana

Joanne M. Pierce, College of the Holy Cross, Worcester, Massachusetts

Patricia Plovanich, University of San Diego, San Diego, California

William Reiser, s.j., College of the Holy Cross, Worcester, Massachusetts

Jeannette Rodríguez, Seattle University, Seattle, Washington

Jean-Pierre Ruiz, Saint John's University, Jamaica, New York

Herbert J. Ryan, s.j., Loyola Marymount University, Los Angeles, California

John R. Sachs, s.j., Weston School of Theology, Cambridge, Massachusetts

Todd A. Salzman, Creighton University, Omaha, Nebraska

Mathew N. Schmalz, College of the Holy Cross, Worcester, Massachusetts

Brian Stiltner, Sacred Heart University, Fairfield, Connecticut

Meghan T. Sweeney, Boston College, Chestnut Hill, Massachusetts

Jesse Thomas, University of San Diego, San Diego, California

Karma Lekshe Tsomo, University of San Diego, San Diego, California

Thomas Worcester, s.j., College of the Holy Cross, Worcester, Massachusetts